Presented

To:

By:

On:

New International Reader's Version

A Beginner's Guide *to the* Bible *for* Kids

NIrV Tiny Theologians Bible
Ancillary Content Copyright © 2026 by Tiny Theologians
Illustrations Copyright © 2026 by Zondervan
All rights reserved

The Holy Bible, New International Reader's Version®, NIrV®
Copyright © 1995, 1996, 1998, 2014 by Biblica, Inc.®
Used by permission. All rights reserved worldwide.

Published by Zondervan, 2026
3950 Sparks Drive SE, Suite 101, Grand Rapids, Michigan 49546, USA
www.Zondervan.com

This Bible was set in the Zondervan NIrV Typeface, created at the 2K/DENMARK type foundry.

"New International Reader's Version" and "NIrV" are registered trademarks of Biblica, Inc.®
Used by permission.

Maps by International Mapping. Copyright © 2009, 2011 by Zondervan. All rights reserved.

Published in association with the literary agency of Wolgemuth & Wilson.

Library of Congress Catalog Card Number 2025937033

The NIrV® text may be quoted in any form (written, visual, electronic or audio), up to and inclusive of five hundred (500) verses without the express written permission of the publisher, providing the verses quoted do not amount to a complete book of the Bible nor do the verses quoted account for twenty-five percent (25%) or more of the total text of the work in which they are quoted. For such uses, notice of copyright must appear on the title or copyright page as follows:

> Scripture quotations taken from The Holy Bible, *New International Reader's Version®*, *NIrV®*
> Copyright © 1995, 1996, 1998, 2014 by Biblica, Inc.® Used by permission. All rights reserved worldwide.
>
> The "NIrV" and "New International Reader's Version" are trademarks registered in the United States Patent and Trademark Office by Biblica, Inc.®

When quotations from the NIrV® text are used by a local church in non-saleable media such as church bulletins, orders of service, posters, or are displayed to the public by projection devices, or similar materials, a complete copyright notice is not required, but the title or the initials (NIrV) must appear at the end of each quotation. Any commentary or other biblical reference work produced for commercial sale that uses the NIrV® text must obtain written permission for use of the NIrV® text.

Permission requests for commercial use that exceeds the above guidelines, please go to www.harpercollinschristian.com/permissions

Permission requests that exceed the above General Use Guidelines must be directed to and approved in writing by Biblica, Inc.® Please send permission requests through the contact link at Biblica.com, or by mail to Biblica, Inc.®, Attn: Rights and Permissions, 300 General Palmer Drive, Palmer Lake, CO 80133, USA.

Any Internet addresses (websites, blogs, etc.) and telephone numbers in this Bible are offered as a resource. They are not intended in any way to be or imply an endorsement by Zondervan, nor does Zondervan vouch for the content of these sites and numbers for the life of the Bible. All rights reserved.

Without limiting the exclusive rights of any author, contributor or the publisher of this publication, any unauthorized use of this publication to train generative artificial intelligence (AI) technologies is expressly prohibited. HarperCollins also exercise their rights under Article 4(3) of the Digital Single Market Directive 2019/790 and expressly reserve this publication from the text and data mining exception.

HarperCollins Publishers, Macken House, 39/40 Mayor Street Upper, Dublin 1, D01 C9W8, Ireland (https://www.harpercollins.com)

Printed in Bangalore, India

26 27 28 29 30 31 32 33 34 /BPI/ 15 14 13 12 11 10 9 8 7 6 5 4 3 2 1

A portion of the purchase price of your NIrV® Bible is provided to Biblica so together we support the mission of *Transforming lives through God's Word.*

Biblica provides God's Word to people through translation, publishing and Bible engagement in Africa, Asia Pacific, Europe, Latin America, Middle East, and North America. Through its worldwide reach, Biblica engages people with God's Word so that their lives are transformed through a relationship with Jesus Christ.

TABLE OF CONTENTS

The Bible is the most amazing book ever written! It's like a library of individual books that, when put together, tell one great big story.

The books of the Bible are organized into two categories: Old Testament books and New Testament books. The books are also organized into six genres, which you can read more about on page vi. If you don't know where to find a certain book of the Bible, you can look in the table of contents below to find the page number where that book begins!

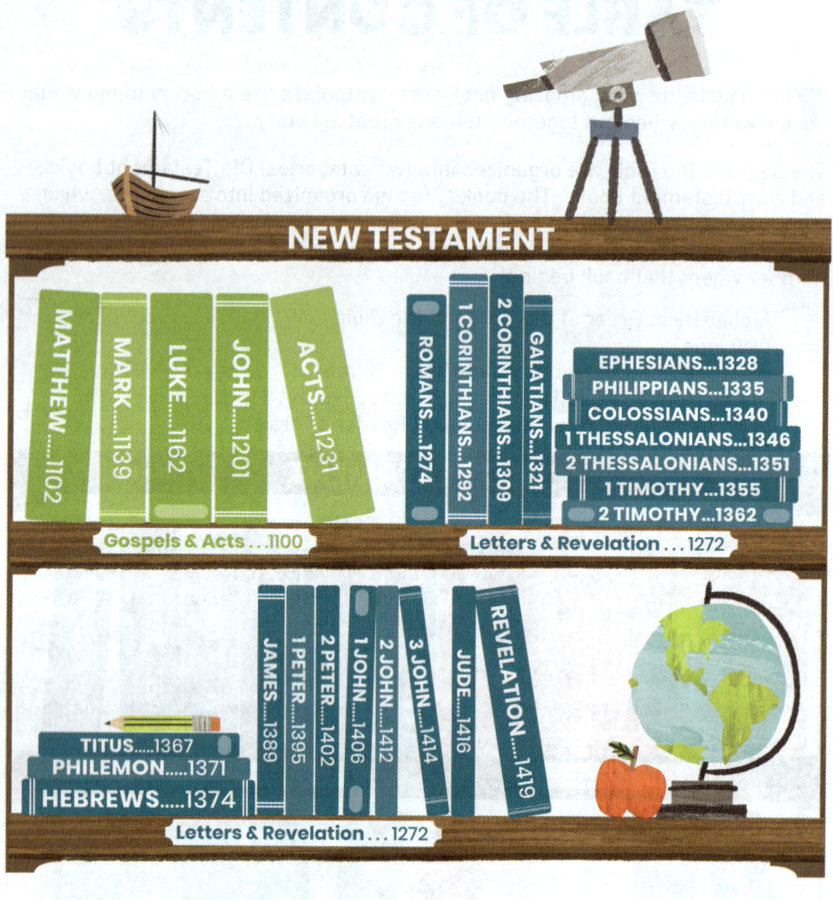
NEW TESTAMENT
MATTHEW.....1102
MARK.....1139
LUKE.....1162
JOHN.....1201
ACTS.....1231
ROMANS.....1274
1 CORINTHIANS...1292
2 CORINTHIANS...1309
GALATIANS...1321
EPHESIANS...1328
PHILIPPIANS...1335
COLOSSIANS...1340
1 THESSALONIANS...1346
2 THESSALONIANS...1351
1 TIMOTHY...1355
2 TIMOTHY...1362
Gospels & Acts . . . 1100
Letters & Revelation . . . 1272
TITUS.....1367
PHILEMON.....1371
HEBREWS.....1374
JAMES.....1389
1 PETER.....1395
2 PETER.....1402
1 JOHN.....1406
2 JOHN.....1412
3 JOHN.....1414
JUDE.....1416
REVELATION.....1419
Letters & Revelation . . . 1272

ALPHABETICAL ORDER OF THE BOOKS OF THE BIBLE

The books of the New Testament are indicated by *italics*.

WELCOME

Welcome to the *NIrV Tiny Theologians Bible*.

Are you curious about God? Do you wonder what his purpose is for your life? The features in this Bible were written to help you understand the basics of faith as you grow in your relationship with God and his Word.

The *NIrV Tiny Theologians Bible* will teach you how to navigate God's Word as your guide and learn more about God's character, purposes, and promises. Before you begin your adventure through the *NIrV Tiny Theologians Bible*, take a moment to read about each feature.

Features

Biblical Genres

All books are written in different styles called genres. A book's genre tells us how it is meant to be read. Some examples of literary genres are poetry, mystery, nonfiction (based on facts), fiction (not based on facts), and history.

The Bible includes 66 books. Each book is written with a unique style and fits within a particular genre. The biblical genres include **Law & Covenant**, **Old Testament History**, **Wisdom & Poetry**, **Prophecy**, the **Gospels & Acts**, and **Letters & Revelation**.

Knowing which genre each book of the Bible was written in helps us to read each book the way the author intended. Look for the genre at the top of each page.

Book Introductions

Each book introduction gives an overview of that book of the Bible. At the top of every book introduction is the name of the author (if we know who it was!). For example, Jesus' disciple Matthew wrote the book of Matthew. Other times the author is unknown. What is amazing is that God worked through ordinary people to write his Holy Word.

Who Is God?

Every book of the Bible helps us see God—from beginning to end. Shortly after each book introduction, you will discover who God is in that book. The God you read about in the Bible is the same God who is with you today!

in **Genesis?**

God is the Creator, the only one who has all power. He has no beginning and will have no end.

Pointing Us to Jesus

The Bible includes many people and things whose purpose is to represent the Savior, Jesus Christ. Every page of God's Word reveals our need for a Savior, God's promise to send a Savior and God's promise fulfilled in Jesus. This feature helps us understand more of who he is and how the entire Bible points to him.

My God Is . . .

The first step in building a relationship with God is knowing who he is. "My God Is . . ." will tell you more about his character. While there are ways we can be like God, there are also ways he is different from us. The ways we can be like God are marked with a **blue** circle next to the kid, and the ways he is different from us are marked with a **purple** circle next to the kid.

Names of God

God is so big and so amazing that one name can't fully explain him. Each of his names tells us something different about him and his great love for us. When we pray, we can call God one of his many names and thank him for all he has done.

NAMES of GOD

Jesus Is the Savior

The Bible tells us that sin separates us from God and makes us unable to see our need for God—even our need for a Savior. But God, who is rich in mercy, reveals or shows us our need for a Savior. God promised from the very beginning to send a Savior to pay the penalty for our sin (see Genesis 3:15). The Savior God sent was his very own Son, Jesus, who died and rose again so that we can live with him forever. Jesus promised that one day he will return and make wrong things right again.

Basics of Faith Q&A

Do you ever wonder, *How did God create the world?* or *Where can I turn when I'm afraid?* These questions and more are answered throughout this Bible. Each question is followed by an answer and a verse to find, showing you how to turn to God's Word to find truth.

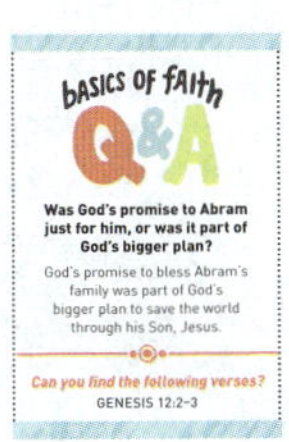

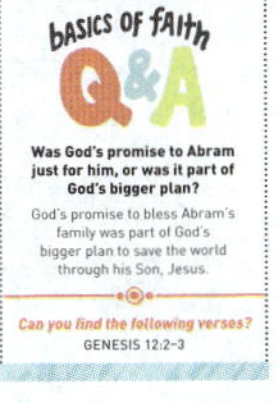

Key Verses

Knowing God's Word will help you on your journey of faith. Try memorizing the key verses and recalling them throughout the day.

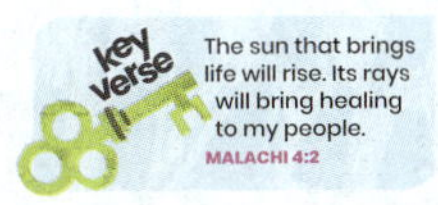

Paul's Missionary Journeys

God used a lot of people to spread the good news about Jesus around the world. One person we read about in the New Testament is named Paul. After Paul became a Christian, he traveled to different cities and regions as a missionary telling people about Jesus. During his travels as a missionary, he wrote many of the books included in the New Testament. By reading about his missionary journeys, starting on page 1233, we learn how the gospel spread and how more people learned to love and follow Jesus.

Glossary

The Bible uses a lot of words that may not be familiar to you. That's okay! The glossary at the back of this Bible includes many words used throughout the Bible, along with simple definitions that explain the meaning of a word. When you come across a word you don't know, turn to the glossary, starting on page 1441. You just might find the explanation you're looking for.

Maps

The maps at the back of this Bible will help you better understand where each of the events in the Bible took place. Spend time reviewing these real places, starting on page 1451.

WHAT ARE CHAPTER NUMBERS AND VERSE NUMBERS, AND HOW DO I USE THEM?

The Bible is full of stories about different people, places, and events. Imagine you're telling your friend about a story you read in the Bible. You know it's a story they will want to read too! How do you tell them where to find that story in the Bible? After all, the Bible has 66 books, 1,189 chapters, and 31,102 verses!

Here is good news: You can tell your friend where to find a story in their Bible by giving them the **name of the book**, the **chapter number**, and the **verse number**. This is called a Bible reference. It's kind of like an address.

Chapter Number

JOHN 3:16

Book Name — Verse Number

Chapter numbers are the big numbers you see throughout each book of the Bible. The chapter numbers in this Bible are in a color. Some books of the Bible have a lot of chapters. (Psalms has the most chapters with 150!) Look for the big numbers to know what chapter you are reading.

Verse numbers are the small numbers you see throughout each book of the Bible. The verse numbers in this Bible are in black. A verse can have just a few words or many words. Every chapter in the Bible includes several verses. Look for the small numbers to know what verse you are reading.

Chapter Number — Verse Numbers

The Beginning

1 In the beginning, God created the
heavens and the earth. 2 The earth
didn't have any shape. And it was empty. There was darkness over the surface
of the waves. At that time, the Spirit of
God was hovering over the waters.

3 God said, "Let there be light." And
there was light. 4 God saw that the light
was good. He separated the light from
the darkness. 5 God called the light
"day." He called the darkness "night."
There was evening, and there was
morning. It was day one.

In books with only one chapter, there is no big chapter number—only small verse numbers, and the Bible reference has just one number—the verse number. Books with only one chapter include Obadiah, Philemon, 2 John, 3 John, and Jude.

PHILEMON 1

Book Name — Verse Number

A WORD ABOUT THE NEW INTERNATIONAL READER'S VERSION

Have You Ever Heard of the New International Version?

We call it the NIV. Many people read the NIV. In fact, more people read the NIV than any other English Bible. They like it because it's easy to read and understand.

And now we are happy to give you another Bible that's easy to read and understand. It's the New International Reader's Version. We call it the NIrV.

Who Will Enjoy Reading the New International Reader's Version?

People who are just starting to read will understand and enjoy the NIrV. Children will be able to read it and understand it. So will older people who are learning how to read. People who are reading the Bible for the first time will be able to enjoy reading the NIrV. So will people who have a hard time understanding what they read. And so will people who use English as their second language. We hope this Bible will be just right for you.

How Is the NIrV Different From the NIV?

The NIrV is based on the NIV. The NIV Committee on Bible Translation (CBT) didn't produce the NIrV. But a few of us who worked on the NIrV are members of CBT. We worked hard to make the NIrV possible. We used the words of the NIV when we could. When the words of the NIV were too long, we used shorter words. We tried to use words that are easy to understand. We also made the sentences of the NIV much shorter.

Why did we do all these things? Because we wanted to make the NIrV very easy to read and understand.

What Other Helps Does the NIrV Have?

We decided to give you a lot of other help too. For example, sometimes a verse is quoted from another place in the Bible. When it is, we tell you the Bible book, chapter and verse it comes from. We put that information right after the verse that quotes from another place.

We separated each chapter into shorter sections. We gave a title to almost every chapter. Sometimes we even gave a title to a section. We did these things to help you understand what the chapter or section is all about.

Another example of a helpful change has to do with the word "Selah" in the Psalms. What this Hebrew word means is still not clear. So, for now, this word is not helpful for readers. The NIV has moved the word to the bottom of the page. We have followed the NIV and removed this Hebrew word from the NIrV. Perhaps one day we will learn what this word means. But until then, the Psalms are easier to read and understand without it.

Sometimes the writers of the Bible used more than one name for the same person or place. For example, in the New Testament the Sea of Galilee is also called the Sea of Gennesaret. Sometimes it is also called the Sea of Tiberias. But in the NIrV we decided to call it the Sea of Galilee everywhere it appears. We called it that because that is its most familiar name.

We also wanted to help you learn the names of people and places in the Bible. So sometimes we provided names even in verses where those names don't actually appear. For example, sometimes the Bible says "the River" where it means "the Euphrates River." In those places, we used the full name "the Euphrates River." Sometimes the word "Pharaoh" in the Bible means "Pharaoh Hophra." In those places, we used his full name "Pharaoh Hophra." We did all these things in order to make the NIrV as clear as possible.

Does the NIrV Say What the First Writers of the Bible Said?

We wanted the NIrV to say just what the first writers of the Bible said. So we kept checking the Greek New Testament as we did our work. That's because the New Testament's first writers used Greek. We also kept checking the Hebrew Old Testament as we did our work. That's because the Old Testament's first writers used Hebrew.

We used the best copies of the Greek New Testament. We also used the best copies of the Hebrew Old Testament. Older English Bibles couldn't use those copies because they had not yet been found. The oldest copies are best because they are closer in time to the ones the first Bible writers wrote. That's why we kept checking the older copies instead of the newer ones.

Some newer copies of the Greek New Testament added several verses that the older ones don't have. Sometimes it's several verses in a row. This occurs at Mark 16:9–20 and John 7:53—8:11. We have included these verses in the NIrV. Sometimes the newer copies added only a single verse. An example is Mark 9:44. That verse is not in the oldest Greek New Testaments. So we put the verse number 43/44 right before Mark 9:43. You can look on the list below for Mark 9:44 and locate the verse that was added.

Verses That Were Not Found in Oldest Greek New Testaments

Matthew 17:21 . . . . . But that kind does not go out except by prayer and fasting.

Matthew 18:11 . . . . . The Son of Man came to save what was lost.

Matthew 23:14 . . . . . How terrible for you, teachers of the law and Pharisees! You pretenders! You take over the houses of widows. You say long prayers to show off. So God will punish you much more.

Mark 7:16 . . . . Everyone who has ears to hear should listen.

Mark 9:44 . . . . In hell, / " 'the worms don't die, / and the fire doesn't go out.'

Mark 9:46 . . . . In hell, / " 'the worms don't die, / and the fire doesn't go out.'

Mark 11:26 . . . . But if you do not forgive, your Father who is in heaven will not forgive your sins either.

Mark 15:28 . . . . Scripture came true. It says, "And he was counted among those who disobey the law."

Luke 17:36	Two men will be in the field. One will be taken and the other left.
Luke 23:17	It was Pilate's duty to let one prisoner go free for them at the Feast.
John 5:4	From time to time an angel of the Lord would come down. The angel would stir up the waters. The first disabled person to go into the pool after it was stirred would be healed.
Acts 8:37	Philip said, "If you believe with all your heart, you can." The official answered, "I believe that Jesus Christ is the Son of God."
Acts 15:34	But Silas decided to remain there.
Acts 24:7	But Lysias, the commander, came. By using a lot of force, he took Paul from our hands.
Acts 28:29	After he said that, the Jews left. They were arguing strongly among themselves.
Romans 16:24	May the grace of our Lord Jesus Christ be with all of you. Amen.

What Is Our Prayer for You?

The Lord has blessed the New International Version in a wonderful way. He has used it to help millions of Bible readers. Many people have put their faith in Jesus after reading it. Many others have become stronger believers because they have read it.

We hope and pray that the New International Reader's Version will help you in the same way. If that happens, we will give God all the glory.

A Word About This Edition

This edition of the New International Reader's Version has been revised to include the changes of the New International Version. Over the years, many helpful changes have been made to the New International Version. Those changes were made because our understanding of the original writings is better. Those changes also include changes that have taken place in the English language. We wanted the New International Reader's Version to include those helpful changes as well. We wanted the New International Reader's Version to be as clear and correct as possible.

We want to thank the people who helped us prepare this new edition. They are Jeannine Brown from Bethel Seminary St. Paul, Yvonne Van Ee from Calvin College, Michael Williams from Calvin Theological Seminary, and Ron Youngblood from Bethel Seminary San Diego. We also want to thank the people at Biblica who encouraged and supported this work.

Old Testament

The first five books in the Old Testament are known as Law and Covenant. They begin with the creation of the world and tell us about the special relationship God had with the people of Israel. These books include stories of how individual people, and even the whole nation of Israel, lived (or didn't live!) in relationship with the God who created them and who made them his own.

These books also give details about God's laws, or commands, for his people and the ways he related to his people through agreements, or promises, known as "covenants." The problem was, because of their sinful nature, the people could not obey God perfectly. But God consistently showed them both mercy and grace.

The way we know we are reading the books of Law and Covenant is by the words God speaks through the author. For example, God often says something like, "Because you are my people, you must live in this way. I will bless you when you obey, and I will discipline you when you disobey. But even when you disobey, you will always be my people."

Law & Covenant
GENESIS
EXODUS
LEVITICUS
NUMBERS
DEUTERONOMY
Lampstand
Table for the Holy Bread
Water Basin
Altar for Burnt Offerings

GENESIS

Author: Moses

The word *genesis* means "beginning," and that's what this book is all about. Genesis tells us the story of the very beginning of the world and the God who has no beginning.

God made the entire universe and created human beings to have a special relationship with him. Though the first people, Adam and Eve, broke their relationship with God through disobedience, God made a promise: One day he would send a Savior who would save people from their sin.

Law & Covenant

Sadly, human beings continued to sin, so God told a man named Noah to build an ark to protect his family and a few of each type of animal from a great big flood. When the floodwaters went down, God put a rainbow in the sky as a reminder that he would never again destroy the earth through a flood.

God also made a promise to a man named Abram, who was later called Abraham. God said that through Abraham's family, the entire world would be blessed (see Genesis 12:2–3). Abraham struggled to trust God, but God was faithful to his promise. Genesis 3:15 is the first time we hear about God's promised Savior, but it is certainly not the last.

The Beginning

1 In the beginning, God created the
heavens and the earth. 2 The earth
didn't have any shape. And it was empty. There was darkness over the surface
of the waves. At that time, the Spirit of
God was hovering over the waters.

3 God said, "Let there be light." And
there was light. 4 God saw that the light
was good. He separated the light from
the darkness. 5 God called the light
"day." He called the darkness "night."
There was evening, and there was
morning. It was day one.

6 God said, "Let there be a huge space
between the waters. Let it separate
water from water." 7 And that's exactly
what happened. God made the huge
space between the waters. He separated
the water under the space from the water above it. 8 God called the huge space
"sky." There was evening, and there was
morning. It was day two.

9 God said, "Let the water under the
sky be gathered into one place. Let dry
ground appear." And that's exactly what

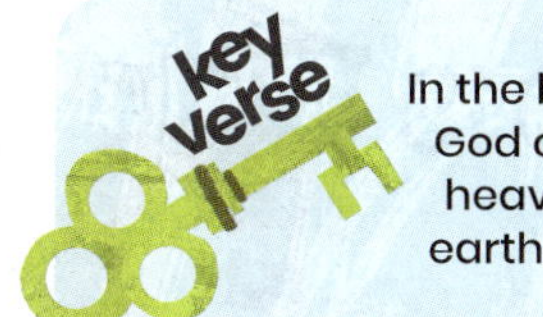

In the beginning, God created the heavens and the earth. **GENESIS 1:1**

happened. 10 God called the dry ground
"land." He called all the water that was
gathered together "seas." And God saw
that it was good.

11 Then God said, "Let the land produce plants. Let them produce their
own seeds. And let there be trees on
the land that grow fruit with seeds in
it. Let each kind of plant or tree have its
own kind of seeds." And that's exactly
what happened. 12 So the land produced
plants. Each kind of plant had its own
kind of seeds. And the land produced
trees that grew fruit with seeds in it.
Each kind of tree had its own kind of
seeds. God saw that it was good. 13 There
was evening, and there was morning.
It was day three.

14 God said, "Let there be lights in the
huge space of the sky. Let them separate

CREATIVE

My GOD IS...

God has a limitless imagination to create wonderful things.

Have you ever looked at something God made and wondered, "How did God think of that?" Think of how mother kangaroos carry their babies in a pocket on the front of their bodies. Or how flamingos stand on one leg at a time and have knees that bend the opposite direction of ours. Think about the ocean, which is filled with all kinds of creatures that swim and jump and light up in the dark depths of the sea.

All creation was God's idea; no one told him what to make. He made everything we can see with his infinite creativity—including you! Each person is specially made by God, and when we create things—like drawings or songs or silly dances—that brings him glory (see Ephesians 2:10).

in Genesis?

God is the Creator, the only one who has all power. He has no beginning and will have no end.

the day from the night. Let the lights set the times for the holy celebrations and the days and the years. 15 Let them be lights in the huge space of the sky to give light on the earth." And that's exactly what happened. 16 God made two great lights. He made the larger light to rule over the day and the smaller light to rule over the night. He also made the stars. 17 God put the lights in the huge space of the sky to give light on the earth. 18 He put them there to rule over the day and the night. He put them there to separate light from darkness. God saw that it was good. 19 There was evening, and there was morning. It was day four.

20 God said, "Let the seas be filled with living things. Let birds fly above the earth across the huge space of the sky." 21 So God created the great sea creatures. He created every kind of living thing that fills the seas and moves about in them. He created every kind of bird that flies. And God saw that it was good. 22 God blessed them. He said, "Have little ones so that there will be many of you. Fill the water in the seas. Let there be more and more birds on the earth." 23 There was evening, and there was morning. It was day five.

24 God said, "Let the land produce every kind of living creature. Let there be livestock, and creatures that move along the ground, and wild animals." And that's exactly what happened. 25 God made every kind of wild animal. He made every kind of livestock. He made every kind of creature that moves along the ground. And God saw that it was good.

26 Then God said, "Let us make human beings so that they are like us. Let them rule over the fish in the seas and the birds in the sky. Let them rule over the livestock and all the wild animals. And let them rule over all the creatures that move along the ground."

27 So God created human beings in his
own likeness.
He created them to be like
himself.
He created them as male and
female.

28 God blessed them. He said to them, "Have children so that there will be many of you. Fill the earth and bring it under your control. Rule over the fish in the seas and the birds in the sky. Rule over every living creature that moves along the ground."

29 Then God said, "I am giving you every plant on the face of the whole earth that produces its own seeds. I am giving you every tree that has fruit with seeds in it. All of them will be given to you for food. 30 I am giving every green plant as food for all the land animals and for all the birds in the sky. I am also giving the plants to all the creatures that move along the ground. I am giving them to every living thing that breathes." And that's exactly what happened.

31 God saw everything he had made. And it was very good. There was evening, and there was morning. It was day six.

2 So the heavens and the earth and everything in them were completed.

2 By the seventh day God had finished the work he had been doing. So on that day he rested from all his work. 3 God blessed the seventh day and made it holy. He blessed it because on that day he rested from all the work he had done.

Adam and Eve

4 Here is the story of the heavens and the earth when they were created. The LORD God made the earth and the heavens.

5 At that time, bushes had not yet appeared on the earth. Plants had not started to grow. The LORD God had not sent rain on the earth. And there was no

one to farm the land. 6 But streams came from the earth. They watered the entire surface of the ground. 7 Then the LORD God formed a man. He made him out of the dust of the ground. God breathed the breath of life into him. And the man became a living person.

8 The LORD God had planted a garden in the east in Eden. He put in the garden the man he had formed. 9 The LORD God made every kind of tree grow out of the ground. The trees were pleasing to look at. Their fruit was good to eat. There were two trees in the middle of the garden. One of them had fruit that let people live forever. The other had fruit that let people tell the difference between good and evil.

10 A river watered the garden. It flowed out of Eden. From there the river separated into four other rivers. 11 The name of the first river is the Pishon. It winds through the whole land of Havilah. Gold is found there. 12 The gold of that land is good. Onyx and sweet-smelling resin are also found there. 13 The name of the second river is the Gihon. It winds through the whole land of Cush. 14 The name of the third river is the Tigris. It runs along the east side of Ashur. And the fourth river is called the Euphrates.

15 The LORD God put the man in the Garden of Eden. He put him there to farm its land and take care of it. 16 The LORD God gave the man a command. He said, "You may eat fruit from any tree in the garden. 17 But you must not eat the fruit from the tree of the knowledge of good and evil. If you do, you will certainly die."

18 The LORD God said, "It is not good for the man to be alone. I will make a helper who is just right for him."

19 The LORD God had formed all the wild animals and all the birds in the sky. He had made all of them out of the ground. He brought them to the man to see what names he would give them. And the name the man gave each living creature became its name. 20 So the man gave names to all the livestock, all the birds in the sky, and all the wild animals.

But Adam didn't find a helper that was just right for him. 21 So the LORD God caused him to fall into a deep sleep. While the man was sleeping, the LORD God took out one of the man's ribs. Then the LORD God closed the opening in the man's side. 22 Then the LORD God made a woman. He made her from the rib he had taken out of the man. And the LORD God brought her to the man.

23 The man said,

"Her bones have come from my
bones.
Her body has come from my
body.
She will be named 'woman,'
because she was taken out of a
man."

24 That's why a man leaves his father and mother and is joined to his wife. The two of them become one.

25 Adam and his wife were both naked. They didn't feel any shame.

Adam and Eve Fall Into Sin

3 The serpent was more clever than any of the wild animals the LORD God had made. The serpent said to the woman, "Did God really say, 'You must not eat fruit from any tree in the garden'?"

2 The woman said to the serpent, "We may eat fruit from the trees in the garden. 3 But God did say, 'You must not eat the fruit from the tree in the middle of the garden. Do not even touch it. If you do, you will die.' "

4 "You will certainly not die," the serpent said to the woman. 5 "God knows that when you eat fruit from that tree, you will know things you have never known before. Like God, you will be able to tell the difference between good and evil."

6 The woman saw that the tree's fruit was good to eat and pleasing to look at. She also saw that it would make a person wise. So she took some of the fruit and ate it. She also gave some to her husband, who was with her. And he ate it. 7 Then both of them knew things they had never known before. They realized they were naked. So they sewed together fig leaves and made clothes for themselves.

8 Then the man and his wife heard the LORD God walking in the garden. It was during the coolest time of the day. They hid from the LORD God among the trees of the garden. 9 But the LORD

God called out to the man. "Where are
you?" he asked.
[10] "I heard you in the garden," the
man answered. "I was afraid, because
I was naked. So I hid."
[11] The LORD God said, "Who told you
that you were naked? Have you eaten
fruit from the tree I commanded you
not to eat from?"
[12] The man said, "It's the fault of the
woman you put here with me. She gave
me some fruit from the tree. And I ate it."
[13] Then the LORD God said to the woman, "What have you done?"
The woman said, "The serpent tricked
me. That's why I ate the fruit."
[14] So the LORD God spoke to the serpent. He said, "Because you have done
this,

"You are set apart from all livestock
and all wild animals.
I am putting a curse on you.
You will crawl on your belly.
You will eat dust
all the days of your life.

[15] I will make you and the woman
hate each other.
Your children and her children
will be enemies.
Her son will crush your head.
And you will bite his heel."

[16] The LORD God said to the woman,

"I will increase your pain when you
give birth.
You will be in great pain when
you have children.
You will long for your husband.
And he will rule over you."

[17] The LORD God said to Adam, "You
listened to your wife's suggestion. You
ate fruit from the tree I warned you
about. I said, 'You must not eat its fruit.'

"So I am putting a curse on the
ground because of what you
did.
All the days of your life you will
have to work hard.

It will be painful for you to get food
from the ground. [18] You will eat
plants from the field,
even though the ground
produces thorns and prickly
weeds.
[19] You will have to work hard and
sweat a lot
to produce the food you eat.
You were made out of the ground.
You will return to it when you die.
You are dust,
and you will return to dust."

[20] Adam named his wife Eve. She
would become the mother of every
living person.
[21] The LORD God made clothes out of
animal skins for Adam and his wife to
wear. [22] The LORD God said, "Just like
one of us, the man can now tell the
difference between good and evil. He
must not be allowed to reach out and
pick fruit from the tree of life and eat
it. If he does, he will live forever." [23] So
the LORD God drove the man out of the
Garden of Eden. He sent the man to
farm the ground he had been made
from. [24] The LORD God drove him out
and then placed angels on the east side
of the garden. He also placed there a
flaming sword that flashed back and
forth. The angels and the sword guarded the way to the tree of life.

Cain and Abel

4 Adam loved his wife Eve and slept
with her. She became pregnant
and gave birth to Cain. She said, "With
the LORD's help I have had a baby boy."
[2] Later she gave birth to his brother Abel.
Abel took care of sheep. Cain farmed
the land. [3] After some time, Cain gathered some things he had grown. He
brought them as an offering to the
LORD. [4] And Abel also brought an offering. He brought the fattest parts of
some animals from his flock. They were
the first animals born to their mothers.
The LORD was pleased with Abel and his
offering. [5] But he wasn't pleased with

pointing us to JESUS: Adam

The first man who ever lived was named Adam. He and his wife, Eve, were made in the image of God. This was God's way of telling Adam and Eve that he created them to have a special relationship with him—a relationship that was different from God's relationship with any of the other created things. Adam and Eve were living proof of God's desire to have a relationship with people.

One day, God's enemy showed up in the Garden of Eden disguised as a serpent. He told Eve a terrible lie. He said that God didn't want what was best for her and Adam. Both Adam and Eve believed the serpent and decided to disobey God. Their disobedience brought sin into the world, which broke all of creation's relationship with God and each other. But soon after Adam and Eve disobeyed, God made them a promise: One day a Savior would come who would make people right with God again. The Savior would be a truer and better Adam.

Jesus was the truer and better Adam, and he fully bore God's image in the world! He was the exact representation of God the Father, and he was living proof of God's goodness. Jesus kept all of God's promises and will one day defeat, or overcome, the deceiving serpent forever. Everything that broke through the first Adam's disobedience was brought back together through Jesus', the second Adam's, obedience to the Father.

Cain and his offering. So Cain became
very angry, and his face was sad.
6 Then the LORD said to Cain, "Why
are you angry? Why are you looking
so sad? 7 Do what is right and then you
will be accepted. If you don't do what
is right, sin is waiting at your door to
grab you. It desires to control you. But
you must rule over it."
8 Cain said to his brother Abel, "Let's
go out to the field." So they went out.
There Cain attacked his brother Abel
and killed him.
9 Then the LORD said to Cain, "Where
is your brother Abel?"
"I don't know," Cain replied. "Am I
supposed to take care of my brother?"
10 The LORD said, "What have you
done? Listen! Your brother's blood is crying out to me from the ground. 11 So I am
putting a curse on you. I am driving you
away from this ground. It has opened its
mouth to receive your brother's blood
from your hand. 12 When you farm the
land, it will not produce its crops for you
anymore. You will be a restless person
who wanders around on the earth."
13 Cain said to the LORD, "You are
punishing me more than I can take.
14 Today you are driving me away from
the land. I will be hidden from you.
I'll be a restless person who wanders
around on the earth. Anyone who finds
me will kill me."
15 But the LORD said to him, "No. Anyone who kills you will be paid back sev-
en times." The LORD put a mark on Cain.
Then anyone who found him wouldn't
kill him. 16 So Cain went away from the
LORD. He lived in the land of Nod. It was
east of Eden.
17 Cain loved his wife and slept with
her. She became pregnant and gave
birth to Enoch. At that time Cain was
building a city. He named it after his son
Enoch. 18 Enoch had a son named Irad.
Irad was the father of Mehujael. Mehujael was the father of Methushael. And
Methushael was the father of Lamech.
19 Lamech married two women. One
was named Adah, and the other was
named Zillah. 20 Adah gave birth to
Jabal. He was the father of people who
live in tents and raise livestock. 21 His
brother's name was Jubal. He was the
father of everyone who plays stringed
instruments and wind instruments.
22 Zillah also had a son. His name was
Tubal-Cain. He made all kinds of tools
out of bronze and iron. Tubal-Cain's
sister was Naamah.
23 Lamech said to his wives,

"Adah and Zillah, listen to me!
  You wives of Lamech, hear my
    words!
I have killed a man because he
    wounded me.
  I have killed a young man
    because he hurt me.
24 Anyone who would have killed
    Cain would have been paid
    back seven times.
  But anyone who hurts me will be
    paid back 77 times."

25 Adam slept with his wife again. She
gave birth to a son and named him Seth.
She said, "God has given me another
child. He will take the place of Abel,
because Cain killed him." 26 Seth also
had a son and named him Enosh.
Then people began to call on the
name of the LORD.

The Family Line of Adam

5 Here is the written story of Adam's
family line.

When God created human beings, he
made them to be like him. 2 He created them as male and female, and he
blessed them. He called them "human
beings" when they were created.

3 When Adam was 130 years old, he
had a son who was like him. He
named him Seth. 4 Adam lived
800 years after Seth was born.
He also had other sons and
daughters. 5 Adam lived a total
of 930 years. And then he died.
6 Seth lived 105 years. Then he
became the father of Enosh.
7 Seth lived 807 years after Enosh
was born. He also had other sons
and daughters. 8 Seth lived a
total of 912 years. And then he
died.
9 Enosh lived 90 years. Then he
became the father of Kenan.
10 Enosh lived 815 years after
Kenan was born. He also had
other sons and daughters.
11 Enosh lived a total of 905 years.
And then he died.

[12]Kenan lived 70 years. Then he became the father of Mahalalel. [13]Kenan lived 840 years after Mahalalel was born. He also had other sons and daughters. [14]Kenan lived a total of 910 years. And then he died.

[15]Mahalalel lived 65 years. Then he became the father of Jared. [16]Mahalalel lived 830 years after Jared was born. He also had other sons and daughters. [17]Mahalalel lived a total of 895 years. And then he died.

[18]Jared lived 162 years. Then he became the father of Enoch. [19]Jared lived 800 years after Enoch was born. He also had other sons and daughters. [20]Jared lived a total of 962 years. And then he died.

[21]Enoch lived 65 years. Then he became the father of Methuselah. [22]Enoch walked faithfully with God 300 years after Methuselah was born. He also had other sons and daughters. [23]Enoch lived a total of 365 years. [24]Enoch walked faithfully with God. And then he couldn't be found, because God took him from this life.

[25]Methuselah lived 187 years. Then he became the father of Lamech. [26]Methuselah lived 782 years after Lamech was born. He also had other sons and daughters. [27]Methuselah lived a total of 969 years. And then he died.

[28]Lamech lived 182 years. Then he had a son [29]and named him Noah. Lamech said, "He will comfort us when we are working. He'll comfort us when our hands work so hard they hurt. We have to work hard because the LORD put a curse on the ground." [30]Lamech lived 595 years after Noah was born. He also had other sons and daughters. [31]Lamech lived a total of 777 years. And then he died.

[32]After Noah was 500 years old, he became the father of Shem, Ham and Japheth.

The Sins of Everyone on Earth

6 There began to be many human beings on the earth. And daughters were born to them. [2]The sons of God saw that the daughters of human beings were beautiful. So they married any of them they chose. [3]Then the LORD said, "My Spirit will not struggle with human beings forever. They will have only 120 years to live."

[4]The Nephilim were on the earth in those days. That was when the sons of God went to the daughters of human beings. Children were born to them. The Nephilim were famous heroes who lived long ago. Nephilim were also on the earth later on.

[5]The LORD saw how bad the sins of everyone on earth had become. They only thought about evil things. [6]The LORD was very sad that he had made human beings on the earth. His heart was filled with pain. [7]So the LORD said, "I created human beings, but I will wipe them out. I will also destroy the animals, the birds in the sky, and the creatures that move along the ground. I am very sad that I have made human beings." [8]But the LORD was very pleased with Noah.

Noah and the Flood

[9]Here is the story of Noah's family line.

Noah was a godly man. He was without blame among the people of his time. He walked faithfully with God. [10]Noah had three sons. Their names were Shem, Ham and Japheth.

[11]The earth was very sinful in God's eyes. It was full of people who did mean and harmful things. [12]God saw how sinful the earth had become. All its people were living very sinful lives. [13]So God said to Noah, "I am going to put an end to everyone. They have filled the earth with their harmful acts. I am certainly going to destroy them and the earth. [14]So make yourself an ark out of cypress wood. Make rooms in it. Cover it with tar inside and out. [15]Here is how I want you to build it. The ark has to be 450 feet long. It has to be 75 feet wide and 45 feet high. [16]Make a roof for it. Leave below the roof an opening all the way around that is a foot and a half high. Put a door in one side of the ark. Make lower, middle and upper decks. [17]I am going to bring a flood

on the earth. It will destroy all life under the sky. It will destroy every living creature that breathes. Everything on earth will die. 18 But I will make my covenant with you. You will go into the ark. Your sons and your wife and your sons' wives will enter it with you. 19 Bring a male and a female of every living thing into the ark. They will be kept alive with you. 20 Two of every kind of bird will come to you. Two of every kind of animal will also come to you. And so will two of every kind of creature that moves along the ground. All of them will be kept alive with you. 21 Take every kind of food that you will need. Store it away as food for you and them."

22 Noah did everything just as God commanded him.

7 Then the LORD said to Noah, "Go into the ark with your whole family. I know that you are a godly man among the people of today. 2 Take seven pairs of every kind of 'clean' animal with you. Take a male and a female of each kind. Take one pair of every kind of animal that is not 'clean.' Take a male and a female of each kind. 3 Also take seven pairs of every kind of bird. Take a male and a female of each kind. Then every kind will be kept alive. They can spread out again over the whole earth. 4 Seven days from now I will send rain on the earth. It will rain for 40 days and 40 nights. I will destroy from the face of the earth every living creature I have made."

5 Noah did everything the LORD commanded him to do.

6 Noah was 600 years old when the flood came on the earth. 7 He and his sons entered the ark. His wife and his sons' wives went with them. They entered the ark to escape the waters of the flood. 8 Male and female pairs of "clean" animals and pairs of animals that were not "clean" came to Noah. So did male and female pairs of birds and of all the creatures that move along the ground. 9 All of them came to Noah and entered the ark. Everything happened just as God had commanded Noah. 10 After seven days the flood came on the earth.

11 Noah was 600 years old. It was the 17th day of the second month of the year. On that day all of the springs at the bottom of the oceans burst open. God opened the windows of the sky. 12 Rain fell on the earth for 40 days and 40 nights.

13 On that same day Noah entered the ark together with his sons Shem, Ham and Japheth. Noah's wife and the wives of his three sons also entered it. 14 They had every kind of wild animal with them. They had every kind of livestock, creature that moves along the ground, and bird that flies. 15 Pairs of all living creatures that breathe came to Noah and entered the ark. 16 The animals going in were male and female of every living thing. Everything happened just as God had commanded Noah. Then the LORD shut him in.

17 For 40 days the flood kept coming on the earth. As the waters rose higher, they lifted the ark high above the earth. 18 The waters rose higher and higher on the earth. And the ark floated on the water. 19 The waters rose on the earth until all the high mountains under the entire sky were covered. 20 The waters continued to rise until they covered the mountains by more than 20 feet. 21 Every living thing that moved on land died. The birds, the livestock and the wild animals died. All of the creatures that fill the earth also died. And so did every human being. 22 Every breathing thing on dry land died. 23 Every living thing on earth was wiped out. People and animals were destroyed. The creatures that move along the ground and the birds in the sky were wiped out. Everything on earth was destroyed. Only Noah and those with him in the ark were left.

24 The waters flooded the earth for 150 days.

8 But God showed concern for Noah. He also showed concern for all the wild animals and livestock that were with Noah in the ark. So God sent a wind to sweep over the earth. And the waters began to go down. 2 The springs at the bottom of the oceans had been closed. The windows of the sky had also been closed. And the rain had stopped falling from the sky. 3 The water on the earth continued to go down. At the end of the 150 days the water had gone down. 4 On the 17th day of the seventh month, the ark came to rest on the mountains of Ararat. 5 The waters continued to go down until the tenth month. On the first day of that month, the tops of the mountains could be seen.

6 After 40 days Noah opened a window he had made in the ark. 7 He sent
out a raven. It kept flying back and
forth until the water on the earth had
dried up. 8 Then Noah sent out a dove.
He wanted to see if the water on the surface of the ground had gone down. 9 But
the dove couldn't find any place to rest.
Water still covered the whole surface of
the earth. So the dove returned to Noah
in the ark. Noah reached out his hand
and took the dove in. He brought it back
to himself in the ark. 10 He waited seven
more days. Then he sent out the dove
again from the ark. 11 In the evening
the dove returned to him. There in its
beak was a freshly picked olive leaf! So
Noah knew that the water on the earth
had gone down. 12 He waited seven more
days. Then he sent out the dove again.
But this time it didn't return to him.

13 It was the first day of the first month
of Noah's 601st year. The water on the
earth had dried up. Then Noah removed
the covering from the ark. He saw that the
surface of the ground was dry. 14 By the
27th day of the second month the earth
was completely dry.

15 Then God said to Noah, 16 "Come out
of the ark. Bring your wife and your
sons and their wives with you. 17 Bring
out every kind of living thing that is
with you. Bring the birds, the animals,
and all the creatures that move along
the ground. Then they can multiply
on the earth. They can have little ones
and the number of them can increase."

18 So Noah came out of the ark. His
sons and his wife and his sons' wives
were with him. 19 All the animals came
out of the ark. The creatures that move
along the ground also came out. So did
all the birds. Everything that moves
on land came out of the ark, one kind
after another.

20 Then Noah built an altar to honor
the LORD. He took some of the "clean"
animals and birds. He sacrificed them
on the altar as burnt offerings. 21 The
smell of the offerings pleased the LORD.
He said to himself, "I will never put a
curse on the ground again because of
human beings. I will not do it even
though their hearts are always directed toward evil. Their thoughts are evil
from the time they are young. I will
never destroy all living things again,
as I have just done.

22 "As long as the earth lasts,
there will always be a time to
plant
and a time to gather the crops.
As long as the earth lasts,
there will always be cold and heat.
There will always be summer and
winter,
day and night."

God Makes a Covenant With Noah

9 Then God blessed Noah and his
sons. He said to them, "Have children so that there are many of you. Fill
the earth. 2 All the land animals will be
afraid of you. All the birds in the sky
will be afraid of you. Every creature
that moves along the ground will be
afraid of you. So will every fish in the
seas. Every living thing is put under
your control. 3 Everything that lives and
moves about will be food for you. I have
already given you the green plants for
food. Now I am giving you everything.

4 "But you must not eat meat that
still has blood in it. 5 I will certainly
hold someone accountable if you are
murdered. I will even hold animals
accountable if they kill you. I will also
hold anyone accountable who murders
another person.

6 "Anyone who murders a human
being
will be killed by a human being.
That is because I have made
human beings
so that they are like me.

7 Have children so that there will be
many of you. Multiply and become
many on the earth."

8 Then God spoke to Noah and to his
sons who were with him. He said, 9 "I am
now making my covenant with you and
with all your children who will be born
after you. 10 I am making it also with
every living creature that was with you
in the ark. I am making my covenant
with the birds, the livestock and all the
wild animals. I am making it with all
the creatures that came out of the ark
with you. In fact, I am making it with
every living thing on earth. 11 Here is
my covenant I am making with you.
The waters of a flood will never again

destroy all life. A flood will never again
destroy the earth."
[12] God continued, "My covenant is
between me and you and every living
creature with you. It is a covenant for
all time to come. Here is the sign of the
covenant I am making. [13] I have put my
rainbow in the clouds. It will be the sign
of the covenant between me and the
earth. [14] Sometimes when I bring clouds
over the earth, a rainbow will appear in
them. [15] Then I will remember my covenant between me and you and every
kind of living creature. The waters will
never again become a flood to destroy
all life. [16] When the rainbow appears in
the clouds, I will see it. I will remember
that my covenant will last forever. It is
a covenant between me and every kind
of living creature on earth."
[17] So God said to Noah, "The rainbow
is the sign of my covenant. I have made
my covenant between me and all life
on earth."

The Sons of Noah

[18] The sons of Noah who came out of
the ark were Shem, Ham and Japheth.
Ham was the father of Canaan. [19] The
people who were scattered over the
earth came from Noah's three sons.
[20] Noah was a man who farmed the
land. He decided to plant a field that
produced grapes for making wine.
[21] When he drank some of the wine, it
made him drunk. Then he lay down
inside his tent without any clothes on.
[22] Ham saw his father naked. Then Ham,
the father of Canaan, went outside and
told his two brothers. [23] But Shem and
Japheth picked up a piece of clothing
and laid it across their shoulders. Then
they walked backward into the tent.
They covered their father's body. They
turned their faces away because they
didn't want to see their father naked.
[24] Then Noah woke up from his sleep
that was caused by the wine. He found

pointing us to JESUS: Noah

The people in Noah's time lived in ways that dishonored God. Their wickedness deserved punishment. But even though the people God created had forgotten about him, God never forgot about them. God showed his grace to a man named Noah by giving him a special job. God told Noah that because of sin he was going to send so much water that it would flood the entire earth. Noah was to build a huge boat called an ark.

Noah obeyed God and built an ark. When the floodwaters came, all living creatures that were not on the ark were destroyed, but Noah's ark saved his family, two of almost every kind of animal, and seven pairs of a few special animals.

After the floodwaters went down, God painted the first-ever rainbow in the sky and promised never again to destroy the earth with a flood (see Genesis 9:8–17). This is called the Noahic covenant. The rainbow looked like a warrior's bow pulled back and ready to shoot an arrow. But instead of pointing down at God's creation, the arrow pointed straight at the heart of heaven. With the arrow pointed at heaven, God seemed to be telling his people that one day he would take on their responsibility of being obedient, even when it was very difficult.

Just as Noah's obedience to God led to salvation for Noah's family and the animals on the ark, Jesus' obedience to the Father provides salvation to those who put their faith in Jesus.

out what his youngest son had done to
him. 25 He said,

"May a curse be put on Canaan!
He will be the lowest of slaves to
his brothers."

26 Noah also said,

"May the LORD, the God of Shem,
be praised.
May Canaan be the slave of
Shem.
27 May God add land to Japheth's
territory.
May Japheth live in the tents of
Shem.
And may Canaan be the slave of
Japheth."

28 After the flood Noah lived 350 years.
29 Noah lived a total of 950 years. And
then he died.

A List of Nations

10 Here is the story of Shem, Ham and Japheth. They were Noah's sons. After the flood, they also had sons.

The Sons of Japheth

2 The sons of Japheth were
Gomer, Magog, Madai, Javan,
Tubal, Meshek and Tiras.
3 The sons of Gomer were
Ashkenaz, Riphath and Togarmah.
4 The sons of Javan were
Elishah, Tarshish, the Kittites
and the Rodanites. 5 From these
people came the families who
lived near the Mediterranean
Sea. Each tribe and nation then
spread out into its own territory
and had its own language.

The Sons of Ham

6 The sons of Ham were
Cush, Egypt, Put and Canaan.

7 The sons of Cush were
Seba, Havilah, Sabtah, Raamah
and Sabteka.
The sons of Raamah were
Sheba and Dedan.
8 Cush was the father of Nimrod.
Nimrod became a mighty hero on
the earth. 9 He was a mighty hunter
in the LORD's eyes. That's why people
sometimes compare others with
Nimrod. They say, "They are like
Nimrod, who was a mighty hunter
in the LORD's eyes." 10 The first capital
cities of Nimrod's kingdom were
Babylon, Uruk, Akkad and Kalneh.
These cities were in the land of
Babylon. 11 From that land he went
to Assyria. There he built Nineveh,
Rehoboth Ir and Calah. 12 He also
built Resen, which is between
Nineveh and Calah. Nineveh is the
most famous city.
13 Egypt was the father of
the Ludites, Anamites, Lehabites,
Naphtuhites, 14 Pathrusites,
Kasluhites and Caphtorites.
The Philistines came from the
Kasluhites.
15 Canaan was the father of Sidon.
Sidon was his oldest son. Canaan
was also the father of the
Hittites, 16 Jebusites, Amorites
and Girgashites. 17 And he was
the father of the Hivites, Arkites,
Sinites, 18 Arvadites, Zemarites
and Hamathites.
Later the Canaanite tribes
scattered. 19 The borders of
Canaan reached from Sidon
toward Gerar all the way to
Gaza. Then they continued
toward Sodom, Gomorrah,
Admah and Zeboyim all the way
to Lasha.
20 These are the sons of Ham. They are
listed by their tribes and languages
in their territories and nations.

The Sons of Shem

21 Sons were also born to Shem,
Japheth's younger brother. All the
sons of Eber belonged to Shem's
family line.
22 The sons of Shem were
Elam, Ashur, Arphaxad, Lud and
Aram.
23 The sons of Aram were
Uz, Hul, Gether and Meshek.
24 Arphaxad was the father of Shelah.
Shelah was the father of Eber.
25 Eber had two sons.
One was named Peleg. That's
because the earth was divided
up in his time. His brother was
named Joktan.
26 Joktan was the father of
Almodad, Sheleph, Hazarmaveth,
Jerah, 27 Hadoram, Uzal, Diklah,
28 Obal, Abimael, Sheba, 29 Ophir,
Havilah and Jobab. They were all
sons of Joktan.
30 The area where they lived
stretched from Mesha toward
Sephar. It was in the eastern hill
country.
31 These are the sons of Shem. They are
listed by their tribes and languages
in their territories and nations.

32 These are the tribes of Noah's sons.
They are listed by their family
lines within their nations. From
them the nations spread out over
the earth after the flood.

The Tower of Babel

11 The whole world had only one
language, and everyone spoke
it. 2 They moved to the east and found
a broad valley in Babylon. There they
made their home.
3 They said to one another, "Come on!
Let's make bricks and bake them well."
They used bricks instead of stones. They
used tar to hold the bricks together.
4 Then they said, "Come on! Let's build
a city for ourselves. Let's build a tower
that reaches to the sky. We'll make a
name for ourselves. Then we won't be
scattered over the whole earth."
5 But the LORD came down to see the
city and the tower the people were
building. 6 He said, "All these people are
united and speak the same language.
That is why they can do all this. Now
they will be able to do anything they
plan. 7 Come on! Let us go down and
mix up their language. Then they will
not be able to understand one another."
8 So the LORD scattered them from
there over the whole earth. And they
stopped building the city. 9 There the
LORD mixed up the language of the
whole world. That's why the city was

called Babel. From there the LORD scattered them over the whole earth.

The Family Line of Shem

[10] Here is the story of Shem's family line.

It was two years after the flood. When Shem was 100 years old, he became the father of Arphaxad. [11] After Arphaxad was born, Shem lived 500 years and had other sons and daughters.
[12] When Arphaxad had lived 35 years, he became the father of Shelah. [13] After Shelah was born, Arphaxad lived 403 years and had other sons and daughters.
[14] When Shelah had lived 30 years, he became the father of Eber. [15] After Eber was born, Shelah lived 403 years and had other sons and daughters.
[16] When Eber had lived 34 years, he became the father of Peleg. [17] After Peleg was born, Eber lived 430 years and had other sons and daughters.
[18] When Peleg had lived 30 years, he became the father of Reu. [19] After Reu was born, Peleg lived 209 years and had other sons and daughters.
[20] When Reu had lived 32 years, he became the father of Serug. [21] After Serug was born, Reu lived 207 years and had other sons and daughters.
[22] When Serug had lived 30 years, he became the father of Nahor. [23] After Nahor was born, Serug lived 200 years and had other sons and daughters.
[24] When Nahor had lived 29 years, he became the father of Terah. [25] After Terah was born, Nahor lived 119 years and had other sons and daughters.
[26] After Terah was 70 years old, he became the father of Abram, Nahor and Haran.

The Family Line of Abram

[27] Here is the story of Terah's family line.

Terah became the father of Abram, Nahor and Haran. And Haran became the father of Lot. [28] Haran died in the city of Ur in Babylonia, the land where he was born. Haran died while his father Terah was still alive. [29] Abram and Nahor both got married. The name of Abram's wife was Sarai. The name of Nahor's wife was Milkah, the daughter of Haran. Haran was the father of Milkah and Iscah. [30] But Sarai wasn't able to have children.

[31] Terah left Ur in Babylon. He took with him his son Abram and his grandson Lot, the son of Haran. Terah also took his daughter-in-law Sarai, the wife of his son Abram. All of them left together to go to Canaan. But when they came to Harran, they made their home there.

[32] Terah lived for 205 years. And then he died in Harran.

Was God's promise to Abram just for him, or was it part of God's bigger plan?

God's promise to bless Abram's family was part of God's bigger plan to save the world through his Son, Jesus.

Can you find the following verses?

GENESIS 12:2–3

God Chooses Abram

12 The LORD had said to Abram, "Go from your country, your people and your father's family. Go to the land I will show you.

[2] "I will make you into a great nation.
And I will bless you.
I will make your name great.
You will be a blessing to others.
[3] I will bless those who bless you.
I will put a curse on anyone who puts a curse on you.

All nations on earth
will be blessed because of you."

[4] So Abram went, just as the LORD had
told him. Lot went with him. Abram
was 75 years old when he left Harran.
[5] He took his wife Sarai and his nephew
Lot. They took all the people and possessions they had acquired in Harran.
They started out for the land of Canaan.
And they arrived there.

[6] Abram traveled through the land.
He went as far as the large tree of Moreh
at Shechem. At that time the Canaanites
were living in the land. [7] The LORD appeared to Abram at Shechem. He said,
"I will give this land to your family who
comes after you." So Abram built an
altar there to honor the LORD, who had
appeared to him.

[8] From there, Abram went on toward
the hills east of Bethel. He set up his tent
there. Bethel was to the west, and Ai was
to the east. Abram built an altar there
and called on the name of the LORD.

[9] Then Abram left and continued
south toward the Negev Desert.

Abram Goes to Egypt

[10] At that time there was not enough
food in the land. So Abram went down
to Egypt to live there for a while. [11] As he
was about to enter Egypt, he spoke to
his wife Sarai. He said, "I know what a
beautiful woman you are. [12] The people
of Egypt will see you and say, 'This is his
wife.' Then they will kill me. But they
will let you live. [13] Tell them you are
my sister. Then I'll be treated well and
my life will be spared because of you."

[14] Abram arrived in Egypt. The Egyptians saw that Sarai was a very beautiful woman. [15] When Pharaoh's officials
saw her, they told Pharaoh how beautiful she was. So she was taken into his
palace. [16] Pharaoh treated Abram well
because of her. So Abram gained more
sheep and cattle and male and female
donkeys. He also gained more male
and female servants and some camels.

[17]But the LORD sent terrible sicknesses on Pharaoh and everyone in his palace. The LORD did it because of Abram's wife Sarai. [18]So Pharaoh sent for Abram. "What have you done to me?" he said. "Why didn't you tell me she was your wife? [19]Why did you say she was your sister? That's why I took her to be my wife. Now then, here's your wife. Take her and go!" [20]Then Pharaoh gave orders to his men about Abram. They sent him on his way. So he left with his wife and everything he had.

Abram and Lot Separate

13 Abram went up from Egypt to the Negev Desert. He took his wife and everything he had. Lot went with him. [2]Abram had become very rich. He had a lot of livestock and silver and gold.

[3]Abram left the Negev Desert. He went from place to place until he came to Bethel. Then he came to the place between Bethel and Ai where his tent had been earlier. [4]There he called on the name of the LORD at the altar he had built.

[5]Lot was moving around with Abram. Lot also had flocks and herds and tents. [6]But the land didn't have enough food for both Abram and Lot. They had large herds and many servants, so they weren't able to stay together. [7]The people who took care of Abram's herds and those who took care of Lot's herds began to argue. The Canaanites and Perizzites were also living in the land at that time.

[8]So Abram said to Lot, "Let's not argue with each other. The people taking care of your herds and those taking care of mine shouldn't argue with one another either. After all, we're part of the same family. [9]Isn't the whole land in front of you? Let's separate. If you go to the left, I'll go to the right. If you go to the right, I'll go to the left."

[10]Lot looked around. He saw that the whole Jordan River valley toward the town of Zoar had plenty of water. It was like the garden of the LORD, like the land of Egypt. This was before the

pointing us to JESUS: Abraham

God called Abraham (first known as Abram) into a special relationship with himself called a covenant. In this covenant, called the Abrahamic covenant, God gave Abraham commands and promises. He commanded Abraham to leave his homeland and follow God into a land that God would give him as his new home. God promised to make Abraham's family members as many as the stars in the sky and the grains of sand on the seashore (see Genesis 22:17). His descendants, or family members, would be a blessing to the entire world.

Abraham obeyed God and left his homeland, but then he and his wife had a problem. They didn't have any children, and they were old enough to be great-grandparents! It seemed impossible to them for God to give them a baby of their own. Abraham and Sarah struggled to believe God, but God kept his promise. At the right time, Abraham and Sarah had a son named Isaac.

Many years later, another Son would be born into Abraham's family. His name was Jesus. He was the great-great-great-great- (and many more "greats") grandson of Abraham. Just as Abraham left his home to fulfill God's promise, Jesus, too, would leave his home in heaven to fulfill God's promise to bless the entire world. Those who put their faith in Jesus are promised an eternal home in heaven.

LORD destroyed Sodom and Gomorrah.
11 So Lot chose the whole Jordan River
valley for himself. Then he started out
toward the east. The two men separated. 12 Abram lived in the land of Canaan.
Lot lived among the cities of the Jordan
River valley. He set up his tents near
Sodom. 13 The people of Sodom were
evil. They were sinning greatly against
the LORD.
14 The LORD spoke to Abram after Lot
had left him. He said, "Look around
from where you are. Look north and
south, east and west. 15 I will give you
all the land you see. I will give it forever
to you and your family who comes after
you. 16 I will make them like the dust of
the earth. Can dust be counted? If it can,
then your family can be counted. 17 Go!
Walk through the land. See how long
and wide it is. I am giving it to you."
18 So Abram went to live near the large
trees of Mamre at Hebron. There he
pitched his tents and built an altar to
honor the LORD.

Abram Saves Lot

14 Amraphel was the king of Babylon. Arioch was the king of
Ellasar. Kedorlaomer was the king of
Elam. And Tidal was the king of Goyim.
2 They went to war against five other
kings. They were Bera king of Sodom,
Birsha king of Gomorrah, Shinab king of
Admah, Shemeber king of Zeboyim, and
the king of Bela. Bela was also called
Zoar. 3 These five kings all gathered their
armies together in the Valley of Siddim.
It was also called the valley of the Dead
Sea. 4 For 12 years Kedorlaomer had
ruled over them. But in the 13th year
they opposed him.
5 So in the 14th year, Kedorlaomer
and the kings who helped him went to
war. They won the battle against the
Rephaites in Ashteroth Karnaim. They
also won the battle against the Zuzites
in Ham and the Emites in Shaveh Kiriathaim. 6 They did the same thing to the
Horites in the hill country of Seir. They
marched all the way to El Paran near
the desert. 7 Then they turned back and
went to En Mishpat. En Mishpat was
also called Kadesh. They took over the
whole territory of the Amalekites. They
also won the battle against the Amorites
who were living in Hazezon Tamar.
8 Then the kings of Sodom, Gomorrah,
Admah, Zeboyim and Bela marched
out. Bela was also called Zoar. They
lined up their armies for battle in the
Valley of Siddim. 9 They got ready to
fight against Kedorlaomer king of
Elam, Tidal king of Goyim, Amraphel
king of Babylonia, and Arioch king of
Ellasar. There were four kings against
five. 10 The Valley of Siddim was full
of tar pits. The kings of Sodom and
Gomorrah ran away from the battle.
Some of their men fell into the pits, but
the rest escaped to the hills. 11 The four
kings took all the things that belonged
to Sodom and Gomorrah. They also
took all their food and then left. 12 They
carried away Abram's nephew Lot and
the things he owned. Lot was living in
Sodom at that time.
13 A man escaped and came to report
everything to Abram. Abram was a Hebrew. He was living near the large trees
of Mamre the Amorite. Mamre was a
brother of Eshkol and Aner. All of them
helped Abram. 14 Abram heard that Lot
had been captured. So he called out his
318 trained men. All of them were sons
of his servants. Abram and his men
chased their enemies as far as Dan.
15 During the night Abram separated
his men into groups. They attacked
their enemies and drove them away.
They chased them north of Damascus
as far as Hobah. 16 Abram took back
everything the kings had taken. He
brought back his nephew Lot and the
things Lot owned. He also brought back
the women and the other people.
17 After Abram won the battle over
Kedorlaomer and the kings who helped
him, he returned home. The king of
Sodom came out to meet him in the
Valley of Shaveh. It was also called the
King's Valley.
18 Melchizedek was the king of Jerusalem. He brought out bread and wine.
He was the priest of the Most High God.
19 He gave a blessing to Abram. He said,

"May the Most High God bless
Abram.
May the Creator of heaven and
earth bless him.
20 Give praise to the Most High God.
He gave your enemies into your
hand."

Then Abram gave Melchizedek a tenth
of everything.
21 The king of Sodom said to Abram,
"Give me the people. Keep everything
else for yourself."
22 But Abram said to the king of Sodom, "I have raised my hand to make
a promise to the LORD. He is the Most
High God. He is the Creator of heaven
and earth. 23 I've said I will not accept
anything that belongs to you. I will
not take even a thread or the strap of
a sandal. You will never be able to say,
'I made Abram rich.' 24 I'll accept only
what my men have eaten and what belongs to Aner, Eshkol and Mamre. These
three men went with me. Let them have
their share."

God Makes a Covenant With Abram

15 Some time later, Abram had a
vision. The LORD said to him,

"Abram, do not be afraid.
I am like a shield to you.
I am your very great reward."

2 But Abram said, "LORD and King,
what can you give me? I still don't have
any children. My servant Eliezer comes
from Damascus. When I die, he will get
everything I own." 3 Abram continued,
"You haven't given me any children.
So this servant of mine will get everything I own."
4 Then a message from the LORD came
to Abram. The LORD said, "When you
die, what you have will not go to this
man. You will have a son of your own.
He will get everything you have." 5 The
LORD took Abram outside and said,
"Look up at the sky. Count the stars, if
you can." Then he said to him, "That's
how many children will be born into
your family."
6 Abram believed the LORD. The LORD
was pleased with Abram because he
believed. So Abram's faith made him
right with the LORD.
7 He also said to Abram, "I am the
LORD. I brought you out of Ur in the land
of Babylon. I will give you this land to
have as your very own."
8 But Abram said, "LORD and King,
how can I know I will have this land
as my own?"
9 So the LORD said to him, "Bring me
a young cow, a goat and a ram. Each
must be three years old. Bring a dove
and a young pigeon along with them."
10 Abram brought all of them to the
LORD. Abram cut them in two and
placed the halves opposite each other.
But he didn't cut the birds in half. 11 Then
large birds came down to eat the dead
bodies of the animals and birds. But
Abram chased the large birds away.
12 As the sun was going down, Abram
fell into a deep sleep. A thick and scary
darkness covered him. 13 Then the LORD
said to him, "You can be sure of what
I am about to tell you. For 400 years,
your family who comes after you will
be strangers in another country. They
will become slaves there and will be
treated badly. 14 But I will punish the
nation that makes them slaves. After
that, they will leave with many possessions. 15 But you will die in peace. You
will join the members of your family
who have already died. And you will
be buried when you are very old. 16 Your
children's grandchildren will come back
here. That's because the sin of the Amorites has not yet reached the point
where I must punish them."
17 The sun set and it became dark.
Then a burning torch and a pot filled
with smoking coals appeared. They
passed between the pieces of the animals that had been cut in two. 18 On
that day the LORD made a covenant
with Abram. He said, "I am giving
this land to your family who comes
after you. It reaches from the River of
Egypt to the great Euphrates River.
19 It includes the land of the Kenites,
Kenizzites, Kadmonites, 20 Hittites, Perizzites and Rephaites. 21 The Amorites,
Canaanites, Girgashites and Jebusites
also live there."

Hagar and Ishmael

16 Abram's wife Sarai had never
had any children by him. But she
had a female slave from Egypt named
Hagar. 2 So she said to Abram, "The LORD
has kept me from having children. Go
and sleep with my slave. Maybe I can
have a family through her."
Abram agreed to what Sarai had
said. 3 His wife Sarai gave him her slave
Hagar to be his wife. That was after

he had been living in Canaan for ten
years. 4 Then he slept with Hagar, and
she became pregnant.

When Hagar knew she was pregnant,
she began to look down on the woman
who owned her. 5 Then Sarai said to
Abram, "It's your fault that I'm suffering like this. I put my slave in your
arms. Now that she knows she's pregnant, she looks down on me. May the
LORD judge between you and me. May
he decide which of us is right."

6 "Your slave belongs to you," Abram
said. "Do with her what you think is
best." Then Sarai treated Hagar badly.
So Hagar ran away from her.

7 The angel of the LORD found Hagar
near a spring of water in the desert.
The spring was beside the road to Shur.
8 The angel said, "Hagar, you are Sarai's slave. Where have you come from?
Where are you going?"

"I'm running away from my owner
Sarai," she answered.

9 Then the angel of the LORD told her,
"Go back to the woman who owns you.
Obey her." 10 The angel continued, "I
will give you and your family many
children. There will be more of them
than anyone can count."

11 The angel of the LORD also said to
her,

"You are now pregnant
  and will have a son.
You will name him Ishmael,
  because the LORD has heard
    about your suffering.
12 He will be like a wild donkey.
  He will use his power against
    everyone,
  and everyone will be against
    him.
  He will not get along with any of
    his family."

13 She gave a name to the LORD who
spoke to her. She called him "You are the
God who sees me." That's because she
said, "I have now seen the One who sees
me." 14 That's why the well was named
Beer Lahai Roi. It's still there, between
Kadesh and Bered.

15 So Hagar had a son by Abram and
Abram gave him the name Ishmael.
16 Abram was 86 years old when Hagar
had Ishmael by him.

The Covenant of Circumcision

17 When Abram was 99 years old, the
LORD appeared to him. He said,
"I am the Mighty God. Walk faithfully
with me. Live in a way that pleases me.
2 I will now act on my covenant between
me and you. I will greatly increase the
number of your children after you."

3 Abram fell with his face to the
ground. God said to him, 4 "This is my
covenant with you. You will be the father of many nations. 5 You will not be
called Abram anymore. Your name will
be Abraham, because I have made you
a father of many nations. 6 I will greatly
increase the number of your children
after you. Nations and kings will come
from you. 7 I will make my covenant
with you last forever. It will be between
me and you and your family after you
for all time to come. I will be your God.
And I will be the God of all your family after you. 8 You are now living in
Canaan as an outsider. But I will give
you the whole land of Canaan. You will
own it forever and so will all your family after you. And I will be their God."

9 Then God said to Abraham, "You
must keep my covenant. You and your
family after you must keep it for all
time to come. 10 Here is my covenant
that you and your family after you
must keep. You and every male among
you must be circumcised. 11 That will be
the sign of the covenant between me
and you. 12 It must be done for all time
to come. Every male among you who
is eight days old must be circumcised.
That includes those who are born into
your own family or outside it. It also
includes those bought with money from
a stranger. 13 So any male born into your
family or bought with your money must
be circumcised. My covenant will last
forever. Your body will have the mark
of my covenant on it. 14 Any male who
has not been circumcised will be separated from his people. He has broken
my covenant."

15 God also said to Abraham, "Do not
continue to call your wife by the name
Sarai. Her name will be Sarah. 16 I will
give her my blessing. You can be sure
that I will give you a son by her. I will
bless her so that she will be the mother
of nations. Kings of nations will come
from her."

17 Abraham fell with his face to the
ground. He laughed and said to himself, "Can a 100-year-old man have
a son? Can Sarah have a child at the
age of 90?" 18 Abraham said to God, "I
really wish Ishmael could receive your
blessing!"
19 Then God said, "Yes, I will bless Ishmael. But your wife Sarah will have a
son by you. And you will name him
Isaac. I will establish my covenant with
him. That covenant will last forever.
It will be for Isaac and his family after him. 20 I have heard what you said
about Ishmael. I will surely bless him.
I will make his family very large. He
will be the father of 12 rulers. And I will
make him into a great nation. 21 But I
will establish my covenant with Isaac.
By this time next year, Sarah will have
a son by you." 22 When God had finished
speaking with Abraham, God left him.
23 On that same day Abraham circumcised his son Ishmael. He also circumcised every male who was born into
his family or bought with his money.
He did exactly as God had told him.
24 Abraham was 99 years old when he
was circumcised. 25 His son Ishmael was
13. 26 Abraham and his son Ishmael were
both circumcised on that same day.
27 And every male in Abraham's household was circumcised along with him.
That included those born into his family
or bought from a stranger.

Three Men Visit Abraham

18 The LORD appeared to Abraham
near the large trees of Mamre.
Abraham was sitting at the entrance to
his tent. It was the hottest time of the
day. 2 Abraham looked up and saw three
men standing nearby. So he quickly left
the entrance to his tent to greet them.
He bowed low to the ground.
3 He said, "My lord, if you are pleased
with me, don't pass me by. 4 Let me get
you some water. Then all of you can
wash your feet and rest under this tree.
5 Let me get you something to eat to give
you strength. Then you can go on your
way. I want to do this for you now that
you have come to me."
"All right," they answered. "Do as
you say."
6 So Abraham hurried into the tent
to Sarah. "Quick!" he said. "Get about
36 pounds of the finest flour. Prepare it
and bake some bread."
7 Then he ran over to the herd. He
picked out a choice, tender calf. He gave
it to a servant, who hurried to prepare it.
8 Then he brought some butter and milk
and the calf that had been prepared. He
served them to the three men. While
they ate, he stood near them under
a tree.
9 "Where is your wife Sarah?" they
asked him.
"Over there in the tent," he said.
10 Then one of them said, "I will surely
return to you about this time next year.
Your wife Sarah will have a son."
Sarah was listening at the entrance
to the tent, which was behind him.
11 Abraham and Sarah were already
very old. Sarah was too old to have a
baby. 12 So she laughed to herself. She
thought, "I'm worn out, and my husband is old. Can I really know the joy
of having a baby?"
13 Then the LORD said to Abraham,
"Why did Sarah laugh? Why did she say,
'Will I really have a baby, now that I am
old?' 14 Is anything too hard for me? I
will return to you at the appointed time
next year. Sarah will have a son."
15 Sarah was afraid. So she lied and
said, "I didn't laugh."
But the LORD said, "Yes, you laughed."

Abraham Pleads for Sodom

16 The men got up to leave. They looked
down toward Sodom. Abraham walked
along with them to see them on their
way. 17 Then the LORD said, "Should I hide
from Abraham what I am about to do?
18 He will certainly become a great and
powerful nation. All nations on earth
will be blessed because of him. 19 I have
chosen him. He must direct his children
to live in the way that pleases me. And he
must direct the members of his family
after him to do the same. So he must
guide all of them in doing what is right
and fair. Then I, the LORD, will do for
Abraham what I have promised him."
20 The LORD also said, "The cries
against Sodom and Gomorrah are very
great. Their sin is so bad 21 that I will go
down and see for myself. I want to see
if what they have done is as bad as the
cries that have reached me. If it is not,
then I will know."

22 The men turned away and went toward Sodom. But Abraham remained
standing in front of the LORD. 23 Then
Abraham came up to him. He said, "Will
you sweep away godly people along with
those who are evil? 24 What if there are 50
godly people in the city? Will you really
sweep it away? Won't you spare the place
because of the 50 godly people in it? 25 You
would never kill godly people along with
those who are evil, would you? Would you
treat them all alike? You would never do
anything like that! Won't the Judge of the
whole earth do what is right?"

26 The LORD said, "If I find 50 godly
people in the city of Sodom, I will spare
it. I will spare the whole place because
of them."

27 Then Abraham spoke up again. He
said, "I have been very bold to speak to
the Lord. After all, I'm only dust and
ashes. 28 What if the number of godly
people is five fewer than 50? Will you
destroy the whole city because there
are five fewer people?"

"If I find 45 there," he said, "I will not
destroy it."

29 Once again Abraham spoke to him. He
asked, "What if only 40 are found there?"

He said, "If there are 40, I will not do it."

30 Then Abraham said, "Lord, please
don't be angry with me. Let me speak.
What if only 30 can be found there?"

He answered, "If I find 30, I will not
do it."

31 Abraham said, "I have been very
bold to speak to the Lord. What if only
20 can be found there?"

He said, "If I find 20, I will not destroy it."

32 Then he said, "Lord, please don't
be angry with me. Let me speak just
one more time. What if only ten can
be found there?"

He answered, "If I find ten, I will not
destroy it."

33 When the LORD had finished speaking with Abraham, he left. And Abraham returned home.

The LORD Destroys Sodom and Gomorrah

19 The two angels arrived at Sodom
in the evening. Lot was sitting
near the gate of the city. When Lot saw
the angels, he got up to greet them. He
bowed down with his face to the ground.
2 "My lords," he said, "please come to
my house. You can wash your feet and
spend the night there. Then you can
go on your way early in the morning."

"No," they answered. "We'll spend the
night in the town square."

3 But Lot wouldn't give up. So they
went with him and entered his house.
He prepared a meal for them. He baked
bread without using yeast. And they ate.
4 Before Lot and his guests had gone to
bed, all the men came from every part
of the city of Sodom. Young and old men
alike surrounded the house. 5 They called
out to Lot. They said, "Where are the men
who came to you tonight? Bring them out
to us. We want to have sex with them."

6 Lot went outside to meet them. He
shut the door behind him. 7 He said, "No,
my friends. Don't do such an evil thing.
8 Look, I have two daughters that no
man has ever slept with. I'll bring them
out to you now. Then do to them what
you want to. But don't do anything to
these men. I've brought them inside so
they can be safe."

9 "Get out of our way!" the men of
Sodom replied to Lot. "You came here as
an outsider. Now you want to act like a
judge! We'll treat you worse than them."
They kept trying to force Lot to open
the door. Then they moved forward to
break it down.

10 But the angels inside reached out
and pulled Lot back into the house and
shut the door. 11 Then they made the
men who were at the door of the house
blind. They blinded both young and old
men so that they couldn't find the door.

12 The two angels said to Lot, "Do you
have any other family members here?
Do you have sons-in-law, sons, daughters or any other relatives in the city?
Get them out of here! 13 We are going
to destroy this place. Many have cried
out to the LORD against the people of
this city. So he has sent us to destroy it."

14 Then Lot went out and spoke to his
sons-in-law. They had promised to marry his daughters. He said, "Hurry up!
Get out of this place! The LORD is about
to destroy the city!" But his sons-in-law
thought he was joking.

15 The sun was coming up. So the angels tried to get Lot to leave. They said,
"Hurry up! Take your wife and your two
daughters who are here. Get out! If you

don't, you will be swept away when the city is destroyed."

16 Lot didn't move right away. So the men grabbed him by the hand. They also took hold of the hands of his wife and two daughters. They led all of them safely out of the city. The LORD had mercy on them. 17 As soon as the angels had brought them out, one of them spoke. He said, "Run for your lives! Don't look back! Don't stop anywhere in the valley! Run to the mountains! If you don't, you will be swept away!"

18 But Lot said to them, "No, my lords! Please! 19 You have done me a big favor. You have been very kind to me by sparing my life. But I can't run to the mountains. I won't be able to escape this horrible thing that's going to happen. And then I'll die. 20 Look, here's a town near enough to run to. It's small. Let me run to it. It's very small, isn't it? Then my life will be spared."

21 The LORD said to Lot, "All right. I will also give you what you are asking for. I will not destroy the town you are talking about. 22 But run there quickly. I can't do anything until you reach it." The town was named Zoar. Zoar means Small.

23 By the time Lot reached Zoar, the sun had risen over the land. 24 Then the LORD sent down burning sulfur. It came down like rain on Sodom and Gomorrah. It came from the LORD. It came out of the sky. 25 The LORD destroyed these cities and the whole valley. All the people who were living in the cities were wiped out. So were the plants in the land. 26 But Lot's wife looked back. When she did, she became a pillar made out of salt.

27 Early the next morning Abraham got up. He returned to the place where he had stood in front of the LORD. 28 He looked down toward Sodom and Gomorrah and the whole valley. He saw thick smoke rising from the land. It looked like smoke from a furnace.

29 So when God destroyed the cities of the valley, he showed concern for Abraham. He brought Lot out safely when he destroyed the cities where Lot had lived.

Lot and His Daughters

30 Lot and his two daughters left Zoar. They went to live in the mountains because Lot was afraid to stay in Zoar. So he and his daughters lived in a cave. 31 One day the older daughter spoke to the younger one. She said, "Our father is old. People all over the earth have men to marry and have children with. We do not. 32 So let's get our father to drink wine. Then we can sleep with him. We can use our father to continue our family line."

33 That night they got their father to drink wine. Then the older daughter went in and slept with him. He wasn't aware when she lay down or when she got up.

34 The next day the older daughter spoke to the younger one again. She said, "Last night I slept with my father. Let's get him to drink wine again tonight. Then you go in and sleep with him. We can use our father to continue our family line." 35 So they got their father to drink wine that night also. Then the younger daughter slept with him. Again he wasn't aware when she lay down or when she got up.

36 So both of Lot's daughters became pregnant by their father. 37 The older daughter had a son. She named him Moab. He's the father of the Moabites of today. 38 The younger daughter also had a son. She named him Ben-Ammi. He's the father of the Ammonites of today.

Abraham and Abimelek

20 Abraham moved south into the Negev Desert. He lived between Kadesh and Shur. For a while he stayed in Gerar. 2 There Abraham said about his wife Sarah, "She's my sister." Then Abimelek, the king of Gerar, sent for Sarah and took her.

3 So God appeared to Abimelek in a dream one night. He said to him, "You are as good as dead because of the woman you have taken. She is already married."

4 But Abimelek hadn't gone near her. So he said, "Lord, will you destroy a nation that hasn't done anything wrong? 5 Didn't Abraham say to me, 'She's my sister'? And didn't she also say, 'He's my brother'? I had no idea I was doing anything wrong."

6 Then God spoke to him in the dream. He said, "Yes, I know you had no idea you were doing anything wrong. So I have kept you from sinning against me. That is why I did not let you touch

her. 7 Now return the man's wife to him.
He is a prophet. So he will pray for you,
and you will live. But what if you do
not return her? Then you can be sure
that you and all your people will die."
8 Early the next morning Abimelek
sent for all his officials. When he told
them everything that had happened,
they were really afraid. 9 Then Abimelek called Abraham in. Abimelek said,
"What have you done to us? Have I done
something wrong to you? Why have you
brought so much guilt on me and my
kingdom? You have done things to me
that should never be done." 10 Abimelek
also asked Abraham, "Why did you
do this?"
11 Abraham replied, "I thought, 'There
is no respect for God in this place. They
will kill me because of my wife.' 12 Besides, she really is my sister. She's the
daughter of my father, but not the
daughter of my mother. And she became my wife. 13 God had me wander
away from my father's house. So I said
to her, 'Here is how you can show your
love to me. Everywhere we go, say about
me, "He's my brother." ' "
14 Then Abimelek gave Abraham sheep
and cattle and male and female slaves.
He also returned his wife Sarah to him.
15 Abimelek said, "Here is my land. Live
anywhere you want to."
16 He said to Sarah, "I'm giving your
brother 25 pounds of silver. This will
show everyone with you that I am sorry
for what I did to you. You haven't done
anything wrong."
17 Then Abraham prayed to God, and
God healed Abimelek. He also healed his
wife and his female slaves so they could
have children again. 18 The LORD had
kept all the women in Abimelek's house
from having children. He had done it
because of Abraham's wife Sarah.

Isaac Is Born

21 The LORD was gracious to Sarah,
just as he had said he would be.
The LORD did for Sarah what he had
promised to do. 2 Sarah became pregnant. She had a son by Abraham when
he was old. The child was born at the exact time God had promised. 3 Abraham
gave the name Isaac to the son Sarah
had by him. 4 When his son Isaac was
eight days old, Abraham circumcised

him. He did it exactly as God had commanded him. 5 Abraham was 100 years
old when his son Isaac was born to him.
6 Sarah said, "God has given laughter to me. Everyone who hears about
this will laugh with me." 7 She also said,
"Who would have said to Abraham that
Sarah would breast-feed children? But
I've had a son by him when he is old."

Abraham Sends Hagar and Ishmael Away

8 Isaac grew. The time came for his
mother to stop breast-feeding him.
On that day Abraham prepared a big
celebration. 9 But Sarah saw Ishmael
making fun of Isaac. Ishmael was the
son Hagar had by Abraham. Hagar was
Sarah's Egyptian slave. 10 Sarah said to
Abraham, "Get rid of that slave woman!
Get rid of her son! That woman's son will
never have a share of the family's property. All of it belongs to my son Isaac."
11 What Sarah said upset Abraham
very much. After all, Ishmael was his
son. 12 But God said to Abraham, "Do
not be so upset about the boy and your
slave Hagar. Listen to what Sarah tells
you, because your family line will
continue through Isaac. 13 I will also
make the son of your slave into a nation. I will do it because he is your child."
14 Early the next morning Abraham
got some food and a bottle of water. The
bottle was made out of animal skin.
He gave the food and water to Hagar,
placing them on her shoulders. Then he
sent her away with the boy. She went
on her way and wandered in the Desert
of Beersheba.
15 When the water in the bottle was
gone, she put the boy under a bush.
16 Then she sat down about as far away
as a person can shoot an arrow. She
thought, "I can't stand to watch the boy
die." As she sat there, she began to sob.
17 God heard the boy crying. Then
the angel of God called out to Hagar
from heaven. He said to her, "What is
the matter, Hagar? Do not be afraid.
God has heard the boy crying as he
lies there. 18 Lift up the boy and take
him by the hand. I will make him into
a great nation."
19 Then God opened Hagar's eyes, and
she saw a well of water. So she went and
filled the bottle with water and gave the
boy a drink.

pointing us to JESUS: Isaac

Isaac was the promised son of Abraham and Sarah. One day God commanded Abraham to do something that seemed downright awful. God told Abraham to sacrifice Isaac. This command likely filled Abraham with many questions, such as "Why would God want my son to die?" and "How will God keep his promise of making us a big family if our only son dies?"

Yet Abraham continued to trust God. He believed that God could do anything, and so he set out to sacrifice his only son, whom he loved so much. Isaac lay down on the altar, and just when Abraham was about to kill Isaac, God stopped him. God told Abraham, "Do not harm him . . . I know that you would do anything for [me]. You have not held back from me your son, your only son" (Genesis 22:12). Then God provided a ram to be sacrificed instead of Isaac.

One day, another Son of Promise—Jesus, the Son of God—would come. He would willingly lay down his life on the cross so that you and I could be in a right relationship with the Father. Because we could not pay the penalty for our sin on our own, Jesus (like the ram) was the sacrifice God provided.

20 God was with the boy as he grew up. He lived in the desert and learned to shoot a bow and arrow. 21 While he was living in the Desert of Paran, his mother got a wife for him from Egypt.

The Agreement at Beersheba

22 At that time Abimelek and his army commander, Phicol, spoke to Abraham. They said to Abraham, "God is with you in everything you do. 23 Now make a promise to me here while God is watching. Give me your word that you will treat me fairly. Promise that you will treat my children and their children the same way. I've been kind to you. Now you be kind to me and the country where you are living as an outsider."

24 Abraham said, "I give you my word that I'll do it."

25 Then Abraham complained to Abimelek that his servants had taken over a well of water. 26 But Abimelek said, "I don't know who has done this. You didn't tell me. And today is the first time I heard about it."

27 So Abraham gave Abimelek sheep and cattle. The two men came to an agreement. 28 Then Abraham picked out seven female lambs from his flock. 29 Abimelek asked Abraham, "What's the meaning of these seven female lambs? Why have you picked them out and set them apart?"

30 Abraham replied, "Accept the seven lambs from me. They will be a witness that I dug this well."

31 So that place was named Beersheba. That's because there the two men came to an agreement.

32 After the agreement had been made at Beersheba, Abimelek went back to the land of the Philistines. His army commander, Phicol, went with him. 33 Abraham planted a tamarisk tree in Beersheba. There he called on the name of the LORD, the God who lives forever. 34 Abraham stayed in the land of the Philistines for a long time.

God Tests Abraham

22 Some time later God tested Abraham. He said to him, "Abraham!"

"Here I am," Abraham replied.

2 Then God said, "Take your son, your only son. He is the one you love. Take Isaac. Go to the place called Moriah. Give your son to me there as a burnt offering. Sacrifice him on the mountain I will show you."

3 Early the next morning Abraham got up and loaded his donkey. He took two of his servants and his son Isaac with him. He cut enough wood for the burnt offering. Then he started out for the place God had shown him. 4 On the third day Abraham saw the place a long way off. 5 He said to his servants, "Stay here with the donkey. I and the boy will go over there and worship. Then we'll come back to you."

6 Abraham had his son Isaac carry the wood for the burnt offering. He himself carried the fire and the knife. And the two of them walked on together. 7 Then Isaac said to his father Abraham, "Father?"

"Yes, my son?" Abraham replied.

"The fire and wood are here," Isaac said. "But where is the lamb for the burnt offering?"

8 Abraham answered, "God himself will provide the lamb for the burnt offering, my son." And the two of them walked on together.

9 They reached the place God had shown Abraham. There Abraham built an altar. He arranged the wood on it. He tied up his son Isaac. Abraham placed him on the altar, on top of the wood. 10 Then he reached out his hand. He picked up the knife to kill his son. 11 But the angel of the LORD called out to him from heaven. He said, "Abraham! Abraham!"

"Here I am," Abraham replied.

12 "Do not lay a hand on the boy," he said. "Do not harm him. Now I know that you would do anything for God. You have not held back from me your son, your only son."

13 Abraham looked around. There in a bush he saw a ram caught by its horns. He went over and took the ram. He sacrificed it as a burnt offering instead of his son. 14 So Abraham named that place The LORD Will Provide. To this day people say, "It will be provided on the mountain of the LORD."

15 The angel of the LORD called out to Abraham from heaven a second time. 16 He said, "I am giving you my word that I will bless you. I will bless you because of what you have done," announces the LORD. "You have not held back your son, your only son. 17 So I

will certainly bless you. I will make the
children born into your family as many
as the stars in the sky. I will make them
as many as the grains of sand on the
seashore. They will take over the cities
of their enemies. 18 All nations on earth
will be blessed because of your children.
All these things will happen because
you have obeyed me."
19 Then Abraham returned to his servants. They started out together for
Beersheba. And Abraham stayed in
Beersheba.

Nahor's Sons

20 Some time later Abraham was
told, "Milkah has become a
mother. She has had sons by
your brother Nahor.
21 Uz was born first. Then came his
brother Buz.
Kemuel was born next. He
became the father of Aram.
22 Milkah's other sons are Kesed,
Hazo, Pildash, Jidlaph and
Bethuel."
23 Bethuel became the father of
Rebekah.
Milkah had the eight sons by
Abraham's brother Nahor.

24 Nahor had a concubine named
Reumah. She also had sons.
They were Tebah, Gaham,
Tahash and Maakah.

Sarah Dies

23 Sarah lived to be 127 years
old. 2 She died at Kiriath Arba.
Kiriath Arba is also called Hebron. It's
in the land of Canaan. Sarah's death
made Abraham very sad. He went to
the place where her body was lying.
There he wept over her.
3 Then Abraham got up from beside
his wife's body. He said to the Hittites,
4 "I'm an outsider. I'm a stranger among
you. Sell me some property where I can
bury those in my family who die. Then
I can bury my wife."
5 The Hittites replied to Abraham,
6 "Sir, listen to us. You are a mighty
prince among us. Bury your wife in
the best place we have to bury our dead.
None of us will refuse to sell you a place
to bury her."
7 Then Abraham bowed down in front
of the Hittites, the people of the land.
8 He said to them, "If you are willing to
let me bury my wife, then listen to me.
Speak to Zohar's son Ephron for me.
9 Ask him to sell me the cave of Machpelah. It belongs to him and is at the
end of his field. Ask him to sell it to me
for the full price. I want it as a place to
bury my dead wife among you."
10 Ephron the Hittite was sitting there
among his people. He replied to Abraham. All of the Hittites who had come to
the gate of his city heard him. 11 "No, sir,"
Ephron said. "Listen to me. I will give
you the field. I'll also give you the cave
that's in the field. I will give it to you in
front of my people. Bury your wife."
12 Again Abraham bowed down in
front of the people of the land. 13 He
spoke to Ephron so they could hear him.
He said, "Please listen to me. I'll pay
the price of the field. Accept it from me.
Then I can bury my wife there."
14 Ephron answered Abraham, 15 "Sir,
listen to me. The land is worth ten
pounds of silver. But what's that between the two of us? Bury your wife."
16 Abraham agreed to Ephron's offer.
He weighed out for Ephron the price
he had named. The Hittites there had
heard the amount. The price was ten
pounds of silver. Abraham measured
it by the weights that were used by
merchants.
17 So Ephron sold his field to Abraham.
The field was in Machpelah near Mamre.
Abraham bought the field and the cave
that was in it. He also bought all the trees
that were inside the borders of the field.
Everything was sold 18 to Abraham as his
property. He bought it in front of all the
Hittites who had come to the gate of the
city. 19 Then Abraham buried his wife
Sarah. He buried her in the cave in the
field of Machpelah near Mamre in the
land of Canaan. Mamre is at Hebron.
20 So the field and the cave that was in
it were sold to Abraham by the Hittites.
The property became a place to bury
those who died in his family.

Abraham's Servant Finds a Wife for Isaac

24 By that time Abraham was very
old. The LORD had blessed Abraham in every way. 2 The best servant in
his house was in charge of everything
Abraham had. Abraham said to him,

"Put your hand under my thigh. 3 The LORD is the God of heaven and the God of earth. I want you to make a promise to me in his name. I'm living among the people of Canaan. But I want you to promise me that you won't get a wife for my son from their daughters. 4 Instead, promise me that you will go to my country and to my own relatives. Get a wife for my son Isaac from there."

5 The servant asked Abraham, "What if the woman doesn't want to come back with me to this land? Then should I take your son back to the country you came from?"

6 "Make sure you don't take my son back there," Abraham said. 7 "The LORD, the God of heaven, took me away from my father's family. He brought me out of my own land. He made me a promise. He said, 'I will give this land to your family after you.' The LORD will send his angel ahead of you. So you will be able to get a wife for my son from there. 8 The woman may not want to come back with you. If she doesn't, you will be free from your promise. But don't take my son back there." 9 So the servant put his hand under Abraham's thigh. He promised to do what his master wanted.

10 The servant chose ten of his master's camels and left. He loaded the camels with all kinds of good things from his master. He started out for Aram Naharaim and made his way to the town of Nahor. 11 He stopped near the well outside the town. There he made the camels get down on their knees. It was almost evening, the time when women go out to get water.

12 Then he prayed, "LORD, you are the God of my master Abraham. Make me successful today. Be kind to my master Abraham. 13 I'm standing beside this spring. The daughters of the people who live in the town are coming out here to get water. 14 I will speak to a young woman. I'll say to her, 'Please lower your jar so I can have a drink.' Suppose she says, 'Have a drink of water, and I'll get some for your camels too.' Then let her be the one you have chosen for your servant Isaac. That's how I'll know you have been kind to my master."

15 Before he had finished praying, Rebekah came out. She was carrying a jar on her shoulder. She was the daughter of Milkah's son Bethuel. Milkah was the wife of Abraham's brother Nahor. 16 The young woman was very beautiful. No man had ever slept with her. She went down to the spring. She filled her jar and came up again.

17 The servant hurried to meet her. He said, "Please give me a little water from your jar."

18 "Have a drink, sir," she said. She quickly lowered the jar to her hands and gave him a drink.

19 After she had given him a drink, she said, "I'll get water for your camels too. I'll keep doing it until they have had enough to drink." 20 So she quickly emptied her jar into the stone tub. Then she ran back to the well to get more water. She got enough for all his camels. 21 The man didn't say a word. He watched her closely. He wanted to learn whether the LORD had given him success on the journey he had made.

22 The camels finished drinking. Then the man took out a gold nose ring. It weighed about a fifth of an ounce. He also took out two gold bracelets. They weighed about four ounces. 23 Then he asked, "Whose daughter are you? And please tell me something else. Is there room in your father's house for us? Can we spend the night there?"

24 She answered, "I'm the daughter of Bethuel. He's the son Milkah had by Nahor." 25 She continued, "We have plenty of straw and feed for your camels. We also have room for you to spend the night."

26 Then the man bowed down and worshiped the LORD. 27 He said, "I praise the LORD, the God of my master Abraham. The LORD hasn't stopped being kind and faithful to my master. The LORD has led me on this journey. He has brought me to the house of my master's relatives."

28 The young woman ran home. She told her mother's family what had happened. 29 Rebekah had a brother named Laban. He hurried out to the spring to meet the man. 30 Laban had seen the nose ring. He had seen the bracelets on his sister's arms. And he had heard Rebekah tell what the man had said to her. So Laban went out to the man. He found him standing by the camels near the spring. 31 "The LORD has given

you his blessing," he said. "So come with
me. Why are you standing out here? I've
prepared my house for you. I also have
a place for the camels."
32 So the man went to the house. The
camels were unloaded. Straw and feed
were brought for the camels. And water
was brought for him and his men to
wash their feet. 33 Then food was placed
in front of him. But he said, "I won't eat
until I've told you what I have to say."
"Then tell us," Laban said.
34 So he said, "I am Abraham's servant.
35 The LORD has blessed my master greatly, and he has become rich. The LORD has
given him sheep and cattle, silver and
gold. He has also given him male and female servants, camels and donkeys. 36 My
master's wife Sarah had a son by him
when she was old. He has given that son
everything he owns. 37 My master made
me promise him. He said, 'I'm living in
the land of the people of Canaan. But
promise me that you won't get a wife for
my son from their daughters. 38 Instead,
go to my father's family and to my own
relatives. Get a wife for my son there.'
39 "Then I asked my master, 'What if
the woman won't come back with me?'
40 "He replied, 'I have walked faithfully with the LORD. He will send his
angel with you. He will give you success
on your journey. So you will be able to
get a wife for my son. She will be from
my own relatives and from my father's
family. 41 When you go to my relatives,
suppose they refuse to give her to you.
Then you will be free from the promise
you made to me.'
42 "Today I came to the spring. I said,
'LORD, you are the God of my master
Abraham. Please make me successful
on this journey I've made. 43 I'm standing beside this spring. A young woman
will come out to get water. I'll say to her,
"Please let me drink a little water from
your jar." 44 Suppose she says, "Have a
drink of water, and I'll get some for your
camels too." Then let her be the one the
LORD has chosen for my master's son.'
45 "Before I finished praying in my
heart, Rebekah came out. She was carrying a jar on her shoulder. She went
down to the spring and got water. I said
to her, 'Please give me a drink.'
46 "She quickly lowered her jar from
her shoulder. She said, 'Have a drink, and
I'll get water for your camels too.' So I
drank. She also got water for the camels.
47 "I asked her, 'Whose daughter are
you?'
"She said, 'The daughter of Bethuel.
He's the son Milkah had by Nahor.'
"Then I put the ring in her nose. I
put the bracelets on her arms. 48 And I
bowed down and worshiped the LORD.
I praised the LORD, the God of my master Abraham. He had led me on the
right road. He had led me to get for
my master's son the granddaughter
of my master's brother. 49 Now will you
be kind and faithful to my master? If
you will, tell me. And if you won't, tell
me. Then I'll know which way to turn."
50 Laban and Bethuel answered, "The
LORD has done all of this. We can't say
anything to you one way or the other.
51 Here is Rebekah. Take her and go. Let
her become the wife of your master's
son, just as the LORD has said."
52 Abraham's servant heard what they
said. So he bowed down to the LORD with
his face to the ground. 53 He brought
out gold and silver jewelry and arti-
cles of clothing. He gave all of them to
Rebekah. He also gave expensive gifts
to her brother and her mother. 54 Then
Abraham's servant and the men who
were with him ate and drank. They
spent the night there.
When they got up the next morning,
Abraham's servant said, "Send me back
to my master."
55 But her brother and her mother
replied, "Let the young woman stay
with us ten days or so. Then you can go."
56 But he said to them, "Don't make
me wait. The LORD has given me success
on my journey. Send me on my way so
I can go to my master."
57 Then they said, "Let's get Rebekah and
ask her about it." 58 So they sent for her
and asked, "Will you go with this man?"
"Yes, I'll go," she said.
59 So they sent their sister Rebekah on
her way with Abraham's servant and his
men. They also sent Rebekah's servant
with her. 60 And they gave Rebekah
their blessing. They said to her,

"Dear sister, may your family grow
  by thousands and thousands.
May they take over
  the cities of their enemies."

61 Then Rebekah and her female servants got ready. They got on their camels
to go back with the man. So Abraham's
servant took Rebekah and left.
62 By that time Isaac had come from
Beer Lahai Roi. He was living in the
Negev Desert. 63 One evening he went
out to the field. He wanted to spend
some time thinking. When he looked up,
he saw camels approaching. 64 Rebekah
also looked up and saw Isaac. She got
down from her camel. 65 She asked the
servant, "Who is that man in the field
coming to meet us?"

"He's my master," the servant answered. So she covered her face with
her veil.

66 Then the servant told Isaac everything he had done. 67 Isaac brought Rebekah into the tent that had belonged
to his mother Sarah. And he married
Rebekah. She became his wife, and he
loved her. So Isaac was comforted after
his mother died.

Abraham Dies

25 Abraham had married another
woman. Her name was Keturah.
2 She had Zimran, Jokshan, Medan, Midian, Ishbak and Shuah by Abraham.
3 Jokshan was the father of Sheba and
Dedan. The children of Dedan were the
Ashurites, the Letushites and the Leum-
mites. 4 The sons of Midian were Ephah,
Epher, Hanok, Abida and Eldaah. All
of them were members of Keturah's
family line.

5 Abraham left everything he owned
to Isaac. 6 But while he was still living,
he gave gifts to the sons of his concubines. Then he sent them away from
his son Isaac. He sent them to the land
of the east.

7 Abraham lived a total of 175 years. 8 He
took his last breath and died when he was
very old. He had lived a very long time.
Then he joined the members of his family
who had already died. 9 Abraham's sons
Isaac and Ishmael buried him. They put
his body in the cave of Machpelah near
Mamre. It was in the field of Ephron, the
son of Zohar the Hittite. 10 Abraham had
bought the field from the Hittites. He was
buried there with his wife Sarah. 11 After
Abraham died, God blessed his son Isaac.
At that time Isaac was living near Beer
Lahai Roi.

The Sons of Ishmael

12 Here is the story of the family line
of Abraham's son Ishmael. Hagar gave
birth to Ishmael by Abraham. Hagar
was Sarah's slave from Egypt.

13 Here are the names of the sons
of Ishmael. They are listed in the
order they were born.
Nebaioth was Ishmael's oldest son.
Then came Kedar, Adbeel, Mibsam,
14 Mishma, Dumah, Massa,
15 Hadad, Tema, Jetur,
Naphish and Kedemah.

16 All of them were Ishmael's sons.
They were rulers of 12 tribes. They
all lived in their own settlements
and camps.

17 Ishmael lived a total of 137 years.
Then he took his last breath and died.
He joined the members of his family
who had already died. 18 His children
settled in the area between Havilah
and Shur. It was near the eastern border of Egypt, as you go toward Ashur.
Ishmael's children weren't friendly toward any of the tribes related to them.

Jacob and Esau

19 Here is the story of the family line
of Abraham's son Isaac.

Abraham was the father of Isaac.
20 Isaac was 40 years old when he married Rebekah. She was the daughter of
Bethuel, the Aramean from Paddan
Aram. She was also the sister of Laban,
the Aramean.

21 Rebekah couldn't have children.
So Isaac prayed to the LORD for her.
And the LORD answered his prayer. His
wife Rebekah became pregnant. 22 The
babies struggled with each other inside
her. She said, "Why is this happening to
me?" So she went to ask the LORD what
she should do.

23 The LORD said to her,

"Two nations are in your body.
Two tribes that are now inside
you will be separated.
One nation will be stronger than
the other.
The older son will serve the
younger one."

24 The time came for Rebekah to have
her babies. There were twin boys in

her body. [25]The first one to come out was red. His whole body was covered with hair. So they named him Esau. [26]Then his brother came out. His hand was holding onto Esau's heel. So he was named Jacob. Isaac was 60 years old when Rebekah had them.

[27]The boys grew up. Esau became a skillful hunter. He liked the open country. But Jacob was content to stay at home among the tents. [28]Isaac liked the meat of wild animals. So Esau was his favorite son. But Rebekah's favorite was Jacob.

[29]One day Jacob was cooking some stew. Esau came in from the open country. He was very hungry. [30]He said to Jacob, "Quick! I'm very hungry! Let me have some of that red stew!" That's why he was also named Edom.

[31]Jacob replied, "First sell me the rights that belong to you as the oldest son in the family."

[32]"Look, I'm dying of hunger," Esau said. "What good are those rights to me?"

[33]But Jacob said, "First promise to sell me your rights." So Esau promised to do it. He sold Jacob all the rights that belonged to him as the oldest son.

[34]Then Jacob gave Esau some bread and some lentil stew. Esau ate and drank. Then he got up and left.

So Esau didn't value the rights that belonged to him as the oldest son.

Isaac and Abimelek

26 There was very little food in the land. The same thing had been true earlier, in Abraham's time. Isaac went to Abimelek in Gerar. Abimelek was the king of the Philistines. [2]The LORD appeared to Isaac and said, "Do not go down to Egypt. Live in the land where I tell you to live. [3]Stay there for a while. I will be with you and give you my blessing. I will give all these lands to you and your children after you. And I will keep my word that I gave to your father Abraham. [4]I will make your children after you as many as the stars in the sky. And I will give them all these lands. All nations on earth will be blessed because of your children. [5]I will do all these things because Abraham obeyed me. He did everything I required. He kept my commands, my rules and my instructions." [6]So Isaac stayed in Gerar.

[7]The men of that place asked him about his wife. He said, "She's my sister." He was afraid to say, "She's my wife." He thought, "The men of this place might kill me because of Rebekah. She's a beautiful woman."

[8]Isaac had been there a long time. One day Abimelek, the king of the Philistines, looked down from a window. He saw Isaac hugging and kissing his wife Rebekah. [9]So Abimelek sent for Isaac. He said, "She's really your wife, isn't she? Why did you say she was your sister?"

Isaac answered him, "I thought I might lose my life because of her."

[10]Then Abimelek said, "What have you done to us? What if one of the men slept with your wife? Then you would have made us guilty."

[11]So Abimelek gave orders to all the people. He said, "Anyone who harms this man or his wife will surely be put to death."

[12]Isaac planted crops in that land. That same year he gathered 100 times more than he planted. That was because the LORD blessed him. [13]Isaac became rich. His wealth continued to grow until he became very rich. [14]He had many flocks and herds and servants. Isaac had so much that the Philistines became jealous of him. [15]So they stopped up all the wells the servants of his father Abraham had dug. They filled them with dirt.

[16]Then Abimelek said to Isaac, "Move away from us. You have become too powerful for us."

[17]So Isaac moved away from there. He camped in the Valley of Gerar, where he made his home. [18]Isaac opened up the wells again. They had been dug in the time of his father Abraham. The Philistines had stopped them up after Abraham died. Isaac gave the wells the same names his father had given them.

[19]Isaac's servants dug wells in the valley. There they discovered fresh water. [20]But the people of Gerar who took care of their own herds argued with the people who took care of Isaac's herds. "The water is ours!" the people of Gerar said. So Isaac named the well Esek. That's because they argued with him. [21]Then Isaac's servants dug another well. They argued about that one too.

So he named it Sitnah. 22 Isaac moved
on from there and dug another well.
But no one argued about that one. So
he named it Rehoboth. He said, "Now
the LORD has given us room. Now we
will be successful in the land."
23 From there Isaac went up to Beersheba. 24 That night the LORD appeared
to him. He said, "I am the God of your
father Abraham. Do not be afraid. I am
with you. I will bless you. I will increase
the number of your children because of
my servant Abraham."
25 Isaac built an altar there and worshiped the LORD. There he set up his
tent. And there his servants dug a well.
26 During that time, Abimelek had
come to him from Gerar. His personal
adviser, Ahuzzath, had come with him.
So had his army commander, Phicol.
27 Isaac asked them, "Why have you
come to me? You were angry with me
and sent me away."
28 They answered, "We saw clearly
that the LORD was with you. So we said,
'There should be an agreement between
us and you.' We want to make a peace
treaty with you. 29 Give us your word
that you won't harm us. We didn't harm
you. We always treated you well. We
sent you away peacefully. And now the
LORD has blessed you."
30 Then Isaac had a feast prepared for
them. They ate and drank. 31 Early the
next morning the men made a treaty
with each other. Then Isaac sent the
men of Gerar on their way. And they
left peacefully.
32 That day Isaac's servants came to
him. They told him about the well they
had dug. They said, "We've found water!"
33 So he named it Shibah. To this day the
name of the town has been Beersheba.

Jacob Takes Esau's Blessing

34 When Esau was 40 years old, he got
married to Judith. She was the daughter
of Beeri the Hittite. Esau also married
Basemath. She was the daughter of
Elon the Hittite. 35 Isaac and Rebekah
became very upset because Esau had
married Hittite women.

27 Isaac had become old. His eyes
were so weak he couldn't see
anymore. One day he called for his
older son Esau. He said to him, "My son."
"Here I am," he answered.
2 Isaac said, "I'm an old man now. And
I don't know when I'll die. 3 Now then,
get your weapons. Get your bow and arrows. Go out to the open country. Hunt
some wild animals for me. 4 Prepare for
me the kind of tasty food I like. Bring
it to me to eat. Then I'll give you my
blessing before I die."
5 Rebekah was listening when Isaac
spoke to his son Esau. Esau left for the
open country. He went to hunt for a
wild animal and bring it back. 6 Then
Rebekah said to her son Jacob, "Look,
I heard your father speaking to your
brother Esau. 7 He said, 'Bring me a wild
animal. Prepare some tasty food for me
to eat. Then I'll give you my blessing
before I die. The LORD will be my witness.' " 8 Rebekah continued, "My son,
listen carefully. Do what I tell you. 9 Go
out to the flock. Bring me two of the
finest young goats. I will prepare tasty
food for your father. I'll make it just the
way he likes it. 10 I want you to take it to
your father to eat. Then he'll give you
his blessing before he dies."
11 Jacob said to his mother Rebekah,
"My brother Esau's body is covered with
hair. But my skin is smooth. 12 What if
my father touches me? He would know I
was trying to trick him. He would curse
me instead of giving me a blessing."
13 His mother said to him, "My son, let
the curse be on me. Just do what I say.
Go and get the goats for me."
14 So he went and got the goats. He
brought them to his mother. And she
prepared some tasty food. She made
it just the way his father liked it. 15 The
clothes of her older son Esau were in
her house. She took Esau's best clothes
and put them on her younger son Jacob.
16 She covered his hands with the skins of
the goats. She also covered the smooth
part of his neck with them. 17 Then she
handed to her son Jacob the tasty food
and the bread she had made.
18 He went to his father and said, "My
father."
"Yes, my son," Isaac answered. "Who
is it?"
19 Jacob said to his father, "I'm your
oldest son Esau. I've done as you told
me. Please sit up. Eat some of my wild
meat. Then give me your blessing."
20 Isaac asked his son, "How did you
find it so quickly, my son?"

"The LORD your God gave me success,"
he replied.
21 Then Isaac said to Jacob, "Come
near so I can touch you, my son. I want
to know whether you really are my
son Esau."
22 Jacob went close to his father. Isaac
touched him and said, "The voice is the
voice of Jacob. But the hands are the
hands of Esau." 23 Isaac didn't recognize
Jacob. Jacob's hands were covered with
hair like those of his brother Esau. So
Isaac blessed him. 24 "Are you really my
son Esau?" he asked.

"I am," Jacob replied.
25 Isaac said, "My son, bring me some
of your wild meat to eat. Then I'll give
you my blessing."

Jacob brought it to him. So Isaac
ate. Jacob also brought some wine.
And Isaac drank. 26 Then Jacob's father Isaac said to him, "Come here, my
son. Kiss me."
27 So Jacob went to him and kissed
him. When Isaac smelled the clothes, he
gave Jacob his blessing. He said,

"It really is the smell of my son.
It's like the smell of a field
that the LORD has blessed.
28 May God give you dew from
heaven.
May he give you the richness of
the earth.
May he give you plenty of grain
and fresh wine.
29 May nations serve you.
May they bow down to you.
Rule over your brothers.
May the sons of your mother bow
down to you.
May those who curse you be cursed.
And may those who bless you be
blessed."

30 When Isaac finished blessing him,
Jacob left his father. Just then his brother Esau came in from hunting. 31 He too
prepared some tasty food. He brought it
to his father. Then Esau said to him, "My
father, please sit up. Eat some of my
wild meat. Then give me your blessing."
32 His father Isaac asked him, "Who
are you?"

"I'm your son," he answered. "I'm
Esau, your oldest son."
33 Isaac began to shake all over. He
said, "Then who hunted a wild animal
and brought it to me? I ate it just before
you came. I gave him my blessing. And
he will certainly be blessed!"
34 Esau heard his father's words. Then
he yelled loudly and bitterly. He said
to his father, "Bless me! Bless me too,
my father!"
35 But Isaac said, "Your brother came
and tricked me. He took your blessing."
36 Esau said, "Isn't Jacob just the right
name for him? This is the second time
he has taken advantage of me. First,
he took my rights as the oldest son.
And now he's taken my blessing!" Then
Esau asked, "Haven't you saved any
blessing for me?"
37 Isaac answered Esau, "I've made
him ruler over you. I've made all his
relatives serve him. And I've provided
him with grain and fresh wine. So what
can I possibly do for you, my son?"
38 Esau said to his father, "Do you
have only one blessing, my father?
Bless me too, my father!" Then Esau
wept loudly.
39 His father Isaac answered him,

"You will live far away from the
fruit of the earth.
You will live far away from the
dew of heaven above.
40 You will live by using the sword.
And you will serve your brother.
But you will grow restless.
Then you will throw off the
heavy load
he has caused you to carry."

41 Esau was angry with Jacob. He was
angry because of the blessing his father
had given to Jacob. He said to himself,
"The days of sorrow over my father's
death are near. Then I'll kill my brother
Jacob."
42 Rebekah was told what her older
son Esau had said. So she sent for her
younger son Jacob. She said to him,
"Your brother Esau is planning to get
back at you by killing you. 43 Now then,
my son, do what I say. Run away at once
to my brother Laban in Harran. 44 Stay
with him until your brother's anger
calms down. 45 When he forgets what
you did to him, I'll let you know. Then
you can come back from there. Why
should I lose both of you in one day?"
46 Then Rebekah spoke to Isaac. She
said, "I'm sick of living because of Esau's

Hittite wives. Suppose Jacob also marries a Hittite woman. If he does, my life
won't be worth living."

28 So Isaac called for Jacob and
blessed him. Then he command-
ed him, "Don't get married to a Canaanite woman. 2 Go at once to Paddan Aram.
Go to the house of your mother's father
Bethuel. Find a wife for yourself there.
Take her from among the daughters
of your mother's brother Laban. 3 May
the Mighty God bless you. May he give
you children. May he make your family
larger until you become a community
of nations. 4 May he give you and your
children after you the blessing he gave
to Abraham. Then you can take over the
land where you now live as an outsider. It's the land God gave to Abraham."
5 Isaac sent Jacob on his way. Jacob went
to Paddan Aram. He went to Laban, the
son of Bethuel the Aramean. Laban was
Rebekah's brother. And Rebekah was the
mother of Jacob and Esau.

6 Esau found out that Isaac had
blessed Jacob and had sent him to
Paddan Aram. Isaac wanted him to get
a wife from there. Esau heard that when
Isaac blessed Jacob, he commanded him,
"Don't get married to a woman from
Canaan." 7 Esau also learned that Jacob
had obeyed his father and mother and
had gone to Paddan Aram. 8 Then Esau
realized how much his father Isaac disliked Canaanite women. 9 So he went to
Ishmael and married Mahalath. She was
the sister of Nebaioth and the daughter
of Abraham's son Ishmael. Esau added
her to the wives he already had.

Jacob Has a Dream at Bethel

10 Jacob left Beersheba and started
out for Harran. 11 He reached a certain
place and stopped for the night. The
sun had already set. He took one of
the stones there and placed it under his
head. Then he lay down to sleep. 12 In a
dream he saw a stairway standing on

the earth. Its top reached to heaven.
The angels of God were going up and
coming down on it. 13 The LORD stood
beside the stairway. He said, "I am the
LORD. I am the God of your grandfather
Abraham and the God of Isaac. I will
give you and your children after you
the land you are lying on. 14 They will
be like the dust of the earth that can't
be counted. They will spread out to the
west and to the east. They will spread
out to the north and to the south. All nations on earth will be blessed because of
you and your children after you. 15 I am
with you. I will watch over you everywhere you go. And I will bring you back
to this land. I will not leave you until I
have done what I have promised you."
16 Jacob woke up from his sleep. Then
he thought, "The LORD is surely in this
place. And I didn't even know it." 17 Jacob was afraid. He said, "How holy this
place is! This must be the house of God.
This is the gate of heaven."
18 Early the next morning Jacob took
the stone he had placed under his head.
He set it up as a sacred stone. And he
poured olive oil on top of it. 19 He named
that place Bethel. But the city used to
be called Luz.
20 Then Jacob made a promise. He
said, "May God be with me. May he
watch over me on this journey I'm taking. May he give me food to eat and
clothes to wear. 21 May he do as he has
promised so that I can return safely
to my father's home. Then you, LORD,
will be my God. 22 This stone I've set up
as a sacred stone will be God's house.
And I'll give you a tenth of everything
you give me."

Jacob Arrives in Paddan Aram

29 Then Jacob continued on his
journey. He came to the land
where the eastern tribes lived. 2 There
he saw a well in the open country. Three
flocks of sheep were lying near it. The

pointing us to JESUS: Jacob

When Isaac grew up and married, he and his wife had twin boys named Esau and Jacob. Esau was the older brother; he was strong and skilled as a hunter. Jacob was the younger brother; he enjoyed learning how to cook at home.

In those days, most of the family inheritance, or wealth, was usually passed down to the oldest son because he would need it to continue to care for the family like his father did. But in this family, God did something surprising. God told Isaac's wife, Rebekah, that he had chosen *Jacob* to carry on the family name and receive the family inheritance. While the rest of the people in that culture would have chosen Esau, God chose Jacob.

Many generations later, God's people would still be waiting for the promised Savior and King to arrive. And once again, God would do something surprising. While everyone expected a strong warrior, Jesus came humbly as a baby. While everyone would have looked for a king who was born in a royal palace or came from a famous family, Jesus was born to a mother and father no one had ever heard of. But even though Jesus wasn't the Savior and King the world would have chosen, he is the Savior and King we all need. Through his death and resurrection, Jesus brings us into his own family. He offers us his family name, makes us sons and daughters of God, and shares his inheritance with us.

flocks were given water from the well.
The stone over the opening of the well
was large. 3 All the flocks would gather there. The shepherds would roll the
stone away from the well's opening.
They would give water to the sheep.
Then they would put the stone back in
its place over the opening of the well.
4 Jacob asked the shepherds, "My
friends, where are you from?"
"We're from Harran," they replied.
5 He said to them, "Do you know Nahor's grandson Laban?"
"Yes, we know him," they answered.
6 Then Jacob asked them, "How is he?"
"He's fine," they said. "Here comes
his daughter Rachel with the sheep."
7 "Look," he said, "the sun is still high
in the sky. It's not time for the flocks
to be brought together. Give water to
the sheep and take them back to the
grasslands."
8 "We can't," they replied. "We have to
wait until all the flocks are brought together. The stone has to be rolled away
from the opening of the well. Then we'll
give water to the sheep."
9 He was still talking with them when
Rachel came with her father's sheep.
It was her job to take care of the flock.
10 Rachel was the daughter of Laban,
Jacob's uncle. When Jacob saw Rachel
with Laban's sheep, he went over to the
well. He rolled the stone away from the
opening. He gave water to his uncle's
sheep. 11 Jacob kissed Rachel. Then he
began to cry because he was so happy.
12 He had told Rachel he was a relative
of her father. He had also said he was
Rebekah's son. Rachel ran and told her
father what Jacob had said.
13 As soon as Laban heard the news
about his sister's son Jacob, he hurried
to meet him. Laban hugged Jacob and
kissed him. Then Laban brought him to
his home. There Jacob told him everything. 14 Then Laban said to him, "You
are my own flesh and blood."

Jacob Marries Leah and Rachel

Jacob stayed with Laban for a whole
month. 15 Then Laban said to him, "You
are one of my relatives. But is that any
reason for you to work for me for nothing? Tell me what your pay should be."
16 Laban had two daughters. The
name of the older one was Leah. And the
name of the younger one was Rachel.
17 Leah was plain, but Rachel was beautiful. She had a nice figure. 18 Jacob was
in love with Rachel. He said to Laban,
"I'll work for you for seven years so I can
marry your younger daughter Rachel."
19 Laban said, "It's better for me to
give her to you than to some other man.
Stay here with me." 20 So Jacob worked
for seven years so he could marry Rachel. But they seemed like only a few
days to him because he loved her so
much.
21 Then Jacob said to Laban, "Give me
my wife. I've completed my time. I want
to sleep with her."
22 So Laban brought all the people
of the place together and had a feast
prepared. 23 But when evening came, he
gave his daughter Leah to Jacob. And
Jacob slept with her. 24 Laban gave his
female servant Zilpah to his daughter
as her servant.
25 When Jacob woke up the next morning, there was Leah next to him! So he
said to Laban, "What have you done to
me? I worked for you so I could marry
Rachel, didn't I? Why did you trick me?"
26 Laban replied, "It isn't our practice here to give the younger daughter to be married before the older one.
27 Complete this daughter's wedding
week. Then we'll give you the younger
one also. But you will have to work for
another seven years."
28 So Jacob completed the week with
Leah. Then Laban gave him his daughter Rachel to be his wife. 29 Laban gave
his female servant Bilhah to his daughter Rachel as her servant. 30 Jacob slept
with Rachel also. He loved Rachel more
than he loved Leah. And he worked for
Laban for another seven years.

Jacob Becomes the Father of Many Children

31 The LORD saw that Jacob didn't love
Leah as much as he loved Rachel. So
he let Leah have children. But Rachel
wasn't able to have children. 32 Leah
became pregnant. She had a son. She
named him Reuben. She said, "The LORD
has seen me suffer. Surely my husband
will love me now."
33 She became pregnant again. She
had a son. Then she said, "The LORD
heard that Jacob doesn't love me very

much. That's why the LORD gave me this
one too." So she named him Simeon.
34 She became pregnant again. She
had a son. Then she said, "Now at last
my husband will value me. I have had
three sons by him." So the boy was
named Levi.
35 She became pregnant again. She
had a son. Then she said, "This time I'll
praise the LORD." So she named him Judah. Then she stopped having children.

30 Rachel saw that she wasn't having any children by Jacob. So she
became jealous of her sister. She said
to Jacob, "Give me children, or I'll die!"
2 Jacob became angry with her. He
said, "Do you think I'm God? He's the
one who has kept you from having
children."
3 Then she said, "Here's my servant
Bilhah. Sleep with her so that she can
have children for me. Then I too can
have a family through her."
4 So Rachel gave Jacob her servant
Bilhah as a wife. Jacob slept with her.
5 And Bilhah became pregnant. She had
a son by him. 6 Then Rachel said, "God
has stood up for my rights. He has listened to my prayer and given me a son."
So she named him Dan.
7 Rachel's servant Bilhah became
pregnant again. She had a second son
by Jacob. 8 Then Rachel said, "I've had
a great struggle with my sister. Now
I've won." So she named him Naphtali.
9 Leah saw that she had stopped having children. So she gave her servant
Zilpah to Jacob as a wife. 10 Leah's servant Zilpah had a son by Jacob. 11 Then
Leah said, "What good fortune!" So she
named him Gad.
12 Leah's servant Zilpah had a second
son by Jacob. 13 Then Leah said, "I'm so
happy! The women will call me happy."
So she named him Asher.
14 While the wheat harvest was being
gathered, Reuben went out into the
fields. He found some mandrake plants.
He brought them to his mother Leah.
Rachel said to Leah, "Please give me
some of your son's mandrakes."
15 But Leah said to her, "Isn't it enough
that you took my husband away? Are you
going to take my son's mandrakes too?"
Rachel said, "All right. Jacob can sleep
with you tonight if you give me your
son's mandrakes."
16 Jacob came in from the fields that
evening. Leah went out to meet him.
"You have to sleep with me tonight," she
said. "I've traded my son's mandrakes
for that time with you." So he slept with
her that night.
17 God listened to Leah. She became
pregnant and had a fifth son by Jacob.
18 Then Leah said, "God has rewarded me
because I gave my female servant to my
husband." So she named the boy Issachar.
19 Leah became pregnant again. She
had a sixth son by Jacob. 20 Then Leah
said, "God has given me a priceless gift.
This time my husband will treat me
with honor. I've had six sons by him."
So she named the boy Zebulun.
21 Some time later she had a daughter.
She named her Dinah.
22 Then God listened to Rachel. He
showed concern for her. He made it possible for her to have children. 23 She became pregnant and had a son. Then she
said, "God has taken away my shame."
24 She said, "May the LORD give me another son." So she named him Joseph.

Jacob Becomes the Owner of Large Flocks

25 After Rachel had Joseph, Jacob
spoke to Laban. He said, "Send me on
my way. I want to go back to my own
home and country. 26 Give me my wives
and children. I worked for you to get
them. So I'll be on my way. You know
how much work I've done for you."
27 But Laban said to him, "If you are
pleased with me, stay here. I've discovered that the LORD has blessed me
because of you." 28 He continued, "Name
your pay. I'll give it to you."
29 Jacob said to him, "You know how
hard I've worked for you. You know that
your livestock has done better under
my care. 30 You had only a little before
I came. But that little has become a lot.
The LORD has blessed you everywhere
I've been. But when can I do something
for my own family?"
31 "What should I give you?" Laban
asked.
"Don't give me anything," Jacob replied. "Just do one thing for me. Then
I'll go on taking care of your flocks
and watching over them. 32 Let me go
through all your flocks today. Let me
remove every speckled or spotted sheep.

Let me remove every dark-colored lamb. Let me remove every speckled or spotted goat. They will be my pay. 33 My honesty will be a witness about me in days to come. It will be a witness every time you check on what you have paid me. Suppose I have a goat that doesn't have speckles or spots. Or suppose I have a lamb that isn't dark colored. Then it will be considered stolen."

34 "I agree," said Laban. "Let's do what you have said." 35 That same day Laban removed all the male goats that had stripes or spots. He removed all the female goats that had speckles or spots. They were the ones that had white on them. He also removed all the dark-colored lambs. He had his sons take care of them. 36 Then he put a journey of three days between himself and Jacob. But Jacob continued to take care of the rest of Laban's flocks.

37 Jacob took freshly cut branches from poplar, almond and plane trees. He made white stripes on the branches by peeling off their bark. 38 Then he placed the peeled branches in all the stone tubs where the animals drank water. He placed them there so they would be right in front of the flocks when they came to drink. The flocks were ready to mate when they came to drink. 39 So they mated in front of the branches. And the flocks gave birth to striped, speckled or spotted little ones. 40 Jacob put the little ones of the flock to one side by themselves. But he made the older ones face the striped and dark-colored animals that belonged to Laban. In that way, he made separate flocks for himself. He didn't put them with Laban's animals. 41 Every time the stronger females were ready to mate, Jacob would place the branches in the stone tubs. He would place them in front of the animals so they would mate near the branches. 42 But if the animals were weak, he wouldn't place the branches there. So the weak animals went to Laban. And the strong ones went to Jacob. 43 That's how Jacob became very rich. He became the owner of large flocks. He also had many male and female servants. And he had many camels and donkeys.

Jacob Runs Away From Laban

31 Jacob heard what Laban's sons were saying. "Jacob has taken everything our father owned," they said. "He has gained all this wealth from what belonged to our father." 2 Jacob noticed that Laban's feelings toward him had changed.

3 Then the LORD spoke to Jacob. He said, "Go back to your father's land and to your relatives. I will be with you."

4 So Jacob sent word to Rachel and Leah. He told them to come out to the fields where his flocks were. 5 He said to them, "I see that your father's feelings toward me have changed. But the God of my father has been with me. 6 You know that I've worked for your father with all my strength. 7 But your father has cheated me. He has changed my pay ten times. In spite of everything that's happened, God hasn't let him harm me. 8 Sometimes Laban would say, 'The speckled ones will be your pay.' Then all the flocks had little ones with speckles. At other times he would say, 'The striped ones will be your pay.' Then all the flocks had little ones with stripes. 9 So God has taken away your father's livestock and given them to me.

10 "Once during the mating season I had a dream. In my dream I looked and saw male goats mating with the flock. The goats had stripes, speckles or spots. 11 The angel of God said to me in the dream, 'Jacob.' I answered, 'Here I am.' 12 He said, 'Look around you. See the male goats mating with the flock. All of them have stripes, speckles or spots. That's because I have seen everything that Laban has been doing to you. 13 I am the God of Bethel. That is where you poured olive oil on a sacred stone. There you made a promise to me. Now leave this land. Go back to your own land.'"

14 Rachel and Leah replied, "Do we still have any share of our father's property? 15 Doesn't our father think of us as outsiders? First he sold us. Now he has used up what he was paid for us. 16 All the wealth God took away from our father really belongs to us and our children. So do what God has told you to do."

17 Then Jacob put his children and wives on camels. 18 He drove all his livestock ahead of him. He also took with him everything he had acquired in

Paddan Aram. He left to go to his father
Isaac in the land of Canaan.
19 Laban had gone to clip the wool
from his sheep. While he was gone,
Rachel stole the statues of the family
gods that belonged to her father. 20 And
that's not all. Jacob tricked Laban, the
Aramean. He didn't tell him he was
running away. 21 So Jacob ran off with
everything he had. He crossed the Euphrates River. And he headed for the
hill country of Gilead.

Laban Chases Jacob

22 On the third day Laban was told
that Jacob had run away. 23 He took his
relatives with him and went after Jacob.
Seven days later he caught up with him
in the hill country of Gilead. 24 Then
God came to Laban, the Aramean, in
a dream at night. He said to him, "Be
careful. Do not say anything to Jacob,
whether it is good or bad."
25 Jacob had set up his tent in the hill
country of Gilead. That's where Laban
caught up with him. Laban and his relatives camped there too. 26 Laban said
to Jacob, "What have you done? You
have tricked me. You have taken my
daughters away like prisoners of war.
27 Why did you run away in secret and
trick me? Why didn't you tell me? Then
I could have sent you away happily.
We could have sung to the music of
tambourines and harps. 28 You didn't
even let me kiss my grandchildren and
my daughters goodbye. You have done
a foolish thing. 29 I have the power to
harm you. But last night the God of
your father spoke to me. He said, 'Be
careful. Do not say anything to Jacob,
whether it is good or bad.' 30 Now you
have run away. You longed to go back
to your father's home. But why did you
have to steal the statues of my gods?"
31 Jacob answered Laban, "I was
afraid. I thought you would take your
daughters away from me by force. 32 But
if you find anyone who has the statues of your gods, that person will not
remain alive. While our relatives are
watching, look for yourself. See if there's
anything of yours here with me. If you
find anything belonging to you, take it."
But Jacob didn't know that Rachel had
stolen the statues.
33 So Laban went into Jacob's tent
and Leah's tent. He went into the tent
of their two female servants. But he
didn't find anything. After he came out
of Leah's tent, he entered Rachel's tent.
34 Rachel was the one who had taken the
statues of Laban's family gods. She had
put them inside her camel's saddle. She
was sitting on them. Laban searched the
whole tent. But he didn't find anything.
35 Rachel said to her father, "I'm sorry,
sir. I can't get up for you right now. But
don't be angry with me. I'm having my
monthly period." So he searched everywhere but couldn't find the statues
of his gods.
36 Jacob was very angry with Laban.
"What is my crime?" he asked. "What
have I done to you that you hunt me
down like this? 37 You have searched
through all my things. What have you
found that belongs to your family? Put it
here in front of your relatives and mine.
Let them decide between the two of us.
38 "I've been with you for 20 years now.
The little ones of your sheep and goats
were not dead when they were born. I
haven't eaten rams from your flocks. 39 I
didn't bring you animals torn apart by
wild beasts. I made up for the loss myself. Also, you made me pay for anything
stolen by day or night. 40 And what was
my life like? The heat burned me in the
daytime. And it was so cold at night that
I froze. I couldn't sleep. 41 That's what it
was like for the 20 years I was living
with you. I worked for 14 years to marry your two daughters. I worked for six
years to get my share of your flocks.
You changed my pay ten times. 42 But
the God of my father was with me. He is
the God of Abraham and the God Isaac
worshiped. If he hadn't been with me,
you would surely have sent me away
without anything to show for all my
work. But God has seen my hard times.
He has seen all the work my hands have
done. So last night he warned you."
43 Laban answered Jacob, "The wom-
en are my daughters. The children are
my children. The flocks are my flocks.
Everything you see is mine. But what
can I do today about these daughters of
mine? What can I do about the children
they've had? 44 Come now. Let's make a
formal agreement, you and I. Let it be
a witness between us."

[45]So Jacob set up a stone as a way to
remember. [46]He said to his relatives,
"Get some stones." So they took stones
and put them in a pile. And they ate
there by it. [47]Laban named the pile of
stones Jegar Sahadutha. Jacob named
it Galeed.
[48]Laban said, "This pile of stones
is a witness between you and me today." That's why it was named Galeed.
[49]It was also called Mizpah. That's because Laban said, "May the LORD keep
watch between you and me when we
are away from each other. [50]Don't treat
my daughters badly. Don't get married
to any women besides my daughters.
There isn't anyone here to see what
we're doing. But remember that God is
a witness between you and me."
[51]Laban also said to Jacob, "Here is
this pile of stones. And here is this stone
I've set up. I've set them up between you
and me. [52]This pile is a witness. And this
stone is a witness. They are witnesses
that I won't go past this pile to harm you.
And they are witnesses that you won't
go past this pile and this stone to harm
me. [53]The God of Abraham and Nahor
is also the God of their father. May their
God decide which of us is right."
So Jacob made a promise using the
name of the God his father Isaac worshiped. [54]He offered a sacrifice there
in the hill country. And he invited his
relatives to a meal. After they had eat-
en, they spent the night there.
[55]Early the next morning Laban
kissed his grandchildren and his daughters. He gave them his blessing. Then he
left and returned home.

Jacob Gets Ready to Meet Esau

32 Jacob also went on his way.
The angels of God met him.
[2]Jacob saw them. He said, "This is the
army of God!" So he named that place
Mahanaim.
[3]Jacob sent messengers ahead of him
to his brother Esau. Esau lived in the
land of Seir. It was also called the country of Edom. [4]Jacob told the messengers
what to do. He said, "Here's what you
must tell my master Esau. 'Your servant Jacob says, "I've been staying with
Laban. I've remained there until now.
[5]I have cattle and donkeys and sheep
and goats. I also have male and female
servants. Now I'm sending this message
to you. I hope I can please you." ' "
[6]The messengers came back to Jacob.
They said, "We went to your brother
Esau. He's coming now to meet you. He
has 400 men with him."
[7]Jacob was very worried and afraid.
So he separated the people with him
into two groups. He also separated
the flocks and herds and camels. [8]He
thought, "Esau might come and attack
one group. If he does, the group that's
left can escape."
[9]Then Jacob prayed, "You are the
God of my grandfather Abraham. You
are the God of my father Isaac. LORD,
you are the one who said to me, 'Go
back to your country and your relatives.
Then I will give you success.' [10]You have
been very kind and faithful to me. But
I'm not worthy of any of this. When I
crossed this Jordan River, all I had was
my walking stick. But now I've become
two camps. [11]Please save me from the
hand of my brother Esau. I'm afraid
he'll come and attack me and the mothers with their children. [12]But you have
said, 'I will surely give you success. I
will make your children as many as the
grains of sand on the seashore. People
will not be able to count them.' "
[13]Jacob spent the night there. He
chose a gift for his brother Esau from
what he had with him. [14]He chose 200
female goats and 20 male goats. He
chose 200 female sheep and 20 male
sheep. [15]He chose 30 female camels
with their little ones. He chose 40 cows
and ten bulls. And he chose 20 female
donkeys and ten male donkeys. [16]He
put each herd by itself. Then he put his
servants in charge of them. He said to
his servants, "Go on ahead of me. Keep
some space between the herds."
[17]Jacob spoke to his servant who was
leading the way. He said, "My brother
Esau will meet you. He'll ask, 'Who is
your master? Where are you going? And
who owns all these animals in front of
you?' [18]Then say to Esau, 'They belong
to your servant Jacob. They are a gift
to you from him. And Jacob is coming
behind us.' "
[19]He also spoke to the second and
third servants. He told them and all
the others who followed the herds what
to do. He said, "Say the same thing to

Esau when you meet him. 20 Make sure you say, 'Your servant Jacob is coming behind us.'" Jacob was thinking, "I'll make peace with him with these gifts I'm sending on ahead. When I see him later, maybe he'll welcome me." 21 So Jacob's gifts went on ahead of him. But he himself spent the night in the camp.

Jacob Wrestles With God

22 That night Jacob got up. He took his two wives, his two female servants and his 11 sons and sent them across the Jabbok River. 23 After they had crossed the stream, he sent over everything he owned. 24 So Jacob was left alone. A man wrestled with him until morning. 25 The man saw that he couldn't win. So he touched the inside of Jacob's hip. As Jacob wrestled with the man, Jacob's hip was twisted. 26 Then the man said, "Let me go. It is morning."

But Jacob replied, "I won't let you go unless you bless me."

27 The man asked him, "What is your name?"

"Jacob," he answered.

28 Then the man said, "Your name will not be Jacob anymore. Instead, it will be Israel. You have wrestled with God and with people. And you have won."

29 Jacob said, "Please tell me your name."

But he replied, "Why do you want to know my name?" Then he blessed Jacob there.

30 So Jacob named the place Peniel. He said, "I saw God face to face. But I'm still alive!"

31 The sun rose above Jacob as he passed by Peniel. He was limping because of his hip. 32 That's why the Israelites don't eat the meat attached to the inside of an animal's hip. They don't eat it to this day. It's because the inside of Jacob's hip was touched.

Jacob Meets Esau

33 Jacob looked and saw Esau coming with his 400 men! So Jacob separated the children. He put them with Leah, Rachel and the two female servants. 2 He put the servants and their children in front. He put Leah and her children next. And he put Rachel and Joseph last. 3 He himself went on ahead. As he came near his brother, he bowed down to the ground seven times.

4 But Esau ran to meet Jacob. He hugged him and threw his arms around his neck. He kissed him, and they cried for joy. 5 Then Esau looked around and saw the women and children. "Who are these people with you?" he asked.

Jacob answered, "They are the children God has so kindly given to me."

6 Then the female servants and their children came near and bowed down. 7 Next, Leah and her children came and bowed down. Last of all came Joseph and Rachel. They bowed down too.

8 Esau asked, "Why did you send all those herds I saw?"

"I hoped I could do something to please you," Jacob replied.

9 But Esau said, "I already have plenty, my brother. Keep what you have for yourself."

10 "No, please!" said Jacob. "If I've pleased you, accept this gift from me. Seeing your face is like seeing the face of God. You have welcomed me so kindly. 11 Please accept the present that was brought to you. God has given me so much. I have everything I need." Jacob wouldn't give in. So Esau accepted it.

12 Then Esau said, "Let's be on our way. I'll go with you."

13 But Jacob said to him, "You know that the children are young. You also know that I have to take care of the cows and female sheep that are feeding their little ones. If the animals are driven hard for just one day, all of them will die. 14 So you go on ahead of me. I'll move along only as fast as the flocks and herds and the children can go. I'll go slowly until I come to you in Seir."

15 Esau said, "Then let me leave some of my men with you."

"Why do that?" Jacob asked. "I just hope I've pleased you."

16 So that day Esau started on his way back to Seir. 17 But Jacob went to Sukkoth. There he built a place for himself. He also made shelters for his livestock. That's why the place is named Sukkoth.

18 After Jacob came from Paddan Aram, he arrived safely at the city of Shechem in Canaan. He camped where he could see the city. 19 For 100 pieces of silver he bought a piece of land. He got it from Hamor's sons. Hamor was the father of Shechem. Jacob set up his tent on that piece of land. 20 He also set up an altar there. He named it El Elohe Israel.

Simeon and Levi Kill the Men of Shechem

34 Dinah was the daughter Leah
had by Jacob. Dinah went out
to visit the women of the land. [2] Hamor,
the Hivite, was the ruler of that area.
When his son Shechem saw Dinah, he
took her and raped her. [3] Then he longed
for Jacob's daughter Dinah. He fell in
love with her and spoke tenderly to her.
[4] Shechem said to his father Hamor, "Get
me that young woman. I want her to
be my wife."
[5] Jacob heard that his daughter Dinah had been raped. His sons were in
the fields with his livestock. So he did
nothing about it until they came home.
[6] Then Shechem's father Hamor went
out to talk with Jacob. [7] Jacob's sons had
come in from the fields. They came as
soon as they heard what had happened.
They were shocked and very angry.
Shechem had done a very terrible thing.
He had forced Jacob's daughter to have
sex with him. He had done something
that should never be done in Israel.
[8] But Hamor said to Jacob and his
sons, "My son Shechem wants your
daughter. Please give her to him to be
his wife. [9] Let your people and ours get
married to each other. Give us your
daughters as our wives. You can have
our daughters as your wives. [10] You can
live among us. Here is the land. Live in
it. Trade in it. Buy property in it."
[11] Then Shechem spoke to Dinah's father and brothers. He said, "I want to
please you. I'll give you anything you
ask for. [12] Make the price for the bride as
high as you want to. I'll pay you whatever you ask. Just give me the young
woman. I want to marry her."
[13] Their sister Dinah had been raped.
So Jacob's sons lied to Shechem and his
father Hamor. [14] They said to them, "We
can't do it. We can't give our sister to a man
who isn't circumcised. That would bring
shame on us. [15] We'll agree, but only on one
condition. You will have to become like us.
You will have to circumcise all your males.
[16] Then we'll give you our daughters as
your wives. And we'll take your daughters
as our wives. We'll live among you and
become one big family with you. [17] But if
you won't agree to be circumcised, then
we'll take our sister and go."
[18] Their offer seemed good to Hamor
and his son Shechem. [19] The young man
was the most honored of all his father's
family. He didn't lose any time in doing
what Dinah's father and brothers had
said, because he was delighted with
Jacob's daughter. [20] Hamor and his son
Shechem went to the city gate. They
spoke to the other men there. [21] "These
men are friendly toward us," they said.
"Let them live in our land. Let them

My GOD IS...

ALL-POWERFUL

God is not just very powerful or even the most powerful. *All* power belongs to him. Nothing is too difficult for him (see Jeremiah 32:17). There is nothing he can't handle. God created the world and keeps the world going each day with his limitless power.

Do you know what else is awesome about God? He does everything out of love. He wants what is best for us, so he uses his power to strengthen us and help us.

Knowing that God is all-powerful and cares for the needs of all creatures means we can trust him to care for us, watch over us, and provide for all our needs.

trade in it. The land has plenty of room for them. We can marry their daughters. And they can marry ours. 22 But they will agree to live with us as one big family only on one condition. All our males must be circumcised, just as they are. 23 Won't their livestock and their property belong to us? Won't all their animals become ours? So let's say yes to them. Then they'll live among us."

24 All the men who went out through the city gate agreed with Hamor and his son Shechem. So every male in the city was circumcised.

25 Three days later, all of them were still in pain. Then Simeon and Levi took their swords. They were Jacob's sons and Dinah's brothers. They attacked the city when the people didn't expect it. They killed every male. 26 They also used their swords to kill Hamor and his son Shechem. Then they took Dinah from Shechem's house and left. 27 Jacob's other sons found the dead bodies. They robbed the city where their sister had been raped. 28 They took the flocks and herds and donkeys. They took everything in the city and in the fields. 29 They carried everything away. And they took all the women and children. They took away everything in the houses.

30 Then Jacob said to Simeon and Levi, "You have brought trouble on me. Now I'm like a very bad smell to the Canaanites and Perizzites who live in this land. There aren't many of us. They may join together against me and attack me. Then I and my family will be destroyed."

31 But they replied, "Should Shechem have treated our sister like a prostitute?"

Jacob Returns to Bethel

35 Then God said to Jacob, "Go up to Bethel and live there. Build an altar there to honor me. That's where I appeared to you when you were running away from your brother Esau."

2 So Jacob spoke to his family and to everyone with him. He said, "Get rid of the statues of false gods you have with you. Make yourselves pure by washing and changing your clothes. 3 Come, let's go up to Bethel. There I'll build an altar to honor God. He answered me when I was in trouble. He's been with me everywhere I've gone." 4 So they gave Jacob all the statues of false gods they had. They also gave him their earrings. Jacob buried those things under the oak tree at Shechem. 5 Then Jacob and everyone with him started out. The terror of God fell on the towns all around them. So no one chased them.

6 Jacob and all the people with him came to Luz. Luz is also called Bethel. It's in the land of Canaan. 7 Jacob built an altar at Luz. He named the place El Bethel. There God made himself known to Jacob when he was running away from his brother.

8 Rebekah's attendant Deborah died. They buried her body under the oak tree outside Bethel. So it was called Allon Bakuth.

9 After Jacob returned from Paddan Aram, God appeared to him again. And God blessed him. 10 God said to him, "Your name is Jacob. But you will not be called Jacob anymore. Your name will be Israel." So he named him Israel.

11 God said to him, "I am the Mighty God. Have children so that there will be many of you. You will become the father of a nation and a community of nations. Your later family will include kings. 12 I am giving you the land I gave to Abraham and Isaac. I will also give it to your children after you." 13 Then God left him at the place where he had talked with him.

14 Jacob set up a sacred stone at the place where God had talked with him. He poured out a drink offering on it. He also poured olive oil on it. 15 Jacob named the place Bethel. That's where God had talked with him.

Rachel and Isaac Die

16 They moved on from Bethel. Ephrath wasn't very far away when Rachel began to have a baby. She was having a very hard time of it. 17 The woman who helped her saw that she was having problems. So she said to Rachel, "Don't be afraid. You have another son." 18 But Rachel was dying. As she took her last breath, she named her son Ben-Oni. But his father named him Benjamin.

19 So Rachel died. She was buried beside the road to Ephrath. Ephrath was also called Bethlehem. 20 Jacob set up

a stone marker over her tomb. To this
day, the stone marks the place where
Rachel was buried.
21 Israel moved on again. He set up
his tent beyond Migdal Eder. 22 While
Israel was living in that area, Reuben
went in and slept with Bilhah. She was
the concubine of Reuben's father. And
Israel heard about it.

Here are the 12 sons Jacob had.

23 Leah was the mother of
Reuben, Jacob's oldest son.
Her other sons were Simeon,
Levi, Judah, Issachar and
Zebulun.
24 The sons of Rachel were
Joseph and Benjamin.
25 The sons of Rachel's female servant
Bilhah were
Dan and Naphtali.
26 The sons of Leah's female servant
Zilpah were
Gad and Asher.

These were Jacob's sons. They were
born in Paddan Aram.

27 Jacob came home to his father Isaac
in Mamre. Mamre is near Kiriath Arba,
where Abraham and Isaac had stayed.
The place is also called Hebron. 28 Isaac
lived 180 years. 29 Then he took his last
breath and died. He was very old when
he joined the members of his family
who had already died. His sons Esau
and Jacob buried him.

The Family Line of Esau

36 Here is the story of the family line of Esau. Esau was also
called Edom.

2 Esau got his wives from among the
women of Canaan. He married Adah,
the daughter of Elon the Hittite. He also
married Oholibamah, the daughter of
Anah and the granddaughter of Zibeon
the Hivite. 3 And he married Basemath,
the daughter of Ishmael and the sister
of Nebaioth.
4 Adah had Eliphaz by Esau. Basemath had Reuel. 5 Oholibamah had
Jeush, Jalam and Korah. All of them
were Esau's sons. They were born in
Canaan.
6 Esau moved to a land far away from
his brother Jacob. Esau took with him
his wives, his sons and daughters, and
all the people who lived with him. He
also took his livestock and all his other
animals. He took everything he had
acquired in Canaan. 7 Jacob and Esau
owned so much that they couldn't remain together. There wasn't enough
land for both of them. They had too
much livestock. 8 So Esau made his
home in the hill country of Seir. Esau
was also called Edom.

9 Here is the story of the family
line of Esau. He's the father of the
people of Edom. They live in the
hill country of Seir.

10 Here are the names of Esau's sons.
They are Eliphaz, the son of
Esau's wife Adah, and Reuel, the
son of Esau's wife Basemath.
11 The sons of Eliphaz were
Teman, Omar, Zepho, Gatam and
Kenaz. 12 Esau's son Eliphaz also
had a concubine named Timna.
She had Amalek by Eliphaz.
They were grandsons of Esau's
wife Adah.
13 The sons of Reuel were
Nahath, Zerah, Shammah and
Mizzah. They were grandsons
of Esau's wife Basemath.
14 Esau's wife Oholibamah was
the daughter of Anah and the
granddaughter of Zibeon.
She had Jeush, Jalam and Korah
by Esau.

15 Here are the chiefs among Esau's
sons.
Eliphaz was Esau's oldest son. The
sons of Eliphaz were
Chiefs Teman, Omar, Zepho,
Kenaz, 16 Korah, Gatam and
Amalek. They were the chiefs in
Edom who were sons of Eliphaz.
They were Adah's grandsons.
17 The sons of Esau's son Reuel were
Chiefs Nahath, Zerah, Shammah
and Mizzah. They were the
chiefs in Edom who were sons
of Reuel. They were grandsons
of Esau's wife Basemath.
18 The sons of Esau's wife Oholibamah
were
Chiefs Jeush, Jalam and Korah.
They were the chiefs who were
sons of Esau's wife Oholibamah.
She was Anah's daughter.

19 That was the family line of Esau. And these were the chiefs. Esau was also called Edom.

20 Seir, the Horite, had sons living in the same area.
They were Lotan, Shobal, Zibeon, Anah, 21 Dishon, Ezer and Dishan. These sons of Seir in Edom were Horite chiefs.
22 The sons of Lotan were
Hori and Homam. Timna was Lotan's sister.
23 The sons of Shobal were
Alvan, Manahath, Ebal, Shepho and Onam.
24 The sons of Zibeon were
Aiah and Anah. He was the Anah who discovered the hot springs of water in the desert. He found them while he was taking care of the donkeys that belonged to his father Zibeon.
25 The children of Anah were
Dishon and Oholibamah. Oholibamah was the daughter of Anah.
26 The sons of Dishon were
Hemdan, Eshban, Ithran and Keran.
27 The sons of Ezer were
Bilhan, Zaavan and Akan.
28 The sons of Dishan were
Uz and Aran.
29 The Horite chiefs were
Lotan, Shobal, Zibeon, Anah,
30 Dishon, Ezer and Dishan.
They were the Horite chiefs in the land of Seir. They are listed tribe by tribe.

The Rulers of Edom

31 Before Israel had a king, there were kings who ruled in Edom.
32 Bela became the king of Edom. Bela was the son of Beor. Bela's city was called Dinhabah.
33 When Bela died, Jobab became the next king. Jobab was the son of Zerah from Bozrah.
34 When Jobab died, Husham became the next king. Husham was from the land of the Temanites.
35 When Husham died, Hadad became the next king. Hadad was the son of Bedad. Hadad had won the battle over Midian in the country of Moab. Hadad's city was called Avith.
36 When Hadad died, Samlah became the next king. Samlah was from Masrekah.
37 When Samlah died, Shaul became the next king. Shaul was from Rehoboth on the river.
38 When Shaul died, Baal-Hanan became the next king. Baal-Hanan was the son of Akbor.
39 When Baal-Hanan died, Hadad became the next king. Hadad's city was called Pau. His wife's name was Mehetabel. She was Matred's daughter. Matred was the daughter of Me-Zahab.

40 Here are the chiefs in the family line of Esau. They are listed by name as chiefs in charge of their tribes and territories. They are
Timna, Alvah, Jetheth,
41 Oholibamah, Elah, Pinon,
42 Kenaz, Teman, Mibzar,
43 Magdiel and Iram.
They were the chiefs of Edom. They ruled over their settlements in the land where they lived.

That's the end of the story of the family line of Esau. He was the father of the people of Edom.

Joseph Has Two Dreams

37 Jacob lived in the land of Canaan. It's the land where his father had stayed.

2 Here is the story of the family line of Jacob.

Joseph was a young man. He was 17 years old. He was taking care of the flocks with some of his brothers. They were the sons of Bilhah and the sons of Zilpah, the wives of his father Jacob. Joseph brought their father a bad report about his brothers.
3 Israel loved Joseph more than any of his other sons. That's because Joseph had been born to him when he was old. Israel made him a beautiful robe. 4 Jo-
seph's brothers saw that their father loved him more than any of them. So they hated Joseph. They couldn't even speak one kind word to him.
5 Joseph had a dream. When he told it to his brothers, they hated him even

more. 6 He said to them, "Listen to the
dream I had. 7 We were tying up bundles
of grain out in the field. Suddenly my
bundle stood up straight. Your bundles
gathered around my bundle and bowed
down to it."
8 His brothers said to him, "Do you
plan to be king over us? Will you really
rule over us?" So they hated him even
more because of his dream. They didn't
like what he had said.
9 Then Joseph had another dream.
He told it to his brothers. "Listen," he
said. "I had another dream. This time
the sun and moon and 11 stars were
bowing down to me."
10 He told his father as well as his brothers. Then his father rebuked him. He said,
"What about this dream you had? Will
your mother and I and your brothers
really do that? Will we really come and
bow down to the ground in front of you?"
11 His brothers were jealous of him. But his
father kept the dreams in mind.

Joseph Is Sold by His Brothers

12 Joseph's brothers had gone to
take care of their father's flocks near
Shechem. 13 Israel said to Joseph, "As
you know, your brothers are taking care
of the flocks near Shechem. Come. I'm
going to send you to them."
"All right," Joseph replied.
14 So Israel said to him, "Go to your
brothers. See how they are doing. Also
see how the flocks are doing. Then come
back and tell me." So he sent him away
from the Hebron Valley.
Joseph arrived at Shechem. 15 A man
found him wandering around in the

fields. He asked Joseph, "What are you looking for?"
16 He replied, "I'm looking for my brothers. Can you tell me where they are taking care of their flocks?"
17 "They've moved on from here," the man answered. "I heard them say, 'Let's go to Dothan.'"

So Joseph went to look for his brothers. He found them near Dothan.
18 But they saw him a long way off. Before he reached them, they made plans to kill him.
19 "Here comes that dreamer!" they said to one another.
20 "Come. Let's kill him. Let's throw him into one of these empty wells. Let's say that a wild animal ate him up. Then we'll see whether his dreams will come true."
21 Reuben heard them talking. He tried to save Joseph from them. "Let's not take his life," he said.
22 "Don't spill any of his blood. Throw him into this empty well here in the desert. But don't harm him yourselves." Reuben said that to save Joseph from them. He was hoping he could take him back to his father.
23 When Joseph came to his brothers, he was wearing his beautiful robe. They took it away from him.
24 And they threw him into the well. The well was empty. There wasn't any water in it.
25 Then they sat down to eat their meal. As they did, they saw some Ishmaelite traders coming from Gilead. Their camels were loaded with spices, lotion and myrrh. They were on their way to take them down to Egypt.

pointing us to JESUS: Joseph

Joseph was one of Jacob's 12 sons. Joseph's brothers were jealous of the special treatment their dad gave Joseph. So they decided to sell Joseph into slavery for 20 pieces of silver.

While Joseph was a slave in Egypt, he was blamed for something he didn't do. Even though the story of what happened wasn't true, Joseph went to prison. But while he was in prison, God was preparing Joseph to be a part of his plan.

One day, Pharaoh started having strange dreams. He didn't know what they meant. One of Pharaoh's servants remembered that Joseph could explain the meaning of dreams. The servant went and got Joseph out of prison and brought him to Pharaoh. Joseph told Pharaoh that a huge famine was coming to the land of Egypt and there wouldn't be enough food. Pharaoh was amazed by Joseph's wisdom and skill, so he made Joseph the second-highest ruler in Egypt!

When the famine came, everyone was hungry, including Joseph's brothers. On one of their trips from the land of Canaan to Egypt to buy grain, they found out that Joseph had become a leader in Egypt. They were afraid that Joseph would treat them unkindly, just as they had treated him. But Joseph forgave them and gave them plenty of grain and food for their journey home.

Joseph's story points God's people to the coming Savior, Jesus. He would be treated unkindly, sold for 30 pieces of silver, and nailed to a cross because of the sins of others. But he, too, would show grace to all who ask him for forgiveness.

26 Judah said to his brothers, "What will we gain if we kill our brother and try to cover up what we've done? 27 Come. Let's sell him to these traders. Let's not harm him ourselves. After all, he's our brother. He's our own flesh and blood." Judah's brothers agreed with him.

28 The traders from Midian came by. Joseph's brothers pulled him up out of the well. They sold him to the Ishmaelite traders for eight ounces of silver. Then the traders took him to Egypt.

29 Later, Reuben came back to the empty well. He saw that Joseph wasn't there. He was so upset that he tore his clothes. 30 He went back to his brothers and said, "The boy isn't there! Now what should I do?"

31 Then they got Joseph's beautiful robe. They killed a goat and dipped the robe in the blood. 32 They took the robe back to their father. They said, "We found this. Take a look at it. See if it's your son's robe."

33 Jacob recognized it. He said, "It's my son's robe! A wild animal has eaten him up. Joseph must have been torn to pieces."

34 Jacob tore his clothes. He put on the rough clothing people wear when they're sad. Then he mourned for his son many days. 35 All Jacob's other sons and daughters came to comfort him. But they weren't able to. He said, "I will continue to mourn until I go down into the grave to be with my son." So Joseph's father mourned for him.

36 But the traders from Midian sold Joseph to Potiphar in Egypt. Potiphar was one of Pharaoh's officials. He was the captain of the palace guard.

Judah and Tamar

38 At that time, Judah left his brothers. He went down to stay with a man named Hirah from the town of Adullam. 2 There Judah met the daughter of a man from Canaan. His name was Shua. Judah married her and slept with her. 3 She became pregnant and had a son. They named him Er. 4 She became pregnant again and had another son. She named him Onan. 5 She had still another son. She named him Shelah. He was born at Kezib.

6 Judah got a wife for his oldest son Er. Her name was Tamar. 7 But Judah's oldest son Er was evil in the LORD's eyes. So the LORD put him to death.

8 Then Judah said to Onan, "Sleep with your brother's wife. After all, you are her brother-in-law. So carry out your duty to her. Provide children for your brother." 9 But Onan knew that the children wouldn't belong to him. So every time he slept with his brother's wife, he spilled his semen on the ground. He did it so he wouldn't provide children for his brother. 10 What he did was evil in the LORD's eyes. So the LORD put him to death also.

11 Then Judah spoke to his daughter-in-law Tamar. He said, "Live as a widow in your father's home. Wait there until my son Shelah grows up." Judah was thinking, "Shelah might die too, just like his brothers." So Tamar went to live in her father's home.

12 After a long time Judah's wife died. She was the daughter of Shua. When Judah got over his sadness, he went up to Timnah. His friend Hirah from Adullam went with him. Men were clipping the wool from Judah's sheep at Timnah.

13 Tamar was told, "Your father-in-law is on his way to Timnah to clip the wool from his sheep." 14 So she took off her widow's clothes. She covered her face with a veil so people wouldn't know who she was. Then she sat down at the entrance to Enaim. Enaim is on the road to Timnah. Tamar knew that Shelah had grown up. But she hadn't been given to him as his wife.

15 Judah saw her. He thought she was a prostitute because she had covered her face with a veil. 16 He didn't realize that she was his daughter-in-law. He went over to her by the side of the road. He said, "Come. Let me sleep with you."

"What will you give me to sleep with you?" she asked.

17 "I'll send you a young goat from my flock," he said.

"Will you give me something that belongs to you?" she asked. "I'll keep it until you send the goat."

18 He said, "What should I give you?"

"Give me your official seal and the string that it hangs from," she answered. "And give me your walking stick." So he gave them to her. Then he slept with her. And she became pregnant by him. 19 After she left, she took off her veil. She put on her widow's clothes again.

20 Judah sent his friend Hirah with the young goat he had promised. He wanted to get back what he had given to the woman. But his friend Hirah couldn't find her. 21 He asked the men who lived at Enaim, "Where's the temple prostitute? She used to sit beside the road here."

"There hasn't been any temple prostitute here," they said.

22 So Hirah went back to Judah. He said, "I couldn't find her. Besides, the men who lived there didn't know anything about her. They said, 'There hasn't been any temple prostitute here.' "

23 Then Judah said, "Let her keep what she has. I don't want people making fun of us. After all, I did send her this young goat. We can't help it if you couldn't find her."

24 About three months later people brought word to Judah. They said, "Your daughter-in-law Tamar is guilty of being a prostitute. Now she's pregnant."

Judah said, "Bring her out! Have her burned to death!"

25 As Tamar was being brought out, she sent a message to her father-in-law. She said, "I am pregnant by the man who owns these." She continued, "Do you recognize this seal and string and walking stick? Do you know who they belong to?"

26 Judah recognized them. He said, "She's a better person than I am. I should have given her to my son Shelah, but I didn't." Judah never slept with Tamar again.

27 The time came for Tamar to have her baby. There were twin boys inside her. 28 As the babies were being born, one of them stuck out his hand. So the woman helping Tamar took a bright red thread. The woman tied it on the baby's wrist. She said, "This one came out first." 29 But he pulled his hand back, and his brother came out first instead. She said, "Just look at how you have forced your way out!" So he was called Perez. 30 Then his brother, who had the red thread on his wrist, came out. So he was named Zerah.

Joseph and the Wife of Potiphar

39 Joseph had been taken down to Egypt. An Egyptian named Potiphar had bought him from the Ishmaelite traders who had taken him there. Potiphar was one of Pharaoh's officials. He was the captain of the palace guard.

2 The LORD was with Joseph. He gave him great success. Joseph lived in Potiphar's house. 3 Joseph's master saw that the LORD was with him. He saw that the LORD made Joseph successful in everything he did. 4 So Potiphar was pleased with Joseph and made him his attendant. He put Joseph in charge of his house. He trusted Joseph to take care of everything he owned. 5 From that time on, the LORD blessed Potiphar's family and servants because of Joseph. He blessed everything Potiphar had in his house and field. 6 So Joseph took good care of everything Potiphar owned. With Joseph in charge, Potiphar didn't have to worry about anything except the food he ate.

Joseph was strong and handsome. 7 After a while, his master's wife noticed Joseph. She said to him, "Come to bed with me!"

8 But he refused. "My master has put me in charge," he told her. "Now he doesn't have to worry about anything in the house. He trusts me to take care of everything he owns. 9 No one in this house is in a higher position than I am. My master hasn't held anything back from me, except you. You are his wife. So how could I do an evil thing like that? How could I sin against God?" 10 She spoke to Joseph day after day. But he told her he wouldn't go to bed with her. He didn't even want to be with her.

11 One day Joseph went into the house to take care of his duties. None of the family servants was inside. 12 Potiphar's wife grabbed him by his coat. "Come to bed with me!" she said. But he left his coat in her hand. And he ran out of the house.

13 She saw that he had left his coat in her hand and had run out of the house. 14 So she called her servants. "Look," she said to them, "this Hebrew slave has been brought here to make fun of us! He came in here to force me to have sex with him. But I screamed for help. 15 He heard my scream. So he left his coat beside me and ran out of the house."

16 She kept Joseph's coat with her until Potiphar came home. 17 Then she told him her story. She said, "That Hebrew slave you brought us came to me to rape me. 18 But I screamed for help. So he left his coat beside me and ran out of the house."

19 Potiphar's wife told him, "That's
how your slave treated me." When Joseph's master heard her story, he became very angry. 20 So he put Joseph
in prison. It was the place where the
king's prisoners were kept.
While Joseph was there in the prison,
21 the LORD was with him. He was kind to
him. So the man running the prison was
pleased with Joseph. 22 He put Joseph
in charge of all the prisoners. He made
him responsible for everything done
there. 23 The man who ran the prison
didn't pay attention to anything in
Joseph's care. That's because the LORD
was with Joseph. He gave Joseph success
in everything he did.

The Wine Taster and the Baker

40 Some time later, the Egyptian
king's baker and wine taster
did something their master didn't like.
2 So Pharaoh became angry with his
two officials, the chief wine taster and
the chief baker. 3 He put them in prison in the house of the captain of the
palace guard. It was the same prison
where Joseph was kept. 4 The captain
put Joseph in charge of those men. So
Joseph took care of them.
Some time passed while they were in
prison. 5 Then each of the two men had
a dream. The men were the Egyptian
king's baker and wine taster. They were
being held in prison. Both of them had
dreams the same night. Each of their
dreams had its own meaning.
6 Joseph came to them the next morning. He saw that they were sad. 7 They
were Pharaoh's officials, and they were
in prison with Joseph in his master's
house. So he asked them, "Why do you
look so sad today?"
8 "We both had dreams," they answered.
"But no one can tell us what they mean."
Then Joseph said to them, "Only God
knows what dreams mean. Tell me your
dreams."
9 So the chief wine taster told Joseph
his dream. He said to him, "In my dream
I saw a vine in front of me. 10 There were
three branches on the vine. As soon as
it budded, it flowered. And bunches of
ripe grapes grew on it. 11 Pharaoh's cup
was in my hand. I took the grapes. I
squeezed them into Pharaoh's cup. Then
I put the cup in his hand."
12 "Here's what your dream means,"
Joseph said to him. "The three branches
are three days. 13 In three days Pharaoh
will let you out of prison. He'll give your
job back to you. And you will put Pharaoh's
cup in his hand. That's what you used to
do when you were his wine taster. 14 But
when everything is going well with you,
remember me. Do me a favor. Speak to
Pharaoh about me. Get me out of this prison. 15 I was taken away from the land of
the Hebrews by force. Even here I haven't
done anything to be put in prison for."
16 The chief baker saw that Joseph had
given a positive meaning to the wine
taster's dream. So he said to Joseph, "I
had a dream too. There were three baskets of bread on my head. 17 All kinds of
baked goods for Pharaoh were in the top
basket. But the birds were eating them
out of the basket on my head."
18 "Here's what your dream means,"
Joseph said. "The three baskets are
three days. 19 In three days Pharaoh
will cut your head off. Then he will stick
a pole through your body and set the
pole up. The birds will eat your flesh."
20 The third day was Pharaoh's birthday. He had a feast prepared for all his
officials. He brought the chief wine taster
and the chief baker out of prison. He
did it in front of his officials. 21 He gave
the chief wine taster's job back to him.
Once again the wine taster put the cup
into Pharaoh's hand. 22 But Pharaoh had
a pole stuck through the chief baker's
body. Then he had the pole set up. Everything happened just as Joseph had told
them when he explained their dreams.
23 But the chief wine taster didn't remember Joseph. In fact, he forgot all
about him.

Pharaoh Has Two Dreams

41 When two full years had passed,
Pharaoh had a dream. In his
dream, he was standing by the Nile
River. 2 Seven cows came up out of the
river. They looked healthy and fat. They
were eating some of the tall grass growing along the river. 3 After them, seven
other cows came up out of the Nile. They
looked ugly and skinny. They were
standing beside the other cows on the
riverbank. 4 The ugly, skinny cows ate
up the seven cows that looked healthy
and fat. Then Pharaoh woke up.

5 He fell asleep again and had a second dream. In that dream, seven heads of grain were growing on one stem. They were healthy and good. 6 After them, seven other heads of grain came up. They were thin and dried up by the east wind. 7 The thin heads of grain swallowed up the seven healthy, full heads. Then Pharaoh woke up. It had been a dream.

8 In the morning he was worried. So he sent for all the magicians and wise men of Egypt. Pharaoh told them his dreams. But no one could tell him what they meant.

9 Then the chief wine taster spoke up. He said to Pharaoh, "Now I remember that I've done something wrong. 10 Pharaoh was once angry with his servants. He put me and the chief baker in prison. We were in the house of the captain of the palace guard. 11 Each of us had a dream the same night. Each dream had its own meaning. 12 A young Hebrew servant was there with us. He was a servant of the captain of the guard. We told him our dreams. And he explained them to us. He told each of us the meaning of our dreams. 13 Things turned out exactly as he said they would. I was given back my job. The other man had a pole stuck through his body."

14 So Pharaoh sent for Joseph. He was quickly brought out of the prison. Joseph shaved and changed his clothes. Then he came to Pharaoh.

15 Pharaoh said to Joseph, "I had a dream. No one can tell me what it means. But I've heard that when you hear a dream you can explain it."

16 "I can't do it," Joseph replied to Pharaoh. "But God will give Pharaoh the answer he wants."

17 Then Pharaoh told Joseph what he had dreamed. He said, "I was standing on the bank of the Nile River. 18 Seven cows came up out of the river. They were fat and looked healthy. They were eating the tall grass growing along the river. 19 After them, seven other cows came up. They were bony and very ugly and thin. I had never seen such ugly cows in the whole land of Egypt. 20 The thin, ugly cows ate up the seven fat cows that came up first. 21 But no one could tell that the thin cows had eaten the fat cows. That's because the thin cows looked just as ugly as they had before. Then I woke up.

22 "In my dream I also saw seven heads of grain. They were full and good. They were all growing on one stem. 23 After them, seven other heads of grain came up. They were weak and thin and dried up by the east wind. 24 The thin heads of grain swallowed up the seven good heads. I told my dream to the magicians. But none of them could explain it to me."

25 Then Joseph said to Pharaoh, "Both of Pharaoh's dreams have the same meaning. God has shown Pharaoh what he is about to do. 26 The seven good cows are seven years. And the seven good heads of grain are seven years. Both dreams mean the same thing. 27 The seven thin, ugly cows that came up later are seven years. So are the seven worthless heads of grain dried up by the east wind. They are seven years when there won't be enough food.

28 "It's just as I said to Pharaoh. God has shown Pharaoh what he's about to do. 29 Seven years with plenty of food are coming to the whole land of Egypt. 30 But seven years when there won't be enough food will follow them. Then everyone will forget about all the food Egypt had. Terrible hunger will destroy the land. 31 There won't be anything left to remind people of the years when there was plenty of food in the land. That's how bad the hunger that follows will be. 32 God gave the dream to Pharaoh in two forms. That's because the matter has been firmly decided by God. And it's because God will do it soon.

33 "So Pharaoh should look for a wise and understanding man. He should put him in charge of the land of Egypt. 34 Pharaoh should appoint officials to be in charge of the land. They should take a fifth of the harvest in Egypt during the seven years when there's plenty of food. 35 They should collect all the extra food of the good years that are coming. Pharaoh should give them authority to store up the grain. They should keep it in the cities for food. 36 The grain should be stored up for the country to use later. It will be needed during the seven years when there isn't enough food in Egypt. Then the country won't be destroyed

just because it doesn't have enough
food."
37 The plan seemed good to Pharaoh
and all his officials. 38 So Pharaoh said
to them, "The spirit of God is in this
man. We can't find anyone else like
him, can we?"
39 Then Pharaoh said to Joseph, "God
has made all this known to you. No one
is as wise and understanding as you are.
40 You will be in charge of my palace. All
my people must obey your orders. I will
be greater than you only because I'm
the one who sits on the throne."

Joseph Is Put in Charge of Egypt

41 So Pharaoh said to Joseph, "I'm putting you in charge of the whole land of
Egypt." 42 Then Pharaoh took from his
finger the ring he used to give his official stamp. He put it on Joseph's finger.
He dressed him in robes made out of
fine linen. He put a gold chain around
Joseph's neck. 43 He also had him ride
in a chariot. Joseph was now next in
command after Pharaoh. People went
in front of Joseph and shouted, "Get
down on your knees!" By doing all these
things, Pharaoh put Joseph in charge
of the whole land of Egypt.
44 Then Pharaoh said to Joseph, "I
am Pharaoh. But unless you give an
order, no one will do anything in the
whole land of Egypt." 45 Pharaoh gave
Joseph the name Zaphenath-Paneah.
He gave Joseph a wife. She was Asenath,
the daughter of Potiphera. Potiphera
was the priest of On. Joseph traveled
all over the land of Egypt.
46 Joseph was 30 years old when he
began serving Pharaoh, the king of
Egypt. He left Pharaoh's palace and
traveled all over Egypt. 47 During the
seven years there was plenty of food.
The land produced more than the people
needed. 48 Joseph collected all the extra
food produced in those seven years in
Egypt. He stored it in the cities. In each
city he stored up the food grown in the
fields around it. 49 Joseph stored up huge
amounts of grain. There was as much of
it as sand by the sea. There was so much
grain it couldn't be measured. So Joseph
stopped keeping records of it.
50 Before the years when there wasn't
enough food, two sons were born to
Joseph. He had them by Asenath, the
daughter of Potiphera. Potiphera was
the priest of On. 51 Joseph named his
first son Manasseh. That's because he
said, "God has made me forget all my
trouble and my father's whole family."
52 He named the second son Ephraim.
That's because he said, "God has given
me children in the land where I've suffered so much."
53 The seven years when there was
plenty of food in Egypt came to an end.
54 Then the seven years when there wasn't
enough food began. It happened just as
Joseph had said it would. There wasn't
enough food in any of the other lands. But
in the whole land of Egypt there was food.
55 When all the people of Egypt began to
get hungry, they cried out to Pharaoh
for food. He told all the Egyptians, "Go
to Joseph. Do what he tells you."
56 There wasn't enough food anywhere in the country. So Joseph opened
the storerooms. He sold grain to the
Egyptians because people were very
hungry all over Egypt. 57 People from
all over the world came to Egypt. They
came to buy grain from Joseph. That's
because people were very hungry
everywhere.

Joseph's Brothers Go Down to Egypt

42 Jacob found out that there was
grain in Egypt. So he said to his
sons, "Why do you just keep looking
at one another?" 2 He continued, "I've
heard there's grain in Egypt. Go down
there. Buy some for us. Then we'll live
and not die."
3 So ten of Joseph's brothers went
down to Egypt to buy grain there.
4 But Jacob didn't send Joseph's brother Benjamin with them. He was afraid
Benjamin might be harmed. 5 Israel's
sons were among the people who went
to buy grain. There wasn't enough food
in the land of Canaan.
6 Joseph was the governor of the land.
He was the one who sold grain to all its
people. When Joseph's brothers arrived,
they bowed down to him with their faces to the ground. 7 As soon as Joseph
saw his brothers, he recognized them.
But he pretended to be a stranger. He
spoke to them in a mean way. "Where
do you come from?" he asked.
"From the land of Canaan," they replied. "We've come to buy food."

8 Joseph recognized his brothers, but they didn't recognize him. 9 Then Joseph remembered his dreams about them. So he said to them, "You are spies! You have come to see the places where our land isn't guarded very well."

10 "No, sir," they answered. "We've come to buy food. 11 All of us are the sons of one man. We're honest men. We aren't spies."

12 "No!" he said to them. "You have come to see the places where our land isn't guarded very well."

13 But they replied, "We were 12 brothers. All of us were the sons of one man. He lives in the land of Canaan. Our youngest brother is now with our father. And one brother is gone."

14 Joseph said to them, "I still say you are spies! 15 So I'm going to test you. And here's the test. You can be sure that you won't leave this place unless your youngest brother comes here. You can be just as sure of this as you are sure that Pharaoh lives. I give you my word that you won't leave here unless your brother comes. 16 Send one of you back to get your brother. The rest of you will be kept in prison. I'll test your words. Then we'll find out whether you are telling the truth. You can be sure that Pharaoh lives. And you can be just as sure that if you aren't telling the truth, we'll know that you are spies!" 17 So Joseph kept all of them under guard for three days.

18 On the third day, Joseph spoke to them again. He said, "Do what I say. Then you will live, because I have respect for God. 19 If you are honest men, let one of your brothers stay here in prison. The rest of you may go and take grain back to your hungry families. 20 But you must bring your youngest brother to me. That will prove that your words are true. Then you won't die." So they did what he said.

21 They said to one another, "God is surely punishing us because of our brother. We saw how upset he was when he begged us to let him live. But we wouldn't listen. That's why all this trouble has come to us."

22 Reuben replied, "Didn't I tell you not to sin against the boy? But you wouldn't listen! Now we're being paid back for killing him." 23 They didn't realize that Joseph could understand what they were saying. He was using someone else to explain their words to him in the Egyptian language.

24 Joseph turned away from his brothers and began to weep. Then he came back and spoke to them again. He had Simeon taken and tied up right there in front of them.

25 Joseph gave orders to have their bags filled with grain. He had each man's money put back into his sack. He also made sure they were given food for their journey. 26 Then the brothers loaded their grain on their donkeys and left.

27 When night came, they stopped. One of them opened his sack to get feed for his donkey. He saw his money in the top of his sack. 28 "My money has been given back," he said to his brothers. "Here it is in my sack."

They had a sinking feeling in their hearts. They began to tremble. They turned to one another and said, "What has God done to us?"

29 They came to their father Jacob in the land of Canaan. They told him everything that had happened to them. They said, 30 "The man who is the governor of the land spoke to us in a mean way. He treated us as if we were spying on the land. 31 But we said to him, 'We're honest men. We aren't spies. 32 We were 12 brothers. All of us were the sons of one father. But now one brother is gone. And our youngest brother is with our father in Canaan.'

33 "Then the man who is the governor of the land spoke to us. He said, 'Here's how I will know whether you are honest men. Leave one of your brothers here with me. Take food for your hungry families and go. 34 But bring your youngest brother to me. Then I'll know that you are honest men and not spies. I'll give your brother back to you. And you will be free to trade in the land.' "

35 They began emptying their sacks. There in each man's sack was his bag of money! When they and their father saw the money bags, they were scared to death. 36 Their father Jacob said to them, "You have taken my children away from me. Joseph is gone. Simeon is gone. Now you want to take Benjamin. Everything is going against me!"

37 Then Reuben spoke to his father.
He said, "You can put both of my sons
to death if I don't bring Benjamin back
to you. Trust me to take care of him. I'll
bring him back."
38 But Jacob said, "My son will not
go down there with you. His brother is
dead. He's the only one left here with
me. Suppose he's harmed on the journey you are taking. Then I would die
as a sad old man."

Joseph's Brothers Go Down to Egypt Again

43 There still wasn't enough food
anywhere in the land. 2 After a
while Jacob's family had eaten all the
grain the brothers had brought from
Egypt. So their father said to them, "Go
back. Buy us a little more food."
3 But Judah said to him, "The man
gave us a strong warning. He said, 'You
won't see my face again unless your
brother Benjamin is with you.' 4 So send
our brother along with us. Then we'll
go down and buy food for you. 5 If you
won't send him, we won't go down. The
man said to us, 'You won't see my face
again unless your brother is with you.' "
6 Israel asked, "Why did you bring
this trouble to me? Why did you tell the
man you had another brother?"
7 They replied, "The man questioned
us closely about ourselves and our family. He asked us, 'Is your father still living? Do you have another brother?' We
just answered his questions. How could
we possibly know he would say, 'Bring
your brother down here'?"
8 Judah spoke to Israel his father.
"Send the boy along with me," he said.
"We'll go right away. Then we and you
and our children will live and not die.
9 I myself promise to keep Benjamin
safe. You can blame me if I don't bring
him back to you. I'll set him right here
in front of you. If I don't, you can put
the blame on me for the rest of my life.
10 As it is, we've already waited too long.
We could have made the trip to Egypt
and back twice by now."
11 Then their father Israel spoke to
them. He said, "If that's the way it has
to be, then do what I tell you. Put some
of the best things from our land in your
bags. Take them down to the man as a
gift. Take some lotion and a little honey.
Take some spices and myrrh. Take some
pistachio nuts and almonds. 12 Take
twice the amount of money with you.
You have to give back the money that
was put in your sacks. Maybe it was
a mistake. 13 Also take your brother.
Go back to the man at once. 14 May the
Mighty God cause him to show you mercy. May the man let your other brother
and Benjamin come back with you. And
if I lose my sons, I lose them."
15 So the men took the gifts. They took
twice the amount of money. They also
took Benjamin. They hurried down to
Egypt and went to Joseph. 16 When Joseph saw Benjamin with them, he spoke
to the manager of his house. "Take these
men to my house," he said. "Kill an animal and prepare a meal. I want them
to eat with me at noon."
17 The manager did what Joseph told
him to do. He took the men to Joseph's
house. 18 They were frightened when
they were taken to Joseph's house. They
thought, "We were brought here because of the money that was put back
in our sacks the first time. He wants to
attack us and overpower us. Then he can
hold us as slaves and take our donkeys."
19 So they went up to Joseph's manager. They spoke to him at the entrance
to the house. 20 "Please, sir," they said.
"We came down here the first time to
buy food. 21 We opened our sacks at the
place where we stopped for the night.
Each of us found in our sacks the exact
amount of the money we had paid. So
we've brought it back with us. 22 We've
also brought more money with us to
buy food. We don't know who put our
money in our sacks."
23 "It's all right," the manager said.
"Don't be afraid. Your God, the God of
your father, has given you riches in your
sacks. I received your money." Then he
brought Simeon out to them.
24 The manager took the men into
Joseph's house. He gave them water to
wash their feet. He provided feed for
their donkeys. 25 The brothers prepared
their gifts for Joseph. He was planning
to arrive at noon. They had heard that
they were going to eat there.
26 When Joseph came home, they gave
him the gifts they had brought into the
house. They bowed down low in front of
him. 27 He asked them how they were.

Then he said, "How is your old father you told me about? Is he still living?"

28 They replied, "Your servant our father is still alive and well." And they bowed down to show him honor.

29 Joseph looked around. Then he saw his brother Benjamin, his own mother's son. He asked, "Is this your youngest brother? Is he the one you told me about?" He continued, "May God be gracious to you, my son." 30 It moved him deeply to see his brother. So Joseph hurried out and looked for a place to cry. He went into his own room and cried there.

31 Then he washed his face and came out. He calmed down and said, "Serve the food."

32 They served Joseph by himself. They served the brothers by themselves. They also served the Egyptians who ate with Joseph by themselves. Because of their beliefs, Egyptians couldn't eat with Hebrews. 33 The brothers had been given places in front of Joseph. They had been seated in the order of their ages, from the oldest to the youngest. That made them look at each other in great surprise. 34 While they were eating, some food was brought to them from Joseph's table. Benjamin was given five times as much as anyone else. So all Joseph's brothers ate and drank a lot with him.

A Silver Cup in a Sack

44 Joseph told the manager of his house what to do. "Fill the men's sacks with as much food as they can carry," he said. "Put each man's money in his sack. 2 Then put my silver cup in the youngest one's sack. Put it there along with the money he paid for his grain." So the manager did what Joseph told him to do.

3 When morning came, the men were sent on their way with their donkeys. 4 They hadn't gone very far from the city when Joseph spoke to his manager. "Go after those men right away," he said. "Catch up with them. Say to them, 'My master was good to you. Why have you paid him back by doing evil? 5 Isn't this the cup my master drinks from? Doesn't he also use it to find things out? You have done an evil thing.' "

6 When the manager caught up with them, he told them what Joseph had said. 7 But they said to him, "Why do you say these things? We would never do anything like that! 8 We even brought back to you from Canaan the money we found in our sacks. So why would we steal silver or gold from your master's house? 9 If you find out that any of us has the cup, he will die. And the rest of us will become your slaves."

10 "All right, then," he said. "As you wish. The one found to have the cup will become my slave. But the rest of you will not be blamed."

11 Each of them quickly put his sack down on the ground and opened it. 12 Then the manager started to search. He began with the oldest and ended with the youngest. The cup was found in Benjamin's sack. 13 When that happened, they were so upset they tore their clothes. Then all of them loaded their donkeys and went back to the city.

14 Joseph was still in the house when Judah and his brothers came in. They threw themselves down on the ground in front of him. 15 Joseph said to them, "What have you done? Don't you know that a man like me has ways to find things out?"

16 "What can we say to you?" Judah replied. "What can we say? How can we prove we haven't done anything wrong? God has shown you that we are guilty. We are now your slaves. All of us are, including the one found to have the cup."

17 But Joseph said, "I would never do anything like that! Only the man found to have the cup will become my slave. The rest of you may go back to your father in peace."

18 Then Judah went up to him. He said, "Please, sir. Let me speak a word to you. Don't be angry with me, even though you are equal to Pharaoh himself. 19 You asked us, 'Do you have a father or a brother?' 20 We answered, 'We have an old father. A young son was born to him when he was old. His brother is dead. He's the only one of his mother's sons left. And his father loves him.'

21 "Then you said to us, 'Bring him down to me. I want to see him for myself.' 22 We said to you, 'The boy can't leave his father. If he does, his father will die.' 23 But you told us, 'Your youngest brother must come down here with

you. If he doesn't, you won't see my face
again.' 24 So we went back to my father.
We told him what you had said.
25 "Then our father said, 'Go back.
Buy a little more food.' 26 But we said,
'We can't go down. We'll only go if our
youngest brother goes there with us. We
can't even see the man's face unless our
youngest brother goes with us.'
27 "Your servant my father said to us,
'You know that my wife had two sons by
me. 28 One of them went away from me.
And I said, "He must have been torn to
pieces." I haven't seen him since. 29 What
if you take this one from me too and he
is harmed? Then you would cause me to
die as a sad old man. I would go down
into the grave full of pain and suffering.'
30 "So now, what will happen if the
boy isn't with us when I go back to my
father? His life depends on the boy's
life. 31 When he sees that the boy isn't
with us, he'll die. Because of us, he'll go
down into the grave as a sad old man.
32 I promised my father I would keep
the boy safe. I said, 'Father, I'll bring
him back to you. If I don't, you can put
the blame on me for the rest of my life.'
33 "Now then, please let me stay here.
Let me be your slave in place of the boy.
Let the boy return with his brothers.
34 How can I go back to my father if
the boy isn't with me? No! Don't let me
see the pain and suffering that would
come to my father."

Joseph Tells His Brothers Who He Is

45 Joseph couldn't control himself anymore in front of all his
attendants. He cried out, "Have everyone leave me!" So there wasn't anyone
with Joseph when he told his brothers
who he was. 2 He wept so loudly that
the Egyptians heard him. Everyone in
Pharaoh's house heard about it.
3 Joseph said to his brothers, "I am
Joseph! Is my father still alive?" But his
brothers weren't able to answer him.
They were too afraid of him.
4 Joseph said to his brothers, "Come
close to me." So they did. Then he said,
"I am your brother Joseph. I'm the one
you sold into Egypt. 5 But don't be upset.
And don't be angry with yourselves
because you sold me here. God sent
me ahead of you to save many lives.
6 For two years now, there hasn't been
enough food in the land. And for the
next five years, people won't be plowing or gathering crops. 7 But God sent
me ahead of you to keep some of you
alive on earth. He sent me here to save
your lives by an act of mighty power.
8 "So then, it wasn't you who sent me
here. It was God. He made me like a
father to Pharaoh. He made me master
of Pharaoh's entire house. God made
me ruler of the whole land of Egypt.
9 Now hurry back to my father. Say to
him, 'Your son Joseph says, "God has
made me master of the whole land of
Egypt. Come down to me. Don't waste
any time. 10 You will live in the area of
Goshen. You, your children and grandchildren, your flocks and herds, and
everything you have will be near me.
11 There I will provide everything you
need. There are still five years to come
when there won't be enough food. If you
don't come down here, you and your
family and everyone who belongs to
you will lose everything." '
12 "My brothers, I am Joseph. You can
see for yourselves that I am the one
speaking to you. My brother Benjamin
can see it too. 13 Tell my father about all
the honor given to me in Egypt. Tell him
about everything you have seen. And
bring my father down here quickly."
14 Then Joseph threw his arms around
his brother Benjamin and wept. Benjamin also hugged him and wept.
15 Joseph kissed all his brothers and
wept over them. After that, his brothers talked with him.
16 The news reached Pharaoh's palace
that Joseph's brothers had come. Pharaoh and all his officials were pleased.
17 Pharaoh said to Joseph, "Here's what
I want you to tell your brothers. Say to
them, 'Load your animals. Return to the
land of Canaan. 18 Bring your father and
your families back to me. I'll give you
the best land in Egypt. You can enjoy
all the good things in the land.'
19 "And here's something else I want
you to tell them. Say to them, 'Take some
carts from Egypt. Your children and your
wives can use them. Get your father and
come back. 20 Don't worry about the
things you have back there. The best of
everything in Egypt will belong to you.' "
21 Then the sons of Israel did so. Joseph gave them carts, as Pharaoh had

commanded. He also gave them supplies
for their journey. 22 He gave new clothes
to each of them. But he gave Benjamin
more than seven pounds of silver. He
also gave him five sets of clothes. 23 He
sent his father ten male donkeys loaded with the best things from Egypt. He
also sent ten female donkeys loaded
with grain and bread and other supplies
for his journey. 24 Then Joseph sent his
brothers away. As they were leaving he
said to them, "Don't argue on the way!"
25 So they went up out of Egypt. They
came to their father Jacob in the land
of Canaan. 26 They told him, "Joseph is
still alive! In fact, he is ruler of the whole
land of Egypt." Jacob was shocked. He
didn't believe them. 27 So they told him
everything Joseph had said to them.
Jacob saw the carts Joseph had sent
to carry him back. That gave new life
to their father Jacob. 28 Israel said, "I
believe it now! My son Joseph is still
alive. I'll go and see him before I die."

Jacob Goes Down to Egypt

46 So Israel started out with everything that belonged to him.
When he reached Beersheba, he offered
sacrifices to the God of his father Isaac.
2 God spoke to Israel in a vision at
night. "Jacob! Jacob!" he said.
"Here I am," Jacob replied.
3 "I am God. I am the God of your father," he said. "Do not be afraid to go
down to Egypt. There I will make you
into a great nation. 4 I will go down to
Egypt with you. I will surely bring you
back again. And when you die, Joseph
will close your eyes with his own hand."
5 Then Jacob left Beersheba. Israel's
sons put their father Jacob and their families in the carts that Pharaoh had sent to
carry him. 6 So Jacob and his whole family went to Egypt. They took their livestock
with them. And they took everything
they had acquired in Canaan. 7 Jacob
brought his sons and grandsons with
him to Egypt. He also brought his daughters and granddaughters. He brought his
whole family with him.

8 Here are the names of Israel's
children and grandchildren who
went to Egypt. Jacob and his whole
family are included.

Reuben was Jacob's oldest son.

9 The sons of Reuben were
Hanok, Pallu, Hezron and Karmi.
10 The sons of Simeon were
Jemuel, Jamin, Ohad, Jakin,
Zohar and Shaul. Shaul was the
son of a woman from Canaan.
11 The sons of Levi were
Gershon, Kohath and Merari.
12 The sons of Judah were
Er, Onan, Shelah, Perez and
Zerah. But Er and Onan had died
in the land of Canaan.
The sons of Perez were
Hezron and Hamul.
13 The sons of Issachar were
Tola, Puah, Jashub and Shimron.
14 The sons of Zebulun were
Sered, Elon and Jahleel.
15 These were the sons and grandsons
born to Jacob and Leah in Paddan
Aram. Leah also had a daughter by
Jacob. Her name was Dinah. The
total number of people in the family
line of Jacob and Leah was 33.

16 The sons of Gad were
Zephon, Haggi, Shuni, Ezbon,
Eri, Arodi and Areli.
17 The sons of Asher were
Imnah, Ishvah, Ishvi and Beriah.
Their sister was Serah.
The sons of Beriah were
Heber and Malkiel.
18 These were the children and
grandchildren born to Jacob and
Zilpah. Laban had given Zilpah
to his daughter Leah. The total
number of people in the family
line of Jacob and Zilpah was 16.

19 The sons of Jacob's wife Rachel
were
Joseph and Benjamin.
20 In Egypt, Asenath had Manasseh and Ephraim by Joseph.
Asenath was the daughter of
Potiphera. Potiphera was the
priest of On.
21 The sons of Benjamin were
Bela, Beker, Ashbel, Gera,
Naaman, Ehi, Rosh, Muppim,
Huppim and Ard.
22 These were the sons and grandsons
born to Jacob and Rachel. The total
number of people in the family
line of Jacob and Rachel was 14.

23 The son of Dan was
Hushim.

24 The sons of Naphtali were
Jahziel, Guni, Jezer and Shillem.
25 These were the sons and grandsons
born to Jacob and Bilhah. Laban
had given Bilhah to his daughter
Rachel. The total number of people
in the family line of Jacob and
Bilhah was seven.

26 The total number of people who
went to Egypt with Jacob was 66.
That number includes only his
own children and grandchildren.
It doesn't include his sons' wives or
his grandsons' wives. 27 The total
number of the members of Jacob's
family who went to Egypt was 70.
That includes the two sons who
had been born to Joseph in Egypt.

28 Jacob sent Judah ahead of him to
Joseph. He sent him to get directions to
Goshen. And so they arrived in the area
of Goshen. 29 Then Joseph had his servants get his chariot ready. He went to
Goshen to meet his father Israel. As soon
as he came to his father, Joseph threw
his arms around him. Then Joseph wept
for a long time.

30 Israel said to Joseph, "I have seen
for myself that you are still alive. Now
I'm ready to die."

31 Then Joseph spoke to his brothers
and to the rest of his father's family. He
said, "I will go up and speak to Pharaoh.
I'll say to him, 'My brothers and the rest
of my father's family have come to me.
They were living in the land of Canaan.
32 The men are shepherds. They take
care of livestock. They've brought along
their flocks and herds and everything
they own.' 33 Pharaoh will send for you.
He'll ask, 'What do you do for a living?'
34 You should answer, 'We've taken care
of livestock from the time we were boys.
We've done just as our fathers did.' It's
the practice of the people of Egypt not
to mix with shepherds. So Pharaoh will
let you settle in the area of Goshen."

47 Joseph went to Pharaoh. He told
him, "My father and brothers
have come from the land of Canaan.
They've brought along their flocks and
herds and everything they own. They are
now in Goshen." 2 Joseph had chosen five
of his brothers to meet with Pharaoh.

3 Pharaoh asked the brothers, "What
do you do for a living?"

"We're shepherds," they replied to
Pharaoh. "And that's what our fathers
were." 4 They also said to him, "We've
come to live in Egypt for a while. There
isn't enough food anywhere in Canaan.
There isn't any grass for our flocks. So
please let us live in Goshen."

5 Pharaoh said to Joseph, "Your father
and your brothers have come to you.
6 The land of Egypt is open to you. Let
your father and brothers live in the
best part of the land. Let them live in
Goshen. Do any of them have special
skills? If they do, put them in charge
of my own livestock."

7 Then Joseph brought his father Jacob in to meet Pharaoh. Jacob gave
Pharaoh his blessing. 8 Then Pharaoh
asked him, "How old are you?"

9 Jacob said to Pharaoh, "The years of
my journey through life are 130. My years
have been few and hard. They aren't as
many as the years of my father and
grandfather before me." 10 Jacob gave
Pharaoh his blessing. Then he left him.

11 So Joseph helped his father and his
brothers make their homes in Egypt. He
gave them property in the best part of
the land, just as Pharaoh had directed
him to do. That part was known as the
territory of Rameses. 12 Joseph also provided food for his father and brothers.
He provided for them and the rest of his
father's family. He gave them enough
for all their children.

Joseph Saves Many Lives

13 But there wasn't any food in the
whole area. In fact, there wasn't enough
food anywhere. The people of Egypt
and Canaan lost their strength because
there wasn't enough food to go around.
14 Joseph collected all the money in Egypt
and Canaan. People paid it to him for
the grain they were buying. And Joseph
brought it to Pharaoh's palace. 15 When
the money of the people of Egypt and Canaan was gone, all the Egyptians came
to Joseph. They said, "Give us food. What
good would it do you to watch us all die?
Our money is all gone."

16 "Then bring your livestock," said
Joseph. "You say your money is gone.
So I'll trade you food for your livestock."
17 They brought their livestock to Joseph.
He traded them food for their animals.
They gave him their horses, sheep,

goats, cattle and donkeys. He helped
the people live through that year by
trading them food for all their livestock.
18 When that year was over, they came
to him the next year. They said, "We
can't hide the truth from you. Our money is gone. Our livestock belongs to you.
We don't have anything left to give you
except our bodies and our land. 19 What
good would it do you to watch us die?
Why should our land be destroyed?
Trade us food for ourselves and our
land. Then we and our land will belong
to Pharaoh. Give us some seeds so we
can live and not die. We don't want the
land to become a desert."
20 So Joseph bought all the land in
Egypt for Pharaoh. All the people of
Egypt sold their fields. They did that
because there wasn't enough food anywhere. So the land became Pharaoh's.
21 Joseph made the people slaves from
one end of Egypt to the other. 22 But Joseph didn't buy the land that belonged
to the priests. They received a regular
share of food from Pharaoh. They had
enough food from what Pharaoh gave
them. That's why they didn't have to
sell their land.
23 Joseph said to the people, "I've
bought you and your land today for
Pharaoh. So here are some seeds for
you to plant in the ground. 24 But when
the crop comes in, give a fifth of it to
Pharaoh. Keep the other four-fifths for
yourselves. They will be seeds for the
fields. And they will be food for yourselves, your children, and the other
people who live with you."
25 "You have saved our lives," they
said. "If you are pleased with us, we
will be Pharaoh's slaves."
26 So Joseph made a law about land in
Egypt. It's still the law today. A fifth of
the produce belongs to Pharaoh. Only
the land belonging to the priests didn't
become Pharaoh's.
27 The people of Israel lived in Egypt
in the area of Goshen. They received
property there. They had children and
so became many.
28 Jacob lived 17 years in Egypt. He
lived a total of 147 years. 29 The time
came near for Israel to die. So he sent
for his son Joseph. He said to him, "If
you are pleased with me, put your hand
under my thigh. Promise me that you
will be kind and faithful to me. Don't
bury me in Egypt. 30 When I join the
members of my family who have already died, carry me out of Egypt. Bury
me where they are buried."
"I'll do exactly as you say," Joseph said.
31 "Give me your word that you will do
it," Jacob said. So Joseph gave him his
word. And Israel worshiped God as he
leaned on the top of his walking stick.

Ephraim and Manasseh

48 Some time later Joseph was
told, "Your father is sick." So
he took his two sons Manasseh and
Ephraim along with him. 2 Jacob was
told, "Your son Joseph has come to you."
So Israel became stronger and sat up
in bed.
3 Jacob said to Joseph, "The Mighty
God appeared to me at Luz in the land of
Canaan. He blessed me there. 4 He said
to me, 'I am going to give you children.
I will make your family very large. I
will make you a community of nations.
And I will give this land to your children
after you. It will belong to them forever.'
5 "Now then, two sons were born to
you in Egypt. It happened before I came
to you here. They will be counted as
my own sons. Ephraim and Manasseh will belong to me, in the same way
that Reuben and Simeon belong to me.
6 Any children born to you after them
will belong to you. Any territory they
receive will come from the land that will
be given to Ephraim and Manasseh. 7 As
I was returning from Paddan, Rachel
died. It made me very sad. She died in
the land of Canaan while we were still
on the way. We weren't very far away
from Ephrath. So I buried her body there
beside the road to Ephrath." Ephrath
was also called Bethlehem.
8 Israel saw Joseph's sons. He asked,
"Who are they?"
9 "They are the sons God has given me
here," Joseph said to his father.
Then Israel said, "Bring them to me.
I want to give them my blessing."
10 Israel's eyes were weak because he
was old. He couldn't see very well. So Joseph brought his sons close to him. His
father kissed them and hugged them.
11 Israel said to Joseph, "I never
thought I'd see your face again. But now
God has let me see your children too."

12 Then Joseph lifted his sons off Israel's knees. Joseph bowed down with
his face to the ground. 13 He placed
Ephraim on his right, toward Israel's
left hand. He placed Manasseh on his
left, toward Israel's right hand. Then
he brought them close to Israel. 14 But
Israel reached out his right hand and
put it on Ephraim's head. He did it even
though Ephraim was the younger son.
He crossed his arms and put his left
hand on Manasseh's head. He did it even
though Manasseh was the older son.
15 Then Israel gave Joseph his blessing. He said,

"May God bless these boys.
He is the God of my grandfather
Abraham and my father Isaac.
They walked faithfully with him.
He is the God who has been my
shepherd
all my life right up to this day.
16 He is the Angel who has saved me
from all harm.
May he bless these boys.
May they be called by my name.
May they also be called by the
names of my grandfather
Abraham and my father Isaac.
And may the number of them
greatly increase
on the earth."

17 Joseph saw his father putting his
right hand on Ephraim's head. And
Joseph didn't like it. So he took hold
of his father's hand to move it over to
Manasseh's head. 18 Joseph said to him,
"No, my father. Here's my older son. Put
your right hand on his head."
19 But his father wouldn't do it. He
said, "I know, my son. I know. He too will
become a nation. He too will become
great. But his younger brother will be
greater than he is. His children after
him will become a group of nations."
20 On that day, Jacob gave them his
blessing. He said,

"The people of Israel will bless
others in your name.
They will say, 'May God
make you like Ephraim and
Manasseh.'"

So he put Ephraim ahead of Manasseh.
21 Then Israel said to Joseph, "I'm
about to die. But God will be with all of
you. He'll take you back to the land of
your fathers. 22 But to you, Joseph, I am
giving more land than your brothers.
I'm giving you the land I took from
the Amorites. I took it with my sword
and bow."

Jacob Gives Blessings to His Sons

49 Then Jacob sent for his sons.
He said, "Gather around me so
I can tell you what will happen to you
in days to come.

2 "Sons of Jacob, come together and
listen.
Listen to your father Israel.

3 "Reuben, you are my oldest son.
You were my first child. You were
the first sign of my strength.
You were first in honor. You were
first in power.
4 But you are as unsteady as water.
So you won't be first anymore.
You had sex with my concubine
on my bed.
You lay on my couch and made it
'unclean.'

5 "Simeon and Levi are brothers.
Their swords have killed a lot of
people.
6 I won't share in their plans.
I won't have anything to do with
them.
They became angry and killed
people.
They cut the legs of oxen just for
the fun of it.
7 May the LORD put a curse on them
because of their terrible anger.
I will scatter them in Jacob's land.
I will spread them around in
Israel.

8 "Judah, your brothers will praise you.
Your enemies will be brought
under your control.
Your father's sons will bow down
to you.
9 Judah, you are like a lion's cub.
You return from hunting, my son.
Like a lion, you lie down and sleep.
You are like a mother lion. Who
dares to wake you up?
10 The right to rule will not leave
Judah.
The ruler's scepter will not be
taken from between his feet.

It will be his until the king it
belongs to will come.
The nations will obey that king.
11 He will tie his donkey to a vine.
He will tie his colt to the very best
branch.
He will wash his clothes in wine.
He will wash his robes in the red
juice of grapes.
12 His eyes will be darker than wine.
His teeth will be whiter than
milk.

13 "Zebulun will live by the seashore.
He will become a safe harbor for
ships.
His border will go out toward
Sidon.

14 "Issachar is like a wild donkey
lying down among the sheep
pens.
15 He sees how good his resting
place is.
He sees that his land is pleasant.
So he will carry a heavy load on his
back.
He will obey when he's forced to
work.

16 "Dan will do what is fair for his
people.
He will do it as one of the tribes
of Israel.
17 Dan will be a snake by the side of
the road.
He will be a poisonous snake
along the path.
It bites the horse's heels
so that the rider falls off
backward.

18 "LORD, I look to you to save me.

19 "Gad will be attacked by a group of
robbers.
But he will attack them as they
run away.

20 "Asher's food will be rich and sweet.
He will provide food that even a
king would enjoy.

21 "Naphtali is a female deer set free
and gives birth to beautiful
fawns.

22 "Joseph is a vine that grows a lot of
fruit.
It grows close by a spring.
Its branches climb over a wall.
23 Mean people shot arrows at him.
They shot at him because they
were angry.
24 But his bow remained steady.
His strong arms moved freely.
The hand of the Mighty God of
Jacob was with him.
The Shepherd, the Rock of Israel,
stood by him.
25 Joseph, your father's God helps you.
The Mighty God blesses you.
He gives you blessings from the sky
above.
He gives you blessings from the
deep springs below.
He blesses you with children and
with a mother's milk.
26 Your father's blessings are great.
They are greater than the
blessings from the age-old
mountains.
They are greater than the gifts
from the ancient hills.
Let all those blessings rest on the
head of Joseph.
Let them rest on the head of the
one who is prince among his
brothers.

27 "Benjamin is a hungry wolf.
In the morning he eats what he
has killed.
In the evening he shares what he
has stolen."

28 All these are the 12 tribes of Israel.
That's what their father said to them
when he blessed them. He gave each
one the blessing that was just right for
him.

Jacob Dies

29 Then Jacob gave directions to his
sons. He said, "I'm about to join the
members of my family who have already died. Bury me with them in the
cave in the field of Ephron, the Hittite.
30 The cave is in the field of Machpelah
near Mamre in Canaan. Abraham had
bought it as a place where he could bury
his wife's body. He had bought the cave
and the field from Ephron, the Hittite.
31 The bodies of Abraham and his wife
Sarah were buried there. So were the
bodies of Isaac and his wife Rebekah.
I also buried Leah's body there. 32 Abraham bought the field and the cave from
the Hittites."

33 When Jacob had finished telling his
sons what to do, he pulled his feet up
into his bed. Then he took his last breath
and died. He joined the members of his
family who had already died.

50 Joseph threw himself on his
father's body. He wept over him
and kissed him. 2 Then Joseph talked
to the doctors who served him. He told
them to prepare the body of his father
Israel to be buried. So the doctors prepared it. 3 They took 40 days to do it.
They needed that much time to prepare
a body in the right way. The Egyptians
mourned for Jacob 70 days.

4 After the days of sadness had passed,
Joseph went to Pharaoh's officials. He
said to them, "If you are pleased with
me, speak to Pharaoh for me. Tell him,
5 'My father made me give my word to
him. He said, "I'm about to die. Bury
me in the tomb I dug for myself in the
land of Canaan." So let me go there and
bury my father. Then I'll come back.' "

6 Pharaoh said, "Go there and bury
your father. Do what he made you
promise to do."

7 So Joseph went to Canaan to bury his
father. All Pharaoh's officials went with
him. They were the important people of
his court and all the leaders of Egypt.
8 Joseph's family also went. His brothers
and all the rest of his father's family went. Only their children and their
flocks and herds were left in Goshen.
9 Chariots and horsemen also went up
with him. It was a very large group.

10 They came to Atad, a place where
grain was processed. It was near the
Jordan River. There they sobbed loudly and bitterly. Joseph set apart seven
days of sadness to honor his father's
memory. 11 The Canaanites living in
that area saw how sad all of them were.
They said, "The Egyptians are having a
very special service for the dead." That's
why that place near the Jordan River is
called Abel of the Egyptians.

12 So Jacob's sons did exactly as he
had commanded them. 13 They carried his body to the land of Canaan.
They buried it in the cave in the field
of Machpelah near Mamre. Abraham
had bought the cave as a place where
he could bury his wife's body. He had
bought the cave and the field from
Ephron, the Hittite. 14 After Joseph
buried his father, he went back to
Egypt. His brothers and all the others
who had gone to help him bury his
father went back with him.

Joseph Calms His Brothers' Fears

15 Now that their father was dead,
Joseph's brothers were worried. They
said, "Remember all the bad things
we did to Joseph? What if he decides to
hold those things against us? What if he
pays us back for them?" 16 So they sent
a message to Joseph. They said, "Your
father gave us directions before he died.
17 He said, 'Here's what you must say to
Joseph. Tell him, "I'm asking you to forgive your brothers. Forgive the terrible
things they did to you. Forgive them
for treating you so badly." ' Now then,
please forgive our sins. We serve the God
of your father." When their message
came to Joseph, he wept.

18 Then his brothers came and threw
themselves down in front of him. "We
are your slaves," they said.

19 But Joseph said to them, "Don't be
afraid. Do you think I'm God? 20 You
planned to harm me. But God planned
it for good. He planned to do what is
now being done. He wanted to save
many lives. 21 So then, don't be afraid.
I'll provide for you and your children."
He calmed their fears. And he spoke in
a kind way to them.

Joseph Dies

22 Joseph stayed in Egypt, along with
all his father's family. He lived 110 years.
23 He lived long enough to see Ephraim's
children and grandchildren. When the
children of Makir were born, they were
placed on Joseph's knees and counted
as his own children. Makir was the son
of Manasseh.

24 Joseph said to his brothers, "I'm
about to die. But God will surely come
to help you. He'll take you up out of
this land. He'll bring you to the land he
promised to give to Abraham, Isaac and
Jacob." 25 Joseph made the Israelites
promise him. He said, "God will surely
come to help you. Then you must carry
my bones up from this place."

26 So Joseph died at the age of 110.
They prepared his body to be buried.
Then he was placed in a casket in Egypt.

EXODUS

Author: Moses

Abraham's family grew until it was so big that it could make up an entire nation! His family members were called Israelites. The book of Exodus tells us how God promised to help the Israelites enter the promised land, known as Canaan. They had been enslaved in Egypt by Pharaoh, but God promised to set them free through his servant Moses.

Moses, however, was afraid to talk to Pharaoh alone, so God sent Moses' brother, Aaron, with Moses to speak to Pharaoh. But Pharaoh did not listen to them. God displayed his power in Egypt by sending ten plagues; these plagues showed the Egyptians that the God of Israel was the only true God and the gods they worshiped were nothing more than idols. Though Pharaoh tried to recapture the Israelites, God miraculously parted the Red Sea and defeated their enemies so the Israelites would be free from slavery.

Law & Covenant

It wasn't long before the Israelites began grumbling and complaining instead of trusting God to provide for them. On their journey across the Desert of Sinai, they came to a place called Mount Sinai where Moses received the Ten Commandments, and God formed a relationship, or covenant, with the people of Israel (see Exodus 20:1–17). In this covenant, God promised to make his people a holy nation. He told them that as they walked in obedience, he would bless them, and that if they disobeyed his commands, they would experience the consequences of their disobedience. Once again, God reminded his people that one day he was going to send a Savior who would set them free from their sin by his own sacrifice.

The Israelites Become Slaves in Egypt

1 Here are the names of Israel's
children who went to Egypt
with Jacob. Each one went with
his family. 2 Jacob's sons were

Reuben, Simeon, Levi, Judah,
3 Issachar, Zebulun, Benjamin,
4 Dan, Naphtali,
Gad and Asher.

5 The total number of Jacob's
children and grandchildren was
70. Joseph was already in Egypt.

6 Joseph and all his brothers died. So
did all their children. 7 The people of
Israel had many children. The number
of them greatly increased. There were so
many of them that they filled the land.
8 Then a new king came to power in
Egypt. Joseph didn't mean anything
to him. 9 "Look," he said to his people.
"The Israelites are far too many for
us. 10 Come. We must deal with them
carefully. If we don't, there will be even
more of them. Then if war breaks out,
they'll join our enemies. They'll fight
against us and leave the country."
11 So the Egyptians put slave drivers over the people of Israel. The slave
drivers treated them badly and made
them work hard. The Israelites built
the cities of Pithom and Rameses so
Pharaoh could store things there. 12 But
the worse the slave drivers treated the
Israelites, the more Israelites there
were. So the Egyptians became afraid
of them. 13 They made them work hard.
They didn't show them any pity. 14 The
people suffered because of their hard
labor. The slave drivers forced them to
work with bricks and mud. And they
made them do all kinds of work in the
fields. The Egyptians didn't show them
any pity at all. They made them work
very hard.
15 There were two Hebrew women
named Shiphrah and Puah. They
helped other women having babies. The
king of Egypt spoke to them. He said,
16 "You are the ones who help the other
Hebrew women. Watch them when they
get into a sitting position to have their
babies. Kill the boys. Let the girls live."
17 But Shiphrah and Puah had respect
for God. They didn't do what the king of

in Exodus?

God is the Deliverer, the one who saves his people from their enemies and from their sin.

Egypt had told them to do. They let the
boys live. 18 Then the king of Egypt sent
for the women. He asked them, "Why
have you done this? Why have you let
the boys live?"
19 The women answered Pharaoh,
"Hebrew women are not like the women
of Egypt. They are strong. They have
their babies before we get there."
20 So God was kind to Shiphrah and
Puah. And the number of Israelites
became even greater. 21 Shiphrah and
Puah had respect for God. So he gave
them families of their own.
22 Then Pharaoh gave an order to all
his people. He said, "You must throw
every Hebrew baby boy into the Nile
River. But let every Hebrew baby girl
live."

Moses Is Born

2 A man and a woman from the tribe
of Levi got married. 2 She became
pregnant and had a son by her husband. She saw that her baby was a fine
child. And she hid him for three months.
3 After that, she couldn't hide him any
longer. So she got a basket made out of
the stems of tall grass. She coated the
basket with tar. She placed the child in
the basket. Then she put it in the tall
grass that grew along the bank of the
Nile River. 4 The child's sister wasn't
very far away. She wanted to see what
would happen to him.
5 Pharaoh's daughter went down to
the Nile River to take a bath. Her attendants were walking along the river

bank. She saw the basket in the tall grass. So she sent her female slave to get it. 6 When she opened it, Pharaoh's daughter saw the baby. He was crying. She felt sorry for him. "This is one of the Hebrew babies," she said.

7 Then his sister spoke to Pharaoh's daughter. She asked, "Do you want me to go and get one of the Hebrew women? She could breast-feed the baby for you."

8 "Yes. Go," she answered. So the girl went and got the baby's mother. 9 Pharaoh's daughter said to her, "Take this baby and feed him for me. I'll pay you." So the woman took the baby and fed him. 10 When the child grew older, she took him to Pharaoh's daughter. And he became her son. She named him Moses. She said, "I pulled him out of the water."

Moses Escapes to Midian

11 Moses grew up. One day, he went out to where his own people were. He watched them while they were hard at work. He saw an Egyptian hitting a Hebrew man. The man was one of Moses' own people. 12 Moses looked around and didn't see anyone. So he killed the Egyptian. Then he hid his body in the sand. 13 The next day Moses went out again. He saw two Hebrew men fighting. He asked the one who had started the fight a question. He said, "Why are you hitting another Hebrew man?"

14 The man said, "Who made you ruler and judge over us? Are you thinking about killing me as you killed the Egyptian?" Then Moses became afraid. He thought, "People must have heard about what I did."

15 When Pharaoh heard about what had happened, he tried to kill Moses. But Moses escaped from Pharaoh and went to live in Midian. There he sat down by a well. 16 A priest of Midian had seven daughters. They came to fill the stone tubs with water. They wanted to give water to their father's flock. 17 Some shepherds came along and chased the girls away. But Moses got up and helped them. Then he gave water to their flock.

18 The girls returned to their father Reuel. He asked them, "Why have you returned so early today?"

19 They answered, "An Egyptian saved us from the shepherds. He even got water for us and gave it to the flock."

20 "Where is he?" Reuel asked his daughters. "Why did you leave him? Invite him to have something to eat."

21 Moses agreed to stay with the man. And the man gave his daughter Zipporah to Moses to be his wife. 22 Zipporah had a son by him. Moses named him Gershom. That's because Moses said, "I'm an outsider in a strange land."

23 After a long time, the king of Egypt died. The people of Israel groaned because they were slaves. They also cried out to God. Their cry for help went up to him. 24 God heard their groans. He remembered his covenant with Abraham, Isaac and Jacob. 25 So God looked on the Israelites with concern for them.

Moses and the Burning Bush

3 Moses was taking care of the flock of his father-in-law Jethro. Jethro was the priest of Midian. Moses led the flock to the western side of the desert. He came to Horeb. It was the mountain of God. 2 There the angel of the LORD appeared to him from inside a burning bush. Moses saw that the bush was on fire. But it didn't burn up. 3 So Moses thought, "I'll go over and see this strange sight. Why doesn't the bush burn up?"

4 The LORD saw that Moses had gone over to look. So God spoke to him from inside the bush. He called out, "Moses! Moses!"

"Here I am," Moses said.

5 "Do not come any closer," God said. "Take off your sandals. The place you are standing on is holy ground." 6 He continued, "I am the God of your father. I am the God of Abraham. I am the God of Isaac. And I am the God of Jacob." When Moses heard that, he turned his face away. He was afraid to look at God.

7 The LORD said, "I have seen how my people are suffering in Egypt. I have heard them cry out because of their slave drivers. I am concerned about their suffering. 8 So I have come down to save them from the Egyptians. I will bring them up out of that land. I will bring them into a good land. It has a lot of room. It is a land that has plenty of milk and honey. The Canaanites, Hittites, Amorites, Perizzites, Hivites and Jebusites live there. 9 And now Israel's cry for help has reached me. I have seen how badly the Egyptians are treating them. 10 So

SELF-SUFFICIENT

God doesn't depend on anyone or anything to live. He has always existed and doesn't need anything to sustain him. He is sustained by his own power. This is one of the many ways God is different from creation.

All created things depend on God for their existence, and they also depend on other things God created in order to live (see Romans 11:35–36). In other words, you were created by God, and without God creating you, you would not exist. You also need food, water, sleep, and many other things to live each day. God doesn't depend on *anything* or *anyone* else!

MY GOD IS...

God is with us for every step we take, and he gives us our every breath. We need to depend on him to care for us and lead us to walk in his ways.

now, go. I am sending you to Pharaoh.
I want you to bring the Israelites out of
Egypt. They are my people."
[11] But Moses spoke to God. "Who am I
that I should go to Pharaoh?" he said.
"Who am I that I should bring the Israelites out of Egypt?"
[12] God said, "I will be with you. I will
give you a sign. It will prove that I have
sent you. When you have brought the
people out of Egypt, all of you will worship me on this mountain."
[13] Moses said to God, "Suppose I go to
the people of Israel. Suppose I say to
them, 'The God of your fathers has sent
me to you.' And suppose they ask me,
'What is his name?' Then what should
I tell them?"
[14] God said to Moses, "I AM WHO I AM.
Here is what you must say to the Israelites. Tell them, 'I AM has sent me to you.'"
[15] God also said to Moses, "Say to the
Israelites, 'The LORD is the God of your
fathers. He has sent me to you. He is the
God of Abraham. He is the God of Isaac.
And he is the God of Jacob.' My name
will always be The LORD. Call me this
name for all time to come.

[16] "Go. Gather the elders of Israel
together. Say to them, 'The LORD, the
God of your fathers, appeared to me.
He is the God of Abraham, Isaac and
Jacob. God said, "I have watched over
you. I have seen what the Egyptians
have done to you.
[17] I have promised
to bring you up out of Egypt where you
are suffering. I will bring you into the
land of the Canaanites, Hittites, Amorites, Perizzites, Hivites and Jebusites.
It is a land that has plenty of milk and
honey."'
[18] "The elders of Israel will listen to
you. Then you and the elders must go to
the king of Egypt. You must say to him,
'The LORD has met with us. He is the God
of the Hebrews. Let us take a journey
that lasts about three days. We want to
go into the desert to offer sacrifices to
the LORD our God.'
[19] But I know that the
king of Egypt will not let you and your
people go. Only a mighty hand could
make him do that.
[20] So I will reach out
my hand. I will strike the Egyptians
with all the amazing things I will do.
After that, their king will let you go.

21 “I will cause the Egyptians to treat
you in a kind way. Then when you leave,
you will not go with your hands empty.
22 Every woman should ask her neighbor
and any woman living in her house for
things made out of silver and gold. Ask
them for clothes too. Put them on your
children. In that way, you will take the
wealth of Egypt along with you.”

Signs for Moses to Do

4 Moses answered, “What if the elders of Israel won't believe me?
What if they won't listen to me? Suppose
they say, ‘The LORD didn't appear to
you.’ Then what should I do?”

2 The LORD said to him, “What do you
have in your hand?”

“A walking stick,” he said.

3 The LORD said, “Throw it on the
ground.”

So Moses threw it on the ground. It
turned into a snake. He ran away from
it. 4 Then the LORD said to Moses, “Reach
your hand out. Take the snake by the
tail.” So he reached out and grabbed
the snake. It turned back into a walking
stick in his hand. 5 The LORD said, “When
they see this sign, they will believe that
I appeared to you. I am the LORD, the
God of their fathers. I am the God of
Abraham. I am the God of Isaac. And I
am the God of Jacob.”

6 Then the LORD said, “Put your hand
inside your coat.” So Moses put his hand

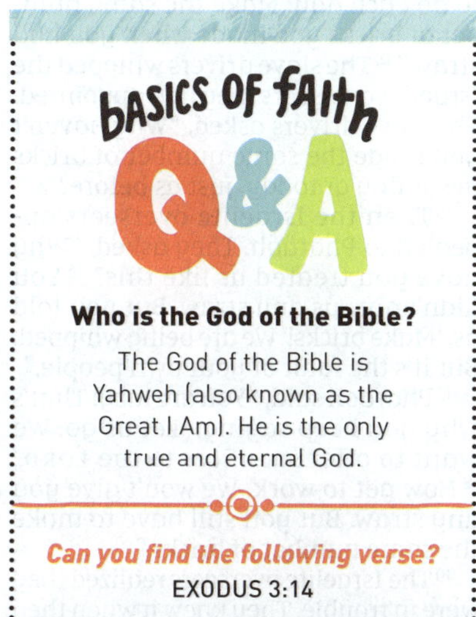

inside his coat. When he took it out, the
skin had become as white as snow. His
hand was covered with a skin disease.

7 “Now put it back into your coat,” the
LORD said. So Moses put his hand back
into his coat. When he took it out, the
skin was healthy again. His hand was
like the rest of his skin.

8 Then the LORD said, “Suppose they
do not believe you or pay attention to
the first sign. Then maybe they will
believe the second one. 9 But suppose
they do not believe either sign. Suppose
they will not listen to you. Then get
some water from the Nile River. Pour it
on the dry ground. The water you take
from the river will turn into blood on
the ground.”

10 Moses spoke to the LORD. He said,
“Lord, I've never been a good speaker.
And I haven't gotten any better since
you spoke to me. I don't speak very
well at all.”

11 The LORD said to him, “Who makes
human beings able to talk? Who makes
them unable to hear or speak? Who
makes them able to see? Who makes
them blind? It is I, the LORD. 12 Now go.
I will help you speak. I will teach you
what to say.”

13 But Moses said, “Lord, please send
someone else to do it.”

14 Then the LORD became very angry
with Moses. He said, “What about your
brother, Aaron the Levite? I know he can
speak well. He is already on his way to
meet you. He will be glad to see you.
15 Speak to him. Tell him what to say. I
will help both of you speak. I will teach
you what to do. 16 He will speak to the
people for you. He will be like your mouth.
And you will be like God to him. 17 But take
this walking stick in your hand. You will
be able to do signs with it.”

Moses Returns to Egypt

18 Then Moses went back to his father-
in-law Jethro. He said to him, “Let me
return to my own people in Egypt. I
want to see if any of them are still alive.”

Jethro said, “Go. I hope everything
goes well with you.”

19 The LORD had said to Moses in Midian, “Go back to Egypt. All those who
wanted to kill you are dead.” 20 So Moses
got his wife and sons. He put them on
a donkey. Together they started back

to Egypt. And he took the walking stick in his hand. It was the stick God would use in a powerful way.

21 The LORD spoke to Moses. He said, "When you return to Egypt, do all the amazing things I have given you the power to do. Do them in the sight of Pharaoh. But I will make him stubborn. He will not let the people go. 22 Then say to Pharaoh, 'The LORD says, "Israel is like an oldest son to me. 23 I told you, 'Let my son go. Then he will be able to worship me.' But you refused to let him go. So I will kill your oldest son." ' "

24 On the way to Egypt, Moses stopped for the night. There the LORD met him and was about to kill him. 25 But Zipporah got a knife made out of flint. She circumcised her son with it. Then she touched Moses' feet with the skin she had cut off. "Surely, you are a husband who has forced me to spill my son's blood," she said. 26 So the LORD didn't kill Moses. When she said "husband who has forced me to spill my son's blood," she was talking about circumcision.

27 The LORD said to Aaron, "Go into the desert to see Moses." So Aaron greeted Moses at the mountain of God and kissed him. 28 Then Moses told Aaron everything the LORD had sent him to say. Moses also told him about all the signs the LORD had commanded him to do.

29 Moses and Aaron gathered all the elders of Israel together. 30 Aaron told them everything the LORD had said to Moses. He also performed the signs in the sight of the people. 31 And they believed. They heard that the LORD was concerned about them. He had seen their suffering. So they bowed down and worshiped him.

Bricks Without Straw

5 Later on, Moses and Aaron went to Pharaoh. They said, "The LORD is the God of Israel. He says, 'Let my people go. Then they will be able to hold a feast to honor me in the desert.' "

2 Pharaoh said, "Who is the LORD? Why should I obey him? Why should I let Israel go? I don't even know the LORD. And I won't let Israel go."

3 Then Moses and Aaron said, "The God of the Hebrews has met with us. Now let us take a journey that lasts about three days. We want to go into the desert to offer sacrifices to the LORD our God. If we don't, he might strike us with plagues. Or he might let us be killed by swords."

4 But the king of Egypt said, "Moses and Aaron, why are you taking the people away from their work? Get back to work!" 5 Pharaoh continued, "There are large numbers of your people in the land. But you are stopping them from working."

6 That same day Pharaoh gave orders to the slave drivers and the overseers in charge of the people. 7 He said, "Don't give the people any more straw to make bricks. Let them go and get their own straw. 8 But require them to make the same number of bricks as before. Don't lower the number they have to make. They are lazy. That's why they are crying out, 'Let us go. We want to offer sacrifices to our God.' 9 Make them work harder. Then they will be too busy to pay attention to lies."

10 The slave drivers and the overseers left. They said to the people, "Pharaoh says, 'I won't give you any more straw. 11 Go and get your own straw anywhere you can find it. But you still have to make the same number of bricks.' " 12 So the people scattered all over Egypt. They went to gather any pieces of straw left in the fields. 13 Pharaoh's slave drivers kept making the people work hard. They said, "Finish the work you are required to do each day. Make the same number of bricks you made when you had straw." 14 The slave drivers whipped the Israelite overseers they had appointed. The slave drivers asked, "Why haven't you made the same number of bricks yesterday or today, just as before?"

15 Then the Israelite overseers appealed to Pharaoh. They asked, "Why have you treated us like this? 16 You didn't give us any straw. But you told us, 'Make bricks!' We are being whipped. But it's the fault of your own people."

17 Pharaoh said, "You are lazy! That's why you keep saying, 'Let us go. We want to offer sacrifices to the LORD.' 18 Now get to work. We won't give you any straw. But you still have to make the same number of bricks."

19 The Israelite overseers realized they were in trouble. They knew it when they were told, "Don't reduce the number of

bricks you are required to make each day." 20 When they left Pharaoh, they found Moses and Aaron waiting to meet them. 21 They said to Moses and Aaron, "We want the LORD to look at what you have done! We want him to judge you for it! We are like a very bad smell to Pharaoh and his officials. You have given them an excuse to kill us with their swords."

The LORD Promises to Save the Israelites

22 Moses returned to talk to the LORD. He said to him, "Why, Lord? Why have you brought trouble on these people? Is this why you sent me? 23 I went to Pharaoh to speak to him in your name. Ever since then, he has brought nothing but trouble on these people. And you haven't saved your people at all."

6 Then the LORD said to Moses, "Now you will see what I will do to Pharaoh. Because of my powerful hand, he will let the people of Israel go. Because of my mighty hand, he will drive them out of his country."

2 God continued, "I am the LORD. 3 I appeared to Abraham, Isaac and Jacob as the Mighty God. But I did not show them the full meaning of my name, The LORD. 4 I also made my covenant with them. I promised to give them the land of Canaan. That is where they lived as outsiders. 5 Also, I have heard the groans of the Israelites. The Egyptians are keeping them as slaves. But I have remembered my covenant.

6 "So tell the people of Israel, 'I am the LORD. I will throw off the heavy load the Egyptians have put on your shoulders. I will set you free from being slaves to them. I will reach out my arm and save you with mighty acts when I judge Egypt. 7 I will take you to be my own people. I will be your God. I throw off the load the Egyptians have put on your shoulders. Then you will know that I am the LORD your God. 8 I will bring you to the land I promised to give to Abraham, Isaac and Jacob. I lifted up my hand and promised it to them. The land will belong to you. I am the LORD.' "

9 Moses reported these things to the Israelites. But they didn't listen to him. That's because they had lost all hope and had to work very hard.

10 Then the LORD said to Moses, 11 "Go. Tell Pharaoh, the king of Egypt, to let the people of Israel leave his country."

12 But Moses said to the LORD, "The people won't listen to me. So why would Pharaoh listen to me? After all, I don't speak very well."

The Family Record of Moses and Aaron

13 The LORD had spoken to Moses and Aaron. He had talked with them about the Israelites and about Pharaoh, the king of Egypt. He had commanded Moses and Aaron to bring the people of Israel out of Egypt.

14 Here were the leaders of the family groups of Reuben, Simeon and Levi.
Reuben was the oldest son of Israel.
Reuben's sons were
Hanok, Pallu, Hezron and Karmi.
These were the family groups of Reuben.

15 The sons of Simeon were
Jemuel, Jamin, Ohad, Jakin, Zohar and Shaul. Shaul was the son of a woman from Canaan.
These were the family groups of Simeon.

16 Here are the names of the sons of Levi written in their family record. They were
Gershon, Kohath and Merari.
Levi lived for 137 years.
17 The sons of Gershon, by their family groups, were
Libni and Shimei.
18 The sons of Kohath were
Amram, Izhar, Hebron and Uzziel.
Kohath lived for 133 years.
19 The sons of Merari were
Mahli and Mushi.
These are the family groups of Levi written in their family record.

20 Amram married his father's sister Jochebed. Aaron and Moses were members of Amram's family line.
Amram lived for 137 years.
21 The sons of Izhar were
Korah, Nepheg and Zikri.
22 The sons of Uzziel were
Mishael, Elzaphan and Sithri.

23 Aaron married Elisheba. She was the daughter of Amminadab and the sister of Nahshon. She had Nadab, Abihu, Eleazar and Ithamar by Aaron.

24 The sons of Korah were
Assir, Elkanah and Abiasaph.
These were the family groups of Korah.

25 Eleazar, the son of Aaron, married one of the daughters of Putiel. She had Phinehas by Eleazar.
These are the leaders of the families of Levi. Their names are written in their family records.

26 The LORD had spoken to this same Aaron and Moses. He had told them, "Bring the Israelites out of Egypt like an army on the march." 27 They spoke to Pharaoh, the king of Egypt, about bringing the people of Israel out of Egypt. It was this same Moses and Aaron.

Aaron Speaks for Moses

28 The LORD had spoken to Moses in Egypt. 29 He had told him, "I am the LORD. Tell Pharaoh, the king of Egypt, everything I tell you."

30 But Moses said to the LORD, "I don't speak very well. So why would Pharaoh listen to me?"

7 Then the LORD said to Moses, "I have made you like God to Pharaoh. And your brother Aaron will be like a prophet to you. 2 You must say everything I command you to say. Then your brother Aaron must tell Pharaoh to let the people of Israel leave his country. 3 But I will make Pharaoh stubborn. I will multiply the signs and amazing things I will do in Egypt. 4 In spite of that, he will not listen to you. So I will use my powerful hand against Egypt. When I judge them with mighty acts, I will bring my people Israel out like an army on the march. 5 Then the Egyptians will know that I am the LORD. I will reach out my powerful hand against them. I will bring the people of Israel out of Egypt."

6 Moses and Aaron did exactly as the LORD had commanded them. 7 Moses was 80 years old and Aaron was 83 when they spoke to Pharaoh.

Aaron's Walking Stick Becomes a Snake

8 The LORD spoke to Moses and Aaron. 9 He said, "Pharaoh will say to you, 'Do a miracle.' When he does, speak to Aaron. Tell him, 'Take your walking stick and throw it down in front of Pharaoh.' It will turn into a snake."

10 So Moses and Aaron went to Pharaoh. They did exactly as the LORD had commanded them. Aaron threw the stick down in front of Pharaoh and his officials. It turned into a snake. 11 Then Pharaoh sent for wise men and people who do evil magic. By doing their magic tricks, the Egyptian magicians did the same things Aaron had done. 12 Each one threw down his walking stick. Each stick turned into a snake. But Aaron's walking stick swallowed theirs up. 13 In spite of that, Pharaoh became stubborn. He wouldn't listen to them, just as the LORD had said.

The Plague of Blood

14 Then the LORD said to Moses, "Pharaoh is very stubborn. He refuses to let the people go. 15 In the morning Pharaoh will go down to the Nile River. Go and meet him on the bank of the river. Take in your hand the walking stick that turned into a snake. 16 Say to Pharaoh, 'The LORD, the God of the Hebrews, has sent me to you. He says, "Let my people go. Then they will be able to worship me in the desert. But up to now you have not listened." 17 The LORD says, "Here is how you will know that I am the LORD. I will strike the water of the Nile River with the walking stick that is in my hand. The river will turn into blood. 18 The fish in the river will die. The river will stink. The Egyptians will not be able to drink its water." ' "

19 The LORD said to Moses, "Tell Aaron, 'Get your walking stick. Reach your hand out over the waters of Egypt. The streams, canals, ponds and all the lakes will turn into blood. There will be blood everywhere in Egypt. It will even be in the wooden buckets and stone jars.' "

20 Moses and Aaron did exactly as the LORD had commanded them. Aaron held out his staff in front of Pharaoh and his officials. He struck the water of the Nile River. And all the water turned into blood. 21 The fish in the Nile died.

The river smelled so bad the Egyptians
couldn't drink its water. There was blood
everywhere in Egypt.
22 But the Egyptian magicians did
the same things by doing their magic
tricks. So Pharaoh became stubborn.
He wouldn't listen to Moses and Aaron,
just as the LORD had said. 23 Even that
miracle didn't change Pharaoh's mind.
In fact, he turned around and went into
his palace. 24 All the Egyptians dug holes
near the Nile River to get drinking water.
They couldn't drink water from the river.

The Plague of Frogs

25 Seven days passed after the LORD
8 struck the Nile River. 1 Then the
LORD said to Moses, "Go to Pharaoh.
Tell him, 'The LORD says, "Let my people
go. Then they will be able to worship me.
2 If you refuse to let them go, I will send
a plague of frogs on your whole country.
3 The Nile River will be full of frogs. They
will come up into your palace. You will
have frogs in your bedroom and on
your bed. They will be in the homes of
your officials and your people. They will
be in your ovens and in the bowls for
kneading your bread. 4 The frogs will
be on you, your people and all your
officials." ' "
5 Then the LORD spoke to Moses.
He said, "Tell Aaron, 'Reach out your
hand. Hold your walking stick over the
streams, canals and ponds. Make frogs
come up on the land of Egypt.' "
6 So Aaron reached out his hand over
the waters of Egypt. The frogs came
up and covered the land. 7 But the magicians did the same things by doing
their magic tricks. They also made frogs
come up on the land of Egypt.
8 Pharaoh sent for Moses and Aaron.
He said to them, "Pray to the LORD to
take the frogs away from me and my
people. Then I'll let your people go to
offer sacrifices to the LORD."
9 Moses said to Pharaoh, "You can
have the honor of setting the time for
me to pray. I will pray for you, your
officials and your people. I'll pray that
the frogs will leave you and your homes.
The only frogs left will be the ones in
the Nile River."
10 "Tomorrow," Pharaoh said.
Moses replied, "It will happen just as
you say. Then you will know that there is
no one like the LORD our God. 11 The frogs
will leave you and your houses. They will
leave your officials and your people. The
frogs will remain only in the Nile River."
12 Moses and Aaron left Pharaoh. Then
Moses cried out to the LORD about the
frogs he had brought on Pharaoh. 13 And
the LORD did what Moses asked. The
frogs died in the houses, courtyards and
fields. 14 The Egyptians piled them up.
The land smelled very bad because of
them. 15 But when Pharaoh saw that the
frogs were dead, he became stubborn.
He wouldn't listen to Moses and Aaron,
just as the LORD had said.

The Plague of Gnats

16 Then the LORD spoke to Moses. He
said, "Tell Aaron, 'Reach out your walking stick. Strike the dust on the ground
with it.' Then all over the land of Egypt
the dust will turn into gnats." 17 So they
did it. Aaron reached out the stick that
was in his hand. He struck the dust on
the ground with it. The dust all over
the land of Egypt turned into gnats.
They landed on people and animals
alike. 18 The magicians tried to produce
gnats by doing their magic tricks. But
they couldn't.
The gnats stayed on people and animals everywhere. 19 So the magicians
said to Pharaoh, "God's powerful finger
has done this." But Pharaoh remained
stubborn. He wouldn't listen, just as the
LORD had said.

The Plague of Flies

20 Then the LORD spoke to Moses. He
said, "Get up early in the morning. Talk
to Pharaoh as he goes down to the Nile
River. Say to him, 'The LORD says, "Let
my people go. Then they will be able
to worship me. 21 If you do not let my
people go, I will send large numbers of
flies. I will send them on you and your
officials. I will send them on your people
and into your homes. The houses of the
Egyptians will be full of flies. Even the
ground will be covered with them.
22 " ' "But on that day I will treat the
area of Goshen differently from yours.
That is where my people live. There
will not be large numbers of flies in
Goshen. Then you will know that I, the
LORD, am in this land. 23 I will treat my
people differently from yours. This sign
will take place tomorrow." ' "

24 So the LORD did it. Huge numbers of
flies poured into Pharaoh's palace. They
came into the homes of his officials. All
over Egypt the flies destroyed the land.
25 Then Pharaoh sent for Moses and
Aaron. He said to them, "Go. Offer sacrifices to your God here in the land."
26 But Moses said, "That wouldn't be
right. The sacrifices we offer to the LORD
our God wouldn't be accepted by the
Egyptians because of their beliefs. For that
reason, they would throw stones at us and
try to kill us. 27 We have to take a journey
that lasts about three days. We want to
go into the desert to offer sacrifices to the
LORD our God, just as he commands us."
28 Pharaoh said, "I will let you and
your people go to offer sacrifices. You
can offer them to the LORD your God in
the desert. But you must not go very far.
Now pray for me."
29 Moses replied, "As soon as I leave
you, I will pray to the LORD. Tomorrow
the flies will leave you. They will also
leave your officials and your people.
Just be sure you don't try to trick us
again. Let the people go to offer sacrifices to the LORD."
30 Then Moses left Pharaoh and
prayed to the LORD. 31 And the LORD
did what Moses asked. The flies left
Pharaoh, his officials and his people.
Not one fly remained. 32 But Pharaoh
became stubborn this time also. He
wouldn't let the people go.

The Plague on Livestock

9 Then the LORD spoke to Moses. He
said, "Go to Pharaoh. Tell him, 'The
LORD, the God of the Hebrews, says, "Let
my people go. Then they will be able to
worship me. 2 Do not refuse to let them
go. Do not keep holding them back.
3 If you refuse, my powerful hand will
bring a terrible plague on you. I will
strike your livestock in the fields. I
will strike your horses, donkeys, camels,
cattle, sheep and goats. 4 But I will treat
Israel's livestock differently from yours.
No animal that belongs to the people
of Israel will die." ' "
5 The LORD set a time for the plague.
He said, "Tomorrow I will send it on the
land." 6 So the next day the LORD sent it.
All the livestock of the Egyptians died.
But not one animal that belonged to the
Israelites died. 7 Pharaoh searched and
found out what had happened. He discovered that not even one animal that
belonged to the Israelites had died. But
he was still very stubborn. He wouldn't
let the people go.

The Plague of Boils

8 Then the LORD spoke to Moses and
Aaron. He said, "Take handfuls of ashes
from a furnace. Have Moses toss them
into the air in front of Pharaoh. 9 The
ashes will turn into fine dust over the
whole land of Egypt. Then painful boils
will break out on people and animals
all over the land. Their bodies will be
covered with them."
10 So Moses and Aaron took ashes
from a furnace and stood in front of
Pharaoh. Moses tossed them into the
air. Then boils broke out on people and
animals alike. 11 The bodies of all the
Egyptians were covered with boils. The
magicians couldn't stand in front of
Moses because of the boils that were
all over them. 12 But the LORD made
Pharaoh stubborn. Pharaoh wouldn't
listen to Moses and Aaron, just as the
LORD had said to Moses.

The Plague of Hail

13 Then the LORD spoke to Moses. He
said, "Get up early in the morning. Go
to Pharaoh and say to him, 'The LORD,
the God of the Hebrews, says, "Let my
people go. Then they will be able to
worship me. 14 If you do not let them go,
I will send the full force of my plagues
against you this time. They will strike
your officials and your people. Then
you will know that there is no one
like me in the whole earth. 15 By now
I could have reached out my hand. I
could have struck you and your people
with a plague that would have wiped
you off the earth. 16 But I had a special
reason for making you king. I decided
to show you my power. I wanted my
name to become known everywhere
on earth. 17 But you are still against my
people. You will not let them go. 18 So
at this time tomorrow I will send the
worst hailstorm ever to fall on Egypt in
its entire history. 19 Give an order now
to bring your livestock inside to a safe
place. Bring in everything that is outside. The hail will fall on all the people
and animals that are left outside. They
will die." ' "

20 The officials of Pharaoh who had respect for what the LORD had said obeyed him. They hurried to bring their slaves and their livestock inside. 21 But others didn't pay attention to what the LORD had said. They left their slaves and livestock outside.

22 Then the LORD spoke to Moses. He said, "Reach out your hand toward the sky. Then hail will fall all over Egypt. It will beat down on people and animals alike. It will strike everything growing in the fields of Egypt." 23 Moses reached out his walking stick toward the sky. Then the LORD sent thunder and hail. Lightning flashed down to the ground. The LORD rained hail on the land of Egypt. 24 Hail fell and lightning flashed back and forth. It was the worst storm in Egypt's entire history. 25 Hail struck everything in the fields all over Egypt. It fell on people and animals alike. It beat down everything growing in the fields. It tore all the leaves off the trees. 26 The only place it didn't hail was in the area of Goshen. That's where the people of Israel were.

27 Then Pharaoh sent for Moses and Aaron. "This time I've sinned," he said to them. "The LORD has done what is right. I and my people have done what is wrong. 28 Pray to the LORD, because we've had enough thunder and hail. I'll let you and your people go. You don't have to stay here any longer."

29 Moses replied, "When I've left the city, I'll lift up my hands and pray to the LORD. The thunder will stop. There won't be any more hail. Then you will know that the earth belongs to the LORD. 30 But I know that you and your officials still don't have any respect for the LORD God."

31 The barley was ripe. The flax was in bloom. So they were both destroyed. 32 But the wheat and spelt weren't destroyed. That's because they ripen later.

33 Then Moses left Pharaoh and went out of the city. Moses lifted up his hands and prayed to the LORD. The thunder and hail stopped. The rain didn't pour down on the land any longer. 34 Pharaoh saw that the rain, hail and thunder had stopped. So he sinned again. He and his officials became stubborn. 35 So Pharaoh was stubborn. He wouldn't let the people of Israel go, just as the LORD had said through Moses.

The Plague of Locusts

10 Then the LORD said to Moses, "Go to Pharaoh. I have made him stubborn. I have also made his officials stubborn so I can perform my signs among them. 2 Then you will be able to tell your children and grandchildren how hard I was on the Egyptians. You can tell them I performed my signs among the people of Egypt. And all of you will know that I am the LORD."

3 So Moses and Aaron went to Pharaoh. They said to him, "The LORD, the God of the Hebrews, says, 'How long will you refuse to obey me? Let my people go. Then they will be able to worship me. 4 If you refuse to let them go, I will bring locusts into your country tomorrow. 5 They will cover the ground so that it can't be seen. They will eat what little you have left after the hail. That includes every tree growing in your fields. 6 They will fill your houses. They will be in the homes of all your officials and your people. Your parents and your people before them have never seen anything like it as long as they have lived here.' " Then Moses turned around and left Pharaoh.

7 Pharaoh's officials said to him, "How long will this man be a trap for us? Let the people go. Then they'll be able to worship the LORD their God. After everything that's happened, don't you realize that Egypt is destroyed?"

8 Moses and Aaron were brought back to Pharaoh. "Go. Worship the LORD your God," he said. "But tell me who will be going."

9 Moses answered, "We'll go with our young people and old people. We'll go with our sons and daughters. We'll take our flocks and herds. We are supposed to hold a feast to honor the LORD."

10 Pharaoh said, "Suppose I ever let you go, along with your women and children. Then the LORD really will be with all of you! Clearly you are planning to do something bad. 11 No! I'll only allow the men to go and worship the LORD. After all, that's what you have been asking for." Then Pharaoh drove Moses and Aaron out of his sight.

12 The LORD said to Moses, "Reach out your hand over Egypt so that locusts cover the land. They will eat up everything growing in the fields. They will eat up everything left by the hail."

[13] So Moses reached out his walking
stick over Egypt. Then the LORD made
an east wind blow across the land. It
blew all that day and all that night.
By morning the wind had brought the
locusts. [14] Large numbers of them came
down in every part of Egypt. There had
never been a plague of locusts like it
before. And there will never be one
like it again. [15] The locusts covered the
ground until it was black. They ate up
everything left after the hail. They ate
up everything growing in the fields.
They ate up the fruit on the trees. There
was nothing green left on any tree or
plant in the whole land of Egypt.
[16] Pharaoh quickly sent for Moses and
Aaron. He said, "I have sinned against
the LORD your God. I've also sinned
against you. [17] Now forgive my sin one
more time. Pray to the LORD your God to
take this deadly plague away from me."
[18] After Moses left Pharaoh, he prayed
to the LORD. [19] The LORD changed the
wind to a very strong west wind. It
picked up the locusts. It blew them into
the Red Sea. Not even one locust was
left anywhere in Egypt. [20] But the LORD
made Pharaoh stubborn. So Pharaoh
wouldn't let the people of Israel go.

The Plague of Darkness

[21] The LORD spoke to Moses. He said,
"Reach out your hand toward the sky so
that darkness spreads over Egypt. It will
be so dark that people can feel it." [22] So
Moses reached out his hand toward the
sky. Then complete darkness covered
Egypt for three days. [23] No one could
see anyone else or go anywhere for
three days. But all the people of Israel
had light where they lived.
[24] Then Pharaoh sent for Moses. He said
to him, "Go. Worship the LORD. Even your
women and children can go with you.
Just leave your flocks and herds behind."
[25] But Moses said, "You must allow us
to take our animals. We need to offer
them as sacrifices and burnt offerings
to the LORD our God. [26] Our livestock
must also go with us. We have to use
some of them to worship the LORD our
God. We can't leave even one animal
behind. Until we get there, we won't
know what we are supposed to use to
worship the LORD."

27 But the LORD made Pharaoh stubborn. So he wouldn't let the people go.
28 Pharaoh said to Moses, "Get out of
my sight! Make sure you don't come to
see me again! If you do, you will die."
29 "I'll do just as you say," Moses replied.
"I will never come to see you again."

The LORD Announces the Tenth Plague

11 The LORD had spoken to Moses. He
had said, "I will bring one more
plague on Pharaoh and on Egypt. After
that, he will let you and your people go.
When he does, he will drive every one of
you away. 2 Tell the men and women
alike to ask their neighbors for things
made out of silver and gold." 3 The LORD
caused the Egyptians to treat the Israelites in a kind way. Pharaoh's officials and
the people had great respect for Moses.
4 Moses told Pharaoh, "The LORD says,
'About midnight I will go through every
part of Egypt. 5 Every oldest son in Egypt
will die. The oldest son of Pharaoh, who
sits on the throne, will die. The oldest son
of every female slave, who works at her
hand mill, will die. All the male animals
born first to their mothers among the
cattle will also die. 6 There will be loud
crying all over Egypt. It will be worse
than it's ever been before. And nothing
like it will ever be heard again. 7 But
among the Israelites not even one dog
will bark at any person or animal.' Then
you will know that the LORD treats Egypt
differently from us. 8 All your officials
will come and bow down to me. They will
say, 'Go, you and all the people who follow you!' After that, I will leave." Moses
was very angry when he left Pharaoh.
9 The LORD had spoken to Moses. He
had said, "Pharaoh will refuse to listen
to you. So I will multiply the amazing
things I will do in Egypt." 10 Moses and
Aaron performed all these amazing
things in the sight of Pharaoh. But
the LORD made Pharaoh stubborn. He
wouldn't let the people of Israel go out
of his country.

The First Passover Sacrifice

12 The LORD spoke to Moses and
Aaron in Egypt. 2 He said, "From
now on, this month will be your first
month. Each of your years will begin

pointing us to JESUS: The Passover Lamb

When God's people, the Israelites, were still enslaved in Egypt, God gave them what seemed to be a very strange command. He told them to sacrifice a lamb that had no flaws and to paint the doorframe of their home with the blood from the lamb. God told the people of Israel that the final sign of his power to the Egyptians who had enslaved them would be a plague of death. But God also promised that all those who painted the doorframe of their home with the blood of the lamb would be spared, or saved, and the oldest son in the family would not die. And that's exactly what happened: God sent death to visit all of Egypt, and the oldest son in every home that was marked with the blood of the lamb did not die. Those homes were "passed over" by God when the destroying angel carried out the plague of death (see Exodus 12:23).

Through the events of Passover, God was pointing his people toward the coming Savior. Jesus would be the perfect, spotless Lamb who would die so that sinners could be made right with God. He promises that all who put their faith in him are saved by the blood of his sacrifice. They are eternally secure and have no need to fear death because they will live with Jesus forever!

with it. [3]Speak to the whole community of Israel. Tell them that on the tenth day of this month each man must get a lamb from his flock. A lamb should be chosen for each family and home. [4]Suppose there are not enough people in your family to eat a whole lamb. Then you must share some of it with your nearest neighbor. You must add up the total number of people there are. You must decide how much lamb is needed for each person. [5]The animals you choose must be males that are a year old. They must not have any flaws. You may choose either sheep or goats. [6]Take care of them until the 14th day of the month. Then the whole community of Israel must kill them when the sun goes down. [7]Take some of the blood. Put it on the sides and tops of the doorframes of the houses where you eat the lambs. [8]That same night eat the meat cooked over a fire. Also eat bitter plants. And eat bread made without yeast. [9]Do not eat the meat when it is raw. Don't boil it in water. Instead, cook it over a fire. Cook the head, legs and inside parts. [10]Do not leave any of it until morning. If some is left over until morning, burn it up. [11]Eat the meat while your coat is tucked into your belt. Put your sandals on your feet. Take your walking stick in your hand. Eat the food quickly. It is the LORD's Passover.

[12]"That same night I will pass through Egypt. I will strike down all those born first among the people and animals. And I will judge all the gods of Egypt. I am the LORD. [13]The blood on your houses will be a sign for you. When I see the blood, I will pass over you. No deadly plague will touch you when I strike Egypt.

[14]"Always remember this day. You and your children after you must celebrate this day as a feast to honor the LORD. You must do this for all time to come. It is a law that will last forever. [15]For seven days eat bread made without yeast. On the first day remove the yeast from your homes. For the next seven days, anyone who eats anything with yeast in it must be separated from Israel. [16]On the first and seventh days, come together for a sacred assembly. Do not work at all on these days. The only thing you are allowed to do is prepare food for everyone to eat.

[17]"Celebrate the Feast of Unleavened Bread. I brought you out of Egypt on this very day like an army on the march. It is a law that will last for all time to come. [18]In the first month eat bread made without yeast. Eat it from the evening of the 14th day until the evening of the 21st day. [19]For seven days do not let any yeast be found in your homes. Anyone who eats anything with yeast in it must be separated from the community of Israel. That applies to outsiders and Israelites alike. [20]Do not eat anything made with yeast. No matter where you live, eat bread made without yeast."

[21]Then Moses sent for all the elders of Israel. He said to them, "Go at once. Choose the animals for your families. Each family must kill a Passover lamb. [22]Get a branch of a hyssop plant. Dip it into the blood in the bowl. Put some of the blood on the top and on both sides of the doorframe. None of you can go out of the door of your house until morning. [23]The LORD will go through the land to strike down the Egyptians. He'll see the blood on the top and sides of the doorframe. He will pass over that house. He won't let the destroying angel enter your homes to strike you down.

[24]"Obey all these directions. It's a law for you and your children after you for all time to come. [25]The LORD will give you the land, just as he promised. When you enter it, keep this holy day. [26]Your children will ask you, 'What does this holy day mean to you?' [27]Tell them, 'It's the Passover sacrifice to honor the LORD. He passed over the houses of the Israelites in Egypt. He spared our homes when he struck down the Egyptians.'" Then the Israelites bowed down and worshiped. [28]They did just what the LORD commanded Moses and Aaron.

[29]At midnight the LORD struck down every oldest son in Egypt. He killed the oldest son of Pharaoh, who sat on the throne. He killed all the oldest sons of prisoners. He also killed all the male animals born first to their mothers among the livestock. [30]Pharaoh and all his officials got up during the night. So did all the Egyptians. There was loud crying in Egypt because someone had died in every home.

The Exodus

[31] During the night, Pharaoh sent for Moses and Aaron. He said to them, "Get out of here! You and the Israelites, leave my people! Go. Worship the LORD, just as you have asked. [32] Go. Take your flocks and herds, just as you have said. And also give me your blessing."

[33] The Egyptians begged the people of Israel to hurry up and leave the country. "If you don't," they said, "we'll all die!" [34] So the people took their dough before the yeast was added to it. They carried it on their shoulders in bowls for kneading bread. The bowls were wrapped in clothes. [35] They did just as Moses had directed them. They asked the Egyptians for things made out of silver and gold. They also asked them for clothes. [36] The LORD had caused the Egyptians to treat the Israelites in a kind way. So the Egyptians gave them what they asked for. The Israelites took many expensive things that belonged to the Egyptians.

[37] The Israelites traveled from Rameses to Sukkoth. There were about 600,000 men old enough to go into battle. The women and children went with them. [38] So did many other people. The Israelites also took large flocks and herds with them. [39] The Israelites brought dough from Egypt. With it they baked loaves of bread without yeast. The dough didn't have any yeast in it. That's because the people had been driven out of Egypt before they had time to prepare their food.

[40] The Israelites lived in Egypt for 430 years. [41] Then all the LORD's people marched out of Egypt like an army. That happened at the end of the 430 years, to the exact day. [42] The LORD kept watch that night to bring them out of Egypt. So on that same night every year all the Israelites must keep watch. They must do it to honor the LORD for all time to come.

Rules for the Passover

[43] The LORD said to Moses and Aaron, "Here are the rules for the Passover meal.

"No one from another country is allowed to eat it. [44] Any slave you have bought is allowed to eat it after you have circumcised him. [45] But a hired worker or someone who lives with you for a short time is not allowed to eat it. [46] "It must be eaten inside the house. Do not take any of the meat outside. Do not break any of the bones. [47] The whole community of Israel must celebrate the Passover.

[48] "Suppose an outsider living among you wants to celebrate the LORD's Passover. Then all the males in that home must be circumcised. After that, the person can take part, just like an Israelite. Only circumcised males may eat it. [49] The same law applies to Israelites and to outsiders living among you."

[50] All the people of Israel did just what the LORD had commanded Moses and Aaron. [51] On that day the LORD brought the Israelites out of Egypt like an army on the march.

Setting Apart the Oldest Sons

13 The LORD said to Moses, [2] "Set apart for me the first boy born in every family. The oldest son of every Israelite mother belongs to me. Every male animal born first to its mother also belongs to me."

[3] Then Moses said to the people, "Remember this day. It's the day you came out of Egypt. That's the land where you were slaves. The LORD used his mighty hand to bring you out of Egypt. Don't eat anything with yeast in it. [4] You are leaving today. It's the month of Aviv. [5] The LORD will bring you into the land of the Canaanites, Hittites, Amorites, Hivites and Jebusites. He promised your people of long ago that he would give that land to you. It's a land that has plenty of milk and honey. When you get there, celebrate this holy day in this month. [6] For seven days eat bread made without yeast. On the seventh day hold a feast to honor the LORD. [7] Eat bread made without yeast during those seven days. Nothing with yeast in it should be found among you. No yeast should be seen anywhere inside your borders. [8] On that day talk to your child. Say, 'I'm doing this because of what the LORD did for me when I came out of Egypt.' [9] When you celebrate this holy day, it will be like a mark on your hand. It will be like a reminder on your forehead. This law of the LORD must be on your lips. The LORD used his mighty hand to bring you out of Egypt. [10] Obey this law at the appointed time year after year.

[11]"The LORD will bring you into
the land of Canaan. He will give it to
you, just as he promised he would. He
gave his word to you and your people
of long ago. [12]After you arrive in the
land, give to the LORD the oldest son of
every mother. Every male animal born
first to its mother among your livestock
belongs to the LORD. [13]By sacrificing a
lamb, buy back every male donkey born
first to its mother. But if you don't buy
the donkey back, break its neck. Buy
back every oldest son.

[14]"In days to come, your child will ask
you, 'What does this mean?' Say to them,
'The LORD used his mighty hand to bring
us out of Egypt. That's the land where we
were slaves. [15]Pharaoh was stubborn. He
refused to let us go. So the LORD killed
every oldest son in Egypt. He also killed
all those born first among the people
and animals. That's why I sacrifice to the
LORD every male animal born first. And
that's why I buy back each of my oldest
sons for the LORD.' [16]This holy day will be
like a mark on your hand. It will be like
a sign on your forehead. It will remind
you that the LORD used his mighty hand
to bring us out of Egypt."

Israel Goes Through the Red Sea

[17]Pharaoh let the people go. The
shortest road from Goshen to Canaan
went through the Philistine country.
But God didn't lead them that way. God
said, "If they have to go into battle, they
might change their minds. They might
return to Egypt." [18]So God led the people
toward the Red Sea by taking them on a
road through the desert. The Israelites
were ready for battle when they went
up out of Egypt.

[19]Moses took the bones of Joseph
along with him. Joseph had made the
Israelites give their word to do this. He
had said, "God will surely come to help
you. When he does, you must carry my
bones up from this place with you."
(Genesis 50:25)

[20]The people left Sukkoth. They
camped at Etham on the edge of the
desert. [21]By day the LORD went ahead of
them in a pillar of cloud. It guided them
on their way. At night he led them with
a pillar of fire. It gave them light. So they
could travel by day or at night. [22]The pillar of cloud didn't leave its place in front
of the people during the day. And the
pillar of fire didn't leave its place at night.

pointing us to JESUS: Moses

God continued to keep his promise to make Abraham's family into a great big family. In fact, Abraham's family had grown so big that the ruler of Egypt, Pharaoh, felt threatened by the people and made all of them slaves in Egypt. God's people were slaves for years, but just when it seemed like they would never be free, God called Moses to lead his people into freedom.

God commanded Moses to tell Pharaoh, "Let my people go" (Exodus 5:1). But Pharaoh would not listen. Again and again Moses told Pharaoh to set God's people free, and again and again Pharaoh refused. God even sent ten plagues on the Egyptians to show Pharaoh that he was the one true God and that all of Egypt's gods were fake and powerless. After the last plague on Egypt, Moses led God's people to the Red Sea, where God miraculously parted the water and set the people free.

God promised his people that a greater Deliverer than Moses would come. That Savior is Jesus, the greater and better deliverer who sets us free from slavery to sin and invites us into new life with him.

14 Then the LORD spoke to Moses.
2 He said, "Tell the people of Israel
to turn back. Have them camp near Pi
Hahiroth between Migdol and the Red
Sea. They must camp by the sea, right
across from Baal Zephon. 3 Pharaoh
will think, 'The Israelites are wandering around the land. They don't know
which way to go. The desert is all around
them.' 4 I will make Pharaoh stubborn.
He will chase them. But I will gain glory
for myself because of what will happen
to Pharaoh and his whole army. And the
Egyptians will know that I am the LORD."
So the Israelites camped by the Red Sea.
5 The king of Egypt was told that the
people had escaped. Then Pharaoh and
his officials changed their minds about
them. They said, "What have we done?
We've let the people of Israel go! We've
lost our slaves and all the work they
used to do for us!" 6 So he had his chariot
made ready. He took his army with him.
7 He took 600 of the best chariots in
Egypt. He also took along all the other
chariots. Officers were in charge of all
of them. 8 The LORD made Pharaoh, the
king of Egypt, stubborn. So he chased
the Israelites as they were marching
out boldly. 9 The Egyptians went after the Israelites. All Pharaoh's horses
and chariots and horsemen and troops
chased them. They caught up with the
Israelites as they camped by the sea.
The Israelites were near Pi Hahiroth,
across from Baal Zephon.
10 As Pharaoh approached, the Israelites looked back. There were the Egyptians marching after them! The Israelites
were terrified. They cried out to the LORD.
11 They said to Moses, "Why did you bring
us to the desert to die? Weren't there any
graves in Egypt? What have you done
to us by bringing us out of Egypt? 12 We
told you in Egypt, 'Leave us alone. Let us
serve the Egyptians.' It would have been
better for us to serve the Egyptians than
to die here in the desert!"
13 Moses answered the people. He said,
"Don't be afraid. Stand firm. You will
see how the LORD will save you today.
Do you see those Egyptians? You will
never see them again. 14 The LORD will
fight for you. Just be still."
15 Then the LORD spoke to Moses. He
said, "Why are you crying out to me?
Tell the people of Israel to move on.
16 Hold out your walking stick. Reach

out your hand over the Red Sea to divide the water. Then the people can go
through the sea on dry ground. 17 I will
make the Egyptians stubborn. They
will go in after the Israelites. I will gain
glory for myself because of what will
happen to Pharaoh, his army, chariots
and horsemen. 18 The Egyptians will
know that I am the LORD. I will gain glory because of what will happen to Pharaoh, his chariots and his horsemen."

19 The angel of God had been traveling
in front of Israel's army. Now he moved
back and went behind them. The pillar
of cloud also moved away from in front
of them. Now it stood behind them. 20 It
came between the armies of Egypt and
Israel. All through the night the cloud
brought darkness to one side and light
to the other. Neither army went near
the other all night long.

21 Then Moses reached out his hand
over the Red Sea. All that night the LORD
pushed the sea back with a strong east
wind. He turned the sea into dry land.
The waters were divided. 22 The people
of Israel went through the sea on dry
ground. There was a wall of water on
their right side and on their left.

23 The Egyptians chased them. All Pharaoh's horses and chariots and horsemen
followed them into the sea. 24 Near the
end of the night the LORD looked down
from the pillar of fire and cloud. He saw
the Egyptian army and threw it into a
panic. 25 He jammed the wheels of their
chariots. That made the chariots hard to
drive. The Egyptians said, "Let's get away
from the Israelites! The LORD is fighting
for Israel against Egypt."

26 Then the LORD spoke to Moses. He
said, "Reach out your hand over the sea.
The waters will flow back over the Egyptians and their chariots and horsemen."
27 So Moses reached out his hand over
the sea. At sunrise the sea went back
to its place. The Egyptians tried to run
away from the sea. But the LORD swept
them into it. 28 The water flowed back
and covered the chariots and horsemen.
It covered the entire army of Pharaoh
that had followed the people of Israel
into the sea. Not one of the Egyptians
was left.

29 But the Israelites went through the
sea on dry ground. There was a wall of
water on their right side and on their left.
30 That day the LORD saved Israel from
the power of Egypt. The Israelites saw
the Egyptians lying dead on the shore.
31 The Israelites saw the amazing power
the LORD showed against the Egyptians.
So the Israelites had great respect for the
LORD and put their trust in him. They
also put their trust in his servant Moses.

The Song of Moses and Miriam

15 Here is the song that Moses and
the people of Israel sang to the
LORD. They said,

"I will sing to the LORD.
He is greatly honored.
He has thrown Pharaoh's horses
and chariot drivers
into the Red Sea.
2 The LORD gives me strength and
protects me.
He has saved me.
He is my God, I will praise him.
He is my father's God, and I will
honor him.
3 The LORD goes into battle.
The LORD is his name.
4 He has thrown Pharaoh's chariots
and army
into the Red Sea.
Pharaoh's best officers
drowned in the sea.
5 The deep waters covered them.
They sank to the bottom like a
stone.
6 "LORD, your right hand
was majestic and powerful.
LORD, your right hand
destroyed your enemies.
7 Because of your great majesty,
you threw down those who
opposed you.
Your burning anger blazed out.
It burned them up like straw.
8 The powerful blast from your nose
piled up the waters.
The rushing waters stood firm like
a wall.
The deep waters stood up in the
middle of the sea.
9 "Your enemies bragged,
'We will chase Israel and will
catch them.
We'll divide up what we take from
them.
We'll eat them alive.

We'll pull our swords out.
  Our powerful hands will destroy
   them.'
10 But you blew with your breath.
  The Red Sea covered your
   enemies.
They sank like lead
  in the mighty waters.

11 "LORD, who among the gods is like
   you?
  Who is like you?
You are majestic and holy.
  Your glory fills me with wonder.
  You do amazing things.
12 You reach out your right hand.
  The earth swallows up your
   enemies.
13 "Because your love is faithful,
  you will lead the people you have
   set free.
Because you are so strong,
  you will guide them to the holy
   place where you live.
14 The nations will hear about it and
   tremble.
  Pain and suffering will take hold
   of the Philistines.
15 The chiefs of Edom will be terrified.
  The leaders of Moab will tremble
   with fear.
The people of Canaan will melt
   away.
16 Fear and terror will fall on them.
Your powerful arm
  will make them as still as a stone.
Then your people will pass by,
   LORD.
  Then the people you created will
   pass by.
17 You will bring them in.
  You will plant them on the
   mountain you gave them.
LORD, you have made that place
   your home.
  Lord, your hands have made
   your holy place secure.
18 "The LORD rules
  for ever and ever."

19 Pharaoh's horses, chariots and
horsemen went into the Red Sea. The
LORD brought the waters of the sea
back over them. But the people of Israel
walked through the sea on dry ground.
20 Aaron's sister Miriam was a prophet.
She took a tambourine in her hand. All
the women followed her. They played
tambourines and danced. 21 Miriam
sang to them,

"Sing to the LORD.
  He is greatly honored.
He has thrown Pharaoh's horses
  and chariot drivers
  into the Red Sea."

The Waters of Marah and Elim

22 Then Moses led Israel away from
the Red Sea. They went into the Desert
of Shur. For three days they traveled in
the desert. They didn't find any water
there. 23 When they came to Marah, they
couldn't drink its water. It was bitter.
That's why the place is named Marah.
24 The people told Moses they weren't
happy with him. They said, "What are
we supposed to drink?"
25 Then Moses cried out to the LORD.
The LORD showed him a stick. Moses
threw it into the water. The water became fit to drink.

There the LORD gave a ruling and
instruction for the people. And there he
tested them. 26 He said, "I am the LORD
your God. Listen carefully to me. Do
what is right in my eyes. Pay attention
to my commands. Obey all my rules.
If you do, I will not send on you any of
the sicknesses I sent on the Egyptians.
I am the LORD who heals you."
27 The people came to Elim. It had 12
springs and 70 palm trees. They camped
there near the water.

The LORD Gives Israel Food Every Day

16 The whole community of Israel
started out from Elim. They came
to the Desert of Sin. It was between Elim
and Sinai. They arrived there on the
15th day of the second month after they
had come out of Egypt. 2 In the desert
the whole community told Moses and
Aaron they weren't happy with them.
3 The Israelites said to them, "We wish
the LORD had put us to death in Egypt.
There we sat around pots of meat. We
ate all the food we wanted. But you
have brought us out into this desert.
You must want this entire community
to die of hunger."
4 Then the LORD spoke to Moses. He
said, "I will rain down bread from
heaven for you. The people must go
out each day. Have them gather enough

bread for that day. Here is how I will test them. I will see if they will follow my directions. 5 On the sixth day they must prepare what they bring in. On that day they must gather twice as much as on the other days."

6 So Moses and Aaron spoke to all the people of Israel. They said, "In the evening you will know that the LORD brought you out of Egypt. 7 And in the morning you will see the glory of the LORD. He has heard you say you aren't happy with him. Who are we? Why are you telling us you aren't happy with us?" 8 Moses also said, "You will know that the LORD has heard you speak against him. He will give you meat to eat in the evening. He'll give you all the bread you want in the morning. But who are we? You aren't speaking against us. You are speaking against the LORD."

9 Then Moses told Aaron, "Talk to the whole community of Israel. Say to them, 'Come to the LORD. He has heard you speak against him.' "

10 While Aaron was talking to the whole community of Israel, they looked toward the desert. There was the glory of the LORD appearing in the cloud!

11 The LORD said to Moses, 12 "I have heard the people of Israel talking about how unhappy they are. Tell them, 'When the sun goes down, you will eat meat. In the morning you will be filled with bread. Then you will know that I am the LORD your God.' "

13 That evening quail came and covered the camp. In the morning the ground around the camp was covered with dew. 14 When the dew was gone, thin flakes appeared on the desert floor. They looked like frost on the ground. 15 The people of Israel saw the flakes. They asked each other, "What's that?" They didn't know what it was.

Moses said to them, "It's the bread the LORD has given you to eat. 16 Here is what the LORD has commanded. He has said, 'Everyone should gather as much as they need. Take three pounds for each person who lives in your tent.' "

17 The people of Israel did as they were told. Some gathered a lot, and some gathered a little. 18 When they measured it out, the one who gathered a lot didn't have too much. And the one who gathered a little had enough. Everyone gathered only what they needed.

19 Then Moses said to them, "Don't keep any of it until morning."

20 Some of them didn't pay any attention to Moses. They kept part of it until morning. But it was full of maggots and began to stink. So Moses became angry with them.

21 Each morning everyone gathered as much as they needed. But by the hottest time of the day, the thin flakes had melted away. 22 On the sixth day, the people gathered twice as much. It amounted to six pounds for each person. The leaders of the community came and reported that to Moses. 23 He said to them, "Here is what the LORD commanded. He said, 'Tomorrow will be a day of rest. It will be a holy Sabbath day. It will be set apart for the LORD. So bake what you want to bake. Boil what you want to boil. Save what is left. Keep it until morning.' "

24 So they saved it until morning, just as Moses commanded. It didn't stink or get maggots in it. 25 "Eat it today," Moses said. "Today is a Sabbath day to honor the LORD. You won't find any flakes on the ground today. 26 Gather them for six days. But on the seventh day there won't be any. It's the Sabbath day."

27 In spite of what Moses said, some of the people went out on the seventh day to gather the flakes. But they didn't find any. 28 Then the LORD spoke to Moses. He said, "How long will all of you refuse to obey my commands and my teachings? 29 Keep in mind that I have given you the Sabbath day. That is why on the sixth day I give you bread for two days. Everyone must stay where they are on the seventh day. No one can go out." 30 So the people rested on the seventh day.

31 The people of Israel called the bread manna. It was white like coriander seeds. It tasted like wafers made with honey. 32 Moses said, "Here is what the LORD has commanded. He has said, 'Get three pounds of manna. Keep it for all time to come. Then those who live after you will see the bread I gave you to eat in the desert. I gave it to you when I brought you out of Egypt.' "

33 So Moses said to Aaron, "Get a jar. Put three pounds of manna in it. Then place it in front of the LORD. Keep it there for all time to come."

34 Aaron did exactly as the LORD had
commanded Moses. He put the manna
with the tablets of the covenant law.
He put it there so it would be kept for
all time to come. 35 The Israelites ate
manna for 40 years. They ate it until
they came to a land where people were
living. They ate it until they reached the
border of Canaan.
36 The jar had three pounds of manna
in it.

Water Out of the Rock

17 The whole community of Israel
started out from the Desert of Sin.
They traveled from place to place, just
as the LORD commanded. They camped
at Rephidim. But there wasn't any water
for the people to drink. 2 So they argued
with Moses. They said, "Give us water
to drink."
Moses replied, "Why are you arguing with me? Why are you testing the
LORD?"
3 But the people were thirsty for water
there. So they told Moses they weren't
happy with him. They said, "Why did
you bring us up out of Egypt? Did you
want us, our children and our livestock
to die of thirst?"
4 Then Moses cried out to the LORD.
He said, "What am I going to do with
these people? They are almost ready
to kill me by throwing stones at me."
5 The LORD answered Moses. "Go out
in front of the people. Take some of the
elders of Israel along with you. Take in
your hand the walking stick you used
when you struck the Nile River. Go. 6 I will
stand there in front of you by the rock at
Mount Horeb. Hit the rock. Then water
will come out of it for the people to drink."
So Moses hit the rock while the elders of
Israel watched. 7 Moses called the place
Massah and Meribah. That's because the
people of Israel argued with him there.
They also tested the LORD. They asked,
"Is the LORD among us or not?"

Joshua Wins the Battle Over the Amalekites

8 The Amalekites came and attacked
the Israelites at Rephidim. 9 Moses said
to Joshua, "Choose some of our men.
Then go out and fight against the Amalekites. Tomorrow I will stand on top
of the hill. I'll stand there holding the
walking stick God gave me."
10 So Joshua fought against the Amalekites, just as Moses had ordered. Moses, Aaron and Hur went to the top of the
hill. 11 As long as Moses held up his hand,
the Israelites were winning. But every
time he lowered his hands, the Amalekites began to win. 12 When Moses' arms
got tired, Aaron and Hur got a stone
and put it under him. Then he sat on it.
Aaron and Hur held up his hands. Aaron
was on one side, and Hur was on the
other. Moses' hands remained steady
until sunset. 13 So Joshua destroyed the
Amalekite army with swords.
14 Then the LORD said to Moses, "This
is something to be remembered. So
write it on a scroll. Make sure Joshua
knows you have done it. I will completely erase the memory of the Amalekites
from the earth."
15 Then Moses built an altar. He called
it The LORD Is My Banner. 16 He said, "The
Amalekites opposed the authority of the
LORD. So the LORD will fight against the
Amalekites for all time to come."

Jethro Visits Moses

18 Moses' father-in-law Jethro was
the priest of Midian. He heard
about everything God had done for
Moses and for his people Israel. Jethro
heard how the LORD had brought Israel
out of Egypt.
2 Moses had sent his wife Zipporah to
his father-in-law. So Jethro welcomed
her 3 and her two sons. One son was
named Gershom. That's because Moses
had said, "I'm an outsider in a strange
land." 4 The other was named Eliezer.
That's because Moses had said, "My
father's God helped me. He saved me
from Pharaoh's sword."
5 Moses' father-in-law Jethro came
to Moses in the desert. Moses' sons
and wife came with Jethro. Moses was
camped near the mountain of God.
6 Jethro had sent a message to him. It
said, "I, your father-in-law Jethro, am
coming to you. I'm bringing your wife
and her two sons."
7 So Moses went out to meet his
father-in-law. Moses bowed down and
kissed him. They greeted each other.
Then they went into the tent. 8 Moses
told Jethro everything the LORD had
done to Pharaoh and the Egyptians.
The LORD did all of this because of how

much he loved Israel. Moses told Jethro
about all their hard times along the
way. He told him about how the LORD
had saved them.
9 Jethro was delighted to hear about
all the good things the LORD had done
for Israel. He heard about how God had
saved them from the power of the Egyptians. 10 He said, "I praise the LORD. He
saved you and your people from the
power of the Egyptians and of Pharaoh.
11 Now I know that the LORD is greater
than all other gods. See what he did
to those who looked down on Israel."
12 Then Moses' father-in-law Jethro
brought a burnt offering and other
sacrifices to God. Aaron came with all
the elders of Israel. They ate a meal with
Moses' father-in-law in the sight of God.
13 The next day Moses took his seat
to serve the people as their judge. They
stood around him from morning until
evening. 14 His father-in-law saw everything Moses was doing for the people.
So he said, "Aren't you trying to do too
much for the people? You are the only
judge. And all these people are standing around you from morning until
evening."
15 Moses answered, "The people come
to me to find out what God wants them
to do. 16 Anytime they don't agree with
one another, they come to me. I decide
between them. I tell them about God's
rules and instructions."
17 Moses' father-in-law replied, "What
you are doing isn't good. 18 You will just
get worn out. And so will these people
who come to you. There's too much work
for you. You can't possibly handle it by
yourself. 19 Listen to me. I'll give you some
advice, and may God be with you. You
must speak to God for the people. Take
their problems to him. 20 Teach them his
rules and instructions. Show them how
to live and what to do. 21 But choose men
of ability from all the people. They must
have respect for God. You must be able to
trust them. They must not try to get money by cheating others. Appoint them as
officials over thousands, hundreds, fifties
and tens. 22 Let them serve the people as
judges. But have them bring every hard
case to you. They can decide the easy
ones themselves. That will make your
load lighter. They will share it with you.
23 If this is what God wants and if you
do it, then you will be able to carry the
load. And all these people will go home
satisfied."
24 Moses listened to his father-in-law.
He did everything Jethro said. 25 He
chose men of ability from the whole
community of Israel. He made them
leaders of the people. They became officials over thousands, hundreds, fifties
and tens. 26 They judged the people at
all times. They brought the hard cases
to Moses. But they decided the easy
ones themselves.
27 Moses sent his father-in-law on
his way. So Jethro returned to his own
country.

Israel Comes to Mount Sinai

19 Exactly three months after
the people of Israel left Egypt,
they came to the Desert of Sinai. 2 After they started out from Rephidim,
they entered the Desert of Sinai. They
camped there in the desert in front of
the mountain.
3 Then Moses went up to God. The
LORD called out to him from the mountain. He said, "Here is what I want you to
say to my people, who belong to Jacob's
family. Tell the Israelites, 4 'You have
seen for yourselves what I did to Egypt.
You saw how I carried you on the wings
of eagles and brought you to myself.
5 Now obey me completely. Keep my
covenant. If you do, then out of all the
nations you will be my special treasure.
The whole earth is mine. 6 But you will
be a kingdom of priests to serve me. You
will be my holy nation.' That is what
you must tell the Israelites."
7 So Moses went back. He sent for the
elders of the people. He explained to
them everything the LORD had commanded him to say. 8 All the people
answered together. They said, "We will
do everything the LORD has said." So
Moses brought their answer back to
the LORD.
9 The LORD spoke to Moses. He said,
"I am going to come to you in a thick
cloud. The people will hear me speaking
with you. They will always put their
trust in you." Then Moses told the LORD
what the people had said.
10 The LORD said to Moses, "Go to the
people. Today and tomorrow set them
apart for me. Have them wash their

clothes. 11 Have the people ready by the
third day. On that day the LORD will come
down on Mount Sinai. Everyone will see
it. 12 Put limits for the people around the
mountain. Tell them, 'Be careful that you
do not go near the mountain. Do not even
touch the foot of it. Whoever touches the
mountain must be put to death. 13 Do not
lay a hand on any of them. Kill them
with stones or shoot them with arrows.
Whether they are people or animals, do
not let them live.' They may go near the
mountain only when the ram's horn gives
out a long blast."

14 Moses went down the mountain to
the people. After he set them apart for the
LORD, they washed their clothes. 15 Then
he spoke to the people. He said, "Get
ready for the third day. Don't have sex."

16 On the morning of the third day
there was thunder and lightning. A thick
cloud covered the mountain. A trumpet
gave out a very loud blast. Everyone in
the camp trembled with fear. 17 Then
Moses led the people out of the camp
to meet with God. They stood at the
foot of the mountain. 18 Smoke covered
Mount Sinai, because the LORD came
down on it in fire. The smoke rose up
from it like smoke from a furnace. The
whole mountain trembled and shook.
19 The sound of the trumpet got louder
and louder. Then Moses spoke. And the
voice of God answered him.

20 The LORD came down to the top of
Mount Sinai. He told Moses to come to
the top of the mountain. So Moses went
up. 21 The LORD said to him, "Go down and
warn the people. They must not force
their way through to see the LORD. If they
do, many of them will die. 22 The priests
approach the LORD when they serve him.
But even they must set themselves apart
for the LORD. If they do not, his anger
will break out against them."

23 Moses said to the LORD, "The people
can't come up Mount Sinai. You yourself
warned us. You said, 'Put limits around
the mountain. Set it apart as holy.'"

24 The LORD replied, "Go down. Bring
Aaron up with you. But the priests and
the people must not force their way
through. They must not come up to the
LORD. If they do, his anger will break
out against them."

25 So Moses went down to the people
and told them.

God Gives His People the Ten Commandments

20 Here are all the words God
spoke. He said,

2 "I am the LORD your God. I brought
you out of Egypt. That is the land
where you were slaves.

3 "Do not put any other gods in place
of me.

4 "Do not make for yourself statues
of gods that look like anything
in the sky. They may not look
like anything on the earth or
in the waters either. 5 Do not
bow down to them or worship
them. I, the LORD your God, am
a jealous God. I cause the sins
of the parents to affect their
children. I will cause the sins
of those who hate me to affect
even their grandchildren and
great-grandchildren. 6 But for
all time to come I show love to
all those who love me and keep
my commandments.

7 "Do not misuse the name of the
LORD your God. The LORD will
find guilty anyone who misuses
his name.

8 "Remember to keep the Sabbath
day holy. 9 Do all your work
in six days. 10 But the seventh
day is a sabbath to honor the
LORD your God. Do not do any
work on that day. The same
command applies to your sons
and daughters, your male and
female servants, and your
animals. It also applies to any
outsiders who live in your towns.
11 In six days the LORD made the
heavens, the earth, the sea and
everything in them. But he
rested on the seventh day. So
the LORD blessed the Sabbath
day and made it holy.

12 "Honor your father and mother.
Then you will live a long time
in the land the LORD your God
is giving you.

13 "Do not murder.

14 "Do not commit adultery.

15 "Do not steal.

16 "Do not be a false witness against
your neighbor.

17 "Do not want to have anything your neighbor owns. Do not want to have your neighbor's house, wife, male or female servant, ox or donkey."

18 The people saw the thunder and lightning. They heard the trumpet. They saw the mountain covered with smoke. They trembled with fear and stayed a long way off. 19 They said to Moses, "Speak to us yourself. Then we'll listen. But don't let God speak to us. If he does, we'll die."

20 Moses said to the people, "Don't be afraid. God has come to test you. He wants you to have respect for him. That will keep you from sinning."

21 Moses approached the thick darkness where God was. But the people remained a long way off.

Worship the LORD

22 Then the LORD said to Moses, "Here is what you must tell the people of Israel. Say to them, 'You have seen for yourselves what I said to you from heaven. 23 Do not put any other gods in place of me. Do not make silver or gold statues of them for yourselves.

24 " 'Make an altar out of dirt for me. Sacrifice your burnt offerings and friendship offerings on it. Sacrifice your sheep, goats and cattle on it. I will come to you and bless you everywhere I cause my name to be honored. 25 If you make an altar out of stones to honor me, do not build it with blocks of stone. You will make it "unclean" if you use a tool on it. 26 Do not walk up steps to my altar. If you do, someone might see your naked body under your robes.'

Other Laws

21 "Here are the laws you must explain to the people of Israel.

Set Your Hebrew Servants Free

2 "Suppose you buy a Hebrew servant. He must serve you for six years. But in the seventh year, you must set him free. He does not have to pay anything. 3 If he does not have a wife when he comes, he must go free alone. But if he has a wife when he comes, she must go with him. 4 Suppose his master gives him a wife. And suppose she has sons or daughters by him. Then only the man will go free. The woman and her children will belong to her master.

5 "But suppose the servant says, 'I love my master and my wife and children. I don't want to go free.' 6 Then his master must take him to the judges. His master must take him to the door or doorpost of his master's house. His master must poke a hole through his servant's earlobe into the door or doorpost. Then he will become his servant for life.

7 "Suppose a man sells his daughter as a servant. Then she can't go free as male servants do. 8 But what if the master who has chosen her does not like her? Then he must let the man buy her back. He has no right to sell her to strangers. He has broken his promise to her. 9 What if he chooses her to marry his son? Then he must grant her the rights of a daughter. 10 What if her master marries another woman? He must still give the first one her food and clothes and sleep with her. 11 If he does not provide her with those three things, she can go free. She does not have to pay anything.

Laws About Harming Others

12 "Anyone who hits and kills someone else must be put to death. 13 Suppose they did not do it on purpose. Suppose I let it happen. Then they can escape to a place I will choose. 14 But suppose they kill someone on purpose. Then take them away from my altar and put them to death.

15 "Anyone who attacks their father or mother must be put to death.

16 "Anyone who kidnaps and sells another person must be put to death. If they still have the person with them when they are caught, they must be put to death.

17 "Anyone who asks for something bad to happen to their father or mother must be put to death.

18 "Suppose two people get into a fight and argue with each other. One hits the other with a stone or his fist. And the person who was hit does not die but has to stay in bed. 19 And later that person gets up and walks around outside with a walking stick. Then the person who hit the other person will not be held responsible. But that person must pay the one who was hurt for the time spent in bed. The one who hit the

other person must be sure that person
is completely healed.

20“Suppose a person beats their male
or female slave to death with a club.
That person must be punished. 21But
they will not be punished if the slave
gets up after a day or two. After all, the
slave is their property.

22“Suppose some people are fighting
and one of them hits a pregnant woman. And suppose she has her baby early
but is not badly hurt. Then the one who
hurt her must pay a fine. That person
must pay what the woman’s husband
asks for and the court allows. 23But if
someone is badly hurt, a life must be
taken for a life. 24An eye must be put
out for an eye. A tooth must be knocked
out for a tooth. A hand must be cut off
for a hand and a foot for a foot. 25A burn
must be given for a burn, a wound for a
wound, and a bruise for a bruise.

26“Suppose an owner hits a male or
female slave in the eye and destroys it.
Then the owner must let the slave go
free to pay for the eye. 27Suppose an
owner knocks out the tooth of a male
or female slave. Then he must let the
slave go free to pay for the tooth.

28“Suppose a bull kills a man or woman with its horns. Then you must kill the
bull by throwing stones at it. Its meat
must not be eaten. But the owner of
the bull will not be held accountable.
29But suppose the bull has had the habit
of attacking people. And suppose the
owner has been warned but has not
kept it fenced in. Then if it kills a man or
woman, you must kill it with stones. The
owner must also be put to death. 30But
suppose payment is required of him
instead. Then the owner can save his life
by paying what is required. 31The same
law applies if the bull wounds a son or
daughter with its horns. 32Suppose the
bull wounds a male or female slave.
Then the owner must pay the slave’s
master about 12 ounces of silver. You
must kill the bull with stones.

33“Suppose someone uncovers a pit
or digs one and does not cover it. And
suppose an ox or donkey falls into it.
34Then the person who opened the pit
must pay the animal’s owner for the
loss. The dead animal will belong to
the person who opened the pit.

35“Suppose someone’s bull wounds
a neighbor’s bull and it dies. Then the
owner and the neighbor must sell the
live one. And they must share the money and the dead animal equally. 36But
suppose people knew that the bull had
the habit of attacking. And suppose the
owner did not keep it fenced in. Then
the owner must give another animal to
pay for the dead animal. And the dead
animal will belong to the owner.

Laws About Keeping Property Safe

22 “Suppose someone steals an ox
or a sheep. And suppose that
person kills it or sells it. Then the thief
must pay back five oxen for the ox. Or
the thief must pay back four sheep for
the sheep.

2“Suppose you catch a thief breaking
into your house at night. And suppose
you hit the thief and the thief dies. Then
you are not guilty of murder. 3But suppose it happens after the sun has come
up. Then you are guilty of murder.

“Anyone who steals must pay for
whatever they steal. But suppose the
thief does not have anything. Then the
thief must be sold to pay for what was
stolen. 4What if the stolen ox, donkey or
sheep is found alive with the thief? Then
the thief must pay back twice as much.

5“Suppose someone lets their livestock eat grass in someone else’s field
or vineyard. Then they must pay that
person back from the best crops of their
own field or vineyard.

6“Suppose a fire breaks out and
spreads into bushes. Suppose it burns
cut and stacked grain or grain that is
still growing. Or suppose it burns the
whole field. Then the one who started
the fire must pay for the loss.

7“Suppose someone gives a neighbor silver or other things to keep safe.
And suppose they are stolen from the
neighbor’s house. The thief, if caught,
must pay back twice as much as was
stolen. 8But suppose the thief is not
found. Then the neighbor must go to
the judges. They will decide whether the
neighbor has stolen the other person’s
property. 9Suppose you have an ox,
donkey, sheep or clothing that does not
belong to you. Or you have other property lost by someone else. And suppose
someone says, ‘That belongs to me.’

Then both people must bring their case
to the judges. The one the judges decide
is guilty must pay back twice as much
to the other person.
10 “Suppose someone asks their neighbor to take care of a donkey, ox, sheep
or any other animal. And suppose the
animal dies or gets hurt. Or suppose it
is stolen while no one is looking. 11 Then
the problem will be settled by promising the LORD to tell the truth. Suppose
the neighbor says, ‘I didn’t steal your
property.’ Then the owner must accept
what the neighbor says. No payment
is required. 12 But suppose the animal
really was stolen. Then the neighbor
must pay the owner back. 13 Or suppose
it was torn to pieces by a wild animal.
Then the neighbor must bring in what
is left as proof. No payment is required.
14 “Suppose someone borrows an animal from their neighbor. And it gets
hurt or dies while the owner is not there.
Then the borrower must pay for it. 15 But
suppose the owner is with the animal.
Then the borrower will not have to pay.
If the borrower hired the animal, the
money paid to hire it covers the loss.

Laws About Social Problems

16 “Suppose a man meets a virgin who
is not engaged. And he talks her into
having sex with him. Then he must
pay her father the price for a bride. And
he must marry her. 17 But suppose her
father absolutely refuses to give her to
him. Then he must still pay the price for
getting married to a virgin.
18 “Do not let a woman who does evil
magic stay alive. Put her to death.
19 “Anyone who has sex with an animal must be put to death.
20 “Anyone who sacrifices to any god
other than the LORD must be destroyed.
21 “Do not treat outsiders badly. Do
not give them a hard time. Remember,
you were outsiders in Egypt.
22 “Do not take advantage of widows. Do not take advantage of children
whose fathers have died. 23 If you do,
they might cry out to me. I will certainly
hear them. 24 And I will get angry. I
will kill you with a sword. Your wives
will become widows. Your children’s
fathers will die.
25 “Suppose you lend money to one
of my people among you who is in
need. Then do not treat it like a business deal. Do not charge any interest
at all. 26 Suppose your neighbor owes
you money and gives you a coat as a
promise to pay it back. Then return it
by sunset. 27 That coat is the only thing
your neighbor owns to wear or sleep in.
When they cry out to me, I will listen,
because I am loving and kind.
28 “Do not speak evil things against
God. Do not curse the ruler of your people.
29 “Do not keep for yourself your grain
offerings or wine offerings.
“You must give me the oldest of your
sons. 30 Do the same with your cattle
and sheep. Let them stay with their
mothers for seven days. But give them
to me on the eighth day.
31 “I want you to be my holy people.
So do not eat the meat of any animal
that has been torn by wild animals.
Throw it to the dogs.

Laws About Mercy and Fairness

23 “Do not spread reports that are
false. Do not help a guilty person by telling lies in court.
2 “Do not follow the crowd when they
do what is wrong. When you are a witness in court, do not turn what is right
into what is wrong. Do not go along
with the crowd. 3 Do not show favor to
a poor person in court.
4 “Suppose you come across your enemy’s ox or donkey wandering away.
Then be sure to return it. 5 Suppose you
see that the donkey of someone who
hates you has fallen down under its
load. Then do not leave it there. Be sure
you help them with it.
6 “Be fair to your poor people in their
court cases. 7 Do not have anything to do
with a false charge. Do not put to death
people not guilty of doing anything
wrong. I will not let guilty people go free.
8 “Do not take money from people
who want special favors. It makes you
blind to the truth. It twists the words
of good people.
9 “Do not treat outsiders badly. You
yourselves know how it feels to be outsiders. Remember, you were outsiders
in Egypt.

Sabbath Laws

10 “For six years plant your fields and
gather your crops. 11 But during the seventh year do not plow your land or use

it. Then the poor people among you can get food from it. The wild animals can eat what is left over. Do the same thing with your vineyards and your groves of olive trees.
12 "Do all your work in six days. But do not do any work on the seventh day. Then your oxen and donkeys can rest. The slaves born in your house can be renewed. And so can the outsiders who live among you.
13 "Be careful to do everything I have said to you. Do not speak the names of other gods. Do not even let them be heard on your lips.

Laws About Celebrating the Three Main Feasts

14 "Three times a year you must celebrate a feast in my honor.
15 "Celebrate the Feast of Unleavened Bread. For seven days, eat bread made without yeast, just as I commanded you. Do it at the appointed time in the month of Aviv. You came out of Egypt in that month.

"You must not come to worship me with your hands empty.
16 "Celebrate the Feast of Weeks. Bring the first share of your crops from your fields.

"Celebrate the Feast of Booths. Hold it in the fall when you gather in your crops from your fields.
17 "Three times a year all your men must come to worship me. I am your LORD and King.
18 "Do not include anything made with yeast when you offer me the blood of a sacrifice.

"Suppose the fat from sacrifices is left over from my feasts. Then do not keep it until morning.
19 "Bring the best of the first share of your crops to my house. I am the LORD your God.

"Do not cook a young goat in its mother's milk.

God's Angel Will Prepare the Way

20 "I am sending an angel ahead of you. He will guard you along the way. He will bring you to the place I have prepared.
21 Pay attention to him. Listen to what he says. Do not refuse to obey him. He will not forgive you if you turn against him. He has my full authority.
22 Listen carefully to what he says. Do everything I say. Then I will be an enemy to your enemies. I will fight against those who fight against you.
23 My angel will go ahead of you. He will bring you into the land of the Amorites, Hittites, Perizzites, Canaanites, Hivites and Jebusites. I will wipe them out.
24 Do not do what they do. Do not bow down to their gods or worship them. You must destroy the statues of their gods. You must break their sacred stones to pieces.
25 Worship the LORD your God. Then he will bless your food and water. I, the LORD, will take away any sickness you may have.
26 In your land no woman will give birth to a dead baby. Every woman will be able to have children. I will give you a long life.
27 "I will send my terror ahead of you. I will throw every nation you meet into a panic. I will make all your enemies turn their backs and run away.
28 I will send hornets ahead of you. They will drive the Hivites, Canaanites and Hittites out of your way.
29 But I will not drive them out in just one year. If I did, the land would be deserted. There would be too many wild animals for you.
30 I will drive them out ahead of you little by little. I will do that until there are enough of you to take control of the land.
31 "I will make your borders secure from the Red Sea to the Mediterranean Sea. They will go from the desert to the Euphrates River. I will hand over to you the people who live in the land. You will drive them out to make room for yourselves.
32 Do not make a covenant with them or with their gods.
33 Do not let them live in your land. If you do, they will cause you to sin against me. If you worship their gods, that will certainly be a trap for you."

The Blood of the Covenant

24 The LORD said to Moses, "You and Aaron, Nadab and Abihu, and 70 of the elders of Israel must come to worship the LORD. Do not come close when you worship.
2 Only Moses can come close to me. The others must not come near. And the people may not go up with him."
3 Moses went and told the people all the LORD's words and laws. They answered with one voice. They said, "We will do everything the LORD has

told us to do." 4Then Moses wrote down
everything the LORD had said.

Moses got up early the next morning. He built an altar at the foot of the
mountain. He set up 12 stone pillars.
They stood for the 12 tribes of Israel.
5Then he sent young Israelite men
to sacrifice burnt offerings. They also
sacrificed young bulls as friendship
offerings to the LORD. 6Moses put half
of the blood in bowls. He splashed the
other half against the altar. 7Then he
took the Book of the Covenant and read
it to the people. They answered, "We will
do everything the LORD has told us to
do. We will obey him."

8Then Moses took the blood and
sprinkled it on the people. He said,
"This is the blood that puts the covenant into effect. The LORD has made
this covenant with you in keeping with
all these words."

9Moses and Aaron, Nadab and Abihu, and the 70 elders of Israel went up.
10They saw the God of Israel. Under his
feet was something like a street made
out of lapis lazuli. It was as bright blue
as the sky itself. 11But God didn't destroy
those Israelite leaders when they saw
him. They ate and drank.

12The LORD said to Moses, "Come up
to me on the mountain. Stay here. I will
give you the stone tablets. They contain
the law and commandments I have
written to teach the people."

13Then Moses and Joshua, his helper,
started out. Moses went up on the mountain of God. 14He said to the elders, "Wait
for us here until we come back to you.
Aaron and Hur are with you. Anyone
who has a problem can go to them."

15Moses went up on the mountain.
Then the cloud covered it. 16The glory of the LORD settled on Mount Sinai. The cloud covered the mountain
for six days. On the seventh day the
LORD called out to Moses from inside
the cloud. 17The people of Israel saw
the glory of the LORD. It looked like a
fire burning on top of the mountain.
18Moses entered the cloud as he went
on up the mountain. He stayed on the
mountain for 40 days and 40 nights.

Offerings for the Holy Tent

25 The LORD said to Moses, 2"Tell
the people of Israel to bring
me an offering. You must receive the
offering for me from everyone whose
hearts move them to give.

3 "Here are the offerings you must
receive from them.

"gold, silver and bronze
4 blue, purple and bright red yarn
and fine linen
goat hair
5 ram skins that are dyed red
another kind of strong leather
acacia wood
6 olive oil for the lights
spices for the anointing oil and for
the sweet-smelling incense
7 onyx stones and other jewels for
the linen apron and chest cloth

8 "Have them make a sacred tent for
me. I will live among them. 9 Make the
holy tent and everything that belongs
to it. Make them exactly like the pattern
I will show you.

The Ark of the Covenant Law

10 "Have them make an ark out of
acacia wood. It must be a chest three
feet nine inches long and two feet three
inches wide and high. 11 Cover it inside
and outside with pure gold. Put a strip
of gold around it. 12 Make four gold rings
for it. Join them to its four bottom corners. Put two rings on one side and two
rings on the other. 13 Then make poles
out of acacia wood. Cover them with
gold. 14 Put the poles through the rings
on the sides of the ark to carry it. 15 The
poles must remain in the rings of the
ark. Do not remove them. 16 I will give
you the tablets of the covenant law.
When I do, put them into the ark.

17 "Make its cover out of pure gold. The
cover is the place where sin will be paid
for. Make it three feet nine inches long
and two feet three inches wide. 18 Make
two cherubim out of hammered gold at
the ends of the cover. 19 Put one of the cherubim on each end of it. Make the cherubim
part of the cover itself. 20 They must have
their wings spread up over the cover. The
cherubim must face each other and look
toward the cover. 21 Place the cover on top
of the ark. I will give you the tablets of the
covenant law. Put them in the ark. 22 The
ark is where the tablets of the covenant
law are kept. I will meet with you above
the cover between the two cherubim that
are over the ark. There I will give you all
my commands for the Israelites.

The Table for the Holy Bread

23 "Make a table out of acacia wood.
Make it three feet long, one foot six

pointing us to JESUS: The Ark of the Covenant

When God commanded his people to build the holy tent, he also gave them instructions for building the ark of the covenant. This was a specially designed box overlaid with gold that featured two cherubim on the top. God said he would meet with his people between the two cherubim. Inside the box were three things: (1) the gold jar of manna, (2) Aaron's walking stick, and (3) the stone tablets with the Ten Commandments written on them (see Hebrews 9:4).

The gold jar of manna represented the bread that God miraculously provided for his people to eat when they wandered in the wilderness. Aaron's walking stick was what one of the high priests carried, and it reminded the people that Aaron was chosen by God to lead God's people. The stone tablets with the Ten Commandments written on them reminded the people of their covenant with God.

When Jesus came, he was the bread of life, the truer and better high priest, and the Savior who could keep God's law perfectly. Through Jesus, we can meet, or pray, and talk with God at any time on any day.

inches wide and two feet three inches high. [24] Cover it with pure gold. Put a strip of gold around it. [25] Also make a rim around it three inches wide. Put a strip of gold around the rim. [26] Make four gold rings for the table. Join them to the four corners, where the four legs are. [27] The rings must be close to the rim. They must hold the poles that will be used to carry the table. [28] Make the poles out of acacia wood. Cover them with gold. Use them to carry the table. [29] Make its plates and dishes out of pure gold. Also make its pitchers and bowls out of pure gold. Use the pitchers and bowls to pour out drink offerings. [30] Put the holy bread on the table. It must be near my holy throne on the ark of the covenant law at all times.

The Gold Lampstand

[31] "Make a lampstand out of pure gold. Hammer out its base and stem. Its buds, blossoms and cups must branch out from it. They must be part of the lampstand itself. [32] Six branches must come out from the sides of the lampstand. Make three on one side and three on the other. [33] On one branch make three cups that are shaped like almond flowers with buds and blossoms. Then put three on the next branch. Do the same with all six branches that come out from the lampstand. [34] On the lampstand there must be four cups that are shaped like almond flowers with buds and blossoms. [35] One bud must be under the first pair of branches that come out from the lampstand. Put a second bud under the second pair. And put a third bud under the third pair. Make a total of six branches. [36] The buds and branches must come out from the lampstand. The whole lampstand must be one piece hammered out of pure gold.

[37] "Then make its seven lamps. Set them up on it so that they light the space in front of it. [38] The trays and wick cutters must be made out of pure gold. [39] Use 75 pounds of pure gold to make the lampstand and everything used with it. [40] Be sure to make everything just like the pattern I showed you on the mountain.

pointing us to JESUS: The Holy Tent

God made a promise to his people that he would lead them to a place that would be their home. He had prepared to give them the promised land known as Canaan. But soon after the Israelites left Egypt, they did not believe God's promise and disobeyed him. So God said they would have to wait before entering the promised land. During their time of waiting, they wandered in the wilderness.

God led the people with a cloud during the day and a fire at night, but he wanted to be even closer to them so they could seek him, worship him, and be made right with him. The people lived in tents because they moved around a lot. So God gave them a gift: He told Moses to build a holy tent where God's presence would live. God said to build *him* a tentlike home. The holy tent would be God's movable house; it would go with the Israelites as they traveled from place to place. Wherever they pitched their tents, they would set the holy tent right in the middle of the camp. The holy tent was a reminder that God was with them.

Jesus is the truer and better house of God's presence, and he came to dwell among us. Jesus' disciple John wrote in John 1:14, "The Word became a human being. He made his home with us." God loves his people so much that he desires to be *with* them.

The Holy Tent

26 "Make ten curtains out of finely
twisted linen for the holy tent.
Make them with blue, purple and bright
red yarn. Have a skilled worker sew
cherubim into the pattern. 2 Make all
the curtains the same size. They must
be 42 feet long and six feet wide. 3 Join
five of the curtains together. Do the
same thing with the other five. 4 Make
loops out of blue strips of cloth along
the edge of the end curtain in one set.
Do the same thing with the end curtain
in the other set. 5 Make 50 loops on the
end curtain of the one set. Do the same
thing on the end curtain of the other set.
Put the loops across from each other.
6 Make 50 gold hooks. Use them to join
the curtains together so that the holy
tent is all one piece.

7 "Make a total of 11 curtains out of
goat hair to put over the holy tent.
8 Make all 11 curtains the same size.
They must be 45 feet long and six feet
wide. 9 Join five of the curtains together
into one set. Do the same thing with
the other six. Fold the sixth curtain in
half at the front of the tent. 10 Make 50
loops along the edge of the end curtain
in the one set. Do the same thing with
the other set. 11 Then make 50 bronze
hooks. Put them in the loops to join the
tent together all in one piece. 12 Let the
extra half curtain hang down at the rear
of the holy tent. 13 The tent curtains will
be 18 inches longer on both sides. What
is left over will hang over the sides of
the holy tent and cover it. 14 Make a
covering for the tent. Make it out of ram
skins that are dyed red. Put a covering
of the other strong leather over that.

15 "Make frames out of acacia wood
for the holy tent. 16 Make each frame 15
feet long and two feet three inches wide.
17 Add two small wooden pins to each
frame. Make the pins stick out so that
they are even with each other. Make all
the frames for the holy tent in the same
way. 18 Make 20 frames for the south side
of the holy tent. 19 And make 40 silver
bases to go under them. Make two bases
for each frame. Put one under each pin

that sticks out. 20 For the north side of
the holy tent make 20 frames 21 and 40
silver bases. Put two bases under each
frame. 22 Make six frames for the west
end of the holy tent. 23 Make two frames
for the corners at the far end. 24 At those
two corners the frames must be double
from top to bottom. They must be fitted
into a single ring. Make both of them the
same. 25 There will be eight frames and
16 silver bases. There will be two bases
under each frame.

26 "Also make crossbars out of acacia
wood. Make five for the frames on one
side of the holy tent. 27 Make five for
the frames on the other side. And make
five for the frames on the west, at the
far end of the holy tent. 28 The center
crossbar must reach from end to end
at the middle of the frames. 29 Cover
the frames with gold. Make gold rings
to hold the crossbars. Also cover the
crossbars with gold.

30 "Set up the holy tent in keeping with
the plan I showed you on the mountain.

31 "Make a curtain out of blue, purple
and bright red yarn and finely twisted
linen. Have a skilled worker sew cherubim
into the pattern. 32 Hang the curtain with
gold hooks on four posts that are made
out of acacia wood. Cover the posts with
gold. Stand them on four silver bases.
33 Hang the curtain from the hooks. Place
the ark of the covenant law behind the
curtain. The curtain will separate the
Holy Room from the Most Holy Room.
34 Put the cover on the ark of the covenant
law in the Most Holy Room. The cover will
be the place where sin is paid for. 35 Place
the table outside the curtain on the north
side of the holy tent. And put the lampstand across from it on the south side.

36 "Make a curtain for the entrance
to the tent. Make it out of blue, purple
and bright red yarn and finely twisted
linen. Have a person who sews skillfully make it. 37 Make gold hooks for the
curtain. Make five posts out of acacia
wood. Cover them with gold. And make
five bronze bases for them.

The Altar for Burnt Offerings

27 "Build an altar out of acacia
wood. It must be four feet six
inches high and seven feet six inches
square. 2 Make a horn stick out from each
of its upper four corners. The horns and
the altar must be all one piece. Cover the
altar with bronze. 3 Make everything for
the altar out of bronze. Make its pots
to remove the ashes. Make its shovels,
sprinkling bowls, meat forks, and pans
for carrying ashes. 4 Make a bronze grate
for the altar. Make a bronze ring for each
of the four corners of the grate. 5 Put the
grate halfway up the altar on the inside.
6 Make poles out of acacia wood for the
altar. Cover them with bronze. 7 Put the
poles through the rings. They will be
on two sides of the altar for carrying
it. 8 Make the altar out of boards. Leave
it hollow. It must look just like what I
showed you on the mountain.

The Courtyard

9 "Make a courtyard for the holy tent.
The south side must be 150 feet long. It
must have curtains that are made out
of finely twisted linen. 10 The curtains
must be hung on 20 posts that have 20
bronze bases. The posts must have silver
hooks and bands on them. 11 The north
side must also be about 150 feet long. It
must have curtains with 20 posts that
have 20 bronze bases. The posts must
have silver hooks and bands on them.

12 "The west end of the courtyard must
be 75 feet wide. It must have curtains
with ten posts that have ten bases. 13 The
east end of the courtyard, toward the
sunrise, must also be 75 feet wide. 14 On
one side of the entrance you must put
curtains that are 22 feet six inches long.
Hang them on three posts. Each post
must have a base. 15 On the other side
you must also put curtains that are
22 feet six inches long. Hang them on
three posts. Each post must have a base.

16 "For the entrance to the courtyard,
provide a curtain 30 feet long. Make it
out of blue, purple and bright red yarn
and finely twisted linen. Have someone
who sews skillfully make it. Hang it
on four posts. Each post must have a
base. 17 All the posts that are around
the courtyard must have silver bands
and hooks. They must also have bronze
bases. 18 The courtyard must be 150 feet
long and 75 feet wide. It must have curtains that are made out of finely twisted
linen. They must be seven feet six inches
high. The posts must have bronze bases.
19 Make out of bronze all the other things
used for any purpose in the holy tent.

That includes all the tent stakes for the tent and the courtyard.

Oil for the Lampstand

20 “Command the Israelites to bring you clear oil made from pressed olives. Use it to keep the lamps burning and giving light. 21 Aaron and his sons must keep the lamps burning in the tent of meeting. The lamps will be outside the curtain in front of the tablets of the covenant law. The lamps must be kept burning in front of the LORD from evening until morning. This is a law for the Israelites that will last for all time to come.

The Clothes for the Priests

28 “Have your brother Aaron brought to you from among the Israelites. His sons Nadab, Abihu, Eleazar and Ithamar must also be brought. They will serve me as priests. 2 Make sacred clothes for your brother Aaron. When he is wearing them, people will honor him. They will have respect for him. 3 Speak to all the skilled workers. I have given them the skill to do this kind of work. Tell them to make clothes for Aaron. He will wear them when he is set apart to serve me as priest. 4 The workers must make a chest cloth, a linen apron and an outer robe. They must also make an inner robe, a turban and a belt. They must make sacred clothes for your brother Aaron and his sons. Then they will serve me as priests. 5 Have the workers use thin gold wire, and blue, purple and bright red yarn, and fine linen.

The Linen Apron

6 “Make the linen apron out of thin gold wire, and out of blue, purple and bright red yarn, and out of finely twisted linen. Have a skilled worker make it. 7 It must have two shoulder straps joined to two of its corners. 8 Its skillfully made waistband must be like the apron. The waistband must be part of the apron itself. Make the waistband out of thin gold wire, and out of blue, purple and bright red yarn, and out of finely twisted linen.

9 “Get two onyx stones. Carve the names of the sons of Israel on them. 10 Arrange them in the order of their birth. Carve six names on one stone and six on the other. 11 Carve the names of the sons of Israel on the two stones the way a jewel cutter would carve them. Then put the stones in fancy gold settings. 12 Connect them to the shoulder straps of the linen apron. The stones will stand for the sons of Israel. Aaron must carry the names on his shoulders as a constant reminder while he is serving the LORD. 13 Make fancy gold settings. 14 Make two braided chains out of pure gold. Make them like ropes. Join the chains to the settings.

The Chest Cloth

15 “Make a chest cloth that will be used for making decisions. Have a skilled worker make it. Make it like the linen apron. Use thin gold wire, and blue, purple and bright red yarn, and finely twisted linen. 16 Make it nine inches square. Fold it in half. 17 Put four rows of valuable jewels on it. Put carnelian, chrysolite and beryl in the first row. 18 Put turquoise, lapis lazuli and emerald in the second row. 19 Put jacinth, agate and amethyst in the third row. 20 And put topaz, onyx and jasper in the fourth row. Put them in fancy gold settings. 21 Use a total of 12 stones. Use one for each of the names of the sons of Israel. Each stone must be carved with the name of one of the 12 tribes.

22 “Make braided chains out of pure gold for the chest cloth. Make them like ropes. 23 Make two gold rings for the chest cloth. Connect them to two corners of it. 24 Join the two gold chains to the rings at the corners of the chest cloth. 25 Join the other ends of the chains to the two settings. Join them to the shoulder straps on the front of the linen apron. 26 Make two gold rings. Connect them to the other two corners of the chest cloth. Put them on the inside edge next to the apron. 27 Make two more gold rings. Connect them to the bottom of the shoulder straps on the front of the apron. Put them close to the seam. Put them right above the waistband of the apron. 28 The rings of the chest cloth must be tied to the rings of the apron. Tie them to the waistband with blue cord. Then the chest cloth will not swing out from the linen apron.

29 “When Aaron enters the Holy Room, he will carry the names of the sons of Israel over his heart. Their names will

be on the chest cloth of decision. They
will be a continuing reminder while he
is serving the LORD. 30 Also put the Urim
and Thummim into the chest cloth.
Then they will be over Aaron's heart
when he comes to serve the LORD. In
that way, Aaron will always have what
he needs to make decisions for the people of Israel. He will carry the Urim and
Thummim over his heart while he is
serving the LORD.

More Clothes for the Priests

31 "Make the outer robe of the linen
apron completely out of blue cloth. 32 In
the center of the robe, make an opening
for the head of the priest. Make an edge
like a collar around the opening. Then it
will not tear. 33 Make pomegranates out
of blue, purple and bright red yarn. Sew
them around the hem of the robe. Sew
gold bells between them. 34 Sew a gold
bell between every two pomegranates
all around the hem of the robe. 35 Aaron
must wear the robe when he serves as
priest. The bells will jingle when he enters the Holy Room while he is serving
the LORD. And they will jingle when he
goes out. Then he will not die.
36 "Make a plate out of pure gold.
Carve words on it as if it were an official
seal. Carve the words

SET APART FOR THE LORD.

37 Tie the plate to the front of the turban
with a blue cord. 38 Aaron must wear
this plate on his forehead all the time.
He will be held responsible for all the
sacred gifts the Israelites set apart. Then
the LORD will accept the gifts.
39 "Make the inner robe out of fine
linen. And make the turban out of fine
linen. The belt must be made by a person who sews skillfully. 40 Make inner
robes, belts and caps for Aaron's sons.
When they are wearing them, people
will honor his sons. They will also have
respect for them. 41 Put all these clothes
on your brother Aaron and his sons.
Then pour olive oil on them and prepare
them to serve me. Set them apart to
serve me as priests.
42 "Make linen underwear that reaches from the waist to the thigh. 43 Aaron
and the priests in his family line must
wear it when they enter the tent of
meeting. They must also wear it when
they approach the altar to serve in the
Holy Room. Then they will not be found
guilty and die.

"For all time to come, that will be
a law for Aaron and the priests in his
family line.

Directions for Setting Apart the Priests

29 "Here is what you must do to set
apart Aaron and his sons to serve
me as priests. Get a young bull and two
rams. They must not have any flaws.
2 Get the finest wheat flour. Make round
loaves of bread that do not have yeast in
them. Make thick loaves of bread that do
not have yeast in them. Mix olive oil into
the thick loaves of bread. Also make thin
loaves of bread that do not have yeast
in them. Brush the thin loaves with olive
oil. 3 Put everything in a basket. Offer
them along with the bull and the two
rams. 4 Then bring Aaron and his sons
to the entrance to the tent of meeting.
Wash them with water. 5 Take the inner
robe, the outer robe of the linen apron,
the apron itself and the chest cloth. Dress
Aaron in them. Take the skillfully made
waistband and tie the apron on him with
it. 6 Put the turban on his head. Connect
the sacred plate to the turban. 7 Take the
anointing oil and pour it on his head.
8 Bring his sons and dress them in their
inner robes. 9 Put caps on their heads. Tie
belts on Aaron and his sons. The work of
the priests belongs to them. This is my
law that will last for all time to come.

"Then you must prepare Aaron and
his sons to serve me.

10 "Bring the bull to the front of the
tent of meeting. Have Aaron and his
sons place their hands on its head. 11 Kill
it in front of the LORD at the entrance to
the tent of meeting. 12 Dip your finger
into some of the bull's blood. Put it on
the horns that stick out from the upper
four corners of the altar. Pour the rest
of it out at the base of the altar. 13 Then
take all the fat on the inside parts. Take
the long part of the liver. Get both kidneys with the fat on them. And burn all
of it on the altar. 14 But burn the bull's
meat, hide and guts outside the camp.
It is a sin offering.

15 "Get one of the rams. Have Aaron
and his sons place their hands on its
head. 16 Kill it. Take the blood and splash

it against the sides of the altar. 17 Cut the ram into pieces. Wash the inside parts and the legs. Put them with the head and the other pieces. 18 Then burn the whole ram on the altar. It is a burnt offering to me. It has a pleasant smell. It is a food offering presented to the LORD.

19 "Get the other ram. Have Aaron and his sons place their hands on its head. 20 Kill it. Put some of its blood on the right earlobes of Aaron and his sons. Put some on the thumbs of their right hands. Also put some on the big toes of their right feet. Then splash the blood against the sides of the altar. 21 Get some of the blood from the altar. Also get some of the anointing oil. Sprinkle both of them on Aaron and his clothes and on his sons and their clothes. Then he and his sons and their clothes will be set apart to serve the LORD.

22 "Here is what you must take from this second ram. Take the fat, the fat tail and the fat around the inside parts. Take the long part of the liver. Also take both kidneys with the fat on them, and the right thigh. It is the ram you must use when you prepare the priests to serve the LORD. 23 Get one round loaf of bread and one thick loaf of bread with olive oil mixed in. Also get one thin loaf of bread. Take them from the basket of bread made without yeast. It is the one in front of the LORD. 24 Put all these things in the hands of Aaron and his sons. Tell them to lift them up and wave them in front of the LORD as a wave offering. 25 Then take all these things from their hands. Burn them on the altar along with the burnt offering. Its smell pleases the LORD. It is a food offering presented to the LORD. 26 Get the breast of the ram used when you prepare Aaron to serve the LORD. Wave it in front of the LORD as a wave offering. It will be your share of the meat.

27 "Here are the parts of the second ram that belong to Aaron and his sons. You must set apart the breast that was waved and the thigh that was offered. 28 It will be the regular share from the Israelites for Aaron and his sons. The people must give it to the LORD from their friendship offerings.

29 "Aaron's sacred clothes will belong to his sons who will come after him. Then they can wear them when you anoint them and prepare them to serve the LORD. 30 The son who comes after Aaron as priest must wear them seven days. He will come and serve in the Holy Room in the tent of meeting.

31 "Get the ram sacrificed when you prepare Aaron and his sons to serve the LORD. Cook the meat in a sacred place. 32 Aaron and his sons must eat the ram's meat. And they must eat the bread in the basket. They must eat all of it at the entrance to the tent of meeting. 33 These are the offerings to pay for their sins. They must eat them. The offerings must be made when Aaron and his sons are set apart and prepared to serve the LORD. No one else can eat them. They are sacred. 34 When you prepare Aaron and his sons to serve me, you will sacrifice the ram and the bread. If any parts of the ram or bread are left until morning, burn them up. They must not be eaten. They are sacred.

35 "Do everything I have commanded you to do for Aaron and his sons. Take seven days when you prepare them to serve the LORD. 36 Sacrifice a bull each day. It is a sin offering to pay for their sins. Make the altar pure. Pour olive oil on it to set it apart. 37 Take seven days to make the altar pure. Set it apart. Then the altar will be a very holy place. Anything that touches it will be holy.

38 "Every day sacrifice on the altar two lambs that are a year old. 39 Sacrifice one in the morning and the other one when the sun goes down. 40 Along with the first lamb, offer three and a half pounds of fine flour. Mix it with a quart of oil made from pressed olives. Along with that, sacrifice a quart of wine as a drink offering. 41 Sacrifice the other lamb when the sun goes down. Sacrifice it along with the same grain offering and its drink offering as you do in the morning. It has a pleasant smell. It is a food offering presented to the LORD.

42 "For all time to come, this burnt offering must be sacrificed regularly. Sacrifice it at the entrance to the tent of meeting in front of the LORD. There I will meet with you and speak to you. 43 There I will also meet with the people of Israel. My glory will make the place holy.

44 "So I will set apart the tent of meeting and the altar. And I will set

apart Aaron and his sons to serve me
as priests. 45 Then I will live among the
people of Israel. And I will be their God.
46 They will know that I am the LORD
their God. They will know that I brought
them out of Egypt so I could live among
them. I am the LORD their God.

The Altar for Burning Incense

30 "Make an altar for burning
incense. Make it out of acacia
wood. 2 It must be one and a half feet
square and three feet high. Make a horn
stick out from each of its upper four corners. 3 Cover the top, sides and horns with
pure gold. Put a strip of gold around it.
4 Make two gold rings for the altar below
the strip. Put the rings across from each
other. They will hold the poles that are
used to carry it. 5 Make the poles out
of acacia wood. Cover them with gold.
6 Put the altar in front of the curtain
that hangs in front of the ark. The ark
is where the tablets of the covenant law
are kept. The ark will have a cover. It will
be the place where sin is paid for. There
I will meet with you.

7 "Aaron must burn sweet-smelling
incense on the altar. He must do it every morning when he takes care of the
lamps. 8 He must burn incense again
when he lights the lamps at sunset.
Incense must be burned regularly in
front of the LORD. Do it for all time to
come. 9 Do not burn any other incense
on the altar. Do not use the altar for
burnt offerings or grain offerings. And
do not pour drink offerings on it. 10 Once
a year Aaron must put the blood of a
sin offering on the horns of the altar.
He must do this to make the altar pure.
He must do this on the day Israel's sin
is paid for. Do this for all time to come.
The altar is a very holy place to me."

Money to Pay for the People's Lives

11 Then the LORD spoke to Moses. He
said, 12 "Make a list of the Israelites
and count them. When you do, each
one must pay the LORD for his life at
the time he is counted. Then a plague
will not come on them when you count
them. 13 Each one counted must pay a
fifth of an ounce of silver. It must be
weighed out in keeping with the standard weights that are used in the sacred
tent. The payment is an offering to the
LORD. 14 Each one counted must be 20
years old or more. He must give an offering to the LORD. 15 When you make
the offering, rich people must not give
more than a fifth of an ounce of silver.
And poor people must not give less.
The offering you give to the LORD will

pay for your lives. [16] Receive the money from the people of Israel. Use it for any purpose in the tent of meeting. It will remind the people that they are paying me for their lives."

The Large Bowl for Washing

[17] Then the LORD spoke to Moses. He said, [18] "Make a large bronze bowl for washing. Make a bronze stand to put it on. Place the bowl between the tent of meeting and the altar. Put water in it. [19] Aaron and his sons must wash their hands and feet with water from it. [20] When they enter the tent of meeting, they must wash with water so that they will not die. They will come to the altar to serve me. They will bring a food offering to the LORD. [21] When they do, they must wash their hands and feet so that they will not die. For all time to come, that will be a law for Aaron and the priests in his family line."

Anointing Oil

[22] Then the LORD said to Moses, [23] "Get some fine spices. Get 12 pounds eight ounces of liquid myrrh. Get six pounds four ounces of sweet-smelling cinnamon and the same amount of sweet-smelling calamus. [24] Also get 12 pounds eight ounces of cassia. All the spices must be weighed out in keeping with the standard weights that are used in the sacred tent. And get a gallon of olive oil. [25] Have a person who makes perfume mix everything into a sacred anointing oil. It will smell sweet. [26] Then use it to anoint the tent of meeting and the ark where the tablets of the covenant law are kept. [27] Anoint the table for the holy bread and all its things. Anoint the lampstand and the things that are used with it. Anoint the altar for burning incense. [28] Anoint the altar for burnt offerings and all its tools. And anoint the large bowl together with its stand. [29] You must set them apart so that they will be very holy. Anything that touches them will be holy.

[30] "Anoint Aaron and his sons. Set them apart so that they can serve me as priests. [31] Say to the people of Israel, 'This will be my sacred anointing oil for all time to come. [32] Do not pour it on anyone else's body. Do not make any other oil in the same way. It is sacred. So you must think of it as sacred. [33] Suppose a person makes perfume in the same way. And suppose that person puts it on someone who is not a priest. Then that person must be separated from their people.' "

pointing us to JESUS: The High Priest

God came and dwelled among his people in the holy tent and then in the temple, but that doesn't mean God's people could just enter his dwelling place at any time or in any way they desired. God is holy, which means he is perfect and pure. Sin cannot be in his presence. So how did God's people, who are sinful, approach him? God gave them instructions for how to approach him, and part of these instructions included a priest. A priest was a representative who would approach God on behalf of the people. The priest would offer sacrifices to God, ask for forgiveness for the people's sins, and pray for them.

Jesus is the truer and better high priest who represents God's people before the Father. Jesus promised that all who believe in him and receive him by faith are welcomed into the presence of God.

Paul wrote in the New Testament that Jesus, who has all power and authority, prays for all who are united to him in faith (see Romans 8:34). In other words, Jesus approaches the Father on our behalf to ask for forgiveness for our sins and to pray for us.

Incense

34 Then the LORD said to Moses, "Get
some sweet-smelling spices. Get some
gum resin, onycha and galbanum. Also
get some pure frankincense. Make sure
everything is in equal amounts. 35 Have
a person who makes perfume mix it all
up into a sweet-smelling incense. It must
have salt in it. It will be pure and sacred.
36 Grind some of it into powder. Place it
in front of the ark of the covenant law in
the tent of meeting. There I will meet with
you. The incense will be very holy to you.
37 Do not make any incense for yourselves
in the same way. Think of it as holy to the
LORD. 38 Whoever makes incense in the
same way to enjoy its sweet smell must
be separated from their people."

Bezalel and Oholiab

31 Then the LORD spoke to Moses.
2 He said, "I have chosen Bezalel,
the son of Uri. Uri is the son of Hur. Bezalel is from the tribe of Judah. 3 I have
filled him with the Spirit of God. I have
filled Bezalel with wisdom, with understanding, with knowledge and with all
kinds of skill. 4 He can make beautiful
patterns in gold, silver and bronze. 5 He
can cut and set stones. He can work
with wood. In fact, he can work in all
kinds of crafts. 6 I have also appointed
Oholiab, the son of Ahisamak, to help
him. Oholiab is from the tribe of Dan.

"I have given ability to all the
skilled workers. They can make
everything I have commanded you
to make. Here is the complete list.

7 "the tent of meeting
the ark where the tablets of the
covenant law are kept
the cover for the ark
8 the table for the holy bread and
its things
the pure gold lampstand and
everything used with it
the altar for burning incense
9 the altar for burnt offerings and
all its tools
the large bowl with its stand
10 the sacred clothes for Aaron the
priest and the clothes for his
sons when they serve as priests
11 the anointing oil
and the sweet-smelling incense for
the Holy Room

"The skilled workers must make
them just as I commanded you."

The Sabbath Day

12 Then the LORD spoke to Moses. 13 He
said, "Tell the people of Israel, 'You must
always keep my Sabbath days. That will
be the sign of the covenant I have made
between me and you for all time to
come. Then you will know that I am the
LORD. I am the one who makes you holy.
14 " 'Keep the Sabbath day. It is holy
to you. Those who misuse it must be
put to death. Those who do any work on
that day must be separated from their
people. 15 Do your work in six days. But
the seventh day is a day of sabbath rest.
You must rest on it. It is set apart for the
LORD. Those who work on the Sabbath
day must be put to death. 16 The Israelites
must keep the Sabbath day. They must
celebrate it for all time to come. It will
be a covenant that lasts forever. 17 It will
be the sign of the covenant I have made
between me and the Israelites forever.
The LORD made the heavens and the
earth in six days. But on the seventh day
he did not work. He rested.' "
18 The LORD finished speaking to Moses on Mount Sinai. Then he gave him
the two tablets of the covenant law.
They were made out of stone. The words
on them were written by the finger of
God.

Israel Worships a Golden Calf

32 The people saw that Moses took
a long time to come down from
the mountain. So they gathered around
Aaron. They said to him, "Come. Make
us a god that will lead us. This fellow
Moses brought us up out of Egypt. But
we don't know what has happened to
him."
2 Aaron answered them, "Take the
gold earrings off your wives, your sons
and your daughters. Bring the earrings
to me." 3 So all the people took off their
earrings. They brought them to Aaron.
4 He took what they gave him and made
it into a metal statue of a god. It looked
like a calf. Aaron shaped it with a tool.
Then the people said, "Israel, here is
your god who brought you up out of
Egypt."
5 When Aaron saw what they were doing, he built an altar in front of the calf.
He said, "Tomorrow will be a feast day

to honor the LORD." 6 So the next day the people got up early. They sacrificed burnt offerings and brought friendship offerings. They sat down to eat and drink. Then they got up to dance wildly in front of their god.

7 The LORD spoke to Moses. He said, "Go down. Your people you brought up out of Egypt have become very sinful. 8 They have quickly turned away from what I commanded them. They have made themselves a metal statue of a god in the shape of a calf. They have bowed down and sacrificed to it. And they have said, 'Israel, here is your god who brought you up out of Egypt.'

9 "I have seen these people," the LORD said to Moses. "They are stubborn. 10 Now leave me alone. I will destroy them because of my great anger. Then I will make you into a great nation."

11 But Moses asked the LORD his God to have mercy on the people. "LORD," he said, "why should you destroy your people in anger? You used your great power and mighty hand to bring them out of Egypt. 12 Why should the Egyptians say, 'He brought them out to hurt them. He wanted to kill them in the mountains. He wanted to wipe them off the face of the earth'? Turn away from your great anger. Please take pity on your people. Don't destroy them! 13 Remember your servants Abraham, Isaac and Israel. You made a promise to them in your own name. You said, 'I will make your children after you as many as the stars in the sky. I will give them all this land I promised them. It will belong to them forever.' " 14 Then the LORD took pity on his people. He didn't destroy them as he had said he would.

15 Moses turned and went down the mountain. He had the two tablets of the covenant law in his hands. Words were written on both sides of the tablets, front and back. 16 The tablets were the work of God. The words had been written by God. They had been carved on the tablets.

17 Joshua heard the noise of the people shouting. So he said to Moses, "It sounds like war in the camp."

18 Moses replied,

"It's not the sound of winning.
  It's not the sound of losing.
  It's the sound of singing that I
    hear."

19 As Moses approached the camp, he saw the calf. He also saw the people dancing. So he was very angry. He threw the tablets out of his hands. They broke into pieces at the foot of the mountain. 20 He took the calf the people had made. He burned it in the fire. Then he ground it into powder. He scattered it on the water. And he made the Israelites drink it.

21 He said to Aaron, "What did these people do to you? How did they make you lead them into such terrible sin?"

22 "Please don't be angry," Aaron answered. "You know how these people like to do what is evil. 23 They said to me, 'Make us a god that will lead us. This fellow Moses brought us up out of Egypt. But we don't know what has happened to him.' 24 So I told them, 'Anyone who has any gold jewelry, take it off.' They gave me the gold. I threw it into the fire. And out came this calf!"

25 Moses saw that the people were running wild. Aaron had let them get out of control. The people had become a joke to their enemies. 26 Moses stood at the entrance to the camp. He said, "Anyone on the LORD's side, come to me." All the Levites joined him.

27 Then he spoke to them. He said, "The LORD, the God of Israel, says, 'Each man must put on his sword. Then he must go back and forth through the camp from one end to the other. Each man must kill his brother and friend and neighbor.' " 28 The Levites did as Moses commanded. About 3,000 of the people died that day. 29 Then Moses said to the Levites, "You have been set apart for the LORD today. You fought against your own sons and brothers. And he has blessed you this day."

30 The next day Moses said to the people, "You have committed a terrible sin. But now I will go up to the LORD. Maybe if I pray to him, he will forgive your sin."

31 So Moses went back to the LORD. He said, "These people have committed a terrible sin. They have made a god out of gold for themselves. 32 Now please forgive their sin. But if you won't, then erase my name out of the book you have written."

33 The LORD replied to Moses. The LORD said, "I will erase out of my book only the names of those who have sinned against me. 34 Now go. Lead the people to the place I spoke about. My angel will

go ahead of you. But when the time
comes for me to punish, I will punish
them for their sin."
35 The LORD struck the people with a
plague. That's because of what they did
with the calf Aaron had made.

33 Then the LORD said to Moses,
"Leave this place. You and the
people you brought up out of Egypt must
leave it. Go up to the land I promised to
give to Abraham, Isaac and Jacob. I said
to them, 'I will give it to your children
after you.' 2 I will send an angel ahead
of you. I will drive out the Canaanites,
Amorites, Hittites, Perizzites, Hivites and
Jebusites. 3 Go up to the land that has
plenty of milk and honey. But I will not
go with you. You are stubborn. I might
destroy you on the way."
4 When the people heard these painful
words, they began to mourn. No one
put on any jewelry. 5 The LORD had said
to Moses, "Tell the Israelites, 'You are
stubborn. If I went with you even for
a moment, I might destroy you. Now
take off your jewelry. Then I will decide
what to do with you.'" 6 So the people
took off their jewelry at Mount Horeb.

The Tent of Meeting

7 Moses used to take a tent and set it
up far outside the camp. He called it the
"tent of meeting." Anyone who wanted
to ask the LORD a question would go to
the tent of meeting outside the camp.
8 When Moses would go out to the tent,
everyone would get up and stand at
the entrances to their tents. They would
watch Moses until he entered the tent.
9 As Moses would go into the tent, the
pillar of cloud would come down. It
would stay at the entrance while the
LORD spoke with Moses. 10 The people
would see the pillar of cloud standing
at the entrance to the tent. Then all
of them would stand and worship at
the entrances to their tents. 11 The LORD
would speak to Moses face to face like
one would speak to a friend. Then Moses
would return to the camp. But Joshua,
his young helper, didn't leave the tent.
Joshua was the son of Nun.

Moses and the Glory of the LORD

12 Moses said to the LORD, "You have
been telling me, 'Lead these people.'
But you haven't let me know whom
you will send with me. You have said, 'I

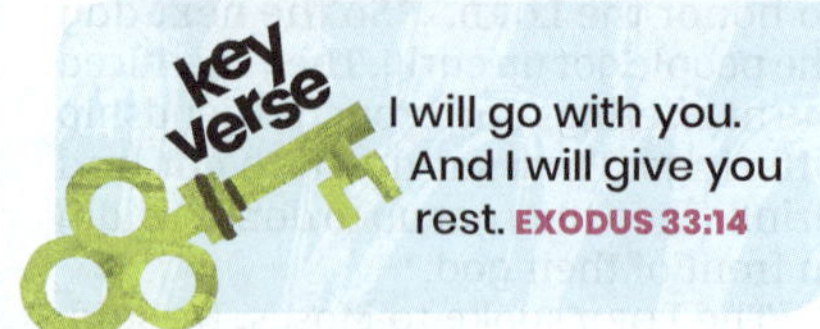

know your name. I know all about you.
And I am pleased with you.' 13 If you are
pleased with me, teach me more about
yourself. Then I can know you. And I can
continue to please you. Remember that
this nation is your people."
14 The LORD replied, "I will go with
you. And I will give you rest."
15 Then Moses said to him, "If you
don't go with us, don't send us up from
here. 16 How will anyone know that you
are pleased with me and your people?
You must go with us. How else will we
be different from all the other people
on the face of the earth?"
17 The LORD said to Moses, "I will do
exactly what you have asked. I am
pleased with you. And I know your
name. I know all about you."
18 Then Moses said, "Now show me
your glory."
19 The LORD said, "I will make all my
goodness pass in front of you. And I will
announce my name, the LORD, in front of
you. I will have mercy on whom I have
mercy. And I will show love to those I
love. 20 But you can't see my face," he
said. "No one can see me and stay alive."
21 The LORD continued, "There is a place
near me where you can stand on a rock.
22 When my glory passes by, I will put you
in an opening in the rock. I will cover you
with my hand until I have passed by.
23 Then I will remove my hand. You will see
my back. But my face must not be seen."

The New Stone Tablets

34 The LORD said to Moses, "Cut
out two stone tablets that are
just like the first ones. I will write on
them the words that were on the first
tablets, which you broke. 2 Be ready in
the morning. Then come up on Mount
Sinai. Meet with me there on top of the
mountain. 3 No one must come with
you. No one must be seen anywhere on
the mountain. Not even the flocks and
herds must be allowed to eat grass in
front of the mountain."

[4]So Moses carved out two stone
tablets just like the first ones. Early in
the morning he went up Mount Sinai.
He carried the two stone tablets in his
hands. He did as the LORD had commanded him to do. [5]Then the LORD
came down in the cloud. He stood
there with Moses and announced his
name, the LORD. [6]As he passed in front
of Moses, he called out. He said, "I am
the LORD, the LORD. I am the God who
is tender and kind. I am gracious. I am
slow to get angry. I am faithful and full
of love. [7]I continue to show my love to
thousands of people. I forgive those
who do evil. I forgive those who refuse
to obey me. And I forgive those who sin.
But I do not let guilty people go without
punishing them. I cause the sins of the
parents to affect their children, grandchildren and great-grandchildren."

[8]Moses bowed down to the ground at
once and worshiped. [9]"Lord," he said,
"if you are pleased with me, then go
with us. Even though these people are
stubborn, forgive the evil things we
have done. Forgive our sin. And accept
us as your people."

[10]Then the LORD said, "I am making a
covenant with you. I will do wonderful
things in front of all your people. I will
do amazing things that have never been
done before in any nation in the whole
world. The people you live among will
see the things that I, the LORD, will do for
you. And they will see how wonderful
those things really are. [11]Obey what I
command you today. I will drive out
the Amorites, Canaanites, Hittites, Perizzites, Hivites and Jebusites to make
room for you. [12]Be careful. Do not make
a peace treaty with those who live in the
land where you are going. They will be
a trap to you. [13]Break down their altars.
Smash their sacred stones. Cut down the
poles they use to worship the female
god named Asherah. [14]Do not worship
any other god. The LORD is a jealous
God. In fact, his name is Jealous.

[15]"Be careful not to make a peace
treaty with the people living in the land.
They commit sin by offering sacrifices
to their gods. They will invite you to eat
their sacrifices, and you will do it. [16]You
will choose some of their daughters as
wives for your sons. And those daughters will commit sin by worshiping their
gods. Then they will lead your sons to
do the same thing.

[17]"Do not make any statues of gods.

JEALOUS

God deeply desires what is best for us, and he knows that the very best thing for us is to have a relationship with him and to worship him alone.

When we think of jealousy, we usually think of a selfish person who wants something for themselves. Have you ever felt jealous of a friend's new bike or your sibling's new toy? That feeling of jealousy means we want something we don't have.

When God says that he is jealous for his people, he means that he wants people to worship him alone (see Exodus 34:14). He saved people from their sin because he loves them, and he deserves their worship and attention. When people worship God alone, they experience joy and peace as God intended.

18 "Celebrate the Feast of Unleavened Bread. For seven days eat bread made without yeast, just as I commanded you. Do it at the appointed time in the month of Aviv. You came out of Egypt in that month.

19 "Every male animal born first to its mother belongs to me. That includes your livestock. It includes herds and flocks alike. 20 Sacrifice a lamb to buy back every male donkey born first to its mother. But if you do not buy the donkey back, break its neck. Buy back all your oldest sons.

"You must not come to worship me with your hands empty.

21 "Do your work in six days. But you must rest on the seventh day. Even when you are plowing your land or gathering your crops, you must rest on the seventh day.

22 "Celebrate the Feast of Weeks. Bring the first share of your wheat crop. Celebrate the Feast of Booths. Hold it in the fall. 23 Three times a year all your men must come to worship me. I am your LORD and King, the God of Israel. 24 I will drive out nations ahead of you. I will increase your territory. Go up three times a year to worship me. While you are doing that, I will keep others from wanting to take any of your land for themselves. I am the LORD your God.

25 "Do not include anything made with yeast when you offer me the blood of a sacrifice. You must not keep any of the meat from the sacrifice of the Passover Feast until morning.

26 "Bring the best of the first share of your crops to the house of the LORD your God.

"Do not cook a young goat in its mother's milk."

27 Then the LORD said to Moses, "Write down the words I have spoken. I have made a covenant with you and with Israel in keeping with those words." 28 Moses was there with the LORD for 40 days and 40 nights. He didn't eat any food or drink any water. The LORD wrote on the tablets the words of the covenant law. Those words are the Ten Commandments.

The Face of Moses Shines

29 Moses came down from Mount Sinai. He had the two tablets of the covenant law in his hands. His face was shining because he had spoken with the LORD. But he didn't realize it. 30 Aaron and all the people of Israel saw Moses. His face was shining. So they were afraid to come near him. 31 But Moses called out to them. So Aaron and all the leaders of the community came to him. And Moses spoke to them. 32 After that, all the Israelites came near him. And he gave them all the commands the LORD had given him on Mount Sinai.

33 Moses finished speaking to them. Then he covered his face with a veil. 34 But when he would go to speak with the LORD, he would remove the veil. He would keep it off until he came out. Then he would tell the people what the LORD had commanded. 35 They would see that his face was shining. So Moses would cover his face with the veil again. He would keep it on until he went in again to speak with the LORD.

Rules for the Sabbath Day

35 Moses gathered the whole community of Israel together. He said to them, "Here are the things the LORD has commanded you to do. 2 You must do your work in six days. But the seventh day will be your holy day. It will be a day of sabbath rest to honor the LORD. You must rest on it. Anyone who does any work on it must be put to death. 3 Do not even light a fire in any of your homes on the Sabbath day."

Supplies for the Holy Tent

4 Moses spoke to the whole community of Israel. He said, "Here is what the LORD has commanded. 5 Take an offering for the LORD from what you have. Those who want to can bring an offering to the LORD. Here is what they can bring.

"gold, silver and bronze
6 blue, purple and bright red yarn
and fine linen
goat hair
7 ram skins that are dyed red
another kind of strong leather
acacia wood
8 olive oil for the lights
spices for the anointing oil and for
the sweet-smelling incense
9 onyx stones and other jewels for
the linen apron and the chest
cloth

10 "All the skilled workers among you
must come. They must make everything
the LORD has commanded 11 for the holy
tent and its covering. Here is what they
must make.

"hooks, frames, crossbars, posts
and bases
12 the ark of the covenant law, the
poles and cover for the ark, and
the curtain that hides the ark
13 the table for the holy bread, the
poles and all the things for the
table, and the holy bread
14 the lampstand for light and
everything used with it, the
lamps, and the olive oil that
gives light
15 the altar for burning incense, the
poles for the altar, the anointing
oil and the sweet-smelling
incense
the curtain for the entrance to the
holy tent
16 the altar for burnt offerings with
its bronze grate, its poles and all
its tools
the large bronze bowl with its
stand
17 the curtains of the courtyard with
their posts and bases, and the
curtain for the entrance to the
courtyard
18 the ropes and tent stakes for the
holy tent and for the courtyard
19 and the sacred clothes for Aaron
the priest and the clothes for his
sons when they serve as priests"

20 Then the whole community of Israel left Moses. 21 Everyone who wanted
to give offerings to the LORD brought
them to him. The offerings were for the
work on the tent of meeting. They were
also for the sacred clothes and for any
other purpose at the tent. 22 Every man
and woman who wanted to give came.
They brought gold jewelry of all kinds.
They brought pins, earrings, rings and
other jewelry. All of them gave their
gold as a wave offering to the LORD.
23 People brought what they had. They
brought blue, purple or bright red yarn
or fine linen. They brought goat hair,
ram skins dyed red, or the other kind
of strong leather. 24 Some brought silver
or bronze as an offering to the LORD.
Others brought acacia wood for any
part of the work. 25 All the skilled wom-
en spun yarn with their hands. They
brought blue, purple or bright red yarn
or fine linen. 26 All the skilled women
who wanted to spin the goat hair did so.
27 The leaders brought onyx stones and
other jewels for the linen apron and the
chest cloth. 28 They also brought spices
and olive oil. They brought them for
the light, for the anointing oil, and for
the sweet-smelling incense. 29 All the
men and women of Israel who wanted
to bring offerings to the LORD brought
them to him. The offerings were for all
the work the LORD had commanded
Moses to tell them to do.

Bezalel and Oholiab

30 Then Moses spoke to the people of
Israel. He said, "The LORD has chosen
Bezalel, the son of Uri. Uri is the son of
Hur. Bezalel is from the tribe of Judah.
31 The LORD has filled him with the Spirit
of God. He has filled him with wisdom,
with understanding, with knowledge
and with all kinds of skill. 32 Bezalel
can make beautiful patterns in gold,
silver and bronze. 33 He can cut and set
stones. He can work with wood. In fact,
he can work in all kinds of arts and
crafts. 34 And the LORD has given both
him and Oholiab the ability to teach
others. Oholiab, the son of Ahisamak,
is from the tribe of Dan. 35 The LORD has
filled Bezalel and Oholiab with skill to
do all kinds of work. They can carve
things and make patterns. They can sew
skillfully with blue, purple and bright
red yarn and on fine linen. They use
thread to make beautiful cloth. Both
of them have the skill to work in all
36 kinds of crafts. 1 Bezalel and
Oholiab must do the work just
as the LORD has commanded. So must
every skilled worker to whom the LORD
has given skill and ability. They know
how to do all the work for every purpose
connected with the sacred tent. And that
includes setting it up."

2 Then Moses sent for Bezalel and
Oholiab. He sent for every skilled worker
to whom the LORD had given ability and
who wanted to come and do the work.
3 They received from Moses all the offerings the people of Israel had brought.
They had brought the offerings for all
the work for every purpose connected

with the holy tent. That included setting it up. The people kept bringing the offerings they chose to give. They brought them morning after morning. 4 So all the skilled workers working on the holy tent stopped what they were doing. 5 They said to Moses, "The LORD commanded us to do the work. And the people are bringing more than enough for us to do it."

6 Then Moses gave an order. A message was sent through the whole camp. It said, "No man or woman should make anything else and offer it for the holy tent." And so the people were kept from bringing more offerings. 7 There was already more than enough to do all the work.

The Holy Tent

8 All the skilled workers made the holy tent. They made ten curtains out of finely twisted linen. They made them with blue, purple and bright red yarn. A skilled worker sewed cherubim into the pattern. 9 All the curtains were the same size. They were 42 feet long and six feet wide. 10 The workers joined five of the curtains together. They did the same thing with the other five. 11 Then they made loops out of blue strips of cloth along the edge of the end curtain in one set. They did the same thing with the end curtain in the other set. 12 They also made 50 loops on the end curtain of the one set. They did the same thing on the end curtain of the other set. They put the loops across from each other. 13 Then they made 50 gold hooks. They used them to join the two sets of curtains together so that the holy tent was all one piece.

14 The workers made a total of 11 curtains out of goat hair to put over the holy tent. 15 All 11 curtains were the same size. They were 45 feet long and six feet wide. 16 The workers joined five of the curtains together into one set. They did the same thing with the other six. 17 Then they made 50 loops along the edge of the end curtain in the one set. They did the same thing with the other set. 18 They made 50 bronze hooks. They used them to join the tent together all in one piece. 19 They made a covering for the tent. They made it out of ram skins dyed red. Over that, they put a covering of another kind of strong leather.

20 The workers made frames out of acacia wood for the holy tent. 21 Each frame was about 15 feet long and two feet three inches wide. 22 The workers added two small wooden pins to each frame. The pins stuck out so that they were even with each other. The workers made all the frames of the holy tent in the same way. 23 The workers made 20 frames for the south side of the holy tent. 24 And they made 40 silver bases to go under them. They made two bases for each frame. They put one under each pin that stuck out. 25 For the north side of the holy tent they made 20 frames 26 and 40 silver bases. They put two bases under each frame. 27 The workers made six frames for the west end of the holy tent. 28 They made two frames for the corners of the holy tent at the far end. 29 At those two corners the frames were double from top to bottom. They were fitted into a single ring. The workers made both of them the same. 30 So there were eight frames and 16 silver bases. There were two bases under each frame.

31 The workers also made crossbars out of acacia wood. They made five for the frames on one side of the holy tent. 32 They made five for the frames on the other side. And they made five for the frames on the west, at the far end of the holy tent. 33 The center crossbar reached from end to end at the middle of the frames. 34 The workers covered the frames with gold. They made gold rings to hold the crossbars. They also covered the crossbars with gold.

35 They made the curtain out of blue, purple and bright red yarn and finely twisted linen. A skilled worker sewed cherubim into the pattern. 36 The workers made four posts out of acacia wood for the curtain. They covered the posts with gold. They made gold hooks and four silver bases for the posts. 37 For the entrance to the tent the workers made a curtain. They made it out of blue, purple and bright red yarn and finely twisted linen. A person who sewed skillfully made it. 38 The workers made five posts with hooks for the curtains. They covered the tops of the posts and their bands with gold. And they made five bronze bases for them.

The Ark of the Covenant Law

37 Bezalel made the ark of the covenant law out of acacia wood. It was three feet nine inches long and two feet three inches wide and high. 2 He covered it inside and outside with pure gold. He put a strip of gold around it. 3 He made four gold rings for it. He joined them to its four bottom corners. He put two rings on one side and two rings on the other. 4 Then he made poles out of acacia wood. He covered them with gold. 5 He put the poles through the rings on the sides of the ark to carry it.

6 He made its cover out of pure gold. It was three feet nine inches long and two feet three inches wide. The cover is the place where sin is paid for. 7 Then he made two cherubim out of hammered gold at the ends of the cover. 8 He put one of the cherubim on each end of it. 9 He made them as part of the cover itself. Their wings spread up over the cover. The cherubim faced each other and looked toward the cover.

The Table for the Holy Bread

10 The workers made the table out of acacia wood. It was three feet long, one foot six inches wide and two feet three inches high. 11 Then they covered it with pure gold. They put a strip of gold around it. 12 They also made a rim around it three inches wide. They put a strip of gold around the rim. 13 They made four gold rings for the table. They joined them to the four corners, where the four legs were. 14 The rings were close to the rim. The rings held the poles used to carry the table. 15 The workers made the poles out of acacia wood. They covered them with gold. 16 They made plates, dishes and bowls out of pure gold for the table. They also made pure gold pitchers to pour out drink offerings.

The Gold Lampstand

17 The workers made the lampstand out of pure gold. They hammered out its base and stem. Its buds, blossoms and cups branched out from it. 18 Six branches came out from the sides of the lampstand. There were three on one side and three on the other. 19 On one branch there were three cups shaped like almond flowers with buds and blossoms. There were three on the next branch. In fact, there were three on each of the six branches that came out from the lampstand. 20 On the lampstand there were four cups shaped like almond flowers with buds and blossoms. 21 One bud was under the first pair of branches that came out from the lampstand. A second bud was under the second pair. And a third bud was under the third pair. There was a total of six branches. 22 The buds and branches came out from the lampstand. The whole lampstand was one piece hammered out of pure gold.

23 The workers made its seven lamps out of pure gold. They also made its trays and wick cutters out of pure gold. 24 They used 75 pounds of pure gold to make the lampstand and everything used with it.

The Altar for Burning Incense

25 The workers made the altar for burning incense. They made it out of acacia wood. It was about one foot six inches square and three feet high. A horn stuck out from each of its upper four corners. 26 The workers covered the top, sides and horns with pure gold. They put a strip of gold around it. 27 They made two gold rings below the strip. They put the rings on the sides across from each other. The rings held the poles used to carry it. 28 The workers made the poles out of acacia wood. They covered them with gold.

29 They also made the sacred anointing oil and the pure, sweet-smelling incense. A person who makes perfume made them.

The Altar for Burnt Offerings

38 The workers built the altar for burnt offerings out of acacia wood. It was four feet six inches high and seven feet six inches square. 2 They made a horn stick out from each of its four upper corners. They covered the altar with bronze. 3 They made all its tools out of bronze. They made its pots, shovels, sprinkling bowls, meat forks, and pans for carrying ashes. 4 They made a bronze grate for the altar. They put the grate halfway up the altar on the inside. 5 They made a bronze ring for each of the four corners of the grate. 6 They made poles out of acacia wood. They covered them with bronze. 7 They put the poles through the rings. The poles were on two sides of the altar for carrying it. The workers made the altar out of boards. They left it hollow.

The Large Bowl for Washing

8 The workers made the large bronze bowl and its bronze stand. They made them out of bronze mirrors. The mirrors belonged to the women who served at the entrance to the tent of meeting.

The Courtyard

9 Next, the workers made the courtyard. The south side was 150 feet long. It had curtains made out of finely twisted linen. 10 The curtains had 20 posts and 20 bronze bases. The posts had silver hooks and bands on them. 11 The north side was also 150 feet long. Its curtains had 20 posts and 20 bronze bases. The posts had silver hooks and bands on them.

12 The west end was 75 feet wide. It had curtains with ten posts and ten bases. The posts had silver hooks and bands on them. 13 The east end, toward the sunrise, was also 75 feet wide. 14 Curtains 22 feet six inches long were on one side of the entrance to the courtyard. They were hung on three posts. Each post had a base. 15 Curtains 22 feet six inches long were also on the other side of the entrance. They were hung on three posts. Each post had a base. 16 All the curtains around the courtyard were made out of finely twisted linen. 17 The bases for the posts were made out of bronze. The hooks and bands on the posts were made out of silver. Their tops were covered with silver. So all the posts of the courtyard had silver bands.

18 The curtain for the courtyard entrance was made out of blue, purple and bright red yarn and finely twisted linen. A person who sewed skillfully made it. It was 30 feet long. Like the curtains of the courtyard, it was seven feet six inches high. 19 It had four posts and four bronze bases. Their hooks and bands were made out of silver. Their tops were covered with silver. 20 All the tent stakes of the holy tent were made out of bronze. So were all the stakes of the courtyard around it.

The Amounts of the Metals Used

21 Here are the amounts of the metals used for the holy tent, where the tablets of the covenant law were kept. Moses commanded the Levites to record the amounts. The Levites did the work under the direction of Ithamar. Ithamar was the son of Aaron the priest. 22 Bezalel, the son of Uri, made everything the LORD had commanded Moses. Uri was the son of Hur. Bezalel was from the tribe of Judah. 23 Oholiab, the son of Ahisamak, helped Bezalel. Oholiab was from the tribe of Dan. He could carve things and make patterns. And he could sew skillfully with blue, purple and bright red yarn and on fine linen. 24 The total weight of the gold from the wave offering was more than a ton. It was weighed out in keeping with the standard weights used in the sacred tent. The gold was used for all the work done in connection with the sacred tent.

25 The silver received from the men in the community who were listed and counted weighed almost four tons. It was weighed out in keeping with the weights used in the sacred tent. 26 It amounted to a fifth of an ounce for each person. It was weighed out in keeping with the weights used in the sacred tent. The silver was received from the men who had been listed and counted. All of them were 20 years old or more. Their total number was 603,550. 27 The four tons of silver were used to make the bases for the holy tent and for the curtain. The 100 bases were made from the four tons. Each base used more than 75 pounds of silver. 28 The workers used 45 pounds to make the hooks for the posts, to cover the tops of the posts, and to make their bands.

29 The bronze from the wave offering weighed two and a half tons. 30 The workers used some of it to make the bases for the entrance to the tent of meeting. They used some for the bronze altar for burnt offerings and its bronze grate and all its tools. 31 They used some for the bases for the courtyard around the holy tent. They used some for the bases for the courtyard entrance. And they used the rest to make all the tent stakes for the holy tent and the courtyard around it.

The Clothes for the Priests

39 The workers made clothes from the blue, purple and bright red yarn. The clothes were worn by the priests who served in the holy tent. The workers also made sacred clothes for Aaron. They made them just as the LORD had commanded Moses.

The Linen Apron

2 The workers made the linen apron. They made it out of thin gold wire, and of blue, purple and bright red yarn, and of finely twisted linen. 3 They hammered out thin sheets of gold. They cut it into thin wire. Then they sewed it into the blue, purple and bright red yarn and fine linen. Skilled workers made it. 4 The workers made shoulder straps for the apron. The straps were joined to two of its corners. 5 Its skillfully made waistband was made like the apron. The waistband was part of the apron itself. It was made out of thin gold wire, and out of blue, purple and bright red yarn, and out of finely twisted linen. The workers made it just as the LORD had commanded Moses.

6 They put the onyx stones in fancy gold settings. They carved the names of the sons of Israel on the stones. They did it the way a jewel cutter would carve them. 7 Then they connected them to the shoulder straps of the linen apron. The stones stood for the sons of Israel and were a constant reminder for them. The workers did those things just as the LORD had commanded Moses.

The Chest Cloth

8 Skilled workers made the chest cloth. They made it like the linen apron. They used thin gold wire, and blue, purple and bright red yarn, and finely twisted linen. 9 The chest cloth was nine inches square. It was folded in half. 10 The workers put four rows of valuable jewels on it. Carnelian, chrysolite and beryl were in the first row. 11 Turquoise, lapis lazuli and emerald were in the second row. 12 Jacinth, agate and amethyst were in the third row. 13 And topaz, onyx and jasper were in the fourth row. The workers put them in fancy gold settings. 14 They used a total of 12 stones. There was one stone for each of the names of the sons of Israel. Each stone was carved with the name of one of the 12 tribes.

15 The workers made braided chains out of pure gold for the chest cloth. They made them like ropes. 16 They made two fancy gold settings and two gold rings. They connected them to two corners of the chest cloth. 17 They joined the two gold chains to the rings at the corners of the chest cloth. 18 They joined the other ends of the chains to the two settings. They joined them to the shoulder straps on the front of the linen apron. 19 The workers made two gold rings. They connected them to the other two corners of the chest cloth. They put them on the inside edge next to the apron. 20 Then they made two more gold rings. They connected them to the bottom of the shoulder straps on the front of the apron. They put them close to the seam. They put them right above the waistband of the apron. 21 They tied the rings of the chest cloth to the rings of the apron with blue cord. That connected it to the waistband. Then the chest cloth would not swing out from the linen apron. The workers did those things just as the LORD had commanded Moses.

More Clothes for the Priests

22 The workers made the outer robe of the linen apron completely out of blue cloth. The cloth was made by a skillful person. 23 The workers made an opening in the center of the robe. They made an edge like a collar around the opening. Then it couldn't tear. 24 They made pomegranates out of blue, purple and bright red yarn and finely twisted linen. They sewed them around the hem of the robe. 25 They made bells out of pure gold. They sewed them around the hem between the pomegranates. 26 They sewed a bell between every two pomegranates all around the hem of the robe. Aaron had to wear the robe when he served as priest. That's what the LORD commanded Moses.

27 The workers made inner robes out of fine linen for Aaron and his sons. The linen cloth was made by a skillful person. 28 The workers also made the turban out of fine linen. And they made the caps and the underwear out of finely twisted linen. 29 The belt was made out of finely twisted linen and blue, purple and bright red yarn. A person who

sewed skillfully made it. The workers
did those things just as the LORD had
commanded Moses.
30 They made the plate out of pure
gold. It was a sacred crown. On the plate,
they carved the words

SET APART FOR THE LORD.

31 Then they tied the plate to the turban
with a blue cord. They did those things
just as the LORD had commanded Moses.

The Holy Tent Is Completed

32 So all the work on the holy tent,
the tent of meeting, was completed.
The Israelites did everything just as the
LORD had commanded Moses. 33 Then
they brought the holy tent to Moses
along with everything that belonged
to it. Here are the things they brought:

hooks, frames, crossbars, posts and bases
34 the covering of ram skins dyed red, the covering of another kind of strong leather and the curtain that hides the ark
35 the ark where the tablets of the covenant law are kept, the poles and the cover for the ark
36 the table for the holy bread with all its things and the holy bread
37 the pure gold lampstand with its row of lamps and everything used with it, and the olive oil that gives light
38 the gold altar for burning incense, the anointing oil and the sweet-smelling incense
the curtain for the entrance to the tent
39 the bronze altar for burnt offerings with its bronze grate, its poles and all its tools
the large bowl with its stand
40 the curtains of the courtyard with their posts and bases, and the curtain for the entrance to the courtyard
the ropes and tent stakes for the courtyard
everything that belongs to the holy tent, the tent of meeting
41 and the sacred clothes for Aaron the priest and the clothes for his sons when they serve as priests

42 The Israelites had done all the work
just as the LORD had commanded Moses.
43 Moses looked over the work carefully.
He saw that the workers had done it just
as the LORD had commanded. So Moses
gave them his blessing.

Moses Sets Up the Holy Tent

40 Then the LORD said to Moses,
2 "Set up the holy tent, the tent
of meeting. Set it up on the first day
of the first month. 3 Place in it the ark
where the tablets of the covenant law
are kept. Hide the ark with the curtain. 4 Bring in the table for the holy
bread. Arrange the loaves of bread
on it. Then bring in the lampstand.
Set up its lamps. 5 Place the gold altar
for burning incense in front of the ark
where the tablets of the covenant law
are kept. Put up the curtain at the entrance to the holy tent.
6 "Place the altar for burnt offerings
in front of the entrance to the holy tent,
the tent of meeting. 7 Place the large
bowl between the tent of meeting and
the altar. Put water in the bowl. 8 Set
up the courtyard around the holy tent.
Put the curtain at the entrance to the
courtyard.
9 "Get the anointing oil. Anoint the
holy tent and everything in it. Set apart
the holy tent and everything that belongs to it. Then it will be holy. 10 Anoint
the altar for burnt offerings and all its
tools. Set apart the altar. Then it will
be a very holy place. 11 Anoint the large
bowl and its stand. Set them apart.
12 "Bring Aaron and his sons to the
entrance to the tent of meeting. Wash
them with water. 13 Dress Aaron in the
sacred clothes. Anoint him and set him
apart. Then he will be able to serve me
as priest. 14 Bring his sons and dress
them in their inner robes. 15 Anoint them
just as you anointed their father. Then
they will be able to serve me as priests.
They will be anointed to do the work of
priests. That work will last for all time
to come." 16 Moses did everything just as
the LORD had commanded him.
17 So the holy tent was set up. It was
the first day of the first month in the
second year. 18 Moses set up the holy
tent. He put the bases in place. He put
the frames in them. He put in the crossbars. He set up the posts. 19 He spread

the holy tent over the frames. Then he
put the coverings over the tent. Moses
did it as the LORD had commanded him.
[20] He got the tablets of the covenant
law. He placed them in the ark. He put
the poles through its rings. And he put
the cover on it. The cover was the place
where sin is paid for. [21] Moses brought
the ark into the holy tent. He hung the
curtain to hide the ark where the tablets
of the covenant law are kept. Moses did
it as the LORD had commanded him.
[22] Moses placed the table for the holy
bread in the tent of meeting. It was on
the north side of the holy tent outside
the curtain. [23] He arranged the loaves
of bread on it in the sight of the LORD.
Moses did it as the LORD had commanded him.
[24] Moses placed the lampstand in the
tent of meeting. It stood across from
the table on the south side of the holy
tent. [25] He set up the lamps in front of
the LORD. Moses did it as the LORD had
commanded him.
[26] Moses placed the gold altar for
burning incense in the tent of meeting. He placed it in front of the curtain.
[27] He burned sweet-smelling incense on
it. Moses did it as the LORD had commanded him.
[28] Then Moses put up the curtain at
the entrance to the holy tent. [29] He set
the altar for burnt offerings near the
entrance to the holy tent, the tent of
meeting. He sacrificed burnt offerings
and grain offerings on it. Moses did it as
the LORD had commanded him.
[30] Moses placed the large bowl between the tent of meeting and the altar.
He put water in the bowl for washing.
[31] Moses and Aaron and his sons used
it to wash their hands and feet. [32] They
washed whenever they entered the tent
of meeting or approached the altar.
They did it as the LORD had commanded
Moses.
[33] Then Moses set up the courtyard
around the holy tent and altar. He put
up the curtain at the entrance to the
courtyard. And so Moses completed
the work.

The Glory of the LORD

[34] Then the cloud covered the tent of
meeting. The glory of the LORD filled
the holy tent. [35] Moses couldn't enter
the tent of meeting because the cloud
had settled on it. The glory of the LORD
filled the holy tent.
[36] The Israelites continued their
travels. Whenever the cloud lifted from
above the holy tent, they started out.
[37] But if the cloud didn't lift, they did not
start out. They stayed until the day it
lifted. [38] So the cloud of the LORD was
above the holy tent during the day.
Fire was in the cloud at night. All the
Israelites could see the cloud during
all their travels.

LEVITICUS

Author: Moses

Once the Israelites were set free from slavery, they had to learn how to live as God's people. They didn't know how to live as people marked by God's presence; they only knew what it was like to be slaves in Egypt! In the book of Leviticus, God gave the Israelites a set of laws and taught them that he is holy. This means that God is pure and set apart, and because God is holy, God's people should be holy too (see Leviticus 21:8).

Law & Covenant

The laws God gave the Israelites taught them how to worship him and live in a way that mirrored his character. Since the Israelites were God's special people, he wanted to live among them and have a relationship with them. So he made them a promise: He would come and dwell among them in the holy tent. However, no one, not even Moses, was pure enough to enter God's presence in the holy tent. The Israelites needed priests to go before God on their behalf and ask for the forgiveness of their sins.

The laws also included promises: If God's people followed his ways, they would be blessed, and if they broke his commands, they would experience the consequences. This relationship between God and his people is called a *covenant*. God knew that his people wouldn't always keep his covenant, but he planned to one day send a Savior who would keep God's laws perfectly on their behalf.

Rules for Burnt Offerings

1 The LORD called out to Moses. He spoke to him from the tent of meeting. He said, 2 "Speak to the Israelites. Tell them, 'Suppose anyone among you brings an offering to the LORD. They must bring an animal from their herd or flock.

3 " 'If someone brings a burnt offering from the herd, they must offer a male animal. It must not have any flaws. They must bring it to the entrance to the tent of meeting. Then the LORD will accept it. 4 They must place their hand on the head of the burnt offering. Then the LORD will accept it in place of them. It will pay for their sin. 5 The young bull must be killed there in the sight of the LORD. Then the priests in Aaron's family line must bring its blood to the altar. They must splash it against the sides of the altar. The altar stands at the entrance to the tent of meeting. 6 The skin must be removed from the animal brought for the burnt offering. Then the animal must be cut into pieces. 7 The priests in Aaron's family line must build a fire on the altar. They must place wood on the fire. 8 Then they must place the pieces of the animal on the burning wood on the altar. The pieces include the head and the fat. 9 The inside parts of the animal must be washed with water. The legs must also be washed. The priest must burn all of it on the altar. It is a burnt offering. It is a food offering. Its smell pleases the LORD.

10 " 'If someone offers a burnt offering from the flock, it must be a male animal. It can be a sheep or a goat. It must not have any flaws. 11 They must kill it at the north side of the altar in the sight of the LORD. The priests in Aaron's family line must splash its blood against the sides of the altar. 12 They must cut the animal into pieces. The priest must place the pieces on the burning wood on the altar. The pieces include the head and the fat. 13 They must wash the inside parts with water. The legs must also be washed. The priest must bring all the parts to the altar. He must burn them there. It is a burnt offering. It is a food offering. Its smell pleases the LORD.

14 " 'If someone offers to the LORD a burnt offering of birds, it must be a dove or a young pigeon. 15 The priest must bring it to the altar. He must twist its head off. Then he must burn the rest of the bird on the altar. Its blood must be emptied out on the side of the altar. 16 The priest must remove the small bag inside the bird's throat. He must also remove the feathers. Then he must throw them to the east side of the altar. That is where the ashes are. 17 He must take hold of the wings of the bird and tear it open. But he must not tear it in two. Then the priest will burn it on the wood burning on the altar. It is a burnt offering. It is a food offering. Its smell pleases the LORD.

Rules for Grain Offerings

2 " 'Suppose anyone brings a grain offering to the LORD. Then their offering must be made out of the finest flour. They must pour olive oil on it. They must also put incense on it. 2 They must take it to the priests in Aaron's family line. A priest must take a handful of the flour and oil. He must mix them with all the incense. Then he must burn that part on the altar. It will be a reminder that all good things come from the LORD. It is a food offering. Its smell pleases the LORD. 3 The rest of the grain offering belongs to Aaron and to the priests in his family line. It is a very holy part of the food offerings presented to the LORD.

4 " 'If you bring a grain offering baked in an oven, make it out of the finest flour. It can be thick loaves of bread made without yeast. Mix them with olive oil. Or it can be thin loaves of bread that are made without yeast. Spread olive oil on them. 5 If your grain offering is cooked on a metal plate, make your offering out of the finest flour. Mix it with oil. Make it without yeast. 6 Break it into pieces. Pour oil on it. It is a grain offering. 7 If your grain offering is cooked in a pan, make your offering out of the finest flour and some olive oil. 8 Bring to the LORD your grain offering made out of all these things. Give it to the priest. He must take it to the altar. 9 All good things come from the LORD. The priest must take out the part of the grain offering that reminds you of this. He must burn it on the altar. It is a food offering. Its smell pleases the LORD. 10 The rest of the grain offering belongs to Aaron and the priests in his

family line. It is a very holy part of the food offerings presented to the LORD.

11 " 'Every grain offering you bring to the LORD must be made without yeast. You must not add any yeast or honey to a food offering presented to the LORD. 12 You can bring them to the LORD as an offering of the first share of food you gather or produce. But they must not be offered on the altar as a pleasant smell. 13 Put salt on all your grain offerings. Salt stands for the lasting covenant between you and your God. So do not leave it out of your grain offerings. Add salt to all your offerings.

14 " 'Suppose you bring to the LORD a grain offering of the first share of your food. Then offer crushed heads of your first grain that have been cooked in fire. 15 Put olive oil and incense on the grain. It is a grain offering. 16 The priest must burn part of the crushed grain and the oil. It will remind you that all good things come from the LORD. The priest must burn it together with all the incense. It is a food offering presented to the LORD.

Rules for Friendship Offerings

3 " 'Suppose someone brings a friendship offering. If they offer an animal from the herd, it can be either male or female. It must not have any flaws. They must offer it in the sight of the LORD. 2 They must place their hand on the animal's head. It must be killed at the entrance to the tent of meeting. Then the priests in Aaron's family line must splash the blood against the sides of the altar. 3 Part of the friendship offering must be given to the LORD as a food offering. It must include all the fat that is connected to them. 4 It must include both kidneys with the fat on them next to the lower back muscles. It must also include the long part of the liver. All of it must be removed together with the kidneys. 5 Then the priests in Aaron's family line must burn it on the altar. They must burn it on top of the burnt offering that is lying on the burning wood. It is a food offering. Its smell pleases the LORD.

6 " 'Suppose someone brings an animal from the flock as a friendship offering to the LORD. It can be either male or female. It must not have any flaws. 7 If they bring a lamb, they must

in Leviticus?

God is the Holy One. This means that he is perfect and never has sinned nor ever will sin.

offer it in the sight of the LORD. 8 They must place their hand on the lamb's head. It must be killed there in front of the tent of meeting. Then the priests in Aaron's family line must splash its blood against the sides of the altar. 9 Part of the offering must be brought as a sacrifice presented to the LORD. It must include the lamb's fat and the entire fat tail cut off close to the backbone. It must include all the fat that is connected to them. 10 It must include both kidneys with the fat on them next to the lower back muscles. The offering must also include the long part of the liver. That must be removed together with the kidneys. 11 Then the priest must burn the offering on the altar as food. It is a food offering presented to the LORD.

12 " 'If someone brings a goat, they must offer it in the sight of the LORD. 13 They must place their hand on its head. It must be killed there in front of the tent of meeting. Then the priests in Aaron's family line must splash its blood against the sides of the altar. 14 Part of the offering must be brought as a food offering presented to the LORD. It must include all the fat that is connected to them. 15 It must include both kidneys with the fat on them next to the lower back muscles. It must also include the long part of the liver. That must be removed together with the kidneys. 16 Then the priest must burn the offering on the altar as food. It is a

food offering. It has a pleasant smell.
All the fat belongs to the LORD.
17 " 'You must not eat any fat or any
blood. That is a law that will last for
all time to come. It applies no matter
where you live.' "

Rules for Sin Offerings

4 The LORD spoke to Moses. He said,
2 "Speak to the Israelites. Tell them,
'Suppose someone sins without meaning to. And that person does something
the LORD commands us not to do.
3 " 'Suppose it is the anointed priest
who sins. And suppose he brings guilt on
the people. Then he must bring a young
bull to the LORD. It must not have any
flaws. He must bring it as a sin offering
for the sin he has committed. 4 He must
bring the bull to the entrance to the tent
of meeting in the sight of the LORD. He
must place his hand on its head. He must
kill it there in the sight of the LORD. 5 Then
the anointed priest must take some of the
bull's blood. He must carry it into the
tent of meeting. 6 He must dip his finger
into the blood. He must sprinkle some of
it seven times in the sight of the LORD.
He must do it in front of the curtain of
the Most Holy Room. 7 Then the priest
must put some of the blood on the horns
of the altar for burning incense. The
horns stick out from the upper four corners of the altar. The incense burned on
that altar has a sweet smell. The altar
stands in front of the LORD in the tent of
meeting. The priest must pour out the
rest of the bull's blood at the bottom of
the altar for burnt offerings. That altar
stands at the entrance to the tent. 8 He
must remove all the fat from the bull
for the sin offering. It includes the fat
that is connected to the inside parts. 9 It
includes both kidneys with the fat on
them next to the lower back muscles. It
also includes the long part of the liver.
He must remove all of it together with
the kidneys. 10 He must remove it in the
same way the fat is removed from an
ox sacrificed as a friendship offering.
Then the priest must burn all of it on
the altar for burnt offerings. 11 But the
bull's hide must be taken away. So must
all its meat. So must its head and legs.
And so must its inside parts and guts.
12 In other words, all the rest of the bull
must be taken away. The priest must
take it outside the camp. He must take
it to a "clean" place. He must take it to
the place where the ashes are thrown.
Then he must burn it there in a wood
fire on a pile of ashes.
13 " 'Or suppose the whole community
of Israel sins without meaning to. They
do something the LORD commands us
not to do. Suppose they realize their
guilt. 14 And suppose their sin becomes
known. Then they must bring a young
bull as a sin offering. They must offer
it in front of the tent of meeting. 15 The
elders of the community must place
their hands on the bull's head in the
sight of the LORD. The bull must be
killed in the sight of the LORD. 16 Then
the anointed priest must take some of
the bull's blood into the tent of meeting.
17 He must dip his finger into the blood.
He must sprinkle it seven times in the
sight of the LORD. He must do it in front
of the curtain. 18 He must put some of
the blood on the horns that stick out
from the upper four corners of the altar.
The altar stands in front of the LORD
in the tent of meeting. The priest must
pour out the rest of the blood at the
bottom of the altar for burnt offerings.
That altar stands at the entrance to the
tent. 19 He must remove all the fat from
the bull. He must burn it on the altar.
20 He must do the same thing with that
bull as he did with the bull for the sin
offering. When he does, he will pay for
the sin of the community. And they will
be forgiven. 21 Then he must take the
bull outside the camp. He must burn it
just as he burned the first bull. It is the
sin offering for the whole community.
22 " 'Or suppose a leader sins without
meaning to. He disobeys any of the
commands of the LORD his God. 23 And
suppose he realizes his guilt and his sin
becomes known. Then he must bring an
offering. It must be a male goat. It must
not have any flaws. 24 He must place his
hand on the goat's head. He must kill
it. He must do it at the place where the
animals for burnt offerings are killed
in the sight of the LORD. His offering is
a sin offering. 25 Then the priest must
dip his finger into some of the blood of
the sin offering. He must put it on the
horns that stick out from the upper four
corners of the altar for burnt offerings.
He must pour out the rest of the blood at

the bottom of the altar. 26 He must burn
all the fat on the altar. He must burn it
in the same way he burned the fat of
the friendship offering. When he does,
he will pay for the sin of the leader. And
the leader will be forgiven.
27 “ ‘Or suppose someone in the community sins without meaning to. They
disobey any of the LORD’s commands.
28 And suppose they realize their guilt
and their sin becomes known. Then they
must bring an offering for the sin they
have committed. It must be a female
goat. It must not have any flaws. 29 They
must place their hand on the head of
the animal for the sin offering. It must
be killed at the place where the animals
for burnt offerings are killed. 30 Then the
priest must dip his finger into some of
the blood. He must put it on the horns
that stick out from the upper four corners of the altar for burnt offerings. He
must pour out the rest of the blood at the
bottom of the altar. 31 They must remove
all the fat in the same way the fat is
removed from the friendship offering.
The priest must burn it on the altar. Its
smell pleases the LORD. When the priest
burns the offering, he will pay for their
sin. And they will be forgiven.
32 “ ‘Suppose someone brings a lamb
as their sin offering. Then they must
bring a female animal. It must not have
any flaws. 33 They must place their hand
on its head. They must kill it as a sin
offering. They must do it at the place
where the animals for burnt offerings
are killed. 34 Then the priest must dip
his finger into some of the blood of
the sin offering. He must put it on the
horns that stick out from the upper four
corners of the altar for burnt offerings.
He must pour out the rest of the blood
at the bottom of the altar. 35 They must
remove all the fat in the same way the
fat is removed from the lamb for the
friendship offering. The priest must
burn it on the altar on top of the food
offerings presented to the LORD. When
he does, he will pay for the sin they have
committed. And they will be forgiven.
5 “ ‘Suppose someone has been called
as a witness to something they
have seen or learned about. Then if
they do not tell what they know, they
have sinned. And they will be held responsible for it.
2 “ ‘Or suppose someone touches something not “clean.” It could be the dead
bodies of wild animals or of livestock.
Or it could be the dead bodies of creatures that move along the ground. Even
though those people are not aware that
they touched them, they have become
“unclean.” And they are guilty. 3 Or suppose they touch something “unclean”
that comes from a human being. It
could be anything that would make
them “unclean.” Suppose they are not
aware that they touched it. When they
find out about it, they will be guilty. 4 Or
suppose someone makes a promise to do
something without thinking it through.
It does not matter what they promised.
It does not matter whether they made
the promise without thinking about
it carefully. And suppose they are not
aware that they did not think it through.
When they find out about it, they will
be guilty. 5 When someone is guilty in
any of those ways, they must admit
they have sinned. 6 They must bring a
sin offering to pay for the sin they have
committed. They must bring to the LORD
a female lamb or goat from the flock.
The priest will sacrifice the animal. That
will pay for the person’s sin.
7 “ ‘Suppose they can’t afford a lamb.
Then they must get two doves or two
young pigeons. They must bring them
to the LORD to pay for their sin. One of
them is for a sin offering. The other is
for a burnt offering. 8 They must bring
them to the priest. The priest will offer
the one for the sin offering first. He must
twist its head. But he must not twist it
off completely. 9 Then he must splash
some of the blood of the sin offering
against the side of the altar. He must
empty out the rest of the blood at the
bottom of the altar. It is a sin offering.
10 Then the priest will offer the other
bird as a burnt offering. He must do it
in the way the law requires. That will
pay for the sin they have committed.
And they will be forgiven.
11 “ ‘But suppose they can’t afford two
doves or two young pigeons. Then they
must bring three and a half pounds of
the finest flour as an offering for their
sin. It is a sin offering. They must not
put olive oil or incense on it. That is
because it is a sin offering. 12 They must
bring it to the priest. The priest must

take a handful of it. He must burn that
part on the altar. It will be a reminder
that all good things come from the
LORD. The priest must burn it on top
of the food offerings presented to the
LORD. It is a sin offering. [13]In that way
the priest will pay for any of the sins
they have committed. And they will be
forgiven. The rest of the offering will
belong to the priest. It is the same as in
the case of the grain offering.' "

Rules for Guilt Offerings

[14]The LORD spoke to Moses. He said,
[15]"Suppose someone is unfaithful to me
and sins. And they do it without meaning to. Here is how they sin against me or
my priests. They refuse to give the priests
one of the holy things set apart for them.
Then they must bring me a ram from
the flock. It must not have any flaws. It
must be worth the required amount of
silver. The silver must be weighed out in
keeping with the standard weights that
are used in the sacred tent. The ram is
a guilt offering. It will pay for their sin.
[16]They must also pay for the holy thing
they refused to give. They must add a
fifth of its value to it. They must give
all of it to the priest. The priest will pay
for their sin with the ram. It is a guilt
offering. And they will be forgiven.

[17]"Suppose someone sins by doing
something I command them not to do.
Even though they do not know it, they are
guilty. They will be held responsible for
it. [18]They must bring to the priest a ram
from the flock as a guilt offering. It must
not have any flaws. And it must be worth
the required amount of money. The priest
will sacrifice the animal. That will pay
for what they have done wrong without
meaning to. And they will be forgiven. [19]It
is a guilt offering. They have been guilty
of doing wrong against me."

6 The LORD spoke to Moses. He said,
[2]"Suppose someone sins by not
being faithful to me. They do it by
tricking their neighbors. They trick
them in connection with something
their neighbors have placed in their
care. They steal from their neighbors.
Or they cheat them. [3]Or they find something their neighbors have lost and
then tell a lie about it. Or they go to
court. They promise to tell the truth. But
instead they tell a lie when they are a
witness about it. Or they lie when they
are witnesses about any other sin like
those sins. [4]When they sin in any of
these ways and realize their guilt, they
must return what they stole. They must
give back what they took by cheating
their neighbors. They must return what
their neighbors placed in their care.
They must return the lost property they
found. [5]They must return anything
they told a lie about when they were
witnesses in court. They must pay back
everything in full. They must add a fifth
of its value to it. They must give all of it
to the owner on the day they bring their
guilt offering. [6]He must bring their guilt
offering to the priest to pay for their
sin. It is an offering to me. They must
bring a ram from the flock. It must not
have any flaws. It must be worth the
required amount of money. [7]The priest
will sacrifice the ram to pay for their sin.
He will do it in my sight. And they will
be forgiven for any of the things they
did that made them guilty."

More Rules for Burnt Offerings

[8]The LORD spoke to Moses. He said,
[9]"Give Aaron and the priests in his family line a command. Tell them, 'Here are
some more rules for burnt offerings.
The burnt offering must remain on
the altar through the whole night. The
fire on the altar must be kept burning
until morning. [10]The priest must put
on his linen clothes. He must put on
linen underwear next to his body. He
must remove the ashes of the burnt
offering that the fire has burned up
on the altar. He must place them beside the altar. [11]Then he must take his
clothes off and put others on. He must
carry the ashes outside the camp to a
"clean" place. [12]The fire on the altar
must be kept burning. It must not go
out. Every morning the priest must add
more wood to the fire. He must place the
burnt offering on the fire. He must burn
the fat of the friendship offerings on it.
[13]The fire must be kept burning on the
altar all the time. It must not go out.

More Rules for Grain Offerings

[14]" 'Here are some more rules for
grain offerings. The priests in Aaron's
family line must bring the grain offering to the LORD in front of the altar.
[15]The priest must take a handful of the

finest flour and olive oil. He must add to it all the incense on the grain offering. He must burn that part on the altar. It will remind him that all good things come from the LORD. Its smell pleases
the LORD. 16 Aaron and the priests in his family line will eat the rest of it. But they must eat it without yeast in the holy area. They must eat it in the courtyard of the tent of meeting. 17 It must
not be baked with yeast added to it. The LORD has given it to the priests as their share of the food offerings presented to him. It is very holy, just like the sin offering and the guilt offering. 18 Any
priests in Aaron's family line can eat it. It is their share of the food offerings presented to the LORD. It is their share for all time to come. Anyone who touches these offerings will become holy.'"
19 The LORD spoke to Moses. He said,
20 "On the day each high priest in Aaron's family line is anointed, he must bring an offering to me. He must bring three and a half pounds of the finest flour as a regular grain offering. He must bring half of it in the morning. He must bring the other half in the evening. 21 Mix it with olive oil. Cook it on
a metal plate. Break it in pieces. Bring it as a grain offering. Its smell pleases the LORD. 22 The son of Aaron who will
become the next high priest after him will prepare the grain offering. It is the share that must be given to the LORD for all time to come. It must be completely burned up. 23 Every grain offering a high
priest offers must be completely burned up. It must not be eaten."

More Rules for Sin Offerings

24 The LORD spoke to Moses. He said,
25 "Speak to Aaron and the priests in his family line. Tell them, 'Here are some more rules for sin offerings. You must kill the animal for the sin offering in the sight of the LORD. Kill it in the place where the burnt offering is killed. It is very holy. 26 The priest who offers it will
eat it. He must eat it in the holy area. He must eat it in the courtyard of the tent of meeting. 27 Anyone who touch-
es any of its meat will become holy. Suppose some of the blood is spilled on someone's clothes. Then you must wash them in the holy area. 28 Break
the clay pot the meat is cooked in. But suppose you cook it in a bronze pot. Then you must scrub the pot and rinse it with water. 29 Any male in a priest's
family may eat the meat. It is very holy.
30 But suppose some of the blood of a sin offering is brought into the tent of

pointing us to JESUS: Sacrificial System

God gave his people the law along with instructions for how to worship him. He reminded them that their sin separated them from God and that only by the blood of a sacrifice could they be made right with him again. God instructed the people to take a perfect animal, one without a single spot or blemish, and sacrifice it on the altar. The animal would be a visible reminder to God's people that sin leads to death, just as God said it would at the very beginning.

God's people would have to sacrifice animals every time they sinned and didn't keep God's law. But one day there would be a final sacrifice. God himself would provide the perfect, sinless, ultimate sacrifice for our sins. His Son, Jesus, would lay down his life on the altar, dying on the cross so that all who put their faith in him will have their sins forgiven forever.

meeting. And that blood is brought into the Holy Room to pay for sin. Then that sin offering must not be eaten. It must be burned up.

More Rules for Guilt Offerings

7 " 'Here are some more rules for
guilt offerings. The guilt offering
is very holy. 2 You must kill the animal
for the guilt offering where you kill the
animal for the burnt offering. Splash
its blood against the sides of the altar.
3 Offer all its fat. It must include the fat
tail and the fat that covers the inside
parts. 4 It must include both kidneys
with the fat on them next to the lower
back muscles. It must also include the
long part of the liver. Remove all of it
together with the kidneys. 5 The priest
must burn all of it on the altar. It is a
food offering presented to the LORD. It is
a guilt offering. 6 Any male in a priest's
family can eat it. But he must eat it in
the holy area. It is very holy.

7 " 'The same law applies to the sin
offering and the guilt offering. Both of
them belong to the priest who offers
them to pay for sin. 8 The priest who
offers a burnt offering for anyone can
keep its hide for himself. 9 Every grain
offering baked in an oven belongs to
the priest who offers it. So does every
grain offering cooked in a pan or on a
metal plate. 10 Every grain offering belongs equally to all the priests in Aaron's
family line. That is true whether it is
mixed with olive oil or it is dry.

More Rules for Friendship Offerings

11 " 'Here are some more rules for
friendship offerings anyone may bring
to the LORD.

12 " 'Suppose they offer a friendship
offering to show they are thankful. Then
together with the thank offering they
must offer thick loaves of bread. They
must make them without yeast.
They must mix them with olive oil. Or
they must offer thin loaves of bread
made without yeast. They must spread
olive oil on them. Or they must offer
thick loaves of bread made out of the
finest flour. They must add olive oil to
it. They must work the flour and prepare it well. 13 They must bring another
friendship offering along with their
thank offering. It should be thick loaves
of bread made with yeast. 14 They must
bring one of each kind of bread as an
offering. One kind is made with yeast.
The other is not. Both of them are a gift
to the LORD. They belong to the priest
who splashes the blood of the friendship
offering against the altar. 15 The person

must eat the meat from their thank offering on the day they offer it. They must not leave any of it until morning.

16 “ ‘But suppose they bring a friendship offering to keep a promise they have made. Or suppose they bring an offering they choose to give. Then they must eat the sacrifice on the day they offer it. But if anything is left over, they may eat it the next day. 17 They must burn up any meat from the sacrifice left over until the third day. 18 Suppose they eat any meat from the friendship offering on the third day. Then the LORD will not accept the offering. He will not accept it as a gift from them. It is not pure. If they eat any of it, they will be held responsible for it.

19 “ ‘They must not eat meat that touches anything “unclean.” They must burn it up. Anyone “clean” may eat any other meat. 20 But suppose an “unclean” person eats any meat from the friendship offering that belongs to the LORD. Then they will be separated from their people. 21 Suppose someone touches something “unclean.” It does not matter whether it comes from a human being who is not “clean.” It does not matter whether it comes from an “unclean” animal. It does not matter whether it comes from something hated and “unclean.” And suppose they eat any of the meat from the friendship offering that belongs to the LORD. Then they will be separated from their people.’ ”

Israel Must Not Eat Fat or Blood

22 The LORD spoke to Moses. He said, 23 “Speak to the Israelites. Tell them, ‘Do not eat any of the fat of cattle, sheep or goats. 24 Do not eat the fat of any animal found dead. Do not eat the fat of an animal that wild animals have torn apart. But you can use the fat for any other purpose. 25 Suppose an animal has been sacrificed as a food offering to the LORD. No one may eat its fat. If they do, they will be separated from their people. 26 No matter where you live, do not eat the blood of any bird or animal. 27 Anyone who eats blood must be separated from their people.’ ”

The Share That Belongs to the Priests

28 The LORD spoke to Moses. He said, 29 “Speak to the Israelites. Tell them, ‘Suppose someone brings a friendship offering to the LORD. Then they must bring part of it as their special gift to the LORD. 30 They must bring it with their own hands. It is a food offering presented to the LORD. They must bring the fat together with the breast. They must lift the breast up and wave it in front of the LORD as a wave offering. 31 The priest will burn the fat on the altar. But the breast belongs to Aaron and the priests in his family line. 32 Give the right thigh from your friendship offerings to the priest as a gift. 33 The priest who offers the blood and fat from the friendship offering must be given the right thigh. It is his share. 34 I, the LORD, have taken the breast that is waved and the thigh that is given. I have taken them from the friendship offerings of the Israelites. And I have given them to Aaron the priest and the priests in his family line. The offerings will be their share from the Israelites for all time to come.’ ”

35 That is the part of the food offerings presented to the LORD. It is given to Aaron and the priests in his family line. It was given to Aaron and his sons on the day they were set apart to serve the LORD as priests. 36 On the day they were anointed, the LORD commanded the Israelites to give that part to them. For all time to come, it will be the share of Aaron and the priests in his family line.

37 These are the rules for burnt offerings, grain offerings, sin offerings, guilt offerings and friendship offerings. They are also the rules for the offerings that are given when priests are being prepared to serve the LORD. 38 They are the rules the LORD gave Moses on Mount Sinai. He gave them on the day he commanded the Israelites to bring their offerings to the LORD. That took place in the Sinai Desert.

Preparing the Priests to Serve the LORD

8 The LORD spoke to Moses. He said, 2 “Bring Aaron and his sons to the entrance to the tent of meeting. Bring their clothes and the anointing oil. Bring the bull for the sin offering. Also bring two rams. And bring the basket with the bread made without yeast. 3 Then gather the whole community at the entrance to the tent of meeting.” 4 Moses did just as the LORD had commanded him. All the

people gathered together at the entrance
to the tent of meeting.
5 Moses said to the people, "Here is
what the LORD has commanded us to
do." 6 Then Moses brought Aaron and
his sons to the people. He washed Aaron
and his sons with water. 7 He put the
inner robe on Aaron. He tied the belt
around him. He dressed him in the outer
robe. He put the linen apron on him.
He took the skillfully made waistband
and tied the apron on him with it. He
wanted to make sure it was securely tied
to him. 8 Moses placed the chest cloth on
Aaron. He put the Urim and Thummim
in the chest cloth. 9 Then he placed the
turban on Aaron's head. On the front of
the turban he put the gold plate. It was
a sacred crown. Moses did everything
just as the LORD had commanded him.
10 Then Moses took the anointing oil
and poured it on the holy tent. He also
poured it on everything in it. That's how
he set apart those things for the LORD.
11 He sprinkled some of the oil on the altar
seven times. He poured oil on the altar
and all its tools. He poured it on the large
bowl and its stand. He did it to set them
apart. 12 He poured some of the anointing
oil on Aaron's head. He anointed him to
set him apart to serve the LORD. 13 Then
Moses brought Aaron's sons to the people. He put the inner robes on them. He
tied belts around them. He put caps on
their heads. He did everything just as
the LORD had commanded him.
14 Then he brought the bull for the
sin offering. Aaron and his sons placed
their hands on its head. 15 Moses killed
the bull. He dipped his finger into some
of the blood. He put it on the horns that
stick out from the upper four corners
of the altar. He did it to make the altar
pure. He poured out the rest of the blood
at the bottom of the altar. So he set
it apart to make it pure. 16 Moses also
removed all the fat around the inside
parts of the bull. He removed the long
part of the liver. He took both kidneys
and their fat. Then he burned all of it
on the altar. 17 But he burned the rest of
the bull outside the camp. He burned up
its hide, its meat and its guts. He did it
just as the LORD had commanded him.
18 Then Moses brought the ram for the
burnt offering. Aaron and his sons placed
their hands on its head. 19 Moses killed
the ram. He splashed the blood against
the sides of the altar. 20 He cut the ram
into pieces. He burned the head, the
other pieces and the fat. 21 He washed the
inside parts and the legs with water. He
burned the whole ram on the altar as a
burnt offering. It had a pleasant smell.
It was a food offering presented to the
LORD. Moses did everything just as the
LORD had commanded him.
22 Then he brought the other ram. It
was sacrificed to prepare the priests for
serving the LORD. Aaron and his sons
placed their hands on its head. 23 Moses
killed the ram. He put some of its blood
on Aaron's right earlobe. He put some
on the thumb of Aaron's right hand. He
also put some on the big toe of Aaron's
right foot. 24 Then Moses brought Aaron's
sons to the people. He put some of the
blood on their right earlobes. He put
some on the thumbs of their right hands.
He also put some on the big toes of their
right feet. Then he splashed the rest of
the blood against the sides of the altar.
25 He removed the fat, the fat tail and
all the fat around the inside parts. He
removed the long part of the liver. He
removed both kidneys and their fat.
And he removed the right thigh. 26 Then
he took a thick loaf of bread from the
basket of bread made without yeast.
The basket was in front of the LORD.
Moses took a thick loaf of bread made
with olive oil. He also took a thin loaf of
bread. He put all of it on the fat parts of
the ram and on its right thigh. 27 He put
everything in the hands of Aaron and his
sons. He told them to lift it up and wave
it in front of the LORD as a wave offering.
28 Then Moses took it from their hands.
He burned it on the altar on top of the
burnt offering. It was the offering that
was sacrificed to prepare the priests for
serving the LORD. It had a pleasant smell.
It was a food offering presented to the
LORD. 29 Moses also lifted up the ram's
breast and waved it in front of the LORD
as a wave offering. The breast was Moses'
share of the ram that was sacrificed to
prepare the priests for serving the LORD.
Moses did everything just as the LORD
had commanded him.
30 Then Moses took some of the anointing oil. He also took some of the blood
from the altar. He sprinkled some of the
oil and blood on Aaron and his clothes.

He also sprinkled some on Aaron's sons
and their clothes. That's how he set apart
Aaron and his clothes. And that's how he
set apart Aaron's sons and their clothes.
31 Then Moses spoke to Aaron and his
sons. He said, "Cook the meat at the
entrance to the tent of meeting. Eat it
there along with the bread from the
basket of the offerings that are brought
to prepare the priests for serving the
LORD. Do it just as I was commanded.
I was told, 'Aaron and his sons must
eat it.' 32 Then burn up the rest of the
meat and the bread. 33 Don't leave the
entrance to the tent of meeting for
seven days. Don't leave until the days
that are required to prepare you for
serving the LORD have been completed.
Stay here for the full seven days. 34 The
LORD commanded what has been done
here today. It was done to pay for your
sin. 35 Stay at the entrance to the tent of
meeting for seven days. Stay here day
and night. Do what the LORD requires.
Then you won't die. That's the command the LORD gave me."
36 So Aaron and his sons did everything just as the LORD had commanded
through Moses.

The Priests Offer Sacrifices

9 On the eighth day Moses sent for
Aaron, his sons and the elders of Israel. 2 He said to Aaron, "Bring a bull calf
for your sin offering. Bring a ram for
your burnt offering. They must not have
any flaws. Offer them to the LORD. 3 Then
speak to the Israelites. Tell them, 'Bring
a male goat for a sin offering. Bring a
calf and a lamb for a burnt offering.
Both of them must be a year old. They
must not have any flaws. 4 Bring an
ox and a ram for a friendship offering.
Sacrifice all of them to the LORD. Also
bring a grain offering. Mix it with olive
oil. Today the LORD will appear to you.' "
5 The people got the things Moses
commanded them to get. They took
them to the front of the tent of meeting.
The whole community came up close to
the tent. They stood there in front of the
LORD. 6 Then Moses said, "You have done
what the LORD has commanded. So the
glory of the LORD will appear to you."
7 Moses said to Aaron, "Come to the
altar. Sacrifice your sin offering and
your burnt offering. Pay for your sin
and the sin of the people. Sacrifice the
people's offering. Pay for their sin. Do
just as the LORD has commanded."
8 So Aaron came to the altar. He killed
the calf as a sin offering for himself.
9 His sons brought its blood to him. He
dipped his finger into the blood. He put
some on the horns that stick out from
the upper four corners of the altar. He
poured out the rest of the blood at the
bottom of the altar. 10 He burned the
fat and the kidneys on the altar. He
also burned the long part of the liver.
All these parts were from the sin offering. Aaron did just as the LORD had
commanded Moses. 11 He burned up the
meat and the hide outside the camp.
12 Then he killed the animal for the
burnt offering. His sons handed him its
blood. He splashed it against the sides of
the altar. 13 They handed him the burnt
offering piece by piece. It included the
animal's head. Aaron burned everything
on the altar. 14 He washed the inside parts
and the legs. He burned them on top of
the burnt offering on the altar.
15 Then Aaron brought the people's
offering. He took the goat for their sin
offering and killed it. He offered it for a
sin offering. He did just as he had done
with his own sin offering.
16 He brought the animal for the burnt
offering. He offered it in the way the law
requires. 17 He also brought the grain
offering. He took a handful of it and
burned it on the altar. It was in addition
to that morning's burnt offering.
18 Aaron killed the ox and the ram
as the friendship offering for the people. His sons handed him the blood.
He splashed it against the sides of the
altar. 19 His sons also brought the fat
parts of the ox and the ram. They included the fat tail and the layer of fat.
They also included the kidneys and the
long part of the liver. 20 Aaron's sons
placed everything on the breasts of the
animals. Aaron burned the fat on the
altar. 21 He lifted up the breasts and
the right thigh and waved them in front
of the LORD as a wave offering. He did it
just as Moses had commanded.
22 Then Aaron lifted up his hands
toward the people. He gave them a
blessing. He had already sacrificed the
sin offering, the burnt offering and the

friendship offering. So he stepped down from the altar.

[23] Moses and Aaron went into the tent of meeting. When they came out, they gave the people a blessing. The glory of the LORD appeared to all the people. [24] The LORD sent fire on the altar. The fire burned up the burnt offering along with the fat parts. All the people saw it. Then they shouted for joy. They fell with their faces to the ground.

The LORD Kills Nadab and Abihu

10 Nadab and Abihu were two of Aaron's sons. They got their shallow cups for burning incense. They put fire in them. They added incense to it. They made an offering to the LORD by using fire that wasn't allowed. They did it against his command. [2] So the LORD sent fire on them. It burned them up. They died in front of the LORD. [3] Then Moses spoke to Aaron. He said, "That's what the LORD was talking about when he said,

" 'Among those who approach me
  I will show that I am holy.
In the sight of all the people
  I will be honored.' "

So Aaron remained silent.

[4] Moses sent for Mishael and Elzaphan. They were sons of Aaron's uncle Uzziel. Moses said to them, "Come here. Carry the bodies of your cousins outside the camp. Take them away from in front of the Holy Room." [5] So they came and carried them outside the camp. It was just as Moses had ordered. The bodies of Nadab and Abihu still had their inner robes on them.

[6] Moses spoke to Aaron and to Eleazar and Ithamar. They were Aaron's sons. Moses said, "Don't let your hair hang loose. Don't tear your clothes. If you do, you will die. And the LORD will be angry with the whole community. But all the Israelites are allowed to show they are sad. They are your relatives. They may mourn for those the LORD has destroyed with fire. [7] Don't leave the entrance to the tent of meeting. If you do, you will die. That's because the LORD's anointing oil has made you holy." So they did what Moses told them to do.

[8] Then the LORD spoke to Aaron. He said, [9] "You and your sons will go into the tent of meeting. When you do, you must not drink any kind of wine. If you do, you will die. This is a law that will last for all time to come. [10] This is so that you can tell the difference between what is holy and what is not. You must be able to tell the difference between what is 'clean' and what is not. [11] Then you will be able to teach the Israelites all the rules I have given them through Moses."

[12] Moses spoke to Aaron and to Eleazar and Ithamar. They were Aaron's two remaining sons. Moses said, "Take the grain offering left over from the food offerings presented to the LORD. It is very holy. Make bread without yeast from it. Eat it beside the altar. [13] Eat it in the holy area. It's your share and your sons' share of the food offerings presented to the LORD. These rules are in keeping with the command the LORD gave me. [14] But you and your sons and your daughters can eat the breast that was waved. You can also eat the thigh that was offered. Eat them in a 'clean' place. They have been given to you and your children. They are your share of the friendship offerings the Israelites bring. [15] The thigh that was offered must be brought together with the fat parts of the food offerings. The breast that was waved must be brought in the same way. All of it must be lifted up and waved in front of the LORD as a wave offering. It will be the share for you and your children for all time to come. That's what the LORD has commanded."

[16] Moses asked about the goat that was brought as the sin offering. He found out that it had been burned up. So he became angry with Eleazar and Ithamar. They were Aaron's two remaining sons. Moses asked them, [17] "Why didn't you eat the sin offering in a place near the Holy Room? The offering is very holy. It was given to you to take the people's guilt away. It paid for their sin in the sight of the LORD. [18] The blood of the offering wasn't taken into the Holy Room. So you should have eaten the goat in a place near the Holy Room. That's what I commanded."

[19] Aaron replied to Moses, "Today the people sacrificed their sin offering to the LORD. They also sacrificed their burnt offerings to him. But a terrible thing has happened to me. Two of my sons have died. Would the LORD have been

pleased if I had eaten the sin offering
today?" [20]When Moses heard that, he
was satisfied.

"Clean" and "Unclean" Food

11 The LORD spoke to Moses and Aaron. He said to them, [2]"Speak to the
Israelites. Tell them, 'Many animals live
on land. Here are the only ones you can
eat. [3]You can eat any animal that has
hooves that are separated completely
in two. But it must also chew the cud.
[4]" 'Some animals only chew the cud.
Some only have hooves that are separated
in two. You must not eat those animals.
Camels chew the cud. But their hooves
are not separated in two. So they are "unclean" for you. [5]Rock badgers chew the
cud. But their hooves are not separated
in two. So they are "unclean" for you.
[6]Rabbits chew the cud. But their hooves
are not separated in two. So they are "unclean" for you. [7]Pigs have hooves that are
separated completely in two. But they do
not chew the cud. So they are "unclean" for
you. [8]You must not eat the meat of those
animals. You must not even touch their
dead bodies. They are "unclean" for you.
[9]" 'Many creatures live in the water of
the oceans and streams. You can eat all
those that have fins and scales. [10]Treat
as "unclean" all the creatures in the
oceans or streams that do not have fins
and scales. That includes all those that
move together in groups and all those
that do not. [11]Treat them as "unclean."
Do not eat their meat. Treat their dead
bodies as "unclean." [12]Regard as "unclean" everything that lives in the water
that does not have fins and scales.
[13]" 'Here are the birds you must treat
as "unclean." Do not eat them because
they are "unclean." The birds include
eagles, vultures and black vultures.
[14]They include red kites and all kinds
of black kites. [15]They include all kinds
of ravens. [16]They include horned owls,
screech owls, gulls and all kinds of
hawks. [17]They include little owls, cormorants and great owls. [18]They include
white owls, desert owls and ospreys.
[19]They also include storks, hoopoes,
bats and all kinds of herons.
[20]" 'Treat as "unclean" every flying
insect that walks on all fours. [21]But you
can eat some flying insects that walk
on all fours. Their legs have joints so
they can hop on the ground. [22]Here are
the insects you can eat. You can eat all
kinds of locusts, katydids, crickets and
grasshoppers. [23]Treat as "unclean" every
other creature with wings and four legs.
[24]" 'You will make yourselves "unclean" if you eat these things. If you
touch their dead bodies, you will be
"unclean" until evening. [25]If a person
picks up one of their dead bodies, that
person must wash their clothes. They
will be "unclean" until evening.
[26]" 'Suppose an animal has hooves
that are not separated completely in
two. Or suppose an animal does not
chew the cud. Then these animals are
"unclean" for you. If you touch the
dead body of any of them, you will be
"unclean." [27]Many animals walk on
all fours. But those that walk on their
paws are "unclean" for you. Anyone
who touches their dead bodies will be
"unclean" until evening. [28]If a person
picks up their dead bodies, that person
must wash their clothes. They will be
"unclean" until evening. These animals
are "unclean" for you.
[29]" 'Many animals move along the
ground. Here are the ones that are "unclean" for you. They include weasels,
rats and all kinds of large lizards. [30]They
also include geckos, monitor lizards, wall
lizards, skinks and chameleons. [31]These
are the animals that move around on
the ground that are "unclean" for you.
If you touch their dead bodies, you will
be "unclean" until evening. [32]Suppose
one of them dies and falls on something.
Then that thing will be "unclean." It does
not matter what it is used for. It does not
matter whether it is made out of wood,
cloth, hide or rough cloth. Put it in water.
It will be "unclean" until evening. After
that, it will be "clean." [33]Suppose one of
these animals falls into a clay pot. Then
everything in the pot will be "unclean."
You must break the pot. [34]Any food that
could be eaten but has water on it that
came from that pot is "unclean." And
any liquid that could be drunk from it
is "unclean." [35]Anything that the dead
body of one of these animals falls on
becomes "unclean." If it is an oven or
cooking pot, break it. It is "unclean."
And you must consider it "unclean."
[36]But a spring or a well for collecting
water remains "clean." That is true even

if the dead body of one of these animals falls into it. But anyone who touches the dead body is not "clean." 37 If the dead body falls on any seeds that have not been planted yet, the seeds remain "clean." 38 But suppose water has already been put on the seeds. And suppose the dead body falls on them. Then they are "unclean" for you.

39 " 'Suppose an animal you are allowed to eat dies. If anyone touches its dead body, they will be "unclean" until evening. 40 If they eat part of the dead body, they must wash their clothes. They will be "unclean" until evening. If they pick up the dead body, they must wash their clothes. They will be "unclean" until evening.

41 " 'Treat as "unclean" every creature that moves along the ground. Do not eat it. 42 Do not eat any of these creatures. It does not matter whether they move on their bellies. It does not matter whether they walk on all fours or on many feet. It is "unclean." 43 Do not make yourselves "unclean" by eating any of these animals. Do not make yourselves "unclean" because of them. Do not let them make you "unclean." 44 I am the LORD your God. Set yourselves apart. Be holy, because I am holy. Do not make yourselves "unclean" by eating any creatures that move around on the ground. 45 I am the LORD. I brought you up out of Egypt to be your God. So be holy, because I am holy.

46 " 'These are the rules about animals and birds. These are the rules about every living thing that moves around in the water. And these are the rules about every creature that moves along the ground. 47 You must be able to tell the difference between what is "clean" and what is not. You must also be able to tell the difference between living creatures that can be eaten and those that can't.' "

Becoming "Clean" After Having a Baby

12 The LORD spoke to Moses. He said, 2 "Speak to the Israelites. Tell them, 'Suppose a woman becomes pregnant and has a baby boy. Then she will be "unclean" for seven days. It is the same as when she is "unclean" during her monthly period. 3 On the eighth day the boy must be circumcised. 4 After that, the woman must wait for 33 days to be made pure from her bleeding. She must not touch anything sacred until the 33 days are over. During that time she must not go to the sacred tent. 5 But suppose she has a baby girl. Then she will be "unclean" for two weeks. It is the same as during her period. After the two weeks, she must wait for 66 days to be made pure from her bleeding.

6 " 'After she has waited the required number of days to be made pure, she must bring two offerings. She must take them to the priest at the entrance to the tent of meeting. She must bring a lamb a year old for a burnt offering. She must also bring a young pigeon or a dove for a sin offering. 7 The priest must offer them to the LORD. They will pay for her sin. Then she will be "clean" from her bleeding.

" 'These are the rules for a woman who has a baby boy or girl. 8 But suppose she can't afford a lamb. Then she must bring two doves or two young pigeons. One is for a burnt offering. The other is for a sin offering. The priest will sacrifice those offerings. That will pay for her sin. And she will be "clean." ' "

Rules About Skin Diseases

13 The LORD spoke to Moses and Aaron. He told them to say to the people, 2 "Suppose someone's skin has a swelling or a rash or a shiny spot. And suppose it could become a skin disease. Then they must be brought to the priest Aaron. Or they must be brought to a priest in Aaron's family line. 3 The priest must look carefully at the sore on the person's skin. He must see whether the hair in the sore has turned white. He must also see whether the sore seems to be under the skin. If the sore is white and is under the skin, it is a skin disease. When the priest looks that person over carefully, he must announce that the person is 'unclean.' 4 Suppose the shiny spot on the skin is white but does not seem to be under the skin. And suppose the hair in the spot has not turned white. Then the priest must make the person stay away from everyone else for seven days. 5 On the seventh day the priest must look carefully at the sore again. Suppose it has not changed and has not spread in the skin. Then the priest must make the person stay away from everyone else for another seven days. 6 On the seventh day the priest must look carefully at the sore again. If it has faded and has not spread, he must announce that the person is 'clean.' It is only a rash. That person must wash their clothes. They will be 'clean.' 7 But suppose the rash spreads in the skin after they have shown themselves to the priest a second time. Then they must appear in front of the priest again. 8 The priest must look carefully at the sore. If the rash has spread, he must announce that the person is 'unclean.' They have a skin disease.

9 "When anyone has a skin disease, they must be brought to the priest. 10 The priest must look them over carefully. Suppose there is a white swelling in the skin. Suppose it has turned the hair white. And suppose there are open sores in the swelling. 11 Then the person has a skin disease that will never go away. The priest must announce that they are 'unclean.' The priest must not make them stay away from everyone else. They are already 'unclean.'

12 "Suppose the disease breaks out all over their skin. And suppose it covers them from head to foot, as far as the priest can tell. 13 Then the priest must look them over carefully. If the disease has covered their whole body, the priest must announce that they are 'clean.' All their skin has turned white. So they are 'clean.' 14 But when open sores appear on their skin, they will not be 'clean.' 15 When the priest sees the open sores, he must announce that they are 'unclean.' The open sores are not 'clean.' They have a skin disease. 16 But if the open sores change and turn white, they must go to the priest. 17 The priest must look them over carefully. If the sores have turned white, the priest must announce that the person is 'clean.' Then they will be 'clean.'

18 "Suppose someone has a boil on their skin and it heals. 19 And suppose a white swelling or shiny pink spot appears where the boil was. Then they must show themselves to the priest. 20 The priest must look at the boil carefully. Suppose it seems to be under the skin. And suppose the hair in it has turned white. Then the priest must announce that the person is 'unclean.' A skin disease has broken out where the boil was. 21 But suppose that when the priest looks at the boil carefully, there is no white hair in it. The boil is not under the skin. And it has faded. Then the priest must make the person stay away from everyone else for seven days. 22 If the boil is spreading in the skin, the priest must announce that the person is 'unclean.' They have a skin disease. 23 But suppose the spot has not changed. And suppose it has not spread. Then it is only a scar from the boil. And the priest must announce that the person is 'clean.'

24 "Suppose someone has a burn on their skin. And suppose a white or shiny pink spot shows up in the open sores of the burn. 25 Then the priest must look at the spot carefully. Suppose the hair in it has turned white. And suppose the spot seems to be under the skin. Then the person has a skin disease. It has broken out where they were burned. The priest must announce that the person is 'unclean.' They have a skin disease. 26 But suppose the priest looks at the spot carefully. Suppose there is no white hair in it. Suppose the spot is not under the skin. And suppose it has faded. Then the priest must make the person stay away from everyone else for seven days. 27 On the seventh day the priest must look them over carefully. If the spot is spreading in the skin, the priest must announce that the person is 'unclean.' They have a skin disease. 28 But suppose the spot has not changed. It has not spread in the skin. And it has faded. Then the burn has caused it to swell. The priest must announce that the person is 'clean.' It is only a scar from the burn.

29 "Suppose a man or woman has a sore on their head or chin. 30 Then the priest must look at the sore carefully. Suppose it seems to be under the skin. And suppose the hair in the sore is yellow and thin. Then the priest must announce that the person is 'unclean.' The sore is a skin disease on the head or chin. 31 But suppose the priest looks carefully at the sore. It does not seem to be under the skin. And there is no black hair in it. Then the priest must make the person stay away from everyone else for seven days. 32 On the seventh day the priest must look at the sore carefully. Suppose it has not spread in the skin. It does not have any yellow hair in it. And

it does not seem to be under the skin.
33 Then the man or woman must shave
their head. But they must not shave the
area where the disease is. And the priest
must make them stay away from everyone else for another seven days. 34 On
the seventh day the priest must look at
the sore carefully. Suppose it has not
spread in the skin. And suppose it does
not seem to be under the skin. Then the
priest must announce that the person
is 'clean.' They must wash their clothes.
They will be 'clean.' 35 But suppose the
sore spreads in the skin after the priest
announces that the person is 'clean.'
36 Then the priest must look them over
carefully. Suppose the sore has spread.
Then the priest does not have to look
for yellow hair. The person is 'unclean.'
37 But suppose the sore has stopped and
black hair has grown there, as far as
the priest can tell. Then the person is
healed and is 'clean.' The priest must
announce that they are 'clean.'

38 "Suppose a man or woman has
white spots on the skin. 39 Then the
priest must look at them carefully.
Suppose he sees that the spots are dull
white. Then a harmless rash has broken
out on the skin. That person is 'clean.'

40 "Suppose a man loses all the hair
on his head. Then he is 'clean.' 41 Suppose
he loses only the hair on the front of his
head. Then he is 'clean.' 42 But suppose he
has a shiny pink sore on his head where
his hair was. Then he has a skin disease.
It is breaking out on his whole head or
on the front of his head. 43 The priest
must look him over carefully. Suppose
the swollen sore on his head or on the
front of it is pink and shiny. And suppose
it looks like a skin disease. 44 Then he has
a skin disease. He is 'unclean.' The priest
must announce that the man is 'unclean.'
That's because he has a sore on his head.

45 "Suppose someone has a skin disease that makes them 'unclean.' Then
they must wear torn clothes. They must
let their hair hang loose. They must
cover the lower part of their face. They
must cry out, 'Unclean! Unclean!' 46 As
long as they have the disease, they remain 'unclean.' They must live alone.
They must live outside the camp.

Rules About Mold

47 "Suppose some clothes have mold
on them. The clothes could be made
out of wool or linen. 48 Or there could be
cloth woven or knitted out of linen or
wool. There could be pieces of leather. Or
there could be things that are made out
of leather. 49 And suppose the mold on the
clothes or on the woven or knitted cloth
looks green or red. Or suppose the green
or red mold is on the pieces of leather or
the leather goods. Then it is mold that
spreads. It must be shown to the priest.
50 The priest must look at it carefully.
He must keep the thing with the mold
on it away from everything else for sev-
en days. 51 On the seventh day he must
look at it carefully. Suppose the mold has
spread in the clothes or in the woven or
knitted cloth. Or suppose it has spread
on the pieces of leather or on the leather
goods. Then it is mold that destroys. The
thing is 'unclean.' 52 The priest must burn
everything with the mold in it. He must
burn the clothes or the woven or knitted cloth made out of wool or linen. He
must burn the leather goods. The mold
destroys. So everything must be burned.

53 "But suppose the priest looks at the
thing carefully. The mold has not spread
in the clothes. And it has not spread in
the woven or knitted cloth or in the leather goods. 54 Then he will order someone
to wash the thing with the mold on it.
After that, the priest must keep that
thing away from everything else for
another seven days. 55 After the thing
with the mold on it has been washed,
the priest must look at it again carefully. Suppose the way the mold looks
has not changed. Then even though the
mold has not spread, it is 'unclean.' Burn
it. It does not matter which side of the
thing the mold is on. 56 But suppose the
priest looks at it carefully. And suppose
the mold has faded after the thing has
been washed. Then the priest must tear
out the part with mold on it. He must
tear it out of the clothes or leather. He
must tear it out of the woven or knitted
cloth. 57 But suppose it shows up again
in the clothes. Or suppose it shows up
again in the woven or knitted cloth or in
the leather goods. Then it is spreading.
Everything with the mold on it must be
burned. 58 The clothes that have been
washed and do not have any more mold

on them must be washed again. So must
the woven or knitted cloth or the leather
goods. Then they will be 'clean.'"
59 These are the rules about what to
do with anything with mold on it. They
apply to clothes that are made out of
wool or linen. They apply to woven and
knitted cloth and to leather goods. They
give a priest directions about when to
announce whether something is "clean"
or "unclean."

Making People "Clean" From Skin Diseases

14 The LORD spoke to Moses. He told
him to say to the people, 2 "Here
are the rules for making anyone 'clean'
who has had a skin disease. They apply
when the person is brought to the priest.
3 The priest must go outside the camp.
He must look the person over carefully.
Suppose they have been healed of their
skin disease. 4 Then the priest will order
someone to bring him two live 'clean'
birds. He will also order someone to
bring him some cedar wood, bright red
yarn and branches of a hyssop plant.
All these things will be used to make
the person 'clean.' 5 The priest will order
someone to kill one of the birds. It must
be killed over fresh water in a clay pot.
6 Then the priest must take the live bird.
He must dip it into the blood of the bird
killed over the fresh water. He must dip
it into the blood together with the cedar
wood, the bright red yarn and the hyssop
plant. 7 The priest will sprinkle the blood
on the person who had the skin disease.
That will make them 'clean.' The priest
must sprinkle them seven times. Then
the priest must announce that they are
'clean.' After that, the priest must let the
live bird go free in the open fields.
8 "The person must also wash their
clothes to be made 'clean.' They must
shave off all their hair. They must take
a bath. Then they will be 'clean.' After
that, they may come into the camp. But
they must stay outside their tent for
seven days. 9 On the seventh day they
must shave off all their hair. They must
shave their head. They must shave off
their beard. They must also shave off
their eyebrows and the rest of their hair.
They must wash their clothes. They must
take a bath. Then they will be 'clean.'
10 "On the eighth day they must bring
two male lambs and one female lamb
as an offering. The female must be a
year old. The lambs must not have any
flaws. They must also bring 11 pounds
of the finest flour as a grain offering.
They must mix it with olive oil. They
must also bring 11 ounces of oil. 11 The
priest who announces that the person
is 'clean' must bring them and their
offerings to me. He must do it at the
entrance to the tent of meeting.
12 "Then the priest must take one of the
male lambs. He must offer it as a guilt
offering. He must offer it along with 11
ounces of oil. He must lift all of it up and
wave it in front of me as a wave offering.
13 He must kill the lamb in the holy area
where sin offerings and burnt offerings
are killed. The guilt offering belongs to
the priest, just as the sin offering does.
The guilt offering is very holy. 14 The
priest must take some of the blood from
the guilt offering and put it on the person's right earlobe. He must put some on
the thumb of their right hand. He must
also put some on the big toe of their right
foot. 15 Then the priest must take some of
the oil and pour it into his own left hand.
16 He must dip his right forefinger into
the oil in his hand. He must use his finger
to sprinkle some of the oil in front of me
seven times. 17 The priest must put some
of the oil in his hand on the same places
he put the blood of the guilt offering.
He must put some on the person's right
earlobe. He must put some on the thumb
of their right hand. He must put some
on the big toe of their right foot. 18 He
must put on their head the rest of the oil
in his hand. It will pay for the person's
sin in my sight.
19 "Then the priest must sacrifice the
sin offering. It will pay for the person's
sin. They will be made 'clean' after being
'unclean.' After that, the priest will kill
the burnt offering. 20 He will offer it on
the altar. He will offer it together with the
grain offering. It will pay for the person's
sin. Then they will be 'clean.'
21 "But suppose they are poor. Suppose
they can't afford all these offerings. Then
they must bring one male lamb as a guilt
offering. It must be lifted up and waved
in front of me to pay for their sin. They
must also bring three and a half pounds
of the finest flour along with the lamb.

They must mix the flour with olive oil. It is a grain offering. They must offer it along with 11 ounces of oil. [22]They must also bring two doves or two young pigeons that they can afford. One is for a sin offering. The other is for a burnt offering.

[23]"On the eighth day they must bring them to the priest so they can be made 'clean.' They must bring them to the entrance to the tent of meeting. They must do it in my sight. [24]The priest must take the lamb for the guilt offering. He must take it together with the 11 ounces of oil. He must lift all of it up and wave it in front of me as a wave offering. [25]He must kill the lamb for the guilt offering. He must take some of its blood and put it on the person's right earlobe. He must put some on the thumb of their right hand. He must also put some on the big toe of their right foot. [26]The priest must pour some of the oil into his own left hand. [27]He must dip his right forefinger into the oil in his hand. He must use his finger to sprinkle some of it seven times in front of me. [28]Here is what he must do with some of the oil in his hand. He must put it on the same places where he put the blood of the guilt offering. He must put some on the person's right earlobe. He must put some on the thumb of their right hand. He must also put some on the big toe of their right foot. [29]He must put on their head the rest of the oil in his hand. It will pay for the person's sin in my sight. [30]The priest will sacrifice the doves or the young pigeons that the person can afford. [31]One is for a sin offering. The other is for a burnt offering. The priest must offer them together with the grain offering. In that way he will pay for the person's sin in my sight. He will do it to make them 'clean.'"

[32]These are the rules for anyone who has a skin disease. They are for people who can't afford the regular offerings that are required to make them "clean."

Making Things "Clean" From Mold

[33]The LORD spoke to Moses and Aaron. He told them to say to the people, [34]"You will enter the land of Canaan. I am giving it to you as your own. When you enter it, suppose I put mold in one of your houses. And suppose the mold spreads. [35]Then the owner of that house must go and speak to the priest. He must say, 'I've seen something that looks like mold in my house.' [36]The priest must order everything to be taken out of the house. It must be done before he goes in to look carefully at the mold. If it is not done, the priest must announce that everything in the house is 'unclean.' After the house is empty the priest must go in and check it. [37]He must look carefully at the mold on the walls. Suppose it looks as if it has green or red dents in it. And suppose the dents look as if they are behind the surface of the wall. [38]Then the priest must go out the door. He must close the house up for seven days. [39]On the seventh day the priest will return to check the house. Suppose the mold on the walls has spread. [40]Then he must order someone to tear out the stones that have mold on them. He must have them thrown into an 'unclean' place outside the town. [41]He must have all the inside walls of the house scraped. Everything scraped off must be dumped into an 'unclean' place outside the town. [42]Then other stones must be put in the place of the stones that had mold on them. The inside walls of the house must be coated with new clay.

[43]"Suppose the stones have been torn out. The house has been scraped. And the walls have been coated with new clay. But the mold appears again. [44]Then the priest must go and look things over carefully. Suppose the mold has spread in the house. Then it is the kind of mold that destroys things. The house is not 'clean.' [45]It must be torn down. The stones, the wood and all the clay coating must be torn out. All of it must be taken out of the town to an 'unclean' place.

[46]"Suppose someone goes into the house while it is closed up. Then they will be 'unclean' until evening. [47]If they sleep or eat in the house, they must wash their clothes.

[48]"But suppose the priest comes to look things over carefully. And suppose the mold has not spread after the walls had been coated with new clay. Then he will announce that the house is 'clean.' The mold is gone. [49]To make the house pure, the priest must get two birds. He must also get some cedar wood, bright red yarn and branches of a hyssop plant. [50]He must kill one of the birds over fresh water in a clay pot. [51]Then he must take the cedar wood, the hyssop plant, the

bright red yarn and the live bird. He must dip all of them into the blood of the dead bird. He must also dip them into the fresh water. He must sprinkle the house seven times. 52 The priest will use the blood and the water to make the house pure. He will use the live bird to make it pure. He will also use the cedar wood, the hyssop plant and the bright red yarn to make it pure. 53 Then he must let the live bird go free in the open fields outside the town. In that way he will make the house pure. It will be 'clean.' "

54 These are the rules for skin diseases. They apply to sores. 55 They apply to mold in clothes or in houses. 56 They also apply to swellings, rashes or shiny red spots on the skin. 57 Use these rules to decide whether something is "clean" or not.

These are the rules for skin diseases and for mold.

Rules About Liquid Body Wastes

15 The LORD said to Moses and Aaron, 2 "Speak to the Israelites. Tell them, 'Suppose liquid waste is flowing out of a man's body. That liquid is not "clean." 3 It does not matter whether it continues to flow out of his body or is blocked. It will make him "unclean." Here is how his liquid body waste will make him "unclean."

4 " 'Any bed the man who has the flow of liquid body waste lies on will be "unclean." Anything he sits on will be "unclean." 5 Anyone who touches the man's bed must wash their clothes. They must take a bath. They will be "unclean" until evening. 6 Suppose someone sits on something the man sat on. Then they must wash their clothes. They must take a bath. They will be "unclean" until evening.

7 " 'Suppose someone touches the man who has the flow of liquid body waste. Then they must wash their clothes. They must take a bath. They will be "unclean" until evening.

8 " 'Suppose someone is "clean." And suppose the man who has the flow of liquid waste spits on them. Then they must wash their clothes. They must take a bath. They will be "unclean" until evening.

9 " 'Everything the man sits on when he is riding will be "unclean." 10 Suppose someone touches any of the things that were under him. Then they will be "unclean" until evening. Even if they pick up those things, they must wash their clothes. They must take a bath. They will be "unclean" until evening.

11 " 'Suppose the man who has the liquid flow touches someone. And suppose he does it without rinsing his hands with water. Then the person he touched must wash their clothes. They must take a bath. They will be "unclean" until evening.

12 " 'Suppose the man touches a clay pot. Then that pot must be broken. Any wooden thing he touches must be rinsed with water.

13 " 'Suppose the man has been healed from his liquid flow. Then he must wait seven days. He must wash his clothes. He must take a bath in fresh water. After that, he will be "clean." 14 On the eighth day he must get two doves or two young pigeons. He must come to the LORD at the entrance to the tent of meeting. There he must give the birds to the priest. 15 The priest must sacrifice them. One is for a sin offering. The other is for a burnt offering. In that way the priest will pay for the man's sin in the sight of the LORD. He will do it because the man had a liquid flow.

16 " 'Suppose semen flows from a man's body. Then he must wash his whole body with water. He will be "unclean" until evening. 17 Suppose clothes or leather have semen on them. Then they must be washed with water. They will be "unclean" until evening. 18 Suppose a man sleeps with a woman. And suppose semen flows from his body and touches both of them. Then they must take a bath. They will be "unclean" until evening.

19 " 'Suppose a woman is having her regular monthly period. Then for seven days she will be "unclean." Anyone who touches her will be "unclean" until evening.

20 " 'Anything she lies on during her period will be "unclean." Anything she sits on will be "unclean." 21 Anyone who touches her bed must wash their clothes. They must take a bath. They will be "unclean" until evening. 22 Anyone who touches anything she sits on must wash their clothes. They must take a bath. They will be "unclean" until evening. 23 It does not matter whether it was her bed or anything she was sitting

on. If anyone touches it, they will be "unclean" until evening.

24 " 'Suppose a man sleeps with that woman. And suppose blood from her monthly period touches him. Then he will be "unclean" for seven days. Any bed he lies on will be "unclean."

25 " 'Suppose blood flows from a woman's body for many days. And it happens at a time other than her monthly period. Or blood keeps flowing after her period is over. Then she will be "unclean" as long as the blood continues to flow. She will be "unclean," just as she is during the days of her period. 26 Any bed she lies on while her blood continues to flow will be "unclean." It is the same as it is when she is having her period. Anything she sits on will be "unclean." 27 If anyone touches those things, they will be "unclean." They must wash their clothes. They must take a bath. They will be "unclean" until evening.

28 " 'Suppose the woman has been healed from her flow of blood. Then she must wait seven days. After that, she will be "clean." 29 On the eighth day she must get two doves or two young pigeons. She must bring them to the priest at the entrance to the tent of meeting. 30 The priest must sacrifice them. One is for a sin offering. The other is for a burnt offering. In that way he will pay for her sin in the sight of the LORD. He will do it because her flow of blood made her "unclean."

31 " 'You must keep the Israelites away from things that make them "unclean." Then they will not die for being "unclean." And they will not die for making the place "unclean" where I, the LORD, live. It is in the middle of the camp.' "

32 These are the rules for a man who has liquid waste flowing out of his body. They apply to a man made "unclean" by semen that flows from his body. 33 They apply to a woman having her monthly period. They apply to a man or woman who has a liquid flow. And they apply to a man who sleeps with a woman who is "unclean."

The Day When Sin Is Paid For

16 The LORD spoke to Moses after two of Aaron's sons had died. They were the sons who died when they came near the LORD. 2 The LORD said to Moses, "Speak to your brother Aaron. Tell him not to come into the Most Holy Room just anytime he wants to. Tell him not to come behind the curtain in front of the cover of the ark. The cover is the place where sin is paid for. If he comes behind the curtain, he will die. That is because I appear in the cloud over the cover.

3 "Aaron must not enter the area of the Most Holy Room without bringing a sacrifice. He must bring a young bull for a sin offering. He must also bring a ram for a burnt offering. 4 He must put on the sacred inner robe made out of linen. He must wear linen underwear next to his body. He must tie the linen belt around him. And he must put the linen turban on his head. Those are sacred clothes. So he must take a bath before he puts them on. 5 The community of Israel must give him two male goats and a ram. The goats are for a sin offering. The ram is for a burnt offering.

6 "Aaron must offer the bull for his own sin offering. It will pay for his own sin and the sin of his whole family. 7 Then he must take the two goats and bring them to me at the entrance to the tent of meeting. 8 He must cast lots for the two goats. One lot is for me. The other is for the goat that carries the people's sins away. 9 Aaron must bring the goat chosen for me by lot. He must sacrifice it for a sin offering. 10 But the goat chosen by the other lot must remain alive. First, it must be brought in to me to pay for the people's sins. Then, it must be sent into the desert as a goat that carries the people's sins away.

11 "Aaron must bring the bull for his own sin offering. It will pay for his own sin and the sin of his whole family. He must kill the bull for his own sin offering. 12 He must take a shallow cup full of burning coals from the altar in my sight. He must get two handfuls of incense completely ground up. The incense must smell sweet. He must take the cup and the incense behind the curtain. 13 He must put the incense on the fire in my sight. The smoke from the incense will hide the cover of the ark where the tablets of the covenant law are kept. The cover is the place where sin is paid for. Aaron must burn the incense so that he will not die. 14 He must dip his finger in the bull's blood. He must

sprinkle it on the front of the cover of
the ark. He must sprinkle some in front
of the cover. He must do it seven times.
15 "Then Aaron must kill the goat for
the sin offering for the people. He must
take its blood behind the curtain. There
he must do the same thing with it as
he did with the bull's blood. He must
sprinkle it on the cover of the ark. He
must also sprinkle some in front of it.
16 That is how he will make the Most
Holy Room pure. He must do it because
the Israelites are not 'clean.' They have
not obeyed me. They have also committed other sins. Aaron must do the
same for the tent of meeting because
it stands in the middle of the camp.
And the camp is 'unclean.' 17 Aaron will
go into the Most Holy Room to pay for
the people's sin. While Aaron is there,
no one may be in the tent of meeting.
No one may enter the tent until Aaron
comes out. He will not come out until
he has paid for his own sin and the sin
of his whole family. He will not come
out until he has also paid for the sin of
the whole community of Israel.
18 "Then he will come out to the altar
for burnt offerings. It is in front of the
tent where the ark of the LORD is. He will
make the altar pure and clean. He will
take some of the bull's blood and some
of the goat's blood. Then he will put the
blood on all the horns that stick out
from the upper four corners of the altar.
19 He will sprinkle some of the blood on
it with his finger seven times. He will do
it to make the altar pure. He will do it
to set it apart from the Israelites. They
are 'unclean.'
20 "Aaron will finish making the Most
Holy Room pure and 'clean.' He will
finish making the tent of meeting and
the altar pure. Then he will bring out
the live goat. 21 He must place both of
his hands on its head. While he does
that, he must tell me about all the sins
the Israelites have committed. He must
tell me about all their evil acts and the
times they did not obey me. In that way
he puts their sins on the goat's head.
Then he will send the goat away into the
desert. The goat will be led away by a
man appointed to do it. 22 The goat will
carry all their sins on itself to a place
where there are no people. And the man
will set the goat free in the desert.
23 "Then Aaron must go into the tent
of meeting. He must take off the linen
clothes he put on before he entered the
Most Holy Room. He must leave them
there. 24 He must take a bath in the holy
area. And he must put on his regular
clothes. Then he will come out and sacrifice the burnt offering for himself. He
will also sacrifice the burnt offering for
the people. That will pay for his own sin
and the people's sin. 25 He will also burn
the fat of the sin offering on the altar.
26 "The man who sets free the goat
that carries the people's sins away must
wash his clothes. He must take a bath.
After that, he can come back into the
camp. 27 The bull and the goat for the
sin offerings must be taken outside
the camp. Their blood was brought into
the Most Holy Room. It paid for sin. The
hides, meat and guts of the animals
must be burned up. 28 The man who
burns them must wash his clothes. He
must take a bath. After that, he can
come back into the camp.
29 "Here is a law for you that will last
for all time to come. On the tenth day
of the seventh month you must not eat
anything. You must not do any work. It
does not matter whether you are Israelites or outsiders. 30 On that day your sin
will be paid for. You will be made pure
and clean. You will be clean from all your
sins in my sight. 31 That day is a sabbath
for you. You must rest on it. You must not
eat anything on that day. This is a law
that will last for all time to come. 32 The
high priest must pay for sin. He must
make everything pure and clean. He has
been anointed and prepared to become
the next high priest after his father. He
must put on the sacred clothes that are
made out of linen. 33 He must make the
Most Holy Room, the tent of meeting and
the altar pure. And he must pay for the
sin of the priests and all the members
of the community.
34 "Here is a law for you that will last
for all time to come. Once a year you
must pay for all the sin of the Israelites."
So it was done, just as the LORD commanded Moses.

Do Not Eat Meat With Blood in It

17 The LORD said to Moses, 2 "Speak to Aaron and his sons. Speak to all the Israelites. Tell them, 'Here is what the LORD has commanded. He has said, 3 "Suppose someone sacrifices an ox, a lamb or a goat. They sacrifice it in the camp or outside of it. 4 They do it instead of bringing the animal to the entrance to the tent of meeting. They sacrifice it instead of giving it as an offering to me in front of my holy tent. Then they will be thought of as guilty of spilling blood. Because they have done that, they must be separated from their people. 5 The Israelites are now making sacrifices in the open fields. But they must bring their sacrifices to the priest. They must bring them to me at the entrance to the tent of meeting. There they must sacrifice them as friendship offerings. 6 The priest must splash the blood against my altar. It is the altar at the entrance to the tent of meeting. He must burn the fat. Its smell will please me. 7 The Israelites must stop offering any of their sacrifices to statues of gods that look like goats. When they offer sacrifices to those statues, they are not faithful to me. This is a law for them that will last for all time to come." '

8 "Tell them, 'Suppose someone offers a burnt offering or sacrifice. It does not matter whether they are an Israelite or an outsider. 9 And suppose they do not bring it to the entrance to the tent of meeting to sacrifice it to me. Then they must be separated from their people.

10 " 'Suppose someone eats meat that still has blood in it. It does not matter whether they are an Israelite or an outsider. I will turn against them if they eat it. I will separate them from their people. 11 The life of each creature is in its blood. So I have given you the blood of animals to pay for your sin on the altar. Blood is life. That is why blood pays for your sin. 12 So I say to the Israelites, "You must not eat meat that still has blood in it. And an outsider who lives among you must not eat it either."

13 " 'Suppose any of you hunts any animal or bird that can be eaten. It does not matter whether you are an Israelite or an outsider. You must let the blood flow out of the animal or bird. You must cover the blood with dirt. 14 That is because every creature's life is its blood. And that is why I have said to the Israelites, "You must not eat any creature's meat that still has blood in it. Every creature's life is its blood. Anyone who eats that kind of meat must be separated from the community of Israel."

15 " 'Suppose someone eats anything found dead or torn apart by wild animals. It does not matter whether they are an Israelite or an outsider. They must wash their clothes. They must take a bath. They will be "unclean" until evening. After that, they will be "clean." 16 But suppose they do not wash their clothes. And suppose they do not take a bath. Then they will be held responsible for what they have done.' "

Do Not Commit Sexual Sins

18 The LORD spoke to Moses. He said, 2 "Speak to the Israelites. Tell them, 'I am the LORD your God. 3 Do not do what the people of Egypt do. You used to live there. And do not do what the people of Canaan do. I am bringing you into their land. Do not follow their practices. 4 Obey my laws. Be careful to follow my rules. I am the LORD your God. 5 Keep my rules and laws. The one who obeys them will benefit from living by them. I am the LORD.

6 " 'Do not have sex with any of your close relatives. I am the LORD.

7 " 'Do not bring shame on your father by having sex with your mother. Do not have sex with her. She is your mother.

8 " 'Do not have sex with any other wife of your father. That would bring shame on your father.

9 " 'Do not have sex with your sister. It does not matter whether she is your father's daughter or your mother's daughter. It does not matter whether she was born in the same home as you were or somewhere else.

10 " 'Do not have sex with your son's daughter or your daughter's daughter. That would bring shame on you.

11 " 'Do not have sex with the daughter of your father's wife. She was born to your father. She is your sister.

12 " 'Do not have sex with your father's sister. She is a close relative on your father's side.

13" 'Do not have sex with your mother's sister. She is a close relative on your mother's side.

14" 'Do not bring shame on your father's brother by having sex with his wife. She is your aunt.

15" 'Do not have sex with your daughter-in-law. She is your son's wife. Do not have sex with her.

16" 'Do not have sex with your brother's wife. That would bring shame on your brother.

17" 'Do not have sex with both a woman and her daughter. Do not have sex with either her son's daughter or her daughter's daughter. They are close relatives on her side. Having sex with them is an evil thing.

18" 'Do not take your wife's sister as another wife and have sex with her. Do not do it while your wife is still living.

19" 'Do not have sex with a woman during her monthly period. She is "unclean" at that time.

20" 'Do not have sex with your neighbor's wife. That would make you "unclean."

21" 'Do not hand over any of your children to be sacrificed to the god Molek. That would be treating my name as if it were not holy. I am the LORD your God.

22" 'Do not have sex with a man as you would have sex with a woman. I hate that.

23" 'Do not have sex with an animal. Do not make yourself "unclean" by doing that. A woman must not offer herself to an animal to have sex with it. That is a wrong use of sex.

24" 'Do not make yourselves "unclean" in any of these ways. That is how other nations became "unclean." So I am going to drive those nations out of
the land to make room for you. 25 Even
their land was not "clean." So I punished it because of its sin. The land itself threw
out the people who lived there. 26 But
you must keep my rules and my laws. You must not do any of the things I hate. It does not matter whether you
are Israelites or outsiders. 27 All these
things were done by the people who lived in the land before you. That is how
the land became "unclean." 28 If you
make the land "unclean," it will throw you out. It will get rid of you just as it got rid of the nations there before you.

29" 'Suppose you do any of the things I hate. Then you must be separated
from your people. 30 Do exactly what
I require. When you arrive in Canaan, do not follow any of the practices of its people. I hate the things they do. Do not make yourselves "unclean" by doing them. I am the LORD your God.' "

Other Laws

19 The LORD spoke to Moses. He said,
2 "Speak to the whole community of Israel. Tell them, 'Be holy, because I am holy. I am the LORD your God.

3" 'All of you must have respect for your mother and father. You must always keep my Sabbath days. I am the LORD your God.

4" 'Do not turn away from me to worship statues of gods. Do not make for yourselves metal statues of gods. I am the LORD your God.

5" 'Suppose you sacrifice a friendship offering to me. Then do it in the right
way. And I will accept it from you. 6 You
must eat it on the same day you sacrifice it or on the next day. Anything left over
until the third day must be burned up. 7 If
you eat any of it on the third day, it is not
pure. I will not accept it. 8 Whoever eats
it will be held responsible. They have misused what is holy to me. They will be separated from their people.

9" 'Suppose you are harvesting your crops. Then do not harvest all the way to the edges of your field. And do not
pick up the grain you missed. 10 Do not
go over your vineyard a second time. Do not pick up the grapes that have fallen to the ground. Leave them for poor people and outsiders. I am the LORD your God.

11" 'Do not steal.

" 'Do not tell lies.

" 'Do not cheat one another.

12" 'Do not give your word in my name and then be a false witness. That would be treating the name of your God as if it were not holy. I am the LORD.

13" 'Do not cheat your neighbor. Do not rob him.

“ ‘Do not hold back the pay of a hired
worker until morning.
14 “ ‘Do not ask for bad things to happen to deaf people. Do not put anything
in front of blind people that will make
them trip. Instead, have respect for me.
I am the LORD your God.
15 “ ‘Do not make something wrong
appear to be right. Treat poor people
and rich people in the same way. Do not
favor one person over another. Instead,
judge everyone fairly.
16 “ ‘Do not go around spreading lies
among your people.
“ ‘Do not do anything that puts your
neighbor’s life in danger. I am the LORD.
17 “ ‘Do not hate another Israelite in
your heart. Correct your neighbor boldly when they do something wrong. Then
you will not share their guilt.
18 “ ‘Do not try to get even. Do not hold
anything against any of your people.
Instead, love your neighbor as you love
yourself. I am the LORD.
19 “ ‘Obey my rules.
“ ‘Do not let different kinds of animals
mate with each other.
“ ‘Do not mix two kinds of seeds and
then plant them in your field.
“ ‘Do not wear clothes that are made
out of two kinds of cloth.
20 “ ‘Suppose a man sleeps with a female slave. But she and another man
have promised to get married to each
other. And her freedom has not yet been
paid for or given to her. Then she and the
man who slept with her must be punished. But they must not be put to death,
because she had not been set free. 21 The
man must bring a ram to the entrance
to the tent of meeting. It is for a guilt
offering to me. 22 The priest must take
the ram for the guilt offering. He must
sacrifice it to pay for the man’s sin in
my sight. Then his sin will be forgiven.
23 “ ‘When you enter the land, suppose
you plant a fruit tree. Then do not eat its
fruit for the first three years. The fruit
is “unclean.” 24 In the fourth year all
the fruit will be holy. Offer it as a way
of showing praise to me. 25 But in the
fifth year you can eat the fruit. Then
you will gather more and more fruit. I
am the LORD your God.
26 “ ‘Do not eat any meat that still
has blood in it.

“ ‘Do not practice any kind of evil
magic.
27 “ ‘Do not cut the hair on the sides
of your head. Do not clip off the edges
of your beard.
28 “ ‘Do not make cuts on your bodies
when someone dies. Do not put marks
on your skin. I am the LORD.
29 “ ‘Do not dishonor your daughter’s
body by making a prostitute out of her.
If you do, the Israelites will start going
to prostitutes. The land will be filled
with evil.
30 “ ‘You must always keep my Sabbath days. Have respect for my sacred
tent. I am the LORD.
31 “ ‘Do not look for advice from people
who get messages from those who have
died. Do not go to people who talk to
the spirits of the dead. If you do, they
will make you “unclean.” I am the LORD
your God.
32 “ ‘Stand up in order to show your
respect for old people. Also have respect
for me. I am the LORD your God.
33 “ ‘Suppose an outsider lives with
you in your land. Then do not treat
them badly. 34 Treat them as if they
were one of your own people. Love them
as you love yourself. Remember that all
of you were outsiders in Egypt. I am the
LORD your God.
35 “ ‘Be honest when you measure
lengths, weights or amounts. 36 Use
honest scales and honest weights. Use
honest dry measures. And use honest
liquid measures. I am the LORD your
God. I brought you out of Egypt.
37 “ ‘Obey all my rules and laws. Follow
them. I am the LORD.’ ”

Israel Will Be Punished for Their Sins

20 The LORD spoke to Moses. He
said, 2 “Say to the Israelites,
‘Suppose a person sacrifices one of
his children to the god Molek. It does
not matter whether that person is an
Israelite or an outsider who lives in
Israel. He must be put to death. The
members of the community must kill
him by throwing stones at him. 3 I will
turn against that man. I will separate
him from his people. That’s because
he has sacrificed his child to Molek. He
has made my sacred tent “unclean.”
He has treated my name as if it were
not holy. 4 Suppose the members of the

community act like they don't know that the man has sacrificed his child to Molek. And suppose they don't put him to death. 5 Then I will turn against that man and his family. I will separate them from their people. I will also separate all those who follow him by joining themselves to Molek. They are not faithful to me.

6 " 'Suppose someone looks for advice from people who get messages from those who have died. Or they go to people who talk to the spirits of the dead. And they do what those people say. Then they have not been faithful to me. So I will turn against them. I will separate them from their people.

7 " 'Set yourselves apart for me. Be holy, because I am the LORD your God. 8 Obey my rules. Follow them. I am the LORD. I make you holy.

9 " 'Anyone who asks for bad things to happen to their father or mother must be put to death. They have cursed their father or mother. So anything that happens to them will be their own fault.

10 " 'Suppose a man commits adultery with his neighbor's wife. Then the man and the woman must be put to death.

11 " 'Suppose a man has sex with his father's wife. Then he has brought shame on his father. The man and the woman must be put to death. Anything that happens to them will be their own fault.

12 " 'Suppose a man has sex with his daughter-in-law. Then they must be put to death. They have used sex in the wrong way. Anything that happens to them will be their own fault.

13 " 'Suppose a man has sex with another man as he would have sex with a woman. I hate what they have done. They must be put to death. Anything that happens to them will be their own fault.

14 " 'Suppose a man gets married to both a woman and her mother. That is evil. All of them must be burned to death. Then there will not be any evil among you.

15 " 'Suppose a man has sex with an animal. Then he must be put to death. You must also kill the animal.

16 " 'Suppose a woman has sex with an animal. Then kill the woman and the animal. They must be put to death. Anything that happens to them will be their own fault.

17 " 'Suppose a man gets married to his sister and has sex with her. That is a shameful thing to do. It does not matter whether she is the daughter of his father or of his mother. They must be separated from their community in front of everyone. That man has brought shame on his sister. He will be responsible for what he has done.

18 " 'Suppose a man has sex with a woman during her monthly period. He has uncovered the place where her bleeding was coming from. And she has let him do it. So both of them must be separated from their people.

19 " 'Do not have sex with the sister of either your mother or your father. That would bring shame on a close relative. Both of you would be held responsible for what you have done.

20 " 'Suppose a man has sex with his aunt. Then he has brought shame on his uncle. Both of them will be held accountable for what they have done. They will die without having any children.

21 " 'Suppose a man gets married to his brother's wife. That is something that should never be done. He has brought shame on his brother. Neither of them will have any children.

22 " 'Obey all my rules and laws. Follow them. Then the land where I am bringing you to live will not throw you out. 23 To make room for you, I am going to drive out the nations that are in the land. You must not follow the practices of those nations. I hated those nations because they did all those things. 24 But I said to you, "You will take over their land as your own. I will give it to you. It will belong to you. It is a land that has plenty of milk and honey." I am the LORD your God. I have set you apart from the other nations.

25 " 'So you must be able to tell the difference between animals that are "clean" and those that are not. You must know which birds are "clean" and which are not. Do not make yourselves "unclean" by eating any "unclean" animal or bird. Do not make yourselves "unclean" by eating anything that moves along the ground. I have set all of them apart as "unclean" for you. 26 You must be holy. You must be set apart to me. I am the LORD. I am holy. I have set you apart from the other nations to be my own people.

27 " 'Suppose a man or woman gets messages from those who have died. Or suppose a man or woman talks to the spirits of the dead. Then you must put that man or woman to death. You must kill them by throwing stones at them. Anything that happens to them will be their own fault.' "

Rules for Priests

21 The LORD said to Moses, "Speak to the priests, the sons of Aaron. Tell them, 'A priest must not make himself "unclean" by going near the dead body of any of his people. 2 But he can go near the body of a close relative. It could be his mother, father, son, daughter or brother. 3 He can also go near a sister who is not married. She would have depended on him because she did not have a husband. The priest can make himself "unclean" by going near her body. 4 But he must not make himself "unclean" by going near the bodies of people only related to him by marriage. Going near them would make him "unclean."

5 " 'Priests must not shave any part of their heads. They must not shave off the edges of their beards. They must not make cuts on their bodies when someone dies. 6 Priests must be holy. They must be set apart for me. I am their God. They must not treat my name as if it were not holy. They must be holy because they bring food offerings to me. That is my food.

7 " 'They must not get married to women who are "unclean" because they are prostitutes. They must not marry women who are divorced from their husbands. That is because priests are holy. They are set apart for me. I am their God. 8 Consider them as holy, because they offer up food to me. Consider them as holy, because I am holy. I am the LORD. I make you holy.

9 " 'Suppose a priest's daughter makes herself "unclean" by becoming a prostitute. Then she brings shame on her father. She must be burned to death.

10 " 'The high priest is the one among his brothers whose head has been anointed with olive oil. He has been appointed to wear the priest's clothes. When someone dies, the high priest must not let his own hair hang loose. He must not tear his clothes to show how sad he is. 11 He must not enter a place where there is a dead body. He must not make himself "unclean," even if his father or mother dies. 12 He must not leave the sacred tent of the LORD to take part in burying a body. That would bring shame on the tent. The anointing oil has set the high priest apart. I am the LORD.

13 " 'The woman the high priest gets married to must be a virgin. 14 He must not marry a widow or a woman who is divorced. He must not marry a woman who is "unclean" because she is a prostitute. He must only marry a virgin. She must come from his own people. 15 If he doesn't marry a virgin, he makes the children he has by her "unclean." I am the LORD. I make him holy.' "

16 The LORD said to Moses, 17 "Speak to Aaron. Tell him, 'No man in your family line with any flaws may come near to offer food to the LORD. This is true for all time to come. 18 No man who has any flaws can come near. No man who is blind or disabled can come. No man whose body is scarred or twisted can come. 19 No man whose foot or hand is disabled can come. 20 No man whose back is bent can come. No man who is too short can come. No man who has anything wrong with his eyes can come.

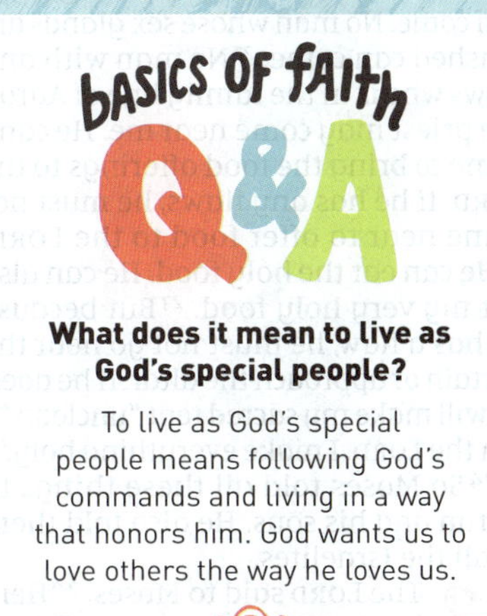

Can you find the following verse?
LEVITICUS 20:26

No man who has boils or running sores
can come. No man whose sex glands are
crushed can come. 21 No man with any
flaws who is in the family line of Aaron
the priest may come near me. He can't
come to bring the food offerings to the
LORD. If he has any flaws, he must not
come near to offer food to the LORD.
22 He can eat the holy food. He can also
eat my very holy food. 23 But because
he has a flaw, he must not go near the
curtain or approach the altar. If he does,
he will make my sacred tent "unclean." I
am the LORD. I make everything holy.' "

24 So Moses told all these things to
Aaron and his sons. He also told them
to all the Israelites.

22 The LORD said to Moses, 2 "Here
is what I want you to tell Aaron and his sons. Tell them to treat the
sacred offerings with respect. They are
the offerings the Israelites set apart to
honor me. So Aaron and his sons must
never treat my name as if it were not
holy. I am the LORD.

3 "Say to them, 'Suppose a man in
your family line is "unclean." And suppose he comes near the sacred offerings.
They are the offerings the Israelites
set apart to honor me. That man must
not be allowed to serve me as a priest.
That applies for all time to come. I am
the LORD.

4 " 'Suppose a man in Aaron's family
line has a skin disease. Or suppose liquid
waste is flowing out of his body. Then
he can't eat the sacred offerings until
he is made pure and clean. Suppose he
touches something made "unclean" by
coming near a dead body. Or suppose
he touches someone who has semen
flowing from his body. Then he will
be "unclean." 5 Or suppose he touches
any crawling thing that makes him
"unclean." Or suppose he touches any
person who makes him "unclean." It
does not matter what "unclean" thing
he touches. It will make him "unclean."
6 The one who touches anything of that
kind will be "unclean" until evening. He
must not eat any of the sacred offerings
unless he has taken a bath. 7 When the
sun goes down, he will be "clean." After
that, he can eat the sacred offerings.
They are his food. 8 He must not eat
anything found dead or torn apart by
wild animals. If he does, it will make
him "unclean." I am the LORD.

9 " 'The priests must do what I require.
But suppose they make fun of what I require. Then they will become guilty and
die. I am the LORD. I make them holy.

10 " 'Only a member of a priest's family can eat the sacred offering. The guest
of a priest can't eat it. A priest's hired
worker can't eat it either. 11 But suppose
a priest buys a slave with money. Or
suppose slaves are born in his house.
Then they can eat the sacred food.
12 Suppose a priest's daughter marries
someone who is not a priest. Then she
can't eat any of the food brought as a
sacred gift. 13 But suppose the priest's
daughter becomes a widow or is divorced. She does not have any children.
And she returns to live in her father's
house, where she lived when she was
young. Then she can eat her father's
food. But a person who does not belong
to a priest's family can't eat any of it.

14 " 'Suppose someone eats a sacred
offering by mistake. Then they must
pay back the priest for the offering.
They must also add a fifth of its value
to it. 15 The priests must not allow the
sacred offerings to become "unclean."
They are the offerings the Israelites
bring to the LORD. 16 The priests must
not allow the offerings to become "unclean" by letting the people eat them.
If they do, they will bring guilt on the
people. They will have to pay for what
they have done. I am the LORD. I make
them holy.' "

Sacrifices the LORD Does Not Accept

17 The LORD spoke to Moses. He said,
18 "Speak to Aaron and his sons. Speak to
all the Israelites. Tell them, 'Suppose any
of you brings a gift for a burnt offering
to the LORD. It does not matter whether
you are an Israelite or an outsider who
lives in Israel. It does not matter whether
you bring the offering to keep a promise
or because you choose to give it. 19 You
must bring a male animal without any
flaws if you want the LORD to accept it
from you. It does not matter whether it
is from your cattle, sheep or goats. 20 Do
not bring an animal that has any flaws.
If you do, the LORD will not accept it from
you. 21 Suppose any of you brings an
animal for a friendship offering to the

LORD. Then it must not have any flaws at all. If it does, the LORD will not accept it. It does not matter whether the animal is from your herd or flock. It does not matter whether you bring it to keep a promise or because you choose to give it. 22 Do not offer a blind animal to the LORD. Do not bring a hurt or wounded animal. And do not offer one that has warts or boils or running sores. Do not place any of them on the altar as a food offering presented to the LORD. 23 But suppose you bring an offering you choose to give. Then you can bring an ox or a sheep whose body is twisted or too small. But the LORD will not accept it if you offer it to keep a promise. 24 You must not offer the LORD a male animal whose sex glands have been hurt. The glands also must not be crushed, torn or cut. You must not offer that kind of animal in your own land. 25 And you must not accept that kind of animal from someone who comes from another land. You must not offer it as food for your God. He will not accept it from you. Its body is twisted and has flaws.' "

26 The LORD spoke to Moses. He said, 27 "When a calf, lamb or goat is born, it must remain with its mother for seven days. From the eighth day on, I will accept it as a food offering presented to me. 28 Do not kill a cow and its calf on the same day. Do not kill a female sheep and its lamb on the same day.

29 "Sacrifice a thank offering to me in the right way. Then I will accept it from you. 30 You must eat it that same day. Do not leave any of it until morning. I am the LORD.

31 "Obey my commands. Follow them. I am the LORD. 32 Do not treat my name as if it were not holy. The Israelites must recognize me as the holy God. I am the LORD. I made you holy. 33 I brought you out of Egypt to be your God. I am the LORD."

The Appointed Feast Days

23 The LORD said to Moses, 2 "Speak to the Israelites. Tell them, 'Here are my appointed feast days. They are the appointed feast days of the LORD. Tell the people that they must come together for these sacred assemblies.

The Sabbath Day

3 " 'There are six days when you can work. But the seventh day is a day of sabbath rest. You must rest on it. Come together on that sacred day. You must not do any work on it. No matter where you live, it is a Sabbath day to honor the LORD.

Passover and Unleavened Bread

4 " 'Here are the LORD's appointed feasts. Tell the people that they must come together for these sacred gatherings at their appointed times. 5 The LORD's Passover begins when the sun goes down on the 14th day of the first month. 6 The LORD's Feast of Unleavened Bread begins on the 15th day of that month. For seven days you must eat bread made without yeast. 7 On the first day you must come together for a special service. Do not do any regular work on that day. 8 On each of the seven days bring a food offering to the LORD. On the seventh day come together for a special service. Do not do any regular work on that day.' "

The First Share of Israel's Crops Belongs to the LORD

9 The LORD said to Moses, 10 "Speak to the Israelites. Tell them, 'When you enter the land I am going to give you, bring an offering to the LORD. Gather your crops. Bring the first bundle of grain to the priest. 11 He must lift up the grain and wave it in front of the LORD. Then the LORD will accept it from you. The priest must wave it on the day after the Sabbath. 12 On the day he waves the grain for you, you must sacrifice a burnt offering to me. It must be a lamb that does not have any flaws. It must be a year old. 13 You must bring it together with its grain offering. The grain offering must be seven pounds of the finest flour. Mix it with olive oil. It is a food offering presented to the LORD. It has a pleasant smell. You must offer a drink offering along with the burnt offering. It must be a quart of wine. 14 You must not eat any bread until the day you bring your offering to the LORD your God. You must not eat any cooked grain or any of your first grain until that time. This is a law that will last for all time to come. It applies no matter where you live.

The Feast of Weeks

15 " 'The day you brought the grain for the wave offering was the day after the Sabbath. Count off seven full weeks from that day. 16 Count off 50 days up to the day after the seventh Sabbath. On that day bring to the LORD an offering of your first grain. 17 Bring two loaves of bread that are made with seven pounds of the finest flour. They must be baked with yeast. Bring them to me as a wave offering from the first share of your crops. That applies no matter where you live. 18 Together with the bread, bring seven male lambs. Each lamb must be a year old. It must not have any flaws. Also bring one young bull and two rams. They will be a burnt offering to the LORD. They will be offered together with their grain offerings and drink offerings. They are food offerings. Their smell pleases the LORD. 19 Then sacrifice one male goat for a sin offering. Also sacrifice two lambs for a friendship offering. Each of the lambs must be a year old. 20 The priest must lift up the two lambs and wave them in front of me as a wave offering. He must offer them together with the bread made out of the first share of your crops. They are a sacred offering to the LORD. They will be given to the priest. 21 On that same day tell the people that they must come together for a special worship service. They must not do any regular work. That is a law that will last for all time to come. It applies no matter where you live.

22 " 'Suppose you are gathering your crops. Then do not harvest all the way to the edges of your field. And do not pick up the grain you missed. Leave some for the poor people and the outsiders who live among you. I am the LORD your God.' "

The Feast of Trumpets

23 The LORD said to Moses, 24 "Say to the Israelites, 'On the first day of the seventh month you must have a day of sabbath rest. It must be a special service announced with trumpet blasts. 25 Do not do any regular work on that day. Instead, bring a food offering to the LORD.' "

The Day When Sin Is Paid For

26 The LORD spoke to Moses. He said, 27 "The tenth day of the seventh month is the day when sin is paid for. Come together for a special service. Do not eat any food. Bring a food offering to the LORD. 28 Do not do any work on that day. It is the day when sin is paid for. On that day your sin will be paid for in my sight. I am the LORD your God. 29 Suppose you do eat food on that day. Then you will be separated from your people. 30 I will destroy anyone among your people who does any work on that day. 31 You must not do any work at all. This is a law that will last for all time to come. It applies no matter where you live. 32 That day is a day of sabbath rest for you. You must rest on it. You must not eat anything on that day. You must follow the rules of the sabbath rest. Follow them from the evening of the ninth day of the month until the following evening."

The Feast of Booths

33 The LORD said to Moses, 34 "Say to the Israelites, 'On the 15th day of the seventh month the LORD's Feast of Booths begins. It lasts for seven days. 35 On the first day you must come together for a special service. Do not do any regular work on that day. 36 On each of the seven days bring a food offering to the LORD. On the eighth day come together for a special service. Bring a food offering to the LORD. That special service is the closing service. Do not do any regular work on that day.

37 " 'These are the LORD's appointed feasts. Tell the people that they must come together for these sacred assemblies. During those times, the people must bring food offerings to the LORD. They are burnt offerings and grain offerings. They are sacrifices and drink offerings. Each offering must be brought at its required time. 38 The offerings are in addition to those of the days of sabbath rest. The offerings are also in addition to your gifts and anything you have promised. They are also in addition to all the offerings you choose to give to the LORD.

39 " 'Begin with the 15th day of the seventh month. That is after you have gathered your crops. On that day celebrate the LORD's Feast of Booths for seven days. The first day is a day of rest. The eighth day is also a day of rest.

40 On the first day you must get branches from palms, willows and other leafy trees. You must be filled with joy in front of the LORD your God for seven days. 41 Celebrate the LORD's Feast of Booths for seven days each year. This is a law that will last for all time to come. Celebrate the feast in the seventh month. 42 Live in booths for seven days. All the Israelites must live in booths. 43 Then your children after you will know that I made the Israelites live in booths. I made them do it after I brought them out of Egypt. I am the LORD your God.' "

44 So Moses announced to the Israelites the appointed feasts of the LORD.

Olive Oil, Bread and Incense

24 The LORD said to Moses, 2 "Command the Israelites to bring you clear oil made from pressed olives. Use it to keep the lamps burning and giving light all the time. 3 Aaron must take care of the lamps in front of the LORD from evening until morning all the time. This is a law that will last for all time to come. The lamps are outside the curtain in front of the tablets of the covenant law in the tent of meeting. 4 The lamps are on the pure gold lampstand in front of the LORD. They must be taken care of all the time.

5 "Get the finest flour and bake 12 loaves of bread. Use seven pounds of flour for each loaf. 6 Arrange them in two stacks. Put six loaves in each stack on the table made out of pure gold. The table stands in front of the LORD. 7 By each stack put some pure incense. It will remind you that all good things come from the LORD. Burn the incense in place of the bread. The incense is a food offering presented to the LORD. 8 The bread must be set out in front of the LORD regularly. Do it every Sabbath day. It will be Israel's duty to provide it for all time to come. 9 The bread belongs to Aaron and his sons. They must eat it in the holy area. It is a very holy part of their regular share of the food offerings presented to the LORD."

A Person Who Speaks Evil Is Put to Death

10 There was a man who had an Israelite mother. His father was born in Egypt. The man went out among the Israelites. A fight broke out in the camp between him and an Israelite. 11 The son of the Israelite woman spoke evil things against the LORD by using a curse. So the people brought him to Moses. The name of the man's mother was Shelomith. She was the daughter of Dibri. Dibri was from the tribe of Dan. 12 The people kept her son under guard until they could find out what the LORD wanted them to do.

13 Then the LORD spoke to Moses. He said, 14 "Get the man who spoke evil things against the LORD. Take him outside the camp. All those who heard him say those things must place their hands on his head. Then the whole community must kill him by throwing stones at him. 15 Say to the Israelites, 'Anyone who curses me will be held accountable. 16 Anyone who speaks evil things against my Name must be put to death. The whole community must kill them by throwing stones at them. It does not matter whether they are an outsider or an Israelite. When they speak evil things against my Name, they must be put to death.

17 " 'Anyone who kills another human being must be put to death. 18 Anyone who kills someone's animal must pay its owner. A life must be taken for a life. 19 Suppose someone hurts their neighbor. Then what they have done must be done to them. 20 A bone must be broken for a bone. An eye must be put out for an eye. A tooth must be knocked out for a tooth. The one who has hurt his neighbor must be hurt in the same way. 21 Whoever kills an animal must pay its owner. But if they kill a human being, they must be put to death. 22 The same law applies whether they are an outsider or an Israelite. I am the LORD your God.' "

23 Then Moses spoke to the Israelites. They got the man who had spoken evil things against the LORD. They took him outside the camp. There they killed him by throwing stones at him. The Israelites did just as the LORD had commanded Moses.

The Sabbath Year

25 The LORD spoke to Moses at Mount Sinai. He said, 2 "Speak to the Israelites. Tell them, 'You will enter the land I am going to give you. When you do, you must honor the

LORD every seventh year by not farming the land that year. 3 For six years plant your fields. Trim the branches in your vineyards and gather your crops. 4 But the seventh year must be a year of sabbath rest for the land. The land must rest during it. It is a sabbath year to honor the LORD. Do not plant your fields. Do not trim the branches in your vineyards. 5 Do not gather what grows without being planted. And do not gather the grapes from the vines you have not taken care of. The land must have a year of rest. 6 Anything the land produces during the sabbath year will be food for you. It will be for you and your male and female servants. Your hired workers will eat it. So will people who live with you for a while. 7 And so will your livestock and the wild animals that are in your land. Anything the land produces can be eaten.

The Year of Jubilee

8 " 'Count off seven sabbath years. Count off seven times seven years. The seven sabbath years add up to a total of 49 years. 9 The tenth day of the seventh month is the day when sin is paid for. On that day blow the trumpet all through your land. 10 Set the 50th year apart. Announce freedom all over the land to everyone who lives there. The 50th year will be a Year of Jubilee for you. Each of you must return to your own family property. And each of you must return to your own tribe. 11 The 50th year will be a Year of Jubilee for you. Do not plant anything. Do not gather what grows without being planted. And do not gather the grapes from the vines you have not taken care of. 12 It is a Year of Jubilee. It will be holy for you. Eat only what the fields produce.

13 " 'In the Year of Jubilee all of you must return to your own property.

14 " 'Suppose you sell land to any of your own people. Or you buy land from them. Then do not take advantage of each other. 15 The price you pay must be based on the number of years since the last Year of Jubilee. Here is how the price you charge must be decided. It must be based on the number of years left for gathering crops before the next Year of Jubilee. 16 When there are many years left, you must raise the price. When there are only a few years left, you must lower the price. That is because what is really being sold to you is the number of crops the land will produce. 17 Do not take advantage of each other. Instead, have respect for your God. I am the LORD your God.

18 " 'Follow my rules. Be careful to obey my laws. Then you will live safely in the land. 19 The land will produce its fruit. You will eat as much as you want. And you will live there in safety. 20 Suppose you say, "In the seventh year we will not plant anything or gather our crops. So what will we eat?" 21 I will send you a great blessing in the sixth year. The land will produce enough for three years. 22 While you plant during the eighth year, you will eat food from the old crop. You will continue to eat food from it until the crops from the ninth year are gathered.

23 " 'The land must not be sold without a way of getting it back. That is because it belongs to me. You are only outsiders and strangers in my land. 24 You must make sure that you can buy the land back. That applies to all the land that belongs to you.

25 " 'Suppose one of your own people becomes poor. And suppose they have to sell some of their land. Then their nearest relative must come and buy back what they have sold. 26 But suppose they do not have anyone to buy it back for them. And suppose things go well for them and they earn enough money to buy it back themselves. 27 Then they must decide how much the crops have become worth since the time they sold the land. They must take that amount off the price the land was sold for. They must give the one selling it back to them the money that is left. Then they can go back to their own property. 28 But suppose they have not earned enough money to pay them back. Then the buyer they sold the land to will keep it until the Year of Jubilee. At that time it will be returned to them. Then they can go back to their property.

29 " 'Suppose someone sells a house in a city that has a wall around it. Then for a full year after they sell it they have the right to buy it back. 30 But suppose they do not buy it back before the full year has passed. Then the house in the

walled city will continue to belong to the buyer and the buyer's children. It will not be returned to the seller in the Year of Jubilee. 31 But houses in villages that do not have walls around them must be treated like property outside walled cities. Those houses can be bought back at any time. And they must be returned in the Year of Jubilee.

32 " 'The Levites always have the right to buy back their houses in the towns that belong to them. 33 So their property among the Israelites can be bought back. That applies to a house sold in any of their towns. Any house that is sold must be returned to its original owner in the Year of Jubilee. That is because the houses of the Levites will always belong to them. 34 But the grasslands around their towns must never be sold. They will belong to them for all time to come.

35 " 'Suppose any of your own people become poor. And suppose they can't take care of themselves. Then help them just as you would help an outsider or a stranger. In that way, the poor can continue to live among you. 36 Do not charge them interest of any kind. Instead, have respect for God. Then those who have become poor can continue to live among you. 37 If you lend them money, you must not charge them interest. And you must not sell them food for more than it cost you. 38 I am the LORD your God. I brought you out of Egypt. I did it to give you the land of Canaan. I wanted to be your God.

39 " 'Suppose any of your own people become poor. And suppose they sell themselves to you. Then do not make them work as slaves. 40 You must treat them like hired workers. Or you must treat them like those living among you for a while. They must work for you until the Year of Jubilee. 41 Then they and their children must be set free. They will go back to their own tribes. They will go back to the property their people have always owned. 42 The Israelites are my servants. I brought them out of Egypt. So they must not be sold as slaves. 43 Show them pity when you rule over them. Have respect for God.

44 " 'You must get your male and female slaves from the nations that are around you. You can buy slaves from them. 45 You can also buy as slaves some of the people living among you for a while. You can also buy members of their families born among you. They will become your property. 46 You can leave them to your children as their share of your property. You can make them slaves for life. But when you rule over your own people, you must be kind to them.

47 " 'Suppose an outsider living among you for a while becomes rich. Then suppose any of your own people become poor. Then they sell themselves to the outsider living among you. Or they sell themselves to a member of the outsider's family. 48 Then they keep the right to buy themselves back after they have sold themselves. One of their relatives can buy them back. 49 An uncle or a cousin can buy them back after they have sold themselves. In fact, any relative in their tribe can do it. Or suppose things go well for them. Then they can buy themselves back. 50 They and their buyer must count the number of years from the time of the sale up to the Year of Jubilee. The price for their freedom must be based on the amount paid to a hired man for that number of years. 51 Suppose there are many years until the Year of Jubilee. Then for their freedom they must pay a larger share of the price paid for them. 52 But suppose there are only a few years left until the Year of Jubilee. Then they must count the number of years that are left. The payment for their freedom must be based on that number. 53 They must be treated as workers hired from year to year. You must make sure that those they must work for are kind to them when they rule over them.

54 " 'Suppose they are not bought back in any of those ways. Then they and their children must still be set free in the Year of Jubilee. 55 That's because the Israelites belong to me. They are my servants. I brought them out of Egypt. I am the LORD your God.

Rewards for Obeying the LORD

26 " 'Do not make statues of gods for yourselves. Do not set up a likeness of a god or a sacred stone for yourselves. Do not place a carved stone in your land and bow down in front of it. I am the LORD your God.

2 " 'You must always keep my Sabbath
days. Have respect for my sacred tent.
I am the LORD.

3 " 'Follow my rules. Be careful to obey
my commands. 4 Then I will send you
rain at the right time. The ground will
produce its crops. The trees will bear
their fruit. 5 You will continue to harvest your grain until you gather your
grapes. You will continue to gather your
grapes until you plant your crops. You
will have all you want to eat. And you
will live in safety in your land.

6 " 'I will give you peace in the land.
You will be able to sleep because no one
will make you afraid. I will remove wild
animals from the land. There will not
be any war in your country. 7 You will
hunt down your enemies. You will kill
them with your swords. 8 Five of you
will chase 100. And 100 of you will chase
10,000. You will kill your enemies with
your swords.

9 " 'I will bless you. I will give you
many children so that there will be
many of you. And I will be faithful to the
covenant I made with you. 10 You will
still be eating last year's crops when you
will have to make room for new crops.
11 I will live among you. I will not turn
away from you. 12 I will walk among
you. I will be your God. And you will be
my people. 13 I am the LORD your God. I
brought you out of Egypt. I did not want
you to be slaves in Egypt anymore. I
threw off your heavy load. I helped you
walk with your heads held high.

Punishment for Not Obeying the LORD

14 " 'On the other hand, suppose you
do not listen to me. Suppose you do not
carry out all my commands. 15 Suppose
you say no to my rules and turn away
from my laws. And suppose you break
my covenant by failing to carry out all
my commands. 16 Then here is what I
will do to you. All at once I will bring
terror on you. I will send sicknesses
that will make you weak. I will send
fever that will destroy your sight. It
will slowly take your strength away.
When you plant seeds, it will not do
you any good. Instead, your enemies
will eat what you have planted. 17 I will
turn against you. Then your enemies
will win the battle over you. Those who
hate you will rule over you. You will run
away even when no one is chasing you.

18 " 'After all that, suppose you still
will not listen to me. Then I will punish
you for your sins seven times. 19 I will
break down your stubborn pride. I will
make the sky above you like iron, and
it will not rain. I will make the ground
under you like bronze, and you will not
be able to farm it. 20 You will work with
all your strength, but it will not do you
any good. That is because your soil will
not produce any crops. The trees of your
land will not bear any fruit.

21 " 'Suppose you continue to be my
enemy. And suppose you still refuse to
listen to me. Then I will multiply your
troubles many times because of your
sins. 22 I will send wild animals against
you. They will kill your children. They
will destroy your cattle. There will be
so few of you left that your roads will
be deserted.

23 " 'After all those things, suppose
you still do not accept my warnings.
And suppose you continue to be my
enemy. 24 Then I myself will be your
enemy. I will make you suffer again
and again for your sins. 25 I will send war
against you to punish you for breaking my covenant. When you go back
into your cities, I will send a plague
among you. You will be handed over
to your enemies. 26 I will cut off your
supply of bread. Ten women will need
only one oven to bake your bread. They
will weigh out the bread piece by piece.
Even when you eat all of it, it will not
be enough to satisfy you.

27 " 'After all that, suppose you still
do not listen to me. And suppose you
continue to be my enemy. 28 Then I
will be angry with you. I will be your
enemy. I myself will again punish you
for your sins over and over. 29 You will
eat the dead bodies of your sons. You
will also eat the dead bodies of your
daughters. 30 I will destroy the high
places where you worship other gods.
I will pull down your incense altars. I
will pile up your dead bodies on the
lifeless statues of your gods. And I will
turn away from you. 31 I will completely
destroy your cities. I will destroy your
places of worship. The pleasant smell
of your offerings will not give me any
delight. 32 I myself will destroy your

land so completely that your enemies
who live there will be shocked. 33 I will
scatter you among the nations. I will
pull out my sword and hunt you down.
Your land and your cities will be completely destroyed. 34 Then the deserted
land will enjoy its sabbath years. It will
rest. It will not be farmed. It will enjoy
its sabbaths. But you will become prisoners in the country of your enemies.
35 The land will rest the whole time it is
deserted. It was not able to rest during
the sabbaths you lived in it.

36 " 'Some of you will be left in the
lands of your enemies. I will fill your
hearts with fear. The sound of a leaf
blown by the wind will scare you away.
You will run as if you were escaping
from swords. You will fall down, even
though no one is chasing you. 37 You will
trip over one another as if you were running away from the battle. You will run
away, even though no one is chasing
you. You will not be able to stand and
fight against your enemies. 38 While you
are still scattered among the nations,
you will die. The lands of your enemies
will destroy you. 39 You who are left in
those lands will become weaker and
weaker. You will die because of your
sins and the sins of your people who
lived before you.

40 " 'But suppose you admit that both
you and your people who lived before
you have sinned. You admit the evil
and dishonest things you have done
against me. And you admit you have
become my enemy. 41 What you did
made me become your enemy. I let
your enemies take you into their land.
But suppose you stop being stubborn.
You stop being proud. And you pay for
your sin. 42 Then I will remember my
covenant with Jacob. I will remember
my covenant with Isaac. I will remember my covenant with Abraham. I will
remember what I said to them about the
land. 43 You will leave the land. It will
enjoy its sabbaths while it lies deserted
because you are not there. You will pay
for your sins because you said no to my
laws. You turned away from my rules.
44 But even after all that, I will not say
no to you or turn away from you. I will
not destroy you completely in the land
of your enemies. I will not break my
covenant with you. I am the LORD your
God. 45 Because of you, I will remember
the covenant I made with the people of
Israel who lived before you. I brought
them out of Egypt to be their God. The
nations saw me do it. I am the LORD.' "

46 These are the orders, the laws and
the rules of the covenant the LORD made
on Mount Sinai. He made it between
himself and the Israelites through
Moses.

Keep Your Promises to the LORD

27 The LORD said to Moses, 2 "Speak
to the Israelites. Tell them, 'Suppose someone makes a special promise
to set a person apart to serve the LORD.
Here is how much it will cost to set that
person free from the promise to serve.
3 The cost for a male between the ages of
twenty and sixty is 20 ounces of silver.
It must be weighed out in keeping with
the standard weights that are used in
the sacred tent. 4 The cost for a female
of the same age is 12 ounces of silver.
5 The cost for a male between the ages
of five and twenty is 8 ounces of silver.
The cost for a female of the same age is
4 ounces of silver. 6 The cost for a male
between the ages of one month and five
years is 2 ounces of silver. The cost for
a female of the same age is 1 ounce of
silver. 7 The cost for a male who is sixty
years old or more is 6 ounces of silver.
The cost for a female of the same age
is 4 ounces of silver. 8 But suppose the
one who makes the special promise is
too poor to pay the required amount.
Then they must bring to the priest the
person who will be set free. The priest
will decide the right value for that person. It will be based on how much the
one who makes the promise can afford.

9 " 'Suppose what they promised is
an animal that the LORD will accept as
an offering. Then the animal given to
the LORD becomes holy. 10 The one who
makes the promise must not trade it.
They must not trade a good animal for
a bad one. And they must not trade a
bad animal for a good one. Suppose
they choose one animal instead of another. Then both animals become holy.
11 Suppose the animal they promised
is not "clean." Suppose the LORD will
not accept it as an offering. Then the
animal must be brought to the priest.
12 He will decide whether it is good or

bad. Its value will be what he decides it will be. 13 Suppose the owner wants to buy the animal back. Then a fifth must be added to its cost.

14 " 'Suppose someone sets apart their house as something holy to the LORD. Then the priest will decide whether it is good or bad. Its value will remain what he decides it will be. 15 Suppose the person sets apart their house. And suppose later they want to buy it back. Then they must add a fifth to its value. The house will belong to them again.

16 " 'Suppose someone sets apart a piece of their family's land to the LORD. Then here is how its value must be decided. It must be based on the number of seeds that are required to grow a full crop on it. That value will be 20 ounces of silver for every 300 pounds of barley seeds. 17 Suppose they set apart their field during the Year of Jubilee. Then the value that has been decided will not be changed. 18 But suppose they set apart their field after the Year of Jubilee. Then here is how the priest will decide its value. It will be based on the number of years that are left until the next Year of Jubilee. The value decided will be reduced. 19 Suppose the one who set apart their field wants to buy it back. Then they must add a fifth to its value. The field will belong to them again. 20 But suppose they do not buy back the field. Instead, suppose they sell it to someone else. Then they can never buy it back. 21 When the field is set free in the Year of Jubilee, it will become holy. It will be like a field set apart to the LORD. It will become the property of the priests.

22 " 'Suppose someone sets apart to the LORD a field they have bought. And suppose it is not part of their family's land. 23 Then here is how the priest will decide its value. It will be based on the number of years that are left until the Year of Jubilee. The owner must pay that value on the day it is decided. The money is holy. It is set apart for the LORD. 24 In the Year of Jubilee the field will go back to the person it was bought from. That person is the one who had owned the land before. 25 Every amount of money must be weighed out in keeping with the standard weights used in the sacred tent.

26 " 'But no one can set apart the first male animal born to its mother. That animal already belongs to the LORD. It does not matter whether it is an ox or a sheep. It belongs to the LORD. 27 Suppose it is an "unclean" animal. Then the owner may buy it back at the value that has been decided. And they must add a fifth to its value. But suppose it is not bought back. Then it must be sold at the value that has been decided.

28 " 'But nothing a person owns and sets apart to the LORD can be sold or bought back. It does not matter whether it is a human being or an animal or a family's land. Everything set apart to the LORD is very holy to him.

29 " 'No one set apart in a special way to be destroyed can be bought back. They must be put to death.

30 " 'A tenth of everything the land produces belongs to the LORD. That includes grain from the soil and fruit from the trees. It is holy. It is set apart for him. 31 Suppose someone wants to buy back some of their tenth. Then they must add a fifth of the cost to it. 32 Every tenth part of herds and flocks will be holy. They will be set apart for the LORD. That includes every tenth animal that its shepherd marks with his wooden staff. 33 No one may pick out the good animals from the bad. They must not choose one animal instead of another. But if anyone does, both animals become holy. They can't be bought back.' "

34 The LORD gave Moses all these commands on Mount Sinai for the Israelites.

NUMBERS

Author: Moses

After God gave Moses the Ten Commandments, he told Moses to count all the people in Israel. That's why this book is called Numbers. The nation of Israel was preparing to cross the desert and enter into the promised land. However, the Israelites needed to trust God because they didn't know where to go or where their new home would be. God reminded the Israelites of the promise he had made to Abraham long ago—God would lead them into a land that would be their new home. God also reminded them of the covenant he had made with them, including the blessings they would experience if they obeyed him and the consequences they would experience if they disobeyed him.

Law & Covenant

Unfortunately, the Israelites did not trust God; they wanted to follow their own plan and do things their own way. Because of their rebellion, they experienced a serious consequence: They wandered in the desert for forty years. God called his people to obey, but over and over they rebelled against him, and their disobedience had consequences. God mercifully called them to repent, but they lost their opportunity to enter the promised land until a new generation of Israelites was born who would choose to trust God. Once again, God promised that one day a Savior would come.

The Men of Israel Are Counted

1 The LORD spoke to Moses in the tent
of meeting. It happened in the Desert
of Sinai. The LORD spoke to him on the
first day of the second month. It was the
second year after the Israelites came
out of Egypt. The LORD said, 2 “Count all
the men of Israel. Make a list of them by
their tribes and families. List every man
by name. List them one by one. 3 Count
all the men able to serve in the army.
They must be 20 years old or more. I
want you and Aaron to make a list of
them group by group. 4 One man from
each tribe must help you. Those who
help must be the heads of their families.

5 “Here are the names of the men
who must help you.

“From the tribe of Reuben will
come Elizur, the son of Shedeur.
6 From the tribe of Simeon will
come Shelumiel, the son of
Zurishaddai.
7 From the tribe of Judah will
come Nahshon, the son of
Amminadab.
8 From the tribe of Issachar will
come Nethanel, the son of Zuar.
9 From the tribe of Zebulun will
come Eliab, the son of Helon.
10 From the tribe of Ephraim will
come Elishama, the son of
Ammihud.
From the tribe of Manasseh will
come Gamaliel, the son of
Pedahzur.
Ephraim and Manasseh are
Joseph’s two sons.
11 From the tribe of Benjamin will
come Abidan, the son of Gideoni.
12 From the tribe of Dan will
come Ahiezer, the son of
Ammishaddai.
13 From the tribe of Asher will come
Pagiel, the son of Okran.
14 From the tribe of Gad will come
Eliasaph, the son of Deuel.
15 From the tribe of Naphtali will
come Ahira, the son of Enan.”

16 These were the men appointed
from the community. They were
the leaders of the tribes of their
people. They were the heads of the
major families in Israel.

17 Moses and Aaron went and got the
men whose names had been given to
them. 18 Then Moses and Aaron gathered all the men of Israel together. It
was the first day of the second month.
The people wrote down the tribe and
family they belonged to. The men 20
years old or more were listed by name.
They were listed one by one. 19 Everything was done just as the LORD had
commanded Moses. So Moses counted
them in the Desert of Sinai.

20 Here is the number of men from
the tribe of Reuben. He is Israel’s
oldest son.
All the men able to serve in
the army were counted. They
were 20 years old or more. They
were listed by name. They were
listed one by one. They were
listed according to the records
of their tribes and families.
21 The number from the tribe of
Reuben was 46,500.

22 Here is the number of men from
the tribe of Simeon.
All the men able to serve in
the army were counted. They
were 20 years old or more. They
were listed by name. They were
listed one by one. They were
listed according to the records
of their tribes and families.
23 The number from the tribe of
Simeon was 59,300.

24 Here is the number of men from
the tribe of Gad.
All the men able to serve in
the army were counted. They
were 20 years old or more. They
were listed by name. They were
listed according to the records of
their tribes and families. 25 The
number from the tribe of Gad
was 45,650.

26 Here is the number of men from
the tribe of Judah.
All the men able to serve in
the army were counted. They
were 20 years old or more. They
were listed by name. They were
listed according to the records of
their tribes and families. 27 The
number from the tribe of Judah
was 74,600.

28 Here is the number of men from the tribe of Issachar.
All the men able to serve in the army were counted. They were 20 years old or more. They were listed by name. They were listed according to the records of their tribes and families.
29 The number from the tribe of Issachar was 54,400.

30 Here is the number of men from the tribe of Zebulun.
All the men able to serve in the army were counted. They were 20 years old or more. They were listed by name. They were listed according to the records of their tribes and families.
31 The number from the tribe of Zebulun was 57,400.

32 Here is the number of men from the tribe of Ephraim. He is the son of Joseph.
All the men able to serve in the army were counted. They were 20 years old or more. They were listed by name. They were listed according to the records of their tribes and families.
33 The number from the tribe of Ephraim was 40,500.

34 Here is the number of men from the tribe of Manasseh. He is the son of Joseph.
All the men able to serve in the army were counted. They were 20 years old or more. They were listed by name. They were listed according to the records of their tribes and families.
35 The number from the tribe of Manasseh was 32,200.

36 Here is the number of men from the tribe of Benjamin.
All the men able to serve in the army were counted. They were 20 years old or more. They were listed by name. They were listed according to the records of their tribes and families.
37 The number from the tribe of Benjamin was 35,400.

38 Here is the number of men from the tribe of Dan.
All the men able to serve in the army were counted. They were 20 years old or more. They were listed by name. They were listed according to the records of their tribes and families.
39 The number from the tribe of Dan was 62,700.

40 Here is the number of men from the tribe of Asher.
All the men able to serve in the army were counted. They were 20 years old or more. They were listed by name. They were listed according to the records of their tribes and families.
41 The number from the tribe of Asher was 41,500.

42 Here is the number of men from the tribe of Naphtali.
All the men able to serve in the army were counted. They were 20 years old or more. They were listed by name. They were listed according to the records of their tribes and families.
43 The number from the tribe of Naphtali was 53,400.

44 These were the men counted by Moses and Aaron. The 12 leaders of Israel helped them. There was one leader from each tribe.
45 The men who were counted were able to serve in Israel's army. All of them were 20 years old or more. They were counted family by family.
46 The total number of men was 603,550.

47 But the families of the tribe of Levi were not counted along with the others.
48 The LORD had spoken to Moses. He had said,
49 "You must not count the men from the tribe of Levi. Do not include them when you list the other men of Israel.
50 Instead, put the Levites in charge of the holy tent. That is where the tablets of the covenant law are kept. The Levites will be in charge of everything that belongs to the holy tent. They must carry the tent and everything that belongs to it. They must take care of it. They must set up camp around it.
51 When the holy tent must be moved, the Levites must take it down. And when the tent must be set up, the Levites must do it. Anyone else who

approaches it must be put to death.
[52] The Israelites must set up their tents
by military groups. All of them must
be in their own camps under their own
flags. [53] But the Levites must set up their
tents around the holy tent. That's where
the tablets of the covenant law are kept.
Then I will not be angry with the community of Israel. The Levites will be
responsible for taking care of the tent."

[54] The Israelites did everything just
as the LORD had commanded Moses.

The Tribes Camp Around the Tent of Meeting

2 The LORD spoke to Moses and Aaron.
He said, [2] "The Israelites must camp
around the tent of meeting. But they
must not camp too close to it. All of
them must camp under their flags and
under the banners of their families."

[3] The groups of the camp of Judah must be on the east side. They must set up camp toward the sunrise. They must camp under their flag. The leader of the tribe of Judah is Nahshon, the son of Amminadab. [4] There are 74,600 men in Nahshon's group.

[5] The tribe of Issachar will camp next to them. The leader of the tribe of Issachar is Nethanel, the son of Zuar. [6] There are 54,400 men in Nethanel's group.

[7] The tribe of Zebulun will be next. The leader of the tribe of Zebulun is Eliab, the son of Helon. [8] There are 57,400 men in Eliab's group.

[9] So a total of 186,400 men will be set apart for the camp of Judah. They will be arranged group by group. They will start out first.

[10] The groups of the camp of Reuben will be on the south side. They will be under their flag. The leader of the tribe of Reuben is Elizur, the son of Shedeur. [11] There are 46,500 men in Elizur's group.

[12] The tribe of Simeon will camp next to them. The leader of the tribe of Simeon is Shelumiel, the son of Zurishaddai. [13] There are 59,300 men in Shelumiel's group.

[14] The tribe of Gad will be next. The leader of the tribe of Gad is Eliasaph, the son of Deuel. [15] There are 45,650 men in Eliasaph's group.

[16] So a total of 151,450 men will be set apart for the camp of Reuben. They will be arranged group by group. They will start out second.

[17] Then the camp of the Levites will start out. The tent of meeting will go with them. They will march in the middle of the other camps. They will start out in the same order as they do when they set up camp. Each one will be in their own place under their flag.

[18] The groups of the camp of Ephraim will be on the west side. They will be under their flag. The leader of the tribe of Ephraim is Elishama, the son of Ammihud. [19] There are 40,500 men in Elishama's group.

[20] The tribe of Manasseh will be next to them. The leader of the tribe of Manasseh is Gamaliel, the son of Pedahzur. [21] There are 32,200 men in Gamaliel's group.

[22] The tribe of Benjamin will be next. The leader of the tribe of Benjamin is Abidan, the son of Gideoni. [23] There are 35,400 men in Abidan's group.

[24] So a total of 108,100 men will be set apart for the camp of Ephraim. They will be arranged group by group. They will start out third.

[25] The groups of the camp of Dan will be on the north side. They will be under their flag. The leader of the tribe of Dan is Ahiezer, the son of Ammishaddai. [26] There are 62,700 men in Ahiezer's group.

[27] The tribe of Asher will camp next to them. The leader of the tribe of Asher is Pagiel, the son of Okran. [28] There are 41,500 men in Pagiel's group.

[29] The tribe of Naphtali will be next. The leader of the tribe of Naphtali is Ahira, the son of Enan. [30] There are 53,400 men in Ahira's group.

[31] So a total of 157,600 men will be set apart for the camp of Dan. They will start out last. They will march under their flags.

[32] Those are the men of Israel. They were counted according to their families. The total number of all the men in the camps is 603,550, group by group. [33] But the Levites weren't counted along with the other men of Israel. That's what the LORD had commanded Moses.

[34] So the Israelites did everything the LORD had commanded Moses. That's the way they set up camp under their flags. And that's the way they started out. Each of them marched out with their own tribe and family.

The Levites

3 Here is the story of the family line of Aaron and Moses. It belongs to the time when the LORD spoke to Moses at Mount Sinai.

[2] Aaron's oldest son was Nadab. Aaron's other sons were Abihu, Eleazar and Ithamar. [3] Those were the names of Aaron's sons. They were the anointed priests. They were given authority to serve the LORD as priests. [4] But Nadab and Abihu made an offering to the LORD by using fire that wasn't allowed. So they died in front of him. That happened in the Desert of Sinai. They didn't have any sons. Only Eleazar and Ithamar served as priests while their father Aaron was living.

[5] The LORD spoke to Moses. He said, [6] "Bring the men of the tribe of Levi to Aaron the priest. They will help him. [7] They must work at the tent of meeting for Aaron and for the whole community. They must do what needs to be done at the holy tent. [8] They must take care of everything connected with the tent of meeting. When they do, they are acting for all the Israelites. [9] Give the Levites to Aaron and his sons. They are the men of Israel who must be given completely to him. [10] Appoint Aaron and his sons to serve as priests. Anyone else who approaches the sacred tent must be put to death."

[11] The LORD also said to Moses, [12] "I have taken the Levites from among the Israelites. I have taken them in place of the son born first to each woman in Israel. The Levites belong to me. [13] That's because every male born first to a mother is mine. In Egypt I struck down all the males born first. I did it when I set apart for myself every male born first

in Numbers?

God is the Trustworthy Guide. He faithfully leads his people into a life of joy and purpose.

to a mother in Israel. That is true for men and animals alike. They belong to me. I am the LORD."

[14] The LORD spoke to Moses in the Desert of Sinai. He said, [15] "Count the Levites by their family groups. Count every male a month old or more." [16] So Moses counted them. He did just as the word of the LORD had commanded him.

[17] The sons of Levi were
Gershon, Kohath and Merari.
[18] The major families from Gershon were
Libni and Shimei.
[19] The major families from Kohath were
Amram, Izhar, Hebron and Uzziel.
[20] The major families from Merari were
Mahli and Mushi.

These were the major families of the Levites.

[21] The families of Libni and Shimei belonged to the family of Gershon.
[22] All the males a month old or more were counted. There were 7,500 of them.
[23] The families of Gershon had to camp on the west side. They had to camp behind the holy tent.
[24] The leader of the families of Gershon was Eliasaph, the son of Lael.
[25] Here are the duties of the families of Gershon at the tent of meeting. They were responsible

for taking care of the holy tent and its coverings. They took care of the curtain at the entrance to the tent of meeting. 26 They took care of the curtains of the courtyard. And they took care of the curtain at the entrance to the courtyard. The courtyard was all around the holy tent and altar. The families of Gershon also took care of the ropes. In fact, they had to take care of everything connected with the use of all those things.

27 The families of Amram, Izhar, Hebron and Uzziel belonged to the family of Kohath.
28 All the males a month old or more were counted. There were 8,600 of them.
The families of Kohath were responsible for taking care of the sacred tent.
29 They had to camp on the south side of the holy tent.
30 The leader of the families of Kohath was Elizaphan, the son of Uzziel.
31 They were responsible for taking care of the ark of the covenant law. They took care of the table for the holy bread. They took care of the lampstand and the two altars. They took care of the things used for serving in the sacred tent. They also took care of the inner curtain. In fact, they had to take care of everything connected with the use of all those things.
32 The chief leader of the Levites was Eleazar. He was the son of Aaron the priest. Eleazar was appointed over those responsible for taking care of the sacred tent.

33 The families of Mahli and Mushi belonged to the family of Merari.
34 All the males a month old or more were counted. There were 6,200 of them.
35 The leader of the families of Merari was Zuriel, the son of Abihail.
The families of Merari had to camp on the north side of the holy tent.
36 They were responsible for taking care of the frames of the tent. They took care of its crossbars, posts and bases. They took care of all its supplies. In fact, they had to take care of everything connected with the use of all those things. 37 They also took care of the posts of the courtyard around the holy tent. And they took care of the bases, tent stakes and ropes.

38 Moses, Aaron and Aaron's sons had to camp to the east of the holy tent. They had to camp toward the sunrise in front of the tent of meeting.
They were responsible for taking care of the sacred tent. They had to do it for the Israelites.
Anyone else who approached the tent would be put to death.

39 The total number of the Levite males was 22,000. They were counted family by family. Every male a month old or more was counted. Moses and Aaron counted them, just as the LORD had commanded.

40 The LORD said to Moses, "Count all the Israelite males born first in their families. Count all those a month old or more. Make a list of their names. 41 Take the Levites for me in their place. And take the livestock of the Levites in place of all the male animals in Israel born first to their mothers. I am the LORD."

42 So Moses counted all the oldest sons in Israel. He did just as the LORD had commanded him. 43 There were 22,273 of those sons a month old or more. They were listed by name.

44 The LORD also said to Moses, 45 "Take the Levites in place of all the males born first in Israel. Also take the livestock of the Levites in place of the livestock of Israel. The Levites belong to me. I am the LORD. 46 But there are 273 more males born first in Israel than there are male Levites. 47 Collect two ounces of silver for each of them. Weigh it out according to the standard weights used in the sacred tent. 48 Give the silver to Aaron and his sons. It will buy the freedom of the additional sons in Israel."

49 So Moses collected the silver from the additional sons in Israel to buy their freedom. The Levites took the place

of all the others. 50 Moses collected 35
pounds of silver. It was weighed out
according to the weights used in the
sacred tent. Moses collected it from the
oldest sons in Israel. 51 He gave the silver
to Aaron and his sons. He did just as the
LORD had commanded him.

The Families of Kohath

4 The LORD said to Moses and Aaron,
2 "Count the Levites who belong
to the families of Kohath. Make a list
of them family by family. 3 Count all
the men 30 to 50 years old. Those are
the men who must come and serve at the
tent of meeting.

4 "Here is the work the men of Kohath
must do at the tent of meeting. They
must take care of the things that are
very holy. 5 When the camp is ready
to move, Aaron and his sons must go
into the tent. They must take down the
curtain that hides the ark where the
tablets of the covenant law are kept.
They must cover the ark with the curtain. 6 Then they must cover that with
strong leather. They must spread a solid
blue cloth over the leather. And they
must put the poles in place.

7 "They must spread a blue cloth over
the table for the holy bread. They must
put the plates, dishes and bowls on the
cloth. They must also put the jars for
drink offerings on it. The bread that is
always kept there must remain on it.
8 They must spread a bright red cloth
over everything. Then they must cover
that with the strong leather. And they
must put the poles of the table in place.

9 "They must get a blue cloth. With
it they must cover the lampstand that
gives light. They must also cover its
lamps, trays and wick cutters. And they
must cover all its jars. The jars are for
the olive oil used in the lampstand.
10 Then Aaron and his sons must wrap
the lampstand and all the things used
with it. They must cover it with the
strong leather. And they must put it
on a frame to carry it.

11 "They must spread a blue cloth over
the gold altar for burning incense. They
must cover that with the strong leather.
And they must put the poles of the altar
in place.

12 "They must get all the things used
for serving in the sacred tent. They must
wrap them in a blue cloth. They must
cover that with the strong leather. Then
they must put those things on a frame
to carry them.

13 "They must remove the ashes from
the bronze altar for burnt offerings.
They must spread a purple cloth over it.
14 Then they must place all the tools on
it. The tools are used for serving at the
altar. They include the pans for carrying
ashes. They also include the meat forks,
shovels and sprinkling bowls. Aaron
and his sons must cover the altar with
the strong leather. And they must put
its poles in place.

15 "Aaron and his sons must cover all
the holy things that belong to the holy
tent. Only then are the men of Kohath to
come and carry everything. They must
do so only when the camp is ready to
move. But they must not touch the holy
things. If they do, they will die. The men
of Kohath must carry everything in the
tent of meeting.

16 "Eleazar the priest will be in charge
of the olive oil for the light. He is the son
of Aaron. Eleazar will be in charge of the
sweet-smelling incense. He will be in
charge of the regular grain offering and
the anointing oil. He will be in charge
of the entire holy tent. He will also be in
charge of everything in it. That includes
all the things that belong to the tent."

17 The LORD spoke to Moses and Aaron.
He said, 18 "Make sure that the Kohath
families are not destroyed from among
the Levites. 19 I want them to live and not
die when they come near the very holy
things. So here is what you must do for
them. Aaron and his sons must go into
the sacred tent and tell each man what
to do. They must tell each man what to
carry. 20 But the men of Kohath must
not go in and look at the holy things.
They must not look at them even for a
moment. If they do, they will die."

The Families of Gershon

21 The LORD said to Moses, 22 "Count
the families of Gershon. Make a list of
them family by family. 23 Count all the
men 30 to 50 years old. Those are the
men who must come and serve at
the tent of meeting.

24 "Here is how the families of Gershon
must serve. They must carry things.
25 They must carry the curtains of the

holy tent of meeting. They must carry its covering and the outside covering of strong leather. They must carry the curtains that cover the entrance to
the tent of meeting. 26 They must carry the curtains of the courtyard. The courtyard is all around the holy tent and altar. They must carry the curtain for the entrance. They must carry the ropes. They must also carry all the supplies used for any purpose in the tent. The families of Gershon must do everything that needs
to be done with those things. 27 All their work must be done under the direction of Aaron and his sons. That includes carrying and everything else they do. Aaron and his sons must tell them what
to carry. And that will be their work. 28 It is what the families of Gershon must do at the tent of meeting. They must work under the direction of Ithamar the priest. He is the son of Aaron.

The Families of Merari

29 "Count the families of Merari.
Count them family by family. 30 Count all the men 30 to 50 years old. Those are the men who must come and serve at the
tent of meeting. 31 Here is the work they must do at the tent of meeting. They must carry the frames of the holy tent. They must carry its crossbars, posts
and bases. 32 They must also carry the posts of the courtyard. The courtyard is all around the holy tent. And they must carry the bases for the posts as well as their tent stakes and ropes. They must also carry all the supplies and everything connected with their use. Tell
each man exactly what to carry. 33 That is the work the families of Merari must do at the tent of meeting. They must work under the direction of Ithamar the priest. He is the son of Aaron."

Counting the Families of the Levites

34 Moses, Aaron and the leaders of the community counted the men of Kohath. They counted them family by family.

35 They counted all the men from 30 to 50 years old. They were the men who came and served at the
tent of meeting. 36 There were 2,750 men. They were counted
family by family. 37 That was the total of all the men in the families of Kohath who served at the tent of meeting. Moses and Aaron counted them. They did just as the LORD had commanded through Moses.

38 The men of Gershon were counted family by family.

39 All the men from 30 to 50 years old were counted. They were the men who came and served at the
tent of meeting. 40 There were 2,630 men. They were counted
family by family. 41 That was the total of the men in the families of Gershon who served at the tent of meeting. Moses and Aaron counted them. They did just as the LORD had commanded.

42 The men of Merari were counted family by family.

43 All the men from 30 to 50 years old were counted. They were the men who came and served at the
tent of meeting. 44 There were 3,200 men. They were counted
family by family. 45 That was the total of the men in the families of Merari. Moses and Aaron counted them. They did just as the LORD had commanded through Moses.

46 So Moses and Aaron counted all the Levites. The leaders of Israel helped them. They counted the
Levites family by family. 47 All the men from 30 to 50 years old were counted. They were the men who came and served at the tent of meeting. They were also supposed
to carry it. 48 The total number of
men was 8,580. 49 Everything was done as the LORD had commanded through Moses. Each man was given his work. And each one was told what to carry.

So they were counted, just as the LORD had commanded Moses.

Making the Camp Pure

5 The LORD spoke to Moses. He said,
2 "Tell the Israelites that certain people must be sent away from the camp. Command them to send away anyone who has a skin disease. They must send away all those who have liquid waste coming from their bodies.

And they must send away those who are 'unclean' because they have touched a dead body. 3 That applies to men and women alike. Send them out of the camp. They must not make their camp 'unclean.' That is where I live among them." 4 So the Israelites did what the LORD commanded. They sent out of the camp those who were "unclean." They did just as the LORD had directed Moses.

Sins Against Others Must Be Paid For

5 The LORD said to Moses, 6 "Speak to the Israelites. Say to them, 'Suppose a man or woman does something wrong to someone else. Then that person is not being faithful to the LORD. People like that are guilty. 7 They must admit they have committed a sin. They must pay in full for what they did wrong. And they must add a fifth of the value to it. Then they must give all of it to the person they have sinned against. 8 But suppose that person has died. And suppose that person does not have a close relative who can be paid for the sin that was committed. Then what is paid belongs to the LORD. It must be given to the priest. A ram must be given along with it. The ram must be sacrificed to the LORD to pay for the sin. 9 All the sacred gifts the Israelites bring to a priest will belong to him. 10 Sacred gifts belong to their owners. But what they give to the priest will belong to the priest.' "

The Test for an Unfaithful Wife

11 Then the LORD spoke to Moses again. He said, 12 "Speak to the Israelites. Say to them, 'Suppose a man's wife goes astray. And suppose she is not faithful to her husband. 13 Suppose another man has sex with her. And suppose this is hidden from her husband. No one knows she is not "clean." So there is no witness against her. And she has not been caught in the act. 14 Suppose her husband becomes jealous. He does not trust his wife, and she is really "unclean." Or suppose he does not trust her even though she is "clean." 15 Then he must take his wife to the priest. He must also bring an offering. It must be eight cups of barley flour. The offering is for his wife. He must not pour olive oil on it. And he must not put incense on it. It is a grain offering for being jealous. It calls attention to the wrong thing a person has done.

16 " 'The priest must have her stand in front of the LORD. 17 He must pour some holy water into a clay jar. He must get some dust from the floor of the holy tent. And he must put it into the water. 18 The priest must have the woman stand in front of the LORD. Then he must untie her hair. He must place in her hands the offering that calls attention to the wrong thing a person has done. It is the grain offering for being jealous. The priest must keep the bitter water with him. It is the water that brings a curse. 19 Then the priest must have the woman give her word. He must say to her, "Suppose no other man has had sex with you. And suppose you haven't gone astray. You have kept yourself pure while you are married to your husband. Then may the bitter water that brings a curse not harm you. 20 But suppose you have gone astray while you are married to your husband. You have made yourself 'unclean.' You have had sex with a man who isn't your husband." 21 At that point the priest must put the woman under the curse that will come if she breaks her word. He must say, "May the LORD cause you to become a curse among your people. You will become a curse when the LORD makes your body unable to have children. 22 May this water that brings a curse enter your body. May it make your body unable to have children."

" 'Then the woman must say, "Amen. Let it happen."

23 " 'The priest must write the curses on a scroll. He must wash them off in the bitter water. 24 It is the water he will make the woman drink. It is bitter water that brings a curse. It will enter her body. And it will cause her to suffer bitterly. 25 The priest must take from her hands the grain offering for being jealous. He must lift it up and wave it in front of the LORD. He must bring it to the altar. 26 Then the priest must take a handful of the grain offering. It is the offering that calls attention to the wrong thing a person has done. The priest must burn it on the altar. After that, he must have the woman drink the water. 27 Suppose she has made herself "unclean." She has not been faithful to

her husband. And she has drunk the
water that brings a curse. Then it will go
into her body. It will cause her to suffer
bitterly. It will make her body unable to
have children. She will become a curse.
28 Suppose the woman has not made
herself "unclean." But suppose she is
"clean." Then she will be free of guilt.
And she will be able to have children.

29 " 'This is the law about being jealous. It applies to a woman who has gone
astray. She has made herself "unclean"
while she is married to her husband.
30 And it applies to a man who becomes
jealous. He has doubts about his wife.
The priest must have her stand in front
of the LORD. He must apply the entire
law to her. 31 The husband will not be
guilty of doing anything wrong. But the
woman will be punished for her sin.' "

Becoming a Nazirite

6 The LORD said to Moses, 2 "Say to
the Israelites, 'Suppose a man or
woman wants to make a special promise. They want to set themselves apart
to the LORD for a certain period of time.
They want to be Nazirites. 3 Then they
must not drink any kind of wine. They
must not drink vinegar made out of
wine of any kind. They must not drink
grape juice. They must not eat grapes or
raisins. 4 As long as they are Nazirites,
they must not eat anything grapevines
produce. They must not even eat the
seeds or skins of grapes.

5 " 'They must not use razors on
their heads. They must not cut their
hair during the whole time they have
set themselves apart to the LORD. They
must be holy until that time is over.
They must let the hair on their heads
grow long.

6 " 'And they must not go near a dead
body during that whole time. 7 But what
if their father or mother dies? Or what
if their brother or sister dies? Then they
must not make themselves "unclean"
because of them. The hair on their
heads shows they are set apart for God.
8 During the whole time they are set
apart they are holy to the LORD.

9 " 'Suppose someone dies suddenly in
front of them. That makes the hair they
have set apart to the LORD "unclean." So
they must shave their heads on the day
they will be made "clean." That is the
seventh day. 10 Then on the eighth day
they must bring two doves. Or they can
bring two young pigeons. They must
bring them to the priest. He will be at
the entrance to the tent of meeting. 11 The
priest must offer one of the birds as a sin
offering. And he must offer the other as
a burnt offering. The sacrifices will pay
for the sin of the Nazirite man or woman.
They sinned by being near a dead body.
That same day they must make their
heads holy again. 12 They must set themselves apart to the LORD again. They must
do it for the same period of time they had
agreed to at first. And they must bring a
male lamb a year old as a guilt offering.
The days before that do not count. That
is because they became "unclean" during
the time they were set apart.

13 " 'The time when the Nazirites are
set apart will come to an end. Here is the
law that applies to them at that time.
They must be brought to the entrance to
the tent of meeting. 14 There they must
present their offerings to the LORD. They
must bring a male lamb a year old.
It must not have any flaws. It is for a
burnt offering. Then they must bring
a female lamb a year old. It must not
have any flaws. It is for a sin offering.
And they must bring a ram that does
not have any flaws. It is for a friendship offering. 15 They must sacrifice
the offerings together with their grain
offerings and drink offerings. And they
must also bring a basket of bread made
with the finest flour. The bread must be
made without yeast. The offering must
include thick loaves with olive oil mixed
in. And it must also include thin loaves
brushed with olive oil.

16 " 'The priest must bring all these
things to the LORD. He must sacrifice the
sin offering and the burnt offering. 17 He
must bring the basket of bread made
without yeast. And he must sacrifice
the ram. It will be a friendship offering
to the LORD. The priest must bring it
together with its grain offering and
drink offering.

18 " 'Then the Nazirites must shave
off the hair that shows they have set
themselves apart to the LORD. They
must do it at the entrance to the tent
of meeting. And they must put the hair
in the fire that burns the sacrifice of the
friendship offering.

19 " 'After the Nazirites have shaved off
their hair, the priest must take a boiled
shoulder of the ram. He must remove one
thick loaf and one thin loaf from the basket. They must be made without yeast.
And he must place the shoulder and
the bread in the hands of the Nazirites.
20 Then he must lift up the shoulder and
bread and wave them in front of the LORD.
They are a wave offering. They are holy
and belong to the priest. Other parts of
the ram belong to the priest as well. They
are the breast that was waved and the
thigh that was offered. After the offering
is waved, the Nazirites may drink wine.
21 " 'This is the law of the Nazirites.
They promise to sacrifice offerings
to the LORD. They do it when they set
themselves apart. And they should
bring anything else they can afford.
They must fulfill the promises they have
made. They must do so according to the
law of the Nazirites.' "

How the Priests Bless the People

22 The LORD spoke to Moses. He said,
23 "Tell Aaron and his sons, 'Here is how
I want you to bless the Israelites. Say
to them,

24 " ' "May the LORD bless you
and take good care of you.
25 May the LORD smile on you
and be gracious to you.
26 May the LORD look on you with
favor
and give you peace." '

27 "In that way they will put the blessing of my name on the Israelites. And I
will bless them."

key verses

May the LORD bless you and take good care of you. May the LORD smile on you and be gracious to you. May the LORD look on you with favor and give you peace. NUMBERS 6:24–26

Israel's Leaders Bring Offerings for the Holy Tent

7 Moses finished setting up the holy
tent. Then he anointed it with olive
oil. He set it apart to the LORD. He did
the same thing with everything that
belonged to it. He also anointed the
altar. And he set apart to the LORD the
altar and all its tools. 2 Then the leaders
of Israel brought their offerings. The
leaders were the heads of the families.
They were the leaders of the tribes. They
were in charge of the men who had
been counted. 3 They brought gifts to the
LORD. They brought six covered carts
and 12 oxen. Each leader gave an ox.
And every two leaders gave a cart. They
put their gifts in front of the holy tent.
4 The LORD said to Moses, 5 "Accept
the gifts from the leaders. I want their
gifts to be used in the work at the tent of
meeting. Give them to the Levites. They
need them to do their work."
6 So Moses gave the carts and the oxen
to the Levites. 7 He gave two carts and
four oxen to the men from the family
of Gershon. They needed them to do
their work. 8 He gave four carts and
eight oxen to the men from the family
of Merari. They needed them to do their
work. All these men were under the
direction of Ithamar the priest. He was
the son of Aaron. 9 But Moses didn't give
any carts or oxen to the men from the
family of Kohath. They had to carry the
holy things on their shoulders. They
were responsible for the holy things.
10 When the altar was anointed, the
leaders brought their offerings. They
placed them in front of the altar. They
brought their offerings in order to set
apart the altar. 11 The LORD had spoken
to Moses. He had said, "Each day one
leader must bring his offering. He must
bring it in order to set apart the altar."

12 On the first day Nahshon, the
son of Amminadab, brought his
offering. Nahshon was from the
tribe of Judah.
13 He brought:
one silver plate and one silver
sprinkling bowl. The plate
weighed three pounds four
ounces. The sprinkling bowl
weighed one pound 12 ounces.
Both were weighed according
to the standard weights used in
the sacred tent. Each plate and
bowl was filled with the finest
flour mixed with olive oil. It was
a grain offering.

14 He brought one gold dish that weighed four ounces. It was filled with incense.
15 Nahshon brought one young bull, one ram, and one male lamb a year old. They would be sacrificed as a burnt offering.
16 He brought one male goat to be sacrificed as a sin offering.
17 He brought two oxen, five rams and five male goats. He also brought five male lambs a year old. All of them would be sacrificed as a friendship offering.

That was everything that Nahshon, the son of Amminadab, brought as his offering.

18 On the second day Nethanel, the son of Zuar, brought his offering. Nethanel was the leader of the tribe of Issachar.
19 He brought:
one silver plate and one silver sprinkling bowl. The plate weighed three pounds four ounces. The sprinkling bowl weighed one pound 12 ounces. Both were weighed according to the standard weights used in the sacred tent. Each plate and bowl was filled with the finest flour mixed with olive oil. It was a grain offering.
20 He brought one gold dish that weighed four ounces. It was filled with incense.
21 Nethanel brought one young bull, one ram, and one male lamb a year old. They would be sacrificed as a burnt offering.
22 He brought one male goat to be sacrificed as a sin offering.
23 He brought two oxen, five rams and five male goats. He also brought five male lambs a year old. All of them would be sacrificed as a friendship offering.

That was everything that Nethanel, the son of Zuar, brought as his offering.

24 On the third day Eliab, the son of Helon, brought his offering. Eliab was the leader of the people of Zebulun.
25 He brought:
one silver plate and one silver sprinkling bowl. The plate weighed three pounds four ounces. The sprinkling bowl weighed one pound 12 ounces. Both were weighed according to the standard weights used in the sacred tent. Each plate and bowl was filled with the finest flour mixed with olive oil. It was a grain offering.
26 He brought one gold dish that weighed four ounces. It was filled with incense.
27 Eliab brought one young bull, one ram, and one male lamb a year old. They would be sacrificed as a burnt offering.
28 He brought one male goat to be sacrificed as a sin offering.
29 He brought two oxen, five rams and five male goats. He also brought five male lambs a year old. All of them would be sacrificed as a friendship offering.

That was everything that Eliab, the son of Helon, brought as his offering.

30 On the fourth day Elizur, the son of Shedeur, brought his offering. Elizur was the leader of the people of Reuben.
31 He brought:
one silver plate and one silver sprinkling bowl. The plate weighed three pounds four ounces. The sprinkling bowl weighed one pound 12 ounces. Both were weighed according to the standard weights used in the sacred tent. Each plate and bowl was filled with the finest flour mixed with olive oil. It was a grain offering.
32 He brought one gold dish that weighed four ounces. It was filled with incense.
33 Elizur brought one young bull, one ram, and one male lamb a year old. They would be sacrificed as a burnt offering.
34 He brought one male goat to be sacrificed as a sin offering.
35 He brought two oxen, five rams and five male goats. He also

brought five male lambs a
year old. All of them would be
sacrificed as a friendship offering.
That was everything that Elizur,
the son of Shedeur, brought as his
offering.

36 On the fifth day Shelumiel, the
son of Zurishaddai, brought his
offering. Shelumiel was the leader
of the people of Simeon.
37 He brought:
one silver plate and one silver
sprinkling bowl. The plate
weighed three pounds four
ounces. The sprinkling bowl
weighed one pound 12 ounces.
Both were weighed according
to the standard weights used in
the sacred tent. Each plate and
bowl was filled with the finest
flour mixed with olive oil. It was
a grain offering.
38 He brought one gold dish that
weighed four ounces. It was
filled with incense.
39 Shelumiel brought one young
bull, one ram, and one male
lamb a year old. They would be
sacrificed as a burnt offering.
40 He brought one male goat to be
sacrificed as a sin offering.
41 He brought two oxen, five
rams and five male goats. He
also brought five male lambs
a year old. All of them would
be sacrificed as a friendship
offering.
That was everything that
Shelumiel, the son of Zurishaddai,
brought as his offering.

42 On the sixth day Eliasaph, the
son of Deuel, brought his offering.
Eliasaph was the leader of the
people of Gad.
43 He brought:
one silver plate and one silver
sprinkling bowl. The plate
weighed three pounds four
ounces. The sprinkling bowl
weighed one pound 12 ounces.
Both were weighed according
to the standard weights used in
the sacred tent. Each plate and
bowl was filled with the finest
flour mixed with olive oil. It was
a grain offering.
44 He brought one gold dish that
weighed four ounces. It was
filled with incense.
45 Eliasaph brought one young
bull, one ram, and one male
lamb a year old. They would be
sacrificed as a burnt offering.
46 He brought one male goat to be
sacrificed as a sin offering.
47 He brought two oxen, five
rams and five male goats. He
also brought five male lambs
a year old. All of them would
be sacrificed as a friendship
offering.
That was everything that Eliasaph,
the son of Deuel, brought as his
offering.

48 On the seventh day Elishama,
the son of Ammihud, brought his
offering. Elishama was the leader
of the people of Ephraim.
49 He brought:
one silver plate and one silver
sprinkling bowl. The plate
weighed three pounds four
ounces. The sprinkling bowl
weighed one pound 12 ounces.
Both were weighed according
to the standard weights used in
the sacred tent. Each plate and
bowl was filled with the finest
flour mixed with olive oil. It was
a grain offering.
50 He brought one gold dish that
weighed four ounces. It was
filled with incense.
51 Elishama brought one young
bull, one ram, and one male
lamb a year old. They would be
sacrificed as a burnt offering.
52 He brought one male goat to be
sacrificed as a sin offering.
53 He brought two oxen, five
rams and five male goats. He
also brought five male lambs
a year old. All of them would
be sacrificed as a friendship
offering.
That was everything that
Elishama, the son of Ammihud,
brought as his offering.

54 On the eighth day Gamaliel, the
son of Pedahzur, brought his
offering. Gamaliel was the leader
of the people of Manasseh.

55 He brought:
one silver plate and one silver sprinkling bowl. The plate weighed three pounds four ounces. The sprinkling bowl weighed one pound 12 ounces. Both were weighed according to the standard weights used in the sacred tent. Each plate and bowl was filled with the finest flour mixed with olive oil. It was a grain offering.
56 He brought one gold dish that weighed four ounces. It was filled with incense.
57 Gamaliel brought one young bull, one ram, and one male lamb a year old. They would be sacrificed as a burnt offering.
58 He brought one male goat to be sacrificed as a sin offering.
59 He brought two oxen, five rams and five male goats. He also brought five male lambs a year old. All of them would be sacrificed as a friendship offering.

That was everything that Gamaliel, the son of Pedahzur, brought as his offering.

60 On the ninth day Abidan, the son of Gideoni, brought his offering. Abidan was the leader of the people of Benjamin.
61 He brought:
one silver plate and one silver sprinkling bowl. The plate weighed three pounds four ounces. The sprinkling bowl weighed one pound 12 ounces. Both were weighed according to the standard weights used in the sacred tent. Each plate and bowl was filled with the finest flour mixed with olive oil. It was a grain offering.
62 He brought one gold dish that weighed four ounces. It was filled with incense.
63 Abidan brought one young bull, one ram, and one male lamb a year old. They would be sacrificed as a burnt offering.
64 He brought one male goat to be sacrificed as a sin offering.
65 He brought two oxen, five rams and five male goats. He also brought five male lambs a year old. All of them would be sacrificed as a friendship offering.

That was everything that Abidan, the son of Gideoni, brought as his offering.

66 On the tenth day Ahiezer, the son of Ammishaddai, brought his offering. Ahiezer was the leader of the people of Dan.
67 He brought:
one silver plate and one silver sprinkling bowl. The plate weighed three pounds four ounces. The sprinkling bowl weighed one pound 12 ounces. Both were weighed according to the standard weights used in the sacred tent. Each plate and bowl was filled with the finest flour mixed with olive oil. It was a grain offering.
68 He brought one gold dish that weighed four ounces. It was filled with incense.
69 Ahiezer brought one young bull, one ram, and one male lamb a year old. They would be sacrificed as a burnt offering.
70 He brought one male goat to be sacrificed as a sin offering.
71 He brought two oxen, five rams and five male goats. He also brought five male lambs a year old. All of them would be sacrificed as a friendship offering.

That was everything that Ahiezer, the son of Ammishaddai, brought as his offering.

72 On the eleventh day Pagiel, the son of Okran, brought his offering. Pagiel was the leader of the people of Asher.
73 He brought:
one silver plate and one silver sprinkling bowl. The plate weighed three pounds four ounces. The sprinkling bowl weighed one pound 12 ounces. Both were weighed according to the standard weights used in the sacred tent. Each plate and bowl was filled with the finest flour mixed with olive oil. It was a grain offering.

74 He brought one gold dish that weighed four ounces. It was filled with incense.
75 Pagiel brought one young bull, one ram, and one male lamb a year old. They would be sacrificed as a burnt offering.
76 He brought one male goat to be sacrificed as a sin offering.
77 He brought two oxen, five rams and five male goats. He also brought five male lambs a year old. All of them would be sacrificed as a friendship offering.
That was everything that Pagiel, the son of Okran, brought as his offering.
78 On the twelfth day Ahira, the son of Enan, brought his offering. Ahira was the leader of the people of Naphtali.
79 He brought:
one silver plate and one silver sprinkling bowl. The plate weighed three pounds four ounces. The sprinkling bowl weighed one pound 12 ounces. Both were weighed according to the standard weights used in the sacred tent. Each plate and bowl was filled with the finest flour mixed with olive oil. It was a grain offering.
80 He brought one gold dish that weighed four ounces. It was filled with incense.
81 Ahira brought one young bull, one ram, and one male lamb a year old. They would be sacrificed as a burnt offering.
82 He brought one male goat to be sacrificed as a sin offering.
83 He brought two oxen, five rams and five male goats. He also brought five male lambs a year old. All of them would be sacrificed as a friendship offering.
That was everything that Ahira, the son of Enan, brought as his offering.
84 Those were the offerings the Israelite leaders brought. They gave them to set the altar apart when it was anointed with olive oil.
They gave 12 silver plates, 12 silver sprinkling bowls and 12 gold
dishes. 85 Each plate weighed three pounds four ounces. Each sprinkling bowl weighed one pound 12 ounces. The total weight of the silver dishes was 60 pounds. Everything was weighed according to the standard weights used in the
sacred tent. 86 Each of the 12 gold dishes weighed four ounces. They were filled with incense. They were weighed according to the weights used in the sacred tent. The total weight of the gold dishes was three pounds.
87 The leaders brought 12 young bulls, 12 rams and 12 male lambs a year old. That was the total number of animals they gave for the burnt offering. They gave them together with the grain offering. They brought 12 male goats for the sin offering.
88 The leaders brought 24 oxen, 60 rams, 60 male goats and 60 male lambs a year old. That was the total number of animals sacrificed as the friendship offering.
Those were the offerings they brought to set apart the altar. The leaders brought them after the altar was anointed with oil.

89 Moses entered the tent of meeting. He wanted to speak with the LORD. There Moses heard the LORD talking to him. The LORD's voice was speaking to him from between the two cherubim. The cherubim were over the place where sin is paid for. It was the cover on the ark where the tablets of the covenant law were kept. In this way the LORD spoke to Moses.

Aaron Sets Up the Lamps

8 The LORD said to Moses, 2 "Say to
Aaron, 'Set up the seven lamps. They will light up the area in front of the lampstand.' "
3 So Aaron did it. He set up the lamps so that they faced forward on the lampstand. He did just as the LORD had commanded Moses. 4 The lampstand was made out of hammered gold. From its

base to its blooms it was made out of hammered gold. The lampstand was made exactly like the pattern the LORD had shown Moses.

Moses Sets Apart the Levites

5 The LORD spoke to Moses. He said, 6 "Take the Levites from among all the Israelites. Make them 'clean' in the usual way. 7 Here is how to make them pure. Sprinkle the special water on them. Then have them shave their whole bodies. Also have them wash their clothes. That is how they will make themselves pure. 8 Have them get a young bull along with its grain offering. The offering must be made out of the finest flour mixed with olive oil. Then you must get a second young bull. You must sacrifice it as a sin offering. 9 Bring the Levites to the front of the tent of meeting. Gather the whole community of Israel together. 10 You must bring the Levites to me. The Israelites must place their hands on them. 11 Aaron must bring the Levites to me. They are a wave offering from the Israelites. That is how they will be set apart to do my work.

12 "Then I want the Levites to place their hands on the heads of the bulls. They must sacrifice one bull as a sin offering to me. And they must sacrifice the other as a burnt offering. The blood of the bulls will pay for the sin of the Levites. 13 Have the Levites stand in front of Aaron and his sons. Then give them as a wave offering to me. 14 That is how I want you to set apart the Levites from the other Israelites. The Levites will belong to me.

15 "Make the Levites pure. Give them to me as a wave offering. Then they must come to do their work at the tent of meeting. 16 They are the Israelites who will be given to me completely. I have taken them to be my own. I have taken them in place of every son born first in his family in Israel. 17 Every male born first in Israel belongs to me. That is true whether it is a human or an animal. In Egypt I struck down all the males born first to their mothers. Then I set apart for myself all the males born first in Israel. 18 And I have taken the Levites in place of all the sons born first in Israel. 19 I have given the Levites as gifts to Aaron and his sons. I have taken them from among all the Israelites. I have appointed them to do the work at the tent of meeting. They will do it in place of the Israelites. That is how they will keep the Israelites from being guilty when they go near the sacred tent. Then no plague will strike the Israelites when they go near the tent."

20 So Moses and Aaron and all the Israelites did with the Levites just as the LORD had commanded Moses. 21 The Levites made themselves pure. They washed their clothes. Then Aaron gave them to the LORD as a wave offering. That's how he paid for their sin to make them pure. 22 After that, the Levites came to do their work at the tent of meeting. They worked under the direction of Aaron and his sons. And so Moses and Aaron and the whole community of Israel did with the Levites just as the LORD had commanded Moses.

23 The LORD said to Moses, 24 "Here is what the Levites must do. Men 25 years old or more must come and take part in the work at the tent of meeting. 25 But when they reach the age of 50, they must not work any longer. They must stop doing their regular work. 26 They can help their brothers with their duties at the tent of meeting. But they themselves should not do the work. That is how you must direct the Levites to do their work."

Israel Celebrates the Passover Feast

9 The LORD spoke to Moses in the Desert of Sinai. It was the first month of the second year after the people came out of Egypt. He said, 2 "Tell the Israelites to celebrate the Passover Feast. Have them do it at the appointed time. 3 Celebrate it when the sun goes down on the 14th day of this month. Obey all its rules and laws."

4 So Moses told the Israelites to celebrate the Passover Feast. 5 They did it in the Desert of Sinai. They celebrated it when the sun went down on the 14th day of the first month. The Israelites did everything just as the LORD had commanded Moses.

6 But some of them couldn't celebrate the Passover Feast on that day. That's because they weren't "clean." They had gone near a dead body. So they came to Moses and Aaron that same day.

7 They said to Moses, “We went near a
dead body. So we aren’t ‘clean.’ But why
should we be kept from bringing the
LORD’s offering at the appointed time?
Why shouldn’t we bring it along with
the other Israelites?”
8 Moses answered them, “Wait until I
find out what the LORD wants you to do.”
9 Then the LORD spoke to Moses. He
said, 10 “Tell the Israelites, ‘Suppose any
of you or your children are “unclean”
because they have gone near a dead
body. Or suppose they are away on a
journey. They must still celebrate the
LORD’s Passover. 11 They must celebrate
it on the 14th day of the second month.
They must do so when the sun goes
down. They must eat the lamb together
with bread made without yeast. They
must eat it with bitter plants. 12 They
must not leave any of it until morning.
They must not break any of its bones.
When they celebrate the Passover Feast,
they must follow all the rules. 13 But
suppose someone is “clean” and not
on a journey. And they fail to celebrate
the Passover Feast. Then they must
be separated from the community of
Israel. They did not bring the LORD’s
offering at the appointed time. They
will be punished for their sin.
14 “ ‘What if there is an outsider living
among you? And what if they want to
celebrate the LORD’s Passover? Then
they must obey its rules and laws. You
must have the same laws for outsiders
as you do for the Israelites.’ ”

The Cloud Covers the Holy Tent

15 The holy tent was set up. It was the
tent where the tablets of the covenant
law were kept. On the day it was set
up, the cloud covered it. From evening
until morning the cloud above the tent
looked like fire. 16 That’s what continued to happen. The cloud covered the
tent. At night the cloud looked like fire.
17 When the cloud lifted from its place
above the tent, the Israelites started out.
Where the cloud settled, the Israelites
camped. 18 When the LORD gave the
command, the Israelites started out.
And when he gave the command, they
camped. As long as the cloud stayed
above the holy tent, they remained in
camp. 19 Sometimes the cloud remained
above the tent for a long time. Then the
Israelites obeyed the LORD’s order. They
didn’t start out. 20 Sometimes the cloud
was above the tent for only a few days.
When the LORD would give the command, they would camp. And when he
would give the command, they would
start out. 21 Sometimes the cloud stayed
only from evening until morning. When
it lifted in the morning, they started out.
It didn’t matter whether it was day or
night. When the cloud lifted, the people
started out. 22 It didn’t matter whether
the cloud stayed above the holy tent
for two days or a month or a year. The
Israelites would remain in camp. They
wouldn’t start out. But when the cloud
lifted, they would start out. 23 When the
LORD gave the command, they camped.
And when he gave the command, they
started out. They obeyed the LORD’s
order. They obeyed him, just as he had
commanded them through Moses.

The Silver Trumpets

10 The LORD said to Moses, 2 “Make
two trumpets out of hammered
silver. Blow them when you want the
community to gather together. And
blow them when you want the camps
to start out. 3 When both trumpets are
blown, the whole community must
gather in front of you. They must come
to the entrance to the tent of meeting.
4 Suppose only one trumpet is blown.
Then the leaders must gather in front of
you. They are the heads of the tribes of
Israel. 5 When a trumpet blast is blown,
the tribes camped on the east side must
start out. 6 When the second blast is
blown, the camps on the south side
must start out. The blast will tell them
when to start. 7 Blow the trumpets to
gather the people together. But do not
use the same kind of blast.
8 “The sons of Aaron, the priests, must
blow the trumpets. That is a law for
you and your children after you for all
time to come. 9 Suppose you go into
battle in your own land. And suppose
it is against an enemy who is treating
you badly. Then blow a blast on the
trumpets. If you do, I will remember
you. I will save you from your enemies.
I am the LORD your God. 10 You must
also blow the trumpets when you are
happy. Blow them at your appointed
feasts. Blow them at your New Moon

feasts. Blow them when you sacrifice your burnt offerings. Blow them when you sacrifice your friendship offerings. They will remind me of you. I am the LORD your God."

The Israelites Leave the Sinai Desert

11 It was the 20th day of the second month of the second year. On that day the cloud began to move. It went up from above the holy tent where the tablets of the covenant law were kept. 12 Then the Israelites started out from the Desert of Sinai. They traveled from place to place. They kept going until the cloud came to rest in the Desert of Paran. 13 The first time they started out, the LORD commanded Moses to tell them to do it. And they did it.

14 The groups of the camp of Judah went first. They marched out under their flag. Nahshon was their commander. He was the son of Amminadab. 15 Nethanel was over the group of the tribe of Issachar. Nethanel was the son of Zuar. 16 Eliab was over the group of the tribe of Zebulun. Eliab was the son of Helon. 17 The holy tent was taken down. The men of Gershon and Merari started out. They carried the tent.

18 The groups of the camp of Reuben went next. They marched out under their flag. Elizur was their commander. He was the son of Shedeur. 19 Shelumiel was over the group of the tribe of Simeon. Shelumiel was the son of Zurishaddai. 20 Eliasaph was over the group of the tribe of Gad. Eliasaph was the son of Deuel. 21 The men of Kohath started out. They carried the holy things. The holy tent had to be set up before they arrived.

22 The groups of the camp of Ephraim went next. They marched out under their flag. Elishama was their commander. He was the son of Ammihud. 23 Gamaliel was over the group of the tribe of Manasseh. Gamaliel was the son of Pedahzur. 24 Abidan was over the group of the tribe of Benjamin. Abidan was the son of Gideoni.

25 Finally, the groups of the camp of Dan started out. They marched out under their flag. They followed behind all the other groups and guarded them. Ahiezer was their commander. He was the son of Ammishaddai. 26 Pagiel was over the group of the tribe of Asher. Pagiel was the son of Okran. 27 Ahira was over the group of the tribe of Naphtali. Ahira was the son of Enan. 28 As the groups of Israel started out, that was the order they marched in.

29 Moses spoke to Hobab, the son of Reuel. Reuel was Moses' father-in-law. Reuel was from Midian. Moses said to Hobab, "We're starting out for the place the LORD promised to us. He said to us, 'I will give it to you.' So come with us. We'll treat you well. The LORD has promised to give good things to Israel."

30 Hobab answered, "No. I can't go. I'm going back to my own land. I'm returning to my own people."

31 But Moses said, "Please don't leave us. You know where we should camp in the desert. You can be our guide. 32 So come with us. The LORD will give us good things. We'll share them with you."

33 So they started out from the mountain of the LORD. They traveled for three days. The ark of the covenant of the LORD went in front of them during those three days. It went ahead of them to find a place for them to rest. 34 They started out from the camp by day. And the cloud of the LORD was above them.

35 When the ark started out, Moses said,

"LORD, rise up!
Let your enemies be scattered.
Let them run away from you."

36 When the ark stopped, Moses said,

"LORD, return.
Return to the many thousands of people in Israel."

The LORD Sends Fire Among the People

11 The people weren't happy about the hard times they were having. The LORD heard what they were saying. It made him very angry. Then the LORD sent fire on them. It blazed out among the people. It burned up some of the outer edges of the camp. 2 The people cried out to Moses. Then he prayed to the LORD. And the fire died down. 3 So that place was named Taberah. That's because fire from the LORD had blazed out among them there.

The LORD Sends Quail for the People to Eat

4 Some people with them began to
wish for other food. Again the Israelites
began to cry out. They said, "We wish
we had meat to eat. 5 We remember
the fish we ate in Egypt. It didn't cost
us anything. We also remember the
cucumbers, melons, leeks, onions and
garlic. 6 But now we've lost all interest
in eating. We never see anything but
this manna!"

7 The manna was like coriander seeds.
It looked like sap from a tree. 8 The people went around gathering it. Then they
ground it up in a small mill they held
in their hands. Or they crushed it in a
stone bowl. They cooked it in a pot. Or
they made loaves out of it. It tasted like
something made with olive oil. 9 When
the dew came down on the camp at
night, the manna also came down.

10 Moses heard people from every
family crying at the entrances to their
tents. The LORD became very angry.
So Moses became upset. 11 He asked the
LORD, "Why have you brought this trouble on me? Why aren't you pleased with
me? Why have you loaded me down
with the troubles of all these people?
12 Am I like a mother to them? Are they
my children? Why do you tell me to
carry them in my arms? Do I have to
carry them the way a nurse carries a
baby? Do I have to carry them to the
land you promised? You promised the
land to their people of long ago. 13 Where
can I get meat for all these people? They
keep crying out to me. They say, 'Give
us meat to eat!' 14 I can't carry all these
people by myself. The load is too heavy
for me. 15 Is this how you are going to
treat me? If you are pleased with me,
just put me to death right now. Don't let
me live if I have to see myself destroyed
anyway."

16 The LORD said to Moses, "Bring me
70 of Israel's elders. Bring men that you
know are leaders and officials among
the people. Have them come to the tent
of meeting. I want them to stand there
with you. 17 I will come down and speak
with you there. I will take some of the
power of the Spirit that is on you. And I
will put it on them. They will share the
responsibility of these people with you.
Then you will not have to carry it alone.

18 "Tell the people, 'Set yourselves
apart for tomorrow. At that time you
will eat meat. The LORD heard you when
you cried out. You said, "We wish we had
meat to eat. We were better off in Egypt."
Now the LORD will give you meat. And
you will eat it. 19 You will not eat it for just
one or two days. You will not eat it for
just five, ten or 20 days. 20 Instead, you
will eat it for a whole month. You will eat
it until it comes out of your noses. You
will eat it until you hate it. The LORD is
among you. But you have turned your
back on him. You have cried out while
he was listening. You have said, "Why
did we ever leave Egypt?"'"

21 But Moses said to the LORD, "Here I
am among 600,000 men on the march.
And you say, 'I will give them meat
to eat for a whole month'! 22 Would
they have enough if flocks and herds
were killed for them? Would they have
enough even if all the fish in the ocean
were caught for them?"

23 The LORD answered Moses, "Am I not
strong enough? Now you will see whether what I say will come true for you."

24 So Moses went out. He told the
people what the LORD had said. He
gathered 70 of their elders together.
He had them stand around the tent of
meeting. 25 Then the LORD came down
in the cloud. He spoke with Moses. He
took some of the power of the Spirit
that was on Moses. And he put it on
the 70 elders. When the Spirit came on
them, they prophesied. But they didn't
do it again.

26 Two men had remained in the
camp. Their names were Eldad and
Medad. They were listed among the
elders. But they didn't go out to the tent
of meeting. In spite of that, the Spirit
came on them too. So they prophesied
in the camp. 27 A young man ran up to
Moses. He said, "Eldad and Medad are
prophesying in the camp."

28 Joshua spoke up. He was the son
of Nun. Joshua had been Moses' helper
from the time he was young. He said,
"Moses! Please stop them!"

29 But Moses replied, "Are you jealous
for me? I wish that all the LORD's people
were prophets. And I wish that the LORD
would put his Spirit on them." 30 Then
Moses and the elders of Israel returned
to the camp.

31 The LORD sent out a wind. It drove
quail in from the Red Sea. It scattered
them all around the camp. They were
about three feet above the ground. They
could be seen in every direction as far as
a person could walk in a day. 32 The people went out all day and gathered quail.
They gathered them all night and all
the next day. No one gathered less than
60 bushels. Then they spread the quail
out all around the camp. 33 But while the
meat was still in their mouths, the LORD
acted. Before the people could swallow
it, he became very angry with them. He
struck them with a terrible plague. 34 So
the place was named Kibroth Hattaavah.
That's where the bodies of the people who
had wished for other food were buried.
35 From Kibroth Hattaavah the people
traveled to Hazeroth. And they stayed
there.

Miriam and Aaron Speak Against Moses

12 Miriam and Aaron began to say
bad things about Moses. That's
because Moses had married a woman
from Cush. 2 "Has the LORD spoken only
through Moses?" they asked. "Hasn't
he also spoken through us?" The LORD
heard what they said.
3 Moses was a very humble man. In
fact, he was more humble than anyone
else on the face of the earth.
4 The LORD spoke to Moses, Aaron and
Miriam. He said, "All three of you, come
out to the tent of meeting." So they did.
5 Then the LORD came down in a pillar
of cloud. He stood at the entrance to the
tent. And he told Aaron and Miriam to
come to him. The two of them stepped
forward. 6 Then the LORD said, "Listen
to my words.

"Suppose there is a prophet among
you.
I, the LORD, make myself known
to them in visions.
I speak to them in dreams.
7 But this is not true of my servant
Moses.
He is faithful in everything he
does in my house.
8 With Moses I speak face to face.
I speak with him clearly. I do not
speak in riddles.
I let him see something of what I
look like.
So why were you not afraid
to speak against my servant
Moses?"

9 The LORD was very angry with them.
And he left them.
10 When the cloud went up from above
the tent, there stood Miriam. She had a
disease that made her skin as white as
snow. Aaron turned toward her. He saw
that she had a skin disease. 11 So he said to
Moses, "We have committed a very foolish
sin. Please don't hold it against us. 12 Don't
let Miriam be like a baby that was born
dead. Don't let her look like a dead baby
whose body is half eaten away."
13 So Moses cried out to the LORD. He
said, "Please, God, heal her!"
14 The LORD answered Moses. He said,
"Suppose her father had spit in her face.
Then she would have been put to shame
for seven days. So keep her outside the
camp for seven days. After that, you can
bring her back." 15 So Miriam was kept
outside the camp for seven days. The
people didn't move on until she was
brought back.
16 After that, the people left Hazeroth.
They camped in the Desert of Paran.

Twelve Men Check Out the Land of Canaan

13 The LORD said to Moses, 2 "Send
some men to check out the land
of Canaan. I am giving it to the Israelites. Send one leader from each of
Israel's tribes."
3 So Moses sent them out from the
Desert of Paran. He sent them as the
LORD had commanded. All of them were
leaders of the Israelites.

4 Here are their names.

There was Shammua from the
tribe of Reuben. Shammua was
the son of Zakkur.
5 There was Shaphat from the tribe
of Simeon. Shaphat was the son
of Hori.
6 There was Caleb from the tribe
of Judah. Caleb was the son of
Jephunneh.
7 There was Igal from the tribe of
Issachar. Igal was the son of
Joseph.
8 There was Hoshea from the tribe
of Ephraim. Hoshea was the son
of Nun.

9 There was Palti from the tribe of
Benjamin. Palti was the son of
Raphu.
10 There was Gaddiel from the tribe
of Zebulun. Gaddiel was the son
of Sodi.
11 There was Gaddi from the tribe of
Manasseh. Gaddi was the son
of Susi. Manasseh was a tribe
of Joseph.
12 There was Ammiel from the tribe
of Dan. Ammiel was the son of
Gemalli.
13 There was Sethur from the tribe
of Asher. Sethur was the son of
Michael.
14 There was Nahbi from the tribe of
Naphtali. Nahbi was the son of
Vophsi.
15 There was Geuel from the tribe of
Gad. Geuel was the son of Maki.

16 Those are the men Moses sent to
check out the land. He gave the
name Joshua to Hoshea, the son
of Nun.

17 Moses sent the 12 men to check out
Canaan. He said, "Go up through the
Negev Desert. Go on into the central
hill country. 18 See what the land is like.
See whether the people who live there
are strong or weak. See whether they
are few or many. 19 What kind of land
do they live in? Is it good or bad? What
kind of towns do they live in? Do the
towns have high walls around them or
not? 20 How is the soil? Is it rich land or
poor land? Are there trees in it or not?
Do your best to bring back some of the
fruit of the land." It was the season for
the first ripe grapes.
21 So the men went up and checked out
the land. They went from the Desert of
Zin as far as Rehob. It was in the direction of Lebo Hamath. 22 They went up
through the Negev Desert and came to
Hebron. That's where Ahiman, Sheshai
and Talmai lived. They belonged to the
family line of Anak. Hebron had been
built seven years before Zoan. Zoan
was a city in Egypt. 23 The men came
to the Valley of Eshkol. There they cut
off a branch that had a single bunch
of grapes on it. Two of them carried it
on a pole between them. They carried
some pomegranates and figs along with
it. 24 That place was called the Valley of
Eshkol. That's because the men of Israel
cut off a bunch of grapes there. 25 At the
end of 40 days, the men returned from
checking out the land.

The Men Report on What They Found

26 The men came back to Moses, Aaron
and the whole community of Israel. The
people were at Kadesh in the Desert of
Paran. There the men reported to Moses and Aaron and all the people. They
showed them the fruit of the land. 27 They
gave Moses their report. They said, "We
went into the land you sent us to. It really does have plenty of milk and honey!
Here's some fruit from the land. 28 But the
people who live there are powerful. Their
cities have high walls around them and
are very large. We even saw members
of the family line of Anak there. 29 The
Amalekites live in the Negev Desert. The
Hittites, Jebusites and Amorites live in the
central hill country. The Canaanites live
near the Mediterranean Sea. They also
live along the Jordan River."
30 Then Caleb interrupted the men
speaking to Moses. He said, "We should
go up and take the land. We can certainly do it."
31 But the men who had gone up with
him spoke. They said, "We can't attack
those people. They are stronger than
we are." 32 The men spread a bad report
about the land among the Israelites.
They said, "The land we checked out destroys those who live in it. All the people
we saw there are very big and tall. 33 We
saw the Nephilim there. We seemed like
grasshoppers in our own eyes. And that's
also how we seemed to them." The family
line of Anak came from the Nephilim.

The People Refuse to Obey the LORD

14 That night all the members of the
community raised their voices.
They wept out loud. 2 The Israelites spoke
against Moses and Aaron. The whole
community said to them, "We wish we
had died in Egypt or even in this desert.
3 Why is the LORD bringing us to this
land? We're going to be killed by swords.
Our enemies will capture our wives and
children. Wouldn't it be better for us to
go back to Egypt?" 4 They said to one
another, "We should choose another
leader. We should go back to Egypt."
5 Then Moses and Aaron fell with their
faces to the ground. They did it in front

of the whole community of Israel gathered there. 6Joshua, the son of Nun, tore
his clothes. So did Caleb, the son of Jephunneh. Joshua and Caleb were two of
the men who had checked out the land.
7They spoke to the whole community of
Israel. They said, "We passed through
the land and checked it out. It's very
good. 8If the LORD is pleased with us,
he'll lead us into that land. It's a land
that has plenty of milk and honey. He'll
give it to us. 9But don't refuse to obey
him. And don't be afraid of the people
of the land. We will swallow them up.
The LORD is with us. So nothing can save
them. Don't be afraid of them."
10But all the people talked about
killing Joshua and Caleb by throwing
stones at them. Then the glory of the
LORD appeared at the tent of meeting.
All the Israelites saw it. 11The LORD said
to Moses, "How long will these people
not respect me? How long will they refuse to believe in me? They refuse even
though I have done many signs among
them. 12So I will strike them down with
a plague. I will destroy them. But I will
make you into a greater and stronger
nation than they are."
13Moses said to the LORD, "Then the
Egyptians will hear about it. You used
your power to bring these people up
from among them. 14And the Egyptians
will tell the people who live in Canaan
about it. LORD, they have already heard
a lot about you. They've heard that you
are with these people. They've heard
that you have been seen face to face.
They've been told that your cloud stays
over them. They've heard that you go in
front of them in a pillar of cloud by day.
They've been told that you go in front of
them in a pillar of fire at night. 15Suppose
you put all these people to death and
leave none alive. Then the nations who
have heard these things about you will
talk. They'll say, 16'The LORD promised
to give these people the land of Canaan.
But he wasn't able to bring them into it.
So he killed them in the desert.'
17"Now, Lord, show your strength. You
have said, 18'I am the LORD. I am slow
to get angry. I am full of love. I forgive
those who sin. I forgive those who refuse
to obey. But I do not let guilty people
go without punishing them. I cause
the sin of the parents to affect their
children, grandchildren and great-
grandchildren.' 19LORD, your love is
great. So forgive the sin of these people.
Forgive them just as you have done
from the time they left Egypt until now."
20The LORD replied, "I have forgiven
them, just as you asked. 21You can be sure
that I live. You can be just as sure that my
glory fills the whole earth. 22And here is
what you can be just as sure of. Not one of
these people will see the land I promised
to give them. They have seen my glory.
They have seen the signs I did in Egypt.
And they have seen what I did in the
desert. But they did not obey me. And
they have tested me ten times. 23So not
even one of them will ever see the land I
promised to give to their people of long
ago. The person who has not respected
me will never see it. 24But my servant
Caleb has a different spirit. He follows me
with his whole heart. So I will bring him
into the land he went to. And his children
after him will receive land there. 25The
Amalekites and the Canaanites are living
in the valleys. So turn back tomorrow.
Start out toward the desert. Go along the
way that leads to the Red Sea."
26The LORD said to Moses and Aaron,
27"How long will this evil community
speak against me? I have heard these
Israelites talk about how unhappy they
are. 28So tell them, 'Here is what I am
announcing. I am the LORD. You can be
sure that I live. And here is what you can
be just as sure of. I will do to you the very
thing that I heard you say. 29You will die
in this desert. Every one of you 20 years
old or more will die. Every one of you who
was counted in the list of the people will
die. Every one of you who has spoken out
against me will be wiped out. 30I lifted up
my hand and promised to make this land
your home. But now not all of you will
enter the land. Caleb, the son of Jephunneh, will enter it. So will Joshua, the son
of Nun. They are the only ones who will
enter the land. 31You have said that your
enemies would capture your children. But
I will bring your children in to enjoy the
land you have turned your backs on. 32As
for you, you will die in the desert. 33Your
children will be shepherds here for 40
years. They will suffer because you were
not faithful. They will suffer until the last
of your bodies lies here in the desert. 34For
40 years you will suffer for your sins. That

is one year for each of the 40 days you checked out the land. You will know what it is like to have me against you.' 35 I, the LORD, have spoken. I will surely do these things to this entire evil community of Israel. They have joined together against me. They will meet their end in this desert. They will die here."

36 So the LORD struck down the men Moses had sent to check out the land. They had returned and had spread a bad report about the land. And that had made the whole community speak out against Moses. 37 Those men were to blame for spreading the bad report. So the LORD struck them down. They died of a plague. 38 Only two of the men who went to check out the land remained alive. One of them was Joshua, the son of Nun. The other was Caleb, the son of Jephunneh.

39 Moses reported to all the Israelites what the LORD had said. And they became very sad. 40 Early the next morning they set out for the highest point in the hill country. "We have sinned," they said. "Now we are ready to go up to the land the LORD promised to give us."

41 But Moses said, "Why aren't you obeying the LORD's command? You won't succeed. 42 So don't go up. The LORD isn't with you. Your enemies will win the battle over you. 43 The Amalekites and the Canaanites will meet you on the field of battle. You have turned away from the LORD. So he won't be with you. And you will be killed by swords."

44 But they wouldn't listen. They still went up toward the highest point in the hill country. They went up even though Moses didn't move from the camp. They went even though the ark of the LORD's covenant didn't move from the camp. 45 Then the Amalekites and the Canaanites who lived in that hill country came down. They attacked the Israelites. They won the battle over them. They chased the Israelites all the way to Hormah.

Other Offerings

15 Here is what the LORD said to Moses. 2 "Say to the Israelites, 'You are going to enter the land I am giving you as a home. 3 When you do, you will present food offerings to the LORD. The animals must come from your herd or flock. The smell of the offerings will please the LORD. They can be either burnt offerings or sacrifices. They can be either for special promises or for feast offerings. Or they can be for offerings you choose to give. 4 With each of the offerings, the person who brings it must present to the LORD a grain offering. It must be eight cups of the finest flour. It must be mixed with a quart of olive oil. 5 Also prepare a quart of wine as a drink offering. You must present it with each lamb that you bring for the burnt offering or the sacrifice.

6 " 'Prepare a grain offering to present along with a ram. The grain offering must be 16 cups of the finest flour. It must be mixed with two and a half pints of olive oil. 7 You must bring two and a half pints of wine as a drink offering. Offer everything as a smell that pleases the LORD.

8 " 'Suppose you prepare a young bull as a burnt offering or sacrifice. You prepare it to keep a special promise to the LORD. Or you prepare it to present as a friendship offering. 9 Then bring a grain offering with the bull. The grain offering must be 24 cups of the finest flour. It must be mixed with two quarts of olive oil. 10 Also bring two quarts of wine as a drink offering. It will be a food offering. Its smell will please the LORD. 11 Each bull or ram must be prepared in the same way. Each lamb or young goat must also be prepared in that way. 12 Do it for each animal. Do it for as many animals as you prepare.

13 " 'Everyone in Israel must do those things in that way. He must do them when he presents a food offering. The smell of offerings like that pleases the LORD. 14 Everyone must always do what the law requires. It does not matter whether they are an outsider or anyone else living among you. They must do exactly as you do when they present a food offering. The smell of offerings like that pleases the LORD. 15 The community must have the same rules for you and for any outsider living among you. This law will last for all time to come. In the sight of the LORD, the law applies both to you and any outsider. 16 The same laws and rules will apply to you and to any outsider living among you.' "

17 The LORD said to Moses, 18 "Speak to the Israelites. Say to them, 'You are going to enter the land I am taking you to. 19 You will eat its food. When you do, present part of it as an offering to the LORD. 20 Present a loaf made from the

first flour you grind. Present it as an offering from the threshing floor. 21 You
must present the offering to the LORD. You
must present it from the first grain you
grind. You must do it for all time to come.

Offerings for Sins That Aren't Committed on Purpose

22 " 'Suppose you as a community fail
to keep any of the commands the LORD
gave Moses. And suppose you do it without meaning to. 23 That applies to any of
the commands the LORD told Moses to
give you. And they are in effect from the
day the LORD gave them and for all time
to come. 24 Suppose the community sins
without meaning to. And suppose they
do not know they have sinned. Then the
whole community must offer a young
bull. They must sacrifice it for a burnt
offering. Its smell will please the LORD.
Along with it, they must offer its required
grain offering and drink offering. They
must also sacrifice a male goat for a sin
offering. 25 With it the priest will pay for
the sin of the whole community of Israel.
Then they will be forgiven. They did not
mean to commit that sin. And they have
presented to the LORD a food offering
for the wrong thing they did. They have
brought a sin offering with it. 26 The LORD
will forgive the whole community of
Israel and the outsiders living among
them. All the people had a part in the sin,
even though they did not mean to do it.

27 " 'But suppose just one person sins
without meaning to. Then that person
must bring a female goat for a sin offering. It must be a year old. 28 With it
the priest will pay for the person's sin
in front of the LORD. The priest will do
it for the one who did wrong by sinning
without meaning to. When the sin is
paid for, that person will be forgiven.
29 The same law applies to everyone
who sins without meaning to. It does
not matter whether they are an Israelite
or an outsider.

30 " 'But suppose someone sins on
purpose. It does not matter whether
they are an Israelite or an outsider.
They speak evil things against the
LORD. They must be separated from the
community of Israel. 31 They have not
respected what the LORD has said. They
have broken the LORD's commands.
They must certainly be separated from
the community. They are still guilty.' "

A Man Works on the Sabbath Day

32 The Israelites were in the desert.
One Sabbath day, people saw a man
gathering wood. 33 They brought him
to Moses and Aaron and the whole
community. 34 They kept him under
guard. It wasn't clear what should be
done to him. 35 Then the LORD said to
Moses, "The man must die. The whole
community must kill him by throwing
stones at him. They must do it outside
the camp." 36 So the people took the man
outside the camp. There they killed him
by throwing stones at him. They did just
as the LORD had commanded Moses.

Tassels on Clothes

37 The LORD said to Moses, 38 "Say to
the Israelites, 'You must make tassels
on the corners of your clothes. A blue
cord must be on each tassel. You must
do it for all time to come. 39 You will have
the tassels to look at. They will remind
you to obey all the LORD's commands.
Then you will be faithful to him. You
will not chase after what your own
hearts and eyes wish for. 40 You will
remember to obey all my commands.
And you will be set apart for your God.
41 I am the LORD your God. I brought
you out of Egypt to be your God. I am
the LORD your God.' "

Korah, Dathan and Abiram

16 Korah was the son of Izhar, the son
of Kohath. Kohath was the son of
Levi. Korah and certain men from the
tribe of Reuben turned against Moses. The
men from Reuben were Dathan, Abiram
and On. Dathan and Abiram were the
sons of Eliab. On was the son of Peleth.
2 All those men rose up against Moses.
And 250 men of Israel joined them. All
of them were known as leaders in the
community. They had been appointed
as members of the ruling body. 3 They
came as a group to oppose Moses and
Aaron. They said to Moses and Aaron,
"You have gone too far! The whole community is holy. Every one in it is holy.
And the LORD is with them. So why do you
put yourselves above the LORD's people?"

4 When Moses heard what they said,
he fell with his face to the ground. 5 Then
he spoke to Korah and all his followers.

He said, "In the morning the LORD will show who belongs to him. He will show who is holy. He'll bring that person near him. He'll bring the man he chooses near him. 6 Korah, here's what you and all your followers must do. Get some shallow cups for burning incense. 7 Tomorrow put burning coals and incense in them. Offer it to the LORD. The man the LORD chooses will be the one who is holy. You Levites have gone too far!"

8 Moses also said to Korah, "Listen, you Levites! 9 The God of Israel has separated you from the rest of the community of Israel. He has brought you near him to work at the LORD's holy tent. He has given you to the people so that you can serve them. Isn't all that enough for you? 10 He has already brought you and all the other Levites near him. But now you want to be priests too. 11 You and all your followers have joined together against the LORD. Why are you telling Aaron you aren't happy with him?"

12 Then Moses sent for Dathan and Abiram, the sons of Eliab. But they said, "We won't come! 13 You have brought us up out of a land that has plenty of milk and honey. You have brought us here to kill us in this desert. Isn't that enough? Now do you also want to act as if you were ruling over us? 14 Besides, you haven't brought us into a land that has plenty of milk and honey. You haven't given us fields and vineyards of our own. Do you want to treat these men like slaves? No! We won't come!"

15 Then Moses became very angry. He said to the LORD, "Don't accept their offering. I haven't taken even a donkey from them. In fact, I haven't done anything wrong to any of them."

16 Moses said to Korah, "You and all your followers must stand in front of the LORD tomorrow. You must appear there along with Aaron. 17 Each man must get his shallow cup. He must put incense in it. There will be a total of 250 incense cups. Each man must bring his cup to the LORD. You and Aaron must also bring your cups." 18 So each of them got his cup. He put burning coals and incense in it. All the men came with Moses and Aaron. They stood at the entrance to the tent of meeting. 19 Korah gathered all his followers together at the entrance to the tent. They opposed Moses and Aaron. Then the glory of the LORD appeared to the whole community. 20 The LORD said to Moses and Aaron, 21 "Separate yourselves from these people. Then I can put an end to all of them at once."

22 But Moses and Aaron fell with their faces to the ground. They cried out, "God, you are the God who gives life and breath to all living things. Will you be angry with the whole community when only one man sins?"

23 Then the LORD spoke to Moses. He said, 24 "Tell the community, 'Move away from the tents of Korah, Dathan and Abiram.' "

25 Moses got up. He went to Dathan and Abiram. The elders of Israel followed him. 26 Moses warned the community. He said, "Move away from the tents of these evil men! Don't touch anything that belongs to them. If you do, the LORD will sweep you away because of all their sins." 27 So they moved away from the tents of Korah, Dathan and Abiram. Dathan and Abiram had already come out. They were standing at the entrances to their tents. Their wives, children and little ones were standing there with them.

28 Then Moses said, "What is about to happen wasn't my idea. The LORD has sent me to do everything I'm doing. Here is how you will know I'm telling you the truth. 29 These men won't die a natural death. Something will happen to them that doesn't usually happen to people. If what I'm telling you doesn't happen, then you will know that the LORD hasn't sent me. 30 But the LORD will make something totally new happen. The ground will open its mouth and swallow them up. It will swallow up everything that belongs to them. They will be buried alive. When that happens, you will know that these men have disrespected the LORD."

31 As soon as Moses finished saying all these words, what he had said came true. The ground under them broke open. 32 It opened its mouth. It swallowed up those men. In fact, it swallowed up everyone who lived in their houses. It swallowed all Korah's men. And it swallowed up everything they owned. 33 They went down into the grave alive. Everything they owned went down with them. The ground closed over them and they died. And so they disappeared from the

community. 34 All the Israelites around them heard their cries. They ran away from them. They shouted, "The ground is going to swallow us up too!"

35 Then the LORD sent down fire. It burned up the 250 men offering the incense.

36 The LORD said to Moses, 37 "Speak to Eleazar the priest. He is the son of Aaron. Remind him that the shallow cups are holy. He must take them out of the ashes. He must scatter the burning coals away from there. 38 The men who sinned used those cups. And it cost them their lives. Hammer the cups into bronze sheets that will cover the altar. The cups were offered to the LORD. They have become holy. Let them serve as a warning to the Israelites."

39 So the priest Eleazar collected the bronze incense cups. They had been brought by the men who had been burned to death. He had them hammered out to cover the altar. 40 He did just as the LORD had directed Moses to tell him to do. The covering would be a reminder to the Israelites. It would remind them that no one except a son of Aaron should come and burn incense to the LORD. If people other than priests did that, they would become like Korah and his followers.

41 The next day the whole community of Israel told Moses and Aaron they weren't happy with them. "You have killed the LORD's people," they said.

42 The community gathered together to oppose Moses and Aaron. The people walked toward the tent of meeting. Suddenly the cloud covered it. The glory of the LORD appeared. 43 Then Moses and Aaron went to the front of the tent of meeting. 44 The LORD said to Moses, 45 "Get away from these people. Then I can put an end to all of them at once." And Moses and Aaron fell with their faces to the ground.

46 Moses said to Aaron, "Take your incense cup. Put incense in it. And put burning coals from the altar in it. Then hurry to the people and pay for their sin. The LORD has begun to show his anger. The plague has started." 47 So Aaron did as Moses said. He ran in among the people. The plague had already started among them. But Aaron offered the incense and paid for their sin. 48 He stood between those alive and those dead. And the plague stopped. 49 But 14,700 people died from the plague. That doesn't include those who had died because of what Korah did. 50 Then Aaron returned to Moses at the entrance to the tent of meeting. The plague had stopped.

Aaron's Walking Stick Produces Buds

17 The LORD said to Moses, 2 "Speak to the Israelites. Get 12 walking sticks from them. Get one from the leader of each of Israel's tribes. Write the name of each man on his walking stick. 3 Write Aaron's name on Levi's walking stick. There must be one stick for the head of each of Israel's tribes. 4 Put the walking sticks in the tent of meeting. Place them in front of the ark where the tablets of the covenant law are kept. That is where I meet with you. 5 The walking stick that belongs to the man I choose will begin to grow new shoots. The Israelites are never happy with what you do. I will put an end to what they are saying."

6 So Moses spoke to the Israelites. Their leaders gave him 12 walking sticks. They gave one for the leader of each of Israel's tribes. Aaron's walking stick was among them. 7 Moses put the sticks in front of the LORD in the tent where the tablets of the covenant law were kept.

8 The next day Moses entered the tent. He looked at Aaron's walking stick. It stood for the tribe of Levi. Moses saw that it had begun to grow new shoots. It had also produced buds and flowers and almonds. 9 Then Moses brought out all the walking sticks from in front of the LORD. He brought them to all the Israelites. They looked at them. And each man took his own walking stick.

10 The LORD said to Moses, "Put Aaron's walking stick back in front of the ark where the tablets of the covenant law are kept. The stick will be kept there as a warning to those who refuse to obey. They are never happy with what I do. Aaron's walking stick will put an end to what they are saying. Then they will not die." 11 Moses did just as the LORD commanded him.

12 The Israelites said to Moses, "We'll die! We are lost! All of us are lost! 13 Anyone who even comes near the LORD's holy tent will die. Are all of us going to die?"

Duties of Priests and Levites

18 The LORD spoke to Aaron. He said, "You, your sons and your family are in charge of the sacred tent. You will be responsible for sins connected with the tent. And you and your sons alone will be responsible for sins connected with the office of priest. 2 Bring the Levites from your tribe to join you. They will help you when you and your sons serve at the tent of meeting. That is where the tablets of the covenant law are kept. 3 The Levites will work for you. They must do everything that needs to be done at the tent. But they must not go near anything that belongs to the sacred tent. And they must not go near the altar. If they do, they and you will die. 4 They will help you take care of the tent of meeting. They will join you in all the work at the tent. No one else can come near you there.

5 "You will be responsible for taking care of the sacred tent and the altar. Then I will not be angry with the Israelites again. 6 I myself have chosen the Levites. I have chosen them from among the Israelites. They are a gift to you. I have set them apart to do the work at the tent of meeting. 7 But only you and your sons can serve as priests. Only you and your sons can work with everything at the altar and behind the curtain. I am letting you serve as priests. It is a gift from me. Anyone else who comes near the sacred tent must be put to death."

Offerings for Priests and Levites

8 Then the LORD spoke to Aaron. He said, "I have put you in charge of the offerings brought to me. The Israelites will give me holy offerings. I will give all their offerings to you and your sons. They are the part that belongs to you. They are your share for all time to come. 9 You will have a part of the very holy offerings. It is the part not burned in the fire. That part belongs to you and your sons. You will have a part of all the gifts the people bring me as very holy offerings. It does not matter whether they are grain offerings or sin offerings or guilt offerings. 10 Eat your part as something that is very holy. Every male will eat it. You must consider it holy.

11 "Part of the gifts the Israelites bring as wave offerings will be set aside. That part will also belong to you. I will give it to you and your sons and daughters. It is your share for all time to come. Everyone in your home who is 'clean' can eat it.

12 "I will give you all the finest olive oil and grain the people give me. And I will give you all the finest fresh wine they give me. They give all those things as the first share of their harvest. 13 All the first shares of the harvest they bring me will belong to you. Everyone in your home who is 'clean' can eat it.

14 "Everything in Israel that is set apart to me belongs to you. 15 Offer to me every male born first to its mother. It belongs to you. That includes humans and animals alike. But you must buy back every oldest son. Suppose certain animals are 'unclean.' Then you must buy back every male born first to its mother. 16 When they are a month old, you must buy them back. You must pay the price to buy them back. The price is set at two ounces of silver. It must be weighed out according to the standard weights used in the sacred tent.

17 "But you must not buy back any male calf, sheep or goat born first. They are holy. Splash their blood against the altar. And burn their fat as a food offering. Its smell pleases me. 18 The meat will belong to you. It is just like the breast and the right thigh of the wave offering. Those parts belong to you. 19 Part of the holy offerings the Israelites bring to me will be set aside. No matter what it is, I will give it to you and your sons and daughters. It is your share for all time to come. It is a covenant of salt from me. The salt means that the covenant will last for all time to come for you and your children."

20 The LORD spoke to Aaron. He said, "You will not receive any part of the land I am giving to Israel. You will not have any share among them. I am your share. I am what you will receive among the Israelites.

21 "The Israelites will give me a tenth of everything they produce. And I will give it to the Levites. They serve at the tent of meeting. I will give them the tenth for the work they do there. 22 From now on the Israelites must not go near the tent of meeting. If they do, they will be punished for their sin. They will die. 23 The Levites will do the work at the tent of meeting. They will be responsible for

any sins connected with the tent. This is a law that will last for all time to come. The Levites will not receive any share among the Israelites. 24 Instead, I will give the Levites the tenth as their share. It is the tenth that the Israelites bring me as an offering. That is why I said the Levites would not have any share of land among the Israelites."

25 The LORD said to Moses, 26 "Speak to the Levites. Say to them, 'You will receive the tenth from the Israelites. I will give it to you as your share. When I do, you must give a tenth of that tenth as an offering to the LORD. 27 Your offering will be considered as if you gave grain from a threshing floor. It will be considered as juice from a winepress. 28 In that way, you also will bring an offering to the LORD. You will bring it from the tenth you receive from the Israelites. You must give the LORD's part to the priest Aaron. You must bring it from the tenth you receive. 29 You must bring to the LORD a part of everything given to you. It must be the best and holiest part.'

30 "Say to the Levites, 'You must bring the best part. Then it will be considered as if you gave grain from a threshing floor. It will be considered as juice from a winepress. 31 You and your families can eat the rest of it anywhere. It is your pay for your work at the tent of meeting. 32 Bring the best part of what you receive. Then you will not be guilty of holding anything back. You will not make the holy offerings of the Israelites "unclean." You will not die.' "

The Special Water That Makes People "Clean"

19 The LORD spoke to Moses and Aaron. He said, 2 "Here is what the law I have commanded requires. Tell the Israelites to bring you a young red cow. It must not have any flaws at all. It must never have pulled a load. 3 Give it to Eleazar the priest. It must be taken outside the camp and killed in front of him. 4 Then Eleazar the priest must put some of its blood on his finger. He must sprinkle the blood toward the front of the tent of meeting. He must do it seven times. 5 While he watches, the young cow must be burned. Its hide, meat, blood and guts must be burned. 6 The priest must get some cedar wood, branches of a hyssop plant, and bright red wool. He must throw them on the young cow as it burns. 7 After that, the priest must wash his clothes. He must also take a bath. Then he can come into the camp. But he will be 'unclean' until evening. 8 The man who burns the young cow must wash his clothes. He must also take a bath. He too will be 'unclean' until evening.

9 "A man who is 'clean' will gather up the ashes of the young cow. He must put them in a place that is 'clean.' The place must be outside the camp. The ashes must be kept by the community of Israel. They will be added to the special water. The water will be used to make people pure from their sin. 10 The man who gathers up the ashes of the young cow must wash his clothes. He too will be 'unclean' until evening. This law is for the Israelites. It is also for the outsiders living among them. The law will last for all time to come.

11 "Anyone who touches a dead person's body will be 'unclean' for seven days. 12 They must make themselves pure and 'clean' with the special water. They must do it on the third day. They must also do it on the seventh day. Then they will be 'clean.' But suppose they do not make themselves pure and 'clean' on the third and seventh days. Then they will not be 'clean.' 13 Anyone who touches a dead person's body and does not make themselves pure and 'clean' makes my holy tent 'unclean.' They must be separated from Israel. The special water has not been sprinkled on them. So they are 'unclean.' And they remain 'unclean.'

14 "Here is the law that applies when a person dies in a tent. Anyone who enters the tent will be 'unclean' for seven days. Anyone in the tent will also be 'unclean' for seven days. 15 And anything in it that is open and has no lid will be 'unclean.'

16 "Suppose someone is out in the country. And suppose they touch someone who has been killed by a sword. Or they touch someone who has died a natural death. Or they touch a human bone or a grave. Then anyone who touches any of those things will be 'unclean' for seven days.

17 "Here is what I want you to do for someone who is 'unclean.' Put some ashes from the burned young cow into

a jar. Pour fresh water on the ashes. 18 Then a man who is 'clean' must dip branches of a hyssop plant in the water. He must sprinkle the tent with it. Everything that belongs to the tent must be sprinkled with it. The people in the tent must also be sprinkled. Anyone who has touched a human bone or a grave must be sprinkled. So must anyone who has touched someone who has been killed. And so must anyone who has touched someone who has died a natural death. 19 The man who is 'clean' must sprinkle those who are 'unclean.' That must be done on the third and seventh days. On the seventh day those who are 'unclean' must be made pure and 'clean.' Those being made 'clean' must wash their clothes. They must take a bath. Then that evening they will be 'clean.' 20 But what if those who are 'unclean' do not make themselves pure and 'clean?' Then they must be separated from the community. They have made my holy tent 'unclean.' The special water has not been sprinkled on them. They are 'unclean.' 21 This law will apply to all those people for all time to come.

"The man who sprinkles the special water must also wash his clothes. Anyone who touches the water will be 'unclean' until evening. 22 Anything that an 'unclean' person touches becomes 'unclean.' And anyone who touches it becomes 'unclean' until evening."

The Lord Gives Israel Water Out of the Rock

20 In the first month the whole community of Israel arrived at the Desert of Zin. They stayed at Kadesh. Miriam died and was buried there.

2 The people didn't have any water. So they gathered together to oppose Moses and Aaron. 3 They argued with Moses. They said, "We wish we had died when our people fell dead in front of the Lord. 4 Why did you bring the Lord's people into this desert? We and our livestock will die here. 5 Why did you bring us up out of Egypt? Why did you bring us to this terrible place? It doesn't have any grain or figs. It doesn't have any grapes or pomegranates. There isn't even any water for us to drink!"

6 Moses and Aaron left the people. They went to the entrance to the tent of meeting. There they fell with their faces to the ground. Then the glory of the Lord appeared to them. 7 The Lord said to Moses, 8 "Get your walking stick. You and your brother Aaron gather the people together. Then speak to that rock while everyone is watching. It will pour out its water. You will bring water out of the rock for the community. Then they and their livestock can drink it."

9 So Moses took the walking stick from the tent. He did just as the Lord had commanded him. 10 He and Aaron gathered the people together in front of the rock. Moses said to them, "Listen, you who refuse to obey! Do we have to bring water out of this rock for you?" 11 Then Moses raised his arm. He hit the rock twice with his walking stick. Water poured out. And the people and their livestock drank it.

12 But the Lord spoke to Moses and Aaron. He said, "You did not trust in me enough to honor me. You did not honor me as the holy God in front of the Israelites. So you will not bring this community into the land I am giving them."

13 Those were the waters of Meribah. That's where the Israelites argued with the Lord. And that's where he was proven to be holy among them.

Edom Doesn't Let Israel Pass Through Its Territory

14 Moses sent messengers from Kadesh to the king of Edom. The messengers said,

> "The nation of Israel is your brother. They say, 'You know about all the hard times we've had. 15 Long ago our people went down into Egypt. We lived there for many years. The Egyptians treated us and our people badly. 16 But we cried out to the Lord. He heard our cry. He sent an angel and brought us out of Egypt.
>
> " 'Now here we are at the town of Kadesh. It's on the edge of your territory. 17 Please let us pass through your country. We won't go through any field or vineyard. We won't drink water from any well. We'll travel along the King's Highway. We won't turn to the right or the left. We'll just go straight through your territory.' "

[18] But the people of Edom answered,

"We won't let you pass through here. If you try to, we'll march out against you. We'll attack you with our swords."

[19] The Israelites replied,

"We'll go along the main road. We and our livestock won't drink any of your water. If we do, we'll pay for it. We only want to walk through your country. That's all we ask."

[20] Again the people of Edom answered,

"We won't let you pass through here."

Then the people of Edom marched out
against them. They came with a large
and powerful army. [21] Edom refused to
let Israel go through their territory. So
Israel turned away from them.

Aaron Dies

[22] The whole community of Israel
started out from Kadesh. They arrived
at Mount Hor. [23] It was near the border
of Edom. There the LORD spoke to Moses
and Aaron. He said, [24] "Aaron will join the
members of his family who have already
died. He will not enter the land I am giving to the Israelites. Both of you refused
to obey my command. You did it at the
waters of Meribah. [25] So get Aaron and
his son Eleazar. Take them up Mount Hor.
[26] Take Aaron's official robes off of him.
Put them on his son Eleazar. Aaron will
die on Mount Hor. He will join the members of his family who have already died."
[27] Moses did just as the LORD had commanded. The three men went up Mount
Hor while the whole community was
watching. [28] Moses took Aaron's official
robes off of him. He put them on Aaron's
son Eleazar. And Aaron died there on
top of the mountain. Then Moses and
Eleazar came down from the mountain.
[29] The whole community found out that
Aaron had died. So all the Israelites
mourned for him for 30 days.

Israel Destroys Arad

21 The Canaanite king of the city of
Arad lived in the Negev Desert.
He heard that Israel was coming along
the road to Atharim. So he attacked the

Israelites. He captured some of them.
2 Then Israel made a promise to the
LORD. They said, "Hand these people
over to us. If you do, we will set their
cities apart to you in a special way to
be destroyed." 3 The LORD gave Israel
what they asked for. He handed the
Canaanites over to them. Israel completely destroyed them and their towns.
So that place was named Hormah.

Moses Makes a Bronze Snake

4 The Israelites traveled from Mount Hor
along the way to the Red Sea. They wanted
to go around Edom. But they grew tired on
the way. 5 So they spoke against God and
against Moses. They said, "Why have you
brought us up out of Egypt? Do you want
us to die here in the desert? We don't have
any bread! We don't have any water! And
we hate this awful food!"
6 Then the LORD sent poisonous
snakes among the Israelites. The snakes
bit them. Many of the people died. 7 The
others came to Moses. They said, "We
sinned when we spoke against the LORD
and against you. Pray that the LORD
will take the snakes away from us." So
Moses prayed for the people.
8 The LORD said to Moses, "Make a
snake. Put it up on a pole. Then anyone
who is bitten can look at it and remain
alive." 9 So Moses made a bronze snake.
He put it up on a pole. Then anyone who
was bitten by a snake and looked at the
bronze snake remained alive.

The People Continue On to Moab

10 The Israelites moved on. They
camped at Oboth. 11 Then they started
out from Oboth. They camped in Iye
Abarim. It's in the desert on the eastern border of Moab. 12 From there they
moved on. They camped in the Zered
Valley. 13 They started out from there
and camped by the Arnon River. It's in
the desert that spreads out into the territory of the Amorites. The Arnon is the
border of Moab. It's between Moab and
the Amorites. 14 Here is what the Book
of the Wars of the LORD says about it.

"Sing about Zahab in Suphah and
the valleys.
Sing about the Arnon 15 and the
slopes of the valleys.

pointing us to JESUS: The Bronze Snake

After God's people, the Israelites, had been set free from slavery in Egypt, they were free to worship God. He cared for them in the wilderness and made a way for them to escape Pharaoh's army by miraculously parting the Red Sea. But the Israelites were forgetful people. They disobeyed God's commands and forgot his promises time and time again. When they disobeyed, they experienced earthly consequences for their sin.

One time, when God's people were walking in disobedience, they experienced a severe consequence: Poisonous snakes visited their camp and bit many of the people. This consequence made them afraid! How would they recover?

Just when things looked the very worst, God provided a way for them to be healed. He told Moses to make a snake and lift it up on a pole. God promised that anyone who was bitten could look at the bronze snake and be healed (see Numbers 21:8–9).

This event pointed God's people toward Jesus, who would be hung on a pole made of wood—what we know as the cross. Jesus hung on the cross as the final and ultimate payment for our sins. He promises that all who look to him for salvation will be saved!

They lead to the settlement
called Ar.
They lie along the border of Moab."
16 From there the Israelites continued
on to Beer. That was the well where the
LORD spoke to Moses. He said, "Gather
the people together. I will give them
water to drink."
17 Then Israel sang a song. They said,

"Spring up, you well!
Sing about it.
18 Sing about the well the princes dug.
Sing about the well the nobles of
the people dug.
All their rulers were holding their
scepters and walking sticks."

Then the Israelites went from the desert
to Mattanah. 19 They went from Mattanah to Nahaliel. They went from
Nahaliel to Bamoth. 20 And they went
from Bamoth to a valley in Moab. It's
the valley where the highest slopes of
Pisgah look out over a dry and empty
land.

Israel Wins the Battle Over Sihon and Og

21 The Israelites sent messengers to
speak to Sihon. He was the king of the
Amorites. The messengers said to him,

22 "Let us pass through your
country. We won't go off the road
into any field or vineyard. We won't
drink water from any well. We'll
travel along the King's Highway.
We'll just go straight through your
territory."

23 But Sihon wouldn't let Israel pass
through his territory. He gathered his
whole army together. Then he marched
out into the desert against Israel. When
he reached Jahaz, he fought against
Israel. 24 But Israel put him to death
with their swords. They took over his
land. They took everything from the
Arnon River to the Jabbok River. But
they didn't take over any of the land
of the Ammonites. That's because the
Ammonites had built strong forts along
their border. 25 The Israelites captured
all the cities of the Amorites. Then they
settled down in them. They captured the
city of Heshbon. They also captured all
the settlements around it. 26 Sihon, the
king of the Amorites, ruled in Heshbon.
He had fought against an earlier king
of Moab. Sihon had taken from him all
his land all the way to the Arnon River.
27 That's why the poets say,

"Come to Heshbon. Let it be built
again.
Let Sihon's city be made as good
as new.
28 "Fire went out from Heshbon.
A blaze went out from the city of
Sihon.
It burned up Ar in Moab.
It burned up the citizens who
lived on Arnon's hills.
29 Moab, how terrible it is for you!
People of Chemosh, you are
destroyed!
Chemosh has deserted his sons and
daughters.
His sons have run away from the
battle.
His daughters have become
prisoners.
He has handed all of them over
to Sihon,
the king of the Amorites.

30 "But we have taken them over.
Heshbon's rule has been
destroyed all the way to Dibon.
We have destroyed them as far as
Nophah.
Nophah goes all the way to
Medeba."

31 So Israel settled in the land of the
Amorites.
32 Moses sent spies to the city of Jazer.
The Israelites captured the settlements
around it. They drove out the Amorites
who were there. 33 Then they turned and
went up along the road toward Bashan.
Og was the king of Bashan. He and his
whole army marched out. They went to
fight against Israel at Edrei.
34 The LORD said to Moses, "Do not be
afraid of Og. I have handed him over to
you. I have given you his whole army. I
have also given you his land. Do to him
what you did to Sihon, the king of the
Amorites. He ruled in Heshbon."
35 So the Israelites struck down Og and
his sons. And they wiped out his whole
army. They didn't leave anyone alive.
They took over his land for themselves.

Balak Sends For Balaam

22 Then the Israelites traveled to the plains of Moab. They camped along the Jordan River across from Jericho.

2 Balak saw everything that Israel had done to the Amorites. Balak was the son of Zippor. 3 The Moabites were terrified because there were so many Israelites. In fact, the Moabites were filled with panic because of the Israelites.

4 The Moabites spoke to the elders of Midian. They said, "This huge mob is going to destroy everything around us. They'll lick it up as an ox licks up all the grass in the fields."

Balak, the son of Zippor, was the king of Moab at that time. 5 He sent messengers to get Balaam. Balaam was the son of Beor. Balaam was at the city of Pethor near the Euphrates River. Pethor was in the land where Balaam had been born. Balak told the messengers to say to Balaam,

> "A nation has come out of Egypt. They are covering the face of the land. They've set up camp next to me. 6 So come and put a curse on these people. They are too powerful for me. Maybe I'll be able to win the battle over them. Maybe I'll be able to drive them out of the land. I know that whoever you bless is blessed. And I know that whoever you curse is cursed."

7 The elders of Moab and Midian left. They took with them the money they knew Balaam would ask for. They wanted him to use evil magic to figure things out for them. They came to where Balaam was. And they told him what Balak had said.

8 "Spend the night here," Balaam said to them. "I'll report back to you with the answer the LORD gives me." So the Moabite officials stayed with him.

9 God came to Balaam. He asked, "Who are these men with you?"

10 Balaam said to God, "Balak king of Moab, the son of Zippor, sent me a message. 11 He said, 'A nation has come out of Egypt. They are covering the whole surface of the land. So come and put a curse on them for me. Maybe I'll be able to fight them. Maybe I'll be able to drive them away.' "

12 But God said to Balaam, "Do not go with them. You must not put a curse on those people. I have blessed them."

NEVER-FAILING

MY GOD IS...

God will never fail us. If God says he will do something, he does it. If God makes a promise, he keeps it. Sometimes people forget what they said or break a promise, but God never will, which means his Word is also trustworthy. Even though we may feel disappointed because things don't turn out the way we hoped they would, we can open God's Word, the Bible, and find everlasting hope because God's Word never fails (see Isaiah 55:10–11).

Can you find a promise God made in the Bible? (Hint: See Genesis 9:11.) Even though we might think God is taking too long or has forgotten what he said, we must remember that he is faithful to his Word. God's never-failing character assures us that he will do *all* that he has promised.

13 The next morning Balaam got up.
He said to Balak's officials, "Go back to
your own country. The LORD won't let
me go with you."
14 So the Moabite officials returned
to Balak. They said, "Balaam wouldn't
come with us."
15 Then Balak sent other officials.
They were more important than the
first ones. And there were more of them.
16 They came to Balaam. They said,

> "Balak, the son of Zippor, says,
> 'Don't let anything keep you from
> coming to me. 17 I'll make you very
> rich. I'll do anything you say. So
> come and put a curse on those
> people for me.'"

18 But Balaam gave them his answer.
He said, "Balak could give me all the silver
and gold in his palace. Even then, I still
couldn't do anything at all that goes beyond what the LORD my God commands.
19 Now spend the night here so that I can
find out what else the LORD will tell me."
20 That night God came to Balaam.
He said, "These men have come to get
you. So go with them. But do only what
I tell you to do."

Balaam's Donkey

21 Balaam got up in the morning. He
put a saddle on his donkey. Then he went
with the Moabite officials. 22 But God
was very angry when Balaam went. So
the angel of the LORD stood in the road
to oppose him. Balaam was riding on
his donkey. His two servants were with
him. 23 The donkey saw the angel of the
LORD standing in the road. The angel
was holding a sword. He was ready for
battle. So the donkey left the road and
went into a field. Balaam hit the donkey.
He wanted to get it back on the road.
24 Then the angel of the LORD stood in
a narrow path. The path went through
the vineyards. There were walls on both
sides. 25 The donkey saw the angel of the
LORD. So it moved close to the wall. It
crushed Balaam's foot against the wall.
So he hit the donkey again.
26 Then the angel of the LORD moved
on ahead. He stood in a narrow place.
There was no room to turn, either right
or left. 27 The donkey saw the angel of
the LORD. So it lay down under Balaam.
That made him angry. He hit the donkey
with his walking stick. 28 Then the LORD
opened the donkey's mouth. It said to
Balaam, "What have I done to you? Why
did you hit me these three times?"
29 Balaam answered the donkey. He
said, "You have made me look foolish!
I wish I had a sword in my hand. If I
did, I'd kill you right now."
30 The donkey said to Balaam, "I'm
your own donkey. I'm the one you have
always ridden. Haven't you been riding
me to this very day? Have I ever made
you look foolish before?"
"No," he said.
31 Then the LORD opened Balaam's
eyes. He saw the angel of the LORD
standing in the road. He saw that the
angel was holding a sword. The angel
was ready for battle. So Balaam bowed
down. He fell with his face to the ground.
32 The angel of the LORD spoke to him.
He asked him, "Why have you hit your
donkey three times? I have come here
to oppose you. What you are doing is
foolish. 33 The donkey saw me. It turned
away from me three times. Suppose
it had not turned away. Then I would
certainly have killed you by now. But I
would have spared the donkey."
34 Balaam said to the angel of the
LORD, "I have sinned. I didn't realize you
were standing in the road to oppose me.
Tell me whether you are pleased with
me. If you aren't, I'll go back."
35 The angel of the LORD said to Balaam, "Go with the men. But say only
what I tell you to say." So Balaam went
with Balak's officials.
36 Balak heard that Balaam was coming. So he went out to meet him. They
met at a Moabite town near the Arnon
River. The town was on the border of
Balak's territory. 37 Balak said to Balaam,
"Didn't I send messengers to you? I wanted you to come quickly. So why didn't
you come? I can make you very rich."
38 "Well, I've come to you now," Balaam replied. "But I can't say whatever
I please. I can only speak the words God
puts in my mouth."
39 Then Balaam went with Balak to
Kiriath Huzoth. 40 Balak sacrificed cattle
and sheep. He gave some to Balaam. He
also gave some to the officials with him.
41 The next morning Balak took Balaam
up to Bamoth Baal. From there he could
see the outer edges of the Israelite camp.

Balaam's First Message From God

23 Balaam said to Balak, "Build
me seven altars here. Prepare
seven bulls and seven rams for me to
sacrifice." 2 Balak did just as Balaam
said. The two of them offered a bull and
a ram on each altar.

3 Then Balaam said to Balak, "Stay
here beside your offering. I'll go and try
to find out what the LORD wants me to
do. Maybe he'll come and meet with me.
Then I'll tell you what he says to me."
So Balaam went off to a bare hilltop.

4 God met with him there. Balaam
said, "I've prepared seven altars. On
each altar I've offered a bull and a ram."

5 The LORD put a message in Balaam's
mouth. The LORD said, "Go back to Balak. Give him my message."

6 So Balaam went back to him. He
found Balak standing beside his offering. All the Moabite officials were with
him. 7 Then Balaam spoke the message
he had received from God. He said,

"Balak brought me from the land
of Aram.
The king of Moab sent for me
from the mountains in the east.
'Come,' he said. 'Put a curse on
Jacob's people for me.
Come. Speak against Israel.'
8 But how can I put a curse on
people God hasn't cursed?
How can I speak against
people the LORD hasn't spoken
against?
9 I see them from the rocky peaks.
I view them from the hills.
I see a group of people who live by
themselves.
They don't consider themselves
to be one of the nations.
10 Jacob's people are like the dust of
the earth.
Can dust be counted?
Who can count even a fourth of
the Israelites?
Let me die as godly people die.
Let my death be like theirs!"

11 Balak said to Balaam, "What have
you done to me? I brought you here
to put a curse on my enemies! But all
you have done is give them a blessing!"

12 He answered, "I have to speak only
the words the LORD puts in my mouth."

Balaam's Second Message From God

13 Then Balak said to Balaam, "Come
with me to another place. You can see
the Israelites from there. You won't see
all of them. You will only see the outer
edges of their camp. From there, put a
curse on them for me." 14 So Balak took
Balaam to the field of Zophim. It was
on the highest slopes of Pisgah. There
Balak built seven altars. He offered a
bull and a ram on each altar.

15 Balaam said to Balak, "Stay here
beside your offering. I'll meet with the
LORD over there."

16 The LORD met with Balaam. He put
a message in Balaam's mouth. The LORD
said, "Go back to Balak. Give him my
message."

17 So Balaam went to Balak. He found
him standing beside his offering. The
Moabite officials were with him. Balak
asked him, "What did the LORD say?"

18 Then Balaam spoke the message he
had received from God. He said,

"Balak, rise up and listen.
Son of Zippor, hear me.
19 God isn't a mere human. He can't lie.
He isn't a human being. He
doesn't change his mind.
He speaks, and then he acts.
He makes a promise, and then he
keeps it.

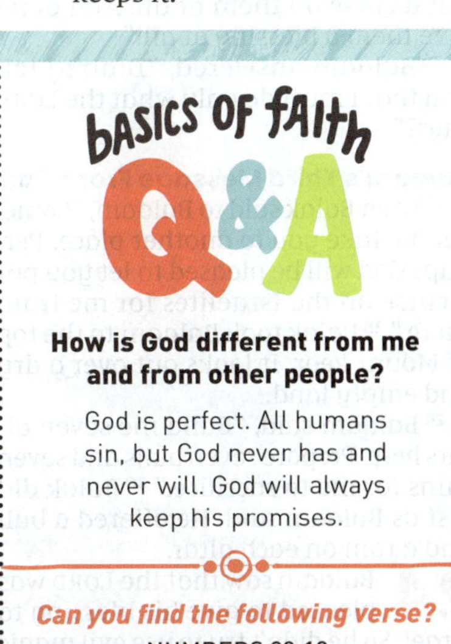

How is God different from me and from other people?

God is perfect. All humans sin, but God never has and never will. God will always keep his promises.

Can you find the following verse?

NUMBERS 23:19

20 He has commanded me to bless
Israel.
He has given them his blessing.
And I can't change it.

21 "I don't see any trouble coming on
the people of Jacob.
I don't see any suffering in Israel.
The LORD their God is with them.
The shout of the King is among
them.
22 God brought them out of Egypt.
They are as strong as a wild ox.
23 There isn't any magic that can hurt
the people of Jacob.
No one can use magic words to
harm Israel.
Here is what will be said about the
people of Jacob.
Here is what will be said about
Israel.
People will say, 'See what God
has done!'
24 The Israelites are going to wake up
like a female lion.
They are going to get up like a
male lion.
They are like a lion that won't rest
until it eats what it has caught.
They are like a lion that won't rest
until it drinks the blood of what
it has killed."

25 Then Balak said to Balaam, "Don't
put a curse on them at all! And don't
give them a blessing at all!"
26 Balaam answered, "Didn't I tell
you that I must do only what the LORD
says?"

Balaam's Third Message From God

27 Then Balak said to Balaam, "Come.
Let me take you to another place. Perhaps God will be pleased to let you put
a curse on the Israelites for me from
there." 28 Balak took Balaam to the top
of Mount Peor. It looks out over a dry
and empty land.
29 Balaam said, "Build me seven altars here. Prepare seven bulls and seven
rams for me to sacrifice." 30 Balak did
just as Balaam said. He offered a bull
and a ram on each altar.

24 Balaam saw that the LORD was
pleased to give his blessing to
Israel. So he didn't try to use evil magic
as he had done at other times. Instead,
he turned and looked toward the desert.
2 He looked out and saw Israel. They had
set up their camps tribe by tribe. The
Spirit of God came on him. 3 Balaam
spoke the message he had received from
God. He said,

"Here is the message God gave
Balaam, the son of Beor.
It's the message God gave to the
one who sees clearly.
4 It's the message God gave to the one
who hears the words of God.
He sees a vision from the Mighty
One.
He falls down flat with his face
toward the ground.
His eyes have been opened by
the LORD.

5 "People of Jacob, your tents are
very beautiful.
Israel, the places where you live
are very beautiful.

6 "They spread out like valleys.
They are like gardens beside a
river.
They are like aloes the LORD has
planted.
They are like cedar trees beside a
stream.
7 Their water buckets will run over.
Their seeds will have plenty of
water.

"Their king will be greater than
King Agag.
Their kingdom will be honored.

8 "God brought them out of Egypt.
They are as strong as a wild ox.
They destroy nations at war with
them.
They break their bones in pieces.
They wound them with their
arrows.
9 Like a male lion they lie down and
sleep.
They are like a female lion.
Who dares to wake them up?

"May those who bless you be blessed!
May those who curse you be
cursed!"

10 Then Balak became very angry with
Balaam. He slapped his hands together.
He said to Balaam, "I sent for you to put
a curse on my enemies. But you have
given them a blessing three times. 11 Get
out of here right away! Go home! I said

I'd make you very rich. But the LORD has kept you from getting rich."

12 Balaam answered Balak, "Here is
what I told the messengers you sent
me. 13 I said, 'Balak could give me all
the silver and gold in his palace. Even if I wanted to, I still couldn't do anything at all that goes beyond what the LORD commands. I must say only what the
LORD tells me to say.' 14 Now I'm going
back to my people. But come. Let me warn you about what these people will do to your people in days to come."

Balaam's Fourth Message From God

15 Then Balaam spoke the message he
had received from God. He said,

"Here is the message God gave
Balaam, the son of Beor.
It's the message God gave to the
one who sees clearly.
16 It's the message God gave to the one
who hears the words of God.
The Most High God has given him
knowledge.
He sees a vision from the Mighty One.
He falls down flat with his face
toward the ground.
His eyes have been opened by
the LORD.

17 "I see him, but I don't see him now.
I view him, but he isn't near.
A star will come from among the
people of Jacob.
A king will rise up out of Israel.
He'll crush the foreheads of the
people of Moab.
He'll crush the heads of all the
people of Sheth.
18 He'll win the battle over Edom.
He'll win the battle over his
enemy Seir.
But Israel will grow strong.
19 A ruler will come from among the
people of Jacob.
He'll destroy those from the city
who are still alive."

Balaam's Fifth Message From God

20 Then Balaam saw the Amalekites.
He spoke the message he had received from God. He said,

"Amalek was the first nation to
attack Israel.
But their end will be total
destruction."

Balaam's Sixth Message From God

21 Then Balaam saw the Kenites. He
spoke the message he had received from God. He said,

"The place where you live is safe.
Your nest is on a high cliff.
22 But you Kenites will be destroyed.
Ashur will take you as prisoners."

Balaam's Seventh Message From God

23 Then Balaam spoke the message he
had received from God. He said,

"Who can live when God does this?
24 Ships will come from the shores
of Cyprus.
They will bring Ashur and Eber
under their control.
But they themselves will also be
destroyed."

25 Then Balaam got up and returned
home. And Balak went on his way.

Moab Leads Israel Astray

25 Israel was staying in Shittim. The men of Israel began to commit sexual sins with the women
of Moab. 2 The women invited the men
to feasts and sacrifices to honor their gods. The people ate the sacrifices and bowed down in front of the statues of
those gods. 3 So Israel joined in worshiping the god named Baal that was worshiped at Peor. The LORD became very angry with Israel.

4 The LORD said to Moses, "Take all the
leaders of these people. Kill them. Put their dead bodies out in the open. I want to see you do it in the middle of the day. Then I will not be angry with Israel."

5 So Moses spoke to Israel's judges. He
said, "Some of your people have joined in worshiping the god named Baal that is worshiped at Peor. Each of you must kill the people in your tribe who have done that."

6 Then an Israelite man brought into
the camp a Midianite woman. He did it right in front of the eyes of Moses and the whole community of Israel. They were weeping at the entrance to the tent
of meeting. 7 Phinehas was a priest. He
was the son of Eleazar, the son of Aaron. When Phinehas saw what had happened, he left the people. He took a spear in his
hand. 8 He followed the man into the

tent. Phinehas stuck the spear through the man and into the woman's stomach. Then the LORD stopped the plague against the Israelites. 9 But the plague had already killed 24,000 of them.

10 The LORD said to Moses, 11 "Phinehas is a priest. He is the son of Eleazar, the son of Aaron. Phinehas has turned my anger away from the Israelites. I am committed to making sure I am honored among them. And he is as committed as I am. So even though I was angry with them, I did not put an end to them. 12 So tell Phinehas I am making my covenant with him. It is my promise to give him peace. 13 He and his sons after him will have a covenant to be priests forever. That is because he was committed to making sure that I, his God, was honored. In that way he paid for the sin of the Israelites."

14 The name of the Israelite man who was killed was Zimri. He was the son of Salu. Zimri was killed along with the Midianite woman. Salu was a family leader in the tribe of Simeon. 15 The name of the Midianite woman who was killed was Kozbi. She was the daughter of Zur. He was the chief of a Midianite family.

16 The LORD spoke to Moses. He said, 17 "Treat the Midianites just as you would treat enemies. Kill them. 18 After all, they treated you like enemies. They tricked you into worshiping the god named Baal that is worshiped at Peor. They also tricked you because of what Kozbi did. She was the woman killed when the plague came that was connected with Peor. Kozbi was the daughter of a Midianite leader."

The Men of Israel Are Counted a Second Time

26 After the plague, the LORD spoke to Moses and Eleazar the priest. Eleazar was the son of Aaron. The LORD said, 2 "Count all the men of Israel. Make a list of them by their families. Count all the men who are able to serve in Israel's army. They must be 20 years old or more." 3 At that time the Israelites were on the plains of Moab. They were by the Jordan River across from Jericho. Moses and Eleazar the priest spoke with them. They said, 4 "Count all the men 20 years old or more. Do it just as the LORD commanded Moses."

Here are the men of Israel who came out of Egypt.

5 Reuben was Israel's oldest son.
Here are the names of his sons.
The Hanokite family came from Hanok.
The Palluite family came from Pallu.
6 The Hezronite family came from Hezron.
The Karmite family came from Karmi.
7 These were the families of Reuben.
The number of men was 43,730.

8 Eliab was the son of Pallu. 9 Eliab's sons were Nemuel, Dathan and Abiram. Dathan and Abiram were the same community officials who refused to obey Moses and Aaron. They were among the followers of Korah who refused to obey the LORD. 10 The ground opened its mouth. It swallowed them up along with Korah. The followers of Korah died when fire burned up 250 men. Their deaths were a warning to the rest of Israel. 11 But the family line of Korah didn't die out completely.

12 Here are the names of Simeon's sons. They are listed by their families.
The Nemuelite family came from Nemuel.
The Jaminite family came from Jamin.
The Jakinite family came from Jakin.
13 The Zerahite family came from Zerah.
The Shaulite family came from Shaul.
14 These were the families of Simeon.
The number of the men counted was 22,200.

15 Here are the names of Gad's sons.
They are listed by their families.
The Zephonite family came from Zephon.
The Haggite family came from Haggi.
The Shunite family came from Shuni.
16 The Oznite family came from Ozni.
The Erite family came from Eri.

[17] The Arodite family came from Arodi.
The Arelite family came from Areli.
[18] These were the families of Gad. The number of the men counted was 40,500.
[19] Er and Onan were sons of Judah. But they died in Canaan.
[20] Here are the names of Judah's sons. They are listed by their families.
The Shelanite family came from Shelah.
The Perezite family came from Perez.
The Zerahite family came from Zerah.
[21] Here are the names of the sons of Perez.
The Hezronite family came from Hezron.
The Hamulite family came from Hamul.
[22] These were the families of Judah. The number of the men counted was 76,500.

[23] Here are the names of Issachar's sons. They are listed by their families.
The Tolaite family came from Tola.
The Puite family came from Puah.
[24] The Jashubite family came from Jashub.
The Shimronite family came from Shimron.
[25] These were the families of Issachar. The number of the men counted was 64,300.

[26] Here are the names of Zebulun's sons. They are listed by their families.
The Seredite family came from Sered.
The Elonite family came from Elon.
The Jahleelite family came from Jahleel.
[27] These were the families of Zebulun. The number of the men counted was 60,500.

[28] Here are the names of Joseph's sons. They are listed by their families. The families came from Manasseh and Ephraim, the sons of Joseph.
[29] Here are the names of Manasseh's sons.
The Makirite family came from Makir. Makir was the father of Gilead.
The Gileadite family came from Gilead.
[30] Here are the names of Gilead's sons.
The Iezerite family came from Iezer.
The Helekite family came from Helek.
[31] The Asrielite family came from Asriel.
The Shechemite family came from Shechem.
[32] The Shemidaite family came from Shemida.
The Hepherite family came from Hepher.
[33] Zelophehad was the son of Hepher. Zelophehad didn't have any sons. All he had was daughters. Their names were Mahlah, Noah, Hoglah, Milkah and Tirzah.
[34] These were the families of Manasseh. The number of the men counted was 52,700.
[35] Here are the names of Ephraim's sons. They are listed by their families.
The Shuthelahite family came from Shuthelah.
The Bekerite family came from Beker.
The Tahanite family came from Tahan.
[36] The sons of Shuthelah were the Eranite family. They came from Eran.
[37] These were the families of Ephraim. The number of the men counted was 32,500.
These were the sons of Joseph. They are listed by their families.

[38] Here are the names of Benjamin's sons. They are listed by their families.
The Belaite family came from Bela.
The Ashbelite family came from Ashbel.

The Ahiramite family came from Ahiram.
39 The Shuphamite family came from Shupham.
The Huphamite family came from Hupham.
40 Bela's sons came from Ard and Naaman.
The Ardite family came from Ard.
The Naamite family came from Naaman.
41 These were the families of Benjamin. The number of the men counted was 45,600.

42 Here is the name of Dan's son. He is listed by his family.
The Shuhamite family came from Shuham.
This was the family of Dan. 43 All
the men in Dan's family were Shuhamites. The number of the men counted was 64,400.

44 Here are the names of Asher's sons. They are listed by their families.
The Imnite family came from Imnah.
The Ishvite family came from Ishvi.
The Beriite family came from Beriah.
45 Here are the names of the families that came from Beriah's sons.
The Heberite family came from Heber.
The Malkielite family came from Malkiel.
46 Asher also had a daughter named Serah.
47 These were the families of Asher. The number of the men counted was 53,400.

48 Here are the names of Naphtali's sons. They are listed by their families.
The Jahzeelite family came from Jahzeel.
The Gunite family came from Guni.
49 The Jezerite family came from Jezer.
The Shillemite family came from Shillem.
50 These were the families of Naphtali. The number of the men counted was 45,400.

51 The total number of the men of Israel was 601,730.

52 The LORD said to Moses, 53 "I will
give the land to them. The amount of
land each family receives will be based
on the number of its men. 54 Give a
larger share to a larger family. Give a
smaller share to a smaller family. Each
family will receive its share based on
the number of men listed in it.
55 "Be sure that you cast lots when
you give out the land. What each family
receives will be based on the number of
men listed in its tribe. 56 Cast lots when
you give out each share. Cast lots for
the larger and smaller families alike."

57 Here are the names of the Levites. They are listed by their families.
The Gershonite family came from Gershon.
The Kohathite family came from Kohath.
The Merarite family came from Merari.
58 Here are the names of the other Levite families. They are
the Libnite family,
the Hebronite family,
the Mahlite family,
the Mushite family,
the Korahite family.
Amram came from the Kohathite
family. 59 The name of Amram's
wife was Jochebed. She was from
the family line of Levi. She was
born to the Levites in Egypt.
Aaron, Moses and their sister
Miriam were born in the family
line of Amram and Jochebed.
60 Aaron was the father of Nadab
and Abihu. He was also the
father of Eleazar and Ithamar.
61 But Nadab and Abihu made an
offering to the LORD by using fire
that wasn't allowed. So they died.

62 The number of male Levites a month old or more was 23,000. They weren't listed along with the other men of Israel. That's because they didn't receive a share among them.

63 These are the men counted by Moses and Eleazar the priest. At that time the

Israelites were on the plains of Moab. They were by the Jordan River across from Jericho. 64 The men of Israel had been counted before in the Sinai Desert by Moses and Aaron the priest. But not one of them was among the men counted this time. 65 The LORD had told the Israelites at Kadesh Barnea that they would certainly die in the desert. Not one of them was left alive except Caleb and Joshua. Caleb was the son of Jephunneh, and Joshua was the son of Nun.

Zelophehad's Daughters

27 The daughters of Zelophehad belonged to the family groups of Manasseh. Zelophehad was the son of Hepher. Hepher was the son of Gilead. Gilead was the son of Makir. Makir was the son of Manasseh. And Manasseh was the son of Joseph. The names of Zelophehad's daughters were Mahlah, Noah, Hoglah, Milkah and Tirzah. They approached 2 the entrance to the tent of meeting. There they stood in front of Moses and Eleazar the priest. The leaders and the whole community were there too. Zelophehad's daughters said, 3 "Our father died in the Sinai Desert. But he wasn't one of the men who followed Korah. He wasn't one of those who joined together against the LORD. Our father died because of his own sin. He didn't leave any sons. 4 Why should our father's name disappear from his family just because he didn't have a son? Give us property among our father's relatives."

5 So Moses brought their case to the LORD. 6 The LORD said to him, 7 "What Zelophehad's daughters are saying is right. You must certainly give them property. Give them a share among their father's relatives. Give their father's property to them.

8 "Say to the Israelites, 'Suppose a man dies who doesn't have a son. Then give his property to his daughter. 9 Suppose the man doesn't have a daughter. Then give his property to his brothers. 10 Suppose the man doesn't have any brothers. Then give his property to his father's brothers. 11 Suppose his father doesn't have any brothers. Then give his property to the nearest male relative in his family group. It will belong to him. That is what the law will require of the Israelites. It is just as the LORD commanded me.' "

Joshua Becomes Israel's New Leader

12 Then the LORD said to Moses, "Go up this mountain in the Abarim Range. See the land I have given the Israelites. 13 After you have seen it, you too will join the members of your family who have already died. You will die, just as your brother Aaron did. 14 The community refused to obey me at the waters of Meribah Kadesh in the Desert of Zin. At that time, you and Aaron did not obey my command. You did not honor me in front of them as the holy God."

15 Moses spoke to the LORD. He said, 16 "LORD, you are the God who gives life and breath to all living things. Please put someone in charge of this community. 17 Have that person lead them and take care of them. Then your people won't be like sheep without a shepherd."

18 So the LORD said to Moses, "Joshua, the son of Nun, has the ability to be a wise leader. Get him and place your hand on him. 19 Have him stand in front of Eleazar the priest and the whole community. Put him in charge while everyone is watching. 20 Give him some of your authority. Then the whole community of Israel will obey him. 21 Joshua will stand in front of Eleazar the priest. Eleazar will help him make decisions. Eleazar will get help from me by using the Urim. Joshua and the whole community of Israel must not make any move at all unless I command them to."

22 Moses did just as the LORD commanded him. He got Joshua and had him stand in front of Eleazar the priest and the whole community. 23 Then Moses placed his hands on Joshua. And he put him in charge of the people. He did just as the LORD had directed through Moses.

Offerings That Israel Must Bring Each Day

28 The LORD said to Moses, 2 "Here is a command I want you to give the Israelites. Tell them, 'Make sure to present to me my food offerings. Do it at the appointed time. Their smell will please me.' 3 Tell them, 'Here is the food offering you must present to the LORD. Present to him two lambs a year old. They must not have any flaws. Present them as a regular burnt offering each day. 4 Offer one lamb in the morning. Offer the other when the sun goes down.

5 Present a grain offering along with them. It must have eight cups of the finest flour. Mix it with a quart of oil made from pressed olives. 6 It is the regular burnt offering. The LORD established it at Mount Sinai. It has a pleasant smell. It is a food offering presented to the LORD. 7 Along with that, offer a quart of wine as a drink offering. It must be given along with each lamb. Pour out the drink offering to the LORD at the sacred tent. 8 Offer the second lamb when the sun goes down. Sacrifice it along with the same kind of grain offering and drink offering that you present in the morning. It is a food offering. Its smell pleases the LORD.

Offerings That Israel Must Bring on the Sabbath Day

9 " 'On the Sabbath day, make an offering of two lambs. They must be a year old. They must not have any flaws. Sacrifice them along with their drink offering. Sacrifice them along with a grain offering of 16 cups of the finest flour. Mix it with olive oil. 10 It is the burnt offering for every Sabbath day. It is in addition to the regular burnt offering and its drink offering.

Offerings That Israel Must Bring Every Month

11 " 'On the first day of every month, bring to the LORD a burnt offering. Bring two young bulls and one ram. Also bring seven male lambs a year old. They must not have any flaws. 12 Present a grain offering along with each bull. It must have 24 cups of the finest flour. Mix it with olive oil. Present a grain offering along with the ram. It must have 16 cups of the finest flour. Mix it with oil. 13 Present a grain offering along with each lamb. It must have eight cups of the finest flour. Mix it with oil. It is for a burnt offering. It has a pleasant smell. It is a food offering presented to the LORD. 14 Present a drink offering along with each bull. It must have two quarts of wine. Offer two and a half pints along with the ram. And offer one quart along with each lamb. It is the burnt offering for each month. It must be made on the day of each New Moon feast during the year. 15 One male goat must be sacrificed to the LORD as a sin offering. It is in addition to the regular burnt offering and its drink offering.

The Passover Feast

16 " 'The LORD's Passover Feast must be held on the 14th day of the first month. 17 On the 15th day of the month there must be a feast. For seven days eat bread made without yeast. 18 On the first day come together for a special service. Do not do any regular work. 19 Present to the LORD a food offering. Present a burnt offering of two young bulls and one ram. Also present seven male lambs a year old. They must not have any flaws. 20 Present a grain offering along with each bull. The offering must have 24 cups of the finest flour. Mix it with olive oil. Offer 16 cups along with the ram. 21 Offer eight cups along with each of the seven lambs. 22 Include a male goat as a sin offering. It will pay for your sin. 23 Offer everything in addition to the regular morning burnt offering. 24 Present the food offering every day for seven days. The smell of the offering will please the LORD. You must present the offering in addition to the regular burnt offering and its drink offering. 25 On the seventh day come together for a special service. Do not do any regular work.

The Feast of Weeks

26 " 'On the day you gather the first share of your crops, present to the LORD an offering of your first grain. Do it during the Feast of Weeks. Come together for a special service. Do not do any regular work. 27 Sacrifice a burnt offering of two young bulls and one ram. Also sacrifice seven male lambs a year old. The smell of the offering will please the LORD. 28 Present a grain offering along with each bull. It must have 24 cups of the finest flour. Mix it with olive oil. Offer 16 cups along with the ram. 29 Offer eight cups along with each of the seven lambs. 30 Include a male goat to pay for your sin. 31 Present everything along with the drink offerings. Do it in addition to the regular burnt offering and its grain offering. Be sure the animals do not have any flaws.

The Feast of Trumpets

29 " 'On the first day of the seventh month, come together for a special service. Do not do any regular work. Blow the trumpets on that day. 2 Sacrifice a burnt offering. Its smell will please the LORD. Sacrifice one young bull and one

ram. Also sacrifice seven male lambs a
year old. They must not have any flaws.
3 Present a grain offering along with the
bull. It must have 24 cups of the finest
flour. Mix it with olive oil. Offer 16 cups
along with the ram. 4 Offer eight cups
along with each of the seven lambs.
5 Include a male goat as a sin offering.
It will pay for your sin. 6 Each month
and each day you must sacrifice burnt
offerings. Sacrifice them along with their
grain offerings and drink offerings as
they are required. The offerings for the
Feast of Trumpets are in addition to the
monthly and daily burnt offerings. They
are food offerings presented to the LORD.
They have a pleasant smell.

The Day When Sin Is Paid For

7 " 'On the tenth day of the seventh
month, come together for a special
service. You must not eat anything on
that day. You must not do any work on
it. 8 Sacrifice a burnt offering. Its smell
will please the LORD. Sacrifice one young
bull and one ram. Also sacrifice seven
male lambs a year old. They must not
have any flaws. 9 Present a grain offering
along with the bull. The offering must
have 24 cups of the finest flour. Mix it
with olive oil. Offer 16 cups along with
the ram. 10 Offer eight cups along with
each of the seven lambs. 11 Include a male
goat as a sin offering. It is in addition
to the offering that pays for sin. It is in
addition to the regular burnt offering
along with its grain offering. It is also in
addition to their drink offerings.

The Feast of Booths

12 " 'On the 15th day of the seventh
month, come together for a special service. Do not do any regular work. Celebrate the Feast of Booths for seven days to
honor the LORD. 13 Present a food offering.
Its smell will please the LORD. Sacrifice
a burnt offering of 13 young bulls and
two rams. Also sacrifice 14 male lambs a
year old. They must not have any flaws.
14 Present a grain offering along with each
of the 13 bulls. It must have 24 cups of the
finest flour. Mix it with olive oil. Offer 16
cups along with each of the two rams.
15 Offer eight cups along with each of the
14 lambs. 16 Include a male goat as a sin
offering. It is in addition to the regular
burnt offering. It is also in addition to its
grain offering and drink offering.

17 " 'On the second day sacrifice 12
young bulls and two rams. Also sacrifice
14 male lambs a year old. They must not
have any flaws. 18 Present their grain
offerings and drink offerings. Present
them along with the bulls, rams and
lambs. Present them according to the
required number. 19 Include a male goat
as a sin offering. It is in addition to the
regular burnt offering along with its
grain offering. It is also in addition to
their drink offerings.

20 " 'On the third day sacrifice 11 bulls
and two rams. Also sacrifice 14 male
lambs a year old. They must not have
any flaws. 21 Present their grain offerings and drink offerings. Present them
along with the bulls, rams and lambs.
Present them according to the required
number. 22 Include a male goat as a sin
offering. It is in addition to the regular
burnt offering. It is also in addition to
its grain offering and drink offering.

23 " 'On the fourth day sacrifice ten
bulls and two rams. Also sacrifice 14 male
lambs a year old. They must not have
any flaws. 24 Present their grain offerings
and drink offerings. Present them along
with the bulls, rams and lambs. Present
them according to the required number.
25 Include a male goat as a sin offering.
It is in addition to the regular burnt offering. It is also in addition to its grain
offering and drink offering.

26 " 'On the fifth day sacrifice nine bulls
and two rams. Also sacrifice 14 male
lambs a year old. They must not have
any flaws. 27 Present their grain offerings
and drink offerings. Present them along
with the bulls, rams and lambs. Present
them according to the required number.
28 Include a male goat as a sin offering.
It is in addition to the regular burnt offering. It is also in addition to its grain
offering and drink offering.

29 " 'On the sixth day sacrifice eight
bulls and two rams. Also sacrifice 14 male
lambs a year old. They must not have
any flaws. 30 Present their grain offerings
and drink offerings. Present them along
with the bulls, rams and lambs. Present
them according to the required number.
31 Include a male goat as a sin offering.
It is in addition to the regular burnt offering. It is also in addition to its grain
offering and drink offering.

32 " 'On the seventh day sacrifice seven bulls and two rams. Also sacrifice 14 male lambs a year old. They must not have any flaws. 33 Present their grain offerings and drink offerings. Present them along with the bulls, rams and lambs. Present them according to the required number. 34 Include a male goat as a sin offering. It is in addition to the regular burnt offering. It is also in addition to its grain offering and drink offering.

35 " 'On the eighth day come together for a closing sacred service. Do not do any regular work. 36 Present a food offering. Its smell will please the LORD. Sacrifice a burnt offering of one bull and one ram. Also sacrifice seven male lambs a year old. They must not have any flaws. 37 Present their grain offerings and drink offerings. Present them along with the bull, the ram and the lambs. Present them according to the required number. 38 Include a male goat as a sin offering. It is in addition to the regular burnt offering. It is also in addition to its grain offering and drink offering.

39 " 'Here are the offerings you must present to the LORD at your appointed feasts. They are burnt offerings, grain offerings, drink offerings and friendship offerings. They are in addition to the offerings you bring to keep a special promise you make to the LORD. They are also in addition to the offerings you choose to give.' "

40 Moses told the Israelites everything the LORD had commanded him.

Special Promises

30 Moses spoke to the heads of the tribes of Israel. He said, "Here is what the LORD commands. 2 Suppose a man makes a special promise to the LORD. Or suppose he gives his word to do something. Then he must keep his promise. He must do everything he said he would do.

3 "Suppose a young woman is still living in her father's house. She makes a special promise to the LORD. Or she gives her word to do something. 4 Suppose her father hears about her promise. And he doesn't say anything to her about it. Then she must keep her promise. She must do what she agreed to do. 5 But suppose her father doesn't allow her to keep her promises when he hears about them. Then she doesn't have to do what she promised or agreed to do. The LORD will set her free. He'll do it because her father hasn't allowed her to keep her promises.

6 "Suppose she gets married after she makes a special promise. Or she gets married after agreeing to do something without thinking it through. 7 Suppose her husband hears about what she did. And he doesn't say anything to her about it. Then she must keep her promise. She must do what she agreed to do. 8 But suppose her husband doesn't allow her to keep her promises when he hears about them. Then she doesn't have to do what she promised. She doesn't have to do what she agreed to do without thinking it through. The LORD will set her free.

9 "Suppose a widow makes a special promise. Or suppose she gives her word to do something. Then she must keep her promise. She must do what she agreed to do. The same rules apply to a woman who has been divorced.

10 "Suppose a woman living with her husband makes a special promise. Or she gives her word to do something. 11 Suppose her husband hears about what she did. He doesn't say anything to her about it. And he doesn't try to stop her from keeping her promises. Then she must keep all of them. She must do what she agreed to do. 12 But suppose her husband doesn't allow her to keep her promises when he hears about them. Then she doesn't have to do what she promised. She doesn't have to do what she agreed to do. Her husband has kept her from doing what she said she would do. The LORD will set her free. 13 Her husband can let her keep any special promise she makes. Or he can refuse to let her keep it. Suppose she gives her word not to eat anything. Then her husband can let her keep her promise. Or he can refuse to let her keep it. 14 But suppose day after day her husband doesn't say anything to her about what she did. Then he lets her keep all her promises. He lets her do everything she agreed to do. That's because he didn't say anything to her when he heard about what she had done. 15 But suppose some time after he hears about her promises he doesn't let her

keep them. Then she will be guilty. But he will bear the consequences for her guilt."

16 These are the rules the LORD gave Moses about a man and his wife. And these are the rules the LORD gave about a father and his young daughter still living at home.

The LORD Punishes the Midianites

31 The LORD spoke to Moses. He said, 2 "Pay the Midianites back for what they did to the Israelites. After that, you will join the members of your family who have already died."

3 So Moses said to the people, "Prepare some of your men for battle. They must go to war against Midian. They will carry out the LORD's plan to punish Midian. 4 Send 1,000 men from each of the tribes of Israel into battle." 5 So Moses prepared 12,000 men for battle. There were 1,000 from each tribe. They came from the families of Israel. 6 Moses sent them into battle. He sent 1,000 from each tribe. Phinehas the priest went along with them. Phinehas was the son of Eleazar. Phinehas took some things from the sacred tent with him. He also took the trumpets. The trumpet blasts would tell the people what to do and when to do it.

7 They fought against Midian, just as the LORD had commanded Moses. They killed every man. 8 Evi, Rekem, Zur, Hur and Reba were among the men they killed. Those men were the five kings of Midian. The Israelites also killed Balaam with their swords. Balaam was the son of Beor. 9 The Israelites captured the Midianite women and children. They took for themselves all the herds, flocks and goods. 10 They burned down all the towns where the Midianites lived. They also burned all their camps. 11 They carried off everything they had taken. That included the people and the animals. 12 They brought back to Israel's camp the prisoners and everything else they had taken. They took them to Moses and to Eleazar the priest. They brought them to the whole community. Israel was camped on the plains of Moab. They were by the Jordan River across from Jericho.

13 Moses and Eleazar the priest went to meet them outside the camp. So did all the leaders of the community. 14 Moses was angry with the officers of the army who had returned from the battle. Some of them were the commanders of thousands of men. Others were the commanders of hundreds.

15 "Have you let all the women remain alive?" Moses asked them. 16 "The women followed Balaam's advice. They caused the Israelites to be unfaithful to the LORD. The people worshiped the god named Baal that was worshiped at Peor. So a plague struck them. 17 Kill all the boys. And kill every woman who has slept with a man. 18 But save for yourselves every woman who has never slept with a man.

19 "Anyone who has killed a person must stay outside the camp for seven days. And anyone who has touched a person who was killed must do the same thing. On the third and seventh days you must make yourselves pure. You must also make your prisoners pure. 20 Make all your clothes pure and 'clean.' Everything made out of leather, goat hair or wood must be made pure and 'clean.' "

21 Then Eleazar the priest spoke to the soldiers who had gone into battle. He said, "Here is what the law the LORD gave Moses requires. 22 All your gold, silver, bronze, iron, tin and lead 23 must be put through fire. So must everything else that doesn't burn up. Then those things will be 'clean.' But they must also be made pure with the special water. In fact, everything that won't burn up must be put through that water. 24 On the seventh day wash your clothes. And you will be 'clean.' Then you can come into the camp."

The People Divide Up What They Had Taken

25 The LORD spoke to Moses. He said, 26 "Here is what you and Eleazar the priest and the family leaders of the community must do. You must count all the people and animals you captured. 27 Divide up some of what you took with the soldiers who fought in the battle. Divide up the rest with the others in the community. 28 Set apart a gift for me. Take something from the soldiers who fought in the battle. Set apart one out of every 500 people, cattle, donkeys or sheep. 29 Take my gift from the soldiers' half. Give it to Eleazar the priest. It is my share. 30 Also take something from the half that belongs to the Israelites. Choose one out of every 50 people, cattle,

donkeys, sheep or other animals. Give
them to the Levites. They are responsible
for taking care of my holy tent." 31 So
Moses and Eleazar the priest did just as
the LORD had commanded Moses.
32 What the soldiers took included 675,000 sheep. 33 There were also
72,000 cattle 34 and 61,000 donkeys.
35 And there were 32,000 women who
had never slept with a man.

36 Here is the half that belonged to
those who had fought in the battle.

There were 337,500 sheep. 37 From
among them, the LORD's gift
was 675.
38 There were 36,000 cattle. From
among them, the LORD's gift
was 72.
39 There were 30,500 donkeys. From
among them, the LORD's gift
was 61.
40 There were 16,000 women. From
among them, the LORD's gift
was 32.

41 Moses gave the gift to Eleazar the
priest. It was the LORD's share. Moses did
just as the LORD had commanded him.
42 The other half belonged to the Israelites. Moses set it apart from what
belonged to the fighting men. 43 The
community's half was 337,500 sheep,
44 36,000 cattle, 45 30,500 donkeys 46 and
16,000 women. 47 Moses chose one out of
every 50 people and animals. He gave
them to the Levites. They were accountable for taking care of the LORD's holy
tent. Moses did just as the LORD had
commanded him.
48 Then the army officers went to
Moses. Some of them were the commanders of thousands of men. Others
were the commanders of hundreds.
49 All of them said to Moses, "We have
counted the soldiers under our command. Not a single one is missing. 50 So
we've brought an offering to the LORD.
We've brought the gold each of us took
in the battle. That includes armbands,
bracelets, rings, earrings and necklaces.
We've brought them in front of the LORD
to pay for our sin."
51 Moses and Eleazar the priest accepted the beautiful gold things from
the army officers. 52 The gold received
from the commanders of thousands and
commanders of hundreds weighed 420
pounds. Moses and Eleazar offered all of
it as a gift to the LORD. 53 Each soldier had
taken things from the battle for himself.
54 Moses and Eleazar the priest accepted
the gold from all the commanders. They
brought it into the tent of meeting. It
reminded the LORD of the Israelites.

The Tribes on the East Side of the Jordan River

32 The tribes of Reuben and Gad
had very large herds and flocks.
They looked at the lands of Jazer and
Gilead. They saw that those lands were
just right for livestock. 2 So they came to
Moses and Eleazar the priest. They also
came to the leaders of the community.
They said, 3 "We have seen the cities
of Ataroth, Dibon, Jazer, Nimrah and
Heshbon. We've seen Elealeh, Sebam,
Nebo and Beon. 4 All of them are in the
land the LORD has brought under Israel's control. This land is just right for
livestock. And we have livestock. 5 We
hope you are pleased with us," they continued. "If you are, please give us this
land. Then it will belong to us. But don't
make us go across the Jordan River."
6 Moses spoke to the people of Gad
and Reuben. He said, "Should the rest of
us go to war while you stay here? 7 The
LORD has given the land of Canaan to
the Israelites. So why would you want
to keep them from going over into it?
8 That's what your fathers did. I sent
them from Kadesh Barnea to check out
the land. 9 They went up to the Valley of
Eshkol and looked at the land. Then they
talked the Israelites out of entering the
land the LORD had given them. 10 The
LORD's anger was stirred up that day.
So he made a promise. He said, 11 'Not
one of those who were 20 years old or
more when they came up out of Egypt
will see the land. They have not followed
me with their whole heart. I promised
to give the land to Abraham, Isaac and
Jacob. 12 But not one of the people who
came up out of Egypt will see the land
except Caleb and Joshua. Caleb is the son
of Jephunneh, the Kenizzite. And Joshua is the son of Nun. They will see the
land. They followed the LORD with their
whole heart.' 13 The LORD became very
angry with Israel. He made them wander
around in the desert for 40 years. They

wandered until all the people who had done evil in his sight had died.

14 “Now here you are, you bunch of sinners! You have taken the place of your fathers. And you are making the LORD even angrier with Israel. 15 What if you turn away from following him? Then he'll leave all these people in the desert again. And it will be your fault when they are destroyed.”

16 Then they came up to Moses. They said, “We would like to build pens here for our livestock. We would also like to build cities for our women and children. 17 But we will prepare ourselves for battle. We're even ready to go ahead of the Israelites. We'll march out with them until we've brought them to their place. While we're gone, our women and children will live in cities that have high walls around them. That will keep them safe from the people living in this land. 18 We won't return to our homes until each of the Israelites has received their share of the land. 19 We won't receive any share with them on the west side of the Jordan River. We've already received our share here on the east side.”

20 Then Moses said to them, “Do what you have promised to do. Get ready to fight for the LORD. 21 Prepare yourselves and go across the Jordan River. Fight for the LORD until he has driven out his enemies in front of him. 22 When the land is under the LORD's control, you can come back here. Your duty to the LORD and Israel will be over. Then the LORD will give you this land as your own.

23 “But what if you fail to do your duty? Then you will be sinning against the LORD. And you may be sure that your sin will be discovered. It will be brought out into the open. 24 So build up cities for your women and children. Make sheep pens for your flocks. But do what you have promised to do.”

25 The people of Gad and Reuben spoke to Moses. They said, “We will do just as you command. 26 Our children and wives will remain here in the cities of Gilead. So will our flocks and herds. 27 But we will prepare ourselves for battle. We'll go across the Jordan River and fight for the LORD. We will do just as you have said.”

28 Then Moses gave orders about them to Eleazar the priest. He gave the same orders to Joshua, the son of Nun. He also spoke to the family leaders of the Israelite tribes. 29 He said, “The men of Gad and Reuben must get ready for battle. They must go across the Jordan River with you. They must help you fight for the LORD. They must stay with you until the land has been brought under your control. If they do, you must give them the land of Gilead as their own. 30 But what if they don't get ready for battle? What if they don't go across the Jordan with you? Then they must accept a share with you in Canaan.”

31 The people of Gad and Reuben gave their answer. They said, “We will do what the LORD has said. 32 We'll get ready for battle. We'll go across the Jordan into Canaan. We'll fight for the LORD there. But the property we receive will be on this side of the Jordan River.”

33 Then Moses gave their land to them. He gave it to the tribes of Gad and Reuben and half of the tribe of Manasseh. Manasseh was Joseph's son. One part of that land had belonged to the kingdom of Sihon. He was the king of the Amorites. The other part had belonged to the kingdom of Og. He was the king of Bashan. Moses gave that whole land to those two and a half tribes. It included its cities and the territory around them.

34 The people of Gad built up the cities of Dibon, Ataroth and Aroer. 35 They built up Atroth Shophan, Jazer, Jogbehah, 36 Beth Nimrah and Beth Haran. They built a high wall around each of those cities. They also built sheep pens for their flocks. 37 The people of Reuben built up Heshbon, Elealeh and Kiriathaim. 38 They also built up Nebo, Baal Meon and Sibmah. They gave new names to the cities they had built up.

39 The people of Makir, the son of Manasseh, went to the land of Gilead. They captured it. They drove out the Amorites living there. 40 So Moses gave Gilead to the people of Makir, the son of Manasseh. And they settled there. 41 Jair was from the family line of Manasseh. Jair captured Gilead's settlements. He called them Havvoth Jair. 42 Nobah captured Kenath and the settlements around it. He named it after himself.

The Places Where Israel Camped During Their Journey

33 Here are the places where the
Israelites camped during their
journey. When they came out of Egypt,
they marched in groups like an army.
Moses and Aaron led them. 2 The LORD
commanded Moses to record their journey. Here are the places where they
camped.

3 The Israelites started out from
Rameses on the 15th day of the first
month. It was the day after the Passover Feast. They marched out boldly
in plain sight of all the Egyptians.
4 The Egyptians were burying all
their oldest sons. The LORD had
struck them down. He had done it
when he punished their gods.

5 The Israelites left Rameses and
camped at Sukkoth.

6 They left Sukkoth and camped
at Etham. Etham was on the edge
of the desert.

7 They left Etham and turned
back to Pi Hahiroth. It was east of
Baal Zephon. They camped near
Migdol.

8 They left Pi Hahiroth. Then they
passed through the Red Sea into
the desert. They traveled for three
days in the Desert of Etham. Then
they camped at Marah.

9 They left Marah and went to
Elim. Twelve springs and 70 palm
trees were there. So they camped
at Elim.

10 They left Elim and camped by
the Red Sea.

11 They left the Red Sea and
camped in the Desert of Sin.

12 They left the Desert of Sin and
camped at Dophkah.

13 They left Dophkah and camped
at Alush.

14 They left Alush and camped at
Rephidim. But there was no water
there for the people to drink.

15 They left Rephidim and
camped in the Desert of Sinai.

16 They left the Desert of Sinai
and camped at Kibroth Hattaavah.

17 They left Kibroth Hattaavah
and camped at Hazeroth.

18 They left Hazeroth and camped
at Rithmah.

19 They left Rithmah and camped
at Rimmon Perez.

20 They left Rimmon Perez and
camped at Libnah.

21 They left Libnah and camped
at Rissah.

22 They left Rissah and camped
at Kehelathah.

23 They left Kehelathah and
camped at Mount Shepher.

24 They left Mount Shepher and
camped at Haradah.

25 They left Haradah and camped
at Makheloth.

26 They left Makheloth and
camped at Tahath.

27 They left Tahath and camped
at Terah.

28 They left Terah and camped
at Mithkah.

29 They left Mithkah and camped
at Hashmonah.

30 They left Hashmonah and
camped at Moseroth.

31 They left Moseroth and camped
at Bene Jaakan.

32 They left Bene Jaakan and
camped at Hor Haggidgad.

33 They left Hor Haggidgad and
camped at Jotbathah.

34 They left Jotbathah and
camped at Abronah.

35 They left Abronah and camped
at Ezion Geber.

36 They left Ezion Geber and
camped at Kadesh. Kadesh was in
the Desert of Zin.

37 They left Kadesh and camped
at Mount Hor. It was on the border
of Edom. 38 Aaron the priest went
up Mount Hor when the LORD commanded him to. That's where he
died. It happened on the first day
of the fifth month. It was the 40th
year after the Israelites came out
of Egypt. 39 Aaron was 123 years old
when he died on Mount Hor.

40 The Canaanite king of Arad
lived in the Negev Desert in Canaan. He heard that the Israelites
were coming.

41 They left Mount Hor and
camped at Zalmonah.

42 They left Zalmonah and
camped at Punon.

43 They left Punon and camped
at Oboth.

44 They left Oboth and camped
at Iye Abarim. It was on the border
of Moab.
45 They left Iye Abarim and
camped at Dibon Gad.
46 They left Dibon Gad and
camped at Almon Diblathaim.
47 They left Almon Diblathaim
and camped in the mountains of
Abarim near Nebo.
48 They left the mountains of
Abarim and camped on the plains
of Moab. That area was by the
Jordan River across from Jericho.
49 They camped there along the
Jordan River from Beth Jeshimoth
to Abel Shittim.

50 On the plains of Moab the LORD spoke
to Moses. He spoke to him by the Jordan
River across from Jericho. The LORD said,
51 "Speak to the Israelites. Tell them, 'Go
across the Jordan River into Canaan.
52 Drive out all those living in the land.
The statues of their gods are made out of
stone and metal. Destroy all those statues.
And destroy all the high places where they
are worshiped. 53 Take the land as your
own. Make your homes in it. I have given
it to you. 54 Cast lots when you divide up
the land. Do it based on the number of
people in each tribe and family. Give a
larger share to a larger group. And give a
smaller group a smaller share. The share
they receive by casting lots will belong to
them. Give out the shares based on the
number of people in Israel's tribes.
55 " 'But suppose you do not drive out
the people living in the land. Then those
you allow to remain there will become
like needles in your eyes. They will become like thorns in your sides. They will
give you trouble in the land where you
will live. 56 Then I will do to you what I
plan to do to them.' "

Israel Arrives at the Borders of Canaan

34 The LORD said to Moses,
2 "Give the Israelites a
command. Tell them, 'You are going
to enter Canaan. The land will be
given to you as your own. Here are
the borders it must have.

3 " 'Your southern border will include
part of the Desert of Zin. It will
be along the border of Edom.
Your southern border will start
in the east from the southern
end of the Dead Sea. 4 It will cross
south of Scorpion Pass. It will
continue on to Zin. From there it
will go south of Kadesh Barnea.
Then it will go to Hazar Addar
and over to Azmon. 5 There it
will turn and join the Wadi of
Egypt. It will come to an end at
the Mediterranean Sea.
6 Your western border will be the coast
of the Mediterranean Sea. That
will be your border on the west.
7 For your northern border, run a
line from the Mediterranean Sea
to Mount Hor. 8 Continue it from
Mount Hor to Lebo Hamath.
Then the border will go to Zedad.
9 It will continue to Ziphron. It
will come to an end at Hazar
Enan. That will be your border
on the north.
10 For your eastern border, run a line
from Hazar Enan to Shepham.
11 The border will go down from
Shepham to Riblah. Riblah is on
the east side of Ain. From there
the border will continue along the
slopes east of the Sea of Galilee.
12 Then the border will go down
along the Jordan River. It will
come to an end at the Dead Sea.

" 'That will be your land. And those
will be its borders on every side.' "

13 Moses gave the Israelites a command. He said, "Cast lots when you
divide up the land. Each tribe will have
its own share. The LORD has ordered it
to be given to the nine and a half tribes.
14 The families of the tribes of Reuben
and Gad have already received their
shares. The families of half of the tribe
of Manasseh have also received their
share. 15 Those two and a half tribes
have received their shares east of the
Jordan River. It flows near Jericho. Their
land is toward the sunrise."
16 The LORD spoke to Moses. He said,
17 "Here are the names of the men who
will give out the shares of the land to
your people. They are Eleazar the priest
and Joshua, the son of Nun. 18 Also appoint one leader from each of the nine
and a half tribes. They will help you
give out the land.

19 "Here are their names.

"Caleb, the son of Jephunneh, is from the tribe of Judah.
20 Shemuel, the son of Ammihud, is from the tribe of Simeon.
21 Elidad, the son of Kislon, is from the tribe of Benjamin.
22 Bukki, the son of Jogli, is the leader from the tribe of Dan.
23 Hanniel, the son of Ephod, is the leader from the tribe of Manasseh. Manasseh was the son of Joseph.
24 Kemuel, the son of Shiphtan, is the leader from the tribe of Ephraim. Ephraim was the son of Joseph.
25 Elizaphan, the son of Parnak, is the leader from the tribe of Zebulun.
26 Paltiel, the son of Azzan, is the leader from the tribe of Issachar.
27 Ahihud, the son of Shelomi, is the leader from the tribe of Asher.
28 Pedahel, the son of Ammihud, is the leader from the tribe of Naphtali."

29 These are the men the LORD commanded to give out the shares of the land. They were commanded to give them to Israel in the land of Canaan.

The Levites Receive Their Towns

35 On the plains of Moab, the LORD
spoke to Moses. It was by the Jordan River across from Jericho. The LORD
said, 2 "Command the Israelites to give
the Levites towns to live in. The towns
must come from the shares of land the
people will have as their own. Also give
the Levites the grasslands around the
towns. 3 Then the Levites will have towns
to live in. They will also have grasslands
for their cattle and all their other livestock.
4 "The grasslands around each town
you give them will go out to 1,500 feet
from the town wall. 5 Outside each town,
the east side will measure 3,000 feet. So
will the south side, the west side and
the north side. The town must be in
the center. And the Levites will own the
grasslands around each town.

Cities to Run to for Safety

6 "Six of the towns you give the Levites
will be cities to go to for safety. A person
who has killed someone can run to one
of them. Also give the Levites 42 other
towns. 7 You must give the Levites a total
of 48 towns. Also give them the grasslands around those towns. 8 The towns
you give the Levites must come from the
land the Israelites have as their own. So
the number you give from each tribe will
depend on the size of that tribe's share.
Take many towns from a tribe that has
many towns. But take only a few towns
from a tribe that has only a few."
9 Then the LORD said to Moses, 10 "Speak
to the Israelites. Tell them, 'You will soon
go across the Jordan River. You will enter
Canaan. 11 When you do, choose the cities
to go to for safety. People who have killed
someone by accident can run to one of
those cities. 12 They will be places of safety
for them. People will be safe there from
those who want to kill them. Then anyone
charged with murder will not die before
their case has been brought to the community court. 13 Six towns will be the cities
you can go to for safety. 14 Three will be
east of the Jordan River. The other three
will be in Canaan. 15 Those six towns will
be places where the Israelites can go for
safety. Outsiders living in Israel can also
go to them for safety. So anyone who
has killed another person by accident
can run there.
16 " 'Suppose a person uses an iron
object to hit and kill someone. Then
that person is a murderer and must be
put to death. 17 Or suppose a person is
holding a stone that could kill. And they
use it to hit and kill someone. Then that
person is a murderer and must be put to
death. 18 Or suppose a person is holding a
wooden object that could kill. And they
use it to hit and kill someone. Then that
person is a murderer and must be put
to death. 19 The dead person's nearest
male relative must kill the murderer.
When he meets up with him, he must
kill the murderer. 20 What if a person
makes evil plans against someone else?
And what if that person pushes them
so that they die? Or what if that person
throws something at them so that they
die? 21 Or what if that person hits another
person with a fist so that the other dies?
Then the person who does any of those
things must be put to death. That person
is a murderer. The dead person's nearest
male relative must kill the murderer.
When he meets up with him, he must
kill the murderer.

[22]" 'But what if a person suddenly pushes someone else without being angry? Or what if that person throws something at someone else without meaning to? [23]Or what if that person does not see the other person and drops a stone on them that kills them? He was not the dead person's enemy. He did not mean to harm them. [24]Then the court must decide between the person who did the act and the nearest male relative of the one who was killed. Here are the rules the court must follow. [25]The court must provide a safe place for the person accused of murder. It must keep the one accused of murder safe from those who want to kill them. The court must send the accused person back to the city they ran to for safety. The accused person must stay there until the high priest dies. That priest has been anointed with holy oil.

[26]" 'But suppose the accused person goes outside that city. [27]And suppose the dead person's nearest male relative finds them outside the city. Then the relative can kill the accused person. The relative will not be guilty of murder. [28]The accused person must stay in that city until the high priest dies. Only then may they return home.

[29]" 'This is what the law requires of you for all time to come. It will apply to you no matter where you live.

[30]" 'Suppose a person kills someone. Then that person must be put to death as a murderer. But do it only when there are witnesses who can tell what happened. Do not put anyone to death if only one witness tells what happened.

[31]" 'Do not accept payment for a murderer's life. A murderer deserves to die. They must certainly be put to death.

[32]" 'Do not accept payment for anyone who has run to a city for safety. Do not let them buy their freedom to return home. They must not go back and live on their own land before the high priest dies.

[33]" 'Do not pollute the land where you are. Murder pollutes the land. Only one thing can pay to remove the pollution in the land where murder has been committed. The blood of the one who spilled another's blood must be spilled. [34]So do not make the land where you live "unclean," because I live there too. I, the LORD, live among the Israelites.' "

The Property Zelophehad's Daughters Will Receive

36 The heads of the families of Gilead came to Moses. Gilead was the son of Makir. The family heads were from the tribe of Manasseh. So they were in the family line of Joseph. They spoke to Moses in front of the leaders of the families of Israel. [2]They said, "The LORD commanded you to give shares of the land to the Israelites. He told you to cast lots when you do it. At that time the LORD ordered you to give our brother Zelophehad's share to his daughters. [3]Suppose they marry men from other tribes in Israel. Then their share will be taken away from our family's land. It will be added to the land of the tribe they marry into. So a part of the share given to us will be taken away. [4]The Year of Jubilee for the Israelites will come. Then their share will be added to the land of the tribe they marry into. Their land will be taken away from the share given to our tribe."

[5]Then the LORD gave a command to Moses. He told Moses to give an order to the Israelites. Moses said, "What the tribe in the family line of Joseph is saying is right. [6]Here is what the LORD commands for Zelophehad's daughters. They can marry anyone they want to. But they have to marry someone in their own family's tribe. [7]Property in Israel must not pass from one tribe to another. Everyone in Israel must keep their family's share of their tribe's land. [8]Suppose a daughter in any tribe of Israel receives land from her parents. Then she must marry someone in her father's family and tribe. In that way, every family's share will remain in its family line in Israel. [9]Property can't pass from one tribe to another. Each tribe of Israel must keep the land it receives."

[10]So Zelophehad's daughters did just as the LORD commanded Moses. [11]The names of the daughters were Mahlah, Tirzah, Hoglah, Milkah and Noah. All of them married their cousins on their father's side. [12]They married men in the family line of Manasseh, the son of Joseph. So the land they received remained in their father's family and tribe.

[13]These are the commands and rules the LORD gave through Moses. He gave them to the Israelites on the plains of Moab. They were by the Jordan River across from Jericho.

DEUTERONOMY

Author: Moses

As God was leading his people to the place he promised would be their permanent home, he taught them how to love and obey him. The book of Deuteronomy is a reminder for God's people of what they learned in Leviticus and Numbers—who God is and how to worship him. Moses wrote this book before the people entered the promised land to remind them of what the generations before them had seen and experienced. From how God set his people free from slavery in Egypt to how he gave them the Ten Commandments, the people needed to know about the faithfulness of God.

Law & Covenant

This book also focuses on God's holiness and the importance of the covenant he made with the people of Israel. Sharing these stories of faith was important so that the people would not forget God's promises and turn to other gods. In Deuteronomy, God reminds his people that obedience leads to blessing and disobedience leads to consequences, like wandering in the desert. By obeying God's laws, the people of Israel would experience all God had for them.

God's commands reminded God's people that they could not be holy by their efforts; they needed a Savior to forgive their sins and make them right with God. One day, the Savior would come and obey God's commands perfectly. Through his sacrifice, he would make them right with God.

The LORD Commands Israel to Leave Mount Horeb

1 These are the words Moses spoke to all the Israelites. At that time, they were in the desert east of the Jordan River. It's in the Arabah Valley across from Suph. The people were between Paran and Tophel, Laban, Hazeroth and Dizahab. 2 It takes 11 days to go from Mount Horeb to Kadesh Barnea if you travel on the Mount Seir road.

3 It was the 40th year since the Israelites had left Egypt. On the first day of the 11th month, Moses spoke to them. He told them everything the LORD had commanded him to tell them. 4 They had already won the battle over Sihon. Sihon was the king of the Amorites. He had ruled in Heshbon. Israel had also won the battle over Og at Edrei. Og was the king of Bashan. He had ruled in Ashtaroth.

5 The people were east of the Jordan River in the territory of Moab. There Moses began to explain the law. Here is what he said.

6 The LORD our God spoke to us at Mount Horeb. He said, "You have stayed long enough at this mountain. 7 Take your tents down. Go into the hill country of the Amorites. Go to all the people who are their neighbors. Go to the people who live in the Arabah Valley. Travel to the mountains and the western hills. Go to the people in the Negev Desert and along the coast. Travel to the land of Canaan and to Lebanon. Go as far as the great Euphrates River. 8 I have given you all this land. Go in and take it as your own. The LORD promised he would give the land to your fathers. He promised it to Abraham, Isaac and Jacob. He also said he would give it to their children after them."

Some Officials Are Chosen to Help Moses

9 At that time I spoke to you. I said, "You are too heavy a load for me to carry alone. 10 The LORD your God has caused there to be many of you. Today you are as many as the stars in the sky. 11 The LORD is the God of your people. May he cause there to be a thousand times more of you. May he bless you, just as he promised he would. 12 But I can't handle your problems and troubles all by myself. I can't settle your arguments. 13 So choose some wise men from each of your tribes. They must understand how to give good advice. The people must have respect for them. I will appoint those men to have authority over you."

14 You answered me, "Your suggestion is good."

15 So I chose the leading men of your tribes who were wise and respected. I appointed them to have authority over you. I made them commanders of thousands, hundreds, fifties and tens. I appointed them to be officials over the tribes. 16 Here is what I commanded your judges at that time. I said, "Listen to your people's cases when they argue with one another. Judge them fairly. It doesn't matter whether the case is between two Israelites or between an Israelite and an outsider living among you. 17 When you judge them, treat everyone the same. Listen to those who are important and those who are not. Don't be afraid of anyone. God is the highest judge. Bring me any case that is too hard for you. I'll listen to it." 18 At that time I told you everything you should do.

Twelve Men Check Out the Land of Canaan

19 The LORD our God commanded us to start out from Mount Horeb. So we did. We went toward the hill country of the Amorites. We traveled all through the huge and terrible desert you saw. Finally, we reached Kadesh Barnea. 20 Then I said to you, "You have reached the hill country of the Amorites. The LORD our God is giving it to us. 21 The LORD your God has given you the land. Go up and take it. Do what the LORD says. He's the God of your people. Don't be afraid. Don't lose hope."

22 Then all of you came to me. You said, "Let's send some men ahead of us. They can check out the land for us and bring back a report. They can suggest to us which way to go. They can tell us about the towns we'll come to."

23 That seemed like a good idea to me. So I chose 12 of you. I picked one man from each tribe. 24 They left and went up into the hill country. There they came to the Valley of Eshkol. They checked it out. 25 They got some of the fruit of that land. Then they brought it down to us and gave us their report. They said, "The LORD our God is giving us a good land."

Israel Refuses to Obey the LORD

26 But you wouldn't go up. You refused
to obey the command of the LORD your
God. 27 You spoke against him in your
tents. You said, "The LORD hates us. That's
why he brought us out of Egypt to hand
us over to the Amorites. He wanted to
destroy us. 28 Where can we go? The men
who checked out the land have made us
afraid. They say, 'The people are stronger and taller than we are. The cities are
large. They have walls that reach up to
the sky. We even saw the Anakites there.' "

29 Then I said to you, "Don't be terrified. Don't be afraid of them. 30 The LORD
your God will go ahead of you. He will
fight for you. With your own eyes you
saw how he fought for you in Egypt.
31 You also saw how the LORD your God
brought you through the desert. He
carried you everywhere you went, just
as a father carries his son. And now you
have arrived here."

32 In spite of that, you didn't trust in
the LORD your God. 33 He went ahead
of you on your journey. He was in the
fire at night and in the cloud during the
day. He found places for you to camp.
He showed you the way you should go.

34 The LORD heard what you said. So
he became angry. He made a promise.
He said, 35 "I promised to give this good
land to your people of long ago. But
no one alive today will see it. 36 Only
Caleb will see the land. He is the son of
Jephunneh. I will give him and his children after him the land he walked on.
He followed me with his whole heart."

37 Because of you, the LORD became
angry with me also. He said, "You will
not enter the land either. 38 But Joshua,
the son of Nun, is your helper. Joshua will enter the land. Help him to be
brave. Give him hope. He will lead Israel
to take the land as their own. 39 You said
your little ones would be taken prisoner.
But they will enter the land. They do not
yet know right from wrong. But I will
give them the land. They will take it as
their own. 40 As for you, turn around.
Start out toward the desert. Go along
the road that leads to the Red Sea."

41 Then you replied, "We have sinned
against the LORD. We will go up and
fight. We'll do just as the LORD our God
has commanded us." So all of you got
your swords and put them on. You
thought it would be easy to go up into
the hill country.

42 But the LORD spoke to me. He said,
"Tell them, 'Do not go up and fight. I will
not be with you. Your enemies will win
the battle over you.' "

43 So I told you what the LORD said.
But you wouldn't listen. You refused to
obey his command. You were so filled
with pride that you marched up into the
hill country. 44 The Amorites who lived
in those hills came out and attacked
you. Like large numbers of bees they
chased you. They beat you down from
Seir all the way to Hormah. 45 You came
back and wept in front of the LORD. But
he didn't pay any attention to your
weeping. He wouldn't listen to you. 46 So
you stayed in Kadesh for many years.
You spent a long time in that area.

Israel Wanders in the Desert

2 We turned back and started out toward the desert. We went along the
road that leads to the Red Sea. That's
how the LORD had directed me. For a
long time we made our way around
the hill country of Seir.

2 Then the LORD spoke to me. He said,
3 "You have made your way around this
hill country long enough. So now turn
north. 4 Here are the orders I want you
to give the people. Tell them, 'You are
about to pass through the territory of
your relatives. They are from the family
line of Esau. They live in Seir. They will
be afraid of you. But be very careful. 5 Do
not make them angry. If you do, they will
go to war against you. I will not give you
any of their land. You will not have even
enough to put your foot on. I have given
Esau's people the hill country of Seir as
their own. 6 Pay them with silver for the
food you eat and the water you drink.' "

7 The LORD your God has blessed you
in everything your hands have done.
He watched over you when you traveled
through that huge desert. For these
40 years the LORD your God has been
with you. So you have had everything
you need.

8 We went on past our relatives. They
are from the family line of Esau. They
live in Seir. We turned away from the
Arabah Valley road. It comes up from
Elath and Ezion Geber. We traveled
along the desert road of Moab.

9 Then the LORD said to me, "Do not
attack the Moabites. Do not even make
them angry. If you do, they will go to
war against you. I will not give you any
part of their land. I have given Moab
to the people in the family line of Lot.
I have given it to them as their own."

10 The Emites used to live there. They
were strong people. There were large
numbers of them. They were as tall as
the Anakites. 11 Like the Anakites, they
too were thought of as Rephaites. But
the Moabites called them Emites. 12 The
Horites used to live in Seir. But the people
of Esau drove them out. They destroyed
the Horites to make room for themselves.
Then they settled in their territory. They
did just as Israel has done in the land the
LORD gave them as their own.

13 The LORD said, "Now get up. Go
across the Zered Valley." So we went
across it.

14 Between the time we left Kadesh
Barnea and the time we went across the
Zered Valley, 38 years had passed. By
then, all the fighting men who had been
in our camp from the beginning had
died. The LORD had warned them that
it would happen. 15 He used his power
against them until he had gotten rid of
all of them. Not one was left in the camp.

16 Finally, the last of the fighting men
among the people died. 17 Then the LORD
said to me, 18 "Today you must pass near
the border of Moab. Moab is also called
Ar. 19 When you come to the Ammonites,
do not attack them. Do not make them
angry. If you do, they will go to war
against you. I will not give you any of
their land as your own. I have given it
to the people in the family line of Lot.
I have given it to them as their own."

20 That land was also thought of as
a land of the Rephaites. They used to
live there. But the Ammonites called
them Zamzummites. 21 The Rephaites
were strong people. There were large
numbers of them. They were as tall as
the Anakites. The LORD destroyed the
Rephaites to make room for the Ammonites. So the Ammonites drove them
out. Then they settled in the territory
of the Rephaites. 22 The LORD had done
the same thing for the people of Esau.
They lived in Seir. The LORD destroyed
the Horites to make room for Esau's
people. They drove the Horites out. So
the people of Esau have lived in Seir in
the territory of the Horites to this very
day. 23 The Avvites lived in villages as
far away as Gaza. But people came from
Crete and destroyed the Avvites. Then
the people of Crete made their home in
the territory of the Avvites.

Israel Wins the Battle Over Sihon

24 The LORD said, "Start out and go
across the valley of the Arnon River. I
have handed Sihon over to you. He is
the Amorite king of Heshbon. I have
also given you his country. Begin to
take it as your own. Go to war against
him. 25 This very day I will bring fear
and terror on all the nations because of
you. They will hear about you. They will
tremble with fear. Pain and suffering
will grip them because of you."

26 I sent messengers from the Desert
of Kedemoth. I told them to go to Sihon,
the king of Heshbon. They offered him
peace. They said, 27 "Let us pass through
your country. We'll stay on the main
road. We won't turn off it to one side
or the other. 28 We'll pay you the right
amount of silver for food to eat and water to drink. Just let us walk through your
country. 29 The people of Esau, who live
in Seir, allowed us to do that. The people
of Moab, who live in Ar, also allowed us
to do it. So let us walk through until we
go across the Jordan River. Then we'll
be able to go into the land the LORD
our God is giving us." 30 But Sihon, the
king of Heshbon, refused to let us walk
through. The LORD your God had made
him stubborn in his heart and spirit. The
LORD wanted to hand him over to you.
And that's exactly what he has done.

31 The LORD said to me, "I have begun
to hand Sihon and his country over to
you. So begin the battle to take his land
as your own."

32 Sihon and his whole army came out
to fight against us at Jahaz. 33 But the
LORD our God handed him over to us.
We struck him down together with his
sons and his whole army. 34 At that time
we took all his towns. We completely
destroyed them. We killed all the men,
women and children. We didn't leave
any of them alive. 35 But we took for
ourselves the livestock and everything
else from the towns we had captured.
36 Not a single town was too strong for

in Deuteronomy?

God is the Righteous Ruler. We cannot keep his commands perfectly, but through faith in his Son, Jesus, we can receive his love and grace.

us. That includes all the towns from Aroer on the rim of the Arnon River valley
all the way to Gilead. It also includes the
town in the valley. The LORD our God
gave us all of them. 37 And you obeyed
the LORD's command. You didn't go near
any part of the land of the Ammonites.
That includes the land along the Jabbok
River. It also includes the land around
the towns in the hills.

Israel Wins the Battle Over Og

3 Next, we turned and went up
along the road toward Bashan. Og
marched out with his whole army. They
fought against us at Edrei. Og was the
king of Bashan. 2 The LORD said to me,
"Do not be afraid of Og. I have handed
him over to you. I have also handed over
his whole army and his land. Do to him
what you did to Sihon. Sihon was the
Amorite king who ruled in Heshbon."
3 So the LORD our God also handed
Og, the king of Bashan, and his whole
army over to us. We struck them down.
We didn't leave any of them alive. 4 At
that time we took all his cities. There
were 60 of them. We took the whole
area of Argob. That was Og's kingdom
in Bashan. 5 All those cities had high
walls around them. The city gates
were made secure with heavy metal
bars. There were also large numbers
of villages that didn't have walls. 6 We
completely destroyed them. We did to
them just as we had done to Sihon, the
king of Heshbon. We destroyed all their
cities. We destroyed the men, women
and children. 7 But we kept for ourselves
the livestock and everything else we
took from their cities.
8 So at that time we took the territory
east of the Jordan River. We captured
it from those two Amorite kings. The
territory goes all the way from the Arnon
River valley to Mount Hermon. 9 Hermon
is called Sirion by the people of Sidon.
The Amorites call it Senir. 10 We captured
all the towns on the high plains. We took
the whole land of Gilead. And we captured the whole land of Bashan as far
away as Salekah and Edrei. Those were
towns that belonged to Og's kingdom
in Bashan. 11 Og, the king of Bashan,
was the only Rephaite left. His bed was
decorated with iron. It was more than 13
feet long and six feet wide. It is still in
the Ammonite city of Rabbah.

Moses Divides Up the Land

12 I divided up the land we took over at that
time. I gave the tribes of Reuben and Gad the
territory north of Aroer by the Arnon River
valley. It includes half of the hill country of
Gilead together with its towns. 13 I gave the
rest of Gilead to half of the tribe of Manasseh.
I also gave them the whole land of Bashan,
the kingdom of Og. The whole area of Argob
in Bashan used to be known as a land of
the Rephaites. 14 Jair took the whole area
of Argob. He was from the family line of
Manasseh. Argob goes all the way to the
border of the people of Geshur and Maakah.
It was named after Jair. So Bashan is called
Havvoth Jair to this very day. 15 I gave Gilead
to Makir. 16 But I gave to the tribes of Reuben
and Gad the territory that reaches from
Gilead down to the Arnon River valley. It
goes all the way to the Jabbok River. The
Jabbok is the northern border of Ammon.
The middle of the Arnon River valley is its
southern border. 17 The western border of
Reuben and Gad is the Jordan River in the
Arabah Valley. It reaches from the Sea of
Galilee to the Dead Sea. It runs below the
slopes of Pisgah.
18 Here is the command I gave at that
time to the tribes of Reuben and Gad and
half of the tribe of Manasseh. I said, "The
LORD your God has given you this land
as your very own. But all your strong
men must be prepared for battle. They
must cross over ahead of the rest of the

Israelites. 19 But your wives and children can stay in the towns I've given you. You can keep your livestock there too. I know you have a lot of livestock. 20 The LORD has given you peace and rest. Then let your families and livestock stay in those towns until the LORD gives peace and rest to the other tribes. And let your families stay until the other tribes have taken over the land the LORD your God is giving them. That land is across the Jordan River. After that, each of you may go back to the land I've given you as your very own."

The LORD Will Not Allow Moses to Cross the Jordan River

21 At that time I gave Joshua a command. I said, "Your own eyes have seen everything the LORD your God has done to Sihon and Og. He will do the same thing to all the kingdoms in the land where you are going. 22 Don't be afraid of them. The LORD your God himself will fight for you."

23 At that time I made my appeal to the LORD. I said, 24 "LORD and King, you have begun to show me how great you are. You have shown me how strong your hand is. You do great works and mighty acts. There isn't any god in heaven or on earth who can do what you do. 25 Let me go across the Jordan River. Let me see the good land beyond it. I want to see that fine hill country and Lebanon."

26 But the LORD was angry with me because of what you did. He wouldn't listen to me. "That is enough!" the LORD said. "Do not speak to me anymore about this matter. 27 Go up to the highest slopes of Pisgah. Look west and north and south and east. Look at the land with your own eyes. But you are not going to go across this Jordan River. 28 So appoint Joshua as the new leader. Help him to be brave. Give him hope and strength. He will take these people across the Jordan. You will see the land. But he will lead them into it to take it as their own." 29 So we stayed in the valley near Beth Peor.

Obey the LORD

4 Now, Israel, listen to the rules and laws I'm going to teach you. Obey them and you will live. You will go in and take over the land. The LORD was the God of your people of long ago. He's giving you the land. 2 Don't add to what I'm commanding you. Don't subtract from it either. Instead, obey the commands of the LORD your God that I'm giving you.

3 Your own eyes saw what the LORD your God did at Baal Peor. He destroyed every one of your people who worshiped the Baal that was worshiped at Peor. 4 But all of you who remained true to the LORD your God are still alive today.

5 I have taught you rules and laws, just as the LORD my God commanded me. Obey them in the land you are entering to take as your very own. 6 Be careful to keep them. That will show the nations how wise and understanding you are. They will hear about all these rules. They'll say, "That great nation certainly has wise and understanding people." 7 The LORD our God is near us every time we pray to him. What other nation is great enough to have its gods that close to them? 8 I'm giving you the laws of the LORD today. What other nation is great enough to have rules and laws as fair as these?

9 Don't be careless. Instead, be very careful. Don't forget the things your eyes have seen. As long as you live, don't let them slip from your mind. Teach them to your children and their children after them. 10 Remember the day you stood at Mount Horeb. The LORD your God was there. He said to me, "Bring the people to me to hear my words. I want them to learn to have respect for me as long as they live in the land. I want them to teach my words to their children." 11 You came near and stood at the foot of the mountain. It blazed with fire that reached as high as the very heavens. There were black clouds and deep darkness. 12 Then the LORD spoke to you out of the fire. You heard the sound of his words. But you didn't see any shape or form. You only heard a voice. 13 He announced his covenant to you. That covenant is the Ten Commandments. He commanded you to obey them. Then he wrote them down on two stone tablets. 14 At that time the LORD directed me to teach you his rules and laws. You must obey them in the land you are crossing the Jordan River to take as your own.

Don't Make or Worship Statues of Gods

15 The LORD spoke to you at Mount Horeb out of the fire. But you didn't see

any shape or form that day. So be very careful. [16] Make sure you don't commit a horrible sin. Don't make for yourselves a statue of a god. Don't make a god that looks like a man or woman or anything else. [17] Don't make one that looks like any animal on earth or any bird that flies in the sky. [18] Don't make a statue that looks like any creature that moves along the ground or any fish that swims in the water. [19] When you look up at the heavens, you will see the sun and moon. And you will see huge numbers of stars. Don't let anyone tempt you to bow down to the sun, moon or stars. Don't worship things the LORD your God has provided for all the nations on earth. [20] Egypt was like a furnace that melts iron down and makes it pure. But the LORD took you and brought you out of Egypt. He wanted you to be his very own people. And that's exactly what you are.

[21] The LORD was angry with me because of what you did. He promised that he would never let me go across the Jordan River. He promised that I would never enter that good land. It's the land the LORD your God is giving you as your own. [22] I'll die here in this land. I won't go across the Jordan. But you are about to cross over it. You will take that good land as your own. [23] Be careful. Don't forget the covenant the LORD your God made with you. Don't make for yourselves a statue of any god at all. He has told you not to. So don't do it. [24] The LORD your God is like a fire that burns everything up. He wants you to worship only him.

[25] So don't make a statue of a god. Don't commit that horrible sin. Don't do it even after you have had children and grandchildren. Don't do it even after you have lived in the land a long time. If you do, that will be an evil thing in the sight of the LORD your God. You will make him angry. [26] Today I'm calling out to the heavens and the earth to be witnesses against you. Suppose you do these things. Then you will quickly die in the land you are going across the Jordan River to take over. You won't live there very long. You will certainly be destroyed. [27] The LORD will drive you out of your land. He will scatter you among the nations. Only a few of you will remain alive there. [28] There you will worship gods that men have made out of wood and stone. Those gods can't see, hear, eat or smell. [29] Perhaps while you are there, you will seek the LORD your God. You will find him if you seek him with all your heart and with all your soul. [30] All the things I've told you about might happen to you. And you will be in trouble. But later you will return to the LORD your God. You will obey him. [31] The LORD your God is tender and loving. He won't leave you or destroy you. He won't forget the covenant he made with your people of long ago. He gave his word when he made it.

The LORD Is God

[32] Ask now about the days of long ago. Find out what happened long before your time. Ask about what has happened since the time God created human beings on the earth. Ask from one end of the world to the other. Has anything as great as this ever happened? Has anything like it ever been heard of? [33] You heard the voice of God speaking out of fire. And you lived! Has that happened to any other people? [34] Has any god ever tried to take one nation out of another to be his own? Has any god done it by testing his people? Has any god done it with signs and amazing deeds or with war? Has any god reached out his mighty hand and powerful arm? Or has any god shown his people his great and wonderful acts? The LORD your God did all those things for you in Egypt. With your very own eyes you saw him do them.

[35] The LORD showed you those things so that you might know he is God. There is no other God except him. [36] From heaven he made you hear his voice. He wanted to teach you. On earth he showed you his great fire. You heard his words coming out of the fire. [37] He loved your people of long ago. He chose their children after them. So he brought you out of Egypt. He used his great strength to do it. [38] He drove out nations to make room for you. They were greater and stronger than you are. He will bring you into their land. He wants to give it to you as your very own. The whole land is as good as yours right now.

[39] The LORD is God in heaven above and on the earth below. Today you must agree with that and take it to heart.

There is no other God. 40 I'm giving you
his rules and commands today. Obey
them. Then things will go well with you
and your children after you. You will
live a long time in the land. The LORD
your God is giving you the land for all
time to come.

Cities to Run to for Safety

41 Then Moses set apart three cities
east of the Jordan River. 42 Suppose
someone killed a person they didn't
hate and without meaning to do it. That
person could run to one of those cities
and stay alive. 43 Here are the names
of the cities. Bezer was for the people
of Reuben. It was in the high plains in
the desert. Ramoth was for the people of
Gad. It was in Gilead. Golan was for the
people of Manasseh. It was in Bashan.

Moses Gives the Law to Israel

44 Here is the law Moses gave the Israelites. 45 Here are its terms, rules and
laws. Moses gave them to the people
when they came out of Egypt. 46 They
were now east of the Jordan River in
the valley near Beth Peor. They were
in the land of Sihon, the king of the
Amorites. He ruled in Heshbon. But
Moses and the Israelites won the battle
over him after we came out of Egypt.
47 They captured his land and made it
their own. They also took the land of Og,
the king of Bashan. Sihon and Og were
the two Amorite kings east of the Jordan
River. 48 Their land reached from Aroer
on the rim of the Arnon River valley to
Mount Hermon. 49 It included the whole
Arabah Valley east of the Jordan. It
included land all the way to the Dead
Sea below the slopes of Pisgah.

The Ten Commandments

5 Moses sent for all the Israelites.
Here is what he said to them.

Israel, listen to me. Here are the rules
and laws I'm announcing to you today.
Learn them well. Be sure to obey them.
2 The LORD our God made a covenant
with us at Mount Horeb. 3 He didn't
make it only with our people of long
ago. He also made it with us. In fact, he
made it with all of us who are alive here
today. 4 The LORD spoke to you face to
face. His voice came out of the fire on the
mountain. 5 At that time I stood between
the LORD and you. I announced to you
the LORD's message. I did it because you
were afraid of the fire. You didn't go up
the mountain.

The LORD said,

6 "I am the LORD your God. I brought
you out of Egypt. That is the land
where you were slaves.

7 "Do not put any other gods in place
of me.

8 "Do not make statues of gods that
look like anything in the sky or
on the earth or in the waters.
9 Do not bow down to them or
worship them. I am the LORD
your God. I want you to worship
only me. I cause the sins of the
parents to affect their children.
I will cause the sins of those
who hate me to affect even
their grandchildren and great-
grandchildren. 10 But for all
time to come I show love to all
those who love me and keep my
commandments.

11 "Do not misuse the name of the
LORD your God. The LORD will
find guilty anyone who misuses
his name.

12 "Keep the Sabbath day holy. Do
this just as the LORD your God
has commanded you. 13 Do all
your work in six days. 14 But
the seventh day is a sabbath to
honor the LORD your God. Do not
do any work on that day. The
same command applies to your
sons and daughters, your male
and female servants, your oxen,
your donkeys and your other
animals. It also applies to any
outsiders who live in your towns.
I want your male and female
servants to rest, just as you
do. 15 Remember that you were
slaves in Egypt. The LORD your
God reached out his mighty hand
and powerful arm and brought
you out of there. So the LORD
your God has commanded you
to keep the Sabbath day holy.

16 "Honor your father and mother,
just as the LORD your God has
commanded you. Then you will
live a long time in the land he
is giving you. And things will go
well with you there.

17 "Do not murder.
18 "Do not commit adultery.
19 "Do not steal.
20 "Do not be a false witness against
your neighbor.
21 "Do not want to have your
neighbor's wife. Do not desire
anything your neighbor owns.
Do not desire to have your
neighbor's house or land, male
or female servant, ox or donkey."
22 These are the commandments the
LORD announced in a loud voice to your
whole community. He gave them to you
there on the mountain. He spoke out
of the fire, cloud and deep darkness.
He didn't add anything else. Then he
wrote the commandments on two stone
tablets. And he gave them to me.
23 The mountain was blazing with
fire. You heard the voice coming out of
the darkness. So your elders and all the
leaders of your tribes came to me. 24 You
said, "The LORD our God has shown us
his glory and majesty. We have heard
his voice coming out of the fire. Today
we have seen that a person can still
stay alive even if God speaks with them.
25 But why should we die? This great fire
will burn us up. We'll die if we hear the
voice of the LORD our God again. 26 We
have heard the voice of the living God.
We've heard him speaking out of the
fire. Has any other human being ever
heard him speak like that and stayed
alive? 27 Go near and listen to everything
the LORD our God says. Then tell us what
he tells you. We will listen and obey."
28 The LORD heard you when you
spoke to me. He said to me, "I have
heard what these people said to you.
Everything they said was good. 29 But
I wish they would always have respect
for me in their hearts. I wish they would
always obey all my commands. Then
things would go well with them and
their children forever.
30 "Go and tell them to return to their
tents. 31 But you stay here with me. Then
I will give you all my commands, rules
and laws. You must teach the people to
obey them in the land I am giving them
as their very own."
32 So be careful to do what the LORD
your God has commanded you. Don't turn
away from his commands to the right or
the left. 33 Live exactly as the LORD your
God has commanded you to live. Then
you will enjoy life in the land you will
soon own. Things will go well with you
there. You will live there for a long time.

Love the LORD Your God

6 The LORD your God has directed me
to teach you his commands, rules
and laws. Obey them in the land you
will take over when you go across the
Jordan River. 2 Then you, your children
and their children after them will honor
the LORD your God as long as you live.
Obey all his rules and commands I'm
giving you. If you do, you will enjoy long
life. 3 Israel, listen to me. Make sure you
obey me. Then things will go well with
you. The number of your people will
increase greatly in a land that has plenty
of milk and honey. That's what the LORD,
the God of your parents, promised you.
4 Israel, listen to me. The LORD is our
God. The LORD is the one and only God.
5 Love the LORD your God with all your
heart and with all your soul. Love him
with all your strength. 6 The commandments I give you today must be in your
hearts. 7 Make sure your children learn
them. Talk about them when you are at
home. Talk about them when you walk
along the road. Speak about them when
you go to bed. And speak about them
when you get up. 8 Write them down and
tie them on your hands as a reminder.
Also tie them on your foreheads. 9 Write
them on the doorframes of your houses.
Also write them on your gates.

10 The LORD your God will bring you
into the land of Canaan. He gave his
word. He promised he would give the
land to your fathers, to Abraham, Isaac
and Jacob. The land has large, wealthy
cities you didn't build. 11 It has houses
filled with all kinds of good things you
didn't provide. The land has wells you
didn't dig. And it has vineyards and
groves of olive trees you didn't plant.
You will have plenty to eat. 12 But be

careful that you don't forget the LORD.
Remember that he brought you out
of Egypt. That's the land where you
were slaves.
13 Worship the LORD your God. He is
the only one you should serve. When
you make promises, do so in his name.
14 Don't serve the gods of the nations
around you. 15 The LORD your God is
among you. He wants you to worship
only him. If you worship other gods,
God will be very angry with you. And
he will destroy you from the face of the
land. 16 Don't test the LORD your God as
you did at Massah. 17 Be sure to obey the
LORD's commands. Obey the terms and
rules he has given you. 18 Do what is
right and good in the LORD's eyes. Then
things will go well with you. You will go
in and take over the land. It's the good
land the LORD promised to your people
of long ago. 19 You will drive out all your
enemies to make room for you. That's
what the LORD said would happen.
20 Later on, your child might ask you,
"What is the meaning of the terms,
rules and laws the LORD our God has
commanded you to obey?" 21 If they do
ask you, tell them, "We were Pharaoh's
slaves in Egypt. But the LORD used his
mighty hand to bring us out of Egypt.
22 With our own eyes we saw the LORD
send amazing signs. They were great
and terrible. He sent them on Egypt
and Pharaoh and everyone in his house.
23 But the LORD brought us out of Egypt.
He planned to bring us into the land of
Canaan and give it to us. It's the land
he promised to our people of long ago.
24 The LORD our God commanded us to
obey all his rules. He commanded us
to honor him. If we do, we will always
succeed and be kept alive. That's what
is happening today. 25 We must make
sure we obey the whole law in the sight
of the LORD our God. That's what he has
commanded us to do. If we obey his law,
we'll be doing what he requires of us."

The LORD Will Drive Out Many Nations

7 The LORD your God will bring you
into the land. You are going to enter
it and take it as your own. He'll drive out
many nations to make room for you.
He'll drive out the Hittites, Girgashites,
Amorites, Canaanites, Perizzites, Hivites
and Jebusites. Those seven nations are
larger and stronger than you are. 2 The
LORD your God will hand them over to
you. You will win the battle over them.
You must completely destroy them.
Don't make a peace treaty with
them. Don't show them any mercy.
3 Don't marry any of their people. Don't
give your daughters to their sons. And
don't take their daughters for your
sons. 4 If you do, those people will turn
your children away from serving the
LORD. Then your children will serve
other gods. The LORD will be very angry with you. He will quickly destroy
you. 5 So here is what you must do to
those people. Break down their altars.
Smash their sacred stones. Cut down
the poles they use to worship the female
god named Asherah. Burn the statues
of their gods in the fire. 6 You are a holy
nation. The LORD your God has set you
apart for himself. He has chosen you
to be his special treasure. He chose
you out of all the nations on the face
of the earth to be his people.
7 The LORD chose you because he loved
you very much. He didn't choose you because you had more people than other
nations. In fact, you had the smallest
number of all. 8 The LORD chose you
because he loved you. He wanted to
keep the promise he had made to your

Are there many gods?

There are many who claim to be gods, but there is only one true God—the God of the Bible. God is called the "Trinity" because he is three persons in one.

Can you find the following verse?
DEUTERONOMY 6:4

people of long ago. That's why he used his mighty hand to bring you out of Egypt. He bought you back from the land where you were slaves. He set you free from the power of Pharaoh, the
king of Egypt. [9] So I want you to realize that the LORD your God is God. He is the faithful God. He keeps his covenant for all time to come. He keeps it with those who love him and obey his commandments. He shows them his love. [10] But
he will pay back those who hate him. He'll destroy them. He'll quickly pay
back those who hate him. [11] So be careful
to obey the commands, rules and laws I'm giving you today.

[12] Pay attention to the laws of the LORD your God. Be careful to obey them. Then he will keep his covenant of love with you. That's what he promised to your
people of long ago. [13] The LORD will love you and bless you. He'll cause there to be many of you. He'll give you many children. He'll bless the crops of your land. He'll give you plenty of grain, olive oil and fresh wine. He'll bless your herds with many calves. He'll give your flocks many lambs. He'll do all these things for you in the land of Canaan. It's the land he promised your people of long ago
that he would give you. [14] He will bless
you more than any other nation. All your men and women will have children. All your livestock will have little ones. [15] The
LORD will keep you from getting sick. He won't send on you any of the horrible sicknesses you saw all around you in Egypt. But he'll send them on everyone
who hates you. [16] You must destroy all
the nations the LORD your God hands over to you. Don't feel sorry for them. Don't serve their gods. If you do, they will be a trap for you.

[17] You might say to yourselves, "These nations are stronger than we are. How
can we drive them out?" [18] But don't be
afraid of them. Be sure to remember what the LORD your God did to Pharaoh and all the Egyptians. [19] With your
own eyes you saw what the LORD did to them. You saw the signs and amazing things he did. He reached out his mighty hand and powerful arm. The LORD your God used all those things to bring you out. You are now afraid of the nations that are in the land the LORD promised you. But the LORD your God will do to them the same things he did to Egypt.
[20] The LORD your God will also send hornets among those nations. Some of the people left alive will hide from
you. But even they will die. [21] So don't
be terrified by them. The LORD your God is with you. He is a great and wonderful
God. [22] The LORD your God will drive out
those nations to make room for you. But

My GOD IS... FAITHFUL

God does exactly what he says he is going to do. Can you think of a time when someone said they were going to share a toy with you, and they did? When God makes a promise, he keeps it (see Numbers 23:19).

Throughout the Bible, we read about the many promises God made to his people. For example, God promised to be with us always, to provide for our needs, and to send a Savior who would take away the sin of the world. And do you know what? God has done everything he said he would do. His faithfulness means he is trustworthy, and he will guide us to be faithful too.

he will do it little by little. You won't be
allowed to get rid of them all at once. If
you did, wild animals would multiply
all around you. 23 But the LORD your
God will hand those nations over to
you. He will throw them into a panic
until they are destroyed. 24 He will hand
their kings over to you. You will wipe out
their names from the earth. No one will
be able to stand up against you. You
will destroy them. 25 Burn the statues
of their gods in the fire. Don't wish for
the silver and gold on those statues.
Don't take it for yourselves. If you do,
it will be a trap for you. The LORD your
God hates it. 26 Don't bring anything he
hates into your house. If you do, you
will be completely destroyed along with
it. So hate it with all your heart. It is set
apart to be destroyed.

Remember What the LORD Has Done

8 Make sure you obey every command I'm giving you today. Then
you will live, and there will be many of
you. You will enter the land and take
it as your own. It's the land the LORD
promised to your people of long ago.
2 Remember how the LORD your God led
you all the way. He guided you in the
desert for these 40 years. He wanted
to take your pride away. He wanted
to test you to know what was in your
hearts. He wanted to see whether you
would obey his commands. 3 He took
your pride away. He let you go hungry. Then he gave you manna to eat.
You and your parents had never even
known anything about manna before.
He tested you to teach you that man
doesn't live only on bread. He also
lives on every word that comes from
the mouth of the LORD. 4 Your clothes
didn't wear out during these 40 years.
Your feet didn't swell. 5 Here is what I
want you to know in your hearts. The
LORD your God guides you, just as parents guide their children.

6 Obey the commands of the LORD
your God. Live as he wants you to live.
Have respect for him. 7 The LORD your
God is bringing you into a good land. It
has brooks, streams and deep springs
of water. Those springs flow in its valleys and hills. 8 It has wheat, barley,
vines, fig trees, pomegranates, olive
oil and honey. 9 There is plenty of food
in that land. You will have everything
you need. Its rocks have iron in them.
And you can dig copper out of its hills.

10 When you have eaten and are satisfied, praise the LORD your God. Praise
him for the good land he has given you.
11 Make sure you don't forget the LORD
your God. Don't fail to obey his commands, laws and rules. I'm giving them
to you today. 12 But suppose you don't
obey his commands. And suppose you
have plenty to eat. You build fine houses
and live in them. 13 The number of your
herds and flocks increases. You also get
more and more silver and gold. And
everything you have multiplies. 14 Then
your hearts will become proud. And you
will forget the LORD your God. The LORD
brought you out of Egypt. That's the
land where you were slaves. 15 He led
you through that huge and terrible
desert. It was a dry land. It didn't have
any water. It had poisonous snakes and
scorpions. The LORD gave you water out
of solid rock. 16 He gave you manna to
eat in the desert. Your people had never
even known anything about manna
before. The LORD took your pride away.
He tested you. He did it so that things
would go well with you in the end. 17 You
might say to yourself, "My power and
my strong hands have made me rich."
18 But remember the LORD your God. He
gives you the ability to produce wealth.
That shows he stands by the terms of the
covenant he made with you. He promised it to your people of long ago. And
he's still faithful to his covenant today.

19 Don't forget the LORD your God.
Don't serve other gods. Don't worship
them and bow down to them. I am a
witness against you today that if you
do, you will certainly be destroyed.
20 You will be destroyed just like the
nations the LORD your God is destroying
to make room for you. That's what will
happen if you don't obey him.

Why the LORD Gave Canaan to Israel

9 Israel, listen to me. You are now
about to go across the Jordan River.
You will take over the land of the nations that live there. Those nations are
greater and stronger than you are. Their
large cities have walls that reach up to
the sky. 2 The people who live there are
Anakites. They are strong and tall. You

know all about them. You have heard
people say, "Who can stand up against
the Anakites?" 3 But today you can be
sure the LORD your God will go over
there ahead of you. He is like a fire that
will burn them up. He'll destroy them.
He'll bring them under your control.
You will drive them out. You will put an
end to them quickly, just as the LORD
has promised you.

4 The LORD your God will drive them
out to make room for you. When he does,
don't say to yourself, "The LORD has done
it because I am godly. That's why he
brought me here to take over this land."
That isn't true. The LORD is going to drive
out those nations to make room for you
because they are very evil. 5 You are not
going in to take over their land because
you have done what is right or honest.
It's because those nations are so evil.
That's why the LORD your God will drive
them out to make room for you. He will
do what he said he would do. He made
a promise to your fathers, to Abraham,
Isaac and Jacob. 6 The LORD your God
is giving you this good land to take as
your own. But you must understand that
it isn't because you are a godly nation.
In fact, you are stubborn.

Israel Worshiped the Golden Calf

7 Here is something you must remember. Never forget it. You made
the LORD your God angry in the desert. You refused to obey him from the
day you left Egypt until you arrived
here. 8 At Mount Horeb you made the
LORD angry enough to destroy you.
9 I went up the mountain. I went there
to receive the tablets of the covenant
law. They were made out of stone. It
was the covenant the LORD had made
with you. I stayed on the mountain for
40 days and 40 nights. I didn't eat any
food or drink any water. 10 The LORD
gave me two stone tablets. The words
on them were written by the finger of
God. All the commandments the LORD
gave you were written on the tablets.
He announced them to you out of the
fire on the mountain. He wrote them on
the day you gathered together there.

11 The 40 days and 40 nights came to
an end. Then the LORD gave me the two
stone tablets. They were the tablets of
the covenant law. 12 The LORD told me,
"Go down from here right away. The
people you brought out of Egypt have
become very sinful. They have quickly
turned away from what I commanded
them. They have made a statue of a god
for themselves."

13 The LORD also said to me, "I have
seen these people. They are so stubborn!
14 Do not try to stop me. I am going to
destroy them. I will wipe them out from
the earth. Then I will make you into a
great nation. Your people will be stronger than they were. There will be more
of you than there were of them."

15 So I turned and went down the
mountain. It was blazing with fire. I
was carrying the two tablets of the
covenant law. 16 When I looked, I saw
that you had sinned against the LORD
your God. You had made for yourselves
a metal statue of a god. It looked like a
calf. You had quickly turned away from
the path the LORD had commanded you
to follow. 17 So I threw the two tablets
out of my hands. You watched them
break into pieces.

18 Then once again I fell down flat in
front of the LORD with my face toward
the ground. I lay there for 40 days and
40 nights. I didn't eat any food or drink
any water. You had committed a terrible sin. You had done an evil thing in the
LORD's sight. You had made him angry.
19 I was afraid of the LORD's great anger.
He was so angry with you he wanted
to destroy you. But the LORD listened
to me again. 20 And he was so angry
with Aaron he wanted to destroy him
too. But at that time I prayed for Aaron. 21 I also got that sinful calf you had
made. I burned it in the fire. I crushed
it and ground it into fine powder. Then
I threw the powder into a stream that
was flowing down the mountain.

22 You also made the LORD angry
at Taberah, Massah and Kibroth
Hattaavah.

23 The LORD sent you out from Kadesh
Barnea. He said, "Go up and take over the
land I have given you." But you refused
to do what the LORD your God had commanded you to do. You didn't trust him
or obey him. 24 You have been refusing to
obey the LORD as long as I've known you.

25 I lay down in front of the LORD
with my face toward the ground for 40
days and 40 nights. I did it because the

LORD had said he would destroy you. [26] I prayed to him. "LORD and King," I said, "don't destroy your people. They belong to you. You set them free by your great power. You used your mighty hand to bring them out of Egypt. [27] Remember your servants Abraham, Isaac and Jacob. Forgive the Israelites for being so stubborn. Don't judge them for the evil and sinful things they've done. [28] If you do, the Egyptians will say, 'The LORD wasn't able to take them into the land he had promised to give them. He hated them. So he brought them out of Egypt to put them to death in the desert.' [29] But they are your people. They belong to you. You used your great power to bring them out of Egypt. You reached out your mighty arm and saved them."

The New Stone Tablets

10 At that time the LORD spoke to me. He said, "Carve out two stone tablets, just like the first ones. Then come up to me on the mountain. Also make a wooden ark. [2] I will write on the tablets the words that were on the first tablets, which you broke. Then you must put the tablets in the ark."

[3] So I made the ark out of acacia wood. I carved out two stone tablets that were just like the first ones. I went up the mountain. I carried the two tablets in my hands. [4] The LORD wrote on the tablets what he had written before. It was the Ten Commandments. He had announced them to you out of the fire on the mountain. It was on the day you had gathered together there. So the LORD gave the tablets to me. [5] Then I came back down the mountain. I put the tablets in the ark I had made, just as the LORD had commanded me. And that's where they are now.

[6] Remember how the Israelites traveled from the wells of Bene Jaakan to Moserah. That's where Aaron died. And his body was buried there. His son Eleazar became the next priest after him. [7] From Moserah the people traveled to Gudgodah. Then they went on to Jotbathah. That land has streams of water. [8] At that time the LORD set the tribe of Levi apart. He appointed them to carry the ark of the covenant of the LORD. He wanted them to serve him. He told them to bless the people in his name. And they still do it today. [9] That's why the Levites don't have any part of the land the LORD gave the other tribes in Israel. They don't have any share among them. The LORD himself is their share. That's what the LORD your God told them.

[10] I had stayed on the mountain for 40 days and 40 nights, just as I did the first time. The LORD listened to me that time also. He didn't want to destroy you. [11] "Go," the LORD said to me. "Lead the people on their way. Then they can enter the land and take it over. I have given my word. I promised I would give the land to their fathers, to Abraham, Isaac and Jacob."

Honor the LORD

[12] And now, Israel, what is the LORD your God asking you to do? Honor him. Live exactly as he wants you to live. Love him. Serve him with all your heart and with all your soul. [13] Obey the LORD's commands and rules. I'm giving them to you today for your own good.

[14] The heavens belong to the LORD your God. Even the highest heavens belong to him. He owns the earth and everything in it. [15] But the LORD loved your people of long ago very much. You are their children. And he chose you above all the other nations. His love and his promise remain with you to this very day. [16] So don't be stubborn anymore. Obey the LORD. [17] The LORD your God is the greatest God of all. He is the greatest LORD of all. He is the great God. He is mighty and wonderful. He treats everyone the same. He doesn't accept any money from those who want special favors. [18] He stands up for widows and for children whose fathers have died. He loves outsiders living among you. He gives them food and clothes. [19] So you also must love outsiders. Remember that you yourselves were outsiders in Egypt. [20] Honor the LORD your God. Serve him. Remain true to him. When you make promises, do so in his name. [21] He is the one you should praise. He's your God. With your own eyes you saw the great and amazing things he did for you. [22] Long ago, your people went down into Egypt. The total number of them was 70. And now the LORD your God has made you as many as the stars in the sky.

Love and Obey the LORD

11 Love the LORD your God. Do what
he requires. Always obey his rules,
laws and commands. 2 Remember today
that your children weren't the ones the
LORD your God guided and corrected.
They didn't see his majesty. They weren't
in Egypt when he reached out his mighty
hand and powerful arm. 3 They didn't
see the signs and the other things he
did in Egypt. They didn't see what he
did to Pharaoh, the king of Egypt, and to
his whole country. 4 They weren't there
when the LORD destroyed the army of
Egypt and its horses and chariots. He
swept the waters of the Red Sea over
the Egyptians while they were chasing
you. He wiped them out forever. 5 Your
children didn't see what he did for you
in the desert before you arrived here.
6 They didn't see what he did to Dathan
and Abiram, the sons of Eliab. Eliab
was from the tribe of Reuben. The earth
opened its mouth right in the middle
of the Israelite camp. It swallowed up
Dathan and Abiram. It swallowed them
up together with their families, tents
and every living thing that belonged to
them. 7 But with your own eyes you saw
all the great things the LORD has done.

8 So obey all the commands I'm giving you today. Then you will be strong
enough to go in and take over the land.
You will go across the Jordan River and
take the land as your own. 9 You will
live there for a long time. It's the land
the LORD promised to give to Abraham,
Isaac and Jacob and their children after
them. He gave his word when he made
that promise. The land has plenty of
milk and honey. 10 You will enter it
and take it over. It isn't like the land
of Egypt. That's where you came from.
You planted your seeds there. You had
to water them, just as you have to water
a vegetable garden. 11 But you will soon
go across the Jordan River. The land you
are going to take over has mountains
and valleys in it. It drinks rain from
heaven. 12 It's a land the LORD your God
takes care of. His eyes always look on it
with favor. He watches over it from the
beginning of the year to its end.

13 So be faithful. Obey the commands
the LORD your God is giving you today.
Love him. Serve him with all your heart
and with all your soul. 14 Then the LORD
will send rain on your land at the right
time. He'll send rain in the fall and in
the spring. You will be able to gather
your grain. You will also be able to make
olive oil and fresh wine. 15 He'll provide
grass in the fields for your cattle. You
will have plenty to eat.

16 But be careful. Don't let anyone
tempt you to do something wrong. Don't
turn away and worship other gods. Don't
bow down to them. 17 If you do, the LORD
will be very angry with you. He'll close
up the sky. It won't rain. The ground
won't produce its crops. Soon you will
die. You won't live to enjoy the good
land the LORD is giving you. 18 So keep
my words in your hearts and minds.
Write them down and tie them on your
hands as a reminder. Also tie them on
your foreheads. 19 Teach them to your
children. Talk about them when you
are at home. Talk about them when you
walk along the road. Speak about them
when you go to bed. And speak about
them when you get up. 20 Write them
on the doorframes of your houses. Also
write them on your gates. 21 Then you
and your children will live for a long time
in the land. The LORD promised to give
the land to Abraham, Isaac and Jacob.
Your family line will continue as long
as the heavens remain above the earth.

22 So be careful. Obey all the commands I'm giving you to follow. Love
the LORD your God. Live exactly as he
wants you to live. Remain true to him.
23 Then the LORD will drive out all the
nations to make room for you. They are
larger and stronger than you are. But
you will take their land. 24 Every place
you walk on will belong to you. Your
territory will go all the way from the
desert to Lebanon. It will go from the
Euphrates River to the Mediterranean
Sea. 25 No one will be able to stand up
against you. The LORD your God will
throw the whole land into a panic because of you. He'll do it everywhere you
go, just as he promised you.

26 Listen to me. I'm setting a blessing
and a curse in front of you today. 27 I'm
giving you the commands of the LORD
your God today. You will be blessed if you
obey them. 28 But you will be cursed if
you don't obey them. So don't turn away
from the path I'm now commanding you
to take. Don't turn away by worshiping

other gods you didn't know before. [29]The LORD your God will bring you into the land to take it over. When he does, you must announce the blessings from Mount Gerizim. You must announce the curses from Mount Ebal. [30]As you know, those mountains are across the Jordan River. They are on the west side of the Jordan toward the setting sun. They are near the large trees of Moreh. The mountains are in the territory of the Canaanites, who live in the Arabah Valley near Gilgal. [31]You are about to go across the Jordan River. You will enter the land and take it over. The LORD your God is giving it to you. You will take it over and live there. [32]When you do, make sure you obey all the rules and laws I'm giving you today.

Worship Only Where the LORD Wants You To

12 Here are the rules and laws you must obey. Be careful to obey them in the land the LORD has given you to take as your own. He's the God of your people who lived long ago. Obey these rules and laws as long as you live in the land. [2]You will soon drive the nations out of it. Completely destroy all the places where they worship their gods. Destroy them on the high mountains, on the hills and under every green tree. [3]Break down their altars. Smash their sacred stones. Burn up the poles they use to worship the female god named Asherah. Cut down the statues of their gods. Wipe out the names of their gods from those places.

[4]You must not worship the LORD your God the way those nations worship their gods. [5]Instead, go to the special place he will choose from among all your tribes. He will put his Name there. That's where you must go. [6]Take your burnt offerings and sacrifices to that place. Bring your special gifts and a tenth of everything you produce. Take with you what you have promised to give. Bring any other offerings you choose to give. And bring the male animals among your livestock that were born first to their mothers. [7]You and your families will eat at the place the LORD your God will choose. He will be with you there. You will find joy in everything you have done. That's because he has blessed you. [8]You must not do as we're doing here today. All of us are doing only what we think is right. [9]That's because you haven't yet reached the place the LORD is giving you. Your God will give you peace and rest there. [10]But first you will go across the Jordan River. You will settle in the land he's giving you. It will belong to you as your share. He will give you peace and rest from all your enemies around you. You will live in safety. [11]The LORD your God will choose a special place. He will put his Name there. That's where you must bring everything I command you to bring. That includes your burnt offerings and sacrifices. It includes your special gifts and a tenth of everything you produce. It also includes all the things of value that you promised to give to the LORD. [12]Be filled with joy there in the sight of the LORD your God. Your children should also be joyful. So should your male and female servants. And so should the Levites from your towns. The Levites won't receive any part of the land as their share. [13]Be careful not to sacrifice your burnt offerings anywhere you want to. [14]Offer them only at the place the LORD will choose in one of your tribes. There you must obey everything I command you.

[15]But you can kill your animals in any of your towns. You can eat as much of the meat as you want to. You can eat it as if it were antelope or deer meat. That is part of the blessing the LORD your God is giving you. Those who are "clean" and those who are not can eat it. [16]But you must not eat meat that still has blood in it. Pour the blood out on the ground like water. [17]Here are the things you must not eat in your own towns. You must not eat the tenth part of your grain, olive oil and fresh wine. It belongs to the LORD. You must not eat the male animals among your livestock that were born first to their mothers. Don't eat anything you have promised to give. Don't eat any offerings you have chosen to give. And you must not eat any of your special gifts. [18]Instead, you must eat all those things in the sight of the LORD your God. Do it at the place he will choose. You, your children, your male and female servants and the Levites from your towns can eat them. Be filled with joy in the sight of the LORD

your God. Be joyful in everything you do. 19 Don't forget to take care of the Levites as long as you live in your land.

20 The LORD your God will increase your territory, just as he has promised you. When he does, you might get hungry for meat. You might say, "I'd really like some meat." Then you can eat as much of it as you want to. 21 The LORD your God will choose a special place. He will put his Name there. But suppose that place is too far away from you. Then you can kill animals from the herds and flocks the LORD has given you. Do it just as I have commanded you. In your own towns you can eat as much of the meat as you want to. 22 Eat it as you would eat antelope or deer meat. Those who are "clean" and those who are not can eat it. 23 But be sure you don't eat meat that still has blood in it. The blood is the animal's life. So you must not eat the life along with the meat. 24 You must not eat the blood. Pour it out on the ground like water. 25 Don't eat it. Then things will go well with you and your children after you. You will be doing what is right in the eyes of the LORD.

26 But go to the place the LORD will choose. Take with you the things you have set apart for him. Bring what you have promised to give him. 27 Sacrifice your burnt offerings on the altar of the LORD your God. Offer the meat and the blood there. The blood of your sacrifices must be poured out beside his altar. But you can eat the meat. 28 Make sure you obey all the rules I'm giving you. Then things will always go well with you and your children after you. That's because you will be doing what is good and right in the eyes of the LORD your God.

29 You are about to attack the land and take it over as your own. When you do, the LORD your God will destroy the nations who live there. He will do it to make room for you. You will drive them out. You will settle in their land. 30 They will be destroyed to make room for you. But when they are destroyed, be careful. Don't be trapped. Don't ask questions about their gods. Don't say, "How do these nations serve their gods? We'll do it in the same way." 31 You must not worship the LORD your God the way they worship their gods. When they worship, they do all kinds of evil things the LORD hates. They even burn up their children in the fire as sacrifices to their gods.

32 Be sure you do everything I am commanding you to do. Do not add anything to my commands. And do not take anything away from them.

Do Not Worship Other Gods

13 Suppose a prophet appears among you. Or someone comes who uses dreams to tell what's going to happen. He tells you that a sign or something amazing is going to take place. 2 The sign or amazing thing he has spoken about might really take place. And then the prophet might say, "Let's serve other gods. Let's worship them." But you haven't known anything about those gods before. 3 So you must not listen to what that prophet or dreamer has said. The LORD your God is testing you. He wants to know whether you love him with all your heart and with all your soul. 4 You must worship him. You must honor him. Keep his commands. Obey him. Serve him. Remain true to him. 5 That prophet or dreamer must be put to death. He told you not to obey the LORD your God. The LORD brought you out of Egypt. He set you free from the land where you were slaves. He commanded you to live the way he wants you to. But that prophet or dreamer has tried to get you to be unfaithful to the LORD. Get rid of that evil person.

6 Suppose your very own brother or sister secretly tempts you to do something wrong. Or your child or the wife you love tempts you. Or your closest friend does it. Suppose one of them says, "Let's go and worship other gods." But you and your people of long ago hadn't known anything about those gods before. 7 They are the gods of the nations around you. Those nations might be near or far away. In fact, they might reach from one end of the land to the other. 8 Don't give in to those who are tempting you. Don't listen to them. Don't feel sorry for them. Don't spare them or save them. 9 You must certainly put them to death. You must be the first to throw stones at them. Then all the people must do the same thing. 10 Put them to death by throwing stones at them. They tried to turn you away from the LORD your God. He brought you out

of Egypt. That's the land where you
were slaves. 11 After you kill those who
tempted you, all the Israelites will hear
about it. And they will be too scared to
do an evil thing like that again.
12 The LORD your God is giving you
towns to live in. But suppose you hear
something bad about one of those towns.
13 You hear that people who cause trouble have appeared among you. They've
tried to get the people of their town to
do something wrong. They've said, "Let's
go and worship other gods." But you
haven't known anything about those
gods before. 14 So you must ask people
some questions. You must check out
the matter carefully. If it's true, an evil
thing has really happened among you.
It's something the LORD hates. 15 Then
you must certainly kill with your swords
everyone who lives in that town. You
must destroy it completely. You must
wipe out its people and livestock. 16 You
must gather all the goods of that town
into the middle of the main street. You
must burn the town completely. You
must burn up everything in it. It's a
whole burnt offering to the LORD your
God. The town must remain a pile of
stones forever. It must never be built
again. 17 Don't keep anything that should
be destroyed. Then the LORD will turn
away from his great anger. He will show
you mercy. He'll have deep concern for
you. He'll cause there to be many of you.
That's what he promised your people
of long ago. He gave his word when he
made the promise. 18 The LORD your God
will do those things if you obey him. I'm
giving you his commands today. And
you must obey all of them. You must
do what is right in his eyes.

"Clean" and "Unclean" Food

14 You are the children of the LORD
your God. Don't cut yourselves to
honor the dead. Don't shave the front
of your heads to honor the dead. 2 You
are a holy nation. The LORD your God
has set you apart for himself. He has
chosen you to be his special treasure.
He chose you out of all the nations on
the face of the earth.
3 Don't eat anything the LORD hates.
4 Here are the only animals you can eat.
You can eat oxen, sheep, goats, 5 deer,
gazelles, roe deer, wild goats, ibexes,
antelope and mountain sheep. 6 You can
eat any animal that has a divided hoof.
But it must also chew the cud. 7 Some
animals only chew the cud. Others only
have a divided hoof. The camel, rabbit
and rock badger chew the cud, but they
don't have a divided hoof. So you can't
eat them. They are not "clean" for you.
8 Pigs aren't "clean" for you either. They
have a divided hoof, but they don't chew
the cud. So don't eat their meat. And
don't touch their dead bodies.
9 Many creatures live in water. You
can eat all the ones that have fins and
scales. 10 But don't eat anything that
doesn't have fins and scales. It isn't
"clean" for you.
11 You can eat any "clean" bird. 12 But
there are many birds you can't eat. They
include eagles, vultures, and black vultures. 13 They include red kites, black kites
and all kinds of falcons. 14 They include
all kinds of ravens. 15 They include horned
owls, screech owls, gulls and all kinds of
hawks. 16 They include little owls, great
owls, white owls 17 and desert owls. They
include ospreys and cormorants. 18 They
include storks and all kinds of herons.
They also include hoopoes and bats.
19 All flying insects are "unclean" for
you. So don't eat them. 20 But you can
eat any creature that has wings and
is "clean."
21 If you find something that's already
dead, don't eat it. You can give it to an
outsider living in any of your towns.
They may eat it. Or you can sell it to
someone from another country. But you
are a holy nation. The LORD your God
has set you apart for himself.

Don't cook a young goat in its mother's milk.

Give a Tenth of What You Produce

22 Be sure to set apart a tenth of everything your fields produce each year.
23 Here are the things you should eat
in the sight of the LORD your God. You
should eat a tenth part of your grain,
olive oil and fresh wine. You should
also eat the male animals among your
livestock that were born first to their
mothers. Eat all these things at the
special place the LORD your God will
choose. He will put his Name there. You
will learn to honor him always. 24 But
suppose the place the LORD will choose

for his Name is too far away from you. And suppose your God has blessed you. And your tenth part is too heavy for you to carry. 25 Then sell it for silver. Take the silver with you. Go to the place the LORD your God will choose. 26 Use the silver to buy anything you like. It can be cattle or sheep. It can be any kind of wine. In fact, it can be anything else you wish. Then you and your family can eat there in the sight of the LORD your God. You can be filled with joy. 27 Don't forget to take care of the Levites who will live in your towns. They won't receive any part of the land as their share.

28 At the end of every three years, bring a tenth of everything you produce that year. Store it in your towns. 29 Then the Levites can come and eat. That's because they won't receive any part of the land as their share. The outsiders and widows who live in your towns can come. So can the children whose fathers have died. Everyone can have plenty to eat. Then the LORD your God will bless you in everything you do.

The Year for Forgiving People What They Owe

15 At the end of every seven years you must forgive people what they owe you. 2 Have you made a loan to one of your own people? Then forgive what is owed to you. You can't require that person to pay you back. The LORD's time to forgive what is owed has been announced. 3 You can require someone from another nation to pay you back. But you must forgive what any of your own people owes you. 4 There shouldn't be any poor people among you. The LORD will greatly bless you in the land he is giving you. You will take it over as your own. 5 The LORD your God will bless you if you obey him completely. Be careful to follow all the commands I'm giving you today. 6 The LORD your God will bless you, just as he has promised. You will lend money to many nations. But you won't have to borrow from any of them. You will rule over many nations. But none of them will rule over you.

7 Suppose someone is poor among you. And suppose they live in one of the towns in the land the LORD your God is giving you. Then don't be mean to them. They are poor. So don't hold back money from them. 8 Instead, open your hands and lend them what they need. Do it freely. 9 Be careful not to have an evil thought in your mind. Don't say to yourself, "The seventh year will soon be here. It's the year for forgiving people what they owe." If you think like that, you might treat the needy people among you badly. You might not give them anything. Then they might make their appeal to the LORD against you. And he will find you guilty of sin. 10 So give freely to needy people. Let your heart be tender toward them. Then the LORD your God will bless you in all your work. He will bless you in everything you do. 11 There will always be poor people in the land. So I'm commanding you to give freely to those who are poor and needy in your land. Open your hands to them.

Set Your Hebrew Servants Free

12 Suppose any Hebrew men or women sell themselves to you. If they do, they will serve you for six years. Then in the seventh year you must let them go free. 13 But when you set them free, don't send them away without anything to show for all their work. 14 Freely give them some animals from your flock. Also give them some of your grain and wine. The LORD your God has blessed you richly. Give to them as he has given to you. 15 Remember that you were slaves in Egypt. The LORD your God set you free. That's why I'm giving you this command today.

16 But suppose your servant says to you, "I don't want to leave you." He loves you and your family. And you are taking good care of him. 17 Then take him to the door of your house. Poke a hole through his earlobe into the doorpost. And he will become your servant for life. Do the same with your female servant.

18 Don't think you are being cheated when you set your servants free. After all, they have served you for six years. The service of each of them has been worth twice as much as the service of a hired worker. And the LORD your God will bless you in everything you do.

Male Animals Born First to Their Mothers

19 Set apart every male animal among your livestock that was born first to its

mother. Set it apart to the LORD your
God. Don't put a firstborn cow to work.
Don't clip the wool from a firstborn sheep.
20 Each year you and your family must
eat them. Do it in front of the LORD your
God at the place he will choose. 21 Suppose
an animal has something wrong with it.
It might not be able to see or walk. Or it
might have a bad flaw. Then you must
not sacrifice it to the LORD your God. 22 You
must eat it in your own towns. Those who
are "clean" and those who are "unclean"
can eat it. Eat it as if it were antelope or
deer meat. 23 But you must not eat meat
that still has blood in it. Pour the blood
out on the ground like water.

The Passover Feast

16 Celebrate the Passover Feast of
the LORD your God in the month
of Aviv. In that month he brought you
out of Egypt at night. 2 Sacrifice an animal from your flock or herd. It is the
Passover sacrifice to honor the LORD
your God. Sacrifice it at the special place
the LORD will choose. He will put his
Name there. 3 Don't eat the animal along
with bread made with yeast. Instead,
for seven days eat bread made without
yeast. It's the bread that reminds you of
how much you suffered. Remember that
you left Egypt in a hurry. Remember
it all the days of your life. Don't forget
the day you left Egypt. 4 Don't keep any
yeast anywhere in your land for seven
days. You will sacrifice the Passover
animal on the evening of the first day.
Do not let any of its meat be left over
until the next morning.
5 You must not sacrifice the Passover
animal in just any town the LORD your
God is giving you. 6 Sacrifice it only in
the special place he will choose for his
Name. Sacrifice it there in the evening
when the sun goes down. Do it on the
same day every year. Be sure it's the day
you left Egypt. 7 Cook the animal and
eat it. Do it at the place the LORD your
God will choose. Then in the morning
return to your tents. 8 For six days eat
bread made without yeast. On the seventh day come together for a service to
honor the LORD your God. Don't do any
work on that day.

The Feast of Weeks

9 Count off seven weeks from the time
you begin to cut your grain in the field.
10 Then celebrate the Feast of Weeks to
honor the LORD your God. Give to the
LORD anything you choose to give as an
offering. Give, just as the LORD has given
to you. 11 Be filled with joy in the sight of
the LORD your God. Be joyful at the special
place he will choose for his Name. You,
your children, and your male and female
servants should be joyful. So should the
Levites living in your towns. So should
the outsiders and widows living among
you. And so should the children whose
fathers have died. 12 Remember that you
were slaves in Egypt. Be careful to obey
the rules I'm giving you.

The Feast of Booths

13 Gather the grain from your threshing floors. Take the fresh wine from
your winepresses. Then celebrate the
Feast of Booths for seven days. 14 Be
filled with joy at your feast. You, your
children, and your male and female
servants should be joyful. So should the
Levites, the outsiders, and the widows
living in your towns. And so should the
children whose fathers have died. 15 For
seven days celebrate the feast to honor
the LORD your God. Do it at the place
he will choose. The LORD will bless you
when you gather all your crops. He'll
bless you in everything you do. And
you will be full of joy. 16 All your men
must appear in front of the LORD your
God at the holy tent. They must go to
the place he will choose. They must do it
three times a year. They must go there
to celebrate the Feast of Unleavened
Bread, the Feast of Weeks and the Feast
of Booths. None of your men should
appear in front of the LORD without
bringing something with him. 17 Each of
you must bring a gift. Give to the LORD
your God, just as he has given to you.

Appoint Judges and Officials

18 Appoint judges and officials for
each of your tribes. Do it in every town
the LORD your God is giving you. They
must judge the people fairly. 19 Do what
is right. Treat everyone the same. Don't
take money from people who want special favors. It makes those who are wise
close their eyes to the truth. It twists the
words of those who have done nothing
wrong. 20 Do only what is right. Then
you will live. You will take over the land
the LORD your God is giving you.

Don't Worship Other Gods

21 Don't set up a wooden pole used to worship the female god named Asherah. Don't set it up beside the altar you build to worship the LORD your God. 22 Don't set up a sacred stone to honor another god. The LORD your God hates Asherah poles and sacred stones.

17 Suppose an ox or sheep has anything at all wrong with it. Then don't sacrifice it to the LORD your God. He hates it.

2 Someone living among you might do what is evil in the sight of the LORD your God. It might happen in one of the towns the LORD is giving you. That person is breaking the LORD's covenant. 3 The person might have worshiped or bowed down to other gods. That person might have bowed down to the sun or moon or stars in the sky. I have commanded you not to do these things. 4 When you hear that people have done something like that, check the matter out carefully. If it's true, an evil thing has been done in Israel. The LORD hates that. 5 So take the person who has done that evil thing to your city gate. Put that person to death by throwing stones at them. 6 Two or three witnesses are required to put someone to death. No one can be put to death because of what only one witness says. Two or three witnesses are required. 7 The witnesses must throw the first stones. Then the rest of the people must also throw stones. Get rid of that evil person.

Law Courts

8 People will bring their cases to your courts. But some cases will be too hard for you to judge. They might be about murders, attacks or other crimes. Then take those hard cases to the place the LORD your God will choose. 9 Go to a priest, who is a Levite. And go to the judge who is in office at that time. Ask them for their decision. They will give it to you. 10 They'll hand down their decisions at the place the LORD will choose. You must do what they decide. Be careful to do everything they tell you to do. 11 Act according to whatever they teach you. Accept the decisions they give you. Don't turn away from what they tell you. Don't turn to the right or the left. 12 Someone might show that they don't respect the judge. Or they will show that they don't respect the priest. The priest will serve the LORD your God at the place God will choose. If anyone doesn't show respect for these people, that person must be put to death. Remove that evil person from Israel. 13 All the Israelites will hear about it. And they will be afraid to disrespect a judge or priest again.

Appoint the King the LORD Chooses

14 You will enter the land the LORD your God is giving you. You will take it as your own. You will make your homes in it. When you do, you will say, "Let's appoint a king over us, just like all the nations around us." 15 When that happens, make sure you appoint over yourselves a king the LORD your God chooses. He must be from among your own people. Don't appoint over yourselves someone from another country. Don't choose anyone who isn't from one of the tribes of Israel. 16 The king must not get large numbers of horses for himself. He must not make the people return to Egypt to get more horses. The LORD has told you, "You must not go back there again." 17 The king must not have many wives. If he does, they will lead him astray. He must not store up large amounts of silver and gold.

18 When he sits on the throne of his kingdom, he must make for himself a copy of the law. He must write on a scroll the law that I am teaching you. He must copy it from the scroll of a priest, who is a Levite. 19 The king must keep the scroll close to him at all times. He must read it all the days of his life. Then he can learn to have respect for the LORD his God. He can carefully obey all the words of this law and these rules. 20 He won't think of himself as being better than his people are. He won't turn away from the law. He won't turn to the right or the left. Then he and his sons after him will rule over his kingdom in Israel for a long time.

Offerings for Priests and Levites

18 The priests, who are Levites, won't receive any part of the land of Israel. That also applies to the whole tribe of Levi. They will eat the food offerings presented to the LORD. That will be their share. 2 They won't have any part of the land the LORD gave the other tribes in Israel. The LORD himself is their share, just as he promised them.

3 Anyone who sacrifices a bull or a sheep owes a share of it to the priests. Their share is the shoulder, the inside parts and the meat from the head. 4 You must give the priests the first share of the harvest of your grain, olive oil and fresh wine. You must also give them the first wool you clip from your sheep. 5 The LORD your God has chosen the Levites and their sons after them to serve him in his name always. He hasn't chosen priests from any of your other tribes.

6 Sometimes a Levite will move from the town in Israel where he's living. And he will come to the place the LORD will choose. He'll do it because he really wants to. 7 Then he can serve in the name of the LORD his God. He'll be like all the other Levites who serve the LORD there. 8 He must have an equal share of the good things they have. That applies even if he has already received money by selling things his family owned.

Practices the LORD Hates

9 You will enter the land the LORD your God is giving you. When you do, don't copy the practices of the nations there. The LORD hates those practices. 10 Here are things you must not do. Don't sacrifice your children in the fire to other gods. Don't practice any kind of evil magic at all. Don't use magic to try to explain the meaning of warnings in the sky or of any other signs. Don't take part in worshiping evil powers. 11 Don't put a spell on anyone. Don't get messages from those who have died. Don't talk to the spirits of the dead. Don't get advice from the dead. 12 The LORD your God hates it when anyone does these things. The nations in the land he's giving you do these things he hates. So he will drive out those nations to make room for you. 13 You must be without blame in the sight of the LORD your God.

The Prophet of the LORD

14 You will take over the nations that are in the land the LORD is giving you. They listen to those who practice all kinds of evil magic. But you belong to the LORD your God. He says you must not do these things. 15 The LORD your God will raise up for you a prophet like me. He will be one of your own people. You must listen to him. 16 At Mount Horeb you asked the LORD your God for a prophet. You asked him on the day you gathered together. You said, "We don't want to hear the voice of the LORD our God. We don't want to see this great fire anymore. If we do, we'll die."

17 The LORD said to me, "What they are saying is good. 18 I will raise up for them a prophet like you. He will be one of their own people. I will put my words in his mouth. He will tell them everything I command him to say. 19 The prophet will speak in my name. But someone might not listen to what I say through the prophet. I will hold that person responsible for not listening. 20 But suppose a prophet dares to speak in my name something I have not commanded. Or he speaks in the name of other gods. Then that prophet must be put to death."

21 You will say to yourselves, "How can we know when a message hasn't been spoken by the LORD?" 22 Sometimes a prophet will announce something in the name of the LORD. And it won't take place or come true. Then that's a message the LORD hasn't told him to speak. That prophet has dared to speak on his own authority. So don't be afraid of what he says.

Cities to Run to for Safety

19 The LORD your God will destroy the nations whose land he is giving you. You will drive them out. And you will make your homes in their towns and their houses. 2 When you do, set apart for yourselves three cities in the land. It's the land the LORD your God is giving you to take as your own. 3 Figure out the distances and then separate the land into three parts. Then anyone who kills another person can run to one of these cities for safety. They are in the land the LORD your God is giving you as your own.

4 Here is the rule about a person who kills someone. That person can run to one of those cities for safety. The rule applies to anyone who kills a neighbor they didn't hate and didn't mean to kill. 5 For example, suppose a man goes into a forest with his neighbor to cut wood. When he swings his ax to chop down a tree, the head of the ax flies off. And it hits his neighbor and kills him. Then that man can run to one of those cities and save his life. 6 If he doesn't go to one of those cities, the dead man's nearest

male relative might become very angry. He might chase the man. If the city is too far away, he might catch him and kill him. But the man running to the city isn't worthy of death, because he didn't hate his neighbor. 7 That's why I command you to set apart for yourselves three cities.

8 The LORD your God will increase the size of your territory. He promised your people of long ago that he would do it. He will give you the whole land he promised them. 9 But he'll do it only if you are careful to obey all the laws I'm commanding you today. I command you to love the LORD your God. You must always live as he wants you to live. Suppose you are careful to obey, and the LORD your God gives you more land. Then you must set apart three more cities. 10 Do it to protect those not guilty of murder. Then you won't spill their blood in your land. It's the land the LORD your God is giving you as your own.

11 But suppose a man hates his neighbor. So he hides and waits for him. Then he attacks him and kills him. And he runs to one of those cities for safety. 12 If he does, the elders of his own town must send for him. He must be brought back from the city. He must be handed over to the dead man's nearest male relative. Then the relative will kill him. 13 Don't feel sorry for him. He has killed someone who hadn't done anything wrong. Crimes like that must be punished in Israel. Then things will go well with you.

14 Don't move your neighbor's boundary stone. It was set up by people who lived there before you. It marks the border of a field in the land you will receive as your own. The LORD your God is giving you that land. You will take it over.

Witnesses

15 Suppose someone is charged with committing a crime of any kind. Then one witness won't be enough to prove that person is guilty. Every matter must be proved by the words of two or three witnesses.

16 Suppose a witness who tells lies goes to court and brings charges against someone. The witness says someone committed a crime. 17 Then the two people in the case must stand in front of the LORD. They must stand in front of the priests and the judges who are in office at that time. 18 The judges must check out the matter carefully. And suppose the witness is proved to be lying. Then he has said something false in court against another Israelite. 19 So do to the lying witness what he tried to do to the other person. Get rid of that evil witness. 20 The rest of the people will hear about it. And they will be afraid. They won't allow such an evil thing to be done among them again. 21 Don't feel sorry for that evil person. A life must be taken for a life. An eye must be put out for an eye. A tooth must be knocked out for a tooth. A hand must be cut off for a hand and a foot for a foot.

Going to War

20 When you go to war against your enemies, you might see that they have horses and chariots. They might even have an army stronger than yours. But don't be afraid of them. The LORD your God will be with you. After all, he brought you up out of Egypt. 2 Just before you go into battle, the priest will come forward. He'll speak to the army. 3 He'll say, "Men of Israel, listen to me. Today you are going into battle against your enemies. Don't be scared. Don't be afraid. Don't panic or be terrified by them. 4 The LORD your God is going with you. He'll fight for you. He'll help you win the battle over your enemies."

5 The officers will speak to the army. They will say, "Has anyone built a new house and not started to live in it? Let him go home. If he doesn't, he might die in battle. Then someone else will live in his house. 6 Has anyone planted a vineyard and not started to enjoy it? Let him go home. If he doesn't, he might die in battle. Then someone else will enjoy his vineyard. 7 Has anyone promised to be married to a woman but hasn't done it yet? Let him go home. If he doesn't, he might die in battle. Then someone else will marry her." 8 The officers will continue, "Is anyone afraid or scared? Let him go home. Then the other soldiers won't lose hope too." 9 The officers will finish speaking to the army. When they do, they'll appoint commanders over it.

10 Suppose you march up to attack a city. Before you attack it, offer to make peace with its people. 11 Suppose they

accept your offer and open their gates. Then force all the people in the city to be your slaves. They will have to work for you. 12 But suppose they refuse your offer of peace and prepare for battle. Then surround that city. Get ready to attack it. 13 The LORD your God will hand it over to you. When he does, kill all the men with your swords. 14 But you can take the women and children for yourselves. You can also take the livestock and everything else in the city. What you have captured from your enemies you can use for yourselves. The LORD your God has given it to you. 15 That's how you must treat all the cities far away from you. Those cities don't belong to the nations that are nearby.

16 But what about the cities the LORD your God is giving you as your own? Kill everything that breathes in those cities. 17 Completely destroy them. Wipe out the Hittites, Amorites, Canaanites, Perizzites, Hivites and Jebusites. That's what the LORD your God commanded you to do. 18 If you don't destroy them, they'll teach you to do all the things the LORD hates. He hates the way they worship their gods. If you do those things, you will sin against the LORD your God.

19 Suppose you surround a city and get ready to attack it. And suppose you fight against it for a long time in order to capture it. Then don't chop down its trees and destroy them. You can eat their fruit. So don't cut them down. Are the trees people? So why should you attack them? 20 But you can cut down trees that you know aren't fruit trees. You can build war machines out of their wood. You can use them until you capture the city you are fighting against.

What to Do When You Don't Know Who Killed Someone

21 Suppose you find someone who has been killed. The body is lying in a field in the land the LORD your God is giving you as your own. But no one knows who the killer was. 2 Then your elders and judges will go out to the field. They will measure the distance from the body to the nearby towns. 3 The elders from the town that is nearest to the body will get a young cow. It must never have been used for work. It must never have pulled a load. 4 The elders must lead it down into a valley. The valley must not have been farmed. There must be a stream flowing through it. There in the valley the elders must break the cow's neck. 5 The priests, who are sons of Levi, will step forward. The LORD your God has chosen them to serve him. He wants them to bless the people in his name. He wants them to decide all cases that have to do with people arguing and attacking others. 6 Then all the elders from the town that is nearest to the body will wash their hands. They will wash them over the young cow whose neck they broke in the valley. 7 They'll say to the LORD, "We didn't kill that person. We didn't see it happen. 8 Accept this payment for the sin of your people Israel. LORD, you have set your people free. Don't hold them guilty for spilling the blood of someone who hasn't done anything wrong." That will pay for the death of that person. 9 So you will get rid of the guilt of killing someone who didn't do anything wrong. That's because you have done what is right in the LORD's eyes.

Marrying a Woman Who Is Your Prisoner

10 Suppose you go to war against your enemies. And the LORD your God hands them over to you and you take them as prisoners. 11 Then you notice a beautiful woman among them. If you like her, you may marry her. 12 Bring her home. Have her shave her head and cut her nails. 13 Have her throw away the clothes she was wearing when she was captured. Let her live in your house and mourn the loss of her parents for a full month. Then you can go to her and be her husband. And she will be your wife. 14 But suppose you aren't pleased with her. Then let her go where she wants to. You must not sell her. You must not treat her as a slave. You have already brought shame on her.

The Rights of the Oldest Son

15 Suppose a man has two wives. He loves one but not the other. And both of them have sons by him. But the oldest son is the son of the wife the man doesn't love. 16 Someday he'll leave his property to his sons. When he does, he must not give the rights of the oldest son to the son of the wife he loves. He must give those rights to his oldest son. He must do it even though his oldest son is the

son of the wife he doesn't love. 17 He must
recognize the full rights of the oldest son.
He must do it, even though that son is
the son of the wife he doesn't love. He
must give that son a double share of
everything he has. That son is the first
sign of his father's strength. So the rights
of the oldest son belong to him.

A Stubborn Son

18 Suppose someone has a very stubborn son. He doesn't obey his father
and mother. And he won't listen to them
when they try to correct him. 19 Then
his parents will take hold of him and
bring him to the elders at the gate of
his town. 20 They will say to the elders,
"This son of ours is very stubborn. He
won't obey us. He eats too much. He's
always getting drunk." 21 Then all the
people in his town will put him to death
by throwing stones at him. Get rid of
that evil person. All the Israelites will
hear about it. And they will be afraid
to disobey their parents.

Several Other Laws

22 Suppose someone is put to death
for a crime worthy of death. And a pole
is stuck through their body and set up
where people can see it. 23 Then you
must not leave the body on the pole all
night. Make sure you bury it that same
day. Everyone who is hung on a pole is
under God's curse. You must not make
the land "unclean." The LORD your God
is giving it to you as your own.

22 Suppose you see your neighbor's
ox or sheep wandering away.
Then don't act as if you didn't see it.
Instead, make sure you take it back to
its owner. 2 Its owner might not live near
you. Or you might not know who owns
it. So take the animal home with you.
Keep it until the owner comes looking
for it. Then give it back to them. 3 Do the
same thing if you find their donkey,
coat or anything they have lost. Don't
act as if you didn't see it.

4 Suppose you see your neighbor's
donkey or ox that has fallen down on
the road. Then don't act as if you didn't
see it. Help the owner get it up on its
feet again.

5 A woman must not wear men's
clothes. And a man must not wear
women's clothes. The LORD your God
hates it when anyone does this.

6 Suppose you happen to find a bird's
nest beside the road. It might be in a
tree or on the ground. And suppose the
mother bird is sitting on her little birds or
on the eggs. Then don't take the mother
along with the little ones. 7 You can take
the little ones. But make sure you let the
mother go. Then things will go well with
you. You will live for a long time.

8 If you build a new house, put a low
wall around the edge of your roof. Then
you won't be responsible if someone
falls off your roof and dies.

9 Don't plant two kinds of seeds in
your vineyard. If you do, the crops you
grow there will be impure. Your grapes
will also be impure.

10 Don't let an ox and a donkey pull
the same plow together.

11 Don't wear clothes made out of wool
and linen woven together.

12 Make tassels on the four corners of
the coat you wear.

Breaking Marriage Laws

13 Suppose a man marries a woman
and sleeps with her. But then he doesn't
like her. 14 So he tells lies about her and
says she's a bad woman. He says, "I
married this woman. But when I slept
with her, I discovered she wasn't a virgin." 15 Then the young woman's parents
must bring proof that she was a virgin.
They must give the proof to the elders
at the gate of the town. 16 Her father will
speak to the elders. He'll say, "I gave my
daughter to this man to be his wife. But
he doesn't like her. 17 So now he has told
lies about her. He has said, 'I discovered
that your daughter wasn't a virgin.' But
here's the proof that my daughter was a
virgin." Then her parents will show the
elders of the town the cloth that has her
blood on it. 18 The elders will punish the
man. 19 They'll make him weigh out two
and a half pounds of silver. They'll give
it to the young woman's father. That's
because the man has said an Israelite
virgin is a bad woman. She will continue
to be his wife. He must not divorce her
as long as he lives.

20 But suppose the charge is true. And
there isn't any proof that the young
woman was a virgin. 21 Then she must be
brought to the door of her father's house.
There the people of her town will put her
to death by throwing stones at her. She

has done a very terrible thing in Israel. She has slept with a man before she was married. Get rid of that evil person.

[22]Suppose a man is seen sleeping with another man's wife. Then the man and the woman must both die. Get rid of those evil people.

[23]Suppose a man happens to see a virgin in a town. And she has promised to marry another man. But the man who happens to see her sleeps with her.
[24]Then you must take both of them to the gate of that town. You must put them to death by throwing stones at them. You must kill the young woman because she was in a town and didn't scream for help. And you must kill the man because he slept with another man's wife. Get rid of those evil people.

[25]But suppose a man happens to see a young woman out in the country. And she has promised to marry another man. But the man who happens to see her rapes her. Then only the man who has
done that will die. [26]Don't do anything to the woman. She hasn't committed a sin worthy of death. That case is like the case of someone who attacks and murders a neighbor. [27]The man found the young woman out in the country. And she screamed for help. But there wasn't anyone around who could save her.

[28]Suppose a man happens to see a virgin who hasn't promised to marry another man. And the man who happens to see her rapes her. But some-
one discovers them. [29]Then the man must weigh out 20 ounces of silver. He must give it to her father. The man must marry the young woman, because he raped her. And he can never divorce her as long as he lives.

[30]A man must not marry his stepmother. He must not bring shame on his father by sleeping with her.

Who Can Join in Worship With the LORD's People?

23 No man whose sex organs have been crushed or cut can join in worship with the LORD's people.

[2]No one born to an unmarried woman can join in worship with the LORD's people. That also applies to the person's children for all time to come.

[3]The people of Ammon and Moab can't join in worship with the LORD's people. That also applies to their children after them for all time to come.
[4]The Ammonites and Moabites didn't come to meet you with food and water on your way out of Egypt. They even hired Balaam from Pethor in Aram Naharaim to put a curse on you. Balaam
was the son of Beor. [5]The LORD your God wouldn't listen to Balaam. Instead, he turned the curse into a blessing for you.
He did it because he loves you. [6]So don't make a peace treaty with the Ammonites and Moabites as long as you live.

[7]Don't hate the people of Edom. They are your relatives. Don't hate the people of Egypt. After all, you lived as outsiders in
their country. [8]The great-grandchildren of the Edomites and Egyptians can join in worship with the LORD's people.

Keep the Camp of the Soldiers Pure and "Clean"

[9]There will be times when you are at war with your enemies. And your soldiers will be in camp. Then keep away from anything that isn't pure and
"clean." [10]Suppose semen flows from the body of one of your soldiers during the night. Then that will make him "unclean." He must go outside the camp and
stay there. [11]But as evening approaches, he must wash himself. When the sun goes down, he can return to the camp.

[12]Choose a place outside the camp
where you can go to the toilet. [13]Keep a shovel among your tools. When you go to the toilet, dig a hole. Then cover up
your waste. [14]The LORD your God walks around in your camp. He's there to keep you safe. He's also there to hand your enemies over to you. So your camp must be holy. Then he won't see anything among you that is shameful. He won't turn away from you.

Several Other Laws

[15]If a slave comes to you for safety, don't hand them over to their master.
[16]Let them live among you anywhere they want to. Let them live in any town they choose. Don't treat them badly.

[17]A man or woman in Israel must not
become a temple prostitute. [18]The LORD your God hates the money that men and women get for being prostitutes. So don't take that money into the house of the LORD to pay what you promised to give.

19 Don't charge your own people any interest. Don't charge them when they borrow money, food or anything else. 20 You can charge interest to people from another country. But don't charge your own people. Then the LORD your God will bless you in everything you do. He will bless you in the land you are entering to take as your own.

21 Don't put off giving to the LORD your God everything you promise him. He will certainly require it from you. And you will be guilty of committing a sin. 22 But if you don't make a promise, you won't be guilty. 23 Make sure you do what you promised to do. With your own mouth you made the promise to the LORD your God. No one forced you to do it.

24 When you enter your neighbor's vineyard, you can eat all the grapes you want. But don't put any of them in your basket. 25 When you enter your neighbor's field, you can pick heads of grain. But don't cut down their standing grain.

24 Suppose a man marries a woman. But later he decides he doesn't like her. He finds something shameful about her. So he gives her a letter of divorce and sends her away from his house. 2 Then after she leaves his house she becomes another man's wife. 3 But her second husband doesn't like her either. So he gives her a letter of divorce and sends her away from his house. Or perhaps he dies. 4 Then her first husband isn't allowed to marry her again. The LORD would hate that. When her first husband divorced her, she became "unclean." Don't bring sin on the land the LORD your God is giving you as your own.

5 Suppose a man has just married his wife. Then don't send him into battle. Don't give him any other duty either. He's free to stay home for one year. He needs time to make his new wife happy.

6 Someone might borrow money from you and give you two millstones to keep until you are paid back. Don't keep them. Don't even keep the upper one. That person needs both millstones to make a living.

7 Suppose someone is caught kidnapping another Israelite. And they sell or treat that person as a slave. Then the kidnapper must die. Get rid of that evil person.

8 What about skin diseases? Be very careful to do exactly what the priests, who are Levites, tell you to do. You must be careful to obey the commands I've given them. 9 Remember what the LORD your God did to Miriam on your way out of Egypt.

10 Suppose your neighbor borrows something from you. And he offers you something to keep until you get paid back. Then don't go into their house to get it. 11 Stay outside. Let the neighbor bring it out to you. 12 The neighbor might be poor. You might be given their coat to keep until you get paid back. Don't go to sleep while you still have it. 13 Return it before the sun goes down. They need it to sleep in and will thank you for returning it. The LORD your God will see it and know that you have done the right thing.

14 Don't take advantage of any hired worker who is poor and needy. That applies to your own people. It also applies to outsiders living in one of your towns. 15 Give them their pay every day. They are poor and are counting on it. If you don't pay them, they might cry out to the LORD against you. Then you will be guilty of committing a sin.

16 Parents must not be put to death because of what their children do. And children must not be put to death because of what their parents do. People must die because of their own sins.

17 Do what is right and fair for outsiders and for children whose fathers have died. Suppose a widow borrows something from you. And she offers to give you her coat until she pays you back. Don't take it. 18 Remember that you were slaves in Egypt. Remember that the LORD your God set you free from there. That's why I'm commanding you to do those things.

19 When you are gathering crops in your field, you might leave some grain behind by mistake. Don't go back to get it. Leave it behind for outsiders and widows. Leave it for children whose fathers have died. Then the LORD your God will bless you in everything you do. 20 When you knock olives off your trees, don't go back over the branches a second time. Leave what remains for outsiders and widows. Leave it for children

whose fathers have died. 21 When you
pick grapes in your vineyard, don't go
back over the vines a second time. Leave
what remains for outsiders and widows.
Leave it for children whose fathers have
died. 22 Remember that you were slaves
in Egypt. That's why I'm commanding
you to do these things.

25 Suppose two people don't agree
about something. Then they
must take their case to court. The judges
will decide the case. They will let the
one who isn't guilty go free. And they
will punish the one who is guilty. 2 The
guilty one might have done something
that's worthy of a beating. Then the
judge will make them lie down and be
beaten with a whip right there in court.
The number of strokes should fit the
crime. 3 But the judge must not give the
guilty person more than 40 strokes. If
more than that are used, you will have
disrespected your Israelite neighbor.

4 Don't stop an ox from eating while
you use it to separate grain from straw.

5 Suppose two brothers are living near
each other. And one of them dies without
having a son. Then his widow must not
marry anyone outside the family. Her
husband's brother should marry her.
That's what a brother-in-law is supposed
to do. 6 Her first baby boy will be named
after her first husband. Then the dead
man's name will continue in Israel.

7 But suppose the man doesn't want to
marry his brother's wife. Then she will
go to the elders at the gate of the town.
She will say, "My husband's brother
refuses to keep his brother's name alive
in Israel. He won't do for me what a
brother-in-law is supposed to do." 8 Then
the elders in his town will send for him.
They will talk to him. But he still might
say, "I don't want to marry her." 9 Then
his brother's widow will go up to him
in front of the elders. She'll pull one
of his sandals off his foot. She'll spit in
his face. And she'll say, "That's what
we do to a man who won't build up his
brother's family line." 10 That man's
family line will be known in Israel as
The Family of the Man Whose Sandal
Was Pulled Off.

11 Suppose two men are fighting. And
the wife of one of them comes to save her
husband from his attacker. So she reaches out and grabs hold of his attacker's
private parts. 12 Then you must cut off
her hand. Don't feel sorry for her.

13 Don't have two different scales.
Don't have scales that cause things to
seem heavier or lighter than they really
are. 14 And don't have two different sets
of measures. Don't have measures that
cause things to seem larger or smaller
than they really are. 15 You must use
weights and measures that are honest
and exact. Then you will live a long time
in the land the LORD your God is giving
you. 16 He hates anyone who cheats.

17 Remember what the Amalekites
did to you on your way out of Egypt.
18 You were tired and worn out. They
met up with you on your journey. They
attacked everyone who was lagging
behind. They didn't have any respect
for God. 19 The LORD your God will give
you peace and rest from all the enemies
around you. He'll do this in the land he's
giving you to take over as your very
own. No one on earth will mention the
Amalekites ever again because you will
destroy them. Do not forget!

Give the LORD His Share

26 You will enter the land the LORD
your God is giving you as your
own. You will take it over. You will make
your homes in the land. 2 When you do,
get some of the first share of everything
your soil produces. Put it in a basket.
It's from the land the LORD your God is
giving you. Take your gifts and go to
the special place he will choose. He will
put his Name there. 3 Speak to the priest
in office at that time. Tell him, "I announce today to the LORD your God that
I have come to this land. It's the land he
promised to give us. He promised it to
our people of long ago." 4 The priest will
receive the basket from you. He'll set it
down in front of the altar of the LORD
your God. 5 Then you will speak while
the LORD is listening. You will say, "My
father Jacob was a wanderer from the
land of Aram. He went down into Egypt
with a few people. He lived there and
became the father of a great nation. It
had huge numbers of people. 6 But the
people of Egypt treated us badly. They
made us suffer. They made us work
very hard. 7 Then we cried out to the
LORD. He is the God of our people who
lived long ago. He heard our voice. He

saw how much we were suffering. The Egyptians were treating us badly. They were making us work very hard. 8 So the LORD used his mighty hand and powerful arm to bring us out of Egypt. He did great and terrifying things. He did signs and amazing things. 9 He brought us to this place. He gave us this land. It's a land that has plenty of milk and honey. 10 Now, LORD, I'm bringing you the first share of crops from the soil. After all, you have given them to me." Place the basket in front of the LORD your God. Bow down to him. 11 Then you and the Levites and the outsiders among you will be full of joy. You will enjoy all the good things the LORD your God has given to you and your family.

12 You will set apart a tenth of everything you produce in the third year. That's the year for giving the tenth to people who have greater needs. You will give it to the Levites, outsiders and widows. You will also give it to children whose fathers have died. Then all of them will have plenty to eat in your towns. 13 Speak to the LORD your God. Say to him, "I have taken your sacred share from my house. I have given it to the Levites, outsiders and widows. I have also given it to children whose fathers have died. I've done everything you commanded me to do. I haven't stopped obeying your commands. I haven't forgotten any of them. 14 I haven't eaten any part of your sacred share while I mourned over someone who had died. I haven't taken any of it from my house while I was 'unclean.' And I haven't offered any of it to the dead. LORD my God, I've obeyed you. I've done everything you commanded me to do. 15 Look down from the holy place where you live in heaven. Bless your people Israel. Bless the land you have given us. It's the land you promised to give to our people of long ago. It's a land that has plenty of milk and honey."

Obey the LORD's Commands

16 This day the LORD your God commands you to obey all these rules and laws. Be careful to obey them with all your heart and with all your soul. 17 Today you have announced that the LORD is your God. You have said you would live exactly as he wants you to live. You have agreed to keep his rules, commands and laws. And you have said you would listen to him. 18 Today the LORD has announced that you are his people. He has said that you are his special treasure. He promised that you would be. He has told you to keep all his commands. 19 He has announced that he will make you famous. He'll give you more praise and honor than all the other nations he has made. And he has said that you will be a holy nation. The LORD your God has set you apart for himself. That's exactly what he promised to do.

The Altar on Mount Ebal

27 Moses and the elders of Israel gave commands to the people. They said, "Obey all the commands we're giving you today. 2 You will go across the Jordan River. You will enter the land the LORD your God is giving you. When you do, set up some large stones. Put a coat of plaster on them. 3 Write all the words of this law on them. Do it when you have crossed over into the land the LORD your God is giving you. It's a land that has plenty of milk and honey. The LORD is the God of your people of long ago. He promised you that you would enter the land. 4 After you have gone across the Jordan, set up those stones on Mount Ebal. Put a coat of plaster on them. We're commanding you today to do that. 5 Build an altar there to honor the LORD your God. Make it out of stones. Don't use any iron tool on them. 6 Use stones you find in the fields to build his altar. Then offer burnt offerings on it to the LORD your God. 7 Sacrifice friendship offerings there. Eat them and be filled with joy in the sight of the LORD your God. 8 You must write all the words of this law on the stones you have set up. Write the words very clearly."

Curses for Not Obeying the LORD

9 Then Moses and the priests, who are Levites, spoke to all the Israelites. They said, "Israel, be quiet! Listen! You have now become the people of the LORD your God. 10 Obey him. Obey his commands and rules that we're giving you today."

11 Here are the commands Moses gave the people that same day.

12 You will go across the Jordan River. When you do, six tribes will stand on Mount Gerizim to bless the people.

Those tribes are Simeon, Levi, Judah,
Issachar, Joseph and Benjamin. 13 The
other six tribes will stand on Mount Ebal
to announce some curses. Those tribes
are Reuben, Gad, Asher, Zebulun, Dan
and Naphtali.
14 The Levites will speak to all the
Israelites in a loud voice. The Levites
will say,
15 "May anyone who makes a statue
of a god and sets it up in secret be under
the LORD's curse. That statue is made by
a skilled worker. And the LORD hates it."
Then all the people will say,
"Amen!"
16 "May anyone who brings shame
on their father or mother be under the
LORD's curse."
Then all the people will say,
"Amen!"
17 "May anyone who moves their
neighbor's boundary stone be under
the LORD's curse."
Then all the people will say,
"Amen!"
18 "May anyone who leads blind people down the wrong road be under the
LORD's curse."
Then all the people will say,
"Amen!"
19 "May anyone who treats unfairly
outsiders, widows, and children whose
fathers have died be under the LORD's
curse."
Then all the people will say,
"Amen!"
20 "May anyone who sleeps with his
stepmother be under the LORD's curse.
That man brings shame on his father
by doing that."
Then all the people will say,
"Amen!"
21 "May anyone who has sex with
animals be under the LORD's curse."
Then all the people will say,
"Amen!"
22 "May anyone who sleeps with
his sister be under the LORD's curse. It
doesn't matter whether she is his full
sister or his half sister."
Then all the people will say,
"Amen!"
23 "May anyone who sleeps with his
mother-in-law be under the LORD's
curse."
Then all the people will say,
"Amen!"
24 "May anyone who kills their neighbor secretly be under the LORD's curse."
Then all the people will say,
"Amen!"
25 "May anyone who accepts money
to kill someone who isn't guilty of doing
anything wrong be under the LORD's
curse."
Then all the people will say,
"Amen!"
26 "May anyone who doesn't honor
the words of this law by obeying them
be under the LORD's curse."
Then all the people will say,
"Amen!"

Blessings for Obeying the LORD

28 Make sure you obey the LORD
your God completely. Be careful
to obey all his commands. I'm giving
them to you today. If you do these
things, the LORD will honor you more
than all the other nations on earth. 2 If
you obey the LORD your God, here are
the blessings that will come to you and
remain with you.

3 You will be blessed in the cities. You will be blessed out in the
country.
4 Your children will be blessed.
Your crops will be blessed. The
young animals among your livestock will be blessed. That includes
your calves and lambs.
5 Your baskets and bread pans
will be blessed.
6 You will be blessed no matter
where you go.

7 Enemies will rise up against you. But
the LORD will help you win the battle
over them. They will come at you from
one direction. But they'll run away from
you in every direction.
8 The LORD your God will bless your
barns with plenty of grain and other food.
He will bless everything you do. He'll bless
you in the land he's giving you.
9 The LORD your God will make you
his holy people. He will set you apart
for himself. He promised to do this. He
promised to do it if you would keep
his commands and live exactly as he
wants you to live. 10 All the nations on
earth will see that you belong to the
LORD. And they will be afraid of you.
11 The LORD will give you more than you

need. You will have many children. Your livestock will have many little ones. Your crops will do very well. All of that will happen in the land he promised to give you. He promised this to your people of long ago.

12The LORD will open up the heavens. That's where he stores his riches. He will send rain on your land at just the right time. He'll bless everything you do. You will lend money to many nations. But you won't have to borrow from any of them. 13The LORD your God will make you leaders, not followers. Pay attention to his commands that I'm giving you today. Be careful to obey them. Then you will always be on top. You will never be on the bottom. 14Don't turn away from any of the commands I'm giving you today. Don't turn to the right or the left. Don't follow other gods. Don't worship them.

Curses for Not Obeying the LORD

15But suppose you don't obey the LORD your God. And you aren't careful to obey all his commands and rules I'm giving you today. Then he will send curses on you. They'll catch up with you. Here are those curses.

16You will be cursed in the cities. You will be cursed out in the country.
17Your baskets and bread pans will be cursed.
18Your children will be cursed. Your crops will be cursed. Your calves and lambs will be cursed.
19You will be cursed no matter where you go.

20The LORD will send curses on you. You won't know what's going on. In everything you do, he will be angry with you. You will be destroyed suddenly and completely. This will happen because you did an evil thing when you deserted the LORD. 21He will send all kinds of sicknesses on you. He'll send them until he has destroyed you. He'll remove you from the land you are entering to take as your own. 22The LORD will make you sick and very weak. He will strike you with fever and swelling. He'll send burning heat. There won't be any rain. The hot winds will completely dry up your crops. All those things will happen until you die. 23The sky above you will be like bronze. The ground beneath you will be like iron. 24The LORD will turn the rain of your country into dust and powder. It will come down from the skies until you are destroyed.

25The LORD will help your enemies win the battle over you. You will come at them from one direction. But you will run away from them in every direction. All the kingdoms on earth will be completely shocked when they see you. 26Birds and wild animals will eat up your dead bodies. There won't be anyone left to scare them away. 27The LORD will send boils on you, just like the ones he sent on the Egyptians. You will have growths in your bodies and boils on your skin. You will itch all over. No one will be able to heal you. 28The LORD will make you lose your mind. He will make you blind. You won't know what's going on. 29Even at noon you will have to feel your way around like a blind person in the dark. You won't have success in anything you do. Day after day you will be robbed and treated badly. No one will be able to save you.

30You and a woman will promise to marry each other. But another man will take her and rape her. You will build a house. But you won't live in it. You will plant a vineyard. But you won't eat a single grape from it. 31Your ox will be killed right in front of your eyes. But you won't eat any of it. Your donkey will be taken away from you by force. And you will never get it back. Your sheep will be given to your enemies. No one will be able to save them. 32Your children will be given to another nation. Day after day you will watch for them to come back. But you will only wear out your eyes. You won't be able to help your children. 33A nation you don't know anything about will eat what you work to produce on your land. You will only be treated badly as long as you live. 34The things you see will make you lose your mind. 35The LORD will send painful boils on your knees and legs. No one will be able to heal them. They will cover you from head to toe.

36The LORD will drive you out of the land. And he will drive out the king you place over yourselves. All of you will go to another nation. You and your people of long ago didn't know anything about them. There you will worship other gods. They will be made out of wood and stone. 37 You will look very bad to all the nations where the LORD sends you. They will be completely shocked when they see you. They will mock you and make fun of you.

38 You will plant many seeds in your field. But you will gather very little food. Locusts will eat it up. 39 You will plant vineyards and take care of them. But you won't drink the wine. You won't gather the grapes. Worms will eat them up. 40 You will have olive trees through your whole country. But you won't use the oil. The olives will drop off the trees. 41 You will have children. But you won't be able to keep them. They'll be taken away as prisoners. 42 Large numbers of locusts will eat up the leaves on all your trees. They will also eat up the crops on your land.

43 Outsiders who live among you will become your leaders. They will rise higher and higher. But you will sink lower and lower. 44 They will lend money to you. But you won't be able to lend money to them. They will be the leaders. But you will be the followers.

45 The LORD your God will send all these curses on you. They will follow you everywhere. They'll catch up with you. You will be under the LORD's curse until you are destroyed. That's because you didn't obey him. You didn't keep the commands and rules he gave you. 46 These curses will remain as signs and awful judgments against you and your children after you forever. 47 You didn't serve the LORD your God with joy and gladness when times were good. 48 So he will send enemies against you. You will have to serve them. You will be hungry and thirsty. You will be naked and poor. The LORD will put the iron chains of slavery around your necks until he has destroyed you.

49 The LORD will bring a nation against you from far away. It will come from the ends of the earth. It will dive down on you like an eagle. You won't understand that nation's language. 50 Its people will look mean. They won't have any respect for old people. They won't show any kindness to young people. 51 They will eat up the young animals among your livestock. They'll eat up the crops on your land. They'll destroy you. They won't leave you any grain, olive oil or fresh wine. They won't leave you any calves or lambs. They'll destroy you. 52 They'll surround all the cities throughout your whole land. They'll attack those cities until the high, strong walls you trust in fall down. That's what will happen to the cities in the land the LORD your God is giving you.

53 Your enemies will surround you and attack you. They will make you suffer greatly. So you will eat your own children. You will eat the dead bodies of the sons and daughters the LORD your God has given you. 54 There may be a gentle and caring man among you. But he will treat his own brother badly. He'll be just as mean to the wife he loves and to any of his children who are still alive. 55 He won't give to a single one of them any part of the dead bodies of his children that he's eating. It will be all he has left to eat. That's how much your enemies will make you suffer when they surround all your cities and attack them. 56 There may be a gentle and caring woman among you. She wouldn't even touch the ground with her feet without first putting her sandals on. But she will not share anything with the husband she loves. She won't share with her own children either. 57 She will eat what comes out of her body after she has a baby. Then she'll even eat her baby. She won't share it with anyone in her family. In her great hunger she'll plan to eat it in secret. There won't be anything else for her to eat because the city she lives in will be surrounded. That's an example of how much your enemies will make you suffer when they are attacking your cities.

58 Be careful to follow all the words of this law. They are written in this scroll. Have respect for the glorious and wonderful name of the LORD your God. If you don't, 59 he will send terrible plagues on you and your children after you. He'll send horrible and lasting troubles. He'll make you very sick for a long time. 60 He'll bring on you all the sicknesses you were afraid of getting when you were in Egypt. You won't be able to get rid of them. 61 The LORD will also bring on you all other kinds of sickness and trouble. I haven't even written those down in this Book of the Law. You will be destroyed. 62 At one time you

were as many as the stars in the sky.
But there will only be a few of you left.
That's because you didn't obey the LORD
your God. 63 It pleased the LORD to give
you success and to cause there to be
many of you. But it will please him just
as much to wipe you out and destroy
you. You will be removed from the land
you are entering to take as your own.
64 Then the LORD will scatter you
among all the nations. He'll spread
you around from one end of the earth
to the other. There you will worship
statues of gods made out of wood and
stone. You and your people of long ago
hadn't known anything about those
gods. 65 Among those nations you won't
find any peace. There won't be any place
where you can make your home and
rest your feet. The LORD will give you
minds filled with worry. He'll give you
eyes worn out from looking for help.
You won't have any hope in your hearts.
66 Your lives will always be in danger.
You will be filled with fear night and
day. You will never be sure you are safe.
67 In the morning you will say, "We wish
it were evening!" In the evening you will
say, "We wish it were morning!" Your
hearts will be filled with fear. The things
you see will terrify you. 68 The LORD will
send you back to Egypt in ships. He'll
send you on a journey I said you should
never have to make again. You will offer
to sell yourselves to your enemies as
slaves in Egypt. But no one will buy you.

Obey the Terms of the Covenant

29 Here are the terms of the covenant the LORD commanded
Moses to make with the Israelites in
Moab. The terms were added to the
covenant he had made with them at
Mount Horeb.
2 Moses sent for all the Israelites. Here
is what he said to them.

With your own eyes you have seen
everything the LORD did in Egypt to
Pharaoh. You have seen what he did to
all Pharaoh's officials and to his whole
land. 3 With your own eyes you saw how
the LORD really made them suffer. You
saw the signs and amazing things he did.
4 But to this day the LORD hasn't given
you a mind that understands. He hasn't
given you eyes that see. He hasn't given
you ears that hear. 5 Yet the LORD says, "I
led you through the desert for 40 years.
During that time your clothes didn't wear
out. The sandals on your feet didn't wear
out either. 6 You didn't eat any bread.
You didn't drink any kind of wine. I did
all these things because I wanted you
to know that I am the LORD your God."
7 When you got here, Sihon and Og
came out to fight against us. Sihon was
the king of Heshbon. And Og was the king
of Bashan. But we won the battle over
them. 8 We took their land. We gave it to
the tribes of Reuben and Gad and half
of the tribe of Manasseh as their share.
9 Be careful to obey the terms of this
covenant. Then you will have success in
everything you do. 10 Today all of you are
standing here in the sight of the LORD
your God. Your leaders and chief men are
here. Your elders and officials are here.
So are all the other men of Israel. 11 Your
children and wives are here with you
too. So are the outsiders living in your
camps. They chop your wood and carry
your water. 12 All of you are standing
here in order to enter into a covenant
with the LORD your God. He is making
the covenant with you today. He's giving
you his word. 13 Today he wants to show
you that you are his people and that he
is your God. That's what he promised to
Abraham, Isaac and Jacob. 14 I'm making
this covenant and the promise that goes
along with it. I'm making this covenant
with you. 15 You are standing here with
us today in front of the LORD our God.
And I'm also making this covenant with
those who aren't here today.
16 You yourselves know how we lived
in Egypt. You also know how we passed
through other countries on the way
here. 17 You saw the statues of their
gods made out of wood, stone, silver
and gold. The LORD hates those statues.
18 Make sure there isn't a man or woman
among your families or tribes who turns
away from the LORD our God. No one
must worship the gods of those nations.
Make sure that kind of worship doesn't
spread like bitter poison through your
whole community.
19 Some people who worship those
gods will hear the promise that seals
the covenant I'm making. They think
they can escape trouble by what they're
saying. They say, "We'll be safe, even
though we're stubborn and go our own

way." But they will bring trouble on
the whole land. 20 The LORD will never
be willing to forgive those people. His
great anger will blaze out against them.
All the curses I've written down in this
book will fall on them. And the LORD will
erase any mention of them from the
earth. 21 He will find those people in all
the tribes of Israel and give them nothing but trouble. That will agree with all
the curses of the covenant. They are
written down in this Book of the Law.

22 Even your children's children will
see the troubles that have fallen on the
land. They'll see the sicknesses the LORD
has brought on it. People who come from
countries far away will also see those
things. 23 The whole land will be burned
up. Nothing but salt and sulfur will be left.
Nothing will be planted there. Nothing
will grow there. In fact, nothing will even
start to grow there. The land will be like
Sodom, Gomorrah, Admah and Zeboyim
after they were destroyed. The LORD wiped
out those cities because he was very angry.
24 All the nations will ask, "Why has the
LORD done this to the land? What could
have made him so very angry?"

25 And they will hear the answer, "It's
because the people living there have
broken the covenant of the LORD. He's
the God of their people of long ago. He
made that covenant with them when
he brought them out of Egypt. 26 They
went off and worshiped other gods.
They bowed down to them. They hadn't
known anything about those gods before. The LORD hadn't given those gods
to them. 27 So the LORD became very
angry with this land. He brought on it
all the curses written down in this book.
28 The LORD's anger blazed out against
his people. So he pulled them up out of
their land. He threw them into another
land. And that's where they are now."

29 The LORD our God keeps certain
things hidden. But he makes other
things known to us and to our children
forever. He does it so we can obey all the
words of this law.

The LORD Will Bless His People

30 I have told you about all these
blessings and curses. The LORD
your God will bring them on you. Then
you will think carefully about the blessings and curses. You will think about
them everywhere the LORD your God
scatters you among the nations. 2 You
and your children will return to the
LORD your God. You will obey him with
all your heart and with all your soul.
That will be according to everything I'm
commanding you today. 3 When all that
happens, the LORD your God will bless
you with great success again. He will be
very kind to you. He'll bring you back
from all the nations where he scattered
you. 4 Suppose you have been forced to
go away to the farthest land on earth.
The LORD your God will bring you back
even from there. 5 He will bring you to
the land that belonged to your people
of long ago. You will take it over. He'll
make you better off than your people
were. He'll cause there to be more of you
than there were of them. 6 The LORD your
God will keep you from being stubborn.
He'll do the same thing for your children
and their children. Then you will love
him with all your heart and with all your
soul. And you will live. 7 The LORD your
God will put all these curses on your enemies. They hated you and hunted you
down. 8 You will obey the LORD again.
You will obey all his commands that
I'm giving you today. 9 Then the LORD
your God will give you great success in
everything you do. You will have many
children. Your livestock will have many
little ones. Your crops will do very well.
The LORD will take delight in you again.
He'll give you success. That's what he did
for your people of long ago. 10 But you
must obey the LORD your God. You must
keep his commands and rules. They are
written in this Book of the Law. You must
turn to the LORD your God with all your
heart and with all your soul.

Choose Life, Not Death

11 What I'm commanding you today
is not too hard for you. It isn't beyond
your reach. 12 It isn't up in heaven. So
you don't have to ask, "Who will go
up into heaven to get it? Who will announce it to us so we can obey it?" 13 And
it isn't beyond the ocean. So you don't
have to ask, "Who will go across the
ocean to get it? Who will announce it to
us so we can obey it?" 14 No, the message
isn't far away at all. In fact, it's really
near you. It's in your mouth and in your
heart so that you can obey it.

15 Today I'm giving you a choice.
You can have life and success. Or you
can have death and harm. 16 I'm commanding you today to love the LORD
your God. I'm commanding you to live
exactly as he wants you to live. You
must obey his commands, rules and
laws. Then you will live. There will be
many of you. The LORD your God will
bless you in the land you are entering
to take as your own.
17 Don't let your hearts turn away
from the LORD. Instead, obey him. Don't
let yourselves be drawn away to other
gods. And don't bow down to them and
worship them. 18 If you do, I announce
to you this day that you will certainly
be destroyed. You are about to go across
the Jordan River and take over the land.
But you won't live there very long.
19 I'm calling for the heavens and the
earth to be witnesses against you this
very day. I'm offering you the choice
of life or death. You can choose either
blessings or curses. But I want you to
choose life. Then you and your children
will live. 20 And you will love the LORD
your God. You will obey him. You will
remain true to him. The LORD is your
very life. He will give you many years
in the land. He promised to give that
land to your fathers, to Abraham, Isaac
and Jacob.

Joshua Becomes the New Leader

31 Here are the words Moses spoke
to all the Israelites. 2 He said, "I
am now 120 years old. I'm not able to
lead you anymore. The LORD has said
to me, 'You will not go across the Jordan
River.' 3 The LORD your God himself will
go across ahead of you. He'll destroy the
nations there in order to make room for
you. You will take over their land. Joshua
will also go across ahead of you, just as
the LORD said he would. 4 The LORD will
do to those nations what he did to Sihon
and Og. He destroyed those Amorite
kings along with their land. 5 The LORD
will hand those nations over to you. Then
you must do to them everything I've
commanded you to do. 6 Be strong and
brave. Don't be afraid of them. Don't be
terrified because of them. The LORD your
God will go with you. He will never leave
you. He'll never desert you."
7 Then Moses sent for Joshua. Moses
spoke to him in front of all the Israelites.

He said, "Be strong and brave. You must
go with these people. They are going into
the land the LORD promised to give to
their people of long ago. You must divide
it up among them. They will each receive
their share. [8]The LORD himself will go
ahead of you. He will be with you. He
will never leave you. He'll never desert
you. So don't be afraid. Don't lose hope."

The Law Must Be Read to the People

[9]Moses wrote down this law. He gave
it to the priests, who are sons of Levi.
They carried the ark of the covenant
of the LORD. He also gave the law to all
the elders of Israel. [10]Then Moses commanded them, "You must read this law
at the end of every seven years. Do it in
the year when you forgive people what
they owe. Read it during the Feast of
Booths. [11]That's when all the Israelites
come to appear in front of the LORD
your God at the holy tent. It will be at
the place he will choose. You must read
this law to them. [12]Gather the people
together. Gather the men, women and
children. Also bring together the outsiders living in your towns. Then they
can listen and learn to have respect
for the LORD your God. And they'll be
careful to obey all the words of this law.
[13]Their children must hear it read too.
They don't know this law yet. They too
must learn to have respect for the LORD
your God. They must honor him as long
as you live in the land. You are about
to go across the Jordan River and take
that land as your very own."

The Israelites Will Refuse to Obey the LORD

[14]The LORD said to Moses, "The day
when you will die is near. Have Joshua go to the tent of meeting. Join him
there. That is where I will appoint him
as the new leader." So Joshua and Moses
went to the tent of meeting.
[15]Then the LORD appeared at the tent
in a pillar of cloud. It stood over the entrance to the tent. [16]The LORD spoke to
Moses. He said, "You are going to join
the members of your family who have
already died. The Israelites will not
be faithful to me. They will soon join
themselves to the false gods that are
worshiped in the land they are entering. The people will desert me. They will
break the covenant I made with them.

pointing us to JESUS: The Law

When God's people were first set free from slavery (remember the story of Moses?), God brought them out of Egypt and into the wilderness to live as his own special people. But there was a problem: God's people had no idea how to live as his people. They had only ever lived as slaves to Pharaoh. They didn't know how to walk with God or live in a way that pleased him. So God gave them a gift known as the Law.

The Law expressed God's heart and character and invited God's people to reflect his character in the world. The Law showed God's people how to be merciful as he is merciful and how to be just as he is just (see Exodus 20–23). This is called the Mosaic covenant.

God knew his people couldn't keep the Law perfectly. But one day, the Savior would come who would keep the Law of God perfectly and would die in our place, rising again so that we could be made right with God forever. When we put our faith in Jesus, we are given the Spirit of God to help us grow each day to reflect God's heart and character.

17 In that day I will become angry with
them. I will desert them. I will turn my
face away from them. And they will be
destroyed. Many horrible troubles and
hard times will come on them. On that
day they will say, 'Trouble has come on
us. Our God isn't with us!' 18 I will certainly turn away from them on that day. I
will do it because they did a very evil
thing when they turned to other gods.
19 "I want you to write down a song and
teach it to the Israelites. Have them sing
it. It will be my witness against them.
20 I will bring them into a land that has
plenty of milk and honey. I promised the
land to their people of long ago. In that
land they will eat until they have had
enough. They will get fat. When they do,
they will turn to other gods and worship
them. They will turn their backs on me.
They will break my covenant. 21 Many
horrible troubles and hard times will
come on them. Then the song I am giving
you will be a witness against them. That
is because the song will not be forgotten
by their children and their children's
children. I know what they are likely to
do. I know it even before I bring them
into the land I promised them." 22 So that
day Moses wrote the song down. And
Moses taught it to the Israelites.
23 The LORD gave a command to Joshua, the son of Nun. He said, "Be strong
and brave. You will bring the Israelites
into the land I promised them. I myself
will be with you."
24 Moses finished writing the words of
this law in a book. He wrote them down
from beginning to end. 25 Then he gave a
command to the Levites who carried the
ark of the covenant of the LORD. Moses
said, 26 "Take this Book of the Law. Place
it beside the ark of the covenant of the
LORD your God. It will remain there as a
witness against you. 27 I know how you
refuse to obey the LORD. I know how
stubborn you are. You have refused to
obey him while I've been living among
you. So you will certainly refuse to obey
him after I'm dead! 28 Gather together
all the elders of your tribes and all your
officials. Bring them to me. Then I can
speak these words to them. I can call
for the heavens and the earth to be
witnesses against them. 29 I know that
after I'm dead you will certainly become
very sinful. You will turn away from the
path I've commanded you to take. In
days to come, trouble will fall on you.
That's because you will do what is evil
in the sight of the LORD. You will make
him very angry because of the statues
of gods your hands have made."

The Song of Moses

30 Moses spoke the words of this song
from beginning to end. The whole community of Israel heard them. Here is
what he said.

32 Heavens, listen to me. Then I
will speak.
Earth, hear the words of my
mouth.
2 Let my teaching fall like rain.
Let my words come down like
dew.
Let them be like raindrops on new
grass.
Let them be like rain on tender
plants.

3 I will make known the name of the
LORD.
Praise God! How great he is!
4 He is the Rock. His works are perfect.
All his ways are right.
He is faithful. He doesn't do
anything wrong.
He is honest and fair.

5 Israel, you have sinned against
him very much.
It's too bad for you that you
aren't his children anymore.
You have become a twisted and
evil nation.
6 Is that how you thank the LORD?
You aren't wise. You are foolish.
Remember, he's your Father. He's
your Creator.
He made you. He formed you.

7 Remember the days of long ago.
Think about what the LORD did
through those many years.
Ask your father. He will tell you.
Ask your elders. They'll explain it
to you.
8 The Most High God gave the
nations their lands.
He divided up the human race.
He set up borders for the nations.
He did it based on the number
of the angels in his heavenly
court.

9 The LORD's people are his share.
Jacob is the nation he has received.
10 The LORD found Israel in a desert.
He found them in an empty and windy land.
He took care of them and kept them safe.
He guarded them as he would guard his own eyes.
11 He was like an eagle that stirs up its nest.
It hovers over its little ones.
It spreads out its wings to catch them.
It carries them up in the air on its feathers.
12 The LORD was the only one who led Israel.
No other god was with them.

13 The LORD made them ride on the highest places in the land.
He fed them what grew in the fields.
He gave them the sweetest honey.
He fed them olive oil from a rocky hillside.
14 He gave them butter and milk from the herds and flocks.
He fed them the fattest lambs and goats.
He gave them the best of Bashan's rams.
He fed them the finest wheat.
They drank the bubbling red juice of grapes.

15 When Israel grew fat, they became stubborn.
When they were filled with food, they became fat and heavy.
They left the God who made them.
They turned away from the Rock who saved them.
16 They made him jealous by serving false gods.
They made him angry by worshiping statues of gods.
He hated those gods.
17 The people sacrificed to those false gods, not to God.
They hadn't known anything about those false gods.
Those gods were new to them.
Their people of long ago didn't worship them.
18 But then they deserted the Rock. He was their Father.
They forgot the God who created them.
19 When the LORD saw this, he turned away from them.
His sons and daughters made him angry.
20 "I will turn my face away from them," he said.
"I will see what will happen to them in the end.
They are sinful people.
They are unfaithful children.
21 They made me jealous by serving what is not even a god.
They made me angry by worshiping worthless statues of gods.
I will use people who are not a nation to make them jealous.
A nation that has no understanding will make them angry.
22 My anger will start a fire.
It will burn all the way down to the kingdom of the dead.
It will eat up the earth and its crops.
It will set the base of the mountains on fire.

23 "I will pile troubles on my people.
I will shoot all my arrows at them.
24 I will send them hunger. It will make them weak.
I will send terrible sickness. I will send deadly plagues.
I will send wild animals that will tear them apart.
Snakes that glide through the dust will bite them.
25 In the streets their children will be killed by swords.
Their homes will be filled with terror.
The young men and women will die.
The babies and old people will die.
26 I said I would scatter them.
I said I would erase their name from human memory.
27 But I was afraid their enemies would make fun of that.
I was afraid their attackers would not understand.

I was sure they would say, 'We're
the ones who've beaten them!
The LORD isn't the one who did it.'"
28 Israel is a nation that doesn't have
any sense.
They can't understand anything.
29 I wish they were wise. Then they
would understand what's
coming.
They'd realize what would
happen to them in the end.
30 How could one person chase a
thousand?
How could two make ten
thousand run away?
It couldn't happen unless their Rock
had deserted them.
It couldn't take place unless the
LORD had given them up.
31 Their rock is not like our Rock.
Even our enemies know that.
32 Their vine comes from the vines of
Sodom.
It comes from the vineyards of
Gomorrah.
Their grapes are filled with poison.
Their bunches of grapes taste
bitter.
33 Their wine is like the poison of
snakes.
It's like the deadly poison of
cobras.

34 The LORD says, "I have kept all
those terrible things stored
away.
I have kept them sealed up in my
strongbox.
35 I punish people. I will pay them
back.
The time will come when their
feet will slip.
Their day of trouble is near.
Very soon they will be
destroyed."

36 The LORD will come to the aid of his
people.
He'll show tender love to those
who serve him.
He will know when their strength is
gone.
He'll see that no one at all is left.
37 He'll say, "Where are their gods
now?
Where is the rock they went to for
safety?
38 Where are the gods who ate the fat
of their sacrifices?
Where are the gods who drank
the wine of their drink
offerings?
Let those gods rise up to help you!
Let them keep you safe!
39 "Look! I am the One!
There is no other God except me.
I put some people to death. I bring
others to life.
I have wounded, and I will heal.
No one can save you from my
power.
40 I raise my hand to heaven. Here is
the promise I make.
You can be sure that I live
forever.
41 And you can be just as sure
that I will sharpen my flashing
sword.
My hand will hold it when I
judge.
I will get even with my enemies.
I will pay back those who hate
me.
42 I will make my arrows drip with
blood.
My sword will destroy people.
It will kill some. It will even kill
prisoners.
It will cut off the heads of enemy
leaders."

43 You nations, be full of joy. Be joyful
together with God's people.
The LORD will get even with his
enemies.
He will pay them back for killing
those who serve him.
He will wipe away the sin of his
land and people.

44 Moses spoke all the words of this
song to the people. Joshua, the son of
Nun, was with him. 45 Moses finished
speaking all these words to all the Israelites. 46 Then he said to them, "Think
carefully about all the words I have
announced to you today. I want you to
command your children to be careful
to obey all the words of this law. 47 They
aren't just useless words for you. They
are your very life. If you obey them,
you will live in the land for a long time.
It's the land you are going across the
Jordan River to take as your own."

Moses Will Die on Mount Nebo

48 On that same day the LORD said to
Moses, 49 "Go up into the Abarim mountains. Go to Mount Nebo in Moab. It is across from Jericho. From there look out over Canaan. It is the land I am giving the Israelites to take as their own.
50 You will die there on the mountain you have climbed. You will join the members of your family who have already died. In the same way, your brother Aaron died on Mount Hor. He joined the members of his family who had already died.
51 You and Aaron disobeyed me in front of the Israelites. It happened at the waters of Meribah Kadesh in the Desert of Zin. You did not honor me among the Israelites as the holy God.
52 So you will see the land, but only from far away. You will not enter the land I am giving to the Israelites."

Moses Blesses the Tribes

33 Here is the blessing that Moses, the man of God, gave to the Israelites before he died.
2 He said,

"The LORD came from Mount Sinai.
  Like the rising sun, he shone on his people from Mount Seir.
  He shone on them from Mount Paran.
He came with large numbers of angels.
  He came from his mountain slopes in the south.
3 LORD, I'm sure you love your people.
  All the holy ones are in your hands.
At your feet all of them bow down.
  And you teach them.
4 They learn the law Moses gave us.
  It belongs to the community of the people of Jacob.
5 The LORD was king over Israel
  when the leaders of the people came together.
  The tribes of Israel were also there."

6 Here's what Moses said about Reuben.

"Let Reuben live. Don't let him die.
  And do not let his people be few."

7 Here's what Moses said about Judah.

"LORD, listen to Judah cry out.
  Bring him to his people.
By his own power he stands up for himself.
  LORD, help him fight against his enemies!"

8 Here's what Moses said about Levi.

"Your Thummim and Urim belong
  to your faithful servant.
  You tested him at Massah.
  You argued with him at the waters of Meribah.
9 Levi didn't show special favor to anyone.
  He did not spare his father and mother.
  He didn't excuse his relatives or his children.
But he watched over your word.
  He guarded your covenant.
10 He teaches your rules to the people of Jacob.
  He teaches your law to Israel.
He offers incense to you.
  He sacrifices whole burnt offerings on your altar.
11 LORD, bless all his skills.
  Be pleased with everything he does.
Destroy those who rise up against him.
  Strike down his enemies until they can't get up."

12 Here's what Moses said about Benjamin.

"Let the one the LORD loves rest safely in him.
  The LORD guards him all day long.
  The one the LORD loves rests in his arms."

13 Here's what Moses said about Joseph.

"May the LORD bless Joseph's land.
  May he bless it with dew from the highest heavens.
  May he bless it with water from the deepest oceans.
14 May he bless it with the best crops
  the sun can produce.
  May he bless it with the finest crops the moon can give.
15 May he bless it with the best
  products of the age-old mountains.
  May he bless it with the many crops of the ancient hills.

16 May he bless it with the best gifts
that fill the earth.
May he bless it with the favor of
the God who spoke out of the
burning bush.
Let all these blessings rest on the
head of Joseph.
Let them rest on the head of the
one who is prince among his
brothers.
17 His glory is like the glory of a bull
born first to its mother.
His horns are like the horns of a
wild ox.
He will use them to destroy the
nations.
He'll wipe out the nations that
are very far away.
The ten thousands of men in
Ephraim's army are like the
bull and the ox.
So are the thousands in the army
of Manasseh."

18 Here's what Moses said about Zebulun and Issachar.

"Zebulun, be filled with joy when
you go out.
Issachar, be joyful in your tents.
19 You will call for other people to go
to the mountain.
There you will offer the sacrifices
of those who do what is right.
You will enjoy the many good
things your ships bring you.
You will enjoy treasures that are
hidden in the sand."

20 Here's what Moses said about Gad.

"May the God who gives Gad more
land be praised!
Gad lives there like a lion
that tears off arms and heads.
21 He chose the best land for his
livestock.
The leader's share was kept for him.
The leaders of the people came
together.
Then Gad carried out the LORD's
holy plan.
He carried out the LORD's
decisions for Israel."

22 Here's what Moses said about Dan.

"Dan is like a lion's cub
that charges out of the land of
Bashan."

23 Here's what Moses said about Naphtali.

"The LORD greatly favors Naphtali.
The LORD fills him with his
blessing.
Naphtali's land will reach south
to the Sea of Galilee."

24 Here's what Moses said about Asher.

"Asher is the most blessed of sons.
Let his brothers be kind to him.
Let Asher wash his feet with olive
oil.
25 The bars of his gates will be made
out of iron and bronze.
His strength will last as long as
he lives.

26 "There is no one like the God of
Israel.
He rides across the heavens to
help you.
He rides on the clouds in his
glory.
27 God lives forever! You can run to
him for safety.
His powerful arms are always
there to carry you.
He will drive out your enemies to
make room for you.
He'll say to you, 'Destroy them!'
28 So Israel will live in safety.
Jacob will live secure
in a land that has grain and fresh
wine.
There the heavens drop their dew.
29 Israel, how blessed you are!
Who is like you?
The LORD has saved you.
He keeps you safe. He helps you.
He's like a glorious sword to you.
Your enemies will bow down to you
in fear.
You will walk on the highest
places of their lands."

Moses Dies

34 Moses climbed Mount Nebo.
He went up from the plains of
Moab to the highest slopes of Pisgah.
It's across from Jericho. At Pisgah the
LORD showed him the whole land from
Gilead all the way to Dan. 2 Moses saw
the whole land of Naphtali. He saw the
territory of Ephraim and Manasseh.
The LORD showed him the whole land of
Judah all the way to the Mediterranean

Sea. [3] Moses saw the Negev Desert. He
saw the whole area from the Valley
of Jericho all the way to Zoar. Jericho
was also known as The City of Palm
Trees. [4] Then the LORD spoke to Moses.
He said, "This is the land I promised to
Abraham, Isaac and Jacob. I told them,
'I will give this land to your children
and their children.' Moses, I have let
you see it with your own eyes. But you
will not go across the Jordan River to
enter it."

[5] Moses, the servant of the LORD, died
there in Moab. It happened just as the
LORD had said. [6] The LORD buried the
body of Moses in Moab. His grave is in
the valley across from Beth Peor. But to
this day no one knows where his grave
is. [7] Moses was 120 years old when he
died. But his eyesight was still good.
He was still very strong. [8] The Israelites
mourned over Moses on the plains of
Moab for 30 days. They did it until their
time for weeping and crying was over.

[9] Joshua, the son of Nun, was filled
with wisdom. That's because Moses
had placed his hands on him. So the
Israelites listened to Joshua. They did
what the LORD had commanded Moses.

[10] Since then, Israel has never had a
prophet like Moses. The LORD knew him
face to face. [11] Moses did many signs
and amazing things. The LORD had sent
him to do them in Egypt. Moses did
them against Pharaoh, against all his
officials and against his whole land.
[12] No one has ever had the mighty power
Moses had. No one has ever done the
wonderful acts he did in the sight of
all the Israelites.

Old Testament History

JOSHUA
JUDGES
RUTH
1 SAMUEL
2 SAMUEL
1 KINGS
2 KINGS

1 CHRONICLES
2 CHRONICLES
EZRA
NEHEMIAH
ESTHER

There are 12 books about the history of God's people in the Old Testament. These books include true stories about events that happened long ago and the people who followed God both in faith and in faithlessness. In Old Testament History, we read about kings and conquerors, priests and prophets, battles and blessings.

Starting in Joshua, we learn about the way the people of Israel entered the promised land and the leaders God appointed to deliver his people. God called judges to free the people from their enemies and restore them. Despite the people's disobedience, God remained faithful and steadfast, committed to fulfilling his good purposes.

We can tell we're reading Old Testament History when a book begins by naming people and places. This is a way of reminding us that these stories took place long ago, and even though some of them seem strange to us, they tell of real people and real events. Naming the person who was king when the book was written or naming where an event took place is the writer's way of saying, *Everything in this book is true! All of it really happened!*

JOSHUA

Author: We don't know.

Israel's new leader, Joshua, had heard God's promises to the generations who had gone before him and believed God would be faithful to give the Israelites a new home. The problem was that the land God promised to give the Israelites was occupied by people called Canaanites. In faith, Joshua led God's people into battles, such as the battle of Jericho, that they knew they could not win on their own (see Joshua 6). The Canaanite enemies had bigger and stronger armies than the Israelites. Driving out the idol-worshiping Canaanites had seemed hopeless to God's people! But the Israelites who entered the promised land learned that when they were obedient to God, they experienced victory. When they were disobedient, they lost the battle. The book of Joshua tells how God faithfully helped his people enter the promised land—a place they could finally call home.

Old Testament History

Victory over the Canaanites reminded the people of Israel that they could never save themselves; they needed God to be their Savior. One day he would send his ultimate Warrior—a truer and better Joshua—who would bring them home to be with him eternally. Jesus would be the ultimate victor who would defeat our enemies—sin and death—and make a way for us to live forever with God.

Joshua Becomes Israel's Leader

1 Moses, the servant of the LORD, died. After that, the LORD spoke to Joshua, the son of Nun. Joshua was Moses' helper. The LORD said to Joshua, 2 "My servant Moses is dead. Now then, I want you and all these people to get ready to go across the Jordan River. I want all of you to go into the land I am about to give to the Israelites. 3 I will give all of you every place you walk on, just as I promised Moses. 4 Your territory will reach from the Negev Desert all the way to Lebanon. The great Euphrates River will be to the east. The Mediterranean Sea will be to the west. Your territory will include all the Hittite country. 5 Joshua, no one will be able to oppose you as long as you live. I will be with you, just as I was with Moses. I will never leave you. I will never desert you. 6 Be strong and brave. You will lead these people. They will take the land as their very own. It is the land I promised to give their people of long ago.

7 "Be strong and very brave. Make sure you obey the whole law my servant Moses gave you. Do not turn away from it to the right or the left. Then you will have success everywhere you go. 8 Never stop reading this Book of the Law. Day and night you must think about what it says. Make sure you do everything written in it. Then things will go well with you. And you will have great success. 9 Here is what I am commanding you to do. Be strong and brave. Do not be afraid. Do not lose hope. I am the LORD your God. I will be with you everywhere you go."

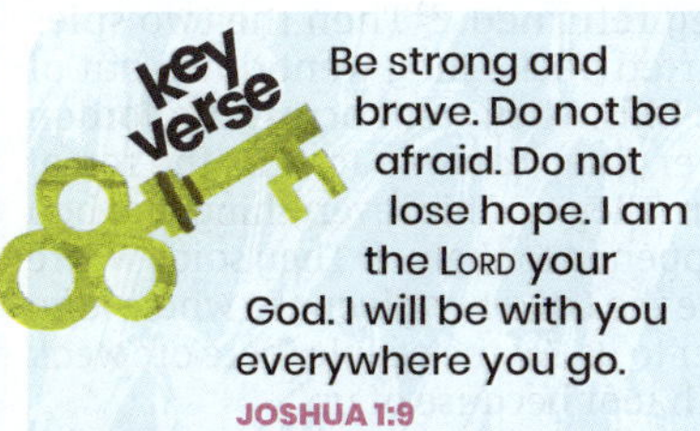

Be strong and brave. Do not be afraid. Do not lose hope. I am the LORD your God. I will be with you everywhere you go.

JOSHUA 1:9

10 So Joshua gave orders to the officers of the people. He said, 11 "Go through the camp. Tell the people, 'Get your supplies ready. Three days from now you will go across the Jordan River right here. You will go in and take over the land.

in Joshua?

God is the Victorious Warrior, the one who defeats the enemy so we can walk in victory.

The LORD your God is giving it to you as your very own.'"

12 Joshua also spoke to the tribes of Reuben and Gad and half of the tribe of Manasseh. He said to them, 13 "Remember what Moses, the servant of the LORD, commanded you. He said, 'The LORD your God is giving you this land. It's a place where you can make your homes and live in peace and rest.' 14 Your wives, children and livestock can stay here east of the Jordan River. Moses gave you this land. But all your fighting men must get ready for battle. They must go across ahead of the other tribes. You must help them 15 until the LORD gives them rest. In the same way, he has already given you rest. You must help them until they also have taken over their land. It's the land the LORD your God is giving them. After that, you can come back here. Then you can live in your own land. It's the land that Moses, the servant of the LORD, gave you east of the Jordan River. It's toward the sunrise."

16 Then the tribes of Reuben and Gad and half of the tribe of Manasseh answered Joshua. They said, "We'll do what you have commanded us to do. We'll go where you send us. 17 We obeyed Moses completely. And we'll obey you just as completely. But may the LORD your God be with you, just as he was with Moses. 18 Suppose people question your authority. And suppose they refuse to obey anything you command them to do. Then they will be put to death. Just be strong and brave!"

Rahab Helps the Spies

2 Joshua, the son of Nun, sent two spies from Shittim. He sent them in secret. He said to them, "Go and look over the land. Most of all, check out Jericho." So they went to Jericho. They stayed at the house of a prostitute. Her name was Rahab.

2 The king of Jericho was told, "Look! Some of the Israelites have come here tonight. They've come to check out the land." 3 So the king sent a message to Rahab. It said, "Bring out the men who came into your house. They've come to check out the whole land."

4 But the woman had hidden the two men. She said, "It's true that the men came here. But I didn't know where they had come from. 5 They left at sunset, when it was time to close the city gate. I don't know which way they went. Go after them quickly. You might catch up with them." 6 But in fact she had taken them up on the roof. There she had hidden them under some flax she had piled up. 7 The king's men left to hunt down the spies. They took the road that leads to where the Jordan River can be crossed. As soon as they had gone out of the city, the gate was shut.

8 Rahab went up on the roof before the spies settled down for the night. 9 She said to them, "I know that the LORD has given you this land. We are very much afraid of you. Everyone who lives in this country is weak with fear because of you. 10 We've heard how the LORD dried up the Red Sea for you when you came out of Egypt. We've heard what you did to Sihon and Og, the two Amorite kings. They ruled east of the Jordan River. You completely destroyed them. 11 When we heard about it, we were terrified. Because of you, we aren't brave anymore. The LORD your God is the God who rules in heaven above and on the earth below.

12 "Now then, please give me your word. Promise me in the name of the LORD that you will be kind to my family. I've been kind to you. Promise me 13 that you will spare the lives of my father and mother. Spare my brothers and sisters. Also spare everyone in their families. Promise that you won't put any of us to death."

14 So the men made a promise to her. "If you save our lives, we'll save yours," they said. "Just don't tell anyone what we're doing. Then we'll be kind and faithful to you when the LORD gives us the land."

15 The house Rahab lived in was part of the city wall. So she let the spies down by a rope through the window. 16 She said to them, "Go up into the hills. The men chasing you won't be able to find you. Hide yourselves there for three days until they return. Then you can go on your way."

17 The spies had said to her, "You made us give our word. But we won't keep our promise 18 unless you do what we say. When we enter the land, you must tie this bright red rope in the window. Tie it in the window you let us down through. Bring your father and mother into your house. Also bring in your brothers and everyone else in your family. 19 None of you must go out into the street. If you do, anything that happens to you will be your own fault. We won't be responsible. But if anyone hurts someone who is inside the house with you, it will be our fault. We will be responsible. 20 Don't tell anyone what we're doing. If you do, we won't have to keep the promise you asked us to make."

21 "I agree," Rahab replied. "I'll do as you say."

So she sent them away, and they left. Then she tied the bright red rope in the window.

22 When the spies left, they went up into the hills. They stayed there for three days. By that time the men chasing them had searched all along the road. They couldn't find them. So they returned. 23 Then the two spies started back. They went down out of the hills. They went across the Jordan River. They came to Joshua, the son of Nun. They told him everything that had happened to them. 24 They said, "We're sure the LORD has given the whole land over to us. All the people there are weak with fear because of us."

Israel Goes Across the Jordan River

3 Early one morning Joshua and all the Israelites started out from Shittim. They went down to the Jordan River. They camped there before they went across it. 2 After three days the officers went all through the camp. 3 They

gave orders to the people. They said,
“Watch for the ark of the covenant of
the LORD your God. The priests, who are
Levites, will be carrying it. When you see
it, you must move out from where you
are and follow it. 4 Then you will know
which way to go. You have never gone
this way before. But don’t go near the ark.
Stay about 1,000 yards away from it.”
5 Joshua said to the people, “Set yourselves apart to the LORD. Tomorrow he’ll
do amazing things among you.”
6 Joshua said to the priests, “Go and get
the ark of the covenant. Walk on ahead
of the people.” So they went and got it.
Then they walked on ahead of them.
7 The LORD said to Joshua, “Today I
will begin to honor you in the eyes of all
the Israelites. Then they will know that
I am with you, just as I was with Moses.
8 Speak to the priests who carry the ark
of the covenant. Tell them, ‘When you
reach the edge of the Jordan River, go
into the water and stand there.’ ”
9 Joshua said to the Israelites, “Come
here. Listen to what the LORD your God
is saying. 10 You will soon know that the
living God is among you. He will certainly drive out the people now living
in the land. He’ll do it to make room
for you. He’ll drive out the Canaanites,
Hittites, Hivites, Perizzites, Girgashites,
Amorites and Jebusites. 11 The ark will
go into the Jordan River ahead of you.
It’s the ark of the covenant of the Lord
of the whole earth. 12 Choose 12 men
from the tribes of Israel. Choose one
from each tribe. 13 The priests will carry
the ark of the LORD. He’s the Lord of the
whole earth. As soon as the priests step
into the Jordan, it will stop flowing. The
water that’s coming down the river will
pile up in one place. That’s how you will
know that the living God is among you.”
14 So the people took their tents down.
They prepared to go across the Jordan
River. The priests carrying the ark of
the covenant went ahead of them. 15 The
water of the Jordan was going over its
banks. It always does that at the time
the crops are being gathered. The priests
came to the river. Their feet touched the
water’s edge. 16 Right away the water
coming down the river stopped flowing.
It piled up far away at a town called
Adam near Zarethan. The water flowing
down to the Dead Sea was completely cut
off. So the people went across the Jordan
River opposite Jericho. 17 The priests carried the ark of the covenant of the LORD.
They stopped in the middle of the river
and stood on dry ground. They stayed
there until the whole nation of Israel
had gone across on dry ground.

4 After the whole nation had gone
across the Jordan River, the LORD
spoke to Joshua. He said, 2 “Choose 12
men from among the people. Choose
one from each tribe. 3 Tell them to get
12 stones from the middle of the river.
They must pick them up from right
where the priests stood. They must carry the stones over with all of you. And
they must put them down at the place
where you will stay tonight.”
4 So Joshua called together the 12
men he had appointed from among
the Israelites. There was one man from
each tribe. 5 He said to them, “Go back
to the middle of the Jordan River. Go to
where the ark of the LORD your God is.
Each one of you must pick up a stone.
You must carry it on your shoulder.
There will be as many stones as there
are tribes in Israel. 6 The stones will
serve as a reminder to you. In days to
come, your children will ask you, ‘What
do these stones mean?’ 7 Tell them that
the LORD cut off the flow of water in
the Jordan River. Tell them its water
stopped flowing when the ark of the
covenant of the LORD went across. The
stones will always remind the Israelites
of what happened there.”
8 So the Israelites did as Joshua commanded them. They took 12 stones from
the middle of the Jordan River. There was
one stone for each of the tribes of Israel.
It was just as the LORD had told Joshua.
The people carried the stones with them
to their camp. There they put them down.
9 Joshua also piled up 12 stones in the
middle of the river. He piled them up
right where the priests who carried the
ark of the covenant had stood. And they
are still there to this very day.
10 The priests who carried the ark remained standing in the middle of the
Jordan River. They stayed there until the
people had done everything the LORD had
commanded Joshua. It was just as Moses
had directed Joshua. All the people went
across quickly. 11 As soon as they did, the
ark of the LORD and the priests also went

across to the other side. The people were
watching them. 12 Among the people who
went across the river were men from the
tribes of Reuben and Gad and half of the
tribe of Manasseh. The men were ready
for battle. They went across ahead of the
rest of the Israelites. It was just as Moses
had directed them. 13 There were about
40,000 of them. All of them were ready
for battle. They went across in front of
the ark of the LORD. They marched to
the plains around Jericho. They were
prepared to go to war.

14 That day the LORD honored Joshua
in the eyes of all the Israelites. They had
respect for Joshua as long as he lived.
They respected him just as much as
they had respected Moses.

15 Then the LORD spoke to Joshua. He
said, 16 "Command the priests to come
up out of the Jordan River. They are
carrying the ark where the tablets of
the covenant law are kept."

17 So Joshua gave a command to the
priests. He said, "Come up out of the
Jordan River."

18 Then the priests came up out of the
river. They were carrying the ark of the
covenant of the LORD. As soon as they
stepped out on dry ground, the water of
the Jordan began to flow again. It went
over its banks, just as it had done before.

19 On the tenth day of the first month
the people went up out of the Jordan
River. They camped at Gilgal on the
eastern border of Jericho. 20 Joshua set
up the 12 stones at Gilgal. They were the
ones the people had taken out of the
Jordan. 21 Then he spoke to the Israelites.
He said, "In days to come, your children
after you will ask their parents, 'What
do these stones mean?' 22 Their parents
must tell them, 'Israel went across the
Jordan River on dry ground.' 23 The LORD
your God dried up the Jordan for you
until you had gone across it. He did to
the Jordan River the same thing he had
done to the Red Sea. He dried up the Red
Sea ahead of us until we had gone across
it. 24 He did it so that all the nations on
earth would know that he is powerful.
He did it so that you would always have
respect for the LORD your God."

5 All the Amorite and Canaanite
kings heard how the LORD had
dried up the Jordan River. They heard
how he had dried it up for the Israelites
until they had gone across it. The Amorite kings lived west of the Jordan.
The kings of Canaan lived along the
Mediterranean Sea. When all those
kings heard what the LORD had done,
they were terrified. They weren't brave
enough to face the Israelites anymore.

Circumcision and Passover at Gilgal

2 At that time the LORD said to Joshua, "Make knives out of flint. Use them
to circumcise the men of Israel." 3 So
Joshua made knives out of flint. Then
he used them to circumcise the men of
Israel at Gibeath Haaraloth.

4 Here is why Joshua circumcised
them. All the men who came out of Egypt
had died. They died while they were
wandering through the Sinai Desert.
They were the men old enough to serve
in the army. 5 All the men who came out
had been circumcised. But all the men
born in the desert during the journey
from Egypt hadn't been circumcised.
6 The Israelites had moved around in the
desert for 40 years. By the end of that
time all the men old enough to serve in
the army when they left Egypt had died.
That's because they hadn't obeyed the
LORD. He had made a promise to them.
He had told them they wouldn't see the
land. It's the land he had promised to
their people to give us. It's a land that has
plenty of milk and honey. 7 Because they
hadn't obeyed him, he raised up their
sons to take their place. They were the
ones Joshua circumcised. They hadn't
been circumcised yet. That's because
no one had circumcised them during
the journey. 8 So Joshua circumcised all
those men. The whole nation remained
in the camp until the men were healed.

9 Then the LORD spoke to Joshua. He
said, "Today I have taken away from
you the shame of being slaves in Egypt."
That's why the place where the men
were circumcised has been called Gilgal
to this very day.

10 The Israelites celebrated the Passover Feast. They observed it on the
evening of the 14th day of the month.
They did it while they were camped at
Gilgal on the plains around Jericho.
11 The day after the Passover, they ate
some of the food grown in the land.
On that same day they ate grain that
had been cooked. They also ate bread

made without yeast. 12 The manna stopped coming down the day after they ate the food grown in the land. The Israelites didn't have manna anymore. Instead, that year they ate food grown in Canaan.

Israel Captures Jericho

13 When Joshua was near Jericho, he looked up and saw a man standing in front of him. The man was holding a sword. He was ready for battle. Joshua went up to him. He asked, "Are you on our side? Or are you on the side of our enemies?"

14 "I am not on either side," he replied. "I have come as the commander of the LORD's army." Then Joshua fell with his face to the ground. He asked the man, "What message does my Lord have for me?"

15 The commander of the LORD's army replied, "Take off your sandals. The place you are standing on is holy ground." So Joshua took them off.

6 The gates of Jericho were shut tight and guarded closely because of the Israelites. No one went out. No one came in.

2 Then the LORD said to Joshua, "I have handed Jericho over to you. I have also handed over to you its king and its fighting men. 3 March around the city once with all your fighting men. In fact, do it for six days. 4 Have seven priests get trumpets made out of rams' horns. They must carry them in front of the ark. On the seventh day, march around the city seven times. Tell the priests to blow the trumpets as you march. 5 You will hear them blow a long blast on the trumpets. When you do, tell the whole army to give a loud shout. The wall of the city will fall down. Then the whole army will march up to the city. Everyone will go straight in."

6 So Joshua, the son of Nun, called for the priests. He said to them, "Go and get the ark of the covenant of the LORD. I want seven of you to carry trumpets in front of it." 7 He gave an order to the army. He said, "Move out! March around the city. Some of the fighting men must march in front of the ark of the LORD."

8 When Joshua had spoken to the men, the seven priests went forward. They were carrying the seven trumpets as they marched in front of the ark of the LORD. They were blowing the trumpets. The ark of the LORD's covenant was carried behind the priests. 9 Some of the fighting men marched ahead of the priests who were blowing the trumpets. The others followed behind the ark and guarded all the priests. That whole time the priests were blowing the trumpets. 10 But Joshua had given an order to the army. He had said, "Don't give a war cry. Don't raise your voices. Don't say a word until the day I tell you to shout. Then shout!" 11 So he had the ark of the LORD carried around the city once. Then the army returned to camp. They spent the night there.

12 Joshua got up early the next morning. The priests went and got the ark of the LORD. 13 The seven priests carrying the seven trumpets started out. They marched in front of the ark of the LORD. They blew the trumpets. Some of the fighting men marched ahead of them. The others followed behind the ark and guarded all of them. The priests kept blowing the trumpets. 14 On the second day they marched around the city once. Then the army returned to camp. They did all those things for six days.

15 On the seventh day, they got up at sunrise. They marched around the city, just as they had done before. But on that day they went around it seven times. 16 On the seventh time around, the priests blew a long blast on the trumpets. Then Joshua gave a command to the army. He said, "Shout! The LORD has given you the city! 17 The city and everything in it must be set apart to the LORD to be destroyed. But the prostitute Rahab and all those with her in her house must be spared. That's because she hid the spies we sent. 18 But keep away from the things that have been set apart to the LORD. If you take any of them, you will be destroyed. And you will bring trouble on the camp of Israel. You will cause it to be destroyed. 19 All the silver and gold is holy. It is set apart to the LORD. So are all the things made out of bronze and iron. All those things must be added to the treasures kept in the LORD's house."

20 The priests blew the trumpets. As soon as the army heard the sound, they gave a loud shout. Then the wall fell down. Everyone charged straight in. So they took the city. 21 They set it apart to the LORD to be destroyed.

They destroyed every living thing in it with their swords. They killed men and women. They wiped out young people and old people. They destroyed cattle, sheep and donkeys.
[22]Then Joshua spoke to the two men who had gone in to check out the land. He said, "Go into the prostitute's house. Bring her out. Also bring out everyone with her. That's what you promised
her you would do." [23]So the young men
who had checked out the land went into Rahab's house. They brought her out along with her parents and brothers and sisters. They brought out everyone else there with her. They put them in a place outside the camp of Israel.
[24]Then they burned the whole city and everything in it. But they added the silver and gold to the treasures kept in the LORD's house. They also put there the things made out of bronze and
iron. [25]But Joshua spared the prosti-
tute Rahab. He spared her family. He also spared everyone else in the house with her. He did it because she hid the spies he had sent to Jericho. Rahab lives among the Israelites to this day.

[26]At that time Joshua made a promise and called down a curse. He said, "May the person who tries to rebuild this city of Jericho be under the LORD's curse.

"If that person lays its foundations,
it will cost the life of his oldest son.
If he sets up its gates,
it will cost the life of his youngest son."

[27]So the LORD was with Joshua. And Joshua became famous everywhere in the land.

Achan Sins Against the LORD

7 But the Israelites weren't faithful to the LORD. They didn't destroy what had been set apart to him. So they did not do what they had been told to do. Achan had taken some of those things. So the LORD became very angry with Israel. Achan was the son of Karmi. Karmi was the son of Zimri. And Zimri was the son of Zerah. Achan and all his relatives were from the tribe of Judah.
[2]Joshua sent men from Jericho to
Ai. Ai is near Beth Aven east of Bethel.

pointing us to JESUS: Joshua

Joshua was called to lead God's people, the Israelites, at a time when no one really wanted to lead them. God's people were on their way to the land God had promised to give them as their home, but there was a problem: A great big city full of their enemies was in the way! This city, called Jericho, was full of strong warriors and people who mocked the Israelites and their God.

Joshua looked to God for direction and provision. He did exactly what God commanded, and God miraculously knocked down the city's walls. The Israelites never could have conquered Jericho on their own, but God was with them and helped them overcome their enemies. Then Joshua was able to lead God's people into the land God had promised to give them.

Generations later, Jesus would come and be the truer and better leader of God's people. Through Jesus' death and resurrection, the enemies of God's people—sin and death—would be destroyed. Jesus leads those who put their faith in him into the eternal promised land, known as heaven.

Joshua told the men, "Go up and check
out the area around Ai." So the men
went up and checked it out.
3 Then they returned to Joshua. They
said, "The whole army doesn't have to
go up and attack Ai. Send only two or
three thousand men. They can take the
city. Don't make the whole army go up
there. Only a few people live in Ai." 4 So
only about 3,000 troops went up. But
the men of Ai drove them away. 5 They
chased the Israelites from the city gate
all the way to Shebarim. They killed
about 36 of them on the way down. So
the Israelites were terrified.
6 Joshua and the elders of Israel became sad. Joshua tore his clothes. He fell
in front of the ark of the LORD with his
face to the ground. He remained there
until evening. The elders did the same
thing. They also sprinkled dust on their
heads. 7 Joshua said, "LORD and King,
why did you ever bring these people
across the Jordan River? Did you want
to hand us over to the Amorites? Did
you want them to destroy us? I wish we
had been content to stay on the other
side of the Jordan! 8 Lord, our enemies
have driven us away. What can I say?
9 The Canaanites will hear about it.
So will everyone else in the country.
They will surround us. They'll erase any
mention of our name from the face of
the earth. Then what will you do when
people don't honor your great name
anymore?"
10 The LORD said to Joshua, "Get up!
What are you doing down there on your
face? 11 Israel has sinned. I made a covenant with them. I commanded them
to keep it. But they have broken it. They
have taken some of the things that had
been set apart to me in a special way to
be destroyed. They have stolen. They
have lied. They have taken the things
they stole and have put them with their
own things. 12 That is why the Israelites
can't stand up against their enemies.
They turn their backs and run. That's
because I have decided to let them be destroyed. You must destroy the things you
took that had been set apart to me. If you
do not, I will not be with you anymore.
13 "Go and set the people apart. Tell
them, 'Make yourselves pure. Get ready
for tomorrow. Here is what the LORD, the

God of Israel, wants you to do. He says, “People of Israel, you have kept some of the things that had been set apart to me to be destroyed. You can't stand up against your enemies until you get rid of those things.”

14 “ ‘In the morning, come forward tribe by tribe. The tribe the LORD chooses will come forward group by group. The group the LORD chooses will come forward family by family. And the men in the family the LORD chooses will come forward one by one. 15 Whoever is caught with the things that had been set apart to the LORD will be destroyed by fire. Everything that belongs to that person will also be destroyed. He has broken the LORD's covenant. He has done a very terrible thing in Israel!' ”

16 Early the next morning Joshua had Israel come forward by tribes. The tribe of Judah was chosen. 17 The groups of Judah came forward. The group of Zerah was chosen. Joshua had the group of Zerah come forward by families. The family of Zimri was chosen. 18 He had their men come forward one by one. Achan was chosen. Achan was the son of Karmi. Karmi was the son of Zimri. And Zimri was the son of Zerah. Zerah was from the tribe of Judah.

19 Joshua said to Achan, “My son, the LORD is the God of Israel. So give him glory and honor him by telling the truth! Tell me what you have done. Don't hide it from me.”

20 Achan replied, “It's true! I've sinned against the LORD, the God of Israel. Here is what I've done. 21 I saw a beautiful robe from Babylonia among the things we had taken. I saw five pounds of silver. And I saw a gold bar that weighed 20 ounces. I wanted them, so I took them. I hid them in the ground inside my tent. The silver is on the bottom.”

22 So Joshua sent some messengers. They ran to Achan's tent. And there was everything, hidden in his tent! The silver was on the bottom. 23 They brought the things out of the tent. They took them to Joshua and all the Israelites. And they spread them out in the sight of the LORD.

24 Then Joshua and all the people grabbed Achan, the son of Zerah. They took the silver, the robe and the gold bar. They took Achan's sons and daughters. They took his cattle, donkeys and sheep. They also took his tent and everything he had. They carried all of it out to the Valley of Achor. 25 Joshua said to Achan, “Why have you brought this trouble on us? The LORD will bring trouble on you today.”

Then all the people killed Achan by throwing stones at him. They also killed the rest of his family with stones. They burned all of them up. 26 They placed a large pile of rocks on top of Achan's body. The place has been called the Valley of Achor ever since. That pile is still there to this day. After the people killed Achan, the LORD was no longer angry with them.

Israel Destroys Ai

8 Then the LORD said to Joshua, “Do not be afraid. Do not lose hope. Go up and attack Ai. Take the whole army with you. I have handed the king of Ai over to you. I have given you his people, his city and his land. 2 Remember what you did to Jericho and its king. You will do the same thing to Ai and its king. But this time you can keep for yourselves the livestock and everything else you take from them. Have some of your fighting men hide behind the city and take them by surprise.”

3 So Joshua and the whole army moved out to attack Ai. He chose 30,000 of his best fighting men. He sent them out at night. 4 He gave them orders. He said, “Listen carefully to what I'm saying. You must hide behind the city. Don't go very far away from it. All of you must be ready to attack it. 5 I and all those with me will march up to the city. The men of Ai will come out to fight against us, just as they did before. Then we'll run away from them. 6 They'll chase us until we've drawn them away from the city. They'll say, ‘They are running away from us, just as they did before.' When we run away from them, 7 come out of your hiding place. Capture the city. The LORD your God will hand it over to you. 8 When you have taken it, set it on fire. Do what the LORD has commanded. Make sure you obey my orders.”

9 Then Joshua sent them away. They went to the place where they had planned to hide. They hid in a place west of Ai. It was between Bethel and Ai. But Joshua spent that night with his troops.

10 Early the next morning Joshua
brought together his army. He and the
leaders of Israel marched in front of
them to Ai. 11 The whole army that was
with him marched up to the city. They
stopped in front of it. They set up camp
north of Ai. There was a valley between
them and the city. 12 Joshua had chosen
about 5,000 soldiers. He had ordered
them to hide in a place west of Ai. It
was between Bethel and Ai. 13 The men
took up their battle positions. All the
men in the camp north of the city took
up their positions. So did those who
were supposed to hide west of the city.
That night Joshua went into the valley.

14 The king of Ai saw what the troops
with Joshua were doing. So the king and
all his men hurried out of the city early in
the morning. They marched out to meet
Israel in battle. They went to a place that
looked out over the Arabah Valley. The
king didn't know that some of Israel's
fighting men were hiding behind the city.
15 Joshua and all his men let the men of Ai
drive them back. The Israelites ran away
toward the desert. 16 All the men of Ai were
called out to chase them. They chased
Joshua. So they were drawn away from
the city. 17 Not even one man remained
in Ai or Bethel. All of them went out to
chase Israel. When they did, they left the
city wide open.

18 Then the LORD said to Joshua, "Hold
out toward Ai the javelin that is in your
hand. I will give the city to you." So
Joshua held out toward the city the
javelin in his hand. 19 As soon as he did,
the men hiding behind the city got up
quickly. They came out of their hiding places and rushed forward. They
entered the city and captured it. They
quickly set it on fire.

20 The men of Ai looked back. They
saw smoke rising up from the city into
the sky. But they couldn't escape in
any direction. The Israelites had been
running away toward the desert. But
now they turned around to face those
chasing them. 21 Joshua and all his men
saw that the men who had been hiding
behind the city had captured it. They
also saw that smoke was going up from
it. So they turned around and attacked
the men of Ai. 22 The men who had set Ai
on fire came out of the city. They also
fought against the men of Ai. So the
men of Ai were caught in the middle.
The army of Israel was on both sides
of them. Israel struck them down. They
didn't let anyone remain alive or get
away. 23 But they captured the king of
Ai alive. They brought him to Joshua.

24 Israel finished killing all the men
of Ai. They destroyed them in the fields
and in the desert where they had chased
them. They struck down every one of
them with their swords. Then all the
Israelites returned to Ai. And they killed
those who were left in it. 25 The total
number of men and women they killed
that day was 12,000. The Israelites put
to death all the people of Ai. 26 Joshua
continued to hold out his javelin toward
Ai. He didn't lower his hand until he and
his men had totally destroyed everyone
who lived there. 27 But this time Israel
kept for themselves the livestock and
everything else they had taken from
the city. The LORD had directed Joshua
to let them do it.

28 So Joshua burned down Ai. He tore
it down so it could never be built again.
It has been deserted to this very day.
29 Joshua killed the king of Ai. He stuck a
pole through the body. Then he set it up
where people could see it. He left it there
until evening. At sunset, Joshua ordered
his men to remove the body from the
pole. He told them to throw the body
down at the entrance of the city gate.
They put a large pile of rocks over the
body. That pile is still there to this day.

Joshua Reads the Book of the Law to the People

30 Joshua built an altar to honor the
LORD, the God of Israel. He built it on
Mount Ebal. 31 Moses, the servant of the
LORD, had commanded the Israelites to
do that. Joshua built the altar according
to what is written in the Book of the
Law of Moses. Joshua built the altar
out of stones that iron tools had never
touched. Then the people offered on the
altar burnt offerings to the LORD. They
also sacrificed friendship offerings on
it. 32 Joshua copied the law of Moses on
stones. He did it while all the Israelites
were watching. 33 They were standing
on both sides of the ark of the covenant
of the LORD. All the Israelites, including
outsiders and citizens, were there. Israel's elders, officials and judges were also

there. All of them faced the priests, who were Levites. They were carrying the ark. Half of the people stood in front of Mount Gerizim. The other half stood in front of Mount Ebal. Moses, the servant of the LORD, had earlier told them to do it. Moses told them to do it when he had given directions to bless the Israelites.
34 Then Joshua read all the words of the law out loud. He read the blessings and the curses. He read them just as they are written in the Book of the Law.
35 Joshua read every word Moses had commanded. He read them to the whole community of Israel. That included the women and children. It also included the outsiders living among them.

The People of Gibeon Trick Israel

9 All the kings who ruled west of the Jordan River heard about the battles Israel had won. That included the kings who ruled in the central hill country and the western hills. It also included those who ruled along the entire coast of the Mediterranean Sea all the way to Lebanon. They were the kings of the Hittites, Amorites, Canaanites,
Perizzites, Hivites and Jebusites. 2 They
brought their armies together to fight against Joshua and Israel.
3 The people of Gibeon heard about what Joshua had done to Jericho and
Ai. 4 So they decided to trick the Israelites. They packed supplies as if they were going on a long trip. They loaded their donkeys with old sacks and old wineskins. The wineskins were cracked
but had been mended. 5 They put worn-out sandals on their feet. The sandals had been patched. They also wore old clothes. All the bread they took along
was dry and moldy. 6 They went to Joshua in the camp at Gilgal. They spoke to him and the Israelites. They said, "We've come from a country that's far away. Make a peace treaty with us."
7 The Israelites said to the Hivites, "But suppose you live close to us. If you do, we can't make a peace treaty with you."
8 "We'll serve you," they said to Joshua.

But Joshua asked, "Who are you? Where do you come from?"
9 They answered, "We've come from a country that's very far away. We've come because the LORD your God is famous. We've heard reports about him. We've heard about everything he did in Egypt.
10 We've heard about everything he did to Sihon and Og. They were the two kings of the Amorites. They ruled east of the Jordan River. Sihon was the king of Heshbon. Og was the king of Bashan. He ruled in
Ashtaroth. 11 Our elders and all the people living in our country spoke to us. They said, 'Take supplies for your trip. Go and meet the Israelites. Say to them, "We'll serve you. Make a peace treaty with us." '
12 Look at our bread. It was warm when we packed it. We packed it at home the day we left to come and see you. But look at
how dry and moldy it is now. 13 When we filled these wineskins, they were new. But look at how cracked they are now. And our clothes and sandals are worn out because we've traveled so far."
14 The Israelites looked over the supplies those people had brought. But they didn't
ask the LORD what they should do. 15 Joshua made a peace treaty with the people who had come. He agreed to let them live. The leaders of the community gave their word that they agreed with the treaty.
16 So the Israelites made a peace treaty with the people of Gibeon. But three days later they heard that the people
of Gibeon lived close to them. 17 So the Israelites started out to go to the cities of those people. On the third day they came to Gibeon, Kephirah, Beeroth and
Kiriath Jearim. 18 But they didn't attack those cities. That's because the leaders of the community had given their word and made a peace treaty with them. They had given their word in the name of the LORD, the God of Israel.

The whole community told the leaders
they weren't happy with them. 19 But all the leaders answered, "We've made a peace treaty with them. We've given our word in the name of the LORD, the God of Israel. So we can't touch them now.
20 But here is what we'll do to them. We'll let them live. Then the LORD won't be angry with us because we didn't keep our
promise." 21 They continued, "Let them live. But make them cut wood and carry water to serve the whole community." So the leaders kept their promise to them.
22 Joshua sent for the people of Gibeon. He said to them, "Why did you trick us? You said, 'We live far away from you.'
But in fact you live close to us. 23 So now

you are under a curse. You will always
serve us. You will always cut wood and
carry water for the house of my God."
24 They answered Joshua, "We were
clearly told what the LORD your God
had commanded his servant Moses to
do. He commanded him to give you
the whole land. He also ordered him to
wipe out all its people to make room for
you. So we were afraid you would kill
us. That's why we tricked you. 25 We are
now under your control. Do to us what
you think is good and right."
26 So Joshua saved the people of
Gibeon. He didn't let the Israelites kill
them. 27 That day he made them cut
wood and carry water. They had to
serve the community of Israel. They
also had to do work connected with the
altar of the LORD. The altar would be at
the place the LORD would choose. And
they still serve the Israelites to this day.

The Sun Stands Still

10 Adoni-Zedek was the king of Jerusalem. He heard that Joshua
had captured Ai. He found out that the
city had been set apart to the LORD in a
special way to be destroyed. He heard
that Joshua had done to Ai and its king
the same thing he had done to Jericho
and its king. Adoni-Zedek heard that
the people of Gibeon had made a peace
treaty with Israel. He also found out
that they were living among the Israelites. 2 The things he heard alarmed
him and his people very much. That's
because Gibeon was an important city.
It was like one of the royal cities. It was
larger than Ai. All its men were good
soldiers. 3 So Adoni-Zedek, the king of
Jerusalem, made an appeal to Hoham,
the king of Hebron. He appealed to Pi-
ram, the king of Jarmuth. He appealed
to Japhia, the king of Lachish. He also
made an appeal to Debir, the king of
Eglon. 4 "Come up and help me attack
Gibeon," he said. "Its people have made
peace with Joshua and the Israelites."
5 Then the kings of Jerusalem, Hebron, Jarmuth, Lachish and Eglon gathered their armies together. Those five
Amorite kings moved all their troops
into position to fight against Gibeon.
Then they attacked it.
6 Joshua was in the camp at Gilgal.
The people of Gibeon sent a message
to him there. They said, "Don't desert
us. We serve you. Come up to us quickly! Save us! Help us! All the Amorite
kings from the central hill country have
gathered their armies together to fight
against us."
7 So Joshua marched up from Gilgal
with his whole army. The army included all his best fighting men. 8 The
LORD said to Joshua, "Do not be afraid
of them. I have handed them over to
you. Not one of them will be able to
fight against you and win."
9 Joshua marched all night from
Gilgal. He took the Amorite armies by
surprise. 10 The LORD threw them into a
panic as Israel marched toward them.
Then Joshua and the Israelites won a
complete victory over them at Gibeon.
The Israelites chased them along the
road that goes up to Beth Horon. They
struck them down all the way to Azekah
and Makkedah. 11 The Amorites tried
to escape as Israel marched toward
them. They ran down the road from
Beth Horon to Azekah. Then the LORD
threw large hailstones down on them.
The hailstones killed more of them than
the swords of the Israelites did.
12 So the LORD gave the Amorites over
to Israel. On that day Joshua spoke to
the LORD while the Israelites were listening. He said,

"Sun, stand still over Gibeon.
  And you, moon, stand still over
    the Valley of Aijalon."
13 So the sun stood still.
  The moon stopped.
  They didn't move again until the
    nation won the battle over its
    enemies.

You can read about it in the Book of
Jashar.
The sun stopped in the middle of the
sky. It didn't go down for about a full
day. 14 There has never been a day like
it before or since. It was a day when the
LORD listened to a mere human being.
Surely the LORD was fighting for Israel!
15 Joshua and his whole army returned to the camp at Gilgal.

Joshua Kills the Five Amorite Kings

16 The five Amorite kings had run
away. They had hidden in the cave at
Makkedah. 17 Joshua was told that the

five kings had been found. He was also told that they were hiding in the cave at Makkedah. 18 He said, "Roll some large rocks up to the opening of the cave. Put some men there to guard it. 19 But keep on going! Chase your enemies! Attack them from behind. Don't let them get back to their cities. The LORD your God has handed them over to you."

20 So Joshua and the men of Israel had complete victory over them. They killed almost every one of them. But a few escaped. They went back to their cities that had high walls around them. 21 Then Israel's whole army returned safely to Joshua. He was in the camp at Makkedah. No one in the land dared to say anything against the Israelites.

22 Joshua said, "Open up the cave. Bring those five kings out to me." 23 So Joshua's men brought the kings out of the cave. They were the kings of Jerusalem, Hebron, Jarmuth, Lachish and Eglon. 24 The men brought them to Joshua. Then he sent for all the men of Israel. He spoke to the army commanders who had come with him. He said, "Come here. Put your feet on the necks of these kings." So they came forward and placed their feet on the necks of the kings.

25 Joshua said to them, "Don't be afraid. Don't lose hope. Be strong and brave. This is what the LORD will do to all the enemies you are going to fight." 26 Joshua put the five kings to death. He stuck a pole through each of their bodies. Then he set the poles up where people could see the bodies. He left them there until evening.

27 At sunset Joshua ordered his men to take down the bodies. So they took them down from the poles and threw them into the cave where the kings had been hiding. They placed large rocks at the opening of the cave. And the rocks are still there to this day.

The Campaign Against the Cities in the South

28 That day Joshua captured Makkedah. He cut down its people and their king. He totally destroyed everyone in it. He didn't leave anyone alive. He did to the king of Makkedah the same thing he had done to the king of Jericho.

29 Joshua moved on from Makkedah to Libnah. Israel's whole army went with him. They attacked Libnah. 30 The LORD also handed that city and its king over to Israel. Joshua destroyed the city. He and his men killed everyone in it with their swords. He didn't leave anyone alive there. He did to its king the same thing he had done to the king of Jericho.

31 Joshua moved on from Libnah to Lachish. Israel's whole army went with him. The men took up their battle positions. Then Joshua attacked Lachish. 32 The LORD handed it over to Israel. Joshua captured the city on the second day of the battle. He destroyed the city. He and his men killed everyone in it with their swords. He had done the same thing to Libnah. 33 While all that was happening, Horam had come up to help Lachish. He was the king of Gezer. But Joshua won the battle over him and his army. No one was left alive.

34 Joshua moved on from Lachish to Eglon. Israel's whole army went with him. They took up their battle positions. Then they attacked Eglon. 35 They captured it that same day. They totally destroyed everyone in it with their swords. They had done the same thing to Lachish.

36 Joshua went up from Eglon to Hebron. Israel's whole army went with him. Then they attacked Hebron. 37 They captured the city. They destroyed it and its villages. They killed all its people and their king with their swords. They didn't leave anyone alive. They totally destroyed the city and everyone in it. They had done the same thing at Eglon.

38 Joshua turned back and attacked Debir. Israel's whole army went with him. 39 They captured the city, its king and its villages. They totally destroyed everyone in Debir with their swords. They didn't leave anyone alive. They did to Debir and its king the same thing they had done to Libnah and its king. They had also done the same thing to Hebron.

40 So Joshua brought the whole area under his control. That included the central hill country and the Negev Desert. It included the western hills and the mountain slopes. It also included all the kings in that whole area. Joshua didn't leave anyone alive. He totally destroyed everyone who breathed. He did just as the LORD, the God of Israel, had commanded. 41 Joshua brought

everyone from Kadesh Barnea to Gaza under his control. He did the same thing to everyone from the whole area of Goshen to Gibeon. 42 He won the battle over all those kings and their lands. He did it in one campaign. That's because the LORD, the God of Israel, fought for Israel.

43 Then Joshua returned to the camp at Gilgal. Israel's whole army went with him.

The Campaign Against the Cities in the North

11 Jabin was the king of Hazor. He heard about the battles Israel had won. So he sent a message to Jobab. Jobab was the king of Madon. Jabin sent the same message to the kings of Shimron and Akshaph. 2 He also sent it to many other kings. Some ruled in the mountains in the north. Some ruled in the Arabah Valley south of Kinnereth. Others ruled in the western hills. Still others ruled in Naphoth Dor in the west. 3 Jabin sent the same message to the people of east Canaan and west Canaan. He sent it to the Amorites, Hittites, Perizzites and Jebusites. They lived in the central hill country. He also sent it to the Hivites who lived below Mount Hermon in the area of Mizpah. 4 Those kings marched out with all their troops. They had a large number of horses and chariots. It was a huge army. The fighting men were as many as the grains of sand on the seashore. 5 All those kings gathered their armies together to fight against Israel. They set up camp together at the Waters of Merom.

6 The LORD said to Joshua, "Do not be afraid of them. By this time tomorrow I will hand all of them over to Israel. All of them will be killed. You must cut the legs of their horses. You must burn their chariots."

7 So Joshua and his whole army attacked them suddenly. They fought against them at the Waters of Merom. 8 The LORD handed them over to Israel. The Israelites won the battle over them. They hunted them down all the way to Greater Sidon. They chased them to Misrephoth Maim. They chased them to the Valley of Mizpah in the east. Not one of them was left alive. 9 Joshua did to them what the LORD had ordered him to do. He cut the legs of their horses. He burned up their chariots.

10 At that time Joshua turned back. He captured Hazor. He killed its king with his sword. Hazor was the most important city in all those kingdoms. 11 The army of Israel killed everyone in Hazor with their swords. Its people had been set apart to the LORD to be destroyed. Israel's army didn't spare anyone who breathed. Then Joshua burned down the city.

12 Joshua captured all those royal cities and their kings. He and his men killed everyone in those cities with their swords. He totally destroyed them. He did just as Moses, the servant of the LORD, had commanded. 13 Many cities were built on top of earlier cities that had been destroyed. Israel didn't burn any of those except Hazor. Joshua burned it down. 14 The army of Israel kept for themselves the livestock and everything else they took from those cities. But they killed all the people with their swords. They completely destroyed them. They didn't spare anyone who breathed. 15 The LORD had commanded his servant Moses to do all these things. Moses had passed that command on to Joshua. And Joshua carried it out. He did everything the LORD had commanded Moses.

16 So Joshua captured the whole land. He took over the central hill country and the whole Negev Desert. He took over the whole area of Goshen. He took over the western hills. He took over the Arabah Valley. He took over the mountains of Israel and the hills around them. 17 He took over the area that begins at Mount Halak, which rises toward Seir. The area ends at Baal Gad in the Valley of Lebanon below Mount Hermon. Joshua captured the kings who ruled over that whole land. He put them to death. 18 He fought battles against all those kings for a long time. 19 Only the Hivites who lived in Gibeon made a peace treaty with the Israelites. No other city made a treaty with them. So Israel captured all those cities in battle. 20 The LORD himself made their people stubborn. He made them go to war against Israel so he could totally destroy them. He wanted to wipe them out. He didn't show them any mercy.

The LORD had commanded Moses to
destroy the Canaanites.
[21]At that time Joshua went and
destroyed the Anakites. They lived
all through the hill country of Judah
and Israel. They lived in Hebron, Debir
and Anab. Joshua totally destroyed
the Anakites and their towns. [22]There
weren't any Anakites left alive in Israel's territory. But a few were left alive
in Gaza, Gath and Ashdod.
[23]So Joshua captured the whole land,
just as the LORD had directed Moses.
Joshua gave the land to Israel as their
very own. He divided it up and gave
each tribe its share. Then the land had
peace and rest.

Israel Wins the Battle Over the Kings in the Land

12 The Israelites took over the
territory east of the Jordan
River. The land they captured
reached from the Arnon River valley
to Mount Hermon. It included the
whole east side of the Arabah Valley.
Israel won the battle over the kings
of that whole territory. Here are the
lands Israel captured from the kings
they won the battle over.

[2]They took over the land of Sihon.
He was the king of the Amorites.
He ruled in Heshbon.
The land he ruled over begins at
Aroer. Aroer is on the rim of the
Arnon River valley. Sihon ruled
from the middle of the valley to
the Jabbok River. The Jabbok is
the border of Ammon. Sihon's
territory included half of Gilead.
[3]He also ruled over the east side
of the Arabah Valley. That land
begins at the Sea of Galilee. It
goes to the Dead Sea and over
to Beth Jeshimoth. Then it
goes south, below the slopes of
Pisgah.
[4]Israel also took over the territory of
Og. He was the king of Bashan.
He was one of the last of the
Rephaites. He ruled in Ashtaroth
and Edrei.
[5]He ruled over Mount Hermon,
Salekah and the whole land of
Bashan. Og's kingdom reached
all the way to the border of
Geshur and Maakah. He ruled
over half of Gilead. His land
reached the border of Sihon, the
king of Heshbon.

[6]Moses was the servant of the LORD.
Moses and the Israelites won the
battle over those two kings. He
gave their land to the tribes of
Reuben and Gad and half of the
tribe of Manasseh. He gave it to
them as their share.

[7]Joshua and the Israelites won the
battle over the kings who ruled west
of the Jordan River. The lands of those
kings reached from Baal Gad in the Valley of Lebanon to Mount Halak, which
rises toward Seir. Joshua gave their
lands to the tribes of Israel as their very
own. He divided them up and gave each
tribe its share. [8]Those lands included
the central hill country, the western
hills and the Arabah Valley. They also
included the mountain slopes, the
Desert of Judah and the Negev Desert.
Those lands belonged to the Hittites,
Amorites, Canaanites, Perizzites, Hivites and Jebusites.

Here are the kings Israel won the
battle over.

[9]the king of Jericho one
the king of Ai, which is near
Bethel one
[10]the king of Jerusalem one
the king of Hebron one
[11]the king of Jarmuth one
the king of Lachish one
[12]the king of Eglon one
the king of Gezer one
[13]the king of Debir one
the king of Geder one
[14]the king of Hormah one
the king of Arad one
[15]the king of Libnah one
the king of Adullam one
[16]the king of Makkedah one
the king of Bethel one
[17]the king of Tappuah one
the king of Hepher one
[18]the king of Aphek one
the king of Lasharon one
[19]the king of Madon one
the king of Hazor one
[20]the king of Shimron Meron one
the king of Akshaph one
[21]the king of Taanach one
the king of Megiddo one

22 the king of Kedesh one
the king of Jokneam in
Carmel one
23 the king of Dor in Naphoth
Dor one
the king of Goyim in Gilgal one
24 the king of Tirzah one
The total number of kings was 31.

The Land That Remained to Be Taken Over

13 Joshua was now very old. The
LORD said to him, "You are very
old. And there are still very large areas
of land that have not yet been taken
over.

2 "Here is the land that remains to
be taken over.

"It includes all the areas of
Philistia and Geshur. 3 Those
areas begin at the Shihor River
in the eastern part of Egypt.
They go to the territory of
Ekron in the north. All that land
is considered Canaanite even
though it is controlled by five
Philistine rulers. They rule over
Gaza, Ashdod, Ashkelon, Gath
and Ekron.
The Avvites 4 live south of them.
The rest of the land of Canaan that
remains to be taken over reaches
from Arah all the way to Aphek.
Arah belongs to the people of
Sidon. The land that remains
to be taken reaches the border
of Amorite territory.
5 It includes the area of Byblos.
It also includes all of Lebanon to
the east. It reaches from Baal
Gad below Mount Hermon all
the way to Lebo Hamath.

6 "I myself will drive out all the people who live in the mountain areas.
Those areas reach from Lebanon to
Misrephoth Maim. They include the
area where all the people of Sidon live.
I myself will drive out those people to
make room for the Israelites. Make
sure you set that land apart for Israel.
Give it to them as their share, just as I
have directed you. 7 Divide it up among
the nine tribes and half of the tribe of
Manasseh. Give each tribe its share."

Land for the Tribes East of the Jordan River

8 The other half of Manasseh's tribe
had already received the share of
land Moses had given them. Their
share was east of the Jordan River.
The tribes of Reuben and Gad had
already received their share too.
Moses, the servant of the LORD,
had given it to them.
9 That land starts at Aroer on the
rim of the Arnon River valley. It
includes the town in the middle
of the valley. It includes the high
plains of Medeba all the way
to Dibon. 10 It also includes all
the towns of Sihon, the king of
the Amorites. He had ruled in
Heshbon. That area reaches to
the border of Ammon.
11 It also includes Gilead. It includes
the territory of Geshur and
Maakah. It includes Mount
Hermon and the whole land of
Bashan all the way to Salekah.
12 So it includes the entire
kingdom of Og in Bashan. Og
had ruled in Ashtaroth and
Edrei. He was the last of the
Rephaites. Moses had won the
battle over Sihon and Og. He had
taken over their land. 13 But the
Israelites didn't drive out the
people of Geshur and Maakah.
So they continue to live among
the Israelites to this day.

14 Moses hadn't given any share of
the land to the tribe of Levi.
That's because the food offerings
are their share. Those offerings
are presented to the LORD, the
God of Israel. Moses gave the
Levites what he had promised
them.

15 Here is what Moses had given to
the tribe of Reuben, according to
its family groups.
16 Their territory starts at Aroer on the
rim of the Arnon River valley. It
includes the town in the middle
of the valley. It includes all of
the high plains near Medeba.
17 It includes Heshbon and all
its towns on those plains. Those
towns include Dibon, Bamoth
Baal, Beth Baal Meon, 18 Jahaz,

Kedemoth and Mephaath.
19 They include Kiriathaim,
Sibmah and Zereth Shahar on
the hill in the valley. 20 They
also include Beth Peor, Beth
Jeshimoth and the slopes of
Pisgah. 21 All those towns are on
the high plains. The territory
includes the whole kingdom of
Sihon, the king of the Amorites.
He had ruled in Heshbon. Moses
had won the battle over him and
over the chiefs of Midian. Those
chiefs were Evi, Rekem, Zur, Hur
and Reba. They were princes who
helped Sihon fight against Israel.
They lived in that country. 22 The
Israelites killed many of them in
battle. They also killed Balaam
with their swords. He was the son
of Beor. Balaam had used evil
magic to find out what was going
to happen.

23 The border of the tribe of Reuben
was the bank of the Jordan River.
All those towns and their villages
were given to the tribe of Reuben
as their very own. Each family
group received its share.

24 Here is what Moses had given to
the tribe of Gad, according to its
family groups.

25 Their territory includes Jazer and
all the towns of Gilead. It includes
half of the country of Ammon
all the way to Aroer, which was
near Rabbah. 26 Their territory
reaches from Heshbon to Ramath
Mizpah and Betonim. It reaches
from Mahanaim to the territory
of Debir. 27 In the valley their
land includes Beth Haram, Beth
Nimrah, Sukkoth and Zaphon.
It also includes the rest of the
kingdom of Sihon. He was the
king of Heshbon. His kingdom
included the east side of the
Jordan River. It reached up to the
south end of the Sea of Galilee.

28 All those towns and their villages
were given to the tribe of Gad as
their very own. Each family group
received its share.

29 Here is what Moses had given
to half of the tribe of Manasseh,
according to its family groups. It's
what Moses had given to half of
Manasseh's family line.

30 Their territory starts at Mahanaim.
It includes the whole land of
Bashan. That was the entire
kingdom of Og, the king of
Bashan. Manasseh's territory
includes all the 60 towns of
Jair in Bashan. 31 It includes
half of the land of Gilead. It also
includes Ashtaroth and Edrei.
They were the royal cities of Og
in Bashan.

That land was given to half of
the family line of Makir. He was
the son of Manasseh. Each family
group received its share.

32 Those were the shares of land Moses
had given the eastern tribes when
he was in the plains of Moab. The
plains are across the Jordan River
east of Jericho. 33 But Moses hadn't
given any share to the tribe of Levi.
The LORD, the God of Israel, is their
share. Moses gave the Levites what
he had promised them.

Land for the Tribes West of the Jordan River

14 The rest of the tribes of Israel
received their shares of land in
Canaan. Eleazar the priest and Joshua,
the son of Nun, decided what each of
the tribes should receive. The leaders
of the tribes helped them make these
decisions. 2 The shares of nine tribes
and half of the tribe of Manasseh were
decided by casting lots. That's what the
LORD had commanded through Moses.
3 Moses had given two tribes and the
other half of the tribe of Manasseh their
shares east of the Jordan River. But
Moses had not given the Levites a share
among the other tribes. 4 Manasseh
and Ephraim were the sons of Joseph.
They had become two tribes. The Levites
didn't receive any share of the land.
They only received towns to live in and
grasslands for their flocks and herds.
5 So the Israelites divided up the land,
just as the LORD had commanded Moses.

Joshua Gives Hebron to Caleb

6 The people of Judah approached
Joshua at Gilgal. Caleb, the son of Je-
phunneh the Kenizzite, spoke to Joshua.
He said, "You know what the LORD said

to Moses, the man of God. He spoke to
him at Kadesh Barnea about you and
me. 7 Moses, the servant of the LORD,
sent me from Kadesh Barnea to check
out the land. I was 40 years old at that
time. I brought back an honest report
to him. I told him exactly what I had
seen. 8 Several other men of Israel went
up with me. What they reported terrified the people. But I followed the LORD
my God with my whole heart. 9 So on
that day Moses made a promise to me.
He said, 'The land you have walked on
will be your share. It will be the share
of your children forever. That's because
you have followed the LORD my God with
your whole heart.' *(Deuteronomy 1:36)*

10 "The LORD has done just as he
promised. He made the promise while
Israel was wandering around in the
desert. That was 45 years ago. He has
kept me alive all this time. So here I am
today, 85 years old! 11 I'm still as strong
today as I was the day Moses sent me
out. I'm just as able to go out to battle
now as I was then. 12 So give me this
hill country. The LORD promised it to
me that day. At that time you yourself
heard that the Anakites were living
there. You also heard that their cities
were large and had high walls around
them. But I'll drive them out, just as the
LORD said I would. He will help me do it."

13 Then Joshua blessed Caleb, the son
of Jephunneh. He gave him Hebron
as his share. 14 So ever since that time
Hebron has belonged to Caleb, the son
of Jephunneh the Kenizzite. That's because he followed the LORD, the God of
Israel, with his whole heart. 15 Hebron
used to be called Kiriath Arba. It was
named after Arba. He was the greatest
man among the Anakites.

So the land had peace and rest.

Land Is Given to Judah

15 Land was given to the tribe
of Judah, according to its
family groups. It reached down
to the territory of Edom. It went
as far south as the Desert of Zin.

2 Judah's border on the south started
from the bay at the south end
of the Dead Sea. 3 It went across
to the south of Scorpion Pass.
It continued on to Zin. It went
over to the south of Kadesh
Barnea. Then it ran past Hezron
up to Addar. It curved around
to Karka. 4 It then went along
to Azmon. There it joined the
Wadi of Egypt and ended at the
Mediterranean Sea. That was
the southern border of Judah.

5 The border on the east was the
Dead Sea. It went north all the
way to where the Jordan River
enters the sea.

The border on the north started at
the bay of the Dead Sea. That's
where the Jordan River enters
the sea. 6 From there it went up to
Beth Hoglah. It continued north
of Beth Arabah to the Stone of
Bohan, the son of Reuben. 7 Then
it went from the Valley of Achor
up to Debir. It turned north to
Gilgal. Gilgal faces the Pass of
Adummim south of the valley.
The border continued along
to the springs of En Shemesh.
It came to an end at En Rogel.
8 Then it ran up the Valley of Ben
Hinnom. It went along the south
slope of Jerusalem. From there it
climbed to the top of the hill west
of the Hinnom Valley. The hill is
also at the north end of the Valley
of Rephaim. 9 From the top of the
hill the border headed toward the
springs of Nephtoah. It went to
the towns near Mount Ephron.
It went down toward Kiriath
Jearim. 10 Then it curved west
from Kiriath Jearim to Mount
Seir. It ran along the north slope
of Mount Kesalon. It continued
down to Beth Shemesh and
crossed over to Timnah. 11 It went
to the north slope of Ekron. Then
it turned toward Shikkeron. It
passed along to Mount Baalah
and reached Jabneel. The
border came to an end at the
Mediterranean Sea.

12 The border on the west was the
coastline of the Mediterranean
Sea.

Those were the borders of the
family groups of the tribe of Judah.

13 Joshua gave a part of Judah's share of
land to Caleb, the son of Jephunneh. That
was according to the LORD's command to

Joshua. The share Caleb received was the
city of Hebron. It was also called Kiriath
Arba. Anak came from the family line of
Arba. 14 Caleb drove three Anakites out
of Hebron. Their names were Sheshai,
Ahiman and Talmai. They were from the
family line of Anak. 15 From Hebron, Caleb
marched out against the people living in
Debir. It used to be called Kiriath Sepher.
16 Caleb said, "I will give my daughter
Aksah to be married. She'll be the wife
of the man who attacks and captures
Kiriath Sepher." 17 Othniel captured it. So
Caleb gave his daughter Aksah to him to
be his wife. Othniel was the son of Kenaz.
He was Caleb's brother.

18 One day Aksah came to Othniel.
She begged him to ask her father for
a field. When she got off her donkey,
Caleb spoke to her. He asked, "What
can I do for you?"

19 She replied, "Do me a special favor.
You have given me some land in the
Negev Desert. Give me springs of water
also." So Caleb gave her the upper and
lower springs.

20 Here is the share of land given to
the tribe of Judah, according to its
family groups.

21 The towns farthest south that
were given to Judah were in the
Negev Desert. They were near
the border of Edom. Here is a
list of those towns.
Kabzeel, Eder, Jagur, 22 Kinah,
Dimonah, Adadah, 23 Kedesh,
Hazor, Ithnan, 24 Ziph, Telem,
Bealoth, 25 Hazor Hadattah, Hazor,
26 Amam, Shema, Moladah,
27 Hazar Gaddah, Heshmon, Beth
Pelet, 28 Hazar Shual, Beersheba,
Biziothiah, 29 Baalah, Iyim, Ezem,
30 Eltolad, Kesil, Hormah, 31 Ziklag,
Madmannah, Sansannah,
32 Lebaoth, Shilhim, Ain and
Rimmon. The total number of
towns was 29. Some of them had
villages near them.

33 Towns were also given to Judah in
the western hills. Here is a list of
those towns.
Eshtaol, Zorah, Ashnah, 34 Zanoah,
En Gannim, Tappuah, Enam,
35 Jarmuth, Adullam, Sokoh,
Azekah, 36 Shaaraim, Adithaim
and Gederah. Gederah is also
called Gederothaim. The total
number of towns was 14. Some
of them had villages near them.

37 Here's another list of towns given
to Judah in the western hills.
Zenan, Hadashah, Migdal Gad,
38 Dilean, Mizpah, Joktheel,
39 Lachish, Bozkath, Eglon,
40 Kabbon, Lahmas, Kitlish,
41 Gederoth, Beth Dagon, Naamah
and Makkedah. The total number
of towns was 16. Some of them
had villages near them.

42 Here's another list of towns given
to Judah in the western hills.
Libnah, Ether, Ashan, 43 Iphtah,
Ashnah, Nezib, 44 Keilah, Akzib
and Mareshah. The total number
of towns was nine. Some of them
had villages near them.

45 Judah was also given Ekron and
the settlements and villages
around it. 46 West of Ekron, Judah
was given all the settlements and
villages near Ashdod. 47 Judah
was given Ashdod and the
settlements and villages around
it. And Judah was given Gaza
and its settlements and villages.
Judah's territory went all the
way to the Wadi of Egypt and
the coast of the Mediterranean
Sea.

48 Towns were also given to Judah in
the central hill country. Here is
a list of those towns.
Shamir, Jattir, Sokoh, 49 Dannah,
Debir, 50 Anab, Eshtemoh, Anim,
51 Goshen, Holon and Giloh. The
total number of towns was 11. Some
of them had villages near them.

52 Here's another list of towns given
to Judah in the central hill
country.
Arab, Dumah, Eshan, 53 Janim, Beth
Tappuah, Aphekah, 54 Humtah,
Hebron and Zior. The total number
of towns was nine. Some of them
had villages near them.

55 Here's another list of towns given to
Judah in the central hill country.
Maon, Carmel, Ziph, Juttah,
56 Jezreel, Jokdeam, Zanoah,
57 Kain, Gibeah and Timnah.
The total number of towns was
ten. Some of them had villages
near them.

58 Here's another list of towns given
to Judah in the central hill
country.
Halhul, Beth Zur, Gedor,
59 Maarath, Beth Anoth and
Eltekon. The total number of
towns was six. Some of them
had villages near them.
60 Here's another list of towns given to
Judah in the central hill country.
Kiriath Jearim and Rabbah. The
total number of towns was two.
They had villages near them.
61 Towns were also given to Judah in
the desert. Here is a list of those
towns.
Beth Arabah, Middin, Sekakah,
62 Nibshan, the City of Salt and
En Gedi. The total number of
towns was six. Some of them
had villages near them.

63 Judah couldn't drive out the Jeb-
usites who were living in Jerusalem.
So they live there with the people of
Judah to this day.

Land Is Given to Ephraim and Manasseh

16 The land given to the two
tribes in the family line
of Joseph began at the Jordan
River. Their border started east
of the springs of Jericho. It went
up from there through the desert
into the hill country of Bethel.
2 Bethel is also called Luz. From
Bethel the border crossed over to
Ataroth. That's where the Arkites
live. 3 Then it went west down to
the territory of the Japhletites.
It went all the way to the area
of Lower Beth Horon. It went on
to Gezer. The border came to an
end at the Mediterranean Sea.
4 The tribes of Manasseh and
Ephraim were from the family
line of Joseph. So they received
that land as their share.

5 Here is the territory given to the
tribe of Ephraim, according to its
family groups.

The border of their share of land
started at Ataroth Addar in
the east. It went to Upper Beth
Horon. 6 It continued toward
the Mediterranean Sea. From
Mikmethath on the north, it
curved toward the east. It went
to Taanath Shiloh. It passed by
Taanath Shiloh to Janoah on the
east. 7 Then it went down from
Janoah to Ataroth and Naarah. It
touched Jericho and came to an
end at the Jordan River. 8 From
Tappuah the border went west to
the Kanah Valley. It came to an
end at the Mediterranean Sea.
That was the land given to the
tribe of Ephraim. Each family
group received its share.
9 The tribe of Ephraim was also
given other towns and villages
that were set apart for them.
Those towns and villages were
in the share of land given to the
tribe of Manasseh.

10 The people of Ephraim didn't drive
out the Canaanites living in Gezer. The
Canaanites live among the people of
Ephraim to this day. But they are forced
to work hard for the people of Ephraim.

17 Land was given to the tribe of
Manasseh. It was given to Makir.
Manasseh was Joseph's oldest son. Makir
was Manasseh's oldest son. The people
of Gilead came from the family line of
Makir. The people of Gilead had received
the lands of Gilead and Bashan. That's
because the people of Makir were great
soldiers. 2 So land was given to the rest of
the people of Manasseh. It was given to
the family groups of Abiezer, Helek, Asriel, Shechem, Hepher and Shemida. They
were the other men in the family line
of Manasseh, the son of Joseph. Those
were their names by their family groups.
3 Makir was the son of Manasseh. Gilead was the son of Makir. Hepher was the
son of Gilead. And Zelophehad was the
son of Hepher. Zelophehad didn't have
any sons. He only had daughters. Their
names were Mahlah, Noah, Hoglah,
Milkah and Tirzah. 4 The daughters of
Zelophehad went to Eleazar the priest
and to Joshua, the son of Nun. They also
went to the other leaders. They said,
"The LORD commanded Moses to give
us our share of land among our male
relatives." So Joshua gave them land
along with their male relatives. That
was according to what the LORD had

commanded. 5 Manasseh's share was
made up of ten pieces of land. That land
was in addition to Gilead and Bashan
east of the Jordan River. 6 So the five
granddaughters of Hepher in the family
line of Manasseh received land, just as
the other five sons of Manasseh did. The
land of Gilead belonged to the rest of
the family line of Manasseh.

7 The territory of Manasseh reached
from Asher to Mikmethath.
Mikmethath was east of Shechem.
The border ran south from
Mikmethath. The people living
at En Tappuah were inside the
border. 8 Manasseh had the land
around Tappuah. But the town of
Tappuah itself was on the border
of Manasseh's land. It belonged
to the people of Ephraim. 9 The
border continued south to the
Kanah Valley. Some of the
towns that belonged to Ephraim
were located among the towns
of Manasseh. But the border of
Manasseh was the north side of
the valley. The border came to
an end at the Mediterranean Sea.
10 The land on the south belonged
to Ephraim. The land on the
north belonged to Manasseh. The
territory of Manasseh reached
the Mediterranean Sea. The tribe
of Asher was the border on the
north. The tribe of Issachar was
the border on the east.
11 Inside the land given to Issachar
and Asher, the towns of Beth
Shan and Ibleam belonged to
Manasseh. The towns of Dor,
Endor, Taanach and Megiddo
and their people also belonged
to Manasseh. Manasseh was
given all those towns and the
settlements around them. The
third town in the list was also
called Naphoth Dor.

12 But the people of Manasseh weren't
able to take over those towns. That's
because the Canaanites had made up
their minds to live in that area. 13 The
Israelites grew stronger. Then they
forced the Canaanites to work hard
for them. But they didn't drive them
out completely.

14 The people in the family line of Joseph spoke to Joshua. They said, "Why
have you given us only one share of the
land to have as our own? There are large
numbers of us. The LORD has blessed
us greatly."

15 "That's true," Joshua said. "There
are large numbers of you. And the hill
country of Ephraim is too small for you.
So go up into the forest. Clear out some
land for yourselves in the territory of
the Perizzites and Rephaites."

16 The people in Joseph's family line replied, "The hill country isn't big enough for
us. And all the Canaanites who live in the
plains use chariots that have iron parts.
They include the people of Beth Shan and
its settlements. They also include the people who live in the Valley of Jezreel."

17 Joshua spoke again to the people in
Joseph's family line. He said to the people of Ephraim and Manasseh, "There
are large numbers of you. And you are
very powerful. You will have more than
one piece of land. 18 You will also have
the central hill country. It's covered
with trees. Cut them down and clear
the land. That whole land from one
end to the other will belong to you. The
Canaanites use chariots that have iron
parts. And those people are strong. But
you can drive them out."

The Rest of the Land Is Divided Up

18 The whole community of Israel gathered together at Shiloh.
They set up the tent of meeting there.
The country was brought under their
control. 2 But there were still seven tribes
in Israel who had not yet received their
shares of land.

3 So Joshua spoke to the Israelites. He
said, "The LORD, the God of your people,
has given you this land. How long will
you wait before you begin to take it over?
4 Appoint three men from each tribe. I'll
send them to map out the land. Then
they'll write a report about its features.
The report will point out the share of
land each tribe will receive. Then the
men will return to me. 5 You must divide
the land up into seven shares. Judah
must remain in its territory in the south.
The people in Joseph's family line must
remain in their territory in the north.
6 Write reports about the features of
those seven shares of land. Bring them

here to me. Then I'll cast lots for you
in the sight of the LORD our God. 7 But
the Levites don't get any share of your
land. That's because their share is to
serve the LORD as priests. The tribes of
Gad and Reuben and half of the tribe of
Manasseh have already received their
shares. They are on the east side of the
Jordan River. Moses, the servant of the
LORD, gave their shares to them."
8 The men started out on their way
to map out the land. Joshua directed
them, "Go and map out the land. Write
a report about its features. Then return
to me. I'll cast lots for you here at Shiloh
in the sight of the LORD." 9 So the men
left and went through the land. They
wrote a report about its features on a
scroll. It showed how they divided up
the land into seven shares. It listed the
towns in each share. The men returned
to Joshua in the camp at Shiloh.

10 Then Joshua cast lots for them in
Shiloh in the sight of the LORD. There
he gave out a share of land to each
of the remaining tribes in Israel.

Land Is Given to Benjamin

11 The first lot drawn out was for the
tribe of Benjamin, according to its
family groups. The territory they
were given was located between
the tribes of the people of Judah
and the people of Joseph. Here are
the borders of Benjamin's territory.
12 On the north side their border
started at the Jordan River. It
went past the north slope of
Jericho. Then it headed west
into the central hill country. It
came to an end at the Desert
of Beth Aven. 13 From there the
border crossed to the south slope
of Bethel. Then it went down to
Ataroth Addar on the hill south
of Lower Beth Horon.
14 From the hill that faces Beth Horon
on the south the border turned
south. Then the border went
along the west side of the hill.
It came to an end at Kiriath
Jearim. That town belongs to
the people of Judah. That was
the border on the west.
15 The border on the south side started
at the west edge of Kiriath Jearim.
It came to an end at the springs of
Nephtoah. 16 It went down to the
foot of the hill that faces the Valley
of Ben Hinnom. The hill is north of
the Valley of Rephaim. The border
continued down the Hinnom
Valley. It went along the south
slope of Jerusalem, where the
people of Jebus live. It continued
on to En Rogel. 17 Then it curved
north. It went to En Shemesh. It
continued on to Geliloth. Geliloth
faces the Pass of Adummim. The
border ran down to the Stone of
Bohan, the son of Reuben. 18 It
continued to the north slope of
Beth Arabah. It went on down into
the Arabah Valley. 19 From there
it went to the north slope of Beth
Hoglah. It came to an end at the
north bay of the Dead Sea. That's
where the Jordan River flows into
the Dead Sea. That was the border
on the south.
20 The Jordan River formed the
border on the east side.

Those were the borders that
marked out on all sides the land
the family groups of Benjamin
received as their share.

21 Here is a list of towns given to the
tribe of Benjamin, according to
its family groups.
Jericho, Beth Hoglah, Emek
Keziz, 22 Beth Arabah, Zemaraim,
Bethel, 23 Avvim, Parah, Ophrah,
24 Kephar Ammoni, Ophni and
Geba. The total number of towns
and their villages was 12.
25 Here is another list of towns given
to Benjamin.
Gibeon, Ramah, Beeroth,
26 Mizpah, Kephirah, Mozah,
27 Rekem, Irpeel, Taralah,
28 Zelah, Haeleph, Jerusalem,
Gibeah and Kiriath. The total
number of towns and their
villages was 14.

That was the share of land the
family groups of Benjamin received.

Land Is Given to Simeon

19 The second lot drawn out
was for the tribe of Simeon,
according to its family groups. The
share of land they were given was
in the territory of Judah.

[2] Here is what Simeon's share included.
Beersheba, Moladah, [3] Hazar
Shual, Balah, Ezem, [4] Eltolad,
Bethul, Hormah, [5] Ziklag, Beth
Markaboth, Hazar Susah, [6] Beth
Lebaoth and Sharuhen. The total
number of towns was 13. Some of
them had villages near them.
[7] Here's another list of towns given
to Simeon.
Ain, Rimmon, Ether and Ashan.
The total number of towns was
four. Some of them had villages
near them. [8] The towns and
all the villages around them
reached all the way to Ramah
in the Negev Desert.
That was the share of land the tribe
of Simeon received, according to its
family groups. [9] Simeon's share of
land was taken from Judah's share.
That's because Judah had more land
than they needed. So the people of
Simeon received their share of land
inside the territory of Judah.

Land Is Given to Zebulun

[10] The third lot drawn out was for
the tribe of Zebulun, according
to its family groups. Here are the
borders of Zebulun's territory.
The border of their share of land
went as far as Sarid. [11] It ran
west to Maralah and touched
Dabbesheth. It reached to the
valley near Jokneam. [12] It turned
east from Sarid toward the
sunrise. It went to the territory
of Kisloth Tabor. It went on to
Daberath and up to Japhia.
[13] Then it continued east to
Gath Hepher and Eth Kazin. It
came to an end at Rimmon and
turned toward Neah. [14] There the
border went around on the north
to Hannathon. It came to an end
at the Valley of Iphtah El.
[15] Zebulun's territory included
Kattath, Nahalal, Shimron,
Idalah and Bethlehem.
The total number of towns was 12.
Some of them had villages near
them.
[16] Those towns and their villages
were Zebulun's share, according
to its family groups.

Land Is Given to Issachar

[17] The fourth lot drawn out was for
the tribe of Issachar, according to
its family groups. [18] Here is what
Issachar's share included.
Jezreel, Kesulloth, Shunem,
[19] Hapharaim, Shion, Anaha-
rath, [20] Rabbith, Kishion, Ebez,
[21] Remeth, En Gannim, En Had-
dah and Beth Pazzez.
[22] The border touched Tabor,
Shahazumah and Beth Shemesh.
It came to an end at the Jordan
River.
The total number of towns was 16.
Some of them had villages near
them.
[23] Those towns and their villages
were the share the tribe of Issachar
received, according to its family
groups.

Land Is Given to Asher

[24] The fifth lot drawn out was for
the tribe of Asher, according to
its family groups. [25] Here is what
Asher's share included.
Helkath, Hali, Beten, Akshaph,
[26] Allammelek, Amad and Mishal.
On the west the border touched
Carmel and Shihor Libnath.
[27] Then it turned east toward Beth
Dagon. It touched Zebulun and
the Valley of Iphtah El. It went
north to Beth Emek and Neiel. It
went past Kabul on the left. [28] It
went to Abdon, Rehob, Hammon
and Kanah. It reached all the way
to Greater Sidon. [29] The border
then turned back toward Ramah.
It went to Tyre, a city that had
high walls around it. It turned
toward Hosah. It came to an end
at the Mediterranean Sea in the
area of Akzib, [30] Ummah, Aphek
and Rehob.
The total number of towns was 22.
Some of them had villages near
them.
[31] Those towns and their villages
were the share the tribe of Asher
received, according to its family
groups.

Land Is Given to Naphtali

[32] The sixth lot drawn out was for
Naphtali, according to its family
groups.

33 Their border started at Heleph and
the large tree in Zaanannim.
It went past Adami Nekeb and
Jabneel. It went to Lakkum and
came to an end at the Jordan
River. 34 The border ran west
through Aznoth Tabor. It came
to an end at Hukkok. It touched
Zebulun on the south. It touched
Asher on the west. It touched the
Jordan on the east.

35 The towns that had high walls
around them were Ziddim, Zer,
Hammath, Rakkath, Kinnereth,
36 Adamah, Ramah, Hazor,
37 Kedesh, Edrei, En Hazor,
38 Iron, Migdal El, Horem, Beth
Anath and Beth Shemesh.

The total number of towns was 19.
Some of them had villages near
them.

39 Those towns and their villages
were the share the tribe of Naphtali
received, according to its family
groups.

Land Is Given to Dan

40 The seventh lot drawn out was for
the tribe of Dan, according to its
family groups. 41 Here is what Dan's
share of land included.

Zorah, Eshtaol, Ir Shemesh,
42 Shaalabbin, Aijalon, Ithlah,
43 Elon, Timnah, Ekron,
44 Eltekeh, Gibbethon, Baalath,
45 Jehud, Bene Berak, Gath
Rimmon, 46 Me Jarkon and
Rakkon. Dan's share included
the area that faces Joppa.

47 The people of Dan lost their
territory. So they went up and
attacked Leshem. They captured
it. They killed its people with their
swords. Then they moved into
Leshem and made their homes
there. They named it Dan. That's
because they traced their family
line back to him.

48 All those towns and their villages
were the share the tribe of Dan
received, according to its family
groups.

Land Is Given to Joshua

49 The Israelites finished dividing
up the shares of land the tribes
received. Then they gave a
share to Joshua, the son of Nun.

50 They did what the LORD had
commanded them to do. They
gave Joshua the town he asked
for. It was Timnath Serah in the
hill country of Ephraim. He built
up the town and made his home
there.

51 All those territories were given
out by casting lots at Shiloh. The
lots were drawn out by Eleazar
the priest and by Joshua, the son
of Nun. The leaders of the tribes of
Israel helped them. The lots were
drawn out in front of the LORD at
the entrance to the tent of meeting.
So the work of dividing up the land
was finished.

Cities to Run to for Safety

20 Then the LORD spoke to Joshua.
He said, 2 "Tell the Israelites to
choose the cities to go to for safety, just
as I directed you through Moses. 3 Anyone who kills a person by accident can
run there for safety. So can anyone who
kills a person without meaning to. The
one charged with murder will be kept
safe from the nearest male relative of the
person killed. 4 Suppose those who are
charged with murder run for safety to
one of these cities. Then they must stand
in the entrance of the city gate. They
must state their case in front of the elders
of that city. The elders must let them
come into their city. The elders must provide a place for them to live in their city.
5 Suppose the nearest male relative of
the person killed chases the one charged
with murder. Then the elders must not
hand them over to that relative. That's
because that person didn't mean to kill
their neighbor. They didn't make evil
plans to do it. 6 They must stay in that
city until their case has been brought to
the community court. They must stay
there until the high priest serving at
that time dies. Then they can go back
to their own home. They can return to
the town they ran away from."

7 So the Israelites set apart Kedesh in
Galilee. It's in the hill country of Naph-
tali. They set apart Shechem. It's in the
hill country of Ephraim. They set apart
Kiriath Arba. It's in the hill country of
Judah. Kiriath Arba is also called He-
bron. 8 On the east side of the Jordan
River near Jericho they chose Bezer.

It's in the desert on the high plains. It's in the territory of the tribe of Reuben. They chose Ramoth in Gilead. It's in the territory of the tribe of Gad. They chose Golan in the land of Bashan. It's in the territory of the tribe of Manasseh.
9 Suppose you kill someone by accident. Or another Israelite does it. Or an outsider who lives among you does it. Then any of you can run for safety to one of these cities that have been chosen. There you won't be killed by the nearest male relative of the person killed by accident. First your case must be brought to the community court.

Towns Are Given to the Levites

21 The leaders of the Levite family groups approached Eleazar the priest and Joshua, the son of Nun. They also approached the leaders of the family groups of Israel's other tribes.
2 They went to all of them at Shiloh in Canaan. They said to them, "Give us towns to live in. Also give us grasslands for our livestock. That's what the LORD commanded through Moses."

3 So the Israelites gave the Levites towns and grasslands out of their own shares of land. They did what the LORD had commanded. Here are the towns the Levites were given.

4 The first lot drawn out was for the people of Kohath, according to their family groups. Some of the Levites came from the family line of Aaron the priest. They were given 13 towns from the tribes of Judah, Simeon and Benjamin.

5 The rest of Kohath's family groups were given ten towns. Those towns were from the family groups of the tribes of Ephraim and Dan and half of the tribe of Manasseh.

6 The family groups of Gershon were given 13 towns. Those towns were from the family groups of the tribes of Issachar, Asher and Naphtali and half of the tribe of Manasseh. That part of Manasseh was in the land of Bashan.

7 The family groups of Merari received 12 towns from the tribes of Reuben, Gad and Zebulun. Each family group received its share.

8 So the Israelites gave those towns and their grasslands to the Levites. They did what the LORD had commanded through Moses.

9 Some towns were given from the territories of the tribes of Judah
and Simeon. 10 The Israelites
gave them to the members of the family line of Aaron. The towns were given to the family groups of Kohath. They were Levites. The first lot drawn out was for them. Here are the towns the family groups of Kohath were given.

11 The Israelites gave them Kiriath Arba and the grasslands around it. Kiriath Arba is also called Hebron. It's in the hill country of Judah. Anak came from
the family line of Arba. 12 But
Israel had already given away the fields and villages around the city. They had given them to Caleb as his share. Caleb was
the son of Jephunneh. 13 So they
gave Hebron to the members of the family line of Aaron the priest. Hebron was a city where anyone charged with murder could go for safety. They also
gave them Libnah, 14 Jattir,
Eshtemoa, 15 Holon, Debir, 16 Ain,
Juttah and Beth Shemesh. They gave those towns and their grasslands to the family groups of Kohath. The total number of towns from the tribes of Judah and Simeon came to nine.

17 The Israelites gave some towns from the tribe of Benjamin to the family groups of Kohath. The towns were Gibeon, Geba,
18 Anathoth and Almon. The total number of these towns and their grasslands came to four.

19 So the total number of towns and their grasslands given to the priests in Aaron's family line came to 13.

20 There were other family groups of Kohath among the Levites. They were given towns from the tribe of Ephraim. Here are the towns those

other family groups of Kohath were given.

21 In the hill country of Ephraim they were given
Shechem. It was a city where anyone charged with murder could go for safety. They were also given Gezer, 22 Kibzaim and Beth Horon. The total number of these towns and their grasslands came to four.

23 From the tribe of Dan they received
Eltekeh, Gibbethon, 24 Aijalon and Gath Rimmon. The total number of these towns and their grasslands came to four.

25 From half of the tribe of Manasseh they received
Taanach and Gath Rimmon. The total number of these towns and their grasslands came to two.

26 So all these ten towns and their grasslands were given to the other family groups of Kohath.

27 Here are the towns given to the family groups of Gershon among the Levites.
From half of the tribe of Manasseh they received
Golan in the land of Bashan. Golan was a city where anyone charged with murder could go for safety. They also received Be Eshterah. The total number of these towns and their grasslands came to two.

28 From the tribe of Issachar they received
Kishion, Daberath, 29 Jarmuth and En Gannim. The total number of these towns and their grasslands came to four.

30 From the tribe of Asher they received
Mishal, Abdon, 31 Helkath and Rehob. The total number of these towns and their grasslands came to four.

32 From the tribe of Naphtali they received
Kedesh in Galilee. Kedesh was a city where anyone charged with murder could go for safety. They also received Hammoth Dor and Kartan. The total number of these towns and their grasslands came to three.

33 So the total number of towns and their grasslands given to the family groups of Gershon came to 13.

34 The rest of the Levites were from the family groups of Merari. Here are the towns they were given.
From the tribe of Zebulun they received
Jokneam, Kartah, 35 Dimnah and Nahalal. The total number of these towns and their grasslands came to four.

36 From the tribe of Reuben they received
Bezer, Jahaz, 37 Kedemoth and Mephaath. The total number of these towns and their grasslands came to four.

38 From the tribe of Gad they received
Ramoth in Gilead. Ramoth was a city where anyone charged with murder could go for safety. They also received Mahanaim, 39 Heshbon and Jazer. The total number of these towns and their grasslands came to four.

40 So the total number of towns given to the family groups of Merari came to 12. That concludes the list of towns the rest of the Levites received.

41 The total number of Levite towns and their grasslands in the territory given to Israel came to 48. 42 Each of those towns had grasslands around it. That was true of all of them.

43 So the LORD gave Israel all the land he had promised to give to Abraham, Isaac and Jacob. And Israel took it over. Then they made their homes there. 44 The LORD gave them peace and rest on every side. He had promised their people of long ago that he would do that. Not one of Israel's enemies was able to fight against them and win. The LORD handed all their enemies over to them. 45 The LORD kept all the good promises he had made to the Israelites. Every one of them came true.

The Eastern Tribes Return Home

22 Joshua sent for the tribes of Reuben and Gad and half of the tribe of Manasseh. 2 He said to them, "You have done everything that Moses, the servant of the LORD, commanded. You have also

obeyed everything I commanded. 3 For
a long time now you haven't deserted
the other Israelites. Instead, you have
done what the LORD your God sent you
to do. You have obeyed him right up to
this day. 4 Now the LORD your God has
given the other tribes peace and rest.
That's what he promised to do. So return
to your homes. They are in the land that
Moses, the servant of the LORD, gave you.
It's on the east side of the Jordan River.
5 Be very careful to obey the law that
Moses, the servant of the LORD, gave you.
He commanded you to love the LORD
your God. He told you to live exactly as
the LORD wants you to. He told you to
obey the LORD's commands. He told you
to remain faithful to the LORD. And he
told you to serve the LORD with all your
heart and with all your soul."

6 Joshua gave the eastern tribes his
blessing. Then he sent them home. So
they went. 7 Moses had given land in
Bashan to half of the tribe of Manasseh.
Joshua had given land to the other half
of the tribe. He had given it to them
along with the other tribes on the west
side of the Jordan River. When Joshua sent them home, he blessed them.
8 He said, "Return to your homes. Take
your great wealth with you. Return
with your large herds of livestock. Take
your silver, gold, bronze and iron with
you. Return with all the extra clothes
you acquired. Divide up the things you
have taken from your enemies. Share
them with your people."

9 So the tribes of Reuben and Gad
and half of the tribe of Manasseh went
home. They left the other Israelites at
Shiloh in Canaan. They returned to
Gilead. That was their own land. They
had acquired it according to the LORD's
command through Moses.

10 The tribes of Reuben and Gad and
half of the tribe of Manasseh came to
Geliloth. It was near the Jordan River in
the land of Canaan. They built a large
altar there by the Jordan. 11 The rest of
the Israelites heard that the eastern
tribes had built the altar. They heard
that it had been built on the border
of Canaan at Geliloth. It was near the
Jordan River on the west side. 12 So the
whole community of Israel gathered
together at Shiloh. They decided to go
to war against the eastern tribes.

13 The Israelites sent Phinehas the priest
to the land of Gilead. Phinehas was the
son of Eleazar. They sent him to the tribes
of Reuben and Gad and half of the tribe
of Manasseh. 14 They sent ten of their
leaders with him. There was one from
each of the tribes of Israel. Each man was
the leader of a family group among the
larger family groups of Israel.

15 Those leaders went to the tribes of
Reuben and Gad and half of the tribe
of Manasseh. Those tribes were in the
land of Gilead. The leaders said to them,
16 "We're speaking for the LORD's whole
community. How could you disobey the
God of Israel like this? How could you
turn away from the LORD? How could
you disobey him by building an altar
for yourselves? 17 Don't you remember
how we sinned at Peor? The LORD struck
us with a plague because of what we
did. Up to this day we're still suffering
because of that sin. 18 Are you turning
away from the LORD now?

"Suppose you disobey the LORD today. If you do, he'll be angry with the
whole community of Israel tomorrow.
19 If your own land is 'unclean,' come
over to the LORD's land. It's where his
holy tent stands. Share our land with
us. But don't disobey the LORD. Don't
turn against us by building an altar
for yourselves. Don't build any altar
other than the altar of the LORD our
God. 20 Remember what happened to
Achan, the son of Zerah. Achan wasn't
faithful to the LORD. He took the things
that had been set apart to the LORD in a
special way to be destroyed. Didn't the
whole community of Israel experience
the LORD's anger? Achan wasn't the only
one who died because of his sin."

21 Then the tribes of Reuben and Gad
and half of the tribe of Manasseh replied.
They answered the leaders of the family
groups of Israel. 22 They said, "The Mighty
One, God, the LORD! The Mighty One, God,
the LORD! He knows! And we want Israel
to know! Have we opposed the LORD?
Have we refused to obey him? If we have,
don't spare us today. 23 Have we built
our own altar so we can turn away from
the LORD? Have we built it to offer burnt
offerings and grain offerings on it? Have
we built it to sacrifice friendship offerings
on it? If we have, may the LORD himself
hold us accountable.

[24]"No! We built it because we were afraid. Someday your children might speak to our children. We were afraid they might say, 'What do you have to do with the LORD? What do you have to do with the God of Israel? [25]The LORD has made the Jordan River a border between us and you. You people of Reuben! You people of Gad! You don't have anything to do with the LORD.' If your children say that, they might cause our children to stop worshiping the LORD.

[26]"That's why we said to ourselves, 'Let's get ready and build an altar. But let's not build it to offer burnt offerings or sacrifices on it.' [27]So just the opposite is true. The altar will be a witness between us and you. It will be a witness between our children and yours after us. It will also be a witness that we will worship the LORD at his sacred tent. We'll worship him there with our burnt offerings, sacrifices and friendship offerings. Then in days to come your children won't be able to say to ours, 'You don't have anything to do with the LORD.'

[28]"So we said to ourselves, 'Suppose they say that to us sometime. Or suppose they say it to our children after us. Then we'll answer, "Look at this altar. It's exactly like the LORD's altar. Our people built it. They didn't build it to offer burnt offerings and sacrifices on it. Instead, they built it to be a witness between us and you."'

[29]"We would never refuse to obey the LORD. We would never turn away from him now. We wouldn't build an altar to offer burnt offerings, grain offerings and sacrifices on it. We wouldn't use any altar other than the altar of the LORD our God. That altar stands in front of his holy tent."

[30]Phinehas the priest heard what the tribes of Reuben, Gad and Manasseh had to say. The leaders of the family groups of the community of Israel heard it too. All of them were pleased with what they heard. [31]Phinehas the priest spoke to the tribes of Reuben, Gad and Manasseh. Phinehas was the son of Eleazar. He said, "Today we know that the LORD is with us. That's because you have been faithful to him in this matter. Now you have saved the Israelites from the LORD's anger against them."

[32]Then Phinehas the priest, the son of Eleazar, returned to Canaan. So did the leaders. All of them went back from their meeting with the tribes of Reuben and Gad in Gilead. They brought a report back to the Israelites. [33]The people were glad to hear the report. They praised God. They didn't talk anymore about going to war against the eastern tribes. And they didn't talk anymore about destroying the country where the tribes of Reuben and Gad lived.

[34]The tribes of Reuben and Gad gave the altar a name. They called it A Witness Between Us that the LORD is God.

Joshua Says Goodbye to the Leaders

23 A long time had passed. The LORD had given Israel peace and rest from all their enemies around them. By that time Joshua was very old. [2]So he sent for all the elders, leaders, judges and officials of Israel. He said to them, "I'm very old. [3]You yourselves have seen everything the LORD your God has done. You have seen what he's done to all these nations because of you. The LORD your God fought for you. [4]Remember how I've given you all the land of the nations that remain here. I've given each of your tribes a share of it. It's the land of the nations I conquered. It's between the Jordan River and the Mediterranean Sea in the west. [5]The LORD your God himself will drive those nations out of your way. He will push them out to make room for you. You will take over their land, just as the LORD your God promised you.

[6]"Be very strong. Be careful to obey everything written in the Book of the Law of Moses. Don't turn away from it to the right or the left. [7]Don't have anything to do with the nations that remain among you. Don't use the names of their gods for any reason at all. Don't give your word and make promises in their names. You must not serve them. You must not bow down to them. [8]You must remain true to the LORD your God, just as you have done until now.

[9]"The LORD has driven out great and powerful nations to make room for you. To this day no one has been able to fight against you and win. [10]One of you can chase a thousand away. That's because

the LORD your God fights for you, just as he promised he would. 11 So be very careful to love the LORD your God.

12 "But suppose you turn away from him. You mix with the people who are left alive in the nations that remain among you. Later, you and they get married to each other. And you do other kinds of things with them. 13 Then you can be sure of what the LORD your God will do. He won't drive out those nations to make room for you anymore. Instead, they will become traps and snares for you. They will be like whips on your backs. They will be like thorns in your eyes. All that will continue until you are destroyed. It will continue until you are removed from this good land. It's the land the LORD your God has given you.

14 "Now I'm about to die, just as everyone else on earth does. The LORD your God has kept all the good promises he gave you. Every one of them has come true. Not one has failed to come true. And you know that with all your heart and soul. 15 Every good thing has come to pass that the LORD your God has promised you. So you know that he can also bring against you all the evil things he has warned you about. He'll do it until he has destroyed you. He'll do it until he has removed you from this good land. It's the land he has given you. 16 Suppose you break the covenant the LORD your God made with you. He commanded you to obey it. But suppose you go and serve other gods. And you bow down to them. Then the LORD will be very angry with you. You will quickly be destroyed. You will be removed from the good land he has given you."

The Covenant Is Renewed at Shechem

24 Joshua gathered all Israel's tribes together at Shechem. He sent for the elders, leaders, judges and officials of Israel. They came and stood there in the sight of God.

2 Joshua spoke to all the people. He said, "The LORD is the God of Israel. He says, 'Long ago your people lived east of the Euphrates River. They worshiped other gods there. Your people included Terah. He was the father of Abraham and Nahor. 3 I took your father Abraham from the land east of the Euphrates. I led him all through Canaan. I gave him many children and grandchildren. I gave him Isaac. 4 To Isaac I gave Jacob and Esau. I gave the hill country of Seir to Esau. But Jacob and his family went down to Egypt.

5 " 'Then I sent Moses and Aaron. I made the people of Egypt suffer because of the plagues I sent on them. But I brought you out of Egypt. 6 When I brought your people out, they came to the Red Sea. The people of Egypt chased them with chariots and with men on horses. They chased them all the way to the sea. 7 But your people cried out to me for help. So I put darkness between you and the people of Egypt. I swept them into the sea. It completely covered them. Your own eyes saw what I did to them. After that, you lived in the desert for a long time.

8 " 'I brought you to the land of the Amorites. They lived east of the Jordan River. They fought against you. But I handed them over to you. I destroyed them to make room for you. Then you took over their land. 9 Balak, the son of Zippor, prepared to fight against Israel. Balak was the king of Moab. He sent for Balaam, the son of Beor. Balak wanted Balaam to put a curse on you. 10 But I would not listen to Balaam's curses. So he blessed you again and again. And I saved you from his power.

11 " 'Then you went across the Jordan River. You came to Jericho. Its people fought against you. So did the Amorites, Perizzites, Canaanites, Hittites, Girgashites, Hivites and Jebusites. But I handed them over to you. 12 I sent hornets ahead of you. They drove your enemies out to make room for you. That included the two Amorite kings. You did not do that with your own swords and bows. 13 So I gave you a land you had never farmed. I gave you cities you had not built. You are now living in them. And you are eating the fruit of vineyards and olive trees you did not plant.'

14 "So have respect for the LORD. Serve him. Be completely faithful to him. Throw away the gods your people worshiped east of the Euphrates River and in Egypt. Serve the LORD. 15 But suppose you don't want to serve him. Then choose for yourselves right now

whom you will serve. You can choose
the gods your people served east of the
Euphrates River. Or you can serve the
gods of the Amorites. After all, you are
living in their land. But as for me and
my family, we will serve the LORD."
16 Then the people answered Joshua,
"We would never desert the LORD! We
would never serve other gods! 17 The
LORD our God himself brought us
and our parents up out of Egypt. He
brought us out of that land where we
were slaves. With our own eyes, we saw
those great signs he did. He kept us safe
on our entire journey. He kept us safe
as we traveled through all the nations.
18 He drove them out to make room for
us. That included the Amorites. They
also lived in the land. We too will serve
the LORD. That's because he is our God."
19 Joshua said to the people, "You
aren't able to serve the LORD. He is a
holy God. He is a jealous God. He won't
forgive you when you disobey him. He
won't forgive you when you sin against
him. 20 Suppose you desert the LORD.
Suppose you serve the gods that people
in other lands serve. If you do, he will
turn against you. He will bring trouble on you. He will destroy you, even
though he has been good to you."
21 But the people said to Joshua, "No!
We will serve the LORD."
22 Then Joshua said, "You are witnesses against yourselves. You have said
that you have chosen to serve the LORD."
"Yes. We are witnesses," they replied.
23 "Now then," said Joshua, "throw
away the statues of the gods that are
among you. People from other lands
serve those gods. Give yourselves completely to the LORD. He is the God of
Israel."
24 Then the people said to Joshua,
"We will serve the LORD our God. We
will obey him."
25 On that day Joshua made a covenant for the people. There at Shechem
he reminded them of its rules and laws.
26 He recorded these things in the Book
of the Law of God. Then he got a large
stone. He set it up in Shechem under the
oak tree. It was near the place that had
been set apart for the LORD.
27 "Look!" he said to all the people.
"This stone will be a witness against
us. It has heard all the words the LORD

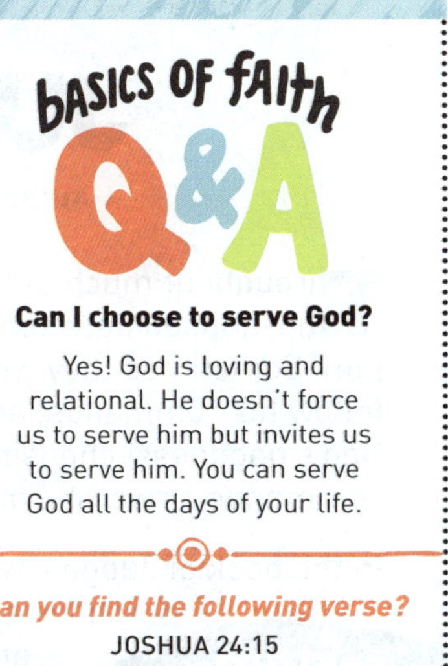

has spoken to us. Suppose you aren't
faithful to your God. Then the stone
will be a witness against you."
28 Joshua sent the people away. He
sent all of them to their own shares
of land.

Joshua Is Buried in the Promised Land

29 Then Joshua, the servant of the
LORD, died. He was the son of Nun. He
was 110 years old when he died. 30 His
people buried him at Timnath Serah on
his own property. It's north of Mount
Gaash in the hill country of Ephraim.
31 Israel served the LORD as long as
Joshua lived. They also served him as
long as the elders lived. Those were the
elders who lived longer than Joshua
did. They had seen for themselves everything the LORD had done for Israel.
32 The Israelites had brought Joseph's
bones up from Egypt. They buried his
bones at Shechem in the piece of land
Jacob had bought. He had bought it
from the sons of Hamor. He had paid
100 pieces of silver for it. Hamor was
the father of Shechem. That piece of
land became the share that belonged
to Joseph's children after him.
33 Aaron's son Eleazar died. He was
buried at Gibeah in the hill country
of Ephraim. Gibeah had been given to
Eleazar's son Phinehas.

JUDGES

Author: We don't know.

Throughout much of Israel's history, the Israelites flip-flopped between believing God and not believing him. Sometimes they would believe God's promises and follow his commands, and sometimes they would doubt God's goodness, choosing to disobey him by breaking his commands or worshiping false gods.

In the book of Judges, we read about the Israelites choosing to adopt the ways of the Canaanites and do what they wanted instead of what God wanted. God responded by allowing them to suffer the consequences for their sins. Then he sent leaders, called judges, to rescue his people.

Old Testament History

The judges were men and women chosen by God to deliver God's people from their enemies. God raised up judges in response to the people's cry for help. Throughout this book, we see God's people cycle through disobeying God, suffering at the hands of their enemies, crying out for help, and being rescued by God. The judges themselves were imperfect and sometimes corrupt, but they served as a reminder that one day God was going to send the perfect and final Savior who would rescue humanity and draw people close to God. Jesus would be the perfect Judge, fulfilling God's promises by defeating sin and death and making God's people right with him again.

The Israelites Fight Against the Remaining Canaanites

1 Joshua died. After that, the Israelites spoke to the LORD. They asked him, "Who of us will go up first and fight against the Canaanites?"

2 The LORD answered, "The tribe of Judah will go up. I have handed the land over to them."

3 Then the men of Judah spoke to their fellow Israelites, the men of Simeon. They said, "Come up with us. Come into the territory Joshua gave us. Help us fight against the Canaanites. Then we'll go with you into your territory." So the men of Simeon went with them.

4 When the men of Judah attacked, the LORD helped them. He handed the Canaanites and Perizzites over to them. They struck down 10,000 men at Bezek. 5 The men of Judah found Adoni-Bezek there. They fought against him. They struck down the Canaanites and Perizzites. 6 But Adoni-Bezek ran away. The men of Judah chased him and caught him. Then they cut off his thumbs and big toes.

7 Adoni-Bezek said, "I cut off the thumbs and big toes of 70 kings. I made them pick up scraps under my table. Now God has paid me back for what I did to them." The men of Judah brought Adoni-Bezek to Jerusalem. That's where he died.

8 The men of Judah attacked Jerusalem and captured it. They set the city on fire. They killed its people with their swords.

9 After that, the men of Judah went down to fight against some Canaanites. Those Canaanites were living in the central hill country. They also fought against those living in the Negev Desert and the western hills. 10 Then the men of Judah marched out against the Canaanites living in Hebron. Hebron used to be called Kiriath Arba. The men of Judah won the battle over Sheshai, Ahiman and Talmai. 11 From Hebron they marched out against the people living in Debir. It used to be called Kiriath Sepher.

12 Caleb said, "I will give my daughter Aksah to be married. I'll give her to the man who attacks and captures Kiriath Sepher." 13 Othniel captured it. So Caleb gave his daughter Aksah to him to be his wife. Othniel was the son of Kenaz. He was Caleb's younger brother.

14 One day Aksah came to Othniel. She begged him to ask her father for a field. When she got off her donkey, Caleb asked her, "What can I do for you?"

15 She replied, "Do me a special favor. You have given me some land in the Negev Desert. Give me springs of water also." So Caleb gave her the upper and lower springs.

16 Moses' father-in-law was a Kenite. His family went up from Jericho. Jericho was also known as the City of Palm Trees. His family went up with the people of Judah to the Desert of Judah. They went there to live among its people. Those people were living in the Negev Desert near Arad.

17 The men of Judah marched out with their fellow Israelites, the men of Simeon. They attacked the people of Canaan living in Zephath. They set the city apart to the LORD in a special way to be destroyed. That's why the city was called Hormah. 18 The men of Judah captured Gaza, Ashkelon and Ekron. They also captured the territory around each of those cities.

19 The LORD was with the men of Judah. They took over the central hill country. But they weren't able to drive the people out of the plains. That's because those people used chariots that had some iron parts. 20 Moses had promised to give Hebron to Caleb. So Hebron was given to Caleb. He drove the three sons of Anak out of it. 21 But the people of Benjamin did not drive out the Jebusites living in Jerusalem. So to this day they live there with the people of Benjamin.

22 The tribes of Joseph attacked Bethel. The LORD was with them. 23 They sent men to Bethel to check it out. It used to be called Luz. 24 Those who were sent saw a man coming out of the city. They said to him, "Show us how to get into the city. If you do, we'll see that you are treated well." 25 So he showed them how to get in. The men of Joseph killed the people in the city with their swords. But they spared the man from Bethel. They also spared his whole family. 26 Then he went to the land of the Hittites. He built a city there. He called it Luz. That's still its name to this day.

27 But the tribe of Manasseh didn't drive out the people of Beth Shan. They

didn't drive out the people of Taanach, Dor, Ibleam and Megiddo. And they didn't drive out the people of the settlements that are around those cities either. That's because the Canaanites had made up their minds to continue living in that land. 28 Later, Israel became stronger. Then they forced the Canaanites to work hard for them. But Israel never drove them out completely. 29 The tribe of Ephraim didn't drive out the Canaanites living in Gezer. So the Canaanites continued to live there among them. 30 The tribe of Zebulun didn't drive out the Canaanites living in Kitron and Nahalol. So these Canaanites lived among them. But the people of Zebulun forced the Canaanites to work hard for them. 31 The tribe of Asher didn't drive out the people living in Akko and Sidon. They didn't drive out the people of Ahlab, Akzib, Helbah, Aphek and Rehob. 32 So the people of Asher lived among the Canaanites who were in the land. 33 The tribe of Naphtali didn't drive out the people living in Beth Shemesh and Beth Anath. So the people of Naphtali lived among the Canaanites who were in the land. The people of Beth Shemesh and Beth Anath were forced to work hard for them. 34 The Amorites made the people of Dan stay in the central hill country. They didn't let them come down into the plain. 35 The Amorites made up their minds to stay in Mount Heres. They also stayed in Aijalon and Shaalbim. But the power of the tribes of Joseph grew. Then the Amorites were forced to work hard for them. 36 The border of the Amorites started at Scorpion Pass. It went to Sela and even past it.

The Angel of the LORD Warns Israel at Bokim

2 The angel of the LORD went up from Gilgal to Bokim. There he said to the Israelites, "I brought you up out of Egypt. I led you into this land. It is the land I promised to give to Abraham, Isaac and Jacob. At that time I said, 'I will never break the covenant I made with you. 2 So you must not make a covenant with the people of this land. Instead, you must tear down their altars.' But you have disobeyed me. Why did you do it? 3 I have said something else. I said, 'I will not drive out those people to make room for you. They and their gods will become traps for you.' "

4 The angel of the LORD spoke these things to all the Israelites. Then the people wept out loud. 5 So that place was called Bokim. The people offered sacrifices there to the LORD.

The People Disobey the LORD and Lose Their Battles

6 Joshua sent the Israelites away. Then they went to take over the land. All of them went to their own shares of land. 7 The people served the LORD as long as Joshua lived. They also served him as long as the elders lived. Those were the elders who lived longer than Joshua did. They had seen all the great things the LORD had done for Israel.

8 Joshua, the servant of the LORD, died. He was the son of Nun. He was 110 years old when he died. 9 His people buried him on his own property at Timnath Heres. It's north of Mount Gaash in the hill country of Ephraim.

10 All the people of Joshua's time joined the members of their families who had already died. Then those who were born after them grew up. They didn't know the LORD and what he had done for Israel. 11 The Israelites did what was evil in the sight of the LORD. They served gods that were named Baal. 12 They deserted the LORD, the God of their people. He had brought them out of Egypt. But now the Israelites served other gods and worshiped them. They served the gods of the nations that were around them. They made the LORD angry 13 because they deserted him. They served Baal. They also served female gods that were named Ashtoreth. 14 The LORD became angry with the Israelites. So he handed them over to robbers. The robbers stole everything from them. The LORD handed the Israelites over to their enemies all around them. Israel wasn't able to fight against them anymore and win. 15 When the Israelites went out to fight, the LORD's power was against them. He let their enemies win the battle over them. The LORD had warned them that it would happen. And now they were suffering terribly.

16 Then the LORD gave them leaders. The leaders saved them from the power of those robbers. 17 But the people wouldn't listen to their leaders. They weren't

in Judges?

God is the Perfect Judge who lovingly gives us commands, enables us to obey him, and forgives our sin when we disobey.

faithful to the LORD. They served other
gods and worshiped them. They didn't
obey the LORD's commands as their people before them had done. They quickly
turned away from the path their people
had taken. 18 When the LORD gave them a
leader, he was with that leader. The LORD
saved the people from the power of their
enemies. He did it as long as the leader
lived. The LORD felt very sorry for the
people. They groaned because of what
their enemies did to them. Their enemies
treated them badly. 19 But when the leader died, the people returned to their evil
ways. The things they did were even more
sinful than the things their people before
them had done. They served other gods
and worshiped them. They refused to
give up their evil practices. They wouldn't
change their stubborn ways.
20 So the LORD became very angry
with the Israelites. He said, "This nation
has broken my covenant. I made it with
their people of long ago. But this nation
has not listened to me. 21 Joshua left
some nations in the land when he died.
I will no longer drive out those nations
to make room for Israel. 22 I will use
those nations to test Israel. I will see
whether Israel will live the way I, the
LORD, want them to. I will see whether
they will be like their people of long ago.
I will see whether they will follow my
path." 23 The LORD had let those nations
remain in the land. He didn't drive them
out right away. He didn't hand them
over to Joshua.

3 The LORD left some nations in the
land. He left them to test the Israelites who hadn't lived through any of the
wars in Canaan. 2 He wanted to teach
the men in Israel who had never been in
battle before. He wanted them to learn
how to fight. 3 So he left the five rulers
of the Philistines. He left the people of
Canaan and the people of Sidon. He
left the Hivites living in the Lebanon
mountains. They lived in the area between Mount Baal Hermon and Lebo
Hamath. 4 The LORD left those nations
where they were to test the Israelites.
He wanted to see whether they would
obey his commands. He had given those
commands through Moses to their people of long ago.
5 So the Israelites lived among the Canaanites, Hittites, Amorites, Perizzites,
Hivites and Jebusites. 6 They married
the daughters of those people. They
gave their own daughters to the sons
of those people. And they served the
gods of those people.

Othniel

7 The Israelites did what was evil in
the sight of the LORD. They forgot the
LORD their God. They served gods that
were named Baal. They also served
female gods that were named Asherah.
8 So the LORD was very angry with Israel.
He handed them over to the power of
Cushan-Rishathaim, the king of Aram
Naharaim. For eight years Israel was
under his rule. 9 They cried out to the
LORD. Then he provided someone to save
them. The man's name was Othniel, the
son of Kenaz. He was Caleb's younger
brother. 10 The Spirit of the LORD came
on Othniel. So he became Israel's leader.
He went to war. The LORD handed over
to him Cushan-Rishathaim, the king of
Aram. Othniel won the battle over him.
11 So the land was at peace for 40 years.
Then Othniel, the son of Kenaz, died.

Ehud

12 Again the Israelites did what was
evil in the sight of the LORD. So the LORD
gave Eglon power over Israel. Eglon
was the king of Moab. 13 He got the Ammonites and Amalekites to join him.
All of them came and attacked Israel.
They captured Jericho. Jericho was also
known as The City of Palm Trees. 14 For

18 years the Israelites were under the rule of Eglon, the king of Moab.

15 Again the Israelites cried out to the Lord. Then he provided someone to save them. The man's name was Ehud, the son of Gera. Ehud was left-handed. He was from the tribe of Benjamin. The Israelites sent Ehud to Eglon, the king of Moab. They sent him to give the king what he required them to bring him. 16 Ehud had made a sword that had two edges. It was about a foot and a half long. He tied it to his right leg under his clothes. 17 Eglon, the king of Moab, was a very fat man. Ehud gave him the gift he had brought. 18 After that, Ehud sent away those who had carried it. 19 When he came to the place where some statues of gods stood near Gilgal, Ehud went back to Eglon. He said, "Your Majesty, I have a secret message for you."

The king said to his attendants, "Leave us!" And all his attendants left him.

20 Then Ehud approached him. King Eglon was sitting alone in the upstairs room of his palace. Ehud said, "I have a message from God for you." So the king got up from his seat. 21 Then Ehud reached out his left hand. He pulled out the sword tied to his right leg. He stuck it into the king's stomach. 22 Even the handle sank in after the blade. Eglon sagged and fell to the floor. Ehud didn't pull out the sword. And the fat closed over it. 23 Ehud went out to the porch. He shut the doors of the upstairs room behind him. Then he locked them.

24 After he had gone, the servants came. They found the doors of the upstairs room locked. They said, "Eglon must be going to the toilet in the inside room of the palace." 25 They waited for a long time. They waited so long they became worried. But the king still didn't open the doors of the room. So they took a key and unlocked them. There they saw their king. He had fallen to the floor and was dead.

26 While Eglon's servants had been waiting, Ehud had gotten away. He passed by the statues of gods and escaped to Seirah. 27 There in the hill country of Ephraim he blew a trumpet. Then he led the Israelites down from the hills.

28 "Follow me," Ehud ordered. "The Lord has handed your enemy Moab over to you." So they followed him down. They took over the only places where people could go across the Jordan River to get to Moab. They didn't let anyone go across. 29 At that time they struck down about 10,000 men of Moab. All those men were strong and powerful. But not even one escaped. 30 That day Moab was brought under the rule of Israel. So the land was at peace for 80 years.

Shamgar

31 After Ehud, Shamgar became the next leader. He was the son of Anath. Shamgar struck down 600 Philistines with a large, pointed stick used to drive oxen. He too saved Israel.

Deborah

4 After Ehud died, the Israelites once again did what was evil in the sight of the Lord. 2 So the Lord handed them over to the power of Jabin. He was a king in Canaan. He ruled in Hazor. The commander of his army was Sisera. He lived in Harosheth Haggoyim. 3 Jabin used 900 chariots that had some iron parts. He treated the Israelites very badly for 20 years. So they cried out to the Lord for help.

4 Deborah was a prophet. She was the wife of Lappidoth. She was leading Israel at that time. 5 Under the Palm Tree of Deborah she served the people as their judge. That place was between Ramah and Bethel in the hill country of Ephraim. The Israelites went up to her there. They came to have her decide cases for them. She settled matters between them. 6 Deborah sent for Barak. He was the son of Abinoam. Barak was from Kedesh in the land of Naphtali. Deborah said to Barak, "The Lord, the God of Israel, is giving you a command. He says, 'Go! Take 10,000 men from the tribes of Naphtali and Zebulun with you. Then lead them up to Mount Tabor. 7 I will lead Sisera into a trap. He is the commander of Jabin's army. I will bring him, his chariots and his troops to the Kishon River. There I will hand him over to you.' "

8 Barak said to her, "If you go with me, I'll go. But if you don't go with me, I won't go."

9 "All right," Deborah said. "I'll go with you. But because of the way you are

doing this, you won't receive any hon-
or. Instead, the LORD will hand Sisera
over to a woman." So Deborah went to
Kedesh with Barak. 10 There he sent for
men from Zebulun and Naphtali. And
10,000 men followed him into battle.
Deborah also went with him.

11 Heber, the Kenite, had left the other
Kenites. They came from the family line
of Hobab. He was the brother-in-law of
Moses. Heber set up his tent by the large
tree in Zaanannim near Kedesh.

12 Sisera was told that Barak, the son
of Abinoam, had gone up to Mount
Tabor. 13 So Sisera gathered together
his 900 chariots that had some iron
parts. He also gathered together all his
men. He brought them from Harosheth
Haggoyim to the Kishon River.

14 Then Deborah said to Barak, "Go!
Today the LORD will hand Sisera over to
you. Hasn't the LORD gone ahead of you?"
So Barak went down Mount Tabor. His
10,000 men followed him. 15 As Barak's
men marched out, the LORD drove Sisera
away from the field of battle. The LORD
scattered all of Sisera's chariots. Barak's
men struck down Sisera's army with
their swords. Sisera got down from his
chariot. He ran away on foot.

16 Barak chased Sisera's chariots and
army. Barak chased them all the way
to Harosheth Haggoyim. All of Sisera's
troops were killed by swords. Not even
one was left. 17 But Sisera ran away on
foot. He ran to the tent of Jael. She was the
wife of Heber, the Kenite. Sisera ran there
because there was a treaty between Heber's family and Jabin, the king of Hazor.

18 Jael went out to meet Sisera. "Come
in, sir," she said. "Come right in. Don't
be afraid." So he entered her tent. Then
she covered him with a blanket.

19 "I'm thirsty," he said. "Please give
me some water." So Jael opened a bottle
of milk. The bottle was made out of
animal skin. She gave him a drink of
milk. Then she covered him up again.

20 "Stand in the doorway of the tent,"
he told her. "Someone might come by
and ask you, 'Is anyone in there?' If that
happens, say 'No.' "

21 But Heber's wife Jael picked up a
tent stake and a hammer. She went quietly over to Sisera. He was lying there,
fast asleep. He was very tired. She drove
the stake through his head right into
the ground. So he died.

22 Just then Barak came by because
he was chasing Sisera. Jael went out
to meet him. "Come right in," she said.
"I'll show you the man you are looking
for." So he went in with her. Sisera was
lying there with the stake through his
head. He was dead.

23 On that day God brought Jabin under Israel's control. He was a king in
Canaan. 24 Israel's power grew stronger
and stronger against King Jabin. The
Israelites became so strong that they
destroyed him.

The Song of Deborah

5 On that day Deborah and Barak
sang a song. Barak was the son of
Abinoam. Here is what Deborah and
Barak sang.

2 "The princes in Israel lead the way.
The people follow them just
because they want to.
When this happens, praise the
LORD!

3 "Kings, hear this! Rulers, listen!
I will sing to the LORD.
I will praise the LORD in song. He
is the God of Israel.

I will sing to the LORD. I will praise the LORD in song. He is the God of Israel. JUDGES 5:3

4 "LORD, you went out from Seir.
You marched out from the land
of Edom.
The earth shook. The heavens
poured.
The clouds poured down their
water.
5 The mountains shook because of the
LORD. He was at Mount Sinai.
They shook because of the LORD.
He is the God of Israel.

6 "The main roads were deserted.
So travelers used the winding
paths.
That happened in the days of
Shamgar, the son of Anath.
It happened in the days of Jael.

7 Those who lived in the villages of
Israel would not fight.
They held back until I, Deborah,
came.
I came as a mother in Israel.
8 War came to the city gates. Then
God chose new leaders.
But no shields or spears were seen
anywhere.
There weren't any among 40,000
men in Israel.
9 My heart is with the princes in Israel.
It's with the people who follow
them just because they want to.
Praise the LORD!

10 "Some of you ride on white donkeys.
Some of you sit on your saddle
blankets.
Some of you walk along the road.
Think about 11 the voices of the
singers at the watering places.
They sing about the victories of
the LORD.
They sing about the victories of his
people who live in Israel's villages.

"The people of the LORD
went down to the city gates.
12 'Wake up, Deborah! Wake up!' they
said.
'Wake up! Wake up! Begin to sing!
Barak, get up!
Son of Abinoam, capture your
prisoners!'

13 "The nobles who were left came
down.
The people of the LORD
came down to me against the
powerful enemy.
14 Some came from the part
of Ephraim where some
Amalekites lived.
Some from Benjamin were
with the people who followed
Ephraim.
Captains came down from Makir.
Those who rule like commanders
came down from Zebulun.
15 The princes of Issachar were with
Deborah.
The men of Issachar were with
Barak.
They went into the valley under
his command.
In the territories of Reuben,
men looked deeply into their
hearts.
16 Why did they stay among the
sheep pens?
Why did they stay to hear
shepherds whistling for the
flocks?

In the territories of Reuben,
men looked deeply into their hearts.
17 Gilead stayed east of the Jordan River.
Why did Dan stay near the ships?
The men of Asher remained on the coast of the Mediterranean Sea.
They stayed in their safe harbors.
18 The people of Zebulun put their very lives in danger.
So did Naphtali on the hillside fields.

19 "Kings came and fought.
The kings of Canaan fought
at Taanach by the streams of Megiddo.
But they didn't carry away any silver.
They didn't take anything at all.
20 From the heavens the stars fought.
From the sky they fought against Sisera.
21 The Kishon River swept them away.
The Kishon is a very old river.
My spirit, march on! Be strong!
22 The hooves of the horses pounded like thunder.
The powerful horses of our enemies galloped away.
23 'Let Meroz be cursed,' said the angel of the LORD.
'Let bitter curses fall on its people.
They did not come to help the LORD.
They did not come to help him
against our powerful enemies.'

24 "May Jael be the most blessed woman of all.
May the wife of Heber, the Kenite, be blessed.
May she be the most blessed woman
of all those who live in tents.
25 Sisera asked for water. She gave him milk.
In a bowl fit for nobles she brought him buttermilk.
26 Her hand reached out for a tent stake.
Her right hand reached for a hammer.
She hit Sisera. She crushed his head.
She drove the stake right through his head.
27 He sank down. He fell at her feet.
He was lying there.
At her feet he sank down. He fell.
He fell where he sank down.
That's where he died.

28 "Sisera's mother looked out through the window.
From behind the wooden screen she cried out.

pointing us to JESUS: The Judges

The people of Israel were worshiping idols and being treated poorly by their enemies. So God raised up judges at different times to deliver his people, who had disobeyed his commands. The judge's job was to deliver God's people from their enemies and restore the land to peace. In the end, although the judges rescued God's people temporarily, everyone still did what they wanted instead of what God wanted. The people needed a better deliverer.

The judges were meant to point God's people toward Jesus, who Scripture tells us is the ultimate and final deliverer of all people. But Jesus didn't just deliver the people for a short time. He delivered his people forever—and from our ultimate enemies, sin and death!—when he took our place as he died on the cross. Jesus redeemed us from sin and rescued us from eternal judgment, making peace between us and God. Now, by putting our faith in Jesus, we can live freely with God forever!

'Why is his chariot taking so long to
get here?' she said.
'Why can't I hear the noise of his
chariots yet?'
29 Her wisest ladies answer her.
And here's what she keeps saying
to herself.
30 She says, 'They must be finding
riches to bring back.
They must be dividing them up.
Each man is getting a woman or
two.
They are giving colorful clothes
to Sisera.
The clothes are very beautiful.
He will bring some for me to wear.
The men must be finding many
things to bring home.'

31 "LORD, may all your enemies be
destroyed.
But may all who love you be like
the morning sun.
May they be like the sun when it
shines the brightest."

So the land was at peace for 40 years.

Gideon

6 The Israelites did what was evil in
the sight of the LORD. So for seven
years he handed them over to the people of Midian. 2 The Midianites treated
the Israelites very badly. That's why
they made hiding places for themselves.
They hid in holes in the mountains.
They also hid in caves and in other safe
places. 3 Each year the people planted
their crops. When they did, the Midianites came into the country and attacked
it. So did the Amalekites and other
tribes from the east. 4 They camped on
the land. They destroyed the crops all
the way to Gaza. They didn't spare any
living thing for Israel. They didn't spare
sheep or cattle or donkeys. 5 The Midianites came up with their livestock and
tents. They came like huge numbers of
locusts. It was impossible to count the
men and their camels. They came into
the land to destroy it. 6 The Midianites
made the Israelites very poor. So they
cried out to the LORD for help.

7 They cried out to the LORD because
of what the Midianites had done. 8 So
he sent a prophet to Israel. The prophet
said, "The LORD is the God of Israel. He
says, 'I brought you up out of Egypt.
That is the land where you were slaves.
9 I saved you from the power of the
Egyptians. I saved you from all those
who were treating you badly. I drove
out the Canaanites to make room for
you. I gave you their land. 10 I said to
you, "I am the LORD your God. You are
now living in the land of the Amorites.
Do not worship their gods." But you
have not listened to me.' "

11 The angel of the LORD came. He sat
down under an oak tree in Ophrah. The
tree belonged to Joash. He was from
the family line of Abiezer. Gideon
was threshing wheat in a winepress
at Ophrah. He was the son of Joash.
Gideon was threshing in a winepress
to hide the wheat from the Midianites.
12 The angel of the LORD appeared to
Gideon. He said, "Mighty warrior, the
LORD is with you."

13 "Pardon me, sir," Gideon replied,
"you say the LORD is with us. Then why
has all this happened to us? Where are
all the wonderful things he has done?
Our people of long ago told us about
them. They said, 'Didn't the LORD bring
us up out of Egypt?' But now the LORD
has deserted us. He has handed us over
to Midian."

14 The LORD turned to Gideon. He said
to him, "You are strong. Go and save
Israel from the power of Midian. I am
sending you."

15 "Pardon me, sir," Gideon replied,
"but how can I possibly save Israel?
My family group is the weakest in the
tribe of Manasseh. And I'm the least
important member of my family."

16 The LORD answered, "I will be with
you. So you will strike down the Midianites. You will leave no one alive."

17 Gideon replied, "If you are pleased
with me, give me a special sign. Then
I'll know that it's really you talking to
me. 18 Please don't go away until I come
back. I'll bring my offering and set it
down in front of you."

The LORD said, "I will wait until you
return."

19 Gideon went inside and prepared
a young goat. From 36 pounds of flour
he made bread without using yeast.
He put the meat in a basket. In a pot
he put soup made from the meat. Then
he brought all of it and offered it to the
LORD under the oak tree.

20 The angel of God said to Gideon,
"Take the meat and the bread. Place
them on this rock. Then pour out the
soup." So Gideon did it. 21 The angel of
the LORD had a walking stick in his hand.
With the tip of the stick he touched the
meat and the bread. Fire blazed out of
the rock. It burned up the meat and the
bread. Then the angel of the LORD disappeared. 22 Gideon realized it was the
angel of the LORD. He cried out, "Oh no,
my LORD and King, I have seen the angel
of the LORD face to face!"
23 But the LORD said to him, "May
peace be with you! Do not be afraid.
You are not going to die."
24 So Gideon built an altar there to
honor the LORD. He called it The LORD
Is Peace. It still stands in Ophrah to
this day. Ophrah is in the territory that
belongs to the family line of Abiezer.
25 That same night the LORD spoke to
Gideon. He said, "Get the second bull
from your father's herd. Get the one
that is seven years old. Tear down the
altar your father built to honor the god
named Baal. Cut down the pole beside
it. The pole is used to worship the female
god named Asherah. 26 Then build the
right kind of altar. Build it to honor

BASICS OF FAITH Q&A

How can I trust God when I can't see him?

God is always at work, even though you can't see him. Someday we will see him, but for now you can read about the way the angel of the Lord appeared to Gideon and choose to trust God by faith.

Can you find the following verse?

JUDGES 6:12

the LORD your God. Build it on top of
this hill. Then use the wood from the
Asherah pole you cut down. Sacrifice
the second bull as a burnt offering."
27 So Gideon went and got ten of his
servants. He did just as the LORD had
told him. But he was afraid of his family. He was also afraid of the people in
the town. So he did everything at night
instead of during the day.
28 In the morning the people in the
town got up. They saw that Baal's altar
had been torn down. The Asherah pole
beside it had been cut down. And the
second bull had been sacrificed on the
new altar that had been built.
29 They asked each other, "Who did
this?"

They looked into the matter carefully.
Someone told them, "Gideon, the son of
Joash, did it."
30 The people in the town spoke to
Joash. They ordered him, "Bring your
son out here. He must die. He has torn
down Baal's altar. He has cut down the
Asherah pole beside it."
31 But Joash replied to the angry
crowd around him. He asked, "Are you
going to stand up for Baal? Are you
trying to save him? Those who stand up
for him will be put to death by morning!
Is Baal really a god? If he is, he can
stand up for himself when someone
tears down his altar." 32 That's why they
gave Gideon the name Jerub-Baal on
that day. Gideon had torn down Baal's
altar. So they said, "Let Baal take his
stand against him."
33 All the Midianites and Amalekites
gathered their armies together. Other
tribes from the east joined them. All of
them went across the Jordan River. They
camped in the Valley of Jezreel. 34 Then
the Spirit of the LORD came on Gideon.
So Gideon blew a trumpet to send for the
men of Abiezer. He told them to follow
him. 35 He sent messengers all through
Manasseh's territory. He called for the
men of Manasseh to fight. He also sent
messengers to the men of Asher, Zebulun and Naphtali. So all those men went
up to join the others.
36 Gideon said to God, "You promised you would use me to save Israel. 37 Please do something for me. I'll
put a piece of wool on the threshing
floor. Suppose dew is only on the wool

tomorrow morning. And suppose the
ground all around it is dry. Then I will
know that you will use me to save Israel.
I'll know that your promise will come
true." 38 And that's what happened.
Gideon got up early the next day. He
squeezed the dew out of the wool. The
water filled a bowl.

39 Then Gideon said to God, "Don't be
angry with me. Let me ask you for just
one more thing. Let me use the wool for
one more test. But this time make the
wool dry. And let the ground be covered
with dew." 40 So that night God did it.
Only the wool was dry. The ground all
around it was covered with dew.

Gideon Wins the Battle Over the Midianites

7 Early in the morning Jerub-Baal
and all his men camped at the
spring of Harod. Jerub-Baal was another name for Gideon. The camp of
Midian was north of Gideon's camp. It
was in the valley near the hill of Moreh.
2 The LORD said to Gideon, "I want to
hand Midian over to you. But you have
too many men for me to do that. Then
Israel might brag, 'My own strength
has saved me.' 3 So here is what I want
you to announce to the army. Tell them,
'Those who tremble with fear can turn
back. They can leave Mount Gilead.' " So
22,000 men left. But 10,000 remained.

4 The LORD said to Gideon, "There are
still too many men. So take them down
to the water. There I will reduce the
number of them for you. If I say, 'This
one will go with you,' he will go. But if
I say, 'That one will not go with you,'
he will not go."

5 So Gideon took the men down to
the water. There the LORD said to him,
"Some men will drink the way dogs
do. They will lap up the water with
their tongues. Separate them from
those who get down on their knees to
drink." 6 Three hundred men brought
up the water to their mouths with their
hands. And they lapped it up the way
dogs do. All the rest got down on their
knees to drink.

7 The LORD spoke to Gideon. He said,
"With the help of the 300 men who
lapped up the water I will save you. I
will hand the Midianites over to you.
Let all the other men go home." 8 So
Gideon sent those Israelites home. But
he kept the 300 men. They took over
the supplies and trumpets the others
had left.

The Midianites had set up their camp
in the valley below where Gideon was.
9 During that night the LORD said to Gideon, "Get up. Go down against the camp.
I am going to hand it over to you. 10 But
what if you are afraid to attack? Then
go down to the camp with your servant
Purah. 11 Listen to what they are saying.
After that, you will not be afraid to attack
the camp." So Gideon and his servant Purah went down to the edge of the camp.
12 The Midianites had set up their camp
in the valley. So had the Amalekites and
all the other tribes from the east. There
were so many of them that they looked
like huge numbers of locusts. Like the
grains of sand on the seashore, their
camels couldn't be counted.

13 Gideon arrived just as a man was
telling a friend about his dream. "I
had a dream," he was saying. "A round
loaf of barley bread came rolling into
the camp of Midian. It hit a tent with
great force. The tent turned over and
fell down flat."

14 His friend replied, "That can only be
the sword of Gideon, the son of Joash.
Gideon is from Israel. God has handed
the Midianites over to him. He has given
him the whole camp."

15 Gideon heard the man explain what
the dream meant. Then Gideon bowed
down and worshiped. He returned to the
camp of Israel. He called out, "Get up! The
LORD has handed the Midianites over to
you." 16 Gideon separated the 300 men into
three fighting groups. He put a trumpet
and an empty jar into the hands of each
man. And he put a torch inside each jar.

17 "Watch me," he told them. "Do what
I do. I'll go to the edge of the enemy
camp. Then do exactly as I do. 18 I and
everyone with me will blow our trumpets. Then blow your trumpets from
your positions all around the camp.
And shout the battle cry, 'For the LORD
and for Gideon!' "

19 Gideon and the 100 men with him
reached the edge of the enemy camp.
It was about ten o'clock at night. It was
just after the guard had been changed.
Gideon and his men blew their trumpets. They broke the jars that were in

their hands. 20 The three fighting groups blew their trumpets. They smashed their jars. They held their torches in their left hands. They held in their right hands the trumpets they were going to blow. Then they shouted the battle cry, "A sword for the LORD and for Gideon!" 21 Each man stayed in his position around the camp. But all the Midianites ran away in fear. They were crying out as they ran.

22 When the 300 trumpets were blown, the LORD caused all the men in the enemy camp to start fighting one another. They attacked one another with their swords. The army ran away to Beth Shittah toward Zererah. They ran all the way to the border of Abel Meholah near Tabbath. 23 Israelites from the tribes of Naphtali, Asher and all of Manasseh were called out. They chased the Midianites. 24 Gideon sent messengers through the entire hill country of Ephraim. They said, "Come on down against the Midianites. Take control of the waters of the Jordan River before they get there. Do it all the way to Beth Barah."

So all the men of Ephraim were called out. They took control of the waters of the Jordan all the way to Beth Barah. 25 They also captured Oreb and Zeeb. Those men were two of the Midianite leaders. The men of Ephraim killed Oreb at the rock of Oreb. They killed Zeeb at the winepress of Zeeb. They chased the Midianites. And they brought the heads of Oreb and Zeeb to Gideon. He was by the Jordan River.

Zebah and Zalmunna

8 The men of Ephraim asked Gideon, "Why have you treated us like this? Why didn't you ask us to help you when you went out to fight against Midian?" In anger they challenged Gideon.

2 But he answered them, "What I've done isn't anything compared to what you have done. Ephraim's grapes have been gathered. Isn't what is left over better than all the grapes that have been gathered from Abiezer's vines? 3 God handed Oreb and Zeeb over to you. They were Midianite leaders. So what was I able to do compared to what you did?" After Gideon had said that, they didn't feel angry with him anymore.

4 Gideon and his 300 men were very tired. But they kept on chasing their enemies. They came to the Jordan River and went across it. 5 Gideon said to the men of Sukkoth, "Give my troops some bread. They are worn out. And I'm still chasing Zebah and Zalmunna. They are the kings of Midian."

6 But the officials of Sukkoth objected. They said, "Have you already killed Zebah and Zalmunna? Have you cut their hands off and brought them back to prove it? If you haven't, why should we give bread to your troops?"

7 Gideon replied, "The LORD will hand Zebah and Zalmunna over to me. When he does, I'll tear your skin with thorns from desert bushes."

8 From there Gideon went up to Peniel. He asked its men for the same thing. But they answered as the men of Sukkoth had. 9 So he said to the men of Peniel, "I'll be back after I've won the battle. Then I'll tear down this tower."

10 Zebah and Zalmunna were in Karkor. They had an army of about 15,000 men. That's all that were left of the armies of the tribes from the east. About 120,000 men who carried swords had died in battle. 11 Gideon went up the trail the people of the desert had made. It ran east of Nobah and Jogbehah. He attacked the army by surprise. 12 Zebah and Zalmunna ran away. They were the two kings of Midian. Gideon chased them and captured them. He destroyed their whole army.

13 Then Gideon, the son of Joash, returned from the battle. He came back through the Pass of Heres. 14 He caught a young man from Sukkoth. He asked him about the elders of the town. The young man wrote down for him the names of Sukkoth's 77 officials. 15 Then Gideon came and said to the men of Sukkoth, "Here are Zebah and Zalmunna. You made fun of me because of them. You said, 'Have you already killed Zebah and Zalmunna? Have you cut their hands off and brought them back to prove it? If you haven't, why should we give bread to your tired men?'" 16 Gideon went and got the elders of the town. Then he taught the men of Sukkoth a lesson. He tore their skin with thorns from desert bushes. 17 He also pulled down the tower at Peniel. He killed the men in the town.

[18]Then he spoke to Zebah and Zalmunna. He asked, "What were the men like that you killed at Tabor?"

"Men like you," they answered. "Each one walked as if he were a prince."

[19]Gideon replied, "Those were my brothers. They were the sons of my own mother. You can be sure that the LORD lives. And you can be just as sure that if you had spared their lives, I wouldn't kill you." [20]Then Gideon turned to his oldest son Jether. He said, "Kill them!" But Jether didn't pull out his sword. He was only a boy. So he was afraid.

[21]Zebah and Zalmunna said, "Come on. Do it yourself. 'The older the man, the stronger he is.'" So Gideon stepped forward and killed them. Then he took the gold chains off the necks of their camels.

Gideon's Linen Apron

[22]The Israelites said to Gideon, "Rule over us. We want you, your son and your grandson to be our rulers. You have saved us from the power of Midian."

[23]But Gideon told them, "I will not rule over you. My son won't rule over you either. The LORD will rule over you." [24]He continued, "I do ask one thing. I want each of you to give me an earring. I'm talking about the earrings you took from your enemies." It was the practice of the people in the family line of Ishmael to wear gold earrings.

[25]The Israelites said, "We'll be glad to give them to you." So they spread out a piece of clothing. Each of them threw a ring on it from what he had taken. [26]The weight of the gold rings Gideon asked for was 43 pounds. That didn't include the moon-shaped necklaces the kings of Midian had worn. It didn't include their other necklaces or their purple clothes. And it didn't include the gold chains that had been on the necks of their camels. [27]Gideon made an object out of all the gold. It looked like the linen apron the high priest of Israel wore. Gideon placed it in Ophrah. That was his hometown. All the Israelites worshiped it there. They weren't faithful to the LORD. So the gold object became a trap to Gideon and his family.

Gideon Dies

[28]Israel brought Midian under their control. Midian wasn't able to attack Israel anymore. So the land was at peace for 40 years. The peace lasted as long as Gideon was living.

[29]Jerub-Baal, the son of Joash, went back home to live. Jerub-Baal was another name for Gideon. [30]He had 70 sons of his own. That's because he had many wives. [31]And he had a concubine who lived in Shechem. She also had a son by him. Gideon named that son Abimelek. [32]Gideon, the son of Joash, died when he was very old. He was buried in the tomb of his father Joash in Ophrah. Ophrah was in the territory that belonged to the family line of Abiezer.

[33]As soon as Gideon had died, the Israelites began serving and worshiping gods that were named Baal. Israel wasn't faithful to the LORD. They worshiped Baal-Berith as their god. [34]They forgot what the LORD their God had done for them. He had saved them from the power of their enemies all around them. [35]Jerub-Baal had done many good things for the Israelites. But they weren't faithful to his family. Jerub-Baal was another name for Gideon.

Abimelek

9 Abimelek was the son of Jerub-Baal. He went to his mother's brothers in Shechem. He spoke to them and to all the members of his mother's family group. He said, [2]"Speak to all the citizens of Shechem. Tell them, 'You can have all 70 of Jerub-Baal's sons rule over you. Or you can have just one man rule over you. Which would you rather have?' Remember, I'm your own flesh and blood."

[3]The brothers told all of that to the citizens of Shechem. Then the people decided to follow Abimelek. They said, "He's related to us." [4]They gave him 28 ounces of silver. They had taken it from the temple of the god named Baal-Berith. Abimelek used it to hire some men. They were wild and weren't good for anything. They became his followers. [5]Abimelek went to his father's home in Ophrah. There on a big rock he murdered his 70 brothers. All of them were the sons of Jerub-Baal. But Jotham escaped by hiding. He was Jerub-Baal's youngest son. [6]All the citizens of Shechem and Beth Millo came together. They gathered at the stone pillar that was beside the large tree in Shechem. They wanted to crown Abimelek as their king.

7 Jotham was told about it. So he
climbed up on top of Mount Gerizim.
He shouted down to them, "Citizens of
Shechem! Listen to me! Then God will
listen to you. 8 One day the trees went
out to anoint a king for themselves.
They said to an olive tree, 'Be our king.'
9 "But the olive tree answered, 'Should
I give up my olive oil? It's used to honor
gods and people alike. Should I give that
up just to rule over the trees?'
10 "Next, the trees said to a fig tree,
'Come and be our king.'
11 "But the fig tree replied, 'Should I
give up my fruit? It's so good and sweet.
Should I give that up just to rule over
the trees?'
12 "Then the trees said to a vine, 'Come
and be our king.'
13 "But the vine answered, 'Should I
give up my wine? It cheers up gods and
people alike. Should I give that up just
to rule over the trees?'
14 "Finally, all the trees spoke to a
bush that had thorns. They said, 'Come
and be our king.'
15 "The bush asked the trees, 'Do you
really want to anoint me as king over
you? If you do, come and rest in my
shade. But if you don't, I will destroy
you! Fire will come out of me and burn
up the cedar trees of Lebanon!'
16 "Did you act in an honest way when
you made Abimelek your king? Did you
really do the right thing? Have you been
fair to Jerub-Baal and his family? Have
you given him the honor he's worthy
of? 17 Remember that my father fought
for you. He put his life in danger for
you. He saved you from the power of
Midian. 18 But today you have turned
against my father's family. You have
murdered his 70 sons on a big rock.
Abimelek is only the son of my father's
female slave. But you have made him
king over the citizens of Shechem. You
have done that because he's related to
you. 19 Have you citizens of Shechem
and Beth Millo acted in an honest way
toward Jerub-Baal? Have you done
the right thing to his family today?
If you have, may you be happy with
Abimelek! And may he be happy with
you! 20 But if you haven't, let fire come
out from Abimelek and burn you up!
And let fire come out from you and burn
Abimelek up!"
21 Then Jotham ran away. He escaped
to a town named Beer. He lived there
because he was afraid of his brother
Abimelek.
22 Abimelek ruled over Israel for three
years. 23 Then God stirred up trouble
between Abimelek and the citizens of
Shechem. So they turned against Abimelek. They decided not to follow him
anymore. 24 God made that happen
because of what Abimelek had done
to Jerub-Baal's 70 sons. He had spilled
their blood. God wanted to punish their
brother Abimelek for doing that. He
also wanted to punish the citizens of
Shechem. They had helped Abimelek
murder his brothers. 25 The citizens of
Shechem didn't want Abimelek to be
their ruler anymore. So they hid some
men on top of the hills. They wanted
them to attack and rob everyone who
passed by. Abimelek was told about it.
26 Gaal and his relatives moved into
Shechem. Gaal was the son of Ebed. The
citizens of Shechem put their trust in Gaal.
27 The people of Shechem went out into
the fields. They gathered the grapes. They
pressed the juice out of them by stomping
on them. Then they held a feast in the
temple of their god. While they were eating and drinking, they cursed Abimelek.
28 Then Gaal, the son of Ebed, said, "Who
is Abimelek? And who is Shechem? Why
should we citizens of Shechem be under
Abimelek's rule? Isn't he Jerub-Baal's
son? Isn't Zebul his helper? It would be
better to serve the family of Hamor. He
was the father of Shechem. So why should
we serve Abimelek? 29 I wish these people
were under my command. Then I would
get rid of Abimelek. I would say to him,
'Call out your whole army!' "
30 Zebul was the governor of Shechem.
He heard about what Gaal, the son of
Ebed, had said. So he was very angry.
31 Zebul secretly sent messengers to
Abimelek. They said, "Gaal, the son of
Ebed, has come to Shechem. His relatives have come with him. They are stirring up the city against you. 32 So come
with your men during the night. Hide
in the fields and wait. 33 In the morning
at sunrise, attack the city. Gaal and his
men will come out against you. Then
take that opportunity to attack them."
34 So Abimelek and all his troops started out at night. They went into their

hiding places near Shechem. Abimelek had separated them into four fighting groups. 35 Gaal, the son of Ebed, had already gone out. He was standing at the entrance of the city gate. He had arrived there just as Abimelek and his troops came out of their hiding places.

36 Gaal saw them. He said to Zebul, "Look! People are coming down from the tops of the mountains!"

Zebul replied, "You are wrong. Those aren't people. They are just the shadows of the mountains."

37 But Gaal spoke up again. He said, "Look! People are coming down from the central hill. Another group is coming from the direction of the fortune tellers' tree."

38 Then Zebul said to Gaal, "Where is your big talk now? You said, 'Who is Abimelek? Why should we be under his rule?' Aren't these the people you made fun of? Go out and fight against them!"

39 So Gaal led the citizens out of Shechem. They fought against Abimelek. 40 He chased Gaal from the field of battle. Abimelek chased them all the way to the entrance of the city gate. Many men were killed as they ran away. 41 Abimelek stayed in Arumah. And Zebul drove Gaal and his relatives out of Shechem.

42 The next day the people of Shechem went out to work in the fields. Abimelek was told about it. 43 So he gathered his men together. He separated them into three fighting groups. Then he hid them in the fields and told them to wait. When he saw the people coming out of the city, he got up to attack them. 44 Abimelek and the men with him ran forward. They placed themselves at the entrance of the city gate. Then the other two groups attacked the people in the fields. There they struck them down. 45 Abimelek kept up his attack against the city all day long. He didn't stop until he had captured it. Then he killed its people. He destroyed the city. He scattered salt on it to make sure that nothing would be able to grow there.

46 The citizens in the tower of Shechem heard about what was happening. So they went to the safest place in the temple of the god named El-Berith. 47 Abimelek heard that they had gathered together there. 48 He and all his men went up Mount Zalmon. He got an ax and cut off some branches. He carried them on his shoulders. He ordered the men with him to do the same thing. "Quick!" he said. "Do what you have seen me do!" 49 So all the men cut branches and followed Abimelek. They piled them against the place where the people had gone for safety. Then they set the place on fire with the people still inside. There were about 1,000 men and women in the tower of Shechem. All of them died.

50 Next, Abimelek went to Thebez. He surrounded it. Then he attacked it and captured it. 51 But inside the city there was a strong tower. All the people in the city had run to it for safety. All the men and women had gone into it. They had locked themselves in. They had climbed up on the roof of the tower. 52 Abimelek went to the tower and attacked it. He approached the entrance to the tower to set it on fire. 53 But a woman dropped a large millstone on him. It broke his head open.

54 He quickly called out to the man carrying his armor. He said, "Pull out your sword and kill me. Then people can't say, 'A woman killed him.' " So his servant stuck his sword through him. And Abimelek died. 55 When the Israelites saw he was dead, they went home.

56 That's how God punished Abimelek for the evil thing he had done to his father. He had murdered his 70 brothers. 57 God also made the people of Shechem pay for all the evil things they had done. The curse of Jotham came down on them. He was the son of Jerub-Baal.

Tola

10 Tola rose up to save Israel. That happened after the time of Abimelek. Tola was from the tribe of Issachar. He was the son of Puah, who was the son of Dodo. Tola lived in Shamir. It's in the hill country of Ephraim. 2 Tola led Israel for 23 years. After he died, he was buried in Shamir.

Jair

3 Jair became the leader after Tola. Jair was from the land of Gilead. He led Israel for 22 years. 4 He had 30 sons. They rode on 30 donkeys. His sons controlled 30 towns in Gilead. Those towns are called Havvoth Jair to this day. 5 After Jair died, he was buried in Kamon.

Jephthah

[6]Once again the Israelites did what was evil in the sight of the LORD. They served gods that were named Baal. They served female gods that were named Ashtoreth. They worshiped the gods of Aram and Sidon. They served the gods of Moab and Ammon. They also worshiped the gods of the Philistines. The Israelites deserted the LORD. They didn't serve him anymore. [7]So the LORD became very angry with them. He handed them over to the Philistines and the Ammonites. [8]That year they broke Israel's power completely. They treated the Israelites badly for 18 years. The people who did this lived east of the Jordan River. They lived in Gilead. That was the land of the Amorites. [9]The Ammonites also went across the Jordan. They crossed over to fight against the tribes of Judah, Benjamin and Ephraim. Israel was suffering terribly. [10]Then the Israelites cried out to the LORD. They said, "We have sinned against you. We have deserted our God. We have served gods that are named Baal."

[11]The LORD replied, "The Egyptians and Amorites treated you badly. So did the Ammonites and Philistines. [12]And so did the Amalekites and the people of Sidon and Maon. Each time you cried out to me for help. And I saved you from their power. [13]But you have deserted me. You have served other gods. So I will not save you anymore. [14]Go and cry out to the gods you have chosen. Let them save you when you get into trouble!"

[15]But the Israelites replied to the LORD, "We have sinned. Do to us what you think is best. But please save us now." [16]Then they got rid of the false gods that were among them. They served the LORD. And he couldn't stand to see Israel suffer anymore.

[17]The Ammonites were called together to fight. They camped in the land of Gilead. Then the Israelites gathered together. They camped at the city of Mizpah. [18]The leaders of Gilead spoke to one another. They said, "Who will lead the attack against the Ammonites? That person will be the ruler of all the people who live in Gilead."

11 Jephthah was a mighty warrior. He was from the land of Gilead. His father's name was Gilead. Jephthah's mother was a prostitute. [2]Gilead's wife also had sons by him. When they had grown up, they drove Jephthah away. "You aren't going to get any share of our family's property," they said. "You are the son of another woman." [3]So Jephthah ran away from his brothers. He made his home in the land of Tob. A group of men who weren't good for anything gathered around him there. And they followed him.

[4]Some time later, the Ammonites were fighting against Israel. [5]So the elders of Gilead went to get Jephthah from the land of Tob. [6]"Come with us," they said. "Be our commander. Then we can fight against the Ammonites."

[7]Jephthah said to them, "Didn't you hate me? Didn't you drive me away from my father's house? Why are you coming to me only when you are in trouble?"

[8]The elders of Gilead replied to him. "You are right," they said. "That's why we're turning to you now. Come with us and fight against the Ammonites. Then you will rule over all of us who live in Gilead."

[9]Jephthah said, "Suppose you take me back to fight against the Ammonites. And suppose the LORD gives me victory over them. Then will I really be your leader?"

[10]The elders of Gilead replied, "The LORD is our witness. We'll certainly do as you say." [11]So Jephthah went with the elders of Gilead. And the people made him their leader and commander. He went to Mizpah. There he repeated to the LORD everything he had said.

[12]Then Jephthah sent messengers to the king of Ammon. They asked, "What do you have against me? Why have you attacked my country?"

[13]The king of Ammon answered Jephthah's messengers. He said, "Israel came up out of Egypt. At that time they took my land away. They took all the land between the Arnon River and the Jabbok River. It reached all the way to the Jordan River. Now give it back. Then there will be peace."

[14]Jephthah sent messengers back to the king of Ammon. [15]They said,

> "Here is what Jephthah says to you. Israel didn't take the land of Moab. They didn't take the land of Ammon. [16]When Israel came up out of Egypt, they went through the

desert to the Red Sea. From there
they went on to Kadesh. [17] Then
Israel sent messengers to the king
of Edom. They said, 'Please let us go
through your country.' But the king
of Edom wouldn't listen to them.
They sent the same message to the
king of Moab. But he refused too.
So Israel stayed at Kadesh.

[18] "Next, they traveled through
the desert. They traveled along the
borders of the lands of Edom and
Moab. They passed along the east
side of the country of Moab. They
camped on the other side of the
Arnon River. They didn't enter the
territory of Moab. The Arnon River
was Moab's border.

[19] "Then Israel sent messengers
to Sihon. He was the king of the
Amorites. He ruled in Heshbon.
They said to him, 'Let us pass
through your country to our own
land.' [20] But Sihon didn't trust Israel to pass through his territory.
Instead, he gathered all his troops
together. They camped at Jahaz.
And they fought against Israel.

[21] "Then the LORD, the God of Israel, handed Sihon and his whole
army over to Israel. Israel won the
battle over them. Amorites were
living in the country at that time.
And Israel took over all their land.
[22] Israel captured all the land between the Arnon River and the Jabbok River. It reached from the desert
all the way to the Jordan River.

[23] "The LORD, the God of Israel, has driven the Amorites out
to make room for his people. So
what right do you have to take it
over? [24] You will take what your god
Chemosh gives you, won't you? In
the same way, we will take over
what the LORD our God has giv-
en us. [25] Are you any better than
Balak, the son of Zippor? Balak
was the king of Moab. Did he ever
argue with Israel? Did he ever fight
against them? [26] For 300 years Israel has been living in Heshbon
and Aroer. They have been living
in the settlements around those
cities. They have also been living
in all the towns along the Arnon
River. Why didn't you take those
places back during that time? [27] I
haven't done anything wrong to
you. But you are doing something
wrong to me. You have gone to war
against me. The LORD is the Judge.
So let him decide our case today.
Let him settle matters between the
Israelites and the Ammonites."

[28] But the king of Ammon didn't pay
any attention to the message Jephthah
sent him.

[29] Then the Spirit of the LORD came
on Jephthah. He went across the territories of Gilead and Manasseh. He
passed through Mizpah in the land
of Gilead. From there he attacked the
people of Ammon. [30] Jephthah made
a promise to the LORD. Jephthah said,
"Hand the Ammonites over to me. [31] If
you do, here's what I'll do when I come
back from winning the battle. Anything
that comes out the door of my house to
meet me will belong to the LORD. I will
sacrifice it as a burnt offering."

[32] Then Jephthah went over to fight
against the Ammonites. The LORD
handed them over to him. [33] Jephthah
destroyed 20 towns between Aroer and
the area of Minnith. He destroyed them
all the way to Abel Keramim. So Israel
brought Ammon under their control.

[34] Jephthah returned to his home in
Mizpah. And guess who came out to
meet him. It was his daughter! She was
dancing to the beat of tambourines.
She was his only child. He didn't have
any other sons or daughters. [35] When
Jephthah saw her, he was so upset that
he tore his clothes. He cried out, "Oh no,
my daughter! You have filled me with
trouble and sorrow. I've made a promise
to the LORD. And I can't break it."

[36] "My father," she replied, "you have
given your word to the LORD. So do to
me just what you promised to do. The
Ammonites were your enemies. And the
LORD has paid them back for what they
did to you. [37] But please do one thing
for me," she continued. "Give me two
months to wander around in the hills. Let
me weep there with my friends. I want to
do that because I'll never get married."

[38] "You may go," he said. He let her
go for two months. She and her friends
went into the hills. They were filled with
sadness because she would never get

married. 39 After the two months were
over, she returned to her father. He did
to her just what he had promised to do.
And she was a virgin.

So that became a practice in Israel.
40 Each year the young women of Israel
go away for four days. They do it in
honor of the daughter of Jephthah. He
was from the land of Gilead.

Jephthah Wins the Battle Over Ephraim

12 The troops of Ephraim were called
out. The troops went across the
Jordan River to Zaphon. When they
arrived, they said to Jephthah, "You
went to fight against the Ammonites.
Why didn't you ask us to go with you?
We're going to burn down your house
over your head."

2 Jephthah answered, "I and my people were taking part in a great struggle.
We were at war with the Ammonites. I
asked you for help. But you didn't come
to save me from their power. 3 I saw that
you wouldn't help. So I put my own life
in danger. I went across the Jordan to
fight against the Ammonites. The LORD
helped me win the battle over them. So
why have you come up today to fight
against me?"

4 Then Jephthah called the men of
Gilead together. They fought against
Ephraim. The men of Gilead struck them
down. The people of Ephraim had said,
"You people of Gilead are nothing but
deserters from Ephraim and Manasseh."
5 The men of Gilead captured the places where people go across the Jordan
River to get to Ephraim. Some men of
Ephraim weren't killed in the battle.
When they arrived at the river, they
would say, "Let us go across." Then the
men of Gilead would ask each one, "Are
you from Ephraim?" Suppose he replied,
"No." 6 Then they would say, "All right.
Say 'Shibboleth.'" If he said "Sibboleth,"
the way he said the word would give him
away. He couldn't say it correctly. So
they would grab him. Then they would
kill him at one of the places where people go across the Jordan. At that time,
42,000 men of Ephraim were killed.

7 Jephthah led Israel for six years.
Then he died. He was buried in a town
in Gilead. Jephthah was from the land
of Gilead.

Ibzan, Elon and Abdon

8 After Jephthah, Ibzan from Bethlehem led Israel. 9 He had 30 sons and 30
daughters. He gave his daughters to be
married to men who were outside his
family group. He brought in 30 young
women to be married to his sons. Those
women also came from outside his family group. Ibzan led Israel for seven
years. 10 Then he died. He was buried
in Bethlehem.

11 After Ibzan, Elon led Israel. He was
from the tribe of Zebulun. Elon led Israel
for ten years. 12 Then he died. He was
buried in Aijalon. It was in the land of
Zebulun.

13 After Elon, Abdon led Israel. Abdon was the son of Hillel. Abdon was
from Pirathon. 14 He had 40 sons and
30 grandsons. They rode on 70 donkeys.
Abdon led Israel for eight years. 15 Then
he died. He was buried at Pirathon in
Ephraim. Pirathon was in the hill country of the Amalekites. Abdon was the
son of Hillel.

Samson Is Born

13 Once again the Israelites did
what was evil in the sight of the
LORD. So the LORD handed them over to
the Philistines for 40 years.

2 A certain man from Zorah was
named Manoah. He was from the tribe
of Dan. Manoah had a wife who wasn't
able to have children. 3 The angel of the
LORD appeared to Manoah's wife. He
said, "You are not able to have children.
But you are going to become pregnant.
You will have a baby boy. 4 Make sure
you do not drink any kind of wine. Also
make sure you do not eat anything that
is 'unclean.' 5 You will become pregnant.
You will have a son. The hair on his head
must never be cut. That is because the
boy will be a Nazirite. He will be set
apart to God from the day he is born. He
will take the lead in saving Israel from
the power of the Philistines."

6 Then the woman went to her husband. She told him, "A man of God came
to me. He looked like an angel of God.
His appearance was so amazing that
it filled me with great wonder. I didn't
ask him where he came from. And he
didn't tell me his name. 7 But he said to
me, 'You will become pregnant. You will
have a son. So do not drink any kind

of wine. Do not eat anything that is
"unclean." That is because the boy will
be a Nazirite. He will belong to God in
a special way from the day he is born
until the day he dies.' "
8 Then Manoah prayed to the LORD.
He said, "Pardon your servant, Lord. I
beg you to let the man of God you sent
to us come again. He told us we would
have a son. We want the man of God
to teach us how to bring up the boy."
9 God heard Manoah. And the angel
of God came again to the woman. He
came while she was out in the field. But
her husband Manoah wasn't with her.
10 The woman hurried to her husband.
She told him, "He's here! The man who
appeared to me the other day is here!"
11 Manoah got up and followed his
wife. When he came to the man, he
spoke to him. He said, "Are you the man
who talked to my wife?"
"I am," he replied.
12 So Manoah asked him, "What will
happen when your words come true?
What rules should we follow for the
boy's life and work?"
13 The angel of the LORD answered
him. He said, "Your wife must do everything I have told her to do. 14 She
must not eat anything that comes from
grapevines. She must not drink any
kind of wine. She must not eat anything
that is 'unclean.' She must do everything I have commanded her to do."
15 Manoah said to the angel of the LORD,
"We would like you to stay and eat. We
want to prepare a young goat for you."
16 The angel of the LORD replied, "Even
if I stay, I will not eat any of your food.
But if you still want to prepare a burnt
offering, you must offer it to the LORD."
Manoah didn't realize it was the angel
of the LORD.
17 Then Manoah asked the angel of the
LORD a question. "What is your name?"
he said. "We want to honor you when
your word comes true."
18 The angel replied, "Why are you
asking me what my name is? You would
not be able to understand it." 19 Manoah
got a young goat. He brought it along
with the grain offering. He sacrificed it
on a rock to the LORD. Then the LORD did
an amazing thing. It happened while
Manoah and his wife were watching.
20 A flame blazed up from the altar
toward heaven. The angel of the LORD
rose up in the flame. When Manoah and
his wife saw it, they fell with their faces
to the ground. 21 The angel of the LORD
didn't show himself again to Manoah
and his wife. Then Manoah realized it
was the angel of the LORD.
22 "We're going to die!" he said to his
wife. "We've seen God!"
23 But his wife answered, "The LORD
doesn't want to kill us. If he did, he
wouldn't have accepted a burnt offering and a grain offering from us. He
wouldn't have shown us all these things.
He wouldn't have told us we're going to
have a son."
24 Later, the woman had a baby boy.
She named him Samson. As he grew
up, the LORD blessed him. 25 The Spirit
of the LORD began to work in his life.
It happened while he was in Mahaneh
Dan. That place is between Zorah and
Eshtaol.

Samson Marries a Philistine Woman

14 Samson went down to Timnah.
There he saw a young Philistine
woman. 2 When he returned, he spoke
to his father and mother. He said, "I've
seen a Philistine woman in Timnah. Get
her for me. I want her to be my wife."
3 His father and mother replied, "Can't
we find a wife for you among your relatives? Isn't there one among any of
our people? Do you have to go to the
Philistines to get a wife? They aren't
God's people. They haven't even been
circumcised."
But Samson said to his father, "Get
her for me. She's the right one for me."
4 Samson's parents didn't know that
the LORD wanted things to happen
this way. He was working out his plans
against the Philistines. That's because
the Philistines were ruling over Israel
at that time.
5 Samson went down to Timnah. His
father and mother went with him. They
approached the vineyards of Timnah.
Suddenly a young lion came roaring
toward Samson. 6 Then the Spirit of
the LORD came powerfully on Samson.
So he tore the lion apart with his bare
hands. He did it as easily as he might
have torn a young goat apart. But he
didn't tell his father or mother what

he had done. 7 Then he went down and
talked with the woman. He liked her.
8 Some time later, he was going back
to marry her. But he turned off the road
to look at the lion's dead body. He saw
large numbers of bees and some honey
in it. 9 He dug out the honey with his
hands. He ate it as he walked along.
Then he joined his parents again. He
gave them some honey. They ate it too.
But he didn't tell them he had taken it
from the lion's dead body.
10 Samson's father went down to
see the woman. Samson had a feast
prepared there. He was following the
practice of young men when they married their wives. 11 When the people saw
Samson, they gave him 30 men to be
his companions.
12 "Let me tell you a riddle," Samson
said to the companions. "The feast will
last for seven days. Give me the answer
to the riddle before the feast ends. If you
do, I'll give you 30 linen shirts. I'll also
give you 30 sets of clothes. 13 But suppose you can't give me the answer. Then
you must give me 30 linen shirts. You
must also give me 30 sets of clothes."
"Tell us your riddle," they said. "Let's
hear it."
14 Samson replied,

"Out of the eater came something
to eat.
Out of the strong came
something sweet."

For three days they couldn't give him
the answer.
15 On the fourth day they spoke to
Samson's wife. "Get your husband to
explain the riddle for us," they said.
"If you don't, we'll burn you to death.
We'll burn up everyone in your family. Did you invite us here to steal our
property?"
16 Then Samson's wife threw herself
on him. She sobbed, "You hate me! You
don't really love me. You have given my
people a riddle. But you haven't told me
the answer."
"I haven't even explained it to my
father or mother," he replied. "So why
should I explain it to you?" 17 She cried
during the whole seven days the feast
was going on. So on the seventh day he
finally told her the answer to the riddle.
That's because she kept on asking him
to tell her. Then she explained the riddle
to her people.
18 Before sunset on the seventh day
of the feast the men of the town spoke
to Samson. They said,

"What is sweeter than honey?
What is stronger than a lion?"

Samson said to them,

"You have plowed with my young
cow.
If you hadn't, you wouldn't
have known the answer to my
riddle."

19 Then the Spirit of the LORD came
powerfully on Samson. He went down
to Ashkelon. He struck down 30 of their
men. He took everything they had with
them. And he gave their clothes to those
who had explained the riddle. Samson
was very angry as he returned to his
father's home. 20 Samson's wife was giv-
en to someone else. She was given to a
companion of Samson. The companion
had helped him at the feast.

Samson Gets Even With the Philistines

15 Later on, Samson went to visit his
wife. He took a young goat with
him. He went at the time the wheat was
being gathered. He said, "I'm going to
my wife's room." But her father wouldn't
let him go in.
2 Her father said, "I was sure you hated her. So I gave her to your companion.
Isn't her younger sister more beautiful?
Take her instead."
3 Samson said to them, "This time I
have a right to get even with the Philistines. I'm going to hurt them badly."
4 So he went out and caught 300 foxes.
He tied them in pairs by their tails. Then
he tied a torch to each pair of tails. 5 He
lit the torches. He let the foxes loose in
the fields of grain that belonged to the
Philistines. He burned up the grain that
had been cut and stacked. He burned up
the grain that was still growing. He also
burned up the vineyards and olive trees.
6 The Philistines asked, "Who did
this?" They were told, "Samson did.
He's the son-in-law of the man from
Timnah. Samson did it because his wife
was given to his companion."

So the Philistines went up and burned
the woman and her father to death.
7 Samson said to the Philistines, "Is that
how you act? Then I promise I won't stop
until I pay you back." 8 He struck them
down with heavy blows. He killed many
of them. Then he went down and stayed
in a cave. It was in the rock of Etam.
9 The Philistines went up and camped
in Judah. They spread out near Lehi.
10 The people of Judah asked, "Why have
you come to fight against us?"
"We've come to take Samson as our
prisoner," they answered. "We want to
do to him what he did to us."
11 Then 3,000 men from Judah went
to get Samson. They went down to the
cave in the rock of Etam. They said to
Samson, "Don't you realize the Philistines are ruling over us? What have you
done to us?"
Samson answered, "I only did to them
what they did to me."
12 The men of Judah said to him,
"We've come to tie you up. We're going
to hand you over to the Philistines."
Samson said, "Promise me you won't
kill me yourselves."
13 "We agree," they answered. "We'll
only tie you up and hand you over to
them. We won't kill you." So they tied
him up with two new ropes. They led
him up from the rock. 14 Samson approached Lehi. The Philistines came
toward him shouting. Then the Spirit
of the LORD came powerfully on Samson. The ropes on his arms became like
burned thread. They dropped off his
hands. 15 He found a fresh jawbone of a
donkey. He grabbed it and struck down
1,000 men.
16 Then Samson said,

"By using a donkey's jawbone
  I've made them look like
    donkeys.
By using a donkey's jawbone
  I've struck down 1,000 men."

17 Samson finished speaking. Then he
threw the jawbone away. That's why
the place was called Ramath Lehi.
18 Samson was very thirsty. So he
cried out to the LORD. He said, "You
have helped me win this great battle.
Do I have to die of thirst now? Must I fall
into the power of people who haven't
even been circumcised? They aren't
your people." 19 Then God opened up the
hollow place in Lehi. Water came out of
it. When Samson drank the water, his
strength returned. He felt as good as
new. So the spring was called En Hak-
kore. It's still there in Lehi.
20 Samson led Israel for 20 years. In
those days the Philistines were in the land.

Samson and Delilah

16 One day Samson went to Gaza.
There he saw a prostitute. He
went in to spend the night with her.
2 The people of Gaza were told, "Samson is here!" So they surrounded the
place. They hid and waited for him at
the city gate all night long. They didn't
make any move against him during
the night. They said, "Let's wait until
the sun comes up. Then we'll kill him."
3 But Samson stayed there only until
the middle of the night. Then he got up.
He took hold of the doors of the city gate.
He also took hold of the two doorposts. He
tore them loose, together with their metal
bar. He picked them up and put them on
his shoulders. Then he carried them to the
top of the hill that faces Hebron.
4 Some time later, Samson fell in love
again. The woman lived in the Valley
of Sorek. Her name was Delilah. 5 The
rulers of the Philistines went to her.
They said, "See if you can get him to
tell you the secret of why he's so strong.
Find out how we can overpower him.
Then we can tie him up. We can bring
him under our control. Each of us will
give you 28 pounds of silver."
6 So Delilah said to Samson, "Tell me
the secret of why you are so strong.
Tell me how you can be tied up and
controlled."
7 Samson answered her, "Let someone
tie me up with seven new bowstrings.
They must be strings that aren't completely dry. Then I'll become as weak
as any other man."
8 So the Philistine rulers brought sev-
en new bowstrings to her. They weren't
completely dry. Delilah tied Samson
up with them. 9 Men were hiding in the
room. She called out to him, "Samson!
The Philistines are attacking you!" But
he snapped the bowstrings easily. They
were like pieces of string that had come
too close to a flame. So the secret of
why he was so strong wasn't discovered.

10 Delilah spoke to Samson again.
"You have made me look foolish," she
said. "You told me a lie. Come on. Tell
me how you can be tied up."
11 Samson said, "Let someone tie me
tightly with new ropes. They must be
ropes that have never been used. Then
I'll become as weak as any other man."
12 So Delilah got some new ropes. She
tied him up with them. Men were hiding
in the room. She called out to him, "Samson! The Philistines are attacking you!"
But he snapped the ropes off his arms.
They fell off just as if they were threads.
13 Delilah spoke to Samson again. "All
this time you have been making me
look foolish," she said. "You have been
telling me lies. This time really tell me
how you can be tied up."

He replied, "Weave the seven braids
of my hair into the cloth on a loom.
Then tighten the cloth with a pin. If you
do, I'll become as weak as any other
man." So while Samson was sleeping,
Delilah took hold of the seven braids of
his hair. She wove them into the cloth
on a loom. 14 Then she tightened the
cloth with a pin.

Again she called out to him, "Samson!
The Philistines are attacking you!" He
woke up from his sleep. He pulled up
the pin and the loom, together with
the cloth.
15 Then she said to him, "How can you
say, 'I love you'? You won't even share
your secret with me. This is the third
time you have made me look foolish.
And you still haven't told me the secret of why you are so strong." 16 She
continued to pester him day after day.
She nagged him until he was sick and
tired of it.
17 So he told her everything. He said,
"My hair has never been cut. That's
because I've been a Nazirite since the
day I was born. A Nazirite is set apart
to God. If you shave my head, I won't
be strong anymore. I'll become as weak
as any other man."
18 Delilah realized he had told her
everything. So she sent a message to
the Philistine rulers. She said, "Come
back one more time. He has told me everything." So the rulers returned. They
brought the silver with them. 19 Delilah
got Samson to go to sleep on her lap.
Then she called for someone to shave off
the seven braids of his hair. That's how
she began to bring Samson under her
control. And he wasn't strong anymore.
20 She called out, "Samson! The Philistines are attacking you!"

He woke up from his sleep. He
thought, "I'll go out just as I did before.
I'll shake myself free." But he didn't
know that the LORD had left him.
21 Then the Philistines grabbed him.
They poked his eyes out. They took him
down to Gaza. They put bronze chains
around him. Then they made him grind
grain in the prison. 22 His head had been
shaved. But the hair on it began to grow
again.

Samson Dies

23 The rulers of the Philistines gathered together. They were going to offer a
great sacrifice to their god Dagon. They
were going to celebrate. They said, "Our
god has handed our enemy Samson
over to us."
24 When the people saw Samson, they
praised their god. They said,

"Our god has handed our enemy
over to us.
Our enemy has destroyed our
land.
He has killed large numbers of
our people."

25 After they had drunk a lot of wine,
they shouted, "Bring Samson out. Let
him put on a show for us." So they called
Samson out of the prison. He put on a
show for them.

They had him stand near the temple
pillars. 26 Then he spoke to the servant
who was holding his hand. He said,
"Put me where I can feel the pillars. I'm
talking about the ones that hold up the
temple. I want to lean against them."
27 The temple was crowded with men
and women. All the Philistine rulers were
there. About 3,000 men and women were
on the roof. They were watching Samson
put on a show. 28 Then he prayed to the
LORD. Samson said, "LORD and King,
show me that you still have concern for
me. Please, God, make me strong just
one more time. Let me pay the Philistines back for what they did to my two
eyes. Let me do it with only one blow."
29 Then Samson reached toward the two
pillars that were in the middle of the

temple. They were the ones that held up the temple. He put his right hand on one of them. He put his left hand on the other. He leaned hard against them. 30 Samson said, "Let me die together with the Philistines!" Then he pushed with all his might. The temple came down on the rulers. It fell on all the people in it. So Samson killed many more Philistines when he died than he did while he lived. 31 Then his brothers went down to get him. So did his father's whole family. All of them brought Samson back home. They buried him in the tomb of his father Manoah. It's between Zorah and Eshtaol. Samson had led Israel for 20 years.

Micah's False Gods

17 A man named Micah lived in the hill country of Ephraim. 2 He said to his mother, "Someone took 28 pounds of silver from you. I heard you curse the one who took it. I have the silver with me. I'm the one who took it."

Then his mother said, "My son, may the LORD bless you!"

3 He gave the 28 pounds of silver back to his mother. She said to him, "I'm making a promise to set apart my silver to the LORD. My son, I want you to use it to cover a statue of a god made out of wood or stone. That's why I'll give the silver back to you."

4 Micah gave the silver back to his mother. Then she gave five pounds of it to a skilled worker who made things out of silver. He used the silver for the statue. The statue was put in Micah's house.

5 That same Micah had a small temple. He made a sacred linen apron and some statues of his family gods. He appointed one of his sons to serve as his priest. 6 In those days Israel didn't have a king. The people did anything they thought was right.

7 A young Levite had been living in land that belonged to the tribe of Judah. He was from Bethlehem in Judah. 8 He left that town to look for some other place to stay. On his way he came to Micah's house. It was in the hill country of Ephraim.

9 Micah asked him, "Where are you from?"

"I'm a Levite," he said. "I'm from Bethlehem in Judah. I'm looking for a place to stay."

10 Then Micah said to him, "Live with me. Be my father and priest. I'll give you four ounces of silver a year. I'll also give you clothes and food." 11 So the Levite agreed to live with him. The young man became just like one of Micah's sons to him. 12 Then Micah appointed the Levite to serve as his priest. He lived in Micah's house. 13 Micah said, "Now I know that the LORD will be good to me. This Levite has become my priest."

The People of Dan Make Their Homes in Laish

18 In those days Israel didn't have a king.

And in those days the tribe of Dan was looking for a place where they could make their homes. They hadn't been able to take over their own share of land among the tribes of Israel. 2 So the people of Dan sent out five of their leading men from Zorah and Eshtaol. They told the men to look over the land and check it out. Those men did it for all the people of Dan. Those people told the men, "Go. Check out the land."

So they entered the hill country of Ephraim. They went to the house of Micah. That's where they spent the night. 3 When they came near Micah's house, they recognized a voice. It was the voice of the young Levite. So they turned off the road and stopped there. They asked him, "Who brought you here? What are you doing in this place? Why are you here?"

4 The Levite told them what Micah had done for him. He said, "He has hired me. I'm his priest."

5 Then they said to him, "Please ask God for advice. Try to find out whether we'll have success on our journey."

6 The priest answered them, "Go in peace. The LORD is pleased with your journey."

7 So the five men left. They came to Laish. There they saw that the people felt secure. They were living in safety. Like the people in Sidon, they were at peace. Their land had everything they needed. Things were going very well for them. They lived a long way from the people of Sidon. And they didn't think they would ever need help from anyone else.

8 The men returned to Zorah and Eshtaol. Their people asked them, "What did you find out?"

9 They answered, "Come on! Let's attack them! We've seen the land, and it is very good. Aren't you going to do something? Don't wait any longer. Go there and take it over. 10 When you get there, you will find people who aren't expecting anything bad to happen to them. Their land has plenty of room. God has handed it over to you. It's a land that has everything you will ever need."

11 So 600 men from the tribe of Dan started out from Zorah and Eshtaol. They were prepared for battle. 12 On their way they set up camp. Their camp was near Kiriath Jearim in Judah. That's why the place is called Mahaneh Dan to this day. It's west of Kiriath Jearim. 13 From there they went to the hill country of Ephraim. They came to Micah's house.

14 Then the five men who had looked over the land of Laish spoke to the other members of their tribe. They said, "Don't you know that one of these houses has a sacred linen apron in it? Some statues of family gods are there. That house also has another statue of a god covered with silver. Now you know what to do." 15 So they turned off the road and stopped there. They went to the house of the young Levite. He was at Micah's place. They greeted the young man. 16 The 600 men from Dan stood at the entrance of the gate. They were prepared for battle. 17 The five men who had looked over the land went inside. They took the statue covered with silver. They also took the family gods and the linen apron. During that time, the priest stood at the entrance of the gate. The 600 men stood there with him. They were prepared for battle.

18 When the five men went into Micah's house and took all those things, the priest spoke to them. He asked, "What are you doing?"

19 They answered him, "Be quiet! Don't say a word. Come with us. Be our father and priest. You can serve a whole tribe and family group in Israel as our priest. Isn't that better than serving just one man's family?" 20 The priest was very pleased. He took the linen apron and the family gods. He also took the statue of the god that was covered with silver. Then the priest left with the people. 21 They put their little children and their livestock in front of them. They also put everything else they owned in front of them. And they turned and went on their way.

22 The men who lived near Micah were called together. Then they left and caught up with the people of Dan. That's because Dan's people hadn't gone very far from Micah's house. 23 Those who lived near Micah shouted at them. The people of Dan turned around and asked Micah, "What's the matter with you? Why did you call out your men to fight against us?"

24 He replied, "You took away the gods I made. And you took away my priest. What do I have left? So how can you ask, 'What's the matter with you?' "

25 The people of Dan answered, "Don't argue with us. Some of the men may get angry and attack you. Then you and your family will lose your lives." 26 So the people of Dan went on their way. Micah saw that they were too strong for him. So he turned around and went back home.

27 The people of Dan took what Micah had made. They also took his priest. They continued on their way to Laish. They went there to fight against a people who were at peace and secure. The people of Dan struck them down with their swords. They burned down their city. 28 No one could save those people and their city. They lived a long way from Sidon. And they didn't think they would ever need help from anyone else. Their city was located in a valley near Beth Rehob.

The people of Dan rebuilt the city. Then they made their homes there. 29 They named it Dan. That's because they traced their family line back to Dan. He was a son of Israel. The city used to be called Laish. 30 There the people of Dan set up for themselves the statue of the god that was covered with silver. Jonathan and his sons were priests for the tribe of Dan. Jonathan was the son of Gershom, the son of Moses. Jonathan and his sons were priests until the time when the land was captured. 31 The people of Dan continued to use the statue Micah had made. They used it during the whole time the house of God was in Shiloh.

A Levite and His Concubine

19 In those days Israel didn't have a king.

There was a Levite who lived deep in the hill country of Ephraim. He got a concubine from Bethlehem in Judah. 2 But she wasn't faithful to him. She left him. She went back to her parents' home in Bethlehem in Judah. She stayed there for four months. 3 Then her husband went to see her. He tried to talk her into coming back with him. He had his servant and two donkeys with him. She took her husband into her parents' home. When her father saw him, he gladly welcomed him. 4 His father-in-law, the woman's father, begged him to stay. So the Levite remained with him for three days. He ate, drank and slept there.

5 On the fourth day they got up early. The Levite prepared to leave. But the woman's father said to his son-in-law, "Have something to eat. It will give you strength. Then you can go on your way." 6 So the two of them sat down. They ate and drank together. After that, the woman's father said, "Please stay tonight. Enjoy yourself." 7 The man got up to go. But his father-in-law talked him into staying. So he stayed there that night. 8 On the morning of the fifth day, the Levite got up to go. But the woman's father said, "Have something to eat. It will give you strength. Wait until this afternoon!" So the two of them ate together.

9 Then the man got up to leave. His concubine and his servant got up when he did. But his father-in-law, the woman's father, spoke to him again. "Look," he said. "It's almost evening. The day is nearly over. So spend another night here. Please stay. Enjoy yourself. Early tomorrow morning you can get up and go back home." 10 But the man didn't want to stay another night. So he left. He went toward Jebus. Jebus is also called Jerusalem. The Levite had his two donkeys and his concubine with him. The donkeys had saddles on them.

11 By the time the travelers came near Jebus, the day was almost over. So the servant said to his master, "Come. Let's stop at this Jebusite city. Let's spend the night here."

12 His master replied, "No. We won't go into any city where strangers live. The people there aren't Israelites. We'll continue on to Gibeah." 13 He added, "Come. Let's try to reach Gibeah or Ramah. We can spend the night in one of those places." 14 So they continued on. As they came near Gibeah in Benjamin, the sun went down. 15 They stopped there to spend the night. They went to the city's main street and sat down. But no one took them home for the night.

16 That evening an old man came into the city. He had been working in the fields. He was from the hill country of Ephraim. But he was living in Gibeah. The people who lived there were from the tribe of Benjamin. 17 The old man saw the traveler in the main street. He asked, "Where are you going? Where did you come from?"

18 The Levite answered, "We've come from Bethlehem in Judah. We're on our way to Ephraim. I live deep in the hill country there. I've been to Bethlehem. Now I'm going to the house of the LORD. But no one has taken me home for the night. 19 We have straw and feed for our donkeys. We have food and wine for ourselves. We have enough for me, the woman and the young man with us. We don't need anything."

20 "You are welcome at my house," the old man said. "I'd be happy to supply anything you might need. But don't spend the night in the street." 21 So the old man took him into his house and fed his donkeys. After the travelers had washed their feet, they had something to eat and drink.

22 They were inside enjoying themselves. But some of the evil men who lived in the city surrounded the house. They pounded on the door. They shouted to the old man who owned the house. They said, "Bring out the man who came to your house. We want to have sex with him."

23 The owner of the house went outside. He said to them, "No, my friends. Don't do such an evil thing. This man is my guest. So don't do this terrible thing. 24 Look, here is my virgin daughter. And here's the Levite's concubine. I'll bring them out to you now. You can have them. Do to them what you want to. But don't do such a terrible thing to this man."

25 The men wouldn't listen to him. So the Levite sent his concubine out to them. They forced her to have sex with

them. They raped her all night long.
As the night was ending, they let her
go. 26 At sunrise she went back to the
house where her master was staying.
She fell down at the door. She stayed
there until daylight.

27 Later that morning her master got
up. He opened the door of the house. He
stepped out to continue on his way. But
his concubine was lying there. She had
fallen at the doorway of the house. Her
hands were reaching out toward the
door. 28 He said to her, "Get up. Let's go."
But there wasn't any answer. Then he
put her dead body on his donkey. And
he started out for home.

29 When he reached home, he got a
knife. He cut up his concubine. He cut
her into 12 pieces. He sent them into all
the territories of Israel. 30 Everyone who
saw it spoke to one another. They said,
"Nothing like this has ever been seen or
done before. Nothing like this has happened since the day the Israelites came
up out of Egypt. Just imagine! We must
do something! So let's hear your ideas!"

The Israelites Punish the Tribe of Benjamin

20 Then all the Israelites came
out. They came from the whole
land between Dan and Beersheba. They
also came from the land of Gilead. All
of them gathered together in front of
the LORD at Mizpah. 2 The leaders of all
the tribes of Israel came. They took their
places among the people of God gathered together. There were 400,000 men
carrying swords. 3 The tribe of Benjamin
heard that the Israelites had gone up
to Mizpah. The Israelites said, "Tell us
how this awful thing happened."

4 So the Levite spoke. He was the
husband of the woman who had been
murdered. He said, "I and my concubine
went to Gibeah in Benjamin. We spent
the night there. 5 During the night the
men of Gibeah came after me. They surrounded the house. They were planning
to kill me. They raped my concubine,
and she died. 6 I took my concubine and
cut her into pieces. I sent one piece to
each part of Israel's territory. I did it
because the men of Gibeah had done
a very terrible thing in Israel. 7 All you
men of Israel, speak up now. Tell me
what you have decided to do."

8 All the men got up together. They
said, "None of us will go home. Not one
of us will return to his house. 9 Here is
what we'll do to Gibeah. We'll cast lots
to tell us how to attack the city. 10 We'll
take ten men out of every 100 from
all the tribes of Israel. We'll take 100
from every 1,000. We'll take 1,000 from
every 10,000. The men we take will get
supplies for the army. Then the army
will go to Gibeah in Benjamin. They'll
give Gibeah exactly what they should
get because of the terrible thing they
did in Israel." 11 So all the men of Israel
came together to fight against the city.

12 The tribes of Israel sent people to
carry a message through the whole
tribe of Benjamin. They said, "What
about this awful crime that was committed among you? 13 Hand over to us
those evil men of Gibeah. We'll put them
to death. In that way we'll get rid of
those evil people."

But the people of Benjamin wouldn't
listen to the other Israelites. 14 They
came together at Gibeah from their
towns. They came to fight against the
other Israelites. 15 Right away the people
of Benjamin gathered together 26,000
men from their towns. They were carrying swords. These men were added
to the 700 capable young men from
Gibeah. 16 Among all these men there
were 700 who were left-handed. Each
of them could sling a stone at a hair
and not miss.

17 Israel gathered 400,000 men together. They were carrying swords. All
of them were trained for battle. That
number didn't include the tribe of
Benjamin.

18 The Israelites went up to Bethel.
There they asked God, "Who should go
up first and fight against the people of
Benjamin?"

The LORD answered, "The tribe of
Judah will go first."

19 The next morning the Israelites
got up. They set up camp near Gibeah. 20 The Israelites went out to fight
against the men of Benjamin. They
took up their battle positions against
them at Gibeah. 21 The men of Benjamin
came out of Gibeah. They killed 22,000
Israelites on the field of battle that day.
22 But the Israelites cheered one another
on. They again took up their positions

in the places where they had been the first day. 23 The Israelites went and wept in front of the LORD until evening. They asked the LORD, "Should we go up again to fight against the men of Benjamin? They are our fellow Israelites."

The LORD answered, "Go up and fight against them."

24 The Israelites came near the men of Benjamin on the second day. 25 The men of Benjamin came out from Gibeah to oppose them. That time they killed 18,000 more Israelites. All the men who died had been carrying swords.

26 Then all the Israelites, the whole army, went up to Bethel. They sat there and wept in front of the LORD. They didn't eat anything that day until evening. Then they brought burnt offerings and friendship offerings to the LORD. 27 Again the Israelites spoke to the LORD. In those days the ark of the covenant of God was there. 28 Phinehas was serving as priest at the ark. He was the son of Eleazar. Eleazar was the son of Aaron. The Israelites asked, "Should we go up again to fight against the men of Benjamin? They are our fellow Israelites."

The LORD answered, "Go. Tomorrow I will hand them over to you."

29 Then Israel hid some men and had them wait all around Gibeah. 30 They went up to fight against the men of Benjamin on the third day. They took up their positions against Gibeah, just as they had done before. 31 The men of Benjamin came out to fight against them. They were drawn away from the city. They began to wound and kill the Israelites just as they had done before. About 30 men fell in battle. They fell in the open fields and on the roads. One of the roads led to Bethel. The other led to Gibeah. 32 The men of Benjamin said, "We're winning the battle over them, just as we did before." But the men of Israel said, "Let's pull back. Let's draw them away from the city to the roads."

33 All the men of Israel moved away from their places. They took up new battle positions at Baal Tamar. The men who had been hiding charged out. They came from west of Gibeah. 34 Then 10,000 of Israel's capable young men attacked Gibeah. The men of Benjamin didn't realize they were about to be destroyed. The fighting was very heavy. 35 The LORD helped Israel win the battle over Benjamin. On that day the Israelites struck down 25,100 men of Benjamin. All the men who died had been carrying swords. 36 Then the men of Benjamin saw that they had lost the battle.

The men of Israel had moved away from their positions in front of Benjamin. They had depended on the men they had hidden near Gibeah. 37 Suddenly those men who had been hiding rushed into Gibeah. They spread out. Then they killed everyone in the city with their swords. 38 The Israelites had made a plan with those who had been hiding. They had told them to send up a large cloud of smoke from the city. 39 Then the Israelites would turn around and attack.

The men of Benjamin had begun to wound and kill the men of Israel. They had struck down about 30 of them. They had said, "We're winning the battle over them, just as we did the first time." 40 But a large cloud of smoke began to go up from the city. The men of Benjamin turned around. They saw the whole city going up in smoke. 41 Then the Israelites turned around and attacked them. The men of Benjamin were terrified. They realized they were going to be destroyed. 42 So they ran away from the men of Israel. They ran toward the desert. But they couldn't escape the battle. Other Israelites came out of the towns. There they struck down the men of Benjamin. 43 Here's how it happened. The Israelites had surrounded them. They had chased them and easily caught up with them east of Gibeah. 44 So 18,000 men of Benjamin fell in battle. All of them were brave fighters. 45 Some men of Benjamin turned back. They ran toward the desert to the rock of Rimmon. As they did, the Israelites struck down 5,000 of them along the roads. They kept chasing the men of Benjamin all the way to Gidom. Along the way they struck down 2,000 more.

46 On that day 25,000 men of Benjamin fell in battle. They had been carrying swords. All of them were brave fighters. 47 But 600 of them turned back. They ran into the desert to the rock of Rimmon. They stayed there for four months. 48 The men of Israel went back to Benjamin. In all the towns they

killed the people with their swords. They even killed the animals. So they killed everything they found. They set on fire all the towns they came to.

Wives for the Men of Benjamin

21 The men of Israel had made a promise at Mizpah. They had said, "Not one of us will give his daughter to be married to a man from Benjamin."

2 The people went to Bethel. They sat there until evening in front of God. They wept loudly and bitterly. 3 "LORD, you are the God of Israel," they cried. "Why has this happened to Israel? Why is one tribe missing from Israel today?"

4 Early the next day the people built an altar. They brought burnt offerings and friendship offerings.

5 Then the Israelites asked, "Has anyone failed to come here in front of the LORD? Is anyone missing from all the tribes of Israel?" The people had made a promise. They had said that anyone who failed to come to Mizpah in front of the LORD must be put to death.

6 The Israelites were very sad because of what had happened to the tribe of Benjamin. After all, they were their fellow Israelites. "Today one tribe has been cut off from Israel," they said. 7 "How can we provide wives for the men who are left? We've made a promise in front of the LORD. We've promised not to give any of our daughters to be married to them." 8 Then they asked, "Has any tribe of Israel failed to come here to Mizpah in front of the LORD?" They discovered that no one from Jabesh Gilead had come. No one from there had gathered together with the others in the camp. 9 They counted the people. They found that none of the people of Jabesh Gilead had come to Mizpah.

10 So the community sent 12,000 fighting men to Jabesh Gilead. They directed them to take their swords and kill those living there. That included the women and children. 11 "Here is what you must do," they said. "Kill every male. Also kill every woman who is not a virgin." 12 They found 400 young women in Jabesh Gilead who had never slept with a man. So they took them to the camp at Shiloh in Canaan.

13 Then the whole community sent an offer of peace to the men of Benjamin. The men were at the rock of Rimmon. 14 So the men of Benjamin returned at that time. They were given the women of Jabesh Gilead who had been spared. But there weren't enough women for all of them.

15 The people were very sad because of what had happened to the tribe of Benjamin. The LORD had left a gap in the tribes of Israel. They weren't complete without Benjamin. 16 The elders of the community spoke up. They said, "All the women of Benjamin have been wiped out. So how will we find wives for the men who are left? 17 The men of Benjamin who are still alive need to have children," they said. "If they don't, a tribe of Israel will be wiped out. 18 But we can't give them our daughters to be their wives. We Israelites have made a promise. We've said, 'May anyone who gives a wife to a man from Benjamin be under the LORD's curse.' 19 Look, a feast is celebrated every year in Shiloh to honor the LORD. Shiloh is north of Bethel. It's east of the road that goes from Bethel to Shechem. It's south of Lebonah."

20 So they told the men of Benjamin what to do. They said, "Go. Hide in the vineyards 21 and watch. The young women of Shiloh will come out. They'll join in the dancing. When they do, run out of the vineyards. Each of you grab a young woman from Shiloh to be your wife. Then return to the land of Benjamin. 22 Their fathers or brothers might not be happy with what we're doing. If they aren't, we'll say to them, 'Do us a favor. Help the men of Benjamin. We didn't get wives for them during the battle. You aren't guilty of doing anything wrong. After all, you didn't give your daughters to them. Your daughters were stolen from you.' "

23 So that's what the men of Benjamin did. While the young women were dancing, each man caught one. He carried her away to be his wife. Then the men returned to their own share of land. They built the towns again. They made their homes in them.

24 At that time the Israelites also left. They went home to their tribes and family groups. Each one went to his own share of land.

25 In those days Israel didn't have a king. The people did anything they thought was right.

RUTH

Author: We don't know.

Old Testament History

The book of Ruth tells about a woman named Naomi who lost everything: She lost her home, her husband, and her family. During a time when food was hard to find in Israel, Naomi, her husband, and their two sons moved to a nearby nation so that they would have plenty to eat. While they were living there, Naomi's sons both married non-Israelite women. For a while, everything seemed to be going well for Naomi's family! But then Naomi's husband and two sons died. One of her daughters-in-law went back to her family, but Naomi's other daughter-in-law, Ruth, promised to stay with Naomi for the rest of her life.

Ruth willingly returned to Israel with Naomi and decided to worship the one true God even though she didn't know what would happen next in her life. God was kind and merciful to Ruth, giving her a new home and a new family through a loving man named Boaz. His name means "strength" because he was the person God chose to redeem Naomi and Ruth's lives. Boaz pointed God's people to the Redeemer, Jesus, who would take away all sadness and loneliness and give them a home with him forever. And do you know what's really special? Through Ruth and Boaz's family, Jesus would eventually be born.

Naomi Loses Her Husband and Sons

1 There was a time when Israel didn't
have kings to rule over them. But they
had leaders to help them. This is a story
about some things that happened during
that time. There wasn't enough food in
the land of Judah. So a man went to live
for a while in the country of Moab. He
was from Bethlehem in Judah. His wife
and two sons went with him. 2 The man's
name was Elimelek. His wife's name was
Naomi. The names of his two sons were
Mahlon and Kilion. They were Ephrathites
whose home had been in Bethlehem in
Judah. They went to Moab and lived there.
3 Naomi's husband Elimelek died. So
she was left with her two sons. 4 They
married women from Moab. One was
named Orpah. The other was named
Ruth. Naomi's family lived in Moab for
about ten years. 5 Then Mahlon and Kilion also died. So Naomi was left without
her two sons and her husband.

Naomi and Ruth Return to Bethlehem

6 While Naomi was in Moab, she
heard that the LORD had helped his
people. He had begun to provide food
for them again. So Naomi and her two
daughters-in-law prepared to go from
Moab back to her home. 7 She left the
place where she had been living. Her
daughters-in-law went with her. They
started out on the road that would take
them back to the land of Judah.
8 Naomi said to her two daughters-
in-law, "Both of you go back. Each of
you go to your own mother's home. You
were kind to your husbands, who have
died. You have also been kind to me. So
may the LORD be just as kind to you.
9 May the LORD help each of you find
rest in the home of another husband."
Then she kissed them goodbye. They
broke down and wept loudly. 10 They said to
her, "We'll go back to your people with you."
11 But Naomi said, "Go home, my
daughters. Why would you want to come
with me? Am I going to have any more
sons who could become your husbands?
12 Go home, my daughters. I'm too old to
have another husband. Suppose I thought
there was still some hope for me. Suppose
I married a man tonight. And later I had
sons by him. 13 Would you wait until they
grew up? Would you stay single until you
could marry them? No, my daughters. My
life is more bitter than yours. The LORD's
power has turned against me!"
14 When they heard that, they broke
down and wept again. Then Orpah
kissed her mother-in-law goodbye. But
Ruth held on to her.
15 "Look," said Naomi. "Your sister-in-
law is going back to her people and her
gods. Go back with her."
16 But Ruth replied, "Don't try to make
me leave you and go back. Where you
go I'll go. Where you stay I'll stay. Your
people will be my people. Your God will

in Ruth?

God is the Family Protector, the one who cares for his people and gives them a place in his family.

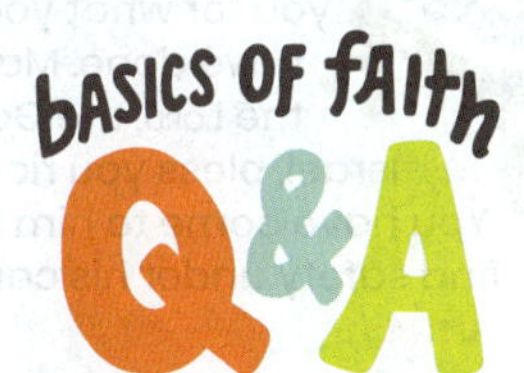

Is anyone welcome in God's family?

God invites everyone to follow him and be included in his special family. Ruth was not originally part of God's special family, but she chose to put her faith in God.

Can you find the following verse?

RUTH 1:16

be my God. 17 Where you die I'll die. And
there my body will be buried. I won't
let even death separate you from me.
If I do, may the LORD punish me greatly." 18 Naomi realized that Ruth had
made up her mind to go with her. So
she stopped trying to make her go back.
19 The two women continued on their
way. At last they arrived in Bethlehem.
The whole town was stirred up because
of them. The women in the town asked,
"Can this possibly be Naomi?"
20 "Don't call me Naomi," she told
them. "Call me Mara. The Mighty One
has made my life very bitter. 21 I was
full when I went away. But the LORD
has brought me back empty. So why
are you calling me Naomi? The LORD
has made me suffer. The Mighty One
has brought trouble on me."
22 So Naomi returned from Moab.
Ruth, her daughter-in-law from Moab,
came with her. They arrived in Bethlehem just when people were beginning
to harvest the barley.

Ruth Meets Boaz in the Grain Field

2 Naomi had a relative on her husband's side of the family. The relative's name was Boaz. He was a very
important man from the family of
Elimelek.
2 Ruth, who was from Moab, spoke
to Naomi. Ruth said, "Let me go out to
the fields. I'll pick up the grain that has
been left. I'll do it behind anyone who
is pleased with me."
Naomi said to her, "My daughter, go
ahead." 3 So Ruth went out to a field
and began to pick up grain. She worked
behind those cutting and gathering the
grain. As it turned out, she was working
in a field that belonged to Boaz. He was
from the family of Elimelek.
4 Just then Boaz arrived from Bethlehem. He greeted those cutting and
gathering the grain. He said, "May the
LORD be with you!"
"And may the LORD bless you!" they
replied.
5 Boaz spoke to the man in charge of
his workers. He asked, "Who does that
young woman belong to?"
6 The man replied, "She's from Moab.
She came back from there with Naomi.
7 The young woman said, 'Please let me
walk behind the workers. Let me pick
up the grain that is left.' She came into
the field. She has kept on working here
from morning until now. She took only
one short rest in the shade."
8 So Boaz said to Ruth, "Dear woman,
listen to me. Don't pick up grain in any
other field. Don't go anywhere else. Stay
here with the women who work for me.
9 Keep your eye on the field where the
men are cutting grain. Walk behind the
women who are gathering it. Pick up
the grain that is left. I've told the men
not to bother you. When you are thirsty,
go and get a drink. Take water from the
jars the men have filled."
10 When Ruth heard that, she bowed
down with her face to the ground. She
asked him, "Why are you being so kind
to me? In fact, why are you even no-
ticing me? I'm from another country."
11 Boaz replied, "I've been told all about
you. I've heard about everything you
have done for your mother-in-law since
your husband died. I know that you left
your father and mother. I know that you
left your country. You came to live with
people you didn't know before. 12 May
the LORD reward you for what you have
done. May the LORD, the God of Israel,
bless you richly. You have come to him
to find safety under his care."

key verse

May the LORD reward you for what you have done. May the LORD, the God of Israel, bless you richly. You have come to him to find safety under his care.

RUTH 2:12

13 "Sir, I hope you will continue to be
kind to me," Ruth said. "You have made
me feel safe. You have spoken kindly to
me. And I'm not even as important as
one of your servants!"
14 When it was time to eat, Boaz spoke
to Ruth again. "Come over here," he
said. "Have some bread. Dip it in the
wine vinegar."
She sat down with the workers. Then
Boaz offered her some grain that had
been cooked. She ate all she wanted.
She even had some left over. 15 Ruth got
up to pick up more grain. Then Boaz
gave orders to his men. He said, "Let

her take some stalks from what the women have tied up. Don't tell her she can't. 16 Even pull out some stalks for her. Leave them for her to pick up. Don't tell her she shouldn't do it."

17 So Ruth picked up grain in the field until evening. Then she separated the barley from the straw. The barley weighed 30 pounds. 18 She carried it back to town. Her mother-in-law saw how much she had gathered. Ruth also brought out the food left over from the lunch Boaz had given her. She gave it to Naomi.

19 Her mother-in-law asked her, "Where did you pick up grain today? Where did you work? May the man who noticed you be blessed!"

Then Ruth told her about the man whose field she had worked in. "The name of the man I worked with today is Boaz," she said.

20 "May the LORD bless him!" Naomi said to her daughter-in-law. "The LORD is still being kind to those who are living and those who are dead." She continued, "That man is a close relative of ours. He's one of our family protectors."

21 Then Ruth, who was from Moab, said, "He told me more. He even said, 'Stay with my workers until they have finished bringing in all my grain.' "

22 Naomi replied to her daughter-in-law Ruth. She said, "That will be good for you, my daughter. Go with the women who work for him. You might be harmed if you go to someone else's field."

23 So Ruth stayed close to the women who worked for Boaz as she picked up grain. She worked until the time when all the barley and wheat had been harvested. And she lived with her mother-in-law.

Ruth and Boaz at the Threshing Floor

3 One day Ruth's mother-in-law Naomi spoke to her. She said, "My daughter, I must find a home for you. It should be a place where you will be provided for. 2 You have been working with the women who work for Boaz. He's a relative of ours. Tonight he'll be separating the straw from his barley on the threshing floor. 3 So wash yourself. Put on some perfume. And put on your best clothes. Then go down to the threshing floor. But don't let Boaz know you are there. Wait until he has finished eating and drinking. 4 Notice where he lies down. Then go over and uncover his feet. Lie down there. He'll tell you what to do."

5 "I'll do everything you say," Ruth answered. 6 So she went down to the threshing floor. She did everything her mother-in-law had told her to do.

7 When Boaz had finished eating and drinking, he was in a good mood. He went over to lie down at the far end of the grain pile. Then Ruth approached quietly. She uncovered his feet and lay down there. 8 In the middle of the night, something surprised Boaz and woke him up. He turned and found a woman lying there at his feet!

9 "Who are you?" he asked.

"I'm Ruth," she said. "You are my family protector. So take good care of me by making me your wife."

10 "Dear woman, may the LORD bless you," he replied. "You are showing even more kindness now than you did earlier. You didn't run after the younger men, whether they were rich or poor. 11 Dear woman, don't be afraid. I'll do for you everything you ask. All the people of my town know that you are an excellent woman. 12 It's true that I'm a relative of yours. But there's a family protector who is more closely related to you than I am. 13 So stay here for the night. In the morning if he wants to help you, good. Let him help you. But if he doesn't want to, then I'll do it. You can be sure that the LORD lives. And you can be just as sure that I'll help you. Lie down here until morning."

14 So she stayed at his feet until morning. But she got up before anyone could be recognized. Boaz thought, "No one must know that a woman came to the threshing floor."

15 He said to Ruth, "Bring me the coat you have around you. Hold it out." So she did. He poured more than fifty pounds of barley into it and helped her pick it up. Then he went back to town.

16 Ruth came to her mother-in-law. Naomi asked, "How did it go, my daughter?"

Then Ruth told her everything Boaz had done for her. 17 She said, "He gave me all this barley. He said, 'Don't go back to your mother-in-law with your hands empty.' "

[18] Naomi said, "My daughter, sit down
until you find out what happens. The
man won't rest until he settles the whole
matter today."

Boaz Marries Ruth

4 Boaz went up to the town gate and
sat down there. Right then, the
family protector he had talked about
came by. Then Boaz said, "Come over
here, my friend. Sit down." So the man
went over and sat down.
[2] Boaz brought ten of the elders of
the town together. He said, "Sit down
here." So they did. [3] Then he spoke to the
family protector. He said, "Naomi has
come back from Moab. She's selling the
piece of land that belonged to our relative Elimelek. [4] I thought I should bring
the matter to your attention. I suggest
that you buy the land. Buy it while those
sitting here and the elders of my people
are looking on as witnesses. If you are
willing to buy it back, do it. But if you
aren't, tell me. Then I'll know. No one
has the right to buy it back except you.
And I'm next in line."
"I'll buy it," he said.
[5] Then Boaz said, "When you buy the
property from Naomi, you must also
marry Ruth. She is from Moab and is
the dead man's widow. So you must
marry her. That's because his property
must continue to belong to his family."
[6] When the family protector heard
that, he said, "Then I can't buy the land.
If I did, I might put my own property
in danger. So you buy it. I can't do it."
[7] In earlier times in Israel, there was
a certain practice. It was used when
family land was bought back and
changed owners. The practice made
the sale final. One person would take
his sandal off and give it to the other.
That was how people in Israel showed
that a business matter had been settled.
[8] So the family protector said to Boaz,
"Buy it yourself." And he took his sandal
off.
[9] Then Boaz said to the elders and
all the people, "Today you are witnesses. You have seen that I have bought
land from Naomi. I have bought all the
property that had belonged to Elimelek,
Kilion and Mahlon. [10] I've also taken
Ruth, who is from Moab, to become my
wife. She is Mahlon's widow. I've decided
to marry her so the dead man's name
will stay with his property. Now his
name won't disappear from his family
line or from his hometown. Today you
are witnesses!"
[11] Then the elders and all the people
at the gate said, "We are witnesses.
The woman is coming into your home.
May the LORD make her like Rachel
and Leah. Together they built up the
family of Israel. May you be an important person in Ephrathah. May you be
famous in Bethlehem. [12] The LORD will
give you children through this young
woman. May your family be like the
family of Perez. He was the son Tamar
had by Judah."

Naomi Gains a Son

[13] So Boaz married Ruth. Then he slept
with her. The LORD blessed her so that
she became pregnant. And she had a
son. [14] The women said to Naomi, "We
praise the LORD. Today he has provided
a family protector for you. May this
child become famous all over Israel!
[15] He will make your life new again. He'll
take care of you when you are old. He's
the son of your very own daughter-in-
law. She loves you. She is better to you
than seven sons."
[16] Then Naomi took the child in
her arms and took care of him. [17] The
women living there said, "Naomi has
a son!" They named him Obed. He was
the father of Jesse. Jesse was the father
of David.

[18] Here is the family line of Perez.

Perez was the father of Hezron.
[19] Hezron was the father of Ram.
Ram was the father of Amminadab.
[20] Amminadab was the father of
Nahshon.
Nahshon was the father of Salmon.
[21] Salmon was the father of Boaz.
Boaz was the father of Obed.
[22] Obed was the father of Jesse.
And Jesse was the father of David.

1 SAMUEL

Author: We don't know.

When the people of Israel were living in their new home, the promised land, God gave them a judge and a prophet named Samuel. He had a very special job: Samuel would speak to the Israelites on God's behalf and lead them to do what God commanded. His main job was to remind God's people that God was their true and perfect King. The Israelites were supposed to live under God's perfect leadership, but they wanted to be like everyone else. When the people of Israel looked at the nations surrounding them and saw that other nations had a king, they demanded that God give them a human king they could see, serve, and follow (see 1 Samuel 8:4–22).

God responded by giving the people of Israel what they wanted. He chose a tall, handsome man named Saul to be king, but Saul turned out to be a terrible, prideful king. Even though Saul looked impressive on the outside, his heart was far from God. The next man God chose was named David. When King David obeyed God, things went well for him and the people of Israel. God used these kings to teach his people something very important: While people care a lot about what others look like on the outside, God cares about people's hearts.

Old Testament History

Samuel Is Born

1 A certain man from Ramathaim
in the hill country of Ephraim was
named Elkanah. He was the son of Jeroham. Jeroham was the son of Elihu.
Elihu was the son of Tohu. Tohu was the
son of Zuph. Elkanah belonged to the
family line of Zuph. Elkanah lived in
the territory of Ephraim. 2 Elkanah had
two wives. One was named Hannah. The
other was named Peninnah. Peninnah
had children, but Hannah didn't.
3 Year after year Elkanah went up
from his town to Shiloh. He went there
to worship and sacrifice to the LORD who
rules over all. Hophni and Phinehas
served as priests of the LORD at Shiloh.
They were the two sons of Eli. 4 Every
year at Shiloh, the day would come for
Elkanah to offer a sacrifice. On that day,
he would give a share of the meat to his
wife Peninnah. He would also give a
share to each of her sons and daughters.
5 But he would give two shares of meat
to Hannah. That's because he loved her.
He also gave her two shares because
the LORD had kept her from having
children. 6 Peninnah teased Hannah
to make her angry. She did it because
the LORD had kept Hannah from having
children. 7 Peninnah teased Hannah
year after year. Every time Hannah
would go up to the house of the LORD,
Elkanah's other wife would tease her.
She would keep doing it until Hannah
cried and wouldn't eat. 8 Her husband
Elkanah would say to her, "Hannah,
why are you crying? Why don't you eat?
Why are you so unhappy? Don't I mean
more to you than ten sons?"
9 One time when they had finished
eating and drinking in Shiloh, Hannah
stood up. Eli the priest was sitting on
his chair by the doorpost of the LORD's
house. 10 Hannah was very sad. She wept
and wept. She prayed to the LORD. 11 She
made a promise to him. She said, "LORD,
you rule over all. Please see how I'm
suffering! Show concern for me! Don't
forget about me! Please give me a son!
If you do, I'll give him back to the LORD.
Then he will serve the LORD all the days
of his life. He'll never use a razor on his
head. He'll never cut his hair."
12 As Hannah kept on praying to the
LORD, Eli watched her lips. 13 She was
praying in her heart. Her lips were
moving. But she wasn't making a sound.
Eli thought Hannah was drunk. 14 He
said to her, "How long are you going to
stay drunk? Stop drinking your wine."
15 "That's not true, sir," Hannah replied. "I'm a woman who is deeply
troubled. I haven't been drinking wine
or beer. I was telling the LORD all my
troubles. 16 Don't think of me as an evil
woman. I've been praying here because
I'm very sad. My pain is so great."
17 Eli answered, "Go in peace. May the
God of Israel give you what you have
asked him for."
18 She said, "May you be pleased with
me." Then she left and had something
to eat. Her face wasn't sad anymore.
19 Early the next morning Elkanah
and his family got up. They worshiped
the LORD. Then they went back to their
home in Ramah. Elkanah slept with
his wife Hannah. And the LORD blessed
her. 20 So after some time, Hannah became pregnant. She had a baby boy.
She said, "I asked the LORD for him."
So she named him Samuel.

Hannah Gives Samuel to the LORD

21 Elkanah went up to Shiloh to offer
the yearly sacrifice to the LORD. He also
went there to keep a promise he had
made. His whole family went with him.
22 But Hannah didn't go. She said to her
husband, "When the boy doesn't need
me to breast-feed him anymore, I'll
take him to the LORD's house. I'll give
him to the LORD there. He'll stay there
for the rest of his life."
23 Her husband Elkanah told her, "Do
what you think is best. Stay here at
home until Samuel doesn't need you
to breast-feed him anymore. May the
LORD make his promise to you come
true." So Hannah stayed home. She
breast-fed her son until he didn't need
her milk anymore.
24 When the boy didn't need her to
breast-feed him anymore, she took him
with her to Shiloh. She took him there
even though he was still very young. She
brought him to the LORD's house. She
brought along a bull that was three years
old. She brought 36 pounds of flour. She
also brought a bottle of wine. The bottle
was made out of animal skin. 25 After the
bull was sacrificed, Elkanah and Hannah
brought the boy to Eli. 26 Hannah said

to Eli, "Pardon me, sir. I'm the woman who stood here beside you praying to the LORD. And that's just as sure as you are alive. 27 I prayed for this child. The LORD has given me what I asked him for. 28 So now I'm giving him to the LORD. As long as he lives he'll be given to the LORD." And there Eli worshiped the LORD.

Hannah's Prayer

2 Then Hannah prayed. She said,

"The LORD has filled my heart with joy.
He has made me strong.
I can laugh at my enemies.
I'm so glad he saved me.

2 "There isn't anyone holy like the LORD.
There isn't anyone except him.
There isn't any Rock like our God.

3 "Don't keep talking so proudly.
Don't let your mouth say such proud things.
The LORD is a God who knows everything.
He judges everything people do.

4 "The bows of great heroes are broken.
But those who trip and fall are made strong.
5 Those who used to be full have to work for food.
But those who used to be hungry aren't hungry anymore.
The woman who couldn't have children has seven of them now.
But the woman who has had many children is sad now because hers have died.

6 "The LORD causes people to die. He also gives people life.
He brings people down to the grave. He also brings people up from death.
7 The LORD makes people poor. He also makes people rich.
He brings people down. He also lifts people up.
8 He raises poor people up from the trash pile.
He lifts needy people out of the ashes.
He lets them sit with princes.
He gives them places of honor.

God is the Coming King. He came through his Son, Jesus, humbly serving others as the perfect King who would rule forever.

"The foundations of the earth belong to the LORD.
On them he has set the world.
9 He guards the paths of his faithful servants.
But evil people will lie silent in their dark graves.

"People don't win just because they are strong.
10 Those who oppose the LORD will be totally destroyed.
The Most High God will thunder from heaven.
The LORD will judge the earth from one end to the other.

"He will give power to his king.
He will give honor to his anointed one."

11 Then Elkanah went home to Ramah.
But the boy Samuel served the LORD
under the direction of Eli the priest.

Eli's Evil Sons

12 Eli's sons were good for nothing.
They didn't honor the LORD. 13 When any
of the people came to offer a sacrifice,
here is what the priests would do. While
the meat was being boiled, the servant
of the priest would come with a large
fork in his hand. 14 He would stick the
fork into the pan or pot or small or large
kettle. Then the priest would take for
himself everything the fork brought
up. That's how Eli's sons treated all the
Israelites who came to Shiloh. 15 Even

before the fat was burned, the priest's
servant would come over. He would
speak to the person who was offering
the sacrifice. He would say, "Give the
priest some meat to cook. He won't accept boiled meat from you. He'll only
accept raw meat."
16 Sometimes the person would say to
him, "Let the fat be burned first. Then
take what you want." But the servant
would answer, "No. Hand it over right
now. If you don't, I'll take it away from
you by force."
17 That sin of Eli's sons was very great in
the LORD's sight. That's because they were
not treating his offering with respect.
18 But the boy Samuel served the LORD.
He wore a sacred linen apron. 19 Each
year his mother made him a little robe.
She took it to him when she went up to
Shiloh with her husband. She did it when
her husband went to offer the yearly
sacrifice. 20 Eli would bless Elkanah and
his wife. He would say, "May the LORD
give you children by this woman. May
they take the place of the boy she prayed
for and gave to the LORD." Then they
would go home. 21 The LORD was gracious
to Hannah. Over a period of years she
had three more sons and two daughters.
During that whole time the boy Samuel
grew up serving the LORD.
22 Eli was very old. He kept hearing
about everything his sons were doing
to all the Israelites. He also heard how
his sons were sleeping with the women
who served at the entrance to the tent
of meeting. 23 So Eli said to his sons,
"Why are you doing these things? All
the people are telling me about the evil
things you are doing. 24 No, my sons.
The report I hear isn't good. And it's
spreading among the LORD's people. 25 If
a person sins against someone else, God
can help that sinner. But if anyone sins
against the LORD, who can help them?"
In spite of what their father Eli said, his
sons didn't pay any attention to his
warning. That's because the LORD had
already decided to put them to death.
26 The boy Samuel continued to grow
stronger. He also became more and more
pleasing to the LORD and to people.

Prophecy Against Eli's Family

27 A man of God came to Eli. He told
him, "The LORD says, 'I made myself
clearly known to your relatives who
lived long ago. I did it when they were
in Egypt under Pharaoh's rule. 28 At that
time, I chose Aaron from your family
line to be my priest. I chose him out
of all the tribes of Israel. I told him to
go up to my altar. I told him to burn
incense. I chose him to wear a linen
apron when he served me. I also gave
his family all the food offerings presented by the Israelites. 29 Why don't you
treat my sacrifices and offerings with
respect? I require them to be brought
to the house where I live. Why do you
honor your sons more than me? Why
do you fatten yourselves on the best
parts of every offering that is made by
my people Israel?'
30 "The LORD is the God of Israel. He
announced, 'I promised that members
of your family line would serve me as
priests forever.' But now the LORD announces, 'I will not let that happen! I
will honor those who honor me. But
I will turn away from those who look
down on me. 31 The time is coming when
I will cut your life short. I will also cut
short the lives of those in your family
line of priests. No one in your family
line will grow old. 32 You will see nothing
but trouble in the house where I live.
Good things will still happen to Israel.
But no one in your family line will ever
grow old. 33 I will prevent the members
of your family from serving me at my
altar. I will destroy the eyesight of all
of you I allow to live. I will also cause
you to lose your strength. And everyone
in your family line will die while they
are still young.
34 " 'Something is going to happen to
your two sons, Hophni and Phinehas.
When it does, it will show you that what
I am saying is true. They will both die
on the same day. 35 I will raise up for
myself a faithful priest. He will do what
my heart and mind want him to do.
I will make his family line of priests
very secure. They will always serve as
priests to my anointed king. 36 Everyone
left in your family line will come and
bow down to him. They will beg him
for a piece of silver and a loaf of bread.
They will say, "Please give me a place
to serve among the priests. Then I can
have food to eat." ' "

The LORD Calls Out to Samuel

3 The boy Samuel served the LORD
under the direction of Eli. In those
days the LORD didn't give many messages to his people. He didn't give them
many visions.
[2]One night Eli was lying down in his
usual place. His eyes were becoming so
weak he couldn't see very well. [3]Samuel
was lying down in the LORD's house.
That's where the ark of God was kept.
The lamp of God was still burning. [4]The
LORD called out to Samuel.

Samuel answered, "Here I am." [5]He
ran over to Eli and said, "Here I am. You
called out to me."

But Eli said, "I didn't call you. Go back
and lie down." So he went and lay down.
[6]Again the LORD called out, "Samuel!"
Samuel got up and went to Eli. He said,
"Here I am. You called out to me."

"My son," Eli said, "I didn't call you.
Go back and lie down."
[7]Samuel didn't know the LORD yet.
That's because the LORD still hadn't
given him a message.
[8]The LORD called out for the third
time. He said, "Samuel!" Samuel got
up and went to Eli. He said, "Here I am.
You called out to me."

Then Eli realized that the LORD was
calling the boy. [9]So Eli told Samuel,
"Go and lie down. If someone calls out
to you again, say, 'Speak, LORD. I'm
listening.' " So Samuel went and lay
down in his place.
[10]The LORD came and stood there.
He called out, just as he had done the
other times. He said, "Samuel! Samuel!"

Then Samuel replied, "Speak. I'm
listening."
[11]The LORD said to Samuel, "Pay attention! I am about to do something
terrible in Israel. It will make the ears of
everyone who hears about it tingle. [12]At
that time I will do everything to Eli and
his family that I said I would. I will finish
what I have started. [13]I told Eli I would
punish his family forever. He knew his
sons were sinning. He knew they were
saying bad things about me. In spite of
that, he did not stop them. [14]So I made a
promise to the family of Eli. I said, 'The
sins of Eli's family will never be paid
for by bringing sacrifices or offerings.' "
[15]Samuel lay down until morning.
Then he opened the doors of the LORD's
house. He was afraid to tell Eli about the
vision he had received. [16]But Eli called
out to him. He said, "Samuel, my son."

Samuel answered, "Here I am."
[17]"What did the LORD say to you?" Eli
asked. "Don't hide from me anything
he told you. If you do, may God punish
you greatly." [18]So Samuel told him everything. He didn't hide anything from
him. Then Eli said, "He is the LORD. Let
him do what he thinks is best."
[19]As Samuel grew up, the LORD was
with him. He made everything Samuel
said come true. [20]So all the Israelites
recognized that Samuel really was a
prophet of the LORD. Everyone from
Dan all the way to Beersheba knew
it. [21]The LORD continued to appear at
Shiloh. There he made himself known
to Samuel through the messages he
gave him.

4 And Samuel gave those messages
to all the Israelites.

The Philistines Capture the Ark

The Israelites went out to fight against
the Philistines. The Israelites camped
at Ebenezer. The Philistines camped at
Aphek. [2]The Philistines brought their
forces together to fight against Israel. As
the fighting spread, the Israelites lost the
battle to the Philistines. The Philistines
killed about 4,000 of them on the field
of battle. [3]The rest of the Israelite soldiers returned to camp. Then the elders
asked them, "Why did the LORD let the
Philistines win the battle over us today?
Let's bring the ark of the LORD's covenant
from Shiloh. Let's take it with us. Then
the LORD will save us from the power of
our enemies."
[4]So the people sent men to Shiloh.
They brought back the ark of the LORD's
covenant law. He sits there on his throne
between the cherubim. The LORD is the
one who rules over all. Eli's two sons,
Hophni and Phinehas, were with the
ark of God's covenant law. The ark was
in Shiloh.
[5]The ark of the LORD's covenant law
was brought into the camp. Then all
the Israelites shouted so loudly that the
ground shook. [6]The Philistines heard
the noise. They asked, "What's all that
shouting about in the Hebrew camp?"

Then the Philistines found out that the
ark of the LORD had come into the camp.

7 So they were afraid. "A god has come into
their camp," they said. "Oh no! Nothing
like this has ever happened before. 8 How
terrible it will be for us! Who will save us
from the power of these mighty gods?
They struck down the people of Egypt in
the desert. They sent all kinds of plagues
on them. 9 Philistines, be strong! Fight like
men! If you don't, you will come under the
control of the Hebrews. You will become
their slaves, just as they have been your
slaves. Fight like men!"

10 So the Philistines fought. The Israelites lost the battle, and every man
ran back to his tent. A large number
of them were killed. Israel lost 30,000
soldiers who were on foot. 11 The ark of
God was captured. And Eli's two sons
Hophni and Phinehas died.

Eli Dies

12 That same day a man from the tribe
of Benjamin ran from the front lines
of the battle. He went to Shiloh. His
clothes were torn. He had dust on his
head. 13 When he arrived, there was Eli
sitting on his chair. He was by the side of
the road. He was watching because his
heart was really concerned about the
ark of God. The man entered the town
and told everyone what had happened.
Then the whole town cried out.

14 Eli heard the people crying out.
He asked, "What's the meaning of all
this noise?"

The man hurried over to Eli. 15 Eli was
98 years old. His eyes were so bad he
couldn't see. 16 The man told Eli, "I've
just come from the front lines of the battle. I just ran away from there today."

Eli asked, "What happened, son?"

17 The man who brought the news
replied, "Israel ran away from the
Philistines. Large numbers of men
in the army were wounded or killed.
Your two sons Hophni and Phinehas
are also dead. And the ark of God has
been captured."

18 When the man spoke about the ark
of God, Eli fell backward off his chair.
He had been sitting by the side of the
gate. When he fell, he broke his neck
and died. He was old and fat. He had
led Israel for 40 years.

19 The wife of Phinehas was pregnant.
She was Eli's daughter-in-law. It was
near the time for her baby to be born.
She heard the news that the ark of God
had been captured. She heard that her
father-in-law and her husband were
dead. So she went into labor and had
her baby. Her pain was more than she
could bear. 20 As she was dying, the
women helping her spoke up. They
said, "Don't be afraid. You have had
a son." But she didn't reply. She didn't
pay any attention.

21 She named the boy Ichabod. She
said, "The God of glory has left Israel."
She said it because the ark of God had
been captured. She also said it because
her father-in-law and her husband had
died. 22 She said, "The God of glory has
left Israel." She said it because the ark
of God had been captured.

The Ark in Ashdod and Ekron

5 The Philistines had captured the
ark of God. They took it from
Ebenezer to Ashdod. 2 They carried the
ark into the temple of their god Dagon.
They set it down beside the statue of
Dagon. 3 The people of Ashdod got up
early the next day. They saw the statue
of Dagon. There it was, lying on the
ground! It had fallen on its face in front
of the ark of the LORD. So they picked up
the statue of Dagon. They put it back in
its place. 4 But the following morning
when they got up, they saw the statue
of Dagon. There it was, lying on the
ground again! It had fallen on its face
in front of the ark of the LORD. Its head
and hands had been broken off. Only
the body of the statue was left. Its head
and hands were lying in the doorway
of the temple. 5 That's why to this day
no one steps on the bottom part of the
doorway of Dagon's temple at Ashdod.
Not even the priests of Dagon step there.

6 The LORD's power was against the
people of Ashdod and the settlements
near it. He destroyed them. He made
them suffer with growths in their bodies. 7 The people of Ashdod saw what was
happening. They said, "The ark of the
god of Israel must not stay here with us.
His power is against us and against our
god Dagon." 8 So they called together all
the rulers of the Philistines. They asked
them, "What should we do with the ark
of the god of Israel?"

The rulers answered, "Have the ark
moved to Gath." So they moved it.

9 But after the people of Ashdod had
moved the ark, the LORD's power was
against Gath. That threw its people into
a great panic. The LORD made them
break out with growths in their bodies.
It happened to young people and old
people alike. 10 So the ark of God was
sent to Ekron.

As the ark was entering Ekron, the
people of the city cried out. They shouted, "They've brought the ark of the god
of Israel to us. They want to kill us and
our people." 11 So they called together all
the rulers of the Philistines. They said,
"Send the ark of the god of Israel away.
Let it go back to its own place. If you
don't, it will kill us and our people." The
death of so many people had filled the
city with panic. God's power was against
the city. 12 Those who didn't die suffered
with growths in their bodies. The people
of Ekron cried out to heaven for help.

The Philistines Return the Ark to Israel

6 The ark of the LORD had been in Philistine territory for seven months.
2 The Philistines called for the priests
and for those who practice evil magic.
They wanted their advice. They said to
them, "What should we do with the ark
of the LORD? Tell us how we should send
it back to its place."

3 They answered, "If you return the
ark of the god of Israel, don't send it
back to him without a gift. Be sure you
send a guilt offering to their god along
with it. Then you will be healed. You will
find out why his power has continued
to be against you."

4 The Philistines asked, "What guilt
offering should we send to him?"

Their advisers replied, "There are five
Philistine rulers. So send five gold rats.
Also send five gold models of the growths
in your bodies. Do it because the same
plague has struck you and your rulers
alike. 5 Make models of the rats and the
growths that are destroying the country.
Give honor to Israel's god. Then perhaps
his power will no longer be against you,
your gods and your land. 6 Why are you
stubborn, as Pharaoh and the people of
Egypt were? Israel's god was very hard
on them. Only then did they send the
Israelites out. Only then did they let
them go on their way.

7 "Now then, get a new cart ready. Get
two cows that have just had calves. Be
sure the cows have never pulled a cart
before. Tie the cart to them. But take
their calves away and put them in a
pen. 8 Then put the ark of the LORD on
the cart. Put the gold models in a chest
beside the ark. Send them back to the
LORD as a guilt offering. Send the cart
on its way. 9 But keep an eye on the cart.
See if it goes up toward Beth Shemesh
to its own territory. If it does, then it's
the LORD who has brought this horrible
trouble on us. But if it doesn't, then we'll
know it wasn't his hand that struck us.
We'll know it happened to us by chance."

10 So that's what they did. They took
the two cows and tied the cart to them.
They put the calves in a pen. 11 They
placed the ark of the LORD on the cart.
They put the chest there along with it.
The chest held the gold models of the
rats and of the growths. 12 Then the cows
went straight up toward Beth Shemesh.
They stayed on the road. They were
mooing all the way. They didn't turn
to the right or the left. The Philistine
rulers followed them all the way to the
border of Beth Shemesh.

13 The people of Beth Shemesh were
working in the valley. They were gathering their wheat crop. They looked up
and saw the ark. When they saw it, they
were filled with joy. 14 The cart came to
the field of Joshua of Beth Shemesh. It
stopped there beside a large rock. The
people chopped up the wood the cart
was made out of. They sacrificed the
cows as a burnt offering to the LORD.
15 Some Levites had taken the ark of the
LORD off the cart. They had also taken
off the chest that held the gold models.
They placed them on the large rock. On
that day the people of Beth Shemesh
offered burnt offerings to the LORD.
They also made sacrifices to him. 16 The
five Philistine rulers saw everything
that happened. On that same day they
returned to Ekron.

17 The Philistines sent gold models of
growths as a guilt offering to the LORD.
There was one each for Ashdod, Gaza,
Ashkelon, Gath and Ekron. 18 They also
sent five gold models of rats. There was
one for each of the Philistine towns that
belonged to the five rulers. Each of those
towns had high walls around it. The

towns also had country villages around
them. The Levites set the ark of the LORD
on the large rock. To this day the rock is
a witness to what happened there. It's
in the field of Joshua of Beth Shemesh.
19 But some of the people of Beth
Shemesh looked into the ark of the
LORD. So he struck them down. He put 70
of them to death. The rest of the people
were filled with sorrow. That's because
the LORD had killed so many of them.
20 The people of Beth Shemesh said,
"The LORD is a holy God. Who can stand
in front of him? Where can the ark go
up to from here?"
21 Then messengers were sent to the
people of Kiriath Jearim. The messengers said, "The Philistines have returned
the ark of the LORD. Come down and
7 take it up to your town." 1 So the
men of Kiriath Jearim came and
got the ark of the LORD. They brought
it up to Abinadab's house on the hill.
They set his son Eleazar apart to guard
the ark. 2 The ark remained at Kiriath
Jearim for a long time. It was there for
a full 20 years.

Samuel Brings the Philistines Under Israel's Control

Then all the Israelites turned back
to the LORD. 3 So Samuel spoke to all
the Israelites. He said, "Do you really
want to return to the LORD with all your
hearts? If you do, get rid of your false
gods. Get rid of your statues of female
gods that are named Ashtoreth. Commit
yourselves to the LORD. Serve him only.
Then he will save you from the power
of the Philistines." 4 So the Israelites put
away their statues of gods that were
named Baal. They put away their statues of female gods that were named
Ashtoreth. They served the LORD only.
5 Then Samuel said, "Gather all the
Israelites together at Mizpah. I will pray
to the LORD for you." 6 When the people
had come together at Mizpah, they went
to the well and got water. They poured it
out in front of the LORD. On that day they
didn't eat any food. They admitted they
had sinned. They said, "We've sinned
against the LORD." Samuel was serving
as the leader of Israel at Mizpah.
7 The Philistines heard that Israel
had gathered together at Mizpah. So
the Philistine rulers came up to attack
them. When the Israelites heard about
it, they were afraid. 8 They said to Samuel, "Don't stop crying out to the LORD
our God to help us. Keep praying that
he'll save us from the power of the
Philistines." 9 Then Samuel got a very
young lamb. He sacrificed it as a whole
burnt offering to the LORD. He cried out
to the LORD to help Israel. And the LORD
answered his prayer.
10 The Philistines came near to attack
Israel. At that time Samuel was sacrificing
the burnt offering. But that day the LORD
thundered loudly against the Philistines.
He threw them into such a panic that the
Israelites were able to chase them away.
11 The men of Israel rushed out of Mizpah.
They chased the Philistines all the way to
a point below Beth Kar. They killed them
all along the way.
12 Then Samuel got a big stone. He
set it up between Mizpah and Shen. He
named it Ebenezer. He said, "The LORD
has helped us every step of the way."
13 So the Philistines were brought
under Israel's control. The Philistines
didn't attack their territory again. The
LORD used his power against the Philistines as long as Samuel lived. 14 The
Philistines had captured many towns
between Ekron and Gath. But they had
to give all of them back. Israel took back
the territories near those towns from
the control of the Philistines. During
that time Israel and the Amorites were
friendly toward each other.
15 Samuel continued to lead Israel
all the days of his life. 16 From year to
year he traveled from Bethel to Gilgal
to Mizpah. He served Israel as judge in
all those places. 17 But he always went
back to Ramah. That's where his home
was. He served Israel as judge there too.
And he built an altar there to honor
the LORD.

Israel Asks for a King

8 When Samuel became old, he appointed his sons as Israel's leaders.
2 The name of his oldest son was Joel.
The name of his second son was Abijah.
They served as judges at Beersheba.
3 But his sons didn't live as he did. They
were only interested in making money.
They accepted money from people who
wanted special favors. They made things
that were wrong appear to be right.

4 So all the elders of Israel gathered together. They came to Samuel at Ramah.
5 They said to him, "You are old. Your
sons don't live as you do. So appoint a
king to lead us. We want a king just like
the kings all the other nations have."
6 Samuel wasn't pleased when they
said, "Give us a king to lead us." So he
prayed to the LORD. 7 The LORD told
him, "Listen to everything the people
are saying to you. You are not the one
they have turned their backs on. I am
the one they do not want as their king.
8 They are doing just as they have always done. They have deserted me
and served other gods. They have done
that from the time I brought them up
out of Egypt until this day. Now they
are deserting you too. 9 Let them have
what they want. But give them a strong
warning. Let them know what the king
who rules over them will expect to be
done for him."
10 Samuel told the people who were
asking him for a king everything the
LORD had said. 11 Samuel told them,
"Here's what the king who rules over
you will expect to be done for him. He
will take your sons. He'll make them
serve with his chariots and horses.
They will run in front of his chariots.
12 He'll choose some of your sons to be
commanders of thousands of men.
Some will be commanders of fifties.
Others will have to plow his fields and
gather his crops. Still others will have
to make weapons of war and parts
for his chariots. 13 He'll also take your
daughters. Some will have to make
perfume. Others will be forced to cook
and bake. 14 He will take away your best
fields and vineyards and olive groves.
He'll give them to his attendants. 15 He
will take a tenth of your grain and a
tenth of your grapes. He'll give it to his
officials and attendants. 16 He will also
take your male and female servants.
He'll take your best cattle and donkeys.
He'll use all of them any way he wants
to. 17 He will take a tenth of your sheep
and goats. You yourselves will become
his slaves. 18 When that time comes, you
will cry out for help because of the king
you have chosen. But the LORD won't
answer you at that time."
19 In spite of what Samuel said, the
people refused to listen to him. "No!"
they said. "We want a king to rule over
us. 20 Then we'll be like all the other
nations. We'll have a king to lead us.
He'll go out at the head of our armies
and fight our battles."
21 Samuel heard everything the people said. He told the LORD about it. 22 The
LORD answered, "Listen to them. Give
them a king."
Then Samuel said to the Israelites,
"Each of you go back to your own town."

Samuel Anoints Saul to Be Israel's King

9 There was a man named Kish from
the tribe of Benjamin. Kish was a
very important person. He was the son
of Abiel, the son of Zeror. Zeror was the
son of Bekorath, the son of Aphiah from
the tribe of Benjamin. 2 Kish had a son
named Saul. Saul was a handsome
young man. He was more handsome
than anyone in Israel. And he was a
head taller than anyone else.
3 The donkeys that belonged to Saul's
father Kish were lost. So Kish spoke to
his son Saul. He said, "Go and look for
the donkeys. Take one of the servants
with you." 4 Saul and his servant went
through the hill country of Ephraim.
They also went through the area around
Shalisha. But they didn't find the donkeys. So they went on into the area of
Shaalim. But the donkeys weren't there
either. Then Saul went through the territory of Benjamin. But they still didn't
find the donkeys.
5 When Saul and the servant with him
reached the area of Zuph, Saul spoke to
the servant. He said, "Come on. Let's go
back. If we don't, my father will stop
thinking about the donkeys. Instead,
he'll start worrying about us."
6 But the servant replied, "There's
a man of God here in Ramah. People
have a lot of respect for him. Everything
he says comes true. So let's go and see
him now. Perhaps he'll tell us which
way to go."
7 Saul said to his servant, "If we go
to see the man, what can we give him?
There isn't any food in our sacks. We
don't have a gift for the man of God.
So what can we give him?"
8 The servant answered Saul again.
"Look," he said. "I've got a tenth of an
ounce of silver. I'll give it to the man

of God. Then maybe he'll tell us which
way to go." 9In Israel, prophets used to
be called seers. So if someone wanted
to ask God for advice, they would say,
"Come on. Let's go to the seer."
10Saul said to his servant, "That's a
good idea. Come on. Let's go and ask the
seer." So they started out for the town
where the man of God lived.
11They were going up the hill toward
the town. Along the way they met some
young women who were coming out to
get water from the well. Saul and his
servant asked them, "Is the seer here?"
12"Yes, he is," they answered. "In fact,
he's just up ahead of you. So hurry along.
He has just come to our town today. The
people are going to offer a sacrifice at
the high place where they worship. 13As
soon as you enter the town, you will find
him. He'll be there until he goes up to
the high place to eat. The people won't
start eating until he gets there. He must
bless the sacrifice first. After that, those
who are invited will eat. So go on up. You
should find him there just about now."
14They went up to the town. As they
were entering it, they saw Samuel. He
was coming toward them. He was on
his way up to the high place.
15The LORD had spoken to Samuel
the day before Saul came. He had said,
16"About this time tomorrow I will send
you a man. He is from the land of Benjamin. Anoint him to be the king of my
people Israel. He will save them from
the power of the Philistines. I have seen
how much my people are suffering.
Their cry for help has reached me."
17When Samuel saw a man coming
toward him, the LORD spoke to Samuel
again. He said, "He is the man I told you
about. His name is Saul. He will govern
my people."
18Saul approached Samuel at the gate
of the town. He asked Samuel, "Can
you please show me the seer's house?"
19"I'm the seer," Samuel replied. "Go
on up to the high place ahead of me. I
want you and your servant to eat with
me today. Tomorrow morning I'll tell
you what's on your mind. Then I'll send
you on your way. 20Don't worry about
the donkeys you lost three days ago.
They've already been found. But who
do all the Israelites want? You and your
father's whole family!"
21Saul answered, "But I'm from the
tribe of Benjamin. It's the smallest tribe
in Israel. And my family group is the least
important in the whole tribe of Benjamin.
So why are you saying that to me?"
22Then Samuel brought Saul and his
servant into the room where they would
be eating. He seated them at the head
table. About 30 people had been invited.
23Samuel said to the cook, "Bring the
piece of meat I gave you. It's the one I
told you to put to one side."
24So the cook went and got a choice
piece of thigh. He set it in front of Saul.
Samuel said, "Here is what has been
kept for you. Eat it. It was put to one
side for you for this special occasion.
We've saved it for you ever since I invited the guests." And Saul ate with
Samuel that day.
25They came down from the high
place to the town. After that, Samuel
talked with Saul on the roof of Samuel's house. 26The next day they got
up at about the time the sun was rising.
Samuel called out to Saul on the roof.
He said, "Get ready. Then I'll send you
on your way." So Saul got ready. And
he and Samuel went outside together.
27As they were on their way down to
the edge of town, Samuel spoke to Saul.
He said, "Tell the servant to go ahead
of us." So the servant went on ahead.
Then Samuel continued, "Stay here for a
while. I'll give you a message from God."
10 Then Samuel took a bottle of
olive oil. He poured it on Saul's
head and kissed him. He said, "The LORD
has anointed you to be the king of his
people. 2When you leave me today,
you will meet two men. They will be
near Rachel's tomb at Zelzah on the
border of Benjamin. They'll say to you,
'The donkeys you have been looking for
have been found. Now your father has
stopped thinking about them. Instead,
he's worried about you. He's asking,
"What can I do to find my son?"'
3"You will go on from Zelzah until
you come to the large tree at Tabor.
Three men will meet you there. They'll
be on their way up to Bethel to worship
God. One of them will be carrying three
young goats. Another will be carrying
three loaves of bread. A third will be
carrying a bottle of wine. It will be a
bottle made out of animal skin. 4The

men will greet you. They'll offer you
two loaves of bread. You will accept the
loaves from them.

5 "After that, you will go to Gibeah
of God. Some Philistine soldiers are
stationed there. As you approach the
town, you will meet a group of prophets.
They'll be coming down from the high
place where they worship. People will
be playing lyres, tambourines, flutes
and harps at the head of the group. The
prophets will be prophesying. 6 The Spirit
of the LORD will come powerfully on you.
Then you will prophesy along with them.
You will become a different person. 7 All
these things will happen. Then do what
you want to do. God is with you.

8 "Go down ahead of me to Gilgal. You
can be sure that I'll come down to you
there. I'll come and sacrifice burnt offerings and friendship offerings. But you
must wait there for seven days until I
come to you. Then I'll tell you what to do."

Saul Becomes King of Israel

9 As Saul turned to leave Samuel, God
changed Saul's heart. All these things
happened that day. 10 When Saul and
his servant arrived at Gibeah, a group
of prophets met Saul. Then the Spirit of
God came powerfully on him. He prophesied along with them. 11 Those who had
known Saul before saw him prophesying
with the prophets. They asked one another, "What has happened to the son of
Kish? Is Saul also one of the prophets?"

12 A man who lived in Gibeah answered, "Yes, he is. In fact, he's their
leader." That's why people say, "Is Saul
also one of the prophets?" 13 After Saul
stopped prophesying, he went to the
high place to worship.

14 Later, Saul's uncle spoke to him and
his servant. He asked, "Where have you
been?"

"Looking for the donkeys," Saul said.
"But we couldn't find them. So we went
to Samuel."

15 Saul's uncle said, "Tell me what
Samuel said to you."

16 Saul replied, "He told us the donkeys had been found." But Saul didn't
tell his uncle that Samuel had said he
would become king.

17 Samuel sent a message to the Israelites. He told them to meet with the
LORD at Mizpah. 18 He said to them, "The
LORD is the God of Israel. He says, 'Israel,
I brought you up out of Egypt. I saved
you from their power. I also saved you
from the power of all the kingdoms that
had treated you badly.' 19 But now you
have turned your backs on your God.
He saves you out of all your trouble
and suffering. In spite of that, you have
said, 'We refuse to listen. Place a king
over us.' So now gather together to meet
with the LORD. Do it tribe by tribe and
family group by family group."

20 Then Samuel had each tribe of Israel
come forward. The tribe of Benjamin was
chosen by casting lots. 21 Next he had the
tribe of Benjamin come forward, family
group by family group. Matri's group
was chosen. Finally Saul, the son of Kish,
was chosen. But when people looked for
him, they realized he wasn't there. 22 They
needed more help from the LORD. So they
asked him, "Has the man come here yet?"

The LORD said, "Yes. He has hidden
himself among the supplies."

23 So they ran over there and brought
him out. When he stood up, the people
saw that he was a head taller than any
of them. 24 Samuel spoke to all the people. He said, "Look at the man the LORD
has chosen! There isn't anyone like him
among all the people."

Then the people shouted, "May the
king live a long time!"

25 Samuel explained to the people
the rights and duties of the king who
ruled over them. He wrote them down
in a book. He placed it in front of the
LORD in the holy tent. Then he sent the
people away. He sent each of them to
their own homes.

26 Saul also went to his home in Gibeah. Some brave men whose hearts God
had touched went with Saul. 27 But some
people who wanted to stir up trouble
said, "How can this fellow save us?" They
looked down on him. They didn't bring
him any gifts. But Saul kept quiet about it.

Saul Rescues the City of Jabesh Gilead

11 Nahash was the king of Ammon. He and his army went up
to Jabesh Gilead. They surrounded it
and got ready to attack it. All the men
of Jabesh spoke to Nahash. They said,
"Make a peace treaty with us. Then we'll
be under your control."

2 Nahash, the king of Ammon, replied,
"I will make a peace treaty with you.
But I'll do it only on one condition. You
must let me put out the right eye of
every one of you. I want to bring shame
on the whole nation of Israel."
3 The elders of Jabesh said to him,
"Give us seven days to report back to
you. We'll send messengers all through
Israel. If no one comes to save us, we'll
hand ourselves over to you."
4 The messengers came to Gibeah of
Saul. They reported to the people the
terms Nahash had required. Then all
the people wept out loud. 5 Just then
Saul was coming in from the fields. He
was walking behind his oxen. He asked,
"What's wrong with everyone? Why are
they weeping?" He was told what the
men of Jabesh had said.
6 When Saul heard their words, the
Spirit of God came powerfully on him.
He became very angry. 7 He got a pair of
oxen and cut them into pieces. He sent
the pieces by messengers all through
Israel. They announced, "You must follow Saul and Samuel. If you don't, this
is what will happen to your oxen." The
terror of the LORD fell on the people.
So all of them came together with one
purpose in mind. 8 Saul brought his army
together at Bezek. There were 300,000
men from Israel and 30,000 from Judah.
9 The messengers who had come were
told, "Go back and report to the men of
Jabesh Gilead. Tell them, 'By the hottest
time of the day tomorrow, you will be
rescued.' " The messengers went and
reported it to the men of Jabesh. It made
those men very happy. 10 They said to
the people of Ammon, "Tomorrow we'll
hand ourselves over to you. Then you
can do to us whatever you like."
11 The next day Saul separated his
men into three groups. While it was still
dark, they broke into the camp of the
Ammonite army. They kept killing the
men of Ammon until the hottest time
of the day. Those who got away were
scattered. There weren't two of them
left together anywhere.

The People Agree to Have Saul as King

12 The people said to Samuel, "Who
asked, 'Is Saul going to rule over us?'
Turn these men over to us. We'll put
them to death."
13 But Saul said, "No one will be put
to death today! After all, this is the day
the LORD has rescued Israel."
14 Then Samuel said to the people,
"Come on. Let's go to Gilgal. There we'll
agree again to have Saul as our king."
15 So all the people went to Gilgal. There,
with the LORD as witness, they made
Saul their king. There they sacrificed
friendship offerings to the LORD. And
there Saul and all the Israelites celebrated with great joy.

Samuel's Final Speech to Israel

12 Samuel spoke to all the Israelites.
He said, "I've done everything
you asked me to do. I've placed a king
over you. 2 Now you have a king as your
leader. But I'm old. My hair is gray. My
sons are here with you. I've been your
leader from the time I was young until
this day. 3 Here I stand. Bring charges
against me if you can. The LORD is a
witness. And so is his anointed king.
Whose ox have I taken? Whose donkey
have I taken? Have I cheated anyone?
Have I treated anyone badly? Have
I accepted money from anyone who
wanted special favors? If I've done any
of these things, I'll make it right."
4 "You haven't cheated us," they replied. "You haven't treated us badly. You
haven't taken anything from anyone."
5 Samuel said to them, "The LORD is a
witness against you this day. And so is
his anointed king. They are witnesses
that I haven't taken anything from any
of you."
"The LORD is a witness," they said.
6 Then Samuel said to the people,
"The LORD appointed Moses and Aaron.
He brought out of Egypt your people
who lived long ago. 7 Now then, stand
here. I'm going to remind you of all the
good things the LORD has done for you
and your people. He is a witness.
8 "After Jacob's family entered Egypt,
they cried out to the LORD for help.
The LORD sent Moses and Aaron. They
brought your people out of Egypt. They
had them make their homes in this land.
9 "But the people forgot the LORD their
God. So he put them under the control
of Sisera. Sisera was the commander of
the army of Hazor. The LORD also put

the Israelites under the control of the Philistines and the king of Moab. All those nations fought against Israel. [10] So the people cried out to the LORD. They said, 'We have sinned. We've deserted the LORD. We've served gods that are named Baal. We've served female gods that are named Ashtoreth. But save us now from the power of our enemies. Then we will serve you.' [11] The LORD sent Gideon, Barak, Jephthah and me. He saved you from the power of your enemies who were all around you. So you lived in safety.

[12] "But then you saw that Nahash, the king of Ammon, was about to attack you. So you said to me, 'No! We want a king to rule over us.' You said it even though the LORD your God was your king. [13] Now here is the king you have chosen. He's the one you asked for. The LORD has placed a king over you. [14] But you must have respect for the LORD. You must serve him and obey him. You must not say no to his commands. Both you and the king who rules over you must obey the LORD your God. If you do, that's good. [15] But you must not disobey him. You must not say no to his commands. If you do, his power will be against you. That's what happened to your people who lived before you.

[16] "So stand still. Watch the great thing the LORD is about to do right here in front of you! [17] It's time to gather in the wheat, isn't it? I'll call out to the LORD to send thunder and rain. Then you will realize what an evil thing you did in the sight of the LORD. You shouldn't have asked for a king."

[18] Samuel called out to the LORD. That same day the LORD sent thunder and rain. So all the people had great respect for the LORD and for Samuel.

[19] They said to Samuel, "Pray to the LORD your God for us. Pray that we won't die because we asked for a king. That was an evil thing to do. We added it to all our other sins."

[20] "Don't be afraid," Samuel replied. "It's true that you have done all these evil things. But don't turn away from the LORD. Serve him with all your heart. [21] Don't turn away and worship statues of gods. They are useless. They can't do you any good. They can't save you either. They are completely useless. [22] But the LORD will be true to his great name. He won't turn his back on his people. That's because he was pleased to make you his own people. [23] I would never sin against the LORD by failing to pray for you. I'll teach you to live in a way that is good and right. [24] But be sure to have respect for the LORD. Serve him faithfully. Do it with all your heart. Think about the great things he has done for you. [25] But don't be stubborn. Don't continue to do what is evil. If you do, both you and your king will be destroyed."

Samuel Judges Saul's Sin

13 Saul was 30 years old when he became king. He ruled over Israel for 42 years.

[2] Saul chose 3,000 of Israel's men. Two thousand of them were with him at Mikmash and in the hill country of Bethel. One thousand were with Jonathan at Gibeah in the land of Benjamin. Saul sent the rest back to their homes.

[3] Some Philistine soldiers were stationed at Geba. Jonathan attacked them. The other Philistines heard about it. Saul announced, "Let the Hebrew people hear about what has happened!" He had trumpets blown all through the land. [4] So all the Israelites heard the news. They were told, "Saul has attacked the Philistine army camp at Geba. Now the Philistines can't stand the Israelites." The Israelites were called out to join Saul at Gilgal.

[5] The Philistines gathered together to fight against Israel. They had 3,000 chariots and 6,000 chariot drivers. Their soldiers were as many as the grains of sand on the seashore. They went up and camped at Mikmash. It was east of Beth Aven. [6] The Israelites saw that their army was in deep trouble. So they hid in caves. They hid among bushes and rocks. They also hid in pits and empty wells. [7] Some of them even went across the Jordan River. They went to the lands of Gad and Gilead.

Saul remained at Gilgal. All the troops with him were shaking with fear. [8] He waited seven days, just as Samuel had told him to. But Samuel didn't come to Gilgal. And Saul's men began to scatter. [9] So he said, "Bring me the burnt offering and the friendship offerings." Then he offered up the burnt offering. 10 Just as Saul finished offering the sacrifice, Samuel arrived. Saul went out to greet him.

11 "What have you done?" asked Samuel.

Saul replied, "I saw that the men were scattering. I saw that the Philistines were gathering together at Mikmash. You didn't come when you said you would. 12 So I thought, 'Now the Philistines will come down to attack me at Gilgal. And I haven't asked the LORD for his blessing.' So I felt I had to sacrifice the burnt offering."

13 "You have done a foolish thing," Samuel said. "You haven't obeyed the command the LORD your God gave you. If you had, he would have made your kingdom secure over Israel for all time to come. 14 But now your kingdom won't last. The LORD has already looked for a man who is dear to his heart. He has appointed him king of his people. That's because you haven't obeyed the LORD's command."

15 Then Samuel left Gilgal and went up to Gibeah in the land of Benjamin. Saul counted the men who were with him. The total number was about 600.

Israel Doesn't Have Weapons

16 Saul and his son Jonathan were staying in Gibeah in the land of Benjamin. The men who remained in the army were there with them. At the same time, the Philistines camped at Mikmash. 17 Three groups of soldiers went out from the Philistine camp to attack Israel. One group turned and went toward Ophrah in the area of Shual. 18 Another went toward Beth Horon. The third went toward the border that looked out over the Valley of Zeboim. That valley faces the desert.

19 There weren't any blacksmiths in the whole land of Israel. That's because the Philistines had said, "The Hebrews might hire them to make swords or spears!" 20 So all the Israelites had to go down to the Philistines. They had to go to them to get their plows, hoes, axes and sickles sharpened. 21 It cost a fourth of an ounce of silver to sharpen a plow or a hoe. It cost an eighth of an ounce to sharpen a pitchfork or an axe. That's also what it cost to put new tips on the large sticks used to drive oxen.

22 So the Israelite soldiers went out to battle without swords or spears in their hands. That was true for all of Saul's and Jonathan's soldiers. Only Saul and his son Jonathan had those weapons.

Jonathan Attacks the Philistines

23 A group of Philistine soldiers had gone out to the pass at Mikmash.

14

1 One day Jonathan, the son of Saul, spoke to the young man carrying his armor. "Come on," he said. "Let's go over to the Philistine army camp on the other side of the pass." But he didn't tell his father about it.

2 Saul was staying just outside Gibeah. He was under a pomegranate tree in Migron. He had about 600 men with him. 3 Ahijah was one of them. He was wearing a sacred linen apron. He was a son of Ichabod's brother Ahitub. Ahitub was the son of Eli's son Phinehas. Eli had been the LORD's priest in Shiloh. No one was aware that Jonathan had left.

4 Jonathan planned to go across the pass to reach the Philistine camp. But there was a cliff on each side of the pass. One cliff was called Bozez. The other was called Seneh. 5 One cliff stood on the north side of the pass toward Mikmash. The other stood on the south side toward Geba.

6 Jonathan spoke to the young man carrying his armor. He said, "Come on. Let's go over to the camp of those fellows who aren't circumcised. Perhaps the LORD will help us. If he does, it won't matter how many or how few of us there are. That won't keep the LORD from saving us."

7 "Go ahead," the young man said. "Do everything you have in mind. I'm with you all the way."

8 Jonathan said, "Come on, then. We'll go across the pass toward the Philistines and let them see us. 9 Suppose they say to us, 'Wait there until we come to you.' Then we'll stay where we are. We won't go up to them. 10 But suppose they say, 'Come up to us.' Then we'll climb up. That will show us that the LORD has handed them over to us."

11 So Jonathan and the young man let the soldiers in the Philistine camp see them. "Look!" said the Philistines. "Some of the Hebrews are crawling out of the holes they were hiding in." 12 The

men in the Philistine camp shouted to Jonathan and the young man carrying his armor. They said, "Come on up here. We'll teach you a thing or two."

So Jonathan said to the young man, "Climb up after me. The LORD has handed them over to Israel."

13 Using his hands and feet, Jonathan climbed up. The young man was right behind him. Jonathan struck down the Philistines. The young man followed him and killed those who were still alive.
14 In that first attack, Jonathan and the young man killed about 20 men. They did it in an area of about half an acre.

Israel Chases the Philistines Away

15 Then panic struck the whole Philistine army. It struck those who were in the camp and those in the field. It struck those who were at the edge of the camp. It also struck those who were in the groups that had been sent out to attack Israel. The ground shook. It was a panic that God had sent.

16 Saul's lookouts at Gibeah in the land of Benjamin saw what was happening. They saw the Philistine army
melting away in all directions. 17 Then
Saul spoke to the men with him. He said, "Bring the troops together. See who has left our camp." When they did, they discovered that Jonathan and the young man carrying his armor weren't there.

18 Saul said to Ahijah the priest, "Bring the ark of God." At that time it was with
the Israelites. 19 While Saul was talking
to the priest, the noise in the Philistine camp got louder and louder. So Saul said to the priest, "Stop what you are doing."

20 Then Saul and all his men gathered together. They went to the battle. They saw that the Philistines were in total disorder. They were striking one another with their swords.
21 At an earlier
time some of the Hebrews had been on the side of the Philistines. They had gone up with them to their camp. But now they changed sides. They joined the Israelites who were with Saul and
Jonathan. 22 Some of the Israelites had
hidden in the hill country of Ephraim. They heard that the Philistines were running away. They quickly joined the
battle and chased after them. 23 So on
that day the LORD saved Israel. And the fighting continued on past Beth Aven.

Jonathan Eats Honey

24 The Israelites became very hungry that day. That's because Saul had forced the army to make a promise. He had said, "None of you must eat any food before evening comes. You must not eat until I've paid my enemies back for what they did. If you do, may you be under a curse!" So none of the troops ate any food at all.

25 The whole army entered the woods.
There was honey on the ground. 26 When
they went into the woods, they saw the honey dripping out of a honeycomb. No one put any of the honey in his mouth. They were afraid of the curse that would
come if they broke their promise. 27 But
Jonathan hadn't heard that his father had forced the army to make a promise. Jonathan had a long stick in his hand. He reached out and dipped the end of it into the honeycomb. He put some honey in his mouth. It gave him new
life. 28 Then one of the soldiers told him,
"Your father forced the army to make a promise that everyone must obey. He said, 'None of you must eat any food today. If you do, may you be under a curse!' That's why the men are weak and ready to faint."

29 Jonathan said, "My father has made trouble for the country. See how I gained new life after I tasted a little
of this honey. 30 Our soldiers took food
from their enemies today. Suppose they had eaten some of it. How much better off they would have been! Even more Philistines would have been killed."

31 That day the Israelites struck down the Philistines. They killed them from Mikmash to Aijalon. By that time
they were tired and worn out. 32 They
grabbed what they had taken from their enemies. They killed some of the sheep, cattle and calves right there on the ground. They ate the meat while
the blood was still in it. 33 Then someone
said to Saul, "Look! The men are sinning against the LORD. They're eating meat that still has blood in it."

Saul said to them, "You have broken your promise. Roll a large stone over
here at once." 34 He continued, "Go out
among the men. Tell them, 'Each of you bring me your cattle and sheep. Kill them here and eat them. Don't sin against the LORD by eating meat that still has blood in it.' "

So that night everyone brought the ox he had taken and killed it there. [35]Then Saul built an altar to honor the LORD. It was the first time he had done that.

[36]Saul said, "Let's go down and chase after the Philistines tonight. Let's not leave even one of them alive. Let's take everything they have before morning."

"Do what you think is best," they replied.

But the priest said, "Let's ask God for advice first."

[37]So Saul asked God, "Should I go down and chase after the Philistines? Will you hand them over to Israel?" But God didn't answer him that day.

[38]Saul said to the leaders of the army, "Come here. Let's find out what sin has been committed today. [39]The LORD is the one who rescues Israel. You can be sure that the LORD lives. And you can be just as sure that the sinner must die. He must die even if he's my son Jonathan." But no one said anything.

[40]Then Saul said to all the Israelites, "You stand over there. I and my son Jonathan will stand over here."

"Do what you think is best," they replied.

[41]Then Saul prayed to the LORD, the God of Israel. He said, "Why haven't you answered your servant today? If I or my son Jonathan is to blame, answer with Urim. But if the Israelites are to blame, answer with Thummim." Jonathan and Saul were chosen by casting lots. The other men were cleared of blame. [42]Saul said, "Cast the lot to find out whether I or my son Jonathan is to blame." And Jonathan was chosen.

[43]Then Saul said to Jonathan, "Tell me what you have done."

So Jonathan told him, "I used the end of my stick to get a little honey and taste it. And now do I have to die?"

[44]Saul said, "Jonathan, I must certainly put you to death. If I don't, may God punish me greatly."

[45]But the men said to Saul, "Should Jonathan be put to death? Never! He has saved Israel in a wonderful way. He did it today with God's help. You can be sure that the LORD lives. And you can be just as sure that not even one hair on Jonathan's head will fall to the ground." So the men rescued Jonathan. He wasn't put to death.

[46]Then Saul stopped chasing the Philistines. They went back to their own land.

[47]After Saul became the king of Israel, he fought against Israel's enemies who were all around them. He went to war against Moab, Ammon and Edom. He fought against the kings of Zobah and the Philistines. No matter where he went, he punished his enemies. [48]He fought bravely. He won the battle over the Amalekites. He saved Israel from the power of those who had carried off what belonged to Israel.

Saul's Family

[49]Saul's sons were Jonathan, Ishvi and Malki-Shua. Saul's older daughter was named Merab. His younger daughter was named Michal. [50]Saul's wife was named Ahinoam. She was the daughter of Ahimaaz. The commander of Saul's army was named Abner. He was the son of Ner. Ner was Saul's uncle. [51]Saul's father Kish and Abner's father Ner were sons of Abiel.

[52]As long as Saul was king, he had to fight hard against the Philistines. So every time Saul saw a strong or brave man, he took him into his army.

The LORD Is Sad That He Made Saul King

15 Samuel said to Saul, "The LORD sent me to anoint you as king over his people Israel. So listen now to a message from him. [2]The LORD who rules over all says, 'I will punish the Amalekites because of what they did to Israel. As the Israelites came up from Egypt, the Amalekites attacked them. [3]Now go. Attack the Amalekites. Completely destroy all that belongs to them. Do not spare the Amalekites. Put the men and women to death. Put the children and babies to death. Also kill the cattle, sheep, camels and donkeys.'"

[4]So Saul brought his men together at Telaim. The total number was 200,000 soldiers on foot from Israel and 10,000 from Judah. [5]Saul went to the city of Amalek. Then Saul had some of his men hide and wait in the valley. [6]Then Saul said to the Kenites, "You were kind to all the Israelites when they came up out of Egypt. Get away from the Amalekites. Then I won't have to destroy you along with them." So the Kenites moved away from the Amalekites.

7 Saul attacked the Amalekites. He
struck them down all the way from
Havilah to Shur. Shur was near the
eastern border of Egypt. 8 Saul captured
Agag, the king of the Amalekites. But
he and his men totally destroyed with
their swords all Agag's people. 9 So Saul
and the army spared Agag. They spared
the best of the sheep and cattle. They
spared the fat calves and lambs. They
spared everything that was valuable.
They weren't willing to completely
destroy any of those things. But they
totally destroyed everything that was
worthless and weak.
10 Then the LORD gave Samuel a message. He said, 11 "I am very sad I have
made Saul king. He has turned away
from me. He has not done what I directed him to do." When Samuel heard
that, he was angry. He cried out to the
LORD during that whole night.
12 Early the next morning Samuel got
up. He went to see Saul. But Samuel was
told, "Saul went to Carmel. There he set
up a monument in his own honor. Now
he has gone on down to Gilgal."
13 When Samuel got there, Saul said,
"May the LORD bless you. I've done what
he directed me to do."
14 But Samuel said, "Then why do I
hear the baaing of sheep? Why do I hear
the mooing of cattle?"
15 Saul answered, "The soldiers
brought them from the Amalekites.
They spared the best of the sheep and
cattle. They did it to sacrifice them to
the LORD your God. But we totally destroyed everything else."
16 "That's enough!" Samuel said to
Saul. "Let me tell you what the LORD
said to me last night."
"Tell me," Saul replied.
17 Samuel said, "There was a time
when you didn't think you were important. But you became the leader of
the tribes of Israel. The LORD anointed
you to be king over Israel. 18 He sent you
to do something for him. He said, 'Go
and completely destroy the Amalekites.
Go and destroy those evil people. Fight
against them until you have wiped
them out.' 19 Why didn't you obey the
LORD? Why did you keep for yourselves
what you had taken from your enemies? Why did you do what is evil in
the sight of the LORD?"

20 "But I did obey the LORD," Saul said.
"I went to do what he sent me to do. I
completely destroyed the Amalekites. I
brought back Agag, their king. 21 The soldiers took sheep and cattle from what
had been taken from our enemies. They
took the best of what had been set apart
to God. They wanted to sacrifice them
to the LORD your God at Gilgal."
22 But Samuel replied,

"What pleases the LORD more?
Burnt offerings and sacrifices, or
obeying the LORD?
It is better to obey than to offer a
sacrifice.
It is better to do what he says
than to offer the fat of rams.
23 Refusing to obey the LORD is as
sinful as using evil magic.
Being proud is as evil as
worshiping statues of gods.
You have refused to do what the
LORD told you to do.
So he has refused to have you as
king."

It is better to obey than to offer a sacrifice.
1 SAMUEL 15:22

24 Then Saul said to Samuel, "I have
sinned. I've broken the LORD's command. I haven't done what you directed
me to do. I was afraid of the men. So I
did what they said I should do. 25 Now
I beg you, forgive my sin. Come back
into town with me so I can worship the
LORD."
26 But Samuel said to him, "I won't go
back with you. You have refused to do
what the LORD told you to do. So he has
refused to have you as king over Israel!"
27 Samuel turned to leave. But Saul
grabbed the hem of his robe, and it tore.
28 Samuel said to Saul, "The LORD has
torn the kingdom of Israel away from
you today. He has given it to one of your
neighbors. He has given it to someone
better than you. 29 The God who is the
Glory of Israel does not lie. He doesn't
change his mind. That's because he
isn't a mere human being. If he were,
he might change his mind."

[30] Saul replied, "I have sinned. But
please honor me in front of the elders of
my people and in front of Israel. Come
back with me so I can worship the LORD
your God." [31] So Samuel went back with
Saul. And Saul worshiped the LORD.
[32] Then Samuel said, "Bring me Agag,
the king of the Amalekites."
Agag was in chains when he came
to Samuel. Agag thought, "The time
for me to be put to death must have
passed by now."
[33] But Samuel said,

"Your sword has killed the children
of other women.
So the child of your mother will
be killed."

Samuel put Agag to death at Gilgal in
front of the LORD.
[34] Then Samuel left to go to Ramah.
But Saul went up to his home in Gibeah
of Saul. [35] Until the day Samuel died, he
didn't go to see Saul again. Samuel was
filled with sorrow because of Saul. And
the LORD was very sad he had made
Saul king over Israel.

Samuel Anoints David to Be Israel's King

16 The LORD said to Samuel, "How
long will you be filled with sorrow because of Saul? I have refused to
have him as king over Israel. Fill your
animal horn with olive oil and go on
your way. I am sending you to Jesse
in Bethlehem. I have chosen one of his
sons to be king."
[2] But Samuel said, "How can I go?
Suppose Saul hears about it. Then he'll
kill me."
The LORD said, "Take a young cow
with you. Tell the elders of Bethlehem,
'I've come to offer a sacrifice to the
LORD.' [3] Invite Jesse to the sacrifice.
Then I will show you what to do. You
must anoint for me the one I point out
to you."
[4] Samuel did what the LORD said. He
arrived at Bethlehem. The elders of the
town met him. They were trembling
with fear. They asked, "Have you come
in peace?"
[5] Samuel replied, "Yes, I've come in
peace. I've come to offer a sacrifice to
the LORD. Set yourselves apart to him

and come to the sacrifice with me." Then
he set Jesse and his sons apart to the
LORD. He invited them to the sacrifice.
6 When they arrived, Samuel saw Eliab. He thought, "This has to be the one
the LORD wants me to anoint for him."
7 But the LORD said to Samuel, "Do not
consider how handsome or tall he is. I
have not chosen him. The LORD does not
look at the things people look at. People
look at the outside of a person. But the
LORD looks at what is in the heart."
8 Then Jesse called for Abinadab. He
had him walk in front of Samuel. But
Samuel said, "The LORD hasn't chosen
him either." 9 Then Jesse had Shammah walk by. But Samuel said, "The
LORD hasn't chosen him either." 10 Jesse
had seven of his sons walk in front of
Samuel. But Samuel said to him, "The
LORD hasn't chosen any of them." 11 So
he asked Jesse, "Are these the only sons
you have?"

"No," Jesse answered. "My youngest son is taking care of the sheep."

Samuel said, "Send for him. We won't sit down to eat until he arrives."

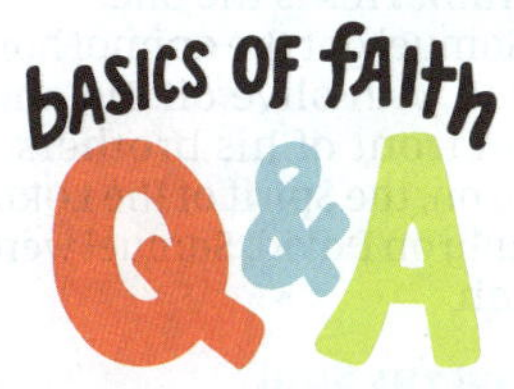

What about me matters most to God?

God cares most about your heart. People look at what a person looks like on the outside, but God looks at your character, or the ways in which you live to honor him.

Can you find the following verse?

1 SAMUEL 16:7

12 So Jesse sent for his son and had
him brought in. He looked very healthy.
He had a fine appearance and handsome features.

pointing us to JESUS: David

Israel had many kings. Some were good, some were bad, and some were really, really bad. The good kings reminded God's people of his promises and encouraged them to walk in his ways. The bad kings led God's people to worship idols and forget the ways and promises of God.

The people of Israel had a favorite king of all, and his name was David. He was a shepherd, a songwriter, and the youngest brother in his family. God chose David to be Israel's king. In fact, God promised David that someone in his family line would sit on the throne forever (see 2 Samuel 7:16). This is called the Davidic covenant.

However, David was human, and he sinned. Even though he was Israel's best king, he still failed to be a perfect king. He reminded God's people that a truer and better King was coming.

Jesus would be the eternal and forever King of God's people. Jesus would never break God's commands, and he would fulfill God's requirement for a perfect sacrifice to pay for sin. Jesus was also born into David's family line, just as God said he would be, and he is the King who reigns forever!

Then the LORD said, "Get up and
anoint him. This is the one."
13 So Samuel got the animal horn that
was filled with olive oil. He anointed
David in front of his brothers. From
that day on, the Spirit of the LORD came
powerfully on David. Samuel went back
to Ramah.

David Serves Saul

14 The Spirit of the LORD had left Saul.
And an evil spirit sent by the LORD terrified him.
15 Saul's attendants said to him, "An
evil spirit sent by God is terrifying you.
16 Give us an order to look for someone
who can play the harp. He will play it
when the evil spirit sent by God comes
on you. Then you will feel better."
17 So Saul said to his attendants, "Find
someone who plays the harp well. Bring
him to me."
18 One of the servants said, "I've seen
someone who knows how to play the
harp. He is a son of Jesse from Bethlehem. He's a brave man. He would make
a good soldier. He's a good speaker.
He's very handsome. And the LORD is
with him."
19 Then Saul sent messengers to Jesse. He said, "Send me your son David,
the one who takes care of your sheep."
20 So Jesse got some bread and a bottle
of wine. The bottle was made out of
animal skin. He also got a young goat.
He loaded everything on the back of a
donkey. He sent all of it to Saul with
his son David.
21 David went to Saul and began to
serve him. Saul liked him very much.
David became one of the men who carried Saul's armor. 22 Saul sent a message
to Jesse. Saul said, "Let David stay here.
I want him to serve me. I'm pleased
with him."
23 When the evil spirit sent by God
would come on Saul, David would get
his harp and play it. That would help
Saul. He would feel better, and the evil
spirit would leave him.

David and Goliath

17 The Philistines gathered their
army together for war. They came
to Sokoh in Judah. They set up camp at
Ephes Dammim. It was between Sokoh
and Azekah. 2 Saul and the army of Israel gathered together. They camped in
the Valley of Elah. They lined up their
men to fight against the Philistines.
3 The Philistine army was camped on
one hill. Israel's army was on another.
The valley was between them.
4 A mighty hero named Goliath came
out of the Philistine camp. He was from
Gath. He was more than nine feet tall.
5 He had a bronze helmet on his head.
He wore bronze armor that weighed 125
pounds. 6 On his legs he wore bronze
guards. He carried a bronze javelin
on his back. 7 His spear was as big as a
weaver's rod. Its iron point weighed 15
pounds. The man who carried his shield
walked along in front of him.
8 Goliath stood there and shouted to
the soldiers of Israel. He said, "Why do
you come out and line up for battle?
I'm a Philistine. You are servants of
Saul. Choose one of your men. Have
him come down and face me. 9 If he's
able to fight and kill me, we'll become
your slaves. But if I win and kill him,
you will become our slaves and serve
us." 10 Goliath continued, "This day I
dare the soldiers of Israel to send a man
down to fight against me." 11 Saul and
the whole army of Israel heard what
the Philistine said. They were terrified.
12 David was the son of an Ephrathite
whose name was Jesse. Jesse was from
Bethlehem in Judah and had eight sons.
When Saul was king, Jesse was already
very old. 13 Jesse's three oldest sons had followed Saul into battle. The oldest son was
Eliab. The second was Abinadab. The third
was Shammah. 14 David was the youngest.
The three oldest sons followed Saul. 15 But
David went back and forth from Saul's
camp to Bethlehem. He went to Bethlehem
to take care of his father's sheep.
16 Every morning and evening Goliath
came forward and stood there. He did
it for 40 days.
17 Jesse said to his son David, "Get at
least half a bushel of grain that has
been cooked. Also get ten loaves of
bread. Take all of it to your brothers.
Hurry to their camp. 18 Take along these
ten chunks of cheese to the commander
of their military group. Find out how
your brothers are doing. Bring me back
some word about them. 19 They are with
Saul and all the men of Israel. They are
in the Valley of Elah. They are fighting
against the Philistines."

20 Early in the morning David left
his father's flock in the care of a shepherd. David loaded up the food and
started out, just as Jesse had directed.
David reached the camp as the army
was going out to its battle positions.
The soldiers were shouting the war cry.
21 The Israelites and the Philistines were
lining up their armies for battle. The
armies were facing each other. 22 David
left what he had brought with the man
who took care of the supplies. He ran to
the battle lines and asked his brothers
how they were. 23 As David was talking
with them, Goliath stepped forward
from his line. Goliath was a mighty
Philistine hero from Gath. He again
dared someone to fight him, and David
heard it. 24 Whenever Israel's army saw
Goliath, all of them ran away from him.
That's because they were so afraid.

25 The Israelites had been saying,
"Just look at how this man keeps daring
Israel to fight him! The king will make
the man who kills Goliath very wealthy.
The king will also give his own daughter
to be that man's wife. The king won't
require anyone in the man's family to
pay any taxes in Israel."

26 David spoke to the men standing
near him. He asked them, "What will
be done for the man who kills this Philistine? Goliath is bringing shame on
Israel. What will be done for the one
who removes it? This Philistine isn't
even circumcised. He dares the armies
of the living God to fight him. Who does
he think he is?"

27 The men told David what Israel's
soldiers had been saying. The men told
him what would be done for the man
who killed Goliath.

28 David's oldest brother Eliab heard
him speaking with the men. So Eliab became very angry with him. Eliab asked
David, "Why have you come down here?
Who is taking care of those few sheep
in the desert for you? I know how proud
you are. I know how evil your heart is.
The only reason you came down here
was to watch the battle."

29 "What have I done now?" said David. "Can't I even speak?" 30 Then he
turned away to speak to some other
men. He asked them the same question
he had asked before. And they gave
him the same answer. 31 Someone heard
what David said and reported it to Saul.
So Saul sent for David.

32 David said to Saul, "Don't let anyone lose hope because of that Philistine.
I'll go out and fight him."

33 Saul replied, "You aren't able to go
out there and fight that Philistine. You
are too young. He's been a warrior ever
since he was a boy."

34 But David said to Saul, "I've been
taking care of my father's sheep. Sometimes a lion or a bear would come and
carry off a sheep from the flock. 35 Then
I would go after it and hit it. I would
save the sheep it was carrying in its
mouth. If it turned around to attack
me, I would grab its hair. I would strike
it down and kill it. 36 In fact, I've killed
both a lion and a bear. I'll do the same
thing to this Philistine. He isn't even
circumcised. He has dared the armies of
the living God to fight him. 37 The LORD
saved me from the paw of the lion. He
saved me from the paw of the bear. And
he'll save me from the powerful hand
of this Philistine too."

Saul said to David, "Go. And may the
LORD be with you."

38 Then Saul dressed David in his
own military clothes. He put a coat of
armor on him. He put a bronze helmet
on his head. 39 David put on Saul's sword
over his clothes. He walked around for
a while in all that armor because he
wasn't used to it.

"I can't go out there in all this armor,"
he said to Saul. "I'm not used to it." So
he took it off. 40 Then David picked up
his wooden staff. He went down to a
stream and chose five smooth stones. He
put them in the pocket of his shepherd's
bag. Then he took his sling in his hand
and approached Goliath.

41 At that same time, the Philistine
kept coming closer to David. The man
carrying Goliath's shield walked along
in front of him. 42 Goliath looked David
over. He saw how young he was. He
also saw how healthy and handsome
he was. And he hated him. 43 He said
to David, "Why are you coming at me
with sticks? Do you think I'm only a
dog?" The Philistine cursed David in the
name of his gods. 44 "Come over here,"
he said. "I'll feed your body to the birds
and wild animals!"

45 David said to Goliath, "You are coming to fight against me with a sword, a spear and a javelin. But I'm coming against you in the name of the LORD who rules over all. He is the God of the armies of Israel. He's the one you have dared to fight against. 46 This day the LORD will give me the victory over you. I'll strike you down. I'll cut your head off. This day I'll feed the bodies of the Philistine army to the birds and wild animals. Then the whole world will know there is a God in Israel. 47 The LORD doesn't rescue people by using a sword or a spear. And everyone here will know it. The battle belongs to the LORD. He will hand all of you over to us."

48 As the Philistine moved closer to attack him, David ran quickly to the battle line to meet him. 49 He reached into his bag. He took out a stone. He put it in his sling. He slung it at Goliath. The stone hit him on the forehead and sank into it. He fell to the ground on his face.

50 So David won the fight against Goliath with a sling and a stone. He struck down the Philistine and killed him. He did it without even using a sword.

51 David ran and stood over him. He picked up Goliath's sword and cut off his head with it.

The Philistines saw that their hero was dead. So they turned around and ran away. 52 Then the men of Israel and Judah shouted and rushed forward. They chased the Philistines to the entrance of Gath. They chased them to the gates of Ekron. Bodies of dead Philistines were scattered all along the road to Gath and Ekron. That's the road that leads to Shaaraim. 53 Israel's army returned from chasing the Philistines. They had taken everything from the Philistine camp.

54 David picked up Goliath's head. He brought it to Jerusalem. He put Goliath's weapons in his own tent.

55 Saul had been watching David as he went out to meet the Philistine. He spoke to Abner, the commander of the army. Saul said to him, "Abner, whose son is that young man?"

Abner replied, "Your Majesty, I don't know. And that's just as sure as you are alive."

56 The king said, "Find out whose son that young man is."

57 After David killed Goliath, he returned to the camp. Then Abner brought him to Saul. David was still carrying Goliath's head.

58 "Young man, whose son are you?" Saul asked him.

David said, "I'm the son of Jesse from Bethlehem."

Saul's Growing Fear of David

18 David finished talking with Saul. After that, Jonathan and David became close friends. Jonathan loved David just as he loved himself. 2 From that time on, Saul kept David with him. He didn't let him return home to his family. 3 Jonathan made a covenant with David because he loved him just as he loved himself. 4 Jonathan took off the robe he was wearing and gave it to David. He also gave him his military clothes. He even gave him his sword, his bow and his belt.

5 David did everything Saul sent him to do. He did it so well that Saul gave him a high rank in the army. That pleased Saul's whole army, including his officers.

6 After David had killed Goliath, the men of Israel returned home. The women came out of all the towns of Israel to meet King Saul. They danced and sang joyful songs. They played harps and tambourines. 7 As they danced, they sang,

"Saul has killed thousands of men.
David has killed tens of
thousands."

8 That song made Saul very angry. It really upset him. He said to himself, "They are saying David has killed tens of thousands of men. But they are saying I've killed only thousands. The only thing left for him to get is the kingdom itself." 9 From that time on, Saul watched David closely.

10 The next day an evil spirit sent by God came powerfully on Saul. Saul began to prophesy in his house. At that same time David began to play the harp, just as he usually did. Saul was holding a spear. 11 He threw it at David. As he did, he said to himself, "I'll pin David to the wall." But David got away from him twice.

12 The LORD had left Saul and was with David. So Saul was afraid of David.

13 He sent David away. He put him in
command of 1,000 men. David led the
troops in battle. 14 In everything he did,
he was very successful. That's because
the LORD was with him. 15 When Saul saw
how successful David was, he became
afraid of him. 16 But all the troops of
Israel and Judah loved David. That's
because he led them in battle.

17 Saul said to David, "Here is my older
daughter Merab. I'll give her to you to
be your wife. Just serve me bravely and
fight the LORD's battles." Saul said to
himself, "I won't have to lift my hand
to strike him down. The Philistines will
do that!"

18 But David said to Saul, "Who am
I? Is anyone in my whole family that
important in Israel? Am I worthy to
become the king's son-in-law?" 19 The
time came for Saul to give his daughter
Merab to David. Instead, Saul gave her
to Adriel from Meholah to be his wife.

20 Saul's daughter Michal was in
love with David. When they told Saul
about it, he was pleased. 21 "I'll give her
to David to be his wife," Saul said to
himself. "Then maybe she'll trap him.
And maybe the Philistines will strike
him down." So Saul said to David, "Now
you have a second chance to become
my son-in-law."

22 Then Saul gave an order to his attendants. He said, "Speak to David in
private. Tell him, 'The king likes you.
All his attendants love you. So become
his son-in-law.' "

23 Saul's attendants spoke those very
words to David. But David said, "Do you
think it's a small thing to become the
king's son-in-law? I'm only a poor man.
I'm not very well known."

24 Saul's attendants told him what
David had said. 25 Saul said, "Tell David, 'Here's the price the king wants
for the bride. He wants you to kill 100
Philistines. Then bring back the skins
you cut off when you circumcise them.
That's how Saul will get even with his
enemies.' " Saul hoped that the Philistines would strike David down.

26 Saul's attendants also told David
those things. Then David was pleased to
become the king's son-in-law. So before
the wedding day, 27 David and his men
went out and killed 200 Philistines.
They circumcised the Philistines. Then
David brought back all the skins. They
counted out the full number and gave
them to the king. By doing that, David
could become the king's son-in-law. So
Saul gave David his daughter Michal
to be his wife.

28 Saul realized that the LORD was
with David. He also realized that his
daughter Michal loved David. 29 So Saul
became even more afraid of him. As
long as Saul lived, he remained David's
enemy.

30 The Philistine commanders kept on
going out to battle. Every time they did,
David had more success against them
than the rest of Saul's officers. So his
name became well known.

Saul Tries to Kill David

19 Saul told his son Jonathan and
all the attendants to kill David.
But Jonathan liked David very much.
2 So Jonathan warned him, "My father
Saul is looking for a chance to kill you.
Be very careful tomorrow morning.
Find a place to hide and stay there.
3 My father and I will come and stand
in the field where you are hiding. I'll
speak to him about you. Then I'll tell
you what I find out."

4 Jonathan told his father Saul some
good things about David. He said to
him, "Please don't do anything to harm
David. He hasn't done anything to harm
you. And what he's done has helped
you a lot. 5 He put his own life in danger when he killed Goliath. The LORD
used him to win a great battle for the
whole nation of Israel. When you saw
it, you were glad. So why would you do
anything to harm a man like David? He
isn't guilty of doing anything to harm
you. Why would you want to kill him
without any reason?"

6 Saul paid attention to Jonathan.
Saul made a promise. He said, "You
can be sure that the LORD lives. And
you can be just as sure that David will
not be put to death."

7 So Jonathan sent for David and told
him everything he and Saul had said.
Then he brought David to Saul. David
served Saul as he had done before.

8 Once more war broke out. So David
went out and fought against the Philistines. He struck them down with so much
force that they ran away from him.

9 But an evil spirit sent by the LORD came on Saul. It happened as he was sitting in his house and holding his spear. While David was playing the harp, 10 Saul tried to pin him to the wall with his spear. But David got away from him just as Saul drove the spear into the wall. That night David escaped.

11 Saul sent some men to watch David's house. He told them to kill David the next morning. But David's wife Michal warned him. She said, "You must run for your life tonight. If you don't, tomorrow you will be killed." 12 So Michal helped David escape through a window. He ran and got away. 13 Then Michal got a statue of a god. She laid it on David's bed. She covered it with clothes. And she put some goat hair at the place where David's head would have been.

14 Saul sent the men to capture David. But Michal told them, "He's sick."

15 Then Saul sent the men back to see David. He told them, "Bring him up here to me in his bed. Then I'll kill him." 16 But when the men entered, the only thing they found in the bed was the statue. Some goat hair was at the place where David's head would have been.

17 Saul said to Michal, "Why did you trick me like this? Why did you help my enemy escape?"

Michal told him, "He said to me, 'Help me get away. If you don't, I'll kill you.' "

18 After David had run away and escaped, he went to Samuel at Ramah. He told him everything Saul had done to him. Then David and Samuel went to Naioth and stayed there. 19 Saul was told, "David is in Naioth at Ramah." 20 So Saul sent some men to capture him. When they got there, they saw a group of prophets who were prophesying. Samuel was standing there as their leader. Then the Spirit of God came on Saul's men. So they also began to prophesy. 21 Saul was told about it. So he sent some more men. They began to prophesy too. Saul sent some men a third time. And they also began to prophesy. 22 Finally, Saul decided to go to Ramah himself. He went to the large well at Seku. He asked some people, "Where are Samuel and David?"

"Over in Naioth at Ramah," they said.

23 So Saul went to Naioth at Ramah. But the Spirit of God even came on him. He walked along and prophesied until he came to Naioth. 24 There he took off his clothes. Then he also prophesied in front of Samuel. He lay there without his clothes on all that day and night. That's why people say, "Is Saul also one of the prophets?"

David and Jonathan

20 David was in Naioth at Ramah. He ran away from there to where Jonathan was. He asked him, "What have I done? What crime have I committed? I haven't done anything to harm your father. So why is he trying to kill me?"

2 "That will never happen!" Jonathan replied. "You aren't going to die! My father doesn't do anything at all without letting me know. So why would he hide this from me? He isn't going to kill you!"

3 But David strongly disagreed. He said, "Your father knows very well that you are pleased with me. He has said to himself, 'I don't want Jonathan to know I'm planning to kill David. If he finds out, he'll be very sad.' But I'm very close to being killed. And that's just as sure as the LORD and you are alive."

4 Jonathan said to David, "I'll do anything you want me to do for you."

5 So David said, "Tomorrow is the time for the New Moon feast. I'm supposed to eat with the king. But let me go and hide in the field. I'll stay there until the evening of the day after tomorrow. 6 Your father might miss me. If he does, then tell him, 'David begged me to let him hurry home to Bethlehem. A yearly sacrifice is being offered there for his whole family group.' 7 Your father might say, 'That's all right.' If he does, it will mean I'm safe. But he might become very angry. If he does, you can be sure he's made up his mind to harm me. 8 Please be kind to me. You have made a covenant with me in front of the LORD. If I'm guilty, kill me yourself! Don't hand me over to your father!"

9 "I would never do that!" Jonathan said. "Suppose I had even the smallest clue that my father had made up his mind to harm you. Then I would tell you."

10 David asked, "Who will tell me if your father answers you in a mean way?"

11 “Come on,” Jonathan said. “Let’s
go out to the field.” So they went there
together.
12 Then Jonathan spoke to David.
He said, “I promise you that I’ll find
out what my father is planning to do.
I’ll find out by this time the day after
tomorrow. The LORD, the God of Israel,
is my witness. Suppose my father has
kind feelings toward you. Then I’ll send
you a message and let you know. 13 But
suppose he wants to harm you. And I
don’t let you know about it. Suppose I
don’t help you get away in peace. Then
may the LORD punish me greatly. May
he be with you, just as he has been with
my father. 14 But always be kind to me,
just as the LORD is. Be kind to me as long
as I live. Then I won’t be killed. 15 And
never stop being kind to my family.
Don’t stop even when the LORD has cut
off every one of your enemies from the
face of the earth.”
16 So Jonathan made a covenant of
friendship with David and his family.
He said, “May the LORD hold David’s
enemies responsible for what they’ve
done.” 17 Jonathan had David promise
his friendship again because he loved
him. In fact, Jonathan loved David just
as he loved himself.
18 Then Jonathan said to David, “Tomorrow is the time for the New Moon
feast. You will be missed, because your
seat at the table will be empty. 19 Go to
the place where you hid when all this
trouble began. Go there the day after
tomorrow, when evening is approaching. There’s a stone out there called Ezel.
20 Wait by it. I’ll shoot three arrows to
one side of the stone. I’ll pretend I’m
practicing my shooting. 21 Then I’ll
send a boy out there. I’ll tell him, ‘Go
and find the arrows.’ Suppose I say to
him, ‘The arrows are on this side of you.
Bring them here.’ Then come. That will
mean you are safe. You won’t be in any
danger. And that’s just as sure as the
LORD is alive. 22 But suppose I tell the
boy, ‘The arrows are far beyond you.’
Then go. That will mean the LORD is
sending you away. 23 And remember
what we talked about. Remember that
the LORD is a witness between you and
me forever.”
24 So David hid in the field. When
the time for the New Moon feast came,
the king sat down to eat. 25 He sat in
his usual place by the wall. Jonathan
sat across from him. Abner sat next
to Saul. But David’s place was empty.
26 Saul didn’t say anything that day.
He said to himself, “Something must
have happened to David to make him
‘unclean.’ That must be why he isn’t
here.” 27 But the next day, David’s place
was empty again. It was the second day
of the month. Finally, Saul spoke to his
son Jonathan. He said, “Why hasn’t the
son of Jesse come to the meal? He hasn’t
been here yesterday or today.”
28 Jonathan replied, “David begged
me to let him go to Bethlehem. 29 He
said, ‘Let me go. Our family is offering
a sacrifice in the town. My brother has
ordered me to be there. Are you pleased
with me? If you are, let me go and see
my brothers.’ That’s why he hasn’t come
to eat at your table.”
30 Saul became very angry with Jonathan. He said to him, “You are an evil
son. You have refused to obey me. I
know that you are on the side of Jesse’s
son. You should be ashamed of that.
And your mother should be ashamed of
having a son like you. 31 You will never
be king as long as Jesse’s son lives on
this earth. And you will never have a
kingdom either. So send someone to
bring the son of Jesse to me. He must
die!”
32 “Why do you want to put him to
death?” Jonathan asked his father.
“What has he done?” 33 But Saul threw
his spear at Jonathan to kill him. Then
Jonathan knew that his father wanted
to kill David.
34 So Jonathan got up from the table.
He was very angry. On that second day
of the feast, he refused to eat. He was
very sad that his father was treating
David so badly.
35 The next morning Jonathan went
out to the field to meet David. He took
a young boy with him. 36 He said to the
boy, “Run and find the arrows I shoot.”
As the boy ran, Jonathan shot an arrow far beyond him. 37 The boy came
to the place where Jonathan’s arrow
had fallen. Then Jonathan shouted to
him, “The arrow went far beyond you,
didn’t it?” 38 He continued, “Hurry up!
Run fast! Don’t stop!” The boy picked up
the arrow and returned to his master.

39 The boy didn't know what was going
on. Only Jonathan and David knew.
40 Jonathan gave his weapons to the
boy. He told him, "Go back to town. Take
the weapons with you."
41 After the boy had gone, David got
up from the south side of the stone.
He bowed down in front of Jonathan
with his face to the ground. He did it
three times. Then they kissed each other
and cried. But David cried more than
Jonathan did.
42 Jonathan said to David, "Go in
peace. In the name of the LORD we've
promised to be friends. We have said,
'The LORD is a witness between you
and me. He's a witness between your
children and my children forever.'"
Then David left, and Jonathan went
back to the town.

David at Nob

21 David went to Ahimelek the priest
at Nob. Ahimelek trembled with
fear when he met him. He asked David,
"Why are you alone? Why isn't anyone
with you?"
2 David answered Ahimelek the priest,
"The king gave me a special job to do.
He said to me, 'I don't want anyone
to know what I'm sending you to do.
So don't say anything about it.' I've
told my men to meet me at a certain
place. 3 Do you have anything for us to
eat? Give me five loaves of bread, or
anything else you can find."
4 But the priest answered David, "I don't
have any bread that isn't holy. I only have
some holy bread here. But it's for men
who haven't slept with women recently."
5 David replied, "Well, we haven't slept
with women recently. That's the way it
is every time I lead my men out to battle. We keep ourselves holy even when
we do jobs that aren't holy. And that's
even more true today." 6 So the priest
gave him the holy bread. It was the only
bread he had. It had been removed from
the table that was in front of the LORD.
On the same day, hot bread had been
put in its place.
7 One of Saul's servants was there that
day. He had been made to stay at the
holy tent for a while. He was Doeg from
Edom. Doeg was Saul's chief shepherd.
8 David asked Ahimelek, "Don't you
have a spear or sword here? I haven't
brought my sword or any other weapon.
That's because the job the king gave
me to do had to be done right away."
9 The priest replied, "The sword of
Goliath, the Philistine, is here. You killed
him in the Valley of Elah. His sword
is wrapped in a cloth. It's behind the
sacred linen apron. If you want it, take
it. It's the only sword here."
David said, "There isn't any sword
like it. Give it to me."

David at Gath

10 That day David ran away from Saul.
He went to Achish, the king of Gath. 11 But
the servants of Achish spoke to him. They
said, "Isn't this David, the king of the
land? Isn't he the one the Israelites sing
about when they dance? They sing,

"'Saul has killed thousands of men.
David has killed tens of
thousands.'"

12 David paid close attention to what
the servants were saying. He became
very much afraid of what Achish, the
king of Gath, might do. 13 So he pretended to be out of his mind when he was
with them. As long as he was in Gath,
he acted like a crazy person. He made
marks on the doors of the city gate. He
let spit run down his beard.
14 Achish said to his servants, "Just
look at the man! He's out of his mind!
Why are you bringing him to me?
15 Don't I have enough crazy people
around me already? So why do you
have to bring this fellow here? Just look
at how he's carrying on in front of me!
Why do you have to bring this man into
my house?"

David at Adullam and Mizpah

22 David left Gath and escaped to
the cave of Adullam. His brothers and the other members of his family
heard about it. So they went down to
join him there. 2 Everyone who was in
trouble or owed money or was unhappy
gathered around him. He became their
commander. About 400 men were with
him.
3 From there David went to Mizpah in
Moab. He spoke to the king of Moab. He
said, "Please let my father and mother
come and stay with you. Let them stay
until I learn what God will do for me."
4 So David left his parents with the king

of Moab. They stayed with him as long
as David was in his usual place of safety.
5 But the prophet Gad spoke to David.
He said, "Don't stay in your usual place
of safety. Go into the land of Judah."
So David left and went to the forest of
Hereth.

Saul Kills the Priests at Nob

6 Saul heard that the place where David and his men were hiding had been
discovered. Saul was sitting under a
tamarisk tree on the hill at Gibeah. He
was holding his spear. All his officials
were standing at his side. 7 Saul said to
them, "Men of Benjamin, listen to me!
Do you think Jesse's son will give all of
you fields and vineyards? Do you think
he'll make some of you commanders of
thousands of men? Do you think he'll
make the rest of you commanders of
hundreds? 8 Is that why all of you have
joined together against me? No one
tells me when my son makes a covenant with Jesse's son. None of you is
concerned about me. No one tells me
that my son has stirred up Jesse's son
to hide and wait to attack me. But that's
exactly what's happening now."
9 Doeg was standing with Saul's officials. He was from Edom. He said, "I
saw Jesse's son David come to Ahimelek
at Nob. Ahimelek is the son of Ahitub.
10 Ahimelek asked the LORD a question
for David. He also gave him food and
the sword of Goliath, the Philistine."
11 Then the king sent for the priest
Ahimelek, the son of Ahitub. The king
also sent for all the men in his family.
They were the priests at Nob. All of them
came to the king. 12 Saul said, "Son of
Ahitub, listen to me."
"Yes, master," he answered.
13 Saul said to him, "Why have you
and Jesse's son joined together against
me? Why did you give him bread and a
sword? Why did you ask God a question
for him? Now he has turned against
me. He is hiding and waiting to attack
me right now."
14 Ahimelek answered the king, "David is faithful to you. In fact, he's more
faithful to you than anyone else who
serves you. He's your own son-in-law.
He's the captain of your own personal
guards. He's highly respected by everyone in your palace. 15 Was that day
the first time I asked God a question for
him? Of course not! Please don't bring
charges against me. Please don't bring
charges against anyone in my family.
I don't know anything at all about this
whole matter."
16 But the king said, "Ahimelek, you
will certainly be put to death. You and
your whole family will be put to death."
17 Then the king gave an order to the
guards at his side. He said, "Go and
kill the priests of the LORD. They are
on David's side too. They knew he was
running away from me. And they didn't
even tell me."
But the king's officials wouldn't raise
a hand to strike down the priests of
the LORD.
18 Then the king ordered Doeg, "You
go and strike down the priests." So
Doeg, the Edomite, went and struck
them down. That day he killed 85 priests
who wore linen aprons. 19 He also killed
the people of Nob with his sword. Nob
was a town where priests lived. Doeg
killed its men and women. He killed its
children and babies. He also destroyed
its cattle, donkeys and sheep.
20 But Abiathar, a son of Ahimelek,
escaped. Ahimelek was the son of
Ahitub. Abiathar ran away and joined
David. 21 He told David that Saul had
killed the priests of the LORD. 22 Then
David said to Abiathar, "One day I was
at Nob. I saw Doeg, the Edomite, there. I
knew he would be sure to tell Saul. Your
whole family has been killed. And I'm
responsible for it. 23 So stay with me.
Don't be afraid. The man who wants to
kill you wants to kill me too. You will
be safe with me."

David Saves the People of Keilah

23 David was told, "The Philistines
are fighting against the town of
Keilah. They are stealing grain from
the threshing floors." 2 So he asked the
LORD for advice. He said, "Should I go
and attack those Philistines?"
The LORD answered him, "Go and
attack them. Save Keilah."
3 But David's men said to him, "We're
afraid here in Judah. Suppose we go to
Keilah and fight against the Philistine
army. Then we'll be even more afraid."
4 Once again David asked the LORD
what he should do. The LORD answered

him, "Go down to Keilah. I am going to hand the Philistines over to you." 5 So David and his men went to Keilah. They fought against the Philistines and carried off their livestock. David wounded and killed large numbers of Philistines. And he saved the people of Keilah. 6 Abiathar, the son of Ahimelek, had brought down the sacred linen apron with him from Nob. He did it when he ran away to David at Keilah.

Saul Chases David

7 Saul was told that David had gone to Keilah. He said, "God has handed him over to me. David has trapped himself by entering a town that has gates with metal bars." 8 So Saul brought together all his soldiers to go to battle. He ordered them to go down to Keilah. He told them to surround David and his men. He told them to get ready to attack them.

9 David learned that Saul was planning to attack him. So he said to Abiathar the priest, "Bring the linen apron." 10 Then David said, "LORD, you are the God of Israel. I know for sure that Saul plans to come to Keilah. He plans to destroy the town because of me. 11 Will the citizens of Keilah hand me over to him? Will Saul come down here, as I've heard he would? LORD, you are the God of Israel. Please answer me."

The LORD said, "He will come down."

12 Again David asked, "Will the citizens of Keilah hand me and my men over to Saul?"

And the LORD said, "They will."

13 So David and his men left Keilah. The total number of them was about 600. They kept moving from place to place. Saul was told that David had escaped from Keilah. So he didn't go there.

14 Sometimes David stayed in places of safety in the desert. At other times he stayed in the hills of the Desert of Ziph. Day after day Saul looked for him. But God didn't hand David over to him.

15 David was at Horesh in the Desert of Ziph. There he learned that Saul had come out to kill him. 16 Saul's son Jonathan went to David at Horesh. He told David that God would make him strong. 17 "Don't be afraid," he said. "My father Saul won't harm you. You will be king over Israel. And I will be next in command. Even my father Saul knows this." 18 The two of them made a covenant of friendship in front of the LORD. Then Jonathan went home. But David remained at Horesh.

19 The people of Ziph went up to Saul at Gibeah. They said, "David is hiding among us. He's hiding in places of safety at Horesh. Horesh is south of Jeshimon on the hill of Hakilah. 20 Your Majesty, come down when it pleases you to come. It will be our duty to hand David over to you."

21 Saul replied, "May the LORD bless you because you were concerned about me. 22 Make sure you are right. Go and check things out again. Find out where David usually goes. Find out who has seen him there. People tell me he's very tricky. 23 Find out about all the hiding places he uses. Come back to me with all the facts. I'll go with you. Suppose he's in the area. Then I'll track him down among all the family groups of Judah."

24 So they started out. They went to Ziph ahead of Saul. David and his men were in the Desert of Maon. Maon is south of Jeshimon in the Arabah Valley. 25 Saul and his men started out to look for David. David was told about it. So he went down to a rock in the Desert of Maon to hide. Saul heard he was there. So he went into the Desert of Maon to chase David.

26 Saul was going along one side of the mountain. David and his men were on the other side. They were hurrying to get away from Saul. Saul and his army were closing in on David and his men. They were about to capture them. 27 Just then a messenger came to Saul. He said, "Come quickly! The Philistines are attacking the land." 28 So Saul stopped chasing David. He went to fight against the Philistines. That's why they call that place Sela Hammahlekoth. 29 David left that place. He went and lived in places of safety near En Gedi.

David Doesn't Kill Saul When He Has the Chance

24 Saul returned from chasing the Philistines. Then he was told, "David is in the Desert of En Gedi." 2 So Saul took 3,000 of the best soldiers from the whole nation of Israel. He started

out to look for David and his men. He
planned to look near the Rocky Cliffs
of the Wild Goats.
3 He came to some sheep pens along
the way. A cave was there. Saul went in
to go to the toilet. David and his men
were far back in the cave. 4 David's men
said, "This is the day the LORD told you
about. He said to you, 'I will hand your
enemy over to you. Then you can deal
with him as you want to.' " So David
came up close to Saul without being
seen. He cut off a corner of Saul's robe.
5 Later, David felt sorry that he had
cut off a corner of Saul's robe. 6 He said
to his men, "May the LORD keep me
from doing a thing like that again to my
master. He is the LORD's anointed king.
So I promise that I will never lay my
hand on him. The LORD has anointed
him." 7 David said that to correct his
men. He wanted them to know that they
should never suggest harming the king.
He didn't allow them to attack Saul. So
Saul left the cave and went on his way.
8 Then David went out of the cave.
He called out to Saul, "King Saul! My
master!" When Saul looked behind him,
David bowed down. He lay down flat
with his face toward the ground. 9 He
said to Saul, "Why do you listen when
men say, 'David is trying to harm you'?
10 This day you have seen with your own
eyes how the LORD handed you over to
me in the cave. Some of my men begged
me to kill you. But I didn't. I said, 'I will
never lay my hand on my master. He
is the LORD's anointed king.' 11 Look,
my father! Look at this piece of your
robe in my hand! I cut off the corner
of your robe. But I didn't kill you. See,
there is nothing in my hand that shows
I am guilty of doing anything wrong. I
haven't turned against you. I haven't
done anything to harm you. But you are
hunting me down. You want to kill me.
12 May the LORD judge between you and
me. And may the LORD pay you back
because of the wrong things you have
done to me. But I won't do anything to
hurt you. 13 People say, 'Evil acts come
from those who do evil.' So I won't do
anything to hurt you.
14 "King Saul, who are you trying to
catch? Who do you think you are chasing? I'm nothing but a dead dog or a
flea! 15 May the LORD be our judge. May
he decide between us. May he consider
my case and stand up for me. May he
show that I'm not guilty of doing anything wrong. May he save me from you."
16 When David finished speaking, Saul
asked him a question. He said, "My son
David, is that your voice?" And Saul
wept out loud. 17 "You are a better person
than I am," he said. "You have treated
me well. But I've treated you badly.
18 You have just now told me about the
good things you did to me. The LORD
handed me over to you. But you didn't
kill me. 19 Suppose a man finds his enemy. He doesn't let him get away without
harming him. May the LORD reward
you with many good things. May he do
it because of the way you treated me
today. 20 I know for sure that you will be
king. I know that the kingdom of Israel
will be made secure under your control.
21 Now make a promise in the name of
the LORD. Promise me that you won't kill
the children of my family. Also promise
me that you won't wipe out my name
from my family line."
22 So David made that promise to
Saul. Then Saul returned home. But
David and his men went up to his usual
place of safety.

David, Nabal and Abigail

25 When Samuel died, the whole
nation of Israel gathered together. They were filled with sorrow
because he was dead. They buried him
at his home in Ramah. Then David went
down into the Desert of Paran.
2 A certain man in Maon was very
wealthy. He owned property there at
Carmel. He had 1,000 goats and 3,000
sheep. He was clipping the wool off the
sheep in Carmel. 3 His name was Nabal.
His wife's name was Abigail. She was
a wise and beautiful woman. But her
husband was rude and mean in the
way he treated others. He was from the
family of Caleb.
4 David was staying in the Desert of
Paran. While he was there, he heard
that Nabal was clipping the wool off
his sheep. 5 So he sent for ten young
men. He said to them, "Go up to Nabal
at Carmel. Greet him for me. 6 Say to
him, 'May you live a long time! May
everything go well with you and your

family! And may things go well with
everything that belongs to you!
[7]" 'I hear that you are clipping the
wool off your sheep. When your shepherds were with us, we treated them
well. The whole time they were at Carmel nothing that belonged to them was
stolen. [8]Ask your own servants. They'll
tell you. We've come to you now at a
happy time of the year. Please be kind
to my men. Please give me and my men
anything you can find for us.' "
[9]When David's men arrived, they
gave Nabal the message from David.
Then they waited.
[10]Nabal answered David's servants,
"Who is this David? Who is this son
of Jesse? Many servants are running
away from their masters these days.
[11]Why should I give away my bread
and water? Why should I give away the
meat I've prepared for those who clip
the wool off my sheep? Why should I
give food to men who come from who
knows where?"
[12]So David's men turned around and
went back. When they arrived, they
reported to David every word Nabal had
spoken. [13]David said to his men, "Each
of you put on your swords!" So they did.
David put his sword on too. About 400
men went up with David. Two hundred
men stayed behind with the supplies.
[14]One of the servants warned Abigail, Nabal's wife. He said, "David sent
some messengers from the desert to
give his greetings to our master. But
Nabal shouted at them and was rude
to them. [15]David's men had been very
good to us. They treated us well. The
whole time we were near them out in
the fields, nothing was stolen. [16]We were
taking care of our sheep near them.
During that time, they were like a wall
around us night and day. They kept us
safe. [17]Now think it over. See what you
can do. Horrible trouble will soon come
to our master and his whole family. He's
such an evil man that no one can even
talk to him."
[18]Abigail didn't waste any time. She
got 200 loaves of bread and two bottles
of wine. The bottles were made out of
animal skins. She got five sheep that
were ready to be cooked. She got a bushel of grain that had been cooked. She
got 100 raisin cakes. And she got 200
cakes of pressed figs. She loaded all of it
on the backs of donkeys. [19]Then she told
her servants, "Go on ahead. I'll follow
you." But she didn't tell her husband
Nabal about it.
[20]Abigail rode her donkey into a
mountain valley. There she saw David
and his men. They were coming down
toward her. [21]David had just said, "Everything we've done hasn't been worth
a thing! I watched over that fellow's
property in the desert. I made sure none
of it was stolen. But he has paid me back
evil for good. [22]I won't leave even one
of his men alive until morning. If I do,
may God punish me greatly!"
[23]When Abigail saw David, she quickly got off her donkey. She bowed down
in front of David with her face toward
the ground. [24]She fell at his feet. She
said, "Pardon your servant, sir. Please
let me speak to you. Listen to what I'm
saying. Let me take the blame myself.
[25]Please don't pay any attention to
that evil man Nabal. His name means
Foolish Person. And that's exactly what
he is. He's always doing foolish things.
I'm sorry I didn't get a chance to see the
men you sent. [26]Sir, the LORD has kept
you from killing Nabal and his men.
He has kept you from using your own
hands to get even. So may what's about
to happen to Nabal happen to all your
enemies. May it happen to everyone
who wants to harm you. And may it
happen just as surely as the LORD your
God and you are alive. [27]I've brought
a gift for you. Give it to the men who
follow you.
[28]"Please forgive me if I shouldn't
have done that. The LORD your God will
certainly give you and your family line
a kingdom that will last. That's because
you fight the LORD's battles. You won't
do anything wrong as long as you live.
[29]Someone may chase you and try to
kill you. But the LORD your God will keep
your life safe like a treasure hidden in
a bag. And he'll destroy your enemies.
Their lives will be thrown away, just as
a stone is thrown from a sling. [30]The
LORD will do for you every good thing
he promised to do. He'll appoint you
ruler over Israel. [31]When that happens,
you won't have this heavy load on your
mind. You won't have to worry about
how you killed people without any

reason. You won't have to worry about
how you got even. The LORD your God
will give you success. When that happens, please remember me."
32 David said to Abigail, "Give praise
to the LORD. He is the God of Israel. He
has sent you today to find me. 33 May
the LORD bless you for what you have
done. You have shown a lot of good
sense. You have kept me from killing
Nabal and his men this day. You have
kept me from using my own hands to
get even. 34 It's a good thing you came
quickly to meet me. If you hadn't come,
not one of Nabal's men would have been
left alive by sunrise. And that's just as
sure as the LORD, the God of Israel, is
alive. He has kept me from harming
you."
35 Then David accepted from her what
she had brought him. He said, "Go home
in peace. I've heard your words. I'll do
what you have asked."
36 Abigail went back to Nabal. He was
having a dinner party in the house. It
was the kind of dinner a king would
have. He had been drinking too much
wine. He was very drunk. So she didn't
tell him anything at all until sunrise.
37 The next morning Nabal wasn't drunk
anymore. Then his wife told him everything. When she did, his heart grew
weak. He became like a stone. 38 About
ten days later, the LORD struck Nabal
down. And he died.
39 David heard that Nabal was dead.
So he said, "Give praise to the LORD.
Nabal was rude to me. But the LORD
stood up for me. He has kept me from
doing something wrong. He has paid
Nabal back for the wrong things he did."
Then David sent a message to Abigail.
He asked her to become his wife. 40 His
servants went to Carmel. They said to
Abigail, "David has sent us to you. He
wants you to come back with us and
become his wife."
41 Abigail bowed down with her face
toward the ground. She said, "I am your
servant. I'm ready to serve him. I'm
ready to wash the feet of his servants."
42 Abigail quickly got on a donkey and
went with David's messengers. Her five
female servants went with her. She became David's wife. 43 David had also
married Ahinoam from Jezreel. Both of
them became his wives. 44 But Saul had
given his daughter Michal, David's first
wife, to Paltiel. Paltiel was from Gallim.
He was the son of Laish.

Once Again David Doesn't Kill Saul When He Has the Chance

26 Some people from Ziph went
to Saul at Gibeah. They said,
"David is hiding on the hill of Hakilah.
It faces Jeshimon."
2 So Saul went down to the Desert of
Ziph. He took 3,000 of the best soldiers
in Israel with him. They went to the
desert to look for David. 3 Saul set up his
camp beside the road. It was on the hill
of Hakilah facing Jeshimon. But David
stayed in the desert. He saw that Saul
had followed him there. 4 So he sent out
scouts. From them he learned that Saul
had arrived.
5 Then David started out. He went to
the place where Saul had camped. He
saw where Saul and Abner were lying
down. Saul was lying inside the camp.
The army was camped all around him.
Abner was commander of the army. He
was the son of Ner.
6 Then David spoke to Ahimelek, the
Hittite. He also spoke to Joab's brother
Abishai, the son of Zeruiah. He asked
them, "Who will go down with me into
the camp to Saul?"
"I'll go with you," said Abishai.
7 So that night David and Abishai
went into the camp. They found Saul
lying asleep inside the camp. His spear
was stuck in the ground near his head.
Abner and the soldiers were lying asleep
around him.
8 Abishai said to David, "Today God
has handed your enemy over to you.
So let me pin him to the ground. I can
do it with one jab of the spear. I won't
even have to strike him twice."
9 But David said to Abishai, "Don't
destroy him! No one can do any harm
to the LORD's anointed king and not
be guilty. 10 You can be sure that the
LORD lives," he said. "And you can be
just as sure that the LORD himself will
strike Saul down. Perhaps he'll die a
natural death. Or perhaps he'll go into
battle and be killed. 11 May the LORD
keep me from doing anything to harm
his anointed king. Now get the spear
and water jug that are near his head.
Then let's leave."

12 So David took the spear and water jug that were near Saul's head. Then he and Abishai left. No one saw them. No one knew about what they had done. In fact, no one even woke up. Everyone was sleeping. That's because the LORD had put them into a deep sleep.

13 David went across to the other side of the valley. He stood on top of a hill far away from Saul's camp. There was a wide space between them. 14 He called out to the army and to Abner, the son of Ner. He said, "Abner! Aren't you going to answer me?"

Abner replied, "Who is calling out to the king?"

15 David said, "You are a great soldier, aren't you? There isn't anyone else like you in Israel. So why didn't you guard the king? He's your master, isn't he? Someone came into the camp to destroy him. 16 You didn't guard him. And that isn't good. You can be sure that the LORD lives. And you can be just as sure that you and your men must die. That's because you didn't guard your master. He's the LORD's anointed king. Look around you. Where are the king's spear and water jug that were near his head?"

17 Saul recognized David's voice. He said, "My son David, is that your voice?"

David replied, "Yes it is, King Saul, my master." 18 He continued, "Why are you chasing me? What evil thing have I done? What am I guilty of? 19 King Saul, please listen to what I'm saying. Was it the LORD who made you angry with me? If it was, may he accept my offering. Was it people who made you angry at me? If it was, may the LORD see them cursed. They have driven me today from my share of the LORD's land. By doing that, they might as well have said, 'Go and serve other gods.' 20 Don't spill my blood on the ground far away from where the LORD lives. King Saul, you have come out to look for nothing but a flea. It's as if you were hunting a partridge in the mountains."

21 Then Saul said, "I have sinned. My son David, come back. Today you thought my life was very special. So I won't try to harm you again. I've really acted like a foolish person. I've made a huge mistake."

22 "Here's your spear," David answered. "Send one of your young men over to get it. 23 The LORD rewards everyone for doing what is right and being faithful. He handed you over to me today. But I wouldn't harm you. You are the LORD's anointed king. 24 Today I thought your life had great value. In the same way, may the LORD think of my life as having great value. May he save me from all trouble."

25 Then Saul said to David, "May the LORD bless you, David my son. You will do great things. You will also have great success."

So David went on his way. And Saul returned home.

David Among the Philistines

27 David thought, "Some day Saul will destroy me. So the best thing I can do is escape. I'll go to the land of the Philistines. Then Saul will stop looking for me everywhere in Israel. His hand won't be able to reach me."

2 So David and his 600 men left Israel. They went to Achish, the king of Gath. He was the son of Maok. 3 David and his men made their homes in Gath near Achish. Each of David's men had his family with him. David had his two wives with him. They were Ahinoam from Jezreel and Abigail from Carmel. Abigail was Nabal's widow. 4 Saul was told that David had run away to Gath. So he didn't look for David anymore.

5 David said to Achish, "If you are pleased with me, give me a place in one of your country towns. I can live there. I don't really need to live near you in the royal city."

6 So on that day Achish gave David the town of Ziklag. It has belonged to the kings of Judah ever since that time. 7 David lived in Philistine territory for a year and four months.

8 Sometimes David and his men would go up and attack the Geshurites. At other times they would attack the Girzites or the Amalekites. All those people had lived in the land that reached all the way to Shur and Egypt. They had been there for a long time. 9 When David would attack an area, he wouldn't leave a man or woman alive. But he would take their sheep, cattle, donkeys, camels and clothes. Then he would return to Achish.

10 Achish would ask, "Who did you at-
tack today?" David would answer, "The
people who live in the Negev Desert of
Judah." Or he would answer, "The peo-
ple in the Negev Desert of Jerahmeel."
Or he would answer, "The people in the
Negev Desert of the Kenites." 11 David
wouldn't leave a man or woman alive
to be brought back to Gath. He thought,
"They might tell on us. They might tell
Achish who we really attacked." That's
what David did as long as he lived in
Philistine territory. 12 Achish trusted
David. He thought, "David's own people,
the Israelites, can't stand him anymore.
So he'll be my servant for life."

28 While David was living in Ziklag,
the Philistines gathered their
army together. They planned to fight
against Israel. Achish said to David,
"Here is what you must understand.
You and your men must march out with
me and my army."

2 David said, "I understand. You will
see for yourself what I can do."

Achish replied, "All right. I'll make
you my own personal guard for life."

Saul and the Woman at Endor

3 Samuel had died. The whole nation
of Israel was filled with sorrow because
he was dead. They had buried him in his
own town of Ramah. Saul had thrown
out of the land people who get messages
from those who have died. He had also
thrown out people who talk to the spirits
of the dead.

4 The Philistines gathered together
and set up camp at Shunem. At the
same time, Saul gathered together
all the Israelites. They set up camp at
Gilboa. 5 When Saul saw the Philistine
army, he was afraid. Terror filled his
heart. 6 He asked the LORD for advice.
But the LORD didn't answer him through
dreams or prophets. He didn't answer
him when Saul had the priest cast lots
by using the Urim. 7 Saul spoke to his
attendants. He said, "Find me a woman who gets messages from those who
have died. Then I can go and ask her
some questions."

"There's a woman like that in Endor,"
they said.

8 Saul put on different clothes so people wouldn't know who he was. At night
he and two of his men went to see the
woman. "I want you to talk to a spirit
for me," he said. "Bring up the spirit of
the dead person I choose."

9 But the woman said to him, "By now
you must know what Saul has done.
He has removed everyone who gets
messages from those who have died.
He has also removed everyone who
talks to the spirits of the dead. He has
thrown all of them out of the land. Why
are you trying to trap me? Why do you
want to have me put to death?"

10 Saul made a promise in the name
of the LORD. He said to the woman, "You
can be sure that the LORD lives. And you
can be just as sure that you won't be
punished for helping me."

11 Then the woman asked, "Whose
spirit should I bring up for you?"

"Bring Samuel up," he said.

12 When the woman saw Samuel, she
let out a loud scream. She said to Saul,
"Why have you tricked me? You are
King Saul!"

13 He said to her, "Don't be afraid. Tell
me what you see."

The woman said, "I see a ghostly
figure. He's coming up out of the earth."

14 "What does he look like?" Saul
asked.

"An old man wearing a robe is coming
up," she said.

Then Saul knew it was Samuel. He
bowed down. He lay down flat with his
face toward the ground.

15 Samuel said to Saul, "Why have
you troubled me by bringing me up
from the dead?"

"I'm having big problems," Saul said.
"The Philistines are fighting against
me. God has left me. He doesn't answer
me anymore. He doesn't speak to me
through prophets or dreams. So I've
called on you to tell me what to do."

16 Samuel said, "The LORD has left you.
He has become your enemy. So why are
you asking me what you should do?
17 The LORD has spoken through me and
has done what he said he would do.
The LORD has torn the kingdom out
of your hands. He has given it to one
of your neighbors. He has given it to
David. 18 You didn't obey the LORD. You
didn't show his great anger against
the Amalekites by destroying them.
So he's punishing you today. 19 He will
hand both Israel and you over to the

Philistines. Tomorrow you and your
sons will be down here with me. The
LORD will also hand Israel's army over
to the Philistines."
20 Immediately Saul fell flat on the
ground. What Samuel had said filled
Saul with fear. His strength was gone.
He hadn't eaten anything all that day
and all that night.
21 The woman went over to Saul because she saw that he was very upset.
She said, "Look, I've obeyed you. I put
my own life in danger by doing what
you told me to do. 22 So please listen to
me. Let me give you some food. Eat it.
Then you will have the strength to go
on your way."
23 But he refused. He said, "I don't
want anything to eat."

Then his men joined the woman in
begging him to eat. Finally, he paid
attention to them. He got up from the
ground and sat on a couch.
24 The woman had a fat calf at her
house. She killed it at once. She got
some flour. She mixed it and baked
some bread that didn't have any yeast
in it. 25 Then she set the food in front of
Saul and his men. They ate it. That same
night they got up and left.

Achish Sends David Back to Ziklag

29 The Philistines gathered their
whole army together at Aphek.
Israel's army camped by the spring of
water at Jezreel. 2 The Philistine rulers
marched out in groups of hundreds and
thousands. David and his men were
marching with Achish behind the others. 3 The commanders of the Philistines
asked, "Why are these Hebrews here?"

Achish replied, "That's David, isn't it?
Wasn't he an officer of Saul, the king of
Israel? He has already been with me for
more than a year. I haven't found any
fault in him. That's been true from the
day he left Saul until now."
4 But the Philistine commanders
were angry with Achish. They said,
"Send David back. Let him return to
the town you gave him. He must not
go with us into battle. If he does, he'll
turn against us during the fighting.
In fact, he might even cut off the
heads of our own men. What better
way could he choose to win back his
master's favor? 5 Isn't David the one
the Israelites sang about when they
danced? They sang,

"'Saul has killed thousands of men.
David has killed tens of
thousands.'"

6 So Achish called David over to him.
He said, "You have been faithful to me.
And that's just as sure as the LORD is
alive. I would be pleased to have you
serve with me in the army. I haven't
found any fault in you. That's been
true from the day you came to me
until today. But the Philistine rulers
aren't pleased to have you come along.
7 So now go back home in peace. Don't
do anything that wouldn't please the
Philistine rulers."
8 "But what have I done?" asked David. "What have you found against me
from the day I came to you until now?
Why can't I go and fight against your
enemies? After all, you are my king
and master."
9 Achish answered, "You have been
as pleasing to me as an angel of God.
But the Philistine commanders have
said, 'We don't want David to go up with
us into battle.' 10 So get up early in the
morning. Take with you the men who
used to serve Saul. Leave as soon as the
sun begins to come up."
11 So David and his men got up early
in the morning. They went back to the
land of the Philistines. And the Philistines went up to Jezreel.

David Destroys the Amalekites

30 On the third day David and
his men arrived in Ziklag. The
Amalekites had attacked the people
of the Negev Desert. They had also attacked Ziklag and burned it. 2 They had
captured the women and everyone else
in Ziklag. They had taken as prisoners
young people and old people alike. But
they didn't kill any of them. Instead,
they carried them off as they went on
their way.
3 David and his men reached Ziklag.
They saw that it had been destroyed
by fire. They found out that their wives
and sons and daughters had been captured. 4 So David and his men began to
weep out loud. They wept until they
couldn't weep anymore. 5 David's two
wives had been captured. Their names

were Ahinoam from Jezreel and Abigail
from Carmel. Abigail was Nabal's widow. 6 David was greatly troubled. His
men were even talking about killing
him by throwing stones at him. All of
them were very bitter because their
sons and daughters had been taken
away. But David was made strong by
the LORD his God.

7 Then David spoke to Abiathar the
priest, the son of Ahimelek. He said,
"Bring me the linen apron." Abiathar
brought it to him. 8 David asked the
LORD for advice. He said, "Should I chase
after the men who attacked Ziklag? If I
do, will I catch up with them?"

"Chase after them," the LORD answered. "You will certainly catch up
with them. You will succeed in saving
those who were captured."

9 David and his 600 men came to
the Besor Valley. Some of them stayed
behind there. 10 That's because 200 of
them were too tired to go across the
valley. But David and the other 400
continued the chase.

11 David's men found an Egyptian
in a field. They brought him to David.
They gave him water to drink and food
to eat. 12 They gave him part of a cake
of pressed figs. They also gave him
two raisin cakes. After he ate them, he
felt as good as new. That's because he
hadn't eaten any food for three days
and three nights. He hadn't drunk any
water during that time either.

13 David asked him, "Who do you
belong to? Where do you come from?"

The man said, "I'm from Egypt. I'm
the slave of an Amalekite. My master
deserted me when I became ill three
days ago. 14 We attacked the people in
the Negev Desert of the Kerethites. We
attacked the territory that belongs to
Judah. We attacked the people in the
Negev Desert of Caleb. And we burned
Ziklag."

15 David asked him, "Can you lead me
down to the men who attacked Ziklag?"

He answered, "Make a promise to me
in the name of God. Promise that you
won't kill me. Promise that you won't
hand me over to my master. Then I'll
take you down to them."

16 He led David down to where the
men were. They were scattered all over
the countryside. They were eating and
drinking and dancing wildly. That's
because they had taken a large amount
of goods from those they had attacked.
They had taken it from the land of the
Philistines and from the people of Judah. 17 David fought against them from
sunset until the evening of the next
day. None of them escaped except 400
young men. They rode off on camels
and got away. 18 David got everything
back that the Amalekites had taken.
That included his two wives. 19 Nothing
was missing. Not one young person or
old person or boy or girl was missing.
None of the goods or anything else the
Amalekites had taken was missing.
David brought everything back. 20 He
brought back all the flocks and herds.
His men drove them on ahead of the
other livestock. They said, "Here's what
David has captured."

21 Then David came to the 200 men
who had been too tired to follow him.
They had been left behind in the Besor
Valley. They came out to welcome David
and the men with him. As David and
his men approached, he asked them
how they were. 22 But some of the men
who had gone out with David were evil.
They wanted to stir up trouble. They
said, "The 200 men didn't go out into
battle with us. So we won't share with
them the goods we brought back. But
each man can take his wife and children
and go home."

23 David replied, "No, my friends. You
must not hold back their share of what
the LORD has given us. He has kept us
safe. He has handed over to us the men
who attacked us. 24 So no one will pay
any attention to what you are saying.
Each man who stayed with the supplies
will receive the same share as each man
who went down to the battle. Everyone's
share will be the same." 25 David made
that a law and a rule for Israel. It has
been followed from that day until now.

26 David reached Ziklag. He sent some
of the goods to the elders of Judah. They
were his friends. He said, "Here's a gift
for you. It's part of the things we took
from the LORD's enemies."

27 David sent some goods to the elders
in Bethel, Ramoth Negev and Jattir.
28 He sent some to the elders in Aroer,
Siphmoth, Eshtemoa 29 and Rakal. He
sent some to the elders in the towns of

the Jerahmeelites and Kenites. 30 He
sent some to the elders in Hormah, Bor
Ashan, Athak 31 and Hebron. He also
sent some to the elders in all the other
places where he and his men had wandered around.

Saul Takes His Own Life

31 The Philistines fought against
the Israelites. The Israelites ran
away from them. But many Israelites
were killed on Mount Gilboa. 2 The Philistines kept chasing Saul and his sons.
They killed his sons Jonathan, Abinadab and Malki-Shua. 3 The fighting
was heavy around Saul. Men who were
armed with bows and arrows caught up
with him. They shot their arrows at him
and wounded him badly.
4 Saul spoke to the man carrying his
armor. He said, "Pull out your sword.
Stick it through me. If you don't, these
fellows who aren't circumcised will
come. They'll stick their swords through
me and hurt me badly."
But the man was terrified. He wouldn't
do it. So Saul took his own sword and fell
on it. 5 The man saw that Saul was dead.
So he fell on his own sword and died with
him. 6 Saul and his three sons died together that same day. The man who carried
his armor also died with them that day.
So did all of Saul's men.
7 The Israelites who lived along the
valley saw that their army had run
away. So did those who lived across
the Jordan River. They saw that Saul
and his sons were dead. So they left
their towns and ran away. Then the
Philistines came and made their homes
in them.
8 The day after the Philistines had
won the battle, they came to take what
they wanted from the dead bodies. They
found Saul and his three sons dead on
Mount Gilboa. 9 So they cut off Saul's
head. They took his armor from his
body. Then they sent messengers
through the whole land of the Philistines. They announced the news in the
temple where they had set up statues
of their gods. They also announced it
among their people. 10 They put Saul's
armor in the temple where they had
set up statues of female gods that were
named Ashtoreth. They hung his body
up on the wall of Beth Shan.
11 The people of Jabesh Gilead heard
about what the Philistines had done to
Saul. 12 So all their brave men marched
through the night to Beth Shan. They
took down the bodies of Saul and
his sons from the wall of Beth Shan.
They brought them to Jabesh. There
they burned them. 13 Then they got
the bones of Saul and his sons and
buried them under a tamarisk tree at
Jabesh. They didn't eat anything for
seven days.

2 SAMUEL

Author: We don't know.

If you were an Israelite when David was king, you probably wouldn't have thought he was the best choice. After all, he had seven older brothers. David was the youngest son in his family and had spent most of his life caring for sheep. But David was willing to do whatever God asked. And since God was looking for a king who would follow him, obey his commands, and humbly worship him, God asked the prophet Samuel to anoint David as king.

David loved God and led God's people in obedience to the law. He was a brave and kind king. In fact, David was the very best king Israel would ever have. Generations after David died, God's people would look back and think about just how wonderful life was when David was king. But even though David was a good king, he failed to be a perfect king. He let God's people down through sin and disobedience in his own life. Though King David failed to lead the Israelites in perfect faithfulness, God reminded his people that one day he would send a Savior who would be the perfect and final King forever and ever.

Old Testament History

David Hears That Saul Has Died

1 After Saul died, David returned to Ziklag. He had won the battle over the Amalekites. He stayed in Ziklag for two days. 2 On the third day a man arrived from Saul's camp. His clothes were torn. He had dust on his head. When he came to David, he fell to the ground to show him respect.

3 "Where have you come from?" David asked him.

He answered, "I've escaped from Israel's camp."

4 "What happened?" David asked. "Tell me."

He said, "Israel's men ran away from the battle. Many of them were killed. Saul and his son Jonathan are dead."

5 David spoke to the young man who brought him the report. He asked him, "How do you know that Saul and his son Jonathan are dead?"

6 "I just happened to be there on Mount Gilboa," the young man said. "Saul was there too. He was leaning on his spear. The enemy chariots and chariot drivers had almost caught up with him. 7 Then he turned around and saw me. He called out to me. I said, 'What do you want me to do?'

8 "He asked me, 'Who are you?'

" 'An Amalekite,' I answered.

9 "Then he said to me, 'Stand here by me and kill me! I'm close to death, but I'm still alive.'

10 "So I stood beside him and killed him. I did it because I knew that after he had lost the battle he would be killed anyway. So I took the crown that was on his head. I also took his armband. I've brought them here to you. You are my master."

11 Then David tore his clothes. And all his men tore their clothes. 12 All of them were filled with sadness. They mourned over the whole nation of Israel. They didn't eat anything until evening. That's because Saul and Jonathan and the LORD's army had been killed by swords.

13 David spoke to the young man who had brought him the report. He asked, "Where are you from?"

"I'm the son of an outsider, an Amalekite," he answered.

14 David asked him, "Why weren't you afraid to lift your hand to kill the LORD's anointed king?"

15 Then David called for one of his men. He said, "Go! Strike him down!" So he struck the man down, and the man died. 16 That's because David had said to him, "Anything that happens to you will be your own fault. What your own mouth has spoken is a witness against you. You said, 'I killed the LORD's anointed king.' "

David's Song of Sadness About Saul and Jonathan

17 David sang a song of sadness about Saul and his son Jonathan. 18 He ordered that it be taught to the people of Judah. It is a song that is played on a stringed instrument. It is written down in the Book of Jashar. David sang,

19 "Israel, a gazelle lies dead on your hills.
Your mighty men have fallen.

20 "Don't announce it in Gath.
Don't tell it in the streets of Ashkelon.
If you do, the daughters of the Philistines will be glad.
The daughters of men who haven't been circumcised will be joyful.

21 "Mountains of Gilboa,
may no dew or rain fall on you.
May no showers fall on your hillside fields.
The shield of the mighty king wasn't respected there.
The shield of Saul lies there. It isn't rubbed with oil anymore.
22 The bow of Jonathan didn't turn back.
The sword of Saul didn't return without being satisfied.
They spilled the blood of their enemies.
They killed mighty men.

23 "When they lived, Saul and Jonathan were loved and respected.
When they died, they were not parted.
They were faster than eagles.
They were stronger than lions.

24 "Daughters of Israel, mourn over Saul.
He dressed you in the finest clothes.
He decorated your clothes with ornaments of gold.

25 "Your mighty men have fallen in
battle.
Jonathan lies dead on your hills.
26 My brother Jonathan, I'm filled
with sadness because of you.
You were very special to me.
Your love for me was wonderful.
It was more wonderful than the
love of women.

27 "Israel's mighty men have fallen.
Their weapons of war are
broken."

David Is Anointed to Be King Over Judah

2 After Saul and Jonathan died,
David asked the LORD for advice.
"Should I go up to one of the towns of
Judah?" he asked.

The LORD said, "Go up."

David asked, "Where should I go?"

"To Hebron," the LORD answered.

2 So David went up there with his two
wives. Their names were Ahinoam from
Jezreel and Abigail from Carmel. Abigail
was Nabal's widow. 3 David also took his
men and their families with him. They
made their homes in Hebron and its
towns. 4 Then the men of Judah came to
Hebron. There they anointed David to be
king over the people of Judah.

David was told that the men from
Jabesh Gilead had buried Saul's body.
5 So he sent messengers to them to speak
for him. The messengers said, "You were
kind to bury the body of your master
Saul. May the LORD bless you for that.
6 And may he now be kind and faithful
to you. David will treat you well for
being kind to Saul's body. 7 Now then,
be strong and brave. Your master Saul
is dead. And the people of Judah have
anointed David to be king over them."

The Armies of David and Saul Fight Each Other

8 Abner, the son of Ner, was commander of Saul's army. Abner had brought
Saul's son Ish-Bosheth to Mahanaim.
9 There Abner made Ish-Bosheth king
over Gilead, Ashuri and Jezreel. He also
made him king over Ephraim, Benjamin
and other areas of Israel.

10 Ish-Bosheth was 40 years old when
he became king over Israel. He ruled
for two years. But the people of Judah
remained faithful to David. 11 David was

in 2 Samuel?

God is the Eternal Hope. In his mercy and kindness, God promised that one day the true and perfect King—King Jesus—would come and reign forever.

king in Hebron over the people of Judah
for seven and a half years.

12 Abner, the son of Ner, left Mahanaim and went to Gibeon. The men of
Ish-Bosheth, the son of Saul, went with
him. 13 Joab, the son of Zeruiah, and
David's men also went out. All of them
met at the pool in Gibeon. One group sat
down on one side of the pool. The other
group sat on the other side.

14 Then Abner said to Joab, "Let's have
some of the young men get up and fight.
Let's tell them to fight hand to hand in
front of us."

"All right. Let them do it," Joab said.
15 So the young men stood up and
were counted off. There were 12 on the
side of Benjamin and Saul's son Ish-
Bosheth. And there were 12 on David's
side. 16 Each man grabbed one of his
enemies by the head. Each one stuck
his dagger into the other man's side.
And all of them fell down together and
died. So that place in Gibeon was named
Helkath Hazzurim.

17 The fighting that day was very
heavy. Abner and the Israelites lost
the battle to David's men.

18 The three sons of Zeruiah were there.
Their names were Joab, Abishai and
Asahel. Asahel was as quick on his feet
as a wild antelope. 19 He chased Abner.
He didn't turn to the right or the left as
he chased him. 20 Abner looked behind
him. He asked, "Asahel, is that you?"

"It is," he answered.

[21]Then Abner said to him, "Turn to the right or the left. Fight one of the young men. Take his weapons away from him." But Asahel wouldn't stop chasing him.
[22]Again Abner warned Asahel, "Stop chasing me! If you don't, I'll strike you down. Then how could I look your brother Joab in the face?"
[23]But Asahel refused to give up the chase. So Abner drove the dull end of his spear into Asahel's stomach. The spear came out through his back. He fell and died right there on the spot. Every man stopped when he came to the place where Asahel had fallen and died.
[24]But Joab and Abishai chased Abner. As the sun was going down, they came to the hill of Ammah. It was near Giah on the way to the dry and empty land close to Gibeon.
[25]The men of Benjamin gathered in a group around Abner. They took their stand on top of a hill.
[26]Abner called out to Joab, "Do you want our swords to keep on killing us off? Don't you know that all this fighting will end in bitter feelings? How long will it be before you order your men to stop chasing their fellow Israelites?"
[27]Joab answered, "It's a good thing you spoke up. If you hadn't, the men would have kept on chasing them until morning. And that's just as sure as God is alive."
[28]So Joab blew a trumpet. All the troops stopped. They didn't chase Israel anymore. They didn't fight anymore either.
[29]All that night Abner and his men marched through the Arabah Valley. They went across the Jordan River. All morning long they kept on going. Finally, they came to Mahanaim.
[30]Then Joab stopped chasing Abner. He gathered together the whole army. Besides Asahel, only 19 of David's men were missing.
[31]But David's men had killed 360 men from Benjamin who were with Abner.
[32]They got Asahel's body and buried it in his father's tomb at Bethlehem. Then Joab and his men marched all night. They arrived at Hebron at sunrise.

3 The war between Saul's royal house and David's royal house lasted a long time. David grew stronger and stronger. But the royal house of Saul grew weaker and weaker.

[2]Sons were born to David in Hebron.

His first son was Amnon. Amnon's mother was Ahinoam from Jezreel.
[3]His second son was Kileab. Kileab's mother was Abigail. She was Nabal's widow from Carmel.
The third son was Absalom. His mother was Maakah. She was the daughter of Talmai, the king of Geshur.
[4]The fourth son was Adonijah. His mother was Haggith.
The fifth son was Shephatiah. His mother was Abital.
[5]The sixth son was Ithream. His mother was David's wife Eglah.

Those sons were born to David in Hebron.

Abner Goes Over to David's Side

[6]The fighting continued between David's royal house and Saul's royal house. Abner gained more and more power in the royal house of Saul.
[7]While Saul was still alive, he had a concubine named Rizpah. She was the daughter of Aiah. Ish-Bosheth said to Abner, "Why did you sleep with my father's concubine?"
[8]Abner was very angry because of what Ish-Bosheth said. So Abner answered, "Do you think I'm only a dog's head? Am I on Judah's side? To this day I've been faithful to the royal house of your father Saul. I've been faithful to his family and friends. I haven't handed you over to David. But now you claim that I've sinned with this woman!
[9]I will do for David what the LORD promised him. If I don't, may God punish me greatly.
[10]I'll take the kingdom away from Saul's royal house. I'll set up the throne of David's kingdom over Israel and Judah. He will rule from Dan all the way to Beersheba."
[11]Ish-Bosheth didn't dare to say another word to Abner. He was much too afraid of him.
[12]Then Abner sent messengers to David to speak for him. They said, "Who will rule over this land? Make a covenant with me. Then I'll help you bring all the Israelites over to your side."
[13]"Good," said David. "I will make a covenant with you. But there's one thing I want you to do. Bring Saul's daughter Michal to me. Don't come to see me unless she's with you."
[14]Then

David sent messengers to Saul's son Ish-
Bosheth. He ordered them to say, "Give
me my wife Michal. She was promised
to me. I paid for her the price that was
demanded. I paid for her with the skins
of 100 circumcised Philistines."
15 So Ish-Bosheth gave the order. He
sent men who took Michal away from
her husband Paltiel. Paltiel was the son
of Laish. 16 But her husband followed
her to Bahurim. He was crying all the
way. Then Abner said to him, "Go back
home!" So he did.
17 Abner talked with the elders of Israel. He said, "For some time you have
wanted to make David your king. 18 Now
do it! The LORD made a promise to David. He said, 'I will rescue my people
Israel from the power of the Philistines.
I will also rescue them from all their
enemies. I will rescue them through
my servant David.' "
19 Abner also spoke to the people of
Benjamin in person. Then he went to
Hebron to tell David everything. He told
him what Israel and all the people of
Benjamin wanted to do. 20 Abner had 20
men with him. They came to David at
Hebron. So David prepared a feast for
Abner and his men. 21 Then Abner said to
David, "Let me go right now. I'll gather
together all the Israelites for you. After
all, you are now my king and master.
The people can make a covenant with
you. Then you can rule over everyone
you want to." So David sent Abner away.
And he went in peace.

Joab Murders Abner

22 Just then David's men and Joab
came back from attacking their enemies. They brought with them the large
amount of goods they had taken. But
Abner wasn't with David in Hebron anymore. That's because David had sent
him away, and he had gone in peace.
23 Joab and all the soldiers with him arrived. Then he was told that Abner, the
son of Ner, had come to see the king. He
was told that the king had sent Abner
away. He was also told that Abner had
gone in peace.
24 So Joab went to the king. He said,
"What have you done? Abner came to
you. Why did you let him get away?
Now he's gone! 25 You know what Abner,
the son of Ner, is like. He came to trick
you. He wanted to watch your every
move. He came to find out everything
you are doing."
26 Then Joab left David. He sent messengers to get Abner. They brought
Abner back from the well of Sirah. But
David didn't know about it. 27 When
Abner returned to Hebron, Joab took
him to one side. He brought him into an
inside room. Joab acted as if he wanted
to speak to him in private. But he really
wanted to get even with him. That's
because Abner had spilled the blood of
Joab's brother Asahel. So Joab stabbed
Abner in the stomach, and he died.
28 Later on, David heard about it. He
said, "I and the people of my kingdom
aren't guilty of spilling the blood of Abner, the son of Ner. We are free of blame
forever in the sight of the LORD. 29 May
Joab and his whole family line be held
accountable for spilling Abner's blood!
May Joab's family never be without
someone who has an open sore or skin
disease. May his family never be without
someone who has to use a crutch to walk.
May his family never be without someone who gets killed by a sword. And may
his family never be without someone
who doesn't have enough to eat."
30 Joab and his brother Abishai murdered Abner. They did it because he had
killed their brother Asahel in the battle
at Gibeon.
31 David spoke to Joab and all the
people with him. He said, "Tear your
clothes. Put on the rough clothing people wear when they're sad. Mourn when
you walk in front of Abner's body." King
David himself walked behind it. 32 Abner's body was buried in Hebron. The
king wept out loud at Abner's tomb. So
did the rest of the people.
33 King David sang a song of sadness
over Abner. He said,

"Should Abner have died as sinful
people do?
34 His hands were not tied.
His feet were not chained.
He died as if he had been killed by
evil people."

All the people mourned over Abner
again.
35 Then all of them came and begged
David to eat something. They wanted
him to eat while it was still day. But

David made a promise. He said, "I won't taste bread or anything else before the sun goes down. If I do, may God punish me greatly!"

36 All the people heard his promise and were pleased. In fact, everything the king did pleased them. 37 So on that day all the people there and all the Israelites understood. They knew that the king didn't have anything to do with the murder of Abner, the son of Ner.

38 The king spoke to his men. He said, "Don't you realize that a great commander has died in Israel today? 39 I'm the anointed king. But today I'm weak. These sons of Zeruiah are too powerful for me. May the LORD pay back the one who killed Abner! May he pay him back for the evil thing he has done!"

Ish-Bosheth Is Murdered

4 Ish-Bosheth, the son of Saul, heard that Abner had died in Hebron. Then he wasn't so brave anymore. And all the Israelites became alarmed. 2 Two men in Ish-Bosheth's army led small fighting groups that attacked their enemies. The names of the men were Baanah and Rekab. They were sons of Rimmon from the town of Beeroth. Rimmon was from the tribe of Benjamin. Beeroth is considered to be part of Benjamin. 3 That's because the people who used to live in Beeroth had run away to Gittaim. They have lived there as outsiders to this day.

4 Jonathan, the son of Saul, had a son named Mephibosheth. Both of Mephibosheth's feet were hurt. He was five years old when the news that Saul and Jonathan had died came from Jezreel. His nurse picked him up and ran. But as she hurried to get away, he fell down. That's how his feet were hurt.

5 Rekab and Baanah started out for the house of Ish-Bosheth. They were the sons of Rimmon from Beeroth. They arrived there during the hottest time of the day. Ish-Bosheth was taking his early afternoon nap. 6 Rekab and his brother Baanah went into the inside part of the house. They acted as if they were going to get some wheat. Instead, they stabbed Ish-Bosheth in the stomach. Then they slipped away.

7 They had gone into the house while Ish-Bosheth was lying on his bed in his bedroom. They stabbed him and killed him. Then they cut off his head and took it with them. They traveled all night through the Arabah Valley. 8 They brought the head of Ish-Bosheth to King David at Hebron. They said to him, "Here's the head of Ish-Bosheth, the son of Saul. Saul was your enemy. He often tried to kill you. Today the LORD has paid back Saul and his family. He has let you get even with them. You are our king and master."

9 David gave an answer to Rekab and his brother Baanah. They were the sons of Rimmon from Beeroth. David said, "The LORD has saved me from every trouble. 10 Someone once told me, 'Saul is dead.' He thought he was bringing me good news. But I grabbed him. I had him put to death in Ziklag. That's the reward I gave him for his news! And that's just as sure as the LORD is alive. 11 Now you evil men have killed a man in his own house. He hadn't done anything wrong. You killed him while he was lying on his own bed. You spilled his blood. So shouldn't I spill your blood? Shouldn't I wipe you off the face of the earth?"

12 Then David gave an order to his men. They killed Rekab and Baanah. They cut off their hands and feet. They hung their bodies by the pool in Hebron. But they buried the head of Ish-Bosheth in Abner's tomb at Hebron.

David Becomes King Over Israel

5 All the tribes of Israel came to see David at Hebron. They said, "We are your own flesh and blood. 2 In the past, Saul was our king. But you led Israel on their military campaigns. And the LORD said to you, 'You will be the shepherd over my people Israel. You will become their ruler.' "

3 All the elders of Israel came to see King David at Hebron. There the king made a covenant with them in front of the LORD. They anointed David as king over Israel.

4 David was 30 years old when he became king. He ruled for 40 years. 5 In Hebron he ruled over Judah for seven and a half years. In Jerusalem he ruled over all of Israel and Judah for 33 years.

David Captures Jerusalem

6 The king and his men marched to Jerusalem. They went to attack the

Jebusites who lived there. The Jebusites
said to David, "You won't get in here.
Even people who can't see or walk can
keep you from coming in." The Jebusites
thought, "David can't get in here." 7 But
David captured the fort of Zion. It became known as the City of David.
8 On that day David had said, "Someone might win the battle over the
Jebusites. But they will have to crawl
through the water tunnel to get into
the city. That's the only way they can
reach those enemies of mine that you
say can't see or walk." That's why people
say, "Those who 'can't see or walk' won't
enter David's palace."
9 David moved into the fort. He called
it the City of David. He built up the area
around the fort. He filled in the low places. He started at the bottom and worked
his way up. 10 David became more and
more powerful. That's because the LORD
God who rules over all was with him.
11 Hiram was king of Tyre. He sent
messengers to David. He sent cedar logs
along with them. He also sent skilled
workers. They worked with wood and
stone. They built a palace for David.
12 Then David knew that the LORD had
made his position as king secure. He
knew that he had made him king over
the whole nation of Israel. He knew
that the LORD had greatly honored his
kingdom. The LORD had done it because
the Israelites were his people.
13 After David left Hebron, he got more
concubines and wives in Jerusalem.
More sons and daughters were born to
him there. 14 Here is a list of the children
who were born to him in Jerusalem.
Their names were Shammua, Shobab,
Nathan, Solomon, 15 Ibhar, Elishua,
Nepheg, Japhia, 16 Elishama, Eliada
and Eliphelet.

David Wins the Battle Over the Philistines

17 The Philistines heard that David
had been anointed king over Israel.
So their whole army went to look for
him. But David heard about it. He went
down to his usual place of safety. 18 The
Philistines had come and spread out in
the Valley of Rephaim. 19 So David asked
the LORD for advice. He said, "Should I
go and attack the Philistines? Will you
hand them over to me?"
The LORD answered him, "Go. I will
surely hand over the Philistines to you."
20 So David went to Baal Perazim.
There he won the battle over the Philistines. He said, "The LORD has broken
through against my enemies when I've
attacked them. He has broken through
just as water breaks through a dam."
That's why the place was called Baal
Perazim. 21 The Philistines left the statues of their gods there. So David and his
men carried off the statues.
22 Once more the Philistines came up.
They spread out in the Valley of Rephaim.
23 So David asked the LORD for advice.
The LORD answered, "Do not go straight
up. Instead, circle around behind them.
Attack them in front of the poplar trees.
24 Listen for the sound of marching in
the tops of the trees. Then move quickly.
The sound will mean that I have gone
out in front of you. I will strike down the
Philistine army." 25 So David did just as
the LORD had commanded him. He struck
down the Philistines. He struck them
down from Gibeon all the way to Gezer.

David Brings the Ark to Jerusalem

6 Again David brought together the
best soldiers in Israel. The total
number was 30,000. 2 He and all his
men went to Baalah in Judah. They
wanted to bring the ark of God up to
Jerusalem from there. The ark is named
after the LORD. He is the LORD who rules
over all. He sits on his throne between
the cherubim that are on the ark. 3 The
ark of God was placed on a new cart.
Then it was brought from Abinadab's
house, which was on a hill. Uzzah and
Ahio were guiding the cart. They were
the sons of Abinadab. 4 The ark of God
was on the cart. Ahio was walking in
front of it. 5 David was celebrating with
all his might in front of the LORD. So
was the whole community of Israel. All
of them were playing castanets, harps,
lyres, tambourines, rattles and cymbals.
6 They came to the threshing floor of
Nakon. The oxen nearly fell there. So
Uzzah reached out and took hold of the
ark of God. 7 Then the LORD was very
angry with Uzzah. That's because what
Uzzah did showed that he didn't have
any respect for the LORD. So God struck
him down. He died there beside the ark
of God.

8 David was angry because the LORD's
great anger had broken out against
Uzzah. That's why the place is still called
Perez Uzzah to this day.
9 David was afraid of the LORD that
day. He asked, "How can the ark of the
LORD ever be brought to me?" 10 He didn't
want to take the ark of the LORD to be
with him in the City of David. Instead,
he took it to the house of Obed-Edom.
Obed-Edom was from Gath. 11 The ark
of the LORD remained in Obed-Edom's
house for three months. And the LORD
blessed him and his whole family.
12 King David was told, "The LORD has
blessed the family of Obed-Edom. He has
also blessed everything that belongs to
him. That's because the ark of God is
in Obed-Edom's house." So David went
down there to bring up the ark. With
great joy he brought it up from the house
of Obed-Edom. He took it to the City of
David. 13 Those carrying the ark of the
LORD took six steps forward. Then David
sacrificed a bull and a fat calf. 14 David
was wearing a sacred linen apron. He
danced in front of the LORD with all his
might. 15 He did it while he was bringing up the ark of the LORD. The whole
community of Israel helped him bring
it up. They shouted. They blew trumpets.
16 The ark of the LORD was brought
into the City of David. Saul's daughter
Michal was watching from a window.
She saw King David leaping and dancing in front of the LORD. That made her
hate him in her heart.
17 The ark of the LORD was brought
into Jerusalem. It was put in its place
in the tent David had set up for it. David
sacrificed burnt offerings and friendship offerings to the LORD. 18 After he
finished sacrificing those offerings, he
blessed the people in the name of the
LORD who rules over all. 19 He gave to
each Israelite man and woman a loaf
of bread. He also gave each one a date
cake and a raisin cake. Then all the
people went home.
20 David returned home to bless his
family. Saul's daughter Michal came
out to meet him. She said, "You are the
king of Israel. You have really brought
honor to yourself today, haven't you?
You have gone around half-naked right
in front of the female slaves of your
officials. You acted like a fool!"
21 David said to Michal, "I did it to honor
the LORD. He chose me instead of your father or anyone else in Saul's family. The
LORD appointed me ruler over his people
Israel. I will celebrate to honor the LORD.
22 And that's not all. I will bring even less
honor to myself. I will bring even more
shame on myself. But those female slaves
you spoke about will honor me."
23 Saul's daughter Michal didn't have
any children as long as she lived.

God's Promise to David

7 The king moved into his palace. The
LORD had given him peace and rest
from all his enemies around him. 2 Then
the king spoke to Nathan the prophet.
He said, "Here I am, living in a house
that has beautiful cedar walls. But the
ark of God remains in a tent."
3 Nathan replied to the king, "Go
ahead and do what you want to. The
LORD is with you."
4 But that night the word of the LORD
came to Nathan. The LORD said,
5 "Go and speak to my servant David. Tell him, 'The LORD says, "Are
you the one to build me a house to
live in? 6 I brought the Israelites up
out of Egypt. But I have not lived in
a house from then until now. I have
been moving from place to place. I
have been living in a tent. 7 I have
moved from place to place with all
the Israelites. I commanded their
rulers to be shepherds over them.
I never asked any of those rulers,
'Why haven't you built me a house
that has beautiful cedar walls?'" '
8 "So tell my servant David, 'The
LORD who rules over all says, "I took
you away from the grasslands.
That's where you were taking care
of your father's sheep and goats.
I made you ruler over my people
Israel. 9 I have been with you everywhere you have gone. I have destroyed all your enemies. Now I will
make you famous. Your name will
be just as respected as the names
of the most important people on
earth. 10 I will provide a place where
my people Israel can live. I will
plant them in the land. Then they
will have a home of their own. They
will not be bothered anymore. Evil
people will no longer crush them,

as they did at first. [11]That is what
your enemies have done ever since
I appointed leaders over my people
Israel. But I will give you peace and
rest from all of them.

"'"I tell you that I, the LORD, will
set up a royal house for you. [12]Some
day your life will come to an end.
You will join the members of your
family who have already died. Then
I will make one of your own sons the
next king after you. And I will make
his kingdom secure. [13]He is the one
who will build a house where I will
put my Name. I will set up the
throne of his kingdom. It will last
forever. [14]I will be his father. And he
will be my son. When he does what
is wrong, I will use other men to beat
him with rods and whips. [15]I took
my love away from Saul. I removed
him from being king. You were there
when I did it. But I will never take
my love away from your son. [16]Your
royal house and your kingdom will
last forever in my sight. Your throne
will last forever."'"

[17]Nathan reported to David all the
words that the LORD had spoken to him.

David's Prayer to the LORD

[18]Then King David went into the holy
tent. He sat down in front of the LORD.
He said,

"LORD and King, who am I? My
family isn't important. So why
have you brought me this far? [19]I
would have thought that you had
already done more than enough
for me. But now, LORD and King,
you have also said what will happen to my royal house in days to
come. And, my LORD and King, this
promise is for a mere human being!

[20]"What more can I say to you?
LORD and King, you know all about
me. [21]You have done a wonderful
thing. You have made it known to
me. You have done it because that's
what you said you would do. It's exactly what you wanted to do for me.

[22]"LORD and King, how great
you are! There isn't anyone like
you. There isn't any God but you.
We have heard about it with our
own ears. [23]Who is like your people
Israel? God, we are the one nation
on earth you have saved. You have
set us free for yourself. Your name
has become famous. You have done
great and wonderful things. You
have driven out nations and their
gods to make room for your people. You saved us when you set us
free from Egypt. [24]You made Israel your very own people forever.
LORD, you have become our God.

[25]"And now, LORD God, keep forever the promise you have made to
me and my royal house. Do exactly
as you promised. [26]Then your name
will be honored forever. People will
say, 'The LORD rules over all. He is
God over Israel.' My royal house will
be made secure in your sight.

[27]"LORD who rules over all, you
are the God of Israel. Here's what
you have shown me. You told me,
'I will build you a royal house.' So
I can boldly pray this prayer to
you. [28]LORD and King, you are God!
Your covenant can be trusted. You
have promised many good things
to me. [29]Now please bless my royal
house. Then it will continue forever
in your sight. LORD and King, you
have spoken. Because you have
given my royal house your blessing, it will be blessed forever."

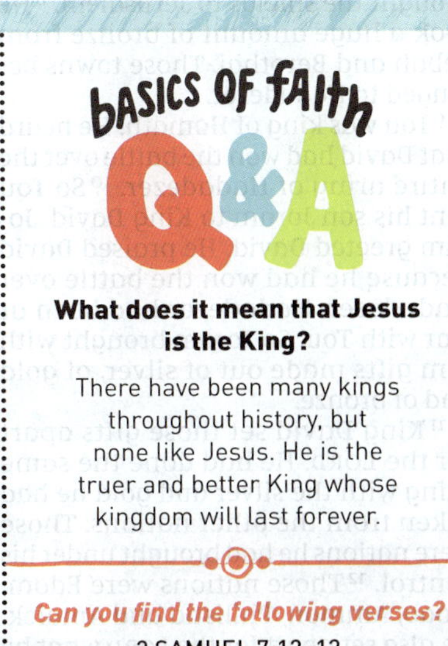

What does it mean that Jesus is the King?

There have been many kings throughout history, but none like Jesus. He is the truer and better King whose kingdom will last forever.

Can you find the following verses?

2 SAMUEL 7:12–13

David Wins Many Battles

8 While David was king of Israel, he won many battles over the Philistines. He brought them under his control. He took Metheg Ammah away from them.

2 David also won the battle over the people of Moab. He made them lie down on the ground. Then he measured them off with a piece of rope. He put two-thirds of them to death. He let the other third remain alive. So the Moabites were brought under David's rule. They gave him the gifts he required them to bring him.

3 David fought against Hadadezer, the son of Rehob. Hadadezer was king of Zobah. He had gone to repair his monument at the Euphrates River. 4 David captured 1,000 of Hadadezer's chariots, 7,000 chariot riders and 20,000 soldiers on foot. He cut the legs of all but 100 of the chariot horses.

5 The Arameans of Damascus came to help Hadadezer, the king of Zobah. But David struck down 22,000 of them. 6 He stationed some soldiers in the Aramean kingdom of Damascus. The people of Aram were brought under his rule. They gave him the gifts he required them to bring him. The LORD helped David win his battles everywhere he went.

7 David took the gold shields that belonged to the officers of Hadadezer. He brought the shields to Jerusalem. 8 He took a huge amount of bronze from Tebah and Berothai. Those towns belonged to Hadadezer.

9 Tou was king of Hamath. He heard that David had won the battle over the entire army of Hadadezer. 10 So Tou sent his son Joram to King David. Joram greeted David. He praised David because he had won the battle over Hadadezer. Hadadezer had been at war with Tou. So Joram brought with him gifts made out of silver, of gold and of bronze.

11 King David set those gifts apart for the LORD. He had done the same thing with the silver and gold he had taken from the other nations. Those were nations he had brought under his control. 12 Those nations were Edom, Moab, Ammon, Philistia and Amalek. He also set apart for the LORD what he had taken from Hadadezer, the son of Rehob. Hadadezer was king of Zobah.

13 David returned after he had struck down 18,000 men of Edom in the Valley of Salt. He became famous for doing it.

14 He stationed some soldiers all through Edom. The whole nation of Edom was brought under David's rule. The LORD helped him win his battles everywhere he went.

David's Officials

15 David ruled over the whole nation of Israel. He did what was fair and right for all his people. 16 Joab, the son of Zeruiah, was commander over the army. Jehoshaphat, the son of Ahilud, kept the records. 17 Zadok, the son of Ahitub, was a priest. Ahimelek, the son of Abiathar, was also a priest. Seraiah was the secretary. 18 Benaiah, the son of Jehoiada, was commander over the Kerethites and Pelethites. And David's sons were priests.

David and Mephibosheth

9 David asked, "Is anyone left from the royal house of Saul? If there is, I want to be kind to him because of Jonathan."

2 Ziba was a servant in Saul's family. David sent for him to come and see him. The king said to him, "Are you Ziba?"

"I'm ready to serve you," he replied.

3 The king asked, "Isn't there anyone still alive from the royal house of Saul? God has been very kind to me. I would like to be kind to that person in the same way."

Ziba answered the king, "A son of Jonathan is still living. Both of his feet were hurt so that he can't walk."

4 "Where is he?" the king asked.

Ziba answered, "He's in the town of Lo Debar. He's staying at the house of Makir, the son of Ammiel."

5 So King David had Mephibosheth brought from Makir's house in Lo Debar.

6 Mephibosheth came to David. He was the son of Jonathan, the son of Saul. Mephibosheth bowed down to David to show him respect.

David said, "Mephibosheth!"

"I'm ready to serve you," he replied.

7 "Don't be afraid," David told him. "You can be sure that I will be kind to you because of your father Jonathan. I'll give back to you all the land that belonged to your grandfather Saul. And I'll always provide what you need."

8 Mephibosheth bowed down to David. He said, "Who am I? Why should
you pay attention to me? I'm nothing
but a dead dog."
9 Then the king sent for Saul's servant
Ziba. He said to him, "I'm giving your
master's grandson everything that belonged to Saul and his family. 10 You
and your sons and your servants must
farm the land for him. You must bring
in the crops. Then he'll be taken care of.
I'll always provide what he needs." Ziba
had 15 sons and 20 servants.
11 Then Ziba said to the king, "I'll do
anything you command me to do. You
are my king and master." So David provided what Mephibosheth needed. He
treated him like one of the king's sons.
12 Mephibosheth had a young son
named Mika. All the members of Ziba's family became servants of Mephibosheth. 13 Mephibosheth lived in
Jerusalem. The king always provided
what he needed. Both of his feet were
hurt so that he could not walk.

David Wins the Victory Over the Ammonites

10 The king of Ammon died. His
son Hanun became the next king
after him. 2 David thought, "I'm going
to be kind to Hanun. His father Nahash
was kind to me." So David sent messengers to Hanun. He wanted them to tell
Hanun how sad he was that Hanun's
father had died.
David's messengers went to the land
of Ammon. 3 The Ammonite commanders spoke to their master Hanun. They
said, "David has sent messengers to
tell you he is sad. They say he wants to
honor your father. But the real reason
they've come is to look the city over.
They want to destroy it." 4 So Hanun
grabbed David's messengers. He shaved
off half of each man's beard. He cut
their clothes off just below the waist
and left them half naked. Then he sent
them away.
5 David was told about it. So he sent
messengers to his men because they were
filled with shame. King David said to
them, "Stay at Jericho until your beards
grow out again. Then come back here."
6 The Ammonites realized that what
they had done had made David very
angry with them. So they hired 20,000
Aramean soldiers who were on foot. The
soldiers came from Beth Rehob and
Zobah. The Ammonites also hired the
king of Maakah and 1,000 men. And
they hired 12,000 men from Tob.
7 David heard about it. So he sent
Joab out with the entire army of Israel's fighting men. 8 The Ammonites
marched out. They took up their battle
positions at the entrance of their city
gate. The Arameans of Zobah and Rehob gathered their troops together in
the open country. So did the men of Tob
and Maakah.
9 Joab saw that there were lines of
soldiers in front of him and behind him.
So he chose some of the best troops in Israel. He sent them to march out against
the Arameans. 10 He put the rest of the
men under the command of his brother Abishai. Joab sent them to march
out against the Ammonites. 11 He said,
"Suppose the Arameans are too strong
for me. Then you must come and help
me. But suppose the Ammonites are
too strong for you. Then I'll come and
help you. 12 Be strong. Let's be brave as
we fight for our people and the cities
of our God. The LORD will do what he
thinks is best."

The LORD will do what he thinks is best. **2 SAMUEL 10:12**

13 Then Joab and the troops with him
marched out to attack the Arameans.
They ran away from him. 14 The Ammonites realized that the Arameans
were running away. So they ran away
from Abishai. They went inside the city.
After Joab had fought against the Ammonites, he went back to Jerusalem.
15 The Arameans saw that they had
been driven away by Israel. So they
brought their troops together. 16 Hadadezer had some Arameans brought
from east of the Euphrates River. They
went to Helam under the command
of Shobak. He was the commander of
Hadadezer's army.
17 David was told about it. So he gathered the whole army of Israel together.
They went across the Jordan River to

Helam. The Arameans lined up their soldiers to go to war against David. They began to fight against him. 18 But then they ran away from Israel. David killed 700 of their chariot riders. He killed 40,000 of their soldiers who were on foot. He also struck down Shobak, the commander of their army. Shobak died there. 19 All the kings who were under the rule of Hadadezer saw that Israel had won the battle over them. So they made a peace treaty with the Israelites. They were brought under Israel's rule.

After that, the Arameans were afraid to help the Ammonites anymore.

David and Bathsheba

11 It was spring. It was the time when kings go off to war. So David sent Joab out with the king's special troops and the whole army of Israel. They destroyed the Ammonites. They marched to the city of Rabbah. They surrounded it and got ready to attack it. But David remained in Jerusalem.

2 One evening David got up from his bed. He walked around on the roof of his palace. From the roof he saw a woman taking a bath. She was very beautiful. 3 David sent a messenger to find out who she was. The messenger returned and said, "She is Bathsheba. She's the daughter of Eliam. She's the wife of Uriah. He's a Hittite." 4 Then David sent messengers to get her. She came to him. And he slept with her. Then she went back home. All of that took place after she had already made herself "clean" from her monthly period. 5 Later, Bathsheba found out she was pregnant. She sent a message to David. She said, "I'm pregnant."

6 So David sent a message to Joab. David said, "Send me Uriah, the Hittite." Joab sent him to David. 7 Uriah came to David. David asked him how Joab and the soldiers were doing. He also asked him how the war was going. 8 David said to Uriah, "Go home and enjoy some time with your wife." So Uriah left the palace. Then the king sent him a gift. 9 But Uriah didn't go home. Instead, he slept at the entrance to the palace. He stayed there with all his master's servants.

10 David was told, "Uriah didn't go home." So he sent for Uriah. David said to him, "You have been away for a long time. Why didn't you go home?"

11 Uriah said to David, "The ark and the army of Israel and Judah are out there in tents. My commander Joab and your special troops are camped in the open country. How could I go to my house to eat and drink? How could I go there and sleep with my wife? I could never do a thing like that. And that's just as sure as you are alive!"

12 Then David said to him, "Stay here one more day. Tomorrow I'll send you back to the battle." So Uriah remained in Jerusalem that day and the next. 13 David invited Uriah to eat and drink with him. David got him drunk. But Uriah still didn't go home. In the evening he went out and slept on his mat. He stayed there among his master's servants.

14 The next morning David wrote a letter to Joab. He sent it along with Uriah. 15 In it he wrote, "Put Uriah out in front. That's where the fighting is the heaviest. Then pull your men back from him. When you do, the Ammonites will strike him down and kill him."

16 So Joab attacked the city. He put Uriah at a place where he knew the strongest enemy fighters were. 17 The troops came out of the city. They fought against Joab. Some of the men in David's army were killed. Uriah, the Hittite, also died.

18 Joab sent David a full report of the battle. 19 He told the messenger, "Tell the king everything that happened in the battle. When you are finished, 20 his anger might explode. He might ask you, 'Why did you go so close to the city to fight against it? Didn't you know that the enemy soldiers would shoot arrows down from the wall? 21 Don't you remember how Abimelek, the son of Jerub-Besheth, was killed? A woman dropped a large millstone on him from the wall. That's how he died in Thebez. So why did you go so close to the wall?' If the king asks you that, tell him, 'And your servant Uriah, the Hittite, is also dead.' "

22 The messenger started out for Jerusalem. When he arrived there, he told David everything Joab had sent him to say. 23 The messenger said to David, "The men in the city were more powerful than we were. They came out to fight against us in the open. But we

drove them back to the entrance of the
city gate. 24 Then those who were armed
with bows shot arrows at us from the
wall. Some of your special troops were
killed. Your servant Uriah, the Hittite,
is also dead."

25 David told the messenger, "Tell
Joab, 'Don't get upset over what happened. Swords kill one person as well
as another. So keep on attacking the
city. Destroy it.' Tell that to Joab. It will
cheer him up."

26 Uriah's wife heard that her husband was dead. She mourned over him.
27 When her time of sadness was over,
David had her brought to his house. She
became his wife. And she had a son by
him. But the LORD wasn't pleased with
what David had done.

Nathan Tells David He Has Sinned

12 The LORD sent the prophet Nathan to David. When Nathan
came to him, he said, "Two men lived
in the same town. One was rich. The
other was poor. 2 The rich man had a
very large number of sheep and cattle.
3 But all the poor man had was one little female lamb. He had bought it. He
raised it. It grew up with him and his
children. It shared his food. It drank
from his cup. It even slept in his arms.
It was just like a daughter to him.

4 "One day a traveler came to the rich
man. The rich man wanted to prepare a
meal for him. But he didn't want to kill
one of his own sheep or cattle. Instead,
he took the little female lamb that belonged to the poor man. Then the rich
man cooked it for the traveler who had
come to him."

5 David was very angry with the rich
man. He said to Nathan, "The man who
did this must die! And that's just as sure
as the LORD is alive. 6 The man must
pay back four times as much as that
lamb was worth. How could he do such
a thing? And he wasn't even sorry he
had done it."

7 Then Nathan said to David, "You
are the man! The LORD, the God of Israel, says, 'I anointed you king over
Israel. I saved you from Saul. 8 I gave
you everything that belonged to your
master Saul. I even put his wives into
your arms. I made you king over all the
people of Israel and Judah. And if all
of that had not been enough for you, I
would have given you even more. 9 Why
did you turn your back on what I told
you to do? You did what is evil in my
sight. You made sure that Uriah, the
Hittite, would be killed in battle. You
took his wife to be your own. You let
the men of Ammon kill him with their
swords. 10 So time after time members
of your own royal house will be killed
with swords. That's because you turned
your back on me. You took the wife of
Uriah, the Hittite, to be your own.'

11 "The LORD also says, 'I am going to
bring trouble on you. It will come from
your own family. I will take your wives
away. Your own eyes will see it. I will
give your wives to a man who is close
to you. He will sleep with them in the
middle of the day. 12 You committed
your sins in secret. But I will make sure
that the man commits his sin in the
middle of the day. Everyone in Israel
will see it.' "

13 Then David said to Nathan, "I have
sinned against the LORD."

Nathan replied, "The LORD has taken
away your sin. You aren't going to die.
14 But you have dared to show great
disrespect for the LORD. So the son who
has been born to you will die."

15 Nathan went home. Then the LORD
made David's child very sick. That was
the child David had by Uriah's wife.
16 David begged God to heal the child.
David didn't eat anything. He spent his
nights lying on the ground. He put on
the rough clothes people wear when
they're sad. 17 His most trusted servants
stood beside him. They wanted him to
get up from the ground. But he refused
to do it. And he wouldn't eat any food
with them.

18 On the seventh day the child died.
David's attendants were afraid to tell
him the child was dead. They thought,
"While the child was still alive, we spoke
to David. But he wouldn't listen to us.
So how can we now tell him the child is
dead? He might do something terrible
to himself."

19 David saw that his attendants were
whispering to one another. Then he
realized the child was dead. "Has the
child died?" he asked.

"Yes," they replied. "He's dead."

20 Then David got up from the ground. After he washed himself, he put on lotions. He changed his clothes. He went into the house of the LORD and worshiped him. Then he went to his own house. He asked for some food. They served it to him. And he ate it.

21 His attendants asked him, "Why are you acting like this? While the child was still alive, you wouldn't eat anything. You cried a lot. But now that the child is dead, you get up and eat!"

22 He answered, "While the child was still alive, I didn't eat anything. And I cried a lot. I thought, 'Who knows? The LORD might have mercy on me. He might let the child live.' 23 But now he's dead. So why should I continue to go without food? Can I bring him back to life again? Someday I'll go to him. But he won't return to me."

24 Then David comforted his wife Bathsheba. He went to her and slept with her. Some time later she had a son. He was given the name Solomon. The LORD loved him. 25 So the LORD sent a message through Nathan the prophet. The LORD said, "Name the boy Jedidiah."

26 During that time, Joab fought against Rabbah. It was the royal city of the Ammonites. It had high walls around it. Joab was about to capture it. 27 He sent messengers to David. He told them to say, "I have fought against Rabbah. I've taken control of its water supply. 28 So bring the rest of the troops together. Surround the city and get ready to attack it. Then capture it. If you don't, I'll capture it myself. Then it will be named after me."

29 So David brought together the whole army and went to Rabbah. He attacked it and captured it. 30 David took the gold crown off the head of the king of Ammon. Then the crown was placed on David's head. The crown weighed 75 pounds. It had jewels in it. David took a huge amount of goods from the city. 31 He brought out the people who were there. He made them work with saws and iron picks and axes. He forced them to make bricks. David did that to all the towns in Ammon. Then he and his entire army returned to Jerusalem.

Amnon and Tamar

13 Some time later, David's son Amnon fell in love with Tamar. She was the beautiful sister of Absalom. He was another one of David's sons.

2 Amnon wanted his sister Tamar so much that it made him sick. She was a virgin, and it seemed impossible for him to do what he wanted with her.

3 Amnon had an adviser named Jonadab. He was the son of David's brother Shimeah. Jonadab was a very clever man. 4 He asked Amnon, "You are the king's son, aren't you? So why do you look so worn out every morning? Won't you tell me?"

Amnon answered, "I'm in love with Tamar. She's the sister of my brother Absalom."

5 "Go to bed," Jonadab said. "Pretend to be sick. Your father will come to see you. When he does, tell him, 'I would like my sister Tamar to come and give me something to eat. Let her prepare the food right here in front of me where I can watch her. Then she can feed it to me.' "

6 So Amnon went to bed. He pretended to be sick. The king came to see him. Amnon said to him, "I would like my sister Tamar to come here. I want to watch her make some special bread. Then she can feed it to me."

7 David sent a message to Tamar at the palace. He said, "Go to your brother Amnon's house. Prepare some food for him." 8 So Tamar went to the house of her brother Amnon. He was lying in bed. She got some dough and mixed it. She shaped the bread right there in front of him. And she baked it. 9 Then she took the bread out of the pan and served it to him. But he refused to eat it.

"Send everyone out of here," Amnon said. So everyone left him. 10 Then he said to Tamar, "Bring the food here into my bedroom. Please feed it to me." So Tamar picked up the bread she had prepared. She brought it to her brother Amnon in his bedroom. 11 She took it to him so he could eat it. But he grabbed her. He said, "My sister, come to bed with me."

12 "No, my brother!" she said to him. "Don't force me! An evil thing like that should never be done in Israel! Don't do it! 13 What about me? How could I ever get rid of my shame? And what about you? You would be as foolish as any evil person

in Israel. Please speak to the king. He
won't keep me from marrying you." 14 But
Amnon refused to listen to her. He was
stronger than she was. So he raped her.

15 Then Amnon hated Tamar very
much. In fact, he hated her more than
he had loved her before. He said to her,
"Get up! Get out!"

16 "No!" she said to him. "Don't send
me away. That would be worse than
what you have already done to me."

But he refused to listen to her. 17 He
sent for his personal servant. He said,
"Get this woman out of my sight. Lock
the door behind her." 18 So his servant
threw her out. Then he locked the door
behind her. Tamar was wearing a beautiful robe. It was the kind of robe the virgin
daughters of the king wore. 19 She put
ashes on her head. She tore the beautiful
robe she was wearing. She put her hands
on her head and went away. She was
weeping out loud as she went.

20 When her brother Absalom saw her,
he spoke to her. He said, "Has Amnon,
that brother of yours, forced you to go
to bed with him? My sister, don't let it
upset you. Don't let it bother you. He's
your brother." After that, Tamar lived
in her brother Absalom's house. She
was very lonely.

21 King David heard about everything
that had happened. So he became very
angry. 22 And Absalom never said a
word of any kind to Amnon. He hated
Amnon because he had brought shame
on his sister Tamar.

Absalom Kills Amnon

23 Two years later, Absalom invited all
the king's sons to come to Baal Hazor.
It was near the border of Ephraim. The
workers who clipped the wool off Absalom's sheep were there. 24 Absalom
went to the king. He said, "I've had my
workers come to clip the wool. Will you
and your attendants please join me?"

25 "No, my son," the king replied. "All
of us shouldn't go. It would be too much
trouble for you." Although Absalom
begged him, the king still refused to
go. But he gave Absalom his blessing.

26 Then Absalom said, "If you won't
come, please let my brother Amnon
come with us."

The king asked him, "Why should he
go with you?" 27 But Absalom begged
him. So the king sent Amnon with him.
He also sent the rest of his sons.

28 Absalom ordered his men, "Listen!
When Amnon has had too much wine
to drink, I'll say to you, 'Strike Amnon
down.' When I do, kill him. Don't be
afraid. I've given you an order, haven't
I? Be strong and brave." 29 So Absalom's
men killed Amnon, just as Absalom had
ordered. Then all the king's sons got on
their mules and rode away.

30 While they were on their way, a
report came to David. It said, "Absalom
has struck down all your sons. Not one
of them is left alive." 31 The king stood
up and tore his clothes. Then he lay
down on the ground. All his attendants
stood near him. They had also torn their
clothes.

32 Jonadab, the son of David's brother Shimeah, spoke up. He said, "You
shouldn't think that all the princes have
been killed. The only one who is dead
is Amnon. Absalom had planned to kill
him ever since the day Amnon raped
his sister Tamar. 33 You are my king and
master. You shouldn't be concerned
about this report. It's not true that all
your sons are dead. The only one who
is dead is Amnon."

34 While all of that was taking place,
Absalom ran away.

The man on guard duty at Jerusalem looked up. He saw many people
coming on the road west of him. They
were coming down the side of the hill.
He went and spoke to the king. He said,
"I see men coming down the road from
Horonaim. They are coming down the
side of the hill."

35 Jonadab said to the king, "See, your
sons are coming. It has happened just
as I said it would."

36 As he finished speaking, the king's
sons came in. They were weeping out
loud. The king and all his attendants
were also weeping very bitterly.

37 When Absalom ran away, he went
to Talmai, the son of Ammihud. Talmai was king of Geshur. King David
mourned many days for his son Amnon.
38 So Absalom ran away and went
to Geshur. He stayed there for three
years. 39 After some time the king got
over his sorrow because of Amnon's
death. Then King David longed to go
to Absalom.

Absalom Returns to Jerusalem

14 Joab, the son of Zeruiah, knew that the king longed to see Absalom. 2 So Joab sent someone to Tekoa to have a wise woman brought back from there. Joab said to her, "Pretend you are filled with sadness. Put on the rough clothing people wear when they're sad. Don't use any makeup. Act like a woman who has spent many days mourning for someone who has died. 3 Then go to the king. Give him the message I'm about to give you." And Joab told her what to say.

4 The woman from Tekoa went to the king. She bowed down with her face toward the ground. She did it to show him respect. She said, "Your Majesty, please help me!"

5 The king asked her, "What's bothering you?"

She said, "I'm a widow. My husband is dead. 6 I had two sons. They got into a fight with each other in a field. No one was there to separate them. One of my sons struck down the other one and killed him. 7 Now my whole family group has risen up against me. They say, 'Hand over the one who struck down his brother. Then we can put him to death for killing his brother. That will also get rid of the one who will receive the family property.' They want to kill the only living son I have left, just as someone would put out a burning coal. That would leave my husband without any son on the face of the earth to carry on the family name."

8 The king said to the woman, "Go home. I'll give an order to make sure you are taken care of."

9 But the woman from Tekoa said to him, "You are my king and master. Please pardon me and my family. You and your royal family won't be guilty of doing anything wrong."

10 The king replied, "If people give you any trouble, bring them to me. They won't bother you again."

11 She said, "Please pray to the LORD your God. Pray that he will keep our nearest male relative from killing my other son. Then my son won't be destroyed."

"You can be sure that the LORD lives," the king said. "And you can be just as sure that not one hair of your son's head will fall to the ground."

12 Then the woman said, "King David, please let me say something else to you."

"Go ahead," he replied.

13 The woman said, "You are the king. So why have you done something that brings so much harm on God's people? When you do that, you hand down a sentence against yourself. You won't let the son you drove away come back. 14 All of us must die. We are like water spilled on the ground. It can't be put back into the jar. But that is not what God desires. Instead, he finds a way to bring back anyone who was driven away from him.

15 "King David, I've come here to say this to you now. I've done it because people have made me afraid. I thought, 'I'll go and speak to the king. Perhaps he'll do what I'm asking. 16 A man is trying to separate me and my son from the property God gave us. Perhaps the king will agree to save me from that man.'

17 "So now I'm saying, 'May what you have told me prevent that man from doing what he wants. You are like an angel of God. You know what is good and what is evil. May the LORD your God be with you.' "

18 Then the king said to the woman, "I'm going to ask you a question. I want you to tell me the truth."

"Please ask me anything you want to," the woman said.

19 The king asked, "Joab told you to say all of this, didn't he?"

The woman answered, "What you have told me is exactly right. And that's just as sure as you are alive. It's true that Joab directed me to do this. He told me everything he wanted me to say. 20 He did it to change the way things now are. You are as wise as an angel of God. You know everything that happens in the land."

21 Later the king said to Joab, "All right. I'll do what you want. Go. Bring back the young man Absalom."

22 Joab bowed down with his face toward the ground. He did it to honor the king. And he asked God to bless the king. He said, "You are my king and master. Today I know that you are pleased with me. You have given me what I asked for."

23 Then Joab went to Geshur. He brought Absalom back to Jerusalem.

24 But the king said, "He must go to his
own house. I don't want him to come
and see me." So Absalom went to his
own house. He didn't go to see the king.
25 In the whole land of Israel there
wasn't any man as handsome as Absalom was. That's why everyone praised
him. From the top of his head to the
bottom of his feet he didn't have any
flaws. 26 He used to cut his hair once a
year when it became too heavy for him.
Then he would weigh it. It weighed five
pounds in keeping with the standard
weights used in the palace.
27 Three sons and a daughter were
born to Absalom. His daughter's name
was Tamar. She became a beautiful
woman.
28 Absalom lived in Jerusalem for two
years without going to see the king.
29 Then Absalom sent for Joab. He wanted to send Joab to the king. But Joab
refused to come to Absalom. So Absalom
sent for him a second time. But Joab still
refused to come. 30 Then Absalom said
to his servants, "Joab's field is next to
mine. He has barley growing there. Go
and set it on fire." So Absalom's servants
set the field on fire.
31 Joab finally went to Absalom's
house. He said to Absalom, "Why did
your servants set my field on fire?"
32 Absalom said to Joab, "I sent a message to you. I said, 'Come here. I want
to send you to the king. I want you to
ask him for me, "Why did you bring me
back from Geshur? I would be better off
if I were still there!" ' Now then, I want to
go and see the king. If I'm guilty of doing
anything wrong, let him put me to death."
33 So Joab went to the king and told
him that. Then the king sent for Absalom. He came in and bowed down to the
king with his face toward the ground.
And the king kissed Absalom.

Absalom Makes Secret Plans Against David

15 Some time later, Absalom got a
chariot and horses for himself.
He also got 50 men to run in front of
him. 2 He would get up early. He would
stand by the side of the road that led to
the city gate. Sometimes a person would
come with a case for the king to decide.
Then Absalom would call out to him,
"What town are you from?" He would
answer, "I'm from one of the tribes of
Israel." 3 Absalom would say, "Look,
your claims are based on the law. So you
have every right to make them. But the
king doesn't have anyone here who can
listen to your case." 4 Absalom would
continue, "I wish I were appointed judge
in the land! Then anyone who has a case
or a claim could come to me. I would
make sure they are treated fairly."
5 Sometimes people would approach
Absalom and bow down to him. Then
he would reach out his hand. He would
take hold of them and kiss them. 6 Absalom did that to all the Israelites who
came to the king with their cases or
claims. That's why the hearts of the
people were turned toward him.
7 After Absalom had lived in Jerusalem for four years, he went and spoke to
the king. He said, "Let me go to Hebron.
I want to keep a promise I made to the
LORD. 8 When I was living at Geshur in
Aram, I made a promise. I said, 'If the
LORD takes me back to Jerusalem, I'll
go to Hebron and worship him there.' "
9 The king said to him, "Go in peace."
So he went to Hebron.
10 Then Absalom sent messengers
secretly to all the tribes of Israel. They
said, "Listen for the sound of trumpets.
As soon as you hear them, say, 'Absalom has become king in Hebron.' "
11 Absalom had taken 200 men from
Jerusalem with him to Hebron. He had
invited them to be his guests. They went
without having any idea what was going to happen. 12 While Absalom was
offering sacrifices, he sent for Ahithophel. Ahithophel was David's adviser.
He came to Absalom from Giloh, his
hometown. The number of people who
followed Absalom kept growing. So he
became more and more able to carry
out his plans against David.

David Runs Away From Absalom

13 A messenger came and spoke to
David. He told him, "The hearts of the
Israelites are turned toward Absalom."
14 Then David spoke to all his officials
who were with him in Jerusalem. He said,
"Come on! We have to leave right away!
If we don't, none of us will escape from
Absalom. He'll move quickly to catch up
with us. He'll destroy us. His men will kill
everyone in the city with their swords."

[15]The king's officials answered him, "You are our king and master. We're ready to do anything you want."
[16]The king started out. Everyone in his whole family went with him. But he left ten concubines behind to take care of the palace.
[17]So the king and all those with him left. They stopped at the edge of the city.
[18]All of David's officials marched past him. All the Kerethites and Pelethites marched along with them. And all of the 600 men who had come with him from Gath marched in front of him.
[19]The king spoke to Ittai. He was from Gath. The king said to him, "Why do you want to come along with us? Go back. Stay with King Absalom. You are an outsider. You left your own country.
[20]You came to join me only a short time ago. So why should I make you wander around with us now? I don't even know where I'm going. So go on back. Take your people with you. And may the LORD be kind and faithful to you."
[21]But Ittai replied to the king, "You are my king and master. I want to be where you are. It doesn't matter whether I live or die. And that's just as sure as the LORD and you are alive."
[22]David said to Ittai, "Go ahead then. Keep marching with my men." So Ittai, the Gittite, kept marching. All his men and their families marched with him.
[23]All the people in the countryside wept out loud as David and all his followers passed by. The king went across the Kidron Valley. He and all the people with him moved on toward the desert.
[24]Zadok also went with them. Some of the Levites went with him. They were carrying the ark of the covenant of God. They set down the ark. Abiathar offered sacrifices until all the people had left the city.
[25]Then the king said to Zadok, "Take the ark of God back into the city. If the LORD is pleased with me, he'll bring me back. He'll let me see the ark again. He'll also let me see Jerusalem again. That's the place where he lives.
[26]But suppose he says, 'I am not pleased with you.' Then I accept that. Let him do to me what he thinks is best."
[27]The king said again to Zadok the priest, "Do you understand? Go back to the city with my blessing. Take your son Ahimaaz with you. Also take Abiathar and his son Jonathan with you.
[28]I'll wait at the place in the desert where we can go across the Jordan River. I'll wait there until you send word to let me know what's happening."
[29]So Zadok and Abiathar took the ark of God back to Jerusalem. They stayed there.
[30]But David went on up the Mount of Olives. He was weeping as he went. His head was covered, and he was barefoot. All the people with him covered their heads too. And they were weeping as they went up.
[31]David had been told, "Ahithophel, along with Absalom, is one of the people making secret plans against you." So David prayed, "LORD, make Ahithophel's advice look foolish."
[32]David arrived at the top of the Mount of Olives. That's where people used to worship God. Hushai, the Arkite, was there to meet him. His robe was torn. There was dust on his head.
[33]David said to him, "If you go with me, you will be too much trouble for me.
[34]So return to the city. Say to Absalom, 'Your Majesty, I'll be your servant. In the past, I was your father's servant. But now I'll be your servant.' If you do that, you can help me by making sure Ahithophel's advice fails.
[35]Zadok and Abiathar, the priests, will be there with you. Tell them everything you hear in the king's palace.
[36]They have their sons Ahimaaz and Jonathan there with them. Send them to tell me everything you hear."
[37]So David's trusted friend Hushai went to Jerusalem. He arrived just as Absalom was entering the city.

David and Ziba

16 David went just beyond the top of the Mount of Olives. Ziba was waiting there to meet him. He was Mephibosheth's manager. He had several donkeys with saddles on them. They were carrying 200 loaves of bread and 100 raisin cakes. They were also carrying 100 fig cakes and a bottle of wine. The bottle was made out of animal skin.
[2]The king asked Ziba, "Why have you brought all these things?"

Ziba answered, "The donkeys are for the king's family to ride on. The bread and fruit are for the people to eat. The wine will make those who get tired in the desert feel like new again."

[3]Then the king asked, "Where is your
master's grandson Mephibosheth?"
Ziba said to him, "He's staying in Jerusalem. He thinks, 'Today the Israelites
will cause me to rule once again over
my grandfather Saul's kingdom.'"
[4]Then the king said to Ziba, "Everything that belonged to Mephibosheth
belongs to you now."
"You are my king and master," Ziba
said. "I make myself humble in front
of you. I bow down to you. May you be
pleased with me."

Shimei Curses David

[5]King David approached Bahurim. As
he did, a man came out toward him. The
man was from the same family group
that Saul was from. His name was Shimei.
He was the son of Gera. As he came out
of the town, he cursed David. [6]He threw
stones at David and all his officials. He
did it even though all the troops and the
special guard were there. They were to
the right and left of David. [7]As Shimei
cursed, he said, "Get out! Get out, you
murderer! You are a worthless and evil
man! [8]You spilled the blood of a lot of
people in Saul's family. You took over
his kingdom. Now the LORD is paying
you back. He has handed the kingdom
over to your son Absalom. You have been
destroyed because you are a murderer!"
[9]Then Abishai, the son of Zeruiah,
spoke to the king. He said, "King David,
why should we let this dead dog curse
you? Let me go over there. I'll cut off
his head."
[10]But the king said, "You and Joab
are sons of Zeruiah. What does this have
to do with you? Maybe the LORD said to
him, 'Curse David.' If he did, who can ask
him, 'Why are you doing this?'"
[11]Then David spoke to Abishai and all
his officials. He said, "My very own son
Absalom is trying to kill me. How much
more should this man from Benjamin
want to kill me! Leave him alone. Let
him curse. The LORD has told him to do
it. [12]Maybe the LORD will see how much
I'm suffering. Maybe he'll bring back to
me his covenant blessing instead of his
curse I'm hearing today."
[13]So David and his men kept going
along the road. At the same time, Shimei
was going along the hillside across from
him. He was cursing David as he went.
He was throwing stones at David. He
was showering him with dirt. [14]The king
and all the people with him came to the
place they had planned to go to. They
were very tired. So David rested there.

Ahithophel and Hushai Give Advice to Absalom

[15]During that time, Absalom and
all the men of Israel came to Jerusalem. Ahithophel was with him. [16]Then
Hushai, the Arkite, went to Absalom. He
said to him, "May the king live a long
time! May the king live a long time!"
Hushai was David's trusted friend.
[17]Absalom said to Hushai, "So this is
the way you show love to your friend?
If he's your friend, why didn't you go
with him?"
[18]Hushai said to Absalom, "Why
should I? You are the one the LORD has
chosen. These people and all the men
of Israel have also chosen you. I want
to be on your side. I want to stay with
you. [19]After all, who else should I serve?
Shouldn't I serve the king's son? I will
serve you, just as I served your father."
[20]Absalom said to Ahithophel, "Give
us your advice. What should we do?"
[21]Ahithophel answered, "Your father
left some concubines behind to take
care of the palace. Go and sleep with
them. Then all the Israelites will hear
about it. They will hear that you have
made your father hate you. Everyone
with you will be encouraged to give you
more support." [22]So they set up a tent
for Absalom on the roof of the palace.
He went in and slept with his father's
concubines. Everyone in Israel saw it.
[23]In those days the advice Ahithophel
gave was as good as advice from someone who asks God for guidance. That's
what David and Absalom thought about
all of Ahithophel's advice.

17 One day Ahithophel said to Absalom, "Here's what I suggest.
Choose 12,000 men. Start out tonight
and go after David. [2]Attack him while
he's tired and weak. Fill him with terror. Then all the people with him will
run away. Don't strike down anyone
except the king. [3]Bring all the other
people back. After the man you want
to kill is dead, everyone else will return
to you. And none of the people will be
harmed." [4]Ahithophel's plan seemed

good to Absalom. It also seemed good to all the elders of Israel.

[5] But Absalom said, “Send for Hushai, the Arkite. Then we can find out what he suggests as well.” [6] Hushai came to him. Absalom said, “Ahithophel has given us his advice. Should we do what he says? If we shouldn’t, tell us what you would do.”

[7] Hushai replied to Absalom, “The advice Ahithophel has given you isn’t good this time. [8] You know your father and his men. They are fighters. They are as strong as a wild bear whose cubs have been stolen from her. Besides, your father really knows how to fight. He won’t spend the night with his troops. [9] In fact, he’s probably hiding in a cave or some other place right now. Suppose he attacks your troops first. When people hear about it, they’ll say, ‘Many of the troops who followed Absalom have been killed.’ [10] Then the hearts of your soldiers will melt away in fear. Even those as brave as a lion will be terrified. That’s because everyone in Israel knows that your father is a fighter. They know that those with him are brave.

[11] “So here’s what I suggest. Bring together all the men of Israel from the town of Dan all the way to Beersheba. They are as many as the grains of sand on the seashore. You yourself should lead them into battle. [12] Then we’ll attack David no matter where we find him. As dew completely covers the ground, we’ll completely overpower his entire army. We won’t leave him or any of his men alive. [13] He might try to get away by going into a city. If he does, all of us will bring ropes to that city. We’ll drag the whole city down into the valley. Not even a pebble of that city will be left.”

[14] Absalom and all the men of Israel agreed. They said, “The advice of Hushai, the Arkite, is better than the advice of Ahithophel.” The LORD had decided that Ahithophel’s good advice would fail. The LORD wanted to bring horrible trouble on Absalom.

[15] Hushai spoke to Zadok and Abiathar, the priests. He said, “Ahithophel has given advice to Absalom and the elders of Israel. He suggested that they should do one thing. But I suggested something else. [16] Send a message right away. Tell David, ‘Don’t spend the night in the desert at a place where people cross the Jordan River. Make sure you go on across. If you don’t, you and all the people with you will be swallowed up.’ ”

[17] Jonathan and Ahimaaz were staying at En Rogel just outside Jerusalem. They knew they would be in danger if anyone saw them entering the city. A female servant was supposed to go and tell them what had happened. Then they were supposed to go and tell King David. [18] But a young man saw Jonathan and Ahimaaz and told Absalom about it. So the two men left right away. They went to the house of a man in Bahurim. He had a well in his courtyard. They climbed down into it. [19] The man’s wife got a covering and spread it out over the opening of the well. Then she scattered grain on the covering. So no one knew that the men were hiding in the well.

[20] Absalom’s men came to the house. They asked the woman, “Where are Ahimaaz and Jonathan?”

She answered, “They went across the brook.” When the men looked around, they didn’t find anyone. So they returned to Jerusalem.

[21] After they had gone, Jonathan and Ahimaaz climbed out of the well. They went to tell King David what they had found out. They said to him, “Go across the river right away. Ahithophel has told Absalom how to come after you and strike you down.” [22] So David and all the people with him started out. They went across the Jordan River. By sunrise, everyone had crossed over.

[23] Ahithophel saw that his advice wasn’t being followed. So he put a saddle on his donkey. He started out for his house in his hometown. When he arrived, he made everything ready for his death. He made out his will. Then he killed himself. And so he died and was buried in his father’s tomb.

Absalom Dies

[24] David went to Mahanaim. Absalom went across the Jordan River with all the men of Israel. [25] Absalom had made Amasa commander of the army in place of Joab. Amasa was the son of Jether. Jether belonged to the family line of Ishmael. He had married Abigail. She was the daughter of Nahash and the

sister of Zeruiah. Zeruiah was the mother of Joab. 26 Absalom and the Israelites
camped in the land of Gilead.
27 David came to Mahanaim. Shobi,
the son of Nahash, met him there. Shobi
was from Rabbah in the land of Ammon.
Makir, the son of Ammiel from Lo Debar,
met him there too. So did Barzillai from
Rogelim in the land of Gilead. 28 They
brought beds, bowls and clay pots. They
brought wheat, barley, flour, and grain
that had been cooked. They brought
beans and lentils. 29 They brought honey, butter, sheep, and cheese that was
made from cows' milk. They brought
all that food for David and his people
to eat. They said, "These people have
become tired. They've become hungry
and thirsty in the desert."

18 David brought together the men
with him. He appointed commanders of thousands over some of
them. He appointed commanders of
hundreds over the others. 2 Then David
sent out his troops in military groups.
One group was under the command of
Joab. Another was under Joab's brother
Abishai, the son of Zeruiah. The last was
under Ittai, the Gittite. The king told the
troops, "You can be sure that I myself
will march out with you."
3 But the men said, "You must not
march out. If we are forced to run away,
our enemies won't care about us. Even if
half of us die, they won't care. But you
are worth 10,000 of us. So it would be
better for you to stay here in the city.
Then you can send us help if we need it."
4 The king said, "I'll do what you think
is best."
So the king stood beside the city gate.
His whole army marched out in groups
of hundreds and groups of thousands.
5 The king gave an order to Joab, Abishai
and Ittai. He commanded them, "Be
gentle with the young man Absalom.
Do it for me." All the troops heard the
king give the commanders that order
about Absalom.
6 David's army marched out of the
city to fight against Israel. The battle
took place in the forest of Ephraim.
7 There David's men won the battle over
Israel's army. A huge number of men
were wounded or killed that day. The
total number was 20,000. 8 The fighting
spread out over the whole countryside.
But more men were killed in the forest
that day than out in the open.
9 Absalom happened to come across
some of David's men. He was riding his
mule. The mule went under the thick
branches of a large oak tree. Absalom's
hair got caught in the tree. He was left
hanging in the air. The mule he was
riding kept on going.
10 One of David's men saw what had
happened. He told Joab, "I just saw Absalom hanging in an oak tree."
11 Joab said to the man, "What! You
saw him? Why didn't you strike him
down right there? Then I would have
had to give you four ounces of silver
and a soldier's belt."
12 But the man replied, "I wouldn't do
anything to hurt the king's son. I wouldn't
do it even for 25 pounds of silver. We heard
the king's command to you and Abishai
and Ittai. He said, 'Be careful not to hurt
the young man Absalom. Do it for me.'
13 Suppose I had put my life in danger by
killing him. The king would have found
out about it. Nothing is hidden from him.
And you wouldn't have stood up for me."
14 Joab said, "I'm not going to waste
any more time on you." So he got three
javelins. Then he went over and plunged
them into Absalom's heart. He did it
while Absalom was still hanging there
alive in the oak tree. 15 Ten of the men
carrying Joab's armor surrounded Absalom. They struck him and killed him.
16 Then Joab blew his trumpet. He ordered his troops to stop chasing Israel's
army. 17 Joab's men threw Absalom into
a big pit in the forest. They covered him
with a large pile of rocks. While all of
that was going on, all the Israelites ran
back to their homes.
18 Earlier in his life Absalom had set
up a pillar in the King's Valley. He had
put it up as a monument to himself. He
thought, "I don't have a son to carry on
the memory of my name." So he named
the pillar after himself. It is still called
Absalom's Monument to this day.

David Mourns Over Absalom

19 Ahimaaz, the son of Zadok, said to
Joab, "Let me run and take the news to
the king. Let me tell him that the LORD
has shown that David is in the right.
The LORD has done this by saving David
from his enemies."

20 “I don’t want you to take the news to
the king today,” Joab told him. “You can
do it some other time. But you must not
do it today, because the king’s son is dead.”
21 Then Joab said to a man from Cush,
“Go. Tell the king what you have seen.”
The man bowed down in front of Joab.
Then he ran off.
22 Ahimaaz, the son of Zadok, spoke
again to Joab. He said, “I don’t care
what happens to me. Please let me run
behind the man from Cush.”
But Joab replied, “My son, why do you
want to go? You don’t have any news
that will bring you a reward.”
23 He said, “I don’t care what happens.
I want to run.”
So Joab said, “Run!” Then Ahimaaz
ran across the plain of the Jordan River.
As he ran, he passed the man from Cush.
24 David was sitting in the area between the inner and outer gates of the
city. The man on guard duty went up
to the roof over the entrance of the gate
by the wall. As he looked out, he saw
someone running alone. 25 The guard
called out to the king and reported it.
The king said, “If the runner is alone,
he must be bringing good news.” The
runner came closer and closer.
26 Then the man on guard duty saw
another runner. He called out to the
man guarding the gate. He said, “Look!
There’s another man running alone!”
The king said, “He must be bringing
good news too.”
27 The man on guard duty said, “I can
see that the first one runs like Ahimaaz,
the son of Zadok.”
“He’s a good man,” the king said.
“He’s bringing good news.”
28 Then Ahimaaz called out to the king,
“Everything’s all right!” He bowed down
in front of the king with his face toward
the ground. He said, “You are my king
and master. Give praise to the LORD your
God! He has handed over to you those
who lifted their hands to kill you.”
29 The king asked, “Is the young man
Absalom safe?”
Ahimaaz answered, “I saw total disorder. I saw it just as Joab was about to
send the king’s servant and me to you.
But I don’t know what it was all about.”
30 The king said, “Stand over there
and wait.” So he stepped over to one
side and stood there.
31 Then the man from Cush arrived.
He said, “You are my king and master.
I’m bringing you some good news. The
LORD has shown that you are in the
right. He has done this by rescuing you
today from all those trying to kill you.”
32 The king asked the man from Cush,
“Is the young man Absalom safe?”
The man replied, “King David, may
your enemies be like that young man.
May all those who rise up to harm you
be like him.”
33 The king was very upset. He went
up to the room over the entrance of the
gate and wept. As he went, he said, “My
son Absalom! My son, my son Absalom!
I wish I had died instead of you. Absalom! My son, my son!”

19 Someone told Joab, “The king is
weeping and mourning for Absalom. He’s filled with sadness because
his son has died.” 2 The army had won
a great battle that day. But their joy
turned into sadness. That’s because
someone had told the troops, “The king
is filled with sorrow because his son is
dead.” 3 The men came quietly into the
city that day. They were like fighting
men who are ashamed because they’ve
run away from a battle. 4 The king covered his face. He cried loudly, “My son
Absalom! Absalom, my son, my son!”
5 Then Joab went into the king’s house.
He said to him, “Today you have made
all your men feel ashamed. They have
just saved your life. They have saved the
lives of your sons and daughters. And
they have saved the lives of your wives
and concubines. 6 You love those who hate
you. You hate those who love you. The
commanders and their troops don’t mean
anything to you. You made that very clear
today. I can see that you would be pleased
if Absalom were alive today and all of us
were dead. 7 Now go out there and cheer up
your men. If you don’t, you won’t have any
of them left with you by sunset. That will
be worse for you than all the troubles you
have ever had in your whole life. That’s
what I promise you in the LORD’s name.”
8 So the king got up and took his seat
in the entrance of the city gate. His men
were told, “The king is sitting in the
entrance of the gate.” Then all of them
came and stood in front of him.
While all of that was going on, the
Israelites had run back to their homes.

David Returns to Jerusalem

[9] People from all the tribes of Israel
began to argue among themselves.
They were saying, "The king saved
us from the power of our enemies. He
saved us from the power of the Philistines. But now he has left the country
to escape from Absalom. [10] We anointed
Absalom to rule over us. But he has
died in battle. So why aren't any of you
talking about bringing the king back?"

[11] King David sent a message to Zadok
and Abiathar, the priests. David said,
"Speak to the elders of Judah. Tell them
I said, 'News has reached me where
I'm staying. People all over Israel are
talking about bringing me back to my
palace. Why should you be the last to
do something about it? [12] You are my
relatives. You are my own flesh and
blood. So why should you be the last to
bring me back?' [13] Say to Amasa, 'Aren't
you my own flesh and blood? You will
be the commander of my army for life
in place of Joab. If that isn't true, may
God punish me greatly.' "

[14] So the hearts of all the men of Judah were turned toward David. All of
them had the same purpose in mind.
They sent a message to the king. They
said, "We want you to come back. We
want all your men to come back too."
[15] Then the king returned. He went as
far as the Jordan River.

The men of Judah had come to Gilgal
to welcome the king back. They had
come to bring him across the Jordan.
[16] Shimei, the son of Gera, was among
them. Shimei was from Bahurim in the
territory of Benjamin. He hurried down
to welcome King David back. [17] There
were 1,000 people from Benjamin with
him. Ziba, the manager of Saul's house,
was with him too. And so were Ziba's 15
sons and 20 servants. All of them rushed
down to the Jordan River. That's where
the king was. [18] They went across at
the place where people usually cross
it. Then they brought the king's family
back over with them. They were ready
to do anything he wanted them to do.

Shimei, the son of Gera, had also
gone across the Jordan. When he did,
he fell down flat with his face toward
the ground in front of the king. [19] He
said to him, "You are my king and master. Please don't hold me guilty. Please
forgive me for the wrong things I did
on the day you left Jerusalem. Please
forget all about them. [20] I know I've
sinned. But today I've come down here
to welcome you. I'm the first member of
Joseph's whole family to do it."

[21] Then Abishai, the son of Zeruiah,
said, "Shouldn't Shimei be put to death
for what he did? He cursed you. And you
are the LORD's anointed king."

[22] But David replied, "You and Joab are
sons of Zeruiah. What does this have to
do with you? What right do you have to
interfere? Should anyone be put to death
in Israel today? Don't I know that today I
am king over Israel again?" [23] So the king
made a promise to Shimei. He said to
him, "You aren't going to be put to death."

[24] Mephibosheth was Saul's grandson.
He had also gone down to welcome the
king back. He had not taken care of his
feet. He hadn't trimmed his mustache or
washed his clothes. He hadn't done any of
those things from the day the king left Jerusalem until the day he returned safely.
[25] He came from Jerusalem to welcome the
king. The king asked him, "Mephibosheth,
why didn't you go with me?"

[26] He said, "You are my king and master. I'm not able to walk. So I thought,
'I'll have a saddle put on my donkey. I'll
ride on it. Then I can go with the king.'
But my servant Ziba turned against me.
[27] He has told you lies about me. King
David, you are like an angel of God. So
do what you wish. [28] You should have
put all the members of my grandfather's family to death, including me.
Instead, you always provided what I
needed. So what right do I have to make
any more appeals to you?"

[29] The king said to him, "You don't
have to say anything else. I order you
and Ziba to divide up Saul's land between you."

[30] Mephibosheth said to the king, "I'm
happy that you have returned home
safely. So just let Ziba have everything."

[31] Barzillai had also come down to go
across the Jordan River with the king.
He wanted to send the king on his way
from there. Barzillai was from Rogelim
in the land of Gilead. [32] He was very old.
He was 80 years old. He had given the
king everything he needed while the
king was staying in Mahanaim. That's
because Barzillai was very wealthy.

33 The king said to Barzillai, "Come
across the river with me. Stay with me
in Jerusalem. I'll take good care of you."
34 But Barzillai said to the king, "I
won't live for many more years. So why
should I go up to Jerusalem with you?
35 I'm already 80 years old. I can hardly tell the difference between what is
enjoyable and what isn't. I can hardly
taste what I eat and drink. I can't even
hear the voices of male and female singers anymore. So why should I add my
problems to yours? 36 I'll go across the
Jordan River with you for a little way.
Why should you reward me by taking
care of me? 37 Let me go back home.
Then I can die in my own town. I can be
buried there in the tomb of my father
and mother. But let Kimham take my
place. Let him go across the river with
you. Do for him whatever you wish."
38 The king said, "Kimham will go
across with me. I'll do for him whatever
you wish. And I'll do for you anything
you wish."
39 So all the people went across the
Jordan River. Then the king crossed
over. The king kissed Barzillai and said
goodbye to him. And Barzillai went
back home.
40 After the king had gone across the
river, he went to Gilgal. Kimham had
gone across with him. All the troops of
Judah and half of the troops of Israel
had taken the king across.
41 Soon all the men of Israel were
coming to the king. They were saying
to him, "Why did the men of Judah
take you away from us? They are our
relatives. What right did they have to
bring you and your family across the
Jordan River? What right did they have
to bring all your men over with you?"
42 All the men of Judah answered the
men of Israel. They said, "We did that
because the king is our close relative. So
why should you be angry about what
happened? Have we eaten any of the
king's food? Have we taken anything
for ourselves?"
43 Then the men of Israel answered
the men of Judah. They said, "We have
ten of the 12 tribes in the kingdom. So
we have a stronger claim on David than
you have. Why then are you acting as
if you hate us? Weren't we the first ones
to talk about bringing back our king?"

But the men of Judah argued their
side even more forcefully than the men
of Israel.

Sheba Urges Israel Not to Follow David

20 An evil man who always stirred
up trouble happened to be in Gilgal. His name was Sheba, the son of Bikri.
Sheba was from the tribe of Benjamin.
He blew his trumpet. Then he shouted,

"We don't have any share in
David's kingdom!
Jesse's son is not our king!
Men of Israel, every one of you
go back home!"

2 So all the men of Israel deserted
David. They followed Sheba, the son
of Bikri. But the men of Judah stayed
with their king. They remained with
him from the Jordan River all the way
to Jerusalem.
3 David returned to his palace in Jerusalem. He had left ten concubines there
to take care of the palace. He put them
in a house and kept them under guard.
He gave them what they needed. But
he didn't sleep with them. They were
kept under guard until the day they
died. They lived as if they were widows.
4 The king said to Amasa, "Send for
the men of Judah. Tell them to come
to me within three days. And be here
yourself." 5 So Amasa went to get the
men of Judah. But he took longer than
the time the king had set for him.
6 David said to Abishai, "Sheba, the
son of Bikri, will do more harm to
us than Absalom ever did. Take my
men and go after him. If you don't,
he'll find cities that have high walls
around them. He'll go into one of them
and escape from us." 7 So Joab's men
marched out with the Kerethites and
Pelethites. They went out with all the
mighty soldiers. All of them were under
Abishai's command. They marched out
from Jerusalem and went after Sheba,
the son of Bikri.
8 They arrived at the great rock in
Gibeon. Amasa went there to welcome
them. Joab was wearing his military
clothes. Over them at his waist he had
strapped on a belt that held a dagger.
As he stepped forward, he secretly took
the dagger out.

9 Joab said to Amasa, "How are you,
my friend?" Then Joab reached out his
right hand. He took hold of Amasa's
beard to kiss him. 10 Amasa didn't notice
the dagger in Joab's left hand. Joab stuck
it into his stomach. His insides spilled out
on the ground. Joab didn't have to stab
him again. Amasa was already dead.
Then Joab and his brother Abishai went
after Sheba, the son of Bikri.

11 One of Joab's men stood beside
Amasa's body. He said to the other men,
"Are you pleased with Joab? Are you on
David's side? Then follow Joab!" 12 Amasa's body lay covered with his blood in
the middle of the road. The man saw
that all the troops stopped there. He
realized that everyone was stopping
to look at Amasa's body. So he dragged
it from the road into a field. Then he
threw some clothes on top of it. 13 After
that happened, everyone continued on
with Joab. They went after Sheba, the
son of Bikri.

14 Sheba passed through all the territory of the tribes of Israel. He arrived
at the city of Abel Beth Maakah. He had
gone through the entire area of the
Bikrites. They had gathered together
and followed him. 15 Joab and all his
troops came to Abel Beth Maakah. They
surrounded it because Sheba was there.
They built a ramp up to the city. It stood
against the outer wall. They pounded
the wall with huge logs to bring it down.
16 While that was going on, a wise woman called out from the city. She shouted,
"Listen! Listen! Tell Joab to come here.
I want to speak to him." 17 So Joab went
toward her. She asked, "Are you Joab?"

"I am," he answered.

She said, "Listen to what I have to say."

"I'm listening," he said.

18 She continued, "Long ago people
used to say, 'Get your answer at Abel.'
And that would settle the matter. 19 We
are the most peaceful and faithful people in Israel. You are trying to destroy
a city that is like a mother in Israel.
Why do you want to swallow up what
belongs to the LORD?"

20 "I would never do anything like
that!" Joab said. "I would never swallow up or destroy what belongs to the
LORD! 21 That isn't what I have in mind
at all. There's a man named Sheba, the
son of Bikri, in your city. He's from the
hill country of Ephraim. He's trying to
kill King David. Hand that man over to
me. Then I'll pull my men back from
your city."

The woman said to Joab, "We'll throw
his head down to you from the wall."

22 Then the woman gave her wise advice to all the people in the city. They cut
off the head of Sheba, the son of Bikri.
They threw it down to Joab. So he blew
his trumpet. Then his men pulled back
from the city. Each of them returned to
his home. And Joab went back to the
king in Jerusalem.

David's Officials

23 Joab was commander over Israel's
entire army.
Benaiah, the son of Jehoiada, was
commander over the Kerethites
and Pelethites.
24 Adoniram was in charge of those
who were forced to work hard.
Jehoshaphat, the son of Ahilud,
kept the records.
25 Sheva was the secretary.
Zadok and Abiathar were priests.
26 Ira, the Jairite, was David's priest.

David Makes Things Right for the People of Gibeon

21 For three years in a row there
wasn't enough food in the land.
That was while David was king. So
David asked the LORD why he wasn't
blessing his people. The LORD said, "It is
because Saul and his family committed
murder. He put the people of Gibeon
to death."

2 The people of Gibeon weren't a part
of Israel. Instead, they were some of
the Amorites who were still left alive.
The Israelites had promised to spare
them. But Saul had tried to put an end
to them. That's because he wanted to
make Israel and Judah strong. So now
King David sent for the people of Gibeon
and spoke to them. 3 He asked them,
"What would you like me to do for you?
How can I make up for the wrong things
that were done to you? I want you to
be able to pray that the LORD will once
again bless his land."

4 The people of Gibeon answered him.
They said, "No amount of silver or gold
can make up for what Saul and his family did to us. And we can't put anyone
in Israel to death."

"What do you want me to do for you?" David asked.

5 They answered the king, "Saul nearly destroyed us. He made plans to wipe us out. We don't have anywhere to live in Israel. 6 So let seven of the males in his family line be given to us. We'll kill them. We'll put their dead bodies out in the open in the sight of the LORD. We'll do it at Gibeah of Saul. Saul was the LORD's chosen king."

So King David said, "I'll give seven males to you."

7 The king spared Mephibosheth. He was the son of Jonathan and the grandson of Saul. David had made a promise in front of the LORD. He had promised to be kind to Jonathan and the family line of his father Saul. 8 But the king chose Armoni and another Mephibosheth. They were the two sons of Aiah's daughter Rizpah. Saul was their father. The king also chose the five sons of Saul's daughter Merab. Adriel, the son of Barzillai, was their father. Adriel was from Meholah. 9 King David handed them over to the people of Gibeon. They killed them. They put their dead bodies out in the open on a hill in the sight of the LORD. All seven of them died together. They were put to death during the first days of the harvest. It happened just when people were beginning to harvest the barley.

10 Aiah's daughter Rizpah took some rough cloth people wear when they're sad. She spread it out for herself on a rock. She stayed there from the beginning of the harvest until it rained. The rain poured down from the sky on the dead bodies of the seven males. She didn't let the birds touch them by day. She didn't let the wild animals touch them at night. 11 Someone told David what Rizpah had done. She was Aiah's daughter and Saul's concubine. 12 David went and got the bones of Saul and his son Jonathan. He got them from the citizens of Jabesh Gilead. They had stolen their bodies from the main street in Beth Shan. That's where the Philistines had hung their bodies up on the city wall. They had done it after they struck Saul down on Mount Gilboa. 13 David brought the bones of Saul and his son Jonathan from Jabesh Gilead. The bones of the seven males who had been killed and put out in the open were also gathered up.

14 The bones of Saul and his son Jonathan were buried in the tomb of Saul's father Kish. The tomb was at Zela in the territory of Benjamin. Everything the king commanded was done. After that, God answered prayer and blessed the land.

Wars Against the Philistines

15 Once again there was a battle between the Philistines and Israel. David went down with his men to fight against the Philistines. He became very tired. 16 Ishbi-Benob belonged to the family line of Rapha. The tip of his bronze spear weighed seven and a half pounds. He was also armed with a new sword. He said he would kill David. 17 But Abishai, the son of Zeruiah, came to save David. He struck down the Philistine and killed him. Then David's men made a promise. They said to David, "We never want you to go out with us to battle again. You are the lamp of Israel's kingdom. We want that lamp to keep on burning brightly."

18 There was another battle against the Philistines. It took place at Gob. At that time Sibbekai killed Saph. Sibbekai was a Hushathite. Saph was from the family line of Rapha.

19 In another battle against the Philistines at Gob, Elhanan killed Goliath's brother. Elhanan was the son of Jair from Bethlehem. Goliath was from the city of Gath. His spear was as big as a weaver's rod.

20 There was still another battle. It took place at Gath. A huge man lived there. He had six fingers on each hand and six toes on each foot. So the total number of his toes and fingers was 24. He was also from the family of Rapha. 21 He made fun of Israel. So Jonathan killed him. Jonathan was the son of David's brother Shimeah.

22 Those four Philistine men lived in Gath. They were from the family line of Rapha. David and his men killed them.

David's Song of Praise

22 David sang the words of this song to the LORD. He sang them when the LORD saved him from the power of all his enemies and of Saul. 2 He said,

"The LORD is my rock and my fort.
He is the God who saves me.
3 My God is my rock. I go to him for safety.
He is like a shield to me. He's the power that saves me.
He's my place of safety. I go to him for help. He's my Savior.
He saves me from those who want to hurt me.
4 I called out to the LORD. He is worthy of praise.
He saved me from my enemies.

5 "The waves of death were all around me.
A destroying flood swept over me.
6 The ropes of the grave were tight around me.
Death set its trap in front of me.
7 When I was in trouble I called out to the LORD.
I called out to my God.
From his temple he heard my voice.
My cry for help reached his ears.

8 "The earth trembled and shook.
The pillars of the heavens rocked back and forth.
They trembled because the LORD was angry.
9 Smoke came out of his nose.
Flames of fire came out of his mouth.
Burning coals blazed out of it.
10 He opened the heavens and came down.
Dark clouds were under his feet.
11 He got on the cherubim and flew.
The wings of the wind lifted him up.
12 He covered himself with darkness.
The dark rain clouds of the sky were like a tent around him.
13 From the brightness all around him flashes of lightning blazed out.
14 The LORD thundered from heaven.
The voice of the Most High God was heard.
15 He shot his arrows and scattered the enemy.
He sent flashes of lightning and chased them away.
16 The bottom of the sea could be seen.
The foundations of the earth were uncovered.
It happened when the LORD's anger blazed out.
It came like a blast of breath from his nose.

17 "He reached down from heaven. He took hold of me.
He lifted me out of deep waters.
18 He saved me from my powerful enemies.
He set me free from those who were too strong for me.
19 They stood up to me when I was in trouble.
But the LORD helped me.
20 He brought me out into a wide and safe place.
He saved me because he was pleased with me.

21 "The LORD has been good to me because I do what is right.
He has rewarded me because I lead a pure life.
22 I have lived the way the LORD wanted me to.
I'm not guilty of turning away from my God.
23 I keep all his laws in mind.
I haven't turned away from his commands.
24 He knows that I am without blame.
He knows I've kept myself from sinning.
25 The LORD has rewarded me for doing what is right.
He has rewarded me because I haven't done anything wrong.

26 "LORD, to those who are faithful you show that you are faithful.
To those who are without blame you show that you are without blame.
27 To those who are pure you show that you are pure.
But to those whose paths are crooked you show that you are clever.
28 You save those who aren't proud.
But you watch the proud to bring them down.
29 LORD, you are my lamp.
You bring light into my darkness.
30 With your help I can attack a troop of soldiers.
With the help of my God I can climb over a wall.

PERFECT

God has no flaws. He will never make a mistake, and he will never break a promise. God never has sinned, and he never will. He is perfect in all his ways.

Have you ever said something unkind that you wish you hadn't said? All people have sinned, or acted in ways that don't please God. We are not perfect like God.

But God loves us, and in his perfect love, he sent a perfect Savior, Jesus (see John 3:16). We are safe and secure in God's love as we learn to follow him.

31 "God's way is perfect.
The LORD's word doesn't have any flaws.
He protects like a shield
all who go to him for safety.
32 Who is God except the LORD?
Who is the Rock except our God?
33 God gives me strength for the battle.
He keeps my way secure.
34 He makes my feet like the feet of a deer.
He causes me to stand on the highest places.
35 He trains my hands to fight every battle.
My arms can bend a bow of bronze.
36 LORD, you shield me with your saving help.
Your help has made me great.
37 You give me a wide path to walk in
so that I don't twist my ankles.

38 "I chased my enemies and crushed them.
I didn't turn back until they were destroyed.
39 I crushed them completely so that they couldn't get up.
They fell under my feet.
40 LORD, you gave me strength to fight the battle.
You caused my enemies to be humble in front of me.
41 You made them turn their backs and run away.
So I destroyed my enemies.
42 They cried out for help. But there was no one to save them.
They called out to the LORD. But he didn't answer them.
43 I beat them as fine as the dust of the earth.
I pounded them and walked on them like mud in the |streets.

44 "You saved me when people attacked me.
You have kept me as the ruler over nations.
People I didn't know serve me now.
45 People from other lands bow down to me in fear.
As soon as they hear about me, they obey me.
46 All of them give up hope.
They come trembling out of their hiding places.

47 "The LORD lives! Give praise to my Rock!
Give honor to my God, the Rock!
He is my Savior!

48 He is the God who pays back my
enemies.
He brings the nations under my
control.
49 He sets me free from my
enemies.
You have honored me more than
them.
You have saved me from a man
who wanted to hurt me.
50 LORD, I will praise you among the
nations.
I will sing your praise.
51 He gives his king great victories.
He shows his faithful love to his
anointed king.
He shows it to David and his
family forever."

David's Last Words

23 Here are David's last words. He
said,

"I am David, the son of Jesse. God
has given me a message.
The Most High God has greatly
honored me.
The God of Jacob anointed me as
king.
I am the hero of Israel's songs.

2 "The Spirit of the LORD spoke
through me.
I spoke his word with my tongue.
3 The God of Israel spoke.
The Rock of Israel said to me,
'A king must rule over people in a
way that is right.
He must have respect for God
when he rules.
4 Then he will be like the light of
morning at sunrise
when there aren't any clouds.
He will be like the bright sun after
rain
that makes grass grow on the
earth.'

5 "Suppose my royal family was not
right with God.
Then he would not have made a
covenant with me that will last
forever.
Every part of it was well prepared
and made secure.
Then God would not have saved me
completely
or given me everything I longed
for.
6 But evil people are like thorns that
are thrown away.
You can't pick them up with your
hands.
7 Even if you touch them,
you must use an iron tool or a
spear.
Thorns are burned up right
where they are."

David's Mighty Warriors

8 Here are the names of David's
mighty warriors.
Josheb-Basshebeth was chief of the
three mighty warriors. He was a Tahke-
monite. He used his spear against 800
men. He killed all of them at one time.
9 Next to him was Eleazar. He was one
of the three mighty warriors. He was
the son of Dodai, the Ahohite. Eleazar
was with David at Pas Dammim. That's
where Israel's army made fun of the
Philistines who were gathered there for
battle. Then the Israelites pulled back.
10 But Eleazar stayed right where he
was. He struck down the Philistines until his hand grew tired. But he still held
on to his sword. The LORD helped him
win a great battle that day. The troops
returned to Eleazar. They came back
to him only to take what they wanted
from the dead bodies.
11 Next to him was Shammah, the
son of Agee. Shammah was a Hararite.
The Philistines gathered together at
a place where there was a field full of
lentils. Israel's troops ran away from
the Philistines. 12 But Shammah took
his stand in the middle of the field. He
didn't let the Philistines capture it. He
struck them down. The LORD helped
him win a great battle.
13 David was at the cave of Adullam.
During harvest time, three of the 30
chief warriors came down to him there.
A group of Philistines was camped in
the Valley of Rephaim. 14 At that time
David was in his usual place of safety.
Some Philistine troops were stationed at
Bethlehem. 15 David longed for a drink of
water. He said, "I wish someone would
get me water from the well near the gate
of Bethlehem." 16 So the three mighty
warriors fought their way past the Philistine guards. They got some water from
the well near the gate of Bethlehem.
They took the water back to David. But

David refused to drink it. Instead, he
poured it out as a drink offering to the
LORD. 17 "LORD, I would never drink that
water!" David said. "It stands for the
blood of these men. They put their lives
in danger by going to Bethlehem to get
it." So David wouldn't drink it.

Those were some of the brave things
the three mighty warriors did.

18 Abishai was chief over the three
mighty warriors. He was the brother
of Joab, the son of Zeruiah. He used his
spear against 300 men. He killed all of
them. So he became as famous as the
three mighty warriors were. 19 In fact,
he was even more honored than the
three mighty warriors. He became their
commander. But he wasn't included
among them.

20 Benaiah was a great hero from
Kabzeel. He was the son of Jehoiada.
Benaiah did many brave things. He
struck down two of Moab's best warriors. He also went down into a pit on a
snowy day. He killed a lion there. 21 And
he struck down a huge Egyptian. The
Egyptian was holding a spear. Benaiah
went out to fight against him with a
club. He grabbed the spear out of the
Egyptian's hand. Then he killed him
with it. 22 Those were some of the brave
things Benaiah, the son of Jehoiada,
did. He too was as famous as the three
mighty warriors were. 23 He was honored
more than any of the thirty chief warriors. But he wasn't included among the
three mighty warriors. David put him
in charge of his own personal guards.

24 Here is a list of David's men who were among the thirty chief warriors.

Asahel, the brother of Joab
Elhanan, the son of Dodo, from Bethlehem
25 Shammah, the Harodite
Elika, the Harodite
26 Helez, the Paltite
Ira, the son of Ikkesh, from Tekoa
27 Abiezer from Anathoth
Sibbekai, the Hushathite
28 Zalmon, the Ahohite
Maharai from Netophah
29 Heled, the son of Baanah, from Netophah
Ithai, the son of Ribai, from Gibeah in Benjamin
30 Benaiah from Pirathon
Hiddai from the valleys of Gaash
31 Abi-Albon, the Arbathite
Azmaveth, the Barhumite
32 Eliahba, the Shaalbonite
the sons of Jashen
Jonathan, 33 the son of Shammah, the Hararite
Ahiam, the son of Sharar, the Hararite
34 Eliphelet, the son of Ahasbai, the Maakathite
Eliam, the son of Ahithophel, from Giloh
35 Hezro from Carmel
Paarai, the Arbite
36 Igal, the son of Nathan, from Zobah
the son of Hagri
37 Zelek from Ammon
Naharai from Beeroth, who carried the armor of Joab, the son of Zeruiah
38 Ira, the Ithrite
Gareb, the Ithrite
39 and Uriah, the Hittite

The total number of men was 37.

David Counts His Fighting Men

24 The LORD was very angry with
Israel. He stirred up David
against them. He said, "Go! Count the
men of Israel and Judah."

2 So the king spoke to Joab and the
army commanders with him. He said,
"Go all through the territories of the
tribes of Israel. Go from the town of
Dan all the way to Beersheba. Count
the fighting men. Then I'll know how
many there are."

3 Joab replied to the king. He said,
"King David, you are my master. May
the LORD your God multiply the troops
100 times. And may you live to see it.
But why would you want me to count
the fighting men?"

4 The king's word had more authority
than the word of Joab and the army
commanders. That was true in spite
of what Joab had said. So they left the
king and went out to count the fighting
men of Israel.

5 They went across the Jordan River.
They camped south of the town in the
middle of the Arnon River valley near
Aroer. Then they went through Gad and
continued on to Jazer. 6 They went to

Gilead and the area of Tahtim Hodshi. They continued to Dan Jaan and on around toward Sidon. 7 Then they went toward the fort of Tyre. They went to all the towns of the Hivites and Canaanites. Finally, they went on to Beersheba. It was in the Negev Desert of Judah.

8 They finished going through the entire land. Then they came back to Jerusalem. They had been gone for nine months and 20 days.

9 Joab reported to the king how many fighting men he had counted. In Israel there were 800,000 men who were able to handle a sword. In Judah there were 500,000.

10 David felt sorry that he had counted the fighting men. So he said to the LORD, "I committed a great sin when I counted Judah and Israel's men. LORD, I beg you to take away my guilt. I've done a very foolish thing."

11 Before David got up the next morning, a message from the LORD came to Gad the prophet. He was David's seer. The message said, 12 "Go and tell David, 'The LORD says, "I could punish you in three different ways. Choose one of them for me to use against you." ' "

13 So Gad went to David. He said to him, "Take your choice. Do you want three years when there won't be enough food in your land? Or do you want three months when you will run away from your enemies while they chase you? Or do you want three days when there will be a plague in your land? Think it over. Then take your pick. Tell me how to answer the one who sent me."

14 David said to Gad, "I'm suffering terribly. Let us fall into the hands of the LORD. His mercy is great. But don't let me fall into human hands."

15 So the LORD sent a plague on Israel. It lasted from that morning until he decided to end it. From Dan all the way to Beersheba 70,000 people died. 16 The angel reached his hand out to destroy Jerusalem. But the LORD stopped sending the plague. So he spoke to the angel who was making the people suffer. He said, "That is enough! Do not kill any more people." The angel of the LORD was at Araunah's threshing floor. Araunah was from the city of Jebus.

17 David saw the angel who was striking down the people. David said to the LORD, "I'm the one who has sinned. I'm the one who has done what is wrong. I'm like a shepherd for these people. These people are like sheep. What have they done? Let your judgment be on me and my family."

David Builds an Altar

18 On that day Gad went to David. Gad said to him, "Go up to the threshing floor of Araunah, the Jebusite. Build an altar there to honor the LORD." 19 So David went up and did it. He did what the LORD had commanded through Gad. 20 Araunah looked and saw the king and his officials coming toward him. So he went out to welcome them. He bowed down to the king with his face toward the ground.

21 Araunah said, "King David, you are my master. Why have you come to see me?"

"To buy your threshing floor," David answered. "I want to build an altar there to honor the LORD. When I do, the plague on the people will be stopped."

22 Araunah said to David, "Take anything you wish. Offer it up. Here are oxen for the burnt offering. Here are threshing sleds. And here are wooden collars from the necks of the oxen. Use all the wood to burn the offering. 23 Your Majesty, I'll give all of it to you." Araunah continued, "And may the LORD your God accept you."

24 But the king replied to Araunah, "No. I want to pay you for it. I won't sacrifice to the LORD my God burnt offerings that haven't cost me anything."

So David bought the threshing floor and the oxen. He paid 20 ounces of silver for them. 25 David built an altar there to honor the LORD. He sacrificed burnt offerings and friendship offerings. Then the LORD answered David's prayer and blessed the land. The plague on Israel was stopped.

1 KINGS

Author: We don't know.

After David was king, the nation of Israel had a time of peace under a good king named Solomon (David's son). Solomon was a very wise king who led God's people with justice. Solomon was so wise, in fact, that other nations came to him to learn from him and hear what he had to say.

Like David, Solomon did not always obey God, but he led God's people to build a special place in Israel, called the temple, where God would come and dwell among his people. This was like the holy tent, but it had a firm foundation, reminding Israel that God had made his home among them.

Old Testament History

Solomon reminded God's people that they were to worship only the Lord. But after Solomon died, the kingdom of Israel split into two kingdoms: The northern kingdom was called Israel, and the southern kingdom was called Judah. Most of the kings who ruled these nations did not listen to or obey God at all. The kings led the people away from God by saying things like, "Go ahead, worship false gods; the Lord won't mind at all!" But they were wrong. Ever since the beginning, God has wanted his people to worship him alone because he is the only true God. God sent a prophet named Elijah to tell the people, "Stop worshiping false gods! Worship the one true God!"

Adonijah Makes Himself King

1 King David was now very old. He
couldn't keep warm even when blankets were spread over him. 2 So his attendants spoke to him. They said, "You
are our king and master. Please let us
try to find a young virgin to serve you.
She can take care of you. She can lie
down beside you to keep you warm."
3 So David's attendants looked all over
Israel for a beautiful young woman.
They found Abishag. She was from the
town of Shunem. They brought her to the
king. 4 The woman was very beautiful.
She took care of the king and served him.
But the king didn't have sex with her.
5 Adonijah was the son of David and
his wife Haggith. He came forward and
announced, "I'm going to be the next
king." So he got chariots and horses
ready. He also got 50 men to run in
front of him. 6 His father had never
tried to stop him from doing what he
wanted to. His father had never asked
him, "Why are you acting the way you
do?" Adonijah was also very handsome.
Now that Absalom was dead, Adonijah
was David's oldest son.
7 Adonijah talked things over with
Joab, the son of Zeruiah. He also talked
with Abiathar the priest. They agreed
to help him. 8 But Zadok the priest and
Benaiah, the son of Jehoiada, didn't join
Adonijah. Nathan the prophet didn't
join him. Shimei and Rei didn't join him.
And neither did David's special guard.
9 Adonijah sacrificed sheep, cattle
and fat calves. He sacrificed them at
the Stone of Zoheleth near En Rogel.
He invited all his brothers, the king's
sons, and all the royal officials of Judah.
10 But he didn't invite Benaiah or Nathan
the prophet. He didn't invite the special
guard or his brother Solomon either.
11 Nathan asked Solomon's mother
Bathsheba, "Haven't you heard? Adonijah, the son of Haggith, has made himself king. And King David doesn't know
anything about it. 12 So let me tell you
what to do to save your life. It will also
save the life of your son Solomon. 13 Go
in and see King David. Say to him, 'You
are my king and master. You promised
me, "You can be sure that your son Solomon will be king after me. He will sit
on my throne." If that's really true, why
has Adonijah become king?' 14 While you

in 1 Kings?

God is the One True God. He alone is worthy of our worship.

are still talking to the king, I'll come in
and support what you have said."
15 So Bathsheba went to see the old
king in his room. Abishag, the Shunammite, was taking care of him there.
16 Bathsheba bowed low in front of the
king.
"What do you want?" the king asked.
17 She said to him, "My master, you
made a promise in the name of the LORD
your God. You promised me, 'Your son
Solomon will be king after me. He will
sit on my throne.' 18 But now Adonijah
has made himself king. And you don't
even know about it. 19 He has sacrificed
large numbers of cattle, fat calves and
sheep. He has invited all the king's sons.
He has also invited Abiathar the priest
and Joab, the commander of the army.
But he hasn't invited your son Solomon.
20 You are my king and master. All the
Israelites are watching to see what you
will do. They want to find out from you
who will sit on the throne after you. 21 If
you don't do something, I and my son
Solomon will be treated like people who
have committed crimes. That will happen as soon as you join the members
of your family who have already died."
22 While she was still speaking with
the king, Nathan the prophet arrived.
23 The king was told, "Nathan the prophet is here." So Nathan went to the king.
He bowed down with his face toward
the ground.
24 Nathan said, "You are my king
and master. Have you announced that
Adonijah will be king after you? Have
you said he will sit on your throne?
25 Today he has gone down outside the

city. He has sacrificed large numbers
of cattle, fat calves and sheep. He has
invited all the king's sons. He has also
invited the commanders of the army
and Abiathar the priest. Even now they
are eating and drinking with him. They
are saying, 'May King Adonijah live a
long time!' 26 But he didn't invite me. He
didn't invite Zadok the priest or Benaiah, the son of Jehoiada. He didn't invite
your son Solomon either. 27 King David,
have you allowed all of that to happen?
Did you do it without letting us know
about it? Why didn't you tell us who is
going to sit on your throne after you?"

David Makes Solomon King

28 King David said, "Tell Bathsheba
to come in." So she came and stood in
front of the king.
29 Then the king made a promise. He
said, "The LORD has saved me from all
my troubles. You can be sure that he
lives. 30 And you can be just as sure I
will do what I promised. This is the day
I will do what I promised in the name
of the LORD. He is the God of Israel. I
promised you that your son Solomon
would be king after me. He will sit on
my throne in my place."
31 Then Bathsheba bowed down in
front of the king. Her face was toward
the ground. She said, "King David, you
are my master. May you live forever!"
32 King David said, "Tell Zadok the
priest and Nathan the prophet to come
in. Also tell Benaiah, the son of Jehoiada, to come." So they came to the king.
33 He said to them, "Take my officials
with you. Have my son Solomon get
on my own mule. Take him down to the
Gihon spring. 34 Have Zadok the priest
and Nathan the prophet anoint him as
king over Israel there. Blow a trumpet.
Shout, 'May King Solomon live a long
time!' 35 Then come back up to the city
with him. Have him sit on my throne.
He will rule in my place. I've appointed
him ruler over Israel and Judah."
36 Benaiah, the son of Jehoiada, answered the king. "Amen!" he said. "May
the LORD your God make it come true.
37 You are my king and master. The LORD
has been with you. May he also be with
Solomon. King David, may the LORD
make Solomon's kingdom even greater
than yours!"
38 So Zadok the priest and Nathan
the prophet left the palace. Benaiah,
the son of Jehoiada, went with them.
So did the Kerethites and Pelethites.
They had Solomon get on King David's
mule. And they brought him down to
the Gihon spring. 39 Zadok the priest
had taken an animal horn from the
sacred tent. The horn was filled with
olive oil. He anointed Solomon with the
oil. A trumpet was blown. All the people
shouted, "May King Solomon live a long
time!" 40 Then they went up toward the
city. Solomon was leading the way. The
people were playing flutes. They were
filled with great joy. The ground shook
because of all the noise.
41 Adonijah and all his guests heard
it. They were just finishing their meal.
Joab heard the sound of the trumpet.
So he asked, "What does all this noise
in the city mean?"
42 While Joab was still speaking, Jonathan arrived. Jonathan was the son
of Abiathar the priest. Adonijah said,
"Come in. I have respect for you. You
must be bringing good news."
43 "No! I'm not!" Jonathan answered.
"Our master King David has made Solomon king. 44 David sent Zadok the priest
and Nathan the prophet along with Solomon. He also sent Benaiah, the son of
Jehoiada, with him. He sent the Kerethites and Pelethites with him too. They
put him on the king's mule. 45 They took
him down to the Gihon spring. There
Zadok the priest and Nathan the prophet
anointed him as king. Now they've gone
back up to the city. They were cheering
all the way. The city is filled with the
sound of it. That's the noise you hear.
46 And that's not all. Solomon has taken
his seat on the royal throne. 47 The royal
officials came to give their blessing to our
master King David. They said, 'May your
God make Solomon's name more famous
than yours! May he make Solomon's
kingdom greater than yours!' While King
David was sitting on his bed, he bowed in
worship. 48 He said, 'I praise the LORD. He
is the God of Israel. He has let me live to
see my son sitting on my throne today
as the next king.' "
49 When all Adonijah's guests heard
that, they were terrified. So they got up
and scattered. 50 Adonijah was afraid of
what Solomon might do to him. So he

went and grabbed the horns of the altar for burnt offerings. Those horns stuck out from its upper corners. 51 Then Solomon was told, "King Solomon, Adonijah is afraid of you. He's holding onto the horns of the altar. He says, 'I want King Solomon to make a promise today. I want him to promise that he won't kill me with his sword.' "

52 Solomon replied, "Let him show that he's a man people can respect. Then not even one hair on his head will fall to the ground. But if I find out he's done something evil, he will die." 53 King Solomon got some men to bring Adonijah down from the altar. He came and bowed down to King Solomon. Solomon said, "Go on home."

David Gives Orders to Solomon

2 The time came near for David to die. So he gave orders to his son Solomon.

2 He said, "I'm about to die, just as everyone else on earth does. So be strong. Show how brave you are. 3 Do everything the LORD your God requires. Live the way he wants you to. Obey his orders and commands. Keep his laws and rules. Do everything written in the Law of Moses. Then you will have success in everything you do. You will succeed everywhere you go. 4 The LORD will keep the promise he made to me. He said, 'Your sons must be careful about how they live. They must be faithful to me with all their heart and soul. Then you will always have a son from your family line to sit on the throne of Israel.'

5 "You yourself know what Joab, the son of Zeruiah, did to me. You know that he killed Abner, the son of Ner, and Amasa, the son of Jether. They were the two commanders of Israel's armies. He killed them in a time of peace. It wasn't a time of war. Joab spilled the blood of Abner and Amasa. With that blood he stained the belt around his waist. He also stained the sandals on his feet. 6 You are wise. So I leave him in your hands. Just don't let him live to become an old man. Don't let him die peacefully.

7 "But be kind to the sons of Barzillai from Gilead. Provide what they need. They were faithful to me when I had to run away from your brother Absalom.

8 "Don't forget that Shimei, the son of Gera, is still around. He's from Bahurim in the territory of Benjamin. Shimei cursed me bitterly. He did it on the day I went to Mahanaim. Later, he came down to welcome me at the Jordan River. At that time I made a promise in the name of the LORD. I promised Shimei, 'I won't put you to death with my sword.' 9 But now I want you to think of him as guilty. You are wise. You will know what to do to him. Don't let him live to become an old man. Put him to death."

10 David joined the members of his family who had already died. He was buried in the City of David. 11 He had ruled over Israel for 40 years. He ruled for seven years in Hebron. Then he ruled for 33 years in Jerusalem. 12 So Solomon sat on the throne of his father David. His position as king was made secure.

Solomon's Kingdom Is Made Secure

13 Adonijah was the son of David's wife Haggith. He went to Bathsheba. She was Solomon's mother. She asked Adonijah, "Have you come in peace?"

He answered, "Yes. I've come in peace." 14 He continued, "I want to ask you something."

"Go ahead," she replied.

15 He said, "As you know, the kingdom belonged to me. The whole nation of Israel thought of me as their king. But now things have changed. The kingdom belongs to my brother. The LORD has given it to him. 16 But I have a favor to ask of you. Don't say no to me."

"Go ahead," she said.

17 So he continued, "Please ask King Solomon for a favor. He won't say no to you. Ask him to give me Abishag from Shunem to be my wife."

18 "All right," Bathsheba replied. "I'll speak to the king for you."

19 So Bathsheba went to King Solomon. She went to him to speak for Adonijah. The king stood up to greet her. He bowed down to her. Then he sat down on his throne. He had a throne brought for his mother. She sat down at his right side.

20 "I have one small favor to ask of you," she said. "Don't say no to me."

The king replied, "Mother, go ahead and ask. I won't say no to you."

21 She said, "Let your brother Adonijah
marry Abishag, the Shunammite."
22 King Solomon answered his mother, "Why are you asking me to give
Abishag, the Shunammite, to Adonijah?
You might as well ask me to give him
the whole kingdom! After all, he's my
older brother. And he doesn't want the
kingdom only for himself. He also wants
it for Abiathar the priest and for Joab,
the son of Zeruiah."
23 Then King Solomon made a promise in the name of the LORD. He said,
"Adonijah will pay with his life because
of what he has asked for. If he doesn't,
may God punish me greatly. 24 The LORD
has made my position as king secure.
I'm sitting on the throne of my father
David. The LORD has built a royal house
for me, just as he promised. You can
be sure that the LORD lives. And you
can be just as sure that Adonijah will
be put to death today." 25 So King Solomon gave the order to Benaiah, the
son of Jehoiada. Benaiah struck down
Adonijah, and he died.
26 The king spoke to Abiathar the
priest. He said, "Go back to your fields
in Anathoth. You should really be put
to death. But I won't have it done now.
That's because you carried the ark of the
LORD and King. You did it for my father
David. You shared all of his hard times."
27 So Solomon wouldn't let Abiathar
serve as a priest of the LORD anymore.
That's how the message the LORD had
spoken at Shiloh came true. He had
spoken it about the family of Eli.
28 News of what Solomon had done
reached Joab. Joab had never made
evil plans along with Absalom. But he
had joined Adonijah. So he ran to the
tent of the LORD. He grabbed the horns
that stuck out from the upper corners
of the altar for burnt offerings. 29 King
Solomon was told that Joab had run to
the tent. He was also told that Joab was
by the altar. Then Solomon gave the
order to Benaiah, the son of Jehoiada.
He told him, "Go! Strike him down!"
30 So Benaiah entered the tent of the
LORD. He said to Joab, "The king says,
'Come on out!' "
But Joab answered, "No. I'd rather
die here."
Benaiah told the king what Joab had
said to him.
31 Then the king commanded Benaiah, "Do what he says. Strike him down
and bury him. Then I and my family
line won't be held accountable for the
blood Joab spilled. He killed people
who weren't guilty of doing anything
wrong. 32 The LORD will pay him back
for the blood he spilled. Joab attacked
two men. He killed them with his sword.
And my father David didn't even know
anything about it. Joab killed Abner, the
son of Ner. Abner was the commander
of Israel's army. Joab also killed Amasa, the son of Jether. Amasa was the
commander of Judah's army. Abner
and Amasa were better men than Joab
is. They were more honest than he is.
33 May Joab and his children after him
be held forever accountable for spilling
the blood of Abner and Amasa. But may
David and his children after him enjoy
the LORD's peace and rest forever. May
the LORD also give his peace to David's
royal house and kingdom forever."
34 So Benaiah, the son of Jehoiada,
went up to the LORD's tent. There he
struck down Joab. And he killed him.
Joab was buried at his home out in
the country. 35 The king put Benaiah
in charge of the army. Benaiah took
Joab's place. The king also put Zadok
the priest in Abiathar's place.
36 Then the king sent for Shimei. He
said to him, "Build yourself a house in
Jerusalem. Live there. Don't go anywhere else. 37 You must not leave the
city and go across the Kidron Valley.
If you do, you can be sure you will die.
And it will be your own fault."
38 Shimei replied to the king, "You are
my king and master. What you say is
good. I'll do it." Shimei stayed in Jerusalem for a long time.
39 Three years after Solomon had
talked with Shimei, two of Shimei's
slaves ran off. They went to Achish, the
king of Gath. He was the son of Maakah.
Shimei was told, "Your slaves are in
Gath." 40 When Shimei heard that, he
put a saddle on his donkey. Then he
went to Achish at Gath to look for his
slaves. Shimei found them and brought
them back from Gath.
41 Solomon was told that Shimei had
left Jerusalem. He was told he had gone
to Gath and had returned. 42 So the king
sent for Shimei. He said to him, "Didn't

I force you to make a promise in the name of the LORD? Didn't I warn you? I said, 'You must not leave the city and go somewhere else. If you do, you can be sure you will die.' At that time you said to me, 'What you say is good. I'll obey your command.' [43] So why didn't you keep your promise to the LORD? Why didn't you obey the command I gave you?"

[44] The king continued, "You know all the wrong things you did to my father David. In your heart you know them. Now the LORD will pay you back for what you did. [45] But I will be blessed. The LORD will make David's kingdom secure forever."

[46] Then the king gave the order to Benaiah, the son of Jehoiada. Benaiah left the palace and struck down Shimei. And he died.

So the kingdom was now made secure in Solomon's hands.

Solomon Asks God for Wisdom

3 Solomon and Pharaoh, the king of Egypt, agreed to help each other. So Solomon married Pharaoh's daughter. He brought her to the City of David. She stayed there until he finished building his palace, the LORD's temple, and the wall around Jerusalem. [2] But the people continued to offer sacrifices at the high places where they worshiped. That's because a temple hadn't been built yet where the LORD would put his Name. [3] Solomon showed his love for the LORD. He did it by obeying the laws his father David had taught him. But Solomon offered sacrifices at the high places. He also burned incense there.

[4] King Solomon went to the city of Gibeon to offer sacrifices. That's where the most important high place was. There he offered 1,000 burnt offerings on the altar. [5] The LORD appeared to Solomon at Gibeon. He spoke to him in a dream during the night. God said, "Ask for anything you want me to give you."

[6] Solomon answered, "You have been very kind to my father David, your servant. That's because he was faithful to you. He did what was right. His heart was honest. And you have continued to be very kind to him. You have given him a son to sit on his throne this day.

[7] "LORD my God, you have now made me king. You have put me in the place of my father David. But I'm only a little child. I don't know how to carry out my duties. [8] I'm here among the people you have chosen. They are a great nation. They are more than anyone can count. [9] So give me a heart that understands. Then I can rule over your people. I can tell the difference between what is right and what is wrong. Who can possibly rule over this great nation of yours?"

[10] The Lord was pleased that Solomon had asked for that. [11] So God said to him, "You have not asked to live for a long time. You have not asked to be wealthy. You have not even asked to have your enemies killed. Instead, you have asked for wisdom. You want to do what is right and fair when you judge people. Because that is what you have asked for, [12] I will give it to you. I will give you a wise and understanding heart. So here is what will be true of you. There has never been anyone like you. And there never will be. [13] And that is not all. I will give you what you have not asked for. I will give you wealth and honor. As long as you live, no other king will be as great as you are. [14] Live the way I want you to. Obey my laws and commands, just as your father David did. Then I will let you live for a long time." [15] Solomon woke up. He realized he had been dreaming.

He returned to Jerusalem. He stood in front of the ark of the Lord's covenant. He sacrificed burnt offerings and friendship offerings. Then he gave a feast for all his officials.

A Wise Ruling

[16] Two prostitutes came to the king. They stood in front of him. [17] One of them said, "Pardon me, my master, this woman and I live in the same house. I had a baby while she was there with me. [18] Three days after my child was born, this woman also had a baby. We were alone. There wasn't anyone in the house but the two of us.

[19] "During the night this woman's baby died. It happened because she was lying on top of him. [20] So she got up in the middle of the night. She took my son from my side while I was asleep. She put him by her breast. Then she put her dead son by my breast. [21] The next morning, I got up to nurse my son. But he was dead! I looked at him closely

in the morning light. And I saw that it
wasn't my baby."
22 The other woman said, "No! The
living baby is my son. The dead one
belongs to you."
But the first woman said, "No! The
dead baby is yours. The living one belongs to me." So they argued in front
of the king.
23 The king said, "One of you says,
'My son is alive. Your son is dead.' The
other one says, 'No! Your son is dead.
Mine is alive.' "
24 He continued, "Bring me a sword."
So a sword was brought to him. 25 Then
he gave an order. He said, "Cut the living
child in two. Give half to one woman
and half to the other."
26 The woman whose son was alive
was filled with deep love for her son.
She said to the king, "My master, please
give her the living baby! Don't kill him!"
But the other woman said, "Neither
one of us will have him. Cut him in two!"
27 Then the king made his decision. He
said, "Give the living baby to the first
woman. Don't kill him. She's his mother."
28 All the Israelites heard about the
decision the king had given. That gave
them great respect for him. They saw
that God had given him wisdom. They
knew that Solomon would do what was
right and fair when he judged people.

Solomon's Officials and Governors

4 So King Solomon ruled over the
whole nation of Israel.

2 Here are the names of his chief
officials.

Azariah was the priest. He was the
son of Zadok.
3 Elihoreph and Ahijah were
secretaries. They were the sons
of Shisha.
Jehoshaphat kept the records. He
was the son of Ahilud.
4 Benaiah was the commander
in chief. He was the son of
Jehoiada.
Zadok and Abiathar were priests.
5 Azariah was in charge of the local
governors. He was the son of
Nathan.
Zabud was a priest. He was also the
king's adviser. He was the son of
Nathan.
6 Ahishar was in charge of the palace.
Adoniram was in charge of those
who were forced to work for the
king. He was the son of Abda.

7 Solomon had 12 local governors over
the whole land of Israel. They provided supplies for the king and the royal
family. Each governor had to provide
supplies for one month out of each year.
8 Here are their names and areas.

Ben-Hur's area was the hill country
of Ephraim.
9 Ben-Deker's area was Makaz,
Shaalbim, Beth Shemesh and
Elon Bethhanan.
10 Ben-Hesed's area was Arubboth.
Sokoh and the whole land of
Hepher were included in his
area.
11 Ben-Abinadab's area was Naphoth
Dor. He married Solomon's
daughter Taphath.
12 Baana's area was Taanach,
Megiddo and the whole territory
of Beth Shan. Beth Shan was
next to Zarethan below Jezreel.
Baana's area reached from
Beth Shan all the way to Abel
Meholah. It also went across to
Jokmeam. Baana was the son
of Ahilud.
13 Ben-Geber's area was Ramoth
Gilead. The settlements of Jair,
the son of Manasseh, were
included in his area in Gilead.
The area of Argob in Bashan was
also included. That area had 60
large cities that had high walls
around them. The city gates
were made secure with heavy
bronze bars.
14 Ahinadab's area was Mahanaim.
He was the son of Iddo.
15 Ahimaaz's area was Naphtali. He
had married Basemath. She was
Solomon's daughter.
16 Baana's area was Asher and Aloth.
He was the son of Hushai.
17 Jehoshaphat's area was Issachar.
He was the son of Paruah.
18 Shimei's area was Benjamin. He
was the son of Ela.
19 Geber's area was Gilead. He was the
only governor over the area. He
was the son of Uri. Gilead had
been the country of Sihon and

Og. Sihon had been king of the
Amorites. Og had been king of
Bashan.

Solomon's Daily Supplies

[20]There were many people in Judah
and Israel. In fact, they were as many
as the grains of sand on the seashore.
They ate, drank and were happy. [21]Solo-
mon ruled over all the kingdoms from
the Euphrates River to the land of the
Philistines. He ruled as far as the border
of Egypt. All those countries brought the
gifts he required them to bring him. And
Solomon ruled over those countries for
his whole life.

[22]Here are the supplies Solomon
required every day.

five and a half tons of the finest
flour
11 tons of meal
[23]ten oxen that had been fed by hand
20 oxen that had been fed on
grasslands
100 sheep and goats
deer, antelopes and roebucks
the finest birds

[24]Solomon ruled over all the kingdoms that were west of the Euphrates
River. He ruled from Tiphsah all the way
to Gaza. And he had peace and rest on
every side. [25]While Solomon was king,
Judah and Israel lived in safety. They
were secure from Dan all the way to
Beersheba. Everyone had their own
vine and their own fig tree.
[26]Solomon had 4,000 spaces where
he kept his chariot horses. He had a
total of 12,000 horses.
[27]The local governors provided supplies for King Solomon. They provided
them for all who ate at the king's table.
Each governor provided supplies for
one month every year. The governors
made sure the king had everything he
needed. [28]They also brought barley
and straw for the chariot horses and
the other horses. Each of the governors
brought the amounts required of them.
They brought them to the proper places.

God Makes Solomon Very Wise

[29]God made Solomon very wise. His
understanding couldn't even be measured. It was like the sand on the seashore. People can't measure that either.
[30]Solomon's wisdom was greater than
the wisdom of all the people of the east. It
was greater than all the wisdom of Egypt.
[31]Solomon was wiser than anyone else.
He was wiser than Ethan, the Ezrahite.
He was wiser than Heman, Kalkol and
Darda. They were the sons of Mahol. Solomon became famous in all the nations
around him. [32]He spoke 3,000 proverbs.
He wrote 1,005 songs. [33]He spoke about
plants. He knew everything about them,
from the cedar trees in Lebanon to the
hyssop plants that grow out of walls. He
spoke about animals and birds. He also
spoke about reptiles and fish. [34]The kings
of all the world's nations heard about
how wise Solomon was. So they sent their
people to listen to him.

Solomon Prepares to Build the Temple

5 Hiram was the king of Tyre. He
heard that Solomon had been
anointed as king. He heard that Solomon had become the next king after
his father David. Hiram had always
been David's friend. So Hiram sent his
messengers to Solomon. [2]Then Solomon sent a message back to Hiram.
Solomon said,

[3]"As you know, my father David had to fight many battles. His
enemies attacked him from every
side. So he couldn't build a temple
where the LORD his God would put
his Name. That wouldn't be possible
until the LORD had put his enemies
under his control. [4]But now the LORD
my God has given me peace and rest
on every side. We don't have any
enemies. And we don't have any
other major problems either. [5]So I'm
planning to build a temple. I want to
build it for the Name of the LORD my
God. That's what he told my father
David he wanted me to do. He said,
'I will put your son on the throne in
your place. He will build a temple. I
will put my Name there.'
[6]"So give your men orders to cut
down cedar trees in Lebanon for
me. My men will work with yours.
I'll pay you for your men's work. I'll
pay any amount you decide on. As
you know, we don't have anyone as
skilled in cutting down trees as the
men of Sidon are."

7 When Hiram heard Solomon's message, he was very pleased. He said, "May
the LORD be praised today. He has given
David a wise son to rule over that great
nation."
8 So Hiram sent a message to Solomon. Hiram said,

> "I have received the message
> you sent me. I'll do everything you
> want me to. I'll provide the cedar
> and juniper logs. 9 My men will
> bring them from Lebanon down
> to the Mediterranean Sea. I'll make
> them into rafts. I'll float them to
> the place you want me to. When
> the rafts arrive, I'll separate the
> logs from each other. Then you can
> take them away. And here's what I
> want in return. Provide food for all
> the people in my palace."

10 So Hiram supplied Solomon with all
the cedar and juniper logs he wanted.
11 Solomon gave Hiram 3,600 tons of
wheat as food for the people in his palace. He also gave him 120,000 gallons
of oil made from pressed olives. He did
that for Hiram year after year. 12 The
LORD made Solomon wise, just as he
had promised him. There was peace
between Hiram and Solomon. The two
of them made a peace treaty.
13 King Solomon forced men from all
over Israel to work hard for him. There
were 30,000 of them. 14 He sent them
off to Lebanon in groups of 10,000 each
month. They spent one month in Lebanon. Then they spent two months at
home. Adoniram was in charge of the
people who were forced to work. 15 Solomon had 70,000 people who carried
things. He had 80,000 who cut stones in
the hills. 16 He had 3,300 men in charge
of the project. They also directed the
workers. 17 The people did what the king
commanded. They removed large blocks
of the best quality stone from a rock pit.
They used them to provide a foundation
for the temple. 18 The skilled workers of
Solomon and Hiram cut and prepared
the logs and stones. They would later
be used in building the temple. Workers
from Byblos also helped.

Solomon Builds the Temple

6 Solomon began to build the temple
of the LORD. It was 480 years after
the Israelites came out of Egypt. It was
in the fourth year of Solomon's rule over
Israel. He started in the second month.
That was the month of Ziv.

pointing us to JESUS: Solomon

Solomon was Israel's king after his father, David (remember Israel's favorite king?). Solomon was a good and wise king. Solomon was given the special job of building the temple for God to dwell in. God was going to live among his people, and Solomon was in charge of building the special place where God would meet with his people. Once the temple was finished, God filled it with his glory!

Jesus was born into Solomon's family many generations later, and Jesus was the truer, better, and wiser King of God's people. He didn't just build a place for God to dwell among his people; Jesus *was* the very presence of God living among his people. Through Jesus' death and resurrection, those who follow him are given a promise: One day we will live with God in eternity, where God's glory will never end, and being with him will be our greatest joy!

[2]The temple King Solomon built for
the LORD was 90 feet long. It was 30
feet wide. And it was 45 feet high. [3]The
temple had a porch in front of the main
hall. The porch was as wide as the temple itself. It was 30 feet wide. It came
out 15 feet from the front of the temple.
[4]Solomon made narrow windows high
up in the temple walls. [5]He built side
rooms around the temple. They were
built against the walls of the main hall
and the Most Holy Room. [6]On the first
floor the side rooms were seven and a
half feet wide. On the second floor they
were nine feet wide. And on the third
floor they were ten and a half feet wide.
Solomon made the walls of the temple
thinner as they went up floor by floor.
The result was ledges along the walls.
So the floor beams of the side rooms
rested on the ledges. The beams didn't
go into the temple walls.

[7]All the stones used for building the
temple were shaped where they were
cut. So hammers, chisels and other
iron tools couldn't be heard where the
temple was being built.

[8]The entrance to the first floor was on
the south side of the temple. A stairway
led up to the second floor. From there it
went on up to the third floor. [9]So Solomon built the temple and finished it. He
made its roof out of beams and cedar
boards. [10]He built side rooms all along
the temple. Each room was seven and a
half feet high. They were joined to the
temple by cedar beams.

[11]A message came to Solomon from
the LORD. The LORD said, [12]"You are now
building this temple. Follow my orders.
Keep my rules. Obey all my commands.
Then I will make the promise I gave
your father David come true. I will do
it through you. [13]I will live among my
people Israel. I will not desert them."

[14]So Solomon built the temple and
finished it. [15]He put cedar boards on its
inside walls. He covered them from floor
to ceiling. He covered the temple floor
with juniper boards. [16]He put up a wall
30 feet from the back of the temple. He
made it with cedar boards from floor
to ceiling. That formed a room inside
the temple. It was the Most Holy Room.
[17]The main hall in front of the room
was 60 feet long. [18]The inside of the
temple was covered with cedar wood.
Gourds and open flowers were carved on
the wood. Everything was cedar. There
wasn't any stone showing anywhere.

19 Solomon prepared the Most Holy Room inside the temple. That's where the ark of the covenant of the LORD would be placed. 20 The Most Holy Room was 30 feet long. It was 30 feet wide. And it was 30 feet high. Solomon covered the inside of it with pure gold. He prepared the cedar altar for burning incense. He covered it with gold. 21 Solomon covered the inside of the main hall with pure gold. He placed gold chains across the front of the Most Holy Room. That room was covered with gold. 22 So Solomon covered the inside of the whole temple with gold. He also covered the altar for burning incense with gold. It was right in front of the Most Holy Room.

23 For the Most Holy Room Solomon made a pair of cherubim. He made them out of olive wood. Each cherub was 15 feet high. 24 One wing of the first cherub was seven and a half feet long. The other wing was also seven and a half feet long. So the wings measured 15 feet from tip to tip. 25 The second cherub's wings also measured 15 feet from tip to tip. The two cherubim had the same size and shape. 26 Each cherub was 15 feet high. 27 Solomon placed the cherubim inside the Most Holy Room in the temple. Their wings were spread out. The wing tip of one cherub touched one wall. The wing tip of the other touched the other wall. The tips of their wings touched each other in the middle of the room. 28 Solomon covered the cherubim with gold.

29 On the walls all around the temple he carved cherubim, palm trees and open flowers. He carved them on the walls of the Most Holy Room and the main hall. 30 He also covered the floors of those two rooms with gold.

31 For the entrance to the Most Holy Room he made two doors out of olive wood. Each door was one-fifth of the width of the Most Holy Room. 32 On the two olive wood doors he carved cherubim, palm trees and open flowers. He covered the cherubim and palm trees with hammered gold. 33 In the same way he made olive wood doorposts for the entrance to the main hall. Each doorpost was one-fourth of the width of the hall. 34 He also made two doors out of juniper wood. Each door had two parts. They turned in bases shaped like cups. 35 He carved cherubim, palm trees and open flowers on the doors. He covered the doors with gold. He hammered the gold evenly over the carvings.

36 He used blocks of stone to build a wall around the inside courtyard. The first three layers of the wall were made out of stone. The top layer was made out of beautiful cedar wood.

37 The foundation of the LORD's temple was laid in Solomon's fourth year. It was in the month of Ziv. 38 The temple was finished in his 11th year. It was in the month of Bul. That was the eighth month. Everything was finished just as the plans required. Solomon had spent seven years building the temple.

Solomon Builds His Palace

7 But it took Solomon 13 years to finish constructing his palace and the other buildings related to it. 2 He built the Palace of the Forest of Lebanon. It was 150 feet long. It was 75 feet wide. And it was 45 feet high. It had four rows of cedar columns. They held up beautiful cedar beams. 3 Above the beams was a roof made out of cedar boards. It rested on the columns. There were three rows of beams with 15 in each row. The total number of beams was 45. 4 The windows of the palace were placed high up in the walls. They were in groups of three. And they faced each other. 5 All the doorways had frames shaped like rectangles. They were in front. They were in groups of three. And they faced each other.

6 Solomon made a covered area. It was 75 feet long. And it was 45 feet wide. Its roof was held up by columns. In front of it was a porch. In front of that were pillars and a roof that went out beyond them.

7 Solomon built the throne hall. It was called the Hall of Justice. That's where he would serve as judge. He covered the hall with cedar boards from floor to ceiling. 8 The palace where he would live was set farther back. Its plan was something like the plan for the hall. Solomon had married Pharaoh's daughter. He made a palace for her. It was like the hall.

9 All those buildings were made out of blocks of good quality stone. They were cut to the right size. They were made smooth on their back and front

sides. Those stones were used for the
outside of each building and for the
large courtyard. They were also used
from the foundations up to the roofs.
10 Large blocks of good quality stone
were used for the foundations. Some
were 15 feet long. Others were 12 feet
long. 11 The walls above them were made
out of good quality stones. The stones
were cut to the right size. On top of them
was a layer of cedar beams. 12 The large
courtyard had a wall around it. The first
three layers of the wall were made out of
blocks of stone. The top layer was made
out of beautiful cedar wood. The same
thing was done with the inside courtyard
of the LORD's temple and its porch.

More Facts About the Temple

13 King Solomon sent messengers to
Tyre. He wanted them to bring Huram
back with them. 14 Huram's mother
was a widow. She was from the tribe
of Naphtali. Huram's father was from
Tyre. He was skilled in working with
bronze. Huram also had great skill,
knowledge and understanding in
working with bronze. He came to King
Solomon and did all the work he was
asked to do.

15 Huram made two bronze pillars.
Each of them was 27 feet high. And each
was 18 feet around. 16 Each pillar had
a decorated top made out of bronze.
Each top was seven and a half feet high.
17 Chains that were linked together hung
down from the tops of the pillars. There
were seven chains for each top. 18 Huram
made two rows of pomegranates. They
circled the chains. The pomegranates
decorated the tops of the pillars. Huram
did the same thing for each pillar. 19 The
tops on the pillars of the porch were
shaped like lilies. The lilies were 6 feet
high. 20 On the tops of both pillars were
200 pomegranates. They were in rows
all around the tops. They were above the
part that was shaped like a bowl. And
they were next to the chains. 21 Huram
set the pillars up at the temple porch.
The pillar on the south he named Jakin.
The one on the north he named Boaz.
22 The tops of the pillars were shaped
like lilies. So the work on the pillars
was finished.

23 Huram made a huge metal bowl
for washing. Its shape was round. It
measured 15 feet from rim to rim. It
was seven and a half feet high. And it
was 45 feet around. 24 Below the rim
there was a circle of gourds around the
bowl. In every 18 inches around the bowl
there were ten gourds. The gourds were
arranged in two rows. They were made
as part of the bowl itself.

25 The huge bowl stood on 12 bulls.
Three of them faced north. Three faced
west. Three faced south. And three faced
east. The bowl rested on top of the bulls.
Their rear ends were toward the center.
26 The bowl was three inches thick. Its
rim was like the rim of a cup. The rim
was shaped like the bloom of a lily.
The bowl held 12,000 gallons of water.

27 Huram also made ten stands out of
bronze. They could be moved around.
Each stand was six feet long. It was six
feet wide. And it was four and a half
feet high. 28 Here is how the stands were
made. They had sides that were joined
to posts. 29 On the sides between the
posts were lions, bulls and cherubim.
They were also on all of the posts.
Above and below the lions and bulls
were wreaths made out of hammered
metal. 30 Each stand had four bronze
wheels with bronze axles. Each stand
had a bowl that rested on four supports.
The stand had wreaths on each side.
31 There was a round opening on the
inside of each stand. The opening had
a frame 18 inches deep. The sides were
27 inches high from the top of the opening to the bottom of the base. There
was carving around the opening. The
sides of the stands were square, not
round. 32 The four wheels were under
the sides. The axles of the wheels were
connected to the stand. Each wheel
was 27 inches across. 33 The wheels were
made like chariot wheels. All the axles,
rims, spokes and hubs were made out
of metal.

34 Each stand had four handles on
it. There was one on each corner. They
came out from the stand. 35 At the top
of the stand there was a round band.
It was nine inches deep. The sides and
supports were connected to the top of
the stand. 36 Huram carved cherubim,
lions and palm trees on the sides of
the stands. He also carved them on the
surfaces of the supports. His carving
covered every open space. He had also

carved wreaths all around. 37 That's how
he made the ten stands. All of them were
made in the same molds. And they had
the same size and shape.
38 Then Huram made ten bronze
bowls. Each one held 240 gallons. The
bowls measured six feet across. There
was one bowl for each of the ten stands.
39 He placed five of the stands on the
south side of the temple. He placed
the other five on the north side. He put
the huge bowl on the south side. It was
at the southeast corner of the temple.
40 He also made the pots, shovels and
sprinkling bowls.

So Huram finished all the work he
had started for King Solomon. Here's
what he made for the LORD's temple.

41 He made the two pillars.
He made the two tops for the
pillars. The tops were shaped
like bowls.
He made the two sets of chains
that were linked together. They
decorated the two bowl-shaped
tops of the pillars.
42 He made the 400 pomegranates
for the two sets of chains. There
were two rows of pomegranates
for each chain. They decorated
the bowl-shaped tops of the
pillars.
43 He made the ten stands with their
ten bowls.
44 He made the huge bowl. He made
the 12 bulls that were under it.
45 He made the pots, shovels and
sprinkling bowls.

Huram made all those objects for
King Solomon for the LORD's temple.
He made them out of bronze. Then he
shined them up. 46 The king had made
them in clay molds. It was done on the
plain of the Jordan River between Sukkoth and Zarethan. 47 Solomon didn't
weigh any of those things. There were
too many of them to weigh. No one
even tried to weigh the bronze they
were made out of.
48 Solomon also made everything in
the LORD's temple.

He made the golden altar.
He made the golden table for the
holy bread.
49 He made the pure gold lampstands.
There were five on the right and
five on the left. They were in
front of the Most Holy Room.
He made the gold flowers. He made
the gold lamps and tongs.
50 He made the bowls, wick cutters,
sprinkling bowls, dishes, and
shallow cups for burning
incense. All of them were made
out of pure gold.
He made the gold bases for the
doors of the inside room. That's
the Most Holy Room. He also
made gold bases for the doors
of the main hall of the temple.

51 King Solomon finished all the work
for the LORD's temple. Then he brought
in the things his father David had set
apart for the LORD. They included the
silver and gold and all the other things
for the LORD's temple. Solomon placed
them with the other treasures that were
there.

The Ark Is Brought to the Temple

8 Then King Solomon sent for the elders of Israel. He told them to come
to him in Jerusalem. They included
all the leaders of the tribes. They also
included the chiefs of the families of
Israel. Solomon wanted them to bring
up the ark of the LORD's covenant from
Zion. Zion was the City of David. 2 All
the Israelites came together to where
King Solomon was. It was at the time
of the Feast of Booths. The feast was
held in the month of Ethanim. That's
the seventh month.
3 All the elders of Israel arrived. Then
the priests picked up the ark and carried it. 4 They brought up the ark of the
LORD. They also brought up the tent of
meeting and all the sacred things in
the tent. The priests and Levites carried
everything up. 5 The entire community
of Israel had gathered around King
Solomon. All of them were in front of
the ark. They sacrificed huge numbers
of sheep and cattle. There were so many
animals that they couldn't be recorded.
In fact, they couldn't even be counted.
6 The priests brought the ark of the
LORD's covenant law to its place in the
Most Holy Room of the temple. They
put it under the wings of the cherubim.
7 Their wings were spread out over the
place where the ark was. They covered
the ark. They also covered the poles

used to carry it. 8 The poles were very
long. Their ends could be seen from the
Holy Room in front of the Most Holy
Room. But they couldn't be seen from
outside the Holy Room. They are still
there to this day. 9 There wasn't anything in the ark except the two stone
tablets. Moses had placed them in it at
Mount Horeb. That's where the LORD
had made a covenant with the Israelites. He made it after they came out
of Egypt.

10 The priests left the Holy Room. Then
the cloud filled the temple of the LORD.
11 The priests couldn't do their work because of it. That's because the glory of
the LORD filled his temple.

12 Then Solomon said, "LORD, you
have said you would live in a dark
cloud. 13 As you can see, I've built a
beautiful temple for you. You can live
in it forever."

14 The whole community of Israel
was standing there. The king turned
around and gave them his blessing.
15 Then he said,

"I praise the LORD. He is the God
of Israel. With his own mouth he
made a promise to my father David. With his own powerful hand
he made it come true. He said, 16 'I
brought my people Israel out of
Egypt. Ever since, I haven't chosen
a city in any tribe of Israel where a
temple could be built for my Name.
But I have chosen David to rule over
my people Israel.'

17 "With all his heart my father
David wanted to build a temple. He
wanted to do it so the LORD could
put his Name there. The LORD is
the God of Israel. 18 But the LORD
spoke to my father David. He said,
'With all your heart you wanted
to build a temple for my Name.
It is good that you wanted to do
that. 19 But you will not build the
temple. Instead, your son will build
the temple for my Name. He is your
own flesh and blood.'

20 "The LORD has kept the promise he made. I've become the next
king after my father David. Now
I'm sitting on the throne of Israel.
That's exactly what the LORD promised would happen. I've built the

temple where the LORD will put his
Name. He is the God of Israel. 21 I've
provided a place for the ark there.
The tablets of the LORD's covenant
law are inside it. He made that covenant with our people of long ago.
He made it when he brought them
out of Egypt."

Solomon Prays to Set the Temple Apart to the LORD

22 Then Solomon stood in front of the
LORD's altar. He stood in front of the
whole community of Israel. He spread
out his hands toward heaven. 23 He said,

"LORD, you are the God of Israel.
There is no God like you in heav-
en above or on earth below. You
keep the covenant you made with
us. You show us your love. You do
that when we follow you with all
our hearts. 24 You have kept your
promise to my father David. He
was your servant. With your mouth
you made a promise. With your
powerful hand you have made it
come true. And today we can see it.

25 "LORD, you are the God of Israel. Keep the promises you made to
my father David. Do it for him. He
was your servant. Here is what you
said to him. 'A son from your family
line will sit before me on the throne
of Israel. This will always be true if
your children after you are careful
in everything they do. They must
live in my sight faithfully the way
you have lived.' 26 God of Israel, let
your promise to my father David
come true.

27 "But will you really live on
earth? After all, the heavens can't
hold you. In fact, even the highest
heavens can't hold you. So this
temple I've built certainly can't
hold you! 28 But please pay attention to my prayer. LORD my God,
be ready to help me as I make
my appeal to you. Listen to my

cry for help. Hear the prayer I'm
praying to you today. 29 Let your
eyes look toward this temple night
and day. You said, 'I will put my
Name there.' So please listen to
the prayer I'm praying toward this
place. 30 Hear me when I ask you
to help us. Listen to your people
Israel when they pray toward this
place. Listen to us from heaven. It's
the place where you live. When you
hear us, forgive us.
31 "Suppose someone does something wrong to their neighbor. And
the person who has done something wrong is required to give
their word. They must tell the truth
about what they have done. They
must come and do it in front of
your altar in this temple. 32 When
they do, listen to them from heav-
en. Take action. Judge between the
person and their neighbor. Punish
the guilty one. Do to that person
what they have done to their
neighbor. Deal with the one who
isn't guilty in a way that shows
they are free from blame. That will
prove they aren't guilty.

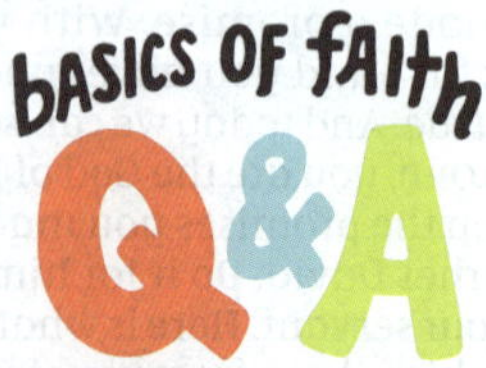

What happens when we disobey God?

When we disobey God's commands, we sin. Sin is anything we say, think, or do that goes against what God says to say, think, or do. Our sin often has consequences, but we can always ask God to forgive us, and he will.

Can you find the following verse?

1 KINGS 8:50

33 "Suppose your people Israel
have lost the battle against their
enemies. And suppose they've
sinned against you. But they turn
back to you and praise your name.
They pray to you in this temple. And
they ask you to help them. 34 Then
listen to them from heaven. Forgive
the sin of your people Israel. Bring
them back to the land you gave to
their people who lived long ago.
35 "Suppose your people have
sinned against you. And because
of that, the sky is closed up and
there isn't any rain. But your people pray toward this place. They
praise you by admitting they've
sinned. And they turn away from
their sin because you have made
them suffer. 36 Then listen to them
from heaven. Forgive the sin of
your people Israel. Teach them the
right way to live. Send rain on the
land you gave them as their share.
37 "Suppose there isn't enough
food in the land. And a plague
strikes the land. The hot winds completely dry up our crops. Or locusts
or grasshoppers come and eat them
up. Or an enemy surrounds one of
our cities and gets ready to attack
it. Or trouble or sickness comes.
38 But suppose one of your people
prays to you. They ask you to help
them. They are aware of how much
their own heart is suffering. And
they spread out their hands toward
this temple to pray. 39 Then listen
to them from heaven. It's the place
where you live. Forgive them. Take
action. Deal with everyone in keeping with everything they do. You
know their hearts. In fact, you are
the only one who knows every human heart. 40 Your people will have
respect for you. They will respect
you as long as they are in the land
you gave our people long ago.
41 "Suppose there are outsiders
who don't belong to your people
Israel. And they have come from
a land far away. They've come because they've heard about your
name. 42 When they get here, they
will find out even more about
your great name. They'll hear
about how you reached out your

mighty hand and powerful arm.
So they'll come and pray toward
this temple. [43]Then listen to them
from heaven. It's the place where
you live. Do what those outsiders
ask you to do. Then all the nations
on earth will know you. They will
have respect for you. They'll respect
you just as your own people Israel
do. They'll know that your Name
is in this house I've built.

[44]"Suppose your people go
to war against their enemies. It
doesn't matter where you send
them. And suppose they pray to
you toward the city you have chosen. They pray toward the temple
I've built for your Name. [45]Then
listen to them from heaven. Listen
to their prayer for your help. Stand
up for them.

[46]"Suppose your people sin
against you. After all, there isn't
anyone who doesn't sin. And suppose you get angry with them. You
hand them over to their enemies.
They take them as prisoners to their
own lands. It doesn't matter whether those lands are near or far away.
[47]But suppose your people change
their ways in the land where they
are held as prisoners. They turn
away from their sins. They beg you
to help them in the land of those
who won the battle over them. They
say, 'We have sinned. We've done
what is wrong. We've done what
is evil.' [48]And they turn back to
you with all their heart and soul.
Suppose it happens in the land
of their enemies who took them
away as prisoners. There they pray
to you toward the land you gave
their people long ago. They pray
toward the city you have chosen.
And they pray toward the temple
I've built for your Name. [49]Then
listen to them from heaven. It's the
place where you live. Listen to their
prayer. Listen to them when they
ask you to help them. Stand up for
them. [50]Your people have sinned
against you. Please forgive them.
Forgive them for all the wrong
things they've done against you.
And make those who won the battle
over them show mercy to them.
[51]After all, they are your people.
They belong to you. You brought
them out of Egypt. You brought
them out of that furnace that melts
iron down and makes it pure.

[52]"Let your eyes be open to me
when I ask you to help us. Let them
be open to your people Israel when
they ask you to help them. Pay attention to them every time they cry out
to you. [53]After all, you chose them
out of all the nations in the world.
You made them your very own
people. You did it just as you had
announced through your servant
Moses. That's when you brought out
of Egypt our people of long ago. You
are our LORD and King."

[54]Solomon finished praying. He finished asking the LORD to help his people. Then he got up from in front of the
LORD's altar. He had been down on his
knees with his hands spread out toward
heaven. [55]He stood in front of the whole
community of Israel. He blessed them
with a loud voice. He said,

[56]"I praise the LORD. He has
given peace and rest to his people Israel. That's exactly what he
promised to do. He gave his people
good promises through his servant
Moses. Every single word of those
promises has come true. [57]May the
LORD our God be with us, just as he
was with our people who lived long
ago. May he never leave us. May he
never desert us. [58]May he turn our
hearts to him. Then we will live the
way he wants us to. We'll obey the
commands, rules and directions
he gave our people of long ago.
[59]I've prayed these words to the
LORD our God. May he keep them
close to him day and night. May
he stand up for me. May he also
stand up for his people Israel. May
he give us what we need every day.
[60]Then all the nations on earth will
know that the LORD is God. They'll
know that there isn't any other
god. [61]And may you commit your
lives completely to the LORD our
God. May you live by his rules. May
you obey his commands. May you
always do as you are doing now."

The Temple Is Set Apart to the LORD

62 Then the king and the whole community of Israel offered sacrifices to the
LORD. 63 Solomon sacrificed friendship
offerings to the LORD. He sacrificed
22,000 oxen. He also sacrificed 120,000
sheep and goats. So the king and the
whole community set the temple of the
LORD apart to him.
64 On that same day the king set the
middle area of the courtyard apart to
the LORD. It was in front of the LORD's
temple. There Solomon sacrificed burnt
offerings and grain offerings. He also
sacrificed the fat of the friendship offerings there. He did it there because
the bronze altar that stood in front of
the LORD was too small. It wasn't big
enough to hold all the burnt offerings,
the grain offerings and the fat of the
friendship offerings.
65 At that time Solomon celebrated
the Feast of Booths. The whole community of Israel was with him. It was
a huge crowd. People came from as far
away as Lebo Hamath and the Wadi of
Egypt. For seven days they celebrated
in front of the LORD our God. The feast
continued for seven more days. That
made a total of 14 days. 66 On the following day Solomon sent the people
away. They asked the LORD to bless the
king. Then they went home. The people
were glad. Their hearts were full of joy.
That's because the LORD had done so
many good things for his servant David
and his people Israel.

The LORD Appears to Solomon

9 Solomon finished building the
LORD's temple and the royal palace.
He had accomplished everything he
had planned to do. 2 The LORD appeared
to him a second time. He had already
appeared to him at Gibeon. 3 The LORD
said to him,

"I have heard you pray to me.
I have heard you ask me to help
you. You have built this temple.
I have set it apart for myself. My
Name will be there forever. My eyes
and my heart will always be there.
4 "But you must walk faithfully
with me, just as your father David
did. Your heart must be honest. It
must be without blame. Do everything I command you to do. Obey
my rules and laws. 5 Then I will set
up your royal throne over Israel forever. I promised your father David
I would do that. I said to him, 'You
will always have a son from your
family line on the throne of Israel.'
6 "But suppose all of you turn
away from me. Or your children
turn away from me. You refuse to
obey the commands and rules I
have given you. And you go off to
serve other gods and worship them.
7 Then I will remove Israel from the
land. It is the land I gave them. I
will turn my back on this temple.
I will do it even though I have set
it apart for my Name to be there.
Then Israel will be hated by all the
nations. They will laugh and joke
about Israel. 8 This temple will become a pile of stones. All those who
pass by it will be shocked. They will
make fun of it. And they will say,
'Why has the LORD done a thing
like this to this land and temple?'
9 People will answer, 'Because they
have deserted the LORD their God.
He brought out of Egypt their people of long ago. But they have been
holding on to other gods. They've
been worshiping them. They've
been serving them. That's why the
LORD has brought all this horrible
trouble on them.' "

Other Things Solomon Did

10 Solomon built the LORD's temple
and the royal palace. It took him 20
years to construct those two buildings.
11 King Solomon gave 20 towns in Galilee
to Hiram, the king of Tyre. That's because Hiram had provided him with all
the cedar and juniper logs he wanted.
He had also provided Solomon with
all the gold he wanted. 12 Hiram went
from Tyre to see the towns Solomon had
given him. But he wasn't pleased with
them. 13 "My friend," he asked, "what
have you given me? What kind of towns
are these?" So he called them the Land
of Kabul. And that's what they are still
called to this day. 14 Hiram had sent
four and a half tons of gold to Solomon.
15 King Solomon forced people to work
hard for him. Here is a record of what
they did. They built the LORD's temple
and Solomon's palace. They filled in the

low places. They rebuilt the wall of Jerusalem. They built up Hazor, Megiddo and Gezer. [16] Pharaoh, the king of Egypt, had attacked Gezer and captured it. He had set it on fire. He had killed the Canaanites who lived there. Then he had given Gezer as a wedding gift to his daughter. She was Solomon's wife. [17] Solomon rebuilt Gezer. He built up Lower Beth Horon [18] and Baalath. He built up Tadmor in the desert. All those towns were in his land. [19] He built up all the cities where he could store things. He also built up the towns for his chariots and horses. He built anything he wanted to build in Jerusalem, Lebanon and all the territory he ruled over.

[20] There were still many people left in the land who weren't Israelites. They included Amorites, Hittites, Perizzites, Hivites and Jebusites. [21] They were children of the people who had lived in the land before the Israelites came. Those people had been set apart to the LORD in a special way to be destroyed. But the Israelites hadn't been able to kill all of them. Solomon forced them to work very hard as his slaves. And they still work for Israel as slaves to this day. [22] But Solomon didn't force any of the Israelites to work as his slaves. Instead, some were his fighting men. Others were his government officials, his officers and his captains. Others were commanders of his chariots and chariot drivers. [23] Still others were the chief officials in charge of Solomon's projects. There were 550 officials in charge of those who did the work.

[24] Pharaoh's daughter moved from the City of David up to the palace Solomon had built for her. After that, he filled in the low places near the palace.

[25] Three times a year Solomon sacrificed burnt offerings and friendship offerings. He sacrificed them on the altar he had built to honor the LORD. Along with the offerings, he burned incense to the LORD. So he carried out his duties for the temple.

[26] King Solomon also built ships at Ezion Geber. It's near Elath in Edom. It's on the shore of the Red Sea. [27] Hiram sent his men to serve on the ships together with Solomon's men. Hiram's sailors knew the sea. [28] All of them sailed to Ophir. They brought back 16 tons of gold. They gave it to King Solomon.

The Queen of Sheba Visits Solomon

10 The queen of Sheba heard about how famous Solomon was. She also heard about how he served and worshiped the LORD. So she came to test Solomon with hard questions. [2] She arrived in Jerusalem with a very large group of attendants. Her camels were carrying spices, huge amounts of gold, and valuable jewels. She came to Solomon and asked him about everything she wanted to know. [3] Solomon answered all her questions. There wasn't anything too hard for the king to explain to her. [4] So the queen of Sheba saw how very wise Solomon was. She saw the palace he had built. [5] She saw the food on his table. She saw his officials sitting there. She saw the robes of the servants who waited on everyone. She saw his wine tasters. And she saw the burnt offerings Solomon sacrificed at the LORD's temple. She could hardly believe everything she had seen.

[6] She said to the king, "Back in my own country I heard a report about you. I heard about how much you had accomplished. I also heard about how wise you are. Everything I heard is true. [7] But I didn't believe those things. So I came to see for myself. And now I believe it! You are twice as wise and wealthy as people say you are. The report I heard doesn't even begin to tell the whole story about you. [8] How happy your people must be! How happy your officials must be! They always get to serve you and hear the wise things you say. [9] May the LORD your God be praised. He takes great delight in you. He placed you on the throne of Israel. The LORD will love Israel for all time to come. That's why he has made you king. He knows that you will do what is fair and right."

[10] She gave the king four and a half tons of gold. She also gave him huge amounts of spices and valuable jewels. No one would ever bring to King Solomon as many spices as the queen of Sheba gave him.

[11] Hiram's ships brought gold from Ophir. From there they also brought huge amounts of almugwood and valuable jewels. [12] The king used the almugwood to make supports for the

LORD's temple and the royal palace. He also used it to make harps and lyres for those who played the music. That much almugwood has never been brought into Judah or seen there since that day.
[13] King Solomon gave the queen of Sheba everything she wanted and asked for. That was in addition to what he had given her out of his royal riches. Then she left. She returned to her own country with her attendants.

Solomon's Greatness

[14] Each year Solomon received 25 tons of gold. [15] That didn't include the money brought in by business and trade. It also didn't include the money from all the kings of Arabia and the governors of the territories.

[16] King Solomon made 200 large shields out of hammered gold. Each one weighed 15 pounds. [17] He also made 300 small shields out of hammered gold. Each one weighed seven and a half pounds. The king put all the shields in the Palace of the Forest of Lebanon.
[18] Then he made a large throne. It was covered with ivory. And that was covered with fine gold. [19] The throne had six steps. Its back had a rounded top. The throne had armrests on both sides of the seat. A statue of a lion stood on each side of the throne. [20] Twelve lions stood on the six steps. There was one at each end of each step. Nothing like that throne had ever been made for any other kingdom. [21] All of King Solomon's cups were made out of gold. All the things used in the Palace of the Forest of Lebanon were made out of pure gold. Nothing was made out of silver. When Solomon was king, silver wasn't considered to be worth very much. [22] He had many ships that carried goods to be traded. His ships went to sea along with Hiram's ships. Once every three years the ships returned. They brought gold, silver, ivory, apes and peacocks.
[23] King Solomon was richer than all the other kings on earth. He was also wiser than they were. [24] People from the whole world wanted to meet Solomon in person. They wanted to see for themselves how wise God had made him. [25] Year after year, everyone who came to him brought a gift. They brought gifts made out of silver and gold. They brought robes, weapons and spices. They also brought horses and mules.
[26] Solomon had 1,400 chariots and 12,000 horses. He kept some of his horses and chariots in the chariot cities. He kept the others with him in Jerusalem. [27] The king made silver as common in Jerusalem as stones. He made cedar wood as common there as sycamore-fig trees in the western hills. [28] Solomon got horses from Egypt and from Kue. The royal traders bought them from Kue at the current price. [29] They weighed out 15 pounds of silver for a chariot from Egypt. And they weighed out almost four pounds of silver for a horse. They also sold horses and chariots to all the kings of the Hittites and the kings of the Arameans.

Solomon's Wives

11 King Solomon loved many women besides Pharaoh's daughter. They were from other lands. They were Moabites, Ammonites, Edomites, Sidonians and Hittites. [2] The LORD had warned Israel about women from other nations. He had said, "You must not marry them. If you do, you can be sure they will turn your hearts toward their gods." But Solomon continued to love them anyway. He wouldn't give them up. [3] He had 700 wives who came from royal families. And he had 300 concubines. His wives led him astray. [4] As Solomon grew older, his wives turned his heart toward other gods. He didn't follow the LORD his God with all his heart. So he wasn't like his father David. [5] Solomon worshiped Ashtoreth. Ashtoreth was the female god of the Sidonians. He also worshiped Molek. Molek was the god of the Ammonites. The LORD hated that god. [6] Solomon did what was evil in the sight of the LORD. He didn't completely obey the LORD. He didn't do what his father David had done.
[7] There is a hill east of Jerusalem. Solomon built a high place for worshiping Chemosh there. He built a high place for worshiping Molek there too. Chemosh was the god of Moab. Molek was the god of Ammon. The LORD hated both of those gods. [8] Solomon also built high places so that all his wives from other nations could worship their gods. Those women burned incense and offered sacrifices to their gods.

9 The LORD became angry with Solomon. That's because his heart had
turned away from the LORD, the God
of Israel. He had appeared to Solomon
twice. 10 He had commanded Solomon not to worship other gods. But
Solomon didn't obey the LORD. 11 So
the LORD said to Solomon, "You have
chosen not to keep my covenant. You
have decided not to obey my rules. I
commanded you to do what I told you.
But you did not do it. So you can be
absolutely sure I will tear the kingdom
away from you. I will give it to one of
your officials. 12 But I will not do that
while you are still living. Because of
your father David I will wait. I will tear
the kingdom out of your son's hand.
13 But I will not tear the whole kingdom
away from him. I will give him one of
the tribes because of my servant David.
I will also do it because of Jerusalem.
That is the city I have chosen."

Solomon's Enemies

14 Then the LORD brought an enemy
against Solomon. The enemy's name
was Hadad. He was from Edom. In
fact, he belonged to the royal family
of Edom. 15 David had fought against
Edom. Joab had been the commander
of the army. He had gone up to bury
the dead bodies of the Israelites who
had been killed in battle. At that time
he had struck down all the men in
Edom. 16 In fact, Joab and all the men
of Israel stayed there for six months.
During that time they destroyed all
the men in Edom. 17 But when Hadad
was only a boy, he ran away to Egypt.
Some officials from Edom went with
him. They had served Hadad's father.
18 They started out from Midian and
went to Paran. They took some people
from Paran with them. Then they went
to Egypt. They went to Pharaoh, the
king of Egypt. He gave Hadad a house
and some land. He also supplied him
with food.

19 Pharaoh was very pleased with
Hadad. Pharaoh's wife was Queen Tahpenes. He gave Hadad her sister to be
his wife. 20 The sister of Tahpenes had
a son by Hadad. The baby was named
Genubath. Tahpenes brought him up in
the royal palace. Genubath lived there
with Pharaoh's own children.

21 Hadad heard that David had joined
the members of his family who had
already died. He also heard that Joab,
the commander of the army, was dead.
Hadad heard those things while he was
in Egypt. He said to Pharaoh, "Let me
go. I want to return to my own country."

22 "Why do you want to go back to
your own country?" Pharaoh asked.
"Don't you have everything you need
right here?"

"Yes," Hadad replied. "But I want you
to let me go anyway!"

23 God brought another enemy
against Solomon. The enemy's name
was Rezon. He was the son of Eliada.
Rezon had run away from his master
Hadadezer, the king of Zobah. 24 David
had destroyed Zobah's army. Then Rezon gathered together some men to
follow him. He became their leader.
They went to Damascus where they
made their homes. They also took control of Damascus. 25 Rezon was Israel's
enemy as long as Solomon was living.
Rezon added to the trouble Hadad had
caused. So Rezon ruled in Aram. He was
Israel's enemy.

Jeroboam Refuses to Follow Solomon

26 Jeroboam refused to follow King
Solomon. He was one of Solomon's
officials. He was from Zeredah in the
territory of Ephraim. His father was
Nebat. His mother was a widow named
Zeruah.

27 Here is the story of how Jeroboam
refused to follow the king. Solomon had
filled in the low places near the palace.
He had also repaired the wall of the city
of his father David. 28 Jeroboam was a
very important young man. Solomon
saw how well he did his work. So he
put him in charge of all the workers in
northern Israel.

29 About that time Jeroboam was going out of Jerusalem. Ahijah the prophet
met him on the road. Ahijah was from
Shiloh. He was wearing a new coat. The
two of them were all alone out in the
country. 30 Ahijah grabbed the new coat
he had on. He tore it up into 12 pieces.
31 Then he said to Jeroboam, "Take ten
pieces for yourself. The LORD is the God
of Israel. He says, 'I am going to tear
the kingdom out of Solomon's hand. I

will give you ten of its tribes. 32 Solomon will have one of its tribes. I will let him keep it because of my servant David and because of Jerusalem. I have chosen that city out of all the cities in the tribes of Israel. 33 I will do these things because the tribes have deserted me. They have worshiped Ashtoreth, the female god of the people of Sidon. They have worshiped Chemosh, the god of the people of Moab. And they have worshiped Molek, the god of the people of Ammon. They have not lived the way I wanted them to. They have not done what is right in my eyes. They have not obeyed my rules and laws as Solomon's father David did.

34 " 'But I will not take the whole kingdom out of Solomon's hand. I have made him ruler all the days of his life. I have done it because of my servant David. I chose him, and he obeyed my commands and rules. 35 I will take the kingdom out of his son's hands. And I will give you ten of the tribes. 36 I will give one of the tribes to David's son. Then my servant David will always have a son on his throne in Jerusalem. The lamp of David's kingdom will always burn brightly in my sight. Jerusalem is the city I chose for my Name. 37 But I will make you king over Israel. You will rule over everything your heart desires. So you will be the king of Israel. 38 Do everything I command you to do. Live the way I want you to. Do what is right in my eyes. Obey my rules and commands. That is what my servant David did. If you do those things, I will be with you. I will build you a kingdom. It will last as long as the one I built for David. I will give Israel to you. 39 I will punish David's family because of what Solomon has done. But I will not punish them forever.' "

40 Solomon tried to kill Jeroboam. But Jeroboam ran away to Egypt. He went to Shishak, the king of Egypt. He stayed there until Solomon died.

Solomon Dies

41 The other events of Solomon's rule are written down. Everything he did and the wisdom he showed are written down. They are written in the official records of Solomon. 42 Solomon ruled in Jerusalem over the whole nation of Israel for 40 years. 43 Then he joined the members of his family who had already died. He was buried in the city of his father David. Solomon's son Rehoboam became the next king after him.

Israel Refuses to Follow Rehoboam

12 Rehoboam went to the city of Shechem. All the Israelites had gone there to make him king. 2 Jeroboam heard about it. He was the son of Nebat. Jeroboam was still in Egypt at that time. He had gone there for safety. He wanted to get away from King Solomon. But now he returned from Egypt. 3 So the people sent for Jeroboam. He and the whole community of Israel went to Rehoboam. They said to him, 4 "Your father put a heavy load on our shoulders. But now make our hard work easier. Make the heavy load on us lighter. Then we'll serve you."

5 Rehoboam answered, "Go away for three days. Then come back to me." So the people went away.

6 King Rehoboam asked the elders for advice. They had served his father Solomon while he was still living. Rehoboam asked them, "What advice can you give me? How should I answer these people?"

7 They replied, "Serve them today. Give them what they are asking for. Then they'll always serve you."

8 But Rehoboam didn't accept the advice the elders gave him. Instead, he asked for advice from the young men. They had grown up with him and were now serving him. 9 He asked them, "What's your advice? How should I answer these people? They say to me, 'Make the load your father put on our shoulders lighter.' "

10 The young men who had grown up with him gave their answer. They replied, "These people have said to you, 'Your father put a heavy load on our shoulders. Make it lighter.' Now tell them, 'My little finger is stronger than my father's legs. 11 My father put a heavy load on your shoulders. But I'll make it even heavier. My father beat you with whips. But I'll beat you with bigger whips.' "

12 Three days later Jeroboam and all the people returned to Rehoboam. That's because the king had said, "Come back to me in three days." 13 The king

answered the people in a mean way. He didn't accept the advice the elders had given him. [14]Instead, he followed the advice of the young men. He said, "My father put a heavy load on your shoulders. But I'll make it even heavier. My father beat you with whips. But I'll beat you with bigger whips." [15]So the king didn't listen to the people. That's because the LORD had planned it that way. What he had said through Ahijah came true. Ahijah had spoken the LORD's message to Jeroboam, the son of Nebat. Ahijah was from Shiloh.

[16]All the Israelites saw that the king refused to listen to them. So they answered the king. They said,

"We don't have any share in
David's royal family.
We don't have any share in
Jesse's son.
People of Israel, let's go back to our
homes.
David's royal family, take care of
your own kingdom!"

So the Israelites went home. [17]But Rehoboam still ruled over the Israelites living in the towns of Judah.

[18]Adoniram was in charge of those who were forced to work hard for King Rehoboam. The king sent him out among all the Israelites. But they killed Adoniram by throwing stones at him. King Rehoboam was able to get away in his chariot. He escaped to Jerusalem. [19]Israel has refused to follow the royal family of David to this day.

[20]All the Israelites heard that Jeroboam had returned. They sent for him. They wanted him to meet with the whole community. Then they made him king over the entire nation of Israel. Only the tribe of Judah remained true to David's royal family.

[21]Rehoboam arrived in Jerusalem. He brought together 180,000 capable young men from Judah and the tribe of Benjamin. He had decided to go to war against Israel. Solomon's son Rehoboam wanted his fighting men to get the kingdom of Israel back for him.

[22]But a message from God came to Shemaiah. He was a man of God. God said to him, [23]"Speak to Solomon's son Rehoboam, the king of Judah. Speak to all Judah and the tribe of Benjamin. Also speak to the rest of the people. Tell all of them, [24]'The LORD says, "Do not go up to fight against the Israelites. They are your relatives. I want every one of you to go back home. Things have happened exactly the way I planned them." ' " So the fighting men obeyed the LORD's message. They went home again, just as he had ordered.

Golden Calves at Bethel and Dan

[25]Jeroboam built up the walls of Shechem. It was in the hill country of Ephraim. Jeroboam made Shechem his home. From there he went out and built up Peniel.

[26]Jeroboam thought, "My kingdom still isn't secure. It could very easily go back to the royal family of David. [27]Suppose the Israelites go up to Jerusalem to offer sacrifices at the LORD's temple. If they do, they will again decide to follow Rehoboam as their master. Then they'll kill me. They'll return to King Rehoboam. He is king of Judah."

[28]So King Jeroboam asked for advice. Then he made two golden statues that looked like calves. He said to the people, "It's too hard for you to go up to Jerusalem. Israel, here are your gods who brought you up out of Egypt." [29]He set up one statue in Bethel. He set up the other one in Dan. [30]What Jeroboam did was sinful. And it caused Israel to sin. The people came to worship the statue at Bethel. They went all the way to Dan to worship the statue that was there.

[31]Jeroboam built temples for worshiping gods on high places. He appointed all kinds of people as priests. They didn't even have to be Levites. [32]He established a feast. It was on the 15th day of the eighth month. He wanted to make it like the Feast of Booths that was held in Judah. Jeroboam built an altar at Bethel. He offered sacrifices on it. He sacrificed to the calves he had made. He also put priests in Bethel. He did it at the high places he had made. [33]He offered sacrifices on the altar he had built at Bethel. It was on the 15th day of the eighth month. That's the month he had chosen for it. So he established the feast for the Israelites. And he went up to the altar to sacrifice offerings.

A Man of God From Judah

13 A man of God went from Judah
to Bethel. He had received a
message from the LORD. He arrived in
Bethel just as Jeroboam was standing
by the altar to offer a sacrifice. 2 The
man cried out. He shouted a message
from the LORD against the altar. He
said, "Altar! Altar! The LORD says, 'A
son named Josiah will be born into the
royal family of David. Altar, listen to
me! Josiah will sacrifice the priests of
the high places on you. They will be the
children of the priests who are offering
sacrifices here. So human bones will be
burned on you.' " 3 That same day the
man of God spoke about a miraculous
sign. He said, "Here is the sign the LORD
has announced. This altar will be broken to pieces. The ashes on it will be
spilled out."

4 The man of God announced that
message against the altar at Bethel.
When King Jeroboam heard it, he
reached out his hand from the altar.
He said, "Grab him!" But as he reached
out his hand toward the man, it dried
up. He couldn't even pull it back. 5 Also,
the altar broke into pieces. Its ashes
spilled out. That happened in keeping
with the miraculous sign the man of
God had announced. He had received
a message from the LORD.

6 King Jeroboam spoke to the man
of God. He said, "Pray to the LORD your
God for me. Pray that my hand will be
as good as new again." So the man of
God prayed to the LORD for the king.
And the king's hand became as good
as new. It was just as healthy as it had
been before.

7 The king said to the man of God,
"Come home with me for a meal. I'll
give you a gift."

8 But the man of God replied to the
king. He said, "What if you were to give
me half of what you own? Even then I
wouldn't go with you. I wouldn't eat
bread or drink water here. 9 The LORD
gave me a command. He said, 'Do not
eat bread or drink water there. Do not
return the same way you came.' " 10 So
he took another road. He didn't go back
on the same road he had taken when
he came to Bethel.

11 An old prophet was living in Bethel.
His sons came and spoke to him. They
told him everything the man of God
had done there that day. They also
told their father what the man had
said to the king. 12 Their father asked
them, "Which way did he go?" His sons
showed him the road the man of God
from Judah had taken. 13 So he said to
his sons, "Put a saddle on the donkey
for me." When they had done it, he got
on the donkey. 14 He traveled on the
same road the man of God had taken.
He found the man sitting under an oak
tree. He asked him, "Are you the man of
God who came from Judah?"

"I am," he replied.

15 So the prophet said to him, "Come
home with me. I'll give you something
to eat."

16 The man of God said, "I can't go
back to Bethel with you. I can't eat
bread or drink water with you there.
17 I've received a message from the LORD.
He told me, 'Do not eat bread or drink
water there. Do not return the same
way you came.' "

18 The old prophet answered, "I'm also
a prophet, just like you. An angel gave
me a message from the LORD. The message said, 'Bring the man of God back
with you to your house. Then he can eat
bread and drink water with you.' " But
the old prophet was telling him a lie.
19 The man of God returned with him.
He ate and drank in his house.

20 They were sitting at the table. The
LORD gave a message to the old prophet
who had brought the man of God back.
21 He cried out to the man who had come
from Judah. He told him, "The LORD says,
'You have not done what I told you to
do. You have not obeyed the command I
gave you. I am the LORD your God. 22 You
came back here and ate bread and drank
water. You did it in the place where I
told you not to. So your body will not be
buried in your family tomb.' "

23 The man of God finished eating and
drinking. Then the old prophet who had
brought him back put a saddle on the
man's donkey for him. 24 And the man
went on his way. A lion attacked him on
the road and killed him. His body was
left lying on the road. The donkey and
the lion were standing beside it. 25 Some
people passed by. They saw the body
lying on the road. They saw the lion
standing beside the body. Then they

went and reported it in the city where the old prophet lived.

26 The prophet who had brought the man back from his journey heard about what had happened. He said, "It's the man of God. He didn't do what the LORD told him to do. So the LORD has given him over to the lion. The lion has attacked him and killed him. Everything has happened just as the LORD's message had warned him it would."

27 The old prophet said to his sons, "Put a saddle on the donkey for me." So
they did. 28 Then he went out. He found the body of the man of God lying on the road. The donkey and the lion were standing beside it. The lion hadn't eaten the body. It hadn't attacked the donkey
either. 29 So the prophet picked up the man's body. He put it on the donkey. He brought it back to his own city. He wanted to mourn for him and bury him.
30 Then he placed the body in his own tomb. People mourned for him. They said, "Oh, no, my friend! My dear friend!"

31 After the old prophet had buried the man of God, he spoke to his sons. He said, "When I die, bury me in the grave where the man of God is buried.
Put my bones next to his bones. 32 I
want you to do that because he announced a message from the LORD. He spoke against the altar in Bethel. He also spoke against all the temples that are on the high places. They are in the towns of Samaria. What the man of God said will certainly come true."

33 Even after all of that happened, Jeroboam still didn't change his evil ways. Once more he appointed priests for the high places. He made priests out of all kinds of people. In fact, he let anyone become a priest who wanted to. He set them apart to serve at the high
places. 34 All of that was the great sin the royal family of Jeroboam committed. It led to their fall from power. Because of it, they were destroyed from the face of the earth.

Ahijah's Prophecy Against Jeroboam

14 At that time Abijah became sick.
He was the son of Jeroboam.
2 Jeroboam said to his wife, "Go. Put on some different clothes. Then no one will recognize you as my wife. Go to Shiloh. That's where Ahijah the prophet is. He told me I would be king over the
Israelites. 3 Take ten loaves of bread with you. Take some cakes and a jar of honey. Go to him. He'll tell you what will
happen to our son." 4 So Jeroboam's wife did what he said. She went to Ahijah's house in Shiloh.

Ahijah couldn't see. He was blind
because he was so old. 5 But the LORD had told Ahijah, "Jeroboam's wife is coming. Her son is sick. She'll ask you about him. Give her the answer I give you. When she arrives, she'll pretend to be someone else."

6 Ahijah heard the sound of her footsteps at the door. He said, "Come in. I know that you are Jeroboam's wife. Why are you pretending to be someone else? I have some bad news for you.
7 Go. Tell Jeroboam that the LORD has a message for him. The LORD is the God of Israel. He says, 'I chose you from among the people. I appointed you king over
my people Israel. 8 I tore the kingdom away from the royal house of David. I gave it to you. But you have not been like my servant David. He obeyed my commands. He followed me with all his heart. He did only what was right in my
eyes. 9 You have done more evil things than all those who lived before you. You have made other gods for yourself. You have made statues of gods out of metal. You have made me very angry. You have turned your back on me.

10 " 'Because of that, I am going to bring horrible trouble on your royal house. I will cut off from you every male in Israel. It does not matter whether they are slaves or free. I will burn up your royal house, just as someone burns up trash. I will burn it until it
is all gone. 11 Some of the people who belong to you will die in the city. Dogs will eat them up. Others will die in the country. The birds will eat them. The LORD has spoken!'

12 "Now go back home. When you
enter your city, your son will die. 13 All the Israelites will mourn for him. Then he will be buried. He is the only one who belongs to Jeroboam who will be buried. That is because he is the only one in Jeroboam's royal house in whom I have found anything good. I am the LORD, the God of Israel.

14 "I will choose for myself a king over Israel. He will destroy the family of Jeroboam. This day your son will die. Even now this is beginning to happen. 15 I, the LORD, will strike down Israel. Israel will be like tall grass swaying in the water. I will pull Israel up from this good land by the roots. I gave it to their people who lived long ago. I will scatter Israel to the east side of the Euphrates River. That is because they made the LORD very angry. They made poles used to worship the female god named Asherah. 16 I will give Israel up because of the sins Jeroboam has committed. He has also caused Israel to commit those same sins."

17 Then Jeroboam's wife got up and left. She went to the city of Tirzah. As soon as she stepped through the doorway of the house, her son died. 18 He was buried and all the Israelites mourned for him. That's what the LORD had said would happen. He had said it through his servant, Ahijah the prophet.

19 The other events of Jeroboam's rule are written down. His wars and how he ruled are written down. They are written in the official records of the kings of Israel. 20 Jeroboam ruled for 22 years. Then he joined the members of his family who had already died. Jeroboam's son Nadab became the next king after him.

Rehoboam King of Judah

21 Rehoboam was king in Judah. He was the son of Solomon. Rehoboam was 41 years old when he became king. He ruled for 17 years in Jerusalem. It was the city the LORD had chosen out of all the cities in the tribes of Israel. He wanted to put his Name there. Rehoboam's mother was Naamah from Ammon.

22 The people of Judah did what was evil in the sight of the LORD. The sins they had committed made the LORD angry. The LORD was angry because they refused to worship only him. They did more to make him angry than their people who lived before them had done. 23 Judah also set up for themselves high places for worship. They set up sacred stones. They set up poles used to worship the female god named Asherah. They did it on every high hill and under every green tree. 24 There were even male prostitutes at the temples in the land. The people took part in all the practices of other nations. The LORD hated those practices. He had driven those nations out to make room for the Israelites.

25 Shishak attacked Jerusalem. It was in the fifth year that Rehoboam was king. Shishak was king of Egypt. 26 He carried away the treasures of the LORD's temple. He also carried away the treasures of the royal palace. He took everything. That included all the gold shields Solomon had made. 27 So King Rehoboam made bronze shields to take their place. He gave them to the commanders of the guards on duty at the entrance to the royal palace. 28 Every time the king went to the LORD's temple, the guards carried the shields. Later, they took them back to the room where they were kept.

29 The other events of Rehoboam's rule are written down. Everything he did is written in the official records of the kings of Judah. 30 Rehoboam and Jeroboam were always at war with each other. 31 Rehoboam joined the members of his family who had already died. He was buried in his family tomb in the City of David. His mother was Naamah from Ammon. Rehoboam's son Abijah became the next king after him.

Abijah King of Judah

15 Abijah became king of Judah. It was in the 18th year of Jeroboam's rule over Israel. Jeroboam was the son of Nebat. 2 Abijah ruled in Jerusalem for three years. His mother's name was Maakah. She was Abishalom's daughter.

3 Abijah committed all the sins his father had committed before him. Abijah didn't obey the LORD his God with all his heart. He didn't do what King David had done. 4 But the LORD still kept the lamp of Abijah's kingdom burning brightly in Jerusalem. He did it by giving him a son to be the next king after him. He also did it by making Jerusalem strong. The LORD did those things because of David. 5 David had done what was right in the sight of the LORD. He had kept all the LORD's commands. He had obeyed them all the days of his life. But he hadn't

obeyed the LORD in the case of Uriah,
the Hittite.
6 There was war between Abijah and
Jeroboam all through Abijah's life. 7 The
other events of Abijah's rule are written down. Everything he did is written
down. All these things are written in the
official records of the kings of Judah.
There was war between Abijah and Jeroboam. 8 Abijah joined the members of
his family who had already died. He
was buried in the City of David. Abijah's
son Asa became the next king after him.

Asa King of Judah

9 Asa became king of Judah. It was in
the 20th year that Jeroboam was king
of Israel. 10 Asa ruled in Jerusalem for
41 years. His grandmother's name was
Maakah. She was Abishalom's daughter.
11 Asa did what was right in the sight
of the LORD. That's what King David
had done. 12 Asa threw out of the land
the male prostitutes who were at the
temples. He got rid of all the statues of
gods made by his people of long ago.
13 He even removed his grandmother
Maakah from her position as queen
mother. That's because she had made
a pole used to worship the female god
named Asherah. The LORD hated it. So
Asa cut it down. He burned it in the
Kidron Valley. 14 Asa didn't remove the
high places from Israel. But he committed his whole life completely to
the LORD. 15 He and his father had set
apart silver, gold and other things to
the LORD. Asa brought them into the
LORD's temple.
16 There was war between Asa and
Baasha, the king of Israel. It lasted the
whole time they were kings. 17 Baasha
was king of Israel. He marched out
against Judah. Baasha built up the
walls of Ramah. He did it to keep people
from leaving or entering the territory
of Asa, the king of Judah.
18 Asa took all the silver and gold
left among the treasures of the LORD's
temple and his own palace. He put his
officials in charge of it. He sent the officials to Ben-Hadad. Ben-Hadad was
king of Aram. He was ruling in Damascus. He was the son of Tabrimmon and
the grandson of Hezion. 19 "Let's make
a peace treaty between us," Asa said.
"My father and your father had made
a peace treaty between them. Now I'm
sending you a gift of silver and gold.
So break your treaty with Baasha, the
king of Israel. Then he'll go back home."
20 Ben-Hadad agreed with King Asa.
He sent his army commanders against
the towns of Israel. He captured Ijon,
Dan, Abel Beth Maakah and the whole
area of Kinnereth in addition to Naphtali. 21 Baasha heard about it. So he
stopped building up Ramah. He went
back home to Tirzah. 22 Then King Asa
gave an order to all the men of Judah.
Everyone was required to help. They
carried away from Ramah the stones
and wood Baasha had been using there.
King Asa used them to build up Geba in
the territory of Benjamin. He also used
them to build up Mizpah.
23 All the other events of Asa's rule
are written down, including the cities
he built. Everything he did is written
in the official records of the kings of
Judah. But when Asa became old, his
feet began to give him trouble. 24 He
joined the members of his family who
had already died. He was buried in his
family tomb. It was in the city of King
David. Asa's son Jehoshaphat became
the next king after him.

Nadab King of Israel

25 Nadab became king of Israel. It was
in the second year that Asa was king
of Judah. Nadab ruled over Israel for
two years. He was the son of Jeroboam.
26 Nadab did what was evil in the sight
of the LORD. He lived the way his father
had lived. He committed the same sin
his father Jeroboam had caused Israel
to commit.
27 Baasha was from the tribe of Issachar. He was the son of Ahijah. Baasha made plans against Nadab and
struck him down at Gibbethon. It was
a Philistine town. Baasha struck him
down while Nadab and all the men of
Israel were getting ready to attack Gibbethon. 28 He killed Nadab in the third
year that Asa was king of Judah. Baasha became the next king after Nadab.
29 As soon as Baasha became king,
he killed Jeroboam's whole family. He
didn't leave any of them alive. He destroyed every one of them. He did what
the LORD had said would happen. The
LORD had spoken that message through

his servant Ahijah from Shiloh. 30 The LORD judged Jeroboam's family because of the sins Jeroboam had committed. He had also caused Israel to commit those same sins. He had made the LORD very angry. The LORD is the God of Israel.

31 The other events of Nadab's rule are written down. Everything he did is written in the official records of the kings of Israel. 32 There was war between Asa and Baasha, the king of Israel. It lasted the whole time they were kings.

Baasha King of Israel

33 Baasha became king of Israel in Tirzah. It was in the third year that Asa was king of Judah. Baasha ruled for 24 years. He was the son of Ahijah. 34 Baasha did what was evil in the sight of the LORD. He lived the way Jeroboam had lived. He committed the same sin Jeroboam had caused Israel to commit.

16 The LORD's message about Baasha came to Jehu, the son of Hanani. Here is what the LORD said about Baasha. 2 "I lifted you up from the dust. I appointed you king over my people Israel. But you lived the way Jeroboam had lived. You also caused my people Israel to sin. And their sins made me very angry. 3 So I am about to destroy you, Baasha, and your royal house. I will make your house like the royal house of Jeroboam, the son of Nebat. 4 Some of the people who belong to you will die in the city. Dogs will eat them up. Others will die in the country. The birds will eat them."

5 The other events of Baasha's rule are written down. What he did and what he accomplished are written in the official records of the kings of Israel. 6 Baasha joined the members of his family who had already died. He was buried in Tirzah. Baasha's son Elah became the next king after him.

7 The LORD's message came through the prophet Jehu, the son of Hanani. It was against Baasha and his royal house. Baasha had done all kinds of evil things in the sight of the LORD. Baasha had also destroyed the royal house of Jeroboam. What Baasha did had made the LORD very angry. So Baasha had become as sinful as the royal house of Jeroboam had been.

Elah King of Israel

8 Elah became king of Israel. It was in the 26th year that Asa was king of Judah. Elah ruled in Tirzah for two years. He was the son of Baasha.

9 Zimri was one of Elah's officials. He commanded half of Elah's chariot drivers. He made plans against Elah. Elah was in Tirzah at the time. He was getting drunk in the home of Arza. Arza was in charge of the palace at Tirzah. 10 Zimri came in. He struck Elah down and killed him. It was in the 27th year of Asa, the king of Judah. Zimri became the next king after Elah.

11 As soon as Zimri was seated on the throne as king, he killed off Baasha's whole family. He didn't even spare one male. It didn't matter whether it was a relative or a friend. 12 So Zimri destroyed the whole family of Baasha. That's what the LORD had said would happen. He had spoken against Baasha through Jehu the prophet. 13 Baasha and his son Elah had committed all kinds of sin. They had also caused Israel to commit the same sins. So Israel made the LORD very angry. They did it by worshiping worthless statues of gods. The LORD is the God of Israel.

14 The other events of Elah's rule are written down. Everything he did is written in the official records of the kings of Israel.

Zimri King of Israel

15 Zimri ruled in Tirzah for seven days. It was in the 27th year that Asa was king of Judah. The army of Israel had set up camp near Gibbethon. It was a Philistine town. 16 The Israelites in the camp heard that Zimri had made plans against King Elah. They also heard that Zimri had murdered him. So they announced that Omri was king over Israel. He was the commander of the army. They made him king that day in the camp. 17 Then Omri and all his men pulled back from Gibbethon. They marched to Tirzah and surrounded it. They attacked it and captured it. 18 Zimri saw that they had taken over the city. So he went into the safest place in the royal palace. He set the palace on fire all around him. He died there 19 because of the sins he had committed. He had done what was evil in the sight of the LORD. He had lived the way Jeroboam had lived. He had

committed the same sin Jeroboam had
caused Israel to commit.
20 The other events of Zimri's rule
are written down. The way he turned
against King Elah and killed him is written down. All these things are written in
the official records of the kings of Israel.

Omri King of Israel

21 The Israelites divided up into two
groups. Half of them wanted Tibni to
be king. He was the son of Ginath. The
other half wanted Omri. 22 But Omri's
followers were stronger than those of
Tibni, the son of Ginath. So Tibni died.
And Omri began to rule.
23 Omri became king of Israel. It
was in the 31st year that Asa was king
of Judah. Omri ruled for 12 years. He
ruled in Tirzah for six of those years.
24 He bought the hill of Samaria from
Shemer. He weighed out 150 pounds of
silver for it. Then he built a city on the
hill. He called it Samaria. He named it
after Shemer. Shemer had owned the
hill before him.
25 But Omri did what was evil in the
sight of the LORD. He sinned more than
all the kings who had ruled before him.
26 He lived the way Jeroboam, the son
of Nebat, had lived. He committed the
same sin Jeroboam had caused Israel
to commit. Israel made the LORD very
angry. They did it by worshiping worthless statues of gods. The LORD is the
God of Israel.
27 The other events of Omri's rule are
written down. Everything he did and
the things he accomplished are written
in the official records of the kings of
Israel. 28 Omri joined the members of
his family who had already died. He
was buried in Samaria. Omri's son Ahab
became the next king after him.

Ahab King of Israel

29 Ahab became king of Israel. It was
in the 38th year that Asa was king of Judah. Ahab ruled over Israel in Samaria
for 22 years. He was the son of Omri.
30 Ahab, the son of Omri, did what was
evil in the sight of the LORD. He did more
evil things than any of the kings who
had ruled before him. 31 He thought it
was only a small thing to commit the
sins Jeroboam, the son of Nebat, had
committed. Ahab also married Jezebel.
She was Ethbaal's daughter. Ethbaal
was king of the people of Sidon. Ahab
began to serve the god named Baal
and worship him. 32 He set up an altar
to honor Baal. He set it up in the temple
of Baal that he built in Samaria. 33 Ahab
also made a pole used to worship the
female god named Asherah. He made
the LORD very angry. Ahab did more to
make him angry than all the kings of
Israel had done before him. The LORD
is the God of Israel.
34 In Ahab's time, Hiel from Bethel
rebuilt Jericho. When he laid its foundations, it cost him the life of his oldest son
Abiram. When he set up its gates, it cost
him the life of his youngest son Segub.
That's what the LORD had said would
happen. He had spoken it through Joshua, the son of Nun.

Elijah Announces No Dew or Rain

17 Elijah was from Tishbe in the land
of Gilead. He said to Ahab, "I serve
the LORD. He is the God of Israel. You can
be sure that he lives. And you can be just
as sure that there won't be any dew or
rain on the whole land. There won't be
any during the next few years. It won't
come until I say so."

Elijah Is Fed by Ravens

2 Then a message came to Elijah from
the LORD. He said, 3 "Leave this place. Go
east and hide in the Kerith Valley. It is
east of the Jordan River. 4 You will drink
water from the brook. I have directed
some ravens to supply you with food
there."
5 So Elijah did what the LORD had
told him to do. He went to the Kerith
Valley. It was east of the Jordan River.
He stayed there. 6 The ravens brought
him bread and meat in the morning.
They also brought him bread and meat
in the evening. He drank water from
the brook.

Elijah and the Widow at Zarephath

7 Some time later the brook dried up.
It hadn't rained in the land for quite a
while. 8 A message came to Elijah from
the LORD. He said, 9 "Go right away to
Zarephath in the region of Sidon. Stay
there. I have directed a widow there to
supply you with food." 10 So Elijah went
to Zarephath. He came to the town gate.
A widow was there gathering sticks. He
called out to her. He asked, "Would you

bring me a little water in a jar? I need a
drink." 11 She went to get the water. Then
he called out to her, "Please bring me a
piece of bread too."
12 "I don't have any bread," she replied. "And that's just as sure as the
LORD your God is alive. All I have is a small amount of flour in a jar and a little olive oil in a jug. I'm gathering a few sticks to take home. I'll make one last meal for myself and my son. We'll eat it. After that, we'll die."
13 Elijah said to her, "Don't be afraid. Go home. Do what you have said. But first make a small loaf of bread for me. Make it out of what you have. Bring it to me. Then make some for yourself
and your son. 14 The LORD is the God of
Israel. He says, 'The jar of flour will not be used up. The jug will always have oil in it. You will have flour and oil until the day the LORD sends rain on the land.' "
15 She went away and did what Elijah had told her to do. So Elijah had food every day. There was also food for the
woman and her family. 16 The jar of
flour wasn't used up. The jug always had oil in it. That's what the LORD had said would happen. He had spoken that message through Elijah.

17 Some time later the son of the woman who owned the house became sick. He got worse and worse. Finally he
stopped breathing. 18 The woman said
to Elijah, "You are a man of God. What do you have against me? Did you come to bring my sin out into the open? Did you come to kill my son?"
19 "Give me your son," Elijah replied. He took him from her arms. He carried him to the upstairs room where he was staying. He put him down on his bed.
20 Then Elijah cried out to the LORD. He said, "LORD my God, I'm staying with this widow. Have you brought pain and sorrow even to her? Have you caused
her son to die?" 21 Then he lay down on
the boy three times. He cried out to the LORD. He said, "LORD my God, give this boy's life back to him!"
22 The LORD answered Elijah's prayer. He gave the boy's life back to him. So
the boy lived. 23 Elijah picked up the boy.
He carried him down from the upstairs room into the house. He gave him to his mother. He said, "Look! Your son is alive!"
24 Then the woman said to Elijah, "Now I know that you are a man of God. I know that the message you have brought from the LORD is true."

Elijah and Obadiah

18 It was now three years since it
had rained. A message came
to Elijah from the LORD. He said, "Go.
Speak to Ahab. Then I will send rain
on the land." 2 So Elijah went to speak
to Ahab.

There wasn't enough food in Samaria.
The people there were very hungry.
3 Ahab had sent for Obadiah. He was in
charge of Ahab's palace. Obadiah had
great respect for the LORD. 4 Ahab's wife
Jezebel had been killing off the LORD's
prophets. So Obadiah had hidden 100
prophets in two caves. He had put 50
in each cave. He had supplied them
with food and water. 5 Ahab had said
to Obadiah, "Go through the land. Go
to all the valleys and springs of water.
Maybe we can find some grass there. It
will keep the horses and mules alive.
Then we won't have to kill any of our
animals." 6 So they decided where each
of them would look. Ahab went in one
direction. Obadiah went in another.

7 As Obadiah was walking along, Eli-
jah met him. Obadiah recognized him.
He bowed down to the ground. He said,
"My master Elijah! Is it really you?"

8 "Yes," he replied. "Go and tell your
master Ahab, 'Elijah is here.' "

9 "What have I done wrong?" asked
Obadiah. "Why are you handing me
over to Ahab to be put to death? 10 My
master has sent people to look for you
everywhere. There isn't a nation or
kingdom where he hasn't sent someone to look for you. Suppose a nation
or kingdom would claim you weren't
there. Then Ahab would make them
give their word that they couldn't find
you. And that's just as sure as the LORD
your God is alive. 11 But now you are
telling me to go to my master. You want
me to say, 'Elijah is here.' 12 But the Spirit of the LORD might carry you away
when I leave you. Then I won't know
where you are. If I go and tell Ahab
and he doesn't find you, he'll kill me.
But I've worshiped the LORD ever since
I was young. 13 My master, haven't you
heard what I did? Jezebel was killing
the LORD's prophets. But I hid 100 of
them in two caves. I put 50 in each cave.
I supplied them with food and water.
14 And now you are telling me to go to
my master Ahab. You want me to say to
him, 'Elijah is here.' Ahab will kill me!"

pointing us to JESUS: Elijah

Elijah was a prophet of God. His name means "My God is Yahweh." Elijah's job as a prophet was to teach God's people about the one true God and remind them to walk in God's ways. To carry out this job, God called Elijah to remind the people of God's power.

Through Elijah, God did many miracles. God worked through him to provide food when there was none and even to raise the dead back to life. Amazingly, Elijah went to heaven even though he never actually died!

Elijah's story points to the coming Savior, Jesus. He would feed many people when there was no food, he would raise the dead, and he himself would rise back to life. In what is known as the *ascension*, Jesus was taken up into heaven to live with God the Father forever. Jesus is preparing a wonderful place for his people to come and live with him too.

[15]Elijah said, "I serve the LORD who rules over all. You can be sure that he lives. And you can be sure that I will speak to Ahab today."

Elijah on Mount Carmel

[16]Obadiah went back to Ahab. He told Ahab that Elijah wanted to see him. So
Ahab went to where Elijah was. [17]When
he saw Elijah, he said to him, "Is that you? You are always stirring up trouble in Israel."

[18]"I haven't made trouble for Israel," Elijah replied. "But you and your father's family have. You have turned away from the LORD's commands. You have followed gods that are named
Baal. [19]Now send for people from all
over Israel. Tell them to meet me on Mount Carmel. And bring the 450 prophets of the god named Baal. Also bring the 400 prophets of the female god named Asherah. All of them eat at Jezebel's table."

[20]So Ahab sent that message all through Israel. He gathered the prophets together on Mount Carmel. [21]Elijah
went there and stood in front of the people. He said, "How long will it take you to make up your minds? If the LORD is the one and only God, worship him. But if Baal is the one and only God, worship him."

The people didn't say anything.

[22]Then Elijah said to them, "I'm the only one of the LORD's prophets left. But
Baal has 450 prophets. [23]Get two bulls
for us. Let Baal's prophets choose one for themselves. Let them cut it into pieces. Then let them put it on the wood. But don't let them set fire to it. I'll prepare the other bull. I'll put it on the wood. But
I won't set fire to it. [24]Then you pray to
your god. And I'll pray to the LORD. The god who answers by sending fire down is the one and only God."

Then all the people said, "What you are saying is good."

[25]Elijah said to the prophets of Baal, "Choose one of the bulls. There are many of you. So prepare your bull first. Pray to your god. But don't light the
fire." [26]So they prepared the bull they
had been given.

They prayed to Baal from morning until noon. "Baal! Answer us!" they shouted. But there wasn't any reply. No one answered. Then they danced around the altar they had made.

[27]At noon Elijah began to tease them. "Shout louder!" he said. "I'm sure Baal is a god! Perhaps he has too much to think about. Or maybe he has gone to the toilet. Or perhaps he's away on a trip. Maybe he's sleeping. You might have to
wake him up." [28]So they shouted louder.
They cut themselves with swords and spears until their blood flowed. That's what they usually did when things really
looked hopeless. [29]It was now past
noon. The prophets of Baal continued to prophesy with all their might. They did it until the time came to offer the evening sacrifice. But there wasn't any reply. No one answered. No one paid any attention.

[30]Then Elijah said to all the people, "Come here to me." So they went to him. He rebuilt the altar of the LORD. It had
been torn down. [31]Elijah got 12 stones.
There was one for each tribe in the family line of Jacob. The LORD's message had come to Jacob. It had said, "Your name
will be Israel." [32]Elijah used the stones
to build an altar to honor the LORD. He dug a ditch around it. The ditch was large enough to hold 24 pounds of seeds.
[33]He arranged the wood for the fire. He
cut the bull into pieces. He placed the pieces on the wood. Then he said to some of the people, "Fill four large jars with water. Pour it on the offering and the wood." So they did.

[34]"Do it again," he said. So they did
it again.

"Do it a third time," he ordered. And
they did it the third time. [35]The water
ran down around the altar. It even filled the ditch.

[36]When it was time to offer the
evening sacrifice, the prophet Elijah stepped forward. He prayed, "LORD, you are the God of Abraham, Isaac and Israel. Today let everyone know that you are God in Israel. Let them know I'm your servant. Let them know I've done all these things because you commanded me to. [37]Answer me. LORD, answer
me. Then these people will know that you are the one and only God. They'll know that you are turning their hearts back to you again."

[38]The fire of the LORD came down. It
burned up the sacrifice. It burned up

the wood and the stones and the soil.
It even dried up the water in the ditch.
39 All the people saw it. Then they fell
down flat with their faces toward the
ground. They cried out, "The LORD is
the one and only God! The LORD is the
one and only God!"
40 Then Elijah commanded them,
"Grab the prophets of Baal. Don't let a
single one of them get away!" So they
grabbed them. Elijah had them brought
down to the Kishon Valley. There he had
them put to death.
41 Elijah said to Ahab, "Go. Eat and
drink. I can hear the sound of a heavy
rain." 42 So Ahab went off to eat and
drink. But Elijah climbed to the top of
Mount Carmel. He bent down toward
the ground. Then he put his face between his knees.
43 "Go and look toward the sea," he told
his servant. So he went up and looked.
"I don't see anything there," he said.
Seven times Elijah said, "Go back."
44 The seventh time the servant said,
"I see a cloud. It's as small as a man's
hand. It's coming up over the sea."
Elijah said, "Go to Ahab. Tell him, 'Tie
your chariot to your horse. Go down
to Jezreel before the rain stops you.' "
45 Black clouds filled the sky. The wind
came up, and a heavy rain began to fall.
Ahab rode off to Jezreel. 46 The power of
the LORD came on Elijah. He tucked his
coat into his belt. And he ran ahead of
Ahab all the way to Jezreel.

Elijah Runs Away to Mount Horeb

19 Ahab told Jezebel everything
Elijah had done. He told her how
Elijah had killed all the prophets of
Baal with his sword. 2 So Jezebel sent
a message to Elijah. She said, "You
can be sure that I will kill you, just as
I killed the other prophets. I'll do it by
this time tomorrow. If I don't, may the
gods punish me greatly."
3 Elijah was afraid. So he ran for his
life. He came to Beersheba in Judah. He
left his servant there. 4 Then he traveled
for one day into the desert. He came to
a small bush. He sat down under it. He
prayed that he would die. "LORD, I've
had enough," he said. "Take my life. I'm
no better than my people of long ago."
5 Then he lay down under the bush. And
he fell asleep.
Suddenly an angel touched him. The
angel said, "Get up and eat." 6 Elijah
looked around. Near his head he saw
some bread. It had been baked over
hot coals. A jar of water was also there.
So Elijah ate and drank. Then he lay
down again.
7 The angel of the LORD came to him
a second time. He touched him and
said, "Get up and eat. Your journey will
be long and hard." 8 So he got up. He
ate and drank. The food gave him new
strength. He traveled for 40 days and 40
nights. He kept going until he arrived
at Horeb. It was the mountain of God.
9 There he went into a cave and spent
the night.

The LORD Appears to Elijah

A message came to Elijah from the
LORD. He said, "Elijah, what are you
doing here?"
10 He replied, "LORD God who rules
over all, I've been very committed to
you. The Israelites have turned their
backs on your covenant. They have
torn down your altars. They've put your
prophets to death with their swords. I'm
the only one left. And they are trying
to kill me."
11 The LORD said, "Go out. Stand on the
mountain in front of me. I am going
to pass by."
As the LORD approached, a very powerful wind tore the mountains apart. It
broke up the rocks. But the LORD wasn't
in the wind. After the wind there was
an earthquake. But the LORD wasn't in
the earthquake. 12 After the earthquake
a fire came. But the LORD wasn't in the
fire. And after the fire there was only
a gentle whisper. 13 When Elijah heard
it, he pulled his coat over his face. He
went out and stood at the entrance to
the cave.
Then a voice said to him, "Elijah, what
are you doing here?"
14 He replied, "LORD God who rules
over all, I've been very committed to
you. The Israelites have turned their
backs on your covenant. They have
torn down your altars. They've put your
prophets to death with their swords. I'm
the only one left. And they are trying
to kill me."
15 The LORD said to him, "Go back
the way you came. Go to the Desert of

Damascus. When you get there, anoint Hazael as king over Aram. 16 Also anoint Jehu as king over Israel. He is the son of Nimshi. And anoint Elisha from Abel Meholah as the next prophet after you. He is the son of Shaphat. 17 Jehu will put to death anyone who escapes Hazael's sword. And Elisha will put to death anyone who escapes Jehu's sword. 18 But I will keep 7,000 people in Israel for myself. They have not bowed down to Baal. And they have not kissed him."

The LORD Chooses Elisha

19 Elijah left Mount Horeb. He saw Elisha, the son of Shaphat. Elisha was plowing in a field. He was driving the last of 12 pairs of oxen. Elijah went up to him. He threw his coat around him. 20 Then Elisha left his oxen. He ran after Elijah. "Let me kiss my father and mother goodbye," he said. "Then I'll come with you."

"Go back," Elijah replied. "What have I done to you?"

21 So Elisha left him and went back. He got his two oxen and killed them. He burned the plow to cook the meat. He gave it to the people, and they ate it. Then he started to follow Elijah. He became Elijah's servant.

Ben-Hadad Attacks Samaria

20 Ben-Hadad brought his whole army together. He was king of Aram. He went up to Samaria. He took 32 kings and their horses and chariots with him. All of them surrounded Samaria and attacked it. 2 Ben-Hadad sent messengers into the city. They spoke to Ahab, the king of Israel. They told him, "Ben-Hadad says, 3 'Your silver and gold belong to me. The best of your wives and children also belong to me.' "

4 The king of Israel replied, "What you say is true. You are my king and master. I belong to you. And everything I have belongs to you."

5 The messengers came again. They told Ahab, "Ben-Hadad says, 'I commanded you to give me your silver and gold. I also commanded you to give me your wives and children. 6 But now I'm going to send my officials to you. They will come about this time tomorrow. They'll search your palace. They'll search the houses of your officials. They'll take everything you value. And they'll carry it all away.' "

7 The king of Israel sent for all the elders of the land. He said to them, "This man is really looking for trouble! He sent for my wives and children. He sent for my silver and gold. And I agreed to give them to him."

8 All the elders and people answered, "Don't listen to him. Don't agree to give him what he wants."

9 So Ahab replied to Ben-Hadad's messengers. He said, "Tell my king and master, 'I will do everything you commanded me to do the first time. But this time, I can't do what you want me to do.' " They took Ahab's answer back to Ben-Hadad.

10 Then Ben-Hadad sent another message to Ahab. Ben-Hadad said, "There won't be enough dust left in Samaria to give each of my followers even a handful. If there is, may the gods punish me greatly."

11 The king of Israel replied. He said, "Tell him, 'Someone who puts his armor on shouldn't brag like someone who takes it off.' "

12 Ben-Hadad and the kings were in their tents drinking. That's when he heard the message. He ordered his men, "Get ready to attack." So they prepared to attack the city.

Ahab Wins the Battle Over Ben-Hadad

13 During that time a prophet came to Ahab, the king of Israel. He announced, "The LORD says, 'Do you see this huge army? I will hand it over to you today. Then you will know that I am the LORD.' "

14 "But who will do it?" Ahab asked.

The prophet answered, "The LORD says, 'The junior officers who are under the area commanders will do it.' "

"And who will start the battle?" Ahab asked.

The prophet answered, "You will."

15 So Ahab sent for the junior officers who were under the area commanders. The total number of officers was 232. Ahab gathered together the rest of the Israelites. The total number of them was 7,000. 16 They started out at noon. At that time Ben-Hadad and the 32 kings helping him were in their tents.

They were getting drunk. 17 The junior
officers who were under Ahab's area
commanders marched out first.
Ben-Hadad had sent out scouts. They
came back and reported, "Men are
marching against us from Samaria."
18 Ben-Hadad said, "They might be
coming to make peace. If they are, take
them alive. Or they might be coming to
make war. If they are, take them alive."
19 The junior officers marched out of
the city. The army was right behind
them. 20 Each man struck down the
one fighting against him. When that
happened, the army of Aram ran away.
The Israelites chased them. But Ben-
Hadad, the king of Aram, escaped on a
horse. Some of his horsemen escaped
with him. 21 The king of Israel attacked
them. He overpowered the horses and
chariots. Large numbers of the men of
Aram were wounded or killed.
22 After that, the prophet came to the
king of Israel again. The prophet said,
"Make your position stronger. Do what
needs to be done. Next spring the king
of Aram will attack you again."
23 During that time, the officials of the
king of Aram gave him advice. They
said, "The gods of Israel are gods of the
hills. That's why they were too strong
for us. But suppose we fight them on the
plains. Then we'll certainly be stronger
than they are. 24 Here's what you should
do. Don't let any of the kings continue
as military leaders. Have other officers
take their places. 25 You must also put
another army together. It should be just
like the one you lost. It should have the
same number of horses and chariots.
Then we'll be able to fight against Israel
on the plains. And we'll certainly be
stronger than they are." Ben-Hadad
agreed with their advice. He did what
they suggested.
26 The next spring Ben-Hadad brought
together the men of Aram. They went up
to the city of Aphek to fight against Israel. 27 The Israelites were also brought
together. They were given supplies.
They marched out to fight against
their enemies. Israel's army camped
across from Aram's army. The Israelites
looked like two small flocks of goats
that had become separated from the
others. But the men of Aram covered
the countryside.
28 The man of God came up to the
king of Israel again. He told him, "The
LORD says, 'The men of Aram think the
LORD is a god of the hills. They do not
think he is a god of the valleys. So I, the
LORD, will hand their huge army over
to you. Then you will know that I am
the LORD.' "
29 For seven days the two armies
camped across from each other. On
the seventh day the battle began. The
Israelites wounded or killed 100,000 Aramean soldiers who were on foot. That
happened in a single day. 30 The rest
of the men of Aram escaped to the city
of Aphek. Its wall fell down on 27,000 of
them. Ben-Hadad ran to the city. He hid
in a secret room.
31 His officials said to him, "Look,
we've heard that the kings of Israel
often show mercy. So let's go to the king
of Israel. Let's wear the rough clothing
people wear when they're sad. Let's tie
ropes around our heads. Perhaps Ahab
will spare your life."
32 So they wore rough clothing. They
tied ropes around their heads. Then
they went to the king of Israel. They told
him, "Your servant Ben-Hadad says,
'Please let me live.' "
The king answered, "Is he still alive?
He used to be my friend."
33 The men thought that was good
news. So they quickly used the word
Ahab had used. "Yes! Your friend
Ben-Hadad!" they said.
"Go and get him," the king said.
Ben-Hadad came out of the secret room.
Then Ahab had him get into his chariot.
34 "I'll return the cities my father took
from your father," Ben-Hadad offered.
"You can set up your own market areas
in Damascus. That's what my father did
in Samaria."
Ahab said, "If we sign a peace treaty,
I'll set you free." So Ben-Hadad made a
treaty with him. Then Ahab let him go.

A Prophet Accuses Ahab

35 There was a group of people called
the group of the prophets. A message
from the LORD came to one of their
members. He said to his companion,
"Strike me down with your weapon."
But he wouldn't do it.
36 The prophet said, "You haven't
obeyed the LORD. So as soon as you

leave me, a lion will kill you." The companion went away. And a lion found him and killed him.

37 The prophet found another man. He said, "Please strike me down." So the man struck him down and wounded him. 38 Then the prophet went and stood by the road. He waited for the king to come by. He pulled his headband down over his eyes so no one would recognize him. 39 The king passed by. Then the prophet called out to him. He said, "I went into the middle of the battle. Someone came to me with a prisoner. He said, 'Guard this man. Don't let him get away. If he does, you will pay for his life with yours. Or you can pay 75 pounds of silver.' 40 While I was busy here and there, the man disappeared."

The king of Israel spoke to him. He told him, "What you've just said is what will happen to you."

41 Then the prophet quickly removed the headband from his eyes. The king of Israel recognized him as one of the prophets. 42 He told the king, "The LORD says, 'You have set a man free. But I had said he should be set apart to the LORD in a special way to be destroyed. So you must pay for his life with yours. You must pay for his people's lives with the lives of your people.' " 43 The king of Israel was angry. He was in a bad mood. He went back to his palace in Samaria.

Naboth's Vineyard

21 Some time later King Ahab wanted a certain vineyard. It belonged to Naboth from Jezreel. The vineyard was in Jezreel. It was close to the palace of Ahab, the king of Samaria. 2 Ahab said to Naboth, "Let me have your vineyard. It's close to my palace. I want to use it for a vegetable garden. I'll trade you a better vineyard for it. Or, if you prefer, I'll pay you what it's worth."

3 But Naboth replied, "May the LORD keep me from giving you the land my family handed down to me."

4 So Ahab went home. He was angry. He was in a bad mood because of what Naboth from Jezreel had said. He had told Ahab, "I won't give you the land my family handed down to me." So Ahab lay on his bed. He was in a very bad mood. He wouldn't even eat anything.

5 His wife Jezebel came in. She asked him, "Why are you in such a bad mood? Why won't you eat anything?"

6 He answered her, "Because I spoke to Naboth from Jezreel. I said, 'Sell me your vineyard. Or, if you prefer, I'll give you another vineyard in its place.' But he said, 'I won't sell you my vineyard.' "

7 His wife Jezebel said, "Is this how the king of Israel acts? Get up! Eat something! Cheer up. I'll get you the vineyard of Naboth from Jezreel."

8 So she wrote some letters in Ahab's name. She stamped them with his royal seal. Then she sent them to the elders and nobles who lived in the city where Naboth lived. 9 In those letters she wrote,

> "Announce a day when people are supposed to go without eating. Have Naboth sit in an important place among the people. 10 But put two worthless and evil men in seats across from him. Have them bring charges that he has cursed God and the king. Then take him out of the city. Kill him by throwing stones at him."

11 So the elders and nobles who lived in that city did what Jezebel wanted. They did everything she directed in the letters she had written to them. 12 They announced a day of fasting. They had Naboth sit in an important place among the people. 13 Then two worthless and evil men came and sat across from him. They brought charges against Naboth in front of the people. The two men said, "Naboth has cursed God and the king." So they took him outside the city. They killed him by throwing stones at him. 14 Then they sent a message to Jezebel. They said, "Naboth is dead. We killed him by throwing stones at him."

15 Jezebel heard that Naboth had been killed. As soon as she heard it, she said to Ahab, "Get up. Take over the vineyard of Naboth from Jezreel. It's the one he wouldn't sell to you. He isn't alive anymore. He's dead." 16 Ahab heard that Naboth was dead. So Ahab got up and went down to take over Naboth's vineyard.

17 Then a message from the LORD came to Elijah, who was from Tishbe. The LORD said, 18 "Go down to see Ahab, the king of Israel. He rules in Samaria.

You will find him in Naboth's vineyard.
Ahab has gone there to take it over.
19 Tell him, 'The LORD says, "Haven't you
murdered a man? Haven't you taken
over his property?" ' Then tell Ahab, 'The
LORD says, "Dogs licked up Naboth's
blood. In that same place dogs will lick
up your blood. Yes, I said your blood!" ' "
20 Ahab said to Elijah, "My enemy!
You have found me!"
"I have found you," he answered.
"That's because you gave yourself over
to do evil things. You did what was evil
in the sight of the LORD. 21 So the LORD
says, 'I am going to bring horrible trouble on you. I will destroy your children
after you. I will destroy every male in
Israel who is related to you. It does not
matter whether they are slaves or free.
22 I will make your royal house like the
house of Jeroboam, the son of Nebat. I
will make it like the house of Baasha, the
son of Ahijah. You have made me very
angry. You have caused Israel to sin.'
23 "The LORD also says, 'Dogs will eat
up Jezebel near the wall of Jezreel.'
24 "Some of the people who belong to
Ahab will die in the city. Dogs will eat
them up. Others will die in the country.
The birds will eat them."
25 There was never anyone like Ahab.
He gave himself over to do what was evil
in the sight of the LORD. His wife Jezebel
talked him into it. 26 He acted in the
most evil way. He worshiped statues of
gods. He was like the Amorites. The LORD
drove them out to make room for Israel.
27 When Ahab heard what Elijah had
said, he tore his clothes. He put on
the rough clothing people wear when
they're sad. He went without eating.
He even slept in his clothes. He went
around looking sad.
28 Then a message from the LORD
came to Elijah, who was from Tishbe.
The LORD said, 29 "Have you seen how
Ahab has made himself humble in my
sight? Because he has done that, I will
not bring trouble on him while he lives.
But I will bring it on his royal house
when his son is king."

Micaiah Prophesies Against Ahab

22 For three years there wasn't any
war between Aram and Israel.
2 In the third year Jehoshaphat went
down to see Ahab, the king of Israel.
Jehoshaphat was king of Judah. 3 The
king of Israel had spoken to his officials. He had said, "Don't you know that
Ramoth Gilead belongs to us? And we
aren't even doing anything to take it
back from the king of Aram."
4 So Ahab asked Jehoshaphat, "Will
you go with me to fight against Ramoth
Gilead?"
Jehoshaphat replied to the king of
Israel, "Yes. I'll go with you. My men
will go with you. My horses will also
go with you." 5 Jehoshaphat continued,
"First ask the LORD for advice."
6 So the king of Israel brought about
400 prophets together. He asked them,
"Should I go to war against Ramoth
Gilead? Or should I stay here?"
"Go," they answered. "The Lord will
hand it over to you."
7 But Jehoshaphat asked, "Is there
no longer a prophet of the LORD here?
If there is, ask him what we should do."
8 The king of Israel answered Jehoshaphat. He said, "There is still one
other man we can go to. We can ask
the LORD for advice through him. But I
hate him. He never prophesies anything
good about me. He only prophesies bad
things. His name is Micaiah. He's the
son of Imlah."
"You shouldn't say bad things about
him," Jehoshaphat replied.
9 So the king of Israel called for one
of his officials. He told him, "Bring Micaiah, the son of Imlah, right away."
10 The king of Israel and Jehoshaphat,
the king of Judah, were wearing their
royal robes. They were sitting on their
thrones at the threshing floor. It was
near the entrance of the gate of Samaria.
All the prophets were prophesying in
front of them. 11 Zedekiah was the son
of Kenaanah. Zedekiah had made horns
out of iron. They looked like animal
horns. He announced, "The LORD says,
'With these horns you will drive back the
men of Aram until they are destroyed.' "
12 All the other prophets were prophesying the same thing. "Attack Ramoth
Gilead," they said. "Win the battle over
it. The LORD will hand it over to you."
13 A messenger went to get Micaiah.
He said to him, "Look. The other prophets agree. All of them are saying the
king will have success. So agree with
them. Say the same thing they do."

14 But Micaiah said, "You can be sure
that the LORD lives. And here is something you can be just as sure of. I can
only tell the king what the LORD tells
me to say."

15 When Micaiah arrived, the king
spoke to him. He asked, "Should we go
to war against Ramoth Gilead, or not?"

"Attack," he answered. "You will win.
The LORD will hand Ramoth Gilead over
to you."

16 The king said to him, "I've made
you promise to tell the truth many
times before. So don't tell me anything
but the truth in the name of the LORD."

17 Then Micaiah answered, "I saw
all the Israelites scattered on the hills.
They were like sheep that didn't have a
shepherd. The LORD said, 'These people
do not have a master. Let each of them
go home in peace.' "

18 The king of Israel spoke to Jehoshaphat. He said, "Didn't I tell you he
never prophesies anything good about
me? He only prophesies bad things."

19 Micaiah continued, "Listen to the
LORD's message. I saw the LORD sitting
on his throne. All the angels of heaven
were standing around him. Some were
standing at his right side. The others
were standing at his left side. 20 The
LORD said, 'Who will get Ahab to attack
Ramoth Gilead? I want him to die there.'

"One angel suggested one thing.
Another suggested something else.
21 Finally, a spirit came forward and
stood in front of the LORD. The spirit
said, 'I'll get Ahab to do it.'

22 " 'How?' the LORD asked.

"The spirit said, 'I'll go out and put
lies in the mouths of all his prophets.'

" 'You will have success in getting
Ahab to attack Ramoth Gilead,' said
the LORD. 'Go and do it.'

23 "So the LORD has put lies in the
mouths of all your prophets. He has
said that great harm will come to you."

24 Then Zedekiah, the son of Kenaanah, went up and slapped Micaiah
in the face. Zedekiah asked Micaiah, "Do
you think the spirit sent by the LORD
left me? Do you think that spirit went
to speak to you?"

25 Micaiah replied, "You will find out
on the day you go to hide in an inside
room to save your life."

26 Then the king of Israel gave an
order. He said, "Take Micaiah away.
Send him back to Amon. Amon is the
ruler of the city of Samaria. And send
him back to Joash. Joash is a member
of the royal court. 27 Tell him, 'The king
says, "Put this fellow in prison. Don't
give him anything but bread and water
until I return safely." ' "

28 Micaiah announced, "Do you really
think you will return safely? If you do,
the LORD hasn't spoken through me." He
continued, "All of you people, remember
what I've said!"

Ahab Is Killed at Ramoth Gilead

29 So the king of Israel went up to Ramoth Gilead. Jehoshaphat, the king of
Judah, went there too. 30 The king of
Israel spoke to Jehoshaphat. He said,
"I'll go into battle wearing different
clothes. Then people won't recognize
me. But you wear your royal robes."
So the king of Israel put on different
clothes. Then he went into battle.

31 The king of Aram had given an order to his 32 chariot commanders. He
had said, "Fight only against the king
of Israel. Don't fight against anyone
else." 32 The chariot commanders saw
Jehoshaphat. They thought, "That has
to be the king of Israel." So they turned
to attack him. But Jehoshaphat cried
out. 33 Then the commanders saw he
wasn't the king of Israel after all. So
they stopped chasing him.

34 But someone shot an arrow without
taking aim. The arrow hit the king of
Israel between the parts of his armor.
The king told his chariot driver, "Turn
the chariot around. Get me out of this
battle. I've been wounded." 35 All day
long the battle continued. The king
kept himself standing up by leaning
against the inside of his chariot. He kept
his face toward the men of Aram. The
blood from his wound ran down onto
the floor of the chariot. That evening
he died. 36 As the sun was setting, a cry
spread through the army. "Every man
must go to his own town!" they said.
"Every man must go to his own land!"

37 So the king died. He was brought
to Samaria. They buried him there.
38 They washed the chariot at a pool in
Samaria. It was where the prostitutes
took baths. The dogs licked up Ahab's

blood. It happened exactly as the LORD
had said it would.
39 The other events of Ahab's rule
are written down. Everything he did
is written down. That includes the palace he built and decorated with ivory.
It also includes the cities he built up
and put high walls around. All these
things are written in the official records
of the kings of Israel. 40 Ahab joined the
members of his family who had already
died. Ahab's son Ahaziah became the
next king after him.

Jehoshaphat King of Judah

41 Jehoshaphat began to rule over
Judah. It was in the fourth year that
Ahab was king of Israel. Jehoshaphat
was the son of Asa. 42 Jehoshaphat was
35 years old when he became king. He
ruled in Jerusalem for 25 years. His
mother's name was Azubah. She was
the daughter of Shilhi. 43 Jehoshaphat
followed all the ways of his father Asa.
He didn't wander away from them. He
did what was right in the sight of the
LORD. But the high places weren't removed. The people continued to offer
sacrifices and burn incense at them.
44 Jehoshaphat was also at peace with
the king of Israel.
45 The other events of Jehoshaphat's
rule are written down. The brave things
he did in battle and everything else
he accomplished are written down.
All these things are written in the official records of the kings of Judah.
46 Jehoshaphat got rid of the rest of
the male prostitutes who were at the
temples. They had remained in the land
even after the rule of his father Asa. 47 At
that time Edom didn't have a king. An
area governor was in charge.
48 Jehoshaphat built many ships that
he used to carry goods to be traded. The
ships were supposed to go to Ophir for
gold. But they never had a chance to
sail. They were wrecked at Ezion Geber.
49 At that time Ahaziah, the son of Ahab,
spoke to Jehoshaphat. He said, "Let my
men sail with yours." But Jehoshaphat
refused.
50 Jehoshaphat joined the members
of his family who had already died. He
was buried in the family tomb in the
city of King David. Jehoshaphat's son
Jehoram became the next king after
him.

Ahaziah King of Israel

51 Ahaziah became king of Israel in
Samaria. It was in the 17th year that Jehoshaphat was king of Judah. Ahaziah
ruled over Israel for two years. He was
the son of Ahab. 52 Ahaziah did what
was evil in the sight of the LORD. He
lived the way his father and mother had
lived. He lived the way Jeroboam, the
son of Nebat, had lived. Jeroboam had
caused Israel to sin. 53 Ahaziah served
and worshiped the god named Baal. He
made the LORD, the God of Israel, very
angry. That's exactly what Ahaziah's
father had done.

2 KINGS

Author: We don't know.

Both Israel's and Judah's kings continued to sin and disobey God. They led God's people to turn away from him and disobey his commands. God sent prophets to tell his people to turn back to him. The prophets reminded God's people of God's promises and urged them to repent. But the people didn't listen. They wanted to do things their own way, not God's way.

Old Testament History

Eventually, both nations, Israel and Judah, fell captive to other nations. The Assyrians captured the people of Israel, and the Babylonians captured the people of Judah. The temple was destroyed, and God allowed his people to experience the consequences of their sinful choices. But even then, when things were terrible for the people of God, the prophets reminded God's people that one day the very best, perfect King was going to come and make everything right again. Even when they were far from home and far from God, he did not forget them. God is patient with his people and faithful to his promises.

The LORD Judges Ahaziah

1 After King Ahab died, Moab refused
to remain under Israel's control.
2 Ahaziah had fallen through the window of his upstairs room in Samaria.
He had hurt himself. So he sent messengers to ask the god named Baal-Zebub
for advice. Baal-Zebub was the god of
the city of Ekron. Ahaziah said to the
messengers, "Go and ask Baal-Zebub
whether I will get well again."
3 But the angel of the LORD spoke to
Elijah, who was from Tishbe. The angel
said, "Go up to see the messengers of
Ahaziah, the king of Samaria. Tell them,
'You are on your way to ask Baal-Zebub
for advice. He is the god of Ekron. Are
you going there to pray to that god?
Do you think there is no God in Israel?'
4 The LORD says to Ahaziah, 'You will
never leave the bed you are lying on.
You can be sure that you will die!' " So
Elijah went to see the messengers.
5 They returned to the king. He asked
them, "Why have you come back?"
6 "A man met us on our way there,"
they replied. "He said to us, 'Go back to
the king who sent you. Tell him, "The
LORD says, 'You are sending messengers
to ask Baal-Zebub for advice. He is the
god of Ekron. Are you going there to
pray to that god? Do you think there is
no God in Israel? You will never leave
the bed you are lying on. You can be
sure that you will die!' " ' "
7 The king asked the messengers,
"What kind of man came to see you?
Who told you these things?"
8 They replied, "He was wearing
clothes made out of hair. He had a
leather belt around his waist."
The king said, "That was Elijah from
Tishbe."
9 Then Ahaziah sent a captain to
Elijah. The captain had his group of
50 fighting men with him. Elijah was
sitting on top of a hill. The captain went
up to him. He said to Elijah, "Man of
God, the king says, 'Come down!' "
10 Elijah answered the captain, "If
I'm really a man of God, may fire come
down from heaven! May it burn up you
and your 50 men!" Then fire came down
from heaven. It burned up the captain
and his men.
11 After that happened, the king sent
another captain to Elijah. The captain
had his 50 men with him. He said to Elijah, "Man of God, the king says, 'Come
down at once!' "
12 Elijah replied, "If I'm really a man
of God, may fire come down from heav-
en! May it burn up you and your 50
men!" Then the fire of God came down
from heaven. It burned up the captain
and his 50 men.
13 So the king sent a third captain with
his 50 men. The captain went up to Elijah.
He fell on his knees in front of him. "Man
of God," he begged, "please have respect
for my life! Please have respect for the
lives of these 50 men! 14 Fire has come
down from heaven. It has burned up the
first two captains and all their men. But
please have respect for my life!"
15 The angel of the LORD said to Elijah, "Go down along with him. Don't
be afraid of him." So Elijah got up and
went down to the king with the captain.
16 Elijah told the king, "The LORD
says, 'You have sent messengers to ask
Baal-Zebub for advice. He is the god of
Ekron. Did you go there to pray to that
god for advice? Do you think there is no
God in Israel? You will never leave the
bed you are lying on. You can be sure
that you will die!' " 17 So King Ahaziah
died. It happened just as the LORD had
said it would. He had spoken that message through Elijah.
Ahaziah didn't have any sons. So Joram, his younger brother, became the
next king after him. It was the second
year of Jehoram, the king of Judah.
Jehoram was the son of Jehoshaphat.
18 All the other events of Ahaziah's rule
are written down. Everything he did
is written in the official records of the
kings of Israel.

Elijah Is Taken Up to Heaven

2 Elijah and Elisha were on their way
from Gilgal. The LORD was going
to use a strong wind to take Elijah up
to heaven. 2 Elijah said to Elisha, "Stay
here. The LORD has sent me to Bethel."
But Elisha said, "I won't leave you. And
that's just as sure as the LORD and you
are alive." So they went down to Bethel.
3 There was a group of prophets at
Bethel. They came out to where Elisha
was. They asked him, "Do you know what
the LORD is going to do? He's going to
take your master away from you today."

in 2 Kings?

God is the True Ruler. Though God's people were divided between two earthly rulers, God's rule and reign were for their greatest good.

"Yes, I know," Elisha replied. "So be
quiet."
4 Then Elijah said to him, "Stay here,
Elisha. The LORD has sent me to Jericho."
Elisha replied, "I won't leave you.
And that's just as sure as the LORD and
you are alive." So they went to Jericho.
5 There was a group of prophets at Jericho. They went up to where Elisha was.
They asked him, "Do you know what the
LORD is going to do? He's going to take
your master away from you today."
"Yes, I know," Elisha replied. "So be
quiet."
6 Then Elijah said to him, "Stay here.
The LORD has sent me to the Jordan
River."
Elisha replied, "I won't leave you. And
that's just as sure as the LORD and you
are alive." So the two of them walked on.
7 Fifty men from the group of prophets followed them. The men stopped and
stood not far away from them. They
faced the place where Elijah and Elisha
had stopped at the Jordan River. 8 Elijah
rolled up his coat. Then he struck the
water with it. The water parted to the
right and to the left. The two of them
went across the river on dry ground.
9 After they had gone across, Elijah
said to Elisha, "Tell me. What can I do for
you before I'm taken away from you?"
"Please give me a double share of
your spirit," Elisha replied.
10 "You have asked me for something
that's very hard to do," Elijah said. "But
suppose you see me when I'm taken
away from you. Then you will receive
what you have asked for. If you don't
see me, you won't receive it."
11 They kept walking along and
talking together. Suddenly there appeared a chariot and horses made of
fire. The chariot and horses came between the two men. Then Elijah went up
to heaven in a strong wind. 12 Elisha saw
it and cried out to Elijah, "My father!
You are like a father to me! You, Elijah,
are the true chariots and horsemen of
Israel!" Elisha didn't see Elijah anymore. Then Elisha took hold of his own
garment and tore it in two.
13 He picked up the coat that had fall-
en from Elijah. He went back and stood
on the bank of the Jordan River. 14 Then
he struck the water with Elijah's coat.
"Where is the power of the LORD?" he
asked. "Where is the power of the God
of Elijah?" When Elisha struck the water,
it parted to the right and to the left. He
went across the river.
15 The group of prophets from Jericho
were watching. They said, "The spirit of
Elijah has been given to Elisha." They
went over to Elisha. They bowed down to
him with their faces toward the ground.
16 "Look," they said. "We have 50 capable men. Let them go and look for your
master. Perhaps the Spirit of the LORD
has lifted him up. Maybe he has put him
down on a mountain or in a valley."
"No," Elisha replied. "Don't send
them."
17 But they kept asking until he felt he
couldn't say no. So he said, "Send them."
And they sent 50 men. They looked for
Elijah for three days. But they didn't
find him. 18 So they returned to Elisha.
He was staying in Jericho. Elisha said
to them, "Didn't I tell you not to go?"

Elisha Makes Jericho's Water Pure

19 The people of Jericho said to Elisha,
"Look. This town has a good location.
You can see that for yourself. But the
spring of water here is bad. So the land
doesn't produce anything."
20 "Bring me a new bowl," Elisha said.
"Put some salt in it." So they brought
it to him.
21 Then he went out to the spring. He
threw the salt into it. He told the people,
"The LORD says, 'I have made this water
pure. It will never cause death again. It

will never keep the land from producing
crops again.' " 22 The water has stayed
pure to this day. That's what Elisha had
said would happen.

Some Boys Make Fun of Elisha

23 Elisha left Jericho and went up
to Bethel. He was walking along the
road. Some boys came out of the town.
They made fun of him. "Get out of here,
baldy!" they said. "Get out of here!
You don't even have any hair on your
head!" 24 He turned around and looked
at them. And he asked for bad things to
happen to them. He did it in the name
of the LORD. Then two bears came out
of the woods. They attacked 42 of the
boys. 25 Elisha went on to Mount Carmel.
From there he returned to Samaria.

Moab's King Refuses to Obey Israel's King

3 Joram became king of Israel in
Samaria. It was in the 18th year
that Jehoshaphat was king of Judah.
Joram ruled for 12 years. He was the
son of Ahab. 2 Joram did what was evil
in the sight of the LORD. But he wasn't
as bad as his father and mother had
been. Joram's father had made a sacred
stone used to worship the god named
Baal. Joram got rid of it. 3 But he kept
on committing the sins of Jeroboam,
the son of Nebat. Jeroboam had also
caused Israel to commit those same
sins. Joram didn't turn away from them.
4 Mesha raised sheep. He was king of
Moab. He had to pay the king of Israel
100,000 lambs a year. He also had to
pay him with the wool of 100,000 rams
a year. 5 After Ahab died, Moab's king
refused to obey the next king of Israel.
6 So at that time King Joram started out
from Samaria. He gathered together
all of Israel's troops. 7 He also sent a
message to Jehoshaphat, the king of
Judah. Joram said, "The king of Moab
is refusing to obey me. Will you go with
me to fight against Moab?"
"Yes. I'll go with you," Jehoshaphat
replied. "My men will go with you. My
horses will also go with you."
8 "What road should we take to attack
Moab?" Joram asked.
"The one that goes through the Desert
of Edom," Jehoshaphat answered.
9 So the king of Israel marched out.
The king of Judah and the king of Edom
went with him. Their armies marched
around the southern end of the Dead
Sea. After seven days they ran out of
water. There wasn't any water for the
men or their animals.
10 "What should we do now?" exclaimed the king of Israel. "The LORD
has called us three kings together. Did
he do it only to hand us over to Moab?"
11 But Jehoshaphat asked, "Isn't there
a prophet of the LORD here? Can't we
ask the LORD for advice through him?"
An officer of the king of Israel answered, "Elisha is here. He's the son of
Shaphat. Elisha used to serve Elijah."
12 Jehoshaphat said, "The LORD speaks
through him." So the king of Israel went
down to see Elisha. Jehoshaphat and
the king of Edom also went there.
13 Elisha said to the king of Israel,
"Why do you want to come to me? Go
to your father's prophets. Go to your
mother's prophets."
"No," the king of Israel answered.
"The LORD called us three kings together. He did it to hand us over to Moab."
14 Elisha said, "I serve the LORD who
rules over all. You can be sure that he
lives. And you can be just as sure that I
have respect for Jehoshaphat, the king
of Judah. If I didn't, I wouldn't pay any
attention to you. 15 But now bring me
someone who plays the harp."
While that person was playing the
harp, the LORD's power came on Elisha.
16 Elisha announced, "The LORD says, 'I
will fill this valley with pools of water.'
17 This will happen because the LORD says,
'You will not see wind or rain. But this
valley will be filled with water. Then you,
your cattle and your other animals will
have water to drink.' 18 This is an easy
thing for the LORD to do. He will also hand
Moab over to you. 19 You will destroy every city that has high walls around it.
You will destroy every major town. You
will cut down every good tree. You will
stop up all the springs of water. And you
will cover every good field with stones."
20 The next day, the time came to
offer the morning sacrifice. And then
it happened! Water was flowing from
the direction of Edom! In fact, the land
was filled with water!
21 Now all the people of Moab had
heard that the kings had come to fight
against them. So the king of Moab sent

for all Moab's fighting men. It didn't matter whether they were young or old. He sent for everyone who could carry a weapon. All of them were stationed at the border.
[22]They got up early in the morning. The sun was already shining on the water. Across the way, the water looked red to the men of Moab. It looked like blood.
[23]"That's blood!" they said. "Those kings must have fought and killed each other. Let's go, Moab! Let's take everything that has any value."
[24]So the men of Moab went to the camp of Israel. Just as they arrived there, the men of Israel got ready to fight. They fought against the men of Moab until those men ran away. The men of Israel marched into the land and attacked it. They killed the people of Moab.
[25]They destroyed the towns. Each man threw a large stone on every good field. They did that until the fields were covered. They stopped up all the springs of water. And they cut down every good tree. The only town left with any stones in place was Kir Hareseth. But some of the Israelites armed with slings surrounded it. Then they attacked it.
[26]The king of Moab saw that the battle had gone against him. So he took with him 700 men who had swords. They tried to break through the battle lines to the king of Edom. But they couldn't do it.
[27]Then the king of Moab took his oldest son. He was the son who would become the next king of Moab. But the king offered his son as a sacrifice on the city wall. That shocked and terrified the men of Israel. So they pulled back and returned to their own land.

Elisha Provides Olive Oil for a Widow

4 The wife of a man from the group of the prophets cried out to Elisha. She said, "My husband is dead. You know how much respect he had for the LORD. But he owed money to someone. And now that person is coming to take my two boys away. They will become his slaves."
[2]Elisha replied to her, "How can I help you? Tell me. What do you have in your house?"

"I don't have anything there at all," she said. "All I have is a small jar of olive oil."
[3]Elisha said, "Go around to all your neighbors. Ask them for empty jars. Get as many as you can.
[4]Then go inside your house. Shut the door behind you and your sons. Pour oil into all the jars. As each jar is filled, put it over to one side."
[5]The woman left him. Then she shut the door behind her and her sons. They

pointing us to JESUS: Elisha

Elisha was a prophet of God who lived at the same time as Elijah. He did many of the same things Elijah did to show God's people the power of God. Elisha's ministry also included ministry to outsiders. He cared for widows (women whose husbands had died), Gentiles (those who were not Israelites), and the poor. Elisha's ministry reminded God's people that God cares about all people.

Jesus was the Savior who came to bring God's promise of salvation to the entire world. Just like Elisha, Jesus cared for those whom others would have overlooked: widows, the poor, and those who were sick. Not only did Jesus care for them during his time on earth, but he also gave his life on the cross so that anyone who believes in him can be welcomed into the family of God.

brought the jars to her. And she kept
pouring. 6 When all the jars were full,
she spoke to one of her sons. She said,
"Bring me another jar."

But he replied, "There aren't any
more left." Then the oil stopped flowing.

7 She went and told the man of God
about it. He said, "Go and sell the oil.
Pay what you owe. You and your sons
can live on what is left."

The Son of a Woman From Shunem Is Brought Back to Life

8 One day Elisha went to the town of
Shunem. A rich woman lived there. She
begged him to stay and have a meal. So
every time he came by, he stopped there
to eat. 9 The woman said to her husband,
"That man often comes by here. I know
that he is a holy man of God. 10 Let's make
a small room for him on the roof. We'll
put a bed and a table in it. We'll also put
a chair and a lamp in it. Then he can stay
there when he comes to visit us."

11 One day Elisha came. He went up
to his room and lay down there. 12 He
said to his servant Gehazi, "Go and get
the woman from Shunem." So he did.
She stood in front of Elisha. 13 He said
to Gehazi, "Tell her, 'You have gone to
a lot of trouble for us. Now what can we
do for you? Can we speak to the king for
you? Or can we speak to the commander
of the army for you?'"

She replied, "I live among my own
people. I have everything I need here."

14 After she left, Elisha asked Gehazi,
"What can we do for her?"

Gehazi said, "She doesn't have a son.
And her husband is old."

15 Then Elisha said, "Bring her here
again." So he did. She stood in the
doorway. 16 "You will hold a son in your
arms," Elisha said. "It will be about this
time next year."

"No, my master!" she objected. "You are
a man of God. So please don't lie to me!"

17 But the woman became pregnant.
She had a baby boy. It happened the next
year about that same time. That's exactly
what Elisha had told her would happen.

18 The child grew. One day he went out
to get his father. His father was with the
people who were gathering the crops.
19 The boy said to his father, "My head
hurts! It really hurts!"

His father told a servant, "Carry him
to his mother." 20 The servant lifted up
the boy. He carried him to his mother.
The boy sat on her lap until noon. Then
he died. 21 She went up to the room on
the roof. There she laid him on the bed

of the man of God. Then she shut the door and went out.

22 She sent for her husband. She said, "Please send me one of the servants and a donkey. Then I can go quickly to the man of God and return."

23 "Why do you want to go to him today?" he asked. "It isn't the time for the New Moon feast. It isn't the Sabbath day."

"Don't let that bother you," she said.

24 She put a saddle on her donkey. She said to her servant, "Let's go. Don't slow down for me unless I tell you to." 25 So she started out. She came to Mount Carmel. That's where the man of God was.

When she was still a long way off, he saw her coming. He said to his servant Gehazi, "Look! There's the woman from Shunem! 26 Run out there to meet her. Ask her, 'Are you all right? Is your husband all right? Is your child all right?' "

"Everything is all right," she said.

27 She came to the man of God at the mountain. Then she took hold of his feet. Gehazi came over to push her away. But the man of God said, "Leave her alone! She is suffering terribly. But the LORD hasn't told me the reason for it. He has hidden it from me."

28 "My master, did I ask you for a son?" she said. "Didn't I tell you, 'Don't make me hope for something that won't happen'?"

29 Elisha said to Gehazi, "Tuck your coat into your belt. Take my walking stick and run to Shunem. Don't say hello to anyone you see. If anyone says hello to you, don't answer. Lay my walking stick on the boy's face."

30 But the child's mother said, "I won't leave you. And that's just as sure as the LORD and you are alive." So Elisha got up and followed her.

31 Gehazi went on ahead. He laid Elisha's walking stick on the boy's face. But there wasn't any sound. The boy didn't move at all. So Gehazi went back to Elisha. He told him, "The boy hasn't awakened."

32 Elisha arrived at the house. The boy was dead. He was lying on Elisha's bed. 33 Elisha went into the room. He shut the door. He was alone with the boy. He prayed to the LORD. 34 Then Elisha got on the bed. He lay down on the boy. His mouth touched the boy's mouth. His eyes touched the boy's eyes. And his hands touched the boy's hands. As Elisha lay on the boy, the boy's body grew warm. 35 Elisha turned away. He walked back and forth in the room. Then he got on the bed again. He lay down on the boy once more. The boy sneezed seven times. After that, he opened his eyes.

36 Elisha sent for Gehazi. He said to him, "Go and get the woman from Shunem." So he did. When she came, Elisha said, "Take your son." 37 She came in and fell at Elisha's feet. She bowed down with her face toward the ground. Then she took her son and went out.

Deadly Food in a Pot

38 Elisha returned to Gilgal. There wasn't enough food to eat in that area. The group of the prophets was meeting with Elisha. So he said to his servant, "Put the large pot over the fire. Cook some stew for these prophets."

39 One of them went out into the fields to gather herbs. He found a wild vine and picked some of its gourds. He picked as many as he could fit in his coat. Then he cut them up and put them into the pot of stew. But no one knew what they were. 40 The stew was poured out for the men. They began to eat it. But then they cried out, "Man of God, the food in that pot will kill us!" They couldn't eat it.

41 Elisha said, "Get some flour." He put it in the pot. He said, "Serve it to the men to eat." Then there wasn't anything in the pot that could harm them.

Elisha Feeds 100 People

42 A man came from Baal Shalishah. He brought the man of God 20 loaves of barley bread. They had been baked from the first grain that had ripened. The man also brought some heads of new grain. "Give this food to the people to eat," Elisha said.

43 "How can I put this in front of 100 men?" his servant asked.

But Elisha answered, "Give it to the people to eat. Do it because the LORD says, 'They will eat and have some left over.' " 44 Then the servant put the food in front of them. They ate it and had some left over. It happened just as the LORD had said it would.

Naaman Is Healed of a Skin Disease

5 Naaman was army commander
of the king of Aram. He was very
important to his master and was highly
respected. That's because the LORD had
helped him win the battle over Aram's
enemies. He was a brave soldier. But he
had a skin disease.
2Groups of soldiers from Aram had
marched out. They had captured a young
girl from Israel. She became a servant of
Naaman's wife. 3The young girl spoke to
the woman she was serving. She said, "I
wish my master would go and see the
prophet who is in Samaria. He would heal
my master of his skin disease."
4Naaman went to see his own master.
He told him what the girl from Israel
had said. 5"I think you should go," the
king of Aram replied. "I'll give you a
letter to take to the king of Israel." So
Naaman left. He took 750 pounds of
silver with him. He also took 150 pounds
of gold. And he took ten sets of clothes.
6He carried the letter to the king of Israel. It said, "I'm sending my servant
Naaman to you with this letter. I want
you to heal him of his skin disease."
7The king of Israel read the letter. As
soon as he did, he tore his royal robes.
He said, "Am I God? Can I kill people
and bring them back to life? Why does
this fellow send someone to me to be
healed of his skin disease? He must be
trying to pick a fight with me!"
8Elisha, the man of God, heard that
the king of Israel had torn his robes. So
he sent the king a message. Elisha said,
"Why have you torn your robes? Tell the
man to come to me. Then he will know
there is a prophet in Israel." 9So Naaman
went to see Elisha. He took his horses and
chariots with him. He stopped at the door
of Elisha's house. 10Elisha sent a messenger out to him. The messenger said, "Go!
Wash yourself in the Jordan River seven
times. Then your skin will be healed. You
will be pure and 'clean' again."
11But Naaman went away angry. He
said, "I was sure Elisha would come out
to me. I thought he would stand there
and pray to the LORD his God. I thought
he would wave his hand over my skin.
Then I would be healed. 12And what
about the Abana and Pharpar rivers
of Damascus? Aren't they better than
all the rivers of Israel? Couldn't I wash
in the rivers of Damascus and be made
pure and 'clean'?" So he turned and
went away. He was very angry.
13Naaman's servants went over to him.
They said, "You are like a father to us.
What if Elisha the prophet had told you
to do some great thing? Wouldn't you
have done it? But he only said, 'Wash
yourself. Then you will be pure and
"clean." ' You should be even more willing to do that!" 14So Naaman went down
to the Jordan River. He dipped himself in
it seven times. He did exactly what the
man of God had told him to do. Then his
skin was made pure again. It became
"clean" like the skin of a young boy.
15Naaman and all his attendants
went back to the man of God. Naaman
stood in front of Elisha. Naaman said,
"Now I know that there is no God anywhere in the whole world except in
Israel. So please accept a gift from me."
16The prophet answered, "I serve the
LORD. You can be sure that he lives. And
you can be just as sure that I won't accept
a gift from you." Even though Naaman
begged him to take it, Elisha wouldn't.
17"I can see that you won't accept a
gift from me," said Naaman. "But please
let me have some soil from your land.
Give me as much as a pair of mules can
carry. Here's why I want it. I won't ever
bring burnt offerings and sacrifices to
any other god again. I'll bring them
only to the LORD. I'll worship him on his
own soil. 18But there is one thing I hope
the LORD will forgive me for. From time
to time my master will enter the temple
to bow down to his god Rimmon. When
he does, he'll lean on my arm. Then I'll
have to bow down there also. I hope the
LORD will forgive me for that."
19"Go in peace," Elisha said.
Naaman started out on his way. 20Ge-
hazi was the servant of Elisha, the man of
God. Gehazi said to himself, "My master
was too easy on Naaman from Aram. He
should have accepted the gift Naaman
brought. I'm going to run after him. I'm
going to get something from him. And
that's just as sure as the LORD is alive."
21Gehazi hurried after Naaman.
Naaman saw him running toward him.
So he got down from the chariot to greet
him. "Is everything all right?" he asked.
22"Everything is all right," Gehazi
answered. "My master sent me to say,

'Two young men from the group of the prophets have just come to me. They've come from the hill country of Ephraim. Please give them 75 pounds of silver and two sets of clothes.' "

23 "I wish you would take twice as much silver," said Naaman. He begged Gehazi to accept it. Then Naaman tied up 150 pounds of silver in two bags. He also gave Gehazi two sets of clothes. He gave all of it to two of his own servants. They carried it ahead of Gehazi. 24 Gehazi came to the hill where Elisha lived. Then the servants handed the things over to Gehazi. He put them away in Elisha's house. He sent the men away, and they left. 25 Then he went back inside the house. He stood in front of his master Elisha.

"Gehazi, where have you been?" Elisha asked.

"I didn't go anywhere," Gehazi answered.

26 But Elisha said to him, "Didn't my spirit go with you? I know that the man got down from his chariot to greet you. Is this the time for you to accept money or clothes? Is it the time to take olive groves, vineyards, flocks or herds? Is it the time to accept male and female slaves? 27 You and your children after you will have Naaman's skin disease forever." Then Gehazi left Elisha. And he had Naaman's skin disease. His skin had become as white as snow.

An Ax Blade Floats

6 The group of the prophets said to Elisha, "Look. The place where we meet with you is too small for us. 2 We would like to go to the Jordan River. Each of us can get some wood there. We want to build a place there for us to meet."

Elisha said, "Go."

3 Then one of them said, "Won't you please come with us?"

"I will," Elisha replied. 4 And he went with them.

They went to the Jordan River. There they began to cut down trees. 5 One of them was cutting down a tree. The iron blade of his ax fell into the water. "Oh no, master!" he cried out. "This ax was borrowed!"

6 The man of God asked, "Where did the blade fall?" He showed Elisha the place. Then Elisha cut a stick and threw it there. That made the iron blade float. 7 "Take it out of the water," he said. So the man reached out and took it.

Elisha Makes the Soldiers of Aram Blind

8 The king of Aram was at war with Israel. He talked things over with his officers. Then he said, "I'm going to set up my camp in a certain place."

9 Elisha, the man of God, sent a message to the king of Israel. Elisha said, "Try to stay away from that place. Aram's army is going to be down there." 10 The king of Israel checked on the place the man of God had told him about. Time after time Elisha warned the king. So the king was on guard in those places.

11 All of that made the king of Aram very angry. He sent for his officers. He said to them, "Tell me! Which of us is on the side of the king of Israel?"

12 "You are my king and master," said one of his officers. "None of us is on Israel's side. But Elisha is a prophet in Israel. He tells the king of Israel even the words you speak in your own bedroom."

13 "Go and find out where he is," the king ordered. "Then I can send my men and capture him." The report came back. The officers said, "He's in Dothan." 14 Then the king sent horses and chariots and a strong army there. They went at night and surrounded the city.

15 The servant of the man of God got up the next morning. He went out early. He saw that an army with horses and chariots had surrounded the city. "Oh no, my master!" the servant said. "What can we do?"

16 "Don't be afraid," the prophet answered. "Those who are with us are more than those who are with them."

17 Elisha prayed, "LORD, open my servant's eyes so that he can see." Then the LORD opened his eyes. Elisha's servant looked up and saw the hills. He saw that Elisha was surrounded by horses and chariots made of fire.

18 Aram's army came down toward Elisha. Then he prayed to the LORD, "Make these soldiers blind." So the LORD made them blind, just as Elisha had prayed.

19 Elisha told them, "This isn't the right road. This isn't the right city. Follow me. I'll lead you to the man you are looking for." He led them to Samaria.

20 They entered the city. Then Elisha
said, "LORD, open the eyes of these men.
Help them see again." Then the LORD
opened their eyes. They looked around.
And there they were, inside Samaria!
21 The king of Israel saw them. So he
asked Elisha, "Should I kill them? I need
your advice. You are like a father to me.
Should I kill them?"
22 "Don't kill them," he answered.
"Would you kill people you have captured with your own sword or bow?
Put some food and water in front of
them. Then they can eat and drink.
They can go back to their master." 23 So
the king of Israel prepared a great feast
for them. After they had finished eating
and drinking, he sent them away. They
returned to their master. So the groups
of fighting men from Aram stopped
attacking Israel's territory.

Aram's Army Attacks Samaria and People Go Hungry

24 Some time later, Ben-Hadad gathered his entire army together. Ben-Hadad
was the king of Aram. His army marched
up and surrounded Samaria. Then they
attacked it. 25 There wasn't enough food
anywhere in the city. It was surrounded
for so long that people had to weigh out
two pounds of silver for a donkey's head.
They had to weigh out two ounces of
silver for half a pint of seed pods.
26 One day the king of Israel was
walking on top of the city wall. A woman cried out to him, "You are my king
and master. Please help me!"
27 The king replied, "If the LORD
doesn't help you, where can I get help
for you? From the threshing floor?
From the winepress?" 28 He continued,
"What's wrong?"

She answered, "A woman said to me,
'Give up your son. Then we can eat him
today. Tomorrow we'll eat my son.' 29 So
we cooked my son. Then we ate him.
The next day I said to her, 'Give up your
son. Then we can eat him.' But she had
hidden him."
30 When the king heard the woman's words, he tore his royal robes. As
he walked along the wall, the people
looked up at him. They saw that under
his robes he was wearing the rough
clothing people wear when they're sad.
31 He said, "I'll cut the head of Shaphat's
son Elisha off his shoulders today. If I
don't, may God punish me greatly!"
32 Elisha was sitting in his house.
The elders were sitting there with him.
The king went to see Elisha. He sent
a messenger on ahead of him. Before
the messenger arrived, Elisha spoke
to the elders. He said, "That murderer
is sending someone here to cut off my
head. Can't you see that? When the
messenger comes, close the door. Hold
it shut against him. Can't you hear his
master's footsteps right behind him?"
33 Elisha was still talking to the elders
when the messenger came down to him.

The king also arrived. He said, "The
LORD has sent this horrible trouble on
us. Why should I wait any longer for
him to help us?"

7 Elisha replied, "Listen to a message
from the LORD. He says, 'About this
time tomorrow, flour won't cost very
much. Even 12 pounds of the finest flour
will cost less than half of an ounce of
silver. You will also be able to buy 20
pounds of barley for the same price.
That's all you will have to pay for those
things at the gate of Samaria.' "
2 The king was leaning on an officer's
arm. The officer spoke to the man of
God. The officer said, "Suppose the LORD
opens the sky and pours down food on
us. Even if he does, could what you are
saying really happen?"

"You will see it with your own eyes,"
answered Elisha. "But you won't eat
any of it!"

The Attack on Samaria Ends

3 There were four men who had a skin
disease. They were at the entrance of the
gate of Samaria. They said to one another, "Why should we stay here until we
die? 4 Suppose we say, 'We'll go into the
city.' There isn't any food there, and we'll
die. But if we stay here, we'll die anyway.
So let's go over to Aram's army camp.
Let's give ourselves up. If they spare us,
we'll live. If they kill us, we'll die."
5 At sunset they got up and went to
Aram's army camp. They arrived at the
edge of it. But no one was there. 6 The
Lord had caused the soldiers of Aram
to hear a noise. It sounded like chariots
and horses and a huge army. So the
soldiers said to one another, "Listen!
The king of Israel has hired the Hittite

and Egyptian kings. He has paid them to attack us!" 7 So the soldiers of Aram had run away at sunset. They had left their tents and horses and donkeys behind. They had left the camp just as it was. And they had run for their lives.

8 The men who had a skin disease arrived at the edge of the camp. They entered one of the tents. They ate and drank. Then they took silver, gold and clothes. They went off and hid them. They returned and entered another tent. They took some things from it and hid them also.

9 But then they said to one another, "What we're doing isn't right. This is a day of good news. And we're keeping it to ourselves. If we wait until sunrise, we'll be punished. Let's go at once. Let's report this to the royal palace."

10 So they went. They called out to the people who were guarding the city gates. They told them, "We went into Aram's army camp. No one was there. We didn't hear anyone. The horses and donkeys were still tied up. The tents were left just as they were." 11 The people who guarded the gates shouted the news. It was reported inside the palace.

12 The king of Israel got up in the night. He spoke to his officers. He said, "I'll tell you what the men of Aram have done to us. They know we are very hungry. So they have left the camp to hide in the countryside. They are thinking, 'We are sure they'll come out. Then we'll take them alive. And we'll get into the city.' "

13 One of the king's officers said, "A few horses are still left in the city. Have some men get five of them. Those men won't be any worse off than all the other Israelites who are left here. In fact, all of us will soon be dead anyway. So let's send the men to find out what happened."

14 The men chose two chariots and their horses. The king sent them out to look for Aram's army. He commanded the drivers, "Go and find out what has happened." 15 They followed the trail of Aram's soldiers all the way to the Jordan River. They found clothes and supplies all along the road. The soldiers had thrown them down when they ran away. So the men who were sent out returned. They reported to the king what they had seen. 16 Then the people went out of the city. They took everything of value from Aram's army camp. So 12 pounds of the finest flour sold for less than half of an ounce of silver. And 20 pounds of barley sold for the same price. That's exactly what the LORD had said would happen.

17 The king had put an officer in charge of the city gate. He was the officer on whose arm the king leaned. On their way out of the city, the people knocked the officer down. In the entrance of the gate he was crushed as they walked on top of him. And so he died. That's exactly what the man of God had said would happen. He had said it when the king came down to his house. 18 What Elisha, the man of God, had told the king came true. Elisha had said, "About this time tomorrow, flour won't cost very much. Even 12 pounds of the finest flour will cost less than half of an ounce of silver. You will also be able to buy 20 pounds of barley for the same price. That's all you will have to pay for those things at the gate of Samaria."

19 The officer had spoken to the man of God. The officer had said, "Suppose the LORD opens the sky and pours down food on us. Even if he does, could what you are saying really happen?" The man of God had replied, "You will see it with your own eyes. But you won't eat any of it!" 20 And that's exactly what happened to the officer. On their way out of the city, the people knocked him down. In the entrance of the gate he was crushed as they walked on top of him. And so he died.

The Woman From Shunem Gets Her Land Back

8 Elisha had brought a woman's son back to life. He had said to her, "Go away with your family. Stay for a while anywhere you can. The LORD has decided that there won't be enough food in the land. That will be true for seven years." 2 The woman did just as the man of God told her to. She and her family went away. They stayed in the land of the Philistines for seven years.

3 The seven years passed. Then she came back from the land of the Philistines. She went to the king of Israel. She wanted to ask him to get her house and land back. 4 The king was talking to Gehazi. Gehazi was the servant of the

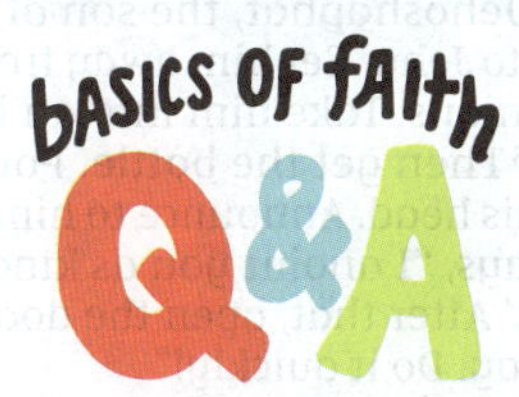

Does God keep his promises?

God always keeps his promises. Sometimes people break promises and don't do what they say they're going to do, but God is always faithful. He keeps his promises even when people disobey him.

Can you find the following verse?
2 KINGS 8:19

man of God. The king had said, "Tell me
about all the great things Elisha has
done." 5 Gehazi was telling the king how
Elisha had brought a dead boy back to
life. Just then the woman came to ask
the king to get her house and land back.
She was the woman whose son Elisha
had brought back to life.
Gehazi said, "King Joram, this is the
woman I've been telling you about.
And this is her son. He's the one Elisha
brought back to life." 6 The king asked
the woman about her house and land.
And she told him.
Then he appointed an official to look
into her case. The king told him, "Give
her back everything that belonged to
her. That includes all the money that was
earned from her land. It was earned from
the day she left the country until now."

Hazael Murders Ben-Hadad

7 Elisha went to Damascus. Ben-
Hadad was sick. He was king of Aram.
The king was told, "The man of God
has come all the way up here." 8 Then
the king said to Hazael, "Take a gift
with you. Go and see the man of God.
Ask him for the LORD's advice. Ask him
whether I will get well again."
9 Hazael went to see Elisha. Hazael
took 40 camels with him as a gift. The
camels were loaded with all the finest
goods of Damascus. Hazael went into
Elisha's house and stood in front of him.
Hazael said, "Ben-Hadad has sent me.
He is the king of Aram. He asks, 'Will I
get well again?' "
10 Elisha answered, "Go and tell him,
'Yes. You will get well again.' But the
LORD has shown me that he will in fact
die." 11 Elisha stared at him without
looking away. He did it until Hazael
felt uncomfortable. Then the man of
God began to weep.
12 "Why are you weeping?" asked Hazael.
"Because I know how much harm you
will do to the people of Israel," Elisha
answered. "You will set fire to their cities that have high walls around them.
You will kill their young men with your
swords. You will smash their little children on the ground. You will rip open
their pregnant women."
13 Hazael said, "How could I possibly
do a thing like that? I'm nothing but a
dog. I don't have that kind of power."
"You will become king of Aram," Elisha answered. "That's what the LORD
has shown me."
14 Then Hazael left Elisha and returned to his master. Ben-Hadad asked,
"What did Elisha say to you?" Hazael
replied, "He told me you would get well
again." 15 But the next day Hazael got
a thick cloth. He soaked it in water. He
spread it over the king's face. He held it
there until the king died. Then Hazael
became the next king after him.

Jehoram King of Judah

16 Jehoram began to rule as king over
Judah. It was in the fifth year that Joram was king of Israel. Joram was the
son of Ahab. Jehoram was the son of
Jehoshaphat. 17 Jehoram was 32 years
old when he became king. He ruled in
Jerusalem for eight years. 18 He followed
the ways of the kings of Israel, just as
the royal family of Ahab had done. In
fact, he married a daughter of Ahab.
Jehoram did what was evil in the sight
of the LORD. 19 But the LORD didn't want to
destroy Judah. That's because the LORD
had made a covenant with his servant
David. The LORD had promised to keep
the lamp of David's kingdom burning
brightly. The LORD had promised that for
him and his children after him forever.

20 When Jehoram was king over Judah,
Edom refused to remain under Judah's
control. Edom set up their own king. 21 So
Jehoram went to Zair. He took all his
chariots with him. The men of Edom
surrounded him and his chariot commanders. He got up at night and fought
his way out. But his army ran back home.
22 To this day Edom has refused to remain
under Judah's control. When Jehoram
was Judah's king, Libnah also refused
to remain under the control of Judah.

23 The other events of Jehoram's rule
are written down. Everything he did
is written in the official records of the
kings of Judah. 24 Jehoram joined the
members of his family who had already
died. He was buried in the family tomb
in the City of David. Jehoram's son Ahaziah became the next king after him.

Ahaziah King of Judah

25 Ahaziah began to rule as king over
Judah. It was in the 12th year that Joram
was king of Israel. Joram was the son of
Ahab. Ahaziah was the son of Jehoram.
26 Ahaziah was 22 years old when he
became king. He ruled in Jerusalem
for one year. His mother's name was
Athaliah. She was a granddaughter of
Omri. Omri had been the king of Israel.
27 Ahaziah followed the ways of the royal
family of Ahab. Ahaziah did what was
evil in the sight of the LORD, just as the
family of Ahab had done. That's because
he had married into Ahab's family.

28 Ahaziah joined forces with Joram.
They went to war against Hazael at
Ramoth Gilead. Joram was the son of
Ahab. Hazael was king of Aram. The
soldiers of Aram wounded King Joram.
29 So he returned to Jezreel to give his
wounds time to heal. The soldiers of
Aram had wounded him at Ramoth
in his battle against Hazael, the king
of Aram.

Ahaziah, the son of Jehoram, went
down to Jezreel. He went there to see
Joram. That's because Joram had been
wounded. Ahaziah was king of Judah.
Joram was the son of Ahab.

Jehu Is Anointed as King of Israel

9 Elisha the prophet sent for a man
from the group of the prophets.
Elisha said to him, "Tuck your coat into
your belt. Take this bottle of olive oil
with you. Go to Ramoth Gilead. 2 When
you get there, look for Jehu. He's the
son of Jehoshaphat, the son of Nimshi. Go to Jehu. Get him away from his
companions. Take him into an inside
room. 3 Then get the bottle. Pour the
oil on his head. Announce to him, 'The
LORD says, "I anoint you as king over
Israel." ' After that, open the door and
run away. Do it quickly!"

4 So the young prophet went to Ramoth Gilead. 5 When he arrived, he
found the army officers sitting together. "Commander, I have a message for
you," he said.

"For which one of us?" asked Jehu.

"For you, commander," he replied.

6 Jehu got up and went into the house.
Then the prophet poured the oil on Jehu's head. He announced, "The LORD is
the God of Israel. He says, 'I am anointing you as king over the LORD's people
Israel. 7 You must destroy the royal house
of your master Ahab. I will pay them
back for spilling the blood of my servants
the prophets. I will also pay them back
for the blood of all the LORD's servants
that Jezebel spilled. 8 The whole house
of Ahab will die out. I will destroy every
male in Israel who is related to Ahab. It
does not matter whether they are slaves
or free. 9 I will make Ahab's royal house
like the house of Jeroboam, the son of
Nebat. I will make it like the house of
Baasha, the son of Ahijah. 10 Dogs will eat
up Jezebel on a piece of land at Jezreel.
No one will bury her.' " Then the prophet
opened the door and ran away.

11 Jehu went out to where the other
officers were. One of them asked him,
"Is everything all right? Why did that
crazy man come to you?"

"You know the man. You know the
kinds of things he says," Jehu replied.

12 "That's not true!" they said. "Tell us."

Jehu said, "Here is what he told me.
He announced, 'The LORD says, "I am
anointing you as king over Israel." ' "

13 The officers quickly grabbed their
coats. They spread them out under Jehu
on the bare steps of the house. Then
they blew a trumpet. They shouted,
"Jehu is king!"

Jehu Kills Joram and Ahaziah

14 Jehu was the son of Jehoshaphat, the
son of Nimshi. Jehu made plans against
Joram. During that time Joram and

Israel's whole army had been guarding Ramoth Gilead. They had been guarding it against Hazael, the king of Aram. 15 But King Joram had returned to Jezreel. He had gone there to give his wounds time to heal. The soldiers of Aram had wounded him in his battle against Hazael, the king of Aram. Jehu said to his men, "Do you want to make me king? If you do, don't let anyone sneak out of the city. Don't let them go and tell the news in Jezreel." 16 Then Jehu got into his chariot. He rode off to Jezreel. Joram was resting there. And Ahaziah, the king of Judah, had gone down to see him.

17 A lookout was standing on the roof of the tower in Jezreel. He saw Jehu's troops approaching. So he called out, "I see some troops coming."

"Get a horseman," Joram ordered. "Send him to ride out to them. Have him ask, 'Are you coming in peace?' "

18 The horseman rode out to where Jehu was. He said, "The king asks, 'Are you coming in peace?' "

"What do you know about peace?" Jehu answered. "Get in line behind me."

The lookout reported, "The messenger has reached them. But he isn't coming back."

19 So the king sent out a second horseman. When he came to them, he said, "The king asks, 'Are you coming in peace?' "

Jehu replied, "What do you know about peace? Get in line behind me."

20 The lookout reported, "The second messenger has reached them. But he isn't coming back either. The one driving the chariot drives like Jehu, the son of Nimshi. He's driving like a crazy person."

21 "Get my chariot ready," King Joram ordered. When it was ready, he rode out. Ahaziah, the king of Judah, rode out with him. Each of them was in his own chariot. They both went to meet Jehu. They met him at the piece of land that had belonged to Naboth from Jezreel. 22 When Joram saw Jehu he asked, "Have you come here in peace, Jehu?"

"Your mother Jezebel worships statues of gods," Jehu replied. "She also worships evil powers. The evil things she does have spread everywhere. As long as all of that goes on, how can there be peace?"

23 Joram turned around and tried to get away. He called out, "It's treason, Ahaziah!"

24 Then Jehu shot an arrow at Joram. It hit him between the shoulders. It went through his heart. He sank down slowly in his chariot. 25 Jehu spoke to Bidkar, his chariot officer. Jehu said, "Pick Joram up. Throw him on the field that belonged to Naboth from Jezreel. Remember how you and I were riding together in chariots behind Joram's father Ahab? It was when the LORD spoke this prophecy against him. The LORD announced, 26 'Yesterday I saw the blood of Naboth and the blood of his sons. You can be sure that I will make you pay for it on this piece of land.' So pick Joram up. Throw him on that piece of land. That's what the LORD said would happen."

27 Ahaziah, the king of Judah, saw what had happened. So he tried to get away. He went up the road toward Beth Haggan. Jehu chased him. He shouted, "Kill him too!" Jehu's men wounded Ahaziah in his chariot. It happened on the way up to Gur near Ibleam. But Ahaziah escaped to Megiddo. And that's where he died. 28 Ahaziah's servants took him to Jerusalem in his chariot. They buried him in his family tomb in the City of David. 29 Ahaziah had become king of Judah. It was in the 11th year of Joram, the son of Ahab.

Jehu Kills Jezebel

30 Jehu went to Jezreel. Jezebel heard about it. So she put makeup on her eyes and fixed her hair. Then she looked out of a window. 31 Jehu entered the gate below. Jezebel said to him, "You are just like Zimri. You murdered your master. Have you come here in peace?"

32 Jehu looked up at the window. "Who is on my side?" he called out. "Who?" Two or three officials looked down at him. 33 "Throw her down!" Jehu said. So they threw her down. Some of her blood splashed on the wall. Some of it splashed on Jehu's chariot horses as they ran over her.

34 Jehu went inside. He ate and drank. "The LORD put a curse on that woman," he said. "Take proper care of her body. Bury her. After all, she was a king's daughter." 35 So they went out to bury her. But all they found was her head,

feet and hands. 36 They went back and
reported it to Jehu. He told them, "That's
what the LORD said would happen. He
announced it through his servant Elijah, who was from Tishbe. He said, 'On
a piece of land at Jezreel, dogs will eat
up Jezebel's body. 37 Her body will end
up as garbage on that piece of land. So
no one will be able to say, "Here's where
Jezebel is buried." ' "

Jehu Wipes Out Ahab's Royal House

10 Ahab's royal family in the city of
Samaria had a total of 70 sons.
Jehu wrote some letters to the officials
of the city. He also sent them to the
elders there. And he sent them to the
people who took care of Ahab's children.
Jehu said, 2 "Your master's sons are with
you. You also have chariots and horses
and weapons. And you are living in
a city that has high walls around it.
As soon as you read this letter, here's
what I want you to do. 3 Choose the
best and most respected son of your
master. Place him on his father Joram's
throne. Then fight for your master's
royal house."

4 The leaders of Samaria were terri-
fied. They said, "King Joram and King
Ahaziah couldn't stand up against Jehu.
So how can we?"

5 The city governor and the person in
charge of the palace sent a message to
Jehu. The message was also from the
elders and the people who took care of
Ahab's children. In the message, they
said, "We will serve you. We'll do anything you say. We won't appoint anyone
to be king. Do what you think is best."

6 Then Jehu wrote them a second letter. He said, "You say you are on my
side. You say you will obey me. If you
really mean it, bring me the heads of
your master's sons. Meet me in Jezreel
by this time tomorrow."

There were 70 royal princes. They
were with the most important men of
the city. Those men were in charge of
raising them. 7 When Jehu's letter arrived, the men went and got the princes.
They killed all 70 of them. They put their
heads in baskets. Then they sent them
to Jehu in Jezreel. 8 When the messenger
arrived, he spoke to Jehu. He told him,
"The heads of the princes have been
brought here."

Then Jehu ordered his men, "Put
them in two piles. Stack them up at the
entrance of the city gate until morning."

9 The next morning Jehu went out.
He stood in front of all the people. He
said, "You aren't guilty of doing anything wrong. I'm the one who made
plans against my master Joram. I killed
him. But who killed all these? 10 I want
you to know that the LORD has spoken
against Ahab's royal house. Not a word
of what he has said will fail. The LORD
has done exactly what he announced
through his servant Elijah." 11 So Jehu
killed everyone from Ahab's family who
was in Jezreel. He also killed all Ahab's
chief men. And he killed Ahab's close
friends and his priests. He didn't leave
anyone alive in Ahab's family.

12 Then Jehu started out for Samaria.
At Beth Eked of the Shepherds, 13 he saw
some people. They were relatives of
Ahaziah, the king of Judah. Jehu asked
them, "Who are you?"

They said, "We are Ahaziah's relatives. We've come down to visit the
families of the king and of his mother."

14 "Take them alive!" Jehu ordered.
So his men took them alive. Then they
killed them by the well of Beth Eked.
They killed a total of 42 of them. Jehu
didn't leave anyone alive.

15 Jehu left there. On the way he met
Jehonadab. He was the son of Rekab.
Jehonadab was on his way to see Jehu.
Jehu greeted him. He asked, "Are you
my friend? You know I'm your friend."

"I am," Jehonadab answered.

"If that's true," said Jehu, "hold out
your hand." So he did. Then Jehu helped
him up into the chariot. 16 Jehu said,
"Come along with me. See how committed I am to serve the LORD." Jehu had
Jehonadab ride along in his chariot.

17 Jehu came to Samaria. He killed everyone there who was left from Ahab's
family. And so he completely destroyed
Ahab's royal house. That's what the
LORD had said would happen. He had
spoken that message to Elijah.

Jehu Kills the People Who Serve Baal

18 Then Jehu brought together all the
people. He said to them, "Ahab served the
god named Baal a little. I will serve him
a lot. 19 Send for all of Baal's prophets.
Also send for all his priests and the others

who serve him. Make sure that not a
single one is missing. I'm going to hold
a great sacrifice to honor Baal. Anyone
who doesn't come will be killed." But Jehu
was lying to them. He was planning to
destroy everyone who served Baal.
20 Jehu said, "Call everyone together to honor Baal." So they did. 21 Then
he sent a message all through Israel.
All those who served Baal came. Not a
single one of them stayed away. They
crowded into Baal's temple. It was full
from one end to the other. 22 Jehu spoke
to the one who took care of the sacred
robes. He told him, "Bring robes for everyone who serves Baal." So he brought
the robes out for them.
23 Then Jehu went into Baal's temple.
Jehonadab, the son of Rekab, went with
him. Jehu said to those who served Baal,
"Look around. Make sure that no one
who serves the LORD is here with you.
Make sure only those who serve Baal are
here." 24 So they went in to offer sacrifices
and burnt offerings. Jehu had stationed
80 men outside. He warned them, "I'm
placing some men in your hands. Don't
let a single one of them escape. If you
do, you will pay for his life with yours."
25 Jehu finished sacrificing the burnt
offering. As soon as he did, he gave an
order to the guards and officers. He
commanded them, "Go inside and kill
everyone. Don't let a single one of them
escape." So they cut them down with
their swords. The guards and officers
threw the bodies outside. Then they entered the most sacred area inside Baal's
temple. 26 They brought the sacred stone
of Baal outside. They burned it up. 27 So
they destroyed Baal's sacred stone. They
also tore down Baal's temple. People
have used it as a public toilet to this day.
28 So Jehu destroyed the worship of
the god named Baal in Israel. 29 But
he didn't turn away from the sins of
Jeroboam, the son of Nebat. Jeroboam
had caused Israel to commit those same
sins. Jehu worshiped the golden calves
at Bethel and Dan.
30 The LORD said to Jehu, "You have
done well. You have accomplished what
is right in my eyes. You have done to
Ahab's royal house everything I wanted
you to do. So your sons after you will
sit on the throne of Israel. They will
rule until the time of your children's
grandchildren." 31 But Jehu wasn't careful to obey the law of the LORD. He didn't
obey the God of Israel with all his heart.
He didn't turn away from the sins of
Jeroboam. Jeroboam had caused Israel
to commit those same sins.
32 In those days the LORD began to
make the kingdom of Israel smaller.
Hazael gained control over many parts
of Israel. He gained control over all their
territory 33 east of the Jordan River. It
included the whole land of Gilead from
Aroer by the Arnon River valley all the
way to Bashan. That was the territory
of Gad, Reuben and Manasseh.
34 The other events of Jehu's rule are
written down. Everything he did and
accomplished is written in the official
records of the kings of Israel.
35 Jehu joined the members of his family who had already died. He was buried
in Samaria. His son Jehoahaz became
the next king after him. 36 Jehu had ruled
over Israel in Samaria for 28 years.

Athaliah and Joash

11 Athaliah was Ahaziah's mother.
She saw that her son was dead. So
she began to destroy the whole royal
house of Judah. 2 But Jehosheba went
and got Joash, the son of Ahaziah.
Jehosheba was the daughter of King
Jehoram and the sister of Ahaziah. She
stole Joash away from among the royal
princes. All of them were about to be
murdered. She put Joash and his nurse
in a bedroom. That's how she hid him
from Athaliah. And that's why Athaliah
didn't kill him. 3 The child remained hidden with his nurse at the LORD's temple
for six years. Athaliah ruled over the
land during that time.
4 In the seventh year Jehoiada the
priest sent for the commanders of military groups of 100 men. They were the
commanders over the Carites and the
guards. Jehoiada had them brought to
him at the temple of the LORD. He made
a covenant with them. At the temple
he made them promise to be faithful.
Then he showed them the king's son.
5 He gave them a command. He said,
"Here's what you must do. There are
five groups of you. Some of you are in
the three groups that are going on duty
on the Sabbath day. A third of you must
guard the royal palace. 6 A third of you

must guard the Sur Gate. And a third of you must guard the gate that is behind the guard. All of you must take turns guarding the temple. 7 The rest of you are in the other two groups. Normally you are not on duty on the Sabbath day. But you also must guard the temple for the king. 8 Station yourselves around the king. Each of you must have his weapon in his hand. Anyone else who approaches your groups must be put to death. Stay close to the king no matter where he goes."

9 The commanders of the military groups did just as Jehoiada the priest ordered. Each commander got his men and came to Jehoiada. Some of the men were going on duty on the Sabbath day. Others were going off duty. 10 Then Jehoiada gave weapons to the commanders. He gave them spears and shields. The weapons had belonged to King David. They had been in the LORD's temple. 11 The guards stationed themselves around the new king. Each of them had his weapon in his hand. They were near the altar and the temple. They stood from the south side of the temple to its north side.

12 Jehoiada brought out Ahaziah's son. He put the crown on him. He gave him a copy of the covenant. And he announced that Joash was king. Jehoiada and his sons anointed him. The people clapped their hands. Then they shouted, "May the king live a long time!"

13 Athaliah heard the noise the guards and the people were making. So she went to the people at the LORD's temple. 14 She looked, and there was the king! He was standing next to the pillar. That was the usual practice. The officers and trumpet players were standing beside the king. All the people of the land were filled with joy. They were blowing trumpets. Then Athaliah tore her royal robes. She called out, "Treason! It's treason!"

15 Jehoiada the priest gave an order to the commanders of the military groups of 100 men. The commanders were in charge of the troops. He said to them, "Bring her away from the temple between the line of guards. Use your swords to kill anyone who follows her." The priest had said, "She must not be put to death at the LORD's temple." 16 So they grabbed her as she reached the place where the horses enter the palace grounds. There she was put to death.

17 Then Jehoiada made a covenant between the LORD and the king and people. He had the king and people promise that they would be the LORD's people. Jehoiada also made a covenant between the king and the people. 18 All the people of the land went to Baal's temple. They tore it down. They smashed to pieces the altars and the statues of gods. They killed Mattan in front of the altars. He was the priest of Baal.

Then Jehoiada the priest stationed guards at the temple of the LORD. 19 Jehoiada took with him the commanders of groups of 100 men. They were the commanders over the Carites and the guards. He also took with him all the people of the land. All of them brought the new king down from the LORD's temple. They went into the palace. They entered it by going through the gate of the guards. Then the king sat down on the royal throne. 20 All the people of the land were filled with joy. And the city was calm. That's because Athaliah had been killed with a sword at the palace.

21 Joash was seven years old when he became king.

Joash Repairs the Temple

12 Joash became king of Judah. It was in the seventh year of Jehu's rule. Joash ruled in Jerusalem for 40 years. His mother's name was Zibiah. She was from Beersheba. 2 Joash did what was right in the eyes of the LORD. Joash lived that way as long as Jehoiada the priest was teaching him. 3 But the high places weren't removed. The people continued to offer sacrifices and burn incense there.

4 Joash spoke to the priests. He said, "Collect all the money the people bring as sacred offerings to the LORD's temple. That includes the money collected when the men who are able to serve in the army are counted. It includes the money received from people who make a special promise to the LORD. It also includes the money people bring to the temple just because they want to. 5 Let each priest receive the money from one of the people in charge of the temple's treasures. Then use all of that money to repair the temple where it needs it."

6 It was now the 23rd year of the rule of King Joash. And the priests still hadn't repaired the temple. 7 So the king sent for Jehoiada the priest and the other priests. He asked them, "Why aren't you repairing the temple where it needs it? Don't take any more money from the people in charge of the treasures. Instead, hand it over so the temple can be repaired." 8 The priests agreed that they wouldn't collect any more money from the people. They also agreed that they wouldn't repair the temple themselves.

9 Jehoiada the priest got a chest. He drilled a hole in its lid. He placed the chest beside the altar for burnt offerings. The chest was on the right side as people enter the LORD's temple. Some priests guarded the entrance. They put into the chest all the money the people brought to the temple. 10 From time to time there was a large amount of money in the chest. When that happened, the royal secretary and the high priest came. They counted the money the people had brought to the temple. Then they put it into bags. 11 After they added it all up, they used it to repair the temple. They gave it to the men who had been put in charge of the work. Those men used it to pay the workers. They paid the builders and those who worked with wood. 12 They paid those who cut stones and those who laid them. They bought lumber and blocks of stone. So they used the money to repair the LORD's temple. They also paid all the other costs to make the temple like new again.

13 The money the people brought to the LORD's temple wasn't used to make silver bowls. It wasn't used for wick cutters, sprinkling bowls or trumpets. And it wasn't used for any other things made out of gold or silver. 14 Instead, it was paid to the workers. They used it to repair the temple. 15 The royal secretary and the high priest didn't require a report from those who were in charge of the work. That's because they were completely honest. They always paid the workers. 16 Money was received from people who brought guilt offerings and sin offerings. But it wasn't taken to the LORD's temple. It belonged to the priests.

17 About that time Hazael, the king of Aram, went up and attacked Gath. Then he captured it. After that, he turned back to attack Jerusalem. 18 But Joash, the king of Judah, didn't want to go to war. So he took all the sacred objects. They had been set apart to the LORD by the kings who had ruled over Judah before him. Those kings were Jehoshaphat, Jehoram and Ahaziah. Joash took the gifts he himself had set apart. He took all the gold that was among the temple treasures. He also took all the gold from the royal palace. He sent all those things to Hazael, the king of Aram. Then Hazael pulled his army back from Jerusalem.

19 The other events of the rule of Joash are written down. Everything he did is written in the official records of the kings of Judah. 20 The officials of Joash made evil plans against him. They killed him at Beth Millo. It happened on the road that goes down to Silla. 21 The officials who murdered him were Jozabad and Jehozabad. Jozabad was the son of Shimeath. Jehozabad was the son of Shomer. After Joash died, he was buried in the family tomb in the City of David. Joash's son Amaziah became the next king after him.

Jehoahaz King of Israel

13 Jehoahaz became king of Israel in Samaria. It was in the 23rd year of the rule of Joash, the king of Judah. Jehoahaz ruled for 17 years. Joash was the son of Ahaziah. Jehoahaz was the son of Jehu. 2 Jehoahaz did what was evil in the eyes of the LORD. He committed the sins Jeroboam, the son of Nebat, had committed. Jeroboam had caused Israel to commit those same sins. Jehoahaz didn't turn away from them. 3 So the LORD was very angry with Israel. For a long time he kept them under the power of Hazael, the king of Aram. The LORD also kept them under the power of his son Ben-Hadad.

4 Then Jehoahaz asked the LORD for help. The LORD listened to him. The LORD saw how badly the king of Aram was treating Israel. 5 The LORD provided someone to save Israel. And they escaped from the power of Aram. So the Israelites lived in their own homes, just as they had before. 6 But the people didn't turn away from the sins of the royal house of Jeroboam. He had caused Israel to commit those same sins. The people continued to commit them. And the pole used to

worship the female god named Asherah
remained standing in Samaria.
7 The army of Jehoahaz had almost
nothing left. All it had was 50 horsemen,
10 chariots and 10,000 soldiers on foot.
The king of Aram had destroyed the rest
of them. He had made them like dust
at threshing time.
8 The other events of the rule of Jehoahaz are written down. Everything he
did and accomplished is written in the
official records of the kings of Israel.
9 Jehoahaz joined the members of his
family who had already died. He was
buried in Samaria. Jehoahaz's son Jehoash became the next king after him.

Jehoash King of Israel

10 Jehoash became king of Israel in
Samaria. It was in the 37th year that
Joash was king of Judah. Jehoash ruled
for 16 years. He was the son of Jehoahaz.
11 Jehoash did what was evil in the eyes
of the LORD. Jehoash didn't turn away
from any of the sins of Jeroboam, the
son of Nebat. Jeroboam had caused
Israel to commit those same sins. And
Jehoash continued to commit them.
12 The other events of the rule of Jehoash are written down. That includes
his war against Amaziah, the king of
Judah. Everything he did and accomplished is written in the official records of
the kings of Israel. 13 Jehoash joined the
members of his family who had already
died. He was buried in the royal tombs
in Samaria. Jeroboam became the next
king on Israel's throne after him.
14 Elisha had been suffering from a
sickness. Later he would die from it.
Jehoash, the king of Israel, went down
to see him. Jehoash wept over him. "My
father!" he cried. "You are like a father
to me! You, Elisha, are the true chariots
and horsemen of Israel!"
15 Elisha said to Jehoash, "Get a bow
and some arrows." So he did. 16 "Hold
the bow in your hands," Elisha said to
the king of Israel. So Jehoash took hold
of the bow. Then Elisha put his hands
on the king's hands.
17 "Open the east window," Elisha said.
So he did. "Shoot!" Elisha said. So he
shot. "That's the LORD's arrow!" Elisha
announced. "It means you will win the
battle over Aram! You will completely
destroy the men of Aram at Aphek."
18 Elisha continued, "Get some arrows." So the king did. Elisha told him,
"Strike the ground." Jehoash struck it
three times. Then he stopped. 19 The
man of God was angry with him. He
said, "You should have struck the
ground five or six times. Then you
would have won the war over Aram.
You would have completely destroyed
them. But now you will win only three
battles over them."
20 Elisha died and was buried.
Some robbers from Moab used to enter the country of Israel every spring.
21 One day some Israelites were burying
a man. Suddenly they saw a group of
robbers. So they threw the man's body
into Elisha's tomb. The body touched
Elisha's bones. When it did, the man
came back to life again. He stood up
on his feet.
22 Hazael, the king of Aram, treated
Israel badly. He did it the whole time
Jehoahaz was king. 23 But the LORD
helped Israel. He was tender and kind
to them. He showed concern for them.
He did all these things because of the
covenant he had made with Abraham,
Isaac and Jacob. To this day he hasn't
been willing to destroy Israel. And he
hasn't driven them out of his land.
24 Hazael, the king of Aram, died. His
son Ben-Hadad became the next king
after him. 25 Then Jehoash won back
some towns from Ben-Hadad, the son of
Hazael. Ben-Hadad had captured them
in battle from Jehoahaz, the father of
Jehoash. Jehoash won three battles
over Ben-Hadad. So Jehoash won back
the Israelite towns.

Amaziah King of Judah

14 Amaziah began to rule as king
over Judah. It was in the second
year that Jehoash was king of Israel. He
was the son of Jehoahaz. Amaziah was
the son of Joash. 2 Amaziah was 25 years
old when he became king. He ruled in
Jerusalem for 29 years. His mother's
name was Jehoaddan. She was from
Jerusalem. 3 Amaziah did what was
right in the eyes of the LORD. But he
didn't do what King David had done. He
always followed the example of his father Joash. 4 But the high places weren't
removed. The people continued to offer
sacrifices and burn incense there.

[5]The kingdom was firmly under his
control. So he put to death the officials
who had murdered his father, the
king. [6]But he didn't put their children
to death. He obeyed what is written in
the Book of the Law of Moses. There
the LORD commanded, "Parents must
not be put to death because of what
their children do. And children must not
be put to death because of what their
parents do. People must die because
of their own sins." *(Deuteronomy 24:16)*
[7]Amaziah won the battle over 10,000
men of Edom. It happened in the Valley
of Salt. During the battle he captured
the town of Sela. He called it Joktheel.
That's the name it still has to this day.
[8]After the battle, Amaziah sent messengers to Jehoash, the king of Israel.
Jehoash was the son of Jehoahaz, the
son of Jehu. Amaziah said, "Come on.
Let us face each other in battle."

[9]But Jehoash, the king of Israel, answered Amaziah, the king of Judah.
Jehoash said, "A thorn bush in Lebanon
sent a message to a cedar tree there. The
thorn bush said, 'Give your daughter to
be married to my son.' Then a wild animal in Lebanon came along. It crushed
the thorn bush by walking on it. [10]It's
true that you have won the battle over
Edom. So you are proud. Enjoy your
success while you can. But stay home
and enjoy it! Why ask for trouble? Why
bring yourself crashing down? Why
bring Judah down with you?"

[11]But Amaziah wouldn't listen. So
Jehoash, the king of Israel, attacked.
He and Amaziah, the king of Judah,
faced each other in battle. The battle
took place at Beth Shemesh in Judah.
[12]Israel drove Judah away. Every man
ran home. [13]Jehoash king of Israel
captured Amaziah king of Judah at
Beth Shemesh. Amaziah was the son
of Joash. Joash was the son of Ahaziah.
Jehoash went to Jerusalem. He broke
down part of its wall. It's the part that
went from the Ephraim Gate to the
Corner Gate. That part of the wall was
600 feet long. [14]Jehoash took all the
gold, silver and objects that were in the
LORD's temple. He also took all those
same kinds of things that were among
the treasures of the royal palace. And
he took prisoners. Then he returned to
Samaria.

[15]The other events of the rule of Jehoash are written down. That includes
his war against Amaziah, the king of
Judah. Everything he did and accomplished is written in the official records
of the kings of Israel. [16]Jehoash joined
the members of his family who had
already died. He was buried in Samaria
in the royal tombs of Israel. Jehoash's
son Jeroboam became the next king
after him.

[17]Amaziah king of Judah lived for 15
years after Jehoash king of Israel died.
Amaziah was the son of Joash. Jehoash
was the son of Jehoahaz. [18]The other
events of Amaziah's rule are written
down. They are written in the official
records of the kings of Judah.

[19]Some people made evil plans
against Amaziah in Jerusalem. So he
ran away to Lachish. But they sent men
to Lachish after him. There they killed
him. [20]His body was brought back on a
horse. Then he was buried in the family
tomb in Jerusalem, the City of David.

[21]All the people of Judah made Uzziah
king. He was 16 years old. They made
him king in place of his father Amaziah.
[22]Uzziah rebuilt Elath. He brought it
under Judah's control again. He did it
after Amaziah joined the members of
his family who had already died.

Jeroboam II King of Israel

[23]Jeroboam became king of Israel
in Samaria. It was in the 15th year that
Amaziah was king of Judah. Jeroboam
ruled for 41 years. Amaziah was the
son of Joash. Jeroboam was the son
of Jehoash. [24]Jeroboam did what was
evil in the eyes of the LORD. He didn't
turn away from any of the sins the
earlier Jeroboam, the son of Nebat,
had committed. That Jeroboam had
caused Israel to commit those same
sins. [25]Jeroboam, the son of Jehoash,
made the borders of Israel the same as
they were before. They reached from
Lebo Hamath all the way to the Dead
Sea. That's what the LORD, the God of
Israel, had said would happen. He had
spoken that message through his servant Jonah. Jonah the prophet was the
son of Amittai. Jonah was from the town
of Gath Hepher.

[26]The LORD had seen how much everyone in Israel was suffering. It didn't

matter whether they were slaves or free. They didn't have anyone to help them. 27 The LORD hadn't said he would wipe out Israel's name from the earth. So he saved them by the power of Jeroboam, the son of Jehoash.

28 The other events of the rule of Jeroboam are written down. What he and his army accomplished is written down. That includes how he brought Damascus and Hamath back under Israel's control. Damascus and Hamath had belonged to the territory of Judah. Everything he did is written in the official records of the kings of Israel. 29 Jeroboam joined the members of his family who had already died. He was buried in the royal tombs of Israel. Jeroboam's son Zechariah became the next king after him.

Uzziah King of Judah

15 Uzziah began to rule as king over Judah. It was in the 27th year that Jeroboam was king of Israel. Uzziah was the son of Amaziah. 2 Uzziah was 16 years old when he became king. He ruled in Jerusalem for 52 years. His mother's name was Jekoliah. She was from Jerusalem. 3 Uzziah did what was right in the eyes of the LORD, just as his father Amaziah had done. 4 But the high places weren't removed. The people continued to offer sacrifices and burn incense there.

5 The LORD caused King Uzziah to suffer from a skin disease until the day he died. He lived in a separate house. His son Jotham was in charge of the palace. Jotham ruled over the people of the land.

6 The other events of the rule of Uzziah are written down. Everything he did is written in the official records of the kings of Judah. 7 Uzziah joined the members of his family who had already died. He was buried near them in the City of David. Uzziah's son Jotham became the next king after him.

Zechariah King of Israel

8 Zechariah became king of Israel in Samaria. It was in the 38th year that Uzziah was king of Judah. Zechariah ruled for six months. He was the son of Jeroboam, the son of Jehoash. 9 Zechariah did what was evil in the eyes of the LORD. He did what the kings of Israel before him had done. He didn't turn away from the sins Jeroboam, the son of Nebat, had committed. Jeroboam had caused Israel to commit those same sins.

10 Shallum made evil plans against Zechariah. He attacked Zechariah in front of the people and killed him. Then he became the next king after him. Shallum was the son of Jabesh. 11 The other events of the rule of Zechariah are written down. They are written in the official records of the kings of Israel. 12 What happened to Zechariah is what the LORD said would happen. He had spoken that message to Jehu. The LORD had said, "Your sons after you will sit on the throne of Israel. They will rule until the time of your children's grandchildren." *(2 Kings 10:30)*

Shallum King of Israel

13 Shallum became king of Israel. It was in the 39th year that Uzziah was king of Judah. Shallum ruled in Samaria for one month. He was the son of Jabesh. 14 Menahem went from Tirzah up to Samaria. There he attacked Shallum, the son of Jabesh. Menahem killed him and became the next king after him. Menahem was the son of Gadi.

15 The other events of Shallum's rule are written down. The evil things he planned are written down. All these things are written in the official records of the kings of Israel.

16 At that time Menahem started out from Tirzah and attacked Tiphsah. He attacked everyone in the city and the area around it. That's because they refused to open their gates for him. He destroyed Tiphsah. He ripped open all their pregnant women.

Menahem King of Israel

17 Menahem became king of Israel. It was in the 39th year that Uzziah was king of Judah. Menahem ruled in Samaria for ten years. He was the son of Gadi. 18 Menahem did what was evil in the eyes of the LORD. During his entire rule he didn't turn away from the sins Jeroboam, the son of Nebat, had committed. Jeroboam had caused Israel to commit those same sins.

19 Then Tiglath-Pileser marched into the land of Israel. He was king of Assyria. Menahem gave him 38 tons of

silver to get his help. He wanted to make his control over the kingdom stronger. 20 Menahem forced Israel to give him that money. Every wealthy person had to give him 20 ounces of silver. All of it went to the king of Assyria. So he pulled his troops back. He didn't stay in the land anymore.

21 The other events of the rule of Menahem are written down. Everything he did is written in the official records of the kings of Israel. 22 Menahem joined the members of his family who had already died. Menahem's son Pekahiah became the next king after him.

Pekahiah King of Israel

23 Pekahiah became king of Israel in Samaria. It was in the 50th year that Uzziah was king of Judah. Pekahiah ruled for two years. He was the son of Menahem. 24 Pekahiah did what was evil in the eyes of the LORD. He didn't turn away from the sins Jeroboam, the son of Nebat, had committed. Jeroboam had caused Israel to commit those same sins. 25 One of Pekahiah's chief officers was Pekah. He was the son of Remaliah. Pekah made evil plans against Pekahiah. He took 50 men from Gilead with him and killed Pekahiah. Pekah also killed Argob and Arieh. He killed all of them in the safest place in the royal palace at Samaria. So Pekah killed Pekahiah. He became the next king after him.

26 The other events of the rule of Pekahiah are written down. Everything he did is written in the official records of the kings of Israel.

Pekah King of Israel

27 Pekah became king of Israel in Samaria. It was in the 52nd year that Uzziah was king of Judah. Pekah ruled for 20 years. He was the son of Remaliah. 28 Pekah did what was evil in the eyes of the LORD. He didn't turn away from the sins Jeroboam, the son of Nebat, had committed. Jeroboam had caused Israel to commit those same sins.

29 During the rule of Pekah, the king of Israel, Tiglath-Pileser marched into the land again. He was king of Assyria. He captured the towns of Ijon, Abel Beth Maakah, Janoah, Kedesh and Hazor. He also captured the lands of Gilead and Galilee. That included the whole territory of Naphtali. He took the people away from their own land. He sent them off to Assyria. 30 Then Hoshea made evil plans against Pekah, the son of Remaliah. Hoshea was the son of Elah. Hoshea attacked Pekah and killed him. Then Hoshea became the next king after him. It was in the 20th year of the rule of Jotham, the son of Uzziah.

31 The other events of the rule of Pekah are written down. Everything he did is written in the official records of the kings of Israel.

Jotham King of Judah

32 Jotham began to rule as king over Judah. It was in the second year that Pekah was king of Israel. He was the son of Remaliah. Jotham was the son of Uzziah. 33 Jotham was 25 years old when he became king. He ruled in Jerusalem for 16 years. His mother's name was Jerusha. She was the daughter of Zadok. 34 Jotham did what was right in the eyes of the LORD, just as his father Uzziah had done. 35 But the high places weren't removed. The people continued to offer sacrifices and burn incense there. Jotham rebuilt the Upper Gate of the LORD's temple.

36 The other events of the rule of Jotham are written down. Everything he did is written in the official records of the kings of Judah. 37 In those days the LORD began to send Rezin and Pekah against Judah. Rezin was king of Aram. Pekah was the son of Remaliah. 38 Jotham joined the members of his family who had already died. He was buried in the family tomb in the city of King David. Jotham's son Ahaz became the next king after him.

Ahaz King of Judah

16 Ahaz began to rule as king over Judah. It was in the 17th year of the rule of Pekah, the son of Remaliah. Ahaz was the son of Jotham. 2 Ahaz was 20 years old when he became king. He ruled in Jerusalem for 16 years. Ahaz didn't do what was right in the eyes of the LORD his God. He didn't do what King David had done. 3 He followed the ways of the kings of Israel. He even sacrificed his son in the fire to another god. He followed the practices of the nations. The LORD hated those practices. He had driven out those nations to make room for the Israelites. 4 Ahaz

offered sacrifices and burned incense
at the high places. He also did it on the
tops of hills and under every green tree.
5 Rezin and Pekah marched up to Jerusalem and surrounded it. Rezin was
king of Aram. Pekah, the son of Remaliah, was king of Israel. They attacked
Ahaz. But they couldn't overpower him.
6 At that time Rezin, the king of Aram,
won back Elath for Aram. He drove out
the people of Judah. Then the people of
Edom moved into Elath. And they still
live there to this day.
7 Ahaz sent messengers to Tiglath-
Pileser. He was king of Assyria. The message of Ahaz said, "I am your servant.
You are my master. Come up and save
me from the power of the kings of Aram
and Israel. They are attacking me." 8 Ahaz
took the silver and gold that were in the
LORD's temple. He also took the silver
and gold that were among the treasures
in the royal palace. He sent all of it as a
gift to the king of Assyria. 9 So the king of
Assyria did what Ahaz asked him to do.
He attacked the city of Damascus and
captured it. He sent its people away to
Kir. And he put Rezin to death.
10 Then King Ahaz went to Damascus.
He went there to see Tiglath-Pileser, the
king of Assyria. Ahaz saw an altar in Damascus. He sent a drawing of it to Uriah
the priest. Ahaz also sent him plans for
building it. 11 So Uriah the priest built an
altar. He followed all the plans King Ahaz
had sent from Damascus. He finished it
before Ahaz returned. 12 The king came
back from Damascus. When he saw the
altar, he approached it. Then he offered
sacrifices on it. 13 He offered up his burnt
offering and grain offering. He poured
out his drink offering. And he splashed
the blood from his friendship offerings
against the altar. 14 The bronze altar for
burnt offerings stood in front of the LORD.
It was between the new altar and the
LORD's temple. Ahaz took the bronze altar
away from the front of the temple. He
put it on the north side of the new altar.
15 Then King Ahaz gave orders to Uriah
the priest. He said, "Offer sacrifices on
the large new altar. Offer the morning
burnt offering and the evening grain offering. Offer my burnt offering and my
grain offering. Offer the burnt offering
of all the people of the land. Offer their
grain offering and their drink offering.
Splash against this altar the blood from
all the burnt offerings and sacrifices.
But I will use the bronze altar to look
for advice and direction." 16 Uriah the
priest did just as King Ahaz had ordered.
17 Ahaz cut off the sides of the bronze
stands. He removed the bowls from the
stands. He removed the huge bowl from
the bronze bulls it stood on. He placed
the bowl on a stone base. 18 He took
away the covered area that had been
used on the Sabbath day. It had been
built at the LORD's temple. He removed
the royal entrance that was outside
the temple. Ahaz did all these things
to honor the king of Assyria.
19 The other events of the rule of Ahaz
are written down. Everything he did
is written in the official records of the
kings of Judah. 20 Ahaz joined the members of his family who had already died.
He was buried in the family tomb in
the City of David. Ahaz's son Hezekiah
became the next king after him.

Hoshea the Last King of Israel

17 Hoshea became king of Israel in
Samaria. It was in the 12th year
that Ahaz was king of Judah. Hoshea
ruled for nine years. He was the son of
Elah. 2 Hoshea did what was evil in the
eyes of the LORD. But he wasn't as evil as
the kings of Israel who ruled before him.
3 Shalmaneser came up to attack
Hoshea. Shalmaneser was king of Assyria. He had been Hoshea's master.
He had forced Hoshea to bring him
gifts. 4 But the king of Assyria found
out that Hoshea had turned against
him. Hoshea had sent messengers to
So, the king of Egypt. Hoshea didn't
send gifts to the king of Assyria anymore. He had been sending them every year. So Shalmaneser grabbed him
and put him in prison. 5 The king of
Assyria marched into the whole land
of Israel. He marched to Samaria and
surrounded it for three years. From
time to time he attacked it. 6 Finally,
the king of Assyria captured Samaria.
It was in the ninth year of Hoshea. The
king of Assyria took the Israelites away
from their own land. He sent them off
to Assyria. He made some of them live
in Halah. He made others live in Gozan
on the Habor River. And he made others
live in the towns of the Medes.

Israel Is Forced to Leave the Land Because of Sin

7 All of this took place because the
Israelites had sinned against the LORD
their God. He had brought them up out
of Egypt. He had brought them out from
under the power of Pharaoh, the king of
Egypt. But they worshiped other gods.
8 The LORD had driven out other nations
to make room for Israel. But they followed the evil practices of those nations.
They also followed the practices that
the kings of Israel had started. 9 The
Israelites did things in secret against
the LORD their God. What they did wasn't
right. They built high places for worship
in all their towns. They built them at
lookout towers. They also built them at
cities that had high walls around them.
10 They set up sacred stones. And they set
up poles used to worship the female god
named Asherah. They did that on every
high hill and under every green tree.
11 The LORD had driven out nations to
make room for Israel. But the Israelites
burned incense at every high place, just
as those nations had done. The Israelites did evil things that made the LORD
very angry. 12 They worshiped statues of
gods. They did it even though the LORD
had said, "Do not do that." 13 The LORD
warned Israel and Judah through all his
prophets and seers. He said, "Turn from
your evil ways. Keep my commands
and rules. Obey every part of my Law.
I commanded your people who lived
long ago to obey it. And I gave it to you
through my servants the prophets."
14 But the people wouldn't listen. They
were as stubborn as their people of long
ago had been. Those people didn't trust
in the LORD their God. 15 They refused to
obey his rules. They broke the covenant
he had made with them. They didn't
pay any attention to the rules he had
warned them to keep. They worshiped
worthless statues of gods. Then they
themselves became worthless. They
followed the example of the nations
around them. They did it even though
the LORD had ordered them not to. He
had said, "Do not do as they do."
16 They turned away from all the
commands of the LORD their God.
They made two statues of gods for
themselves. The statues were shaped
like calves. They made a pole used to
worship the female god named Asherah. They bowed down to all the stars.
And they worshiped the god named
Baal. 17 They sacrificed their sons and
daughters in the fire. They practiced
all kinds of evil magic. They gave up
following God's rules. They did only
what was evil in the eyes of the LORD.
All these things made him very angry.
18 So the LORD was very angry with
Israel. He removed them from his land.
Only the tribe of Judah was left. 19 And
even Judah didn't obey the commands
of the LORD their God. They followed
the practices Israel had started. 20 So
the LORD turned his back on all the
people of Israel. He made them suffer.
He handed them over to people who
stole everything they had. And finally
he threw them out of his land.
21 The LORD took control of Israel
away from the royal house of David.
The Israelites made Jeroboam, the son
of Nebat, their king. Jeroboam tried to
get Israel to stop following the LORD.
He caused them to commit a terrible
sin. 22 The Israelites were stubborn.
They continued to commit all the sins
Jeroboam had committed. They didn't
turn away from them. 23 So the LORD
removed them from his land. That's
what he had warned them he would
do. He had given that warning through
all his servants the prophets. So the
people of Israel were taken away from
their country. They were forced to go to
Assyria. And that's where they still are.

Assyria Makes Other People Live in Samaria

24 The king of Assyria brought people from Babylon, Kuthah, Avva, Hamath and Sepharvaim. He made all
of them live in the towns of Samaria.
They took the place of the people of
Israel. They lived in all the towns of
Samaria. 25 When they first lived there,
they didn't worship the LORD. So he sent
lions among them. And the lions killed
some of the people. 26 A report was given
to the king of Assyria. He was told, "You
forced people to leave their own homes
and live in the towns of Samaria. But
they don't know what the god of that
country requires. So he has sent lions
among them. And the lions are killing

the people off. That's because the people don't know what that god requires."

27 Then the king of Assyria gave an order. He said, "Get one of the priests you captured from Samaria. Send him back to live there. Have him teach the people what the god of that land requires." 28 So a priest went back to live in Bethel. He was one of the priests who had been forced to leave Samaria. He taught the people of Bethel how to worship the LORD.

29 In spite of that, the people from each nation made statues of their own gods. They made them in all the towns where they had been forced to live. They set up those statues in small temples. The people of Samaria had built the temples at the high places. 30 The people from Babylon made statues of the god named Sukkoth Benoth. Those from Kuthah made statues of the god named Nergal. Those from Hamath made statues of the god named Ashima. 31 The Avvites made statues of the gods named Nibhaz and Tartak. The Sepharvites sacrificed their children in the fire to the gods named Adrammelek and Anammelek. They were the gods of Sepharvaim. 32 So the people of Samaria worshiped the LORD. But they also appointed all kinds of their own people to be their priests. The priests served in the small temples at the high places. 33 The people worshiped the LORD. But they also served their own gods. They followed the evil practices of the nations they had been taken from.

34 The people of Samaria are still stubborn. They continue in their old practices to this day. And now they don't even worship the LORD. They don't follow his directions and rules. They don't obey his laws and commands. The LORD had given all these laws to the family of Jacob. He gave the name Israel to Jacob. 35 The LORD made a covenant with the Israelites. At that time he commanded them, "Do not worship any other gods. Do not bow down to them. Do not serve them or sacrifice to them. 36 The LORD is the one you must worship. The LORD brought you up out of Egypt by his great power. He saved you by reaching out his mighty arm. You must bow down only to him. You must offer sacrifices only to him. 37 You must always be careful to follow his directions and rules. You must obey the laws and commands he wrote for you. Do not worship other gods. 38 Do not forget the covenant I made with you. And remember, you must not worship other gods. 39 Instead, worship the LORD your God. He will save you from the powerful hand of all your enemies."

40 But the people wouldn't listen. Instead, they were stubborn. They continued in their old practices. 41 They worshiped the LORD. But at the same time, they served the statues of their gods. And to this day their children and grandchildren continue to do what their people before them did.

Hezekiah King of Judah

18 Hezekiah began to rule as king over Judah. It was in the third year that Hoshea was king of Israel. He was the son of Elah. Hezekiah was the son of Ahaz. 2 Hezekiah was 25 years old when he became king. He ruled in Jerusalem for 29 years. His mother's name was Abijah. She was the daughter of Zechariah. 3 Hezekiah did what was right in the eyes of the LORD, just as King David had done. 4 Hezekiah removed the high places. He smashed the sacred stones. He cut down the poles used to worship the female god named Asherah. He broke into pieces the bronze snake Moses had made. Up to that time the Israelites had been burning incense to it. They called it Nehushtan.

5 Hezekiah trusted in the LORD, the God of Israel. There was no one like Hezekiah among all the kings of Judah. There was no king like him either before him or after him. 6 Hezekiah remained faithful to the LORD. He didn't stop serving him. He obeyed the commands the LORD had given Moses. 7 The LORD was with Hezekiah. Because of that, Hezekiah was successful in everything he did. He refused to remain under the control of the king of Assyria. He didn't serve him. 8 He won the war against the Philistines. He won battles at their lookout towers. He won battles at their cities that had high walls around them. He won battles against the Philistines all the way to Gaza and its territory.

9 Shalmaneser marched to Samaria and surrounded it. It was in the fourth year of King Hezekiah. That was the

seventh year of Hoshea, the king of Israel. Hoshea was the son of Elah. Shalmaneser was king of Assyria. 10 At the end of three years the army of Assyria captured Samaria. That happened in the sixth year of Hezekiah's rule. It was the ninth year of the rule of Hoshea, the king of Israel. 11 The king of Assyria took the people of Israel away from their own land. He sent them off to Assyria. He made some of them live in Halah. He made others live in Gozan on the Habor River. And he made others live in the towns of the Medes. 12 These things happened because the Israelites hadn't obeyed the LORD their God. They had broken the covenant he had made with them. They had refused to do everything Moses, the servant of the LORD, had commanded. They hadn't paid any attention to those commands. They hadn't obeyed them.

13 Sennacherib attacked and captured all the cities of Judah that had high walls around them. It was in the 14th year of the rule of Hezekiah. Sennacherib was king of Assyria. 14 Hezekiah, the king of Judah, sent a message to the king of Assyria at Lachish. Hezekiah said, "I have done what is wrong. Pull your troops back from me. Then I'll pay you anything you ask me to." The king of Assyria forced Hezekiah, the king of Judah, to give him 11 tons of silver. Hezekiah also had to give him one ton of gold. 15 So Hezekiah gave him all the silver in the LORD's temple. He also gave him all the silver among the treasures in the royal palace.

16 Hezekiah, the king of Judah, had covered the doors and doorposts of the LORD's temple with gold. But now he had to strip it off. He had to give it to the king of Assyria.

Sennacherib Warns Jerusalem

17 The king of Assyria sent his highest commander from Lachish to King Hezekiah at Jerusalem. He also sent his chief officer and his field commander along with a large army. All of them came up to Jerusalem. They stopped at the channel that brings water from the Upper Pool. The channel was on the road to the Washerman's Field. 18 The Assyrians called for King Hezekiah. Eliakim, Shebna and Joah went out to them. Eliakim, the son of Hilkiah, was in charge of the palace. Shebna was the secretary. Joah, the son of Asaph, kept the records.

19 The field commander said to them, "Give Hezekiah this message. Tell him,

> " 'Sennacherib is the great king of Assyria. He says, "Why are you putting your faith in what your king says? 20 You say you have a military plan. You say you have a strong army. But your words don't mean anything. Who are you depending on? Why don't you want to stay under my control? 21 Look, I know you are depending on Egypt. Why are you doing that? Egypt is nothing but a broken papyrus stem. Try leaning on it. It will only cut your hand. Pharaoh, the king of Egypt, is just like that to everyone who depends on him. 22 But suppose you say to me, 'We are depending on the LORD our God.' Didn't Hezekiah remove your god's high places and altars? Didn't Hezekiah say to the people of Judah and Jerusalem, 'You must worship at the altar in Jerusalem'?
>
> 23 " ' "Go ahead and make a deal with my master, the king of Assyria. I'll give you 2,000 horses. But only if you can put riders on them! 24 You are depending on Egypt for chariots and horsemen. You can't drive away even the least important officer among my master's officials. 25 Besides, do you think I've come without receiving a message from the LORD? Have I come to attack and destroy this place without a message from him? The LORD himself told me to march out against your country. He told me to destroy it." ' "

26 Then Shebna, Joah and Eliakim, the son of Hilkiah, spoke to the field commander. They said, "Please speak to us in the Aramaic language. We understand it. Don't speak to us in Hebrew. If you do, the people sitting on the city wall will be able to understand you."

27 But the commander replied, "My master sent me to say these things. Are these words only for your master and you to hear? Aren't they also for the people sitting on the wall? They are

going to suffer just like you. They'll have to eat their own waste. They'll have to drink their own urine."

28 Then the commander stood up and spoke in the Hebrew language. He called out, "Pay attention to what the great king of Assyria is telling you. 29 He says, 'Don't let Hezekiah trick you. He can't save you from my power. 30 Don't let Hezekiah talk you into trusting in the LORD. Don't believe him when he says, "You can be sure that the LORD will save us. This city will not be handed over to the king of Assyria." '

31 "Don't listen to Hezekiah. The king of Assyria says, 'Make a peace treaty with me. Come over to my side. Then each one of you will eat fruit from your own vine and fig tree. Each one of you will drink water from your own well. 32 You will do that until I come back. Then I'll take you to a land just like yours. It's a land that has a lot of grain and fresh wine. It has plenty of bread and vineyards. It has olive trees and honey. So choose life! Don't choose death!'

"Don't pay any attention to Hezekiah. He's telling you a lie when he says, 'The LORD will save us.' 33 Has the god of any nation ever saved his land from the power of the king of Assyria? 34 Where are the gods of Hamath and Arpad? Where are the gods of Sepharvaim, Hena and Ivvah? Have they saved Samaria from my power? 35 Which one of all the gods of those countries has been able to save his land from me? So how can the LORD save Jerusalem from my power?"

36 But the people remained silent. They didn't say anything. That's because King Hezekiah had commanded, "Don't answer him."

37 Then Eliakim, the son of Hilkiah, went to Hezekiah. Eliakim was in charge of the palace. Shebna the secretary went with him. So did Joah, the son of Asaph. Joah kept the records. All of them went to Hezekiah with their clothes torn. They told him what the field commander had said.

Isaiah Prophesies That Jerusalem Will Be Saved

19 When King Hezekiah heard what the field commander had said, he tore his clothes. He put on the rough clothing people wear when they're sad. Then he went into the LORD's temple. 2 Hezekiah sent Eliakim, who was in charge of the palace, to Isaiah the prophet. Isaiah was the son of Amoz. Hezekiah also sent to Isaiah the leading priests and Shebna the secretary. All of them were wearing the same rough clothing. 3 They told Isaiah, "Hezekiah says, 'Today we're in great trouble. The LORD is warning us. He's bringing shame on us. Sometimes babies come to the moment when they should be born. But their mothers aren't strong enough to allow them to be born. Today we are like those mothers. We aren't strong enough to save ourselves. 4 Perhaps the LORD your God will hear everything the field commander has said. His master, the king of Assyria, has sent him to make fun of the living God. Maybe the LORD your God will punish him for what he has heard him say. So pray for the remaining people who are still alive here.' "

5 King Hezekiah's officials came to Isaiah. 6 Then Isaiah said to them, "Tell your master, 'The LORD says, "Do not be afraid of what you have heard. The officers of the king of Assyria have spoken evil things against me. 7 Listen! I will send him news from his own country. It will make him want to return home. There I will have him killed by a sword." ' "

8 The field commander heard that the king of Assyria had left Lachish. So the commander pulled his troops back from Jerusalem. He went to join the king. He found out that the king was fighting against Libnah.

9 During that time Sennacherib received a report. He was told that Tirhakah was marching out to fight against him. Tirhakah was the king of Cush. Sennacherib sent messengers again to Hezekiah with a letter. Sennacherib said, 10 "Tell Hezekiah, the king of Judah, 'Don't let the god you depend on trick you. He says, "Jerusalem will not be handed over to the king of Assyria." But don't believe him. 11 I'm sure you have heard about what the kings of Assyria have done to all the other countries. They have destroyed them completely. So do you think you will be saved? 12 The kings who ruled before me destroyed many nations. Did

the gods of those nations save them?
Did the gods of Gozan, Harran or Rezeph
save them? What about the gods of the
people of Eden who were in Tel Assar?
13 Where is the king of Hamath? Where is
the king of Arpad? Where are the kings
of Lair, Sepharvaim, Hena and Ivvah?'"

Hezekiah's Prayer

14 When Hezekiah received the letter
from the messengers, he read it. Then he
went up to the LORD's temple. There he
spread the letter out in front of the LORD.
15 Hezekiah prayed to the LORD. He said,
"LORD, you are the God of Israel. You sit
on your throne between the cherubim.
You alone are God over all the kingdoms
on earth. You have made heaven and
earth. 16 Listen, LORD. Hear us. Open
your eyes, LORD. Look at the trouble
we're in. Listen to what Sennacherib is
saying. You are the living God. And he
dares to make fun of you!

You alone are God over all the kingdoms on earth. You have made heaven and earth. 2 KINGS 19:15

17 "LORD, it's true that the kings of
Assyria have completely destroyed
many nations and their lands. 18 They
have thrown the statues of the gods of
those nations into the fire. And they
have destroyed them. That's because
they weren't really gods at all. They
were nothing but statues made out of
wood and stone. They were made by
human hands. 19 LORD our God, save us
from the power of Sennacherib. Then
all the kingdoms of the earth will know
that you alone are the LORD. You alone
are God."

Isaiah Prophesies That Sennacherib Will Fall From Power

20 Isaiah sent a message to Hezekiah.
Isaiah was the son of Amoz. Isaiah said,
"The LORD is the God of Israel. The LORD
says, 'I have heard your prayer about
Sennacherib, the king of Assyria.' 21 Here
is the message the LORD has spoken
against him. The LORD says,

"'You will not win the battle over
Zion.
Its people hate you and make
fun of you.
The people of Jerusalem lift up
their heads proudly
as you run away.
22 Who have you laughed at?
Who have you spoken evil things
against?
Who have you raised your voice
against?
Who have you looked at so
proudly?
You have done it against me.
I am the Holy One of Israel!
23 Through your messengers
you have dared to make fun of
the Lord.
And you have said,
"I have many chariots.
With them I have gone to the tops
of the mountains.
I've climbed the highest
mountains in Lebanon.
I've cut down its tallest cedar
trees.
I've cut down the best of its
juniper trees.
I've reached its farthest parts.
I've reached its finest forests.
24 I've dug wells in strange lands.
I've drunk the water from them.
I've walked through all of Egypt's
streams.
I've dried up every one of them."
25 "'But I, the LORD, say, "Haven't you
heard what I have done?
Long ago I arranged for you to
do all of that.
In days of old I planned it.
Now I have made it happen.
You have turned cities with high
walls
into piles of stone.
26 Their people do not have any
power left.
They are troubled and put to
shame.
They are like plants in the field.
They are like new green plants.
They are like grass that grows on a
roof.
It dries up before it is completely
grown.

27 “ ‘ “But I know where you are.
I know when you come and go.
I know how very angry you are
with me.
28 You roar against me and brag.
And I have heard your bragging.
So I will put my hook in your nose.
I will put my bit in your mouth.
And I will make you go home
by the same way you came.” ’ ”

29 The LORD said, “Hezekiah, here is
a miraculous sign for you.

“This year you will eat what grows
by itself.
In the second year you will eat
what grows from that.
But in the third year you will plant
your crops and gather them in.
You will plant your grapevines
and eat their fruit.
30 Those who remain from the
kingdom of Judah will be like
plants.
Once more they will put down
roots and produce fruit.
31 Out of Jerusalem will come those
who remain.
Out of Mount Zion will come
those who survive.

“The LORD’s great love will make
sure that happens.
He rules over all.

32 “Here is a message from me about
the king of Assyria. The LORD says,

“ ‘The king of Assyria will not enter
this city.
He will not even shoot an arrow
at it.
He will not come near it with a shield.
He will not build a ramp in order
to climb over its walls.
33 By the same way he came he will
go home.
He will not enter this city,’
announces the LORD.
34 ‘I will guard this city and save it.
I will do it for myself. And I will
do it for my servant David.’ ”

35 That night the angel of the LORD
went into the camp of the Assyrians.
He put to death 185,000 people there.
The people of Jerusalem got up the next
morning and looked out at the camp.
There were all the dead bodies! 36 So
Sennacherib, the king of Assyria, took
the army tents down. Then he left. He
returned to Nineveh and stayed there.
37 One day Sennacherib was worshiping
in the temple of his god Nisrok. His sons
Adrammelek and Sharezer killed him
with their swords. Then they escaped to
the land of Ararat. Esarhaddon became
the next king after his father Sennacherib.

Hezekiah Becomes Sick

20 In those days Hezekiah became
very sick. He was about to die.
Isaiah the prophet, the son of Amoz,
went to him. Isaiah told Hezekiah, “The
LORD says, ‘Put everything in order.
Make out your will. You are going to
die soon. You will not get well again.’ ”
2 Hezekiah turned his face toward the
wall. He prayed to the LORD. He said,
3 “LORD, please remember how faithful
I’ve been to you. I’ve lived the way you
wanted me to. I’ve served you with all
my heart. I’ve done what is good in
your sight.” And Hezekiah wept bitterly.
4 Isaiah was leaving the middle courtyard. Before he had left it, a message
came to him from the LORD. He said,
5 “Go back and speak to Hezekiah. He
is the ruler of my people. Tell him, ‘The
LORD, the God of King David, says, “I
have heard your prayer. I have seen
your tears. And I will heal you. On the
third day from now you will go up to my
temple. 6 I will add 15 years to your life.
And I will save you and this city from the
power of the king of Assyria. I will guard
this city. I will do it for myself. And I will
do it for my servant David.” ’ ”
7 Then Isaiah said, “Press some figs
together. Spread them on a piece of
cloth.” So that’s what they did. Then
they applied it to Hezekiah’s boil. And
he got well again.
8 Hezekiah had said to Isaiah, “You
say the LORD will heal me. You say that
I’ll go up to his temple on the third day
from now. What will the sign be to prove
he’ll really do that?”
9 Isaiah answered, “The LORD will do
what he has promised. Here is his sign
to you. Do you want the shadow the
sun makes to go forward ten steps? Or
do you want it to go back ten steps?”
10 “It’s easy for the shadow to go forward ten steps,” said Hezekiah. “So have
it go back ten steps.”

[11]Then Isaiah the prophet called out to the LORD. And the LORD made the shadow go back ten steps. It went back the ten steps it had gone down on the stairway Ahaz had made.

Messengers Come From Babylon to Hezekiah

[12]At that time Marduk-Baladan, the king of Babylon, sent Hezekiah letters and a gift. He had heard that Hezekiah had been sick. Marduk-Baladan was the son of Baladan. [13]Hezekiah received the messengers. He showed them everything in his storerooms. He showed them the silver and gold. He showed them the spices and the fine olive oil. He showed them where he kept his weapons. And he showed them all his treasures. In fact, he showed them everything in his palace and in his whole kingdom.

[14]Then Isaiah the prophet went to King Hezekiah. He asked him, "What did those men say? Where did they come from?"

"They came from a land far away," Hezekiah said. "They came from Babylon."

[15]The prophet asked, "What did they see in your palace?"

"They saw everything in my palace," Hezekiah said. "I showed them all my treasures."

[16]Then Isaiah said to Hezekiah, "Listen to the LORD's message. He says, [17]'You can be sure the time will come when everything in your palace will be carried off to Babylon. Everything the kings before you have stored up until this day will be taken away. There will not be anything left,' says the LORD. [18]'Some of the members of your family line will be taken away. They will be your own flesh and blood. They will include the children who will be born into your family line in years to come. And they will serve the king of Babylon in his palace.' "

[19]"The message the LORD has spoken through you is good," Hezekiah replied. He thought, "There will be peace and safety while I'm still living."

[20]The other events of the rule of Hezekiah are written down. That includes how he made the pool and the tunnel. He used them to bring water into Jerusalem. Everything he accomplished is written in the official records of the kings of Judah. [21]Hezekiah joined the members of his family who had already died. Hezekiah's son Manasseh became the next king after him.

Manasseh King of Judah

21 Manasseh was 12 years old when he became king. He ruled in Jerusalem for 55 years. His mother's name was Hephzibah. [2]Manasseh did what was evil in the eyes of the LORD. He followed the practices of the nations. The LORD hated those practices. He had driven those nations out to make room for the Israelites. [3]Manasseh rebuilt the high places. His father Hezekiah had destroyed them. Manasseh also set up altars to the god named Baal. He made a pole used to worship the female god named Asherah. Ahab, the king of Israel, had done those same things. Manasseh even bowed down to all the stars. And he worshiped them. [4]He built altars in the LORD's temple. The LORD had said about his temple, "I will put my Name there in Jerusalem." [5]In the two courtyards of the LORD's temple Manasseh built altars to honor all the stars. [6]He sacrificed his own son in the fire to another god. He practiced all kinds of evil magic. He got messages from those who had died. He talked to the spirits of the dead. He did many things that were evil in the eyes of the LORD. Manasseh made the LORD very angry.

[7]Manasseh had carved a pole used to worship the female god named Asherah. He put it in the temple. The LORD had spoken to David and his son Solomon about the temple. He had said, "My Name will be in this temple and in Jerusalem forever. Out of all the cities in the tribes of Israel I have chosen Jerusalem. [8]I gave this land to your people who lived long ago. I will not make the Israelites wander away from it again. But they must be careful to do everything I commanded them. They must obey the whole Law that my servant Moses gave them." [9]But the people didn't pay any attention. Manasseh led them astray. They did more evil things than the nations the LORD had destroyed. He had destroyed them to make room for the Israelites.

[10]The LORD spoke through his servants the prophets. He said, [11]"Manasseh, the

king of Judah, has committed terrible sins. I hate them. Manasseh has done more evil things than the Amorites who were in the land before him. And he has led Judah to commit sin by worshiping his statues of gods. 12 I am the LORD, the God of Israel. I tell you, 'I am going to bring trouble on Jerusalem and Judah. It will be so horrible that the ears of everyone who hears about it will tingle. 13 I will measure out punishment against Jerusalem, just as I did against Samaria. I used a plumb line against the royal family of Ahab. I used it to prove that they did not measure up to my standards. I will use the same plumb line against Jerusalem. I will wipe out Jerusalem, just as someone wipes a dish. I will wipe it and turn it upside down. 14 I will desert those who remain among my people. I will hand them over to their enemies. All their enemies will rob them. 15 That's because my people have done what is evil in my sight. They have made me very angry. They have done that from the day their own people came out of Egypt until this day.' "

16 Manasseh also spilled the blood of many people who weren't guilty of doing anything wrong. He spilled so much blood that he filled Jerusalem with it from one end of the city to the other. And he caused Judah to commit sin. So they also did what was evil in the eyes of the LORD.

17 The other events of the rule of Manasseh are written down. That includes the sin he committed. Everything he did is written in the official records of the kings of Judah. 18 Manasseh joined the members of his family who had already died. He was buried in his palace garden. It was called the garden of Uzza. Manasseh's son Amon became the next king after him.

Amon King of Judah

19 Amon was 22 years old when he became king. He ruled in Jerusalem for two years. His mother's name was Meshullemeth. She was the daughter of Haruz. She was from Jotbah. 20 Amon did what was evil in the eyes of the LORD, just as his father Manasseh had done. 21 He lived the way his father had lived. He worshiped the statues of the gods his father had worshiped. He bowed down to them. 22 He deserted the LORD, the God of his people. He didn't obey the LORD.

23 Amon's officials made plans against him. They murdered the king in his palace. 24 Then the people of the land killed all those officials who had made plans against King Amon. Then the people of the land made his son Josiah king in his place.

25 The other events of the rule of Amon are written down. Everything he did is written in the official records of the kings of Judah. 26 Amon was buried in his grave in the garden of Uzza. Amon's son Josiah became the next king after him.

Hilkiah Finds the Book of the Law

22 Josiah was eight years old when he became king. He ruled in Jerusalem for 31 years. His mother's name was Jedidah. She was the daughter of Adaiah. She was from Bozkath. 2 Josiah did what was right in the eyes of the LORD. He lived the way King David had lived. He didn't turn away from it to the right or the left.

3 King Josiah sent his secretary Shaphan to the LORD's temple. It was in the 18th year of Josiah's rule. Shaphan was the son of Azaliah. Azaliah was the son of Meshullam. Josiah said, 4 "Go up to Hilkiah the high priest. Have him add up the money that has been brought into the LORD's temple. The men who guard the doors have collected it from the people. 5 Have them put all the money in the care of certain men. These men have been put in charge of the work on the LORD's temple. Have them pay the workers who repair it. 6 Have them pay the builders and those who work with wood. Have them pay those who lay the stones. Also have them buy lumber and blocks of stone to repair the temple. 7 But they don't have to report how they use the money that is given to them. That's because they are completely honest."

8 Hilkiah the high priest spoke to Shaphan the secretary. Hilkiah said, "I've found the Book of the Law in the LORD's temple." Hilkiah gave it to Shaphan, who read it. 9 Then Shaphan went to King Josiah. Shaphan told him, "Your officials have paid out the money that was in the LORD's temple. They've

put it in the care of the workers and directors there." 10 Shaphan continued, "Hilkiah the priest has given me a book." Shaphan read some of it to the king.

11 The king heard the words of the Book of the Law. When he did, he tore his royal robes. 12 He gave orders to Hilkiah the priest, Ahikam, Akbor, Shaphan the secretary and Asaiah. Ahikam was the son of Shaphan. Akbor was the son of Micaiah. And Asaiah was the king's attendant. Josiah commanded them, 13 "Go. Ask the LORD for advice. Ask him about what is written in this book that has been found. Do it for me. Also do it for the people and the whole nation of Judah. The LORD is very angry with us. That's because our people who have lived before us didn't obey the words of this book. They didn't do everything written there about us."

14 Hilkiah the priest went to speak to Huldah the prophet. So did Ahikam, Akbor, Shaphan and Asaiah. Huldah was the wife of Shallum. Shallum was the son of Tikvah. Tikvah was the son of Harhas. Shallum took care of the sacred robes. Huldah lived in the New Quarter of Jerusalem.

15 Huldah said to them, "The LORD is the God of Israel. He says, 'Here is what you must tell the man who sent you to me. 16 Tell him, "The LORD says, 'I am going to bring horrible trouble on this place and its people. Everything written in the book the king of Judah has read will take place. 17 That's because the people have deserted me. They have burned incense to other gods. They have made me very angry because of the statues of gods their hands have made. So my anger will burn like a fire against this place. And the fire of my anger will not be put out.' " ' 18 The king of Judah sent you to ask the LORD for advice. Tell him, 'The LORD is the God of Israel. He has a message for you about the things you heard. He says, 19 "Your heart was tender. You made yourself humble in the eyes of the LORD. You heard what I spoke against this place and its people. I said they would be under a curse. I told them they would be destroyed. You tore your royal robes and wept in front of me. And I have heard you," announces the LORD. 20 "You will join the members of your family who have already died. You will be buried in peace. Your eyes will not see all the trouble I am going to bring on this place." ' "

Huldah's answer was taken back to the king.

Josiah Promises Again to Obey the Covenant

23 Then the king called together all the elders of Judah and Jerusalem. 2 He went up to the LORD's temple. The people of Judah and Jerusalem went with him. So did the priests and prophets. All of them went, from the least important of them to the most important. The king had all the words of the Book of the Covenant read to them. The book had been found in the LORD's temple. 3 The king stood next to his pillar. He agreed to the terms of the covenant in front of the LORD. The king promised to serve the LORD and obey his commands, directions and rules. He promised to obey them with all his heart and with all his soul. So he agreed to the terms of the covenant written down in that book. Then all the people committed themselves to the covenant as well.

4 Certain things in the LORD's temple had been made to honor other gods. They were the god named Baal, the female god named Asherah and all the stars in the sky. The king ordered Hilkiah the high priest to remove those things. The king ordered the priests who were next in rank and the men who guarded the doors to help Hilkiah. Josiah took those things that had been in the LORD's temple and burned them outside Jerusalem. He burned them in the fields in the Kidron Valley. And he took the ashes to Bethel. 5 Josiah got rid of the priests who served other gods. The kings of Judah had appointed those priests to burn incense. They burned the incense on the high places of the towns of Judah. And they burned it on the high places around Jerusalem. They burned incense to honor Baal and the sun and moon. They burned it to honor all the stars. 6 Josiah removed the Asherah pole from the LORD's temple. It had been used to worship the female god named Asherah. He took it to the Kidron Valley outside Jerusalem. There he burned it. He ground it into powder.

And he scattered it over the graves of the ordinary people. 7 He also tore down the rooms where the male temple prostitutes stayed. Those rooms were in the LORD's temple. Women had made cloth for Asherah in them.

8 Josiah brought all the priests from the towns of Judah and destroyed the high places. He destroyed them from Geba all the way to Beersheba. The priests had burned incense on them. Josiah broke down the gate at the entrance of the Gate of Joshua. It was on the left side of Jerusalem's city gate. Joshua was the city governor. 9 The priests of the high places didn't serve at the LORD's altar in Jerusalem. In spite of that, they ate with the other priests. All of them ate bread made without yeast.

10 Josiah destroyed the high place at Topheth in the Valley of Ben Hinnom. He didn't want anyone to use the high place to sacrifice his son or daughter in the fire to the god named Molek. 11 Josiah removed the statues of horses from the entrance to the LORD's temple. The kings of Judah had set them apart to honor the sun. The statues were in the courtyard. They were near the room of an official named Nathan-Melek. Josiah burned the chariots that had been set apart to honor the sun.

12 He pulled down the altars the kings of Judah had set up. They had put them on the palace roof near the upstairs room of Ahaz. Josiah also pulled down the altars Manasseh had built. They were in the two courtyards of the LORD's temple. Josiah removed the altars from there. He smashed them to pieces. Then he threw the broken pieces into the Kidron Valley. 13 The king also destroyed the high places that were east of Jerusalem. They were at the southern end of the Mount of Olives. They were the ones Solomon, the king of Israel, had built. He had built a high place for worshiping Ashtoreth. She was the evil female god of the people of Sidon. Solomon had also built one for worshiping Chemosh. He was the evil god of Moab. And Solomon had built one for worshiping Molek. He was the god of the people of Ammon. The LORD hated that god. 14 Josiah smashed the sacred stones. He cut down the poles used to worship the female god named Asherah. Then he covered all those places with human bones.

15 There was an altar at Bethel. It was at the high place made by Jeroboam, the son of Nebat. Jeroboam had caused Israel to commit sin. Even that altar and high place were destroyed by Josiah. He burned the high place. He ground it into powder. He also burned the Asherah pole. 16 Then Josiah looked around. He saw the tombs on the side of the hill. He had the bones removed from them. And he burned them on the altar to make it "unclean." That's what the LORD had said would happen. He had spoken that message through a man of God. The man had announced those things long before they took place.

17 The king asked, "What's that stone on the grave over there?"

The people of the city said, "It marks the tomb where the man of God is buried. He came from Judah. He spoke against the altar at Bethel. He announced the very things you have done to it."

18 "Leave it alone," Josiah said. "Don't let anyone touch his bones." So they spared his bones. They also spared the bones of the prophet who had come from the northern kingdom of Israel.

19 Josiah did in the rest of the northern kingdom the same things he had done at Bethel. He removed all the small temples at the high places. He made them "unclean." The kings of Israel had built them in the towns of the northern kingdom. The people in those towns had made the LORD very angry. 20 Josiah killed all the priests of those high places on the altars. He burned human bones on the altars. Then he went back to Jerusalem.

21 The king gave an order to all the people. He said, "Celebrate the Passover Feast to honor the LORD your God. Do what is written in this Book of the Covenant." 22 A Passover Feast like that one had not been held for a long time. There hadn't been any like it in the days of the judges who led Israel. And there hadn't been any like it during the whole time the kings of Israel and Judah were ruling. 23 King Josiah celebrated the Passover Feast in Jerusalem to honor the LORD. It was in the 18th year of his rule.

24 And that's not all. Josiah got rid of
those who got messages from people
who had died. He got rid of those who
talked to the spirits of people who had
died. He got rid of the statues of family
gods and the statues of other gods. He
got rid of everything else the LORD hates
that was in Judah and Jerusalem. He
did it to carry out what the law required.
That law was written in the book that
Hilkiah the priest had found in the
LORD's temple. 25 There was no king like
Josiah either before him or after him.
None of them turned to the LORD as he
did. He obeyed the LORD with all his
heart and all his soul. He obeyed him
with all his strength. He did everything
the Law of Moses required.

26 In spite of that, the LORD didn't
turn away from his great anger against
Judah. That's because of everything
Manasseh had done to make him very
angry. 27 So the LORD said, "I will remove
Judah from my land. I will do to them
what I did to Israel. I will turn my back
on Jerusalem. It is the city I chose. I
will also turn my back on this temple.
I spoke about it. I said, 'I will put my
Name there.'" *(1 Kings 8:29)*

28 The other events of the rule of Josiah are written down. Everything he
did is written in the official records of
the kings of Judah.

29 Pharaoh Necho was king of Egypt.
He marched up to the Euphrates River.
He went there to help the king of Assyria. It happened while Josiah was king.
Josiah marched out to meet Necho in
battle. When Necho saw him at Megiddo, he killed him. 30 Josiah's servants
brought his body in a chariot from
Megiddo to Jerusalem. They buried him
in his own tomb. Then the people of
the land went and got Jehoahaz. They
anointed him as king in place of his
father Josiah.

Jehoahaz King of Judah

31 Jehoahaz was 23 years old when he
became king. He ruled in Jerusalem for
three months. His mother's name was
Hamutal. She was the daughter of Jeremiah. She was from Libnah. 32 Jehoahaz
did what was evil in the eyes of the LORD.
He did just as the kings who had ruled
before him had done. 33 Pharaoh Necho
put him in chains at Riblah in the land
of Hamath. That kept him from ruling
in Jerusalem. Necho made the people
of Judah pay him a tax of almost four
tons of silver and 75 pounds of gold.
34 Pharaoh Necho made Eliakim king in
place of his father Josiah. Necho changed
Eliakim's name to Jehoiakim. But he took
Jehoahaz with him to Egypt. And that's
where Jehoahaz died. 35 Jehoiakim paid
Pharaoh Necho the silver and gold he
required. To get the money, Jehoiakim
taxed the land. He forced the people to
give him the silver and gold. He made
each one pay him what he required.

Jehoiakim King of Judah

36 Jehoiakim was 25 years old when
he became king. He ruled in Jerusalem
for 11 years. His mother's name was Ze-
bidah. She was the daughter of Pedaiah.
She was from Rumah. 37 Jehoiakim did
what was evil in the eyes of the LORD.
He did just as the kings who had ruled
before him had done.

24 During Jehoiakim's rule, Nebuchadnezzar marched into the
land and attacked it. He was king of
Babylon. He became Jehoiakim's master for three years. But then Jehoiakim
decided he didn't want to remain under
Nebuchadnezzar's control. 2 The LORD
sent robbers against Jehoiakim from
Babylon, Aram, Moab and Ammon.
He sent them to destroy Judah. That's
what the LORD had said would happen.
He had spoken that message through
his servants the prophets. 3 These things
happened to Judah in keeping with
what the LORD had commanded. He
brought enemies against his people in
order to remove them from his land. He
removed them because of all the sins
Manasseh had committed. 4 Manasseh
had spilled the blood of many people
who weren't guilty of doing anything
wrong. In fact, he spilled so much of
their blood that he filled Jerusalem with
it. So the LORD refused to forgive him.

5 The other events of the rule of Jehoiakim are written down. Everything
he did is written in the official records of
the kings of Judah. 6 Jehoiakim joined
the members of his family who had already died. Jehoiakim's son Jehoiachin
became the next king after him.

7 The king of Egypt didn't march out
from his own country again. That's

because the king of Babylon had taken so much of his territory. It reached from the Wadi of Egypt all the way to the Euphrates River.

Jehoiachin King of Judah

[8]Jehoiachin was 18 years old when he became king. He ruled in Jerusalem for three months. His mother's name was Nehushta. She was the daughter of Elnathan. She was from Jerusalem. [9]Jehoiachin did what was evil in the eyes of the LORD. He did just as his father Jehoiakim had done.

[10]At that time the officers of Nebuchadnezzar, the king of Babylon, marched to Jerusalem. They surrounded it and got ready to attack it. [11]Nebuchadnezzar himself came up to the city. He arrived while his officers were attacking it. [12]Jehoiachin, the king of Judah, handed himself over to Nebuchadnezzar. Jehoiachin's mother did the same thing. And so did all his attendants, nobles and officials.

The king of Babylon took Jehoiachin away as his prisoner. It was in the eighth year of Nebuchadnezzar's rule. [13]Nebuchadnezzar removed the treasures from the LORD's temple. He also removed the treasures from the royal palace. He cut up the gold objects that Solomon, the king of Israel, had made for the temple. That's what the LORD had announced would happen. [14]Nebuchadnezzar took all the people of Jerusalem to the land of Babylon as prisoners. That included all the officers and fighting men. It also included all the skilled workers. The total number of prisoners was 10,000. Only the poorest people were left in the land.

[15]Nebuchadnezzar took Jehoiachin to Babylon as his prisoner. He also took the king's mother from Jerusalem to Babylon. And he took Jehoiachin's wives, his officials and the most important people of the land. [16]The king also forced the whole army of 7,000 soldiers to go away to the land of Babylon. Those men were strong and able to go to war. And the king forced 1,000 skilled workers to go to Babylon. [17]Nebuchadnezzar made Jehoiachin's uncle Mattaniah king in his place. And Nebuchadnezzar changed Mattaniah's name to Zedekiah.

Zedekiah King of Judah

[18]Zedekiah was 21 years old when he became king. He ruled in Jerusalem for 11 years. His mother's name was Hamutal. She was the daughter of Jeremiah. She was from Libnah. [19]Zedekiah did what was evil in the eyes of the LORD. He did just as Jehoiakim had done. [20]The enemies of Jerusalem and Judah attacked them because the LORD was angry. In the end the LORD threw them out of his land.

The Fall of Jerusalem

Zedekiah also refused to remain under the control of Nebuchadnezzar.

25 Nebuchadnezzar was king of Babylon. He marched out against Jerusalem. His whole army went with him. It was in the ninth year of the rule of Zedekiah. It was on the tenth day of the tenth month. Nebuchadnezzar set up camp outside the city. He brought in war machines all around it. [2]It was surrounded until the 11th year of King Zedekiah's rule.

[3]By the ninth day of the fourth month, there wasn't any food left in the city. So the people didn't have anything to eat. [4]Then the Babylonians broke through the city wall. Judah's whole army ran away at night. They went out through the gate between the two walls near the king's garden. They escaped even though the Babylonians surrounded the city. Judah's army ran toward the Arabah Valley. [5]But the Babylonian army chased King Zedekiah. They caught up with him in the plains near Jericho. All his soldiers were separated from him. They had scattered in every direction. [6]The king was captured.

He was taken to the king of Babylon at Riblah. That's where Nebuchadnezzar decided how he would be punished. [7]Nebuchadnezzar's men killed the sons of Zedekiah. They forced him to watch it with his own eyes. Then they poked out his eyes. They put him in bronze chains. And they took him to Babylon.

[8]Nebuzaradan was an official of the king of Babylon. In fact, he was commander of the royal guard. He came to Jerusalem. It was in the 19th year that Nebuchadnezzar was king of Babylon. It was on the seventh day of the fifth month. [9]Nebuzaradan set the LORD's

temple on fire. He also set fire to the
royal palace and all the houses in Jerusalem. He burned down every important
building. 10 The whole Babylonian army
broke down the walls around Jerusalem.
That's what the commander told them
to do. 11 Some people still remained in the
city. But Nebuzaradan the commander
took them away as prisoners. He also
took the rest of the people of the land.
That included those who had joined the
king of Babylon. 12 But the commander
left behind some of the poorest people
of the land. He told them to work in the
vineyards and fields.

13 The Babylonian army destroyed the
LORD's temple. They broke the bronze
pillars into pieces. They broke up the
bronze stands that could be moved
around. And they broke up the huge
bronze bowl. Then they carried the
bronze away to Babylon. 14 They also
took away the pots, shovels, wick cutters and dishes. They took away all the
bronze objects used for any purpose in
the temple. 15 The commander of the
royal guard took away the shallow cups
for burning incense. He took away the
sprinkling bowls. So he took away everything made out of pure gold or silver.

16 The bronze was more than anyone
could weigh. It included the bronze from
the two pillars, the huge bowl and the
stands. Solomon had made all those
things for the LORD's temple. 17 Each
pillar was 27 feet high. The bronze top of
one pillar was four and a half feet high.
It was decorated with a set of bronze
chains and pomegranates all around it.
The other pillar was just like it. It also
had a set of chains.

18 The commander of the guard took
some prisoners. They included Seraiah
the chief priest and Zephaniah the priest
who was next in rank. They also included
the three men who guarded the temple
doors. 19 Some people were still left in the
city. The commander took as a prisoner the officer who was in charge of the
fighting men. He took the five men who
gave advice to the king. He also took
the secretary. He was the chief officer in
charge of getting the people of the land
to serve in the army. And he took 60 of
those people serving in the army who
were still in the city. 20 Nebuzaradan the
commander took all of them away. He
brought them to the king of Babylon at
Riblah. 21 There the king had them put to
death. Riblah was in the land of Hamath.

So the people of Judah were taken as
prisoners. They were taken far away
from their own land.

22 Nebuchadnezzar, the king of Babylon,
had left some people behind in Judah.
He appointed Gedaliah to govern them.
Gedaliah was the son of Ahikam. Ahikam
was the son of Shaphan. 23 All of Judah's
army officers and their men heard about
what had happened. They heard that the
king had appointed Gedaliah as governor.
So they came to Gedaliah at Mizpah. Ishmael, the son of Nethaniah, came. So did
Johanan, the son of Kareah. Seraiah, the
son of Tanhumeth, also came. And so did
Jaazaniah, the son of the Maakathite. All
their men came too. Seraiah was from
Netophah. 24 Gedaliah promised to help
them and their men. He spoke in a kind
way to them. He said, "Don't be afraid
of the Babylonian officials. Make your
homes in the land of Judah. Serve the
king of Babylon. Then things will go well
with you."

25 But in the seventh month Ishmael,
the son of Nethaniah, came with ten men.
He killed Gedaliah. He also killed the people of Judah and the Babylonians who
were with Gedaliah at Mizpah. Nethaniah
was the son of Elishama. Ishmael was a
member of the royal family. 26 After he
had killed Gedaliah, all the people ran
away to Egypt. Everyone from the least
important of them to the most important
ran away. The army officers went with
them. All of them went to Egypt because
they were afraid of the Babylonians.

Jehoiachin Is Set Free

27 Awel-Marduk set Jehoiachin, the
king of Judah, free from prison. It was
in the 37th year after Jehoiachin had
been taken away to Babylon. It was also
the year Awel-Marduk became king of
Babylon. It was on the 27th day of the
12th month. 28 Awel-Marduk spoke kindly
to Jehoiachin. He gave him a place of
honor. Other kings were with Jehoiachin
in Babylon. But his place was more important than theirs. 29 So Jehoiachin put
his prison clothes away. For the rest of
Jehoiachin's life the king provided what
he needed. 30 The king did that for Jehoiachin day by day as long as he lived.

1 CHRONICLES

Author: Ezra (we think)

The books of 1 and 2 Chronicles give us a big-picture look at God's story from the first people God created through Israel's history as a nation. The books are written as though we are zooming out to see what God had done since the beginning of creation.

First Chronicles tells us the family tree of God's people, particularly King David's family. This book also reminds us that God has been faithful to his people in every generation and shows that through David's descendants, the forever King would come!

First Chronicles also tells of God's promise to come and live among his people, as well as King David's desire to build the temple. It was a project King David couldn't wait to get started on! But David didn't get to participate in the actual construction of the temple. Instead, God told David that he had chosen David's son Solomon to complete this very special project. On every page of this book, we are reminded of what set God's people apart from all the nations that surrounded them: It was God's presence! That's why the temple was important to God's people. The temple would identify them as God's special, set-apart people.

Old Testament History

A List of Names From Adam to Abraham

A List of Names From Adam to the Sons of Noah

1 Adam, Seth, Enosh,
2 Kenan, Mahalalel, Jared,
3 Enoch, Methuselah, Lamech, Noah.

4 The sons of Noah were Shem, Ham and Japheth.

The Sons of Japheth

5 The sons of Japheth were
Gomer, Magog, Madai, Javan, Tubal, Meshek and Tiras.
6 The sons of Gomer were
Ashkenaz, Riphath and Togarmah.
7 The sons of Javan were
Elishah, Tarshish, the Kittites and the Rodanites.

The Sons of Ham

8 The sons of Ham were
Cush, Egypt, Put and Canaan.
9 The sons of Cush were
Seba, Havilah, Sabta, Raamah and Sabteka.
The sons of Raamah were
Sheba and Dedan.
10 Cush was the father of
Nimrod. Nimrod became a mighty hero on the earth.
11 Egypt was the father of
the Ludites, Anamites, Lehabites
and Naphtuhites. 12 He was also
the father of the Pathrusites, Kasluhites and Caphtorites. The Philistines came from the family line of the Kasluhites.
13 Canaan was the father of Sidon.
Sidon was his oldest son.
Canaan was also the father
of the Hittites, 14 Jebusites,
Amorites and Girgashites. 15 And
he was the father of the Hivites,
Arkites, Sinites, 16 Arvadites,
Zemarites and Hamathites.

The Sons of Shem

17 The sons of Shem were
Elam, Ashur, Arphaxad, Lud and Aram.
The sons of Aram were
Uz, Hul, Gether and Meshek.
18 Arphaxad was the father of Shelah.
Shelah was the father of Eber.
19 Eber was the father of two sons.
One was named Peleg. That's because the earth was divided up in his time. His brother was named Joktan.
20 Joktan was the father of
Almodad, Sheleph, Hazarmaveth
and Jerah. 21 He was also the
father of Hadoram, Uzal, Diklah,
22 Obal, Abimael, Sheba, 23 Ophir,
Havilah and Jobab. All of them were sons of Joktan.

24 Shem, Arphaxad, Shelah,
25 Eber, Peleg, Reu,
26 Serug, Nahor, Terah,
27 Abram. Abram was also called Abraham.

The Family of Abraham

28 The sons of Abraham were Isaac and Ishmael.

The Family Line of Hagar

29 Here are the members of the family line of Hagar.
Nebaioth was Ishmael's oldest son. Then came Kedar, Adbeel,
Mibsam, 30 Mishma, Dumah,
Massa, Hadad, Tema, 31 Jetur,
Naphish and Kedemah.
All of them were Ishmael's sons.

The Family Line of Keturah

32 Here are the sons born to Abraham's concubine Keturah.
They were Zimran, Jokshan, Medan, Midian, Ishbak and Shuah.
The sons of Jokshan were
Sheba and Dedan.
33 The sons of Midian were
Ephah, Epher, Hanok, Abida and Eldaah.
All of them were from the family line of Keturah.

The Family Line of Sarah

34 Abraham was the father of Isaac.
The sons of Isaac were
Esau and Israel.

The Sons of Esau

35 The sons of Esau were
Eliphaz, Reuel, Jeush, Jalam and Korah.
36 The sons of Eliphaz were
Teman, Omar, Zepho, Gatam and Kenaz.

Timna had Amalek by Eliphaz.
37 The sons of Reuel were
Nahath, Zerah, Shammah and Mizzah.

The People of Seir in Edom

38 The sons of Seir were
Lotan, Shobal, Zibeon, Anah, Dishon, Ezer and Dishan.
39 The sons of Lotan were
Hori and Homam. Timna was Lotan's sister.
40 The sons of Shobal were
Alvan, Manahath, Ebal, Shepho and Onam.
The sons of Zibeon were
Aiah and Anah.
41 The son of Anah was
Dishon.
The sons of Dishon were
Hemdan, Eshban, Ithran and Keran.
42 The sons of Ezer were
Bilhan, Zaavan and Akan.
The sons of Dishan were
Uz and Aran.

The Rulers of Edom

43 Before Israel had a king, there were kings who ruled in Edom.
Bela was the son of Beor. Bela's city was called Dinhabah.
44 When Bela died, Jobab became the next king. Jobab was the son of Zerah from Bozrah.
45 When Jobab died, Husham became the next king. Husham was from the land of the people of Teman.
46 When Husham died, Hadad became the next king. Hadad was the son of Bedad. Hadad had won the battle over Midian in the country of Moab. Hadad's city was called Avith.
47 When Hadad died, Samlah became the next king. Samlah was from Masrekah.
48 When Samlah died, Shaul became the next king. Shaul was from the town of Rehoboth. It was by a river.
49 When Shaul died, Baal-Hanan became the next king. Baal-Hanan was the son of Akbor.
50 When Baal-Hanan died, Hadad became the next king. Hadad's city was called Pau. His wife's name was Mehetabel. She was the daughter of Matred. Matred was the daughter of Me-Zahab.
51 Hadad also died.

The chiefs of Edom were
Timna, Alvah, Jetheth, 52 Oholibamah, Elah, Pinon, 53 Kenaz, Teman, Mibzar, 54 Magdiel and Iram.
They were the chiefs of Edom.

The Sons of Israel

2 Here are the names of the sons of Israel. Reuben, Simeon, Levi, Judah, Issachar, Zebulun,
2 Dan, Joseph, Benjamin, Naphtali, Gad, Asher.

The Family of Judah

The Family Line From Judah's Sons to Hezron's Sons

3 The sons of Judah were
Er, Onan and Shelah. A woman from Canaan had these three sons by him. She was the daughter of Shua.
Er was Judah's oldest son. He was evil in the LORD's sight. So the LORD put him to death.
4 Tamar was Judah's daughter-in-law. She had Perez and Zerah by him.
The total number of Judah's sons was five.

5 The sons of Perez were
Hezron and Hamul.
6 The sons of Zerah were
Zimri, Ethan, Heman, Kalkol and Darda. The total number of Zerah's sons was five.
7 The son of Karmi was Achar.
He brought trouble on Israel. Some things that had been set apart to the LORD in a special way to be destroyed. He took some of those things. When he did that, he disobeyed the LORD's command.
8 The son of Ethan was
Azariah.
9 Hezron was the father of
Jerahmeel, Ram and Caleb.

The Family Line of Ram

10 Ram was the father of Amminadab.
Amminadab was the father of Nahshon. Nahshon was the leader of the people of Judah.

11 Nahshon was the father of Salmon.
Salmon was the father of Boaz.
12 Boaz was the father of Obed.
And Obed was the father of Jesse.

13 Jesse's first son was
Eliab. His second son was
Abinadab.
The third was Shimea. 14 The
fourth was Nethanel.
The fifth was Raddai. 15 The sixth
was Ozem.
And the seventh was David.
16 Their sisters were Zeruiah and
Abigail.
Zeruiah's three sons were
Abishai, Joab and Asahel.
17 Abigail was the mother of
Amasa. Amasa's father was
Jether. Jether belonged to the
family line of Ishmael.

The Family Line of Caleb

18 Caleb was the son of Hezron.
Caleb's wife Azubah had children
by him. Jerioth also had children
by him. Azubah's sons were
Jesher, Shobab and Ardon.
19 When Azubah died, Caleb married
Ephrath. She had Hur by him.
20 Hur was the father of Uri. And
Uri was the father of Bezalel.

21 When he was 60 years old, Hezron
married the daughter of Makir.
Makir was the father of Gilead.
Hezron slept with his wife, and
she had Segub by him.
22 Segub was the father of Jair. Jair
controlled 23 towns in Gilead.
23 But Geshur and Aram captured
Havvoth Jair. They also captured
Kenath and the settlements
around it. The total number of
towns captured was 60.
Hezron, Segub and Jair belonged
to the family line of Makir. Makir
was the father of Gilead.
24 Hezron died in Caleb Ephrathah.
Abijah was Hezron's wife. She
had Ashhur by him. Ashhur was
born after Hezron died. Ashhur
was the father of Tekoa.

The Family Line of Jerahmeel

25 Here are the sons of Jerahmeel. He
was the oldest son of Hezron.
Ram was Jerahmeel's oldest
son. Then came Bunah, Oren,

in 1 Chronicles?

God is our True Identity. Following God makes us who we are as Christians. His presence in our lives defines who we are and how we live.

Ozem and Ahijah. 26 Jerahmeel
had another wife. Her name was
Atarah. She was the mother of
Onam.
27 Here are the sons of Ram. He was
the oldest son of Jerahmeel. The
sons of Ram were
Maaz, Jamin and Eker.
28 The sons of Onam were
Shammai and Jada.
The sons of Shammai were
Nadab and Abishur. 29 Abishur's
wife was named Abihail. She
had Ahban and Molid by him.
30 The sons of Nadab were
Seled and Appaim. Seled died
without having any children.
31 The son of Appaim was
Ishi. Ishi was the father of Sheshan.
Sheshan was the father of Ahlai.
32 The sons of Jada were
Jether and Jonathan. Jada was
Shammai's brother. Jether died
without having any children.
33 The sons of Jonathan were
Peleth and Zaza.
They belonged to the family line
of Jerahmeel.

34 Sheshan didn't have any sons. All
he had was daughters.
He had a servant from Egypt
named Jarha. 35 Sheshan gave
his daughter to be married to
his servant Jarha. She had Attai
by Jarha.
36 Attai was the father of Nathan.
Nathan was the father of Zabad.

37 Zabad was the father of Ephlal.
Ephlal was the father of Obed.
38 Obed was the father of Jehu.
Jehu was the father of Azariah.
39 Azariah was the father of Helez.
Helez was the father of Eleasah.
40 Eleasah was the father of Sismai.
Sismai was the father of Shallum.
41 Shallum was the father of Jekamiah.
And Jekamiah was the father of Elishama.

The Family Groups of Caleb

42 Caleb was the brother of Jerahmeel.
Caleb's oldest son was Mesha.
Mesha was the father of Ziph.
Caleb had another son named Mareshah. Mareshah was the father of Hebron.
43 The sons of Hebron were
Korah, Tappuah, Rekem and Shema.
44 Shema was the father of Raham.
Raham was the father of Jorkeam.
Rekem was the father of Shammai.
45 The son of Shammai was Maon.
Maon was the father of Beth Zur.
46 Caleb had a concubine named Ephah.
She was the mother of Haran, Moza and Gazez.
Haran was the father of Gazez.
47 The sons of Jahdai were
Regem, Jotham, Geshan, Pelet, Ephah and Shaaph.
48 Caleb had a concubine named Maakah.
She was the mother of Sheber and Tirhanah.
49 She was also the mother of Shaaph and Sheva. Shaaph was the father of Madmannah.
Sheva was the father of Makbenah and Gibea.
Caleb's daughter was Aksah.
50 All of them belonged to the family line of Caleb.

Hur was the oldest son of Ephrathah.
Hur was the brother of Shobal.
Shobal was the father of Kiriath
Jearim. 51 Hur was the father of
Salma. Salma was the father of Bethlehem. Hur was also the father of Hareph. Hareph was the father of Beth Gader.
52 Here is the family line of Shobal, the father of Kiriath Jearim. It included
Haroeh and half of the people of
Manahath. 53 It also included the
family groups of Kiriath Jearim. They were the Ithrites, Puthites, Shumathites and Mishraites. The people of Zorah and Eshtaol belonged to these family groups.
54 Here is the family line of Salma. It included
Bethlehem, the people of Netophah, Atroth Beth Joab, half of the people of Manahath, and
the Zorites. 55 It also included the
family groups of secretaries who lived at Jabez. They were the Tirathites, Shimeathites and Sucathites. They were the Kenites who belonged to the family line of Hammath. Hammath was the father of the family line of Rekab.

The Sons of David

3 Here are the sons of David who were born to him in Hebron.

His first son was Amnon. Amnon's mother was Ahinoam from Jezreel.
The second son was Daniel. His mother was Abigail from Carmel.
2 The third son was Absalom. His mother was Maakah. She was the daughter of Talmai, the king of Geshur.
The fourth son was Adonijah. His mother was Haggith.
3 The fifth son was Shephatiah. His mother was Abital.
The sixth son was Ithream. David's wife Eglah had Ithream by him.

4 These six sons were born to David in Hebron. He ruled there for seven and a half years.

After that, he ruled in Jerusalem
for 33 years. 5 Children were born
to him there.

They included Shammua, Shobab, Nathan and Solomon. The mother of these four sons was Bathsheba. She was the daughter of Ammiel.

[6]David's children also included
Ibhar, Elishua, Eliphelet, [7]Nogah,
Nepheg, Japhia, [8]Elishama,
Eliada and Eliphelet. There were
nine of them.

[9]David was the father of all these
sons. His concubines also had sons
by him. David's sons had a sister
named Tamar.

The Kings of Judah

[10]Solomon's son was Rehoboam.
Abijah was the son of Rehoboam.
Asa was the son of Abijah.
Jehoshaphat was the son of Asa.
[11]Jehoram was the son of Jehoshaphat.
Ahaziah was the son of Jehoram.
Joash was the son of Ahaziah.
[12]Amaziah was the son of Joash.
Azariah was the son of Amaziah.
Jotham was the son of Azariah.
[13]Ahaz was the son of Jotham.
Hezekiah was the son of Ahaz.
Manasseh was the son of Hezekiah.
[14]Amon was the son of Manasseh.
Josiah was the son of Amon.
[15]Josiah's first son was Johanan.
Jehoiakim was his second son.
Zedekiah was the third son.
Shallum was the fourth son.
[16]The next king after Jehoiakim was
his son Jehoiachin.
After that, Josiah's son Zedekiah
became king.

The Royal Family Line After Jehoiachin

[17]Here are the members of the family
line of Jehoiachin. He was taken
as a prisoner to Babylon.
His sons were Shealtiel,
[18]Malkiram, Pedaiah, Shenaz-
zar, Jekamiah, Hoshama and
Nedabiah.
[19]The sons of Pedaiah were
Zerubbabel and Shimei.
The sons of Zerubbabel were
Meshullam and Hananiah.
Shelomith was their sister.
[20]There were also five other
sons. They were Hashubah,
Ohel, Berekiah, Hasadiah and
Jushab-Hesed.
[21]The family line of Hananiah
included
Pelatiah and Jeshaiah. It also
included the sons of Rephaiah,
Arnan, Obadiah and Shekaniah.
[22]The family line of Shekaniah
included
Shemaiah and his sons. They
were Hattush, Igal, Bariah,
Neariah and Shaphat. The total
number of men was six.
[23]The sons of Neariah were
Elioenai, Hizkiah and Azrikam.
The total number of sons was
three.
[24]The sons of Elioenai were
Hodaviah, Eliashib, Pelaiah,
Akkub, Johanan, Delaiah and
Anani. The total number of sons
was seven.

Other Family Groups of Judah

4 The family line of Judah
included
Perez, Hezron, Karmi, Hur and
Shobal.
[2]Reaiah was the son of Shobal and
the father of Jahath. Jahath was
the father of Ahumai and Lahad.
These were the family groups of
the people of Zorah.
[3]The sons of Etam were
Jezreel, Ishma and Idbash. Their
sister was named Hazzelelponi.
[4]Penuel was the father of Gedor.
Ezer was the father of Hushah.
These people belonged to the
family line of Hur. He was
the oldest son of Ephrathah and
the father of Bethlehem.

[5]Ashhur was the father of Tekoa.
Ashhur had two wives. Their
names were Helah and Naarah.
[6]Naarah had Ahuzzam, Hepher,
Temeni and Haahashtari by
Ashhur. They belonged to the
family line of Naarah.
[7]The sons of Helah were
Zereth, Zohar, Ethnan [8]and Koz.
Koz was the father of Anub and
Hazzobebah. He was also the
father of the family groups of
Aharhel. Aharhel was the son
of Harum.

[9]Jabez was more respected than his
brothers. His mother had named him
Jabez. She had said, "I was in a lot of
pain when he was born." [10]Jabez cried
out to the God of Israel. He said, "I wish
you would bless me. I wish you would
give me more territory. Let your power

protect me. Keep me from harm. Then
I won't have any pain." God gave him
what he asked for.

11 Kelub was the brother of Shuhah
and the father of Mehir. Mehir
was the father of Eshton. 12 Eshton
was the father of Beth Rapha,
Paseah and Tehinnah. Tehinnah
was the father of Ir Nahash. These
were the men of Rekah.

13 The sons of Kenaz were
Othniel and Seraiah.
The sons of Othniel were
Hathath and Meonothai.
14 Meonothai was the father of
Ophrah.
Seraiah was the father of Joab.
Joab was the father of Ge
Harashim. Ge Harashim was
called by that name because all
its people were skilled workers.
15 The sons of Caleb were
Iru, Elah and Naam. Caleb was
the son of Jephunneh.
The son of Elah was
Kenaz.
16 The sons of Jehallelel were
Ziph, Ziphah, Tiria and Asarel.
17 The sons of Ezrah were
Jether, Mered, Epher and Jalon.
One of Mered's wives had Miriam,
Shammai and Ishbah by
him. Ishbah was the father of
Eshtemoa. 18 These were the
children of Pharaoh's daughter
Bithiah. Mered had married her.
His wife from the tribe of Judah
had Jered, Heber and Jekuthiel
by him. Jered was the father of
Gedor. Heber was the father of
Soko. Jekuthiel was the father
of Zanoah.
19 Hodiah's wife was the sister of
Naham. Her sons were
the father of Keilah the Garmite
and Eshtemoa the Maakathite.
20 The sons of Shimon were
Amnon, Rinnah, Ben-Hanan and
Tilon.
The family line of Ishi included
Zoheth and Ben-Zoheth.
21 Shelah was the son of Judah. The
sons of Shelah were
Er and Laadah. Er was the father
of Lekah. Laadah was the father
of Mareshah. He was also the
father of the family groups of
the linen workers who lived in
Beth Ashbea.
22 Other sons of Shelah were Jokim,
Joash, Saraph and the men of
Kozeba. Moab and Jashubi
Lehem were ruled by sons of
Shelah. The records of all these
matters are very old. 23 Some of
Shelah's sons were potters who
lived in Netaim and Gederah.
They stayed there and worked
for the king.

The Family Line of Simeon

24 The family line of Simeon included
Nemuel, Jamin, Jarib, Zerah and
Shaul. 25 Shallum was Shaul's
son. Mibsam was Shallum's son.
Mishma was Mibsam's son.
26 The family line of Mishma
included Hammuel. Hammuel
was Mishma's son. Zakkur was
Hammuel's son. Shimei was
Zakkur's son.

27 Shimei had 16 sons and six daughters. But his brothers didn't have many
children. So their whole family group
didn't have as many people as Judah
had. 28 Shimei's family group lived in
Beersheba, Moladah, Hazar Shual, 29 Bilhah, Ezem, Tolad, 30 Bethuel, Hormah,
Ziklag, 31 Beth Markaboth, Hazar Susim,
Beth Biri and Shaaraim. These were
their towns until David became king.
32 Five of the villages around these towns
were Etam, Ain, Rimmon, Token and
Ashan. 33 The territory of all the villages
around these towns reached all the way
to Baalath. These were their settlements.

The tribe of Simeon kept its own
family history.

34 Simeon's family line included
Meshobab, Jamlech and Joshah.
Joshah was the son of Amaziah.
35 Simeon's family line also included
Joel and Jehu. Jehu was the son
of Joshibiah. Joshibiah was the
son of Seraiah. Seraiah was the
son of Asiel.
36 And the family line included
Elioenai, Jaakobah, Jeshohaiah,
Asaiah, Adiel, Jesimiel, Benaiah
37 and Ziza. Ziza was the son of
Shiphi. Shiphi was the son
of Allon. Allon was the son of

Jedaiah. Jedaiah was the son
of Shimri. And Shimri was the
son of Shemaiah.

38 The men whose names are listed
above were leaders of their family
groups.

Their families greatly increased their
numbers. 39 They spread out all the way to
the edge of Gedor east of the valley. They
looked for grasslands for their flocks.
40 They found grasslands that were rich
and good. The land had plenty of room.
It was peaceful and quiet. Some of the
people of Ham had lived there before.
41 The men whose names are listed
lived at the time when Hezekiah was
king of Judah. They came and attacked
the Hamites in their homes. They also
attacked the Meunites who were there.
And they completely destroyed them.
What happened to them is clear even
to this day. The men of Simeon made
their homes where the Meunites had
lived. That's because in that place there
were enough grasslands for their flocks.
42 Five hundred of these men came into
the hill country of Seir and attacked it.
They were led by Pelatiah, Neariah,
Rephaiah and Uzziel. These four men
were the sons of Ishi. 43 They killed the
rest of the Amalekites who had escaped.
And they still live there to this day.

The Family Line of Reuben

5 Reuben was the oldest son
of Israel. But he slept with
his father's concubine. By doing
that, he made his father's bed
"unclean." That's why his rights
as the oldest son were given to the
sons of Joseph, the son of Israel. So
Reuben isn't listed in the family
history as the one who had the
rights of the oldest son. 2 Judah
also did not have the rights of the
oldest son. Judah didn't have them
even though he was the leader
among his brothers. And a ruler
came from his family line. But the
rights of the oldest son belonged
to Joseph. 3 Reuben was the oldest
son of Israel. Reuben's sons were

Hanok, Pallu, Hezron and Karmi.

4 The family line of Joel includes
his son Shemaiah. Gog was the
son of Shemaiah.
Shimei was the son of Gog.
5 Micah was the son of Shimei.
Reaiah was the son of Micah.
Baal was the son of Reaiah.
6 And Beerah was the son of
Baal. Beerah was a leader of
the people of Reuben. Tiglath-
Pileser took Beerah as a prisoner
to another country. Tiglath-
Pileser was the king of Assyria.
7 Here are the relatives of the family
groups of Reuben. They are
listed in their family history.
They include Chief Jeiel, Zechariah
8 and Bela. Bela was the son of
Azaz. Azaz was the son of Shema.
Shema was the son of Joel.

All of them made their homes in the
area from Aroer to Nebo and Baal Meon.
9 To the east they made their homes
in the land up to the edge of the desert. That desert reaches all the way to
the Euphrates River. They made their
homes there because their livestock had
increased in Gilead.
10 While Saul was king, the people of
Reuben went to war against the Hagrites. They won the battle over them.
Then they lived in the houses of the
Hagrites. The people of Reuben lived in
the entire area east of Gilead.

The Family Line of Gad

11 The people of Gad lived next to the
people of Reuben in Bashan. They
spread out all the way to Salekah.
12 Joel was their chief. Shapham
was next. Then came Janai and
Shaphat in Bashan.
13 Here are their relatives family by
family. They included
Michael, Meshullam, Sheba,
Jorai, Jakan, Zia and Eber. The
total number of them was seven.
14 These were the sons of Abihail.
Abihail was the son of Huri. Huri
was the son of Jaroah. Jaroah
was the son of Gilead. Gilead was
the son of Michael. Michael was
the son of Jeshishai. Jeshishai
was the son of Jahdo. And Jahdo
was the son of Buz.
15 Ahi was the leader of some of the
families of Gad. Ahi was the son
of Abdiel. Abdiel was the son of
Guni.

16 The people of Gad lived in the land
of Gilead. They lived in the villages of
Bashan. They also lived on all the grasslands of Sharon as far as they reached.
17 All these names were written down
in the family history. They were written
during the time when Jotham was king of
Judah and Jeroboam was king of Israel.

18 The tribes of Reuben, Gad and half the
tribe of Manasseh had 44,760 men able
to serve in the army. Each one was able
to handle a shield and sword. Each was
also able to use a bow. Each was trained
for battle. 19 They went to war against
the Hagrites, Jetur, Naphish and Nodab.
20 God helped his people fight against
the Hagrites and all who were helping
them. He handed over all those enemies
to his people. That's because they cried
out to him during the battle. He answered
their prayers, because they trusted in
him. 21 They captured the livestock of the
Hagrites. They captured 50,000 camels,
250,000 sheep and 2,000 donkeys. They
also took 100,000 people as prisoners.
22 Many others were killed, because God
won the battle over them. His people lived
in the land until they themselves were
taken as prisoners to other countries.

The Family Line of Half of the Tribe of Manasseh

23 The people in half of the tribe of
Manasseh became a very large group.
They made their homes in the land from
Bashan to Baal Hermon. Baal Hermon
is also called Senir. Another name for
it is Mount Hermon.
24 Here are the leaders of their families. They included Epher, Ishi, Eliel,
Azriel, Jeremiah, Hodaviah and Jahdiel.
They were brave fighting men. They
were also famous and were leaders
of their families. 25 But they weren't
faithful to the God of their people. They
joined themselves to the gods of the nations of the land and worshiped them.
God had destroyed those nations to
make room for his people. 26 So the God
of Israel stirred up the spirit of Pul. He
was king of Assyria. He was also called
Tiglath-Pileser. He took the tribes of
Reuben and Gad and half of the tribe
of Manasseh to other countries as his
prisoners. He took them to Halah, Habor, Hara and the river of Gozan. And
that's where they still are to this day.

The Family Line of Levi

6 The sons of Levi were
Gershon, Kohath and Merari.
2 The sons of Kohath were
Amram, Izhar, Hebron and
Uzziel.
3 Aaron, Moses and Miriam
were born into the family line
of Amram.
The sons of Aaron were
Nadab, Abihu, Eleazar and
Ithamar.
4 Eleazar was the father of
Phinehas.
Phinehas was the father of
Abishua.
5 Abishua was the father of Bukki.
Bukki was the father of Uzzi.
6 Uzzi was the father of Zerahiah.
Zerahiah was the father of
Meraioth.
7 Meraioth was the father of
Amariah.
Amariah was the father of
Ahitub.
8 Ahitub was the father of Zadok.
Zadok was the father of
Ahimaaz.
9 Ahimaaz was the father of
Azariah.
Azariah was the father of
Johanan.
10 Johanan was the father of
Azariah.
Azariah served as priest in
the temple Solomon built in
Jerusalem.
11 Azariah was the father of
Amariah.
Amariah was the father of
Ahitub.
12 Ahitub was the father of Zadok.
Zadok was the father of Shallum.
13 Shallum was the father of
Hilkiah.
Hilkiah was the father of
Azariah.
14 Azariah was the father of
Seraiah.
And Seraiah was the father of
Jozadak.
15 Jozadak was taken away from
his own land. The LORD took the
people of Judah and Jerusalem
to the land of Babylon. He used
Nebuchadnezzar to take them
there as prisoners.

16 The sons of Levi were
Gershon, Kohath and Merari.
17 The names of the sons of Gershon were
Libni and Shimei.
18 The sons of Kohath were
Amram, Izhar, Hebron and Uzziel.
19 The sons of Merari were
Mahli and Mushi.

Here are the members of the family groups of the Levites. They are listed under the names of their fathers.
20 Gershon was the father of Libni.
Jahath was Libni's son.
Zimmah was Jahath's son.
21 Joah was Zimmah's son.
Iddo was Joah's son.
Zerah was Iddo's son.
And Jeatherai was Zerah's son.
22 The family line of Kohath included his son Amminadab.
Korah was Amminadab's son.
Assir was Korah's son.
23 Elkanah was Assir's son.
Ebiasaph was Elkanah's son.
Assir was Ebiasaph's son.
24 Tahath was Assir's son.
Uriel was Tahath's son.
Uzziah was Uriel's son.
And Shaul was Uzziah's son.
25 The family line of Elkanah included his son Amasai.
Amasai was the father of Ahimoth.
26 Elkanah was Ahimoth's son.
Zophai was Elkanah's son.
Nahath was Zophai's son.
27 Eliab was Nahath's son.
Jeroham was Eliab's son.
Elkanah was Jeroham's son.
And Samuel was Elkanah's son.
28 The sons of Samuel were
his first son Joel
and his second son Abijah.
29 The family line of Merari included his son Mahli.
Libni was Mahli's son.
Shimei was Libni's son.
Uzzah was Shimei's son.
30 Shimea was Uzzah's son.
Haggiah was Shimea's son.
And Asaiah was Haggiah's son.

The Levites Who Were in Charge of the Music

31 Here are the Levites David put in
charge of the music in the house of the
LORD. He did it after the ark was placed
there. 32 The men used their music to
serve in front of the holy tent, the tent
of meeting. They served there until Solomon built the temple of the LORD in Jerusalem. They did their work according to the rules they had been given.

33 Here are the men who served. The list also includes their sons.

The family line of Kohath included
Heman. He led the music.
He was the son of Joel.
Joel was the son of Samuel.
34 Samuel was the son of Elkanah.
Elkanah was the son of Jeroham.
Jeroham was the son of Eliel.
Eliel was the son of Toah.
35 Toah was the son of Zuph.
Zuph was the son of Elkanah.
Elkanah was the son of Mahath.
Mahath was the son of Amasai.
36 Amasai was the son of Elkanah.
Elkanah was the son of Joel.
Joel was the son of Azariah.
Azariah was the son of Zephaniah.
37 Zephaniah was the son of Tahath.
Tahath was the son of Assir.
Assir was the son of Ebiasaph.
Ebiasaph was the son of Korah.
38 Korah was the son of Izhar.
Izhar was the son of Kohath.
Kohath was the son of Levi.
And Levi was the son of Israel.
39 Heman had a relative named Asaph. Asaph served as Heman's helper at his right side.
Asaph was the son of Berekiah.
Berekiah was the son of Shimea.
40 Shimea was the son of Michael.
Michael was the son of Baaseiah.
Baaseiah was the son of Malkijah.
41 Malkijah was the son of Ethni.
Ethni was the son of Zerah.
Zerah was the son of Adaiah.
42 Adaiah was the son of Ethan.
Ethan was the son of Zimmah.
Zimmah was the son of Shimei.
43 Shimei was the son of Jahath.
Jahath was the son of Gershon.
And Gershon was the son of Levi.
44 Here are the Levites in the family line of Merari who served as Heman's helpers at his left side. They were relatives of the Kohathites.

Ethan was the son of Kishi.
Kishi was the son of Abdi.
Abdi was the son of Malluk.
45 Malluk was the son of Hashabiah.
Hashabiah was the son of Amaziah.
Amaziah was the son of Hilkiah.
46 Hilkiah was the son of Amzi.
Amzi was the son of Bani.
Bani was the son of Shemer.
47 Shemer was the son of Mahli.
Mahli was the son of Mushi.
Mushi was the son of Merari.
And Merari was the son of Levi.

48 The rest of the Levites were appointed to do all the other work at
the holy tent. It was the house of God.
49 Aaron and his sons after him brought
the offerings. They sacrificed them on the altar of burnt offering. They also burned incense on the altar of incense. That was part of what they did in the Most Holy Room. That's how they paid for the sin of Israel. They did everything just as Moses, the servant of God, had commanded.

50 Here are the members of the family line of Aaron.
Eleazar was Aaron's son.
Phinehas was Eleazar's son.
Abishua was Phinehas's son.
51 Bukki was Abishua's son.
Uzzi was Bukki's son.
Zerahiah was Uzzi's son.
52 Meraioth was Zerahiah's son.
Amariah was Meraioth's son.
Ahitub was Amariah's son.
53 Zadok was Ahitub's son.
And Ahimaaz was Zadok's son.

54 Here were the places where they made their homes. These places were given to them as their territory. Some were given to the children of Aaron who were from the family group of Kohath. They were given out by casting lots. The first lot was for Kohath.
55 In Judah the Kohathites were given Hebron. They also received the grasslands around Hebron.
56 But the fields and villages around the city were given to Caleb, the son of Jephunneh.
57 So the people in the family line of Aaron received Hebron. It was a city where people could go for safety. Aaron's family line received Libnah, Jattir, Eshtemoa,
58 Hilen and Debir.
59 They also received Ashan, Juttah and Beth Shemesh. They were given all these towns together with their grasslands.
60 From the tribe of Benjamin they received Gibeon, Geba, Alemeth and Anathoth. They received these towns together with their grasslands.
All these towns were handed out to the family groups of Kohath. The total number of towns was 13.

61 The rest of the members of the family line of Kohath were given ten towns. The towns were from the family groups of half of the tribe of Manasseh.
62 The members of the family line of Gershon were given 13 towns. They received them family group by family group. Most of the towns were from the tribes of Issachar, Asher and Naphtali. The rest were from the other half of the tribe of Manasseh. It's in Bashan.
63 The members of the family line of Merari were given 12 towns. They received them family group by family group. The towns were from the tribes of Reuben, Gad and Zebulun.

64 So the Israelites gave the Levites all these towns and their grasslands.

65 They gave other towns to them from the tribes of Judah, Simeon and Benjamin.

66 Some of the family groups of Kohath were given towns from the tribe of Ephraim as their territory.
67 In the hill country of Ephraim they received Shechem. Shechem was a city where people could go for safety. The Kohathites also received Gezer,
68 Jokmeam, Beth Horon,
69 Aijalon and Gath Rimmon. They were given all these towns together with their grasslands.

70 From half of the tribe of Manasseh the people of Israel gave the

towns of Aner and Bileam. They gave them to the rest of the family groups of Kohath. They gave them together with their grasslands.

71 Here is what the members of the family line of Gershon were given.
From half of the tribe of Manasseh they received Golan in Bashan and also Ashtaroth. They received them together with their grasslands.
72 From the tribe of Issachar they received Kedesh, Daberath,
73 Ramoth and Anem. They received them together with their grasslands.
74 From the tribe of Asher they received Mashal, Abdon,
75 Hukok and Rehob. They received them together with their grasslands.
76 From the tribe of Naphtali they received Kedesh in Galilee. They also received Hammon and Kiriathaim. They were given all these towns together with their grasslands.

77 The members of the family line of Merari make up the rest of the Levites. Here is what they were given.
From the tribe of Zebulun they received Jokneam, Kartah, Rimmono and Tabor. They received them together with their grasslands.
78 The tribe of Reuben was across the Jordan River east of Jericho. From that tribe the Merarites received Bezer in the desert, Jahzah,
79 Kedemoth and Mephaath. They received them together with their grasslands.
80 From the tribe of Gad they received Ramoth in Gilead. They also received Mahanaim,
81 Heshbon and Jazer. They received all these towns together with their grasslands.

The Family Line of Issachar

7 The sons of Issachar were
Tola, Puah, Jashub and Shimron. The total number of sons was four.

2 The sons of Tola were
Uzzi, Rephaiah, Jeriel, Jahmai, Ibsam and Samuel. They were the leaders of their families. The total number of fighting men who were listed in the history of the family line of Tola was 22,600. That was when David was king.
3 The son of Uzzi was
Izrahiah.
The sons of Izrahiah were
Michael, Obadiah, Joel and Ishiah. All five of them were chiefs.
4 According to their family history, 36,000 of their men were ready for battle. That's because they had many wives and children.
5 The total number of fighting men who belonged to all the family groups of Issachar was 87,000. The men were listed in their family history.

The Family Line of Benjamin

6 The three sons of Benjamin were
Bela, Beker and Jediael.
7 The sons of Bela were
Ezbon, Uzzi, Uzziel, Jerimoth and Iri. They were the leaders of their families. The total number of sons was five. Their family history listed 22,034 fighting men.
8 The sons of Beker were
Zemirah, Joash, Eliezer, Elioenai, Omri, Jeremoth, Abijah, Anathoth and Alemeth. All of them were the sons of Beker.
9 Their family history listed the leaders of their families. It also listed 20,200 fighting men.
10 The son of Jediael was
Bilhan.
The sons of Bilhan were
Jeush, Benjamin, Ehud, Kenaanah, Zethan, Tarshish and Ahishahar.
11 All these sons of Jediael were the leaders of their families. There were 17,200 fighting men who were ready to go to war.
12 The Shuppites and Huppites belonged to the family line of Ir. The Hushites belonged to the family line of Aher.

The Family Line of Naphtali

[13] The sons of Naphtali were
Jahziel, Guni, Jezer and Shillem.
They belonged to the family line
of Bilhah.

The Family Line of Manasseh

[14] Here is the family line of Manasseh.
He had a concubine who was
from the land of Aram. She had
Asriel and Makir by him. Makir
was the father of Gilead. [15] Makir
married a woman from among
the Huppites and Shuppites. He
had a sister named Maakah.
Another member of Manasseh's
family line was Zelophehad. All
he had was daughters. [16] Makir's
wife Maakah had a son by him.
She named the boy Peresh. He
had a brother named Sheresh.
The sons of Sheresh were Ulam
and Rakem.

[17] The son of Ulam was
Bedan.

These were the members of the
family line of Makir, the son of
Manasseh. Gilead was the son of
Makir.

[18] Gilead's sister was Hammoleketh.
She was the mother of Ishhod,
Abiezer and Mahlah.

[19] The sons of Shemida were
Ahian, Shechem, Likhi and
Aniam.

The Family Line of Ephraim

[20] Here are the members of the
family line of Ephraim.
Shuthelah was Ephraim's son.
Bered was Shuthelah's son.
Tahath was Bered's son.
Eleadah was Tahath's son.
Tahath was Eleadah's son.
[21] Zabad was Tahath's son.
And Shuthelah was Zabad's son.
Men from Gath killed Ezer and
Elead when they went down
to steal their livestock. [22] Their
father Ephraim mourned for
them for many days. His relatives
came to comfort him. [23] Then he
slept with his wife. She became
pregnant and had a baby boy.
Ephraim named him Beriah.
That's because something bad
had happened in his family. [24] His
daughter was Sheerah. She built
Lower and Upper Beth Horon. She
also built Uzzen Sheerah.
[25] Rephah was Beriah's son.
Resheph was Rephah's son.
Telah was Resheph's son.
Tahan was Telah's son.
[26] Ladan was Tahan's son.
Ammihud was Ladan's son.
Elishama was Ammihud's son.
[27] Nun was Elishama's son.
And Joshua was the son of Nun.

[28] The lands and settlements of the
members of Ephraim's line included
Bethel and the villages around it.
Naaran was on the east. Gezer and
its villages were on the west. The
lands and settlements included
Shechem. They also included the
villages around Shechem all the
way to Ayyah and its villages.
[29] Along the borders of Manasseh
were Beth Shan, Taanach, Megiddo
and Dor, together with their
villages. The members of the family
line of Joseph lived in these towns.
Joseph was the son of Israel.

The Family Line of Asher

[30] The sons of Asher were
Imnah, Ishvah, Ishvi and Beriah.
They had a sister named Serah.

[31] The sons of Beriah were
Heber and Malkiel. Malkiel was
the father of Birzaith.

[32] Heber was the father of Japhlet,
Shomer, Hotham and their sister
Shua.

[33] The sons of Japhlet were
Pasak, Bimhal and Ashvath.
They were Japhlet's sons.

[34] The sons of Shomer were
Ahi, Rohgah, Hubbah and Aram.

[35] The sons of Shomer's brother
Helem were
Zophah, Imna, Shelesh and Amal.

[36] The sons of Zophah were
Suah, Harnepher, Shual, Beri,
Imrah, [37] Bezer, Hod, Shamma,
Shilshah, Ithran and Beera.

[38] The sons of Jether were
Jephunneh, Pispah and Ara.

[39] The sons of Ulla were
Arah, Hanniel and Rizia.

[40] All of them were members of the
family line of Asher. They were the
leaders of their families. They were
fine men. They were brave fighting

men. They were outstanding
leaders. The total number of men
who were ready for battle was
26,000. They were listed in their
family history.

The Family History of Saul

8 Benjamin was the father of
Bela. Bela was his first son.
Ashbel was his second son.
Aharah was the third.
2 Nohah was the fourth. And
Rapha was the fifth.
3 The sons of Bela were
Addar, Gera, Abihud, 4 Abishua,
Naaman, Ahoah, 5 Gera,
Shephuphan and Huram.
6 Here are the members of the
family line of Ehud. They were
the leaders of the families who
were living in Geba. Later, they
were taken away from their own
land. They were forced to go to
Manahath. 7 The sons of Ehud
were
Naaman, Ahijah and Gera. Gera
took them away from their land.
He was the father of Uzza and
Ahihud.
8 Sons were born to Shaharaim in
Moab. That happened after he
had divorced his wives Hushim
and Baara. 9 His wife Hodesh had
sons by him. Their names were
Jobab, Zibia, Mesha, Malkam,
10 Jeuz, Sakia and Mirmah. His
sons were the leaders of their
families. 11 His wife Hushim had
Abitub and Elpaal by him.
12 The sons of Elpaal were
Eber, Misham and Shemed.
Shemed built Ono and Lod and
the villages around it. 13 Beriah
and Shema were also sons of
Elpaal. They were the leaders
of the families who were living
in Aijalon. Beriah and Shema
drove out the people who were
living in Gath.
14 Ahio, Shashak, Jeremoth,
15 Zebadiah, Arad, Eder,
16 Michael, Ishpah and Joha were
the sons of Beriah.
17 Zebadiah, Meshullam, Hizki,
Heber, 18 Ishmerai, Izliah and
Jobab were other sons of Elpaal.
19 Jakim, Zikri, Zabdi, 20 Elienai,
Zillethai, Eliel, 21 Adaiah, Beraiah
and Shimrath were the sons of
Shimei.
22 Ishpan, Eber, Eliel, 23 Abdon, Zikri,
Hanan, 24 Hananiah, Elam,
Anthothijah, 25 Iphdeiah and
Penuel were the sons of Shashak.
26 Shamsherai, Shehariah, Athaliah,
27 Jaareshiah, Elijah and Zikri
were the sons of Jeroham.
28 All these men were the leaders of
their families. They were listed as
chiefs in their family history. They
lived in Jerusalem.

29 Jeiel lived in the city of Gibeon. He
was the father of Gibeon.
Jeiel had a wife named Maakah.
30 His oldest son was Abdon. His
other sons were Zur, Kish, Baal,
Ner, Nadab, 31 Gedor, Ahio, Zeker
32 and Mikloth. Mikloth was the
father of Shimeah. Mikloth and
Shimeah also lived in Jerusalem.
They lived near their relatives.
33 Ner was the father of Kish. Kish was
the father of Saul. Saul was the
father of Jonathan, Malki-Shua,
Abinadab and Esh-Baal.
34 The son of Jonathan was
Merib-Baal. Merib-Baal was the
father of Micah.
35 The sons of Micah were
Pithon, Melek, Tarea and
Ahaz. 36 Ahaz was the father
of Jehoaddah. Jehoaddah was
the father of Alemeth, Azmaveth
and Zimri. Zimri was the father
of Moza. 37 Moza was the father
of Binea. Raphah was Binea's
son. Eleasah was Raphah's son.
And Azel was Eleasah's son.
38 Azel had six sons. Their names
were
Azrikam, Bokeru, Ishmael,
Sheariah, Obadiah and Hanan.
All of them were the sons of Azel.
39 Here are the sons of Azel's brother
Eshek.
Ulam was his first son. Jeush was
the second. Eliphelet was the
third. 40 The sons of Ulam were
brave fighting men. They could
use a bow. They had many sons
and grandsons. The total number
of sons and grandsons was 150.
All these men belonged to the
family line of Benjamin.

9 The whole community of Israel was listed in their family histories. They were written down in the records of the kings of Israel and Judah. The people of Judah were taken away from their own land. They were taken as prisoners to Babylon. That's because they weren't faithful to the LORD.

The People Who Lived in Jerusalem

2 The first people who came back from Babylon were some Israelites, priests, Levites and temple servants. They made their homes again in their own towns on their own property.

3 Some of them lived in Jerusalem. They included people from Judah, Benjamin, Ephraim and Manasseh.
4 They included Uthai. He was the son of Ammihud. Ammihud was the son of Omri. Omri was the son of Imri. Imri was the son of Bani. Bani belonged to the family line of Perez. Perez was the son of Judah.
5 The family line of Shelah included his oldest son Asaiah. It also included the sons of Asaiah.
6 The family line of Zerah included Jeuel.
The total number of the people of Judah was 690.

7 The family line of Benjamin included
Sallu. He was the son of Meshullam. Meshullam was the son of Hodaviah. Hodaviah was the son of Hassenuah.
8 Ibneiah was the son of Jeroham.
Elah was the son of Uzzi. Uzzi was the son of Mikri.
Meshullam was the son of Shephatiah. Shephatiah was the son of Reuel. Reuel was the son of Ibnijah.
9 The total number of the people of Benjamin was 956. They were listed in their family history. All these men were the leaders of their families.

10 The family line of the priests included
Jedaiah, Jehoiarib and Jakin.
11 It also included Azariah. He was the son of Hilkiah. Hilkiah was the son of Meshullam. Meshullam was the son of Zadok. Zadok was the son of Meraioth. Meraioth was the son of Ahitub. Azariah was the official who was in charge of the house of God.
12 Adaiah was the son of Jeroham. Jeroham was the son of Pashhur. Pashhur was the son of Malkijah.
Maasai was the son of Adiel. Adiel was the son of Jahzerah. Jahzerah was the son of Meshullam. Meshullam was the son of Meshillemith. Meshillemith was the son of Immer.
13 The total number of priests was 1,760. They were the leaders of their families. They were able men. It was their duty to serve in the house of God.

14 The family line of the Levites included
Shemaiah. He was the son of Hasshub. Hasshub was the son of Azrikam. Azrikam was the son of Hashabiah. Shemaiah belonged to the family line of Merari.
15 The family line of the Levites also included Bakbakkar, Heresh, Galal and Mattaniah. Mattaniah was the son of Mika. Mika was the son of Zikri. Zikri was the son of Asaph.
16 Obadiah was the son of Shemaiah. Shemaiah was the son of Galal. Galal was the son of Jeduthun.
Berekiah was the son of Asa. Asa was the son of Elkanah. He lived in the villages of the people of Netophah.

17 The men who guarded the gates were
Shallum, Akkub, Talmon, Ahiman and other Levites. Shallum was their chief. 18 He was stationed at the King's Gate on the east side. That duty has continued to this day. These guards belonged to the camp of the Levites.
19 Shallum was the son of Kore. Kore was the son of Ebiasaph. Ebiasaph was the son of Korah. Shallum and the other Levites in his family belonged to the family line of Korah. They

had the duty of guarding the
entrances to the tent. From long
ago, their people had the duty
of guarding the entrance to the
house of the LORD.
20 Long ago Phinehas, the son of
Eleazar, was in charge of those
who guarded the gate. And the
LORD was with him.
21 Zechariah guarded the entrance
to the tent of meeting. He was
the son of Meshelemiah.
22 The total number of the men who
were chosen to guard the entrances
was 212. They were listed in their
family history in their villages.

David and Samuel the prophet had
appointed them to their positions. They
appointed them because they trusted
them. 23 These Levites and their children
after them were in charge of guarding
the gates of the house of the LORD. The
house of the LORD was also called the
tent of meeting. 24 The men who guarded the gates were on the four sides of
the tent. They were on the east, west,
north and south sides. 25 From time to
time, their relatives in their villages
had to come to help them. They had to
share their duties for a week at a time.
26 But the four main men who guarded the gates were Levites. They were
trusted with the duty of taking care of
the storerooms and the other rooms in
the house of God. 27 They spent the night
in their positions around the house of
God. That's because they had to guard
it. They were in charge of the key that
opened it each morning.
28 Some Levites were in charge of the
objects that were used when they served
at the temple. They counted the objects
when they were brought in. They also
counted them when they were taken
out. 29 Other Levites were appointed to
take care of all the other things that
belonged to the temple. They also took
care of the special flour, wine, olive
oil, incense and spices. 30 Some of the
priests took care of mixing the spices.
31 There was a Levite named Mattithiah. He was the oldest son of Shallum.
Shallum belonged to the family line
of Korah. Mattithiah was trusted with
the duty of baking the offering bread.
32 The bread was placed on the table
every Sabbath day. Some Levites in the
family line of Kohath were in charge of
preparing the bread.
33 Those who led the music lived in
rooms in the temple. They were the
leaders of their Levite families. Their
only duty was to lead the music. They
had to do that work day and night.
34 All of them were the leaders of
their Levite families. They were listed
as chiefs in their family history. They
lived in Jerusalem.

The Family History of Saul

35 Jeiel lived in the city of Gibeon. He
was the father of Gibeon.
Jeiel had a wife named Maakah.
36 His oldest son was Abdon.
His other sons were Zur, Kish,
Baal, Ner, Nadab, 37 Gedor,
Ahio, Zechariah and Mikloth.
38 Mikloth was the father of
Shimeam. Mikloth and Shimeam
lived near their relatives in
Jerusalem.
39 Ner was the father of Kish. Kish was
the father of Saul. Saul was the
father of Jonathan, Malki-Shua,
Abinadab and Esh-Baal.
40 The son of Jonathan was
Merib-Baal. Merib-Baal was the
father of Micah.
41 The sons of Micah were
Pithon, Melek, Tahrea and Ahaz.
42 Ahaz was the father of Jadah.
Jadah was the father of Alemeth,
Azmaveth and Zimri. Zimri was
the father of Moza. 43 Moza was
the father of Binea. Rephaiah
was Binea's son. Eleasah was
Rephaiah's son. And Azel was
Eleasah's son.
44 Azel had six sons. Their names
were
Azrikam, Bokeru, Ishmael,
Sheariah, Obadiah and Hanan.
They were the sons of Azel.

Saul Takes His Own Life

10 The Philistines fought against Israel. The men of Israel ran away
from them. But many Israelites were
killed on Mount Gilboa. 2 The Philistines
kept chasing Saul and his sons. They
killed his sons Jonathan, Abinadab and
Malki-Shua. 3 The fighting was heavy
around Saul. Men armed with bows
and arrows caught up with him. They

shot their arrows at him and wounded him badly.

4 Saul spoke to the man who was carrying his armor. He said, "Pull out your sword and stick it through me. If you don't, these men who aren't circumcised will come and hurt me badly."

But the man was terrified. He wouldn't do it. So Saul took his own sword and fell on it. 5 The man saw that Saul was dead. So he fell on his own sword and died. 6 Saul and his three sons died. All of them died together.

7 All the Israelites who lived in the valley saw that their army had run away. They saw that Saul and his sons were dead. So the Israelites left their towns and ran away. Then the Philistines came and lived in them.

8 The day after the Philistines had won the battle, they came to take what they wanted from the dead bodies. They found Saul and his sons dead on Mount Gilboa. 9 So they took what they wanted from Saul's body. They cut off his head and took his armor. Then they sent messengers through the whole land of the Philistines. They announced the news to the statues of their gods. They also announced it among their people. 10 They put Saul's armor in the temple of their gods. They hung up his head in the temple of their god Dagon.

11 The people of Jabesh Gilead heard what the Philistines had done to Saul. 12 So all the brave men of Jabesh Gilead went and got the bodies of Saul and his sons. They brought them to Jabesh. Then they buried the bones of Saul and his sons under the great tree that was there. They didn't eat anything for seven days.

13 Saul died because he wasn't faithful to the LORD. He didn't obey the word of the LORD. He even asked for advice from a person who gets messages from people who have died. 14 He didn't ask the LORD for advice. So the LORD put him to death. He turned the kingdom over to David. David was the son of Jesse.

David Becomes King Over Israel

11 The whole community of Israel came together to see David at Hebron. They said, "We are your own flesh and blood. 2 In the past, Saul was our king. But you led the men of Israel in battle. The LORD your God said to you, 'You will be the shepherd over my people Israel. You will become their ruler.'"

3 All the elders of Israel came to see King David at Hebron. There he made a covenant with them in front of the LORD. They anointed David as king over Israel. It happened just as the LORD had promised through Samuel.

David Captures Jerusalem

4 David and all the men of Israel marched to Jerusalem. Jerusalem was also called Jebus. The Jebusites who lived there 5 said to David, "You won't get in here." But David captured the fort of Zion. It became known as the City of David.

6 David had said, "Anyone who leads the attack against the Jebusites will become the commander of Israel's army." Joab went up first. So he became the commander of the army. He was the son of Zeruiah.

7 David moved into the fort. So it was called the City of David. 8 He built up the city around the fort. He filled in the low places. He built a wall around it. During that time, Joab built up the rest of the city. 9 David became more and more powerful. That's because the LORD who rules over all was with him.

David's Mighty Warriors

10 The chiefs of David's mighty warriors and the whole community of Israel helped David greatly. They helped him become king over the entire land. That's exactly what the LORD had promised him. 11 Here is a list of David's mighty warriors.

Jashobeam was chief of the officers. He was a Hakmonite. He used his spear against 300 men. He killed all of them at one time.

12 Next to him was Eleazar. He was one of the three mighty warriors. He was the son of Dodai, the Ahohite. 13 Jashobeam was with David at Pas Dammim. The Philistines had gathered there for battle. Israel's troops ran away from the Philistines. At the place where that happened, there was a field full of barley. 14 The three mighty warriors took their stand in the middle of the field. They didn't let the Philistines capture it. They struck them down. The LORD helped them win a great battle.

[15]David was near the rock at the cave
of Adullam. Three of the 30 chiefs came
down to him there. A group of Philistines
was camped in the Valley of Rephaim.
[16]At that time David was in his usual
place of safety. Some Philistine troops
were stationed at Bethlehem. [17]David
really wanted some water. He said, "I
wish someone would get me a drink
of water from the well near the gate of
Bethlehem!" [18]So the three mighty warriors fought their way past the Philistine
guards. They got some water from the
well near the gate of Bethlehem. They
took the water back to David. But David
refused to drink it. Instead, he poured it
out as a drink offering to the LORD. [19]"I
would never drink that water!" David
said. "It would be like drinking the blood
of these men. They put their lives in danger by going to Bethlehem." The men had
put their lives in danger by bringing the
water back. So David wouldn't drink it.

Those were some of the brave things the three mighty warriors did.

[20]Abishai was chief over the three
mighty warriors. He was the brother of
Joab. Abishai used his spear against 300
men. He killed all of them. So he became
as famous as the three mighty warriors.
[21]He was honored twice as much as the
three mighty warriors. He became their
commander. But he wasn't included
among them.

[22]Benaiah was a great hero from
Kabzeel. He was the son of Jehoiada.
Benaiah did many brave things. He
struck down two of Moab's best fighting
men. He also went down into a pit on a
snowy day. He killed a lion there. [23]And
Benaiah struck down an Egyptian who
was seven and a half feet tall. The Egyptian was holding a spear as big as a
weaver's rod. Benaiah went out to fight
against him with a club. He grabbed the
spear out of the Egyptian's hand. Then
he killed him with it. [24]Those were some
of the brave things Benaiah, the son of
Jehoiada, did. He too was as famous as
the three mighty warriors. [25]He was
honored more than any of the 30 chiefs.
But he wasn't included among the three
mighty warriors. And David put him
in charge of his own personal guards.

[26]Here is a list of David's mighty warriors.

Asahel, the brother of Joab
Elhanan, the son of Dodo, from Bethlehem
[27]Shammoth, the Harorite
Helez, the Pelonite
[28]Ira, the son of Ikkesh, from Tekoa
Abiezer from Anathoth
[29]Sibbekai, the Hushathite
Ilai, the Ahohite
[30]Maharai from Netophah
Heled, the son of Baanah, from Netophah
[31]Ithai, the son of Ribai, from Gibeah in Benjamin
Benaiah from Pirathon
[32]Hurai from the valleys of Gaash
Abiel, the Arbathite
[33]Azmaveth, the Baharumite
Eliahba, the Shaalbonite
[34]the sons of Hashem, the Gizonite
Jonathan, the son of Shagee, the Hararite
[35]Ahiam, the son of Sakar, the Hararite
Eliphal, the son of Ur
[36]Hepher, the Mekerathite
Ahijah, the Pelonite
[37]Hezro from Carmel
Naarai, the son of Ezbai
[38]Joel, the brother of Nathan
Mibhar, the son of Hagri
[39]Zelek from Ammon
Naharai, from Beeroth, who carried the armor of Joab, the son of Zeruiah
[40]Ira, the Ithrite
Gareb, the Ithrite
[41]Uriah, the Hittite
Zabad, the son of Ahlai
[42]Adina, the son of Shiza, the Reubenite, who was chief of the Reubenites and the 30 men with him
[43]Hanan, the son of Maakah
Joshaphat, the Mithnite
[44]Uzzia, the Ashterathite
Shama and Jeiel, the sons of Hotham from Aroer
[45]Jediael, the son of Shimri
his brother Joha, the Tizite
[46]Eliel, the Mahavite
Jeribai and Joshaviah, the sons of Elnaam
Ithmah from Moab
[47]Eliel
Obed
Jaasiel, the Mezobaite

Fighting Men Join David

12 Some fighting men came to David at Ziklag. They were among those who helped him in battle. David had been forced to hide from Saul, the son of Kish.
2 The men were armed with bows. They were able to shoot arrows or throw stones from a sling with either hand. They were relatives of Saul from the tribe of Benjamin. Here is a list of them.

3 Their chief Ahiezer and Joash, the sons of Shemaah the Gibeathite
Jeziel and Pelet, the sons of Azmaveth
Berakah
Jehu from Anathoth
4 Ishmaiah, the Gibeonite, who was a mighty warrior among the 30 chiefs and a leader of the 30 chiefs
Jeremiah
Jahaziel
Johanan
Jozabad from Gederah
5 Eluzai
Jerimoth
Bealiah
Shemariah
Shephatiah, the Haruphite
6 the Korahites Elkanah, Ishiah, Azarel, Joezer and Jashobeam
7 Joelah and Zebadiah, the sons of Jeroham from Gedor

8 Some men of Gad went over to David's side at his usual place of safety
in the desert. They were brave fighting
men. They were ready for battle. They
were able to use shields and spears.
Their faces were like the faces of lions.
They could run as fast as antelopes in
the mountains.

9 Ezer was their chief.
Obadiah was next in command.
Eliab was third.
10 Mishmannah was fourth. Jeremiah was fifth.
11 Attai was sixth. Eliel was seventh.
12 Johanan was eighth. Elzabad was ninth.
13 Jeremiah was tenth. And Makbannai was eleventh.

14 All these men of Gad were army
commanders. The least important of
them was equal to 100 men. The most
important was equal to 1,000. 15 They
went across the Jordan River when it
was flowing over its banks. That happened in the first month of spring. They
chased away everyone who lived in the
valleys. They chased them away from
the east and west sides of the river.
16 Some men from the territories of
Benjamin and Judah also came to David
at his usual place of safety. 17 David
went out to meet them. He said to them,
"Have you come to me in peace? Have
you come to help me? If you have, I'm
ready for you to join me. But suppose
you have come to hand me over to my
enemies when I haven't even harmed
anyone. Then may the God of our people see it and judge you."
18 The Spirit of God came on Amasai.
He was leader of the 30 chiefs. He said,

"David, we belong to you!
Son of Jesse, we're on your side!
May you have great success.
May those who help you also have success.
Your God will help you."

So David welcomed them. He made
them leaders in his army.
19 Some people from the tribe of
Manasseh went over to David's side.
They did this when he marched out
with the Philistines to fight against
Saul. But David and his men didn't help
the Philistines. That's because after all
the Philistine rulers had discussed the
matter, they sent him away. They said,
"Suppose he deserts to his master Saul.
Then our heads will be cut off!" 20 So
David went to Ziklag. Here are the men
of Manasseh who went over to his side.
They were Adnah, Jozabad, Jediael,
Michael, Jozabad, Elihu and Zillethai.
They were leaders of groups of 1,000
men in Manasseh. 21 They helped David
fight against enemy armies. All the
men of Manasseh were brave fighting
men. They were commanders in David's
army. 22 Day after day men came to help
David. Soon he had a large army. It was
like the army of God.

Other Fighting Men Join David at Hebron

23 Large numbers of men came to David at Hebron. They were

prepared for battle. They came to hand Saul's kingdom over to him, just as the LORD had said. Here are the numbers of the men who came.

24 The men from Judah carried shields and spears. They were prepared for battle. The total number of them was 6,800.
25 The fighting men from Simeon were ready for battle. The total number of them was 7,100.
26 The total number of men from Levi was 4,600. [27] They included Jehoiada. He was the leader of the family of Aaron. He came with 3,700 men. [28] The men from Levi also included Zadok. He was a brave young fighter. He came with 22 officers from his family.
29 The men from Benjamin were from Saul's tribe. Most of them had remained faithful to Saul's family until that time. The total number of them was 3,000.
30 The men from Ephraim were brave fighting men. They were famous in their own family groups. The total number of them was 20,800.
31 The men from half of the tribe of Manasseh had been chosen by name to come and make David king. The total number of them was 18,000.
32 The men from Issachar understood what was going on at that time. They knew what Israel should do. The total number of their chiefs was 200. They came with all their relatives who were under their command.
33 The men from Zebulun knew how to fight well. That's because they had done it many times before. They were prepared for battle. They had every kind of weapon. They came to help David with their whole heart. The total number of them was 50,000.
34 The total number of officers from Naphtali was 1,000. They came with 37,000 men who carried shields and spears.
35 The men from Dan were ready for battle. The total number of them was 28,600.
36 The men from Asher knew how to fight well. That's because they had done it many times before. They were prepared for battle. The total number of them was 40,000.
37 The men from the tribes of Reuben, Gad and half the tribe of Manasseh were armed with every kind of weapon. The men came from the east side of the Jordan River. The total number of them was 120,000.

38 All these fighting men offered to serve in the army.

Before they came to Hebron, they
had agreed completely to make David
king over all the Israelites. All the rest
of the people also agreed to make David king. 39 The men spent three days
there with David. They ate and drank
what their families had given them.
40 Their neighbors also brought food.
They brought it on donkeys, camels,
mules and oxen. They came from as
far away as the territories of Issachar,
Zebulun and Naphtali. There was plenty
of flour, fig cakes, raisin cakes, wine,
olive oil, cattle and sheep. The Israelites
brought all these things because they
were so happy.

David Brings Back the Ark

13 David talked with each of his
officers. He wanted to get their
advice. Some of them were commanders
of thousands of men. Others were commanders of hundreds. 2 David spoke to
the whole community of Israel. He said,
"Let's send word to the rest of our people
no matter how far away they live. They
live in all the territories of Israel. Let's
also send word to the priests and Levites
who are with them in their towns and on
their grasslands. Let's invite everyone to
come and join us. Let's do it if it seems
good to you and if that's what the LORD
our God wants. 3 Let's bring the ark of
our God back here to us. We didn't use it
to ask God for advice during the whole
time Saul was king." 4 So that's what
the whole community agreed to do. It
seemed right to them.

5 David gathered together all the
Israelites. They came from the area
between the Shihor River in Egypt and

Lebo Hamath. They came to bring the ark of God from Kiriath Jearim to Jerusalem. 6 David went to Baalah of Judah. The whole community of Israel went with him. Baalah is also called Kiriath Jearim. All the people went there to get the ark of God the LORD. He sits on his throne between the cherubim. The ark is named after the LORD.

7 The ark of God was placed on a new cart. Then it was moved from Abinadab's house. Uzzah and Ahio were guiding it. 8 David was celebrating with all his might in front of God. So was the whole community of Israel. All of them were singing songs. They were also playing harps, lyres, tambourines, cymbals and trumpets.

9 They came to the threshing floor of Kidon. The oxen nearly fell there. So Uzzah reached out his hand to hold the ark steady. 10 Then the LORD became very angry with Uzzah. The LORD struck him down because he had put his hand on the ark. So Uzzah died there in front of God.

11 David was angry because the LORD's great anger had broken out against Uzzah. That's why the place is still called Perez Uzzah to this day.

12 David was afraid of God that day. David asked, "How can I ever bring the ark of God back here to me?" 13 So he didn't take the ark to be with him in the City of David. Instead, he took it to the house of Obed-Edom. Obed-Edom was from Gath. 14 The ark of God remained with the family of Obed-Edom. It stayed in his house for three months. And the LORD blessed his family. He also blessed everything that belonged to him.

David's Palace and Family

14 Hiram was king of Tyre. He sent messengers to David. He sent cedar logs along with them. He also sent skilled workers to build a palace for David. They worked with stone and wood. 2 David knew that the LORD had made his position as king secure. He knew that the LORD had made him king over the whole nation of Israel. He knew that the LORD had greatly honored his kingdom. The LORD had done it because the Israelites were his people.

3 In Jerusalem David married more women. He also became the father of more sons and daughters. 4 Here is a list of the children born to him in Jerusalem. Their names were Shammua, Shobab, Nathan, Solomon, 5 Ibhar, Elishua, Elpelet, 6 Nogah, Nepheg, Japhia, 7 Elishama, Beeliada and Eliphelet.

David Wins the Battle Over the Philistines

8 The Philistines heard that David had been anointed king over the entire nation of Israel. So the whole Philistine army went to look for him. But David heard about it. He went out to where they were. 9 The Philistines had come and attacked the people in the Valley of Rephaim. 10 So David asked God for advice. David asked, "Should I go and attack the Philistines? Will you hand them over to me?"

The LORD answered him, "Go. I will hand them over to you."

11 So David and his men went up to Baal Perazim. There David won the battle over the Philistines. He said, "God has broken through against my enemies, just as water breaks through a dam." That's why the place was called Baal Perazim. 12 The Philistines had left statues of their gods there. So David gave orders to burn them up.

13 Once more the Philistines attacked the people in the valley. 14 So David asked God for advice again. God answered him, "Do not go straight after them. Instead, circle around them. Attack them in front of the poplar trees. 15 Listen for the sound of marching in the tops of the trees. Then move out to fight. The sound will mean that I have gone out in front of you. I will strike down the Philistine army." 16 So David did just as God had commanded him. He and his men struck down the Philistine army. They struck them down from Gibeon all the way to Gezer.

17 So David became famous in every land. The LORD made all the nations afraid of him.

David Brings the Ark to Jerusalem

15 David constructed buildings for himself in the City of David. Then he prepared a place for the ark of God. He set up a tent for it. 2 He said, "Only Levites can carry the ark of God. That's because the LORD chose them to carry his ark. He chose them to serve him forever in front of the place where his throne is."

3 David gathered the whole community of Israel together in Jerusalem. He wanted to carry up the ark of the LORD to the place he had prepared for it.

4 He called together the members of the family line of Aaron. He also called the Levites together. Here are the men who came from the families of the Levites.

5 From the families of Kohath
came the leader Uriel and 120 relatives.
6 From the families of Merari
came the leader Asaiah and 220 relatives.
7 From the families of Gershon
came the leader Joel and 130 relatives.
8 From the families of Elizaphan
came the leader Shemaiah and 200 relatives.
9 From the families of Hebron
came the leader Eliel and 80 relatives.
10 From the families of Uzziel
came the leader Amminadab and 112 relatives.

11 David sent for Zadok and Abiathar, the priests. He also sent for Uriel, Asaiah, Joel, Shemaiah, Eliel and Amminadab. They were Levites. 12 He said to them, "You are the leaders of the families of Levi. You and the other Levites must set yourselves apart to serve the LORD and his people. You must carry up the ark of the LORD. He is the God of Israel. Put the ark in the place I've prepared for it. 13 Remember when the anger of the LORD our God broke out against us? That's because it wasn't you Levites who tried to carry up the ark the first time. We didn't ask the LORD how to do it in the way the law requires." 14 So the priests and Levites set themselves apart. Then they carried up the ark of the LORD. He is the God of Israel. 15 This time the Levites used the poles to carry on their shoulders the ark of God. That's what Moses had commanded in keeping with the word of the LORD.

16 David told the Levite leaders to appoint other Levites as musicians. He wanted them to make a joyful sound with lyres, harps and cymbals.

17 So the Levites appointed Heman, the son of Joel. From his relatives they chose Asaph, the son of Berekiah. Other relatives were from the family of Merari. From them they chose Ethan, the son of Kushaiah. 18 Along with them they chose their relatives who were next in rank. Their names were Zechariah, Jaaziel, Shemiramoth, Jehiel, Unni, Eliab, Benaiah, Maaseiah, Mattithiah, Eliphelehu, Mikneiah, Obed-Edom and Jeiel. They guarded the gates.

19 Heman, Asaph and Ethan played the bronze cymbals. 20 Zechariah, Jaaziel, Shemiramoth, Jehiel, Unni, Eliab, Maaseiah and Benaiah played the lyres according to *alamoth*. 21 Mattithiah, Eliphelehu, Mikneiah, Obed-Edom, Jeiel and Azaziah played the harps according to *sheminith*. 22 Kenaniah was the leader of the Levites. He was in charge of the singing because he was good at it.

23 Berekiah and Elkanah guarded the ark. 24 Some of the priests blew trumpets in front of the ark of God. Their names were Shebaniah, Joshaphat, Nethanel, Amasai, Zechariah, Benaiah and Eliezer. Obed-Edom and Jehiah also helped guard the ark.

25 David and the elders of Israel went to carry up the ark of the covenant of the LORD. So did the commanders of military groups of 1,000 men. With great joy they carried up the ark from the house of Obed-Edom. 26 God had helped the Levites who were carrying the ark of the covenant of the LORD. So seven bulls and seven rams were sacrificed. 27 David was wearing a robe made out of fine linen. So were all the Levites who were carrying the ark. And so were the musicians and the choir director Kenaniah. David was also wearing a sacred linen apron. 28 So the whole community of Israel brought up the ark of the covenant of the LORD. They shouted. They blew rams' horns and trumpets. They played cymbals, lyres and harps.

29 The ark of the covenant of the LORD was brought into the City of David. Saul's daughter Michal was watching from a window. She saw King David dancing and celebrating. That made her hate him in her heart.

Serving God in Front of the Ark

16 The ark of God was carried into Jerusalem. It was put in the tent David had set up for it. The priests brought burnt offerings and friendship

offerings to God. 2 After David finished
sacrificing those offerings, he blessed
the people in the name of the LORD. 3 He
gave to each Israelite man and woman
a loaf of bread. He also gave each one
a date cake and a raisin cake.
4 He appointed some of the Levites
to serve in front of the ark of the LORD.
David wanted them to give honor,
thanks and praise to the LORD. He is
the God of Israel. 5 Asaph was the leader
of those Levites. Zechariah was next in
rank. Then came Jaaziel, Shemiramoth,
Jehiel, Mattithiah, Eliab, Benaiah, Obed-
Edom and Jeiel. They played the lyres
and harps. Asaph played the cymbals.
6 Benaiah and Jahaziel, the priests,
blew the trumpets. They blew them at
regular times in front of the ark of the
covenant of God.

7 That day was the first time David
appointed Asaph and his helpers. He
appointed them to give praise to the
LORD with these words.

8 Give praise to the LORD. Make his
name known.
Tell the nations what he has
done.
9 Sing to him. Sing praise to him.
Tell about all the wonderful
things he has done.
10 Honor him, because his name is
holy.
Let the hearts of those who trust
in the LORD be glad.
11 Look to the LORD and to his
strength.
Always look to him.
12 Remember the wonderful things he
has done.
Remember his miracles and how
he judged our enemies.
13 Remember, you his servants, the
children of Israel.
Remember, you people of Jacob.
Remember, you who are chosen
by God.
14 He is the LORD our God.
He judges the whole earth.
15 He will keep his covenant forever.
He will keep his promise for all
time to come.
16 He will keep the covenant he made
with Abraham.
He will keep the promise he
made to Isaac.
17 He made it stand as a law for Jacob.
He made it stand as a covenant
for Israel. It will last forever.
18 He said, "I will give you the land of
Canaan.
It will belong to you."

19 At first there weren't very many of
God's people.
There were only a few. And they
were strangers in the land.
20 They wandered from nation to
nation.
They wandered from one
kingdom to another.
21 But God didn't allow anyone to
treat them badly.
To keep them safe, he gave a
command to kings.
22 He said to them, "Do not touch my
anointed ones.
Do not harm my prophets."

23 All you people of the earth, sing to
the LORD.
Day after day tell about how he
saves us.
24 Tell the nations about his glory.
Tell all people about the
wonderful things he has done.
25 The LORD is great. He is really
worthy of praise.
People should have respect for
him as the greatest God of all.
26 All the gods of the nations are like
their statues.
They can't do anything.
But the LORD made the heavens.
27 Glory and majesty are all around
him.
Strength and joy are in the place
where he lives.
28 Praise the LORD, all you nations.
Praise the LORD for his glory and
strength.
29 Praise the LORD for the glory that
belongs to him.
Bring an offering and come to him.
Worship the LORD because of his
beauty and holiness.
30 All you people of the earth, tremble
when you are with him.
The world is firmly set in place. It
can't be moved.
31 Let the heavens be filled with joy.
Let the earth be glad.
Let them say among the nations,
"The LORD rules!"

32 Let the ocean and everything in it
roar.
Let the fields and everything in
them be glad.
33 Let the trees in the forest sing with
joy.
They will sing before the LORD.
He will judge the people of the
world.

34 Give thanks to the LORD, because he
is good.
His faithful love continues forever.
35 Cry out, "Save us, God our Savior.
Save us. Bring us back from
among the nations.
Then we will give thanks to you,
because your name is holy.
We will celebrate by praising
you."
36 Give praise to the LORD, the God of
Israel,
for ever and ever.

Then all the people said, "Amen!" They
also said, "Praise the LORD."

37 David left Asaph and his helpers
to serve in front of the ark of the covenant of the LORD. They served there at
regular times. They did it as they were
required to do each day. 38 David also
left Obed-Edom and his 68 helpers to
serve with them. Obed-Edom and Hosah
guarded the gates. Obed-Edom was the
son of Jeduthun.
39 David left Zadok the priest and
some other priests in front of the holy
tent of the LORD. It was at the high place
in Gibeon. 40 David left them there to
sacrifice burnt offerings to the LORD on
the altar every morning and evening.
They did it according to everything
written in the Law of the LORD. That's
the Law he had given to Israel. 41 Heman
and Jeduthun were with the priests. So
were the rest of those who had been
chosen by name and appointed to serve.
They had been chosen to give thanks
to the LORD, "because his faithful love
continues forever." 42 It was the duty of
Heman and Jeduthun to blow the trumpets. They also had the duty of playing
the cymbals and other instruments for
the sacred songs. The sons of Jeduthun
were stationed at one of the gates.
43 All the people left. Everyone went
home. And David returned home to
bless his family.

God Makes a Promise to David

17 David moved into his palace. Then
he spoke to Nathan the prophet.
He said, "Here I am, living in a house
that has beautiful cedar walls. But the
ark of the covenant of the LORD is under
a tent."
2 Nathan replied to David, "Do what
you want to. God is with you."
3 But that night a message came to
Nathan from God. He said,

4 "Go and speak to my servant
David. Tell him, 'The LORD says,
"You are not the one who will build
me a house to live in. 5 I have not
lived in a house from the day I
brought Israel up out of Egypt
until now. I have moved my tent
from one place to another. I have
moved my home from one place
to another. 6 I have moved from
place to place with all the Israelites.
I commanded their leaders to be
shepherds over my people. I never
asked any of those leaders, 'Why
haven't you built me a house that
has beautiful cedar walls?'"'
7 "So tell my servant David, 'The
LORD who rules over all says, "I took
you away from the grasslands.
That is where you were taking care
of your father's sheep and goats. I
appointed you ruler over my people
Israel. 8 I have been with you everywhere you have gone. I destroyed
all your enemies when you were
attacking them. Now I will make
you famous. Your name will be just
as respected as the names of the
most important people on earth.
9 I will provide a place where my
people Israel can live. I will plant
them in the land. Then they will
have a home of their own. They will
not be bothered anymore. Sinful
people will no longer crush them,
as they did at first. 10 That is what
your enemies have done ever since
I appointed leaders over my people
Israel. But I will bring all your enemies under your control.
"'"I tell you that I, the LORD,
will build a royal house for your
family. 11 Some day your life will
come to an end. You will join the
members of your family who have

already died. Then I will give you one of your own sons to become the next king after you. I will make his kingdom secure. [12] He is the one who will build me a house. I will set up his throne. It will last forever. [13] I will be his father. And he will be my son. I took my love away from the man who ruled before you. But I will never take my love away from your son. [14] I will place him over my house and my kingdom forever. His throne will last forever." ' "

[15] Nathan reported to David all the words that the LORD had spoken to him.

David's Prayer

[16] Then King David went into the holy tent. He sat down in front of the LORD. He said,

"LORD God, who am I? My family isn't important. So why have you brought me this far? [17] I would have thought that you had already done more than enough for me. But now, my God, you have spoken about my royal house. You have said what will happen to it in days to come. LORD God, you have treated me as if I were the most honored man of all.

[18] "What more can I say to you for honoring me? You know all about me. [19] LORD, you have done a wonderful thing. You have given me many great promises. All of them are for my good. They are exactly what you wanted to give me.

[20] "LORD, there isn't anyone like you. There isn't any God but you. We have heard about it with our own ears. [21] Who is like your people Israel? God, we are the one nation on earth you have saved. You have set us free for yourself. Your name has become famous. You have done great and wonderful things. You have driven out nations to make room for your people. You saved us when you set us free from Egypt. [22] You made Israel your very own people forever. LORD, you have become our God.

[23] "And now, LORD, let the promise you have made to me and my royal house stand forever. Do exactly as you promised. [24] When your promise comes true, your name will be honored forever. People will say, 'The LORD rules over all. He is the God over Israel. He is Israel's God!' My royal house will be made secure in your sight.

[25] "My God, you have shown me that you will build me a royal house. So I can pray to you boldly. [26] You, LORD, are God! You have promised many good things to me. [27] You have been pleased to bless my royal house. Now it will continue forever in your sight. LORD, you have blessed it. And it will be blessed forever."

David Wins Many Battles

18 While David was king of Israel, he won many battles over the Philistines. He brought them under his control. He took Gath away from the Philistines. He also captured the villages around Gath.

[2] David also won the battle over the people of Moab. They were brought under his rule. They gave him the gifts he required them to bring him.

[3] David fought against Hadadezer in the area of Hamath. Hadadezer was king of Zobah. He had gone to set up his monument at the Euphrates River. [4] David captured 1,000 of Hadadezer's chariots, 7,000 chariot riders and 20,000 soldiers on foot. He cut the legs of all but 100 of the chariot horses.

[5] The Arameans of Damascus came to help Hadadezer, the king of Zobah. But David struck down 22,000 of them. [6] David stationed some soldiers in the Aramean kingdom of Damascus. The people of Aram were brought under his rule. They gave him the gifts he required them to bring him. The LORD helped David win his battles wherever he went.

[7] David took the gold shields carried by the officers of Hadadezer. He brought the shields to Jerusalem. [8] He took a huge amount of bronze from Tebah and Kun. Those towns belonged to Hadadezer. Later, Solomon used the bronze to make the huge bronze bowl for washing. He also used it to make the pillars and many other bronze objects for the temple.

[9] Tou was king of Hamath. He heard that David had won the battle over the

entire army of Hadadezer, the king of Zobah. 10 So Tou sent his son Hadoram to King David. Hadoram greeted David. He praised him because David had won the battle over Hadadezer. Hadadezer had been at war with Tou. So Hadoram brought David all kinds of things made out of gold, of silver and of bronze.

11 King David set those things apart for the LORD. He had done the same thing with the silver and gold he had taken from other nations. The nations were Edom, Moab, Ammon, Philistia and Amalek.

12 Abishai struck down 18,000 men of Edom in the Valley of Salt. Abishai was the son of Zeruiah. 13 Abishai stationed some soldiers in Edom. The whole nation of Edom was brought under his rule. The LORD helped David win his battles wherever he went.

David's Officials

14 David ruled over the whole nation of Israel. He did what was fair and right for all his people.

15 Joab, the son of Zeruiah, was commander over the army.
Jehoshaphat, the son of Ahilud, kept the records.
16 Zadok, the son of Ahitub, was a priest. Ahimelek, the son of Abiathar, was also a priest.
Shavsha was the secretary.
17 Benaiah, the son of Jehoiada, was commander over the Kerethites and Pelethites.
And King David's sons were the chief officials who served at his side.

David Wins the Battle Over the Ammonites

19 Nahash was king of Ammon. After he died, his son became the next king after him. 2 David thought, "I'm going to be kind to Hanun. His father Nahash was kind to me." So David sent messengers to Hanun. He wanted them to tell Hanun how sad he was that Hanun's father had died. David's messengers went to the land of Ammon. They told Hanun how sad David was.

3 The Ammonite commanders spoke to Hanun. They said, "David has sent messengers to tell you he is sad. They say he wants to honor your father. But the real reason they've come is to look the land over. They want to destroy it." 4 So Hanun grabbed David's messengers. He shaved them. He cut off their clothes just below the waist and left them half naked. Then he sent them away.

5 Someone came and told David what had happened to his men. So David sent messengers to them because they were filled with shame. King David said to them, "Stay at Jericho until your beards grow out again. Then come back here."

6 The Ammonites realized that what they had done had made David very angry with them. So Hanun and the Ammonites got 38 tons of silver. They used it to hire chariots and chariot riders from Aram Naharaim, Aram Maakah and Zobah. 7 They hired 32,000 chariots and riders. They also hired the king of Maakah and his troops. All of them came out and camped near Medeba. At the same time the Ammonites brought their troops together from their towns. Then they marched out to fight.

8 David heard about it. So he sent Joab out with the entire army of Israel's fighting men. 9 The Ammonites marched out. They took up their battle positions at the entrance to their city. The kings who came to help them gathered their troops together in the open country.

10 Joab saw that there were lines of soldiers in front of him and behind him. So he chose some of the best troops in Israel. He sent them to march out against the Arameans. 11 He put the rest of the men under the command of his brother Abishai. They were sent to march out against the Ammonites. 12 Joab said, "Suppose the Arameans are too strong for me. Then you must come and help me. But suppose the Ammonites are too strong for you. Then I'll come and help you. 13 Be strong. Let's be brave as we fight for our people and the cities of our God. The LORD will do what he thinks is best."

14 Then Joab and the troops with him marched out to attack the Arameans. They ran away from him. 15 The Ammonites realized that the Arameans were running away. So they also ran away from Joab's brother Abishai. They went inside the city. Then Joab went back to Jerusalem.

BASICS OF FAITH Q&A

When I have sinned, where should I turn?

When you've sinned, it's easy to want to run and hide. But God invites you to run to him. He is merciful and forgives all who come to him in repentance. Repentance is when we choose to turn from our sin and turn toward God.

Can you find the following verse?

1 CHRONICLES 21:13

16 The Arameans saw that they had
been driven away by Israel. So they
sent messengers to get some Arameans
from east of the Euphrates River. The
Arameans were under the command
of Shophak. He was the commander of
Hadadezer's army.
17 David was told about it. So he gathered together the whole army of Israel.
They went across the Jordan River. David marched out against the Arameans.
He lined up his soldiers opposite them.
He lined them up to meet the Arameans
in battle. The Arameans began to fight
against him. 18 But then they ran away
from Israel. David killed 7,000 of their
chariot riders. He killed 40,000 of their
soldiers who were on foot. He also killed
Shophak, the commander of their army.
19 The people who were under the rule
of Hadadezer saw that Israel had won
the battle over them. So they made a
peace treaty with David. They were
brought under his rule.
After that, the Arameans wouldn't
help the Ammonites anymore.

Joab Captures the City of Rabbah

20 In the spring, Joab led Israel's
army out. It was the time when
kings march out to war. Joab destroyed
the land of Ammon. He went to the city
of Rabbah. He surrounded it and got
ready to attack it. But David remained
in Jerusalem. Later, Joab attacked
Rabbah and completely destroyed it.
2 David took the gold crown off the
head of the king of Ammon. The crown
weighed 75 pounds. It had jewels in it.
It was placed on David's head. He took
a huge amount of goods from the city.
3 He brought out the people who were
there. He made them work with saws
and iron picks and axes. David did that
to all the towns in Ammon. Then he and
his entire army returned to Jerusalem.

Israel Goes to War Against the Philistines

4 War broke out at Gezer against the
Philistines. At that time Sibbekai killed
Sippai. So the Philistines were brought
under Israel's control. Sibbekai was a
Hushathite. Sippai was from the family
line of Rapha.
5 In another battle against the Philistines, Elhanan killed Lahmi. Elhanan was the son of Jair. Lahmi was the
brother of Goliath. Goliath was from the
city of Gath. Lahmi's spear was as big
as a weaver's rod.
6 There was still another battle. It took
place at Gath. A huge man lived there. He
had six fingers on each hand and six toes
on each foot. So the total number of his
toes and fingers was 24. He was also from
the family line of Rapha. 7 He made fun of
Israel. So Jonathan killed him. Jonathan
was the son of David's brother Shimea.
8 Those Philistine men lived in Gath.
They were from the family line of Rapha. David and his men killed them.

David Counts His Fighting Men

21 Satan rose up against Israel. He
stirred up David to count the men
of Israel. 2 So David said to Joab and the
commanders of the troops, "Go! Count
the men of Israel from Beersheba all the
way to Dan. Report back to me. Then I'll
know how many there are."
3 Joab replied, "May the LORD multiply his troops 100 times. King David,
you are my master. Aren't all the men
under your control? Why would you
want me to count them? Do you want
to make Israel guilty?"

4 In spite of what Joab said, the king's
order had more authority than Joab's
reply did. So Joab left and went all
through Israel. Then he came back to
Jerusalem. 5 Joab reported to David how
many fighting men he had counted.
In the whole land of Israel there were
1,100,000 men who could use their
swords well. That included 470,000
men in Judah.
6 But Joab didn't include the tribes of
Levi and Benjamin in the total number.
The king's command was sickening to
Joab. 7 It was also evil in the sight of
God. So he punished Israel.
8 Then David said to God, "I committed a great sin when I counted Israel's
men. I beg you to take away my guilt.
I've done a very foolish thing."
9 The LORD spoke to Gad, David's
prophet. The LORD said, 10 "Go and tell
David, 'The LORD says, "I could punish
you in three different ways. Choose one
of them for me to punish you with." ' "
11 So Gad went to David. Gad said to
him, "The LORD says, 'Take your choice.
12 You can have three years when there
will not be enough food in the land.
You can have three months when your
enemies will sweep you away. They will
catch up with you. They will destroy you
with their swords. Or you can have three
days when the sword of the LORD will
punish you. That means there would
be three days of plague in the land. My
angel would strike down people in every
part of Israel.' So take your pick. Tell me
how to answer the one who sent me."
13 David said to Gad, "I'm suffering
terribly. Let me fall into the hands of
the LORD. His mercy is very great. But
don't let me fall into human hands."
14 So the LORD sent a plague on Israel.
And 70,000 Israelites died. 15 God sent
an angel to destroy Jerusalem. But as
the angel was doing it, the LORD saw
it. The LORD decided to end the plague
he had sent. So he spoke to the angel
who was destroying the people. He said,
"That is enough! Do not kill any more
people!" The angel of the LORD was
standing at Araunah's threshing floor.
Araunah was from the city of Jebus.
16 David looked up. He saw the angel
of the LORD standing between heaven
and earth. The angel was holding out
a sword over Jerusalem. David and the
elders fell with their faces to the ground.
They were wearing the rough clothing
people wear when they're sad.
17 David said to God, "I ordered the
fighting men to be counted. I'm the
one who has sinned. I am the shepherd
of these people. I'm the one who has
done what is wrong. These people are
like sheep. What have they done? LORD
my God, punish me and my family. But
don't let this plague continue to strike
your people."

David Builds an Altar

18 Then the angel of the LORD ordered
Gad to tell David to go up to the threshing floor of Araunah, the Jebusite. He
wanted David to build an altar there to
honor the LORD. 19 So David went up and
did it. He obeyed the message that Gad
had spoken in the LORD's name.
20 Araunah was threshing wheat. He
turned and saw the angel. Araunah's
four children were with him. They hid
themselves. 21 David approached the
threshing floor. Araunah looked up and
saw him. So Araunah left the threshing
floor. He bowed down to David with his
face toward the ground.
22 David said to him, "Let me have
the property your threshing floor is
on. I want to build an altar there to
honor the LORD. When I do, the plague
on the people will be stopped. Sell the
threshing floor to me for the full price."
23 Araunah said to David, "Take it!
King David, you are my master. Do what
you please. I'll even provide the oxen
for the burnt offerings. Use boards from
the threshing sleds for the wood. Use the
wheat for the grain offering. I'll give it
all to you."
24 But King David replied to Araunah,
"No! I want to pay the full price. I won't
take what belongs to you and give it
to the LORD. I won't sacrifice a burnt
offering that hasn't cost me anything."
25 So David paid Araunah 15 pounds of
gold for the property. 26 David built an
altar there to honor the LORD. He sacrificed burnt offerings and friendship
offerings. He called out to the LORD.
The LORD answered him by sending
fire from heaven on the altar for burnt
offerings.
27 Then the LORD spoke to the angel.
And the angel put his sword away.

[28]When the angel did that, David was still at the threshing floor of Araunah, the Jebusite. David saw that the LORD had answered him. So he offered sacrifices there. [29]At that time, the LORD's holy tent was at the high place in Gibeon. The altar for burnt offerings was there too. Moses had made the holy tent in the desert. [30]David couldn't go to the tent to pray to God. That's because he was afraid of the sword of the angel of the LORD.

22 David announced, "The house of the LORD God will be built here. Israel's altar for burnt offerings will also be here."

David Makes Plans for Building the Temple

[2]David gave orders to bring together the outsiders who were living in Israel. He appointed some of them to cut stones. He wanted them to prepare blocks of stone for building the house of God. [3]David provided a large amount of iron to make nails. They were for the doors of the gateways and for the fittings. He provided more bronze than anyone could weigh. [4]He also provided more cedar logs than anyone could count. The people of Sidon and Tyre brought large numbers of logs to David.

[5]David said, "My son Solomon is young. He's never done anything like this before. The house that will be built for the LORD should be very grand and wonderful. All the nations should consider it to be famous and beautiful. I'll get things ready for it." So David got many things ready before he died.

[6]Then he sent for his son Solomon. He told him to build a house for the LORD, the God of Israel. [7]David said to Solomon, "My son, with all my heart I wanted to build a house for the LORD my God. That's where his Name will be. [8]But a message from the LORD came to me. It said, 'You have spilled the blood of many people. You have fought many wars. You are not the one who will build a house for my Name. That is because I have seen you spill the blood of many people on the earth. [9]But you are going to have a son. He will be a man of peace. And I will give him peace and rest from all his enemies on every side. His name will be Solomon. I will give Israel peace and quiet while he is king. [10]He will build a house for my Name. He will be my son. And I will be his father. I will make his kingdom secure over Israel. It will last forever.'

[11]"My son, may the LORD be with you. May you have success. May you build the house of the LORD your God, just as he said you would. [12]May the LORD give you good sense. May he give you understanding when he makes you king over Israel. Then you will keep the law of the LORD your God. [13]Be careful to obey the rules and laws the LORD gave Moses for Israel. Then you will have success. Be strong and brave. Don't be afraid. Don't lose hope.

[14]"I've tried very hard to provide for the LORD's temple. I've provided 3,750 tons of gold and 37,500 tons of silver. I've provided more bronze and iron than anyone can weigh. I've also given plenty of wood and stone. You can add to it. [15]You have a lot of workers. You have people who can cut stones and people who can lay the stones. You have people who can work with wood. You also have people who are skilled in every other kind of work. [16]Some of them can work with gold and silver. Others can work with bronze and iron. There are more workers than anyone can count. So begin the work. May the LORD be with you."

[17]Then David ordered all Israel's leaders to help his son Solomon. [18]He said to them, "The LORD your God is with you. He's given you peace and rest on every side. He's handed over to me the people who are living in the land. The land has been brought under the control of the LORD and his people. [19]So be committed to the LORD your God with all your heart and soul. Start building the temple of the LORD God. Then bring the ark of the covenant of the LORD into it. Also bring in the sacred objects that belong to God. The temple will be built for the Name of the LORD."

The Family Line of Levi

23 David had become very old. So he made his son Solomon king over Israel.

[2]He gathered together all the leaders of Israel. He also gathered the priests

and the Levites together. 3 The Levites
who were 30 years old or more were
counted. The total number of men
was 38,000. 4 David said, "From them,
24,000 will be in charge of the work of
the LORD's temple. And 6,000 will be
officials and judges. 5 Another 4,000 will
guard the gates. And 4,000 will praise
the LORD with the instruments of music
I've provided for that purpose."

6 David separated the Levites into
groups. He did it according to
the sons of Levi. The sons were
Gershon, Kohath and Merari.

The Family of Gershon

7 Ladan and Shimei belonged to the
family of Gershon.
8 The sons of Ladan were
Jehiel, Zetham and Joel. Jehiel
was the oldest son. The total
number of sons was three.
9 The sons of Shimei were
Shelomoth, Haziel and Haran.
The total number of sons was
three.
They were the leaders of the
families of Ladan.
10 The sons of Shimei were
Jahath, Ziza, Jeush and Beriah.
The total number of the sons of
Shimei was four.
11 Jahath was the first son. Ziza
was the second son. But Jeush
and Beriah didn't have many
sons. So they were counted as
one family. They had only one
task.

The Family of Kohath

12 The sons of Kohath were
Amram, Izhar, Hebron and
Uzziel. The total number of sons
was four.
13 The sons of Amram were
Aaron and Moses.
Aaron and his family line were
set apart forever as the LORD's
priests. They had the duty of
setting the most holy things
apart to the LORD. They offered
sacrifices to the LORD. They
served him. They gave blessings
in his name forever. 14 The sons
of Moses, the man of God, were
counted as part of the tribe of
Levi.
15 The sons of Moses were
Gershom and Eliezer.
16 Shubael was the oldest son in the
family line of Gershom.
17 Rehabiah was the oldest son in the
family line of Eliezer.
Eliezer didn't have any other sons.
But Rehabiah had a great many
sons.
18 Shelomith was the oldest son of
Izhar.
19 Jeriah was the first son of Hebron.
Amariah was his second
son. Jahaziel was the third.
Jekameam was the fourth.
20 Micah was the first son of Uzziel.
Ishiah was his second son.

The Family of Merari

21 The sons of Merari were
Mahli and Mushi.
The sons of Mahli were
Eleazar and Kish.
22 Eleazar died without having any
sons. All he had was daughters.
They married their cousins. The
cousins were the sons of Kish.
23 The sons of Mushi were
Mahli, Eder and Jerimoth. The
total number of sons was three.

24 Those were the family lines of
Levi. They were recorded under
the names of the family leaders.
Each worker who was 20 years old
or more was counted. They served
in the LORD's temple. 25 David had
said, "The LORD is the God of Israel.
He has given peace and rest to his
people. He has come to Jerusalem
to live there forever. 26 So the
Levites don't need to carry the holy
tent anymore. They don't need to
carry any of its objects anymore.
Those were the things that were
used to serve there." 27 The Levites
who were 20 years old or more
were counted. That was in keeping
with David's final directions.

28 The Levites had the duty of helping
the members of Aaron's family line.
They helped them serve in the LORD's
temple. They were in charge of the
courtyards and the side rooms. They
made all the sacred things pure and
"clean." They also had other duties at
the house of God. 29 They were in charge

of setting the holy bread out on the table. They prepared the special flour for
the grain offerings. They made the thin
loaves without using any yeast. They
did the baking and the mixing. They
measured the amount and size of everything. 30 They stood every morning to
thank and praise the LORD. They did the
same thing every evening. 31 They also
did it every time burnt offerings were
brought to the LORD. Those offerings
were brought every Sabbath day. They
were also brought at every New Moon
feast and during the appointed yearly
feasts. The Levites served in front of
the LORD at regular times. The proper
number of Levites was always used
when they served. They served in the
way the law required.
32 So the Levites carried out their duties for the tent of meeting and for the
Holy Room. They worked under their
relatives who were in the family line
of Aaron. They helped them serve at
the LORD's temple.

The Groups of Priests

24 The priests in the family line
of Aaron were separated into
groups. The groups were separated
according to the sons of Aaron.
The sons of Aaron were Nadab, Abihu,
Eleazar and Ithamar. 2 But Nadab and
Abihu died before their father did. They
didn't have any sons. So Eleazar and
Ithamar served as the priests. 3 With
the help of Zadok and Ahimelek, David
separated the priests into groups. Each
group served in its appointed order and
time. Zadok belonged to the family line
of Eleazar. Ahimelek belonged to the
family line of Ithamar. 4 More leaders
were found among Eleazar's family
line than among Ithamar's. So the
priests were separated into their groups
based on that fact. There were 16 family
leaders from Eleazar's line. There were
eight family leaders from Ithamar's
line. 5 The priests were separated into
their groups by casting lots. That was
the fair way to do it. The priests were
officials of the temple and officials of
God. They came from the family lines
of Eleazar and Ithamar.
6 Shemaiah was a Levite. He was
the son of Nethanel. Shemaiah was
the writer who recorded the names of
the priests. He wrote them down in
front of the king and the officials. The
officials included Zadok the priest and
Ahimelek. Ahimelek was the son of Abiathar. The officials also included the
leaders of the families of the priests and
the Levites. One family was chosen by
lot from Eleazar's group. Then one was
chosen from Ithamar's group.

7 The 1st lot chosen was for Jehoiarib.
The 2nd was for Jedaiah.
8 The 3rd was for Harim.
The 4th was for Seorim.
9 The 5th was for Malkijah.
The 6th was for Mijamin.
10 The 7th was for Hakkoz.
The 8th was for Abijah.
11 The 9th was for Jeshua.
The 10th was for Shekaniah.
12 The 11th was for Eliashib.
The 12th was for Jakim.
13 The 13th was for Huppah.
The 14th was for Jeshebeab.
14 The 15th was for Bilgah.
The 16th was for Immer.
15 The 17th was for Hezir.
The 18th was for Happizzez.
16 The 19th was for Pethahiah.
The 20th was for Jehezkel.
17 The 21st was for Jakin.
The 22nd was for Gamul.
18 The 23rd was for Delaiah.
The 24th was for Maaziah.

19 That was their appointed order for
serving when they entered the LORD's
temple. That order was based on the
rules Aaron had given them long ago.
Everything was done exactly as the
LORD had commanded Aaron. The LORD
is the God of Israel.

The Rest of the Levites

20 Here are the other members of the
family line of Levi.

From the sons of Amram came
Shubael.
From the sons of Shubael came
Jehdeiah.
21 From the sons of Rehabiah came
Ishiah. Ishiah was the oldest.
22 From the people of Izhar came
Shelomoth.
From the sons of Shelomoth
came Jahath.
23 Jeriah was the first son of Hebron.
Amariah was his second

son. Jahaziel was the third. Jekameam was the fourth.
24 The son of Uzziel was Micah. From the sons of Micah came Shamir.
25 The brother of Micah was Ishiah. From the sons of Ishiah came Zechariah.
26 The sons of Merari were Mahli and Mushi.
The son of Jaaziah was Beno.
27 The sons of Merari from Jaaziah were Beno, Shoham, Zakkur and Ibri.
28 From Mahli came Eleazar. Eleazar didn't have any sons.
29 From Kish came Jerahmeel. Jerahmeel was the son of Kish.
30 The sons of Mushi were Mahli, Eder and Jerimoth.

Those were the Levites, family by family.

31 They cast lots just as their relatives had done. Their relatives were in the family line of Aaron. They cast lots in front of King David, Zadok and Ahimelek. They did it in front of the family leaders of the priests. They also did it in front of the family leaders of the Levites. The families of the oldest brother were treated in the same way as the families of the youngest.

The Musicians

25 David and the commanders of the army set apart some of the sons of Asaph, Heman and Jeduthun. They set them apart to serve the LORD by prophesying while harps, lyres and cymbals were being played. Here is the list of the men who served in that way.

2 From the sons of Asaph came Zakkur, Joseph, Nethaniah and Asarelah. The sons of Asaph were under the direction of Asaph. He prophesied under the king's direction.
3 From the sons of Jeduthun came Gedaliah, Zeri, Jeshaiah, Shimei, Hashabiah and Mattithiah. The total number was six. They were under the direction of their father Jeduthun. He prophesied while playing the harp. He used it to thank and praise the LORD.
4 From the sons of Heman came Bukkiah, Mattaniah, Uzziel, Shubael, Jerimoth, Hananiah, Hanani, Eliathah, Giddalti, Romamti-Ezer, Joshbekashah, Mallothi, Hothir and Mahazioth.
5 All of them were sons of the king's prophet Heman. They were given to Heman to bring him honor. That's what God had promised. God gave him 14 sons and three daughters.

6 All of them were under the direction of their father. They played music for the LORD's temple. They served at the house of God by playing cymbals, lyres and harps. Asaph, Jeduthun and Heman were under the king's direction.
7 All of them were trained and skilled in playing music for the LORD. Their total number was 288. That included their relatives. 8 Young and old alike cast lots for their duties. That was true for students as well as teachers.

9 The 1st lot chosen was for Asaph. It was for Joseph and his sons and relatives. The total number was 12.
The 2nd lot was for Gedaliah and his relatives and sons. The total number was 12.
10 The 3rd was for Zakkur and his sons and relatives. The total number was 12.
11 The 4th was for Izri and his sons and relatives. The total number was 12.
12 The 5th was for Nethaniah and his sons and relatives. The total number was 12.
13 The 6th was for Bukkiah and his sons and relatives. The total number was 12.
14 The 7th was for Jesarelah and his sons and relatives. The total number was 12.
15 The 8th was for Jeshaiah and his sons and relatives. The total number was 12.
16 The 9th was for Mattaniah and his sons and relatives. The total number was 12.
17 The 10th was for Shimei and his sons and relatives. The total number was 12.

18 The 11th was for Azarel and his sons and relatives. The total number was 12.
19 The 12th was for Hashabiah and his sons and relatives. The total number was 12.
20 The 13th was for Shubael and his sons and relatives. The total number was 12.
21 The 14th was for Mattithiah and his sons and relatives. The total number was 12.
22 The 15th was for Jerimoth and his sons and relatives. The total number was 12.
23 The 16th was for Hananiah and his sons and relatives. The total number was 12.
24 The 17th was for Joshbekashah and his sons and relatives. The total number was 12.
25 The 18th was for Hanani and his sons and relatives. The total number was 12.
26 The 19th was for Mallothi and his sons and relatives. The total number was 12.
27 The 20th was for Eliathah and his sons and relatives. The total number was 12.
28 The 21st was for Hothir and his sons and relatives. The total number was 12.
29 The 22nd was for Giddalti and his sons and relatives. The total number was 12.
30 The 23rd was for Mahazioth and his sons and relatives. The total number was 12.
31 The 24th was for Romamti-Ezer and his sons and relatives. The total number was 12.

The Men Who Guarded the Gates

26 Here are the groups of men who guarded the gates.

From the family of Korah came Meshelemiah, the son of Kore. Kore was one of the sons of Asaph.
2 Meshelemiah had sons.
Zechariah was his first son.
Jediael was his second son.
Zebadiah was the third.
Jathniel was the fourth.
3 Elam was the fifth.
Jehohanan was the sixth.
And Eliehoenai was the seventh.
4 Obed-Edom also had sons.
Shemaiah was his first son.
Jehozabad was his second son.
Joah was the third.
Sakar was the fourth.
Nethanel was the fifth.
5 Ammiel was the sixth.
Issachar was the seventh.
And Peullethai was the eighth.
God had blessed Obed-Edom.
6 Obed-Edom's son Shemaiah also had sons. They were leaders in their family. That's because they
were men of great ability. 7 The
sons of Shemaiah were
Othni, Rephael, Obed and Elzabad.
Elzabad's relatives Elihu and Semakiah were also capable men.
8 All of them belonged to the family line of Obed-Edom. They and their sons and relatives were capable men. They were strong enough to do their work. The total number of men in the family line of Obed-Edom was 62.
9 Meshelemiah's sons and relatives were capable men. Their total number was 18.

10 Hosah belonged to the family line of Merari. Hosah's first son was Shimri. But Shimri wasn't the oldest son. His father had made him the first.
11 Hilkiah was Hosah's second son.
Tabaliah was the third.
Zechariah was the fourth.
The total number of Hosah's sons and relatives was 13.

12 Those groups of men guarded the gates. They worked under their leaders. They served at the LORD's temple, just as their relatives had
served. 13 Lots were cast for each
gate, family by family. Young and old alike were chosen.
14 The lot chosen for the East Gate was for Shelemiah.
Then lots were cast for his son Zechariah, who gave wise advice. The lot chosen for the North Gate was for Zechariah.
15 The lot chosen for the South Gate was for Obed-Edom. The lot

chosen for the storeroom was for his sons.
16 Lots were chosen for the West Gate and the Shalleketh Gate on the upper road. Those lots were chosen for Shuppim and Hosah.

One guard stood next to another.
17 There were six Levites a day on the east.
There were four a day on the north.
There were four a day on the south.
And there were two at a time at the storeroom.
18 Two Levite guards were at the courtyard to the west. And four were at the road.
19 Those were the groups of the men who guarded the gates. They belonged to the family lines of Korah and Merari.

Other Officials

20 Men were in charge of the treasures
in the house of God. They were the Levite relatives of the men who guarded the gates. These men were also in
charge of other treasures that had been
set apart for God.
21 Ladan was from the family line
of Gershon. Some leaders of families
belonged to Ladan's family line. One of
them was Jehieli. 22 The sons of Jehieli
were Zetham and his brother Joel. They
were in charge of the treasures in the
LORD's temple.

23 Here are the officials who were from the family lines of Amram, Izhar, Hebron and Uzziel.

24 Shubael was from the family line
of Moses' son Gershom. Shubael
was the official in charge of the
treasures. 25 His relatives through
Eliezer included his son Rehabiah.
Jeshaiah was Rehabiah's son.
Joram was Jeshaiah's son. Zikri
was Joram's son. And Shelomith
was Zikri's son.
26 Shelomith and his relatives were
in charge of all the treasures that
had been set apart for God. King
David had set those treasures
apart. Some family leaders had
also set them apart. They were the
commanders of thousands of men
and commanders of hundreds.
The treasures had also been set
apart by other army commanders.
27 Some of the goods that had been
taken in battle were set apart to
repair the LORD's temple. 28 Samuel
the prophet had set apart some
things for God. Saul, the son of
Kish, had set apart other things.
So had Abner, the son of Ner. And
so had Joab, the son of Zeruiah.
All these things and everything
else that had been set apart were
taken care of by Shelomith and his
relatives.
29 From the family line of Izhar came
Kenaniah and his sons. They
were given duties that were
away from the temple. They
were officials and judges over
Israel.
30 From the family line of Hebron
came
Hashabiah and his relatives.
They were capable men. The
total number was 1,700. It was
their duty to serve the king in
Israel west of the Jordan River.
It was also their duty to do all
the LORD's work there. 31 Jeriah
was the chief of the family line
of Hebron. That's based on their
family history.
In the 40th year of David's
rule, a search was made in the
records. That's how capable men
were found in the family line
of Hebron at Jazer in Gilead.
32 Jeriah had 2,700 relatives.
They were capable men and
family leaders. King David had
put them in charge of the tribes
of Reuben and Gad and half of
the tribe of Manasseh. They were
in charge of matters having to
do with God and the king.

The Groups of Fighting Men in the Army

27 Here is the list of the Israelites who served in the
king's army. They included
leaders of families. They included
commanders of thousands of men
and commanders of hundreds. They
also included other officers. All of
them served the king in everything
concerning the army's fighting

groups. These groups were on duty month by month all through the year. The total number of men in each group was 24,000.

2 Jashobeam was in charge of the first fighting group for the first month. He was the son of Zabdiel. The total number of men in Jashobeam's group was 24,000.
3 He belonged to the family line of Perez. He was chief of all the army officers for the first month.

4 Dodai was in charge of the second fighting group for the second month. He belonged to the family line of Ahoah. Mikloth was the leader of Dodai's group. The total number of men in Dodai's group was 24,000.

5 The third army commander for the third month was Benaiah the priest, the son of Jehoiada. Benaiah was the chief. The total number of men in Benaiah's fighting group was 24,000.
6 That same Benaiah was a mighty warrior among the 30 chiefs. In fact, he was leader over the 30 chiefs. His son Ammizabad was in charge of Benaiah's group.

7 The fourth commander for the fourth month was Joab's brother Asahel. Asahel's son Zebadiah was the next commander after him. The total number of men in Asahel's fighting group was 24,000.

8 The fifth commander for the fifth month was Shamhuth. He was an Izrahite. The total number of men in Shamhuth's fighting group was 24,000.

9 The sixth commander for the sixth month was Ira. He was the son of Ikkesh from Tekoa. The total number of men in Ira's fighting group was 24,000.

10 The seventh commander for the seventh month was Helez. He was a Pelonite from Ephraim. The total number of men in Helez's fighting group was 24,000.

11 The eighth commander for the eighth month was Sibbekai. He was a Hushathite from Zerah. The total number of men in Sibbekai's fighting group was 24,000.

12 The ninth commander for the ninth month was Abiezer. He was from Anathoth in Benjamin. The total number of men in Abiezer's fighting group was 24,000.

13 The tenth commander for the tenth month was Maharai. He was a Netophathite from Zerah. The total number of men in Maharai's fighting group was 24,000.

14 The 11th commander for the 11th month was Benaiah. He was from Pirathon in Ephraim. The total number of men in Benaiah's fighting group was 24,000.

15 The 12th commander for the 12th month was Heldai. He was a Netophathite from the family line of Othniel. The total number of men in Heldai's fighting group was 24,000.

The Leaders of the Tribes

16 Here are the leaders of the tribes of Israel.

Over the tribe of Reuben was Eliezer, the son of Zikri.
Over Simeon was Shephatiah, the son of Maakah.
17 Over Levi was Hashabiah, the son of Kemuel.
Over Aaron was Zadok.
18 Over Judah was Elihu. He was David's brother.
Over Issachar was Omri, the son of Michael.
19 Over Zebulun was Ishmaiah, the son of Obadiah.
Over Naphtali was Jerimoth, the son of Azriel.
20 Over Ephraim was Hoshea, the son of Azaziah.
Over half of the tribe of Manasseh was Joel, the son of Pedaiah.
21 Over the half of the tribe of Manasseh in Gilead was Iddo, the son of Zechariah.
Over Benjamin was Jaasiel, the son of Abner.
22 Over Dan was Azarel, the son of Jeroham.

These were the leaders of the tribes of Israel.

23 David didn't count the men who were 20 years old or less. That's because the LORD had promised to make the people of Israel as many as the stars in the sky. 24 Joab, the son of Zeruiah, began to count the men. But he didn't finish. The LORD was angry with Israel because David had begun to count the men. So the number wasn't written down in the official records of King David.

Other Officials of the King

25 Azmaveth was in charge of the royal storerooms. He was the son of Adiel.

Jonathan was in charge of the storerooms in the fields, towns, villages and lookout towers. He was the son of Uzziah.

26 Ezri was in charge of the workers who farmed the land. He was the son of Kelub.

27 Shimei was in charge of the vineyards. He was from Ramah.

Zabdi was in charge of the grapes from the vineyards. He was also in charge of storing the wine. He was a Shiphmite.

28 Baal-Hanan was in charge of the olive trees and sycamore-fig trees in the western hills. He was from Geder.

Joash was in charge of storing the olive oil.

29 Shitrai was in charge of the herds that ate grass in Sharon. He was from Sharon.

Shaphat was in charge of the herds in the valleys. He was the son of Adlai.

30 Obil was in charge of the camels. He was from the family line of Ishmael.

Jehdeiah was in charge of the donkeys. He was from Meronoth.

31 Jaziz was in charge of the flocks. He was a Hagrite.

All these men were the officials in charge of King David's property.

32 Jonathan was David's uncle. He gave good advice. He was a man of understanding. He was also a secretary.

Jehiel took care of the king's sons. He was the son of Hakmoni.

33 Ahithophel was the king's adviser.

Hushai was the king's trusted friend. He was an Arkite.

34 Jehoiada and Abiathar became the next advisers after Ahithophel. Jehoiada was the son of Benaiah.

Joab was the commander of the royal army.

David's Plans for the Temple

28 David asked all the officials
of Israel to come together at
Jerusalem. He sent for the officers who were over the tribes. He sent for the commanders of the military groups who served the king. He sent for the commanders of thousands of men and commanders of hundreds. He sent for the officials who were in charge of all the royal property and livestock. They belonged to the king and his sons. He sent for the palace officials and the warriors. He also sent for all the brave fighting men.

2 King David stood up. He said, "All of
you Israelites, listen to me. With all my
heart I wanted to build a house for the
LORD. I wanted it to be a place of peace
and rest for the ark of the covenant of
the LORD. The ark is the stool for our
God's feet. I made plans to build the
LORD's house. 3 But God said to me, 'You
are not the one who will build a house
for my Name. That is because you are a
fighting man. You have spilled people's
blood.'

4 "But the LORD chose me. He is the
God of Israel. He chose me from my
whole family to be king over Israel forever. He chose Judah to lead the tribes.
From the tribe of Judah he chose my
family. From my father's sons he chose
me. He was pleased to make me king
over the whole nation of Israel. 5 The
LORD has given me many sons. From all
of them he has chosen my son Solomon.
He wants Solomon to sit on the throne
of the LORD's kingdom. He wants him to
rule over Israel. 6 The LORD said to me,
'Your son Solomon is the one who will
build my house and my courtyards. I
have chosen him to be my son. And I
will be his father. 7 I will make his kingdom secure. It will last forever. That
will happen if he continues to obey my
commands and laws. He must continue
to obey them, just as he is doing now.'

8 “So I'm giving you a command in
the sight of all the people of Israel. The
LORD's community is watching. And our
God is listening. I command you to be
careful to follow all the commands of
the LORD your God. Then you will own
this good land. You will pass it on to
your children after you as their share
forever.
9 “My son Solomon, always remember
the God of your father. Serve him with
all your heart. Do it with a mind that
wants to obey him. The LORD looks deep
down inside every heart. He understands every desire and every thought.
If you look to him, you will find him. But
if you desert him, he will turn his back
on you forever. 10 Think about it. The
LORD has chosen you to build a house
as a holy place where he can live. So be
strong. Get to work.”
11 Then David gave his son Solomon
the plans for the porch of the temple. He
gave him the plans for its buildings and
its storerooms. He gave him the plans
for its upper parts and its inside rooms.
He gave him the plans for the place
where sin is paid for and forgiven. 12 He
gave him the plans for everything the
Spirit of the LORD had put in his mind.
There were plans for the courtyards of
the LORD's temple. There were plans
for all the rooms around it. There were
plans for the places where the treasure
of God's temple would be kept. There
were plans for the places where the
things set apart for God would be kept.
13 David told Solomon how to separate
the priests and Levites into groups. He
gave him directions for all the work
they should do when they served in
the LORD's temple. David also showed
Solomon how all the objects should be
used at the temple. 14 Different things
were used for different purposes. David
told Solomon how much gold should be
used for each gold object. He also told
him how much silver should be used for
each silver object. 15 He told him how
much gold should be used to make each
gold lampstand and its lamps. He told
him how much silver should be used
to make each silver lampstand and its
lamps. The amount depended on how
each lampstand would be used. 16 David
told Solomon how much gold should be
used to make each table for holy bread.
He told him how much silver should
be used to make the silver tables. 17 He
told him how much pure gold should
be used to make the forks, sprinkling
bowls and pitchers. He told him how
much gold should be used to make each
gold dish. He told him how much silver
should be used to make each silver dish.
18 And David told Solomon how much
pure gold should be used to make the
altar for burning incense. He also gave
Solomon the plan for the chariot of the
gold cherubim. The cherubim spread
their wings over the ark of the covenant
of the LORD.
19 David said, “I have written everything down. I wrote it all down as the
LORD guided me. He helped me understand every part of the plan.”
20 David also said to his son Solomon,
“Be strong and brave. Get to work. Don't
be afraid. Don't lose hope. The LORD God
is my God. He is with you. He won't fail
you. He won't desert you until all the
work for serving in the LORD's temple
is finished. 21 The groups of the priests
and Levites are ready to do all the work
on God's temple. Every person who is
willing and skilled can help you do
all the work. The officials and all the
people will obey every command you
give them.”

Gifts Are Brought for Building the Temple

29 Then King David spoke to the
whole community. He said,
“God has chosen my son Solomon. But
Solomon is young. He's never done
anything like this before. The task is
huge. This grand and wonderful temple
won't be built for human beings. It will
be built for the LORD God. 2 With all my
riches I've done everything I could for
the temple of my God. I've provided
gold for the gold work and silver for the
silver work. I've provided bronze for the
bronze work and iron for the iron work.
I've given wood for the things that will
be made out of wood. I've given onyx
and turquoise for the settings. I've given
stones of different colors and all kinds
of fine stone and marble. I've provided
everything in huge amounts. 3 With all
my heart I want the temple of my God
to be built. So I'm giving my personal
treasures of gold and silver for it. I'm

adding them to everything else I've provided for the holy temple. 4 I'm giving
110 tons of gold and 260 tons of pure
silver. Cover the walls of the buildings
with it. 5 Use it for the gold work and the
silver work. Use it for everything the
skilled workers will do. How many of
you are willing to set yourselves apart
to the LORD today?"

6 Many people were willing to give.
They included the leaders of families
and the officers of the tribes of Israel. They included the commanders of
thousands of men and commanders
of hundreds. They also included the
officials who were in charge of the king's
work. 7 All of them gave to the work on
God's temple. They gave more than 190
tons of gold and 380 tons of silver. They
also gave 675 tons of bronze and 3,800
tons of iron. 8 Anyone who had valuable
jewels added them to the treasure for
the LORD's temple. Jehiel was in charge
of the temple treasure. He was from the
family line of Gershon. 9 The people
were happy when they saw what their
leaders had been willing to give. The
leaders had given freely. With their
whole heart they had given everything
to the LORD. King David was filled with
joy.

David's Prayer

10 David praised the LORD in front of
the whole community. He said,

"LORD, we give you praise.
  You are the God of our father
    Israel.
  We give you praise for ever and
    ever.
11 LORD, you are great and powerful.
  Glory, majesty and beauty
    belong to you.
  Everything in heaven and on
    earth belongs to you.
LORD, the kingdom belongs to you.
  You are honored as the one who
    rules over all.

key verse

LORD, you are great
and powerful.
Glory, majesty
and beauty
belong to you.
1 CHRONICLES 29:11

12 Wealth and honor come from you.
  You are the ruler of all things.
In your hands are strength and
    power.
  You can give honor and strength
    to everyone.
13 Our God, we give you thanks.
  We praise your glorious name.

14 "But who am I? And who are my
people? Without your help we wouldn't
be able to give this much. Everything
comes from you. We've given back to
you only what comes from you. 15 We are
outsiders and strangers in your sight.
So were all of our people who lived long
ago. Our days on this earth are like a
shadow. We don't have any hope. 16 LORD
our God, we've given more than enough.
We've provided it to build you a temple
where you will put your holy Name. But
all of it comes from you. All of it belongs
to you. 17 My God, I know that you tested
our hearts. And you are pleased when
we are honest. I've given all these things
just because I wanted to. When I did
it, I was completely honest with you.
Your people here have also been willing
to give to you. And I've been happy
to see this. 18 LORD, you are the God of
our fathers Abraham, Isaac and Israel.
Keep these desires and thoughts in the
hearts of your people forever. Keep their
hearts faithful to you. 19 Help my son
Solomon serve you with all his heart.
Then he will keep your commands and
rules. He will do what you require. He'll
do everything to build the grand and
wonderful temple I've provided for."

20 Then David said to the whole community, "Praise the LORD your God." So
all of them praised the LORD. He's the
God of their people who lived long ago.
The whole community bowed low. They
fell down flat with their faces toward
the ground. They did it in front of the
LORD and the king.

Solomon Becomes the Next King

21 The next day they offered sacrifices to the LORD. They brought burnt
offerings to him. They sacrificed 1,000
bulls, 1,000 rams and 1,000 male lambs.
They also brought the required drink
offerings. And they offered many other
sacrifices for the whole community of
Israel. 22 They ate and drank with great
joy that day. They did it in front of the

LORD. Then they announced a second time that Solomon was king. He was the son of David. They anointed Solomon in front of the LORD. They anointed him to be ruler. They also anointed Zadok to be priest.

23 So Solomon sat on the throne of the LORD. He ruled as king in place of his father David. Things went well with him. All the people of Israel obeyed him.
24 All the officers and warriors promised to be completely faithful to King Solomon. So did all of King David's sons.

25 The LORD greatly honored Solomon in the sight of all the people. He gave him royal majesty. Solomon was given more glory than any king over Israel ever had before.

David Dies

26 David was king over the whole nation of Israel. He was the son of Jesse.
27 He ruled over Israel for 40 years. He ruled for seven years in Hebron and for 33 years in Jerusalem. 28 He died when he was very old. He had enjoyed a long life. He had enjoyed wealth and honor. David's son Solomon became the next king after him.

29 The events of King David's rule from beginning to end are written down. They are written in the records of Samuel, Nathan and Gad, the prophets. 30 The records tell all about David's rule and power. They tell about what happened concerning him and Israel and the kingdoms of all the other lands.

2 CHRONICLES

Author: Ezra (we think)

Second Chronicles retells the history of Solomon and the kings who led the people of Judah away from God until they were captured by the Babylonians. This book once again shows the importance of the temple: the place where God himself lived among his people and where the Israelites could come and worship him, being made right with God by offering sacrifices for their sins.

But—like so many times before—the people rejected God. They disobeyed God's commands and forgot his promises. And the consequence for their sin was that another nation, the Babylonians, destroyed the temple. God's people were carried away from their homeland and made slaves again. How could God live among them since the temple was destroyed? How would they find their way back home? How would they ever return to being God's special, set-apart people?

God reminded his people that the temple was always meant to point them toward the Savior who would live among them. Jesus was on his way, and he was going to be the presence of God in this world! Jesus was going to make a way for the whole world to come back home to God.

Solomon Asks God for Wisdom

1 Solomon was the son of David. Solomon made his position secure over his kingdom. The LORD his God was with him. He made Solomon very great.

2 Solomon spoke to the whole community of Israel. He spoke to the commanders of thousands of men and commanders of hundreds. He spoke to the judges and all the leaders in Israel. He spoke to the leaders of Israel's families. 3 Solomon and the whole community went to the high place at Gibeon. That's because God's tent of meeting was there. The LORD's servant Moses had made the tent in the desert. 4 David had carried up the ark of God from Kiriath Jearim. He had it brought to the place he had prepared for it. He had set up a tent for it in Jerusalem. 5 But the bronze altar that Bezalel had made was in Gibeon. Bezalel was the son of Uri. Uri was the son of Hur. The altar was in front of the LORD's holy tent. So Solomon and the whole community asked the LORD for advice in Gibeon. 6 Solomon went up to the bronze altar in front of the LORD at the tent of meeting. Solomon sacrificed 1,000 burnt offerings on the altar.

7 That night God appeared to Solomon. He said to him, "Ask for anything you want me to give you."

8 Solomon answered God, "You were very kind to my father David. Now you have made me king in his place. 9 LORD God, let the promise you gave to my father David come true. You have made me king. My people are as many as the dust of the earth. They can't be counted. 10 Give me wisdom and knowledge. Then I'll be able to lead these people. Without your help, who would be able to rule this great nation of yours?"

11 God said to Solomon, "I am glad that those are the things you really want. You have not asked for wealth, possessions or honor. You have not even asked to have your enemies killed. You have not asked to live for a long time. Instead, you have asked for wisdom and knowledge. You want to be able to rule my people wisely. I have made you king over them. 12 So wisdom and knowledge will be given to you. I will also give you wealth, possessions and honor. You will have more than any king before you ever had. And no king after you will have as much."

13 Then Solomon left the high place at Gibeon. He went from the tent of meeting there to Jerusalem. And he ruled over Israel.

14 Solomon had 1,400 chariots and 12,000 horses. He kept some of them in the chariot cities. He kept others with him in Jerusalem. 15 The king made silver and gold as common in Jerusalem as stones. He made cedar wood as common there as sycamore-fig trees in the western hills. 16 Solomon got horses from Egypt and Kue. The king's buyers purchased them from Kue at the current price. 17 They could get a chariot from Egypt for 15 pounds of silver. They could get a horse for less than four pounds of silver. They sold horses and chariots to all the Hittite and Aramean kings.

Solomon Prepares to Build the Temple

2 Solomon gave orders to build a temple. That's where the LORD would put his Name. Solomon also gave orders to build a royal palace for himself. 2 He chose 70,000 men to carry things. He chose 80,000 to cut stones in the hills. He put 3,600 men in charge of them.

3 Solomon sent a message to Hiram. Hiram was king of Tyre. Solomon said,

> "Send me cedar logs, just as you did for my father David. You sent him cedar to build a palace to live in. 4 Now I'm about to build a temple. The Name of the LORD my God will be there. I'll set the temple apart for him. Sweet-smelling incense will be burned in front of him there. The holy bread will be set out at regular times. Burnt offerings will be sacrificed there every morning and evening. They will be sacrificed every Sabbath day. They will be sacrificed at every New Moon feast. And they will be sacrificed at every yearly appointed feast of the LORD our God. That's a law for Israel that will last for all time to come.
>
> 5 "The temple I'm going to build will be beautiful. That's because our God is greater than all other gods. 6 So who is able to build a temple for him? After all, the heavens can't hold him. In fact, not even the highest heavens can hold him. So who am I to build a temple for

in 2 Chronicles?

God is our Constant Help. Even though the Israelites disobeyed, God made a way for them to return and worship him.

him? It will only be a place to burn sacrifices in front of him.

7 "Send me a man skilled at working with gold, silver, bronze and iron. He must also be able to work with purple, blue and bright red yarn. He must be skilled in the art of carving. Send him to work in Judah and Jerusalem with my skilled workers. My father David provided them to help me.

8 "Also send me cedar, juniper and algum logs from Lebanon. I know that your servants are skilled in cutting wood there. My servants will work with yours. 9 They'll provide me with plenty of lumber. That's because the temple I'm building must be large and beautiful. 10 I'll pay your servants. They will cut the wood. I'll pay them 3,600 tons of wheat that has been ground up. I'll pay them 3,000 tons of barley. I'll also pay them 120,000 gallons of wine and 120,000 gallons of olive oil."

11 King Hiram of Tyre replied to Solomon. He wrote a letter to him. In it Hiram said,

"The LORD loves his people. That's why he has made you their king."

12 Hiram continued,

"I praise the LORD. He is the God of Israel. He made heaven and earth. He has given King David a wise son. You have good sense. You understand what is right. You will build a temple for the LORD. You will also build a palace for yourself.

13 "I'm sending Huram-Abi to you. He is very skillful. 14 His mother was from Dan. His father was from Tyre. He is trained to work with gold, silver, bronze and iron. He knows how to work with stone and wood. He can also work with purple, blue and bright red yarn and fine linen. He's skilled in all kinds of carving. He can follow any pattern you give him. He'll work with your skilled workers. He'll also work with those of your father David. David was my master.

15 "Now please send us what you promised. Send us the wheat, barley, olive oil and wine. 16 And we'll cut all the logs from Lebanon that you need. We'll make rafts out of them. We'll float them by sea down to Joppa. Then you can take them up to Jerusalem."

17 Solomon counted all the outsiders who were living in Israel. He did it after his father David had counted them. There were 153,600 of them. 18 He chose 70,000 to carry things. He chose 80,000 to cut stones in the hills. He put 3,600 men in charge of the people to keep them working.

Solomon Builds the Temple

3 Then Solomon began to build the temple of the LORD. He built it on Mount Moriah in Jerusalem. That's where the LORD had appeared to Solomon's father David. The LORD had appeared at the threshing floor of Araunah. Araunah was from Jebus. David had provided the threshing floor. 2 Solomon began building the temple on the second day of the second month. It was in the fourth year of his rule.

3 Solomon laid the foundation for God's temple. It was 90 feet long and 30 feet wide. Solomon's men followed the standard measure used at that time. 4 The porch in front of the temple was 30 feet across and 30 feet high.

Solomon covered the inside of the temple with pure gold. 5 He covered the inside of the main hall with juniper boards. Then he covered the boards

with fine gold. He decorated the hall
with palm tree patterns and chain patterns. 6 He decorated the temple with
valuable jewels. The gold he used came
from Parvaim. 7 He covered the ceiling
beams, doorframes, walls and doors of
the temple with gold. He carved cherubim on the walls.
8 He built the Most Holy Room. It was
as long as the temple was wide. It was 30
feet long and 30 feet wide. He covered
the inside of the Most Holy Room with
23 tons of fine gold. 9 He also covered
the upper parts with gold. The gold on
the nails weighed 20 ounces.
10 For the Most Holy Room, Solomon
made a pair of carved cherubim. He covered them with gold. 11 The total length
of the cherubim's wings from tip to tip
was 30 feet. One wing of the first cherub
was seven and a half feet long. Its tip
touched the temple wall. The other wing
was also seven and a half feet long. Its
tip touched the wing tip of the other
cherub. 12 In the same way one wing of
the second cherub was seven and a half
feet long. Its tip touched the other temple wall. The other wing was also seven
and a half feet long. Its tip touched the
wing tip of the first cherub. 13 So the total
length of the wings of the two cherubim
was 30 feet from tip to tip. The cherubim
stood facing the main hall.
14 Solomon made the curtain out of
blue, purple and bright red yarn and
fine linen. A skilled worker sewed cherubim into its pattern.
15 For the front of the temple, Solomon
made two pillars. Each pillar was 26 feet
tall. Each had a decorated top seven
and a half feet high. 16 Solomon made
chains that were linked together. He put
them on top of the pillars. He also made
100 pomegranates. He fastened them
to the chains. 17 Solomon set the pillars
up in front of the temple. One was on
the south. The other was on the north.
He named the one on the south Jakin.
The one on the north he named Boaz.

More Facts About the Temple

4 Solomon made a bronze altar 30
feet long, 30 feet wide and 15 feet
high. 2 He made a huge metal bowl for
washing. Its shape was round. It measured 15 feet from rim to rim. It was
seven and a half feet high. And it was 45
feet around. 3 Below the rim there was a
circle of bull figures around the bowl. In
every 18 inches around the bowl there
were ten bulls. The bulls were arranged
in two rows. They were made as part of
the bowl itself.

4 The bowl stood on 12 bulls. Three
of them faced north. Three faced west.
Three faced south. And three faced east.
The bowl rested on top of them. Their
rear ends were toward the center. 5 The
bowl was three inches thick. Its rim
was like the rim of a cup. The rim was
shaped like the bloom of a lily. The bowl
held 18,000 gallons of water.
6 Solomon made ten smaller bowls
for washing. He placed five of them
on the south side of the huge bowl. He
placed the other five on the north side.
The things used for the burnt offerings
were rinsed in the smaller bowls. But the
priests used the huge bowl for washing.
7 Solomon made ten gold lampstands.
He followed the pattern the LORD had
given him. He placed the lampstands
in the temple. He put five of them on
the south side. He put the other five on
the north side.
8 He made ten tables. He placed them
in the temple. He put five of them on
the south side. He put the other five on
the north side. He also made 100 gold
sprinkling bowls.
9 He made the courtyard of the priests.
He also made the large courtyard. He
made doors for it. He covered the doors
with bronze. 10 He placed the huge bowl
on the south side of the courtyard. He
put it at the southeast corner.
11 And Huram also made the pots,
shovels and sprinkling bowls.

So Huram finished the work he had
started for King Solomon. Here's what
he made for God's temple.

12 He made the two pillars.
He made the two tops for the pillars.
The tops were shaped like bowls.
He made the two sets of chains
that were linked together. They
decorated the two bowl-shaped
tops of the pillars.
13 He made the 400 pomegranates for
the two sets of chains. There were
two rows of pomegranates for
each chain. They decorated the
bowl-shaped tops of the pillars.
14 He made the stands and their
bowls.
15 He made the huge bowl. He made
the 12 bulls that were under it.
16 He made the pots, shovels and
meat forks. He also made all
the things used with them.

Huram-Abi made all these objects for
King Solomon for the LORD's temple.
He made them out of bronze. Then he
shined them up. 17 The king had them

pointing us to JESUS: The Temple

The holy tent was God's movable house that the Israelites took with them wherever they went. But one day God told them it was time to build him a permanent home with a rock-solid foundation.

This home was called the temple, and it was a sign to God's people that they were finally home! They had finally settled in the land God had promised to bring his people to all those generations ago. God was going to have the Israelites build him a house with a firm foundation because they weren't going to move around anymore. God's house would now be among them permanently.

The temple was God's promise to always be with his people. He kept that promise by sending Jesus Christ, who is the foundation on which we can build our lives. To those who put their faith in Jesus, God gives his Spirit, the Holy Spirit, to live inside them. The New Testament uses this special Old Testament word, *temple*, to talk about how God's Spirit comes to live within those who are in Christ—all of God's people are the temple of God (see 1 Corinthians 3:16).

made in clay molds. It was done on the
plains of the Jordan River between Sukkoth and Zarethan. 18 Solomon made
huge numbers of these things. There
were too many of them to weigh. In
fact, it was impossible to add up the
weight of all the bronze.
19 Solomon also made all the objects
that were in God's temple.

He made the golden altar.
He made the tables for the holy
bread.
20 He made the pure gold lampstands
and their lamps. The lamps
burned in front of the Most Holy
Room, just as the law required.
21 He made the gold flowers. He made
the gold lamps and tongs. They
were made out of solid gold.
22 He made the wick cutters, sprinkling
bowls, dishes, and shallow cups
for burning incense. All of them
were made out of pure gold.
He made the gold doors of the
temple. They were the inner
doors to the Most Holy Room
and the doors of the main hall.

5 Solomon finished all the work for
the LORD's temple. Then he brought
in the things his father David had set
apart for the LORD. They included the
silver and gold and all the objects for
God's temple. Solomon placed them
there with the other treasures.

The Ark Is Brought to the Temple

2 Then Solomon sent for the elders
of Israel. He told them to come to Jerusalem. They included all the leaders
of the tribes. They also included the
chiefs of the families of Israel. Solomon
wanted them to bring up the ark of the
LORD's covenant from Zion. Zion was the
City of David. 3 All the Israelites came
together to where the king was. It was
at the time of the Feast of Booths. The
feast was held in the seventh month.
4 All the elders of Israel arrived. Then
the Levites picked up the ark and carried it. 5 They brought up the ark. They
also brought up the tent of meeting
and all the sacred things in the tent.
The priests, who were Levites, carried
up everything. 6 The entire community
of Israel had gathered around King
Solomon. All of them were in front of
the ark. They sacrificed huge numbers
of sheep and cattle. There were so many
animals that they couldn't be recorded.
In fact, they couldn't even be counted.
7 The priests brought the ark of the
LORD's covenant to its place in the Most
Holy Room of the temple. They put it
under the wings of the cherubim. 8 The
cherubim's wings were spread out over
the place where the ark was. They covered the ark. They also covered the poles
used to carry it. 9 The poles reached out
from the ark. They were so long that
their ends could be seen from in front of
the Most Holy Room. But they couldn't
be seen from outside the Holy Room.
They are still there to this day. 10 There
wasn't anything in the ark except the
two tablets. Moses had placed them in it
at Mount Horeb. That's where the LORD
had made a covenant with the Israelites.
He made it after they came out of Egypt.
11 The priests left the Holy Room.
All the priests who were there had set
themselves apart to the LORD. It didn't
matter what group they were in. 12 All
the Levites who played music stood near
the east side of the altar. They included Asaph, Heman, Jeduthun and their
sons and relatives. They were dressed in
fine linen. They were playing cymbals,
harps and lyres. They were joined by
120 priests who were blowing trumpets.
13 The trumpet players and other musicians played their instruments together.
They praised the LORD and gave thanks
to him. The singers sang to the music of
the trumpets, cymbals and other instruments. They sang in praise to the LORD,

"The LORD is good.
His faithful love continues
forever."

Then a cloud filled the temple of the
LORD. 14 The priests couldn't do their
work. That's because the cloud of the
LORD's glory filled God's temple.

6 Then Solomon said, "LORD, you
have said you would live in a dark
cloud. 2 I've built a beautiful temple for
you. You can live in it forever."
3 The whole community of Israel was
standing there. The king turned around
and gave them his blessing. 4 Then he
said,

"I praise the LORD. He is the God
of Israel. With his mouth he made

a promise to my father David. With his powerful hands he made it come true. He said, 5 'I brought my people out of Egypt. Since then, a temple for my Name has not been built. I have not chosen a city in any tribe of Israel for that purpose. And I have not chosen anyone to be ruler over my people Israel. 6 But now I have chosen Jerusalem. I will put my Name there. And I have chosen David to rule over my people Israel.'

7 "With all his heart my father David wanted to build a temple. He wanted to do it so the Name of the LORD could be there. The LORD is the God of Israel. 8 But the LORD spoke to my father David. He said, 'With all your heart you wanted to build a temple for my Name. It is good that you wanted to do that. 9 But you will not build the temple. Instead, your son will build the temple for my Name. He is your own flesh and blood.'

10 "The LORD has kept the promise he made. I've become the next king after my father David. Now I'm sitting on the throne of Israel. That's exactly what the LORD promised would happen. I've built the temple for the Name of the LORD. He is the God of Israel. 11 I've placed the ark there. The tablets of the LORD's covenant are inside it. He made that covenant with the people of Israel."

Solomon Prays to Set the Temple Apart to the LORD

12 Then Solomon stood in front of the LORD's altar. He stood in front of the whole community of Israel. He spread out his hands to pray. 13 He had made a bronze stage. It was seven and a half feet long and seven and a half feet wide. It was four and a half feet high. He had placed it in the center of the outer courtyard. He stood on the stage. Then he got down on his knees in front of the whole community of Israel. He spread out his hands toward heaven. 14 He said,

"LORD, you are the God of Israel. There is no God like you in heaven or on earth. You keep the covenant you made with us. You show us your love. You do that when we follow you with all our hearts. 15 You have kept your promise to my father David. He was your servant. With your mouth you made a promise. With your powerful hand you have made it come true. And today we can see it.

16 "LORD, you are the God of Israel. Keep the promises you made to my father David. Do it for him. He was your servant. You said to him, 'You will always have a son from your family line to sit on Israel's throne. He will sit in front of the Most Holy Room, where my own throne is. That will be true only if your children after you are careful in everything they do. They must live the way my law tells them to. That is the way you have lived.' 17 LORD, you are the God of Israel. So let your promise to your servant David come true.

18 "But will God really live on earth with human beings? After all, the heavens can't hold you. In fact, even the highest heavens can't hold you. So this temple I've built certainly can't hold you! 19 But please pay attention to my prayer. LORD my God, be ready to help me as I make my appeal to you. Listen to my cry for help. Hear the prayer I'm praying to you. 20 Let your eyes look toward this temple day and night. You said you would put your Name here. Listen to the prayer I'm praying toward this place. 21 Hear me when I ask you to help us. Listen to your people Israel when they pray toward this place. Listen to us from heaven. It's the place where you live. When you hear us, forgive us.

22 "Suppose someone does something wrong to their neighbor. And the person who has done something wrong is required to give their word. They must tell the truth about what they have done. They must come and do it in front of your altar in this temple. 23 When they do, listen to them from heaven. Take action. Judge between the person and their neighbor. Pay back the guilty one. Do to them what they have done to their neighbor. Deal with the one who isn't guilty in a way that shows they are free from blame. That will prove they aren't guilty.

[24]"Suppose your people Israel have lost the battle against their enemies. And suppose they've sinned against you. But they turn back to you and praise your name. They pray to you in this temple. And they ask you to help them. [25]Then listen to them from heaven. Forgive the sin of your people Israel. Bring them back to the land you gave to them and their people who lived long ago.

[26]"Suppose your people have sinned against you. And because of that, the sky is closed up and there isn't any rain. But your people pray toward this place. They praise you by admitting they've sinned. And they turn away from their sin because you have made them suffer. [27]Then listen to them from heaven. Forgive the sin of your people Israel. Teach them the right way to live. Send rain on the land you gave them as their share.

[28]"Suppose there isn't enough food in the land. And a plague strikes the land. The hot winds completely dry up our crops. Or locusts or grasshoppers come and eat them up. Or enemies surround one of our cities and get ready to attack it. Or trouble or sickness comes. [29]But suppose one of your people prays to you. They ask you to help them. They are aware of how much they are suffering. And they spread out their hands toward this temple to pray. [30]Then listen to them from heaven. It's the place where you live. Forgive them. Deal with everyone in keeping with everything they do. You know their hearts. In fact, you are the only one who knows every human heart. [31]Your people will have respect for you. They will live the way you want them to. They'll live that way as long as they are in the land you gave our people long ago.

[32]"Suppose an outsider who doesn't belong to your people Israel has come from a land far away. They have come because they've heard about your great name. They have heard that you reached out your mighty hand and powerful arm. So they come and pray toward this temple. [33]Then listen to them

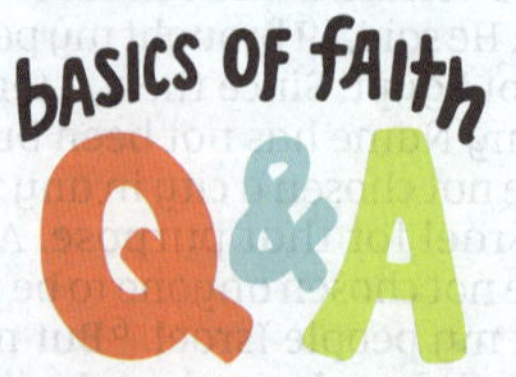

Will God ever give up on me?

No matter what you've done, God loves you and wants to be with you. He continually pursues his people and offers his amazing grace.

Can you find the following verse?

2 CHRONICLES 7:14

from heaven. It's the place where you live. Do what that outsider asks you to do. Then all the nations on earth will know you. They will have respect for you. They'll respect you just as your own people Israel do. They'll know that your Name is in this house I've built.

[34]"Suppose your people go to war against their enemies. It doesn't matter where you send them. And suppose they pray to you toward this city you have chosen. They pray toward the temple I've built for your Name. [35]Then listen to them from heaven. Listen to their prayer. Listen to them when they ask you to help them. Stand up for them.

[36]"Suppose they sin against you. After all, there isn't anyone who doesn't sin. And suppose you get angry with them. You hand them over to their enemies. They take them as prisoners to another land. It doesn't matter whether that land is near or far away. [37]But suppose your people change their ways in the land where they are held as prisoners. They turn away from their sins. They beg you to help them in the land where they are prisoners. They say, 'We have sinned. We've done what is wrong. We've done what is evil.' [38]And they turn back to you with all their heart

and soul. Suppose it happens in the
land where they were taken as prisoners. There they pray toward the
land you gave their people long ago.
They pray toward the city you have
chosen. And they pray toward the
temple I've built for your Name.
39 Then listen to them from heaven.
It's the place where you live. Listen
to their prayer. Listen to them when
they ask you to help them. Stand up
for them. Your people have sinned
against you. Please forgive them.
40 "My God, let your eyes see us.
Let your ears pay attention to the
prayers offered in this place.

41 "LORD God, rise up and come to
your resting place.
Come in together with the ark.
It's the sign of your power.
LORD God, may your priests put
on salvation as if it were
their clothes.
May your faithful people be
glad because you are so good.
42 LORD God, don't turn your back
on your anointed king.
Remember the great love you
promised to your servant
David."

The Temple Is Set Apart to the LORD

7 Solomon finished praying. Then fire
came down from heaven. It burned
up the burnt offering and the sacrifices.
The glory of the LORD filled the temple.
2 The priests couldn't enter the temple of
the LORD because his glory filled it. 3 All
the Israelites saw the fire coming down.
They saw the glory of the LORD above
the temple. So they got down on their
knees in the courtyard with their faces
toward the ground. They worshiped the
LORD. They gave thanks to him and said,

"The LORD is good.
His faithful love continues
forever."

4 Then the king and all the people offered sacrifices to the LORD. 5 King Solomon sacrificed 22,000 oxen and 120,000
sheep and goats. So the king and all the
people set the temple of God apart. 6 The
priests and Levites took their positions.
The Levites played the LORD's musical
instruments. King David had made
them for praising the LORD. They were
used when he gave thanks to the LORD.
He said, "His faithful love continues
forever." Across from where the Levites
were, the priests blew their trumpets.
All the people of Israel were standing.
7 Solomon set the middle area of the
courtyard apart to the LORD. It was in
front of the LORD's temple. There Solomon sacrificed burnt offerings. He also
sacrificed the fat of the friendship offerings there. He did it there because the
bronze altar he had made couldn't hold
it all. It couldn't hold the burnt offerings,
the grain offerings and the fat parts.

His faithful love continues forever.
2 CHRONICLES 7:6

8 At that time Solomon celebrated
the Feast of Booths for seven days. The
whole community of Israel was with
him. It was a huge crowd. People came
from as far away as Lebo Hamath and
the Wadi of Egypt. 9 On the eighth day
they held a special service. For seven
days they had celebrated by setting
the altar apart to honor God. The feast
continued for seven more days. 10 Then
Solomon sent the people home. It was
the 23rd day of the seventh month. The
people were glad. Their hearts were full
of joy. That's because the LORD had done
good things for David and Solomon and
his people Israel.

The LORD Appears to Solomon

11 Solomon finished the LORD's temple
and the royal palace. He had done everything he had planned to do in the LORD's
temple and his own palace. 12 The LORD
appeared to him at night. The LORD said,

"I have heard your prayer. I have
chosen this place for myself. It is
a temple where sacrifices will be
offered.
13 "Suppose I close up the sky
and there isn't any rain. Suppose
I command locusts to eat up the
crops. And I send a plague among
my people. 14 But they make themselves humble in my sight. They
pray and look to me. And they
turn from their evil ways. Then I

will listen to them from heaven.
I will forgive their sin. And I will
heal their land. After all, they are
my people. 15 Now my eyes will see
them. My ears will pay attention to
the prayers they offer in this place.
16 I have chosen this temple. I have
set it apart for myself. My Name
will be there forever. My eyes and
my heart will always be there.

17 "But you must walk faithfully
with me, just as your father David
did. Do everything I command
you to do. Obey my rules and laws.
18 Then I will set up your royal
throne. I made a covenant with your
father David to do that. I said to him,
'You will always have a son from
your family line to rule over Israel.'

19 "But suppose all of you turn
away from me. You refuse to obey
the rules and commands I have
given you. And you go off to serve
other gods and worship them.
20 Then I will remove Israel from
my land. It is the land I gave them.
I will turn my back on this temple.
I will do it even though I have set
it apart for my Name to be there.
I will make all the nations hate it.
They will laugh and joke about it.
21 This temple will become a pile
of stones. All those who pass by it
will be shocked. They will say, 'Why
has the LORD done a thing like this
to this land and temple?' 22 People
will answer, 'Because they have
deserted the LORD. He is the God
of their people who lived long ago.
He brought them out of Egypt. But
they have been holding on to other gods. They've been worshiping
them. They've been serving them.
That's why the LORD has brought
all this horrible trouble on them.' "

Other Things Solomon Did

8 Solomon built the LORD's temple
and his own palace. It took him
20 years to build them. After that,
2 Solomon rebuilt the villages Hiram
had given him. Solomon had Israelites make their homes in them. 3 Then
Solomon went to Hamath Zobah. He
captured it. 4 He also built up Tadmor
in the desert. He built up all the cities
in Hamath where he could store things.
5 He rebuilt Upper Beth Horon and Lower
Beth Horon. He put up high walls around
them. He made their city gates secure
with heavy metal bars. 6 He rebuilt Baalath and all the cities where he could
store things. He also rebuilt all the cities
for his chariots and horses. Solomon
built anything he wanted in Jerusalem,
Lebanon and all the territory he ruled.

7 There were still many people left in
the land who weren't Israelites. They
included Hittites, Amorites, Perizzites,
Hivites and Jebusites. 8 They were children of the people who had lived in
the land before the Israelites came.
The people of Israel hadn't destroyed
them. Solomon forced them to work
very hard as his slaves. And they still
work for Israel to this day. 9 But Solomon didn't force the Israelites to work
as his slaves. Instead, some were his
fighting men. Others were commanders
of his captains, chariots and chariot
drivers. 10 Still others were King Solomon's chief officials. There were 250
officials in charge of the other men.

11 Solomon brought Pharaoh's daughter up from the City of David to the palace he had built for her. Solomon said,
"My wife must not live in the palace of
David, who was the king of Israel. It's
one of the places the ark of the LORD has
entered. That makes it holy."

12 Solomon had built the LORD's altar.
It stood in front of the temple porch. On
that altar Solomon sacrificed burnt offerings to the LORD. 13 Each day he sacrificed what the Law of Moses required. He
sacrificed the required offerings every
Sabbath day. He also sacrificed them
at each New Moon feast and during the
three yearly feasts. Those three were the
Feast of Unleavened Bread, the Feast of
Weeks and the Feast of Booths. 14 Solomon followed the orders his father
David had given him. He appointed the
groups of priests for their duties. He appointed the Levites to lead the people in
praising the LORD. They also helped the
priests do their required tasks each day.
Solomon appointed the groups of men
who guarded all the gates. That's what
David, the man of God, had ordered.
15 The king's commands were followed
completely. They applied to the priests
and Levites. They also applied to the
temple treasure.

16 All of Solomon's work was carried out. It started the day the foundation of the LORD's temple was laid. It ended when the LORD's temple was finished.

17 Solomon went to Ezion Geber and Elath on the coast of Edom. 18 Hiram sent him ships that his own officers commanded. They were sailors who knew the sea. Together with Solomon's men they sailed to Ophir. They brought back 17 tons of gold. They gave it to King Solomon.

The Queen of Sheba Visits Solomon

9 The queen of Sheba heard about how famous Solomon was. So she came to Jerusalem to test him with hard questions. She arrived with a very large group of attendants. Her camels were carrying spices, huge amounts of gold, and valuable jewels. She came to Solomon and asked him about everything she wanted to know. 2 He answered all her questions. There wasn't anything too hard for him to explain to her. 3 So the queen of Sheba saw how wise Solomon was. She saw the palace he had built. 4 She saw the food on his table. She saw his officials sitting there. She saw the robes of the servants who waited on everyone. She saw the robes the wine tasters were wearing. And she saw the burnt offerings Solomon sacrificed at the LORD's temple. She could hardly believe everything she had seen.

5 She said to the king, "Back in my own country I heard a report about you. I heard about how much you had accomplished. I also heard about how wise you are. Everything I heard is true. 6 But I didn't believe what people were saying. So I came to see for myself. And now I believe it! You are twice as wise as people say you are. The report I heard doesn't even begin to tell the whole story about you. 7 How happy your people must be! How happy your officials must be! They always get to serve you and hear the wise things you say. 8 May the LORD your God be praised. He takes great delight in you. He placed you on his throne as king. He put you there to rule for him. Your God loves Israel very much. He longs to take good care of them forever. That's why he has made you king over them. He knows that you will do what is fair and right."

9 She gave the king four and a half tons of gold. She also gave him huge amounts of spices and valuable jewels. There had never been as many spices as the queen of Sheba gave to King Solomon.

10 The servants of Hiram and the servants of Solomon brought gold from Ophir. They also brought algumwood and valuable jewels. 11 The king used the algumwood to make steps for the LORD's temple and the royal palace. He also used it to make harps and lyres for those who played the music. No one had ever seen anything like those instruments in Judah before.

12 King Solomon gave the queen of Sheba everything she wanted and asked for. In fact, he gave her more than she had brought to him. Then she left. She returned to her own country with her attendants.

Solomon's Greatness

13 Each year Solomon received 25 tons of gold. 14 That didn't include the money brought in by business and trade. All the kings of Arabia also brought gold and silver to Solomon. So did the governors of the territories.

15 King Solomon made 200 large shields out of hammered gold. Each one weighed 15 pounds. 16 He also made 300 small shields out of hammered gold. Each one weighed almost eight pounds. The king put all the shields in the Palace of the Forest of Lebanon.

17 Then he made a large throne. It was covered with ivory. And that was covered with pure gold. 18 The throne had six steps. A gold stool for the king's feet was connected to it. The throne had armrests on both sides of the seat. A statue of a lion stood on each side of the throne. 19 Twelve lions stood on the six steps. There was one at each end of each step. Nothing like that throne had ever been made for any other kingdom. 20 All of King Solomon's cups were made out of gold. All the things used in the Palace of the Forest of Lebanon were made out of pure gold. Nothing was made out of silver. When Solomon was king, silver wasn't considered to be worth very much. 21 He had many ships that carried goods to be traded. The crews of those ships were made up

of Hiram's servants. Once every three years the ships returned. They brought gold, silver, ivory, apes and peacocks. 22 King Solomon was richer than all the other kings on earth. He was also wiser than they were. 23 All these kings wanted to meet Solomon in person. They wanted to see for themselves how wise God had made him. 24 Year after year, everyone who came to him brought a gift. They brought gifts made out of silver and gold. They brought robes, weapons and spices. They also brought horses and mules.

25 Solomon had 4,000 spaces where he kept his horses and chariots. He had 12,000 horses. He kept some of his horses and chariots in the chariot cities. He kept the others with him in Jerusalem. 26 Solomon ruled over all the kings from the Euphrates River to the land of the Philistines. He ruled all the way to the border of Egypt. 27 The king made silver as common in Jerusalem as stones. He made cedar wood as common there as sycamore-fig trees in the western hills. 28 Solomon got horses from Egypt. He also got them from many other countries.

Solomon Dies

29 The other events of Solomon's rule from beginning to end are written down. They are written in the records of Nathan the prophet. They are written in the prophecy of Ahijah. He was from Shiloh. They are also written in the records of the visions of Iddo the prophet about Jeroboam. Jeroboam was the son of Nebat. 30 Solomon ruled in Jerusalem over the whole nation of Israel for 40 years. 31 Then he joined the members of his family who had already died. He was buried in the city of his father David. Solomon's son Rehoboam became the next king after him.

Israel Refuses to Follow Rehoboam

10 Rehoboam went to the city of Shechem. All the Israelites had gone there to make him king. 2 Jeroboam heard about it. He was the son of Nebat. Jeroboam was in Egypt at that time. He had gone there for safety. He wanted to get away from King Solomon. But now he returned from Egypt. 3 So the people sent for Jeroboam. He and all the people went to Rehoboam. They said to him, 4 "Your father put a heavy load on our shoulders. But now make our hard work easier. Make the heavy load on us lighter. Then we'll serve you."

5 Rehoboam answered, "Come back to me in three days." So the people went away.

6 Then King Rehoboam asked the elders for advice. They had served his father Solomon while he was still living. Rehoboam asked them, "What advice can you give me? How should I answer these people?"

7 They replied, "Be kind to them. Please them. Give them what they are asking for. Then they'll always serve you."

8 But Rehoboam didn't accept the advice the elders gave him. He asked for advice from the young men who had grown up with him and were now serving him. 9 He asked them, "What's your advice? How should I answer these people? They said to me, 'Make the load your father put on our shoulders lighter.'"

10 The young men who had grown up with him gave their answer. They replied, "The people have said to you, 'Your father put a heavy load on our shoulders. Make it lighter.' Now tell them, 'My little finger is stronger than my father's legs. 11 My father put a heavy load on your shoulders. But I'll make it even heavier. My father beat you with whips. But I'll beat you with bigger whips.'"

12 Three days later Jeroboam and all the people returned to Rehoboam. That's because the king had said, "Come back to me in three days." 13 The king answered them in a mean way. He didn't accept the advice of the elders. 14 Instead, he followed the advice of the young men. He said, "My father put a heavy load on your shoulders. But I'll make it even heavier. My father beat you with whips. But I'll beat you with bigger whips." 15 So the king didn't listen to the people. That's because God had planned it that way. What the LORD had said through Ahijah came true. Ahijah had spoken the LORD's message to Jeroboam, the son of Nebat. Ahijah was from Shiloh.

16 All the Israelites saw that the king refused to listen to them. So they answered the king. They said,

> "We don't have any share in
> David's royal family.
> We don't have any share in
> Jesse's son.
> People of Israel, let's go back to our
> homes.
> David's royal family, take care of
> your own kingdom!"

So all the Israelites went home. 17 But Rehoboam still ruled over the Israelites who were living in the towns of Judah.

18 Adoniram was in charge of those who were forced to work hard for King Rehoboam. The king sent him out among the Israelites. But they killed Adoniram by throwing stones at him. Rehoboam was able to get away in his chariot. He escaped to Jerusalem. 19 Israel has refused to follow the royal family of David to this day.

11 Rehoboam arrived in Jerusalem. He brought together 180,000 capable young men from the tribes of Judah and Benjamin. He had decided to go to war against Israel. He wanted his fighting men to get the kingdom of Israel back for him.

2 But a message came to Shemaiah from the LORD. Shemaiah was a man of God. The LORD said to him, 3 "Speak to Solomon's son Rehoboam, the king of Judah. Speak to all the people of Israel in Judah and Benjamin. Tell them, 4 'The LORD says, "Do not go up to fight against your relatives. I want every one of you to go back home. Things have happened exactly the way I planned them." ' " So the young men obeyed the LORD's message. They turned back. They didn't march out against Jeroboam.

Rehoboam Builds Up Judah's Towns

5 Rehoboam lived in Jerusalem. He made Judah more secure by building up its towns. 6 He built up Bethlehem, Etam, Tekoa, 7 Beth Zur, Soko and Adullam. 8 He also built up Gath, Mareshah, Ziph, 9 Adoraim, Lachish, Azekah, 10 Zorah, Aijalon and Hebron. All of them were cities in Judah and Benjamin that had high walls around them. 11 Rehoboam made those cities even more secure. He put commanders in them. He gave the cities plenty of food, olive oil and wine. 12 He put shields and spears in all those cities. He made them very strong. So he ruled over Judah and Benjamin.

13 The priests and Levites were on Rehoboam's side. They came from their territories all over Israel. 14 The Levites even left their grasslands and other property behind. They came to Judah and Jerusalem. That's because Jeroboam and his sons had refused to accept them as priests of the LORD. 15 Jeroboam had appointed his own priests to serve at the high places. He had made statues of gods that looked like goats and calves. His priests served those gods. 16 Some people from every tribe in Israel followed the Levites to Jerusalem. With all their hearts they wanted to worship the LORD. He is the God of Israel. They came to Jerusalem to offer sacrifices to him. He was the God of their people of long ago. 17 All those who came to Jerusalem made the kingdom of Judah strong. They helped Solomon's son Rehoboam for three years. During that time they lived the way David and Solomon had lived.

Rehoboam's Family

18 Rehoboam married Mahalath. She was the daughter of David's son Jerimoth. Her mother was Abihail. Abihail was the daughter of Jesse's son Eliab. 19 Mahalath had sons by Rehoboam. Their names were Jeush, Shemariah and Zaham. 20 Then Rehoboam married Maakah. She was the daughter of Absalom. She had sons by Rehoboam. Their names were Abijah, Attai, Ziza and Shelomith. 21 Rehoboam loved Absalom's daughter Maakah. In fact, he loved her more than any of his other wives and concubines. He had a total of 18 wives and 60 concubines. And he had a total of 28 sons and 60 daughters.

22 Rehoboam appointed Maakah's son Abijah to be the chief prince among his brothers. He did it because he wanted to make him king. 23 Rehoboam acted wisely. He scattered some of his sons through all the territories of Judah and Benjamin. He put them in all the cities that had high walls around them. He gave them plenty of food and everything else they needed. He also gave them many wives.

Shishak Attacks Jerusalem

12 Rehoboam had made his position as king secure. He had become very strong. Then he turned away from the law of the LORD. So did all the people of Judah. 2 They hadn't been faithful to the LORD. So Shishak attacked Jerusalem. It was in the fifth year that Rehoboam was king. Shishak was king of Egypt. 3 He came with 1,200 chariots and 60,000 horsemen. Troops of Libyans, Sukkites and Cushites came with him from Egypt. There were so many of them they couldn't be counted. 4 Shishak captured the cities of Judah that had high walls around them. He came all the way to Jerusalem.

5 Then Shemaiah the prophet came to Rehoboam and the leaders of Judah. They had gathered together in Jerusalem. They were afraid of Shishak. Shemaiah said to them, "The LORD says, 'You have left me. So now I am leaving you to Shishak.' "

6 The king and the leaders of Israel made themselves humble in the LORD's sight. They said, "The LORD does what is right and fair."

7 The LORD saw they had made themselves humble. So he gave a message to Shemaiah. The LORD said, "They have made themselves humble in my sight. So I will not destroy them. Instead, I will soon save them. Even though I am very angry with Jerusalem, I will not use Shishak to destroy them. 8 But the people of Jerusalem will be brought under his control. Then they will learn the difference between serving me and serving the kings of other lands."

9 Shishak, the king of Egypt, attacked Jerusalem. He carried away the treasures of the LORD's temple. He also carried the treasures of the royal palace away. He took everything. That included the gold shields Solomon had made. 10 So King Rehoboam made bronze shields to take their place. He gave them to the commanders of the guards who were on duty at the entrance to the royal palace. 11 Every time the king went to the LORD's temple, the guards went with him. They carried the shields. Later, they took them back to the room where they were kept.

12 Rehoboam had made himself humble in the LORD's sight. So the LORD turned his anger away from him. Rehoboam wasn't totally destroyed. In fact, some good things happened in Judah.

13 King Rehoboam had made his position secure in Jerusalem. He continued as king. He was 41 years old when he became king. He ruled for 17 years in Jerusalem. It was the city the LORD had chosen out of all the cities in the tribes of Israel. He wanted to put his Name there. The name of Rehoboam's mother was Naamah from Ammon. 14 Rehoboam did what was evil. That's because he hadn't worshiped the LORD with all his heart.

15 The events of Rehoboam's rule from beginning to end are written down. They are written in the records of Shemaiah and Iddo, the prophets. The records deal with family histories. Rehoboam and Jeroboam were always at war with each other. 16 Rehoboam joined the members of his family who had already died. He was buried in the City of David. Rehoboam's son Abijah became the next king after him.

Abijah King of Judah

13 Abijah became king of Judah. It was in the 18th year of Jeroboam's rule over Israel. 2 Abijah ruled in Jerusalem for three years. His mother's name was Maakah. She was a daughter of Uriel. Uriel was from Gibeah.

There was war between Abijah and Jeroboam. 3 Abijah went into battle with an army of 400,000 capable fighting men. Jeroboam lined up his soldiers against them. He had 800,000 able troops.

4 Abijah stood on Mount Zemaraim. It's in the hill country of Ephraim. Abijah said, "Jeroboam and all you Israelites, listen to me! 5 The LORD is the God of Israel. Don't you know that he has placed David and his sons after him on Israel's throne forever? The LORD made a covenant of salt with David. The salt means the covenant will last for all time to come. 6 Jeroboam, the son of Nebat, was an official of David's son Solomon. But he refused to obey his master. 7 Some worthless and evil men gathered around him. They opposed Solomon's son Rehoboam. At that

time Rehoboam was young. He couldn't
make up his mind. He wasn't strong
enough to stand up against those men.
8 "Now you plan to stand up against
the kingdom of the LORD. His kingdom is in the hands of men in David's
family line. It's true that you have a
huge army. You have the statues of the
golden calves that Jeroboam made to
be your gods. 9 But you drove out the
priests of the LORD, the sons of Aaron.
You also drove out the Levites. You appointed your own priests. That's what
the people of other nations do. Anyone
can come and set himself apart. All he
has to do is sacrifice a young bull and
seven rams. Then he becomes a priest
of gods that aren't really gods at all!
10 "But the LORD is our God. We haven't
deserted him. The priests who serve the
LORD belong to the family line of Aaron.
The Levites help them. 11 Every morning
and evening the priests bring burnt
offerings and sweet-smelling incense
to the LORD. They set out the holy bread
on the table. That table is 'clean.' They
light the lamps on the gold lampstand
every evening. We always do what the
LORD our God requires in his law. But
you have deserted him. 12 God is with
us. He's our leader. His priests will blow
their trumpets. They will sound the battle cry against you. People of Israel,
don't fight against the LORD. He's the
God of your people who lived long ago.
You can't possibly succeed."
13 Jeroboam had sent some troops behind Judah's battle lines. He told them
to hide and wait there. He and his men
stayed in front of Judah's lines. 14 Judah
turned and saw that they were being
attacked from the front and from the
back. Then they cried out to the LORD.
The priests blew their trumpets. 15 The
men of Judah shouted the battle cry.
When they did, God drove Jeroboam and
all the Israelites away from Abijah and
Judah. 16 The Israelites ran away from
them. God handed Israel over to Judah.
17 Abijah and his troops wounded and
killed large numbers of them. In fact,
500,000 of Israel's capable men lay dead
or wounded. 18 So at that time the Israelites were brought under Judah's control.
The people of Judah won the battle over
them. That's because they trusted in the
LORD, the God of their people.
19 Abijah chased Jeroboam. He captured from him the towns of Bethel,
Jeshanah and Ephron. He also captured
the villages around them. 20 Jeroboam
didn't get his power back during the
time of Abijah. In fact, the LORD struck
Jeroboam down, and he died.
21 But Abijah grew stronger. He married 14 wives. He had 22 sons and 16
daughters.
22 The other events of Abijah's rule are
written down. The things he did and
said are written in the notes of Iddo
the prophet.

14 Abijah joined the members of his
family who had already died. He
was buried in the City of David. Abijah's
son Asa became the next king after him.
While Asa was king, the country had
peace and rest for ten years.

Asa Becomes King of Judah

2 Asa did what was good and right
in the eyes of the LORD his God. 3 Asa
removed the altars where false gods
were worshiped. He took away the high
places. He smashed the sacred stones.
He cut down the poles used to worship
the female god named Asherah. 4 He
commanded Judah to worship the LORD,
the God of their people. He commanded
them to obey the LORD's laws and commands. 5 Asa removed the high places
and incense altars from every town in
Judah. The kingdom had peace and rest
under his rule. 6 He built up the cities
of Judah that had high walls around
them. The land was at peace. No one
was at war with Asa during those years.
That's because the LORD gave him peace
and rest.
7 "Let's build up our towns," Asa said
to the people of Judah. "Let's put walls
around them. Let's provide them with
towers. Let's make them secure with
gates that have heavy metal bars. The
land still belongs to us. That's because
we've trusted in the LORD our God. We
trusted in him, and he has given us
peace and rest on every side." So they
built. And things went well for them.
8 Asa had an army of 300,000 men
from Judah. They carried spears and
large shields. There were 280,000 men
from Benjamin. They were armed with
bows and small shields. All these men
were brave soldiers.

[9] Zerah marched out against them.
He was from Cush. He had a huge army
of thousands. He also had 300 chariots.
They came all the way to Mareshah.
[10] Asa went out to meet Zerah in battle.
They took up their positions in the Valley of Zephathah. It's near Mareshah.
[11] Then Asa called out to the LORD his
God. He said, "LORD, there isn't anyone
like you. You help the weak against the
strong. LORD our God, help us. We trust
in you. In your name we have come out
to fight against this huge army. LORD,
you are our God. Don't let mere human
beings win the battle over you."
[12] The LORD struck down the men of
Cush for Asa and Judah. The Cushites
ran away. [13] Asa and his army chased
them all the way to Gerar. A large number of Cushites fell down wounded or
dead. So they couldn't fight back. The
LORD and his army crushed them.
The men of Judah carried off a large
amount of goods. [14] They destroyed
all the villages around Gerar. The LORD
had made the people in those villages
afraid of him. The men of Judah took
everything from all the villages. [15] They
also attacked the camps of those who
took care of the herds. They carried off
large numbers of sheep, goats and camels. Then they returned to Jerusalem.

Asa Makes Judah a Better Nation

15 The Spirit of God came on Azariah. He was the son of Oded.
[2] Azariah went out to meet Asa. He
said to him, "Asa and all you people of
Judah and Benjamin, listen to me. The
LORD is with you when you are with
him. If you really look for him, you will
find him. But if you desert him, he will
desert you. [3] For a long time Israel didn't
worship the true God. They didn't have
a priest who taught them. So they didn't
know God's law. [4] But when they were
in trouble, they turned to the LORD, the
God of Israel. When they did, they found
him. [5] In those days it wasn't safe to
travel around. The people who lived in
all the areas of the land were having a
lot of trouble. [6] One nation was crushing
another. One city was crushing another.
That's because God was causing them to
suffer terribly. [7] But be strong. Don't give
up. God will reward you for your work."
[8] Asa heard that prophecy. He paid
attention to the words of Azariah the
prophet, the son of Oded. So Asa became
bolder than ever. He removed the statues of gods from the whole land of Judah
and Benjamin. He also removed them
from the towns he had captured in the
hills of Ephraim. He did it because the
LORD hated those gods. Asa repaired
the altar of the LORD. It was in front of
the porch of the LORD's temple.
[9] Then Asa gathered together all
the people of Judah and Benjamin.
He also gathered together the people
from Ephraim, Manasseh and Simeon
who were living among them. Large
numbers of people had come over to
him from Israel. They came because
they saw that the LORD his God was
with him.
[10] They gathered in Jerusalem. It was
the third month of the 15th year of Asa's
rule. [11] At that time they sacrificed to the
LORD 700 oxen and 7,000 sheep and
goats. The animals were among the
things they had taken after the battle.
[12] They made a covenant to obey the
LORD, the God of their people. They
would obey him with all their heart and
soul. [13] All those who wouldn't obey the
LORD, the God of Israel, would be killed.
It wouldn't matter how important they
were. It wouldn't matter whether they
were men or women. [14] They made
a promise to the LORD. They praised
him out loud. They shouted. They blew
trumpets and horns. [15] All the people of
Judah were happy about the promise
they had made. They turned to God
with all their heart. When they did,
they found him. So the LORD gave them
peace and rest on every side.
[16] King Asa also removed his grandmother Maakah from her position as
queen mother. That's because she had
made a pole used to worship the female
god named Asherah. The LORD hated it.
So Asa cut it down. He broke it up. He
burned it in the Kidron Valley. [17] Asa
didn't remove the high places from
Israel. But he committed his whole life
completely to the LORD. [18] He and his
father had set apart silver, gold and
other things to the LORD. Asa brought
them into God's temple.
[19] There weren't any more wars until
the 35th year of Asa's rule.

Asa's Last Years

16 Baasha was king of Israel. He
marched out against Judah. It
was in the 36th year of Asa's rule over
Judah. Baasha built up the walls of
Ramah. He did it to keep people from
leaving or entering the territory of Asa,
the king of Judah.
2 Asa took the silver and gold from
among the treasures of the LORD's
temple and his own palace. He sent
it to Ben-Hadad. Ben-Hadad was king
of Aram. He was ruling in Damascus.
3 "Let's make a peace treaty between
us," Asa said. "My father and your father
had made a peace treaty between them.
Now I'm sending you silver and gold.
So break your treaty with Baasha, the
king of Israel. Then he'll go back home."
4 Ben-Hadad agreed with King Asa.
He sent his army commanders against
the towns of Israel. His army captured
Ijon, Dan, Abel Maim and all the cities
in Naphtali where Baasha stored things.
5 Baasha heard about it. So he stopped
building up Ramah and left that place.
6 Then King Asa brought all the men of
Judah to Ramah. They carried away
the stones and wood Baasha had been
using. Asa used them to build up Geba
and Mizpah.
7 At that time Hanani the prophet
came to Asa, the king of Judah. He
said to him, "You trusted the king of
Aram. You didn't trust in the LORD your
God. So the army of the king of Aram
has escaped from you. 8 The people of
Cush and Libya had a strong army.
They had large numbers of chariots
and horsemen. But you trusted in the
LORD. So he handed them over to you.
9 The LORD looks out over the whole
earth. He gives strength to those who
commit their lives completely to him.
You have done a foolish thing. From
now on you will be at war."
10 Asa was angry with the prophet
because of what he had said. In fact,
he was so angry he put him in prison.
At the same time, Asa treated some of
his own people very badly.
11 The events of Asa's rule from beginning to end are written down. They
are written in the records of the kings
of Judah and Israel. 12 In the 39th year
of Asa's rule his feet began to hurt. The
pain was terrible. But even though he
was suffering, he didn't look to the LORD
for help. All he did was go to the doctors.
13 In the 41st year of Asa's rule he joined
the members of his family who had
already died. 14 He was buried in a tomb.
He had cut it out for himself in the City
of David. His body was laid on a wooden
frame. It was covered with spices and
different mixes of perfume. A huge fire
was made to honor him.

Jehoshaphat King of Judah

17 Jehoshaphat was the son of Asa.
Jehoshaphat became the next
king after him. He made his kingdom
strong in case Israel would attack him.
2 He placed troops in all the cities of
Judah that had high walls around them.
He stationed some soldiers in Judah. He
also put some in the towns of Ephraim
that his father Asa had captured.
3 The LORD was with Jehoshaphat.
That's because he lived the way King
David had lived. He didn't ask for advice from the gods that were named
Baal. 4 Instead, Jehoshaphat obeyed the
God of his father. He obeyed the LORD's
commands instead of the practices of
Israel. 5 The LORD made the kingdom
secure under Jehoshaphat's control.
All the people of Judah brought gifts
to Jehoshaphat. So he had great wealth
and honor. 6 His heart was committed to
living the way the LORD wanted him to.
He removed the high places from Judah.
He also removed the poles used to worship the female god named Asherah.
7 In the third year of his rule, he
sent his officials to teach in the towns
of Judah. The officials were Ben-Hail,
Obadiah, Zechariah, Nethanel and Micaiah. 8 Some Levites were with them.
Their names were Shemaiah, Nethaniah, Zebadiah, Asahel, Shemiramoth,
Jehonathan, Adonijah, Tobijah and
Tob-Adonijah. Elishama and Jehoram,
the priests, were also with them. 9 They
taught people all through Judah. They
took the Book of the Law of the LORD with
them. They went around to all the towns
of Judah. And they taught the people.
10 All the kingdoms of the lands
around Judah became afraid of the
LORD. So they didn't go to war against
Jehoshaphat. 11 Some Philistines
brought to Jehoshaphat the gifts and
silver he required of them. The Arabs

brought him their flocks. They brought
him 7,700 rams and 7,700 goats.
12 Jehoshaphat became more and
more powerful. He built forts in Judah.
He also built cities in Judah where he
could store things. 13 He had large supplies in the towns of Judah. In Jerusalem he kept men who knew how to fight
well. 14 Here is a list of them, family by
family.

From Judah there were
commanders of groups of 1,000.
One of them was Adnah. He
commanded 300,000 fighting
men.
15 Another was Jehohanan. He
commanded 280,000.
16 Another was Amasiah, the son
of Zikri. Amasiah commanded
200,000. He had offered to serve
the LORD.
17 From Benjamin there were also
commanders.
One of them was Eliada. He was
a brave soldier. He commanded
200,000 men. They were armed
with bows and shields.
18 Another was Jehozabad. He
commanded 180,000 men. They
were prepared for battle.

19 These were the men who served the
king. He stationed some other men in
the cities all through Judah. The cities
had high walls around them.

Micaiah Prophesies Against Ahab

18 Jehoshaphat had great wealth
and honor. He joined forces with
Ahab by marrying Ahab's daughter.
2 Some years later he went down to see
Ahab in Samaria. Ahab killed a lot of
sheep and cattle for Jehoshaphat and
the people with him. Ahab tried to get
Jehoshaphat to attack Ramoth Gilead.
3 Ahab was the king of Israel. He spoke
to Jehoshaphat, the king of Judah. He
asked, "Will you go with me to fight
against Ramoth Gilead?"

Jehoshaphat replied, "Yes. I'll go with
you. My men will also go with your men.
We'll join you in the war." 4 He continued, "First ask the LORD for advice."
5 So the king of Israel brought 400
prophets together. He asked them,
"Should we go to war against Ramoth
Gilead, or not?"

"Go," they answered. "God will hand
it over to you."
6 But Jehoshaphat asked, "Is there
no longer a prophet of the LORD here?
If there is, ask him what we should do."
7 The king of Israel answered Jehoshaphat. He said, "There is still one
prophet we can go to. We can ask the
LORD for advice through him. But I hate
him. He never prophesies anything
good about me. He only prophesies
bad things. His name is Micaiah. He's
the son of Imlah."

"You shouldn't say bad things about
him," Jehoshaphat replied.
8 So the king of Israel called for one
of his officials. He told him, "Bring Micaiah, the son of Imlah, right away."
9 The king of Israel and Jehoshaphat,
the king of Judah, were wearing their
royal robes. They were sitting on their
thrones at the threshing floor. It was
near the entrance of the gate of Samaria. All the prophets were prophesying in front of them. 10 Zedekiah was
the son of Kenaanah. Zedekiah had
made horns out of iron. They looked
like animal horns. He announced, "The
LORD says, 'With these horns you will
drive back the men of Aram until they
are destroyed.' "
11 All the other prophets were prophesying the same thing. "Attack Ramoth
Gilead," they said. "Win the battle over
it. The LORD will hand it over to you."
12 A messenger went to get Micaiah.
He said to him, "Look. The other prophets agree. All of them are saying the
king will have success. So agree with
them. Say the same thing they do."
13 But Micaiah said, "You can be sure
that the LORD lives. And you can be just
as sure that I can only tell the king what
my God says."
14 When Micaiah arrived, the king
spoke to him. He asked, "Should we go
to war against Ramoth Gilead, or not?"

"Attack," he answered. "You will win.
The people of Ramoth Gilead will be
handed over to you."
15 The king said to him, "I've made
you promise to tell the truth many
times before. So don't tell me anything
but the truth in the name of the LORD."
16 Then Micaiah answered, "I saw
all the Israelites scattered on the hills.
They were like sheep that didn't have a

shepherd. The LORD said, 'These people do not have a master. Let each of them go home in peace.' "

17 The king of Israel spoke to Jehoshaphat. He said, "Didn't I tell you he never prophesies anything good about me? He only prophesies bad things."

18 Micaiah continued, "Listen to the LORD's message. I saw the LORD sitting on his throne. Some of the angels of heaven were standing at his right side. The others were standing at his left side. 19 The LORD said, 'Who will get Ahab, the king of Israel, to attack Ramoth Gilead? I want him to die there.'

"One angel suggested one thing. Another suggested something else. 20 Finally, a spirit came forward and stood in front of the LORD. The spirit said, 'I'll get Ahab to do it.'

" 'How?' the LORD asked.

21 "The spirit said, 'I'll go and put lies in the mouths of all his prophets.'

" 'You will have success in getting Ahab to attack Ramoth Gilead,' said the LORD. 'Go and do it.'

22 "So the LORD has put lies in the mouths of your prophets. He has said that great harm will come to you."

23 Then Zedekiah, the son of Kenaanah, went up and slapped Micaiah in the face. Zedekiah asked Micaiah, "Do you think the spirit sent by the LORD left me? Do you think that spirit went to speak to you?"

24 Micaiah replied, "You will find out on the day you go to hide in an inside room to save your life."

25 Then the king of Israel gave an order. He said, "Take Micaiah away. Send him back to Amon. Amon is the ruler of the city of Samaria. And send Micaiah back to Joash. Joash is a member of the royal court. 26 Tell them, 'The king says, "Put this fellow in prison. Don't give him anything but bread and water until I return safely." ' "

27 Micaiah announced, "Do you really think you will return safely? If you do, the LORD hasn't spoken through me." He continued, "All you people, remember what I've said!"

Ahab Is Killed at Ramoth Gilead

28 So the king of Israel went up to Ramoth Gilead. Jehoshaphat, the king of Judah, went there too. 29 The king of Israel spoke to Jehoshaphat. He said, "I'll go into battle wearing different clothes. Then people won't recognize me. But you wear your royal robes." So the king of Israel put on different clothes. Then he went into battle.

30 The king of Aram had given an order to his chariot commanders. He had said, "Fight only against the king of Israel. Don't fight against anyone else." 31 The chariot commanders saw Jehoshaphat. They thought, "That's the king of Israel." So they turned to attack him. But Jehoshaphat cried out. And the LORD helped him. God drew the commanders away from him. 32 They saw he wasn't the king of Israel after all. So they stopped chasing him.

33 But someone shot an arrow without taking aim. The arrow hit the king of Israel between the parts of his armor. The king told the chariot driver, "Turn the chariot around. Get me out of this battle. I've been wounded." 34 All day long the battle continued. The king of Israel kept himself standing up by leaning against the inside of his chariot. He kept his face toward the men of Aram until evening. At sunset he died.

19 Jehoshaphat, the king of Judah, returned safely to his palace in Jerusalem. 2 Jehu the prophet went out to meet him. He was the son of Hanani. Jehu said to the king, "You shouldn't help evil people. You shouldn't love those who hate the LORD. The LORD is angry with you. 3 But there's some good in you. You have removed all the poles in the land used to worship the female god named Asherah. And you have worshiped God with all your heart."

Jehoshaphat Appoints Judges

4 Jehoshaphat lived in Jerusalem. He went out again among the people. He went from Beersheba to the hill country of Ephraim. He turned the people back to the LORD, the God of Israel. 5 Jehoshaphat appointed judges in the land. He put them in all the cities of Judah that had high walls around them. 6 He told the judges, "Think carefully about what you do. After all, you aren't judging for human beings. You are judging for the LORD. He's with you every time you make a decision. 7 Have respect for the LORD. Judge carefully. He

is always right. He treats everyone the same. Our God doesn't want his judges to take money from people who want special favors."

8 In Jerusalem, Jehoshaphat chose some Levites and priests. He also chose some leaders of Israelite families. He appointed all of them to apply the law of the LORD fairly. He wanted them to decide cases. He wanted them to settle matters between people. All those judges lived in Jerusalem. 9 Here are the orders Jehoshaphat gave them. He said, "Have respect for the LORD. Serve him faithfully. Do it with all your heart. 10 Cases will come to you from your people who live in the other cities. The cases might be about murder or other matters dealt with by the law, commands, directions and rules. Warn the people not to sin against the LORD. If you don't warn them, he will be angry with you and your people. Do what I say. Then you won't sin.

11 "Amariah the chief priest will be over you in any matter that concerns the LORD. Zebadiah is the leader of the tribe of Judah. He is the son of Ishmael. Zebadiah will be over you in any matter that concerns the king. The Levites will serve as your officials. Be brave. And may the LORD be with those of you who do well."

Jehoshaphat Wins the Battle Over Moab and Ammon

20 After that, the Moabites, Ammonites and some Meunites went to war against Jehoshaphat.

2 Some people came and told him, "A huge army is coming from Edom to fight against you. They have come across the Dead Sea. They are already in Hazezon Tamar." Hazezon Tamar is also called En Gedi. 3 Jehoshaphat was alarmed. So he decided to ask the LORD for advice. He told all the people of Judah to go without eating. 4 The people came together to ask the LORD for help. In fact, they came from every town in Judah to pray to him.

5 Then Jehoshaphat stood up among the people of Judah and Jerusalem. He was in front of the new courtyard at the LORD's temple. 6 He said,

"LORD, you are the God of our people who lived long ago. You are the God who is in heaven. You rule over all the kingdoms of the nations. You are strong and powerful. No one can fight against you and win. 7 Our God, you drove out the people who lived in this land. You drove them out to make room for your people Israel. You gave this land forever to those who belong to the family line of your friend Abraham. 8 They have lived in this land. They've built a temple here for your Name. They have said, 9 'Suppose trouble comes on us. It doesn't matter whether it's a punishing sword, or plague or hunger. We'll serve you. We'll stand in front of this temple where your Name is. We'll cry out to you when we're in trouble. Then you will hear us. You will save us.'

10 "But here are men from Ammon, Moab and Mount Seir. You wouldn't allow Israel to march in and attack their territory when the Israelites came from Egypt. So Israel turned away from them. They didn't destroy them. 11 See how they are paying us back. They are coming to drive us out. They want to take over the land you gave us as our share. 12 Our God, won't you please judge them? We don't have the power to face this huge army that's attacking us. We don't know what to do. But we're looking to you to help us."

13 All the men of Judah stood there in front of the LORD. Their wives, children and little ones were with them.

14 Then the Spirit of the LORD came on Jahaziel. He was standing among the people of Israel. He was the son of Zechariah. Zechariah was the son of Benaiah. Benaiah was the son of Jeiel. Jeiel was the son of Mattaniah. Jahaziel was a Levite. He was from the family line of Asaph.

15 Jahaziel said, "King Jehoshaphat, listen! All you who live in Judah and Jerusalem, listen! The LORD says to you, 'Do not be afraid. Do not lose hope because of this huge army. The battle is not yours. It is God's. 16 Tomorrow march down against them. They will be climbing up by the Pass of Ziz. You will find them at the end of the valley in

the Desert of Jeruel. 17 You will not have to fight this battle. Take your positions. Stand firm. You will see how the LORD will save you. Judah and Jerusalem, do not be afraid. Do not lose hope. Go out and face them tomorrow. The LORD will be with you.' "

18 Jehoshaphat bowed down with his face toward the ground. All the people of Judah and Jerusalem also bowed down. They worshiped the LORD. 19 Then some Levites from the families of Kohath and Korah stood up. They praised the LORD, the God of Israel. They praised him with very loud voices.

20 Early in the morning all the people left for the Desert of Tekoa. As they started out, Jehoshaphat stood up. He said, "Judah, listen to me! People of Jerusalem, listen to me! Have faith in the LORD your God. He'll take good care of you. Have faith in his prophets. Then you will have success." 21 Jehoshaphat asked the people for advice. Then he appointed men to sing to the LORD. He wanted them to praise the LORD because of his glory and holiness. They marched out in front of the army. They said,

"Give thanks to the LORD.
His faithful love continues
forever."

22 They began to sing and praise him. Then the LORD hid some men and told them to wait. He wanted them to attack the people of Ammon, Moab and Mount Seir. They had gone into Judah and attacked it. But they lost the battle. 23 The Ammonites and Moabites rose up against the men from Mount Seir. They destroyed them. They put an end to them. When they finished killing the men from Seir, they destroyed one another.

24 The men of Judah came to the place that looks out over the desert. They turned to look down at the huge army. But all they saw was dead bodies lying there on the ground. No one had escaped. 25 So Jehoshaphat and his men went down there to carry off anything of value. Among the dead bodies they found a large amount of supplies, clothes and other things of value. There was more than they could take away. There was so much it took three days to collect all of it. 26 On the fourth day they gathered together in the Valley of Berakah. There they praised the LORD. That's why it's called the Valley of Berakah to this day.

27 Then all the men of Judah and Jerusalem returned to Jerusalem. They were filled with joy. Jehoshaphat led them. The LORD had made them happy because all their enemies were dead. 28 They entered Jerusalem and went to the LORD's temple. They were playing harps, lyres and trumpets.

29 All the surrounding kingdoms began to have respect for God. They had heard how the LORD had fought against Israel's enemies. 30 The kingdom of Jehoshaphat was at peace. His God had given him peace and rest on every side.

Jehoshaphat's Rule Comes to an End

31 So Jehoshaphat ruled over Judah. He was 35 years old when he became Judah's king. He ruled in Jerusalem for 25 years. His mother's name was Azubah. She was the daughter of Shilhi. 32 Jehoshaphat followed the ways of his father Asa. He didn't wander away from them. He did what was right in the eyes of the LORD. 33 But the high places weren't removed. The people still hadn't worshiped the God of Israel with all their hearts.

34 The other events of Jehoshaphat's rule from beginning to end are written down. They are written in the official records of Jehu, the son of Hanani. They are written in the records of the kings of Israel.

35 Jehoshaphat king of Judah and Ahaziah king of Israel agreed to be friends. Ahaziah did what was evil. 36 Jehoshaphat agreed with him to build a lot of ships. They were built at Ezion Geber. They carried goods that were traded for other goods. 37 Eliezer was the son of Dodavahu from Mareshah. Eliezer prophesied against Jehoshaphat. He said, "You have joined forces with Ahaziah. So the LORD will destroy what you have made." The ships were wrecked. They were never able to sail or trade goods.

21 Jehoshaphat joined the members of his family who had already died. He was buried in the family tomb in the City of David. Jehoshaphat's son Jehoram became the next king after

him. 2 Jehoram's brothers, the sons
of Jehoshaphat, were Azariah, Jehiel,
Zechariah, Azariahu, Michael and
Shephatiah. All of them were sons of
Jehoshaphat, the king of Israel. 3 Their
father had given them many gifts. He
had given them silver, gold and other things of value. He had also given
them cities in Judah that had high
walls around them. But he had made
Jehoram king. That's because Jehoram
was his oldest son.

Jehoram King of Judah

4 Jehoram made his position secure
over his father's kingdom. Then he
killed all his brothers with his sword.
He also killed some of the officials
of Israel. 5 Jehoram was 32 years old
when he became king. He ruled in Jerusalem for eight years. 6 He followed
the ways of the kings of Israel, just as
the royal family of Ahab had done. In
fact, he married a daughter of Ahab.
Jehoram did what was evil in the eyes
of the LORD. 7 But the LORD didn't want
to destroy the royal family of David.
That's because the LORD had made
a covenant with him. The LORD had
promised to keep the lamp of David's
kingdom burning brightly. The LORD
had promised that for David and his
children after him forever.

8 When Jehoram was king over Judah,
Edom refused to remain under Judah's
control. They set up their own king. 9 So
Jehoram went to Edom. He took his
officers and all his chariots with him.
The men of Edom surrounded him and
his chariot commanders. But he got up
at night and fought his way out. 10 To
this day Edom has refused to remain
under Judah's control.

At that same time, Libnah also refused
to remain under the control of Judah.
That's because Jehoram had deserted
the LORD, the God of his people. 11 Jehoram had also built high places on the
hills of Judah. He had caused the people
of Jerusalem to worship other gods. They
weren't faithful to the LORD. Jehoram
had led Judah down the wrong path.

12 Jehoram received a letter from Elijah the prophet. In it, Elijah said,

"The LORD is the God of your
father David. The LORD says, 'You
have not followed the ways of your
own father Jehoshaphat or of Asa,
the king of Judah. 13 Instead, you
have followed the ways of the kings
of Israel. You have led Judah and
the people of Jerusalem to worship other gods, just as the royal
family of Ahab did. Also, you have
murdered your own brothers. They
were members of your own family.
They were better men than you are.
14 So now the LORD is about to strike
down your people with a heavy
blow. He will strike down your sons,
your wives and everything that
belongs to you. 15 And you yourself
will be very sick for a long time.
The sickness will finally cause your
insides to come out.'"

16 The LORD stirred up the anger of the
Philistines against Jehoram. He also
stirred up the anger of the Arabs. They
lived near the people of Cush. 17 The
Philistines and Arabs attacked Judah.
They went in and carried off all the
goods they found in the king's palace.
They also took his sons and wives. The
only son he had left was Ahaziah. He
was the youngest son.

18 After all of that, the LORD made Jehoram very sick. He couldn't be healed.
19 After he had been sick for two years,
the sickness caused his insides to come
out. He died in great pain. His people
didn't make a funeral fire to honor him.
They had made funeral fires to honor
the kings who ruled before him.

20 Jehoram was 32 years old when he
became king. He ruled in Jerusalem for
eight years. No one was sorry when he
passed away. He was buried in the City
of David. But he wasn't placed in the
tombs of the kings.

Ahaziah King of Judah

22 The people of Jerusalem
made Ahaziah king in place
of Jehoram. Ahaziah was Jehoram's
youngest son. Robbers had come with
the Arabs into Jehoram's camp. The
robbers had killed all his older sons. So
Ahaziah, the king of Judah, began to
rule. He was the son of Jehoram.

2 Ahaziah was 22 years old when he
became king. He ruled in Jerusalem
for one year. His mother's name was
Athaliah. She was a granddaughter
of Omri.

3 Ahaziah also followed the ways of the royal family of Ahab. That's because Ahaziah's mother gave him bad advice. She told him to do what was wrong. 4 So he did what was evil in the eyes of the LORD. He did what the family of Ahab had done. After Ahaziah's father died, the members of Ahab's family became his advisers. That's what destroyed him. 5 He also followed their advice when he joined forces with Joram, the king of Israel. They went to war against Hazael at Ramoth Gilead. Joram was the son of Ahab. Hazael was king of Aram. The soldiers of Aram wounded Joram. 6 So he returned to Jezreel to give his wounds time to heal. His enemies had wounded him at Ramoth in his battle against Hazael, the king of Aram.

Ahaziah, the son of Jehoram, went down to Jezreel. He went there to see Joram. That's because Joram had been wounded. Ahaziah was king of Judah. Joram was the son of Ahab.

7 Through Ahaziah's visit to Joram, God caused Ahaziah to fall from power. When Ahaziah arrived, he rode out with Joram to meet Jehu, the son of Nimshi. The LORD had anointed Jehu to destroy the royal family of Ahab. 8 So Jehu punished Ahab's family, just as the LORD had told him to. While he was doing it, he found the officials of Judah and the sons of Ahaziah's relatives. They had been serving Ahaziah. So Jehu killed them. 9 Then he went to look for Ahaziah. Jehu's men captured him while he was hiding in Samaria. Ahaziah was brought to Jehu and put to death. People buried him, because they said, "He was a grandson of Jehoshaphat, who followed the LORD with all his heart." So no one in the royal family of Ahaziah was powerful enough to keep the kingdom.

Athaliah and Joash

10 Athaliah was Ahaziah's mother. She saw that her son was dead. So she began to wipe out the whole royal family of Judah. 11 But Jehosheba went and got Joash, the son of Ahaziah. Jehosheba was the daughter of King Jehoram. She stole Joash away from among the royal princes. All of them were about to be murdered. She put Joash and his nurse in a bedroom. Jehosheba, the daughter of King Jehoram, was the wife of Jehoiada the priest. She was also Ahaziah's sister. So Jehosheba hid the child from Athaliah. That's why Athaliah couldn't kill him. 12 The child remained hidden with the priest and his wife at God's temple for six years. Athaliah ruled over the land during that time.

23 When Joash was seven years old, Jehoiada showed how strong he was. He made a covenant with the commanders of groups of 100 men. The commanders were Azariah son of Jeroham, Ishmael son of Jehohanan, Azariah son of Obed, Maaseiah son of Adaiah, and Elishaphat son of Zikri. 2 They went all through Judah. They gathered together the Levites and the leaders of Israelite families from all the towns. They came to Jerusalem. 3 The whole community made a covenant with the new king at God's temple.

Jehoiada said to them, "Ahaziah's son will rule over Judah. That's what the LORD promised concerning the family line of David. 4 Here's what I want you to do. A third of you priests and Levites who are going on duty on the Sabbath day must guard the doors. 5 A third of you must guard the royal palace. And a third of you must guard the Foundation Gate. All the other men must guard the courtyards of the LORD's temple. 6 Don't let anyone enter the temple except the priests and Levites who are on duty. They can enter because they are set apart to the LORD. But all the other men must obey the LORD's command not to enter. 7 The Levites must station themselves around the new king. Each man must have his weapon in his hand. Anyone else who enters the temple must be put to death. Stay close to the king no matter where he goes."

8 The Levites did just as Jehoiada the priest ordered. So did all the men of Judah. Each commander got his men. Some of the men were going on duty on the Sabbath day. Others were going off duty. Jehoiada didn't let any of the groups go. 9 Then he gave weapons to the commanders of the groups. He gave them spears, large shields and small shields. The weapons had belonged to King David. They had been in God's temple. 10 Jehoiada stationed all the men around the new king. Each man

had his weapon in his hand. They were
standing near the altar and the temple.
They stood from the south side of the
temple to its north side.
11 Jehoiada and his sons brought
Ahaziah's son out. They put the crown
on him. They gave him a copy of the
covenant. And they announced that
he was king. They anointed him. Then
they shouted, "May the king live a long
time!"
12 Athaliah heard the noise of the
people running and cheering the new
king. So she went to them at the LORD's
temple. 13 She looked, and there was the
king! He was standing next to his pillar
at the entrance. The officers and trumpet
players were standing beside the king.
All the people of the land were filled
with joy. They were blowing trumpets.
Musicians with their musical instruments were leading the songs of praise.
Then Athaliah tore her royal robes. She
shouted, "Treason! It's treason!"
14 Jehoiada the priest sent out the
commanders of the groups of 100 men.
They were in charge of the troops. He
said to them, "Bring her away from the
temple between the line of guards. Use
your swords to kill anyone who follows
her." The priest had said, "Don't put her
to death at the LORD's temple." 15 So they
grabbed her as she reached the entrance
of the Horse Gate on the palace grounds.
There they put her to death.
16 Then Jehoiada made a covenant.
He promised that he, the people and
the king would be the LORD's people.
17 All the people went to Baal's temple.
They tore it down. They smashed the
altars and the statues of gods. They
killed Mattan in front of the altars. He
was the priest of Baal.
18 Then Jehoiada put the priests, who
were Levites, in charge of the LORD's
temple. David had given them their
duties in the temple. He had appointed
them to sacrifice burnt offerings to the
LORD. He wanted them to do it in keeping with what was written in the Law
of Moses. David wanted them to sing
and be full of joy. 19 Jehoiada stationed
guards at the gates of the LORD's temple.
No one who was "unclean" in any way
could enter.
20 Jehoiada took with him the commanders of hundreds, the nobles, the
rulers of the people, and all the people
of the land. He brought the new king
down from the LORD's temple. They
went into the palace through the Upper
Gate. Then they seated the king on the
royal throne. 21 All the people of the
land were filled with joy. And the city
was calm. That's because Athaliah had
been killed by a sword.

Joash Repairs the Temple

24 Joash was seven years old when
he became king. He ruled in
Jerusalem for 40 years. His mother's
name was Zibiah. She was from Beersheba. 2 Joash did what was right in the
eyes of the LORD. Joash lived that way
as long as Jehoiada the priest was alive.
3 Jehoiada chose two wives for Joash.
They had sons and daughters by Joash.
4 Some time later Joash decided to
make the LORD's temple look like new
again. 5 He called together the priests
and Levites. He said to them, "Go to the
towns of Judah. Collect the money that
the nation of Israel owes every year.
Use it to repair the temple of your God.
Do it now." But the Levites didn't do it
right away.
6 So the king sent for Jehoiada the
chief priest. He said to him, "Why
haven't you required the Levites to
bring in the tax from Judah and Jerusalem? It was set up by the LORD's servant
Moses and the whole community of
Israel. It was used for the tent where the
tablets of the covenant law were kept."
7 The children of that evil woman
Athaliah had broken into God's temple.
They had used even its sacred objects
for the gods that were named Baal.
8 King Joash commanded that a
wooden chest be made. It was placed
outside near the gate of the LORD's
temple. 9 Then a message went out
in Judah and Jerusalem. It said that
the people should bring the tax to the
LORD. God's servant Moses had required
Israel to pay that tax when they were
in the desert. 10 All the officials and
people gladly brought their money.
They dropped it into the chest until it
was full. 11 The chest was brought in by
the Levites to the king's officials. Every
time the officials saw there was a large
amount of money in the chest, it was
emptied out. The royal secretary and

the officer of the chief priest came and emptied it. Then they carried it back to its place. They did it regularly. They collected a great amount of money. 12 The king and Jehoiada gave it to the people who were doing the work on the LORD's temple. They hired people who could lay the stones and people who could work with wood. They also hired people who could work with iron and bronze. They hired all of them to repair the temple.

13 The men in charge of the work did their best. The repairs went very well under them. They rebuilt God's temple. They did it in keeping with its original plans. They made the temple even stronger. 14 So they finished the work. Then they brought the rest of the money to the king and Jehoiada. It was used to pay for the objects that were made for the LORD's temple. The objects were used for serving at the temple. They were also used for the burnt offerings. The objects included dishes and other things made out of gold and silver. As long as Jehoiada lived, burnt offerings were sacrificed continually at the LORD's temple.

15 Jehoiada had become very old. He died at the age of 130. 16 He was buried with the kings in the City of David. That's because he had done so many good things in Israel for God and his temple.

The Evil Things Joash Did

17 After Jehoiada died, the officials of Judah came to King Joash. They bowed down to him. He listened to them. 18 They turned their backs on the temple of the LORD, the God of their people. They worshiped poles made to honor the female god named Asherah. They also worshiped statues of other gods. Because Judah and Jerusalem were guilty of sin, God became angry with them. 19 The LORD sent prophets to the people to bring them back to him. The prophets told the people what they were doing wrong. But the people wouldn't listen.

20 Then the Spirit of God came on Zechariah the priest. He was the son of Jehoiada. Zechariah stood in front of the people. He told them, "God says, 'Why do you refuse to obey my commands? You will not have success. You have deserted me. So I have deserted you.'"

21 But the people made evil plans against Zechariah. The king ordered them to kill Zechariah by throwing stones at him. They did it in the courtyard of the LORD's temple. 22 King Joash didn't remember how kind Zechariah's father Jehoiada had been to him. So he killed Jehoiada's son. As Zechariah was dying he said, "May the LORD see this. May he hold you responsible."

23 In the spring, the army of Aram marched into Judah and Jerusalem against Joash. They killed all the leaders of the people. They took a large amount of goods from Judah. They sent it to their king in Damascus. 24 The army of Aram had come with only a few men. But the LORD allowed them to win the battle over a much larger army. Judah had deserted the LORD, the God of their people. That's why the LORD punished Joash. 25 The army of Aram pulled back. They left Joash badly wounded. His officials planned to do evil things to him. That's because he murdered the son of Jehoiada the priest. They killed Joash in his bed. So he died. He was buried in the City of David. But he wasn't placed in the tombs of the kings.

26 Those who made the plans against Joash were Zabad and Jehozabad. Zabad was the son of Shimeath. She was from Ammon. Jehozabad was the son of Shimrith. She was from Moab. 27 The story of the sons of Joash is written in the notes on the records of the kings. The many prophecies about him are written there too. So is the record of how he made God's temple look like new again. Joash's son Amaziah became the next king after him.

Amaziah King of Judah

25 Amaziah was 25 years old when he became king. He ruled in Jerusalem for 29 years. His mother's name was Jehoaddan. She was from Jerusalem. 2 Amaziah did what was right in the eyes of the LORD. But he didn't do it with all his heart. 3 The kingdom was firmly under his control. So he put to death the officials who had murdered his father, the king. 4 But he didn't put their children to death. He obeyed what is written in the Law, the Book of Moses.

There the LORD commanded, "Parents
must not be put to death because of
what their children do. And children
must not be put to death because of
what their parents do. People must die
because of their own sins." *(Deuteronomy 24:16)*

5 Amaziah called the people of Judah
together. He arranged them by families
under commanders of thousands and
commanders of hundreds. He did it for
all the people of Judah and Benjamin.
Then he brought together the men who
were 20 years old or more. He found
out there were 300,000 men who were
able to serve in the army. They could
handle spears and shields. 6 He also
hired 100,000 fighting men from Israel.
He had to pay them almost four tons
of silver.

7 But a man of God came to him. He
said, "Your Majesty, these troops from
Israel must not march out with you.
The LORD is not with Israel. He isn't with
any of the people of Ephraim. 8 Go and
fight bravely in battle if you want to.
But God will destroy you right in front
of your enemies. God has the power to
help you or destroy you."

9 Amaziah asked the man of God,
"But what about all that silver I paid
for these Israelite troops?"

The man of God replied, "The LORD
can give you much more than that."

10 So Amaziah let the troops go who
had come to him from Ephraim. He sent
them home. They were very angry with
Judah. They were still very angry when
they went home.

11 Then Amaziah showed how strong
he was. He led his army to the Valley
of Salt. There he killed 10,000 men of
Seir. 12 The army of Judah also captured
10,000 men alive. The army of Judah
took them to the top of a cliff. Then
they threw them down. All of them were
smashed to pieces.

13 The troops Amaziah had sent back
attacked some towns that belonged to
Judah. Amaziah hadn't allowed the
troops to take part in the war. They
attacked towns from Samaria to Beth
Horon. They killed 3,000 people. They
carried off huge amounts of goods.

14 Amaziah returned from killing the
men of Edom. He brought back the statues of the gods of Seir. He set them up as
his own gods. He bowed down to them.
He burned sacrifices to them. 15 The LORD
was very angry with Amaziah. He sent a
prophet to him. The prophet said, "Why
do you ask the gods of those people for
advice? They couldn't even save their
own people from your power!"

16 While the prophet was still speaking, the king spoke to him. He said, "Did
I ask you for advice? Stop! If you don't,
you will be struck down."

So the prophet stopped. But then he
said, "I know that God has decided to
destroy you. That's because you have
worshiped other gods. You haven't listened to my advice."

17 Amaziah, the king of Judah, spoke
to his advisers. Then he sent a message
to Jehoash, the king of Israel. Jehoash
was the son of Jehoahaz. Jehoahaz
was the son of Jehu. Amaziah dared
Jehoash, "Come on! Let us face each
other in battle!"

18 But Jehoash, the king of Israel, answered Amaziah, the king of Judah.
Jehoash said, "A thorn bush in Lebanon
sent a message to a cedar tree there. The
thorn bush said, 'Give your daughter to
be married to my son.' Then a wild animal in Lebanon came along. It crushed
the thorn bush by walking on it. 19 You
brag that you have won the battle over
Edom. You are very proud. But stay
home! Why ask for trouble? Why bring
yourself crashing down? Why bring
Judah down with you?"

20 But Amaziah wouldn't listen.
That's because God had planned to
hand Judah over to Jehoash. After all,
they had asked the gods of Edom for
advice. 21 So Jehoash, the king of Israel,
attacked. He and Amaziah, the king
of Judah, faced each other in battle.
The battle took place at Beth Shemesh
in Judah. 22 Israel drove Judah away.
Every man ran home. 23 Jehoash king
of Israel captured Amaziah king of
Judah at Beth Shemesh. Amaziah was
the son of Joash. Joash was the son of
Ahaziah. Jehoash brought Amaziah to
Jerusalem. Jehoash broke down part
of its wall. It's the part that went from
the Ephraim Gate to the Corner Gate.
That part of the wall was 600 feet long.
24 Jehoash took all the gold and silver.
He took all the objects he found in God's
temple. Obed-Edom had been in charge

of them. Jehoash also took the palace
treasures and the prisoners. Then he
returned to Samaria.
25 Amaziah king of Judah lived for
15 years after Jehoash king of Israel
died. Amaziah was the son of Joash.
Jehoash was the son of Jehoahaz. 26 The
other events of Amaziah's rule from
beginning to end are written down.
They are written in the records of the
kings of Judah and Israel. 27 Amaziah
turned away from obeying the LORD.
From that time on, some people made
evil plans against him in Jerusalem.
So he ran away to Lachish. But they
sent men after him to Lachish. There
they killed him. 28 His body was brought
back on a horse to Jerusalem, the City
of Judah. There he was buried in the
family tomb.

Uzziah King of Judah

26 All the people of Judah made
Uzziah king. He was 16 years
old. They made him king in place of his
father Amaziah. 2 Uzziah rebuilt Elath.
He brought it under Judah's control
again. He did it after Amaziah joined
the members of his family who had
already died.
3 Uzziah was 16 years old when he became king. He ruled in Jerusalem for 52
years. His mother's name was Jekoliah.
She was from Jerusalem. 4 Uzziah did
what was right in the eyes of the LORD,
just as his father Amaziah had done.
5 He tried to obey God during the days
of Zechariah. Zechariah taught him to
have respect for God. As long as Uzziah
obeyed the LORD, God gave him success.
6 Uzziah went to war against the
Philistines. He broke down the walls
of Gath, Jabneh and Ashdod. Then he
rebuilt some towns that were near Ashdod. He also rebuilt some other towns
where Philistines lived. 7 God helped him
fight against the Philistines. He also
helped him fight against the Meunites
and against the Arabs who lived in
Gur Baal. 8 The Ammonites brought to
Uzziah the gifts he required of them.
He became famous all the way to the
border of Egypt. That's because he had
become very powerful.
9 Uzziah built towers in Jerusalem.
They were at the Corner Gate, the Valley Gate and the angle of the wall. He
made the towers very strong. 10 He also
built towers in the desert. He dug many
wells, because he had a lot of livestock.
The livestock were in the western hills
and on the plains. Uzziah had people
working in his fields and vineyards in
the hills and in the rich lands. That's
because he loved the soil.
11 Uzziah's army was well trained. It
was ready to march out by military
groups according to their numbers. Jeiel
and Maaseiah brought them together.
Jeiel was the secretary. Maaseiah was
the officer. They were under the direction of Hananiah. He was one of the
royal officials. 12 The total number of
family leaders who were over the fighting men was 2,600. 13 An army of 307,500
men was under their command. The
men were trained for war. They were
a powerful force. They helped the king
against his enemies. 14 Uzziah provided
the entire army with shields, spears,
helmets, coats of armor, bows, and
stones for their slings. 15 In Jerusalem
he invented machines to be used on
the towers and on the corners of city
walls. These machines were used by
men who shot arrows from the walls.
The machines were also used by men
to throw large stones from the walls.
Uzziah became famous everywhere.
God greatly helped him until he became
powerful.
16 But after Uzziah became powerful,
his pride brought him down. He wasn't
faithful to the LORD his God. He entered
the LORD's temple to burn incense on the
altar for burning incense. 17 Azariah the
priest followed him in. So did 80 other
brave priests of the LORD. 18 They stood
up to Uzziah. They said, "Uzziah, it isn't
right for you to burn incense to the LORD.
Only the priests are supposed to do that.
They are members of the family line
of Aaron. They have been set apart to
burn incense. So get out of here. Leave
the temple. You haven't been faithful.
The LORD God won't honor you."
19 Uzziah was holding a shallow cup.
He was ready to burn incense in it. He
became angry. He shouted at the priests
in the LORD's temple. He did it near the
altar for burning incense. While he was
shouting, a skin disease suddenly broke
out on his forehead. 20 Azariah the chief
priest and all the other priests looked at

him. They saw that Uzziah had a skin disease on his forehead. So they hurried him out of the temple. Actually, he himself really wanted to leave. He knew that the LORD was making him suffer.

21 King Uzziah had the skin disease until the day he died. He lived in a separate house because he had the disease. And he wasn't allowed to enter the LORD's temple. Uzziah's son Jotham was in charge of the palace. Jotham ruled over the people of the land.

22 The other events of Uzziah's rule from beginning to end were written down by Isaiah the prophet. Isaiah was the son of Amoz. 23 Uzziah joined the members of his family who had already died. He was buried near them in a royal burial ground. People said, "He had a skin disease." Uzziah's son Jotham became the next king after him.

Jotham King of Judah

27 Jotham was 25 years old when he became king. He ruled in Jerusalem for 16 years. His mother's name was Jerusha. She was the daughter of Zadok. 2 Jotham did what was right in the eyes of the LORD, just as his father Uzziah had done. But Jotham didn't enter the LORD's temple as Uzziah had done. The people, however, continued to do very sinful things. 3 Jotham rebuilt the Upper Gate of the LORD's temple. He did a lot of work on the wall at the hill of Ophel. 4 He built towns in the hill country of Judah. He also built forts and towers in areas that had a lot of trees in them.

5 Jotham went to war against the king of Ammon. He won the battle over the Ammonites. That year they paid Jotham almost four tons of silver. They paid him 1,800 tons of wheat and 1,500 tons of barley. They also brought him the same amount in the second and third years.

6 Jotham became powerful. That's because he had worshiped the LORD his God with all his heart.

7 The other events of Jotham's rule are written down. That includes all his wars and the other things he did. All these things are written in the records of the kings of Israel and Judah. 8 Jotham was 25 years old when he became king. He ruled in Jerusalem for 16 years. 9 Jotham joined the members of his family who had already died. He was buried in the City of David. Jotham's son Ahaz became the next king after him.

Ahaz King of Judah

28 Ahaz was 20 years old when he became king. He ruled in Jerusalem for 16 years. He didn't do what was right in the eyes of the LORD. He didn't do what King David had done. 2 He followed the ways of the kings of Israel. He also made statues of gods that were named Baal. 3 He burned sacrifices in the Valley of Ben Hinnom. He sacrificed his children in the fire to other gods. He followed the practices of the nations. The LORD hates these practices. The LORD had driven out those nations to make room for the people of Israel. 4 Ahaz offered sacrifices and burned incense at the high places. He also did it on the tops of hills and under every green tree.

5 So the LORD his God handed him over to the king of Aram. The men of Aram won the battle over him. They took many of his people as prisoners. They brought them to Damascus.

God also handed Ahaz over to Pekah. Pekah was king of Israel. His army wounded or killed many of the troops of Ahaz. 6 In one day Pekah, the son of Remaliah, killed 120,000 soldiers in Judah. That's because Judah had deserted the LORD, the God of their people. 7 Zikri was a fighting man from Ephraim. He killed Maaseiah, Azrikam and Elkanah. Maaseiah was the king's son. Azrikam was the officer who was in charge of the palace. And Elkanah was next in command after the king. 8 The men of Israel captured 200,000 wives, sons and daughters from their relatives in Judah. They also took a large amount of goods. They carried all of it back to Samaria.

9 But a prophet of the LORD was there. His name was Oded. When the army returned to Samaria, he went out to meet them. He said to them, "The LORD is the God of your people. He was very angry with Judah. So he handed them over to you. But you have killed them. Your anger reached all the way to heaven. 10 Now you are planning to make the men and women of Judah and Jerusalem your slaves. But aren't you also

guilty of sins against the LORD your God? 11 Listen to me! You have taken your relatives from Judah as prisoners. The LORD is very angry with you. So send your relatives back."

12 Then some of the leaders in Ephraim stood up to those who were returning from the war. The leaders were Azariah, Berekiah, Jehizkiah and Amasa. Azariah was the son of Jehohanan. Berekiah was the son of Meshillemoth. Jehizkiah was the son of Shallum. And Amasa was the son of Hadlai. 13 "Don't bring those prisoners here," they said. "If you do, we'll be guilty in the sight of the LORD. Do you really want to add to our sin and guilt? We're already very guilty. The LORD is very angry with Israel."

14 So the soldiers gave up the prisoners and the goods they had taken. They did it in front of the officials and the whole community. 15 Azariah, Berekiah, Jehizkiah and Amasa received the prisoners. From the goods that had been taken, they gave clothes to everyone who was naked. They gave them clothes, sandals, food, drink and healing lotion. They put all the weak people on donkeys. They took them back to their relatives at Jericho. Then they returned to Samaria. Jericho was also known as the City of Palm Trees.

16 At that time King Ahaz sent men to the king of Assyria to get help. 17 The men of Edom had come and attacked Judah again. They had carried away prisoners. 18 At the same time the Philistines had attacked towns in the western hills and in the Negev Desert of Judah. They had captured Beth Shemesh, Aijalon and Gederoth. They had also captured Soko, Timnah and Gimzo and the villages around them. They had settled down in all of them. 19 The LORD had made Judah less powerful because of Ahaz, their king. Ahaz had stirred up the people of Judah to do evil things. He hadn't been faithful to the LORD at all. 20 Tiglath-Pileser came to Ahaz. But he gave Ahaz trouble instead of help. Tiglath-Pileser was king of Assyria. 21 Ahaz took some things from the LORD's temple. He also took some from the royal palace and from the officials. He gave all of them to the king of Assyria. But that didn't help Ahaz.

22 When King Ahaz was in trouble, he became even more unfaithful to the LORD. 23 Ahaz offered sacrifices to the gods of Damascus. They had won the battle over him. Ahaz thought, "The gods of the kings of Aram have helped them. So I'll sacrifice to those gods. Then they'll help me." But those gods only caused his ruin. In fact, those gods caused the ruin of the whole nation of Israel.

24 Ahaz gathered together everything that belonged to God's temple. He cut all of it in pieces. Ahaz shut the doors of the LORD's temple. He set up altars at every street corner in Jerusalem. 25 In every town in Judah he built high places. Sacrifices were burned there to other gods. That made the LORD, the God of his people, very angry.

26 The other events of the rule of Ahaz and all his evil practices from beginning to end are written down. They are written in the records of the kings of Judah and Israel. 27 Ahaz joined the members of his family who had already died. He was buried in the city of Jerusalem. But he wasn't placed in the tombs of the kings of Israel. Ahaz's son Hezekiah became the next king after him.

Hezekiah Purifies the Temple

29 Hezekiah was 25 years old when he became king. He ruled in Jerusalem for 29 years. His mother's name was Abijah. She was the daughter of Zechariah. 2 Hezekiah did what was right in the eyes of the LORD, just as King David had done.

3 In the first month of Hezekiah's first year as king, he opened the doors of the LORD's temple. He repaired them. 4 He brought the priests and Levites in. He gathered them together in the open area on the east side of the temple. 5 He said, "Levites, listen to me! Set yourselves apart to the LORD. Set apart the temple of the LORD. He's the God of your people who lived long ago. Remove anything 'unclean' from the temple. 6 Our people weren't faithful. They did what was evil in the eyes of the LORD our God. They deserted him. They turned their faces away from the place where he lives. They turned their backs on him. 7 They also shut the doors of the temple porch. They put the lamps out. They didn't burn incense at the temple.

They didn't sacrifice burnt offerings
there to the God of Israel. 8 So the LORD
has become angry with Judah and Jerusalem. He has made them look so bad
that everyone is shocked when they
see them. They laugh at them. You can
see it with your own eyes. 9 That's why
our fathers have been killed by swords.
That's why our sons and daughters and
wives have become prisoners. 10 So I'm
planning to make a covenant with the
LORD, the God of Israel. Then he'll stop
being angry with us. 11 My sons, don't
fail to obey the LORD. He has chosen
you to stand in front of him and work
for him. He wants you to serve him and
burn incense to him."

12 Here are the Levites who went to work.

Mahath and Joel were from the family line of Kohath.
Mahath was the son of Amasai.
Joel was the son of Azariah.
Kish and Azariah were from the family line of Merari.
Kish was the son of Abdi. Azariah was the son of Jehallelel.
Joah and Eden were from the family line of Gershon.
Joah was the son of Zimmah.
Eden was the son of Joah.
13 Shimri and Jeiel were from the family line of Elizaphan.
Zechariah and Mattaniah were from the family line of Asaph.
14 Jehiel and Shimei were from the family line of Heman.
Shemaiah and Uzziel were from the family line of Jeduthun.

15 All these Levites gathered the other
Levites together. They set themselves
apart to the LORD. Then they went in to
purify the LORD's temple. That's what
the king had ordered them to do. They
did what the LORD told them to. 16 The
priests went into the LORD's temple to
make it pure. They brought out to the
temple courtyard everything that was
"unclean." They had found "unclean"
things in the LORD's temple. The Levites took them and carried them out
to the Kidron Valley. 17 On the first day
of the first month they began to set
everything in the temple apart to the
LORD. By the eighth day of the month
they reached the LORD's porch. For eight
more days they set the LORD's temple
itself apart to him. They finished on the
16th day of the first month.

18 Then they went to King Hezekiah. They reported, "We've purified the
whole temple of the LORD. That includes
the altar for burnt offerings and all its
tools. It also includes the table for the
holy bread and all its objects. 19 We've
prepared all the things King Ahaz had
removed. We've set them apart to the
LORD. Ahaz had removed them while
he was king. He wasn't faithful to the
LORD. Those things are now in front of
the LORD's altar."

20 Early the next morning King Hezekiah gathered together the city officials.
They all went up to the LORD's temple.
21 They brought seven bulls, seven rams,
seven male lambs and seven male goats
with them. They sacrificed the animals
as a sin offering for the kingdom, for
the temple and for Judah. The king
commanded the priests to offer them
on the LORD's altar. The priests were
from the family line of Aaron. 22 They
killed the bulls. Then they splashed
the blood against the altar. Next they
killed the rams and splashed the blood
against the altar. Then they killed the
lambs and splashed the blood against
the altar. 23 The goats for the sin offering
were brought to the king and the whole
community. They placed their hands
on them. 24 Then the priests killed the
goats. They put the blood on the altar
as a sin offering. It paid for the sin of
the whole nation of Israel. The king had
ordered the burnt offering and the sin
offering for the whole nation.

25 Hezekiah stationed the Levites in
the LORD's temple. They had cymbals,
harps and lyres. They did everything in
the way King David, his prophet Gad,
and Nathan the prophet had required.
The LORD had given commands about
all these things through his prophets.
26 So the Levites stood ready with David's musical instruments. And the
priests had their trumpets ready.

27 Hezekiah gave the order to sacrifice
the burnt offering on the altar. The offering began. Singing to the LORD also
began. The singing was accompanied
by the trumpets and by the instruments
of David. He had been king of Israel.
28 The whole community bowed down.

They worshiped the LORD. At the same time the musicians played their musical instruments. The priests blew their trumpets. All of that continued until the burnt offering had been sacrificed.

29 So the offerings were finished. King Hezekiah got down on his knees. He worshiped the LORD. So did everyone who was with him. 30 The king and his officials ordered the Levites to praise the LORD. They used the words of David and Asaph the prophet. They sang praises with joy. They bowed down and worshiped the LORD.

31 Then Hezekiah said, "You have set yourselves apart to the LORD. Come and bring sacrifices and thank offerings to his temple." So the whole community brought sacrifices and thank offerings. Everyone who wanted to brought burnt offerings.

32 The whole community brought 70 bulls, 100 rams and 200 male lambs. They brought all of them as burnt offerings to the LORD. 33 The total number of animals set apart as sacrifices to the LORD was 600 bulls and 3,000 sheep and goats. 34 But there weren't enough priests to skin all the burnt offerings. So their relatives, the Levites, helped them. They worked until the task was finished. By that time other priests had been set apart to the LORD. The Levites had been more careful than the priests when they set themselves apart. 35 There were large numbers of burnt offerings, along with the drink offerings and the fat from the friendship offerings. They were offered along with the burnt offerings.

So the service of the LORD's temple was started up again. 36 Hezekiah and all the people were filled with joy. That's because everything had been done so quickly. God had provided for his people in a wonderful way.

Hezekiah Celebrates the Passover Feast

30 Hezekiah sent a message to all the people of Israel and Judah. He also wrote letters to the tribes of Ephraim and Manasseh. He invited everyone to come to the LORD's temple in Jerusalem. He wanted them to celebrate the Passover Feast to honor the LORD. He is the God of Israel. 2 The king, his officials and the whole community in Jerusalem decided to celebrate the Passover Feast in the second month. 3 They hadn't been able to celebrate it at the regular time. That's because there weren't enough priests who had set themselves apart to the LORD. Also, the people hadn't gathered together in Jerusalem. 4 The plan seemed good to the king and the whole community. 5 They decided to send a message all through Israel. It was sent out from Beersheba all the way to Dan. The message invited the people to come to Jerusalem. It invited them to celebrate the Passover Feast to honor the LORD, the God of Israel. The Passover Feast hadn't been celebrated by large numbers of people for a long time. It hadn't been done in keeping with what was written in the law.

6 Messengers went all through Israel and Judah. They carried letters from the king and his officials. The king had ordered them to do that. The letters said,

> "People of Israel, return to the LORD. He is the God of Abraham, Isaac and Israel. Return to him. Then he will return to you who are left in the land. You have escaped from the power of the kings of Assyria. 7 Don't be like your parents and the rest of your people. They weren't faithful to the LORD, the God of their people. That's why he punished them. He made them look so bad that everyone was shocked when they saw them. You can see it for yourselves. 8 Don't be stubborn. Don't be as your people were. Obey the LORD. Come to his temple. He has set it apart to himself forever. Serve the LORD your God. Then he'll stop being angry with you. 9 Suppose you return to the LORD. Then those who captured your relatives and children will be kind to them. In fact, your relatives and children will come back to this land. The LORD your God is kind and tender. He won't turn away from you if you return to him."

10 The messengers went from town to town in Ephraim and Manasseh. They went all the way to Zebulun. But people laughed and made fun of them. 11 In spite of that, some people from Asher, Manasseh and Zebulun made

God is gracious to his people even though they don't deserve it (see Exodus 34:6). Grace is a free gift of God best seen in the gift of salvation he offers to people through Jesus. But God doesn't just *do* gracious things; he *is* gracious.

Even though we sin and fail to meet God's perfect standard, God willingly and joyfully gives us what we don't deserve. He forgives our sin, provides for our needs, and gives us strength to live in ways that honor him. God's grace toward us teaches us to forgive people when they hurt us.

My GOD IS...

themselves humble. They went to Jerusalem. 12 God helped the people of
Judah. He helped them agree with one
another. So they did what the king and
his officials had ordered. They did what
the LORD told them to do.
13 A very large crowd of people gathered together in Jerusalem. They went
there to celebrate the Feast of Unleavened Bread. It took place in the second
month. 14 They removed the altars in
Jerusalem. They cleared away the altars for burning incense. They threw all
the altars into the Kidron Valley.
15 They killed the Passover lamb on the
14th day of the second month. The priests
and Levites were ashamed of how they
had lived. They set themselves apart to
the LORD. They brought burnt offerings
to his temple. 16 Then they did their regular tasks just as the Law of Moses, the
man of God, required. The Levites gave
the blood of the animals to the priests.
The priests splashed it against the altar. 17 Many people in the crowd hadn't
set themselves apart to the LORD. They
weren't "clean." They couldn't set apart
their lambs to him. So the Levites had to
kill the Passover lambs for all of them.
18 Many people came from Ephraim,
Manasseh, Issachar and Zebulun. Most of
them hadn't made themselves pure and
"clean." But they still ate the Passover
meal. That was against what was written in the law. But Hezekiah prayed for
them. He said, "The LORD is good. May he
forgive everyone 19 who wants to worship
God with all their heart. God is the LORD,
the God of their people. May God forgive
them even if they aren't 'clean' in keeping
with the rules of the temple." 20 The LORD
answered Hezekiah's prayer. He healed
the people.
21 The people of Israel who were in
Jerusalem celebrated the Feast of Unleavened Bread. They celebrated for
seven days with great joy. The Levites
and priests praised the LORD every day.
They praised the LORD with loud musical instruments. The instruments had
been set apart to the LORD.
22 Hezekiah spoke words that gave
hope to all the Levites. They understood
how to serve the LORD well. For the seven
days of the feast they ate the share
given to them. They also sacrificed
friendship offerings. They praised the
LORD, the God of their people.
23 Then the whole community agreed
to celebrate the feast for seven more
days. So for another seven days they
celebrated with joy. 24 Hezekiah, the
king of Judah, provided 1,000 bulls and
7,000 sheep and goats for the community. The officials provided 1,000 bulls and
10,000 sheep and goats for them. A large
number of priests set themselves apart
to the LORD. 25 The entire community of

Judah was filled with joy. So were the
priests and Levites. And so were all the
people who had gathered together from
Israel. That included the outsiders who
had come from Israel. It also included
those who lived in Judah. 26 There was
great joy in Jerusalem. There hadn't
been anything like it in Israel since
the days of Solomon, the son of David.
Solomon had been king of Israel. 27 The
priests and Levites gave their blessing
to the people. God heard them. Their
prayer reached all the way to heaven.
It's the holy place where God lives.

31 The Passover Feast came to an
end. The people of Israel who
were in Jerusalem went out to the towns
of Judah. They smashed the sacred
stones. They cut down the poles used
to worship the female god named Asherah. They destroyed the high places and
the altars. They did those things all
through Judah and Benjamin. They also
did them in Ephraim and Manasseh.
They destroyed all the objects used to
worship other gods. Then the Israelites returned to their own towns and
property.

The People Bring Gifts to the LORD

2 Hezekiah put the priests and Levites
in groups based on their duties. The
priests sacrificed burnt offerings and
friendship offerings. The Levites served
the LORD by giving thanks and singing
praises at the gates of his house. 3 The
king gave some of his own possessions
to the temple. He gave them for the
morning and evening burnt offerings.
He gave them for the burnt offerings
for every Sabbath day. He gave them
for the burnt offerings for every New
Moon feast. And he gave them for
the burnt offerings for every yearly
appointed feast. He did it in keeping
with what is written in the Law of the
LORD. 4 Hezekiah gave an order to the
people who were living in Jerusalem.
He commanded them to give to the
priests and Levites the share they owed
them. Then the priests and Levites could
give their full attention to the Law of
the LORD. 5 The order went out. Right
away the people of Israel began to
give freely. They gave the first share
of the harvest of their grain, fresh wine,
olive oil and honey. They also gave
the first share of everything else their
fields produced. They brought a large
amount. It was a tenth of everything.
6 Here is what the people of Israel and
Judah who lived in the towns of Judah
brought. They brought a tenth of their
herds and flocks. They also brought a
tenth of the holy things they had set
apart to the LORD their God. They put
them in piles. 7 They began doing it
in the third month. They finished in
the seventh month. 8 Hezekiah and his
officials came and saw the piles. When
they did, they praised the LORD. And
they blessed his people Israel.

9 Hezekiah asked the priests and
Levites about the piles. 10 Azariah the
chief priest answered him. He said,
"The people have been bringing their
gifts to the LORD's temple. Ever since
they began to bring them, we've had
enough to eat. We have even had plenty
to spare. That's because the LORD has
blessed his people. So we have a large
amount left over." Azariah was from
the family line of Zadok.

11 Hezekiah gave orders to prepare
storerooms in the LORD's temple. And
it was done. 12 The people were faithful.
They brought in their offerings and
a tenth of everything they produced.
They also brought the gifts they had
set apart to the LORD. Konaniah the
Levite was in charge of everything they
brought. His brother Shimei was next
in command after him. 13 Konaniah and
his brother Shimei had helpers who
worked with them. Their names were
Jehiel, Azaziah, Nahath, Asahel, Jerimoth, Jozabad, Eliel, Ismakiah, Mahath
and Benaiah. King Hezekiah and Azariah had appointed them. Azariah was
the official in charge of God's temple.

14 Kore the Levite guarded the East
Gate. He was in charge of the offerings
people chose to give to God. He handed
out the offerings made to the LORD.
He also handed out the gifts that had
been set apart to the LORD. Kore was
the son of Imnah. 15 Eden, Miniamin,
Jeshua, Shemaiah, Amariah and Shekaniah helped Kore. They were faithful in
helping him in the towns of the priests.
They handed out gifts to their brother
priests, group by group. They gave the
gifts to old men and young men alike.

16 In addition to that, they handed out gifts to the males who were three years old or more. The names of those males were listed in their family history. All of them would enter the LORD's temple. They would carry out their duties each day. Each group did all the different things it was supposed to do. 17 Kore and his Levite companions also handed out gifts to the priests. The priests were listed by their families in their family history. Those Levites also handed out gifts to the Levites who were 20 years old or more. Each group did all the different things it was supposed to do. 18 Those groups included all the little ones, the wives, and the sons and daughters of the whole community. All of them were listed in their family history. They were faithful in setting themselves apart to serve the LORD.

19 Some of the priests lived in other towns or on farms around their towns. They were from the family line of Aaron. Men were chosen by name to hand out shares to those priests. They gave a share to every male among them. They also gave a share to everyone whose name was written down in the family history of the Levites.

20 That's what Hezekiah did all through Judah. He did what was good and right. He was faithful to the LORD his God. 21 He tried to obey his God. He worked for him with all his heart. That's the way he worked in everything he did to serve God's temple. He obeyed the law. He followed the LORD's commands. So he had success.

Sennacherib Warns Jerusalem

32 Hezekiah had been completely faithful to the LORD. However, Sennacherib king of Assyria came and marched into Judah. Sennacherib surrounded the cities that had high walls around them. He got ready to attack them. He thought he could win the battle over them. He thought he could take them for himself. 2 Hezekiah saw that Sennacherib had come to Jerusalem to fight against it. 3 So he asked his officials and military leaders for advice. He asked them about blocking off the water from the springs outside the city. They gave him the advice he asked for. 4 They gathered together a large group of people. They blocked all the springs. They also blocked the stream that flowed through the land. "Why should the kings of Assyria come and find plenty of water?" they asked. 5 Then Hezekiah worked hard repairing all the broken parts of the wall. He built towers on it. He built another wall outside that one. He built up the areas that had been filled in around the City of David. He also made large numbers of weapons and shields.

6 He appointed military officers over the people. He gathered the officers together in front of him in the open area at the city gate. He gave them words of hope. He said, 7 "Be strong. Be brave. Don't be afraid. Don't lose hope. The king of Assyria has a huge army with him. But there's a greater power with us than there is with him. 8 The only thing he has is human strength. But the LORD our God is with us. He will help us. He'll fight our battles." The people had great faith in what Hezekiah, the king of Judah, said.

9 Later Sennacherib, the king of Assyria, and all his forces surrounded Lachish. They prepared to attack it. At that time, Sennacherib sent his officers to Jerusalem. They went there with a message for Hezekiah, the king of Judah. The message was also for all the people of Judah who were there. The message said,

> 10 "Sennacherib, the king of Assyria, says, 'Why are you putting your faith in what your king says? Why do you remain in Jerusalem when you are surrounded? 11 Hezekiah says, "The LORD our God will save us from the power of the king of Assyria." But he isn't telling you the truth. If you listen to him, you will die of hunger and thirst. 12 Didn't Hezekiah himself remove your god's high places and altars? Didn't Hezekiah say to the people of Judah and Jerusalem, "You must worship at one altar. You must burn sacrifices on it"?
>
> 13 " 'Don't you know what I and the kings who ruled before me have done? Don't you know what we've done to all the peoples of the other lands? Were the gods of those nations ever able to save their lands from my power? 14 The kings who

ruled before me destroyed many
nations. Which one of the gods of
those nations has been able to save
his people from me? So how can
your god save you from my power?
15 Don't let Hezekiah trick you. He's
telling you lies. Don't believe him.
No god of any nation or kingdom
has been able to save his people
from my power. No god has been
able to save his people from the
power of the kings who ruled before
me. So your god won't save you
from my power either!' "

16 Sennacherib's officers spoke even
more things against the LORD God and
his servant Hezekiah. 17 The king also
wrote letters against the LORD. His letters made fun of the God of Israel. They
said, "The peoples of other lands have
their gods. But those gods didn't save
their people from my power. So the god
of Hezekiah won't save his people from
my power either." 18 Then the officers
called out in the Hebrew language to
the people of Jerusalem who were on
the wall. They were trying to scare them
and make them afraid. That's because
they wanted to capture the city. 19 They
were comparing the God of Jerusalem
to the gods of the other nations of the
world. But those gods were only statues.
They had been made by human hands.
20 King Hezekiah cried out in prayer
to God in heaven. He prayed about the
problem Jerusalem was facing. So did
Isaiah the prophet. He was the son of
Amoz. 21 The LORD sent an angel. The
angel wiped out all the enemy's fighting
men, commanders and officers. He put
an end to them right there in the camp
of the Assyrian king. So Sennacherib
went back to his own land in shame. He
went into the temple of his god. There
some of his own sons, the people closest
to him, killed him with their swords.

22 So the LORD saved Hezekiah and
the people of Jerusalem. He saved them
from the power of Sennacherib, the king
of Assyria. He also saved them from
all their other enemies. He took care
of them on every side. 23 Many people
brought offerings to Jerusalem for the
LORD. They brought expensive gifts for
Hezekiah, the king of Judah. From then
on, all the nations thought well of him.

Hezekiah's Pride, Success and Death

24 In those days Hezekiah became
sick. He knew he was about to die. So
he prayed to the LORD. And the LORD
answered him. He gave him a miraculous sign. 25 But Hezekiah's heart was
proud. He didn't give thanks for the
many kind things the LORD had done
for him. So the LORD became angry with
him. He also became angry with Judah
and Jerusalem. 26 Then Hezekiah had a
change of heart. He was sorry he had
been proud. The people of Jerusalem
were also sorry they had sinned. So the
LORD wasn't angry with them as long
as Hezekiah was king.

27 Hezekiah was very rich. He received
great honor. He made storerooms for
his silver and gold. He also made them
for his jewels, spices, shields and all
kinds of expensive things. 28 He made
buildings to store the harvest of grain,
fresh wine and olive oil. He made barns
for all kinds of cattle. He made sheep
pens for his flocks. 29 He built villages.
He gained large numbers of flocks and
herds. God had made him very rich.

30 Hezekiah blocked up the upper
opening of the Gihon spring. He directed the water to flow down to the
west side of the City of David. He had
success in everything he did. 31 The rulers of Babylon sent messengers to him.
They asked him about the miraculous
sign that had taken place in the land.
Then God left Hezekiah to test him.
God wanted to know everything in
Hezekiah's heart.

32 Hezekiah did many things that
showed he was faithful to the LORD.
Those things and the other events of
his rule are written down. They are
written in the record of the vision of
the prophet Isaiah, the son of Amoz.
That record is part of the records of the
kings of Judah and Israel. 33 Hezekiah
joined the members of his family who
had already died. He was buried on the
hill where the tombs of David's family
are. The whole nation of Judah honored
him when he died. So did the people of
Jerusalem. Hezekiah's son Manasseh
became the next king after him.

Manasseh King of Judah

33 Manasseh was 12 years old when he became king. He ruled in Jerusalem for 55 years. 2 Manasseh did what was evil in the eyes of the LORD. He followed the practices of the nations. The LORD hated those practices. The LORD had driven out those nations to make room for the Israelites. 3 Manasseh rebuilt the high places. His father Hezekiah had destroyed them. Manasseh also set up altars to the gods that were named Baal. He made poles used to worship the female god named Asherah. He even bowed down to all the stars and worshiped them. 4 He built altars in the LORD's temple. The LORD had said about his temple, "My Name will remain in Jerusalem forever." 5 In the two courtyards of the LORD's temple Manasseh built altars to honor all the stars in the sky. 6 He sacrificed his children in the fire to other gods. He did it in the Valley of Ben Hinnom. He practiced all kinds of evil magic. He took part in worshiping evil powers. He got messages from people who had died. He talked to the spirits of people who have died. He did many things that were evil in the eyes of the LORD. Manasseh made the LORD very angry.

7 Manasseh had carved a statue of a god. He put it in God's temple. God had spoken to David and his son Solomon about the temple. He had said, "My Name will be in this temple and in Jerusalem forever. Out of all the cities in the tribes of Israel I have chosen Jerusalem. 8 I gave this land to your people who lived long ago. I will not make the Israelites leave it again. But they must be careful to do everything I commanded them. They must follow all the laws, directions, and rules I gave them through Moses." 9 But Manasseh led Judah and the people of Jerusalem astray. They did more evil things than the nations the LORD had destroyed to make room for the Israelites.

10 The LORD spoke to Manasseh and his people. But they didn't pay any attention to him. 11 So the LORD brought the army commanders of the king of Assyria against them. They took Manasseh as a prisoner. They put a hook in his nose. They put him in bronze chains. And they took him to Babylon. 12 When Manasseh was in trouble, he asked the LORD his God to help him. He made himself very humble in the sight of the God of his people. 13 Manasseh prayed to him. When he did, the LORD felt sorry for him. He answered his prayer. The LORD brought Manasseh back to Jerusalem and his kingdom. Then Manasseh knew that the LORD is God.

14 After that, Manasseh rebuilt the outer wall of the City of David. It was west of the Gihon spring in the valley. It reached all the way to the entrance of the Fish Gate. It went around the entire hill of Ophel. Manasseh also made the wall much higher. He stationed military commanders in all the cities in Judah that had high walls around them.

15 Manasseh got rid of the false gods. He removed the statue of one of those gods from the LORD's temple. He also removed all the altars he had built on the temple hill and in Jerusalem. He threw them out of the city. 16 Then he made the LORD's altar look like new again. He sacrificed friendship offerings and thank offerings on it. He told the people of Judah to serve the LORD, the God of Israel. 17 The people continued to offer sacrifices at the high places. But they offered them only to the LORD their God.

18 The other events of Manasseh's rule are written down in the official records of the kings of Judah. These records include his prayer to his God. They also include the words the prophets spoke to him in the name of the LORD, the God of Israel. 19 Everything about Manasseh is written in the records of the prophets. That includes his prayer and the fact that God felt sorry for him. It includes everything he did before he made himself humble in the LORD's sight. It includes all his sins and the fact that he wasn't faithful to the LORD. It includes the locations where he built high places. It includes the places where he set up poles used to worship the female god named Asherah. And it includes the places where he set up statues of other gods. 20 Manasseh joined the members of his family who had already died. He was buried in his palace. Manasseh's son Amon became the next king after him.

Amon King of Judah

21 Amon was 22 years old when he became king. He ruled in Jerusalem for two years. 22 Amon did what was evil in the eyes of the LORD, just as his father Manasseh had done. Amon worshiped and offered sacrifices to all the statues of gods that Manasseh had made. 23 He didn't make himself humble in the LORD's sight as his father Manasseh had done. So Amon became even more guilty.

24 Amon's officials made plans against him. They murdered him in his palace. 25 Then the people of the land killed all those who had made plans against King Amon. They made his son Josiah king in his place.

Josiah Makes Judah a Better Nation

34 Josiah was eight years old when he became king. He ruled in Jerusalem for 31 years. 2 He did what was right in the eyes of the LORD. He lived the way King David had lived. He didn't turn away from it to the right or the left.

3 While he was still young, he began to worship the God of King David. It was the eighth year of Josiah's rule. In his 12th year Josiah began to get rid of the high places in Judah and Jerusalem. He removed the poles used to worship the female god named Asherah. He also removed the statues of other false gods. 4 He ordered the altars of the gods that were named Baal to be torn down. Josiah cut to pieces the altars above them that were used for burning incense. He smashed the Asherah poles. He also smashed the statues of other false gods. Josiah broke all of them to pieces. He scattered the pieces over the graves of those who had offered sacrifices to those gods. 5 He burned the bones of the priests on their altars. That's the way he made Judah and Jerusalem pure and "clean." 6 Josiah went to the towns of Manasseh, Ephraim and Simeon. He went all the way to Naphtali. He also went to the destroyed places around all those towns. 7 Everywhere Josiah went he tore down the altars and the Asherah poles. He crushed the statues of gods to powder. He cut to pieces all the altars for burning incense. He destroyed all those things everywhere in Israel. Then he went back to Jerusalem.

8 In the 18th year of Josiah's rule, he decided to make the land and temple pure and "clean." So he sent Shaphan, Maaseiah and Joah to repair the temple of the LORD his God. Shaphan was the son of Azaliah. Maaseiah was ruler of the city. And Joah, the son of Joahaz, kept the records.

9 These men went to Hilkiah the high priest. They gave him the money that had been brought into God's temple. The Levites who guarded the gates had collected it. They had received some of the money from the people of Manasseh and Ephraim. They had also received some from the other people who remained in Israel. The rest of the money came from other people. It came from all the people of Judah and Benjamin and the people living in Jerusalem. 10 Men were appointed to direct the work on the LORD's temple. All the money collected was given to them. These men paid the workers who repaired the temple. They made it look like new again. 11 They also gave money to the builders and those who worked with wood. The workers used it to buy lumber and blocks of stone. The lumber was used for the supports and beams for the buildings. The kings of Judah had let the buildings fall down.

12 The workers were faithful in doing the work. Jahath and Obadiah directed them. They were Levites from the family line of Merari. Zechariah and Meshullam also directed them. They were from the family line of Kohath. The Levites were skilled in playing musical instruments. 13 They were in charge of the laborers. They directed all the workers from job to job. Some of the Levites were secretaries and writers. Other Levites guarded the gates.

Hilkiah Finds the Book of the Law

14 The money that had been taken into the LORD's temple was being brought out. At that time Hilkiah the priest found the Book of the Law of the LORD. It had been given through Moses. 15 Hilkiah spoke to Shaphan the secretary. Hilkiah said, "I've found the Book of the Law in the LORD's temple." Hilkiah gave the book to Shaphan.

16 Then Shaphan took the book to King Josiah. He told him, "Your officials are doing everything they've been asked to do. 17 They have paid out the money that was in the LORD's temple. They've put it in the care of the directors and workers." 18 Shaphan continued, "Hilkiah the priest has given me a book." Shaphan read some of it to the king.

19 The king heard the words of the Law. When he did, he tore his royal robes. 20 He gave orders to Hilkiah, Ahikam, Abdon, Shaphan the secretary and Asaiah. Ahikam was the son of Shaphan. Abdon was the son of Micah. And Asaiah was the king's attendant. Josiah commanded them, 21 "Go. Ask the LORD for advice. Ask him about what is written in this book that has been found. Do it for me. Also do it for the people who remain in Israel and Judah. The LORD has been very angry with us. That's because our people before us didn't obey what the LORD had said. They didn't do everything written in this book."

22 Hilkiah and the people the king had sent with him went to speak to Huldah the prophet. She was the wife of Shallum. Shallum was the son of Tokhath. Tokhath was the son of Hasrah. Shallum took care of the sacred robes. Huldah lived in the New Quarter of Jerusalem.

23 Huldah said to them, "The LORD is the God of Israel. He says, 'Here is what you should tell the man who sent you to me. 24 "The LORD says, 'I am going to bring horrible trouble on this place and its people. There are curses written down in the book that has been read to the king of Judah. All those curses will take place. 25 That's because the people have deserted me. They have burned incense to other gods. They have made me very angry because of everything their hands have made. So my anger will burn like a fire against this place. And the fire of my anger will not be put out.' " ' 26 The king of Judah sent you to ask for advice. Tell him, 'The LORD is the God of Israel. He has a message for you about the things you heard. 27 The LORD says, "Your heart was tender. You made yourself humble in my sight. You heard what I spoke against this place and its people. So you made yourself humble. You tore your royal robes and wept. And I have heard you," announces the LORD. 28 You will join the members of your family who have already died. You will be buried in peace. You will not see all the trouble I am going to bring. I am going to bring trouble on this place and the people who live here.' "

Huldah's answer was taken back to the king.

29 Then the king called together all the elders of Judah and Jerusalem. 30 He went up to the LORD's temple. The people of Judah and Jerusalem went with him. So did the priests and Levites. All of them went, from the least important of them to the most important. The king had all the words of the Book of the Covenant read to them. The book had been found in the LORD's temple. 31 The king stood next to his pillar. He agreed to the terms of the covenant in front of the LORD. The king promised to serve the LORD and obey his commands, directions and rules. He promised to obey them with all his heart and with all his soul. So the king promised to obey the terms of the covenant that were written in that book.

32 Then he had everyone in Jerusalem and in Benjamin commit themselves to the covenant. The people of Jerusalem did it in keeping with the covenant of the God of Israel.

33 Josiah removed all the statues of false gods from the whole territory that belonged to the Israelites. The LORD hated those statues. Josiah had everyone in Israel serve the LORD their God. As long as he lived, they didn't fail to follow the LORD, the God of their people.

Josiah Celebrates the Passover Feast

35 Josiah celebrated the Passover Feast in Jerusalem to honor the LORD. The Passover lamb was killed on the 14th day of the first month. 2 Josiah appointed the priests to their duties. He cheered them up as they served the LORD at his temple. 3 The Levites taught all the people of Israel. The Levites had been set apart to the LORD. Josiah said to them, "Put the sacred ark of the covenant in the temple Solomon built. He was the son of David and king of Israel. The ark must not be carried around on your shoulders. Serve the LORD your

God. Serve his people Israel. 4 Prepare yourselves by families in your groups. Do it based on the directions written by David, the king of Israel, and by his son Solomon.

5 "Stand at the temple. Stand there with a group of Levites for each group of families among your people. 6 Kill the Passover lambs. Set yourselves apart to the LORD. Prepare the lambs for your people. Do what the LORD commanded through Moses."

7 Josiah provided animals for the Passover offerings. He gave them for all the people who were there. He gave a total of 30,000 lambs and goats and 3,000 oxen. He gave all of them from his own possessions.

8 His officials also gave freely. They gave to the people and the priests and Levites. Hilkiah, Zechariah and Jehiel were in charge of God's temple. They gave the priests 2,600 Passover lambs and 300 oxen. 9 Konaniah and his brothers Shemaiah and Nethanel also gave offerings. So did Hashabiah, Jeiel and Jozabad. All of them were the leaders of the Levites. They gave 5,000 Passover lambs and 500 oxen for the Levites.

10 The Passover service was arranged. The priests stood in their places. The Levites were in their groups. That's what the king had ordered. 11 The Passover lambs were killed. The priests splashed against the altar the blood handed to them. The Levites skinned the animals. 12 They set the burnt offerings to one side. These offerings were for the smaller family groups to offer to the LORD. That's what was written in the Book of Moses. The Levites did the same thing with the oxen. 13 They cooked the Passover animals over the fire, just as the law required. They boiled the holy offerings in pots, large kettles and pans. They served the offerings quickly to all the people. 14 After that, they got things ready for themselves and the priests. That's because the priests, who were from the family line of Aaron, were busy until dark. They were sacrificing the burnt offerings and the fat parts. The Levites got things ready for themselves and for the priests, who belonged to Aaron's family line.

15 Those who played music were from the family line of Asaph. They were in the places that had been set up by David, Asaph, Heman and Jeduthun. Jeduthun had been the king's prophet. The guards at each gate didn't have to leave their places. That's because their brother Levites got things ready for them.

16 So at that time the entire service to honor the LORD was carried out. The Passover Feast was celebrated. The burnt offerings were sacrificed on the LORD's altar. That's what King Josiah had ordered. 17 The Israelites who were there celebrated the Passover Feast at that time. They observed the Feast of Unleavened Bread for seven days. 18 The Passover Feast hadn't been observed like that in Israel since the days of Samuel the prophet. None of the kings of Israel had ever celebrated a Passover Feast like Josiah's. He celebrated it with the priests and Levites. All the people of Judah and Israel were there along with the people of Jerusalem. He celebrated it with them too. 19 That Passover Feast was celebrated in the 18th year of Josiah's rule.

Josiah Dies

20 Josiah had put the temple in order. After all of that, Necho went up to fight at Carchemish. He was king of Egypt. Carchemish was on the Euphrates River. Josiah marched out to meet Necho in battle. 21 But Necho sent messengers to him. They said, "Josiah king of Judah, there isn't any trouble between you and me. I'm not attacking you at this time. I'm at war with another country. God told me to hurry. He's with me. So stop opposing him. If you don't, he'll destroy you."

22 But Josiah wouldn't turn away from Necho. Josiah wore different clothes so people wouldn't recognize him. He wanted to go to war against Necho. He wouldn't listen to what God had commanded Necho to say. Instead, Josiah went out to fight him on the plains of Megiddo.

23 Men who had bows shot arrows at King Josiah. After he was hit, he told his officers, "Take me away. I'm badly wounded." 24 So they took him out of his chariot. They put him in his other chariot. They brought him to Jerusalem. There he died. He was buried in the

tombs of his family. All the people of
Judah and Jerusalem mourned for him.
25 Jeremiah wrote songs of sadness
about Josiah. To this day all the male
and female singers remember Josiah
by singing those songs. That became
a practice in Israel. The songs are written down in the Book of the Songs of
Sadness.
26 Josiah did many things that
showed he was faithful to the LORD.
Those things and the other events of
Josiah's rule were in keeping with what
is written in the Law of the LORD. 27 All
the events from beginning to end are
written down. They are written in the
records of the kings of Israel and Judah.

36 1 The people of the land went
and got Jehoahaz. He was the
son of Josiah. The people made Jehoahaz king in Jerusalem in place of his
father.

Jehoahaz King of Judah

2 Jehoahaz was 23 years old when he
became king. He ruled in Jerusalem
for three months. 3 The king of Egypt
removed him from his throne in Jerusalem. The king of Egypt made the
people of Judah pay him a huge tax.
The tax was almost four tons of silver
and 75 pounds of gold. 4 Necho, the king
of Egypt, made Eliakim king over Judah
and Jerusalem. Eliakim was a brother
of Jehoahaz. Necho changed Eliakim's
name to Jehoiakim. But Necho took
Eliakim's brother Jehoahaz with him
to Egypt.

Jehoiakim King of Judah

5 Jehoiakim was 25 years old when
he became king. He ruled in Jerusalem
for 11 years. He did what was evil in the
eyes of the LORD his God. 6 Nebuchadnezzar attacked him. Nebuchadnezzar
was king of Babylon. He put Jehoiakim
in bronze chains. And he took him to
Babylon. 7 Nebuchadnezzar also took to
Babylon objects from the LORD's temple.
He put them in his own temple there.
8 The other events of Jehoiakim's rule
are written in the records of the kings
of Israel and Judah. He did things the
LORD hated. Those things and everything that happened to him are also
written in those records. Jehoiakim's
son Jehoiachin became the next king
after him.

Jehoiachin King of Judah

9 Jehoiachin was 18 years old when he
became king. He ruled in Jerusalem for
three months and ten days. He did what
was evil in the eyes of the LORD. 10 In the
spring, King Nebuchadnezzar sent for
him. He brought him to Babylon. He
also brought things of value from the
LORD's temple. He made Zedekiah king
over Judah and Jerusalem. Zedekiah
was Jehoiachin's uncle.

Zedekiah King of Judah

11 Zedekiah was 21 years old when he
became king. He ruled in Jerusalem for
11 years. 12 He did what was evil in the
eyes of the LORD his God. He didn't pay
any attention to the message the LORD
spoke through Jeremiah the prophet.
13 Zedekiah also refused to remain under
the control of King Nebuchadnezzar.
The king had forced Zedekiah to make
a promise in God's name. But Zedekiah's heart became very stubborn. He
wouldn't turn to the LORD, the God of
Israel. 14 And that's not all. The people
and all the leaders of the priests became more and more unfaithful. They
followed all the practices of the nations.
The LORD hated those practices. The
people and leaders made the LORD's
temple "unclean." The LORD had set the
temple in Jerusalem apart in a special
way for himself.

The Fall of Jerusalem

15 The LORD, the God of Israel, sent
word to his people through his messengers. He sent it to them again and
again. He took pity on his people. He
also took pity on the temple where he
lived. 16 But God's people made fun of
his messengers. They hated his words.
They laughed at his prophets. Finally
the LORD's great anger was stirred up
against his people. Nothing could save
them. 17 The LORD brought the king of
the Babylonians against them. The
Babylonian army killed their young
people with their swords at the temple.
They didn't spare young men or young
women. They didn't spare the old people or weak people either. God handed
all of them over to Nebuchadnezzar.
18 Nebuchadnezzar carried off to Babylon all the objects from God's temple.
Some of those things were large. Others
were small. He carried off the treasures

of the temple. He also carried off the treasures that belonged to the king and his officials. [19] The Babylonians set God's temple on fire. They broke down the wall of Jerusalem. They burned all the palaces. They destroyed everything of value there.

[20] Nebuchadnezzar took the rest of the people to Babylon as prisoners. They had escaped from being killed by swords. They served him and those who ruled after him. That lasted until the kingdom of Persia came to power. [21] The land of Israel enjoyed its sabbath years. It rested. That deserted land wasn't farmed for a full 70 years. What the LORD had spoken through Jeremiah came true.

[22] It was the first year of the rule of Cyrus. He was king of Persia. The LORD inspired him to send a message all through his kingdom. It happened so that what the LORD had spoken through Jeremiah would come true. The message was written down. It said,

[23] "Cyrus, the king of Persia, says,

" 'The LORD is the God of heaven. He has given me all the kingdoms on earth. He has appointed me to build a temple for him at Jerusalem in Judah. Any of his people among you may go up to Jerusalem. And may the LORD their God be with them.' "

EZRA

Author: Ezra (we think)

After the temple was destroyed, God's people found themselves far from home and without hope. They were no longer living as God's special people in the home God had given them; they were lost and living in a foreign country! Everything seemed to have gone wrong, and the Israelites wondered how anything could be made right again. How would God come dwell among them while the temple was a pile of rubble? How could they find their way back home to live with God in their midst?

Old Testament History

When the kingdom of Persia rose to power, the people of Judah (now called Jews) were allowed to return to Jerusalem and begin rebuilding the temple. But it had been so long, the Jews had completely forgotten what it meant to be God's people. They had forgotten who God was and how to worship him. They had forgotten his commands and all his promises to them. As they rebuilt the temple, a scribe named Ezra taught them how to obey God's laws once again. Ezra reminded them of all the things God had said in the past, and he taught them how to follow God in the present. Most importantly, Ezra reminded the Jews that they were created to worship God and that one day something better than the temple would come: the Messiah!

Cyrus Helps the Jews to Return to Jerusalem

1 It was the first year of the rule of
Cyrus. He was king of Persia. The
LORD inspired him to send a message
all through his kingdom. It happened so
that what the LORD had spoken through
Jeremiah would come true. The message was written down. It said,

2 "Cyrus, the king of Persia, says,

" 'The LORD is the God of heaven.
He has given me all the kingdoms
on earth. He has appointed me to
build a temple for him at Jerusalem
in Judah. 3 Any of his people among
you may go up to Jerusalem and
build the LORD's temple. He is the
God of Israel. He is the God who is
in Jerusalem. And may their God be
with them. 4 The people still left alive
in every place must bring gifts to the
people going. They must provide silver and gold to the people going up
to Jerusalem. The people must bring
goods and livestock. They should
also bring any offerings they choose
to. All those gifts will be for God's
temple in Jerusalem.' "

5 Then everyone God had inspired
prepared to go. They wanted to go up to
Jerusalem and build the LORD's temple
there. They included the family leaders of Judah and Benjamin. They also
included the priests and Levites. 6 All
their neighbors helped them. They gave
them silver and gold objects. They gave
them goods and livestock. And they
gave them gifts of great value. All those
things were added to the other offerings
the people chose to give.
7 King Cyrus also brought out the objects that belonged to the LORD's temple.
Nebuchadnezzar had carried them off
from Jerusalem. He had put them in
the temple of his own god. 8 Cyrus, the
king of Persia, told Mithredath to bring
them out. Mithredath was in charge
of the temple treasures. He counted
those objects. Then he gave them to
Sheshbazzar, the prince of Judah.

9 Here is a list of the objects.

There were 30 gold dishes.
There were 1,000 silver dishes.
There were 29 silver pans.
10 There were 30 gold bowls.

in Ezra?

God is the Restorer. God helped his people return to their home, and he was making a way for all people to return to him through the coming Savior.

There were 410 matching silver bowls.
There were 1,000 other objects.

11 The total number of gold and silver
objects was 5,400.

Sheshbazzar brought all of these back with him to Jerusalem. So Sheshbazzar and the Jews who had been forced to leave Judah came up from Babylon to Jerusalem.

The List of the Jews Who Returned to Judah

2 Nebuchadnezzar had taken
many Jews away from the
land of Judah. He had forced them
to go to Babylon as prisoners. Now
they returned to Jerusalem and
Judah. All of them went back to
their own towns. Nebuchadnezzar
was king of Babylon. 2 The leaders
of the Jews included Zerubbabel,
Joshua, Nehemiah, Seraiah and
Reelaiah. They also included
Mordecai, Bilshan, Mispar, Bigvai,
Rehum and Baanah.

Here is a list of the men of Israel who returned home.

3 There were 2,172 from the family
line of Parosh.
4 There were 372 from Shephatiah.
5 There were 775 from Arah.

6 There were 2,812 from Pahath-Moab through the family line of Jeshua and Joab.
7 There were 1,254 from Elam.
8 There were 945 from Zattu.
9 There were 760 from Zakkai.
10 There were 642 from Bani.
11 There were 623 from Bebai.
12 There were 1,222 from Azgad.
13 There were 666 from Adonikam.
14 There were 2,056 from Bigvai.
15 There were 454 from Adin.
16 There were 98 from Ater through the family line of Hezekiah.
17 There were 323 from Bezai.
18 There were 112 from Jorah.
19 There were 223 from Hashum.
20 There were 95 from Gibbar.

21 There were 123 from the men of Bethlehem.
22 There were 56 from Netophah.
23 There were 128 from Anathoth.
24 There were 42 from Azmaveth.
25 There were 743 from Kiriath Jearim, Kephirah and Beeroth.
26 There were 621 from Ramah and Geba.
27 There were 122 from Mikmash.
28 There were 223 from Bethel and Ai.
29 There were 52 from Nebo.
30 There were 156 from Magbish.
31 There were 1,254 from the other Elam.
32 There were 320 from Harim.
33 There were 725 from Lod, Hadid and Ono.
34 There were 345 from Jericho.
35 There were 3,630 from Senaah.

36 Here is a list of the priests.
There were 973 from the family line of Jedaiah through the line of Jeshua.
37 There were 1,052 from Immer.
38 There were 1,247 from Pashhur.
39 There were 1,017 from Harim.

40 Here is a list of the Levites.
There were 74 from the family lines of Jeshua and Kadmiel. Kadmiel was from the line of Hodaviah.

41 Here is a list of the musicians.
There were 128 from the family line of Asaph.

42 Here is a list of the men who guarded the gates.
There were 139 from the family lines of Shallum, Ater, Talmon, Akkub, Hatita and Shobai.

43 Here is a list of the members of the family lines of the temple servants.
Ziha, Hasupha, Tabbaoth,
44 Keros, Siaha, Padon,
45 Lebanah, Hagabah, Akkub,
46 Hagab, Shalmai, Hanan,
47 Giddel, Gahar, Reaiah,
48 Rezin, Nekoda, Gazzam,
49 Uzza, Paseah, Besai,
50 Asnah, Meunim, Nephusim,
51 Bakbuk, Hakupha, Harhur,
52 Bazluth, Mehida, Harsha,
53 Barkos, Sisera, Temah,
54 Neziah, Hatipha
55 Here is a list of the members of the family lines of the servants of Solomon.
Sotai, Hassophereth, Peruda,
56 Jaala, Darkon, Giddel,
57 Shephatiah, Hattil, Pokereth-Hazzebaim, Ami
58 The total number of the members of the family lines of the temple servants and the servants of Solomon was 392.

59 Many people came up to Judah from the towns of Tel Melah, Tel Harsha, Kerub, Addon and Immer. But they weren't able to prove that their families belonged to the people of Israel.
60 There were 652 of them from the family lines of Delaiah, Tobiah and Nekoda.

61 Here is a list of the members of the family lines of the priests.
They were Hobaiah, Hakkoz and Barzillai. Barzillai had married a daughter of Barzillai from Gilead. So he was also called Barzillai.
62 The priests looked for their family records. But they couldn't find them. So they weren't able to serve as priests. They were "unclean."
63 The governor gave them an order. He told them not to eat any of the most sacred food. They had to wait until there was a priest who could use the Urim and Thummim. The priest would use them to find out what the LORD wanted the people to do.

64 The total number of the entire
group that returned was 42,360.
65 That didn't include their 7,337
male and female slaves. There
were also 200 male and female
singers. 66 And there were 736
horses, 245 mules, 67 435 camels
and 6,720 donkeys.

68 All the people arrived at the place
in Jerusalem where the LORD's temple
would be rebuilt. Then some of the leaders of the families brought offerings
they chose to give. They would be used
for rebuilding the house of God. It would
stand in the same place it had been
before. 69 The people gave money for
the work. It was based on how much
they had. They gave 1,100 pounds of
gold. They also gave three tons of silver.
And they gave 100 sets of clothes for
the priests. All of that was added to the
temple treasure.

70 The priests and Levites made their
homes in their own towns. So did the
musicians, the men who guarded the
gates, and the temple servants. The rest
of the Israelites also made their homes
in their own towns.

The People Rebuild the Altar

3 The Israelites had made their
homes in their towns. In the seventh
month all of them gathered together in
Jerusalem. 2 Then Joshua began to build
the altar for burnt offerings to honor
the God of Israel. Joshua was the son
of Jozadak. The other priests helped
Joshua. So did Zerubbabel and his men.
They built the altar according to what is
written in the Law of Moses. Moses was
a man of God. Zerubbabel was the son
of Shealtiel. 3 The people who built the
altar were afraid of the nations around
them. But they built it anyway. They set
it up where it had stood before. They
sacrificed burnt offerings on it to the
LORD. They offered the morning and
evening sacrifices on it. 4 Then they
celebrated the Feast of Booths. They
did it according to what is written in
the Law. They sacrificed the number
of burnt offerings required for each
day. 5 After they celebrated the Feast
of Booths, they sacrificed the regular
burnt offerings. They offered the New
Moon sacrifices. They also offered the
sacrifices for all the appointed sacred
feasts of the LORD. And they sacrificed
the offerings the people chose to give
him. 6 On the first day of the seventh
month they began to offer burnt offerings to the LORD. They did it even
though the foundation of the LORD's
temple hadn't been laid yet.

The People Begin to Rebuild the Temple

7 The people gave money to those
who worked with stone and those who
worked with wood. They gave food and
drink and olive oil to the people of Sidon
and Tyre. Then those people brought
cedar logs down from Lebanon to the
Mediterranean Sea. They floated them
down to Joppa. Cyrus, the king of Persia,
authorized them to do it.

8 It was the second month of the second year after they had arrived at the
house of God in Jerusalem. Zerubbabel,
the son of Shealtiel, began the work.
Joshua, the son of Jozadak, helped him.
So did everyone else. That included the
priests and Levites. It also included the
rest of those who had returned to Jerusalem. They had been prisoners in the
land of Babylon. Levites who were 20
years old or more were appointed to be
in charge of building the LORD's house.
9 Those who joined together to direct the
work included Joshua and his sons and
brothers. They also included Kadmiel
and his sons. And they included the
sons of Henadad and their sons and
brothers. All those men were Levites.
Kadmiel and his sons were members
of the family line of Hodaviah.

10 The builders laid the foundation
of the LORD's temple. Then the priests
came. They were wearing their special
clothes. They brought their trumpets
with them. The Levites who belonged
to the family line of Asaph also came.
They brought their cymbals with them.
The priests and Levites took their places
to praise the LORD. They did everything
just as King David had required them to.
11 They sang to the LORD. They praised
him. They gave thanks to him. They
said,

"The LORD is good.
His faithful love to Israel
continues forever."

Why does God love me?

God loves you because God himself *is* love. His love is selfless and personal. He knows you and chooses you, and his love will never end.

Can you find the following verse?

EZRA 3:11

All the people gave a loud shout. They
praised the LORD. They were glad because the foundation of the LORD's
temple had been laid. 12 But many of
the older priests and Levites and family
leaders wept out loud. They had seen
the first temple. So when they saw the
foundation of the second temple being
laid, they wept. Others shouted with joy.
13 No one could tell the difference between the shouts of joy and the sounds
of weeping. That's because the people
made so much noise. The sound was
heard far away.

Enemies Oppose the Rebuilding of the Temple

4 The people who had returned from
Babylon were building a temple to
honor the LORD. He is the God of Israel.
The enemies of Judah and Benjamin
heard about it. 2 Then those enemies
came to Zerubbabel. The family leaders
of Israel were with him. The enemies
said, "We want to help you build. We're
just like you. We worship your God. We
offer sacrifices to him. We've been doing
that ever since the time of Esarhaddon.
He was king of Assyria. He brought our
people here."
3 Zerubbabel and Joshua answered
them. So did the rest of the family leaders of Israel. They said, "You can't help
us build a temple to honor our God. You
aren't part of us. We'll build it ourselves.
We'll do it to honor the LORD, the God of
Israel. Cyrus, the king of Persia, commanded us to build it."
4 Then the nations around Judah
tried to make its people lose hope. They
wanted to make them afraid to go on
building. 5 So those nations paid some
of the Jewish officials to work against
the people of Judah. They wanted their
plans to fail. They did it during the whole
time Cyrus was king of Persia. They kept
doing it until Darius became king.

Later Enemies Also Oppose the Jews

6 The enemies of the Jews brought
charges against the people of Judah
and Jerusalem. It happened when Xerxes began to rule over Persia.
7 Then Artaxerxes became king of
Persia. During his rule, Bishlam, Mithredath, Tabeel and their friends wrote a
letter to Artaxerxes. It was written in
the Aramaic language. And it used the
Aramaic alphabet.
8 Rehum and Shimshai also wrote a
letter to King Artaxerxes. Rehum was
the commanding officer. Shimshai
was the secretary. Their letter was
against the people of Jerusalem. It said,

9 We, Rehum and Shimshai, are
writing this letter. Rehum is the
commanding officer. Shimshai is
the secretary. Our friends join us
in writing. They include the judges,
officials and managers in charge of
the people from Persia, Uruk and
Babylon. They are also over the
Elamites from Susa. 10 And they
are over those who were forced to
leave their countries. The great
King Ashurbanipal, who is worthy
of honor, forced them to leave. He
moved them to the city of Samaria.
He also moved them to other places
west of the Euphrates River.

11 Here is a copy of the letter sent to
Artaxerxes.

We are sending this letter to you,
King Artaxerxes.

It is from your servants who live
west of the Euphrates River.

12 We want you to know about
the people who left you and have

come up to us. They have gone to Jerusalem and are rebuilding that evil city. It has caused trouble for a long time. Those people are making its walls like new again. They are repairing the foundations.

13 Here is something else we want you to know. Suppose this city is rebuilt. And suppose its walls are made like new again. Then no more taxes, gifts or fees will be collected. And sooner or later there will be less money for you. 14 We owe a lot to you. We don't want to see dishonor brought on you. So we're sending this letter to tell you what is going on. 15 Then you can have a search made in the official records. Have someone check the records of the kings who ruled before you. If you do, you will find out that Jerusalem is an evil city. It causes trouble for kings and countries. For a long time the city has refused to let anyone rule over it. That's why it was destroyed. 16 We want you to know that this city shouldn't be rebuilt. Its walls shouldn't be made like new again. If that happens, you won't have anything left west of the Euphrates River.

17 The king replied,

I am writing this letter to Rehum, the commanding officer. I am also writing it to Shimshai the secretary. And I am writing it to your friends living in Samaria and in other places west of the Euphrates River.

I give you my greetings.

18 The letter you sent us has been read to me. It has been explained to me in my language. 19 I gave an order. I had a search made. Here is what we found out. Jerusalem has a long history of turning against the kings of the countries that have ruled over it. It has refused to remain under their control. It is always stirring up trouble. 20 Jerusalem has had powerful kings. Some of them ruled over everything west of the Euphrates. Taxes, gifts and fees were paid to them. 21 So give an order to those men. Make them stop their work. Then the city won't be rebuilt until I give the order. 22 Pay careful attention to this matter. Why should we let this danger grow? That would not be in our best interests.

23 The copy of the letter of King Artaxerxes was read to Rehum and Shimshai the secretary. It was also read to their friends. Right away they went to the Jews in Jerusalem. They forced them to stop their work.

24 And so the work on the house of God in Jerusalem came to a stop. No more work was done on it until the second year that Darius was king of Persia.

Tattenai's Letter to King Darius

5 Haggai and Zechariah, the prophets, prophesied to the Jews in Judah and Jerusalem. They spoke to them in the name of the God of Israel. God had spoken to those prophets. Zechariah belonged to the family line of Iddo. 2 Zerubbabel, the son of Shealtiel, began to work. So did Joshua, the son of Jozadak. They began to rebuild the house of God in Jerusalem. The prophets of God were right there with them. They were helping them.

3 At that time Tattenai was governor of the land west of the Euphrates River. He and Shethar-Bozenai and their friends went to the Jews. They asked them, "Who authorized you to rebuild this temple? Who told you that you could finish it?" 4 They also asked, "What are the names of the people who are putting up this building?" 5 But the God of the Jews was watching over their elders. So they didn't have to stop their work. First a report would have to be sent to Darius. Then they would have to receive his answer in writing.

6 Here is a copy of the letter sent to King Darius. It was from Tattenai, the governor of the land west of the Euphrates. Shethar-Bozenai joined him in writing it. So did their friends. They were officials of that land. 7 The report they sent to the king said,

We are sending this letter to you, King Darius.

We give you our most friendly greetings.

[8]We want you to know that we went to the land of Judah. We went to the temple of the great God. The people are building it with large stones. They are putting wooden beams in the walls. The people are working hard. The work is moving ahead very quickly under the direction of the people.

[9]We asked the elders some questions. We said to them, "Who authorized you to rebuild this temple? Who told you that you could finish it?" [10]We also asked them what their names were. We wanted to write down the names of their leaders for your information.

[11]Here is the answer they gave us. They said,

"We serve the God of heaven and earth. We are rebuilding the temple that was built many years ago. The great King Solomon built it and finished it. [12]But our people made the God of heaven angry. So he handed them over to Nebuchadnezzar from Chaldea. He was king of Babylon. He destroyed this temple. He forced the Jews to leave their own country. He took them away to Babylon.

[13]"But King Cyrus gave an order to rebuild this house of God. He gave it in the first year he was king of Babylon. [14]He even removed some gold and silver objects from the temple of Babylon. Nebuchadnezzar had brought them there from the house of God in Jerusalem. He had taken them to the temple in Babylon. Then King Cyrus brought the objects out. He gave them to a man named Sheshbazzar. Cyrus had appointed him as governor. [15]Cyrus told him, 'Take these objects with you. Go and put them in the temple in Jerusalem. Rebuild the house of God in the same place where it stood before.'

[16]"So Sheshbazzar made the trip to Jerusalem. He laid the foundations of the house of God there. From that day until now the people have been working on it. But they haven't finished it yet."

[17]If it pleases you, King Darius, let a search be made in the royal records. Search the official records of the kings of Babylon. Find out whether King Cyrus really did give an order to rebuild this house of God in Jerusalem. Then tell us what you decide to do.

King Darius's Reply to Tattenai

6 King Darius gave an order. He had a search made in the official records stored among the treasures at Babylon. [2]A book was found in a safe storeroom at Ecbatana in the land of Media. Here is what was written on it.

This is my official reply to your letter.

[3]In the first year that Cyrus was king, he gave an order. It concerned God's temple in Jerusalem. King Cyrus said,

Rebuild the temple. Then the Jews can offer sacrifices there. Lay its foundations. The temple must be 90 feet high and 90 feet wide. [4]Its walls must have three layers of large stones. They must also have a layer of beautiful wood. Use money from the royal treasures to pay for everything. [5]The gold and silver objects from the house of God must be returned. Nebuchadnezzar had taken them from the first temple in Jerusalem. And he had brought them to Babylon. Now they must be returned to their places in the temple at Jerusalem. They must be put in the house of God there.

[6]Tattenai, you are governor of the land west of the Euphrates River. I want you to stay away from the temple in Jerusalem. I also want you, Shethar-Bozenai, and you other officials of that area to stay away from it. [7]Don't try to stop the work on the temple of God. Let the governor of the Jews and their elders rebuild the house of their God. Let them build it in the same place where it stood before.

[8]Here is what I want you to do for the elders of the Jews. Here is how you must help them to build the house of their God.

Pay all their expenses from the
royal treasures. Use the money
you collect from the people who
live west of the Euphrates. Don't
let the work on the temple stop.
9 Don't fail to give the priests in
Jerusalem what they ask for each
day. Give them what they need.
Give them young bulls, rams and
male lambs. The priests can use
them to sacrifice burnt offerings to
the God of heaven. Also give them
wheat, salt, wine and olive oil.
10 Give them those things so they
can offer sacrifices that please the
God of heaven. And I want them
to pray that things will go well for
me and my sons.
11 Don't change this order. If anyone tries to change it, they must be
put to death. A pole must be pulled
from their house. The pole must be
stuck through their body. Because
that person tried to change my
royal order, their house must be
broken to pieces. 12 God has chosen
to put his Name in the temple at
Jerusalem. May he wipe out any
king or nation that lifts a hand to
change this order. May he also wipe
out anyone who tries to destroy the
temple in Jerusalem.

That's what I have ordered. I am
King Darius. Make sure you carry
out my order.

The Temple Is Completed and Set Apart to God

13 The governor Tattenai and Shethar-
Bozenai carried out King Darius's order.
And so did their friends. 14 The elders of
the Jews continued to build the temple.
They enjoyed great success because of
the preaching of Haggai and Zechariah, the prophets. Zechariah belonged
to the family line of Iddo. The people
finished building the temple. That's
what the God of Israel had commanded
them to do. Cyrus and Darius had given
orders allowing them to do it. Later,
Artaxerxes supplied many things that
were needed in the temple. Those three
men were kings of Persia. 15 So the temple was completed on the third day of
the month of Adar. It was in the sixth
year that Darius was king.
16 When the house of God was set
apart, the people of Israel celebrated
with joy. The priests and Levites joined
them. So did the rest of those who had
returned from the land of Babylon.
17 When the house of God was set apart
to him, the people sacrificed 100 bulls.
They also sacrificed 200 rams and
400 male lambs. As a sin offering for
the whole nation of Israel, the people
sacrificed 12 male goats. One goat was
sacrificed for each tribe in Israel. 18 The
priests were appointed to their groups.
And the Levites were appointed to their
groups. All of them served God at Jerusalem. They served him in keeping with
what is written in the Book of Moses.

The People Celebrate the Passover Feast

19 The people who had returned
from the land of Babylon celebrated
the Passover Feast. It was on the 14th
day of the first month. 20 The priests
and Levites had made themselves pure
and "clean." The Levites killed Passover
lambs for the people who had returned
from Babylon. They also did it for themselves and their relatives, the priests.
21 So the Israelites who had returned
ate the Passover lamb. They ate it together with all those who had separated
themselves from the practices of their
Gentile neighbors. Those practices were
"unclean." The people worshiped the
LORD. He is the God of Israel. 22 For seven
days they celebrated the Feast of Unleavened Bread with joy. That's because
the LORD had filled them with joy. They
were glad because he had changed the
mind of the king of Persia. So the king
had helped them with the work on the
house of the God of Israel.

Ezra Comes to Jerusalem

7 After all these things had happened,
Ezra came up to Jerusalem from
Babylon. It was during the rule of Artaxerxes. He was king of Persia. Ezra
was the son of Seraiah. Seraiah was
the son of Azariah. Azariah was the
son of Hilkiah. 2 Hilkiah was the son of
Shallum. Shallum was the son of Zadok.
Zadok was the son of Ahitub. 3 Ahitub
was the son of Amariah. Amariah was
the son of Azariah. Azariah was the son
of Meraioth. 4 Meraioth was the son of
Zerahiah. Zerahiah was the son of Uzzi.

Uzzi was the son of Bukki. [5]Bukki was
the son of Abishua. Abishua was the
son of Phinehas. Phinehas was the son
of Eleazar. And Eleazar was the son of
Aaron the chief priest. [6]So Ezra came
up from Babylon. He was a teacher
who knew the Law of Moses very well.
The LORD, the God of Israel, had given
Israel that law. The king had given Ezra
everything he asked for. That's because
the LORD his God helped him. [7]Some of
the Israelites came up to Jerusalem too.
They included priests, Levites and musicians. They also included the temple
servants and those who guarded the
temple gates. It was in the seventh year
that Artaxerxes was king.

[8]Ezra arrived in Jerusalem in the
fifth month of the seventh year of the
king's rule. [9]Ezra had begun his journey
from Babylon on the first day of the
first month. He arrived in Jerusalem on
the first day of the fifth month. That's
because God was gracious to him and
helped him. [10]Ezra had committed
himself to study and obey the Law of
the LORD. He also wanted to teach the
LORD's rules and laws in Israel.

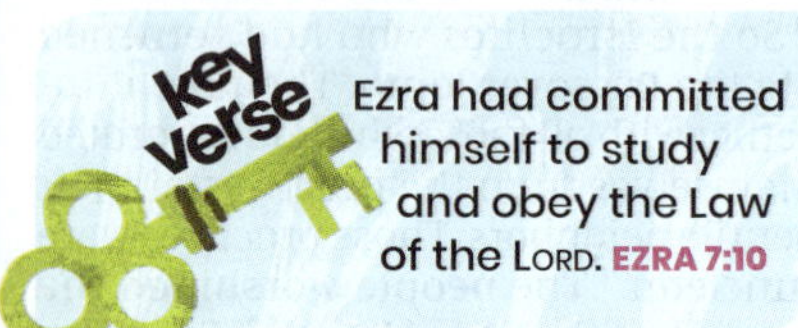

Ezra had committed himself to study and obey the Law of the LORD. EZRA 7:10

King Artaxerxes's Letter to Ezra

[11]Ezra was a priest and teacher of
the Law. He was an educated man. He
knew the LORD's commands and rules
for Israel very well. Here is a copy of
a letter King Artaxerxes had given to
Ezra. It said,

> [12]I, Artaxerxes, am writing this letter. I am the greatest king of all.
>
> I have given it to Ezra the priest. He is the teacher of the Law of the God of heaven.
>
> I give you my greetings.
>
> [13]Ezra, I am giving an order
> about the Israelites in my kingdom. Any of them who want to go
> to Jerusalem with you may go.
> The order also allows priests and
> Levites to go with you. [14]I and my
> seven advisers are sending you to
> see how things are going in Judah
> and Jerusalem. Find out whether
> the people there are obeying the
> Law of your God. You have a copy
> of that law with you. [15]I and my
> advisers have freely given some
> silver and gold to the God of Israel.
> He is the God who lives in Jerusalem. Take that silver and gold with
> you. [16]Also take any other silver
> and gold you can get from the land
> of Babylon. And take the offerings
> the people and priests choose to
> give for the temple of their God in
> Jerusalem. [17]Make sure you use
> the money to buy bulls, rams and
> male lambs. Also buy their grain
> offerings and drink offerings. Then
> sacrifice them on the altar of the
> temple of your God in Jerusalem.
>
> [18]You and the other Jews can do
> what you think is best with the rest
> of the silver and gold. Do what your
> God wants you to do. [19]Give to the
> God of Jerusalem all the things you
> are responsible for. Use them for
> worshiping your God in his temple. [20]You might need to supply
> some other things for the temple
> of your God. If you do, take them
> from among the royal treasures.
>
> [21]I, King Artaxerxes, also give
> this order. It applies to all those
> who are in charge of the treasures
> west of the Euphrates River. Make
> sure you provide anything Ezra the
> priest might ask you to give. He is
> the teacher of the Law of the God
> of heaven. [22]Give Ezra up to three
> and three-fourths tons of silver.
> Give him up to 18 tons of wheat.
> Give him up to 600 gallons of wine
> and up to 600 gallons of olive oil.
> And give him as much salt as he
> needs. [23]Work hard for the temple
> of the God of heaven. Do everything
> he has required. I don't want him
> to be angry with my kingdom and
> the kingdom of my sons. [24]Here is
> something else I want you to know.
> You have no authority to collect
> taxes, gifts or fees from these people. You may not collect them from
> the priests, Levites or musicians.
> You may not collect them from
> those who guard the temple gates.

You may not collect them from the
temple servants. And you may not
collect them from other workers
at the house of God in Jerusalem.
25 Ezra, appoint judges and other
court officials. When you do it, use
the wisdom your God gives you.
Those you appoint should do what
is right and fair when they judge
people. They should do it for everyone who lives west of the Euphrates
River. They should do it for everyone
who knows the laws of your God. And
I want you to teach the people who
don't know those laws. 26 Anyone
who doesn't obey the law of your
God must be punished. The same
thing applies to anyone who doesn't
obey my law. The people must be
punished in keeping with the laws
they have broken. Some of them
must be put to death. Others must be
forced to leave the places where they
live. Others must have their property
taken away from them. Still others
must be put in prison.

27 So here is what I, Ezra, say to you
people of Israel. "Give praise to the LORD.
He is the God of our people who lived long
ago. He has put it in the king's heart to
bring honor to the LORD's temple in Jerusalem. The king has honored the LORD
in his letter. 28 The LORD has been kind
to me. He has caused the king and his
advisers to be kind to me. In fact, all the
king's powerful officials have been kind to
me. The strong hand of the LORD my God
helped me. That gave me new strength.
So I gathered together leaders from Israel
to go up to Jerusalem with me."

The Family Leaders Who Returned to Jerusalem With Ezra

8 Many family leaders came up
to Jerusalem with me from
Babylon. So did others who were
listed with them. It was during the
time when Artaxerxes was king.
Here is a list of those who came.

2 Gershom came from the family
line of Phinehas.
Daniel came from the family line
of Ithamar.
Hattush came from the family line
of David. 3 Hattush also belonged
to the family of Shekaniah.
Zechariah came from the family
line of Parosh. The total number
of men who were listed with him
was 150.
4 Eliehoenai came from the family
line of Pahath-Moab. Eliehoenai
was the son of Zerahiah. The
total number of men with him
was 200.
5 Shekaniah came from the family
line of Zattu. Shekaniah was the
son of Jahaziel. The total number
of men with him was 300.
6 Ebed came from the family line
of Adin. Ebed was the son of
Jonathan. The total number of
men with him was 50.
7 Jeshaiah came from the family
line of Elam. Jeshaiah was
the son of Athaliah. The total
number of men with him was 70.
8 Zebadiah came from the family
line of Shephatiah. Zebadiah
was the son of Michael. The total
number of men with him was 80.
9 Obadiah came from the family line
of Joab. Obadiah was the son of
Jehiel. The total number of men
with him was 218.
10 Shelomith came from the family
line of Bani. Shelomith was
the son of Josiphiah. The total
number of men with him was
160.
11 Zechariah came from the family
line of Bebai. Zechariah was the
son of Bebai. The total number
of men with him was 28.
12 Johanan came from the family
line of Azgad. Johanan was
the son of Hakkatan. The total
number of men with him was
110.
13 Eliphelet, Jeuel and Shemaiah came
from the family line of Adonikam.
Some members of their family
had gone up to Jerusalem before
them. The total number of men
with them was 60.
14 Uthai and Zakkur came from the
family line of Bigvai. The total
number of men with them was 70.

Ezra Leads Many Jews Back to Jerusalem

15 I gathered the people together at
the canal that flows toward Ahava. We

camped there for three days. I looked
for Levites among the people and
priests. But I didn't find any. [16] So I sent
for Eliezer, Ariel, Shemaiah, Elnathan
and Jarib. I also sent for Elnathan, Nathan, Zechariah and Meshullam. All of
them were leaders. And I sent for Joiarib
and Elnathan. They were very well educated. [17] I ordered all those men to go
to Iddo. He was the leader in Kasiphia.
He and his Levite relatives were temple
servants there. I told my men what to
say to them. I wanted Iddo and his Levite relatives to bring some attendants
to us for the house of our God. [18] God was
gracious to us and helped us. So they
brought us Sherebiah, a very capable
man. He came from the family line of
Mahli. Mahli was the son of Levi. Levi
was a son of Israel. They also brought
us Sherebiah's sons and brothers. The
total number of men was 18. [19] And they
brought Hashabiah and his brothers
and nephews. They brought them together with Jeshaiah. He came from the
family line of Merari. The total number
of men was 20. [20] They also brought
220 of the temple servants. That was
a special group David and his officials
had established. They were supposed
to help the Levites. All of them were
listed by name.

[21] By the canal that flows toward Ahava, I announced a fast. I told the people
not to eat any food. In that way, we
made ourselves humble in God's sight.
We prayed that he would give us and
our children a safe journey. We asked
him to keep safe everything we owned.
[22] I was ashamed to ask King Artaxerxes
for soldiers and horsemen. They could
have kept us safe from enemies on the
road. But we had told the king that our
God would keep us safe. We had said,
"Our God is gracious and helps everyone
who looks to him. But he becomes very
angry with anyone who deserts him."
[23] So we didn't eat anything. We prayed
to our God about all these matters. And
he answered our prayers.

[24] Then I set apart 12 of the leading
priests. They were Sherebiah, Hashabiah and ten of their relatives. [25] I weighed
out to them the offering of silver and
gold and other things. They had been
given for the house of our God. The king,
his advisers and officials, and all the
Israelites who were there had given
them. [26] I weighed out 24 tons of silver
and gave it to those men. I weighed
out almost four tons of silver things. I
weighed out almost four tons of gold.
[27] I weighed out 20 gold bowls. They
weighed 19 pounds. I also weighed out
two fine objects. The bronze they were
made out of was highly polished. They
were as priceless as gold.

[28] I said to those men, "You are set
apart to the LORD. So are these things.
The silver and gold were offered to the
LORD by those who chose to give them.
He is the God of your people. [29] Guard all
these things carefully until you weigh
them out. Weigh them in the special
rooms of the LORD's temple in Jerusalem. Do this in front of the leading
priests and the Levites. Make sure the
family leaders of Israel are watching."
[30] Then the priests and Levites received
the silver and gold and sacred objects.
All of them had been weighed out. They
were going to be taken to the house of
our God in Jerusalem.

[31] On the 12th day of the first month
we started out. We left the canal that
flows toward Ahava. And we headed for
Jerusalem. Our God helped us. He kept
us safe from enemies and robbers along
the way. [32] So we arrived in Jerusalem.
There we rested for three days.

[33] On the fourth day we weighed out
the silver and gold. We also weighed
out the sacred objects. We weighed everything in the house of our God. We
handed all of it over to Meremoth the
priest. He was the son of Uriah. Eleazar,
Jozabad and Noadiah were with him.
Eleazar was the son of Phinehas. Jozabad was the son of Jeshua. Noadiah
was the son of Binnui. Jozabad and
Noadiah were Levites. [34] Everything was
listed by number and weight. And the
total weight was recorded at that time.

[35] Then the people sacrificed burnt
offerings to the God of Israel. They had
returned from Babylon. They offered 12
bulls for the whole nation of Israel. They
offered 96 rams and 77 male lambs. All
of that was a burnt offering to the LORD.
They sacrificed 12 male goats as a sin
offering. [36] They also handed over the
king's orders. They gave them to the
royal officials and governors who ruled
over the land west of the Euphrates

River. Then those men helped the people. They also did many things for the
house of God.

Ezra Prays for the People

9 After all these things had been
done, the leaders came to me.
They said, "The people of Israel have
committed sins. Even the priests and
Levites have sinned. They haven't kept
themselves separate from the nations
around them. The LORD hates the practices of those nations. He hates what
the Canaanites, Hittites, Perizzites
and Jebusites do. He also hates what
the Ammonites, Moabites, Egyptians
and Amorites do. 2 The men of Israel
have married the daughters of some of
those people. They've also taken some
of those women for their sons to marry.
So they've mixed our holy nation with
the nations around us. We leaders and
officials have also married women who
don't worship the LORD. By doing this,
we have led the way in breaking our
covenant with the LORD."
3 When I heard that, I tore my inner
robe and my coat. I pulled hair from
my head and beard. I was so shocked
I sat down. 4 Then everyone who trembled with fear at God's words gathered
around me. That's because the people
who had returned from Babylon had
not been faithful. So I was very upset.
I just sat there until the time of the
evening sacrifice.
5 Then I got up. I had been very sad
for quite a while. My inner robe and my
coat were torn. I fell down on my knees.
I spread my hands out to the LORD my
God. 6 I prayed,

"I'm filled with shame and dishonor, my God. I can hardly look to
you and pray. That's because our
sins are piled up above our heads.
Our guilt reaches all the way to
the heavens. 7 We are filled with
it. It has been like that ever since
the days of our people who lived
long ago. Kings of other countries
have killed many of us and our
kings and priests with their swords.
They've forced others to leave their
own land. They've taken them
away as prisoners. They've robbed
others. They've made still others
feel ashamed and dishonored. All
these things have happened to us
because we've committed so many
sins. And that's how things still are
to this day.
8 "But you are the LORD our
God. Now you have shown us your
kindness for a short time. That's
because you have allowed a few
of us to remain here. Your temple
has given us new hope. So you have
made things easier for us. You have
given us a little rest from our slavery. 9 We are still slaves. But you
are our God. You haven't turned
away from us. You haven't left us
in our slavery. You have been kind
to us. The kings of Persia have seen
it. You have given us new life to
repair your temple and rebuild it.
You have given us a place of safety
in Judah and Jerusalem.
10 "You are our God. What can
we say after the way you have
blessed us? We have turned away
from your commands. 11 You gave
us your commands through your
servants the prophets. You said,
'You are entering the land to take it
as your own. The sinful practices of
its people have made the land impure. They have filled it with their
"unclean" acts from one end to the
other. The LORD hates all their practices. 12 So don't let your daughters
marry their sons. And don't let their
daughters marry your sons. Don't
make a peace treaty with them at
any time. Then you will be strong.
You will eat the good things the
land produces. And you will leave
all of it to your children as their
share. They and their children after
them will enjoy it forever.'
13 "Our evil acts and our terrible
sins have brought about the things
that have happened to us. You are
our God. Because we sinned so
much, you should have punished
us even more than you have. But
you have left many of your people
alive. 14 Suppose we don't obey your
commands again. And suppose
we continue to marry people who
commit sins that you hate. If we
do, you will be so angry with us
that you will destroy us. You won't
leave us even a few people. You

won't leave anyone alive. 15 LORD,
you are the God of Israel. You are
holy. You always do what is right.
Today you have left many of your
people alive. Here we are with all
our guilt. You see the guilt of our
sin. Because we have sinned, not
one of us can stand in front of you."

The People Admit They Have Sinned

10 Ezra was praying and admitting to God that his people had
sinned. He was weeping and throwing
himself down in front of the house of
God. Then a large crowd of Israelites
gathered around him. Men, women and
children were there. They too wept bitterly. 2 Shekaniah spoke to Ezra. Shekaniah was the son of Jehiel. He belonged
to the family line of Elam. Shekaniah
said, "We haven't been faithful to our
God. We've married women from the
nations around us. In spite of that, there
is still hope for Israel. 3 So let's make
a covenant in front of our God. Let's
promise to send away all these women
and their children. That's what you have
advised us to do. Those who respect
our God's commands have given us the
same advice. We want to do what the
Law says. 4 Get up, Ezra. This matter is
in your hands. Do what you need to.
We will be behind you all the way. Be
brave and do it."

5 So Ezra got up. He made the leading
priests and Levites and all the Israelites
make a promise. He made them promise they would do what Shekaniah had
suggested. And they made that promise. 6 Then Ezra left the house of God. He
went to Jehohanan's room. Jehohanan
was the son of Eliashib. While Ezra was
there, he didn't eat any food. He didn't
drink any water. That's because he
was filled with sadness. He mourned
because the people weren't faithful to
the LORD's commands. Those people
were the ones who had returned from
the land of Babylon.

7 Then an announcement was sent all
through Judah and Jerusalem. All the
people who had returned were told to
gather together in Jerusalem. 8 They
were supposed to come there before
three days had passed. If they didn't,
they would lose all their property.
They would also be removed from the
community of those who had returned.
That's what the officials and elders had
decided.

9 Before the three days were over, all
the men of Judah and Benjamin had
gathered together in Jerusalem. It was
the 20th day of the ninth month. They
were sitting in the open area in front of
the house of God. They were very upset
by what they knew would happen. And
they were upset because it was raining.
10 Then Ezra the priest stood up. He said,
"You haven't been faithful to the LORD.
You have married women from other
lands. So you have added to Israel's
guilt. 11 Now honor the LORD, the God
of your people. Then do what he wants
you to do. Separate yourselves from the
nations around you. Send away your
wives from other lands."

12 The whole community answered
with a loud voice. They said, "You are
right! We must do as you say. 13 But
there are a lot of people here. And it's
the rainy season. So we can't stand outside. Besides, this matter can't be taken
care of in just a day or two. That's because we have sinned terribly by what
we've done. 14 Our officials can act for
the whole community. Have everyone
in our towns who has married a woman
from another land come at a certain
time. Tell them to come together with
the elders and judges of each town.
Then our God will no longer be angry
with us concerning this whole matter."
15 Only a few men opposed that. They
included Jonathan and Jahzeiah. Meshullam and Shabbethai the Levite
joined them. Jonathan was the son of
Asahel. Jahzeiah was the son of Tikvah.

16 So those who had returned did what
had been suggested. Ezra the priest
chose some family leaders. There was
one from each family group. All of them
were chosen by name. They sat down
to check out each case. They started on
the first day of the tenth month. 17 By
the first day of the first month they
were finished. They had handled all
the cases of the men who had married
women from other lands.

A List of Those Who Had Married Women From Other Lands

18 Among the family lines of the priests, here are the men who had married women from other lands.
Maaseiah, Eliezer, Jarib and Gedaliah
came from the family line of Joshua and his brothers. Joshua was the son of Jozadak. 19 All of them made a firm promise to send their wives away. Each of these men brought a ram from his flock as a guilt offering.
20 Hanani and Zebadiah
came from the family line of Immer.
21 Maaseiah and Elijah
came from the family line of Harim. So did Shemaiah, Jehiel and Uzziah.
22 Elioenai, Maaseiah and Ishmael
came from the family line of Pashhur. So did Nethanel, Jozabad and Elasah.

23 Among the Levites, here are the men who had married women from other lands.
There were Jozabad, Shimei and Kelaiah. There were also Pethahiah, Judah and Eliezer. Kelaiah's other name was Kelita.
24 Eliashib
came from the musicians.
Shallum, Telem and Uri
came from the men who guarded the temple gates.

25 Among the other Israelites, here are the men who had married women from other lands.
Ramiah, Izziah, Malkijah and Mijamin
came from the family line of Parosh. So did Eleazar, Malkijah and Benaiah.
26 Mattaniah, Zechariah and Jehiel
came from the family line of Elam. So did Abdi, Jeremoth and Elijah.
27 Elioenai, Eliashib and Mattaniah
came from the family line of Zattu. So did Jeremoth, Zabad and Aziza.
28 Jehohanan, Hananiah, Zabbai and Athlai
came from the family line of Bebai.
29 Meshullam, Malluk and Adaiah
came from the family line of Bani. So did Jashub, Sheal and Jeremoth.
30 Adna, Kelal, Benaiah and Maaseiah
came from the family line of Pahath-Moab. So did Mattaniah, Bezalel, Binnui and Manasseh.
31 Eliezer, Ishijah, Malkijah, Shemaiah and Shimeon
came from the family line of
Harim. 32 So did Benjamin,
Malluk and Shemariah.
33 Mattenai, Mattattah, Zabad and Eliphelet
came from the family line of Hashum. So did Jeremai, Manasseh and Shimei.
34 Maadai, Amram and Uel
came from the family line of
Bani. 35 So did Benaiah, Bedeiah,
Keluhi, 36 Vaniah, Meremoth,
Eliashib, 37 Mattaniah, Mattenai
and Jaasu.
38 Shimei
came from the family line of
Binnui. 39 So did Shelemiah,
Nathan, Adaiah, 40 Maknad-
ebai, Shashai, Sharai, 41 Azarel,
Shelemiah, Shemariah, 42 Shallum, Amariah and Joseph.
43 Jeiel, Mattithiah, Zabad and Zebina
came from the family line of Nebo. So did Jaddai, Joel and Benaiah.

44 All these men had married women from other lands. Some of them had even had children by those wives.

NEHEMIAH

Author: We don't know (but it might be Ezra).

When the temple was destroyed, the wall around Jerusalem was destroyed as well. The wall was important because it had protected the city from other nations, and it also helped others identify Jerusalem as a special city. God called a man named Nehemiah to return to Jerusalem and lead the people in rebuilding the wall.

Old Testament History

Nehemiah's job was hard: The non-Jews did not like that the wall was being rebuilt, and the Jews did not want to follow God's laws. But Nehemiah, alongside Ezra, led the Jews to finish the city wall and repent of their sins. Nehemiah prayed for God's people and earnestly desired for them to walk in God's ways. Unfortunately, the Jews turned away from God again and went back to doing things their own way.

The book of Nehemiah reminds us of God's grace—even though the Jews disobeyed God and suffered the consequences of their disobedience, God had a plan to restore the nation and was making a way for his people to come home. The people failed to keep their promise, but God would be faithful to keep his promise. One day God would send a Savior who would make a way for God's people to live with him forever.

Nehemiah Prays to the LORD

1 These are the words of Nehemiah. He was the son of Hakaliah.

I was in the fort of Susa. I was there in the 20th year that Artaxerxes was king. It was in the month of Kislev. 2 At that time Hanani came from Judah with some other men. He was one of my brothers. I asked him and the other men about the Jews who were left alive in Judah. They had returned from Babylon. I also asked him about Jerusalem.
3 He and the men with him said to me, "Some of the people who returned are still alive. They are back in the land of Judah. But they are having a hard time. They are ashamed. The wall of Jerusalem is broken down. Its gates have been burned with fire."
4 When I heard about these things, I sat down and wept. For several days I was very sad. I didn't eat any food. And I prayed to the God of heaven. 5 I said,

"LORD, you are the God of heaven. You are a great and wonderful God. You keep the covenant you made with those who love you and obey your commandments. You show them your love. 6 Please pay careful attention to my prayer. See how your people are suffering. Please listen to me. I'm praying to you day and night. I'm praying for the people of Israel. We Israelites have committed sins against you. All of us admit it. I and my family have also sinned against you. 7 We've done some very evil things. We haven't obeyed the commands, rules and laws you gave your servant Moses.
8 "Remember what you told him. You said, 'If you people are not faithful, I will scatter you among the nations. 9 But if you return to me, I will bring you back. If you obey my commands, I will gather you together again. I will bring you back from the farthest places on earth. I will bring you to the special place where I have chosen to put my Name.'
10 "LORD, they are your people. They serve you. You used your great strength and mighty hand to set them free from Egypt. 11 Lord, please pay careful attention to my prayer. Listen to the prayers of all of us. We take delight in bringing honor to your name. Give me success today when I bring my request to King Artaxerxes."

I was the king's wine taster.

in Nehemiah?

God is the Way Maker. It seemed impossible for Israel to return home and rebuild, but God, in his limitless power, made a way.

Artaxerxes Sends Nehemiah to Jerusalem

2 Wine was brought in for King Artaxerxes. It was the month of Nisan in the 20th year of his rule. I got the wine and gave it to him. I hadn't been

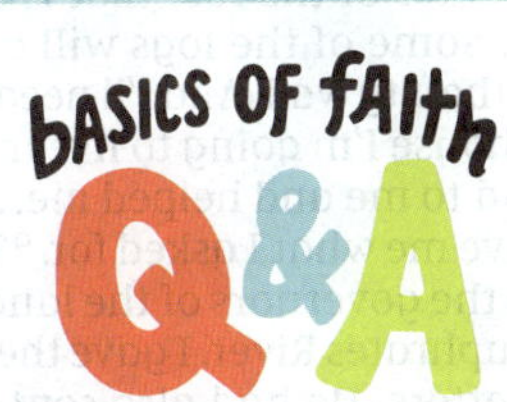

Why should I pray if God already knows what will happen?

God tells us to pray so that we will know how he worked. His plans always happen, but when we pray, we learn to trust God and can thank him for all he has done.

Can you find the following verse?
NEHEMIAH 1:11

sad in front of him before. But now I was. [2] So the king asked me, "Why are you looking so sad? You aren't sick. You must be feeling very sad."

I was really afraid. [3] But I said to the king, "May you live forever! Why shouldn't I look sad? The city where my people of long ago are buried has been destroyed. And fire has burned up its gates."

[4] The king said to me, "What do you want?"

I prayed to the God of heaven. [5] Then I answered the king, "Are you pleased with me, King Artaxerxes? If it pleases you, send me to Judah. Let me go to the city of Jerusalem. That's where my people are buried. I want to rebuild it."

[6] The queen was sitting beside the king. He turned and asked me, "How long will your journey take? When will you get back?" It pleased the king to send me. So I chose a certain time.

[7] I also said to him, "If it pleases you, may I take some letters with me? I want to give them to the governors of the land west of the Euphrates River. Then they'll help me travel safely through their territory until I arrive in Judah. [8] May I also have a letter to Asaph? He takes care of the royal park. I want him to give me some logs so I can make beams out of them. I want to use them for the gates of the fort that is by the temple. Some of the logs will also be used in the city wall. And I'll need some for the house I'm going to live in." God was kind to me and helped me. So the king gave me what I asked for. [9] Then I went to the governors of the land west of the Euphrates River. I gave them the king's letters. He had also sent army officers and horsemen along with me.

God was kind to me and helped me. NEHEMIAH 2:8

[10] Sanballat and Tobiah heard about what was happening. Sanballat was a Horonite. Tobiah was an official from Ammon. They were very upset that someone had come to help the Israelites.

Nehemiah Checks Out the Walls of Jerusalem

[11] I went to Jerusalem and stayed there for three days. [12] Then at night I took a few other people with me to check out the walls. I hadn't told anyone what my God wanted me to do for Jerusalem. There weren't any donkeys with me except the one I was riding on.

[13] That night I went out through the Valley Gate. I went toward the Jackal Well and the Dung Gate. I checked out the walls of Jerusalem. They had been broken down. I also checked the city gates. Fire had burned them up. [14] I moved on toward the Fountain Gate and the King's Pool. But there wasn't enough room for my donkey to get through. [15] It was still night. I went up the Kidron Valley. I kept checking the wall. Finally, I turned back. I went back in through the Valley Gate. [16] The officials didn't know where I had gone or what I had done. That's because I hadn't said anything to anyone yet. I hadn't told the priests or nobles or officials. And I hadn't spoken to any other Jews who would be rebuilding the wall.

[17] I said to them, "You can see the trouble we're in. Jerusalem has been destroyed. Fire has burned up its gates. Come on. Let's rebuild the wall of Jerusalem. Then people won't be ashamed anymore." [18] I also told them how my gracious God was helping me. And I told them what the king had said to me.

They replied, "Let's start rebuilding." So they began that good work.

[19] But Sanballat, the Horonite, heard about it. So did Tobiah, the official from Ammon. Geshem, the Arab, heard about it too. All of them laughed at us. They made fun of us. "What do you think you are doing?" they asked. "Are you turning against the king?"

[20] I answered, "The God of heaven will give us success. We serve him. So we'll start rebuilding the walls. But you don't have any share in Jerusalem. You don't have any claim to it. You don't have any right to worship here."

A List of the People Who Repaired the Wall

3 Eliashib the high priest and the other priests went to work. They rebuilt the Sheep Gate. They set it apart to God. They put its doors in place. They continued to rebuild the wall up to the Tower of the Hundred. They set the tower apart to God. Then they continued to rebuild the wall all the way to the Tower of Hananel. 2 Some men from Jericho rebuilt the next part of the wall. And Zakkur rebuilt the next part. He was the son of Imri.

3 The sons of Hassenaah rebuilt the Fish Gate. They laid its beams. They put in place its doors with their metal bolts and bars. 4 Meremoth repaired the next part of the wall. He was the son of Uriah. Uriah was the son of Hakkoz. Next to Meremoth, Meshullam made some repairs. He was the son of Berekiah. Berekiah was the son of Meshezabel. Next to Meshullam, Zadok also made some repairs. He was the son of Baana. 5 Some men from Tekoa repaired the next part of the wall. But their nobles refused to do any work at all. They didn't pay any attention to the people who were in charge of the work.

6 Joiada and Meshullam repaired the Jeshanah Gate. Joiada was the son of Paseah. Meshullam was the son of Besodeiah. Joiada and Meshullam laid the beams of the gate. They put in place its doors with their metal bolts and bars. 7 Next to them, some men from Gibeon and Mizpah made repairs. They included Melatiah from Gibeon and Jadon from Meronoth. Those places were under the authority of the governor of the land west of the Euphrates River. 8 Uzziel repaired the next part of the wall. He made his living by working with gold. He was the son of Harhaiah. Hananiah made repairs on the next part. He made his living by making perfume. So the wall of Jerusalem was made like new again all the way to the Broad Wall. 9 Rephaiah repaired the next part. He was the son of Hur. Rephaiah ruled over half of the territory where Jerusalem was located. 10 Jedaiah repaired the part of the wall that was across from his house. He was the son of Harumaph. Hattush made repairs next to Jedaiah. Hattush was the son of Hashabneiah. 11 Malkijah and Hasshub repaired another part of the wall. They also repaired the Tower of the Ovens. Malkijah was the son of Harim. Hasshub was the son of Pahath-Moab. 12 Shallum repaired the next part. His daughters helped him. He was the son of Hallohesh. Shallum ruled over the other half of the territory where Jerusalem was located.

13 Hanun repaired the Valley Gate. Some people who lived in Zanoah helped him. They rebuilt it. They put in place its doors with their metal bolts and bars. They also repaired 1,500 feet of the wall. They repaired it all the way to the Dung Gate.

14 Malkijah repaired the Dung Gate. He was the son of Rekab. Malkijah ruled over the territory where Beth Hakkerem was located. He rebuilt the gate. He put in place its doors with their metal bolts and bars.

15 Shallun repaired the Fountain Gate. He was the son of Kol-Hozeh. Shallun ruled over the territory where Mizpah was located. He rebuilt the gate. He put a roof over it. And he put in place the doors of the gate with their metal bolts and bars. He also repaired the wall by the Pool of Siloam. It was near the King's Garden. Shallun repaired the wall as far as the steps that go down from the City of David. 16 Next to Shallun, Nehemiah made some repairs. He was the son of Azbuk. Nehemiah ruled over half of the territory where Beth Zur was located. He repaired the wall up to the part that was across from the tombs of David. He repaired it all the way to the man-made pool and the House of the Heroes.

17 Next to Nehemiah, some Levites made repairs. They worked under the direction of Rehum. He was the son of Bani. Next to Rehum, Hashabiah made repairs for his territory. He ruled over half of the territory where Keilah was located. 18 Next to him, other Levites made some repairs. They worked under the direction of Binnui. He was the son of Henadad. Binnui ruled over the other half of the territory where Keilah was located. 19 Next to Binnui, Ezer repaired another part of the wall. He was the son of Jeshua. Ezer ruled over Mizpah. He

repaired the part across from the place that went up to the storeroom where the weapons were kept. He repaired the wall up to the angle of the wall. 20 Next to Ezer, Baruch worked hard to repair another part of the wall. He was the son of Zabbai. He repaired the part from the angle of the wall to the entrance to Eliashib's house. Eliashib was the high priest. 21 Next to Baruch, Meremoth repaired another part. He was the son of Uriah. Uriah was the son of Hakkoz. Meremoth repaired the part from the entrance to Eliashib's house to the end of the house.

22 Next to Meremoth, some priests from the surrounding area made repairs. 23 Next to them, Benjamin and Hasshub repaired the part of the wall that was in front of their house. Next to them, Azariah repaired the part that was beside his house. He was the son of Maaseiah. Maaseiah was the son of Ananiah. 24 Next to Azariah, Binnui made repairs on another part. Binnui was the son of Henadad. Binnui repaired the wall from Azariah's house to the angle and the corner. 25 Palal worked across from the angle. He was the son of Uzai. Palal also worked across from the tower that was part of the upper palace. It was near the courtyard of the guard. Next to him, Pedaiah made some repairs. He was the son of Parosh. 26 The temple servants who lived on the hill of Ophel helped Pedaiah. They repaired the wall up to the part that was across from the Water Gate. It was toward the east and the palace tower. 27 Next to the temple servants, the men from Tekoa repaired another part. They made repairs from the large palace tower to the wall of Ophel.

28 The priests made repairs above the Horse Gate. Each priest repaired the part of the wall that was in front of his own house. 29 Next to them, Zadok made repairs across from his house. He was the son of Immer. Next to Zadok, Shemaiah made some repairs. He was the son of Shekaniah. Shemaiah guarded the East Gate. 30 Next to him, Hananiah and Hanun repaired another part of the wall. Hananiah was the son of Shelemiah. Hanun was the sixth son of Zalaph. Next to Hananiah and Hanun, Meshullam made some repairs. He was the son of Berekiah. Meshullam repaired the part that was across from where he lived. 31 Next to him, Malkijah made some repairs. He made his living by working with gold. He repaired the wall up to the house of the temple servants and the traders. It was across from the Inspection Gate. He also repaired the wall as far as the room above the corner. 32 The traders and those who made their living by working with gold made some repairs. They repaired the wall from the room above the corner to the Sheep Gate.

Nehemiah's Enemies Oppose the Rebuilding

4 Sanballat heard that we were rebuilding the wall. So he became very angry and upset. He made fun of the Jews. 2 He spoke to his friends and the army of Samaria. He said, "What are those Jews trying to do? Can they make their city wall like new again? Will they offer sacrifices? Can they finish everything in a single day? The stones from their city wall and buildings are piled up like trash. And everything has been badly burned. Can they use those stones to rebuild everything again?"

3 Tobiah from Ammon was at Sanballat's side. He said, "What are they building? They're putting up a stone wall. But suppose a fox climbs on top of it. Even that will break it down!"

4 I prayed to God. I said, "Our God, please listen to our prayer. Some people hate us. They're saying bad things about us. So let others say bad things about them. Let them be carried off like stolen goods. Let them be taken to another country as prisoners. 5 Don't hide your eyes from their guilt. Don't forgive their sins. They have said bad things about the builders."

6 So we rebuilt the wall. We repaired it until all of it was half as high as we wanted it to be. The people worked with all their heart.

7 But Sanballat and Tobiah heard that Jerusalem's walls continued to be repaired. The Arabs, the Ammonites and the people of Ashdod heard about it too. They heard that the gaps in the wall were being filled in. So they were very

angry. 8 All of them made evil plans to come and fight against Jerusalem. They wanted to stir up trouble against it. 9 But we prayed to our God. We put guards on duty day and night to watch out for danger.

10 During that time, the people in Judah spoke up. They said, "The workers are getting weaker and weaker all the time. Broken stones are piled up everywhere. They are in our way. So we can't rebuild the wall."

11 And our enemies said, "We will be right there among them. We'll kill them. We'll put an end to their work. We'll do it before they even know it or see us."

12 Then the Jews who lived near our enemies came to us. They told us ten times, "No matter where you are, they'll attack us."

13 So I stationed some people behind the lowest parts of the wall. That's where our enemies could easily attack us. I stationed the people family by family. They had their swords, spears and bows with them. 14 I looked things over. Then I stood up and spoke to the nobles, the officials and the rest of the people. I said, "Don't be afraid of your enemies. Remember the Lord. He is great and powerful. So fight for your families. Fight for your sons and daughters. Fight for your wives and homes."

15 Our enemies heard that we knew what they were trying to do. They heard that God had blocked their evil plans. So all of us returned to the wall. Each of us did our own work.

16 From that day on, half of my men did the work. The other half were given spears, shields, bows and armor. The officers stationed themselves behind all the people of Judah. 17 The people continued to build the wall. The people who carried supplies did their work with one hand. They held a weapon in the other hand. 18 Each of the builders wore his sword at his side as he worked. But the man who blew the trumpet stayed with me.

19 Then I spoke to the nobles, the officials and the rest of the people. I said, "This is a big job. It covers a lot of territory. We're separated too far from one another along the wall. 20 When you hear the sound of the trumpet, join us at that location. Our God will fight for us!"

21 So we continued the work. Half of the men held spears. We worked from the first light of sunrise until the stars came out at night. 22 At that time I also spoke to the people. I told them, "Have every man and his helper stay inside Jerusalem at night. Then they can guard us at night. And they can work during the day." 23 My relatives and I didn't take off our clothes. My men and the guards didn't take theirs off either. Each man kept his weapon with him, even when he went to get water.

Nehemiah Helps Some Poor People

5 Some men and their wives cried out against their Jewish brothers and sisters. 2 Some of them were saying, "There are now many of us. We have many sons and daughters. We have to get some grain so we can eat and stay alive."

3 Others were saying, "We're being forced to sell our fields, vineyards and homes. We have to do it to buy grain. There isn't enough food for everyone."

4 Still others were saying, "We've had to borrow money. We needed it to pay the king's tax on our fields and vineyards. 5 We belong to the same family lines as the rest of our people. Our children are as good as theirs. But we've had to sell them off as slaves. Some of our daughters have already been made slaves. But we can't do anything about it. That's because our fields and vineyards now belong to others."

6 I heard them when they cried out. And I was very angry when I heard what they were saying. 7 I thought it over for a while. Then I accused the nobles and officials of breaking the law. I told them, "You are charging your own people interest!" So I called together a large group of people to handle the matter. 8 I said, "Our Jewish brothers and sisters were sold to other nations. We've done everything we could to buy them back and bring them home. But look at what you are doing! You are actually selling your own people! Now we'll have to buy them back too!" The people kept quiet. They couldn't think of anything to say.

9 So I continued, "What you are doing isn't right. Shouldn't you show respect for our God? Shouldn't you live in a way that will keep our enemies from saying

bad things about us? 10 I'm lending the people money and grain. So are my relatives and my men. But we must stop charging interest! 11 Give the people's fields back to them. Give them back their vineyards, olive groves and houses. Do it right away. Give everything back to them. Also give them back the one percent on the money, grain, fresh wine and olive oil you have charged them."

12 "We'll give it back," they said. "And we won't require anything more from them. We'll do exactly as you say."

Then I sent for the priests. I made the nobles and officials promise to do what they had said. 13 I also shook out my pockets and emptied them. I said, "Someone might decide not to keep this promise they have made. If that happens, may God shake them out of their house! May he empty them of everything they own!"

The whole community said, "Amen." They praised the LORD. And the leaders did what they had promised to do.

14 And that's not all. I was appointed as governor of Judah in the 20th year that Artaxerxes was king of Persia. I remained in that position until his 32nd year. During those 12 years, I and my relatives didn't eat the food that was provided for my table. 15 But there had been governors before me. They had put a heavy load on the people. They had taken a pound of silver from each of them. They had also taken food and wine from them. Their officials had acted like high and mighty rulers over them. But because of my great respect for God, I didn't act like that. 16 Instead, I spent all my time working on this wall. All my men were gathered there to work on it too. We didn't receive any land for ourselves.

17 Many people ate at my table. They included 150 Jews and officials. They also included leaders who came to us from the nations that were around us. 18 Each day one ox, six of the best sheep and some birds were prepared for me. Every ten days plenty of wine of all kinds was brought in as well. In spite of all that, I never asked for the food that was provided for my table. That's because the people were already paying too many taxes.

19 You are my God. Please remember me and help me. Keep in mind everything I've done for these people.

Nehemiah's Enemies Continue to Oppose the Rebuilding

6 Sanballat, Tobiah and Geshem, the Arab, heard about what I had done. So did the rest of our enemies. All of them heard I had rebuilt the wall. In fact, they heard there weren't any gaps left in it. But up to that time I hadn't put up the gates at the main entrances to the city. 2 Sanballat and Geshem sent me a message. They said, "Come. Let's talk with one another. Let's meet in one of the villages on the plain of Ono."

But they were planning to harm me. 3 So I sent messengers to them with my answer. I replied, "I'm working on a huge project. So I can't get away. Why should the work stop while I leave it? Why should I go down and talk with you?" 4 They sent me the same message four times. And I gave them the same answer each time.

5 Sanballat sent his helper to me a fifth time. He brought the same message. He was carrying a letter that wasn't sealed. 6 It said,

> "A report is going around among the nations. Geshem says it's true. We hear that you and the other Jews are planning to turn against the Persian rulers. And that's why you are building the wall. It's also reported that you are about to become their king. 7 People say that you have even appointed prophets to make an announcement about you. In Jerusalem they are going to say, 'Judah has a king!' That report will get back to the king of Persia. So come. Let's meet together."

8 I sent a reply to Sanballat. I said, "What you are saying isn't really happening. You are just making it up."

9 All of them were trying to frighten us. They thought, "Their hands will get too weak to do the work. So it won't be completed."

But I prayed to God. I said, "Make my hands stronger."

10 One day I went to Shemaiah's house. He was the son of Delaiah. Delaiah was the son of Mehetabel.

Shemaiah had shut himself up in his
home. He said, "Let's go to God's house.
Let's meet inside the temple and close
the doors. Some men are coming at
night to kill you."
11 But I said, "Should a man like me
run away? Should someone like me go
into the temple just to save his life? No!
I won't go!" 12 I realized that God hadn't
sent Shemaiah. Tobiah and Sanballat had hired him. That's why he had
prophesied lies about me. 13 They had
hired him to scare me. They wanted me
to commit a sin by doing what he said.
That would give me a bad name in the
community. People would find fault
with me and my work.

14 You are my God. Remember what
Tobiah and Sanballat have done. Also
remember the prophet Noadiah. She
and the rest of the prophets have been
trying to scare me. 15 So the city wall
was completed on the 25th day of the
month of Elul. It was finished in 52 days.

Nehemiah's Enemies Oppose the Completed Wall

16 All our enemies heard about it. All
the nations around us became afraid.
They weren't sure of themselves anymore. They realized that our God had
helped us finish the work.
17 In those days the nobles of Judah
sent many letters to Tobiah. And replies
from Tobiah came back to them. 18 Many
people in Judah had promised that they
would be faithful to him. That's because
he was Shekaniah's son-in-law. Shekaniah was the son of Arah. Tobiah's son
Jehohanan had married Meshullam's
daughter. Meshullam was the son of
Berekiah. 19 Tobiah's friends kept reporting to me the good things he did. They
also kept telling him what I said. And
Tobiah himself sent letters to scare me.

7 The wall had been rebuilt. I had put
up the gates at the main entrances
to the city. The people who guarded the
gates were appointed to their positions.
So were the musicians and the Levites.
2 I put my brother Hanani in charge
of Jerusalem. Hananiah helped him.
Hananiah was commander of the fort
that was by the temple. Hanani was
an honest man. He had more respect
for God than most people do. 3 I said
to Hanani and Hananiah, "Don't open
the gates of Jerusalem until the hottest
time of the day. Tell the men who guard
the gates to shut them before they go off
duty. Make sure they lock them up tight.
Also appoint as guards some people
who live in Jerusalem. Station some of
them at their appointed places. Station
others near their own homes."

A List of People Who Returned to Judah

4 Jerusalem was large. It had a lot
of room. But only a few people lived
there. The houses hadn't been rebuilt
yet. 5 So my God gave me the idea and
encouraged me to gather the people
together. He also encouraged me to
gather the nobles and officials together
with them. He wanted me to list them
by families. I found the family history
of those who had been the first to return.
Here is what I found written in it.

6 Nebuchadnezzar had taken
many Jews away from the land
of Judah. He had forced them to go
to Babylon as prisoners. Now they
returned to Jerusalem and Judah.
All of them went back to their own
towns. Nebuchadnezzar was king
of Babylon. 7 The leaders of the
Jews included Zerubbabel, Joshua,
Nehemiah, Azariah, Raamiah and
Nahamani. They also included
Mordecai, Bilshan, Mispereth,
Bigvai, Nehum and Baanah.

Here is a list of the men of Israel
who returned home.
8 There were 2,172 from the family
line of Parosh.
9 There were 372 from Shephatiah.
10 There were 652 from Arah.
11 There were 2,818 from Pahath-
Moab through the family line
of Jeshua and Joab.
12 There were 1,254 from Elam.
13 There were 845 from Zattu.
14 There were 760 from Zakkai.
15 There were 648 from Binnui.
16 There were 628 from Bebai.
17 There were 2,322 from Azgad.
18 There were 667 from Adonikam.
19 There were 2,067 from Bigvai.
20 There were 655 from Adin.
21 There were 98 from Ater through
the family line of Hezekiah.
22 There were 328 from Hashum.

23 There were 324 from Bezai.
24 There were 112 from Hariph.
25 There were 95 from Gibeon.

26 There were 188 from the men of Bethlehem and Netophah.
27 There were 128 from Anathoth.
28 There were 42 from Beth Azmaveth.
29 There were 743 from Kiriath Jearim, Kephirah and Beeroth.
30 There were 621 from Ramah and Geba.
31 There were 122 from Mikmash.
32 There were 123 from Bethel and Ai.
33 There were 52 from the other Nebo.
34 There were 1,254 from the other Elam.
35 There were 320 from Harim.
36 There were 345 from Jericho.
37 There were 721 from Lod, Hadid and Ono.
38 There were 3,930 from Senaah.

39 Here is a list of the priests.
There were 973 from the family line of Jedaiah through the line of Jeshua.
40 There were 1,052 from Immer.
41 There were 1,247 from Pashhur.
42 There were 1,017 from Harim.

43 The Levites belonged to
the family line of Jeshua through Kadmiel through the line of Hodaviah. The total number of men was 74.

44 The musicians belonged to
the family line of Asaph. The total number of men was 148.

45 The men who guarded the temple gates belonged to
the family lines of Shallum, Ater, Talmon, Akkub, Hatita and Shobai. The total number of men was 138.

46 Here is a list of the members of the family lines of the temple servants.
Ziha, Hasupha, Tabbaoth,
47 Keros, Sia, Padon,
48 Lebana, Hagaba, Shalmai,
49 Hanan, Giddel, Gahar,
50 Reaiah, Rezin, Nekoda,
51 Gazzam, Uzza, Paseah,
52 Besai, Meunim, Nephusim,
53 Bakbuk, Hakupha, Harhur,
54 Bazluth, Mehida, Harsha,
55 Barkos, Sisera, Temah,
56 Neziah, Hatipha

57 Here is a list of the members of the family lines of the servants of Solomon.
Sotai, Sophereth, Perida,
58 Jaala, Darkon, Giddel,
59 Shephatiah, Hattil,
Pokereth-Hazzebaim, Amon
60 The total number of the members of the family lines of the temple servants and the servants of Solomon was 392.

61 Many people came up to Judah from the towns of Tel Melah, Tel Harsha, Kerub, Addon and Immer. But they weren't able to prove that their families belonged to the people of Israel.
62 There were 642 of them from the family lines of
Delaiah, Tobiah and Nekoda.

63 Here is a list of the members of the family lines of the priests.
They were
Hobaiah, Hakkoz and Barzillai.
Barzillai had married a daughter of Barzillai from Gilead. So he was also called Barzillai.
64 The priests looked for their family records. But they couldn't find them. So they weren't able to serve as priests. They weren't "clean."
65 The governor gave them an order. He told them not to eat any of the most sacred food. They had to wait until there was a priest who could use the Urim and Thummim. The priest would use them to get decisions from the LORD.

66 The total number of the entire group that returned was 42,360.
67 That didn't include their 7,337 male and female slaves. There were also 245 male and female singers.
68 And there were 736 horses, 245 mules,
69 435 camels and 6,720 donkeys.

70 Some of the family leaders helped pay for the work. The governor gave 19 pounds of gold to be added to the temple treasure. He also gave 50 bowls and 530 sets of clothes for the priests.
71 Some of the family leaders gave 375

pounds of gold for the work. They also gave one and a third tons of silver. All of that was added to the temple treasure. 72 The rest of the people gave a total of 375 pounds of gold and one and a fourth tons of silver. They also gave 67 sets of clothes for the priests.

73 The priests and Levites made their homes in their own towns. So did the musicians, the temple servants and the men who guarded the gates. The rest of the Israelites also made their homes in their own towns.

Ezra Reads the Law to the People

The Israelites had made their homes in their towns. In the seventh month, **8** 1 all of them gathered together. They went to the open area in front of the Water Gate. They told Ezra to bring out the Book of the Law of Moses. The LORD had given Israel that Law so they would obey him. Ezra was the teacher of the Law.

2 Ezra the priest brought the Law out to the whole community. It was the first day of the seventh month. The group was made up of men, women, and children old enough to understand what Ezra was going to read. 3 He read the Law to them from sunrise until noon. He did it as he faced the open area in front of the Water Gate. He read it to the men, the women, and the children old enough to understand. And all the people paid careful attention as Ezra was reading the Book of the Law.

4 Ezra, the teacher of the Law, stood on a high wooden stage. It had been built for the occasion. Mattithiah, Shema and Anaiah stood at his right side. So did Uriah, Hilkiah and Maaseiah. Pedaiah, Mishael and Malkijah stood at his left side. So did Hashum, Hashbaddanah, Zechariah and Meshullam.

5 Ezra opened the book. All the people could see him. That's because he was standing above them. As he opened the book, the people stood up. 6 Ezra praised the LORD. He is the great God. All the people lifted up their hands and said, "Amen! Amen!" Then they bowed down. They turned their faces toward the ground and worshiped the LORD.

7 The Levites taught the Law to the people. They remained standing while the Levites taught them. The Levites who were there included Jeshua, Bani, Sherebiah, Jamin, Akkub, Shabbethai and Hodiah. They also included Maaseiah, Kelita, Azariah, Jozabad, Hanan and Pelaiah. 8 All these Levites read to the people parts of the Book of the Law of God. They made it clear to them. They told them what it meant. So the people understood what was being read.

9 Nehemiah was the governor. Ezra was a priest and the teacher of the Law. They spoke up. So did the Levites who were teaching the people. All these men said to the people, "This day is set apart to honor the LORD your God. So don't weep. Don't be sad." All the people had been weeping as they listened to the words of the Law.

10 Nehemiah said, "Go and enjoy some good food and sweet drinks. Send some of it to people who don't have any. This day is holy to our Lord. So don't be sad. The joy of the LORD makes you strong."

11 The Levites calmed all the people down. They said, "Be quiet. This is a holy day. So don't be sad."

12 Then all the people went away to eat and drink. They shared their food with others. They celebrated with great joy. Now they understood the words they had heard. That's because everything had been explained to them.

13 All the family leaders gathered around Ezra, the teacher. So did the priests and Levites. All of them paid attention to the words of the Law. It was the second day of the month. 14 The LORD had given the Law through Moses. He wanted the Israelites to obey it. It is written there that they were supposed to live in booths during the Feast of Booths. That feast was celebrated in the seventh month. 15 They were also supposed to spread the message all through their towns and in Jerusalem. They were supposed to announce, "Go out into the central hill country. Bring back some branches from olive and wild olive trees. Also bring some from myrtle, palm and shade trees. Use the branches to make booths."

16 So the people went out and brought back some branches. They built themselves booths on their own roofs. They made them in their courtyards. They put them up in the courtyards of the house of God. They built them in the

open area in front of the Water Gate.
And they built them in the open area
in front of the Gate of Ephraim. 17 All the
people who had returned from the land
of Babylon made booths. They lived
in them during the Feast of Booths.
They hadn't celebrated the feast with so
much joy for a long time. In fact, they
had never celebrated it like that from
the days of Joshua, the son of Nun, until
that day. So their joy was very great.
18 Day after day, Ezra read parts of
the Book of the Law of God to them. He
read it out loud from the first day to the
last. They celebrated the Feast of Booths
for seven days. On the eighth day they
gathered together. They followed the
required rules for celebrating the feast.

The Israelites Admit They Have Sinned

9 It was the 24th day of the seventh
month. The Israelites gathered together again. They didn't eat any food.
They wore the rough clothing people
wear when they're sad. They put dust on
their heads. 2 The Israelites separated
themselves from everyone else. They
stood and admitted they had sinned.
They also admitted that their people
before them had sinned. 3 They stood
where they were. They listened while
the Levites read parts of the Book of the
Law of the LORD their God. They listened
for a fourth of the day. They spent another fourth of the day admitting their
sins. They also worshiped the LORD their
God. 4 Some people were standing on
the stairs of the Levites. They included
Jeshua, Bani, Kadmiel, Shebaniah, Bunni, Sherebiah, Bani and Kenani. With
loud voices they called out to the LORD
their God. 5 Then some Levites spoke
up. They included Jeshua, Kadmiel,
Bani, Hashabneiah, Sherebiah, Hodiah,
Shebaniah and Pethahiah. They said to
the people, "Stand up. Praise the LORD
your God. He lives for ever and ever!"

So the people said, "LORD, may
your glorious name be praised.
May it be lifted high above every
other name that is blessed and
praised. 6 You are the one and only
LORD. You made the heavens. You
made even the highest heavens.
You created all the stars in the
sky. You created the earth and
everything on it. And you made
the oceans and everything in them.
You give life to everything. Every
living being in heaven worships
you.

7 "You are the LORD God. You
chose Abram. You brought him
out of Ur in the land of Babylon.
You named him Abraham. 8 You
knew that his heart was faithful
to you. And you made a covenant
with him. You promised to give
to his children after him a land of
their own. It was the land of the
Canaanites, Hittites and Amorites.
The Perizzites, Jebusites and Girgashites also lived there. You have
kept your promise. That's because
you always do what is right and
fair.

9 "You saw how our people of
long ago suffered in Egypt. You
heard them cry out to you at the
Red Sea. 10 You sent signs and wonders against Pharaoh. You sent
plagues on all his officials. In fact,
you sent them on all the people of
Egypt. You knew how they treated our people. They looked down
on them. But you made a name
for yourself. That name remains
to this very day. 11 You parted the
waters of the Red Sea for the Israelites. They passed through it on
dry ground. But you threw into
the sea those who chased them.
They sank down like a stone into
the mighty waters. 12 By day you
led the Israelites with a pillar of
cloud. At night you led them with
a pillar of fire. It gave them light
to show them the way you wanted
them to go.

13 "You came down on Mount Sinai. From heaven you spoke to our
people. You gave them rules and
laws. Those laws are right and fair.
You gave them orders and commands that are good. 14 You taught
them about your holy Sabbath day.
You gave them commands, orders
and laws. You did it through your
servant Moses. 15 When the people were hungry, you gave them
bread from heaven. When they
were thirsty, you brought them
water out of a rock. You told them

to go into the land of Canaan. You
told them to take it as their own.
It was the land you had promised
to give them.
16 “But our people before us became proud and stubborn. They
didn’t obey your commands.
17 They refused to listen to you.
They forgot the miracles you had
done among them. So they became
stubborn. When they refused to
obey you, they appointed a leader
for themselves. They wanted to go
back to being slaves in Egypt. But
you are a God who forgives. You are
gracious. You are tender and kind.
You are slow to get angry. You are
full of love. So you didn’t desert
them. 18 They made for themselves
a metal statue of a god that looked
like a calf. They said to one another, ‘Here is your god. He brought
you up out of Egypt.’ And they did
evil things that dishonored you.
But you still didn’t desert them.
19 “Because you loved them so
much, you didn’t leave them in the
desert. During the day the pillar
of cloud didn’t stop guiding them
on their path. At night the pillar
of fire didn’t stop shining on the
way you wanted them to go. 20 You
gave them your good Spirit to teach
them. You didn’t hold back your
manna from their mouths. And you
gave them water when they were
thirsty. 21 For 40 years you took
good care of them in the desert.
They had everything they needed.
Their clothes didn’t wear out. And
their feet didn’t swell up.
22 “You gave them kingdoms
and nations. You even gave them
lands far away. They took over
the country of Sihon. He was the
king of Heshbon. They also took
over the country of Og. He was the
king of Bashan. 23 You gave them
as many children as there are stars
in the sky. You told their parents
to enter the land. You told them to
take it over. And you brought their
children into it. 24 Their children
went into the land. They took it
as their own. You brought the Canaanites under Israel’s control. The
Canaanites lived in the land. But
you handed them over to Israel.
You also handed over their kings
and the other nations in the land
to Israel. You allowed Israel to deal
with them just as they wanted to.
25 Your people captured cities that
had high walls around them. They
also took over the rich land in Canaan. They took houses filled with
all kinds of good things. They took
over wells that had already been
dug. They took many vineyards,
olive groves and fruit trees. They
ate until they were very full and
satisfied. They were filled with joy
because you were so good to them.
26 “But they didn’t obey you.
Instead, they turned against you.
They turned their backs on your
law. They killed your prophets.
The prophets had warned them
to return to you. But they did very
evil things that dishonored you.
27 So you handed them over to
their enemies, who treated them
badly. Then they cried out to you.
From heaven you heard them. You
loved them very much. So you sent
leaders to help them. The leaders
saved them from the power of their
enemies.
28 “Then the people were enjoying peace and rest again. That’s
when they did what you did not
want them to do. Then you handed them over to their enemies. So
their enemies ruled over them.
When they cried out to you again,
you heard them from heaven. You
loved them very much. So you
saved them time after time.
29 “You warned them so that they
would obey your law again. But
they became proud. They didn’t
obey your commands. They sinned
against your rules. You said, ‘Anyone who obeys my rules will live by
them.’ But the people didn’t care
about that. They turned their backs
on you. They became very stubborn. They refused to listen to you.
30 For many years you put up with
them. By your Spirit you warned
them through your prophets. In
spite of that, they didn’t pay any
attention. So you handed them over
to the nations that were around

them. [31] But you loved them very much. So you didn't put an end to them. You didn't desert them. That's because you are a gracious God. You are tender and kind.

[32] "Our God, you are the great God. You are mighty and wonderful. You keep the covenant you made with us. You show us your love. So don't let all our suffering seem like a small thing to you. We've suffered greatly. So have our kings and leaders. So have our priests and prophets. Our people who lived long ago also suffered. And all your people are suffering right now. In fact, we've been suffering from the time of the kings of Assyria until today.
[33] In spite of everything that has happened to us, you have been fair. You have been faithful in what you have done. But we did what was evil. [34] Our kings and leaders didn't follow your law. Our priests and our people before us didn't follow it either. They didn't pay any attention to your commands or rules that you warned them to keep. [35] They didn't serve you. They didn't turn from their evil ways. They didn't obey you even when they had a kingdom. You were very good to them. And they enjoyed it. You gave them a rich land. It had plenty of room in it. But they still didn't serve you.

[36] "Now look at us. We are slaves today. We're slaves in the land you gave our people of long ago. You gave it to them so they could eat its fruit and the other good things it produces. [37] But we have sinned against you. So its great harvest goes to the kings of Persia. You have placed them over us. They rule over our bodies and cattle just as they please. And we are suffering terribly.

The People Agree to Obey God's Law

[38] "So we are making a firm agreement. We're writing it down. Our leaders are putting their official marks on it. And so are our Levites and priests."

10 Here are the names of those who put their official marks on the agreement.

Nehemiah, the son of Hakaliah
He was the governor.
Zedekiah, [2] Seraiah, Azariah, Jeremiah,
[3] Pashhur, Amariah, Malkijah,
[4] Hattush, Shebaniah, Malluk,
[5] Harim, Meremoth, Obadiah,
[6] Daniel, Ginnethon, Baruch,
[7] Meshullam, Abijah, Mijamin,
[8] Maaziah, Bilgai, Shemaiah
They were the priests.
[9] Here are the names of the Levites.
Jeshua, the son of Azaniah,
Binnui, one of the sons of Henadad,
Kadmiel
[10] Here are the names of those who helped them.
Shebaniah, Hodiah, Kelita, Pelaiah, Hanan,
[11] Mika, Rehob, Hashabiah,
[12] Zakkur, Sherebiah, Shebaniah,
[13] Hodiah, Bani, Beninu
[14] Here are the names of the leaders of the people.
Parosh, Pahath-Moab, Elam, Zattu, Bani,
[15] Bunni, Azgad, Bebai,
[16] Adonijah, Bigvai, Adin,
[17] Ater, Hezekiah, Azzur,
[18] Hodiah, Hashum, Bezai,
[19] Hariph, Anathoth, Nebai,
[20] Magpiash, Meshullam, Hezir,
[21] Meshezabel, Zadok, Jaddua,
[22] Pelatiah, Hanan, Anaiah,
[23] Hoshea, Hananiah, Hasshub,
[24] Hallohesh, Pilha, Shobek,
[25] Rehum, Hashabnah, Maaseiah,
[26] Ahiah, Hanan, Anan,
[27] Malluk, Harim, Baanah

[28] The rest of the people gathered together. They included the priests, the Levites and the men who guarded the gates. They included the musicians and temple servants. They also included all the people who separated themselves from the surrounding nations to obey the Law of God. All these men brought their wives with them. And they brought all their sons and daughters who were old enough to understand what was being agreed

to. 29 All the men joined the nobles
of their people. They made a firm
agreement. They made a promise
and said they would be cursed if
they didn't keep it. They promised
to follow the Law of God. It had
been given through Moses, the
servant of God. They promised to
obey carefully all the commands,
rules and laws of the LORD our Lord.
30 Here is what the priests, Levites and people said. "We promise
not to let our daughters marry men
from the nations around us. And we
promise not to let their daughters
marry our sons.
31 "The people around us will
bring goods and grain to sell on
the Sabbath day. But we won't
buy anything from them on the
Sabbath day. In fact, we won't buy
anything from them on any holy
day. Every seventh year we won't
farm the land. And we'll forgive
people what they owe us.
32 "We will be accountable for
carrying out the commands for
serving in the house of our God.
Each of us will give an eighth of
an ounce of silver every year. 33 It
will pay for the holy bread that is
placed on the table in the temple.
It will pay for the regular grain
offerings and burnt offerings. It
will pay for the offerings on the
Sabbath days. It will pay for the
offerings at the New Moon feasts
and at the appointed feasts. It will
pay for the holy offerings. It will
be used for sin offerings to pay for
the sins of Israel. It will also pay
for everything else that needs to
be done at the house of our God.
34 "We are the priests, Levites and
people. Each of our families should
bring a gift of wood to the house of
our God. We have cast lots to decide when they will do that. They
will bring it at certain appointed
times every year. The wood will be
burned on the altar of the LORD our
God. That's what the Law requires.
35 "We will also be accountable
for bringing the first share of our
crops each year. And we'll bring the
first share of every fruit tree. We'll
bring them to the LORD's house.
36 "Each of us will bring our oldest son to the priests who serve
there. We'll also bring the male
animals that were born first to their
mothers among our cattle, herds
and flocks. We'll bring them to the
house of our God. That's what the
Law requires.
37 "We will also bring the first part
of the meal we grind. We'll bring
the first of our grain offerings. We'll
bring the first share of fruit from
all our trees. And we'll bring the
first share of our olive oil and fresh
wine. We'll give all those things
to the priests. They'll put them in
the storerooms of the house of our
God. And we'll give a tenth of our
crops to the Levites. They collect
the tenth shares. They do it in all
the towns where we work. 38 A priest
from Aaron's family line must go
with the Levites when they receive
the tenth shares. And the Levites
must bring a tenth of those shares
up to the house of our God. They
must put it in the rooms where the
treasures are stored. 39 The people
of Israel, including the Levites,
must bring their gifts. They must
bring grain, olive oil and fresh
wine. They must put them in the
storerooms where the objects for
the temple are kept. That's also
where the objects are kept for the
priests serving at the temple, the
musicians and the men who guard
the gates.
"We won't forget to take care of
the house of our God."

People Are Chosen to Live in Jerusalem

11 The leaders of the people made
their homes in Jerusalem. The rest
of the people cast lots. They did it to
choose one person out of every ten of
them. That person was chosen to live
in the holy city of Jerusalem. The other
nine had to stay in their own towns.
2 The people thanked everyone who
agreed to live in Jerusalem.

3 Here are the leaders from different
parts of the country who made
their homes in Jerusalem. Some
Israelites, priests and Levites
lived in the towns of Judah. So did

some temple servants and some
members of the family lines of
Solomon's servants. All of them
lived on their own property in
the towns of Judah. 4 At the same
time, other people from the tribes
of Judah and Benjamin lived in
Jerusalem.

Here are the leaders from the
family line of Judah.
There was Athaiah. He was the
son of Uzziah. Uzziah was the
son of Zechariah. Zechariah was
the son of Amariah. Amariah
was the son of Shephatiah.
Shephatiah was the son of
Mahalalel. Mahalalel belonged
to the family line of Perez.
5 There was also Maaseiah. He
was the son of Baruch. Baruch
was the son of Kol-Hozeh. Kol-
Hozeh was the son of Hazaiah.
Hazaiah was the son of Adaiah.
Adaiah was the son of Joiarib.
Joiarib was the son of Zechariah.
Zechariah belonged to the
family line of Shelah.
6 Many important men who
belonged to the family line of
Perez lived in Jerusalem. The
total number of them was 468.
7 Here are the leaders from the
family line of Benjamin.
There was Sallu. He was the son of
Meshullam. Meshullam was the
son of Joed. Joed was the son of
Pedaiah. Pedaiah was the son
of Kolaiah. Kolaiah was the son
of Maaseiah. Maaseiah was the
son of Ithiel. Ithiel was the son
of Jeshaiah. 8 There were also
Gabbai and Sallai. They were
Sallu's followers. The total
number of men was 928.
9 Joel was their chief officer. He
was the son of Zikri. A man
named Judah was in charge of
the New Quarter of Jerusalem.
He was the son of Hassenuah.
10 Here are the leaders from among
the priests.
There were Jedaiah, Jakin and
the son of Joiarib.
11 There was also Seraiah. He
was the son of Hilkiah. Hilkiah
was the son of Meshullam.
Meshullam was the son of
Zadok. Zadok was the son of
Meraioth. Meraioth was the
son of Ahitub. Ahitub was the
official in charge of God's house.
12 There were also people who
helped them. They carried out
the work for the temple. The
total number of men was 822.
There was also Adaiah. He was
the son of Jeroham. Jeroham
was the son of Pelaliah. Pelaliah
was the son of Amzi. Amzi was
the son of Zechariah. Zechariah
was the son of Pashhur. Pashhur
was the son of Malkijah. 13 There
were also people who helped
Adaiah. They were family
leaders. The total number of
men was 242.
There was also Amashsai. He was
the son of Azarel. Azarel was the
son of Ahzai. Ahzai was the son
of Meshillemoth. Meshillemoth
was the son of Immer. 14 There
were also people who helped
Amashsai. They were important
men. The total number of them
was 128.
Their chief officer was Zabdiel.
He was the son of Haggedolim.
15 Here are the leaders from among
the Levites.
There was Shemaiah. He was the
son of Hasshub. Hasshub was
the son of Azrikam. Azrikam
was the son of Hashabiah.
Hashabiah was the son of Bunni.
16 There were also Shabbethai and
Jozabad. They were two of the
leaders of the Levites. They were
in charge of the work that was
done outside God's house.
17 There was also Mattaniah. He
led in prayer and in giving
thanks. He was the son of Mika.
Mika was the son of Zabdi. Zabdi
was the son of Asaph.
There was also Bakbukiah. He
was second among those who
helped Mattaniah.
And there was Abda. He was the
son of Shammua. Shammua
was the son of Galal. Galal was
the son of Jeduthun.
18 The total number of Levites in
the holy city was 284.

19 Here are the leaders from among
the men who guarded the gates.
There were Akkub, Talmon and
those who helped them. They
stood guard at the gates. The
total number of men was 172.

20 The rest of the Israelites were in
all the towns of Judah. The priests and
Levites were with them. All of them lived
on their own family property.
21 The temple servants lived on the
hill of Ophel. Ziha and Gishpa were in
charge of them.
22 Uzzi was the chief officer of the
Levites in Jerusalem. He was the son
of Bani. Bani was the son of Hashabiah.
Hashabiah was the son of Mattaniah.
Mattaniah was the son of Mika. Uzzi was
one of the members of Asaph's family
line. They were musicians in charge
of the worship services at the house
of God. 23 The musicians received their
orders from the Persian king. He told
them what they should do every day.
24 Pethahiah worked for the king in all
matters that were connected with the
people. He was the son of Meshezabel.
Meshezabel belonged to the family line
of Zerah. Zerah was the son of Judah.
25 Many of the people of Judah lived
in villages that had fields around them.
Some of them lived in Kiriath Arba and
the settlements that were around it.
Others lived in Dibon and its settlements. Others lived in Jekabzeel and
its villages. 26 Others lived in Jeshua,
Moladah and Beth Pelet. 27 Others lived
in Hazar Shual and in Beersheba and
its settlements. 28 Others lived in Ziklag
and in Mekonah and its settlements.
29 Others lived in En Rimmon and Zorah.
Others lived in Jarmuth, 30 Zanoah and
Adullam and their villages. Others lived
in Lachish and its fields. Still others
lived in Azekah and its settlements.
So the people of Judah were living all
the way from Beersheba to the Valley
of Hinnom.
31 Some of the members of the family
line of Benjamin who were from Geba
lived in Mikmash. Others lived in Aija
and in Bethel and its settlements. 32 Others lived in Anathoth, Nob and Ananiah.
33 Others lived in Hazor, Ramah and
Gittaim. 34 Others lived in Hadid, Zeboim
and Neballat. 35 Others lived in Lod and
Ono. Still others lived in Ge Harashim.
36 Some of the groups of the Levites
from Judah made their homes in the
territory of Benjamin.

The Priests and Levites Who Returned to Judah

12 Some priests and Levites
returned to Judah with Zerubbabel and Joshua. Zerubbabel
was the son of Shealtiel. Here are
the names of those priests and
Levites.

Seraiah, Jeremiah, Ezra,
2 Amariah, Malluk, Hattush,
3 Shekaniah, Rehum, Meremoth,
4 Iddo, Ginnethon, Abijah,
5 Mijamin, Moadiah, Bilgah,
6 Shemaiah, Joiarib, Jedaiah,
7 Sallu, Amok, Hilkiah, Jedaiah

All of them were the leaders of
the priests and those who helped
them. They lived in the days of
Joshua.

8 The Levites were Jeshua, Binnui,
Kadmiel, Sherebiah and Judah. There
were also Mattaniah and those who
helped him. They were in charge of the
songs for giving thanks. 9 Bakbukiah
and Unni helped them. They stood
and sang across from them during the
services.

10 Joshua was the father of Joiakim.
Joiakim was the father of Eliashib.
Eliashib was the father of Joiada.
11 Joiada was the father of Jonathan.
And Jonathan was the father of
Jaddua.

12 Here are the names of the family
leaders of the priests. They were
the leaders in the days of Joiakim.

Meraiah was from Seraiah's
family.
Hananiah was from Jeremiah's
family.
13 Meshullam was from Ezra's family.
Jehohanan was from Amariah's
family.
14 Jonathan was from Malluk's
family.
Joseph was from Shekaniah's
family.
15 Adna was from Harim's family.

Helkai was from Meremoth's family.
16 Zechariah was from Iddo's family.
Meshullam was from Ginnethon's family.
17 Zikri was from Abijah's family.
Piltai was from Miniamin's and Moadiah's family.
18 Shammua was from Bilgah's family.
Jehonathan was from Shemaiah's family.
19 Mattenai was from Joiarib's family.
Uzzi was from Jedaiah's family.
20 Kallai was from Sallu's family.
Eber was from Amok's family.
21 Hashabiah was from Hilkiah's family.
And Nethanel was from Jedaiah's family.

22 The names of the family leaders of the Levites in the days of Eliashib, Joiada, Johanan and Jaddua were written down. So were the names of the family leaders of the priests. That happened while Darius ruled over Persia. 23 The names of the leaders in Levi's family line up to the time of Johanan were written down. They were written in the official records. Johanan was the son of Eliashib. 24 The leaders of the Levites were Hashabiah, Sherebiah and Jeshua. Jeshua was the son of Kadmiel. Those who helped them stood across from them to sing praises and give thanks. One group would sing back to the other. That's what David, the man of God, had ordered.

25 Mattaniah, Bakbukiah, Obadiah, Meshullam, Talmon and Akkub stood at the gates of the temple. They guarded the storerooms at the gates. 26 They served in the days of Joiakim. He was the son of Joshua. Joshua was the son of Jozadak. They also served in the days of Nehemiah and Ezra. Nehemiah was the governor. Ezra was a priest and the teacher of the Law.

The Wall of Jerusalem Is Set Apart to God

27 The wall of Jerusalem was set apart to God. For that occasion, the Levites were gathered together from where they lived. They were brought to Jerusalem to celebrate that happy occasion. They celebrated the fact that the wall was being set apart to God. They did it by singing and giving their thanks to him. They celebrated by playing music on cymbals, harps and lyres. 28 The musicians were also brought together. Some of them

came in from the area around Jerusalem.
Others came from the villages where the
people of Netophah lived. 29 Others came
from Beth Gilgal. Still others came from
the area of Geba and Azmaveth. The musicians had built villages for themselves
around Jerusalem. 30 The priests and
Levites made themselves pure. Then they made the people, the gates and the wall pure and "clean."

31 I, Nehemiah, had the leaders of Judah go up on top of the wall. I also appointed two large choirs to sing and give thanks. I told one of them to walk south on top of the wall. That was toward the Dung Gate.
32 Hoshaiah and half of the leaders of Judah followed them.
33 Azariah, Ezra, Meshullam,
34 Judah, Benjamin, Shemaiah and Jeremiah
also followed them.
35 Some priests who had trumpets followed them. So did Zechariah. He was the son of Jonathan. Jonathan was the son of Shemaiah. Shemaiah was the son of Mattaniah. Mattaniah was the son of Micaiah. Micaiah was the son of Zakkur. Zakkur was
the son of Asaph.
36 Those who helped Zechariah also marched along. They were Shemaiah, Azarel, Milalai, Gilalai, Maai, Nethanel, Judah and Hanani. They brought musical instruments with them. That's what David, the man of God, had ordered. Ezra led the group that was marching south. He was the
teacher of the Law.
37 At the Fountain Gate they continued straight up the steps of the City of David. The steps went up to the wall. Then the group passed above the place where David's palace had been. They continued on to the Water Gate on the east.

38 The second choir went north. I followed them on top of the wall. Half of the people went with me. They went past the Tower of the Ovens. They went
to the Broad Wall.
39 They marched over the Gate of Ephraim. They went over the Jeshanah Gate and the Fish Gate. They went past the Tower of Hananel and the Tower of the Hundred. They continued on to the Sheep Gate. At the Gate of the Guard they stopped.

40 Then the two choirs that sang and gave thanks took their places in God's house. So did I. So did half of the officials.
41 And so did the priests. They were Eliakim, Maaseiah, Miniamin, Micaiah, Elioenai, Zechariah and Hananiah. They had their trumpets with them.
42 Maaseiah, Shemaiah, Eleazar, Uzzi, Jehohanan, Malkijah, Elam and Ezer were also there. The choirs sang under

pointing us to JESUS: Nehemiah

God's people worked together to build God a very special house called the temple. One day, after God's people had continued to disobey him over and over and over again, the worst thing they could imagine happened: They were captured by their enemies, and the temple was destroyed! They lived for years away from their home and away from the ruined temple during what is called *the exile*. While they were in exile, they wondered, "When will we be able to go back home?"

Meanwhile, God raised up a new, humble leader. His name was Nehemiah, and he was given the important task of helping God's people rebuild the wall around the city. The wall needed to be rebuilt so that life in God's city could be safe and the people could flourish once again.

Nehemiah represents Jesus, who came to repair and rebuild the world as God intended it to be. Everyone who puts their faith in Jesus can confidently build their life on his strong foundation.

the direction of Jezrahiah. 43 On that
day large numbers of sacrifices were
offered. The people were glad because
God had given them great joy. The
women and children were also very
happy. The joyful sound in Jerusalem
could be heard far away.

Nehemiah Makes Some Final Changes

44 At that time some men were put
in charge of the storerooms. That's
where all the gifts the people brought
were placed. Those gifts included the
first shares of their crops. They also
included a tenth of everything the
Law required. Crops were harvested
from the fields around the towns.
The people had to bring the shares
of those crops that were required
by the Law. They gave them to the
priests and Levites. That's because
the people of Judah were pleased with
the priests and Levites who were serving God. 45 The priests and Levites did
everything their God wanted them to
do. They made things pure and "clean."
The musicians and the men who guarded
the temple gates also served God. Everything was done just as David and
his son Solomon had commanded. 46 A
long time ago there had been directors
for the musicians. There had also been
directors for the songs for giving thanks
and praise to God. It was in the time of
David and Asaph. 47 So now in the days of
Zerubbabel and Nehemiah, all the people
of Israel brought their gifts. They gave
the musicians and the men who guarded
the gates what they were supposed to
give them every day. They also set apart
the shares for the other Levites. And the
Levites set apart the shares for the priests
in the family line of Aaron.

13 At that time the Book of Moses
was read out loud. All the people heard it. It was written there that
no Ammonite or Moabite could ever
become a member of God's community.
2 That's because they hadn't given the
people of Israel food and water. Instead,
they had hired Balaam to put a curse
on them. But our God turned the curse
into a blessing. 3 When that law was
read, the people of Judah obeyed it.
They sent out of Israel everyone who
was from another nation.

4 Eliashib the priest had been put in
charge of the storerooms in the house
of our God. He had worked closely with
Tobiah. 5 He had also provided a large
room for Tobiah. It had been used to
store the grain offerings. The incense
and the objects for the temple had been
put there. And a tenth of the grain, olive
oil and fresh wine had been kept there.
That's what the Law required for the
Levites. That's also what it required
for the musicians and the men who
guarded the temple gates. The gifts
for the priests had been kept there too.

6 But I wasn't in Jerusalem while all
of that was going on. I had returned
to the Persian King Artaxerxes, the
king of Babylon. I went to him in the
32nd year of his rule. Some time later I
asked him to let me return to Jerusalem.
7 When I got back, I learned about the
evil thing Eliashib had done. He had
provided a room for Tobiah. It was in
the courtyards of God's house. 8 So I was
very unhappy. I threw all of Tobiah's
things out of the room. 9 I gave orders to
make the rooms pure and "clean" again.
Then I put the supplies from God's house
back into them. That included the grain
offerings and the incense.

10 I also learned that the shares the
Levites were supposed to receive hadn't
been given to them. So all the Levites
and musicians had to leave their regular temple duties. They had to go back
and farm their own fields. 11 I gave a
warning to the officials. I asked them,
"Why aren't you taking care of God's
house?" Then I brought the Levites and
musicians together. I stationed them
in their proper places. I put them back
to work.

12 All the people of Judah brought a
tenth of the grain, olive oil and fresh
wine. They took it to the storerooms.
13 I put some men in charge of the storerooms. They were Shelemiah, Zadok
and Pedaiah. Shelemiah was a priest.
Zadok was a teacher of the law. And
Pedaiah was a Levite. I made Hanan
their assistant. He was the son of Zakkur. Zakkur was the son of Mattaniah.
I knew that these men could be trusted.
They were put in charge of handing out
the supplies to the other Levites.

14 You are my God. Remember me because of what I've done. I've worked faithfully for your temple and its services. So please don't forget the good things I've done.

15 In those days I saw some people of Judah stomping on grapes in winepresses. They were doing it on the Sabbath day. Other people were bringing in grain. They were loading it on donkeys. Still other people were loading up wine, grapes, figs and other kinds of things. They were bringing all of it into Jerusalem on the Sabbath day. So I warned them not to sell food on that day. 16 People from Tyre who lived in Jerusalem were bringing in fish. In fact, they were bringing in all kinds of goods. They were selling them in Jerusalem on the Sabbath day. The people of Judah were buying them. 17 I gave a warning to the nobles of Judah. I said, "Why are you doing such an evil thing? You are misusing the Sabbath day! 18 Your people of long ago did the very same things. That's why our God has brought all this trouble on us. That's why he's making this city suffer so much. Now you are making him even angrier against Israel. You are misusing the Sabbath day."

19 Evening shadows fell on the gates of Jerusalem before the Sabbath day started. So I ordered the gates to be shut. They had to remain closed until the Sabbath day was over. I stationed some of my own men at the gates. I told them not to let anything be brought in on the Sabbath day. 20 Once or twice some traders and sellers spent the night outside Jerusalem. They were hoping to sell all kinds of goods. 21 But I gave them a warning. I said, "Why are you spending the night by the wall? If you do this again, I'll arrest you." So from that time on they didn't come on the Sabbath day anymore. 22 I commanded the Levites to make themselves pure. Then I told them to go and guard the gates. I wanted the Sabbath day to be kept holy.

You are my God. Remember me because of the good things I've done. Be kind to me according to your great love.

23 In those days I also saw that some men of Judah had married women from Ashdod. Others had married women from Ammon or Moab. 24 Half of their children spoke the language of Ashdod. Or they spoke the language of one of the other nations. They didn't even know how to speak the language of Judah. 25 So I gave them a warning. I cursed them. I beat up some of them. I pulled their hair out. I had them make a promise in God's name. I said, "You must promise not to give your daughters to be married to their sons. You must promise not to let their daughters marry your sons. And you must not marry their daughters either. 26 That's how Solomon, the king of Israel, sinned. He married women from other nations. There wasn't a king like him anywhere. His God loved him. In fact, God made him king over the whole nation of Israel. But even he was led into sin by women from other lands. 27 Now I hear that you too are doing all of the same terrible and evil things. You aren't being faithful to our God. You are marrying women from other lands."

28 One of the sons of Joiada was the son-in-law of Sanballat the Horonite. Joiada, the son of Eliashib, was the high priest. I drove Joiada's son away from me.

29 You are my God. Remember what those priests have done. They have brought shame to their own work. They have also brought shame to the covenant that God made with the priests and Levites long ago.

30 So I made the priests and Levites pure. I made them pure from every practice that had come from other countries and had made them impure. I gave them their duties. Each one had his own job to do. 31 I also made plans for gifts of wood to be brought at certain appointed times. And I made plans for the first share of the crops to be brought.

You are my God. Please remember me with kindness.

ESTHER

Author: We don't know.

While many of God's people returned to the promised land, some of the Jews chose to stay in the land of exile. One day the king of Persia was looking for a woman to be queen of the entire nation. After searching and searching, he found a woman named Esther. She was a Jew who learned about God from her uncle Mordecai. After she became queen, a wicked man named Haman plotted to kill all the Jews living in the land of exile. When Esther discovered his plan, she knew she had to stop him; Esther knew that saving her people was the reason God had allowed her to be the queen. But saving God's people meant Esther would have to be brave and risk her own life. With God's help, she told her husband, the king, about Haman's evil plan. God used Esther to save the entire nation!

Old Testament History

Esther's bravery reminded God's people that even though they were far from home, God never left them alone and without hope. He works through faithful people to accomplish his will. And one day God would send the Savior—the ultimate Chosen One—to save and protect his people.

Vashti Is Removed From Her Position as Queen

1 King Xerxes ruled over the 127 territories in his kingdom. They reached
from India all the way to Cush. Here is
what happened during the time Xerxes
ruled over the whole Persian kingdom.
2 He was ruling from his royal throne in
the fort of Susa. 3 In the third year of his
rule King Xerxes gave a feast. It was for
all his nobles and officials. The military
leaders of Persia and Media were there.
So were the princes and the nobles of
the territories he ruled over.
4 Every day for 180 days he showed
his guests the great wealth of his kingdom. He also showed them how glorious
his kingdom was. 5 When those days
were over, the king gave another feast.
It lasted for seven days. It was held in
the garden of the king's courtyard. It
was for all the people who lived in the
fort of Susa. Everyone from the least important person to the most important
was invited. 6 The garden was decorated
with white and blue linen banners. They
hung from ropes that were made out
of white linen and purple cloth. The
ropes were connected to silver rings
on marble pillars. There were gold and
silver couches in the garden. They were
placed on a floor that was made out
of small stones. The floor had purple
crystal, marble, mother-of-pearl and
other stones of great value. 7 Royal wine
was served in gold cups. Each cup was
different from all the others. There was
plenty of wine. The king always provided as much as his guests wanted.
8 He commanded that they should be
allowed to drink as much or as little as
they wished. He directed all his servants
to give his guests what they asked for.
9 Queen Vashti also gave a feast. Only
women were invited. It was held in the
royal palace of King Xerxes.
10 On the seventh day Xerxes was in
a good mood because he had drunk
a lot of wine. So he gave a command
to the seven officials who served him.
They were Mehuman, Biztha, Harbona,
Bigtha, Abagtha, Zethar and Karkas.
11 King Xerxes told them to bring Queen
Vashti to him. He wanted her to come
wearing her royal crown. He wanted
to show off her beauty to the people
and nobles. She was lovely to look at.

in Esther?

God is the Present One. Even though God's people were far from their home and the temple, God was present with them, just as the Holy Spirit is present with his people today.

12 The attendants told Queen Vashti
what the king had ordered her to do.
But she refused to come. So the king
became very angry.
13 It was the king's practice to ask for
advice about matters of law and fairness. So he spoke with the wise men who
understood what was going on at that
time. 14 They were the men closest to
the king. Their names were Karshena,
Shethar, Admatha, Tarshish, Meres,
Marsena and Memukan. They were the
seven nobles of Persia and Media. They
were the king's special advisers and the
most important men in the kingdom.
15 "You know the law," the king said.
"What should I do to Queen Vashti?
She hasn't obeyed my command. The
officials told her what I ordered her to
do, didn't they?"
16 Then Memukan gave a reply to the
king and the nobles. He said, "Queen
Vashti has done what is wrong. But
she didn't do it only against you, King
Xerxes. She did it also against all the
nobles. And she did it against the people
in all the territories you rule over. 17 All
the women will hear about what the
queen has done. Then they won't respect
their husbands. They'll say, 'King Xerxes
commanded Queen Vashti to be brought
to him. But she wouldn't come.' 18 Here
is what will start today. The leading
women in Persia and Media who have

heard about the queen's actions will act in the same way. They'll disobey all your nobles, just as she disobeyed you. They won't have any respect for their husbands. They won't honor them.

19 "So if it pleases you, send out a royal order. Let it be written down in the laws of Persia and Media. Those laws can never be changed. Let the royal order say that Vashti can never see you again. Also let her position as queen be given to someone who is better than she is. 20 And let your order be announced all through your entire kingdom. Then all women will have respect for their husbands, from the least important to the most important."

21 The king and his nobles were pleased with that advice. So he did what Memukan had suggested. 22 The king sent messages out to every territory in the kingdom. He sent them to each territory in its own writing. He sent them to every nation in its own language. The messages announced that every man should rule over his own family, using his own language.

Esther Becomes Queen of Persia

2 Later, the great anger of King Xerxes calmed down. Then he remembered Vashti and what she had done. He also remembered the royal order he had sent out concerning her. 2 At that time the king's personal attendants made a suggestion. They said, "King Xerxes, let a search be made for some beautiful young virgins for you. 3 Appoint some officials in every territory in your kingdom. Have them bring all these beautiful young women into the fort of Susa. Put them in the special place where the virgins stay. Then put Hegai in charge of them. He's the official who serves you. He's in charge of the women. Let beauty care be given to the new group of women. 4 Then let the young woman who pleases you the most become queen in Vashti's place." The king liked that advice. So he followed it.

5 There was a Jew living in the fort of Susa. He was from the tribe of Benjamin. His name was Mordecai. He was the son of Jair. Jair was the son of Shimei. Shimei was the son of Kish. 6 Nebuchadnezzar had forced Mordecai to leave Jerusalem. He was among the prisoners who were carried off along with Jehoiachin. Jehoiachin had been king of Judah. Nebuchadnezzar was king of Babylon. 7 Mordecai had a cousin named Hadassah. He had raised her because she didn't have a father or mother. Hadassah was also called Esther. She had a lovely figure and was very beautiful. Mordecai had adopted her as his own daughter. He had done it when her father and mother died.

8 After the king's order and law were announced, many young women were brought to the fort of Susa. Hegai was put in charge of them. Esther was also taken to the king's palace. She was put under the control of Hegai. He was in charge of the place where the virgins stayed. 9 Esther pleased him. He showed her how happy he was with her. Right away he provided her with her beauty care and special food. He appointed seven female attendants to help her. They were chosen from the king's palace. He moved her and her attendants into the best part of the place where the virgins stayed.

10 Esther hadn't told anyone who her people were. She hadn't talked about her family. That's because Mordecai had told her not to. 11 Mordecai tried to find out how Esther was getting along. He wanted to know what was happening to her. So he walked back and forth near the courtyard by the place where the virgins stayed. He did it every day.

12 Each young woman had to complete 12 months of beauty care. They used oil of myrrh for six months. And they used perfume and makeup for the other six months. A virgin's turn to go in to King Xerxes could come only after a full 12 months had passed. 13 And here is how she would go to the king. She would be given anything she wanted from the place where the virgins stayed. She could take it with her to the king's palace. 14 In the evening she would go there. In the morning she would leave. Then she would go to the special place where the king's concubines stayed. She would be put under the control of Shaashgaz. He was the king's official who was in charge of the concubines. She would never return to the king unless he was pleased with her. He had to

send for her by name before she could
go to him again.
15 Mordecai had adopted Esther. She
had been the daughter of his uncle
Abihail. Her turn came to go in to the
king. She only asked for what Hegai
suggested. He was the king's official
who was in charge of the place where
the virgins stayed. Everyone who saw
Esther was pleased with her. 16 She was
taken to King Xerxes in the royal house.
It was now the tenth month. That was
the month of Tebeth. It was the seventh
year of the rule of Xerxes.
17 The king liked Esther more than
he liked any of the other women. She
pleased him more than any of the other
virgins. So he put a royal crown on her
head. He made her queen in Vashti's
place. 18 Then the king gave a feast to
honor Esther. All his nobles and officials
were invited. He announced a holiday
all through the territories he ruled over.
He freely gave many gifts in keeping
with his royal wealth.

Mordecai Uncovers a Plan to Kill the King

19 The virgins were gathered together
a second time. At that time Mordecai
was sitting at the palace gate. 20 Esther
had kept her family history a secret.
She hadn't told anyone who her people
were. Mordecai had told her not to. She
continued to follow his directions. That's
what she had always done when he was
bringing her up.
21 Bigthana and Teresh were two of
the king's officers. They guarded the
door of the royal palace. They became
angry with King Xerxes. So they decided to kill him. They made their evil
plans while Mordecai was sitting at
the palace gate. 22 So Mordecai found
out about it and told Queen Esther.
Then she reported it to the king. She
told him that Mordecai had uncovered the plans against him. 23 Some
people checked Esther's report. And
they found out it was true. So the two
officials were put to death. Then poles
were stuck through them. They were
set up where people could see them.
All of that was written in the official
records. It was written down while the
king was watching.

Haman Plans to Destroy the Jews

3 After those events, King Xerxes honored Haman. Haman was the son of
Hammedatha. He was from the family
line of Agag. The king gave Haman a
higher position than he had before. He
gave him a seat of honor. It was higher
than the positions any of the other nobles had. 2 All the royal officials at the
palace gate got down on their knees.
They gave honor to Haman. That's because the king had commanded them to
do it. But Mordecai refused to get down
on his knees. He wouldn't give Haman
any honor at all.
3 The royal officials at the palace gate
asked Mordecai a question. They said,
"Why don't you obey the king's command?" 4 Day after day they spoke to
him. But he still refused to obey. So they
told Haman about it. They wanted to
see whether he would let Mordecai get
away with what he was doing. Mordecai
had told them he was a Jew.
5 Haman noticed that Mordecai
wouldn't get down on his knees. He
wouldn't give Haman any honor. So
Haman was very angry. 6 But he had
found out who Mordecai's people were.
So he didn't want to kill only Mordecai.
He also looked for a way to destroy all
Mordecai's people. They were Jews. He
wanted to kill all of them everywhere
in the kingdom of Xerxes.
7 The lot was cast in front of Haman.
The lot was called Pur. It was cast in the
first month of the 12th year that Xerxes
was king. That month was called Nisan.
The lot was cast to choose a day and a
month. The month chosen was the 12th
month. That month was called Adar.
8 Then Haman said to King Xerxes,
"Certain people are scattered among
the nations. They live in all the territories in your kingdom. They keep themselves separate from everyone else.
Their practices are different from the
practices of all other people. They don't
obey your laws. It really isn't good for
you to put up with them. 9 If it pleases
you, give the order to destroy them. I'll
even add 375 tons of silver to the king's
officials for the royal treasures."
10 So the king took his ring off his finger. The ring had his royal seal on it. He
gave the ring to Haman. Haman was
the son of Hammedatha, the Agagite.

Haman was the enemy of the Jews. 11 “Keep the money,” the king said to Haman. “Do what you want to with those people.”

12 The king sent for the royal secretaries. It was the 13th day of the first month. The secretaries wrote down all Haman’s orders. They wrote them down in the writing of each territory in the kingdom. They also wrote them in the language of each nation. The orders were sent to the royal officials and to the governors of the territories. And the orders were also sent to the nobles of the nations. The orders were written in the name of King Xerxes himself. And they were stamped with his own official mark. 13 They were carried by messengers. They were sent to all the king’s territories. The orders commanded people to destroy, kill and wipe out all the Jews. That included young people and old people alike. It included women and children. All the Jews were supposed to be killed on a single day. That day was the 13th day of the 12th month. It was the month of Adar. The orders also commanded people to take everything that belonged to the Jews. 14 A copy of the order had to be sent out as law. It had to be sent to every territory in the kingdom. It had to be announced to the people of every nation. Then they would be ready for that day.

15 The king commanded the messengers to go out. So they did. The order was sent out from the fort of Susa. Then the king and Haman sat down to drink wine. But the people in the city were bewildered.

Mordecai Talks Esther Into Helping the Jews

4 Mordecai found out about everything that had been done. So he tore his clothes. He put on the rough clothing people wear when they’re sad. He sat down in ashes. Then he went out into the city. He wept out loud. He cried bitter tears. 2 But he only went as far as the palace gate. That’s because no one dressed in that rough clothing was allowed to go through it. 3 All the Jews were very sad. They didn’t eat anything. They wept and cried. Many of them put on the rough clothing people wear when they’re sad. They were lying down in ashes. They did all these things in every territory where the king’s order and law had been sent.

4 Esther’s male and female attendants came to her. They told her about Mordecai. So she became very troubled. She wanted him to take off his rough clothing. So she sent him other clothes to wear. But he wouldn’t accept them. 5 Then Esther sent for Hathak. He was one of the king’s officials. He had been appointed to take care of her. She ordered him to find out what was troubling Mordecai. She wanted to know why he was so upset.

6 So Hathak went out to see Mordecai. He was in the open area in front of the palace gate. 7 Mordecai told him everything that had happened to him. He told him about the exact amount of money Haman had promised to add to the royal treasures. He said Haman wanted it to be used to pay some men to destroy the Jews. 8 Mordecai also gave Hathak a copy of the order. It commanded people to wipe out the Jews. The order had been sent from Susa. Mordecai told Hathak to show the order to Esther. He wanted Hathak to explain it to her. Mordecai told him to tell her to go and beg the king for mercy. Mordecai wanted her to make an appeal to the king for her people.

9 Hathak went back and reported to Esther what Mordecai had said. 10 Then Esther directed him to give an answer to Mordecai. She told him to say, 11 “There is a certain law that everyone knows about. All the king’s officials know about it. The people in the royal territories know about it. It applies to any man or woman who approaches the king in the inner courtyard without being sent for. It says they must be put to death. But there is a way out. Suppose the king reaches out his gold scepter toward them. Then their lives will be spared. But 30 days have gone by since the king sent for me.”

12 Esther’s words were reported to Mordecai. 13 Then he sent back an answer. He said, “You live in the king’s palace. But don’t think that just because you are there you will be the only Jew who will escape. 14 What if you don’t say anything at this time? Then help for the Jews will come from another place.

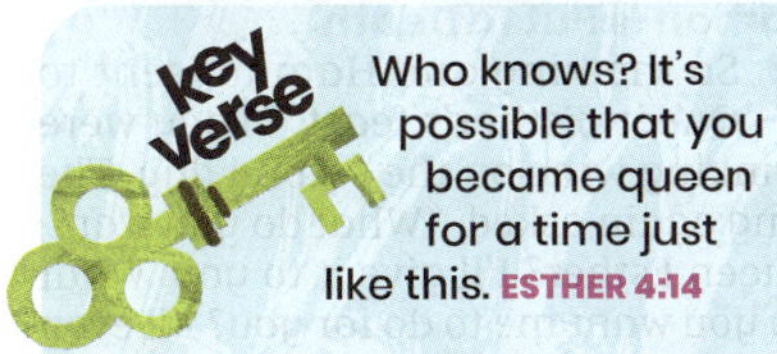

Who knows? It's
possible that you
became queen
for a time just
like this. ESTHER 4:14

But you and your family will die. Who
knows? It's possible that you became
queen for a time just like this."
15 Then Esther sent a reply to Mordecai. She said, 16 "Go. Gather together all
the Jews who are in Susa. And fast for
my benefit. Don't eat or drink anything
for three days. Don't do it night or day.
I and my attendants will fast just as
you do. Then I'll go to the king. I'll do
it even though it's against the law. And
if I have to die, I'll die."
17 So Mordecai went away. He carried
out all Esther's directions.

Esther Asks the King for a Favor

5 On the third day Esther put on her
royal robes. She stood in the inner
courtyard of the palace. It was in front
of the king's hall. The king was sitting
on his royal throne in the hall. He was
facing the entrance. 2 He saw Queen
Esther standing in the courtyard. He
was pleased with her. So he reached out
toward her the gold scepter that was
in his hand. Then Esther approached
him. She touched the tip of the scepter.
3 The king asked, "What is it, Queen
Esther? What do you want? I'll give it
to you. I'll even give you up to half of
my kingdom."
4 Esther replied, "King Xerxes, if it
pleases you, come to a feast today. I've
prepared it for you. Please have Haman
come with you."
5 "Bring Haman at once," the king
said to his servants. "Then we'll do what
Esther asks."
So the king and Haman went to the
feast Esther had prepared. 6 As they
were drinking wine, the king asked
Esther the same question again. He
said, "What do you want? I'll give it to
you. What do you want me to do for
you? I'll even give you up to half of my
kingdom."
7 Esther replied, "Here is what I want.
Here is my appeal to you. 8 I hope you
will be pleased to give me what I want.
And I hope you will be pleased to listen
to my appeal. If you are, I'd like you and
Haman to come tomorrow to the feast
I'll prepare for you. Then I'll answer
your question."

Haman Is Very Angry With Mordecai

9 That day Haman was happy. So he
left the palace in a good mood. But then
he saw Mordecai at the palace gate. He
noticed that Mordecai didn't stand up
when he walked by. In fact, Mordecai
didn't have any respect for him at all.
So he was very angry with him. 10 But
Haman was able to control himself. He
went on home.
Haman called together his friends and
his wife Zeresh. 11 He bragged to them
about how rich he was. He talked about
how many sons he had. He spoke about
all the ways the king had honored him.
He bragged about how the king had giv-
en him a high position. It was higher
than the position of any of the other
nobles and officials. 12 "And that's not
all," Haman added. "I'm the only person
Queen Esther invited to come with the
king to the feast she gave. Now she has
invited me along with the king tomorrow.
13 But even all of that doesn't satisfy me.
I won't be satisfied as long as I see that
Jew Mordecai sitting at the palace gate."
14 Haman's wife Zeresh and all his
friends said to him, "Get a pole. In the
morning, ask the king to have Mordecai put to death. Have the pole stuck
through his body. Set it up at a place
where it will be 75 feet above the ground.
Everyone will be able to see it there. Then
go to the feast with the king. Have a
good time." Haman was delighted with
that suggestion. So he got the pole ready.

The King Honors Mordecai

6 That night the king couldn't sleep.
So he ordered the official records
of his rule to be brought in. He ordered
someone to read them to him. 2 What
Mordecai had done was written there.
He had uncovered the plans of Bigthana
and Teresh. They were two of the king's
officers who guarded the door of the
royal palace. They had decided to kill
King Xerxes.
3 "What great honor has Mordecai
received for doing that?" the king asked.
"Nothing has been done for him," his
attendants answered.

4 The king asked, "Who is in the courtyard?" Haman had just entered the outer courtyard of the palace. He had come to speak to the king about putting Mordecai to death. He wanted to talk about putting Mordecai's body on the pole he had prepared for him.

5 The king's attendants said to him, "Haman is standing in the courtyard."

"Bring him in," the king ordered.

6 Haman entered. Then the king asked him, "What should be done for the man I want to honor?"

Haman said to himself, "Is there anyone the king would rather honor than me?" 7 So he answered the king. He said, "Here is what you should do for the man you want to honor. 8 Have your servants get a royal robe you have worn. Have them bring a horse you have ridden on. Have a royal mark placed on its head. 9 Then give the robe and horse to one of your most noble princes. Let the robe be put on the man you want to honor. Let him be led on the horse through the city streets. Let people announce in front of him, 'This is what is done for the man the king wants to honor!' "

10 "Go right away," the king commanded Haman. "Get the robe. Bring the horse. Do exactly what you have suggested. Do it for Mordecai the Jew. He's sitting out there at the palace gate. Make sure you do everything you have suggested."

11 So Haman got the robe and the horse. He put the robe on Mordecai. And he led him on horseback through the city streets. He walked along in front of him and announced, "This is what is done for the man the king wants to honor!"

12 After that, Mordecai returned to the palace gate. But Haman rushed home. He covered his head because he was very sad. 13 He told his wife Zeresh everything that had happened to him. He also told all his friends.

His advisers and his wife Zeresh spoke to him. They said, "Your fall from power started with Mordecai. He's a Jew. So now you can't stand up against him. You are going to be destroyed!" 14 They were still talking with him when the king's officials arrived. They hurried Haman away to the feast Esther had prepared.

Haman Is Put to Death

7 So the king and Haman went to Queen Esther's feast. 2 They were drinking wine on the second day. The king again asked, "What do you want, Queen Esther? I'll give it to you. What do you want me to do for you? I'll even give you up to half of my kingdom."

3 Then Queen Esther answered, "Your Majesty, I hope you will be pleased to let me live. That's what I want. Please spare my people. That's my appeal to you. 4 My people and I have been sold to be destroyed. We've been sold to be killed and wiped out. Suppose we had only been sold as male and female slaves. Then I wouldn't have said anything. That kind of suffering wouldn't be a good enough reason to bother you."

5 King Xerxes asked Queen Esther, "Who is the man who has dared to do such a thing? And where is he?"

6 Esther said, "The man hates us! He's our enemy! He's this evil Haman!"

Then Haman was terrified in front of the king and queen. 7 The king got up. He was very angry. He left his wine and went out into the palace garden. But Haman realized that the king had already decided what he was going to do to him. So he stayed behind to beg Queen Esther for his life.

8 The king returned from the palace garden to the dinner hall. Just then he saw Haman falling on the couch where Esther was lying.

The king shouted, "Will he even treat the queen like this? Will he harm her while she's right here with me in the palace?"

As soon as the king finished speaking, his men covered Haman's face. 9 Then Harbona said, "There's a pole standing near Haman's house. He has prepared it for Mordecai. Mordecai is the one who spoke up to help you. Haman had planned to have him put to death. He was going to have the pole stuck through his body. Then he was going to set it up at a place where it would be 75 feet above the ground." Harbona was one of the officials who attended the king.

The king said to his men, "Put Haman to death! Stick the pole through his body! Set it up where everyone can see it!" 10 So they did. And they used the pole Haman had prepared for Mordecai. Then the king's anger calmed down.

The King Allows the Jews to Fight for Their Lives

8 That same day King Xerxes gave
Queen Esther everything Haman
had owned. Haman had been the enemy of the Jews. Esther had told the
king that Mordecai was her cousin. So
Mordecai came to see the king. 2 The
king took his ring off. It had his royal
mark on it. He had taken it back from
Haman. Now he gave it to Mordecai.
And Esther put Mordecai in charge of
everything Haman had owned.
3 Esther made another appeal to the
king. She fell at his feet and wept. She
begged him to put an end to the evil
plan of Haman, the Agagite. He had decided to kill the Jews. 4 The king reached
out his gold scepter toward Esther. She
got up and stood in front of him.
5 She said, "King Xerxes, I hope you
will think what I'm asking is the right
thing to do. I hope you are pleased with
me. If you are, and if it pleases you,
let an order be written. Let it take the
place of the messages Haman wrote.
Haman was the son of Hammedatha,
the Agagite. He planned to kill the Jews.
He wrote orders to destroy us in all your
territories. 6 I couldn't stand by and see
the horrible trouble that would fall on
my people! I couldn't stand to see my
family destroyed!"
7 King Xerxes gave a reply to Queen
Esther and Mordecai the Jew. He said,
"Haman attacked the Jews. So I've given
Esther everything he owned. My men
have stuck a pole through his dead
body. And they've set it up where everyone can see it. 8 Now write another
order in my name. Do it for the benefit
of the Jews. Do what seems best to you.
Stamp the order with my royal mark.
Nothing that is written in my name
and stamped with my mark can ever
be changed."
9 Right away the king sent for the
royal secretaries. It was the 23rd day of
the third month. That was the month of
Sivan. They wrote down all Mordecai's
orders to the Jews. They also wrote them
to the royal officials, the governors and
the nobles of the 127 territories in his
kingdom. The territories reached from
India all the way to Cush. The orders
were written down in the writing of
each territory. They were written in the
language of each nation. They were also
written to the Jews in their own writing
and language. 10 Mordecai wrote the
orders in the name of King Xerxes. He
stamped them with the king's royal
mark. He sent them by messengers on
horseback. They rode fast horses that
were raised just for the king.
11 The Jews in every city could now
gather together and fight for their lives.
The king's order gave them that right.
But suppose soldiers from any nation or
territory attacked them, their women or
children. Then the Jews could destroy,
kill and wipe out those soldiers. They
could also take the goods that belonged
to their enemies. 12 A day was appointed
for the Jews to do that in all the king's
territories. It was the 13th day of the 12th
month. That was the month of Adar. 13 A
copy of the order was sent out as law
in every territory. It was announced to
the people of every nation. So the Jews
would be ready on that day. They could
pay back their enemies.
14 The messengers rode on the royal
horses. They raced along. That's what
the king commanded them to do. The
order was also sent out in the fort of
Susa.

Can I be a part of God's work in the world?

Everyone who follows God joins his mission—to spread the good news about Jesus. Just as God used Esther to save Israel, God can use you right where you are to make himself known in the world.

Can you find the following verse?

ESTHER 7:3

The Jews Win the Battle Over Their Enemies

15 Mordecai left the king and went on
his way. Mordecai was wearing royal
clothes when he went. They were blue
and white. He was also wearing a large
gold crown. And he was wearing a purple coat. It was made out of fine linen.
The city of Susa celebrated with great
joy. 16 The Jews were filled with joy and
happiness. They were very glad because
now they were being honored. 17 They
celebrated and enjoyed good food. They
were glad and full of joy. That was true
everywhere the king's order came. It
was true in every territory and every
city. Many people from other nations
announced that they had become Jews.
That's because they were so afraid of
the Jews.

9 The king's order had to be carried
out on the 13th day of the 12th
month. That was the month of Adar.
On that day the enemies of the Jews had
hoped to win the battle over them. But
now everything had changed. The Jews
had gained the advantage over those
who hated them. 2 The Jews gathered
together in their cities. They gathered
in all the territories King Xerxes ruled
over. They came together to attack those
who were trying to destroy them. No
one could stand up against them. The
people from all the other nations were
afraid of them. 3 All the nobles in the
territories helped the Jews. So did the
royal officials, the governors and
the king's officers. That's because they
were so afraid of Mordecai. 4 He was well
known in the palace. His fame spread
all through the territories. So he became
more and more important.

5 The Jews struck down with swords
all their enemies. They killed them and
destroyed them. They did what they
pleased to those who hated them. 6 The
Jews killed 500 men. They destroyed
them in the fort of Susa. 7 They also
killed Parshandatha, Dalphon, Aspatha,
8 Poratha, Adalia, Aridatha, 9 Parmash-
ta, Arisai, Aridai and Vaizatha. 10 They
were the ten sons of Haman. He was
the son of Hammedatha. Haman had
been the enemy of the Jews. They didn't
take anything that belonged to their
enemies.

11 A report was brought to the king
that same day. He was told how many
men had been killed in the fort of Susa.
12 He said to Queen Esther, "The Jews
have killed 500 men. They destroyed
them in the fort of Susa. They also killed
the ten sons of Haman there. What have
they done in the rest of my territories?
Now what do you want? I'll give it to
you. What do you want me to do for
you? I'll do that too."

13 "If it pleases you," Esther answered,
"let the Jews in Susa carry out today's
order tomorrow also. Stick poles
through the dead bodies of Haman's
ten sons. Set them up where everyone
can see them."

14 So the king commanded that it be
done. An order was sent out in Susa.
And the king's men did to the bodies of
Haman's sons everything they were told
to do. 15 The Jews in Susa came together
on the 14th day of the month of Adar.
They put 300 men to death in Susa. But
they didn't take anything that belonged
to those men.

16 During that time, the rest of the
Jews also gathered together. They lived
in the king's territories. They came together to fight for their lives. They didn't
want their enemies to bother them
anymore. They wanted to get some
peace and rest. So they killed 75,000
of their enemies. But they didn't take
anything that belonged to them. 17 It
happened on the 13th of Adar. On the
14th day they rested. They made it a
day to celebrate with great joy. And
they enjoyed good food.

18 But the Jews in Susa had gathered
together on the 13th and 14th. Then on
the 15th they rested. They made it a day
to celebrate with great joy. And they
enjoyed good food.

19 That's why Jews who live out in the
villages celebrate on the 14th of Adar.
They celebrate that day with great joy.
And they enjoy good food. They also
give presents to each other on that day.

Purim Is Celebrated

20 Mordecai wrote down these events.
He sent letters to all the Jews all through
the territories of King Xerxes. It didn't
matter whether the Jews lived nearby
or far away. 21 Mordecai told them to
celebrate the 14th and 15th days of the

month of Adar. He wanted them to do
it every year. 22 Mordecai told the Jews
to celebrate the time when they got rest
from their enemies. That was the month
when their sadness was turned into
joy. It was when their weeping turned
into a day for celebrating. He wrote
the letters to celebrate those days as
times of joy. He wanted the people to
enjoy good food. He told them to give
presents of food to one another. He also
wanted them to give gifts to people who
were poor.
23 So the Jews agreed to continue the
celebrating they had started. They kept
doing what Mordecai had written to
them. 24 Haman was the son of Hammedatha, the Agagite. He had been the
enemy of all the Jews. He had planned
to destroy them. He had cast the lot to
destroy them completely. The lot was
called Pur. 25 But the king had found
out about Haman's evil plan. So the
king had sent out written orders. He
had ordered that Haman's evil plan
against the Jews should happen to him
instead. The king also commanded that
poles be stuck through the dead bodies of Haman and his sons. Then they
should be set up where everyone could
see them. 26 The days the Jews were
celebrating were called Purim. Purim
comes from the word Pur. Pur means
Lot. Now the Jews celebrate these two
days every year. They do it because of
everything that was written in Mordecai's letter. They also do it because of
what they had seen and what had happened to them. 27 So they established
it as a regular practice. They decided
they would always observe these two
days of the year. They would celebrate
in the required way. And they would
celebrate at the appointed time. They
and their children after them would
always observe these days. And so
would all who join them. 28 The days
should be remembered and celebrated.
They should be remembered by every
family for all time to come. They should
be celebrated in every territory and in
every city. The Jews should never stop
celebrating the days of Purim. Their
children after them should always remember these days.
29 So Queen Esther, the daughter
of Abihail, wrote a second letter. She
wrote it together with Mordecai the Jew.
They wanted to give their full authority to this second letter about Purim.
30 Mordecai sent letters to all the Jews
in the 127 territories of the kingdom
of Xerxes. The letters had messages of
kindness and hope in them. 31 The letters
established the days of Purim at their
appointed times. They spoke about
what Mordecai the Jew and Queen
Esther had ordered the people to do.
Everything should be done in keeping
with the directions the Jews had set up
for themselves and their children after
them. The directions applied to their
times of fasting and sadness. 32 Esther's
order established the rules about Purim.
It was written down in the records.

The Greatness of Mordecai

10 King Xerxes required people all
through his kingdom to bring
gifts. King Xerxes required gifts from its
farthest shores. 2 All the king's powerful
and mighty acts are written down. That
includes the whole story of how important Mordecai was. The king had given
him a position of great honor. All these
things are written in the official records
of the kings of Media and Persia. 3 The
position of Mordecai the Jew was second
only to the position of King Xerxes. Mordecai was the most important Jew. All
the other Jews had the highest respect
for him. That's because he worked for
the good of his people. And he spoke up
for the benefit of all the Jews.

The books of Wisdom and Poetry show us how we can live according to God's design. They teach us to see how the world God created points us to worship him. Since God is perfectly wise and because he designed the world, these books guide us in knowing how to think and act in ways that are pleasing to God.

The wisdom books of the Bible teach us how to live following God's ways, such as how to have relationships that honor God, how to be a hard worker, how to use wisely the talents and possessions God has entrusted to us, and much more. The wisdom books are full of practical advice that is still helpful today. Poetry is writing that expresses someone's heart and the heart of God. These beautiful poems can be used as prayers or songs to worship God.

As you read the books of Wisdom and Poetry, you'll find the writer expressing emotions such as sadness, pain, gratitude, joy, hope, and more! Like the writers of these books, we can talk to God about our real thoughts and feelings.

We know we're reading Wisdom and Poetry when there is practical advice or honest expressions of thoughts and feelings. These books remind us to delight in God's creativity and beauty as we learn to follow him.

Wisdom & Poetry

JOB
PSALMS
PROVERBS
ECCLESIASTES
SONG OF SONGS

JOB

Author: We don't know.

Job was a man who loved God and was loved by God. However, God allowed Job to experience great suffering. Job lost everything: His children died, his belongings were stolen, and his body became sick. Job's friends thought his suffering was a result of something he had done. And there were times that Job looked toward heaven and asked, "Why, God? Why have you let me suffer so much?" But God kindly and powerfully reminded Job of something very important: God alone is God, and even when our circumstances are not good, he is still good. Bad things will happen in this world, and God doesn't always stop the suffering. Still, we can trust God's wisdom, justice, and goodness. He promises to stay beside us, giving us the strength to endure when life is very, very hard.

Wisdom & Poetry

Job's innocent suffering points us forward to the ultimate innocent sufferer—Jesus. The Savior was going to give up everything to pay the penalty for our sin. When Jesus' circumstances looked the worst, God promised to do something amazing—he was going to use the darkest day to show his ultimate goodness to the entire world.

The Story Begins

1 There was a man who lived in the land of Uz. His name was Job. He was honest. He did what was right. He had respect for God and avoided evil. 2 Job had seven sons and three daughters. 3 He owned 7,000 sheep and 3,000 camels. He owned 500 pairs of oxen and 500 donkeys. He also had a large number of servants. He was the most important man among all the people in the east.

4 His sons used to give feasts in their homes on their birthdays. They would invite their three sisters to eat and drink with them. 5 The time for enjoying good food would end. Then Job would make plans for his children to be made pure and "clean." He would sacrifice a burnt offering for each of them. He would do it early in the morning. He would think, "Perhaps my children have sinned. Maybe they have spoken evil things against God in their hearts." That's what Job always did for his children when he felt they had sinned.

6 One day angels came to the LORD. Satan also came with them. 7 The LORD said to Satan, "Where have you come from?"

Satan answered, "From traveling all around the earth. I've been going from one end of it to the other."

8 Then the LORD said to Satan, "Have you thought about my servant Job? There isn't anyone on earth like him. He is honest. He does what is right. He has respect for God and avoids evil."

9 "You always give Job everything he needs," Satan replied. "That's why he has respect for you. 10 Haven't you guarded him and his family? Haven't you taken care of everything he has? You have blessed everything he does. His flocks and herds are spread all through the land. 11 But now reach out your hand and strike down everything he has. Then I'm sure he will speak evil things against you. In fact, he'll do it right in front of you."

12 The LORD said to Satan, "All right. I am handing everything he has over to you. But do not touch the man himself."

Then Satan left the LORD and went on his way.

13 One day Job's sons and daughters were at their oldest brother's house. They were enjoying good food and drinking wine. 14 During that time a messenger came to Job. He said, "The oxen were plowing. The donkeys were eating grass near them. 15 Then the Sabeans attacked us and carried off the animals. They killed some of the servants with their swords. I'm the only one who has escaped to tell you!"

16 While he was still speaking, a second messenger came. He said, "God sent lightning from the sky. It struck the sheep and killed them. It burned up some of the servants. I'm the only one who has escaped to tell you!"

17 While he was still speaking, a third messenger came. He said, "The Chaldeans separated themselves into three groups. They attacked your camels and carried them off. They killed the rest of the servants with their swords. I'm the only one who has escaped to tell you!"

18 While he was still speaking, a fourth messenger came. He said, "Your sons and daughters were at their oldest brother's house. They were enjoying good food and drinking wine. 19 Suddenly a strong wind blew in from the desert. It struck the four corners of the house. The house fell down on your children. Now all of them are dead. I'm the only one who has escaped to tell you!"

20 After Job heard all these reports, he got up and tore his robe. He shaved his head. Then he fell to the ground and worshiped the LORD. 21 He said,

"I was born naked.
  And I'll leave here naked.
The LORD has given, and the LORD
    has taken away.
  May the name of the LORD be
    praised."

22 In spite of everything, Job didn't sin by blaming God for doing anything wrong.

2 On another day angels came to the LORD. Satan also came to him along with them. 2 The LORD said to Satan, "Where have you come from?"

Satan answered, "From traveling all around the earth. I've been going from one end of it to the other."

3 Then the LORD said to Satan, "Have you thought about my servant Job? There isn't anyone on earth like him. He is honest. He does what is right. He has respect for God and avoids evil. You tried

in Job?

God is the Sovereign Lord. Even when we are sad or hurt, we can trust him to have our best in mind.

to turn me against him. You wanted me
to destroy him without any reason. But
he still continues to be faithful."
4 Satan replied, "A man will give
everything he has to save himself. So
Job is willing to give up the lives of his
family to save his own life. 5 But now
reach out your hand and strike his flesh
and bones. Then I'm sure he will speak
evil things against you. In fact, he'll do
it right in front of you."
6 The LORD said to Satan, "All right. I
am handing him over to you. But you
must spare his life."
7 Then Satan left the LORD and went
on his way. He sent painful sores on
Job. They covered him from the bottom
of his feet to the top of his head. 8 He
got part of a broken pot. He used it to
scrape his skin. He did it while he was
sitting in ashes.
9 His wife said to him, "Are you still
continuing to be faithful to the LORD?
Speak evil things against him and die!"
10 Job replied, "You are talking like a
foolish woman. We accept good things
from God. So we should also accept
trouble when he sends it."
In spite of everything, Job didn't say
anything that was sinful.

11 Job had three friends named Eliphaz
the Temanite, Bildad the Shuhite, and
Zophar the Naamathite. They heard
about all the troubles that had come
to Job. So they started out from their
homes. They had agreed to meet together. They wanted to go and show their
concern for Job. They wanted to comfort
him. 12 When they got closer to where he
lived, they could see him. But they could
hardly recognize him. They began to
weep out loud. They tore their robes and
sprinkled dust on their heads. 13 Then
they sat down on the ground with him
for seven days and seven nights. No one
said a word to him. That's because they
saw how much he was suffering.

Job Wishes He Had Never Been Born

3 After a while, Job opened his mouth
to speak. He cursed the day he had
been born. 2 He said,

3 "May the day I was born be wiped
out.
May the night be wiped away
when people said, 'A boy is
born!'
4 May that day turn into darkness.
May God in heaven not care
about it.
May no light shine on it.
5 May gloom and total darkness take
it back.
May a cloud settle over it.
May blackness cover it up.
6 May deep darkness take over the
night I was born.
May it not be included among
the days of the year.
May it never appear in any of the
months.
7 May no children ever have been
born on that night.
May no shout of joy be heard in it.
8 May people say evil things about
that day.
May people ready to wake the
sea monster Leviathan say evil
things about that day.
9 May its morning stars become dark.
May it lose all hope of ever
seeing daylight.
May it not see the first light of
the morning sun.
10 It didn't keep my mother from
letting me be born.
It didn't keep my eyes from
seeing trouble.

11 "Why didn't I die when I was born?
Why didn't I die as I came out of
my mother's body?
12 Why was I placed on her knees?
Why did her breasts give me
milk?

13 If all of that hadn't happened,
I would be lying down in peace.
I'd be asleep and at rest in the grave.
14 I'd be with the earth's kings and rulers.
They had built for themselves places that are now destroyed.
15 I'd be with princes who used to have gold.
They had filled their houses with silver.
16 Why wasn't I buried like a baby who was born dead?
Why wasn't I buried like a child who never saw the light of day?
17 In the grave, sinful people don't cause trouble anymore.
And there tired people find rest.
18 Prisoners also enjoy peace there.
They don't hear a slave driver shouting at them anymore.
19 The least important and most important people are there.
And there the slaves are set free from their owners.

20 "Why should those who suffer ever be born?
Why should life be given to those whose spirits are bitter?
21 Why is life given to those who long for death that doesn't come?
Why is it given to those who would rather search for death than for hidden treasure?
22 Why is life given to those who are actually happy and glad when they reach the grave?
23 Why is life given to a man like me?
God hasn't told me what will happen to me.
He has surrounded me with nothing but trouble.
24 Sighs have become my food every day.
Groans pour out of me like water.
25 What I was afraid of has come on me.
What I worried about has happened to me.
26 I don't have any peace and quiet.
I can't find any rest. All I have is trouble."

The First Speech of Eliphaz

4 Then Eliphaz the Temanite replied,

2 "Job, suppose someone tries to talk to you.
Will that make you uneasy?
I can't keep from speaking up.
3 Look, you taught many people.
You made weak hands strong.
4 Your words helped those who had fallen down.
You made shaky knees strong.
5 Now trouble comes to you. And you are unhappy about it.
It strikes you down. And you are afraid.
6 Shouldn't you worship God and trust in him?
Shouldn't your honest life give you hope?

7 "Here's something to think about.
Have people who aren't guilty ever been wiped out?
Have honest people ever been completely destroyed?
8 Here's what I've observed.
People gather a crop from what they plant.
If they plant evil and trouble, that's what they will harvest.
9 The breath of God destroys them.
The blast of his anger wipes them out.
10 Powerful lions might roar and growl.
But their teeth are broken.
11 Lions die because they don't have any food.
Then their cubs are scattered.

12 "A message came to me in secret.
It was as quiet as a whisper.
13 I had a scary dream one night.
I was sound asleep.
14 Fear and trembling seized me.
That made every bone in my body shake.
15 A spirit glided past my face.
The hair on my body stood on end.
16 Then the spirit stopped.
But I couldn't tell what it was.
Something stood there in front of me.
I heard a soft voice.
17 It said, 'Can a human being be more right than God?
Can even a strong man be more pure than the God who made him?

18 God doesn't trust those who serve him.
He even brings charges against his angels.
19 So he'll certainly find fault with human beings.
After all, they are made out of dust.
They can be crushed more easily than a moth.
20 Between sunrise and sunset they are broken to pieces.
Nobody even notices. They disappear forever.
21 Like a tent that falls down, they get weak.
They die because they didn't follow God's wisdom.' "

5 Eliphaz continued,

"Call out if you want to, Job.
But who will answer you?
Which one of the holy angels will you turn to?
2 Anger kills foolish people.
Jealousy destroys those who are childish.
3 I saw that foolish people were having success.
But suddenly harm came to their homes.
4 Their children aren't safe at all.
They lose their case in court.
No one speaks up for them.
5 Hungry people eat up the crops of the foolish.
They even take the food that grows among thorns.
Thirsty people long for the wealth of the foolish.
6 Hard times don't just grow out of the soil.
Trouble doesn't jump out of the ground.
7 People are born to have trouble.
And that's just as sure as sparks fly up.

8 "If I were you, I'd make my appeal to God.
I'd bring my case to be judged by him.
9 He does wonderful things that can't be understood.
He does miracles that can't even be counted.

[10] He sends rain on the earth.
He sends water on the countryside.
[11] He lifts up people who are lowly in spirit.
He lifts up those who are sad.
He keeps them safe.
[12] He stops the evil plans of those who are clever.
The work of their hands doesn't succeed.
[13] Some people think they are so wise.
But God catches them in their own tricks.
He sweeps away the evil plans of sinful people.
[14] Darkness covers them in the daytime.
At noon they feel their way around as if it were night.
[15] God saves needy people from the cutting words of their enemies.
He saves them from their power.
[16] So poor people have hope.
And God shuts the mouths of those who don't treat others fairly.

[17] "Blessed is the person God corrects.
So don't hate the Mighty One's training.
[18] He wounds. But he also bandages up those he wounds.
He harms. But his hands also heal those he harms.
[19] From six troubles he will save you.
Even if you are in trouble seven times, no harm will come to you.
[20] When there isn't enough food, God will keep you from dying.
When you go into battle, he won't let a sword strike you down.
[21] He will keep you safe from words that can hurt you.
You won't need to be afraid when everything is being destroyed.
[22] You will laugh when things are being destroyed.
You will enjoy life even when there isn't enough food.
You won't be afraid of wild animals.
[23] You will make a covenant with the stones in the fields.
They won't keep your crops from growing.
Even wild animals will be at peace with you.

pointing us to JESUS: Job

Job was a man who had everything he wanted. He had a wife he loved and children who brought him joy. He was also very wealthy, with lots of animals and a huge household. He followed and served God faithfully, being careful to keep God's commands. Job was a good man living a good life.

But one day Job lost everything. His flocks and herds were stolen, his children were killed, and his house fell down. Almost everything Job loved was gone in the blink of an eye.

Job's wife said, "Speak evil things against [God] and die!" (Job 2:9). Job's friends told him that he must have done something wrong for these bad things to be happening to him. But Job didn't take the advice of his wife or his friends. Instead, he looked to God, declaring that everything belongs to God and that God is trustworthy even when things don't make sense.

Job's story points us to Jesus, the Son of God and promised Savior. Jesus was the most innocent person and yet suffered many things. Though he never once sinned, he died on a cross for our sins and rose again so that we could be saved through him.

[24]You will know that the tent you live
in is secure.
You will check out your property.
You will see that nothing is
missing.
[25]You can be sure you will have a lot
of children.
They will be as many as the
blades of grass on the earth.
[26]You will go down to the grave
while you are still very strong.
You will be like a crop that is
gathered at the right time.

[27]"We have carefully studied all these
things.
And they are true.
So pay attention to them.
Apply them to yourself."

Job's Reply

6 Job replied,

[2]"I wish my great pain could be
weighed!
I wish all my suffering could be
weighed on scales!
[3]I'm sure it would weigh more than the
grains of sand on the seashore.
No wonder I've been so quick to
speak!
[4]The Mighty One has shot me with
his arrows.
I have to drink their poison.
God's terrors are aimed at me.
[5]Does a wild donkey cry out when it
has enough grass?
Does an ox call out when it has
plenty of food?
[6]Is food that doesn't have any taste
eaten without salt?
Is there any flavor in the sap of a
mallow plant?
[7]I refuse to touch that kind of food.
It makes me sick.

[8]"I wish I could have what I'm
asking for!
I wish God would give me what
I'm hoping for!
[9]I wish he would crush me!
I wish he would just cut off my life!
[10]Then I'd still have one thing to
comfort me.
It would be that I haven't said no
to the Holy One's commands.
That would give me joy in spite
of my pain that never ends.

[11]"I'm so weak that I no longer have
any hope.
Things have gotten so bad that I
can't wait for help anymore.
[12]Am I as strong as stone?
Is my body made out of bronze?
[13]I don't have the power to help
myself.
All hope of success has been
taken away from me.

[14]"A person shouldn't stop being kind
to a friend.
Anyone who does that stops
showing respect for the Mighty
One.
[15]But my friends have stopped being
kind to me.
They are like streams that only
flow for part of the year.
They are like rivers that flow over
their banks
[16]when the ice begins to break up.
The streams rise when the snow
starts to melt.
[17]But they stop flowing when the dry
season comes.
They disappear from their
stream beds when the weather
warms up.
[18]Groups of traders turn away from
their usual paths.
They go off into the dry and
empty land.
And they die there.
[19]Traders from Tema look for water.
Traveling merchants from Sheba
also hope to find it.
[20]They become troubled because they
had expected to find some.
But when they arrive at the
stream beds,
they don't find any water at all.
[21]And now, my friends, you haven't
helped me either.
You see the horrible condition
I'm in.
And that makes you afraid.
[22]I've never said, 'Give me something
to help me.
Use your wealth to set me free.
[23]Save me from the power of my
enemy.
Rescue me from the power of
mean people.'

[24]"Teach me. Then I'll be quiet.
Show me what I've done wrong.

25 Honest words are so painful!
But your reasoning doesn't prove anything.
26 Are you trying to correct what I'm saying?
Are you treating my hopeless words like nothing but wind?
27 You would even cast lots for those whose fathers have died.
You would even trade away your closest friend.

28 "But now please look at me.
Would I tell you a lie right here in front of you?
29 Stop what you are saying. Don't be so unfair.
Think it over again.
You are trying to take my honesty away from me.
30 Has my mouth spoken anything that is evil?
Do my lips say things that are hateful?"

7 Job continued,

"Don't all human beings have to work hard on this earth?
Aren't their days like the days of hired workers?
2 I've been like a slave
who longs for the evening shadows to come.
I've been like a hired worker
who is waiting to be paid.
3 I've been given several months that were useless to me.
My nights have been filled with suffering.
4 When I lie down I think,
'How long will it be before I can get up?'
The night drags on.
I toss and turn until sunrise.
5 My body is covered with worms and sores.
My skin is broken. It has boils all over it.

6 "My days pass by faster than a weaver can work.
They come to an end. I don't have any hope.
7 God, remember that my life is only a breath.
I'll never be happy again.
8 The eyes that see me now won't see me anymore.
You will look for me. But I'll be gone.
9 When a cloud disappears, it's gone forever.
And anyone who goes down to the grave never returns.
10 He never comes home again.
Even his own family doesn't remember him.

11 "So I won't keep quiet.
When I'm suffering greatly, I'll speak out.
When my spirit is bitter, I'll tell you how unhappy I am.
12 Am I the ocean? Am I the sea monster?
If I'm not, why do you guard me so closely?
13 Sometimes I think my bed will comfort me.
I think my couch will keep me from being unhappy.
14 But even then you send me dreams that frighten me.
You send me visions that terrify me.
15 So I would rather choke to death.
That would be better than living in this body of mine.
16 I hate my life. I don't want to live forever.
Leave me alone. My days don't mean anything to me.

17 "What are human beings that you think so much of them?
What are they that you pay so much attention to them?
18 You check up on them every morning.
You test them every moment.
19 Won't you ever look away from me?
Won't you leave me alone even for one second?
20 If I've really sinned, tell me what I've done to you.
You see everything we do.
Why do you shoot your arrows at me?
Have I become a problem to you?
21 Why don't you forgive the wrong things I've done?
Why don't you forgive me for my sins?
I'll soon lie down in the dust of my grave.
You will search for me. But I'll be gone."

The First Speech of Bildad

8 Then Bildad the Shuhite replied,

2 "Job, how long will you talk like that?
Your words don't have any meaning.
3 Does God ever treat people unfairly?
Does the Mighty One make what is wrong
appear to be right?
4 Your children sinned against him.
So he punished them for their sin.
5 But seek God with all your heart.
Make your appeal to the Mighty One.
6 Be pure and honest.
And he will rise up and help you now.
He'll give you everything you had before.
7 In the past, things went well with you.
But in days to come, things will get even better.

8 "Find out what our parents taught.
Discover what those who lived before them learned.
9 After all, we were born only yesterday.
So we don't know anything.
Our days on this earth are like a shadow that disappears.
10 Won't your people of long ago teach you and tell you?
Won't the things they said help you understand?
11 Can grass grow tall where there isn't any swamp?
Can plants grow well where there isn't any water?
12 While they are still growing and haven't been cut,
they dry up faster than grass does.
13 The same thing happens to everyone who forgets God.
The hope of ungodly people dies out.
14 What they trust in is very weak.
What they depend on is like a spider's web.
15 They lean on it, but it falls apart.
They hold on to it, but it gives way.
16 They are like a plant in the sunshine
that receives plenty of water.
It spreads its new growth all over the garden.
17 It wraps its roots around a pile of rocks.
It tries to find places to grow among the stones.
18 But when the plant is pulled up from its spot,
that place says, 'I never saw you.'
19 The life of that plant is sure to dry up.
But from the same soil other plants will grow.

20 "I'm sure God doesn't turn his back on anyone who is honest.
And he doesn't help those who do what is evil.
21 He will fill your mouth with laughter.
Shouts of joy will come from your lips.
22 Your enemies will put on shame as if it were clothes.
The tents of sinful people will be gone."

Job's Reply

9 Job replied,

2 "I'm sure that what you have said is true.
But how can human beings prove to God they are not guilty?
3 They might wish to argue with him.
But they couldn't answer him even once in a thousand times.
4 His wisdom is deep. His power is great.
No one opposes him and comes away unharmed.
5 He moves mountains, and they don't even know it.
When he is angry, he turns them upside down.
6 He shakes the earth loose from its place.
He makes its pillars tremble.
7 When he tells the sun not to shine, it doesn't.
He turns off the light of the stars.
8 He's the only one who can spread out the heavens.
He alone can walk on the waves of the ocean.

9 He made the Big Dipper and Orion.
He created the Pleiades and the southern stars.
10 He does wonderful things that can't be understood.
He does miracles that can't even be counted.
11 When he passes by me, I can't see him.
When he goes past me, I can't recognize him.
12 If he takes something, who can stop him?
Who would dare to ask him, 'What are you doing?'
13 God doesn't hold back his anger.
Even the helpers of the sea monster Rahab
bowed in fear at his feet.

14 "So how can I disagree with God?
How can I possibly argue with him?
15 Even if I hadn't done anything wrong,
I couldn't answer him.
I could only beg my Judge to have mercy on me.
16 Suppose I called out to him and he answered.
I don't believe he'd listen to me.
17 He would send a storm to crush me.
He'd increase my wounds without any reason.
18 He wouldn't let me catch my breath.
He'd make my life very bitter.
19 If it's a matter of strength, he is mighty!
And if it's a matter of being fair,
who would dare to bring charges against him?
20 Even if I hadn't sinned, what I said would prove me guilty.
Even if I were honest, my words would show that I'm wrong.

21 "Even though I'm honest,
I'm not concerned about myself.
I hate my own life.
22 It all amounts to the same thing.
That's why I say,
'God destroys honest people and sinful people alike.'
23 Suppose a plague brings sudden death.
Then he laughs when those who haven't sinned lose hope.
24 Suppose a nation falls into the power of sinful people.
Then God makes its judges blind to the truth.
If he isn't the one doing it, who is?

25 "God, my days race by like a runner.
They fly away without seeing any joy.
26 They speed along like papyrus boats.
They are like eagles swooping down on their food.
27 Suppose I say, 'I'll forget about all my problems.
I'll change my frown into a smile.'
28 Then I'd still be afraid I'd go on suffering.
That's because I know you would say
I had done something wrong.
29 In fact, you have already said I'm guilty.
So why should I struggle without any reason?
30 Suppose I clean myself with soap.
Suppose I wash my hands with cleanser.
31 Even then you would throw me into a muddy pit.
And even my clothes would hate me.

32 "God isn't a mere human being like me. I can't answer him.
We can't take each other to court.
33 I wish someone would settle matters between us.
I wish someone would bring us together.
34 I wish someone would keep God from punishing me.
Then his terror wouldn't frighten me anymore.
35 I would speak up without being afraid of him.
But as things stand now, I can't do that.

10 "I'm sick of living.
So I'll talk openly about my problems.
I'll speak out because my spirit is bitter.
2 I say to God, 'Don't find me guilty.
Instead, tell me what charges you are bringing against me.

3 Does it make you happy when you crush me?
Does it please you to turn your back on what you have made?
While you do those things,
you smile on the plans of sinful people!
4 You don't have human eyes.
You don't see as people see.
5 Your days aren't like the days of a mere human being.
Your years aren't even like the years of a strong man.
6 So you search for my mistakes.
You look for my sin.
7 You already know I'm not guilty.
No one can save me from your power.

8 " 'Your hands shaped me and made me.
So are you going to destroy me now?
9 Remember, you molded me like clay.
So are you going to turn me back into dust?
10 Didn't you pour me out like milk?
Didn't you form me like cheese?
11 Didn't you put skin and flesh on me?
Didn't you sew me together with bones and muscles?
12 You gave me life. You were kind to me.
You took good care of me. You watched over me.

13 " 'But here's what you hid in your heart.
Here's what you had on your mind.
14 If I sinned, you would be watching me.
You wouldn't let me go without punishing me.
15 If I were guilty, how terrible that would be for me!
Even if I haven't sinned,
I can't be proud of what I've done.
That's because I'm so full of shame.
I'm drowning in my suffering.
16 If I become proud, you hunt me down like a lion.
You show your mighty power against me.
17 You bring new witnesses against me.
You become more and more angry with me.
You use your power against me again and again.

18 " 'Why did you bring me out of my mother's body?
I wish I had died before anyone saw me.
19 I wish I'd never been born!
I wish I'd been carried straight from my mother's body to the grave!
20 Aren't my few days almost over?
Leave me so I can have a moment of joy.
21 Turn away before I go to the place I can't return from.
It's the land of gloom and total darkness.
22 It's the land of darkest night
and total darkness and disorder.
There even the light is like darkness.' "

The First Speech of Zophar

11 Then Zophar the Naamathite replied,

2 "Don't all your words require an answer?
I'm sure that what you are saying can't be right.
3 Your useless talk won't keep us quiet.
Someone has to correct you when you make fun of truth.
4 You say to God, 'My beliefs are perfect.
I'm pure in your sight.'
5 I wish God would speak.
I wish he'd answer you.
6 I wish he'd show you the secrets of wisdom.
After all, true wisdom has two sides.
Here's what I want you to know.
God has forgotten some of your sins.

7 "Do you know how deep the mysteries of God are?
Can you discover the limits of the Mighty One's knowledge?
8 They are higher than the heavens above.
What can you do?
They are deeper than the deepest parts of the earth below.
What can you know?
9 They are longer than the earth.
They are wider than the ocean.

10 "Suppose God comes along and
puts you in prison.
Suppose he takes you to court.
Then who can oppose him?
11 He certainly knows when people
tell lies.
When he sees evil, he pays
careful attention to it.
12 A wild donkey's colt can't be born a
human being.
And it's just as impossible that
a person without sense can
become wise.
13 "So commit yourself to God
completely.
Reach out your hands to him for
help.
14 Get rid of all the sin you have.
Don't let anything that is evil
stay in your tent.
15 Then, free of those things, you can
face others.
You can stand firm without being
afraid.
16 You can be sure you will forget
your troubles.
They will be like water that has
flowed on by.
17 Life will be brighter than the sun at
noon.
And darkness will become like
morning.
18 You will be secure, because there is
hope.
You will look around you and
find a safe place to rest.
19 You will lie down, and no one will
make you afraid.
Many people will want you to
help them.
20 But sinful people won't find what
they are looking for.
They won't be able to escape.
All they can hope for is to die."

Job's Reply

12 Job replied,

2 "You people think you are the only
ones who matter!
You are sure that wisdom will die
with you!
3 But I have a brain, just like you.
I'm as clever as you are.
In fact, everyone knows as much
as you do.
4 "My friends laugh at me all the
time,
even though I called out to God
and he answered.
My friends laugh at me,
even though I'm honest and right.
5 People who have an easy life
look down on those who have
problems.
They think trouble comes only to
those whose feet are slipping.
6 Why doesn't anyone bother the
tents of robbers?
Why do those who make God
angry remain secure?
They are in God's hands!
7 "But ask the animals what God
does.
They will teach you.
Or ask the birds in the sky.
They will tell you.
8 Or speak to the earth. It will teach
you.
Or let the fish in the ocean
educate you.
9 Are there any of these creatures
that don't know
what the powerful hand of the
LORD has done?
10 He holds the life of every creature
in his hand.
He controls the breath of every
human being.
11 Our tongues tell us what tastes
good and what doesn't.
And our ears tell us what's true
and what isn't.
12 Old people are wise.
Those who live a long time have
understanding.
13 "Wisdom and power belong to God.
Advice and understanding also
belong to him.
14 What he tears down can't be
rebuilt.
The people he puts in prison can't
be set free.
15 If he holds back the water,
everything dries up.
If he lets the water loose, it floods
the land.
16 Strength and understanding
belong to him.
Those who tell lies and those who
believe them also belong to
him.

17 He removes the wisdom of rulers
and leads them away.
He makes judges look foolish.
18 He sets people free from the chains
that kings put on them.
Then he dresses the kings in the
clothes of slaves.
19 He removes the authority of priests
and leads them away.
He removes from their positions
officials who have been in control
for a long time.
20 He shuts the mouths of trusted
advisers.
He takes away the
understanding of elders.
21 He looks down on proud leaders.
He takes away the strength of
those who are mighty.
22 He tells people the secrets of
darkness.
He brings total darkness out into
the light.
23 He makes nations great, and then
he destroys them.
He makes nations grow, and then
he scatters them.
24 He takes away the understanding
of the leaders of the earth.
He makes them wander in a
desert where no one lives.
25 Without any light, they feel their
way along in darkness.
God makes them unsteady like
those who get drunk.

13 "My eyes have seen everything
God has done.
My ears have heard it and
understood it.
2 What you know, I also know.
I'm as clever as you are.
3 In fact, I long to speak to the
Mighty One.
I want to argue my case with God.
4 But you spread lies about me and
take away my good name.
If you are trying to heal me,
you aren't very good doctors!
5 I wish you would keep your mouths
shut!
Then people would think you
were wise.
6 Listen to my case.
Listen as I make my appeal.
7 Will you say evil things in order to
help God?
Will you tell lies for him?
8 Do you want to be on God's side?
Will you argue his case for him?
9 Would it turn out well if he looked
you over carefully?
Could you fool him as you might
fool human beings?
10 He would certainly hold you
responsible
if you took his side in secret.
11 Wouldn't his glory terrify you?
Wouldn't the fear of him fall on
you?
12 Your sayings are as useless as ashes.
The answers you give are as
weak as clay.

13 "So be quiet and let me speak.
Then I won't care what happens
to me.
14 Why do I put myself in danger?
Why do I take my life in my
hands?
15 Even if God kills me, I'll still put my
hope in him.
I'll argue my case in front of him.
16 No matter how things turn out,
I'm sure I'll still be saved.
After all, no ungodly person
would dare to come into his court.
17 Listen carefully to what I'm saying.
Pay close attention to my words.
18 I've prepared my case.
And I know I'll be proved right.
19 Can others bring charges
against me?
If they can, I'll keep quiet and
die.

20 "God, I won't hide from you.
Here are the only two things I
want.
21 Stop treating me this way.
And stop making me so afraid.
22 Then send for me, and I'll answer.
Or let me speak, and you reply.
23 How many things have I done
wrong?
How many sins have I committed?
Show me my crime. Show me my
sin.
24 Why do you turn your face away
from me?
Why do you think of me as your
enemy?
25 I'm already like a leaf that is blown
by the wind.
Are you going to terrify me even
more?

I'm already like dry straw.
Are you going to keep on chasing me?
26 You write down bitter things against me.
You make me suffer for the sins I committed when I was young.
27 You put my feet in chains.
You watch every step I take.
You do it by putting marks on the bottom of my feet.

28 "People waste away like something that is rotten.
They are like clothes that are eaten by moths.

14 "Human beings have only a few days to live.
Their lives are full of trouble.
2 They grow like flowers, and then they dry up.
They are like shadows that quickly disappear.

3 "God, do you even notice them?
Will you let them appear in your court?
4 Who can bring what is pure from something that isn't pure?
No one!
5 You decide how long anyone will live.
You have established the number of his months.
You have set a limit to the number of his days.
6 So look away from him. Leave him alone.
Let him put in his time like a hired worker.

7 "At least there is hope for a tree.
If it's cut down, it will begin to grow again.
New branches will appear on it.
8 Its roots may grow old in the ground.
Its stump may die in the soil.
9 But when it smells water, it will begin to grow.
It will send out new growth like a plant.
10 No man is like that. When he dies, he is buried in a grave.
He takes his last breath. Then he is gone.
11 Water dries up from lakes.
Riverbeds become empty and dry.
12 In the same way, people lie down and never get up.
People won't wake or rise from their sleep
until the heavens are gone.

13 "I wish you would hide me in a grave!
I wish you would cover me up until your anger passes by!
I wish you would set the time for me to spend in the grave
and then bring me back up!
14 If someone dies, will they live again?
All the days of my hard work
I will wait for the time when you give me new life.
15 You will call out to me, and I will answer you.
You will long for the person your hands have made.
16 Then you will count every step I take.
But you won't keep track of my sin.
17 The wrong things I've done will be sealed up in a bag.
You will wipe out my sins by forgiving them.

18 "A mountain wears away and crumbles.
A rock is moved from its place.
19 Water wears away stones.
Storms wash away soil.
In the same way, you destroy a person's hope.
20 You overpower them completely, and then they're gone.
You change the way they look and send them to their graves.
21 If their children are honored, they don't even know it.
If their children are dishonored, they don't even see it.
22 All they feel is the pain of their own bodies.
They are full of sadness only for themselves."

The Second Speech of Eliphaz

15 Then Eliphaz the Temanite replied,

2 "Job, would a wise person answer with a lot of meaningless talk?
Would they fill their stomach with the hot east wind?

[3] Would they argue with useless
words?
Would they give worthless
speeches?
[4] But you even cause others to lose
their respect for God.
You make it hard for them to be
faithful to him.
[5] Your sin makes you say evil things.
You talk like people who twist
the truth.
[6] Your own mouth judges you, not
mine.
Your own lips witness against
you.

[7] "Are you the first man who was
ever born?
Were you created before the
hills?
[8] Do you listen in when God speaks
with his angels?
Do you think you are the only
wise person?
[9] What do you know that we don't
know?
What understanding do you
have that we don't have?
[10] People who are old and gray are on
our side.
And they are even older than
your parents!
[11] Aren't God's words of comfort
enough for you?
He speaks them to you gently.
[12] Why have you let your wild ideas
carry you away?
Why do your eyes flash with
anger?
[13] Why do you get so angry with God?
Why do words like those pour out
of your mouth?

[14] "Can human beings really be pure?
Can those who are born really be
right with God?
[15] God doesn't trust his holy angels.
Even the heavens aren't pure in
his sight.
[16] So he'll certainly find fault with
human beings.
After all, they are evil and sinful.
They drink up evil as if it were
water.

[17] "Listen to me. I'll explain things to
you.
Let me tell you what I've seen.
[18] I'll tell you what those who are wise
have said.
They don't hide anything they've
received
from their people of long ago.
[19] The land was given only to those
people.
Their wisdom didn't come from
outsiders.
And here's what those who are
wise have said.
[20] Sinful people always suffer pain.
Mean people suffer all their lives.
[21] Terrifying sounds fill their ears.
When everything seems to be
going well,
robbers attack them.
[22] They lose all hope of escaping the
darkness of death.
They will certainly be killed by
swords.
[23] Like vultures, they look around for
food.
They know that the day they will
die is near.
[24] Suffering and pain terrify them.
Their troubles overpower them,
like a king ready to attack his
enemies.
[25] They shake their fists at God.
They brag about themselves and
oppose the Mighty One.
[26] They boldly charge against him
with their thick, strong shields.

[27] "Their faces are very fat.
Their stomachs hang out.
[28] They'll live in towns that have been
destroyed.
They'll live in houses where no
one else lives.
The houses will crumble to
pieces.
[29] They won't be rich anymore. Their
wealth won't last.
Their property will no longer
spread out over the land.
[30] They won't escape the darkness of
death.
A flame will dry up everything
they have.
The breath of God will blow them
away.
[31] Don't let them fool themselves
by trusting in what is worthless.
They won't get anything out of it.

[32] Even before they die, they will
dry up.
No matter what they do, it won't
succeed.
[33] They'll be like vines
that are stripped of their unripe
grapes.
They'll be like olive trees
that drop their flowers.
[34] People who are ungodly won't have
any children.
Fire will burn up the tents of
people who accept money
from those who want special
favors.
[35] Instead of having children,
ungodly people create
suffering.
All they produce is evil.
They are full of lies."

Job's Reply

16 Job replied,
[2] "I've heard many of these things
before.
All of you are terrible at
comforting me!
[3] Your speeches go on forever.
Won't they ever end?
What's wrong with you?
Why do you keep on arguing?
[4] If you and I changed places,
I could say the same things you
are saying.
I could make fine speeches against
you.
I could shake my head at you.
[5] But what I might say would give
you hope.
My words of comfort would help
you.
[6] "If I speak, it doesn't help me.
And if I keep quiet, my pain
doesn't go away.
[7] God has worn me out completely.
He has destroyed my whole
family.
[8] People can see the condition he has
put me in.
My thin body stands as a witness
against me.
[9] God is angry with me.
He attacks me and tears me up.
He grinds his teeth at me.
He stares at me as if he were my
enemy.
[10] People make fun of me.
They slap my face and laugh
at me.
All of them join together
against me.
[11] God has turned me over to sinful
people.
He has handed me over to them.
[12] Everything was going well with me.
But he broke me into pieces like a
clay pot.
He grabbed me by the neck and
crushed me.
He has taken aim at me.
[13] He shoots his arrows at me from
all sides.
Without pity, he stabs me in the
kidneys.
He spills my insides on the
ground.
[14] He smashes through me as if I were
a wall.
He rushes at me like a fighting
man.
[15] "I've sewed rough clothing over my
skin.
All I can do is sit here in the dust.
[16] My face is red from crying.
I have dark circles under my
eyes.
[17] But I haven't harmed anyone.
My prayers to God are pure.
[18] "Earth, please don't cover up my
blood!
May God always hear my cry for
help!
[19] Even now my witness is in heaven.
The one who speaks up for me is
there.
[20] My go-between is my friend
as I pour out my tears to God.
[21] He makes his appeal to God to
help me
as a person pleads for a friend.
[22] "Only a few years will pass by.
Then I'll take the path of no
return.

17 [1] My strength is almost gone.
I won't live much longer.
A grave is waiting for me.
[2] People who make fun of me are all
around me.
I'm forced to watch as they
attack me with their words.

[3]"God, please pay the price to have
me set free.
Who else would put up money
for me?
[4]You have closed the minds of
those who are trying to
comfort me.
They don't understand that I
haven't done anything wrong.
So don't let them win the
argument.
[5]Suppose someone tells lies about
their friends to get a reward.
Then their own children will
suffer for it.

[6]"God has made an example
of me.
People spit in my face.
[7]My eyes have grown weak because
I'm so sad.
My body is so thin it hardly casts
a shadow.
[8]People who claim to be honest
are shocked when they see me.
Those who think they haven't
sinned
are stirred up against me.
They think I'm ungodly.
[9]But godly people will keep doing
what is right.
Those who have clean hands will
grow stronger.

[10]"Come on, all of you! Try again!
I can't find a wise person among
you.
[11]My life is almost over. My plans are
destroyed.
Yet the desires of my heart
[12]turn night into day.
Even though it's dark,
'Light is nearby.'
[13]Suppose the only home I can hope
for is a grave.
And suppose I make my bed in
the darkness of death.
[14]Suppose I say to the grave,
'You are like a father to me.'
And suppose I say to its worms,
'You are like a mother or sister
to me.'
[15]Then what hope do I have?
Who can give me any hope?
[16]Will hope go down to the gates of
death with me?
Will we go down together into
the dust of the grave?"

The Second Speech of Bildad

18 Then Bildad the Shuhite replied,

[2]"Job, when will you stop these
speeches of yours?
Be reasonable! Then we can talk.
[3]Why do you look at us as if we were
cattle?
Why do you think of us as being
stupid?
[4]Your anger is tearing you to pieces.
Does the earth have to be
deserted just to prove you are
right?
Must all the rocks be moved from
their places?

[5]"The lamps of sinful people are
blown out.
Their flames will never burn
again.
[6]The lights in their tents become
dark.
The lamps beside those who are
evil go out.
[7]They walk more slowly than they
used to.
Their own evil plans make them
fall.
[8]Their feet take them into a net.
They wander right into it.
[9]A trap grabs hold of their heels.
It refuses to let them go.
[10]A trap lies in their path.
A rope to catch them is hidden on
the ground.
[11]Terrors alarm them on every side.
They follow them every step of
the way.
[12]Trouble would like to eat them up.
Danger waits for them when they
fall.
[13]It eats away parts of their skin.
Death itself feeds on their arms
and legs.
[14]They are torn away from the safety
of their tents.
They are marched off to the one
who rules over death.
[15]Fire races through their tents.
Burning sulfur is scattered over
their homes.
[16]Their roots dry up under them.
Their branches dry up above them.
[17]No one on earth remembers them.
Their names are forgotten in the
land.

18 They are driven from light into the
place of darkness.
They are thrown out of the
world.
19 Their family dies out among their
people.
No one is left where they used to
live.
20 What has happened to them shocks
the people in the west.
It terrifies the people in the east.
21 Now you know what the homes of
sinners are like.
Those who don't know God live in
places like that."

Job's Reply

19 Job replied,

2 "How long will you people make
me suffer?
How long will you crush me with
your words?
3 You have already accused me
many times.
You have attacked me without
feeling any shame.
4 Suppose it's true that I've gone
down the wrong path.
Then it's my concern, not yours.
5 Suppose you want to place
yourselves above me.
Suppose you want to use my
shame to prove I'm wrong.
6 Then I want you to know that God
hasn't treated me right.
In fact, he has captured me in
his net.

7 "I cry out, 'Someone harmed me!'
But I don't get any reply.
I call out for help.
But I'm not treated fairly.
8 God has blocked my way, and I
can't get through.
He has made my paths so dark I
can't see where I'm going.
9 He has taken my wealth away
from me.
He has stripped me of my
honor.
10 He tears me down on every side
until I'm gone.
He pulls up the roots of my hope
as if I were a tree.
11 His anger burns against me.
He thinks I'm one of his enemies.
12 His troops march toward me in
force.
They come at me from every
direction.
They camp around my tent.

13 "God has caused my family to
desert me.
The people I used to know are
now strangers to me.
14 My relatives have gone away.
My closest friends have
forgotten me.
15 My guests and my female
servants think of me as a
stranger.
They look at me as if I were an
outsider.
16 I send for my servant, but he
doesn't answer.
He doesn't come, even though I
beg him to.
17 My wife can't stand the way my
breath smells.
My own family won't have
anything to do with me.
18 Even little children mock me.
When I appear, they make fun
of me.
19 All my close friends hate me.
Those I love have turned
against me.
20 I'm nothing but skin and bones.
I've barely escaped death.

21 "Have pity on me, my friends!
Please have pity!
God has struck me down with his
powerful hand.
22 Why do you chase after me as he
does?
Aren't you satisfied with
what you have done to me
already?

23 "I wish my words were written
down!
I wish they were written in a
book!
24 I wish they were cut into lead with
an iron tool!
I wish they were carved in rock
forever!
25 I know that my redeemer lives.
In the end he will stand on the
earth.
26 Though my skin will be destroyed,
in my body I'll see God.

key verses I know that my redeemer lives. In the end he will stand on the earth. . . . In my body I'll see God. I myself will see him with my own eyes. I'll see him, and he won't be a stranger to me. JOB 19:25–27

27 I myself will see him with my own eyes.
I'll see him, and he won't be a stranger to me.
How my heart longs for that day!

28 "You might say, 'Let's keep bothering Job.
After all, he's the cause of all his suffering.'
29 But you should be afraid when God comes to judge you.
He'll be angry. He'll punish you with his sword.
Then you will know that he is the Judge."

The Second Speech of Zophar

20 Then Zophar the Naamathite replied,

2 "My troubled thoughts force me to answer you.
That's because I'm very upset.
3 What you have just said dishonors me.
So I really have to reply to you.

4 "I'm sure you must know how things have always been.
They've been that way
ever since human beings were placed on this earth.
5 Those who are evil are happy for only a short time.
The joy of ungodly people lasts only for a moment.
6 Their pride might reach all the way up to the heavens.
Their heads might touch the clouds.
7 But they will disappear forever,
like the waste from their own bodies.
Anyone who has seen them will say,
'Where did they go?'
8 Like a dream they will fly away.
They will never be seen again.
They will be driven away like visions in the night.
9 The eyes that saw them won't see them anymore.
Even their own families won't remember them.
10 Their children must pay back what they took from poor people.
Their own hands must give back the wealth they stole.
11 They might feel young and very strong.
But they will soon lie down in the dust of their graves.

12 "Anything that is evil tastes sweet to them.
They keep it under their tongues for a while.
13 They can't stand to let it go.
So they hold it in their mouths.
14 But their food will turn sour in their stomachs.
It will become like the poison of a serpent inside them.
15 They will spit out the rich food they swallowed.
God will make their stomachs throw it up.
16 They will suck the poison of a serpent.
The fangs of an adder will kill them.
17 They won't enjoy streams that flow with honey.
They won't enjoy rivers that flow with cream.
18 What they worked for they must give back
before they can eat it.
They won't enjoy what they have earned.
19 They've crushed poor people and left them with nothing.
They've taken over houses they didn't even build.

20 "No matter how much they have,
they always long for more.
But their treasure can't save them.
21 There isn't anything left for them to eat up.
Their success won't last.
22 While they are enjoying the good life,
trouble will catch up with them.
Terrible suffering will come on them.

23 When they've filled their stomachs,
God will pour out his great anger on them.
He'll strike them down with blow after blow.
24 They might run away from iron weapons.
But arrows that have bronze tips will wound them.
25 They will pull the arrows out of their backs.
They will remove the shining tips from their livers.
They will be filled with terror.
26 Total darkness hides and waits for their treasures.
God will send a fire that will destroy them.
It will burn up everything that's left in their tents.
27 Heaven will show their guilt to everyone.
The earth will be a witness against them.
28 A flood will carry their houses away.
Rushing water will wash them away
on the day when God judges.
29 Now you know what God will do to sinful people.
Now you know what he has planned for them."

Job's Reply

21 Job replied,

2 "Listen carefully to what I'm saying.
Let that be the comfort you people give me.
3 Put up with me while I speak.
After I've spoken, you can make fun of me!

4 "I'm not arguing with mere human beings.
So why shouldn't I be angry and uneasy?
5 Look at me and be shocked.
Put your hand over your mouth and stop talking!
6 When I think about these things, I'm terrified.
My whole body trembles.
7 Why do sinful people keep on living?
The older they grow, the richer they get.
8 They see their children grow up around them.
They watch their family grow larger.
9 Their homes are safe.
They don't have to be afraid.
God isn't punishing them.
10 Every time their bulls mate, their cows become pregnant.
And the calves don't die before they are born.
11 Sinful people send their children out like a flock of lambs.
Their little ones dance around.
12 They sing to the music of tambourines and lyres.
They have a good time while flutes are being played.
13 Those who are evil spend their years living well.
They go down to their graves in peace.
14 But they say to God, 'Leave us alone!
We don't want to know how you want us to live.
15 Who is the Mighty One? Why should we serve him?
What would we get if we prayed to him?'
16 But they aren't in control of their own success.
So I don't pay any attention to their plans.

17 "How often are their lamps blown out?
How often does trouble come on them?
How often does God punish them when he's angry?
18 How often are they like straw blowing in the wind?
How often are they like tumbleweeds swept away by a storm?
19 People say, 'God stores up the punishment of evil people for their children.'
But let God punish the evil people themselves.
Then they'll learn a lesson from it.
20 Let their own eyes see how they are destroyed.
Let them drink the wine of the Mighty One's anger.
21 What do they care about the families they leave behind?
What do they care about them when their lives come to an end?

[22] "Can anyone teach God anything?
After all, he judges even the angels in heaven.
[23] Some people die while they are still very strong.
They are completely secure. They have an easy life.
[24] They are well fed.
Their bodies are healthy.
[25] Others die while their spirits are bitter.
They've never enjoyed anything good.
[26] Side by side they lie in the dust of death.
The worms in their graves cover all of them.

[27] "I know exactly what you people are thinking.
I know you are planning to do bad things to me.
[28] You are saying to yourselves,
'Where is the great man's house now?
Where are the tents where his evil family lived?'
[29] Haven't you ever asked questions of those who travel?
Haven't you paid any attention to their stories?
[30] They'll tell you that sinful people are spared from the day of trouble.
They'll say that those people are saved from the day when God will judge.
[31] Who speaks against them for the way they act?
Who pays them back for what they've done?
[32] Their bodies will be carried to their graves.
Guards will watch over their tombs.
[33] The soil in the valley will be pleasant
to those who have died.
Many people will walk along behind their bodies.
Many others will walk in front of them.

[34] "So how can you comfort me with your speeches?
They don't make any sense at all.
Your answers are nothing but lies!"

The Third Speech of Eliphaz

22 Then Eliphaz the Temanite replied,

[2] "Can any person be of benefit to God?
Can even a wise person be of any help to him?
[3] Job, what pleasure would it give the Mighty One if you were right?
What would he get if you were completely honest?

[4] "You say you have respect for him.
Is that why he corrects you?
Is that why he brings charges against you?
[5] Haven't you done many evil things?
Don't you sin again and again?
[6] You took clothes away from your relatives
just because they owed you some money.
You left them naked for no reason at all.
[7] You didn't give any water to people who were tired.
You held food back from those who were hungry.
[8] You did it even though you were honored and powerful.
You owned land and lived on it.
[9] But you sent widows away without anything.
You mistreated children whose fathers had died.
[10] That's why traps have been set all around you.
That's why sudden danger terrifies you.
[11] That's why it's so dark you can't even see.
That's why a flood covers you up.

[12] "Isn't God in the highest parts of heaven?
See how high the highest stars are!
[13] But you still say, 'What does God know?
Can he see through the darkest clouds to judge us?
[14] He goes around in the highest heavens.
Thick clouds keep him from seeing us.'
[15] Will you stay on the old path
that sinful people have walked on?

16 They were carried off even before
they died.
Their foundations were washed
away by a flood.
17 They said to God, 'Leave us alone!
What can you do to us, you
Mighty One?'
18 But he was the one who filled their
houses with good things.
So I don't pay any attention to
the plans of evil people.

19 "Those who do what is right are
joyful
when they see sinners destroyed.
Those who haven't done
anything wrong make fun of
them.
20 They say, 'Our enemies are
completely destroyed.
Fire has burned up their wealth.'
21 "Job, obey God and be at peace with
him.
Then he will help you succeed.
22 Do what he teaches you to do.
Keep his words in your heart.
23 If you return to the Mighty One,
you will have what you had
before.
But first you must remove
everything that is evil far from
your tent.
24 You must throw your gold nuggets
away.
You must toss your gold from
Ophir into a valley.
25 Then the Mighty One himself will
be your gold.
He'll be like the finest silver to
you.
26 You will find delight in the Mighty
One.
You will honor God and trust in
him.
27 You will pray to him, and he will
hear you.
You will keep the promises you
made to him.
28 What you decide to do will be done.
Light will shine on the path you
take.
29 When people are brought low you
will say, 'Lift them up!'
Then God will help them.
30 He'll even save those who are guilty.
He'll save them because your
hands are clean."

Job's Reply

23 Job replied,

2 "Even today my problems are more
than I can handle.
In spite of my groans, God's hand
is heavy on me.
3 I wish I knew where I could find him!
I wish I could go to the place
where he lives!
4 I would state my case to him.
I'd give him all my arguments.
5 I'd find out what his answers
would be.
I'd think about what he would
say to me.
6 Would he strongly oppose me?
No. He wouldn't bring charges
against me.
7 There honest people can prove to
him they're not guilty.
There my Judge would tell me once
and for all that I'm not guilty.

8 "But if I go to the east, God isn't
there.
If I go to the west, I don't find him.
9 When he's working in the north, I
don't see him there.
When he turns to the south, I
don't see him there either.
10 But he knows every step I take.
When he has tested me,
I'll come out as pure as gold.
11 My feet have closely followed his
steps.
I've stayed on his path without
turning away.
12 I haven't disobeyed his commands.
I've treasured his words more
than my daily bread.

13 "But he's the only God. Who can
oppose him?
He does anything he wants to do.
14 He carries out his plans against me.
And he still has many other
plans just like them.
15 That's why I'm so terrified.
When I think about all of this,
I'm afraid of him.
16 God has made my heart weak.
The Mighty One has filled me
with terror.
17 But even the darkness of death
won't make me silent.
When the darkness of the grave
covers my face, I won't be quiet.

24

"Why doesn't the Mighty One set a time for judging sinful people?
Why do those who know him have to keep waiting for that day?
2 People move their neighbor's boundary stones.
They steal their neighbor's flocks.
3 They take away the donkeys that belong to children whose fathers have died.
They take a widow's ox until she has paid what she owes.
4 They push those who are needy out of their way.
They force all the poor people in the land to go into hiding.
5 The poor are like wild donkeys in the desert.
They have to go around looking for food.
The dry and empty land provides the only food for their children.
6 The poor go to the fields and get a little grain.
They gather up what is left in the vineyards of sinners.
7 The poor don't have any clothes. So they spend the night naked.
They don't have anything to cover themselves in the cold.
8 They are soaked by mountain rains.
They hug the rocks because they don't have anything to keep them warm.
9 Children whose fathers have died are torn away from their mothers.
A poor person's baby is taken away to pay back what is owed.
10 The poor don't have any clothes.
They go around naked.
They carry bundles of grain, but they still go hungry.
11 They work very hard as they crush olives.
They stomp on grapes in winepresses,
but they are still thirsty.
12 The groans of those who are dying are heard from the city.
Those who are wounded cry out for help.
But God doesn't charge anyone with doing what is wrong.

13 "Some people hate it when daylight comes.
In the daytime they never walk outside.
14 When daylight is gone, murderers get up.
They kill poor people and those who are in need.
In the night they sneak around like robbers.
15 Those who commit adultery wait until the sun goes down.
They think, 'No one will see us.'
They keep their faces hidden.
16 In the dark, thieves break into houses.
But by day they shut themselves in.
They don't want anything to do with the light.
17 Midnight is like morning to them.
The terrors of darkness are their friends.

18 "But sinners are like bubbles on the surface of water.
Their share of the land is under God's curse.
So no one goes to their vineyards.
19 Melted snow disappears when the air is hot and dry.
And sinners disappear when they go down into their graves.
20 Even their mothers forget them.
The worms in their graves eat them up.
No one remembers sinful people anymore.
They are cut down like trees.
21 They mistreat women who aren't able to have children.
They aren't kind to widows.
22 But God is powerful.
He even drags away people who are strong.
When he rises up against them,
they can never be sure they are safe.
23 God might let them rest and feel secure.
But his eyes see how they live.
24 For a little while they are honored.
Then they are gone.
They are brought low.
And they die like everyone else.
They are cut off like heads of grain.

[25] "Who can prove that what I'm
saying is wrong?
Who can prove that my words
aren't true?"

The Third Speech of Bildad

25 Then Bildad the Shuhite replied,

[2] "God is King. He should be feared.
He establishes peace in the
highest parts of heaven.
[3] Can anyone count his troops?
Is there anyone his light doesn't
shine on?
[4] How can human beings be right
with God?
How can mere people really be
pure?
[5] Even the moon isn't bright
and the stars aren't pure in God's
eyes.
[6] So how about human beings? They
are like maggots.
How about mere people? They
are like worms."

Job's Reply

26 Job replied,

[2] "Bildad, you haven't helped people
who aren't strong!
You haven't saved people who
are weak!
[3] You haven't offered advice to those
who aren't wise!
In fact, you haven't understood
anything at all!
[4] Who helped you say these things?
Whose spirit was speaking
through you?

[5] "The spirits of the dead are
suffering greatly.
So are those that are under the
waters.
And so are all those that live in
them.
[6] The place of the dead is naked in
the sight of God.
The grave lies open in front of him.
[7] He spreads out the northern skies
over empty space.
He hangs the earth over nothing.
[8] He wraps up water in his clouds.
They are heavy, but they don't
burst.
[9] He covers the face of the full moon.
He spreads his clouds over it.
[10] He marks out the place where the
sky meets the sea.
He marks out the boundary
between light and darkness.
[11] The pillars of the heavens shake.
They are terrified when his anger
blazes out.
[12] With his power he stirred up the
oceans.
In his wisdom he cut the sea
monster Rahab to pieces.
[13] His breath made the skies bright
and clear.
His hand wounded the serpent
that glides through the sea.
[14] Those are only on the edges of
what he does.
They are only the soft whispers
that we hear from him.
So who can understand how very
powerful he is?"

Job's Final Reply to His Friends

27 Job continued to speak. He said,

[2] "God hasn't treated me fairly.
The Mighty One has made my
life bitter.
You can be sure that God lives.
And here's something else you
can be sure of.
[3] As long as I have life
and God gives me breath,
[4] my mouth won't say evil things.
My lips won't tell lies.
[5] I'll never admit you people are
right.
Until I die, I'll say I'm telling the
truth.
[6] I'll continue to say I'm right.
I'll never let go of that.
I won't blame myself as long as I
live.

[7] "May my enemies suffer like sinful
people!
May my attackers be punished
like those who aren't fair!
[8] What hope do ungodly people have
when their lives are cut short?
What hope do they have when
God takes away their lives?
[9] God won't listen to their cry
when trouble comes on them.
[10] They won't take delight in the
Mighty One.
They'll never call out to God.

[11] "I'll teach all of you about God's
power.
I won't hide the things the
Mighty One does.
[12] You have seen those things
yourselves.
So why do you continue your
useless talk?

[13] "Here's what God does to sinful
people.
Here's what those who are mean
receive from the Mighty One.
[14] All their children will be killed by
swords.
They'll never have enough to eat.
[15] A plague will kill those who are left
alive.
The widows of sinful men
won't even weep over their own
children.
[16] Sinners might store up silver like dust
and clothes like piles of clay.
[17] But people who do what is right will
wear those clothes.
People who haven't done
anything wrong
will divide up that silver.
[18] The house an evil person builds is
like a moth's cocoon.
It's like a hut that's made by
someone on guard duty.
[19] Sinful people lie down wealthy, but
their wealth is taken away.
When they open their eyes,
everything is gone.
[20] Terrors sweep over them like a
flood.
A storm takes them away during
the night.
[21] The east wind carries them off, and
they are gone.
It sweeps them out of their houses.
[22] It blows against them without
mercy.
They try to escape from its power.
[23] It claps its hands and makes fun of
them.
It hisses them out of their
houses."

The Place Where Wisdom Is Found Is Explained

28 There are mines where silver
is found.
There are places where gold is
purified.
[2] Iron is taken out of the earth.
Copper is melted down from ore.
[3] Human beings light up the
darkness.
They search for ore in the
deepest pits.
They look for it in the blackest
darkness.
[4] Far from where people live they cut
a tunnel.
They do it in places where other
people don't go.
Far away from people they swing
back and forth on ropes.
[5] Food grows on the surface of the
earth.
But far below, the earth is
changed as if by fire.
[6] Lapis lazuli is taken from the rocky
earth.
Its dust contains nuggets of
gold.
[7] No bird knows that hidden path.
No falcon's eye has seen it.
[8] Proud animals don't walk on it.
Lions don't prowl there.
[9] Human hands attack the hardest
rock.
Their strong hands uncover the
base of the mountains.
[10] They tunnel through the rock.
Their eyes see all its treasures.
[11] They search the places where the
rivers begin.
They bring hidden things out
into the light.

[12] But where can wisdom be found?
Where does understanding live?
[13] No human being understands how
much it's worth.
It can't be found anywhere in the
world.
[14] The ocean says, "It's not in me."
The sea says, "It's not here
either."
[15] It can't be bought with the finest
gold.
Its price can't be weighed out in
silver.
[16] It can't be bought with gold from
Ophir.
It can't be bought with priceless
onyx or lapis lazuli.
[17] Gold or crystal can't compare
with it.
It can't be bought with jewels
made of gold.

18 Don't bother to talk about coral and
jasper.
Wisdom is worth far more than
rubies.
19 A topaz from Cush can't compare
with it.
It can't be bought with the purest
gold.

20 So where does wisdom come from?
Where does understanding live?
21 It's hidden from the eyes of every
living thing.
Even the birds in the sky can't
find it.
22 Death and the Grave say,
"Only reports about it have
reached our ears."
23 But God understands the way
to it.
He is the only one who knows
where it lives.
24 He sees from one end of the earth
to the other.
He views everything in the world.
25 He made the mighty wind.
He measured out the waters.
26 He gave orders for the rain to fall.
He made paths for the
thunderstorms.
27 Then he looked at wisdom and set
its price.
He established it and tested it.
28 He said to human beings,
"Have respect for the Lord. That
will prove you are wise.
Avoid evil. That will show you
have understanding."

Job's Final Speech

29 Job continued to speak. He said,

2 "How I long for the times when
things were better!
That's when God watched over me.
3 The light of his lamp shone on me.
I walked through darkness by his
light.
4 Those were the best days of my life.
That's when God's friendship
blessed my house.
5 The Mighty One was still with me.
My children were all
around me.
6 The path in front of me was like
sweet cream.
It was as if the rock poured out
olive oil for me.

7 "In those days I went to the city
gate.
I took my seat as a member of
the council.
8 Young people who saw me stepped
to one side.
Old people stood up as I
approached.
9 The leaders stopped speaking.
They covered their mouths with
their hands.
10 The voices of the nobles became
quiet.
Their tongues stuck to the roofs
of their mouths.
11 Everyone who heard me said good
things about me.
Those who saw me honored me.
12 That's because I saved poor people
who cried out for help.
I saved helpless children whose
fathers had died.
13 Those who were dying gave me
their blessing.
I made the hearts of widows sing.
14 I put on a godly life as if it were my
clothes.
Fairness was my robe and my
turban.
15 I was like eyes for those who were
blind.
I was like feet for those who
couldn't walk.
16 I was like a father to needy people.
I stood up for strangers in court.
17 Sinners are like animals that have
powerful teeth.
But I took from their mouths the
people they had caught.

18 "I thought, 'I'll die in my own house.
The days of my life will be as
many as the grains of sand.
19 My roots will reach down to the
water.
The dew will lie all night on my
branches.
20 I will remain healthy and strong.
My bow will stay as good as new
in my hand.'

21 "People wanted to hear what I had
to say.
They waited silently for the
advice I gave them.
22 After I had spoken, they didn't
speak anymore.
My words fell gently on their ears.

[23] They waited for me just as they
would wait for rain showers.
They drank my words just as they
would drink the spring rain.
[24] When I smiled at them, they could
hardly believe it.
The light of my face lifted their
spirits.
[25] I chose the way they should go. I
sat as their chief.
I lived as a king lives among his
troops.
I was like someone who comforts
those who are sad.

30 "But now those who are
younger than I am make fun
of me.
I wouldn't even put their parents
with my sheep dogs!
[2] Their strong hands couldn't give
me any help.
That's because their strength was
gone.
[3] They were weak because they were
needy and hungry.
They wandered through dry and
empty deserts at night.
[4] Among the bushes they gathered
salty plants.
They ate the roots of desert bushes.
[5] They were driven away from
human society.
They were shouted at as if they
were robbers.
[6] They were forced to live in dry
stream beds.
They had to stay among rocks
and in holes in the ground.
[7] Like donkeys they cried out among
the bushes.
There they crowded together and
hid.
[8] They were so foolish that no one
respected them.
They were driven out of the land.

[9] "Now their children laugh at me.
They make fun of me with their
songs.
[10] They hate me. They stay away
from me.
They even dare to spit in my face.
[11] God has made my body weak.
It's like a tent that has fallen
down.
So those children do what they
want to in front of me.
[12] Many people attack me on my
right side.
They lay traps for my feet.
They come at me from every
direction.
[13] They tear up the road I walk on.
They succeed in destroying me.
They say, 'No one can help him.'
[14] They attack me like troops
smashing through a wall.
Among the destroyed buildings
they come rolling in.
[15] Terrors sweep over me.
My honor is driven away as if by
the wind.
My safety vanishes like a cloud.

[16] "Now my life is slipping away.
Days of suffering grab hold of
me.
[17] At night my bones hurt.
My aches and pains never stop.
[18] God's great power becomes like
clothes to me.
He chokes me like the neck of my
shirt.
[19] He throws me down into the mud.
I'm nothing but dust and ashes.

[20] "God, I cry out to you. But you don't
answer me.
I stand up. But all you do is look
at me.
[21] You do mean things to me.
You attack me with your mighty
power.
[22] You pick me up and blow me away
with the wind.
You toss me around in the storm.
[23] I know that you will bring me down
to death.
That's what you have appointed
for everyone.

[24] "No one would crush people
when they cry out for help in
their trouble.
[25] Haven't I wept for those who are in
trouble?
Haven't I felt sorry for poor
people?
[26] I hoped good things would happen,
but something evil came.
I looked for light, but all I saw
was darkness.
[27] My insides are always churning.
Nothing but days of suffering are
ahead of me.

28 My skin has become dark, but the
sun didn't do it.
I stand up in the community and
cry out for help.
29 I've become a brother to wild dogs.
Owls are my companions.
30 My skin grows black and peels.
My body burns with fever.
31 My lyre is tuned to sadness.
My flute makes a sound like
weeping.

31 "I made an agreement with my
eyes.
I promised not to look at a young
woman with impure thoughts.
2 What do we receive from God
above?
What do we get from the Mighty
One in heaven?
3 Sinful people are destroyed.
Trouble comes to those who do
what is wrong.
4 Doesn't God see how I live?
Doesn't he count every step I take?

5 "I haven't told any lies.
My feet haven't hurried to cheat
others.
6 So let God weigh me in honest
scales.
Then he'll know I haven't done
anything wrong.
7 Suppose my steps have turned
away from the right path.
Suppose my heart has wanted
what my eyes have seen.
Or suppose my hands have
become 'unclean.'
8 Then may others eat what I've
planted.
May my crops be pulled up by
the roots.

9 "Suppose my heart has been
tempted by a woman.
Or suppose I've prowled around
my neighbor's home.
10 Then may my wife grind another
man's grain.
May other men sleep with her.
11 Wanting another woman would
have been an evil thing.
It would have been a sin that
should be judged.
12 It's like a fire that burns down to
the grave.
It would have caused my crops to
be pulled up by the roots.

13 "Suppose I haven't treated any of my
male and female servants fairly
when they've brought charges
against me.
14 Then what will I do when God
opposes me?
What answer will I give him
when he asks me to explain
myself?
15 Didn't he who made me make my
servants also?
Didn't the same God form us
inside our mothers?

16 "I haven't said no to what poor
people have wanted.
I haven't let widows lose their
hope.
17 I haven't kept my bread to myself.
I've shared it with children whose
fathers had died.
18 From the time I was young, I've
helped those widows.
I've raised those children as a
father would.
19 Suppose I've seen people dying
because they didn't have enough
clothes.
I've seen needy people
who didn't have enough to keep
warm.
20 And they didn't give me their
blessing
when I warmed them with wool
from my sheep.
21 Suppose I've raised my hand
against children whose fathers
have died.
And I did it because I knew
I had power in the courts.
22 Then let my arm fall from my
shoulder.
Let it be broken off at the joint.
23 I was afraid God would destroy me.
His glory terrifies me.
So I'd never do things like that.

24 "Suppose I've put my trust in gold.
I've said to pure gold, 'You make
me feel secure.'
25 And I'm happy because I'm so
wealthy.
I'm glad because my hands have
earned so much.
26 Suppose I've worshiped the sun in
all its glory.
I've bowed down to the moon in
all its beauty.

27 My heart has been secretly tempted.
My hand has thrown kisses to the sun and moon.
28 Then these things would have been sins that should be judged.
And I wouldn't have been faithful to God in heaven.

29 "I wasn't happy when hard times came to my enemies.
I didn't enjoy seeing the trouble they had.
30 I didn't allow my mouth to sin by asking for bad things to happen to them.
31 The workers in my house always said, 'Job always gives plenty of food to everyone.'
32 No stranger ever had to spend the night in the street.
My door was always open to travelers.
33 I didn't hide my sin as other people do.
I didn't hide my guilt in my heart.
34 I was never afraid of the crowd.
I never worried that my relatives might hate me.
I didn't have to keep quiet or stay inside.

35 "I wish someone would listen to me!
I'm signing my name to everything I've said.
I hope the Mighty One will give me his answer.
I hope the one who brings charges against me will write them down.
36 I'll wear them on my shoulder.
I'll put them on my head like a crown.
37 I'll give that person a report of every step I take.
I'll present it to him like I would to a ruler.

38 "Suppose my land cries out against me.
And all its soil is wet with tears.
39 Suppose I've used up its crops without paying for them.
Or I've broken the spirit of its renters.
40 Then let thorns grow instead of wheat.
Let stinkweed come up instead of barley."

The words of Job end here.

The Speech of Elihu

32 So the three men stopped answering Job, because he thought
he was right. 2 But Elihu the Buzite was
very angry with Job. That's because
Job said he himself was right instead
of God. Elihu was the son of Barakel.
He was from the family of Ram. 3 Elihu
was also very angry with Job's three
friends. They hadn't found any way to
prove that Job was wrong. But they still
said he was guilty. 4 Elihu had waited
before he spoke to Job. That's because
the others were older than he was. 5 But
he saw that the three men didn't have
anything more to say. So he was very
angry.

6 Elihu the Buzite, the son of Barakel,
said,

"I'm young, and you are old.
So I was afraid to tell you what I know.
7 I thought, 'Those who are older should speak first.
Those who have lived for many years should teach people how to be wise.'
8 But the spirit in people gives them understanding.
The breath of the Mighty One gives them wisdom.
9 Older people aren't the only ones who are wise.
They aren't the only ones who understand what is right.

10 "So I'm saying you should listen to me.
I'll tell you what I know.
11 I waited while you men spoke.
I listened to your reasoning.
While you were searching for words,
12 I paid careful attention to you.
But not one of you has proved that Job is wrong.
None of you has answered his arguments.
13 Don't claim, 'We have enough wisdom to answer Job.'
Let God, not a mere man, prove that he's wrong.
14 Job hasn't directed his words against me.
I won't answer him with your arguments.

15 "Job, these men are afraid.
They don't have anything else to say.
They've run out of words.
16 Do I have to keep on waiting, now that they are silent?
They are just standing there with nothing to say.
17 I too have something to say.
I too will tell what I know.
18 I'm full of words.
My spirit inside me forces me to speak.
19 Inside I'm like wine that is bottled up.
I'm like new wineskins ready to burst.
20 I must speak so I can feel better.
I must open my mouth and reply.
21 I'll treat everyone the same.
I won't praise anyone without meaning it.
22 If I weren't honest when I praised people,
my Maker would soon take me from this life.

33 "Job, listen now to my words.
Pay attention to everything I say.
2 I'm about to open my mouth.
My words are on the tip of my tongue.
3 What I say comes from an honest heart.
My lips speak only what I know is true.
4 The Spirit of God has made me.
The breath of the Mighty One gives me life.
5 So answer me if you can.
Stand up and argue your case in front of me.
6 To God I'm just the same as you.
I too am a piece of clay.
7 You don't have to be afraid of me.
My hand won't be too heavy on you.

8 "But I heard what you said.
And here are the exact words I heard.
9 You said, 'I'm pure. I have done no wrong.
I'm clean. I'm free from sin.
10 But God has found fault with me.
He thinks I'm his enemy.
11 He puts my feet in chains.
He watches every step I take.'

12 "But I'm telling you that you aren't right when you talk like that.
After all, God is greater than any human being.
13 Why do you claim that God never answers anybody's questions?
14 He speaks in one way and then another.
But we do not even realize it.
15 He might speak in a dream or in a vision at night.
That's when people are sound asleep in their beds.
16 He might speak in their ears.
His warnings might terrify them.
17 He warns them in order to turn them away from sinning.
He wants to keep them from being proud.
18 He wants to stop them from going down into the grave.
He doesn't want them to be killed by swords.
19 Someone might be punished by suffering in bed.
The pain in their bones might never go away.
20 They might feel so bad they can't eat anything.
They might even hate the finest food.
21 Their body might waste away to nothing.
Their bones might have been hidden.
But now they stick out.
22 They might approach the very edge of the grave.
The messengers of death might come for them.

23 "But suppose there is an angel who will speak up for him.
The angel is very special. He's one out of a thousand.
He will tell that person how to do what is right.
24 That angel will be gracious to them. He'll say to God,
'Spare them from going down into the grave.
I know a way that can set them free.'

25 Then their body is made like new
again.
They become as strong and
healthy as when they were
young.
26 Then that person can pray to God
and be blessed by him.
They will see God's face and
shout for joy.
God will make them well and
happy again.
27 Then that person will come to
others and say,
'I sinned. I made what is wrong
appear to be right.
But I wasn't punished as I should
have been.
28 God has set me free. He has kept
me from going down into the
darkness of the grave.
So I'll live to enjoy the light of life.'

29 "God does all these things to people.
In fact, he does them again and
again.
30 He wants to stop people from going
down into the darkness of the
grave.
Then the light of life will shine on
them.

31 "Pay attention, Job! Listen to me!
Be quiet so I can speak.
32 If you have anything to say,
answer me.
Speak up. I want to help you be
cleared of all charges.
33 But if you don't have anything to
say, listen to me.
Be quiet so I can teach you how
to be wise."

34

Elihu continued,

2 "Hear what I'm saying, you wise
men.
Listen to me, you who have
learned so much.
3 Our tongues tell us what tastes
good and what doesn't.
And our ears tell us what's true
and what isn't.
4 So let's choose for ourselves what is
right.
Let's learn together what is good.

5 "Job says, 'I'm not guilty of doing
anything wrong.
But God doesn't treat me fairly.
6 Even though I'm right,
he thinks I'm a liar.
Even though I'm not guilty,
his arrows give me wounds that
can't be healed.'
7 Is there anyone like Job?
He accuses God as easily as he
drinks water.
8 He's a companion of those who do
evil.
He spends his time with sinful
people.
9 He asks, 'What good is it
to try to please God?'

10 "So listen to me, you men who have
understanding.
God would never do what is evil.
The Mighty One would never do
what is wrong.
11 He pays back everyone for what
they've done.
He gives them exactly what they
should get.
12 It isn't possible for God to do wrong.
The Mighty One would never
treat people unfairly.
13 Who appointed him to rule over the
earth?
Who put him in charge of the
whole world?
14 If he really wanted to,
he could hold back his spirit and
breath.
15 Then everyone would die together.
They would return to the dust.

16 "Job, if you have understanding,
listen to me.
Pay attention to what I'm saying.
17 Can someone who hates to be fair
govern?
Will you bring charges against
the holy and mighty God?
18 He says to kings, 'You are
worthless.'
He says to nobles, 'You are evil.'
19 He doesn't favor princes.
He treats rich people and poor
people the same.
His hands created all of them.
20 They die suddenly in the middle of
the night.
God strikes them down, and they
pass away.
Even people who are mighty are
removed, but not by human
hands.

21 "His eyes see how people live.
He watches every step they take.
22 There is no deep shadow or total darkness
where those who do what is evil can hide.
23 God doesn't need to bring charges against anyone.
He knows they are guilty.
So he doesn't need to have them appear in his court to be judged.
24 He destroys the mighty without asking them questions in court.
Then he sets others up in their places.
25 He knows what they do.
So he crushes them during the night.
26 He punishes them for the sins they commit.
He does it where everyone can see them.
27 That's because they turned away from following him.
They didn't have respect for anything he does.
28 They caused poor people to cry out to him.
He heard the cries of those who were in need.
29 But if he remains silent, who can judge him?
If he turns his face away, who can see him?
He rules over individual people and nations alike.
30 He keeps those who are ungodly from ruling.
He keeps them from laying traps for others.

31 "Someone might say to God,
'I'm guilty of sinning,
but I won't do it anymore.
32 Show me my sins that I'm not aware of.
If I've done what is wrong,
I won't do it again.'
33 But you refuse to turn away from your sins.
So God won't treat you the way you want to be treated.
You must decide, Job. I can't do it for you.
So tell me what you know.

34 "You men who have understanding have spoken.
You wise men who hear me have said to me,
35 'Job doesn't know what he's talking about.
The things he has said don't make any sense.'
36 I wish Job would be given the hardest test possible!
He answered like someone who is evil.
37 To his sin he adds even more sin.
He claps his hands and makes fun of us.
He multiplies his words against God."

35

Elihu continued,

2 "Job, do you think it's fair for you to say,
'I am the one who is right, not God'?
3 You ask him, 'What good is it for me not to sin?
What do I get by not sinning?'

4 "I'd like to reply to you
and to your friends who are with you.
5 Look up at the heavens.
Observe the clouds that are high above you.
6 If you sin, what does that mean to God?
If you sin many times, what does that do to him?
7 If you do what is right, how does that help him?
What does he get from you?
8 The evil things you do only hurt people like yourself.
The right things you do only help other human beings.

9 "People cry out when they are treated badly.
They beg to be set free from the power of those who are over them.
10 But no one says, 'Where is the God who made me?
He gives us songs even during the night.
11 He teaches us more than he teaches the wild animals.
He makes us wiser than the birds in the sky.'

[12] He doesn't answer sinful people
when they cry out to him.
That's because they are so proud.
[13] In fact, God doesn't listen to their
empty cries.
The Mighty One doesn't pay any
attention to them.
[14] So he certainly won't listen to you.
When you say you don't see him,
he won't hear you.
He won't listen when you state your
case to him.
He won't pay attention even if
you wait for him.
[15] When you say his anger never
punishes sin, he won't hear you.
He won't listen when you say he
doesn't pay any attention to
evil.
[16] So you say things that don't mean
anything.
You use a lot of words,
but you don't know what you are
talking about."

36

Elihu continued,

[2] "Put up with me a little longer.
I'll show you I can speak up for
God even more.
[3] I get my knowledge from far away.
I'll announce that the God who
made me is fair.
[4] You can be sure that my words are
true.
One who has perfect knowledge
is talking to you.

[5] "God is mighty, but he doesn't hate
people.
He's mighty, and he knows
exactly what he's going to do.
[6] He doesn't keep alive those who are
evil.
Instead, he gives suffering people
their rights.
[7] He watches over those who do what
is right.
He puts them on thrones as if
they were kings.
He honors them forever.
[8] But some people are held by
chains.
Their pain ties them up like
ropes.
[9] God tells them what they've done.
He tells them they've become
proud and sinned against him.
[10] He makes them listen when he
corrects them.
He commands them to turn
away
from the evil things they've
done.
[11] If they obey him and serve him,
they'll enjoy a long and happy
life.
Things will go well with them.
[12] But if they don't listen to him,
they'll be killed by swords.
They'll die because they didn't
want to know anything about
him.

[13] "Those whose hearts are ungodly
are always angry.
Even when God puts them in
chains,
they don't cry out for help.
[14] They die while they are still young.
They die among the male
prostitutes at the temples.
[15] But God saves suffering people
while they suffer.
He speaks to them while they are
hurting.

[16] "Job, he wants to take you out of
the jaws of trouble.
He wants to bring you to a wide
and safe place.
He'd like to seat you at a table
that is loaded with the best
food.
[17] But now you are loaded down
with the punishment sinners will
receive.
You have been judged fairly.
[18] Be careful that no one tempts you
with riches.
Don't take money from people
who want special favors,
no matter how much it is.
[19] Can your wealth keep you out of
trouble?
Can all your mighty efforts keep
you going?
[20] Don't wish for the night to come
so you can drag people away
from their homes.
[21] Be careful not to do what is evil.
You seem to like evil better than
suffering!

[22] "God is honored because he is so
powerful.
There is no teacher equal to him.

23 Who has told him what he can do?
Who has said to him, 'You have done what is wrong'?
24 Remember to thank him for what he's done.
People have praised him with their songs.
25 Every human being has seen his work.
People can see it from far away.
26 How great God is! We'll never completely understand him.
We'll never find out how long he has lived.

27 "He makes mist rise from the water.
Then it falls as rain into the streams.
28 The clouds pour down their moisture.
Rain showers fall on people everywhere.
29 Who can understand how God spreads out the clouds?
Who can explain how he thunders from his home in heaven?
30 See how he scatters his lightning around him!
He lights up the deepest parts of the ocean.
31 The rain he sends makes things grow for the nations.
He provides them with plenty of food.
32 He holds lightning bolts in his hands.
He commands them to strike their marks.
33 His thunder announces that a storm is coming.
Even the cattle let us know it's approaching.

37 "When I hear the thunder, my heart pounds.
It beats faster inside me.
2 Listen! Listen to the roar of his voice!
Listen to the thunder that comes from him!
3 He sends his lightning across the sky.
It reaches from one end of the earth to the other.
4 Next comes the sound of his roaring thunder.
He thunders with his majestic voice.
When his voice fills the air,
he doesn't hold anything back.
5 God's voice thunders in wonderful ways.
We'll never understand the great things he does.
6 He says to the snow, 'Fall on the earth.'
He tells the rain, 'Pour down your mighty waters.'
7 He stops everyone from working.
He wants them to see his work.
8 The animals go inside.
They remain in their dens.
9 The storm comes out of its storeroom in the heavens.
The cold comes from the driving winds.
10 The breath of God produces ice.
The shallow water freezes over.
11 He loads the clouds with moisture.
He scatters his lightning through them.
12 He directs the clouds to circle above the surface of the whole earth.
They do everything he commands them to do.
13 He tells the clouds to punish people.
Or he brings them to water his earth and show his love.

14 "Job, listen to me.
Stop and think about the wonderful things God does.
15 Do you know how he controls the clouds?
Do you understand how he makes his lightning flash?
16 Do you know how the clouds stay up in the sky?
Do you understand the wonders of the God who has perfect knowledge?
17 Even your clothes are too hot for you
when the land lies quiet under the south wind.
18 Can you help God spread out the skies?
They are as hard as a mirror that's made out of bronze.

19 "Job, tell us what we should say to God.
We can't prepare our case because our minds are dark.

20 Should he be told that I want to
speak?
Would anyone ask to be
destroyed by him?
21 No one can look at the sun.
It's too bright after the wind has
swept the skies clean.
22 Out of the north, God comes in his
shining glory.
He comes in all his wonderful
majesty.
23 We can't reach up to the Mighty One.
He is lifted high because of his
power.
Everything he does is fair and right.
So he doesn't crush people.
24 That's why they have respect for
him.
He cares about all those who are
wise."

The LORD Speaks

38 The LORD spoke to Job out of a
storm. He said,

2 "Who do you think you are to
disagree with my plans?
You do not know what you are
talking about.
3 Get ready to stand up for yourself.
I will ask you some questions.
Then I want you to answer me.

4 "Where were you when I laid the
earth's foundation?
Tell me, if you know.
5 Who measured it? I am sure you
know!
Who stretched a measuring line
across it?
6 What was it built on?
Who laid its most important
stone?
7 When it happened, the morning
stars sang together.
All the angels shouted with joy.

8 "Who created the ocean?
Who caused it to be born?
9 I put clouds over it as if they were
its clothes.
I wrapped it in thick darkness.
10 I set limits for it.
I put its doors and metal bars in
place.
11 I said, 'You can come this far.
But you can't come any farther.
Here is where your proud waves
have to stop.'

12 "Job, have you ever commanded
the morning to come?
Have you ever shown the sun
where to rise?
13 The daylight takes the earth by its
edges
as if it were a blanket.
Then it shakes sinful people out
of it.
14 The earth takes shape like clay
stamped with an official's mark.
Its features stand out
like the different parts of your
clothes.
15 Sinners would rather have
darkness than light.
When the light comes, their
power is broken.

16 "Have you traveled to the springs
at the bottom of the ocean?
Have you walked in its deepest
parts?
17 Have the gates of death been
shown to you?
Have you seen the gates of the
deepest darkness?
18 Do you understand how big the
earth is?
Tell me, if you know all these
things.

19 "Where does light come from?
And where does darkness live?
20 Can you take them to their places?
Do you know the paths to their
houses?
21 I am sure you know! After all, you
were already born!
You have lived so many years!

22 "Have you entered the places where
the snow is kept?
Have you seen the storerooms for
the hail?
23 I store up snow and hail for times
of trouble.
I keep them for days of war and
battle.
24 Where does lightning come from?
Where do the east winds live that
blow across the earth?
25 Who tells the rain where it should fall?
Who makes paths for the
thunderstorms?
26 They bring water to places where
no one lives.
They water deserts that do not
have anyone in them.

How did God create the world?

As we read in the creation story in Genesis, God created the world with his spoken word. He existed before anything or anyone.

Can you find the following verses?

JOB 38:4–7

27 They satisfy the needs of dry and
empty lands.
They make grass start growing
there.
28 Does the rain have a father?
Who is the father of the drops of
dew?
29 Does the ice have a mother?
Who is the mother of the frost
from the heavens?
30 The waters become as hard as
stone.
The surface of the ocean freezes
over.

31 "Can you tie up the cords of the
Pleiades?
Can you untie the belt that Orion
wears?
32 Can you bring out all the stars in
their seasons?
Can you lead out the Big Dipper
and the Little Dipper?
33 Do you know the laws that govern
the heavens?
Can you rule over the earth the
way I do?

34 "Can you give orders to the clouds?
Can you make them pour rain
down on you?
35 Do you send the lightning bolts on
their way?
Do they report to you, 'Here we
are'?
36 Who gives the ibis wisdom?
Who gives the rooster
understanding?
37 Who is wise enough to count the
clouds?
Who can tip over the water jars of
the heavens?
38 I tip them over when the ground
becomes hard.
I do it when the dirt sticks
together.

39 "Do you hunt for food for mother
lions?
Do you satisfy the hunger of their
cubs?
40 Some of them lie low in their dens.
Others lie waiting in the bushes.
41 Who provides food for ravens
when their babies cry out to me?
They wander around because
they do not have anything to
eat.

39 "Job, do you know when
mountain goats have their
babies?
Do you watch when female deer
give birth?
2 Do you count the months until the
animals have their babies?
Do you know the time when they
give birth?
3 They bend their back legs and have
their babies.
Then their labor pains stop.
4 Their little ones grow strong and
healthy in the wild.
They leave and do not come
home again.

5 "Who let the wild donkeys go free?
Who untied their ropes?
6 I gave them the dry and empty
land as their home.
I gave them salt flats to live in.
7 They laugh at all the noise in town.
They do not hear the shouts of
the donkey drivers.
8 They wander over the hills to look
for grass.
They search for anything green
to eat.

9 "Job, will wild oxen agree to serve
you?
Will they stay by your feed box
at night?

10 Can you keep them in straight rows
with harnesses?
Will they plow the valleys behind
you?
11 Will you depend on them for their
great strength?
Will you let them do your heavy
work?
12 Can you trust them to haul in your
grain?
Will they bring it to your
threshing floor?

13 "The wings of ostriches flap with
joy.
But they can't compare with the
wings and feathers of storks.
14 Ostriches lay their eggs on the
ground.
They let them get warm in the
sand.
15 They do not know that something
might step on them.
A wild animal might walk all
over them.
16 Ostriches are mean to their little
ones.
They treat them as if they did
not belong to them.
They do not care that their work
was useless.
17 I did not provide ostriches with
wisdom.
I did not give them good sense.
18 But when they spread their
feathers to run,
they laugh at a horse and its
rider.

19 "Job, do you give horses their
strength?
Do you put flowing manes on
their necks?
20 Do you make them jump like
locusts?
They terrify others with their
proud snorting.
21 They paw the ground wildly.
They are filled with joy.
They charge at their enemies.
22 They laugh at fear. They are not
afraid of anything.
They do not run away from
swords.
23 Many arrows rattle at their sides.
Flashing spears and javelins are
also there.
24 They are so excited that they race
over the ground.
They can't stand still when
trumpets are blown.
25 When they hear the trumpets they
snort, 'Aha!'
They catch the smells of battle
far away.
They hear the shouts of
commanders and the battle
cries.

26 "Job, are you wise enough to teach
hawks where to fly?
They spread their wings and fly
toward the south.
27 Do you command eagles to fly so
high?
They build their nests as high as
they can.
28 They live on cliffs and stay there at
night.
High up on the rocks they think
they are safe.
29 From there they look for their food.
They can see it from far away.
30 Their little ones like to eat blood.
Eagles gather where they see
dead bodies."

40

The LORD continued,

2 "I am the Mighty One.
Will the man who argues with
me correct me?
Let him who brings charges
against me answer me!"

3 Job replied to the LORD,

4 "I'm not worthy. How can I reply to
you?
I'm putting my hand over my
mouth. I'll stop talking.
5 I spoke once. But I really don't have
any answer.
I spoke twice. But I won't say
anything else."

6 Then the LORD spoke to Job out of
the storm. He said,

7 "Get ready to stand up for yourself.
I will ask you some more
questions.
Then I want you to answer me.
8 "Would you dare to claim that I am
not being fair?
Would you judge me in order to
make yourself seem right?

9 Is your arm as powerful as mine is?
Can your voice thunder as mine does?
10 Then put on glory and beauty as if they were your clothes.
Also put on honor and majesty.
11 Let loose your great anger.
Look at those who are proud and bring them low.
12 Look at proud people and make them humble.
Crush evil people right where they are.
13 Bury their bodies together in the dust.
Cover their faces in the grave.
14 Then I myself will admit to you that your own right hand can save you.
15 "Look at Behemoth. It is a huge animal.
I made both of you.
It eats grass like an ox.
16 Look at the strength it has in its hips!
What power it has in the muscles of its stomach!
17 Its tail sways back and forth like a cedar tree.
The tendons of its thighs are close together.
18 Its bones are like tubes made out of bronze.
Its legs are like rods made out of iron.
19 It ranks first among my works.
I made it. I can approach it with my sword.
20 The hills produce food for it.
All the other wild animals play near it.
21 It lies under lotus plants.
It hides in tall grass in the swamps.
22 The lotus plants hide it in their shade.
Poplar trees near streams surround it.
23 It is not afraid when the river roars.
It is secure even when the Jordan River rushes against its mouth.
24 Can anyone capture it by its eyes?
Can anyone trap it and poke a hole through its nose?

41

"Job, can you pull Leviathan out of the sea with a fishhook?
Can you tie down its tongue with a rope?
2 Can you put a rope through its nose?
Can you stick a hook through its jaw?
3 Will it keep begging you for mercy?
Will it speak gently to you?
4 Will it make an agreement with you?
Can you make it your slave for life?
5 Can you make a pet out of it like a bird?
Can you put it on a leash for the young women in your house?
6 Will traders offer you something for it?
Will they divide it up among the merchants?
7 Can you fill its body with harpoons?
Can you throw fishing spears into its head?
8 If you touch it, it will fight you.
Then you will remember never to touch it again!
9 No one can possibly control Leviathan.
Just looking at it will terrify you.
10 No one dares to wake it up.
So who can possibly stand up to me?
11 Who has a claim against me that I must pay?
Everything on earth belongs to me.
12 "Now I will speak about the Leviathan's legs.
I will talk about its strength and its graceful body.
13 Who can strip off its outer coat?
Who would try to pierce its double coat of armor?
14 Who dares to open its jaws?
Its mouth is filled with terrifying teeth.
15 Its back has rows of shields that are close together.
16 Each one is so close to the next one that not even air can pass between them.

[17] They are joined tightly to one
another.
They stick together and can't be
forced apart.
[18] Leviathan's snorting throws out
flashes of light.
Its eyes shine like the first light
of day.
[19] Flames spray out of its mouth.
Sparks of fire shoot out.
[20] Smoke pours out of its nose.
It is like smoke from a boiling pot
over burning grass.
[21] Its breath sets coals on fire.
Flames fly out of its mouth.
[22] Its neck is very strong.
People run to get out of its way.
[23] Its rolls of fat are close together.
They are firm and can't be
moved.
[24] Its chest is as hard as rock.
It is as hard as a lower millstone.
[25] When Leviathan rises up,
even mighty people are terrified.
They run away when it moves
around wildly.
[26] A sword that strikes it has no effect.
Neither does a spear or dart or
javelin.
[27] It treats iron as if it were straw.
It crushes bronze as if it were
rotten wood.
[28] Arrows do not make it run away.
Stones that are thrown from
slings are like straw hitting it.
[29] A club seems like a piece of straw
to it.
It laughs when it hears a javelin
rattling.
[30] Its undersides are like broken
pieces of pottery.
It leaves a trail in the mud like a
threshing sled.
[31] It makes the ocean churn like a
boiling pot.
It stirs up the sea like perfume
someone is making.
[32] It leaves a shiny trail behind it.
You would think the ocean had
white hair.
[33] Nothing on earth is equal to
Leviathan.
That creature is not afraid of
anything.
[34] It looks down on proud people.
It rules over all those who are
proud."

Job's Reply

42 Job replied to the LORD,

[2] "I know that you can do anything.
No one can keep you from doing
what you plan to do.
[3] You asked me, 'Who do you think
you are to disagree with my
plans?
You do not know what you are
talking about.'
I spoke about things I didn't
completely understand.
I talked about things that were
too wonderful for me to know.

[4] "You said, 'Listen now, and I will
speak.
I will ask you some questions.
Then I want you to answer me.'
[5] My ears had heard about you.
But now my own eyes have seen
you.
[6] So I hate myself.
I'm really sorry for what I said
about you.
That's why I'm sitting in dust and
ashes."

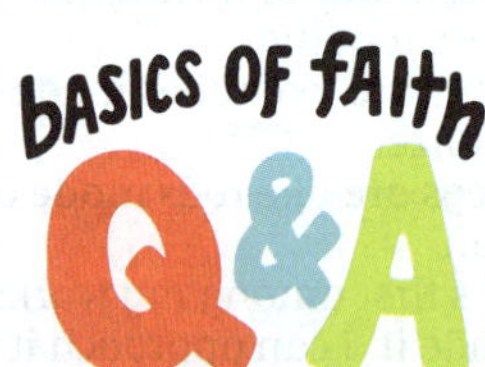

If God is good, why do bad things happen?

God gave humans the ability to choose to obey or disobey him. When Adam and Eve chose disobedience, sin entered the world, bringing death and destruction. We don't always know why bad things happen, but we can trust that God is good and that he is in control.

Can you find the following verses?

JOB 42:2–3

The Story Ends

[7]After the LORD finished speaking to
Job, he spoke to Eliphaz the Temanite. He
said, "I am angry with you and your two
friends. You have not said what is true
about me, as my servant Job has. [8]So
now get seven bulls and seven rams. Go to
my servant Job. Then sacrifice a burnt offering for yourselves. My servant Job will
pray for you. And I will accept his prayer.
I will not punish you for saying the foolish
things you said. You have not said what
is true about me, as my servant Job has."
[9]So Eliphaz the Temanite, Bildad the
Shuhite, and Zophar the Naamathite did
what the LORD told them to do. And the
LORD accepted Job's prayer.

[10]After Job had prayed for his friends,
the LORD made him successful again.
He gave him twice as much as he had
before. [11]All his brothers and sisters and
everyone who had known him before
came to see him. They ate with him in
his house. They showed their concern
for him. They comforted him because
of all the troubles the LORD had brought
on him. Each one gave him a piece of
silver and a gold ring.

[12]The LORD blessed the last part of
Job's life even more than the first part.
He gave Job 14,000 sheep and 6,000
camels. He gave him 1,000 pairs of oxen
and 1,000 donkeys. [13]Job also had seven
sons and three daughters. [14]He named
the first daughter Jemimah. He named
the second Keziah. And he named the
third Keren-Happuch. [15]Job's daughters
were more beautiful than any other
women in the whole land. Their father
gave them a share of property along
with their brothers.

[16]After all of that happened, Job
lived for 140 years. He saw his children, his grandchildren and his great-
grandchildren. [17]And so Job died. He
had lived for a very long time.

PSALMS

Author: Many of the psalms were written by King David, but a lot of people contributed to this book.

Wisdom & Poetry

Psalms is made up of poetic prayers and songs that were written by many authors and compiled into one book. Psalms was a book of songs or prayers for God's people in the Old Testament. They could use this book whether they were having a big gathering or worshiping in their own homes. When they were sad or confused, they could read the prayers to God. When they were full of thanksgiving and praise, they could sing the songs to him. The entire book invites us to take all our emotions to God and shows us how to talk to him whether we are sad, excited, frustrated, afraid, joyful, or worried. Psalms reminds us that our emotions are never too big for God; we can bring them to God and talk to him no matter what we are feeling.

But that's not all. The book of Psalms also has a unifying message. Even though many different people wrote this book, each psalm works together to teach about God's plan to redeem the world through a Savior. In every line of every poem, God was writing one great big message: God's people needed saving, and God was going to be the one to save them.

BOOK I

Psalms 1–41

Psalm 1

1 Blessed is the person who obeys the law of the LORD.
They don't follow the advice of evil people.
They don't make a habit of doing what sinners do.
They don't join those who make fun of the LORD and his law.
2 Instead, the law of the LORD gives them joy.
They think about his law day and night.
3 That kind of person is like a tree that is planted near a stream of water.
It always bears its fruit at the right time.
Its leaves don't dry up.
Everything godly people do turns out well.

4 Sinful people are not like that at all.
They are like straw
that the wind blows away.
5 When the LORD judges them, their life will come to an end.
Sinners won't have any place among those who are godly.

6 The LORD watches over the lives of godly people.
But the lives of sinful people will lead to their death.

Psalm 2

1 Why do the nations plan evil together?
Why do they make useless plans?
2 The kings of the earth rise up against the LORD.
The rulers of the earth join together against his anointed king.
3 "Let us break free from their chains," they say.
"Let us throw off their ropes."
4 The God who sits on his throne in heaven laughs.
The Lord makes fun of those rulers and their plans.
5 When he is angry, he warns them.
When his anger blazes out, he terrifies them.

in Psalms?

God is the Worthy One. He is the only one who deserves our endless praise.

6 He says to them,
"I have placed my king on my holy mountain of Zion."

7 I will announce what the LORD has
promised.

He said to me, "You are my son.
Today I have become your father.
8 Ask me, and I will give the nations to you.
All nations on earth will belong to you.
9 You will break them with an iron scepter.
You will smash them to pieces like clay pots."
10 Kings, be wise!
Rulers of the earth, be warned!
11 Serve the LORD and have respect for him.
Celebrate his rule with trembling.
12 Obey the son completely, or he will be angry.
Your way of life will lead to your death.
His anger can blaze out at any moment.
Blessed are all those who go to him for safety.

Psalm 3

A psalm of David when he ran away from his son Absalom.

1 LORD, I have so many enemies!
So many people are rising up against me!

[2] Many are saying about me,
"God will not save him."

[3] LORD, you are like a shield that
keeps me safe.
You bring me honor. You help me
win the battle.
[4] I call out to the LORD.
He answers me from his holy
mountain.

[5] I lie down and sleep.
I wake up again, because the
LORD takes care of me.
[6] I won't be afraid even though tens
of thousands
attack me on every side.

[7] LORD, rise up!
My God, save me!
Strike all my enemies in the
face.
Break the teeth of sinful
people.

[8] LORD, you are the one who saves.
May your blessing be on your
people.

Psalm 4

For the director of music.
A psalm of David to be played
on stringed instruments.

[1] My faithful God,
answer me when I call out
to you.
Give me rest from my trouble.
Have mercy on me. Hear my
prayer.
[2] How long will you people turn my
glory into shame?
How long will you love what will
certainly fail you?
How long will you pray to statues
of gods?
[3] Remember that the LORD has set
apart his faithful servant for
himself.
The LORD hears me when I call
out to him.

[4] Tremble and do not sin.
When you are in bed,
look deep down inside yourself
and be silent.
[5] Offer to the LORD the sacrifices that
godly people offer.
Trust in him.

[6] LORD, many are asking, "Who will
make us successful?"
LORD, may you do good things
for us.
[7] Fill my heart with joy
when the people have lots of
grain and fresh wine.
[8] In peace I will lie down and sleep.
LORD, you alone keep me safe.

Psalm 5

For the director of music.
A psalm of David to be played
on flutes.

[1] LORD, listen to my words.
Pay attention when I mourn.
[2] My King and my God,
hear me when I cry for help.
I pray to you.
[3] LORD, in the morning you hear my
voice.
In the morning I pray to you.
I wait for you in hope.

[4] For you, God, aren't happy with
anything that is evil.
Those who do what is wrong can't
live where you are.
[5] Those who are proud can't stand in
front of you.
You hate everyone who does
what is evil.
[6] You destroy those who tell lies.
LORD, you hate murderers and
those who cheat others.

[7] Because of your great love
I can come into your house.
With deep respect I bow down
toward your holy temple.
[8] LORD, I have many enemies.
Lead me in your right path.
Make your way smooth and
straight for me.

[9] Not a word from their mouths can
be trusted.
Their hearts are filled with a
desire to hurt others.
Their throats are like open graves.
With their tongues they tell lies.
[10] God, show that they are guilty.
Let their evil plans bring them
down.
Send them away because of their
many sins.
They have refused to obey you.

[11] But let all those who go to you for safety be glad.
Let them always sing for joy.
Spread your cover over them and keep them safe.
Then those who love you will be glad because of you.
[12] Surely, LORD, you bless those who do what is right.
Like a shield, your loving care keeps them safe.

Psalm 6

For the director of music. According to sheminith. *A psalm of David to be played on stringed instruments.*

[1] LORD, don't correct me when you are angry.
Don't punish me when you are very angry.
[2] LORD, have mercy on me. I'm so weak.
LORD, heal me. My body is full of pain.
[3] My soul is very troubled.
LORD, how long will it be until you save me?

[4] LORD, turn to me and help me.
Save me. Your love never fails.
[5] Dead people can't call out your name.
How can they praise you when they are in the grave?

[6] My groaning has worn me out.
All night long my tears flood my bed.
My bed is wet because of my crying.
[7] I'm so sad I can't see very well.
My eyesight gets worse because of all my enemies.

[8] Get away from me, all you who do evil.
The LORD has heard my weeping.
[9] The LORD has heard my cry for his mercy.
The LORD accepts my prayer.
[10] All my enemies will be covered with shame and trouble.
They will turn back in shame. It will happen suddenly.

Psalm 7

A shiggaion *of David. He sang it to the LORD about Cush, who was from the tribe of Benjamin.*

[1] LORD my God, I go to you for safety.
Help me. Save me from all those who are chasing me.
[2] If you don't, they will tear me apart as if they were lions.
They will rip me to pieces so that no one can save me.

[3] LORD my God, suppose I have done something wrong.
Suppose I am guilty.
[4] Or I have done evil to my friend.
Or I have robbed my enemy without any reason.
[5] Then let my enemy chase me and catch me.
Let him stomp me into the ground.
Let him bury me in the dust.

[6] LORD, rise up in your anger.
Rise up against the great anger of my enemies.
My God, wake up. Command that the right thing be done.
[7] Let all the people of the earth gather around you.
Rule over them from your throne in heaven.
[8] LORD, judge all people.
LORD, show that I have done what is right.
Most High God, remember that I am honest.
[9] God, you always do what is right.
You look deep down inside the hearts and minds of people.
Bring to an end the terrible things sinful people do.
Make godly people safe.

[10] The Most High God is like a shield that keeps me safe.
He saves those whose hearts are honest.
[11] God judges fairly.
He shows his anger every day.
[12] If evil people don't change their ways, God will sharpen his sword.
He will get his bow ready to use.
[13] He has prepared his deadly weapons.
He has made his flaming arrows ready.

[14] Whoever is full of evil
plans trouble and ends up telling lies.
[15] Whoever digs a hole and shovels it out
falls into the pit they have made.
[16] The trouble they cause comes back on them.
The terrible things they do will happen to them.
[17] I will give thanks to the LORD
because he does what is right.
I will sing the praises of the
name of the LORD Most High.

Psalm 8

For the director of music. According to gittith. A psalm of David.

[1] LORD, our Lord,
how majestic is your name in the whole earth!

You have set your glory
in the heavens.
[2] You have made sure that children
and infants praise you.
Their praise is a wall
that stops the talk of your enemies.

[3] I think about the heavens.
I think about what your fingers have created.
I think about the moon and stars
that you have set in place.
[4] What are human beings that you think about them?
What is a son of man that you take care of him?
[5] You have made them a little lower than the angels.
You placed on them a crown of glory and honor.

[6] You made human beings rule over
everything your hands created.
You put everything under their control.
[7] They rule over all flocks and herds
and over the wild animals.
[8] They rule over the birds in the sky
and over the fish in the ocean.
They rule over everything that swims in the oceans.

[9] LORD, our Lord,
how majestic is your name in the whole earth!

Psalm 9

For the director of music. A psalm of David to the tune of "The Death of the Son."

[1] LORD, I will give thanks to you with all my heart.
I will tell about all the wonderful things you have done.
[2] I will be glad and full of joy
because of you.
Most High God, I will sing the praises of your name.

key verse LORD, I will give thanks to you with all my heart. I will tell about all the wonderful things you have done. **PSALM 9:1**

[3] My enemies turn back.
They fall down and die right in front of you.
[4] You have proved that I haven't done anything wrong.
You have sat on your throne and judged fairly.
[5] You have punished the nations.
You have destroyed evil people.
You have erased their names
from your book for ever and ever.
[6] My enemies have been destroyed forever.
You have leveled their cities to the ground.
Even the memory of them is gone.

[7] The LORD rules forever.
He has set up his throne so that he can judge people.
[8] He rules the world in keeping with what is right.
He judges all its people fairly.
[9] The LORD is a place of safety for
those who have been treated badly.
He keeps them safe in times of trouble.
[10] LORD, those who know you will
trust in you.
You have never deserted those
who look to you.

11 Sing the praises of the LORD. He
rules from his throne in Zion.
Tell among the nations what he
has done.
12 The God who pays back murderers
remembers.
He doesn't forget the cries of
those who are hurting.
13 LORD, see how badly my enemies
treat me!
Help me! Don't let me go down to
the gates of death!
14 Then I can give praise to you
at the gates of the city of Zion.
There I will be full of joy
because you have saved me.
15 The nations have fallen into the pit
they have dug.
Their feet are caught in the net
they have hidden.
16 The LORD is known to be fair by the
things he does.
Evil people are trapped by what
they have done.
17 Sinful people go down to the place
of the dead.
So do all the nations that forget
God.
18 But God will never forget needy
people.
The hope of those who are
hurting will never die.
19 LORD, rise up. Don't let people win
the battle.
Let the nations come to you and
be judged.
20 LORD, strike them with terror.
Let the nations know they are only
human beings.

Psalm 10

1 LORD, why are you so far away?
Why do you hide yourself in
times of trouble?
2 An evil person is proud and hunts
down those who are weak.
He catches weak people by
making clever plans.
3 He brags about what his heart
desires.
He speaks well of those who
always want more.
He attacks the LORD with his
words.
4 Because he is proud, that evil
person doesn't turn to the LORD.
There is no room for God in any
of his thoughts.
5 Everything always goes well for him.
So he is proud.
He doesn't want to have anything
to do with God's laws.
He makes fun of all his enemies.
6 He says to himself, "I will always be
secure."
He promises himself, "No one will
ever harm me."
7 His mouth is full of lies and
warnings.
With his tongue he speaks evil
and makes trouble.
8 Sinful people hide and wait near
the villages.
From their hiding places they
murder people who aren't
guilty.
They watch in secret for those
they want to attack.
9 They hide and wait like a lion in
the bushes.
From their hiding places they
wait to catch those who are
helpless.
They catch them and drag them
off in their nets.
10 Those they have attacked are
beaten up. They fall to the
ground.
They fall because their attackers
are too strong for them.
11 Sinful people say to themselves,
"God will never notice.
He covers his face. He never
sees us."
12 LORD, rise up! God, show your
power!
Don't forget those who are
helpless.
13 Why do sinful people attack you
with their words?
Why do they say to themselves,
"He won't hold us accountable"?
14 God, you see the problems of people
in trouble.
You take note of their pain. You
do something about it.
So those who are attacked place
themselves in your care.
You help children whose fathers
have died.

[15]Take away the power of sinful people.
Hold them accountable for the evil things they do.
Uncover all the evil they have done.

[16]The LORD is King for ever and ever.
The nations will disappear from his land.
[17]LORD, you hear the desires of those who are hurting.
You cheer them up and give them hope.
You listen to their cries.
[18]You stand up for those whose fathers have died
and for those who have been treated badly.
You do it so that mere human beings made of dust
may not terrify others anymore.

Psalm 11

For the director of music. A psalm of David.

[1]I run to the LORD for safety.
So how can you say to me,
"Fly away like a bird to your mountain.
[2]Look! Evil people are bending their bows.
They are placing their arrows against the strings.
They are planning to shoot from the shadows
at those who have honest hearts.
[3]When law and order are being destroyed,
what can godly people do?"

[4]The LORD is in his holy temple.
The LORD is on his throne in heaven.
He watches everyone on earth.
His eyes study them.
[5]The LORD watches over those who do what is right.
But he really hates sinful people
and those who love to hurt others.
[6]He will pour out flaming coals and burning sulfur
on those who do what is wrong.
A hot and dry wind will destroy them.

[7]The LORD always does what is right.
So he loves it when people do what is fair.
Those who are honest will enjoy his blessing.

Psalm 12

For the director of music. According to sheminith. *A psalm of David.*

[1]Help, LORD! No one does what is right anymore.
Those who are faithful have disappeared from the human race.
[2]Everyone tells lies to their neighbors.
With their lips they praise others,
but they don't really mean it.

[3]May the LORD close all lips that don't mean what they say.
May he stop every tongue that brags.
[4]They say, "What we speak with our tongues will win the battle.
What we say with our lips will keep us safe. No one will have victory over us."

[5]The LORD says, "The poor are being robbed.
Those who are in need groan.
So I will stand up to help them.
I will keep them safe from those who tell lies about them."
[6]The words of the LORD are perfect.
They are like silver made pure in a clay furnace.
They are like gold made pure seven times over.

[7]LORD, you will keep needy people safe.
You will always keep sinners from hurting us.
[8]Proud and sinful people walk around openly
when the evil they do is praised by the human race.

Psalm 13

For the director of music. A psalm of David.

[1]LORD, how long must I wait? Will you forget me forever?
How long will you turn your face away from me?

2 How long must I struggle with my
thoughts?
How long must my heart be sad
day after day?
How long will my enemies keep
winning the battle over me?

3 LORD my God, look at me and
answer me.
Give me new life, or I will die.
4 Then my enemies will say, "We
have beaten him."
They will be filled with joy when
I die.

5 But I trust in your faithful love.
My heart is filled with joy
because you will save me.
6 I will sing praise to the LORD.
He has been so good to me.

Psalm 14

For the director of music.
A psalm of David.

1 Foolish people say in their hearts,
"There is no God."
They do all kinds of horrible and
evil things.
No one does anything good.

2 The LORD looks down from heaven
on all people.
He wants to see if there are any
who understand.
He wants to see if there are any
who trust in God.
3 All of them have turned away.
They have all become evil.
No one does anything good,
no one at all.

4 Do all these people who do evil
know nothing?
They eat up my people as if they
were eating bread.
They never call out to the LORD.
5 But just look at them! They are
filled with terror
because God is among those who
do right.
6 You who do evil keep poor people
from succeeding.
But the LORD is their place of safety.
7 How I pray that the God who saves
Israel will come out of Zion!
Then the LORD will bless his
people with great success again.
So let the people of Jacob be filled
with joy! Let Israel be glad!

Psalm 15

A psalm of David.

1 LORD, who can live in your sacred
tent?
Who can stay on your holy
mountain?

2 Anyone who lives without blame
and does what is right.
They speak the truth from their
heart.
3 They don't tell lies about other
people.
They don't do wrong to their
neighbors.
They don't say anything bad
about them.
4 They hate evil people.
But they honor those who have
respect for the LORD.
They keep their promises even
when it hurts.
They do not change their mind.
5 They lend their money to poor
people without charging
interest.
They don't accept money to
harm those who aren't guilty.

Anyone who lives like that
will always be secure.

Psalm 16

A miktam of David.

1 My God, keep me safe.
I go to you for safety.

2 I say to the LORD, "You are my Lord.
Without you, I don't have
anything that is good."
3 I say about God's people who live in
our land, "They are the noble
ones.
I take great delight in them."
4 Those who run after other gods
will suffer more and more.
I will not pour out offerings of
blood to those gods.
My lips will not speak their names.

5 LORD, you alone are everything I
need.
You make my life secure.

[6]I am very pleased with what you
have given me.
I am very happy with what I've
received from you.

[7]I will praise the LORD. He gives me
good advice.
Even at night my heart teaches me.
[8]I keep my eyes always on the LORD.
He is at my right hand.
So I will always be secure.

[9]So my heart is glad. Joy is on my
tongue.
My body also will be secure.
[10]You will not leave me in the place
of the dead.
You will not let your faithful one
rot away.
[11]You always show me the path of
life.
You will fill me with joy when I
am with you.
You will make me happy forever
at your right hand.

Psalm 17

A prayer of David.

[1]LORD, hear me, because I ask for
what is right.
Listen to my cry for help.
Hear my prayer.
It doesn't come from lips that tell
lies.
[2]When you hand down your
sentence, may it be in my
favor.
May your eyes see what is right.

[3]Look deep down into my heart.
Study me carefully at night and
test me.
You won't find anything wrong.
I have planned nothing evil.
My mouth has not said sinful
things.
[4]Though evil people tried to pay me
to do wrong,
I have not done what they
wanted.
Instead I have done what you
commanded.
[5]My steps have stayed on your paths.
My feet have not slipped.

[6]My God, I call out to you because
you will answer me.
Listen to me. Hear my prayer.
[7]Show me the wonders of your great
love.
By using your great power,
you save those who go to you for
safety from their enemies.
[8]Take good care of me, just as you
would take care of your own
eyes.
Hide me in the shadow of your
wings.
[9]Save me from the sinful people who
want to destroy me.
Save me from my deadly
enemies who are all around me.

[10]They make their hearts hard and
stubborn.
Their mouths speak with pride.
[11]They have tracked me down. They
are all around me.
Their eyes watch for a chance to
throw me to the ground.
[12]They are like a hungry lion,
waiting to attack.
They are like a powerful lion,
hiding in the bushes.

[13]LORD, rise up. Oppose them and
bring them down.
With your sword, save me from
those evil people.
[14]LORD, by your power save me from
people like that.
They belong to this world. They
get their reward in this life.

May what you have stored up for
evil people fill their bellies.
May their children's stomachs be
filled with it.
And may there even be leftovers
for their little ones.
[15]You will show that I am right; I will
enjoy your blessing.
When I wake up, I will be
satisfied because I will see you.

Psalm 18

*For the director of music.
A psalm of David, the servant
of the LORD. He sang the words
of this song to the LORD. He sang
them when the LORD saved him. He
saved him from the power of all his
enemies and of Saul. David said,*

[1]I love you, LORD.
You give me strength.

[2]The LORD is my rock and my place of safety. He is the God who saves me.
My God is my rock. I go to him for safety.
He is like a shield to me. He's the power that saves me. He's my place of safety.
[3]I called out to the LORD. He is worthy of praise.
He saved me from my enemies.

[4]The ropes of death were almost wrapped around me.
A destroying flood swept over me.
[5]The ropes of the grave were tight around me.
Death set its trap in front of me.
[6]When I was in trouble, I called out to the LORD.
I cried to my God for help.
From his temple he heard my voice.
My cry for help reached his ears.

[7]The earth trembled and shook.
The base of the mountains rocked back and forth.
It trembled because the LORD was angry.
[8]Smoke came out of his nose.
Flames of fire came out of his mouth.
Burning coals blazed out of it.
[9]He opened the heavens and came down.
Dark clouds were under his feet.
[10]He stood on the cherubim and flew.
The wings of the wind lifted him up.
[11]He covered himself with darkness.
The dark rain clouds of the sky were like a tent around him.
[12]Clouds came out of the brightness that was all around him.
They came with hailstones and flashes of lightning.
[13]The LORD thundered from heaven.
The voice of the Most High God was heard.
[14]He shot his arrows and scattered our enemies.
He sent great flashes of lightning and chased the enemies away.
[15]The bottom of the sea could be seen.
The foundations of the earth were uncovered.
LORD, it happened when your anger blazed out.
It came like a blast of breath from your nose.

[16]He reached down from heaven. He took hold of me.
He lifted me out of deep waters.
[17]He saved me from my powerful enemies.
He set me free from those who were too strong for me.
[18]They opposed me when I was in trouble.
But the LORD helped me.
[19]He brought me out into a wide and safe place.
He saved me because he was pleased with me.

[20]The LORD has been good to me because I do what is right.
He has rewarded me because I lead a pure life.
[21]I have lived the way the LORD wanted me to.
I am not guilty of turning away from my God.
[22]I keep all his laws in mind.
I haven't turned away from his commands.
[23]He knows that I am without blame.
He knows I've kept myself from sinning.
[24]The LORD has rewarded me for doing what is right.
He has rewarded me because I haven't done anything wrong.

[25]LORD, to those who are faithful you show that you are faithful.
To those who are without blame you show that you are without blame.
[26]To those who are pure you show that you are pure.
But to those whose paths are crooked you show that you are clever.
[27]You save those who aren't proud.
But you bring down those whose eyes are proud.
[28]LORD, you keep the lamp of my life burning brightly.
You are my God. You bring light into my darkness.

29 With your help I can attack a troop
of soldiers.
With the help of my God I can
climb over a wall.

30 God's way is perfect.
The LORD's word doesn't have
any flaws.
He is like a shield
to all who go to him for safety.
31 Who is God except the LORD?
Who is the Rock except our God?
32 God gives me strength for the
battle.
He keeps my way secure.
33 He makes my feet like the feet of a
deer.
He causes me to stand on the
highest places.
34 He trains my hands to fight every
battle.
My arms can bend a bow of
bronze.
35 LORD, you are like a shield that
keeps me safe.
Your strong right hand keeps me
going.
Your help has made me great.
36 You give me a wide path to walk on
so that I don't twist my ankles.

37 I chased my enemies and caught
them.
I didn't turn back until they were
destroyed.
38 I crushed them so that they
couldn't get up.
They fell under my feet.
39 LORD, you gave me strength to fight
the battle.
You made my enemies humble
in front of me.
40 You made them turn their backs
and run away.
So I destroyed my enemies.
41 They cried out for help. But there
was no one to save them.
They called out to the LORD. But
he didn't answer them.
42 I beat them as fine as dust blown
by the wind.
I stomped on them like mud in
the streets.
43 You saved me when my own people
attacked me.
You made me the ruler over
nations.
People I didn't know serve me now.
44 People from other lands bow down
to me in fear.
As soon as they hear me, they
obey me.
45 All of them give up hope.
They come trembling out of their
hiding places.

46 The LORD lives! Give praise to my
Rock!
Give honor to God my Savior!
47 He is the God who pays back my
enemies.
He brings the nations under my
control.
48 He saves me from my
enemies.
You have honored me more than
them.
You have saved me from a man
who wanted to hurt me.
49 LORD, I will praise you among the
nations.
I will sing the praises of your
name.
50 The LORD helps his king win great
battles.
He shows his faithful love to his
anointed king.
He shows it to David and to his
family forever.

Psalm 19

For the director of music.
A psalm of David.

1 The heavens tell about the glory of
God.
The skies show that his hands
created them.
2 Day after day they speak about it.
Night after night they make it
known.
3 But they don't speak or use words.
No sound is heard from them.
4 Yet their voice goes out into the
whole earth.
Their words go out from one end
of the world to the other.

God has set up a tent in the
heavens for the sun.
5 The sun is like a groom leaving
the room of his wedding
night.
The sun is like a great runner
who takes delight in running a
race.

6 It rises at one end of the heavens.
Then it moves across to the other end.
Everything enjoys its warmth.

7 The law of the LORD is perfect.
It gives us new strength.
The laws of the LORD can be trusted.
They make childish people wise.
8 The rules of the LORD are right.
They give joy to our hearts.
The commands of the LORD shine brightly.
They give light to our minds.
9 The law that brings respect for the LORD is pure.
It lasts forever.
The commands the LORD gives are true.
All of them are completely right.
10 They are more priceless than gold.
They have greater value than huge amounts of pure gold.
They are sweeter than honey
that is taken from the honeycomb.
11 Your servant is warned by them.
When people obey them, they are greatly rewarded.

12 But who can know their own mistakes?
Forgive my hidden faults.
13 Also keep me from the sins I want to commit.
May they not be my master.
Then I will be without blame.
I will not be guilty of any great sin against your law.

14 LORD, may these words of my mouth please you.
And may these thoughts of my heart please you also.
You are my Rock and my Redeemer.

Psalm 20

For the director of music.
A psalm of David.

1 May the LORD answer you when you are in trouble.
May the God of Jacob keep you safe.
2 May he send you help from the sacred tent.
May he give you aid from Zion.
3 May he remember all your sacrifices.
May he accept your burnt offerings.
4 May he give you what your heart wishes for.
May he make all your plans succeed.
5 May we shout for joy over your victory.
May we lift up our flags in the name of our God.
May the LORD give you everything you ask for.

6 Now I know that the LORD gives victory to his anointed king.
He answers him from his sacred home in heaven.
The power of God's right hand gives victory to the king.
7 Some trust in chariots. Some trust in horses.
But we trust in the LORD our God.
8 They are brought to their knees and fall down.
But we get up and stand firm.

9 LORD, give victory to the king!
Answer us when we call out to you!

How can we know that the Bible is true?

A lot of evidence throughout history points to the fact that the Bible is true. But most importantly, Scripture encourages us to look around at all God created to learn about him and see how he is at work in the world.

Can you find the following verse?

PSALM 19:1

Psalm 21

For the director of music.
A psalm of David.

1 LORD, the king is filled with joy
because you are strong.
How great is his joy because
you help him win his
battles!
2 You have given him what his heart
wished for.
You haven't kept back from him
what his lips asked for.
3 You came to greet him with rich
blessings.
You placed a crown of pure gold
on his head.
4 He asked you for life, and you gave
it to him.
You promised him days that
would never end.
5 His glory is great because
you helped him win his
battles.
You have honored him with glory
and majesty.
6 You have given him blessings that
will never end.
You have made him glad and
joyful because you are with
him.

7 The king trusts in the LORD.
The faithful love of the Most High
God
will keep the king secure.

8 You, the king, will capture all your
enemies.
Your right hand will take hold of
them.
9 When you appear for battle,
you will burn them up like
they were in a flaming
furnace.
The LORD will swallow them up in
his great anger.
His fire will burn them up.
10 You will wipe their children from
the face of the earth.
You will remove them from the
human race.
11 Your enemies make evil plans
against you.
They think up evil things
to do. But they can't
succeed.
12 You will make them turn their
backs and run away
when you aim your arrows at
them.

13 LORD, may you be honored because
you are strong.
We will sing and praise your
might.

Psalm 22

For the director of music.
A psalm of David to the tune
of "The Doe of the Morning."

1 My God, my God, why have you
deserted me?
Why do you seem so far away
when I need you to save me?
Why do you seem so far away
that you can't hear my
groans?
2 My God, I cry out in the daytime.
But you don't answer.
I cry out at night. But you don't
let me sleep.
3 But you rule from your throne as
the Holy One.
You are the God Israel praises.
4 Our people of long ago put their
trust in you.
They trusted in you, and you
saved them.
5 They cried out to you and were
saved.
They trusted in you, and you
didn't let them down.

6 Everyone treats me like a worm
and not a man.
They hate me and look down
on me.
7 All those who see me laugh
at me.
They shout at me and make fun
of me.
They shake their heads at me.
8 They say, "He trusts in the LORD.
Let the LORD help him.
If the LORD is pleased with him,
let him save him."

9 But you brought me out of my
mother's body.
You made me trust in you
even when I was at my mother's
breast.

[10] From the time I was born, you took
good care of me.
Ever since I came out of my
mother's body, you have been
my God.
[11] Don't be far away from me.
Trouble is near,
and there is no one to help me.

[12] Many enemies are all
around me.
They are like strong bulls from
the land of Bashan.
[13] They are like roaring lions that tear
to pieces what they kill.
They open their mouths wide to
attack me.
[14] My strength is like water that is
poured out on the ground.
I feel as if my bones aren't
connected.
My heart has turned to wax.
It has melted away inside me.
[15] My mouth is dried up like a piece of
broken pottery.
My tongue sticks to the roof of
my mouth.
You bring me down to the edge
of the grave.
[16] A group of sinful people has closed
in on me.
They are all around me like a
pack of dogs.
They have pierced my hands and
my feet.
[17] Everyone can see all my bones
right through my skin.
People stare at me. They laugh
when I suffer.
[18] They divide up my clothes among
them.
They cast lots for what I am
wearing.
[19] LORD, don't be so far away
from me.
You give me strength. Come
quickly to help me.
[20] Save me from being killed by the
sword.
Save the only life I have.
Save me from the power of
those dogs.
[21] Save me from the mouths of those
lions.
Save me from the horns of those
wild oxen.

[22] I will announce your name to my
people.
I will praise you among those
who are gathered to worship
you.
[23] You who have respect for the LORD,
praise him!
All you people of Jacob, honor
him!
All you people of Israel, worship
him!
[24] He has not forgotten the one who is
hurting.
He has not turned away from his
suffering.
He has not turned his face away
from him.
He has listened to his cry for
help.

[25] Because of what you have
done,
I will praise you in the whole
community of those who
worship you.
In front of those who respect you,
I will keep my promises.
[26] Those who are poor will eat and be
satisfied.
Those who seek the LORD will
praise him.
May their hearts be filled with
new hope!
[27] People from one end of the earth to
the other
will remember and turn to the
LORD.
The people of all the nations
will bow down in front of him.
[28] The LORD is King.
He rules over the nations.
[29] All rich people of the earth will
feast and worship God.
All who go down to the grave will
kneel in front of him.
Those who cannot keep
themselves alive will kneel.
[30] Those who are not yet born will
serve him.
Those who are born later will be
told about the Lord.
[31] And they will tell people who have
not yet been born,
"The Lord has done what is
right!"

Psalm 23

A psalm of David.

[1]The LORD is my shepherd. He gives
me everything I need.
[2] He lets me lie down in fields of
green grass.
He leads me beside quiet
waters.
[3] He gives me new strength.
He guides me in the right paths
for the honor of his name.
[4] Even though I walk
through the darkest valley,
I will not be afraid.
You are with me.
Your shepherd's rod and staff
comfort me.

[5] You prepare a feast for me
right in front of my enemies.
You pour oil on my head.
My cup runs over.

Jesus Is the Good Shepherd

Throughout the Bible we read about Jesus being like a good and compassionate shepherd who cares for the sheep in his flock. We are like sheep whom he tenderly guides while he fends off our enemies, provides for us, disciplines us, and safely leads us to our eternal home in heaven. Jesus compares himself to a shepherd who works tirelessly to find a sheep that is lost (see Luke 15:3–7). In the same way, God will look for us when we stray from him, inviting us to come back to him and reminding us that he has promised to care for and protect us.

[6] I am sure that your goodness and
love will follow me
all the days of my life.
And I will live in the house of the
LORD
forever.

Psalm 24

A psalm of David.

[1]The earth belongs to the LORD. And
so does everything in it.
The world belongs to him. And so
do all those who live in it.
[2] He set it firmly on the oceans.
He made it secure on the waters.

[3] Who can go up to the temple on the
mountain of the LORD?
Who can stand in his holy place?
[4] Anyone who has clean hands and a
pure heart.
Anyone who does not trust in the
statue of a god.
Anyone who doesn't use the
name of that god when he
makes a promise.
[5] People like that will receive the
LORD's blessing.
When God their Savior hands
down his sentence, it will be in
their favor.
[6] The people who look to God are like
that.
God of Jacob, they look to you.

[7] Open wide, you gates.
Open up, you ancient doors.
Then the King of glory will come in.
[8] Who is the King of glory?
The LORD, who is strong and
mighty.
The LORD, who is mighty in battle.
[9] Open wide, you gates.
Open wide, you ancient doors.
Then the King of glory will come in.
[10] Who is he, this King of glory?
The LORD who rules over all.
He is the King of glory.

Psalm 25

A psalm of David.

[1] In you, LORD my God, I put my trust.
[2] I trust in you.
Don't let me be put to shame.
Don't let my enemies win the
battle over me.

I refuse to spend time with those
who are evil.
6 I wash my hands to show that I'm
not guilty.
LORD, I come near your altar.
7 I shout my praise to you.
I tell about all the wonderful
things you have done.
8 LORD, I love the house where you
live.
I love the place where your glory is.
9 Don't destroy me together with
sinners.
Don't take away my life along
with murderers.
10 Their hands are always planning to
do evil.
Their right hands are full of
money that has bought their
help.
11 But I live without blame.
Save me from harm and treat me
with kindness.
12 My feet stand on level ground.
In the whole community I will
praise the LORD.

Psalm 27

A psalm of David.

1 The LORD is my light, and he
saves me.
Why should I fear anyone?
The LORD is my place of safety.
Why should I be afraid?
2 My enemies are evil.
They will trip and fall
when they attack me
and try to swallow me up.
3 Even if an army attacks me,
my heart will not be afraid.
Even if war breaks out against me,
I will still trust in God.
4 I'm asking the LORD for only one
thing.
Here is what I want.
I want to live in the house of the
LORD
all the days of my life.
I want to look at the beauty of the
LORD.
I want to worship him in his
temple.
5 When I'm in trouble,
he will keep me safe in his house.
He will hide me in the safety of his
holy tent.
He will put me on a rock that is
very high.
6 Then I will win the battle
over my enemies who are all
around me.
At his holy tent I will offer my
sacrifice with shouts of joy.
I will sing and make music to the
LORD.
7 LORD, hear my voice when I call out
to you.
Treat me with kindness and
answer me.
8 My heart says, "Seek him!"
LORD, I will seek you.
9 Don't turn your face away from me.
Don't turn me away because you
are angry.
You have helped me.
God my Savior, don't say no to me.
Don't desert me.
10 My father and mother may desert
me,
but the LORD will accept me.
11 LORD, teach me your ways.
Lead me along a straight path.
There are many people who treat
me badly.
12 My enemies want to harm me. So
don't turn me over to them.
Witnesses who tell lies are rising
up against me.
They say all sorts of evil things
about me.
13 Here is something I am still sure of.
I will see the LORD's goodness
while I'm still alive.
14 Wait for the LORD.
Be strong and don't lose hope.
Wait for the LORD.

Psalm 28

A psalm of David.

1 LORD, my Rock, I call out to you.
Pay attention to me.
If you remain silent, I will die.
I will be like those who go down
into the grave.
2 Hear my cry for your favor
when I call out to you for help.
Hear me when I lift up my hands in
prayer
toward your Most Holy Room.

[3]Those who put their hope in you
will never be put to shame.
But those who lie to other people
for no reason
will be put to shame.

[4]LORD, show me your ways.
Teach me how to follow you.
[5]Guide me in your truth. Teach me.
You are God my Savior.
I put my hope in you all day long.
[6]LORD, remember your great mercy
and love.
You have shown them to your
people for a long time.
[7]Don't remember the sins I
committed when I was young.
Don't remember how often I
refused to obey you.
Remember me because you
love me.
LORD, you are good.

[8]The LORD is honest and good.
He teaches sinners to walk in his
ways.
[9]He shows those who aren't proud
how to do what is right.
He teaches them his ways.
[10]All the LORD's ways are loving and
faithful
toward those who obey what his
covenant commands.
[11]LORD, be true to your name.
Forgive my sin, even though it is
great.
[12]Who are the people who have
respect for the LORD?
God will teach them the ways
they should choose.
[13]Things will always go well for them.
Their children will be given the
land.
[14]The LORD shares his plans with
those who have respect for him.
He makes his covenant known to
them.
[15]My eyes always look to the LORD.
He alone can set my feet free
from the trap.

[16]Turn to me and help me.
I am lonely and hurting.
[17]Take away the troubles of my
heart.
Set me free from my great pain.
[18]Look at how I'm hurting! See how
much I suffer!
Take away all my sins.

Can I trust God to provide for me?

God is a good shepherd who cares for you, his sheep. He will protect you, lead you, and provide for all your needs.

Can you find the following verse?
PSALM 23:1

[19]Look at how many enemies I have!
See how terrible their hatred is
for me!
[20]Guard my life. Save me.
Don't let me be put to shame.
I go to you for safety.
[21]May my honest and good life keep
me safe.
LORD, I have put my hope in you.

[22]God, set Israel free
from all their troubles!

Psalm 26

A psalm of David.

[1]LORD, when you hand down your
sentence, let it be in my favor.
I have lived without blame.
I have trusted in the LORD.
I have never doubted him.
[2]LORD, test me. Try me out.
Look deep down into my heart
and mind.
[3]I have always remembered your
love that never fails.
I have always depended on the
fact that you are faithful.
[4]I don't spend time with people who
tell lies.
I don't keep company with
pretenders.
[5]I hate to be with a group of sinful
people.

3 Don't drag me away with sinners.
Don't drag me away with those who do evil.
They speak in a friendly way to their neighbors.
But their hearts are full of hate.
4 Pay them back for their evil actions.
Pay them back for what their hands have done.
Give them exactly what they should get.
5 They don't care about the LORD's mighty acts.
They don't care about what his hands have done.
So he will tear them down.
He will never build them up again.
6 Give praise to the LORD.
He has heard my cry for his favor.
7 The LORD gives me strength. He is like a shield that keeps me safe.
My heart trusts in him, and he helps me.
My heart jumps for joy.
With my song I praise him.
8 The LORD gives strength to his people.
He guards and saves his anointed king.
9 Save your people. Bless those who belong to you.
Be their shepherd. Take care of them forever.

Psalm 29

A psalm of David.

1 Praise the LORD, you angels in heaven.
Praise the LORD for his glory and strength.
2 Praise the LORD for the glory that belongs to him.
Worship the LORD because of his beauty and holiness.
3 The voice of the LORD is heard over the waters.
The God of glory thunders.
The LORD thunders over the mighty waters.
4 The voice of the LORD is powerful.
The voice of the LORD is majestic.
5 The voice of the LORD breaks the cedar trees.
The LORD breaks the cedars of Lebanon into pieces.
6 He makes the mountains of Lebanon leap like a calf.
He makes Mount Hermon jump like a young wild ox.

BEAUTIFUL

Who God is and what he creates is beautiful (see Psalm 19:1). The goodness we feel on the inside is beautiful too.

Can you think of something beautiful God created? Perhaps you thought of a butterfly or a bird with bright, colorful wings. Or maybe you thought of majestic mountains with wildflowers growing on the hillsides. You may have even thought of the warm hug you received from a friend! All these things are beautiful, and God made all of them.

The things that God creates are beautiful because God himself is beautiful, and he wants us to share in that beauty with others.

[7] The voice of the LORD strikes
with flashes of lightning.
[8] The voice of the LORD shakes the
desert.
The LORD shakes the Desert of
Kadesh.
[9] The voice of the LORD twists the oak
trees.
It strips the forests bare.
And in his temple everyone cries
out, "Glory!"

[10] The LORD on his throne rules over
the flood.
The LORD rules from his throne
as King forever.
[11] The LORD gives strength to his
people.
The LORD blesses his people with
peace.

Psalm 30

A psalm of David. A song for setting apart the completed temple to God.

[1] LORD, I will give you honor.
You brought me out of deep
trouble.
You didn't give my enemies the
joy of seeing me die.
[2] LORD my God, I called out to you for
help.
And you healed me.
[3] LORD, you brought me up from the
place of the dead.
You kept me from going down
into the pit.

[4] Sing the praises of the LORD, you
who are faithful to him.
Praise him, because his name is
holy.
[5] His anger lasts for only a moment.
But his favor lasts for a person's
whole life.
Weeping can stay for the night.
But joy comes in the morning.

[6] When I felt safe, I said,
"I will always be secure."
[7] LORD, when you gave me your help,
you made Mount Zion stand
firm.
But when you took away your help,
I was terrified.

[8] LORD, I called out to you.
I cried to you for mercy.
[9] I said, "What good will come if I
become silent in death?
What good will come if I go down
into the grave?
Can the dust of my dead body
praise you?
Can it tell how faithful you are?
[10] LORD, hear me. Have mercy
on me.
LORD, help me."

[11] You turned my loud crying into
dancing.
You removed my clothes of
sadness and dressed me with
joy.
[12] So my heart will sing your praises. I
can't keep silent.
LORD, my God, I will praise you
forever.

Psalm 31

For the director of music. A psalm of David.

[1] LORD, I have come to you for
safety.
Don't let me ever be put to
shame.
Save me, because you do what is
right.
[2] Pay attention to me.
Come quickly to help me.
Be the rock I go to for safety.
Be the strong fort that saves me.
[3] You are my rock and my fort.
Lead me and guide me for the
honor of your name.
[4] Keep me free from the trap that is
set for me.
You are my place of safety.
[5] Into your hands I commit my very
life.
LORD, set me free. You are my
faithful God.

[6] I hate those who worship worthless
statues of gods.
But I trust in the LORD.
[7] I will be glad and full of joy
because you love me.
You saw that I was hurting.
You took note of my great pain.
[8] You have not handed me over to
the enemy.
You have put me in a wide and
safe place.

9 LORD, have mercy on me. I'm in
deep trouble.
I'm so sad I can hardly see.
My whole body grows weak with
sadness.
10 Pain has taken over my life.
My years are spent in groaning.
I have no strength because I'm
hurting so much.
My body is getting weaker and
weaker.
11 My neighbors make fun of me
because I have so many enemies.
My closest friends are afraid of me.
People who see me on the street
run away from me.
12 No one remembers me. I might as
well be dead.
I have become like broken pottery.
13 I hear many people whispering,
"There is terror all around him!"
Many have joined together
against me.
They plan to kill me.

14 But I trust in you, LORD.
I say, "You are my God."
15 My whole life is in your hands.
Save me from the hands of my
enemies.
Save me from those who are
chasing me.
16 May you look on me with favor.
Save me because your love is
faithful.
17 LORD, I have cried out to you.
Don't let me be put to shame.
But let sinners be put to shame.
Let them lie silent in the place of
the dead.
18 Their lips tell lies. Let them be
silenced.
They speak with pride against
those who do right.
They make fun of them.

19 You have stored up so many good
things.
You have stored them up for
those who have respect for you.
You give those things while
everyone watches.
You give them to people who run
to you for safety.
20 They are safe because you are with
them.
You hide them from the evil
plans of their enemies.
In your house you keep them safe
from those who bring charges
against them.

21 Give praise to the LORD.
He showed me his wonderful love
when my enemies attacked the
city I was in.
22 I was afraid and said,
"I've been cut off from you!"
But you heard my cry for your favor.
You heard me when I called out
to you for help.

23 Love the LORD, all you who are
faithful to him!
The LORD keeps safe those who
are faithful to him.
But he completely pays back
those who are proud.
24 Be strong, all you who put your
hope in the LORD.
Never give up.

Psalm 32

A maskil of David.

1 Blessed is the person whose lawless
acts are forgiven.
Their sins have been taken away.
2 Blessed is the person whose sin the
LORD never counts against them.
That person doesn't want to
cheat anyone.

3 When I kept silent about my sin,
my body became weak
because I groaned all day long.
4 Day and night
you punished me.
I became weaker and weaker
as I do in the heat of summer.
5 Then I admitted my sin to you.
I didn't cover up the wrong I had
done.
I said, "I will admit my lawless acts
to the LORD."
And you forgave the guilt of my
sin.

6 Let everyone who is faithful pray to
you
while they can still look to you.
When troubles come like a flood,
they certainly won't reach those
who are faithful.
7 You are my hiding place.
You will keep me safe from
trouble.

You will surround me with songs
sung by those who praise you
because you save your people.

8 I will guide you and teach you the
way you should go.
I will give you good advice and
watch over you with love.
9 Don't be like a horse or a mule.
They can't understand anything.
They have to be controlled by bits
and bridles.
If they aren't, they won't come to
you.
10 Sinful people have all kinds of
trouble.
But the LORD's faithful love
is all around those who trust in
him.

11 Be glad because of what the LORD
has done for you.
Be joyful, you who do what is
right!
Sing, all you whose hearts are
honest!

Psalm 33

1 You who are godly, sing with joy to
the LORD.
It is right for honest people to
praise him.
2 With the harp, praise the LORD.
With the lyre that has ten strings,
make music to him.
3 Sing a new song to him.
Play with skill, and shout with
joy.

4 What the LORD says is right and true.
He is faithful in everything he
does.
5 The LORD loves what is right and
fair.
The earth is full of his faithful
love.

6 The heavens were made when the
LORD commanded it to happen.
All the stars were created by the
breath of his mouth.
7 He gathers together the waters of
the sea.
He puts the oceans in their places.
8 Let the whole earth have respect for
the LORD.
Let all the people in the world
honor him.
9 He spoke, and the world came into
being.
He commanded, and it stood firm.
10 The LORD blocks the sinful plans of
the nations.
He keeps them from doing what
they want to do.
11 But the plans of the LORD stand
firm forever.
What he wants to do will last for
all time.

12 Blessed is the nation whose God is
the LORD.
Blessed are the people he chose
to be his own.
13 From heaven the LORD looks down
and sees everyone.
14 From his throne he watches
all those who live on the earth.
15 He creates the hearts of all people.
He is aware of everything they do.
16 A king isn't saved just because his
army is big.
A soldier doesn't escape just
because he is very strong.
17 People can't trust a horse to save
them either.
Though it is very strong, it can't
save them.
18 But the LORD looks with favor on
those who respect him.
He watches over those who put
their hope in his faithful love.
19 He watches over them to save them
from death.
He wants to keep them alive when
there is no food in the land.

20 We wait in hope for the LORD.
He helps us. He is like a shield
that keeps us safe.
21 Our hearts are full of joy because of
him.
We trust in him, because he is
holy.
22 LORD, may your faithful love be
with us.
We put our hope in you.

Psalm 34

A psalm of David when he was with Abimelek and pretended to be out of his mind. Abimelek drove him away, and David left.

1 I will thank the LORD at all times.
My lips will always praise him.

[2] I will find my glory in knowing the
LORD.
Let those who are hurting hear
me and be joyful.
[3] Join me in giving glory to the LORD.
Let us honor him together.

[4] I looked to the LORD, and he
answered me.
He saved me from everything I
was afraid of.
[5] Those who look to him have joyful
faces.
They are never covered with
shame.
[6] This poor man called out, and the
LORD heard him.
He saved him out of all his
troubles.
[7] The angel of the LORD stands guard
around those who have respect
for him.
And he saves them.

[8] Taste and see that the LORD is good.
Blessed is the person who goes to
him for safety.
[9] You holy people of God, have
respect for the LORD.
Those who respect him have
everything they need.
[10] The lions may grow weak and
hungry.
But those who look to the LORD
have every good thing they
need.

[11] My children, come. Listen to me.
I will teach you to have respect
for the LORD.
[12] Do you love life
and want to see many good days?
[13] Then keep your tongues from
speaking evil.
Keep your lips from telling lies.
[14] Turn away from evil, and do good.
Look for peace, and go after it.

[15] The LORD looks with favor on those
who are godly.
His ears are open to their cry.
[16] But the LORD doesn't look with
favor on those who do evil.
He removes all memory of them
from the earth.

[17] Godly people cry out, and the LORD
hears them.
He saves them from all their
troubles.
[18] The LORD is close to those whose
hearts have been broken.
He saves those whose spirits have
been crushed.

[19] The person who does what is right
may have many troubles.
But the LORD saves him from all
of them.
[20] The LORD watches over all his bones.
Not one of them will be broken.

[21] Sinners will be killed by their own
evil.
The enemies of godly people will
be judged.
[22] The LORD will save those who serve
him.
No one who goes to him for
safety will be found guilty.

Psalm 35

A psalm of David.

[1] LORD, stand up against those who
stand up against me.
Fight against those who fight
against me.
[2] Pick up your shield and your
armor.
Rise up and help me.
[3] Get your spear and javelin ready to
fight
against those who are
chasing me.
Say to me, "I will save you."

[4] Let those who are trying to kill me
be brought down in dishonor.
Let those who plan to destroy me
be turned back in terror.
[5] Let them be like straw blowing in
the wind,
while the angel of the LORD
drives them away.
[6] Let their path be dark and slippery,
while the angel of the LORD
chases them.
[7] They set a trap for me without any
reason.
Without any reason they dug a
pit to catch me.
[8] So let them be destroyed without
warning.
Let the trap they set for me catch
them.
Let them fall into the pit and be
destroyed.

9 Then I will be full of joy because of
what the LORD has done.
I will be glad because he has
saved me.
10 My whole being will cry out,
"Who is like you, LORD?
You save poor people from those
who are too strong for them.
You save poor and needy people
from those who rob them."
11 Mean people come forward to
speak against me.
They ask me things I don't know
anything about.
12 They pay me back with evil, even
though I was good to them.
They leave me like someone who
has lost a family member.
13 But when they were sick, I put on
the clothing of sadness.
I made myself humble by going
without food.
My prayers for them weren't
always answered.
14 So I went around crying
as if I were mourning over my
friend or relative.
I bowed my head in sadness
as if I were weeping over my
mother.
15 But when I tripped and fell, they
were all very happy.
Attackers gathered against me
when I didn't even know it.
They kept on telling lies about
me.
16 Like ungodly people, they were
mean and made fun of me.
They ground their teeth at me in
hate.
17 Lord, how much longer will you just
look on?
Save me from their deadly
attacks.
Save the only life I have.
Save me from these lions.
18 I will give you thanks in the whole
community.
Among all your people I will
praise you.

19 Don't let those who are my enemies
without any reason
laugh at me and make fun of me.
Don't let those who hate me
without any reason
wink at me with an evil purpose.
20 They don't speak words of peace.
They make up false charges
against those who live quietly in
the land.
21 They make fun of me.
They say, "With our own eyes we
have seen what you did."

22 LORD, you have seen this. Don't be
silent.
Lord, don't be far away from me.
23 Wake up! Rise up to help me!
My God and Lord, stand up
for me.
24 LORD my God, when you hand
down your sentence, let it be in
my favor.
You always do what is right.
Don't let my enemies have the
joy of seeing me fall.
25 Don't let them think, "That's
exactly what we wanted!"
Don't let them say, "We have
swallowed him up."

26 Let all those who laugh at me
because I'm in trouble
be ashamed and bewildered.
Let all who think they are better
than I am
put on shame and dishonor as if
they were clothes.
27 Let those who are happy when my
name is cleared
shout with joy and gladness.
Let them always say, "May the
LORD be honored.
He is pleased when everything
goes well with the one who
serves him."
28 You always do what is right. My
tongue will speak about it
and praise you all day long.

Psalm 36

For the director of music.
A psalm of David, the servant
of the LORD.

1 I have a message from God in my
heart.
It is about the evil ways of
anyone who sins.
They don't have any respect for
God.
2 They praise themselves so much
that they can't see their sin or
hate it.

3 Their mouths speak words that are
evil and false.
They do not act wisely or do what
is good.
4 Even as they lie in bed they make
evil plans.
They commit themselves to a
sinful way of life.
They never say no to what is
wrong.

5 LORD, your love is as high as the
heavens.
Your faithful love reaches up to
the skies.
6 Your holiness is as great as
the height of the highest
mountains.
You are as honest as the oceans
are deep.
LORD, you keep people and animals
safe.
7 How priceless your faithful
love is!
People find safety in the shadow
of your wings.
8 They eat well because there is more
than enough in your house.
You let them drink from your
river that flows with good
things.
9 You have the fountain of life.
We are filled with light because
you give us light.

10 Keep on loving those who know
you.
Keep on doing right to those
whose hearts are honest.
11 Don't let the feet of those who are
proud step on me.
Don't let the hands of those who
are evil drive me away.
12 See how those who do evil have
fallen!
They are thrown down and can't
get up.

Psalm 37

A psalm of David.

1 Don't be upset because of sinful
people.
Don't be jealous of those who do
wrong.
2 Like grass, they will soon dry up.
Like green plants, they will soon
die.

3 Trust in the LORD and do good.
Then you will live in the land and
enjoy its food.
4 Find your delight in the LORD.
Then he will give you everything
your heart really wants.

5 Commit your life to the LORD.
Here is what he will do if you
trust in him.
6 He will make the reward for your
godly life shine like the dawn.
He will make the proof of your
honest life shine like the sun at
noon.

7 Be still and wait patiently for the
LORD to act.
Don't be upset when other people
succeed.
Don't be upset when they carry
out their evil plans.

8 Turn away from anger and don't
give in to wrath.
Don't be upset, because that only
leads to evil.
9 Sinful people will be destroyed.
But those who put their hope in
the LORD will receive the land.

10 In a little while, there won't be any
more sinners.
Even if you look for them, you
won't be able to find them.
11 But those who are free of pride will
be given the land.
They will enjoy peace and success.

12 Sinful people make plans to harm
those who do what is right.
They grind their teeth at them.
13 But the Lord laughs at those who
do evil.
He knows the day is coming
when he will judge them.

14 Sinners pull out their swords.
They bend their bows.
They want to kill poor and needy
people.
They plan to murder those who
lead honest lives.
15 But they will be killed by their own
swords.
Their own bows will be broken.

16 Those who do what is right may
have very little.
But it's better than the wealth of
many sinners.

17 The power of those who are evil will
be broken.
But the LORD takes good care of
those who do what is right.

18 Those who are without blame
spend their days in the LORD's
care.
What he has given them will last
forever.
19 When trouble comes to them, they
will have what they need.
When there is little food in the
land, they will still have plenty.

20 But sinful people will die.
The LORD's enemies may be like
flowers in the field.
But they will be swallowed up.
They will disappear like smoke.

21 Sinful people borrow and don't pay
back.
But those who are godly give
freely to others.
22 The LORD will give the land to those
he blesses.
But he will destroy those he
curses.

23 The LORD makes secure the
footsteps
of the person who delights in him,
24 Even if that person trips, he won't
fall.
The LORD's hand takes good care
of him.

25 I once was young, and now I'm old.
But I've never seen godly people
deserted.
I've never seen their children
begging for bread.
26 The godly are always giving and
lending freely.
Their children will be a blessing.

27 Turn away from evil and do good.
Then you will live in the land
forever.
28 The LORD loves those who are
honest.
He will not desert those who are
faithful to him.

Those who do wrong will be
completely destroyed.
The children of sinners will die.
29 Those who do what is right will be
given the land.
They will live in it forever.

30 The mouths of those who do what
is right speak words of wisdom.
They say what is honest.
31 God's law is in their hearts.
Their feet do not slip.

32 Those who are evil hide and wait
for godly people.
They want to kill them.
33 But the LORD will not leave the
godly in their power.
He will not let them be found
guilty when they are brought
into court.

34 Put your hope in the LORD.
Live as he wants you to.
He will honor you by giving you
the land.
When sinners are destroyed, you
will see it.

35 I saw a mean and sinful person.
He was doing well, like a green
tree in its own land.
36 But he soon passed away and was
gone.
Even though I looked for him, I
couldn't find him.

37 Consider honest people who are
without blame.
People who seek peace will have
a tomorrow.
38 But all sinners will be destroyed.
Those who are evil won't have a
tomorrow.

39 The LORD saves those who do what
is right.
He is their place of safety when
trouble comes.
40 The LORD helps them and saves
them.
He saves them from sinful people
because they go to him for
safety.

Psalm 38

A psalm of David. A prayer.

1 LORD, don't correct me when you
are angry.
Don't punish me when you are
burning with anger.
2 You have wounded me with your
arrows.
You have struck me with your
hand.

[3]Because of your anger, my whole
body is sick.
Because of my sin, I'm not healthy.
[4]My guilt has become too much
for me.
It is a load too heavy to carry.

[5]My wounds are ugly. They stink.
I've been foolish. I have sinned.
[6]I am bent over. I've been brought
very low.
All day long I go around
weeping.
[7]My back is filled with burning pain.
My whole body is sick.
[8]I am weak and feel as if I've been
broken in pieces.
I groan because of the great pain
in my heart.

[9]Lord, everything I really want is
clearly known to you.
You always hear me when I sigh.
[10]My heart pounds, and my strength
is gone.
My eyes can hardly see.
[11]My friends and companions avoid
me because of my wounds.
My neighbors stay far away from
me.
[12]Those who are trying to kill me set
their traps.
Those who want to harm me talk
about destroying me.
All day long they make their
plans and tell their lies.

[13]Like a deaf person, I can't hear.
Like someone who can't speak, I
can't say a word.
[14]I'm like someone who doesn't hear.
I'm like someone whose mouth
can't make any reply.
[15]LORD, I wait for you to help me.
Lord my God, I know you will
answer.
[16]I said, "Don't let my enemies have
the joy of seeing me fall.
Don't let them brag when my feet
slip."

[17]I am about to fall.
My pain never leaves me.
[18]I admit that I have done wrong.
I am troubled by my sin.
[19]Though I have done nothing to
cause it, many people have
become my enemies.
They hate me without any reason.
[20]They pay me back with evil, even
though I was good to them.
They bring charges against me,
though I try only to do what is
good.

[21]LORD, don't desert me.
My God, don't be far away
from me.
[22]Lord my Savior,
come quickly to help me.

Psalm 39

For the director of music.
For Jeduthun. A psalm of David.

[1]I said, "I will be careful about how I
live.
I will not sin by what I say.
I will keep my mouth closed
when I am near sinful people."
[2]So I was completely silent.
I didn't even say anything good.
But the pain inside me grew
worse.
[3]My heart was deeply troubled.
As I thought about what was
happening to me,
I became even more troubled.
Then I spoke out.

[4]I said, "LORD, show me when my
life will end.
Show me how many days I have
left.
Tell me how short my life will be.
[5]You have given me only a few days
to live.
My whole life doesn't seem like
anything to you.
No one lasts any longer than a
breath.
This is true even for those who
feel secure.
[6]People are only shadows as they go
here and there.
They rush around, but it doesn't
mean anything.
They pile up wealth, but they don't
know who will finally get it.

[7]"Lord, what can I look forward to
now?
You are the only hope I have.
[8]Save me from all the wrong things
I've done.
Don't let foolish people make fun
of me.

[9] I keep silent. I don't open my
    mouth.
  You are the one who has caused
    all this to happen.
[10] Please stop beating me.
  I'm about to die from the blows
    of your hand.
[11] You correct and punish people for
    their sin.
  Then, just as a moth eats cloth,
    you destroy their wealth.
  No one lasts any longer than a
    breath.

[12] "LORD, hear my prayer.
  Listen to my cry for help.
  Pay attention to my weeping.
I'm like an outsider in your home.
  I'm just a stranger, like all my
    family who lived before me.
[13] Leave me alone.
  Let me enjoy life again before I
    die."

Psalm 40

For the director of music.
A psalm of David.

[1] I was patient while I waited for the
    LORD.
  He turned to me and heard my
    cry for help.
[2] I was sliding down into the pit of
    death, and he pulled me out.
  He brought me up out of the mud
    and dirt.
He set my feet on a rock.
  He gave me a firm place to stand
    on.
[3] He gave me a new song to sing.
  It is a hymn of praise to our God.
Many people will see and have
    respect for the LORD.
  They will put their trust in him.
[4] Blessed is the person
  who trusts in the LORD.
They don't trust in proud people.
  Those proud people worship
    statues of gods.
[5] LORD my God,
  no one can compare with you.
You have done many wonderful
    things.
  You have planned to do these
    things for us.
There are too many of them
  for me to talk about.

[6] You didn't want sacrifices and
    offerings.
  You didn't require burnt offerings
    and sin offerings.
  You opened my ears so that I
    could hear you and obey you.
[7] Then I said, "Here I am.
  It is written about me in the
    book.
[8] My God, I have come to do what
    you want.
  Your law is in my heart."

[9] I have told the whole community of
    those who worship you.
  I have told them what you have
    done to save me.
LORD, you know
  that I haven't kept quiet.
[10] I haven't kept to myself that what
    you did for me was right.
  I have spoken about how faithful
    you were when you saved me.
I haven't hidden your love and
    your faithfulness
  from the whole community.
[11] LORD, don't hold back your mercy
    from me.
  May your love and faithfulness
    always keep me safe.
[12] There are more troubles all around
    me than I can count.
  My sins have caught up with me,
    and I can't see any longer.
My sins are more than the hairs of
    my head.
  I have lost all hope.
[13] LORD, please save me.
  LORD, come quickly to help me.
[14] Let all those who are trying to kill
    me be put to shame.
  Let them lose their way.
Let all those who want to destroy me
  be turned back in shame.
[15] Some people make fun of me.
  Let them be shocked when their
    plans fail.
[16] But let all those who seek you
  be joyful and glad because of
    what you have done.
Let those who count on you to save
    them always say,
  "The LORD is great!"

[17] But I am poor and needy.
  May the Lord be concerned
    about me.

You are the God who helps me and
saves me.
You are my God, so don't wait
any longer.

Psalm 41

For the director of music.
A psalm of David.

1 Blessed are those who care about
weak people.
When they are in trouble, the
LORD saves them.
2 The LORD guards them and keeps
them alive.
They are counted among those
who are blessed in the land.
The LORD won't hand them over
to the wishes of their enemies.
3 The LORD will take care of them
when they are lying sick in bed.
He will make them well again.

4 I said, "LORD, have mercy on me.
Heal me, because I have sinned
against you."
5 My enemies are saying bad things
about me.
They say, "When will he die and
his name be forgotten?"
6 When one of them comes to see me,
he says things that aren't true.
At the same time, he thinks up lies
to tell against me.
Then he goes out and spreads
those lies around.

7 All my enemies whisper to each
other about me.
They want something terrible to
happen to me.
8 They say, "He is sick and will die
very soon.
He will never get up from his bed
again."
9 Even my close friend, someone I
trusted, has failed me.
I even shared my bread with
him.

10 But LORD, may you have mercy
on me.
Make me well, so I can pay them
back.
11 Then I will know that you are
pleased with me,
because my enemies haven't won
the battle over me.
12 You will take good care of me
because I've been honest.
You will let me be with you forever.

13 Give praise to the LORD, the God of
Israel,
for ever and ever.
Amen and Amen.

BOOK II

Psalms 42–72

Psalm 42

For the director of music. A maskil
of the Sons of Korah.

1 A deer longs for streams of water.
God, I long for you in the same
way.
2 I am thirsty for God. I am thirsty
for the living God.
When can I go and meet with him?
3 My tears have been my food
day and night.
All day long people say to me,
"Where is your God?"
4 When I remember what has
happened,
I tell God all my troubles.
I remember how I used to walk to
the house of God.
The Mighty One guarded my steps.
We shouted with joy and praised God
as we went along with the joyful
crowd.

5 My spirit, why are you so sad?
Why are you so upset deep down
inside me?
Put your hope in God.
Once again I will have reason to
praise him.
He is my Savior and my God.

6 My spirit is very sad deep down
inside me.
So I will remember you here
where the Jordan River begins.
I will remember you here on the
Hermon mountains
and on Mount Mizar.
7 You have sent wave upon wave of
trouble over me.
It roars down on me like a
waterfall.
All your waves and breakers have
rolled over me.

[8] During the day the LORD sends his
love to me.
During the night I sing about
him.
I say a prayer to the God who
gives me life.

[9] I say to God my Rock,
"Why have you forgotten me?
Why must I go around in sorrow?
Why am I treated so badly by my
enemies?"
[10] My body suffers deadly pain
as my enemies make fun of me.
All day long they say to me,
"Where is your God?"

[11] My spirit, why are you so sad?
Why are you so upset deep down
inside me?
Put your hope in God.
Once again I will have reason to
praise him.
He is my Savior and my God.

Psalm 43

[1] My God, when you hand down your
decision, let it be in my favor.
Stand up for me against an
unfaithful nation.
Save me from those lying and
sinful people.
[2] You are God, my place of safety.
Why have you turned your back
on me?
Why must I go around in sorrow?
Why am I beaten down by my
enemies?
[3] Send me your light and your
faithful care.
Let them lead me.
Let them bring me back to your
holy mountain,
to the place where you live.
[4] Then I will go to the altar of God.
I will go to God. He is my joy and
my delight.
God, you are my God.
I will praise you by playing the
lyre.

[5] My spirit, why are you so sad?
Why are you so upset deep down
inside me?
Put your hope in God.
Once again I will have reason to
praise him.
He is my Savior and my God.

Psalm 44

For the director of music. A maskil *of the Sons of Korah.*

[1] God, we have heard what you did.
Those who came before us have
told us
what you did in their days,
in days long ago.
[2] By your power you drove out the
nations.
You gave our people homes in
the land.
You crushed the people who were
there.
And you made our people do well.
[3] They didn't win the land with their
swords.
They didn't gain success by their
own power.
Your powerful right hand and your
mighty arm gave them victory.
You gave them success because
you loved them.

[4] You are my King and my God.
You give victories to the people of
Jacob.
[5] With your help we push back our
enemies.
By your power we walk all over
them.
[6] I put no trust in my bow.
My sword doesn't bring me victory.
[7] But you give us victory over our
enemies.
You put them to shame.
[8] All day long we talk about how
great God is.
We will praise your name forever.

[9] But now you have turned your back
on us and made us humble.
You don't march out with our
armies anymore.
[10] You made us turn and run from our
enemies.
They have taken what belongs
to us.
[11] You handed us over to be eaten up
like sheep.
You have scattered us among the
nations.
[12] You sold your people for very little.
You didn't gain anything when
you sold them.

[13]You have made us something that
our neighbors laugh at.
Those who live around us make
fun of us and tease us.
[14]The nations make jokes about us.
They shake their heads at us.
[15]All day long I have to live with my
shame.
My face is covered with it.
[16]That's because they laugh at me
and attack me with their words.
They want to get even with me.
[17]All of this happened to us,
even though we had not
forgotten you.
We had not broken the covenant
you made with us.
[18]Our hearts had not turned away
from you.
Our feet had not wandered from
your path.
[19]But you crushed us and left us to
the wild dogs.
You covered us over with deep
darkness.

[20]We didn't forget our God.
We didn't spread out our hands
in prayer to a false god.
[21]If we had, God would have
discovered it.
He knows the secrets of our hearts.
[22]But because of you, we face death
all day long.
We are considered as sheep to be
killed.

[23]Lord, wake up! Why are you sleeping?
Get up! Don't say no to us forever.
[24]Why do you turn your face away
from us?
Why do you forget our pain and
troubles?

[25]We are brought down to the dust.
Our bodies lie flat on the ground.
[26]Rise up and help us.
Save us because of your faithful
love.

Psalm 45

For the director of music. A maskil *of the Sons of Korah. A wedding song to the tune of "Lilies."*

[1]My heart is full of beautiful words
as I say my poem for the king.
My tongue is like the pen of a
skillful writer.

[2]You are the most excellent of men.
Your lips have been given the
ability to speak gracious words.
God has blessed you forever.
[3]Mighty one, put your sword at your
side.
Put on glory and majesty as if
they were your clothes.
[4]In your majesty ride out with power
to fight for what is true, humble
and fair.
Let your right hand do wonderful
things.
[5]Shoot your sharp arrows into the
hearts of your enemies.
Let the nations come under your
control.
[6]Your throne is the very throne of
God.
Your kingdom will last for ever
and ever.
You will rule by treating
everyone fairly.
[7]You love what is right and hate
what is evil.
So your God has placed you
above your companions.
He has filled you with joy by
pouring the sacred oil on your
head.
[8]Myrrh and aloes and cassia make
all your robes smell good.
In palaces decorated with ivory
the music played on stringed
instruments makes you glad.
[9]Daughters of kings are among the
women you honor.
At your right hand is the royal
bride dressed in gold from
Ophir.

[10]Royal bride, listen and pay careful
attention.
Forget about your people and the
home you came from.
[11]Let the king be charmed by your
beauty.
Honor him. He is now your
master.
[12]The people of Tyre will come with
gifts.
Wealthy people will try to gain
your favor.

[13]In her room, the princess looks
glorious.
Her gown has gold threads
running through it.

14 Dressed in beautiful clothes, she is
led to the king.
Her virgin companions follow
her.
They have been brought to be
with her.
15 They are led in with joy and
gladness.
They enter the palace of the king.

16 Your sons will rule just as your
father and grandfather did.
You will make them princes
through the whole land.
17 I will make sure that people will
always remember you.
The nations will praise you for
ever and ever.

Psalm 46

For the director of music. A song of the Sons of Korah. According to alamoth.

1 God is our place of safety. He gives
us strength.
He is always there to help us in
times of trouble.
2 The earth may fall apart.
The mountains may fall into the
middle of the sea.
But we will not be afraid.
3 The waters of the sea may roar and
foam.
The mountains may shake when
the waters rise.
But we will not be afraid.

4 God's blessings are like a river. They
fill the city of God with joy.
That city is the holy place where
the Most High God lives.
5 Because God is there, the city will
not fall.
God will help it at the beginning
of the day.
6 Nations are in disorder. Kingdoms
fall.
God speaks, and the people of the
earth melt in fear.

7 The LORD who rules over all is
with us.
The God of Jacob is like a fort to us.

8 Come and see what the LORD has
done.
See the places he has destroyed
on the earth.
9 He makes wars stop from one end
of the earth to the other.
He breaks every bow. He snaps
every spear.
He burns every shield with fire.
10 He says, "Be still, and know that I
am God.
I will be honored among the
nations.
I will be honored in the earth."

11 The LORD who rules over all is with us.
The God of Jacob is like a fort to us.

Psalm 47

For the director of music. A psalm of the Sons of Korah.

1 Clap your hands, all you nations.
Shout to God with cries of joy.
2 Do this because the LORD Most High
is wonderful.
He is the great King over the
whole earth.
3 He brought nations under our
control.
He made them fall under us.
4 He chose our land for us.
The people of Jacob are proud of
their land,
and God loves them.

5 God went up to his throne while his
people were shouting with joy.
The LORD went up while trumpets
were playing.
6 Sing praises to God. Sing praises.
Sing praises to our King. Sing
praises.

7 God is the King of the whole earth.
Sing a psalm of praise to him.
8 God rules over the nations.
He is seated on his holy throne.
9 The nobles of the nations come
together.
They are now part of the people
of the God of Abraham.
The kings of the earth belong to God.
He is greatly honored.

Psalm 48

A song. A psalm of the Sons of Korah.

1 The LORD is great. He is really
worthy of praise.
Praise him in the city of our God,
his holy mountain.

2 Mount Zion is high and beautiful.
It brings joy to everyone on earth.
Mount Zion is like the highest parts of Mount Zaphon.
It is the city of the Great King.
3 God is there to keep it safe.
He has shown himself to be like a fort to the city.
4 Many kings joined forces.
They entered Israel together.
5 But when they saw Mount Zion, they were amazed.
They ran away in terror.
6 Trembling took hold of them.
They felt pain like a woman giving birth.
7 LORD, you destroyed them like ships of Tarshish
that were torn apart by an east wind.

8 What we heard we have also seen.
We have seen it
in the city of the LORD who rules over all.
We have seen it in the city of our God.
We have heard and seen that God makes it secure forever.
9 God, inside your temple
we think about your faithful love.
10 God, your fame reaches from one end of the earth to the other.
So people praise you from one end of the earth to the other.
You use your power to do what is right.
11 Mount Zion is filled with joy.
The villages of Judah are glad.
That's because you judge fairly.

12 Walk all around Zion.
Count its towers.
13 Think carefully about its outer walls.
Just look at how safe it is!
Then you can tell its people that God keeps them safe.
14 This God is our God for ever and ever.
He will be our guide to the very end.

Psalm 49

For the director of music. A psalm of the Sons of Korah.

1 Hear this, all you nations.
Listen, all you who live in this world.
2 Listen, people, whether you are ordinary or important.
Listen, people, whether you are rich or poor.
3 My mouth will speak wise words.
What I think about in my heart will give you understanding.
4 I will pay attention to a proverb.
I will explain my riddle as I play the harp.

5 Why should I be afraid when trouble comes?
Why should I fear when sinners are all around me?
They are the kind of people who want to take advantage of me.
6 They trust in their wealth.
They brag about how rich they are.
7 No one can pay for the life of anyone else.
No one can give God what that would cost.
8 The price for a life is very high.
No payment is ever enough.
9 No one can pay enough to live forever
and not rot in the grave.

10 Everyone can see that even wise people die.
People who are foolish and who have no sense also pass away.
All of them leave their wealth to others.
11 Their tombs will remain their houses forever.
Their graves will be their homes for all time to come.
Naming lands after themselves won't help either.

12 Even though people may be very rich, they don't live on and on.
They are like the animals. They die.

13 That's what happens to those who trust in themselves.
It also happens to their followers, who agree with what they say.

[14] They are like sheep and will end up
in the grave.
Death will be their shepherd.
But when honest people come to
power, a new day will dawn.
The bodies of sinners will waste
away in the grave.
They will end up far away from
their princely houses.
[15] But God will save me from the place
of the dead.
He will certainly take me to
himself.
[16] Don't get too upset when other
people become rich.
Don't be troubled when they
become more and more
wealthy.
[17] They won't take anything with
them when they die.
Their riches won't go down to the
grave with them.
[18] While they lived, they believed they
were blessed.
People praised them when things
were going well for them.
[19] But they will die, like their people
of long ago.
They will never again see the
light of life.
[20] People who have riches but don't
understand
are like the animals. They die.

Psalm 50

A psalm of Asaph.

[1] The Mighty One, God, the LORD,
speaks.
He calls out to the earth
from the sunrise in the east
to the sunset in the west.
[2] From Zion, perfect and beautiful,
God's glory shines out.
[3] Our God comes, and he won't be
silent.
A burning fire goes ahead of him.
A terrible storm is all around
him.
[4] He calls out to heaven and earth to
be his witnesses.
Then he judges his people.
[5] He says, "Gather this holy people
around me.
They made a covenant with me
by offering a sacrifice."
[6] The heavens announce that what
God decides is right.
That's because he is a God of
justice.
[7] God says, "Listen, my people, and I
will speak.
I will be a witness against you,
Israel.
I am God, your God.
[8] I don't bring charges against you
because of your sacrifices.
I don't bring charges because of
the burnt offerings you always
bring me.
[9] I don't need a bull from your barn.
I don't need goats from your pens.
[10] Every animal in the forest already
belongs to me.
And so do the cattle on a
thousand hills.
[11] I own every bird in the mountains.
The insects in the fields belong to
me.
[12] If I were hungry, I wouldn't tell
you.
The world belongs to me. And so
does everything in it.
[13] Do I eat the meat of bulls?
Do I drink the blood of goats?
[14] Bring me thank offerings, because I
am your God.
Carry out the promises you made
to me, because I am the Most
High God.
[15] Call out to me when trouble comes.
I will save you. And you will
honor me."

[16] But here is what God says to a sinful
person.

"What right do you have to speak
the words of my laws?
How dare you speak the words of
my covenant!
[17] You hate my teaching.
You turn your back on what I
say.
[18] When you see a thief, you join him.
You make friends with those who
commit adultery.
[19] You use your mouth to speak evil.
You use your tongue to spread
lies.
[20] You are a witness against your
brother.
You always tell lies about your
own mother's son.

21 When you did these things, I kept silent.
So you thought I was just like you.
But now I'm going to bring you to court.
I will bring charges against you.

22 "You who forget God, think about this.
If you don't, I will tear you to pieces.
No one will be able to save you.
23 People who sacrifice thank offerings to me honor me.
To those who are without blame I will show my power to save."

Psalm 51

For the director of music. A psalm of David when the prophet Nathan came to him. Nathan came to him after David had committed adultery with Bathsheba.

1 God, have mercy on me
according to your faithful love.
Because your love is so tender and kind,
wipe out my lawless acts.
2 Wash away all the evil things I've done.
Make me pure from my sin.

3 I know the lawless acts I've committed.
I can't forget my sin.
4 You are the one I've really sinned against.
I've done what is evil in your sight.
So you are right when you sentence me.
You are fair when you judge me.
5 I know I've been a sinner ever since I was born.
I've been a sinner ever since my mother became pregnant with me.
6 I know that you wanted faithfulness even when I was in my mother's body.
You taught me wisdom in that secret place.
7 Sprinkle me with hyssop, then I will be clean.
Wash me, then I will be whiter than snow.
8 Let me hear you say, "Your sins are forgiven."
That will bring me joy and gladness.
Let the body you have broken be glad.
9 Take away all my sins.
Wipe away all the evil things I've done.

10 God, create a pure heart in me.
Give me a new spirit that is faithful to you.
11 Don't send me away from you.
Don't take your Holy Spirit away from me.
12 Give me back the joy that comes from being saved by you.
Give me a spirit that obeys you so that I will keep going.
13 Then I will teach your ways to those who commit lawless acts.
And sinners will turn back to you.
14 You are the God who saves me.
I have committed murder.
God, take away my guilt.
Then my tongue will sing about how right you are
no matter what you do.

BASICS OF FAITH Q&A

Can I be good without God?

The Bible teaches us that no one does good on their own. God alone is good. The only way you can do good that brings glory to God is by asking Jesus to give you a pure heart that desires to walk in his ways.

Can you find the following verse?

PSALM 51:10

15 Lord, open my lips so that I can speak.
Then my mouth will praise you.
16 You don't take delight in sacrifice.
If you did, I would bring it.
You don't take pleasure in burnt offerings.
17 The greatest sacrifice you want is a broken spirit.
God, you will gladly accept a heart that is broken because of sadness over sin.
18 May you be pleased to give Zion success.
May it please you to build up the walls of Jerusalem.
19 Then you will delight in the sacrifices of those who do what is right.
Whole burnt offerings will bring delight to you.
And bulls will be offered on your altar.

Psalm 52

For the director of music. A maskil *of David when Doeg, who was from Edom, had gone to Saul. Doeg had told Saul, "David has gone to the house of Ahimelek."*

1 You think you are such a big, strong man!
Why do you brag about the evil things you've done?
You are a dishonor to God all the time.
2 You plan ways to destroy others.
Your tongue is like a blade that has a sharp edge.
You are always telling lies.
3 You love evil instead of good.
You would rather lie than tell the truth.
4 You love to harm others with your words, you liar!
5 So God will destroy you forever.
He will grab you and pluck you from your tent.
He will remove you from this life.
6 Those who do what is right will see it and learn a lesson from it.
They will laugh at you and say,
7 "Just look at this fellow!
He didn't depend on God for his safety.
He put his trust in all his wealth.
He grew strong by destroying others!"
8 But I am like a healthy olive tree.
My roots are deep in the house of God.
I trust in your faithful love for ever and ever.
9 I will praise you forever for what you have done.
I will praise you when I'm with your faithful people.
I will put my hope in you because you are good.

Psalm 53

For the director of music. According to mahalath. *A* maskil *of David.*

1 Foolish people say in their hearts, "There is no God."
They do all kinds of horrible and evil things.
No one does anything good.
2 God looks down from heaven on all people.
He wants to see if there are any who understand.
He wants to see if there are any who trust in God.
3 All of them have turned away.
They have all become evil.
No one does anything good, no one at all.
4 Don't these people who do evil know anything?
They eat up my people as if they were eating bread.
They never call out to God for help.
5 Just look at them! They are filled with terror
even when there is nothing to be afraid of!
People of Israel, God scattered the bones of those who attacked you.
You put them to shame, because God hated them.
6 How I pray that the God who saves Israel will come out of Zion!
God will bless his people with great success again.
Then let the people of Jacob be filled with joy! Let Israel be glad!

Psalm 54

For the director of music. To be played on stringed instruments. A maskil *of David when the men from Ziph had gone to Saul. They had said, "Isn't David hiding among us?"*

1 God, save me by your power.
Set me free by your might.
2 God, hear my prayer.
Listen to what I'm saying.

3 Enemies who are proud are attacking me.
Mean people are trying to kill me.
They don't care about God.

4 But I know that God helps me.
The Lord is the one who keeps me going.

5 My enemies tell lies about me.
Do to them the evil things they planned against me.
God, be faithful and destroy them.

6 I will sacrifice an offering to you just because I choose to.
LORD, I will praise your name because it is good.
7 You have saved me from all my troubles.
With my own eyes I have seen you win the battle over my enemies.

Psalm 55

For the director of music. A maskil *of David to be played on stringed instruments.*

1 God, listen to my prayer.
Pay attention to my cry for help.
2 Hear me and answer me.
My thoughts upset me. I'm very troubled.
3 I'm troubled by what my enemies say about me.
I'm upset because they say they will harm me.
They cause me all kinds of suffering.
When they are angry, they attack me with their words.

4 I feel great pain deep down inside me.
The terrors of death have fallen on me.
5 Fear and trembling have taken hold of me.
Panic has overpowered me.
6 I said, "I wish I had wings like a dove!
Then I would fly away and be at rest.
7 I would escape to a place far away.
I would stay out in the desert.
8 I would hurry to my place of safety.
It would be far away from the winds and storms I'm facing."

9 Lord, confuse the sinners and keep them from understanding one another.
I see people destroying things and fighting in the city.
10 Day and night they prowl around on top of its walls.
The city is full of crime and trouble.
11 Forces that destroy are at work inside it.
Its streets are full of people who cheat others and take advantage of them.

12 If an enemy were making fun of me, I could stand it.
If he were getting ready to oppose me, I could hide.
13 But it's you, someone like myself.
It's my companion, my close friend.
14 We used to enjoy good friendship at the house of God.
We used to walk together among those who came to worship.

15 Let death take my enemies by surprise.
Let them be buried alive, because their hearts and homes are full of evil.

16 But I call out to God.
And the LORD saves me.
17 Evening, morning and noon I groan and cry out.
And he hears my voice.
18 Even though many enemies are fighting against me, he brings me safely back from the battle.
19 God has been on his throne since ancient times and does not change.

He will hear my enemies and
make them humble.
That's because they have no
respect for God.

20 My companion attacks his friends.
He breaks his promise.
21 His talk is as smooth as butter.
But he has war in his heart.
His words flow like olive oil.
But they are like swords ready
for battle.

22 Turn your worries over to the LORD.
He will keep you going.
He will never let godly people be
shaken.
23 God, you will bring sinners
down to the grave.
Murderers and liars
won't live out even half of their
lives.

But I trust in you.

Psalm 56

For the director of music. A miktam *of David after the Philistines had captured him in Gath. To the tune of "A Dove on Distant Oak Trees."*

1 Help me, God. Men are chasing me.
All day long they keep
attacking me.
2 My enemies chase me all day long.
Many proud people are
attacking me.

3 When I'm afraid,
I put my trust in you.
4 I trust in God. I praise his word.
I trust in God. I am not afraid.
What can mere people do to me?

5 All day long they twist my words.
They are always making plans to
destroy me.
6 They get together and hide.
They watch my steps.
They hope to kill me.
7 Because they are so evil, make sure
you don't let them escape.
God, bring down the nations in
your anger.
8 Make a record of my sadness.
List my tears in your book.
Aren't you making a record of
them?
9 My enemies will turn back
when I call out to you for help.
Then I will know that God is on
my side.
10 I trust in God. I praise his word.
I trust in the LORD. I praise his
word.
11 I trust in God. I am not afraid.
What can mere people do to me?

12 God, I have made promises to you.
I will bring my thank offerings to
you.
13 You have saved me from the
darkness of death.
You have kept me from tripping
and falling.
Now I can live with you
in the light of life.

Psalm 57

For the director of music. A miktam *of David when he had run away from Saul into the cave. To the tune of "Do Not Destroy."*

1 Have mercy on me, God. Have
mercy on me.
I go to you for safety.
I will find safety in the shadow of
your wings.
There I will stay until the danger
is gone.

2 I cry out to God Most High.
I cry out to God, and he shows
that I am right.
3 He answers from heaven and
saves me.
He puts to shame those who
chase me.
He shows his love and that he is
faithful.

4 Men who are like lions are all
around me.
I am forced to lie down among
people who are like hungry
animals.
Their teeth are like spears and
arrows.
Their tongues are like sharp
swords.

5 God, may you be honored above
the heavens.
Let your glory be over the whole
earth.

6 My enemies spread a net to catch
me by the feet.
I felt helpless.
They dug a pit in my path.
But they fell into it themselves.

7 God, my heart feels secure.
My heart feels secure.
I will sing and make music to
you.
8 My spirit, wake up!
Harp and lyre, wake up!
I want to sing and make music
before the sun rises.
9 Lord, I will praise you among the
nations.
I will sing about you among the
people of the earth.
10 Great is your love. It reaches to the
heavens.
Your truth reaches to the skies.
11 God, may you be honored above
the heavens.
Let your glory be over the whole
earth.

Psalm 58

For the director of music. A miktam *of David to the tune of "Do Not Destroy."*

1 Are you rulers really fair when you
speak?
Do you judge people honestly?
2 No, in your hearts you plan to be
unfair.
With your hands you do terrible
things on the earth.
3 Even from birth those who are evil
go down the wrong path.
From the day they are born they
go the wrong way and spread
lies.
4 Their words are like the poison of a
snake.
They are like the poison of a
cobra that has covered up its
ears.
5 It won't listen to a snake charmer's
tune,
even if the charmer plays very
well.
6 God, break the teeth in the mouths
of those sinners!
LORD, tear out the sharp teeth of
those lions!
7 Let those people disappear like
water that flows away.
When they draw their bows, let
their arrows fall short of the
target.
8 Let them be like a slug that melts
away as it moves along.
Let them be like a baby that is
born dead and never sees the
sun.
9 Evil people will be swept away
before burning thorns can heat
a pot.
And it doesn't matter if the
thorns are green or dry.
10 Godly people will be glad when
those who have hurt them are
paid back.
They will dip their feet in the
blood of those who do evil.
11 Then people will say,
"The godly will get their reward.
There really is a God who judges
the earth."

Psalm 59

For the director of music. A miktam *of David when Saul had sent men to watch David's house. Saul sent the men to kill David. To the tune of "Do Not Destroy."*

1 God, save me from my enemies.
Keep me safe from people who
are attacking me.
2 Save me from those who do evil.
Save me from people who want
to kill me.
3 See how they hide and wait for me!
LORD, angry people plan to harm
me,
even though I haven't hurt them
in any way or sinned against
them.
4 I haven't done anything wrong to
them. But they are ready to
attack me.
Rise up and help me! Look at
what I'm up against!
5 LORD God who rules over all, rise
up. God of Israel,
punish all the nations.
Don't show any mercy to those
sinful people
who have turned against me.

6 My enemies are like a pack of
barking dogs
that come back to the city in the
evening.
They prowl around the city.
7 Listen to what pours out of their
mouths.
The words from their lips are like
swords.
They think, "Who can hear us?"
8 But you laugh at them, LORD.
You make fun of all those
nations.

9 You give me strength. I look to you.
God, you are like a fort to me.
10 You are my God, and I can
depend on you.
God will march out in front of me.
He will let me look down on those
who tell lies about me.
11 Lord, you are like a shield that
keeps us safe.
Don't kill my enemies all at once.
If you do, my people will forget
about it.
Use your power to pull my enemies
up by the roots like weeds.
Destroy them.
12 They have sinned with their
mouths.
Their lips have spoken evil words.
They have cursed me and lied.
Let them be caught in their pride.
13 Burn them up in your anger.
Burn them up until there isn't
anything left of them.
Then everyone from one end of the
earth to the other will know
that God rules over the people of
Jacob.

14 My enemies are like a pack of
barking dogs
that come back into the city in
the evening.
They prowl around the city.
15 They wander around looking for
food.
They groan if they don't find
something that will satisfy
them.
16 But I will sing about your strength.
In the morning I will sing about
your love.
You are like a fort to me.
You keep me safe in times of
trouble.

17 You give me strength. I sing praise
to you.
God, you are like a fort to me.
You are my God, and I can
depend on you.

Psalm 60

For the director of music. For teaching. A miktam *of David when he fought against Aram Naharaim and Aram Zobah. That was when Joab returned and struck down 12,000 people from Edom in the Valley of Salt. To the tune of "The Lily of the Covenant."*

1 God, you have turned away from
us. You have attacked us.
You have been angry. Now turn
back to us!
2 You have shaken the land and torn
it open.
Fix its cracks, because it is falling
apart.
3 You have shown your people hard
times.
You have made us drink the wine
of your anger.
Now we can't even walk straight.

4 But you lead into battle those who
have respect for you.
You give them a flag to wave
against the enemy's weapons.
5 Save us and help us by your power.
Do this so that those you love
may be saved.
6 God has spoken from his temple.
He has said, "I will win the battle.
Then I will divide up the land
around Shechem.
I will divide up the Valley of
Sukkoth.
7 Gilead belongs to me.
So does the land of Manasseh.
Ephraim is the strongest tribe.
It is like a helmet for my head.
Judah is the royal tribe.
It is like a ruler's scepter.
8 Moab serves me like one who
washes my feet.
I toss my sandal on Edom to
show that I own it.
I shout to Philistia that I have
won the battle."

9 Who will bring me to the city that
has high walls around it?
Who will lead me to the land of
Edom?
10 God, isn't it you, even though
you have now turned away
from us?
Isn't it you, even though you
don't lead our armies into
battle anymore?
11 Help us against our enemies.
The help people give doesn't
amount to anything.
12 With your help we will win the
battle.
You will walk all over our
enemies.

Psalm 61

For the director of music.
A psalm of David to be played
on stringed instruments.

1 God, hear my cry for help.
Listen to my prayer.
2 From a place far away I call out to
you.
I call out as my heart gets
weaker.
Lead me to the safety of a rock
that is high above me.
3 You have always kept me safe from
my enemies.
You are like a strong tower to me.
4 I long to live in your holy tent
forever.
There I find safety in the shadow
of your wings.
5 God, you have heard my promises.
You have given me what belongs
to those who worship you.
6 Add many days to the king's life.
Let him live on and on for many
years.
7 May he always enjoy your blessing
as he rules.
Let your love and truth keep him
safe.
8 Then I will always sing praise to
you.
I will keep my promises day after
day.

Psalm 62

For the director of music.
For Jeduthun. A psalm of David.

1 It is surely true that I find my rest
in God.
He is the God who saves me.
2 It is surely true that he is my rock.
He is the God who saves me.
He is like a fort to me. I will
always be secure.
3 How long will you enemies
attack me?
Will all of you throw me down?
I'm like a leaning wall.
I'm like a fence about to fall.
4 Surely my enemies only want to
pull me down
from my place of honor.
They take delight in telling lies.
They bless me with what they say.
But in their hearts they ask for
bad things to happen to me.
5 Yes, I must find my rest in God.
He is the God who gives me hope.
6 It is surely true that he is my rock
and the God who saves me.
He is like a fort to me, so I will
always be secure.
7 I depend on God to save me and to
honor me.
He is my mighty rock and my
place of safety.
8 Trust in him at all times, you
people.
Tell him all your troubles.
God is our place of safety.
9 Surely ordinary people are only a
breath.
Important people are not what
they seem to be.
If they were weighed on a scale,
they wouldn't amount to
anything.
Together they are only a breath.
10 Don't trust in money you have
taken from others.
Don't put false hope in things
you have stolen.
Even if your riches grow,
don't put your trust in them.
11 God, I have heard you say two
things.
One is that power belongs to you,
God.

12 The other is that your love, Lord,
never ends.
You will reward everyone
in keeping with what they have
done.

Psalm 63

A psalm of David when he was in the Desert of Judah.

1 God, you are my God.
I seek you with all my heart.
With all my strength I thirst for you
in this dry desert
where there isn't any water.
2 I have seen you in the sacred tent.
There I have seen your power
and your glory.
3 Your love is better than life.
So I will bring glory to you with
my lips.
4 I will praise you as long as I live.
I will call on your name when I
lift up my hands in prayer.
5 I will be as satisfied as if I had
eaten the best food there is.
I will sing praise to you with my
mouth.
6 As I lie on my bed I remember you.
I think of you all night long.
7 Because you have helped me,
I sing in the shadow of your
wings.
8 I hold on to you tightly.
Your powerful right hand takes
good care of me.
9 Those who want to kill me will be
destroyed.
They will go down into the grave.
10 They will be killed by swords.
They will become food for wild
dogs.
11 But the king will be filled with joy
because of what God has done.
All those who make promises in
God's name will be able to brag.
But the mouths of liars will be shut.

Psalm 64

For the director of music. A psalm of David.

1 God, hear me as I tell you my
problem.
Don't let my enemies kill me.
2 Hide me from evil people who talk
about how to harm me.
Hide me from those people who
are planning to do evil.
3 They make their tongues like sharp
swords.
They aim their mean words like
deadly arrows.
4 They shoot from their hiding places
at people who aren't guilty.
They shoot quickly and aren't
afraid of being caught.
5 They help one another make evil
plans.
They talk about hiding their
traps.
They say, "Who can see what we
are doing?"
6 They make plans to do what is evil.
They say, "We have thought up a
perfect plan!"
The hearts and minds of people
are so clever!
7 But God will shoot my enemies with
his arrows.
He will suddenly strike them
down.
8 He will turn their own words
against them.
He will destroy them.
All those who see them will shake
their heads
and look down on them.
9 All people will respect God.
They will tell about his works.
They will think about what he
has done.
10 Godly people will be full of joy
because of what the LORD has
done.
They will go to him for safety.
All those whose hearts are honest
will be proud of what he has
done.

Psalm 65

For the director of music. A psalm of David. A song.

1 Our God, we look forward to
praising you in Zion.
We will keep our promises to you.
2 All people will come to you,
because you hear and answer
prayer.

3 When our sins became too much for us,
you forgave our lawless acts.
4 Blessed are those you choose
and bring near to worship you.
You bring us into the courtyards of your holy temple.
There in your house we are filled with all kinds of good things.

5 God our Savior, you answer us with right and wonderful deeds.
People all over the world and beyond the farthest oceans
put their hope in you.
6 You formed the mountains by your power.
You showed how strong you are.
7 You calmed the oceans and their roaring waves.
You calmed the angry words and actions of the nations.
8 Everyone on earth is amazed at the wonderful things you have done.
What you do makes people from one end of the earth to the other sing for joy.

9 You take care of the land and water it.
You make it able to grow many crops.
You fill your streams with water.
You do that to provide the people with grain.
That's what you have decided to do for the land.
10 You water its rows.
You smooth out its bumps.
You soften it with showers.
And you bless its crops.
11 You bring the year to a close with huge crops.
You provide more than enough food.
12 The grass grows thick even in the desert.
The hills are dressed with gladness.
13 The meadows are covered with flocks and herds.
The valleys are dressed with grain.
They sing and shout for joy.

Psalm 66

For the director of music.
A song. A psalm.

1 Shout to God for joy, everyone on earth!
2 Sing about the glory of his name!
Give him glorious praise!
3 Say to God, "What wonderful things you do!
Your power is so great
that your enemies bow down to you in fear.
4 Everyone on earth bows down to you.
They sing praise to you.
They sing the praises of your name."

5 Come and see what God has done.
See what wonderful things he has done for people!
6 He turned the Red Sea into dry land.
The people of Israel passed through the waters on foot.
Come, let us be full of joy because of what he did.
7 He rules by his power forever.
His eyes watch the nations.
Let no one who refuses to obey him rise up against him.

8 Praise our God, all you nations.
Let the sound of the praise you give him be heard.
9 He has kept us alive.
He has kept our feet from slipping.
10 God, you have tested us.
You put us through fire to make us like silver.
11 You put us in prison.
You placed heavy loads on our backs.
12 You let our enemies ride their chariots over our heads.
We went through fire and water.
But you brought us to a place
where we have everything we need.

13 I will come to your temple with burnt offerings.
I will keep my promises to you.
14 I made them with my lips.
My mouth spoke them when I was in trouble.

15 I will sacrifice fat animals to you as burnt offerings.
I will offer rams, bulls and goats to you.
16 Come and hear, all you who have respect for God.
Let me tell you what he has done for me.
17 I cried out to him with my mouth.
I praised him with my tongue.
18 If I had enjoyed having sin in my heart,
the Lord would not have listened.
19 But God has surely listened.
He has heard my prayer.
20 Give praise to God.
He has accepted my prayer.
He has not held back his love from me.

Psalm 67

For the director of music. A psalm. A song to be played on stringed instruments.

1 God, have mercy on us and bless us.
May you be pleased with us.
2 Then your ways will be known on earth.
All nations will see that you have the power to save.
3 God, may the nations praise you.
May all the people on earth praise you.
4 May the nations be glad and sing for joy.
You rule the people of the earth fairly.
You guide the nations of the earth.
5 God, may the nations praise you.
May all the people on earth praise you.

6 The land produces its crops.
God, our God, blesses us.
7 May God continue to bless us.
Then people from one end of the earth to the other
will have respect for him.

Psalm 68

For the director of music. A psalm of David. A song.

1 May God rise up and scatter his enemies.
May they turn and run away from him.
2 May you, God, blow them away like smoke.
As fire melts wax,
so may God destroy sinful people.
3 But may those who do what is right be glad
and filled with joy when they are with him.
May they be happy and joyful.

4 Sing to God, sing praise to his name.
Lift up a song to the God who rides on the clouds.
Be glad when you are with him.
His name is the LORD.
5 God is in his holy temple.
He is a father to children whose fathers have died.
He takes care of women whose husbands have died.
6 God gives lonely people a family.
He sets prisoners free, and they go out singing.
But those who refuse to obey him
live in a land that is baked by the sun.

7 God, you led your people out.
You marched through the desert.
8 The ground shook
when you, the God of Sinai, appeared.
The heavens poured down rain
when you, the God of Israel, appeared.
9 God, you gave us plenty of rain.
You renewed your worn-out land.
10 God, your people made their homes in it.
From all your riches, you provided for those who were poor.

11 The Lord gives the message.
The women who make it known are a huge group.

12 They said, "Kings and armies are running away.
The women at home are dividing up
the things the army took from their enemies.
13 Even while the soldiers sleep near the sheep pens,
God wins the battle for them.
He gives the enemy's silver and gold
to Israel, his dove."
14 The Mighty One has scattered the kings around the land.
It was like snow falling on Mount Zalmon.

15 Mount Bashan is a majestic mountain.
Mount Bashan is a very rocky mountain.
16 Why are you jealous of Mount Zion, you rocky mountain?
That's where God chooses to rule.
That's where the LORD himself will live forever.
17 God has come with tens of thousands of his chariots.
He has come with thousands and thousands of them.
The Lord has come from Mount Sinai.
He has entered his holy place.
18 When he went up to his place on high,
he took many prisoners.
He received gifts from people,
even from those who refused to obey him.
The LORD God went up to live on Mount Zion.

19 Give praise to the Lord. Give praise to God our Savior.
He carries our heavy loads day after day.
20 Our God is a God who saves.
He is the King and the LORD. He saves us from death.

21 God will certainly smash the heads of his enemies.
He will break the hairy heads of those who keep on sinning.
22 The Lord says, "I will bring your enemies from Bashan.
I will bring them up from the bottom of the sea.
23 Then your feet can wade in their blood.
The tongues of your dogs can lick up all the blood they want."

24 God, those who worship you come marching into view.
My God and King, those who follow you have entered the sacred tent.
25 The singers are walking in front.
Next come the musicians.
Young women playing tambourines are with them.
26 The leaders sing, "Praise God among all those who worship him.
Praise the LORD in the community of Israel."
27 The little tribe of Benjamin leads the worshipers.
Next comes the great crowd of Judah's princes.
Then come the princes of Zebulun and the princes of Naphtali.

28 God, show us your power.
Show us your strength.
God, do as you have done before.
29 Do it from your temple at Jerusalem,
where kings will bring you gifts.
30 Give a strong warning to Egypt,
that beast among the tall grass.
It is like a herd of bulls among the calves.
May that beast bow down before you with gifts of silver.
Scatter the nations who like to make war.
31 Messengers will come from Egypt.
The people of Cush will be quick to bring gifts to you.

32 Sing to God, you kingdoms of the earth.
Sing praise to the Lord.
33 He rides across the highest places in heaven.
He rides across the ancient skies above.
He thunders with his mighty voice.
34 Tell how powerful God is.
He rules as king over Israel.
The skies show how powerful he is.

35 How wonderful is God in his holy
place!
The God of Israel gives power and
strength to his people.

Give praise to God!

Psalm 69

For the director of music.
A psalm of David to the tune
of "Lilies."

1 God, save me.
My troubles are like a flood.
I'm up to my neck in them.
2 I'm sinking in deep mud.
I have no firm place to stand.
I am out in deep water.
The waves roll over me.
3 I'm worn out from calling for help.
My throat is very dry.
My eyes grow tired
looking for my God.
4 Those who hate me without any
reason
are more than the hairs on my
head.
Many people who don't have any
reason to be my enemies
are trying to destroy me.
They force me to give back
what I didn't steal.
5 God, you know how foolish I've
been.
My guilt is not hidden from you.
6 Lord, you are the LORD who rules
over all.
May those who put their hope in
you not be dishonored because
of me.
You are the God of Israel.
May those who worship you not
be put to shame because of me.
7 Because of you, people laugh
at me.
My face is covered with shame.
8 I'm an outsider to my own family.
I'm a stranger to my own
mother's children.
9 My great love for your house
destroys me.
Those who make fun of you
make fun of me also.
10 When I weep and go without
eating,
they laugh at me.
11 When I put on rough clothing to
show how sad I am,
people make jokes about me.
12 Those who gather in public places
make fun of me.
Those who get drunk make up
songs about me.

13 But LORD, I pray to you.
May this be the time you
help me.
God, answer me because you love
me so much.
Save me, as you always do.
14 Save me from the trouble I'm in.
It's like slippery mud, so don't let
me sink in it.
Save me from those who hate me.
Save me from the deep water
I'm in.
15 Don't let the floods cover me.
Don't let the deep water swallow
me up.
Don't let the grave close its
mouth over me.
16 LORD, answer me because your love
is so good.
Turn to me because you are so
kind.
17 Don't turn your face away from me.
Answer me quickly. I'm in
trouble.
18 Come near and save me.
Set me free from my enemies.
19 You know how they make fun of me.
They dishonor me and put me to
shame.
You know all about my enemies.
20 They have broken my heart by
saying evil things about me.
It has left me helpless.
I looked for pity, but I didn't find
any.
I looked for someone to comfort
me, but I didn't find anyone.
21 They put bitter spices in my food.
They gave me vinegar when I
was thirsty.

22 Let their feast be a trap and a
snare.
Let my enemies get what's
coming to them.
23 Let their eyes grow weak so they
can't see.
Let their backs be bent forever.
24 Pour out your anger on them.
Let them feel what it is like.

25 May their homes be deserted.
May no one live in their tents.
26 They attack those you have wounded.
They talk about the pain of those you have hurt.
27 Charge them with one crime after another.
Don't save them.
28 May their names be erased from the book of life.
Don't include them in the list of those who do right.

29 I'm in pain. I'm in deep trouble.
God, save me and keep me safe.
30 I will praise God's name by singing to him.
I will bring him glory by giving him thanks.
31 That will please the LORD more than offering him an ox.
It will please him more than offering him a bull with its horns and hooves.
32 Poor people will see it and be glad.
The hearts of those who worship God will be strengthened.
33 The LORD hears those who are in need.
He doesn't forget his people in prison.

34 Let heaven and earth praise him.
Let the oceans and everything that moves in them praise him.
35 God will save Zion.
He will build the cities of Judah again.
Then people will live in them and own the land.
36 The children of those who serve God will receive it.
Those who love him will live there.

Psalm 70

For the director of music.
A prayer of David.

1 God, hurry and save me.
LORD, come quickly and help me.
2 Let those who are trying to kill me be put to shame.
Let them not be honored.
Let all those who want to destroy me
be turned back in shame.
3 Some people make fun of me.
Let them be turned back when their plans fail.
4 But let all those who seek you be joyful and glad because of what you have done.
Let those who want you to save them always say,
"The LORD is great!"

5 But I am poor and needy.
God, come quickly to me.
You are the God who helps me and saves me.
LORD, please don't wait any longer.

Psalm 71

1 LORD, I have gone to you for safety.
Let me never be put to shame.
2 You do what is right, so save me and help me.
Pay attention to me and save me.
3 Be my rock of safety
that I can always go to.
Give the command to save me.
You are my rock and my fort.
4 My God, save me from the power of sinners.
Save me from the hands of those who are mean and evil.

5 You are the King and the LORD. You have always been my hope.
I have trusted in you ever since I was young.
6 From the time I was born I have depended on you.
You brought me out of my mother's body.
I will praise you forever.
7 To many people I am an example of how much you care.
You are my strong place of safety.
8 My mouth is filled with praise for you.
All day long I will talk about your glory.

9 Don't push me away when I'm old.
Don't desert me when my strength is gone.
10 My enemies speak against me.
Those who want to kill me get together and make evil plans.
11 They say, "God has deserted him.
Go after him and grab him.
No one will save him."

12 God, don't be far away from me.
My God, come quickly and
help me.
13 May those who bring charges
against me die in shame.
May those who want to harm me
be covered with shame and
dishonor.

14 But I will always have hope.
I will praise you more and more.
15 I will tell other people about all the
good things you have done.
All day long I will talk about how
you have saved your people.
But there's no way I could say how
many times you've done this.
16 LORD and King, I will come and
announce your mighty acts.
I will announce all the good
things that you alone do.
17 God, ever since I was young you
have taught me.
To this very day I tell about your
wonderful acts.
18 God, don't leave me
even when I'm old and have gray
hair.
Let me live to tell my children
about your power.
Let me tell all of them about your
mighty acts.

19 God, your saving acts reach to the
skies.
You have done great things.
God, who is like you?
20 You have sent many bitter troubles
my way.
But you will give me new life.
Even if I'm almost in the grave,
you will bring me back.
21 You will honor me more and more.
You will comfort me once again.
22 My God, I will use the harp to praise
you
because you are always faithful.
Holy One of Israel,
I will use the lyre to sing praise to
you.
23 My lips will shout with joy
when I sing praise to you.
You have saved me.
24 All day long my tongue will say
that you have done what is right.
Those who wanted to harm me
have been put to shame.
They have not been honored.

Psalm 72

A psalm of Solomon.

1 God, give the king the ability to
judge fairly.
He is your royal son. Help him to
do what is right.
2 May he rule your people in the
right way.
May he be fair to those among
your people who are hurting.
3 May the mountains and the hills
produce rich crops,
because the people will do what
is right.
4 May the king stand up for those
who are hurting.
May he save the children of those
who are in need.
May he crush those who treat
others badly.

5 May the king rule as long as the
sun shines
and the moon gives its light.
May he rule for all time to come.
6 May he be like rain falling on the
fields.
May he be like showers watering
the earth.
7 May godly people do well as long
as he rules.
May they have more than they
need as long as the moon lasts.

8 May the king rule from sea to sea.
May his kingdom reach from the
Euphrates River to the ends of
the earth.
9 May the desert tribes bow down to
him.
May his enemies lick the dust.
10 May the kings of Tarshish and of
places far away
bring him gifts.
May the kings of Sheba and Seba
give him presents.
11 May all kings bow down to him.
May all nations serve him.

12 The king will save needy people
who cry out to him.
He will save those who are
hurting and have no one else to
help.
13 He will take pity on those who are
weak and in need.
He will save them from death.

14 He will save them from people who
treat others badly.
He will save them from people
who do mean things to them.
Their lives are very special to
him.

15 May the king live a long time!
May gold from Sheba be given to
him.
May people always pray for him.
May they ask the LORD to bless
him all day long.
16 May there be plenty of grain
everywhere in the land.
May it sway in the wind on the
tops of the hills.
May the crops grow well, like those
in Lebanon.
May they grow like the grass of
the field.
17 May the king's name be
remembered forever.
May his fame last as long as the
sun shines.

Then all nations will be blessed
because of him.
They will call him blessed.

18 Give praise to the LORD God, the
God of Israel.
Only he can do wonderful things.
19 Give praise to his glorious name
forever.
May his glory fill the whole
earth.
Amen and Amen.

20 The prayers of David, the son of
Jesse, end here.

BOOK III

Psalms 73–89

Psalm 73

A psalm of Asaph.

1 God is truly good to Israel.
He is good to those who have
pure hearts.

2 But my feet had almost slipped.
I had almost tripped and fallen.
3 I saw that proud and sinful people
were doing well.
And I began to long for what
they had.

4 They don't have any troubles.
Their bodies are healthy and
strong.
5 They don't have the problems most
people have.
They don't suffer as other people
do.
6 Their pride is like a necklace.
They put on meanness as if it
were their clothes.
7 Many sins come out of their hard
and stubborn hearts.
There is no limit to the evil things
they can think up.
8 They laugh at others and speak
words of hatred.
They are proud. They warn
others about the harm they can
do to them.
9 They brag as if they owned heaven
itself.
They talk as if they controlled
the earth.
10 So people listen to them.
They lap up their words like
water.
11 They say, "How would God know
what we're doing?
Does the Most High God know
anything?"

12 Here is what sinful people are like.
They don't have a care in the
world.
They keep getting richer and
richer.

13 It seems as if I have kept my heart
pure for no reason.
It didn't do me any good to wash
my hands
to show that I wasn't guilty of
doing anything wrong.
14 Day after day I've been in pain.
God has punished me in a new
way every morning.

15 What if I had talked like that?
Then I wouldn't have been
faithful to God's children.
16 I tried to understand it all.
But it was more than I could
handle.
17 It troubled me until I entered God's
temple.
Then I understood what will
finally happen to bad people.

18 God, I'm sure you will make them
slip and fall.
You will throw them down and
destroy them.
19 It will happen very suddenly.
A terrible death will take them
away completely.
20 A dream goes away when a person
wakes up.
Lord, it will be like that when you
rise up.
It will be as if those people were
only a dream.
21 At one time my heart was sad
and my spirit was bitter.
22 I didn't have any sense. I didn't
know anything.
I acted like a wild animal toward
you.
23 But I am always with you.
You hold me by my right hand.
24 You give me wise advice to
guide me.
And when I die, you will take me
away
into the glory of heaven.
25 I don't have anyone in heaven but
you.
I don't want anything on earth
besides you.
26 My body and my heart may grow
weak.
God, you give strength to my
heart.
You are everything I will ever
need.
27 Those who don't want anything to
do with you will die.
You destroy all those who aren't
faithful to you.
28 But I am close to you. And that's
good.
LORD and King, I have made you
my place of safety.
I will talk about everything you
have done.

Psalm 74

A maskil of Asaph.

1 God, why have you turned your
back on us for so long?
Why are you so angry with us?
We are your very own sheep.
2 Remember the nation that you
chose as your own so long ago.
Remember that you set us free
from slavery to be your very
own people.
Remember Mount Zion, where
you lived.
3 Walk through this place that has
been torn down beyond repair.
See how completely your
enemies have destroyed the
temple!
4 In the place where you used to
meet with us,
your enemies have shouted,
"We've won the battle!"
They have set up their flags to
show they have beaten us.
5 They acted like people cutting
down a forest with axes.
6 They smashed all the beautiful
wooden walls
with their axes and hatchets.
7 They burned your temple to the
ground.
They polluted the place where
your Name is.
8 They had said in their hearts, "We
will crush them completely!"
They burned every place where
you were worshiped in the land.
9 We don't get signs from God
anymore.
There aren't any prophets left.
None of us knows how long that
will last.
10 God, how long will your enemies
make fun of you?
Will they attack you with their
words forever?
11 Why don't you help us? Why do you
hold back your power?
Use your strong power to destroy
your enemies!
12 God, you have been my king for a
long time.
You are the only God who can
save anyone on earth.
13 You parted the waters of the Red
Sea by your power.
You broke the heads of that sea
monster in Egypt.
14 You crushed the heads of the sea
monster Leviathan.
You fed it to the creatures of the
desert.

15 You opened up streams and springs.
You dried up rivers that flow all year long.
16 You rule over the day and the night.
You created the sun and the moon.
17 You decided where the borders of the earth would be.
You made both summer and winter.
18 LORD, remember how your enemies have made fun of you.
Remember how foolish people have attacked you with their words.
19 Don't hand over Israel, your dove, to those wild animals.
Don't forget your suffering people forever.
20 Honor the covenant you made with us.
Horrible things are happening in every dark corner of the land.
21 Don't let your suffering people be put to shame.
May those who are poor and needy praise you.

22 God, rise up. Stand up for your cause.
Remember how foolish people make fun of you all day long.
23 Pay close attention to the shouts of your enemies.
The trouble they cause never stops.

Psalm 75

For the director of music. A psalm of Asaph. A song to the tune of "Do Not Destroy."

1 God, we praise you.
We praise you because you are near to us.
People talk about the wonderful things you have done.
2 You say, "I choose the appointed time to judge people.
And I judge them fairly.
3 When the earth and all its people tremble,
I keep everything from falling to pieces.
4 To the proud I say, 'Don't brag anymore.'
To sinners I say, 'Don't show off your power.
5 Don't show it off against me.
Don't talk back to me.'"

6 No one from east or west or north or south
can judge themselves.
7 God is the one who judges.
He says to one person, "You are guilty."
To another he says, "You are not guilty."
8 In the hand of the LORD is a cup.
It is full of wine mixed with spices.
It is the wine of his anger.
He pours it out. All the evil people on earth
drink it down to the very last drop.

9 I will speak about this forever.
I will sing praise to the God of Jacob.
10 God says, "I will destroy the power of all sinful people.
But I will make godly people more powerful."

Psalm 76

For the director of music. A psalm of Asaph. A song to be played on stringed instruments.

1 In the land of Judah, God is well known.
In Israel, his name is great.
2 His tent is in Jerusalem.
The place where he lives is on Mount Zion.
3 There he broke the deadly arrows of his enemies.
He broke their shields and swords.
He broke their weapons of war.

4 God, you shine like a very bright light.
You are more majestic than mountains full of wild animals.
5 Brave soldiers have been robbed of everything they had.
Now they lie there, sleeping in death.
Not one of them can even lift his hands.

6 God of Jacob, at your command
both horse and chariot lie still.
7 People should have respect for you
alone.
Who can stand in front of you
when you are angry?
8 From heaven you handed down
your sentence.
The land was afraid and became
quiet.
9 God, that happened when you rose
up to judge.
It happened when you came to
save all your suffering people
in the land.
10 Your anger against sinners brings
you praise.
Those who live through your
anger gather to worship you.

11 Make promises to the LORD your
God and keep them.
Let all the neighboring nations
bring gifts to the God who should
be respected.
12 He breaks the proud spirit of rulers.
The kings of the earth have
respect for him.

Psalm 77

For the director of music.
For Jeduthun. A psalm of Asaph.

1 I cried out to God for help.
I cried out to God to hear me.
2 When I was in trouble, I looked to
the Lord for help.
During the night I lifted up my
hands in prayer.
But I refused to be comforted.
3 God, I remembered you, and I
groaned.
I thought about you, and I
became weak.
4 You kept me from going to sleep.
I was so troubled I couldn't
speak.
5 I thought about days gone by.
I thought about the years of long
ago.
6 I remembered how I used to sing
praise to you in the night.
I thought about it, and here is
what I asked myself.

7 "Will the Lord turn away from us
forever?
Won't he ever show us his
kindness again?
8 Has his faithful love disappeared
forever?
Has his promise failed for all
time?
9 Has God forgotten to help us?
Has he held back his tender love
because he was angry?"

10 Then I thought, "Here is what gives
me hope.
For many years the Most High
God showed how powerful
he is.
11 LORD, I will remember what you
did.
Yes, I will remember your
miracles of long ago.
12 I will spend time thinking about
everything you have done.
I will consider all your mighty
acts."

13 God, everything you do is holy.
What god is as great as our God?
14 You are the God who does miracles.
You show your power among the
nations.
15 With your mighty arm you set your
people free.
You set the children of Jacob and
Joseph free.
16 God, the water of the Red Sea saw
you.
It saw you and boiled up.
The deepest waters were stirred
up.
17 The clouds poured down rain.
The skies rumbled with thunder.
Lightning flashed back and forth
like arrows.
18 Your thunder was heard in the
windstorm.
Your lightning lit up the world.
The earth trembled and shook.
19 Your path led through the Red Sea.
You walked through the mighty
waters.
But your footprints were not
seen.
20 You led your people like a flock.
You led them by the hands of
Moses and Aaron.

Psalm 78

A maskil of Asaph.

1 My people, listen to my teaching.
Pay attention to what I say.
2 I will open my mouth and tell a story.
I will speak about things that were hidden.
They happened a long time ago.
3 We have heard about them and we know them.
Our people who lived before us have told us about them.
4 We won't hide them from our children.
We will tell them to those who live after us.
We will tell them what the LORD has done that is worthy of praise.
We will talk about his power and the wonderful things he has done.
5 He gave laws to the people of Jacob.
He gave Israel their law.
He commanded our people who lived before us
to teach his laws to their children.
6 Then those born later would know his laws.
Even their children yet to come would know them.
And they in turn would tell their children.
7 Then they would put their trust in God.
They would not forget what he had done.
They would obey his commands.
8 They would not be like their people who lived long ago.
Those people were stubborn.
They refused to obey God.
They turned away from him.
Their spirits were not faithful to him.

9 The soldiers of Ephraim were armed with bows.
But they ran away on the day of battle.
10 They didn't keep the covenant God had made with them.
They refused to live by his law.
11 They forgot what he had done.
They didn't remember the wonders he had shown them.
12 He did miracles right in front of their people who lived long ago.
At that time they were living in Egypt, in the area of Zoan.
13 God parted the Red Sea and led them through it.
He made the water stand up like a wall.
14 He guided them with the cloud during the day.
He led them with the light of a fire all night long.
15 He broke the rocks open in the desert.
He gave them as much water as there is in the oceans.
16 He brought streams out of a rocky cliff.
He made water flow down like rivers.

17 But they continued to sin against him.
In the desert they refused to obey the Most High God.
18 They were stubborn and tested God.
They ordered him to give them the food they wanted.
19 They spoke against God. They said,
"Can God really put food on a table in the desert?
20 It is true that he struck the rock,
and streams of water poured out.
Huge amounts of water flowed down.
But can he also give us bread?
Can he supply meat for his people?"
21 When the LORD heard what they said, he was very angry.
His anger broke out like fire against the people of Jacob.
He became very angry with Israel.
22 That was because they didn't believe in God.
They didn't trust in his power to save them.
23 But he gave a command to the skies above.
He opened the doors of the heavens.
24 He rained down manna for the people to eat.
He gave them the grain of heaven.

25 Mere human beings ate the bread
of angels.
He sent them all the food they
could eat.
26 He made the east wind blow from
the heavens.
By his power he caused the south
wind to blow.
27 He rained down meat on them like
dust.
He sent them birds like sand on
the seashore.
28 He made the birds come down
inside their camp.
The birds fell all around their
tents.
29 People ate until they couldn't eat
any more.
He gave them what they had
wanted.
30 But even before they had finished
eating, God acted.
He did it while the food was still
in their mouths.
31 His anger rose up against them.
He put to death the strongest
among them.
He struck down Israel's young
men.
32 But even after all that, they kept on
sinning.
Even after the wonderful things
he had done, they still didn't
believe.
33 So he brought their days to an end
like a puff of smoke.
He ended their years with terror.
34 Every time God killed some of
them, the others would seek
him.
They gladly turned back to him
again.
35 They remembered that God was
their Rock.
They remembered that God Most
High had set them free.
36 But they didn't mean it when they
praised him.
They lied to him when they spoke.
37 They turned away from him.
They weren't faithful to the
covenant he had made with
them.
38 But he was full of tender love.
He forgave their sins
and didn't destroy his people.
Time after time he held back his
anger.
He didn't let all his burning
anger blaze out.
39 He remembered that they were
only human.
He remembered they were only a
breath of air
that drifts by and doesn't return.
40 How often they refused to obey him
in the desert!
How often they caused him
sorrow in that dry and empty
land!
41 Again and again they tested God.
They made the Holy One of Israel
sad and angry.
42 They didn't remember his power.
They forgot the day he set them
free
from those who had treated them
so badly.
43 They forgot how he had shown
them his signs in Egypt.
They forgot his miracles in the
area of Zoan.
44 He turned the river of Egypt into
blood.
The people of Egypt couldn't
drink water from their streams.
45 He sent large numbers of flies that
bit them.
He sent frogs that destroyed their
land.
46 He gave their crops to the
grasshoppers.
He gave their food to the locusts.
47 He destroyed their vines with hail.
He destroyed their fig trees with
sleet.
48 He killed their cattle with hail.
Their livestock were struck by
lightning.
49 Because he was so angry with
Egypt, he caused them to have
great trouble.
In his great anger he sent
destroying angels against them.
50 God prepared a path for his anger.
He didn't spare their lives.
He gave them over to the plague.
51 He killed the oldest son of each
family in Egypt.
He struck down the oldest son
in every house in the land of
Ham.

52 But he brought his people out like a flock.
He led them like sheep through the desert.
53 He guided them safely, and they weren't afraid.
But the Red Sea swallowed up their enemies.
54 And so he brought his people to the border of his holy land.
He led them to the central hill country he had taken by his power.
55 He drove out the nations to make room for his people.
He gave to each family a piece of land to pass on to their children.
He gave the tribes of Israel a place to make their homes.

56 But they tested God.
They refused to obey the Most High God.
They didn't keep his laws.
57 They were like their people who lived long ago.
They turned away from him and were not faithful.
They were like a bow that doesn't shoot straight.
They couldn't be trusted.
58 They made God angry by going to their high places.
They made him jealous by worshiping the statues of their gods.
59 When God saw what the people were doing, he was very angry.
He turned away from them completely.
60 He deserted the holy tent at Shiloh.
He left the tent he had set up among his people.
61 He allowed the ark to be captured.
Into the hands of his enemies he sent the ark where his glory rested.
62 He let his people be killed by swords.
He was very angry with them.
63 Fire destroyed their young men.
Their young women had no one to marry.
64 Their priests were killed by swords.
Their widows weren't able to weep.

65 Then the Lord woke up as if he had been sleeping.
He was like a warrior waking up from the deep sleep caused by wine.
66 He drove back his enemies.
He put them to shame that will last forever.
67 He turned his back on the tents of the people of Joseph.
He didn't choose to live in the tribe of Ephraim.
68 Instead, he chose to live in the tribe of Judah.
He chose Mount Zion, which he loved.
69 There he built his holy place as secure as the heavens.
He built it to last forever, like the earth.
70 He chose his servant David.
He took him from the sheep pens.
71 He brought him from tending sheep
to be the shepherd of his people Jacob.
He made him the shepherd of Israel, his special people.
72 David cared for them with a faithful and honest heart.
With skilled hands he led them.

Psalm 79

A psalm of Asaph.

1 God, an army from the nations has attacked your land.
They have polluted your holy temple.
They have completely destroyed Jerusalem.
2 They have left the dead bodies of your people.
They have left them as food for the birds in the sky.
They have left the bodies of your faithful people.
They have left them for the wild animals.
3 They have poured out the blood of your people like water.
It is all around Jerusalem.
No one is left to bury the dead.
4 We are something our neighbors joke about.
The nations around us laugh at us and make fun of us.

5 LORD, how long will you be angry
with us? Will it be forever?
How long will your jealousy burn
like fire?
6 Bring your great anger against the
nations
that don't pay any attention to
you.
Bring it against the kingdoms
that don't worship you.
7 They have swallowed up the people
of Jacob.
They have destroyed Israel's
homeland.
8 Don't hold against us the sins of our
people who lived before us.
May you be quick to show us
your tender love.
We are in great need.

9 God our Savior, help us.
Then glory will come to you.
Save us and forgive our sins.
Then people will honor your name.
10 Why should the nations say,
"Where is their God?"
Show the nations that you punish
those who kill your people.
We want to see it happen.
11 Listen to the groans of the prisoners.
Use your strong arm
to save people sentenced to death.

12 Lord, our neighbors have laughed
at you.
Pay them back seven times for
what they have done.
13 We are your people, your very own
sheep.
We will praise you forever.
For all time to come
we will keep on praising you.

Psalm 80

For the director of music. A psalm of Asaph to the tune of "The Lilies of the Covenant."

1 Shepherd of Israel, hear us.
You lead the people of Joseph
like a flock.
You sit on your throne between
the cherubim.
Show your glory
2 to the people of Ephraim,
Benjamin and Manasseh.
Call your strength into action.
Come and save us.

3 God, make us new again.
May you be pleased with us.
Then we will be saved.

4 LORD God, you rule over all.
How long will you be angry?
Will you be angry with your
people even when they pray to
you?
5 You have given us tears as our
food.
You have made us drink tears by
the bowlful.
6 You have let our neighbors
mock us.
Our enemies laugh at us.

7 God who rules over all, make us
new again.
May you be pleased with us.
Then we will be saved.

8 You brought Israel out of Egypt.
Israel was like a vine.
After you drove the nations out of
Canaan,
you planted the vine in their
land.
9 You prepared the ground for it.
It took root and spread out over
the whole land.
10 The mountains were covered with
its shade.
The shade of its branches covered
the mighty cedar trees.
11 Your vine sent its branches out all
the way to the Mediterranean
Sea.
They reached as far as the
Euphrates River.

12 Why have you broken down the
walls around your vine?
Now all who pass by it can pick
its grapes.
13 Wild pigs from the forest destroy it.
Insects from the fields feed on it.
14 God who rules over all, return to us!
Look down from heaven and
see us!
Watch over your vine.
15 Guard the root you have planted
with your powerful right hand.
Take care of the branch you have
raised up for yourself.

16 Your vine has been cut down and
burned in the fire.
You have been angry with us,
and we are dying.

17 May you honor the people at your
right hand.
May you honor the nation you
have raised up for yourself.
18 Then we won't turn away from you.
Give us new life. We will worship
you.
19 LORD God who rules over all, make
us new again.
May you be pleased with us.
Then we will be saved.

Psalm 81

For the director of music. According to gittith. A psalm of Asaph.

1 Sing joyfully to God! He gives us
strength.
Give a loud shout to the God of
Jacob!
2 Let the music begin. Play the
tambourines.
Play sweet music on harps and
lyres.

3 Blow the ram's horn on the day of
the New Moon feast.
Blow it again when the moon
is full and the Feast of Booths
begins.
4 This is an order given to Israel.
It is a law of the God of Jacob.
5 He gave it as a covenant law for the
people of Joseph.
It was given when God went out
to punish Egypt.
There I heard a voice I didn't
recognize.
6 The voice said, "I removed the load
from your shoulders.
I set your hands free from
carrying heavy baskets.
7 You called out when you were in
trouble, and I saved you.
I answered you out of a
thundercloud.
I tested you at the waters of
Meribah.

8 "My people, listen and I will warn
you.
Israel, I wish you would listen to
me!
9 Don't have anything to do with the
gods of other nations.
Don't bow down and worship any
god other than me.
10 I am the LORD your God.
I brought you up out of Egypt.
Open your mouth wide, and I will
fill it with good things.

11 "But my people wouldn't listen
to me.
Israel wouldn't obey me.
12 So I let them go their own stubborn
way.
I let them follow their own sinful
plans.

13 "I wish my people would listen
to me!
I wish Israel would live as I want
them to live!
14 Then I would quickly bring their
enemies under control.
I would use my power against
their attackers.
15 Those who hate me would bow
down to me in fear.
They would be punished forever.
16 But you would be fed with the
finest wheat.
I would satisfy you with the
sweetest honey."

Psalm 82

A psalm of Asaph.

1 God takes his place at the head of a
large gathering of leaders.
He announces his decisions
among them.

2 He says, "How long will you stand
up for those who aren't fair to
others?
How long will you show mercy to
sinful people?
3 Stand up for the weak and for
children whose fathers have
died.
Protect the rights of people who
are poor or treated badly.
4 Save those who are weak and
needy.
Save them from the power of
sinful people.

5 "You leaders don't know anything.
You don't understand anything.
You are in the dark about what is
right.
Law and order have been
destroyed all over the world.

6 "I said, 'You leaders are like gods.
You are all children of the Most High God.'
7 But you will die, like mere human beings.
You will die like every other leader."

8 God, rise up. Judge the earth.
All the nations belong to you.

Psalm 83

A song. A psalm of Asaph.

1 God, don't remain silent.
Don't refuse to listen.
Do something, God.
2 See how your enemies are growling like dogs.
See how they are rising up against you.
3 They make clever plans against your people.
They make evil plans against those you love.
4 "Come," they say. "Let's destroy that whole nation.
Then the name of Israel won't be remembered anymore."

5 All of them agree on the evil plans they have made.
They join forces against you.
6 Their forces include the people of Edom,
Ishmael, Moab and Hagar.
7 They also include the people of Byblos, Ammon, Amalek,
Philistia and Tyre.
8 Even Assyria has joined them
to give strength to the people of Moab and Ammon.

9 Do to them what you did to the people of Midian.
Do to them what you did to Sisera and Jabin at the Kishon River.
10 Sisera and Jabin died near the town of Endor.
Their bodies were left on the ground like human waste.
11 Do to the nobles of your enemies what you did to Oreb and Zeeb.
Do to all their princes what you did to Zebah and Zalmunna.
12 They said, "Let's take over the grasslands that belong to God."
13 My God, make them like straw that the wind blows away.
Make them like tumbleweed.
14 Destroy them as fire burns up a forest.
Destroy them as a flame sets mountains on fire.
15 Chase them with your mighty winds.
Terrify them with your storm.
16 LORD, put them to shame
so that they will seek you.

17 May they always be filled with terror and shame.
May they die in dishonor.
18 May you, the LORD, let your enemies know who you are.
You alone are the Most High God over the whole earth.

Psalm 84

For the director of music. According to gittith. *A psalm of the Sons of Korah.*

1 LORD who rules over all,
how lovely is the place where you live!
2 I can't wait to be in the courtyards of the LORD's temple.
I really want to be there.
My whole being cries out
for the living God.

3 LORD who rules over all,
even the sparrow has found a home near your altar.
My King and my God,
the swallow also has a nest there,
where she may have her young.
4 Blessed are those who live in your house.
They are always praising you.

5 Blessed are those whose strength comes from you.
They have firmly decided to travel to your temple.
6 As they pass through the dry Valley of Baka,
they make it a place where water flows.
The rain in the fall covers it with pools.
7 Those people get stronger as they go along,
until each of them appears in Zion, where God lives.

8 LORD God who rules over all, hear my prayer.
God of the people of Jacob, listen to me.
9 God, may you be pleased with your anointed king.
You appointed him to be like a shield that keeps us safe.

10 A single day in your courtyards is better
than a thousand anywhere else.
I would rather guard the door of the house of my God
than live in the tents of sinful people.
11 The LORD God is like the sun that gives us light.
He is like a shield that keeps us safe.
The LORD blesses us with favor and honor.
He doesn't hold back anything good
from those whose lives are without blame.

12 LORD who rules over all,
blessed is the person who trusts in you.

Psalm 85

For the director of music.
A psalm of the Sons of Korah.

1 LORD, you were good to your land.
You blessed the people of Jacob with great success again.
2 You forgave the evil things your people did.
You took away all their sins.
3 You stopped being angry with them.
You turned your great anger away from them.

4 God our Savior, make us new again.
Stop being unhappy with us.
5 Will you be angry with us forever?
Will you be angry for all time to come?
6 Won't you give us new life again?
Then we'll be joyful because of what you have done.
7 LORD, show us your faithful love.
Save us.

8 I will listen to what God the LORD says.
He promises peace to his faithful people.
But they must not turn to foolish ways.
9 I know he's ready to save those who have respect for him.
Then his glory can be seen in our land.

10 God's truth and faithful love join together.
His peace and holiness kiss each other.
11 His truth springs up from the earth.
His holiness looks down from heaven.
12 The LORD will certainly give what is good.
Our land will produce its crops.
13 God's holiness leads the way in front of him.
It prepares the way for his coming.

Psalm 86

A prayer of David.

1 LORD, hear me and answer me.
I am poor and needy.
2 Keep my life safe, because I am faithful to you.
Save me, because I trust in you.
You are my God.
3 Lord, have mercy on me.
I call out to you all day long.
4 Bring joy to me.
Lord, I put my trust in you.

5 Lord, you are forgiving and good.
You are full of love for all who call out to you.
6 LORD, hear my prayer.
Listen to my cry for mercy.
7 When I'm in trouble, I will call out to you.
And you will answer me.

8 Lord, there's no one like you among the gods.
No one can do what you do.
9 Lord, all the nations you have made will come and worship you.
They will bring glory to you.
10 You are great. You do wonderful things.
You alone are God.

11 LORD, teach me how you want me to live.
Do this so that I will depend on you, my faithful God.

Give me a heart that doesn't want anything
more than to worship you.
12 Lord my God, I will praise you with all my heart.
I will bring glory to you forever.
13 Great is your love for me.
You have kept me from going down into the place of the dead.

14 God, proud people are attacking me.
A gang of mean people is trying to kill me.
They don't care about you.
15 But Lord, you are a God who is tender and kind.
You are gracious.
You are slow to get angry.
You are faithful and full of love.
16 Come to my aid and have mercy on me.
Show your strength by helping me.
Save me because I serve you just as my mother did.
17 Prove your goodness to me.
Then my enemies will see it and be put to shame.
LORD, you have helped me and given me comfort.

Psalm 87

A psalm of the Sons of Korah. A song.

1 The LORD has built his city
on the holy mountain.
2 He loves the city of Zion
more than all the other places
where the people of Jacob live.
3 City of God,
the LORD says glorious things about you.
4 He says, "I will include Egypt and Babylon
in a list of nations who recognize me as king.
I will also include Philistia and Tyre, along with Cush.
I will say about them, 'They were born in Zion.'"

5 Certainly it will be said about Zion,
"This nation and that nation were born in it.
The Most High God himself will make it secure."
6 Here is what the LORD will write in his list of the nations.
"Each of them was born in Zion."
7 As they make music they will sing,
"Zion, all our blessings come from you."

Psalm 88

For the director of music. According to mahalath leannoth. *A song. A psalm of the Sons of Korah. A* maskil *of Heman the Ezrahite.*

1 LORD, you are the God who saves me.
Day and night I cry out to you.
2 Please hear my prayer.
Pay attention to my cry for help.

3 I have so many troubles
I'm about to die.
4 People think my life is over.
I'm like someone who doesn't have any strength.
5 People treat me as if I were dead.
I'm like those who have been killed and are now in the grave.
You don't even remember them anymore.
They are cut off from your care.

6 It's as if you have put me deep down in the grave.
It's as if you have put me in that deep, dark place.
7 Your great anger lies heavy on me.
All the waves of your anger have crashed over me.
8 You have taken my closest friends away from me.
You have made me sickening to them.
I feel trapped and can't escape.
9 I'm crying so much I can't see very well.

LORD, I call out to you every day.
I lift up my hands to you in prayer.
10 Do you do wonderful things for those who are dead?
Do their spirits rise up and praise you?
11 Do those who are dead speak about your love?
Do those who are in the grave tell how faithful you are?

12 Are your wonderful deeds known in
that dark place?
Are your holy acts known in
that land where the dead are
forgotten?

13 LORD, I cry out to you for help.
In the morning I pray to you.
14 LORD, why do you say no to me?
Why do you turn your face away
from me?

15 I've been in pain ever since I was
young.
I've been close to death.
You have made me suffer terrible
things.
I have lost all hope.
16 Your great anger has swept
over me.
Your terrors have destroyed me.
17 All day long they surround me like
a flood.
They have closed in all around
me.
18 You have taken my friends and
neighbors away from me.
Darkness is my closest friend.

Psalm 89

A maskil of Ethan the Ezrahite.

1 LORD, I will sing about your great
love forever.
For all time to come, I will tell
how faithful you are.
2 I will tell everyone that your love
stands firm forever.
I will tell them that you are
always faithful, even in heaven
itself.

3 You said, "Here is the covenant I
have made with my chosen
one.
Here is the promise I have made
to my servant David.
4 'I will make your family line
continue forever.
I will make your kingdom secure
for all time to come.' "

5 LORD, the heavens praise you for
your wonderful deeds.
When your holy angels gather
together,
they praise you for how faithful
you are.
6 Who in the skies above can
compare with the LORD?
Who among the angels is like the
LORD?
7 God is highly respected among his
holy angels.
He's more wonderful than all
those who are around him.
8 LORD God who rules over all, who is
like you?
LORD, you are mighty. You are
faithful in everything you do.

9 You rule over the stormy sea.
When its waves rise up, you calm
them down.
10 You crushed Egypt and killed her
people.
With your powerful arm you
scattered your enemies.
11 The heavens belong to you. The
earth is yours also.
You made the world and
everything that is in it.
12 You created everything from north
to south.
Mount Tabor and Mount Hermon
sing to you with joy.
13 Your arm is powerful.
Your hand is strong.
Your right hand is mighty.

14 Your kingdom is built on what is
right and fair.
Your faithful love leads the way
in front of you.
15 Blessed are those who have learned
to shout praise to you.
LORD, they live in the light of
your kindness.
16 All day long they are full of joy
because of who you are.
They celebrate the fact that you
do what is right.
17 You bring them glory and give
them strength.
You are pleased to honor our king.
18 Our king is like a shield that keeps
us safe.
He belongs to the LORD.
He belongs to the Holy One of
Israel.

19 You once spoke to your faithful
people in a vision.
You said, "I have given strength
to a soldier.
I have raised up a young man
from among the people.

[20] I have found my servant David.
I have poured my sacred oil on his head.
[21] My powerful hand will keep him going.
My mighty arm will give him strength.
[22] No enemy will have the victory over him.
No evil person will treat him badly.
[23] I will crush the king's enemies.
I will completely destroy them.
[24] I will love him and be faithful to him.
Because of me his power will increase.
[25] I will give him a great kingdom.
It will reach from the Mediterranean Sea to the Euphrates River.
[26] He will call out to me, 'You are my Father.
You are my God. You are my Rock and Savior.'
[27] I will also make him my oldest son.
Among all the kings of the earth, he will be the most important one.
[28] I will continue to love him forever.
I will never break my covenant with him.
[29] I will make his family line continue forever.
His kingdom will last as long as the heavens.

[30] "What if his sons turn away from my laws
and do not follow them?
[31] What if they disobey my orders
and fail to keep my commands?
[32] Then I will punish them for their sins.
I will strike them with a rod.
I will whip them for their evil acts.
[33] But I will not stop loving David.
I will always be faithful to him.
[34] I will not break my covenant.
I will not go back on my word.
[35] Once and for all, I have made a promise.
It is based on my holiness.
And I will not lie to David.
[36] His family line will continue forever.
His kingdom will last as long as the sun.
[37] It will last forever like the moon,
that faithful witness in the sky."

[38] But you have turned your back on your anointed king.
You have been very angry with him.
[39] You have broken the covenant you made with him.
You have thrown your servant's crown into the dirt.
[40] You have broken through the walls around his city.
You have completely destroyed his secure places.
[41] All those who pass by have carried off what belonged to him.
His neighbors make fun of him.
[42] You have made his enemies strong.
You have made all of them happy.
[43] You have made his sword useless.
You have not helped him in battle.
[44] You have put an end to his glory.
You have knocked his throne to the ground.
[45] You have cut short the days of his life.
You have covered him with shame.

[46] LORD, how long will you hide yourself? Will it be forever?
How long will your anger burn like fire?
[47] Remember how short my life is.
You have created all people for such a useless purpose!
[48] Who can live and not die?
Who can escape the power of the grave?
[49] Lord, where is the great love you used to have?
You faithfully promised it to David.
[50] Lord, remember how my enemies have made fun of me.
I've had to put up with mean words from all the nations.
[51] LORD, your enemies have said mean things.
They have laughed at everything your anointed king has done.

[52] Give praise to the LORD forever!
Amen and Amen.

BOOK IV

Psalms 90–106

Psalm 90

A prayer of Moses, the man of God.

1 Lord, from the very beginning
you have been like a home to us.
2 Before you created the whole world
and the mountains were made,
from the beginning to the end
you are God.

3 You turn human beings back to
dust.
You say to them, "Return to
dust."
4 To you a thousand years
are like a day that has just
gone by.
They are like a few hours of the
night.
5 Yet you sweep people away, and
they die.
They are like new grass that
grows in the morning.
6 In the morning it springs up new,
but by evening it's all dried up.

7 Your anger destroys us.
Your burning anger terrifies us.
8 You have put our sins right in front
of you.
You have placed our secret
sins where you can see them
clearly.
9 You have been angry with us all of
our days.
We groan as we come to the end
of our lives.
10 We live to be about 70.
Or we may live to be 80, if we
stay healthy.
But even our best days are filled
with trouble and sorrow.
The years quickly pass, and we
are gone.

11 If only we knew the power of your
anger!
It's as great as the respect we
should have for you.
12 Teach us to realize how short our
lives are.
Then our hearts will become
wise.

13 LORD, please stop punishing us!
How long will you keep it up?
Be kind to us.
14 Satisfy us with your faithful love
every morning.
Then we can sing for joy and be
glad all our days.
15 Make us glad for as many days as
you have made us suffer.
Give us joy for as many years as
we've had trouble.
16 Show us your mighty acts.
Let our children see your glorious
power.

17 May the Lord our God always be
pleased with us.
Lord, make what we do succeed.
Please make what we do succeed.

Psalm 91

1 Whoever rests in the shadow of the
Most High God
will be kept safe by the Mighty
One.
2 I will say about the LORD,
"He is my place of safety.
He is like a fort to me.
He is my God. I trust in him."

3 He will certainly save you from
hidden traps
and from deadly sickness.
4 He will cover you with his wings.
Under the feathers of his wings
you will find safety.
He is faithful. He will keep you
safe like a shield or a tower.
5 You won't have to be afraid of the
terrors that come during the
night.
You won't have to fear the arrows
that come at you during the
day.
6 You won't have to be afraid of the
sickness that attacks in the
darkness.
You won't have to fear the plague
that destroys at noon.
7 A thousand may fall dead at your
side.
Ten thousand may fall near your
right hand.
But no harm will come to you.
8 You will see with your own eyes
how God punishes sinful people.

[9]Suppose you say, "The LORD is the
one who keeps me safe."
Suppose you let the Most High
God be like a home to you.
[10]Then no harm will come to you.
No terrible plague will come near
your tent.
[11]The LORD will command his angels
to take good care of you.
[12]They will lift you up in their hands.
Then you won't trip over a stone.
[13]You will walk on lions and cobras.
You will crush mighty lions and
poisonous snakes.

[14]The LORD says, "I will save the one
who loves me.
I will keep him safe, because he
trusts in me.
[15]He will call out to me, and I will
answer him.
I will be with him in times of
trouble.
I will save him and honor him.
[16]I will give him a long and full life.
I will save him."

Psalm 92

A psalm. A song for the Sabbath day.

[1]LORD, it is good to praise you.
Most High God, it is good to make
music to honor you.
[2]It is good to sing every morning
about your love.
It is good to sing every night
about how faithful you are.
[3]I sing about it to the music of the
lyre that has ten strings.
I sing about it to the music of the
harp.

[4]LORD, you make me glad by your
deeds.
I sing for joy about what you
have done.
[5]LORD, how great are the things
you do!
How wise your thoughts are!
[6]Here is something that people
without sense don't know.
Here is what foolish people don't
understand.
[7]Those who are evil spring up like
grass.
Those who do wrong succeed.
But they will be destroyed
forever.

[8]But LORD, you are honored forever.

[9]LORD, your enemies will certainly
die.
All those who do evil will be
scattered.
[10]You have made me as strong as a
wild ox.
You have poured the finest olive
oil on me.
[11]I've seen my evil enemies destroyed.
I've heard that they have lost the
battle.

[12]Those who do what is right will
grow like a palm tree.
They will grow strong like a
cedar tree in Lebanon.
[13]Their roots will be firm in the house
of the LORD.
They will grow strong and
healthy in the courtyards of
our God.
[14]When they get old, they will still
bear fruit.
Like young trees they will stay
fresh and strong.
[15]They will say to everyone, "The
LORD is honest.
He is my Rock, and there is no
evil in him."

Psalm 93

[1]The LORD rules.
He puts on majesty as if it were
clothes.
The LORD puts on majesty and
strength.
Indeed, the world has been set in
place.
It is firm and secure.
[2]LORD, you began to rule a long time
ago.
You have always existed.

[3]LORD, the seas have lifted up their
voice.
They have lifted up their
pounding waves.
[4]But LORD, you are more powerful
than the roar of the ocean.
You are stronger than the waves
of the sea.
LORD, you are powerful in heaven.

[5]Your laws do not change, LORD.
Your temple will be holy
for all time to come.

Psalm 94

1 The LORD is a God who punishes.
Since you are the one who punishes, come and show your anger.
2 Judge of the earth, rise up.
Pay back proud people for what they have done.
3 LORD, how long will those who are evil be glad?
How long will they be full of joy?

4 Proud words pour out of their mouths.
All those who do evil are always bragging.
5 LORD, they crush your people.
They treat badly those who belong to you.
6 They kill outsiders. They kill widows.
They murder children whose fathers have died.
7 They say, "The LORD doesn't see what's happening.
The God of Jacob doesn't pay any attention to it."
8 You who aren't wise, pay attention.
You foolish people, when will you become wise?
9 Does he who made the ear not hear?
Does he who formed the eye not see?
10 Does he who corrects nations not punish?
Does he who teaches human beings not know anything?
11 The LORD knows what people think.
He knows that their thoughts don't amount to anything.

12 LORD, blessed is the person you correct.
Blessed is the person you teach from your law.
13 You give them rest from times of trouble,
until a pit is dug to trap sinners.
14 The LORD won't say no to his people.
He will never desert those who belong to him.
15 He will again judge people in keeping with what is right.
All those who have honest hearts will follow the right way.

16 Who will rise up for me against sinful people?
Who will stand up for me against those who do evil?
17 Suppose the LORD had not helped me.
Then I would soon have been lying quietly in the grave.
18 I said, "My foot is slipping."
But LORD, your faithful love kept me from falling.
19 I was very worried.
But your comfort brought me joy.

20 Can you have anything to do with rulers who aren't fair?
Can those who make laws that cause suffering be friends of yours?
21 Evil people join together against those who do what is right.
They sentence to death those who aren't guilty of doing anything wrong.
22 But the LORD has become like a fort to me.
My God is my rock. I go to him for safety.
23 He will pay them back for their sins.
He will destroy them for their evil acts.
The LORD our God will destroy them.

Psalm 95

1 Come, let us sing for joy to the LORD.
Let us give a loud shout to the Rock who saves us.
2 Let us come to him and give him thanks.
Let us praise him with music and song.

3 The LORD is the great God.
He is the greatest King.
He rules over all the gods.
4 He owns the deepest parts of the earth.
The mountain peaks belong to him.
5 The ocean is his, because he made it.
He formed the dry land with his hands.

6 Come, let us bow down and worship
him.
Let us fall on our knees in front
of the LORD our Maker.
7 He is our God.
We are the sheep belonging to his
flock.
We are the people he takes good
care of.
If only you would listen to his voice
today.
8 He says, "Don't be stubborn as
you were at Meribah.
Don't be stubborn as you were
that day at Massah in the
desert.
9 There your people of long ago
really tested me.
They did it even though they had
seen what I had done for them.
10 For 40 years I was angry with
them.
I said, 'Their hearts are always
going astray.
They do not know how I want
them to live.'
11 So when I was angry, I made a
promise.
I said, 'They will never enjoy the
rest I planned for them.'"

Psalm 96

1 Sing a new song to the LORD.
All you people of the earth, sing
to the LORD.
2 Sing to the LORD. Praise him.
Day after day tell about how he
saves us.
3 Tell the nations about his glory.
Tell all people about the
wonderful things he has done.
4 The LORD is great. He is really
worthy of praise.
People should have respect for
him as the greatest God of all.
5 All the gods of the nations are like
their statues.
They can't do anything.
But the LORD made the heavens.
6 Glory and majesty are all around
him.
Strength and glory can be seen in
his temple.
7 Praise the LORD, all you nations.
Praise the LORD for his glory and
strength.
8 Praise the LORD for the glory that
belongs to him.
Bring an offering and come into
the courtyards of his temple.
9 Worship the LORD because of his
beauty and holiness.
All you people of the earth,
tremble when you are with
him.
10 Say to the nations, "The LORD
rules."
The world is firmly set in place. It
can't be moved.
The LORD will judge the people of
the world fairly.
11 Let the heavens be full of joy. Let
the earth be glad.
Let the ocean and everything in
it roar.
12 Let the fields and everything in
them be glad.
Let all the trees in the forest sing
for joy.
13 Let all creation be full of joy in
front of the LORD,
because he is coming to judge the
earth.
He will faithfully judge the people
of the world
in keeping with what is right.

Psalm 97

1 The LORD rules. Let the earth be
glad.
Let countries that are far away
be full of joy.
2 Clouds and thick darkness
surround him.
His rule is built on what is right
and fair.
3 The LORD sends fire ahead of him.
It burns up his enemies all
around him.
4 His lightning lights up the world.
The earth sees it and trembles.
5 The mountains melt like wax when
the LORD is near.
He is the Lord of the whole earth.
6 The heavens announce that what
he does is right.
All people everywhere see his
glory.

WORTHY

MY GOD IS...

To have worth is to have value. Have you ever been shopping in a store and looked at the price of a toy? The price tells you what someone thinks the toy is worth, or the value of the toy. God has great value—more than anything we can imagine!—because he is the one true God. There is no one like him. He alone is worthy of all our worship and praise (see Revelation 4:11).

We tell God that we believe he is worthy by praying and telling him how much we love him. We tell God that we believe he is worthy by obeying him. We also tell God that we believe he is worthy by singing praises to him. He is a great and worthy God!

7 All who worship statues of gods
or brag about them are put to shame.
All you gods, worship the LORD!
8 Zion hears about it and is filled with joy.
LORD, the villages of Judah are glad
because of how you judge.
9 LORD, you are the Most High God.
You rule over the whole earth.
You are honored much more than all gods.
10 Let those who love the LORD hate evil.
He guards the lives of those who are faithful to him.
He saves them from the power of sinful people.
11 Good things come to those who do what is right.
Joy comes to those whose hearts are honest.
12 You who are godly, be glad
because of what the LORD has done.
Praise him, because his name is holy.

Psalm 98

A psalm.

1 Sing a new song to the LORD.
He has done wonderful things.
By the power of his right hand and his holy arm
he has saved his people.
2 The LORD has made known his power to save.
He has shown the nations that he does what is right.
3 He has shown his faithful love
to the people of Israel.
People from one end of the earth to the other
have seen that our God has saved us.
4 Shout for joy to the LORD, everyone on earth.
Burst into joyful songs and make music.
5 Make music to the LORD with the harp.
Sing and make music with the harp.
6 Blow the trumpets. Give a blast on the ram's horn.
Shout for joy to the LORD. He is the King.

[7]Let the ocean and everything in it roar.
Let the world and all who live in it shout.
[8]Let the rivers clap their hands.
Let the mountains sing together with joy.
[9]Let them sing to the LORD,
because he is coming to judge the earth.
He will judge the nations of the world
in keeping with what is right and fair.

Psalm 99

[1]The LORD rules.
Let the nations tremble.
He sits on his throne between the cherubim.
Let the earth shake.
[2]Great is the LORD in Zion.
He is honored over all the nations.
[3]Let them praise his great and wonderful name.
He is holy.

[4]The King is mighty and loves justice.
He has set up the rules for fairness.
He has done what is right and fair
for the people of Jacob.
[5]Honor the LORD our God.
Worship at his feet.
He is holy.

[6]Moses and Aaron were two of his priests.
Samuel was one of those who worshiped him.
They called out to the LORD.
And he answered them.
[7]He spoke to them from the pillar of cloud.
They obeyed his laws and the orders he gave them.

[8]LORD our God, you answered them.
You showed Israel that you are a God who forgives.
But when they did wrong, you punished them.
[9]Honor the LORD our God.
Worship at his holy mountain.
The LORD our God is holy.

Psalm 100

A psalm for giving grateful praise.

[1]Shout for joy to the LORD, everyone on earth.
[2] Worship the LORD with gladness.
Come to him with songs of joy.
[3]Know that the LORD is God.
He made us, and we belong to him.
We are his people.
We are the sheep belonging to his flock.

[4]Give thanks as you enter the gates of his temple.
Give praise as you enter its courtyards.
Give thanks to him and praise his name.
[5]The LORD is good. His faithful love continues forever.
It will last for all time to come.

Psalm 101

A psalm of David.

[1]I will sing about your love and fairness.
LORD, I will sing praise to you.
[2]I will be careful to lead a life
that is without blame.
When will you come and help me?

In my own home I will lead a life
that is without blame.
[3] I won't look at anything that is evil and call it good.

I hate the acts of people who aren't faithful to you.
I won't have anything to do with those things.
[4]I will stay away from those whose hearts are twisted.
I won't have anything to do with what is evil.

[5]I will get rid of anyone
who tells lies about their neighbor in secret.
I won't put up with anyone
whose eyes and heart are proud.

[6]I will look with favor on the faithful people in the land.
They will live with me.
Those whose lives are without blame will serve me.

7 No one who lies and cheats
will live in my house.
No one who tells lies
will serve me.

8 Every morning I will get rid of
all the sinful people in the land.
I will remove from the city of the
LORD
everyone who does what is evil.

Psalm 102

A prayer of a suffering person who has become weak. They pour out their problems to the LORD.

1 LORD, hear my prayer.
Listen to my cry for help.
2 Don't turn your face away from me
when I'm in trouble.
Pay attention to me.
When I call out for help, answer
me quickly.

3 My days are disappearing like smoke.
My body burns like glowing coals.
4 My strength has dried up like grass.
I even forget to eat my food.
5 I groan out loud because of my
suffering.
I'm nothing but skin and bones.
6 I'm like a desert owl.
I'm like an owl among destroyed
buildings.
7 I can't sleep. I've become
like a bird alone on a roof.
8 All day long my enemies laugh
at me.
Those who make fun of me use
my name as a curse.
9 I eat ashes as my food.
My tears fall into what I'm
drinking.
10 You were very angry with me.
So you picked me up and threw
me away.
11 The days of my life are like an
evening shadow.
I dry up like grass.

12 But LORD, you are seated on your
throne forever.
Your fame will continue for all
time to come.
13 You will rise up and show deep
concern for Zion.
The time has come for you to
help Zion.
14 The stones of your destroyed city
are priceless to us.
Even its dust brings deep concern
to us.
15 The nations will worship the LORD.
All the kings on earth will respect
his glorious power.
16 The LORD will build Zion again.
He will appear in his glory.
17 He will answer the prayer of those
who don't have anything.
He won't say no to their cry for
help.

18 Let this be written down for those
born after us.
Then people who are not yet
born can praise the LORD.
19 Here is what should be written.
"The LORD looked down from his
temple in heaven.
From heaven he viewed the
earth.
20 He heard the groans of the
prisoners.
He set free those who were
sentenced to death."
21 So people will talk about him in
Zion.
They will praise him in
Jerusalem.
22 Nations and kingdoms
will gather there to worship the
LORD.

23 When I was still young, he took
away my strength.
He wasn't going to let me live
much longer.
24 So I said, "My God, don't let me die
in the middle of my life.
You will live for all time to come.
25 In the beginning you made the
earth secure.
You placed it on its foundations.
Your hands created the heavens.
26 They will pass away. But you will
remain.
They will all wear out like a piece
of clothing.
You will make them like clothes
that are taken off and thrown
away.
27 But you remain the same.
Your years will never end.
28 Our children will live with you.
Their sons and daughters will be
safe in your care."

Psalm 103

A psalm of David.

1 I will praise the LORD.
Deep down inside me, I will praise him.
I will praise him, because his name is holy.
2 I will praise the LORD.
I won't forget anything he does for me.
3 He forgives all my sins.
He heals all my sicknesses.
4 He saves my life from going down into the grave.
His faithful and tender love makes me feel like a king.
5 He satisfies me with the good things I desire.
Then I feel young and strong again, just like an eagle.

6 The LORD does what is right and fair
for all who are treated badly.
7 He told Moses all about his plans.
He let the people of Israel see his mighty acts.
8 The LORD is tender and kind. He is gracious.
He is slow to get angry. He is full of love.
9 He won't keep bringing charges against us.
He won't stay angry with us forever.
10 He doesn't punish us for our sins as much as we should be punished.
He doesn't pay us back in keeping with the evil things we've done.
11 He loves those who have respect for him.
His love is as high as the heavens are above the earth.
12 He has removed our sins from us.
He has removed them as far as the east is from the west.
13 A father is tender and kind to his children.
In the same way, the LORD is tender and kind
to those who have respect for him.
14 He knows what we are made of.
He remembers that we are dust.
15 The life of human beings is like grass.
People grow like the flowers in the field.
16 When the wind blows on them, they are gone.
No one can tell that they had ever been there.
17 But the LORD's love
for those who have respect for him
lasts for ever and ever.
Their children's children will know
that he always does what is right.
18 He always loves those who keep his covenant.
He always does what is right for those who remember to obey his commands.

19 The LORD has set up his throne in heaven.
His kingdom rules over all.
20 Praise the LORD, you angels of his.
Praise him, you mighty ones who carry out his orders and obey his word.
21 Praise the LORD, all you angels in heaven.
Praise him, all you who serve him and do what he wants.
22 Let everything the LORD has made praise him
everywhere in his kingdom.

I will praise the LORD.

Psalm 104

1 I will praise the LORD.

LORD my God, you are very great.
You are dressed in glory and majesty.
2 The LORD wraps himself in light as if it were a robe.
He spreads out the heavens like a tent.
3 He builds his palace high in the heavens.
He makes the clouds serve as his chariot.
He rides on the wings of the wind.
4 He makes the winds serve as his messengers.
He makes flashes of lightning serve him.

5 He placed the earth on its
foundations.
It can never be moved.
6 You, LORD, covered it with the
oceans like a blanket.
The waters covered the mountains.
7 But you commanded the waters,
and they ran away.
At the sound of your thunder
they rushed off.
8 They flowed down the mountains.
They went into the valleys.
They went to the place you
appointed for them.
9 You drew a line they can't cross.
They will never cover the earth
again.
10 The LORD makes springs pour water
into the valleys.
It flows between the mountains.
11 The springs give water to all the
wild animals.
The wild donkeys satisfy their
thirst.
12 The birds in the sky build nests by
the waters.
They sing among the branches.
13 The LORD waters the mountains
from his palace high in the
clouds.
The earth is filled with the things
he has made.
14 He makes grass grow for the cattle
and plants for people to take
care of.
That's how they get food from
the earth.
15 There is wine to make people glad.
There is olive oil to make their
skin glow.
And there is bread to make them
strong.
16 The cedar trees of Lebanon belong
to the LORD.
He planted them and gave them
plenty of water.
17 There the birds make their nests.
The stork has its home in the
juniper trees.
18 The high mountains belong to the
wild goats.
The cliffs are a safe place for the
rock badgers.
19 The LORD made the moon to mark
off the seasons.
The sun knows when to go down.
20 You, LORD, bring darkness, and it
becomes night.
Then all the animals of the forest
prowl around.
21 The lions roar while they hunt.
All their food comes from God.
22 The sun rises, and they slip away.
They return to their dens and lie
down.
23 Then people get up and go to work.
They keep working until evening.
24 LORD, you have made so many
things!
How wise you were when you
made all of them!
The earth is full of your
creatures.
25 Look at the ocean, so big and wide!
It is filled with more creatures
than people can count.
It is filled with living things, from
the largest to the smallest.
26 Ships sail back and forth on it.
Leviathan, the sea monster you
made, plays in it.
27 All creatures depend on you
to give them their food when
they need it.
28 When you give it to them,
they eat it.
When you open your hand,
they are satisfied with good
things.
29 When you turn your face away
from them,
they are terrified.
When you take away their breath,
they die and turn back into dust.
30 When you send your Spirit,
you create them.
You give new life to the ground.
31 May the glory of the LORD continue
forever.
May the LORD be happy with
what he has made.
32 When he looks at the earth, it
trembles.
When he touches the mountains,
they pour out smoke.
33 I will sing to the LORD all my life.
I will sing praise to my God as
long as I live.
34 May these thoughts of mine please
him.
I find my joy in the LORD.

35 But may sinners be gone from the
earth.
May evil people disappear.

I will praise the LORD.

Praise the LORD.

Psalm 105

1 Give praise to the LORD and
announce who he is.
Tell the nations what he has done.
2 Sing to him, sing praise to him.
Tell about all the wonderful
things he has done.
3 Praise him, because his name is holy.
Let the hearts of those who trust
in the LORD be glad.
4 Seek the LORD and the strength he
gives.
Always seek him.

5 Remember the wonderful things he
has done.
Remember his miracles and how
he judged our enemies.
6 Remember what he has done, you
children of his servant Abraham.
Remember it, you people of
Jacob, God's chosen ones.
7 He is the LORD our God.
He judges the whole earth.

8 He will keep his covenant forever.
He will keep his promise for all
time to come.
9 He will keep the covenant he made
with Abraham.
He will keep the promise he
made to Isaac.
10 He made it stand as a law for Jacob.
He made it stand as a covenant
for Israel that will last forever.
11 He said, "I will give you the land of
Canaan.
It will belong to you."

12 At first there weren't very many of
God's people.
There were only a few, and they
were strangers in the land.
13 They wandered from nation to
nation.
They wandered from one
kingdom to another.
14 But God didn't allow anyone to
treat them badly.
To keep them safe, he gave a
command to kings.
15 He said to them, "Do not touch my
anointed ones.
Do not harm my prophets."

16 He made the people in the land go
hungry.
He destroyed all their food
supplies.
17 He sent a man ahead of them into
Egypt.
That man was Joseph. He had
been sold as a slave.
18 The Egyptians put his feet in chains.
They put an iron collar around
his neck.
19 He was in prison until what he said
would happen came true.
The word of the LORD proved that
he was right.
20 The king of Egypt sent for Joseph
and let him out of prison.
The ruler of many nations set
him free.
21 He put Joseph in charge of his palace.
He made him ruler over
everything he owned.
22 Joseph was in charge of teaching
the princes.
He taught the elders how to think
and live wisely.

23 Then the rest of Jacob's family went
to Egypt.
The people of Israel lived as
outsiders in the land of Ham.
24 The LORD gave his people so many
children
that there were too many of
them for their enemies.
25 He made the Egyptians hate his
people.
The Egyptians made evil plans
against them.
26 The LORD sent his servant Moses to
the king of Egypt.
He sent Aaron, his chosen one,
along with him.
27 The LORD gave them the power to
do signs among the Egyptians.
They did his wonders in the land
of Ham.
28 The LORD sent darkness over the
land.
He did it because the Egyptians
had refused to obey his words.
29 He turned their rivers and streams
into blood.
He caused the fish in them to die.

30 Their land was covered with frogs.
Frogs even went into the bedrooms of the rulers.
31 The LORD spoke, and large numbers of flies came.
Gnats filled the whole country.
32 He turned their rain into hail.
Lightning flashed all through their land.
33 He destroyed their vines and fig trees.
He broke down the trees in Egypt.
34 He spoke, and the locusts came.
There were so many of them they couldn't be counted.
35 They ate up every green thing in the land.
They ate up what the land produced.
36 Then he killed the oldest son of every family in Egypt.
He struck down the oldest of all their sons.

37 He brought the people of Israel out of Egypt.
The Egyptians loaded them down with silver and gold.
From among the tribes of Israel no one got tired or fell down.
38 The Egyptians were glad when the people of Israel left.
They were terrified because of Israel.
39 The LORD spread out a cloud to cover his people.
He gave them a fire to light up the night.
40 They asked for meat, and he brought them quail.
He fed them well with manna, the bread of heaven.
41 He broke open a rock, and streams of water poured out.
They flowed like a river in the desert.

42 He remembered the holy promise he had made to his servant Abraham.
43 His chosen people shouted for joy as he brought them out of Egypt.
44 He gave them the lands of other nations.
He let them take over what others had worked for.
45 He did it so they might obey his rules
and follow his laws.

Praise the LORD.

Psalm 106

1 Praise the LORD.

Give thanks to the LORD, because he is good.
His faithful love continues forever.
2 Who can speak enough about the mighty acts of the LORD?
Who can praise him as much as he should be praised?
3 Blessed are those who always do what is fair.
Blessed are those who keep doing what is right.
4 LORD, remember me when you bless your people.
Help me when you save them.
5 Then I will enjoy the good things you give your chosen ones.
I will be joyful together with your people.
I will join them when they praise you.

6 We have sinned, just as our people of long ago did.
We too have done what is evil and wrong.
7 When our people were in Egypt, they forgot about the LORD's miracles.
They didn't remember his many kind acts.
At the Red Sea they refused to obey him.
8 But he saved them for the honor of his name.
He did it to make his mighty power known.
9 He ordered the Red Sea to dry up, and it did.
He led his people through it as if it were a desert.
10 He saved them from the power of their enemies.
He set them free from their control.
11 The waters covered their enemies.
Not one of them escaped alive.
12 Then his people believed his promises
and sang praise to him.

[13] But they soon forgot what he had done.
They didn't wait for what he had planned to happen.
[14] In the desert they longed for food.
In that dry and empty land they tested God.
[15] So he gave them what they asked for.
But he also sent a sickness that killed many of them.
[16] In their camp some of them became jealous of Moses and Aaron.
Aaron had been set apart to serve the LORD.
[17] The ground opened up and swallowed Dathan.
It buried Abiram and his followers.
[18] Fire blazed among all of them.
Flames destroyed those evil people.
[19] At Mount Horeb they made a metal statue of a bull calf.
They worshiped that statue of a god.
[20] They traded their glorious God
for a statue of a bull that eats grass.
[21] They forgot the God who saved them.
They forgot the God who had done great things in Egypt.
[22] They forgot the miracles he did in the land of Ham.
They forgot the wonderful things he did by the Red Sea.
[23] So he said he would destroy them.
But Moses, his chosen one,
stood up for them.
He kept God's anger from destroying them.
[24] Later on, they refused to enter the pleasant land of Canaan.
They didn't believe God's promise.
[25] In their tents they told the LORD
how unhappy they were.
They didn't obey him.
[26] So he lifted up his hand and promised
that he would make them die in the desert.
[27] He promised he would scatter their children's children among the nations.
He would make them die in other lands.
[28] They joined in worshiping the Baal that was worshiped at Peor.
They ate food that had been offered to gods that aren't even alive.
[29] Their evil ways made the LORD angry.
So a plague broke out among them.
[30] But Phinehas stood up and took action.
Then the plague stopped.
[31] What Phinehas did made him right with the LORD.
It will be remembered for all time to come.
[32] By the waters of Meribah the LORD's people made him angry.
Moses got in trouble because of them.
[33] They refused to obey the Spirit of God.
So Moses spoke without thinking.
[34] They didn't destroy the nations in Canaan
as the LORD had commanded them.
[35] Instead, they mixed with those nations
and adopted their ways.
[36] They worshiped statues of their gods.
That became a trap for them.
[37] They sacrificed their sons and daughters
as offerings to false gods.
[38] They killed those who weren't guilty of doing anything wrong.
They killed their own sons and daughters.
They sacrificed them as offerings to statues of the gods of Canaan.
The land became "unclean"
because of the blood of their children.
[39] The people made themselves impure by what they had done.
They weren't faithful to the LORD.
[40] So the LORD became angry with his people.
He turned away from his own children.
[41] He handed them over to the nations.
Their enemies ruled over them.

42 Their enemies treated them badly
and kept them under their power.
43 Many times the LORD saved them.
But they refused to obey him.
So he destroyed them because of
their sins.

44 Yet he heard them when they cried
out.
He paid special attention to their
suffering.
45 Because they were his people, he
remembered his covenant.
Because of his great love, he felt
sorry for them.
46 He made all those who held them
as prisoners
have mercy on them.

47 LORD our God, save us.
Bring us back from among the
nations.
Then we will give thanks to you,
because your name is holy.
We will celebrate by praising
you.

48 Give praise to the LORD, the God of
Israel,
for ever and ever.
Let all the people say, "Amen!"

Praise the LORD.

BOOK V

Psalms 107–150

Psalm 107

1 Give thanks to the LORD, because he
is good.
His faithful love continues
forever.
2 Let those who have been set free by
the LORD tell their story.
He set them free from the power
of the enemy.
3 He brought them back from other
lands.
He brought them back from
east and west, from north and
south.
4 Some of them wandered in deserts
that were dry and empty.
They couldn't find a city where
they could make their homes.
5 They were hungry and thirsty.
Their lives were slipping away.
6 Then they cried out to the LORD
because of their problems.
And he saved them from their
troubles.
7 He led them straight
to a city where they could make
their homes.
8 Let them give thanks to the LORD
for his faithful love.
Let them give thanks for the
wonderful things he does for
people.
9 He gives those who are thirsty all
the water they want.
He gives those who are hungry
all the good food they can eat.

10 Others lived in the deepest
darkness.
They suffered as prisoners in iron
chains.
11 That's because they hadn't obeyed
the commands of God.
They had refused to follow the
plans of the Most High God.
12 So he made them do work that was
hard and bitter.
They tripped and fell, and there
was no one to help them.
13 Then they cried out to the LORD
because of their problems.
And he saved them from their
troubles.
14 He brought them out of the deepest
darkness.
He broke their chains off.
15 Let them give thanks to the LORD
for his faithful love.
Let them give thanks for the
wonderful things he does for
people.
16 He breaks down gates that are
made of bronze.
He cuts through bars that are
made of iron.

17 Others were foolish. They suffered
because of their sins.
They suffered because they
wouldn't obey the LORD.
18 They refused to eat anything.
They came close to passing
through the gates of death.
19 Then they cried out to the LORD
because of their problems.
And he saved them from their
troubles.

20 He gave his command and healed
them.
He saved them from the grave.
21 Let them give thanks to the LORD
for his faithful love.
Let them give thanks for the
wonderful things he does for
people.
22 Let them sacrifice thank offerings.
Let them talk about what he has
done as they sing with joy.

23 Some people sailed out on the
ocean in ships.
They traded goods on the mighty
waters.
24 They saw the works of the LORD.
They saw the wonderful deeds he
did on the ocean.
25 He spoke and stirred up a storm.
It lifted the waves high.
26 They rose up to the heavens. Then
they went down deep into the
ocean.
In that kind of danger the
people's boldness melted away.
27 They were unsteady like people
who have become drunk.
They didn't know what to do.
28 Then they cried out to the LORD
because of their problems.
And he brought them out of their
troubles.
29 He made the storm as quiet as a
whisper.
The waves of the ocean calmed
down.
30 The people were glad when the
ocean became calm.
Then he guided them to the
harbor they were looking for.
31 Let them give thanks to the LORD
for his faithful love.
Let them give thanks for the
wonderful things he does for
people.
32 Let them honor him among his
people who gather for worship.
Let them praise him in the
meeting of the elders.

33 He turned rivers into a desert.
He turned flowing springs into
thirsty ground.
34 He turned land that produced crops
into a salty land where nothing
could grow.
He did it because the people who
lived there were evil.
35 He turned the desert into pools of
water.
He turned the dry and cracked
ground into flowing springs.
36 He brought hungry people there to
live.
They built a city where they
could make their homes.
37 They planted fields and vineyards
that produced large crops.
38 He blessed the people, and they
greatly increased their
numbers.
He kept their herds from getting
smaller.

39 Then the number of God's people
got smaller.
They were made humble by
trouble, suffering and sorrow.
40 The God who looks down on proud
nobles
made them wander in a desert
where no one lives.
41 But he lifted needy people out of
their suffering.
He made their families increase
like flocks of sheep.
42 Honest people see it and are filled
with joy.
But no one who is evil has
anything to say.

43 Let those who are wise pay
attention to these things.
Let them think about the loving
deeds of the LORD.

Psalm 108

A song. A psalm of David.

1 God, my heart feels secure.
I will sing and make music to
you with all my heart.
2 Harp and lyre, wake up!
I want to sing and make music
before the sun rises.
3 LORD, I will praise you among the
nations.
I will sing about you among the
people of the earth.
4 Great is your love. It is higher than
the heavens.
Your truth reaches to the skies.
5 God, may you be honored above
the heavens.
Let your glory be over the whole
earth.

6 Save us. Help us with your powerful
right hand,
so that those you love may be
saved.
7 God has spoken from his temple.
He has said, "I will win the battle.
Then I will divide up the land
around Shechem.
I will divide up the Valley of
Sukkoth.
8 Gilead belongs to me, and so does
the land of Manasseh.
Ephraim is the strongest tribe. It
is like a helmet for my head.
Judah is the royal tribe. It is like
a ruler's scepter.
9 Moab serves me like one who
washes my feet.
I toss my sandal on Edom to
show that I own it.
I shout to Philistia that I have
won the battle."

10 Who will bring me to the city that
has high walls around it?
Who will lead me to the land of
Edom?
11 God, isn't it you, even though you
have now turned away from us?
Isn't it you, even though you
don't lead our armies into
battle anymore?
12 Help us against our enemies.
The help people give doesn't
amount to anything.
13 With your help we will win the
battle.
You will walk all over our
enemies.

Psalm 109

For the director of music.
A psalm of David.

1 God, I praise you.
Don't remain silent.
2 Sinful people who lie and cheat
have spoken against me.
They have used their tongues to
tell lies about me.
3 They gather all around me with
their words of hatred.
They attack me without any
reason.
4 They bring charges against me,
even though I love them
and pray for them.
5 They pay me back with evil for the
good things I do.
They pay back my love with
hatred.

6 Appoint an evil person to take my
enemies to court.
Let him stand at their right hand
and bring charges against
them.
7 When they are tried, let them be
found guilty.
May even their prayers judge
them.
8 May their days be few.
Let others take their places as
leaders.
9 May their children's fathers die.
May their wives become widows.
10 May their children be driven from
their destroyed homes.
May they wander around like
beggars.
11 May everything those people own
be taken away to pay for what
they owe.
May strangers rob them of
everything they've worked for.
12 May no one be kind to them
or take pity on the children they
leave behind.
13 May their family line come to an
end.
May their names be forgotten by
those who live after them.
14 May the LORD remember the evil
things their fathers have done.
May he never erase the sins of
their mothers.
15 May the LORD never forget their sins.
Then he won't let people
remember the names of my
enemies anymore.

16 They never thought about doing
anything kind.
Instead, they drove those who
were poor and needy to their
deaths.
They did the same thing to those
whose hearts were broken.
17 They loved to curse others.
May their curses come back on
them.
They didn't find any pleasure in
giving anyone their blessing.
May no blessing ever come to
them.

18 They cursed others as easily as
they put on clothes.
Cursing was as natural to them
as getting a drink of water
or putting olive oil on their bodies.
19 May their curses cover them like
coats.
May their curses be wrapped
around them like a belt forever.
20 May that be the LORD's way of
paying back
those who bring charges
against me.
May it happen to those who say
evil things about me.

21 But LORD and King,
help me so that you bring honor
to yourself.
Because your love is so good,
save me.
22 I am poor and needy.
My heart is wounded deep down
inside me.
23 I fade away like an evening
shadow.
I'm like a locust that someone
brushes off.
24 My knees are weak because I've
gone without food.
My body is very thin.
25 Those who bring charges against
me laugh at me.
When they see me, they shake
their heads at me.

26 LORD my God, help me.
Save me because of your faithful
love.
27 LORD, let my enemies know that
you yourself have saved me.
You have done it with your own
hand.
28 They may curse me.
But may you bless me.
May those who attack me be put to
shame.
But may I be filled with joy.
29 May those who bring charges
against me be clothed with
dishonor.
May they be wrapped in shame
as if it were a coat.

30 With my mouth I will continually
praise the LORD.
I will praise him when all his
people gather for worship.
31 He stands ready to help those who
need it.
He saves them from those who are
ready to sentence them to death.

17 I will not die but live.
I will talk about what the LORD has done.
18 The LORD has really punished me.
But he didn't let me die.

19 Open for me the gates where the godly can go in.
I will enter and give thanks to the LORD.
20 This is the gate of the LORD.
Only those who do what is right can go through it.
21 LORD, I will give thanks to you,
because you answered me.
You have saved me.

22 The stone the builders didn't accept
has become the most important stone of all.
23 The LORD has done it.
It is wonderful in our eyes.
24 The LORD has done it on this day.
Let us be joyful today and be glad.

25 LORD, save us.
LORD, give us success.
26 Blessed is the one who comes in the name of the LORD.
From the temple of the LORD we bless you.
27 The LORD is God.
He has been good to us.
Take branches in your hands. Join in the march on the day of the feast.
March up to the corners of the altar.

28 You are my God, and I will praise you.
You are my God, and I will honor you.

29 Give thanks to the LORD, because he is good.
His faithful love continues forever.

Psalm 119

א Aleph

1 Blessed are those who live without blame.
They live in keeping with the law of the LORD.
2 Blessed are those who obey his covenant laws.
They trust in him with all their hearts.
3 They don't do anything wrong.
They live as he wants them to live.
4 You have given me rules
that I must obey completely.
5 I hope I will always stand firm
in following your orders.
6 Then I won't be put to shame
when I think about all your commands.
7 I will praise you with an honest heart
as I learn about how fair your decisions are.
8 I will obey your orders.
Please don't leave me all alone.

ב Beth

9 How can a young person keep their life pure?
By living according to your word.
10 I trust in you with all my heart.
Don't let me wander away from your commands.
11 I have hidden your word in my heart
so that I won't sin against you.
12 LORD, I give praise to you.
Teach me your orders.
13 With my lips I talk about
all the decisions you have made.
14 Following your covenant laws gives me joy
just as great riches give joy to others.
15 I spend time thinking about your rules.
I consider how you want me to live.
16 I take delight in your orders.
I won't fail to obey your word.

ג Gimel

17 Be good to me while I am alive.
Do this so that I may obey your word.
18 Open my eyes so that I can see
the wonderful truths in your law.
19 I'm a stranger on earth.
Don't hide your commands from me.
20 My heart is filled with longing
for your laws at all times.
21 You correct proud people. They are under your curse.
They wander away from your commands.
22 I obey your covenant laws.
So don't let evil people laugh at me or hate me.

23 Even if rulers sit together and tell
lies about me,
I will spend time thinking about
your orders.
24 Your covenant laws are my delight.
They give me wise advice.

ד Daleth

25 I lie in the dust. I'm about to die.
Keep me alive as you have
promised.
26 I told you how I've lived, and you
gave me your answer.
Teach me your orders.
27 Help me understand how your
rules direct me to live.
Then I may think deeply about
the wonderful things you have
done.
28 My sadness has worn me out.
Give me strength as you have
promised.
29 Keep me from cheating and telling
lies.
Be kind to me and teach me your
law.
30 I have chosen to be faithful to you.
I put my trust in your laws.
31 LORD, I'm careful to obey your
covenant laws.
Don't let me be put to shame.
32 I am quick to follow your
commands,
because you have added to my
understanding.

ה He

33 LORD, teach me how your orders
direct me to live.
Then I will live that way to the
very end.
34 Help me understand your law so
that I may follow it.
I will obey it with all my heart.
35 Teach me to live as you command,
because that makes me very
happy.
36 Make me want to follow your
covenant laws
instead of wanting to gain things
only for myself.
37 Turn my eyes away from things
that are worthless.
Keep me alive as you have
promised.
38 Keep your promise to me.
Then other people will have
respect for you.
39 Please don't let me be put to
shame.
Your laws are good.
40 I really want to follow your rules.
Keep me alive, because you do
what is right.

ו Waw

41 LORD, show me your faithful love.
Save me as you have promised.
42 Then I can answer anyone who
makes fun of me,
because I trust in your word.
43 Help me always to tell the truth
about how faithful you are.
I have put my hope in your
laws.
44 I will always obey your law,
for ever and ever.
45 I will lead a full and happy life,
because I've tried to obey your
rules.
46 I will talk about your covenant
laws to kings.
I will not be put to shame.
47 I take delight in obeying your
commands
because I love them.
48 I reach out for your commands that
I love.
I do this so that I may think
deeply about your orders.

ז Zayin

49 Remember what you have said
to me.
You have given me hope.
50 Even when I suffer, I am comforted
because you promised to keep
me alive.
51 Proud people make fun of me
without mercy.
But I don't turn away from your
law.
52 LORD, I remember the laws you
gave long ago.
I find comfort in them.
53 I am very angry
because evil people have turned
away from your law.
54 No matter where I live,
I sing about your orders.
55 LORD, during the night I remember
who you are.
That's why I keep your law.
56 I have really done my best
to obey your rules.

ח Heth

57 LORD, you are everything I need.
I have promised to obey your words.
58 I have looked to you with all my heart.
Be kind to me as you have promised.
59 I have thought about the way I live.
And I have decided to follow your covenant laws.
60 I won't waste any time.
I will be quick to obey your commands.
61 Evil people may tie me up with ropes.
But I won't forget to obey your law.
62 At midnight I get up to give you thanks
because your decisions are very fair.
63 I'm a friend to everyone who has respect for you.
I'm a friend to everyone who follows your rules.
64 LORD, the earth is filled with your love.
Teach me your orders.

ט Teth

65 LORD, be good to me
as you have promised.
66 Increase my knowledge and give me good sense,
because I trust your commands.
67 Before I went through suffering, I went down the wrong path.
But now I obey your word.
68 You are good, and what you do is good.
Teach me your orders.
69 The lies of proud people have taken away my good name.
But I follow your rules with all my heart.
70 Their unfeeling hearts are hard and stubborn.
But I take delight in your law.
71 It was good for me to suffer.
That's what helped me to understand your orders.
72 The law you gave is worth more to me
than thousands of pieces of silver and gold.

י Yodh

73 You made me and formed me with your own hands.
Give me understanding so that I can learn your commands.
74 May those who have respect for you be filled with joy when they see me.
I have put my hope in your word.
75 LORD, I know that your laws are right.
You were faithful to your promise when you made me suffer.
76 May your faithful love comfort me as you have promised me.
77 Show me your tender love so that I can live.
I take delight in your law.
78 May proud people be put to shame for treating me badly for no reason.
I will think deeply about your rules.
79 May those who have respect for you come to me.
Then I can teach them your covenant laws.
80 May I follow your orders with all my heart.
Then I won't be put to shame.

כ Kaph

81 I deeply long for you to save me.
I have put my hope in your word.
82 My eyes grow tired looking for what you have promised.
I say, "When will you comfort me?"
83 I'm as useless as a wineskin that smoke has dried up.
But I don't forget to follow your orders.
84 How long do I have to wait?
When will you punish those who attack me?
85 Proud people do what is against your law.
They dig pits for me to fall into.
86 All your commands can be trusted.
Help me, because people attack me without any reason.
87 They almost wiped me off the face of the earth.
But I have not turned away from your rules.
88 Keep me alive, because of your faithful love.
Do this so that I may obey the covenant laws you have given.

ל Lamedh

89 LORD, your word lasts forever.
It stands firm in the heavens.
90 You will be faithful for all time to come.
You made the earth, and it continues to exist.
91 Your laws continue to this very day,
because all things serve you.
92 If I had not taken delight in your law,
I would have died because of my suffering.
93 I will never forget your rules.
You have kept me alive, because I obey them.
94 Save me, because I belong to you.
I've tried to obey your rules.
95 Sinful people are waiting to destroy me.
But I will spend time thinking about your covenant laws.
96 I've learned that everything has its limits.
But your commands are perfect.
They are always there when I need them.

מ Mem

97 LORD, I really love your law!
All day long I spend time thinking about it.
98 Your commands make me wiser than my enemies,
because your commands are always in my heart.
99 I know more than all my teachers do,
because I spend time thinking about your covenant laws.
100 I understand more than the elders do,
because I obey your rules.
101 I've kept my feet from every path that sinners take
so that I might obey your word.
102 I haven't turned away from your laws,
because you yourself have taught me.
103 Your words are very sweet to my taste!
They are sweeter than honey to me.
104 I gain understanding from your rules.
So I hate every path that sinners take.

נ Nun

105 Your word is like a lamp that shows me the way.
It is like a light that guides me.
106 I have made a promise
to follow your laws, because they are right.
107 I have suffered very much.
LORD, keep me alive as you have promised.
108 LORD, accept the praise I freely give you.
Teach me your laws.
109 I keep putting my life in danger.
But I won't forget to obey your law.
110 Evil people have set a trap for me.
But I haven't wandered away from your rules.
111 Your covenant laws are your gift to me forever.
They fill my heart with joy.
112 I have decided to obey your orders
to the very end.

God Is Light

One way the Bible describes God's purity is by saying that he is light. In God, there is no darkness at all; God has no blemish or stain resulting from sin (see 1 John 1:5). God himself is light, which means that God is the one who draws us to himself and helps us know and understand the truth. He reveals to us our need for a Savior and invites us to shine his light to the world around us. Those who join God's family through faith get to live in the light of Christ, resisting sin and walking together with God and other believers.

ס Samekh

113 I hate people who can't make up
their minds.
But I love your law.
114 You are my place of safety.
You are like a shield that keeps
me safe.
I have put my hope in your word.
115 Get away from me, you who do
evil!
Then I can do what my God
commands me to do.
116 My God, keep me going as you
have promised. Then I will live.
Don't let me lose all hope.
117 Take good care of me, and I will be
saved.
I will always honor your orders.
118 You turn your back on all those
who wander away from your
orders.
Their wrong thoughts will be
proved to be wrong.
119 You throw away all the sinners on
earth as if they were trash.
So I love your covenant laws.
120 My body trembles because I have
respect for you.
I have great respect for your laws.

ע Ayin

121 I have done what is right and fair.
So don't leave me to those who
treat me badly.
122 Make sure that everything goes
well with me.
Don't let proud people treat me
badly.
123 My eyes grow tired as I look to you
to save me.
Please save me as you have
promised.
124 Be good to me, because you
love me.
Teach me your orders.
125 I serve you, so help me to
understand what is right.
Then I will understand your
covenant laws.
126 LORD, it's time for you to act.
People are breaking your law.
127 I love your commands more than
gold.
I love them more than pure gold.
128 I consider all your rules to be right.
So I hate every path that sinners
take.

פ Pe

129 Your covenant laws are wonderful.
So I obey them.
130 When your words are made clear,
they bring light.
They bring understanding to
childish people.
131 I open my mouth and pant like a
dog,
because I long to know your
commands.
132 Turn to me and have mercy
on me.
That's what you've always done
for those who love you.
133 Teach me how to live as you have
promised.
Don't let any sin be my master.
134 Set me free from people who treat
me badly.
Then I will obey your rules.
135 Have mercy on me.
Teach me your orders.
136 Streams of tears flow from my eyes,
because people don't obey your
law.

צ Tsadhe

137 LORD, you do what is fair.
And your laws are right.
138 The laws you have made are fair.
They can be completely trusted.
139 My anger is wearing me out,
because my enemies don't pay
any attention to your words.
140 Your promises have proved to be
true.
I love them.
141 I'm not important. People look
down on me.
But I don't forget to obey your
rules.
142 You always do what is right.
And your law is true.
143 I've had my share of trouble and
suffering.
But your commands give me
delight.
144 Your covenant laws are always
right.
Help me to understand them.
Then I will live.

ק Qoph

145 LORD, I call out to you with all my
heart.
Answer me, and I will obey your
orders.

[146] I call out to you.
Save me, and I will keep your covenant laws.
[147] I get up before the sun rises. I cry out for help.
I've put my hope in your word.
[148] My eyes stay open all night long.
I spend my time thinking about your promises.
[149] Listen to me, because you love me.
LORD, keep me alive as you have promised.
[150] Those who think up evil plans are near.
They have wandered far away from your law.
[151] But LORD, you are near.
All your commands are true.
[152] Long ago I learned from your covenant laws
that you made them to last forever.

ר Resh

[153] Look at how I'm suffering!
Save me, because I haven't forgotten to obey your law.
[154] Stand up for me and set me free.
Keep me alive as you have promised.
[155] Those who are evil are far from being saved.
They don't want to obey your orders.
[156] LORD, you have deep concern for me.
Keep me alive as you have promised.
[157] Many enemies attack me.
But I haven't turned away from your covenant laws.
[158] I get very angry when I see people who aren't faithful to you.
They don't obey your word.
[159] See how I love your rules!
LORD, keep me alive, because you love me.
[160] All your words are true.
All your laws are right. They last forever.

ש Sin and Shin

[161] Rulers attack me for no reason.
But I tremble because of your word.
[162] I'm filled with joy because of your promise.
It's like finding a great fortune.
[163] I hate lies with a deep hatred.
But I love your law.
[164] Seven times a day I praise you for your laws, because they are right.
[165] Those who love your law enjoy great peace.
Nothing can make them trip and fall.
[166] LORD, I wait for you to save me.
I follow your commands.
[167] I obey your covenant laws,
because I love them greatly.
[168] I obey your rules and your covenant laws,
because you know all about how I live.

ת Taw

[169] LORD, may you hear my cry.
Give me understanding, just as you said you would.
[170] May you hear my prayer.
Save me, just as you promised.
[171] May my lips pour out praise to you,
because you teach me your orders.
[172] May my tongue sing about your word,
because all your commands are right.
[173] May your hand be ready to help me,
because I have chosen to obey your rules.
[174] LORD, I long for you to save me.
Your law gives me delight.
[175] Let me live so that I can praise you.
May your laws keep me going.
[176] Like a lost sheep, I've gone down the wrong path.
Come and look for me,
because I haven't forgotten to obey your commands.

Psalm 120

A song for those who go up to Jerusalem to worship the LORD.

[1] I call out to the LORD when I'm in trouble,
and he answers me.
[2] LORD, save me from people whose lips tell lies.
Save me from people whose tongues don't tell the truth.
[3] What will the LORD do to you, you lying tongue?
And what more will he do?

4 He will punish you with the sharp
arrows of a soldier.
He will punish you with burning
coals from a desert bush.

5 How terrible it is for me to live
in the tents of the people of
Meshek!
How terrible to live in the tents of
the people of Kedar!
6 I have lived too long
among those who hate peace.
7 I want peace.
But when I speak, they want war.

Psalm 121

A song for those who go up
to Jerusalem to worship the LORD.

1 I look up to the mountains.
Where does my help come from?
2 My help comes from the LORD.
He is the Maker of heaven and
earth.

3 He won't let your foot slip.
He who watches over you won't
get tired.
4 In fact, he who watches over Israel
won't get tired or go to sleep.
5 The LORD watches over you.
The LORD is like a shade tree at
your right hand.
6 The sun won't harm you during the
day.
The moon won't harm you
during the night.

7 The LORD will keep you from every
kind of harm.
He will watch over your life.
8 The LORD will watch over your life
no matter where you go,
both now and forever.

Psalm 122

A song for those who go up
to Jerusalem to worship the LORD.
A psalm of David.

1 I was very glad when they said to me,
"Let us go up to the house of the
LORD."
2 Jerusalem, our feet are standing
inside your gates.

3 Jerusalem is built like a city
where everything is close together.
4 The tribes of the LORD go there to
praise his name.
They do it in keeping with the
law he gave to Israel.
5 The thrones of the family line of
David are there.
That's where the people are
judged.

6 Pray for the peace of Jerusalem.
Say,
"May those who love you be
secure.
7 May there be peace inside your
walls.
May your people be kept safe."
8 I'm concerned for my family and
friends.
So I say to Jerusalem, "May you
enjoy peace."
9 I'm concerned about the house of
the LORD our God.
So I pray that things will go well
with Jerusalem.

Psalm 123

A song for those who go up
to Jerusalem to worship the LORD.

1 I look up and pray to you.
Your throne is in heaven.
2 Slaves depend on their masters.
A female slave depends on the
woman she works for.
In the same way, we depend on the
LORD our God.
We wait for him to have mercy
on us.

3 LORD, have mercy on us. Have
mercy on us,
because people haven't stopped
making fun of us.
4 We have had to put up with a lot
from those who are proud.
They were always laughing
at us.

Psalm 124

A song for those who go up
to Jerusalem to worship the LORD.
A psalm of David.

1 Here is what Israel should say.
Suppose the LORD had not been
on our side.

[2] Suppose the LORD had not been on
our side
when our enemies attacked us.
[3] Suppose he had not been on our
side
when their burning anger blazed
out against us.
Then they would have swallowed
us alive.
[4] They would have been like a flood
that drowned us.
They would have swept over us
like a rushing river.
[5] They would have washed us away
like a swollen stream.
[6] Give praise to the LORD.
He has not let our enemies chew
us up.
[7] We have escaped like a bird
from a hunter's trap.
The trap has been broken,
and we have escaped.
[8] Our help comes from the LORD.
He is the Maker of heaven and
earth.

Psalm 125

*A song for those who go up
to Jerusalem to worship the LORD.*

[1] Those who trust in the LORD are like
Mount Zion.
They will always be secure. They
will last forever.
[2] Like the mountains around
Jerusalem,
the LORD is all around his people
both now and forever.

[3] Evil people will not always rule
the land the LORD gave to those
who do right.
If they did, those who do right
might do what is evil.

[4] LORD, do good to those who are
good.
Do good to those whose hearts
are honest.
[5] But the LORD will drive out those
who have taken crooked paths.
He will drive them out with those
who do evil things.

May Israel enjoy peace.

Psalm 126

*A song for those who go up
to Jerusalem to worship the LORD.*

[1] Our enemies took us away from
Zion.
But when the LORD brought us
home,
it seemed like a dream to us.
[2] Our mouths were filled with laughter.
Our tongues sang with joy.
Then the people of other nations
said,
"The LORD has done great things
for them."
[3] The LORD has done great things
for us.
And we are filled with joy.

[4] LORD, bless us with great success
again,
as rain makes streams flow in
the Negev Desert.
[5] Those who cry as they plant their
crops
will sing with joy when they
gather them in.
[6] Those who go out weeping
as they carry seeds to plant
will come back singing with joy.
They will bring the new crop
back with them.

Psalm 127

*A song for those who go up to
Jerusalem to worship the LORD.
A psalm of Solomon.*

[1] If the LORD doesn't build a house,
the work of the builders is
useless.
If the LORD doesn't watch over a city,
it's useless for those on guard
duty to stand watch over it.
[2] It's useless for you to work from
early morning
until late at night
just to get food to eat.
God provides for those he loves
even while they sleep.

[3] Children are a gift from the LORD.
They are a reward from him.
[4] Children who are born to people
when they are young
are like arrows in the hands of a
soldier.

5 Blessed are those
who have many children.
They won't be put to shame
when they go up against their
enemies in court.

Psalm 128

A song for those who go up to Jerusalem to worship the LORD.

1 Blessed are all those who have
respect for the LORD.
They live as he wants them to live.
2 Your work will give you what you
need.
Blessings and good things will
come to you.
3 As a vine bears a lot of fruit,
so may your wife have many
children by you.
May they sit around your table
like young olive trees.
4 Only a man who has respect for the
LORD
will be blessed like that.
5 May the LORD bless you from Zion.
May you enjoy the good things
that come to Jerusalem
all the days of your life.
6 May you live to see your
grandchildren.

May Israel enjoy peace.

Psalm 129

A song for those who go up to Jerusalem to worship the LORD.

1 Here is what Israel should say.
"My enemies have treated me
badly ever since I was a young
nation.
2 My enemies have treated me
badly ever since I was a young
nation.
But they haven't won the battle.
3 They have made deep wounds in
my back.
It looks like a field a farmer has
plowed.
4 The LORD does what is right.
Sinners had tied me up with
ropes. But the LORD has set me
free."

5 May all those who hate Zion
be driven back in shame.
6 May they be like grass that grows
on the roof of a house.
It dries up before it can grow.
7 There isn't enough of it to fill a
person's hand.
There isn't enough to tie up and
carry away.
8 May no one who passes by say to
those who hate Zion,
"May the blessing of the LORD be
on you.
We bless you in the name of the
LORD."

Psalm 130

A song for those who go up to Jerusalem to worship the LORD.

1 LORD, I cry out to you
because I'm suffering so deeply.
2 Lord, listen to me.
Pay attention to my cry for your
mercy.

3 LORD, suppose you kept a close
watch on sins.
Lord, who then wouldn't be found
guilty?
4 But you forgive.
So we can serve you with respect.

5 With all my heart I wait for the
LORD to help me.
I put my hope in his word.
6 I wait for the Lord to help me.
I want his help more than night
watchmen want the morning
to come.
I'll say it again.
I want his help more than night
watchmen want the morning
to come.
7 Israel, put your hope in the LORD,
because the LORD's love never
fails.
He sets his people completely
free.
8 He himself will set Israel
free from all their sins.

Psalm 131

A song for those who go up to Jerusalem to worship the LORD.

A psalm of David.

1 LORD, my heart isn't proud.
My eyes aren't proud either.

I don't concern myself with
important matters.
I don't concern myself with
things that are too wonderful
for me.
2 I have made myself calm and content
like a young child in its mother's
arms.
Deep down inside me, I am as
content as a young child.

3 Israel, put your hope in the LORD
both now and forever.

Psalm 132

A song for those who go up to Jerusalem to worship the LORD.

1 LORD, remember David
and all the times he didn't do
what he wanted.

2 LORD, he made a promise.
Mighty One of Jacob, he made a
promise to you.
3 He said, "I won't enter my house
or go to bed.
4 I won't let my eyes sleep.
I won't close my eyelids
5 until I find a place for the LORD.
I want to build a house for the
Mighty One of Jacob."

6 Here are the words we heard in
Ephrathah.
We heard them again in the
fields of Kiriath Jearim.
7 "Let us go to the LORD's house.
Let us worship at his feet. Let us
say,
8 'LORD, rise up and come to your
resting place.
Come in together with the ark.
It's the sign of your power.
9 May your priests put on godliness
as if it were their clothes.
May your faithful people sing for
joy.' "

10 In honor of your servant David,
don't turn your back on your
anointed king.

11 The LORD made a promise to David.
It is a firm promise that he will
never break.
He said, "After you die,
I will place one of your own sons
on your throne.
12 If your sons keep my covenant
and the laws I teach them,
then their sons will sit
on your throne for ever and ever."

13 The LORD has chosen Zion.
That's the place where he wants
to live.
14 He has said, "This will be my
resting place for ever and ever.
Here I will sit on my throne,
because that's what I want.
15 I will greatly bless Zion with
everything it needs.
I will give plenty of food to the
poor people living there.
16 I will put salvation on its priests as
if it were their clothes.
God's faithful people will always
sing for joy.

17 "Here in Jerusalem I will raise up a
mighty king from the family of
David.
I will set up the lamp of David's
kingdom for my anointed king.
Its flame will burn brightly forever.
18 I will put shame on his enemies as
if it were their clothes.
But he will wear on his head a
shining crown."

Psalm 133

A song for those who go up to Jerusalem to worship the LORD. A psalm of David.

1 How good and pleasant it is
when God's people live together
in peace!
2 It's like the special olive oil
that was poured on Aaron's head.
It ran down on his beard
and on the collar of his robe.
3 It's as if the dew of Mount Hermon
were falling on Mount Zion.
There the LORD gives his blessing.
He gives life that never ends.

Psalm 134

A song for those who go up to Jerusalem to worship the LORD.

1 All you who serve the LORD, praise
the LORD.
All you who serve at night in the
house of the LORD, praise him.

[2]Lift up your hands in the temple
and praise the LORD.
[3]May the LORD bless you from Zion.
He is the Maker of heaven and earth.

Psalm 135

[1]Praise the LORD.

Praise the name of the LORD.
You who serve the LORD, praise him.
[2]You who serve in the house of the LORD, praise him.
You who serve in the courtyards of the temple of our God, praise him.
[3]Praise the LORD, because he is good.
Sing praise to his name, because that is pleasant.
[4]The LORD has chosen the people of Jacob to be his own.
He has chosen Israel to be his special treasure.
[5]I know that the LORD is great.
I know that our Lord is greater than all gods.
[6]The LORD does anything he wants to do
in the heavens and on the earth.
He does it even in the deepest parts of the oceans.
[7]He makes clouds rise from one end of the earth to the other.
He sends lightning with the rain.
He brings the wind out of his storerooms.

[8]He killed the oldest son of each family in Egypt.
He struck down the oldest males that were born to people and animals.
[9]He did miraculous signs in Egypt.
He did wonders against Pharaoh and everyone who served him.
[10]He destroyed many nations.
He killed mighty kings.
[11]He killed Sihon, the king of the Amorites,
and Og, the king of Bashan.
He killed all the kings of Canaan.
[12]He gave their land as a gift
to his people Israel.

[13]LORD, your name continues forever.
LORD, your fame will last for all time to come.
[14]When the LORD hands down his sentence, it will be in his people's favor.
He will show deep concern for those who serve him.

[15]The statues of the nations' gods are made out of silver and gold.
They are made by human hands.
[16]They have mouths but can't speak.
They have eyes but can't see.
[17]They have ears but can't hear.
They have mouths but can't breathe.
[18]Those who make statues of gods will be like them.
So will all those who trust in them.

[19]People of Israel, praise the LORD.
Priests of Aaron, praise the LORD.
[20]Tribe of Levi, praise the LORD.
You who have respect for the LORD, praise him.
[21]Give praise to the LORD in Zion.
Give praise to the God who lives in Jerusalem.

Praise the LORD.

Psalm 136

[1]Give thanks to the LORD, because he is good.
His faithful love continues forever.
[2]Give thanks to the greatest God of all.
His faithful love continues forever.
[3]Give thanks to the most powerful Lord of all.
His faithful love continues forever.

[4]Give thanks to the only one who can do great miracles.
His faithful love continues forever.
[5]By his understanding he made the heavens.
His faithful love continues forever.
[6]He spread out the earth on the waters.
His faithful love continues forever.
[7]He made the great lights in the sky.
His faithful love continues forever.
[8]He made the sun to rule over the day.
His faithful love continues forever.

9 He made the moon and stars to
rule over the night.
His faithful love continues forever.

10 Give thanks to the God who killed
the oldest son of each family in
Egypt.
His faithful love continues forever.
11 He brought the people of Israel out
of Egypt.
His faithful love continues forever.
12 He did it by reaching out his mighty
hand and powerful arm.
His faithful love continues forever.

13 Give thanks to the God who parted
the waters of the Red Sea.
His faithful love continues forever.
14 He brought Israel through the
middle of it.
His faithful love continues forever.
15 But he swept Pharaoh and his army
into the Red Sea.
His faithful love continues forever.

16 Give thanks to the God who led his
people through the desert.
His faithful love continues forever.
17 He killed great kings.
His faithful love continues forever.
18 He struck down mighty kings.
His faithful love continues forever.
19 He killed Sihon, the king of the
Amorites.
His faithful love continues forever.
20 He killed Og, the king of Bashan.
His faithful love continues forever.
21 He gave their land as a gift.
His faithful love continues forever.
22 He gave it as a gift to his servant
Israel.
His faithful love continues forever.

23 Give thanks to the God who
remembered us when things
were going badly.
His faithful love continues forever.
24 He set us free from our enemies.
His faithful love continues forever.
25 He gives food to every creature.
His faithful love continues forever.

26 Give thanks to the God of heaven.
His faithful love continues forever.

Psalm 137

1 We were sitting by the rivers of
Babylon.
We wept when we remembered
what had happened to Zion.
2 On the nearby poplar trees
we hung up our harps.
3 Those who held us as prisoners
asked us to sing.
Those who enjoyed hurting us
ordered us to sing joyful
songs.
They said, "Sing one of the songs
of Zion to us!"

4 How can we sing the songs of the
LORD
while we are in another land?
5 Jerusalem, if I forget you,
may my right hand never be able
to play the harp again.
6 If I don't remember you,
may my tongue stick to the roof
of my mouth so I can't sing.
May it happen if I don't consider
Jerusalem
to be my greatest joy.

7 LORD, remember what the people of
Edom did
on the day Jerusalem fell.
"Tear it down!" they cried.
"Tear it down to the ground!"

8 People of Babylon, you are
sentenced to be destroyed.
Happy is the person who pays
you back
according to what you have done
to us.
9 Happy is the person who grabs
your babies
and smashes them against the
rocks.

Psalm 138

A psalm of David.

1 LORD, I will praise you with all my
heart.
In front of those who think they
are gods
I will sing praise to you.
2 I will bow down facing your holy
temple.
I will praise your name,
because you are always loving
and faithful.
You have honored your holy word
even more than your own fame.
3 When I called out to you, you
answered me.
You made me strong and
brave.

4 Lord, may all the kings on earth
praise you
when they hear about what you
have decided.
5 Lord, may they sing about what
you have done,
because your glory is great.

6 Though the Lord is high above all,
he cares for the lowly.
Though he is in heaven above, he
sees them on earth below.
7 Trouble is all around me,
but you keep me alive.
You reach out your hand to put a
stop to the anger of my enemies.
With your powerful right hand
you save me.
8 Lord, you will show that I was right
to trust you.
Lord, your faithful love
continues forever.
You have done so much for us, so
don't stop now.

Psalm 139

For the director of music.
A psalm of David.

1 Lord, you have seen what is in my
heart.
You know all about me.
2 You know when I sit down and
when I get up.
You know what I'm thinking
even though you are far away.
3 You know when I go out to work
and when I come back home.
You know exactly how I live.
4 Lord, even before I speak a word,
you know all about it.
5 You are all around me, behind me
and in front of me.
You hold me safe in your hand.
6 I'm amazed at how well you
know me.
It's more than I can understand.
7 How can I get away from your Spirit?
Where can I go to escape from you?
8 If I go up to the heavens, you are
there.
If I lie down in the deepest parts
of the earth, you are also there.
9 Suppose I were to rise with the sun
in the east.
Suppose I travel to the west
where it sinks into the ocean.

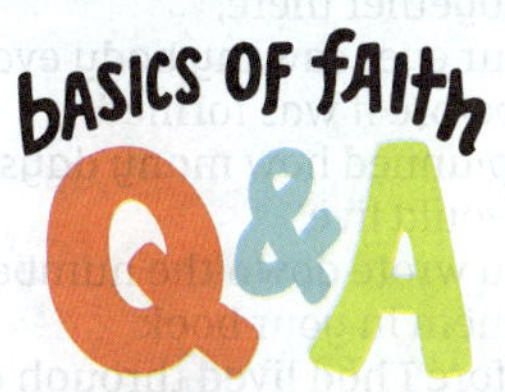

Does God know everything about me?

God sees everything in your heart and knows all about you. He even knows what you're going to say before you say it. God knows you completely and loves you wholeheartedly.

Can you find the following verses?

PSALM 139:1–4

10 Your hand would always be there
to guide me.
Your right hand would still be
holding me close.
11 Suppose I were to say, "I'm sure the
darkness will hide me.
The light around me will become
as dark as night."
12 Even that darkness would not be
dark to you.
The night would shine like the
day,
because darkness is like light to
you.
13 You created the deepest parts of
my being.
You put me together inside my
mother's body.
14 How you made me is amazing and
wonderful.
I praise you for that.
What you have done is wonderful.
I know that very well.
15 None of my bones was hidden from
you
when you made me inside my
mother's body.
That place was as dark as the
deepest parts of the earth.

When you were putting me
together there,
16 your eyes saw my body even
before it was formed.
You planned how many days I
would live.
You wrote down the number of
them in your book
before I had lived through even
one of them.

17 God, your thoughts about me are
priceless.
No one can possibly add them
all up.
18 If I could count them,
they would be more than the
grains of sand.
If I were to fall asleep counting and
then wake up,
you would still be there
with me.

19 God, I wish you would kill the
people who are evil!
I wish those murderers would get
away from me!
20 They are your enemies. They
misuse your name.
They misuse it for their own evil
purposes.
21 LORD, I really hate those who hate
you!
I really hate those who rise up
against you!
22 I have nothing but hatred for them.
I consider them to be my
enemies.

23 God, see what is in my heart.
Know what is there.
Test me.
Know what I'm thinking.
24 See if there's anything in my life
you don't like.
Help me live in the way that is
always right.

Psalm 140

For the director of music.
A psalm of David.

1 LORD, save me from sinful people.
Keep me safe from those who
want to hurt me.
2 They make evil plans in their
hearts.
They are always starting fights.
3 Their tongues are as deadly as the
tongue of a serpent.
The words from their lips are like
the poison of a snake.

My GOD IS...

ALL-PRESENT

God is present everywhere in this world through the Holy Spirit. There is no place in this world where God does not exist. What's more, he is present everywhere at the same time. He is not limited to being in one place at one time, but he is always present everywhere.

The psalmist David reflected on this reality in Psalm 139:8, saying that if he went up to the heavens, God would be there; if he went down to the deepest parts of the earth, God would be there too.

Though humans can be in only one place at a time, that's not true of God. Anywhere we go in this world, God is there. And no matter where we are, we can talk to God through prayer.

4 LORD, keep me safe from the hands of sinful people.
Protect me from those who want to hurt me.
They plan ways to trip me up and make me fall.
5 Proud people have hidden their traps to catch me.
They have spread out their nets.
They have set traps for me along my path.

6 I say to the LORD, "You are my God."
LORD, hear my cry for mercy.
7 LORD and King, you save me because you are strong.
You are like a shield that keeps me safe in the day of battle.
8 LORD, don't give sinners what they want.
Don't let their plans succeed.

9 Those who are all around me proudly raise their heads.
May the trouble they planned for me happen to them.
10 May burning coals fall on people like that.
May they be thrown into the fire.
May they be thrown into muddy pits and never get out.
11 Don't let people who lie about me be secure in the land.
May trouble hunt down those who want to hurt me.

12 I know that the LORD makes sure that poor people are treated fairly.
He stands up for those who are in need.
13 I'm sure that those who do right will praise your name.
Those who are honest will live with you.

Psalm 141

A psalm of David.

1 I call out to you, LORD. Come quickly to help me.
Listen to me when I call out to you.
2 May my prayer come to you like the sweet smell of incense.
When I lift up my hands in prayer, may it be like the evening sacrifice.

3 LORD, guard my mouth.
Keep watch over the door of my lips.
4 Don't let my heart be drawn to what is evil.
Don't let me join with people who do evil.
Don't let me eat their fancy food.

5 If a godly person hit me, it would be an act of kindness.
If they would correct me, it would be like pouring olive oil on my head.
I wouldn't say no to it.

I will always pray against the things that sinful people do.
6 When their rulers are thrown down from the rocky cliffs,
those evil people will realize that my words were true.
7 They will say, "As clumps of dirt are left from plowing up the ground,
so our bones will be scattered near an open grave."

8 But LORD and King, I keep looking to you for help.
I go to you for safety. Don't let me die.
9 Keep me from the traps of those who do evil.
Save me from the traps they have set for me.
10 Let evil people fall into their own nets.
But let me go safely on my way.

Psalm 142

A prayer of David when he was in the cave. A maskil.

1 I call out to the LORD.
I pray to him for mercy.
2 I pour out my problem to him.
I tell him about my trouble.

3 When I grow weak,
you are watching over my life.
In the path where I walk,
people have hidden a trap to catch me.
4 Look and see that no one is on my right side to help me.
No one is concerned about me.
I have no place of safety.
No one cares whether I live or die.

[5] LORD, I cry out to you.
I say, "You are my place of safety.
You are everything I need in this life."
[6] Listen to my cry.
I am in great need.
Save me from those who are chasing me.
They are too strong for me.
[7] My troubles are like a prison.
Set me free so I can praise your name.

Then those who do what is right will gather around me
because you have been good to me.

Psalm 143

A psalm of David.

[1] LORD, hear my prayer.
Listen to my cry for mercy.
You are faithful and right.
Come and help me.
[2] Don't take me to court and judge me,
because in your eyes no living person does what is right.
[3] My enemies chase me.
They crush me down to the ground.
They make me live in the darkness
like those who died long ago.
[4] So I grow weak.
Deep down inside me, I'm afraid.

[5] I remember what happened long ago.
I spend time thinking about all your acts.
I consider what your hands have done.
[6] I spread out my hands to you in prayer.
I'm thirsty for you, just as dry ground is thirsty for rain.

[7] LORD, answer me quickly.
I'm growing weak.
Don't turn your face away from me,
or I will be like those who go down into the grave.
[8] In the morning let me hear about your faithful love,
because I've put my trust in you.
Show me the way I should live,
because I trust you with my life.
[9] LORD, save me from my enemies,
because I go to you for safety.
[10] Teach me to do what you want,
because you are my God.
May your good Spirit
lead me on a level path.

[11] LORD, bring yourself honor by keeping me alive.
Because you do what is right, get me out of trouble.
[12] Because your love is faithful, put an end to my enemies.
Destroy all of them, because I serve you.

Psalm 144

A psalm of David.

[1] Give praise to the LORD, my Rock.
He trains my hands for war.
He trains my fingers for battle.
[2] He is my loving God and is like a fort to me.
He is my place of safety and the God who saves me.
He is like a shield that keeps me safe.
He brings nations under my control.

[3] LORD, what are human beings that you take care of them?
What are mere people that you think about them?
[4] Their lives don't last any longer than a breath.
Their days are like a shadow that quickly disappears.

[5] LORD, open up your heavens and come down.
Touch the mountains, and they will pour out smoke.
[6] Send flashes of lightning and scatter my enemies.
Shoot your arrows and chase them away.
[7] My enemies are like a mighty flood.
Reach down from heaven and save me.
Save me from outsiders who attack me.
[8] They tell all kinds of lies with their mouths.
Even when they make a promise by raising their right hands,
they don't mean it.

9 My God, I will sing a new song to
you.
I will make music to you on a
lyre that has ten strings.
10 You are the God who helps kings
win battles.
You save your servant David.

From death by the sword
11 save me.
Set me free from outsiders who
attack me.
They tell all kinds of lies with their
mouths.
Even when they make a promise
by raising their right hands,
they don't mean it.

12 While our sons are young,
they will be like healthy plants.
Our daughters will be like pillars
that have been made to decorate
a palace.
13 Our storerooms will be filled
with every kind of food.
The sheep in our fields will increase
by thousands.
They will increase by tens of
thousands.
14 Our oxen will pull heavy loads.
None of our city walls will be
broken down.
No one will be carried off as a
prisoner.
No cries of pain will be heard in
our streets.

15 Blessed is the nation about whom
all these things are true.
Blessed is the nation whose God
is the LORD.

Psalm 145

A psalm of praise. A psalm of David.

1 I will honor you, my God the King.
I will praise your name for ever
and ever.
2 Every day I will praise you.
I will praise your name for ever
and ever.

3 LORD, you are great. You are really
worthy of praise.
No one can completely
understand how great you are.
4 Parents praise your works to their
children.
They tell about your mighty acts.
5 They speak about your glorious
majesty.
I will spend time thinking about
your wonderful deeds.
6 They speak about the powerful and
wonderful things you do.
I will talk about the great things
you have done.
7 They celebrate your great
goodness.
They sing for joy about your holy
acts.

8 The LORD is gracious, kind and
tender.
He is slow to get angry and full of
love.
9 The LORD is good to all.
He shows deep concern for
everything he has made.
10 LORD, all your works praise you.
Your faithful people praise you.
11 They tell about your glorious
kingdom.
They speak about your power.
12 Then all people will know about the
mighty things you have done.
They will know about the
glorious majesty of your
kingdom.
13 Your kingdom is a kingdom that
will last forever.
Your rule will continue for all
time to come.

The LORD will keep all his promises.
He is faithful in everything he
does.
14 The LORD takes good care of all
those who fall.
He lifts up all those who feel
helpless.
15 Every living thing looks to you for
food.
You give it to them exactly when
they need it.
16 You open your hand
and satisfy the needs of every
living creature.

17 The LORD is right in everything he
does.
He is faithful in everything he
does.
18 The LORD is ready to help all those
who call out to him.
He helps those who really mean
it when they call out to him.

[19] He satisfies the needs of those who
have respect for him.
He hears their cry and saves
them.
[20] The LORD watches over all those
who love him.
But he will destroy all sinful
people.

[21] I will praise the LORD with my
mouth.
Let every creature praise his holy
name
for ever and ever.

Psalm 146

[1] Praise the LORD.

I will praise the LORD.
[2] I will praise the LORD all my life.
I will sing praise to my God as
long as I live.

[3] Don't put your trust in human
leaders.
Don't trust in people who can't
save you.
[4] When they die, they return to the
ground.
On that day their plans come to
nothing.

[5] Blessed are those who depend on
the God of Jacob for help.
Blessed are those who put their
hope in the LORD their God.
[6] He is the Maker of heaven and
earth and the ocean.
He made everything in them.
He remains faithful forever.
[7] He stands up for those who are
treated badly.
He gives food to hungry people.
The LORD sets prisoners free.
[8] The LORD gives sight to those
who are blind.
The LORD lifts up those who feel
helpless.
The LORD loves those who do
what is right.
[9] The LORD watches over the
outsiders who live in our land.
He takes good care of children
whose fathers have died.
He also takes good care of
widows.
But he causes evil people to fail
in everything they do.

[10] The LORD rules forever.
The God of Zion will rule for all
time to come.

Praise the LORD.

Psalm 147

[1] Praise the LORD.

How good it is to sing praises to our
God!
How pleasant and right it is to
praise him!

[2] The LORD builds up Jerusalem.
He gathers the scattered people
of Israel.
[3] He heals those who have broken
hearts.
He takes care of their wounds.

[4] He decides how many stars there
should be.
He gives each one of them a
name.
[5] Great is our Lord. His power is
mighty.
There is no limit to his
understanding.
[6] The LORD gives strength to those
who aren't proud.
But he throws evil people down
to the ground.

[7] Sing to the LORD and give him
grateful praise.
Make music to our God on the
harp.
[8] He covers the sky with clouds.
He supplies the earth with rain.
He makes grass grow on the hills.
[9] He provides food for the cattle.
He provides for the young ravens
when they cry out.

[10] He doesn't take pleasure in the
strength of horses.
He doesn't take delight in the
strong legs of warriors.
[11] The LORD takes delight in those
who have respect for him.
They put their hope in his
faithful love.

[12] Jerusalem, praise the LORD.
Zion, praise your God.
[13] He makes the metal bars of your
gates stronger.
He blesses the people who live
inside you.

INFINITE

God has no limits. He doesn't need sleep, and he doesn't get hungry. God can be everywhere at the same time, and he knows all things—including every star in the sky. Isn't that amazing? God's power and his strength are infinite, or limitless.

We are not infinite like God. We get hungry, need sleep, and can only know so much. God alone exists beyond the boundaries and limitations of what we know. Isaiah 55:9 says, "[God's] ways are higher than your ways." Yet God will always be the same, and more than anything, he wants us to know that his love for us is limitless.

14 He keeps your borders safe and secure.
He satisfies you with the finest wheat.
15 He sends his command to the earth.
His word arrives there quickly.
16 He spreads the snow like wool.
He scatters the frost like ashes.
17 He throws down his hail like pebbles.
No one can stand his icy blast.
18 He gives his command, and the ice melts.
He stirs up his winds, and the waters flow.
19 He has made his word known to the people of Jacob.
He has made his laws and rules known to Israel.
20 He hasn't done that for any other nation.
They don't know his laws.

Praise the LORD.

Psalm 148

1 Praise the LORD.

Praise the LORD from the heavens.
Praise him in the heavens above.
2 Praise him, all his angels.
Praise him, all his angels in heaven.
3 Praise him, sun and moon.
Praise him, all you shining stars.
4 Praise him, you highest heavens.
Praise him, you waters above the skies.
5 Let all of them praise the name of the LORD,
because at his command they were created.
6 He established them for ever and ever.
He gave them laws they will always have to obey.
7 Praise the LORD from the earth,
you great sea creatures and all the deepest parts of the ocean.
8 Praise him, lightning and hail, snow and clouds.
Praise him, you stormy winds that obey him.
9 Praise him, all you mountains and hills.
Praise him, all you fruit trees and cedar trees.
10 Praise him, all you wild animals and cattle.
Praise him, you small creatures and flying birds.
11 Praise him, you kings of the earth and all nations.
Praise him, all you princes and rulers on earth.

12 Praise him, young men and
women.
Praise him, old men and
children.

13 Let them praise the name of the
LORD.
His name alone is honored.
His glory is higher than the earth
and the heavens.
14 He has given his people a strong
king.
All his faithful people praise him
for that gift.
All the people of Israel are close
to his heart.

Praise the LORD.

Psalm 149

1 Praise the LORD.

Sing a new song to the LORD.
Sing praise to him in the
assembly of his faithful people.

2 Let Israel be filled with joy because
God is their Maker.
Let the people of Zion be glad
because he is their King.
3 Let them praise his name with
dancing.
Let them make music to him
with harps and tambourines.
4 The LORD takes delight in his
people.
He awards with victory those
who are humble.
5 Let his faithful people be filled with
joy because of that honor.
Let them sing for joy even when
they are lying in bed.

6 May they praise God with their
mouths.
May they hold in their hands a
sword that has two edges.
7 Let them pay the nations back.
Let them punish the people of the
earth.
8 Let them put the kings of those
nations in chains.
Let them put their nobles in iron
chains.
9 Let them carry out God's sentence
against those nations.
This will bring glory to all his
faithful people.

Praise the LORD.

Psalm 150

1 Praise the LORD.

Praise God in his holy temple.
Praise him in his mighty
heavens.
2 Praise him for his powerful acts.
Praise him because he is greater
than anything else.
3 Praise him by blowing trumpets.
Praise him with harps and lyres.
4 Praise him with tambourines and
dancing.
Praise him with stringed
instruments and flutes.
5 Praise him with clashing cymbals.
Praise him with clanging
cymbals.

6 Let everything that has breath
praise the LORD.

Praise the LORD.

PROVERBS

Author: King Solomon and other wise men

Wisdom is knowing and doing what is right according to God's Word. A wise person is someone who knows God's character and follows his commands. In this book, the writers explain how to live in ways that please God and lead to good outcomes. The writers of Proverbs teach us who God is and how he created the world. They also tell us about the world we live in, describing the effects of sin. That's why the more we know God and grow in wisdom, the more we'll know what is right. Have you ever looked in a mirror and seen your reflection looking back at you? Proverbs helps us look at our own lives as though we are holding up a mirror to see if we are reflecting God's ways or our own ways.

Wisdom & Poetry

The writers of Proverbs also imagined wisdom as a person. This person calls out to her neighbors: "Do what's right! Follow God's commands!" One day God's people wouldn't have to imagine wisdom as a person because they would be able to look right at the Savior and know: This is God's wisdom in human form. The Savior was coming, and he is the wisdom everyone needs.

PURPOSE

1 These are the proverbs of Solomon. He was the son of David and the king of Israel.

[2] Proverbs teach you wisdom and
instruct you.
They help you understand wise
sayings.
[3] They provide you with instruction
and help you live wisely.
They lead to what is right and
honest and fair.
[4] They give understanding to
childish people.
They give knowledge and good
sense to those who are young.
[5] Let wise people listen and add to
what they have learned.
Let those who understand what
is right get guidance.
[6] What I'm teaching also helps you
understand proverbs and
stories.
It helps you understand the
sayings and riddles of those
who are wise.

[7] If you really want to gain
knowledge, you must begin by
having respect for the LORD.
But foolish people hate wisdom
and instruction.

THINK AND LIVE WISELY

A Warning Against Sinful Men

[8] My son, listen to your father's advice.
Don't turn away from your
mother's teaching.
[9] What they teach you will be like a
beautiful crown on your head.
It will be like a chain to decorate
your neck.

[10] My son, if sinful men tempt you,
don't give in to them.
[11] They might say, "Come along
with us.
Let's hide and wait to kill
someone who hasn't done
anything wrong.
Let's catch some harmless person
in our trap.
[12] Let's swallow them alive, as the
grave does.
Let's swallow them whole, like
those who go down into the pit.

in Proverbs?

God is True Wisdom. God's way is best, and trusting him to lead us helps us grow in faith.

[13] We'll get all kinds of valuable
things.
We'll fill our houses with what we
steal.
[14] Cast lots with us for what they own.
We'll share everything we take
from them."
[15] My son, don't go along with them.
Don't even set your feet on their
paths.
[16] They are always in a hurry to sin.
They are quick to spill someone's
blood.
[17] How useless it is to spread a net
where every bird can see it!
[18] Those who hide and wait will spill
their own blood.
They will be caught in their own
trap.
[19] That's what happens to everyone
who goes after money in the
wrong way.
That kind of money takes away
the life of those who get it.

Wisdom's Warning

[20] Out in the open wisdom calls out.
She raises her voice in a public
place.
[21] On top of the city wall she cries out.
Here is what she says near the
gate of the city.

[22] "How long will you childish people
love your childish ways?
How long will you rude people
enjoy making fun of God and
others?
How long will you foolish people
hate knowledge?

23 Pay attention to my warning!
Then I will pour out my thoughts to you.
I will make known to you my teachings.
24 But you refuse to listen when I call out to you.
No one pays attention when I reach out my hand.
25 You turn away from all my advice.
And you do not accept my warning.
26 So I will laugh at you when you are in danger.
I will make fun of you when hard times come.
27 I will laugh when hard times hit you like a storm.
I will laugh when danger comes your way like a windstorm.
I will make fun of you when suffering and trouble come.

28 "Then you will call to me. But I won't answer.
You will look for me. But you won't find me.
29 You hated knowledge.
You didn't choose to have respect for the LORD.
30 You wouldn't accept my advice.
You turned your backs on my warnings.

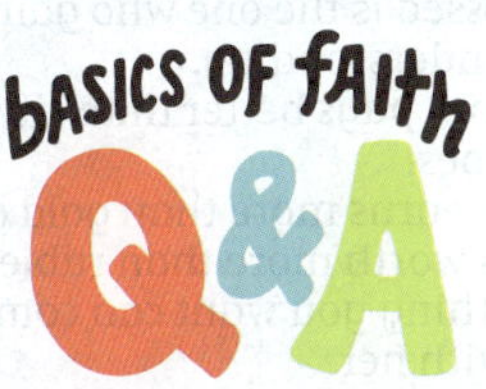

How can I live the very best way?

Choose to live God's way. He is for you, and his ways are the best ways. Ask him for wisdom and learn to do what he tells you.

Can you find the following verse?

PROVERBS 1:7

31 So you will eat the fruit of the way you have lived.
You will choke on the fruit of what you have planned.

32 "The wrong path that childish people take will kill them.
Foolish people will be destroyed by being satisfied with the way they live.
33 But those who listen to me will live in safety.
They will be at ease and have no fear of being harmed."

Good Things Come From Wisdom

2 My son, accept my words.
Store up my commands inside you.
2 Let your ears listen to wisdom.
Apply your heart to understanding.
3 Call out for the ability to be wise.
Cry out for understanding.
4 Look for it as you would look for silver.
Search for it as you would search for hidden treasure.
5 Then you will understand how to have respect for the LORD.
You will find out how to know God.
6 The LORD gives wisdom.
Knowledge and understanding come from his mouth.
7 He stores up success for honest people.
He is like a shield to those who live without blame.
8 He guards the path of those who are honest.
He watches over the way of his faithful ones.

9 You will understand what is right and honest and fair.
You will understand the right way to live.
10 Your heart will become wise.
Your mind will delight in knowledge.
11 Good sense will keep you safe.
Understanding will guard you.

12 Wisdom will save you from the ways of evil men.
It will save you from men who twist their words.

[13] Men like that have left the straight paths
to walk in dark ways.
[14] They take delight in doing what is wrong.
They take joy in twisting everything around.
[15] Their paths are crooked.
Their ways are not straight.

[16] Wisdom will save you from a woman who commits adultery.
It will save you from a sinful woman and her tempting words.
[17] She has left the man she married when she was young.
She has broken the promise she made in front of God.
[18] Surely her house leads down to death.
Her paths lead to the spirits of the dead.
[19] No one who goes to her comes back
or reaches the paths of life.

[20] You will walk in the ways of good people.
You will follow the paths of those who do right.
[21] Honest people will live in the land.
Those who are without blame will remain in it.
[22] But sinners will be cut off from the land.
Those who aren't faithful will be torn away from it.

More Good Things Come From Wisdom

3 My son, do not forget my teaching.
Keep my commands in your heart.
[2] They will help you live for many years.
They will bring you peace and success.

[3] Don't let love and truth ever leave you.
Tie them around your neck.
Write them on the tablet of your heart.
[4] Then you will find favor and a good name
in the eyes of God and people.

[5] Trust in the LORD with all your heart.
Do not depend on your own understanding.
[6] In all your ways obey him.
Then he will make your paths smooth and straight.

key verses

Trust in the LORD with all your heart. Do not depend on your own understanding. In all your ways obey him. Then he will make your paths smooth and straight.
PROVERBS 3:5–6

[7] Don't be wise in your own eyes.
Have respect for the LORD and avoid evil.
[8] That will bring health to your body.
It will make your bones strong.

[9] Honor the LORD with your wealth.
Give him the first share of all your crops.
[10] Then your storerooms will be so full they can't hold everything.
Your huge jars will spill over with fresh wine.

[11] My son, do not hate the LORD's training.
Do not object when he corrects you.
[12] The LORD trains those he loves.
He is like a father who trains the son he is pleased with.

[13] Blessed is the one who finds wisdom.
Blessed is the one who gains understanding.
[14] Wisdom pays better than silver does.
She earns more than gold does.
[15] She is worth more than rubies.
Nothing you want can compare with her.
[16] Long life is in her right hand.
In her left hand are riches and honor.
[17] Her ways are pleasant ways.
All her paths lead to peace.
[18] She is a tree of life to those who take hold of her.
Those who hold her close will be blessed.

[19] By wisdom the LORD laid the earth's foundations.
Through understanding he set the heavens in place.

20 By his knowledge the seas were
separated,
and the clouds dropped their dew.

21 My son, do not let wisdom and
understanding out of your
sight.
Hold on to good sense and the
understanding of what is right.
22 They will be life for you.
They will be like a gracious
necklace around your neck.
23 Then you will go on your way in
safety.
You will not trip and fall.
24 When you lie down, you won't be
afraid.
When you lie down, you will
sleep soundly.
25 Don't be terrified by sudden trouble.
Don't be afraid when sinners are
destroyed.
26 The LORD will be at your side.
He will keep your feet from being
caught in a trap.

27 Don't hold back good from those
who are worthy of it.
Don't hold it back when you can
help.
28 Suppose you already have
something to give.
Don't say to your neighbor,
"Come back tomorrow.
I'll give it to you then."

29 Don't plan to harm your neighbor.
He lives near you and trusts you.
30 Don't bring charges against anyone
for no reason.
They have not harmed you.

31 Don't be jealous of a person who
hurts others.
Don't choose any of their ways.
32 The LORD really hates sinful people.
But he makes honest people his
closest friends.

33 The LORD puts a curse on the
houses of sinners.
But he blesses the homes of those
who do what is right.
34 He makes fun of proud people who
make fun of others.
But he gives grace to those who
are humble and treated badly.
35 Wise people receive honor.
But foolish people get only
shame.

Get Wisdom at Any Cost

4 My sons, listen to a father's
teaching.
Pay attention and gain
understanding.
2 I give you good advice.
So don't turn away from what I
teach you.
3 I, too, was once a young boy in my
father's house.
And my mother loved me deeply.
4 Then my father taught me.
He said to me, "Take hold of my
words with all your heart.
Keep my commands, and you
will live.
5 Get wisdom, and get
understanding.
Don't forget my words or turn
away from them.
6 Stay close to wisdom, and she will
keep you safe.
Love her, and she will watch over
you.
7 To start being wise you must first
get wisdom.
No matter what it costs, get
understanding.
8 Value wisdom highly, and she will
lift you up.
Hold her close, and she will honor
you.
9 She will set a beautiful crown on
your head.
She will give you a glorious
crown."

10 My son, listen. Accept what I say.
Then you will live for many
years.
11 I instruct you in the way of
wisdom.
I lead you along straight paths.
12 When you walk, nothing will slow
you down.
When you run, you won't trip
and fall.
13 Hold on to my teaching and don't
let it go.
Guard it well, because it is your
life.
14 Don't take the path of evil people.
Don't live the way sinners do.
15 Stay away from their path and
don't travel on it.
Turn away from it and go on
your way.

16 Sinners can't rest until they do
what is evil.
They can't sleep until they make
someone sin.
17 They do evil just as easily as they
eat food.
They hurt others as easily as
they drink wine.

18 The path of those who do right is
like the sun in the morning.
It shines brighter and brighter
until the full light of day.
19 But the way of those who do what
is wrong is like deep darkness.
They don't know what makes
them trip and fall.

20 My son, pay attention to what I say.
Listen closely to my words.
21 Don't let them out of your sight.
Keep them in your heart.
22 They are life to those who find them.
They are health to a person's
whole body.
23 Above everything else, guard your
heart.
Everything you do comes from it.
24 Don't speak with twisted words.
Keep evil talk away from your
lips.
25 Let your eyes look straight ahead.
Keep looking right in front of you.
26 Think carefully about the paths
that your feet walk on.
Always choose the right ways.
27 Don't turn to the right or left.
Keep your feet from the path of
evil.

A Warning Against Committing Adultery

5 My son, pay attention to my
wisdom.
Listen carefully to my wise
sayings.
2 Then you will continue to have
good sense.
Your lips will keep on speaking
words of knowledge.
3 A woman who commits adultery
has lips that drip honey.
What she says is smoother than
olive oil.
4 But in the end she is like bitter
poison.
She cuts like a sword that has
two edges.
5 Her feet go down to death.
Her steps lead straight to the
grave.
6 She doesn't give any thought to her
way of life.
Her paths have no direction, but
she doesn't realize it.

7 My sons, listen to me.
Don't turn away from what I say.
8 Stay on a path far away from that
evil woman.
Don't even go near the door of
her house.
9 If you do, you will lose your honor
to other people.
You will give your self-respect to
someone who is mean.
10 Strangers will use up all your
wealth.
Your hard work will make
someone else rich.
11 At the end of your life you will
groan.
Your skin and your body will be
worn out.
12 You will say, "How I hated to take
advice!
How my heart refused to be
corrected!

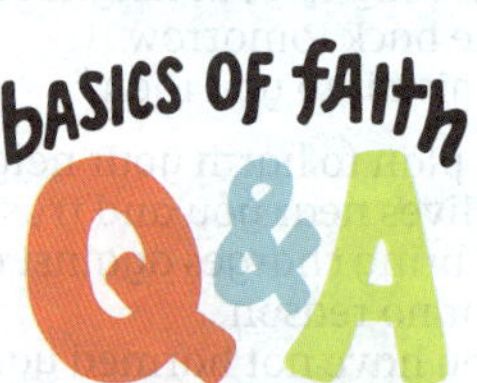

Why does it matter what I believe?

What you believe in your heart matters because it affects your everyday life. What you think about and believe determines your actions or what you do. God wants his people to believe the truth, which is why he gave us his Word.

Can you find the following verse?

PROVERBS 4:23

13 I would not obey my teachers.
I wouldn't listen to those who taught me.
14 I was soon in deep trouble.
It happened right in front of the whole assembly of God's people."

15 Drink water from your own well.
Drink running water from your own spring.
16 Should your springs pour out into the streets?
Should your streams of water pour out in public places?
17 No! Let them belong to you alone.
Never share them with strangers.
18 May your fountain be blessed.
May the wife you married when you were young make you happy.
19 She is like a loving doe, a graceful deer.
May her breasts always satisfy you.
May you always be captured by her love.
20 My son, why be captured by another man's wife?
Why hug a woman who has gone astray?

21 The LORD watches your ways.
He studies all your paths.
22 Sinners are trapped by their own evil acts.
They are held tight by the ropes of their sins.
23 They will die because they refused to be corrected.
Their sins will capture them because they were very foolish.

Warnings Against Foolish Acts

6 My son, don't promise to pay for what your neighbor owes.
Don't agree to pay a stranger's bill.
2 Don't be trapped by what you have said.
Don't be caught by the words of your mouth.
3 Instead, my son, do something to free yourself.
Don't fall into your neighbor's hands.
Go until you can't go anymore.
Don't let your neighbor rest.
4 Don't let your eyes go to sleep.
Don't let your eyelids close.
5 As a deer frees itself from a hunter, free yourself.
As a bird frees itself from a trapper, free yourself.

6 You people who don't want to work, think about the ant!
Consider its ways and be wise!
7 It has no commander.
It has no leader or ruler.
8 But it stores up its food in summer.
It gathers its food at harvest time.
9 You lazy people, how long will you lie there?
When will you get up from your sleep?
10 You might sleep a little or take a little nap.
You might even fold your hands and rest.
11 Then you would be poor, as if someone had robbed you.
You would have little, as if someone had stolen from you.

12 An evil troublemaker
goes around saying twisted things with his mouth.
13 He winks with his eyes.
He makes signals with his feet.
He motions with his fingers.
14 His plans are evil, and he has lies in his heart.
He is always stirring up fights.
15 Trouble will catch up with him in an instant.
He will suddenly be destroyed, and nothing can save him.

16 There are six things the LORD hates.
In fact, he hates seven things.
17 The LORD hates proud eyes,
a lying tongue,
and hands that kill those who aren't guilty.
18 He also hates hearts that make evil plans
and feet that are quick to do evil.
19 He hates any witness who pours out lies
and anyone who stirs up conflict in the community.

A Warning Against Committing Adultery

20 My son, keep your father's
command.
Don't turn away from your
mother's teaching.
21 Always tie them on your heart.
Put them around your neck.
22 When you walk, they will guide
you.
When you sleep, they will watch
over you.
When you wake up, they will
speak to you.
23 Your father's command is like a
lamp.
Your mother's teaching is like a
light.
And whatever instructs and
corrects you
leads to life.
24 It keeps you from your neighbor's
wife.
It keeps you from the smooth
talk of a woman who commits
adultery.
25 Don't hunger in your heart after
her beauty.
Don't let her eyes capture you.
26 A prostitute can be bought for only
a loaf of bread.
But another man's wife hunts
your very life.
27 You can't shovel fire into your lap
without burning your clothes.
28 You can't walk on hot coals
without burning your feet.
29 It's the same for anyone who has
sex with another man's wife.
Anyone who touches her will be
punished.

30 People don't hate a thief who steals
to fill his empty stomach.
31 But when he is caught, he must
pay seven times as much as he
stole.
It may even cost him everything
he has.
32 A man who commits adultery has
no sense.
Anyone who does it destroys
himself.
33 He will be beaten up and
dishonored.
His shame will never be wiped
away.
34 Jealousy stirs up a husband's anger.
He will show no mercy when he
gets even.
35 He won't accept any payment.
He won't take any money, no
matter how much he is offered.

A Warning Against a Woman Who Commits Adultery

7 My son, obey my words.
Store up my commands inside you.
2 Obey my commands and you will
live.
Guard my teachings as you
would guard your own eyes.
3 Tie them on your fingers.
Write them on the tablet of your
heart.
4 Say to wisdom, "You are my sister."
Say to understanding, "You are a
member of my family."
5 They will keep you from a woman
who commits adultery.
They will keep you from the
smooth talk of a sinful wife.

6 I stood at the window of my house.
I looked down through it.
7 Among those who were childish
I saw a young man who had no
sense.
8 He went down the street near that
sinful woman's corner.
He walked toward her house.
9 The sun had gone down, and the
day was fading.
The darkness of night was
falling.

10 A woman came out to meet him.
She was dressed like a prostitute
and had a clever plan.
11 She was wild and pushy.
She never stayed at home.
12 Sometimes she's in the streets.
Sometimes she's at other places.
At every corner she waits.
13 She took hold of the young man
and kissed him.
With a bold face she spoke to
him. She said,

14 "Today I offered what I promised I
would.
At home I have meat left over
from my fellowship offering.
15 So I came out to meet you.
I looked for you and have found
you!

16 I have covered my bed
with colored sheets from Egypt.
17 I've perfumed my bed with spices.
I used myrrh, aloes and cinnamon.
18 Come, let's drink our fill of love until morning.
Let's enjoy ourselves by sleeping together!
19 My husband isn't home.
He's gone on a long journey.
20 He took his bag full of money.
He won't be home for several days."

21 She led him astray with her clever words.
She charmed him with her smooth talk.
22 All at once he followed her.
He was like an ox going to be killed.
He was like a deer stepping into a trap
23 until an arrow struck its liver.
He was like a bird rushing into a trap.
Little did he know it would cost him his life!

24 My sons, listen to me.
Pay attention to what I say.
25 Don't let your hearts turn to her ways.
Don't step onto her paths.
26 She has brought down a lot of men.
She has killed a huge crowd.
27 Her house is a road to the grave.
It leads down to the place of the dead.

Wisdom Calls Out

8 Doesn't wisdom call out?
Doesn't understanding raise her voice?
2 At the highest point along the way,
she takes her place where the paths meet.
3 Beside the gate leading into the city,
she cries out at the entrance. She says,
4 "People, I call out to you.
I raise my voice to all human beings.
5 You who are childish, get some good sense.
You who are foolish, set your hearts on getting it.
6 Listen! I have things to say that you can depend on.
I open my lips to speak what is right.
7 My mouth speaks what is true.
My lips hate evil.
8 All the words of my mouth are honest.
None of them is twisted or sinful.
9 To those who have understanding,
all my words are right.
To those who have found knowledge, they are true.
10 Choose my teaching instead of silver.
Choose knowledge rather than fine gold.
11 Wisdom is worth more than rubies.
Nothing you want can compare with her.

12 "I, wisdom, live together with understanding.
I have knowledge and good sense.
13 To have respect for the LORD is to hate evil.
I hate pride and bragging.
I hate evil ways and twisted words.
14 I have good sense and give good advice.
I have understanding and power.
15 By me kings rule.
Leaders make laws that are fair.
16 By me princes and nobles govern.
It is by me that anyone rules on earth.
17 I love those who love me.
Those who look for me find me.
18 With me are riches and honor.
With me are lasting wealth and success.
19 My fruit is better than fine gold.
My gifts are better than the finest silver.
20 I walk in ways that are honest.
I take paths that are right.
21 I leave riches to those who love me.
I give them more than they have room for.

22 "The LORD created me as the first of his works,
before his acts of long ago.
23 I was formed a long, long time ago.
I was formed at the very beginning,
when the world was created.

24 Before there were any oceans, I was
born.
It was before there were springs
flowing with water.
25 Before the mountains were settled
in place, I was born.
Before there were any hills, I was
born.
26 It happened before the LORD made
the world and its fields.
It was before he made the dust of
the earth.
27 I was there when he set the heavens
in place.
When he marked out the place
where the sky meets the sea, I
was there.
28 That was when he put the clouds
above.
It was when he fixed the ocean
springs in place.
29 It was when he set limits for the sea
so that the waters had to obey
his command.
When the LORD marked out the
foundations of the earth, I was
there.
30 I was constantly at his side.
I was filled with delight day after day.
I was always happy to be with him.
31 His whole world filled me with joy.
I took delight in all human
beings.
32 "My children, listen to me.
Blessed are those who keep my
ways.
33 Listen to my teaching and be wise.
Don't turn away from it.
34 Blessed are those who listen to me.
They watch every day at my
doors.
They wait beside my doorway.
35 Those who find me find life.
They receive blessing from the
LORD.
36 But those who don't find me harm
only themselves.
Everyone who hates me loves
death."

Wisdom and Foolishness Call Out

9 Wisdom has built her house.
She has set up its seven pillars.
2 She has prepared her meat and
mixed her wine.
She has also set her table.
3 She has sent out her servants.
She calls out from the highest
point of the city.

pointing us to JESUS: Lady Wisdom

The book of Proverbs imagines that wisdom looks like a woman who calls out in the streets. She tells men and women, "Listen to me! I'll show you the way to true life. Don't forget God's promises. Walk in his ways and you will live fully." She is called Lady Wisdom because she is a picture of what God's wisdom would look like as a person.

The writers of Proverbs were using their imagination as they wrote about Lady Wisdom, but later, God's people wouldn't have to imagine what God's wisdom looked like as a person. One day, God himself would come in a human body and live among his people. Jesus would walk this earth and live out the wisdom of God for all to see. He would call to all who would listen, "Come to me! I am the way; I am true life. Don't forget God's promises. Walk with me and you will find eternal life."

4 She says, "Let all who are childish
come to my house!"
She speaks to those who have no
sense. She says,
5 "Come and eat my food.
Drink the wine I have mixed.
6 Leave your childish ways and you
will live.
Walk in the way of
understanding."

7 When you correct someone who
makes fun of others, you might
be laughed at.
When you warn a sinner, you
might get hurt.
8 Don't warn those who make fun of
others, or they will hate you.
Warn those who are wise, and
they will love you.
9 Teach a wise person, and they will
become even wiser.
Teach a person who does right,
and they will learn even more.

10 If you want to become wise, you
must begin by respecting the
LORD.
To know the Holy One is to gain
understanding.
11 Through wisdom, you will live a
long time.
Years will be added to your life.
12 If you are wise, your wisdom will
reward you.
If you make fun of others, you
alone will suffer.

13 The woman called Foolishness is
wild.
She is childish and knows
nothing.
14 She sits at the door of her house.
She sits at the highest point of
the city.
15 She calls out to those who pass by.
She calls out to those who go
straight on their way.
She says,
16 "Let all who are childish come to
my house!"
She speaks to those who have no
sense.
17 She says, "Stolen water is sweet.
Food eaten in secret tastes
good!"
18 But they don't know that dead
people are there.
They don't know that her guests
are deep in the place of the
dead.

THE PROVERBS OF SOLOMON

10 These are the proverbs of Solomon.

A wise son makes his father glad.
But a foolish son brings sorrow to his mother.

2 Riches that are gained by sinning aren't worth anything.
But doing what is right saves you from death.

3 The LORD gives those who do right the food they need.
But he lets those who do wrong go hungry.

4 Hands that don't want to work make you poor.
But hands that work hard bring wealth to you.

5 A child who gathers crops in summer is wise.
But a child who sleeps at harvest time brings shame.

6 Blessings are like crowns on the heads of those who do right.
But the trouble caused by what sinners say destroys them.

7 The names of those who do right are used in blessings.
But the names of those who do wrong will rot.

8 A wise heart accepts commands.
But foolish chattering destroys you.

9 Anyone who lives without blame walks safely.
But anyone who takes a crooked path will get caught.

10 An evil wink gets you into trouble.
And foolish chattering destroys you.

11 The mouths of those who do right pour out life like a fountain.
But the mouths of sinners hide their evil plans.

12 Hate stirs up fights.
But love erases all sins by forgiving them.

13 Wisdom is found on the lips of those who understand what is right.
But those who have no sense are punished.

14 Wise people store up knowledge.
But the mouths of foolish people destroy them.

15 The wealth of rich people is like a city that makes them feel safe.
But having nothing destroys those who are poor.

16 People who do what is right earn life.
But sinners earn sin and death.

17 Anyone who pays attention to correction
shows the path to life.
But anyone who refuses to be corrected
leads others down the wrong path.

18 Anyone who hides hatred with lying lips
and spreads lies is foolish.

19 Sin is not ended by using many words.
But those who are wise control their tongues.

20 The tongues of those who do right are like fine silver.
But the hearts of those who do wrong aren't worth very much.

21 The words of those who do right benefit many people.
But those who are foolish die because they have no sense.

22 The blessing of the LORD brings wealth.
And it comes without painful work.

23 A foolish person finds pleasure in evil plans.
But a person who has understanding takes delight in wisdom.

24 What sinners are afraid of will catch up with them.
But those who do right will get what they want.

25 When the storm is over, sinners are gone.
But those who do right stand firm forever.

26 Those who don't want to work hurt
those who send them.
They are like vinegar on the
teeth or smoke in the eyes.

27 Having respect for the LORD leads
to a longer life.
But the years of evil people are
cut short.

28 Those who do right can expect joy.
But the hopes of sinners are
bound to fail.

29 The way of the LORD is a safe place
for those without blame.
But that way destroys those who
do evil.

30 Those who do right will never be
removed from the land.
But those who do wrong will not
remain in it.

31 The mouths of those who do right
produce wisdom.
But tongues that speak twisted
words will be made silent.

32 Those who do right know the
proper thing to say.
But those who do wrong speak
only twisted words.

11 The LORD hates it when people
use scales to cheat others.
But he is delighted when people
use honest weights.

2 When pride comes, shame follows.
But wisdom comes to those who
are not proud.

3 Those who do what is right are
guided by their honest lives.
But those who aren't faithful are
destroyed by their lies.

4 Wealth isn't worth anything when
God judges you.
But doing what is right saves you
from death.

5 The ways of honest people are
made straight because they do
what is right.
But those who do what is wrong are
brought down by their own sins.

6 Godly people are saved by doing
what is right.
But those who aren't faithful are
trapped by evil longings.

7 Hopes placed in human beings will
die with them.
Everything their power promised
comes to nothing.

8 Those who do right are saved from
trouble.
But trouble comes on those who
do wrong.

9 With their words ungodly people
destroy their neighbors.
But those who do what is right
escape because of their
knowledge.

10 When those who do right succeed,
their city is glad.
When those who do wrong die,
people shout for joy.

11 The blessing of honest people
builds up a city.
But the words of sinners destroy
it.

12 Whoever makes fun of their
neighbor has no sense.
But the one who has
understanding controls their
tongue.

13 Those who talk about others will
tell secrets.
But those who can be trusted
keep the secrets of others.

14 Without guidance a nation falls.
But many good advisers can
bring victory to a nation.

15 Whoever promises to pay for
what someone else owes will
certainly suffer.
But a person who doesn't agree
to pay someone else's bill is
safe.

16 A woman who has a kind heart
gains honor.
But men who are not kind gain
only wealth.

17 Those who are kind benefit
themselves.
But mean people bring ruin on
themselves.

18 An evil person really earns
nothing.
But the one who plants what
is right will certainly be
rewarded.

19 Surely right living leads to life.
But whoever runs after evil finds death.

20 The LORD hates those whose hearts are twisted.
But he is pleased with those who live without blame.

21 You can be sure that sinners will be punished.
And you can also be sure that godly people will go free.

22 A beautiful woman who has no sense is like a gold ring in a pig's nose.

23 What godly people long for ends only in what is good.
But what sinners hope for ends only in God's anger.

24 One person gives freely but gets even richer.
Another person doesn't give what they should but gets even poorer.

25 Anyone who gives a lot will succeed.
Anyone who renews others will be renewed.

26 People ask for bad things to happen to those who store up grain for themselves.
But people ask for God's blessing on those who are willing to sell.

27 Anyone who looks for what is good will be blessed.
But bad things will happen to a person who plans to do evil.

28 Those who trust in their riches will fall.
But those who do right will be as healthy as a green leaf.

29 Those who bring ruin on their families will receive nothing but wind.
And foolish people will serve wise people.

30 The fruit that godly people bear is like a tree of life.
And those who are wise save lives.

31 Godly people get what they should get on earth.
So ungodly people and sinners will certainly get what they should get!

12 Anyone who loves correction loves knowledge.
Anyone who hates to be corrected is stupid.

2 The LORD blesses anyone who does good.
But he judges anyone who plans to do evil.

3 No one can become strong and steady by doing evil.
But if people do what is right, they can't be removed from the land.

4 An excellent woman is her husband's crown.
But a wife who brings shame is like sickness in his bones.

5 The plans of godly people are right.
But the advice of sinners will lead you the wrong way.

6 The words of those who are evil hide and wait to spill people's blood.
But the speech of those who are honest saves them from traps like that.

7 Sinners are destroyed and taken away.
But the houses of godly people stand firm.

8 A person is praised for how wise they are.
But people hate anyone who has a twisted mind.

9 Being nobody and having a servant
is better than pretending to be somebody and having no food.

10 Those who do what is right take good care of their animals.
But the kindest acts of those who do wrong are mean.

11 Those who farm their land will have plenty of food.
But those who chase dreams have no sense.

12 Those who do what is wrong are safe for just a while.
But those who do what is right last forever.

13 Those who do evil are trapped by
their sinful talk.
But those who have done no
wrong escape trouble.

14 Many good things come from what
people say.
And the work of their hands
rewards them.

15 The way of foolish people seems
right to them.
But those who are wise listen to
advice.

16 Foolish people are easily upset.
But wise people pay no attention
to hurtful words.

17 An honest witness tells the truth.
But a dishonest witness tells lies.

18 The words of thoughtless people cut
like swords.
But the tongue of wise people
brings healing.

19 Truthful words last forever.
But lies last for only a moment.

20 There are lies in the hearts of those
who plan evil.
But there is joy for those who
work to bring peace.

21 No harm comes to godly people.
But sinners have all the trouble
they can handle.

22 The LORD hates those whose lips
tell lies.
But he is pleased with people
who tell the truth.

23 Wise people keep their knowledge
to themselves.
But the hearts of foolish people
shout foolish things.

24 Hands that work hard will rule.
But people who are lazy will be
forced to work.

25 Worry makes the heart heavy.
But a kind word cheers it up.

26 Godly people are careful about the
friends they choose.
But the way of sinners leads
them down the wrong path.

27 Lazy people do not even cook what
they catch.
But those who work hard eat
their fill of what is hunted.

28 There is life in doing what is right.
Along that path you will never
die.

13

1 A wise son pays attention to
what his father teaches him.
But anyone who makes fun
of others doesn't listen to
warnings.

2 The good things people say benefit
them.
But liars love to hurt others.

3 Those who guard what they say
guard their lives.
But those who speak without
thinking will be destroyed.

4 People who refuse to work want
things and get nothing.
But the desires of people who
work hard are completely
satisfied.

5 Those who do right hate what is
false.
But those who do wrong stink and
bring shame on themselves.

6 Doing right guards those who are
honest.
But evil destroys those who are
sinful.

7 Some people pretend to be rich but
have nothing.
Others pretend to be poor but
have great wealth.

8 A person's riches might save their
life.
But a poor person is not able to
do anything about danger.

9 The lights of godly people shine
brightly.
But the lamps of sinners are
blown out.

10 Where there is arguing, there is pride.
But those who take advice are
wise.

11 Money gained in the wrong way
disappears.
But money gathered little by
little grows.

12 Hope that is put off makes one sick
at heart.
But a desire that is met is like a
tree of life.

13 Anyone who hates what they are
taught will pay for it later.
But a person who respects a
command will be rewarded.

14 The teaching of wise people is like a
fountain that gives life.
It turns those who listen to it
away from the jaws of death.

15 Good judgment wins favor.
But the way of liars leads to their
ruin.

16 Wise people act with knowledge.
But foolish people show how
foolish they are.

17 An evil messenger gets into trouble.
But a trusted messenger brings
healing.

18 Those who turn away from their
training become poor and
ashamed.
But those who accept warnings
are honored.

19 A desire that is met is like
something that tastes sweet.
But foolish people hate to turn
away from evil.

20 Walk with wise people and become
wise.
A companion of foolish people
suffers harm.

21 Hard times chase those who are
sinful.
But those who do right are
rewarded with good things.

22 A good person leaves what they
own to their children and
grandchildren.
But a sinner's wealth is stored up
for those who do right.

23 An unplowed field produces food
for poor people.
But those who treat them badly
destroy it all.

24 Those who don't correct their
children hate them.
But those who love them are
careful to correct them.

25 Those who do right eat until they
are full.
But the stomachs of those who do
wrong go hungry.

14

A wise woman builds her
house.
But a foolish woman tears hers
down with her own hands.

2 Whoever has respect for the LORD
lives a good life.
But those who hate him walk
down an evil path.

3 The proud words of a foolish person
sting like a whip.
But the things wise people say
keep them safe.

4 Where there are no oxen, the feed
box is empty.
But a strong ox brings in huge
harvests.

5 An honest witness does not lie.
But a dishonest witness pours out
lies.

6 Those who make fun of others look
for wisdom and don't find it.
But knowledge comes easily to
those who understand what is
right.

7 Stay away from a foolish person.
You won't find knowledge in
what they say.

8 People are wise and understanding
when they think about the way
they live.
But people are foolish when their
foolish ways trick them.

9 Foolish people laugh at making
things right when they sin.
But honest people try to do the
right thing.

10 Each heart knows its own sadness.
And no one else can share its joy.

11 The houses of sinners will be
destroyed.
But the tents of honest people
will stand firm.

12 There is a way that appears to be
right.
But in the end it leads to death.

13 Even when you laugh, your heart
can be hurting.
And your joy can end in sadness.

14 Those who aren't faithful will be
paid back
for what they've done.

And good people will receive rewards
for how they've lived.

15 A childish person believes
anything.
But a wise person thinks about
how they live.

16 A wise person has respect for the
LORD and avoids evil.
But a foolish person has a bad
temper and yet feels secure.

17 Anyone who gets angry quickly
does foolish things.
And a person who is tricky is
hated.

18 Childish people act in keeping with
their foolish ways.
But knowledge makes wise
people feel like kings.

19 Evil people will bow down in front
of good people.
And those who do wrong will bow
down at the gates of those who
do right.

20 Poor people are avoided even by
their neighbors.
But rich people have many
friends.

21 It is a sin to hate your neighbor.
But blessed is the person who is
kind to those in need.

22 Those who plan evil go down the
wrong path.
But those who plan good find
love and truth.

23 All hard work pays off.
But if all you do is talk, you will
be poor.

24 The wealth of wise people is their
crown.
But the foolish ways of foolish
people lead to what is foolish.

25 An honest witness saves lives.
But a dishonest witness tells lies.

26 Anyone who shows respect for the
LORD has a strong tower.
It will be a safe place for their
children.

27 Respect for the LORD is like a
fountain that gives life.
It turns you away from the jaws
of death.

28 A large population is a king's glory.
But a prince without followers is
destroyed.

29 Anyone who is patient has great
understanding.
But anyone who gets angry
quickly shows how foolish they
are.

30 A peaceful heart gives life to the
body.
But jealousy rots the bones.

31 Anyone who crushes poor people
makes fun of their Maker.
But anyone who is kind to those
in need honors God.

32 When trouble comes, sinners are
brought down.
But godly people seek safety in
God even as they die.

33 Wisdom rests in the hearts of those
who understand what is right.
And even among foolish people
she makes herself known.

34 Doing what is right lifts people up.
But sin brings judgment to any
nation.

35 A king is pleased with a wise
servant.
But a servant who is full of
shame stirs up the king's anger.

15 A gentle answer turns anger
away.
But mean words stir up anger.

2 The tongues of wise people use
knowledge well.
But the mouths of foolish people
pour out foolish words.

3 The eyes of the LORD are
everywhere.
They watch those who are evil
and those who are good.

4 A tongue that calms is like a tree of
life.
But a tongue that tells lies
produces a broken spirit.

5 A foolish person turns their back on
their parent's correction.
But anyone who accepts
correction shows
understanding.

6 The houses of those who do what is
right hold great wealth.
But those who do what is wrong
earn only ruin.

7 The lips of wise people spread
knowledge.
But the hearts of foolish people
are not honest.

8 The LORD hates the sacrifice of
sinful people.
But the prayers of honest people
please him.

9 The LORD hates how sinners live.
But he loves those who run after
what is right.

10 Hard training is in store for anyone
who leaves the right path.
A person who hates to be
corrected will die.

11 Death and the Grave lie open in
front of the LORD.
So human hearts certainly lie
open to him!

12 People who make fun of others
don't like to be corrected.
So they stay away from wise
people.

13 A happy heart makes a face look
cheerful.
But a sad heart produces a
broken spirit.

14 A heart that understands what is
right looks for knowledge.
But the mouths of foolish people
feed on what is foolish.

15 All the days of those who are
crushed are filled with pain
and suffering.
But a cheerful heart enjoys a
good time that never ends.

16 It is better to have respect for the
LORD and have little
than to be rich and have trouble.

17 A few vegetables where there is love
are better than the finest meat
where there is hatred.

18 A person with a bad temper stirs up
conflict.
But a person who is patient
calms things down.

19 The way of people who don't want
to work is blocked with thorns.
But the path of honest people is a
wide road.

20 A wise son makes his father glad.
But a foolish son hates his mother.

21 A person who has no sense enjoys
doing foolish things.
But a person who has
understanding walks straight
ahead.

22 Plans fail without good advice.
But they succeed when there are
many advisers.

23 Joy is found in giving the right
answer.
And how good is a word spoken
at the right time!

24 The path of life leads up for those
who are wise.
It keeps them from going down
to the place of the dead.

25 The LORD tears down the proud
person's house.
But he keeps the widow's
property safe.

26 The LORD hates the thoughts of
sinful people.
But he considers kind words to be
pure.

27 Those who always want more bring
ruin to their households.
But a person who refuses to be
paid to lie will live.

28 The hearts of those who do right
think about how they will
answer.
But the mouths of those who do
wrong pour out evil.

29 The LORD is far away from those
who do wrong.
But he hears the prayers of those
who do right.

30 The cheerful look of a messenger
brings joy to your heart.
And good news gives health to
your body.

31 Whoever listens to a warning that
gives life
will be at home among those
who are wise.

32 Those who turn away from
correction hate themselves.
But anyone who accepts
correction gains understanding.

33 Wisdom teaches you to have
respect for the LORD.
So don't be proud if you want to
be honored.

16 People make plans in their
hearts.
But the LORD puts the correct
answer on their tongues.

2 Everything a person does might
seem pure to them.
But the LORD knows why they do
what they do.

3 Commit to the LORD everything
you do.
Then he will make your plans
succeed.

4 The LORD works everything out to
the proper end.
Even those who do wrong were
made for a day of trouble.

5 The LORD hates all those who have
proud hearts.
You can be sure that they will be
punished.

6 Through love and truth sin is paid
for.
People avoid evil when they have
respect for the LORD.

7 When the way you live pleases the
LORD,
he makes even your enemies live
at peace with you.

8 It is better to have a little and do
right
than to have a lot and be unfair.

9 In their hearts human beings plan
their lives.
But the LORD decides where their
steps will take them.

10 A king speaks as if his words come
from God.
And what he says does not turn
right into wrong.

11 Honest scales and balances belong
to the LORD.
He made all the weights in the
bag.

12 A king hates it when his people do
what is wrong.
A ruler is made secure when they
do what is right.

13 Kings are pleased when what you
say is honest.
They value people who speak
what is right.

14 An angry king can order your death.
But a wise person will try to calm
him down.

15 When a king's face is happy, it
means life.
His favor is like rain in the
spring.

16 It is much better to get wisdom
than gold.
It is much better to choose
understanding than silver.

17 The path of honest people takes
them away from evil.
Those who guard their ways
guard their lives.

18 If you are proud, you will be
destroyed.
If you are proud, you will fall.

19 Suppose you are lowly in spirit
along with those who are
treated badly.
That's better than sharing stolen
goods with those who are
proud.

20 If anyone pays attention to what
they're taught, they will succeed.
Blessed is the person who trusts
in the LORD.

21 Wise hearts are known for
understanding what is right.
Kind words make people want to
learn more.

22 Understanding is like a fountain of
life to those who have it.
But foolish people are punished
for the foolish things they do.

23 The hearts of wise people guide
their mouths.
Their words make people want to
learn more.

24 Kind words are like honey.
They are sweet to the spirit and
bring healing to the body.

25 There is a way that appears to be
right.
But in the end it leads to death.

26 The hunger of workers makes them
work.
Their hunger drives them on.

27 A worthless person plans to do evil
things.
Their words are like a burning fire.

28 A twisted person stirs up conflict.
Anyone who talks about others
separates close friends.

29 A person who wants to hurt others
tries to get them to sin.
That person leads them down a
path that isn't good.

30 Whoever winks with their eye is
planning to do wrong.
Whoever closes their lips tightly
is up to no good.

31 Gray hair is a glorious crown.
You get it by living the right way.

32 It is better to be patient than to fight.
It is better to control your temper
than to take a city.

33 Lots are cast into the lap to make
decisions.
But everything they decide
comes from the LORD.

17 It is better to eat a dry crust of
bread in peace and quiet
than to eat a big dinner in a
house full of fighting.

2 A wise servant will rule over a
shameful child.
He will be given part of the
property as if he were a family
member.

3 Fire tests silver, and heat tests gold.
But the LORD tests our hearts.

4 Evil people listen to lies.
Lying people listen to evil.

5 Anyone who laughs at those who are
poor makes fun of their Maker.
Anyone who is happy when
others suffer will be punished.

6 Grandchildren are like a crown to
older people.
And children are proud of their
parents.

7 Fancy words don't belong in the
mouths of ungodly fools.
And lies certainly don't belong in
the mouths of rulers!

8 Those who give money think it will
buy them favors.
They think that no matter where
they turn, they will succeed.

9 Whoever wants to show love
forgives a wrong.
But those who talk about it
separate close friends.

10 A person who understands what is
right learns more from just a
warning
than a foolish person learns from
100 strokes with a whip.

11 An evil person tries to keep others
from obeying God.
The messenger of death will be
sent against them.

12 It is better to meet a bear whose
cubs have been stolen
than to meet a foolish person
who is acting foolishly.

13 Evil will never leave the house
of anyone who pays back evil for
good.

14 Starting to argue is like making a
crack in a dam.
So drop the matter before a fight
breaks out.

15 The LORD hates two things.
He hates it when the guilty are
set free.
He also hates it when those who
aren't guilty are punished.

16 Why should a foolish person try to
buy wisdom?
They are not even able to
understand it.

17 A friend loves at all times.
They are there to help when
trouble comes.

18 A person who has no sense agrees
to pay what other people owe.
It isn't wise to promise to pay
other people's bills.

19 The one who loves to argue loves to
sin.
The one who builds a high gate is
just asking to be destroyed.

20 If your heart is twisted, you won't
succeed.
If your tongue tells lies, you will
get into trouble.

21 It is sad to have a foolish child.
The parents of a godless fool
have no joy.

22 A cheerful heart makes you healthy.
But a broken spirit dries you up.

23 Anyone who does wrong accepts
favors in secret.
Then they turn what is right into
what is wrong.

24 Anyone who understands what is
right keeps wisdom in view.
But the eyes of a foolish person
look everywhere else.

25 A foolish child makes his father sad
and his mother sorry.

26 It isn't good to fine those who aren't
guilty.
So it certainly isn't good to whip
officials just because they are
honest.

27 Anyone who has knowledge
controls their words.
Anyone who has understanding
is not easily upset.

28 We think even foolish people are
wise if they keep silent.
We think they understand what is
right if they control their tongues.

18 A person who isn't friendly
looks out only for themselves.
They oppose all good sense by
starting fights.

2 Foolish people don't want to
understand.
They take delight in saying only
what they think.

3 People hate it when evil comes.
And they refuse to honor those
who bring shame.

4 The words of a person's mouth are
like deep water.
But the fountain of wisdom is
like a flowing stream.

5 It isn't good to favor those who do
wrong.
That would keep justice from
those who aren't guilty.

6 What foolish people say leads to
arguing.
They are just asking for a beating.

7 The words of foolish people drag
them down.
They are trapped by what they
say.

8 The words of anyone who talks
about others are like tasty bites
of food.
They go deep down inside you.

9 Anyone who doesn't want to work
is like someone who destroys.

10 The name of the LORD is like a
strong tower.
Godly people run to it and are
safe.

11 The wealth of rich people is like a
city that makes them feel safe.
They think of it as a city with
walls that can't be climbed.

12 If a person's heart is proud, they
will be destroyed.
So don't be proud if you want to
be honored.

13 To answer before listening
is foolish and shameful.

14 A cheerful spirit gives strength
even during sickness.
But you can't keep going if you
have a broken spirit.

15 Those whose hearts understand
what is right get knowledge.
That's because the ears of those
who are wise listen for it.

16 A gift opens the door
and helps the giver meet
important people.

17 In court, the first one to speak
seems right.
Then someone else comes
forward and questions him.

18 Casting lots will put a stop to
arguing.
It will keep the strongest enemies
apart.

19 A broken friendship is harder to
handle than a city with high
walls around it.
And arguing is like the locked
gates of a mighty city.

[20] Because of what they say a person
can fill their stomach.
What their words produce can
satisfy them.

[21] Your tongue has the power of life
and death.
Those who love to talk will eat
the fruit of their words.

[22] The one who finds a wife finds what
is good.
He receives favor from the LORD.

[23] Poor people beg for mercy.
But rich people answer in a mean
way.

[24] A person with unfaithful friends
soon comes to ruin.
But there is a friend who sticks
closer than a brother.

19 It is better to be poor and to
live without blame
than to be foolish and to twist
words around.

[2] Getting excited about something
without knowledge isn't good.
It's even worse to be in a hurry
and miss the way.

[3] A person's own foolish acts destroy
their life.
But their heart is angry with the
LORD.

[4] Wealth brings many friends.
But even the closest friend of a
poor person abandons them.

[5] A dishonest witness will be
punished.
And whoever pours out lies will
not go free.

[6] Many try to win the favor of rulers.
And everyone is the friend of a
person who gives gifts.

[7] Poor people are avoided by their
whole family.
Their friends avoid them even
more.
The poor person runs after his
friends to beg for help.
But they can't be found.

[8] Anyone who gets wisdom loves life.
Anyone who values
understanding will soon
succeed.

[9] A dishonest witness will be
punished.
And those who pour out lies will
die.

[10] It isn't proper for a foolish person to
live in great comfort.
And it is much worse when a
slave rules over princes!

[11] A person's wisdom makes them
patient.
They will be honored if they
forgive someone who sins
against them.

[12] A king's anger is like a lion's roar.
But his favor is like dew on the
grass.

[13] A foolish child is a father's ruin.
A nagging wife is like dripping
that never stops.

[14] You will receive houses and wealth
from your parents.
But a wise wife is given by the
LORD.

[15] Anyone who doesn't want to work
sleeps his life away.
And a person who refuses to work
goes hungry.

[16] Those who keep commandments
keep their lives.
But those who don't care how
they live will die.

[17] Anyone who is kind to poor people
lends to the LORD.
God will reward them for what
they have done.

[18] Train your children, because then
there is hope.
Don't do anything to bring about
their deaths.

[19] A person with a bad temper must
pay for it.
If you save them, you will have
to do it again.

[20] Listen to advice and accept
correction.
In the end you will be counted
among those who are wise.

[21] A person may have many plans in
their heart.
But the LORD's purpose wins out
in the end.

22 Everyone longs for love that never
fails.
It is better to be poor than to be a
liar.

23 Having respect for the LORD leads
to life.
Then you will be content and free
from trouble.

24 A person who doesn't want to work
leaves his hand in the dish.
He won't even bring it back up to
his mouth!

25 If you whip a person who makes
fun of others,
childish people will learn to be
wise.
If you warn those who already
understand what is right,
they will gain even more
knowledge.

26 Anyone who robs their father and
drives out their mother
is a child who brings shame and
dishonor.

27 My son, if you stop listening to
what I teach you,
you will wander away from the
words of knowledge.

28 A dishonest witness makes fun of
what is right.
The mouths of those who do
wrong gulp down evil.

29 Those who make fun of others will
be judged.
Foolish people will be punished.

20 Wine causes you to make fun
of others, and beer causes you
to start fights.
Anyone who is led astray by
them is not wise.

2 A king's anger brings terror like a
lion's roar.
Anyone who makes him angry
may lose their life.

3 Avoiding a fight brings honor to a
person.
But every foolish person is quick
to argue.

4 Anyone who refuses to work doesn't
plow in the right season.
When they look for a crop at
harvest time, they don't find it.

5 The purposes of a person's heart
are like deep water.
But one who has understanding
brings them out.

6 Many claim to have love that never
fails.
But who can find a faithful person?

7 Those who do what is right live
without blame.
Blessed are their children after
them.

8 A king sits on his throne to judge.
He gets rid of all evil when he
sees it.

9 No one can say, "I have kept my
heart pure.
I'm 'clean,' and I haven't sinned."

10 The LORD hates two things.
He hates weights that weigh
things heavier or lighter than
they really are.
He also hates measures that
measure things larger or
smaller than they really are.

11 Even small children are known by
their actions.
So is their conduct really pure
and right?

12 The LORD has made two things.
He has made ears that hear.
He has also made eyes that see.

13 Don't love sleep, or you will become
poor.
Stay awake, and you will have
more food than you need.

14 "It's no good. It's no good!" says a
buyer.
Then off they go and brag about
what they bought.

15 There is gold, and there are plenty
of rubies.
But lips that speak knowledge
are a priceless jewel.

16 Take the coat of one who puts up
money for what a stranger owes.
Hold it until you get paid back if
it is done for an outsider.

17 Food gained by cheating tastes
sweet.
But you will end up with a mouth
full of gravel.

18 Plans are made by asking for
guidance.
So if you go to war, get good
advice.

19 A person who talks about others
tells secrets.
So avoid anyone who talks too
much.

20 If anyone asks for bad things to
happen to their father or mother,
that person's lamp will be blown
out in total darkness.

21 Property that you claim too soon
will not be blessed in the end.

22 Don't say, "I'll get even with you for
the wrong you did to me!"
Wait for the LORD, and he will
make things right for you.

23 The LORD hates weights that weigh
things heavier or lighter than
they really are.
Scales that are not honest don't
please him.

24 The LORD directs a person's steps.
So how can anyone understand
their own way?

25 A person is trapped if they make a
hasty promise to God
and only later thinks about what
they said.

26 A wise king gets rid of evil people.
He runs the threshing wheel over
them.

27 The spirit of a person is the lamp of
the LORD.
It lights up what is deep down
inside them.

28 Love and truth keep a king safe.
Faithful love makes his throne
secure.

29 Young men are proud of their
strength.
Gray hair brings honor to old
men.

30 Blows and wounds scrub evil away.
And beatings make you pure
deep down inside.

21 In the LORD's hand the king's
heart is like a stream of water.
The LORD directs it toward all
those who please him.

2 A person might think their own
ways are right.
But the LORD knows what they
are thinking.

3 Do what is right and fair.
The LORD accepts that more than
sacrifices.

4 The proud eyes and hearts of sinful
people are like a field not
plowed.
Those things produce nothing
good.

5 The plans of people who work hard
succeed.
You can be just as sure that those
in a hurry will become poor.

6 A fortune made by people who tell
lies
amounts to nothing and leads to
death.

7 The harmful things that evil people
do will drag them away.
They refuse to do what is right.

8 The path of those who are guilty is
crooked.
But the conduct of those who are
not guilty is honest.

9 It is better to live on a corner of a
roof
than to share a house with a
nagging wife.

10 Sinful people long to do evil.
They don't show their neighbors
any mercy.

11 When you punish someone who
makes fun of others, childish
people get wise.
By paying attention to wise
people, the childish get
knowledge.

12 The Blameless One knows where
sinners live.
And he destroys them.

13 Whoever refuses to listen to the
cries of poor people
will also cry out and not be
answered.

14 A secret gift calms down anger.
A hidden favor softens great
anger.

15 When you do what is fair, you
make godly people glad.
But you terrify those who do
what is evil.

16 Whoever leaves the path of
understanding
ends up with those who are dead.

17 Anyone who loves pleasure will
become poor.
Anyone who loves wine and olive
oil will never be rich.

18 Evil people become the payment
for setting godly people free.
Those who aren't faithful are the
payment for honest people.

19 It is better to live in a desert
than to live with a nagging wife
who loves to argue.

20 Wise people store up the best food
and olive oil.
But foolish people eat up
everything they have.

21 Anyone who wants to be godly and
loving
finds life, success and honor.

22 A wise person can attack a strong
city.
They can pull down the place of
safety its people trust in.

23 Those who are careful about what
they say
keep themselves out of trouble.

24 A proud person is called a mocker.
He thinks much too highly of
himself.

25 Some people will die while they are
still hungry.
That's because their hands refuse
to work.
26 All day long they hunger for more.
But godly people give without
holding back.

27 God hates sacrifices that are
brought by evil people.
He hates it even more when
they bring them for the wrong
reason.

28 Witnesses who aren't honest will
die.
But anyone who listens carefully
will be a successful witness.

29 Sinful people try to look as if they
were bold.
But honest people think about
how they live.

30 No wisdom, wise saying or plan
can succeed against the LORD.

31 You can prepare a horse for the day
of battle.
But the power to win comes from
the LORD.

22 You should want a good name
more than you want great
riches.
To be highly respected is better
than having silver or gold.

2 The LORD made rich people and
poor people.
That's what they have in common.

3 Wise people see danger and go to a
safe place.
But childish people keep going
and suffer for it.

4 Being humble comes from having
respect for the LORD.
This will bring you wealth and
honor and life.

5 Thorns and traps lie in the paths of
evil people.
But those who value their lives
stay far away from them.

6 Start children off on the right path.
And even when they are old, they
will not turn away from it.

7 Rich people rule over those who are
poor.
Borrowers are slaves to lenders.

8 Anyone who plants evil gathers a
harvest of trouble.
Their power to treat others badly
will be destroyed.

9 Those who give freely will be blessed.
That's because they share their
food with those who are poor.

10 If you drive away those who make
fun of others, fighting also goes
away.
Arguing and unkind words will
stop.

11 A person who has a pure and loving
heart and speaks kindly
will be a friend of the king.

12 The eyes of the LORD keep watch
over knowledge.
But he does away with the words
of those who aren't faithful.

13 People who don't want to work say,
"There's a lion outside!"
Or they say, "I'll be murdered if I
go out into the streets!"

14 The mouth of a woman who commits
adultery is like a deep pit.
Any man the LORD is angry with
falls into it.

15 Children are going to do foolish
things.
But correcting them will drive
that foolishness far away.

16 You might treat poor people badly
or give gifts to rich people.
Trying to get rich in these ways
will instead make you poor.

30 SAYINGS OF WISE PEOPLE

Saying 1

17 Pay attention and listen to the
sayings of wise people.
Apply your heart to the sayings I
teach.
18 It is pleasing when you keep them
in your heart.
Have all of them ready on your
lips.
19 You are the one I am teaching today.
That's because I want you to
trust in the LORD.
20 I have written 30 sayings for you.
They will give you knowledge
and good advice.
21 I am teaching you to be honest and
to speak the truth.
Then you can give honest reports
to those you serve.

Saying 2

22 Don't take advantage of poor people
just because they are poor.
Don't treat badly those who are
in need by taking them to
court.
23 The LORD will stand up for them in
court.
He will require the lives of people
who have taken the lives of
those in need.

Saying 3

24 Don't be a friend of a person who
has a bad temper.
Don't go around with a person
who gets angry easily.
25 You might learn their habits.
And then you will be trapped by
them.

Saying 4

26 Don't agree to pay for what
someone else owes.
And don't agree to pay their bills
for them.
27 If you don't have the money to pay,
your bed will be taken right out
from under you!

Saying 5

28 Don't move old boundary stones
set up by your people of long
ago.

Saying 6

29 Do you see someone who does good
work?
That person will serve kings.
That person won't serve officials
of lower rank.

Saying 7

23 When you sit down to eat with
a ruler,
look carefully at what's in front
of you.
2 Put a knife to your throat
if you like to eat too much.
3 Don't long for his fancy food.
It can fool you.

Saying 8

4 Don't wear yourself out to get rich.
Don't trust how wise you think
you are.
5 When you take even a quick look at
riches, they are gone.
They grow wings and fly away
into the sky like an eagle.

Saying 9

6 Don't eat the food of anyone who
doesn't want to share it.
Don't long for his fancy food.
7 He is the kind of person
who is always thinking about
how much it costs.
"Eat and drink," he says to you.
But he doesn't mean it.

[8] You will throw up what little you
have eaten.
You will have wasted your words
of praise.

Saying 10

[9] Don't speak to foolish people.
They will laugh at your wise
words.

Saying 11

[10] Don't move old boundary stones.
Don't try to take over the fields
of children whose fathers have
died.
[11] That's because the God who guards
them is strong.
He will stand up for them in court
against you.

Saying 12

[12] Apply your heart to what you are
taught.
Listen carefully to words of
knowledge.

Saying 13

[13] Don't hold back correction from a
child.
If you correct them, they won't
die.
[14] So correct them.
Then you will save them from
death.

Saying 14

[15] My son, if your heart is wise,
my heart will be very glad.
[16] Deep down inside, I will be happy
when you say what is right.

Saying 15

[17] Do not long for what sinners have.
But always show great respect
for the LORD.
[18] There really is hope for you in days
to come.
So your hope will not be cut off.

Saying 16

[19] My son, listen and be wise.
Set your heart on the right path.
[20] Don't join those who drink too
much wine.
Don't join those who stuff
themselves with meat.
[21] Those who drink or eat too much
will become poor.
If they sleep too much, they'll
have to wear rags.

Saying 17

[22] Listen to your father, who gave you
life.
Don't hate your mother when she
is old.
[23] Buy the truth and don't sell it.
Get wisdom, instruction and
understanding as well.
[24] The father of a godly child is very
happy.
A man who has a wise son is
glad.
[25] May your father and mother be
glad.
May the woman who gave birth
to you be joyful.

Saying 18

[26] My son, give me your heart.
May you be happy living the way
you see me live.
[27] An unfaithful wife is like a deep pit.
A wife who commits adultery is
like a narrow well.
[28] She hides and waits like a thief.
She causes many men to sin.

Saying 19

[29] Who has trouble? Who has sorrow?
Who argues? Who has problems?
Who has wounds for no reason?
Who has red eyes?
[30] Those who spend too much time
with wine.
Or those who like to taste wine
mixed with spices.
[31] Don't look at wine when it is red.
Don't look at it when it bubbles in
the cup.
And don't look at it when it goes
down smoothly.
[32] In the end it bites like a snake.
It bites like a poisonous serpent.
[33] Your eyes will see strange sights.
Your mind will imagine weird
things.
[34] You will feel like someone sleeping
on the ocean.
You will think you are lying
among the ropes in a boat.
[35] "They hit me," you will say. "But
I'm not hurt!
They beat me. But I don't feel it!
When will I wake up
so I can find another drink?"

Saying 20

24 Do not want what evil people have.
Don't long to be with them.
2 In their hearts they plan to hurt others.
With their lips they talk about making trouble.

Saying 21

3 By wisdom a house is built.
Through understanding it is made secure.
4 Through knowledge its rooms are filled
with priceless and beautiful things.

Saying 22

5 Wise people have success by means of great power.
Those who have knowledge gather strength.
6 If you go to war, you surely need guidance.
If you want to win, you need many good advisers.

Saying 23

7 Wisdom is too high for foolish people.
They shouldn't speak when people meet at the city gate to conduct business.

Saying 24

8 Anyone who thinks up sinful things to do
will be known as one who plans evil.
9 Foolish plans are sinful.
People hate those who make fun of others.

Saying 25

10 If you grow weak when trouble comes,
your strength is very small!
11 Save those who are being led away to death.
Hold back those who are about to be killed.
12 Don't say, "But we didn't know anything about this."
Doesn't the God who knows what you are thinking see it?
Doesn't the God who guards your life know it?
He will pay back everyone for what they have done.

Saying 26

13 Eat honey, my son, because it is good.
Honey from a honeycomb has a sweet taste.
14 I want you to know that wisdom is like honey for you.
If you find it, there is hope for you tomorrow.
So your hope will not be cut off.

Saying 27

15 Don't hide and wait like a burglar near a godly person's house.
Don't rob their home.
16 Even if godly people fall down seven times, they always get up.
But those who are evil trip and fall when trouble comes.

Saying 28

17 Don't be happy when your enemy falls.
When he trips, don't let your heart be glad.
18 The LORD will see it, but he won't be pleased.
He might turn his anger away from your enemy.

Saying 29

19 Don't be upset because of evil people.
Don't long for what sinners have.
20 Tomorrow evil people won't have any hope.
The lamps of sinners will be blown out.

Saying 30

21 My son, have respect for the LORD and the king.
Don't join with officials who disobey them.
22 The LORD and the king will suddenly destroy them.
Who knows what trouble those two can bring?

MORE SAYINGS OF WISE PEOPLE

23 Here are more sayings of wise people.

Taking sides in court is not good.
24 A curse will fall on those who say the guilty are not guilty.

Nations will ask for bad things to
happen to them.
People will speak against them.
25 But it will go well with those who
sentence guilty people.
Rich blessings will come to them.

26 An honest answer
is like a kiss on the lips.

27 Put your outdoor work in order.
Get your fields ready.
After that, build your house.

28 Don't be a witness against your
neighbor for no reason.
Would you use your lips to tell lies?
29 Don't say, "I'll do to them what
they have done to me.
I'll get even with them for what
they did."

30 I went past the field of someone
who didn't want to work.
I went past the vineyard of
someone who didn't have any
sense.
31 Thorns had grown up everywhere.
The ground was covered with
weeds.
The stone wall had fallen down.
32 I applied my heart to what I
observed.
I learned a lesson from what I saw.
33 You might sleep a little or take a
little nap.
You might even fold your hands
and rest.
34 Then you would be poor, as if
someone had robbed you.
You would have little, as if
someone had stolen from you.

MORE PROVERBS OF SOLOMON

25 These are more proverbs of
Solomon. They were gathered
together by the men of Hezekiah, the
king of Judah.

2 When God hides a matter, he gets
glory.
When kings figure out a matter,
they get glory.

3 The heavens are high and the earth
is deep.
In the same way, the minds of
kings are impossible to figure
out.

4 Remove the scum from the silver.
Then the master worker can
make something out of it.
5 Remove ungodly officials from
where the king is.
Then the king can make his
throne secure because of the
godliness around him.

6 Don't brag in front of the king.
Don't claim a place among his
great men.
7 Let the king say to you, "Come up
here."
That's better than for him to
shame you in front of his
nobles.

What you have seen with your own
eyes
8 don't bring too quickly to court.
What will you do in the end
if your neighbor puts you to
shame?

9 If you take your neighbor to court,
don't tell others any secrets you
promised to keep.
10 If you do, someone might hear it
and put you to shame.
And the charge against you will
stand.

11 The right ruling at the right time
is like golden apples in silver
jewelry.

12 A wise judge's warning to a
listening ear
is like a gold earring or jewelry
made of fine gold.

13 A messenger trusted by the one
who sends him
is like a drink cooled by snow at
harvest time.
He renews the spirit of his
master.

14 A person who brags about gifts
never given
is like wind and clouds that don't
produce rain.

15 If you are patient, you can win an
official over to your side.
And gentle words can break a
bone.

16 If you find honey, eat just enough.
If you eat too much of it, you will
throw up.

17 Don't go to your neighbor's home
very often.
If they see too much of you, they
will hate you.

18 A person who is a false witness
against a neighbor
is like a club, a sword or a sharp
arrow.

19 Trusting someone who is not
faithful when trouble comes
is like a broken tooth or a
disabled foot.

20 You may sing songs to a troubled
heart.
But that's like taking a coat away
on a cold day.
It's like pouring vinegar on a
wound.

21 If your enemy is hungry, give him
food to eat.
If he is thirsty, give him water to
drink.

22 By doing these things, you will pile
up burning coals on his head.
And the LORD will reward you.

23 Like a north wind that brings rain
you didn't expect
is a crafty tongue that brings
looks of shock.

24 It is better to live on a corner of a
roof
than to share a house with a
nagging wife.

25 Hearing good news from a land far
away
is like drinking cold water when
you are tired.

26 Sometimes godly people give in to
those who are evil.
Then they become like a muddy
spring of water or a polluted well.

27 It isn't good for you to eat too much
honey.
And you shouldn't try to search
out matters too deep for you.

28 A person without self-control
is like a city whose walls are
broken through.

26 It isn't proper to honor a
foolish person.
That's like having snow in
summer or rain at harvest time.

2 A curse given for no reason is like
a wandering bird or a flying
sparrow.
It doesn't go anywhere.

3 A whip is for a horse, and a harness
is for a donkey.
And a beating is for the backs of
foolish people.

4 Don't answer a foolish person in
keeping with their foolish acts.
If you do, you yourself will be
just like them.

5 Answer a foolish person in keeping
with their foolish acts.
If you do not, they will be wise in
their own eyes.

6 Sending a message in the hand of a
foolish person
is like cutting off your feet or
drinking poison.

7 A proverb in the mouth of a foolish
person
is like disabled legs that are
useless.

8 Giving honor to a foolish person
is like tying a stone in a
slingshot.

9 A proverb in the mouth of a foolish
person
is like a thorn in the hand of
someone who is drunk.

10 Anyone who hires a foolish person
or someone who is passing by
is like a person who shoots
arrows at just anybody.

11 Foolish people who do the same
foolish things again
are like a dog that returns to
where it has thrown up.

12 Do you see a person who is wise in
their own eyes?
There is more hope for a foolish
person than for them.

13 A person who doesn't want to work
says, "There's a lion in the road!
There's an angry lion wandering
in the streets!"

14 A person who doesn't want to work
turns over in bed
just like a door that swings back
and forth.

15 A person who doesn't want to work
leaves his hand in his plate.
He acts as if he is too tired to
bring his hand back up to his
mouth.

16 A person who doesn't want to work
is wiser in his own eyes
than seven people who give
careful answers.

17 Don't be quick to get mixed up in
someone else's fight.
That's like grabbing a stray dog
by its ears.

18 Suppose a crazy person shoots
flaming arrows that can kill.
19 Someone who lies to their neighbor
and says, "I was only joking!" is
just like that crazy person.

20 If you don't have wood, your fire
goes out.
If you don't talk about others,
arguing dies down.

21 Coal glows, and wood burns.
And a person who argues stirs up
conflict.

22 The words of anyone who talks
about others are like tasty bites
of food.
They go deep down inside you.

23 Warm words that come from an
evil heart
are like a shiny coating on a clay
pot.

24 Enemies use their words as a mask.
They hide their evil plans in their
hearts.
25 Even though what they say can be
charming, don't believe them.
That's because seven things God
hates fill that person's heart.
26 Their hatred can be hidden by lies.
But their evil plans will be shown
to everyone.

27 Whoever digs a pit will fall into it.
If someone rolls a big stone, it
will roll back on them.

28 A tongue that tells lies hates the
people it hurts.
And words that seem to praise
you destroy you.

27 Don't brag about tomorrow.
You don't know what a day
will bring.

2 Let another person praise you, and
not your own mouth.
Let an outsider praise you, and
not your own lips.

3 Stones are heavy, and sand weighs
a lot.
But letting a foolish person make
you angry is a heavier load
than both of them.

4 Anger is mean, and great anger
overpowers you.
But who can face jealousy?

5 Being warned openly is better
than being loved in secret.

6 Wounds from a friend can be trusted.
But an enemy kisses you many
times.

7 When you are full, you even hate
honey.
When you are hungry, even what
is bitter tastes sweet.

8 Anyone who runs away from home
is like a bird that flies away from
its nest.

9 Perfume and incense bring joy to
your heart.
And the sweetness of a friend
comes from their honest
advice.

10 Don't desert your friend or a friend
of your family.
And don't go to your relative's
house when trouble strikes you.
A neighbor nearby is better than
a relative far away.

11 My son, be wise and bring joy to
my heart.
Then I can answer anyone who
makes fun of me.

12 Wise people see danger and go to a
safe place.
But childish people keep on
going and suffer for it.

13 Take the coat of one who puts up
money for what a stranger
owes.
Hold it until you get paid back if
it is done for an outsider.

14 Suppose you loudly bless your
neighbor early in the morning.
Then you might as well be
cursing him.
15 A nagging wife is like the dripping
of a leaky roof in a rainstorm.
16 Stopping her is like trying to stop
the wind.
It's like trying to grab olive oil
with your hand.
17 As iron sharpens iron,
so one person sharpens another.

18 A person who guards a fig tree will
eat its fruit.
And a person who protects their
master will be honored.

19 When you look into water, you see
a likeness of your face.
When you look into your heart,
you see what you are really
like.

20 Death and the Grave are never
satisfied.
People's eyes are never satisfied
either.

21 Fire tests silver, and heat tests gold.
But people are tested by the
praise they receive.

22 Suppose you could grind a foolish
person in a mill.
Suppose you could grind them as
you would grind grain with a
tool.
Even then you could not remove
their foolishness from them.

23 Be sure you know how your flocks
are doing.
Pay careful attention to your herds.
24 Riches don't last forever.
And a crown is not secure for all
time to come.
25 The hay is removed, and new
growth appears.
The grass from the hills is
gathered in.
26 Then your lambs will provide you
with clothes.
And the money from selling your
goats will buy you a field.
27 You will have plenty of goats' milk
to feed your family.
It will also feed your female
servants.

28 Sinners run away even when
no one is chasing them.
But those who do what is right
are as bold as lions.

2 A country has many rulers when its
people don't obey.
But an understanding ruler
knows how to keep order.

3 A ruler who treats poor people
badly
is like a pounding rain that
leaves no crops.

4 Those who turn away from
instruction praise sinners.
But those who learn from it
oppose them.

5 Sinful people don't understand
what is right.
But those who worship the LORD
understand it completely.

6 It is better to be poor and live
without blame
than to be rich and follow a
crooked path.

7 A child who understands what is
right learns from instruction.
But a child who likes to eat too
much brings shame on his
father.

8 Someone might get rich by taking
interest or profit from poor
people.
But that person only piles up
wealth for someone who will be
kind to poor people.

9 If you don't pay attention to my
instruction,
even your prayers are hated.

10 Those who lead honest people
down an evil path
will fall into their own trap.
But those who are without blame
will receive good things.

11 Rich people may think they are
wise.
But a poor person with
understanding knows that rich
people are fooling themselves.

12 When godly people win, everyone
is very happy.
But when sinners take charge,
everyone hides.

[13]Anyone who hides their sins doesn't
succeed.
But anyone who admits their
sins and gives them up finds
mercy.
[14]Blessed is the one who always
trembles in front of God.
But anyone who makes their
heart stubborn will get into
trouble.
[15]An evil person who rules over
helpless people
is like a roaring lion or an angry
bear.
[16]A ruler who is mean to his people
takes money from them by
force.
But one who hates money gained
in the wrong way will rule a
long time.
[17]Anyone troubled by the guilt of
murder
will seek to escape their guilt by
death.
No one should keep them from it.
[18]Anyone who lives without blame is
kept safe.
But anyone whose path is
crooked will fall into the pit.
[19]Those who work their land will
have plenty of food.
But those who chase dreams will
be very poor.
[20]A faithful person will be richly
blessed.
But anyone who wants to get rich
will be punished.
[21]Favoring one person over another
is not good.
But a person will do wrong for a
piece of bread.
[22]Those who won't share what they
have want to get rich.
They don't know they are going
to be poor.
[23]It is better to warn a person than to
pretend to praise them.
In the end that person will be
more pleased with you.
[24]Anyone who steals from their parents
and says, "It's not wrong,"
is just like someone who destroys.
[25]People who always want more stir
up conflict.
But those who trust in the LORD
will succeed.
[26]Those who trust in themselves are
foolish.
But those who live wisely are
kept safe.
[27]Those who give to poor people will
have all they need.
But those who close their eyes
to the poor will receive many
curses.
[28]When those who are evil take
charge, other people hide.
But when those who are evil die,
godly people grow stronger.

29 Whoever still won't obey after
being warned many times
will suddenly be destroyed.
Nothing can save them.
[2]When those who do right grow
stronger, the people are glad.
But when those who do wrong
become rulers, the people
groan.
[3]A man who loves wisdom makes
his father glad.
But a man who spends time with
prostitutes wastes his father's
wealth.
[4]By doing what is fair, a king makes
a country secure.
But those who only want money
tear it down.
[5]Those who only pretend to praise
their neighbors
are spreading a net to catch
them by the feet.
[6]Sinful people are trapped by their
own sin.
But godly people shout for joy
and are glad.
[7]Those who do what is right want to
treat poor people fairly.
But those who do what is wrong
don't care about the poor.
[8]Those who make fun of others stir
up a city.
But wise people turn anger away.

9 Suppose a wise person goes to court
with a foolish person.
Then the foolish person gets mad
and pokes fun, and there is no
peace.

10 Murderers hate honest people.
They try to kill those who do
what is right.

11 Foolish people let their anger run
wild.
But wise people keep themselves
under control.

12 If rulers listen to lies,
all their officials become evil.

13 The LORD gives sight to the eyes
of poor people and those who
treat others badly.
That's what they both have in
common.

14 If a king judges poor people fairly,
his throne will always be secure.

15 If a child is corrected, they become
wise.
But a child who is not corrected
brings shame to their mother.

16 When those who do wrong grow
stronger, so does sin.
But those who do right will see
them destroyed.

17 If you correct your children, they
will give you peace.
They will bring you the delights
you desire.

18 Where there is no message from
God, people don't control
themselves.
But blessed is the one who obeys
wisdom's instruction.

19 Servants can't be corrected only by
words.
Even if they understand, they
won't obey.

20 Have you seen someone who
speaks without thinking?
There is more hope for foolish
people than for that person.

21 A servant who has been spoiled
from youth
will have no respect for you
later on.

22 An angry person stirs up fights.
And a person with a bad temper
commits many sins.

23 Pride brings a person low.
But those whose spirits are low
will be honored.

24 To help a thief is to become your
own enemy.
When you go to court, you won't
dare to say anything.

25 If you are afraid of people, it will
trap you.
But if you trust in the LORD, he
will keep you safe.

26 Many people want to meet a ruler.
But only the LORD sees that
people are treated fairly.

27 Those who do what is right hate
dishonest people.
Those who do what is wrong hate
honest people.

THE SAYINGS OF AGUR

30 These sayings are the words
of Agur, son of Jakeh. These
sayings came from God.

This man said to Ithiel:

"I am weary, God.
But I can still have success.
2 Surely I am only a dumb animal
and not a man.
I don't understand as other men do.
3 I haven't learned wisdom.
And I don't know the things the
Holy One knows.
4 Who has gone up to heaven and
come down?
Whose hands have gathered up
the wind?
Who has wrapped up the waters in
a coat?
Who has set in place all the
boundaries of the earth?
What is his name? What is his son's
name?
Surely you know!

5 "Every word of God is perfect.
He is like a shield to those who
trust in him.
He keeps them safe.
6 Don't add to his words.
If you do, he will correct you.
He will prove that you are a liar.

7 "LORD, I ask you for two things.
Don't refuse me before I die.
8 Keep lies far away from me.
Don't make me either poor or rich,
but give me only the bread I need
each day.
9 If you don't, I might have too much.
Then I might say I don't know
you.
I might say, 'Who is the LORD?'
Or I might become poor and steal.
Then I would bring shame to the
name of my God.

10 "Don't tell lies about a servant
when you talk to their master.
If you do, they will curse you,
and you will pay for your lies.

11 "Some people curse their fathers.
Others don't bless their mothers.
12 Some are pure in their own eyes.
But their dirty sins haven't been
washed away.
13 Some have eyes that are very proud.
They look down on others.
14 Some people have teeth like
swords.
The teeth in their jaws are as
sharp as knives.
They are ready to eat up the poor
people of the earth.
They are ready to eat up those
who are the most needy.

15 "A leech has two daughters.
They cry out, 'Give! Give!'

"Three things are never satisfied.
Four things never say, 'Enough!'
16 The first is the grave.
The second is a woman who
can't have a baby.
The third is land, which never
gets enough water.
And the fourth is fire, which
never says, 'Enough!'

17 "One person makes fun of their
father.
Another doesn't honor their
mother when she is old.
The ravens of the valley will peck
out their eyes.
Then the vultures will eat them.

18 "Three things are too amazing
for me.
There are four things I don't
understand.
19 The first is the way of an eagle
in the sky.
The second is the way of a
snake on a rock.
The third is the way of a ship
on the ocean.
And the fourth is the way of a
man with a young woman.

PURE

There are no flaws in God's character or nature. He is flawless and pure (see 1 John 3:3). Here's an example: When we talk about a substance like gold being pure, we mean that it is 100 percent gold; there is nothing in it that would make it cloudy or impure. This is how it is with God, except that we're not talking about gold but about righteous character.

God is pure in his character, which means he has no faults. God never has sinned, and we can trust that he never will sin. God's purity sets the standard of righteousness in our lives and makes Jesus the perfect sacrifice for our sin.

MY GOD IS...

20 "This is the way of a woman who
commits adultery.
She eats and wipes her mouth.
Then she says, 'I haven't done
anything wrong.'

21 "Under three things the earth
shakes.
Under four things it can't
stand up.
22 The first is a servant who
becomes a king.
The second is a foolish and
ungodly person who gets
plenty to eat.
23 The third is a mean woman
who gets married.
And the fourth is a servant
who takes the place of the
woman she works for.

24 "Four things on earth are small.
But they are very wise.
25 The first are ants, which aren't
very strong.
But they store up their food in
the summer.
26 The second are hyraxes, which
aren't very powerful.
But they make their home
among the rocks.
27 The third are locusts, which
don't have a king.
But they all march forward in
ranks.
28 And the fourth are lizards,
which your hand can catch.
But you will find them in
kings' palaces.

29 "Three things walk as if they were
kings.
Four things move as kings do.
30 The first is a lion, which is
mighty among the animals.
It doesn't back away from
anything.
31 The second is a rooster, which
walks proudly.
The third is a billy goat.
And the fourth is a king, who is
secure against any who might
oppose him.

32 "Do you do foolish things?
Do you think you are better than
others?
Do you plan evil?
If you do, put your hand over
your mouth and stop talking!
33 If you churn cream, you will
produce butter.
If you twist a nose, you will
produce blood.
And if you stir up anger, you will
produce a fight."

THE SAYINGS OF KING LEMUEL

31 These are the sayings of King
Lemuel. His mother taught them
to him. These sayings came from God.

2 Listen, my son! Listen, my very own
son!
Listen, you who are the answer to
my prayers!
3 Don't waste your strength on
women.
Don't waste it on those who
destroy kings.

4 Lemuel, it isn't good for kings to
drink wine.
It isn't good for rulers to long for
beer.
5 If they do, they might drink
and forget what has been
commanded.
They might take away the rights
of all those who are treated
badly.
6 Let beer be for those who are dying.
Let wine be for those who are sad
and troubled.
7 Let them drink and forget how poor
they are.
Let them forget their suffering.
8 Speak up for those who can't speak
for themselves.
Speak up for the rights of all
those who are poor.
9 Speak up and judge fairly.
Speak up for the rights of those
who are poor and needy.

THE EXCELLENT WOMAN

10 Who can find an excellent woman?
She is worth far more than
rubies.
11 Her husband trusts her completely.
She gives him all the important
things he needs.
12 She brings him good, not harm,
all the days of her life.

13 She chooses wool and flax.
She loves to work with her hands.
14 She is like the ships of traders.
She brings her food from far away.
15 She gets up while it is still night.
She provides food for her family.
She also gives some to her female servants.
16 She considers a field and buys it.
She uses some of the money she earns to plant a vineyard.
17 She gets ready to work hard.
Her arms are strong.
18 She sees that her trading earns a lot of money.
Her lamp doesn't go out at night.
19 With one hand she holds the wool.
With the other she spins the thread.
20 She opens her arms to those who are poor.
She reaches out her hands to those who are needy.
21 When it snows, she's not afraid for her family.
All of them are dressed in the finest clothes.
22 She makes her own bed coverings.
She is dressed in fine linen and purple clothes.
23 Her husband is respected at the city gate.
There he takes his seat among the elders of the land.
24 She makes linen clothes and sells them.
She supplies belts to the traders.
25 She puts on strength and honor as if they were her clothes.
She can laugh at the days that are coming.
26 She speaks wisely.
She teaches faithfully.
27 She watches over family matters.
She is busy all the time.
28 Her children stand up and call her blessed.
Her husband also rises up, and he praises her.
29 He says, "Many women do excellent things.
But you are better than all the others."
30 Charm can fool you. Beauty fades.
But a woman who has respect for the LORD should be praised.
31 Give her honor for all that her hands have done.
Let everything she has done bring praise to her at the city gate.

ECCLESIASTES

Author: We don't know (but it might be King Solomon).

Ecclesiastes is a long poem written by someone called "the Teacher." He had experienced a lot in his life and yet felt empty. It's as though the author of this book looked around and thought, "Everything is the same! Nothing ever changes!" The author used the example of farming to make his point. Farmers, he said, plant seeds every year. They work hard to water those seeds, and they patiently wait for their crops to grow. Finally, the crops are ready for harvest, so the farmers pick their crops. Then what? They have to start all over again the next year! The author laments, or says in a sad way, that everything is always the same; nothing seems to change. There's just more work to be done.

Wisdom & Poetry

Ecclesiastes teaches us that while there are things in this life that can be enjoyed, nothing in this world can satisfy our deepest longings. The best thing we can do with our life is to trust God, follow his commands, and enjoy the good things he gives us.

In calling humans to live in relationship with God and enjoy his gifts, the Teacher points us back to the Garden of Eden before sin and forward to the Marriage Supper of the Lamb, when we will once again dine with our Lord in heaven.

Everything Is Meaningless

1 These are the words of the Teacher. He was the son of David. He was also the king in Jerusalem.

2 "Meaningless! Everything is
meaningless!"
says the Teacher.
"Everything is completely
meaningless!
Nothing has any meaning."

3 What do people get for all their work?
Why do they work so hard on this
earth?
4 People come and people go.
But the earth remains forever.
5 The sun rises. Then it sets.
And then it hurries back to where
it rises.
6 The wind blows to the south.
Then it turns to the north.
Around and around it goes.
It always returns to where it
started.
7 Every stream flows into the ocean.
But the ocean never gets full.
The streams return
to the place they came from.
8 All things are tiresome.
They are more tiresome than
anyone can say.
But our eyes never see enough of
anything.
Our ears never hear enough.
9 Everything that has ever been will
come back again.
Everything that has ever been
done will be done again.
Nothing is new on earth.
10 There isn't anything about which
someone can say,
"Look! Here's something new."
It was already here long ago.
It was here before we were.
11 No one remembers the people of
long ago.
Even those who haven't been
born yet
won't be remembered
by those who will be born after
them.

Wisdom Is Meaningless

12 I, the Teacher, was king over Israel
in Jerusalem. 13 I decided to study things
carefully. I used my wisdom to check
everything out. I looked into everything
that is done on earth. What a heavy
load God has put on human beings!
14 I've seen what is done on this earth.
All of it is meaningless. It's like chasing
the wind.

15 People can't straighten things that
are crooked.
They can't count things that
don't even exist.

16 I said to myself, "Look, I've now
grown wiser than anyone who ruled
over Jerusalem in the past. I have a
lot of wisdom and knowledge." 17 Then
I used my mind to understand what it
really means to be wise. And I wanted
to know what foolish pleasure is all
about. But I found out that it's also like
chasing the wind.

18 A lot of human wisdom leads to a
lot of sorrow.
More knowledge only brings
more sadness.

Pleasure Is Meaningless

2 I said to myself, "Come on. I'll try
out pleasure. I want to find out if it
is good." But it also proved to be meaningless. 2 "Laughter doesn't make any
sense," I said. "And what can pleasure
do for me?" 3 I tried cheering myself up
by drinking wine. I even tried living in a
foolish way. But wisdom was still guiding my mind. I wanted to see what was
good for people to do on earth during
their short lives.

4 So I started some large projects. I
built houses for myself. I planted vineyards. 5 I made gardens and parks. I

in Ecclesiastes?

God is the Gift Giver. God gives his people good gifts to enjoy as they live in relationship with him.

planted all kinds of fruit trees in them.
6 I made lakes to water groves of healthy
trees. 7 I bought male and female slaves.
And I had other slaves who were born
in my house. I also owned more herds
and flocks than anyone in Jerusalem
ever had before. 8 I stored up silver and
gold for myself. I gathered up the treasures of kings and their kingdoms. I got
some male and female singers. I also
got many women for myself. Women
delight the hearts of men. 9 I became
far more important than anyone in
Jerusalem had ever been before. And
in spite of everything, I didn't lose my
wisdom.

10 I gave myself everything my eyes
wanted.
There wasn't any pleasure that I
refused to give myself.
I took delight in everything I did.
And that was what I got for all
my work.
11 But then I looked over everything
my hands had done.
I saw what I had worked so hard
to get.
And nothing had any meaning.
It was like chasing the wind.
Nothing was gained on this
earth.

Wisdom and Foolish Pleasure Are Meaningless

12 I decided to think about wisdom.
I also thought about foolish
pleasure.
What more can a new king do?
Can he do anything more than
others have already done?
13 I saw that wisdom is better than
foolishness,
just as light is better than
darkness.
14 The eyes of a wise person see things
clearly.
A person who is foolish lives in
darkness.
But I finally realized that death
catches up
with both of them.

15 Then I said to myself,
"What happens to a foolish person
will catch up with me too.
So what do I gain by being wise?"
I said to myself,
"That doesn't have any meaning
either."
16 Like a foolish person, a wise person
won't be remembered very
long.
The days have already come
when both of them have been
forgotten.
Like a person who is foolish,
a wise person must die too!

Work Is Meaningless

17 So I hated life. That's because the
work done on this earth made me sad.
None of it has any meaning. It's like
chasing the wind. 18 I hated everything
I had worked for on earth. I'll have to
leave all of it to someone who lives after
me. 19 And who knows whether that person will be wise or foolish? Either way,
they'll take over everything on earth
I've worked so hard for. That doesn't
have any meaning either. 20 So I began
to lose hope because of all my hard
work on this earth. 21 A person might
use wisdom, knowledge and skill to
do their work. But then they have to
leave everything they own to someone
who hasn't worked for it. That doesn't
have any meaning either. In fact, it isn't
fair. 22 What do people get for all their
hard work on earth? What do they get

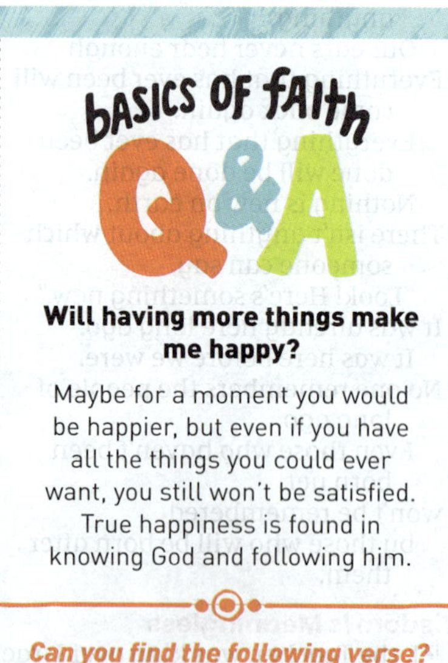

Will having more things make me happy?

Maybe for a moment you would be happier, but even if you have all the things you could ever want, you still won't be satisfied. True happiness is found in knowing God and following him.

Can you find the following verse?
ECCLESIASTES 2:11

for all their worries? [23]As long as they live, their work is nothing but pain and sorrow. Even at night their minds can't rest. That doesn't have any meaning either.

[24]A person can't do anything better than eat, drink and be satisfied with their work. I'm finally seeing that those things also come from the hand of God. [25]Without his help, who can eat or find pleasure? [26]God gives wisdom, knowledge and happiness to the person who pleases him. But to a sinner he gives the task of gathering and storing up wealth. Then the sinner must hand it over to the one who pleases God. That doesn't have any meaning either. It's like chasing the wind.

There Is a Time for Everything

3 There is a time for everything.
There's a time for everything
that is done on earth.

[2]There is a time to be born.
And there's a time to die.
There is a time to plant.
And there's a time to pull up
what is planted.
[3]There is a time to kill.
And there's a time to heal.
There is a time to tear down.
And there's a time to build up.
[4]There is a time to weep.
And there's a time to laugh.
There is a time to be sad.
And there's a time to dance.
[5]There is a time to scatter stones.
And there's a time to gather
them.
There is a time to embrace
someone.
And there's a time not to
embrace.
[6]There is a time to search.
And there's a time to stop
searching.
There is a time to keep.
And there's a time to throw
away.
[7]There is a time to tear.
And there's a time to mend.
There is a time to be silent.
And there's a time to speak.
[8]There is a time to love.
And there's a time to hate.
There is a time for war.
And there's a time for peace.

[9]What do workers get for their hard
work? [10]I've seen the heavy load God
has put on human beings. [11]He has
made everything beautiful in its time.
He has also given people a sense of
who he is. But they can't completely
understand what God has done from
beginning to end. [12]People should be
happy and do good while they live. I
know there's nothing better for them
to do than that. [13]Each of them should
eat and drink. People should be satisfied
with all their hard work. That is God's
gift to them. [14]I know that everything
God does will last forever. Nothing can
be added to it. And nothing can be taken
from it. God does that so people will
have respect for him.

[15]Everything that now exists has
already been.
And what is coming has existed
before.
God will judge those who treat
others badly.

[16]Here's something else I saw on earth.

Where people should be treated
right,
they are treated wrong.
Where people should be treated
fairly,
they are treated unfairly.

[17]I said to myself,

"God will judge
godly and sinful people alike.
He has a time for every act.
He has a time to judge
everything that is done."

[18]I also said to myself, "God tests human beings. He does this so they can see
that in certain ways they are like animals. [19]Surely what happens to animals
happens to people too. Death waits for
people and animals alike. People die,
just as animals do. All of them have the
same breath. People don't have any advantage over animals. Nothing has any
meaning. [20]People and animals go to
the same place. All of them come from
dust. And all of them return to dust.
[21]Who can know whether the spirit of
a person goes up? Who can tell whether
the spirit of an animal goes down into
the earth?"

22 So a person should enjoy their work. That's what God made them for. I saw that there's nothing better for them to do than that. After all, who can show them what will happen after they are gone?

Suffering, Hard Work and No Friends

4 I looked and saw how much people were suffering on this earth.

I saw the tears of those who are suffering.
They don't have anyone to comfort them.
Power is on the side of those who treat them badly.
Those who are suffering don't have anyone to comfort them.
2 Then I announced that those who have already died
are happier than those who are still alive.
3 But someone who hasn't been born yet
is better off than the dead or the living.
That's because that person hasn't seen the evil things
that are done on earth.

4 I also saw that a person works hard and accomplishes a lot. But they do it only because they want what another person has. That doesn't have any meaning either. It's like chasing the wind.

5 Foolish people fold their hands and don't work.
And that destroys them.
6 One handful with peace and quiet
is better than two handfuls with hard work.
Working too hard is like chasing the wind.

7 Again I saw something on earth that didn't mean anything.

8 A man lived all by himself.
He didn't have any sons or brothers.
His hard work never ended.
But he wasn't happy with what he had.
"Who am I working so hard for?" he asked.
"Why don't I get the things I enjoy?"
That doesn't have any meaning either.
In fact, it's a very bad deal!

9 Two people are better than one.
They can help each other in everything they do.
10 Suppose either of them falls down.
Then the one can help the other one up.
But suppose a person falls down
and doesn't have anyone to help them up.
Then feel sorry for that person!
11 Or suppose two people lie down together.
Then they'll keep warm.
But how can one person keep warm alone?
12 One person could be overpowered.
But two people can stand up for themselves.
And a rope made out of three cords isn't easily broken.

Getting Ahead Is Meaningless

13 A poor but wise young man is better
off than an old but foolish king. That
king doesn't pay attention to a warning
anymore. 14 The young man might have
come from prison to become king. Or he
might have been born poor within the
kingdom but still became king. 15 I saw
that everyone was following the young
man who had become the new king. 16 At
first, all the people served him when he
became king. But those who came later
weren't pleased with the way he was
ruling. That doesn't have any meaning
either. It's like chasing the wind.

Keep Your Promise to God

5 Be careful what you say when you go to God's house. Go there to listen. Don't be like foolish people when you offer your sacrifice. They do what is wrong and don't even know it.

2 Don't be too quick to speak.
Don't be in a hurry to say anything to God.
God is in heaven. You are on earth.
So use only a few words when you speak.
3 Many worries result in dreams.
Many words result in foolish talk.

4 When you make a promise to God,
don't wait too long to carry it out. He
isn't pleased with foolish people. So
do what you have promised. 5 It is not
good to make a promise and not keep
it. It is better to make no promise at all.

[6] Don't let your mouth cause you to sin. Don't say to the temple messenger, "My promise was a mistake." Why should God be angry with what you say? Why should he destroy what you have done?
[7] Dreaming too much and talking too much are meaningless. So have respect for God.

Riches Are Meaningless

[8] Suppose you see poor people being mistreated somewhere. And what is being done to them isn't right or fair. Don't be surprised by that. One official is watched by a higher one. Officials who are even higher are watching both of
them. [9] All of them take what the land produces. And the king himself takes his share from the fields.

[10] Anyone who loves money never
has enough.
Anyone who loves wealth is never
satisfied with what they get.
That doesn't have any meaning
either.

[11] As more and more goods are made,
more and more people use
them up.
So how can those goods benefit
their owners?
All they can do is look at them
with desire.

[12] The sleep of a worker is sweet.
It doesn't matter whether they
eat a little or a lot.
But the wealth of rich people
keeps them awake at night.

[13] I've seen something very evil on earth.

It's when wealth is stored up
and then brings harm to its
owners.
[14] It's also when wealth is lost
because of an unwise business
deal.
Then there won't be anything left
for the owners' children.
[15] Everyone is born naked.
They come into the world with
nothing.
And they go out of it with
nothing.
They don't get anything from their
work
that they can take with them.

[16] Here's something else that is very evil.

Everyone is born, and everyone
dies.
And what do they get for their
work?
Nothing. It's like working for the
wind.
[17] All their lives they eat in darkness.
Their lives are full of trouble,
suffering and anger.

[18] I have seen what is good. It is good for a person to eat and drink. It's good for them to be satisfied with their hard work on this earth. That's what they should do during the short life God has given them. That's what God
made them for. [19] Sometimes God gives a person wealth and possessions. God makes it possible for that person to enjoy them. God helps them accept the life he has given them. God helps them to be happy in their work. All these things
are gifts from God. [20] A person like that doesn't have to think about how their life is going. That's because God fills their heart with joy.

6 I've seen another evil thing on this earth. And it's a heavy load on human beings. [2] God gives some people wealth, possessions and honor. They have everything their hearts desire. But God doesn't let them enjoy those things. Instead, strangers enjoy them. This doesn't have any meaning. It's a very evil thing.
[3] A man might have a hundred children. He might live a long time. But suppose he can't enjoy his wealth. And suppose he isn't buried in the proper way. Then it doesn't matter how long he lives. I'm telling you that a baby that is born dead is better off than that man
is. [4] That kind of birth doesn't have any meaning. The baby dies in darkness and leaves this world. And in darkness
it is forgotten. [5] It didn't even see the sun. It didn't know anything at all. But it has more rest than that man does.
[6] And that's true even if he lives for 2,000 years but doesn't get to enjoy his wealth. All people die and go to the grave, don't they?

[7] People eat up everything they work
to get.
But they are never satisfied.

8 What advantage do wise people have
over those who are foolish?
What do poor people gain
by knowing how to act toward
others?
9 Being satisfied with what you have
is better than always wanting
more.
That doesn't have any meaning
either.
It's like chasing the wind.

10 God has already planned what now
exists.
He has already decided what a
human being is.
No one can argue with someone
who is stronger.
11 The more words people use,
the less meaning there is.
And that doesn't help anyone.

12 Who knows what's good for a person? They live for only a few meaningless days. They pass through life like a
shadow. Who can tell them what will
happen on earth after they are gone?

Good Advice About How to Live

7 A good name is better than fine
perfume.
People can learn more from
mourning when someone dies
than from being happy when
someone is born.
2 So it's better to go where people are
mourning
than to go where people are
having a good time.
Everyone will die someday.
Those who are still living
should really think about that.
3 Not being able to figure things out
is better than laughter.
That's because sorrow is good for
the heart.
4 Those who are wise are found
where there is sorrow.
But foolish people are found
where there is pleasure.
5 Pay attention to a wise person's
warning.
That's better than listening to the
songs of those who are foolish.
6 A foolish person's laughter
is like the crackling of thorns
burning under a pot.
That doesn't have any meaning
either.

7 When a wise person takes wealth
by force, they become foolish.
It is sinful to take money from
people who want special favors.
8 The end of a matter is better than
its beginning.
So it's better to be patient than
proud.
9 Don't become angry quickly.
Anger lives in the hearts of
foolish people.

10 Don't say, "Why were things better
in the good old days?"
It isn't wise to ask that kind of
question.

11 Wisdom is a good thing.
It's like getting a share of the
family wealth.
It benefits those who live on this
earth.
12 Wisdom provides safety,
just as money provides safety.
But here's the advantage of wisdom.
It guards those who have it.

13 Think about what God has done.

Who can make straight
what he has made crooked?
14 When times are good, be happy.
But when times are bad, here's
something to think about.
God has made bad times.
He has also made good times.
So no one can find out anything
about what's ahead for them.

15 In my meaningless life here's what
I've seen.

I've seen godly people dying
even though they are godly.
And I've seen sinful people living a
long time
even though they are sinful.
16 Don't claim to be better than you are.
And don't claim to be wiser than
you are.
Why destroy yourself?
17 Don't be too sinful.
And don't be foolish.
Why die before your time comes?
18 It's good to hold on to both of those
things.
Don't let go of either one.
Whoever has respect for God will
avoid
going too far in either direction.

19 Wisdom makes one wise person
more powerful
than ten rulers in a city.
20 It is true that there isn't anyone on
earth
who does only what is right and
never sins.

21 Don't pay attention to everything
people say.
If you do, you might hear your
servant cursing you.
22 Many times you yourself have
cursed others.
Deep down inside, you know
that's true.

23 I used wisdom to test all these things.
I said,

"I've made up my mind to be wise."
But it was more than I could
accomplish.
24 Whatever exists is far away and
very deep.
Who can find it?
25 So I tried to understand wisdom
more completely.
I wanted to study it and figure it
out.
I tried to find out everything I
could about it.
I tried to understand why it's
foolish to be evil.
I wanted to see why choosing
foolishness is so unwise.

26 A woman who hunts a man down
is more painful than death.
Her heart is like a trap.
Her hands are like chains.
A man who pleases God will try to
get away from her.
But she will trap a sinner.

27 "Look," says the Teacher. "Here's
what I've discovered.

"I added one thing to another to
find out
everything I could about wisdom.
28 I searched and searched
but found very little.
I did find one honest man among a
thousand.
But I didn't find one honest
woman among a thousand.
29 Here's the only other thing I found.
God created human beings as
honest.
But they've made many evil plans."

8 Who is like a wise person?
Who knows how to explain
things?
A person's wisdom makes their face
bright.
It softens the look on their face.

Obey the King

2 I'm telling you to obey the king's
command. You promised to serve him.
You made a promise to God. 3 Don't be
in a hurry to quit your job in the palace.
Don't stand up for something the king
doesn't like. He'll do anything he wants
to. 4 The king has the final word. So who
can ask him, "What are you doing?"

5 No one who obeys his command
will be harmed.
Those who are wise will know
the proper time and way to
approach him.
6 There's a proper time and way for
people to do everything.
That's true even though a person
might be suffering greatly.

7 No one knows what lies ahead.
So who can tell someone else
what's going to happen?
8 No one can stop the wind from
blowing.
And no one has the power to
decide when they will die.
No one is let out of the army in
times of war.
And evil won't let go of those who
practice it.

9 I understood all these things. I used
my mind to study everything that's
done on earth. A man sometimes
makes life hard for others. But he ends
up hurting himself. 10 I also saw sinful
people being buried. They used to come
and go from the place of worship. And
others praised them in the city where
they worshiped. That doesn't have any
meaning either.

11 Sometimes the sentence for a crime
isn't carried out quickly. So people make
plans to commit even more crimes. 12 An
evil person may be guilty of a hundred
crimes. Yet they may still live a long
time. But I know that things will go better with those who have great respect for
God. 13 Sinful people don't respect God.
So things won't go well with them. Like a
shadow, they won't be around very long.

14 Here's something else on this earth
that doesn't have any meaning. Sometimes godly people get what sinful people should receive. And sinful people
get what godly people should receive.
Here's what I'm telling you. That doesn't
have any meaning either. 15 So I advise
everyone to enjoy life. A person on this
earth can't do anything better than eat
and drink and be glad. Then they will
enjoy their work. They'll be happy all
the days of the life God has given them
on earth.
16 I used my mind to understand what
it really means to be wise. I wanted to
observe the hard work people do on
earth. They don't close their eyes and go
to sleep day or night. 17 I saw everything
God has done. No one can understand
what happens on earth. People might
try very hard to figure it out. But they
still can't discover what it all means.
Wise people might claim they know. But
they can't really understand it either.

Everyone Dies

9 I thought about all these things.
I realized that those who are wise
and do what is right are under God's
control. What they do is also under his
control. But no one knows whether they
will be loved or hated. 2 Everyone will
die someday. Death comes to godly and
sinful people alike. It comes to good and
bad people alike. It comes to "clean"
and "unclean" people alike. Those who
offer sacrifices and those who don't offer
them also die.

A good person dies,
  and so does a sinner.
Those who make promises die.
  So do those who are afraid to
    make them.

3 Here's what is so bad about everything that happens on this earth. Death
catches up with all of us. Also, the hearts
of people are full of evil. They live in
foolish pleasure. After that, they join
those who have already died. 4 Anyone
who is still living has hope. Even a live
dog is better off than a dead lion!

5 People who are still alive know
    they'll die.
  But those who have died don't
    know anything.
They don't receive any more
    rewards.
  And even their name is forgotten.
6 Their love, hate and jealousy
    disappear.
  They will never share again
  in anything that happens on
    earth.

7 Go and enjoy your food. Be joyful as
you drink your wine. God has already
approved what you do. 8 Always wear
white clothes to show you are happy.
Anoint your head with olive oil. 9 You
love your wife. So enjoy life with her.
Do it all the days of this meaningless
life God has given you on earth. That's
what he made you for. That's what you
get for all your hard work on earth. 10 No
matter what you do, work at it with all
your might. Remember, you are going
to the place of the dead. And there isn't
any work or planning or knowledge or
wisdom there.
11 Here's something else I've seen on
this earth.

Races aren't always won by those
    who run fast.
  Battles aren't always won by
    those who are strong.
Wise people don't always have
    plenty of food.
  Clever people aren't always
    wealthy.
  Those who have learned a lot
    aren't always successful.
God controls the timing of every
    event.
  He also controls how things turn
    out.

12 No one knows when trouble will
come to them.

Fish are caught in nets.
  Birds are taken in traps.
And people are trapped by hard
    times
  that come when they don't
    expect them.

Being Wise Is Better Than Being Foolish

13 Here's something else I saw on this
earth. I saw an example of wisdom that
touched me deeply. 14 There was once a
small city. Only a few people lived there.
A powerful king attacked it. He brought

in war machines all around it. [15] A certain man lived in that city. He was poor
but wise. He used his wisdom to save the
city. But no one remembered that poor
man. [16] So I said, "It's better to be wise
than to be powerful." But people look
down on the poor man's wisdom. No
one pays any attention to what he says.

[17] People should listen to the quiet
words
of those who are wise.
That's better than paying attention
to the shouts
of a ruler of foolish people.
[18] Wisdom is better than weapons of
war.
But one sinner destroys a lot of
good.

10 Dead flies give perfume a bad
smell.
And a little foolishness can make
a lot of wisdom useless.
[2] The hearts of wise people lead
them on the right path.
But the hearts of foolish people
take them down the wrong
path.
[3] Foolish people don't have any sense
at all.
They show everyone they are
foolish.
They do it even when they are
walking along the road.
[4] Suppose a ruler gets very angry
with you.
If he does, don't quit your job in
the palace.
Being calm can overcome what
you have done against him.

[5] Here's something evil I've seen on
this earth.
And it's the kind of mistake that
rulers make.
[6] Foolish people are given many
important jobs.
Rich people are given
unimportant ones.
[7] I've seen slaves on horseback.
I've also seen princes who were
forced to walk as if they were
slaves.

[8] Anyone who digs a pit might fall
into it.
Anyone who breaks through a
wall might be bitten by a snake.
[9] Anyone who removes stones from
rock pits might get hurt.
Anyone who cuts logs might get
wounded.

[10] Suppose the blade of an ax is dull.
And its edge hasn't been
sharpened.
Then more effort is needed to
use it.
But skill will bring success.

[11] Suppose a snake bites before it is
charmed.
Then the snake charmer receives
no payment.

[12] Wise people say gracious things.
But foolish people are destroyed
by what their own lips speak.
[13] At first what they say is foolish.
In the end their words are very
evil.
[14] They talk too much.

No one knows what lies ahead.
Who can tell someone else what
will happen after they are
gone?

[15] The work foolish people do makes
them tired.
They don't even know the way to
town.

[16] How terrible it is for a land whose
king used to be a servant!
How terrible if its princes get
drunk in the morning!
[17] How blessed is the land whose
king was born into the royal
family!
How blessed if its princes eat and
drink at the proper time!
How blessed if they eat and drink
to become strong and not to get
drunk!

[18] When a person won't work, the roof
falls down.
Because of hands that aren't
busy, the house leaks.

[19] People laugh at a dinner party.
And wine makes life happy.
People think money can buy
everything.

[20] Don't say bad things about the
king.
Don't even think about those
things.

Don't curse rich people.
Don't even curse them in your bedroom.
A bird might fly away and carry your words.
It might report what you said.

Do Many Things to Succeed

11 Sell your grain in the market overseas.
After a while you might earn something from it.
2 Try to succeed by doing many things.
After all, you don't know what great trouble might come on the land.

3 Clouds that are full of water pour rain down on the earth.
A tree might fall to the south or the north.
It will stay in the place where it falls.
4 Anyone who keeps on watching the wind won't plant seeds.
Anyone who keeps looking at the clouds won't gather crops.
5 You don't know the path the wind takes.
You don't know how a baby is made inside its mother.
So you can't understand how God works either.
He made everything.
6 In the morning plant your seeds.
In the evening keep your hands busy.
You don't know what will succeed.
It may be one or the other.
Or both might do equally well.

Remember Your Creator While You Are Young

7 Light is sweet.
People enjoy being out in the sun.
8 No matter how many years anyone might live,
let them enjoy all of them.
But let them remember the dark days.
There will be many of those.
Nothing that's going to happen will have any meaning.

9 You young people, be happy while you are still young.
Let your heart be joyful while you are still strong.
Do what your heart tells you to do.
Go after what your eyes look at.
But I want you to know that God will judge you for everything you do.
10 So drive worry out of your heart.
Get rid of all your troubles.
Being young and strong doesn't have any meaning.

12 Remember your Creator.
Remember him while you are still young.
Think about him before your times of trouble come.
The years will come when you will say,
"I don't find any pleasure in them."

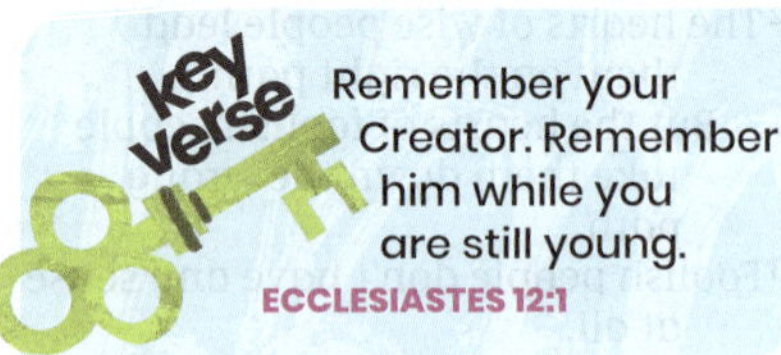

2 That's when the sunlight will become dark.
The moon and the stars will also grow dark.
And the clouds will return after it rains.
3 Remember your Creator before those who guard the house tremble with old age.
That's when strong men will be bent over.
The women who grind grain will stop because there are so few of them left.
Those who look through the windows won't be able to see very well.
4 Remember your Creator before the front doors are closed.
That's when the sound of grinding will fade away.
Old people will rise up when they hear birds singing.
But they will barely hear any of their songs.

5 Remember your Creator before you
become afraid of places that
are too high.
You will also be terrified because
of danger in the streets.
Remember your Creator before the
almond trees have buds on
them.
That's when grasshoppers will
drag themselves along.
Old people will lose their desire.
That's when people will go to their
dark homes in the grave.
And those who mourn for the
dead will walk around in the
streets.

6 Remember your Creator before the
silver cord is cut.
Remember him before the golden
bowl is broken.
The wheel will be broken at the
well.
The pitcher will be smashed at
the spring.
7 Remember your Creator before you
return to the dust you came
from.
Remember him before your spirit
goes back to God who gave it.

8 "Meaningless! Everything is
meaningless!"
says the Teacher.
"Nothing has any meaning."

Have Respect for God and Obey His Commandments

9 The Teacher was wise. He gave
knowledge to people. He tried out
many proverbs. He thought about them
carefully. Then he wrote them down in
order. 10 He did his best to find just the
right words. And what he wrote was
honest and true.

11 The sayings of those who are wise
move people to take action. Their collected sayings are like nails pounded in
firm and deep. These sayings are given
to us by one shepherd. 12 My son, be
careful not to pay attention to anything
added to them.

Books will never stop being written.
Too much studying makes people
tired.

13 Everything has now been heard.
And here's the final thing I want
to say.
Have respect for God and obey his
commandments.
This is what he expects of all
human beings.
14 God will judge everything
people do.
That includes everything they
try to hide.
He'll judge everything, whether
it's good or evil.

SONG OF SONGS

Author: King Solomon (we think)

Song of Songs is a love letter between a husband and a wife. In the letter, the husband and wife tell each other how much they love each other and talk about all the things they love about each other. The husband tells his wife how much he loves the way she looks and smells and how much she means to him. And the wife tells her husband that she enjoys being with him and misses him when he's away. She says that she loves the way God created him.

Wisdom & Poetry

Song of Songs reminds us that God designed marriage to be enjoyed! The author of this book wants us to know that marriage is a gift created by God and should be received with gratitude. Throughout the Bible, we learn that a joyful marriage is about a man and a woman who love each other and who both love God. Marriage is a way we can faithfully love and be loved just like God loves us. When we read Song of Songs, we can be reminded that God loves us so much that he sent a Savior to make a way for us to have a relationship with him forever.

1 This is the greatest song Solomon ever wrote.

A Shulammite woman says to King Solomon

2 "I long for your lips to kiss me!
Your love makes me happier than wine does.
3 The lotion you have on pleases me.
Your name is like perfume that is poured out.
No wonder the young women love you!
4 Take me away with you. Let us hurry!
King Solomon, bring me into your palace."

The other women say

"King Solomon, you fill us with joy.
You make us happy.
We praise your love more than we praise wine."

The woman says to the king

"It is right for them to love you!

5 "Women of Jerusalem,
my skin is dark but lovely.
It is dark like the tents in Kedar.
It's like the curtains of Solomon's tent.
6 Don't stare at me because I'm dark.
The sun has made my skin look like this.
My brothers were angry with me.
They made me take care of the vineyards.
I haven't even taken care of my own vineyard.

7 "King Solomon, I love you.
So tell me where you take care of your flock.
Tell me where you rest your sheep at noon.
Why should I have to act like a prostitute
near the flocks of your friends?"

The other women say

8 "You are the most beautiful woman of all.
Don't you know where to find the king?
Follow the tracks the sheep make.
Take care of your young goats
near the tents of the shepherds."

King Solomon says to the Shulammite woman

9 "You are my love.
You are like a mare among Pharaoh's chariot horses.
10 Your earrings make your cheeks even more beautiful.
Your strings of jewels make your neck even more lovely.
11 We will make gold earrings for you.
We'll decorate them with silver."

The woman says

12 "The king was at his table.
My perfume gave off a sweet smell.
13 The one who loves me is like a small bag of myrrh
resting between my breasts.
14 He is like henna flowers
from the vineyards of En Gedi."

The king says

15 "You are so beautiful, my love!
So beautiful!
Your eyes are like doves."

The woman says

16 "You are so handsome, my love!
So charming!
The green field is our bed."

The king says

17 "Cedar trees above us are the beams of our house.
Fir trees overhead are its rafters."

The woman says

2 "I am like a rose on the coast of Sharon.
I'm like a lily in the valleys."

The king says

2 "My love, among the young women
you are like a lily among thorns."

in Song of Songs?

God is the Truest Love, the only one who will ever love us perfectly.

The woman says

3 "My love, among the young men
you are like an apple tree among
the trees of the forest.
I'm happy to sit in your shade.
Your fruit tastes so sweet to me.
4 Lead me to the dinner hall.
Let your banner of love be lifted
high above me.
5 Give me some raisins to make me
strong.
Give me some apples to make me
feel like new again.
Our love has made me weak.
6 Your left arm is under my head.
Your right arm is around me.
7 Women of Jerusalem, make me a
promise.
Let the antelopes and the does
serve as witnesses.
Don't stir up love.
Don't wake it up until it's ready.

8 "Listen! I hear my love!
Look! Here he comes!
He's leaping across the mountains.
He's coming over the hills.
9 The one who loves me is like an
antelope or a young deer.
Look! There he stands behind our
wall.
He's gazing through the window.
He's peering through the screen.
10 He said to me, 'Rise up, my love.
Come with me, my beautiful one.
11 Look! The winter is past.
The rains are over and gone.
12 Flowers are appearing on the earth.
The season for singing has come.
The cooing of doves
is heard in our land.
13 The fig trees are producing their
early fruit.
The flowers on the vines are
giving off their sweet smell.
Rise up and come, my love.
Come with me, my beautiful
one.' "

The king says

14 "You are like a dove in an opening
in the rocks.
You are like a dove in a hiding
place on a mountainside.
Show me your face.
Let me hear your voice.
Your voice is so sweet.
Your face is so lovely.
15 Catch the foxes for us.
Catch the little foxes.
They destroy our vineyards.
The vineyards are in bloom."

The woman says

16 "My love belongs to me, and I
belong to him.
Like an antelope, he eats among
the lilies.
17 Until the day begins
and the shadows fade away,
turn to me, my love.
Be like an antelope
or like a young deer
on the rocky hills.

My love belongs to me, and I belong to him.
SONG OF SONGS 2:16

3 "All night long on my bed
I searched for the one my heart
loves.
I looked for him but didn't find him.
2 I will get up and go around in the
city.
I'll look through all of its streets.
I'll search for the one my heart
loves.
So I looked for him but didn't find
him.
3 Those on guard duty found me
as they were walking around in
the city.
'Have you seen the one my heart
loves?' I asked.
4 As soon as I had passed by them
I found the one my heart loves.
I threw my arms around him and
didn't let him go
until I had brought him to my
mother's house.
I took him to my mother's room.
5 Women of Jerusalem, make me a
promise.
Let the antelopes and the does
serve as witnesses.
Don't stir up love.
Don't wake it up until it's ready.

6 "Who is this man coming up from
the desert
like a column of smoke?

He smells like myrrh and incense
made from all the spices of the
trader.
7 Look! There's Solomon's movable
throne.
Sixty soldiers accompany it.
They have been chosen from the
best warriors in Israel.
8 All of them are wearing swords.
They have fought many battles.
Each one has his sword at his side.
Each is prepared for the terrors of
the night.
9 King Solomon made the movable
throne for himself.
He made it out of wood from
Lebanon.
10 He formed its posts out of silver.
He made its base out of gold.
Its seat was covered with purple
cloth.
It was decorated inside with love.
Women of Jerusalem, 11 come out.

"Look, you women of Zion.
Look at King Solomon wearing
his crown.
His mother placed it on him.
She did it on his wedding day.
His heart was full of joy."

The king says to the Shulammite woman

4 "You are so beautiful, my love!
So beautiful!
Your eyes behind your veil are
like doves.
Your hair flows like a flock of black
goats
coming down from the hills of
Gilead.
2 Your teeth are as clean as a flock of
sheep.
Their wool has just been clipped.
They have just come up from
being washed.
Each of your teeth has its twin.
Not one of them is alone.
3 Your lips are like a bright red
ribbon.
Your mouth is so lovely.
Your cheeks behind your veil
are like the halves of a
pomegranate.
4 Your neck is strong and beautiful
like the tower of David.
That tower is built with rows of
stones.
A thousand shields are hanging
on it.
All of them belong to mighty
soldiers.
5 Your breasts are lovely.
They are like two young
antelopes
that eat among the lilies.
6 I will go to the mountain of myrrh.
I'll go to the hill of incense.
I'll stay there until the day begins
and the shadows fade away.
7 Every part of you is so beautiful,
my love.
There is no flaw in you.

8 "Come with me from Lebanon, my
bride.
Come with me from Lebanon.
Come down from the top of Mount
Amana.
Come down from the top of Senir.
Come to me from the peak of
Mount Hermon.
Leave the dens where the lions live.
Leave the places in the
mountains where the leopards
stay.
9 My bride, you have stolen my heart
with one glance of your eyes.
My sister, you have stolen my heart
with one jewel in your necklace.
10 My bride, your love is so delightful.
My sister, your love makes me
happier than wine does.
Your perfume smells better than
any spice.
11 Your lips are as sweet as honey, my
bride.
Milk and honey are under your
tongue.
Your clothes smell like the cedar
trees in Lebanon.
12 My bride, you are like a garden
that is locked up.
My sister, you are like a spring
of water that has a fence
around it.
You are like a fountain that is
sealed up.
13 You are like trees whose branches
are loaded
with pomegranates, fine fruits,
henna and nard,
14 with nard and saffron, cane and
cinnamon.

You are like every kind of incense
tree.
You have myrrh, aloes
and all the finest spices.
15 You are like a fountain in a garden.
You are like a well of flowing
water
streaming down from Lebanon."

The woman says

16 "Wake up, north wind!
Come, south wind!
Blow on my garden.
Then its sweet smell will spread
everywhere.
Let my love come into his garden.
Let him taste its fine fruits."

The king says

5 "My bride, I have come into my
garden.
My sister, I've gathered my
myrrh and my spice.
I've eaten my honeycomb and my
honey.
I've drunk my wine and my milk."

The other women say to the Shulammite woman and to Solomon

"Friends, eat and drink.
Drink up all the love you want."

The woman says

2 "I slept, but my heart was awake.
Listen! The one who loves me is
knocking.
He says, 'My sister, I love you.
Open up so I can come in.
You are my dove.
You are perfect in every way.
My head is soaked with dew.
The night air has made my hair
wet.'
3 "But I've taken off my robe.
Must I put it on again?
I've washed my feet.
Must I get them dirty again?
4 My love put his hand through the
opening.
My heart began to pound for
him.
5 I got up to open the door for my
love.
My hands dripped with myrrh.
It flowed from my fingers
onto the handles of the lock.
6 I opened the door for my love.
But he had left and was gone.
My heart sank because he had left.
I looked for him but didn't find
him.
I called out to him, but he didn't
answer.
7 Those on guard duty found me
as they were walking around in
the city.
They beat me. They hurt me.
Those on guard duty at the walls
took my coat away from me.
8 Women of Jerusalem, make me a
promise.
If you find the one who loves me,
tell him our love has made me
weak."

The other women say

9 "You are the most beautiful woman
of all.
How is the one you love better
than others?
How is he better than anyone else?
Why do you ask us to make you
this promise?"

The woman says

10 "The one who loves me is tanned
and handsome.
He's the finest man among 10,000.
11 His head is like the purest gold.
His hair is wavy and as black as a
raven.
12 His eyes are like doves
by streams of water.
They look as if they've been
washed in milk.
They are set like jewels in his head.
13 His cheeks are like beds of spice
giving off perfume.
His lips are like lilies
dripping with myrrh.
14 His arms are like rods of gold
set with topaz.
His body is like polished ivory
decorated with lapis lazuli.
15 His legs are like pillars of marble
set on bases of pure gold.
He looks like the finest cedar tree
in the mountains of Lebanon.
16 His mouth is very sweet.
Everything about him is
delightful.
That's what the one who loves me is
like.
That's what my friend is like,
women of Jerusalem."

The other women say

6 "You are the most beautiful
woman of all.
Where has the one who loves you
gone?
Which way did he turn?
We'll help you look for him."

The woman says

2 "My love has gone down to his
garden.
He's gone to the beds of spices.
He's eating in the gardens.
He's gathering lilies.
3 I belong to my love, and he belongs
to me.
He's eating among the lilies."

The king says

4 "My love, you are as beautiful as
the city of Tirzah.
You are as lovely as Jerusalem.
You are as majestic as troops
carrying their banners.
5 Turn your eyes away from me.
They overpower me.
Your hair flows like a flock of black
goats
coming down from the hills of
Gilead.
6 Your teeth are as clean as a flock of
sheep
coming up from being washed.
Each of your teeth has its twin.
Not one of them is missing.
7 Your cheeks behind your veil
are like the halves of a
pomegranate.
8 There might be 60 queens and 80
concubines.
There might be more virgins
than anyone can count.
9 But you are my perfect dove.
There isn't anyone like you.
You are your mother's favorite
daughter.
The young women see you and call
you blessed.
The queens and concubines
praise you."

The other women say

10 "Who is this woman?
She is like the sunrise in all its glory.
She is as beautiful as the moon.
She is as bright as the sun.
She is as majestic as the stars
traveling across the sky."

The king says

11 "I went down to a grove of nut
trees.
I wanted to look at the new
plants growing in the valley.
I wanted to find out whether the
vines had budded.
I wanted to see if the
pomegranate trees had
bloomed.
12 Before I realized it,
I was among the royal chariots
of my people."

The other women say

13 "Come back to us.
Come back, Shulammite woman.
Come back to us.
Come back. Then we can look at
you."

The king says to the women

"Why do you want to look at the
Shulammite woman
as you would watch a dancer at
Mahanaim?"

The king says to the Shulammite woman

7 "You are like a prince's daughter.
Your feet in sandals are so
beautiful.
Your graceful legs are like jewels.
The hands of an artist must have
shaped them.
2 Your navel is like a round bowl
that always has mixed wine in it.
Your waist is like a mound of wheat
surrounded by lilies.
3 Your two breasts are lovely.
They are like two young
antelopes.
4 Your neck is smooth and beautiful
like an ivory tower.
Your eyes are like the pools of
Heshbon
by the gate of Bath Rabbim.
Your nose is like the towering
mountains of Lebanon
that face the city of Damascus.
5 Your head is like a crown on you.
It is as beautiful as Mount
Carmel.
Your hair is as smooth as purple
silk.
I am captured by your flowing
curls.

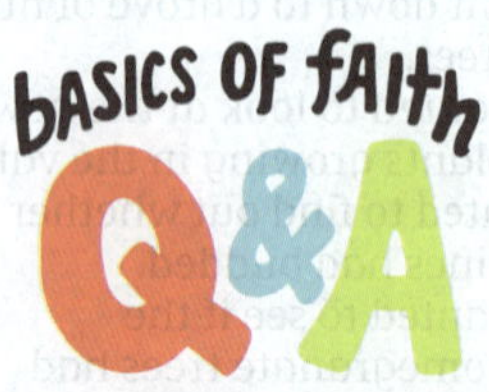

How powerful is love?

True love is one of the most powerful things in the world. God's love for us keeps us close to his heart, and in love God promises that he will never let us go.

Can you find the following verse?

SONG OF SONGS 8:6

6 You are so beautiful! You please me
 so much!
 You are so delightful, my love!
7 You are as graceful as a palm
 tree.
 Your breasts are as sweet as the
 freshest fruit.
8 I said, 'I will climb the palm tree.
 I'll take hold of its fruit.'
May your breasts be as sweet as
 grapes on the vine.
 May your breath smell like the
 tastiest apples.
9 May your lips be like the finest
 wine."

The woman says

"May my wine go straight to you,
 my love.
 May it flow gently over our lips
 as we sleep.
10 "I belong to you, my love.
 And you long for me.
11 Come, my love. Let's go to the
 country.
 Let's spend the night in the
 villages.
12 Let's go out to the vineyards
 early.
 Let's go and see if the vines have
 budded.
Let's find out whether their flowers
 have opened.
 Let's see if the pomegranate trees
 are blooming.
 There I will give you my love.
13 The mandrake flowers give off their
 strong smell.
 All the best things are waiting
 for us,
new and old alike.
 I've stored them up for you, my
 love.

8 "I wish you were like a brother
 to me.
 I wish my mother's breasts had
 nursed you.
Then if I found you outside,
 I could kiss you.
 No one would look down on me.
2 I'd bring you to my mother's
 house.
 She taught me everything I
 know.
I'd give you spiced wine to drink.
 It's the juice of my
 pomegranates.
3 Your left arm is under my head.
 Your right arm is around me.
4 Women of Jerusalem, make me a
 promise.
 Don't stir up love.
 Don't wake it up until it's ready."

The other women say

5 "Who is this woman coming up
 from the desert?
 She's leaning on the one who
 loves her."

The woman says to the king

"Under the apple tree I woke
 you up.
 That's where your mother
 became pregnant with you.
 She went into labor, and you
 were born there.
6 Hold me close to your heart where
 your royal seal is worn.
 Keep me as close to yourself as
 the bracelet on your arm.
My love for you is so strong it won't
 let you go.
 Love is as powerful as death.
 Love's jealousy is as strong as the
 grave.
Love is like a blazing fire.
 Love burns like a mighty flame.

7 No amount of water can put it out.
Rivers can't sweep it away.
Suppose someone offers
all their wealth to buy love.
That won't even come close to being enough."

The woman's brothers say

8 "We have a little sister.
Her breasts are still small.
What should we do for our sister
when she gets engaged?
9 If she were a wall,
we'd build silver towers on her.
If she were a door,
we'd cover her with cedar boards."

The woman says to the king

10 "I am a wall.
My breasts are like well-built towers.
So in your eyes I've become
like someone who makes you happy.
11 Solomon, you had a vineyard in Baal Hamon.
You rented your vineyard to others.
They had to pay 25 pounds
of silver for its fruit.
12 But I can give my own vineyard to anyone I want to.
So I give my 25 pounds of silver to you, Solomon.
Give 5 pounds to those who take care of its fruit."

The king says

13 "My love, you live in the gardens.
My friends listen for your voice.
But let me hear it now."

The woman says

14 "Come away with me, my love.
Be like an antelope
or like a young deer
on mountains that are full of spices."

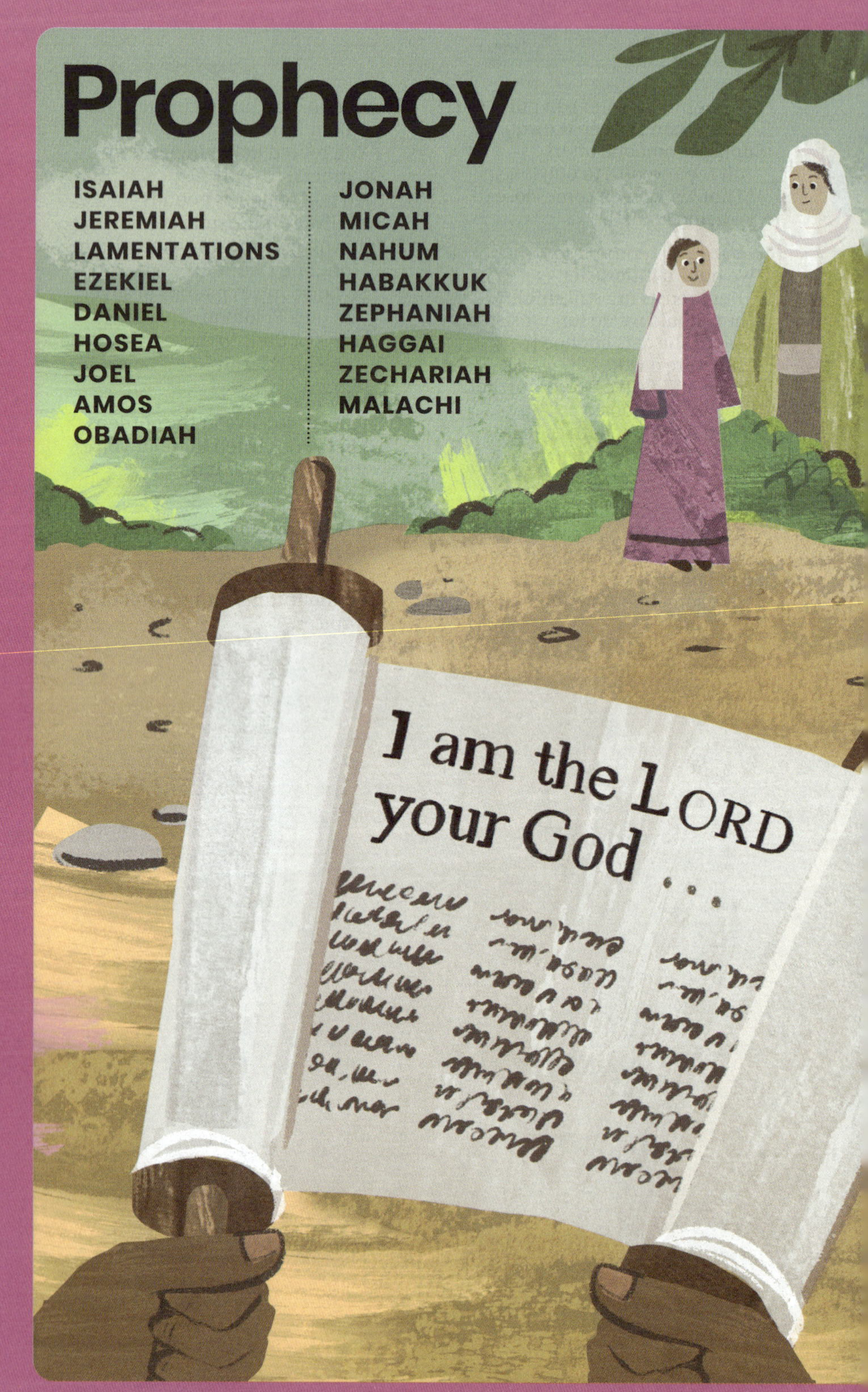
Prophecy
ISAIAH
JEREMIAH
LAMENTATIONS
EZEKIEL
DANIEL
HOSEA
JOEL
AMOS
OBADIAH
JONAH
MICAH
NAHUM
HABAKKUK
ZEPHANIAH
HAGGAI
ZECHARIAH
MALACHI
I am the LORD your God . . .

The books of Prophecy tell us about God's continued faithfulness despite his people's disobedience. Over and over, God's people forgot what he said and broke his laws.

In response, God gave his people prophets. The prophets were to speak on God's behalf, reminding the people of God's promises and commands. They called the people to repent and turn away from their sinful ways because God is holy and cannot be near sin. The bad news was that God would have to judge his people. But the good news was that God promised to restore his people by sending a Savior to pay the penalty for sin and make his people right with him again. This was the most special message: The Savior was on his way!

Even though the people were not faithful to obey God's commands, God kept his promises. While we don't know who wrote some of the books of Prophecy in the Old Testament, we can know we're reading Prophecy when we read about God's messages and visions given to his prophets to call God's people to repent, or turn away from their sin, and turn back to God. He wanted to bless them in the most amazing way!

ISAIAH

Author: Isaiah

Isaiah lived among God's people and was given a very special job: He was one of God's prophets. God asked Isaiah to speak to the people of Israel on his behalf. God was going to give Isaiah a message, and Isaiah's job was to share the message with the nation of Israel. The message God gave Isaiah to share was this: The Savior is coming! But he may not be exactly what you expect.

Prophecy

I am the LORD your God . . .

Through Isaiah, God told his people about his holiness and justice and said that the coming Savior would fulfill all his promises. The Savior would make God's sinful people right with him. But this Savior wasn't going to defeat the earthly enemies of God's people (like many of them thought he would). The Savior wasn't going to be a triumphant king born in a palace like they imagined. Instead, the Savior would come and suffer in their place to save them from their sin. He would be humiliated and treated unjustly before dying for sins he never committed. This wasn't at all what God's people were expecting, but Isaiah boldly proclaimed that when the Savior came, he would be better than the people of Israel ever could have imagined!

1 Here is the vision about Judah and Jerusalem that Isaiah saw. It came to him when Uzziah, Jotham, Ahaz and Hezekiah were ruling. They were kings of Judah. Isaiah was the son of Amoz.

The Nation Refuses to Obey the LORD

2 Listen to me, you heavens! Pay
attention to me, earth!
The LORD has said,
"I raised children. I brought
them up.
But they have refused to obey me.
3 The ox knows its master.
The donkey knows where its
owner feeds it.
But Israel does not know me.
My people do not understand me."

4 How terrible it will be for this sinful
nation!
They are loaded down with guilt.
They are people who do nothing
but evil.
They are children who are
always sinning.
They have deserted the LORD.
They have turned against the
Holy One of Israel.
They have turned their backs on
him.

5 Israel, why do you want to be
beaten all the time?
Why do you always refuse to
obey the LORD?
Your head is covered with wounds.
Your whole heart is weak.
6 There isn't a healthy spot on your
body.
You are not healthy from the
bottom of your feet to the top
of your head.
You have nothing but wounds, cuts
and open sores.
They haven't been cleaned up or
bandaged
or treated with olive oil.

7 Your country has been deserted.
Your cities have been burned
down.
The food from your fields is being
eaten up by outsiders.
They are doing it right in front of
you.
Your land has been completely
destroyed.
It looks as if strangers have
taken it over.
8 The city of Zion is left like a shed
where someone stands guard in
a vineyard.
It is left like a hut in a cucumber
field.
It's like a city being attacked.
9 The LORD who rules over all
has let some people live through
that time of trouble.
If he hadn't, we would have become
like Sodom.
We would have been like
Gomorrah.

10 Rulers of Sodom,
hear the LORD's message.
People of Gomorrah,
listen to the instruction of our
God.
11 "Do you think I need any more of
your sacrifices?"
asks the LORD.
"I have more than enough of your
burnt offerings.
I have more than enough of rams
and the fat of your fattest
animals.
I do not find any pleasure
in the blood of your bulls, lambs
and goats.
12 Who asked you to bring all these
animals
when you come to worship me?
Who asked you and your animals
to walk all over my courtyards?
13 Stop bringing offerings that do not
mean anything to me!
I hate your incense.
I can't stand your worthless
gatherings.
I can't stand the way you
celebrate your New Moon feasts,
Sabbath days and special
services.
14 Your New Moon feasts and your
other appointed feasts
I hate with my whole being.
They have become a heavy load
to me.
I am tired of carrying it.
15 You might spread out your hands
toward me when you pray.
But I do not look at you.
You might even offer many prayers.
But I am not listening to them.

Your hands are covered with the
blood of the people you have
murdered.
16 So wash and make yourselves
clean.
Get your evil actions out of my
sight!
Stop doing what is wrong!
17 Learn to do what is right!
Treat people fairly.
Help those who are treated badly.
Stand up in court for children
whose fathers have died.
And do the same thing for
widows.

18 "Come. Let us settle this matter,"
says the LORD.
"Even though your sins are bright
red,
they will be as white as snow.
Even though they are deep red,
they will be white like wool.
19 But you have to be willing to
change and obey me.
If you are, you will eat the good
things that grow on the land.
20 But if you are not willing to obey me,
you will be killed by swords."
The LORD has spoken.
21 See how the faithful city of
Jerusalem
has become like a prostitute!
Once it was full of people who
treated others fairly.
Those who did what was right
used to live in it.
But now murderers live there!
22 Jerusalem, your silver isn't pure
anymore.
Your best wine has been made
weak with water.
23 Your rulers refuse to obey the LORD.
They join forces with robbers.
All of them love to accept money
from those who want special
favors.
They are always looking for gifts
from other people.
They don't stand up in court for
children whose fathers have
died.
They don't do it for widows
either.
24 The Lord is the Mighty One of
Israel.
The LORD who rules over all
announces,
"Israel, you have become my
enemies.
I will act against you in my
anger.
I will pay you back for what you
have done.
25 I will turn my power against you.
I will make you completely
'clean.'
I will remove everything that is
not pure.
26 I will give you leaders like the ones
you had long ago.
I will give you rulers like those
you had at the beginning.
Then you will be called
the City That Does What Is
Right.
You will also be called the
Faithful City."

27 Zion will be saved when justice is
done.
Those who are sorry for their sins
will be saved
when what is right is done.
28 But sinners and those who refuse
to obey the LORD will be
destroyed.
And those who desert the LORD
will die.

29 "Israel, you take delight in
worshiping among the sacred
oak trees.
You will be full of shame for
doing that.
You have chosen to worship in the
sacred gardens.
You will be dishonored for doing
that.
30 You will be like an oak tree whose
leaves are dying.
You will be like a garden that
doesn't have any water.
31 Your strongest men will become
like dry pieces of wood.
Their worship of other gods
will be the spark that lights the
fire.
Everything will be burned up.
No one will be there to put the
fire out."

People From Many Nations Will Worship at Mount Zion

2 Here is a vision that Isaiah, the son of Amoz, saw about Judah and Jerusalem.

2 In the last days
the mountain where the LORD's
temple is located will be
famous.
It will be the highest mountain of
all.
It will be raised above the hills.
All the nations will go to it.

3 People from many nations will go there. They will say,

"Come. Let us go up to the LORD's
mountain.
Let's go to the temple of Jacob's
God.
He will teach us how we should live.
Then we will live the way he
wants us to."
The law of the LORD will be taught
at Zion.
His message will go out from
Jerusalem.
4 He will judge between the nations.
He'll settle problems among
many of them.
They will hammer their swords into
plows.
They'll hammer their spears into
pruning tools.
Nations will not go to war against
one another.
They won't even train to fight
anymore.

5 People of Jacob, come.
Let us live the way the LORD has
taught us to.

The Day of the LORD Is Coming

6 LORD, you have deserted the people
of Jacob.
They are your people.
The land is full of false beliefs from
the east.
The people practice evil magic,
just as the Philistines do.
They do what ungodly people do.
7 Their land is full of silver and gold.
There is no end to their treasures.
Their land is full of horses.
There is no end to their chariots.
8 Their land is full of statues of gods.

in Isaiah?

God is the Unexpected King. The Savior would come in a way that God's people weren't looking for. He would come as a suffering servant who would die for their sins.

Their people bow down to what
their own hands have made.
They bow down to what their
fingers have shaped.
9 So people will be brought low.
Everyone will be made humble.
Do not forgive them.

10 Go and hide in caves in the rocks,
you people!
Hide in holes in the ground.
Hide from the terrifying presence
of the LORD!
Hide when he comes in glory and
majesty!
11 Anyone who brags will be brought
low.
Anyone who is proud will be
made humble.
The LORD alone will be honored
at that time.

12 The LORD who rules over all has set
apart a day when he will judge.
He has set it apart for all those
who are proud and think they
are important.
He has set it apart for all those who
brag about themselves.
All of them will be brought low.
13 The LORD has set that day apart for
all the cedar trees in Lebanon.
They are very tall.
He has set that day apart for all
the oak trees in Bashan.

[14] He has set it apart for all the towering mountains.
He has set it apart for all the high hills.
[15] He has set it apart for every high tower
and every strong wall.
[16] He has set it apart for every trading ship
and every beautiful boat.
[17] Anyone who brags will be brought low.
Anyone who is proud will be made humble.
The LORD alone will be honored at that time.
[18] And the statues of gods will totally disappear.

[19] People will run and hide in caves in the rocks.
They will go into holes in the ground.
They will run away from the terrifying presence of the LORD.
They will run when he comes in glory and majesty.
When he comes, he will shake the earth.
[20] People had made some statues of gods out of silver.
They had made others out of gold.
Then they worshiped them.
But when the LORD comes,
they will throw the statues away to the moles and bats.
[21] Those people will run and hide in caves in the rocks.
They will go into holes in the cliffs.
They will run away from the terrifying presence of the LORD.
They will run when he comes in glory and majesty.
When he comes, he will shake the earth.

[22] Stop trusting in mere human beings, who can't help you.
They only live for a little while.
What good are they?

The LORD Will Judge Jerusalem and Judah

3 Here is what the LORD who rules over all is about to do.
The Lord will take away from Jerusalem and Judah
supplies and help alike.
He will take away all the supplies of food and water.
[2] He'll take away heroes and soldiers.
He'll take away judges and prophets.
He'll take away fortune tellers and elders.
[3] He'll take away captains of groups of 50 men.
He'll take away government leaders.
He'll take away advisers, skilled workers
and those who are clever at doing evil magic.

[4] The LORD will make mere youths their leaders.
Children will rule over them.
[5] People will treat one another badly.
They will fight against one another.
They will fight against their neighbors.
Young people will attack old people.
Ordinary people will attack those who are more important.

[6] A man will grab one of his brothers in his father's house. He will say,
"You have a coat. So you be our leader.
Take charge of all these broken-down buildings!"
[7] But at that time the brother will cry out,
"I can't help you.
I don't have any food or clothing in my house.
Don't make me the leader of these people."

[8] Jerusalem is about to fall.
And so is Judah.
They say and do things against the LORD.
They dare to disobey him to his very face.
[9] The look on their faces is a witness against them.
They show off their sin, just as the people of Sodom did.
They don't even try to hide it.
How terrible it will be for them!
They have brought trouble on themselves.

[10]Tell those who do what is right that
things will go well with them.
They will enjoy the results of the
good things they've done.
[11]But how terrible it will be for those
who do what is evil!
Trouble is about to fall on them.
They will be paid back for the
evil things they've done.

[12]Those who are young treat my
people badly.
Women rule over them.
My people, your leaders have taken
you down the wrong path.
They have turned you away from
the right path.
[13]The LORD takes his place in court.
He stands up to judge the people.
[14]He judges the elders and leaders of
his people.
He says to them,
"My people are like a vineyard.
You have destroyed them.
The things you have taken from
poor people are in your houses.
[15]What do you mean by crushing my
people?
Why are you grinding the faces
of the poor into the dirt?"
announces the Lord. He is the
LORD who rules over all.

[16]The LORD continues,
"The women in Zion are very
proud.
They walk along with their noses in
the air.
They tease men with their eyes.
They sway their hips as they walk
along.
Little chains jingle on their
ankles.
[17]So I will put sores on the heads of
Zion's women.
And I will remove the hair from
their heads."

[18]At that time the Lord will take away
the beautiful things they wear. He will
take away their decorations, headbands
and moon-shaped necklaces. [19]He'll
take away their earrings, bracelets and
veils. [20]He'll remove their headdresses,
anklets and belts. He'll take away their
perfume bottles and charms. [21]He'll
remove the rings they wear on their
fingers and in their noses. [22]He'll take
away their fine robes and their capes
and coats. He'll take away their purses
[23]and mirrors. And he'll take away their
linen clothes, turbans and shawls.

[24]Instead of smelling sweet,
the women will smell bad.
Instead of wearing belts,
they will wear ropes.
Instead of having beautiful hair,
they won't have any hair at all.
Instead of wearing fine clothes,
they'll wear rough clothes to
show how sad they are.
Instead of being beautiful,
on their bodies they'll have the
marks of their owners.
[25]Jerusalem, your men will be killed
by swords.
Your soldiers will die in battle.
[26]The city of Zion will be very sad.
Like a widow, she will lose
everything.
She will sit on the ground and
mourn.

4 [1]At that time seven women
will grab hold of one man.
They'll say to him, "We will eat our
own food.
We'll provide our own clothes.
Just let us become your wives.
Take away our shame!"

The Branch of the LORD

[2]At that time Israel's king will be
beautiful and glorious. He will be called
The Branch of the LORD. The fruit of the
land will be the pride and glory of those
who are still left alive in Israel. [3]Those
who are left in Zion will be called holy.
They will be recorded among those who
are alive in Jerusalem. [4]The Lord will
wash away the sin of the women in
Zion. He will clean up the blood that was
spilled there. He will judge those who
spilled that blood. His burning anger
will blaze out at them. [5]Then the LORD
will create over Jerusalem a cloud of
smoke by day. He will also create a glow
of flaming fire at night. The cloud and
fire will appear over all of Mount Zion.
They will also appear over the people
who gather together there. The LORD's
glory will be like a tent over everything.
[6]It will cover the people and give them
shade from the hot sun all day long. It
will be a safe place where they can hide
from storms and rain.

The Song of the Vineyard

5 I will sing a song for the LORD.
He is the one I love.
It's a song about his vineyard Israel.
The one I love had a vineyard.
It was on a hillside that had rich soil.
2 He dug up the soil and removed its stones.
He planted the very best vines in it.
He built a lookout tower there.
He also cut out a winepress for it.
Then he kept looking for a crop of good grapes.
But the vineyard produced only bad fruit.

3 So the LORD said, "People of Jerusalem and Judah,
you be the judge between me and my vineyard.
4 What more could I have done for my vineyard?
I did everything I could.
I kept looking for a crop of good grapes.
So why did it produce only bad ones?
5 Now I will tell you
what I am going to do to my vineyard.
I will take away its fence.
And the vineyard will be destroyed.
I will break down its wall.
And people will walk all over my vineyard.
6 I will turn my vineyard into a dry and empty desert.
It will not be pruned or taken care of.
Thorns and bushes will grow there.
I will command the clouds
not to rain on it."
7 The vineyard of the LORD who rules over all
is the nation of Israel.
The people of Judah
are the vines he took delight in.
He kept looking for them to do what is fair.
But all he saw was blood being spilled.
He kept looking for them to do what is right.
But all he heard were cries of suffering.

The LORD Judges His Vineyard

8 How terrible it will be for you who get too many houses!
How terrible for you who get too many fields!
Finally there won't be any space left in the land.
Then you will live all alone.

9 I heard the LORD who rules over all
announce a message. He said,
"You can be sure that the great houses will become empty.
The fine homes will be left with no one living in them.
10 A ten-acre vineyard will produce only six gallons of wine.
360 pounds of seeds will produce only 36 pounds of grain."

11 How terrible it will be for those who get up early in the morning
to start drinking!
How terrible for those who stay up late at night
until they are drunk with wine!
12 They have harps and lyres at their banquets.
They have tambourines, flutes and wine.
But they don't have any concern for the mighty acts of the LORD.
They don't have any respect for what his power has done.
13 So my people will be taken away as prisoners.
That's because they don't understand what the LORD has done.
Their nobles will die of hunger.
The rest of the people won't have any water to drink.
14 So Death opens its jaws to receive them.
Its mouth is open wide to swallow them up.
Their nobles and the rest of the people will go down into it.
They will go there together with all those who have wild parties.
15 So people will be brought low.
Everyone will be made humble.
Those who brag will be brought down.

[16] But the LORD who rules over all will
be honored
because he judges fairly.
The holy God will prove that he is
holy
by doing what is right.
[17] Then sheep will graze as if they
were in their own grasslands.
Lambs will eat grass among the
destroyed buildings
where rich people used to live.

[18] How terrible it will be for those who
continue to sin
and lie about it!
How terrible for those who keep on
doing what is evil
as if they were tied to it!
[19] How terrible for those who say,
"Let God hurry up and do what
he says he will.
We want to see it happen.
Let us see the plan of the Holy One
of Israel.
We want to know what it is."

[20] How terrible it will be for those who
say
that what is evil is good!
How terrible for those who say
that what is good is evil!
How terrible for those who say
that darkness is light
and light is darkness!
How terrible for those who say
that what is bitter is sweet
and what is sweet is bitter!

[21] How terrible it will be for those who
think they are wise!
How terrible for those who think
they are really clever!

[22] How terrible it will be for those
who are heroes at drinking wine!
How terrible for those
who are heroes at mixing drinks!
[23] How terrible for those
who take money to set guilty
people free!
How terrible for those
who don't treat good people fairly!
[24] Flames of fire burn up straw.
Dry grass sinks down into those
flames.
Evil people will be like plants
whose roots rot away.
They will be like flowers that are
blown away like dust.
That's because they have said no to
the law of the LORD who rules
over all.
They have turned against the
message of the Holy One of
Israel.
[25] So the LORD is angry with his
people.
He raises his hand against them
and strikes them down.
The mountains shake.
The bodies of dead people lie in
the streets like trash.

Even then, the LORD is still angry.
His hand is still raised against
them.

[26] He lifts up a banner to gather the
nations that are far away.
He whistles for them to come
from the farthest places on earth.
Here they come.
They are moving very quickly.
[27] None of them grows tired.
None of them falls down.
None of them sleeps or even
takes a nap.
All of them are ready for battle.
Every belt is pulled tight.
Not a single sandal strap is
broken.
[28] The enemies' arrows are sharp.
All their bows are ready.
The hooves of their horses are as
hard as rock.
Their chariot wheels turn like a
twister.
[29] The sound of their army is like the
roar of lions.
It's like the roar of young lions.
They growl as they capture what
they were chasing.
They carry it off.
No one can take it away from
them.
[30] At that time the enemy army will
roar over Israel.
It will sound like the roaring of
the ocean.
If someone looks at the land of
Israel,
there is only darkness and
trouble.
The clouds will make even the
sun become dark.

The Lord Appoints Isaiah to Speak for Him

6 In the year that King Uzziah died, I
saw the Lord. He was seated on his
throne. His long robe filled the temple.
He was highly honored. 2 Above him
were seraphs. Each of them had six
wings. With two wings they covered
their faces. With two wings they covered
their feet. And with two wings they were
flying. 3 They were calling out to one
another. They were saying,

"Holy, holy, holy is the LORD who
rules over all.
The whole earth is full of his
glory."

4 The sound of their voices caused the
stone doorframe to shake. The temple
was filled with smoke.
5 "How terrible it is for me!" I cried out.
"I'm about to be destroyed! My mouth
speaks sinful words. And I live among
people who speak sinful words. Now I
have seen the King with my own eyes.
He is the LORD who rules over all."
6 A seraph flew over to me. He was
holding a hot coal. He had used tongs to
take it from the altar. 7 He touched my
mouth with the coal. He said, "This has
touched your lips. Your guilt has been
taken away. Your sin has been paid for."
8 Then I heard the voice of the Lord.
He said, "Who will I send? Who will go
for us?"
I said, "Here I am. Send me!"
9 So he said, "Go and speak to these
people. Tell them,

" 'You will hear but never
understand.
You will see but never know what
you are seeing.'
10 Make the hearts of these people
stubborn.
Plug up their ears.
Close their eyes.
Otherwise they might see with their
eyes.
They might hear with their
ears.
They might understand with
their hearts.
And they might turn to me and be
healed."

11 Then I said, "Lord, how long will it
be like that?"
He answered,

"It will last until the cities of Israel
are destroyed.
It will last until no one is living in
them.
It will last until the houses are
deserted.
The fields will be completely
destroyed.
12 It will last until the LORD has sent
everyone far away.
The land will be totally deserted.
13 Suppose only a tenth of the people
remain there.
Even then the land will be
completely destroyed again.
But when oak trees and terebinth
trees
are cut down, stumps are left.
And my holy people will be like
stumps
that begin to grow again."

The Sign of Immanuel

7 Ahaz was king of Judah. Rezin was
king of Aram. And Pekah was king
of Israel. Rezin and Pekah marched up
to fight against Jerusalem. But they
couldn't overpower it. Ahaz was the son
of Jotham and the grandson of Uzziah.
Pekah was the son of Remaliah.

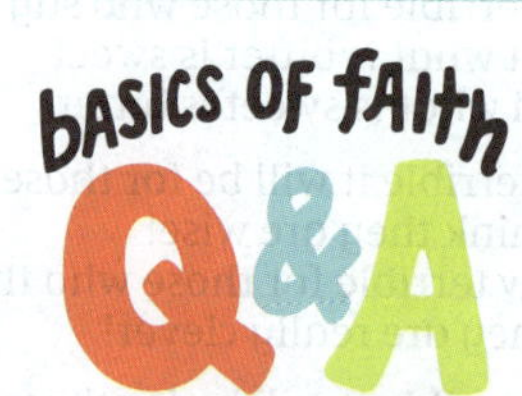

Can God use me to make him known even when I am young?

Yes! God wants to use you right where you are to make himself known in the world. No matter your age, you can share God's love with others and tell others all about him.

Can you find the following verse?

ISAIAH 6:8

2 The royal family of Ahaz was told,
“The army of Aram has joined forces with
Ephraim’s army.” So the hearts of Ahaz
and his people trembled with fear. They
shook just as trees in the forest shake
when the wind blows through them.
3 The LORD said to Isaiah, “Go out
and see Ahaz. Take your son Shear-
Jashub with you. Meet Ahaz at the
end of the channel that brings water
from the Upper Pool. It is on the road
to the Washerman’s Field. 4 Tell Ahaz,
‘Be careful. Stay calm. Do not be afraid.
Do not lose hope because of the great
anger of Rezin, Aram and the son of
Remaliah. After all, they are nothing
but two pieces of smoking firewood.
5 Aram, Ephraim and Remaliah’s son
have planned to destroy you. They said,
6 “Let’s march into Judah and attack it.
Let’s tear everything down. Then we can
share the land among ourselves. And
we can make Tabeel’s son king over
it.” 7 But I am the LORD and King. I say,

“ ‘ “That will not happen.
It will not take place.
8 The capital of Aram is Damascus.
And the ruler of Damascus is
only Rezin.
Do not worry about the people of
Ephraim.
They will be too crushed to be
considered a people.
That will happen before 65 years
are over.
9 The capital of Ephraim is Samaria.
And the ruler of Samaria is only
Remaliah’s son.
If you do not stand firm in your
faith,
you will not stand at all.” ’ ”

10 The LORD spoke to Ahaz through
Isaiah again. He said, 11 “I am the LORD
your God. Ask me to give you a sign. It
can be anything in the deepest grave
or in the highest heaven.”
12 But Ahaz said, “I won’t ask. I won’t
test the LORD.”
13 Then Isaiah said, “Listen, you members of the royal family of David! Isn’t
it enough for you to test the patience
of human beings? Are you also going
to test the patience of my God? 14 The
Lord himself will give you a sign. The
virgin is going to have a baby. She will
give birth to a son. And he will be called
Immanuel. 15 He will still be very young
when he can decide between right and
wrong. 16 Even before then, the lands of
the two kings you fear will be ruined.
17 The LORD will also bring the king of
Assyria against you. And he will bring
him against your people and the whole
royal family. That will be a time of trouble. It will be unlike any since the people
of Ephraim broke away from Judah.”

The LORD Uses Assyria to Judge Judah

18 At that time the LORD will whistle
for the Egyptians. They will come like
flies from the Nile River in Egypt. He will
also whistle for the Assyrians. They will
come from their country like bees. 19 All
of them will come and camp in the deep
valleys. They will camp in caves in the
rocks. And they’ll camp near bushes and
water holes. 20 At that time the Lord will
use the Assyrians to punish you. Ahaz
had hired them earlier from east of the
Euphrates River. Now their king will
be like a razor in the Lord’s hand. He
will shave the hair from your head and
private parts. He will also shave off your
beards. 21 At that time a person may
only be able to keep alive one young
cow and two goats. 22 But they will give
plenty of milk to live on. In fact, everyone left in the land will only have
milk curds and honey to eat. 23 The land
used to have vineyards with 1,000 vines
worth 25 pounds of silver. But soon the
whole land will be covered with thorns
and bushes. 24 Hunters will go there with
bows and arrows. That’s because it will
be covered with bushes and thorns. 25 All
the hills used to be plowed with hoes.
But you won’t go there anymore. That’s
because you will be afraid of the thorns
and bushes. Cattle will be turned loose
on those hills. Sheep will also run there.

Isaiah and His Children Are Signs

8 The LORD said to me, “Get a large
sheet of paper. Write ‘Maher-
Shalal-Hash-Baz’ on it with a pen.” 2 So I
sent for Zechariah and Uriah the priest.
Zechariah is the son of Jeberekiah. Zechariah and Uriah were witnesses for me
whom I could trust. 3 Then I went and
slept with my wife, who was a prophet.
She became pregnant and had a baby
boy. The LORD said to me, “Name him
Maher-Shalal-Hash-Baz. 4 The king of

Assyria will carry off the wealth of Damascus. He will also carry away the goods that were taken from Samaria. That will happen before the boy knows how to say 'My father' or 'My mother.' "

5 The LORD continued,

6 "I am like the gently flowing
stream of Siloam.
But the people of Judah have
turned their backs on me.
They are filled with joy because of
the fall of Rezin
and the son of Remaliah.
7 So I am about to bring against
these people
the king of Assyria and his whole
army.
The Assyrians will be like the
mighty Euphrates River
when it is flooding.
They will run over everything in
their path.
8 They will sweep on into Judah like
a flood.
They will pass through Judah
and reach all the way to
Jerusalem.
Immanuel, they will attack your
land like an eagle.
Their wings will spread out and
cover it."

9 Sound the battle cry, you nations!
But you will be torn apart.
Listen, all you lands far away!
Prepare for battle! But you will be
torn apart.
Prepare for battle! But you will be
torn apart.
10 Make your battle plans! But you
won't succeed.
Give your orders! But they won't
be carried out.
That's because God is with us.

11 The LORD speaks to me while his
powerful hand is on me. He is warning
me not to live the way these people
live. He says,

12 "People of Judah, do not agree with
those who say
Isaiah is guilty of treason.
Do not fear what they fear.
Do not be afraid.
13 The LORD rules over all.
So you must think about him as
holy.
You must have respect for him.
You must fear him.
14 Then the LORD will be a holy place
of safety for you.
But that's not true for many
people in Israel and Judah.
He will be a stone that causes
them to trip.
He will be a rock that makes
them fall.
And for the people of Jerusalem
he will be a trap and a snare.
15 Many of them will trip.
They will fall and be broken.
They will be trapped and
captured."

16 Tie up and seal this warning
that the LORD said to you
through me.
Preserve among my followers
what he taught you through me.
17 I will wait for the LORD.
He is turning his face away from
Jacob's people.
I will put my trust in him.

18 Here I am. Here are the children the
LORD has given me. We are signs and
reminders to Israel from the LORD who
rules over all. He lives on Mount Zion.

The Darkness Turns to Light

19 There are people who get messages
from those who have died. But these people only whisper words that are barely
heard. Suppose someone tells you to ask
for advice from these people. Shouldn't
you ask for advice from your God instead?
Why should you get advice from dead
people to help those who are alive? 20 Follow what the LORD taught you and said to
you through me. People who don't speak
in keeping with these words will have no
hope in the morning. 21 They will suffer
and be hungry. They'll wander through
the land. When they are very hungry,
they will become angry. They'll look up
toward heaven. They'll ask for bad things
to happen to their king and their God.
22 Then they will look at the earth. They'll
see nothing but suffering and darkness.
They'll see terrible sadness. They'll be
driven into total darkness.

9 But there won't be any more sadness for those who were suffering.
In the past the LORD brought shame on
the land of Zebulun. He also brought

shame on the land of Naphtali. But in days to come he will honor Galilee, where people from other nations live. He will honor the land along the Mediterranean Sea. And he will honor the territory east of the Jordan River.

2 The people who are now living in darkness
will see a great light.
They are now living in a very dark land.
But a light will shine on them.
3 LORD, you will make our nation larger.
You will increase their joy.
They will show you how glad they are.
They will be as glad as people are at harvest time.
They will be as glad as warriors are
when they share the things they've taken after a battle.
4 You set Israel free from Midian long ago.
In the same way, you will break
the heavy yoke that weighs Israel down.
You will break the wooden beams that are on their shoulders.
You will break the rods of those who strike them down.
5 Every fighting man's boot that he wore in battle will be burned up.
So will every piece of clothing covered with blood.
All of them will be thrown into the fire.
6 A child will be born to us.
A son will be given to us.
He will rule over us.
And he will be called
Wonderful Adviser and Mighty God.
He will also be called Father Who Lives Forever
and Prince Who Brings Peace.
7 There will be no limit to how great his authority is.
The peace he brings will never end.
He will rule on David's throne
and over his kingdom.
He will make the kingdom strong and secure.
His rule will be based on what is fair and right.
It will last forever.
The LORD's great love will make sure that happens.
He rules over all.

The LORD Is Angry With Israel

8 The Lord has sent a message against Jacob's people.
He will punish Israel.
9 All the people will know about it.
Ephraim's people and those who live in Samaria will know about it.
Their hearts are very proud.
They say,
10 "The brick buildings have fallen down.
But we will rebuild them with blocks of stone.
The fig trees have been chopped down.
But we'll plant cedar trees in place of them."
11 In spite of that, the LORD has made Rezin's enemies stronger.
He has stirred up Assyria to fight against Israel.
12 Arameans from the east
have opened their mouths and swallowed up Israel.
So have Philistines from the west.

Even then, the LORD is still angry.
His hand is still raised against them.

13 But his people have not returned
to the God who struck them down.
They haven't turned for help
to the LORD who rules over all.
14 So he will cut off from Israel heads and tails alike.
In a single day he will cut off palm branches and tall grass alike.
The palm branches are the people who rule over others.
The tall grass is the people who bow down to them.
15 The elders and important leaders are the heads.
The prophets who teach lies are the tails.
16 Those who guide the people of Israel are leading them down the wrong path.
So those who follow them aren't on the right road.

17 The Lord will not be pleased with
the young men.
He won't take pity on widows
and on children whose fathers
have died.
All of them are ungodly and evil.
They say foolish things with their
mouths.
Even then, the LORD is still angry.
His hand is still raised against
them.

18 What is evil burns like a fire.
It burns up bushes and thorns.
It sets the forest on fire.
It sends up a huge column of
smoke.
19 The LORD rules over all.
When he gets angry, he will burn
up the land.
The people will burn in the fire.
They will not spare one another.
20 People will eat up everything they
can find on their right.
But they'll still be hungry.
They will eat everything they can
find on their left.
But they won't be satisfied.
So they will eat the dead bodies of
their children.
21 That's what Manasseh's people
will do to Ephraim.
And that's what Ephraim's people
will do to Manasseh.
Together they will turn against
Judah.
Even then, the LORD is still angry.
His hand is still raised against
them.

10 How terrible it will be for you
who make laws that aren't fair!
How terrible for you
who write laws that make life
hard for others!
2 You take away the rights of poor
people.
You hold back what is fair from
my people who are suffering.
You take for yourselves what
belongs to widows.
You rob children whose fathers
have died.
3 What will you do on the day when
the LORD punishes you?
On that day trouble will come
from far away.
Who will you run to for help?
Who will you trust your riches
with?
4 All you can do is bow down in fear
among the prisoners.
All you can do is fall among
those who have died in battle.
Even then, the LORD is still angry.
His hand is still raised against
them.

The LORD Will Judge Assyria

5 The LORD says, "How terrible it will
be for the people of Assyria!
They are the war club that carries
out my anger.
6 I will send them against the
ungodly nation of Judah.
I will order them to fight against
my own people.
My people make me angry.
I will order Assyria to take their
goods and carry them away.
I will order Assyria to walk on my
people
as if they were walking on mud.
7 But that is not what the king of
Assyria plans.
It is not what he has in mind.
His purpose is to destroy many
nations.
His purpose is to put an end to
them.
8 'Aren't all my commanders kings?'
he says.
9 'I took over Kalno just as I took
Carchemish.
I took over Hamath just as I did
Arpad.
I took Samaria just as I did
Damascus.
10 My powerful hand grabbed hold of
kingdoms
whose people worship statues of
gods.
They had more gods than
Jerusalem and Samaria did.
11 I took over Samaria and its statues
of gods.
In the same way, I will take
Jerusalem and its gods.' "

12 The Lord will finish everything he
has planned to do against Mount Zion
and Jerusalem. Then he'll say, "Now I
will punish the king of Assyria. I will
punish him because his heart and his

eyes are so proud. [13]The king of Assyria says,

"'By my power
I have taken over all these nations.
I am very wise.
I have great understanding.
I have wiped out the borders between nations.
I've taken their treasures.
Like a great hero I've brought their kings under my control.
[14]I've taken the wealth of the nations.
It was as easy as reaching into a bird's nest.
I've gathered the riches of all these countries.
It was as easy as gathering eggs that have been left in a nest.
Not a single baby bird flapped its wings.
Not one of them opened its mouth to chirp.'"

[15]Does an ax claim to be more important
than the person who swings it?
Does a saw brag that it is better
than the one who uses it?
That would be like a stick
swinging the person who picks it up!
It would be like a war club
waving the one who carries it!
[16]So the LORD who rules over all will send a sickness.
The Lord will send it on the king of Assyria's strong fighting men.
It will make them weaker and weaker.
The army he was so proud of will be completely destroyed.
It will be as if it had been burned up in a fire.
[17]The LORD is the Light of Israel.
He will become a fire.
Israel's Holy One will become a flame.
In a single day he will burn up all Assyria's bushes.
He will destroy all their thorns.
[18]He will completely destroy the beauty
of their forests and rich farm lands.
The Assyrian army will be like a sick person
who becomes weaker and weaker.
[19]It will be like the trees of their forests.
So few of them will be left standing
that even a child could count them.

The Israelites Who Are Left Alive

[20]In days to come, some people will still be left alive in Israel.
They will be from Jacob's family line.
But they won't depend any longer on
the nation that struck them down.
Instead, they will truly depend on the LORD.
He is the Holy One of Israel.
[21]The people of Jacob who are still alive
will return to the Mighty God.
[22]Israel, your people might be as many as the grains of sand by the sea.
But only a few of them will return.
The LORD has handed down a death sentence.
He will destroy his people.
What he does is right.
[23]The LORD who rules over all will carry out his sentence.
The Lord will destroy the whole land.

[24]The LORD rules over all. The Lord says,

"My people who live in Zion,
do not be afraid of the Assyrian army.
They beat you with rods.
They lift up war clubs against you,
just as the Egyptians did.
[25]Very soon I will not be angry with you anymore.
I will turn my anger against the Assyrians.
I will destroy them."

[26]The LORD who rules over all will beat them with a whip.
He will strike them down as he struck down Midian at the rock of Oreb.

And he will stretch out his walking
stick over the waters.
That's what he did in Egypt.
27 People of Zion, in days to come he
will help you.
He will lift the heavy load of the
Assyrians from your shoulders.
He will remove their yokes from
your necks.
Their yokes will be broken
because you have become so strong.
28 The Assyrian army has entered the
town of Aiath.
They have passed through
Migron.
They have stored up supplies at
Mikmash.
29 They have marched through the
pass there. They said,
"Let's camp for the night at Geba."
The people of Ramah tremble with
fear.
Those who live in Gibeah of Saul
run away.
30 Town of Gallim, cry out!
Laishah, listen!
Poor Anathoth!
31 The people of Madmenah are
running away.
Those who live in Gebim are
hiding.
32 Today the Assyrians have stopped
at Nob.
They are shaking their fists
at Mount Zion in the city of
Jerusalem.

33 The Assyrian soldiers are like trees
in a forest.
The LORD who rules over all
will chop them down.
The Lord will cut off their branches
with his great power.
He will chop the tall trees down.
He will cut down even the highest
ones.
34 The Mighty One will chop down the
forest with his ax.
He will cut down the cedar trees
in Lebanon.

A Branch Will Come From Jesse's Family Line

11 Jesse's family is like a tree that
has been cut down.
A new little tree will grow from
its stump.
From its roots a Branch will grow
and produce fruit.
2 The Spirit of the LORD will rest on
that Branch.
The Spirit will help him to be
wise and understanding.
The Spirit will help him make wise
plans and carry them out.
The Spirit will help him know the
LORD and have respect for him.
3 The Branch will take delight
in respecting the LORD.

He will not judge things only by the
way they look.
He won't make decisions based
simply on what people say.
4 He will always do what is right
when he judges those who are in
need.
He'll be completely fair
when he makes decisions about
poor people.
When he commands that people be
punished,
it will happen.
When he orders that evil people be
put to death,
it will take place.
5 He will put on godliness as if it were
his belt.
He'll wear faithfulness around
his waist.

6 Wolves will live with lambs.
Leopards will lie down with
goats.
Calves and lions will eat together.
And little children will lead them
around.
7 Cows will eat with bears.
Their little ones will lie down
together.
And lions will eat straw like
oxen.
8 A baby will play near a hole where
cobras live.
A young child will put its hand
into a nest
where poisonous snakes live.
9 None of those animals will harm or
destroy anything or anyone
on my holy mountain of Zion.
The oceans are full of water.
In the same way, the earth will
be filled
with the knowledge of the LORD.

[10]At that time, here is what the man
who is called the Root of Jesse will do. He
will be like a banner that brings nations
together. They will come to him. And the
place where he rules will be glorious. [11]At
that time the Lord will reach out his hand.
He will gather his people a second time.
He will bring back those who are left alive.
He'll bring them back from Assyria, Lower
Egypt, Upper Egypt and Cush. He'll bring
them from Elam, Babylon and Hamath.
He will also bring them from the islands
of the Mediterranean Sea.

[12]He will lift up a banner.
It will show the nations that he is gathering the people of Israel.
He'll bring back those who had been taken away as prisoners.
He'll gather together the scattered people of Judah.
He'll bring them back from all four directions.
[13]Ephraim's people won't be jealous anymore.
Judah's attackers will be destroyed.
Ephraim won't be jealous of Judah.
And Judah won't attack Ephraim.
[14]Together they will rush down the slopes of Philistia to the west.
They'll take what belongs to the people of the east.
They'll take over Edom and Moab.
The people of Ammon will be under their control.
[15]The LORD will dry up the Red Sea in Egypt.
By his power he'll send a burning wind
to sweep over the Euphrates River.
He will break it up into many streams.
Then people will be able to go across it wearing sandals.
[16]There was a road the people of Israel used
when they came up from Egypt.
In the same way, there will be a wide road coming out of Assyria.
It will be used by the LORD's people who are left alive there.

Two Songs of Praise

12 In days to come, the people of Israel will sing,

"LORD, we will praise you.
You were angry with us.
But now your anger has turned away from us.
And you have brought us comfort.
[2]God, you are the one who saves us.
We will trust in you.
Then we won't be afraid.
LORD, you are the one who gives us strength.
You are the one who keeps us safe.
LORD, you have saved us."
[3]People of Israel, he will save you.
That will bring you joy like water brought up from wells.

[4]In days to come, the people of Israel
will sing,

"Give praise to the LORD. Make his name known.
Tell the nations what he has done.
Announce how honored he is.
[5]Sing to the LORD. He has done glorious things.
Let it be known all over the world.
[6]People of Zion, give a loud shout!
Sing for joy!
The Holy One of Israel is among you.
And he is great."

Give praise to the LORD. Make his name known. Tell the nations what he has done. ISAIAH 12:4

A Prophecy Against Babylon

13 Here is the prophecy against Babylon that Isaiah, the son of Amoz, saw.

[2]Lift up a banner on the top of a bare hill.
Shout to the enemy soldiers.
Wave for them to enter the gates that are used by the nobles of Babylon.
[3]The LORD has commanded the soldiers he prepared for battle.
He has sent for them to carry out his anger against Babylon.
They will be happy when he wins the battle for them.

[4]Listen! I hear a noise in the mountains.
It sounds like a huge crowd.
Listen! I hear a loud noise among the kingdoms.
It sounds like nations gathering together.
The LORD who rules over all is bringing
an army together for war.
[5]They come from lands far away.
They come from the farthest places on earth.
The LORD and those weapons of his anger
are coming to destroy the whole country of Babylon.

[6]Cry out! The day of the LORD is near.
The Mighty One is coming to destroy the Babylonians.
[7]Their hands won't be able to help them.
Everyone's heart will melt away in fear.
[8]The people will be filled with terror.
Pain and suffering will grab hold of them.
They will groan with pain like a woman having a baby.
They'll look at one another in terror.
Their faces will burn with shame.

[9]The day of the LORD is coming.
It will be a terrible day.
The LORD's burning anger will blaze out.
He will make the land dry and empty.
He'll destroy the sinners in it.
[10]All the stars in the sky
will stop giving their light.
The sun will be darkened as soon as it rises.
The moon will not shine.
[11]The LORD will punish the world
because it is so evil.
He will punish evil people for their sins.
He'll put an end to the bragging of those who are proud.
He'll bring down the pride of those who don't show any pity.
[12]He'll make people harder to find than pure gold.
They will be harder to find than gold from Ophir.
[13]He will make the heavens tremble.
He'll shake the earth out of its place.
The LORD who rules over all will show how angry he is.
At that time his burning anger will blaze out.

[14]Outsiders who live in Babylon will scatter
like antelope that are chased by a hunter.
They are like sheep that don't have a shepherd.
All of them will return to their own people.
They will run back to their own countries.
[15]Those who are captured will have spears stuck through them.
Those who are caught will be killed by swords.
[16]Their babies will be smashed to pieces right in front of their eyes.
Their houses will be robbed.
Their wives will be raped.

[17]The LORD will stir up the Medes to attack the Babylonians.
They aren't interested in getting silver.
They don't want gold.
[18]Instead, they will use their bows and arrows
to strike down the young men.
They won't even show any mercy to babies.
They won't take pity on children.
[19]The city of Babylon is the jewel of kingdoms.
It is the pride and glory of the Babylonians.
But God will destroy it
just as he did Sodom and Gomorrah.
[20]No one will ever live in Babylon again.
No one will live there for all time to come.
Those who wander in the desert will never set up their tents there.
Shepherds will never rest their flocks there.
[21]But desert creatures will lie down there.
Wild dogs will fill its houses.
Owls will live there.
Wild goats will jump around in it.

22 Hyenas will live in its forts.
Wild dogs will live in its beautiful palaces.
The time for Babylon to be punished is near.
Its days are numbered.

14 The LORD will show tender love toward Jacob's people.
Once again he will choose Israel.
He'll give them homes in their own land.
Outsiders will join them.
They and the people of Jacob will become one people.
2 Nations will help Israel return to their own land.
Israel will possess other nations.
They will serve Israel as male and female servants in the LORD's land.
The Israelites will make prisoners of those who had held them as prisoners.
Israel will rule over those who had crushed them.

3 The LORD will put an end to Israel's
suffering and trouble. They will no longer be forced to do hard labor. At that
time, 4 they will make fun of the king
of Babylon. They will say,

"See how the one who crushed others has fallen!
See how his anger has come to an end!
5 The LORD has taken away the authority of evil people.
He has broken the power of rulers.
6 When they became angry, they struck down nations.
Their blows never stopped.
In their anger they brought nations under their control.
They attacked them again and again.
7 All the lands now enjoy peace and rest.
They break out into singing.
8 Even the juniper trees show how happy they are.
The cedar trees of Lebanon celebrate too.
They say, 'Babylon, you have fallen.
Now no one comes and cuts us down.'
9 "King of Babylon, many people in the place of the dead are really excited.
They're excited about meeting you when you go down there.
The spirits of the dead get up to welcome you.
At one time all of them were leaders in the world.
They were kings over the nations.
They get up from their thrones.
10 All of them call out to you.
They say,
'You have become weak, just as we are.
You have become like us.'
11 Your grand show of power has been brought down to the grave.
The noise of your harps has come down here along with your power.
Maggots are spread out under you.
Worms cover you.

12 "King of Babylon, you thought you were the bright morning star.
But now you have fallen from heaven!
You once brought down nations.
But now you have been thrown down to the earth!
13 You said in your heart,
'I will go up to the heavens.
I'll raise my throne above the stars of God.
I'll sit as king on the mountain where the gods meet.
I'll set up my throne on the highest slopes of Mount Zaphon.
14 I will rise above the tops of the clouds.
I'll make myself like the Most High God.'
15 But now you have been brought down to the place of the dead.
You have been thrown into the deepest part of the pit.

16 "Those who see you stare at you.
They think about what has happened to you.
They say to themselves,
'Is this the man who shook the earth?
Is he the one who made kingdoms tremble with fear?
17 Did he turn the world into a desert?
Did he destroy its cities?
Did he refuse to let his prisoners go home?'

18 "All the kings of the nations are buried with honor.
Each of them lies in his own tomb.
19 But you have been thrown out of your tomb.
You are like a branch that is cut off and thrown away.
You are covered with the bodies of those who have been killed by swords.
You have been tossed into a stony pit along with them.
You are like a dead body that people have walked on.
20 You won't be buried like other kings.
That's because you have destroyed your land.
You have killed your people.

"Let the children of that evil man be killed.
Let none of them be left to carry on the family name.
21 So prepare a place to kill his children.
Kill them because of the sins of the rulers
who lived before them.
They must not rise to power.
They must not rule over the world.
They must not cover the earth with their cities."

22 "I will rise up against them," announces the LORD who rules over all.
"I will destroy Babylon.
It will not be remembered anymore.
No one will be left alive there.
I will destroy its people and their children after them,"
announces the LORD.
23 "I will turn it into a place where nothing but owls can live.
I will turn it into a swamp.
I will sweep through it like a broom and destroy everything,"
announces the LORD who rules over all.

24 The LORD who rules over all has
made a promise. He has said,

"You can be sure that what I have planned will happen.
What I have decided will take place.
25 I will crush the Assyrians in my land.
On my mountains I will walk all over them.
The yokes they put on my people will be removed.
The heavy load they put on their shoulders will be taken away."
26 That's how the LORD carries out his plan all over the world.
That's how he reaches out his powerful hand to punish all the nations.
27 The LORD who rules over all has planned it.
Who can stop him?
He has reached out his powerful hand.
Who can keep him from using it?

A Prophecy Against the Philistines

28 This prophecy came to me from
the LORD in the year King Ahaz died.
The LORD said,

29 "The rod of Assyria has struck all of you Philistines.
But do not be glad that it is broken.
That rod is like a snake that will produce an even more poisonous snake.
It will produce a darting, poisonous serpent.
30 Even the poorest people in Israel will have plenty to eat.
Those who are in need will lie down in safety.
But I will destroy your families.
They will die of hunger.
I will kill any of them who are still left alive.

31 "Cities of Philistia, cry out for help!
Scream in pain!
All you Philistines, melt away in fear!
An army is coming from the north in a cloud of dust.
No one in its ranks is falling behind.
32 What answer should be given to the messengers from that nation?
Tell them, 'The LORD has made Zion secure.
His suffering people will find safety there.' "

A Prophecy Against Moab

15 Here is a prophecy against Moab that the LORD gave me.

The city of Ar in Moab is destroyed.
It happened in a single night.
Kir in Moab is also destroyed.
It happened in a single night.
2 The people of Dibon go up to their temple to worship.
They go to their high places to weep.
The people of Moab cry over the cities of Nebo and Medeba.
All their heads are shaved.
All their beards have been cut off.
3 In the streets they wear the rough clothing people wear when they're sad.
On their roofs and in the market places
all of them are crying.
They fall down flat with their faces toward the ground.
And they weep.
4 The people of Heshbon and Elealeh cry out.
Their voices are heard all the way to Jahaz.
So the fighting men of Moab cry out.
Their hearts are weak.

5 My heart cries out over Moab.
Some who run away get as far as Zoar.
Others run all the way to Eglath Shelishiyah.
Others go up the hill to Luhith.
They are weeping as they go.
Still others travel the road to Horonaim.
They sing a song of sadness because their town is being destroyed.
6 The waters at Nimrim are dried up.
And so is the grass.
The plants have died.
Nothing green is left.
7 The people are trying to escape through the Valley of the Poplar Trees.
They are carrying with them the wealth
they have collected and stored up.
8 Their loud cries echo along the border of Moab.
They reach as far as Eglaim.
Their songs of sadness reach all the way to Beer Elim.
9 The waters of the city of Dimon are full of blood.
But the LORD will bring even more trouble on Dimon.
He will bring lions against those who run away from Moab.
They will also attack those who remain in the land.

16 People of Moab, send lambs as a gift
to the ruler of Judah.
Send them from Sela.
Send them across the desert.
Send them to Mount Zion in the city of Jerusalem.
2 The women of Moab are at the places where people go across the Arnon River.
They are like birds that flap their wings
when they are pushed from their nest.

3 The Moabites say to the rulers of Judah,
"Make up your mind. Make a decision.
Cover us with your shadow.
Make it like night even at noon.
Hide those of us who are running away.
Don't turn them over to their enemies.
4 Let those who have run away from Moab stay with you.
Keep them safe from those who are trying to destroy them."
Those who crush others will be destroyed.
The killing will stop.
The attackers will disappear from the earth.
5 A man from the royal house of David will sit on Judah's throne.
He will rule with faithful love.
When he judges he will do what is fair.
He will be quick to do what is right.

6 We have heard all about Moab's pride.
We have heard how very proud they are.
They think they are so much better than others.

They brag about themselves.
But all their bragging is nothing but empty words.

7 So the people of Moab cry out.
All of them cry over their country.
Sing a song of sadness.
Weep that you can no longer enjoy the raisin cakes of Kir Hareseth.
8 The fields of Heshbon dry up.
So do the vines of Sibmah.
The rulers of the nations have walked all over its finest vines.
Those vines once reached as far as Jazer.
They spread out toward the desert.
Their new growth went all the way to the Dead Sea.
9 Jazer weeps for the vines of Sibmah.
And so do I.
Heshbon and Elealeh, I soak you with my tears!
There isn't any ripe fruit for people to shout about.
There isn't any harvest to make them happy.
10 Joy and gladness are taken away from the orchards.
No one sings or shouts in the vineyards.
No one stomps on grapes at the winepresses.
That's because the LORD has put an end to the shouting.
11 My heart mourns over Moab like a song of sadness played on a harp.
Deep down inside me I mourn over Kir Hareseth.
12 Moab's people go to their high place to pray.
But all they do is wear themselves out.
Their god Chemosh can't help them at all.

13 That's the message the LORD has
already spoken against Moab. 14 But
now he says, "In exactly three years,
people will look down on Moab's glory.
Now Moab has many people. But by
that time only a few of them will be
left alive. And even they will be weak."

Prophecies Against Damascus and Israel

17 Here is a prophecy against Damascus that the LORD gave me. He said,

"Damascus will not be a city anymore.
Instead, all its buildings will be knocked down.
2 The cities of Aroer will be deserted.
They will be left to the flocks that lie down there.
No one will make them afraid.
3 Ephraim's people will no longer have cities with high walls around them.
Royal power will disappear from Damascus.
Those who are left alive in Aram will be like the glory of the people of Israel,"
announces the LORD who rules over all.

4 "In days to come, the glory of Jacob's people will fade.
Their strength will get weaker and weaker.
5 It will be as when workers cut and gather grain
in the Valley of Rephaim.
They gather up stalks in their arms.
Only a few heads of grain are left.
6 In the same way, only a few people will be left alive.
It will be as when workers knock olives off the trees.
Only two or three olives are left on the highest branches.
Four or five at most are left on the limbs that produce fruit,"
announces the LORD, the God of Israel.

7 In days to come, people will look to their Maker for help.
They will turn their eyes to the Holy One of Israel.
8 They won't trust in the altars
they made with their own hands.
They won't pay any attention to the poles they used
to worship the female god named Asherah.
And they won't depend on the incense altars
they made with their own fingers.

9 At that time the strong cities in Israel
will be deserted. They will be as they were
when the Israelites drove the Canaanites
away. They will be like places that are
taken over by bushes and weeds. The
whole land will become dry and empty.

10 Israel, you have forgotten God, who saves you.
You have not remembered the Rock, who keeps you safe.
You might set out the finest plants.
You might plant vines from other lands.
11 The plants might start to grow on the day you set them out.
The vines might begin to bud on the morning you plant them.
But even if they do, there won't be any harvest.
Instead, there will be sickness and pain that won't go away.

12 How terrible it will be for the nations that attack us!
The noise of their armies is like the sound of the ocean.
How terrible it will be for the nations who fight against us!
They are as loud as huge waves crashing on the shore.
13 They sound like the roar of rushing waters.
But when the LORD speaks out against them, they run far away.
The wind blows them away like straw on the hills.
A strong wind drives them along like tumbleweeds.
14 In the evening, the nations terrify us.
But before morning comes, they are gone.
That's what happens to those who steal our goods.
That's what happens to those who take what belongs to us.

A Prophecy Against Cush

18 How terrible it will be for the land
whose armies are like large numbers of flying insects!
That land is along the rivers of Cush.
2 Its people send messengers on the Nile River.
They travel over the water in papyrus boats.
Messengers, hurry back home!
Go back to your people,
who are tall and have smooth skin.
Everyone is afraid of them.
They are warriors whose language is different from ours.
Their land is divided up by rivers.

3 Pay attention, all you people of the world!
Listen, all you who live on earth!
Banners will be lifted up on the mountains.
And you will see them.
Trumpets will be blown.
And you will hear them.
4 The LORD says to me,
"I will look down from heaven, where I live.
I will be as quiet as summer heat in the sunshine.
I will be as quiet as a cloud of dew in the heat of harvest."
5 A farmer cuts off new growth with pruning knives.
He cuts down spreading branches and takes them away.
He does it before the grapes are harvested.
That's when the blooms are gone and the grapes are ripe.
In the same way, the LORD will cut off the nations
that are gathered against his people.
6 Their dead bodies will be left for the birds of the mountains to eat.
They will be left for the wild animals.
The birds will eat the dead bodies all summer long.
The wild animals will eat them all through the winter.

7 At that time gifts will be brought to
the LORD who rules over all.

The people who are tall and have smooth skin will bring them.
Everyone is afraid of those people.
They are warriors whose language is different from ours.
Their land is divided up by rivers.

They will bring their gifts to Mount Zion.
That's where the LORD who rules over
all has put his Name.

A Prophecy Against Egypt

19 Here is a prophecy against Egypt
that the LORD gave me.

The LORD is coming to Egypt.
He's riding on a cloud that moves very fast.
The statues of the gods in Egypt
tremble with fear because of him.
The hearts of the people there
melt with fear.

2 The LORD says, "I will stir up one
Egyptian against another.
Relatives will fight against
relatives.
Neighbors will fight against one
another.
Cities will fight against cities.
Kingdoms will fight against one
another.
3 The people of Egypt will lose hope.
I will keep them from doing what
they plan to do.
They will ask their gods for advice.
They will turn to the spirits of
dead people for help.
They will go to people who get
messages from those who have
died.
They will ask for advice from
people who talk to the spirits of
the dead.
4 I will hand the Egyptians over
to a mean and unkind master.
A powerful king will rule over
them," announces the LORD.
He is the LORD who rules over all.

5 The waters of the Nile River will
dry up.
The bottom of it will be cracked
and dry.
6 Its canals will stink.
And the streams of Egypt will get
smaller and smaller
until they dry up.
The tall grass that grows along the
river will dry up.
7 So will the plants along the
banks of the Nile.
Even the planted fields along the
Nile will dry up.
Everything that grows there will
blow away and disappear.
8 The fishermen will moan.
All those who drop hooks into the
Nile will weep.
Those who throw their nets on the
water
will become very sad.
9 Those who make clothes out of flax
will lose hope.
So will those who weave fine
linen.
10 Those who work with cloth will be
unhappy.
And all those who work for
money will be sick at heart.

11 The officials of the city of Zoan are
very foolish.
Pharaoh's wise men give advice
that doesn't make any sense.
How can they dare to say to
Pharaoh,
"We're among the wise men"?
How can they say to him,
"We're like the advisers to the
kings of long ago"?

12 Pharaoh, where are your wise men
now?
Let them tell you
what the LORD who rules over all
has planned against Egypt.
13 The officials of Zoan have become
foolish.
The leaders of Memphis have
been lied to.
The most important leaders in
Egypt
have led its people astray.
14 The LORD has given them
a spirit that makes them feel
dizzy.
They make Egypt unsteady in
everything it does.
Egypt is like a person who drinks
too much.
He throws up and then walks
around in the mess he's made.
15 No one in Egypt can do anything to
help them.
Its elders and important leaders
can't help them.
Its prophets and priests can't do
anything.
Those who rule over others can't
help.
And those who bow down to
them can't help either.

16 In days to come, the people of Egypt
will become weak. The LORD who rules
over all will raise his hand against
them. Then they will tremble with fear.

17 The people of Judah will bring terror
to the Egyptians. Everyone in Egypt
who hears the name of Judah will be
terrified. That's because of what the
LORD who rules over all is planning to
do to them.
18 At that time the people of five cities
in Egypt will worship the LORD. He is
the LORD who rules over all. They will
use the Hebrew language when they
worship him. They will promise to be
faithful to him. One of those cities will
be called the City of the Sun.
19 At that time there will be an altar to
the LORD in the middle of Egypt. There
will be a monument to him at its border. 20 They will remind people that the
LORD who rules over all is worshiped in
Egypt. The people there will cry out to
the LORD. They will cry out because of
those who treat them badly. He will send
someone to stand up for them and save
them. And he will set them free. 21 So the
LORD will make himself known to the
people of Egypt. At that time they will
recognize that he is the LORD. They will
worship him by bringing sacrifices and
grain offerings to him. They will make
promises to the LORD. And they will keep
them. 22 The LORD will strike Egypt with
a plague. But then he will heal them.
They will turn to the LORD. And he will
answer their prayers and heal them.
23 At that time there will be a wide
road from Egypt to Assyria. The people of Assyria will go to Egypt. And
the people of Egypt will go to Assyria.
The people of Egypt and Assyria will
worship the LORD together. 24 At that
time Egypt, Assyria and Israel will be a
blessing to the whole earth. 25 The LORD
who rules over all will bless those three
nations. He will say, "Let the Egyptians
be blessed. They are my people. Let the
Assyrians be blessed. My hands created
them. And let the Israelites be blessed.
They are my very own people."

A Prophecy Against Egypt and Cush

20 Sargon, the king of Assyria, sent
his highest commander to the
city of Ashdod. He attacked it and captured it. 2 Three years earlier the LORD
had spoken to Isaiah, the son of Amoz.
The LORD had said, "Take off the rough
clothing you are wearing. And take off
your sandals." So Isaiah did. He went
around barefoot and naked.
3 After Ashdod was captured, the
LORD said, "My servant Isaiah has gone
around barefoot and naked for three
years. He is a sign and reminder to
Egypt and Cush about what will happen
to them. 4 The king of Assyria will lead
prisoners away from Egypt and Cush.
Young people and old people alike will
be taken away. Like Isaiah, they will be
barefoot and naked. Their backsides
will be bare. So the Egyptians will be
put to shame. 5 People trusted in Cush
to help them. They bragged about what
Egypt could do for them. But they will
lose heart and be put to shame. 6 At that
time the people who live on the coast
of Philistia will speak up. They will say,
'See what has happened to those we depended on! We ran to them for help. We
wanted them to save us from the king
of Assyria. Now how can we escape?' "

A Prophecy Against Babylon

21 Here is a prophecy against Babylon that the LORD gave me. Babylon is known as the Desert by the Sea.

An attack is coming through the
desert.
It is coming from a land of terror.
It's sweeping along like a
windstorm blowing across the
Negev Desert.

2 I have seen a vision about
something terrible that will
happen.
People are turning against
Babylon.
Robbers are taking its goods.
Elamites, attack the city! Medes,
surround it!
The LORD will put an end to all
the suffering Babylon has
caused.

3 The vision fills my body with pain.
Pains take hold of me.
They are like the pains of a
woman having a baby.
I am shaken by what I hear.
I'm terrified by what I see.
4 My heart grows weak.
Fear makes me tremble.
I longed for evening to come.
But it brought me horror instead
of rest.

[5] In my vision the Babylonians set
the tables.
They spread out the rugs.
They eat and drink.
Get up, you officers!
Rub your shields with oil!
[6] The Lord said to me,
"Go. Put a guard on duty on
Jerusalem's walls.
Have him report what he sees.
[7] Tell him to watch for chariots
that are pulled by teams of
horses.
Tell him to watch for men riding on
donkeys or camels.
Make sure he stays awake.
Make sure he stays wide awake."

[8] "My master!" the guard shouts back.
"Day after day I stand here on the
lookout tower.
Every night I stay here on duty.
[9] Look! Here comes a man in a
chariot!
It's being pulled by a team of
horses.
He's calling out the news,
'Babylon has fallen! It has fallen!
All the statues of its gods
lie broken in pieces on the
ground!' "

[10] My people, you have been crushed
like grain on a threshing floor.
But now I'm telling you the good
news I've heard.
It comes from the LORD who rules
over all.
He is the God of Israel.

A Prophecy Against Edom

[11] Here is a prophecy against Edom
that the LORD gave me.

Someone is calling out to me from
the land of Seir. He says,
"Guard, when will the night be
over?
Guard, how soon will it end?"
[12] The guard answers,
"Morning is coming, but the
night will return.
If you want to ask again,
come back and ask."

A Prophecy Against Arabia

[13] Here is a prophecy against Arabia
that the LORD gave me.

He told me to give orders to traders
from Dedan.
They were camping in the bushes
of Arabia.
[14] I told them to bring water for
those who are thirsty.
I also gave orders to those who live
in Tema.
I told them to bring food for
those who are running away.
[15] They are running away from where
the fighting is heaviest.
That's where the swords are
ready to strike.
That's where the bows are ready
to shoot.

[16] The Lord spoke to me. He said, "In
exactly one year, Kedar's splendor will
come to an end. [17] Only a few of Kedar's
soldiers who shoot arrows will be left
alive." The LORD has spoken. He is the
God of Israel.

A Prophecy Against Jerusalem

22 Here is a prophecy against Jerusalem that the LORD gave me.
Jerusalem is also known as the Valley
of Vision.

People of Jerusalem, what's the
matter with you?
Why have all of you gone up on
the roofs of your houses?
[2] Why is your town so full of noise?
Why is your city so full of the
sound of wild parties?
Those among you who died weren't
killed by swords.
They didn't die in battle.
[3] All your leaders have run away.
They've been captured without a
single arrow being shot.
All you who were caught were
taken away as prisoners.
You ran off while your enemies
were still far away.
[4] So I said, "Leave me alone.
Let me weep bitter tears.
Don't try to comfort me.
My people have been destroyed."

[5] The LORD who rules over all sent
the noise of battle against you.
The Lord brought disorder and
terror
to the Valley of Vision.
The walls of the city were knocked
down.

Cries for help were heard in the
mountains.
6 Soldiers from Elam came armed
with bows and arrows.
They came with their chariots
and horses.
Soldiers from Kir got their shields
ready.
7 Your rich valleys filled up with
chariots.
Horsemen took up their battle
positions at your city gates.
8 The Lord made Judah a place
where it wasn't safe to live
anymore.

At that time, you depended
on the weapons in the Palace of
the Forest of Lebanon.
9 You saw that the walls of the City of
David
were broken through in many
places.
You stored up water
in the Lower Pool.
10 You picked out the weaker
buildings in Jerusalem.
You tore them down and used
their stones
to strengthen the city walls
against attack.
11 You built a pool between the two
walls.
You used it to save the water
that was running down from the
Old Pool.
But you didn't look to the God who
made it all possible.
You didn't pay any attention to
the God
who planned everything long
ago.
12 The LORD who rules over all
called out to you at that time.
The Lord told you to weep and cry.
He told you to tear your hair out.
And he told you to put on the
rough clothing people wear
when they're sad.
13 Instead, you are enjoying
yourselves at wild parties!
You are killing cattle and sheep.
You are eating their meat and
drinking wine.
You are saying, "Let's eat and
drink,
because tomorrow we'll die."

14 I heard the LORD who rules over all
speaking. "Your sin can never be paid
for as long as you live," says the Lord.

15 The LORD who rules over all speaks.
The Lord says,

"Go and speak to Shebna, the head
servant.
He is in charge of the palace. Tell
him,
16 'What are you doing here outside
the city?
Who allowed you to cut out a
tomb for yourself here?
Who said you could carve out your
grave on the hillside?
Who allowed you to cut out your
resting place in the rock?
17 " 'Watch out, you mighty man!
The LORD is about to grab you.
He is about to throw you away.
18 He will roll you up tightly like a ball.
He will throw you into a very
large country.
There you will die.
And that's where the chariots
you were so proud of will be.
Those chariots will then bring
nothing but shame on your
master's family!
19 The LORD will remove you from
your job.
You will be brought down from
your high position.

20 " 'At that time he will send for his
servant Eliakim. He is the son of Hilkiah.
21 The LORD will put your robe on Eliakim.
He will tie your belt around him. He
will hand your authority over to him.
Eliakim will be like a father to the people
of Jerusalem and Judah. 22 The LORD
will give Eliakim the key of authority
in David's royal house. No one can shut
what he opens. And no one can open
what he shuts. 23 The LORD will set him
firmly in place like a peg driven into a
wall. He will hold a position of honor in
his family. 24 The good name of his whole
family will depend on him. They will be
like bowls and jars hanging on a peg.

25 " 'But a new day is coming,' " announces the LORD who rules over all. " 'At
that time the peg that was driven into the
wall will give way. It will break off and
fall down. And the heavy load hanging
on it will also fall.' " The LORD has spoken.

A Prophecy Against Tyre

23 Here is a prophecy against Tyre that the LORD gave me.

Men in the ships of Tarshish, cry out!
The city of Tyre is destroyed.
Its houses and harbor are gone.
That's the message you have received
from the island of Cyprus.

2 People on the island of Tyre, be silent.
Traders from the city of Sidon, be quiet.
Those who sail on the Mediterranean Sea have made you rich.
3 Grain from Egypt
came across the mighty waters.
The harvest of the Nile River brought wealth to Tyre.
It became the market place of the nations.

4 Sidon, be ashamed. Mighty Tyre out in the sea, be ashamed.
The sea has spoken. It has said,
"It's as if I had never felt labor pains or had children.
It's as if I had never brought up sons or daughters.
It's as if the city of Tyre had never existed."
5 The Egyptians will hear about what has happened to Tyre.
They'll be very sad and troubled.

6 People of the island of Tyre, cry out!
Go across the sea to Tarshish.
7 Just look at Tyre.
It's no longer the old, old city that was known for its wild parties.
It no longer sends its people out to make their homes in lands far away.
8 Tyre was a city that produced kings.
Its traders were princes.
They were honored all over the earth.
So who planned to destroy such a city?
9 The LORD who rules over all planned to do it.
He wanted to bring down all its pride and glory.
He wanted to shame those who were honored all over the earth.

10 People of Tarshish, farm your land as they do along the Nile River.
That's because you don't have a harbor anymore.
11 The LORD has reached his powerful hand out over the sea.
He has made its kingdoms tremble with fear.
He has given a command concerning Phoenicia.
He has ordered that its forts be destroyed.
12 He said, "No more wild parties for you!
People of Sidon, you are now destroyed!

"Leave your city. Go across the sea to Cyprus.
Even there you will not find any rest."
13 Look at the land of the Babylonians.
No one lives there anymore.
The Assyrians have turned it into a place for desert creatures.
They built their towers in order to attack it.
They took everything out of its forts.
They knocked down all its buildings.

14 Men in the ships of Tarshish, cry out!
Mighty Tyre is destroyed!

15 A time is coming when people will
forget about Tyre for 70 years. That's
the length of a king's life. But at the
end of those 70 years, Tyre will be like
the prostitute that people sing about.
They say,

16 "Forgotten prostitute, pick up a harp.
Walk through the city.
Play the harp well. Sing many songs.
Then you will be remembered."

17 At the end of the 70 years, the LORD
will punish Tyre. He will let it return to its
way of life as a prostitute. It will earn its
living with all the kingdoms on the face
of the earth. 18 But the money it earns

will be set apart for the LORD. The money won't be stored up or kept for Tyre. Instead, it will go to those who live the way the LORD wants them to. It will pay for plenty of food and fine clothes for them.

The LORD Will Destroy the Earth

24 The LORD is going to completely destroy everything on earth.
He will twist its surface.
He'll scatter those who live on it.
2 Priests and people alike will suffer.
So will masters and their servants.
And so will women and their female servants.
Sellers and buyers alike will suffer.
So will those who borrow and those who lend.
And so will those who owe money and those who lend it.
3 The earth will be completely destroyed.
Everything of value will be taken out of it.
That's what the LORD has said.

4 The earth will dry up completely.
The world will dry up and waste away.
The heavens will fade away along with the earth.
5 The earth is polluted by its people.
They haven't obeyed the laws of the LORD.
They haven't done what he told them to do.
They've broken the covenant that will last forever.
6 So the LORD will send a curse on the earth.
Its people will pay for what they've done.
They will be burned up.
Very few of them will be left.
7 The vines and fresh wine will dry up completely.
Those who used to have a good time will groan.
8 The happy sounds of tambourines will be gone.
The noise of those who enjoy wild parties will stop.
The joyful music of harps will become silent.
9 People will no longer sing as they drink wine.
Beer will taste bitter to those who drink it.
10 Destroyed cities will lie empty.
People will lock themselves inside their houses.
11 In the streets people will cry out for wine.
All joy will turn into sadness.
All joyful sounds will be driven out of the earth.
12 All the buildings will be knocked down.
Every city gate will be smashed to pieces.
13 That's how it will be on the earth.
And that's how it will be among the nations.
It will be as when workers knock all but a few olives off the trees.
It will be like a vine that has only a few grapes left after the harvest.

14 Those who are left alive will shout for joy.
People from the west will praise the LORD because he is the King.
15 So give glory to him, you who live in the east.
Honor the name of the LORD, you who are in the islands of the sea.
He is the God of Israel.
16 From one end of the earth to the other we hear singing.
People are saying,
"Give glory to the God who always does what is right."

But I said, "I feel very bad.
I'm getting weaker and weaker.
How terrible it is for me!
People turn against one another.
They can't be trusted.
So they turn against one another."
17 Listen, you people of the earth.
Terror, a pit and a trap are waiting for you.
18 Anyone who runs away from the terror
will fall into the pit.
Anyone who climbs out of the pit will be caught in the trap.

The LORD will open the windows of the skies.
He will flood the land.
The foundations of the earth will shake.

19 The earth will be broken up.
It will split open.
It will be shaken to pieces.
20 The earth will be unsteady like someone who is drunk.
It will sway like a tent in the wind.
Its sin will weigh so heavily on it that it will fall.
It will never get up again.

21 At that time the LORD will punish the spiritual forces of evil in the heavens above.
He will also punish the kings on the earth below.
22 They will be brought together like prisoners in chains.
They'll be locked up in prison.
After many days the LORD will punish them.
23 The LORD who rules over all will rule on Mount Zion in Jerusalem.
The elders of the city will be there.
They will see his great glory.
His rule will be so glorious that the sun and moon
will be too ashamed to shine.

A Song of Praise to the LORD

25 LORD, you are my God.
I will honor you.
I will praise your name.
You have been perfectly faithful.
You have done wonderful things.
You had planned them long ago.
2 You have turned cities into piles of trash.
You have pulled down the high walls that were around them.
You have destroyed our enemies' forts.
They will never be rebuilt.
3 Powerful nations will honor you.
Even sinful people from their cities will have respect for you.
4 Poor people have come to you for safety.
You have kept needy people safe when they were in trouble.
You have been a place to hide when storms came.
You have been a shade from the heat of the sun.
Evil people attack us.
They are like a storm beating against a wall.
5 They are like the heat of the desert.
You stopped the noisy shouts of our enemies.
You kept them from winning the battle over us and singing about it.
You are like the shadow of a cloud that cools the earth.
6 On Mount Zion the LORD who rules over all will prepare
a feast for all the nations.
The best and richest foods
and the finest aged wines will be served.
7 On that mountain the LORD will destroy
the veil of sadness that covers all the nations.
He will destroy the gloom that is spread over everyone.
8 He will swallow up death forever.
The LORD and King will wipe away the tears
from everyone's face.
He will remove the shame of his people
from the whole earth.
The LORD has spoken.

9 At that time they will say,

"He is our God.
We trusted in him, and he saved us.
He is the LORD. We trusted in him.
Let us be filled with joy because he saved us."

10 The LORD's power will keep Mount Zion safe.
But the people of Moab will be crushed in their land.
They will be crushed just as straw is crushed in animal waste.
11 They will try to swim their way out of it.
They will spread out their hands in it,
just as swimmers spread out their hands to swim.
But God will bring down Moab's pride.
None of their skill will help them.
12 He will pull down their high, strong walls.
He will bring them down to the ground.
He'll bring them right down to the dust.

Another Song of Praise

26 At that time a song will be sung in the land of Judah. It will say,

"We have a strong city.
God's saving power surrounds it like walls and towers.
2 Open its gates
so that those who do what is right can enter.
They are the people who remain faithful to God.
3 LORD, you will give perfect peace
to those who commit themselves to be faithful to you.
That's because they trust in you.

4 "Trust in the LORD forever.
The LORD himself is the Rock.
The LORD will keep us safe forever.
5 He brings down those who are proud.
He pulls down cities that have high walls.
They fall down flat on the ground.
He throws them down to the dust.
6 The feet of those who were treated badly stomp on them.
Those who were poor walk all over them."

7 The path of godly people is level.
You are the God who does what is right.
You make their way smooth.
8 LORD, we are living the way your laws command us to live.
We are waiting for you to act.
We want your honor and fame to be known.
9 My heart longs for you at night.
My spirit longs for you in the morning.
You will come and judge the earth.
Then the people of the world will learn to do what is right.
10 Sometimes grace is shown to sinful people.
But they still don't learn to do what is right.
They keep on doing evil even in a land where others are honest and fair.
They don't have any respect for the majesty of the LORD.
11 LORD, you have raised your hand high to punish them.
But they don't even see it.
Let them see how much you love your people.
Then they will be put to shame.
Let the fire you are saving for your enemies burn them up.

12 LORD, you give us peace.
You are the one who has done everything we've accomplished.
13 LORD, you are our God.
Other masters besides you have ruled over us.
But your name is the only one we honor.
14 Those other masters are now dead.
They will never live again.
Their spirits won't rise from the dead.
You punished them and destroyed them.
You wiped out all memory of them.
15 LORD, you have made our nation grow.
You have made it larger.
You have gained glory for yourself.
You have increased the size of our land.

16 LORD, when your people were suffering, they came to you.
When you punished them,
they could barely whisper a prayer.
17 LORD, you made us like a woman who is about to have a baby.
She groans and cries out in pain.
18 We were pregnant and groaned with pain.
But nothing was born.
We didn't bring your saving power to the earth.
And the people of the world have not come to life.

19 LORD, your people who have died will live again.
Their bodies will rise from the dead.
Let those who lie in the grave wake up and shout for joy.
You give life, LORD, like the dew of the morning.
So the earth will give up its dead people.

[20]My people, go into your houses.
Shut the doors behind you.
Hide yourselves for a little while.
Do it until the LORD's anger is over.
[21]He is coming from the place where he lives.
He will punish the people of the earth for their sins.
The blood spilled on the earth will be brought out into the open.
The ground will no longer hide those who have been killed.

Israel Will Be Saved

27 At that time
the LORD will punish Leviathan with his sword.
His great, powerful and deadly sword will punish
the serpent that glides through the sea.
He will kill that twisting sea monster.

[2]At that time the LORD will sing about
his fruitful vineyard. He will say,

[3]"I am the LORD. I watch over my vineyard.
I water it all the time.
I guard it day and night.
I do it so no one can harm it.
[4]I am not angry with my vineyard.
I wish thorns and bushes would come up in it.
Then I would march out against them in battle.
I would set all of them on fire.
[5]So the enemies of my people should come to me for safety.
They should make peace with me.
I will say it again.
They should make peace with me."
[6]In days to come, Jacob's people will put down roots like a vine.
Israel will bud and bloom.
They will fill the whole world with fruit.

[7]The LORD struck down those who struck down Israel.
But he hasn't punished Israel as much.
The LORD killed those who killed many of his people.
But he hasn't punished his people as much.
[8]The LORD will use war to punish Israel.
He will make them leave their land.
With a strong blast of his anger he will drive them out.
It will be as if the east wind were blowing.
[9]The people of Jacob will have to pay for their sin.
Here is how they will show that their sin has been removed.
They will make all the altar stones like limestone.
They will crush them to pieces.
No poles used to worship the female god named Asherah will be left standing.
No incense altars will be left either.
[10]Cities that have high walls around them will become empty.
They will be settlements with no one in them.
They will be like a desert.
Calves will eat and lie down in them.
They will strip bare the branches of their trees.
[11]When their twigs are dry, they will be broken off.
Then women will come and make fires with them.
The people of Jacob don't understand the LORD.
So the God who made them won't be concerned about them.
Their Creator won't be kind to them.

[12]At that time the LORD will separate
Israel from other people. He will gather
the Israelites together one by one. He
will gather them from the Euphrates
River to the Wadi of Egypt. [13]At that
time a loud trumpet will be blown.
Those who were dying in Assyria will
come and worship the LORD. So will
those who were taken away to Egypt.
All of them will worship the LORD on his
holy mountain in Jerusalem.

The LORD Will Judge the Leaders of Ephraim and Judah

28 How terrible it will be for the city of Samaria!
It sits on a hill like a wreath of flowers.

The leaders of Ephraim are drunk.
They take pride in their city.
It sits above a valley that has rich soil.
How terrible it will be for the glorious beauty of that fading flower!
2 The Lord will bring the strong and powerful king of Assyria against Samaria.
The Lord will throw that city down to the ground with great force.
It will be like a hailstorm.
It will be like a wind that destroys everything.
It will be like a driving rain and a flooding storm.
3 That city is like a wreath.
The leaders of Ephraim are drunk.
They take pride in their city.
But its enemies will walk all over it.
4 It sits on a hill above a rich valley.
The city is like a wreath of flowers whose glorious beauty is fading away.
But it will become like figs that are ripe before harvest.
As soon as people see them,
they pick them and swallow them.

5 At that time the LORD who rules over all
will be like a glorious crown.
He will be like a beautiful wreath
for those of his people who will be left alive.
6 He will help those
who are fair when they judge.
He will give strength to those
who turn back their enemies at the city gate.

7 Israel's leaders are drunk from wine.
They can't walk straight.
They are drunk from beer.
They are unsteady on their feet.
Priests and prophets drink beer.
They can't walk straight.
They are mixed up from drinking too much wine.
They drink too much beer.
They are unsteady on their feet.
The prophets see visions but don't really understand them.
The priests aren't able to make good decisions.
8 They throw up. All the tables are covered
with the mess they've made.
There isn't one spot on the tables
that isn't smelly and dirty.

9 The LORD's people are making fun of him. They say,
"Who does he think he's trying to teach?
Who does he think he's explaining his message to?
Is it to children who do not need their mother's milk anymore?
Is it to those who have just been taken from her breast?
10 Here is how he teaches.
Do this and do that.
There is a rule for this and a rule for that.
Learn a little here and learn a little there."

11 All right then, these people won't listen to me.
So God will speak to them.
He will speak by using people who speak unfamiliar languages.
He will speak by using the mouths of strangers.
12 He said to his people,
"I am offering you a resting place.
Let those who are tired rest."
He continued, "I am offering you a place of peace and quiet."
But they wouldn't listen.
13 So then, here is what the LORD's message will become to them.
Do this and do that.
There is a rule for this and a rule for that.
Learn a little here and learn a little there.
So when they try to go forward,
they'll fall back and be wounded.
They'll be trapped and captured.

14 Listen to the LORD's message,
you who make fun of the truth.
Listen, you who rule over these people in Jerusalem.
15 You brag, "We have entered into a covenant with the place of the dead.
We have made an agreement with the grave.

When a terrible plague comes to
punish us,
it can't touch us.
That's because we depend on lies to
keep us safe.
We hide behind what isn't true."

16 So the LORD and King speaks. He
says,

"Look! I am laying a stone in Zion.
It is a stone that has been tested.
It is the most important stone for a
firm foundation.
The one who depends on that
stone will never be shaken.
17 I will use a measuring line to prove
that you have not been fair.
I will use a plumb line to prove
that you have not done what is
right.
Hail will sweep away the lies you
depend on to keep you safe.
Water will flood your hiding
place.
18 Your covenant with death will be
called off.
The agreement you made with
the place of the dead will not
stand.
When the terrible plague comes to
punish you,
you will be struck down by it.
19 As often as it comes, it will carry
you away.
Morning after morning, day and
night,
it will come to punish you."

If you understand this message,
it will bring you absolute terror.
20 You will be like someone whose bed
is too short to lie down on.
You will be like those whose
blankets are too small to wrap
themselves in.
21 The LORD will rise up to judge, just
as he did at Mount Perazim.
He will get up to act, just as he
did in the Valley of Gibeon.
He'll do his work, but it will be
strange work.
He'll carry out his task, but it will
be an unexpected one.
22 Now stop making fun of me.
If you don't, your chains will
become heavier.
The LORD who rules over all has
spoken to me.
The Lord has told me he has
ordered that the whole land be
destroyed.

23 Listen and hear my voice.
Pay attention to what I'm saying.
24 When a farmer plows in order to
plant, does he plow without
stopping?
Does he keep on breaking up the
soil and making the field level?
25 When he's made the surface even,
doesn't he plant caraway seeds?
Doesn't he scatter cumin seeds?
Doesn't he plant wheat in its proper
place?
Doesn't he plant barley where it
belongs?
Doesn't he plant spelt along the
edge of the field?
26 His God directs him.
He teaches him the right way to
do his work.

27 Caraway seeds are beaten out with
a rod.
They aren't separated out under
a threshing sled.
Cumin seeds are beaten out with a
stick.
The wheel of a cart isn't rolled
over them.
28 Grain must be ground up to make
bread.
A farmer separates it out.
But he doesn't go on doing it
forever.
He drives the wheels of a threshing
cart over it.
But he doesn't use horses to grind
the grain.
29 All these insights come from the
LORD who rules over all.
His advice is wonderful. His
wisdom is glorious.

The LORD Will Judge Jerusalem

29 Jerusalem, how terrible it will
be for you!
Ariel, you are the city where
David made his home.
The years will come and go.
Keep on celebrating your regular
feasts.
2 The LORD says, "Ariel, I will
surround you.
Jerusalem, I will get ready to
attack you.

Your people will mourn.
They will sing songs of sadness.
I will make you like the front of an altar
covered with blood.
3 I will be like an army camped against you on all sides.
I will surround you with towers in order to attack you.
I will build my ramps all around you and set up my ladders.
4 You will be brought down to the grave.
You will speak from deep down inside the ground.
Your words will be barely heard out of the dust.
Your voice will sound like the voice of a ghost
coming from under the ground.
Your words will sound like a whisper out of the dust."

5 Jerusalem, all your enemies will become like fine dust.
Their terrifying armies will become like straw
that the wind blows away.
All of a sudden, in an instant,
6 the LORD who rules over all will come.
He will come with thunder, earthquakes and a lot of noise.
He'll bring windstorms and rainstorms with him.
He'll send a blazing fire that will burn up everything.

7 Armies from all the nations will fight against Ariel.
They will attack it and its fort.
They'll surround it completely.
But suddenly those armies will disappear like a dream.
They will vanish like a vision in the night.
8 It will be as when a hungry person dreams of eating,
but wakes up still hungry.
It will be as when a thirsty person dreams of drinking,
but wakes up weak and still thirsty.
In the same way, the armies from all the nations
that fight against Mount Zion will disappear.

9 People of Jerusalem, be shocked and amazed.
Make yourselves blind so you can't see anything.
Get drunk, but not from wine.
Be unsteady on your feet, but not because of beer.
10 The LORD has made you fall into a deep sleep.
He has closed the eyes of your prophets.
He has covered the heads of your seers so they can't see.

11 For you, this whole vision is like
words that are sealed up in a scroll.
Suppose you give it to someone who can
read. And suppose you say, "Please read
this for us." Then they'll answer, "I can't.
It's sealed up." 12 Or suppose you give the
scroll to someone who can't read. And
suppose you say, "Please read this for
us." Then they'll answer, "I don't know
how to read."

13 The Lord says,

"These people worship me only with their words.
They honor me by what they say.
But their hearts are far away from me.
Their worship doesn't mean anything to me.
They teach nothing but human rules that they have been taught.
14 So once more I will shock these people
with many wonderful acts.
I will destroy the wisdom of those who think they are so wise.
I will do away with the cleverness of those who think they are so smart."
15 How terrible it will be for people who try hard
to hide their plans from the LORD!
They do their work in darkness.
They think, "Who sees us? Who will know?"
16 They turn everything upside down.
How silly they are to think that potters are like the clay they work with!
Can what is made say to the one who made it,
"You didn't make me"?

Can the pot say to the potter,
"You don't know anything"?

17 In a very short time, Lebanon
will be turned into rich farm lands.
The rich farm lands will seem like a forest.
18 At that time those who can't hear
will hear what is read from the scroll.
Those who are blind will come
out of gloom and darkness.
They will be able to see.
19 Those who aren't proud will once
again find their joy in the LORD.
And those who are in need will
find their joy in the Holy One of Israel.
20 Those who don't show any pity will vanish.
Those who make fun of others will disappear.
All those who look for ways to do
what is evil will be cut off.
21 Without any proof, they claim that
a person is guilty.
In court they try to trap
the one who speaks up for others.
By using dishonest witnesses they
keep people who aren't guilty
from being treated fairly.

22 Long ago the LORD saved Abraham
from trouble. Now he says to Jacob's
people,

"You will not be ashamed anymore.
Your faces will no longer grow
pale with fear.
23 You will see your children living
among you.
I myself will give you those
children.
Then you will honor my name.
You will recognize how holy
I am.
I am the Holy One of Jacob.
You will have great respect for me.
I am the God of Israel.
24 I will give understanding to you
who find yourselves going
astray.
You who are always speaking
against others
will accept what I teach you."

The LORD Will Judge His Stubborn People

30 "How terrible it will be for these
stubborn children of mine!"
announces the LORD.
"How terrible for those who carry out
plans that did not come from me!
Their agreement with Egypt did
not come from my Spirit.
So they pile up one sin on top of
another.
2 They go down to Egypt
without asking me for advice.
They look to Pharaoh to help them.
They ask Egypt to keep them safe.
3 But looking to Pharaoh will only
bring them shame.
Asking Egypt for help will bring
them dishonor.
4 Their officials have gone to the city
of Zoan.
Their messengers have arrived in
Hanes.
5 But the people of Judah will be put
to shame.
That's because they are trusting in
a nation that is useless to them.
Egypt will not bring them any help
or advantage.
Instead, it will bring them shame
and dishonor."

6 Here is a prophecy the LORD gave me
about the animals in the Negev Desert.

Judah's messengers carry their
riches on the backs of donkeys.
They carry their treasures on the
humps of camels.
They travel through a land of
danger and suffering.
It's a land filled with lions.
Poisonous snakes are also there.
The messengers travel to a nation
that can't do them any good.
7 They travel to Egypt, whose help is
totally useless.
That's why I call it Rahab the
Do-Nothing.

8 The LORD said to me, "Go now.
Write on a tablet for the people of
Judah
what I am about to say.
Also write it on a scroll.
In days to come
it will be a witness that lasts
forever.

9 That's because these people of
Judah refuse to obey me.
They are children who tell lies.
They will not listen to what I
want to teach them.
10 They say to the seers,
'Don't see any more visions!'
They say to the prophets,
'Don't give us any more visions of
what is right!
Tell us pleasant things.
Prophesy things we want to hear
even if they aren't true.
11 Get out of our way!
Get off our path!
Keep the Holy One of Israel away
from us!' "

12 So the Holy One of Israel speaks.
He says,

"You have turned your backs on
what I have said.
You have depended on telling
people lies.
You have crushed others.
13 Those sins are like cracks in a high
wall.
They get bigger and bigger.
Suddenly the wall breaks apart.
Then it quickly falls down.
14 It breaks into small pieces like a
clay pot.
It breaks up completely.
Not one piece is left big enough
for taking coals from a fireplace.
Not one piece is left for dipping
water out of a well."

15 The LORD and King is the Holy One
of Israel. He says,

"You will find peace and rest
when you turn away from your
sins and depend on me.
You will receive the strength you
need
when you stay calm and trust
in me.
But you do not want to do what I
tell you to.
16 You said, 'No. We'll escape on
horses.'
So you will have to escape!
You said, 'We'll ride off on fast
horses.'
So those who chase you will use
faster horses!
17 When one of them dares you to
fight,
a thousand of you will run away.
When five of them dare you,
all of you will run away.
So few of you will be left that you
will be
like a flagpole on top of a
mountain.
You will be like only one banner
on a hill."

18 But the LORD wants to have mercy
on you.
So he will rise up to give you his
tender love.
The LORD is a God who is always
fair.
Blessed are all those who wait for
him to act!

19 People of Zion, who live in Jerusalem, you won't weep anymore. When
you cry out to the LORD for help, he
will have mercy on you. As soon as he
hears you, he'll answer you. 20 He might
treat you like prisoners. You might eat
the bread of trouble. You might drink
the water of suffering. But he will be
your Teacher. He won't hide himself
anymore. You will see him with your
own eyes. 21 You will hear your Teacher's voice behind you. You will hear it
whether you turn to the right or the
left. It will say, "Here is the path I want
you to take. So walk on it." 22 Then you
will get rid of the silver statues of your
gods. You won't have anything to do
with the gold statues either. All of them
are "unclean." So you will throw them
away like dirty rags. You will say to
them, "Get away from us!"

23 The LORD will send rain on the seeds
you plant in the ground. The crops that
grow will be rich and plentiful. At that
time your cattle will eat grass in rolling
meadows. 24 The oxen and donkeys that
work the soil will eat the finest feed and
crushed grain. The farmers will use pitch-
forks and shovels to separate it from the
straw. 25 At that time the towers of your
enemies will fall down. Their soldiers will
die. Streams of water will flow on every
high mountain and hill. 26 The moon will
shine like the sun. And the sunlight will
be seven times brighter than usual. It
will be like the light of seven full days.
That will happen when the LORD

bandages and heals the wounds and bruises he has brought on his people.

27 The LORD will come from far away
in all his power and glory.
He will show his burning anger.
Thick clouds of smoke will be all around him.
His mouth will speak angry words.
The words from his tongue will be like a destroying fire.
28 His breath will be like a rushing flood
that rises up to the neck.
He'll separate out the nations he is going to destroy.
He'll place a bit in their jaws.
It will lead them down the road to death.
29 You will sing
as you do on the night you celebrate a holy feast.
Your hearts will be filled with joy.
You will be as joyful as people playing their flutes
as they go up to the mountain of the LORD.
He is the Rock of Israel.
30 The LORD will cause people to hear his powerful voice.
He will make them see his arm coming down to punish them.
It will come down with burning anger and destroying fire.
It will come down with rain, thunderstorms and hail.
31 The voice of the LORD will tear the Assyrians apart.
He will strike them down with his scepter.
32 He will strike them
with his club to punish them.
Each time he does, his people will celebrate
with the music of harps and tambourines.
He will use his powerful arm
to strike down the Assyrians in battle.
33 In the Valley of Ben Hinnom,
Topheth has been prepared for a long time.
It has been made ready for the king of Assyria.
Its fire pit has been made deep and wide.
It has plenty of wood for the fire.
The breath of the LORD
will be like a stream of burning sulfur.
It will set the wood on fire.

The LORD Will Judge Those Who Depend on Egypt

31 How terrible it will be for those
who go down to Egypt for help!
How terrible for those who depend on horses!
They trust in how many chariots they have.
They trust in how strong their horsemen are.
But they don't look to the Holy One of Israel.
They don't ask the LORD for his help.
2 He too is wise. He can bring horrible trouble.
He does what he says he'll do.
He'll rise up against that evil nation.
He'll fight against those who help them.
3 The men of Egypt are only human beings.
They aren't God.
Their horses are only flesh and blood.
They aren't spirits.
The LORD will reach out his powerful hand
to punish everyone.
The Egyptians provide help.
But they will be tripped up.
The people of Judah receive the help.
But they will fall down.
All of them will be destroyed.

4 The LORD says to me,

"A powerful lion stands over its food and growls.
A lot of shepherds can be brought together to drive it away.
But the lion is not frightened by their shouts.
It is not upset by the noise they make.
In the same way, I will come down from heaven.
I will fight on Mount Zion and on its hills.
Nothing will drive me away.
I am the LORD who rules over all.

5 Like a bird hovering over its nest, I
will guard Jerusalem.
I will keep it safe.
I will 'pass over' it and save it.
I am the LORD who rules over all."

6 People of Israel, return to the LORD.
He's the God you have so strongly opposed. 7 You sinned when you made
your gods out of silver and gold. The
time will come when all of you will turn
away from them.

8 The LORD says, "The Assyrians will
be killed by swords.
But the swords that kill them will
not be used by human beings.
The Assyrians will run away from
those swords.
But their young men will be
caught
and forced to work hard.
9 Their hiding places will be destroyed
when terror strikes them.
Their commanders will see their
enemy's battle flags.
Then they will be filled with panic,"
announces the LORD.
His fire blazes out from Mount Zion.
His furnace burns in Jerusalem.

The King Who Will Do What Is Right

32 A king will come who will do
what is right.
His officials will govern fairly.
2 Each official will be like a place to
get out of the wind.
He will be like a place to hide
from storms.
He'll be like streams of water
flowing in the desert.
He'll be like the shadow of a huge
rock in a dry and thirsty land.
3 Then the eyes of those who see
won't be closed anymore.
The ears of those who hear will
listen to the truth.
4 People who are afraid will know
and understand.
Tongues that stutter will speak
clearly.
5 Foolish people won't be considered
noble anymore.
Those who are worthless won't be
highly respected.
6 Foolish people say foolish things.
Their minds are set on doing evil
things.
They don't do what is right.
They tell lies about the LORD.
They don't give hungry people any
food.
They don't let thirsty people have
any water.
7 Those who are worthless use sinful
methods.
They make evil plans against
poor people.
They destroy them with their lies.
They do it even when those
people are right.
8 But those who are noble make
noble plans.
And by doing noble things they
succeed.

The Sinful Women in Jerusalem

9 You women who are so contented,
pay attention to me.
You who feel so secure,
listen to what I have to say.
10 You feel secure now.
But in a little over a year you will
tremble with fear.
The grape harvest will fail.
There won't be any fruit.
11 So tremble, you contented women.
Tremble with fear, you who feel
so secure.
Take off your fine clothes.
Wrap yourselves in rags.
12 Beat your chests to show how sad
you are.
The pleasant fields have been
destroyed.
The fruitful vines have dried up.
13 My people's land is overgrown with
thorns and bushes.
Mourn for all the houses that
were once filled with joy.
Cry over this city that used to be
full of wild parties.
14 The royal palace will be left empty.
The noisy city will be deserted.
The fort and lookout tower will
become
a dry and empty desert forever.
Donkeys will enjoy being there.
Flocks will eat there.
15 That will continue until the Holy
Spirit
is poured out on us from heaven.
Then the desert will be turned into
rich farm lands.
The rich farm lands will seem
like a forest.

[16]In the desert, the LORD will make
sure people do what is right.
In the rich farm lands he will
make sure they treat one
another fairly.
[17]Doing what is right will bring peace
and rest.
When my people do that, they
will stay calm
and trust in the LORD forever.
[18]They will live in a peaceful land.
Their homes will be secure.
They will enjoy peace and quiet.
[19]Hail might strip the forests bare.
Cities might be completely
destroyed.
[20]But how blessed you people will be!
You will plant your seeds by
every stream.
You will let your cattle and donkeys
wander anywhere they want to.

Trouble for Assyria and Help for God's People

33 How terrible it will be for you,
you who destroy others!
Assyria, you haven't been
destroyed yet.
How terrible for you, you who turn
against others!
Others haven't turned against
you yet.
When you stop destroying,
you will be destroyed.
When you stop turning against
others,
others will turn against you.

[2]LORD, have mercy on us.
We long for you to help us.
Make us strong every morning.
Save us when we're in trouble.
[3]At the roar of your army, the
nations run away.
When you rise up against them,
they scatter.
[4]Nations, what you have taken in
battle is destroyed.
It's as if young locusts had eaten
it up.
Like large numbers of locusts,
people rush to get it.
[5]The LORD is honored. He lives in
heaven.
He will make sure Zion's people
only do what is fair and right.
[6]He will be the firm foundation for
their entire lives.
He will give them all the wisdom,
knowledge and saving power
they will ever need.
Respect for the LORD is the key to
that treasure.

[7]Look! Judah's brave men cry out
loud in the streets.
The messengers who were sent to
bring peace weep bitter tears.
[8]The wide roads are deserted.
No one travels on them.
Our peace treaty with Assyria is
broken.
Those who witnessed it are
looked down on.
No one is respected.
[9]The land dries up and wastes away.
Lebanon is full of shame and
dries up.
The rich land of Sharon is like the
Arabah Desert.
The trees of Bashan and Carmel
drop their leaves.

[10]"Now I will take action," says the
LORD.
"Now I will be honored.
Now I will be respected.
[11]Assyria, your plans and actions are
like straw.
Your anger is a fire that will
destroy you.
[12]The nations will be burned to
ashes.
They will be like bushes that are
cut down and set on fire.

[13]"You nations far away, listen to
what I have done!
My people who are near,
recognize how powerful I am!
[14]The sinners in Zion are terrified.
They tremble with fear.
They say, 'Who of us can live
through the LORD's destroying
fire?
Who of us can live through the
fire that burns forever?'
[15]People must do what is right.
They must be honest and tell the
truth.
They must not get rich by cheating
others.
Their hands must not receive
money from those who want
special favors.

They must not let their ears listen
to plans to commit murder.
They must close their eyes to
even thinking about doing
what is evil.
16 People like that will be kept safe.
It will be as if they were living on
high mountains.
It will be as if they were living in
a mountain fort.
They will have all the food they
need.
And they will never run out of
water."

17 People of Judah, you will see
the king in all his glory and
majesty.
You will view his kingdom
spreading far and wide.
18 You will think about what used to
terrify you.
You will say to yourself,
"Where is that chief officer of
Assyria?
Where is the one who forced us to
send gifts to his king?
Where is the officer in charge of
the towers
that were used when we were
attacked?"
19 You won't see those proud people
anymore.
They spoke a strange language.
None of us could understand it.

20 Just look at Zion! It's the city
where we celebrate our regular
feasts.
Turn your eyes toward
Jerusalem.
It will be a peaceful place to live in.
It will be like a tent that will
never be moved.
Its stakes will never be pulled up.
None of its ropes will be broken.
21 There the LORD will be our Mighty
One.
It will be like a place of wide
rivers and streams.
No boat with oars will travel on
them.
No mighty ship will sail on them.
22 That's because the LORD is our
judge.
The LORD gives us our law.
The LORD is our king.
He will save us.

23 The ropes on your ship hang loose.
The mast isn't very secure.
The sail isn't spread out.
But the LORD will strike down the
Assyrians.
Then a large amount of goods
will be taken from them and
divided up.
Even people who are disabled
will carry off some of it.
24 No one living in Zion will ever say
again, "I'm sick."
And the sins of those who live
there will be forgiven.

The LORD Will Judge the Nations

34 Nations, come near and listen
to me!
Pay attention to what I'm about
to say.
Let the earth and everything in it
listen.
Let the world and everything that
comes out of it pay attention.
2 The LORD is angry with all the
nations.
His anger is against all their
armies.
He will totally destroy them.
He will have them killed.
3 Those who are killed won't be
buried.
Their dead bodies will be thrown
on the ground.
They will stink.
Their blood will cover the
mountains.
4 All the stars in the sky will vanish.
The heavens will be rolled up like
a scroll.
All the stars in the sky will fall like
dried-up leaves from a vine.
They will drop like wrinkled figs
from a fig tree.

5 The sword of the LORD will finish its
deadly work in the sky.
Then it will come down to strike
Edom.
He will totally destroy that
nation.
6 His sword will be red with blood.
It will be covered with fat.
The blood will flow like the blood
of lambs and goats being
sacrificed.
The fat will be like the fat
taken from the kidneys of rams.

That's because the LORD will offer a sacrifice
in the city of Bozrah.
He will kill many people in the land of Edom.
7 The people and their leaders will be killed
like wild oxen and young bulls.
Their land will be wet with their blood.
The dust will be covered with their fat.
8 That's because the LORD has set aside a day to pay Edom back.
He has set aside a year to pay them back. He will pay them back for what they did to Zion.
9 The streams of Edom will be turned into tar.
Its dust will be turned into blazing sulfur.
Its land will become burning tar.
10 The fire will keep burning night and day.
It can't be put out.
Its smoke will go up forever.
Edom will lie empty for all time to come.
No one will ever travel through it again.
11 The desert owl and screech owl will make it their home.
The great owl and the raven will build their nests there.
God will use his measuring line
to show how completely Edom will be destroyed.
He will use his plumb line
to show how empty Edom will become.
12 Edom's nobles won't have anything left there
that can be called a kingdom.
All its princes will vanish.
13 Thorns will cover its forts.
Bushes and weeds will cover its safest places.
It will become a home for wild dogs.
It will become a place where owls live.
14 Desert creatures will meet with hyenas.
Wild goats will call out to each other.
Night creatures will also lie down there.
They will find places where they can rest.
15 Owls will make their nests and lay their eggs there.
And they will hatch them.
They will take care of their little ones
under the shadow of their wings.
Male and female falcons will also gather there.

16 Look in the book of the LORD. Here
is what you will read there.

None of those animals will be missing.
Male and female alike will be there.
The LORD himself has commanded it.
And his Spirit will gather them together.
17 The LORD will decide what part of the land goes to each animal.
Then he will give each one its share.
It will belong to them forever.
And they will live there for all time to come.

The Joy of the LORD's People

35 The desert and the dry ground will be glad.
The dry places will be full of joy.
Flowers will grow there.
Like the first crocus in the spring,
2 the desert will bloom with flowers.
It will be very glad and shout for joy.
The glorious beauty of Lebanon will be given to it.
It will be as beautiful as the rich lands
of Carmel and Sharon.
Everyone will see the glory of the LORD.
They will see the beauty of our God.
3 Strengthen the hands of those who are weak.
Help those whose knees give way.
4 Say to those whose hearts are afraid,
"Be strong and do not fear.

Your God will come.
He will pay your enemies back.
He will come to save you."
5 Then the eyes of those who are blind will be opened.
The ears of those who can't hear will be unplugged.
6 Those who can't walk will leap like a deer.
And those who can't speak will shout for joy.
Water will pour out in dry places.
Streams will flow in the desert.
7 The burning sand will become a pool of water.
The thirsty ground will become bubbling springs.
In the places where wild dogs once lay down,
tall grass and papyrus will grow.

8 A wide road will go through the land.
It will be called the Way of Holiness.
Only those who lead a holy life can use it.
"Unclean" and foolish people can't walk on it.
9 No lions will use it.
No hungry wild animals will be on it.
None of them will be there.
Only people who have been set free will walk on it.
10 Those the LORD has saved will return to their land.
They will sing as they enter the city of Zion.
Joy that lasts forever will be like beautiful crowns on their heads.
They will be filled with gladness and joy.
Sorrow and sighing will be gone.

Sennacherib Warns Jerusalem

36 Sennacherib attacked and captured all the cities of Judah that
had high walls around them. It was in
the 14th year of the rule of Hezekiah.
Sennacherib was king of Assyria. 2 He
sent his field commander from Lachish
to King Hezekiah at Jerusalem. He sent
him along with a large army. The commander stopped at the channel that
brings water from the Upper Pool. It
was on the road to the Washerman's
Field. 3 Eliakim, Shebna and Joah went
out to him. Eliakim, the son of Hilkiah,
was in charge of the palace. Shebna was
the secretary. Joah, the son of Asaph,
kept the records.
4 The field commander said to them,
"Give Hezekiah this message. Tell him,

" 'Sennacherib is the great king
of Assyria. He says, "Why are you
putting your faith in what your king
says? 5 You say you have a military
plan. You say you have a strong
army. But your words don't mean
anything. Who are you depending
on? Why don't you want to stay under my control? 6 Look, I know you
are depending on Egypt. Why are
you doing that? Egypt is nothing but
a broken papyrus stem. Try leaning on it. It will only cut your hand.
Pharaoh, the king of Egypt, is just
like that to everyone who depends
on him. 7 But suppose you say to me,
'We are depending on the LORD our
God.' Didn't Hezekiah remove your
god's high places and altars? Didn't
Hezekiah say to the people of Judah
and Jerusalem, 'You must worship
at the altar in Jerusalem'?
8 " ' "Come on. Make a deal with
my master, the king of Assyria. I'll
give you 2,000 horses. But only if
you can put riders on them! 9 You
are depending on Egypt for chariots and horsemen. You can't drive
away even the least important officer among my master's officials.
10 Besides, do you think I've come
without being sent by the LORD?
Have I come to attack and destroy
this land without receiving a message from him? The LORD himself
told me to march out against your
country. He told me to destroy it." ' "

11 Then Eliakim, Shebna and Joah
spoke to the field commander. They
said, "Please speak to us in the Aramaic language. We understand it. Don't
speak to us in Hebrew. If you do, the
people on the wall will be able to understand you."
12 But the commander replied, "My
master sent me to say these things.
Are these words only for your master
and you to hear? Aren't they also for

the people sitting on the wall? They are
going to suffer just like you. They'll have
to eat their own waste. They'll have to
drink their own urine."
13 Then the commander stood up and
spoke in the Hebrew language. He called
out, "Pay attention to what the great
king of Assyria is telling you. 14 He says,
'Don't let Hezekiah trick you. He can't
save you! 15 Don't let Hezekiah talk you
into trusting in the LORD. Don't believe
him when he says, "You can be sure that
the LORD will save us. This city will not
be handed over to the king of Assyria." '
16 "Don't listen to Hezekiah. The king of
Assyria says, 'Make a peace treaty with
me. Come over to my side. Then each one
of you will eat fruit from your own vine
and fig tree. Each one of you will drink
water from your own well. 17 You will do
that until I come back. Then I'll take you
to a land just like yours. It's a land that
has a lot of grain and fresh wine. It has
plenty of bread and vineyards.
18 " 'Don't let Hezekiah fool you. He's
telling you a lie when he says, "The
LORD will save us." Have the gods of any
nations ever saved their lands from the
power of the king of Assyria? 19 Where
are the gods of Hamath and Arpad?
Where are the gods of Sepharvaim?
Have they saved Samaria from my
power? 20 Which one of all the gods of
those countries has been able to save
their lands from me? So how can the
LORD save Jerusalem from my power?' "
21 But the people remained silent.
They didn't say anything. That's because King Hezekiah had commanded,
"Don't answer him."
22 Then Eliakim, the son of Hilkiah, went to Hezekiah. Eliakim was in
charge of the palace. Shebna the secretary went with him. So did Joah, the
son of Asaph. Joah kept the records. All
of them went to Hezekiah with their
clothes torn. They told him what the
field commander had said.

Isaiah Prophesies That Jerusalem Will Be Saved

37 When King Hezekiah heard what
the field commander had said,
he tore his clothes. He put on the rough
clothing people wear when they're sad.
Then he went into the LORD's temple.
2 Hezekiah sent Eliakim, who was in
charge of the palace, to Isaiah the prophet, the son of Amoz. He also sent the
leading priests and Shebna the secretary
to him. All of them were wearing rough
clothing. 3 They told Isaiah, "Hezekiah
says, 'Today we're in great trouble. The
LORD is warning us. He's bringing shame
on us. Sometimes babies come to the
moment when they should be born. But
their mothers aren't strong enough to
give birth to them. Today we are like
those mothers. We aren't strong enough
to save ourselves. 4 Perhaps the LORD
your God will hear everything the field
commander has said. His master, the
king of Assyria, has sent him to make
fun of the living God. Maybe the LORD
your God will punish him for what he
has heard him say. So pray for the remaining people who are still alive here.' "
5 King Hezekiah's officials came to
Isaiah. 6 Then he said to them, "Tell
your master, 'The LORD says, "Do not
be afraid of what you have heard. The
officers who are under the king of Assyria have spoken evil things against
me. 7 Listen! I will send him news from
his own country. It will make him want
to return home. There I will have him
cut down by a sword." ' "
8 The field commander heard that the
king of Assyria had left Lachish. So the
commander pulled his troops back from
Jerusalem. He went to join the king. He
found out that the king was fighting
against Libnah.
9 During that time Sennacherib
received a report. He was told that
Tirhakah was marching out to fight
against him. Tirhakah was the king
of Cush. When Sennacherib heard the
report, he sent messengers again to
Hezekiah with a letter. It said, 10 "Tell
Hezekiah, the king of Judah, 'Don't let
the god you depend on trick you. He
says, "Jerusalem will not be handed
over to the king of Assyria." But don't
believe him. 11 I'm sure you have heard
about what the kings of Assyria have
done to all the other countries. They
have destroyed them completely. So
do you think you will be saved? 12 The
kings who ruled before me destroyed
many nations. Did the gods of those
nations save them? Did the gods of
Gozan, Harran or Rezeph save them?
What about the gods of the people of

Eden who were in Tel Assar? [13]Where is
the king of Hamath? Where is the king
of Arpad? Where are the kings of Lair,
Sepharvaim, Hena and Ivvah?' "

Hezekiah Prays to the LORD

[14]When Hezekiah received the letter
from the messengers, he read it. Then
he went up to the LORD's temple. There
he spread the letter out in front of the
LORD. [15]Hezekiah prayed to the LORD. He
said, [16]"LORD who rules over all, you are
the God of Israel. You sit on your throne
between the cherubim. You alone are God
over all the kingdoms on earth. You have
made heaven and earth. [17]Listen, LORD.
Hear us. Open your eyes, LORD. Look at
the trouble we're in. Listen to what Sennacherib is saying. You are the living
God. And he dares to make fun of you!

[18]"LORD, it's true that the kings of
Assyria have completely destroyed
many nations and their lands. [19]They
have thrown the statues of the gods of
those nations into the fire. And they
have destroyed them. That's because
they weren't really gods at all. They
were nothing but statues made out of
wood and stone. They were made by
human hands. [20]LORD our God, save
us from the power of Sennacherib. Then
all the kingdoms of the earth will know
that you are the only God."

Sennacherib Falls From Power

[21]Isaiah sent a message to Hezekiah. Isaiah said, "The LORD is the God
of Israel. He says, 'You have prayed
to me about Sennacherib, the king of
Assyria. [22]So here is the message the
LORD has spoken against him. The LORD
is telling him,

" ' "You will not win the battle over
Zion.
Its people hate you and make
fun of you.
The people of Jerusalem lift up
their heads proudly
as you run away.
[23]Who have you laughed at?
Who have you spoken evil things
against?
Who have you raised your voice
against?
Who have you looked at so proudly?
You have done it against me.
I am the Holy One of Israel!
[24]Through your messengers
you have laughed at me again
and again.
And you have said,
'I have many chariots.
With them I have climbed to the
tops of the mountains.
I've climbed the highest
mountains in Lebanon.
I've cut down its tallest cedar trees.
I've cut down the best of its
juniper trees.
I've reached its farthest mountains.
I've reached its finest forests.
[25]I've dug wells in other lands.
I've drunk the water from them.
I've walked through all the streams
of Egypt.
I've dried up every one of them.'

[26]" ' "But I, the LORD, say, 'Haven't
you heard what I have done?
Long ago I arranged for you to
do this.
In days of old I planned it.
Now I have made it happen.
You have turned cities with high
walls
into piles of stone.
[27]Their people do not have any
power left.
They are troubled and put to
shame.
They are like plants in the field.
They are like new green plants.
They are like grass that grows on a
roof.
It dries up before it is completely
grown.

[28]" ' " 'But I know where you are.
I know when you come and go.
I know how very angry you are
with me.
[29]You roar against me and brag.
And I have heard your bragging.
So I will put my hook in your nose.
I will put my bit in your mouth.
And I will make you go home
by the same way you came.' " ' "

[30]The LORD said, "Hezekiah, here is
a sign for you.

"This year you will eat what grows
by itself.
Next year you will eat what
grows from that.

But in the third year you will plant
your crops and gather them in.
You will plant your grapevines
and eat their fruit.
31 The people of the kingdom of
Judah who are still alive will be
like plants.
Once more they will put down
roots and produce fruit.
32 Out of Jerusalem will come the
people who remain.
Out of Mount Zion will come
those who are still left alive.
My great love will make sure that
happens.
I rule over all.

33 "Here is a message from me about
the king of Assyria. I say,

" 'He will not enter this city.
He will not even shoot an arrow
at it.
He will not come near it with a
shield.
He will not build a ramp in order
to climb over its walls.
34 By the way that he came he will go
home.
He will not enter this city,'
announces the LORD.
35 'I will guard this city and save it.
I will do it for myself.
And I will do it for my servant
David.' "

36 Then the angel of the LORD went
into the camp of the Assyrians. He put to
death 185,000 soldiers there. The people
of Jerusalem got up the next morning.
They looked out and saw all the dead
bodies. 37 So Sennacherib, the king of
Assyria, took the army tents down.
Then he left. He returned to Nineveh
and stayed there.
38 One day Sennacherib was worshiping in the temple of his god Nisrok. His
sons Adrammelek and Sharezer killed
him with their swords. Then they escaped to the land of Ararat. Esarhaddon
became the next king after his father
Sennacherib.

Hezekiah Becomes Sick and Is Healed

38 In those days Hezekiah became very sick. He knew he
was about to die. Isaiah went to see
him. Isaiah was the son of Amoz. Isaiah
told Hezekiah, "The LORD says, 'Put
everything in order. Make out your will.
You are going to die soon. You will not
get well again.' "
2 Hezekiah turned his face toward the
wall. He prayed to the LORD. He said,
3 "LORD, please remember how faithful
I've been to you. I've lived the way you
wanted me to. I've served you with all
my heart. I've done what is good in
your sight." And Hezekiah wept bitterly.
4 A message from the LORD came to
Isaiah. The LORD said, 5 "Go and speak
to Hezekiah. Tell him, 'The LORD, the
God of King David, says, "I have heard
your prayer. I have seen your tears. I
will add 15 years to your life. 6 And I will
save you and this city from the power of
the king of Assyria. I will guard this city.
7 " ' "Here is a sign from me. It will
show you that I will heal you, just as
I promised I would. 8 The shadow that
was made by the sun has gone down
ten steps on the stairway of Ahaz. I will
make it go back up those ten steps." ' "
So the shadow went back up the ten
steps it had gone down.
9 Here is a song of praise that was
written by Hezekiah, the king of Judah.
He wrote it after he was sick and had
gotten well again.

10 I said, "I'm enjoying the best years
of my life.
Must I now go through the gates
of death?
Will the rest of my years be taken
away from me?"
11 I said, "LORD, I'll never see you
again
while I'm still alive.
I'll never see people anymore.
I'll never again be with those
who live in this world.
12 My body is like a shepherd's tent.
It has been pulled down and
carried off.
My life is like a piece of cloth that
I've rolled up.
You have cut it off from the loom.
In a short period of time you
have brought my life to an end.
13 I waited patiently until sunrise.
But like a lion you broke all my
bones.
In a short period of time you
have brought my life to an end.

[14] I cried softly like a weak little bird.
I sounded like a dove as I mourned.
My eyes grew tired as I looked up toward heaven.
Lord, my life is in danger. Please come and help me!

[15] "But what can I say?
You have promised to heal me.
And you yourself have done it.
Once I was proud and bitter.
But now I will live the rest of my life free of pride.

[16] Lord, people find the will to live because you keep your promises.
And my spirit also finds life in your promises.
You brought me back to health.
You let me live.

[17] I'm sure it was for my benefit that I suffered such great pain.
You love me. You kept me from going down into the pit of death.
You have put all my sins behind your back.

[18] People in the grave can't praise you.
Dead people can't sing praise to you.
Those who go down to the grave can't hope for you to be faithful to them.

[19] It is those who are alive who praise you.
And that's what I'm doing today.
Parents tell their children about how faithful you are.

[20] "The LORD will save me.
So we will sing and play music on stringed instruments.
We will sing all the days of our lives in the LORD's temple."

[21] When Hezekiah was sick, Isaiah had
said, "Press some figs together. Spread
them on a piece of cloth. Apply them
to Hezekiah's boil. Then he'll get well
again."

[22] At that time Hezekiah had asked,
"What will the sign be to prove I'll go
up to the LORD's temple?" That's when
the LORD had made the shadow go back
ten steps.

Messengers Come From Babylon to Hezekiah

39 At that time Marduk-Baladan,
the king of Babylon, sent Hezekiah letters and a gift. He had heard
that Hezekiah had been sick but had
gotten well again. Marduk-Baladan was
the son of Baladan. [2] Hezekiah gladly
received the messengers. He showed
them what was in his storerooms. He
showed them the silver and gold. He
took them to where the spices and the
fine olive oil were kept. He showed them
where he kept all his weapons. And he
showed them all his treasures. In fact,
he showed them everything that was in
his palace and in his whole kingdom.

[3] Then Isaiah the prophet went to
King Hezekiah. Isaiah asked him,
"What did those men say? Where did
they come from?"

"They came from a land far away,"
Hezekiah said. "They came to me from
Babylon."

[4] Isaiah asked, "What did they see in
your palace?"

"They saw everything in my palace,"
Hezekiah said. "I showed them all my
treasures."

[5] Then Isaiah said to Hezekiah, "Listen
to the message of the LORD who rules
over all. He says, [6] 'You can be sure the
time will come when everything in your
palace will be carried off to Babylon.
Everything the kings before you have
stored up until this day will be taken
away. There will not be anything left,'
says the LORD. [7] 'Some of the members
of your family line will be taken away.
They will be your own flesh and blood.
They will include the children who will be
born into your family line. And they will
serve the king of Babylon in his palace.'"

[8] "The message the LORD has spoken
through you is good," Hezekiah replied.
He thought, "There will be peace and
safety while I'm still living."

God Comforts His People

40 "Comfort my people," says your God.
"Comfort them.

[2] Speak tenderly to the people of Jerusalem.
Announce to them that their hard labor has been completed.

Tell them that their sin has been
paid for.
Tell them the LORD has punished
them enough
for all their sins."

3 A messenger is calling out,
"In the desert prepare
the way for the LORD.
Make a straight road through it
for our God.
4 Every valley will be filled in.
Every mountain and hill will be
made level.
The rough ground will be smoothed
out.
The rocky places will be made
flat.
5 Then the glory of the LORD will
appear.
And everyone will see it together.
The LORD has spoken."

6 Another messenger says, "Cry out."
And I said, "What should I cry?"
"Cry out, 'All people are like grass.
They don't stay faithful to me
any longer than wildflowers
last.
7 The grass dries up. The flowers fall
to the ground.
That happens when the LORD
makes his wind blow on them.
So people are just like grass.
8 The grass dries up. The flowers fall
to the ground.
But what our God says will stand
forever.' "

9 Zion, you are bringing good news
to your people.
Go up on a high mountain and
announce it.
Jerusalem, you are bringing good
news to them.
Shout the message loudly.
Shout it out loud. Don't be afraid.
Say to the towns of Judah,
"Your God is coming!"
10 The LORD and King is coming with
power.
He rules with a powerful arm.
He has set his people free.
He is bringing them back as his
reward.
He has won the battle over their
enemies.
11 He takes care of his flock like a
shepherd.
He gathers the lambs in his arms.
He carries them close to his heart.
He gently leads those that have
little ones.

12 Who has measured the oceans by
using the palm of his hand?
Who has used the width of his
hand to mark off the sky?
Who has measured out the dust of
the earth in a basket?
Who has weighed the mountains
on scales?
Who has weighed the hills in a
balance?
13 Who can ever understand the Spirit
of the LORD?
Who can ever give him advice?
14 Did the LORD have to ask anyone to
help him understand?
Did he have to ask someone to
teach him the right way?
Who taught him what he knows?
Who showed him how to
understand?

15 The nations are only a drop in a
bucket to him.
He considers them as nothing but
dust on the scales.
He weighs the islands as if they
were only fine dust.
16 Lebanon doesn't have enough trees
to keep his altar fires burning.
It doesn't have enough animals
to sacrifice as burnt offerings to
him.
17 To him, all the nations don't
amount to anything.
He considers them to be
worthless.
In fact, they are less than
nothing in his sight.

18 So who will you compare God with?
Is there any other god like him?
19 Will you compare him with a statue
of a god?
Anyone who works with metal
can make a statue.
Then another worker covers it with
gold
and makes silver chains for it.
20 But someone who is too poor to
bring that kind of offering
will choose some wood that won't
rot.

Then they look for a skilled worker.
They pay the worker to make a statue of a god that won't fall over.

21 Don't you know who made everything?
Haven't you heard about him?
Hasn't it been told to you from the beginning?
Haven't you understood it ever since the earth was made?
22 God sits on his throne high above the earth.
Its people look like grasshoppers to him.
He spreads out the heavens like a cover.
He sets it up like a tent to live in.
23 He takes the power of princes away from them.
He reduces the rulers of this world to nothing.
24 They are planted.
They are scattered like seeds.
They put down roots in the ground.
But as soon as that happens, God blows on them and they dry up.
Then a windstorm sweeps them away like straw.

25 "So who will you compare me with?
Who is equal to me?" says the Holy One.
26 Look up toward the sky.
Who created everything you see?
The LORD causes the stars to come out at night one by one.
He calls out each one of them by name.
His power and strength are great.
So none of the stars is missing.

27 Family of Jacob, why do you complain,
"The LORD doesn't notice our condition"?
People of Israel, why do you say,
"Our God doesn't pay any attention to our rightful claims"?
28 Don't you know who made everything?
Haven't you heard about him?
The LORD is the God who lives forever.
He created everything on earth.
He won't become worn out or get tired.
No one will ever know how great his understanding is.
29 He gives strength to those who are tired.
He gives power to those who are weak.
30 Even young people become worn out and get tired.
Even the best of them trip and fall.
31 But those who trust in the LORD will receive new strength.
They will fly as high as eagles.
They will run and not get tired.
They will walk and not grow weak.

The LORD Helps Israel

41 The LORD says, "People who live on the islands,
come and stand quietly in front of me.
Let the nations gain new strength in order to state their case.
Let them come forward and speak.
Let us go to court and find out who is right.

2 "Who has stirred up a king from the east?
Who has helped him win his battles?
I hand nations over to him.
I bring kings under his control.
He turns them into dust with his sword.
With his bow he turns them into straw blowing in the wind.
3 He hunts them down. Then he moves on unharmed.
He travels so fast that his feet don't seem to touch the ground.
4 Who has made that happen? Who has carried it out?
Who has created all the people who have ever lived?
I, the LORD, have done it.
I was with the first of them.
And I will be with the last of them."

5 The people on the islands have seen that king coming.
And it has made them afraid.
People tremble with fear from one end of the earth to the other.

They come and gather together.
6 They help one another.
They say to one another, "Be strong!"
7 One skilled worker makes a statue of a god.
Another covers it with gold.
The first worker says to the second, "You have done a good job."
Another worker smooths out the metal with a hammer.
Still another gives the statue its final shape.
The one who hammers says to the one who shapes,
"You have done a good job."
Then they nail the statue down so it won't fall over.

8 The LORD says, "People of Israel, you are my servants.
Family of Jacob, I have chosen you.
You are the children of my friend Abraham.
9 I gathered you from one end of the earth to the other.
From the farthest places on earth I brought you together.
I said, 'You are my servants.'
I have chosen you.
I have not turned my back on you.
10 So do not be afraid. I am with you.
Do not be terrified. I am your God.
I will make you strong and help you.
I will hold you safe in my hands.
I always do what is right.
11 "All those who are angry with you will be put to shame.
And they will be dishonored.
Those who oppose you will be destroyed.
And they will vanish.
12 You might search for your enemies.
But you will not find them.
Those who go to war against you will completely disappear.
13 I am the LORD your God.
I take hold of your right hand.
I say to you, 'Do not be afraid.
I will help you.'
14 Family of Jacob, you are as weak as a worm.
But do not be afraid.
People of Israel, there are only a few of you.
But do not be afraid.
I myself will help you," announces the LORD.
He is the one who sets his people free.
He is the Holy One of Israel.
15 He says, "I will make you into a threshing sled.
It will be new and sharp.
It will have many teeth.
You will grind the mountains down and crush them.
You will turn the hills into nothing but straw.
16 You will toss them in the air.
A strong wind will catch them and blow them away.
You will be glad because I will make that happen.
You will praise me.
I am the Holy One of Israel.

17 "Those who are poor and needy search for water.
But there isn't any.
Their tongues are dry because they are thirsty.
But I will help them. I am the LORD.
I will not desert them.
I am Israel's God.
18 I will make streams flow on the bare hilltops.
I will make springs come up in the valleys.
I will turn the desert into pools of water.
I will turn the dry and cracked ground into flowing springs.
19 I will make trees grow in the desert.
I will plant cedar and acacia trees there.
I will plant myrtle and olive trees there.
I will make juniper trees grow in the dry and empty desert.
I will plant fir and cypress trees there.
20 Then people will see and know that my powerful hand has done it.
They will consider and understand that I have created it.
I am the Holy One of Israel."

21 The LORD says to the nations and
their gods,
"State your case."
Jacob's King says to them,
"Prove your case to me.
22 Tell us, you false gods,
what is going to happen.
Tell us what happened in the past.
Then we can check it out
and see if it is really true.
Or announce to us the things that
will take place.
23 Tell us what will happen in the
days ahead.
Then we will know that you are
gods.
Do something. It does not matter
whether it is good or bad.
Then we will be terrified and
filled with fear.
24 But you false gods are less than
nothing.
Your actions are completely
worthless.
I hate it when people worship
you.

25 "I have stirred up a king
who will come from the north.
He lives in the east.
He will bring honor to me.
He walks all over rulers as if they
were mud.
He steps on them just as a potter
stomps on clay.
26 Which one of you false gods said
those things
would happen before they did?
Who told us about them
so we could know them?
Who told us ahead of time?
Who told us so we could say,
'You are right'?
None of you false gods told us
about them.
None of you told us ahead of
time.
In fact, no one heard you say
anything at all.
27 I was the first to tell Zion.
I said, 'Look! The people of Israel
are coming back!'
I sent a messenger to Jerusalem
with the good news.
28 I look, but there is no one
among the gods that can give me
advice.
None of them can answer
when I ask them the simplest
question.
29 So they are not really gods at all.
What they do does not amount to
anything.
They are as useless as wind.

The LORD's Chosen Servant

42 "Here is my servant. I take
good care of him.
I have chosen him. I am very
pleased with him.
I will put my Spirit on him.
He will bring justice to the
nations.
2 He will not shout or cry out.
He will not raise his voice in the
streets.
3 He will not break a bent twig.
He will not put out a dimly
burning flame.
He will be faithful and make
everything right.
4 He will not grow weak or lose hope.
He will not give up until he brings
justice to the earth.
The islands will put their hope in
his teaching."

5 God created the heavens and
stretches them out.
The LORD spreads out the earth
with everything that grows
on it.
He gives breath to its people.
He gives life to those who walk
on it.
He says to his servant,
6 "I, the LORD, have chosen you to do
what is right.
I will take hold of your hand.
I will keep you safe.
You will put into effect my
covenant with the people of
Israel.
And you will be a light for the
Gentiles.
7 You will open eyes that can't see.
You will set prisoners free.
Those who sit in darkness will
come out of their cells.

8 "I am the LORD. That is my name!
I will not let any other god share
my glory.
I will not let statues of gods share
my praise.

[9] What I said would happen has
taken place.
Now I announce new things to you.
Before they even begin to happen,
I announce them to you."

A Song of Praise to the LORD

[10] Sing a new song to the LORD.
Sing praise to him from one end
of the earth to the other.
Sing, you who sail out on the ocean.
Sing, all you creatures in it.
Sing, you islands.
Sing, all you who live there.
[11] Let the desert and its towns raise
their voices.
Let those who live in the
settlements of Kedar be glad.
Let the people of Sela sing for joy.
Let them shout from the tops of
the mountains.
[12] Let them give glory to the LORD.
Let them praise him in the islands.
[13] The LORD will march out like a
mighty warrior.
He will stir up his anger like a
soldier getting ready to fight.
He will shout the battle cry.
And he will win the battle over
his enemies.

[14] The LORD says, "For a long time I
have kept silent.
I have been calm and quiet.
But now, like a woman having a
baby,
I cry out. I gasp and pant.
[15] I will completely destroy the
mountains and hills.
I will dry up everything that
grows there.
I will turn rivers into dry land.
I will dry up the pools.
[16] Israel is blind.
So I will lead them along paths
they had not known before.
I will guide them on roads they are
not familiar with.
I will turn the darkness into light
as they travel.
I will make the rough places
smooth.
Those are the things I will do.
I will not desert my people.
[17] Some people trust in statues of gods.
They say to them, 'You are our
gods.'
But they will be dishonored.
They will be put to shame.

Israel Can't See or Hear

[18] "Israel, listen to me! You can hear,
but you do not understand.
Look to me! You can see,
but you do not know what you
are seeing.
[19] The people of Israel serve me. But
who is more blind than they are?
Who is more deaf than the
messengers I send?
Who is more blind than the one
who has promised to be
faithful to me?
Who is more blind than the
servant of the LORD?
[20] Israel, you have seen many things.
But you do not pay any attention
to me.
Your ears are open.
But you do not listen to anything
I say."
[21] The LORD wanted his people to see
how great and glorious his law is.
He wanted to show them
that he always does what is
right.
[22] Enemies have carried off
everything they own.
All my people are trapped in pits
or hidden away in prisons.
They themselves have become like
stolen goods.
No one can save them.
They have been carried off.
And there is no one who will say,
"Send them back."

[23] Family of Jacob, who among you
will listen to what I'm saying?
People of Israel, which one of you
will pay close attention in days
to come?
[24] Who allowed you to be carried off
like stolen goods?
Who handed you over to robbers?
The LORD did it!
We have sinned against him.
Israel, you wouldn't follow his
ways.
You didn't obey his law.
[25] So he poured out his great anger on
you.
He had many of you killed in
battle.
You were surrounded by flames.
But you didn't realize what was
happening.

Many of you were destroyed.
But you didn't learn anything
from it.

The LORD Saves Israel

43 Family of Jacob, the LORD
created you.
People of Israel, he formed you.
He says, "Do not be afraid.
I will set you free.
I will send for you by name.
You belong to me.
2 You will pass through deep waters.
But I will be with you.
You will pass through the rivers.
But their waters will not sweep
over you.
You will walk through fire.
But you will not be burned.
The flames will not harm you.
3 I am the LORD your God.
I am the Holy One of Israel.
I am the one who saves you.
I will give up Egypt to set you free.
I will give up Cush and Seba for
you.
4 You are priceless to me.
I love you and honor you.
So I will trade other people for you.
I will give up other nations to
save your lives.
5 Do not be afraid. I am with you.
I will bring your people back
from the east.
I will gather you from the west.
6 I will say to the north, 'Let them go!'
And I will say to the south, 'Do
not hold them back.'
Bring my sons from far away.
Bring my daughters from the
farthest places on earth.
7 Bring back everyone who belongs
to me.
I created them to bring glory
to me.
I formed them and made them."
8 Lead my people into court.
They have eyes but can't see.
Bring those who have ears but
can't hear.
9 All the nations are gathering
together.
All of them are coming.
Which one of their gods said ahead
of time
that the people of Israel would
return?
Which of them told us anything
at all about the past?
Let them bring in their witnesses to
prove they were right.
Then others will hear them. And
they will say,
"What they said is true."
10 "People of Israel, you are my
witnesses," announces the LORD.
"I have chosen you to be my
servant.
I wanted you to know me and
believe in me.
I wanted you to understand that
I am the one and only God.
Before me, there was no other god
at all.
And there will not be any god
after me.
11 I am the one and only LORD.
I am the only one who can save
you.
12 I have made known what would
happen.
I saved you. I have told you
about it.

Jesus Is the Savior

The Bible tells us that sin separates us from God and makes us unable to see our need for God—even our need for a Savior. But God, who is rich in mercy, reveals or shows us our need for a Savior. God promised from the very beginning to send a Savior to pay the penalty for our sin (see Genesis 3:15). The Savior God sent was his very own Son, Jesus, who died and rose again so that we can live with him forever. Jesus promised that one day he will return and make wrong things right again.

I did this. It was not some other god
you worship.
You are my witnesses that I am
God," announces the LORD.
13 "And that is not all! I have always
been God,
and I always will be.
No one can save people from my
power.
When I do something, who can
undo it?"

The LORD Is Full of Mercy but Israel Is Unfaithful

14 The LORD sets his people free.
He is the Holy One of Israel. He
says,
"People of Israel, I will send an
army to Babylon to save you.
I will cause all the Babylonians
to run away.
They will try to escape in the
ships they were so proud of.
15 I am your LORD and King.
I am your Holy One.
I created you."

16 Long ago the LORD opened
a way for his people to go
through the Red Sea.
He made a path through the
mighty waters.
17 He caused Egypt to send out its
chariots and horses.
He sent its entire army to its
death.
Its soldiers lay down there.
They never got up again.
They were destroyed.
They were blown out like a dimly
burning flame.
But the LORD says,
18 "Forget the things that happened
in the past.
Do not keep on thinking about
them.
19 I am about to do something new.
It is beginning to happen even
now.
Don't you see it coming?
I am going to make a way for you
to go through the desert.
I will make streams of water in
the dry and empty land.
20 Even wild dogs and owls honor me.
That is because I provide water in
the desert
for my people to drink.
I cause streams to flow in the dry
and empty land
for my chosen ones.
21 I do it for the people I made for
myself.
I want them to sing praise to me.
22 "Family of Jacob, you have not
prayed to me as you should.
People of Israel, you have not
worn yourselves out for me.
23 You have not brought me sheep for
burnt offerings.
You have not honored me with
your sacrifices.
I have not loaded you down
by requiring grain offerings.
I have not made you tired
by requiring you to burn incense.
24 But you have not bought any
sweet-smelling cane for me.
You have not given me the fattest
parts
of your animal sacrifices.
Instead, you have loaded me down
with your sins.
You have made me tired with the
wrong things you have done.
25 "I am the one who wipes out your
lawless acts.
I do it because of who I am.
I will not remember your sins
anymore.
26 But let us go to court together.
Remind me of what you have
done.
State your case.
Prove to me that you are not
guilty.
27 Your father Jacob sinned.
The people I sent to teach you
refused to obey me.
28 So I put the high officials of your
temple to shame.
I let Jacob's family be totally
destroyed.
And I let people make fun of Israel.

The LORD Chooses Israel

44 "Family of Jacob, listen to
me. You are my servant.
People of Israel, I have chosen
you.
2 I made you. I formed you when
you were born as a nation.
I will help you.
So listen to what I am saying.

Family of Jacob, do not be afraid.
You are my servant.
People of Israel, I have chosen you.
3 I will pour out water on the thirsty land.
I will make streams flow on the dry ground.
I will pour out my Spirit on your children.
I will pour out my blessing on their children after them.
4 They will spring up like grass in a meadow.
They will grow like poplar trees near flowing streams.
5 Some will say, 'We belong to the LORD.'
Others will call themselves by Jacob's name.
Still others will write on their hands,
'We belong to the LORD.'
And they will be called by the name of Israel.

Worship the LORD, Not False Gods

6 "I am Israel's King. I set them free.
I am the LORD who rules over all.
So listen to what I am saying.
I am the first and the last.
I am the one and only God.
7 Who is like me? Let him come forward and speak boldly.
Let him tell me everything that has happened
since I created my people long ago.
And let him tell me what has not happened yet.
Let him announce ahead of time what is going to take place.
8 Do not tremble with fear. Do not be afraid.
Didn't I announce everything that has happened?
Didn't I tell you about it long ago?
You are my witnesses. Is there any other God but me?
No! There is no other Rock. I do not know even one."
9 Those who make statues of gods don't amount to anything.
And the statues they think so much of are worthless.
Those who would speak up for them are blind.
They don't know anything.
So they will be put to shame.
10 People make statues of gods.
But those gods can't do any good.
11 People who do that will be put to shame.
Those who make statues of gods are mere human beings.
Let all of them come together and state their case.
They will be terrified and put to shame.
12 A blacksmith gets his tool.
He uses it to shape metal over the burning coals.
He uses his hammers to make a statue of a god.
He forms it with his powerful arm.
He gets hungry and loses his strength.
He doesn't drink any water.
He gets weaker and weaker.
13 A carpenter measures a piece of wood with a line.
He draws a pattern on it with a marker.
He cuts out a statue with sharp tools.
He marks it with compasses.
He shapes it into the form of a beautiful human being.
He does this so he can put it in a temple.
14 He cuts down a cedar tree.
Or perhaps he takes a cypress or an oak tree.
It might be a tree that grew in the forest.
Or it might be a pine tree he planted.
And the rain made it grow.
15 A man gets wood from trees to burn.
He uses some of it to warm himself.
He starts a fire and bakes bread.
But he also uses some of it to make a god and worship it.
He makes a statue of a god and bows down to it.
16 He burns half of the wood in the fire.
He prepares a meal over it.
He cooks meat over it.
He eats until he is full.

He also warms himself. He says,
"Good! I'm getting warm.
The fire is nice and hot."
17 From the rest of the wood he makes a statue.
It becomes his god.
He bows down and worships it.
He prays to it. He says,
"Save me! You are my god!"
18 People like that don't even know what they are doing.
Their eyes are shut so that they can't see the truth.
Their minds are closed so that they can't understand it.
19 No one even stops to think about this.
No one has any sense or understanding.
If anyone did, they would say,
"I used half of the wood for fuel.
I even baked bread over the fire.
I cooked meat. Then I ate it.
Should I now make a statue of a god out of the wood that's left over?
Should I bow down to a block of wood?
The LORD would hate that."
20 That's as foolish as eating ashes!
The mind of someone like that has led him astray.
He can't save himself.
He can't bring himself to say,
"This thing I'm holding in my right hand
isn't really a god at all."
21 The LORD says, "Family of Jacob, remember these things.
People of Israel, you are my servant.
I have made you. You are my servant.
Israel, I will not forget you.
22 I will sweep your sins away as if they were a cloud.
I will blow them away as if they were the morning mist.
Return to me.
Then I will set you free."
23 Sing for joy, you heavens!
The LORD does wonderful things.
Shout out loud, you earth!
Burst into song, you mountains!
Sing, you forests and all your trees!
The LORD sets the family of Jacob free.
He shows his glory in Israel.

People Will Live in Jerusalem Again

24 The LORD says,
"People of Israel, I set you free.
I formed you when you were born as a nation.

"I am the LORD. I am the Maker of everything.
I alone stretch out the heavens.
I spread out the earth by myself.

25 "Some prophets are not really prophets at all.
I show that their signs are fake.
I make those who practice evil magic look foolish.
I destroy the learning of those who think they are wise.
Their knowledge does not make any sense at all.
26 I make the words of my servants the prophets come true.
I carry out what my messengers say will happen.

"I say about Jerusalem,
'My people will live there again.'
I say about the towns of Judah,
'They will be rebuilt.'
I say about their broken-down buildings,
'I will make them like new again.'
27 I say to the deep waters,
'Dry up. Let your streams become dry.'
28 I say about Cyrus,
'He is my shepherd.
He will accomplish everything I want him to.
He will say about Jerusalem,
"Let it be rebuilt."
And he will say about the temple,
"Let its foundations be laid." ' "

45 "Cyrus is my anointed king.
I take hold of his right hand.
I give him the power
to bring nations under his control.
I help him strip kings of their power
to go to war against him.
I break city gates open so he can go through them.
I say to him,
2 'I will march out ahead of you.
I will make the mountains level.
I will break down bronze gates.
I will cut through their heavy iron bars.

3 I will give you treasures that are
hidden away.
I will give you riches that are
stored up in secret places.
Then you will know that I am the
LORD.
I am the God of Israel.
I am sending for you by name.
4 Cyrus, I am sending for you by
name.
I am doing it for the good of the
family of Jacob.
They are my servant.
I am doing it for Israel.
They are my chosen people.
You do not know anything
about me.
But I am giving you a title of
honor.
5 I am the LORD. There is no other
LORD.
I am the one and only God.
You do not know anything
about me.
But I will make you strong.
6 Then people will know there is no
God but me.
Everyone from where the sun
rises in the east
to where it sets in the west will
know it.
I am the LORD.
There is no other LORD.
7 I cause light to shine. I also create
darkness.
I bring good times. I also create
hard times.
I do all these things. I am the LORD.

8 " 'Rain down my godliness, you
heavens above.
Let the clouds shower it down.
Let the earth open wide to receive it.
Let freedom spring to life.
Let godliness grow richly along
with it.
I have created all these things.
I am the LORD.' "

9 How terrible it will be for anyone
who argues with their Maker!
They are like a broken piece of
pottery lying on the ground.
Does clay say to a potter,
"What are you making?"
Does a pot say,
"The potter doesn't have any
skill"?
10 How terrible it will be for anyone
who says to a father,
"Why did you give me life?"
How terrible for anyone who says
to a mother,
"Why have you brought me into
the world?"

11 The LORD is the Holy One of Israel.
He made them.
He says to them,
"Are you asking me about what
will happen to my children?
Are you telling me what I should
do with what my hands have
made?
12 I made the earth.
I created human beings to live
there.
My own hands spread out the
heavens.
I put all the stars in their places.
13 I will stir up Cyrus and help him
win his battles.
I will make all his roads straight.
He will rebuild Jerusalem.
My people have been taken away
from their country.
But he will set them free.
I will not pay him to do it.
He will not receive a reward
for it,"
says the LORD who rules over all.

14 The LORD says to the people of
Jerusalem,
"You will get everything Egypt
produces.
You will receive everything the
people of Cush
and the tall Sabeans get in trade.
All of it will belong to you.
And all these people will walk
behind you as slaves.
They will be put in chains and
come over to you.
They will bow down to you.
They will admit,
'God is with you.
There is no other God.' "

15 You are a God who has been hiding
yourself.
You are the God of Israel. You
save us.
16 All those who make statues of gods
will be put to shame.
They will be dishonored.

They will be led away in shame
together.
17 But the LORD will save Israel.
He will save them forever.
They will never be put to shame or
dishonored.
That will be true for all time to
come.
18 The LORD created the heavens.
He is God.
He formed the earth and made it.
He set it firmly in place.
He didn't create it to be empty.
Instead, he formed it for people
to live on.
He says, "I am the LORD.
There is no other LORD.
19 I have not spoken in secret.
I have not spoken from a dark
place.
I have not said to Jacob's people,
'It is useless to look for me.'
I am the LORD. I always speak the
truth.
I always say what is right.

20 "Come together, you people of the
nations
who escaped from Babylon.
Gather together and come into
court.
Only people who do not know
anything
would carry around gods that
are made out of wood.
They pray to false gods that can't
save them.
21 Tell me what will happen. State
your case.
Talk it over together.
Who spoke long ago about what
would happen?
Who said it a long time ago?
I did. I am the LORD.
I am the one and only God.
I always do what is right.
I am the one who saves.
There is no God but me.

22 "All you who live anywhere on earth,
turn to me and be saved.
I am God. There is no other God.
23 I have made a promise in my own
name.
I have spoken with complete
honesty.
I will not take back a single word.
I said,
'Everyone will kneel down to me.
Everyone's mouth will make
promises in my name.'
24 They will say, 'The LORD is the only
one who can save us.
Only he can make us strong.' "
All those who have been angry with
the LORD will come to him.
And they will be put to shame.
25 But the LORD will save all the
people of Israel.
And so they will boast about the
LORD.

The False Gods of Babylon

46 The gods named Bel and Nebo
are brought down in shame.
The statues of them are being
carried away on the backs of
animals.
They used to be carried around
by the people who worshiped
them.
But now they've become a heavy
load for tired animals.
2 The gods named Bel and Nebo are
brought down in shame together.
They aren't able to save their
own statues.
They themselves are carried off
as prisoners.

3 The LORD says, "Family of Jacob,
listen to me.
Pay attention, you people of
Israel who are left alive.
I have taken good care of you since
your life began.
I have carried you since you were
born as a nation.
4 I will continue to carry you even
when you are old.
I will take good care of you even
when your hair is gray.
I have made you, and I will carry
you.
I will take care of you, and I will
save you.
I am the LORD.

5 "Who will you compare me with?
Who is equal to me?
What am I like?
Who can you compare me with?
6 Some people pour out gold from
their bags.
They weigh out silver on the
scales.

They hire someone who works with
gold to make it into a god.
They bow down to it and
worship it.
7 They lift it up on their shoulders
and carry it.
They set it up in its place, and
there it stands.
It can't move from that spot.
Someone might cry out to it.
But it does not answer.
It can't save them from their
troubles.
8 So remember this, you who refuse
to obey me.
Keep it in your minds and hearts.

9 "Remember what happened in the
past.
Think about what took place
long ago.
I am God. There is no other God.
I am God. There is no one like me.
10 Before something even happens, I
announce how it will end.
In fact, from times long ago I
announced what was still to
come.
I say, 'My plan will succeed.
I will do anything I want to do.'
11 I will send for a man from the east
to carry out my plan.
From a land far away, he will come
like a bird that kills its food.
I will bring about what I have said.
I will do what I have planned.
12 Listen to me, you stubborn people.
Pay attention, you who now refuse
to do what I have said is right.
13 The time is almost here for me to
make everything right.
It is not far away.
The time for me to save you will
not be put off.
I will save the city of Zion.
I will bring honor to Israel.

Babylon Will Fall

47 "City of Babylon,
go down and sit in the dust.
Leave your throne and sit on the
ground.
Queen city of the Babylonians,
your life will not be comfortable
and easy anymore.
2 Get millstones and grind some
flour like a female slave.
Take off your veil.
Lift up your skirts. Make your legs
bare.
Wade through the streams.
3 Everyone will see your naked body.
Everyone will see your shame.
I will pay you back for what you
did.
I will not spare any of your
people."

4 The one who sets us free is the Holy
One of Israel.
His name is the LORD Who Rules
Over All.

5 The LORD says, "Queen city of the
Babylonians,
go into a dark prison. Sit there
quietly.
You will not be called
the queen of kingdoms anymore.
6 I was angry with my people.
I treated them as if they did not
belong to me.
I handed them over to you.
And you did not show them any
pity.
You even placed heavy loads on
their old people.
7 You said, 'I am queen forever!'
But you did not think about what
you were doing.
You did not consider how things
might turn out.

8 "So listen, you who love pleasure.
You think you are safe and
secure.
You say to yourself,
'I am like a god.
No one is greater than I am.
I'll never be a widow.
And my children will never be
taken away from me.'
9 But both of these things will
happen to you in a moment.
They will take place on a single
day.
You will lose your children.
And you will become a widow.
That is what will happen to you.
All your evil magic
and powerful spells will not save
you.
10 You have felt secure in your evil
ways.
You have said, 'No one sees what
I'm doing.'

Your wisdom and knowledge lead
you astray.
You say to yourself,
'I am like a god. No one is greater
than I am.'
11 So horrible trouble will come on you.
You will not know how to use your
evil magic to make it go away.
Great trouble will fall on you.
No amount of money can keep it
away.
Something terrible will happen to
you all at once.
You will not see it coming ahead
of time.

12 "So keep on casting your magic
spells.
Keep on practicing your evil
magic.
You have been doing those things
ever since you were a child.
Perhaps they will help you.
Maybe they will scare your
enemies away.
13 All the advice you have received
has only worn you out!
Let those who study the heavens
come forward.
They claim to know what is going
to happen
by watching the stars every month.
So let them save you from the
trouble
that is coming on you.
14 They are just like straw.
Fire will burn them up.
They can't even save themselves
from the powerful flames.
These are not like coals that can
warm anyone.
This is not like a fire to sit by.
15 They can't do you any good.
You have done business with
them ever since you were a
child.
You have always asked them for
advice.
All of them are bewildered and
continue in their own ways.
None of them can save you."

Israel Is Stubborn

48 People of Jacob, listen to me.
You are called by the name
of Israel.
You come from the family line of
Judah.
You make promises in the name of
the LORD.
You pray to Israel's God.
But you aren't honest.
You don't mean what you say.
2 You call yourselves citizens of the
holy city of Jerusalem.
You say you depend on Israel's
God.
His name is the LORD Who Rules
Over All. He says,
3 "Long ago I told you ahead of time
what would happen.
I announced it and made it
known.
Then all of a sudden I acted.
And those things took place.
4 I knew how stubborn you were.
Your neck muscles were as
unbending as iron.
Your forehead was as hard as
bronze.
5 So I told you those things long ago.
Before they happened I
announced them to you.
I did it so you would not be able to
say,
'My statues of gods did them.
My wooden and metal gods
made them happen.'
6 You have heard me tell you these
things.
Think about all of them.
Won't you admit they have taken
place?
"From now on I will tell you about
new things that will happen.
I have not made them known to
you before.
7 These things are taking place right
now.
They did not happen long ago.
You have not heard of them
before today.
So you can't say,
'Oh, yes. I already knew about
them.'
8 You have not heard or understood
what I said.
Your ears have been plugged up
for a long time.
I knew very well that you would
turn against me.
From the day you were born, you
have refused to obey me.

9 For the honor of my own name I
wait to show my anger.
I hold it back from you so people
will continue to praise me.
I do not want to destroy you
completely.
10 I have tested you in the furnace of
suffering.
I have tried to make you pure.
But I did not use as much heat as
it takes to make silver pure.
11 I tried to purify you for my own
honor.
I did it for the honor of my name.
How can I let myself be dishonored?
I will not give up my glory to any
other god.

Israel Is Set Free

12 "Family of Jacob, listen to me.
People of Israel, pay attention.
I have chosen you.
I am the first and the last.
I am the LORD.
13 With my own hand I laid the
foundations of the earth.
With my right hand I spread out
the heavens.
When I send for them,
they come and stand ready to
obey me.

14 "People of Israel, come together
and listen to me.
What other god has said ahead of
time that certain things would
happen?
I have chosen Cyrus.
He will carry out my plans
against Babylon.
He will use his power against the
Babylonians.
15 I myself have spoken.
I have chosen him to carry out
my purpose.
I will bring him to Babylon.
He will succeed in what I tell him
to do.

16 "Come close and listen to me.

"From the first time I said Cyrus
was coming,
I did not do it in secret.
When he comes, I will be there."

The LORD and King has filled me
with his Spirit.
People of Israel, he has sent me
to you.

17 The LORD is the Holy One of Israel.
He sets his people free. He says to
them,
"I am the LORD your God.
I teach you what is best for you.
I direct you in the way you
should go.
18 I wish you would pay attention to
my commands.
If you did, peace would flow over
you like a river.
Godliness would sweep over you
like the waves of the ocean.
19 Your family would be like the sand.
Your children after you would be
as many as the grains of sand
by the sea.
It would be impossible to count
them.
I would always accept the members
of your family line.
They would never disappear or
be destroyed."

20 People of Israel, leave Babylon!
Hurry up and get away from the
Babylonians!
Here is what I want you to
announce.
Make it known with shouts of
joy.
Send the news out from one end of
the earth to the other.
Say, "The LORD has set free his
servant Jacob."
21 They didn't get thirsty when he led
them through the deserts.
He made water flow out of the
rock for them.
He broke the rock open,
and water came out of it.

22 "There is no peace for those who
are evil," says the LORD.

The Servant of the LORD

49 People who live on the
islands, listen to me.
Pay attention, you nations far
away.
Before I was born the LORD chose
me to serve him.
Before I was born the LORD spoke
my name.
2 He made my words like a sharp
sword.
He hid me in the palm of his
hand.

He made me into a sharpened
arrow.
He took good care of me and kept
me safe.
3 He said to me, "You are my true
servant Israel.
I will show my glory through
you."
4 But I said, "In spite of my hard
work,
I feel as if I haven't accomplished
anything.
I've used up all my strength.
It seems as if everything I've
done is worthless.
But the LORD will give me what I
should receive.
My God will reward me."

5 The LORD formed me in my
mother's body to be his
servant.
He wanted me to bring the
family of Jacob back to him.
He wanted me to gather the people
of Israel to himself.
The LORD will honor me.
My God will give me strength.

6 Here is what the LORD says to me.
"It is not enough for you as my
servant
to bring the tribes of Jacob back
to their land.
It is not enough for you to bring
back
the people of Israel I have kept
alive.
I will also make you a light for the
Gentiles.
Then you will make it possible
for the whole world to be
saved."

7 The LORD sets his people free.
He is the Holy One of Israel.
He speaks to his servant, who is
looked down on and hated by
the nations.
He speaks to the servant of
rulers. He says to him,
"Kings will see you and stand up to
honor you.
Princes will see you and bow
down to show you their respect.
I am the LORD. I am faithful.
I am the Holy One of Israel.
I have chosen you."

Israel Is Brought Back to Their Land

8 The LORD says to his servant,
"When it is time to have mercy on
you, I will answer your prayers.
When it is time to save you, I will
help you.
I will keep you safe.
You will put into effect my
covenant with the people of
Israel.
Then their land will be made like
new again.
Each tribe will be sent back to its
territory that was left empty.
9 I want you to say to the prisoners,
'Come out.'
Tell those who are in their dark
cells, 'You are free!'

"On their way home they will eat
beside the roads.
They will find plenty to eat on
every bare hill.
10 They will not get hungry or thirsty.
The heat from the desert sun will
not beat down on them.
The God who has tender love for
them will guide them.
Like a shepherd, he will lead
them beside springs of water.
11 I will make roads across the
mountains.
I will build wide roads for my
people.
12 They will come from far away.
Some of them will come from the
north.
Others will come from the west.
Still others will come from Aswan
in the south."

13 Shout for joy, you heavens!
Be glad, you earth!
Burst into song, you mountains!
The LORD will comfort his people.
He will show his tender love to
those who are suffering.

14 But the city of Zion said, "The LORD
has deserted me.
The Lord has forgotten me."

15 The LORD answers, "Can a mother
forget the baby
who is nursing at her breast?
Can she stop having tender love
for the child who was born to her?
She might forget her child.
But I will not forget you.

16 I have written your name on the palms of my hands.
Your walls are never out of my sight.
17 Your people will hurry back.
Those who destroyed you so completely will leave you.
18 Look up. Look all around you.
All your people are getting together
to come back to you.
You can be sure that I live,"
announces the LORD.
"And you can be just as sure that your people
will be like decorations you will wear.
Like a bride, you will wear them proudly.

19 "Zion, you were destroyed. Your land was left empty.
It was turned into a dry and empty desert.
But now you will be too small to hold all your people.
And those who destroyed you will be far away.
20 The children born during your time of sorrow
will speak to you. They will say,
'This city is too small for us.
Give us more space to live in.'
21 Then you will say to yourself,
'Whose children are these?
I lost my children.
And I couldn't have any more.
My children were taken far away from me.
And no one wanted them.
Who brought these children up?
I was left all alone.
So where have these children come from?' "

22 The LORD and King continues,
"I will call out to the nations.
I will give a signal to them.
They will bring back your sons in their arms.
They will carry your daughters on their hips.
23 Their kings will become like fathers to you.
Their queens will be like mothers who nurse you.
They will bow down to you with their faces toward the ground.
They will kiss the dust at your feet to show you their respect.
Then you will know that I am the LORD.
Those who put their hope in me will not be ashamed."

24 Can goods that were stolen by soldiers be taken away from them?
Can prisoners be set free from the powerful Babylonians?
25 "Yes, they can," the LORD answers.

"Prisoners will be taken away from soldiers.
Stolen goods will be taken back from the powerful Babylonians.
Zion, I will fight against those who fight against you.
And I will save your people.
26 I will make those who treat you badly eat the flesh of others.
They will drink blood and get drunk on it as if it were wine.
Then everyone on earth will know that I am the one who saves you.
I am the LORD. I set you free.
I am the Mighty One of Jacob."

Israel Sins but the LORD's Servant Obeys

50 The LORD says to the people in Jerusalem,

"Do you think I divorced your people who lived before you?
Is that why I sent them away?
If it is, show me the letter of divorce.
I did not sell you into slavery to pay someone I owe.
You were sold because you sinned against me.
Your people were sent away because of their lawless acts.
2 When I came to save you, why didn't anyone welcome me?
When I called out to you, why didn't anyone answer me?
Wasn't I powerful enough to set you free?
Wasn't I strong enough to save you?
I dry up the sea with a single command.
I turn rivers into a desert.

Then fish rot because they do not
have any water.
They die because they are thirsty.
3 I make the sky turn dark.
It looks as if it's dressed in
clothing sad people wear."

4 The LORD and King has taught me
what to say.
He has taught me how to help
those who are tired.
He wakes me up every morning.
He makes me want to listen like
a good student.
5 The LORD and King has unplugged
my ears.
I've always obeyed him.
I haven't turned away from him.
6 I let my enemies beat me on my
bare back.
I let them pull the hair out of my
beard.
I didn't turn my face away
when they made fun of me and
spit on me.
7 The LORD and King helps me.
He won't let me be dishonored.
So I've made up my mind to keep
on serving him.
I know he won't let me be put to
shame.
8 He is near. He will prove I haven't
done anything wrong.
So who will bring charges
against me?
Let's face each other in court!
Who can bring charges against me?
Let him come and face me!
9 The LORD and King helps me.
So who will judge me?
My enemies will be like clothes that
moths have eaten up.
My enemies will disappear.

10 Does anyone among you have
respect for the LORD?
Does anyone obey the message
of the LORD's servant?
Let the person who walks in the dark
trust in the LORD.
Let the one who doesn't have any
light to guide them
depend on their God.
11 But all you sinners who light fires
should go ahead and walk in
their light.
You who carry flaming torches
should walk in their light.
Here's what I'm going to do to you.
I'll make you lie down in great
pain.

The LORD's Saving Power for Zion Lasts Forever

51 The LORD says, "Listen to me, you
who want to do what is right.
Pay attention, you who look to me.
Consider the rock you were cut
out of.
Think about the rock pit you
were dug from.
2 Consider Abraham. He is the father
of your people.
Think about Sarah. She is your
mother.
When I chose Abraham, he did not
have any children.
But I blessed him and gave him
many of them.
3 You can be sure that I will comfort
Zion's people.
I will look with loving concern on
all their destroyed buildings.
I will make their deserts like Eden.
I will make their dry and empty
land like the garden of the LORD.
Joy and gladness will be there.
People will sing and give thanks
to me.

4 "Listen to me, my people.
Pay attention, my nation.
My instruction will go out to the
nations.
I make everything right.
That will be a guiding light for
them.
5 The time for me to set you free is
near.
I will soon save you.
My powerful arm will make
everything right among the
nations.
The islands will put their hope
in me.
They will wait for my powerful
arm to act.
6 Look up toward the heavens.
Then look at the earth.
The heavens will vanish like smoke.
The earth will wear out like
clothes.
Those who live there will die like
flies.
But I will save you forever.
My saving power will never end.

7 "Listen to me, you who know what
is right.
Pay attention, you who have
taken my instruction to heart.
Do not be afraid when mere human
beings make fun of you.
Do not be terrified when they
laugh at you.
8 They will be like clothes that moths
have eaten up.
They will be like wool that worms
have chewed up.
But my saving power will last
forever.
I will save you for all time to come."

9 Wake up, arm of the LORD!
Wake up!
Dress yourself with strength as if
it were your clothes!
Wake up, just as you did in the
past.
Wake up, as you did long ago.
Didn't you cut Rahab to pieces?
Didn't you stab that sea monster
to death?
10 Didn't you dry up the Red Sea?
Didn't you dry up those deep
waters?
You made a road on the bottom of
that sea.
Then those who were set free
went across.
11 Those the LORD has saved will
return to their land.
They will sing as they enter the
city of Zion.
Joy that lasts forever will be
like beautiful crowns on their
heads.
They will be filled with gladness
and joy.
Sorrow and sighing will be gone.

12 The LORD says to his people,
"I comfort you because of who
I am.
Why are you afraid of mere human
beings?
They are like grass that dries up.
13 How can you forget me? I made you.
I stretch out the heavens.
I lay the foundations of the earth.
Why are you terrified every day?
Is it because those who are angry
with you are crushing you?
Is it because they are trying to
destroy you?
Their anger can't harm you
anymore.
14 You prisoners who are so afraid
will soon be set free.
You will not die in your prison cells.
You will not go without food.
15 I am the LORD your God.
I stir up the ocean. I make its
waves roar.
My name is the LORD Who Rules
Over All.
16 I have put my words in your mouth.
I have kept you safe in the palm
of my hand.
I set the heavens in place.
I laid the foundations of the earth.
I say to Zion, 'You are my
people.' "

The Cup of the LORD's Great Anger

17 Wake up, Jerusalem!
Wake up! Get up!
The LORD has handed you the cup
of his great anger.
And you have drunk from it.
That cup makes people unsteady
on their feet.
And you have drunk from it to
the very last drop.
18 Among all the children who were
born to you
there was none to guide you.
Among all the children you
brought up
there was none to lead you by
the hand.
19 Nothing but trouble has come to
you.
You have been wiped out and
destroyed.
And you have suffered hunger
and war.
No one feels sorry for you.
No one can comfort you.
20 Your children have fainted.
They lie helpless at every street
corner.
They are like antelope that have
been caught in a net.
They have felt the full force of the
LORD's great anger.
Jerusalem, your God had to warn
them strongly.

21 So listen to me, you suffering
people of Jerusalem.
You have been made drunk, but
not by drinking wine.

[22] Your LORD and King speaks.
He is your God.
He stands up for his people. He says,
"I have taken from you the cup
of my great anger.
It made you unsteady on your
feet.
But you will never drink
from that cup again.
[23] Instead, I will give it to those who
made you suffer.
They said to you,
'Fall down flat on the ground.
Then we can walk all over you.'
And that is exactly what you did.
You made your back like a street
to be walked on."

52 Wake up! Zion, wake up!
Dress yourself with strength
as if it were your clothes.
Holy city of Jerusalem,
put on your clothes of glory.
Those who haven't been circumcised
will never enter you again.
Neither will those who are
"unclean."
[2] Get up, Jerusalem! Shake off your
dust.
Take your place on your throne.
Captured people of Zion,
remove the chains from your neck.
[3] The LORD says,
"When you were sold as slaves, no
one paid anything for you.
Now no one will pay any money
to set you free."
[4] The LORD and King continues,
"Long ago my people went down to
Egypt.
They lived there for a while.
Later, Assyria crushed them
without any reason.
[5] "Now look at what has happened to
them," announces the LORD.
"Once again my people have been
taken away.
And no one paid anything for them.
Those who rule over them brag
about it,"
announces the LORD.
"All day long without stopping,
people speak evil things against
my name.
[6] So the day will come when my
people will really know the
meaning of my name.
They will know what kind of God
I am.
They will know that I told them
ahead of time they would
return to their land.
They will know that it was I."

[7] What a beautiful sight it is
to see messengers coming with
good news!
How beautiful to see them coming
down from the mountains
with a message about peace!
How wonderful it is when they
bring the good news
that we are saved!
How wonderful when they say to
Zion,
"Your God rules!"
[8] Listen! Those on guard duty are
shouting out the message.
With their own eyes
they see the LORD returning to
Zion.
So they shout for joy.
[9] Burst into songs of joy together,
you broken-down buildings in
Jerusalem.
The LORD has comforted his
people.
He has set Jerusalem free.
[10] The LORD will use the power of his
holy arm to save his people.
All the nations will see him do it.
Everyone from one end of the
earth to the other will see it.

[11] You who carry the objects that
belong to the LORD's temple,
leave Babylon!
Leave it! Get out of there!
Don't touch anything that isn't
pure and "clean."
Come out of Babylon and be
pure.
[12] But this time you won't have to
leave in a hurry.
You won't have to rush away.
The LORD will go ahead of you and
lead you.
The God of Israel will follow
behind you and guard you.

The Suffering and Glory of the LORD's Servant

13 The LORD says, "My servant will act wisely and accomplish his task.
He will be highly honored. He will be greatly respected.
14 Many people were shocked when they saw him.
He was so scarred that he no longer looked like a person.
His body was so twisted that he did not look like a human being anymore.
15 But many nations will be surprised when they see what he has done.
Kings will be so amazed that they will not be able to say anything.
They will understand things they were never told.
They will know the meaning of things they never heard."

53 Who has believed what we've been saying?
Who has seen the LORD's saving power?
2 His servant grew up like a tender young plant.
He grew like a root coming up out of dry ground.
He didn't have any beauty or majesty that made us notice him.
There wasn't anything special about the way he looked that drew us to him.
3 People looked down on him. They didn't accept him.
He knew all about pain and suffering.
He was like someone people turn their faces away from.
We looked down on him. We didn't have any respect for him.
4 He suffered the things we should have suffered.
He took on himself the pain that should have been ours.
But we thought God was punishing him.
We thought God was wounding him and making him suffer.
5 But the servant was pierced because we had sinned.
He was crushed because we had done what was evil.
He was punished to make us whole again.
His wounds have healed us.
6 All of us are like sheep. We have wandered away from God.
All of us have turned to our own way.
And the LORD has placed on his servant
the sins of all of us.

7 He was treated badly and made to suffer.
But he didn't open his mouth.
He was led away like a lamb to be killed.
Sheep are silent while their wool is being cut off.
In the same way, he didn't open his mouth.
8 He was arrested and sentenced to death.
Then he was taken away.
He was cut off from this life.
He was punished for the sins of my people.
Who among those who were living at that time
tried to stop what was happening?
9 He was given a grave with those who were evil.
But his body was buried in the tomb of a rich man.
He was killed even though he hadn't harmed anyone.
And he had never lied to anyone.

10 The LORD says, "It was my plan to crush him
and cause him to suffer.
I made his life an offering to pay for sin.
But he will see all his children after him.
In fact, he will continue to live.
My plan will be brought about through him.
11 After he has suffered, he will see the light of life.
And he will be satisfied.
My godly servant will make many people godly
because of what he will accomplish.
He will be punished for their sins.
12 So I will give him a place of honor among those who are great.
He will be rewarded just like others who win the battle.

That's because he was willing to
give his life as a sacrifice.
He was counted among those
who had committed crimes.
He took the sins of many people on
himself.
And he gave his life for those who
had done what is wrong."

Jerusalem Will Be Glorious

54 "Jerusalem, sing!
You are now like a woman
who never had a child.
Burst into song! Shout for joy!
You who have never had labor
pains,
you are now all alone.
But you will have more children
than a woman who still has a
husband,"
says the LORD.
2 "Make a large area for your tent.
Spread out its curtains.
Go ahead and make your tent
wider.
Make its ropes longer.
Drive the stakes down deeper.
3 You will spread out to the right and
the left.
Your children after you will drive
out the nations that are now
living in your land.
They will make their homes in
the deserted cities of those
nations.
4 "Do not be afraid. You will not be
put to shame anymore.
Do not be afraid of being
dishonored.
People will no longer make fun of
you.
You will forget the time when you
suffered as slaves in Egypt.
You will no longer remember the
shame
of being a widow in Babylon.
5 I made you. I am now your husband.
My name is the LORD Who Rules
Over All.
I am the Holy One of Israel.
I have set you free.
I am the God of the whole earth.
6 You were like a wife who was deserted.
And her heart was broken.
You were like a wife who married
young.
And her husband sent her away.
But now I am calling you to come
back," says your God.
7 "For a brief moment I left you.
But because I love you so much, I
will bring you back.
8 For a moment I turned my face
away from you.
I was very angry with you.
But I will show you my loving concern.
My faithful love will continue
forever,"
says the LORD. He is the one who
set you free.

9 "During Noah's time I made a
promise.
I said I would never cover the
earth with water again.
In the same way, I have promised
not to be angry with you.
I will never punish you again.
10 The mountains might shake.
The hills might be removed.
But my faithful love for you will
never be shaken.
And my covenant that promises
peace to you will never be
removed,"
says the LORD. He shows you his
loving concern.

11 "Suffering city, you have been
beaten by storms.
You have not been comforted.
I will rebuild you with turquoise
stones.
I will rebuild your foundations
with lapis lazuli.
12 I will line the top of your city wall
with rubies.
I will make your gates out of
gleaming jewels.
And I will make all your walls
out of precious stones.
13 I will teach all your children.
And they will enjoy great peace.
14 When you do what is right,
you will be made secure.
Your leaders will not be mean to
you.
You will not have anything to be
afraid of.
You will not be terrified anymore.
Terror will not come near you.
15 People might attack you. But I will
not be the cause of it.
Those who attack you will give
themselves up to you.

16 "I created blacksmiths.
They fan the coals into flames of fire.
They make weapons that are fit for their work.
I also created those who destroy others.
17 But no weapon used against you will succeed.
People might bring charges against you.
But you will prove that they are wrong.
Those are the things I do for my servants.
I make everything right for them,"
announces the LORD.

The LORD Invites Thirsty People to Come to Him

55 "Come, all you who are thirsty.
Come and drink the water I offer to you.
You who do not have any money, come.
Buy and eat the grain I give you.
Come and buy wine and milk.
You will not have to pay anything for it.
2 Why spend money on what is not food?
Why work for what does not satisfy you?
Listen carefully to me.
Then you will eat what is good.
You will enjoy the richest food there is.
3 Listen and come to me.
Pay attention to me.
Then you will live.
I will make a covenant with you that will last forever.
I will give you my faithful love.
I promised it to David.
4 I made him a witness to the nations.
He became a ruler and commander over them.
5 You too will send for nations you do not know.
Even though you do not know them,
they will come running to you.
That is what I will do. I am the LORD your God.
I am the Holy One of Israel.
I have honored you."

6 Turn to the LORD before it's too late.
Call out to him while he's still ready to help you.
7 Let those who are evil stop doing evil things.
And let them quit thinking evil thoughts.
Let them turn to the LORD.

TRANSCENDENT

My GOD is...

When we say God is "transcendent," we mean that God is far beyond us in all ways. He is not created, and he has always existed. All humans, on the other hand, are created by God. We have limited understanding, which means we cannot fully grasp who God is in his nature and character (see 1 Corinthians 2:9). We can study God our whole lives yet never fully wrap our minds around him, because he is beyond our understanding.

God transcends, or goes beyond, our ability to fully know him because he is greater than we are. In fact, God can listen to everyone's prayers at the same time. Isn't that amazing? God is deserving of all glory, honor, and praise.

The LORD will show them his
tender love.
Let them turn to our God.
He is always ready to forgive.

8 "My thoughts are not like your
thoughts.
And your ways are not like my
ways,"
announces the LORD.
9 "The heavens are higher than the
earth.
And my ways are higher than
your ways.
My thoughts are higher than
your thoughts.
10 The rain and the snow
come down from the sky.
They do not return to it
without watering the earth.
They make plants come up and grow.
The plants produce seeds for
farmers.
They also produce food for
people to eat.
11 The words I speak are like that.
They will not return to me
without producing results.
They will accomplish what I want
them to.
They will do exactly what I sent
them to do.

12 "My people, you will go out of
Babylon with joy.
You will be led out of it in peace.
The mountains and hills
will burst into song as you go.
And all the trees in the fields
will clap their hands.
13 Juniper trees will grow where there
used to be bushes that had
thorns on them.
And myrtle trees will grow where
there used to be thorns.
That will bring me great fame.
It will be a lasting reminder of
what I can do.
It will stand forever."

The LORD Will Save Those Who Come to Him

56 The LORD says,

"Do what is fair and right.
I will soon come and save you.
Soon everyone will know that
what I do is right.
2 Blessed is the person who does
what I want them to.
They are faithful in keeping the
Sabbath day.
They do not misuse it.
They do not do what is evil on
that day."

3 Suppose an outsider wants to
follow the LORD.
Then that person shouldn't say,
"The LORD won't accept me as
one of his people."
And a eunuch shouldn't say,
"I'm like a dry tree
that doesn't bear any fruit."
4 The LORD says,

"Suppose some eunuchs keep my
Sabbath days.
They choose to do what
pleases me.
And they are faithful in keeping
my covenant.
5 Then I will set up a monument in
the area of my temple.
Their names will be written on it.
That will be better for them than
having sons and daughters.
The names of the eunuchs will be
remembered forever.
They will never be forgotten.

6 "Suppose outsiders want to
follow me
and serve me.
They want to love me
and worship me.
They keep the Sabbath day and do
not misuse it.
And they are faithful in keeping
my covenant.
7 Then I will bring them to my holy
mountain of Zion.
I will give them joy in my house.
They can pray there.
I will accept their burnt offerings
and sacrifices on my altar.
My house will be called
a house where people from all
nations can pray."
8 The LORD and King will gather
those who were taken away from
their homes in Israel.
He announces, "I will gather them
to myself.
And I will gather others to join
them."

The LORD Judges Israel's Evil Leaders

9 Come, all you enemy nations!
Come like wild animals.
Come and destroy like animals
in the forest.
10 Israel's prophets are blind.
They don't know the LORD.
All of them are like watchdogs that
can't even bark.
They just lie around and dream.
They love to sleep.
11 They are like dogs that love to eat.
They never get enough.
They are like shepherds who don't
have any understanding.
All of them do as they please.
They only look for what they can
get for themselves.
12 "Come!" they shout. "Let's get some
wine!
Let's drink all the beer we can!
Tomorrow we'll do the same thing.
And that will be even better than
today."

57 Those who are right with God
die.
And no one really cares about it.
People who are faithful to the LORD
are swept away by trouble.
And no one understands why
that happens
to those who do what is right.
2 Those who lead honest lives
will enjoy peace and rest when
they die.
3 The LORD says, "Come here,
you children of women who
practice evil magic!
You are children of prostitutes
and those who commit
adultery.
4 Who are you making fun of?
Who are you laughing at?
Who are you sticking your
tongue out at?
You are people who refuse to
obey me.
You are just a bunch of liars!
5 You burn with sinful desire among
the oak trees.
You worship your gods under
every green tree.
You sacrifice your children in the
valleys.
You also do it under the cliffs.
6 You have chosen some of the
smooth stones in the valleys to
be your gods.
You have joined yourselves to
them.
You have even poured out drink
offerings to them.
You have given grain offerings to
them.
So why should I take pity on you?
7 You have made your bed on a very
high hill.
You went up there to offer your
sacrifices.
8 You have set up statues to remind
you of your gods.
You have put them behind your
doors and doorposts.
You deserted me. You invited other
lovers into your bed.
You climbed into it and
welcomed them.
You made a deal with them.
And you looked with desire at
their naked bodies.
9 You took olive oil to the god named
Molek.
You took a lot of perfume along
with you.
You sent your messengers to places
far away.
You even sent them down to the
place of the dead.
10 You wore yourself out with all your
efforts.
But you would not say, 'It's
hopeless.'
You received new strength.
So you did not give up.
11 "Who are you so afraid of
that you have not been faithful
to me?
You have not remembered me.
What you do doesn't even bother
you.
I have not punished you for a long
time.
That is why you are not afraid of me.
12 You have not done what is right or
good.
I will let everyone know about it.
And that will not be of any
benefit to you.
13 Go ahead and cry out for help to all
the statues of your gods.
See if they can save you!

The wind will carry them off.
Just a puff of air will blow them away.
But anyone who comes to me for safety
will receive the land.
They will possess my holy mountain of Zion."

The LORD Comforts People Who Are Sorry for Their Sins

14 A messenger says,

"Build up the road! Build it up! Get it ready!
Remove anything that would keep my people from coming back."
15 The God who is highly honored lives forever.
His name is holy. He says,
"I live in a high and holy place.
But I also live with anyone who turns away from their sins.
I live with anyone who is not proud.
I give new life to them.
I give it to anyone who turns away from their sins.
16 I will not find fault with my people forever.
I will not always be angry with them.
If I were, I would cause their spirits to grow weak.
The people I created would faint away.
17 I was very angry with them.
They always longed for more and more of everything.
So I punished them for that sin.
I turned my face away from them because I was angry.
But they kept on wanting their own way.
18 I have seen what they have done.
But I will heal them.
I will guide them.
I will give those who mourn in Israel the comfort they had before.
19 Then they will praise me.
I will give perfect peace to those who are far away and those who are near.
And I will heal them," says the LORD.
20 But those who are evil are like the rolling sea.
It never rests.
Its waves toss up mud and sand.
21 "There is no peace for those who are evil," says my God.

What True Worship Is All About

58 The LORD told me,

"Shout out loud. Do not hold back.
Raise your voice like a trumpet.
Tell my people that they have refused to obey me.
Tell the family of Jacob how much they have sinned.
2 Day after day they worship me.
They seem ready and willing to know how I want them to live.
They act as if they were a nation that does what is right.
They act as if they have not turned away from my commands.
They claim to want me to give them fair decisions.
They seem ready and willing to come near and worship me.
3 'We have gone without food,' they say.
'Why haven't you noticed it?
We have made ourselves suffer.
Why haven't you paid any attention to us?'

"On the day when you fast, you do as you please.
You take advantage of all your workers.
4 When you fast, it ends in arguing and fighting.
You hit one another with your fists.
That is an evil thing to do.
The way you are now fasting keeps your prayers from being heard in heaven.
5 Do you think that is the way I want you to fast?
Is it only a time for people to make themselves suffer?
Is it only for people to bow their heads like tall grass bent by the wind?
Is it only for people to lie down in ashes and clothes of mourning?
Is that what you call a fast?
Do you think I can accept that?

6 "Here is the way I want you to fast.

"Set free those who are held by
chains without any reason.
Untie the ropes that hold people
as slaves.
Set free those who are crushed.
Break every evil chain.
7 Share your food with hungry people.
Provide homeless people with a
place to stay.
Give naked people clothes to wear.
Provide for the needs of your
own family.
8 Then the light of my blessing will
shine on you like the rising sun.
I will heal you quickly.
I will march out ahead of you.
And my glory will follow behind
you and guard you.
That's because I always do what
is right.
9 You will call out to me for help.
And I will answer you.
You will cry out.
And I will say, 'Here I am.'

"Get rid of the chains you use to
hold others down.
Stop pointing your finger at
others as if they had done
something wrong.
Stop saying harmful things
about them.
10 Work hard to feed hungry people.
Satisfy the needs of those who
are crushed.
Then my blessing will light up your
darkness.
And the night of your suffering
will become as bright as the
noonday sun.
11 I will always guide you.
I will satisfy your needs in a land
baked by the sun.
I will make you stronger.
You will be like a garden that has
plenty of water.
You will be like a spring whose
water never runs dry.
12 Your people will rebuild the cities
that were destroyed long ago.
And you will build again on the
old foundations.
You will be called One Who Repairs
Broken Walls.
You will be called One Who Makes
City Streets Like New Again.

13 "Do not work on the Sabbath day.
Do not do just anything you want
to on my holy day.
Make the Sabbath a day you can
enjoy.
Honor the LORD's holy day.
Do not work on it.
Do not do just anything you
want to.
Do not talk about things that are
worthless.
14 Then you will find your joy in me.
I will give you control over the most
important places in the land.
And you will enjoy all the good things
in the land I gave your father
Jacob."
The LORD has spoken.

The LORD Sets His People Free

59 People of Israel, the LORD's arm
is not too weak to save you.
His ears aren't too deaf to hear
your cry for help.
2 But your sins have separated you
from your God.
They have caused him to turn his
face away from you.
So he won't listen to you.
3 Your hands and fingers are stained
with blood.
You are guilty of committing
murder.
Your mouth has told lies.
Your tongue says evil things.
4 People aren't fair when they
present cases in court.
They aren't honest when they
state their case.
They depend on weak arguments.
They tell lies.
They plan to make trouble.
Then they carry it out.
5 The plans they make are like the
eggs of poisonous snakes.
Anyone who eats those eggs will
die.
When one of them is broken, a
snake comes out.
6 Those people weave their evil plans
together like a spider's web.
But the webs they make can't be
used as clothes.
They can't cover themselves with
what they make.
Their acts are evil.
They do things to harm others.

[7]They are always in a hurry to sin.
They run quickly to murder those who aren't guilty.
They love to think up evil plans.
They leave a trail of harmful actions.
[8]They don't know how to live at peace with others.
What they do isn't fair.
They lead twisted lives.
No one who lives like that will enjoy peace and rest.
[9]We aren't being treated fairly.
We haven't been set free yet.
The God who always does what is right
hasn't come to help us.
We look for light, but we see nothing but darkness.
We look for brightness, but we walk in deep shadows.
[10]Like blind people we feel our way along the wall.
We are like those who can't see.
At noon we trip and fall as if the sun had already set.
Compared to those who are healthy, we are like dead people.
[11]All of us growl like hungry bears.
We sound like doves as we mourn.
We want the LORD to do what is fair and save us.
But he doesn't do it.
We long for him to set us free.
But the time for that seems far away.
[12]That's because we've done so many things he considers wrong.
Our sins prove that we are guilty.
The wrong things we've done are always troubling us.
We admit that we have sinned.
[13]We've refused to obey the LORD.
We've made evil plans against him.
We've turned our backs on our God.
We've stirred up conflict and refused to follow him.
We've told lies that came from our own minds.
[14]So people stop others from doing what is fair.
They keep them from doing what is right.
No one tells the truth in court anymore.
No one is honest there.
[15]In fact, truth can't be found anywhere.
Those who refuse to do evil are attacked.
The LORD sees that people aren't treating others fairly.
That makes him unhappy.
[16]He sees that there is no one who helps his people.
He is shocked that no one stands up for them.
So he will use his own powerful arm to save them.
He has the strength to do it because he is holy.
[17]He will put the armor of holiness on his chest.
He'll put the helmet of salvation on his head.
He'll pay people back for the wrong things they do.
He'll wrap himself in anger as if it were a coat.
[18]He will pay his enemies back for what they have done.
He'll pour his anger out on them.
He'll punish those who attack him.
He'll give the people in the islands what they have coming to them.
[19]People in the west will show respect for the LORD's name.
People in the east will worship him because of his glory.
The LORD will come like a rushing river that was held back.
His breath will drive it along.
[20]"I set my people free. I will come to Mount Zion.
I will come to those in Jacob's family who turn away from their sins,"
announces the LORD.

[21]"Here is the covenant I will make
with them," says the LORD. "My Spirit
is on you and will not leave you. I have
put my words in your mouth. They will
never leave your mouth. And they will
never leave the mouths of your children
or their children after them. That will be
true for all time to come," says the LORD.

Zion Will Be Glorious

60 "People of Jerusalem, get up.
Shine, because your light has come.
The glory of the LORD will shine on you.
2 Darkness covers the earth.
Thick darkness spreads over the nations.
But I will rise and shine on you.
My glory will appear over you.
3 Nations will come to your light.
Kings will come to the brightness of your new day.

4 "Look up. Look all around you.
All your people are getting together to come back to you.
Your sons will come from far away.
Your daughters will be carried on the hip like little children.
5 Then your face will glow with joy.
Your heart will beat fast because you are so happy.
Wealth from across the ocean will be brought to you.
The riches of the nations will come to you.
6 Herds of young camels will cover your land.
They will come from Midian and Ephah.
They will also come from Sheba.
They'll carry gold and incense.
And people will shout praises to me.
7 All of Kedar's flocks will be gathered to you.
The rams of Nebaioth will serve as your sacrifices.
I will accept them as offerings on my altar.
That is how I will bring honor to my glorious temple.

8 "Whose ships are these that sail along like clouds?
They fly like doves to their nests.
9 People from the islands are coming to me.
The ships of Tarshish are out in front.
They are bringing your children back from far away.
Your children are bringing their silver and gold with them.
They are coming to honor me.
I am the LORD your God.
I am the Holy One of Israel.
I have honored you.

10 "People from other lands will rebuild your walls.
Their kings will serve you.
When I was angry with you, I struck you.
But now I will show you my tender love.
11 Your gates will always stand open.
They will never be shut, day or night.
Then people can bring you the wealth of the nations.
Their kings will come along with them.
12 The nation or kingdom that will not serve you will be destroyed.
It will be completely wiped out.

13 "Lebanon's glorious trees will be brought to you.
Its junipers, firs and cypress trees will be brought.
They will be used to make my temple beautiful.
And I will bring glory to the place where my throne is.
14 The children of those who crush you will come and bow down to you.
All those who hate you will kneel down at your feet.
Jerusalem, they will call you the City of the LORD.
They will name you Zion, the City of the Holy One of Israel.

15 "You have been deserted and hated.
No one even travels through you.
But I will make you into something to be proud of forever.
You will be a place of joy for all time to come.
16 You will get everything you need from kings and nations.
You will be like children who are nursing
at their mother's breasts.
Then you will know that I am the one who saves you.
I am the LORD. I set you free.
I am the Mighty One of Jacob.
17 Instead of bronze I will bring you gold.
In place of iron I will give you silver.
Instead of wood I will bring you bronze.
In place of stones I will give you iron.

I will make peace govern you.
I will make godliness rule over you.
18 People will no longer harm one another in your land.
They will not wipe out or destroy anything inside your borders.
You will call your walls Salvation.
And you will name your gates Praise.
19 You will not need the light of the sun by day anymore.
The bright light of the moon will no longer have to shine on you.
I will be your light forever.
My glory will shine on you.
I am the LORD your God.
20 Your sun will never set again.
Your moon will never lose its light.
I will be your light forever.
Your days of sorrow will come to an end.
21 Then all your people will do what is right.
The land will belong to them forever.
They will be like a young tree I have planted.
My hands have created them.
They will show how glorious I am.
22 The smallest family among you will become a tribe.
The smallest tribe will become a mighty nation.
I am the LORD.
When it is the right time, I will act quickly."

The Year When the LORD Sets His People Free

61 The Spirit of the LORD and King is on me.
The LORD has anointed me
to announce good news to poor people.
He has sent me to comfort
those whose hearts have been broken.
He has sent me to announce freedom
for those who have been captured.
He wants me to set prisoners free
from their dark cells.
2 He has sent me to announce the year
when he will set his people free.
He wants me to announce the day
when he will pay his enemies back.
Our God has sent me to comfort all
those who are sad.
3 He wants me to help those in Zion who are filled with sorrow.
I will put beautiful crowns on their heads
in place of ashes.
I will anoint them with olive oil to give them joy
instead of sorrow.
I will give them a spirit of praise
in place of a spirit of sadness.
They will be like oak trees that are strong and straight.
The LORD himself will plant them in the land.
That will show how glorious he is.

4 They will rebuild the places that were destroyed long ago.
They will repair the buildings that have been broken down for many years.
They will make the destroyed cities like new again.
They have been broken down for a very long time.
5 Outsiders will serve you by taking care of your flocks.
People from other lands will work in your fields and vineyards.
6 You will be called priests of the LORD.
You will be named workers for our God.
You will enjoy the wealth of nations.
You will brag about getting their riches.

7 Instead of being put to shame
you will receive a double share of wealth.
Instead of being dishonored
you will be glad to be in your land.
You will receive a double share of riches there.
And you'll be filled with joy that will last forever.

8 The LORD says, "I love those who do what is right.
I hate it when people steal and do other sinful things.

So I will be faithful to my people.
And I will bless them.
I will make a covenant with them
that will last forever.
9 Their children after them will be
famous among the nations.
Their families will be praised by
people everywhere.
All those who see them will agree
that I have blessed them."

10 The people of Jerusalem will say,
"We take great delight in the LORD.
We are joyful because we belong
to our God.
He has dressed us with salvation as
if it were our clothes.
He has put robes of godliness on us.
We are like a groom who is dressed
up for his wedding.
We are like a bride who decorates
herself with her jewels.
11 The soil makes the young plant
come up.
A garden causes seeds to grow.
In the same way, the LORD and
King will make godliness grow.
And all the nations will praise him."

The LORD Gives Zion a New Name

62 The LORD says, "For the good
of Zion I will not keep silent.
For Jerusalem's benefit I will not
remain quiet.
I will not keep silent until what I
will do for them
shines like the sunrise.
I will not remain quiet until they
are saved
and shine like a blazing torch.
2 Jerusalem, the nations will see
that I have made everything
right for you.
All their kings will see your glory.
You will be called by a new name.
I myself will give it to you.
3 You will be like a glorious crown in
my strong hand.
You will be like a royal crown in
my powerful hand.
4 People will not call you Deserted
anymore.
They will no longer name your
land Empty.
Instead, you will be called One the
LORD Delights In.
Your land will be named Married
One.
That's because the LORD will take
delight in you.
And your land will be married.
5 As a young man marries a young
woman,
so your Builder will marry you.
As a groom is happy with his bride,
so your God will be full of joy
over you."

6 Jerusalem, I have stationed guards
on your walls.
They must never be silent day or
night.
You who call out to the LORD
must not give yourselves any rest.
7 And don't give him any rest
until he makes Jerusalem secure.
Don't give him any peace
until people all over the earth
praise that city.

8 The LORD has made a promise.
He has lifted up his right hand
and mighty arm.
He has promised, "I will never give
your grain
to your enemies for food again.
Outsiders will never again drink
the fresh wine
you have worked so hard for.
9 Instead, those who gather the grain
will eat it themselves.
And they will praise me.
Those who gather grapes to make
the wine will enjoy it.
They will drink it in the
courtyards of my temple."

10 Go out through your gates, people
of Jerusalem! Go out!
Prepare the way for the rest of
your people to return.
Build up the road! Build it up!
Remove the stones.
Raise a banner over the city
for the nations to see.

11 The LORD has announced a
message
from one end of the earth to the
other.
He has said, "Tell the people of
Zion,
'Look! Your Savior is coming!
He is bringing his people back as
his reward.
He has won the battle over their
enemies.'"

[12]They will be called the Holy People.
They will be called the People the LORD Set Free.
And Jerusalem will be named the City the LORD Cares About.
It will be named the City No Longer Deserted.

God Will Save His People and Punish Their Enemies

63 Who is this man coming from the city of Bozrah in Edom?
His clothes are stained bright red.
Who is he? He is dressed up in all his glory.
He is marching toward us with great strength.

The LORD answers, "It is I.
I have won the battle.
I am mighty.
I have saved my people."

[2]Why are your clothes red?
They look as if you have been stomping
on grapes in a winepress.
[3]The LORD answers, "I have been stomping on the nations
as if they were grapes.
No one was there to help me.
I walked all over the nations because I was angry.
That is why I stomped on them.
Their blood splashed all over my clothes.
So my clothes were stained bright red.
[4]I decided it was time to pay back Israel's enemies.
The year for me to set my people free had come.
[5]I looked around, but no one was there to help me.
I was shocked that no one gave me any help.
So I used my own power to save my people.
I had the strength to do it because I was angry.
[6]I walked all over the nations because I was angry with them.
I made them drink from the cup of my great anger.
I poured out their blood on the ground."

Isaiah Praises the LORD and Prays to Him

[7]I will talk about the kind things the LORD has done.
I'll praise him for everything he's done for us.
He has done many good things for the nation of Israel.
That's because he loves us and is very kind to us.
[8]In the past he said, "They are my people.
They are children who will be faithful to me."
So he saved them.
[9]When they suffered, he suffered with them.
He sent his angel to save them.
He set them free because he is loving and kind.
He lifted them up and carried them.
He did it again and again in days long ago.
[10]But they refused to obey him.
They made his Holy Spirit sad.
So he turned against them and became their enemy.
He himself fought against them.

[11]Then his people remembered what he did long ago.
They recalled the days of Moses and his people.
They asked, "Where is the God who brought
Israel through the Red Sea?
Moses led them as the shepherd of his flock.
Where is the God who put
his Holy Spirit among them?
[12]He used his glorious and powerful arm
to help Moses.
He parted the waters of the sea in front of them.
That mighty act made him famous forever.
[13]He led them through that deep sea.
Like a horse in open country,
they didn't trip and fall.
[14]They were like cattle that are taken down to the plains.
They were given rest by the Spirit of the LORD."
That's how he guided his people.
So he made a glorious name for himself.

15 LORD, look down from heaven.
Look down from your holy and glorious throne.
Where is your great love for us?
Where is your power?
Why don't you show us
your tender love and concern?
16 You are our Father.
Abraham might not accept us as his children.
Jacob might not recognize us as his family.
But you are our Father, LORD.
Your name is One Who Always Sets Us Free.
17 LORD, why do you let us wander away from you?
Why do you let us become so stubborn
that we don't respect you?
Come back and help us.
We are the tribes that belong to you.
18 For a little while your holy people possessed the land.
But now our enemies have torn your temple down.
19 We are like people you never ruled over.
We are like those who don't belong to you.

64 I wish you would open up your heavens
and come down to us!
I wish the mountains would tremble
when you show your power!
2 Be like a fire that causes twigs to burn.
It also makes water boil.
So come down and make yourself known to your enemies.
Cause the nations to shake with fear
when they see your power!
3 Long ago you did some wonderful things we didn't expect.
You came down, and the mountains trembled
when you showed your power.
4 No one's ears have ever heard of a God like you.
No one's eyes have ever seen a God who is greater than you.
No God but you acts for the good
of those who trust in him.
5 You come to help those who enjoy doing what is right.

God Is the Potter

God created us, and he knows everything about each one of us. He is called the Potter, and we are the clay (see Isaiah 64:8). God molds us, or shapes us, to be more like Jesus.

The Bible uses the image of a potter working with clay as a way to describe how God uniquely shapes us for the work he calls us to do. Each day God is forming us by the power of his Spirit to make our lives reflect more of his character. Because God is the Potter and we are the clay, we yield, or surrender, to his work in our lives.

You help those who thank you for teaching them how to live.
But when we continued to disobey you,
you became angry with us.
So how can we be saved?
6 All of us have become like someone who is "unclean."
All the good things we do are like dirty rags to you.
All of us are like leaves that have dried up.
Our sins sweep us away like the wind.
7 No one prays to you.
No one asks you for help.
You have turned your face away from us.
You have let us feel the effects of our sins.

8 LORD, you are our Father.
We are the clay. You are the potter.
Your hands made all of us.

[9] Don't be so angry with us, LORD.
Don't remember our sins anymore.
Please have mercy on us.
All of us belong to you.
[10] Your sacred cities have become a desert.
Even Zion is a desert.
Jerusalem is a dry and empty place.
[11] Our people of long ago used to praise you in our holy and glorious temple.
But now it has been burned down.
Everything we treasured has been destroyed.
[12] LORD, won't you help us even after everything that's happened?
Will you keep silent and punish us more than we can stand?

The LORD Judges and Saves

65 The LORD says, "I made myself known to those who were not asking for me.
I was found by those who were not trying to find me.
I spoke to a nation that did not pray to me.
'Here I am,' I said. 'Here I am.'
[2] All day long I have held out my hands
to welcome a stubborn nation.
They lead sinful lives.
They go where their evil thoughts take them.
[3] They are always making me very angry.
They do it right in front of me.
They offer sacrifices in the gardens of other gods.
They burn incense on altars that are made out of bricks.
[4] They sit among the graves.
They spend their nights talking to the spirits of the dead.
They eat the meat of pigs.
Their cooking pots hold soup that has 'unclean' meat in it.
[5] They say, 'Keep away! Don't come near us!
We are too sacred for you!'
Those people are like smoke in my nose.
They are like a fire that keeps burning all day.
[6] "I will judge them. I have even written it down.
I will not keep silent.
Instead, I will pay them back for all their sins.
[7] I will punish them for their sins.
I will also punish them for the sins of their people before them."
This is what the LORD says.
"They burned sacrifices on the mountains.
They disobeyed me by worshiping other gods on the hills.
So I will make sure they are fully punished
for all the sins they have committed."

[8] The LORD says,

"Sometimes juice is still left in grapes that have been crushed.
So people say, 'Don't destroy them.'
They are still of some benefit."
That is what I will do for the good of those who serve me.
I will not destroy all my people.
[9] I will give children
to the families of Jacob and Judah.
They will possess my entire land.
My chosen people will be given all of it.
Those who serve me will live there.
[10] Their flocks will eat in the rich grasslands of Sharon.
Their herds will rest in the Valley of Achor.
That is what I will do for my people who follow me.

[11] "But some of you have deserted me.
You no longer worship on my holy mountain of Zion.
You spread a table for the god called Good Fortune.
You offer bowls of mixed wine to the god named Fate.
[12] So I will make it your fate to be killed by swords.
All of you will die in the battle.
That's because I called out to you,
but you did not answer me.
I spoke to you, but you did not listen.
You did what is evil in my sight.
You chose to do what does not please me."

[13] So the LORD and King says,

"Those who serve me will have food
to eat.
But you will be hungry.
My servants will have plenty to drink.
But you will be thirsty.
Those who serve me will be full of
joy.
But you will be put to shame.
[14] My servants will sing
with joy in their hearts.
But you will cry out
because of the great pain in your
hearts.
You will cry because your spirits
are sad.
[15] My chosen ones will use your names
when they curse others.
I am your LORD and King.
I will put you to death.
But I will give new names to
those who serve me.
[16] They will ask me to bless their land.
They will do it in my name.
I am the one true God.
They will make promises in their
land.
They will do it in my name.
I am the one true God.
The troubles of the past will be
forgotten.
They will be hidden from my eyes.

The LORD Will Create New Heavens and a New Earth

[17] "I will create new heavens and a
new earth.
The things that have happened
before will not be remembered.
They will not even enter your
minds.
[18] So be glad and full of joy forever
because of what I will create.
I will cause others to take delight in
Jerusalem.
They will be filled with joy
when they see its people.
[19] And I will be full of joy because of
Jerusalem.
I will take delight in my people.
Weeping and crying
will not be heard there anymore.
[20] "Babies in Jerusalem will no longer
live only a few days.
Old people will not fail
to live for a very long time.
Those who live to the age of 100
will be thought of as mere
children when they die.
Those who die before they are 100
will be considered as having
been under God's curse.
[21] My people will build houses and
live in them.
They will plant vineyards and
eat their fruit.
[22] They will no longer build houses
only to have others live in them.
They will no longer plant crops
only to have others eat them.
My people will live to be as old as
trees.
My chosen ones will enjoy for a
long time
the things they have worked for.
[23] Their work will not be worthless
anymore.
They will not have children who
are sure to face sudden terror.
Instead, I will bless them.
I will also bless their children
after them.
[24] Even before they call out to me, I
will answer them.
While they are still speaking, I
will hear them.
[25] Wolves and lambs will eat together.
Lions will eat straw like oxen.
Serpents will eat nothing but dust.
None of those animals will harm or
destroy
anything or anyone on my holy
mountain of Zion,"
says the LORD.

The LORD Judges Some People and Blesses Others

66 The LORD says,

"Heaven is my throne.
The earth is under my control.
So how could you ever build a
house for me?
Where would my resting place be?
[2] Didn't I make everything by my
power?
That is how all things were created,"
announces the LORD.

"The people I value are not proud.
They are sorry for the wrong
things they have done.
They have great respect for what
I say.

[3]But others are not like that.
They sacrifice bulls to me,
but at the same time they kill people.
They offer lambs to me,
but they also sacrifice dogs to other gods.
They bring grain offerings to me,
but they also offer pig's blood to other gods.
They burn incense to me,
but they also worship statues of gods.
They have chosen to go their own way.
They take delight in things I hate.
[4]So I have also made a choice.
I will make them suffer greatly.
I will bring on them what they are afraid of.
When I called out to them, no one answered me.
When I spoke to them, no one listened.
They did what is evil in my sight.
They chose to do what displeases me."

[5]Listen to the word of the LORD.
Listen, you who tremble with fear when he speaks. He says,
"Some of your own people hate you.
They turn their backs on you because you are faithful to me.
They make fun of you and say,
'Let the LORD show his glory by saving you.
Then we can see how happy you are.'
But they will be put to shame.
[6]Hear the loud sounds coming from the city!
Listen to the noise coming from the temple!
I am the one causing it.
I am paying back my enemies for everything they have done.

[7]"Zion is like a woman who has a baby
before she goes into labor.
She has a son
even before her labor pains begin.
[8]Who has ever heard of anything like that?
Who has ever seen such a thing?
Can a country be born in a day?
Can a nation be created in a moment?
But as soon as Zion goes into labor,
there are many more of her people.
[9]Zion, would I bring you to the moment of birth
and not let it happen?"
says the LORD.
"Would I close up a mother's body
when it is time for her baby to be born?"
says your God.
[10]"Be glad along with Jerusalem, all you who love her.
Be filled with joy because of her.
Take great delight in her,
all you who mourn over her.
[11]You will nurse at her comforting breasts.
And you will be satisfied.
You will drink until you are full.
And you will delight in her rich and plentiful supply."

[12]The LORD continues,

"I will cause peace to flow over her like a river.
I will make the wealth of nations sweep over her like a flooding stream.
You will nurse and be carried in her arms.
You will play on her lap.
[13]As a mother comforts her child,
I will comfort you.
You will find comfort in Jerusalem."
[14]When you see that happen, your hearts will be filled with joy.
Just as grass grows quickly, you will succeed.
The LORD will show his power to those who serve him.
But he will pour out his anger on his enemies.
[15]The LORD will judge them with fire.
His chariots are coming like a windstorm.
He will pour out his burning anger on his enemies.
It will blaze out like flames of fire.
[16]The LORD will judge with fire and with his sword.
He will judge all people.
He will put many people to death.

17 "Some people set themselves apart
and make themselves pure. They do it
so they can go into the gardens to worship other gods. They follow what the
worship leader tells them to do. They
are among those who eat the meat
of pigs and rats. They also eat other
'unclean' things. Those people and the
one they follow will come to a horrible
end," announces the LORD.
18 "They have planned to do many
evil things. And they have carried out
their plans. So I will come and gather
the people of every nation and language. They will see my glory when
I act.
19 "I will give them a sign. I will send
to the nations some of those who are
left alive. I will send some of them to
the people of Tarshish, Libya and Lydia, who are famous for using bows. I
will send others to Tubal and Greece.
And I will send still others to islands
far away. The people who live there
have not heard about my fame. They
have not seen my glory. But when I act,
those I send will tell the nations about
my glory. 20 And they will bring back
all the people of Israel from all those
nations. They will bring them to my
holy mountain in Jerusalem. My people
will ride on horses, mules and camels.
They will come in chariots and wagons,"
says the LORD. "Those messengers will
bring my people as an offering to me.
They will bring them to my temple,
just as the Israelites bring their grain
offerings in bowls that are 'clean.' 21 And
I will choose some of them to be priests
and Levites," says the LORD.

22 "I will make new heavens and a
new earth. And they will last forever,"
announces the LORD. "In the same way,
your name and your children after you
will last forever. 23 Everyone will come
and bow down to me. They will do it
at every New Moon feast and on every
Sabbath day," says the LORD. 24 "When
they go out of Jerusalem, they will see
the dead bodies of those who refused
to obey me. The worms that eat their
bodies will not die. The fire that burns
them will not be put out. It will make
everyone sick just to look at them."

JEREMIAH

Author: Jeremiah

Jeremiah was another one of God's prophets. Just like Isaiah, Jeremiah received a special message from God, but this message was for the people of Judah. They were disobeying God and doing what pleased themselves instead of God. The message God gave Jeremiah for the people of Judah was this: Repent! To repent means to turn around—to stop running toward sin and run back to God. The people had been worshiping other gods and didn't seem to care about the one true God. They had gone their own way and wanted to make their own rules. If the people did not repent, they would be captured by the Babylonians. And that's exactly what happened.

Prophecy

I am the LORD your God . . .

Through Jeremiah, God told his people that he would give them a new covenant. God said, "I will put my law in their minds. I will write it on their hearts" (Jeremiah 31:33). God promised that the way back to him was always open to them. If they repented of their sin, God would forgive them and welcome them back into relationship with him.

Jeremiah's message pointed God's people toward the Savior. One day God promised to send the Savior to restore his people and be everyone's way back to God.

1 These are the words Jeremiah received from the LORD. Jeremiah was
the son of Hilkiah. Jeremiah was one of
the priests at Anathoth. That's a town
in the territory of Benjamin. 2 A message
from the LORD came to Jeremiah. It
came in the 13th year that Josiah was
king over Judah. Josiah was the son of
Amon. 3 After Josiah, his son Jehoiakim
was king over Judah. The LORD's message also came to Jeremiah during the
whole time Jehoiakim ruled. The LORD
continued to speak to Jeremiah while
Zedekiah was king over Judah. He did
this until the fifth month of the 11th
year of Zedekiah's rule. That's when the
people of Jerusalem were forced to leave
their country. Zedekiah was the son
of Josiah. Here is what Jeremiah said.

The LORD Appoints Jeremiah to Speak for Him

4 A message from the LORD came to
me. The LORD said,

5 "Before I formed you in your
mother's body I chose you.
Before you were born I set you
apart to serve me.
I appointed you to be a prophet
to the nations."

6 "You are my LORD and King," I said. "I
don't know how to speak. I'm too young."
7 But the LORD said to me, "Do not say,
'I'm too young.' You must go to everyone
I send you to. You must say everything I
command you to say. 8 Do not be afraid
of the people I send you to. I am with
you. I will save you," announces the LORD.
9 Then the LORD reached out his hand.
He touched my mouth and spoke to me.
He said, "I have put my words in your
mouth. 10 Today I am appointing you to
speak to nations and kingdoms. I give
you authority to pull them up by the
roots and tear them down. I give you
authority to destroy them and crush
them. I give you authority to build them
up and plant them."
11 A message from the LORD came to
me. The LORD asked me, "What do you
see, Jeremiah?"
"The branch of an almond tree," I
replied.
12 The LORD said to me, "You have seen
correctly. I am watching to see that my
word comes true."
13 Another message from the LORD
came to me. The LORD asked me, "What
do you see?"
"A pot that has boiling water in it," I
answered. "It's leaning toward us from
the north."
14 The LORD said to me, "Something
very bad will be poured out on everyone
who lives in this land. It will come from
the north. 15 I am about to send for all
the armies in the northern kingdoms,"
announces the LORD.

"Their kings will come to
Jerusalem.
They will set up their thrones at
the very gates of the city.
They will attack all the walls that
surround the city.
They will go to war against all
the towns of Judah.
16 I will judge my people.
They have done many evil things.
They have deserted me.
They have burned incense to other
gods.
They have worshiped the gods
their own hands have made.

17 "So get ready! Stand up! Tell them
everything I command you to. Do not
let them terrify you. If you do, I will
terrify you in front of them. 18 Today
I have made you like a city that has a
high wall around it. I have made you
like an iron pillar and a bronze wall.
Now you can stand up against the whole
land. You can stand against the kings
and officials of Judah. You can stand
against its priests and its people. 19 They
will fight against you. But they will not
win the battle over you. I am with you.
I will save you," announces the LORD.

Israel Deserts the LORD

2 A message from the LORD came to
me. The LORD said, 2 "Go. Announce
my message to the people in Jerusalem.
I want everyone to hear it. Tell them,

"Here is what the LORD says.
" 'I remember how faithful you
were to me when you were
young.
You loved me as if you were my
bride.
You followed me through the desert.
Nothing had been planted there.

[3] Your people were holy to me.
They were the first share of my harvest.
All those who destroyed them were held guilty.
And trouble came to their enemies,'"
announces the LORD.

[4] People of Jacob, hear the LORD's message.
Listen, all you tribes of Israel.

[5] The LORD says,

"What did your people of long ago find wrong with me?
Why did they wander so far away from me?
They worshiped worthless statues of gods.
Then they themselves became worthless.
[6] They did not ask, 'Where is the LORD?
He brought us up out of Egypt.
He led us through a dry and empty land.
He guided us through deserts and deep valleys.
It was a land of total darkness where there wasn't any rain.
No one lived or traveled there.'
[7] But I brought you into a land that has rich soil.
I gave you its fruit and its finest food.
In spite of that, you made my land impure.
You turned it into something I hate.
[8] The priests did not ask,
'Where is the LORD?'
Those who taught my law did not know me.
The leaders refused to obey me.
The prophets prophesied in the name of Baal.
They worshiped worthless statues of gods.
[9] "So I am bringing charges against you again,"
announces the LORD.
"And I will bring charges against your children's children.
[10] Go over to the coasts of Cyprus and look.
Send people to the land of Kedar and have them look closely.
See if there has ever been anything like this.
[11] Has a nation ever changed its gods?
Actually, they are not even gods at all.
But my people have traded away their glorious God.
They have traded me for worthless statues of gods.
[12] Sky above, be shocked over this.
Tremble with horror,"
announces the LORD.
[13] "My people have sinned twice.
They have deserted me,
even though I am the spring of water that gives life.
And they have dug their own wells.
But those wells are broken.
They can't hold any water.
[14] Are you people of Israel servants?
You were not born as slaves, were you?
Then why have you been carried off like stolen goods?
[15] Lions have roared.
They have growled at you.
They have destroyed your land.
Your towns are burned and deserted.
[16] The men of Memphis and Tahpanhes have cracked your skulls.
[17] Haven't you brought this on yourselves?
I am the LORD your God, but you deserted me.
You left me even while I was leading you.
[18] Why do you go to Egypt
to drink water from the Nile River?
Why do you go to Assyria
to drink from the Euphrates River?
[19] You will be punished because you have sinned.
You will be corrected for turning away from me.
I am the LORD your God.
If you desert me, bad things will happen to you.
If you do not respect me, you will suffer bitterly.
I want you to understand that,"
announces the LORD who rules over all.

[20] "Long ago you broke off the yoke I put on you.
You tore off the ropes I tied you up with.
You said, 'I won't serve you!'

In fact, on every high hill
you lay down like a prostitute.
You worshiped other gods under
every green tree.
21 You were like a good vine when I
planted you.
You were a healthy plant.
Then how did you turn against me?
How did you become a bad, wild
vine?
22 You might wash yourself with soap.
You might use plenty of strong
soap.
But I can still see the stains your
guilt covers you with,"
announces the LORD and King.
23 "You say, 'I am "clean."
I haven't followed the gods that
are named Baal.'
How can you say that?
Remember how you acted in the
valley.
Consider what you have done.
You are like a female camel
running quickly here and
there.
24 You are like a wild donkey that
lives in the desert.
She smells the wind when she
longs for a mate.
Who can hold her back?
The males that run after her do not
need to wear themselves out.
At mating time they will easily
find her.
25 Do not run after other gods
until your sandals are worn out
and your throat is dry.
But you said, 'It's no use!
I love those gods.
I must go after them.'
26 "A thief is dishonored when he is
caught.
And you people of Israel are
filled with shame.
Your kings and officials are
dishonored.
So are your priests and your
prophets.
27 You say to a piece of wood, 'You are
my father.'
You say to a stone, 'You are my
mother.'
You have turned your backs to me.
You refuse to look at me.
But when you are in trouble, you
say,
'Come and save us!'
28 Then where are the gods you made
for yourselves?
Let them come when you are in
trouble!
Let them save you if they can!
Judah, you have as many gods
as you have towns.
29 "Why do you bring charges
against me?
All of you have refused to obey me,"
announces the LORD.
30 "I punished your people. But it did
not do them any good.
They did not pay attention when
they were corrected.
You have killed your prophets by
swords.
You have swallowed them up like
a hungry lion.

31 "You who are now living, consider
my message. I am saying,

"Have I been like a desert to Israel?
Have I been like a land of deep
darkness?
Why do my people say, 'We are free
to wander.
We won't come to you anymore'?
32 Does a young woman forget all
about her jewelry?
Does a bride forget her wedding
jewels?
But my people have forgotten me
more days than anyone can
count.
33 You are very skilled at chasing
after love!
Even the worst of women can
learn from how you act.
34 The blood of those you have killed
is on your clothes.
You have destroyed poor people
who were not guilty.
You did not catch them in the act
of breaking in.
In spite of all this,
35 you say, 'I'm not guilty of doing
anything wrong.
The LORD isn't angry with me.'
But I will judge you.
That's because you say, 'I haven't
sinned.'
36 Why do you keep on
changing your ways so much?

Assyria did not help you.
And Egypt will not help you either.
37 So you will also leave Egypt
with your hands tied together
above your heads.
I have turned my back on those
you trust.
They will not help you.

3 "Suppose a man divorces his wife.
What if she then marries another
man?
Should her first husband return to
her again?
If he does, won't the land become
completely 'unclean'?
People of Israel, you have lived like
a prostitute.
You have loved many other gods.
So do you think you can return to
me now?"
announces the LORD.
2 "Look up at the bare hilltops.
Is there any place where you
have not worshiped other gods?
You have been unfaithful to
me like a wife committing
adultery.
By the side of the road you sat
waiting for lovers.
You sat there like someone who
wanders in the desert.
You have made the land impure.
You are like a sinful prostitute.
3 So I have held back the showers.
I have kept the spring rains from
falling.
But you still have the bold face of a
prostitute.
You refuse to blush with shame.
4 You have just now called out to me.
You said,
'My Father, you have been my friend
ever since I was young.
5 Will you always be angry with me?
Will your anger continue
forever?'
This is how you talk.
But you do all the evil things you
can."

Israel Is Not Faithful to the LORD

6 During the time Josiah was king,
the LORD spoke to me. He said, "Have
you seen what the people of Israel have
done? They have not been faithful to
me. They have committed adultery with
other gods. They worshiped them on
every high hill and under every green
tree. 7 I thought that after they had done
all this, they would return to me. But
they did not. Their sister nation Judah
saw them doing this. And they were
not faithful to me either. 8 I gave Israel
their letter of divorce. I sent them away
because they were unfaithful to me so
many times. But I saw that their sister
nation Judah did not have any respect
for me. They were not faithful to me
either. They also went out and committed adultery with other gods. 9 Israel
was not faithful to me, but that did not
bother them at all. They made the land
'unclean.' They worshiped gods that
were made out of stone and wood. 10 In
spite of all this, their sister nation Judah
did not come back to me. They were
not faithful to me either. They did not
return with all their heart. They only
pretended to," announces the LORD.
11 The LORD said to me, "Israel and
Judah have not been faithful to me. But
Israel was not as bad as Judah was. 12 Go.
Announce this message to the people
in the north. Tell them,

" 'Israel, you have not been
faithful,' announces the LORD.
'Return to me. Then I will do
good things for you again.
That's because I am faithful,'
announces the LORD.

in Jeremiah?

God is the Forgiving One. Even when God's people forgot about him and walked in disobedience, God reminded them that he would welcome them again if they turned toward him.

'I will not be angry with you
forever.
13 Admit that you are guilty of doing
what is wrong.
You have refused to obey me.
I am the LORD your God.
You have committed adultery with
other gods.
You worshiped them under every
green tree.
And you have not obeyed me,'"
announces the LORD.

14 "You people have not been faithful,"
announces the LORD. "Return to me. I
am your husband. I will choose one of
you from each town. I will choose two
from each territory. And I will bring
you to the city of Zion. 15 Then I will
give you shepherds who are dear to
my heart. Their knowledge and understanding will help them lead you. 16 In
those days there will be many more of
you in the land," announces the LORD.
"Then people will not talk about the ark
of the covenant of the LORD anymore.
It will never enter their minds. They
will not remember it. The ark will not
be missed. And another one will not
be made. 17 At that time they will call
Jerusalem The Throne of the LORD. All
the nations will gather together there.
They will go there to honor me. They
will no longer do what their stubborn
and evil hearts want them to do. 18 In
those days the people of Judah will join
the people of Israel. Together they will
come from a land in the north. They will
come to the land I gave to your people
of long ago. I wanted them to have it
as their very own.
19 "I myself said,

"'I would gladly treat you like my
children.
I would give you a pleasant land.
It is the most beautiful land any
nation could have.'
I thought you would call me
'Father.'
I hoped you would always obey me.
20 But you people are like a woman
who is not faithful to her
husband.
Israel, you have not been faithful
to me,"
announces the LORD.

21 A cry is heard on the bare hilltops.
The people of Israel are weeping
and begging for help.
That's because their lives are so
twisted.
They've forgotten the LORD their
God.

22 "You have not been faithful,"
says the LORD.
"Return to me. I will heal you.
Then you will not turn away
from me anymore."

"Yes," the people say. "We will come
to you.
You are the LORD our God.
23 The gods we worship on the hills
and mountains are useless.
You are the LORD our God.
You are the only one who can
save us.
24 From our earliest years shameful
gods have harmed us.
They have eaten up everything
our people of long ago worked
for.
They have eaten up our flocks and
herds.
They've destroyed our sons and
daughters.
25 Let us lie down in our shame.
Let our dishonor cover us.
You are the LORD our God. But we
have sinned against you.
We and our people of long ago
have sinned.
We haven't obeyed you
from our earliest years until
now."

4 "If you, Israel, will return,"
announces the LORD,
"then return to me.
Put the statues of your gods out of
my sight.
I hate them.
Stop going astray.
2 Make all your promises in my
name.
When you promise say, 'You can
be sure that the LORD is alive.'
Be truthful, fair and honest when
you make these promises.
Then the nations will ask for
blessings from me.
And they will boast about me."

[3]Here is what the LORD is telling the people of Judah and Jerusalem. He says,

"Your hearts are as hard as a field
that has not been plowed.
So change your ways and produce
good crops.
Do not plant seeds among
thorns.
[4]People of Judah and you who live
in Jerusalem, obey me.
Do not let your hearts be
stubborn.
If you do, my anger will blaze out
against you.
It will burn like fire because of
the evil things you have done.
No one will be able to put it out.

Trouble Will Come From the North

[5]"Announce my message in Judah.
Tell it in Jerusalem.
Say, 'Blow trumpets all through
the land!'
Give a loud shout and say,
'Gather together!
Let's run to cities that have high
walls around them!'
[6]Warn everyone to go to Zion!
Run for safety! Do not wait!
I am bringing trouble from the
north.
Everything will be totally
destroyed."
[7]Lions have come out of their dens.
Those who destroy nations have
begun to march out.
They have left their place
to destroy your land completely.
Your towns will be broken to pieces.
No one will live in them.
[8]So put on the clothes of sadness.
Mourn and weep over what has
happened.
The LORD hasn't turned
his great anger away from us.
[9]"A dark day is coming," announces
the LORD.
"The king and his officials will
lose hope.
The priests will be shocked.
And the prophets will be terrified."

[10]Then I said, "You are my LORD and
King. You have completely tricked the
people of Judah and Jerusalem! You
have told them, 'You will have peace
and rest.' But swords are pointed at
our throats!"
[11]At that time the people of Judah and
Jerusalem will be warned. They will be
told, "A hot and dry wind is coming, my
people. It is blowing toward you from
the bare hilltops in the desert. But it
does not separate straw from grain. [12]It
is much too strong for that. The wind
is coming from me. I am making my
decision against you."

[13]Look! Our enemies are approaching
like the clouds.
Their chariots are coming like a
strong wind.
Their horses are faster than eagles.
How terrible it will be for us!
We'll be destroyed!
[14]People of Jerusalem, wash your
sins from your hearts and be
saved.
How long will you hold on to
your evil thoughts?
[15]A voice is speaking all the way from
the city of Dan.
From the hills of Ephraim it
announces
that trouble is coming.
[16]"Tell the nations.
Make an announcement
concerning Jerusalem.
Say, 'An army will attack Judah.
It is coming from a land far
away.
It will shout a war cry
against the cities of Judah.
[17]It will surround them like people
who guard a field.
Judah has refused to obey me,'"
announces the LORD.
[18]"The army will attack you
because of your conduct and
actions.
This is how you will be punished.
It will be so bitter!
It will cut deep down into your
hearts!"

[19]I'm suffering! I'm really suffering!
I'm hurting badly.
My heart is suffering so much!
It's pounding inside me.
I can't keep silent.
I've heard the sound of trumpets.
I've heard the battle cry.
[20]One trouble follows another.

The whole land is destroyed.
In an instant my tents are gone.
My home disappears in a moment.
21 How long must I look at our enemy's battle flag?
How long must I hear the sound of the trumpets?

22 The LORD says, "My people are foolish.
They do not know me.
They are children who do not have any sense.
They have no understanding at all.
They are skilled in doing what is evil.
They do not know how to do what is good."

23 I looked at the earth.
It didn't have any shape. And it was empty.
I looked at the sky.
Its light was gone.
24 I looked at the mountains.
They were shaking.
All the hills were swaying.
25 I looked. And there weren't any people.
Every bird in the sky had flown away.
26 I looked. And the fruitful land had become a desert.
All its towns were destroyed.
The LORD had done all this because of his great anger.

27 The LORD says,

"The whole land will be destroyed.
But I will not destroy it completely.
28 So the earth will be filled with sadness.
The sky above will grow dark.
I have spoken, and I will not take pity on them.
I have made my decision, and I will not change my mind."

29 People can hear the sound of horsemen.
Men armed with bows are coming.
The people in every town run away.
Some of them go into the bushes.
Others climb up among the rocks.
All the towns are deserted.
No one is living in them.
30 What are you doing, you who are destroyed?
Why do you dress yourself in bright red clothes?
Why do you put on jewels of gold?
Why do you put makeup on your eyes?
You make yourself beautiful for no reason at all.
Your lovers hate you.
They want to kill you.

31 I hear a cry like the cry of a woman having a baby.
I hear a groan like someone having her first child.
It's the cry of the people of Zion struggling to breathe.
They reach out their hands and say,
"Help us! We're fainting!
Murderers are about to kill us!"

No One Is Honest

5 The LORD says, "Go up and down the streets of Jerusalem.
Look around.
Think about what you see.
Search through the market.
See if you can find one honest person who tries to be truthful.
If you can, I will forgive this city.
2 They make their promises in my name.
They say, 'You can be sure that the LORD is alive.'
But their promises can't be trusted."

3 LORD, don't your eyes look for truth?
You struck down your people.
But they didn't feel any pain.
You crushed them.
But they refused to be corrected.
They made their faces harder than stone.
They refused to turn away from their sins.
4 I thought, "The people of Jerusalem are foolish.
They don't know how the LORD wants them to live.
They don't know what their God requires of them.

5 So I will go to the leaders.
I'll speak to them.
They should know how the LORD
wants them to live.
They must know what their God
requires of them."
But all of them had broken off
the yoke the LORD had put on
them.
They had torn off the ropes he
had tied them up with.
6 So a lion from the forest will attack
them.
A wolf from the desert will
destroy them.
A leopard will hide and wait near
their towns.
It will tear to pieces anyone who
dares to go out.
Again and again they have refused
to obey the LORD.
They have turned away from
him many times.

7 The LORD says, "Jerusalem, why
should I forgive you?
Your people have deserted me.
They have made their promises in
the names of gods
that are not really gods at all.
I supplied everything they needed.
But they committed adultery.
Large crowds went to the houses
of prostitutes.
8 Your people are like stallions that
have plenty to eat.
Their sinful desires are out of control.
Each of them goes after another
man's wife.
9 Shouldn't I punish them for this?"
announces the LORD.
"Shouldn't I pay back the nation
that does these things?

10 "Armies of Babylon, go through their
vineyards and destroy them.
But do not destroy them
completely.

Strip off their branches.
These people do not belong to me.
11 The people of Israel and the people of Judah
have not been faithful to me at all,"
announces the LORD.
12 They have told lies about the LORD.
They said, "He won't do anything!
No harm will come to us.
We will never see war or be hungry.
13 The prophets are nothing but wind.
Their message doesn't come from the LORD.
So let what they say will happen be done to them."

14 The LORD God rules over all. He says to me,

"The people have spoken these words.
So my words will be like fire in your mouth.
I will make the people like wood.
And the fire will burn them up."

15 "People of Israel, listen to me,"
announces the LORD.
"I am bringing against you
a nation from far away.
It is an old nation. And it will last for a long time.
Its people speak a language you do not know.
You can't understand what they are saying.
16 The bags they carry their arrows in
are like an open grave.
All their soldiers are mighty.
17 They will eat up your crops and your food.
They will strike down your sons and daughters.
They will kill your sheep and cattle.
They will destroy your vines and fig trees.
You trust in your cities that have high walls around them.
But the people in them will be killed by swords.

pointing us to JESUS: Jeremiah

Jeremiah was a prophet of God. He spoke to the nation of Judah on behalf of God. His job was very important: He was to remind God's people to walk in God's ways and to keep God's commands. If the people did this, they would be blessed. But God's people refused.

Jeremiah watched those around him disobey God time and time again, and he watched them suffer the consequences of their disobedience. When Jeremiah saw this, he wept! In fact, Jeremiah cried so much that he became known as "the Weeping Prophet." He cried and cried and cried over the disobedience all around him because he cared so deeply for the people and wanted them to worship the one true God. It grieved Jeremiah to see how they rebelled against God, treated others unjustly, and worshiped idols. Jeremiah told the people of Judah that one day, God would send a Savior who would forgive their disobedience and make them right with God again (see Jeremiah 31:31–34).

Generations later, Jesus came as the Savior whom Jeremiah had prophesied would come. And like Jeremiah, Jesus wept over the people's sin. Seeing so many people turning away from God caused Jesus great sadness and grief. But Jesus willingly died on the cross to pay the penalty for sin. He rose again, overcoming sin and death so that all who come to him in faith and repentance are made right with God. This is called the new covenant.

18 "In spite of that, even in those days
I will not destroy you completely," announces the LORD. 19 " 'Jeremiah,' the
people will ask, 'Why has the LORD our
God done all this to us?' Then you will
tell them, 'You have deserted the LORD.
You have served other gods in your own
land. So now you will serve another
nation in a land that is not your own.'

20 "Here is what I want you to
announce
to the people of Jacob.
Tell it in Judah.
Tell them I say,
21 'Listen to this, you foolish people,
who do not have any sense.
You have eyes, but you do not see.
You have ears, but you do not
hear.
22 Shouldn't you have respect for me?'
announces the LORD.
'Shouldn't you tremble with fear
in front of me?
I made the sand to hold the ocean
back.
It will do that forever.
The ocean can't go past it.
The waves might roll, but they can't
sweep over it.
They might roar, but they can't
go across it.
23 But you people have stubborn hearts.
You refuse to obey me.
You have turned away from me.
You have gone astray.
24 You do not say to yourselves,
"Let us have respect for the LORD
our God.
He sends rain in the fall and the
spring.
He promises us that the harvest
will come
at the same time each year."
25 But the things you have done wrong
have robbed you of these gifts.
Your sins have kept these good things
far away from you.'

26 "Jeremiah, some of my people are
evil.
They hide and wait just as people
hide to catch birds.
They set traps for people.
27 A hunter uses tricks to fill his cage
with birds.
And my people have filled their
houses with a lot of goods.
They have become rich and
powerful.
28 They have grown fat and heavy.
There is no limit to the evil things
they do.
In court they do not seek justice.
They don't protect the rights of
children whose fathers have
died.
They do not stand up for poor
people.
29 Shouldn't I punish them for this?"
announces the LORD.
"Shouldn't I pay back the
nation that does these things?

30 "Something horrible and shocking
has happened in the land.
31 The prophets prophesy lies.
The priests rule by their own
authority.
And my people love it this way.
But what will you do in the end?"

The Babylonians Will Attack Jerusalem

6 The LORD says, "People of
Benjamin, run for safety!
Run away from Jerusalem!
Blow trumpets in the city of Tekoa!
Warn everyone in Beth Hakkerem!
Horrible trouble is coming from the
north.
The Babylonians will destroy
everything with awful power.
2 I will destroy the city of Zion,
even though it is very beautiful.
3 Shepherds will come against it with
their flocks.
They will set up their tents
around it.
All of them will take care of their
own sheep."

4 The Babylonians say, "Prepare for
battle against Judah!
Get up! Let's attack them at noon!
But the daylight is fading.
The shadows of evening are
getting longer.
5 So get up! Let's attack them at night!
Let's destroy their strongest forts!"

6 The LORD who rules over all speaks
to the Babylonians. He says,

"Cut down some trees.
Use the wood to build ramps
against Jerusalem's walls.

I must punish that city.
It is filled with people who treat others badly.
7 Wells keep giving fresh water.
And Jerusalem keeps on sinning.
Its people are always fighting and causing trouble.
When I look at them,
I see nothing but sickness and wounds.
8 Jerusalem, listen to my warning.
If you do not, I will turn away from you.
Your land will become a desert.
No one will be able to live there."

9 The LORD rules over all. He says to me,

"People gather the few grapes left on a vine.
So let Israel's enemies gather the few people left alive in the land
Look carefully at the branches again.
Do this like someone who gathers the last few grapes."

10 Who can I speak to? Who can I warn?
Who will even listen to me?
Their ears are closed
so they can't hear.
The LORD's message displeases them.
They don't take any delight in it.
11 But the LORD's anger burns inside me.
I can no longer hold it in.

The LORD says to me, "Pour out my anger on the children in the street.
Pour it out on the young men who are gathered together.
Husband and wife alike will be caught in it.
So will those who are very old.
12 I will reach out my hand against those who live in the land,"
announces the LORD.
"Then their houses will be turned over to others.
So will their fields and their wives.
13 Everyone wants to get richer and richer,
from the least important of them to the most important.
Prophets and priests alike
try to fool everyone they can.
14 They bandage the wounds of my people
as if they were not very deep.
'Peace, peace,' they say.
But there isn't any peace.
15 Are they ashamed of their hateful actions?
No. They do not feel any shame at all.
They do not even know how to blush.
So they will fall like others who have already fallen.
They will be brought down when I punish them,"
says the LORD.

16 The LORD tells the people of Judah,

"Stand where the roads cross, and look around.
Ask where the old paths are.
Ask for the good path, and walk on it.
Then your hearts will find rest in me.
But you said, 'We won't walk on it.'
17 I appointed prophets to warn you. I said,
'Listen to the sound of the trumpets!'
But you said, 'We won't listen.'
18 So pay attention, you nations.
You are witnesses for me.
Watch what will happen to my people.
19 Earth, pay attention.
I am going to bring trouble on them.
I will punish them because of the evil things they have done.
They have not listened to my words.
They have said no to my law.
20 What do I care about incense from the land of Sheba?
Why should I bother with sweet-smelling cane from a land far away?
I do not accept your burnt offerings.
Your sacrifices do not please me."

21 So the LORD says,

"I will bring an army against the people of Judah.
Parents and children alike will trip and fall.
Neighbors and friends will die."

[22]The LORD says to Jerusalem,

"Look! An army is coming
from the land of the north.
I am stirring up a great nation.
Its army is coming from a land
that is very far away.
[23]Its soldiers are armed with bows
and spears.
They are mean. They do not
show any mercy at all.
They come riding in on their
horses.
They sound like the roaring
ocean.
They are lined up for battle.
They are marching out
to attack you, city of Zion."

[24]We have heard reports about them.
And our hands can't help us.
We are suffering greatly.
It's like the pain of a woman
having a baby.
[25]Don't go out to the fields.
Don't walk on the roads.
Our enemies have swords.
And there is terror on every side.
[26]My people, put on the clothes of
sadness.
Roll among the ashes.
Mourn with bitter weeping
just as you would mourn for an
only son.
The one who is going to destroy us
will come suddenly.

[27]The LORD says to me, "I have made
you like one who tests metals.
My people are the ore.
I want you to watch them
and test the way they live.
[28]All of them are used to
disobeying me.
They go around telling lies about
others.
They are like bronze mixed with
iron.
All of them do very sinful things.
[29]The fire is made very hot
so the lead will burn away.
But it is impossible to make these
people pure.
Those who are evil are not
removed.
[30]They are like silver that is thrown
away.
That is because I have not
accepted them."

Worshiping Other Gods Is Worthless

7 A message from the LORD came to
Jeremiah. The LORD said, [2]"Stand
at the gate of my house. Announce my
message to the people there. Say,

"'Listen to the LORD's message, all
you people of Judah. You always come
through these gates to worship the LORD.
[3]The God of Israel is speaking to you.
He is the LORD who rules over all. He
says, "Change the way you live and act.
Then I will let you live in this place. [4]Do
not trust in lies. Do not say, 'This is the
temple of the LORD! This is the temple of
the LORD! This is the temple of the LORD!'
[5]You must really change the way you
live and act. Treat one another fairly.
[6]Do not treat outsiders or widows badly
in this place. Do not take advantage
of children whose fathers have died.
Do not kill those who are not guilty of
doing anything wrong. Do not worship
other gods. That will only bring harm to
you. [7]If you obey me, I will let you live
in this place. It is the land I gave your
people of long ago. It was promised to
them for ever and ever. [8]But look! You
are trusting in worthless lies.

[9]"'"You continue to steal and commit
murder. You commit adultery. You tell
lies in court. You burn incense to Baal.
You worship other gods you didn't know
before. [10]Then you come and stand in
front of me. You keep coming to this
house where I have put my Name. You
say, 'We are safe.' You think you are safe
when you do so many things I hate. [11]My
Name is in this house. But you have
made it a den for robbers! I have been
watching you!" announces the LORD.

[12]"'"Go now to the town of Shiloh.
Go to the place where I first made a
home for my Name. See what I did to
it because of the evil things my people
Israel were doing. [13]I spoke to you again
and again," announces the LORD. "I
warned you while you were doing all
these things. But you did not listen. I
called out to you. But you did not answer. [14]So what I did to Shiloh I will
now do to the house where my Name
is. It is the temple you trust in. It is the
place I gave to you and your people of
long ago. [15]But I will throw you out of
my land. That is exactly what I did to
the people of Ephraim. And they are
your relatives."'

16 "Jeremiah, do not pray for these
people. Do not make any appeal or request for them. Do not beg me. I will not
listen to you. 17 Don't you see what they
are doing? They are worshiping other
gods in the towns of Judah. They are
offering sacrifices to them in the streets
of Jerusalem. 18 The children go out and
gather wood. The fathers light the fire.
The women mix the dough. They make
flat cakes of bread to offer to the female
god called the Queen of Heaven. They
pour out drink offerings to other gods.
That makes me very angry. 19 But am I
the one they are hurting?" announces the
LORD. "Aren't they only harming themselves? They should be ashamed of it."
20 So the LORD and King says, "I will
pour out my burning anger on this
place. It will strike people and animals
alike. It will destroy the trees in the
fields and the crops in your land. It will
burn, and no one will be able to put
it out."
21 The LORD who rules over all is the
God of Israel. He says, "Go ahead! Add
your burnt offerings to your other sacrifices. Eat the meat yourselves! 22 When
I brought your people out of Egypt, I
spoke to them. But I did not just give
them commands about burnt offerings
and sacrifices. 23 I also gave them another command. I said, 'Obey me. Then
I will be your God. And you will be my
people. Live the way I command you to
live. Then things will go well with you.'
24 But they did not listen. They refused to
pay any attention to me. Instead, they
did what their stubborn and evil hearts
wanted them to do. They went backward
and not forward. 25 Again and again I
sent my servants the prophets to you.
They came to you day after day. They
prophesied from the time your people
left Egypt until now. 26 But your people
of long ago did not listen. They refused
to pay any attention to me. They were
stubborn. They did more evil things
than their people who lived before them.
27 "Jeremiah, when you tell them all
this, they will not listen to you. When
you call out to them, they will not answer. 28 So say to them, 'You are a nation
that has not obeyed the LORD your God.
You did not pay attention when you
were corrected. Truth has died out. You
do not tell the truth anymore.' "
29 The LORD says to the people of Jerusalem, "Cut off your hair. Throw it
away. Sing a song of sadness on the
bare hilltops. I am very angry with you.
I have turned my back on you. I have
deserted you.

The Valley of Death

30 "The people of Judah have done
what is evil in my eyes," announces the
LORD. "They have set up statues of their
gods. They have worshiped them in the
house where my Name is. They have
made my house 'unclean.' I hate those
statues. 31 The people have built the high
places of Topheth in the Valley of Ben
Hinnom. There they worship other gods.
And there they sacrifice their children in
the fire. That is something I did not command. It did not even enter my mind.
32 So watch out!" announces the LORD.
"The days are coming when people will
not call it Topheth anymore. And they
will not call it the Valley of Ben Hinnom
either. Instead, they will call it the Valley
of Death. They will bury the dead bodies
of some people in Topheth. But they will
run out of room. 33 Then they will not be
able to bury the bodies of other people
there. So the bodies will become food
for birds and wild animals. And no one
will scare them away. 34 I will put an end
to the sounds of joy and gladness. The
voices of brides and grooms will not be
heard anymore. There will be no sounds
of joy in the towns of Judah. And there
will be no joy in the streets of Jerusalem.
The land will become a desert.

8 "At that time the tombs will be
opened," announces the LORD. "The
bones of the kings and officials of Judah
will be brought out. The bones of the
priests and prophets will be removed. So
will the bones of the people of Jerusalem. 2 They will lie outside under the sun,
moon and all the stars. All these people
had loved and served these things. They
had followed them and worshiped them.
They had asked them for advice. So the
bones of these people will not be gathered up or buried again. Instead, they
will be like human waste lying there on
the ground. 3 Everyone left alive in this
evil nation will want to die rather than
live. That is what they will long for in
the lands where I force them to go." The
LORD who rules over all announces this.

The LORD Punishes His Sinful People

4 "Jeremiah, tell them, 'The LORD says,

" ' "When people fall down, don't
they get up again?
When someone turns away, don't
they come back?
5 Then why have the people of
Jerusalem turned away
from me?
Why do they always turn away?
They keep on telling lies.
They refuse to come back to me.
6 I have listened carefully.
But they do not say what is right.
They refuse to turn away from
their sins.
None of them says, 'What have I
done?'
Each of them goes their own way.
They are like horses charging
into battle.
7 Storks know when to fly south.
So do doves, swifts and thrushes.
But my people do not know
what I require them to do.
8 " ' "How can you people say, 'We are
wise.
We have the law of the LORD'?
Actually, the teachers of the law
have told lies about it.
Their pens have not written what
is true.
9 Those who think they are wise will
be put to shame.
They will become terrified. They
will be trapped.
They have not accepted my
message.
So what kind of wisdom do they
have?
10 I will give their wives to other men.
I will give their fields to new
owners.
Everyone wants to get richer and
richer.
Everyone is greedy, from the
least important to the most
important.
Prophets and priests alike
try to fool everyone they can.
11 They bandage the wounds of my
people
as if they were not very deep.
'Peace, peace,' they say.
But there isn't any peace.
12 Are they ashamed of their hateful
actions?
No. They do not feel any shame
at all.
They do not even know how to
blush.
So they will fall like others who
have already fallen.
They will be brought down when
I punish them,"
says the LORD.

13 " ' "I will take away their harvest,"
announces the LORD.
"There will not be any grapes on
the vines.
The trees will not bear any figs.
The leaves on the trees will
dry up.
What I have given my people
will be taken away from them." ' "

14 Why are we sitting here?
Let's gather together!
Let's run to the cities that have high
walls around them!
Let's die there!
The LORD our God has sentenced us
to death.
He has given us poisoned water
to drink.
That's because we've sinned
against him.
15 We hoped peace would come.
But nothing good has happened
to us.
We hoped we would finally be
healed.
But there is only terror.
16 When our enemy's horses snort,
the noise is heard all the way
from the city of Dan.
When their stallions neigh,
the whole land trembles with fear.
They have come to destroy
the land and everything in it.
The city and everyone who lives
there will be destroyed.

17 "People of Judah, I will send
poisonous snakes among you.
No one will be able to charm them.
And they will bite you,"
announces the LORD.

18 LORD, my heart is weak inside me.
You comfort me when I'm sad.
19 Listen to the cries of my people
from a land far away.

They cry out, "Isn't the LORD in Zion?
Isn't its King there anymore?"
The LORD says, "Why have they made me so angry
by worshiping their wooden gods?
Why have they made me angry with their worthless statues
of gods from other lands?"
20 The people say, "The harvest is over.
The summer has ended.
And we still haven't been saved."
21 My people are crushed, so I am crushed.
I mourn, and I am filled with horror.
22 Isn't there any healing lotion in Gilead?
Isn't there a doctor there?
Then why doesn't someone heal
the wounds of my people?

9

1 I wish my head were a spring of water!
I wish my eyes were a fountain of tears!
I would weep day and night
for my people who have been killed.
2 I wish I had somewhere to go in the desert
where a traveler could stay!
Then I could leave my people.
I could get away from them.
All of them commit adultery by worshiping other gods.
They aren't faithful to the LORD.
3 "They get ready to use
their tongues like bows,"
announces the LORD.
"Their mouths shoot out lies like arrows.
They tell lies to gain power in the land.
They go from one sin to another.
They do not pay any attention to me.
4 Be on guard against your friends.
Do not trust the members of your own family.
Every one of them cheats.
Every friend tells lies.
5 One friend cheats another.
No one tells the truth.
They have taught their tongues how to lie.
They wear themselves out sinning.
6 Jeremiah, you live among people who tell lies.
When they lie, they refuse to pay any attention to me,"
announces the LORD.

7 So the LORD who rules over all says,
"I will put them through the fire to test them.
What else can I do?
My people are so sinful!
8 Their tongues are like deadly arrows.
They tell lies.
With their mouths all of them
speak kindly to their neighbors.
But in their hearts they set traps for them.
9 Shouldn't I punish them for this?"
announces the LORD.
"Shouldn't I pay back the nation
that does these things?"
10 I will cry and mourn over the mountains.
I will sing a song of sadness
about the desert grasslands.
They are dry and empty. No one travels through them.
The mooing of cattle isn't heard there.
The birds have flown away.
All the animals are gone.
11 The LORD says, "I will knock down
all of Jerusalem's buildings.
I will make it a home for wild dogs.
The towns of Judah will be
completely destroyed.
No one will be able to live in them."

12 Who is wise enough to understand
these things? Who has been taught by
the LORD? Who can explain them? Why
has the land been destroyed so completely? Why has it become like a desert
that no one can go across?
13 The LORD answered me, "Because
my people have turned away from my
law. I gave it to them. But they have
not kept it. They have not obeyed me.
14 Instead, they have done what their
stubborn hearts wanted them to do.

They have worshiped the gods that are
named Baal. They have done what their
people have taught them to do through
the years." 15 So now the LORD who rules
over all speaks. He is the God of Israel. He says, "I will make these people
eat bitter food. I will make them drink
poisoned water. 16 I will scatter them
among the nations. They and their
people before them didn't know about
these nations. With swords I will chase
these people. I will hunt them down
until I have destroyed them."

17 The LORD rules over all. He says,

"Here is something I want you to
think about.
Send for the women who mourn
for the dead.
Send for the most skilled among
them."

18 Let them come quickly
and weep for us.
Let them cry until tears flow from
our eyes.
Let them weep until water pours
out of our eyes.
19 People are heard weeping in Zion.
They are saying, "We are
destroyed!
We are filled with shame!
We must leave our land.
Our houses have been torn
down."
20 You women, hear the LORD's
message.
Listen to what he's saying.
Teach your daughters how to
mourn for the dead.
Teach one another a song of
sadness.
21 Death has climbed in through our
windows.
It has entered our forts.
Death has removed the children
from the streets.
It has taken the young men out
of the market.

22 Say, "The LORD announces,

" 'Dead bodies will be like human
waste
lying in the open fields.
They will lie there like grain
that is cut down at harvest time.
No one will gather them up.' "

23 The LORD says,

"Do not let wise people brag about
how wise they are.
Do not let strong people boast
about how strong they are.
Do not let rich people brag about
how rich they are.
24 But here is what the one who brags
should boast about.
They should brag that they have
the understanding to know me.
I want them to know that I am the
LORD.
No matter what I do on earth, I
am always kind, fair and right.
And I take delight in this,"
announces the LORD.

25 "The days are coming when I will
judge people," announces the LORD.
"I will punish all those who are circumcised only in their bodies. 26 That
includes the people of Egypt, Judah,
Edom, Ammon and Moab. It also includes all those who live in the desert
in places far away. None of the people
in these nations is really circumcised.
And not even the people of Israel are
circumcised in their hearts."

The LORD Is the Only True God

10 People of Israel, listen to what
the LORD is telling you. 2 He says,

"Do not follow the practices of other
nations.
Do not be terrified by warnings
in the sky.
Do not be afraid, even though the
nations are terrified by them.
3 The practices of these nations are
worthless.
People cut a tree out of the forest.
A skilled worker shapes the wood
with a sharp tool.
4 Others decorate it with silver and
gold.
They use a hammer to nail it to
the floor.
They want to keep it from falling
down.
5 The statues of their gods can't
speak.
They are like scarecrows in a
field of cucumbers.
Their statues have to be carried
around
because they can't walk.

So do not be afraid of their gods.
They can't do you any harm.
And they can't do you any good either."

6 LORD, no one is like you.
You are great.
You are mighty and powerful.
7 King of the nations,
everyone should have respect for you.
That's what people should give you.
Among all the wise leaders of the nations
there is no one like you.
No one can compare with you in all their kingdoms.
8 All of them are foolish. They don't have any sense.
They think they are taught by worthless wooden gods.
9 Hammered silver is brought from Tarshish.
Gold is brought from Uphaz.
People skilled in working with wood and gold make a statue.
Then they put blue and purple clothes on it.
The whole thing is made by skilled workers.
10 But you are the only true God.
You are the only living God.
You are the King who rules forever.
When you are angry, the earth trembles with fear.
The nations can't stand up under your anger.

11 The LORD speaks to the Jews living
in Babylon. He says, "Here is what you
must tell the people of the nations. Tell
them, 'Your gods did not make the heavens and the earth. In fact, these gods
will disappear from the earth. They
will vanish from under the heavens.' "

12 But God used his power to make the earth.
His wisdom set the world in place.
His understanding spread out the heavens.
13 When he thunders, the waters in the heavens roar.
He makes clouds rise from one end of the earth to the other.
He sends lightning along with the rain.
He brings the wind out from his storerooms.

14 No one has any sense or knows anything at all.
Everyone who works with gold is put to shame by his gods.
The metal gods he has made are fakes.
They can't even breathe.
15 They are worthless things that people make fun of.
When the LORD judges them, they will be destroyed.
16 The God of Jacob is not like them.
He gives his people everything they need.
He made everything that exists.
And that includes Israel.
They are the people who belong to him.
His name is the LORD Who Rules Over All.

The Land Will Be Destroyed

17 People of Jerusalem, your enemies have surrounded you.
They are attacking you.
So gather up what belongs to you.
Then leave the land.
18 The LORD says,
"I am about to throw out of this land
everyone who lives in it.
I will bring trouble on them.
They will be captured."
19 How terrible it will be for me!
I've been wounded!
And my wound can't be healed!
In spite of that, I said to myself,
"I'm sick. But I'll have to put up with it."
20 Jerusalem is like a tent that has been destroyed.
All its ropes have snapped.
My people have gone away from me.
Now no one is left to set up my tent.
I have no one to set up my shelter.
21 The leaders of my people are like shepherds
who don't have any sense.
They don't ask the LORD for advice.

That's why they don't succeed.
And that's why their whole flock
is scattered like sheep.
22 Listen! A message is coming!
I hear the sound of a great army
marching down from the north!
It will turn Judah's towns into a
desert.
They will become a home for wild
dogs.

Jeremiah Prays to the Lord

23 Lord, I know that a person doesn't
control their own life.
They don't direct their own steps.
24 Correct me, Lord, but please be fair.
Don't correct me when you are
angry.
If you do, nothing will be left of me.
25 Pour out your great anger on the
nations.
They don't pay any attention to
you.
They refuse to worship you.
They have destroyed the people of
Jacob.
They've wiped them out
completely.
They've also destroyed the land
they lived in.

The Lord's People Have Broken His Covenant

11 A message from the Lord came to
Jeremiah. The Lord said, 2 "Listen
to the terms of the covenant I made
with my people of long ago. Tell Judah
the terms still apply to them. Tell those
who live in Jerusalem that they must
obey them too. 3 I am the Lord, the God
of Israel. So let the people know what
I want them to do. Here is what I want
you to tell them. 'May the person who
does not obey the terms of the covenant
be under my curse. 4 I gave those terms
to your people of long ago. That was
when I brought them out of Egypt. I
saved them out of that furnace that
melts down iron and makes it pure.' I
said, 'Obey me. Do everything I command you to do. Then you will be my
people. And I will be your God. 5 I raised
my hand and made a promise to your
people of long ago. I promised them I
would give them a land that had plenty
of milk and honey.' It is the land you
own today. I kept my promise."
I replied, "Amen, Lord."
6 The Lord said to me, "Here is what
I want you to announce in the towns
of Judah. Say it also in the streets of
Jerusalem. Tell the people, 'Listen to
the terms of my covenant. Obey them.
7 Long ago I brought your people up
from Egypt. From that time until today,
I warned them again and again. I said,
"Obey me." 8 But they did not listen.
They did not pay any attention to me.
Instead, they did what their stubborn
and evil hearts wanted them to do. So
I brought down on them all the curses
of the covenant. I commanded them to
obey it. But they refused.' "
9 The Lord continued, "The people of
Judah have made some evil plans. So
have those who live in Jerusalem. 10 All
of them have returned to the sins their
people of long ago committed. Those
people refused to listen to what I told
them. And now the people of Israel and
Judah alike have worshiped other gods
and served them. They have broken the
covenant I made with their people who
lived before them. 11 So I say, 'I will bring
trouble on them. They will not be able
to escape it. They will cry out to me. But
I will not listen to them. 12 The people of
Jerusalem and of the towns of Judah
will cry out. They will cry out to the gods
they burn incense to. But those gods will
not help them at all when trouble strikes
them. 13 Judah, you have as many gods
as you have towns. And in Jerusalem
you have set up as many altars as there
are streets. You are burning incense to
that shameful god named Baal.'
14 "Jeremiah, do not pray for these
people. Do not make any appeal or
request for them. They will call out to
me when they are in trouble. But I will
not listen to them.

15 "I love the people of Judah.
But they are working out their evil
plans along with many others.
So what are they doing in my
temple?
Can meat that is offered to me keep
me from punishing you?
When you do evil things, you get
a lot of pleasure from them."

16 People of Judah, the Lord once
called you a healthy olive tree.
He thought its fruit was
beautiful.

But now he will come with the roar
of a mighty storm.
He will set the tree on fire.
And its branches will be broken.

17 The LORD who rules over all planted you. But now he has ordered your enemies to destroy you. The people of Israel and Judah have both done what is evil. They have made the LORD very angry by burning incense to Baal.

Jeremiah's Enemies Make Evil Plans Against Him

18 The LORD told me about the evil plans of my enemies. That's how I knew about them. He showed me what they were
doing. 19 I had been like a gentle lamb led off to be killed. I didn't realize they had made plans against me. They had said,

"Let's destroy the tree and its fruit.
Let's take away his life.
Then his name won't be
remembered anymore."
20 But LORD, you rule over all.
You always judge fairly.
You test people's hearts and minds.
So pay them back for what they've
done.
I've committed my cause to you.

21 The LORD says, "Jeremiah, here is what I am telling you about the people of Anathoth. They say they're going to kill you. They are saying, 'Don't prophesy in the LORD's name. If you do, we
will kill you with our own hands.'" 22 So
the LORD who rules over all says, "I will punish them. Their young men will be killed by swords. Their sons and daughters will die of hunger.
23 Only a few
people will be left alive. I will judge the people of Anathoth. I will destroy them when the time comes to punish them."

Jeremiah Complains to the LORD

12 LORD, when I bring a matter to
you,
you always do what is right.
But now I would like to speak with
you
about whether you are being fair.
Why are sinful people successful?
Why do those who can't be
trusted have an easy life?
2 You have planted them.
Their roots are deep in the ground.
They grow and produce fruit.
They honor you by what they say.
But their hearts are far away
from you.
3 LORD, you know me and see me.
You test my thoughts about you.
Drag those people off like sheep to
be killed!
Set them apart for the day of
their death!
4 How long will the land be thirsty
for water?
How long will the grass in every
field be dry?
The people who live in the land are
evil.
So the animals and birds have died.
And that's not all. The people are
saying,
"The LORD won't see what
happens to us."

The LORD Answers Jeremiah

5 The LORD says, "Suppose you have
raced against people.
And suppose they have worn you
out.
Then how would you be able to
race against horses?
Suppose you feel safe only in open
country.
Then how would you get along
in the bushes near the Jordan
River?
6 Even your relatives have turned
against you.
They are members of your own
family.
They have shouted loudly at you.
They might say nice things about
you.
But do not trust them.

7 "I will turn my back on my people.
I will desert my land.
I love the people of Judah.
In spite of that, I will hand them
over to their enemies.
8 My land has become to me
like a lion in the forest.
It roars at me.
So I hate it.
9 My own land has become like a
spotted hawk.
And other hawks surround it and
attack it.
Come, all you wild animals!
Gather together!
Come together to eat up my land.

10 Many shepherds will destroy my
vineyard.
They will walk all over it.
They will turn my pleasant
vineyard
into a dry and empty land.
11 My vineyard will become a desert.
It will be dry and empty in my
sight.
The whole land will be completely
destroyed.
And no one even cares.
12 Many will come to destroy it.
They will gather on the bare
hilltops in the desert.
I will use them as my sword to
destroy my people.
They will kill them from one end
of the land to the other.
No one will be safe.
13 People will plant wheat. But all
they will gather is thorns.
They will wear themselves
out. But they will not have
anything to show for it.
I am very angry with them.
So they will be ashamed of the
crop they gather."

14 Here is what the LORD says. "All my
evil neighbors have taken over the land
I gave my people Israel. So I will pull
them up by their roots from the lands
they live in. And I will pull up the roots of
the people of Judah from among them.
15 But after I pull up those nations, I will
give my tender love to them again. I will
bring all of them back to their own lands.
I will take all of them back to their own
countries. 16 Suppose those nations learn
to follow the practices of my people. And
they make their promises in my name.
When they promise, they say, 'You can
be sure that the LORD is alive.' They do
this just as they once taught my people
to make promises in Baal's name. Then I
will give them a place among my people.
17 But what if one of those nations does
not listen? Then you can be sure of this.
I will pull it up by the roots and destroy
it," announces the LORD.

A Linen Belt

13 The LORD said to me, "Go and buy
a linen belt. Put it around your
waist. But do not let it get wet." 2 So I
bought a belt, just as the LORD had told
me to do. And I put it around my waist.

3 Then another message from the
LORD came to me. The LORD said, 4 "Take
off the belt you bought and are wearing
around your waist. Go to Perath. Hide
the belt there in a crack in the rocks."
5 So I went and hid it at Perath. I did just
as the LORD had told me to do.

6 Many days later the LORD said to
me, "Go to Perath. Get the belt I told
you to hide there." 7 So I went to Perath.
I dug up the belt. I took it from the place
where I had hidden it. But it had rotted.
It was completely useless.

8 Then another message from the LORD
came to me. The LORD said, 9 "In the same
way, I will destroy Judah's pride. And I
will destroy the great pride of Jerusalem.
10 These people are evil. They refuse to
listen to what I say. They do what their
stubborn hearts want them to do. They
chase after other gods. They serve them
and worship them. So they will be like
this belt. They will be completely useless.
11 A belt is tied around a person's waist.
In the same way, I tied all the people of
Israel to me. I also tied all the people of
Judah to me like a belt. I wanted them to
be my people. They should have brought
me fame and praise and honor. But they
have not listened to me," announces
the LORD.

Wineskins

12 "Tell them, 'The LORD is the God of
Israel. He says, "Every wineskin should
be filled with wine." ' Here is what the
people might say to you. 'Don't we know
that every wineskin should be filled with
wine?' 13 If they do, here is what you must
tell them. 'The LORD says, "I am going
to fill with wine everyone who lives in
this land. I will make the kings who sit
on David's throne drunk. And I will fill
with wine the priests, the prophets and
everyone who lives in Jerusalem. 14 I
will smash them against one another. I
will punish parents and children alike,"
announces the LORD. "I will not feel sorry for them. I will not show them any
kindness. My tender love for them will
not keep me from destroying them." ' "

Judah Will Be Taken Away From Their Land

15 People of Judah, listen to me.
Pay attention and don't be
proud.
The LORD has spoken.

16 Give glory to the LORD your God.
Honor him before he sends
darkness to cover the land.
Do this before you trip and fall
on the darkened hills.
You hope that light will come.
But he will turn it into thick
darkness.
He will change it to deep
shadows.
17 If you don't listen,
I will weep in secret.
Because you are so proud,
I will weep bitterly.
Tears will flow from my eyes.
The LORD's flock will be taken
away as prisoners.

18 Speak to the king and his mother.
Tell them,
"Come down from your thrones.
Your glorious crowns
are about to fall from your heads."
19 The gates of the cities in the Negev
Desert will be shut tight.
There won't be anyone to open
them.
Everyone in Judah will be carried
away as prisoners.
You will be completely taken
away.

20 Jerusalem, look up!
Your enemies are coming from
the north.
Where is the flock you were
supposed to take care of?
Where are the sheep you were so
proud of?
21 You have worked hard to make
special friends.
But the LORD will let them rule
over you.
Then what will you say?
Suffering will take hold of you.
It will be like the pain of a
woman having a baby.
22 Suppose you ask yourself,
"Why has this happened to me?"
It's because you have committed so
many sins.
That's the reason your skirt has
been torn off.
That's why your body has been
treated so badly.
23 Can people from Ethiopia change
their skin?
Can leopards change their spots?
It's the same with you.
You have always done what is
evil.
So how can you do what is good?

24 The LORD says, "I will scatter you
like straw
that the desert wind blows away.
25 This is what will happen to you.
I have appointed it for you,"
announces the LORD.
"You have forgotten me.
You have trusted in other gods.
26 So I will pull your skirt up over your
face.
Then people will see the shame
of your naked body.
27 They will see that you have not
been faithful to me.
You have committed adultery
with other gods.
And you have acted like a prostitute
who does not have any shame.
I have seen what you did
on the hills and in the fields.
And I hate it.
How terrible it will be for you,
Jerusalem!
How long will you choose to be
'unclean'?"

War and Hunger

14 A message from the LORD came
to Jeremiah. He told Jeremiah
there wouldn't be any rain in the land.
The LORD said,

2 "Judah is filled with sadness.
Its cities are wasting away.
The people weep for the land.
Crying is heard in Jerusalem.
3 The nobles send their servants to
get water.
They go to the wells.
But they do not find any water.
They return with empty jars.
They are terrified. They do not
have any hope.
They cover their heads.
4 The ground is dry and cracked.
There isn't any rain in the
land.
The farmers are terrified.
They cover their heads.
5 Even the female deer in the fields
desert their newborn fawns.
There isn't any grass to eat.

[6]Wild donkeys stand on the bare
hilltops.
They long for water as wild
dogs do.
Their eyesight fails
because they do not have any
food to eat."
[7]LORD, our sins are a witness
against us.
But do something for the honor
of your name.
We have often turned away from
you.
We've sinned against you.
[8]You are Israel's only hope.
You save us when we're in
trouble.
Why are you like a stranger to us?
Why are you like a traveler who
stays for only one night?
[9]Why are you like a man taken by
surprise?
Why are you like a soldier who
can't save anyone?
LORD, you are among us.
And we are your people.
Please don't desert us!

[10]The LORD gave Jeremiah a message
about these people. The LORD said,

"They really love to wander away
from me.
Their feet go down the wrong
path.
I do not accept these people.
I will remember the evil things
they have done.
I will punish them for their sins."

[11]The LORD continued, "Do not pray
that things will go well with them.
[12]Even if they go without food, I will
not listen to their cry for help. They
might sacrifice burnt offerings and
grain offerings. But I will not accept
them. Instead, I will destroy them with
war, hunger and plague."
[13]But I said, "LORD and King, the
prophets keep telling them something
else. They say, 'You won't have to suffer from war or hunger. Instead, the
LORD will give you peace and rest in
this place.'"
[14]Then the LORD said to me, "The
prophets are prophesying lies in my
name. I have not sent them or appointed them. I have not even spoken
to them. Everything they tell you about
their visions or secret knowledge is a lie.
They pretend to bring you messages
from other gods. They try to get you
to believe their own mistaken ideas.
[15]So here is what I am saying about
the prophets who are prophesying in
my name. I did not send them. But they
are saying, 'No war or hunger will come
to this land.' Those same prophets will
die because of war and hunger. [16]And
the people they are prophesying to will
be thrown out into the streets of Jerusalem. They will die because of hunger
and war. No one will bury them. No
one will bury their wives and children.
I will pour out trouble on them. That is
exactly what they should get.
[17]"Jeremiah, give them this message.
Tell them,

" 'Let tears flow from my eyes.
Let them pour out night and day.
Never let them stop.
The people of my own nation
have suffered a terrible wound.
They have been crushed.
[18]Suppose I go into the country.
Then I see people who have been
killed by swords.
Or suppose I go into the city.
Then I see people who have died
of hunger.
Prophet and priest alike have gone
to a land
they hadn't known about before.'"

[19]LORD, have you completely turned
your back on Judah?
Do you hate the city of Zion?
Why have you made us suffer?
We can't be healed.
We hoped peace would come.
But nothing good has happened
to us.
We hoped we would finally be
healed.
But all we got was terror.
[20]LORD, we admit we've done evil
things.
We also admit that our people of
long ago were guilty.
It's true that we've sinned
against you.
[21]For the honor of your name, don't
turn your back on us.
Don't bring shame on your
glorious throne in the temple.

Remember the covenant you made
with us.
Please don't break it.
22 Do any of the worthless gods of the
nations bring rain?
Do the skies send down showers
all by themselves?
No. LORD our God, you send the
rain.
So we put our hope in you.
You are the one who does all
these things.

15 Then the LORD said to me, "Suppose Moses and Samuel were
standing in front of me. Even then my
heart would not feel sorry for these
people. Send them away from me! Let
them go! 2 Suppose these people ask
you, 'Where should we go?' Then tell
them, 'The LORD says,

" ' "Those I have appointed to die
will die.
Those I have appointed to be killed
by swords
will be killed by swords.
Those I have appointed to die of
hunger
will die of hunger.
Those I have appointed to be taken
away as prisoners
will be taken away." '

3 "I will send four kinds of destroyers
against them," announces the LORD.
"Swords will kill them. Dogs will drag
them away. Birds will eat them up. And
wild animals will destroy them. 4 I will
make all the kingdoms on earth hate
them. That will happen because of what
Manasseh did in Jerusalem. He was
king of Judah and the son of Hezekiah.

5 "Jerusalem, who will have pity on
you?
Who will mourn for you?
Who will stop to ask how you are
doing?
6 You have said no to me,"
announces the LORD.
"You keep on turning away
from me.
So I will reach out and destroy you.
I am tired of showing you pity.
7 I will stand at the city gates of the
land.
I will separate the straw from the
grain.
I will destroy my people. I will
bring great sorrow on them.
They have not changed their ways.
8 I will increase the number of their
widows.
There will be more of them
than the grains of sand on the
seashore.
At noon I will bring a destroyer
against the mothers of the young
men among my people.
All at once I will bring down on them
great suffering and terror.
9 Mothers who have many children
will grow weak.
They will take their last breath.
The sun will set on them while it is
still day.
They will be dishonored and put
to shame.
All those who are left alive I will kill
by swords.
I will have their enemies do this,"
announces the LORD.

10 My mother, I wish I had never been
born!
The whole land opposes me.
They fight against me.
I haven't made loans to anyone.
And I haven't borrowed
anything.
But everyone curses me anyway.

11 The LORD said,

"Jeremiah, I will keep you safe for a
good purpose.
I will make your enemies ask you
to pray for them.
They will make their appeal to you
when they are in great trouble.

12 "People of Judah, the armies of
Babylon
will come from the north.
They are as strong as iron and
bronze.
Can anyone break their power?
13 I will give away your wealth and
your treasures.
Your enemies will carry off
everything.
And they will not pay anything
for it.
That will happen because you have
sinned so much.
You have done it throughout
your country.

14 I will make you slaves to your
enemies.
You will serve them in a land
you have not known about
before.
My anger will start a fire
that will burn you up."

15 LORD, you understand how much
I'm suffering.
Show concern for me. Take care
of me.
Pay back those who are trying to
harm me.
You are patient. Don't take my life
away from me.
Think about how much shame I
suffer because of you.
16 When I received your words, I ate
them.
They filled me with joy.
My heart took delight in them.
LORD God who rules over all,
I belong to you.
17 I never sat around with those who
go to wild parties.
I never had a good time with them.
I sat alone because you had put
your powerful hand on me.
Your anger against sin was
burning inside me.
18 Why does my pain never end?
Why is my wound so deep?
Why can't I ever get well?
To me you are like a stream that
runs dry.
You are like a spring that doesn't
have any water.

19 So the LORD says to Jeremiah,
"If you turn away from your sins, I
will heal you.
And then you will be able to
serve me.
Speak words that are worthy, not
worthless.
Then you will be speaking
for me.
Let these people turn to you.
But you must not turn to them.
20 I will make you like a wall to them.
I will make you like a strong
bronze wall.
The people will fight against you.
But they will not overcome you.
I am with you.
I will save you,"
announces the LORD.
21 "I will save you from the hands of
evil people.
I will set you free from those who
treat you badly."

Times of Trouble Are Coming

16 A message from the LORD came
to me. He said, 2 "Jeremiah, you
must not get married. You must not
have any sons or daughters in this land."
3 Here is the LORD's message about the
children born in this place. He says
about them and their parents, 4 "Some
of them will die of deadly sicknesses. No
one will mourn for them. Their bodies
will not be buried. Instead, they will be
like human waste lying there on the
ground. Others will die because of war
and hunger. Their bodies will not be
buried. Instead, they will become food
for the birds and the wild animals."
5 The LORD says, "Jeremiah, suppose a
meal is being served because someone
has died. Do not enter any house where
that is happening. Do not go there to
mourn or to comfort the family. I will
not bless these people anymore. I have
taken my love and pity away from
them," announces the LORD. 6 "Important and unimportant people alike will
die in this land. Their bodies will not be
buried. No one will mourn for them. No
one will cut themselves or shave their
head for the dead. 7 No one will offer food
or drink to comfort those who mourn
for the dead. No one will do this even if
someone's father or mother has died.
8 "Do not enter a house where a feast
is being held. Do not sit down there to
eat and drink. 9 I am the LORD who rules
over all. I am the God of Israel. I am
telling you, 'In your days I will judge
your people. You will see it with your
own eyes. I will put an end to the sounds
of joy and gladness here in Jerusalem.
The voices of brides and grooms will
not be heard anymore.'
10 "Tell these people all these things.
They will ask you, 'Why has the LORD
decided to send so much trouble on us?
We haven't done anything wrong. We
haven't committed any sins against the
LORD our God.' 11 When they say this,
here is what you should tell them. 'I did
it because your people of long ago deserted me,' announces the LORD. 'They
followed other gods. They served them

and worshiped them. They deserted
me. They did not obey my law. 12 But
you have done more evil things than
they did. All of you are doing what your
stubborn and evil hearts want you to do.
You are not obeying me. 13 So I will throw
you out of this land. I will send you away
to another land. Neither you nor your
people of long ago have known about it.
There you will serve other gods day and
night. And I will not give you any help.'

14 "But a new day is coming," announces the LORD. "At that time here
is what people will no longer say. 'As
sure as he is alive, the LORD brought
the Israelites up out of Egypt.' 15 Instead,
they will say, 'The LORD brought the
Israelites up out of the land of the north.
He gathered them out of all the countries where he had forced them to go.
And that's just as sure as he is alive.' I
will bring them back to the land I gave
their people of long ago.

16 "But now I will send for many fishermen," announces the LORD. "They will
catch some of these people. After that,
I will send for many hunters. They will
hunt down the others on every mountain and hill. They will bring them out
of the cracks in the rocks. 17 My eyes see
everything these people do. What they
do is not hidden from me. I always see
their sin. 18 I will pay them back double
for their sin and the evil things they
have done. They have made my land
'unclean.' They have set up lifeless statues of their evil gods. They have filled
my land with them. I hate those gods."

19 LORD, you give me strength.
You are like a fort to me.
When I'm in trouble,
I go to you for safety.
The nations will come to you
from one end of the earth to the other.
They will gather together and say,
"Our people of long ago didn't own anything
except statues of gods.
The statues were worthless.
They didn't do them any good.
20 Do human beings really make their own gods?
Yes. But they aren't really gods at all!"

21 The LORD says, "So I will teach them about myself.
This time I will show them
how powerful and mighty I am.
Then they will know
that I am the LORD.

17

"Judah's sin is carved with an iron tool.
It is written with the flint point of the tool.
It is carved on the tablets of their hearts.
It is written on the horns that stick out
from the corners of their altars.
2 Even their children offer sacrifices
to other gods on those altars.
They use the poles that were made
to worship the female god named Asherah.
They worship strange gods beside the green trees
and on the high hills.
3 I will give away my holy Mount Zion to the Babylonians.
Your enemies will carry off your wealth
and all your treasures.
I will give away your high places.
That will happen because you have sinned.
You have done it throughout your country.
4 You will lose the land I gave you.
And it will be your own fault.
I will make you slaves to your enemies.
You will serve them in a land you didn't know about before.
You have set my anger on fire.
It will burn forever."

5 The LORD says,

"Those who trust in human beings are under my curse.
They depend on human strength.
Their hearts turn away from me.
6 They will be like a bush in a dry and empty land.
They will not enjoy success when it comes.
They will live in dry places in the desert.
It is a land of salt where no one else lives.

[7]"But I will bless anyone who trusts in me.
I will do good things for the person who depends on me.
[8]They will be like a tree planted near water.
It sends out its roots beside a stream.
It is not afraid when heat comes.
Its leaves are always green.
It does not worry when there is no rain.
It always bears fruit."

[9]A human heart is more dishonest than anything else.
It can't be healed.
Who can understand it?

[10]The LORD says, "I look deep down inside human hearts.
I see what is in people's minds.
I reward each person in keeping with their conduct.
I bless them based on what they have done."

[11]Some people get rich by doing sinful things.
They are like a partridge that hatches eggs it didn't lay.
When their lives are half over, their riches will desert them.
In the end they will prove how foolish they have been.

[12]Our temple is where the LORD's glorious throne is.
From the beginning it has been high and lifted up.
[13]LORD, you are Israel's only hope.
Everyone who deserts you will be put to shame.
The names of those who turn away from you will be listed among the dead.
LORD, they have deserted you.
You are the spring of water that gives life.
[14]LORD, heal me. Then I will be healed.
Save me from my enemies. Then I will be saved.
You are the one I praise.
[15]They keep saying to me,
"What has happened to the message the LORD gave you?
Let it come true right now!"

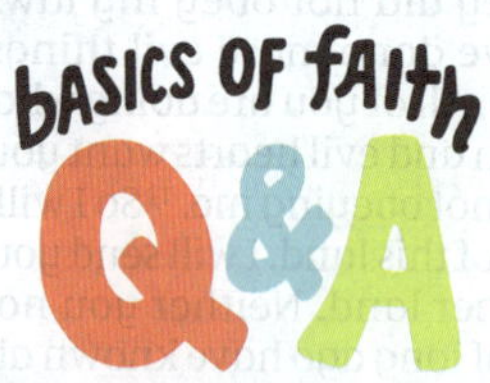

Should I follow my heart?

Your heart, or thoughts and feelings, doesn't always tell you the truth and can lead you away from God. Ask God to give you a new, pure heart and choose to follow him instead.

Can you find the following verse?
JEREMIAH 17:9

[16]I haven't run away from being the shepherd of your people.
You know I haven't wanted the day of Jerusalem's fall to come.
You are aware of every word that comes from my lips.
[17]Don't be a terror to me.
When I'm in trouble, I go to you for safety.
[18]Let those who attack me be put to shame.
But keep me from shame.
Let them be terrified.
But keep me from terror.
Bring the day of trouble on them.
Destroy them once and for all.

Keep the Sabbath Day Holy

[19]The LORD said to me, "Go. Stand at
the city gate called the Gate of the People.
That is where the kings of Judah go in and
out. Then stand at all the other gates of
Jerusalem. [20]Say, 'Listen to the LORD's
message, you kings of Judah and all you
people of Judah and Jerusalem. You always come through these gates. [21]The
LORD says, "Make sure you do not carry
a load on the Sabbath day. Do not bring
it through the gates of Jerusalem. [22]Do
not bring a load out of your houses on
the Sabbath day. Do not do any work on
that day. Instead, keep the Sabbath day
holy. Do as I commanded your people of

long ago. 23 But they did not listen. They
did not pay any attention to me. They
were stubborn. They would not listen
or pay attention when I corrected them.
24 Be careful to obey me," announces the
LORD. "Do not bring a load through the
gates of this city on the Sabbath day.
Instead, keep the Sabbath day holy. Do
not do any work on it. 25 Then kings who
sit on David's throne will come through
the gates of this city. They and their officials will come riding in chariots and
on horses. The people of Judah and Jerusalem will come along with them. And
this city will always have people living
in it. 26 Some will come from the towns of
Judah. And some will come in from the
villages around Jerusalem. Others will
come from the territory of Benjamin. And
others will come in from the western hills.
Still others will come from the central hill
country and the Negev Desert. All of them
will bring burnt offerings and sacrifices.
They will come bringing grain offerings,
incense and thank offerings. They will
take all these offerings to my house. 27 But
what if you do not obey me? Suppose you
do not keep the Sabbath day holy. And
suppose you carry a load through the
gates of Jerusalem on the Sabbath day.
Then I will start a fire that can't be put out.
It will begin at the gates of Jerusalem. It
will destroy its mighty towers." ' "

The LORD Sends Jeremiah to the Potter's House

18 A message from the LORD came
to me. He said, 2 "Jeremiah, go
down to the potter's house. I will give
you my message there." 3 So I went
down to the potter's house. I saw him
working at his wheel. 4 His hands were
shaping a pot out of clay. But he saw
that something was wrong with it. So he
formed it into another pot. He shaped
it in the way that seemed best to him.

5 Then the LORD's message came to me.
6 "People of Israel, I can do with you just
as this potter does," announces the LORD.
"The clay is in the potter's hand. And you
are in my hand, people of Israel. 7 Suppose I announce that something will
happen to a nation or kingdom. Suppose
I announce that it will be pulled up by
the roots. And I announce that it will be
torn down and destroyed. 8 But suppose
the nation I warned turns away from
its sins. Then I will not do what I said I
would. I will not bring trouble on it as I
had planned. 9 But suppose I announce
that a nation or kingdom is going to be
built up and planted. 10 And then it does
what is evil in my eyes. It does not obey
me. Then I will think again about the
good things I had wanted to do for it.

11 "So speak to the people of Judah and
Jerusalem. Tell them, 'The LORD says,
"Look! I am making plans against you.
I am going to bring trouble on you. So
each one of you must turn from your
evil ways. Change the way you live and
act." ' 12 But they will reply, 'It's no use.
We will continue to do what we've already planned. All of us will do what our
stubborn and evil hearts want us to do.' "

13 So the LORD says,

"Ask the nations a question. Say to
them,
'Who has ever heard anything
like this?
The people of Israel have done
a very horrible thing.
14 Does the snow ever disappear
from Lebanon's rocky slopes?
Do its cool waters ever stop
flowing from places far away?
15 But my people have forgotten me.
They burn incense to worthless
gods.
Their gods made them trip and fall
as they walked on the old paths.
They made them use side roads
instead of roads that were built
up.
16 So their land will become a horrible
thing.
People will make fun of it again
and again.
All those who pass by it will be
shocked.
They will shake their heads.
17 I will sweep over my people like a
wind from the east.
I will use the Babylonians to
scatter them.
I will show them my back and not
my face.
I will desert them when their day
of trouble comes.' "

18 They said, "Come on. Let's make
plans against Jeremiah. We'll still have
priests to teach us the law. We'll always
have wise people to give us advice. We'll

have prophets to bring us messages
from the LORD. So come on. Let's speak
out against Jeremiah. We shouldn't pay
any attention to what he says."

19 LORD, please listen to me!
Hear what my enemies are
saying about me!
20 Should the good things I've done be
paid back with evil?
But my enemies have dug a pit
for me.
Remember that I stood in front of
you
and spoke up for them.
I tried to turn your anger away
from them.
21 So let their children die of hunger.
Let my enemies be killed in war.
Let their wives lose their children
and husbands.
Let their men be put to death.
Let their young men be killed in
battle.
22 Bring their enemies against them
without warning.
Let cries be heard from their
houses.
They have dug a pit to capture me.
They have hidden traps for my
feet.
23 But LORD, you know
all about their plans to kill me.
Don't forgive their crimes.
Don't erase their sins from your
sight.
Destroy my enemies.
Punish them when the time to
show your anger comes.

19 The LORD said to Jeremiah, "Go
and buy a clay jar from a potter.
Take along some of the elders of the
people. Also tell some of the priests to
go with you. 2 Go out to the Valley of Ben
Hinnom. Stand near the entrance of the
gate where broken pieces of pottery
are thrown away. There announce the
message I give you. 3 Tell the people,
'Listen to the LORD's message, you kings
of Judah and people of Jerusalem. The
LORD who rules over all is the God of
Israel. He says, "Listen! I am going to
bring trouble on Jerusalem. It will be
so horrible that it will make the ears
of everyone who hears about it ring.
4 My people have deserted me. They
have made this city a place where other
gods are worshiped. They have burned
incense to them here. They, their people
of long ago and the kings of Judah had
never known these gods. My people
have also filled this place with the blood
of those who aren't guilty. 5 They have
built the high places where they worship
Baal. There they sacrifice their children
in the fire as offerings to Baal. That is
something I did not command or talk
about. It did not even enter my mind.
6 So watch out!" announces the LORD.
"The days are coming when people will
not call this place Topheth anymore.
And they will not call it the Valley of
Ben Hinnom either. Instead, they will
call it the Valley of Death.
7 " ' "In this place I will make the plans
of Judah and Jerusalem as useless as
a broken jar. I will use their enemies
to kill my people by swords. They will
die at the hands of those who want to
take their lives. I will give their dead
bodies as food to the birds and the wild
animals. 8 I will completely destroy this
city. I will make it a horrible thing. People will make fun of it. All those who
pass by it will be shocked. They will
laugh at its people because of all their
wounds. 9 I will make the people of this
city eat their sons and daughters. And
they will eat one another. They will
do this because things will be so bad
during the attack. The enemies who
want to take their lives will bring all
this trouble on them." '

10 "Jeremiah, break the jar while
those who go with you are watching.
11 Tell them, 'Here is what the LORD who
rules over all says. "This potter's jar is
smashed and can't be repaired. And I
will smash this nation and this city.
People will bury their dead in Topheth.
But they will run out of room. 12 Here is
what I will do to Jerusalem and those
who live here," ' announces the LORD. ' "I
will make this city like Topheth. 13 The
houses in Jerusalem will be made 'unclean' like Topheth. So will the houses
of the kings of Judah. All these people
burned incense on their roofs to all the
stars. They poured out drink offerings
to other gods." ' "

14 Then Jeremiah returned from
Topheth. That's where the LORD had sent
him to prophesy. Jeremiah stood in the
courtyard of the LORD's temple. He spoke

to all the people. He said, [15]"The LORD
who rules over all is the God of Israel.
He says, 'Listen! I am going to punish
this city and all the villages around it.
I am going to bring against them all
the trouble I have announced. That's
because my people were stubborn. They
would not listen to what I said.'"

Jeremiah and Pashhur

20 Pashhur the priest was the official in charge of the LORD's
temple. He was the son of Immer.
Pashhur heard Jeremiah prophesying
that Jerusalem would be destroyed. [2]So
he had Jeremiah the prophet beaten.
Then Pashhur put him in prison at the
Upper Gate of Benjamin at the LORD's
temple. [3]The next day Pashhur set him
free. Jeremiah said to him, "The LORD's
name for you isn't Pashhur. The LORD's
name for you is Terror on Every Side.
[4]The LORD says to you, 'I will make you
a terror to yourself. You will also be a
terror to all your friends. With your
own eyes you will see them die. Their
enemies will kill them with swords. I
will hand over all the people of Judah
to the king of Babylon. He will carry
them away to Babylon or kill them
with swords. [5]I will hand over all the
wealth of this city to Judah's enemies.
I will give them all its products and
everything of value. I will turn over to
them all the treasures that belonged to
the kings of Judah. They will take these
things and carry them off to Babylon.
[6]Pashhur, you and everyone who lives
in your house will also be forced to go
there. You have prophesied lies to all
your friends. So all of you will die and
be buried in Babylon.'"

Jeremiah Complains to the LORD

[7]You tricked me, LORD, and I was
tricked.
You overpowered me and won.
People make fun of me all day
long.
Everyone laughs at me.
[8]Every time I speak, I cry out.
All you ever tell me to talk about
is fighting and trouble.
Your message has brought me
nothing but dishonor.
It has made me suffer shame all
day long.
[9]Sometimes I think, "I won't talk
about his message anymore.
I'll never speak in his name
again."
But then your message burns in my
heart.
It's like a fire deep inside my
bones.
I'm tired of holding it in.
In fact, I can't.
[10]I hear many people whispering,
"There is terror on every side!
Bring charges against Jeremiah!
Let's bring charges against
him!"
All my friends
are waiting for me to slip.
They are saying, "Perhaps he will
be tricked
into making a mistake.
Then we'll win out over him.
We'll get even with him."
[11]But you are with me like a mighty
warrior.
So those who are trying to harm
me will trip and fall.
They won't win out over me.
They will fail. They'll be totally put
to shame.
Their dishonor will never be
forgotten.

[12]LORD, you rule over all.
You test those who do what is
right.
You see what is in people's hearts
and minds.
So pay them back for what they've
done.
I've committed my cause to you.

[13]Sing to the LORD, you people!
Give praise to him!
He saves the lives of people in need.
He saves them from the power of
sinful people.

[14]May the day I was born be cursed!
May the day I was born to my
mother not be blessed!
[15]May the man who brought my
father the news be cursed!
He's the one who made my father
very glad.
He said, "You have had a baby!
It's a boy!"
[16]May that man be like the towns
the LORD destroyed without pity.

May that man hear loud weeping
in the morning.
May he hear a battle cry at noon.
17 He should have killed me in my
mother's body.
He should have made my mother
my grave.
He should have let her body stay
large forever.
18 Why did I ever come out of my
mother's body?
I've seen nothing but trouble and
sorrow.
My days will end in shame.

The LORD Refuses Zedekiah's Appeal

21 A message from the LORD came
to Jeremiah. It came when King
Zedekiah sent Pashhur to Jeremiah.
Pashhur was the son of Malkijah. Zedekiah sent Zephaniah the priest along
with him. Zephaniah was the son of
Maaseiah. They said to Jeremiah, 2 "Ask
the LORD to help us. Nebuchadnezzar
king of Babylon is attacking us. In the
past the LORD did wonderful things for
us. Maybe he'll do them again. Then
Nebuchadnezzar will pull his armies
back from us."

3 But Jeremiah answered them, "Tell
Zedekiah and his people, 4 'The LORD is
the God of Israel. He says, "The king of
Babylon and his armies are all around
this city. They are getting ready to attack you. You have weapons of war in
your hands to fight against them. But I
am about to turn your weapons against
you. And I will bring your enemies inside this city. 5 I myself will fight against
you. I will reach out my powerful hand
and mighty arm. I will come against
you with all my great anger. 6 I will
strike down those who live in this city. I
will kill people and animals alike. They
will die of a terrible plague. 7 After that,
I will hand you over to your enemies.
They want to kill you," announces the
LORD. "I will hand over Zedekiah, the
king of Judah, and his officials. I will
also hand over the people in this city
who live through the plague, war and
hunger. All of them will be handed over
to Nebuchadnezzar, the king of Babylon. He will kill them with swords. He
will show them no mercy. He will not
feel sorry for them. In fact, he will not
have any concern for them at all." '

8 "Tell the people, 'The LORD says,
"I am offering you a choice. You can
choose the way that leads to life. Or
you can choose the way that leads to
death. 9 Those who stay in this city will
die of war, hunger or plague. But suppose some go out and give themselves
up to the Babylonians attacking you.
They will live. They will escape with
their lives. 10 I have decided to do this
city harm and not good," announces
the LORD. "It will be handed over to the
king of Babylon. And he will destroy it
with fire." '

11 "Also speak to Judah's royal family.
Tell them, 'Listen to the LORD's message.
12 Here is what the LORD says to you who
belong to David's royal house.

" ' "Every morning do what is right
and fair.
Save those who have been
robbed.
Set them free from the people
who have treated them badly.
If you do not, my anger will blaze
out against you.
It will burn like fire because of
the evil things you have done.
No one will be able to put it out.
13 Jerusalem, I am against you,"
announces the LORD.
"You live above this valley.
You are on a high, rocky plain.
And you say, 'Who can come
against us?
Who can enter our place of
safety?'
14 But I will punish you in keeping
with what you have done,"
announces the LORD.
"I will start a fire in your forests.
It will burn down everything
around you." ' "

The LORD Judges Evil Kings

22 The LORD said to Jeremiah, "Go
down to the palace of the king
of Judah. Announce my message there.
Tell him, 2 'King of Judah, listen to the
LORD's message. You are sitting on
David's throne. You and your officials
and your people come through these
gates. 3 The LORD says, "Do what is fair
and right. Save those who have been
robbed. Set them free from the people who have treated them badly. Do
not do anything wrong to outsiders or

widows in this place. Do not harm children whose fathers have died. Do not
kill those who are not guilty of doing
anything wrong. 4 Be careful to obey
these commands. Then kings who sit
on David's throne will come through
the gates of this palace. They will come
riding in chariots and on horses. Their
officials and their people will come
along with them. 5 But suppose you do
not obey these commands," announces
the LORD. "Then I promise you that this
palace will be destroyed. You can be
as sure of this promise as you are sure
that I live." ' "

6 The LORD speaks about the palace
of the king of Judah. He says,

"You are like the land of Gilead
to me.
You are like the highest
mountain in Lebanon.
But I will make you like a desert.
You will become like towns that
no one lives in.
7 I will send destroyers against you.
All of them will come with their
weapons.
They will cut up your fine cedar
beams.
They will throw them into the
fire.

8 "People from many nations will pass
by this city. They will ask one another,
'Why has the LORD done such a thing
to this great city?' 9 And the answer will
be, 'This happened because of what its
people have done. They have turned
away from the covenant the LORD
their God made with them. They have
worshiped other gods. And they have
served them.' "

10 Don't weep over dead King Josiah.
Don't be sad because he's gone.
Instead, weep bitterly over King
Jehoahaz.
He was forced to leave his
country.
He will never return.
He'll never see his own land
again.

11 Jehoahaz became king of Judah after
his father Josiah. But he has gone away
from this place. That's because the LORD
says about him, "He will never return.
12 He will die in Egypt. That is where he
was taken as a prisoner. He will not see
this land again."

13 The LORD says, "How terrible it will
be for King Jehoiakim!
He builds his palace
by mistreating his people.
He builds its upstairs rooms
with money gained by sinning.
He makes his own people work for
nothing.
He does not pay them for what
they do.
14 He says, 'I will build myself a great
palace.
It will have large rooms upstairs.'
So he makes big windows in it.
He covers its walls with cedar
boards.
He decorates it with red paint.

15 "Jehoiakim, does having more and
more cedar boards
make you a king?
Your father Josiah had enough to
eat and drink.
He did what was right and fair.
So everything went well with
him.
16 He stood up for those who were
poor or needy.
So everything went well with him.
That is what it means to know me,"
announces the LORD.
17 "Jehoiakim, the only thing on your
mind
is to get rich by cheating others.
You would even kill people who are
not guilty
of doing anything wrong.
You would mistreat them.
You would take everything they
own."

18 So the LORD speaks about King Jehoiakim, the son of Josiah. He says,

"His people will not mourn for him.
They will not say,
'My poor brother! My poor sister!'
They will not mourn for him.
They will not say,
'My poor master! How sad that
his glory is gone!'
19 In fact, he will be buried like a
donkey.
His body will be dragged away
and thrown
outside the gates of Jerusalem."

20 The LORD says, "People of
Jerusalem, go up to Lebanon.
Cry out for help.
Let your voice be heard in the
land of Bashan.
Cry out from the mountains of
Abarim.
All those who were going to help
you are crushed.
21 When you felt secure, I warned you.
But you said, 'I won't listen!'
You have acted like that ever since
you were young.
You have not obeyed me.
22 The wind will drive away all your
shepherds.
All those who were going to
help you will be carried off as
prisoners.
Then you will be dishonored and
put to shame.
That will happen because you
have been so sinful.
23 Some of you live in Jerusalem in the
Palace of the Forest of Lebanon.
You are comfortable in your
cedar buildings.
But you will groan when pain
comes on you.
It will be like the pain of a
woman having a baby.

24 "King Jehoiachin, you are the son
of Jehoiakim," announces the LORD.
"Suppose you were a ring on my right
hand. And suppose the ring even had
my royal mark on it. Then I would still
pull you off my finger. And that is just
as sure as I am alive. 25 I will hand you
over to those who want to kill you. I will
hand you over to people you are afraid
of. I will give you to Nebuchadnezzar,
the king of Babylon. I will hand you
over to his armies. 26 I will throw you
out into another country. I will throw
your mother out. Neither of you was
born in that country. But both of you
will die there. 27 You will never come
back to the land you long to return to."

28 This man Jehoiachin is like a
broken pot.
Everyone hates him. No one
wants him.
Why will he and his children be
thrown out of this land?
Why will they be sent to a land
they don't know about?
29 Land, land, land,
listen to the LORD's message!
30 The LORD says,
"Let the record say that this man
did not have any children.
Let it report that he did not have
any success in life.
None of his children will have
success either.
None of them will sit on David's
throne.
None of them will ever rule over
Judah.

The Godly Branch

23 "How terrible it will be for the
shepherds who lead my people
astray!" announces the LORD. "They are
destroying and scattering the sheep
that belong to my flock." 2 So the LORD,
the God of Israel, speaks to the shepherds who take care of my people. He
tells them, "You have scattered my
sheep. You have driven them away. You
have not taken good care of them. So I
will punish you for the evil things you
have done," announces the LORD. 3 "I
myself will gather together those who
are left alive in my flock. I will gather
them out of all the countries where I
have driven them. And I will bring them
back to their own land. There my sheep
will have many lambs. There will be
many more of them. 4 I will place shepherds over them who will take good care
of them. My sheep will not be afraid or
terrified anymore. And none of them
will be missing," announces the LORD.

5 "A new day is coming," announces
the LORD.
"At that time I will raise up for
David's royal line
a godly Branch.
He will be a King who will rule
wisely.
He will do what is fair and right
in the land.
6 In his days Judah will be saved.
Israel will live in safety.
And the Branch will be called
The LORD Who Makes Us Right
With Himself.

7 Other days are also coming," announces the LORD. "At that time people will
no longer say, 'The LORD brought the
Israelites up out of Egypt. And that's just

as sure as he is alive.' 8 Instead, they will
say, 'The LORD brought the Israelites up
out of the land of the north. He gathered
them out of all the countries where he
had forced them to go. And that's just
as sure as he is alive.' Then they will live
in their own land."

Prophets Who Tell Lies

9 Here is my message about the
prophets.

My heart is broken inside me.
All my bones tremble with fear.
I am like a man who is drunk.
I am like a strong man who has had too much wine.
That's what the LORD's holy words have done to me.
10 The land is full of people
who aren't faithful to the LORD.
Now the land is under his curse.
And that's why it is thirsty for water.
That's why the desert grasslands are dry.
The prophets are leading sinful lives.
They don't use their power in the right way.

11 "Prophets and priests alike are ungodly,"
announces the LORD.
"Even in my temple I find them sinning.
12 So their path will become slippery.
They will be thrown out into darkness.
There they will fall.
I will bring trouble on them
when the time to punish them comes,"
announces the LORD.

13 "Among the prophets of Samaria
I saw something I can't stand.
They were prophesying in the name of Baal.
They were leading my people Israel astray.
14 I have also seen something horrible
among Jerusalem's prophets.
They are not faithful to me.
They are not living by the truth.
They strengthen the hands of those who do evil.
So not one of them turns from their sinful ways.
All of them are like the people of Sodom to me.
They are just like the people of Gomorrah."

15 So the LORD who rules over all
speaks about the prophets. He says,

"I will make them eat bitter food.
I will make them drink poisoned water.
The prophets of Jerusalem have spread
their ungodly ways all through the land."

16 The LORD who rules over all says to
the people of Judah,

"Do not listen to what the prophets are saying to you.
They fill you with false hopes.
They talk about visions that come from their own minds.
What they say does not come from my mouth.
17 They keep speaking to those who hate me. They say,
'The LORD says you will have peace.'
They speak to all those who do
what their stubborn hearts want them to do.
They tell them, 'No harm will come to you.'
18 But which of them has ever stood in my courts?
Have they been there to see a vision or hear my message?
Who has listened and heard my message there?
19 A storm will burst out
because of my great anger.
A windstorm will sweep down
on the heads of sinful people.
20 My anger will not turn back.
I will accomplish everything
I plan to do.
In days to come
you will understand it clearly.
21 I did not send these prophets.
But they have run to tell you their message anyway.
I did not speak to them.
But they have still prophesied.
22 Suppose they had stood in my courts.
Then they would have announced my message to my people.

They would have turned my people
from their evil ways.
They would have turned them
away from their sins.

23 “Am I only a God who is nearby?”
announces the LORD.
“Am I not a God who is also far
away?
24 Who can hide in secret places
so that I can't see them?”
announces the LORD.
“Don't I fill heaven and earth?”
announces the LORD.

25 “I have heard what the prophets
are saying. They prophesy lies in my
name. They say, ‘I had a dream! The
LORD has given me a dream!’ 26 How
long will that continue in the hearts
of these prophets who tell lies? They
try to get others to believe their own
mistaken ideas. 27 They tell one another
their dreams. They think that will make
my people forget my name. In the same
way, their people of long ago forgot my
name when they worshiped Baal. 28 Let
the prophet who has a dream describe
the dream. But let the one who has my
message speak it faithfully. Your prophets have given you straw to eat instead
of grain,” announces the LORD. 29 “My
message is like fire,” announces the
LORD. “It is like a hammer that breaks
a rock in pieces.

30 “So I am against these prophets,”
announces the LORD. “I am against
those who steal messages from one
another. They claim that the messages
come from me. 31 Yes,” announces the
LORD. “I am against the prophets who
speak their own words. But they still
say, ‘Here is what the LORD says.’ 32 I
am against prophets who talk about
dreams that did not come from me,”
announces the LORD. “They tell foolish
lies. Their lies lead my people astray.
But I did not send these prophets. I did
not appoint them. They do not help
my people in the least,” announces the
LORD.

Prophets Who Give Messages That Are Not From the LORD

33 “Jeremiah, these people might ask
you a question. Or a prophet or priest
might do this. They might ask, ‘What
message have you received from the
LORD?’ Then tell them, ‘You ask, “What
message?” Here it is. “I will desert you,”
announces the LORD.’ 34 A prophet or
priest might make a claim. Or someone
else might do this. He might claim, ‘This
is a message from the LORD.’ Then I will
punish them and their family. 35 Here
is what each of you people keeps on
saying to your friends and other Israelites. You ask, ‘What is the LORD's
answer?’ Or you ask, ‘What has the LORD
spoken?’ 36 But you must not talk about
‘a message from the LORD’ again. That's
because each person's own words become their message. And so you twist
the LORD's words. He is the living God.
He is the LORD who rules over all. And
he is our God. 37 Here is what you keep
saying to a prophet. You ask, ‘What
is the LORD's answer to you?’ Or you
ask, ‘What has the LORD spoken?’ 38 You
claim, ‘This is a message from the LORD.’
But here is what the LORD says. ‘You
used the words, “This is a message from
the LORD.” But I told you that you must
not claim, “This is a message from the
LORD.” ’ 39 So you can be sure I will forget
you. I will throw you out of my sight. I
will also destroy the city I gave you and
your people of long ago. 40 I will bring
on you shame that will last forever. It
will never be forgotten.”

Judah Is Like Two Baskets of Figs

24 King Jehoiachin was forced to
leave Jerusalem. He was the son
of Jehoiakim. Jehoiachin was taken to
Babylon by Nebuchadnezzar, the king
of Babylon. The officials and all the
skilled workers were forced to leave with
him. After they left, the LORD showed me
two baskets of figs. They were in front
of his temple. 2 One basket had very
good figs in it. They were like figs that
ripen early. The other basket had very
bad figs in it. In fact, they were so bad
they couldn't even be eaten.

3 Then the LORD asked me, “What do
you see, Jeremiah?”

“Figs,” I answered. “The good ones
are very good. But the others are so bad
they can't be eaten.”

4 Then a message from the LORD came
to me. The LORD said, 5 “I am the LORD,
the God of Israel. I say, ‘I consider the
people who were forced to leave Judah
to be like these good figs. I sent them

away from this place. I forced them to go to Babylon. 6 My eyes will watch over them. I will be good to them. And I will bring them back to this land. I will build them up. I will not tear them down. I will plant them. I will not pull them up by the roots. 7 I will change their hearts. Then they will know that I am the LORD. They will be my people. And I will be their God. They will return to me with all their heart.

8 " 'But there are also bad figs. In fact, they are so bad they can't be eaten,' says the LORD. 'Zedekiah, the king of Judah, is like these bad figs. So are his officials and the people of Jerusalem who are still left alive. I will punish them whether they remain in this land or live in Egypt. 9 I will make all the kingdoms on earth displeased with them. In fact, they will hate them a great deal. They will shake their heads at them. They will curse them and make fun of them. All this will happen no matter where I force them to go. 10 I will send war, hunger and plague against them. They will be destroyed from the land I gave them and their people of long ago.' "

Seventy Years in Babylon

25 A message from the LORD about all the people of Judah came to Jeremiah. It came in the fourth year that Jehoiakim was the king of Judah. It was the first year that Nebuchadnezzar was the king of Babylon. Jehoiakim was the son of Josiah. 2 Jeremiah, the LORD's prophet, spoke to all the people of Judah and Jerusalem. He said, 3 "For 23 years the LORD's messages have been coming to me. They began to come in the 13th year that Josiah was king of Judah. He was the son of Amon. The LORD's messages still come to me today. I've spoken to you people again and again. But you haven't listened to me.

4 "The LORD has sent all his servants the prophets to you. They've come to you again and again. But you haven't listened. You haven't paid any attention to them. 5 They said, 'Each of you must turn from your evil ways and practices. Then you can stay in the land forever. It's the land the LORD gave you and your people of long ago. 6 Don't follow other gods. Don't serve them or worship them. Don't make the LORD angry with the gods your own hands have made. Then he won't harm you.'

7 " 'But you did not listen to me,' announces the LORD. 'You have made me very angry with the gods your hands have made. And you have brought harm on yourselves.'

8 "The LORD who rules over all says, 'You have not listened to my words. 9 So I will send for all the nations in the north. And I will send for my servant Nebuchadnezzar, the king of Babylon,' announces the LORD. 'I will bring all of them against this land and against you who live here. They will march out against all the nations that are around this land. I will set apart Judah and the nations around it in a special way to be destroyed. People will be shocked because of them. And they will make fun of them. Those nations will be destroyed forever. 10 I will put an end to the sounds of joy and gladness. I will put an end to the voices of brides and grooms. The sound of grinding millstones will not be heard anymore. And lamps will not be lit anymore. 11 This whole country will become dry and empty. And these nations will serve the king of Babylon for 70 years.

12 " 'But I will punish that king and his nation because they are guilty. I will do this when the 70 years are over,' announces the LORD. 'I will make that land a desert forever. 13 I have spoken against that land. And I will make all these things happen to it. Everything will happen that is written in this book. And I will make everything Jeremiah prophesied against all the nations come true. 14 The people of Babylon will become slaves of many other nations and great kings. I will pay them back for what they have done.' "

The Cup of God's Great Anger

15 The LORD is the God of Israel. He said to me, "Take this cup from my hand. It is filled with the wine of my great anger. Make all the nations to which I send you drink it. 16 When they drink it, they will not even be able to walk straight. It will drive them out of their minds. I am going to send war against them." 17 So I took the cup from the LORD's hand. I made all the nations to which he sent me drink from it.

[18] He sent me to Judah's kings and officials. He told me to go to Jerusalem and the towns of Judah. He wanted me to tell them they would be destroyed. Then people would be shocked because of them. They would make fun of them. They would use their name in a curse. And that's how things still are today.
[19] Here is a list of the other kings and nations he sent me to.
Pharaoh, the king of Egypt
his attendants, his officials, all his people
[20] all the people from other lands who lived there
all the kings of Uz
the Philistine kings of Ashkelon, Gaza and Ekron
the Philistines still living in Ashdod
[21] Edom, Moab, Ammon
[22] all the kings of Tyre and Sidon
the kings of the islands and other lands along the Mediterranean Sea
[23] Dedan, Teman, Buz
all the other places far away in the east
[24] all the kings of Arabia
all the other kings of people who live in the desert
[25] all the kings of Zimri, Elam and Media
[26] all the kings in the north, near and far

So he sent me to all the kingdoms on the face of the earth, one after the other. They will all drink from the cup of the LORD's anger. After they drink, the king of Babylon will drink from it too.

[27] The LORD says, "Tell them, 'The LORD who rules over all is the God of Israel. He says, "Drink from this cup. Get drunk and throw up. Fall down and do not get up again. I am going to send war against you." ' [28] But they might refuse to take the cup from your hand. They might not want to drink from it. Then tell them, 'The LORD who rules over all says, "You must drink from it!
[29] I am beginning to bring trouble on the city where I have put my Name. You might think you will not be punished. But you will certainly be punished. I am sending war against everyone who lives on earth," announces the LORD who rules over all.'

[30] "Jeremiah, prophesy against them. Tell them,

" 'The LORD will roar from heaven like a lion.
His voice will sound like thunder from his holy temple there.
He will roar loudly against his land.
He will shout like those who stomp on grapes in winepresses.
He will shout against everyone who lives on earth.
[31] The noise of battle will be heard from one end of the earth to the other.
That's because the LORD will bring charges against the nations.
He will judge every human being.
He will kill sinful people with his sword,' "
announces the LORD.

[32] The LORD who rules over all says,

"Look! Horrible trouble is spreading from one nation to another.
A mighty storm is rising.
It is coming from a place that is very far away."

[33] At that time those the LORD kills will be lying around everywhere. They will be found from one end of the earth to the other. No one will mourn for them. Their dead bodies will not be gathered up or buried. Instead, they will be like human waste lying there on the ground.

[34] Weep and cry, you shepherds.
Roll in the dust, you leaders of the flock.
Your time to be killed has come.
You will fall like the best of the rams.
[35] The shepherds won't have any place to run to.
The leaders of the flock won't be able to escape.
[36] Listen to the cries of the shepherds.
Hear the weeping of the leaders of the flock.
The LORD is destroying their grasslands.
[37] Their peaceful meadows will be completely destroyed because of the LORD's great anger.

38 Like a lion he will leave his den.
  The land of those leaders will
    become a desert.
 That's because the sword of the
    LORD brings great harm.
  His anger will burn against
    them.

Jeremiah's Enemies Try to Have Him Killed

26 A message from the LORD came to Jeremiah. It was shortly after Jehoiakim became king of Judah. He was the son of Josiah. 2 The LORD said to Jeremiah, "Stand in the courtyard of my house. Speak to the people of the towns in Judah. Speak to all those who come to worship in my house. Tell them everything I command you. Do not leave out a single word. 3 Perhaps they will listen. Maybe they will turn from their evil ways. Then I will not do what I said I would. I will not bring trouble on them. I had planned to punish them because of the evil things they had done. 4 Tell them, 'The LORD says, "Listen to me. Obey my law that I gave you. 5 And listen to the words my servants the prophets are speaking. I have sent them to you again and again. But you have not listened to them. 6 So I will make this house like Shiloh. All the nations on earth will use the name of this city in a curse." ' "

7 Jeremiah spoke these words in the LORD's house. The priests, the prophets and all the people heard him. 8 Jeremiah finished telling all the people everything the LORD had commanded him to say. But as soon as he did, the priests, the prophets and all the people grabbed him. They said, "You must die! 9 Why do you prophesy these things in the LORD's name? Why do you say that this house will become like Shiloh? Why do you say that this city will be empty and deserted?" And all the people crowded around Jeremiah in the LORD's house.

10 The officials of Judah heard what had happened. So they went up from the royal palace to the LORD's house. There they took their places at the entrance of the New Gate. 11 Then the priests and prophets spoke to the officials and all the people. They said, "This man should be sentenced to death. He has prophesied against this city. You have heard it with your own ears!"

12 Then Jeremiah spoke to all the officials and people. He said, "The LORD sent me to prophesy against this house and this city. He told me to say everything you have heard. 13 So change the way you live and act. Obey the LORD your God. Then he won't do what he said he would. He won't bring on you the trouble he said he would bring. 14 As for me, I'm in your hands. Do to me what you think is good and right. 15 But you can be sure of one thing. If you put me to death, you will be held responsible for spilling my blood. And I haven't even done anything wrong. You will bring guilt on yourselves and this city and those who live in it. The LORD has sent me to you. He wanted me to say all these things so you could hear them. And that's the truth."

16 Then the officials and all the people spoke to the priests and prophets. They said, "This man shouldn't be sentenced to death! He has spoken to us in the name of the LORD our God."

17 Some of the elders of the land stepped forward. They spoke to the whole community gathered there. They said, 18 "Micah from Moresheth prophesied. It was during the time Hezekiah was king over Judah. Micah spoke to all the people of Judah. He told them, 'The LORD who rules over all says,

" ' "Zion will be plowed up like a
    field.
  Jerusalem will be turned into a
    pile of trash.
  The temple hill will be covered
    with bushes and weeds." '
    (Micah 3:12)

19 Did King Hezekiah or anyone else in Judah put Micah to death? Hezekiah had respect for the LORD and tried to please him. And the LORD didn't judge Jerusalem as he said he would. He didn't bring on it the trouble he said he would bring. But we are about to bring horrible trouble on ourselves!"

20 Uriah was another man who prophesied in the name of the LORD. He was from Kiriath Jearim. He was the son of Shemaiah. Uriah prophesied against this city and this land. He said the same things Jeremiah did. 21 King Jehoiakim and all his officers and officials heard Uriah's words. So the king decided to

put him to death. But Uriah heard about
it. He was afraid. And he ran away to
Egypt. 22 So King Jehoiakim sent Elnathan to Egypt. He also sent some
other men along with him. Elnathan
was the son of Akbor. 23 Those men
brought Uriah out of Egypt. They took
him to King Jehoiakim. Then the king
had Uriah struck down with a sword.
He had Uriah's body thrown into one
of the graves of the ordinary people.
24 In spite of that, Ahikam stood up
for Jeremiah. Ahikam was the son of
Shaphan. Because of Ahikam, Jeremiah
wasn't handed over to the people to be
put to death.

Judah Will Serve Nebuchadnezzar

27 A message from the LORD came
to Jeremiah. It was shortly after
Zedekiah became king of Judah. He
was the son of Josiah. 2 The LORD said,
"Make a yoke out of ropes and wooden
boards. Put it on your neck. 3 Then write
down a message for the kings of Edom,
Moab, Ammon, Tyre and Sidon. Give
it to their messengers who have come
to Jerusalem. They have come to see
Zedekiah, the king of Judah. 4 Give them
a message for the kings who sent them.
It should say, 'The LORD who rules over
all is the God of Israel. He says, "Here is
what I want you to tell your masters.
5 I reached out my great and powerful
arm. I made the earth. I made its people
and animals. And I can give the earth to
anyone I please. 6 Now I will hand over
all your countries to my servant Nebuchadnezzar. He is the king of Babylon.
I will put even the wild animals under
his control. 7 All the nations will serve
him and his son and grandson. After
that, I will judge his land. Then many
nations and great kings will make him
serve them.
8 " ' "But suppose any nation or kingdom will not serve Nebuchadnezzar,
the king of Babylon. And suppose it
refuses to put its neck under his yoke.
Then I will punish that nation with war,
hunger and plague," announces the
LORD. "I will punish it until his powerful
hand destroys it. 9 So do not listen to
your prophets. Do not listen to those
who claim to have secret knowledge.
Do not listen to those who try to explain
your dreams. Do not listen to those who
get messages from people who have
died. Do not listen to those who practice
evil magic. All of them will tell you,
'You won't serve the king of Babylon.'
10 But they prophesy lies to you. If you
listen to them, you will be removed far
away from your lands. I will drive you
away from them. And you will die. 11 But
suppose any nation will put its neck
under the yoke of the king of Babylon.
And suppose it serves him. Then I will
let that nation remain in its own land.
I will let its people plow the land and
live there," ' " announces the LORD.
12 I gave the same message to Zedekiah, the king of Judah. I said, "Put
your neck under the yoke of the king
of Babylon. Obey him. Serve his people.
Then you will live. 13 Why should you
and your people die? Why should you
die of war, hunger and plague? That's
what the LORD said would happen to
any nation that won't serve the king
of Babylon. 14 Don't listen to the words
of the prophets who say to you, 'You
won't serve the king of Babylon.' They
are prophesying lies to you. 15 'I have not
sent them,' announces the LORD. 'They
are prophesying lies in my name. So I
will drive you away from your land.
And you will die. So will the prophets
who prophesy to you.' "
16 Then I spoke to the priests and all
these people. I said, "The LORD says, 'Do
not listen to the prophets who speak to
you. They say, "Very soon the objects
from the LORD's house will be brought
back from Babylon." Those prophets are
prophesying lies to you. 17 Do not listen
to them. Serve the king of Babylon.
Then you will live. Why should this city
be destroyed? 18 If they are prophets and
have received a message from me, let
them pray to me. I am the LORD who
rules over all. Those prophets should
pray that what is still in Jerusalem will
remain here. They should pray that
the objects in my house and the king's
palace will not be taken to Babylon.
19 I am the LORD who rules over all. Do
you know what these objects are? They
include the two pillars in front of the
temple. They include the huge bronze
bowl. They include the bronze stands
that can be moved around. And they
include the other things left in this city.
20 Nebuchadnezzar, the king of Babylon,

did not take these things away at first. That was when he took King Jehoiachin from Jerusalem to Babylon. Jehoiachin is the son of Jehoiakim. Nebuchadnezzar also took all the nobles of Judah and Jerusalem along with Jehoiachin. 21 I am the LORD who rules over all. I am the God of Israel. Here is what will happen to the things that are left in my house, the king's palace and Jerusalem. 22 They will be taken to Babylon. They will remain there until the day I come for them,' announces the LORD. 'Then I will bring them back. I will return them to this place.' "

The False Prophet Hananiah Opposes Jeremiah

28 The false prophet Hananiah spoke to me, Jeremiah, in the LORD's house. Hananiah was from Gibeon. He was the son of Azzur. It was shortly after Zedekiah became king of Judah. It was in the fifth month of his fourth year. In front of the priests and all the people Hananiah spoke to me. He said, 2 "The LORD who rules over all is the God of Israel. He says, 'I will break the yoke of the king of Babylon. 3 Nebuchadnezzar, the king of Babylon, removed all the objects that belong to my house. He took them to Babylon. Before two years are over, I will bring them back to this place. 4 I will also bring King Jehoiachin back. He is the son of Jehoiakim. And I will bring back all the others who were taken from Judah to Babylon,' announces the LORD. 'I will break the yoke of the king of Babylon.' "

5 Then Jeremiah the prophet replied to the false prophet Hananiah. Jeremiah spoke to him in front of the priests and all the people. They were standing in the LORD's house. 6 Jeremiah said, "Amen, Hananiah! May the LORD do those things! May he make the words you have prophesied come true. May he bring back from Babylon the objects that belong to the LORD's house. May he bring back to this place all the people who were taken away. 7 But listen to what I have to say. I want you and all the people to hear it. 8 There have been prophets long before you and I were ever born. They have prophesied against many countries and great kingdoms. They have spoken about war, trouble and plague. 9 But what if a prophet says peace will come? And suppose peace really does come? Only then will he be recognized as a prophet truly sent by the LORD."

10 The false prophet Hananiah took the yoke off the neck of Jeremiah the prophet. Then Hananiah broke the yoke. 11 In front of all the people he said, "The LORD says, 'In the same way, I will break the yoke of Nebuchadnezzar, the king of Babylon. Before two years are over, I will remove it from the necks of all the nations.' " When Jeremiah the prophet heard this, he went on his way.

12 A message from the LORD came to Jeremiah. It was after the false prophet Hananiah had broken the yoke off Jeremiah's neck. The message said, 13 "Go. Tell Hananiah, 'The LORD says, "You have broken a wooden yoke. But in its place you will get an iron yoke." 14 The LORD who rules over all is the God of Israel. He says, "I will put an iron yoke on the necks of all these nations. I will make them serve Nebuchadnezzar, the king of Babylon. So they will serve him. I will even give him control over the wild animals." ' "

15 Then Jeremiah the prophet spoke to the false prophet Hananiah. Jeremiah said, "Listen, Hananiah! The LORD hasn't sent you. But you have tricked these people. Now they trust in lies. 16 So the LORD says, 'I am about to remove you from the face of the earth. Before this year is over, you will die. You have taught the people to turn against me.' "

17 In the seventh month of that very year, the false prophet Hananiah died.

Jeremiah's Letter to the Jews in Babylon

29 Jeremiah the prophet sent a letter from Jerusalem to Babylon. It was for the Jewish elders still alive there. It was also for the priests and prophets in Babylon. And it was for all the other people Nebuchadnezzar had taken from Jerusalem to Babylon. 2 It was sent to them after King Jehoiachin had been forced to leave Jerusalem. His mother and the court officials were taken with him. The leaders of Judah and Jerusalem had been forced to go to Babylon. All the skilled workers had also been forced to go. 3 Jeremiah gave

the letter to Elasah and Gemariah. Elasah was the son of Shaphan. Gemariah
was the son of Hilkiah. Zedekiah, the
king of Judah, had sent Elasah and
Gemariah to King Nebuchadnezzar in
Babylon. Here is what the letter said.

4 The LORD who rules over all is
the God of Israel. He speaks to all
those he forced to go from Jerusalem to Babylon. He says, 5 "Build
houses and make your homes
there. Plant gardens and eat what
they produce. 6 Get married. Have
sons and daughters. Find wives for
your sons. Give your daughters to
be married. Then they too can have
sons and daughters. Let there be
many more of you and not fewer.
7 Also work for the success of the
city I have sent you to. Pray to the
LORD for that city. If it succeeds,
you too will enjoy success." 8 The
LORD who rules over all is the God
of Israel. He says, "Do not let the
prophets trick you. Do not be fooled
by those who claim to have secret
knowledge. Do not listen to people
who try to explain their dreams to
you. 9 All of them are prophesying
lies to you in my name. I have not
sent them," announces the LORD.
10 The LORD says, "You will be
forced to live in Babylon for 70
years. After they are over, I will
come to you. My good promise to
you will come true. I will bring you
back home. 11 I know the plans I
have for you," announces the LORD.
"I want you to enjoy success. I do
not plan to harm you. I will give
you hope for the years to come.
12 Then you will call out to me. You
will come and pray to me. And I will
listen to you. 13 When you look for
me with all your heart, you will find
me. 14 I will be found by you," announces the LORD. "And I will bring
you back from where you were tak-
en as prisoners. I will gather you

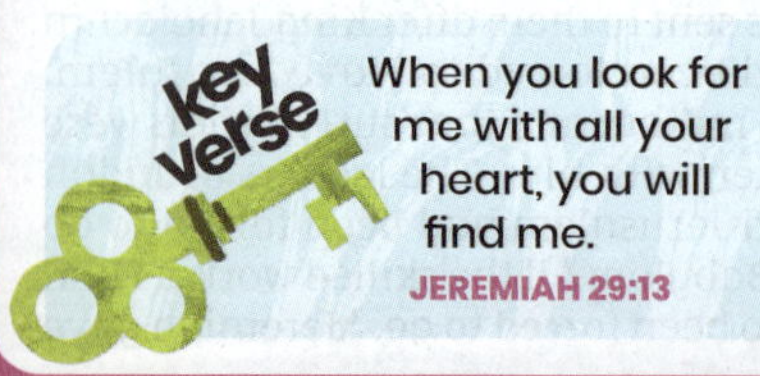

from all the nations. I will gather
you from the places where I have
forced you to go," announces the
LORD. "I will bring you back to the
place I sent you away from."
15 You might say, "The LORD has
given us prophets in Babylon."
16 But here is what the LORD says
about the king who now sits on
David's throne. He also says it
about all the people who remain
in this city. And he says it about all
those who did not go with you to
Babylon. 17 The LORD who rules over
all says, "I will send war, hunger
and plague against them. I will
make them like bad figs. They are
so bad they can't be eaten. 18 I will
hunt them down with war, hunger and plague. I will make all the
kingdoms on earth displeased with
them. They will use their name in a
curse. All the nations where I drive
them will be shocked at them. They
will make fun of them. And they
will bring shame on them. 19 That's
because they have not listened to
my words," announces the LORD.
"I sent messages to them again
and again. I sent them through
my servants the prophets. And you
who were taken to Babylon have
not listened either," announces
the LORD.

20 So listen to the LORD's message. Listen, all you whom he has
sent away from Jerusalem to Babylon. 21 The LORD who rules over all
is the God of Israel. He speaks about
Ahab and Zedekiah. Ahab is the son
of Kolaiah. Zedekiah is the son of
Maaseiah. They are prophesying
lies to you in my name. The LORD
says about Ahab and Zedekiah, "I
will hand them over to Nebuchadnezzar, the king of Babylon. He will
put them to death. You will see it
with your own eyes. 22 Because of
what happens to them, people will
use their names when they curse
someone. All those who have been
taken from Judah to Babylon will
use their names in that way. They
will say, 'May the LORD treat you
like Zedekiah and Ahab. The king
of Babylon burned them in the fire.'
23 That will happen because they

have done awful things in Israel.
They have committed adultery
with their neighbors' wives. They
have spoken lies in my name. I
did not give them the authority
to speak those things. I know what
they have done. And I am a witness
to it," announces the LORD.

Shemaiah Opposes Jeremiah

24 Tell Shemaiah, the Nehelamite,
25 "The LORD who rules over all is the God
of Israel. He says, 'You sent letters in your
own name to all the people in Jerusalem.
You also sent them to Zephaniah the
priest. He is the son of Maaseiah. And
you sent them to all the other priests. You
said to Zephaniah, 26 "The LORD has appointed you priest in place of Jehoiada.
He has put you in charge of the LORD's
house. You are supposed to arrest any
crazy person who claims to be a prophet.
You should put him in prison. You should
put iron bands around his neck. 27 So why
haven't you punished Jeremiah from
Anathoth? He claims to be a prophet
among you. 28 He has sent a message to
us in Babylon. It says, 'You will be there
a long time. So build houses and make
your homes there. Plant gardens and eat
what they produce.' " ' "

29 But Zephaniah the priest read the
letter to me. 30 Then a message from
the LORD came to me. The LORD said,
31 "Send a message to all the people
who were taken away. Tell them, 'The
LORD speaks about Shemaiah, the
Nehelamite. He says, "Shemaiah has
prophesied to you. But I did not send
him. He has made you trust in lies. 32 So
I say, 'I will certainly punish Shemaiah,
the Nehelamite. I will also punish his
children after him. He will not have any
children left among these people. I will
do good things for my people. But he
will not see them,' " ' " announces the
LORD. " ' " 'That's because he has taught
people to turn against me.' " ' "

Israel Will Return to the LORD

30 A message from the LORD came
to Jeremiah. The LORD said, 2 "I
am the LORD. I am the God of Israel. I
say, 'Write in a book all the words I have
spoken to you. 3 A new day is coming,' "
announces the LORD. " 'At that time I will
bring my people Israel and Judah back
from where they have been taken as
prisoners. I will bring them back to this
land. I gave it to their people of long ago
to have as their own,' " says the LORD.

4 Here are the words the LORD spoke
about Israel and Judah. He said, 5 "I am
the LORD. I say,

" 'Cries of fear are heard.
There is terror. There isn't any
peace.
6 Ask and see.
Can a man give birth to children?
Then why do I see every strong
man
with his hands on his stomach?
Each of them is acting like a
woman having a baby.
Every face is as pale as death.
7 How awful that day will be!
No other day will be like it.
It will be a time of trouble for the
people of Jacob.
But they will be saved out of it.

8 " 'At that time I will break the yoke
off their necks,'
announces the LORD who rules
over all.
'I will tear off the ropes that hold
them.
People from other lands will not
make them slaves anymore.
9 Instead, they will serve me.
And they will serve David their
king.
I will raise him up for them.
I am the LORD their God.

10 " 'People of Jacob, do not be afraid.
You are my servant.
Israel, do not be terrified,' "
announces the LORD.
" 'You can be sure that I will save you.
I will bring you out of a place far
away.
I will bring your children back
from the land where they were
taken.
Your people will have peace and
security again.
And no one will make them
afraid.
11 I am with you. I will save you,' "
announces the LORD.
" 'I will completely destroy all the
nations
among which I scatter you.
But I will not completely destroy
you.

I will correct you. But I will be fair.
I will not let you go without any punishment.' "

12 The LORD says,
"Your wound can't be cured.
Your pain can't be healed.
13 No one will stand up for you.
There isn't any medicine for your sore.
There isn't any healing for you.
14 All those who were going to help you have forgotten you.
They do not care about you.
I have struck you as if I were your enemy.
I have punished you as if I were very mean.
That is because your guilt is so great.
You have sinned so much.
15 Why do you cry out about your wound?
Your pain can't be healed.
Your guilt is very great.
And you have committed many sins.
That is why I have done all these things to you.

16 "But everyone who destroys you will be destroyed.
All your enemies will be forced to leave their countries.
Those who steal from you will be stolen from.
I will take the belongings of those who take things from you.
17 But I will make you healthy again.
I will heal your wounds,"
announces the LORD.
"That's because you have been thrown out.
You are called Zion, the one no one cares about."

18 The LORD says,
"I will bless Jacob's people with great success again.
I will show tender love to Israel.
Jerusalem will be rebuilt where it was destroyed.
The palace will stand in its proper place.
19 From those places the songs of people giving thanks will be heard.
The sound of great joy will come from there.
I will cause there to be more of my people.
There will not be fewer of them.
I will bring them honor.
People will have respect for them.
20 Things will be as they used to be for Jacob's people.
I will make their community firm and secure.
I will punish everyone who treats them badly.
21 Their leader will be one of their own people.
Their ruler will rise up from among them.
I will bring him near.
And he will come close to me.
He will commit himself to serve me,"
announces the LORD.
22 "So you will be my people.
And I will be your God."

23 A storm will burst out because of the LORD's great anger.
A strong wind will sweep down on the heads of evil people.
24 The LORD's great anger won't turn back.
He will accomplish everything his heart plans to do.
In days to come
you will understand this.

31 "At that time I will be the God
of all the families of Israel," announces the LORD. "And they will be
my people."

2 The LORD says,
"Some of my people will live through
everything their enemies do to them.
They will find help in the desert.
I will come to give peace and rest to Israel."

3 The LORD appeared to us in the past.
He said,
"I have loved you with a love that lasts forever.
I have kept on loving you with a kindness that never fails.
4 I will build you up again.
Nation of Israel, you will be rebuilt.

Once again you will use your
tambourines to celebrate.
You will go out and dance with
joy.
5 Once again you will plant
vineyards
on the hills of Samaria.
Farmers will plant them.
They will enjoy their fruit.
6 There will be a day when those on
guard duty will cry out.
They will stand on the hills of
Ephraim.
And they will shout,
'Come! Let's go up to Zion.
Let's go up to where the LORD our
God is.' "

7 The LORD says,

"Sing for joy because the people of
Jacob are blessed.
Shout because the LORD has
made them the greatest nation.
Make your praises heard.
Say, 'LORD, save your people.
Save the people who are left alive
in Israel.'
8 I will bring them from the land of
the north.
I will gather them from one end
of the earth to the other.
Even those who are blind and those
who can't walk
will be among them.
Pregnant women and women
having their babies
will be among them also.
Many of them will return.
9 Their eyes will be filled with tears
as they come.
They will pray as I bring them
back.
I will lead them beside streams of
water.
I will lead them on a level path
where they will not trip or fall.
I am Israel's father.
And Ephraim is my oldest son.

10 "Listen to my message, you nations.
Announce it on shores far away.
Say, 'He who scattered Israel will
gather them.
He will watch over his flock like a
shepherd.'
11 I will set the people of Jacob free.
I will save them from those who
are stronger than they are.
12 They will come and shout for joy on
Mount Zion.
They will be joyful because of
everything I give them.
I give them grain, olive oil and
fresh wine.
I give them the young animals in
their flocks and herds.
Israel will be like a garden that has
plenty of water.
And they will not be sad
anymore.
13 Then young women will dance and
be glad.
And so will the men, young and
old alike.
I will turn their mourning into
gladness.
I will comfort them.
And I will give them joy instead
of sorrow.
14 I will satisfy the priests. I will give
them more than enough.
And my people will be filled with
the good things I give them,"
announces the LORD.

15 The LORD says,

"A voice is heard in Ramah.
It is the sound of weeping and
deep sadness.
Rachel is weeping for her children.
She refuses to be comforted,
because they are gone."

16 The LORD says,

"Do not weep anymore.
Do not let tears fall from your
eyes.
I will reward you for your work,"
announces the LORD.
"Your children will return from
the land of the enemy.
17 So there is hope for your children,"
announces the LORD.
"Your children will return to their
own land.

18 "I have heard the groans of
Ephraim's people. They say,
'You corrected us like a calf you
were training.
And we have been trained.
Bring us back to you, and we will
come back.
You are the LORD our God.
19 After we wandered away from you,
we turned away from our sins.

After we learned our lesson,
we beat our chests in sorrow.
We were full of shame.
What we did when we were
young brought dishonor on us.'
20 Aren't the people of Ephraim my
dear children?
Aren't they the children I take
delight in?
I often speak against them.
But I still remember them.
So my heart longs for them.
I love them with a tender love,"
announces the LORD.

21 The LORD says, "Put up road signs.
Set up stones to show the way.
Look carefully for the highway.
Look for the road you will take.
Return, people of Israel.
Return to your towns.
22 How long will you wander,
my people Israel, who are not
faithful to me?
I will create a new thing on earth.
The woman will return to the
man."

23 The LORD who rules over all is the God
of Israel. He says, "I will bring them back
from the place where they were taken.
Here is what the people in Judah and its
towns will say once again. 'May the LORD
bless you, you successful city. Sacred
mountain, may he bless you.' 24 People
will live together in Judah and all its
towns. Farmers and shepherds will live
there. 25 I will give rest to those who are
tired. I will satisfy those who are weak."

26 When I heard this, I woke up and
looked around. My sleep had been
pleasant to me.

27 Here is what the LORD announces. "The days are coming when I will
plant the kingdoms of Israel and Judah
again. I will plant them with children
and young animals. 28 I watched over
Israel and Judah to pull them up by the
roots. I tore them down. I crushed them.
I destroyed them. I brought horrible
trouble on them. But now I will watch
over them to build them up and plant
them," announces the LORD. 29 "In those
days people will no longer say,

" 'The parents have eaten sour
grapes.
But the children have a bitter
taste in their mouths.'

30 Instead, everyone will die for their
own sin. The one who eats sour grapes
will taste how bitter they are.

31 "The days are coming," announces
the LORD.
"I will make a new covenant
with the people of Israel.
I will also make it with the
people of Judah.
32 It will not be like the covenant
I made with their people of long
ago.
That was when I took them by the
hand.
I led them out of Egypt.
But they broke my covenant.
They did it even though I was
like a husband to them,"
announces the LORD.
33 "This is the covenant I will make
with Israel
after that time," announces the
LORD.
"I will put my law in their minds.
I will write it on their hearts.
I will be their God.
And they will be my people.
34 They will not need to teach their
neighbor anymore.
And they will not need to teach
one another anymore.
They will not need to say, 'Know
the LORD.'
That's because everyone will know me.
From the least important of them
to the most important,
all of them will know me,"
announces the LORD.
"I will forgive their evil ways.
I will not remember their sins
anymore."

35 The LORD speaks.

He makes the sun
shine by day.
He orders the moon and stars
to shine at night.
He stirs up the ocean.
He makes its waves roar.
His name is the LORD Who Rules
Over All.
36 "Suppose my orders for creation
disappear from my sight,"
announces the LORD.
"Only then will the people of Israel
stop being
a nation in my sight."

37 The LORD says,

"Suppose the sky above could be
measured.
Suppose the foundations of
the earth below could be
completely discovered.
Only then would I turn away the
people of Israel.
Even though they have
committed many sins,
I will still accept them,"
announces the LORD.

38 "The days are coming," announces
the LORD. "At that time Jerusalem will
be rebuilt for me. It will be rebuilt from
the Tower of Hananel to the Corner Gate.
39 The measuring line will reach out
from there. It will go straight to the hill
of Gareb. Then it will turn and reach as
far as Goah. 40 There is a valley where
dead bodies and ashes are thrown. That
whole valley will be holy to me. The side
of the Kidron Valley east of the city will
be holy to me. It will be holy all the way
to the corner of the Horse Gate. The city
will never again be pulled up by the
roots. It will never be destroyed."

Jeremiah Buys a Field

32 A message from the LORD came
to Jeremiah. It came in the 10th
year that Zedekiah was king of Judah.
It was in the 18th year of the rule of
Nebuchadnezzar. 2 The armies of the
king of Babylon were getting ready to
attack Jerusalem. Jeremiah the prophet
was being held as a prisoner. He was
kept in the courtyard of the guard. It
was part of Judah's royal palace.

3 Zedekiah, the king of Judah, had
made Jeremiah a prisoner there. Zedekiah had said to him, "Why do you prophesy as you do? You say, 'The LORD says,
"I am about to hand over this city to the
king of Babylon. He will capture it. 4 Zedekiah, the king of Judah, will not escape
from the powerful hands of the armies
of Babylon. He will certainly be handed
over to the king of Babylon. Zedekiah will
speak with him face to face. He will see
him with his own eyes. 5 Nebuchadnezzar
will take Zedekiah to Babylon. Zedekiah
will remain there until I deal with him,"
announces the LORD. "Suppose you fight
against the armies of Babylon. If you do,
you will not succeed." ' "

6 Jeremiah said, "A message from
the LORD came to me. The LORD said,
7 'Hanamel is going to come to you. He is
the son of your uncle Shallum. Hanamel
will say, "Buy my field at Anathoth. You
are my closest relative. So it's your right
and duty to buy it." '

8 "Then my cousin Hanamel came to
me. I was in the courtyard of the guard.
It happened just as the LORD had said it
would. Hanamel said, 'Buy my field at
Anathoth. It is in the territory of Benjamin. It is your right to buy it and own
it. So buy it for yourself.'

"I knew that this was the LORD's message. 9 So I bought the field at Anathoth
from my cousin Hanamel. I weighed out
seven ounces of silver for him. 10 I signed
and sealed the deed of purchase. I had
some people witness everything. And
I weighed out the silver on the scales.
11 There were two copies of the deed. One
was sealed and the other wasn't. The
deed included the terms and conditions
of the sale. 12 I gave Baruch the copies of
the deed. My cousin Hanamel saw me
do this. The witnesses who had signed
the deed were there too. So were all the
Jews who were sitting in the courtyard
of the guard. Baruch was the son of
Neriah. Neriah was the son of Mahseiah.

13 "I gave Baruch directions in front
of all of them. I said, 14 'The LORD who
rules over all is the God of Israel. He
says, "Take this deed of purchase. Take
the sealed and unsealed copies. Put
them in a clay jar. Then they will last
a long time." 15 The LORD who rules over
all is the God of Israel. He says, "Houses, fields and vineyards will again be
bought in this land." '

16 "I gave the deed of purchase to Baruch, the son of Neriah. Then I prayed
to the LORD. I said,

17 " 'LORD and King, you have
reached out your great and powerful arm. You have made the
heavens and the earth. Nothing is
too hard for you. 18 You show your
love to thousands of people. But
you cause the sins of parents to
affect even their children. Great
and powerful God, your name is
the LORD Who Rules Over All. 19 Your
purposes are great. Your acts are
mighty. Your eyes see everything

people do. You reward each one
of them in keeping with their conduct. You do this based on what
they have done. 20 You performed
signs and wonders in Egypt. And
you have continued to do them
to this day. You have done them
in Israel and among all people.
You are still known for doing them.
21 You brought your people Israel
out of Egypt. You did it with signs
and wonders. You reached out
your mighty hand and powerful
arm. You did great and wonderful
things. 22 You gave Israel this land
that you promised to their people
of long ago. It is a land that has
plenty of milk and honey. 23 Israel
came in and took it over. But they
did not obey you. They didn't follow your law. They didn't do what
you commanded them to do. So
you brought all this trouble on
them.

24 " 'See how ramps are built up
against Jerusalem's walls to attack
it. The city will be handed over to
the armies of Babylon. They are
attacking it. It will fall because of
war, hunger and plague. What you
said would happen is now happening, as you can see. 25 LORD and
King, the city will be handed over
to the armies of Babylon. In spite
of that, you tell me to buy a field.
You say, "Pay for it with silver. And
have the sale witnessed." ' "

26 Then a message from the LORD
came to Jeremiah. The LORD said, 27 "I
am the LORD. I am the God of all people.
Is anything too hard for me?" 28 So the
LORD says, "I am about to hand this
city over to the armies of Babylon. I
will give it to Nebuchadnezzar, the king
of Babylon. He will capture it. 29 The
armies of Babylon are now attacking
this city. They will come in and set it
on fire. They will burn it down. They
will burn down the houses where the
people made me very angry. They
burned incense on their roofs to the
god named Baal. And they poured out
drink offerings to other gods.

30 "The people of Israel and Judah
have done nothing but evil in my eyes.
They have done it since the nation was
young. In fact, they have done nothing
but make me very angry. They have
worshiped statues of gods their own
hands have made," announces the
LORD. 31 "This city has always stirred
up my great anger. It has done it since
the day it was built. Now I must remove
it from my sight. 32 The people of Israel
and Judah have made me very angry.
They have done many evil things. They,
their kings and officials have sinned. So
have their priests and prophets. And the
people of Judah and Jerusalem have
also sinned. 33 They turned their backs
to me. They would not face me. I taught
them again and again. But they would
not listen or pay attention when they
were corrected. 34 They set up the hateful statues of their gods. They did it in
the house where I have put my Name.
They made my house 'unclean.' 35 The
people built high places for Baal in the
Valley of Ben Hinnom. That is where
they sacrifice their children to Molek
in the fire. That is something I did not
command. It did not even enter my
mind. They did something I hate. They
made Judah sin."

36 Here is what you people of Judah
are saying about this city. "By war, hunger and plague it will be handed over to
the king of Babylon." But here is what
the LORD, the God of Israel, says. 37 "You
can be sure that I will gather my people again. I will send them away when
my burning anger blazes out against
them. But I will bring them back to this
place. And I will let them live in safety.
38 They will be my people. And I will be
their God. 39 I will give them a single
purpose in life. Then, they will always
have respect for me. Then all will go
well for them. And it will also go well
for their children after them. 40 I will
make a covenant with them that will
last forever. I promise that I will never
stop doing good to them. I will cause
them to respect me. Then they will never
turn away from me again. 41 I will take
pleasure in doing good things for them.
I will certainly plant them in this land.
I will do these things with all my heart
and soul."

42 The LORD says, "I have brought all
this horrible trouble on these people.
But now I will give them all the good
things I have promised them. 43 Once

more fields will be bought in this land. It is the land about which you now say, 'It is a dry and empty desert. It doesn't have any people or animals in it. It has been handed over to the armies of Babylon.' 44 Fields will be bought with silver. Deeds will be signed, sealed and witnessed. That will be done in the territory of Benjamin. It will be done in the villages around Jerusalem and in the towns of Judah. It will also be done in the towns of the central hill country. And it will be done in the towns of the western hills and the Negev Desert. I will bless their people with great success again," announces the LORD.

The LORD Promises to Heal His People

33 Jeremiah was still being held as a prisoner. He was kept in the courtyard of the guard. Then another message from the LORD came to him. The LORD said, 2 "I made the earth. I formed it. And I set it in place. The LORD is my name. 3 Call out to me. I will answer you. I will tell you great things you do not know. And unless I do, you wouldn't be able to find out about them." 4 The LORD is the God of Israel. He speaks about the houses in Jerusalem. He talks about the royal palaces of Judah. The people had torn down many of them. They had used their stones to strengthen the city walls against attack. 5 That was during their fight with the armies of Babylon. The LORD says, "The houses will be filled with dead bodies. They will be the bodies of the people I will kill. I will kill them when I am very angry with them. I will hide my face from this city. That's because its people have committed so many sins.

6 "But now I will bring health and healing to Jerusalem. I will heal my people. I will let them enjoy great peace and security. 7 I will bring Judah and Israel back from the places where they have been taken. I will build up the nation again. It will be just as it was before. 8 I will wash from its people all the sins they have committed against me. And I will forgive all the sins they committed when they turned away from me. 9 Then this city will bring me fame, joy, praise and honor. All the nations on earth will hear about the good things I do for this city. They will see the great success and peace I give it. Then they will be filled with wonder. And they will tremble with fear."

10 The LORD says, "You say about this place, 'It's a dry and empty desert. It doesn't have any people or animals in it.' The towns of Judah and the streets of Jerusalem are now deserted. So they do not have any people or animals living in them. But happy sounds will be heard there once more. 11 They will be the sounds of joy and gladness. The voices of brides and grooms will fill the streets. And the voices of those who bring thank offerings to my house will be heard there. They will say,

"'Give thanks to the LORD who rules
over all,
because he is good.
His faithful love continues
forever.'

That's because I will bless this land with great success again. It will be as it was before," says the LORD.

12 The LORD who rules over all says, "This place is a desert. It does not have any people or animals in it. But there will again be grasslands near all its towns. Shepherds will rest their flocks there. 13 Flocks will again pass under the hands of shepherds as they count their sheep," says the LORD. "That will be done in the towns of the central hill country. It will be done in the western hills and the Negev Desert. It will be done in the territory of Benjamin. And it will be done in the villages around Jerusalem and in the towns of Judah.

14 "The days are coming," announces the LORD. "At that time I will fulfill my good promise to my people. I made it to the people of Israel and Judah.

15 "Here is what I will do in those days
and at that time.
I will make a godly Branch grow
from David's royal line.
He will do what is fair and right
in the land.
16 In those days Judah will be saved.
Jerusalem will live in safety.
And it will be called
The LORD Who Makes Us Right
With Himself."

17 The LORD says, "David will always have a son to sit on the throne of

Israel. 18 The priests, who are Levites,
will always have a man to serve me.
He will sacrifice burnt offerings. He will
burn grain offerings. And he will offer
sacrifices."

19 A message from the LORD came to
Jeremiah. 20 The LORD said, "Could you
ever break my covenant with the day?
Could you ever break my covenant with
the night? Could you ever stop day and
night from coming at their appointed
times? 21 Only then could my covenant
with my servant David be broken. Only
then could my covenant with the Levites who serve me as priests be broken.
Only then would David no longer have
someone from his family line to rule on
his throne. 22 Here is what I will do for
my servant David. And here is what I
will do for the Levites who serve me. I
will make their children after them as
many as the stars in the sky. And I will
make them as many as the grains of
sand on the seashore. It will be impossible to count them."

23 A message from the LORD came to
Jeremiah. The LORD said, 24 "Haven't
you noticed what these people are saying? They say, 'The LORD once chose the
two kingdoms of Israel and Judah. But
now he has turned his back on them.'
So they hate my people. They do not
think of them as a nation anymore.
25 I say, 'What if I had not made my
covenant with day and night? What if I
had not established the laws of heaven
and earth? 26 Only then would I turn my
back on the children of Jacob and my
servant David. Only then would I not
choose one of David's sons to rule over
the children of Abraham, Isaac and
Jacob. But I will bless my people with
great success again. I will love them
with tender love.' "

Zedekiah Is Warned

34 Nebuchadnezzar, the king of
Babylon, and all his armies
were fighting against Jerusalem. They
were also fighting against all the towns
around it. All the kingdoms and nations Nebuchadnezzar ruled over were
helping him. At that time a message
from the LORD came to Jeremiah. The
LORD said, 2 "I am the LORD, the God
of Israel. Go to Zedekiah, the king of
Judah. Tell him, 'The LORD says, "I am
about to hand this city over to the king
of Babylon. He will burn it down. 3 You
will not escape from his power. You will
certainly be captured. You will be handed over to him. You will see the king of
Babylon with your own eyes. He will
speak with you face to face. And you
will go to Babylon.

4 " ' "But listen to the LORD's promise
to you, Zedekiah king of Judah. I say
that you will not be killed by a sword.
5 You will die in a peaceful way. People
made fires to honor the kings who died
before you. In the same way, they will
make a fire in your honor. They will
mourn for you. They will say, 'My poor
master!' I myself make this promise,"
announces the LORD.' "

6 Then Jeremiah the prophet told all
this to King Zedekiah in Jerusalem. 7 At
that time Nebuchadnezzar's armies
were fighting against Jerusalem. They
were also fighting against Lachish and
Azekah. These two cities were still holding out. They were the only cities left in
Judah that had high walls around them.

The People Set Their Slaves Free

8 A message from the LORD came to
Jeremiah. King Zedekiah had made a
covenant with all the people in Jerusalem. He had told them to set their Hebrew slaves free. 9 All of them had to do
this. That applied to male and female
slaves alike. No one was allowed to hold
another Hebrew as a slave. 10 So all the
officials and people entered into this
covenant. They agreed to set their male
and female slaves free. They agreed
not to hold them as slaves anymore.
Instead, they set them free. 11 But later
they changed their minds. They took
back the people they had set free. They
made them slaves again.

12 Then a message from the LORD
came to Jeremiah. 13 The LORD is the
God of Israel. He says, "I made a covenant with your people of long ago. I
brought them out of Egypt. That is the
land where they were slaves. I said,
14 'Every seventh year you must set your
people free. Each of you must set free all
the Hebrews who have sold themselves
to you. Let them serve you for six years.
Then you must let them go free.' *(Deuteronomy 15:12)* But your people of long
ago did not listen to me. They did not

pay any attention to me. 15 Recently you
turned away from your sins. You did
what is right in my eyes. Each of you set
your Hebrew slaves free. You even made
a covenant in front of me. You did it in
the house where I have put my Name.
16 But now you have turned around. You
have treated my name as if it were not
holy. Each of you has taken back your
male and female slaves. You had set
them free to go where they wished. But
now you have forced them to become
your slaves again."

17 So the LORD says, "You have not
obeyed me. You have not set your
Hebrew slaves free. So now I will set
you free," announces the LORD. "I will
set you free to be destroyed by war,
plague and hunger. I will make all the
kingdoms on earth displeased with you.
18 Those people who have broken my
covenant will be punished. They have
not lived up to the terms of the covenant
they made in front of me. When you
made that covenant, you cut a calf in
two. Then you walked between its pieces. Now I will cut you to pieces. 19 That
includes all of you who walked between
the pieces of the calf. It includes the
leaders of Judah and Jerusalem, the
court officials and the priests. It also
includes some of the people of the land.
20 So I will hand over all those people
to their enemies who want to kill them.
Their dead bodies will become food for
the birds and the wild animals.

21 "I will hand over King Zedekiah
and his officials to their enemies. I will
hand them over to those who want to
kill them. I will hand them over to the
armies of the king of Babylon. They
have now pulled back from you. 22 But
I am going to give an order," announces
the LORD. "I will bring them back to this
city. They will fight against it. They will
capture it and burn it down. And I will
completely destroy the towns of Judah.
No one will be able to live there."

The Family Line of Rekab

35 A message from the LORD came
to Jeremiah. It came during the
time Jehoiakim was king over Judah.
Jehoiakim was the son of Josiah. The
message said, 2 "Go to the members of
the family line of Rekab. Invite them
to come to one of the side rooms in my
house. Then give them wine to drink."

3 So I went to get Jaazaniah. He was
the son of Jeremiah. Jeremiah was the
son of Habazziniah. I also went to get
Jaazaniah's brothers and all his sons.
That included all the members of the
family line of Rekab. 4 I brought them
into the LORD's house. I took them into
the room of the sons of Hanan. He was
the son of Igdaliah. He was also a man
of God. His room was next to the room
of the officials. Their room was above
the room of Maaseiah. He was the son
of Shallum. He also was one of those
who guarded the temple doors. 5 Then
I got bowls full of wine and some cups. I
set them down in front of the men from
the family line of Rekab. I said to them,
"Drink some wine."

6 But they replied, "We don't drink
wine. That's because Jehonadab gave
us a command. He was the son of Rekab.
He was also one of our own people
from long ago. He commanded, 'You
and your children after you must never drink wine. 7 Also you must never
build houses. You must never plant
crops or vineyards. You must never
have any of these things. Instead, you
must always live in tents. Then you
will live a long time in the land where
you are wandering around.' 8 We have
done everything Jehonadab, the son
of Rekab, commanded us to do. So we
and our wives and our children have
never drunk wine. 9 We have never built
houses to live in. We've never had vineyards, fields or crops. 10 We've always
lived in tents. We've completely obeyed
everything Jehonadab commanded our
people of long ago. 11 But Nebuchadnezzar, the king of Babylon, marched into
this land. Then we said, 'Come. We must
go to Jerusalem. There we can escape
the armies of Babylon and Aram.' So we
have remained in Jerusalem."

12 Then a message from the LORD
came to Jeremiah. It said, 13 "The LORD
who rules over all is the God of Israel.
He says, 'Go. Speak to the people of Judah and Jerusalem. Tell them, "Won't
you ever learn a lesson? Won't you
ever obey my words?" announces the
LORD. 14 "Jehonadab, the son of Rekab,
ordered his children not to drink wine.
And they have kept his command. To

this day they do not drink wine. They obey the command Jehonadab gave their people long ago. But I have spoken to you again and again. In spite of that, you have not obeyed me. [15]Again and again I sent all my servants the prophets to you. They said, 'Each of you must turn from your evil ways. You must change the way you act. Do not worship other gods. Do not serve them. Then you will live in the land. I gave it to you and your people of long ago.' But you have not paid any attention. You have not listened to me. [16]The children of Jehonadab, the son of Rekab, have obeyed the command Jehonadab gave them long ago. But the people of Judah have not obeyed me." ' "

[17]So the LORD God who rules over all speaks. The God of Israel says, "Listen! I am going to bring horrible trouble on Judah. I will also bring it on everyone who lives in Jerusalem. I will bring on them every trouble I said I would. I spoke to them. But they did not listen. I called out to them. But they did not answer."

[18]Then Jeremiah spoke to the members of the family line of Rekab. Jeremiah said, "The LORD who rules over all is the God of Israel. He says, 'You have obeyed the command Jehonadab gave your people of long ago. You have followed all his directions. You have done everything he ordered.' [19]So the LORD who rules over all speaks. The God of Israel says, 'Jehonadab, the son of Rekab, will always have someone from his family line to serve me.' "

Jehoiakim Burns Up Jeremiah's Scroll

36 A message from the LORD came to Jeremiah. It came in the fourth year that Jehoiakim was king of Judah. He was the son of Josiah. The message said, [2]"Get a scroll. Write on it all the words I have spoken to you. Write down what I have said about Israel, Judah and all the other nations. Write what I have said to you from the time of King Josiah until now. [3]The people of Judah will hear about all the trouble I plan to bring on them. Maybe then each of them will turn from their evil ways. If they do, I will forgive their sins and the evil things they have done."

[4]So Jeremiah sent for Baruch, the son of Neriah. Jeremiah told him to write down all the words the LORD had spoken to him. And Baruch wrote them on the scroll. [5]Then Jeremiah said to him, "I'm not allowed to go to the LORD's temple. [6]So you go there. Go on a day when the people are fasting. Read to them from the scroll. Read the words of the LORD you wrote down as I gave them to you. Read them to all the people of Judah who come in from their towns. [7]They will hear what the LORD will do to them when his burning anger blazes out against them. Then perhaps they will pray to him. And maybe each of them will turn from their evil ways."

[8]Baruch, the son of Neriah, did everything Jeremiah the prophet told him to do. He went to the LORD's temple. There he read the words of the LORD from the scroll. [9]It was in the fifth year that Jehoiakim, the son of Josiah, was king of Judah. It was the ninth month of that year. A time of fasting at the LORD's temple had been ordered. All the people in Jerusalem were told to take part in it. So were those who had come in from the towns of Judah. [10]Baruch read to all the people who were at the LORD's temple. He read Jeremiah's words from the scroll. He was in the room of Gemariah the secretary. It was located in the upper courtyard at the entrance of the New Gate of the temple. Gemariah was the son of Shaphan.

[11]Micaiah was the son of Gemariah, the son of Shaphan. Micaiah heard Baruch reading all the LORD's words that were written on the scroll. [12]Then he went down to the secretary's room in the royal palace. All the officials were sitting there. They included the secretary Elishama and Delaiah, the son of Shemaiah. Elnathan, the son of Akbor, was also there. So was Gemariah, the son of Shaphan. Zedekiah, the son of Hananiah, was there too. And so were all the other officials. [13]Micaiah told all of them what he had heard. He told them everything Baruch had read to the people from the scroll. [14]All the officials sent Jehudi to speak to Baruch, the son of Neriah. Jehudi was the son of Nethaniah. Nethaniah was the son of Shelemiah. Shelemiah was the son of Cushi. Jehudi said to Baruch, "Come.

Bring the scroll you have read to the
people." So Baruch went to them. He
carried the scroll with him. 15 The officials said to him, "Please sit down. Read
the scroll to us."

So Baruch read it to them. 16 They
heard all its words. Then they looked
at one another in fear. They said to
Baruch, "We must report all these words
to the king." 17 They said to Baruch, "Tell
us. How did you happen to write all
these things? Did Jeremiah tell you to
do this?"

18 "Yes," Baruch replied. "He told me
to write down all these words. So I wrote
them in ink on the scroll."

19 Then the officials spoke to Baruch.
They said, "You and Jeremiah must go
and hide. Don't let anyone know where
you are."

20 The officials put the scroll in the
room of Elishama the secretary. Then
they went to the king in the courtyard.
They reported everything to him. 21 The
king sent Jehudi to get the scroll. Jehudi
brought it from the room of Elishama
the secretary. Jehudi read it to the king.
All the officials were standing beside the
king. So they heard it too. 22 It was the
ninth month. The king was sitting in his
winter apartment. A fire was burning
in the fire pot in front of him. 23 Jehudi
read three or four sections from the
scroll. Then the king cut them off with
a secretary's knife. He threw them into
the fire pot. He did that until the entire
scroll was burned up in the fire. 24 The
king and some of his attendants heard
all these words. But they weren't afraid.
They didn't tear their clothes. 25 Elnathan, Delaiah and Gemariah begged
the king not to burn the scroll. But he
wouldn't listen to them. 26 Instead, the
king commanded three men to arrest
Baruch the secretary and Jeremiah
the prophet. But the LORD had hidden
them. The three men were Jerahmeel,
Seraiah and Shelemiah. Jerahmeel was
a member of the royal court. Seraiah
was the son of Azriel. And Shelemiah
was the son of Abdeel.

27 A message from the LORD came to
Jeremiah. It came after the king burned
the scroll. On the scroll were the words
Baruch had written down. Jeremiah
had told him to write them. The message said, 28 "Get another scroll. Write
on it all the words that were on the first
one. King Jehoiakim burned that one
up. 29 Also tell King Jehoiakim, 'The
LORD says, "You burned that scroll. You
said to Baruch, 'Why did you write that
the king of Babylon would certainly
come? Why did you write that he would
destroy this land? And why did you
write that he would remove from it
people and animals alike?' " 30 So now
the LORD has something to say about
Jehoiakim, the king of Judah. He says,
"No one from Jehoiakim's family line
will sit on David's throne. Jehoiakim's
body will be thrown out. It will lie
outside in the heat by day and in the
frost at night. 31 I will punish him and
his children and his attendants. I will
punish them for their sinful ways. I will
bring on them all the trouble I said I
would. And I will bring it on the people
of Jerusalem and Judah. They have not
listened to me." ' "

32 So Jeremiah got another scroll. He
gave it to Baruch the secretary. He was
the son of Neriah. Jeremiah told Baruch
what to write on it. Baruch wrote down
all the words that were on the scroll
King Jehoiakim had burned up in the
fire. And many more words were written
on it. They were similar to those that
had already been written.

Jeremiah Is Put in Prison

37 Nebuchadnezzar, the king of
Babylon, appointed Zedekiah
to be king of Judah. He was the son
of Josiah. Zedekiah ruled in place of
Jehoiachin, the son of Jehoiakim. 2 Zedekiah and his attendants didn't pay
any attention to what the LORD had
said through Jeremiah the prophet.
And the people of the land didn't pay
any attention either.

3 But King Zedekiah sent Jehukal to
Jeremiah the prophet. Zedekiah sent
Zephaniah the priest along with him.
Jehukal was the son of Shelemiah.
Zephaniah was the son of Maaseiah.
Jehukal and Zephaniah brought the
king's message to Jeremiah. It said,
"Please pray to the LORD our God for us."

4 At that time Jeremiah was free to
come and go among the people. Jeremiah had not yet been put in prison.
5 The armies of Babylon were attacking
Jerusalem. They received a report that

Pharaoh's army had marched out of Egypt to help Zedekiah. So armies of Babylon pulled back from Jerusalem.

6 A message from the LORD came to Jeremiah. 7 The LORD is the God of Israel. He says, "The king of Judah has sent you to ask me for advice. Tell him, 'Pharaoh's army has marched out to help you. But it will go back to its own land. It will return to Egypt. 8 Then the armies of Babylon will come back here. They will attack this city. They will capture it. Then they will burn it down.'

9 "The LORD says, 'Do not fool yourselves. You think, "The Babylonians will leave us alone." But they will not! 10 Suppose you destroy all the armies of Babylon that are attacking you. Suppose only wounded men are left in their tents. Even then they will come out and burn down this city.' "

11 The armies of Babylon had pulled back from Jerusalem because of Pharaoh's army. 12 So Jeremiah started to leave the city. He was planning to go to the territory of Benjamin. Jeremiah wanted to get his share of the property among the people there. 13 He got as far as the Benjamin Gate. But the captain of the guard arrested him. He said, "You are going over to the side of the Babylonians!" The captain's name was Irijah, the son of Shelemiah. Shelemiah was the son of Hananiah.

14 Jeremiah said to Irijah, "That isn't true! I'm not going to the side of the Babylonians." But Irijah wouldn't listen to him. Instead, he arrested Jeremiah. He brought Jeremiah to the officials. 15 They were angry with him. So they had him beaten. Then they took him to the house of Jonathan the secretary. It had been made into a prison. That's where they put Jeremiah.

16 Jeremiah was put into a prison cell below ground level. He remained there a long time. 17 Then King Zedekiah sent for him. King Zedekiah had Jeremiah brought to the palace. There the king spoke to him in private. The king asked, "Do you have a message from the LORD for me?"

"Yes," Jeremiah replied. "You will be handed over to the king of Babylon."

18 Then Jeremiah continued, "Why have you put me in prison? What crime have I committed against you? What have I done to your attendants or these people? 19 Where are your prophets who prophesied to you? They said, 'The king of Babylon won't attack you. He won't march into this land.' 20 But now please listen, my king and master. Let me make my appeal to you. Please don't send me back to the house of Jonathan the secretary. If you do, I'll die there."

21 Then King Zedekiah gave the order. His men put Jeremiah in the courtyard of the guard. They gave him a loaf of bread from the street of the bakers. They did it every day until all the bread in the city was gone. So Jeremiah remained in the courtyard of the guard.

Jeremiah Is Thrown Into an Empty Well

38 Shephatiah, Gedaliah, Jehukal and Pashhur heard what Jeremiah was telling all the people. Shephatiah was the son of Mattan. Gedaliah was the son of Pashhur. Jehukal was the son of Shelemiah. And Pashhur was the son of Malkijah. These four men heard Jeremiah say, 2 "The LORD says, 'Those who stay in this city will die of war, hunger or plague. But those who go over to the side of the Babylonians will live. They will escape with their lives. They will remain alive.' 3 The LORD also says, 'This city will certainly be handed over to the armies of the king of Babylon. They will capture it.' "

4 Then these officials said to the king, "This man should be put to death. What he says is making the soldiers who are left in this city lose hope. It's making all the people lose hope too. He isn't interested in what is best for the people. In fact, he's trying to destroy them."

5 "He's in your hands," King Zedekiah answered. "I can't do anything to oppose you."

6 So they took Jeremiah and put him into an empty well. It belonged to Malkijah. He was a member of the royal court. His well was in the courtyard of the guard. Zedekiah's men lowered Jeremiah by ropes into the well. It didn't have any water in it. All it had was mud. And Jeremiah sank down into the mud.

7 Ebed-Melek was an official in the royal palace. He was from the land of Cush. He heard that Jeremiah had been put into the well. The king was sitting by

the Benjamin Gate at that time. 8 Ebed-Melek went out of the palace. He said to the king, 9 "My king and master, everything these men have done to Jeremiah the prophet is evil. They have thrown him into an empty well. Soon there won't be any more bread in the city. Then he'll starve to death."

10 So the king gave an order to Ebed-Melek the Cushite. He said, "Take with you 30 men from here. Lift Jeremiah the prophet out of the well before he dies."

11 Then Ebed-Melek took the men with him. He went to a room in the palace. It was under the place where the treasures were stored. He got some old rags and worn-out clothes from there. Then he let them down with ropes to Jeremiah in the well. 12 Ebed-Melek the Cushite told Jeremiah what to do. Ebed-Melek said, "Put these old rags and worn-out clothes under your arms. They'll pad the ropes." So Jeremiah did. 13 Then the men pulled him up with the ropes. They lifted him out of the well. And Jeremiah remained in the courtyard of the guard.

Zedekiah Questions Jeremiah Again

14 Then King Zedekiah sent for Jeremiah the prophet. The king had him brought to the third entrance to the LORD's temple. "I want to ask you something," the king said to Jeremiah. "Don't hide anything from me."

15 Jeremiah said to Zedekiah, "Suppose I give you an answer. You will kill me, won't you? Suppose I give you good advice. You won't listen to me, will you?"

16 But King Zedekiah promised Jeremiah secretly, "I won't kill you. And I won't hand you over to those who want to kill you. That's just as sure as the LORD is alive. He's the one who has given us breath."

17 So Jeremiah said to Zedekiah, "The LORD God who rules over all is the God of Israel. He says, 'Give yourself up to the officers of the king of Babylon. Then your life will be spared. And this city will not be burned down. You and your family will remain alive. 18 But what if you do not give yourself up to them? Then this city will be handed over to the Babylonians. They will burn it down. And you yourself will not escape from them.' "

19 King Zedekiah said to Jeremiah, "I'm afraid of some of the Jews. They are the ones who have gone over to the side of the Babylonians. The Babylonians might hand me over to them. And those Jews will treat me badly."

20 "They won't hand you over to them," Jeremiah replied. "Obey the LORD. Do what I tell you to do. Then things will go well with you. Your life will be spared. 21 Don't refuse to give yourself up. The LORD has shown me what will happen if you do. 22 All the women who are left in your palace will be brought out. They'll be given to the officials of the king of Babylon. Those women will say to you,

" 'Your trusted friends have tricked
you.
They have gotten the best of you.
Your feet are sunk down in the
mud.
Your friends have deserted you.'

23 "All your wives and children will be brought out to the Babylonians. You yourself won't escape from them. You will be captured by the king of Babylon. And this city will be burned down."

24 Then Zedekiah said to Jeremiah, "Don't let anyone know about the talk we've had. If you do, you might die. 25 Suppose the officials find out that I've talked with you. And suppose they come to you and say, 'Tell us what you said to the king. Tell us what the king said to you. Don't hide it from us. If you do, we'll kill you.' 26 Then tell them, 'I was begging the king not to send me back to Jonathan's house. I don't want to die there.' "

27 All the officials came to Jeremiah. And they questioned him. He told them everything the king had ordered him to say. None of them had heard what he told the king. So they didn't say anything else to him.

28 Jeremiah remained in the courtyard of the guard. He stayed there until the day Jerusalem was captured.

Jerusalem Is Destroyed

39 Here is how Jerusalem was captured. 1 Nebuchadnezzar, the king of Babylon, marched out against Jerusalem. He came with all his armies and attacked it. It was in the ninth year

that Zedekiah was king of Judah. It
was in the tenth month. [2]The city wall
was broken through. It happened on
the ninth day of the fourth month. It
was in the 11th year of Zedekiah's rule.
[3]All the officials of the king of Babylon
came. They took seats near the Middle
Gate. Nergal-Sharezer from Samgar was
there. Nebo-Sarsekim, a chief officer,
was also there. So was Nergal-Sharezer,
a high official. And all the other officials
of the king of Babylon were there too.
[4]King Zedekiah and all the soldiers saw
them. Then they ran away. They left the
city at night. They went by way of the
king's garden. They went out through
the gate between the two walls. And
they headed toward the Arabah Valley.
[5]But the armies of Babylon chased
them. They caught up with Zedekiah in
the plains near Jericho. They captured
him there. And they took him to Nebuchadnezzar, the king of Babylon. He was
at Riblah in the land of Hamath. That's
where Nebuchadnezzar decided how
Zedekiah would be punished. [6]The king
of Babylon killed the sons of Zedekiah
at Riblah. He forced Zedekiah to watch
it with his own eyes. He also killed all
the nobles of Judah. [7]Then he poked out
Zedekiah's eyes. He put him in bronze
chains. And he took him to Babylon.
[8]The Babylonians set the royal palace on fire. They also set fire to the houses of the people. And they broke down
the walls of Jerusalem. [9]Nebuzaradan
was commander of the royal guard.
Some people still remained in the city.
But he took them away to Babylon as
prisoners. He also took along those who
had gone over to his side. And he took
the rest of the people. [10]Nebuzaradan,
the commander of the guard, left some
of the poor people of Judah behind.
They didn't own anything. So at that
time he gave them vineyards and fields.
[11]Nebuchadnezzar, the king of Babylon, had given orders about Jeremiah.
He had given them to Nebuzaradan,
the commander of the royal guard.
Nebuchadnezzar had said, [12]"Take him.
Look after him. Don't harm him. Do
for him anything he asks." [13]So that's
what Nebuzaradan, the commander
of the guard, did. Nebushazban and
Nergal-Sharezer were with him. So
were all the other officers of the king
of Babylon. Nebushazban was a chief
officer. Nergal-Sharezer was a high official. All these men [14]sent for Jeremiah.
They had him taken out of the courtyard of the guard. They turned him over
to Gedaliah. Gedaliah was the son of
Ahikam, the son of Shaphan. They told
Gedaliah to take Jeremiah back to his
home. So Jeremiah remained among
his own people.
[15]A message from the LORD came to
Jeremiah. It came while he was being
kept in the courtyard of the guard. The
LORD said, [16]"Go. Speak to Ebed-Melek
the Cushite. Tell him, 'The LORD who
rules over all is the God of Israel. He
says, "I am about to make the words
I spoke against this city come true. I
will not give success to it. Instead, I will
bring horrible trouble on it. At that time
my words will come true. You will see
it with your own eyes. [17]But I will save
you on that day," announces the LORD.
"You will not be handed over to those
you are afraid of. [18]I will save you. You
will not be killed by a sword. Instead,
you will escape with your life. That's
because you trust in me," announces
the LORD.'"

Jeremiah Is Set Free From His Chains

40 A message from the LORD
came to Jeremiah. It came
after Nebuzaradan, the commander
of the royal guard, had set him free at
Ramah. Jeremiah was being held by
chains when Nebuzaradan found him.
Jeremiah was among all the prisoners
from Jerusalem and Judah. They were
being taken to Babylon. [2]But the commander of the guard found Jeremiah.
The commander said to him, "The LORD
your God ordered that this place be destroyed. [3]And now he has brought it
about. He has done exactly what he
said he would do. All these things have
happened because you people sinned
against the LORD. You didn't obey him.
[4]But today I'm setting you free from the
chains on your wrists. Come with me to
Babylon if you want to. I'll take good
care of you there. But if you don't want
to come, then don't. The whole country
lies in front of you. Go anywhere you
want to." [5]But before Jeremiah turned
to go, Nebuzaradan continued, "Go back
to Gedaliah, the son of Ahikam. The

king of Babylon has appointed Gedaliah to be over the towns of Judah. Go and
live with him among your people. Or go
anywhere else you want to." Ahikam
was the son of Shaphan.

The commander gave Jeremiah food
and water. He also gave him a gift. Then
he let Jeremiah go. 6 So Jeremiah went
to Mizpah to see Gedaliah, the son of
Ahikam. Jeremiah stayed with him.
Jeremiah lived among the people who
were left behind in the land.

Gedaliah Is Murdered

7 Some of Judah's army officers and
their men were still in the open country.
They heard that the king of Babylon
had appointed Gedaliah as governor
over Judah. Gedaliah was the son of
Ahikam. The king had put Gedaliah in
charge of the men, women and children who were still there. They were
the poorest people in the land. They
hadn't been taken to Babylon. 8 When
the army officers and their men heard
these things, they came to Gedaliah at
Mizpah. Ishmael, the son of Nethaniah,
came. So did Johanan and Jonathan,
the sons of Kareah. Seraiah, the son
of Tanhumeth, also came. The sons
of Ephai from Netophah came too.
And so did Jaazaniah, the son of the
Maakathite. All their men came with
them. 9 Gedaliah, the son of Ahikam,
the son of Shaphan, made a promise.
He made the promise to give hope to all
these men. He spoke in a kind way to
them. He said, "Don't be afraid to serve
the Babylonians. Make your homes in
the land of Judah. Serve the king of
Babylon. Then things will go well with
you. 10 I myself will stay at Mizpah. I'll
speak for you to the officials of Babylon
who come to us. But you must harvest
the wine, summer fruit and olive oil. Put
them in your jars. Store them up. And
live in the towns you have taken over."

11 All the Jews in Moab, Ammon and
Edom heard what had happened. So did
the Jews in all the other countries. They
heard that the king of Babylon had left
some people behind in Judah. They also
heard that he had appointed Gedaliah,
the son of Ahikam, as governor over
them. Ahikam was the son of Shaphan.
12 When they heard these things, all of
them came back to the land of Judah.
They went to Gedaliah at Mizpah. They
came from all the countries where they
had been scattered. And they harvested
a large amount of wine and summer
fruit.

13 Johanan and all the other army
officers still in the open country came
to Gedaliah at Mizpah. Johanan was the
son of Kareah. 14 The officers spoke to
Gedaliah. They said, "Don't you know
that Baalis has sent someone to take
your life? Baalis is the king of Ammon.
He has sent Ishmael, the son of Nethaniah." But Gedaliah, the son of Ahikam,
didn't believe them.

15 Then Johanan, the son of Kareah,
spoke in private to Gedaliah in Mizpah.
He said, "Let me go and kill Ishmael,
the son of Nethaniah. No one will know
about it. Why should he take your life?
Why should he cause all the Jews gathered around you to be scattered? Why
should he cause the people who remain
in Judah to die?"

16 But Gedaliah, the son of Ahikam,
spoke to Johanan, the son of Kareah. He
said, "Don't do an awful thing like that!
What you are saying about Ishmael
isn't true."

41 In the seventh month Ishmael
came with ten men to Gedaliah,
the son of Ahikam, at Mizpah. Ishmael
was the son of Nethaniah. Nethaniah
was the son of Elishama. Ishmael was
a member of the royal family. He had
been one of the king's officers. Ishmael
and his ten men were eating together at
Mizpah. 2 They got up and struck down
Gedaliah, the son of Ahikam, with their
swords. They killed him even though
the king of Babylon had appointed him
as governor over Judah. Ahikam was
the son of Shaphan. 3 Ishmael also killed
all the men of Judah who were with
Gedaliah at Mizpah. And he killed the
Babylonian soldiers who were there.

4 On the next day, people still hadn't
found out that Gedaliah had been murdered. 5 On that day 80 men came from
Shechem, Shiloh and Samaria. They
had shaved off their beards. They had
torn their clothes. And they had cut
themselves. They brought grain offerings and incense with them. They took
them to the LORD's house. 6 Ishmael,
the son of Nethaniah, went out from
Mizpah to meet them. He was weeping

as he went. When he met them, he said,
"Come to Gedaliah, the son of Ahikam."
7 They went with him into the city. Then
Ishmael, the son of Nethaniah, and the
men who were with him killed them.
And they threw them into an empty
well. 8 But ten of the men had spoken
to Ishmael. They had said, "Don't kill
us! We have some wheat and barley.
We also have olive oil and honey. We've
hidden all of it in a field." So he didn't kill
them along with the others. 9 But he had
thrown into the empty well all the bodies
of the men he had killed. That included
Gedaliah's body. The well was the one
King Asa had made. He had made it
when he strengthened Mizpah against
attack by Baasha, the king of Israel.
Ishmael, the son of Nethaniah, filled it
with the bodies of those he had killed.

10 Nebuzaradan was the commander
of the royal guard. He had appointed
Gedaliah son of Ahikam over all the
people at Mizpah. But Ishmael made
prisoners of the people left at Mizpah.
These prisoners included women who
were members of the royal court. The
prisoners also included everyone else
left at Mizpah. Then Ishmael started
out to go across the Jordan River to the
land of Ammon.

11 Johanan, the son of Kareah, was told
what had happened. And so were all
the other army officers with him. They
heard about all the crimes Ishmael, the
son of Nethaniah, had committed. 12 So
they brought all their men together.
Then they went to fight against Ishmael,
the son of Nethaniah. They caught up
with him near the large pool in Gibeon.
13 Ishmael had many people with him.
They saw Johanan, the son of Kareah.
And they saw the other army officers
who were with him. So the people who
had been forced to go with Ishmael were
glad. 14 Ishmael had taken those people
from Mizpah as prisoners. But now they
turned and went over to the side of Johanan, the son of Kareah. 15 But Ishmael,
the son of Nethaniah, and eight of his
men escaped from Johanan. They ran
away to the land of Ammon.

Some Jews Take Jeremiah to Egypt

16 Then Johanan, the son of Kareah,
led away all the people of Mizpah who
were still alive. All the other army
officers with Johanan helped him do
this. He had taken them away from
Ishmael, the son of Nethaniah. That
happened after Ishmael had murdered
Gedaliah, the son of Ahikam. The people Johanan had taken away included
soldiers, women, children and court
officials. He had brought them from
Gibeon. 17 They went on their way. They
stopped at Geruth Kimham near Bethlehem. They were going to Egypt. 18 They
wanted to get away from the Babylonians. They were afraid of them. That's
because Ishmael, the son of Nethaniah,
had killed Gedaliah, the son of Ahikam.
The king of Babylon had appointed
Gedaliah as governor over Judah.

42 Then all the army officers approached Jeremiah. They included Johanan, the son of Kareah, and
Jezaniah, the son of Hoshaiah. All the
people from the least important of them
to the most important also came. 2 All
of them said to Jeremiah the prophet,
"Please listen to our appeal. Pray to the
LORD your God. Pray for all of us who
are left here. Once there were many of
us. But as you can see, only a few of us
are left now. 3 So pray to the LORD your
God. Pray that he'll tell us where we
should go. Pray that he'll tell us what
we should do."

4 "I've heard you," Jeremiah the
prophet replied. "I'll certainly pray to
the LORD your God. I'll do what you
have asked me to do. In fact, I'll tell you
everything the LORD says. I won't keep
anything back from you."

5 Then they said to Jeremiah, "We'll
do everything the LORD your God sends
you to tell us to do. If we don't, may he
be a true and faithful witness against
us. 6 It doesn't matter whether what you
say is in our favor or not. We're asking
you to pray to the LORD our God. And
we'll obey him. Things will go well with
us. That's because we will obey the LORD
our God."

7 Ten days later a message came to
Jeremiah from the LORD. 8 So Jeremiah
sent for Johanan, the son of Kareah,
and all the other army officers with
him. Jeremiah also gathered together
all the people from the least important
of them to the most important. 9 He
said to all of them, "The LORD is the
God of Israel. You asked me to present

your appeal to him. He told me, 10 'Stay
in this land. Then I will build you up.
I will not tear you down. I will plant
you. I will not pull you up by the roots.
I have decided to stop bringing trouble
on you. 11 Do not be afraid of the king
of Babylon. You are afraid of him now.
Do not be,' announces the LORD. 'I am
with you. I will keep you safe. I will save
you from his power. 12 I will show you
my loving concern. Then he will have
concern for you. And he will let you
return to your land.'

13 "But suppose you say, 'We won't
stay in this land.' If you do, you will be
disobeying the LORD your God. 14 And
suppose you say, 'No! We'll go and live
in Egypt. There we won't have to face
war anymore. We won't hear the trumpets of war. And we won't get hungry.'
15 Then listen to what the LORD says to
you who are left in Judah. He is the
LORD who rules over all. He is the God
of Israel. He says, 'Have you already
made up your minds to go to Egypt? Are
you going to make your homes there?
16 Then the war you fear will catch up
with you there. The hunger you are
afraid of will follow you into Egypt.
And you will die there. 17 In fact, that
will happen to all those who go and
make their homes in Egypt. All of them
will die of war, hunger and plague. Not
one of them will live. None of them will
escape the trouble I will bring on them.'
18 He is the LORD who rules over all. He
is the God of Israel. He says, 'My great
anger has been poured out on those who
used to live in Jerusalem. In the same
way, it will be poured out on you when
you go to Egypt. People will use your
name in a curse. They will be shocked at
you. They will say bad things about you.
And they will say you are shameful. You
will never see this place again.'

19 "The LORD has spoken to you who
are left in Judah. He has said, 'Do not
go to Egypt.' Here is something you can
be sure of. I am warning you about it
today. 20 You made a big mistake when
you asked me to pray to the LORD your
God. You said, 'Pray to the LORD our
God for us. Tell us everything he says.
We'll do it.' 21 I have told you today what
the LORD your God wants you to do.
But you still haven't obeyed him. You
haven't done anything he sent me to
tell you to do. 22 So here is something
else you can be sure of. You will die of
war, hunger and plague. You want to
go and make your homes in Egypt. But
you will die there."

43 Jeremiah finished telling the
people everything the LORD
their God had said. Jeremiah told them
everything the LORD had sent him to
tell them. 2 After that, Azariah, the son
of Hoshaiah, and Johanan, the son of
Kareah, spoke to Jeremiah. And all the
proud men joined them. They said, "You
are lying! The LORD our God hasn't sent
you to speak to us. He hasn't told you
to say, 'You must not go to Egypt and
make your homes there.' 3 But Baruch,
the son of Neriah, is turning you against
us. He wants us to be handed over to
the Babylonians. Then they can kill us.
Or they can take us away to Babylon."

4 So Johanan, the son of Kareah, disobeyed the LORD's command. So did
all the other army officers and all the
people. They didn't stay in the land of
Judah. 5 Instead Johanan, the son of
Kareah, and all the other army officers
led away all the people who were left
in Judah. Those people had returned
to Judah from all the nations where
they had been scattered. 6 Johanan
and the other officers also led away
many people Nebuzaradan had left at
Mizpah. They included men, women
and children. They also included the
king's daughters. Nebuzaradan had left
them with Gedaliah, the son of Ahikam.
They also took Jeremiah the prophet
and Baruch son of Neriah along with
them. Nebuzaradan was commander
of the royal guard. Ahikam was the
son of Shaphan. 7 So the Jewish leaders
disobeyed the LORD. They took everyone to Egypt. They went all the way to
Tahpanhes.

8 In Tahpanhes a message from the
LORD came to Jeremiah. The LORD said,
9 "Make sure the Jews are watching you.
Then get some large stones. Go to the
entrance to Pharaoh's house in Tahpanhes. Bury the stones in the clay under
the brick walkway there. 10 Then tell the
Jews, 'The LORD who rules over all is the
God of Israel. He says, "I will send for
my servant Nebuchadnezzar, the king
of Babylon. And I will set his throne
over these stones that are buried here.

He will set up his royal tent over them.
11 He will come and attack Egypt. He will
bring death to those I have appointed to
die. He will take away as prisoners those
I have appointed to be taken away. And
he will kill with swords those I have
appointed to be killed. 12 He will set the
temples of the gods of Egypt on fire. He
will burn down their temples. He will
take away the statues of their gods.
Nebuchadnezzar will be like a shepherd
who picks his coat clean of lice. Nebuchadnezzar will pick Egypt clean and
then depart. 13 At Heliopolis in Egypt he
will smash the sacred pillars to pieces.
And he will burn down the temples of
the gods of Egypt." ' "

Worshiping Other Gods Brings Horrible Trouble

44 A message from the LORD came
to Jeremiah. It was about all
the Jews living in Lower Egypt. They
were living in Migdol, Tahpanhes and
Memphis. It was also about all the Jews
living in Upper Egypt. 2 The LORD who
rules over all is the God of Israel. He
said, "You saw all the trouble I brought
on Jerusalem. I also brought it on all
the towns in Judah. Today they lie
there deserted and destroyed. 3 That's
because of the evil things their people
did. They made me very angry. They
burned incense to other gods. And they
worshiped them. They and you and
your people of long ago never knew
those gods. 4 Again and again I sent my
servants the prophets. They said, 'Don't
worship other gods! The LORD hates it!'
5 But the people didn't listen. They didn't
pay any attention. They didn't turn
from their sinful ways. They didn't stop
burning incense to other gods. 6 So my
burning anger was poured out. It blazed
out against the towns of Judah and the
streets of Jerusalem. It made them the
dry and empty places they are today."

7 The LORD God who rules over all
is the God of Israel. He says, "Why do
you want to bring all this trouble on
yourselves? You are removing from
Judah its men and women, its children
and babies. Not one of you will be left.
8 Why do you want to make me angry
with the gods your hands have made?
Why do you burn incense to the gods
of Egypt, where you now live? You will
destroy yourselves. All the nations on
earth will use your name as a curse.
They will say you are shameful. 9 Have
you forgotten the evil things done by
your people of long ago? The kings
and queens of Judah did those same
things. So did you and your wives. They
were done in the land of Judah and
the streets of Jerusalem. 10 To this day
the people of Judah have not made
themselves humble in my sight. They
have not shown any respect for me.
They have not obeyed my law. They
have not followed the rules I gave you
and your people of long ago."

11 The LORD who rules over all is the
God of Israel. He says, "I have decided
to bring horrible trouble on you. I will
destroy the whole land of Judah. 12 I will
destroy the people of Judah who are
left. They had decided to go to Egypt
and make their homes there. But all
of them will die in Egypt. They will die
of war or hunger. All of them will die,
from the least important of them to the
most important. They will die of war or
hunger. People will use their name as
a curse. They will be shocked at them.
They will say bad things about them.
And they will say they are shameful.
13 I will use war, hunger and plague to
punish the Jews who live in Egypt. I
punished Jerusalem in the same way.
14 None of the people of Judah who have
gone to live in Egypt will escape. Not
one of them will live to return to Judah.
They long to return and live there. But
only a few will escape from Egypt and
go back."

15 All the Jews who were living in
Lower and Upper Egypt gathered to
give Jeremiah their answer. A large
crowd had come together. It included
men who knew that their wives were
burning incense to other gods. Their
wives were there with them. All of them
said to Jeremiah, 16 "We won't listen to
the message you have spoken to us in
the LORD's name! 17 We will certainly do
everything we said we would. We'll burn
incense to the female god called the
Queen of Heaven. We'll pour out drink
offerings to her. We'll do just as we and
our people of long ago have done. Our
kings and our officials also did it. All of
us did it in the towns of Judah and the
streets of Jerusalem. At that time we

had plenty of food. We were well off. We didn't suffer any harm. 18 But then we stopped burning incense to the Queen of Heaven. We stopped pouring out drink offerings to her. And ever since that time we haven't had anything. Instead, we've been dying of war and hunger."

19 The women added, "We burned incense to the Queen of Heaven. We poured out drink offerings to her. And our husbands knew we were making cakes that looked like her. They knew we were pouring out drink offerings to her."

20 Then Jeremiah spoke to all the people who were answering him. He spoke to men and women alike. He said, 21 "Didn't the LORD know you were burning incense in the towns of Judah? Didn't he care that you were also doing it in the streets of Jerusalem? You and your people of long ago were doing it. Your kings and officials were doing it too. So were the rest of the people in the land. 22 The LORD couldn't put up any longer with the evil things you were doing. He hated the things you did. So your land became a curse. It became a dry and empty desert. No one lived there. And that's the way it still is today. 23 You have burned incense to other gods. You have sinned against the LORD. You haven't obeyed him or his law. You haven't followed his rules. You haven't lived up to the terms of the covenant he made with you. That's why all this trouble has come on you. You have seen it with your own eyes."

24 Then Jeremiah spoke to all the people. That included the women. He said, "All you people of Judah in Egypt, listen to the LORD's message. 25 The LORD who rules over all is the God of Israel. He says, 'You and your wives have done what you promised you would do. You said, "We will certainly keep the promises we made to the Queen of Heaven. We'll burn incense to her. We'll pour out drink offerings to her." '

"Go ahead then. Do what you said you would! Keep your promises! 26 But listen to the LORD's message. Listen, all you Jews living in Egypt. 'I make a promise by my own great name,' says the LORD. 'Here is what I promise. "No one from Judah who lives anywhere in Egypt will ever again pray in my name. None of them will ever make this promise. They will never say, 'You can be sure that the LORD and King is alive.' " 27 I am watching over them to do them harm and not good. The Jews in Egypt will die of war and hunger until all of them are destroyed. 28 Some will not be killed. They will return to Judah from Egypt. But they will be very few. Then all the people of Judah who came to live in Egypt will know the truth. They will know whether what I say or what they say will come true.

29 " 'I will give you a sign that I will punish you in this place,' announces the LORD. 'Then you can be sure that my warnings of harm against you will come true.' 30 The LORD says, 'I am going to hand over Pharaoh Hophra king of Egypt. I will hand him over to his enemies who want to kill him. In the same way, I handed over King Zedekiah to Nebuchadnezzar, the king of Babylon. He was the enemy who wanted to kill Zedekiah.' "

The LORD Speaks to Baruch

45 Jeremiah talked to Baruch, the son of Neriah. It was in the fourth year that Jehoiakim, the son of Josiah, was king of Judah. It was when Baruch had written down on a scroll the words Jeremiah the prophet told him to write. Jeremiah had said, 2 "The LORD is the God of Israel. Baruch, he says to you, 3 'You have said, "How terrible it is for me! The LORD has added sorrow to my pain. I'm worn out from all my groaning. I can't find any rest." ' 4 But here is what the LORD has told me to say to you, Baruch. 'The LORD says, "I will destroy what I have built up. I will pull up by the roots what I have planted. I will do this throughout the earth. 5 So should you seek great things for yourself? Do not seek them. I will bring trouble on everyone," announces the LORD. "But no matter where you go, I will let you escape with your life." ' "

A Message About Egypt

46 A message from the LORD came to Jeremiah the prophet. It was about the nations.

2 Here is what the LORD says about Egypt.

Here is his message against the army of Pharaoh Necho. He was king of Egypt. Nebuchadnezzar, the king of Babylon, won the battle over Necho's army. That happened at Carchemish on the Euphrates River. It was in the fourth year that Jehoiakim was king of Judah. He was the son of Josiah. The message says,

3 "Egyptians, prepare your shields!
Prepare large and small shields alike!
March out for battle!
4 Get the horses and chariots ready to ride!
Take up your battle positions!
Put on your helmets!
Shine up your spears!
Put on your armor!
5 What do I see?
The Egyptians are terrified.
They are pulling back.
Their soldiers are losing.
They run away as fast as they can.
They do not look back.
There is terror on every side,"
announces the LORD.
6 "Those who run fast can't get away.
Those who are strong can't escape.
In the north by the Euphrates River
they trip and fall.

7 "Who is this that rises like the Nile River?
Who rises like rivers of rushing waters?
8 Egypt rises like the Nile River.
It rises like rivers of rushing waters.
Egypt says, 'I will rise and cover the earth.
I'll destroy cities and their people.'
9 Charge, you horses!
Drive fast, you chariot drivers!
March on, you soldiers!
March on, you men of Cush and Put who carry shields.
March on, you men of Lydia who shoot arrows.
10 But that day belongs to me.
I am the LORD who rules over all.
It is a day for me to pay back my enemies.
My sword will eat until it is satisfied.
It will drink until it is not thirsty for blood anymore.
I am the Lord. I am the LORD who rules over all.
I will offer a sacrifice.
I will offer it in the land of the north
by the Euphrates River.

11 "People of Egypt,
go up to Gilead and get some healing lotion.
You may try many medicines, but you will not be healed.
There isn't any healing for you.
12 The nations will hear about your shame.
Your cries of pain will fill the earth.
One soldier will trip over another.
Both of them will fall down together."

13 Nebuchadnezzar, the king of Babylon, was coming to attack Egypt. Here is the message the LORD spoke to Jeremiah the prophet about it. He said,

14 "Egyptians, here is what I want you to announce in your land.
Announce it in the city of Migdol.
Also announce it in Memphis and Tahpanhes.
Say, 'Take up your battle positions!
Get ready!
The sword eats up those around you.'
15 Why are your soldiers lying on the ground?
They can't stand, because I bring them down.
16 They will trip again and again.
They will fall over one another.
They will say, 'Get up. Let's go back home.
Let's return to our own people and our own lands.
Let's get away from the swords
that will bring us great harm.'
17 The Egyptian soldiers will cry out,
'Pharaoh, our king, is only a loud noise.
He has missed his chance to win the battle.'

18 "I am the King.
My name is the LORD Who Rules Over All.
Someone will come who is like
Mount Tabor among the mountains.
He is like Mount Carmel by the
Mediterranean Sea.

And that is just as sure as I am alive,"
announces the King.
19 "So pack your belongings, you who live in Egypt.
You will be taken away from your land.
Memphis will be completely destroyed.
Its buildings will be broken down.
No one will live there.

20 "Egypt is like a beautiful young cow.
But Nebuchadnezzar is coming against her from the north.
He will bite her like a fly.
21 Hired soldiers are in Egypt's army.
They are like fat calves.
All of them will turn and run away.
They will not hold their positions.
The day of trouble is coming on them.
The time for them to be punished is near.
22 The Egyptians will hiss like a snake that is trying to get away.
A powerful army will advance against them.
Their enemies will come against them with axes.
They will be like those who cut down trees.
23 Egypt is like a thick forest.
But they will chop it down,"
announces the LORD.
"There are more of their enemies than there are locusts.
In fact, they can't even be counted.
24 The nation of Egypt will be put to shame.
It will be handed over to the people of the north."

25 The LORD who rules over all is the
God of Israel. He says, "I am about
to punish Amon, the god of Thebes. I
will also punish Pharaoh. I will punish
Egypt and its gods and kings. And I will
punish those who depend on Pharaoh.
26 I will hand them over to those who
want to kill them. I will give them to
Nebuchadnezzar, the king of Babylon,
and his officers. But later, many people
will live in Egypt again as in times past,"
announces the LORD.

27 "People of Jacob, do not be afraid.
You are my servant.
Israel, do not be terrified.
I will bring you safely out of a place far away.
I will bring your children back
from the land where they were taken.
Your people will have peace and security again.
And no one will make them afraid.
28 People of Jacob, do not be afraid.
You are my servant.
I am with you,"
announces the LORD.
"I will completely destroy all the nations
among which I scatter you.
But I will not completely destroy you.
I will correct you. But I will be fair.
I will not let you go without any punishment."

A Message About the Philistines

47 A message from the LORD came to Jeremiah the prophet. It was about the Philistines before Pharaoh attacked the city of Gaza.

2 The LORD said,

"The armies of Babylon are like waters rising in the north.
They will become a great flood.
They will flow over the land and everything in it.
They will flow over the towns and those who live in them.
The people will cry out.
All those who live in the land will weep.
3 They will weep when they hear galloping horses.
They will weep at the noise of enemy chariots.
They will weep at the rumble of their wheels.
Parents will not even try to help their children.
Their hands will not be able to help them.
4 The day has come
to destroy all the Philistines.
The time has come to remove all those
who could help Tyre and Sidon.

I am about to destroy the
Philistines.
I will not leave anyone alive
who came from the coasts of
Crete.
5 The people of Gaza will be so sad
they will shave their heads.
And Ashkelon's people will be
silent.
You who remain on the plain,
how long will you cut yourselves?
6 " 'Sword of the LORD!' you cry out.
'How long will it be until you
rest?
Return to the place you came from.
Stop killing us! Be still!'
7 But how can his sword rest
when the LORD has given it a
command?
He has ordered it
to attack Ashkelon and the
Philistine coast."

A Message About Moab

48 Here is what the LORD says
about Moab.
The LORD who rules over all is the God
of Israel. He says,

"How terrible it will be for the city
of Nebo!
It will be destroyed.
Kiriathaim will be captured.
It will be put to shame.
Its fort will be broken down.
It will be put to shame.
2 Moab will not be praised anymore.
In Heshbon people will plan its
fall from power.
They will say, 'Come. Let's put an
end to that nation.'
City of Madmen, you too will be
silent.
My sword will hunt you down.
3 Cries of sorrow come from
Horonaim.
The town is being completely
destroyed.
4 Moab will be broken.
Her little ones will cry out.
5 The people go up the hill to Luhith.
They are weeping bitterly as
they go.
Loud cries are heard on the road
down to Horonaim.
People cry out because the town
is being destroyed.
6 People of Moab, run away! Run for
your lives!
Become like a lonely bush in the
desert.
7 You trust in the things you can do.
You trust in your riches.
So you too will be taken away as
prisoners.
Your god named Chemosh will be
carried away.
So will its priests and officials.
8 The one who is going to destroy you
will come against every town.
Not even one of them will escape.
The valley and the high plain
will be destroyed.
The LORD has spoken.
9 Sprinkle salt all over Moab.
It will be completely destroyed.
Its towns will be a dry and empty
desert.
No one will live in them.

10 "May anyone who is lazy when
they do the LORD's work
be under my curse!
May anyone who keeps their sword
from killing
be under my curse!

11 "Moab has been at peace and rest
from its earliest days.
It is like wine that has not been
shaken up.
It has not been poured from one jar
to another.
Moab's people have not been
taken away from their land.
They are like wine that tastes as it
always did.
Its smell has not changed at all.
12 But other days are coming,"
announces the LORD.
"At that time I will send people who
pour wine from pitchers.
They will pour Moab out like wine.
They will empty its pitchers.
They will smash its jars.
13 Then Moab's people will be
ashamed of their god named
Chemosh.
They will be ashamed just as the
people of Israel were
when they trusted in their false
god at Bethel.
14 "How can you say, 'We are soldiers.
We are men who are brave in
battle'?

15 Moab will be destroyed.
Its enemies will march into its towns.
Its finest young men will die in battle,"
announces the King.
His name is the LORD Who Rules Over All.
16 "The fall of Moab is near.
Its time of trouble will come quickly.
17 All you who live around it, mourn for its people.
Be sad, you who know how famous Moab is.
Say, 'Its powerful ruler's scepter is broken!
His glorious scepter is smashed.'

18 "Come down from your glorious city, you who live in Dibon.
Come and sit on the thirsty ground.
The one who destroys Moab
will come up and attack you.
Your enemies will destroy your cities
that have high walls around them.
19 Stand by the road and watch,
you who live in Aroer.
Ask the men who are running away.
Ask the women who are escaping.
Ask them, 'What has happened?'
20 Moab has been put to shame.
It has been destroyed.
Weep and cry out!
Tell everyone Moab has been destroyed.
Announce it by the Arnon River.
21 The high plain has been judged.
So have Holon, Jahzah and Mephaath.
22 Dibon, Nebo and Beth Diblathaim have been judged.
23 So have Kiriathaim, Beth Gamul and Beth Meon.
24 Kerioth and Bozrah have also been judged.
And so have all the towns of Moab, far and near alike.
25 Moab's power is gone.
Its strength is broken,"
announces the LORD.

26 "Moab's people think they are better than I am.
So let their enemies make them drunk.
Let the people get sick and throw up.
Let them roll around in the mess they have made.
Let people laugh at them.
27 Moab, you laughed at Israel, didn't you?
Were Israel's people caught among robbers?
Is that why you shake your head at them?
Is that why you make fun of them
every time you talk about them?
28 Leave your towns,
you who live in Moab.
Go and live among the rocks.
Be like a dove that makes its nest
at the entrance of a cave.

29 "We have heard all about Moab's pride.
We have heard how very proud they are.
They think they are so much better than others.
Their pride reaches deep down inside their hearts.
30 I know how rude they are.
But it will not get them anywhere," announces the LORD.
"Their bragging does not accomplish anything.
31 So I weep over Moab.
I cry for all Moab's people.
I groan for the people of Kir Hareseth.
32 I weep for you as Jazer weeps,
you vines of Sibmah.
Your branches used to spread out.
They went all the way down to the Dead Sea.
They reached as far as the sea of Jazer.
The one who destroys your country
has taken away your grapes and ripe fruit.
33 Joy has left your orchards.
Gladness is gone from your fields.
I have stopped the flow of juice from your winepresses.
No one stomps on your grapes with shouts of joy.
There are shouts.
But they are not shouts of joy.

34 "The sound of their cry rises from
Heshbon.
It rises as far as Elealeh and Jahaz.
It rises from Zoar.
It goes all the way to Horonaim
and Eglath Shelishiyah.
Even the waters at Nimrim are
dried up.
35 In Moab people sacrifice offerings
on the high places.
They burn incense to their gods.
But I will put an end to those people,"
announces the LORD.
36 "Like a flute my heart sings a song
of sadness for Moab.
It sings like a flute for the people
of Kir Hareseth.
The wealth they had acquired is
gone.
37 Every head is shaved.
Every beard is cut off.
Every hand is cut.
And every waist is covered with
the clothes of sadness.
38 Weeping is the only sound in Moab.
It is heard on all its roofs.
It is heard in the market.
I have broken Moab
like a jar that no one wants,"
announces the LORD.
39 "How broken Moab is! How the
people weep!
They turn away from others
because they are so ashamed.
All those around them laugh at them.
They are shocked at them."

40 The LORD says,

"Look! Nebuchadnezzar is like an
eagle diving down.
He is spreading his wings over
Moab.
41 Kerioth will be captured.
Its forts will be taken.
At that time the hearts of Moab's
soldiers will tremble in fear.
They will be like the heart of a
woman having a baby.
42 Moab will be destroyed as a nation.
That is because its people thought
they were better than the LORD.
43 You people of Moab,"
announces the LORD,
"terror, a pit and a trap are
waiting for you.
44 Anyone who runs away from the
terror
will fall into the pit.
Anyone who climbs out of the pit
will be caught in the trap.
The time is coming
when I will punish Moab,"
announces the LORD.

45 "In the shadow of Heshbon
those who are trying to escape
stand helpless.
A fire has blazed out from Heshbon.
Flames have come out from
Sihon's city.
It burns the foreheads of Moab's
people.
It burns the skulls of those who
brag loudly.
46 How terrible it will be for you, Moab!
Those who worship Chemosh are
destroyed.
Your sons are being taken to
another country.
Your daughters are taken away
as prisoners.

47 "But in days to come
I will bless Moab with great
success again,"
announces the LORD.

This ends the report about how the
LORD would judge Moab.

A Message About Ammon

49 Here is what the LORD says
about the people of Ammon.

He says,

"Doesn't Israel have any sons?
Doesn't Israel have anyone
to take over the family property?
Then why has the god named
Molek taken over Gad?
Why do those who worship him
live in its towns?
2 But a new day is coming,"
announces the LORD.
"At that time I will sound the battle
cry.
I will sound it against Rabbah in
the land of Ammon.
It will become a pile of
broken-down buildings.
The villages around it will be set
on fire.
Then Israel will drive out
those who drove her out,"
says the LORD.
3 "Heshbon, weep for Ai! It is destroyed!
Cry out, you who live in Rabbah!

Put on the clothes of sadness and mourn.
Run here and there inside the walls.
Your god named Molek will be carried away.
So will its priests and officials.
4 Why do you brag about your valleys?
You brag that they produce so many crops.
Ammon, you are an unfaithful country.
You trust in your riches.
You say,
'Who will attack me?'
5 I will bring terror on you.
It will come from all those around you,"
announces the Lord. He is the LORD who rules over all.
"Every one of you will be driven away.
No one will bring back those who escape.

6 "But after that, I will bless the people of Ammon
with great success again,"
announces the LORD.

A Message About Edom

7 Here is what the LORD says about Edom.

The LORD who rules over all says,

"Isn't there wisdom in the town of Teman anymore?
Can't those who are wise give advice?
Has their wisdom disappeared completely?
8 Turn around and run away, you who live in Dedan.
Hide in deep caves.
I will bring trouble on Esau's family line.
I will do this at the time I punish them.
9 Edom, suppose grape pickers came to harvest your vines.
They would still leave a few grapes.
Suppose robbers came at night.
They would steal only as much as they wanted.
10 But I will strip everything away from Esau's people.
I will uncover their hiding places.
They will not be able to hide anywhere.
Their army is destroyed.
Their friends and neighbors are destroyed.
So there is no one to say,
11 'Leave your children whose fathers have died.
I will keep them alive.
Your widows can also depend on me.' "

12 The LORD says, "What if those who
do not have to drink the cup must drink
it anyway? Then shouldn't you be punished? You will certainly be punished.
You must drink the cup. 13 I make a
promise in my own name. Bozrah will
be destroyed," announces the LORD.
"People will be shocked at it. They will
say Bozrah is a shameful place. They
will use its name as a curse. And all its
towns will be destroyed forever."

14 I've heard a message from the LORD.
A messenger was sent to the nations. The LORD told him to say,
"Gather yourselves together to attack Edom!
Prepare for battle!"

15 The LORD says to Edom, "I will make you weak among the nations.
They will hate you.
16 You live in the safety of the rocks.
You live on top of the hills.
But the terror you stir up has now turned against you.
Your proud heart has tricked you.
You build your nest as high as an eagle does.
But I will bring you down from there,"
announces the LORD.
17 "People of Edom,
all those who pass by you will be shocked.
They will make fun of you
because of all your wounds.
18 Sodom and Gomorrah were destroyed.
So were the towns that were near them,"
says the LORD.

"You will be just like them.
No one will live in your land.
No human beings will stay there.

19 "I will be like a lion coming up
from the bushes by the Jordan River.
I will hunt in rich grasslands.
I will chase you from your land in an instant.
What nation will I choose to do this?
Which one will I appoint?
Is anyone like me?
Who would dare to argue with me?
What leader can stand against me?"

20 So listen to what the LORD has planned
against the people of Edom.
Hear what he has planned
against those who live in Teman.
Edom's young people will be dragged away.
Their grasslands will be shocked at their fate.

21 When the earth hears Edom fall, it will shake.
The people's cries will be heard
all the way to the Red Sea.

22 Look! An enemy is coming.
It's like an eagle diving down.
It will spread its wings over Bozrah.
At that time the hearts of Edom's soldiers
will tremble in fear.
They'll be like the heart of a woman having a baby.

A Message About Damascus

23 Here is what the LORD says about
Damascus. He says,

"The people of Hamath and Arpad are terrified.
They have heard bad news.
They have lost all hope.
They are troubled like the rolling sea.

24 The people of Damascus have become weak.
They have turned to run away.
Panic has taken hold of them.
Suffering and pain have taken hold of them.
Their pain is like the pain of a woman having a baby.

25 Why hasn't the famous city been deserted?
It is the town I take delight in.

26 You can be sure its young men will fall dead in the streets.
All its soldiers will be put to death at that time,"
announces the LORD who rules over all.

27 "I will set the walls of Damascus on fire.
It will burn down the strong towers of King Ben-Hadad."

A Message About Kedar and Hazor

28 Here is what the LORD says about
the people of Kedar and the kingdoms
of Hazor. Nebuchadnezzar, the king of
Babylon, was planning to attack them.

The LORD says to the armies of Babylon,

"Prepare for battle. Attack Kedar.
Destroy the people of the east.

29 Their tents and flocks will be taken away from them.
Their tents will be carried off.
All their goods and camels will be stolen.
People will shout to them,
'There is terror on every side!'

30 "Run away quickly!
You who live in Hazor, stay in deep caves,"
announces the LORD.
"Nebuchadnezzar, the king of Babylon,
has made plans against you.
He has decided to attack you.

31 "Armies of Babylon, prepare for battle.
Attack a nation that feels secure.
Its people do not have any worries,"
announces the LORD.
"That nation does not have gates or bars that lock them.
Its people live far from danger.

32 Their camels will be stolen.
Their large herds will be taken away.
I will scatter to the winds those who are in places far away.

I will bring trouble on them from every side,"
announces the LORD.
33 "Hazor will become a home for wild dogs.
It will be a dry and empty desert forever.
No one will live in that land.
No human beings will stay there."

A Message About Elam

34 A message from the LORD came to Jeremiah the prophet. It was about Elam. It came shortly after Zedekiah became king of Judah.

35 The LORD who rules over all said,

"Elam's bow is the secret of its strength.
But I will break it.
36 I will bring the four winds against Elam.
I will bring them from all four directions.
I will scatter Elam's people to the four winds.
They will be taken away
to every nation on earth.
37 I will use Elam's enemies to smash them.
Those who want to kill them will kill them.
I will bring trouble on Elam's people.
My anger will be great against them,"
announces the LORD.
"I will chase them with swords.
I will hunt them down
until I have destroyed them.
38 I will set up my throne in Elam.
I will destroy its king and officials,"
announces the LORD.

39 "But in days to come I will bless Elam with great success again,"
announces the LORD.

A Message About Babylon

50 Here is the message the LORD spoke through Jeremiah the prophet. It was about the city of Babylon and the land of Babylon. He said,

2 "Announce this message among the nations.
Lift up a banner.
Let the nations hear the message.
Do not keep anything back.
Say, 'Babylon will be captured.
The god named Bel will be put to shame.
The god named Marduk will be filled with terror.
Babylon's gods will be put to shame.
The gods its people made will be filled with terror.'
3 A nation from the north will attack it.
That nation will destroy Babylon.
No one will live there.
People and animals alike will run away.

4 "The days are coming,"
announces the LORD.
"At that time the people of Israel and Judah will gather together.
They will come in tears to me.
I am the LORD their God.
5 They will ask how to get to Zion.
Then they will turn their faces toward it.
They will come and join themselves to me.
They will enter into the covenant I make with them.
It will last forever.
It will never be forgotten.

6 "My people have been like lost sheep.
Their shepherds have led them astray.
They have caused them to wander in the mountains.
They have wandered over mountains and hills.
They have forgotten that I am their true resting place.
7 Everyone who found them destroyed them.
Their enemies said, 'We aren't guilty.
They sinned against the LORD.
He gave them everything they needed.
He has always been Israel's hope.'

8 "People of Judah, run away from Babylon.
Leave the land of Babylon.
Be like the goats that lead the flock.
9 I will stir up great nations
that will join forces against Babylon.
I will bring them from the land of the north.

They will take up their battle
positions against Babylon.
They will come from the north
and capture it.
Their arrows will be like skilled
soldiers.
They will not miss their mark.
10 So the riches of Babylon will be
taken away.
All those who steal from it will
have more than enough,"
announces the LORD.

11 "People of Babylon, you have
stolen what belongs to me.
That has made you glad and full
of joy.
You dance around like a young cow
on a threshing floor.
You neigh like stallions.
12 Because of that, you will bring
great shame on your land.
Your whole nation will be
dishonored.
It will become the least important
of the nations.
It will become a dry and empty
desert.
13 Because I am angry with it, no one
will live there.
It will be completely deserted.
All those who pass by Babylon will
be shocked.
They will make fun of it because
of all its wounds.

14 "All you who shoot arrows,
take up your battle positions
around Babylon.
Shoot at it! Do not spare any arrows!
Its people have sinned against me.
15 Shout against them on every side!
They are giving up.
The towers of the city are falling.
Its walls are being pulled down.
The LORD is paying back its people.
So pay them back yourselves.
Do to them what they have done
to others.
16 Do not leave anyone in Babylon to
plant the fields.
Do not leave anyone to harvest
the grain.
Let each of them return to their
own people.
Let them run away to their own
land.
If they don't, their enemy's sword
will bring them great harm.

17 "Israel is like a scattered flock
that lions have chased away.
The first lion that ate them up
was the king of Assyria.
The last one that broke their bones
was Nebuchadnezzar, the king of
Babylon."

18 The LORD who rules over all is the
God of Israel. He says,

"I punished the king of Assyria.
In the same way, I will punish
the king of Babylon and his land.
19 But I will bring Israel back to their
own grasslands.
I will feed them on Mount Carmel
and in Bashan.
I will satisfy their hunger
on the hills of Ephraim and
Gilead.
20 The days are coming,"
announces the LORD.
"At that time people will search for
Israel's guilt.
But they will not find any.
They will search for Judah's sins.
But they will not find any.
That is because I will forgive the
people I have spared.

21 "Enemies of Babylon, attack their
land of Merathaim.
Make war against those who live
in Pekod.
Chase them and kill them. Destroy
them completely,"
announces the LORD.
"Do everything I have
commanded you to do.
22 The noise of battle is heard in the
land.
It is the noise of a great city
being destroyed!
23 It has been broken to pieces.
It was the hammer that broke the
whole earth.
How empty Babylon is among
the nations!
24 Babylon, I set a trap for you.
And you were caught before you
knew it.
You were found and captured.
That is because you opposed me.
25 I have opened up my storeroom.
I have brought out the weapons I
use when I am angry.
I am the LORD and King who rules
over all.

I have work to do in the land of
the Babylonians.
26 So come against it from far away.
Open up its storerooms.
Stack everything up like piles of
grain.
Completely destroy that country.
Do not leave anyone alive there.
27 Kill all Babylon's strongest warriors.
Let them die in battle.
How terrible it will be for them!
Their time to be judged has come.
Now they will be punished.
28 Listen to those who have escaped.
Listen to those who have
returned from Babylon.
They are announcing in Zion
how I have paid Babylon back.
I have paid it back for destroying
my temple.

29 "Send for men armed with bows
and arrows.
Send them against Babylon.
Set up camp all around it.
Do not let anyone escape.
Pay it back for what its people have
done.
Do to them what they have done
to others.
They have dared to disobey me.
I am the Holy One of Israel.
30 You can be sure its young men will
fall dead in the streets.
All its soldiers will be put to
death at that time,"
announces the LORD.
31 "Proud Babylonians, I am against
you,"
announces the Lord.
The LORD who rules over all says,
"Your day to be judged has come.
It is time for you to be punished.
32 You proud people will trip and fall.
No one will help you up.
I will start a fire in your towns.
It will burn up everyone around
you."

33 The LORD who rules over all says,

"The people of Israel are being
treated badly.
So are the people of Judah.
Those who have captured them are
holding them.
They refuse to let them go.
34 But I am strong and will save them.
My name is the LORD Who Rules
Over All.
I will stand up for them.
I will bring peace and rest to
their land.
But I will bring trouble to those
who live in Babylon.

35 "A sword is coming against the
Babylonians!"
announces the LORD.
"It is coming against those who live
in Babylon.
It is coming against their officials
and wise men.
36 A sword is coming against their
prophets.
But they are not really prophets
at all!
So they will look foolish.
A sword is coming against their
soldiers!
They will be filled with terror.
37 A sword is coming against their
horses and chariots!
It is coming against all the hired
soldiers in their armies.
They will become weak.
A sword is coming against their
treasures!
They will be stolen.
38 There will not be any rain for their
rivers.
So they will dry up.
Those things will happen because
their land is full of statues of gods.
Those gods will go crazy with
terror.

39 "Desert creatures and hyenas will
live in Babylon.
And so will owls.
People will never live there again.
It will not be lived in for all time
to come.
40 I destroyed Sodom and Gomorrah.
I also destroyed the towns that
were near them,"
announces the LORD.
"Babylon will be just like them.
No one will live there.
No human beings will stay there.

41 "Look! An army is coming from the
north.
I am stirring up a great nation
and many kings.
They are coming from a land
that is very far away.

42 Their soldiers are armed with bows
and spears.
They are mean.
They do not show any mercy at
all.
They come riding in on their
horses.
They sound like the roaring
ocean.
They are lined up for battle.
They are coming to attack you,
city of Babylon.
43 The king of Babylon has heard
reports about them.
His hands can't help him.
He is in great pain.
It is like the pain of a woman
having a baby.
44 I will be like a lion coming up from
the bushes by the Jordan River.
I will hunt in rich grasslands.
I will chase the people of Babylon
from their land in an instant.
What nation will I choose to do
this?
Which one will I appoint?
Is anyone like me? Who would dare
to argue with me?
What leader can stand against
me?"
45 So listen to what the LORD has
planned against Babylon.
Hear what he has planned
against the land of the
Babylonians.
Their young people will be dragged
away.
Their grasslands will be shocked
at their fate.
46 At the news of Babylon's capture,
the earth will shake.
The people's cries will be heard
among the nations.

51 The LORD says,

"I will stir up the spirits of
destroyers.
They will march out against
Babylon and its people.
2 I will send other nations against it
to separate the straw from the
grain.
I will send them to destroy
Babylon completely.
They will oppose it on every side.
At that time it will be destroyed.
3 Do not let its soldiers get their bows
ready to use.
Do not let them put on their
armor.
Do not spare their young men.
Destroy their armies completely.
4 They will fall down dead in
Babylon.
They will receive deadly wounds
in its streets.
5 The land of Israel and Judah is full
of guilt.
Its people have sinned against me.
But I have not deserted them. I am
their God.
I am the LORD who rules over all.
I am the Holy One of Israel.

6 "People of Judah, run away from
Babylon!
Run for your lives!
Do not be destroyed because of
the sins of its people.
It is time for me to pay them back.
I will punish them for what they
have done.
7 Babylon was like a gold cup in my
hand.
That city made the whole earth
drunk.
The nations drank its wine.
So now they have gone crazy.
8 Babylon will suddenly fall and be
broken.
Weep for it!
Get healing lotion for its pain.
Perhaps it can be healed.

9 "The nations say, 'We would have
healed Babylon.
But it can't be healed.
So let's leave it. Let's each go to our
own land.
Babylon's sins reach all the way
to the skies.
They rise up as high as the
heavens.'

10 "The people of Judah say,
'The LORD has made things right
for us again.
So come. Let's tell in Zion
what the LORD our God has done.'

11 "I have stirred up you kings of the
Medes.
So sharpen your arrows!
Get your shields!
I plan to destroy Babylon.

I will pay the Babylonians back.
They have destroyed my temple.
12 Lift up a banner! Attack Babylon's walls!
Put more guards on duty!
Station more of them to watch over you!
Hide and wait to attack them!
I will do what I have planned.
I will do what I have decided to do
against the people of Babylon.
13 You who live by the rivers of Babylon,
your end has come.
You who are rich in treasures,
it is time for you to be destroyed.
14 I am the LORD who rules over all.
I have made a promise in my own name.
I have said, 'I will certainly fill your land with soldiers.
They will be as many as a huge number of locusts.
They will win the battle over you.
They will shout for joy.'

15 "I used my power to make the earth.
I used my wisdom to set the world in place.
I used my understanding to spread out the heavens.
16 When I thunder, the waters in the heavens roar.
I make clouds rise from one end of the earth to the other.
I send lightning with the rain.
I bring out the wind from my storerooms.

17 "No one has any sense.
No one knows anything.
Everyone who works with gold is put to shame
by his wooden gods.
His metal gods are fakes.
They can't even breathe.
18 They are worthless, and people make fun of them.
When I judge them, they will be destroyed.
19 But I, the God of Jacob, am not like them.
I give my people everything they need.
I can do this because I made everything, including Israel.
They are the people who belong to me.
My name is the LORD Who Rules Over All.

20 "Babylon, you are my war club.
You are my weapon for battle.
I use you to destroy nations.
I use you to wipe out kingdoms.
21 I use you to destroy horses and their riders.
I use you to destroy chariots and their drivers.
22 I use you to destroy men and women.
I use you to destroy old people and young people.
I use you to destroy young men and young women.
23 I use you to destroy shepherds and their flocks.
I use you to destroy farmers and their oxen.
I use you to destroy governors and officials.

24 "Judah, I will pay Babylon back.
You will see it with your own eyes. I
will pay back all those who live in Babylon. I will pay them back for all the
wrong things they have done in Zion,"
announces the LORD.

25 "Babylon, I am against you.
Your kingdom is like a destroying mountain.
You have destroyed the whole earth,"
announces the LORD.
"I will reach out my hand against you.
I will roll you off the cliffs.
I will make you like a mountain that has been burned up.
26 No rock will be taken from you to be used
as the most important stone for a building.
No stones will be taken from you to be used for a foundation.
Your land will be empty forever,"
announces the LORD.

27 "Nations, lift up a banner in the land of Babylon!
Blow a trumpet among yourselves!
Prepare yourselves for battle against Babylon.

Send the kingdoms
of Ararat, Minni and Ashkenaz
against it.
Appoint a commander against it.
Send many horses against it.
Let them be as many as a huge
number of locusts.
28 Prepare yourselves for battle
against Babylon.
Prepare the kings of the Medes.
Prepare their governors and all
their officials.
Prepare all the countries they
rule over.
29 The Babylonians tremble and
shake with fear.
My plans against them stand
firm.
I plan to destroy their land
completely.
Then no one will live there.
30 Babylon's soldiers have stopped
fighting.
They remain in their forts.
Their strength is all gone.
They have become weak.
Their buildings are set on fire.
The metal bars that lock their
gates are broken.
31 One messenger after another
comes to the king of Babylon.
All of them announce that
his entire city is captured.
32 The places where people go across
the Euphrates River have been
captured.
The swamps have been set on fire.
And the soldiers are terrified."

33 The LORD who rules over all is the
God of Israel. He says,

"The city of Babylon is like a
threshing floor
when cattle are walking on it.
The time to destroy it will soon
come."

34 The people of Jerusalem say,
"Nebuchadnezzar, the king of
Babylon, has destroyed us.
He has thrown us into a panic.
He has emptied us out like a jar.
Like a snake he has swallowed
us up.
He has filled his stomach with
our rich food.
Then he has spit us out of his
mouth."

35 The people continue, "May the
people of Babylon
pay for the harmful things they
have done to us.
May those who live in Babylon
pay for spilling the blood of our
people."
That's what the people who live
in Zion say.

36 So the LORD says,

"I will stand up for you.
I will pay the Babylonians back
for what they did to you.
I will dry up their water supply.
I will make their springs run dry.
37 Babylon will have all its buildings
knocked down.
It will be a home for wild dogs.
No one will live there.
People will be shocked at it.
They will make fun of it.
38 All its people roar like young lions.
They growl like lion cubs.
39 They are stirred up.
So I will set a feast in front of
them.
I will make them drunk.
And they will shout and laugh.
But then they will lie down and
die.
They will never wake up,"
announces the LORD.
40 "I will lead them down like lambs
to be put to death.
They will be like rams and goats
that have been killed.

41 "Babylon will be captured!
The whole earth was very proud
of it.
But it will be taken over by others!
It will be a deserted place among
the nations.
42 Babylon's enemies will sweep over
it like an ocean.
Like roaring waves they will
cover it.
43 The towns of Babylon will be
empty.
It will become a dry and desert
land.
No one will live there.
No one will even travel through it.
44 I will punish the god named Bel in
Babylon.
I will make Bel spit out what he
has swallowed.

The nations will not come and
worship him anymore.
And Babylon's walls will fall down.

45 "Come out of there, my people!
Run for your lives!
Run away from my great anger.
46 You will hear about terrible things
that are happening in Babylon.
But do not lose hope. Do not be
afraid.
You will hear one thing this year.
And you will hear something else
next year.
You will hear about awful things in
the land.
You will hear about one ruler
fighting against another.
47 I will punish the gods of Babylon.
That time will certainly come.
Then the whole land will be full of
shame.
Its people will lie down and die
there.
48 So heaven and earth and
everything in them will shout
for joy.
They will be glad because of
what will happen to Babylon.
Armies will attack it from the
north.
And they will destroy it,"
announces the LORD.

49 "Babylon's people have killed my
people Israel.
They have also killed people all
over the earth.
So now Babylon itself must fall.
50 You who have not been killed in the
war against Babylon,
leave! Do not wait!
In a land far away remember me.
And think about Jerusalem."

51 The people of Judah reply, "No one
honors us anymore.
People make fun of us.
Our faces are covered with
shame.
People from other lands have
entered
the holy places of the LORD's
house."

52 "But the days are coming,"
announces the LORD.
"At that time I will punish the
gods of Babylon.
And all through its land
wounded people will groan.
53 What if Babylon reached all the
way to the heavens?
What if it made its high walls
even stronger?
I would still send destroyers
against it,"
announces the LORD.

54 "The noise of people screaming
comes from Babylon.
A terrible sound comes from its
land.
It is the sound of a mighty city
being destroyed.
55 I will destroy Babylon.
I will put an end to all its noise.
Waves of enemies will sweep
through it like great waters.
The roar of their voices will fill
the air.
56 A destroying army will come
against Babylon.
The soldiers in the city will be
captured.
Their bows will be broken.
I am the LORD God who pays people
back.
I will pay them back in full.
57 I will make Babylon's officials and
wise men drunk.
I will do the same thing to its
governors, officers and soldiers.
They will lie down and die. They
will never wake up,"
announces the King. His name is
the LORD Who Rules Over All.

58 The LORD who rules over all says,

"Babylon's thick walls will fall
down flat.
Its high gates will be set on fire.
The nations wear themselves out
for no reason at all.
Their hard work will only be
burned up in the flames."

59 Jeremiah the prophet gave a message to the staff officer Seraiah, the
son of Neriah. Neriah was the son of
Mahseiah. Jeremiah told Seraiah to
take the message with him to Babylon.
Seraiah went there with Zedekiah, the
king of Judah. He left in the fourth year
of Zedekiah's rule. 60 Jeremiah had written about all the trouble that would
come on Babylon. He had written it

down on a scroll. It included everything
that had been recorded about Babylon.
61 Jeremiah said to Seraiah, "When you
get to Babylon, here's what I want you
to do. Make sure that you read all these
words out loud. 62 Then say, 'LORD, you
have said you will destroy this place.
You have said that no people or animals
will live here. It will be empty forever.'
63 Finish reading the scroll. Tie a stone
to it. Throw it into the Euphrates River.
64 Then say, 'In the same way, Babylon
will sink down. It will never rise again.
That is because I will bring such horrible
trouble on it. And its people will fall
along with it.' "

The words of Jeremiah end here.

Nebuchadnezzar Destroys Jerusalem

52 Zedekiah was 21 years old when
he became king. He ruled in Jerusalem for 11 years. His mother's name
was Hamutal. She was the daughter of
Jeremiah. She was from Libnah. 2 Zedekiah did what was evil in the eyes of
the LORD. He did just as Jehoiakim had
done. 3 The enemies of Jerusalem and
Judah attacked them because the LORD
was angry. In the end he threw them
out of his land.

Zedekiah refused to obey the king
of Babylon.

4 Nebuchadnezzar was the king of
Babylon. He marched out against Jerusalem. All his armies went with him.
It was in the ninth year of the rule of
Zedekiah. It was on the tenth day of the
tenth month. The armies set up camp
outside the city. They set up ladders and
built ramps and towers all around it. 5 It
was surrounded until the 11th year of
King Zedekiah's rule.

6 By the ninth day of the fourth
month, there wasn't any food left in the
city. So the people didn't have anything
to eat. 7 Then the Babylonians broke
through the city wall. Judah's whole
army ran away. They left the city at
night. They went out through the gate
between the two walls that were near
the king's garden. They escaped even
though the Babylonians surrounded the
city. Judah's army ran toward the Arabah Valley. 8 But the armies of Babylon
chased King Zedekiah. They caught up
with him in the plains near Jericho. All
his soldiers were separated from him.
They had scattered in every direction.
9 The king was captured.

He was taken to the king of Babylon
at Riblah. Riblah was in the land of
Hamath. That's where Nebuchadnezzar
decided how Zedekiah would be punished. 10 At Riblah the king of Babylon
killed the sons of Zedekiah. He forced
him to watch it with his own eyes. Nebuchadnezzar also killed all the officials of
Judah. 11 Then he poked out Zedekiah's
eyes. He put him in bronze chains. And
he took him to Babylon. There he put
Zedekiah in prison until the day he died.

12 Nebuzaradan served the king of
Babylon. In fact, he was commander of
the royal guard. He came to Jerusalem.
It was in the 19th year that Nebuchadnezzar was king of Babylon. It was on
the tenth day of the fifth month. 13 Nebuzaradan set the LORD's temple on fire.
He also set fire to the royal palace and
all the houses in Jerusalem. He burned
down every important building. 14 The
armies of Babylon broke down all the
walls around Jerusalem. That's what
the commander told them to do. 15 Some
of the poorest people still remained in
the city along with the others. But the
commander Nebuzaradan took them
away as prisoners. He also took the rest
of the skilled workers. That included
the people who had joined the king of
Babylon. 16 But Nebuzaradan left the
rest of the poorest people of the land
behind. He told them to work in the
vineyards and fields.

17 The armies of Babylon destroyed
the LORD's temple. They broke the
bronze pillars into pieces. They broke
up the bronze stands that could be
moved around. And they broke up the
huge bronze bowl. Then they carried
away all the bronze to Babylon. 18 They
also took away the pots, shovels, wick
cutters, sprinkling bowls and dishes.
They took away all the bronze objects
that were used for any purpose in the
temple. 19 The commander of the royal
guard took away the bowls and the
shallow cups for burning incense. He
took away the sprinkling bowls, the
pots, the lampstands and the dishes.
He took away the bowls used for drink
offerings. So he took away everything
made out of pure gold or silver.

20 The bronze was more than anyone
could weigh. It included the bronze from
the two pillars. It included the bronze
from the huge bowl and the 12 bronze
bulls under it. It also included the stands.
King Solomon had made all those things
for the LORD's temple. 21 Each pillar was 27
feet high and 18 feet around. The pillars
were hollow. The metal in each of them
was three inches thick. 22 The bronze
top of one pillar was seven and a half
feet high. It was decorated with a set
of bronze chains and pomegranates all
around it. The other pillar was just like
it. It also had pomegranates. 23 There
were 96 pomegranates on the sides of
each of the two tops. The total number of
pomegranates above the bronze chains
around each top was 100.

24 The commander of the guard took
many prisoners. They included Seraiah
the chief priest and Zephaniah the priest
who reported to him. They also included
the three men who guarded the temple
doors. 25 Some people were still left in the
city. The commander took as a prisoner
the officer in charge of the fighting men.
He took the seven men who gave advice
to the king. He also took the secretary
who was the chief officer in charge of
getting the people of the land to serve
in the army. There were 60 people of the
land still in the city. 26 The commander
Nebuzaradan took all of them away. He
brought them to the king of Babylon at
Riblah. 27 There the king had them put to
death. Riblah was in the land of Hamath.

So the people of Judah were taken as
prisoners. They were taken far away
from their own land.

28 Here is the number of the people
Nebuchadnezzar took to Babylon
as prisoners.

In the seventh year of his rule,
he took 3,023 Jews.
29 In his 18th year,
he took 832 people from
Jerusalem.
30 In Nebuchadnezzar's 23rd year,
Nebuzaradan, the commander
of the royal guard, took 745 Jews
to Babylon.

The total number of people taken
to Babylon was 4,600.

Jehoiachin Is Set Free

31 Awel-Marduk set Jehoiachin, the
king of Judah, free from prison. It was
in the 37th year after Jehoiachin had
been taken away to Babylon. It was
also the year Awel-Marduk became king
of Babylon. It was on the 25th day of
the 12th month. 32 Awel-Marduk spoke
kindly to Jehoiachin. He gave him a
place of honor. Other kings were with
Jehoiachin in Babylon. But his place
was more important than theirs. 33 So
Jehoiachin put away his prison clothes.
For the rest of Jehoiachin's life the king
of Babylon provided what he needed.
34 The king did that for Jehoiachin day
by day as long as he lived. He did it until
the day Jehoiachin died.

LAMENTATIONS

Author: We don't know (but it might be Jeremiah).

Do you remember when God's people did whatever they wanted and lost everything they had, including the temple? Because of their sin and disobedience, Israel was completely devastated. They went from living in the land God had given them, worshiping him in the temple, and enjoying fellowship with him and each other to being slaves in a foreign land! Everything changed because of their disobedience.

Prophecy

The book of Lamentations was written during this sad time in Israel's history. And it was written differently than most of the other books. Instead of retelling the story of what happened, Lamentations tells how sad the author feels when people run away from God. The book is like a long sad song sharing what it feels like to lose everything because of sin. God's people were sad because they disobeyed and were sent far from him and far from home.

The author lamented, or told how deeply upset he was, because everything seemed to be falling apart. But the author also reminded God's people that his mercies never end (see Lamentations 3:22–23). And one day his mercies would be shown through the Savior.

1 The city of Jerusalem is so empty!
She used to be full of people.
But now she's like a woman whose
husband has died.
She used to be great among the
nations.
She was like a queen among the
kingdoms.
But now she is a slave.

2 Jerusalem weeps bitterly at night.
Tears run down her cheeks.
None of her friends comforts her.
All those who were going to help her
have turned against her.
They have become her enemies.

3 After Judah's people had suffered
greatly,
they were taken away as prisoners.
Now they live among the nations.
They can't find any place to rest.
All those who were chasing them
have caught up with them.
And they can't get away.

4 The roads to Zion are empty.
No one travels to her appointed
feasts.
All the public places near her gates
are deserted.
Her priests groan.
Her young women are sad.
And Zion herself weeps bitterly.

5 Her enemies have become her
masters.
They have an easy life.
The LORD has brought suffering to
Jerusalem
because her people have
committed so many sins.
Her children have been taken away
as prisoners.
Her enemies have forced her
people to leave their homes.

6 The city of Zion used to be full of
glory.
But now her glory has faded away.
Her princes are like deer.
They can't find anything to eat.
They are almost too weak to get
away
from those who hunt them down.

7 Jerusalem's people are suffering
and wandering.
They remember all the treasures
they used to have.

in Lamentations?

God is the Merciful Judge. God doesn't let sin go unpunished, yet his mercy is unending.

But they fell into the hands of their
enemies.
And no one was there to help
them.
Their enemies looked at them.
They laughed because Jerusalem
had been destroyed.

8 Her people have committed many
sins.
They have become impure.
All those who honored Jerusalem
now look down on her.
They all look at her as if she were
a naked woman.
The city groans and turns away
in shame.

9 Her skirts are dirty.
She didn't think about how
things might turn out.
Her fall from power amazed
everyone.
And no one was there to comfort
her.
She said, "LORD, please pay attention
to how much I'm suffering.
My enemies have won the battle
over me."

10 Jerusalem's enemies took away
all her treasures.
Her people saw outsiders
enter her temple.
The LORD had commanded them
not to do that.

11 All Jerusalem's people groan
as they search for bread.
They trade their treasures for food
just to stay alive.

Jerusalem says, "LORD, look at me.
Think about my condition.
Everyone looks down on me."

12 Jerusalem also says, "All you who are passing by,
don't you care about what has happened to me?
Just look at my condition.
Has anyone suffered the way I have?
The LORD has brought all this on me.
He has made me suffer.
His anger has burned against me.

13 "He sent down fire from heaven.
It went deep down into my bones.
He spread a net to catch me by the feet.
He stopped me right where I was.
He made me empty.
I am sick all the time.

14 "My sins have been made into a heavy yoke.
They were woven together by his hands.
They have been placed on my neck.
The Lord has taken away my strength.
He has handed me over to my enemies.
I can't win the battle over them.

15 "The Lord has refused to accept any of my soldiers.
He has sent for an army
to crush my young men.
I am like grapes in the Lord's winepress.
He has stomped on me,
even though I am his very own.

16 "That's why I am weeping.
Tears are flowing from my eyes.
No one is near to comfort me.
No one can heal my spirit.
My children don't have anything.
My enemies are much too strong for me."

17 Zion reaches out her hands.
But no one is there to comfort her people.
The LORD has ordered that
the neighbors of Jacob's people
would become their enemies.
Jerusalem has become impure among them.

18 Jerusalem says, "The LORD always does what is right.
But I refused to obey his commands.
Listen, all you nations.
Pay attention to how much I'm suffering.
My young men and women
have been taken away as prisoners.

19 "I called out to those who were going to help me.
But they turned against me.
My priests and elders
died in the city.
They were searching for food
just to stay alive.

20 "LORD, see how upset I am!
I am suffering deep down inside.
My heart is troubled.
Again and again I have refused to obey you.
Outside the city, people are being killed by swords.
Inside, there is nothing but death.

21 "People have heard me groan.
But no one is here to comfort me.
My enemies have heard about all my troubles.
What you have done makes them happy.
So please judge them, just as you said you would.
Let them become like me.

22 "Please pay attention to all their sinful ways.
Punish them as you have punished me.
You judged me because I had committed so many sins.
I groan all the time.
And my heart is weak."

2 See how the Lord covered the city of Zion
with the cloud of his anger!
He threw Israel's glory down
from heaven to earth.
When he was angry, he turned his back
on his own city.

2 Without pity the Lord swallowed up
all the homes of Jacob's people.
When he was angry, he tore down
the forts of the people of Judah.

He brought down their kingdom
and princes
to the ground in dishonor.

3 When he was very angry,
he took away Israel's power.
He pulled back his powerful right
hand
as the enemy approached.
His burning anger blazed out in
Jacob's land.
It burned up everything near it.

4 Like an enemy the Lord got his bow
ready to use.
He had a sword in his right hand.
Like an enemy he destroyed
everything that used to be
pleasing to him.
His anger blazed out like fire.
It burned up the homes in the
city of Zion.

5 The Lord was like an enemy.
He swallowed up Israel.
He swallowed up all of its palaces.
He destroyed its forts.
He filled the people of Judah
with sorrow and sadness.

6 The LORD's temple was like a
garden.
But he completely destroyed it.
He destroyed the place
where he used to meet with his
people.
He made Zion's people forget
their appointed feasts and
Sabbath days.
When he was very angry, he turned
his back on
king and priest alike.

7 The Lord deserted his altar.
He left his temple.
He gave the walls of Jerusalem's
palaces
into the hands of her enemies.
They shouted loudly in the house
of the LORD.
You would have thought it was
the day
of an appointed feast.

8 The LORD decided to tear down
the walls around the city of Zion.
He measured out what he wanted
to destroy.
Then he destroyed Jerusalem by
his power.
He made even her towers and walls
sing songs of sadness.
All of them fell down.

9 Her gates sank down into the
ground.
He broke the metal bars that
locked her gates, and he
destroyed them.
Her king and princes were taken
away to other nations.
There is no law anymore.
Jerusalem's prophets no longer
receive
visions from the LORD.

10 The elders of the city of Zion
sit silently on the ground.
They have sprinkled dust on their
heads.
They've put on the clothes of
sadness.
The young women of Jerusalem
have bowed their heads toward
the ground.

11 I've cried so much I can't see very
well.
I'm suffering deep down inside.
My heart is broken
because my people are
destroyed.
Children and babies are fainting
in the streets of the city.

12 They say to their mothers,
"Where can we find something to
eat and drink?"
They faint like wounded soldiers
in the streets of the city.
Their lives are slipping away
in their mothers' arms.

13 City of Jerusalem, what can I say
about you?
What can I compare you to?
People of Zion, what are you like?
I want to comfort you.
Your wound is as deep as the ocean.
Who can heal you?

14 The visions of your prophets were
lies.
They weren't worth anything.
They didn't show you the sins you
had committed.
So that's why you were captured.
The messages they gave you were
lies.
They led you astray.

15 All those who pass by
clap their hands and make fun of you.
They laugh at you and shake their heads
at the city of Jerusalem.
They say, "Could that be the city
that was called perfect and beautiful?
Is that the city that brought joy
to everyone on earth?"
16 All your enemies open their mouths
wide against you.
They laugh at you and grind their teeth.
They say, "We have swallowed
up Jerusalem's people.
This is the day we've waited for.
And we've lived to see it."
17 The LORD has done what he planned to do.
He has made what he said come true.
He gave the command long ago.
He has destroyed you without pity.
He has let your enemies laugh at you.
He has made them stronger than you are.
18 People in the city of Zion,
cry out from your heart to the Lord.
Let your tears flow like a river
day and night.
Don't stop at all.
Don't give your eyes any rest.
19 Get up. Cry out as the night begins.
Tell the Lord all your troubles.
Lift up your hands to him.
Pray that the lives of your
children will be spared.
At every street corner they faint
because they are so hungry.
20 Jerusalem says, "LORD, look at me.
Think about my condition.
Have you ever treated anyone
else like this?
Should women have to eat their babies?
Should they eat the children
they've taken care of?
Should priests and prophets be killed
in your own temple?
21 "Young people and old people alike
lie dead in the dust of my streets.
My young men and women
have been killed by swords.
You killed them when you were angry.
You put them to death without pity.
22 "You sent for terrors to come
against me on every side.
It was as if you were inviting
people to enjoy a feast day.
Because you were angry, no one escaped.
No one was left alive.
I took good care of my children and
brought them up.
But my enemies have destroyed them."

3

I am a man who has suffered greatly.
The LORD has used the Babylonians
to punish my people.
2 He has driven me away. He has made me walk
in darkness instead of light.
3 He has turned his powerful hand against me.
He has done it again and again,
all day long.
4 He has worn out my body.
He has broken my bones.
5 He has surrounded me and attacked me.
He has made me suffer bitterly.
He has made things hard for me.
6 He has made me live in darkness
like those who are dead and gone.
7 He has built walls around me, so I can't escape.
He has put heavy chains on me.
8 I call out and cry for help.
But he won't listen to me when I pray.
9 He has put up a stone wall to block my way.
He has made my paths crooked.
10 He has been like a bear waiting to attack me.
He has been like a lion hiding in the bushes.
11 He has dragged me off the path.
He has torn me to pieces.
And he has left me helpless.

12 He has gotten his bow ready to use.
He has shot his arrows at me.

13 The arrows from his bag
have gone through my heart.
14 My people laugh at me all the time.
They sing and make fun of me
all day long.
15 The LORD has made my life bitter.
He has made me suffer bitterly.

16 He made me chew stones that
broke my teeth.
He has walked all over me in the
dust.
17 I have lost all hope of ever having
any peace.
I've forgotten what good times
are like.
18 So I say, "My glory has faded
away.
My hope in the LORD is gone."

19 I remember how I suffered and
wandered.
I remember how bitter my life
was.
20 I remember it very well.
My spirit is very sad deep down
inside me.
21 But here is something else I
remember.
And it gives me hope.

22 The LORD loves us very much.
So we haven't been completely
destroyed.
His loving concern never fails.
23 His great love is new every
morning.
LORD, how faithful you are!
24 I say to myself, "The LORD is
everything I will ever need.
So I will put my hope in him."

25 The LORD is good to those who put
their hope in him.
He is good to those who look to
him.
26 It is good when people wait
quietly
for the LORD to save them.
27 It is good for a man to carry a
heavy load of suffering
while he is young.

28 Let him sit alone and not say
anything.
The LORD has placed that load on
him.
29 Let him bury his face in the dust.
There might still be hope for him.
30 Let him turn his cheek toward
those who would slap him.
Let him be filled with shame.

31 The Lord doesn't turn his back
on people forever.
32 He might bring suffering.
But he will also show loving
concern.
How great his faithful love is!
33 He doesn't want to bring pain
or suffering to anyone.

34 Every time people crush prisoners
under their feet,
the Lord knows all about it.
35 When people refuse to give
someone what they should,
the Most High God knows it.
36 When people don't treat someone
fairly,
the Lord knows it.

37 Suppose people order something to
happen.
It won't happen unless the Lord
has planned it.
38 Troubles and good things alike
come to people
because the Most High God has
commanded them to come.

If I ask God to forgive me, will he ever reject me?

God promises to forgive you when you confess your sin to him. He doesn't run out of patience; he loves you very much.

Can you find the following verses?

LAMENTATIONS 3:22–23

39 A person who is still alive shouldn't
blame God
when God punishes them for
their sins.
40 Let's take a good look at the way
we're living.
Let's return to the LORD.
41 Let's lift up our hands to God in
heaven.
Let's pray to him with all our
hearts.
42 Let's say, "We have sinned.
We've refused to obey you.
And you haven't forgiven us.
43 "You have covered yourself with
the cloud of your anger.
You have chased us.
You have killed us without pity.
44 You have covered yourself with the
cloud of your anger.
Our prayers can't get through to
you.
45 You have made us become like
trash and garbage
among the nations.
46 "All our enemies have opened their
mouths wide
to swallow us up.
47 We are terrified and trapped.
We are broken and destroyed."
48 Streams of tears flow from my eyes.
That's because my people are
destroyed.
49 Tears will never stop flowing from
my eyes.
My eyes can't get any rest.
50 I'll weep until the LORD looks down
from heaven.
I'll cry until he notices my tears.
51 What I see brings pain to my spirit.
All the women of my city are
mourning.
52 Those who were my enemies for no
reason at all
hunted me down as if I were a bird.
53 They tried to end my life
by throwing me into a deep pit.
They threw stones down at me.
54 The water rose and covered my
head.
I thought I was going to die.
55 LORD, I called out to you.
I called out from the bottom of
the pit.
56 I prayed, "Please don't close your
ears
to my cry for help."
And you heard my appeal.
57 You came near when I called out to
you.
You said, "Do not be afraid."
58 Lord, you stood up for me in court.
You saved my life and set me
free.
59 LORD, you have seen the wrong
things
people have done to me.
Stand up for me again!
60 You have seen how my enemies
have tried to get even with me.
You know all about their plans
against me.
61 LORD, you have heard them laugh
at me.
You know all about their plans
against me.
62 You have heard my enemies
whispering among themselves.
They speak against me all day
long.
63 Just look at them sitting and
standing there!
They sing and make fun of me.
64 LORD, pay them back.
Punish them for what their
hands have done.
65 Cover their minds with a veil.
Put a curse on them!
66 LORD, get angry with them and
hunt them down.
Wipe them off the face of the
earth.

4 Look at how the gold has lost its
brightness!
See how dull the fine gold has
become!
The sacred jewels are scattered
at every street corner.
2 The priceless children of Zion
were worth their weight in gold.
But now they are thought of as clay
pots
made by the hands of a potter.
3 Even wild dogs
nurse their young pups.
But my people are as mean
as ostriches in the desert.

4 When the babies get thirsty,
their tongues stick to the roofs of their mouths.
When the children beg for bread,
no one gives them any.

5 Those who once ate fine food
are dying in the streets.
Those who wore royal clothes
are now lying on piles of trash.

6 My people have been punished
more than Sodom was.
It was destroyed in a moment.
No one offered it a helping hand.

7 Jerusalem's princes were brighter than snow.
They were whiter than milk.
Their bodies were redder than rubies.
They looked like lapis lazuli.

8 But now they are blacker than coal.
No one even recognizes them in the streets.
Their skin is wrinkled on their bones.
It has become as dry as a stick.

9 Those killed by swords are better off
than those who die of hunger.
Those who are hungry waste away to nothing.
They don't have any food from the fields.

10 With their own hands, loving mothers
have had to cook even their own children.
They ate their children
when my people were destroyed.

11 The LORD has become very angry.
He has poured out his burning anger.
He started a fire in Zion.
It burned its foundations.

12 The kings of the earth couldn't believe what was happening.
Neither could any of the peoples of the world.
Enemies actually attacked and entered
the gates of Jerusalem.

13 It happened because Jerusalem's prophets had sinned.
Her priests had done evil things.
All of them spilled the blood
of those who did what was right.

14 Now those prophets and priests
have to feel their way along the streets
as if they were blind.
The blood of those they killed has made them "unclean."
So no one dares to touch their clothes.

15 "Go away! You are 'unclean'!"
people cry out to them.
"Go away! Get out of here!
Don't touch us!"
So they run away and wander around.
Then people among the nations say,
"They can't stay here anymore."

16 The LORD himself has scattered them.
He doesn't watch over them anymore.
No one shows the priests any respect.
No one honors the elders.

17 And that's not all. Our eyes grew tired.
We looked for help that never came.
We watched from our towers.
We kept looking for a nation that couldn't save us.

18 People hunted us down no matter where we went.
We couldn't even walk in our streets.
Our end was near, so we only had a few days to live.
Our end had come.

19 Those who were hunting us down were faster
than eagles in the sky.
They chased us over the mountains.
They hid and waited for us in the desert.

20 Zedekiah, the LORD's anointed king,
was our last hope.
But he was caught in their traps.
We thought he would keep us safe.
We expected to continue living among the nations.

[21]People of Edom, be joyful.
You who live in the land of Uz, be glad.
But the cup of the LORD's anger will also be passed to you.
Then you will become drunk.
Your clothes will be stripped off.

[22]People of Zion, the time for you to be punished
will come to an end.
The LORD won't keep you away from your land any longer.
But he will punish your sin, people of Edom.
He will show everyone the evil things you have done.

5 LORD, think about what has happened to us.
Look at the shame our enemies have brought on us.
[2]The land you gave us has been turned over to outsiders.
Our homes have been given to strangers.
[3]Our fathers have been killed.
Our mothers don't have husbands.
[4]We have to buy the water we drink.
We have to pay for the wood we use.
[5]Those who chase us are right behind us.
We're tired and can't get any rest.
[6]We put ourselves under the control of Egypt and Assyria
just to get enough bread.
[7]Our people of long ago sinned.
And they are now dead.
We are being punished because of their sins.
[8]Slaves rule over us.
No one can set us free
from their power.
[9]We put our lives in danger just to get some bread to eat.
Robbers in the desert might kill us with their swords.
[10]Our skin is as hot as an oven.
We are so hungry we're burning up with fever.

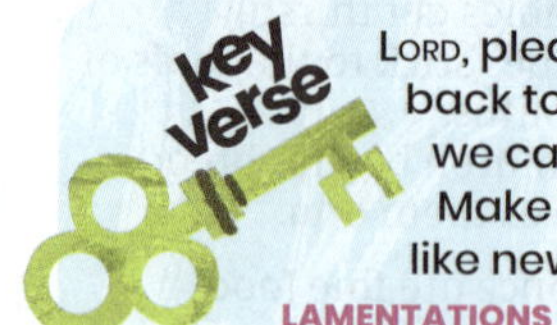

LORD, please bring us back to you. Then we can return. Make our lives like new again.
LAMENTATIONS 5:21

[11]Our women have been treated badly in Zion.
Our virgins have been treated badly in the towns of Judah.
[12]Our princes have been hung up by their hands.
No one shows our elders any respect.
[13]Our young men are forced to grind grain at the mill.
Our boys almost fall down
as they carry heavy loads of wood.
[14]Our elders don't go to the city gate anymore.
Our young men have stopped playing their music.
[15]There isn't any joy in our hearts.
Our dancing has turned into mourning.
[16]All of our honor is gone.
How terrible it is for us because we have sinned!
[17]So our hearts are weak.
Our eyes can't see very clearly.
[18]Mount Zion has been deserted.
Wild dogs are prowling all around on it.

[19]LORD, you rule forever.
Your throne will last for all time to come.
[20]Why do you always forget us?
Why have you deserted us for so long?
[21]LORD, please bring us back to you.
Then we can return.
Make our lives like new again.
[22]Or have you completely turned away from us?
Are you really that angry with us?

EZEKIEL

Author: Ezekiel

Ezekiel was a prophet of God who lived during the time in Israel's history when the Babylonians took captive part of the nation of Israel. God's people were far from home and far from God. They were living in a foreign land, surrounded by false gods. God had spoken to his people through many prophets, telling the people to repent and return to him, but they didn't listen. They insisted on doing things their own way rather than God's way. God said their hearts were like rocks or stones—hard toward God and unmoving in their disobedience.

Through Ezekiel, God warned that if the people continued in their sin and did not repent, they would experience consequences. Through Ezekiel, God also gave the people a message of hope: He promised that he would give them hearts that were sensitive to him to replace their hearts of stone (see Ezekiel 36:26). God was going to show them compassion by helping them listen to and obey his commands. Ezekiel's words reminded God's people that one day God would send the Savior to make all things right again: both for the nation of Israel and for all who put their trust in him.

Prophecy

I am the LORD your God . . .

The LORD Gives Ezekiel Visions of His Glory

1 I was 30 years old. I was with my people. We had been taken away from our country. We were by the Kebar River in the land of Babylon. On the fifth day of the fourth month, the heavens were opened. I saw visions of God.

2 It was the fifth day of the month. Jehoiachin had been king of Judah. It was the fifth year since he had been brought to Babylon as a prisoner. 3 A message from the LORD came to me. I was by the Kebar River in Babylon. The power of the LORD came on me there. I am Ezekiel the priest, the son of Buzi.

4 I looked up and saw a windstorm coming from the north. I saw a huge cloud. The fire of lightning was flashing out of it. Bright light surrounded it. The center of the fire looked like glowing metal. 5 I saw in the fire something that looked like four living creatures. They appeared to have the shape of a human being. 6 But each of them had four faces and four wings. 7 Their legs were straight. Their feet looked like the feet of a calf. They were as bright as polished bronze. 8 The creatures had human hands under their wings on their four sides. All four of them had faces and wings. 9 The wings of one touched the wings of another. Each of the creatures went straight ahead. They didn't change their direction as they moved.

10 Here's what their faces looked like. Each of the four creatures had the face of a human being. On the right side each had the face of a lion. On the left each had the face of an ox. Each one also had an eagle's face. 11 That's what their faces looked like. They each had two wings that spread out and lifted up. Each wing touched the wing of another creature on either side. They each had two other wings that covered their bodies. 12 All the creatures went straight ahead. Anywhere their spirits would lead them to go, they would go. They didn't change their direction as they went. 13 The living creatures looked like burning coals of fire or like torches. Fire moved back and forth among the creatures. It was bright. Lightning flashed out of it. 14 The creatures raced back and forth like flashes of lightning.

15 As I looked at the living creatures, I saw wheels on the ground beside them. Each creature had four faces. 16 Here's how the wheels looked and worked. They gleamed like topaz. All four of them looked alike. Each one seemed to be made like a wheel inside another wheel at right angles. 17 The wheels could go in any one of the four directions the creatures faced. The wheels didn't change their direction as the creatures moved. 18 Their rims were high and terrifying. All four rims were full of eyes all the way around them.

19 When the living creatures moved, the wheels beside them moved. When the creatures rose from the ground, the wheels also rose. 20 Anywhere their spirits would lead them to go, they would go. And the wheels would rise along with them. That's because the spirits of the living creatures were in the wheels. 21 When the living creatures moved, the wheels also moved. When the creatures stood still, they also stood still. When the creatures rose from the ground, the wheels rose along with them. That's because the spirits of the living creatures were in the wheels.

22 Something that looked like a huge space was spread out above the heads of the living creatures. It gleamed like crystal. It was terrifying. 23 The wings of the creatures were spread out under the space. They reached out toward one another. Each creature had two wings covering its body. 24 When the living creatures moved, I heard the sound of their wings. It was like the roar of rushing waters. It sounded like the thundering voice of the Mighty God. It was like the loud noise an army makes. When the creatures stood still, they lowered their wings.

25 Then a voice came from above the huge space over their heads. They stood with their wings lowered. 26 Above the space over their heads was something that looked like a throne made out of lapis lazuli. On the throne high above was a figure that appeared to be a man. 27 From his waist up he looked like glowing metal that was full of fire. From his waist down he looked like fire. Bright light surrounded him. 28 The glow around him looked like a rainbow in the clouds on a rainy day.

That's what the glory of the LORD looked like. When I saw it, I fell with my face toward the ground. Then I heard the voice of someone speaking.

The LORD Appoints Ezekiel to Speak for Him

2 He said to me, "Son of man, stand up on your feet. I will speak to you." 2 As he spoke, the Spirit of the LORD came into me. He raised me to my feet. I heard him speaking to me.

3 He said, "Son of man, I am sending you to the people of Israel. That nation has refused to obey me. They have turned against me. They and their people of long ago have been against me to this day. 4 The people I am sending you to are very stubborn. Tell them, 'Here is what the LORD and King says.' 5 They might listen, or they might not. After all, they refuse to obey me. But whether they listen or not, they will know that a prophet was among them. 6 Son of man, do not be afraid of them or of what they say. Do not be afraid, even if thorns and bushes are all around you. Do not be afraid, even if you live among scorpions. Do not be afraid of what they say. Do not be terrified by them. They always refuse to obey me. 7 You must give them my message. They might listen, or they might not. After all, they refuse to obey me. 8 Son of man, listen to what I tell you. Do not be like those who refuse to obey me. Open your mouth. Eat what I give you."

9 Then I looked up. I saw a hand reach out to me. A scroll was in it. 10 He unrolled it in front of me. Both sides had words written on them. They spoke about sadness, sorrow and trouble.

3 The LORD said to me, "Son of man, eat what is in front of you. Eat this scroll. Then go and speak to the people of Israel." 2 So I opened my mouth. And he gave me the scroll to eat.

3 Then he said to me, "Son of man, eat this scroll I am giving you. Fill your stomach with it." So I ate it. And it tasted as sweet as honey in my mouth.

4 Then he said to me, "Son of man, go to the people of Israel. Give them my message. 5 I am not sending you to people who speak another language that is hard to learn. Instead, I am sending you to the people of Israel. 6 You are not being sent to many nations whose people speak other

in Ezekiel?

God is the Transforming One. Only God can take a hard heart and make it soft again, displaying his transforming power.

languages that are hard to learn. You would not be able to understand them. Suppose I had sent you to them. Then they certainly would have listened to you. 7 But the people of Israel do not want to listen to you. That is because they do not want to listen to me. All the Israelites are very stubborn. 8 But I will make you just as stubborn as they are. 9 I will make you very brave. So do not be afraid of them. Do not let them terrify you, even though they refuse to obey me."

10 He continued, "Son of man, listen carefully. Take to heart everything I tell you. 11 Go now to your own people who were brought here as prisoners. Speak to them. Tell them, 'Here is what the LORD and King says.' Speak to them whether they listen or not."

12 Then the Spirit of the LORD lifted me up. I heard a loud rumbling sound behind me. The sound was made when the glory of the LORD rose up. It rose up from the place it had been standing. 13 The sound was made by the wings of the living creatures. They were brushing against one another. The sound was also made by the wheels beside them. It was a loud rumbling sound. 14 Then the Spirit lifted me up and took me away. My spirit was bitter. I was very angry. The power of the LORD was on me. 15 I came to my people who had been brought as prisoners to Tel Aviv. It was near the Kebar River. I went to where they were living. There I sat among them for seven days. I was very sad and scared about everything that had happened.

The LORD Has Appointed Ezekiel to Warn Israel

16 After seven days, a message from the LORD came to me. 17 The LORD said, "Son of man, I have appointed you as a prophet to warn the people of Israel. So listen to my message. Give them a warning from me. 18 Suppose I say to a sinful person, 'You can be sure you will die.' And you do not warn them. You do not try to get them to change their evil ways in order to save their life. Then that sinful person will die because they have sinned. And I will hold you responsible for their death. 19 But suppose you do warn that sinful person. And they do not turn away from their sin or their evil ways. Then they will die because they have sinned. But you will have saved yourself.

20 "Or suppose a godly person turns away from their godliness and does what is evil. And suppose I put something in their way that will trip them up. Then they will die. Since you did not warn them, they will die for their sin. The godly things that person did will not be remembered. And I will hold you responsible for their death. 21 But suppose you do warn a godly person not to sin. And they do not sin. Then you can be sure that they will live because they listened to your warning. And you will have saved yourself."

22 The power of the LORD was on me. He said, "Get up. Go out to the plain. I will speak to you there." 23 So I got up and went out to the plain. The glory of the LORD was standing there. It was just like the glory I had seen by the Kebar River. So I fell with my face toward the ground.

24 Then the Spirit of the LORD came into me. He raised me to my feet. He said to me, "Go, son of man. Shut yourself inside your house. 25 Some people will tie you up with ropes. So you will not be able to go out among your people. 26 I will make your tongue stick to the roof of your mouth. Then you will be silent. You will not be able to correct them. That's because they always refuse to obey me. 27 But later I will speak to you. I will open your mouth. Then you will tell them, 'Here is what the LORD and King says.' Those who listen will listen. And those who refuse to listen will refuse. They always refuse to obey me.

An Attack on Jerusalem Is Pictured

4 "Son of man, get a block of clay. Put it in front of you. Draw the city of Jerusalem on it. 2 Then pretend to surround it and attack it. Make some little models of war machines. Build a ramp up to it. Set camps up around it. Surround it with models of logs to be used for knocking down its gates. 3 Then get an iron pan. Put it between you and the city. Pretend it is an iron wall. Turn your face toward the city. It will be under attack when you begin to attack it. That will show the people of Israel what is going to happen to Jerusalem.

4 "Next, lie down on your left side. Pretend that you are putting Israel's sin on yourself. Keep their sin on you for the number of days you lie on your side. 5 Let each day you lie there stand for one year of their sin. So you will keep Israel's sin on you for 390 days.

6 "After you have finished this, lie down again. This time lie on your right side. Pretend that you are putting Judah's sin on yourself. Lie there for 40 days. That is one day for each year of their sin. 7 Next, turn your face toward the model of Jerusalem under attack. Uncover your arm as if you were a soldier ready to fight. Prophesy against the city. 8 I will tie you up with ropes. Then you will not be able to turn from one side to the other. You will stay that way until you have finished attacking Jerusalem.

9 "Get some wheat and barley. Also get some beans and lentils. And get some millet and spelt. Put everything in a storage jar. Use it to make some bread for yourself. Eat it during the 390 days you are lying down on your side. 10 Weigh out eight ounces of food to eat each day. Eat it at your regular mealtimes. 11 Also measure out two-thirds of a quart of water. Drink it at your regular mealtimes. 12 Eat your food as you would eat a loaf of barley bread. Bake it over human waste in front of the people." 13 The LORD said, "That is how the people of Israel will eat 'unclean' food. They will eat it in the nations where I will drive them."

14 Then I said, "No, LORD and King! I won't do this! I've never eaten anything 'unclean.' From the time I was young

until now, I've never eaten anything
that was found dead. And I've never
eaten anything torn apart by wild animals. 'Unclean' meat has never entered
my mouth."
15 "All right," he said. "I will let you bake
your bread over waste from cows. You
can use that instead of human waste."
16 He continued, "Son of man, I am
about to cut off the food supply in Jerusalem. The people will be worried
as they eat their tiny share of food.
They will not have any hope as they
drink their tiny share of water. 17 There
will be very little food and water. The
people will be shocked as they look at
one another. They will become weaker
and weaker because of their sin.

God's Judgment Will Be Like a Barber's Razor

5 "Son of man, get a sharp sword. Use
it as a barber's razor. Shave your
head and beard with it. Then get a set
of scales and weigh the hair. Separate it
into three piles. 2 Burn up a third of the
hair inside the city. Do this when you
stop attacking the model of Jerusalem.
Next, get another third of the hair. Strike
it with a sword all around the city. Then
scatter the last third to the winds. That
is because I will chase the people with
a sword that is ready to strike them
down. 3 But save a few hairs. Tuck them
away in the clothes you are wearing.
4 Next, get a few more hairs. Throw them
into the fire. Burn them up. The fire will
spread to all the people of Israel."
5 The LORD and King says, "What you
do with the hair stands for what I will do
with Jerusalem's people. I have placed
that city in the center of the nations.
Countries are all around it. 6 But its people are sinful. They have refused to obey
my laws and rules. They have turned
their backs on my laws. They have not
followed my rules. These people are
worse than the nations and countries
around them."
7 The LORD and King continues, "You
people have been worse than the nations around you. You have not lived
by my rules or kept my laws. You have
not even lived up to the standards of
the nations around you."
8 The LORD and King continues, "Jerusalem, I myself am against you. I will
punish you in the sight of the nations.
9 I will do to you what I have never
done before and will never do again.
That is because you worship statues
of gods. I hate them. 10 So parents will
eat their own children inside the city.
And children will eat their parents. I
will punish you. And I will scatter to the
winds anyone who is left alive. 11 You
have made my temple 'unclean.' You
have set up statues of all your evil gods.
You have done other things I hate. So I
will cut you off just like Ezekiel cut off
his hair. I will not spare you or feel sorry
for you. And that is just as sure as I am
alive," announces the LORD and King.
12 A third of your people will die of the
plague inside your walls. Or they will die
of hunger there. Another third will be
killed by swords outside your walls. And
I will scatter the last third of your people
to the winds. I will chase them with a
sword that is ready to strike them down.
13 "Then I will not be angry anymore.
My great anger against them will die
down. And I will be satisfied. Then
they will know that I have spoken with
strong feelings. And my great anger
toward them will come to an end. I am
the LORD.
14 "I will destroy you. I will bring
shame on you in the sight of the nations
around you. All those who pass by will
see it. 15 You will be put to shame. The
nations will make fun of you. You will
serve as a warning to others. They will
be shocked when they see you. So I
will punish you because I am very angry
with you. You will feel the sting of my
warning. I have spoken. I am the LORD.
16 I will shoot at you with my deadly, destroying arrows of hunger. I will shoot to
kill. I will bring more and more hunger
on you. I will cut off your food supply.
17 I will send hunger and wild animals
against you. They will destroy all your
children. Plague and murder will sweep
over you. And I will send swords to kill
you. I have spoken. I am the LORD."

Ezekiel Prophesies Against the Mountains of Israel

6 A message from the LORD came to
me. The LORD said, 2 "Son of man,
turn your attention to the mountains
of Israel. Prophesy against them.
3 Say, 'Mountains of Israel, listen to the

message of the LORD and King. Here is
what he says to the mountains and hills.
And here is what he says to the canyons
and valleys. He tells them, "I will send
swords to kill your people. I will destroy
the high places where you worship other
gods. 4 Your altars will be torn down.
Your incense altars will be smashed.
And I will kill your people in front of
the statues of your gods. 5 I will put the
dead bodies of Israelites in front of those
statues. I will scatter your bones around
your altars. 6 No matter where you live,
the towns will be destroyed. The high
places will be torn down. So your altars will be completely destroyed. The
statues of your gods will be smashed to
pieces. Your incense altars will be broken
down. And everything you have made
will be wiped out. 7 Your people will fall
down dead among you. Then you will
know that I am the LORD.
8 " ' "But I will spare some of you. Some
will escape from being killed by swords.
You will be scattered among other lands
and nations. 9 You will be taken away to
those nations as prisoners. Those of you
who escape will remember me. You will
recall how much pain your unfaithful
hearts gave me. You turned away from
me. Your eyes longed to see the statues
of your gods. You will hate yourselves
because of all the evil things you have
done. I hate those things too. 10 You will
know that I am the LORD. I said I would
bring trouble on you. And my warning
came true." ' "
11 The LORD and King said to me, "Clap
your hands. Stamp your feet. Cry out,
'How sad!' Do this because the people of
Israel have done so many evil things.
I hate those things. Israel will be destroyed by war, hunger and plague.
12 The one who is far away will die of
the plague. The one who is near will
be killed by swords. Anyone who is left
alive and is spared will die of hunger.
And in this way I will pour out my great
anger on them. 13 Then they will know
that I am the LORD. Their people will lie
dead among the statues of their gods
around their altars. Their bodies will
lie on every high hill and every moun-
taintop. They will lie under every green
tree and leafy oak tree. They used to
offer sweet-smelling incense to all their
gods at those places. 14 I will reach out
my powerful hand against them. The
land will become dry and empty. Those
people will live from the desert all the
way to Diblah. They will know that I
am the LORD."

The End Has Come

7 A message from the LORD came to
me. The LORD said, 2 "Son of man,
I am the LORD and King. I say to the
land of Israel, 'The end has come! It has
come on the four corners of the land.
3 The end has now come for you. I will
pour out my anger on you. I will judge
you based on how you have lived. I will
pay you back for all your evil practices.
I hate them.
4 " 'I will not feel sorry for you. I will
not spare you. You can be sure that I will
pay you back for how you have lived.
I will judge you for your evil practices.
I hate them. You will know that I am
the LORD.'
5 "I am the LORD and King. I say, 'Horrible trouble is coming! No one has ever
heard of anything like it. It is here!
6 " 'The end has come! The end has
come! It has stirred itself up against you.
It is here! 7 Death has come on you who
live in the land. The time for you to be
destroyed has come. The day when it will
happen is near. There is no joy on your
mountains. There is nothing but panic.
8 " 'I am about to pour out all my
great anger on you. I will judge you
based on how you have lived. I will pay
you back for all your evil practices. I
hate them.
9 " 'I will not feel sorry for you. I will
not spare you. I will pay you back for
how you have lived. I will judge you for
your evil practices. I hate them. You will
know that I am the one who strikes you
down. I am the LORD.
10 " 'The day for me to punish you is
here! It is here! Death has arrived. The
time is ripe for you to be judged. Your
pride has grown so much that you will
be destroyed. 11 Your mean and harmful
acts have become like a rod. I will use
it to punish those who do evil. None of
them will be left. None of their wealth
or anything of value will remain.
12 " 'The time has come! The day has
arrived! I will soon pour out my great
anger on the whole crowd of you. Do
not let the buyer be happy. Do not let

the seller be sad. 13 The seller will not get
back the land that was sold. That will
be true as long as both the buyer and
seller are alive.
“ ‘Ezekiel, the vision I gave you about
that whole crowd will come true. They
have committed many sins. So not one
of them will be able to save their life.
14 They have blown trumpets. They have
made everything ready. But no one will
go into battle. I will soon pour out my
great anger on the whole crowd.
15 “ ‘There is trouble everywhere. War
is outside the city. Plague and hunger
are inside it. Those out in the country
will die in battle. Those in the city will be
destroyed by hunger and plague. 16 All
those who escape and are left alive will
run to the mountains. They will sound
like doves of the valley when they cry
over their sins.
17 “ ‘Their hands will be powerless to
help them. They will wet themselves.
18 They will put on the rough clothing
people wear when they're sad. They will
put on terror as if it were their clothes.
Every face will be covered with shame.
Every head will be shaved.
19 “ ‘They will throw their silver into the
streets. They will treat their gold like an
“unclean” thing. Their silver and gold
won't be able to save them on the day
I pour out my anger. It will not be able
to satisfy their hunger. Their stomachs
can't be filled with it. Their silver and
gold have tripped them up. It has made
them fall into sin. 20 My people were so
proud of their beautiful jewelry. They
used it to make statues of their evil gods.
I hate those gods. So I will turn their
jewelry into an “unclean” thing for them.
21 “ ‘I will hand over their wealth to
outsiders. I will turn it over to sinful people in other countries. They will make
it “unclean.” 22 I will turn my face away
from my people. Robbers will make
“unclean” the temple I love. They will
enter it and make it “unclean.”
23 “ ‘Ezekiel, get ready to put my people in chains. The land is full of murderers. They are harming one another
all over Jerusalem. 24 I will bring the
most evil nations against them. They
will take over the houses in the city. I
will put an end to the pride of those
who are mighty. Their holy places will
be made “unclean.”
25 “ ‘When terror comes, they will look
for peace. But there will not be any.
26 Trouble after trouble will come. One
report will follow another. But they will
not be true. The people will go searching
for a vision from the prophets. But there
will not be any. The teaching of the law
by the priests will be gone. Advice from
the elders will come to an end.
27 “ ‘The king will be filled with sadness. The princes will lose all hope. The
hands of the people of the land will
tremble. I will punish them based on
how they have lived. I will judge them
by their own standards. Then they will
know that I am the LORD.’ ”

The People Worship Other Gods in the Temple

8 It was the sixth year since King
Jehoiachin had been brought to
Babylon as a prisoner. On the fifth day
of the sixth month, I was sitting in my
house. The elders of Judah were sitting
there with me. The power of the LORD
and King came on me there. 2 I looked
up and saw a figure that appeared to be
human. From his waist down he looked
like fire. From his waist up he looked as
bright as glowing metal. 3 He reached
out what appeared to be a hand. He took
hold of me by the hair of my head. The
Spirit of the LORD lifted me up between
earth and heaven. In visions God gave
me, the Spirit took me to Jerusalem.
He brought me to the entrance of the
north gate of the inner courtyard. The
statue of a god was standing there. It
made God very angry. 4 There in front
of me was the glory of the God of Israel.
It looked just as it did in the vision I had
seen on the plain.
5 Then the LORD said to me, “Son of
man, look toward the north.” So I did.
I saw a statue that made God angry. It
was in the entrance of the gate north
of the altar.
6 He said to me, “Son of man, do you
see what the Israelites are doing here?
They are doing things I hate very much.
Those things will cause me to go far
away from my temple. But you will see
things I hate even more.”
7 Then he brought me to the entrance
to the courtyard. I looked up and saw
a hole in the wall. 8 He said to me, “Son

of man, dig into the wall." So I did. And I saw a door there.

9 He continued, "Go through it. Look at the evil things they are doing here. I hate those things." 10 So I went in and looked. All over the walls were pictures of all kinds of crawling things and "unclean" animals. The LORD hates it when people worship those things. There were also carvings of the gods of the people of Israel. 11 In front of them stood 70 elders of Israel. Jaazaniah was standing there among them. He is the son of Shaphan. Each elder was holding a shallow cup. A sweet-smelling cloud of incense was rising from the cups.

12 The LORD spoke to me. He said, "Son of man, do you see what the elders of Israel are doing in the dark? Each of them is in his own room worshiping his own god. They say, 'The LORD doesn't see us. He has deserted the land.' " 13 He continued, "You will see them doing things I hate even more."

14 Then he brought me to the entrance of the north gate of the LORD's house. I saw women sitting there. They were mourning for the god named Tammuz. 15 The LORD said to me, "Son of man, do you see what they are doing? You will see things I hate even more."

16 Then he brought me into the inner courtyard of the LORD's house. About 25 men were there. They were at the entrance to the LORD's temple between the porch and the altar. Their backs were turned toward the temple. Their faces were turned toward the east. And they were bowing down to the sun.

17 He said to me, "Son of man, have you seen all of this? The people of Judah are doing things here that I hate. This is a very serious matter. They are harming one another all through the land. They continue to make me very angry. Just look at them making fun of me! 18 So I am angry with them. I will punish them. I will not spare them or feel sorry for them. They might even shout in my ears. But I will not listen to them."

The LORD Judges Those Who Worship Other Gods

9 Then I heard the LORD call out in a loud voice. He said, "Bring here those who are appointed to bring my judgment on the city. Make sure each of them has a weapon in his hand." 2 I saw six men coming from the direction of the upper gate. It faces north. Each of them had a deadly weapon in his hand. A man wearing linen clothes came along with them. He was carrying a writing kit at his side. They came in and stood beside the bronze altar.

3 The glory of the God of Israel had been above the cherubim. It moved from there to the doorway of the temple. Then the LORD called to the man who was dressed in linen clothes. He had the writing kit. 4 The LORD said to him, "Go all through Jerusalem. Look for those who are sad and sorry about all the things being done there. I hate those things. Put a mark on the foreheads of those people."

5 I heard him speak to the six men. He said, "Follow him through the city. Do not show any pity or concern. 6 Kill the old men and women, the young men and women, and the children. But do not touch anyone who has the mark. Start at my temple." So they began with the old men who were in front of the temple.

7 Then he said to the men, "Make the temple 'unclean.' Fill the courtyards with dead bodies. Go!" So they went out and started killing people all through the city. 8 While they were doing it, I was left alone. I fell with my face toward the ground. I cried out, "LORD and King, are you going to destroy all the Israelites who are still left alive? Will you pour out your great anger on all those who remain in Jerusalem?"

9 He answered me, "The sin of Israel and Judah is very great. The land is full of murderers. Its people are not being fair to one another anywhere in Jerusalem. They say, 'The LORD has deserted the land. He doesn't see us.' 10 So I will not spare them or feel sorry for them. Anything that happens to them will be their own fault."

11 Then the man wearing linen clothes returned. He had the writing kit. He reported, "I've done what you commanded."

The Glory of the LORD Moves Out of the Temple

10 I looked up and saw something that appeared to be a throne made out of lapis lazuli. It was above the huge space that was spread out over the heads of the cherubim. 2 The LORD spoke to the man who was wearing linen clothes. He said, "Go in among the wheels beneath the cherubim. Fill your hands with burning coals from the fire that is among the cherubim. Scatter the coals over the city." As I watched, he went in.

3 The cherubim were standing on the south side of the temple when the man went in. A cloud filled the inner courtyard. 4 Then the glory of the LORD rose from above the cherubim. It moved to the doorway of the temple. The cloud filled the temple. And the courtyard was full of the brightness of the glory of the LORD. 5 The sound the wings of the cherubim made could be heard as far away as the outer courtyard. It was like the voice of the Mighty God when he speaks.

6 The LORD gave a command to the man who was dressed in linen clothes. He said, "Get some coals of fire from among the wheels. Take them from among the cherubim." So the man went in and stood beside a wheel. 7 Then one of the cherubim reached out his hand. He picked up some of the burning coals that were among the wheels. He handed them to the man who was wearing linen clothes. The man took them and left. 8 I saw what looked like human hands. They were under the wings of the cherubim.

9 I looked up and saw four wheels beside the cherubim. One wheel was beside each of them. The wheels gleamed like topaz. 10 All four of them looked alike. Each wheel appeared to be inside another wheel at right angles. 11 The wheels could go in any one of the four directions the cherubim faced. The wheels didn't change their direction as the cherubim moved. The cherubim went in the direction their heads faced. They didn't change their direction as they moved. 12 Their whole bodies were completely covered with eyes. That included their backs, hands and wings. Their four wheels were covered with eyes too. 13 I heard someone tell the wheels to start spinning around. 14 Each of the cherubim had four faces. One face was the face of a cherub. The second was the face of a human being. The third was the face of a lion. And the fourth was an eagle's face.

15 The cherubim rose from the ground. They were the same living creatures I had seen by the Kebar River. 16 When the cherubim moved, the wheels beside them moved. The cherubim spread their wings to rise from the ground. As they did, the wheels didn't leave their side. 17 When the cherubim stood still, the wheels also stood still. When the cherubim rose, the wheels rose along with them. That's because the spirits of the living creatures were in the wheels.

18 Then the glory of the LORD moved away from the doorway of the temple. It stopped above the cherubim. 19 While I watched, they spread their wings. They rose from the ground. As they went, the wheels went along with them. They stopped at the entrance of the east gate of the LORD's house. And the glory of the God of Israel was above them.

20 These were the same living creatures I had seen by the Kebar River. I had seen them beneath the God of Israel. I realized that they were cherubim. 21 Each one had four faces and four wings. Under their wings was what looked like human hands. 22 Their faces looked the same as the ones I had seen by the Kebar River. Each of the cherubim went straight ahead.

The LORD's Judgment of Jerusalem Is Certain

11 Then the Spirit of the LORD lifted me up. He brought me to the east gate of the LORD's house. There were 25 men at the entrance of the gate. I saw Jaazaniah and Pelatiah among them. They were leaders of the people. Jaazaniah is the son of Azzur. Pelatiah is the son of Benaiah. 2 The LORD said to me, "Son of man, these men are making evil plans. They are giving bad advice to the city. 3 They say, 'Haven't our houses just been built again? The city is like a pot used for cooking. And we are the meat in it.' 4 So prophesy against them. Prophesy, son of man."

5 Then the Spirit of the LORD came on me. He told me to tell them, "The LORD says, 'You leaders in Israel, that is what you are saying. But I know what you are thinking. 6 You have killed many people in this city. In fact, you have filled its streets with dead bodies.'

7 “So the LORD and King says, ‘The bodies you have thrown there are the meat. And the city is the cooking pot. But I will drive you out of it. 8 You are afraid of the swords of war. But I will bring them against you,’ announces the LORD and King. 9 ‘I will drive you out of the city. I will hand you over to outsiders. And I will punish you. 10 You will be killed by swords. I will judge you at the borders of Israel. Then you will know that I am the LORD. 11 This city will not be a pot for you. And you will not be the meat in it. I will judge you at the borders of Israel. 12 Then you will know that I am the LORD. You have not obeyed my rules. You have not kept my laws. Instead, you have lived by the standards of the nations around you.’ ”

13 Pelatiah, the son of Benaiah, died as I was prophesying. Then I fell with my face toward the ground. I cried out in a loud voice. I said, “LORD and King, will you destroy all the Israelites who are still left alive?”

The LORD Will Bring His People Back Home

14 A message from the LORD came to me. The LORD said, 15 “Son of man, the people of Jerusalem have spoken about you. They have spoken about the others the Babylonians have taken away. They have also spoken about all the other people of Israel. The people of Jerusalem have said, ‘Those people are far away from the LORD. This land was given to us. And it belongs to us.’

16 “So tell them, ‘The LORD and King says, “I sent some of my people far away among the nations. I scattered them among the countries. But for a little while I have been their temple in the countries where they have gone.” ’

17 “Tell them, ‘The LORD and King says, “I will gather you from the nations. I will bring you back from the countries where you have been scattered. I will give you back the land of Israel.” ’

18 “They will return to it. They will remove all its statues of evil gods. I hate those gods. 19 I will give my people hearts that are completely committed to me. I will give them a new spirit that is faithful to me. I will remove their stubborn hearts from them. And I will give them hearts that obey me. 20 Then they will follow my rules. They will be careful to keep my laws. They will be my people. And I will be their God. 21 But some people have hearts that are committed to worshiping the statues of their evil gods. I hate those gods. Anything that happens to those people will be their own fault,” announces the LORD and King.

22 Then the cherubim spread their wings. The wheels were beside them. The glory of the God of Israel was above them. 23 The glory of the LORD went up from the city. It stopped above the Mount of Olives east of the city. 24 The Spirit of God lifted me up. He took me to those who had been brought to Babylon as prisoners. These are the things that happened in the visions the Spirit gave me.

Then the visions I had seen were gone. 25 I told my people everything the LORD had shown me.

Ezekiel Gives a Picture of What Will Happen

12 A message from the LORD came to me. The LORD said, 2 “Son of man, you are living among people who refuse to obey me. They have eyes that can see. But they do not really see. They have ears that can hear. But they do not really hear. They refuse to obey me.

3 “Son of man, pack your belongings as if you were going on a long trip. Leave in the daytime. Let the people see you. Start out from where you are. Go to another place. Perhaps they will understand the meaning of what you are doing. But they will still refuse to obey me. 4 Bring out your belongings packed for a long trip. Do this during the daytime. Let the people see you. Then in the evening, pretend you are being forced to leave home. Let the people see you. 5 While the people are watching, dig through the mud bricks of your house. Then take your belongings out through the hole in the wall. 6 Put them on your shoulder. Carry them out at sunset. Let the people see you. Cover your face so you can’t see the land. All of that will show the Israelites what is going to happen to them.”

7 So I did just as he commanded me. During the day I brought out my things as if I were going on a long trip. In the

evening I dug through the wall of my
house with my hands. At sunset I took
my belongings out. I put them on my
shoulders. The people watched what I
was doing.
8 In the morning a message from
the LORD came to me. The LORD said,
9 "Son of man, didn't the Israelites ask
you, 'What are you doing?' They always
refuse to obey me.
10 "Tell them, 'The LORD and King
says, "This prophecy is about Zedekiah, the prince in Jerusalem. It is also
about all the Israelites who still live
there." ' 11 Tell them, 'The things I've
done are a picture of what's going to
happen to you.
" 'So what I've done will happen
to you. You will be forced to leave
home. You will be taken to Babylon as
prisoners.'
12 "The prince among them will put
his things on his shoulder and leave.
He will do this at sunset. Someone will
dig a hole in the city wall for him to go
through. He will cover his face so he
can't see the land. 13 I will spread out my
net to catch him. He will be caught in
my trap. I will bring him to Babylon. It
is the land where the Chaldeans live. But
he will not see it. He will die there. 14 I
will scatter to the winds all those around
him. I will scatter his officials and all
his troops. And I will chase them with a
sword that is ready to strike them down.
15 "They will know that I am the LORD
when I scatter them among the nations.
I will send them to other countries. 16 But
I will spare a few of them. I will save
them from war, hunger and plague. In
those countries they will admit they
have done all kinds of evil things. I hate
those things. They will know that I am
the LORD."
17 A message from the LORD came
to me. The LORD said, 18 "Son of man,
tremble with fear as you eat your
food. Tremble as you drink your water.
19 Speak to the people of the land. Say to
them, 'Here is what the LORD and King
says. He says this about those who live
in Jerusalem and Israel. "They will be
worried as they eat their food. They will
not have any hope as they drink their
water. Their land will be stripped of
everything in it because all those who
live there are harming one another.
20 The towns where people live will be
completely destroyed. The land will
become a dry and empty desert. Then
you will know that I am the LORD." ' "

The LORD's Judgment Will Come Soon

21 A message from the LORD came to
me. The LORD said, 22 "Son of man, you
have a proverb in the land of Israel.
It says, 'The days go by, and not even
one vision comes true.' 23 Tell them, 'The
LORD and King says, "I am going to put
an end to this proverb. They will not use
that saying in Israel anymore." ' Tell
them, 'The days are coming soon when
every vision will come true. 24 There will
be no more false visions. People will no
longer use magic to find out whether
good things are going to happen in
Israel. 25 I am the LORD. So I will say
what I want to. And it will come true
when I want it to. In your days I will do
everything I say I will. But you people
always refuse to obey me,' announces
the LORD and King."
26 A message from the LORD came to
me. The LORD said, 27 "Son of man, the
Israelites are saying, 'The vision Ezekiel
sees won't come true for many years.
He is prophesying about a time that is
a long way off.'
28 "So tell them, 'The LORD and King
says, "Everything I say will come true.
It will happen when I want it to," announces the LORD and King.' "

The LORD Punishes Those Who Pretend to Be True Prophets

13 A message from the LORD came
to me. The LORD said, 2 "Son of
man, prophesy against those who are
now prophesying in Israel. What they
prophesy comes out of their own minds.
Tell them, 'Listen to the LORD's message!
3 The LORD and King says, "How terrible it will be for you foolish prophets!
You say what your own minds tell you
to. Your visions do not come from me.
4 Israel, your prophets are like wild dogs
that live among broken-down buildings. 5 You have not repaired the cracks
in the city wall for the people of Israel.
So it will not stand firm in the battle
on the day I judge you. 6 The visions
of those prophets are false. They use
magic to try to find out what is going to
happen. But their magic tricks are lies.
They say, 'The LORD announces.' But I

have not sent them. In spite of that,
they expect him to make their words
come true. 7 You prophets have seen
false visions. You have used magic to try
to find out what is going to happen. But
your magic tricks are lies. So you lied
when you said, 'The LORD announces.' I
did not even speak to you at all."
8 " 'The LORD and King says, "I am
against you prophets. Your messages
are false. Your visions do not come
true," announces the LORD and King.
9 "Israel, my power will be against the
prophets who see false visions. Their
magic tricks are lies. They will not be
among the leaders of my people. They
will not be listed in the records of Israel.
In fact, they will not even enter the land.
Then you will know that I am the LORD
and King.
10 " ' "They lead my people away from
me. They say, 'Peace.' But there isn't any
peace. They are like people who build
a weak wall. They try to cover up the
weakness by painting the wall white.
11 Tell those who do this that their wall
is going to fall. Heavy rains will come.
I will send hailstones crashing down.
Powerful winds will blow. 12 The wall will
fall down. Then people will ask them,
'Now where is the paint you covered
it with?' "
13 " 'So the LORD and King speaks. He
says, "When I am very angry, I will
send a powerful wind. Hailstones and
heavy rains will come. They will fall
with great force. 14 I will tear down the
wall you prophets painted over. I will
knock it down. The only thing left will
be its foundation. When it falls, you
will be destroyed along with it. Then
you will know that I am the LORD. 15 So
I will pour out all my great anger on
the wall. I will also send it against you
prophets who painted it. I will say to
you, 'The wall is gone. You who painted
it will be gone too. 16 You prophets of
Israel prophesied to Jerusalem. You
saw visions of peace for its people. But
there wasn't any peace,' announces the
LORD and King." '
17 "Son of man, turn your attention to
the daughters of your people. What they
prophesy comes out of their own minds.
So prophesy against them. 18 Tell them,
'Here is what the LORD and King says.
"How terrible it will be for you women
who sew magic charms to put around
your wrists! You make veils of different
lengths to put on your heads. You do
these things to trap people. You trap
my people. But you will also be trapped.
19 You have treated me as if I were not
holy. You did it among my very own
people. You did it for a few handfuls
of barley and scraps of bread. You told
lies to my people. They like to listen to
lies. You killed those who should have
lived. And you spared those who should
have died."
20 " 'So the LORD and King says, "I
am against your magic charms. You
use them to trap people as if they were
birds. I will tear them off your arms. I
will set free the people you trap like
birds. 21 I will tear your veils off your
heads. I will save my people from your
power. They will no longer be under
your control. Then you will know that
I am the LORD. 22 I had not made godly
people sad. But when you told them
lies, you made them lose all hope. You
advised sinful people not to turn from
their evil ways. You did not want them
to save their lives. 23 So you will never
see false visions again. You will not use
your magic tricks anymore. I will save
my people from your power. Then you
will know that I am the LORD." ' "

The LORD Judges Those Who Worship Other Gods

14 Some of the elders of Israel came
to see me. They sat down with
me. 2 Then a message from the LORD
came to me. The LORD said, 3 "Son of
man, these men have thought about
nothing but other gods. They have
fallen into the evil trap of worshiping
them. Should I let these men ask me
for any advice? 4 Speak to them. Tell
them, 'The LORD and King says, "Suppose any of the Israelites think about
other gods. And they fall into the evil
trap of worshiping them. Then they go
to a prophet to ask for advice. If they do,
I myself will tell the prophet to answer
them in keeping with their worship of
many gods. 5 I will win back the hearts
of the people of Israel. All of them have
deserted me for their other gods." '
6 "So speak to the people of Israel.
Tell them, 'The LORD and King says,
"Turn away from your sins! Also turn

away from your gods. Give up all the evil things you have done. I hate them.

7 " ' "Suppose any of the Israelites or any outsiders who live in Israel separate themselves from me. And they think about other gods. They fall into the evil trap of worshiping them. Then they go to a prophet to ask me for advice. If they do, I myself will tell the prophet to answer them. 8 I will turn against them. I will make an example out of them. People will talk about the bad things that happen to them. I will remove them from you. Then you will know that I am the LORD.

9 " ' "Suppose that prophet is stirred up to give a prophecy. Then I am the one who has stirred him up. And I will reach out my powerful hand against him. I will destroy him from among my people Israel. 10 The prophet will be as much to blame as the one who asks him for advice. Both of them will be guilty. 11 Then the people of Israel will no longer wander away from me. And they will not make themselves 'unclean' anymore with their many sins. They will be my people. And I will be their God," ' announces the LORD and King."

Jerusalem Can't Escape the LORD's Judgment

12 A message from the LORD came to me. The LORD said, 13 "Son of man, suppose the people in a certain country sin against me. And they are not faithful to me. So I reach out my powerful hand against them. I cut off their food supply. I make them very hungry. I kill them and their animals. 14 And suppose Noah, Daniel and Job were in that country. Then these three men could save only themselves by doing what is right," announces the LORD and King.

15 "Or suppose I send wild animals through that country. And they kill all its children. It becomes a dry and empty desert. No one can pass through it because of the animals. 16 And suppose these three men were in that country. Then they could not save their own sons or daughters. They alone would be saved. But the land would become a dry and empty desert. And that is just as sure as I am alive," announces the LORD and King.

17 "Or suppose I send swords to kill the people in that country. And I say, 'Let swords sweep all through the land.' And I kill its people and their animals. 18 And suppose these three men were in that country. Then they could not save their own sons or daughters. They alone would be saved. And that is just as sure as I am alive," announces the LORD and King.

19 "Or suppose I send a plague into that land. And I pour out my great anger on it by spilling blood. I kill its people and their animals. 20 And suppose Noah, Daniel and Job were in that land. Then they could not save their own sons or daughters. They could save only themselves by doing what is right. And that is just as sure as I am alive," announces the LORD and King.

21 The LORD and King says, "It will get much worse. I will punish Jerusalem in four horrible ways. There will be war, hunger, wild animals and plague. They will destroy the people and their animals. 22 But some people will be left alive. Some children will be brought out of the city. They will come to you. You will see how they act and the way they live. And you will be comforted in spite of all the trouble I brought on Jerusalem. 23 You will be comforted when you see how they act and the way they live. Then you will know that I did not do anything there without a reason," announces the LORD and King.

Jerusalem Is Like a Useless Vine

15 A message from the LORD came to me. Here is what the LORD said. 2 "Son of man, how is the wood of a vine different from the wood of any tree in the forest? 3 Can its wood ever be made into anything useful? Can pegs be made from it to hang things on? 4 Suppose it is thrown in the fire to be burned. And the fire burns both ends and blackens the middle. Then is the wood useful for anything? 5 It was not useful when it was whole. So how can it be made into something useful now? The fire has burned it and blackened it."

6 Here is what the LORD and King says. "Instead of the wood of any tree in the forest, I have given the vine to burn in the fire. I will treat the people who live in Jerusalem the same way. 7 I will turn

against them. They might have come out of the fire. But the fire will destroy them anyway. I will turn against them. Then you will know that I am the LORD. 8 I will make the land a dry and empty desert. My people have not been faithful to me," announces the LORD and King.

Jerusalem Is Like an Unfaithful Wife

16 A message from the LORD came to me. The LORD said, 2 "Son of man, tell the people of Jerusalem the evil things they have done. I hate those things. 3 Tell them, 'The LORD and King speaks to Jerusalem. He says, "Your history in the land of Canaan goes back a long way. Your father was an Amorite. Your mother was a Hittite. 4 On the day you were born your cord was not cut. You were not washed with water to clean you up. You were not rubbed with salt. And you were not wrapped in large strips of cloth. 5 No one took pity on you. No one was concerned enough to do any of these things for you. Instead, you were thrown out into an open field. You were hated on the day you were born.

6 " ' "I was passing by. I saw you kicking around in your blood. As you were lying there, I said to you, 'Live!' 7 I made you grow like a plant in a field. Soon you had grown up. You became a young adult. Your breasts had formed. Your hair had grown. But you were completely naked.

8 " ' "Later, I was passing by again. I looked at you. I saw that you were old enough for love. So I married you and took good care of you. I covered your naked body. I made a firm promise to you. I entered into a covenant with you. And you became mine," announces the LORD and King.

9 " ' "I bathed you with water. I washed the blood off you. And I put lotions on you. 10 I put a beautiful dress on you. I gave you sandals made out of fine leather. I dressed you in fine linen. I covered you with expensive clothes. 11 I decorated you with jewelry. I put bracelets on your arms. I gave you a necklace for your neck. 12 I put rings on your nose and ears. And I gave you a beautiful crown for your head. 13 So you were decorated with gold and silver. Your clothes were made out of fine linen. They were made out of expensive and beautiful cloth. Your food was made out of honey, olive oil and the finest flour. You became very beautiful. You became a queen. 14 You were so beautiful that your fame spread among the nations. The glory I had given you made your beauty perfect," announces the LORD and King.

15 " ' "But you trusted in your beauty. You used your fame to become a prostitute. You offered your body freely to anyone who passed by. In fact, you gave yourself to anyone who wanted you. 16 You used some of your clothes to make high places colorful. That is where people worshiped other gods. You were a prostitute there. You went to your lover and he took your beauty. 17 I had given you fine jewelry. It was made out of gold and silver. You used it to make for yourself statues of male gods. You worshiped those gods. You were not faithful to me. 18 You put your beautiful clothes on them. You offered my oil and incense to them. 19 You also offered them food. It was made out of olive oil, honey and the finest flour. I had given it to you to eat. You offered it as sweet-smelling incense to them. That is what you did," announces the LORD and King.

20 " ' "Then you took your sons and daughters who belonged to me. And you sacrificed them as food to other gods. Wasn't it enough for you to be a prostitute? 21 You killed my children. You sacrificed them to other gods. 22 You did not remember the days when you were young. At that time you were completely naked. You were kicking around in your blood. But now you have done evil things. I hate them. You have worshiped other gods. You have not been faithful to me.

23 " ' "How terrible it will be for you!" announces the LORD and King. "How terrible for you! You continued to sin against me. 24 Your people built up mounds for themselves in every market. They put little places of worship on them. 25 They set them up at every street corner. Jerusalem, you misused your beauty. You offered your body to anyone who passed by. You did it again and again. 26 You committed shameful acts with the people of Egypt. They were your neighbors who were ready to have

sex with you. You offered yourself to
them again and again. That made me
very angry. [27] So I reached out my powerful hand against you. I made your
territory smaller. I handed you over
to your Philistine enemies. The people
in their towns were shocked by your
impure conduct. [28] You also committed
shameful acts with the people of Assyria. Nothing ever seemed to satisfy you.
You could never get enough. [29] Then
you offered yourself to the people of
Babylon. But that did not satisfy you
either. There are many traders in the
land of Babylon.

[30] " ' "I am filled with great anger
against you," announces the LORD and
King. "Just look at all the things you
are doing! You are acting like a prostitute who has no shame at all. [31] Your
people built up mounds at every street
corner. You put little places of worship
on them in every market. But you did
not really act like a prostitute. That's
because you refused to let your lovers
pay you anything.

[32] " ' "You unfaithful wife! You would
rather be with strangers than with your
own husband! [33] Every prostitute receives gifts. Instead, you give gifts to
all your lovers. You offer them money
to come to you from everywhere. You
want them to sleep with you. You are
not faithful to me. [34] As a prostitute,
you are the opposite of others. No one
runs after you to sleep with you. You
are exactly the opposite. You pay them.
They do not pay you." ' "

[35] You prostitute, listen to the LORD's
message. [36] The LORD and King says,
"You poured out your desire on your
lovers. You took off your clothing and
slept with them. You did it again and
again. You worshiped other gods. I hate
them. You even sacrificed your children
to them. [37] So I am going to gather together all the lovers you found pleasure
with. They include those you loved and
those you hated. I will gather them
against you from everywhere. I will
take your clothes off right in front of
them. Then they will see you completely
naked. [38] I will hand down my sentence
against you. You will be punished like
women who commit adultery and sacrifice their children to other gods. I am
so angry with you. So I will sentence
you to death for everything you have
done. [39] Then I will hand you over to
your lovers. They will tear down those
mounds you built. They will destroy the
little places of worship you put on them.
They will take your clothes off. They will
remove your fine jewelry. And they will
leave you completely naked. [40] They
will bring a crowd against you. The
crowd will put you to death by throwing
stones at you. And they will chop you
to pieces with their swords. [41] They will
burn down your houses and punish you.
Many women will see it. I will not let
you be a prostitute anymore. You will
no longer pay your lovers. [42] Then my
great anger against you will die down.
My jealous anger will turn away from
you. I will be calm. I will not be angry
anymore.

[43] "You did not remember the days
when you were young. The things you
did made me very angry. So anything
that happens to you will be your own
fault," announces the LORD and King.
"You added impure conduct to all the
other evil things you did. I hate all those
things.

[44] "All those who use proverbs will
use this one about you. They will say,
'Like mother, like daughter.' [45] You are
a true daughter of your mother. She
hated her husband and children. And
you are a true sister of your sisters. They
hated their husbands and children. Your
mother was a Hittite. Your father was
an Amorite. [46] Your older sister was
Samaria. She lived north of you with
her daughters. Your younger sister was
Sodom. She lived south of you with her
daughters. [47] You lived exactly the way
they did. You copied their evil practices.
I hate those practices. Everything you
did was so sinful that you soon became
even worse than they were. [48] Your sister
Sodom and her daughters never did
what you and your daughters have
done. And that is just as sure as I am
alive," announces the LORD and King.

[49] "Here is the sin your sister Sodom
committed. She and her daughters were
proud. They ate too much. They were
not concerned about others. They did
not help those who were poor and in
need. [50] They were very proud. They
did many things that were evil in my
eyes. I hated those things. So I got rid of

Sodom and her daughters, just as you have seen. 51 Samaria did not commit half the sins you did. You sinned even more than they did. I hate those sins. Compared to what you did, you made your sisters seem godly. 52 So you will be dishonored. You have given your sisters an excuse for what they did. Your sins were far worse than theirs. In fact, your sisters appear to be more godly than you. So then, be ashamed. You will be dishonored. You have made them appear to be godly.

53 "I will not only give you back what you had before. I will also do the same thing for Sodom and her daughters. And I will do the same for Samaria and her daughters. 54 That will make you feel dishonored. You will be ashamed of everything you have done. You have made them feel better because you sinned more and were punished more than they were. 55 Your sisters Sodom and Samaria and their daughters will return to what they were before. And you and your daughters will return to what you were before. 56 In the past you would not even mention your sister Sodom. You were proud at that time. 57 That was before your sin was uncovered. Now the daughters of Edom make fun of you. So do all her neighbors and the daughters of the Philistines. Everyone who lives around you hates you. 58 You will be punished for your impure conduct. I will also punish you for the other evil things you have done. I hate all those things," announces the LORD.

59 The LORD and King says, "I will punish you in keeping with what you have done. I sealed with a promise the covenant I made with you. You hated that promise. And you broke my covenant. 60 But I will remember my covenant with you. I made it with you when you were young. Now I will make a new covenant with you. It will last forever. 61 Then you will remember how you have lived. You will be ashamed when I give you Samaria and Sodom. Samaria is your older sister. Sodom is your younger one. I will give them and their daughters to you as daughters. That can't happen based on my old covenant with you. 62 So I will make my new covenant with you. Then you will know that I am the LORD. 63 I will pay for all the sins you have committed. Then you will remember what you have done. You will be ashamed of it. Because of your shame, you will never speak against me again," announces the LORD and King.

Two Eagles and a Vine

17 A message from the LORD came to me. The LORD said, 2 "Son of man, tell the people of Israel a story about their kings. Let them know what will happen to them. 3 Tell them, 'The LORD and King says, "A great eagle came to the city of 'Lebanon.' It had powerful wings and a lot of long feathers. The feathers were colorful and beautiful. The eagle landed in the top of a cedar tree. 4 It broke off the highest twig. The eagle carried it away to the land of Babylon. There are many traders in that land. The eagle planted the twig in the city of Babylon.

5 " ' "Then it took from the land a seed that had just sprouted. It put it in rich soil near plenty of water. It planted the seed like a willow tree. 6 The seed grew into a low, spreading vine. Its branches turned toward the eagle. And its roots remained under the eagle. So the seed became a vine. It produced branches and put out leaves.

7 " ' "But there was another great eagle. It also had powerful wings and a lot of feathers. The vine now sent out its roots toward that eagle. It sent them out from the place where it was planted. And it reached out its branches to the eagle for water. 8 The seed had been planted in good soil near plenty of water. Then it could produce branches and bear fruit. It could become a beautiful vine." '

9 "Ezekiel, tell the Israelites, 'The LORD and King asks, "Will the vine grow? Won't it be pulled up by its roots? Won't all its fruit be stripped off? Won't it dry up? All its new growth will dry up. It will not take a strong arm or many people to pull it up. 10 It has been planted, but will it grow? No. It will dry up completely when the east wind strikes it. It will dry up in the place where it grew." ' "

11 A message from the LORD came to me. The LORD said, 12 "These people refuse to obey me. Ask them, 'Don't you know what these things mean?'

Tell them, 'Nebuchadnezzar went to
Jerusalem. He was the king of Babylon.
He carried off King Jehoiachin and the
nobles. He brought them back with him
to the city of Babylon. [13]Then Nebuchadnezzar made a peace treaty with
Zedekiah. He was a member of Jerusalem's royal family. Nebuchadnezzar
made him promise he would keep the
treaty. He also took away the leading
men of the land as prisoners. [14]He did it
to bring down their kingdom. It would
not rise again. In fact, it would be able
to last only by keeping his treaty. [15]But
Zedekiah turned against him. He sent
messengers to Egypt. They went there
to get horses and a large army. Will he
succeed? Will he who does things like
that escape? Can he break the peace
treaty and still escape?

[16]" 'Zedekiah will die in Babylon,' announces the LORD and King. 'And that is
just as sure as I am alive. He will die in
the land of King Nebuchadnezzar, who
put him on the throne. Zedekiah didn't
keep his promise to Nebuchadnezzar
and broke his treaty. [17]So Nebuchadnezzar will build ramps against the
walls of Jerusalem. He will set up war
machines to destroy many lives. Pharaoh will not be able to help Zedekiah
during the war. The huge and mighty
army of Egypt will not be of any help.
[18]Zedekiah didn't keep his promise to
Nebuchadnezzar and broke his treaty.
Zedekiah had made a firm promise to
keep it. But he broke it anyway. So he
will not escape.

[19]" 'The LORD and King says, "Zedekiah didn't keep the promise he made
in my name. He broke the treaty. So I
will pay him back. And that is just as
sure as I am alive. [20]I will spread out
my net to catch him. He will be caught
in my trap. I will bring him to Babylon.
I will judge him there because he was
not faithful to me. [21]All Zedekiah's best
troops will be killed by swords. Those
who are left alive will be scattered to
the winds. Then you will know that I
have spoken. I am the LORD."

[22]" 'The LORD and King says, "I myself
will get a twig from the very top of a
cedar tree and plant it. I will break off
the highest twig. I will plant it on a very
high mountain. [23]I will plant it on the
high mountains of Israel. It will produce
branches and bear fruit. It will become
a beautiful cedar tree. All kinds of birds
will make their nests in it. They will live
in the shade of its branches. [24]All the
trees in the forest will know that I bring
down tall trees. I make short trees grow
tall. I dry up green trees. And I make
dry trees green."

" 'I have spoken. I will do this. I am
the LORD.' "

People Will Die Because of Their Own Sins

18 A message from the LORD came to
me. The LORD said, [2]"You people
have a proverb about the land of Israel.
What do you mean by it? It says,

" 'The parents eat sour grapes.
But the children have a bitter
taste in their mouths.'

[3]"You will not use that proverb in
Israel anymore," announces the LORD
and King. "And that is just as sure as
I am alive. [4]Everyone belongs to me.
Parents and children alike belong to
me. A person will die because of their
own sins.

[5]"Suppose there is a godly man
who does what is fair and right.
[6]And he does not eat at the
mountain temples.
He does not worship the statues
of Israel's gods.
He does not sleep with another
man's wife.
He does not have sex with his
own wife
during her monthly period.
[7]He does not treat anyone badly.
Instead, he always returns things
he takes
to make sure loans are paid back.
He does not steal.
Instead, he gives his food to
hungry people.
He provides clothes for those who
are naked.
[8]He does not charge interest when
he lends money to them.
He does not make money from
them.
He keeps himself from doing
what is wrong.
He judges cases fairly.
[9]He obeys my rules.
He is faithful in keeping my laws.

He always does what is right.
You can be sure he will live,"
announces the LORD and King.

[10] "But suppose he has a mean son
who harms other people. The son commits murder. Or he does some other
things that are wrong. [11] Suppose he
does these things even though his father
never did.

"Suppose the son eats at the
mountain temples.
And he sleeps with another
man's wife.
[12] He treats poor and needy people
badly.
He steals.
He does not pay back what he
owes.
He worships statues of gods.
He does other things I hate.
[13] He charges interest when he
lends money to poor people. He
makes money from them.

Will a man like that live? He will not!
He must be put to death. And what happens to him will be his own fault. He did
many things I hate.

[14] "But suppose this son has a son of
his own. And the son sees all the sins
his father commits. He sees them, but
he does not do them.

[15] "Suppose he does not eat at the
mountain temples.
And he does not worship the
statues of Israel's gods.
He does not sleep with another
man's wife.
[16] He does not treat anyone badly.
He does not make people give
him something
to prove they will pay back what
they owe him.
He does not steal.
Instead, he gives his food to
hungry people.
He provides clothes for those who
are naked.
[17] He keeps himself from committing
sins.
He does not charge interest when
he lends money to poor people.
He does not make money from
them.
He keeps my laws and obeys my
rules.

He will not die because of his father's
sin. You can be sure he will live. [18] But
his father will die because of his own
sin. He got rich by cheating others. He
robbed his relatives. He also did what
was wrong among his people.

[19] "But you still ask, 'Is the son guilty
along with his father?' No! The son did
what was fair and right. He was careful
to obey all my rules. So you can be sure
he will live. [20] A person will die because
of their own sins. A child will not be
guilty because of what their parent did.
And a parent will not be guilty because
of what their child did. The right things
a godly person does will be added to
their account. The wrong things a sinful
person does will be charged against
them.

[21] "But suppose a sinful person turns
away from all the sins they have committed. And they obey all my rules.
They do what is fair and right. Then
you can be sure they will live. They
will not die. [22] None of the sins they
have committed will be held against
them. Because of the godly things they
have done, they will live. [23] When sinful
people die, it does not give me any joy,"
announces the LORD and King. "But
when they turn away from their sins
and live, that makes me very happy.

[24] "Suppose a godly person stops doing what is right. And they sin. They
do the same evil things a sinful person
does. They do things I hate. Then they
will not live. I will not remember any of
the right things they have done. They
have not been faithful to me. They have
also committed many other sins. So
they are guilty. They will die.

[25] "But you say, 'What the Lord does
isn't fair.' Listen to me, you Israelites.
What I do is always fair. What you do
is not. [26] Suppose a godly person stops
doing what is right. And they sin. Then
they will die because of it. They will
die because of the sin they have committed. [27] But suppose a sinful person
turns away from the evil things they
have done. And they do what is fair
and right. Then they will save their life.
[28] They think about all the evil things
they have done. And they turn away
from them. So you can be sure they
will live. They will not die. [29] But the
Israelites still say, 'What the Lord does

isn't fair.' People of Israel, what I do is
always fair. What you do is not.
30 "So I will judge you Israelites. I will
judge each of you in keeping with what
you have done," announces the LORD
and King. "Turn away from your sins!
Turn away from all the evil things you
have done. Then sin will not bring you
down. 31 Get rid of all the evil things
you have done. Let me give you a new
heart and a new spirit. Then you will
be faithful to me. Why should you die,
people of Israel? 32 When anyone dies,
it does not give me any joy," announces
the LORD and King. "So turn away from
your sins. Then you will live!

A Song of Sadness About Israel's Princes

19 "Sing a song of sadness about
Israel's princes. 2 Say to Israel,

" 'You were like a mother lion to
your princes.
She lay down among the lions.
She brought up her cubs.
3 One of them was Jehoahaz.
He became a strong lion.
He learned to tear apart what he
caught.
And he became a man-eater.
4 The nations heard about him.
They trapped him in their pit.
They put hooks in his face.
And they led him away to Egypt.

5 " 'The mother lion looked and
waited.
But all her hope was gone.
So she got another one of her cubs.
She made him into a strong lion.
6 He prowled with the lions.
He became very strong.
He learned to tear apart what he
caught.
And he became a man-eater.
7 He broke down their forts.
He completely destroyed their
towns.
The land and all those who were
in it
were terrified when he roared.
8 Then nations came against him.
They came from all around him.
They spread out their net to catch
him.
He was trapped in their pit.
9 They used hooks to pull him into a
cage.
They brought him to the king of
Babylon.
They put him in prison.
So his roar was not heard
anymore
on the mountains of Israel.

10 " 'Israel, you were like a vine in a
vineyard.
It was planted near water.
It had a lot of fruit and many
branches.
There was plenty of water.
11 Its branches were strong.
Each was good enough to be
made into a ruler's scepter.
The vine grew high
above all the leaves.
It stood out because it was so tall
and had so many branches.
12 But Nebuchadnezzar became
angry.
He pulled it up by its roots.
He threw it to the ground.
The east wind dried it up.
Its fruit was stripped off.
Its strong branches dried up.
And fire destroyed them.
13 Now it is planted in the Babylonian
desert.
It is in a dry and thirsty land.
14 One of its main branches was
Zedekiah.
Fire spread from it and burned
up its fruit.
None of its branches is good enough
to be made into a ruler's scepter.'

This is a song of sadness. And that is
how it should be used."

The LORD Judges Sinful Israel

20 It was the seventh year since
King Jehoiachin had been
brought to Babylon as a prisoner. On
the tenth day of the fifth month, some
of the elders of Israel came to ask the
LORD for advice. They sat down with me.
2 Then a message from the LORD came
to me. The LORD said, 3 "Son of man,
speak to the elders of Israel. Tell them,
'The LORD and King says, "Have you
come to ask me for advice? I will not
let you do that," announces the LORD
and King. "And that is just as sure as
I am alive."'

4 “Are you going to judge them, son
of man? Will you judge them? Tell them
the evil things done by their people
of long ago. I hate those things. 5 Tell
them, ‘The LORD and King says, “I chose
Israel. On that day I raised my hand
and made a promise. I made a promise
to the members of Jacob’s family line. I
made myself known to them in Egypt. I
raised my hand and told them, ‘I am the
LORD your God.’ 6 On that day I promised
I would bring them out of Egypt. I told
them I would take them to a land I had
found for them. It had plenty of milk
and honey. It was the most beautiful
land of all. 7 I said to them, ‘Each of
you must get rid of the statues of the
evil gods you worship. Do not make
yourselves “unclean” by worshiping the
gods of Egypt. I am the LORD your God.’

8 “ ‘ “But they refused to obey me.
They would not listen to me. They did
not get rid of the evil gods they worshiped. And they did not turn away
from Egypt’s gods. So I said I would
pour out all my great anger on them
in Egypt. 9 I wanted my name to be
honored. So I brought my people out
of Egypt. I did it to keep my name from
being treated as if it were not holy. I
didn’t want this to happen in front of
the nations around my people. I had
made myself known to Israel in the
sight of those nations. 10 So I led them
out of Egypt. I brought them into the
Desert of Sinai. 11 I gave them my rules.
I made my laws known to them. The
person who obeys them will live by
them. 12 I also told them to observe my
Sabbath days. That is the sign of the
covenant I made with them. I wanted
them to know that I made them holy.
I am the LORD.

13 “ ‘ “But in the desert the people of
Israel refused to obey me. They did not
follow my rules. They turned their backs
on my laws. The person who obeys them
will live by them. They totally misused
my Sabbath days. So I said I would pour
out my great anger on them. I would destroy them in the desert. 14 But I wanted
my name to be honored. I kept it from
being treated as if it were not holy. I
did not want that to happen in front of
the nations. They had seen me bring
Israel out of Egypt. 15 I also raised my
hand and made a promise in the desert.
I told my people I would not bring them
into the land I had given them. It had
plenty of milk and honey. It was the
most beautiful land of all. 16 But they
turned their backs on my laws. They
did not obey my rules. They misused
my Sabbath days. Their hearts were
committed to worshiping the statues of
their gods. 17 Then I felt sorry for them.
So I did not destroy them. I did not put
an end to them in the desert. 18 I spoke to
their children there. I said, ‘Do not follow
the rules your parents gave you. Do not
obey their laws. Do not make yourselves
“unclean” by worshiping their gods. 19 I
am the LORD your God. So follow my
rules. Be careful to obey my laws. 20 Keep
my Sabbath days holy. That is the sign
of the covenant I made with you. You
will know that I am the LORD your God.’

21 “ ‘ “But their children refused to
obey me. They did not follow my rules.
They were not careful to keep my laws.
The person who obeys them will live by
them. They misused my Sabbath days.
So I said I would pour out all my great
anger on them in the desert. 22 But I kept
myself from punishing them at that
time. I wanted my name to be honored.
So I kept it from being treated as if it
were not holy. I did not want that to
happen in front of the nations. They
had seen me bring Israel out of Egypt.
23 I also raised my hand and made a
promise in the desert. I told my people I
would scatter them among the nations.
I would send them to other countries.
24 They had not obeyed my laws. They
had turned their backs on my rules.
They had misused my Sabbath days.
They only wanted to worship the statues of their parents’ gods. 25 So I let them
follow other rules. Those other rules
were not good. I let them have laws they
could not live by. 26 I let them become
‘unclean’ by offering sacrifices to other
gods. They even sacrificed the first male
child born in each family. I wanted to
fill them with horror. Then they would
know that I am the LORD.” ’

27 “Son of man, speak to the people of
Israel. Tell them, ‘The LORD and King
says, “Your people spoke evil things
against me long ago. They were unfaithful to me. 28 But I brought them
into the land. I had promised to give
the land to them. Then they offered

sacrifices that made me very angry.
They did it on every high hill and under
every green tree. There they brought
their sweet-smelling incense. And there
they poured out their drink offerings.
29 Then I said to them, 'What is this high
place you go to?' " ' " That high place is
called Bamah to this day.

The LORD Makes Israel New Again

30 The LORD said to me, "Speak to the
Israelites. Tell them, 'Here is what the
LORD and King says. "Are you going to
make yourselves 'unclean' the way your
people of long ago did? Are you also
going to want to worship the statues of
their evil gods? 31 You make yourselves
'unclean' by offering sacrifices to other
gods. You even sacrifice your children in
the fire. You continue to do these things
to this day. People of Israel, should I let
you ask me for advice? I will not let you
do that," announces the LORD and King.
"And that is just as sure as I am alive.
32 " ' "You say, 'We want to be like the
other nations. We want to be like all the
other people in the world. They serve
gods made out of wood and stone.' But
what you have in mind will never happen. 33 I will rule over you by reaching
out my mighty hand and powerful arm.
I will pour my great anger out on you,"
announces the LORD and King. "And
that is just as sure as I am alive. 34 I will
bring you back from the nations. I will
gather you together from the countries
where you have been scattered. I will
reach out my mighty hand and powerful arm. I will pour my great anger
out on you. 35 I will send you among
the nations. There I will judge you face
to face. It will be as if I were judging
you in the desert again. 36 Long ago,
I judged your people in the desert of
Egypt. In the same way, I will judge
you," announces the LORD and King.
37 "I will take note of you as you pass under my shepherd's stick. I will separate
those who obey me from those who do
not. And I will give the blessings of the
covenant to those of you who obey me.
38 I will get rid of those among you who
turn against me. They refuse to obey
me. I will bring them out of the land
where they are living. But they will not
enter the land of Israel. Then you will
know that I am the LORD.
39 " ' "People of Israel, the LORD and
King says, 'Go, every one of you! Serve
your gods. But later you will listen to
me. You will no longer treat my name
as if it were not holy. You will not offer sacrifices to other gods anymore.
40 People of Israel, you will all serve me,'
announces the LORD and King. 'You will
serve me on my high and holy mountain in Jerusalem. There I will accept
you. I will require your offerings and
your finest gifts. I want you to bring
them along with all your other holy
sacrifices. 41 I will bring you back from
the nations. I will gather you together
from the countries where you have been
scattered. Then I will accept you as if
you were sweet-smelling incense. I will
show that I am holy among you. The
nations will see it. 42 I will bring you
into the land of Israel. Then you will
know that I am the LORD. Long ago I
raised my hand and made a promise.
I promised to give that land to your
people of long ago. 43 There you will
remember your conduct. You will think
about everything you did that made
you "unclean." And you will hate yourselves because of all the evil things you
have done. 44 People of Israel, I will deal
with you for the honor of my name. I
will not deal with you based on your
evil conduct and sinful practices. Then
you will know that I am the LORD,' announces the LORD and King." ' "

Ezekiel Prophesies Against the South

45 A message from the LORD came to
me. The LORD said, 46 "Son of man, turn
your attention to Judah in the south.
Preach against it. Prophesy against its
forests. 47 Tell them, 'Listen to the LORD's
message. The LORD and King says, "I
am about to set you on fire. The fire
will destroy all your trees. It will burn
down green trees and dry trees alike.
The blazing flame will not be put out.
The faces of everyone from south to
north will be burned by it. 48 Everyone
will see that I started the fire. It will not
be put out. I am the LORD." ' "
49 Then I said, "LORD and King, people
are talking about me. They are saying,
'Isn't he just telling stories?' "

God Uses the Babylonians to Judge Israel

21 A message from the LORD came to me. The LORD said, 2 "Son of man, turn your attention to Jerusalem. Preach against the temple. Prophesy against the land of Israel. 3 Tell them, 'The LORD says, "I am against you. I will pull out my sword. I will remove from you godly people and sinful people alike. 4 Because I am going to remove them, my sword will be ready to use. I will strike down everyone from south to north. 5 Then all people will know that I have pulled out my sword. I will not put it back. I am the LORD." '

6 "Groan, son of man! Groan in front of your people. Groan with a broken heart and bitter sorrow. 7 They will ask you, 'Why are you groaning?' Then you will say, 'Because of the news that is coming. The hearts of all the people will melt away in fear. Their hands will not be able to help them. Their spirits will grow weak. And they will be so afraid they'll wet themselves.' The news is coming! You can be sure those things will happen," announces the LORD and King.

8 A message from the LORD came to me. The LORD said, 9 "Son of man, prophesy. Say, 'The Lord says,

" ' "A sword! A sword!
A sharp and shiny sword is
coming from Babylon!
10 It is sharpened to kill people.
It flashes like lightning." ' "

The people say, "Should we take delight in the scepter of the LORD's royal son? The sword looks down on every scepter like this." 11 The LORD says,

"I have told Nebuchadnezzar to
shine his sword.
It is in his hand.
It has been sharpened and shined.
It is ready for the killer's hand.
12 Son of man, cry out and weep.
The sword is against my people.
It is against all the princes of
Israel.
It will kill them
along with the rest of my people.
So beat your chest in sorrow.

13 "You can be sure that testing will come. Why does the sword look down on the scepter? Because even the scepter will not continue to rule," announces the LORD and King.

14 "Son of man, prophesy.
Clap your hands.
Let the sword strike twice.
Let it strike even three times.
It is a sword to kill people.
It is a sword to kill many people.
It is closing in on them from
every side.
15 People's hearts will melt away in
fear.
Many will be wounded or killed.
I have prepared the sword to kill
people
at all their city gates.
Look! It strikes like lightning.
It is in the killer's hand.
16 Sword, cut to the right.
Then cut to the left.
Strike down people everywhere
your blade is turned.
17 I too will clap my hands.
I won't be so angry anymore.
I have spoken. I am the LORD."

18 A message from the LORD came to
me. The LORD said, 19 "Son of man, mark
out on a map two roads for the sword
to take. The sword belongs to the king
of Babylon. Both roads start from the
same country. Put up a sign where the
road turns off to the city of Rabbah.
20 Mark out one road for the sword to
take against Rabbah in Ammon. Mark
out another against Judah and the walls
of Jerusalem. 21 The king of Babylon will
stop at the place where the two roads
meet. He will look for a special sign. He
will cast lots by pulling arrows out of
a bag. He will ask his gods for advice.
And he will look carefully at the liver
of a sheep. 22 His right hand will pull
out the arrow for Jerusalem. There he
will get huge logs ready to knock down
its gates. He will give the command to
kill its people. He will sound the battle
cry. He will build a ramp up to the city
wall. He will bring in his war machines.
23 The decision to attack Jerusalem will
seem like the wrong advice to those who
made a treaty with Nebuchadnezzar.
But he will remind them that they are
guilty. And he will take them away as
prisoners."

24 So the LORD and King says, "You
people have reminded everyone of

how guilty you are. You have done it
by refusing to obey me or any other
authority. Everything you do clearly
shows how sinful you are. So you will
be taken away as prisoners."
25 King Zedekiah, your day has come.
You are an unholy and evil prince in
Israel. The day for you to be punished
is here. 26 The LORD and King says, "Take
off your turban. Remove your crown.
Things will not be as they were in the
past. Those who are considered not
important will be honored. And those
who are honored will be considered not
important. 27 Jerusalem will fall. I will
destroy it. It will not be rebuilt until the
true king comes. After all, the kingdom
belongs to him. I will give it to him.
28 "Son of man, prophesy. Say, 'The
LORD and King speaks about the Ammonites. He also talks about the way
they laugh because of Jerusalem's fall.
He says,

" ' "A sword! A sword!
Nebuchadnezzar's sword is ready to kill you.
It is shined to destroy you.
It flashes like lightning.
29 The visions of your prophets are false.
They use magic to try to find out what is going to happen to you.
But their magic tricks are lies.
The sword will strike the necks of you sinful people.
You will be killed.
The day for you to be punished has finally come.
Your time is up.
30 Ammon, return your sword to its place.
In the land where you were created, I will judge you.
That is where you came from.
31 I will pour out my anger on you.
I will breathe out my burning anger against you.
I will hand you over to mean people.
They are skilled at destroying others.
32 You will be burned in the fire.
Your blood will be spilled in your land.
You will not be remembered anymore.
I have spoken. I am the LORD." ' "

The LORD Judges Jerusalem for Its Sins

22 A message from the LORD came
to me. The LORD said,
2 "Son of man, are you going to judge
Jerusalem? Will you judge this city that
has so many murderers in it? Then tell
its people they have done many evil
things. I hate those things. 3 Tell them,
'The LORD and King says, "Your city
brings death on itself. You spill blood
inside its walls. You make yourselves
'unclean' by making statues of gods.
4 You are guilty of spilling blood. Your
statues have made you 'unclean.' You
have brought your days to a close. The
end of your years has come. So the
nations will make fun of you. All
the countries will laugh at you. 5 Those
who are near you will tell jokes about
you. So will those who are far away.
Trouble fills the streets of your sinful city.
6 " ' "The princes of Israel are in your
city. All of them use their power to spill
blood. 7 They have made fun of fathers
and mothers alike. They have crushed
outsiders. They have treated badly the
children whose fathers have died. They
have done the same thing to widows.
8 You have looked down on the holy
things that were set apart to me. You
have misused my Sabbath days. 9 You
have spread lies about others so you
can spill someone's blood. You eat at the
mountain temples. You commit impure
acts. 10 You bring shame on your fathers
by having sex with their wives. You have
sex with women during their monthly
period. That is when they are 'unclean.'
11 One of you has sex with another man's
wife. I hate that sin. Another brings
shame on his daughter-in-law by having sex with her. Still another has sex
with his sister, even though she is his
own father's daughter. 12 You accept
money from people who want special
favors. You do this to spill someone's
blood. You charge interest to poor
people when you lend them money.
You make money from them. You get
rich by cheating your neighbors. And
you have forgotten me," announces the
LORD and King.
13 " ' "I will clap my hands because I
am so angry. You got rich by cheating
others. You spilled blood inside the walls

of your city. [14]Will you be brave on the day I deal with you? Will you be strong at that time? I have spoken. I will do this. I am the LORD. [15]I will scatter you among the nations. I will send you to other countries. I will put an end to your 'uncleanness.' [16]You will be 'unclean' in the sight of the nations. Then you will know that I am the LORD.' "

[17]A message from the LORD came to me. The LORD said, [18]"Son of man, the people of Israel have become like scum to me. All of them are like the copper, tin, iron and lead left inside a furnace. They are only the scum that is removed from silver." [19]So the LORD and King says, "People of Israel, all of you have become like scum. So I will gather you together in Jerusalem. [20]People put silver, copper, iron, lead and tin into a furnace. They melt it with a blazing fire. In the same way, I will gather you. I will pour out my burning anger on you. I will put you inside the city and melt you. [21]I will gather you together. My burning anger will blaze out at you. And you will be melted inside Jerusalem. [22]Silver is melted in a furnace. And you will be melted inside the city. Then you will know that I have poured out my burning anger on you. I am the LORD."

[23]Another message from the LORD came to me. The LORD said, [24]"Son of man, speak to the land. Tell it, 'You have not been washed clean with rain. That's because I am angry with you.' [25]Ezekiel, the princes of the land are like a roaring lion that tears its food apart. They eat people up. They take treasures and other valuable things. They cause many women in the land to become widows. [26]Its priests break my law. They treat things set apart to me as if they were not holy. They treat holy and common things as if they were the same. They teach that there is no difference between things that are 'clean' and things that are not. They refuse to keep my Sabbath days. So they treat me as if I were not holy. [27]The officials in the land are like wolves that tear their food apart. They spill blood and kill people to get rich. [28]The prophets cover up these acts for them. The visions of these prophets are false. They use magic to try to find out what is going to happen. But their magic tricks are lies. They say, 'The LORD and King says.' But I have not spoken to them. [29]The people of the land get rich by cheating others. They steal. They crush those who are poor and in need. They treat outsiders badly. They refuse to be fair to them.

[30]"I looked for someone among them who would stand up for Jerusalem. I tried to find someone who would pray to me for the land. Then I would not have to destroy it. But I could not find anyone who would pray for it. [31]So I will pour out my anger on its people. I will destroy them because of my great anger against them. And anything that happens to them will be their own fault," announces the LORD and King.

Samaria and Jerusalem Are Like Two Impure Sisters

23 A message from the LORD came to me. The LORD said, [2]"Son of man, once there were two women. They had the same mother. [3]They became prostitutes in Egypt. They have been unfaithful to me since they were young. In that land they allowed their breasts to be touched. They permitted their virgin breasts to be kissed. [4]The older sister was named Oholah. The younger one was Oholibah. They belonged to me. Sons and daughters were born to them. Oholah stands for Samaria. And Oholibah stands for Jerusalem.

[5]"Oholah was unfaithful to me even while she still belonged to me. She longed for her Assyrian lovers. They included soldiers [6]who wore blue uniforms. They also included governors and commanders. All of them were young and handsome. They rode horses. [7]She gave herself as a prostitute to all Assyria's finest warriors. She made herself impure with the statues of the gods of everyone she longed for. [8]She started being a prostitute in Egypt. And she never stopped. When she was young, men had sex with her. They kissed her virgin breasts. They used up all their sinful desires on her.

[9]"So I handed her over to her Assyrian lovers. She longed for them. [10]They stripped her naked. They took away her sons and daughters. And they killed her with their swords. Other women laughed when that happened. I was the one who had punished her.

11 “Her sister Oholibah saw it. But her
evil desire for sexual sin was worse than
her sister’s. 12 She too longed for the men
of Assyria. They included governors and
commanders. They included soldiers
who wore fancy uniforms. They also
included men who rode horses. All of
them were young and handsome. 13 I
saw that she too made herself impure.
So both sisters did the same evil things.

14 “But Oholibah went even further
with her sexual sins. She saw pictures
of men drawn on a wall. They were
figures of Babylonians drawn in red.
15 They had belts around their waists.
They wore flowing turbans on their
heads. All of them looked like Babylonian chariot officers. They were from
the land of the Chaldeans. 16 As soon as
she saw the pictures, she longed for the
men. So she sent messengers to them in
Babylon. 17 Then the Babylonians came
to her. They went to bed with her. They
had sex with her. They made her impure
when they had sex with her. After they
did it, she became sick of them. So she
turned away from them. 18 She acted
like a prostitute who had no shame
at all. She openly showed her naked
body. I became sick of what she was
doing. So I turned away from her. I had
also turned away from her sister. 19 But
Oholibah offered her body to her lovers
again and again. She remembered the
days when she was a young prostitute
in Egypt. 20 There she had longed for her
lovers. Their private parts seemed as big
as those of donkeys. And their flow of
semen appeared to be as much as that
of horses. 21 So you wanted to return to
the days when you were young. You
longed for the time when you first became impure in Egypt. That was when
you allowed your breasts to be kissed.
And you permitted your young breasts
to be touched.”

22 So the LORD and King says, “Oholibah, I will stir up your lovers against
you. You became sick of them. You
turned away from them. But I will
bring them against you from every
side. 23 They include the Babylonians
and all the Chaldeans. They include the
men from Pekod, Shoa and Koa. They
also include all the Assyrians. They are
young and handsome. Some of them
are governors and commanders. Others
are chariot officers. Still others are very
high officials. All of them ride horses.
24 So a huge army will come against you
with weapons, chariots and wagons.
They will take up positions against you
on every side. They will carry large and
small shields. They will wear helmets.
I will turn you over to them to be punished. They will punish you in their own
way. 25 I will pour out my jealous anger
on you. And the army’s anger will burn
against you. They will cut off your noses
and ears. Some of you who are left will
be killed by swords. They will take away
your sons and daughters. Others of you
who are left will be burned up. 26 The
army will also strip off your clothes.
They will take your fine jewelry away
from you. 27 You became an impure
prostitute in Egypt. But I will put a stop
to all of that. You will no longer want
to do any of it. You will not remember
Egypt anymore.”

28 The LORD and King says, “I am
about to hand you over to people you
hate. You became sick of them. You
turned away from them. 29 They will
punish you because they hate you so
much. They will take away from you
everything you have worked for. They
will leave you completely naked. Then
everyone will see that you are a prostitute who has no shame at all. You
were impure. You offered your body to
your lovers again and again. 30 That is
why you will be punished. You longed
for lovers in other nations. You made
yourself impure by worshiping their
gods. 31 You did the same things your
sister Oholah did. So I will put her cup
in your hand. It is filled with the wine
of my anger.”

32 The LORD and King says to Oholibah,

“You will drink from your sister’s
cup.
It is large and deep.
It is filled with the wine of my
anger.
So others will laugh at you.
They will make fun of you.
33 You will become drunk and sad.
The cup of my anger will
completely destroy you.
It is the same cup your sister
Samaria drank from.

34 You will drink from it until it is
empty.
Then you will chew on its pieces.
And you will claw at your breasts.
I have spoken," announces the LORD
and King.

35 So the LORD and King says, "You
have forgotten me. You have turned
your back on me. You have been impure. You have acted like a prostitute.
So I will punish you."

36 The LORD said to me, "Son of man,
are you going to judge Oholah and Oholibah? Then tell them they have done
many evil things. I hate those things.
37 They have committed adultery. Their
hands are covered with the blood of
the people they have murdered. They
have worshiped other gods. They have
not been faithful to me. They have
even sacrificed their children as food
to other gods. Those children belonged
to me. 38 Here are some other things
the sisters have done to me. They have
made my temple 'unclean.' They have
misused my Sabbath days. 39 They
have sacrificed their children to their
gods. On that same day they entered
my temple and made it 'unclean.' That
is what they have done in my house.

40 "They even sent messengers to
bring men from far away. When the
men arrived, Oholibah took a bath.
She put makeup on her eyes. She put
her jewelry on. 41 She sat down on a
beautiful couch. A table was in front of
it. There she put the incense and olive
oil that belonged to me.

42 "The noise of a carefree crowd
was all around her. Men who drink too
much were brought from the desert.
Other men were brought along with
them. They put bracelets on the wrists
of the two sisters. They put beautiful
crowns on their heads. 43 Then I spoke
about Oholibah. She was worn out by
adultery. I said, 'Let them use her as a
prostitute. After all, that is what she is.'
44 So they slept with her. In fact, they
slept with both of these impure women,
Oholah and Oholibah. They slept with
them just as men sleep with prostitutes.
45 But judges who are right with God
will sentence the sisters to be punished.
They will be punished in the same way
as women who commit adultery and
murder. After all, they have committed
adultery. And their hands are covered
with the blood of the people they have
murdered."

46 The LORD and King says, "Bring an
angry crowd against the sisters. Hand
them over to those who will terrify them
and steal everything they have. 47 The
crowd will kill them by throwing stones
at them. They will use swords to cut
them down. They will kill their sons and
daughters. And they will burn down
their houses.

48 "So I will put an end to impurity
in the land. Then all its women will be
warned. They will not want to be like the
sisters. 49 Those sisters will be punished
because of the impure things they have
done. They will be judged because they
have worshiped other gods. Then they
will know that I am the LORD and King."

Jerusalem Is Like a Cooking Pot

24 It was the ninth year since King
Jehoiachin had been brought
to Babylon as a prisoner. On the tenth
day of the tenth month, a message from
the LORD came to me. The LORD said,
2 "Son of man, write down today's date.
The king of Babylon has surrounded
Jerusalem and attacked it today. 3 Your
people refuse to obey me. So tell them
a story. Say to them, 'The LORD and
King told me,

" ' "Put a cooking pot on the fire.
Pour water into it.
4 Put pieces of meat in it.
Use all the best pieces.
Use the leg and shoulder.
Fill it with the best bones.
5 Pick the finest animal in the flock.
Pile wood under the pot to cook
the bones.
Bring the water to a boil.
Cook the bones in it." ' "

6 The LORD and King says,

"How terrible it will be for this city!
It has so many murderers in it.
How terrible for the pot that is
coated with scum!
The scum on it will not go away.
Take the meat out of the pot piece
by piece.
Take it out in whatever order it
comes.

7 "The blood Jerusalem's people
spilled is inside its walls.
They poured it out on a bare
rock.
They did not pour it on the ground.
If they had, dust would have
covered it up.
8 So I put their blood on the bare
rock.
I did not want it to be covered up.
I poured out my great anger on
them.
I paid them back."

9 So the LORD and King said to me,

"How terrible it will be for this city!
It has so many murderers in it.
I too will pile the wood high.
10 So pile on the wood.
Light the fire.
Cook the meat well.
Mix in the spices.
Let the bones be blackened.
11 Then set the empty pot on the
coals.
Let it get hot. Let its copper glow.
Then what is not pure in it will
melt.
Its scum will be burned away.
12 But it can't be cleaned up.
Its thick scum has not been
removed.
Even fire can't burn it off.

13 "Jerusalem, you are really impure.
I tried to clean you up. But you would
not let me make you pure. So you will
not be clean again until I am no longer
so angry with you.

14 "I have spoken. The time has come
for me to act. I will not hold back. I will
not feel sorry for you. I will do what
I said I would do. You will be judged
for your conduct and actions. I am the
LORD," announces the LORD and King.

Ezekiel's Wife Dies

15 A message from the LORD came to
me. The LORD said, 16 "Son of man, I
will take away from you the wife you
delight in. It will happen very soon. But
do not sing songs of sadness. Do not let
any tears flow from your eyes. 17 Groan
quietly. Do not mourn for your wife
when she dies. Keep your turban on
your head. Keep your sandals on your
feet. Do not cover your mustache and
beard. Do not eat the food people eat
to comfort them when someone dies."

18 So I spoke to my people in the morning. And in the evening my wife died.
The next morning I did what I had been
commanded to do.

19 Then the people said to me, "Tell us
what these things have to do with us.
Why are you acting like this?"

20 So I told them. I said, "A message
from the LORD came to me. The LORD
said, 21 'Speak to the people of Israel. Tell
them, "The LORD and King says, 'I am
about to make my temple "unclean." I
will let the Babylonians burn it down.
It is the beautiful building you are so
proud of. You take delight in it. You
love it. The sons and daughters you left
behind will be killed by swords. 22 So
do what Ezekiel did. Do not cover your
mustache and beard. Do not eat the
food people eat to comfort them when
someone dies. 23 Keep your turbans on
your heads. Keep your sandals on your
feet. Do not mourn or weep. You will
waste away because you have sinned
so much. You will groan among yourselves. 24 What Ezekiel has done will
show you what is going to happen to
you. You will do just as he has done.
Then you will know that I am the LORD
and King.'"'

25 "Son of man, I will take away their
beautiful temple. It is their joy and glory. They take delight in it. Their hearts
long for it. I will also take away their
sons and daughters. 26 On the day I destroy everything, a man will escape.
He will come and tell you the news.
27 At that time I will open your mouth.
Then you will no longer be silent. You
will speak with the man. That will show
them what will happen to them. And
they will know that I am the LORD."

A Prophecy Against Ammon

25 A message from the LORD came
to me. The LORD said, 2 "Son of
man, turn your attention to the Ammonites. Prophesy against them. 3 Tell
them, 'Listen to the message of the LORD
and King. He says, "You laughed when
my temple was made 'unclean.' You
also laughed when the land of Israel
was completely destroyed. You mocked
the people of Judah when they were
taken away as prisoners. 4 So I am

going to hand you over to the people
of the east. They will set up their tents
in your land. They will camp among
you. They will eat your fruit. They will
drink your milk. 5 I will turn the city
of Rabbah into grasslands for camels.
Ammon will become a resting place for
sheep. Then you will know that I am the
LORD.' " 6 The LORD and King says, "You
clapped your hands. You stamped your
feet. Deep down inside, you hated the
land of Israel. You were glad because of
what happened to it. 7 So I will reach out
my powerful hand against you. I will
give you and everything you have to
the nations. I will bring you to an end
among the nations. I will destroy you.
Then you will know that I am the LORD."

A Prophecy Against Moab

8 The LORD and King says, "Moab and
Edom said, 'Look! Judah has become
like all the other nations.' 9 So I will let
Moab's enemies attack its lower hills.
They will begin at the border towns.
Those towns include Beth Jeshimoth,
Baal Meon and Kiriathaim. They are
the glory of that land. 10 I will hand
Moab over to the people of the east. I
will also give the Ammonites to them.
And the Ammonites will no longer be
remembered among the nations. 11 I will
punish Moab. Then they will know that
I am the LORD."

A Prophecy Against Edom

12 The LORD and King says, "Edom
got even with Judah. That made Edom
very guilty." 13 The LORD continues, "I
will reach out my hand against Edom.
I will kill its people and their animals. I
will completely destroy it. They will be
killed by swords from Teman all the way
to Dedan. 14 I will use my people Israel to
pay Edom back. They will punish Edom
because my anger against it is great.
They will know how I pay back my enemies," announces the LORD and King.

A Prophecy Against the Philistines

15 The LORD and King says, "Deep
down inside them, the Philistines hated
Judah. So the Philistines tried to get
even with them. They had been Judah's
enemies for many years. So they tried
to destroy them." 16 The LORD continues, "I am about to reach out my hand
against the Philistines. I will wipe out
the Kerethites. I will destroy those who
remain along the coast. 17 You can be
sure that I will pay them back. I will
punish them because my anger against
them is great. When I pay them back,
they will know that I am the LORD."

A Prophecy Against Tyre

26 It was the first day of the 11th
month. It was the 12th year
since King Jehoiachin had been brought
to Babylon as a prisoner. A message
from the LORD came to me. The LORD
said, 2 "Son of man, Tyre laughed because of what happened to Jerusalem.
The people of Tyre said, 'Jerusalem is
the gateway to the nations. But the gate
is broken. Its doors have swung open to
us. Jerusalem has been destroyed. So
now we will succeed.' " 3 The LORD and
King says, "But I am against you, Tyre.
I will bring many nations against you.
They will come in like the waves of the
sea. 4 They will destroy your walls. They
will pull down your towers. I will clear
away the stones of your broken-down
buildings. I will turn you into nothing
but a bare rock. 5 Out in the Mediterranean Sea your island city will become a
place to spread fishnets. I have spoken,"
announces the LORD and King. "The
nations will take you and everything
you have. 6 Your settlements on the
coast will be destroyed by war. Then you
will know that I am the LORD."

7 The LORD and King says, "From the
north I am going to bring Nebuchadnezzar against Tyre. He is the king of
Babylon. He is the greatest king of all.
He will come with horses and chariots.
Horsemen and a great army will be
brought along with him. 8 He will go
to war against you. He will destroy
your settlements on the coast. He will
bring in war machines to attack you. A
ramp will be built up to your walls. He
will raise his shields against you. 9 He
will use huge logs to knock down your
walls. He will destroy your towers with
his weapons. 10 He will have so many
horses that they will cover you with
dust. Your walls will shake because of
the noise of his war horses, wagons and
chariots. He will enter your gates, just
as men enter a city whose walls have
been broken through. 11 The hooves of
his horses will pound in your streets. His

swords will kill your people. Your strong
pillars will fall to the ground. [12] His men
will take away from you your wealth
and anything else you have. They will
pull down your walls. They will completely destroy your fine houses. They
will throw the stones and lumber of
your broken-down buildings into the
sea. [13] I will put an end to your noisy
songs. No one will hear the music of
your harps anymore. [14] I will turn you
into nothing but a bare rock. You will
become a place to spread fishnets. You
will never be rebuilt. I have spoken.
I am the LORD," announces the LORD
and King.

[15] The LORD and King speaks to Tyre.
He says, "The lands along the coast will
shake because of the sound of your fall.
Wounded people will groan because
so many are dying there. [16] Then all
the princes along the coast will step
down from their thrones. They will put
their robes away. They will take off their
beautiful clothes. They will sit on the
ground. They will put on terror as if
it were their clothes. They will tremble with fear all the time. They will be
shocked because of what has happened
to you. [17] Then they will sing a song of
sadness about you. They will say to you,

"'Famous city, you have been
completely destroyed!
You were filled with sea traders.
You and your citizens
were a mighty power on the seas.
You terrified everyone
who lived in you.
[18] The lands along the coast trembled
with fear
when you fell.
The islands in the sea
were terrified when you were
destroyed.'"

[19] The LORD and King says to Tyre, "I
will turn you into an empty city. You
will be like cities where no one lives anymore. I will cause the ocean to sweep
over you. Its mighty waters will cover
you. [20] So I will bring you down together
with those who go down into the grave.
The people there lived long ago. You
will have to live in the earth below. It
will be like living in buildings that were
destroyed many years ago. You will go
down into the grave along with others.
And you will never come back. You will
not take your place in this world again.
[21] I will bring you to a horrible end. You
will be gone forever. People will look
for you. But they will never find you,"
announces the LORD and King.

A Song of Sadness About Tyre

27 A message from the LORD came
to me. The LORD said, [2] "Son of
man, sing a song of sadness about Tyre.
[3] It is located at the gateway to the Mediterranean Sea. It does business with
nations on many coasts. Say to it, 'The
LORD and King says,

"'"Tyre, you say,
'I am perfect and beautiful.'
[4] You were like a ship that ruled over
the high seas.
Your builders made you perfect
and beautiful.
[5] They cut all your lumber
from juniper trees on Mount
Hermon.
They used a cedar tree from Lebanon
to make a mast for you.
[6] They made your oars
out of oak trees from Bashan.
They made your deck out of
cypress wood
from the coasts of Cyprus.
They decorated it with ivory.
[7] Your sail was made out of beautiful
Egyptian linen.
It served as your banner.
Your shades were made out of blue
and purple cloth.
They were from the coasts of
Elishah.
[8] Men from Sidon and Arvad
manned your oars.
Tyre, your sailors were skillful.
[9] Very skilled workers from Byblos
were on board.
They kept you waterproof.
All the ships on the sea and their
sailors
came up beside you.
They brought their goods to
trade for yours.

[10] "'"Men from Persia, Lydia and Put
served as soldiers in your army,
city of Tyre.
They hung their shields and
helmets on your walls.
That brought glory to you.

11 Men from Arvad and Helek
guarded your walls on every
side.
Men from Gammad
were in your towers.
They hung their shields around
your walls.
They made you perfect and
beautiful.

12 “ ‘ “Tarshish did business with you
because you had so much wealth. They
traded silver, iron, tin and lead for your
goods.

13 “ ‘ “Greece, Tubal and Meshek did
business with you. They traded human
beings and bronze objects for your
products.

14 “ ‘ “Men from Beth Togarmah traded chariot horses, war horses and mules
for your goods.

15 “ ‘ “Men from Rhodes did business
with you. Many lands along the coast
bought goods from you. They paid you
with ivory tusks and ebony wood.

16 “ ‘ “Aram did business with you
because you had so many products
for sale. They traded turquoise, purple
cloth and needlework for your goods.
They also traded fine linen, coral and
rubies for them.

17 “ ‘ “Judah and Israel did business
with you. They traded wheat from Minnith, sweets, honey, olive oil and lotion
for your products.

18 “ ‘ “Damascus did business with
you. That's because you had so many
products and so much wealth. They
traded to you wine from Helbon and
wool from Zahar. 19 They also traded
to you casks of wine from Izal. You
traded to them wrought iron, cassia
and calamus.

20 “ ‘ “Dedan traded saddle blankets
to you.

21 “ ‘ “Arabia and all the princes of
Kedar bought goods from you. They
traded you lambs, rams and goats for
them.

22 “ ‘ “Traders from Sheba and
Raamah did business with you. They
traded the finest spices, jewels and gold
for your goods.

23 “ ‘ “Harran, Kanneh and Eden did
business with you. So did traders from
Sheba, Ashur and Kilmad. 24 In your
market they traded beautiful clothes,
blue cloth, and needlework to you. They
also traded colorful rugs that had twisted cords and tight knots.

25 “ ‘ “The ships of Tarshish
carry your products.
You are like a ship filled with a
heavy load
as you sail the sea.
26 The sailors who man your oars take
you
out to the high seas.
But the east wind will break you in
pieces
far out at sea.
27 You will be wrecked on that day.
Your wealth, goods and products
will sink deep into the sea.
So will your sailors, officers,
carpenters,
traders and all your soldiers.
Anyone else on board will sink
too.
28 The lands along the coast will
shake
when your sailors cry out.
29 All those who man the oars
will desert their ships.
The sailors and all the officers
will stand on the shore.
30 They will raise their voices.
They will cry bitterly over you.
They will sprinkle dust on their
heads.
They will roll in ashes.
31 They will shave their heads
because of you.
And they will put on the clothes
of sadness.
They will weep over you.
Their spirits will be greatly troubled.
They will be very sad.
32 As they weep and mourn over you,
they will sing a song of sadness
about you.
They will say, ‘Who was ever like
Tyre?
It was destroyed in the sea.’
33 Your goods went out on the seas.
You supplied many nations with
what they needed.
You had so much wealth and so
many products.
You made the kings of the earth
rich.
34 Now the sea has torn you apart.
You have sunk deep down into it.

Your products and all your people
have gone down with you.
35 All those who live in the lands
along the coast
are shocked because of what has
happened to you.
Their kings tremble with fear.
Their faces are twisted in horror.
36 The traders among the nations
laugh at you.
You have come to a horrible end.
And you will be gone forever." ' "

A Prophecy Against the King of Tyre

28 A message from the LORD came
to me. The LORD said, 2 "Son of
man, speak to Ethbaal. He is the ruler of
Tyre. Tell him, 'The LORD and King says,

" ' "In your proud heart
you say, 'I am a god.
I sit on the throne of a god
in the Mediterranean Sea.'
But you are only a human being.
You are not a god.
In spite of that, you think you
are as wise as a god.
3 Are you wiser than Daniel?
Isn't even one secret hidden from
you?
4 You are wise and understanding.
So you have become very
wealthy.
You have piled up gold and silver
among your treasures.
5 You have used your great skill in
trading
to increase your wealth.
You are very rich.
So your heart has become
proud." ' "

6 The LORD and King says,
"You think you are wise.
In fact, you claim to be as wise as
a god.
7 So I am going to bring outsiders
against you.
They will not show you any pity
at all.
They will use their swords against
your beauty and wisdom.
They will strike down your
shining glory.
8 They will bring you down to the
grave.
You will die a horrible death
in the middle of the sea.
9 Then will you say, 'I am a god'?
Will you say that to those who
kill you?
You will be only a human being to
those who kill you.
You will not be a god to them.
10 You will die just like those who
have not been circumcised.
Outsiders will kill you.

I have spoken," announces the LORD
and King.

11 A message from the LORD came to
me. The LORD said, 12 "Son of man, sing a
song of sadness about the king of Tyre.
Tell him, 'The LORD and King says,

" ' "You were the model of
perfection.
You were full of wisdom.
You were perfect and beautiful.
13 You were in Eden.
It was my garden.
All kinds of jewels decorated you.
Here is a list of them:
carnelian, chrysolite and
emerald,
topaz, onyx and jasper,
lapis lazuli, turquoise and beryl.
Your settings and mountings were
made out of gold.
On the day you were created,
they were prepared.
14 I appointed you to be like a
guardian angel.
I anointed you for that purpose.
You were on my holy mountain.
You walked among the gleaming
jewels.
15 Your conduct was without blame
from the day you were created.
But soon you began to sin.
16 You traded with many nations.
You harmed people everywhere.
And you sinned.
So I sent you away from my
mountain in shame.
Guardian angel, I drove you
away
from among the gleaming
jewels.
17 You thought you were so handsome
that it made your heart proud.
You thought you were so glorious
that it spoiled your wisdom.
So I threw you down to the earth.
I made an example out of you in
front of kings.

18 Your many sins and dishonest
trade
made your holy places impure.
So I made you go up in flames.
I turned you into nothing but
ashes on the ground.
I let everyone see it.
19 All the nations that knew you
are shocked because of what
happened to you.
You have come to a horrible end.
And you will be gone forever." ' "

A Prophecy Against Sidon

20 A message from the LORD came
to me. The LORD said, 21 "Son of man,
turn your attention to the city of Sidon.
Prophesy against it. 22 Say, 'The LORD
and King says,

" ' "Sidon, I am against your people.
Among you I will display my
glory.
I will punish your people.
Among you I will prove that I am
holy.
Then you will know that I am the
LORD.
23 I will send a plague on you.
I will make blood flow in your
streets.
Those who are killed will fall inside
you.
Swords will strike your people on
every side.
Then they will know that I am
the LORD.

24 " ' "The people of Israel will no longer have neighbors who hate them.
Those neighbors will not be like sharp
and painful thorns anymore. Then Israel will know that I am the LORD and
King." ' "
25 The LORD and King says, "I will
gather the people of Israel together
from the nations where they have been
scattered. That will prove that I am
holy. I will let the nations see it. Then
Israel will live in their own land. I gave
it to my servant Jacob. 26 My people
will live there in safety. They will build
houses. They will plant vineyards. They
will live in safety. I will punish all their
neighbors who told lies about them.
Then Israel will know that I am the
LORD their God."

A Prophecy Against Egypt

29 It was the tenth year since King
Jehoiachin had been brought to
Babylon as a prisoner. On the 12th day
of the tenth month, a message from
the LORD came to me. The LORD said,
2 "Son of man, turn your attention to
Pharaoh Hophra. He is king of Egypt.
Prophesy against him and the whole
land of Egypt. 3 Tell him, 'The LORD and
King says,

" ' "Pharaoh Hophra, I am against
you.
King of Egypt, you are like a
huge monster
lying among your streams.
You say, 'The Nile River belongs
to me.
I made it for myself.'
4 But I will put hooks in your jaws.
I will make the fish in your
streams
stick to your scales.
I will pull you out from among
your streams.
All the fish will stick to your
scales.
5 I will leave you out in the desert.
All the fish in your streams
will be there with you.
You will fall down in an open field.
You will not be picked up.
I will feed you to the wild animals
and to the birds in the sky.

6 Then everyone who lives in Egypt will
know that I am the LORD.

" ' "You have been like a walking stick
made out of a papyrus stem. The people
of Israel tried to lean on you. 7 They took
hold of you. But you broke under their
weight. You tore open their shoulders.
The people of Israel leaned on you. But
you snapped in two. And their backs
were broken." ' "
8 So the LORD and King says, "I will
send Nebuchadnezzar's sword against
you. He will kill people and animals
alike. 9 Egypt will become a dry and
empty desert. Then your people will
know that I am the LORD.
"You said, 'The Nile River belongs
to me. I made it for myself.' 10 So I am
against you and your streams. I will
destroy the land of Egypt. I will turn
it into a dry and empty desert from
Migdol all the way to Aswan. I will

destroy everything as far as the border
of Cush. 11 No people or animals will
travel through Egypt. No one will even
live there for 40 years. 12 Egypt will be
more empty than any other land. Its
destroyed cities will lie empty for 40
years. I will scatter the people of Egypt
among the nations. I will send them to
other countries."

13 But here is what the LORD and King
says. "At the end of 40 years I will gather the Egyptians together. I will bring
them back from the nations where they
were scattered. 14 I will bring them back
from where they were taken as prisoners. I will return them to Upper Egypt.
That is where their families came from.
There they will be an unimportant kingdom. 15 Egypt will be the least important
kingdom of all. It will never place itself
above the other nations again. I will
make it very weak. Then it will never again rule over the nations. 16 The
people of Israel will no longer trust in
Egypt. Instead, Egypt will remind them
of how they sinned when they turned
to it for help. Then they will know that
I am the LORD and King."

17 It was the 27th year since King Jehoiachin had been brought to Babylon
as a prisoner. On the first day of the first
month, a message from the LORD came
to me. Here is what the LORD said. 18 "Son
of man, King Nebuchadnezzar drove his
army in a hard military campaign.
The campaign was against Tyre. Their
helmets rubbed their heads bare. The
heavy loads they carried made their
shoulders raw. But he and his army did
not gain anything from the campaign
he led against Tyre. 19 So I am going to
give Egypt to Nebuchadnezzar, the king
of Babylon. He will carry off its wealth.
He will take away anything else they
have. He will give it to his army. 20 I
have given Egypt to him as a reward
for his efforts. After all, he and his army
attacked Egypt because I told them to,"
announces the LORD and King.

21 "When Nebuchadnezzar wins the
battle over Egypt, I will make the Israelites strong again. Ezekiel, I will open
your mouth. And you will be able to
speak to them. Then they will know
that I am the LORD."

30

A message from the LORD came
to me. The LORD said, 2 "Son of
man, prophesy. Say, 'The LORD and
King says,

" ' "Cry out,
'A terrible day is coming!'
3 The day is near.
The day of the LORD is coming.
It will be a cloudy day.
The nations have been sentenced
to die.
4 I will send Nebuchadnezzar's sword
against Egypt.
Cush will suffer terribly.
Many will die in Egypt.
Then its wealth will be carried
away.
Its foundations will be torn
down.

5 The people of Cush, Libya, Lydia, Kub
and the whole land of Arabia will be
killed by swords. So will the Jews who
live in Egypt. They went there from
the covenant land of Israel. And the
Egyptians will die too." ' "

6 The LORD says,

"Those who were going to help
Egypt will die.
The strength Egypt was so proud
of will fail.
Its people will be killed by swords
from Migdol all the way to
Aswan,"
announces the LORD and King.
7 "Egypt will be more empty than
any other land.
Its cities will be completely
destroyed.
8 I will set Egypt on fire.
All those who came to help it will
be crushed.
Then they will know that I am
the LORD.

9 "At that time I will send messengers
out in ships. They will terrify the people
of Cush who are so contented. Cush will
suffer greatly when Egypt falls. And you
can be sure it will fall."

10 The LORD and King says,

"I will put an end to the huge
armies of Egypt.
I will use Nebuchadnezzar, the
king of Babylon, to do this.

[11] He and his armies will attack the
land and destroy it.
They will not show its people any
pity at all.
They will use their swords against
Egypt.
They will fill the land with dead
bodies.
[12] I will dry up the waters of the Nile
River.
I will sell the land to an evil
nation.
I will use the power of outsiders
to destroy the land and
everything in it.

I have spoken. I am the LORD."

[13] The LORD and King says,

"I will destroy the statues of Egypt's
gods.
I will put an end to the gods
the people in Memphis worship.
Egypt will not have princes
anymore.
I will spread fear all through the
land.
[14] I will completely destroy Upper
Egypt.
I will set Zoan on fire.
I will punish Thebes.
[15] I will pour out my burning anger
on Pelusium.
It is a fort in eastern Egypt.
I will wipe out the huge army of
Thebes.
[16] I will set Egypt on fire.
Pelusium will groan with terrible
pain.
Thebes will be ripped apart.
Memphis will suffer greatly
because of everything that
happens.
[17] The young men of Heliopolis and
Bubastis
will be killed by swords.
Their people will be taken away
as prisoners.
[18] I will break Egypt's power over
other lands.
That will be a dark day for
Tahpanhes.
There the strength Egypt was so
proud of
will come to an end.
Egypt will be covered with clouds.
The people in its villages
will be taken away as prisoners.
[19] So I will punish Egypt.
Then they will know that I am
the LORD."

[20] It was the 11th year since King Jehoiachin had been brought to Babylon
as a prisoner. On the seventh day of the
first month, a message from the LORD
came to me. The LORD said, [21] "Son of
man, I have broken the powerful arm
of Pharaoh Hophra, the king of Egypt.
No bandages have been put on his arm
to heal it. It has not been put in a cast.
So his arm will not be strong enough to
use a sword. [22] I am against Pharaoh,
the king of Egypt. I will break both his
arms. I will break his healthy arm and
his broken one. His sword will fall from
his hand. [23] I will scatter the people of
Egypt among the nations. I will send
them to other countries. [24] I will make
the arms of the king of Babylon stronger. I will put my sword in his hand. But
I will break the arms of Pharaoh. And he
will groan in front of Nebuchadnezzar.
He will cry out like someone dying from
his wounds. [25] I will make the arms of
the king of Babylon stronger. But the
arms of Pharaoh will not be able to help
Egypt. I will put my sword in Nebuchadnezzar's hand. He will get ready to use
it against Egypt. Then they will know
that I am the LORD. [26] I will scatter the
Egyptians among the nations. I will
send them to other countries. Then they
will know that I am the LORD."

31 It was the 11th year since King
Jehoiachin had been brought to
Babylon as a prisoner. On the first day
of the third month, a message from the
LORD came to me. The LORD said, [2] "Son
of man, speak to Pharaoh Hophra, the
king of Egypt. Also speak to his huge
army. Tell him,

" 'Who can be compared with your
majesty?
[3] Think about what happened to
Assyria.
Once it was like a cedar tree in
Lebanon.
It had beautiful branches
that provided shade for the
forest.
It grew very high.
Its top was above all the leaves.
[4] The waters fed it.
Deep springs made it grow tall.

Their streams flowed
all around its base.
They made their way
to all the trees in the fields.
5 So it grew higher
than any other tree in the fields.
It grew more limbs.
Its branches grew long.
They spread because they had
plenty of water.
6 All the birds in the sky
made their nests in its limbs.
All the wild animals
had their babies under its
branches.
All the great nations
lived in its shade.
7 Its spreading branches
made it majestic and beautiful.
Its roots went down deep
to where there was plenty of
water.
8 The cedar trees in my garden
were no match for it.
The juniper trees
could not equal its limbs.
The plane trees
could not compare with its
branches.
No tree in my garden
could match its beauty.
9 I gave it many branches.
They made it beautiful.
All the trees in my Garden of Eden
were jealous of it.' "

10 So the LORD and King says, "The
great cedar tree grew very high. Its top
was above all the leaves. It was proud
of how tall it was. 11 So I handed it over
to the Babylonian ruler of the nations.
I wanted him to punish it because it
was so evil. I decided to get rid of it.
12 The Babylonians cut it down and left
it there. They did not show it any pity
at all. Some of its branches fell on the
mountains. Others fell in all the valleys. The branches lay broken in all the
stream beds in the land. All the nations
on earth came out from under its shade.
And they went on their way. 13 All the
birds settled on the fallen tree. All the
wild animals lived among its branches.
14 So trees that receive plenty of water
must never grow so high that it makes
them proud. Their tops must never be
above the rest of the leaves. No other
trees that receive a lot of water must
ever grow that high. They are appointed
to die and go down into the earth below.
They will join human beings, who go
down to the place of the dead."

15 The LORD and King says, "Assyria
was like a cedar tree. But I brought it
down to the place of the dead. On that
day I dried up the deep springs of water
and covered them. I held its streams
back. I shut off its rich supply of water.
Because of that, Lebanon was dressed in
gloom as if it were clothes. All the trees
in the fields dried up. 16 I brought the
cedar tree down to the place of the dead.
It joined the other nations that go down
there. I made the nations on earth shake
because of the sound of its fall. Then
all the trees of Eden were comforted
in the earth below. That included the
finest and best trees in Lebanon. And
it included all the trees that received
plenty of water. 17 Others also went down
along with the cedar tree into the place
of the dead. They included those who
had been killed by swords. They also
included the armed men among the
nations who lived in its shade.

18 "Which one of the trees of Eden can
be compared with you? What tree is as
glorious and majestic as you are? But
you too will be brought down to the
earth below. There you will join the trees
of Eden. You will lie down with those
who have not been circumcised. You
will be among those who were killed
by swords.

"That is what will happen to Pharaoh
and his huge armies," announces the
LORD and King.

32 It was the 12th year since King
Jehoiachin had been brought to
Babylon as a prisoner. On the first day
of the 12th month, a message from the
LORD came to me. The LORD said, 2 "Son
of man, sing a song of sadness about
Pharaoh Hophra, the king of Egypt.
Tell him,

" 'You are like a lion among the
nations.
You are like a monster in the sea.
You move around wildly in your
rivers.
You churn the water with your
feet.
You make the streams muddy.' "

[3]The LORD and King says,

"I will use a large crowd of people
to throw my net over you.
They will pull you up in it.
[4]Then I will throw you on the land.
I will toss you into an open field.
I will let all the birds in the sky
settle on you.
I will let all the wild animals eat
you up.
[5]I will scatter the parts of your body
all over the mountains.
I will fill the valleys with your
remains.
[6]I will soak the land with your
blood.
It will flow all the way to the
mountains.
The valleys will be filled with the
parts of your body.
[7]When I wipe you out,
I will put a cover over the
heavens.
I will darken the stars.
I will cover the sun with a cloud.
The moon will stop shining.
[8]I will darken all the bright lights
in the sky above you.
I will bring darkness over your
land,"
announces the LORD and King.
[9]"The hearts of many people will be
troubled.
That is because I will destroy you
among the nations.
You had never known anything
about those lands before.
[10]Many nations will be shocked
when they see what has
happened to you.
Their kings will tremble with fear
when they find out about it.
I will get ready to use
Nebuchadnezzar
as my sword against them.
On the day you fall from power,
each of the kings will tremble
with fear.
Each will be afraid he is the next
to die."

[11]The LORD and King says,

"I will send against you
the sword of the king of Babylon.
[12]I will destroy your huge army.
They will be killed by the swords
of Babylon's mighty soldiers.
The soldiers will not show them
any pity.
They will bring Egypt down in all
its pride.
Its huge armies will be thrown
down.
[13]I will destroy all its cattle
from the places where they have
plenty of water.
Human feet will never stir up the
water again.
The hooves of cattle will not
make it muddy anymore.
[14]I will let the waters of Egypt settle.
I will make its streams flow like
olive oil,"
announces the LORD and King.
[15]"I will turn Egypt into an empty
land.
I will strip away everything in it.
I will strike down everyone who
lives there.
Then they will know that I am
the LORD."

[16]"That is the song of sadness people
will sing about Egypt. Women from
other nations will sing it. They will
weep over Egypt and its huge armies,"
announces the LORD and King.

[17]A message from the LORD came to
me. King Jehoiachin had been brought
to Babylon as a prisoner. On the 15th
day of a month 12 years after that, the
message came. The LORD said, [18]"Son of
man, weep over the huge army of Egypt.
Tell the Egyptians they will go down
into the earth below. The women singers
from the other mighty nations will go
down into the grave along with them
and others. [19]Tell them, 'Are you any
better than others? Since you are not,
go down there. Lie down with those who
have not been circumcised.' [20]They will
fall dead among those who were killed
by swords. Nebuchadnezzar is ready to
use his sword against them. Let Egypt
be dragged off together with its huge
armies. [21]The mighty leaders who are
already in the place of the dead will talk
about Egypt. They will also speak about
the nations that were going to help it.
They will say, 'They have come down
here. They are lying down with those
who had not been circumcised. They
are here with those who were killed
by swords.'

22 “Assyria is there with its whole
army. Its king is surrounded by the
graves of all its people who were killed
by swords. 23 Their graves are deep down
in the pit. Assyria’s army lies around the
grave of its king. All those who spread
terror while they were alive are now
dead. They were killed by swords.
24 “Elam is also there. Its huge armies
lie around the grave of its king. All those
who spread terror while they were alive
are now dead. They were killed by
swords. They had not been circumcised.
They went down into the earth below.
Their shame is like the shame of others
who go down into the grave. 25 A bed is
made for Elam’s king among the dead.
His huge armies lie around his grave.
They had not been circumcised. They
were killed by swords. They had spread
terror while they were alive. So now
their shame is like the shame of others
who go down into the grave. They lie
down among the dead.
26 “Meshek and Tubal are also there.
Their huge armies lie around the graves
of their kings. None of them had been
circumcised. They had spread their terror while they were alive. So they were
killed by swords. 27 But they do not lie
down with the other dead soldiers of
long ago. Those soldiers and their weapons had gone down into the place of
the dead. Their swords had been placed
under their heads. Their shields rest on
their bones. The soldiers of Meshek and
Tubal do not lie down with them. This is
true even though they had also spread
terror while they were alive.
28 “Pharaoh Hophra, you too will be
broken. You will lie down among those
who had not been circumcised. You will
be there with those who were killed by
swords.
29 “Edom is also there. So are its kings
and all its princes. In spite of their power, they lie down with those who were
killed by swords. They lie down with
those who had not been circumcised.
They are there with others who went
down into the grave.
30 “All the princes of the north are
there too. So are all the people of Sidon.
They went down into the grave in dishonor. While they were alive, they used
their power to spread terror. They had
never been circumcised. But now they
lie down there with those who were
killed by swords. Their shame is like
the shame of others who go down into
the grave.
31 “Pharaoh and his whole army will
see all of them. That will comfort him
even though his huge armies were
killed by swords.” This is what the LORD
and King announces. 32 “I let Pharaoh
spread terror while he was alive. But
now he and his huge armies will be
buried with those who had not been
circumcised. They will lie down there
with those who were killed by swords,”
announces the LORD and King.

The LORD Again Appoints Ezekiel to Warn Israel

33 A message from the LORD came
to me. The LORD said, 2 “Son of
man, speak to your people. Tell them,
‘Suppose I send enemies against a land.
And its people choose one of their men
to stand guard. 3 He sees the enemies
coming against the land. He blows a
trumpet to warn the people. 4 Someone
hears the trumpet. But they do not pay
any attention to the warning. The enemies come and kill them. Then what
happens to them will be their own fault.
5 They heard the sound of the trumpet.
But they did not pay any attention
to the warning. So what happened to
them was their own fault. If they had
paid attention, they would have saved
themselves. 6 But suppose the guard sees
the enemies coming. And he does not
blow the trumpet to warn the people.
The enemies come and kill one of them.
Then their life has been taken away from
them because they sinned. But I will hold
the guard responsible for their death.’
7 “Son of man, I have appointed you
as a prophet to warn the people of Israel. So listen to my message. Give them
a warning from me. 8 Suppose I say to
a sinful person, ‘You can be sure that
you will die.’ And suppose you do not
try to get them to change their ways.
Then they will die because they have
sinned. And I will hold you responsible
for their death. 9 But suppose you do
warn that sinful person. You tell them
to change their ways. But they do not
change. Then they will die because they
have sinned. But you will have saved
yourself.

10 "Son of man, speak to the Israelites. Tell them, 'You are saying, "Our sins and the wrong things we have done weigh us down. We are wasting away because we have sinned so much. So how can we live?"' 11 Tell them, 'When sinful people die, it does not give me any joy. But when they turn away from their sins and live, that makes me very happy. And that is just as sure as I am alive,' announces the LORD and King. 'So turn away from your sins! Change your evil ways! Why should you die, people of Israel?'

12 "Son of man, speak to your people. Tell them, 'Suppose a godly person does not obey the LORD. Then the right things that person has done in the past count for nothing. Suppose a sinful person turns away from doing wrong things. Then the wrong things that person has done in the past won't bring them judgment. A godly person who sins won't be allowed to live. That's true even though they used to do right things.' 13 Suppose I tell a godly person that they will live. And they trust in the fact that they used to do what is right. But now they do what is evil. Then I will not remember any of the right things they have done. They will die because they have done so many evil things. 14 Suppose I say to a sinful person, 'You can be sure you will die.' And then they turn away from their sin. They do what is fair and right. 15 They return things they take to make sure loans are repaid. They give back what they have stolen. They obey my rules that give life. They do not do what is evil. Then you can be sure they will live. They will not die. 16 None of the sins they have committed will be held against them. They have done what is fair and right. So you can be sure they will live.

17 "In spite of that, your people say, 'What the Lord does isn't fair.' But it is what you do that is not fair. 18 Suppose a godly person stops doing what is right. And they do what is evil. Then they will die because of it. 19 But suppose a sinful person turns away from the evil things they have done. And they do what is fair and right. Then they will live by doing that. 20 In spite of that, you Israelites say, 'What the Lord does isn't fair.' But I will judge each of you based on how you have lived."

The LORD Explains Why Jerusalem Fell

21 It was the 12th year since we had been brought to Babylon as prisoners. On the fifth day of the tenth month, a man who had escaped from Jerusalem came to bring me a report. He said, "The city has fallen!" 22 The evening before the man arrived, the power of the LORD came on me. He opened my mouth before the man came to me in the morning. So my mouth was opened. I was no longer silent.

23 Then a message from the LORD came to me. The LORD said, 24 "Son of man, here is what the people living in Israel's broken-down buildings are saying. 'Abraham was only one man. But he owned the land. We are many people. The land must certainly belong to us.' 25 So tell them, 'The LORD and King says, "You eat meat that still has blood in it. You worship your statues of gods. You commit murder. So should you still possess the land? 26 You depend on your swords. You do things I hate. Each one of you sleeps with your neighbor's wife. So should you still possess the land?"'

27 "Tell them, 'Here is what the LORD and King says. "The people who are left in those broken-down buildings will be killed by swords. Wild animals will eat up those who are out in the country. Those who are in caves and other safe places will die of a plague. And that is just as sure as I am alive. 28 I will turn the land into a dry and empty desert. The strength Jerusalem is so proud of will come to an end. The mountains of Israel will be deserted. No one will travel across them. 29 So I will turn the land into a dry and empty desert. I will punish my people because of all the evil things they have done. I hate those things. Then they will know that I am the LORD."'

30 "Son of man, your people are talking about you. They are getting together by the walls of their houses and at their doors. They are saying to one another, 'Come. Listen to the LORD's message.' 31 My people come to you, just as they usually do. They sit in front of you. They hear what you say. But they do not put it into practice. With their mouths they say they love me. But in their hearts they want what belongs to others. They try to get rich by cheating

them. 32 You are nothing more to them than someone who sings love songs. They say you have a beautiful voice. They think you play an instrument well. They hear what you say. But they do not put it into practice.

33 "Everything I have told you will come true. You can be sure of it. Then the people will know that a prophet has been among them."

The LORD Will Be the Shepherd of His People

34 A message from the LORD came to me. The LORD said, 2 "Son of man, prophesy against the shepherds of Israel. Tell them, 'The LORD and King says, "How terrible it will be for you shepherds of Israel! You only take care of yourselves. You should take good care of your flocks. 3 Instead, you eat the butter. You dress yourselves with the wool. You kill the finest animals. But you do not take care of your flocks. 4 You have not made the weak ones in the flock stronger. You have not healed the sick. You have not bandaged those who are hurt. You have not brought back those who have wandered away. You have not searched for the lost. When you ruled over them, you were mean to them. You treated them badly. 5 So they were scattered because they did not have a shepherd. They became food for all of the wild animals. 6 My sheep wandered all over the mountains and high hills. They were scattered over the whole earth. No one searched for them. No one looked for them."

7 " 'Shepherds, listen to the LORD's message. He says, 8 "My flock does not have a shepherd. Many of my sheep have been stolen. They have become food for all the wild animals. My shepherds did not care for my sheep. They did not even search for them. Instead, they only took care of themselves. And that is just as sure as I am alive," announces the LORD and King. 9 Shepherds, listen to the LORD's message. 10 The LORD and King says, "I am against the shepherds. I will hold them responsible for my flock. I will stop them from taking care of the flock. Then they will not be able to feed themselves anymore. I will save my flock from their mouths. My sheep will no longer be food for them." ' "

11 The LORD and King says, "I myself will search for my sheep. I will look after them. 12 A shepherd looks after his scattered flock when he is with them. And I will look after my sheep. I will save them from all the places where they were scattered on a dark and cloudy day. 13 I will bring them out from among the nations. I will gather them together from other countries. I will bring them into their own land. There they will eat grass on the mountains and in the valleys. And they will eat in all the fields of Israel. 14 I will take care of them in the best grasslands. They will eat grass on the highest mountains of Israel. There they will lie down in the finest grasslands. They will eat grass in the best places on Israel's mountains. 15 I myself will take care of my sheep. I will let them lie down in safety," announces the LORD and King. 16 "I will search for the lost. I will bring back those who have wandered away. I will bandage the ones who are hurt. I will make the weak ones stronger. But I will destroy those who are fat and strong. I will take good care of my sheep. I will treat them fairly."

17 The LORD and King says, "You are my flock. I will judge between one sheep and another. I will judge between rams and goats. 18 You already eat in the best grasslands. Must you also stomp all over the other fields? You already drink clear water. Must you also make the rest of the water muddy with your feet? 19 Must my flock have to eat the grass you have stomped on? Must they drink the water you have made muddy?"

20 So the LORD and King speaks to them. He says, "I myself will judge between the fat sheep and the skinny sheep. 21 You push the other sheep around with your hips and shoulders. You use your horns to butt all the weak sheep. Finally, you drive them away. 22 But I will save my sheep. They will not be carried off anymore. I will judge between one sheep and another. 23 I will place one shepherd over them. He will belong to the family line of my servant David. He will take good care of them. He will look after them. He will be their shepherd. 24 I am the LORD. I will be their God. And my servant from David's family line will be the prince among them. I have spoken. I am the LORD.

25 “I will make a covenant with them. It promises to give them peace. I will get rid of the wild animals in the land. Then my sheep can live safely in the desert. They can sleep in the forests. 26 I will make them and the places surrounding my holy mountain of Zion a blessing. I will send down rain at the right time. There will be showers of blessing. 27 The trees will bear their fruit. And the ground will produce its crops. The people will be secure in their land. I will break the chains that hold them. I will save them from the power of those who made them slaves. Then they will know that I am the LORD. 28 The nations will not carry them off anymore. Wild animals will no longer eat them up. They will live in safety. And no one will make them afraid. 29 I will give them a land that is famous for its crops. They will never again be hungry there. The nations will not make fun of them anymore. 30 Then they will know that I am with them. I am the LORD their God. And the Israelites will know that they are my people,” announces the LORD and King. 31 “You are my sheep. You belong to my flock. And I am your God,” announces the LORD and King.

A Prophecy Against Edom

35 A message from the LORD came to me. The LORD said, 2 “Son of man, turn your attention to Mount Seir. Prophesy against it. 3 Tell it, ‘The LORD and King says, “Mount Seir, I am against you. I will reach out my powerful hand against you. I will turn you into a dry and empty desert. 4 I will destroy your towns. Your land will become empty. Then you will know that I am the LORD.

5 “ ‘ “People of Edom, you have been Israel’s enemies for a long time. You let many Israelites be killed by swords when they were in great trouble. At that time I used Nebuchadnezzar to punish them and destroy them completely. 6 Now I will hand you over to murderers. They will hunt you down. You murdered others. So murderers will chase you. And that is just as sure as I am alive,” announces the LORD and King. 7 “I will turn Mount Seir into a dry and empty desert. No one will be able to go anywhere or do anything there. 8 I will fill your mountains with dead bodies. Some of those who are killed by swords will fall down dead on your hills. Others will die in your valleys and in all your canyons. 9 I will make your land empty forever. No one will live in your towns. Then you will know that I am the LORD.

10 “ ‘ “You said, ‘The nations of Israel and Judah will belong to us. We will take them over.’ You said that, even though I was there. I am the LORD. 11 You were full of anger, jealousy and hatred toward my people. So I will punish you. When I judge you, they will know that I am the LORD. And that is just as sure as I am alive,” announces the LORD and King. 12 “You will know that I have heard all the terrible things you said. You said them about those who live in the mountains of Israel. You made fun of them. You said, ‘They have been destroyed. They’ve been handed over to us. Let’s wipe them out.’ 13 You bragged that you were better than I am. You spoke against me. You did not hold anything back. But I heard it.” ’ ” 14 The LORD and King says, “The whole earth will be glad. But I will make your land empty. 15 You were happy when the land of Israel became empty. So I will treat you in the same way. Mount Seir, you will be empty. So will the whole land of Edom. Then you will know that I am the LORD.”

A Prophecy of Hope for the Mountains of Israel

36 “Son of man, prophesy to the mountains of Israel. Tell them, ‘Mountains of Israel, listen to the LORD’s message. 2 The LORD and King says, “Your enemies made fun of you. They bragged, ‘The hills you lived in for a long time belong to us now.’ ” ’ 3 Ezekiel, prophesy. Say, ‘The LORD and King says, “Your enemies destroyed you. They crushed you from every side. So the rest of the nations took over your land. People talked about you. They told lies about you.” ’ ” 4 Mountains of Israel, listen to the message of the LORD and King. He speaks to you mountains, hills, canyons and valleys. He speaks to you destroyed cities and deserted towns. The rest of the nations around you took away from you everything of value. They made fun of you. 5 So the LORD and King says, “I am very angry with those nations. I have spoken against them and the whole land of Edom. They were very happy when they took over my land. Deep down inside them, they hated Israel. They wanted to take its grasslands. 6 Ezekiel, prophesy about the land of Israel. Speak to the mountains, hills, canyons and valleys. Tell them, ‘The LORD and King says, “I have a jealous anger against the nations. They have laughed at you.” 7 So the LORD and King says, “I raise my hand and make a promise. I promise that the nations around you will also be laughed at.

8 “ ‘ “Mountains of Israel, you will produce branches and bear fruit for my people Israel. They will come home soon. 9 I am concerned about you. I will do good things for you. Farmers will plow your ground. They will plant seeds in it. 10 I will cause many people to live in Israel. The towns will no longer be empty. Their broken-down houses will be rebuilt. 11 I will cause many people and animals to live in you, Israel. They will have many babies. I will cause people to make their homes in your towns, just as I did in the past. I will help you succeed more than ever before. Then you will know that I am the LORD. 12 I will let my people Israel live there again. They will possess you. They will receive you as their own. You will never take their children away from them again.” ’ ”

13 The LORD and King says, “People say to you mountains, ‘You destroy people. You let your nation’s children be taken away.’ 14 But I will not let you destroy people anymore. I will no longer let your nation’s children be taken away,” announces the LORD and King. 15 “You will not have to listen to the nations laughing at you anymore. People will no longer make fun of you. You will not let your nation fall,” announces the LORD and King.

Israel Will Surely Be Rebuilt

16 Another message from the LORD came to me. The LORD said, 17 “Son of man, the people of Israel used to live in their own land. But they made it ‘unclean’ because of how they acted and the way they lived. To me they were ‘unclean’ like a woman having her monthly period. 18 They spilled people’s blood in the land. They made the land ‘unclean’ by worshiping other gods. So I poured out my great anger on them. 19 I scattered them among the nations. I sent them to other countries. I judged them based on how they acted and on how they lived. 20 They treated my name as if it were not holy. They did it everywhere they went among the nations. People said about them, ‘They are the LORD’s people. But they were forced to leave his land.’ 21 I was concerned about my holy name. The people of Israel treated it as if it were not holy. They did it everywhere they went among the nations.

22 “So tell the Israelites, ‘The LORD and King speaks. He says, “People of Israel, I will not take action for your benefit. Instead, I will act for the honor of my holy name. You have treated it as if it were not holy. You did it everywhere you went among the nations. 23 But I will show everyone how holy my great name is. You have treated it as if it were not holy. So I will use you to prove to the nations how holy I am. Then they will know that I am the LORD,” announces the LORD and King.

24 “ ‘ “I will take you out of the nations. I will gather you together from all the countries. I will bring you back into your own land. 25 I will sprinkle pure water on you. Then you will be ‘clean.’ I will make you completely pure and ‘clean.’ I will take all the statues of your gods away from you. 26 I will give you new hearts. I will give you a new spirit that is faithful to me. I will remove your stubborn hearts from you. I will give you hearts that obey me. 27 I will put my Spirit in you. I will make you want to obey my rules. I want you to be careful to keep my laws. 28 Then you will live in the land I gave your people of long ago. You will be my people. And I will be your God. 29 I will save you from all your ‘uncleanness.’ I will give you plenty of grain. You will have more than enough. So you will never be hungry again. 30 I will multiply the fruit on your trees. I will increase the crops in your fields. Then the nations will no longer make fun of you because you are hungry. 31 You will remember your evil ways

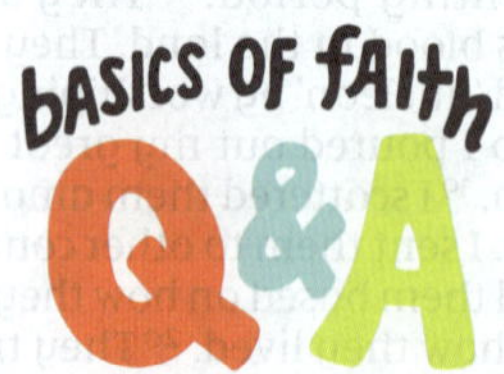

What if I don't want to obey God's commands?

None of us desire to obey God on our own. When we ask God to save us, he gives us a new heart, and his Spirit helps us obey his commands. If you don't feel like you want to obey God, ask him to help you. He is ready and eager to help you obey him.

Can you find the following verses?

EZEKIEL 36:26–27

and the sinful things you have done. You will hate yourselves because you have sinned so much. I also hate your evil practices. 32 I want you to know that I am not doing those things for your benefit," announces the LORD and King. "People of Israel, you should be ashamed of yourselves! Your conduct has brought dishonor to you." ' "

33 The LORD and King says, "I will make you pure from all your sins. On that day I will give you homes in your towns again. Your broken-down houses will be rebuilt. 34 The dry and empty land will be farmed again. Everyone who passes through it will see that it is no longer empty. 35 They will say, 'This land was completely destroyed. But now it's like the Garden of Eden. The cities were full of broken-down buildings. They were destroyed and empty. But now they have high walls around them. And people live in them.' 36 Then the nations that remain around you will know that I have rebuilt what was once destroyed. I have planted again the fields that were once empty. I have spoken. And I will do this. I am the LORD."

37 The LORD and King says, "Once again I will answer Israel's prayer. Here is what I will do for them. I will multiply them as if they were sheep. 38 Large flocks of animals are sacrificed at Jerusalem during the appointed feasts there. In the same way, the destroyed cities will be filled with flocks of people. Then they will know that I am the LORD."

The Valley of Dry Bones

37 The power of the LORD came on me. His Spirit brought me away from my home. He put me down in the middle of a valley. It was full of bones. 2 He led me back and forth among them. I saw a huge number of bones in the valley. The bones were very dry. 3 The LORD asked me, "Son of man, can these bones live?"

I said, "LORD and King, you are the only one who knows."

4 Then he said to me, "Prophesy to these bones. Tell them, 'Dry bones, listen to the LORD's message. 5 The LORD and King speaks to you. He says, "I will put breath in you. Then you will come to life again. 6 I will attach tendons to you. I will put flesh on you. I will cover you with skin. So I will put breath in you. And you will come to life again. Then you will know that I am the LORD." ' "

7 So I prophesied just as the LORD commanded me to. As I was prophesying, I heard a noise. It was a rattling sound. The bones came together. One bone connected itself to another. 8 I saw tendons and flesh appear on them. Skin covered them. But there was no breath in them.

9 Then the LORD said to me, "Prophesy to the breath. Prophesy, son of man. Tell it, 'The LORD and King says, "Breath, come from all four directions. Go into these people who have been killed. Then they can live." ' " 10 So I prophesied just as he commanded me to. And breath entered them. Then they came to life again. They stood up on their feet. They were like a huge army.

11 Then the LORD said to me, "Son of man, these bones stand for all the people of Israel. The people say, 'Our bones are dried up. We've lost all hope. We are destroyed.' 12 So prophesy. Tell them, 'The LORD and King says, "My people, I am going to open up your graves. I am

going to bring you out of them. I will
take you back to the land of Israel. 13So I
will open up your graves and bring you
out of them. Then you will know that I
am the LORD. You are my people. 14I will
put my Spirit in you. And you will live
again. I will settle you in your own land.
Then you will know that I have spoken.
I have done it," announces the LORD.' "

Israel Will Be One Nation Under One King

15A message from the LORD came to
me. The LORD said, 16"Son of man, get
a stick of wood. Write on it, 'Belonging
to the tribe of Judah and the Israelites
who are connected with it.' Then get
another stick. Write on it, 'Ephraim's
stick. Belonging to the tribes of Joseph
and all the Israelites connected with
them.' 17Join them together into one
stick in your hand.

18"Your people will ask you, 'What
do you mean by this?' 19Tell them, 'The
LORD and King says, "I am going to
get the stick of Joseph and the Israelites connected with it. That stick is
in Ephraim's hand. I am going to join
it to Judah's stick. I will make them
a single stick of wood in my hand." '
20Show them the sticks you wrote on.
21Tell them, 'The LORD and King says,
"I will take the Israelites out of the
nations where they have gone. I will
gather them together from all around. I
will bring them back to their own land.
22There I will make them one nation.
They will live on the mountains of Israel. All of them will have one king. They
will never be two nations again. They
will never again be separated into two
kingdoms. 23They will no longer make
themselves 'unclean' by worshiping
any of their evil gods. They will not do
wrong things anymore. They always
turn away from me. But I will save them
from that sin. I will make them pure and
'clean.' They will be my people. And I
will be their God.

24" ' "A man who belongs to the family
line of my servant David will be their
king. All of them will have one shepherd. They will obey my laws. And they
will be careful to keep my rules. 25They
will live in the land I gave to my servant
Jacob. That is where your people of long
ago lived. They, their children, their
children's children, and their children
after them will live there forever. And
my servant from David's family line will
be their prince forever. 26I will make
a covenant with them. It promises to
give them peace. The covenant will last
forever. I will make them my people.
And I will cause there to be many of
them. I will put my temple among them
forever. 27I will live with them. I will be
their God. And they will be my people.
28My temple will be among them forever. Then the nations will know that
I make Israel holy. I am the LORD." ' "

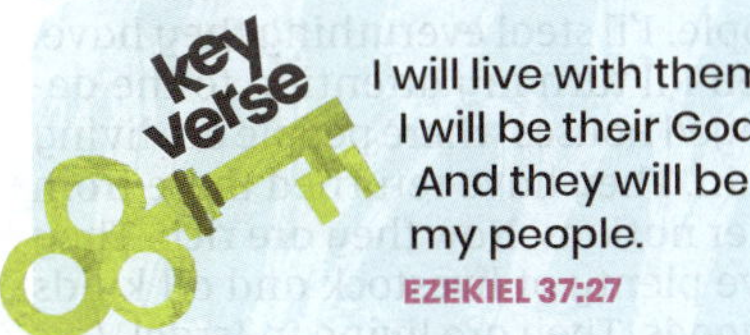

The LORD Will Have Great Victory Over the Nations

38 A message from the LORD came
to me. The LORD said, 2"Son of
man, turn your attention to Gog. He is
from the land of Magog. He is the chief
prince of Meshek and Tubal. Prophesy against him. 3Tell him, 'The LORD
and King says, "Gog, I am against you.
You are the chief prince of Meshek and
Tubal. 4But I will turn you around. I
will put hooks in your jaws. I will bring
you out of your land along with your
whole army. Your horses will come with
you. Your horsemen will be completely
armed. Your huge army will carry large
and small shields. All of them will be
ready to use their swords. 5The men
of Persia, Cush and Put will march out
with them. All of them will have shields
and helmets. 6Gomer and all its troops
will be there too. Beth Togarmah from
the far north will also come with all
its troops. Many nations will help you.

7" ' "Get ready. Be prepared. Take
command of the huge armies gathered
around you. 8After many years you
will be called together to fight. Later,
you will march into a land that has
not had war for a while. Its people were
gathered together from many nations.
They came to the mountains of Israel.
No one had lived in those mountains
for a long time. So the people had been

brought back from other nations. Now all the people live in safety. [9]You, all your troops and the many nations with you will march up to attack them. All of you will advance like a storm. You will be like a cloud covering their land.”

[10]“ ‘The LORD and King says, “At that time some ideas will come to you. You will make evil plans. [11]You will say, ‘I will march out against a land whose villages don’t have walls around them. I’ll attack those peaceful people. I’ll do this when they aren’t expecting it. None of their villages has walls or gates with metal bars on them. [12]I will rob those people. I’ll steal everything they have. Then I’ll turn my attention to the destroyed houses where people are living again. They have returned there from other nations. Now they are rich. They have plenty of livestock and all kinds of goods. They are living in Israel. It is the center of the earth.’ [13]The people of Sheba and Dedan will speak to you. So will the traders of Tarshish and all its villages. They will say, ‘Have you come to rob us? Have you gathered your huge army together to steal our silver and gold? Are you going to take away from us our livestock and goods? Do you plan to carry off everything we have?’ ” ’

[14]“Son of man, prophesy. Tell Gog, ‘The LORD and King says, “A time is coming when my people Israel will be living in safety. You will see that it is a good time to attack them. [15]So you will come from your place in the far north. Many nations will join you. All their men will be riding on horses. You will have a huge and mighty army. [16]They will advance against my people Israel. They will be like a cloud covering their land. Gog, in days to come I will bring you against my land. Then the nations will know me. I will use you to prove to them how holy I am.”

[17]“ ‘Here is what the LORD and King says to Gog. “In the past I spoke about you through my servants, the prophets of Israel. At that time they prophesied for years that I would bring you against them. [18]Here is what will happen in days to come. You will attack the land of Israel. That will stir up my burning anger,” announces the LORD and King. [19]“At that time my burning anger will blaze out at you. There will be a great earthquake in the land of Israel. [20]The fish in the sea, the birds in the sky and the wild animals will tremble with fear. They will tremble with fear because of what I will do. So will every creature that moves along the ground. And so will all the people on earth. The mountains will come crashing down. The cliffs will break into pieces. Every wall will fall to the ground. [21]I will punish you on all my mountains,” announces the LORD and King. “Your men will use their swords against one another. [22]I will judge you. I will send a plague against you. A lot of blood will be spilled. I will send heavy rain, hailstones and burning sulfur down to the earth. They will fall on you and your troops. They will also come down on the many nations that are helping you. [23]That will show how great and holy I am. I will make myself known to many nations. Then they will know that I am the LORD.” ’

39 “Son of man, prophesy against Gog. Tell him, ‘The LORD and King says, “Gog, I am against you. You are the chief prince of Meshek and Tubal. [2]But I will turn you around. I will drag you along. I will bring you from the far north. I will send you against the mountains of Israel. [3]Then I will knock your bow out of your left hand. I will make your arrows drop from your right hand. [4]You will fall dead on the mountains of Israel. You and all your troops will die there. So will the nations that join you. I will feed you to all kinds of birds that eat dead bodies. So they and the wild animals will eat you up. [5]You will fall dead in the open fields. I have spoken,” announces the LORD and King. [6]“I will send fire on the land of Magog. It will burn up the people who live in safety on the coast. So they will know that I am the LORD.

[7]“ ‘ “I will make my holy name known among my people Israel. I will no longer let them treat my name as if it were not holy. Then the nations will know that I am the Holy One in Israel. I am the LORD. [8]The day I will judge you is coming. You can be sure of it,” announces the LORD and King. “It is the day I have spoken about.

[9]“ ‘ “At that time those who live in the towns of Israel will go out and light a fire. They will use it to burn up

the weapons. That includes small and
large shields. It also includes bows and
arrows, war clubs and spears. It will
take seven years to burn all of them
up. 10 People will not gather wood from
the fields. They will not cut down the
forests. Instead, they will burn the
weapons. And they will rob those who
robbed them. They will steal from those
who stole from them," announces the
LORD and King.

11 " ' "Gog, at that time I will bury
you in a grave in Israel. It will be in
the valley where people travel east of
the Dead Sea. It will block the path of
travelers. That's because you and your
huge armies will be buried there. So it
will be called the Valley of Gog's Armies.

12 " ' "It will take seven months for the
Israelites to bury the bodies. They will
do this to make the land 'clean' again.
13 All the people in the land will bury
them. The day that I show how glorious
I am will be a time to remember." This
is what the LORD and King announces.
14 "People will keep being hired to make
the land 'clean' again. They will go all
through it. They and others will bury
any bodies lying on the ground.

" ' "After the seven months they will
search even more carefully. 15 As they
go through the land here is what they'll
do. When anyone sees a bone, they will
put a marker beside it. Then those who
dig the graves will take the bone to the
Valley of Gog's Armies. There they will
bury it. 16 That is how they will make
the land 'clean' again." ' " Also a town
called Gog's Armies is near there.

17 The LORD and King said to me, "Son
of man, speak to every kind of bird.
Call out to all the wild animals. Tell
them, 'Gather together. Come from everywhere. Gather around the sacrifice
I am preparing for you. It is the great
sacrifice on the mountains of Israel.
There you will eat human bodies and
drink human blood. 18 You will eat the
bodies of mighty men. You will drink
the blood of the princes of the earth.
You will eat their bodies and drink their
blood. You will do this as if they were
rams and lambs, goats and bulls. You
will enjoy it as if you were eating the
fattest animals from Bashan. 19 So I am
preparing a sacrifice for you. You will
eat fat until you are completely full. You
will drink blood until you are drunk.
20 At my table you will eat horses, riders,
mighty men and soldiers until you are
full,' announces the LORD and King.

21 " 'I will show all the nations my
glory. They will see how I punish them
when I use my power against them.
22 From that time on, the people of Israel
will know that I am the LORD their God.
23 The nations will know that the people
of Israel were taken away as prisoners
because they sinned against me. They
were not faithful to me. So I turned my
face away from them. I handed them
over to their enemies. All of them were
killed by swords. 24 I punished them
because they were "unclean." They
did many things that were wrong. So
I turned my face away from them.' "

25 The LORD and King says, "I will now
cause the people of Jacob to recover from
my judgment. I will show my tender love
for all the people of Israel. I will make
sure that my name is kept holy. 26 My
people will forget the shameful things
they have done. They will not remember
all the ways they were unfaithful to me.
They used to live in safety in their land.
At that time no one made them afraid.
27 So I will bring them back from the
nations. I will gather them from the
countries of their enemies. And I will
use them to prove to many nations how
holy I am. 28 Then they will know that I
am the LORD their God. I let the nations
take my people away as prisoners. But
now I will bring them back to their own
land. I will not leave anyone behind. 29 I
will no longer turn my face away from
the people of Israel. I will pour out my
Spirit on them," announces the LORD
and King.

The New Temple Area

40 It was the 14th year after Jerusalem had been captured. We
had been brought to Babylon as prisoners. It was the tenth day of a month
near the beginning of the 25th year
after that. On that day the power of the
LORD came on me. He took me back to
my land. 2 In visions God gave me, he
brought me to the land of Israel. He
set me on a very high mountain. Some
buildings were on the south side of it.
They looked like a city. 3 He took me
there. I saw a man who appeared to be

made out of bronze. He was standing at the gate of the outer courtyard. He was holding a linen measuring tape and a
measuring rod. [4]The man said to me, "Son of man, look carefully and listen closely. Pay attention to everything I show you. That is why the LORD brought you here. Tell the people of Israel everything you see."

The East Gate to the Outer Courtyard

[5]I saw a wall that completely surrounded the temple area. The measuring rod in the man's hand was 11 feet long. He measured the wall with it. The wall was as thick and as high as one measuring rod.

[6]Then the man went to the east gate. He climbed its steps. He measured the
gateway. It was one rod wide. [7]The rooms where the guards stood were one rod long and one rod wide. The walls between the rooms were almost nine feet thick. The gateway next to the porch was one rod wide. The porch faced the front of the temple.

[8]Then the man measured the porch of
the gateway. [9]It was 14 feet wide. Each of its doorposts was three and a half feet thick. The porch of the gateway faced the front of the temple.

[10]Inside the east gate were three rooms on each side. All the rooms were the same size. The walls on each side of the rooms had the same thickness.
[11]Then the man measured the entrance of the gateway. It was 18 feet wide and
23 feet long. [12]In front of each room was a wall. It was 21 inches high. The rooms measured 11 feet on each side.
[13]Then he measured the gateway from the back wall of one room to the back wall of the room across from it. It was 44 feet from the top of one wall to the
top of the other. [14]He measured along the front of the side walls all around the inside of the gateway. The total was 105 feet. That didn't include the porch
that faced the courtyard. [15]It was 88 feet from the entrance of the gateway
to the far end of its porch. [16]The rooms and their side walls inside the gateway had narrow openings on top of them. So did the porch. All the openings faced the inside. The front of each side wall was decorated with a palm tree.

The Outer Courtyard

[17]Then the man brought me into the outer courtyard. There I saw some rooms and a sidewalk. They had been built all around the courtyard. Along
the sidewalk were 30 rooms. [18]The sidewalk went all the way up to the sides of the gateways. It was as wide as they were long. This was the lower sidewalk.
[19]Then he measured from the inside of the lower gateway to the outside of the inner courtyard. The east side measured 175 feet. So did the north side.

The North Gate

[20]Then the man measured the north gate. He wanted to show me how long and wide it was. The gate led into the
outer courtyard. [21]It had three rooms on each side. Their side walls and porch measured the same as the ones at the first gateway. They measured 88 feet
long and 44 feet wide. [22]Its openings, porch and palm tree decorations measured the same as the ones at the east gate. Seven steps led up to the north gate.
Its porch was across from them. [23]The inner courtyard had a gate. It faced the gate on the north. It was just like the east gate. He measured from one gate to the one across from it. The total was 175 feet.

The South Gate

[24]Then the man led me to the south side of the courtyard. There I saw the south gate. He measured its doorposts and porch. They measured the same as
the others. [25]The gateway and its porch had narrow openings all around. The openings were the same as the others had. The side walls and porch measured
88 feet long and 44 feet wide. [26]Seven steps led up to it. Its porch was across from them. The front of each side wall
was decorated with a palm tree. [27]The inner courtyard also had a gate that faced south. The man measured from this gate to the outer gate on the south side. The total was 175 feet.

The Gates to the Inner Courtyard

[28]Then the man brought me into the inner courtyard. We went through the south gate. He measured it. It was
the same size as the others. [29]Its rooms, side walls and porch measured the same as the ones at the other gateways. The gateway and its porch had openings

all around. The side walls and porch
measured 88 feet long and 44 feet wide.
30 The porches of the gateways around
the inner courtyard were 44 feet wide
and nine feet long. 31 Its porch faced the
outer courtyard. Palm trees decorated
its doorposts. Eight steps led up to it.
32 Then the man brought me to the
east side of the inner courtyard. There
he measured the gateway. It was the
same size as the others. 33 Its rooms, side
walls and porch measured the same
as the ones at the other gateways. The
gateway and its porch had openings all
around. The side walls and porch measured 88 feet long and 44 feet wide. 34 Its
porch faced the outer courtyard. Each
doorpost was decorated with a palm
tree. Eight steps led up to the porch.
35 Then the man brought me to the
north gate. He measured it. It was the
same size as the others. 36 Its rooms, side
walls and porch measured the same as
the ones at the other gateways. It had
openings all around. The side walls and
the porch measured 88 feet long and 44
feet wide. 37 The porch faced the outer
courtyard. Each doorpost was decorated
with a palm tree. Eight steps led up to
the porch.

The Rooms for Preparing Sacrifices

38 A room with a doorway was by the
porch of each inner gateway. The burnt
offerings were washed there. 39 On each
side of the porch of the gateway were two
tables. The burnt offerings were killed
on them. So were the sin offerings and
guilt offerings. 40 Two more tables were
by the outer wall of the gateway porch.
They were near the steps at the entrance
of the north gateway. Two more tables
were on the other side of the steps. 41 So
there were four tables on each side of
the gateway. The total number of tables
was eight. Animals for sacrifice were
killed on all of them. 42 There were also
four other tables for the burnt offerings.
They were made out of blocks of stone.
Each table was two and a half feet long
and two and a half feet wide. And each
was almost two feet high. The tools for
killing the burnt offerings and other
sacrifices were placed on them. 43 Large
hooks hung on the walls all around. Each
was three inches long. The meat of the
offerings was placed on the tables.

The Rooms for the Priests

44 Near the inner gates were two
rooms. They were in the inner courtyard. One room was next to the north
gate. It faced south. The other one was
next to the south gate. It faced north.
45 The man said to me, "The room that
faces south is for the priests who guard
the temple. 46 The one that faces north
is for the priests who guard the altar. All
these priests are the sons of Zadok. They
are the only Levites who can approach
the LORD to serve him."
47 Then the man measured the courtyard. It was square. It measured 175 feet
long and 175 feet wide. And the altar was
in front of the temple.

The New Temple

48 The man brought me to the porch of
the temple. He measured the doorposts
of the porch. Each of them was almost
nine feet wide. The entrance was 24 and
a half feet wide. Each of the side walls
was a little over five feet wide. 49 The
porch was 35 feet wide. It was 21 feet
from front to back. It was reached by
some stairs. Pillars were on each side
of the doorposts.

41 Then the man brought me to the
main hall. There he measured
the doorposts. Each of them was 11 feet
wide. 2 The entrance was 18 feet wide.
Each of its side walls was almost nine
feet wide. He also measured the main
hall. It was 70 feet long and 35 feet wide.
3 Then he went into the Most Holy
Room. There he measured the doorposts
at the entrance. Each one of them was
three and a half feet wide. The entrance
itself was 11 feet wide. Each of its side
walls was a little over 12 feet wide. 4 He
also measured the Most Holy Room. It
was 35 feet long and 35 feet wide. He said
to me, "This is the Most Holy Room." It
was beyond the back wall of the main
hall.
5 Then the man measured the wall
of the temple. It was 11 feet thick. Each
side room around the temple was sev-
en feet wide. 6 The side rooms were on
three floors. There were 30 rooms on
each floor. Ledges had been built all
around the wall of the temple. So the
floor beams of the side rooms rested
on the ledges. The beams didn't go into
the temple wall. 7 The side rooms of the

temple were wider as we went up floor
by floor. A stairway went from the lowest floor all the way up to the top floor.
It passed through the middle floor.
8 I saw that the temple had a raised
base all around it. The base formed the
foundation of the side rooms. It was as
long as one measuring rod. So it was 11
feet long. 9 The outer wall of each side
room was almost nine feet thick. The
open area between the side rooms of the
temple 10 and the priests' rooms was 35
feet wide. It went all around the temple.
11 The side rooms had entrances from the
open area. One was on the north side.
Another was on the south. The base next
to the open area was almost nine feet
wide all around.
12 There was a large building right
behind the temple. It was on the west
side of the outer courtyard. It was 123
feet wide. Its wall was almost nine feet
thick all around. And it was 158 feet
long.
13 Then the man measured the temple.
It was 175 feet long. The open area and
the large building behind the temple
also measured 175 feet. 14 The east side
of the inner courtyard was 175 feet wide.
That included the front of the temple.
15 Then the man measured the building that was on the west side of the outer courtyard. It was behind the temple.
It was 175 feet long. That included the
walkways of the building on each side.
The main hall and the Most Holy
Room were covered with wood. 16 And
the porch that faced the inner courtyard was covered with wood. So were
the gateways, narrow openings and
walkways around these three places.
The gateways and everything beyond
them were covered with wood. The floor,
the wall up to the openings, and the
openings themselves were also covered. 17 The area above the outside of
the entrance to the Most Holy Room was
decorated. There were also decorations
all around the walls of the Most Holy
Room. 18 Carved cherubim and palm
trees were used in the decorations. Each
cherub had a palm tree next to it. And
each palm tree had a cherub next to it.
Each cherub had two faces. 19 One was
the face of a human being. It looked
toward the palm tree on one side. The
other was the face of a lion. It looked
toward the palm tree on the other side.
The decorations were carved all around
the whole temple. 20 Cherubim and
palm trees decorated the wall of the
main hall. They were carved from the
floor all the way up to the area above
the entrance.
21 The main hall had a doorframe
shaped like a rectangle. So did the Most
Holy Room. 22 A wooden altar stood in
the main hall. It was a little over five feet
high. It was three and a half feet long
and three and a half feet wide. Its corners, base and sides were made out of
wood. The man said to me, "This is the
table that stands in front of the LORD."
23 The main hall had double doors. So
did the Most Holy Room. 24 Each door
had two parts that could swing back
and forth. 25 Cherubim and palm trees
were carved on the doors of the main
hall. The decorations were like the ones
on the walls. A wooden roof went out beyond the front of the porch. 26 The side
walls of the porch had narrow openings
on top of them. Palm trees were carved
on each side. A wooden roof went out
beyond the entrance to each side room
of the temple.

The Rooms for the Priests

42 Then the man led me north into
the outer courtyard of the temple. He brought me to the rooms that
were across from the inner courtyard.
They were across from the outer wall
of the temple on the north side. 2 The
rooms were in a building north of the
temple. The building had a door that
faced north. It was 175 feet long. It was
88 feet wide. 3 One row of rooms was
next to the inner courtyard. The other
row was across from the sidewalk of
the outer courtyard. Each room was
35 feet long. Walkways in front of each
row faced each other on all three floors.
4 Between the two rows was an inner
sidewalk. It was 18 feet wide and 175 feet
long. Each of the rooms had a door on
the north side. 5 The rooms on the top
floor were narrower than the others.
The walkways took up more space from
these rooms. The walkways took up
less space from the rooms on the other
two floors. 6 The courtyards had pillars.
But the rooms on the top floor didn't.
So their floor space was smaller than

the space in the rooms on the other
floors. [7]The building had an outer wall.
It was even with the outer row of rooms
and with the outer courtyard. The wall
continued east of the outer row for 88
feet. [8]So there were two rows of rooms.
The row next to the outer courtyard
was 88 feet long. The one closest to the
temple was 175 feet long. [9]The first floor
of the building had an entrance on the
east side. It led to the outer courtyard.

[10]There were also two rows of rooms
in a building next to the south side of
the inner courtyard. The building was
across from the south wall of the outer
courtyard. [11]Between the two rows was
an inner sidewalk. The rooms were like
the ones in the north building. They
were as long and wide as the rooms on
the north. The doorways of the rooms
on the south were like the ones on the
north. [12]People entered the south rooms
through the doorway at the east end of
the inner sidewalk. The south wall continued east of the outer row of rooms.

[13]The man said to me, "The north
and south rooms face the inner courtyard. They are the priests' rooms. That
is where the priests who approach the
LORD will eat the very holy offerings.
They will also store them there. That
includes the grain offerings, sin offerings and guilt offerings. This place is
holy. [14]The priests who enter these holy
rooms must leave behind the clothes
they served in. Then they can go into
the outer courtyard. The clothes they
served in are holy. So the priests must
put other clothes on. They have to do
that before they go near the places
where other people go."

[15]The man finished measuring what
was inside the temple area. Then he
led me out through the east gate. He
measured all around the area. [16]He
measured the east side with his measuring rod. It was 875 feet long. [17]He
measured the north side. It was 875 feet
long. [18]He measured the south side. It
was 875 feet long. [19]Finally, he turned
and measured the west side. It was 875
feet long. [20]So he measured the area on
all four sides. It had a wall around it.
The wall was 875 feet long and 875 feet
wide. It separated what was holy from
what was not.

The Glory of God Returns to the Temple

43 Then the man brought me to
the east gate. [2]There I saw the
glory of the God of Israel. He was coming from the east. His voice was like the
roar of rushing waters. His glory made
the land shine brightly. [3]The vision
I saw was like the one I had when he
came to destroy the city. It was also
like the visions I had seen by the Kebar
River. I fell with my face toward the
ground. [4]The glory of the LORD entered
the temple through the east gate. [5]Then
the Spirit lifted me up. He brought me
into the inner courtyard. The glory of
the LORD filled the temple.

[6]The man was standing beside me. I
heard someone speaking to me from inside the temple. [7]He said, "Son of man,
this is the place where my throne is. The
stool for my feet is also here. I will live
here among the people of Israel forever.
They will never again treat my name as
if it were not holy. They and their kings
will not serve other gods anymore. The
people will no longer make funeral offerings for their kings. [8]The people of
Israel placed their own doorway next to
my holy doorway. They put their doorposts right beside mine. Nothing but a
thin wall separated us. They treated my
name as if it were not holy. I hated it
when they did that. So I became angry
with them and destroyed them. [9]Now
let them stop serving other gods. Let
them stop making funeral offerings for
their kings. If they obey me, I will live
among them forever.

[10]"Son of man, tell the people of Israel
about the temple. Then they will be
ashamed of their sins. Let them think
carefully about how perfect it is. [11]What
if they are ashamed of everything they
have done? Then show them all the
plans of the temple. Explain to them
how it is laid out. Tell them about its
exits and entrances. Show them exactly
what it will look like. Give them all its
rules and laws. Write everything down
so they can see it. Then they will be
faithful to its plan. And they will obey
all its rules.

[12]"Here is the law of the temple. The
whole area on top of Mount Zion will be
very holy. That is the law of the temple."

The Great Altar Is Rebuilt

13 The man said, "Here is the size of the altar. The standard measurement I am using is 21 inches. The altar has a drain on the ground. The drain is 21 inches deep and 21 inches wide. It has a rim that is nine inches wide around the edge. Here is how high the altar is. 14 From the drain to the lower ledge is three and a half feet. The lower ledge goes around the altar and is 21 inches wide. From the lower ledge to the upper ledge is seven feet. The upper ledge also goes around the altar and is 21 inches wide. 15 The top part of the altar is where the sacrifices are burned. It is seven feet high. A horn sticks out from each of its four corners. 16 The top part of the altar is square. It is 21 feet long and 21 feet wide. 17 The upper ledge is also square. It is 25 feet long and 25 feet wide. The drain goes all the way around the altar. The rim of the drain is 11 inches wide. The steps leading up to the top of the altar face east."

18 Then the man said to me, "Son of man, the LORD and King speaks. He says, 'Here are the rules for the altar when it is built. Follow them when you sacrifice burnt offerings and splash blood against it. 19 Give a young bull to the priests as a sin offering. They are Levites from the family of Zadok. They approach me to serve me,' announces the LORD and King. 20 'Get some of the bull's blood. Put it on the four horns of the altar. Also put it on the four corners of the upper ledge of the altar and all around the rim. That will make the altar pure and "clean." 21 Use the bull for the sin offering. Burn it in the proper place outside the temple.

22 " 'On the second day offer a male goat. It must not have any flaws. It is a sin offering to make the altar pure and "clean." So do the same thing with the goat that you did with the bull. 23 When you finish making the altar pure, offer a young bull and a ram from the flock. They must not have any flaws. 24 Offer them to me. The priests must sprinkle salt on them. Then they must sacrifice them as a burnt offering to me.

25 " 'Provide a male goat each day for seven days. It is a sin offering. Also provide a young bull and a ram from the flock. They must not have any flaws. 26 For seven days the priests must make the altar pure and "clean." That is how they will set it apart to me. 27 From the eighth day on, the priests must bring your burnt offerings and friendship offerings. They must sacrifice them on the altar. Then I will accept you,' announces the LORD and King."

The Priesthood Will Be Established Again

44 Then the man brought me back to the outer gate of the temple. It was the one that faced east. It was shut. 2 The LORD said to me, "This gate must remain shut. It must not be opened. No one can enter through it. It must remain shut because I have entered through it. I am the God of Israel. 3 The prince is the only one who can sit in the gateway. There he can eat in front of me. He must enter through the porch of the gateway. And he must go out the same way."

4 Then the man brought me through the north gate. He took me to the front of the temple. I looked up and saw the glory of the LORD. It filled his temple. I fell with my face toward the ground.

5 The LORD said to me, "Son of man, pay attention. Look carefully. Listen closely to everything I tell you. I'm telling you about all the rules and instructions concerning my temple. Pay attention to the entrance to the temple and to all its exits. 6 Speak to the people of Israel. They refuse to obey me. Tell them, 'Here is what the LORD and King says. "People of Israel, I have had enough of your evil practices. I hate them. 7 You brought outsiders into my temple. They were not circumcised. Their hearts were stubborn. You made my temple 'unclean.' But you offered me food, fat and blood anyway. When you did all these things, you broke the covenant I made with you. I hated all the evil things you did. 8 You did not do what I told you to. You did not take care of my holy things. Instead, you put other people in charge of my temple." ' " 9 The LORD and King says, "No outsider whose heart is stubborn can enter my temple. They have not been circumcised. Even if they live among the people of Israel they can't enter my temple.

[10] "Some Levites wandered far away from me when Israel went astray. They worshiped the statues of their gods. So they will be punished because they have sinned. [11] They might serve in my temple. They might be in charge of its gates. They might kill the burnt offerings and sacrifices for the people. And they might stand in front of the people and serve them in other ways. [12] But these Levites served the people of Israel. They served while the Israelites were worshiping the statues of their gods. They made the people fall into sin. So I raised my hand and made a promise. I warned them that I would punish them because of their sin," announces the LORD and King. [13] "They must not approach me to serve me as priests. They must not come near any of my holy things. They must stay away from my very holy offerings. They did many things they should have been ashamed of. I hated those things. [14] But I will still appoint them to guard the temple. They will guard it for all the work that has to be done there.

[15] "But the priests must approach me to serve me. They are Levites from Zadok's family line. They guarded my temple when the people of Israel turned away from me. These priests must serve me by offering sacrifices of fat and blood," announces the LORD and King. [16] "They are the only ones who can enter my temple. Only they can come near to serve me as guards.

[17] "They will enter the gates of the inner courtyard. When they do, they must wear linen clothes. They will serve at the gates of the inner courtyard or inside the temple. When they do, they must not wear any clothes made out of wool. [18] They must have linen turbans on their heads. They must wear linen underwear around their waists. They must not wear anything that makes them sweat. [19] They will go into the outer courtyard where the people are. When they do, they must take off the clothes they have been serving in. They must leave them in the sacred rooms. And they must put other clothes on. Then the people will not be made holy if they happen to touch the priests' clothes.

[20] "The priests must not shave their heads. They must not let their hair grow long. They must keep it cut short. [21] No priest may drink wine when he enters the inner courtyard. [22] They must not get married to widows or divorced women. They may only marry Israelite virgins or the widows of priests. [23] The priests must teach my people the difference between what is holy and what is not. They must show them how to tell the difference between what is 'clean' and what is not.

[24] "When people do not agree, the priests must serve as judges between them. They must make their decisions based on my laws. They must obey my laws and rules for all my appointed feasts. And they must keep my Sabbath days holy.

[25] "A priest must not make himself 'unclean' by going near a dead person. But suppose the dead person was his father or mother. Or suppose it was his son or daughter or brother or unmarried sister. Then the priest may make himself 'unclean.' [26] After he is pure and 'clean' again, he must wait seven days. [27] Then he may go to the inner courtyard to serve in the temple. But when he does, he must sacrifice a sin offering for himself," announces the LORD and King.

[28] "The priests will not receive any part of the land of Israel. I myself will be their only share. [29] They will eat the grain offerings, sin offerings and guilt offerings. Everything in Israel that is set apart to me in a special way will belong to them. [30] The best of every first share of the people's crops will belong to the priests. So will all their special gifts. The people must give the priests the first share of their ground meal. Then I will bless my people's families. [31] The priests must not eat any bird or animal that is found dead. They must not eat anything that wild animals have torn apart.

The LORD Establishes Israel Again

45 "People of Israel, you will divide up the land you will receive. When you do, give me my share of it. It will be a sacred area. It will be eight miles long and six and a half miles wide. The entire area will be holy. [2] The temple area in it will be 875 feet long and 875 feet wide. An 88-foot strip around it will be open land. 3 In the sacred area, measure off a large strip of land. It will be eight miles long and three and a third miles wide. The temple will be in it. It will be the most holy place of all. 4 The large strip will be the sacred share of land for the priests. There they will serve in the temple. And they will approach me to serve me there. Their houses will be built on that land. The holy temple will also be located there. 5 So the Levites will serve in the temple. They will have an area eight miles long and three and a third miles wide. The towns they live in will be located there.

6 "Give the city an area one and two-thirds miles wide and eight miles long. It will be right next to the sacred area. It will belong to all the people of Israel.

7 "The prince will have land on both sides of the sacred area and the city. Its border will run east and west along the land of one of the tribes. 8 The prince will own this land in Israel. And my princes will not crush my people anymore. Instead, they will allow the people of Israel to receive their own share of land. It will be divided up based on their tribes."

9 The LORD and King says, "Princes of Israel, you have gone far enough! Stop hurting others. Do not crush them. Do what is fair and right. Stop taking my people's land away from them," announces the LORD and King. 10 "Use weights and measures that are honest and exact. 11 Use the same standard to measure dry and liquid products. Use a 6-bushel measure for dry products. And use a 60-gallon measure for liquids. 12 Every amount of money must be weighed out in keeping with the standard weights.

13 "You must offer a special gift. It must be six pounds out of every six bushels of grain. 14 Give two and a half quarts out of every 60 gallons of olive oil. 15 Also give one sheep from every flock of 200 sheep. Get them from the grasslands of Israel that receive plenty of water. Use them for grain offerings, burnt offerings and friendship offerings. They will be used to pay for the sin of the people," announces the LORD and King. 16 "All the people in the land will be required to give this special gift. They must give it to the prince in Israel. 17 He must provide the burnt offerings, grain offerings and drink offerings. They will be for the yearly feasts, New Moon feasts and Sabbath days. So they will be for all the appointed feasts of the people of Israel. The prince will provide the sin offerings, grain offerings, burnt offerings and friendship offerings. They will be used to pay for the sin of the Israelites."

18 The LORD and King says, "Get a young bull. It must not have any flaws. Use it to make the temple pure and 'clean.' Do this on the first day of the first month. 19 The priest must get some of the blood from the sin offering. He must put some on the doorposts of the temple. He must apply some to the four corners of the upper ledge of the altar. He must put the rest on the gateposts of the inner courtyard. 20 Do the same thing on the seventh day of the month. Do this for those who sin without meaning to. And do this for those who sin without realizing what they are doing. So you will make the temple pure and 'clean.'

21 "Keep the Passover Feast on the 14th day of the first month. It will last for seven days. During that time you must eat bread made without yeast. 22 The prince must provide a bull as a sin offering. It will be for him and all the people of the land. 23 For each of the seven days of the feast he must provide seven bulls and seven rams. They must not have any flaws. They will be a burnt offering to me. The prince must also provide a male goat for a sin offering. 24 He must bring 35 pounds for each bull or ram. He must also provide four quarts of olive oil for each of them.

25 "The seven days of the feast begin on the 15th day of the seventh month. During those days the prince must provide the same sin offerings, burnt offerings, grain offerings and olive oil."

46 The LORD and King says, "On the six working days of each week you must keep the east gate of the inner courtyard of the temple shut. But open it on Sabbath days and during New Moon feasts. 2 The prince must enter the temple area through the porch of the gateway. He must stand by the gatepost. The priests must sacrifice his burnt offering and friendship offerings.

He must bow down in worship at the
entrance of the gateway. Then he must
leave. But the gate will not be shut until
evening. 3 On Sabbath days and during
New Moon feasts the people of the land
must gather together. They must gather
at the entrance of the temple gateway.
That is where they must worship me.
4 The prince must bring a burnt offering
to me on the Sabbath day. It will be
six male lambs and a ram. They must
not have any flaws. 5 He must offer 35
pounds of grain along with the ram. The
grain he offers along with the lambs can
be as much as he wants to give. He must
also offer four quarts of olive oil for
every 35 pounds of grain. 6 On the day
of the New Moon feast the prince must
make another offering. He must offer a
young bull, six lambs and a ram. They
must not have any flaws. 7 He must offer
35 pounds of grain along with the bull
or ram. The grain he offers along with
the lambs can be as much as he wants
to give. He must also offer four quarts
of olive oil for every 35 pounds of grain.
8 Here is how the prince must enter the
temple area. He must go in through
the porch of the gateway. And he must
leave the same way.

9 "The people of the land must worship me at the appointed feasts. Those
who enter through the north gate must
leave through the south gate. Those
who enter through the south gate must
leave through the north gate. They
must not leave through the same gate
they entered. Each one must go out
the opposite gate. 10 The prince must
be among them. He must go in when
they go in. And he must leave when
they leave. 11 At the yearly feasts and
other appointed feasts there must be
grain offerings. The prince must offer
35 pounds of grain along with a bull or
ram. The grain he offers along with the
lambs can be as much as he wants to
give. He must also offer four quarts of
olive oil for every 35 pounds of grain.

12 "He may also bring another offering to me because he chooses to. It
might be a burnt offering or friendship
offering. When he brings it, the east
gate must be opened for him. He will
bring his offering just as he does on the
Sabbath day. Then he will leave. After
he has gone out, the gate must be shut.

13 "Every day you must provide a lamb
that is a year old. It must not have any
flaws. It is a burnt offering to me. You
must provide it every morning. 14 You
must also offer grain along with it every
morning. Bring six pounds of grain. Also
bring one and a half quarts of olive oil
to make the flour a little wet. So you
will give the grain offering to me. That
will be a law that will last for all time to
come. 15 Provide the lamb, grain offering
and oil every morning. They will be used
for a regular burnt offering."

16 The LORD and King says, "Suppose
the prince makes a gift from his share
of land. And he gives it to one of his
sons. Then the property will also belong
to his sons after him. It will be handed
down to them. 17 But suppose he makes
a gift from his share of land to one of
his servants. Then the servant may keep
it until the Year of Jubilee. After that,
it will be returned to the prince. His
property may be handed down only
to his sons. It belongs to them. 18 The
prince must not take any share of land
that belongs to the people. He must not
drive them off their property. He must
give his sons their share out of his own
property. Then not one of my people
will be separated from their property."

19 The man brought me through the
entrance at the side of the north building. That's where the priests' sacred
rooms were located. He showed me a
place west of the building. 20 He said to
me, "This is where the priests must cook
the guilt offerings and sin offerings.
They must also bake the grain offerings
here. Then they will not have to bring
the offerings into the outer courtyard.
That will keep the people from touching
the offerings and becoming holy."

21 Then the man brought me to the
outer courtyard. He led me around to
its four corners. In each corner I saw
another smaller courtyard. 22 So in the
four corners of the outer courtyard were
walled courtyards. Each one was 70
feet long and 53 feet wide. All of them
were the same size. 23 Around the inside
of each of the four courtyards was a
stone ledge. Places for fire were built all
around under each ledge. 24 The man
said to me, "These are the kitchens.
Those who serve at the temple must
cook the people's sacrifices here."

A River Will Flow From the Temple

47 The man brought me back to the
entrance to the temple. I saw
water flowing east from under a temple
gateway. The temple faced east. The
water was coming down from under the
south side of the temple. It was flowing
south of the altar. 2 Then he brought
me out through the north gate of the
outer courtyard. He led me around the
outside to the outer gate that faced east.
The water was flowing from the south
side of the east gate.

3 Then the man went toward the
east. He had a measuring line in his
hand. He measured off 1,700 feet. He
led me through water that was up to
my ankles. 4 Then he measured off
another 1,700 feet. He led me through
water that was up to my knees. Then
he measured off another 1,700 feet. He
led me through water that was up to my
waist. 5 Then he measured off another
1,700 feet. But now it was a river that
I could not go across. The water had
risen so high that it was deep enough
to swim in. 6 He asked me, "Son of man,
do you see this?"

Then he led me back to the bank of
the river. 7 When I arrived there, I saw
many trees. They were on both sides of
the river. 8 The man said to me, "This
water flows toward the eastern territory. It goes down into the Arabah Valley.
There it enters the Dead Sea. When it
empties into it, the salt water there
becomes fresh. 9 Many creatures will
live where the river flows. It will have
many schools of fish. This water flows
there and makes the salt water fresh.
So where the river flows everything will
live. 10 People will stand along the shore
to fish. From En Gedi all the way to En
Eglaim there will be places for spreading fishnets. The Dead Sea will have
many kinds of fish. They will be like
the fish in the Mediterranean Sea. 11 But
none of the swamps will have fresh
water in them. They will stay salty.
12 Fruit trees of all kinds will grow on
both banks of the river. Their leaves will
not dry up. The trees will always have
fruit on them. Every month they will
bear fruit. The water from the temple
will flow to them. Their fruit will be used
for food. And their leaves will be used
for healing."

The Borders of the Land

13 Here is what the LORD and King
says. "People of Israel, here are the borders of the land that you will divide up.
You will divide up the land among the
12 tribes of Israel. Each tribe will receive
a share. But the family of Joseph will
have two shares. 14 Divide the land into
equal parts. Long ago I raised my hand
and made a promise. I promised to give
the land to your people of long ago. So
all of it will belong to you.

15 "Here are the borders of the land.

"On the north side the border will
start at the Mediterranean Sea.
It will go by the Hethlon road
past Lebo Hamath. Then it will
continue on to Zedad, 16 Berothah
and Sibraim. Sibraim is between
Damascus and Hamath. The
border will reach all the way to
Hazer Hattikon. It is right next
to Hauran. 17 The border will go
from the sea to Hazar Enan. It
will run north of Damascus and
south of Hamath. This will be the
northern border.

18 On the east side the border will run
between Hauran and Damascus.
It will continue along the Jordan
River between Gilead and the
land of Israel. It will reach to
the Dead Sea and all the way to
Tamar. This will be the eastern
border.

19 On the south side the border will
start at Tamar. It will reach all
the way to the waters of Meribah
Kadesh. Then it will run along
the Wadi of Egypt. It will end at
the Mediterranean Sea. This will
be the southern border.

20 On the west side, the Mediterranean
Sea will be the border. It will
go to a point across from Lebo
Hamath. This will be the western
border.

21 "You must divide up this land
among yourselves. Do this based on the
number of men in your tribes. 22 Each
of the tribes must receive a share of the
land. You must also give some land to
the outsiders who live among you and
who have children. Treat them as if
they had been born in Israel. Let them

have some land among your tribes.
23 Outsiders can live in the land of any
tribe. There you must give them their
share," announces the LORD and King.

The Land Will Be Divided Up

48 "Here are the tribes. They
are listed by their names.

"Dan will receive one share of
land. It will be at the northern
border of Israel. The border will
follow the Hethlon road to Lebo
Hamath. Hazar Enan will be
part of the border. So will the
northern border of Damascus
next to Hamath. Dan's northern
border will run from east to west.
2 Asher will receive one share. It will
border the territory of Dan from
east to west.
3 Naphtali will receive one share. It
will border the territory of Asher
from east to west.
4 Manasseh will receive one share.
It will border the territory of
Naphtali from east to west.
5 Ephraim will receive one share.
It will border the territory of
Manasseh from east to west.
6 Reuben will receive one share.
It will border the territory of
Ephraim from east to west.
7 Judah will receive one share. It will
border the territory of Reuben
from east to west.

8 "You must give one share as a special gift to me. It will border the territory
of Judah from east to west. It will be
eight miles wide. It will be as long as
the border of each of the territories of
the tribes. Its border will run from east
to west. The temple will be in the center
of that strip of land.
9 "Give that special share of land to
me. It will be eight miles long and three
and a third miles wide. 10 It will be the
sacred share of land for the priests. It
will be eight miles long on the north
side. It will be three and a third miles
wide on the west side. It will be three
and a third miles wide on the east side.
And it will be eight miles long on the
south side. My temple will be in the
center of it. 11 This share of land will be
for the priests who are set apart to me.
They will come from the family line
of Zadok. The members of that family
served me faithfully. They did not go
astray as the Levites and other Israelites did. 12 Their share of land will be a
special gift to them. It will be part of
the sacred share of the land. It will be
very holy. Its border will run along the
territory of the Levites.
13 "The Levites will receive a share.
It will be next to the territory of the
priests. The Levites' share will be eight
miles long and three and a third miles
wide. 14 They must not sell or trade any
of it. It is the best part of the land. It
must not be handed over to anyone
else. It is set apart to me.
15 "The area that remains is one and
two-thirds miles wide. It is eight miles
long. It will not be holy. The people in
Jerusalem can build houses there. They
can use some of it as grasslands. The
city will be in the center of it. 16 Each of
the four sides of the city will be one and
a half miles long. 17 Each of the four sides
of the city's grasslands will be 440 feet
long. 18 What remains of the area will
be three and a third miles long on the
east and west sides. Its border will run
along the border of the sacred share.
Its crops will supply food for the city
workers. 19 They will farm the area. They
will come from all the tribes of Israel.
20 The entire area will be a square. Each
of its four sides will be eight miles long.
Set the sacred share apart as a special
gift to me. Do the same thing with the
property of the city.
21 "The area that remains on both
sides will belong to the prince. So his
land does not include the sacred share
and the property of the city. The eastern part of his land will reach from the
sacred share all the way to the eastern
border. The western part will reach from
the sacred share to the western border.
The sacred share itself is eight miles
long on its east and west sides. Both
of those areas will be right next to the
borders of the two tribes on the north
and south sides. They will belong to the
prince. The sacred share will be in the
center of them. It will have the temple
in it. 22 The property of the Levites will
lie in the center of the prince's share. So
will the property of the city. The prince's
land will lie between the borders of the
tribes of Judah and Benjamin.

[23]"Here is the land for the rest of the tribes.

"Benjamin will receive one share. It will reach from the eastern border to the western border.
[24]Simeon will receive one share. It will border the territory of Benjamin from east to west.
[25]Issachar will receive one share. It will border the territory of Simeon from east to west.
[26]Zebulun will receive one share. It will border the territory of Issachar from east to west.
[27]Gad will receive one share. It will border the territory of Zebulun from east to west.
[28]The southern border of Gad will run south from Tamar to the waters of Meribah Kadesh. It will continue along the Wadi of Egypt. It will end at the Mediterranean Sea.

[29]"This is the land you must divide among the tribes of Israel. And these will be the shares they will receive," announces the LORD and King.

The Gates of the New City

[30]"Here is a list of the gates of the city.

"Start with its north side. It will be
a mile and a half long. [31]The city
gates will be named after the tribes of Israel. The north side will have three gates. They will be the gates of Reuben, Judah and Levi.
[32]The east side will be a mile and a half long. It will have three gates. They will be the gates of Joseph, Benjamin and Dan.
[33]The south side will be a mile and a half long. It will have three gates. They will be the gates of Simeon, Issachar and Zebulun.
[34]The west side will be a mile and a half long. It will have three gates. They will be the gates of Gad, Asher and Naphtali.

[35]"The city will be six miles around.

"From that time on, its name will be 'The LORD Is There.' "

DANIEL

Author: Daniel

The prophet Daniel (like Ezekiel) was living in Babylon when Judah was taken captive. Daniel served in the king's courts with three of his friends. The king of Babylon, named King Nebuchadnezzar, made a massive gold statue and ordered people to fall down and worship it. Daniel's three friends refused to obey this wicked command because they were determined to worship only the one true God. Daniel and his friends put their lives at risk and were willing to suffer to do what was right, even when that meant being put in a fiery furnace or spending a night in a lions' den.

God gave Daniel a message of hope to share with his people, and God helped Daniel interpret King Nebuchadnezzar's dream about a grand statue that represented Babylon and other nations. In his dream, a giant rock came and crashed into the statue, shattering it to bits. Then the rock grew into a huge mountain that filled the entire earth. Through King Nebuchadnezzar's dream, God was telling his people that one day his kingdom would come and be greater than any other kingdom. God's plan was to bring his kingdom through the promised Savior!

Daniel Is Trained in Babylon

1 It was the third year that Jehoiakim
was king of Judah. Nebuchadnezzar, king of Babylon, came to Jerusalem. His armies surrounded the city
and attacked it. 2 The Lord handed
Jehoiakim, the king of Judah, over to
him. Nebuchadnezzar also took some
of the objects from God's temple. He
carried them off to the temple of his
god in Babylon. He put them among
the treasures of his god.
3 The king gave Ashpenaz an order.
Ashpenaz was the chief of Nebuchadnezzar's court officials. The king told
him to bring him some of the Israelites.
The king wanted them to serve him in
his court. He wanted nobles and men
from the royal family. 4 He was looking
for young men who were healthy and
handsome. They had to be able to learn
anything. They had to be well educated.
They had to have the ability to understand new things quickly and easily.
The king wanted men who could serve
in his palace. Ashpenaz was supposed
to teach them the Babylonian language
and writings. 5 The king had his servants
give them food and wine from his own
table. They received a certain amount
every day. The young men had to be
trained for three years. After that, they
could begin to serve the king.
6 Some of the men chosen were from
Judah. Their names were Daniel, Hananiah, Mishael and Azariah. 7 The chief
official gave them new names. He gave
Daniel the name Belteshazzar. He gave
Hananiah the name Shadrach. He
gave Mishael the name Meshach. And
he gave Azariah the name Abednego.
8 Daniel decided not to make himself
"unclean" by eating the king's food and
drinking his wine. So he asked the chief
official for a favor. He wanted permission not to make himself "unclean"
with the king's food and wine. 9 God
had caused the official to be kind and
friendly to Daniel. 10 But the official
refused to do what Daniel asked for. He
said, "I'm afraid of the king. He is my
master. He has decided what you and
your three friends must eat and drink.
Other young men are the same age as
you. Why should he see you looking
worse than them? When he sees how
you look, he might kill me."

in Daniel?

God is the Mighty One. God's kingdom is the only unshakable, never-ending, never-failing, perfectly good kingdom. God came in Christ and has promised to come again.

11 So Daniel spoke to one of the guards.
The chief official had appointed him
over Daniel, Hananiah, Mishael and
Azariah. 12 Daniel said to him, "Please
test us for ten days. Give us nothing
but vegetables to eat. And give us only
water to drink. 13 Then compare us with
the young men who eat the king's food.
See how we look. After that, do what
you want to." 14 So the guard agreed.
He tested them for ten days.
15 After the ten days Daniel and his
friends looked healthy and well fed. In
fact, they looked better than any of the
young men who ate the king's food. 16 So
the guard didn't require them to eat the
king's special food. He didn't require
them to drink the king's wine either. He
gave them vegetables instead.
17 God gave knowledge and understanding to these four young men.
So they understood all kinds of writings and subjects. And Daniel could
understand all kinds of visions and
dreams.
18 The three years the king had set for
their training ended. So the chief official brought them to Nebuchadnezzar.
19 The king talked with them. He didn't
find anyone equal to Daniel, Hananiah,
Mishael and Azariah. So they began
to serve the king. 20 He asked them for
advice in matters that required wisdom
and understanding. The king always
found their answers to be the best.

Other men in his kingdom claimed to get knowledge by using magic. But the answers of Daniel and his friends were ten times better than theirs.
21 Daniel served in Babylon until the first year Cyrus ruled over the land of Babylon. Cyrus was king of Persia.

Nebuchadnezzar Dreams About a Large Statue

2 In the second year of Nebuchadnezzar's rule, he had a dream. His mind
was troubled. He couldn't sleep. 2 So the
king sent for those who claimed to get knowledge by using magic. He also sent for those who practiced evil magic and those who studied the heavens. He wanted them to tell him what he had dreamed. They came in and stood in
front of the king. 3 He said to them, "I
had a dream. It troubles me. So I want to know what it means."

God Is Our Provider

God is willing and able to care for our needs, and he knows what is best for us (see Philippians 4:19). Sometimes he even gives us the things we want. Plus, listen to this: God is all-powerful! That's why we can tell him our desires and rely on him to meet all our needs. No need in this world is beyond God's ability to provide, and every good gift we receive comes from him (see James 1:17). We can express our gratitude to God by thanking him for who he is and all he has done. In his loving-kindness, God gave us the greatest gift of all: salvation through his Son, Jesus.

4 Then those who studied the heavens answered the king. They spoke in Aramaic. They said, "King Nebuchadnezzar, may you live forever! Tell us what you dreamed. Then we'll explain what it means."
5 The king replied to them, "I have
made up my mind. You must tell me what I dreamed. And you must tell me what it means. If you don't, I'll have you cut to pieces. And I'll have your
houses turned into piles of trash. 6 So
tell me what I dreamed. Explain it to me. Then I'll give you gifts. I'll reward you. I'll give you great honor. So tell me the dream. And tell me what it means."
7 Once more they replied, "King Nebuchadnezzar, tell us what you dreamed. Then we'll tell you what it means."
8 The king answered, "I know what
you are doing. You are trying to gain more time. You realize that I've made
up my mind. 9 You must tell me the
dream. If you don't, you will pay for it. You have gotten together and made evil plans. You hope things will change. So you are telling me lies. But I want you to tell me what I dreamed. Then I'll know that you can tell me what it means."
10 They answered the king, "There is
no one on earth who can do what you are asking! No king has ever asked for anything like that. Not even a king as great and mighty as you has asked for it. Those who get knowledge by using magic have never been asked to do what you are asking. And those who study the heavens haven't been asked
to do it either. 11 What you are asking
is much too hard. No one can tell you what you dreamed except the gods. And they don't live among human beings."
12 That made the king very angry. He
ordered that all the wise men in Babylon be put to death. 13 So the order was
given to kill them. Men were sent out to look for Daniel and his friends. They were also supposed to be put to death.
14 Arioch was the commander of the
king's guard. He went out to put the wise men of Babylon to death. So Daniel spoke to him wisely and carefully.
15 He asked the king's officer, "Why did
Nebuchadnezzar give a terrible order like that?" Then Arioch explained to
Daniel what was going on. 16 When Dan-
iel heard that, he went to the king. He

told him he would explain the dream to
him. But he needed more time.
17 Then Daniel returned to his house.
He explained everything to his friends
Hananiah, Mishael and Azariah. 18 He
asked them to pray that the God of
heaven would give him mercy. He
wanted God to help him understand
the mystery of the king's dream. Then
he and his friends wouldn't be killed
along with Babylon's other wise men.
19 During that night, God gave Daniel a
vision. He showed him what the mystery was all about. Then Daniel praised
the God of heaven. 20 He said,

"May God be praised for ever and
ever!
He is wise and powerful.
21 He changes times and seasons.
He removes some kings from
power.
He causes other kings to rule.
The wisdom of those who are wise
comes from him.
He gives knowledge to those who
have understanding.
22 He explains deep and hidden
things.
He knows what happens in the
darkest places.
And where he is, everything is
light.
23 God of my people of long ago, I
thank and praise you.
You have given me wisdom and
power.
You have made known to me what
we asked you for.
You have shown us the king's
dream."

Daniel Tells the King What His Dream Means

24 Then Daniel went to Arioch. The
king had appointed him to put the wise
men of Babylon to death. Daniel said
to him, "Don't kill the wise men of Babylon. Take me to the king. I'll tell him
what his dream means."
25 So Arioch took Daniel to the king
at once. Arioch said, "I have found a
man among those you brought here
from Judah. He can tell you what your
dream means."
26 Nebuchadnezzar spoke to Daniel,
who was also called Belteshazzar. The
king asked him, "Are you able to tell
me what I saw in my dream? And can
you tell me what it means?"
27 Daniel replied, "You have asked
us to explain a mystery to you. But no
wise man can do that. And those who
try to figure things out by using magic
can't do it either. 28 But there is a God
in heaven who can explain mysteries.
King Nebuchadnezzar, he has shown
you what is going to happen. Here is
what you dreamed while lying in bed.
And here are the visions that passed
through your mind.
29 "Your Majesty, while you were still
in bed your mind was troubled. You
were thinking about things that haven't
happened yet. The God who explains
mysteries showed these things to you.
30 Now the mystery has been explained
to me. But it isn't because I have greater wisdom than anyone else alive. It's
because God wants you to know what
the mystery means, Your Majesty. He
wants you to understand what went
through your mind.
31 "King Nebuchadnezzar, you looked
up and saw a large statue standing in
front of you. It was huge. It shone brightly. And it terrified you. 32 The head of the
statue was made out of pure gold. Its
chest and arms were made out of silver.
Its stomach and thighs were made out of
bronze. 33 Its legs were made out of iron.
And its feet were partly iron and partly
baked clay. 34 While you were watching,
a rock was cut out. But human hands
didn't do it. It struck the statue on its
feet of iron and clay. It smashed them.
35 Then the iron and clay were broken
to pieces. So were the bronze, silver and
gold. All of them were broken to pieces.
They became like straw on a threshing
floor at harvest time. The wind blew
them away without leaving a trace. But
the rock that struck the statue became a
huge mountain. It filled the whole earth.
36 "This was your dream. Now I will
tell you what it means. 37 King Nebuchadnezzar, you are the greatest king

of all. The God of heaven has given you
authority and power. He has given you
might and glory. 38 He has put everyone
under your control. He has also given
you authority over the wild animals
and the birds in the sky. It doesn't
matter where they live. He has made
you ruler over all of them. You are that
head of gold.

39 "After you, another kingdom will
take over. It won't be as powerful as
yours. Next, a third kingdom will rule
over the whole earth. The bronze part
of the statue stands for that kingdom.
40 Finally, there will be a fourth kingdom. It will be as strong as iron. Iron
breaks and smashes everything to pieces. And the fourth kingdom will crush
and break all the others. 41 You saw
that the feet and toes were made out
of iron and baked clay. And the fourth
kingdom will be divided up. But it will
still have some of the strength of iron.
That's why you saw iron mixed with
clay. 42 The toes were partly iron and
partly clay. And the fourth kingdom
will be partly strong and partly weak.
43 You saw the iron mixed with baked
clay. And the fourth kingdom will be
made up of all kinds of people. They
won't hold together any more than iron
mixes with clay.

44 "In the time of those kings, the
God of heaven will set up a kingdom.
It will never be destroyed. And no other
nation will ever take it over. It will crush
all those other kingdoms. It will bring
them to an end. But it will last forever.
45 That's what the vision of the rock
cut out of a mountain means. Human
hands didn't cut out the rock. It broke
the statue to pieces. It smashed the iron,
bronze, clay, silver and gold.

"The great God has shown you what
will take place in days to come. The
dream is true. And you can trust the
meaning of it that I have explained
to you."

46 Then King Nebuchadnezzar bowed
low in front of Daniel. He wanted to
honor him. So he ordered that an offering and incense be offered up to him.
47 The king said to Daniel, "I'm sure your
God is the greatest God of all. He is the
Lord of kings. He explains mysteries.
That's why you were able to explain
the mystery of my dream."

48 Then the king put Daniel in a position of authority. He gave him many
gifts. He made him ruler over the city
of Babylon and the towns around it. He
put him in charge of all its other wise
men. 49 The king also did what Daniel
asked him to. He appointed Shadrach,
Meshach and Abednego to help Daniel
govern Babylon and the towns around
it. Daniel himself remained at the royal
court.

A Gold Statue and a Blazing Furnace

3 King Nebuchadnezzar made a gold
statue. It was 90 feet tall and 9 feet
wide. He set it up on the plain of Dura
near the city of Babylon. 2 Then the king
sent for the royal rulers, high officials
and governors. He sent for the advisers,
treasurers, judges and court officers.
And he sent for all the other officials
of Babylon. He asked them to come to
a special gathering to honor the statue
he had set up. 3 So the royal rulers, high
officials and governors came together.
So did the advisers, treasurers, judges
and court officers. All the other officials
joined them. They came to honor the
statue that King Nebuchadnezzar had
set up. They stood in front of it.

4 Then a messenger called out loudly, "Listen, you people who come from
every nation! Pay attention, you who
speak other languages! Here is what

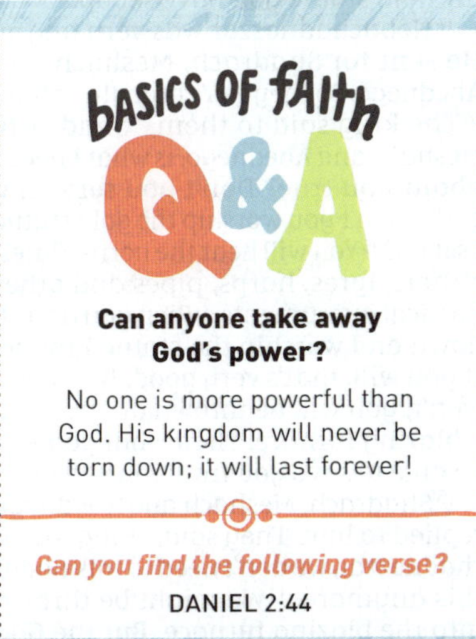

the king commands you to do. [5]You will
soon hear the sound of horns and flutes.
You will hear zithers, lyres, harps and
pipes. In fact, you will hear all kinds of
music. When you do, you must fall down
and worship the gold statue. That is the
statue that King Nebuchadnezzar has
set up. [6]If you don't, you will be thrown
into a blazing furnace right away."
[7]All the people heard the sound of
the horns and flutes. They heard the
zithers, lyres, harps and other musical
instruments. As soon as they did, they
fell down and worshiped Nebuchadnezzar's gold statue. They were people from
all nations no matter what language
they spoke.
[8]At this time some people who studied the heavens came forward. They
spoke against the Jews. [9]They said,
"King Nebuchadnezzar, may you live
forever! [10]Your Majesty has commanded everyone to fall down and worship
the gold statue. You told them to do
it when they heard the horns, flutes,
zithers, lyres, harps, pipes and other
musical instruments. [11]If they didn't,
they would be thrown into a blazing furnace. [12]But you have appointed some
Jews to help Daniel govern Babylon
and the towns around it. Their names
are Shadrach, Meshach and Abednego.
They don't pay any attention to you,
King Nebuchadnezzar. They don't serve
your gods. And they refuse to worship
the gold statue you have set up."
[13]Nebuchadnezzar was very angry.
He sent for Shadrach, Meshach and
Abednego. So they were brought to him.
[14]The king said to them, "Shadrach,
Meshach and Abednego, is what I heard
about you true? Don't you serve my
gods? Don't you worship the gold statue
I set up? [15]You will hear the horns, flutes,
zithers, lyres, harps, pipes and other
musical instruments. When you do, fall
down and worship the statue I made.
If you will, that's very good. But if you
won't, you will be thrown at once into
a blazing furnace. Then what god will
be able to save you from my power?"
[16]Shadrach, Meshach and Abednego
replied to him. They said, "King Nebuchadnezzar, we don't need to talk about
this anymore. [17]We might be thrown
into the blazing furnace. But the God
we serve is able to bring us out of it
alive. He will save us from your power.
[18]But we want you to know this, Your
Majesty. Even if we knew that our God
wouldn't save us, we still wouldn't serve
your gods. We wouldn't worship the gold
statue you set up."
[19]Then Nebuchadnezzar was very angry with Shadrach, Meshach and Abednego. The look on his face changed. And
he ordered that the furnace be heated
seven times hotter than usual. [20]He
also gave some of the strongest soldiers
in his army a command. He ordered
them to tie up Shadrach, Meshach and
Abednego. Then he told his men to
throw them into the blazing furnace.
[21]So they were tied up. Then they were
thrown into the furnace. They were
wearing their robes, pants, turbans and
other clothes. [22]The king's command
was carried out quickly. The furnace
was so hot that its flames killed the
soldiers who threw Shadrach, Meshach
and Abednego into it. [23]So the three
men were firmly tied up. And they fell
into the blazing furnace.
[24]Then King Nebuchadnezzar leaped
to his feet. He was so amazed he asked
his advisers, "Didn't we tie up three
men? Didn't we throw three men into
the fire?"
They replied, "Yes, we did, Your
Majesty."
[25]The king said, "Look! I see four men
walking around in the fire. They aren't
tied up. And the fire hasn't even harmed
them. The fourth man looks like a son
of the gods."
[26]Then the king approached the
opening of the blazing furnace. He
shouted, "Shadrach, Meshach and
Abednego, come out! You who serve
the Most High God, come here!"
So they came out of the fire. [27]The royal rulers, high officials, governors and
advisers crowded around them. They saw
that the fire hadn't harmed their bodies.
Not one hair on their heads was burned.
Their robes weren't burned either. And
they didn't even smell like smoke.
[28]Then Nebuchadnezzar said, "May
the God of Shadrach, Meshach and
Abednego be praised! He has sent his
angel and saved his servants. They
trusted in him. They refused to obey
my command. They were willing to give
up their lives. They would rather die

than serve or worship any god except their own God. 29 No other god can save people this way. So I'm giving an order about the God of Shadrach, Meshach and Abednego. No one may say anything against him. That's true no matter what language they speak. If they say anything against him, they'll be cut to pieces. And their houses will be turned into piles of trash."

30 Then the king honored Shadrach, Meshach and Abednego. He gave them higher positions in the city of Babylon and the towns around it.

Nebuchadnezzar Dreams About a Tree

4 I, King Nebuchadnezzar, am writing this letter.

I am sending it to people who live all over the world. I'm sending it to people of every nation no matter what language they speak.

May you have great success!

2 I am pleased to tell you what has happened. The Most High God has done miraculous signs and wonders for me.

3 His signs are great.
His wonders are mighty.
His kingdom will last forever.
His rule will never end.

4 I was at home in my palace. I was content and very successful. 5 But I had a dream that made me afraid. I was lying in bed. Then dreams and visions passed through my mind. They terrified me. 6 So I commanded that all the wise men in Babylon be brought to me. I wanted them to tell me what my dream meant. 7 Those who try to figure things out by using magic came. So did those who study the heavens. I told all of them what I had dreamed. But they couldn't tell me what it meant. 8 Finally, Daniel came to me. He is called Belteshazzar, after the name of my god. The spirit of the holy gods is in him. I told him my dream.

9 I said, "Belteshazzar, you are chief of the magicians. I know that the spirit of the holy gods is in you. No mystery is too hard for you to figure out. Here is my dream. Tell me what it means. 10 Here are the visions I saw while I was lying in bed. I looked up and saw a tree standing in the middle of the land. It was very tall. 11 It had grown to be large and strong. Its top touched the sky. It could be seen anywhere on earth. 12 Its leaves were beautiful. It had a lot of fruit on it. It provided enough food for people and animals. Under the tree, the wild animals found safety. The birds lived in its branches. Every creature was fed from that tree.

13 "While I was still lying in bed, I looked up. In my visions, I saw a holy one. He was a messenger. He was coming down from heaven. 14 He called out in a loud voice. He said, 'Cut down the tree. Break off its branches. Strip off its leaves. Scatter its fruit. Let the animals under it run away. Let the birds in its branches fly off. 15 But leave the stump with its roots in the ground. Let it stay in the field. Put a band of iron and bronze around it.

" 'Let King Nebuchadnezzar become wet with the dew of heaven. Let him live with the animals among the plants of the earth. 16 Let him no longer have the mind of a man. Instead, let him be given the mind of an animal. Let him stay that way until seven periods of time pass by.

17 " 'The decision is announced by holy messengers. So all who are alive will know that the Most High God is King. He rules over all kingdoms on earth. He gives them to anyone he wants. Sometimes he puts the least important people in charge of them.'

18 "This is the dream I, King Nebuchadnezzar, had. Now tell me what it means, Belteshazzar. None of the wise men in my kingdom can explain it to me. But you can. After all, the spirit of the holy gods is in you."

Daniel Explains Nebuchadnezzar's Dream

19 Daniel, who was also called Belteshazzar, was very bewildered for a while. His thoughts terrified

him. So the king said, "Beltesha z-
zar, don't let the dream or its meaning make you afraid."
Belteshazzar answered, "My master, I wish the dream were about
your enemies! I wish its meaning
had to do with them! 20 You saw a
tree. It grew to be large and strong.
Its top touched the sky. It could be
seen from anywhere on earth. 21 Its
leaves were beautiful. It had a lot
of fruit on it. It provided enough
food for people and animals. Under
the tree, the wild animals found
safety. The birds lived in its branches. 22 Your Majesty, you are that
tree! You have become great and
strong. Your greatness has grown
until it reaches the sky. Your rule
has spread to all parts of the earth.
23 "Your Majesty, you saw a
holy one. He was a messenger. He
came down from heaven. He said,
'Cut down the tree. Destroy it. But
leave the stump with its roots in the
ground. Let it stay in the field. Put
an iron and bronze band around it.
Let King Nebuchadnezzar become
wet with the dew of heaven. Let
him live with the wild animals.
Let him stay that way until seven
periods of time pass by.'
24 "Your Majesty, here is what
your dream means. The Most High
God has given an order against
you. 25 You will be driven away
from people. You will live with the
wild animals. You will eat grass
just as an ox does. You will become
wet with the dew of heaven. Sev-
en periods of time will pass by for
you. Then you will recognize that
the Most High God rules over all
kingdoms on earth. He gives them
to anyone he wants. 26 But he gave
a command to leave the stump of
the tree along with its roots. That
means your kingdom will be given
back to you. It will happen when
you recognize that the God of
heaven rules. 27 So, Your Majesty,
I hope you will accept my advice.
Stop being sinful. Do what is right.
Give up your evil practices. Show
kindness to those who are being
treated badly. Then perhaps things
will continue to go well with you."

Nebuchadnezzar's Dream Comes True

28 All this happened to King
Nebuchadnezzar. 29 It took place
twelve months later. He was walking on the roof of his palace in Babylon. 30 He said, "Isn't this the great
Babylon I have built as a place for
my royal palace? I used my mighty
power to build it. It shows how glorious my majesty is."
31 He was still speaking when
he heard a voice from heaven. It
said, "King Nebuchadnezzar, here
is what has been ordered concerning you. Your royal authority has
been taken from you. 32 You will
be driven away from people. You
will live with the wild animals. You
will eat grass just as an ox does.
Seven periods of time will pass by
for you. Then you will recognize
that the Most High God rules over
all kingdoms on earth. He gives
them to anyone he wants."
33 What had been said about
King Nebuchadnezzar came true
at once. He was driven away from
people. He ate grass just as an ox
does. His body became wet with the
dew of heaven. He stayed that way
until his hair grew like the feathers
of an eagle. His nails became like
the claws of a bird.

34 At the end of that time I, Nebuchadnezzar, looked up toward
heaven. My mind became clear
again. Then I praised the Most High
God. I gave honor and glory to the
God who lives forever.

His rule will last forever.
  His kingdom will never end.
35 He considers all the nations on
  earth
  to be nothing.
He does as he pleases
  with the powers of heaven.
He does what he wants
  with the nations of the earth.
No one can hold back his hand.
  No one can say to him,
  "What have you done?"

36 My honor and glory were
returned to me when my mind
became clear again. The glory of

my kingdom was given back to
me. My advisers and nobles came
to me. And I was put back on my
throne. I became even greater than
I had been before. 37 Now I, Nebuchadnezzar, give praise and honor
and glory to the King of heaven.
Everything he does is right. All his
ways are fair. He is able to bring
down those who live proudly.

A Hand Writes on the Palace Wall

5 King Belshazzar gave a huge banquet. He invited a thousand of his
nobles to it. He drank wine with them.
2 While Belshazzar was drinking his
wine, he gave orders to his servants. He
commanded them to bring in some gold
and silver cups. They were the cups his
father Nebuchadnezzar had taken from
the temple in Jerusalem. Belshazzar
had them brought in so everyone could
drink from them. That included the king
himself, his nobles, his wives and his
concubines. 3 So the servants brought
in the gold cups. The cups had been
taken from God's temple in Jerusalem.
The king and his nobles drank from
them. So did his wives and concubines.
4 As they drank the wine, they praised
their gods. The statues of those gods
were made out of gold, silver, bronze,
iron, wood or stone.

5 Suddenly the fingers of a human
hand appeared. They wrote something
on the plaster of the palace wall. It happened near the lampstand. The king
watched the hand as it wrote. 6 His face
turned pale. He was so afraid that his
legs became weak. And his knees were
knocking together.

7 The king sent for those who try to figure things out by using magic. He also
sent for those who study the heavens.
All of them were wise men in Babylon.
Then the king spoke to them. He said,
"I want one of you to read this writing.
I want you to tell me what it means.
Whoever does this will be dressed in
purple clothes. A gold chain will be put
around his neck. And he will be made
the third highest ruler in the kingdom."

8 Then all the king's wise men came
in. But they couldn't read the writing.
They couldn't tell him what it meant.
9 So King Belshazzar became even more
terrified. His face grew more pale. And
his nobles were bewildered.

10 The queen heard the king and his
nobles talking. So she came into the
dining hall. "King Belshazzar, may you
live forever!" she said. "Don't be afraid!
Don't look so pale! 11 I know a man in
your kingdom who has the spirit of the
holy gods in him. He has understanding
and wisdom and good sense just like
the gods. He was chief of those who
tried to figure things out by using magic. And he was in charge of those who
studied the heavens. Your father, King
Nebuchadnezzar, appointed him to
that position. 12 King Nebuchadnezzar
did this because he saw what the man
could do. This man's name is Daniel.
Your father called him Belteshazzar.
He has a clever mind and knowledge
and understanding. He is also able to
tell what dreams mean. He can explain
riddles and solve hard problems. Send
for him. He'll tell you what the writing
means."

13 So Daniel was brought to the king.
The king said to him, "Are you Daniel?
Are you one of the prisoners my father
the king brought here from Judah? 14 I
have heard that the spirit of the gods
is in you. I've also heard that you have
understanding and good sense and
special wisdom. 15 The wise men and
those who practice magic were brought
to me. They were asked to read this
writing and tell me what it means. But
they couldn't. 16 I have heard that you
are able to explain things and solve
hard problems. I hope you can read
this writing and tell me what it means.
If you can, you will be dressed in purple
clothes. A gold chain will be put around
your neck. And you will be made the
third highest ruler in the kingdom."

17 Then Daniel answered the king.
He said, "You can keep your gifts for
yourself. You can give your rewards to
someone else. But I will read the writing
for you. I'll tell you what it means.

18 "Your Majesty, the Most High God
was good to your father Nebuchadnezzar. He gave him authority and greatness
and glory and honor. 19 God gave him a
high position. Then people from every
nation became afraid of the king. That
was true no matter what language they
spoke. The king put to death anyone he

wanted to. He spared anyone he wanted to spare. He gave high positions to anyone he wanted to. And he brought down anyone he wanted to bring down.
20 But his heart became very stubborn and proud. So he was removed from his royal throne. His glory was stripped away from him.
21 He was driven away from people. He was given the mind of an animal. He lived with the wild donkeys. He ate grass just as an ox does. His body became wet with the dew of heaven. He stayed that way until he recognized that the Most High God rules over all kingdoms on earth. He puts anyone he wants to in charge of them.

22 "But you knew all that, Belshazzar. After all, you are Nebuchadnezzar's son. In spite of that, you are still proud.
23 You have taken your stand against the Lord of heaven. You had your servants bring cups from his temple to you. You and your nobles drank wine from them. So did your wives and concubines. You praised your gods. The statues of those gods are made out of silver, gold, bronze, iron, wood or stone. They can't see or hear or understand anything. But you didn't honor God. He holds in his hand your very life and everything you do.
24 So he sent the hand that wrote on the wall.

25 "Here is what was written.

MENE, MENE, TEKEL, PARSIN

26 "And here is what these words mean.

"The word Mene means that God has limited the time of your rule. He has brought it to an end.

27 "The word Tekel means that you have been weighed on scales. And you haven't measured up to God's standard.

28 "The word Peres means that your authority over your kingdom will be taken away from you. It will be given to the Medes and Persians."

29 Then Belshazzar commanded his servants to dress Daniel in purple clothes. So they did. They put a gold chain around his neck. And he was made the third highest ruler in the kingdom.

30 That very night Belshazzar, the king of Babylon, was killed.
31 His kingdom was given to Darius the Mede. Darius was 62 years old.

Daniel Is Thrown Into a Den of Lions

6 It pleased Darius to appoint 120 royal rulers over his entire kingdom.
2 He placed three leaders over them. One of the leaders was Daniel. The royal rulers were made accountable to the three leaders. Then the king wouldn't lose any of his wealth.
3 Daniel did a better job than the other two leaders or any of the royal rulers. He was an unusually good and able man. So the king planned to put him in charge of the whole kingdom.
4 But the other two leaders and the royal rulers heard about it. So they looked for a reason to bring charges against Daniel. They tried to find something wrong with the way he ran the government. But they weren't able to. They couldn't find any fault with his work. He could always be trusted. He never did anything wrong. And he always did what he was supposed to.
5 Finally these men said, "We want to bring charges against this man Daniel. But it's almost impossible for us to come up with a reason to do it. If we find a reason, it will have to be in connection with the law of his God."

6 So the two leaders and the royal rulers went as a group to the king. They said, "King Darius, may you live forever!
7 All the royal leaders, high officials, royal rulers, advisers and governors want to make a suggestion. We've agreed that you should give an order. And you should make sure it's obeyed. Your Majesty, here is the command you should make your people obey for the next 30 days. Don't let any of your people pray to any god or human being except to you. If they do, throw them into the lions' den.
8 Now give the order. Write it down in the law of the Medes and Persians. Then it can't be changed."
9 So King Darius put the order in writing.

10 Daniel found out that the king had signed the order. In spite of that, he did just as he had always done before. He went home to his upstairs room. Its windows opened toward Jerusalem. He went to his room three times a day to pray. He got down on his knees and gave thanks to his God.
11 Some of the other royal officials went to where Daniel was staying. They saw him praying and asking God for help.
12 So they went to the king. They spoke to him about his

royal order. They said, "Your Majesty,
didn't you sign an official order? It said
that for the next 30 days your people
could pray only to you. They could not
pray to anyone else, whether god or
human being. If they did, they would
be thrown into the lions' den."

The king answered, "The order must
still be obeyed. It's what the law of the
Medes and Persians requires. So it can't
be changed."

13 Then they spoke to the king again.
They said, "Daniel is one of the prisoners from Judah. He doesn't pay any
attention to you, Your Majesty. He
doesn't obey the order you put in writing. He still prays to his God three times
a day." 14 When the king heard this, he
was very upset. He didn't want Daniel
to be harmed in any way. Until sunset,
he did everything he could to save him.

15 Then the men went as a group to
King Darius. They said to him, "Your
Majesty, remember that no order or
command you give can be changed.
That's what the law of the Medes and
Persians requires."

16 So the king gave the order. Daniel
was brought out and thrown into the
lions' den. The king said to him, "You
always serve your God faithfully. So
may he save you!"

17 A stone was brought and placed
over the opening of the den. The king
sealed it with his own special ring. He
also sealed it with the rings of his nobles.
Then nothing could be done to help Daniel. 18 The king returned to his palace. He
didn't eat anything that night. He didn't
ask for anything to be brought to him
for his enjoyment. And he couldn't sleep.

19 As soon as the sun began to rise, the
king got up. He hurried to the lions' den.
20 When he got near it, he called out to
Daniel. His voice was filled with great
concern. He said, "Daniel! You serve
the living God. You always serve him
faithfully. So has he been able to save
you from the lions?"

21 Daniel answered, "Your Majesty,
may you live forever! 22 My God sent his
angel. And his angel shut the mouths
of the lions. They haven't hurt me at
all. That's because I haven't done anything wrong in God's sight. I've never
done anything wrong to you either,
Your Majesty."

23 The king was filled with joy. He
ordered his servants to lift Daniel out
of the den. So they did. They didn't see
any wounds on him. That's because he
had trusted in his God.

24 Then the king gave another order.
The men who had said bad things
about Daniel were brought in. They
were thrown into the lions' den. So
were their wives and children. Before
they hit the bottom of the den, the lions
attacked them. And the lions crushed
all their bones.

25 Then King Darius wrote to people of
all nations, no matter what language
they spoke. He said,

"May you have great success!

26 "I order people in every part of
my kingdom to respect and honor
Daniel's God.

"He is the living God.
He will live forever.
His kingdom will not be
destroyed.
His rule will never end.
27 He sets people free and saves them.
He does miraculous signs and
wonders.
He does them in the heavens
and on the earth.
He has saved Daniel
from the power of the lions."

28 So Daniel had success while Darius
was king. Things went well with Daniel
during the rule of Cyrus, the Persian.

Daniel Has a Dream About Four Animals

7 It was the first year that Belshazzar was king of Babylon. Daniel
had a dream. He was lying in bed. In
his dream, visions passed through his
mind. He wrote down what he saw.

2 Daniel said, "I had a vision at night.
I looked up and saw the four winds of
heaven. They were stirring up the Mediterranean Sea. 3 Four large animals
came up out of the sea. Each one was
different from the others.

4 "The first animal was like a lion. It
had the wings of an eagle. I watched
until its wings were torn off. Then it was
lifted up from the ground. It stood on
two feet like a human being. And the
mind of a human being was given to it.

5 “I saw a second animal. It looked
like a bear. It was raised up on one of
its sides. And it had three ribs between
its teeth. It was told, ‘Get up! Eat meat
until you are full!’
6 “After that, I saw another animal. It
looked like a leopard. On its back were
four wings like the wings of a bird. The
animal I saw had four heads. And it was
given authority to rule.
7 “After that, in my vision I looked up
and saw a fourth animal. It was terrifying and very powerful. It had large iron
teeth. It crushed those it attacked and
ate them up. It stomped on anything
that was left. It was different from the
other animals. And it had ten horns.
8 “I thought about the horns. Then I
saw another horn. It was a little one. It
grew up among the other horns. Three
of the first horns were pulled up by their
roots to make room for it. The little horn
had eyes like the eyes of a human being.
Its mouth was always bragging.
9 “As I watched,

“thrones were set in place.
 The Eternal God took his seat.
His clothes were as white as snow.
 The hair on his head was white
  like wool.
His throne was blazing with fire.
 And flames were all around its
  wheels.
10 A river of fire was flowing.
 It was coming out from in front
  of God.
Thousands and thousands of
  angels served him.
 Millions of them stood in front of
  him.
The court was seated.
 And the books were opened.

11 “Then I continued to watch because
of the way the horn was bragging. I
kept looking until the fourth animal
was killed. I watched until its body
was destroyed. It was thrown into the
blazing fire. 12 The authority of the other
animals had been stripped away from
them. But they were allowed to live for
a period of time.
13 “In my vision I saw one who looked
like a son of man. He was coming with
the clouds of heaven. He approached
the Eternal God. He was led right up
to him. 14 And he was given authority,
glory and a kingdom. People of all nations, no matter what language they
spoke, worshiped him. His authority
will last forever. It will not pass away.
His kingdom will never be destroyed.

An Angel Tells Daniel What His Dream Means

15 “My spirit was troubled. The visions
that passed through my mind upset
me. 16 I approached an angel who was
standing there. I asked him what all
these things really meant.
“So he explained to me what everything meant. 17 He said, ‘The four large
animals stand for four kings. The kings
will appear on the earth. 18 But the holy
people of the Most High God will receive the kingdom. They will possess it
forever. It will belong to them for ever
and ever.’
19 “Then I wanted to know what the
fourth animal stood for. It was different
from the others. It was the most terrifying of all. It had iron teeth and bronze
claws. It crushed everyone it attacked
and ate them up. It stomped on anything that was left. 20 I also wanted to
know about the ten horns on its head.
And I wanted to know about the other
horn that grew up later. It caused three
of the ten horns to fall out. It appeared
to be stronger than the others. It had
eyes. And its mouth was always bragging. 21 I saw that the horn was at war
with God’s holy people. It was winning
the battle over them. 22 But then the
Eternal God came. He decided in favor
of his holy people. So the time came
when the kingdom was given to them.
23 “Here’s how the angel explained it to
me. He said, ‘The fourth animal stands
for a fourth kingdom. It will appear on
earth. It will be different from the other
kingdoms. It will eat up the whole earth.
It will stomp on it and crush it. 24 The
ten horns stand for ten kings. They
will come from the fourth kingdom.
After them another king will appear.
He will be different from the earlier
ones. He’ll bring three kings under his
control. 25 He’ll speak against the Most
High God. He’ll treat God’s holy people
badly. He will try to change the times
and laws that were given by God. God’s
holy people will be placed under his
power for three and a half years.

26 “ ‘But the court will be seated. And the power of that king will be taken away from him. It will be completely destroyed forever. 27 Then the authority, power and greatness of all the kingdoms on earth will be taken from them. And all they had will be given to the holy people of the Most High God. His kingdom will last forever. Every ruler will worship and obey him.’

28 “That's all I saw. My thoughts deeply troubled me. My face turned pale. But I kept those things to myself.”

Daniel Has a Vision About a Ram and a Goat

8 It was the third year of King Belshazzar's rule. After the vision that had already appeared to me, I had another one. 2 In my vision I saw myself in the city of Susa. It has high walls around it. It is in the land of Elam. In the vision I was beside the Ulai Canal. 3 I looked up and saw a ram that had two horns. It was standing beside the canal. Its horns were long. One of them was longer than the other. But that horn grew up later. 4 I watched the ram as it charged toward the west. It also charged toward the north and the south. No animal could stand up against it. Not one of them could save anyone from its power. It did as it pleased. And it became great.

5 I was thinking about all of this. Then a goat suddenly came from the west. It had a large horn between its eyes. The goat raced across the whole earth without even touching the ground. 6 It came toward the ram that had the two horns. It was the ram I had seen standing beside the canal. The goat was very angry. It charged at the ram. 7 I saw it attack the ram with mighty force. It struck the ram and broke the ram's two horns. The ram didn't have the power to stand up against it. The goat knocked the ram to the ground and stomped on it. No one could save the ram from the goat's power. 8 The goat became very great. But when its power was at its greatest, the goat's large horn was broken off. In its place four large horns grew up toward the four winds of heaven.

9 Out of one of the four horns came another horn. It was small at first but became more and more powerful. It grew to the south and to the east and toward the beautiful land of Israel. 10 It grew until it reached the stars in the sky. It threw some of them down to the earth. And it stomped on them. 11 It set itself up to be as great as the commander of the LORD's army. It took away the daily sacrifices from the LORD. And his temple in Jerusalem was thrown down. 12 Because many of the LORD's people refused to obey him, they were handed over to the horn. The daily sacrifices were also given over to it. The horn was successful no matter what it did. And true worship of God was thrown down to the ground.

13 Then I heard a holy angel speaking. Another holy angel spoke to him. He asked, “How long will it take for the vision to come true? When will the daily sacrifices be stopped? When will those who refuse to obey God be destroyed? When will the temple be handed over to an enemy? And when will some of the LORD's people be stomped on?”

14 One of the holy angels said to me, “It will take 2,300 evenings and mornings. Then the temple will be made holy again.”

Gabriel Tells Daniel What His Vision Means

15 I was having the vision. And I was trying to understand it. Then I saw someone who looked like a man. 16 I heard a voice from the Ulai Canal. It called out, “Gabriel, tell Daniel what his vision means.”

17 Gabriel came close to where I was standing. I was terrified and fell down flat with my face toward the ground. Here is what he said to me. “Son of man, I want you to understand the vision. It's about the time of the end.”

18 While he was speaking to me, I was sound asleep. I lay with my face on the ground. Then he touched me. He raised me to my feet.

19 He said, “I am going to tell you what will happen later. It will take place when God is angry. The vision is about the appointed time of the end. 20 You saw a ram that had two horns. It stands for the kings of Media and Persia. 21 The goat stands for the king of Greece. The large horn between its eyes is the first

king. 22 Four horns took the horn's place when it was broken off. They stand for four kingdoms that will come from his nation. But those kingdoms will not be as powerful as his.

23 "Toward the end of their rule, those who refuse to obey God will become completely evil. Then another king will appear. He will have a scary-looking face. He will be a master at making clever plans. 24 He will become very strong. But he will not get that way by his own power. People will be amazed at the way he destroys everything. He will be successful no matter what he does. He will destroy mighty people. Those mighty people are God's holy people. 25 He will tell lies in order to succeed. He will think he is more important than anyone else. When people feel safe, he will destroy many of them. He will stand up against the greatest Prince of all. Then he will be destroyed. But he will not be killed by human beings.

26 "The vision of the evenings and mornings that has been given to you is true. But seal up the vision. It is about a time far off."

27 I, Daniel, was worn out. I was too tired to get up for several days. Then I got up and returned to my work for the king. The vision bewildered me. I couldn't understand it.

Daniel Prays to the LORD

9 It was the first year that Darius was king of Babylon. He was from Media and was the son of Xerxes. 2 In that year I learned from the Scriptures that Jerusalem would remain destroyed for 70 years. That was what the LORD had told Jeremiah the prophet. 3 So I prayed to the Lord God. I begged him. I made many appeals to him. I didn't eat anything. I put on the rough clothing people wear when they're sad. And I sat down in ashes.

4 I prayed to the LORD my God. I admitted that we had sinned. I said,

"Lord, you are a great and wonderful God. You keep the covenant you made with all those who love you and obey your commandments. You show them your love. 5 We have sinned and done what is wrong. We have been evil. We have refused to obey you. We have turned away from your commands and laws. 6 We haven't listened to your servants the prophets. They spoke in your name to our kings, our princes and our people of long ago. They also brought your message to all our people in the land.

7 "Lord, you always do what is right. But we are covered with shame today. We are the people of Judah and Jerusalem. All of us are Israelites, no matter where we live. We are now living in many countries. You scattered us among the nations because we weren't faithful to you. 8 LORD, we are covered with shame. So are our kings and princes, and our people of long ago. We have sinned against you. 9 You are the Lord our God. You show us your tender love. You forgive us. But we have turned against you. 10 You are the LORD our God. But we haven't obeyed you. We haven't kept the laws you gave us through your servants the prophets. 11 All the people of Israel have broken your law and turned away from it. They have refused to obey you.

"Curses and warnings are written down in the Law of Moses. He was your servant. Those curses have been poured out on us. That's because we have sinned against you. 12 The warnings you gave us and our rulers have come true. You have brought great trouble on us. Nothing like what has been done to Jerusalem has ever happened anywhere else on earth. 13 The curses that are written in the Law of Moses have fallen on us. We have received nothing but trouble. You are the LORD our God. But we haven't asked for your favor. We haven't turned away from our sins. We've refused to pay attention to the laws you gave us. 14 LORD, you didn't hold back from bringing this trouble on us. You always do what is right. But we haven't obeyed you.

15 "Lord our God, you used your mighty hand to bring your people out of Egypt. You made a name for yourself. It is still great to this day. But we have sinned. We've done what is wrong. 16 Lord, you saved

your people before. So turn your great anger away from Jerusalem again. After all, it is your city. It's your holy mountain. You have made those who live around us think little of Jerusalem and your people. That's because we have sinned. Our people before us did evil things too.

17 "Our God, hear my prayers. Pay attention to the appeals I make to you. Lord, have mercy on your temple that has been destroyed. Do
it for your own honor. 18 Our God,
please listen to us. The city that belongs to you has been destroyed. Open your eyes and see it. We aren't asking you to answer our prayers because we are godly. Instead, we're asking you to do it because
you love us so much. 19 Lord, please
listen! Lord, please forgive us! Lord, hear our prayers! Take action for your own honor. Our God, please don't wait. Your city and your people belong to you."

Gabriel Tells Daniel About Seventy "Weeks"

20 I was speaking and praying. I was admitting that I and my people Israel had sinned. I was making my appeal to the LORD my God. My appeal was about
his holy mountain of Zion. 21 While I was
still praying, Gabriel came to me. I had seen him in my earlier vision. He flew over to me very quickly. It was about the time when the evening sacrifice is
offered. 22 He helped me understand.
He said, "Daniel, I have come now to help you know and understand these
things. 23 You are highly respected. So
as soon as you began to pray, the LORD gave you a message. I have come to tell you what it is. Here is how you must understand the vision.

24 "The LORD has appointed 70 'weeks' for your people and your holy city. During that time, acts against God's law will be stopped. Sin will come to an end. And the evil things people do will be paid for. Then everyone will always do what is right. Everything that has been made known in visions and prophecies will come true. And the Most Holy Room in the temple will be anointed.

25 "Here is what I want you to know and understand. There will be seven 'weeks.' Then there will be 62 'weeks.' The seven 'weeks' will begin when an order is given to rebuild Jerusalem and make it like new again. At the end of the 62 'weeks,' the Anointed King will come. Jerusalem will have streets and

QUICK TO FORGIVE

MY GOD IS...

When we sin and disobey God, we can ask God to forgive our sins and help us do what honors him. This is called *repentance*. We can tell him that we have sinned and have done what is wrong. We can ask him for his forgiveness and know that, because of Jesus, God will forgive our sins.

We can also ask God for forgiveness right away. We don't have to worry about when God will forgive us, nor do we have to wonder about whether he will forgive us. God forgives anyone who comes to him through Jesus.

In fact, the Bible says God removes our sins as far as the east is from the west (see Psalm 103:12)—that's farther than we can imagine! God's forgiveness for us means we can be quick to forgive others who sin against us.

a water system when it is rebuilt. But that will be done in times of trouble. 26 After the 62 'weeks,' the Anointed King will be put to death. His followers will desert him. And everything he has will be taken away from him. The army of the ruler who will come will destroy the city and the temple. The end will come like a flood. War will continue until the end. The LORD has ordered that many places be destroyed. 27 A covenant will be put into effect with many people for one 'week.' In the middle of the 'week' sacrifices and offerings will come to an end. And at the temple a hated thing that destroys will be set up. It will remain until that ruler who will come is destroyed. Then he will experience what the LORD has ordered."

Daniel Has a Vision About What Will Happen to Israel

10 It was the third year that Cyrus, the king of Persia, ruled over Babylon. At that time I was living in Babylon. There the people called me Belteshazzar. A message from God came to me. It was true. It was about a great war. I had a vision that showed me what it meant.

2 At that time I was very sad for three weeks. 3 I didn't eat any rich food. No meat or wine touched my lips. I didn't use any lotions at all until the three weeks were over.

4 I was standing on the bank of the great Tigris River. It was the 24th day of the first month. 5 I looked up and saw a man dressed in linen clothes. He had a belt around his waist. It was made out of fine gold from Uphaz. 6 His body gleamed like topaz. His face shone like lightning. His eyes were like flaming torches. His arms and legs were as bright as polished bronze. And his voice was like the sound of a large crowd.

7 I was the only one who saw the vision. The people who were there with me didn't see it. But they were so terrified that they ran and hid. 8 So I was left alone as I was watching this great vision. I felt very weak. My face turned as pale as death. And I was helpless. 9 Then I heard the man speak. As I listened to him, I fell sound asleep. My face was toward the ground.

10 A hand touched me. It pulled me up on my hands and knees. I began to tremble with fear. 11 The man said, "Daniel, you are highly respected. Think carefully about what I am going to say to you. And stand up. God has sent me to you." When he said that, I trembled as I stood up.

12 He continued, "Do not be afraid, Daniel. You decided to get more understanding. You made yourself humble as you worshiped your God. Since the first day you did those things, your words were heard. I have come to give you an answer. 13 But the prince of Persia opposed me for 21 days. Then Michael came to help me. He is one of the leaders of the angels. He helped me win the battle over the king of Persia. 14 Now I have come to explain the vision to you. I will tell you what will happen to your people. The vision shows what will take place in days to come."

15 While he was telling me these things, I bowed with my face toward the ground. I wasn't able to speak. 16 Then someone who looked like a man touched my lips. I opened my mouth. I began to speak to the one who was standing in front of me. I said, "My master, I'm greatly troubled because of the vision I've seen. And I feel very weak. 17 How can I talk with you? My strength is gone. In fact, I can hardly breathe."

18 The one who looked like a man touched me again. He gave me strength. 19 "Do not be afraid," he said. "You are highly respected. May peace be with you! Be strong now. Be strong."

When he spoke to me, I became stronger. I said, "Speak, my master. You have given me strength."

20 So he said, "Do you know why I have come to you? Soon I will return to fight against the prince of Persia. When I go, the prince of Greece will come. 21 But first I will tell you what is written in the Book of Truth. No one gives me any help against those princes except Michael. He is your leader.

11 1 I stepped forward to help him and keep him safe. It was the first year that Darius, the Mede, was king.

The Kings of Egypt and Syria

2 "Now then, what I'm about to tell you is true. Three more kings will come to power in Persia. Then a fourth one

will rule. He will be much richer than
all the others. He will use his wealth to
gain power. And he will stir up everyone
against the kingdom of Greece. [3]After
him, a mighty king will come to power.
He will rule with great power and do as
he pleases. [4]Not long after his rule ends,
his kingdom will be broken up. It will be
divided up into four parts. His children
will not receive it when he dies. And it
will not be as strong as his kingdom.
It will be pulled up by the roots. And it
will be given to others.

[5]"The king of Egypt will become
strong. But one of his commanders will
become even stronger. He will rule over
his own kingdom with great power.
[6]After many years, the two kingdoms
will join forces. The daughter of the
next king of Egypt will go to the king of
Syria. She will join forces with him. But
she will not hold on to her power. And
he and his power will not last either. In
those days she and her attendants will
die. They will die when the people she
trusts lie to her. The same thing will
happen to her father and the one who
helped her.

[7]"Someone from her family line will
take her place. He will attack the army
of the next king of Syria. Then he will
enter his fort. He will fight against that
army and win. [8]He will take the metal
statues of their gods. He will also take
away their priceless objects of silver
and gold. He will carry everything off to
Egypt. For many years he will leave the
king of Syria alone. [9]Then the king of
Syria will march into territory that was
controlled by Egypt. After that, he will
return to his own country. [10]His sons
will prepare for war. They will gather
a huge army. It will sweep along like
a mighty flood. The army will fight its
way as far as one of the Egyptian forts.

[11]"Another king of Egypt will march
out with mighty force. He will be very
angry. By then, another person will
have become king in Syria. The king
of Egypt will come to fight against him.
The king of Syria will gather a huge
army. But that army will lose the battle.
[12]His soldiers will be carried off. Then
the king of Egypt will be filled with
pride. He will kill many thousands of
soldiers. But his success will not last.
[13]The king of Syria will bring another
army together. It will be larger than
the first one. After several years, he will
march out with a huge army. It will
have everything it needs for battle.

[14]"In those times many people will
rise up against the next king of Egypt.
Lawless people in your own nation will
refuse to obey him. That is what you
saw in your vision. But they will not
succeed. [15]Then the king of Syria will
go to a certain city that has high walls
around it. He will build ramps against
them. And he will capture that city. The
forces of Egypt will not have the power to stop him. Even their best troops
will not be strong enough to stand up
against him. [16]He will do anything he
wants to. No one will be able to stand up
against him. He will take over the beautiful land of Israel. And he will have the
power to destroy it. [17]The king of Syria
will decide to come with the might of his
entire kingdom. He will join forces with
the king of Egypt. And the king of Syria
will give his daughter to him to become
his wife. The king of Syria will do this
in order to take control of Egypt. But
his plans will not succeed or help him.
[18]Then he will turn his attention to the
lands along the Mediterranean coast.
He will take over many of them. But a
commander will put an end to his proud
actions. He will turn his pride back on
him. [19]After this, the king of Syria will
return to the forts in his own country.
But he will trip and fall. And he will
never be seen again.

[20]"The next king after him will send
someone out to collect taxes. The taxes
will help maintain the glory of his kingdom. But in a few years the king will be
destroyed. It will not happen because
someone becomes angry with him or
kills him in battle.

[21]"After him, another king will take
his place. Many people will hate him.
He will not be honored as a king should
be. He will lead an army into the kingdom when its people feel secure. He will
make clever plans to capture it. [22]Then
he will sweep away a huge army. The
army and a prince of the covenant
will be destroyed. [23]The king of Syria will make an agreement with that
prince. But then the king of Syria will
not keep his word. He will rise to even
greater power with the help of only a

few people. 24 When the people in the richest areas feel secure, he will attack them. He will do what the kings before him could not do. And he will reward his followers with the goods and wealth he takes. He will make clever plans to take over the forts. But that will last for only a short time.

25 "He will become stronger and more confident. He will do that by gathering a large army. Then he will go to war against the next king of Egypt. That king will fight against him with a huge and very powerful army. But the king of Egypt will not be able to stand up against him. So the plans of the king of Syria will succeed. 26 The trusted advisers of the king of Egypt will try to destroy him. His army will be swept away. Many of his soldiers will be wounded or killed. 27 The kings of Syria and Egypt will sit at the same table. But in their hearts they will plan to do what is evil. And they will tell lies to each other. But it will not do them any good. God will put an end to their plans at his appointed time. 28 The king of Syria will return to his own country. He will go back there with great wealth. But he will make evil plans against the holy temple in Jerusalem. He will do a lot of harm to the temple and the people who worship there. Then he will return to his own country.

29 "At God's appointed time, the king of Syria will march south again. But this time things will turn out differently. 30 Roman ships will oppose him. He will lose hope. Then he will turn back. He will take out his anger against the holy temple. And he will do good to the Jews who desert it.

31 "His army will come and make the temple area 'unclean.' They will put a stop to the daily sacrifices. Then they will set up a hated thing that destroys. 32 He will pretend to praise those who have broken the covenant. He will lead them to do what is evil. But the people who know their God will firmly oppose him.

33 "Those who are wise will teach many others. But for a while, some of the wise will be killed by swords. Others will be burned to death. Still others will be made prisoners. Or they will be robbed of everything they have. 34 When that happens, they will receive a little help. Many who are not honest will join them. 35 So some of the wise people will suffer. They will be made pure in the fire. They will be made spotless until the time of the end. It will still come at God's appointed time.

The King Who Honors Himself

36 "A certain king will do as he pleases. He will honor himself. He will put himself above every god. He will say things against the greatest God of all. Those things have never been heard before. He will have success until God is not angry anymore. What God has decided to do must take place. 37 The king will not show any respect for the gods his people have always worshiped. There is a god desired by women. He will not respect that god either. He will not have respect for any god. Instead, he will put himself above all of them. 38 In place of them, he will worship a god of war. He will honor a god his people have not known before. He will give gold and silver to that god. He will bring jewels and expensive gifts to it. 39 He will attack the strongest forts. A new god will help him do it. He will greatly honor those who recognize him as their leader. He will make them rulers over many people. And he will give them land as a reward.

40 "A king in the south will go to war against him. It will happen at the time of the end. The king who will honor himself will rush out against him. He will come with chariots and horsemen. He will attack with a lot of ships. He will lead his army into many countries. He will sweep through them like a flood. 41 He will also march into the beautiful land of Israel. Many countries will fall. But Edom, Moab and the leaders of Ammon will be saved from his mighty hand. 42 His power will reach out into many countries. Even Egypt will not escape. 43 He will gain control of all Egypt's riches. He will take their gold and silver treasures. The people of Libya and Cush will be under his control. 44 But reports from the east and the north will terrify him. He will march out with great anger to destroy many people and wipe them out. 45 He will set up his royal tents. He will put them between the Mediterranean Sea and the beautiful

holy mountain of Zion. But his end will
come. And no one will help him.

The Time of the End

12 "At that time Michael will appear. He is the great prince of the
angels. He guards your people. There
will be a time of terrible suffering.
Things will be worse than at any time
since nations began. But at that time
of suffering your people will be saved.
Their names are written in the book of
life. 2 Many people who lie dead in their
graves will wake up. Some will rise up
to life that will never end. Others will
rise up to shame that will never end.
3 Those who are wise will shine like the
brightness of the sky. Those who lead
many others to do what is right will be
like the stars for ever and ever. 4 But I
want you to roll up this scroll, Daniel.
Seal it until the time of the end. Many
people will go here and there to increase
their knowledge."

5 Then I looked up and saw two other
angels. One was on this side of the Tigris
River. And one was on the other side.
6 The man who was dressed in linen was
above the waters of the river. One of the
angels spoke to him. He asked, "How
long will it be before these amazing
things come true?"

7 The man raised both hands toward
heaven. I heard him make a promise in
the name of the God who lives forever.
He answered me, "Three and a half
years. Then the power of the holy people
will finally be broken. And all these
things will come true."

8 I heard what he said. But I didn't
understand it. So I asked, "My master,
what will come of all this?"

9 He answered, "Go on your way, Daniel. The scroll is rolled up. It is sealed
until the time of the end. 10 Many people will be made pure in the fire. They
will be made spotless. But sinful people
will continue to be evil. Not one sinful
person will understand. But those who
are wise will.

11 "The daily sacrifices will be stopped.
And the hated thing that destroys will
be set up. After that, there will be 1,290
days. 12 Blessed are those who wait for
the 1,335 days and reach the end of them.

13 "Daniel, go on your way until the
end. Your body will rest in the grave.
Then at the end of the days you will
rise from the dead. And you will receive
what God has appointed for you."

HOSEA

Author: Hosea

Throughout Israel's history, God spoke to his people through prophets, calling his people to remember his promises and obey his commands. But God gave one of his prophets a special way to communicate this message. God told a prophet named Hosea to live this message out—to tell Israel God's message, not with words, but with his life.

Prophecy

I am the LORD your God . . .

Hosea had a wife named Gomer whom he loved, but she was unfaithful to him. Gomer left Hosea and chased other men, hoping they would love her back, but they never did. Hosea was heartbroken when Gomer left him, but God told Hosea to go find Gomer, forgive her, pay any of her debts, and bring her back home. God showed Hosea that his love for Gomer was like God's love for his people.

You see, God was demonstrating that even though his people disobeyed him again and again, loving and worshiping other gods instead of him, he continued to forgive them. He showered them with his love and compassion and made a way for them to come back to him. And one day God was going to send the perfect Savior as the ultimate expression of his love and faithfulness.

1 A message from the LORD came to
Hosea, the son of Beeri. The message
came while Uzziah, Jotham, Ahaz and
Hezekiah were kings of Judah. It also
came while Jeroboam was king of Israel. He was the son of Jehoash. Here is
what the LORD said to him.

Hosea's Wife and Children

2 The LORD began to speak through
Hosea. He said to him, "Go. Marry a
woman who has sex with anyone she
wants. Have children with her. Do this
because the people of the land are
like that kind of wife. They have not
been faithful to me." 3 So Hosea married Gomer. She was the daughter of
Diblaim. Gomer became pregnant and
had a son by Hosea.

4 Then the LORD said to Hosea, "Name
him Jezreel. That's because I will soon
punish Jehu's royal family. He killed
many people at the city of Jezreel. So I
will put an end to the kingdom of Israel.
5 At that time I will break their military
power. It will happen in the Valley of
Jezreel."

6 Gomer became pregnant again. She
had a daughter. Then the LORD said
to Hosea, "Name her Lo-Ruhamah."
Lo-Ruhamah means Not Loved. "That's
because I will no longer show love to the
people of Israel. I will not forgive them
anymore. 7 But I will show love to the
people of Judah. And I will save them.
I will not use bows or swords or other
weapons of war to do it. I will not save
them by using horses and horsemen
either. Instead, I will use my own power
to save them. I am the LORD their God.
And I will save them."

8 Later, Gomer stopped nursing Lo-
Ruhamah. After that, she had another
son. 9 Then the LORD said, "Name him
Lo-Ammi." Lo-Ammi means Not My
People. "That's because Israel is no
longer my people. And I am no longer
their God.

10 "But the time will come when the
people of Israel will be like the sand
on the seashore. It can't be measured
or counted. Now it is said about them,
'You are not my people.' But at that
time they will be called 'children of the
living God.' 11 The people of Judah and
Israel will come together again. They
will appoint one leader and come up
out of the land. And Jezreel's day will
be great.

2 "People of Israel, call your brothers
'My people.' And call your sisters
'My loved ones.'

Israel Is Punished and Brought Back to the LORD

2 "Tell your mother she is wrong.
Tell her she is wrong.
She isn't acting like a wife to me
anymore.
She no longer treats me as her
husband.
Tell her to stop looking and acting
like a prostitute.
Tell her not to let her lovers
lie on her breasts anymore.
3 If she doesn't stop it, I will strip her
naked.
I'll make her as bare as she was
on the day she was born.
I'll make her like a desert.
She will become like dry land.
And I'll let her die of thirst.

4 "I won't show my love to her
children.
They are the children of other
men.
5 Their mother hasn't been faithful
to me.
She who became pregnant with
them
has brought shame on herself.
She said, 'I will chase after my lovers.
They give me my food and water.
They provide me with wool and
linen.
They give me olive oil and wine.'
6 So I will block her path with bushes
that have thorns.
I'll build a wall around her.
Then she can't go to her lovers.
7 She will still chase after her lovers.
But she won't catch them.
She'll look for them.
But she won't find them.
Then she'll say,
'I'll go back to my husband.
That's where I was at first.
I was better off then than I am
now.'
8 She wouldn't admit that I was the
one
who gave her everything she had.
I provided her with grain, olive
oil and fresh wine.

I gave her plenty of silver and gold.
But she used it to make statues of Baal.
9 "So I will take away my grain when it gets ripe.
I'll take my fresh wine when it's ready.
I'll take back my wool and my linen.
I gave them to her to cover her naked body.
10 So now I'll uncover her body.
All her lovers will see it.
No one can stop me from punishing her.
11 I will put a stop to the special times she celebrates.
I'll bring an end to the feasts she celebrates each year.
I'll stop her New Moon feasts and her Sabbath days.
I'll bring all her appointed feasts to an end.
12 I will destroy her vines and her fig trees.
She said they were her pay from her lovers.
I'll make them like clumps of bushes and weeds.
Wild animals will eat them up.
13 Israel burned incense to the gods that were named Baal.
I will punish her
for all the times she did that.
She decorated herself with rings and jewelry.
Then she went after her lovers.
But she forgot all about me,"
declares the LORD.

14 "So now I am going to draw her back to me.
I will lead her into the desert.
There I will speak tenderly to her.
15 I will give her back her vineyards.
I will make the Valley of Achor a door of hope for her.
Then she will love me, as she did when she was young.
She will love me just as she did when she came up out of Egypt.

16 "A new day is coming," announces the LORD.
"Israel will call me 'my husband.'
She will no longer call me 'my master.'

in Hosea?

God is the Faithful Husband. God is forgiving, kind, and always loving. He makes a way for all people to return to him through Jesus.

17 She will no longer speak about the gods
that are named Baal.
She will not pray to them for help anymore.
18 At that time I will make a covenant
for the good of my people.
I will make it with the wild animals
and the birds in the sky.
It will also be made with the creatures
that move along the ground.
I will remove bows and swords
and other weapons of war from the land.
Then my people can lie down in safety.
19 I will make Israel my own.
She will belong to me forever.
I will do to her what is right and fair.
I will love her tenderly.
20 I will be faithful to her.
And she will recognize me as the LORD.

21 "So at that time I will answer her,"
announces the LORD.
"I will command the skies
to send rain on the earth.
22 Then the earth will produce grain,
olive oil and fresh wine.
And Israel will be called Jezreel.
That's because I will answer her prayers.

23 I will plant her in the land for
myself.
I will show my love to the one I
called Not My Loved One.
I will say, 'You are my people'
to those who were called Not My
People.
And they will say, 'You are my
God.'"

Hosea Brings His Wife Back to Himself

3 The LORD said to me, "Go. Show
your love to your wife again. She
is loved by another man. And she has
committed adultery. But I want you
to love her just as I love the people of
Israel. They turn to other gods. And they
love to offer raisin cakes to Baal and eat
them. In spite of that, I love my people."
2 So I bought Gomer for six ounces of
silver and 430 pounds of barley. 3 Then
I told her, "You must wait for me for a
long time. You must not be a prostitute.
You must not have sex with any man.
And I will be faithful to you too."
4 So the people of Israel will live for a
long time without a king or prince. They
won't have sacrifices or sacred stones.
They won't have sacred linen aprons or
statues of family gods. 5 After that, the
people of Israel will return to the LORD
their God. They will look to him and to
a king from the family line of David.
In the last days, they will tremble with
fear as they come to the LORD. And they
will receive his full blessing.

The LORD Brings Charges Against Israel

4 People of Israel, listen to the
LORD's message.
He is bringing charges
against you who live in Israel.
He says, "There is no faithfulness
or love in the land.
No one recognizes me as God.
2 People curse one another.
They tell lies and commit
murder.
They steal and commit adultery.
They break all my laws.
They keep spilling the blood of
other people.
3 That is why the land is drying up.
All those who live in it
are getting weaker and weaker.
The wild animals and the birds in
the sky are dying.
So are the fish in the ocean.

4 "But you priests should not blame
the people.
You should not find fault with
one another.
After all, your people
could also bring charges against
you.
5 You trip and fall day and night.
And the prophets fall down along
with you.
So I will destroy your nation.
She is the one who gave birth to
you.
6 My people are destroyed
because they do not know me.

"You priests have refused to obey me.
So I will refuse to accept you as
my priests.
You have not paid any attention to
my law.
So I will not let your children be
my priests.
7 The more priests there were,
the more they sinned against me.
They have traded their glorious
God for that shameful god
named Baal.
8 They live off the sins of my people.
And they want them to keep on
sinning.
9 So here is what I will do.
I will punish people and priests
alike.
I will judge them because of their
sinful lives.
I will pay them back
for the evil things they have done.
10 "My people will eat.
But they will not have enough.
They will have sex with prostitutes.
But they will not have any
children.
That's because they have
deserted me.
They have sex 11 with prostitutes.
They drink old wine and fresh
wine.
Their drinking has destroyed their
ability to understand.
12 My people ask a wooden statue of a
god for advice.
They get answers from a stick of
wood.

They are as unfaithful as
prostitutes.
They are not faithful to their
God.
13 They offer sacrifices on the
mountaintops.
They burn offerings on the hills.
They worship under oak, poplar
and terebinth trees.
The trees provide plenty of
shade.
So your daughters become
prostitutes.
And your daughters-in-law
commit adultery.

14 "I will not punish your daughters
when they become prostitutes.
I will not judge your
daughters-in-law
when they commit adultery.
After all, the men themselves have
sex with sinful women.
They offer sacrifices where
temple prostitutes earn their
living.
People who can't understand will
be destroyed!

15 "Israel, you are not faithful to me.
But I do not want Judah to
become guilty too.

"My people, do not go to Gilgal to
offer sacrifices.
Do not go up to Bethel to worship
other gods.
When you make a promise, do not
say,
'You can be sure that the LORD is
alive.'
16 The people of Israel are stubborn.
They are as stubborn as a young
cow.
So how can I take care of them
like lambs in a meadow?
17 The people of Ephraim have joined
themselves to other gods.
And nothing can be done to help
them.
18 They continue to be unfaithful
to me
even when their drinks are gone.
And their rulers love to do
shameful things.
19 A windstorm will blow all of them
away.
And their sacrifices will bring
shame on them.

The LORD Judges Israel

5 "Listen to me, you priests!
Pay attention, people of Israel!
Listen, you members of the royal
family!
Here is my decision against you.
You have been like a trap at
Mizpah.
You have been like a net spread
out on Mount Tabor.
2 You refuse to obey me.
You are knee-deep in killing.
So I will punish all of you.
3 I know all about the people of
Ephraim.
What Israel is doing is not
hidden from me.
Now they have joined themselves
to other gods.
They have made themselves
'unclean.'

4 "They can't return to me
because they have done so many
evil things.
In their hearts they long to act like
prostitutes.
They do not recognize me as the
LORD.
5 Israel's pride proves that they are
guilty.
The people of Ephraim trip and
fall because they have sinned.
Judah falls down along with them.
6 Israel will come to worship the LORD.
They will bring their animals to
offer as sacrifices.
But they will not find him.
He has turned away from them.
7 They are not faithful to the LORD.
Their children are not his.
When they celebrate their New
Moon feasts,
he will destroy their fields.

8 "My people, blow trumpets in
Gibeah!
Blow horns in Ramah!
Shout the battle cry in Bethel!
Say to the people of Benjamin,
'Lead on into battle!'
9 The people of Ephraim will be
completely destroyed
when it is time for me to punish
them.
They can be sure it will happen.
I am announcing it among their
tribes.

10 Judah's leaders have stolen some land.
They have moved their borders farther north.
So I will pour out my anger on them like a flood of water.
11 Ephraim will soon be crushed.
The Assyrians will stomp all over them.
It will happen because they have made up their minds
to chase after other gods.
12 I will be like a moth to Ephraim.
I will cause Judah to rot away.

13 "The people of Ephraim saw how sick they were.
The people of Judah saw that they were wounded.
Then Ephraim turned to Assyria for help.
They sent gifts to the great King Tiglath-Pileser.
But he is not able to make you well.
He can't heal your wounds.
14 I will be like a lion to Ephraim.
I will attack Judah like a powerful lion.
I will tear them to pieces.
I will drag them off.
Then I will leave them.
No one will be able to save them.
15 I will go back to my lion's den.
I will stay there until they pay the price for their sin.
Then they will turn to me.
They will suffer so much
that they will really want me to help them."

Israel Refuses to Turn Away From Their Sins

6 The people say, "Come.
Let us return to the LORD.
He has torn us to pieces.
But he will heal us.
He has wounded us.
But he'll bandage our wounds.
2 After two days he will give us new life.
On the third day he'll make us like new again.
Then we will enjoy his blessing.
3 Let's recognize him as the LORD.
Let's keep trying to know him.
You can be sure the sun will rise.
And you can be just as sure the LORD will appear.
He will come to renew us like the winter rains.
He will be like the spring rains that water the earth."

4 The LORD says, "Ephraim, what can I do with you?
And what can I do with you, Judah?
Your love for me vanishes like the morning mist.
It soon disappears like the early dew.
5 So I used the words of my prophets to cut you in pieces.
I used my words to put you to death.
Then my judgments blazed out like the sun.
6 I want mercy and not sacrifice.
I want you to recognize me as God
instead of bringing me burnt offerings.
7 Just as at the city of Adam, they disobeyed me,
they have broken the covenant I made with them.
They were not faithful to me there.
8 Ramoth Gilead is a city where sinful people live.
It is stained with footprints of blood.

What does God want from me?

God wants you to love and be faithful to him and others. Being loving and faithful means more to God than anything you could give him.

Can you find the following verse?
HOSEA 6:6

[9]On the road to Shechem, groups of
priests act like robbers.
They hide and wait to attack
people.
They murder them.
So they carry out their evil plans.
[10]I have seen a horrible thing in
Israel.
The people of Ephraim are
unfaithful to their own God.
The people of Israel are 'unclean.'
[11]"People of Judah, I have also
appointed a time
for you to be destroyed.

"I would like to bless my people
with great success again.

7 [1]I would like to heal Israel.
But when I try to, Ephraim's sins
are brought out into the open.
The crimes of Samaria
are made known to everyone.
The people tell lies.
They break into houses and steal.
They rob others in the streets.
[2]But they do not realize
that I remember all the evil
things they do.
Their sins pile up and cover them.
I am always aware of their sins.

[3]"Their evil conduct even makes the
king glad.
Their lies make the princes
happy.
[4]But all the people are unfaithful to
the king.
Their anger against him burns
like the coals in an oven.
The baker does not even need to
stir up the fire
until the dough is ready."

[5]On special days to honor our king,
the princes get drunk with wine.
And the king enjoys the party.
He joins hands with those
who pretend to be faithful to
him.
[6]Their hearts are as hot as an oven.
They make evil plans to get rid of
him.
Their anger burns like a slow fire
all night.
In the morning it blazes out like
a flaming fire.
[7]All of them are as hot as an oven.
They destroy their rulers.
All their kings fall from power.
But none of them calls on the
LORD for help.

[8]The people of Ephraim mix with
the nations.
They are like a thin loaf of bread
that is baked on only one side.
[9]People from other lands make
them weaker and weaker.
But they don't realize it.
Their hair is becoming gray.
But they don't even notice it.
[10]The pride of Israel proves that they
are guilty.
But in spite of everything,
they don't return to the LORD their
God.
They don't go to him for help.

[11]The LORD says,

"The people of Ephraim are like a
dove.
They are easily tricked.
They do not have any sense at all.
First they call out to Egypt for help.
Then they turn to Assyria.
[12]When they send for help,
I will throw my net over them.
I will capture them like the birds in
the sky.
When I hear them gathering like
birds,
I will catch them.
[13]How terrible it will be for them!
They have wandered away
from me.
So they will be destroyed.
That's because they have refused
to obey me.
I long to save them.
But they tell lies about me.
[14]They do not cry out to me from
their hearts.
Instead, they just lie on their
beds and sob.
They cut themselves when they
pray to their gods
for grain and fresh wine.
But they turn away from me.
[15]I brought them up and made them
strong.
But they make evil plans
against me.
[16]I am the Most High God. But they
do not turn to me.
They are like a bow that does not
shoot straight.

Their leaders will be killed by
swords.
They will die because they have
spoken too proudly.
The people of Egypt
will make fun of them."

Israel Will Harvest a Windstorm

8 The LORD said to me,

"Put a trumpet to your lips!
Give a warning to my people!
Assyria is like an eagle.
It is ready to attack my land.
My people have broken the
covenant I made with them.
They have refused to obey my
law.
2 Israel shouts to me,
'We recognize you as our God!'
3 But they have turned away from
what is good.
So an enemy will chase them.
4 My people appoint kings I do not
want.
They choose princes without my
permission.
They use their silver and gold
to make statues of gods.
That is how they destroy
themselves."
5 The LORD says, "People of Samaria,
throw out your god that looks
like a calf!
I am very angry with them.
How long will it be until they are
able
to remain faithful to me?
6 Their calf is not God.
A skilled worker from Israel
made it.
But that calf of Samaria will be
broken to pieces."

7 The LORD says,

"Worshiping other gods is like
worshiping the wind.
It is like planting worthless seeds.
Assyria is like a windstorm.
That is all my people will
harvest.
There are no heads of grain
on the stems that will come up.
So they will not produce any
flour.
Even if they did produce grain,
the Assyrians would eat all of it up.
8 So the people of Israel are
swallowed up.
Now they are among the nations
like something no one wants.
9 They have gone up to Assyria for
help.
They are like a wild donkey
that wanders around by itself.
Ephraim's people have sold
themselves
to their Assyrian lovers.
10 They have sold themselves to the
nations
to get their help.
But now I will gather them together.
They will get weaker and weaker.
The mighty kings of Assyria will
crush them.

11 "Ephraim built many altars where
they sacrificed
sin offerings to other gods.
So their altars have become
places where they commit sin.
12 In my law I wrote down many
things for their good.
But they considered those things
as something strange.
13 They offer sacrifices as gifts to me.
They eat the meat of the animals
they bring.
But the LORD is not pleased with
any of this.
He will remember the evil things
they have done.
He will punish them for their
sins.
And they will return to Egypt.
14 Israel has forgotten the God who
made them.
They have built palaces for
themselves.
Judah has built forts in many
towns.
But I will send down fire on their
cities.
It will burn up their forts."

Israel Will Be Punished

9 Israel, don't be joyful.
Don't be glad as the other nations
are.
You haven't been faithful to your
God.
You love to get paid for being a
prostitute.
Your pay is the grain at every
threshing floor.

[2] But soon there won't be any grain
or wine to feed you.
There won't even be any fresh
wine.
[3] You won't remain in the LORD's
land.
Ephraim, you will return to
Egypt.
You will eat "unclean" food in
Assyria.
[4] You won't pour out wine offerings
to the LORD.
Your sacrifices won't please him.
They'll be like the bread people eat
when someone dies.
Everyone who eats those
sacrifices will be "unclean."
They themselves will have to eat
that kind of food.
They can't bring it into the LORD's
temple.

[5] What will you do when your
appointed feasts come?
What will you do on the LORD's
special days?
[6] Some of you will escape without
being destroyed.
But you will die in Egypt.
Your bodies will be buried at
Memphis.
Weeds will cover your treasures of
silver.
Thorns will grow up in your
tents.
[7] The time when God will punish you
is coming.
The day when he will judge you
is near.
I want Israel to know this.
You have committed many sins.
And you hate me very much.
That's why you think the prophet is
foolish.
You think the person the LORD
speaks through is crazy.
[8] People of Ephraim, the prophet,
along with my God,
is warning you of danger.
But you set traps for him
everywhere he goes.
You hate him so much
you even wait for him in God's
house.
[9] You have sunk very deep into sin,
just as your people did at Gibeah
long ago.
God will remember the evil things
they have done.
He will punish them for their
sins.

[10] The LORD says,

"When I first found Israel,
it was like finding grapes in the
desert.
When I saw your people of long
ago,
it was like seeing the early fruit
on a fig tree.
But then they went to Baal Peor.
There they gave themselves to
that shameful god named Baal.
They became as evil as the god
they loved.
[11] Ephraim's greatness and glory will
be gone.
It will fly away like a bird.
Women will no longer have
children.
They will not be able to get
pregnant.
[12] But suppose they do have children.
Then I will kill every one of them.
How terrible it will be for them
when I turn away from them!
[13] Tyre is planted in a pleasant place.
And so is Ephraim.
But the Assyrians will kill
Ephraim's children."

[14] LORD, what should you do to
Ephraim's people?
Give them women whose babies
die before they are born.
Give them women whose breasts
have no milk.

[15] The LORD says,

"My people did many evil things in
Gilgal.
That is why I hated them there.
They committed many sins.
So I will drive them out of my
land.
I will not love them anymore.
All their leaders refuse to
obey me.
[16] Ephraim is like a worthless plant.
Its roots are dried up.
It does not produce any fruit.
Suppose Ephraim's people have
children.
Then I will kill the children they
love so much."

17 My God will turn his back on his people.
They have not obeyed him.
So they will wander among other nations.

10 Israel was like a spreading vine.
They produced fruit for themselves.
As they grew more fruit,
they built more altars.
As their land became richer,
they made more beautiful the sacred stones they worshiped.
2 Their hearts are dishonest.
So now they must pay for their sins.
The LORD will tear down their altars.
He'll destroy their sacred stones.

3 Then they'll say, "We don't have a king.
That's because we didn't have any respect for the LORD.
But suppose we did have a king.
What could he do for us?"
4 They make a lot of promises.
They make agreements among themselves.
They make promises they don't mean to keep.
So court cases spring up
like poisonous weeds in a plowed field.
5 The people who live in Samaria are filled with fear.
They are afraid for their god that looks like a calf.
They're afraid it will be carried off from Beth Aven, that evil town.
They will mourn over it.
So will the priests who led them to worship it.
The priests were full of joy
because their statue was so glorious.
But it will be captured
and taken far away from them.
6 It will be carried off to Assyria.
The people of Ephraim will be forced
to give it to the great king.
They will be dishonored.
Israel will be ashamed
of its agreements with other nations.
7 Samaria's king will be destroyed.
He will be like a twig swept away by a river.
8 The high places where Israel worshiped other gods
will be destroyed.
That's where they sinned against the LORD.
Thorns and weeds will grow up there.
They will cover the altars.
Then the people will say to the mountains, "Cover us!"
They'll say to the hills, "Fall on us!"

9 The LORD says,

"Israel, you have done evil things
ever since your people sinned at Gibeah long ago.
And you are still doing what is evil.
War will come again
to those who sinned at Gibeah.
10 I will punish them when I want to.
Nations will gather together to fight against them.
They will put them in chains
because they have committed so many sins.
11 Ephraim was like a well-trained young cow.
It loved to thresh grain.
So I will put a yoke
on its pretty neck.
I will make Ephraim do hard work.
Judah also must plow.
So all the people of Jacob
must break up the ground.
12 Your hearts are as hard as a field
that has not been plowed.
If you change your ways,
you will produce good crops.
So plant the seeds of doing what is right.
Then you will harvest the fruit of your faithful love.
It is time to seek the LORD.
When you do, he will come
and shower his blessings on you.
13 But you have planted the seeds of doing what is wrong.
So you have harvested the fruit of your evil conduct.
You have had to eat the fruit of your lies.

You have trusted in your own strength.
You have depended on your many soldiers.
14 But the roar of battle will come against you.
All your forts will be completely destroyed.
It will happen just as Shalman destroyed Beth Arbel in a battle.
Mothers and their children were smashed on the ground.
15 People of Bethel, that will happen to you.
You have committed far too many sins.
When the time comes for me to punish you,
the king of Israel will be completely destroyed."

God Loves Israel

11 The LORD continues,

"When Israel was a young nation, I loved them.
I chose to bring my son out of Egypt.
2 But the more I called out to Israel,
the more they went away from me.
They brought sacrifices to the statues of the gods
that were named Baal.
And they burned incense to them.
3 I taught Ephraim to walk.
I took them up in my arms.
But they did not realize
I was the one who took care of them.
4 I led them with kindness and love.
I was to them like a person who lifts
a little child to their cheek.
I bent down and fed them.

5 "But they refuse to turn away from their sins.
So they will return to Egypt.
And Assyria will rule over them.
6 A sword will flash in their cities.
It will destroy the prophets who teach lies.
It will bring an end to their plans.
7 My people have made up their minds
to turn away from me.
Even if they call me the Most High God,
I will certainly not honor them."
8 The LORD continues,

"People of Ephraim, how can I give you up?
Israel, how can I hand you over to your enemies?
Can I destroy you as I did the town of Admah?
Can I treat you like Zeboyim?
My heart is stirred inside me.
It is filled with pity for you.
9 I will not be so angry with you anymore.
I will not completely destroy you again.
After all, I am God.
I am not a mere man.
I am the Holy One among you.
I will not direct my anger against their cities.
10 I will roar like a lion against my enemies.
Then the LORD's people will follow him.
When he roars, his children will come home trembling with fear.
They will return from the west.
11 They will come from Egypt, trembling like sparrows.
They will return from Assyria, flying in like doves.
I will settle you again in your homes,"
announces the LORD.

Israel Has Sinned

12 The people of Ephraim tell me nothing but lies.
Israel has not been honest with me.
And Judah continues to wander away from God.
They have deserted the faithful Holy One.
12 1 The people of Ephraim look to others for help.
It's like chasing the wind.
The wind they keep chasing is hot and dry.
They tell more and more lies.
They are always hurting others.
They make a peace treaty with Assyria.
They send olive oil to Egypt to get help.

[2] The LORD is bringing charges
against Judah.
He will punish Jacob's people
because of how they act.
He'll pay them back
for the evil things they've done.
[3] Even before Jacob was born,
he was holding on to his brother's
heel.
When he became a man,
he struggled with God.
[4] At Peniel he struggled with the
angel and won.
Jacob wept and begged for his
blessing.
God also met with him at Bethel.
He talked with him there.
[5] He is the LORD God who rules over all.
His name is the LORD.
[6] People of Jacob, you must return to
your God.
You must hold on to love and do
what is fair.
You must trust in your God always.

key verse You must return to your God. You must hold on to love and do what is fair. You must trust in your God always. HOSEA 12:6

[7] You are like a trader who uses
dishonest scales.
You love to cheat others.
[8] People of Ephraim, you brag,
"We are very rich.
We've become wealthy.
And no one can prove we sinned
to gain all this wealth."

[9] The LORD says,

"I have been the LORD your God
ever since you came out of Egypt.
But I will make you live in tents
again.
That is what you did when you
celebrated
the Feast of Booths in the desert.
[10] I spoke to the prophets.
They saw many visions.
I gave you warnings through them."

[11] The people of Gilead are evil!
They aren't worth anything!
Gilgal's people sacrifice bulls to
other gods.
Their altars will become like piles
of stones
on a plowed field.
[12] Jacob ran away to the country of
Aram.
There Israel served Laban to get
a wife.
He took care of sheep to pay for her.
[13] The prophet Moses brought Israel
up from Egypt.
The LORD used him to take care
of them.
[14] But Ephraim's people have made
the LORD very angry.
Their Lord will hold them
accountable for the blood
they've spilled.
He'll pay them back for the
shameful things they've done.

The LORD Is Angry With Israel

13 When the tribe of Ephraim
spoke,
the other tribes trembled with
fear.
Ephraim was honored in Israel.
But its people sinned by worshiping
Baal.
So they were as good as dead.
[2] Now they sin more and more.
They use their silver
to make statues of gods for
themselves.
The statues come from their own
clever ideas.
Skilled workers make all of them.
The people pray to these gods.
They offer human sacrifices to
them.
They kiss the gods that look like
calves.
[3] So these people will vanish like the
morning mist.
They will soon disappear like the
early dew.
They will be like straw
that the wind blows around on a
threshing floor.
They will be like smoke
that escapes through a window.

[4] The LORD says,

"People of Israel, I have been the
LORD your God
ever since you came out of Egypt.

You must not worship any god
but me.
You must not have any savior
except me.
5 I took care of you in the desert.
It was a land of burning heat.
6 I fed them until they were satisfied.
Then they became proud.
They forgot all about me.
7 So I will leap on them like a lion.
I will hide and wait
beside the road like a leopard.
8 I will attack them like a bear
that is robbed of her cubs.
I will rip them wide open.
Like a lion I will eat them up.
Like a wild animal I will tear
them apart.

9 "Israel, you will be destroyed.
I helped you. But you turned
against me.
10 Where is your king?
Wasn't he supposed to save you?
Where are the rulers in all your
towns?
You said, 'Give us a king and
princes.'
11 So I became angry and gave you a
king.
Then I took him away from you.
12 Ephraim's guilt is piling up.
I am keeping a record of all their
sins.
13 They will suffer pain like a woman
having a baby.
They are like foolish children.
It is time for them to be born.
But they don't have the sense
to come out of their mother's
body.

14 "I will set these people free from
the power of the grave.
I will save them from death.
Death, where are your plagues?
Grave, where is your power to
destroy?

"I will no longer pity Ephraim.
15 Even though they are doing well
among the other tribes,
trouble will come to them.
I will send a hot and dry wind from
the east.
It will blow in from the desert.
Their springs will not have any
water.
Their wells will dry up.
All their treasures
will be taken out of their
storerooms.
16 The people of Samaria must pay
for their sins.
They have refused to obey me.
They will be killed by swords.
Their little children will be
smashed on the ground.
Their pregnant women will be
ripped wide open."

The LORD Blesses Those Who Turn Away From Sin

14 Israel, return to the LORD your
God.
Your sins have destroyed you!
2 Tell the LORD you are turning away
from your sins.
Return to him.
Say to him,
"Forgive us for all our sins.
Please be kind to us.
Welcome us back to you.
Then our lips will offer you our
praise.
3 Assyria can't save us.
We won't trust in our war horses.
Our own hands have made statues
of gods.
But we will never call them our
gods again.
We are like children whose fathers
have died.
But you show us your tender
love."

4 Then the LORD will answer,

"My people always wander away
from me.
But I will put an end to that.
My anger has turned away from
them.
Now I will love them freely.
5 I will be like the dew to Israel.
They will bloom like a lily.
They will send their roots down
deep
like a cedar tree in Lebanon.
6 They will spread out like new
branches.
They will be as beautiful as an
olive tree.
They will smell as sweet as the
cedar trees in Lebanon.
7 Once again my people will live
in the safety of my shade.

They will grow like grain.
They will bloom like vines.
And Israel will be as famous
as wine from Lebanon.
8 Ephraim will have nothing more to
do with other gods.
I will answer the prayers of my
people.
I will take good care of them.
I will be like a healthy juniper tree
to them.
All the fruit they bear will come
from me."

9 If someone is wise, they will realize
that what I've said is true.
If they have understanding,
they will know what it means.
The ways of the LORD are right.
People who are right with God
live the way he wants them to.
But those who refuse to obey him
trip and fall.

JOEL

Author: Joel

Joel was a prophet in Judah at a time when a terrible swarm of locusts invaded the land. The locusts ate the crops of the people of Judah, leaving the people hungry and desperate. Joel told God's people that what they were experiencing was a picture of their own rebellion against God. He challenged them to think about their hungry bellies as an example of how hungry they could be for God. Joel also warned them that if they continued in their disobedience, things could get even worse.

But God also gave Joel a message of hope for his people. God told them there was going to be a time of blessing in their future. At this time their hunger for God would be satisfied because God's Spirit was going to be poured out on both young and old, sons and daughters (see Joel 2:28–29). A day was coming when God would judge sin—Joel called this future day "the day of the Lord" (Joel 2:1)—but God also promised to bring restoration.

All the times God saved his people from their enemies were meant to point them toward the coming Savior who would destroy sin and offer salvation to a hungry and desperate world.

1

A message from the LORD came to Joel, the son of Pethuel. Here is what Joel said.

Locusts Attack the Land

2 Elders, listen to me.
Pay attention, all you who live in the land.
Has anything like this ever happened in your whole life?
Did it ever happen to your people who lived long ago?
3 Tell your children about it.
Let them tell their children.
And let their children tell it to those who live after them.
4 The giant locusts have eaten what the common locusts have left.
The young locusts have eaten what the giant locusts have left.
And other locusts have eaten what the young locusts have left.
5 Get up and weep, you people who drink too much!
Cry, all you who drink wine!
Cry because the fresh wine has been taken away from you.
6 The locusts are like a mighty army that has marched into our land.
There are so many of them they can't even be counted.
Their teeth are as sharp as a lion's teeth.
They are like the fangs of a female lion.
7 The locusts have completely destroyed our vines.
They have wiped out our fig trees.
They've stripped off the bark and thrown it away.
They've left the branches bare.
8 My people, mourn like a virgin who is dressed in the clothes of sadness.
She is sad because she has lost the young man she was going to marry.
9 No one brings grain offerings and drink offerings
to the LORD's house anymore.
So the priests who serve the LORD are filled with sorrow.
10 Our fields are wiped out.
The ground is dried up.

God is the Saving One. God offers salvation to all people and gives them his Spirit to help them live by faith.

The grain is destroyed.
The fresh wine is gone.
And there isn't any more olive oil.
11 Farmers, be sad.
Cry, you who grow vines.
Mourn because the wheat and barley are gone.
The crops in the fields are destroyed.
12 The vines and fig trees are dried up.
The pomegranate, palm and apple trees
don't have any fruit on them.
In fact, all the trees in the fields are dried up.
And my people's joy has faded away.

A Call to Mourn

13 Priests, put on the clothing of sadness and mourn.
Cry, you who serve at the altar.
Come, you who serve my God in the temple.
Spend the night dressed in the clothes of sadness.
Weep because no one brings grain offerings and drink offerings
to the house of your God anymore.
14 Announce a holy fast.
Tell the people not to eat anything.
Gather them together for a special service.
Send for the elders
and all who live in the land.

Have them come to the house of
the LORD your God.
And pray to him.

15 The day of the LORD is near.
How sad it will be on that day!
The Mighty One is coming to
destroy you.

16 Our food has been taken away
right in front of our eyes.
There isn't any joy or gladness
in the house of our God.
17 The seeds have dried up in the
ground.
The grain is also gone.
The storerooms have been destroyed.
The barns are broken down.
18 Listen to the cattle groan!
The herds wander around.
They don't have any grass to eat.
The flocks of sheep are also
suffering.

19 LORD, I call out to you.
Fire has burned up the desert
grasslands.
Flames have destroyed all the
trees in the fields.
20 Even the wild animals cry out to
you for help.
The streams of water have dried up.
Fire has burned up the desert
grasslands.

The LORD Sends an Army of Locusts

2 Priests, blow the trumpets in
Zion.
Give a warning on my holy
mountain.
Let everyone who lives in the land
tremble with fear.
The day of the LORD is coming.
It is very near.
2 That day will be dark and sad.
It will be black and cloudy.
A huge army of locusts is coming.
They will spread across the
mountains
like the sun when it rises.
There has never been an army
like it.
And there will never be another
for all time to come.

3 Like fire they eat up everything in
their path.
Behind them it looks as if flames
have burned the land.
In front of them the land is like the
Garden of Eden.
Behind them it is a dry and
empty desert.
Nothing escapes them.
4 They look like horses.
Like war horses they charge ahead.
5 They sound like chariots as they
leap over the mountaintops.
They crackle like fire burning up
dry weeds.
They are like a mighty army
that is ready for battle.

6 When people see them, they
tremble with fear.
All their faces turn pale.
7 The locusts charge ahead like
warriors.
They climb over walls like soldiers.
All of them march in line.
They don't turn to the right or
the left.
8 They don't bump into one another.
Each of them marches straight
ahead.
They charge through everything
that tries to stop them.
But they still stay in line.
9 They attack a city.
They run along its wall.
They climb into houses.
They enter through windows like
robbers.

10 As they march forward, the earth
shakes.
The heavens tremble as they
approach.
The sun and moon grow dark.
And the stars stop shining.
11 The LORD thunders with his mighty
voice
as he leads his army.
He has so many forces they can't
even be counted.
The army that obeys his
commands is mighty.
The day of the LORD is great and
terrifying.
Who can live through it?

Let Your Hearts Be Broken

12 The LORD announces to his people,

"Return to me with all your heart.
There is still time.
Do not eat any food.
Weep and mourn."

[13] Don't just tear your clothes to show
how sad you are.
Let your hearts be broken.
Return to the LORD your God.
He is gracious.
He is tender and kind.
He is slow to get angry.
He is full of love.
He won't bring his judgment.
He won't destroy you.

key verse
Return to the LORD your God. He is gracious. He is tender and kind. He is slow to get angry. He is full of love. JOEL 2:13

[14] Who knows? He might turn toward
you
and not bring his judgment.
He might even give you his
blessing.
Then you can bring grain offerings
and drink offerings
to the LORD your God.

[15] Priests, blow the trumpets in Zion.
Announce a holy fast.
Tell the people not to eat anything.
Gather them together for a
special service.
[16] Bring them together.
Set all of them apart to me.
Bring together the elders.
Gather the children and the
babies
who are still nursing.
Let the groom leave his bedroom.
Let the bride leave their
marriage bed.
[17] Let the priests who serve the LORD
weep.
Let them cry between the temple
porch and the altar.
Let them say, "LORD, spare your
people.
Don't let others make fun of
them.
Don't let the nations laugh at
them.
Don't let them tease your people
and say,
'Where is their God?' "

The LORD Answers the Prayer of His People

[18] Then the LORD was concerned for
his land.
He took pity on his people.

[19] He replied,

"I am sending you grain, olive oil
and fresh wine.
It will be enough to satisfy you
completely.
I will never allow other nations
to make fun of you again.

[20] "I will drive far away from you
the army that comes from the
north.
I will send some of its forces
into a dry and empty land.
Its eastern troops will drown in the
Dead Sea.
Its western troops will drown in
the Mediterranean Sea.
Their dead bodies will stink."

The LORD has done great things.
[21] Land of Judah, don't be afraid.
Be glad and full of joy.
The LORD has done great things.
[22] Wild animals, don't be afraid.
The desert grasslands are
turning green again.
The trees are bearing their fruit.
The vines and fig trees are
producing rich crops.
[23] People of Zion, be glad.
Be joyful because of what the
LORD your God has done.
He has given you the right amount
of rain in the fall.
That's because he is faithful.
He has sent you plenty of showers.
He has sent fall and spring rains
alike,
just as he did before.
[24] Your threshing floors will be
covered with grain.
Olive oil and fresh wine will spill
over
from the places where they are
stored.

[25] The LORD says,

"I sent a great army of locusts to
attack you.
They included common locusts,
giant locusts,
young locusts and other locusts.

I will make up for the years
they ate your crops.
26 You will have plenty to eat.
It will satisfy you completely.
Then you will praise me.
I am the LORD your God.
I have done wonderful things for you.
My people will never again be
put to shame.
27 You will know that I am with you in
Israel.
I am the LORD your God.
There is no other God.
So my people will never again be
put to shame.

The Day of the LORD Is Coming

28 "After that, I will pour out my Spirit
on all people.
Your sons and daughters will
prophesy.
Your old men will have dreams.
Your young men will have
visions.
29 In those days I will pour out my
Spirit
on those who serve me, men and
women alike.
30 I will show wonders in the heavens
and on the earth.
There will be blood and fire and
clouds of smoke.
31 The sun will become dark.
The moon will turn red like
blood.
It will happen before the great
and terrible day of the LORD
comes.
32 Everyone who calls out to me will
be saved.
On Mount Zion and in Jerusalem
some of my people will be left
alive.
I have chosen them.
That is what I have promised.

The LORD Judges the Nations

3 "At that time I will bless Judah
and Jerusalem
with great success again.
2 I will gather together all the
nations.
I will bring them down to the
Valley of Jehoshaphat.
There I will put them on trial.
I will judge them for what they
have done
to my people Israel.
They scattered them among the
nations.
They divided up my land among
themselves.
3 They cast lots for my people.
They sold boys into slavery to get
prostitutes.
They sold girls to buy some wine
to drink.

4 "Tyre and Sidon, why are you doing
things like that to me? And why are you
doing them, all you people in Philistia?
Are you trying to get even with me for
something I have done? If you are, I
will pay you back for it in a quick and
speedy way. 5 You took my silver and
gold. You carried off my finest treasures
to your temples. 6 You sold the people
of Judah and Jerusalem to the Greeks.
You wanted to send them far away from
their own country.

7 "But now I will stir them up into action. I will bring them back from the
places you sold them to. And I will do
to you what you did to them. 8 I will sell
your sons and daughters to the people
of Judah. And they will sell them to the
Sabeans. The Sabeans are a nation that
is far away." The LORD has spoken.

9 Announce this among the nations.
Tell them to prepare for battle.
Nations, get your soldiers ready!
Bring all your fighting men
together
and march out to attack.
10 Hammer your plows into swords.
Hammer your pruning tools into
spears.
Let anyone who is weak say,
"I am strong!"
11 Come quickly, all you surrounding
nations.
Gather together in the Valley of
Jehoshaphat.

LORD, send down your soldiers from
heaven!

12 The LORD says,

"Stir up the nations into action!
Let them march into the valley
where I will judge them.
I will take my seat in court.
I will judge all the surrounding
nations.
13 My soldiers, swing your blades.
The nations are ripe for harvest.

Is there anyone who God will not save?

God promises to save anyone who asks him for salvation. He doesn't turn away anyone who repents of their sin and asks Jesus to be the Lord of their life.

Can you find the following verse?

JOEL 2:32

Come and stomp on them as if they
were grapes.
Crush them until the winepress
of my anger is full.
Do it until the wine spills over
from the places where it is stored.
The nations have committed far
too many sins!"

14 Huge numbers of soldiers are
gathered in the valley
where the LORD will hand down
his sentence.
The day of the LORD is near in
that valley.
15 The sun and moon will become
dark.
The stars won't shine anymore.
16 The LORD will roar like a lion from
Jerusalem.
His voice will sound like thunder
from Zion.
The earth and the heavens will
tremble.
But the LORD will keep the people of
Israel safe.
He will be a place of safety for
them.

The LORD Blesses His People

17 The LORD says,

"You will know that I am the LORD
your God.
I live in Zion.
It is my holy mountain.
Jerusalem will be my holy city.
People from other lands
will never again attack it.

18 "At that time fresh wine will drip
from the mountains.
Milk will flow down from the
hills.
Water will run through all
Judah's valleys.
A fountain will flow out of my
temple.
It will water the places where
acacia trees grow.
19 But Egypt will be deserted.
Edom will become a dry and
empty desert.
They did terrible harm to the
people of Judah.
My people were not guilty of
doing anything wrong.
But Egypt and Edom spilled their
blood anyway.
20 My people will live in Judah and
Jerusalem forever.
The land will be their home for
all time to come.
21 Egypt and Edom have spilled my
people's blood.
Should I let them escape my
judgment?
No, I will not."

The LORD lives in Zion!

AMOS

Author: Amos

Amos was a fig tree farmer and a shepherd who lived in Israel. In some ways he might have seemed like an ordinary Israelite, but God used Amos in extraordinary ways to call his people back to himself. You see, Amos was also a prophet of God. Amos lived during a time when Israel had a horrible king. This king encouraged God's people to worship false gods and idols, and he didn't take care of the poor. Instead, he stored up a bunch of wealth for himself. This king was, in so many ways, the opposite of what God wanted for his people!

Prophecy

I am the LORD your God . . .

God's people were still going through the motions of worshiping God by doing things like making sacrifices, but as soon as the ceremonies were over, they treated other people unfairly. God directed Amos to tell his people: "Your worship is a bunch of baloney! You go through the motions and say you love me, but you don't show me true worship by the way you live." Through sermons, poems, and visions, Amos told God's people to turn from their false worship to true worship. God promised that one day he would send a Savior to change their whole lives for the better.

1 These are the words of Amos. He was a shepherd from the town of Tekoa. Here is the vision he saw concerning Israel. It came to him two years before the earthquake. At that time Uzziah was king of Judah. Jeroboam, the son of Jehoash, was king of Israel. Here are the words of Amos.

2 He said,

"The LORD roars like a lion from
Jerusalem.
His voice sounds like thunder
from Zion.
The grasslands of the shepherds
turn brown.
The top of Mount Carmel dries up."

The LORD Judges Israel's Neighbors

3 The LORD says,

"The people of Damascus have
sinned again and again.
So I will judge them.
They used threshing sleds with iron
teeth
to crush Gilead's people.
4 So I will send fire to destroy the
palace of King Hazael.
It will burn up the forts of his son
Ben-Hadad.
5 I will break down the city gate of
Damascus.
I will kill the king
who lives in the Valley of Aven,
that evil place.
He holds the ruler's scepter in Beth
Eden.
The people of Aram will be taken
away to Kir as prisoners,"
says the LORD.

6 The LORD says,

"The people of Gaza have sinned
again and again.
So I will judge them.
They captured whole communities.
They sold them to Edom.
7 So I will send fire to destroy the
walls of Gaza.
It will burn up its forts.
8 I will kill the king of Ashdod.
He holds the ruler's scepter in
Ashkelon.
I will use my power against Ekron.
Every single Philistine will die,"
says the LORD and King.

9 The LORD says,

"The people of Tyre have sinned
again and again.
So I will judge them.
They captured whole communities.
They sold them to Edom.
They did not honor the treaty
of friendship they had made.
10 So I will send fire to destroy the
walls of Tyre.
It will burn up its forts."

11 The LORD says,

"The people of Edom have sinned
again and again.
So I will judge them.
They chased Israel with swords
that were ready to strike them
down.
They killed the women of the
land.
They were angry all the time.
Their anger was like a fire that
blazed out.
It could not be stopped.
12 So I will send fire to destroy the city
of Teman.
It will burn up Bozrah's forts."

13 The LORD says,

"The people of Ammon have sinned
again and again.
So I will judge them.
They ripped open the pregnant
women in Gilead.
They wanted to add land to their
territory.
14 So I will set fire to destroy the walls
of Rabbah.
It will burn up its forts.
War cries will be heard on that day
of battle.
Strong winds will blow on that
stormy day.
15 Ammon's king will be carried away.
So will his officials,"
says the LORD.

2 The LORD says,

"The people of Moab have sinned
again and again.
So I will judge them.
They burned the bones
of Edom's king to ashes.
2 So I will send fire to destroy Moab.
It will burn up Kerioth's forts.

in Amos?

God is the Refining Fire. God wants his people to be transformed so what they think and believe matches what they say and do. He promises to purify them to be more like him.

Moab will come crashing down
with a loud noise.
War cries will be heard.
So will the blast of trumpets.
3 I will kill Moab's ruler.
I will also kill all its officials,"
says the LORD.

4 The LORD says,

"The people of Judah have sinned
again and again.
So I will judge them.
They have refused to obey my law.
They have not kept my rules.
Other gods have led them astray.
Their people of long ago
worshiped those gods.
5 So I will send fire to destroy Judah.
It will burn up Jerusalem's forts."

The LORD Judges Israel

6 The LORD says,

"The people of Israel have sinned
again and again.
So I will judge them.
They sell into slavery those who
have done no wrong.
They trade needy people
for a mere pair of sandals.
7 They grind the heads of the poor
into the dust of the ground.
They refuse to be fair to those
who are crushed.
A father and his son have sex with
the same girl.
They treat my name as if it were
not holy.
8 They lie down beside every altar on
clothes they have taken.
They lie on those clothes
until the owner pays back what
is owed.
In the house of their God
they drink wine that was paid as
fines.

9 "Yet I destroyed the Amorites
to make room in the land for my
people.
The Amorites were as tall as cedar
trees.
They were as strong as oak trees.
But I cut off their fruit above the
ground
and their roots below it.

10 "People of Israel, I brought you up
out of Egypt.
I led you in the desert for 40
years.
I gave you the land of the
Amorites.
11 I raised up prophets from among
your children.
I also set apart for myself some
of your young people to be
Nazirites.
Isn't that true, people of Israel?"
announces the LORD.
12 "But you made the Nazirites drink
wine.
You commanded the prophets
not to prophesy.

13 "A cart that is loaded with grain
crushes anything it runs over.
In the same way, I will crush you.
14 Your fastest runners will not
escape.
The strongest people will not get
away.
Even soldiers will not be able
to save their own lives.
15 Men who are armed with bows will
lose the battle.
Soldiers who are quick on their
feet will not escape.
Horsemen will not be able
to save their own lives.
16 Even your bravest soldiers
will run away naked on that
day,"
announces the LORD.

The LORD Calls for Witnesses Against Israel

3 People of Israel, listen to the LORD's message. He has spoken his message against you. He has spoken it against the whole family he brought up out of Egypt. He says,

2 "Out of all the families on earth
I have chosen only you.
So I will punish you
because you have committed so many sins."

3 Do two people walk together
unless they've agreed to do so?
4 Does a lion roar in the bushes
when it doesn't have any food?
Does it growl in its den
when it hasn't caught anything?
5 Does a bird fly down to a trap on the ground
when no bait is there?
Does a net spring up from the ground
when it has not caught anything?
6 When someone blows a trumpet in a city,
don't the people tremble with fear?
When trouble comes to a city,
hasn't the LORD caused it?
7 The LORD and King never does anything
without telling his servants the prophets about it.

8 A lion has roared.
Who isn't afraid?
The LORD and King has spoken.
Who can do anything but prophesy?

9 Speak to the people in the forts of Ashdod and Egypt.
Tell them, "Gather together
on the mountains of Samaria.
Look at the great trouble in that city.
Its people are committing many crimes."

10 "They do not know how to do what is right,"
announces the LORD.
"They store up stolen goods in their forts."

11 So the LORD and King says,

"Enemies will take over your land.
They will pull down your places of safety.
They will rob your forts."

12 The LORD says,

"Suppose a shepherd saves only two leg bones
from a lion's mouth.
Or he might save only a piece of an ear.
That is how the Israelites living in Samaria will be saved.
They will only have a board
from a bed
and a piece of cloth
from a couch."

13 "Listen to me," announces the Lord.
"Be a witness against the people of Jacob," says the LORD God who rules over all.

14 "I will punish Israel for their sins.
When I do, I will destroy their altars at Bethel.
The horns that stick out from the upper corners
of their main altar will be cut off.
They will fall to the ground.
15 I will tear down their winter houses.
I will also pull down their summer houses.
The houses they have decorated with ivory will be destroyed.
And their princely houses will be torn down,"
announces the LORD.

Israel Has Not Returned to the LORD

4 Listen to the LORD's message,
you women who live on the hill of Samaria.
You treat poor people badly.
You crush those who are in need.
You say to your husbands,
"Bring us some drinks!"
But you are already as fat
as the cows in Bashan.
2 The LORD and King has made a promise
by his own holy name.
He says, "You can be sure
that the time will come
when your enemies will put hooks in your faces.
They will lead every one of you
away with fishhooks.
3 Each of you will go straight out
through gaps made in the wall.
You will be thrown out toward Harmon,"
announces the LORD.

4 "People of Samaria, go to Bethel
and sin!
Go to Gilgal! Sin there even more!
Bring your sacrifices every morning.
Every third year, bring a tenth
of everything you produce.
5 Bake some bread with yeast.
Burn it as a thank offering.
Brag about the offerings you freely
give.
This is what you Israelites love
to do,"
announces the LORD and King.

6 "I made sure your stomachs were
empty in every city.
You did not have enough bread
in any of your towns.
In spite of that, you still have not
returned to me,"
announces the LORD.

7 "I also held back rain from you.
The time to harvest crops
was still three months away.
I sent rain on one town.
But I held it back from another.
One field had rain.
But another had no rain and
dried up.
8 People wandered from town to
town to look for water.
But they did not get enough to
drink.
In spite of that, you still have not
returned to me,"
announces the LORD.

9 "Many times I kept your gardens
and vineyards from growing.
I sent hot winds to dry them up
completely.
Locusts ate up your fig and olive
trees.
In spite of that, you still have not
returned to me,"
announces the LORD.

10 "I sent plagues on you,
just as I did on Egypt.
I killed your young men by swords.
I also let the horses you had
captured be killed.
I filled your noses with the stink of
your camps.
In spite of that, you still have not
returned to me,"
announces the LORD.

11 "I destroyed some of you,
just as I did Sodom and
Gomorrah.
You were like a burning stick that
was pulled out of the fire.
In spite of that, you still have not
returned to me,"
announces the LORD.

12 "So, people of Israel, I will judge you.
Because I will do that to you,
Israel,
prepare to meet your God!"

13 The LORD forms the mountains.
He creates the wind.
He makes his thoughts known to
human beings.
He turns sunrise into darkness.
He rules over even the highest
places on earth.
His name is the LORD God Who
Rules Over All.

Mourn and Turn Back to the LORD

5 People of Israel, listen to the LORD's
message. Hear my song of sadness
about you. I say,

2 "The people of Israel have fallen.
They will never get up again.
They are deserted in their own land.
No one can lift them up."

3 Here is what the LORD and King says
to Israel.

"A thousand soldiers will march out
from a city.
But only a hundred will return.
A hundred soldiers will march out
from a town.
But only ten will come back."

4 The LORD speaks to the people of
Israel. He says,

"Look to me and live.
5 Do not look to Bethel.
Do not go to Gilgal.
Do not travel to Beersheba.
The people of Gilgal will be taken
away as prisoners.
Nothing will be left of Bethel."

6 Israel, look to the LORD and live.
If you don't, he will sweep
through
the tribes of Joseph like a fire.
It will burn everything up.
And Bethel won't have anyone to
put it out.

7 There are people among you
who turn what is fair into
something bitter.
They throw down to the ground
what is right.
8 The LORD made the Pleiades and
Orion.
He turns midnight into sunrise.
He makes the day fade into night.
He sends for the waters in the
clouds.
Then he pours them out on the
surface of the land.
His name is the LORD.
9 With a flash of light he destroys
places of safety.
He tears down cities
that have high walls around them.
10 There are people among you who
hate anyone who stands for
justice in court.
They hate those who tell the truth.

11 You make poor people pay tax on
their straw.
You also tax their grain.
So, even though you have built
stone houses,
you won't live in them.
You have planted fruitful vineyards.
But you won't drink the wine
they produce.

Where is true life found?

God says that true life is found in him. People often look to things besides God to save them, but nothing in this world has the power to save. Only God offers salvation and true life through his Son, Jesus.

Can you find the following verse?

AMOS 5:4

12 I know how many crimes you have
committed.
You have sinned far too much.

Among you are people who crush
those who have done no wrong.
They accept money from people
who want special favors.
They take away the rights of
poor people in the courts.
13 So those who are wise keep quiet in
times like these.
That's because the times are evil.

14 Look to what is good, not to what is
evil.
Then you will live.
And the LORD God who rules over
all
will be with you,
just as you say he is.
15 Hate evil and love good.
Do what is fair in the courts.
Perhaps the LORD God who rules
over all
will have mercy on you.
After all, you are the only ones left
in the family line of Joseph.

16 The LORD God rules over all. The
Lord says,

"People will weep in all the streets.
They will be very sad in every
market place.
Even farmers will be told to cry
loudly.
People will mourn for the dead.
17 Workers will cry in all the
vineyards.
That's because I will punish you,"
says the LORD.

The Day of the LORD Is Coming

18 How terrible it will be for you
who long for the day of the LORD!
Why do you want it to come?
That day will be dark, not light.
19 It will be like a man running away
from a lion
only to meet a bear.
He enters his house and rests his
hand on a wall
only to be bitten by a snake.
20 The day of the LORD will be dark,
not light.
It will be very black.
There won't be a ray of sunlight
anywhere.

21 The LORD says,

"I hate your holy feasts.
I can't stand them.
Your gatherings stink.
22 You bring me burnt offerings and
grain offerings.
But I will not accept them.
You bring your best friendship
offerings.
But I will not even look at them.
23 Take the noise of your songs away!
I will not listen to the music of
your harps.
24 I want you to treat others fairly.
So let fair treatment roll on
just as a river does!
Always do what is right.
Let right living flow along
like a stream that never runs dry!

Always do what is right. Let right living flow along like a stream that never runs dry! AMOS 5:24

25 "People of Israel, did you bring me
sacrifices and offerings
for 40 years in the desert?
26 Yes. But you have honored the
place
where your king worshiped other
gods.
You have carried the stands
the statues of your gods were on.
You have lifted up the banners
of the stars you worship as
gods.
You made all those things for
yourselves.
27 So I will send you away
as prisoners beyond Damascus,"
says the LORD.
His name is God Who Rules
Over All.

How Terrible for Those Who Feel Secure When They Shouldn't

6 How terrible it will be for you men
who are so contented on Mount
Zion!
How terrible for you who feel secure
on the hill of Samaria!
You are famous men from the
greatest nation.
The people of Israel come to you
for help and advice.
2 Go and look at the city of Kalneh.
Go from there to the great city of
Hamath.
Then go down to Gath in Philistia.
Are those places better off than
your two kingdoms?
Is their land larger than yours?
3 You are trying to avoid the time
when trouble will come.
But you are only bringing closer
the Assyrian rule of terror.
4 You lie down on beds
that are decorated with ivory.
You rest on your couches.
You eat the best lambs
and the fattest calves.
5 You pluck away on your harps as
David did.
You play new songs on musical
instruments.
6 You drink wine by the bowlful.
You use the finest lotions.
But Joseph's people will soon be
destroyed.
And you aren't even sad about it.
7 So you will be among the first
to be taken away as prisoners.
You won't be able to enjoy good
food.
You won't lie around on couches
anymore.

The LORD Hates the Pride of Israel

8 The LORD and King has made a
promise in his own name. He is the LORD
God who rules over all. He announces,

"I hate the pride of Jacob's people.
I can't stand their forts.
I will hand the city of Samaria
and everything in it over to their
enemies."

9 Ten people might be left in one house.
If they are, they will die there. 10 Relatives might come to burn the dead bodies. If they do, they'll have to carry them
out of the house first. They might ask
someone still hiding there, "Is anyone
else here with you?" If the answer is no,
the relatives will go on to say, "Be quiet!
We must not pray in the LORD's name."

11 That's because the LORD has
already given an order.
He will smash large houses to
pieces.

He will crush small houses to bits.
12 Horses don't run on rocky ground.
People don't plow the sea with oxen.
But you have turned fair treatment into poison.
You have turned the fruit of right living into bitterness.
13 You are happy because you captured the town of Lo Debar.
You say, "We were strong enough to take Karnaim too."

14 But the LORD God rules over all. He announces, "People of Israel,
I will stir up a nation against you.
They will crush you from Lebo Hamath
all the way down to the Arabah Valley."

Amos Has Visions of Locusts, Fire and a Plumb Line

7 The LORD and King gave me a vision. He was bringing large numbers of locusts on the land. The king's share had already been harvested. Now the later crops were coming up.
2 The locusts stripped the land clean. Then I cried out, "LORD and King, forgive Israel! How can Jacob's people continue? They are such a weak nation!"
3 So the LORD had pity on them.

"I will let them continue for now," he said.
4 The LORD and King gave me a second vision. He was using fire to punish his people. It dried up the deep waters. It burned the land up.
5 Then I cried out, "LORD and King, please stop! How can Jacob's people continue? They are such a weak nation!"
6 So the LORD had pity on them.

"I will let them continue for now," the LORD and King said.
7 Then the Lord gave me a third vision. He was standing by a wall. It had been built very straight, all the way up and down. He was holding a plumb line.
8 The LORD asked me, "What do you see, Amos?"

"A plumb line," I replied.

Then the Lord said, "Look at what I am doing. I am hanging a plumb line next to my people Israel. It will show how crooked they are. I will no longer spare them.

9 "The high places where Isaac's people worship other gods will be destroyed.
The other places of worship in Israel will also be torn down.
I will use my sword to attack Jeroboam's royal family."

Amaziah Tells Amos to Stop Prophesying

10 Amaziah was priest of Bethel. He sent a message to Jeroboam, the king of Israel. He said, "Amos is making evil plans against you right here in Israel. The people in the land can't stand to listen to what he's saying.
11 Amos is telling them,

" 'Jeroboam will be killed by a sword.
The people of Israel will be taken away as prisoners.
They will be carried off from their own land.' "

12 Then Amaziah said to Amos, "Get out of Israel, you prophet! Go back to the land of Judah. Earn your living there. Do your prophesying there.
13 Don't prophesy here at Bethel anymore. This is where the king worships. The main temple in the kingdom is located here."
14 Amos answered Amaziah, "I was not a prophet. I wasn't even the son of a prophet. I was a shepherd. I also took care of sycamore-fig trees.
15 But the LORD took me away from taking care of the flock. He said to me, 'Go. Prophesy to my people Israel.'
16 Now then, listen to the LORD's message. You say,

" 'Don't prophesy against Israel.
Stop preaching against the people of Isaac.'

17 "But the LORD says,

" 'Your wife will become a prostitute in the city of Bethel.
Your sons and daughters will be killed by swords.
Your land will be measured and divided up.
And you yourself will die in another country.
The people of Israel will surely be taken away as prisoners.
They will be carried off from their own land.' "

Amos Has a Vision of a Basket of Ripe Fruit

8 The LORD and King gave me a vision.
He showed me a basket of ripe fruit.
2 "What do you see, Amos?" he asked.
"A basket of ripe fruit," I replied.
Then the LORD said to me, "The time
is ripe for my people Israel. I will no
longer spare them.
3 "The time is coming when the songs
in the temple will turn to weeping,"
announces the LORD and King. "Many,
many bodies will be thrown everywhere! So be quiet!"

4 Listen to me, you who walk all over
needy people.
You crush those who are poor in
the land.

5 You say,

"When will the New Moon feast be
over?
Then we can sell our grain.
When will the Sabbath day come to
an end?
Then people can buy our wheat."
But you measure out less than the
right amount.
You raise your prices.
You cheat others by using
dishonest scales.
6 You buy poor people to make slaves
out of them.
You buy those who are in need
for a mere pair of sandals.
You even sell the worthless parts
of your wheat.

7 People of Jacob, you are proud that
the LORD is your God. But he has made a
promise in his own name. He says, "I will
never forget anything Israel has done.

8 "The land will tremble because of
what will happen.
Everyone who lives in it will mourn.
So the whole land will rise like the
Nile River.
It will be stirred up.
Then it will settle back down again
like that river in Egypt."

9 The LORD and King announces,

"At that time I will make the sun go
down at noon.
The earth will become dark in
the middle of the day.
10 I will turn your holy feasts into
times for mourning.
I will turn all your songs into
weeping.
You will have to wear the clothing
of sadness.
You will shave your heads.
I will make you mourn as if your
only son had died.
The end of that time will be like a
bitter day."

11 The LORD and King announces,

"The days are coming
when I will send hunger through
the land.
But people will not be hungry for
food.
They will not be thirsty for water.
Instead, they will be hungry
to hear a message from me.
12 People will wander from the Dead
Sea to the Mediterranean.
They will travel from north to
east.
They will look for a message from me.
But they will not find it.

13 "At that time

"the lovely young women and
strong young men
will faint because they are so
thirsty.
14 Some people make promises in the
name of Samaria's god.
That god has led them astray.
Others say, 'People of Dan, you can
be sure
that your god is alive.'
Still others say, 'You can be sure
that Beersheba's god is alive.'
But all these people will fall dead.
They will never get up again."

Israel Will Be Destroyed

9 I saw the Lord standing next to the
altar in the temple. He said to me,

"Strike the tops of the temple
pillars.
Then the heavy stones at the
base of the entrance will shake.
Bring everything down on the
heads of everyone there.
I will kill with my swords
those who are left alive.
None of the Israelites will escape.
None will get away.

2 They might dig down deep.
But my powerful hand will take them out of there.
They might climb up to the heavens.
But I will bring them down from there.
3 They might hide on top of Mount Carmel.
But I will hunt them down
and grab them.
They might hide from me at the bottom of the ocean.
But even there I will command the serpent to bite them.
4 Their enemies might take them away
as prisoners to another country.
But there I will command Israel's enemies
to cut them down with swords.
I will keep my eye on Israel to harm them.
I will not help them."

5 The LORD rules over all.
The Lord touches the earth, and it melts.
Everyone who lives in it mourns.
The whole land rises like the Nile River.
Then it settles back down again
like that river in Egypt.
6 The LORD builds his palace high in the heavens.
He lays its foundation on the earth.
He sends for the waters in the clouds.
Then he pours them out on the surface of the land.
His name is the LORD.

7 "You Israelites are just like
the people of Cush to me,"
announces the LORD.
"I brought Israel up from Egypt.
I also brought the Philistines from Crete
and the Arameans from Kir.

8 "I am the LORD and King.
My eyes are watching the sinful kingdom of Israel.
I will wipe it off the face of the earth.
But I will not totally destroy the people of Jacob,"
announces the LORD.

9 "I will give an order.
I will shake the people of Israel
among all the nations.
They will be like grain that is shaken through a screen.
Not a pebble will fall to the ground.
10 All the sinners among my people
will be killed by swords.
They say, 'Nothing bad will ever happen to us.'

Israel Will Be Made Like New Again

11 "The time will come when I will set up
David's fallen shelter.
I will repair its broken walls.
I will rebuild what was destroyed.
I will make it what it used to be.
12 Then my people will take control of those
who are left alive in Edom.
They will also possess all the nations
that belong to me,"
announces the LORD.
He will do all these things.

13 "The days are coming," announces
the LORD.

"At that time those who plow the land
will catch up with those who harvest the crops.
Those who stomp on grapes
will catch up with those who plant the vines.
Fresh wine will drip from the mountains.
It will flow down from all the hills.
14 I will bring my people Israel back home.
I will bless them with great success again.
They will rebuild the destroyed cities and live in them.
They will plant vineyards and drink the wine they produce.
They will make gardens and eat their fruit.
15 I will plant Israel in their own land.
They will never again be removed
from the land I have given them,"

says the LORD your God.

OBADIAH

Author: Obadiah

When the prophet Obadiah lived in the kingdom of Judah, the neighboring nation was called Edom. The kingdoms of Judah and Edom were supposed to care about each other, but when Judah was attacked by Babylon, Edom looked the other way. The Edomites didn't come to help Judah. Instead, the Edomites took some of the possessions belonging to the people of Judah after they had been attacked and taken away from their homes!

Prophecy

I am the LORD your God . . .

God gave Obadiah a message for Edom—and any nation that wanted to harm his people. God said every nation that was prideful and sought to destroy his people would face his judgment. Obadiah promised that one day God would come and judge every kingdom that set itself up against his perfect kingdom.

God also gave Obadiah a message of hope for anyone who wasn't a part of the kingdom of Judah: Through the coming Savior, God would extend his blessing to the entire world. Though God had called the Israelites to be his special people, his promise of blessing was available to anyone. Obadiah looked forward to the day when the Savior would come and God's promise of salvation would reach every single nation, just like God had promised Abraham long ago.

in Obadiah?

God is the Defender. God delights in shielding all who trust him for protection from their enemies, and he will defend his people from their greatest enemy—sin.

Obadiah's Vision

1 This is the vision about Edom that Obadiah had.

Here is what the LORD and King says about Edom.

We've heard a message from the LORD.
A messenger was sent to the nations.
The LORD told him to say,
"Get up! Let us go and make war against Edom."

2 The LORD says to Edom,

"I will make you weak among the nations.
They will look down on you.
3 You live in the safety of the rocks.
You make your home high up in the mountains.
But your proud heart has tricked you.
So you say to yourself,
'No one can bring me down to the ground.'
4 You have built your home as high as an eagle does.
You have made your nest among the stars.
But I will bring you down from there,"
announces the LORD.

5 "Edom, suppose robbers came to you at night.
They would steal only as much as they wanted.
Suppose grape pickers came to harvest your vines.
They would still leave a few grapes.
But you are facing horrible trouble!
6 People of Esau, everything will be taken away from you.
Your hidden treasures will be stolen.
7 All those who are helping you will force you to leave your country.
Your friends will trick you and overpower you.
Those who eat bread with you will set a trap for you.
But you will not see it."

8 Here is what the LORD announces.
"At that time
I will destroy the wise men of Edom.
I will wipe out the men of understanding
in the mountains of Esau.
9 People of Teman, your soldiers will be terrified.
Everyone in Esau's mountains will be cut down by swords.
10 You did harmful things to the people of Jacob.
They are your relatives.
So you will be covered with shame.
You will be destroyed forever.
11 Outsiders entered the gates of Jerusalem.
They cast lots to see what each one would get.
Strangers carried off its wealth.
When that happened, you just stood there and did nothing.
You were like one of them.
12 That was a time of trouble for your relatives.
So you shouldn't have been happy about what happened to them.
The people of Judah were destroyed.
So you should not have been happy about it.
You should not have laughed at them so much
when they were in trouble.

[13]You should not have marched
through the gates of my people's
city
when they were in trouble.
You shouldn't have been happy
about what happened to them.
You should not have stolen their
wealth
when they were in trouble.
[14]You waited where the roads cross.
You wanted to cut down those
who were running away.
You should not have done that.
You handed over to their enemies
those who were still left alive.
You should not have done that.
They were in trouble.

[15]"The day of the LORD is near
for all the nations.
Others will do to you
what you have done to them.
You will be paid back
for what you have done.

The day of the LORD is near for all the nations.
OBADIAH 15

[16]You Edomites made my holy
mountain of Zion impure
by drinking and celebrating there.
So all the nations will drink
from the cup of my anger.
And they will keep on drinking
from it.
They will vanish.
It will be as if they had never
existed.
[17]But on Mount Zion some of my
people will be left alive.
I will save them.
Zion will be my holy mountain
once again.
And the people of Jacob
will again receive the land as
their own.
[18]They will be like a fire.
Joseph's people will be like a
flame.
The nation of Edom will be like
straw.
Jacob's people will set Edom on
fire and burn it up.

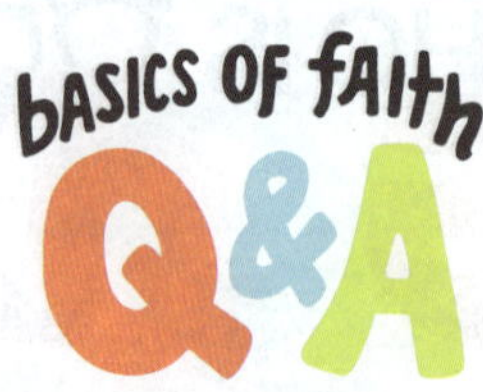

Is God King over everyone, or is he only King over those who follow him?

God is King over the whole world. He allows earthly kingdoms now, but one day God will return and establish his forever kingdom. Then we will see him rule over all nations.

Can you find the following verse?
OBADIAH 21

No one will be left alive
among Esau's people."
The LORD has spoken.

[19]Israelites from the Negev Desert
will take over Esau's mountains.
Israelites from the western hills
will possess the land of the
Philistines.
They'll take over the territories
of Ephraim and Samaria.
Israelites from the tribe of
Benjamin
will possess the land of Gilead.
[20]Some Israelites were forced to leave
their homes.
They'll come back to Canaan and
possess
it all the way to the town of
Zarephath.
Some people from Jerusalem were
taken
to the city of Sepharad.
They'll return and possess
the towns of the Negev Desert.
[21]Leaders from Mount Zion will go
and rule over the mountains of
Esau.
And the kingdom will belong to
the LORD.

JONAH

Author: Jonah

Jonah was a prophet, but unlike other prophetic books that tell us the prophet's message, the book of Jonah is *about* Jonah. He was called by God to go to Nineveh, a city full of Israel's enemies, to tell the people to repent and turn to God. But Jonah didn't obey God; instead, he got on a boat and headed in the opposite direction of Nineveh. A huge storm came, and when Jonah realized it was sent by God, he told the sailors to throw him into the sea to stop the storm. Jonah thought he would die, but instead God sent a big fish to swallow him alive! While in the belly of the fish, Jonah confessed his disobedience to God. Three days later, God caused the fish to vomit Jonah onto dry land. Jonah went to Nineveh and proclaimed God's message to the people: Repent and turn to God! And you know what? The people did, and God forgave them! But once again, Jonah's heart was far from God, and he was upset that God forgave his enemies.

Prophecy

I am the LORD your God . . .

The book of Jonah reminds God's people that God's mercy is big and wide. Through the coming Savior, God would extend his forgiveness to anyone who asked for it—even our enemies.

Jonah Runs Away From the LORD

1 A message from the LORD came to
Jonah, the son of Amittai. The LORD
said, 2 "Go to the great city of Nineveh.
Preach against it. The sins of its people
have come to my attention."
3 But Jonah ran away from the LORD.
He headed for Tarshish. So he went
down to the port of Joppa. There he
found a ship that was going to Tarshish.
He paid the fare and went on board.
Then he sailed for Tarshish. He was
running away from the LORD.
4 But the LORD sent a strong wind over
the Mediterranean Sea. A wild storm
came up. It was so wild that the ship
was in danger of breaking apart. 5 All
the sailors were afraid. Each one cried
out to his own god for help. They threw
the ship's contents into the sea. They
were trying to make the ship lighter.
But Jonah had gone below deck.
There he lay down and fell into a deep
sleep. 6 The captain went down to him
and said, "How can you sleep? Get up
and call out to your god for help! Maybe
he'll pay attention to what's happening
to us. Then we won't die."
7 Here is what the sailors said to one
another. "Someone is to blame for getting us into all this trouble. Come. Let's

in Jonah?

God is the One Who Saves the Undeserving. He not only saved the repentant Ninevites but also extended his grace to Jonah when Jonah failed to obey God.

cast lots to find out who it is." So they
did. And Jonah was picked. 8 They asked
him, "What terrible thing have you done
to bring all this trouble on us? Tell us.
What do you do for a living? Where do
you come from? What is your country?
What people do you belong to?"
9 He answered, "I'm a Hebrew. I worship the LORD. He is the God of heaven.
He made the sea and the dry land."
10 They found out he was running
away from the LORD. That's because
he had told them. Then they became
terrified. So they asked him, "How could
you do a thing like that?"
11 The sea was getting rougher and
rougher. So they asked him, "What should
we do to you to make the sea calm down?"
12 "Pick me up and throw me into the
sea," he replied. "Then it will become
calm. I know it's my fault that this terrible storm has come on you."
13 But the men didn't do what he said.
Instead, they did their best to row back
to land. But they couldn't. The sea got
even rougher than before. 14 Then they

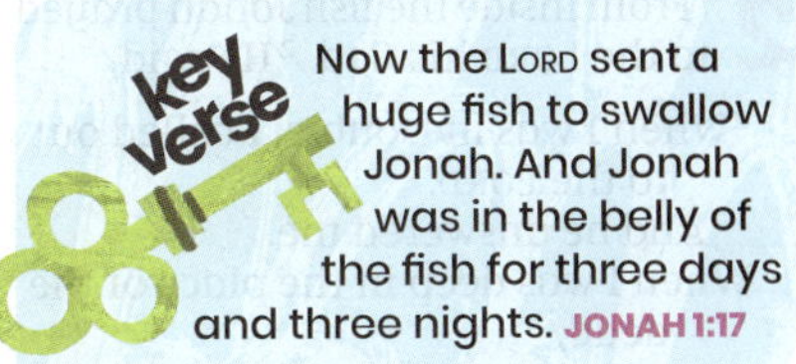

Now the LORD sent a huge fish to swallow Jonah. And Jonah was in the belly of the fish for three days and three nights. JONAH 1:17

cried out to the LORD. They prayed,
"Please, LORD, don't let us die for taking
this man's life. After all, he might not be
guilty of doing anything wrong. So don't
hold us responsible for killing him. LORD,
you always do what you want to." 15 Then
they took Jonah and threw him overboard. And the stormy sea became calm.
16 The men saw what had happened.
Then they began to have great respect
for the LORD. They offered a sacrifice to
him. And they made promises to him.

Jonah Prays to the LORD

17 Now the LORD sent a huge fish to swallow Jonah. And Jonah was in the belly of
the fish for three days and three nights.

pointing us to JESUS: Jonah

Jonah was a prophet, or messenger, who was called by God to go to a city called Nineveh. God told Jonah to tell the people in Nineveh to repent and turn to God. But Jonah didn't want to go because the city of Nineveh was full of Israel's enemies. Jonah didn't like them at all, and he didn't want them to receive the same forgiveness the people of Israel received from God. So Jonah hopped on a ship and headed in the opposite direction from Nineveh.

God sent a great big storm that rocked the ship Jonah was on, and Jonah knew the storm was because of his disobedience. Jonah told the sailors to throw him overboard so the storm would stop. When they did, the water became calm again. Then God sent a huge fish to swallow Jonah whole! Jonah began to pray in the belly of the huge fish, and after three days and three nights, God told the fish to "spit Jonah up onto dry land" (Jonah 2:10). Jonah was given another chance to obey God, and he finally did and went to Nineveh.

Jonah's story points us toward another messenger who willingly obeyed God's command to save the people from their sins. Jesus offered himself as the sacrifice for our sin, and after spending three days and three nights in the belly of the earth (also known as the grave), he rose again in victory!

2 [1]From inside the fish Jonah prayed to the LORD his God. [2]He said,

"When I was in trouble, I called out
to the LORD.
And he answered me.
When I was deep in the place of the
dead,
I called out for help.
And you listened to my cry.
[3]You threw me deep into the
Mediterranean Sea.
I was deep down in its waters.
They were all around me.
All your rolling waves
were sweeping over me.
[4]I said, 'I have been driven away
from you.
But I will look again
toward your holy temple in
Jerusalem.'
[5]I had almost drowned in the
waves.
The deep waters were all
around me.
Seaweed was wrapped around
my head.
[6]I sank down to the bottom of the
mountains.
I thought I had died
and gone down into the grave
forever.
But you are the LORD my God.

Is there anywhere I can go where God cannot help me?

God is all-present, which means he is present everywhere. There is no place in this world where God cannot hear your prayers and help you.

Can you find the following verse?

JONAH 2:2

You brought my life up
from the very edge of the pit of
death.
[7]"When my life was nearly over,
I remembered you, LORD.
My prayer rose up to you.
It reached you in your holy
temple in heaven.
[8]"Some people worship the
worthless statues of their
gods.
They turn away from God's love
for them.
[9]But I will sacrifice a thank offering
to you.
And I will shout with thankful
praise.
I will do what I have promised.
I will say, 'LORD, you are the one
who saves.'"

[10]The LORD gave the fish a command.
And it spit Jonah up onto dry land.

Jonah Goes to Nineveh

3 A message from the LORD came
to Jonah a second time. The LORD
said, [2]"Go to the great city of Nineveh.
Announce to its people the message I
give you."
[3]Jonah obeyed the LORD. He went to
Nineveh. It was a very large city. In fact,
it took about three days to go through it.
[4]Jonah began by going one whole day
into the city. As he went, he announced,
"In 40 days Nineveh will be destroyed."
[5]The people of Nineveh believed God's
warning. So they decided not to eat any
food for a while. And all of them put on
the rough clothing people wear when
they're sad. That's what everyone did,
from the least important of them to the
most important.
[6]Jonah's warning reached the king of
Nineveh. He got up from his throne. He
took off his royal robes. He also dressed
himself in the clothing of sadness. And
then he sat down in the dust. [7]Here is
the message he sent out to the people
of Nineveh.

"I and my nobles give this order.

Don't let people or animals taste anything. That includes your herds and flocks. People and animals must not eat or drink anything. [8]Let people and animals alike be

covered with the clothing of sadness. All of you must call out to God
with all your hearts. Stop doing
what is evil. Don't harm others.
9 Who knows? God might take pity
on us. He might not be angry with
us anymore. Then we won't die."

10 God saw what they did. He saw that
they stopped doing what was evil. So
he took pity on them. He didn't destroy
them as he had said he would.

Jonah Is Angry That the Lord Spares Nineveh

4 But to Jonah this seemed very
wrong. He became angry. 2 He
prayed to the Lord. Here is what Jonah
said to him. "Lord, isn't this exactly
what I thought would happen when I
was still at home? That is what I tried to
prevent by running away to Tarshish.
I knew that you are gracious. You are
tender and kind. You are slow to get
angry. You are full of love. You are a
God who takes pity on people. You don't
want to destroy them. 3 Lord, take away
my life. I'd rather die than live."

4 But the Lord replied, "Is it right for
you to be angry?"

5 Jonah had left the city. He had sat
down at a place east of it. There he put
some branches over his head. He sat in
their shade. He waited to see what would
happen to the city. 6 Then the Lord God
sent a leafy plant and made it grow up
over Jonah. It gave him more shade for
his head. It made him more comfortable.
Jonah was very happy he had the leafy
plant. 7 But before sunrise the next day,
God sent a worm. It chewed the plant so
much that it dried up. 8 When the sun
rose, God sent a burning east wind. The
sun beat down on Jonah's head. It made
him very weak. He wanted to die. So he
said, "I'd rather die than live."

9 But God spoke to Jonah. God said,
"Is it right for you to be angry about
the plant?"

"It is," Jonah said. "In fact, I'm so angry I wish I were dead."

10 But the Lord said, "You have been
concerned about this plant. But you did
not take care of it. You did not make it
grow. It grew up in one night and died
the next. 11 And shouldn't I show concern
for the great city of Nineveh? It has
more than 120,000 people. They can't
tell right from wrong. Nineveh also has
a lot of animals."

MICAH

Author: Micah

Micah was sent by God to tell the people of Israel and Judah that they had broken God's laws and, therefore, their relationship with him. Micah told the people of Israel and Judah that because they failed to act justly and worshiped false gods, they would be punished. But Micah also gave them hope: God would restore them.

Prophecy

God had warned that there would be consequences for their disobedience, but he promised to preserve a group of people. Through them, he would rebuild the nation into his special people once again. This group of people is called a "remnant" in the Old Testament, and the book of Micah tells of just one of many times God preserved a remnant as a display of his mercy and grace.

The book of Micah reminds God's people that God does not take sin lightly, and because he is righteous, God will punish those who break his laws. But it also reminds us that God is a God of grace. And God's greatest display of grace was about to come through the Savior who would be a shepherd-king like David. Jesus would be born in Bethlehem, bear the ultimate punishment for sin, and be raised to life again on the third day.

1 A message from the LORD came to
Micah. He was from the town of
Moresheth. The message came while
Jotham, Ahaz and Hezekiah were kings
of Judah. This is the vision Micah saw
concerning Samaria and Jerusalem.
Here is what he said.

2 Listen to me, all you nations!
Earth and everyone who lives in
it, pay attention!
The LORD and King will be a
witness against you.
The Lord will speak from his holy
temple in heaven.

The LORD Will Judge Samaria and Jerusalem

3 The LORD is about to come down
from his home in heaven.
He rules over even the highest
places on earth.
4 The mountains will melt under him
like wax near a fire.
The valleys will be broken apart
by water rushing down a slope.
5 All this will happen because
Jacob's people have done what is
wrong.
The people of Israel
have committed many sins.
Who is to blame
for the wrong things Jacob has
done?
Samaria!
Who is to blame for the high places
where Judah's people worship
other gods?
Jerusalem!

6 So the LORD says,

"I will turn Samaria into a pile of
trash.
It will become a place for
planting vineyards.
I will dump its stones down into the
valley.
And I will destroy it
down to its very foundations.
7 All the statues of Samaria's gods
will be broken to pieces.
All the gifts its people gave to
temple prostitutes
will be burned with fire.
I will destroy all the statues of its
gods.
Samaria collected gifts that were
paid to temple prostitutes.
So the Assyrians will use the gifts
to pay their own temple
prostitutes."

Micah Weeps Over His People

8 I will weep and mourn because
Samaria will be destroyed.
I'll walk around barefoot and
naked.
I'll bark like a wild dog.
I'll hoot like an owl.
9 Samaria's plague can't be healed.
The plague has spread to Judah.
It has spread right up to the gate of
my people.
It has spread to Jerusalem itself.
10 Don't tell the people of Gath
about it.
Don't let them see you weep.
People in Beth Ophrah, roll in the
dust.
11 You who live in the town of
Shaphir,
leave naked and in shame.
Those who live in Zaanan
won't come out to help you.
The people in Beth Ezel will mourn.
They won't be able to help keep
you safe any longer.
12 Those who live in Maroth will
groan with pain
as they wait for help.
That's because the LORD will bring
trouble on them.
It will reach the very gate of
Jerusalem.
13 You who live in Lachish,
get your fast horses ready to pull
their chariots.
You trust in military power.
Lachish was where sin began
for the people of Zion.
The wrong things Israel did
were also done by you.
14 People of Judah, you might as well
say goodbye
to Moresheth near Gath.
The town of Akzib won't give any
help
to the kings of Israel.
15 An enemy will attack
you who live in Mareshah.
Israel's nobles will have to run
away
and hide in the cave of Adullam.

16 The children you enjoy so much
will be taken away as prisoners.
So shave your heads and mourn.
Make them as bare as the head of a vulture.

People's Plans and God's Plans

2 How terrible it will be for those
who plan to harm others!
How terrible for those who make evil plans
before they even get out of bed!
As soon as daylight comes,
they carry out their plans.
That's because they have the power to do it.
2 If they want fields or houses,
they take them.
They cheat people out of their homes.
They rob them of their property.

3 So the LORD says to them,

"I am planning to send trouble on you.
You will not be able to save yourselves from it.
You will not live so proudly anymore.
It will be a time of trouble.
4 At that time people will make fun of you.
They will tease you by singing a song of sadness.
They will pretend to be you and say,
'We are totally destroyed.
Our enemies have divided up our land.
The LORD has taken it away from us!
He has given our fields to those
who turned against us.'"

5 So you won't even have anyone left
in the LORD's community
who can divide up the land for you.

Some Prophets Aren't Really Prophets at All

6 "Don't prophesy," the people's prophets say.
"Don't prophesy about bad things.
Nothing shameful is going to happen to us."

in Micah?

God is the Shepherd-King. He would send his Son, Jesus, to be a truer and better King David who would take the punishment for his people's sin.

7 People of Jacob, should anyone say,
"The LORD is patient,
so he wouldn't do things like that"?

The LORD replies, "What I promise brings good things
to those who lead honest lives.
8 But lately my people have attacked one another
as if they were enemies.
You strip off the rich robes
from those who happen to pass by.
They thought they were as safe as men
returning from a battle they had won.
9 You drive the women among my people
out of their pleasant homes.
You take away my blessing
from their children forever.
10 Get up! Leave this land!
It is no longer your resting place.
You have made it 'unclean.'
You have completely destroyed it.
11 Suppose a prophet goes around telling lies.
And he prophesies that you will have
plenty of wine and beer.
Then that kind of prophet would be
just right for this nation!

The LORD Promises to Save His People

12 "People of Jacob, I will gather all of you.
I will bring together
you who are still left alive in Israel.
I will gather you together like sheep in a pen.
You will be like a flock in its grasslands.
Your country will be filled with people.
13 I will open the way for you to return.
I will march in front of you.
You will break through the city gates and go free.
I am your King. I will pass through the gates
in front of you.
I, the LORD, will lead the way."

The LORD Warns Israel's Leaders and Prophets

3 Then I said,

"Listen, you leaders of Jacob's people!
Pay attention, you rulers of Israel!
You should want to judge others fairly.
2 But you hate what is good.
And you love what is evil.
You are like someone
who tears the skin off my people.
You pull the meat off their bones.
3 You eat my people's bodies.
You strip off their skin.
You break their bones in pieces.
You chop them up like meat.
You put them in a cooking pot."

4 The time will come when Israel
will cry out to the LORD.
But he won't answer them.
In fact, he'll turn his face away from them.
They have done what is evil.

5 The LORD says,

"The prophets are those
who lead my people astray.
If my people feed them,
the prophets promise them peace.
If my people do not feed them,
the prophets prepare to go to war against them.
6 So night will come on the prophets.
But they will not have any visions.
Darkness will cover them.
But they will not be able
to figure out what is going to happen.
The sun will set on the prophets.
The day will become dark for them.
7 Those who see visions will be put to shame.
Those who try to figure out what is going to happen
will be dishonored.
All of them will cover their faces.
I will not answer them."

8 The Spirit of the LORD
has filled me with power.
He helps me do what is fair.
He makes me brave.
Now I'm prepared to tell Jacob's people
what they've done wrong.
I'm ready to tell Israel they've sinned.
9 Listen to me, you leaders of Jacob's people!
Pay attention, you rulers of Israel!
You hate to do what is fair.
You twist everything that is right.
10 You build up Zion by spilling the blood of others.
You build Jerusalem by doing what is evil.
11 Your judges take money from people
who want special favors.
Your priests teach only if they get paid for it.
Your prophets won't tell fortunes
unless they receive money.
But you still look for the LORD's help.
You say, "The LORD is with us.
No trouble will come on us."
12 So because of what you have done,
Zion will be plowed up like a field.
Jerusalem will be turned into a pile of trash.
The temple hill will be covered
with bushes and weeds.

People From Many Nations Will Worship at the LORD's Mountain

4 In the last days
the mountain where the LORD's
temple is located will be famous.
It will be the highest mountain of
all.
It will be lifted up above the hills.
And nations will go to it.

2 People from many nations will go
there. They will say,
"Come, let us go up to the LORD's
mountain.
Let's go to the temple of Jacob's
God.
He will teach us how we should live.
Then we will live the way he
wants us to."
The law of the LORD will be taught
at Zion.
His message will go out from
Jerusalem.
3 He will judge between people from
many nations.
He'll settle problems among
strong nations everywhere.
They will hammer their swords into
plows.
They'll hammer their spears into
pruning tools.
Nations will not go to war against
one another.
They won't even train to fight
anymore.
4 Everyone will have
their own vine and fig tree.
And no one will make them afraid.
That's what the LORD who rules
over all has promised.
5 Other nations worship and trust in
their gods.
But we will worship and obey the
LORD.
He will be our God for ever and ever.

The LORD's Plan

6 "The time is coming
when I will gather those who are
disabled,"
announces the LORD.
"I will bring together those
who were taken away as
prisoners.
I will gather those I have allowed
to suffer.
7 I will make the disabled my
faithful people.
I will make into a strong nation
those driven away from their
homes.
I will rule over them on Mount Zion.
I will be their King from that
time on and forever.
8 Jerusalem, you used to be
like a guard tower for my flock.
City of Zion, you used to be
a place of safety for my people.
The glorious kingdom you had
before
will be given back to you.
Once again a king will rule over
your people."

9 Why are you crying out so loudly
now?
Don't you have a king?
Has your ruler died?
Is that why pain comes on you
like the pain of a woman having
a baby?
10 People of Zion, groan with pain.
Cry out like a woman having a
baby.
Soon you must leave your city.
You must camp in the open
fields.
You will have to go to the land of
Babylon.
But that's where the LORD will
save you.
There he will set you free
from the power of your enemies.

11 But now many nations
have gathered together to attack
you.
They say, "Let Jerusalem be made
'unclean.'
We want to laugh when Zion
suffers!"
12 But those nations don't know
what the LORD has in mind.
They don't understand his plan.
He has planned to gather them
up like bundles of grain.
He has planned to take them to
his threshing floor.

13 The LORD says,

"People of Zion, get up
and crush your enemies.
I will make you like a
threshing ox.

I will give you iron horns and
bronze hooves.
So you will crush many nations."

They got their money in the wrong
way.
But you will set it apart to the
LORD.
You will give their wealth
to the Lord of the whole earth.

A Promised Ruler Will Come From Bethlehem

5 Jerusalem, you are being
attacked.
So bring your troops together.
Our enemies have surrounded us.
They want to slap the face of
Israel's ruler.

2 The LORD says,

"Bethlehem Ephrathah, you might
not be
an important town in the nation
of Judah.
But out of you will come for me
a ruler over Israel.
His family line goes back
to the early years of your nation.
It goes all the way back
to days of long ago."

3 The LORD will hand over his people
to their enemies.
That will last until the pregnant
woman bears her promised son.
Then the rest of his relatives in
Judah
will return to their land.

4 That promised son will stand firm
and be a shepherd for his flock.
The LORD will give him the strength
to do it.
The LORD his God will give him
the authority to rule.
His people will live safely.
His greatness will reach
from one end of the earth to the
other.

5 And he will be our peace
when the Assyrians attack our
land.
They will march through our forts.
But we will raise up against them
many shepherds.
We'll send out against them
as many commanders as we
need to.

6 They will use their swords to rule
over Assyria.
They'll rule the land of Nimrod
with swords that are ready to
strike.
The Assyrians will march across
our borders
and attack our land.
But the promised ruler will save
us from them.

7 Jacob's people who are still left alive
will be scattered among many
nations.
They will be like dew the LORD has
sent.
Dew doesn't depend on any
human being.
They will be like rain that falls on
the grass.
Rain doesn't wait for someone to
give it orders.

8 So Jacob's people will be scattered
among many nations.
They will be like a lion
among the animals in the forest.
They'll be like a young lion
among flocks of sheep.
Lions attack and tear apart their
prey as they move along.
No one can keep them
from killing what they want.

9 LORD, your power will win the battle
over your enemies.
All of them will be destroyed.

10 "At that time I will destroy
your war horses," announces the
LORD.
"I will smash your chariots.

11 I will destroy the cities in your land.
I will tear down all your forts.

12 I will destroy your worship of evil
powers.
You will no longer be able
to put a spell on anyone.

13 I will destroy the statues of your
gods.
I will take your sacred stones
away from you.
You will no longer bow down
to the gods your hands have
made.

14 I will pull down the poles you used
to worship the female god
named Asherah.
That will happen when I
completely destroy your cities.

15 I will pay back the nations
that have not obeyed me.
I will direct my anger against
them."

The LORD Brings Charges Against Israel

6 Israel, listen to the LORD's message.
He says to me,

"Stand up in court.
Let the mountains serve as
witnesses.
Let the hills hear what you have
to say."

2 Hear the LORD's case, you
mountains.
Listen, you age-old foundations
of the earth.
The LORD has a case against his
people Israel.
He is bringing charges against
them.

3 The LORD says,

"My people, what have I done to
you?
Have I made things too hard for
you? Answer me.

4 I brought your people up out of
Egypt.
I set them free from the land
where they were slaves.
I sent Moses to lead them.
Aaron and Miriam helped him.
5 Remember how Balak, the king of
Moab,
planned to put a curse on your
people.
But Balaam, the son of Beor,
gave them a blessing instead.
Remember their journey from
Shittim to Gilgal.
I want you to know
that I always do what is right."

6 The people of Israel say,

"What should we bring with us
when we go to worship the LORD?
What should we offer the God of
heaven
when we bow down to him?
Should we take burnt offerings to
him?
Should we sacrifice calves
that are a year old?
7 Will the LORD be pleased with
thousands of rams?
Will he take delight in 10,000
rivers of olive oil?
Should we offer our oldest sons
for the wrong things we've done?
Should we sacrifice our own
children
to pay for our sins?"

8 The LORD has shown you what is
good.
He has told you what he requires
of you.
You must act with justice.
You must love to show mercy.
And you must be humble as you
live in the sight of your God.

The LORD Will Punish His Guilty People

9 The LORD is calling out to
Jerusalem.
And it would be wise to pay
attention to him.
He says, "Listen, tribe of Judah
and you people who are gathered
in the city.
10 You sinful people, should I forget
that you got your treasures by
stealing them?

How does God want me to live?

God wants you to act justly, which means treating others with fairness. He wants you to show mercy, which means treating others better than they deserve. He also wants you to live humbly, which means not thinking you're better than anyone else.

Can you find the following verse?

MICAH 6:8

JUST

God is fair, and he knows what is right because he created the world.

He doesn't play favorites by treating some people better than others; he loves everyone the same. When God gives consequences for disobeying him, the consequences are always right. Deuteronomy 32:4 says, "[God] is the Rock. His works are perfect. All his ways are right. He is faithful. He doesn't do anything wrong. He is honest and fair."

Have you ever been treated unfairly? God isn't pleased when people disobey him, but he is never mean or out of control. He is perfectly just and will right every wrong when he comes again.

You use dishonest measures to
cheat others.
I have placed a curse on that
practice.
11 Should I forgive anyone who uses
dishonest scales?
They use weights that weigh
things heavier
or lighter than they really are.
12 The rich people among you harm
others.
You are always telling lies.
You try to fool others by what
you say.
13 So I have begun to strike you
down.
I have begun to destroy you
because you have sinned so
much.
14 You will eat. But you will not be
satisfied.
Your stomachs will still be
empty.
You will try to save what you
can.
But you will not be able to.
If you do save something,
it will be destroyed in battle.
15 You will plant seeds.
But you will not harvest any
crops.
You will press olives.
But you will not use the oil.
You will crush grapes.
But you will not drink the wine
that is made from them.
16 You have followed the evil
practices
of King Omri of Israel.
You have done what the family
of King Ahab did.
You have followed their bad
example.
So I will let you be destroyed.
Others will make fun of you.
The nations will laugh at
you."

Israel's Sin Brings Suffering

7 I'm suffering very much!
I'm like someone who gathers
summer fruit in a vineyard
after the good fruit has already
been picked.
No grapes are left to eat.
None of the early figs I long for
remain.
2 Faithful people have disappeared
from the land.
Those who are honest are gone.
Everyone hides and waits
to spill the blood of others.
They use nets to try and trap one
another.
3 They are very good at doing what
is evil.
Rulers require gifts.

Judges accept money from
people
who want special favors.
Those who are powerful
always get what they want.
All of them make evil plans
together.
4 The best of these people are as
harmful as thorns.
The most honest of them are
even worse.
God has come to punish you.
The time your prophets warned
you about has come.
Panic has taken hold of you.
5 Don't trust your neighbors.
Don't put your faith in your
friends.
Be careful what you say
even to your own wife.
6 Sons don't honor their fathers.
Daughters refuse to obey their
mothers.
Daughters-in-law are against their
mothers-in-law.
A man's enemies are the
members of his own family.

7 But I will look to the LORD.
I'll put my trust in God my
Savior.
He will hear me.

Jerusalem Will Be Rebuilt

8 The people of Jerusalem say,

"Don't laugh when we suffer,
you enemies of ours!
We have fallen.
But we'll get up.
Even though we sit in the dark,
the LORD will give us light.
9 We've sinned against the LORD.
So he is angry with us.
His anger will continue until he
takes up our case.
Then he'll do what is right
for us.
He'll bring us out into the light.
Then we'll see him save us.
10 Our enemies will see it too.
And they will be put to shame.
After all, they said to us,
'Where is the LORD your God?'
But we will see them destroyed.
Soon they will be stomped on
like mud in the streets."

11 People of Jerusalem, the time will
come
when your walls will be rebuilt.
Land will be added to your
territory.
12 At that time your people will come
back to you.
They'll return from Assyria
and the cities of Egypt.
They'll come from the countries
between Egypt and the
Euphrates River.
They'll return from the lands
between the seas.
They'll come back from the
countries
between the mountains.
13 But the rest of the earth will be
deserted.
The people who live in it
have done many evil things.

Prayer and Praise

14 LORD, be like a shepherd to your
people.
Take good care of them.
They are your flock.
They live by themselves
in the safety of a forest.
Rich grasslands are all around
them.
Let them eat grass in Bashan and
Gilead
just as they did long ago.

15 The LORD says to his people,

"I showed you my wonders
when you came out of Egypt long
ago.
In the same way, I will show
them to you again."

16 When the nations see those
wonders,
they will be put to shame.
All their power will be taken
away from them.
They will be so amazed
that they won't be able to speak
or hear.
17 They'll be forced to eat dust like a
snake.
They'll be like creatures
that have to crawl on the
ground.
They'll come out of their dens
trembling with fear.

They'll show respect for the LORD
our God.
They will also have respect for
his people.
18 LORD, who is a God like you?
You forgive sin.
You forgive your people
when they do what is wrong.
You don't stay angry forever.
Instead, you take delight in
showing
your faithful love to them.
19 Once again you will show loving
concern for us.
You will completely wipe out
the evil things we've done.
You will throw all our sins
into the bottom of the sea.

key verse

LORD, who is a God like you? You forgive sin. You forgive your people when they do what is wrong. You don't stay angry forever. Instead, you take delight in showing your faithful love to them. MICAH 7:18

20 You will be faithful to Jacob's people.
You will show your love
to Abraham's children.
You will do what you promised to
do for our people.
You made that promise long ago.

NAHUM

Author: Nahum

Nahum was a prophet of God who spoke about both God's goodness and his judgment against the wicked. The empire of Assyria was prideful and arrogant. The Assyrians hated God's people, the people of Judah, making enemies of them by attacking and warring against them. God gave Nahum a special message: He was going to cause Assyria to fall. Through this, God wanted to remind his people that he had always been the one protecting them from their enemies.

Prophecy

I am the LORD your God . . .

In the book of Nahum, God displays his protection and power by defending the people of Judah from their worst enemies. This showed that no empire is more powerful than God and encouraged the people of Judah that he will be faithful to them in every generation.

Nahum wrote God's message in a series of poems, reminding God's people that God had not forgotten about them and that he would save them from their enemies. Nahum referred to other books in the Old Testament, such as Exodus, Isaiah, and Daniel, to tell how God had never left his people alone but had always been with them.

Though Nahum spoke against the people of Judah's enemies, the Assyrians, his overarching message was much bigger. Nahum reminded God's people that one day God was going to send a Savior who would save them from their ultimate enemy—sin.

1 Here is a prophecy the LORD gave Nahum, who was from the town of Elkosh. The prophecy came in a vision and is written in a book. The prophecy is about Nineveh.

The LORD Is Angry With Nineveh

2 The LORD is a jealous God who
punishes people.
He pays them back for the evil
things they do.
He directs his anger against
them.
The LORD punishes his enemies.
He holds his anger back
until the right time to use it.
3 The LORD is slow to get angry.
But he is very powerful.
The LORD will not let guilty
people go
without punishing them.
When he marches out, he stirs up
winds and storms.
Clouds are the dust kicked up by
his feet.
4 He controls the seas. He dries
them up.
He makes all the rivers run dry.
Bashan and Mount Carmel dry up.
The flowers in Lebanon fade.
5 He causes the mountains to shake.
The hills melt away.

Where can I turn when I'm afraid?

God wants you to turn to him when you're afraid. You can pray to him and ask him for protection. He is a safe place and cares for all who put their trust in him.

Can you find the following verse?
NAHUM 1:7

in Nahum?

God is the Upholder of His People. He is the only one who will never let us down.

The earth trembles because he is
there.
The world and all those who live
in it also tremble.
6 Who can stand firm when his anger
burns?
Who can live when he is
angry?
His anger blazes out like fire.
He smashes the rocks to
pieces.

7 The LORD is good.
When people are in trouble,
they can go to him for safety.
He takes good care of those
who trust in him.
8 But he will destroy Nineveh
with a powerful flood.
He will chase his enemies
into the place of darkness.

9 The LORD will put an end
to anything they plan against
him.
He won't allow Assyria to win the
battle
over his people a second time.
10 His enemies will be tangled up
among thorns.
Their wine will make them
drunk.
They'll be burned up like dry
straw.
11 Nineveh, a king has marched out
from you.
He makes evil plans against the
LORD.
He thinks about how he can do
what is wrong.

[12] The LORD says,

"His army has many soldiers.
Other nations are helping them.
But they will be destroyed and pass away.
Judah, I punished you.
But I will not do it anymore.
[13] Now I will break Assyria's yoke off your neck.
I will tear off the ropes that hold you."

[14] Nineveh, the LORD has given an order concerning you.
He has said, "You will not have any children
to carry on your name.
I will destroy the wooden and metal statues
that are in the temple of your gods.
I will get your grave ready for you.
You are worthless."

[15] Look at the mountains of Judah!
I see a messenger running to bring good news!
He's telling us that peace has come!
People of Judah, celebrate your feasts.
Carry out your promises.
The evil Assyrians won't attack you again.
They'll be completely destroyed.

Look at the mountains of Judah! I see a messenger running to bring good news! He's telling us that peace has come! NAHUM 1:15

The LORD Will Destroy Nineveh

2 Nineveh, armies are coming to attack you.
Guard the forts!
Watch the roads!
Get ready!
Gather all your strength!

[2] Assyria once took everything of value from God's people.
Its army destroyed all their vines.
But the LORD will bring back the glory of Jacob's people.
He'll make Israel glorious again.

[3] The shields of the soldiers are red.
The warriors are dressed in bright red uniforms.
The metal on their chariots flashes when they are prepared for war.
Their spears made out of juniper are ready to use.

LONG-SUFFERING

God wants what is best for us because he is good, and he loves us. Our sin, however, goes against God's nature. In other words, because he is holy, he isn't pleased by sin. Yet, when we sin, God is slow to anger, or long-suffering (see Psalm 145:8–9). When we are not walking in his ways, he humbly suffers with us and is compassionate, or loving, toward us.

God doesn't walk away from us when we disobey. Instead, God walks with us like a good father walks with his children, teaching us and training us to know and follow him. God is long-suffering with us and teaches us how we can be long-suffering with others.

4 The chariots race through the main
streets.
They rush back and forth
through them.
They look like flaming torches.
They dart around like lightning.
5 Nineveh sends for their special
troops.
But they trip and fall on their way.
They run toward the city wall.
They keep their shield in front of
them.
6 The attackers open the gates that
hold back
the waters of the river.
And the palace falls down.
7 The attackers order that Nineveh's
people
be taken away as prisoners.
The female slaves sound like doves
as they mourn.
They beat their chests.
8 Nineveh is like a pool
whose water is draining away.
"Stop running away!" someone
cries out.
But no one turns back.
9 "Steal the silver!" the attackers
shout.
"Grab the gold!"
The supply is endless.
There is plenty of wealth
among all the city's treasures.
10 Nineveh is destroyed, robbed and
stripped!
Hearts melt away in fear.
Knees give way.
Bodies tremble with fear.
Everyone's face turns pale.
11 Assyria is like a lion.
Where is the lions' den now?
Where did they feed their cubs?
Where did all the lions go?
In their den they had nothing to
fear.
12 The lion killed enough for his cubs
to eat.
He choked what he caught for his
mate.
He filled his home with what he
had killed.
He brought to his dens what he
had caught.
13 "Nineveh, I am against you,"
announces the LORD who rules
over all.
"I will burn up your chariots with
fire.
Your young lions will be killed by
swords.
I will leave you nothing on earth
to catch.
The voices of your messengers
will no longer be heard."

The LORD Will Judge Nineveh

3 How terrible it will be for
Nineveh!
It is a city of murderers!
It is full of liars!
It is filled with stolen goods!
The killing never stops!
2 Whips crack!
Wheels clack!
Horses charge!
Chariots rumble!
3 Horsemen attack!
Swords flash!
Spears gleam!
Many people die.
Dead bodies pile up.
They can't even be counted.
People trip over them.
4 All of that was caused by the evil
desires
of the prostitute Nineveh.
That woman who practiced evil
magic
was very beautiful.
She used her sinful charms
to make slaves out of the nations.
She worshiped evil powers
in order to trap others.
5 "Nineveh, I am against you,"
announces the LORD who rules
over all.
"I will pull your skirts up over your
face.
I will show the nations your
naked body.
Kingdoms will make fun of your
shame.
6 I will throw garbage at you.
I will look down on you.
I will make an example out of
you.
7 All those who see you will run away
from you.
They will say, 'Nineveh is
destroyed.
Who will mourn over it?'
Where can I find someone
to comfort your people?"

[8]Nineveh, are you better than Thebes
on the Nile River?
There was water all around that city.
The river helped to keep it safe.
The waters were like a wall
around it.
[9]Cush and Egypt gave it all the
strength it needed.
Put and Libya also helped it.
[10]But Thebes was captured anyway.
Its people were taken away as
prisoners.
Its babies were smashed to pieces
at every street corner.
The Assyrian soldiers cast lots
for all its nobles.
They put them in chains
and made slaves out of them.
[11]People of Nineveh, you too will get
drunk.
You will try to hide from your
enemies.
You will look for a place of safety.

[12]All your forts are like fig trees
that have their first ripe fruit on
them.
When the trees are shaken,
the figs fall into the mouths
of those who eat them.
[13]Look at your troops.
All of them are weak.
The gates of your forts
are wide open to your enemies.
Fire has destroyed the bars that
lock your gates.

[14]Prepare for the attack by storing up
water!
Make your walls as strong as you
can!
Make some bricks out of clay!
Mix the mud to hold them
together!
Use them to repair the walls!
[15]In spite of all your hard work,
fire will burn you up inside your
city.
Your enemies will cut you down
with their swords.
They will destroy you
just as a swarm of locusts eats up
crops.
Multiply like grasshoppers!
Increase your numbers like
locusts!
[16]You have more traders
than the number of stars in the
sky.
But like locusts they strip the
land.
Then they fly away.
[17]Your guards are like grasshoppers.
Your officials are like swarms of
locusts.
They settle in the walls on a cold
day.
But when the sun appears, they fly
away.
And no one knows where
they go.

[18]King of Assyria, your leaders are
asleep.
Your nobles lie down to rest.
Your people are scattered on the
mountains.
No one is left to gather them
together.
[19]Nothing can heal your wounds.
You will die of them.
All those who hear the news about
you clap their hands.
That's because you have fallen
from power.
Is there anyone who has not
suffered
because of how badly you
treated them?

HABAKKUK

Author: Habakkuk

Habakkuk was a prophet of God who lived in the kingdom of Judah just before the nation was attacked by Babylon. When Habakkuk looked around him, he saw his neighbors doing terrible things. They were oppressing the poor, making unfair laws (and then not keeping their own laws), worshiping idols, and bowing down to false gods instead of the one true God. Habakkuk's heart was sad because he didn't understand why God would allow evil, but he learned that even though evil exists, God is loving and powerful.

Prophecy

I am the LORD your God . . .

The book of Habakkuk is a prophetic book, but instead of being filled with messages from God to God's people, this book is like a conversation, or prayer, between Habakkuk and God. Habakkuk told God how discouraging it was to watch the people of Judah break God's laws. And he asked God, "How could you use a nation as wicked as Babylon to punish your own people? Are you still good?" At the end of his prayer, Habakkuk remembered that God had saved his people in the past, and he trusted God to save them in the future. Habakkuk knew that one day God would deliver his people forever.

1 This is a prophecy that Habakkuk the prophet received from the LORD. Here is what Habakkuk said.

Habakkuk Complains to the LORD

2 LORD, how long do I have to call out
for help?
Why don't you listen to me?
How long must I keep telling you
that things are terrible?
Why don't you save us?
3 Why do you make me watch while
people treat others so unfairly?
Why do you put up with the wrong
things
they are doing?
I have to look at death.
People are harming others.
They are arguing and fighting all
the time.
4 The law can't do what it's supposed
to do.
Fairness never comes out on top.
Sinful people surround those
who do what is right.
So people are never treated
fairly.

The LORD Replies to Habakkuk

5 The LORD replies,

"Look at the nations. Watch them.
Be totally amazed at what you
see.
I am going to do something in your
days
that you would never believe.
You would not believe it
even if someone told you about it.
6 I am going to send the armies of
Babylon to attack you.
They are very mean. They move
quickly.
They sweep across the whole earth.
They take over homes
that do not belong to them.

key verse Look at the nations. Watch them. Be totally amazed at what you see. I am going to do something in your days that you would never believe. You would not believe it even if someone told you about it. HABAKKUK 1:5

in Habakkuk?

God is the One Who Hears. Habakkuk's heart was broken over Israel's sin. God heard and responded to Habakkuk's prayers with kindness and compassion.

7 They terrify others.
They do not recognize any laws
but their own.
That is how proud they are.
8 Their horses are faster than leopards.
They are meaner than wolves at
sunset.
Their horsemen charge straight
into battle.
They ride in from far away.
They come down like an eagle
diving for its food.
9 All of them are ready and willing to
destroy others.
Their huge armies advance like a
wind out of the desert.
They gather prisoners like sand.
10 They mock kings
and make fun of rulers.
They laugh at all the cities
that have high walls around them.
They build dirt ramps against the
walls
and capture the cities.
11 They sweep past like the wind.
Then they go on their way.
They are guilty.
They worship their own
strength."

Habakkuk Complains to the LORD Again

12 LORD, haven't you existed forever?
You are my holy God.
You will never die.

Lord, you have appointed the
Babylonians
to punish your people.
My Rock, you have chosen them
to judge us.
13 Your eyes are too pure to look at
what is evil.
You can't put up with the wrong
things people do.
So why do you put up
with those who can't be trusted?
The evil Babylonians swallow up
those who are more godly than
themselves.
So why are you silent?
14 You have made people to be like
the fish in the sea.
They are like the sea creatures
that don't have a ruler.
15 The evil Babylonians pull all of
them up with hooks.
They catch them in their nets.
They gather them up.
So they celebrate.
They are glad.
16 They offer sacrifices to their nets.
They burn incense to them.
Their nets allow them to live in
great comfort.
They enjoy the finest food.
17 Are you going to let them
keep on emptying their nets?
Will they go on destroying nations
without showing them any
mercy?

2 I will go up to the lookout tower.
I'll station myself on the city
wall.
I'll wait to see how the Lord will
reply to me.
Then I'll try to figure out how
his reply answers what I've
complained about.

The Lord Replies to Habakkuk

2 The Lord replies,

"Write down the message I am
giving you.
Write it clearly on the tablets you
use.
Then a messenger can read it
and run to announce it.
3 The message I give you
waits for the time I have
appointed.
It speaks about what is going to
happen.
And all of it will come true.
It might take a while.
But wait for it.
You can be sure it will come.
It will happen when I want it to.

4 "The Babylonians are very proud.
What they want is not good.

"But the person who is godly
will live by his faithfulness.
5 "Wine makes the Babylonians do
foolish things.
They are proud. They never rest.
Like the grave, they are always
hungry for more.
Like death, they are never
satisfied.
They gather all the nations to
themselves.
They take all those people away
as prisoners.

6 "Won't those people laugh at the
Babylonians? Won't they make fun of
them? They will say to them,

" 'How terrible it will be for you
who pile up stolen goods!
You get rich by cheating others.
How long will this go on?'
7 Those you owe money to will
suddenly rise up.
They will wake up
and make you tremble with fear.
Then they will take away
everything you have.
8 You have robbed many nations.
So the nations that are left will
rob you.
You have spilled human blood.
You have destroyed lands and
cities
and everyone in them.

9 "How terrible it will be for the
Babylonians!
They build their kingdom with
money
that they gained by cheating
others.
They have tried to make the
kingdom
as secure as possible.
After all, they did not want to be
destroyed.

[10] They have planned to wipe out
many nations.
But they have brought shame on
their own kingdom.
So they must pay with their own
lives.
[11] The stones in the walls of their
homes will cry out.
And the wooden beams will echo
that cry.

[12] "How terrible it will be for the
Babylonians!
They build cities by spilling the
blood of others.
They establish towns by doing
what is wrong.
[13] I am the LORD who rules over all.
Human effort is no better than
wood that feeds a fire.
So the nations wear themselves
out for nothing.
[14] The oceans are full of water.
In the same way, the earth will
be filled
with the knowledge of my glory.

[15] "How terrible it will be for the
Babylonians!
They give drinks to their
neighbors.
They pour the drinks from wineskins
until their neighbors are drunk.
They want to look at their naked
bodies.
[16] But the Babylonians will be filled
with shame instead of glory.
So now it is their turn to drink
and be stripped of their clothes.
The cup of anger in my powerful
right hand
is going to punish them.
They will be covered with shame
instead of glory.
[17] The harm they have done to
Lebanon
will bring them down.
Because they have killed so many
animals,
animals will terrify them.
They have spilled human blood.
They have destroyed lands and
cities
and everyone in them.

[18] "If someone carves a statue of a
god, what is it worth?
What value is there in a god
that teaches lies?
The one who trusts in this kind of
god
worships his own creation.
He makes statues of gods that
can't speak.
[19] How terrible it will be for the
Babylonians!
They say to a wooden god, 'Come
to life!'
They say to a stone god, 'Wake up!'
Can those gods give advice?
They are covered with gold and
silver.
They can't even breathe."

[20] The LORD is in his holy temple.
Let the whole earth be silent in
front of him.

Habakkuk Prays to the LORD

3 *This is a prayer of Habakkuk the prophet. It is on* shigionoth. *Here is what he said.*

[2] LORD, I know how famous you are.
I have great respect for you
because of your mighty acts.
Do them again for us.
Make them known in our time.
When you are angry,
please have mercy on us.

[3] God came from Teman.
The Holy One came from Mount
Paran.
His glory covered the heavens.
His praise filled the earth.
[4] His glory was like the sunrise.
Rays of light flashed from his
mighty hand.
His power was hidden there.
[5] He sent plagues ahead of him.
Sickness followed behind him.
[6] When he stood up, the earth shook.
When he looked at the nations,
they trembled with fear.
The age-old mountains crumbled.
The ancient hills fell down.
But he marches on forever.
[7] I saw the tents of Cushan in
trouble.
The people of Midian were
suffering greatly.

[8] LORD, were you angry with the
rivers?
Were you angry with the
streams?
Were you angry with the Red Sea?

How can I do hard things?

God will give you strength to do hard things. You don't have to do anything alone. You can always ask God to help you.

Can you find the following verse?
HABAKKUK 3:19

You rode your horses and chariots
to overcome it.
9 You got your bow ready to use.
You asked for many arrows.
You broke up the surface
of the earth with rivers.
10 The mountains saw you and shook.
Floods of water swept by.
The sea roared.
It lifted its waves high.

11 The sun and moon stood still in the
sky.
They stopped because your
flying arrows flashed by.
Your gleaming spear shone like
lightning.
12 When you were angry, you
marched across the earth.
Because of your anger you
destroyed the nations.
13 You came out to set your people
free.
You saved your chosen ones.
You crushed Pharaoh, the leader of
that evil land of Egypt.
You stripped him from head to
foot.
14 His soldiers rushed out to
scatter us.
They were laughing at us.
They thought they would easily
destroy us.
They saw us as weak people who
were trying to hide.
So you wounded Pharaoh's head
with his own spear.
15 Your horses charged into the Red
Sea.
They stirred up the great waters.

16 I listened and my heart pounded.
My lips trembled at the sound.
My bones seemed to rot.
And my legs shook.
But I will be patient.
I'll wait for the day of trouble to
come on Babylon.
It's the nation that is
attacking us.
17 The fig trees might not bud.
The vines might not produce any
grapes.
The olive crop might fail.
The fields might not produce any
food.
There might not be any sheep in
the pens.
There might not be any cattle in
the barns.
18 But I will still be glad
because of what the LORD has
done.
God my Savior fills me with joy.

19 The LORD and King gives me
strength.
He makes my feet like the feet of
a deer.
He helps me walk on the highest
places.

This prayer is for the director of music. It should be sung while being accompanied by stringed instruments.

ZEPHANIAH

Author: Zephaniah

Zephaniah was a prophet of God who lived in the final days of the southern kingdom of Judah. He lived during a time when God's people had turned away (again!) from following God's laws. They were worshiping idols and false gods in temples and robbing each other in the city markets. They were living lives that didn't reflect God's presence in their lives at all! During this time, God gave Zephaniah a message for the people of Judah: All their evil ways were going to come crumbling down. God is holy and just, and he takes sin seriously. The temples to false gods were going to be destroyed, and the markets would be demolished. All nations, including the kingdom of Judah, would be judged according to their disobedience.

Prophecy

But bad news wasn't all Zephaniah had for Judah and the surrounding nations; God also gave him a message of hope. Just as God always does, he pointed all people toward greater hope—the Savior! One day the Savior would come and restore those who humbly repented. Because God is merciful and faithful to his covenant, he promised to establish his kingdom where the perfect King would rule forever.

1 A message from the LORD came to Zephaniah, the son of Cushi. Cushi was the son of Gedaliah. Gedaliah was the son of Amariah. Amariah was the son of King Hezekiah. The LORD spoke to Zephaniah during the rule of Josiah. He was king of Judah and the son of Amon.

The LORD Will Judge the Whole World

2 "I will sweep away everything
from the face of the earth,"
announces the LORD.
3 "I will destroy people and animals
alike.
I will wipe out the birds in the sky
and the fish in the waters.
I will destroy the statues of gods
that cause evil people to sin.
That will happen when I destroy
all human beings on the face of
the earth,"
announces the LORD.
4 "I will reach out my powerful hand
against Judah.
I will punish all those who live in
Jerusalem.
I will destroy from this place
what is left of Baal worship.
The priests who serve other gods
will be removed.
5 I will destroy those who bow down
on their roofs
to worship all the stars.
I will destroy those who make
promises
not only in my name but also in
the name of Molek.
6 I will destroy those who stop
following the LORD.
They no longer look to him or ask
him for advice.
7 Be silent in front of him.
He is the LORD and King.
The day of the LORD is near.
The LORD has prepared a sacrifice.
He has set apart for himself
the people he has invited.
8 When the LORD's sacrifice is ready
to be offered,
I will punish the officials and the
king's sons.
I will also judge all those who follow
the practices of other nations.
9 At that time I will punish
all those who worship other gods.
They fill the temples of their gods
with lies and other harmful things.

God is the Steadfast King. God's justice and mercy never end; he will always be who he says he is.

10 "At that time people at the Fish
Gate in Jerusalem
will cry out," announces the LORD.
"So will those at the New Quarter.
The buildings on the hills will
come crashing down
with a loud noise.
11 Cry out, you who live in the market
places.
All your merchants will be wiped
out.
Those who trade in silver will be
destroyed.
12 At that time I will search Jerusalem
with lamps.
I will punish those who are so
contented.
They are like wine that has not
been shaken up.
They think, 'The LORD won't do
anything.
He won't do anything good or bad.'
13 Their wealth will be stolen.
Their houses will be destroyed.
They will build houses.
But they will not live in them.
They will plant vineyards.
But they will not drink the wine
they produce.
14 The great day of the LORD is near.
In fact, it is coming quickly.
The cries on that day are bitter.
The Mighty Warrior shouts his
battle cry.
15 At that time I will pour out my
anger.
There will be great suffering and
pain.

It will be a day of horrible trouble.
It will be a time of darkness and gloom.
It will be filled with the blackest clouds.
16 Trumpet blasts and battle cries will be heard.
Soldiers will attack cities
that have forts and corner towers.
17 I will bring great trouble on all people.
So they will feel their way around like blind people.
They have sinned against the LORD.
Their blood will be poured out like dust.
Their bodies will lie rotting on the ground.
18 Their silver and gold
won't save them
on the day the LORD pours out his anger.
The whole earth will be burned up
when his jealous anger blazes out.
Everyone who lives on earth
will come to a sudden end."

The LORD Will Judge Judah and Jerusalem Along With the Nations

God Calls Judah to Turn Away From Their Sins

2 Gather together,
you shameful nation of Judah!
Gather yourselves together!
2 Come together before the LORD's judgment arrives.
The day of the LORD's judgment will sweep in
like straw blown by the wind.
Soon the LORD's great anger will come against you.
The day of his wrath will come against you.
3 So look to him, all you people in the land
who worship him faithfully.
You always do what he commands you to do.
Continue to do what is right.
Don't be proud.
Then perhaps the LORD will keep you safe
on the day he pours out his anger on the world.

key verse

So look to him, all
you people in the
land who worship
him faithfully.
You always do what
he commands you to do.
Continue to do what is right.
ZEPHANIAH 2:3

A Message About Philistia

4 Gaza will be deserted.
Ashkelon will be destroyed.
Ashdod will be emptied out at noon.
Ekron will be pulled up by its roots.
5 How terrible it will be for you Kerethites
who live by the Mediterranean Sea!
Philistia, the LORD has spoken against you.
What happened to Canaan will happen to you.

The LORD says, "I will destroy you.
No one will be left."

6 The land by the sea will become grasslands.
It will have wells for shepherds
and pens for flocks.
7 That land will belong to those who are still left alive
among the people of Judah.
They will find grasslands there.
They will take over
the houses in Ashkelon and live in them.
The LORD their God will take care of them.
He will bless them with great success again.

A Message About Moab and Ammon

8 The LORD says,

"I have heard Moab make fun of my people.
The Ammonites also laughed at them.
They told them that bad things
would happen to their land.
9 So Moab will become like Sodom,"
announces the LORD who rules over all.
"Ammon will be like Gomorrah.

Weeds and salt pits will cover those
countries.
They will be dry and empty
deserts forever.
Those who are still left alive among
my people
will take all their valuable
things.
So they will receive those lands
as their own.
And that is just as sure as I am
alive."
The LORD is the God of Israel.

10 Moab and Ammon will be judged
because they are so proud.
They made fun of the LORD's
people.
They laughed at them.
11 The LORD who rules over all will
terrify Moab and Ammon.
He will destroy all the gods on
earth.
Then distant nations will bow down
to him.
All of them will serve him in their
own lands.

A Message About Cush

12 The LORD says, "People of Cush,
you too will die by my sword."

A Message About Assyria

13 The LORD will reach out his powerful
hand against the north.
He will destroy Assyria.
He'll leave Nineveh totally empty.
It will be as dry as a desert.
14 Flocks and herds will lie down
there.
So will creatures of every kind.
Desert owls and screech owls
will rest on its pillars.
The sound of their hooting will
echo through the windows.
The doorways will be full of
trash.
The cedar beams will be showing.
15 Nineveh was a carefree city.
It lived in safety.
It said to itself,
"I am the one!
No one is greater than I am."
But it has been destroyed.
Wild animals make their home
there.
All those who pass by laugh
and shake their fists at it.

A Message About Jerusalem

3 How terrible it will be for
Jerusalem!
Its people crush others.
They refuse to obey the LORD.
They are "unclean."
2 They don't obey anyone.
They don't accept the LORD's
warnings.
They don't trust in him.
They don't ask their God for his
help.
3 Jerusalem's officials are like
roaring lions.
Their rulers are like wolves that
hunt in the evening.
They don't leave anything to eat
in the morning.
4 Their prophets care about nothing.
They can't be trusted.
Their priests make the temple
"unclean."
They break the law they teach
others to obey.
5 In spite of that, the LORD is good to
Jerusalem.
He never does anything that is
wrong.
Every morning he does what is fair.
Each new day he does the right
thing.
But those who do what is wrong
aren't even ashamed of it.

Jerusalem Remains Unrepentant

6 The LORD says to his people,

"I have destroyed other nations.
I have wiped out their forts.
I have left their streets deserted.
No one walks along them.
Their cities are destroyed.
They are deserted and empty.
7 Here is what I thought about
Jerusalem.
'Surely you will have respect for me.
Surely you will accept my warning.'
Then the city you think is safe
would not be destroyed.
And I would not have to punish you
so much.
But they still wanted to go on
sinning
in every way they could.
8 So wait for me to come as judge,"
announces the LORD.
"Wait for the day I will stand up
to witness against all sinners.

I have decided to gather the
nations.
I will bring the kingdoms
together.
And I will pour out all my burning
anger on them.
The fire of my jealous anger
will burn the whole world up.

Israel Will Trust in the LORD

9 "But then I will purify what all the
nations say.
And they will use their words to
worship me.
They will serve me together.
10 My scattered people will come to me
from beyond the rivers of Cush.
They will worship me.
They will bring me offerings.
11 Jerusalem, you have done many
wrong things to me.
But at that time you will not be
put to shame anymore.
That's because I will remove from
this city
those who think so highly of
themselves.
You will never be proud again
on my holy mountain of Zion.
12 But inside your city I will leave
those who are not proud at all.
Those who are still left alive will
trust in the LORD.
13 They will not do anything wrong.

The Bible says God loves me, but how can I know he likes me?

God not only loves you; he delights in you. He likes how he made you. You bring him joy just by being his child.

Can you find the following verse?

ZEPHANIAH 3:17

They will not tell any lies.
They will not say anything to
fool other people.
They will eat and lie down in peace.
And no one will make them
afraid."

14 People of Zion, sing!
Israel, shout loudly!
People of Jerusalem, be glad!
Let your hearts be full of joy.
15 The LORD has stopped punishing you.
He has made your enemies turn
away from you.
The LORD is the King of Israel.
He is with you.
You will never again be afraid
that others will harm you.
16 The time is coming when people
will say to Jerusalem,
"Zion, don't be afraid.
Don't give up.
17 The LORD your God is with you.
He is the Mighty Warrior who saves.
He will take great delight in you.
In his love he will no longer
punish you.
Instead, he will sing for joy
because of you."

18 The LORD says to his people,

"You used to celebrate my
appointed feasts in Jerusalem.
You are sad because you can't do
that anymore.
Other people make fun of you
because of that.
That sadness was a heavy load for
you to carry.
But I will remove that load from
you.
19 At that time I will punish
all those who crushed you.
I will save those among you who
are disabled.
I will gather those who have been
taken away.
I will give them praise and honor
in every land where they have
been put to shame.
20 At that time I will gather you
together.
And I will bring you home.
I will give you honor and praise
among all the nations on earth.
I will bless you with great success
again,"
says the LORD.

HAGGAI

Author: Haggai

Haggai was a prophet of God who lived in Israel when the Jewish exiles were returning from Babylon to rebuild the ruined city of Jerusalem. After experiencing the consequences of their disobedience, the Jews were finally allowed to return to their homeland. Even though they were discouraged and unsure of what life would look like when they returned, they wanted to go home to the land God had given them.

Prophecy

Since the entire city was in shambles, the people started rebuilding their own homes. But Haggai asked the people, "Why are you building your own homes when the temple of God is still a pile of rubble?" God's message to his people through Haggai was this: Even though you're back in your homeland, your hearts still need to change. God wanted his people to seek him first. He wanted the Jews to rebuild the temple first so they could experience his presence. Haggai promised God's people that if they rebuilt God's temple and dedicated their lives to serving him, he would fill the temple with his glory. Haggai also reminded God's people that one day God would build the new Jerusalem, or heaven on earth, where the Savior-King would rule forever.

Haggai Tells His People to Rebuild the LORD's Temple

1 A message from the LORD came to
Haggai the prophet. Haggai gave it
to Zerubbabel and Joshua. Zerubbabel
was governor of Judah and the son of
Shealtiel. Joshua was high priest and
the son of Jozadak. The message came
on the first day of the sixth month of
the second year that Darius was king of
Persia. Here is what Haggai said.
2 Here is what the LORD who rules over
all says. "The people of Judah say, 'It's not
yet time to rebuild the LORD's temple.' "
3 So the message from the LORD came
to me. The LORD said, 4 "My temple is
still destroyed. But you are living in
your houses that have beautiful wooden
walls."
5 The LORD who rules over all says,
"Think carefully about how you are
living. 6 You have planted many seeds.
But the crops you have gathered are
small. So you eat. But you never have
enough. You drink. But you are never
full. You put on your clothes. But you
are not warm. You earn your pay. But
it will not buy everything you need."
7 He continues, "Think carefully
about how you are living. 8 Go up into
the mountains. Bring logs down. Use
them to rebuild the temple, my house.
Then I will enjoy it. And you will honor
me," says the LORD. 9 "You expected a lot.
But you can see what a small amount
it turned out to be. I blew away what
you brought home. I'll tell you why,"
announces the LORD who rules over all.
"Because my temple is still destroyed.
In spite of that, each one of you is busy
with your own house. 10 So because of
what you have done, the heavens have
held back the dew. And the earth has not
produced its crops. 11 I ordered the rain
not to fall on the fields and mountains.
Then the ground did not produce any
grain. There were not enough grapes to
make fresh wine. The trees did not bear
enough olives to make oil. People and
cattle suffered. All your hard work failed."

12 Zerubbabel was the son of Shealtiel.
Joshua the high priest was the son of
Jozadak. They obeyed the LORD their
God. So did all the LORD's people who
were still left alive. The LORD had given
his message to them through me. He

in Haggai?

God is the Deserving One. God is the giver of all things and is worthy of our deepest devotion.

had sent me to speak to them. And the
people had respect for him.
13 Haggai was the LORD's messenger.
So Haggai gave the LORD's message to
the people. He told them, "The LORD announces, 'I am with you.' " 14 So the LORD
stirred up the spirits of Zerubbabel, the
governor of Judah, and Joshua the high
priest. The LORD also stirred up the rest of
the people to help them. Then everyone
began to work on the temple of the LORD
who rules over all. He is their God. 15 It
was the 24th day of the sixth month.

The New Temple Will Be Beautiful

2 In the second year of King Darius,
1 a second message came from the
LORD. It came to Haggai the prophet. The
message came on the 21st day of the seventh month. The LORD said, 2 "Speak to
Zerubbabel, the governor of Judah and
the son of Shealtiel. Also speak to Joshua
the high priest, the son of Jozadak. And
speak to all my people who are still left
alive. Ask them, 3 'Did any of you who
are here see how beautiful this temple
used to be? How does it look to you now?
It doesn't look so good, does it? 4 But
be strong, Zerubbabel,' announces the
LORD. 'Be strong, Joshua. Be strong, all of
you people in the land,' announces the
LORD. 'Start rebuilding. I am with you,'
announces the LORD who rules over all.
5 'That is what I promised you when you
came out of Egypt. My Spirit continues
to be with you. So do not be afraid.' "
6 The LORD says, "In a little while I
will shake the heavens and the earth
once more. I will also shake the ocean
and the dry land. 7 I will shake all the

How did God come to live among his people?

God walked with Adam and Eve in the Garden of Eden. When they sinned, they had to leave God's presence. Later, God's presence lived among his people in the tabernacle and then in the temple—but with special rules. In Jesus, God walked freely among his people again, and today the Holy Spirit lives in everyone who trusts in Jesus.

Can you find the following verse?
HAGGAI 2:9

nations. Then what is desired by all nations will come to my temple. And I will
fill the temple with glory," says the LORD
who rules over all. 8 "The silver belongs
to me. So does the gold," announces
the LORD who rules over all. 9 "The new
temple will be more beautiful than the
first one was," says the LORD. "And in
this place I will bring peace," announces
the LORD who rules over all.

The LORD Will Make His People Pure and "Clean"

10 A third message from the LORD came
to Haggai the prophet. The message
came on the 24th day of the ninth month
of the second year that Darius was king.
11 The LORD who rules over all speaks. He
says, "Ask the priests what the law says.
12 Suppose someone carries holy meat in
the clothes they are wearing. And the
clothes touch some bread or stew. Or they
touch some wine, olive oil or other food.
Then do these things also become holy?"
The priests answered, "No."
13 So Haggai said, "Suppose someone
is made 'unclean' by touching a dead
body. And then they touch one of these
things. Does it become 'unclean' too?"
"Yes," the priests replied. "It does."
14 Then here is what Haggai said. "The
LORD announces, 'That is how I look at
these people and this nation. Anything
they do and anything they sacrifice on
the altar is "unclean."
15 " 'Think carefully about this from
now on. Think about how things were
before the LORD's temple was built. This
was before one stone was laid on top of
another. 16 People went to get 20 measures of grain. But they could find only
10. They went to where the wine was
stored to get 50 measures. But only 20
were there. 17 You worked very hard to
produce all those things. But I struck
them with rot, mold and hail. And you
still did not return to me,' announces the
LORD. 18 It is the 24th day of the ninth
month. From this day on, here is what
you should think carefully about. Think
about the day when the foundation of
my temple was laid. 19 Are any seeds
still left in your barns? Until now, your
vines and fig trees have not produced
any fruit. Your pomegranate and olive
trees have not produced any either.
" 'But from this day on I will bless you.' "

From this day on I will bless you.
HAGGAI 2:19

The LORD Compares Zerubbabel to His Royal Ring

20 A final message from the LORD came
to Haggai. This message also came on
the 24th day of the ninth month. The
LORD said, 21 "Speak to Zerubbabel, the
governor of Judah. Tell him I am going
to shake the heavens and the earth. 22 I
will throw down royal thrones. I will
smash the power of other kingdoms. I
will destroy chariots and their drivers.
Horses and their riders will fall. They will
be killed by the swords of their relatives.
23 " 'Zerubbabel, at that time I will
pick you,' announces the LORD. 'You
are my servant,' announces the LORD.
'You will be like a ring that has my
royal mark on it. I have chosen you,'
announces the LORD who rules over all."

ZECHARIAH

Author: Zechariah

The prophet Zechariah lived during the same time as the prophet Haggai. They shared a similar message: Rebuild God's house, and keep his commands. God wanted his people to return to him with their whole hearts. He wanted them to worship him alone and follow his commands because they loved him. But Zechariah's neighbors were growing weary. They had heard that God was going to come and establish his perfect kingdom—they had been listening to the prophets in every generation promise that the Savior was going to come—but they wondered when he would actually do it. How long would they have to wait? Was the Savior really on his way like God had promised?

Prophecy

I am the LORD your God . . .

Zechariah reminded the Jews of God's promise: One day the true King was going to come, and he would rule forever! Zechariah described the new Jerusalem as a city with a river flowing from it that would give life to Israel and the entire world, just like God promised from the beginning. Not only was God going to restore his people to their home, but he also was promising to come and make his home among them—for their good and for the good of the whole world!

The LORD Wants His People to Return to Him

1 A message from the LORD came to
Zechariah the prophet. Zechariah
was the son of Berekiah. Berekiah was
the son of Iddo. It was the eighth month
of the second year that Darius was king
of Persia. Here is what Zechariah said.
2 The LORD who rules over all was
very angry with your people of long
ago. 3 And now he says to us, "Return
to me. Then I will return to you," announces the LORD. 4 "Do not be like your
people of long ago. The earlier prophets
gave them my message. I said, 'Stop
doing what is evil. Turn away from
your sinful practices.' But they would
not listen to me. They would not pay
any attention," announces the LORD.
5 "Where are those people now? And
what about my prophets? Do they live
forever? 6 I commanded my servants
the prophets what to say. I told them
what I planned to do. But your people
refused to obey me. So I had to punish
them.

"Then they had a change of heart.
They said, 'The LORD who rules over
all has punished us because of how we
have lived. He was fair and right to do
that. He has done to us just what he
decided to do.'"

A Vision of a Horseman Among Some Myrtle Trees

7 A message from the LORD came to
Zechariah the prophet. Zechariah was
the son of Berekiah. Berekiah was the
son of Iddo. The message came during
the second year that Darius was king.
It was the 24th day of the 11th month.
That's the month of Shebat.
8 I had a vision at night. I saw a man
sitting on a red horse. He was standing
among the myrtle trees in a valley.
Behind him were red, brown and white
horses.
9 An angel was talking with me. I
asked him, "Sir, what are these?"

He answered, "I will show you what
they are."
10 Then the man standing among
the myrtle trees spoke. He said, "They
are the messengers the LORD has sent
out. He told them to go all through the
earth."
11 They brought a report to the angel
of the LORD. He was standing among
the myrtle trees. They said to him, "We
have gone all through the earth. We've
found the whole world enjoying peace
and rest."
12 Then the angel of the LORD spoke
up. He said, "LORD, you rule over all.
How long will you keep from showing
your tender love to Jerusalem? How
long will you keep it from the towns
of Judah? You have been angry with
them for 70 years." 13 So the LORD replied with kind and comforting words.
He spoke them to the angel who talked
with me.
14 Then the angel said, "Announce
this message. Say, 'The LORD who rules
over all says, "I am very jealous for my
people in Jerusalem and Zion. 15 And I
am very angry with the nations that
feel secure. I was only a little angry with
my people. But the nations went too far
and tried to wipe them out."
16 " 'So the LORD says, "I will return
to Jerusalem. I will show its people my
tender love. My temple will be rebuilt
there. Workers will use a measuring
line when they rebuild Jerusalem,"
announces the LORD.
17 " 'He says, "My towns will be filled
with good things once more. I will comfort Zion. And I will choose Jerusalem
again." ' "

A Vision of Four Horns and Four Skilled Workers

18 Then I looked up and saw four animal horns. 19 I spoke to the angel who
was talking with me. "What are these
horns?" I asked.

He said, "They are the powerful nations that scattered Judah, Israel and
Jerusalem."
20 Then the LORD showed me four
skilled workers. 21 I asked, "What are
they coming to do?"

He answered, "The horns are the powerful nations that scattered the people
of Judah. That made Judah helpless.
But these four skilled workers have
come to terrify the horns. The workers
will destroy the power of those nations.
Those nations had used their power to
scatter Judah's people."

in Zechariah?

God is the Triumphant One. We can trust him to keep his promises, even when we have been waiting for a very long time.

A Vision of a Man Holding a Measuring Line

2 Then I looked up and saw a man.
He was holding a measuring line.
2 "Where are you going?" I asked.
"To measure Jerusalem," he answered. "I want to find out how wide
and how long it is."
3 The angel who was talking with me
was leaving. At that time, another angel came over to him. 4 He said to him,
"Run! Tell that young man Zechariah,
'Jerusalem will be a city that does not
have any walls around it. It will have
huge numbers of people and animals
in it. 5 And I myself will be like a wall
of fire around it,' announces the LORD.
'I will be the city's glory.'
6 "Israel, I have scattered you," announces the LORD. "I have used the
power of the four winds of heaven to
do it. Come quickly! Run away from the
land of the north," announces the LORD.
7 "Come, people of Zion! Escape, you
who live in Babylon!" 8 The LORD rules
over all. His angel says to Israel, "The
Glorious One has sent me to punish
the nations that have robbed you of
everything. That's because anyone who
hurts you hurts those the LORD loves
and guards. 9 So I will raise my powerful
hand to strike down your enemies. Their
own slaves will rob them of everything.
Then you will know that the LORD who
rules over all has sent me.
10 " 'People of Zion, shout and be glad! I
am coming to live among you,' announces the LORD. 11 'At that time many nations
will join themselves to me. And they will
become my people. I will live among
you,' says the LORD. Then you will know
that the LORD who rules over all has sent
me to you. 12 He will receive Judah as
his share in the holy land. And he will
choose Jerusalem again. 13 All you people
of the world, be still because the LORD
is coming. He is getting ready to come
down from his holy temple in heaven."

A Vision of the High Priest Dressed in Fine Clothes

3 Then the LORD showed me Joshua
the high priest. He was standing in
front of the angel of the LORD. Satan was
standing to the right of Joshua. He was
there to bring charges against the high
priest. 2 The LORD said to Satan, "May
the LORD correct you! He has chosen
Jerusalem. So may he correct you! Isn't
this man Joshua like a burning stick
pulled out of the fire?"
3 Joshua stood in front of the angel.
He was wearing clothes that were very
dirty. 4 The angel spoke to those who
were standing near him. He said, "Take
his dirty clothes off."
He said to Joshua, "I have taken your
sin away. I will put fine clothes on you."
5 I added, "Put a clean turban on his
head." So they did. And they dressed him
while the angel of the LORD stood by.
6 Then the angel spoke to Joshua. He
said, 7 "The LORD who rules over all says,
'You must obey me. You must do what I
have commanded. Then you will rule in
my temple. You will be in charge of my
courtyards. And I will give you a place
among these who are standing here.
8 " 'High Priest Joshua, pay attention!
I want you other priests who are sitting
with Joshua to listen also. All you men
are signs of things to come. I am going
to bring to you my servant the Branch.
9 Look at the stone I have put in front of
Joshua! There are seven eyes on that one
stone. I will carve a message on it,' says
the LORD who rules over all. 'And I will
remove the sin of this land in one day.
10 " 'At that time each of you will invite your neighbors to visit you. They
will sit under your vines and fig trees,'
announces the LORD."

A Vision of the Gold Lampstand and Two Olive Trees

4 Then the angel who was talking with me returned. He woke me up. It was as if I had been asleep. 2 "What do you see?" he asked me.

"I see a solid gold lampstand," I answered. "It has a bowl on top of it. There are seven lamps on it. Seven tubes lead to the lamps. 3 There are two olive trees by the lampstand. One is on its right side. The other is on its left."

4 I asked the angel who was talking with me, "Sir, what are these?"

5 He answered, "Don't you know what they are?"

"No, sir," I replied.

6 So he said to me, "A message from the LORD came to Zerubbabel. The LORD said, 'Your strength will not get my temple rebuilt. Your power will not do it either. Only the power of my Spirit will do it,' says the LORD who rules over all.

7 "So nothing can stop Zerubbabel from completing the temple. Even a mountain of problems will be smoothed out by him. When the temple is finished, he will put its most important stone in place. Then the people will shout, 'God bless it! God bless it!' "

8 Then a message from the LORD came to me. His angel said, 9 "The hands of Zerubbabel have laid the foundation of this temple. His hands will also complete it. Then you will know that the LORD who rules over all has sent me to you.

10 "Do not look down on the small amount of work done on the temple so far. The seven eyes of the LORD look over the whole earth. They will see Zerubbabel holding the most important stone. They will be filled with joy when they see it."

11 Then I said to the angel, "I see two olive trees. One is on the right side of the lampstand. The other is on the left. What are these trees?"

12 I continued, "I also see two olive branches. They are next to the two gold pipes that pour out golden olive oil. What are these branches?"

13 He answered, "Don't you know what they are?"

"No, sir," I said.

14 So he told me, "They are Zerubbabel and Joshua. The Lord of the whole earth has anointed them to serve him."

A Vision of a Flying Scroll

5 I looked up again and saw a flying scroll.

2 "What do you see?" the angel asked me.

"A scroll flying in the air," I replied. "It's 30 feet long and 15 feet wide."

3 He said to me, "A curse sent by the LORD is written on it. It is going out over the whole land. Every thief will be driven out of the land. That is what it says on one side of the scroll. Everyone who lies when promising to tell the truth will also be driven out. That is what it says on the other side. 4 The LORD who rules over all announces, 'I will send the curse out. It will enter the house of the thief. It will also enter the house of anyone who lies when making a promise in my name. It will remain in that house and destroy it completely. It will pull down its beams and stones.' "

A Vision of a Woman in a Basket

5 Then the angel who was talking with me came forward. He said to me, "Look at what is coming."

6 "What is it?" I asked.

"A basket," he replied. "The sins of the people all through the land are in it."

7 Then the basket's cover was lifted up. It was made out of lead. A woman was sitting in the basket! 8 The angel said, "She stands for everything that is evil." Then he pushed her down into the basket. He put the lead cover back over it.

9 I looked up and saw two other women. They had wings like the wings of a stork. A wind sent by the LORD carried them along. They lifted the basket up between heaven and earth.

10 "Where are they taking the basket?" I asked the angel.

11 He replied, "To the country of Babylon. A temple will be built for it. When the temple is ready, the basket will be set there in its place."

A Vision of Four Chariots

6 I looked up again and saw four chariots. They were coming out from between two mountains. The mountains were made out of bronze. 2 The first chariot was pulled by red horses. The second one had black horses. 3 The third had white horses. And the fourth had spotted horses. All

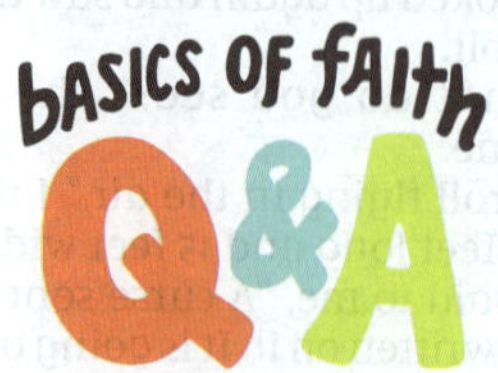

How can I reflect God's character?

No one can reflect God's character simply by trying. You need God to help you. God promises to give you his Spirit to dwell within you so you'll grow to be more like him every day.

Can you find the following verse?

ZECHARIAH 7:9

the horses were powerful. [4]I asked the
angel who was talking with me, "Sir,
what are these?"
[5]The angel answered, "The four spirits of heaven. They are going out to
serve the Lord of the whole world. [6]The
chariot pulled by the black horses is going toward the north country. The one
with the white horses is going toward
the west. And the one with the spotted
horses is going toward the south."
[7]The powerful horses went out. They
were in a hurry to go all over the earth.
The angel said, "Go all through the
earth!" So they did.
[8]Then the LORD called out to me,
"Look! The horses going toward the
north have given my Spirit rest in the
north country."

A Crown Is Given to Joshua

[9]A message from the LORD came to
me. His angel said, [10]"Get some silver
and gold from Heldai, Tobijah and Jedaiah. They have just come back from
Babylon. On that same day go to Josiah's
house. He is the son of Zephaniah. [11]Use
the silver and gold to make a crown. Set
it on the head of Joshua the high priest.
He is the son of Jozadak. [12]Give Joshua a
message from the LORD who rules over
all. He says, 'Here is the man whose
name is the Branch. He will branch out
and build my temple. [13]That is what he
will do. He will be dressed in majesty
as if it were his royal robe. He will sit
as king on his throne. He will also be a
priest there. So he will combine the positions of king and priest in himself.' [14]The
crown will be given to Heldai, Tobijah,
Jedaiah and Zephaniah's son Hen. The
crown will be kept in the LORD's temple.
It will remind everyone that the LORD's
promises will come true. [15]Those who are
far away will come to Jerusalem. They
will help build the LORD's temple. Then
his people will know that the LORD who
rules over all has sent me to them. It will
happen if they are careful to obey the
LORD their God."

Have Justice and Mercy

7 During the fourth year that Darius
was king, a message from the LORD
came to me. It was the fourth day of
the ninth month. That's the month of
Kislev. [2]The people of Bethel wanted to
ask the LORD for his blessing. So they
sent Sharezer and Regem-Melek and
their men. [3]They went to the prophets
and priests at the LORD's temple. They
asked them, "Should we mourn and
go without eating in the fifth month?
That's what we've done for many years."
[4]Then the message came to me from
the LORD who rules over all. He said,
[5]"Ask the priests and all the people in
the land a question for me. Say to them,
'You mourned and fasted in the fifth
and seventh months. You did it for the
past 70 years. But did you really do it
for me? [6]And when you were eating and
drinking, weren't you just enjoying good
food for yourselves? [7]Didn't I tell you the
same thing through the earlier prophets? That was when Jerusalem and the
towns around it were at rest and enjoyed
success. People lived in the Negev Desert
and the western hills at that time.'"
[8]Another message from the LORD
came to me. [9]Here is what the LORD who
rules over all said to his people. "Treat
everyone with justice. Show mercy and
tender concern to one another. [10]Do
not take advantage of widows. Do not
mistreat children whose fathers have
died. Do not be mean to outsiders or
poor people. Do not make evil plans
against one another."

[11] But they refused to pay attention to the LORD. They were stubborn. They turned their backs and covered their ears. [12] They made their hearts as hard as the hardest stone. They wouldn't listen to the law. They wouldn't pay attention to the LORD's messages. So the LORD who rules over all was very angry. After all, his Spirit had spoken to his people through the earlier prophets.

[13] "When I called, they did not listen," says the LORD. "So when they called, I would not listen. [14] I used a windstorm to scatter them among all the nations. They were strangers there. The land they left behind became dry and empty. No one could even travel through it. This is how they turned the pleasant land into a dry and empty desert."

The LORD Promises to Bless Jerusalem

8 A message came to me from the LORD who rules over all.

He said, [2] "I am very jealous for my people in Zion. In fact, I am burning with jealousy for them."

[3] He continued, "I will return to Zion. I will live among my people in Jerusalem. Then Jerusalem will be called the Faithful City. And my mountain will be called the Holy Mountain."

[4] He continued, "Once again old men and women will sit in the streets of Jerusalem. All of them will be using canes because they are old. [5] The city streets will be filled with boys and girls. They will be playing there."

[6] He continued, "All of that might seem hard to believe to the people living then. But it will not be too hard for me."

[7] He continued, "I will save my people. I will gather them from the countries of the east and the west. [8] I will bring them back to live in Jerusalem. They will be my people. I will be their faithful God. I will keep my promises to them."

[9] The LORD who rules over all says to his people, "Now listen to these words, 'Let your hands be strong so that you can rebuild the temple.' This also was said by the prophets Haggai and Zechariah. They spoke to you when the work on my temple began again. [10] Before the work was started again, there was no pay for the people. And there was no money to rent animals. People could not go about their business safely because of their enemies. I had turned all of them against one another. [11] But now I will not punish you who are living at

RIGHTEOUS

God has never done anything wrong and has never sinned. Because God is righteous, we can trust that he will always be just—he will never make a judgment that is unfair.

Imagine you're playing with your friend's toy and you accidently break it. By choosing to tell your friend the truth that you were playing with their toy when it broke, you are being righteous. You are doing what is fair and kind.

God wants his people to grow in righteousness. With the Spirit of God living inside all who believe in Jesus, God's people have the power to live and act in ways that are honest and fair, mirroring God's righteous character (see 2 Timothy 1:7).

My GOD IS...

this time. I will not treat you as I treated
your people before you," announces the
LORD who rules over all.
12 "Your seeds will grow well. Your
vines will bear fruit. The ground will
produce crops for you. And the heavens
will drop their dew on your land. I will
give all these things to those who are
still left alive here. 13 Judah and Israel, in
the past you have been a curse among
the nations. But now I will save you.
You will be a blessing to others. Do not
be afraid. Let your hands be strong so
that you can do my work."
14 The LORD who rules over all says,
"Your people of long ago made me angry. So I decided to bring trouble on
them. I did not show them any pity.
15 But now I plan to do good things to
Jerusalem and Judah again. So do not
be afraid. 16 Here is what you must do.
Speak the truth to one another. Make
true and wise decisions in your courts.
17 Do not make evil plans against one
another. When you promise to tell the
truth, do not lie. Many people love to
do that. But I hate all these things,"
announces the LORD.
18 Another message came to me from
the LORD who rules over all.
He said, 19 "You have established special times to go without eating. They are
your fasts in the fourth, fifth, seventh
and tenth months. They will become
days of joy. They will be happy times
for Judah. It will happen if you take
delight in telling the truth and bringing
about peace."
20 He continued, "Many nations will
still come to you. And those who live in
many cities will also come. 21 The people
who live in one city will go to another
city. They will say, 'Let's go right away
to ask the LORD for his blessing. Let's
look to him as our God. We ourselves
are going.' 22 Large numbers of people
and nations will come to Jerusalem.
They will look to me. They will ask me
to bless them."
23 He continued, "At that time many
people of all nations and languages will
take hold of one Jew. They will grab hold
of the hem of his robe. And they will
say, 'We want to go to Jerusalem with
you. We've heard that God is with you.' "

The LORD Destroys Israel's Enemies

9 This is a prophecy.

It is the LORD's message
against the land of Hadrak.
He will judge Damascus.
That's because all the tribes of
Israel look to him.
So do all other people.
2 The LORD will judge Hamath too.
It's next to Damascus.
He will also punish Tyre and Sidon
even though they are very
clever.
3 Tyre's people have built a fort for
themselves.
They've piled up silver like dust.
They have as much gold as the
dirt in the streets.
4 But the Lord will take away
everything they have.
He'll destroy their power on the
Mediterranean Sea.
And Tyre will be completely
burned up.
5 Ashkelon will see it and become
afraid.
Gaza will groan with pain.
So will Ekron. Its hope will
vanish.
Gaza will no longer have a king.
Ashkelon will be deserted.
6 A people who come from several
nations will take over Ashdod.
The LORD says, "I will put an
end to the pride of the
Philistines.
7 They will no longer drink the blood
of their animal sacrifices.
I will remove the 'unclean' food
from between their teeth.
The Philistines who are left will
belong to our God.
They will become a family group
in Judah.
And Ekron will be like the
Jebusites.
So the Philistines will become
part of Israel.
8 But I will camp at my temple.
I will guard it against enemy
armies.
No one will ever crush my people
again.
I will make sure it does not
happen.

A King Comes to Zion

9 "City of Zion, be full of joy!
People of Jerusalem, shout!
See, your king comes to you.
He always does what is right.
He has won the victory.
He is humble and riding on a donkey.
He is sitting on a donkey's colt.
10 I will take the chariots away from Ephraim.
I will remove the war horses from Jerusalem.
I will break the bows that are used in battle.
Your king will announce peace to the nations.
He will rule from ocean to ocean.
His kingdom will reach from the Euphrates River
to the ends of the earth.
11 I will set your prisoners free
from where their enemies are keeping them.
I will do it because of the blood
that put into effect my covenant with you.
12 Return to your place of safety,
you prisoners who still have hope.
Even now I announce that I will give you back
much more than you had before.
13 I will bend Judah as I bend my bow.
I will make Ephraim's people my arrows.
Zion, I will stir up your sons.
Greece, they will attack your sons.
My people, I will use you as my sword."

The LORD Will Appear

14 Then the LORD will appear over his people.
His arrows will flash like lightning.
The LORD and King will blow the trumpet of his thunder.
He'll march out like a storm in the south.
15 The LORD who rules over all
will be like a shield to his people.
They will destroy their enemies.
They'll use slings to throw stones at them.

key verse City of Zion, be full of joy! People of Jerusalem, shout! See, your king comes to you. He always does what is right. He has won the victory. He is humble and riding on a donkey. He is sitting on a donkey's colt. ZECHARIAH 9:9

They'll drink the blood of their enemies
as if it were wine.
They'll be full like the bowl that is used
for sprinkling the corners of the altar.
16 The LORD their God will save his people on that day.
He will be like a shepherd who saves his flock.
They will gleam in his land
like jewels in a crown.
17 How very beautiful they will be!
Grain and fresh wine
will make the young men and young women strong.

The LORD Will Take Care of Judah

10 People of Judah, ask the LORD
to send rain in the spring.
He is the one who sends the thunderstorms.
He sends down showers of rain on all people.
He gives everyone the plants in the fields.
2 Other gods tell lies.
Those who practice magic
see visions that aren't true.
They tell dreams that fool people.
They give comfort that doesn't do any good.
So the people wander around like sheep.
They are crushed because they don't have a shepherd.

3 The LORD who rules over all says,

"I am very angry with the shepherds.
I will punish the leaders.
The LORD will take care of his flock.
They are the people of Judah.
He will make them like a proud horse in battle.

[4]The most important building stone
will come from the tribe of
Judah.
The tent stake will also come
from it.
And the bow that is used in battle
will come from it.
In fact, every ruler will come
from it.
[5]Together they will be like warriors
in battle.
They will stomp their enemies
into the mud of the streets.
The LORD will be with them.
So they will fight against the
horsemen
and put them to shame.
[6]"I will make the family of Judah
strong.
I will save the tribes of Joseph.
I will bring them back
because I have tender love for
them.
It will be as if
I had not sent them away.
I am the LORD their God.
I will help them.
[7]The people of Ephraim will become
like warriors.
Their hearts will be glad
as if they were drinking wine.
Their children will see it
and be filled with joy.
I will make their hearts glad.
[8]I will signal for my people to come,
and I will gather them in.
I will set them free.
There will be as many of them as
before.
[9]I have scattered them among the
nations.
But in lands far away they will
remember me.
They and their children will be kept
alive.
And they will return.
[10]I will bring them back from Egypt.
I will gather them from Assyria.
I will bring them to Gilead and
Lebanon.
There will not be enough room
for them.
[11]They will pass through a sea of
trouble.
The stormy sea will calm down.
All the deep places in the Nile
River will dry up.
Assyria's pride will be brought
down.
Egypt's right to rule will
disappear.
[12]I will make my people strong.
They will live in safety because
of me,"
announces the LORD.

11 Lebanon, open your doors!
Then fire can burn up your cedar
trees.
[2]Juniper trees, cry out!
The cedar trees have fallen down.
The majestic trees are destroyed.
Cry out, you oak trees of Bashan!
The thick forest has been cut
down.
[3]Listen to the shepherds cry out!
Their rich grasslands are
destroyed.
Listen to the lions roar!
The trees and bushes along the
Jordan River are gone.

The Two Shepherds

[4]The LORD my God says, "Take care of
the sheep that are set apart to be sacrificed. [5]Those who buy them kill them.
And they are not punished for it. Those
who sell them say, 'Praise the LORD!
We're rich!' And their own shepherds
do not spare them. [6]I will no longer
have pity on the people in the land,"
announces the LORD. "I will hand all of
them over to their neighbors and their
king. They will destroy the land. And I
will not save anyone from their power."
[7]So I took care of the sheep set apart
to be sacrificed. I took special care of
those that had been treated badly. Then
I got two shepherd's staffs. I called one
of them Favor. I called the other one
Union. And I took care of the flock. [8]In
one month I got rid of three worthless
shepherds.

The sheep hated me, and I got tired
of them. [9]So I said, "I won't be your
shepherd anymore. Let those of you
who are dying die. Let those who are
passing away pass away. Let those who
are left eat one another up."
[10]Then I got my staff called Favor. I
broke it. That meant the covenant the
LORD had made with all the nations
was broken. [11]It happened that day.

The sheep that had been treated badly were watching me. They knew it was the LORD's message.
[12] I told them, "If you think it is best, give me my pay. But if you don't think so, keep it." So they paid me 30 silver coins.
[13] The LORD said to me, "Throw those coins to the potter." That amount shows how little they valued me! So I threw the 30 silver coins to the potter at the LORD's temple.
[14] Then I broke my second staff called Union. That broke the family connection between Judah and Israel.
[15] The LORD said to me, "Now pretend to be a foolish shepherd. Get the things you need.
[16] I am going to raise up a shepherd over the land. He will not take care of those that are wounded. He will not look for the young ones. He will not heal those that are hurt. He will not feed the healthy ones. Instead, he will eat the best sheep. He will even tear their hooves off.

[17] "How terrible it will be for that
worthless shepherd!
He deserts the flock.
May a sword strike his arm and his
right eye!
May his powerful arm become
weak!
May his right eye be totally
blinded!"

The LORD Will Destroy Jerusalem's Enemies

12 This is a prophecy. It is the LORD's message about Israel.

The LORD spreads out the heavens. He lays the foundation of the earth. He creates the human spirit within a person. He says,
[2] "Jerusalem will be like a cup in my hand. It will make all the surrounding nations drunk from the wine of my anger. Judah will be attacked by its enemies. So will Jerusalem.
[3] At that time all the nations on earth will gather together against Jerusalem. Then it will become like a rock that can't be moved. All the nations that try to move it will only hurt themselves.
[4] On that day I will fill every horse with panic. I will make every rider crazy," announces the LORD. "I will watch over the people of Judah. But I will make all the horses of the nations blind.
[5] Then the family groups of Judah will say in their hearts, 'The people of Jerusalem are strong. That's because the LORD who rules over all is their God.'
[6] "At that time Judah's family groups will be like a fire pot in a pile of wood. They will be like a burning torch among bundles of grain. They will destroy all the surrounding nations on every side. But Jerusalem will remain unharmed in its place.
[7] "I will save the houses in Judah first. The honor of David's family line is great. So is the honor of those who live in Jerusalem. But their honor will not be greater than the honor of the rest of Judah.
[8] At that time I will be like a shield to those who live in Jerusalem. Then even the weakest among them will be great warriors like David. And David's family line will be like the angel of the LORD who leads them.
[9] On that day I will begin to destroy all the nations that attack Jerusalem.

Israel's People Will Mourn Over the One They Pierced

[10] "I will pour out a spirit of grace and prayer on David's family line. I will also send it on those who live in Jerusalem. They will look to me. I am the one they have pierced. They will mourn over me as someone mourns over an only child who has died. They will be full of sorrow over me. Their sorrow will be just like someone's sorrow over an oldest son.
[11] At that time there will be a lot of weeping in Jerusalem. It will be as great as the weeping of the people at Hadad Rimmon. Hadad Rimmon is in the valley of Megiddo. They were weeping over Josiah's death.
[12] Everyone in the land will mourn. Each family will mourn by themselves and their wives by themselves. That will include the family lines of David, Nathan,
[13] Levi, Shimei and
[14] all the others.

The LORD Makes Israel Pure and "Clean"

13 "At that time a fountain will be opened for the benefit of David's family line. It will also bless the others who live in Jerusalem. It will wash away their sins. It will make them pure and 'clean.'
[2] "On that day I will remove the names of other gods from the land. They will

not even be remembered anymore,"
announces the LORD who rules over
all. "I will drive the evil prophets out
of the land. I will get rid of the spirit
that put lies in their mouths. 3 Some
people might still prophesy. But their
own fathers and mothers will speak to
them. They will tell them, 'You must die.
You have told lies in the LORD's name.'
When they prophesy, their own parents
will stab them.

4 "At that time every prophet will be
ashamed of the vision they see. They
will no longer pretend to be a true
prophet. They will not put on clothes
that are made out of hair in order to
trick people. 5 In fact, each one will say,
'I'm not really a prophet. I'm a farmer.
I've farmed the land since I was young.'
6 Suppose someone asks, 'What are
these wounds on your body?' Then they
will answer, 'I was given these wounds
at the house of my friends.'

The Good Shepherd Is Killed and the Sheep Are Scattered

7 "My sword, wake up! Attack my
shepherd!
Attack the man who is close to me,"
announces the LORD who rules
over all.
"Strike down the shepherd.
Then the sheep will be scattered.
And I will turn my hand against
their little ones.
8 Here is what will happen in the
whole land,"
announces the LORD.
"Two-thirds of the people will be
struck down and die.
But one-third will be left.
9 I will put this third in the fire.
I will make them as pure as
silver.
I will test them like gold.
They will call out to me.
And I will answer them.
I will say, 'They are my people.'
And they will say, 'The LORD is
our God.' "

The LORD Will Be King Over the Whole Earth

14 The day of the LORD is coming,
Jerusalem. At that time your enemies will steal everything your people
own. They will divide it up within your
walls.

2 The LORD will gather all the nations
together. They will fight against Jerusalem. They'll capture the city. Its houses
will be robbed. Its women will be raped.
Half of the people will be taken away
as prisoners. But the rest of them won't
be taken. 3 Then the LORD will march
out and fight against those nations.
He will fight as on a day of battle. 4 On
that day he will stand on the Mount of
Olives. It's east of Jerusalem. It will be
split in two from east to west. Half of the
mountain will move north. The other
half will move south. A large valley will
be formed. 5 The people will run away
through that mountain valley. It will
reach all the way to Azel. They'll run
away just as they ran from the earthquake when Uzziah was king of Judah.
Then the LORD my God will come. All the
holy ones will come with him.

6 There won't be any sunlight on that
day. There will be no cold, frosty darkness either. 7 It will be a day unlike any
other. It will be a day known only to the
LORD. It won't be separated into day and
night. After that day is over, there will
be light again.

8 At that time water that gives life will
flow out from Jerusalem. Half of it will
run east into the Dead Sea. The other
half will go west to the Mediterranean
Sea. The water will flow in summer and
winter.

9 The LORD will be king over the whole
earth. On that day there will be one
LORD. His name will be the only name.
10 The whole land south of Jerusalem
will be changed. From Geba to Rimmon
it will become like the Arabah Valley.
But Jerusalem will be raised up high. It
will be raised from the Benjamin Gate to
the First Gate to the Corner Gate. It will
be raised from the Tower of Hananel
to the royal winepresses. And it will
remain in its place. 11 People will live
in it. Jerusalem will never be destroyed
again. It will be secure.

12 The LORD will punish all the nations that fought against Jerusalem.
He'll strike them with a plague. It will
make their bodies rot while they are
still standing on their feet. Their eyes
will rot in their heads. Their tongues will
rot in their mouths. 13 On that day the
LORD will fill people with great panic.
They will grab one another by the hand.

And they'll attack one another. 14 Judah
will also fight at Jerusalem. The wealth
of all the surrounding nations will be
collected. Huge amounts of gold, silver
and clothes will be gathered up. 15 The
same kind of plague will strike the
horses, mules, camels and donkeys. In
fact, it will strike all the animals in the
army camps.

16 But some people from all the nations that have attacked Jerusalem will
still be left alive. All of them will go up
there to worship the King. He is the LORD
who rules over all. Year after year these
people will celebrate the Feast of Booths.
17 Some nations might not go up to Jerusalem to worship the King. If they
don't, they won't have any rain. 18 The
people of Egypt might not go up there
to take part. Then they won't have any
rain either. That's the plague the LORD
will send on the nations that don't go
to celebrate the Feast of Booths. 19 Egypt
will be punished. So will all the other
nations that don't celebrate the feast.

20 On that day "Holy to the LORD" will
be carved on the bells of the horses. The
cooking pots in the LORD's temple will be
just like the sacred bowls in front of the
altar for burnt offerings. 21 Every pot in
Jerusalem and Judah will be set apart
to the LORD. All those who come to offer
sacrifices will get some of the pots and
cook in them. At that time there won't
be any Canaanites in the LORD's temple.
He is the LORD who rules over all.

MALACHI

Author: Malachi

Malachi was a prophet of God who lived in Judah after the Jews returned from Babylon. The Jews had finished rebuilding the temple but still were not worshiping God. They had physically returned home to Jerusalem, but their hearts were far from God. Through Malachi, God called Israel out for being rebellious and forsaking his covenant. But they disagreed with God! They argued with him, insisting they *had* kept his law. They looked at what they had accomplished and thought they were doing well; they thought God should be pleased with them. In response, Malachi listed all the ways the people had been unfaithful while God had been faithful. The book of Malachi lists the sins of God's people, reminding them that in every generation, they had failed to keep God's laws.

Malachi ended this book with a reminder that the day of the Lord was coming soon. He reminded the people that for those who love God, repent of their sins, and worship God alone, the day of the Lord will be the best day ever! On that day, God will judge those who have done evil, but he will take his people home with him forever. Soon—very, very soon!—the Savior was going to come.

1 This is a prophecy. It is the LORD's
message to Israel through Malachi.

Israel Doubts God's Love

2 "Israel, I have loved you," says the
LORD.
"But you ask, 'How have you loved us?'
"Wasn't Esau Jacob's brother?" says
the LORD. "But I chose Jacob 3 instead of
Esau. I have turned Esau's hill country
into a dry and empty land. I left that
land of Edom to the wild dogs in the
desert."
4 Edom might say, "We have been
crushed. But we'll rebuild our cities."
The LORD who rules over all says,
"They might rebuild their cities. But I
will destroy them. They will be called
the Evil Land. My anger will always
remain on them. 5 You will see it with
your own eyes. You will say, 'The LORD is
great! He rules even beyond the borders
of Israel!'

Give Your Best to the LORD

6 "A son honors his father. A slave
honors his master. If I am a father,
where is the honor I should have? If I
am a master, where is the respect you
should give me?" says the LORD who
rules over all.
"You priests look down on me.
"But you ask, 'How have we looked
down on you?'
7 "You sacrifice 'unclean' food on my
altar.
"But you ask, 'How have we made
you "unclean"?'
"You do it by looking down on my
altar. 8 You sacrifice blind animals to
me. Isn't that wrong? You sacrifice disabled or sick animals. Isn't that wrong?
Try offering them to your governor!
Would he be pleased with you? Would
he accept you?" says the LORD who rules
over all.
9 "Now plead with God to be gracious
to us! But as long as you give offerings
like those, how can he accept you?" says
the LORD.
10 "You might as well shut the temple
doors! Then you would not light useless
fires on my altar. I am not pleased with
you," says the LORD. "I will not accept
any of the offerings you bring. 11 My
name will be great among the nations.
They will worship me from where the

in Malachi?

God is the Coming Messiah. In this last book of the Old Testament, God repeats this promise: The Savior is coming. The Promised One is on his way.

sun rises in the east to where it sets in
the west. In every place, incense and
pure offerings will be brought to me.
That's because my name will be great
among the nations," says the LORD.
12 "But you treat my name as if it were
not holy. You say the LORD's altar is
'unclean.' And you look down on its
food. 13 You say, 'What a heavy load our
work is!' And you turn up your nose. You
act as if you hate working for me," says
the LORD who rules over all.
"You bring animals that have been
hurt. Or you bring disabled or sick animals. Then you dare to offer them to
me as sacrifices! Should I accept them
from you?" says the LORD. 14 "Suppose
you have a male sheep or goat that does
not have any flaws. And you promise to
offer it to me. But then you sacrifice an
animal that has flaws. When you do that,
you cheat me. And anyone who cheats
me is under my curse. After all, I am a
great king," says the LORD who rules over
all. "The other nations have respect for
my name. So why don't you respect it?

The LORD Warns the Priests

2 "Now I am giving this warning to
you priests. 2 Listen to it. Honor me
with all your heart," says the LORD who
rules over all. "If you do not, I will send
a curse on you. I will turn your blessings
into curses. In fact, I have already done
that because you have not honored me
with all your heart.

3 "Because of what you have done, I
will punish your children. I will smear
the waste from your sacrifices on your
faces. And you will be carried off to the
dump along with it. 4 You will know that
I have given you this warning. I have
warned you so that my covenant with
Levi will continue," says the LORD who
rules over all. 5 "My covenant promised
Levi life and peace. So I gave them to
him. I required him to respect me. And
he had great respect for my name.
6 True teaching came from his mouth.
Nothing but the truth came from his
lips. He walked with me in peace. He
did what was right. He turned many
people away from their sins.

7 "The lips of a priest should guard
knowledge. After all, he is the messenger of the LORD who rules over all. And
people seek instruction from his mouth.
8 But you have turned away from the
right path. Your teaching has caused
many people to trip and fall. You have
broken my covenant with Levi," says
the LORD who rules over all. 9 "So I have
caused all the people to hate you. They
have lost respect for you. You have not
done what I told you to do. Instead, you
have favored one person over another
in matters of the law."

Breaking the Covenant Through Divorce

10 People of Judah, all of us have one
Father. One God created us. So why do
we break the covenant the LORD made
with our people of long ago? We do this
by being unfaithful to one another.

11 And Judah has been unfaithful. A
hateful thing has been done in Israel and Jerusalem. The LORD loves his
temple. But Judah has made it impure.
Their men have married women who
worship other gods. 12 May the LORD
punish the man who marries a woman like this. It doesn't matter who that
man is. May the LORD who rules over all
remove him from the tents of Jacob's
people. May the LORD remove him even
if he brings an offering to him.

13 Here's something else you do.
You flood the LORD's altar with your
tears. You weep and cry because your
offerings don't please him anymore.
He doesn't accept them with pleasure
from your hands. 14 You ask, "Why?"
It's because the LORD is holding you
responsible. He watches how you treat
the wife you married when you were
young. You have been unfaithful to
her. You did it even though she's your
partner. You promised to stay married
to her. And the LORD was a witness to it.

15 Hasn't the one God made the two
of you one also? Both of you belong to
him in body and spirit. And why has
the one God made you one? Because he
wants his children to be like him. So be
careful. Don't be unfaithful to the wife
you married when you were young.

16 "Suppose a man hates and divorces his wife," says the LORD God of Israel. "Then he is harming the one he
should protect," says the LORD who rules
over all.

So be careful. And don't be unfaithful.

Breaking the Covenant by Treating Others Unfairly

17 You have worn out the LORD by what
you keep saying.

"How have we worn him out?" you
ask.

You have done it by saying, "All
those who do evil things are good in
the LORD's sight. And he is pleased with
them." Or you ask, "Is God really fair?"

3 The LORD who rules over all says,
"I will send my messenger. He will
prepare my way for me. Then suddenly
the Lord you are looking for will come
to his temple. The messenger of the
covenant will come. He is the one you
long for."

2 But who can live through the day
when he comes? Who will be left standing when he appears? He will be like a
fire that makes things pure. He will be
like soap that makes things clean. 3 He
will act like one who makes silver pure.
And he will purify the Levites, just as
gold and silver are purified with fire.
Then these men will bring proper offerings to the LORD. 4 And the offerings of
Judah and Jerusalem will be acceptable
to him. It will be as it was in days and
years gone by.

5 "So I will come and put you on trial.
I will be quick to bring charges against
all of you," says the LORD who rules
over all. "I will bring charges against
you sinful people who do not have any
respect for me. That includes those who

UNCHANGING

God is the same today as he always has been, and he will be the same tomorrow and every day after (see Hebrews 13:8). His character and nature will always be the same. He will never change.

Sometimes we don't know what to expect from people because they respond differently each time something happens to them. But God is not like that—he is always the same, so we always know how he will respond to us.

God's Word never changes, and that means we can trust him to be faithful. The God who made the promises we read in the Bible is the same God who will be faithful to keep those promises today.

practice evil magic. It includes those who commit adultery and those who tell lies in court. It includes those who cheat workers out of their pay. It includes those who treat widows badly. It also includes those who mistreat children whose fathers have died. And it includes those who take away the rights of outsiders in the courts.

If God loves me just the way I am, why should I obey his commands?

God gives his people commands to obey because he loves us and knows what is best for us. His commands are an invitation to live life more fully.

Can you find the following verse?

MALACHI 3:7

Breaking the Covenant by Stealing From God

6 "I am the LORD. I do not change.
That is why I have not destroyed you
members of Jacob's family. 7 You have
turned away from my rules. You have
not obeyed them. You have lived that
way ever since the days of your people
of long ago. Return to me. Then I will
return to you," says the LORD who rules
over all.

"But you ask, 'How can we return?'
8 "Will a mere human being dare to
steal from God? But you rob me!

"You ask, 'How are we robbing you?'

"By holding back your offerings. You
also steal from me when you do not
bring me a tenth of everything you
produce. 9 So you are under my curse.
In fact, your whole nation is under my
curse. That is because you are robbing
me. 10 Bring the entire tenth to the storerooms in my temple. Then there will be
plenty of food. Test me this way," says
the LORD. "Then you will see that I will
throw open the windows of heaven. I

will pour out so many blessings that
you will not have enough room to store
them. [11] I will keep bugs from eating up
your crops. And your grapes will not
drop from the vines before they are
ripe," says the LORD. [12] "Then all the
nations will call you blessed. Your land
will be delightful," says the LORD who
rules over all.

Israel Speaks With Pride Against the LORD

[13] "You have spoken with pride
against me," says the LORD.
"But you ask, 'What have we spoken
against you?'
[14] "You have said, 'It is useless to serve
God. What do we gain by obeying his
laws? And what do we get by pretending
to be sad in front of the LORD? [15] But now
we call proud people blessed. Things
go well with those who do what is evil.
And God doesn't even punish those who
test him.' "

Those Who Respect the LORD

[16] Those who had respect for the LORD
talked with one another. And the LORD
heard them. A list of people and what
they did was written in a book in front of
him. It included the names of those who
respected the LORD and honored him.
[17] "The day is coming when I will
judge," says the LORD who rules over
all. "On that day they will be my special treasure. I will spare them just as
a father loves and spares his son who
serves him. [18] Then once again you will
see the difference between godly people
and sinful people. And you will see the
difference between those who serve me
and those who do not.

The Day of the LORD Is Coming

4 "You can be sure the day of the
LORD is coming. My anger will burn
like a furnace. All those who are proud
will be like straw. So will all those who
do what is evil. The day that is coming
will set them on fire," says the LORD
who rules over all. "Not even a root or
a branch will be left to them. [2] But here
is what will happen for you who have
respect for me. The sun that brings life
will rise. Its rays will bring healing to
my people. You will go out and leap for
joy like calves that have just been fed.
[3] Then you will stomp on sinful people.
They will be like ashes under your feet.
That will happen on the day I judge,"
says the LORD.

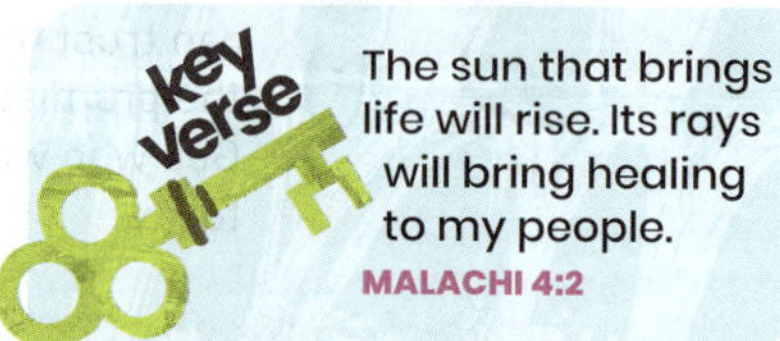

[4] "Remember the law my servant
Moses gave you. Remember the rules
and laws I gave him at Mount Horeb.
They were for the whole nation of
Israel.
[5] "I will send the prophet Elijah to you.
He will come before the day of the LORD
arrives. It will be a great and terrifying
day. [6] Elijah will bring peace between
parents and their children. He will also
bring peace between children and their
parents. If that does not happen, I will
come. And I will completely destroy
the land."

New Testament

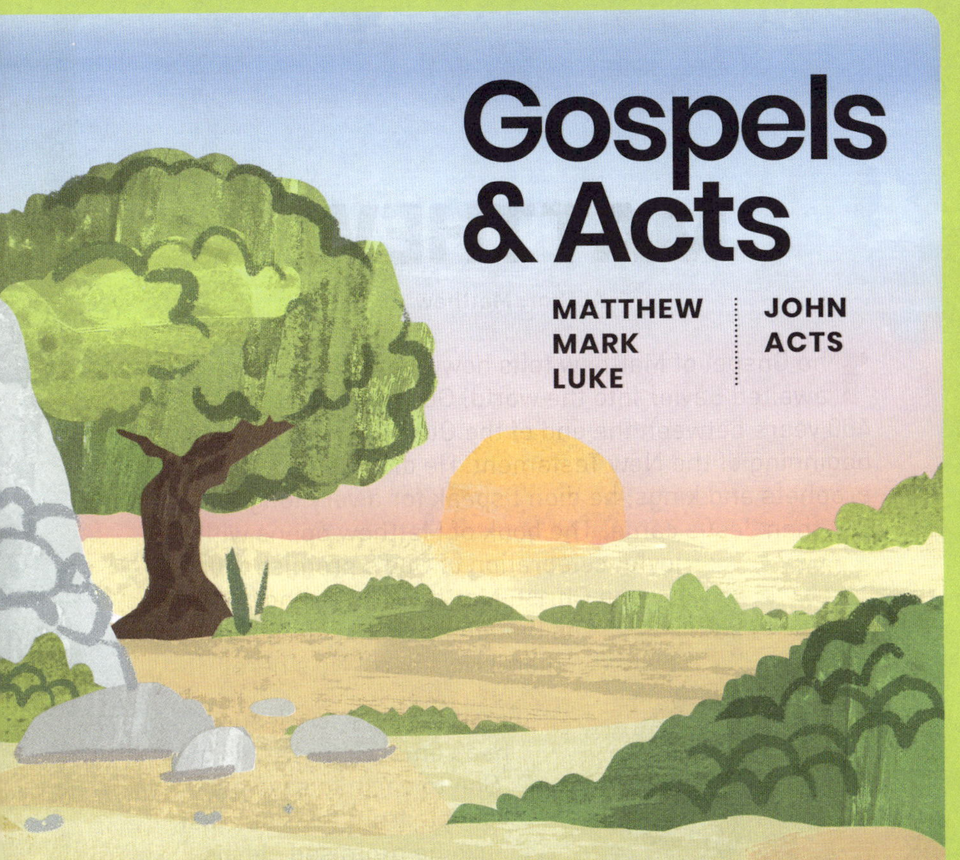

Gospels & Acts

MATTHEW
MARK
LUKE
JOHN
ACTS

The Gospels and Acts include five books written by four different authors: Matthew, Mark, Luke, and John. With the help of the Holy Spirit, the authors of the Gospels wrote down what happened during Jesus' life, ministry, death, and resurrection. They shared what they saw with their own eyes or heard with their own ears, as well as stories from eyewitnesses.

The Gospels include Jesus' teachings about the kingdom of God and true stories of how he healed people who were sick, gave sight to people who were blind, fed thousands of people from a small amount of bread and fish, and so much more! Matthew, Mark, Luke, and John testify, or tell, about how Jesus died on the cross for the sins of all people and how he was raised back to life three days later. In the book of Acts, Luke wrote about the very first church, or gathering of people who follow Jesus, and how the Good News spread all over the world.

We can know we're reading the Gospels and Acts when we read about Jesus' life and ministry, the beginning of the church, and the missionary journeys of apostles like Paul. These books encourage us to put our faith in Jesus and to ask the Holy Spirit to help us accomplish Jesus' mission on earth.

MATTHEW

Author: Matthew

The Gospel of Matthew tells how God sent the long-awaited Savior into the world. God was silent for 400 years between the end of the Old Testament and the beginning of the New Testament. He didn't speak through prophets and kings; he didn't speak for a very long time. But then Jesus came! The book of Matthew opens with a joyful celebration of God's promise fulfilled in Christ. Matthew, the author, wrote as though he was shouting, "He's here! He's here! He's here!"

Gospels & Acts

Finally, the Savior, Jesus, had come! God sent his own Son to earth to save his people from their sin, just like he promised. Jesus walked this earth, healed people of their sicknesses, taught his friends how to be part of God's kingdom, and eventually died on the cross as the ultimate sacrifice for sin. But just like God had promised, the Savior didn't stay in the grave; he rose again and demonstrated his power over death. Matthew wanted to show God's people that the coming of the Savior wasn't something new that God was doing but actually the fulfillment of God's oldest promises. Matthew told the story of Jesus in such a way that he said to Israel, "Jesus is the Messiah you've been waiting for all along!"

The Family Line of Jesus the Messiah

1 This is the written story of the family line of Jesus the Messiah. He is the son of David. He is also the son of Abraham.

2 Abraham was the father of Isaac.
Isaac was the father of Jacob.
Jacob was the father of Judah and his brothers.
3 Judah was the father of Perez and Zerah. Tamar was their mother.
Perez was the father of Hezron.
Hezron was the father of Ram.
4 Ram was the father of Amminadab.
Amminadab was the father of Nahshon.
Nahshon was the father of Salmon.
5 Salmon was the father of Boaz. Rahab was Boaz's mother.
Boaz was the father of Obed. Ruth was Obed's mother.
Obed was the father of Jesse.
6 And Jesse was the father of King David.

David was the father of Solomon. Solomon's mother had been Uriah's wife.
7 Solomon was the father of Rehoboam.
Rehoboam was the father of Abijah.
Abijah was the father of Asa.
8 Asa was the father of Jehoshaphat.
Jehoshaphat was the father of Jehoram.
Jehoram was the father of Uzziah.
9 Uzziah was the father of Jotham.
Jotham was the father of Ahaz.
Ahaz was the father of Hezekiah.
10 Hezekiah was the father of Manasseh.
Manasseh was the father of Amon.
Amon was the father of Josiah.
11 And Josiah was the father of Jeconiah and his brothers. At that time, the Jewish people were forced to go away to Babylon.

12 After this, the family line continued.
Jeconiah was the father of Shealtiel.
Shealtiel was the father of Zerubbabel.
13 Zerubbabel was the father of Abihud.
Abihud was the father of Eliakim.

in Matthew?

God is the Promised Savior. Jesus is the Savior the whole world had been waiting for.

Eliakim was the father of Azor.
14 Azor was the father of Zadok.
Zadok was the father of Akim.
Akim was the father of Elihud.
15 Elihud was the father of Eleazar.
Eleazar was the father of Matthan.
Matthan was the father of Jacob.
16 Jacob was the father of Joseph.
Joseph was the husband of Mary. And Mary was the mother of Jesus, who is called the Messiah.

17 So there were 14 generations from Abraham to David. There were 14 from David until the Jewish people were forced to go away to Babylon. And there were 14 from that time to the Messiah.

Joseph Accepts Jesus as His Son

18 This is how the birth of Jesus the Messiah came about. His mother Mary and Joseph had promised to get married. But before they started to live together, it became clear that she was going to have a baby. She became pregnant by the power of the Holy Spirit.
19 Her husband Joseph was faithful to the law. But he did not want to put her to shame in public. So he planned to divorce her quietly.
20 But as Joseph was thinking about this, an angel of the Lord appeared to him in a dream. The angel said, "Joseph, son of David, don't be afraid to take Mary home as your wife. The baby inside her is from the Holy Spirit. 21 She is going to have a son. You must give him the name Jesus. That's because he will save his people from their sins."

22 All this took place to bring about
what the Lord had said would happen.
He had said through the prophet, 23 "The
virgin is going to have a baby. She will
give birth to a son. And he will be called
Immanuel." *(Isaiah 7:14)* The name Immanuel means "God with us."
24 Joseph woke up. He did what the
angel of the Lord commanded him to
do. He took Mary home as his wife. 25 But
he did not sleep with her until she gave
birth to a son. And Joseph gave him the
name Jesus.

The Wise Men Visit Jesus

2 Jesus was born in Bethlehem in
Judea. This happened while Herod
was king of Judea. After Jesus' birth,
Wise Men from the east came to Jerusalem. 2 They asked, "Where is the
child who has been born to be king of
the Jews? We saw his star when it rose.
Now we have come to worship him."
3 When King Herod heard about it, he
was very upset. Everyone in Jerusalem
was troubled too. 4 So Herod called together all the chief priests of the people.
He also called the teachers of the law.
He asked them where the Messiah was
going to be born. 5 "In Bethlehem in
Judea," they replied. "This is what the
prophet has written. He said,

6 " 'But you, Bethlehem, in the land
of Judah,
are certainly not the least
important among the towns of
Judah.
A ruler will come out of you.
He will rule my people Israel like
a shepherd.' " *(Micah 5:2)*

7 Then Herod secretly called for the
Wise Men. He found out from them
exactly when the star had appeared.
8 He sent them to Bethlehem. He said,
"Go and search carefully for the child.
As soon as you find him, report it to me.
Then I can go and worship him too."
9 After the Wise Men had listened
to the king, they went on their way.
The star they had seen when it rose
went ahead of them. It finally stopped
over the place where the child was.
10 When they saw the star, they were
filled with joy. 11 The Wise Men went
to the house. There they saw the child
with his mother Mary. They bowed
down and worshiped him. Then they
opened their treasures. They gave him
gold, frankincense and myrrh. 12 But
God warned them in a dream not to go
back to Herod. So they returned to their
country on a different road.

Jesus' Family Escapes to Egypt

13 When the Wise Men had left, Joseph
had a dream. In the dream an angel of
the Lord appeared to Joseph. "Get up!"
the angel said. "Take the child and his
mother and escape to Egypt. Stay there
until I tell you to come back. Herod is
going to search for the child. He wants
to kill him."

Jesus Is Immanuel

Immanuel means "God with us." When the first humans, Adam and Eve, lived in the Garden of Eden, God lived among them. But when they sinned, they were separated from God. The consequence, or result, of disobeying God was that they could no longer live in God's presence. But God loved Adam and Eve and all people so much that he made a way to be in his presence again, even though the price was enormous.

In Matthew 1:23, we read that Jesus would come and live among people. He is called Immanuel, "God with us." Jesus' death, his sacrifice, paid the penalty for sin so that the Holy Spirit could live *within* his people, or be "with us." Now, even when we sin, God is still with us because Immanuel drew near to us so that we could have a relationship with him.

[14] So Joseph got up. During the night,
he left for Egypt with the child and his
mother Mary. [15] They stayed there until
King Herod died. So the words the Lord
had spoken through the prophet came
true. He had said, "I brought my son out
of Egypt." *(Hosea 11:1)*

[16] Herod realized that the Wise Men
had tricked him. So he became very
angry. He gave orders about Bethlehem
and the area around it. He ordered all
the boys two years old and under to be
killed. This agreed with the time when
the Wise Men had seen the star. [17] In this
way, the words Jeremiah the prophet
spoke came true. He had said,

[18] "A voice is heard in Ramah.
It's the sound of crying and deep sadness.
Rachel is crying over her children.
She refuses to be comforted,
because they are gone." *(Jeremiah 31:15)*

Jesus' Family Returns to Nazareth

[19] After Herod died, Joseph had a
dream while he was still in Egypt. In the
dream an angel of the Lord appeared
to him. [20] The angel said, "Get up! Take
the child and his mother. Go to the land
of Israel. The people who were trying to
kill the child are dead."

[21] So Joseph got up. He took the child
and his mother Mary back to the land of
Israel. [22] But then he heard that Archelaus was king of Judea. Archelaus was
ruling in place of his father Herod. This
made Joseph afraid to go there. Joseph
had been warned in a dream. So he
went back to the land of Galilee instead.
[23] There he lived in a town called Nazareth. So what the prophets had said
about Jesus came true. They had said
that he would be called a Nazarene.

John the Baptist Prepares the Way

3 In those days John the Baptist
came and preached in the Desert
of Judea. [2] He said, "Turn away from
your sins! The kingdom of heaven has
come near." [3] John is the one Isaiah the
prophet had spoken about. He had said,

"A messenger is calling out in the desert,
'Prepare the way for the Lord.
Make straight paths for him.' "
(Isaiah 40:3)

[4] John's clothes were made out of camel's hair. He had a leather belt around
his waist. His food was locusts and wild
honey. [5] People went out to him from Jerusalem and all Judea. They also came
from the whole area around the Jordan
River. [6] When they confessed their sins,
John baptized them in the Jordan.

[7] John saw many Pharisees and
Sadducees coming to where he was
baptizing. He said to them, "You are
like a nest of poisonous snakes! Who
warned you to escape the coming of
God's anger? [8] Live in a way that shows
you have turned away from your sins.
[9] Don't think you can say to yourselves,
'Abraham is our father.' I tell you, God
can raise up children for Abraham even
from these stones. [10] The ax is ready to
cut the roots of the trees. All the trees
that don't produce good fruit will be cut
down. They will be thrown into the fire.

[11] "I baptize you with water, calling you
to turn away from your sins. But after
me, someone is coming who is more powerful than I am. I'm not worthy to carry
his sandals. He will baptize you with
the Holy Spirit and fire. [12] His pitchfork
is in his hand to clear the straw from his
threshing floor. He will gather his wheat
into the storeroom. But he will burn up
the husks with fire that can't be put out."

Jesus Is Baptized

[13] Jesus came from Galilee to the Jordan River. He wanted to be baptized by
John. [14] But John tried to stop him. So
he told Jesus, "I need to be baptized by
you. So why do you come to me?"

[15] Jesus replied, "Let it be this way for
now. It is right for us to do this. It carries
out God's holy plan." Then John agreed.

[16] As soon as Jesus was baptized, he
came up out of the water. At that moment heaven was opened. Jesus saw
the Spirit of God coming down on him
like a dove. [17] A voice from heaven said,
"This is my Son, and I love him. I am
very pleased with him."

Jesus Is Tempted in the Desert

4 The Holy Spirit led Jesus into the
desert. There the devil tempted
him. [2] After 40 days and 40 nights of going without eating, Jesus was hungry.
[3] The tempter came to him. He said, "If
you are the Son of God, tell these stones
to become bread."

4 Jesus answered, "It is written, 'Man
must not live only on bread. He must
also live on every word that comes from
the mouth of God.' " *(Deuteronomy 8:3)*
5 Then the devil took Jesus to the holy
city. He had him stand on the highest
point of the temple. 6 "If you are the
Son of God," he said, "throw yourself
down. It is written,

" 'The Lord will command his
angels to take good care of you.
They will lift you up in their hands.
Then you won't trip over a
stone.' " *(Psalm 91:11,12)*

7 Jesus answered him, "It is also written, 'Do not test the Lord your God.' "
(Deuteronomy 6:16)
8 Finally, the devil took Jesus to a very
high mountain. He showed him all the
kingdoms of the world and their glory.
9 "If you bow down and worship me," he
said, "I will give you all this."
10 Jesus said to him, "Get away from
me, Satan! It is written, 'Worship the
Lord your God. He is the only one you
should serve.' " *(Deuteronomy 6:13)*
11 Then the devil left Jesus. Angels
came and took care of him.

Jesus Begins to Preach

12 John had been put in prison. When
Jesus heard about this, he returned
to Galilee. 13 Jesus left Nazareth and
went to live in the city of Capernaum.
It was by the lake in the area of Zebulun
and Naphtali. 14 In that way, what the
prophet Isaiah had said came true. He
had said,

15 "Land of Zebulun! Land of
Naphtali!
Galilee, where Gentiles live!
Land along the Mediterranean
Sea! Territory east of the
Jordan River!
16 The people who are now living in
darkness
have seen a great light.
They are now living in a very dark
land.
But a light has shined on them."
(Isaiah 9:1,2)

17 From that time on Jesus began to
preach. "Turn away from your sins!"
he said. "The kingdom of heaven has
come near."

Jesus Chooses His First Disciples

18 One day Jesus was walking beside
the Sea of Galilee. There he saw two
brothers, Simon Peter and his brother
Andrew. They were throwing a net into
the lake, because they were fishermen.
19 "Come and follow me," Jesus said. "I
will send you out to fish for people."
20 At once they left their nets and followed him.
21 Going on from there, he saw two
other brothers. They were James, son
of Zebedee, and his brother John. They
were in a boat with their father Zebedee. As they were preparing their nets,
Jesus called out to them. 22 Right away
they left the boat and their father and
followed Jesus.

Jesus Heals Sick People

23 Jesus went all over Galilee. There he
taught in the synagogues. He preached
the good news of God's kingdom. He
healed every illness and sickness the
people had. 24 News about him spread
all over Syria. People brought to him
all who were ill with different kinds of
sicknesses. Some were suffering great
pain. Others were controlled by demons.
Some were shaking wildly. Others
couldn't move at all. And Jesus healed
all of them. 25 Large crowds followed
him. People came from Galilee, from
the area known as the Ten Cities, and
from Jerusalem and Judea. Others came
from the area across the Jordan River.

Jesus Teaches the Disciples and Crowds

5 Jesus saw the crowds. So he went up
on a mountainside and sat down.
His disciples came to him. 2 Then he
began to teach them.

Jesus Gives Blessings

He said,

3 "Blessed are those who are
spiritually needy.
The kingdom of heaven belongs
to them.
4 Blessed are those who are sad.
They will be comforted.
5 Blessed are those who are humble.
They will be given the earth.
6 Blessed are those who are hungry
and thirsty for what is right.
They will be filled.

[7]Blessed are those who show mercy.
They will be shown mercy.
[8]Blessed are those whose hearts are pure.
They will see God.
[9]Blessed are those who make peace.
They will be called children of God.
[10]Blessed are those who suffer for doing what is right.
The kingdom of heaven belongs to them.

[11]"Blessed are you when people make
fun of you and hurt you because of me.
You are also blessed when they tell all
kinds of evil lies about you because of
me. [12]Be joyful and glad. Your reward in
heaven is great. In the same way, people
hurt the prophets who lived long ago.

Salt and Light

[13]"You are the salt of the earth. But
suppose the salt loses its saltiness. How
can it be made salty again? It is no longer good for anything. It will be thrown
out. People will walk all over it.

[14]"You are the light of the world. A
town built on a hill can't be hidden.
[15]Also, people do not light a lamp and
put it under a bowl. Instead, they put
it on its stand. Then it gives light to
everyone in the house. [16]In the same
way, let your light shine so others can
see it. Then they will see the good things
you do. And they will bring glory to your
Father who is in heaven.

Jesus Fulfills the Law

[17]"Do not think I have come to get rid
of what is written in the Law or in the
Prophets. I have not come to do this.
Instead, I have come to fulfill what is
written. [18]What I'm about to tell you is
true. Heaven and earth will disappear
before the smallest letter disappears
from the Law. Not even the smallest
mark of a pen will disappear from the
Law until everything is completed. [19]Do
not ignore even one of the least important commands. And do not teach others to ignore them. If you do, you will be
called the least important person in the
kingdom of heaven. Instead, practice
and teach these commands. Then you
will be called important in the kingdom
of heaven. [20]Here is what I tell you. You
must be more godly than the Pharisees
and the teachers of the law. If you are
not, you will certainly not enter the
kingdom of heaven.

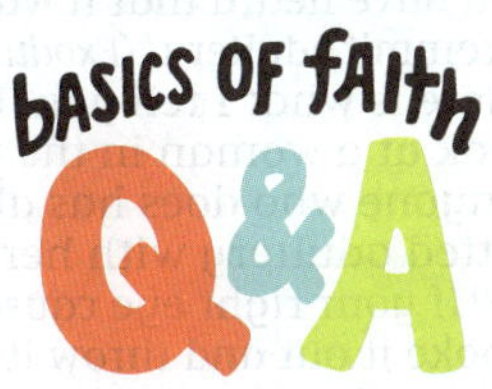

If Jesus saves, what is the point of God's Law?

God gave his people the Law so that they would understand his holiness and be set apart from other nations. He also gave them the Law so that they would see how much they needed a Savior.

Can you find the following verse?

MATTHEW 5:17

Murder

[21]"You have heard what was said to
people who lived long ago. They were
told, 'Do not commit murder. *(Exodus
20:13)* Anyone who murders will be
judged for it.' [22]But here is what I tell
you. Do not be angry with a brother or
sister. Anyone who is angry with them
will be judged. Again, anyone who says
to a brother or sister, 'Raca,' must stand
trial in court. And anyone who says, 'You
fool!' will be in danger of the fire in hell.

[23]"Suppose you are offering your gift
at the altar. And you remember that your
brother or sister has something against
you. [24]Leave your gift in front of the
altar. First go and make peace with them.
Then come back and offer your gift.

[25]"Suppose someone has a claim
against you and is taking you to court.
Settle the matter quickly. Do this while
you are still together on the way. If you
don't, you may be handed over to the
judge. The judge may hand you over
to the officer to be thrown into prison.
[26]What I'm about to tell you is true. You
will not get out until you have paid the
very last penny!

Adultery

27 “You have heard that it was said, ‘Do not commit adultery.’ *(Exodus 20:14)* 28 But here is what I tell you. Do not even look at a woman in the wrong way. Anyone who does has already committed adultery with her in his heart. 29 If your right eye causes you to sin, poke it out and throw it away. Your eye is only one part of your body. It is better to lose an eye than for your whole body to be thrown into hell. 30 If your right hand causes you to sin, cut it off and throw it away. Your hand is only one part of your body. It is better to lose a hand than for your whole body to go into hell.

Divorce

31 “It has been said, ‘Suppose a man divorces his wife. If he does, he must give her a letter of divorce.’ *(Deuteronomy 24:1)* 32 But here is what I tell you. Anyone who divorces his wife makes her a victim of adultery. And anyone who gets married to the divorced woman commits adultery. A man may divorce his wife only if she has not been faithful to him.

Promises

33 “Again, you have heard what was said to your people long ago. They were told, ‘Do not break the promises you make to the Lord. Keep your promises to the Lord that you have made.’ 34 But here is what I tell you. Do not make any promises like that at all. Do not make them in the name of heaven. That is God’s throne. 35 Do not make them in the name of the earth. That is the stool for God’s feet. Do not make them in the name of Jerusalem. That is the city of the Great King. 36 And do not make a promise in your own name. You can’t make even one hair of your head white or black. 37 All you need to say is simply ‘Yes’ or ‘No.’ Anything more than this comes from the evil one.

Be Kind to Others

38 “You have heard that it was said, ‘An eye must be put out for an eye. A tooth must be knocked out for a tooth.’ *(Exodus 21:24; Leviticus 24:20; Deuteronomy 19:21)* 39 But here is what I tell you. Do not fight against an evil person. Suppose someone slaps you on your right cheek. Turn your other cheek to them also. 40 Suppose someone takes you to court to get your shirt. Let them have your coat also. 41 Suppose someone forces you to go one mile. Go two miles with them. 42 Give to the one who asks you for something. Don’t turn away from the one who wants to borrow something from you.

Love Your Enemies

43 “You have heard that it was said, ‘Love your neighbor. *(Leviticus 19:18)* Hate your enemy.’ 44 But here is what I tell you. Love your enemies. Pray for those who hurt you. 45 Then you will be children of your Father who is in heaven. He causes his sun to shine on evil people and good people. He sends rain on those who do right and those who don’t. 46 If you love those who love you, what reward will you get? Even the tax collectors do that. 47 If you greet only your own people, what more are you doing than others? Even people who are ungodly do that. 48 So be perfect, just as your Father in heaven is perfect.

Giving to Needy People

6 “Be careful not to do good deeds in front of other people. Don’t do those deeds to be seen by others. If you do, your Father in heaven will not reward you.

2 “When you give to needy people, do not announce it by having trumpets blown. Do not be like those who only pretend to be holy. They announce what they do in the synagogues and on the streets. They want to be honored by other people. What I’m about to tell you is true. They have received their complete reward. 3 When you give to needy people, don’t let your left hand know what your right hand is doing. 4 Then your giving will be done secretly. Your Father will reward you, because he sees what you do secretly.

Prayer

5 “When you pray, do not be like those who only pretend to be holy. They love to stand and pray in the synagogues and on the street corners. They want to be seen by other people. What I’m about to tell you is true. They have received their complete reward. 6 When you pray, go into your room. Close the door and

pray to your Father, who can't be seen.
Your Father will reward you, because
he sees what you do secretly. 7When
you pray, do not keep talking on and
on. That is what ungodly people do.
They think they will be heard because
they talk a lot. 8Do not be like them.
Your Father knows what you need even
before you ask him.
9"This is how you should pray.

"'Our Father in heaven,
may your name be honored.
10May your kingdom come.
May what you want to happen be
done
on earth as it is done in heaven.
11Give us today our daily bread.
12And forgive us our sins,
just as we also have forgiven
those who sin against us.
13Keep us from sinning when we are
tempted.
Save us from the evil one.'

14Forgive other people when they sin
against you. If you do, your Father who
is in heaven will also forgive you. 15But
if you do not forgive the sins of other
people, your Father will not forgive
your sins.

Fasting

16"When you go without eating, do
not look gloomy like those who only
pretend to be holy. They make their
faces look very sad. They want to
show people they are fasting. What
I'm about to tell you is true. They have
received their complete reward. 17But
when you go without eating, put olive oil on your head. Wash your face.
18Then others will not know that you
are fasting. Only your Father, who can't
be seen, will know it. Your Father will
reward you, because he sees what you
do secretly.

Gather Riches in Heaven

19"Do not gather for yourselves riches
on earth. Moths and rats can destroy
them. Thieves can break in and steal
them. 20Instead, gather for yourselves
riches in heaven. There, moths and rats
do not destroy them. There, thieves
do not break in and steal them. 21Your
heart will be where your riches are.
22"The eye is like a lamp for the body.
Suppose your eyes are healthy. Then
your whole body will be full of light.
23But suppose your eyes can't see well.
Then your whole body will be full of
darkness. If the light inside you is darkness, then it is very dark!
24"No one can serve two masters at
the same time. You will hate one of
them and love the other. Or you will
be faithful to one and dislike the other.
You can't serve God and money at the
same time.

Do Not Worry

25"I tell you, do not worry. Don't worry about your life and what you will
eat or drink. And don't worry about
your body and what you will wear.
Isn't there more to life than eating?
Aren't there more important things
for the body than clothes? 26Look at
the birds of the air. They don't plant
or gather crops. They don't put away
crops in storerooms. But your Father
who is in heaven feeds them. Aren't
you worth much more than they are?
27Can you add even one hour to your
life by worrying?
28"And why do you worry about
clothes? See how the wild flowers grow.
They don't work or make clothing. 29But
here is what I tell you. Not even Solomon in all his royal robes was dressed
like one of these flowers. 30If that is
how God dresses the wild grass, won't
he dress you even better? Your faith is
so small! After all, the grass is here only
today. Tomorrow it is thrown into the
fire. 31So don't worry. Don't say, 'What
will we eat?' Or, 'What will we drink?'
Or, 'What will we wear?' 32People who
are ungodly run after all those things.
Your Father who is in heaven knows
that you need them. 33But put God's
kingdom first. Do what he wants you
to do. Then all those things will also
be given to you. 34So don't worry about
tomorrow. Tomorrow will worry about
itself. Each day has enough trouble of
its own.

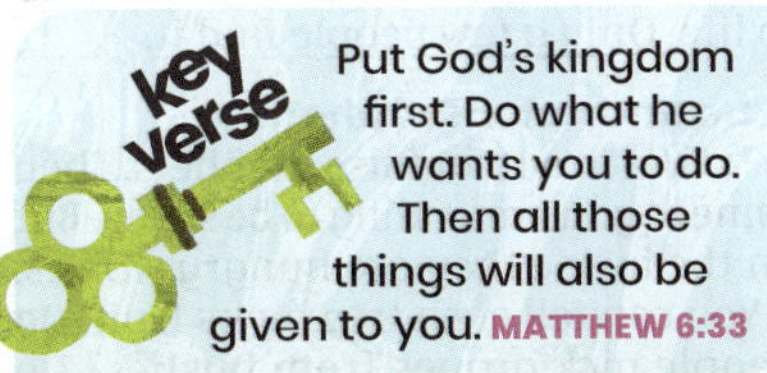

Be Fair When You Judge Other People

7 “Do not judge other people. Then you will not be judged. 2 You will be judged in the same way you judge others. You will be measured in the same way you measure others.

3 “You look at the bit of sawdust in your friend’s eye. But you pay no attention to the piece of wood in your own eye. 4 How can you say to your friend, ‘Let me take the bit of sawdust out of your eye’? How can you say this while there is a piece of wood in your own eye? 5 You pretender! First take the piece of wood out of your own eye. Then you will be able to see clearly to take the bit of sawdust out of your friend’s eye.

6 “Do not give holy things to dogs. Do not throw your pearls to pigs. If you do, they might walk all over them. They might turn around and tear you to pieces.

Ask, Search, Knock

7 “Ask, and it will be given to you. Search, and you will find. Knock, and the door will be opened to you. 8 Everyone who asks will receive. The one who searches will find. The door will be opened to the one who knocks.

9 “Suppose your son asks for bread. Which of you will give him a stone? 10 Or suppose he asks for a fish. Which of you will give him a snake? 11 Even though you are evil, you know how to give good gifts to your children. How much more will your Father who is in heaven give good gifts to those who ask him! 12 In everything, do to others what you would want them to do to you. This is what is written in the Law and in the Prophets.

The Large and Small Gates

13 “Enter God’s kingdom through the narrow gate. The gate is large and the road is wide that leads to ruin. Many people go that way. 14 But the gate is small and the road is narrow that leads to life. Only a few people find it.

True and False Prophets

15 “Watch out for false prophets. They come to you pretending to be sheep. But on the inside they are hungry wolves. 16 You can tell each tree by its fruit. Do people pick grapes from bushes? Do they pick figs from thorns? 17 In the same way, every good tree bears good fruit. But a bad tree bears bad fruit. 18 A good tree can’t bear bad fruit. And a bad tree can’t bear good fruit. 19 Every tree that does not bear good fruit is cut down. It is thrown into the fire. 20 You can tell each tree by its fruit.

True and False Disciples

21 “Not everyone who says to me, ‘Lord, Lord,’ will enter the kingdom of heaven. Only those who do what my Father in heaven wants will enter. 22 Many will say to me on that day, ‘Lord! Lord! Didn’t we prophesy in your name? Didn’t we drive out demons in your name? Didn’t we do many miracles in your name?’ 23 Then I will tell them clearly, ‘I never knew you. Get away from me, you who do evil!’

The Wise and Foolish Builders

24 “So then, everyone who hears my words and puts them into practice is like a wise man. He builds his house on the rock. 25 The rain comes down. The water rises. The winds blow and beat against that house. But it does not fall. It is built on the rock. 26 But everyone who hears my words and does not put them into practice is like a foolish man. He builds his house on sand. 27 The rain comes down. The water rises. The winds blow and beat against that house. And it falls with a loud crash.”

28 Jesus finished saying all these things. The crowds were amazed at his teaching. 29 That’s because he taught like one who had authority. He did not speak like their teachers of the law.

Jesus Heals a Man Who Had a Skin Disease

8 Jesus came down from the mountainside. Large crowds followed him. 2 A man who had a skin disease came and got down on his knees in front of Jesus. He said, “Lord, if you are willing to make me ‘clean,’ you can do it.”

3 Jesus reached out his hand and touched the man. “I am willing to do it,” he said. “Be ‘clean’!” Right away the man was healed of his skin disease. 4 Then Jesus said to him, “Don’t tell anyone. Go and show yourself to the priest, and offer the gift Moses commanded. It will be a witness to everyone.”

A Roman Commander Has Faith

5 When Jesus entered Capernaum,
a Roman commander came to him.
He asked Jesus for help. 6 "Lord," he
said, "my servant lies at home and can't
move. He is suffering terribly."
7 Jesus said, "Shall I come and heal
him?"
8 The commander replied, "Lord, I am
not good enough to have you come into
my house. But just say the word, and
my servant will be healed. 9 I myself
am a man under authority. And I have
soldiers who obey my orders. I tell this
one, 'Go,' and he goes. I tell that one,
'Come,' and he comes. I say to my slave,
'Do this,' and he does it."
10 When Jesus heard this, he was
amazed. He said to those following him,
"What I'm about to tell you is true. In
Israel I have not found anyone whose
faith is so strong. 11 I say to you that
many will come from the east and the
west. They will take their places at the
feast in the kingdom of heaven. They
will sit with Abraham, Isaac and Jacob.
12 But those who think they belong in
the kingdom will be thrown outside,
into the darkness. There they will weep
and grind their teeth."
13 Then Jesus said to the Roman commander, "Go! It will be done just as you
believed it would." And his servant was
healed at that moment.

Jesus Heals Many People

14 When Jesus came into Peter's house,
he saw Peter's mother-in-law. She was
lying in bed. She had a fever. 15 Jesus
touched her hand, and the fever left
her. She got up and began to serve him.
16 When evening came, many people
controlled by demons were brought
to Jesus. He drove out the spirits with
a word. He healed all who were sick.
17 This happened so that what Isaiah
the prophet had said would come true.
He had said,

> "He suffered the things we should
> have suffered.
> He took on himself the sicknesses
> that should have been ours."
> *(Isaiah 53:4)*

The Cost of Following Jesus

18 Jesus saw the crowd around him. So
he gave his disciples orders to go to the
other side of the Sea of Galilee. 19 Then a
teacher of the law came to him. He said,
"Teacher, I will follow you no matter
where you go."
20 Jesus replied, "Foxes have dens.
Birds have nests. But the Son of Man
has no place to lay his head."
21 Another follower said to him, "Lord,
first let me go and bury my father."
22 But Jesus told him, "Follow me. Let
the dead bury their own dead."

Jesus Calms the Storm

23 Jesus got into a boat. His disciples
followed him. 24 Suddenly a terrible
storm came up on the lake. The waves
crashed over the boat. But Jesus was
sleeping. 25 The disciples went and woke
him up. They said, "Lord! Save us! We're
going to drown!"
26 He replied, "Your faith is so small!
Why are you so afraid?" Then Jesus got
up and ordered the winds and the waves
to stop. It became completely calm.
27 The disciples were amazed. They
asked, "What kind of man is this? Even
the winds and the waves obey him!"

Jesus Heals Two Men Controlled by Demons

28 Jesus arrived at the other side of
the lake in the area of the Gadarenes.
Two men controlled by demons met
him. They came from the tombs. The
men were so wild that no one could
pass that way. 29 "Son of God, what do
you want with us?" they shouted. "Have
you come here to punish us before the
time for us to be judged?"
30 Not very far away, a large herd of
pigs was feeding. 31 The demons begged
Jesus, "If you drive us out, send us into
the herd of pigs."
32 Jesus said to them, "Go!" So the demons came out of the men and went
into the pigs. The whole herd rushed
down the steep bank. They ran into the
lake and drowned in the water. 33 Those
who were tending the pigs ran off. They
went into the town and reported all
this. They told the people what had
happened to the men who had been
controlled by demons. 34 Then the whole
town went out to meet Jesus. When they
saw him, they begged him to leave their
area.

Jesus Forgives and Heals a Man Who Could Not Walk

9 Jesus stepped into a boat. He went over to the other side of the lake and came to his own town. 2 Some men brought to him a man who could not walk. He was lying on a mat. Jesus saw that they had faith. So he said to the man, "Don't lose hope, son. Your sins are forgiven."

3 Then some teachers of the law said to themselves, "This fellow is saying a very evil thing!"

4 Jesus knew what they were thinking. So he said, "Why do you have evil thoughts in your hearts? 5 Is it easier to say, 'Your sins are forgiven'? Or to say, 'Get up and walk'? 6 But I want you to know that the Son of Man has authority on earth to forgive sins." So he spoke to the man who could not walk. "Get up," he said. "Take your mat and go home." 7 The man got up and went home. 8 When the crowd saw this, they were filled with wonder. They praised God for giving that kind of authority to a human being.

Jesus Chooses Matthew and Eats With Sinners

9 As Jesus went on from there, he saw a man named Matthew. He was sitting at the tax collector's booth. "Follow me," Jesus told him. Matthew got up and followed him.

10 Later Jesus was having dinner at Matthew's house. Many tax collectors and sinners came. They ate with Jesus and his disciples. 11 The Pharisees saw this. So they asked the disciples, "Why does your teacher eat with tax collectors and sinners?"

12 Jesus heard this. So he said, "Those who are healthy don't need a doctor. Sick people do. 13 Go and learn what this means, 'I want mercy and not sacrifice.' *(Hosea 6:6)* I have not come to get those who think they are right with God to follow me. I have come to get sinners to follow me."

Jesus Is Asked About Fasting

14 One day John's disciples came. They said to Jesus, "We and the Pharisees often go without eating. Why don't your disciples go without eating?"

15 Jesus answered, "How can the guests of the groom be sad while he is with them? The time will come when the groom will be taken away from them. Then they will fast.

16 "People don't sew a patch of new cloth on old clothes. The new piece will pull away from the old. That will make the tear worse. 17 People don't pour new wine into old wineskins. If they do, the skins will burst. The wine will run out, and the wineskins will be destroyed. No, people pour new wine into new wineskins. Then both are saved."

Jesus Heals a Dead Girl and a Suffering Woman

18 While Jesus was saying this, a synagogue leader came. He got down on his knees in front of Jesus. He said, "My daughter has just died. But come and place your hand on her. Then she will live again." 19 Jesus got up and went with him. So did his disciples.

20 Just then a woman came up behind Jesus. She had a sickness that made her bleed. It had lasted for 12 years. She touched the edge of his clothes. 21 She thought, "I only need to touch his clothes. Then I will be healed."

22 Jesus turned and saw her. "Dear woman, don't give up hope," he said. "Your faith has healed you." The woman was healed at that moment.

23 When Jesus entered the synagogue leader's house, he saw the noisy crowd and people playing flutes. 24 He said, "Go away. The girl is not dead. She is sleeping." But they laughed at him. 25 After the crowd had been sent outside, Jesus went in. He took the girl by the hand, and she got up. 26 News about what Jesus had done spread all over that area.

Jesus Heals Two Blind Men

27 As Jesus went on from there, two blind men followed him. They called out, "Have mercy on us, Son of David!"

28 When Jesus went indoors, the blind men came to him. He asked them, "Do you believe that I can do this?"

"Yes, Lord," they replied.

29 Then he touched their eyes. He said, "It will happen to you just as you believed." 30 They could now see again. Jesus strongly warned them, "Be sure that no one knows about this." 31 But

they went out and spread the news. They
talked about him all over that area.
32 While they were going out, another
man was brought to Jesus. A demon
controlled him, and he could not speak.
33 When the demon was driven out, the
man spoke. The crowd was amazed.
They said, "Nothing like this has ever
been seen in Israel."
34 But the Pharisees said, "He drives
out demons by the power of the prince
of demons."

There Are Only a Few Workers

35 Jesus went through all the towns and
villages. He taught in their synagogues.
He preached the good news of the kingdom. And he healed every illness and
sickness. 36 When he saw the crowds, he
felt deep concern for them. They were
treated badly and were helpless, like
sheep without a shepherd. 37 Then Jesus
said to his disciples, "The harvest is huge.
But there are only a few workers. 38 So
ask the Lord of the harvest to send workers out into his harvest field."

Jesus Sends Out the Twelve Disciples

10 Jesus called for his 12 disciples
to come to him. He gave them
authority to drive out evil spirits and to
heal every illness and sickness.

2 Here are the names of the 12
apostles.

First there were Simon Peter and
his brother Andrew.
Then came James, son of Zebedee,
and his brother John.
3 Next were Philip and Bartholomew,
and also Thomas and Matthew the
tax collector.
Two more were James, son of
Alphaeus, and Thaddaeus.
4 The last were Simon the Zealot
and Judas Iscariot. Judas was
the one who was later going to
hand Jesus over to his enemies.

5 Jesus sent these 12 out with the following orders. "Do not go among the
Gentiles," he said. "Do not enter any
town of the Samaritans. 6 Instead, go
to the people of Israel. They are like
sheep that have become lost. 7 As you go,
preach this message, 'The kingdom of
heaven has come near.' 8 Heal those who
are sick. Bring those who are dead back
to life. Make those who have skin diseases 'clean' again. Drive out demons.
You have received freely, so give freely.
9 "Do not get any gold, silver or
copper to take with you in your belts.
10 Do not take a bag for the journey.
Do not take extra clothes or sandals
or walking sticks. A worker should be
given what he needs. 11 When you enter
a town or village, look for someone who
is willing to welcome you. Stay at their
house until you leave. 12 As you enter
the home, greet those who live there.
13 If that home welcomes you, give it
your blessing of peace. If it does not,
don't bless it. 14 Some people may not
welcome you or listen to your words.
If they don't, leave that home or town,
and shake the dust off your feet. 15 What
I'm about to tell you is true. On judgment day it will be easier for Sodom and
Gomorrah than for that town.
16 "I am sending you out like sheep
among wolves. So be as wise as snakes
and as harmless as doves. 17 Watch out!
You will be handed over to the local
courts. You will be whipped in the synagogues. 18 You will be brought to governors and kings because of me. You will
be witnesses to them and to the Gentiles.
19 But when they arrest you, don't worry
about what you will say or how you will
say it. At that time you will be given the
right words to say. 20 It will not be you
speaking. The Spirit of your Father will
be speaking through you.
21 "Brothers will hand over brothers to
be killed. Fathers will hand over their
children. Children will rise up against
their parents and have them put to
death. 22 You will be hated by everyone
because of me. But anyone who remains
strong in the faith will be saved. 23 When
people attack you in one place, escape
to another. What I'm about to tell you is
true. You will not finish going through
the towns of Israel before the Son of
Man comes.
24 "The student is not better than the
teacher. A slave is not better than his
master. 25 It is enough for students to
be like their teachers. And it is enough
for slaves to be like their masters. If
the head of the house has been called
Beelzebul, what can the others who live
there expect?

26 “So don’t be afraid of your enemies.
Everything that is secret will be brought
out into the open. Everything that is
hidden will be uncovered. 27 What I tell
you in the dark, speak in the daylight.
What is whispered in your ear, shout from
the rooftops. 28 Do not be afraid of those
who kill the body but can’t kill the soul.
Instead, be afraid of the one who can destroy both soul and body in hell. 29 Aren’t
two sparrows sold for only a penny? But
not one of them falls to the ground outside
your Father’s care. 30 He even counts every
hair on your head! 31 So don’t be afraid.
You are worth more than many sparrows.
32 “What if someone says in front of
others that they know me? I will also
say in front of my Father who is in
heaven that I know them. 33 But what
if someone says in front of others that
they don’t know me? I will say in front
of my Father who is in heaven that I
don’t know them.
34 “Do not think that I came to bring
peace to the earth. I didn’t come to bring
peace. I came to bring a sword. 35 I have
come to turn

“ ‘sons against their fathers.
Daughters will refuse to obey
their mothers.
Daughters-in-law will be against
their mothers-in-law.
36 A man’s enemies will be the
members of his own family.’
(Micah 7:6)

37 “Anyone who loves their father or
mother more than me is not worthy
of me. Anyone who loves their son or
daughter more than me is not worthy
of me. 38 Whoever does not pick up their
cross and follow me is not worthy of
me. 39 Whoever finds their life will lose
it. Whoever loses their life because of
me will find it.
40 “Anyone who welcomes you welcomes me. And anyone who welcomes
me welcomes the one who sent me.
41 Suppose someone welcomes a prophet
as a prophet. They will receive a prophet’s
reward. And suppose someone welcomes
a godly person as a godly person. They
will receive a godly person’s reward.
42 Suppose someone gives even a cup
of cold water to a little one who follows
me. What I’m about to tell you is true.
That person will certainly be rewarded.”

Jesus and John the Baptist

11 Jesus finished teaching his 12 disciples. Then he went on to teach and
preach in the towns of Galilee.
2 John the Baptist was in prison. When
he heard about the actions of the Messiah, he sent his disciples to him. 3 They
asked Jesus, “Are you the one who is
supposed to come? Or should we look
for someone else?”
4 Jesus replied, “Go back to John. Report to him what you hear and see. 5 Blind
people receive sight. Disabled people
walk. Those who have skin diseases are
made ‘clean.’ Deaf people hear. Those
who are dead are raised to life. And the
good news is preached to those who are
poor. 6 Blessed is anyone who does not
give up their faith because of me.”
7 As John’s disciples were leaving,
Jesus began to speak to the crowd about
John. He said, “What did you go out into
the desert to see? Tall grass waving in
the wind? 8 If not, what did you go out
to see? A man dressed in fine clothes?
No. People who wear fine clothes are
in kings’ palaces. 9 Then what did you
go out to see? A prophet? Yes, I tell you,
and more than a prophet. 10 He is the
one written about in Scripture. It says,

“ ‘I will send my messenger ahead
of you.
He will prepare your way for
you.’ *(Malachi 3:1)*

11 What I’m about to tell you is true.
No one more important than John the
Baptist has ever been born. But the least
important person in the kingdom of
heaven is more important than he is.
12 Since the days of John the Baptist,
the kingdom of heaven has been under
attack. And violent people are taking
hold of it. 13 All the Prophets and the Law
prophesied until John came. 14 If you are
willing to accept it, John is the Elijah
who was supposed to come. 15 Whoever
has ears should listen.
16 “What can I compare today’s people to? They are like children sitting in
the markets and calling out to others.
They say,

17 “ ‘We played the flute for you.
But you didn’t dance.
We sang a funeral song.
But you didn’t become sad.’

18 When John came, he didn't eat or
drink as you do. And people say, 'He has
a demon.' 19 But when the Son of Man
came, he ate and drank as you do. And
people say, 'This fellow is always eating
and drinking far too much. He's a friend
of tax collectors and "sinners."' By wise
actions wisdom is shown to be right."

Towns That Do Not Turn Away From Sin

20 Jesus began to speak against the
towns where he had done most of his
miracles. The people there had not
turned away from their sins. So he
said, 21 "How terrible it will be for you,
Chorazin! How terrible for you, Bethsaida! Suppose the miracles done in
you had been done in Tyre and Sidon.
They would have turned away from
their sins long ago. They would have put
on clothes for mourning. They would
have sat down in ashes. 22 But I tell you
this. On judgment day it will be easier
for Tyre and Sidon than for you. 23 And
what about you, Capernaum? Will you
be lifted to the heavens? No! You will go
down to the place of the dead. Suppose
the miracles done in you had been done
in Sodom. It would still be here today.
24 But I tell you this. On judgment day it
will be easier for Sodom than for you."

Rest for All Who Are Tired

25 At that time Jesus said, "I praise
you, Father. You are Lord of heaven and
earth. You have hidden these things
from wise and educated people. But you
have shown them to little children. 26 Yes,
Father. This is what you wanted to do.

27 "My Father has given all things to
me. The Father is the only one who knows
the Son. And the only ones who know the
Father are the Son and those to whom
the Son chooses to make him known.

28 "Come to me, all you who are tired
and are carrying heavy loads. I will
give you rest. 29 Become my servants
and learn from me. I am gentle and
free of pride. You will find rest for your
souls. 30 Serving me is easy, and my
load is light."

Jesus Is Lord of the Sabbath Day

12 One Sabbath day Jesus walked
through the grainfields. His disciples were hungry. So they began to
break off some heads of grain and eat
them. 2 The Pharisees saw this. They
said to Jesus, "Look! It is against the
Law to do this on the Sabbath day. But
your disciples are doing it anyway!"

3 Jesus answered, "Haven't you read
about what David did? He and his men
were hungry. 4 So he entered the house
of God. He and his men ate the holy
bread. Only priests were allowed to eat
it. 5 Haven't you read the Law? It tells
how every Sabbath day the priests in
the temple have to do their work on that
day. But they are not considered guilty.
6 I tell you that something more important than the temple is here. 7 Scripture
says, 'I want mercy and not sacrifice.'
(Hosea 6:6) You don't know what those
words mean. If you did, you would not
bring charges against those who are not
guilty. 8 The Son of Man is Lord of the
Sabbath day."

9 Going on from that place, Jesus went
into their synagogue. 10 A man with
a weak and twisted hand was there.
The Pharisees were trying to accuse
Jesus of a crime. So they asked him,
"Does the Law allow us to heal on the
Sabbath day?"

11 He said to them, "What if one of
your sheep falls into a pit on the Sabbath day? Won't you take hold of it and
lift it out? 12 A person is worth more than
sheep! So the Law allows us to do good
on the Sabbath day."

13 Then Jesus said to the man, "Stretch
out your hand." So he stretched it out. It
had been made as good as new. It was
just as good as the other hand. 14 But
the Pharisees went out and planned
how to kill Jesus.

God's Chosen Servant

15 Jesus knew all about the Pharisees'
plans. So he left that place. A large
crowd followed him, and he healed all
who were sick. 16 But he warned them
not to tell other people about him. 17 This
was to make what was spoken through
the prophet Isaiah come true. It says,

18 "Here is my servant. I have chosen
him.
He is the one I love. I am very
pleased with him.
I will put my Spirit on him.
He will announce to the nations
that everything will be made
right.

19 He will not argue or cry out.
  No one will hear his voice in the streets.
20 He will not break a bent twig.
  He will not put out a dimly burning flame.
 He will make right win over wrong.
21 The nations will put their hope in him." *(Isaiah 42:1–4)*

Jesus and Beelzebul

22 A man controlled by demons was brought to Jesus. The man was blind and could not speak. Jesus healed him. Then the man could speak and see. 23 All the people were amazed. They said, "Could this be the Son of David?"

24 The Pharisees heard this. So they said, "This fellow drives out demons by the power of Beelzebul, the prince of demons."

25 Jesus knew what they were thinking. So he said to them, "Every kingdom that fights against itself will be destroyed. Every city or family that is divided against itself will not stand. 26 If Satan drives out Satan, he fights against himself. Then how can his kingdom stand? 27 You say I drive out demons by the power of Beelzebul. Then by whose power do your people drive them out? So then, they will be your judges. 28 But suppose I drive out demons by the Spirit of God. Then the kingdom of God has come to you.

29 "Or think about this. How can you enter a strong man's house and just take what the man owns? You must first tie him up. Then you can rob his house.

30 "Anyone who is not with me is against me. Anyone who does not gather sheep with me scatters them. 31 So here is what I tell you. Every kind of sin and every evil word spoken against God will be forgiven. But speaking evil things against the Holy Spirit will not be forgiven. 32 Anyone who speaks a word against the Son of Man will be forgiven. But anyone who speaks against the Holy Spirit will not be forgiven. A person like that won't be forgiven either now or in days to come.

33 "If you make a tree good, its fruit will be good. If you make a tree bad, its fruit will be bad. You can tell a tree by its fruit. 34 You nest of poisonous snakes! How can you who are evil say anything good? Your mouths say everything that is in your hearts. 35 A good man says good things. These come from the good that is stored up inside him. An evil man says evil things. These come from the evil that is stored up inside him. 36 But here is what I tell you. On judgment day, everyone will have to account for every empty word they have spoken. 37 By your words you will be found guilty or not guilty."

The Sign of Jonah

38 Some of the Pharisees and the teachers of the law came to Jesus. They said, "Teacher, we want to see a sign from you."

39 He answered, "Evil and unfaithful people ask for a sign! But none will be given except the sign of the prophet Jonah. 40 Jonah was in the belly of a huge fish for three days and three nights. Something like that will happen to the Son of Man. He will spend three days and three nights in the grave. 41 The men of Nineveh will stand up on judgment day with the people now living. And the Ninevites will prove that these people are guilty. The men of Nineveh turned away from their sins when Jonah preached to them. And now something more important than Jonah is here. 42 The Queen of the South will stand up on judgment day with the people now living. And she will prove that they are guilty. She came from very far away to listen to Solomon's wisdom. And now something more important than Solomon is here.

43 "What happens when an evil spirit comes out of a person? It goes through dry areas looking for a place to rest. But it doesn't find it. 44 Then it says, 'I will return to the house I left.' When it arrives there, it finds the house empty. The house has been swept clean and put in order. 45 Then the evil spirit goes and takes with it seven other spirits more evil than itself. They go in and live there. That person is worse off than before. That is how it will be with the evil people of today."

Jesus' Mother and Brothers

46 While Jesus was still talking to the crowd, his mother and brothers stood outside. They wanted to speak to him. 47 Someone told him, "Your mother and

brothers are standing outside. They
want to speak to you."
48 Jesus replied to him, "Who is my
mother? And who are my brothers?"
49 Jesus pointed to his disciples. He
said, "Here is my mother! Here are my
brothers! 50 Anyone who does what my
Father in heaven wants is my brother
or sister or mother."

The Story of the Farmer

13 That same day Jesus left the
house and sat by the Sea of Galilee. 2 Large crowds gathered around
him. So he got into a boat and sat down.
All the people stood on the shore. 3 Then
he told them many things using stories.
He said, "A farmer went out to plant
his seed. 4 He scattered the seed on the
ground. Some fell on a path. Birds came
and ate it up. 5 Some seed fell on rocky
places, where there wasn't much soil.
The plants came up quickly, because the
soil wasn't deep. 6 When the sun came
up, it burned the plants. They dried
up because they had no roots. 7 Other
seed fell among thorns. The thorns grew
up and crowded out the plants. 8 Still
other seed fell on good soil. It produced
a crop 100, 60 or 30 times more than
what was planted. 9 Whoever has ears
should listen."
10 The disciples came to him. They
asked, "Why do you use stories when
you speak to the people?"
11 He replied, "Because you have been
given the knowledge of the secrets of
the kingdom of heaven. It has not been
given to outsiders. 12 Everyone who has
this kind of knowledge will be given
more knowledge. In fact, they will have
very much. If anyone doesn't have this
kind of knowledge, even what little they
have will be taken away from them.
13 Here is why I use stories when I speak
to the people. I say,

"They look, but they don't really
see.
They listen, but they don't really
hear or understand.

14 In them the words of the prophet
Isaiah come true. He said,

" 'You will hear but never
understand.
You will see but never know what
you are seeing.
15 The hearts of these people have
become stubborn.
They can barely hear with their
ears.
They have closed their eyes.
Otherwise they might see with their
eyes.
They might hear with their ears.
They might understand with
their hearts.
They might turn to the Lord, and
then he would heal them.'
(Isaiah 6:9,10)

16 But blessed are your eyes because
they see. And blessed are your ears because they hear. 17 What I'm about to tell
you is true. Many prophets and godly
people wanted to see what you see. But
they didn't see it. They wanted to hear
what you hear. But they didn't hear it.
18 "Listen! Here is the meaning of the
story of the farmer. 19 People hear the
message about the kingdom but do not
understand it. Then the evil one comes.
He steals what was planted in their
hearts. Those people are like the seed
planted on a path. 20 The seed that fell
on rocky places is like other people. They
hear the message and at once receive it
with joy. 21 But they have no roots. So
they last only a short time. They quickly
fall away from the faith when trouble or
suffering comes because of the message.
22 The seed that fell among the thorns is
like others who hear the message. But
then the worries of this life and the false
promises of wealth crowd it out. They
keep the message from producing fruit.
23 But the seed that fell on good soil is like
those who hear the message and understand it. They produce a crop 100, 60 or
30 times more than the farmer planted."

The Story of the Weeds

24 Jesus told the crowd another story.
"Here is what the kingdom of heaven is
like," he said. "A man planted good seed
in his field. 25 But while everyone was
sleeping, his enemy came. The enemy
planted weeds among the wheat and
then went away. 26 The wheat began
to grow and form grain. At the same
time, weeds appeared.
27 "The owner's slaves came to him.
They said, 'Sir, didn't you plant good
seed in your field? Then where did the
weeds come from?'

[28] " 'An enemy did this,' he replied.
"The slaves asked him, 'Do you want
us to go and pull up the weeds?'
[29] " 'No,' the owner answered. 'While
you are pulling up the weeds, you might
pull up the wheat with them. [30] Let both
grow together until the harvest. At that
time I will tell the workers what to do.
Here is what I will say to them. First
collect the weeds. Tie them in bundles
to be burned. Then gather the wheat.
Bring it into my storeroom.' "

The Stories of the Mustard Seed and the Yeast

[31] Jesus told the crowd another story.
He said, "The kingdom of heaven is
like a mustard seed. Someone took the
seed and planted it in a field. [32] It is the
smallest of all seeds. But when it grows,
it is the largest of all garden plants. It
becomes a tree. Birds come and rest in
its branches."
[33] Jesus told them still another story.
"The kingdom of heaven is like yeast,"
he said. "A woman mixed it into 60
pounds of flour. The yeast worked its
way all through the dough."
[34] Jesus spoke all these things to the
crowd using stories. He did not say anything to them without telling a story.
[35] So the words spoken by the prophet
came true. He had said,

"I will open my mouth and tell
stories.
I will speak about things that
were hidden since the world
was made." *(Psalm 78:2)*

Jesus Explains the Story of the Weeds

[36] Then Jesus left the crowd and went
into the house. His disciples came to
him. They said, "Explain to us the story
of the weeds in the field."
[37] He answered, "The one who planted
the good seed is the Son of Man. [38] The
field is the world. The good seed stands
for the people who belong to the kingdom. The weeds are the people who
belong to the evil one. [39] The enemy who
plants them is the devil. The harvest
is judgment day. And the workers are
angels.
[40] "The weeds are pulled up and
burned in the fire. That is how it will
be on judgment day. [41] The Son of Man
will send out his angels. They will weed
out of his kingdom everything that
causes sin. They will also get rid of all
who do evil. [42] They will throw them
into the blazing furnace. There people
will weep and grind their teeth. [43] Then
God's people will shine like the sun in
their Father's kingdom. Whoever has
ears should listen.

The Stories of the Hidden Treasure and the Pearl

[44] "The kingdom of heaven is like
treasure that was hidden in a field.
When a man found it, he hid it again.
He was very happy. So he went and
sold everything he had. And he bought
that field.
[45] "Again, the kingdom of heaven is
like a trader who was looking for fine
pearls. [46] He found one that was very
valuable. So he went away and sold
everything he had. And he bought that
pearl.

The Story of the Net

[47] "Again, the kingdom of heaven is
like a net. It was let down into the lake.
It caught all kinds of fish. [48] When it was
full, the fishermen pulled it up on the
shore. Then they sat down and gathered
the good fish into baskets. But they
threw the bad fish away. [49] This is how
it will be on judgment day. The angels
will come. They will separate the people
who did what is wrong from those who
did what is right. [50] They will throw the
evil people into the blazing furnace.
There the evil ones will weep and grind
their teeth.
[51] "Do you understand all these
things?" Jesus asked.
"Yes," they replied.
[52] He said to them, "Every teacher of
the law who has become a disciple in
the kingdom of heaven is like the owner
of a house. He brings new treasures out
of his storeroom as well as old ones."

A Prophet Without Honor

[53] Jesus finished telling these stories.
Then he moved on from there. [54] He
came to his hometown of Nazareth.
There he began teaching the people in
their synagogue. They were amazed.
"Where did this man get this wisdom? Where did he get this power to
do miracles?" they asked. [55] "Isn't this

the carpenter's son? Isn't his mother's name Mary? Aren't his brothers James, Joseph, Simon and Judas? 56 Aren't all his sisters with us? Then where did this man get all these things?" 57 They were not pleased with him at all.

But Jesus said to them, "A prophet is honored everywhere except in his own town and in his own home."

58 He did only a few miracles in Nazareth because the people there had no faith.

John the Baptist's Head Is Cut Off

14 At that time Herod, the ruler of Galilee and Perea, heard reports about Jesus. 2 He said to his attendants, "This is John the Baptist. He has risen from the dead! That is why he has the power to do miracles."

3 Herod had arrested John. He had tied him up and put him in prison because of Herodias. She was the wife of Herod's brother Philip. 4 John had been saying to Herod, "It is against the Law for you to have her as your wife." 5 Herod wanted to kill John. But he was afraid of the people, because they thought John was a prophet.

6 On Herod's birthday the daughter of Herodias danced for Herod and his guests. She pleased Herod very much. 7 So he promised to give her anything she asked for. 8 Her mother told her what to say. So the girl said to Herod, "Give me the head of John the Baptist on a big plate." 9 The king was very upset. But he thought of his promise and his dinner guests. So he told one of his men to give her what she asked for. 10 Herod had John's head cut off in the prison. 11 His head was brought in on a big plate and given to the girl. She then carried it to her mother. 12 John's disciples came and took his body and buried it. Then they went and told Jesus.

Jesus Feeds Five Thousand

13 Jesus heard what had happened to John. He wanted to be alone. So he went in a boat to a quiet place. The crowds heard about this. They followed him on foot from the towns. 14 When Jesus came ashore, he saw a large crowd. He felt deep concern for them. He healed their sick people.

15 When it was almost evening, the disciples came to him. "There is nothing here," they said. "It's already getting late. Send the crowds away. They can go and buy some food in the villages."

16 Jesus replied, "They don't need to go away. You give them something to eat."

17 "We have only five loaves of bread and two fish," they answered.

18 "Bring them here to me," he said. 19 Then Jesus directed the people to sit down on the grass. He took the five loaves and the two fish. He looked up to heaven and gave thanks. He broke the loaves into pieces. Then he gave them to the disciples. And the disciples gave them to the people. 20 All of them ate and were satisfied. The disciples picked up 12 baskets of leftover pieces. 21 The number of men who ate was about 5,000. Women and children also ate.

Jesus Walks on the Water

22 Right away Jesus made the disciples get into the boat. He had them go on ahead of him to the other side of the Sea of Galilee. Then he sent the crowd away. 23 After he had sent them away, he went up on a mountainside by himself to pray. Later that night, he was there alone. 24 The boat was already a long way from land. It was being pounded by the waves because the wind was blowing against it.

25 Shortly before dawn, Jesus went out to the disciples. He walked on the lake. 26 They saw him walking on the lake and were terrified. "It's a ghost!" they said. And they cried out in fear.

27 Right away Jesus called out to them, "Be brave! It is I. Don't be afraid."

28 "Lord, is it you?" Peter asked. "If it is, tell me to come to you on the water."

29 "Come," Jesus said.

So Peter got out of the boat. He walked on the water toward Jesus. 30 But when Peter saw the wind, he was afraid. He began to sink. He cried out, "Lord! Save me!"

31 Right away Jesus reached out his hand and caught him. "Your faith is so small!" he said. "Why did you doubt me?"

32 When they climbed into the boat, the wind died down. 33 Then those in the boat worshiped Jesus. They said, "You really are the Son of God!"

34 They crossed over the lake and landed at Gennesaret. 35 The men who lived there recognized Jesus. So they

sent a message all over the nearby
countryside. People brought all those
who were sick to Jesus. 36 They begged
him to let those who were sick just
touch the edge of his clothes. And all
who touched his clothes were healed.

What Makes People "Unclean"?

15 Some Pharisees and some
teachers of the law came from
Jerusalem to see Jesus. They asked,
2 "Why don't your disciples obey what
the elders teach? Your disciples don't
wash their hands before they eat!"

3 Jesus replied, "And why don't you
obey God's command? You would rather
follow your own teachings! 4 God said,
'Honor your father and mother.' *(Exodus 20:12; Deuteronomy 5:16)* He also
said, 'Anyone who asks for bad things to
happen to their father or mother must be
put to death.' *(Exodus 21:17; Leviticus 20:9)*
5 But suppose people have something
that might be used to help their parents.
You allow them to say it is instead 'a gift
set apart for God.' 6 So they do not need to
honor their father or mother with their
gift. You make the word of God useless
in order to follow your own teachings.
7 You pretenders! Isaiah was right when
he prophesied about you. He said,

8 " 'These people honor me by what
they say.
But their hearts are far away
from me.
9 Their worship doesn't mean
anything to me.
They teach nothing but human
rules.' " *(Isaiah 29:13)*

10 Jesus called the crowd to him. He
said, "Listen and understand. 11 What
goes into someone's mouth does not
make them 'unclean.' It's what comes
out of their mouth that makes them
'unclean.' "

12 Then the disciples came to him.
They asked, "Do you know that the
Pharisees were angry when they heard
this?"

13 Jesus replied, "They are plants that
my Father in heaven has not planted.
They will be pulled up by the roots.
14 Leave the Pharisees. They are blind
guides. If one blind person leads another blind person, both of them will
fall into a pit."

15 Peter said, "Explain this to us."

16 "Don't you understand yet?" Jesus
asked them. 17 "Don't you see? Everything that enters the mouth goes into
the stomach. Then it goes out of the
body. 18 But the things that come out of
a person's mouth come from the heart.
Those are the things that make someone 'unclean.' 19 Evil thoughts come
out of a person's heart. So do murder,
adultery, and other sexual sins. And so
do stealing, false witness, and telling
lies about others. 20 Those are the things
that make you 'unclean.' But eating
without washing your hands does not
make you 'unclean.' "

The Faith of a Woman From Canaan

21 Jesus left Galilee and went to the
area of Tyre and Sidon. 22 A woman from
Canaan lived near Tyre and Sidon. She
came to him and cried out, "Lord! Son
of David! Have mercy on me! A demon
controls my daughter. She is suffering
terribly."

23 Jesus did not say a word. So his
disciples came to him. They begged
him, "Send her away. She keeps crying
out after us."

24 Jesus answered, "I was sent only
to the people of Israel. They are like
lost sheep."

25 Then the woman fell to her knees in
front of him. "Lord! Help me!" she said.

26 He replied, "It is not right to take
the children's bread and throw it to the
dogs."

27 "Yes it is, Lord," she said. "Even the
dogs eat the crumbs that fall from their
owner's table."

28 Then Jesus said to her, "Woman,
you have great faith! You will be giv-
en what you are asking for." And her
daughter was healed at that moment.

Jesus Feeds Four Thousand

29 Jesus left there. He walked along
the Sea of Galilee. Then he went up on
a mountainside and sat down. 30 Large
crowds came to him. They brought blind
people and those who could not walk.
They also brought disabled people,
those who could not speak, and many
others. They laid them at his feet, and
he healed them. 31 The people were
amazed. Those who could not speak
were speaking. The disabled were
made well. Those not able to walk were

walking. Those who were blind could
see. So the people praised the God of
Israel.
32 Then Jesus called for his disciples
to come to him. He said, "I feel deep
concern for these people. They have
already been with me three days. They
don't have anything to eat. I don't
want to send them away hungry. If I
do, they will become too weak on their
way home."
33 His disciples answered him. "There
is nothing here," they said. "Where
could we get enough bread to feed this
large crowd?"
34 "How many loaves do you have?"
Jesus asked.
"Seven," they replied, "and a few
small fish."
35 Jesus told the crowd to sit down on
the ground. 36 He took the seven loaves
and the fish and gave thanks. Then
he broke them and gave them to the
disciples. And the disciples passed them
out to the people. 37 All of them ate and
were satisfied. After that, the disciples
picked up seven baskets of leftover
pieces. 38 The number of men who ate
was 4,000. Women and children also
ate. 39 After Jesus had sent the crowd
away, he got into the boat. He went to
the area near Magadan.

Jesus Is Asked for a Sign

16 The Pharisees and Sadducees
came to test Jesus. They asked
him to show them a sign from heaven.
2 He replied, "In the evening you
look at the sky. You say, 'It will be
good weather. The sky is red.' 3 And in
the morning you say, 'Today it will be
stormy. The sky is red and cloudy.' You
know the meaning of what you see in
the sky. But you can't understand the
signs of what is happening right now.
4 An evil and unfaithful people look for
a sign. But none will be given to them
except the sign of Jonah." Then Jesus
left them and went away.

The Yeast of the Pharisees and Sadducees

5 The disciples crossed over to the other side of the lake. They had forgotten
to take bread. 6 "Be careful," Jesus said
to them. "Watch out for the yeast of the
Pharisees and Sadducees."
7 The disciples talked about this
among themselves. They said, "He must
be saying this because we didn't bring
any bread."
8 Jesus knew what they were saying.
So he said, "Your faith is so small! Why
are you talking to each other about having no bread? 9 Don't you understand
yet? Don't you remember the five loaves
for the 5,000? Don't you remember how
many baskets of pieces you gathered?
10 Don't you remember the seven loaves
for the 4,000? Don't you remember how
many baskets of pieces you gathered?
11 How can you possibly not understand?
I wasn't talking to you about bread. But
watch out for the yeast of the Pharisees
and Sadducees." 12 Then the disciples understood that Jesus was not telling them
to watch out for the yeast used in bread.
He was warning them against what the
Pharisees and Sadducees taught.

Peter Says That Jesus Is the Messiah

13 Jesus went to the area of Caesarea
Philippi. There he asked his disciples,
"Who do people say the Son of Man is?"
14 They replied, "Some say John the
Baptist. Others say Elijah. Still others
say Jeremiah, or one of the prophets."
15 "But what about you?" he asked.
"Who do you say I am?"
16 Simon Peter answered, "You are the
Messiah. You are the Son of the living
God."
17 Jesus replied, "Blessed are you,
Simon, son of Jonah! No mere human
showed this to you. My Father in heaven
showed it to you. 18 Here is what I tell
you. You are Peter. On this rock I will
build my church. The gates of hell will
not be strong enough to destroy it. 19 I
will give you the keys to the kingdom
of heaven. What you lock on earth will
be locked in heaven. What you unlock
on earth will be unlocked in heaven."
20 Then Jesus ordered his disciples not
to tell anyone that he was the Messiah.

Jesus Speaks About His Coming Death

21 From that time on Jesus began to
explain to his disciples what would
happen to him. He told them he must
go to Jerusalem. There he must suffer
many things from the elders, the chief
priests and the teachers of the law. He

must be killed and on the third day rise
to life again.
22 Peter took Jesus to one side and
began to scold him. "Never, Lord!" he
said. "This will never happen to you!"
23 Jesus turned and said to Peter, "Get
behind me, Satan! You are standing in
my way. You do not have in mind the
things God cares about. Instead, you
only have in mind the things humans
care about."
24 Then Jesus spoke to his disciples.
He said, "Whoever wants to be my disciple must say no to themselves. They
must pick up their cross and follow
me. 25 Whoever wants to save their life
will lose it. But whoever loses their life
for me will find it. 26 What good is it if
someone gains the whole world but
loses their soul? Or what can anyone
trade for their soul? 27 The Son of Man
is going to come in his Father's glory.
His angels will come with him. And he
will reward everyone in keeping with
what they have done.
28 "What I'm about to tell you is true.
Some who are standing here will not die
before they see the Son of Man coming
in his kingdom."

Jesus' Appearance Is Changed

17 After six days Jesus took Peter,
James, and John the brother of
James with him. He led them up a high
mountain. They were all alone. 2 There
in front of them his appearance was
changed. His face shone like the sun.
His clothes became as white as the light.
3 Just then Moses and Elijah appeared
in front of them. Moses and Elijah were
talking with Jesus.
4 Peter said to Jesus, "Lord, it is good
for us to be here. If you wish, I will put
up three shelters. One will be for you,
one for Moses, and one for Elijah."
5 While Peter was still speaking, a
bright cloud covered them. A voice from
the cloud said, "This is my Son, and I
love him. I am very pleased with him.
Listen to him!"
6 When the disciples heard this, they
were terrified. They fell with their faces
to the ground. 7 But Jesus came and
touched them. "Get up," he said. "Don't
be afraid." 8 When they looked up, they
saw no one except Jesus.
9 They came down the mountain. On
the way down, Jesus told them what to
do. "Don't tell anyone what you have
seen," he said. "Wait until the Son of
Man has been raised from the dead."
10 The disciples asked him, "Why do
the teachers of the law say that Elijah
has to come first?"
11 Jesus replied, "That's right. Elijah is
supposed to come and make all things
new again. 12 But I tell you, Elijah has
already come. People didn't recognize
him. They have done to him everything
they wanted to do. In the same way,
they are going to make the Son of Man
suffer." 13 Then the disciples understood
that Jesus was talking to them about
John the Baptist.

Jesus Heals a Boy Who Is Controlled by a Demon

14 When they came near the crowd,
a man approached Jesus. He got on
his knees in front of him. 15 "Lord," he
said, "have mercy on my son. He shakes
wildly and suffers a great deal. He often
falls into the fire or into the water. 16 I
brought him to your disciples. But they
couldn't heal him."
17 "You unbelieving and evil people!"
Jesus replied. "How long do I have to
stay with you? How long do I have
to put up with you? Bring the boy here
to me." 18 Jesus ordered the demon to
leave the boy, and it came out of him.
He was healed at that moment.
19 Then the disciples came to Jesus in
private. They asked, "Why couldn't we
drive out the demon?"
20-21 He replied, "Because your faith is
much too small. What I'm about to tell
you is true. If you have faith as small
as a mustard seed, it is enough. You can
say to this mountain, 'Move from here
to there.' And it will move. Nothing will
be impossible for you."

Jesus Speaks a Second Time About His Coming Death

22 They came together in Galilee. Then
Jesus said to them, "The Son of Man is
going to be handed over to men. 23 They
will kill him. On the third day he will
rise from the dead." Then the disciples
were filled with deep sadness.

Jesus Pays the Temple Tax

24 Jesus and his disciples arrived in
Capernaum. There the people who collect the temple tax came to Peter. They
asked him, "Doesn't your teacher pay
the temple tax?"

25 "Yes, he does," he replied.

When Peter came into the house,
Jesus spoke first. "What do you think,
Simon?" he asked. "Who do the kings of
the earth collect taxes and fees from?
Do they collect them from their own
children or from others?"

26 "From others," Peter answered.

"Then the children don't have to pay,"
Jesus said to him. 27 "But we don't want
to make them angry. So go to the lake
and throw out your fishing line. Take
the first fish you catch. Open its mouth.
There you will find the exact coin you
need. Take it and give it to them for my
tax and yours."

Who Is the Most Important Person in the Kingdom?

18 At that time the disciples came
to Jesus. They asked him, "Then
who is the most important person in the
kingdom of heaven?"

2 Jesus called a little child over to him.
He had the child stand among them.
3 Jesus said, "What I'm about to tell you
is true. You need to change and become
like little children. If you don't, you will
never enter the kingdom of heaven.
4 Anyone who takes the humble position
of this child is the most important in
the kingdom of heaven. 5 Anyone who
welcomes a little child like this one in
my name welcomes me.

Do Not Cause People to Sin

6 "What if someone causes one of these
little ones who believe in me to sin? If
they do, it would be better for them to
have a large millstone hung around their
neck and be drowned at the bottom of the
sea. 7 How terrible it will be for the world
because of the things that cause people
to sin! Things like that must come. But
how terrible for the person who causes
them! 8 If your hand or foot causes you
to sin, cut it off and throw it away. It
would be better to enter the kingdom of
heaven with only one hand than go into
hell with two hands. It would be better to
enter the kingdom of heaven with only
one foot than go into hell with two feet.
In hell the fire burns forever. 9 If your eye
causes you to sin, poke it out and throw
it away. It would be better to enter the
kingdom of heaven with one eye than
to have two eyes and be thrown into
the fire of hell.

The Story of the Wandering Sheep

10-11 "See that you don't look down on
one of these little ones. Here is what I
tell you. Their angels in heaven are always with my Father who is in heaven.

12 "What do you think? Suppose a
man owns 100 sheep and one of them
wanders away. Won't he leave the 99
sheep on the hills? Won't he go and look
for the one that wandered off? 13 What
I'm about to tell you is true. If he finds
that sheep, he is happier about the one
than about the 99 that didn't wander
off. 14 It is the same with your Father in
heaven. He does not want any of these
little ones to die.

When Someone Sins Against You

15 "If your brother or sister sins against
you, go to them. Tell them what they did
wrong. Keep it between the two of you.
If they listen to you, you have won them
back. 16 But what if they won't listen to
you? Then take one or two others with
you. Scripture says, 'Every matter must
be proved by the words of two or three
witnesses.' *(Deuteronomy 19:15)* 17 But
what if they also refuse to listen to the
witnesses? Then tell it to the church.
And what if they refuse to listen even
to the church? Then don't treat them
as a brother or sister. Treat them as
you would treat an ungodly person or
a tax collector.

18 "What I'm about to tell you is true.
What you lock on earth will be locked
in heaven. What you unlock on earth
will be unlocked in heaven.

19 "Again, here is what I tell you. Suppose two of you on earth agree about
anything you ask for. My Father in
heaven will do it for you. 20 Where two
or three people gather in my name, I
am there with them."

The Servant Who Had No Mercy

21 Peter came to Jesus. He asked,
"Lord, how many times should I forgive
my brother or sister who sins against
me? Up to seven times?"

22 Jesus answered, "I tell you, not
seven times, but 77 times.
23 "The kingdom of heaven is like
a king who wanted to collect all the
money his servants owed him. 24 As the
king began to do it, a man who owed
him 10,000 bags of gold was brought to
him. 25 The man was not able to pay. So
his master gave an order. The man, his
wife, his children, and all he owned had
to be sold to pay back what he owed.
26 "Then the servant fell on his
knees in front of him. 'Give me time,'
he begged. 'I'll pay everything back.'
27 His master felt sorry for him. He forgave him what he owed and let him go.
28 "But then that servant went out and
found one of the other servants who
owed him 100 silver coins. He grabbed
him and began to choke him. 'Pay back
what you owe me!' he said.
29 "The other servant fell on his knees.
'Give me time,' he begged him. 'I'll pay
it back.'
30 "But the first servant refused. Instead, he went and had the man thrown
into prison. The man would be held
there until he could pay back what he
owed. 31 The other servants saw what
had happened and were very angry.
They went and told their master everything that had happened.
32 "Then the master called the first
servant in. 'You evil servant,' he said. 'I
forgave all that you owed me because
you begged me to. 33 Shouldn't you have
had mercy on the other servant just as
I had mercy on you?' 34 In anger his
master handed him over to the jailers.
He would be punished until he paid
back everything he owed.
35 "This is how my Father in heaven
will treat each of you unless you forgive
your brother or sister from your heart."

Jesus Teaches About Divorce

19 When Jesus finished saying these
things, he left Galilee. He went
into the area of Judea on the other side
of the Jordan River. 2 Large crowds followed him. He healed them there.
3 Some Pharisees came to test Jesus.
They asked, "Does the Law allow a man
to divorce his wife for any reason at
all?"
4 Jesus replied, "Haven't you read
that in the beginning the Creator 'made
them male and female'? *(Genesis 1:27)*
5 He said, 'That's why a man will leave
his father and mother and be joined
to his wife. The two will become one.'
(Genesis 2:24) 6 They are no longer two,
but one. So no one should separate what
God has joined together."
7 They asked, "Then why did Moses
command that a man can give his wife
a letter of divorce and send her away?"
8 Jesus replied, "Moses let you divorce
your wives because you were stubborn.
But it was not this way from the beginning. 9 Here is what I tell you. Anyone
who divorces his wife and marries another woman commits adultery. A man
may divorce his wife only if she has not
been faithful to him."
10 Here is what the disciples said to
him. "If that's the way it is between
a husband and wife, it is better not to
get married."
11 Jesus replied, "Not everyone can
accept the idea of staying single. Only
those who have been helped to live
without getting married can accept
it. 12 Some men are not able to have
children because they were born that
way. Some have been made that way
by other people. Others have chosen
to live that way in order to serve the
kingdom of heaven. The one who can
accept this should accept it."

Little Children Are Brought to Jesus

13 Some people brought little children
to Jesus. They wanted him to place his
hands on the children and pray for
them. But the disciples told them not
to do it.
14 Jesus said, "Let the little children
come to me. Don't keep them away. The
kingdom of heaven belongs to people
like them." 15 Jesus placed his hands
on them to bless them. Then he went
on from there.

Rich People and the Kingdom of God

16 Just then, a man came up to Jesus.
He asked, "Teacher, what good thing
must I do to receive eternal life?"
17 "Why do you ask me about what is
good?" Jesus replied. "There is only one
who is good. If you want to enter the
kingdom, obey the commandments."
18 "Which ones?" the man asked.

Jesus said, " 'Do not murder. Do not commit adultery. Do not steal. Do not be a false witness. 19 Honor your father and mother.' *(Exodus 20:12–16; Deuteronomy 5:16–20)* And 'love your neighbor as you love yourself.' " *(Leviticus 19:18)*

20 "I have obeyed all those commandments," the young man said. "What else do I need to do?"

21 Jesus answered, "If you want to be perfect, go and sell everything you have. Give the money to those who are poor. You will have treasure in heaven. Then come and follow me."

22 When the young man heard this, he went away sad. He was very rich.

23 Then Jesus said to his disciples, "What I'm about to tell you is true. It is hard for someone who is rich to enter the kingdom of heaven. 24 Again I tell you, it is hard for a camel to go through the eye of a needle. But it is even harder for someone who is rich to enter the kingdom of God."

25 When the disciples heard this, they were really amazed. They asked, "Then who can be saved?"

26 Jesus looked at them and said, "With people, this is impossible. But with God, all things are possible."

27 Peter answered him, "We have left everything to follow you! What reward will be given to us?"

28 "What I'm about to tell you is true," Jesus said to them. "When all things are made new, the Son of Man will sit on his glorious throne. Then you who have followed me will also sit on 12 thrones. You will judge the 12 tribes of Israel. 29 Suppose anyone has left houses, brothers or sisters, father or mother, husband or wife, children or fields because of me. Anyone who has done that will receive 100 times as much. They will also receive eternal life. 30 But many who are first will be last. And many who are last will be first.

The Story of the Workers in the Vineyard

20 "The kingdom of heaven is like a man who owned land. He went out early in the morning to hire workers for his vineyard. 2 He agreed to give them the usual pay for a day's work. Then he sent them into his vineyard.

3 "About nine o'clock in the morning he went out again. He saw others standing in the market doing nothing. 4 He told them, 'You also go and work in my vineyard. I'll pay you what is right.' 5 So they went.

"He went out again about noon and at three o'clock and did the same thing. 6 About five o'clock he went out and found still others standing around. He asked them, 'Why have you been standing here all day long doing nothing?'

7 " 'Because no one has hired us,' they answered.

"He said to them, 'You also go and work in my vineyard.'

8 "When evening came, the owner of the vineyard spoke to the person who was in charge of the workers. He said, 'Call the workers and give them their pay. Begin with the last ones I hired. Then go on to the first ones.'

9 "The workers who were hired about five o'clock came. Each received the usual day's pay. 10 So when those who were hired first came, they expected to receive more. But each of them also received the usual day's pay. 11 When they received it, they began to complain about the owner. 12 'These people who were hired last worked only one hour,' they said. 'You have paid them the same as us. We have done most of the work and have been in the hot sun all day.'

13 "The owner answered one of them. 'Friend,' he said, 'I'm being fair to you. Didn't you agree to work for the usual day's pay? 14 Take your money and go. I want to give the one I hired last the same pay I gave you. 15 Don't I have the right to do what I want with my own money? Do you feel cheated because I gave so freely to the others?'

16 "So those who are last will be first. And those who are first will be last."

Jesus Speaks a Third Time About His Coming Death

17 Jesus was going up to Jerusalem. On the way, he took his 12 disciples to one side to talk to them. 18 "We are going up to Jerusalem," he said. "The Son of Man will be handed over to the chief priests and the teachers of the law. They will sentence him to death. 19 Then they will hand him over to the Gentiles. The people will make fun of him and whip

him. They will nail him to a cross. On the third day, he will rise from the dead!"

A Mother Asks a Favor of Jesus

20 The mother of Zebedee's sons came to Jesus. Her sons came with her. Getting on her knees, she asked a favor of him.

21 "What do you want?" Jesus asked.

She said, "Promise me that one of my two sons may sit at your right hand in your kingdom. Promise that the other one may sit at your left hand."

22 "You don't know what you're asking for," Jesus said to them. "Can you drink the cup of suffering I am going to drink?"

"We can," they answered.

23 Jesus said to them, "You will certainly drink from my cup. But it is not for me to say who will sit at my right or left hand. These places belong to those my Father has prepared them for."

24 The other ten disciples heard about this. They became angry at the two brothers. 25 Jesus called them together. He said, "You know about the rulers of the Gentiles. They hold power over their people. Their high officials order them around. 26 Don't be like that. Instead, anyone who wants to be important among you must be your servant. 27 And anyone who wants to be first must be your slave. 28 Be like the Son of Man. He did not come to be served. Instead, he came to serve others. He came to give his life as the price for setting many people free."

Two Blind Men Receive Their Sight

29 Jesus and his disciples were leaving Jericho. A large crowd followed him. 30 Two blind men were sitting by the side of the road. They heard that Jesus was going by. So they shouted, "Lord! Son of David! Have mercy on us!"

31 The crowd commanded them to stop. They told them to be quiet. But the two men shouted even louder, "Lord! Son of David! Have mercy on us!"

32 Jesus stopped and called out to them. "What do you want me to do for you?" he asked.

33 "Lord," they answered, "we want to be able to see."

34 Jesus felt deep concern for them. He touched their eyes. Right away they could see. And they followed him.

Jesus Comes to Jerusalem as King

21 As they all approached Jerusalem, they came to Bethphage. It was on the Mount of Olives. Jesus sent out two disciples. 2 He said to them, "Go to the village ahead of you. As soon as you get there, you will find a donkey tied up. Her colt will be with her. Untie them and bring them to me. 3 If anyone says anything to you, say that the Lord needs them. The owner will send them right away."

4 This took place so that what was spoken through the prophet would come true. It says,

> 5 "Say to the city of Zion,
> 'See, your king comes to you.
> He is gentle and riding on a
> donkey.
> He is riding on a donkey's colt.' "
> *(Zechariah 9:9)*

6 The disciples went and did what Jesus told them to do. 7 They brought the donkey and the colt. They placed their coats on them for Jesus to sit on. 8 A very large crowd spread their coats on the road. Others cut branches from the trees and spread them on the road. 9 Some of the people went ahead of him, and some followed. They all shouted,

> "Hosanna to the Son of David!"
>
> "Blessed is the one who comes in
> the name of the Lord!" *(Psalm 118:26)*
>
> "Hosanna in the highest heaven!"

10 When Jesus entered Jerusalem, the whole city was stirred up. The people asked, "Who is this?"

11 The crowds answered, "This is Jesus. He is the prophet from Nazareth in Galilee."

Jesus Clears Out the Temple

12 Jesus entered the temple courtyard. He began to drive out all those who were buying and selling there. He turned over the tables of the people who were exchanging money. He also turned over the benches of those who were selling doves. 13 He said to them, "It is written that the Lord said, 'My house will be called a house where people can pray.' *(Isaiah 56:7)* But you are making it 'a den for robbers.'" *(Jeremiah 7:11)*

14 Blind people and those who were
disabled came to Jesus at the temple.
There he healed them. 15 The chief
priests and the teachers of the law saw
the wonderful things he did. They also
saw the children in the temple courtyard shouting, "Hosanna to the Son of
David!" But when they saw all this, they
became angry.
16 "Do you hear what these children
are saying?" they asked him.
"Yes," replied Jesus. "Haven't you ever
read about it in Scripture? It says,

" 'Lord, you have made sure that
children and infants
praise you.' " *(Psalm 8:2)*

17 Then Jesus left the people and went
out of the city to Bethany. He spent the
night there.

Jesus Makes a Fig Tree Dry Up

18 Early in the morning, Jesus was
on his way back to Jerusalem. He was
hungry. 19 He saw a fig tree by the road.
He went up to it but found nothing on it
except leaves. Then he said to it, "May
you never bear fruit again!" Right away
the tree dried up.
20 When the disciples saw this, they
were amazed. "How did the fig tree dry
up so quickly?" they asked.
21 Jesus replied, "What I'm about to
tell you is true. You must have faith
and not doubt. Then you can do what
was done to the fig tree. And you can
say to this mountain, 'Go and throw
yourself into the sea.' It will be done.
22 If you believe, you will receive what
you ask for when you pray."

The Authority of Jesus Is Questioned

23 Jesus entered the temple courtyard.
While he was teaching there, the chief
priests and the elders of the people
came to him. "By what authority are
you doing these things?" they asked.
"Who gave you this authority?"
24 Jesus replied, "I will also ask you
one question. If you answer me, I will
tell you by what authority I am doing
these things. 25 Where did John's baptism come from? Was it from heaven?
Or did it come from human authority?"
They talked to one another about it.
They said, "If we say, 'From heaven,' he
will ask, 'Then why didn't you believe
him?' 26 But what if we say, 'From human authority'? We are afraid of the
people. Everyone believes that John
was a prophet."
27 So they answered Jesus, "We don't
know."
Jesus said, "Then I won't tell you by
what authority I am doing these things
either.

The Story of the Two Sons

28 "What do you think about this? A
man had two sons. He went to the first
and said, 'Son, go and work today in
the vineyard.'
29 " 'I will not,' the son answered. But
later he changed his mind and went.
30 "Then the father went to the other
son. He said the same thing. The son
answered, 'I will, sir.' But he did not go.
31 "Which of the two sons did what his
father wanted?"
"The first," they answered.
Jesus said to them, "What I'm about
to tell you is true. Tax collectors and
prostitutes will enter the kingdom of
God ahead of you. 32 John came to show
you the right way to live. And you did
not believe him. But the tax collectors
and the prostitutes did. You saw this.
But even then you did not turn away
from your sins and believe him.

The Story of the Renters

33 "Listen to another story. A man who
owned some land planted a vineyard.
He put a wall around it. He dug a pit
for a winepress in it. He also built a
lookout tower. He rented the vineyard
out to some farmers. Then he moved
to another place. 34 When harvest time
approached, he sent his slaves to the
renters. He told the slaves to collect his
share of the fruit.
35 "But the renters grabbed his slaves.
They beat one of them. They killed another. They threw stones at the third
to kill him. 36 Then the man sent other
slaves to the renters. He sent more than
he did the first time. The renters treated
them the same way. 37 Last of all, he sent
his son to them. 'They will respect my
son,' he said.
38 "But the renters saw the son coming. They said to one another, 'This is
the one who will receive all the owner's
property someday. Come, let's kill him.
Then everything will be ours.' 39 So they

took him and threw him out of the vineyard. Then they killed him.
40 "When the owner of the vineyard
comes back, what will he do to those
renters?"
41 "He will destroy those evil people," they replied. "Then he will rent
the vineyard out to other renters. They
will give him his share of the crop at
harvest time."
42 Jesus said to them, "Haven't you
ever read what the Scriptures say,

" 'The stone the builders didn't
accept
has become the most important
stone of all.
The Lord has done it.
It is wonderful in our eyes'?
(Psalm 118:22,23)

43 "So here is what I tell you. The kingdom of God will be taken away from
you. It will be given to people who will
produce its fruit. 44 Anyone who falls on
that stone will be broken to pieces. But
the stone will crush anyone it falls on."
45 The chief priests and the Pharisees
heard Jesus' stories. They knew he was
talking about them. 46 So they looked
for a way to arrest him. But they were
afraid of the crowd. The people believed
that Jesus was a prophet.

The Story of the Wedding Dinner

22 Jesus told them more stories. He
said, 2 "Here is what the kingdom of heaven is like. A king prepared
a wedding dinner for his son. 3 He sent
his slaves to those who had been invited
to the dinner. The slaves told them to
come. But they refused.
4 "Then he sent some more slaves.
He said, 'Tell those who were invited
that I have prepared my dinner. I have
killed my oxen and my fattest cattle.
Everything is ready. Come to the wedding dinner.'
5 "But the people paid no attention.
One went away to his field. Another
went away to his business. 6 The rest
grabbed his slaves. They treated them
badly and then killed them. 7 The king
became very angry. He sent his army
to destroy them. They killed those murderers and burned their city.
8 "Then the king said to his slaves,
'The wedding dinner is ready. But those
I invited were not fit to come. 9 So go to
the street corners. Invite to the dinner
anyone you can find.' 10 So the slaves
went out into the streets. They gathered
all the people they could find, the bad
as well as the good. Soon the wedding
hall was filled with guests.
11 "The king came in to see the guests.
He noticed a man there who was not
wearing wedding clothes. 12 'Friend,' he
asked, 'how did you get in here without
wedding clothes?' The man couldn't
think of anything to say.
13 "Then the king told his slaves, 'Tie
up his hands and feet. Throw him outside into the darkness. Out there people
will weep and grind their teeth.'
14 "Many are invited, but few are
chosen."

Is It Right to Pay the Royal Tax to Caesar?

15 The Pharisees went out. They made
plans to trap Jesus with his own words.
16 They sent their followers to him. They
sent the Herodians with them. "Teacher," they said, "we know that you are
a man of honor. You teach the way of
God truthfully. You don't let others tell
you what to do or say. You don't care
how important they are. 17 Tell us then,
what do you think? Is it right to pay the
royal tax to Caesar or not?"
18 But Jesus knew their evil plans.
He said, "You pretenders! Why are you
trying to trap me? 19 Show me the coin
people use for paying the tax." They
brought him a silver coin. 20 He asked
them, "Whose picture is this? And whose
words?"
21 "Caesar's," they replied.
Then he said to them, "So give back
to Caesar what belongs to Caesar. And
give back to God what belongs to God."
22 When they heard this, they were
amazed. So they left him and went
away.

Marriage When the Dead Rise

23 That same day the Sadducees came
to Jesus with a question. They do not
believe that people rise from the dead.
24 "Teacher," they said, "here is what
Moses told us. If a man dies without
having children, his brother must get
married to the widow. He must provide
children to carry on his brother's name.
25 There were seven brothers among

us. The first one got married and died. Since he had no children, he left his wife to his brother. 26 The same thing happened to the second and third brothers. It happened right on down to the seventh brother. 27 Finally, the woman died. 28 Now then, when the dead rise, whose wife will she be? All seven of them were married to her."

29 Jesus replied, "You are mistaken, because you do not know the Scriptures. And you do not know the power of God. 30 When the dead rise, they won't get married. And their parents won't give them to be married. They will be like the angels in heaven. 31 What about the dead rising? Haven't you read what God said to you? 32 He said, 'I am the God of Abraham. I am the God of Isaac. And I am the God of Jacob.' *(Exodus 3:6)* He is not the God of the dead. He is the God of the living."

33 When the crowds heard this, they were amazed by what he taught.

The Most Important Commandment

34 The Pharisees heard that the Sadducees weren't able to answer Jesus. So the Pharisees got together. 35 One of them was an authority on the law. So he tested Jesus with a question. 36 "Teacher," he asked, "which is the most important commandment in the Law?"

37 Jesus replied, " 'Love the Lord your God with all your heart and with all your soul. Love him with all your mind.' *(Deuteronomy 6:5)* 38 This is the first and most important commandment. 39 And the second is like it. 'Love your neighbor as you love yourself.' *(Leviticus 19:18)* 40 Everything that is written in the Law and the Prophets is based on these two commandments."

Whose Son Is the Messiah?

41 The Pharisees were gathered together. Jesus asked them, 42 "What do you think about the Messiah? Whose son is he?"

"The son of David," they replied.

43 He said to them, "Then why does David call him 'Lord'? The Holy Spirit spoke through David himself. David said,

44 " 'The Lord said to my Lord,
"Sit at my right hand
until I put your enemies
under your control." ' *(Psalm 110:1)*

45 So if David calls him 'Lord,' how can he be David's son?" 46 No one could give any answer to him. From that day on, no one dared to ask him any more questions.

A Warning Against Doing Things for the Wrong Reasons

23 Jesus spoke to the crowds and to his disciples. 2 "The teachers of the law and the Pharisees sit in Moses' seat," he said. 3 "So you must be careful to do everything they say. But don't do what they do. They don't practice what they preach. 4 They tie up heavy loads that are hard to carry. Then they put them on other people's shoulders. But they themselves aren't willing to lift a finger to move them.

5 "Everything they do is done for others to see. On their foreheads and arms they wear little boxes that hold Scripture verses. They make the boxes very wide. And they make the tassels on their coats very long. 6 They love to sit down in the place of honor at dinners. They also love to have the most important seats in the synagogues. 7 They love to be greeted with respect in the markets. They love it when people call them 'Rabbi.'

8 "But you shouldn't be called 'Rabbi.' You have only one Teacher, and you are all brothers. 9 Do not call anyone on earth 'father.' You have one Father, and he is in heaven. 10 You shouldn't be called 'teacher.' You have one Teacher, and he is the Messiah. 11 The most important person among you will be your servant. 12 People who lift themselves up will be made humble. And people who make themselves humble will be lifted up.

How Terrible for the Teachers of the Law and the Pharisees

13-14 "How terrible it will be for you, teachers of the law and Pharisees! You pretenders! You shut the door of the kingdom of heaven in people's faces. You yourselves do not enter. And you will not let those enter who are trying to.

15 "How terrible for you, teachers of the law and Pharisees! You pretenders!

You travel everywhere to win one person to your faith. Then you make them
twice as much a child of hell as you are.
16 "How terrible for you, blind guides!
You say, 'If anyone makes a promise
in the name of the temple, it means
nothing. But anyone who makes a
promise in the name of the gold of the
temple must keep that promise.' 17 You
are blind and foolish! Which is more
important? Is it the gold? Or is it the
temple that makes the gold holy? 18 You
also say, 'If anyone makes a promise in
the name of the altar, it means nothing.
But anyone who makes a promise in the
name of the gift on the altar must keep
that promise.' 19 You are blind! Which
is more important? Is it the gift? Or is
it the altar that makes the gift holy?
20 So anyone making a promise in the
name of the altar makes a promise in
the name of it and everything on it.
21 And anyone making a promise in the
name of the temple makes a promise in
the name of it and the one who lives
in it. 22 And anyone making a promise in
the name of heaven makes a promise in
the name of God's throne and the one
who sits on it.

23 "How terrible for you, teachers of
the law and Pharisees! You pretenders!
You give God a tenth of your spices, like
mint, dill and cumin. But you have not
practiced the more important things of
the law, which are fairness, mercy and
faithfulness. You should have practiced
the last things without failing to do the
first. 24 You blind guides! You remove the
smallest insect from your food. But you
swallow a whole camel!

25 "How terrible for you, teachers of
the law and Pharisees! You pretenders!
You clean the outside of a cup and dish.
But on the inside you are full of greed.
You only want to satisfy yourselves.
26 Blind Pharisee! First clean the inside
of the cup and dish. Then the outside
will also be clean.

27 "How terrible for you, teachers of
the law and Pharisees! You pretenders!
You are like tombs that are painted
white. They look beautiful on the outside. But on the inside they are full of
the bones of the dead. They are also
full of other things that are not pure
and 'clean.' 28 It is the same with you.
On the outside you seem to be doing
what is right. But on the inside you are
full of what is wrong. You pretend to be
what you are not.

29 "How terrible for you, teachers of
the law and Pharisees! You pretenders!
You build tombs for the prophets. You
decorate the graves of the godly. 30 And
you say, 'If we had lived in the days of
those who lived before us, we wouldn't
have done what they did. We wouldn't
have helped to kill the prophets.' 31 So
you are witnesses against yourselves.
You admit that you are the children of
those who murdered the prophets. 32 So
go ahead and finish the sins that those
who lived before you started!

33 "You nest of poisonous snakes! How
will you escape from being sentenced to
hell? 34 So I am sending you prophets,
wise people, and teachers. You will kill
some of them. You will nail some to a
cross. Others you will whip in your synagogues. You will chase them from town
to town. 35 So you will pay for all the
godly people's blood spilled on earth.
I mean from the blood of godly Abel
to the blood of Zechariah, the son of
Berekiah. Zechariah was the one you
murdered between the temple and the
altar. 36 What I'm about to tell you is
true. All this will happen to those who
are now living.

37 "Jerusalem! Jerusalem! You kill the
prophets and throw stones in order to
kill those who are sent to you. Many
times I have wanted to gather your
people together. I have wanted to be
like a hen who gathers her chicks under
her wings. And you would not let me!
38 Look, your house is left empty. 39 I
tell you, you will not see me again until
you say, 'Blessed is the one who comes
in the name of the Lord.' " *(Psalm 118:26)*

When the Temple Will Be Destroyed and the Signs of the End

24 Jesus left the temple. He was
walking away when his disciples came up to him. They wanted to
call his attention to the temple buildings. 2 "Do you see all these things?"
Jesus asked. "What I'm about to tell
you is true. Not one stone here will be
left on top of another. Every stone will
be thrown down."

3 Jesus was sitting on the Mount of
Olives. There the disciples came to him

in private. "Tell us," they said. "When will this happen? And what will be the sign of your coming? What will be the sign of the end?"

4 "Jesus answered, "Keep watch! Be careful that no one fools you. 5 Many will come in my name. They will claim, 'I am the Messiah!' They will fool many people. 6 You will hear about wars. You will also hear people talking about future wars. Don't be alarmed. Those things must happen. But the end still isn't here. 7 Nation will fight against nation. Kingdom will fight against kingdom. People will go hungry. There will be earthquakes in many places. 8 All these are the beginning of birth pains.

9 "Then people will hand you over to be treated badly and killed. All nations will hate you because of me. 10 At that time, many will turn away from their faith. They will hate each other. They will hand each other over to their enemies. 11 Many false prophets will appear. They will fool many people. 12 Because evil will grow, most people's love will grow cold. 13 But the one who remains strong in the faith will be saved. 14 This good news of the kingdom will be preached in the whole world. It will be a witness to all nations. Then the end will come.

15 "The prophet Daniel spoke about 'the hated thing that destroys.' *(Daniel 9:27; 11:31; 12:11)* Someday you will see it standing in the holy place. The reader should understand this. 16 Then those who are in Judea should escape to the mountains. 17 No one on the housetop should go down into the house to take anything out. 18 No one in the field should go back to get their coat. 19 How awful it will be in those days for pregnant women! How awful for nursing mothers! 20 Pray that you will not have to escape in winter or on the Sabbath day. 21 There will be terrible suffering in those days. It will be worse than any other from the beginning of the world until now. And there will never be anything like it again.

22 "If the time had not been cut short, no one would live. But because of God's chosen people, it will be shortened. 23 At that time someone may say to you, 'Look! Here is the Messiah!' Or, 'There he is!' Do not believe it. 24 False messiahs and false prophets will appear. They will do great signs and miracles. They will try to fool God's chosen people if possible. 25 See, I have told you ahead of time.

26 "So if anyone tells you, 'He is a long way out in the desert,' do not go out there. Or if anyone says, 'He is deep inside the house,' do not believe it. 27 Lightning that comes from the east can be seen in the west. It will be the same when the Son of Man comes. 28 The vultures will gather wherever there is a dead body.

29 "Right after the terrible suffering of those days,

" 'The sun will be darkened.
  The moon will not shine.
The stars will fall from the sky.
  The heavenly bodies will be
    shaken.' *(Isaiah 13:10; 34:4)*

30 "Then the sign of the Son of Man will appear in heaven. At that time, all the peoples of the earth will mourn. They will mourn when they see the Son of Man coming on the clouds of heaven. He will come with power and great glory. 31 He will send his angels with a loud trumpet call. They will gather his chosen people from all four directions. They will bring them from one end of the heavens to the other.

32 "Learn a lesson from the fig tree. As soon as its twigs get tender and its leaves come out, you know that summer is near. 33 In the same way, when you see all these things happening, you know that the end is near. It is right at the door. 34 What I'm about to tell you is true. The people living now will certainly not pass away until all these things have happened. 35 Heaven and earth will pass away. But my words will never pass away.

The Day and Hour Are Not Known

36 "But no one knows about that day or hour. Not even the angels in heaven know. The Son does not know. Only the Father knows. 37 Remember how it was in the days of Noah. It will be the same when the Son of Man comes. 38 In the days before the flood, people were eating and drinking. They were getting married. They were giving their daughters to be married. They did all those things right up to the day Noah entered the

ark. [39]They knew nothing about what would happen until the flood came and took them all away. That is how it will be when the Son of Man comes. [40]Two men will be in the field. One will be taken and the other left. [41]Two women will be grinding with a hand mill. One will be taken and the other left.

[42]"So keep watch. You do not know on what day your Lord will come. [43]You must understand something. Suppose the owner of the house knew what time of night the robber was coming. Then he would have kept watch. He would not have let his house be broken into. [44]So you also must be ready. The Son of Man will come at an hour when you don't expect him.

[45]"Suppose a master puts one of his slaves in charge of the other slaves in his house. The slave's job is to give them their food at the right time. The master wants a faithful and wise slave for this. [46]It will be good for the slave if the master finds him doing his job when the master returns. [47]What I'm about to tell you is true. The master will put that slave in charge of everything he owns. [48]But suppose that slave is evil. Suppose he says to himself, 'My master is staying away a long time.' [49]Suppose he begins to beat the other slaves. And suppose he eats and drinks with those who drink too much. [50]The master of that slave will come back on a day the slave doesn't expect him. He will return at an hour the slave does not know. [51]Then the master will cut him to pieces. He will send him to the place where pretenders go. There people will weep and grind their teeth.

The Story of Ten Bridesmaids

25 "Here is what the kingdom of heaven will be like at that time. Ten bridesmaids took their lamps and went out to meet the groom. [2]Five of them were foolish. Five were wise. [3]The foolish ones took their lamps but didn't take any olive oil with them. [4]The wise ones took oil in jars along with their lamps. [5]The groom did not come for a long time. So the bridesmaids all grew tired and fell asleep.

[6]"At midnight someone cried out, 'Here's the groom! Come out to meet him!'

[7]"Then all the bridesmaids woke up and got their lamps ready. [8]The foolish ones said to the wise ones, 'Give us some of your oil. Our lamps are going out.'

[9]" 'No,' they replied. 'There may not be enough for all of us. Instead, go to those who sell oil. Buy some for yourselves.'

[10]"So they went to buy the oil. But while they were on their way, the groom arrived. The bridesmaids who were ready went in with him to the wedding dinner. Then the door was shut.

[11]"Later, the other bridesmaids also came. 'Sir! Sir!' they said. 'Open the door for us!'

[12]"But he replied, 'What I'm about to tell you is true. I don't know you.'

[13]"So keep watch. You do not know the day or the hour that the groom will come.

The Story of Three Slaves

[14]"Again, here is what the kingdom of heaven will be like. A man was going on a journey. He sent for his slaves and put them in charge of his money. [15]He gave five bags of gold to one. He gave two bags to another. And he gave one bag to the third. The man gave each slave the amount of money he knew the slave could take care of. Then he went on his journey. [16]The slave who had received five bags of gold went at once and put his money to work. He earned five bags more. [17]The one with the two bags of gold earned two more. [18]But the man who had received one bag went and dug a hole in the ground. He hid his master's money in it.

[19]"After a long time the master of those slaves returned. He wanted to collect all the money they had earned. [20]The man who had received five bags of gold brought the other five. 'Master,' he said, 'you trusted me with five bags of gold. See, I have earned five more.'

[21]"His master replied, 'You have done well, good and faithful slave! You have been faithful with a few things. I will put you in charge of many things. Come and share your master's happiness!'

[22]"The man with two bags of gold also came. 'Master,' he said, 'you trusted me with two bags of gold. See, I have earned two more.'

23 "His master replied, 'You have done
well, good and faithful slave! You have
been faithful with a few things. I will put
you in charge of many things. Come
and share your master's happiness!'
24 "Then the man who had received
one bag of gold came. 'Master,' he said,
'I knew that you are a hard man. You
harvest where you have not planted.
You gather crops where you have not
scattered seed. 25 So I was afraid. I went
out and hid your gold in the ground.
See, here is what belongs to you.'
26 "His master replied, 'You evil,
lazy slave! So you knew that I harvest
where I have not planted? You knew
that I gather crops where I have not
scattered seed? 27 Well then, you should
have put my money in the bank. When
I returned, I would have received it back
with interest.'
28 "Then his master commanded
the other slaves, 'Take the bag of gold
from him. Give it to the one who has
ten bags. 29 Everyone who has will be
given more. They will have more than
enough. And what about anyone who
doesn't have? Even what they have will
be taken away from them. 30 Throw that
worthless slave outside. There in the
darkness, people will weep and grind
their teeth.'

The Sheep and the Goats

31 "The Son of Man will come in all his
glory. All the angels will come with him.
Then he will sit in glory on his throne.
32 All the nations will be gathered in
front of him. He will separate the people into two groups. He will be like a
shepherd who separates the sheep from
the goats. 33 He will put the sheep to his
right and the goats to his left.
34 "Then the King will speak to those
on his right. He will say, 'My Father
has blessed you. Come and take what
is yours. It is the kingdom prepared for
you since the world was created. 35 I was
hungry. And you gave me something
to eat. I was thirsty. And you gave me
something to drink. I was a stranger. And you invited me in. 36 I needed
clothes. And you gave them to me. I was
sick. And you took care of me. I was in
prison. And you came to visit me.'
37 "Then the people who have done
what is right will answer him. 'Lord,'
they will ask, 'when did we see you
hungry and feed you? When did we
see you thirsty and give you something
to drink? 38 When did we see you as a
stranger and invite you in? When did we
see you needing clothes and give them
to you? 39 When did we see you sick or
in prison and go to visit you?'
40 "The King will reply, 'What I'm
about to tell you is true. Anything you
did for one of the least important of
these brothers and sisters of mine, you
did for me.'
41 "Then he will say to those on his left,
'You are cursed! Go away from me into
the fire that burns forever. It has been
prepared for the devil and his angels. 42 I
was hungry. But you gave me nothing
to eat. I was thirsty. But you gave me
nothing to drink. 43 I was a stranger.
But you did not invite me in. I needed
clothes. But you did not give me any. I
was sick and in prison. But you did not
take care of me.'
44 "They also will answer, 'Lord, when
did we see you hungry or thirsty and
not help you? When did we see you as
a stranger or needing clothes or sick or
in prison and not help you?'
45 "He will reply, 'What I'm about to
tell you is true. Anything you didn't do
for one of the least important of these,
you didn't do for me.'
46 "Then they will go away to be punished forever. But those who have done
what is right will receive eternal life."

The Plan to Kill Jesus

26 Jesus finished saying all these
things. Then he said to his disciples, 2 "As you know, the Passover Feast
is two days away. The Son of Man will
be handed over to be nailed to a cross."
3 Then the chief priests met with the
elders of the people. They met in the
palace of Caiaphas, the high priest.
4 They made plans to arrest Jesus secretly. They wanted to kill him. 5 "But
not during the feast," they said. "The
people may stir up trouble."

A Woman Pours Perfume on Jesus

6 Jesus was in Bethany. He was in the
home of Simon, who had a skin disease.
7 A woman came to Jesus with a special
sealed jar of very expensive perfume.
She poured the perfume on his head
while he was at the table.

8 When the disciples saw this, they became angry. "Why this waste?" they asked. 9 "The perfume could have been sold at a high price. The money could have been given to poor people."

10 Jesus was aware of this. So he said to them, "Why are you bothering this woman? She has done a beautiful thing to me. 11 You will always have poor people with you. But you will not always have me. 12 She poured the perfume on my body to prepare me to be buried. 13 What I'm about to tell you is true. What she has done will be told anywhere this good news is preached all over the world. It will be told in memory of her."

Judas Agrees to Hand Jesus Over

14 One of the 12 disciples went to the chief priests. His name was Judas Iscariot. 15 He asked, "What will you give me if I hand Jesus over to you?" So they counted out 30 silver coins for him. 16 From then on, Judas watched for the right time to hand Jesus over to them.

The Lord's Supper

17 It was the first day of the Feast of Unleavened Bread. The disciples came to Jesus. They asked, "Where do you want us to prepare for you to eat the Passover meal?"

18 He replied, "Go into the city to a certain man. Tell him, 'The Teacher says, "My time is near. I am going to celebrate the Passover at your house with my disciples." ' " 19 So the disciples did what Jesus had told them to do. They prepared the Passover meal.

20 When evening came, Jesus was at the table with his 12 disciples. 21 While they were eating, he said, "What I'm about to tell you is true. One of you will hand me over to my enemies."

22 The disciples became very sad. One after the other, they began to say to him, "Surely you don't mean me, Lord, do you?"

23 Jesus replied, "The one who has dipped his hand into the bowl with me will hand me over. 24 The Son of Man will go just as it is written about him. But how terrible it will be for the one who hands over the Son of Man! It would be better for him if he had not been born."

25 Judas was the one who was going to hand him over. He said, "Surely you don't mean me, Teacher, do you?"

Jesus answered, "You have said so."

26 While they were eating, Jesus took bread. He gave thanks and broke it. He handed it to his disciples and said, "Take this and eat it. This is my body."

27 Then he took a cup. He gave thanks and handed it to them. He said, "All of you drink from it. 28 This is my blood of the covenant. It is poured out to forgive the sins of many people. 29 Here is what I tell you. From now on, I won't drink wine with you again until the day I drink it with you in my Father's kingdom."

30 Then they sang a hymn and went out to the Mount of Olives.

Jesus Says That the Disciples Will Turn Away

31 Jesus told them, "This very night you will all turn away because of me. It is written that the Lord said,

> " 'I will strike the shepherd down.
> Then the sheep of the flock will
> be scattered.' *(Zechariah 13:7)*

32 But after I rise from the dead, I will go ahead of you into Galilee."

33 Peter replied, "All the others may turn away because of you. But I never will."

34 "What I'm about to tell you is true," Jesus answered. "It will happen tonight. Before the rooster crows, you will say three times that you don't know me."

35 But Peter said, "I may have to die with you. But I will never say I don't know you." And all the other disciples said the same thing.

Jesus Prays in Gethsemane

36 Then Jesus went with his disciples to a place called Gethsemane. He said to them, "Sit here while I go over there and pray." 37 He took Peter and the two sons of Zebedee along with him. He began to be sad and troubled. 38 Then he said to them, "My soul is very sad. I feel close to death. Stay here. Keep watch with me."

39 He went a little farther. Then he fell with his face to the ground. He prayed, "My Father, if it is possible, take this cup of suffering away from me. But let what you want be done, not what I want."

40 Then he returned to his disciples
and found them sleeping. "Couldn't
you men keep watch with me for one
hour?" he asked Peter. 41 "Watch and
pray. Then you won't fall into sin when
you are tempted. The spirit is willing,
but the body is weak."
42 Jesus went away a second time. He
prayed, "My Father, is it possible for
this cup to be taken away? But if I must
drink it, may what you want be done."
43 Then he came back. Again he found
them sleeping. They couldn't keep their
eyes open. 44 So he left them and went
away once more. For the third time he
prayed the same thing.
45 Then he returned to the disciples.
He said to them, "Are you still sleeping
and resting? Look! The hour has come.
The Son of Man is about to be handed
over to sinners. 46 Get up! Let us go! Here
comes the one who is handing me over
to them!"

Jesus Is Arrested

47 While Jesus was still speaking,
Judas arrived. He was one of the 12
disciples. A large crowd was with him.
They were carrying swords and clubs.
The chief priests and the elders of the
people had sent them. 48 Judas, who was
going to hand Jesus over, had arranged
a signal with them. "The one I kiss is
the man," he said. "Arrest him." 49 So
Judas went to Jesus at once. He said,
"Greetings, Rabbi!" And he kissed him.
50 Jesus replied, "Friend, do what you
came to do."
Then the men stepped forward. They
grabbed Jesus and arrested him. 51 At
that moment, one of Jesus' companions
reached for his sword. He pulled it out
and struck the slave of the high priest
with it. He cut off the slave's ear.
52 "Put your sword back in its place,"
Jesus said to him. "All who use the sword
will die by the sword. 53 Do you think I
can't ask my Father for help? He would
send an army of more than 70,000 angels right away. 54 But then how would
the Scriptures come true? They say it
must happen in this way."
55 At that time Jesus spoke to the
crowd. "Am I leading a band of armed
men against you?" he asked. "Do you
have to come out with swords and clubs
to capture me? Every day I sat in the
temple courtyard teaching. And you
didn't arrest me. 56 But all this has happened so that the words of the prophets
would come true." Then all the disciples
left him and ran away.

Jesus Is Taken to the Sanhedrin

57 Those who had arrested Jesus took
him to Caiaphas, the high priest. The
teachers of the law and the elders had
come together there. 58 Not too far away,
Peter followed Jesus. He went right up
to the courtyard of the high priest. He
entered and sat down with the guards
to see what would happen.
59 The chief priests and the whole
Sanhedrin were looking for something
to use against Jesus. They wanted to
put him to death. 60 But they did not
find any proof, even though many false
witnesses came forward.
Finally, two other witnesses came forward. 61 They said, "This fellow claimed,
'I am able to destroy the temple of God.
I can build it again in three days.' "
62 Then the high priest stood up. He
asked Jesus, "Aren't you going to answer? What are these charges that these
men are bringing against you?" 63 But
Jesus remained silent.
The high priest said to him, "I am
commanding you in the name of the
living God. May he judge you if you
don't tell the truth. Tell us if you are
the Messiah, the Son of God."
64 "You have said so," Jesus replied.
"But here is what I say to all of you.
From now on, you will see the Son of
Man sitting at the right hand of the
Mighty One. You will see the Son of Man
coming on the clouds of heaven."
65 Then the high priest tore his clothes.
He said, "He has spoken a very evil thing
against God! Why do we need any more
witnesses? You have heard him say this
evil thing. 66 What do you think?"
"He must die!" they answered.
67 Then they spit in his face. They hit
him with their fists. Others slapped him.
68 They said, "Prophesy to us, Messiah!
Who hit you?"

Peter Says He Does Not Know Jesus

69 Peter was sitting out in the courtyard. A female servant came to him.
"You also were with Jesus of Galilee,"
she said.

70 But in front of all of them, Peter said he was not. "I don't know what you're talking about," he said.

71 Then he went out to the gate leading into the courtyard. There another servant saw him. She said to the people, "This fellow was with Jesus of Nazareth."

72 Again he said he was not. With a curse he said, "I don't know the man!"

73 After a little while, those standing there went up to Peter. "You must be one of them," they said. "The way you talk gives you away."

74 Then Peter began to curse and said to them, "I don't know the man!"

Right away a rooster crowed. 75 Then Peter remembered what Jesus had said. "The rooster will crow," Jesus had told him. "Before it does, you will say three times that you don't know me." Peter went outside. He broke down and cried.

Judas Hangs Himself

27 It was early in the morning. All the chief priests and the elders of the people planned how to put Jesus to death. 2 So they tied him up and led him away. Then they handed him over to Pilate, who was the governor.

3 Judas, who had handed him over, saw that Jesus had been sentenced to die. He felt deep shame and sadness for what he had done. So he returned the 30 silver coins to the chief priests and the elders. 4 "I have sinned," he said. "I handed over a man who is not guilty."

"What do we care?" they replied. "That's your problem."

5 So Judas threw the money into the temple and left. Then he went away and hanged himself.

6 The chief priests picked up the coins. They said, "It's against the law to put this money into the temple fund. It is blood money. It has paid for a man's death." 7 So they decided to use the money to buy a potter's field. People from other countries would be buried there. 8 That is why it has been called the Field of Blood to this day. 9 Then the words spoken by Jeremiah the prophet came true. He had said, "They took the 30 silver coins. That price was set for him by the people of Israel. 10 They used the coins to buy a potter's field, just as the Lord commanded me." *(Zechariah 11:12,13; Jeremiah 19:1–13; 32:6–9)*

Jesus Is Brought to Pilate

11 Jesus was standing in front of the governor. The governor asked him, "Are you the king of the Jews?"

"Yes. You have said so," Jesus replied.

12 But when the chief priests and the elders brought charges against him, he did not answer. 13 Then Pilate asked him, "Don't you hear the charges they are bringing against you?" 14 But Jesus made no reply, not even to a single charge. The governor was really amazed.

15 It was the governor's practice at the Passover Feast to let one prisoner go free. The people could choose the one they wanted. 16 At that time they had a well-known prisoner named Jesus Barabbas. 17 So when the crowd gathered, Pilate asked them, "Which one do you want me to set free? Jesus Barabbas? Or Jesus who is called the Messiah?" 18 Pilate knew that the leaders wanted to get their own way. He knew this was why they had handed Jesus over to him.

19 While Pilate was sitting on the judge's seat, his wife sent him a message. It said, "Don't have anything to do with that man. He is not guilty. I have suffered a great deal in a dream today because of him."

20 But the chief priests and the elders talked the crowd into asking for Barabbas and having Jesus put to death.

21 "Which of the two do you want me to set free?" asked the governor.

"Barabbas," they answered.

22 "Then what should I do with Jesus who is called the Messiah?" Pilate asked.

They all answered, "Crucify him!"

23 "Why? What wrong has he done?" asked Pilate.

But they shouted even louder, "Crucify him!"

24 Pilate saw that he wasn't getting anywhere. Instead, the crowd was starting to get angry. So he took water and washed his hands in front of them. "I am not guilty of this man's death," he said. "You are accountable for that!"

25 All the people answered, "Put the blame for his death on us and our children!"

26 Pilate let Barabbas go free. But he had Jesus whipped. Then he handed him over to be nailed to a cross.

The Soldiers Make Fun of Jesus

27 The governor's soldiers took Jesus
into the palace, which was called the
Praetorium. All the rest of the soldiers
gathered around him. 28 They took off
his clothes and put a purple robe on
him. 29 Then they twisted thorns together to make a crown. They placed it on his
head. They put a stick in his right hand.
Then they fell on their knees in front of
him and made fun of him. "We honor
you, king of the Jews!" they said. 30 They
spit on him. They hit him on the head
with the stick again and again. 31 After
they had made fun of him, they took
off the robe. They put his own clothes
back on him. Then they led him away
to nail him to a cross.

Jesus Is Nailed to a Cross

32 On their way out of the city, they
met a man from Cyrene. His name was
Simon. They forced him to carry the
cross. 33 They came to a place called
Golgotha. The word Golgotha means
the Place of the Skull. 34 There they
mixed wine with bitter spices and gave
it to Jesus to drink. After tasting it, he
refused to drink it. 35 When they had
nailed him to the cross, they divided up
his clothes by casting lots. 36 They sat
down and kept watch over him there.
37 Above his head they placed the written charge against him. It read,

THIS IS JESUS, THE KING OF THE JEWS.

38 Two rebels against Rome were crucified with him. One was on his right
and one was on his left. 39 Those who
passed by shouted at Jesus and made
fun of him. They shook their heads
40 and said, "So you are going to destroy the temple and build it again in
three days? Then save yourself! Come
down from the cross, if you are the Son
of God!" 41 In the same way the chief
priests, the teachers of the law and the
elders made fun of him. 42 "He saved
others," they said. "But he can't save
himself! He's the king of Israel! Let him
come down now from the cross! Then we
will believe in him. 43 He trusts in God.
Let God rescue him now if he wants him.
He's the one who said, 'I am the Son of
God.' " 44 In the same way the rebels
who were being crucified with Jesus
also made fun of him.

Jesus Dies

45 From noon until three o'clock, the
whole land was covered with darkness.
46 About three o'clock, Jesus cried out
in a loud voice. He said, *"Eli, Eli, lema
sabachthani?"* This means "My God,
my God, why have you deserted me?"
(Psalm 22:1)

47 Some of those standing there heard
Jesus cry out. They said, "He's calling
for Elijah."

48 Right away one of them ran and
got a sponge. He filled it with wine vinegar and put it on a stick. He offered it
to Jesus to drink. 49 The rest said, "Leave
him alone. Let's see if Elijah comes to
save him."

50 After Jesus cried out again in a loud
voice, he died.

51 At that moment the temple curtain
was torn in two from top to bottom. The
earth shook. The rocks split. 52 Tombs
broke open. The bodies of many holy
people who had died were raised to
life. 53 They came out of the tombs. After
Jesus was raised from the dead, they
went into the holy city. There they appeared to many people.

54 The Roman commander and those
guarding Jesus saw the earthquake and
all that had happened. They were terrified. They exclaimed, "He was surely
the Son of God!"

55 Not very far away, many women
were watching. They had followed Jesus
from Galilee to take care of his needs.
56 Mary Magdalene was among them.
Mary, the mother of James and Joseph,
was also there. So was the mother of
Zebedee's sons.

Jesus Is Buried

57 As evening approached, a rich man
came from the town of Arimathea. His
name was Joseph. He had become a
follower of Jesus. 58 He went to Pilate
and asked for Jesus' body. Pilate ordered that it be given to him. 59 Joseph
took the body and wrapped it in a clean
linen cloth. 60 He placed it in his own
new tomb that he had cut out of the
rock. He rolled a big stone in front of
the entrance to the tomb. Then he went
away. 61 Mary Magdalene and the other
Mary were sitting there across from
the tomb.

The Guards at the Tomb

62 The next day was the day after
Preparation Day. The chief priests and
the Pharisees went to Pilate. 63 "Sir,"
they said, "we remember something
that liar said while he was still alive.
He claimed, 'After three days I will rise
again.' 64 So give the order to make the
tomb secure until the third day. If you
don't, his disciples might come and steal
the body. Then they will tell the people
that Jesus has been raised from the
dead. This last lie will be worse than
the first."

65 "Take some guards with you," Pilate
answered. "Go. Make the tomb as secure
as you can." 66 So they went and made
the tomb secure. They put a royal seal
on the stone and placed some guards
on duty.

Jesus Rises From the Dead

28 The Sabbath day was now over.
It was dawn on the first day of
the week. Mary Magdalene and the
other Mary went to look at the tomb.

2 There was a powerful earthquake.
An angel of the Lord came down from
heaven. The angel went to the tomb. He
rolled back the stone and sat on it. 3 His
body shone like lightning. His clothes
were as white as snow. 4 The guards
were so afraid of him that they shook
and became like dead men.

5 The angel said to the women, "Don't
be afraid. I know that you are looking
for Jesus, who was crucified. 6 He is not
here! He has risen, just as he said he
would! Come and see the place where he
was lying. 7 Go quickly! Tell his disciples,
'He has risen from the dead. He is going
ahead of you into Galilee. There you will
see him.' Now I have told you."

8 So the women hurried away from
the tomb. They were afraid, but they
were filled with joy. They ran to tell the
disciples. 9 Suddenly Jesus met them.
"Greetings!" he said. They came to him,
took hold of his feet and worshiped him.
10 Then Jesus said to them, "Don't be
afraid. Go and tell my brothers to go to
Galilee. There they will see me."

The Guards Report to the Chief Priests

11 While the women were on their way,
some of the guards went into the city.
They reported to the chief priests all
that had happened. 12 When the chief
priests met with the elders, they came
up with a plan. They gave the soldiers
a large amount of money. 13 They told
the soldiers, "We want you to say, 'His
disciples came during the night. They
stole his body while we were sleeping.'
14 If the governor hears this report, we
will pay him off. That will keep you out
of trouble." 15 So the soldiers took the
money and did as they were told. This
story has spread all around among the
Jews to this day.

Jesus' Final Orders to His Disciples

16 Then the 11 disciples went to Galilee.
They went to the mountain where Jesus
had told them to go. 17 When they saw
him, they worshiped him. But some still
had their doubts. 18 Then Jesus came to
them. He said, "All authority in heaven
and on earth has been given to me. 19 So
you must go and make disciples of all
nations. Baptize them in the name of
the Father and of the Son and of the
Holy Spirit. 20 Teach them to obey everything I have commanded you. And
you can be sure that I am always with
you, to the very end."

MARK

Author: John Mark

The Gospel of Mark also tells of the coming of the Savior, Jesus. Mark (called John Mark) was a follower of Jesus and wrote down what he learned about the life and ministry of Jesus so that others could know about Jesus too.

Mark was a friend of Peter and Paul and traveled with them when they were spreading the good news about Jesus. Mark wanted everyone to know what Jesus did, where he went, and how he died and rose again. Mark also wanted everyone to know that what Jesus did changes everything because Jesus is the Son of God. Mark's goal was for those who read his account to know that Jesus was the suffering servant whom Isaiah prophesied, or predicted, would come and die for his people. Mark helps those reading to understand that all the things Jesus did only could have happened if Jesus was who he said he was: the Son of God! In his Gospel, Mark included stories about Jesus' power and teaching, and in every story the theme is the same: Jesus is good news because he is the Son of God who brings salvation!

Gospels & Acts

John the Baptist Prepares the Way

1 This is the beginning of the good news about Jesus the Messiah, the Son of God. 2 Long ago Isaiah the prophet wrote,

> "I will send my messenger ahead of
> you.
> He will prepare your way."
> *(Malachi 3:1)*
>
> 3 "A messenger is calling out in the
> desert,
> 'Prepare the way for the Lord.
> Make straight paths for him.' "
> *(Isaiah 40:3)*

4 And so John the Baptist appeared in the desert. He preached that people should be baptized and turn away from their sins. Then God would forgive them. 5 All the people from the countryside of Judea went out to him. All the people from Jerusalem went too. When they admitted they had sinned, John baptized them in the Jordan River. 6 John wore clothes made out of camel's hair. He had a leather belt around his waist. And he ate locusts and wild honey. 7 Here is what John was preaching. "After me, there is someone coming who is more powerful than I am. I'm not good enough to bend down and untie his sandals. 8 I baptize you with water. But he will baptize you with the Holy Spirit."

Jesus Is Baptized and Tempted

9 At that time Jesus came from Nazareth in Galilee. John baptized Jesus in the Jordan River. 10 Jesus was coming up out of the water. Just then he saw heaven being torn open. Jesus saw the Holy Spirit coming down on him like a dove. 11 A voice spoke to him from heaven. It said, "You are my Son, and I love you. I am very pleased with you."

12 At once the Holy Spirit sent Jesus out into the desert. 13 He was in the desert 40 days. There Satan tempted him. The wild animals didn't harm Jesus. Angels took care of him.

Jesus Preaches the Good News

14 After John was put in prison, Jesus went into Galilee. He preached the good news of God. 15 "The time has come," he said. "The kingdom of God has come near. Turn away from your sins and believe the good news!"

Jesus Chooses His First Disciples

16 One day Jesus was walking beside the Sea of Galilee. There he saw Simon and his brother Andrew. They were throwing a net into the lake. They were fishermen. 17 "Come and follow me," Jesus said. "I will send you out to fish for people." 18 At once they left their nets and followed him.

19 Then Jesus walked a little farther. As he did, he saw James, the son of Zebedee, and his brother John. They were in a boat preparing their nets. 20 Right away he called out to them. They left their father Zebedee in the boat with the hired men. Then they followed Jesus.

Jesus Drives Out an Evil Spirit

21 Jesus and those with him went to Capernaum. When the Sabbath day came, he went into the synagogue. There he began to teach. 22 The people were amazed at his teaching. That's because he taught them like one who had authority. He did not talk like the teachers of the law. 23 Just then a man in their synagogue cried out. He was controlled by an evil spirit. He said, 24 "What do you want with us, Jesus of Nazareth? Have you come to destroy us? I know who you are. You are the Holy One of God!"

25 "Be quiet!" said Jesus firmly. "Come out of him!" 26 The evil spirit shook the man wildly. Then it came out of him with a scream.

27 All the people were amazed. So they asked each other, "What is this? A new teaching! And with so much authority! He even gives orders to evil spirits, and they obey him." 28 News about Jesus spread quickly all over Galilee.

Jesus Heals Many People

29 Jesus and those with him left the synagogue. Right away they went with James and John to the home of Simon and Andrew. 30 Simon's mother-in-law was lying in bed with a fever. They told Jesus about her right away. 31 So he went to her. He took her hand and helped her up. The fever left her. Then she began to serve them.

32 That evening after sunset, the people brought to Jesus all who were sick. They also brought all who were controlled by demons. 33 All the people in town gathered at the door. 34 Jesus healed many of them. They had all

kinds of sicknesses. He also drove out many demons. But he would not let the demons speak, because they knew who he was.

Jesus Prays in a Quiet Place

35 It was very early in the morning and still dark. Jesus got up and left the house. He went to a place where he could be alone. There he prayed. 36 Simon and his friends went to look for Jesus. 37 When they found him, they called out, "Everyone is looking for you!"

38 Jesus replied, "Let's go somewhere else. I want to go to the nearby towns. I must preach there also. That is why I have come." 39 So he traveled all around Galilee. He preached in their synagogues. He also drove out demons.

Jesus Heals a Man Who Had a Skin Disease

40 A man who had a skin disease came to Jesus. On his knees he begged Jesus. He said, "If you are willing to make me 'clean,' you can do it."

41 Jesus became angry. He reached out his hand and touched the man. "I am willing to do it," Jesus said. "Be 'clean'!" 42 Right away the disease left the man, and he was "clean."

43 Jesus sent him away at once. He gave the man a strong warning. 44 "Don't tell this to anyone," he said. "Go and show yourself to the priest. Offer the sacrifices that Moses commanded. It will be a witness to the priest and the people that you are 'clean.'" 45 But the man went out and started talking right away. He spread the news to everyone. So Jesus could no longer enter a town openly. He stayed outside in lonely places. But people still came to him from everywhere.

Jesus Forgives and Heals a Man Who Could Not Walk

2 A few days later, Jesus entered Capernaum again. The people heard that he had come home. 2 So many people gathered that there was no room left. There was not even room outside the door. And Jesus preached the word to them. 3 Four of those who came were carrying a man who could not walk. 4 But they could not get him close to Jesus because of the crowd. So they made a hole by digging through the roof above Jesus. Then they lowered

in Mark?

God is the Miracle Worker. He sent his Son, Jesus, to show his love for us by healing the sick, calming a storm, and feeding five thousand people with five loaves and two fish.

the man through it on a mat. 5 Jesus saw their faith. So he said to the man, "Son, your sins are forgiven."

6 Some teachers of the law were sitting there. They were thinking, 7 "Why is this fellow talking like that? He's saying a very evil thing! Only God can forgive sins!"

8 Right away Jesus knew what they were thinking. So he said to them, "Why are you thinking these things? 9 Is it easier to say to this man, 'Your sins are forgiven'? Or to say, 'Get up, take your mat and walk'? 10 But I want you to know that the Son of Man has authority on earth to forgive sins." So Jesus spoke to the man who could not walk. 11 "I tell you," he said, "get up. Take your mat and go home." 12 The man got up and took his mat. Then he walked away while everyone watched. All the people were amazed. They praised God and said, "We have never seen anything like this!"

Jesus Chooses Levi and Eats With Sinners

13 Once again Jesus went out beside the Sea of Galilee. A large crowd came to him. He began to teach them. 14 As he walked along he saw Levi, the son of Alphaeus. Levi was sitting at the tax collector's booth. "Follow me," Jesus told him. Levi got up and followed him.

15 Later Jesus was having dinner at Levi's house. Many tax collectors and

sinners were eating with him and his disciples. They were part of the large crowd following Jesus. [16] Some teachers of the law who were Pharisees were there. They saw Jesus eating with sinners and tax collectors. So they asked his disciples, "Why does he eat with tax collectors and sinners?"

[17] Jesus heard that. So he said to them, "Those who are healthy don't need a doctor. Sick people do. I have not come to get those who think they are right with God to follow me. I have come to get sinners to follow me."

Jesus Is Asked About Fasting

[18] John's disciples and the Pharisees were going without eating. Some people came to Jesus. They said to him, "John's disciples are fasting. The disciples of the Pharisees are also fasting. But your disciples are not. Why aren't they?"

[19] Jesus answered, "How can the guests of the groom go without eating while he is with them? They will not fast as long as he is with them. [20] But the time will come when the groom will be taken away from them. On that day they will go without eating.

[21] "No one sews a patch of new cloth on old clothes. Otherwise, the new piece will pull away from the old. That will make the tear worse. [22] No one pours new wine into old wineskins. Otherwise, the wine will burst the skins. Then the wine and the wineskins will both be destroyed. No, people pour new wine into new wineskins."

Jesus Is Lord of the Sabbath Day

[23] One Sabbath day Jesus was walking with his disciples through the grainfields. The disciples began to break off some heads of grain. [24] The Pharisees said to Jesus, "Look! It is against the Law to do this on the Sabbath day. Why are your disciples doing it?"

[25] He answered, "Haven't you ever read about what David did? He and his men were hungry. They needed food. [26] It was when Abiathar was high priest. David entered the house of God and ate the holy bread. Only priests were allowed to eat it. David also gave some to his men."

[27] Then Jesus said to them, "The Sabbath day was made for man. Man was not made for the Sabbath day. [28] So the Son of Man is Lord even of the Sabbath day."

Jesus Heals on the Sabbath Day

3 Another time Jesus went into the synagogue. A man with a weak and twisted hand was there. [2] Some Pharisees were trying to find fault with Jesus. They watched him closely. They wanted to see if he would heal the man on the Sabbath day. [3] Jesus spoke to the man with the weak and twisted hand. "Stand up in front of everyone," he said.

[4] Then Jesus asked them, "What does the Law say we should do on the Sabbath day? Should we do good? Or should we do evil? Should we save life? Or should we kill?" But no one answered.

[5] Jesus looked around at them in anger. He was very upset because their hearts were stubborn. Then he said to the man, "Stretch out your hand." He stretched it out, and his hand had become as good as new. [6] Then the Pharisees went out and began to make plans with the Herodians. They wanted to kill Jesus.

Crowds Follow Jesus

[7] Jesus went off to the Sea of Galilee with his disciples. A large crowd from Galilee followed. [8] People heard about all that Jesus was doing. And many came to him. They came from Judea, Jerusalem and Idumea. They came from the lands east of the Jordan River. And they came from the area around Tyre and Sidon. [9] Because of the crowd, Jesus told his disciples to get a small boat ready for him. This would keep the people from crowding him. [10] Jesus had healed many people. So those who were sick were pushing forward to touch him. [11] When people controlled by evil spirits saw him, they fell down in front of him. The spirits shouted, "You are the Son of God!" [12] But Jesus ordered them not to tell people about him.

Jesus Appoints the Twelve Disciples

[13] Jesus went up on a mountainside. He called for certain people to come to him, and they came. [14] He appointed 12 of them so that they would be with him. He would also send them out to preach. [15] And he gave them authority to drive out demons.

[16] So Jesus appointed the 12 disciples.

Simon was one of them. Jesus gave him the name Peter.

17 There were James, son of Zebedee,
and his brother John. Jesus gave
them the name Boanerges.
Boanerges means Sons of Thunder.
18 There were also Andrew,
Philip,
Bartholomew,
Matthew,
Thomas,
and James, son of Alphaeus.
And there were Thaddaeus
and Simon the Zealot.
19 Judas Iscariot was one of them too.
He was the one who was later
going to hand Jesus over to his
enemies.

Jesus Is Accused by Teachers of the Law

20 Jesus entered a house. Again a
crowd gathered. It was so large that
Jesus and his disciples were not even
able to eat. 21 His family heard about
this. So they went to take charge of him.
They said, "He is out of his mind."
22 Some teachers of the law were there.
They had come down from Jerusalem.
They said, "He is controlled by Beelzebul! He is driving out demons by the
power of the prince of demons."
23 So Jesus called them over to him. He
began to speak to them using stories. He
said, "How can Satan drive out Satan?
24 If a kingdom fights against itself, it
can't stand. 25 If a family is divided, it can't
stand. 26 And if Satan fights against himself, and his helpers are divided, he can't
stand. That is the end of him. 27 In fact,
none of you can enter a strong man's
house unless you tie him up first. Then
you can steal things from his house.
28 What I'm about to tell you is true. Everyone's sins and evil words against God
will be forgiven. 29 But whoever speaks evil
things against the Holy Spirit will never
be forgiven. Their guilt will last forever."
30 Jesus said this because the teachers
of the law were saying, "He has an evil
spirit."

Jesus' Mother and Brothers

31 Jesus' mother and brothers came
and stood outside. They sent someone
in to get him. 32 A crowd was sitting
around Jesus. They told him, "Your
mother and your brothers are outside.
They are looking for you."
33 "Who is my mother? Who are my
brothers?" he asked.
34 Then Jesus looked at the people
sitting in a circle around him. He said,
"Here is my mother! Here are my brothers! 35 Anyone who does what God wants
is my brother or sister or mother."

The Story of the Farmer

4 Again Jesus began to teach by the
Sea of Galilee. The crowd that gathered around him was very large. So he
got into a boat. He sat down in it out on
the lake. All the people were along the
shore at the water's edge. 2 He taught
them many things using stories. In his
teaching he said, 3 "Listen! A farmer went
out to plant his seed. 4 He scattered the
seed on the ground. Some fell on a path.
Birds came and ate it up. 5 Some seed fell
on rocky places, where there wasn't much
soil. The plants came up quickly, because
the soil wasn't deep. 6 When the sun came
up, it burned the plants. They dried up
because they had no roots. 7 Other seed
fell among thorns. The thorns grew up
and crowded out the plants. So the plants
did not bear grain. 8 Still other seed fell
on good soil. It grew up and produced a
crop 30, 60, or even 100 times more than
the farmer planted."
9 Then Jesus said, "Whoever has ears
should listen."
10 Later Jesus was alone. The 12 disciples asked him about the stories. So
did the others around him. 11 He told
them, "The secret of God's kingdom
has been given to you. But to outsiders
everything is told using stories. 12 In
that way,

" 'They will see but never know
what they are seeing.
They will hear but never
understand.
Otherwise they might turn and be
forgiven!' " *(Isaiah 6:9,10)*

13 Then Jesus said to them, "Don't you
understand this story? Then how will
you understand any stories of this kind?
14 The seed the farmer plants is God's
message. 15 What is seed scattered on
a path like? The message is planted.
The people hear the message. Then
Satan comes. He takes away the message that was planted in them. 16 And
what is seed scattered on rocky places

like? The people hear the message. At
once they receive it with joy. 17 But they
have no roots. So they last only a short
time. They quickly fall away from the
faith when trouble or suffering comes
because of the message. 18 And what is
seed scattered among thorns like? The
people hear the message. 19 But then
the worries of this life come to them.
Wealth comes with its false promises.
The people also long for other things.
All of these are the kinds of things that
crowd out the message. They keep it
from producing fruit. 20 And what is seed
scattered on good soil like? The people
hear the message. They accept it. They
produce a good crop 30, 60, or even 100
times more than the farmer planted."

A Lamp on a Stand

21 Jesus said to them, "Do you bring
in a lamp to put it under a large bowl
or a bed? Don't you put it on its stand?
22 What is hidden is meant to be seen.
And what is put out of sight is meant to
be brought out into the open. 23 Whoever
has ears should listen."

24 "Think carefully about what you
hear," he said. "As you give, so you will receive. In fact, you will receive even more.
25 Whoever has something will be given
more. Whoever has nothing, even what
they have will be taken away from them."

The Story of the Growing Seed

26 Jesus also said, "Here is what God's
kingdom is like. A farmer scatters seed
on the ground. 27 Night and day the seed
comes up and grows. It happens whether
the farmer sleeps or gets up. He doesn't
know how it happens. 28 All by itself the
soil produces grain. First the stalk comes
up. Then the head appears. Finally, the
full grain appears in the head. 29 Before
long the grain ripens. So the farmer cuts
it down, because the harvest is ready."

The Story of the Mustard Seed

30 Again Jesus said, "What can we
say God's kingdom is like? What story
can we use to explain it? 31 It is like a
mustard seed, which is the smallest of
all seeds on earth. 32 But when you plant
the seed, it grows. It becomes the largest
of all garden plants. Its branches are
so big that birds can rest in its shade."
33 Using many stories like these, Jesus
spoke the word to them. He told them as
much as they could understand. 34 He did
not say anything to them without using
a story. But when he was alone with his
disciples, he explained everything.

Jesus Calms the Storm

35 When evening came, Jesus said to
his disciples, "Let's go over to the other
side of the lake." 36 They left the crowd
behind. And they took him along in a
boat, just as he was. There were also
other boats with him. 37 A wild storm
came up. Waves crashed over the boat.
It was about to sink. 38 Jesus was in the
back, sleeping on a cushion. The disciples woke him up. They said, "Teacher!
Don't you care if we drown?"

39 He got up and ordered the wind to
stop. He said to the waves, "Quiet! Be
still!" Then the wind died down. And it
was completely calm.

40 He said to his disciples, "Why are
you so afraid? Don't you have any faith
at all yet?"

41 They were terrified. They asked
each other, "Who is this? Even the wind
and the waves obey him!"

Jesus Heals a Man Controlled by Demons

5 They went across the Sea of Galilee
to the area of the Gerasenes. 2 Jesus
got out of the boat. A man controlled by
an evil spirit came from the tombs to
meet him. 3 The man lived in the tombs.
No one could keep him tied up anymore.
Not even a chain could hold him. 4 His
hands and feet had often been chained.
But he tore the chains apart. And he
broke the iron cuffs on his ankles. No
one was strong enough to control him.
5 Night and day he screamed among the
tombs and in the hills. He cut himself
with stones.

6 When he saw Jesus a long way off,
he ran to him. He fell on his knees in
front of him. 7 He shouted at the top of
his voice, "Jesus, Son of the Most High
God, what do you want with me? Swear
to God that you won't hurt me!" 8 This
was because Jesus had said to him,
"Come out of this man, you evil spirit!"

9 Then Jesus asked the demon, "What
is your name?"

"My name is Legion," he replied.
"There are many of us." 10 And he
begged Jesus again and again not to
send them out of the area.

11 A large herd of pigs was feeding on the nearby hillside. 12 The demons begged Jesus, "Send us among the pigs. Let us go into them." 13 Jesus allowed it. The evil spirits came out of the man and went into the pigs. There were about 2,000 pigs in the herd. The whole herd rushed down the steep bank. They ran into the lake and drowned.

14 Those who were tending the pigs ran off. They told the people in the town and countryside what had happened. The people went out to see for themselves. 15 Then they came to Jesus. They saw the man who had been controlled by many demons. He was sitting there. He was now dressed and thinking clearly. All this made the people afraid. 16 Those who had seen it told them what had happened to the man. They told about the pigs as well. 17 Then the people began to beg Jesus to leave their area.

18 Jesus was getting into the boat. The man who had been controlled by demons begged to go with him. 19 Jesus did not let him. He said, "Go home to your own people. Tell them how much the Lord has done for you. Tell them how kind he has been to you." 20 So the man went away. In the area known as the Ten Cities, he began to tell how much Jesus had done for him. And all the people were amazed.

Jesus Heals a Dead Girl and a Suffering Woman

21 Jesus went across the Sea of Galilee in a boat. It landed at the other side. There a large crowd gathered around him. 22 Then a man named Jairus came. He was a synagogue leader. When he saw Jesus, he fell at his feet. 23 He begged Jesus, "Please come. My little daughter is dying. Place your hands on her to heal her. Then she will live." 24 So Jesus went with him.

A large group of people followed. They crowded around him. 25 A woman was there who had a sickness that made her bleed. It had lasted for 12 years. 26 She had suffered a great deal, even though she had gone to many doctors. She had spent all the money she had. But she was getting worse, not better. 27 Then she heard about Jesus. She came up behind him in the crowd and touched his clothes. 28 She thought, "I just need to touch his clothes. Then I will be healed." 29 Right away her bleeding stopped. She felt in her body that her suffering was over.

30 At once Jesus knew that power had gone out from him. He turned around in the crowd. He asked, "Who touched my clothes?"

31 "You see the people," his disciples answered. "They are crowding against you. And you still ask, 'Who touched me?' "

32 But Jesus kept looking around. He wanted to see who had touched him. 33 Then the woman came and fell at his feet. She knew what had happened to her. She was shaking with fear. But she told him the whole truth. 34 He said to her, "Dear woman, your faith has healed you. Go in peace. You are free from your suffering."

35 While Jesus was still speaking, some people came from the house of Jairus. He was the synagogue leader. "Your daughter is dead," they said. "Why bother the teacher anymore?"

36 Jesus heard what they were saying. He told the synagogue leader, "Don't be afraid. Just believe."

37 He let only Peter, James, and John, the brother of James, follow him. 38 They came to the home of the synagogue leader. There Jesus saw a lot of confusion. People were crying and sobbing loudly. 39 He went inside. Then he said to them, "Why all this confusion and sobbing? The child is not dead. She is only sleeping." 40 But they laughed at him.

He made them all go outside. He took only the child's father and mother and the disciples who were with him. And he went in where the child was. 41 He took her by the hand. Then he said to her, *"Talitha koum!"* This means, "Little girl, I say to you, get up!" 42 The girl was 12 years old. Right away she stood up and began to walk around. They were totally amazed at this. 43 Jesus gave strict orders not to let anyone know what had happened. And he told them to give her something to eat.

A Prophet Without Honor

6 Jesus left there and went to his hometown of Nazareth. His disciples went with him. 2 When the Sabbath day came, he began to teach in the synagogue. Many who heard him were amazed.

"Where did this man get these things?" they asked. "What's this wisdom that has been given to him? What are these remarkable miracles he is doing? 3 Isn't this the carpenter? Isn't this Mary's son? Isn't this the brother of James, Joseph, Judas and Simon? Aren't his sisters here with us?" They were not pleased with him at all.

4 Jesus said to them, "A prophet is honored everywhere except in his own town. He doesn't receive any honor among his relatives or in his own home." 5 Jesus placed his hands on a few sick people and healed them. But he could not do any other miracles there. 6 He was amazed because they had no faith.

Jesus Sends Out the Twelve Disciples

Jesus went around teaching from village to village. 7 He called the 12 disciples to him. Then he began to send them out two by two. He gave them authority to drive out evil spirits.

8 Here is what he told them to do. "Take only a walking stick for your trip. Do not take bread or a bag. Take no money in your belts. 9 Wear sandals. But do not take extra clothes. 10 When you are invited into a house, stay there until you leave town. 11 Some places may not welcome you or listen to you. If they don't, leave that place and shake the dust off your feet. That will be a witness against the people living there."

12 They went out. And they preached that people should turn away from their sins. 13 They drove out many demons. They poured olive oil on many sick people and healed them.

John the Baptist's Head Is Cut Off

14 King Herod heard about this. Jesus' name had become well known. Some were saying, "John the Baptist has been raised from the dead! That is why he has the power to do miracles."

15 Others said, "He is Elijah."

Still others claimed, "He is a prophet. He is like one of the prophets of long ago."

16 But when Herod heard this, he said, "I had John's head cut off. And now he has been raised from the dead!"

17 In fact, it was Herod himself who had given orders to arrest John. He had him tied up and put in prison. He did this because of Herodias. She was the wife of Herod's brother Philip. But now Herod was married to her. 18 John had been saying to Herod, "It is against the Law for you to be married to your brother's wife." 19 Herodias couldn't forgive John for saying that. She wanted to kill him. But she could not, 20 because Herod was afraid of John. So he kept John safe. Herod knew John was a holy man who did what was right. When Herod heard him, he was very puzzled. But he liked to listen to John.

21 Finally the right time came. Herod gave a banquet on his birthday. He invited his high officials and military leaders. He also invited the most important men in Galilee. 22 Then the daughter of Herodias came in and danced. She pleased Herod and his dinner guests.

The king said to the girl, "Ask me for anything you want. I'll give it to you." 23 And he gave her his promise. He said to her, "Anything you ask for I will give you. I'll give you up to half my kingdom."

24 She went out and said to her mother, "What should I ask for?"

"The head of John the Baptist," she answered.

25 At once the girl hurried to ask the king. She said, "I want you to give me the head of John the Baptist on a big plate right now."

26 The king was very upset. But he thought about his promise and his dinner guests. So he did not want to say no to the girl. 27 He sent a man right away to bring John's head. The man went to the prison and cut off John's head. 28 He brought it back on a big plate. He gave it to the girl, and she gave it to her mother. 29 John's disciples heard about this. So they came and took his body. Then they placed it in a tomb.

Jesus Feeds Five Thousand

30 The apostles gathered around Jesus. They told him all they had done and taught. 31 But many people were coming and going. So they did not even have a chance to eat. Then Jesus said to his apostles, "Come with me by yourselves to a quiet place. You need to get some rest."

32 So they went away by themselves in a boat to a quiet place. 33 But many people who saw them leaving recognized them. They ran from all the towns and got there ahead of them. 34 When Jesus came ashore, he saw a large crowd. He felt deep concern for them. They were

like sheep without a shepherd. So he began teaching them many things.

35 By that time it was late in the day. His disciples came to him. "There is nothing here," they said. "It's already very late. 36 Send the people away. Then they can go to the nearby countryside and villages to buy something to eat."

37 But Jesus answered, "You give them something to eat."

They said to him, "That would take more than half a year's pay! Should we go and spend that much on bread? Are we supposed to feed them?"

38 "How many loaves do you have?" Jesus asked. "Go and see."

When they found out, they said, "Five loaves and two fish."

39 Then Jesus directed them to have all the people sit down in groups on the green grass. 40 So they sat down in groups of 100s and 50s. 41 Jesus took the five loaves and the two fish. He looked up to heaven and gave thanks. He broke the loaves into pieces. Then he gave them to his disciples to pass around to the people. He also divided the two fish among them all. 42 All of them ate and were satisfied. 43 The disciples picked up 12 baskets of broken pieces of bread and fish. 44 The number of men who had eaten was 5,000.

Jesus Walks on the Water

45 Right away Jesus made his disciples get into the boat. He had them go on ahead of him to Bethsaida. Then he sent the crowd away. 46 After leaving them, he went up on a mountainside to pray.

47 Later that night, the boat was in the middle of the Sea of Galilee. Jesus was alone on land. 48 He saw the disciples pulling hard on the oars. The wind was blowing against them. Shortly before dawn, he went out to them. He walked on the lake. When he was about to pass by them, 49 they saw him walking on the lake. They thought he was a ghost, so they cried out. 50 They all saw him and were terrified.

Right away Jesus said to them, "Be brave! It is I. Don't be afraid." 51 Then he climbed into the boat with them. The wind died down. And they were completely amazed. 52 They had not understood about the loaves. They were stubborn.

53 They went across the lake and landed at Gennesaret. There they tied up the boat. 54 As soon as Jesus and his disciples got out, people recognized him. 55 They ran through that whole area to bring to him those who were sick. They carried them on mats to where they heard he was. 56 He went into the villages, the towns and the countryside. Everywhere he went, the people brought the sick to the market areas. Those who were sick begged him to let them touch just the edge of his clothes. And all who touched his clothes were healed.

What Makes People "Unclean"?

7 The Pharisees gathered around Jesus. So did some of the teachers of the law. All of them had come from Jerusalem. 2 They saw some of his disciples eating food with "unclean" hands. That means they were not washed. 3 The Pharisees and all the Jews do not eat unless they wash their hands to make them "clean." That's what the elders teach. 4 When they come from the market, they do not eat unless they wash. And they follow many other teachings. For example, they wash cups, pitchers, and kettles in a special way.

5 So the Pharisees and the teachers of the law questioned Jesus. "Why don't your disciples live by what the elders teach?" they asked. "Why do they eat their food with 'unclean' hands?"

6 He replied, "Isaiah was right. He prophesied about you people who pretend to be good. He said,

" 'These people honor me by what
they say.
But their hearts are far away
from me.
7 Their worship doesn't mean
anything to me.
They teach nothing but human
rules.' *(Isaiah 29:13)*

8 You have let go of God's commands. And you are holding on to teachings that people have made up."

9 Jesus continued speaking, "You have a fine way of setting aside God's commands! You do this so you can follow your own teachings. 10 Moses said, 'Honor your father and mother.' *(Exodus 20:12; Deuteronomy 5:16)* He also said, 'Anyone who asks for bad things to happen to their father

or mother must be put to death.' *(Exodus
21:17; Leviticus 20:9)* 11 But you allow people
to say that what might have been used
to help their parents is Corban. Corban
means A Gift Set Apart for God. 12 So you
no longer let them do anything for their
parents. 13 You make the word of God useless by putting your own teachings in its
place. And you do many things like this."

14 Again Jesus called the crowd to
him. He said, "Listen to me, everyone.
Understand this. 15-16 Nothing outside of
a person can make them 'unclean' by
going into them. It is what comes out
of them that makes them 'unclean.' "

17 Then he left the crowd and entered
the house. His disciples asked him about
this teaching. 18 "Don't you understand?"
Jesus asked. "Don't you see? Nothing
that enters a person from the outside can
make them 'unclean.' 19 It doesn't go into
their heart. It goes into their stomach.
Then it goes out of the body." In saying
this, Jesus was calling all foods "clean."

20 He went on to say, "What comes out
of a person is what makes them 'unclean.'
21 Evil thoughts come from the inside,
from a person's heart. So do sexual sins,
stealing and murder. 22 Adultery, greed,
hate and cheating come from a person's
heart too. So do desires that are not pure,
and wanting what belongs to others. And
so do telling lies about others and being
proud and being foolish. 23 All these evil
things come from inside a person and
make them 'unclean.' "

Jesus Honors a Greek Woman's Faith

24 Jesus went from there to a place
near Tyre. He entered a house. He did
not want anyone to know where he
was. But he could not keep it a secret.
25 Soon a woman heard about him. An
evil spirit controlled her little daughter.
The woman came to Jesus and fell at his
feet. 26 She was a Greek, born in Syrian
Phoenicia. She begged Jesus to drive
the demon out of her daughter.

27 "First let the children eat all they
want," he told her. "It is not right to
take the children's bread and throw it
to the dogs."

28 "Lord," she replied, "even the dogs
under the table eat the children's crumbs."

29 Then he told her, "That was a good
reply. You may go. The demon has left
your daughter."

30 So she went home and found her
child lying on the bed. And the demon
was gone.

Jesus Heals a Man Who Could Not Hear or Speak

31 Then Jesus left the area of Tyre and
went through Sidon. He went down to the
Sea of Galilee and into the area known
as the Ten Cities. 32 There some people
brought a man to Jesus. The man was
deaf and could hardly speak. They begged
Jesus to place his hand on the man.

33 Jesus took the man to one side,
away from the crowd. He put his fingers into the man's ears. Then he spit
and touched the man's tongue. 34 Jesus
looked up to heaven. With a deep sigh,
he said to the man, *"Ephphatha!"* That
means "Be opened!" 35 The man's ears
were opened. His tongue was freed up,
and he began to speak clearly.

36 Jesus ordered the people not to tell
anyone. But the more he did so, the more
they kept talking about it. 37 People were
really amazed. "He has done everything
well," they said. "He even makes deaf
people able to hear. And he makes those
who can't speak able to talk."

Jesus Feeds the Four Thousand

8 During those days another large
crowd gathered. They had nothing
to eat. So Jesus called for his disciples to
come to him. He said, 2 "I feel deep concern for these people. They have already
been with me three days. They don't have
anything to eat. 3 If I send them away
hungry, they will become too weak on
their way home. Some of them have come
from far away."

4 His disciples answered him. "There
is nothing here," they said. "Where
can anyone get enough bread to feed
them?"

5 "How many loaves do you have?"
Jesus asked.

"Seven," they replied.

6 He told the crowd to sit down on
the ground. He took the seven loaves
and gave thanks to God. Then he broke
them and gave them to his disciples. They
passed the pieces of bread around to
the people. 7 The disciples also had a few
small fish. Jesus gave thanks for them too.
He told the disciples to pass them around.
8 The people ate and were satisfied. After
that, the disciples picked up seven baskets

Why does the resurrection of Jesus matter?

Jesus was resurrected, or rose from the dead, after three days. This matters because he conquered sin and death, showing that he was God and the only one who could forgive sin. If he hadn't been resurrected, there would be no forgiveness, no salvation, and no hope of heaven.

Can you find the following verse?
MARK 8:31

of leftover pieces. 9 About 4,000 people
were there. After Jesus sent them away,
10 he got into a boat with his disciples. He
went to the area of Dalmanutha.

11 The Pharisees came and began to
ask Jesus questions. They wanted to
test him. So they asked him for a sign
from heaven. 12 He sighed deeply. He
said, "Why do you people ask for a sign?
What I'm about to tell you is true. No
sign will be given to you." 13 Then he left
them. He got back into the boat and
crossed to the other side of the lake.

The Yeast of the Pharisees and Herod

14 The disciples had forgotten to bring
bread. They had only one loaf with them
in the boat. 15 "Be careful," Jesus warned
them. "Watch out for the yeast of the
Pharisees. And watch out for the yeast
of Herod."

16 They talked about this with each
other. They said, "He must be saying
this because we don't have any bread."

17 Jesus knew what they were saying.
So he asked them, "Why are you talking
about having no bread? Why can't you
see or understand? Are you stubborn?
18 Do you have eyes and still don't see?
Do you have ears and still don't hear?
And don't you remember? 19 Earlier I
broke five loaves for the 5,000. How
many baskets of pieces did you pick up?"

"Twelve," they replied.

20 "Later I broke seven loaves for the
4,000. How many baskets of pieces did
you pick up?"

"Seven," they answered.

21 He said to them, "Can't you understand yet?"

Jesus Heals a Blind Man at Bethsaida

22 Jesus and his disciples came to
Bethsaida. Some people brought a
blind man to him. They begged Jesus
to touch him. 23 He took the blind man
by the hand. Then he led him outside
the village. He spit on the man's eyes
and placed his hands on him. "Do you
see anything?" Jesus asked.

24 The man looked up. He said, "I see
people. They look like trees walking
around."

25 Once more Jesus put his hands
on the man's eyes. Then his eyes were
opened so that he could see again. He
saw everything clearly. 26 Jesus sent
him home. He told him, "Don't even go
into the village."

Peter Says That Jesus Is the Messiah

27 Jesus and his disciples went on to
the villages around Caesarea Philippi.
On the way he asked them, "Who do
people say I am?"

28 They replied, "Some say John the
Baptist. Others say Elijah. Still others
say one of the prophets."

29 "But what about you?" he asked.
"Who do you say I am?"

Peter answered, "You are the Messiah."

30 Jesus warned them not to tell anyone about him.

Jesus Tells About His Coming Death

31 Jesus then began to teach his disciples. He taught them that the Son
of Man must suffer many things. He
taught them that the elders would not
accept him. The chief priests and the
teachers of the law would not accept
him either. He must be killed and after
three days rise again. 32 He spoke clearly

about this. Peter took Jesus to one side
and began to scold him.
33 Jesus turned and looked at his disciples. He scolded Peter. "Get behind me,
Satan!" he said. "You are not thinking
about the things God cares about. Instead, you are thinking only about the
things humans care about."

You Must Pick Up Your Cross

34 Jesus called the crowd to him along
with his disciples. He said, "Whoever
wants to be my disciple must say no
to themselves. They must pick up their
cross and follow me. 35 Whoever wants to
save their life will lose it. But whoever
loses their life for me and for the good
news will save it. 36 What good is it if
someone gains the whole world but
loses their soul? 37 Or what can anyone
trade for their soul? 38 Suppose anyone
is ashamed of me and my words among
these adulterous and sinful people.
Then the Son of Man will be ashamed
of them when he comes in his Father's
glory with the holy angels."

9 Jesus said to them, "What I'm about
to tell you is true. Some who are
standing here will not die before they
see that God's kingdom has come with
power."

Jesus' Appearance Is Changed

2 After six days Jesus took Peter, James
and John with him. He led them up a
high mountain. They were all alone.
There in front of them his appearance
was changed. 3 His clothes became so
white they shone. They were whiter
than anyone in the world could bleach
them. 4 Elijah and Moses appeared in
front of Jesus and his disciples. The two
of them were talking with Jesus.
5 Peter said to Jesus, "Rabbi, it is good
for us to be here. Let us put up three
shelters. One will be for you, one for
Moses, and one for Elijah." 6 Peter didn't
really know what to say, because they
were so afraid.
7 Then a cloud appeared and covered
them. A voice came from the cloud. It
said, "This is my Son, and I love him.
Listen to him!"
8 They looked around. Suddenly they
no longer saw anyone with them except
Jesus.
9 They came down the mountain.
On the way down, Jesus ordered them
not to tell anyone what they had seen.
He told them to wait until the Son of
Man had risen from the dead. 10 So they
kept the matter to themselves. But they
asked each other what "rising from the
dead" meant.
11 Then they asked Jesus, "Why do the
teachers of the law say that Elijah has
to come first?"
12 Jesus replied, "That's right. Elijah
does come first. He makes all things
new again. So why is it written that the
Son of Man must suffer much and not be
accepted? 13 I tell you, Elijah has come.
They have done to him everything they
wanted to do. They did it just as it is
written about him."

Jesus Heals a Boy Who Is Controlled by an Evil Spirit

14 When Jesus and those who were
with him came to the other disciples,
they saw a large crowd around them.
The teachers of the law were arguing
with them. 15 When all the people saw
Jesus, they were filled with wonder. And
they ran to greet him.
16 "What are you arguing with them
about?" Jesus asked.
17 A man in the crowd answered. "Teacher," he said, "I brought you my son. He is
controlled by an evil spirit. Because of
this, my son can't speak anymore. 18 When
the spirit takes hold of him, it throws him
to the ground. He foams at the mouth. He
grinds his teeth. And his body becomes
stiff. I asked your disciples to drive out
the spirit. But they couldn't do it."
19 "You unbelieving people!" Jesus
replied. "How long do I have to stay with
you? How long do I have to put up with
you? Bring the boy to me."
20 So they brought him. As soon as the
spirit saw Jesus, it threw the boy into
a fit. He fell to the ground. He rolled
around and foamed at the mouth.
21 Jesus asked the boy's father, "How
long has he been like this?"
"Since he was a child," he answered.
22 "The spirit has often thrown him into
fire or water to kill him. But if you can do
anything, take pity on us. Please help us."
23 " 'If you can'?" said Jesus. "Everything is possible for the one who believes."
24 Right away the boy's father cried
out, "I do believe! Help me overcome
my unbelief!"

25 Jesus saw that a crowd was running over to see what was happening. Then he ordered the evil spirit to leave the boy. "You spirit that makes him unable to hear and speak!" he said. "I command you, come out of him. Never enter him again."

26 The spirit screamed. It shook the boy wildly. Then it came out of him. The boy looked so lifeless that many people said, "He's dead." 27 But Jesus took him by the hand. He lifted the boy to his feet, and the boy stood up.

28 Jesus went indoors. Then his disciples asked him in private, "Why couldn't we drive out the evil spirit?"

29 He replied, "This kind can come out only by prayer."

Jesus Speaks a Second Time About His Coming Death

30 They left that place and passed through Galilee. Jesus did not want anyone to know where they were. 31 That was because he was teaching his disciples. He said to them, "The Son of Man is going to be handed over to men. They will kill him. After three days he will rise from the dead." 32 But they didn't understand what he meant. And they were afraid to ask him about it.

Who Is the Most Important Person?

33 Jesus and his disciples came to a house in Capernaum. There he asked them, "What were you arguing about on the road?" 34 But they kept quiet. On the way, they had argued about which one of them was the most important person.

35 Jesus sat down and called for the 12 disciples to come to him. Then he said, "Anyone who wants to be first must be the very last. They must be the servant of everyone."

36 Jesus took a little child and had the child stand among them. Then he took the child in his arms. He said to them, 37 "Anyone who welcomes one of these little children in my name welcomes me. And anyone who welcomes me also welcomes the one who sent me."

Anyone Who Is Not Against Us Is for Us

38 "Teacher," said John, "we saw someone driving out demons in your name. We told him to stop, because he was not one of us."

39 "Do not stop him," Jesus said. "For no one who does a miracle in my name can in the next moment say anything bad about me. 40 Anyone who is not against us is for us. 41 What I'm about to tell you is true. Suppose someone gives you a cup of water in my name because you belong to the Messiah. That person will certainly not go without a reward.

Leading People to Sin

42 "What if someone leads one of these little ones who believe in me to sin? If they do, it would be better if a large millstone were hung around their neck and they were thrown into the sea. 43-44 If your hand causes you to sin, cut it off. It would be better for you to enter God's kingdom with only one hand than to go into hell with two hands. In hell the fire never goes out. 45-46 If your foot causes you to sin, cut it off. It would be better to enter God's kingdom with only one foot than to have two feet and be thrown into hell. 47 If your eye causes you to sin, poke it out. It would be better for you to enter God's kingdom with only one eye than to have two eyes and be thrown into hell. 48 In hell,

" 'The worms that eat them do not
die.
The fire is not put out.' *(Isaiah 66:24)*

49 Everyone will be salted with fire.

50 "Salt is good. But suppose it loses its saltiness. How can you make it salty again? Have salt among yourselves. And be at peace with each other."

Jesus Teaches About Divorce

10 Jesus left that place and went into the area of Judea and across the Jordan River. Again crowds of people came to him. As usual, he taught them.

2 Some Pharisees came to test Jesus. They asked, "Does the Law allow a man to divorce his wife?"

3 "What did Moses command you?" he replied.

4 They said, "Moses allowed a man to write a letter of divorce and send her away."

5 "You were stubborn. That's why Moses wrote you this law," Jesus replied. 6 "But at the beginning of creation, God 'made them male and female.' *(Genesis 1:27)* 7 'That's why a man will leave his

father and mother and be joined to his wife. 8 The two of them will become one.' *(Genesis 2:24)* They are no longer two, but one. 9 So no one should separate what God has joined together."

10 When they were in the house again, the disciples asked Jesus about this. 11 He answered, "What if a man divorces his wife and gets married to another woman? He commits adultery against her. 12 And what if she divorces her husband and gets married to another man? She commits adultery."

Little Children Are Brought to Jesus

13 People were bringing little children to Jesus. They wanted him to place his hands on them to bless them. But the disciples told them to stop. 14 When Jesus saw this, he was angry. He said to his disciples, "Let the little children come to me. Don't keep them away. God's kingdom belongs to people like them. 15 What I'm about to tell you is true. Anyone who will not receive God's kingdom like a little child will never enter it." 16 Then he took the children in his arms. He placed his hands on them to bless them.

Rich People and the Kingdom of God

17 As Jesus started on his way, a man ran up to him. He fell on his knees before Jesus. "Good teacher," he said, "what must I do to receive eternal life?"

18 "Why do you call me good?" Jesus answered. "No one is good except God. 19 You know what the commandments say. 'Do not murder. Do not commit adultery. Do not steal. Do not be a false witness. Do not cheat. Honor your father and mother.' " *(Exodus 20:12–16; Deuteronomy 5:16–20)*

20 "Teacher," he said, "I have obeyed all those commandments since I was a boy."

21 Jesus looked at him and loved him. "You are missing one thing," he said. "Go and sell everything you have. Give the money to those who are poor. You will have treasure in heaven. Then come and follow me."

22 The man's face fell. He went away sad, because he was very rich.

23 Jesus looked around. He said to his disciples, "How hard it is for rich people to enter God's kingdom!"

24 The disciples were amazed at his words. But Jesus said again, "Children, how hard it is to enter God's kingdom! 25 Is it hard for a camel to go through the eye of a needle? It is even harder for someone who is rich to enter God's kingdom!"

26 The disciples were even more amazed. They said to each other, "Then who can be saved?"

27 Jesus looked at them and said, "With people, this is impossible. But not with God. All things are possible with God."

28 Then Peter spoke up, "We have left everything to follow you!"

29 "What I'm about to tell you is true," Jesus replied. "Has anyone left home or family or fields for me and the good news? 30 They will receive 100 times as much in this world. They will have homes and families and fields. But they will also be treated badly by others. In the world to come they will live forever. 31 But many who are first will be last. And the last will be first."

Jesus Speaks a Third Time About His Coming Death

32 They were on their way up to Jerusalem. Jesus was leading the way. The disciples were amazed. Those who followed were afraid. Again Jesus took the 12 disciples to one side. He told them what was going to happen to him. 33 "We are going up to Jerusalem," he said. "The Son of Man will be handed over to the chief priests and the teachers of the law. They will sentence him to death. Then they will hand him over to the Gentiles. 34 They will make fun of him and spit on him. They will whip him and kill him. Three days later he will rise from the dead!"

James and John Ask Jesus for a Favor

35 James and John came to Jesus. They were the sons of Zebedee. "Teacher," they said, "we would like to ask you for a favor."

36 "What do you want me to do for you?" he asked.

37 They replied, "Let one of us sit at your right hand in your glorious kingdom. Let the other one sit at your left hand."

38 "You don't know what you're asking for," Jesus said. "Can you drink the cup of suffering I drink? Or can you go through the baptism of suffering I must go through?"

My GOD IS...

Everything God does reflects his goodness (see Psalm 25:8). No matter how hard we try, we can never be good enough to earn our way to God. Jesus, however, lived a perfect life and met God's standard for goodness. Through Jesus, we can have a relationship with God.

Jesus invites those of us who follow him to obey his commands (see John 14:15). With the help of God's Spirit living within us, we can study God's Word, obey God, and worship him in all that we say and do. God's Spirit helps us learn day by day how to live in a way that reflects God's goodness to the world around us.

39 "We can," they answered.
Jesus said to them, "You will drink
the cup I drink. And you will go through
the baptism I go through. 40 But it is not
for me to say who will sit at my right or
left hand. These places belong to those
they are prepared for."
41 The other ten disciples heard about
it. They became angry at James and
John. 42 Jesus called them together. He
said, "You know about those who are
rulers of the Gentiles. They hold power
over their people. Their high officials
order them around. 43 Don't be like
that. Instead, anyone who wants to be
important among you must be your
servant. 44 And anyone who wants to
be first must be the slave of everyone.
45 Even the Son of Man did not come to
be served. Instead, he came to serve
others. He came to give his life as the
price for setting many people free."

Blind Bartimaeus Receives His Sight

46 Jesus and his disciples came to Jericho. They were leaving the city. A large
crowd was with them. A blind man was
sitting by the side of the road begging.
His name was Bartimaeus. Bartimaeus
means Son of Timaeus. 47 He heard that
Jesus of Nazareth was passing by. So he
began to shout, "Jesus! Son of David!
Have mercy on me!"
48 Many people commanded him to
stop. They told him to be quiet. But he
shouted even louder, "Son of David!
Have mercy on me!"
49 Jesus stopped and said, "Call for
him."
So they called out to the blind man,
"Cheer up! Get up on your feet! Jesus
is calling for you." 50 He threw his coat
to one side. Then he jumped to his feet
and came to Jesus.
51 "What do you want me to do for
you?" Jesus asked him.
The blind man said, "Rabbi, I want
to be able to see."
52 "Go," said Jesus. "Your faith has
healed you." Right away he could see.
And he followed Jesus along the road.

Jesus Comes to Jerusalem as King

11 As they all approached Jerusalem, they came to Bethphage and
Bethany at the Mount of Olives. Jesus
sent out two of his disciples. 2 He said
to them, "Go to the village ahead of
you. Just as you enter it, you will find
a donkey's colt tied there. No one has
ever ridden it. Untie it and bring it here.
3 Someone may ask you, 'Why are you
doing this?' If so, say, 'The Lord needs
it. But he will send it back here soon.' "
4 So they left. They found a colt out in
the street. It was tied at a doorway. They
untied it. 5 Some people standing there

asked, "What are you doing? Why are
you untying that colt?" 6 They answered
as Jesus had told them to. So the people
let them go. 7 They brought the colt to
Jesus. They threw their coats over it.
Then he sat on it. 8 Many people spread
their coats on the road. Others spread
branches they had cut in the fields.
9 Those in front and those in back
shouted,

"Hosanna!"

"Blessed is the one who comes in
the name of the Lord!" *(Psalm
118:25,26)*

10 "Blessed is the coming kingdom of
our father David!"

"Hosanna in the highest heaven!"

11 Jesus entered Jerusalem and went
into the temple courtyard. He looked
around at everything. But it was already late. So he went out to Bethany
with the 12 disciples.

Jesus Curses a Fig Tree and Clears Out the Temple Courtyard

12 The next day as Jesus and his disciples were leaving Bethany, they were
hungry. 13 Not too far away, he saw a
fig tree. It was covered with leaves. He
went to find out if it had any fruit. When
he reached it, he found nothing but
leaves. It was not the season for figs.
14 Then Jesus said to the tree, "May no
one ever eat fruit from you again!" And
his disciples heard him say it.

15 When Jesus reached Jerusalem, he
entered the temple courtyard. He began
to drive out those who were buying and
selling there. He turned over the tables
of the people who were exchanging
money. He also turned over the benches
of those who were selling doves. 16 He
would not allow anyone to carry items
for sale through the temple courtyard.
17 Then he taught them. He told them, "It
is written that the Lord said, 'My house
will be called a house where people from
all nations can pray.' *(Isaiah 56:7)* But
you have made it a 'den for robbers.' "
(Jeremiah 7:11)

18 The chief priests and the teachers
of the law heard about this. They began
looking for a way to kill Jesus. They
were afraid of him, because the whole
crowd was amazed at his teaching.

19 When evening came, Jesus and his
disciples left the city.

The Dried-Up Fig Tree

20 In the morning as Jesus and his
disciples walked along, they saw the fig
tree. It was dried up all the way down to
the roots. 21 Peter remembered. He said
to Jesus, "Rabbi, look! The fig tree you
put a curse on has dried up!"

22 "Have faith in God," Jesus said.
23 "What I'm about to tell you is true.
Suppose someone says to this mountain, 'Go and throw yourself into the
sea.' They must not doubt in their heart.
They must believe that what they say
will happen. Then it will be done for
them. 24 So I tell you, when you pray
for something, believe that you have
already received it. Then it will be
yours. 25-26 And when you stand praying, forgive anyone you have anything
against. Then your Father in heaven
will forgive your sins."

The Authority of Jesus Is Questioned

27 Jesus and his disciples arrived again
in Jerusalem. He was walking in the temple courtyard. Then the chief priests came
to him. The teachers of the law and the
elders came too. 28 "By what authority
are you doing these things?" they asked.
"Who gave you authority to do this?"

29 Jesus replied, "I will ask you one
question. Answer me, and I will tell you
by what authority I am doing these
things. 30 Was John's baptism from
heaven? Or did it come from human
authority? Tell me!"

31 They talked to each other about it.
They said, "If we say, 'From heaven,'
he will ask, 'Then why didn't you believe him?' 32 But what if we say, 'From
human authority'?" They were afraid
of the people. Everyone believed that
John really was a prophet.

33 So they answered Jesus, "We don't
know."

Jesus said, "Then I won't tell you by
what authority I am doing these things
either."

The Story of the Renters

12 Jesus began to speak to the people using stories. He said, "A man
planted a vineyard. He put a wall around
it. He dug a pit for a winepress. He also

built a lookout tower. He rented the vineyard out to some farmers. Then he went
to another place. 2At harvest time he
sent a servant to the renters. He told the
servant to collect from them some of the
fruit of the vineyard. 3But they grabbed
the servant and beat him up. Then they
sent him away with nothing. 4So the
man sent another servant to the renters.
They hit this one on the head and treated
him badly. 5The man sent still another
servant. The renters killed him. The man
sent many others. The renters beat up
some of them. They killed the others.
6"The man had one person left to
send. It was his son, and he loved him.
He sent him last of all. He said, 'They
will respect my son.'
7"But the renters said to each other,
'This is the one who will receive all the
owner's property someday. Come, let's
kill him. Then everything will be ours.'
8So they took him and killed him. They
threw him out of the vineyard.
9"What will the owner of the vineyard
do then? He will come and kill those
renters. He will give the vineyard to
others. 10Haven't you read what this
part of Scripture says,

"'The stone the builders didn't
accept
has become the most important
stone of all.
11The Lord has done it.
It is wonderful in our eyes'?"
(Psalm 118:22,23)

12Then the chief priests, the teachers
of the law and the elders looked for a
way to arrest Jesus. They knew he had
told the story against them. But they
were afraid of the crowd. So they left
him and went away.

Is It Right to Pay the Royal Tax to Caesar?

13Later the religious leaders sent
some of the Pharisees and Herodians
to Jesus. They wanted to trap him with
his own words. 14They came to him and
said, "Teacher, we know that you are a
man of honor. You don't let other people
tell you what to do or say. You don't
care how important they are. But you
teach the way of God truthfully. Is it
right to pay the royal tax to Caesar or
not? 15Should we pay or shouldn't we?"

But Jesus knew what they were trying
to do. So he asked, "Why are you trying
to trap me? Bring me a silver coin. Let
me look at it." 16They brought the coin.
He asked them, "Whose picture is this?
And whose words?"

"Caesar's," they replied.

17Then Jesus said to them, "Give back
to Caesar what belongs to Caesar. And
give back to God what belongs to God."

They were amazed at him.

Marriage When the Dead Rise

18The Sadducees came to Jesus with
a question. They do not believe that
people rise from the dead. 19"Teacher,"
they said, "Moses wrote for us about
a man who died and didn't have any
children. But he did leave a wife behind.
That man's brother must get married
to the widow. He must provide children
to carry on his dead brother's name.
20There were seven brothers. The first
one got married. He died without leaving any children. 21The second one got
married to the widow. He also died and
left no child. It was the same with the
third one. 22In fact, none of the seven
left any children. Last of all, the woman
died too. 23When the dead rise, whose
wife will she be? All seven of them were
married to her."

24Jesus replied, "You are mistaken
because you do not know the Scriptures.
And you do not know the power of God.
25When the dead rise, they won't get
married. And their parents won't give
them to be married. They will be like the
angels in heaven. 26What about the dead
rising? Haven't you read in the Book of
Moses the story of the burning bush? God
said to Moses, 'I am the God of Abraham.
I am the God of Isaac. And I am the God
of Jacob.' *(Exodus 3:6)* 27He is not the God
of the dead. He is the God of the living.
You have made a big mistake!"

The Most Important Commandment

28One of the teachers of the law came
and heard the Sadducees arguing. He
noticed that Jesus had given the Sadducees a good answer. So he asked him,
"Which is the most important of all the
commandments?"

29Jesus answered, "Here is the most
important one. Moses said, 'Israel, listen
to me. The Lord is our God. The Lord
is one. 30Love the Lord your God with

all your heart and with all your soul.
Love him with all your mind and with
all your strength.' *(Deuteronomy 6:4,5)*
31 And here is the second one. 'Love your
neighbor as you love yourself.' *(Leviticus
19:18)* There is no commandment more
important than these."

32 "You have spoken well, teacher," the
man replied. "You are right in saying
that God is one. There is no other God but
him. 33 To love God with all your heart and
mind and strength is very important. So
is loving your neighbor as you love yourself. These things are more important
than all burnt offerings and sacrifices."

34 Jesus saw that the man had answered wisely. He said to him, "You
are not far from God's kingdom." From
then on, no one dared to ask Jesus any
more questions.

Whose Son Is the Messiah?

35 Jesus was teaching in the temple
courtyard. He asked, "Why do the teachers of the law say that the Messiah is the
son of David? 36 The Holy Spirit spoke
through David himself. David said,

> " 'The Lord said to my Lord,
> "Sit at my right hand
> until I put your enemies
> under your control." ' *(Psalm 110:1)*

37 David himself calls him 'Lord.' So how
can he be David's son?"

The large crowd listened to Jesus with
delight.

Warning Against the Teachers of the Law

38 As he taught, he said, "Watch out
for the teachers of the law. They like to
walk around in long robes. They like to
be greeted with respect in the market.
39 They love to have the most important
seats in the synagogues. They also love
to have the places of honor at dinners.
40 They take over the houses of widows.
They say long prayers to show off. God
will punish these men very much."

The Widow's Offering

41 Jesus sat down across from the
place where people put their temple
offerings. He watched the crowd putting
their money into the offering boxes.
Many rich people threw large amounts
into them. 42 But a poor widow came
and put in two very small copper coins.
They were worth only a few pennies.

43 Jesus asked his disciples to come
to him. He said, "What I'm about to
tell you is true. That poor widow has
put more into the offering box than all
the others. 44 They all gave a lot because
they are rich. But she gave even though
she is poor. She put in everything she
had. That was all she had to live on."

When the Temple Will Be Destroyed and the Signs of the End

13 Jesus was leaving the temple.
One of his disciples said to him,
"Look, Teacher! What huge stones! What
wonderful buildings!"

2 "Do you see these huge buildings?"
Jesus asked. "Not one stone here will be
left on top of another. Every stone will
be thrown down."

3 Jesus was sitting on the Mount of
Olives, across from the temple. Peter,
James, John and Andrew asked him
a question in private. 4 "Tell us," they
said. "When will these things happen?
And what will be the sign that they are
all about to come true?"

5 Jesus said to them, "Keep watch! Be
careful that no one fools you. 6 Many
will come in my name. They will claim,
'I am he.' They will fool many people.
7 You will hear about wars. You will also
hear people talking about future wars.
Don't be alarmed. These things must
happen. But the end still isn't here. 8 Nation will fight against nation. Kingdom
will fight against kingdom. There will
be earthquakes in many places. People
will go hungry. All these things are the
beginning of birth pains.

9 "Watch out! You will be handed over
to the local courts. You will be whipped in
the synagogues. You will stand in front
of governors and kings because of me. In
that way you will be witnesses to them.
10 The good news has to be preached to
all nations before the end comes. 11 You
will be arrested and brought to trial. But
don't worry ahead of time about what
you will say. Just say what God brings
to your mind at the time. It is not you
speaking, but the Holy Spirit.

12 "Brothers will hand over brothers to
be killed. Fathers will hand over their
children. Children will rise up against
their parents and have them put to

death. 13 Everyone will hate you because of me. But the one who remains strong in the faith will be saved.

14 "You will see 'the hated thing that destroys.' *(Daniel 9:27; 11:31; 12:11)* It will stand where it does not belong. The reader should understand this. Then those who are in Judea should escape to the mountains. 15 No one on the roof should go down into the house to take anything out. 16 No one in the field should go back to get their coat. 17 How awful it will be in those days for pregnant women! How awful for nursing mothers! 18 Pray that this will not happen in winter. 19 Those days will be worse than any others from the time God created the world until now. And there will never be any like them again.

20 "If the Lord had not cut the time short, no one would live. But because of God's chosen people, he has shortened it. 21 At that time someone may say to you, 'Look! Here is the Messiah!' Or, 'Look! There he is!' Do not believe it. 22 False messiahs and false prophets will appear. They will do signs and miracles. They will try to fool God's chosen people if possible. 23 Keep watch! I have told you everything ahead of time.

24 "So in those days there will be terrible suffering. After that, Scripture says,

" 'The sun will be darkened.
  The moon will not shine.
25 The stars will fall from the sky.
  The heavenly bodies will be
    shaken.' *(Isaiah 13:10; 34:4)*

26 "At that time people will see the Son of Man coming in clouds. He will come with great power and glory. 27 He will send his angels. He will gather his chosen people from all four directions. He will bring them from the ends of the earth to the ends of the heavens.

28 "Learn a lesson from the fig tree. As soon as its twigs get tender and its leaves come out, you know that summer is near. 29 In the same way, when you see these things happening, you know that the end is near. It is right at the door. 30 What I'm about to tell you is true. The people living now will certainly not pass away until all those things have happened. 31 Heaven and earth will pass away. But my words will never pass away.

The Day and Hour Are Not Known

32 "But no one knows about that day or hour. Not even the angels in heaven know. The Son does not know. Only the Father knows. 33 Keep watch! Stay awake! You do not know when that time will come. 34 It's like a man going away. He leaves his house and puts his servants in charge. Each one is given a task to do. He tells the one at the door to keep watch.

35 "So keep watch! You do not know when the owner of the house will come back. It may be in the evening or at midnight. It may be when the rooster crows or at dawn. 36 He may come suddenly. So do not let him find you sleeping. 37 What I say to you, I say to everyone. 'Watch!' "

A Woman Pours Perfume on Jesus at Bethany

14 The Passover and the Feast of Unleavened Bread were only two days away. The chief priests and the teachers of the law were plotting to arrest Jesus secretly. They wanted to kill him. 2 "But not during the feast," they said. "The people may stir up trouble."

3 Jesus was in Bethany. He was at the table in the home of Simon, who had a skin disease. A woman came with a special sealed jar. It contained very expensive perfume made out of pure nard. She broke the jar open and poured the perfume on Jesus' head.

4 Some of the people there became angry. They said to one another, "Why waste this perfume? 5 It could have been sold for more than a year's pay. The money could have been given to poor people." So they found fault with the woman.

6 "Leave her alone," Jesus said. "Why are you bothering her? She has done a beautiful thing to me. 7 You will always have poor people with you. You can help them any time you want to. But you will not always have me. 8 She did what she could. She poured perfume on my body to prepare me to be buried. 9 What I'm about to tell you is true. What she has done will be told anywhere the good news is preached all over the world. It will be told in memory of her."

10 Judas Iscariot was one of the 12 disciples. He went to the chief priests to hand Jesus over to them. 11 They were

delighted to hear that he would do this. They promised to give Judas money. So he watched for the right time to hand Jesus over to them.

The Last Supper

12 It was the first day of the Feast of Unleavened Bread. That was the time to sacrifice the Passover lamb. Jesus' disciples asked him, "Where do you want us to go and prepare for you to eat the Passover meal?"

13 So he sent out two of his disciples. He told them, "Go into the city. A man carrying a jar of water will meet you. Follow him. 14 He will enter a house. Say to its owner, 'The Teacher asks, "Where is my guest room? Where can I eat the Passover meal with my disciples?"' 15 He will show you a large upstairs room. It will have furniture and will be ready. Prepare for us to eat there."

16 The disciples left and went into the city. They found things just as Jesus had told them. So they prepared the Passover meal.

17 When evening came, Jesus arrived with the 12 disciples. 18 While they were at the table eating, Jesus said, "What I'm about to tell you is true. One of you who is eating with me will hand me over to my enemies."

19 The disciples became sad. One by one they said to him, "Surely you don't mean me?"

20 "It is one of you," Jesus replied. "It is the one who dips bread into the bowl with me. 21 The Son of Man will go just as it is written about him. But how terrible it will be for the one who hands over the Son of Man! It would be better for him if he had not been born."

22 While they were eating, Jesus took bread. He gave thanks and broke it. He handed it to his disciples and said, "Take it. This is my body."

23 Then he took a cup. He gave thanks and handed it to them. All of them drank from it.

24 "This is my blood of the covenant," he said to them. "It is poured out for many. 25 What I'm about to tell you is true. I won't drink wine with you again until the day I drink it in God's kingdom."

26 Then they sang a hymn and went out to the Mount of Olives.

Jesus Says That the Disciples Will Turn Away

27 "You will all turn away," Jesus told the disciples. "It is written,

> " 'I will strike the shepherd down.
> Then the sheep will be scattered.'
> *(Zechariah 13:7)*

28 But after I rise from the dead, I will go ahead of you into Galilee."

29 Peter said, "All the others may turn away. But I will not."

30 "What I'm about to tell you is true," Jesus answered. "It will happen today, in fact tonight. Before the rooster crows twice, you yourself will say three times that you don't know me."

31 But Peter would not give in. He said, "I may have to die with you. But I will never say I don't know you." And all the others said the same thing.

Jesus Prays in Gethsemane

32 Jesus and his disciples went to a place called Gethsemane. Jesus said to them, "Sit here while I pray." 33 He took Peter, James and John along with him. He began to be very upset and troubled. 34 "My soul is very sad. I feel close to death," he said to them. "Stay here. Keep watch."

35 He went a little farther. Then he fell to the ground. He prayed that, if possible, the hour might pass by him. 36 "*Abba*, Father," he said, "everything is possible for you. Take this cup of suffering away from me. But let what you want be done, not what I want."

37 Then he returned to his disciples and found them sleeping. "Simon," he said to Peter, "are you asleep? Couldn't you keep watch for one hour? 38 Watch and pray. Then you won't fall into sin when you are tempted. The spirit is willing, but the body is weak."

39 Once more Jesus went away and prayed the same thing. 40 Then he came back. Again he found them sleeping. They couldn't keep their eyes open. They did not know what to say to him.

41 Jesus returned the third time. He said to them, "Are you still sleeping and resting? Enough! The hour has come. Look! The Son of Man is about to be handed over to sinners. 42 Get up! Let us go! Here comes the one who is handing me over to them!"

Jesus Is Arrested

43 Just as Jesus was speaking, Judas
appeared. He was one of the 12 disciples.
A crowd was with him. They were carrying swords and clubs. The chief priests,
the teachers of the law, and the elders
had sent them.

44 Judas, who was going to hand Jesus
over, had arranged a signal with them.
"The one I kiss is the man," he said. "Arrest
him and have the guards lead him away."
45 So Judas went to Jesus at once. Judas
said, "Rabbi!" And he kissed Jesus. 46 The
men grabbed Jesus and arrested him.
47 Then one of those standing nearby
pulled his sword out. He struck the servant of the high priest and cut off his ear.

48 "Am I leading a band of armed men
against you?" asked Jesus. "Do you have
to come out with swords and clubs to
capture me? 49 Every day I was with
you. I taught in the temple courtyard,
and you didn't arrest me. But the Scriptures must come true." 50 Then everyone
left him and ran away.

51 A young man was following Jesus.
The man was wearing nothing but a
piece of linen cloth. When the crowd
grabbed him, 52 he ran away naked. He
left his clothing behind.

Jesus Is Taken to the Sanhedrin

53 The crowd took Jesus to the high
priest. All the chief priests, the elders,
and the teachers of the law came together. 54 Not too far away, Peter followed Jesus. He went right into the
courtyard of the high priest. There he
sat with the guards. He warmed himself
at the fire.

55 The chief priests and the whole Sanhedrin were looking for something to
use against Jesus. They wanted to put
him to death. But they did not find any
proof. 56 Many witnesses lied about him.
But their stories did not agree.

57 Then some of them stood up. Here
is what those false witnesses said about
him. 58 "We heard him say, 'I will destroy
this temple made by human hands. In
three days I will build another temple,
not made by human hands.' " 59 But
what they said did not agree.

60 Then the high priest stood up in
front of them. He asked Jesus, "Aren't
you going to answer? What are these
charges these men are bringing against
you?" 61 But Jesus remained silent. He
gave no answer.

Again the high priest asked him, "Are
you the Messiah? Are you the Son of the
Blessed One?"

62 "I am," said Jesus. "And you will see
the Son of Man sitting at the right hand
of the Mighty One. You will see the Son
of Man coming on the clouds of heaven."

63 The high priest tore his clothes.
"Why do we need any more witnesses?"
he asked. 64 "You have heard him say
a very evil thing against God. What do
you think?"

They all found him guilty and said
he must die. 65 Then some began to spit
at him. They blindfolded him. They hit
him with their fists. They said, "Prophesy!" And the guards took him and beat
him.

Peter Says He Does Not Know Jesus

66 Peter was below in the courtyard.
One of the high priest's female servants
came by. 67 When she saw Peter warming himself, she looked closely at him.

"You also were with Jesus, that Nazarene," she said.

68 But Peter said he had not been with
him. "I don't know or understand what
you're talking about," he said. He went
out to the entrance to the courtyard.

69 The servant saw him there. She said
again to those standing around, "This
fellow is one of them." 70 Again he said
he was not.

After a little while, those standing
nearby said to Peter, "You must be one
of them. You are from Galilee."

71 Then Peter began to curse. He said
to them, "I don't know this man you're
talking about!"

72 Right away the rooster crowed the
second time. Then Peter remembered
what Jesus had spoken to him. "The
rooster will crow twice," he had said.
"Before it does, you will say three times
that you don't know me." Peter broke
down and cried.

Jesus Is Brought to Pilate

15 It was very early in the morning.
The chief priests, with the elders,
the teachers of the law, and the whole
Sanhedrin, made their plans. So they
tied Jesus up and led him away. Then
they handed him over to Pilate.

2 "Are you the king of the Jews?" asked Pilate.

"You have said so," Jesus replied.

3 The chief priests brought many charges against him. 4 So Pilate asked him again, "Aren't you going to answer? See how many things they charge you with."

5 But Jesus still did not reply. Pilate was amazed.

6 It was the usual practice at the Passover Feast to let one prisoner go free. The people could choose the one they wanted. 7 A man named Barabbas was in prison. He was there with some other people who had fought against the country's rulers. They had committed murder while they were fighting against the rulers. 8 The crowd came up and asked Pilate to do for them what he usually did.

9 "Do you want me to let the king of the Jews go free?" asked Pilate. 10 He knew that the chief priests had handed Jesus over to him because they wanted to get their own way. 11 But the chief priests stirred up the crowd. So the crowd asked Pilate to let Barabbas go free instead.

12 "Then what should I do with the one you call the king of the Jews?" Pilate asked them.

13 "Crucify him!" the crowd shouted.

14 "Why? What wrong has he done?" asked Pilate.

But they shouted even louder, "Crucify him!"

15 Pilate wanted to satisfy the crowd. So he let Barabbas go free. He ordered that Jesus be whipped. Then he handed him over to be nailed to a cross.

The Soldiers Make Fun of Jesus

16 The soldiers led Jesus away into the palace. It was called the Praetorium. They called together the whole company of soldiers. 17 The soldiers put a purple robe on Jesus. Then they twisted thorns together to make a crown. They placed it on his head. 18 They began to call out to him, "We honor you, king of the Jews!" 19 Again and again they hit him on the head with a stick. They spit on him. They fell on their knees and pretended to honor him. 20 After they had made fun of him, they took off the purple robe. They put his own clothes back on him. Then they led him out to nail him to a cross.

Jesus Is Nailed to a Cross

21 A man named Simon was passing by. He was from Cyrene. He was the father of Alexander and Rufus. Simon was on his way in from the country. The soldiers forced him to carry the cross. 22 They brought Jesus to the place called Golgotha. The word Golgotha means the Place of the Skull. 23 Then they gave him wine mixed with spices. But he did not take it. 24 They nailed him to the cross. Then they divided up his clothes. They cast lots to see what each of them would get.

25 It was nine o'clock in the morning when they crucified him. 26 They wrote out the charge against him. It read,

THE KING OF THE JEWS.

27-28 They crucified with him two rebels against Rome. One was on his right and one was on his left. 29 Those who passed by shouted at Jesus and made fun of him. They shook their heads and said, "So you are going to destroy the temple and build it again in three days? 30 Then come down from the cross! Save yourself!" 31 In the same way the chief priests and the teachers of the law made fun of him among themselves. "He saved others," they said. "But he can't save himself! 32 Let this Messiah, this king of Israel, come down now from the cross! When we see that, we will believe." Those who were being crucified with Jesus also made fun of him.

Jesus Dies

33 At noon, darkness covered the whole land. It lasted three hours. 34 At three o'clock in the afternoon Jesus cried out in a loud voice, *"Eloi, Eloi, lema sabachthani?"* This means "My God, my God, why have you deserted me?" *(Psalm 22:1)*

35 Some of those standing nearby heard Jesus cry out. They said, "Listen! He's calling for Elijah."

36 Someone ran and filled a sponge with wine vinegar. He put it on a stick. He offered it to Jesus to drink. "Leave him alone," he said. "Let's see if Elijah comes to take him down."

37 With a loud cry, Jesus took his last breath.

38 The temple curtain was torn in two from top to bottom. 39 A Roman

commander was standing there in front of Jesus. He saw how Jesus died. Then he said, "This man was surely the Son of God!"

40 Not very far away, some women were watching. Mary Magdalene was among them. Mary, the mother of the younger James and of Joseph, was also there. So was Salome. 41 In Galilee these women had followed Jesus. They had taken care of his needs. Many other women were also there. They had come up with him to Jerusalem.

Jesus Is Buried

42 It was the day before the Sabbath. That day was called Preparation Day. As evening approached, 43 Joseph went boldly to Pilate and asked for Jesus' body. Joseph was from the town of Arimathea. He was a leading member of the Jewish Council. He was waiting for God's kingdom. 44 Pilate was surprised to hear that Jesus was already dead. So he called for the Roman commander. He asked him if Jesus had already died. 45 The commander said it was true. So Pilate gave the body to Joseph. 46 Then Joseph bought some linen cloth. He took down the body and wrapped it in the linen. He put it in a tomb cut out of rock. Then he rolled a stone against the entrance to the tomb. 47 Mary Magdalene and Mary the mother of Joseph saw where Jesus' body had been placed.

Jesus Rises From the Dead

16 The Sabbath day ended. Mary Magdalene, Mary the mother of James, and Salome bought spices. They were going to use them for Jesus' body. 2 Very early on the first day of the week, they were on their way to the tomb. It was just after sunrise. 3 They asked each other, "Who will roll the stone away from the entrance to the tomb?"

4 Then they looked up and saw that the stone had been rolled away. The stone was very large. 5 They entered the tomb. As they did, they saw a young man dressed in a white robe. He was sitting on the right side. They were alarmed.

6 "Don't be alarmed," he said. "You are looking for Jesus the Nazarene, who was crucified. But he has risen! He is not here! See the place where they had put him. 7 Go! Tell his disciples and Peter, 'He is going ahead of you into Galilee. There you will see him. It will be just as he told you.' "

8 The women were shaking and confused. They went out and ran away from the tomb. They said nothing to anyone, because they were afraid.

9 Jesus rose from the dead early on the first day of the week. He appeared first to Mary Magdalene. He had driven seven demons out of her. 10 She went and told those who had been with him. She found them crying. They were very sad. 11 They heard that Jesus was alive and that she had seen him. But they did not believe it.

12 After that, Jesus appeared in a different form to two of them. This happened while they were walking out in the country. 13 The two returned and told the others about it. But the others did not believe them either.

14 Later Jesus appeared to the 11 disciples as they were eating. He spoke firmly to them because they had no faith. They would not believe those who had seen him after he rose from the dead.

15 He said to them, "Go into all the world. Preach the good news to everyone. 16 Anyone who believes and is baptized will be saved. But anyone who does not believe will be punished. 17 Here are the miraculous signs that those who believe will do. In my name they will drive out demons. They will speak in languages they had not known before. 18 They will pick up snakes with their hands. And when they drink deadly poison, it will not hurt them at all. They will place their hands on sick people. And the people will get well."

19 When the Lord Jesus finished speaking to them, he was taken up into heaven. He sat down at the right hand of God. 20 Then the disciples went out and preached everywhere. The Lord worked with them. And he backed up his word by the signs that went with it.

LUKE

Author: Luke

The Gospel of Luke also tells about Jesus' life, ministry, death, and resurrection. Although Matthew, Mark, and John wrote about these things too, Luke wanted to write an account of Jesus' life that showed how God's plan of salvation is for everyone. While others were telling the people of Israel how God had never forgotten his promises to them, Luke wanted to help people see how God's plan of salvation was for more than just Israel—it was for the whole world! Luke wanted everyone reading his Gospel to see how Jesus was the fulfillment of God's promise to Abraham all those generations ago. God's promise to bless Israel was ultimately a plan to bless the whole world (see Genesis 12:2–3)!

Gospels & Acts

Luke wrote the story of Jesus' life in a way that highlights how Jesus loved those who were usually left out—the poor, the sick, and the outcast in society. Through Jesus, God made salvation available to everyone, both Jews and Gentiles (non-Jews). Luke wanted everyone to know: God's desire is for the entire world to come to know him through his Son, Jesus Christ.

Luke Writes an Orderly Report

1 Many people have attempted to write about the things that have taken place among us. 2 Reports of these things were handed down to us. There were people who saw these things for themselves from the beginning. They saw them and then passed the word on. 3 With this in mind, I myself have carefully looked into everything from the beginning. So I also decided to write down an orderly report of exactly what happened. I am doing this for you, most excellent Theophilus. 4 I want you to know that the things you have been taught are true.

The Coming Birth of John the Baptist

5 Herod was king of Judea. During the time he was ruling, there was a priest named Zechariah. He belonged to a group of priests named after Abijah. His wife Elizabeth also came from the family line of Aaron. 6 Both of them did what was right in the sight of God. They obeyed all the Lord's commands and rules faithfully. 7 But they had no children, because Elizabeth was not able to have any. And they were both very old.

8 One day Zechariah's group was on duty. He was serving as a priest in God's temple. 9 He happened to be chosen, in the usual way, to go into the temple of the Lord. There he was supposed to burn incense. 10 The time came for this to be done. All who had gathered to worship were praying outside.

11 Then an angel of the Lord appeared to Zechariah. The angel was standing at the right side of the incense altar. 12 When Zechariah saw him, he was amazed and terrified. 13 But the angel said to him, "Do not be afraid, Zechariah. Your prayer has been heard. Your wife Elizabeth will have a child. It will be a boy, and you must call him John. 14 He will be a joy and delight to you. His birth will make many people very glad. 15 He will be important in the sight of the Lord. He must never drink wine or other such drinks. He will be filled with the Holy Spirit even before he is born. 16 He will bring back many of the people of Israel to the Lord their God. 17 And he will prepare the way for the Lord. He will have the same spirit and power that

in Luke?

God is the Healer of Hearts, the one who welcomes the lowly into his kingdom and heals those who are hurting.

Elijah had. He will bring peace between parents and their children. He will teach people who don't obey to be wise and do what is right. In this way, he will prepare a people who are ready for the Lord."

18 Zechariah asked the angel, "How can I be sure of this? I am an old man, and my wife is old too."

19 The angel said to him, "I am Gabriel. I serve God. I have been sent to speak to you and to tell you this good news. 20 And now you will have to be silent. You will not be able to speak until after John is born. That's because you did not believe my words. They will come true at the time God has chosen."

21 During that time, the people were waiting for Zechariah to come out of the temple. They wondered why he stayed there so long. 22 When he came out, he could not speak to them. They realized he had seen a vision in the temple. They knew this because he kept gesturing to them. He still could not speak.

23 When his time of service was over, he returned home. 24 After that, his wife Elizabeth became pregnant. She stayed at home for five months. 25 "The Lord has done this for me," she said. "In these days, he has been kind to me. He has taken away my shame among the people."

The Coming Birth of Jesus

26 In the sixth month after Elizabeth had become pregnant, God sent the angel Gabriel to Nazareth, a town in Galilee. 27 He was sent to a virgin. The girl was engaged

to a man named Joseph. He came from
the family line of David. The virgin's name
was Mary. 28 The angel greeted her and
said, "The Lord has blessed you in a special way. He is with you."
29 Mary was very upset because of
his words. She wondered what kind of
greeting this could be. 30 But the angel
said to her, "Do not be afraid, Mary.
God is very pleased with you. 31 You will
become pregnant and give birth to a
son. You must call him Jesus. 32 He will
be great and will be called the Son of
the Most High God. The Lord God will
make him a king like his father David
of long ago. 33 The Son of the Most High
God will rule forever over his people.
They are from the family line of Jacob.
That kingdom will never end."
34 "How can this happen?" Mary asked
the angel. "I am a virgin."
35 The angel answered, "The Holy
Spirit will come to you. The power of
the Most High God will cover you. So the
holy one that is born will be called the
Son of God. 36 Your relative Elizabeth
will have a child even though she is
old. People thought she could not have
children. But she has been pregnant for
six months now. 37 That's because what
God says will always come true."
38 "I serve the Lord," Mary answered.
"May it happen to me just as you said it
would." Then the angel left her.

Mary Visits Elizabeth

39 At that time Mary got ready and
hurried to a town in Judea's hill country.
40 There she entered Zechariah's home
and greeted Elizabeth. 41 When Elizabeth
heard Mary's greeting, the baby inside
her jumped. And Elizabeth was filled
with the Holy Spirit. 42 In a loud voice she
called out, "God has blessed you more
than other women. And blessed is the
child you will have! 43 But why is God so
kind to me? Why has the mother of my
Lord come to me? 44 As soon as I heard
the sound of your voice, the baby inside
me jumped for joy. 45 You are a woman
God has blessed. You have believed that
the Lord would keep his promises to you!"

Mary's Song

46 Mary said,

"My soul gives glory to the Lord.
47 My spirit delights in God my
Savior.
48 He has taken note of me
even though I am not considered
important.
From now on all people will call me
blessed.
49 The Mighty One has done great
things for me.
His name is holy.
50 He shows his mercy to those who
have respect for him,
from parent to child down
through the years.
51 He has done mighty things with his
powerful arm.
He has scattered those who
are proud in their deepest
thoughts.
52 He has brought down rulers from
their thrones.
But he has lifted up people who
are not considered important.
53 He has filled with good things those
who are hungry.
But he has sent away empty
those who are rich.
54 He has helped the people of Israel,
who serve him.
He has always remembered to be
kind
55 to Abraham and his children down
through the years.
He has done it just as he
promised to our people of long
ago."

56 Mary stayed with Elizabeth about
three months. Then she returned home.

John the Baptist Is Born

57 The time came for Elizabeth to have
her baby. She gave birth to a son. 58 Her
neighbors and relatives heard that the
Lord had been very kind to her. They
shared her joy.
59 On the eighth day, they came to
have the child circumcised. They were
going to name him Zechariah, like his
father. 60 But his mother spoke up. "No!"
she said. "He must be called John."
61 They said to her, "No one among
your relatives has that name."
62 Then they motioned to his father.
They wanted to find out what he would
like to name the child. 63 He asked for
something to write on. Then he wrote,
"His name is John." Everyone was
amazed. 64 Right away Zechariah could
speak again. Right away he praised

God. [65] All his neighbors were filled with fear and wonder. Throughout Judea's hill country, people were talking about all these things. [66] Everyone who heard this wondered about it. And because the Lord was with John, they asked, "What is this child going to be?"

Zechariah's Song

[67] John's father Zechariah was filled with the Holy Spirit. He prophesied,

[68] "Give praise to the Lord, the God of Israel!
He has come to his people and purchased their freedom.

Give praise to the Lord, the God of Israel! He has come to his people and purchased their freedom. LUKE 1:68

[69] He has acted with great power and has saved us.
He did it for those who are from the family line of his servant David.
[70] Long ago holy prophets said he would do it.
[71] He has saved us from our enemies.
We are rescued from all who hate us.
[72] He has been kind to our people of long ago.
He has remembered his holy covenant.
[73] He made a promise to our father Abraham.
[74] He promised to save us from our enemies.
Then we could serve him without fear.
[75] He wants us to be holy and godly as long as we live.

[76] "And you, my child, will be called a prophet of the Most High God.
You will go ahead of the Lord to prepare the way for him.
[77] You will tell his people how they can be saved.
You will tell them that their sins can be forgiven.
[78] All of that will happen because our God is tender and caring.
His kindness will bring the rising sun to us from heaven.
[79] It will shine on those living in darkness
and in the shadow of death.
It will guide our feet on the path of peace."

[80] The child grew up, and his spirit became strong. He lived in the desert until he appeared openly to Israel.

Jesus Is Born

2 In those days, Caesar Augustus
made a law. It required that a list
be made of everyone in the whole Roman world. [2] It was the first time a list
was made of the people while Quirinius
was governor of Syria. [3] Everyone went
to their own town to be listed.
[4] So Joseph went also. He went from
the town of Nazareth in Galilee to
Judea. That is where Bethlehem, the
town of David, was. Joseph went there
because he belonged to the family line
of David. [5] He went there with Mary to
be listed. Mary was engaged to him. She
was expecting a baby. [6] While Joseph
and Mary were there, the time came for
the child to be born. [7] She gave birth to
her first baby. It was a boy. She wrapped
him in large strips of cloth. Then she
placed him in a manger. That's because
there was no guest room where they
could stay.
[8] There were shepherds living out in
the fields nearby. It was night, and they
were taking care of their sheep. [9] An
angel of the Lord appeared to them.
And the glory of the Lord shone around
them. They were terrified. [10] But the
angel said to them, "Do not be afraid. I
bring you good news. It will bring great
joy for all the people. [11] Today in the
town of David a Savior has been born to
you. He is the Messiah, the Lord. [12] Here
is how you will know I am telling you
the truth. You will find a baby wrapped
in strips of cloth and lying in a manger."
[13] Suddenly a large group of angels
from heaven also appeared. They were
praising God. They said,

[14] "May glory be given to God in the highest heaven!
And may peace be given to those he is pleased with on earth!"

15 The angels left and went into heav-
en. Then the shepherds said to one another, "Let's go to Bethlehem. Let's see
this thing that has happened, which the
Lord has told us about."
16 So they hurried off and found Mary
and Joseph and the baby. The baby was
lying in the manger. 17 After the shepherds had seen him, they told everyone.
They reported what the angel had said
about this child. 18 All who heard it were
amazed at what the shepherds said to
them. 19 But Mary kept all these things
like a secret treasure in her heart. She
thought about them over and over. 20 The
shepherds returned. They gave glory and
praise to God. Everything they had seen
and heard was just as they had been told.
21 When the child was eight days
old, he was circumcised. At the same
time he was named Jesus. This was the
name the angel had given him before
his mother became pregnant.

Joseph and Mary Take Jesus to the Temple

22 The time came for making Mary
"clean" as required by the Law of Moses.
So Joseph and Mary took Jesus to Jerusalem. There they presented him to the
Lord. 23 In the Law of the Lord it says,
"The first boy born in every family must
be set apart for the Lord." *(Exodus 13:2,12)*
24 They also offered a sacrifice. They did
it in keeping with the Law, which says,
"a pair of doves or two young pigeons."
(Leviticus 12:8)
25 In Jerusalem there was a man
named Simeon. He was a good and
godly man. He was waiting for God's
promise to Israel to come true. The
Holy Spirit was with him. 26 The Spirit
had told Simeon that he would not die
before he had seen the Lord's Messiah.
27 The Spirit led him into the temple
courtyard. Then Jesus' parents brought
the child in. They came to do for him
what the Law required. 28 Simeon took
Jesus in his arms and praised God. He
said,

29 "Lord, you are the King over all.
Now let me, your servant, go in
peace.
That is what you promised.
30 My eyes have seen your salvation.
31 You have prepared it in the sight
of all nations.
32 It is a light to be given to the Gentiles.
It will be the glory of your people
Israel."

33 The child's father and mother were
amazed at what was said about him.
34 Then Simeon blessed them. He said to
Mary, Jesus' mother, "This child is going
to cause many people in Israel to fall
and to rise. God has sent him. But many
will speak against him. 35 The thoughts
of many hearts will be known. A sword
will wound your own soul too."
36 There was also a prophet named
Anna. She was the daughter of Penuel
from the tribe of Asher. Anna was very
old. After getting married, she lived with
her husband seven years. 37 Then she
was a widow until she was 84. She never
left the temple. She worshiped night
and day, praying and going without
food. 38 Anna came up to Jesus' family
at that moment. She gave thanks to
God. And she spoke about the child to
all who were looking forward to the
time when Jerusalem would be set free.
39 Joseph and Mary did everything
the Law of the Lord required. Then they
returned to Galilee. They went to their
own town of Nazareth. 40 And the child
grew and became strong. He was very
wise. He was blessed by God's grace.

The Boy Jesus at the Temple

41 Every year Jesus' parents went
to Jerusalem for the Passover Feast.
42 When Jesus was 12 years old, they
went up to the feast as usual. 43 After
the feast was over, his parents left to
go back home. The boy Jesus stayed
behind in Jerusalem. But they were
not aware of it. 44 They thought he was
somewhere in their group. So they traveled on for a day. Then they began to
look for him among their relatives and
friends. 45 They did not find him. So they
went back to Jerusalem to look for him.
46 After three days they found him in the
temple courtyard. He was sitting with
the teachers. He was listening to them
and asking them questions. 47 Everyone
who heard him was amazed at how
much he understood. They also were
amazed at his answers. 48 When his
parents saw him, they were amazed.
His mother said to him, "Son, why have
you treated us like this? Your father

and I have been worried about you. We
have been looking for you everywhere."
49 "Why were you looking for me?"
he asked. "Didn't you know I had to be
in my Father's house?" 50 But they did
not understand what he meant by that.
51 Then he went back to Nazareth
with them, and he obeyed them. But
his mother kept all these things like
a secret treasure in her heart. 52 Jesus
became wiser and stronger. He also
became more and more pleasing to
God and to people.

John the Baptist Prepares the Way

3 Tiberius Caesar had been ruling for
15 years. Pontius Pilate was governor of Judea. Herod was the ruler of
Galilee. His brother Philip was the ruler
of Iturea and Traconitis. Lysanias was
ruler of Abilene. 2 Annas and Caiaphas
were high priests. At that time God's
word came to John, son of Zechariah,
in the desert. 3 He went into all the
countryside around the Jordan River.
There he preached that people should
be baptized and turn away from their
sins. Then God would forgive them.
4 Here is what is written in the book of
Isaiah the prophet. It says,

"A messenger is calling out in the
desert,
'Prepare the way for the Lord.
Make straight paths for him.
5 Every valley will be filled in.
Every mountain and hill will be
made level.
The crooked roads will become
straight.
The rough ways will become
smooth.
6 And all people will see God's
salvation.' " *(Isaiah 40:3–5)*

7 John spoke to the crowds coming to
be baptized by him. He said, "You are
like a nest of poisonous snakes! Who
warned you to escape the coming of
God's anger? 8 Live in a way that shows
you have turned away from your sins.
And don't start saying to yourselves,
'Abraham is our father.' I tell you, God
can raise up children for Abraham even
from these stones. 9 The ax is already
lying at the roots of the trees. All the trees
that don't produce good fruit will be cut
down. They will be thrown into the fire."
10 "Then what should we do?" the
crowd asked.
11 John answered, "Anyone who has
extra clothes should share with the one
who has none. And anyone who has
extra food should do the same."
12 Even tax collectors came to be
baptized. "Teacher," they asked, "what
should we do?"
13 "Don't collect any more than you
are required to," John told them.
14 Then some soldiers asked him, "And
what should we do?"
John replied, "Don't force people
to give you money. Don't bring false
charges against people. Be happy with
your pay."
15 The people were waiting. They were
expecting something. They were all
wondering in their hearts if John might
be the Messiah. 16 John answered them
all, "I baptize you with water. But one
who is more powerful than I am will
come. I'm not good enough to untie the
straps of his sandals. He will baptize
you with the Holy Spirit and fire. 17 His
pitchfork is in his hand to toss the straw
away from his threshing floor. He will
gather the wheat into his barn. But he
will burn up the husks with fire that
can't be put out." 18 John said many
other things to warn the people. He
also announced the good news to them.
19 But John found fault with Herod,
the ruler of Galilee, because of his
marriage to Herodias. She was the
wife of Herod's brother. John also spoke
strongly to Herod about all the other
evil things he had done. 20 So Herod
locked John up in prison. Herod added
this sin to all his others.

The Baptism and Family Line of Jesus

21 When all the people were being
baptized, Jesus was baptized too. And
as he was praying, heaven was opened.
22 The Holy Spirit came to rest on him in
the form of a dove. A voice came from
heaven. It said, "You are my Son, and I
love you. I am very pleased with you."
23 Jesus was about 30 years old when
he began his special work for God and
others. It was thought that he was the
son of Joseph.

Joseph was the son of Heli.
24 Heli was the son of Matthat.

Matthat was the son of Levi.
Levi was the son of Melki.
Melki was the son of Jannai.
Jannai was the son of Joseph.
25 Joseph was the son of Mattathias.
Mattathias was the son of Amos.
Amos was the son of Nahum.
Nahum was the son of Esli.
Esli was the son of Naggai.
26 Naggai was the son of Maath.
Maath was the son of Mattathias.
Mattathias was the son of Semein.
Semein was the son of Josek.
Josek was the son of Joda.
27 Joda was the son of Joanan.
Joanan was the son of Rhesa.
Rhesa was the son of Zerubbabel.
Zerubbabel was the son of Shealtiel.
Shealtiel was the son of Neri.
28 Neri was the son of Melki.
Melki was the son of Addi.
Addi was the son of Cosam.
Cosam was the son of Elmadam.
Elmadam was the son of Er.
29 Er was the son of Joshua.
Joshua was the son of Eliezer.
Eliezer was the son of Jorim.
Jorim was the son of Matthat.
Matthat was the son of Levi.
30 Levi was the son of Simeon.
Simeon was the son of Judah.
Judah was the son of Joseph.
Joseph was the son of Jonam.
Jonam was the son of Eliakim.
31 Eliakim was the son of Melea.
Melea was the son of Menna.
Menna was the son of Mattatha.
Mattatha was the son of Nathan.
Nathan was the son of David.
32 David was the son of Jesse.
Jesse was the son of Obed.
Obed was the son of Boaz.
Boaz was the son of Salmon.
Salmon was the son of Nahshon.
33 Nahshon was the son of
Amminadab.
Amminadab was the son of Ram.
Ram was the son of Hezron.
Hezron was the son of Perez.
Perez was the son of Judah.
34 Judah was the son of Jacob.
Jacob was the son of Isaac.
Isaac was the son of Abraham.
Abraham was the son of Terah.
Terah was the son of Nahor.
35 Nahor was the son of Serug.
Serug was the son of Reu.
Reu was the son of Peleg.
Peleg was the son of Eber.
Eber was the son of Shelah.
36 Shelah was the son of Cainan.
Cainan was the son of Arphaxad.
Arphaxad was the son of Shem.
Shem was the son of Noah.
Noah was the son of Lamech.
37 Lamech was the son of Methuselah.
Methuselah was the son of Enoch.
Enoch was the son of Jared.
Jared was the son of Mahalalel.
Mahalalel was the son of Kenan.
38 Kenan was the son of Enosh.
Enosh was the son of Seth.
Seth was the son of Adam.
Adam was the son of God.

Jesus Is Tempted in the Desert

4 Jesus, full of the Holy Spirit, left
the Jordan River. The Spirit led him
into the desert. 2 There the devil tempted him for 40 days. Jesus ate nothing
during that time. At the end of the 40
days, he was hungry.

3 The devil said to him, "If you are
the Son of God, tell this stone to become
bread."

4 Jesus answered, "It is written, 'Man
must not live only on bread.' " *(Deuteronomy 8:3)*

5 Then the devil led Jesus up to a high
place. In an instant, he showed Jesus all
the kingdoms of the world. 6 He said to
Jesus, "I will give you all their authority
and glory. It has been given to me, and
I can give it to anyone I want to. 7 If you
worship me, it will all be yours."

8 Jesus answered, "It is written, 'Worship the Lord your God. He is the only one
you should serve.' " *(Deuteronomy 6:13)*

9 Then the devil led Jesus to Jerusalem. He had Jesus stand on the highest
point of the temple. "If you are the Son
of God," he said, "throw yourself down
from here. 10 It is written,

" 'The Lord will command his
angels to take good care of you.
11 They will lift you up in their hands.
Then you won't trip over a
stone.' " *(Psalm 91:11,12)*

12 Jesus answered, "Scripture says,
'Do not test the Lord your God.' " *(Deuteronomy 6:16)*

13 When the devil finished all this
tempting, he left Jesus until a better time.

Jesus Is Not Accepted in Nazareth

14 Jesus returned to Galilee in the power of the Holy Spirit. News about him spread through the whole countryside.
15 He was teaching in their synagogues, and everyone praised him.

16 Jesus went to Nazareth, where he had been brought up. On the Sabbath day he went into the synagogue as he usually did. He stood up to read. 17 And the scroll of Isaiah the prophet was handed to him. Jesus unrolled it and found the right place. There it is written,

18 "The Spirit of the Lord is on me.
He has anointed me
to announce the good news to
poor people.
He has sent me to announce
freedom for prisoners.
He has sent me so that the blind
will see again.
He wants me to set free those who
are treated badly.
19 And he has sent me to announce
the year when he will set his
people free." *(Isaiah 61:1,2)*

20 Then Jesus rolled up the scroll. He gave it back to the attendant and sat down. The eyes of everyone in the synagogue were staring at him. 21 He
began by saying to them, "Today this passage of Scripture is coming true as you listen."

22 Everyone said good things about him. They were amazed at the gracious words they heard from his lips. "Isn't this Joseph's son?" they asked.

23 Jesus said, "Here is a saying you will certainly apply to me. 'Doctor, heal yourself!' And you will tell me this. 'Do the things here in your hometown that we heard you did in Capernaum.' "

24 "What I'm about to tell you is true," he continued. "A prophet is not accepted in his hometown. 25 I tell you for sure that there were many widows in Israel in the days of Elijah. And there had been no rain for three and a half years. There wasn't enough food to eat anywhere in the land. 26 But Elijah was not sent to any of those widows. Instead, he was sent to a widow in Zarephath near Sidon. 27 And there were many in Israel who had skin diseases in the days of Elisha the prophet. But not one of them was healed except Naaman the Syrian."

28 All the people in the synagogue were very angry when they heard that.
29 They got up and ran Jesus out of town. They took him to the edge of the hill on which the town was built. They planned to throw him off the cliff. 30 But Jesus walked right through the crowd and went on his way.

Jesus Drives Out an Evil Spirit

31 Then Jesus went to Capernaum, a town in Galilee. On the Sabbath day he taught the people. 32 They were amazed at his teaching, because his words had authority.

33 In the synagogue there was a man controlled by a demon, an evil spirit. He cried out at the top of his voice. 34 "Go away!" he said. "What do you want with us, Jesus of Nazareth? Have you come to destroy us? I know who you are. You are the Holy One of God!"

35 "Be quiet!" Jesus said firmly. "Come out of him!" Then the demon threw the man down in front of everybody. And it came out without hurting him.

36 All the people were amazed. They said to each other, "What he says is amazing! With authority and power

How do we know Jesus was the promised Savior?

In the Old Testament, God gave his people prophecies, or signs, to watch for so that they would know the Savior when he arrived. When Jesus came, he fulfilled every single prophecy, showing that he was the promised Savior.

Can you find the following verses?

LUKE 4:17–21

he gives orders to evil spirits. And they come out!" [37]The news about Jesus spread throughout the whole area.

Jesus Heals Many People

[38]Jesus left the synagogue and went to the home of Simon. At that time, Simon's mother-in-law was suffering from a high fever. So they asked Jesus to help her. [39]He bent over her and commanded the fever to leave, and it left her. She got up right away and began to serve them.

[40]At sunset, people brought to Jesus all who were sick. He placed his hands on each one and healed them. [41]Also, demons came out of many people. The demons shouted, "You are the Son of God!" But he commanded them to be quiet. He would not allow them to speak, because they knew he was the Messiah.

[42]At dawn, Jesus went out to a place where he could be by himself. The people went to look for him. When they found him, they tried to keep him from leaving them. [43]But he said, "I must announce the good news of God's kingdom to the other towns also. That is why I was sent." [44]And he kept on preaching in the synagogues of Judea.

Jesus Chooses His First Disciples

5 One day Jesus was standing by the Sea of Galilee. The people crowded around him and listened to the word of God. [2]Jesus saw two boats at the edge of the water. They had been left there by the fishermen, who were washing their nets. [3]He got into the boat that belonged to Simon. Jesus asked him to go out a little way from shore. Then he sat down in the boat and taught the people.

[4]When he finished speaking, he turned to Simon. Jesus said, "Go out into deep water. Let down the nets so you can catch some fish."

[5]Simon answered, "Master, we've worked hard all night and haven't caught anything. But because you say so, I will let down the nets."

[6]When they had done so, they caught a large number of fish. There were so many that their nets began to break. [7]So they motioned to their partners in the other boat to come and help them. They came and filled both boats so full that they began to sink.

[8]When Simon Peter saw this, he fell at Jesus' knees. "Go away from me, Lord!" he said. "I am a sinful man!" [9]He and everyone with him were amazed at the number of fish they had caught. [10]So were James and John, the sons of Zebedee, who worked with Simon.

Then Jesus said to Simon, "Don't be afraid. From now on you will fish for people." [11]So they pulled their boats up on shore. Then they left everything and followed him.

Jesus Heals a Man Who Had a Skin Disease

[12]While Jesus was in one of the towns, a man came along. He had a skin disease all over his body. When he saw Jesus, the man fell with his face to the ground. He begged him, "Lord, if you are willing to make me 'clean,' you can do it."

[13]Jesus reached out his hand and touched the man. "I am willing to do it," he said. "Be 'clean'!" Right away the disease left him.

[14]Then Jesus ordered him, "Don't tell anyone. Go and show yourself to the priest. Offer the sacrifices that Moses commanded. It will be a witness to the priest and the people that you are 'clean.' "

[15]But the news about Jesus spread even more. So crowds of people came to hear him. They also came to be healed of their sicknesses. [16]But Jesus often went away to be by himself and pray.

Jesus Forgives and Heals a Man Who Could Not Walk

[17]One day Jesus was teaching. Pharisees and teachers of the law were sitting there. They had come from every village of Galilee and from Judea and Jerusalem. They heard that the Lord had given Jesus the power to heal the sick. [18]So some men came carrying a man who could not walk. He was lying on a mat. They tried to take him into the house to place him in front of Jesus. [19]They could not find a way to do this because of the crowd. So they went up on the roof. Then they lowered the man on his mat through the opening in the roof tiles. They lowered him into the middle of the crowd, right in front of Jesus.

[20]When Jesus saw that they had faith,
he spoke to the man. He said, "Friend,
your sins are forgiven."
[21]The Pharisees and the teachers of
the law began to think, "Who is this
fellow who says such an evil thing? Who
can forgive sins but God alone?"
[22]Jesus knew what they were thinking. So he asked, "Why are you thinking these things in your hearts? [23]Is it
easier to say, 'Your sins are forgiven'?
Or to say, 'Get up and walk'? [24]But I
want you to know that the Son of Man
has authority on earth to forgive sins."
So he spoke to the man who could not
walk. "I tell you," he said, "get up. Take
your mat and go home." [25]Right away,
the man stood up in front of them. He
took his mat and went home praising
God. [26]Everyone was amazed and gave
praise to God. They were filled with wonder. They said, "We have seen unusual
things today."

Jesus Chooses Levi and Eats With Sinners

[27]After this, Jesus left the house. He
saw a tax collector sitting at the tax
booth. The man's name was Levi. "Follow me," Jesus said to him. [28]Levi got
up, left everything and followed him.
[29]Then Levi gave a huge banquet
for Jesus at his house. A large crowd of
tax collectors and others were eating
with them. [30]But the Pharisees and
their teachers of the law complained
to Jesus' disciples. They said, "Why do
you eat and drink with tax collectors
and sinners?"
[31]Jesus answered them, "Healthy
people don't need a doctor. Sick people
do. [32]I have not come to get those who
think they are right with God to follow
me. I have come to get sinners to turn
away from their sins."

Jesus Is Asked About Fasting

[33]Some of the people who were there
said to Jesus, "John's disciples often
pray and go without eating. So do the
disciples of the Pharisees. But yours go
on eating and drinking."
[34]Jesus answered, "Can you make
the friends of the groom fast while he
is with them? [35]But the time will come
when the groom will be taken away
from them. In those days they will go
without eating."
[36]Then Jesus gave them an example.
He said, "No one tears a piece out of new
clothes to patch old clothes. Otherwise,
they will tear the new clothes. Also, the
patch from the new clothes will not
match the old clothes. [37]No one pours
new wine into old wineskins. Otherwise,
the new wine will burst the skins. The
wine will run out, and the wineskins
will be destroyed. [38]No, new wine must
be poured into new wineskins. [39]After
drinking old wine, no one wants the
new. They say, 'The old wine is better.'"

Jesus Is Lord of the Sabbath Day

6 One Sabbath day Jesus was walking
through the grainfields. His disciples began to break off some heads of
grain. They rubbed them in their hands
and ate them. [2]Some of the Pharisees
said, "It is against the Law to do this on
the Sabbath day. Why are you doing it?"
[3]Jesus answered them, "Haven't you
ever read about what David did? He and
his men were hungry. [4]He entered the
house of God and took the holy bread.
He ate the bread that only priests were
allowed to eat. David also gave some to
his men." [5]Then Jesus said to them, "The
Son of Man is Lord of the Sabbath day."
[6]On another Sabbath day, Jesus went
into the synagogue and was teaching.
A man whose right hand was weak and
twisted was there. [7]The Pharisees and
the teachers of the law were trying to
find fault with Jesus. So they watched
him closely. They wanted to see if he
would heal on the Sabbath day. [8]But
Jesus knew what they were thinking.
He spoke to the man who had the weak
and twisted hand. "Get up and stand in
front of everyone," he said. So the man
got up and stood there.
[9]Then Jesus said to them, "What
does the Law say we should do on the
Sabbath day? Should we do good? Or
should we do evil? Should we save life?
Or should we destroy it?"
[10]He looked around at all of them.
Then he said to the man, "Stretch out
your hand." He did, and his hand had
been made as good as new. [11]But the
Pharisees and the teachers of the law
were very angry. They began to talk
to one another about what they might
do to Jesus.

Jesus Chooses the Twelve Apostles

[12] On one of those days, Jesus went out
to a mountainside to pray. He spent the
night praying to God. [13] When morning
came, he called for his disciples to come
to him. He chose 12 of them and made
them apostles. Here are their names.

[14] Simon, whom Jesus named Peter,
and his brother Andrew
James
John
Philip
Bartholomew
[15] Matthew
Thomas
James, son of Alphaeus
Simon who was called the Zealot
[16] Judas, son of James
and Judas Iscariot who would later
hand Jesus over to his enemies

Jesus Gives Blessings and Warnings

[17] Jesus went down the mountain with
them and stood on a level place. A large
crowd of his disciples was there. A large
number of other people were there too.
They came from all over Judea, including Jerusalem. They also came from
the coastland around Tyre and Sidon.
[18] They had all come to hear Jesus and
to be healed of their sicknesses. People
who were troubled by evil spirits were
made well. [19] Everyone tried to touch
Jesus. Power was coming from him and
healing them all.

[20] Jesus looked at his disciples. He
said to them,

"Blessed are you who are needy.
God's kingdom belongs to you.
[21] Blessed are you who are hungry
now.
You will be satisfied.
Blessed are you who are sad now.
You will laugh.
[22] Blessed are you when people hate
you,
when they have nothing to do
with you
and say bad things about you,
and when they treat your name
as something evil.
They do all this because you are
followers of the Son of Man.

[23] "The prophets of long ago were
treated the same way. When these
things happen to you, be glad and jump
for joy. You will receive many blessings
in heaven.

[24] "But how terrible it will be for you
who are rich!
You have already had your easy
life.
[25] How terrible for you who are well
fed now!
You will go hungry.
How terrible for you who laugh now!
You will cry and be sad.
[26] How terrible for you when
everyone says good things
about you!
Their people treated the false
prophets the same way long
ago.

Love Your Enemies

[27] "But here is what I tell you who are
listening. Love your enemies. Do good to
those who hate you. [28] Bless those who
call down curses on you. And pray for
those who treat you badly. [29] Suppose
someone slaps you on one cheek. Let
them slap you on the other cheek as
well. Suppose someone takes your coat.
Don't stop them from taking your shirt
as well. [30] Give to everyone who asks
you. And if anyone takes what belongs
to you, don't ask to get it back. [31] Do to
others as you want them to do to you.

[32] "Suppose you love those who love
you. Should anyone praise you for that?
Even sinners love those who love them.
[33] And suppose you do good to those
who are good to you. Should anyone
praise you for that? Even sinners do
that. [34] And suppose you lend money
to those who can pay you back. Should
anyone praise you for that? Even a sinner lends to sinners, expecting them to
pay everything back. [35] But love your
enemies. Do good to them. Lend to them
without expecting to get anything back.
Then you will receive a lot in return. And
you will be children of the Most High
God. He is kind to people who are evil
and are not thankful. [36] So have mercy,
just as your Father has mercy.

Be Fair When You Judge Other People

[37] "If you do not judge other people,
then you will not be judged. If you do
not find others guilty, then you will

not be found guilty. Forgive, and you will be forgiven. 38 Give, and it will be given to you. A good amount will be poured into your lap. It will be pressed down, shaken together, and running over. The same amount you give will be measured out to you."

39 Jesus also gave them another example. He asked, "Can a blind person lead another blind person? Won't they both fall into a pit? 40 The student is not better than the teacher. But everyone who is completely trained will be like their teacher.

41 "You look at the bit of sawdust in your friend's eye. But you pay no attention to the piece of wood in your own eye. 42 How can you say to your friend, 'Let me take the bit of sawdust out of your eye'? How can you say this while there is a piece of wood in your own eye? You pretender! First take the piece of wood out of your own eye. Then you will be able to see clearly to take the bit of sawdust out of your friend's eye.

A Tree and Its Fruit

43 "A good tree doesn't bear bad fruit. And a bad tree doesn't bear good fruit. 44 You can tell each tree by the kind of fruit it bears. People do not pick figs from thorns. And they don't pick grapes from bushes. 45 A good man says good things. These come from the good that is stored up in his heart. An evil man says evil things. These come from the evil that is stored up in his heart. A person's mouth says everything that is in their heart.

The Wise and Foolish Builders

46 "Why do you call me, 'Lord, Lord,' and still don't do what I say? 47 Some people come and listen to me and do what I say. I will show you what they are like. 48 They are like a man who builds a house. He digs down deep and sets it on solid rock. When a flood comes, the river rushes against the house. But the water can't shake it. The house is well built. 49 But here is what happens when people listen to my words and do not obey them. They are like a man who builds a house on soft ground instead of solid rock. The moment the river rushes against that house, it falls down. It is completely destroyed."

A Roman Commander Has Faith

7 Jesus finished saying all these things to the people who were listening. Then he entered Capernaum. 2 There the servant of a Roman commander was sick and about to die. His master thought highly of him. 3 The commander heard about Jesus. So he sent some elders of the Jews to him. He told them to ask Jesus to come and heal his servant. 4 They came to Jesus and begged him, "This man deserves to have you do this. 5 He loves our nation and has built our synagogue." 6 So Jesus went with them.

When Jesus came near the house, the Roman commander sent friends to him. He told them to say, "Lord, don't trouble yourself. I am not good enough to have you come into my house. 7 That is why I did not even think I was fit to come to you. But just say the word, and my servant will be healed. 8 I myself am a man who is under authority. And I have soldiers who obey my orders. I tell this one, 'Go,' and he goes. I tell that one, 'Come,' and he comes. I say to my servant, 'Do this,' and he does it."

9 When Jesus heard this, he was amazed at the commander. Jesus turned to the crowd that was following him. He said, "I tell you, even in Israel I have not found anyone whose faith is so strong." 10 Then the men who had been sent to Jesus returned to the house. They found that the servant was healed.

Jesus Raises a Widow's Son From the Dead

11 Some time later, Jesus went to a town called Nain. His disciples and a large crowd went along with him. 12 He approached the town gate. Just then, a dead person was being carried out. He was the only son of his mother. She was a widow. A large crowd from the town was with her. 13 When the Lord saw her, he felt sorry for her. So he said, "Don't cry."

14 Then he went up and touched the coffin. Those carrying it stood still. Jesus said, "Young man, I say to you, get up!" 15 The dead man sat up and began to talk. Then Jesus gave him back to his mother.

16 The people were all filled with wonder and praised God. "A great prophet

has appeared among us," they said.
"God has come to help his people." 17 This
news about Jesus spread all through
Judea and the whole country.

Jesus and John the Baptist

18 John's disciples told him about all
these things. So he chose two of them.
19 He sent them to the Lord. John told
them to ask him, "Are you the one who
is supposed to come? Or should we look
for someone else?"
20 The men came to Jesus. They said,
"John the Baptist sent us to ask you, 'Are
you the one who is supposed to come?
Or should we look for someone else?' "
21 At that time Jesus healed many
people. They had illnesses, sicknesses
and evil spirits. He also gave sight to
many who were blind. 22 So Jesus replied to the messengers, "Go back to
John. Tell him what you have seen and
heard. Blind people receive sight. Disabled people walk. Those who have skin
diseases are made 'clean.' Deaf people
hear. Those who are dead are raised to
life. And the good news is announced to
those who are poor. 23 Blessed is anyone
who does not give up their faith because
of me."
24 So John's messengers left. Then
Jesus began to speak to the crowd about
John. He said, "What did you go out into
the desert to see? Tall grass waving in
the wind? 25 If not, what did you go out
to see? A man dressed in fine clothes?
No. Those who wear fine clothes and
have many expensive things are in
palaces. 26 Then what did you go out
to see? A prophet? Yes, I tell you, and
more than a prophet. 27 He is the one
written about in Scripture. It says,

" 'I will send my messenger ahead
of you.
He will prepare your way for
you.' *(Malachi 3:1)*

28 I tell you, no one more important
than John has ever been born. But the
least important person in God's kingdom is more important than John is."
29 All the people who heard Jesus'
words agreed that God's way was right.
Even the tax collectors agreed. These
people had all been baptized by John.
30 But the Pharisees and the authorities
on the law did not accept for themselves
God's purpose. So they had not been
baptized by John.
31 Jesus went on to say, "What can I
compare today's people to? What are
they like? 32 They are like children sitting in the market and calling out to
each other. They say,

" 'We played the flute for you.
But you didn't dance.
We sang a funeral song.
But you didn't cry.'

33 That is how it has been with John the
Baptist. When he came to you, he didn't
eat bread or drink wine. And you say,
'He has a demon.' 34 But when the Son
of Man came, he ate and drank as you
do. And you say, 'This fellow is always
eating and drinking far too much. He's
a friend of tax collectors and sinners.'
35 All who follow wisdom prove that
wisdom is right."

A Sinful Woman Pours Perfume on Jesus

36 One of the Pharisees invited Jesus
to have dinner with him. So he went to
the Pharisee's house. He took his place
at the table. 37 There was a woman in
that town who had lived a sinful life.
She learned that Jesus was eating at the
Pharisee's house. So she came there with
a special jar of perfume. 38 She stood
behind Jesus and cried at his feet. And
she began to wet his feet with her tears.
Then she wiped them with her hair.
She kissed them and poured perfume
on them.
39 The Pharisee who had invited Jesus
saw this. He said to himself, "If this man
were a prophet, he would know who is
touching him. He would know what
kind of woman she is. She is a sinner!"
40 Jesus answered him, "Simon, I have
something to tell you."
"Tell me, teacher," he said.
41 "Two people owed money to a certain lender. One owed him 500 silver
coins. The other owed him 50 silver
coins. 42 Neither of them had the money to pay him back. So he let them go
without paying. Which of them will love
him more?"
43 Simon replied, "I suppose the one
who owed the most money."
"You are right," Jesus said.

44 Then he turned toward the woman. He said to Simon, "Do you see this
woman? I came into your house. You
did not give me any water to wash my
feet. But she wet my feet with her tears
and wiped them with her hair. 45 You
did not give me a kiss. But this woman
has not stopped kissing my feet since
I came in. 46 You did not put any olive
oil on my head. But she has poured this
perfume on my feet. 47 So I tell you this.
Her many sins have been forgiven. She
has shown that she understands this
by her great acts of love. But whoever
has been forgiven only a little loves
only a little."

48 Then Jesus said to her, "Your sins
are forgiven."

49 The other guests began to talk
about this among themselves. They
said, "Who is this who even forgives
sins?"

50 Jesus said to the woman, "Your
faith has saved you. Go in peace."

The Story of the Farmer

8 After this, Jesus traveled around
from one town and village to another. He announced the good news of
God's kingdom. His 12 disciples were
with him. 2 So were some women who
had been healed of evil spirits and sicknesses. One was Mary Magdalene. Seven
demons had come out of her. 3 Another
was Joanna, the wife of Chuza. He was
the manager of Herod's household. Su-
sanna and many others were there also.
These women were helping to support
Jesus and the 12 disciples with their
own money.

4 A large crowd gathered together.
People came to Jesus from town after town. As they did, he told a story.
He said, 5 "A farmer went out to plant
his seed. He scattered the seed on the
ground. Some fell on a path. People
walked on it, and the birds ate it up.
6 Some seed fell on rocky ground. When
it grew, the plants dried up because they
had no water. 7 Other seed fell among
thorns. The thorns grew up with it and
crowded out the plants. 8 Still other
seed fell on good soil. It grew up and
produced a crop 100 times more than
the farmer planted."

When Jesus said this, he called out,
"Whoever has ears should listen."

9 His disciples asked him what the
story meant. 10 He said, "You have been
given the chance to understand the secrets of God's kingdom. But to outsiders
I speak by using stories. In that way,

" 'They see, but they will not know
what they are seeing.
They hear, but they will not
understand what they are
hearing.' *(Isaiah 6:9)*

11 "Here is what the story means. The
seed is God's message. 12 The seed on
the path stands for God's message in the
hearts of those who hear. But then
the devil comes. He takes away the
message from their hearts. He does it
so they won't believe. Then they can't
be saved. 13 The seed on rocky ground
stands for those who hear the message
and receive it with joy. But they have no
roots. They believe for a while. But when
they are tested, they fall away from the
faith. 14 The seed that fell among thorns
stands for those who hear the message.
But as they go on their way, they are
choked by life's worries, riches and pleasures. So they do not reach full growth.
15 But the seed on good soil stands for
those with an honest and good heart.
Those people hear the message. They
keep it in their hearts. They remain
faithful and produce a good crop.

A Lamp on a Stand

16 "No one lights a lamp and then
hides it in a clay jar or puts it under
a bed. Instead, they put it on a stand.
Then those who come in can see its light.
17 What is hidden will be seen. And what
is out of sight will be brought into the
open and made known. 18 So be careful
how you listen. Whoever has something
will be given more. Whoever has nothing, even what they think they have will
be taken away from them."

Jesus' Mother and Brothers

19 Jesus' mother and brothers came
to see him. But they could not get near
him because of the crowd. 20 Someone
told him, "Your mother and brothers are
standing outside. They want to see you."

21 He replied, "My mother and brothers are those who hear God's word and
do what it says."

Jesus Calms the Storm

22 One day Jesus said to his disciples, "Let's go over to the other side of the lake." So they got into a boat and left. 23 As they sailed, Jesus fell asleep. A storm came down on the lake. It was so bad that the boat was about to sink. They were in great danger.

24 The disciples went and woke Jesus up. They said, "Master! Master! We're going to drown!"

He got up and ordered the wind and the huge waves to stop. The storm quieted down. It was completely calm. 25 "Where is your faith?" he asked his disciples.

They were amazed and full of fear. They asked one another, "Who is this? He commands even the winds and the waves, and they obey him."

Jesus Heals a Man Controlled by Demons

26 Jesus and his disciples sailed to the area of the Gerasenes across the lake from Galilee. 27 When Jesus stepped on shore, he was met by a man from the town. The man was controlled by demons. For a long time he had not worn clothes or lived in a house. He lived in the tombs. 28 When he saw Jesus, he cried out and fell at his feet. He shouted at the top of his voice, "Jesus, Son of the Most High God, what do you want with me? I beg you, don't hurt me!" 29 This was because Jesus had commanded the evil spirit to come out of the man. Many times the spirit had taken hold of him. The man's hands and feet were chained, and he was kept under guard. But he had broken his chains. And then the demon had forced him to go out into lonely places in the countryside.

30 Jesus asked him, "What is your name?"

"Legion," he replied, because many demons had gone into him. 31 And they begged Jesus again and again not to order them to go into the Abyss.

32 A large herd of pigs was feeding there on the hillside. The demons begged Jesus to let them go into the pigs. And he allowed it. 33 When the demons came out of the man, they went into the pigs. Then the herd rushed down the steep bank. They ran into the lake and drowned.

34 Those who were tending the pigs saw what had happened. They ran off and reported it in the town and countryside. 35 The people went out to see what had happened. Then they came to Jesus. They found the man who was now free of the demons. He was sitting at Jesus' feet. He was dressed and thinking clearly. All this made the people afraid. 36 Those who had seen it told the others how the man who had been controlled by demons was now healed. 37 Then all the people who lived in the area of the Gerasenes asked Jesus to leave them. They were filled with fear. So he got into the boat and left.

38 The man who was now free of the demons begged to go with him. But Jesus sent him away. He said to him, 39 "Return home and tell how much God has done for you." So the man went away. He told people all over town how much Jesus had done for him.

Jesus Heals a Dead Girl and a Suffering Woman

40 When Jesus returned, a crowd welcomed him. They were all expecting him. 41 Then a man named Jairus came. He was a synagogue leader. He fell at Jesus' feet and begged Jesus to come to his house. 42 His only daughter was dying. She was about 12 years old. As Jesus was on his way, the crowds almost crushed him.

43 A woman was there who had a sickness that made her bleed. Her sickness had lasted for 12 years. No one could heal her. 44 She came up behind Jesus and touched the edge of his clothes. Right away her bleeding stopped.

45 "Who touched me?" Jesus asked.

Everyone said they didn't do it. Then Peter said, "Master, the people are crowding and pushing against you."

46 But Jesus said, "Someone touched me. I know that power has gone out from me."

47 The woman realized that people would notice her. Shaking with fear, she came and fell at his feet. In front of everyone, she told why she had touched him. She also told how she had been healed in an instant. 48 Then he said to her, "Dear woman, your faith has healed you. Go in peace."

49 While Jesus was still speaking,
someone came from the house of Jairus.
Jairus was the synagogue leader. "Your
daughter is dead," the messenger said.
"Don't bother the teacher anymore."
50 Hearing this, Jesus said to Jairus,
"Don't be afraid. Just believe. She will
be healed."
51 When he arrived at the house of
Jairus, he did not let everyone go in
with him. He took only Peter, John and
James, and the child's father and mother. 52 During this time, all the people
were crying and sobbing loudly over
the child. "Stop crying!" Jesus said. "She
is not dead. She is sleeping."
53 They laughed at him. They knew
she was dead. 54 But he took her by
the hand and said, "My child, get up!"
55 Her spirit returned, and right away
she stood up. Then Jesus told them to
give her something to eat. 56 Her parents
were amazed. But Jesus ordered them
not to tell anyone what had happened.

Jesus Sends Out the Twelve Disciples

9 Jesus called together the 12 disciples. He gave them power and
authority to drive out all demons and
to heal sicknesses. 2 Then he sent them
out to announce God's kingdom and to
heal those who were sick. 3 He told them,
"Don't take anything for the journey. Do
not take a walking stick or a bag. Do not
take any bread, money or extra clothes.
4 When you are invited into a house,
stay there until you leave town. 5 Some
people may not welcome you. If they
don't, leave their town and shake the
dust off your feet. This will be a witness
against the people living there." 6 So the
12 disciples left. They went from village
to village. They announced the good
news and healed people everywhere.
7 Now Herod, the ruler of Galilee,
heard about everything that was going
on. He was bewildered, because some
were saying that John the Baptist had
been raised from the dead. 8 Others were
saying that Elijah had appeared. Still
others were saying that a prophet of
long ago had come back to life. 9 But
Herod said, "I had John's head cut off. So
who is it that I hear such things about?"
And he tried to see Jesus.

Jesus Feeds the Five Thousand

10 The disciples returned. They told
Jesus what they had done. Then he
took them with him. They went off by
themselves to a town called Bethsaida.
11 But the crowds learned about it and
followed Jesus. He welcomed them and
spoke to them about God's kingdom.
He also healed those who needed to
be healed.
12 Late in the afternoon the 12 disciples came to him. They said, "Send the
crowd away. They can go to the nearby
villages and countryside. There they
can find food and a place to stay. There
is nothing here."
13 Jesus replied, "You give them something to eat."
The disciples answered, "We have
only five loaves of bread and two fish.
We would have to go and buy food for
all this crowd." 14 About 5,000 men were
there.
But Jesus said to his disciples, "Have
them sit down in groups of about 50
each." 15 The disciples did so, and everyone sat down. 16 Jesus took the five
loaves and the two fish. He looked up
to heaven and gave thanks. He broke
them into pieces. Then he gave them
to the disciples to give to the people.
17 All of them ate and were satisfied.
The disciples picked up 12 baskets of
leftover pieces.

Peter Says That Jesus Is the Messiah

18 One day Jesus was praying alone.
Only his disciples were with him. He asked
them, "Who do the crowds say I am?"
19 They replied, "Some say John the
Baptist. Others say Elijah. Still others
say that one of the prophets of long
ago has come back to life."
20 "But what about you?" he asked.
"Who do you say I am?"
Peter answered, "God's Messiah."

Jesus Speaks About His Coming Death

21 Jesus strongly warned them not to
tell this to anyone. 22 He said, "The Son
of Man must suffer many things. The
elders will not accept him. The chief
priests and the teachers of the law
will not accept him either. He must be
killed and on the third day rise from
the dead."

23 Then he said to all of them, "Whoever wants to follow me must say no
to themselves. They must pick up their
cross every day and follow me. 24 Whoever wants to save their life will lose it.
But whoever loses their life for me will
save it. 25 What good is it if someone
gains the whole world but loses or gives
up their very self? 26 Suppose someone is
ashamed of me and my words. The Son
of Man will come in his glory and in the
glory of the Father and the holy angels.
Then he will be ashamed of that person.
27 "What I'm about to tell you is true.
Some who are standing here will not die
before they see God's kingdom."

Jesus' Appearance Is Changed

28 About eight days after Jesus said
this, he went up on a mountain to pray.
He took Peter, John and James with him.
29 As he was praying, the appearance of
his face changed. His clothes became
as bright as a flash of lightning. 30 Two
men, Moses and Elijah, appeared in
shining glory. Jesus and the two of them
talked together. 31 They talked about
how he would be leaving them soon.
This was going to happen in Jerusalem.
32 Peter and his companions had been
very sleepy. But then they became completely awake. They saw Jesus' glory
and the two men standing with him.
33 As the men were leaving Jesus, Peter
spoke up. "Master," he said to him, "it
is good for us to be here. Let us put up
three shelters. One will be for you, one
for Moses, and one for Elijah." Peter
didn't really know what he was saying.
34 While he was speaking, a cloud
appeared and covered them. The disciples were afraid as they entered the
cloud. 35 A voice came from the cloud. It
said, "This is my Son, and I have chosen
him. Listen to him." 36 When the voice
had spoken, they found that Jesus was
alone. The disciples kept quiet about
this. They didn't tell anyone at that
time what they had seen.

Jesus Heals a Boy Who Is Controlled by an Evil Spirit

37 The next day Jesus and those who
were with him came down from the
mountain. A large crowd met Jesus. 38 A
man in the crowd called out. "Teacher,"
he said, "I beg you to look at my son. He
is my only child. 39 A spirit takes hold
of him, and he suddenly screams. It
throws him into fits so that he foams
at the mouth. It hardly ever leaves
him. It is destroying him. 40 I begged
your disciples to drive it out. But they
couldn't do it."
41 "You unbelieving and evil people!"
Jesus replied. "How long do I have to
stay with you? How long do I have to
put up with you?" Then he said to the
man, "Bring your son here."
42 Even while the boy was coming, the
demon threw him into a fit. The boy fell
to the ground. But Jesus ordered the
evil spirit to leave the boy. Then Jesus
healed him and gave him back to his
father. 43 They were all amazed at God's
greatness.

Jesus Speaks a Second Time About His Coming Death

Everyone was wondering about all
that Jesus did. Then Jesus said to his
disciples, 44 "Listen carefully to what I
am about to tell you. The Son of Man
is going to be handed over to men."
45 But they didn't understand what this
meant. That was because it was hidden
from them. And they were afraid to ask
Jesus about it.

Who Is the Most Important Person?

46 The disciples began to argue about
which one of them would be the most
important person. 47 Jesus knew what
they were thinking. So he took a little
child and had the child stand beside
him. 48 Then he spoke to them. "Anyone who welcomes this little child in
my name welcomes me," he said. "And
anyone who welcomes me welcomes the
one who sent me. The one considered
least important among all of you is
really the most important."
49 "Master," said John, "we saw someone driving out demons in your name.
We tried to stop him, because he is not
one of us."
50 "Do not stop him," Jesus said. "Anyone who is not against you is for you."

The Samaritans Do Not Welcome Jesus

51 The time grew near for Jesus to be
taken up to heaven. So he made up
his mind to go to Jerusalem. 52 He sent
messengers on ahead. They went into
a Samaritan village to get things ready

for him. 53 But the people there did not
welcome Jesus. That was because he was
heading for Jerusalem. 54 The disciples
James and John saw this. They asked,
"Lord, do you want us to call down fire
from heaven to destroy them?" 55 But
Jesus turned and commanded them not
to do it. 56 Then Jesus and his disciples
went on to another village.

The Cost of Following Jesus

57 Once Jesus and those who were with
him were walking along the road. A
man said to Jesus, "I will follow you no
matter where you go."

58 Jesus replied, "Foxes have dens.
Birds have nests. But the Son of Man
has no place to lay his head."

59 He said to another man, "Follow me."

But the man replied, "Lord, first let
me go and bury my father."

60 Jesus said to him, "Let dead people
bury their own dead. You go and tell
others about God's kingdom."

61 Still another person said, "I will
follow you, Lord. But first let me go back
and say goodbye to my family."

62 Jesus replied, "Suppose someone
starts to plow and then looks back.
That person is not fit for service in God's
kingdom."

Jesus Sends Out the Seventy-Two

10 After this the Lord appointed 72
others. He sent them out two by
two ahead of him. They went to every
town and place where he was about to
go. 2 He told them, "The harvest is huge,
but the workers are few. So ask the Lord
of the harvest to send out workers into
his harvest field. 3 Go! I am sending you
out like lambs among wolves. 4 Do not
take a purse or bag or sandals. And don't
greet anyone on the road.

5 "When you enter a house, first say,
'May this house be blessed with peace.'
6 If someone there works to bring peace,
your blessing of peace will rest on them.
If not, it will return to you. 7 Stay there,
and eat and drink anything they give
you. Workers are worthy of their pay. Do
not move around from house to house.

8 "When you enter a town and are
welcomed, eat what is given to you.
9 Heal the sick people who are there. Tell
them, 'God's kingdom has come near
to you.' 10 But what if you enter a town
and are not welcomed? Then go into its
streets and say, 11 'We wipe from our feet
even the dust of your town. We do it to
warn you. But here is what you can be
sure of. God's kingdom has come near.'
12 I tell you this. On judgment day it will
be easier for Sodom than for that town.

13 "How terrible it will be for you,
Chorazin! How terrible for you, Bethsaida! Suppose the miracles done in you
had been done in Tyre and Sidon. They
would have turned away from their
sins long ago. They would have put on
the rough clothing people wear when
they're sad. They would have sat down
in ashes. 14 On judgment day it will be
easier for Tyre and Sidon than for you.
15 And what about you, Capernaum? Will
you be lifted up to the heavens? No! You
will go down to the place of the dead.

16 "Whoever listens to you listens to
me. Whoever does not accept you does
not accept me. But whoever does not
accept me does not accept the one who
sent me."

17 The 72 returned with joy. They said,
"Lord, even the demons obey us when
we speak in your name."

18 Jesus replied, "I saw Satan fall
like lightning from heaven. 19 I have
given you authority to walk all over
snakes and scorpions. You will be able
to destroy all the power of the enemy.
Nothing will harm you. 20 But do not
be glad when the evil spirits obey you.
Instead, be glad that your names are
written in heaven."

21 At that time Jesus was full of joy
through the Holy Spirit. He said, "I
praise you, Father. You are Lord of
heaven and earth. You have hidden
these things from wise and educated
people. But you have shown them to
little children. Yes, Father. This is what
you wanted to do.

22 "My Father has given all things
to me. The Father is the only one who
knows who the Son is. And the only
ones who know the Father are the Son
and those to whom the Son chooses to
make the Father known."

23 Then Jesus turned to his disciples.
He said to them in private, "Blessed are
the eyes that see what you see. 24 I tell
you, many prophets and kings wanted
to see what you see. But they didn't see
it. They wanted to hear what you hear.
But they didn't hear it."

The Story of the Good Samaritan

25 One day an authority on the law
stood up to test Jesus. "Teacher," he
asked, "what must I do to receive eternal life?"

26 "What is written in the Law?" Jesus
replied. "How do you understand it?"

27 He answered, " 'Love the Lord
your God with all your heart and with
all your soul. Love him with all your
strength and with all your mind.' *(Deuteronomy 6:5)* And, 'Love your neighbor
as you love yourself.' " *(Leviticus 19:18)*

28 "You have answered correctly," Jesus
replied. "Do that, and you will live."

29 But the man wanted to make himself look good. So he asked Jesus, "And
who is my neighbor?"

30 Jesus replied, "A man was going
down from Jerusalem to Jericho. Robbers attacked him. They stripped off his
clothes and beat him. Then they went
away, leaving him almost dead. 31 A priest
happened to be going down that same
road. When he saw the man, he passed
by on the other side. 32 A Levite also came
by. When he saw the man, he passed by
on the other side too. 33 But a Samaritan
came to the place where the man was.
When he saw the man, he felt sorry for
him. 34 He went to him, poured olive oil
and wine on his wounds and bandaged
them. Then he put the man on his own
donkey. He brought him to an inn and
took care of him. 35 The next day he took
out two silver coins. He gave them to the
owner of the inn. 'Take care of him,' he
said. 'When I return, I will pay you back
for any extra expense you may have.'

36 "Which of the three do you think
was a neighbor to the man who was
attacked by robbers?"

37 The authority on the law replied,
"The one who felt sorry for him."

Jesus told him, "Go and do as he did."

Jesus at the Home of Martha and Mary

38 Jesus and his disciples went on their
way. Jesus came to a village where a
woman named Martha lived. She welcomed him into her home. 39 She had
a sister named Mary. Mary sat at the
Lord's feet listening to what he said.
40 But Martha was busy with all the
things that had to be done. She came
to Jesus and said, "Lord, my sister has
left me to do the work by myself. Don't
you care? Tell her to help me!"

41 "Martha, Martha," the Lord answered. "You are worried and upset
about many things. 42 But few things
are needed. Really, only one thing is
needed. Mary has chosen what is better.
And it will not be taken away from her."

Jesus Teaches About Prayer

11 One day Jesus was praying in a
certain place. When he finished,
one of his disciples spoke to him. "Lord,"
he said, "teach us to pray, just as John
taught his disciples."

2 Jesus said to them, "When you pray,
this is what you should say.

" 'Father,
may your name be honored.
May your kingdom come.
3 Give us each day our daily bread.
4 Forgive us our sins,
as we also forgive everyone who
sins against us.
Keep us from falling into sin when
we are tempted.' "

5 Then Jesus said to them, "Suppose you
have a friend. You go to him at midnight
and say, 'Friend, lend me three loaves of
bread. 6 A friend of mine on a journey has
come to stay with me. I have no food to
give him.' 7 And suppose the one inside
answers, 'Don't bother me. The door is
already locked. My children and I are in
bed. I can't get up and give you anything.'
8 I tell you, that person will not get up.
And he won't give you bread just because
he is your friend. But because you keep
bothering him, he will surely get up. He
will give you as much as you need.

9 "So here is what I say to you. Ask,
and it will be given to you. Search, and
you will find. Knock, and the door will
be opened to you. 10 Everyone who asks
will receive. The one who searches will
find. And the door will be opened to the
one who knocks.

11 "Fathers, suppose your son asks
for a fish. Which of you will give him
a snake instead? 12 Or suppose he asks
for an egg. Which of you will give him
a scorpion? 13 Even though you are evil,
you know how to give good gifts to your
children. How much more will your Father who is in heaven give the Holy
Spirit to those who ask him!"

Jesus and Beelzebul

14 Jesus was driving out a demon. The man who had the demon could not speak. When the demon left, the man began to speak. The crowd was amazed. 15 But some of them said, "Jesus is driving out demons by the power of Beelzebul, the prince of demons." 16 Others tested Jesus by asking for a sign from heaven.

17 Jesus knew what they were thinking. So he said to them, "Any kingdom that fights against itself will be destroyed. A family that is divided against itself will fall. 18 If Satan fights against himself, how can his kingdom stand? I say this because of what you claim. You say I drive out demons by the power of Beelzebul. 19 Suppose I do drive out demons with Beelzebul's help. With whose help do your followers drive them out? So then, they will be your judges. 20 But suppose I drive out demons with the help of God's powerful finger. Then God's kingdom has come upon you.

21 "When a strong man is completely armed and guards his house, what he owns is safe. 22 But when someone stronger attacks, he is overpowered. The attacker takes away the armor the man had trusted in. Then he divides up what he has stolen.

23 "Whoever is not with me is against me. And whoever does not gather with me scatters.

24 "What happens when an evil spirit comes out of a person? It goes through dry areas looking for a place to rest. But it doesn't find it. Then it says, 'I will return to the house I left.' 25 When it arrives there, it finds the house swept clean and put in order. 26 Then the evil spirit goes and takes seven other spirits more evil than itself. They go in and live there. That person is worse off than before."

27 As Jesus was saying these things, a woman in the crowd called out. She shouted, "Blessed is the mother who gave you birth and nursed you."

28 He replied, "Instead, blessed are those who hear God's word and obey it."

The Sign of Jonah

29 As the crowds grew larger, Jesus spoke to them. "The people of today are evil," he said. "They ask for a sign from God. But none will be given except the sign of Jonah. 30 He was a sign from God to the people of Nineveh. In the same way, the Son of Man will be a sign from God to the people of today. 31 The Queen of the South will stand up on judgment day with the people now living. And she will prove that they are guilty. She came from very far away to listen to Solomon's wisdom. And now something more important than Solomon is here. 32 The men of Nineveh will stand up on judgment day with the people now living. And the Ninevites will prove that those people are guilty. The men of Nineveh turned away from their sins when Jonah preached to them. And now something more important than Jonah is here.

The Eye Is the Lamp of the Body

33 "No one lights a lamp and hides it. No one puts it under a bowl. Instead, they put a lamp on its stand. Then those who come in can see the light. 34 Your eye is like a lamp for your body. Suppose your eyes are healthy. Then your whole body also is full of light. But suppose your eyes can't see well. Then your body also is full of darkness. 35 So make sure that the light inside you is not darkness. 36 Suppose your whole body is full of light. And suppose no part of it is dark. Then your body will be full of light. It will be just as when a lamp shines its light on you."

Six Warnings

37 Jesus finished speaking. Then a Pharisee invited him to eat with him. So Jesus went in and took his place at the table. 38 But the Pharisee was surprised. He noticed that Jesus did not wash before the meal.

39 Then the Lord spoke to him. "You Pharisees clean the outside of the cup and dish," he said. "But inside you are full of greed and evil. 40 You foolish people! Didn't the one who made the outside make the inside also? 41 Give freely to poor people to show what is inside you. Then everything will be clean for you.

42 "How terrible it will be for you Pharisees! You give God a tenth of your garden plants, such as mint and rue. But you have forgotten to be fair and to love

God. You should have practiced the last things without failing to do the first.

[43] "How terrible for you Pharisees! You love the most important seats in the synagogues. You love having people greet you with respect in the market.

[44] "How terrible for you! You are like graves that are not marked. People walk over them without knowing it."

[45] An authority on the law spoke to Jesus. He said, "Teacher, when you say things like that, you say bad things about us too."

[46] Jesus replied, "How terrible for you authorities on the law! You put such heavy loads on people that they can hardly carry them. But you yourselves will not lift one finger to help them.

[47] "How terrible for you! You build tombs for the prophets. It was your people of long ago who killed them.
[48] So you show that you agree with what your people did long ago. They killed the prophets, and now you build the prophets' tombs. [49] So God in his wisdom said, 'I will send prophets and apostles to them. They will kill some. And they will try to hurt others.' [50] So the people of today will be punished. They will pay for all the prophets' blood spilled since the world began. [51] I mean from the blood of Abel to the blood of Zechariah. He was killed between the altar and the temple. Yes, I tell you, the people of today will be punished for all these things.

[52] "How terrible for you authorities on the law! You have taken away the key to the door of knowledge. You yourselves have not entered. And you have stood in the way of those who were entering."

[53] When Jesus went outside, the Pharisees and the teachers of the law strongly opposed him. They threw a lot of questions at him. [54] They set traps for him. They wanted to catch him in something he might say.

Jesus Gives Words of Warning and Hope

12 During that time a crowd of many thousands had gathered. There were so many people that they were stepping on one another. Jesus spoke first to his disciples. "Be on your guard against the yeast of the Pharisees," he said. "They just pretend to be godly. [2] Everything that is secret will be brought out into the open. Everything that is hidden will be uncovered.
[3] What you have said in the dark will be heard in the daylight. What you have whispered to someone behind closed doors will be shouted from the rooftops.

[4] "My friends, listen to me. Don't be afraid of those who kill the body but can't do any more than that. [5] I will show you whom you should be afraid of. Be afraid of the one who has the authority to throw you into hell after you have been killed. Yes, I tell you, be afraid of him. [6] Aren't five sparrows sold for two pennies? But God does not forget even one of them. [7] In fact, he even counts every hair on your head! So don't be afraid. You are worth more than many sparrows.

[8] "What about someone who says in front of others that he knows me? I tell you, the Son of Man will say in front of God's angels that he knows that person.
[9] But what about someone who says in front of others that he doesn't know me? I, the Son of Man, will say in front of God's angels that I don't know him.
[10] Everyone who speaks a word against the Son of Man will be forgiven. But anyone who speaks evil things against the Holy Spirit will not be forgiven.

[11] "You will be brought before synagogues, rulers and authorities. But do not worry about how to stand up for yourselves or what to say. [12] The Holy Spirit will teach you at that time what you should say."

The Story of the Rich Fool

[13] Someone in the crowd spoke to Jesus. "Teacher," he said, "tell my brother to divide the family property with me."

[14] Jesus replied, "Friend, who made me a judge or umpire between you?"
[15] Then he said to them, "Watch out! Be on your guard against wanting to have more and more things. Life is not made up of how much a person has."

[16] Then Jesus told them a story. He said, "A certain rich man's land produced a very large crop. [17] He thought to himself, 'What should I do? I don't have any place to store my crops.'

[18] "Then he said, 'This is what I'll do. I will tear down my barns and build bigger ones. I will store my extra grain

in them. [19] I'll say to myself, "You have plenty of grain stored away for many years. Take life easy. Eat, drink and have a good time." '

[20] "But God said to him, 'You foolish man! Tonight I will take your life away from you. Then who will get what you have prepared for yourself?'

[21] "That is how it will be for whoever stores things away for themselves but is not rich in the sight of God."

Do Not Worry

[22] Then Jesus spoke to his disciples. He said, "I tell you, do not worry. Don't worry about your life and what you will eat. And don't worry about your body and what you will wear. [23] There is more to life than eating. There are more important things for the body than clothes. [24] Think about the ravens. They don't plant or gather crops. They don't have any barns at all. But God feeds them. You are worth much more than birds! [25] Can you add even one hour to your life by worrying? [26] You can't do that very little thing. So why worry about the rest?

[27] "Think about how the wild flowers grow. They don't work or make clothing. But here is what I tell you. Not even Solomon in his royal robes was dressed like one of those flowers. [28] If that is how God dresses the wild grass, how much better will he dress you! After all, the grass is here only today. Tomorrow it is thrown into the fire. Your faith is so small! [29] Don't spend time thinking about what you will eat or drink. Don't worry about it. [30] People who are ungodly run after all those things. Your Father knows that you need them. [31] But put God's kingdom first. Then those other things will also be given to you.

[32] "Little flock, do not be afraid. Your Father has been pleased to give you the kingdom. [33] Sell what you own. Give to those who are poor. Provide purses for yourselves that will not wear out. Store up riches in heaven that will never be used up. There, no thief can come near it. There, no moth can destroy it. [34] Your heart will be where your riches are.

Be Ready

[35] "Be dressed and ready to serve. Keep your lamps burning. [36] Be like servants waiting for their master to return from a wedding dinner. When he comes and knocks, they can open the door for him at once. [37] It will be good for those servants whose master finds them ready when he comes. What I'm about to tell you is true. The master will then dress himself so he can serve them. He will have them take their places at the table. And he will come and wait on them. [38] It will be good for those servants whose master finds them ready. It will even be good if he comes in the middle of the night or toward morning. [39] But here is what you must understand. Suppose the owner of the house knew at what hour the robber was coming. He would not have let his house be broken into. [40] You also must be ready. The Son of Man will come at an hour when you don't expect him."

[41] Peter asked, "Lord, are you telling this story to us, or to everyone?"

[42] The Lord answered, "Suppose a master puts one of his servants in charge of his other servants. The servant's job is to give them the food they are to receive at the right time. The master wants a faithful and wise manager for this. [43] It will be good for the servant if the master finds him doing his job when the master returns. [44] What I'm about to tell you is true. The master will put that servant in charge of everything he owns. [45] But suppose the servant says to himself, 'My master is taking a long time to come back.' Suppose that servant begins to beat the other servants, both men and women. Suppose he feeds himself. And suppose he drinks until he gets drunk. [46] The master of that servant will come back on a day the servant doesn't expect him. The master will return at an hour the servant doesn't know. Then the master will cut him to pieces. He will send the servant to the place where unbelievers go.

[47] "Suppose a servant knows the master's wishes. But the servant doesn't get ready and doesn't do what the master wants. Then that servant will receive a heavy beating. [48] But suppose the servant does not know his master's wishes. And suppose the servant does things for which he should be punished. He will receive a lighter beating. Much will be required of everyone who has been given much. Even more will be asked of the person who is supposed to take care of much.

Jesus Will Separate People From One Another

49 "I have come to bring fire on the earth. How I wish the fire had already started! 50 But I have a baptism of suffering to go through. And I must go through it. 51 Do you think I came to bring peace on earth? No, I tell you. I have come to separate people. 52 From now on there will be five members in a family, each one against the other. There will be three against two and two against three. 53 They will be separated. Father will turn against son and son against father. Mother will turn against daughter and daughter against mother. Mother-in-law will turn against daughter-in-law and daughter-in-law against mother-in-law."

Understanding the Meaning of What Is Happening

54 Jesus spoke to the crowd. He said, "You see a cloud rising in the west. Right away you say, 'It's going to rain.' And it does. 55 The south wind blows. So you say, 'It's going to be hot.' And it is. 56 You pretenders! You know how to understand the appearance of the earth and the sky. Why can't you understand the meaning of what is happening right now?

57 "Why don't you judge for yourselves what is right? 58 Suppose someone has a claim against you, and you are on your way to court. Try hard to settle the matter on the way. If you don't, that person may drag you off to the judge. The judge may turn you over to the officer. And the officer may throw you into prison. 59 I tell you, you will not get out until you have paid the very last penny!"

Turn Away From Sin or Die

13 Some people who were there at that time told Jesus about certain Galileans. Pilate had mixed their blood with their sacrifices. 2 Jesus said, "These people from Galilee suffered greatly. Do you think they were worse sinners than all the other Galileans? 3 I tell you, no! But unless you turn away from your sins, you will all die too. 4 Or what about the 18 people in Siloam? They died when the tower fell on them. Do you think they were more guilty than all the others living in Jerusalem? 5 I tell you, no! But unless you turn away from your sins, you will all die too."

6 Then Jesus told a story. "A man had a fig tree," he said. "It was growing in his vineyard. When he went to look for fruit on it, he didn't find any. 7 So he went to the man who took care of the vineyard. He said, 'For three years now I've been coming to look for fruit on this fig tree. But I haven't found any. Cut it down! Why should it use up the soil?'

8 " 'Sir,' the man replied, 'leave it alone for one more year. I'll dig around it and feed it. 9 If it bears fruit next year, fine! If not, then cut it down.' "

Jesus Heals a Disabled Woman on the Sabbath Day

10 Jesus was teaching in one of the synagogues on a Sabbath day. 11 A woman there had been disabled by an evil spirit for 18 years. She was bent over and could not stand up straight. 12 Jesus saw her. He asked her to come to him. He said to her, "Woman, you will no longer be disabled. I am about to set you free." 13 Then he put his hands on her. Right away she stood up straight and praised God.

14 Jesus had healed the woman on the Sabbath day. This made the synagogue leader angry. He told the people, "There are six days for work. So come and be healed on those days. But do not come on the Sabbath day."

15 The Lord answered him, "You pretenders! Doesn't each of you go to the barn and untie your ox or donkey on the Sabbath day? Then don't you lead it out to give it water? 16 This woman is a member of Abraham's family line. But Satan has kept her disabled for 18 long years. Shouldn't she be set free on the Sabbath day from what was keeping her disabled?"

17 When Jesus said this, all those who opposed him were put to shame. But the people were delighted. They loved all the wonderful things he was doing.

The Stories of the Mustard Seed and the Yeast

18 Then Jesus asked, "What is God's kingdom like? What can I compare it to? 19 It is like a mustard seed. Someone took the seed and planted it in a garden.

It grew and became a tree. The birds sat
in its branches."
20 Again he asked, "What can I compare God's kingdom to? 21 It is like yeast
that a woman used. She mixed it into
60 pounds of flour. The yeast worked
its way all through the dough."

The Narrow Door

22 Then Jesus went through the towns
and villages, teaching the people. He
was on his way to Jerusalem. 23 Someone asked him, "Lord, are only a few
people going to be saved?"
He said to them, 24 "Try very hard to
enter through the narrow door. I tell
you, many will try to enter and will not
be able to. 25 The owner of the house will
get up and close the door. Then you will
stand outside knocking and begging.
You will say, 'Sir, open the door for us.'
"But he will answer, 'I don't know you.
And I don't know where you come from.'
26 "Then you will say, 'We ate and
drank with you. You taught in our
streets.'
27 "But he will reply, 'I don't know you.
And I don't know where you come from.
Get away from me, all you who do evil!'
28 "You will weep and grind your teeth
together when you see those who are in
God's kingdom. You will see Abraham,
Isaac and Jacob and all the prophets
there. But you yourselves will be thrown
out. 29 People will come from east and
west and north and south. They will
take their places at the feast in God's
kingdom. 30 Then the last will be first.
And the first will be last."

Jesus' Sadness Over Jerusalem

31 At that time some Pharisees came
to Jesus. They said to him, "Leave this
place. Go somewhere else. Herod wants
to kill you."
32 He replied, "Go and tell that fox,
'I will keep on driving out demons. I
will keep on healing people today and
tomorrow. And on the third day I will
reach my goal.' 33 In any case, I must
keep going today and tomorrow and
the next day. Certainly no prophet can
die outside Jerusalem!
34 "Jerusalem! Jerusalem! You kill the
prophets and throw stones in order to
kill those who are sent to you. Many
times I have wanted to gather your
people together. I have wanted to be
like a hen who gathers her chicks under
her wings. And you would not let me.
35 Look, your house is left empty. I tell
you, you will not see me again until
you say, 'Blessed is the one who comes
in the name of the Lord.' " *(Psalm 118:26)*

Jesus Eats at a Pharisee's House

14 One Sabbath day, Jesus went to
eat in the house of a well-known
Pharisee. While he was there, he was
being carefully watched. 2 In front of
him was a man whose body was badly
swollen. 3 Jesus turned to the Pharisees
and the authorities on the law. He asked
them, "Is it breaking the Law to heal on
the Sabbath day?" 4 But they remained
silent. So Jesus took hold of the man and
healed him. Then he sent him away.
5 He asked them another question. He
said, "Suppose one of you has a child or
an ox that falls into a well on the Sabbath day. Wouldn't you pull it out right
away?" 6 And they had nothing to say.
7 Jesus noticed how the guests picked
the places of honor at the table. So he
told them a story. 8 He said, "Suppose
someone invites you to a wedding feast.
Do not take the place of honor. A person
more important than you may have
been invited. 9 If so, the host who invited
both of you will come to you. He will
say, 'Give this person your seat.' Then
you will be filled with shame. You will
have to take the least important place.
10 But when you are invited, take the
lowest place. Then your host will come
over to you. He will say, 'Friend, move
up to a better place.' Then you will be
honored in front of all the other guests.
11 All those who lift themselves up will
be made humble. And those who make
themselves humble will be lifted up."
12 Then Jesus spoke to his host. "Suppose you give a lunch or a dinner," he
said. "Do not invite your friends, your
brothers or sisters, or your relatives,
or your rich neighbors. If you do, they
may invite you to eat with them. So
you will be paid back. 13 But when you
give a banquet, invite those who are
poor. Also invite those who can't see or
walk. 14 Then you will be blessed. Your
guests can't pay you back. But you will
be paid back when those who are right
with God rise from the dead."

The Story of the Great Banquet

15 One of the people at the table with
Jesus heard him say those things. So he
said to Jesus, "Blessed is the one who
will eat at the feast in God's kingdom."
16 Jesus replied, "A certain man was
preparing a great banquet. He invited
many guests. 17 Then the day of the
banquet arrived. He sent his servant
to those who had been invited. The
servant told them, 'Come. Everything
is ready now.'
18 "But they all had the same idea.
They began to make excuses. The first
one said, 'I have just bought a field. I
have to go and see it. Please excuse me.'
19 "Another said, 'I have just bought
five pairs of oxen. I'm on my way to try
them out. Please excuse me.'
20 "Still another said, 'I just got married, so I can't come.'
21 "The servant came back and reported this to his master. Then the owner of
the house became angry. He ordered
his servant, 'Go out quickly into the
streets and lanes of the town. Bring in
those who are poor. Also bring those
who can't see or walk.'
22 "'Sir,' the servant said, 'what you
ordered has been done. But there is
still room.'
23 "Then the master told his servant,
'Go out to the roads. Go out to the country lanes. Make the people come in. I
want my house to be full. 24 I tell you,
not one of those people who were invited will get a taste of my banquet.'"

The Cost of Being a Disciple

25 Large crowds were traveling with
Jesus. He turned and spoke to them. He
said, 26 "Anyone who comes to me must
hate their father and mother. They
must hate their wife and children. They
must hate their brothers and sisters.
And they must hate even their own life.
Unless they do this, they can't be my
disciple. 27 Whoever doesn't carry their
cross and follow me can't be my disciple.
28 "Suppose one of you wants to build
a tower. Won't you sit down first and
figure out how much it will cost? Then
you will see whether you have enough
money to finish it. 29 Suppose you start
building and are not able to finish. Then
everyone who sees what you have done
will laugh at you. 30 They will say, 'This
person started to build but wasn't able
to finish.'
31 "Or suppose a king is about to go to
war against another king. And suppose
he has 10,000 men, while the other has
20,000 coming against him. Won't he
first sit down and think about whether
he can win? 32 And suppose he decides
he can't win. Then he will send some
men to ask how peace can be made. He
will do this while the other king is still
far away. 33 In the same way, you must
give up everything you have. Those of
you who don't cannot be my disciple.
34 "Salt is good. But suppose it loses
its saltiness. How can it be made salty
again? 35 It is not good for the soil. And
it is not good for the trash pile. It will
be thrown out.
"Whoever has ears should listen."

The Story of the Lost Sheep

15 The tax collectors and sinners
were all gathering around to
hear Jesus. 2 But the Pharisees and the
teachers of the law were whispering
among themselves. They said, "This
man welcomes sinners and eats with
them."
3 Then Jesus told them a story. 4 He
said, "Suppose one of you has 100 sheep
and loses one of them. Won't he leave
the 99 in the open country? Won't he
go and look for the one lost sheep until
he finds it? 5 When he finds it, he will
joyfully put it on his shoulders 6 and
go home. Then he will call his friends
and neighbors together. He will say, 'Be
joyful with me. I have found my lost
sheep.' 7 I tell you, it will be the same
in heaven. There will be great joy when
one sinner turns away from sin. Yes,
there will be more joy than for 99 godly
people who do not need to turn away
from their sins.

The Story of the Lost Coin

8 "Or suppose a woman has ten silver
coins and loses one. Won't she light a
lamp and sweep the house? Won't she
search carefully until she finds the coin?
9 And when she finds it, she will call her
friends and neighbors together. She will
say, 'Be joyful with me. I have found
my lost coin.' 10 I tell you, it is the same
in heaven. There is joy in heaven over
one sinner who turns away from sin."

The Story of the Lost Son

11 Jesus continued, "There was a man
who had two sons. 12 The younger son
spoke to his father. He said, 'Father, give
me my share of the family property.' So
the father divided his property between
his two sons.

13 "Not long after that, the younger
son packed up all he had. Then he left
for a country far away. There he wasted
his money on wild living. 14 He spent
everything he had. Then the whole
country ran low on food. So the son
didn't have what he needed. 15 He went
to work for someone who lived in that
country. That person sent the son to
the fields to feed the pigs. 16 The son
wanted to fill his stomach with the food
the pigs were eating. But no one gave
him anything.

17 "Then he began to think clearly
again. He said, 'How many of my father's hired servants have more than
enough food! But here I am dying from
hunger! 18 I will get up and go back to
my father. I will say to him, "Father, I
have sinned against heaven. And I have
sinned against you. 19 I am no longer fit
to be called your son. Make me like one
of your hired servants." ' 20 So he got up
and went to his father.

"While the son was still a long way off, his father saw him. He was filled with tender love for his son. He ran to him. He threw his arms around him and kissed him.

21 "The son said to him, 'Father, I have
sinned against heaven and against you.
I am no longer fit to be called your son.'

22 "But the father said to his servants,
'Quick! Bring the best robe and put it on
him. Put a ring on his finger and sandals
on his feet. 23 Bring the fattest calf and
kill it. Let's have a feast and celebrate.
24 This son of mine was dead. And now
he is alive again. He was lost. And now
he is found.' So they began to celebrate.

25 "The older son was in the field.
When he came near the house, he heard
music and dancing. 26 So he called one
of the servants. He asked him what
was going on. 27 'Your brother has come
home,' the servant replied. 'Your father
has killed the fattest calf. He has done
this because your brother is back safe
and sound.'

28 "The older brother became angry.
He refused to go in. So his father went
out and begged him. 29 But he answered
his father, 'Look! All these years I've
worked like a slave for you. I have always obeyed your orders. You never
gave me even a young goat so I could
celebrate with my friends. 30 But this
son of yours wasted your money with
some prostitutes. Now he comes home.
And for him you kill the fattest calf!'

31 " 'My son,' the father said, 'you are
always with me. Everything I have is
yours. 32 But we had to celebrate and
be glad. This brother of yours was dead.
And now he is alive again. He was lost.
And now he is found.' "

The Story of the Clever Manager

16 Jesus told his disciples another
story. He said, "There was a rich
man who had a manager. Some said
that the manager was wasting what the
rich man owned. 2 So the rich man told
him to come in. He asked him, 'What is
this I hear about you? Tell me exactly
how you have handled what I own. You
can't be my manager any longer.'

3 "The manager said to himself, 'What
will I do now? My master is taking away
my job. I'm not strong enough to dig.
And I'm too ashamed to beg. 4 I know
what I'm going to do. I'll do something
so that when I lose my job here, people
will welcome me into their houses.'

5 "So he called in each person who
owed his master something. He asked
the first one, 'How much do you owe
my master?'

6 " 'I owe 900 gallons of olive oil,' he
replied.

"The manager told him, 'Take your bill. Sit down quickly and change it to 450 gallons.'

7 "Then he asked the second one, 'And
how much do you owe?'

" 'I owe 1,000 bushels of wheat,' he replied.

"The manager told him, 'Take your bill and change it to 800 bushels.'

8 "The manager had not been honest.
But the master praised him for being
clever. The people of this world are
clever in dealing with those who are
like themselves. They are more clever
than God's people. 9 I tell you, use the
riches of this world to help others. In

that way, you will make friends for yourselves. Then when your riches are gone, you will be welcomed into your eternal home in heaven.

10 "Suppose you can be trusted with something very little. Then you can also be trusted with something very large. But suppose you are not honest with something very little. Then you will also not be honest with something very large. 11 Suppose you have not been worthy of trust in handling worldly wealth. Then who will trust you with true riches? 12 Suppose you have not been worthy of trust in handling someone else's property. Then who will give you property of your own?

13 "No one can serve two masters at the same time. Either you will hate one of them and love the other. Or you will be faithful to one and dislike the other. You can't serve God and money at the same time."

14 The Pharisees loved money. They heard all that Jesus said and made fun of him. 15 Jesus said to them, "You try to make yourselves look good in the eyes of other people. But God knows your hearts. What people think is worth a lot is hated by God.

More Teachings

16 "The teachings of the Law and the Prophets were preached until John the Baptist came. Since then, the good news of God's kingdom is being preached. And everyone is trying very hard to enter it. 17 It is easier for heaven and earth to disappear than for the smallest part of a letter to drop out of the Law.

18 "Anyone who divorces his wife and marries another woman commits adultery. Also, the man who marries a divorced woman commits adultery.

The Rich Man and Lazarus

19 "Once there was a rich man. He was dressed in purple cloth and fine linen. He lived an easy life every day. 20 A man named Lazarus was placed at his gate. Lazarus was a beggar. His body was covered with sores. 21 Even dogs came and licked his sores. All he wanted was to eat what fell from the rich man's table.

22 "The time came when the beggar died. The angels carried him to Abraham's side. The rich man also died and was buried. 23 In the place of the dead, the rich man was suffering terribly. He looked up and saw Abraham far away. Lazarus was by his side. 24 So the rich man called out, 'Father Abraham! Have pity on me! Send Lazarus to dip the tip of his finger in water. Then he can cool my tongue with it. I am in terrible pain in this fire.'

25 "But Abraham replied, 'Son, remember what happened in your lifetime. You received your good things. Lazarus received bad things. Now he is comforted here, and you are in terrible pain. 26 Besides, a wide space has been placed between us and you. So those who want to go from here to you can't go. And no one can cross over from there to us.'

27 "The rich man answered, 'Then I beg you, father Abraham. Send Lazarus to my family. 28 I have five brothers. Let Lazarus warn them. Then they will not come to this place of terrible suffering.'

29 "Abraham replied, 'They have the teachings of Moses and the Prophets. Let your brothers listen to them.'

30 " 'No, father Abraham,' he said. 'But if someone from the dead goes to them, they will turn away from their sins.'

31 "Abraham said to him, 'They do not listen to Moses and the Prophets. So they will not be convinced even if someone rises from the dead.' "

Sin, Faith and Duty

17 Jesus spoke to his disciples. "Things that make people sin are sure to come," he said. "But how terrible it will be for anyone who causes those things to come! 2 Suppose people lead one of these little ones to sin. It would be better for those people to be thrown into the sea with a millstone tied around their neck. 3 So watch what you do.

"If your brother or sister sins against you, tell them they are wrong. Then if they turn away from their sins, forgive them. 4 Suppose they sin against you seven times in one day. And suppose they come back to you each time and say, 'I'm sorry.' You must forgive them."

5 The apostles said to the Lord, "Give us more faith!"

6 He replied, "Suppose you have faith as small as a mustard seed. Then you can say to this mulberry tree, 'Be pulled up. Be planted in the sea.' And it will obey you.

7 “Suppose one of you has a servant
plowing or looking after the sheep. And
suppose the servant came in from the
field. Will you say to him, ‘Come along
now and sit down to eat’? 8 No. Instead,
you will say, ‘Prepare my supper. Get
yourself ready. Wait on me while I eat
and drink. Then after that you can eat
and drink.’ 9 Will you thank the servant
because he did what he was told to do?
10 It’s the same with you. Suppose you
have done everything you were told
to do. Then you should say, ‘We are
not worthy to serve you. We have only
done our duty.’ ”

Jesus Heals Ten Men Who Have a Skin Disease

11 Jesus was on his way to Jerusalem.
He traveled along the border between
Samaria and Galilee. 12 As he was going
into a village, ten men met him. They
had a skin disease. They were standing
close by. 13 And they called out in a loud
voice, “Jesus! Master! Have pity on us!”

14 Jesus saw them and said, “Go. Show
yourselves to the priests.” While they
were on the way, they were healed.

15 When one of them saw that he was
healed, he came back. He praised God
in a loud voice. 16 He threw himself at
Jesus’ feet and thanked him. The man
was a Samaritan.

17 Jesus asked, “Weren’t all ten healed?
Where are the other nine? 18 Didn’t anyone else return and give praise to God
except this outsider?” 19 Then Jesus said
to him, “Get up and go. Your faith has
healed you.”

The Coming of God’s Kingdom

20 Once the Pharisees asked Jesus
when God’s kingdom would come. He
replied, “The coming of God’s kingdom
is not something you can see. 21 People
will not say, ‘Here it is.’ Or, ‘There it is.’
That’s because God’s kingdom is among
you.”

22 Then Jesus spoke to his disciples.
“The time is coming,” he said, “when
you will long to see one of the days of
the Son of Man. But you won’t see it.
23 People will tell you, ‘There he is!’ Or,
‘Here he is!’ Don’t go running off after
them. 24 When the Son of Man comes,
he will be like the lightning. It flashes
and lights up the sky from one end to
the other. 25 But first the Son of Man
must suffer many things. He will not be
accepted by the people of today.

26 “Remember how it was in the days
of Noah. It will be the same when the
Son of Man comes. 27 People were eating
and drinking. They were getting married. They were giving their daughters
to be married. They did all those things
right up to the day Noah entered the
ark. Then the flood came and destroyed
them all.

28 “It was the same in the days of Lot.
People were eating and drinking. They
were buying and selling. They were
planting and building. 29 But on the day
Lot left Sodom, fire and sulfur rained
down from heaven. And all the people
were destroyed.

30 “It will be just like that on the day
the Son of Man is shown to the world.
31 Suppose someone is on the housetop
on that day. And suppose what they
own is inside the house. They should not
go down to get what they own. No one
in the field should go back for anything
either. 32 Remember Lot’s wife! 33 Whoever tries to keep their life will lose it.
Whoever loses their life will keep it. 34 I
tell you, on that night two people will
be in one bed. One person will be taken
and the other left. 35-36 Two women will
be grinding grain together. One will be
taken and the other left.”

37 “Where, Lord?” his disciples asked.

He replied, “The vultures will gather
where there is a dead body.”

The Story of the Widow Who Would Not Give Up

18 Jesus told his disciples a story. He
wanted to show them that they
should always pray and not give up.
2 He said, “In a certain town there was
a judge. He didn’t have any respect for
God or care about what people thought.
3 A widow lived in that town. She came
to the judge again and again. She kept
begging him, ‘Make things right for me.
Someone is treating me badly.’

4 “For some time the judge refused.
But finally he said to himself, ‘I don’t
have any respect for God. I don’t care
about what people think. 5 But this
widow keeps bothering me. So I will
see that things are made right for her.
If I don’t, she will someday come and
attack me!’ ”

[6]The Lord said, "Listen to what the unfair judge says. [7]God's chosen people cry out to him day and night. Won't he make things right for them? Will he keep putting them off? [8]I tell you, God will see that things are made right for them. He will make sure it happens quickly. But when the Son of Man comes, will he find people on earth who have faith?"

The Story of the Pharisee and the Tax Collector

[9]Jesus told a story to some people who were sure they were right with God. They looked down on everyone else. [10]He said to them, "Two men went up to the temple to pray. One was a Pharisee. The other was a tax collector. [11]The Pharisee stood by himself and prayed. 'God, I thank you that I am not like other people,' he said. 'I am not like robbers or those who do other evil things. I am not like those who commit adultery. I am not even like this tax collector. [12]I fast twice a week. And I give a tenth of all I get.'

[13]"But the tax collector stood farther away than the Pharisee. He would not even look up to heaven. He brought his hand to his heart and prayed. He said, 'God, have mercy on me. I am a sinner.'

[14]"I tell you, the tax collector went home accepted by God. But not the Pharisee. All those who lift themselves up will be made humble. And those who make themselves humble will be lifted up."

Little Children Are Brought to Jesus

[15]People were also bringing babies to Jesus. They wanted him to place his hands on the babies. When the disciples saw this, they told the people to stop. [16]But Jesus asked the children to come to him. "Let the little children come to me," he said. "Don't keep them away. God's kingdom belongs to people like them. [17]What I'm about to tell you is true. Anyone who will not receive God's kingdom like a little child will never enter it."

Rich People and the Kingdom of God

[18]A certain ruler asked Jesus a question. "Good teacher," he said, "what must I do to receive eternal life?"

[19]"Why do you call me good?" Jesus answered. "No one is good except God. [20]You know what the commandments say. 'Do not commit adultery. Do not commit murder. Do not steal. Do not be a false witness. Honor your father and mother.' " *(Exodus 20:12–16; Deuteronomy 5:16–20)*

[21]"I have obeyed all those commandments since I was a boy," the ruler said.

[22]When Jesus heard this, he said to him, "You are still missing one thing. Sell everything you have. Give the money to those who are poor. You will have treasure in heaven. Then come and follow me."

[23]When the ruler heard this, he became very sad. He was very rich. [24]Jesus looked at him. Then he said, "How hard it is for rich people to enter God's kingdom! [25]Is it hard for a camel to go through the eye of a needle? It is even harder for someone who is rich to enter God's kingdom!"

[26]Those who heard this asked, "Then who can be saved?"

[27]Jesus replied, "Things that are impossible with people are possible with God."

[28]Peter said to him, "We have left everything we had in order to follow you!"

[29]"What I'm about to tell you is true," Jesus said to them. "Has anyone left home or wife or husband or brothers or sisters or parents or children for God's kingdom? [30]They will receive many times as much in this world. In the world to come they will receive eternal life."

Jesus Speaks a Third Time About His Coming Death

[31]Jesus took the 12 disciples to one side. He told them, "We are going up to Jerusalem. Everything that the prophets wrote about the Son of Man will come true. [32]He will be handed over to the Gentiles. They will make fun of him. They will laugh at him and spit on him. [33]They will whip him and kill him. On the third day, he will rise from the dead!"

[34]The disciples did not understand any of this. Its meaning was hidden from them. So they didn't know what Jesus was talking about.

A Blind Beggar Receives His Sight

[35]Jesus was approaching Jericho. A blind man was sitting by the side of the

road begging. 36 The blind man heard the crowd going by. He asked what was happening. 37 They told him, "Jesus of Nazareth is passing by."

38 So the blind man called out, "Jesus! Son of David! Have mercy on me!"

39 Those who led the way commanded him to stop. They told him to be quiet. But he shouted even louder, "Son of David! Have mercy on me!"

40 Jesus stopped and ordered the man to be brought to him. When the man came near, Jesus spoke to him. 41 "What do you want me to do for you?" Jesus asked.

"Lord, I want to be able to see," the blind man replied.

42 Jesus said to him, "Receive your sight. Your faith has healed you." 43 Right away he could see. He followed Jesus, praising God. When all the people saw it, they also praised God.

Zacchaeus the Tax Collector

19 Jesus entered Jericho and was passing through. 2 A man named Zacchaeus lived there. He was a chief tax collector and was very rich. 3 Zacchaeus wanted to see who Jesus was. But he was a short man. He could not see Jesus because of the crowd. 4 So he ran ahead and climbed a sycamore-fig tree. He wanted to see Jesus, who was coming that way.

5 Jesus reached the spot where Zacchaeus was. He looked up and said, "Zacchaeus, come down at once. I must stay at your house today." 6 So Zacchaeus came down at once and welcomed him gladly.

7 All the people saw this. They began to whisper among themselves. They said, "Jesus has gone to be the guest of a sinner."

8 But Zacchaeus stood up. He said, "Look, Lord! Here and now I give half of what I own to those who are poor. And if I have cheated anybody out of anything, I will pay it back. I will pay back four times the amount I took."

9 Jesus said to Zacchaeus, "Today salvation has come to your house. You are a member of Abraham's family line. 10 The Son of Man came to look for the lost and save them."

The Story of Three Slaves

11 While the people were listening to these things, Jesus told them a story. He was near Jerusalem. The people thought that God's kingdom was going to appear right away. 12 Jesus said, "A man from an important family went to a country far away. He went there to be made king and then return home. 13 So he sent for ten of his slaves. He gave them each about three months' pay. 'Put this money to work until I come back,' he said.

14 "But those he ruled over hated him. They sent some messengers after him. They were sent to say, 'We don't want this man to be our king.'

15 "But he was made king and returned home. Then he sent for the slaves he had given the money to. He wanted to find out what they had earned with it.

16 "The first one came to him. He said, 'Sir, your money has earned ten times as much.'

17 " 'You have done well, my good slave!' his master replied. 'You have been faithful in a very small matter. So I will put you in charge of ten towns.'

18 "The second slave came to his master. He said, 'Sir, your money has earned five times as much.'

19 "His master answered, 'I will put you in charge of five towns.'

20 "Then another slave came. He said, 'Sir, here is your money. I have kept it hidden in a piece of cloth. 21 I was afraid of you. You are a hard man. You take out what you did not put in. You harvest what you did not plant.'

22 "His master replied, 'I will judge you by your own words, you evil slave! So you knew that I am a hard man? You knew that I take out what I did not put in? You knew that I harvest what I did not plant? 23 Then why didn't you put my money in the bank? When I came back, I could have collected it with interest.'

24 "Then he said to those standing by, 'Take his money away from him. Give it to the one who has ten times as much.'

25 " 'Sir,' they said, 'he already has ten times as much!'

26 "He replied, 'I tell you that everyone who has will be given more. But here is what will happen to anyone who has nothing. Even what they have will be taken away from them. 27 And what about my enemies who did not want me to be king over them? Bring them here! Kill them in front of me!' "

Jesus Comes to Jerusalem as King

28 After Jesus had said this, he went on ahead. He was going up to Jerusalem. 29 He approached Bethphage and Bethany. The hill there was called the Mount of Olives. Jesus sent out two of his disciples. He said to them, 30 "Go to the village ahead of you. As soon as you get there, you will find a donkey's colt tied up. No one has ever ridden it. Untie it and bring it here. 31 Someone may ask you, 'Why are you untying it?' If so, say, 'The Lord needs it.'"

32 Those who were sent ahead went and found the young donkey. It was there just as Jesus had told them. 33 They were untying the colt when its owners came. The owners asked them, "Why are you untying the colt?"

34 They replied, "The Lord needs it."

35 Then the disciples brought the colt to Jesus. They threw their coats on the young donkey and put Jesus on it. 36 As he went along, people spread their coats on the road.

37 Jesus came near the place where the road goes down the Mount of Olives. There the whole crowd of disciples began to praise God with joy. In loud voices they praised him for all the miracles they had seen. They shouted,

38 "Blessed is the king who comes in
the name of the Lord!"
(Psalm 118:26)

"May there be peace and glory in
the highest heaven!"

39 Some of the Pharisees in the crowd spoke to Jesus. "Teacher," they said, "tell your disciples to stop!"

40 "I tell you," he replied, "if they keep quiet, the stones will cry out."

41 He approached Jerusalem. When he saw the city, he began to weep. 42 He said, "I wish you had known today what would bring you peace! But now it is hidden from your eyes. 43 The days will come when your enemies will arrive. They will build a wall of dirt up against your city. They will surround you and close you in on every side. 44 You didn't recognize the time when God came to you. So your enemies will smash you to the ground. They will destroy you and all the people inside your walls. They will not leave one stone on top of another."

Jesus Clears Out the Temple

45 Then Jesus entered the temple courtyard. He began to drive out those who were selling there. 46 He told them, "It is written that the Lord said, 'My house will be a house where people can pray.' *(Isaiah 56:7)* But you have made it a 'den for robbers.'" *(Jeremiah 7:11)*

47 Every day Jesus was teaching at the temple. But the chief priests and the teachers of the law were trying to kill him. So were the leaders among the people. 48 But they couldn't find any way to do it. All the people were paying close attention to his words.

The Authority of Jesus Is Questioned

20 One day Jesus was teaching the people in the temple courtyard. He was announcing the good news to them. The chief priests and the teachers of the law came up to him. The elders came with them. 2 "Tell us by what authority you are doing these things," they all said. "Who gave you this authority?"

3 Jesus replied, "I will also ask you a question. Tell me, 4 was John's baptism from heaven? Or did it come from people?"

5 They talked to one another about it. They said, "If we say, 'From heaven,' he will ask, 'Why didn't you believe him?' 6 But if we say, 'From people,' all the people will throw stones at us and kill us. They believe that John was a prophet."

7 So they answered Jesus, "We don't know where John's baptism came from."

8 Jesus said, "Then I won't tell you by what authority I am doing these things either."

The Story of the Renters

9 Jesus went on to tell the people a story. "A man planted a vineyard," he said. "He rented it out to some farmers. Then he went away for a long time. 10 At harvest time he sent a slave to the renters. They were supposed to give him some of the fruit of the vineyard. But the renters beat the slave. Then they sent him away with nothing. 11 So the man sent another slave. They beat that one and treated him badly. They also sent him away with nothing. 12 The man sent a third slave. The renters wounded him and threw him out.

13 "Then the owner of the vineyard
said, 'What should I do? I have a son,
and I love him. I will send him. Maybe
they will respect him.'
14 "But when the renters saw the son,
they talked the matter over. 'This is the
one who will receive all the owner's
property someday,' they said. 'Let's kill
him. Then everything will be ours.' 15 So
they threw him out of the vineyard. And
they killed him.
"What will the owner of the vineyard
do to the renters? 16 He will come and
kill them. He will give the vineyard to
others."
When the people heard this, they
said, "We hope this never happens!"
17 Jesus looked right at them and
said, "Here is something I want you to
explain the meaning of. It is written,

" 'The stone the builders didn't
accept
has become the most important
stone of all.' *(Psalm 118:22)*

18 Everyone who falls on that stone will
be broken to pieces. But the stone will
crush anyone it falls on."
19 The teachers of the law and the
chief priests looked for a way to arrest
Jesus at once. They knew he had told
that story against them. But they were
afraid of the people.

Is It Right to Pay the Royal Tax to Caesar?

20 The religious leaders sent spies to
keep a close watch on Jesus. The spies
pretended to be sincere. They hoped
they could trap Jesus with something
he would say. Then they could hand
him over to the power and authority of
the governor. 21 So the spies questioned
Jesus. "Teacher," they said, "we know
that you speak and teach what is right.
We know you don't favor one person
over another. You teach the way of God
truthfully. 22 Is it right for us to pay
taxes to Caesar or not?"
23 Jesus saw they were trying to trick
him. So he said to them, 24 "Show me a
silver coin. Whose picture and words
are on it?"
"Caesar's," they replied.
25 He said to them, "Then give back
to Caesar what belongs to Caesar. And
give back to God what belongs to God."
26 They were not able to trap him with
what he had said there in front of all
the people. Amazed by his answer, they
became silent.

Marriage When the Dead Rise

27 The Sadducees do not believe that
people rise from the dead. Some of
them came to Jesus with a question.
28 "Teacher," they said, "Moses wrote for
us about a man's brother who dies. Suppose the brother leaves a wife but has
no children. Then the man must marry
the widow. He must provide children
to carry on his dead brother's name.
29 There were seven brothers. The first
one married a woman. He died without
leaving any children. 30 The second one
married her. 31 And then the third one
married her. One after another, the
seven brothers married her. They all
died. None left any children. 32 Finally,
the woman died too. 33 Now then, when
the dead rise, whose wife will she be? All
seven brothers were married to her."
34 Jesus replied, "People in this world
get married. And their parents give
them to be married. 35 But it will not
be like that when the dead rise. Those
who are considered worthy to take part
in the world to come won't get married.
And their parents won't give them to
be married. 36 They can't die anymore.
They are like the angels. They are God's
children. They will be given a new form
of life when the dead rise. 37 Remember the story of Moses and the burning
bush. Even Moses showed that the dead
rise. The Lord said to him, 'I am the God
of Abraham. I am the God of Isaac. And I
am the God of Jacob.' *(Exodus 3:6)* 38 He is
not the God of the dead. He is the God of
the living. In his eyes, everyone is alive."
39 Some of the teachers of the law replied, "You have spoken well, teacher!"
40 And no one dared to ask him any
more questions.

Whose Son Is the Messiah?

41 Jesus said to them, "Why do people
say that the Messiah is the son of David?
42 David himself says in the Book of
Psalms,

" 'The Lord said to my Lord,
"Sit at my right hand
43 until I put your enemies
under your control." ' *(Psalm 110:1)*

44 David calls him 'Lord.' So how can he
be David's son?"

Warning Against the Teachers of the Law

45 All the people were listening. Jesus
said to his disciples, 46 "Watch out for
the teachers of the law. They like to
walk around in long robes. They love to
be greeted with respect in the market.
They love to have the most important
seats in the synagogues. They also love
to have the places of honor at banquets.
47 They take over the houses of widows.
They say long prayers to show off. God
will punish these men very much."

The Widow's Offering

21 As Jesus looked up, he saw rich
people putting their gifts into the
temple offering boxes. 2 He also saw a
poor widow put in two very small copper
coins. 3 "What I'm about to tell you is
true," Jesus said. "That poor widow has
put in more than all the others. 4 All
these other people gave a lot because
they are rich. But even though she is
poor, she put in everything. She had
nothing left to live on."

When the Temple Will Be Destroyed and the Signs of the End

5 Some of Jesus' disciples were talking
about the temple. They spoke about
how it was decorated with beautiful
stones and with gifts that honored God.
But Jesus asked, 6 "Do you see all this?
The time will come when not one stone
will be left on top of another. Every
stone will be thrown down."

7 "Teacher," they asked, "when will
these things happen? And what will
be the sign that they are about to take
place?"

8 Jesus replied, "Keep watch! Be careful that you are not fooled. Many will
come in my name. They will claim, 'I
am he!' And they will say, 'The time is
near!' Do not follow them. 9 Do not be
afraid when you hear about wars and
about fighting against rulers. Those
things must happen first. But the end
will not come right away."

10 Then Jesus said to them, "Nation
will fight against nation. Kingdom will
fight against kingdom. 11 In many places there will be powerful earthquakes.
People will go hungry. There will be
terrible sicknesses. Things will happen
that will make people afraid. There will
be great and miraculous signs from
heaven.

12 "But before all this, people will
arrest you and treat you badly. They
will hand you over to synagogues and
put you in prison. You will be brought
to kings and governors. All this will
happen to you because of my name.
13 And so you will be witnesses about me.
14 But make up your mind not to worry
ahead of time about how to stand up
for yourselves. 15 I will give you words of
wisdom. None of your enemies will be
able to withstand them or prove them
wrong. 16 Even your parents, brothers,
sisters, relatives and friends will hand
you over to the authorities. The authorities will put some of you to death.
17 Everyone will hate you because of me.
18 But not a hair on your head will be
harmed. 19 Remain strong in the faith,
and you will receive eternal life.

20 "A time is coming when you will see
armies surround Jerusalem. Then you
will know that it will soon be destroyed.
21 Those who are in Judea should then
escape to the mountains. Those in the
city should get out. Those in the country
should not enter the city. 22 This is the
time when God will punish Jerusalem.
Everything will come true, just as it has
been written. 23 How awful it will be in
those days for pregnant women! How
awful for nursing mothers! There will
be terrible suffering in the land. There
will be great anger against those people. 24 Some will be killed by the sword.
Others will be taken as prisoners to all
the nations. Jerusalem will be taken
over by Gentiles until the times of the
Gentiles come to an end.

25 "There will be signs in the sun,
moon and stars. The nations of the
earth will be in terrible pain. They will
be puzzled by the roaring and tossing
of the sea. 26 Terror will make people
faint. They will be worried about what
is happening in the world. The sun,
moon and stars will be shaken from
their places. 27 At that time people will
see the Son of Man coming in a cloud. He
will come with power and great glory.
28 When these things begin to take place,
stand up. Hold your head up with joy

and hope. The time when you will be set free will be very close."

29 Jesus told them a story. "Look at the fig tree and all the trees," he said. 30 "When you see leaves appear on the branches, you know that summer is near. 31 In the same way, when you see these things happening, you will know that God's kingdom is near.

32 "What I'm about to tell you is true. The people living now will certainly not pass away until all these things have happened. 33 Heaven and earth will pass away. But my words will never pass away.

34 "Be careful. If you aren't, your hearts will be loaded down with wasteful living, drunkenness and the worries of life. Then the day the Son of Man returns will close on you like a trap. It will happen suddenly. 35 That day will come on every person who lives on the whole earth. 36 Always keep watching. Pray that you will be able to escape all that is about to happen. Also, pray that you will not be judged guilty when the Son of Man comes."

37 Each day Jesus taught at the temple. And each evening he went to spend the night on the hill called the Mount of Olives. 38 All the people came to the temple early in the morning. They wanted to hear Jesus speak.

Judas Agrees to Hand Jesus Over

22 The Feast of Unleavened Bread, called the Passover, was near. 2 The chief priests and the teachers of the law were looking for a way to get rid of Jesus. They were afraid of the people. 3 Then Satan entered Judas, who was called Iscariot. Judas was one of the 12 disciples. 4 He went to the chief priests and the officers of the temple guard. He talked with them about how he could hand Jesus over to them. 5 They were delighted and agreed to give him money. 6 Judas accepted their offer. He watched for the right time to hand Jesus over to them. He wanted to do it when no crowd was around.

The Last Supper

7 Then the day of Unleavened Bread came. That was the time the Passover lamb had to be sacrificed. 8 Jesus sent Peter and John on ahead. "Go," he told them. "Prepare for us to eat the Passover meal."

9 "Where do you want us to prepare for it?" they asked.

10 Jesus replied, "When you enter the city, a man carrying a jar of water will meet you. Follow him to the house he enters. 11 Then say to the owner of the house, 'The Teacher asks, "Where is the guest room? Where can I eat the Passover meal with my disciples?"' 12 He will show you a large upstairs room with furniture already in it. Prepare for us to eat there."

13 Peter and John left. They found things just as Jesus had told them. So they prepared the Passover meal.

14 When the hour came, Jesus and his apostles took their places at the table. 15 He said to them, "I have really looked forward to eating this Passover meal with you. I wanted to do this before I suffer. 16 I tell you, I will not eat the Passover meal again until it is celebrated in God's kingdom."

17 After Jesus took the cup, he gave thanks. He said, "Take this cup and share it among yourselves. 18 I tell you, I will not drink wine with you again until God's kingdom comes."

19 Then Jesus took bread. He gave thanks and broke it. He handed it to them and said, "This is my body. It is given for you. Every time you eat it, do this in memory of me."

20 In the same way, after the supper he took the cup. He said, "This cup is the new covenant in my blood. It is poured out for you. 21 But someone here is going to hand me over to my enemies. His hand is with mine on the table. 22 The Son of Man will go to his death, just as God has already decided. But how terrible it will be for the one who hands him over!" 23 The apostles began to ask one another about this. They wondered which one of them would do it.

24 They also started to argue. They disagreed about which of them was thought to be the most important person. 25 Jesus said to them, "The kings of the Gentiles hold power over their people. And those who order them around call themselves Protectors. 26 But you must not be like that. Instead, the most important among you should be like the youngest. The one who rules should be like the one who serves. 27 Who is more important? Is it the one at the

table, or the one who serves? Isn't it the
one who is at the table? But I am among
you as one who serves. 28 You have stood
by me during my troubles. 29 And I give
you a kingdom, just as my Father gave
me a kingdom. 30 Then you will eat and
drink at my table in my kingdom. And
you will sit on thrones, judging the 12
tribes of Israel.

31 "Simon, Simon! Satan has asked
to sift all of you disciples like wheat.
32 But I have prayed for you, Simon.
I have prayed that your faith will not
fail. When you have turned back, help
your brothers to be strong."

33 But Simon replied, "Lord, I am
ready to go with you to prison and to
death."

34 Jesus answered, "I tell you, Peter,
you will say three times that you don't
know me. And you will do it before the
rooster crows today."

35 Then Jesus asked the disciples, "Did
you need anything when I sent you
without a purse, bag or sandals?"

"Nothing," they answered.

36 He said to them, "But now if you
have a purse, take it. And also take a
bag. If you don't have a sword, sell your
coat and buy one. 37 It is written, 'He was
counted among those who had committed crimes.' *(Isaiah 53:12)* I tell you that
what is written about me must come
true. Yes, it is already coming true."

38 The disciples said, "See, Lord, here
are two swords."

"Two swords are enough!" he replied.

Jesus Prays on the Mount of Olives

39 Jesus went out as usual to the
Mount of Olives. His disciples followed
him. 40 When they reached the place,
Jesus spoke. "Pray that you won't fall
into sin when you are tempted," he said
to them. 41 Then he went a short distance
away from them. There he got down
on his knees and prayed. 42 He said,
"Father, if you are willing, take this
cup of suffering away from me. But do
what you want, not what I want." 43 An
angel from heaven appeared to Jesus
and gave him strength. 44 Because he
was very sad and troubled, he prayed
even harder. His sweat was like drops
of blood falling to the ground.

45 After that, he got up from prayer
and went back to the disciples. He found
them sleeping. They were worn out because they were very sad. 46 "Why are
you sleeping?" he asked them. "Get up!
Pray that you won't fall into sin when
you are tempted."

Jesus Is Arrested

47 While Jesus was still speaking, a
crowd came up. The man named Judas
was leading them. He was one of the 12
disciples. Judas approached Jesus to
kiss him. 48 But Jesus asked him, "Judas,
are you handing over the Son of Man
with a kiss?"

49 Jesus' followers saw what was going
to happen. So they said, "Lord, should
we use our swords against them?" 50 One
of them struck the slave of the high
priest and cut off his right ear.

51 But Jesus answered, "Stop this!" And
he touched the man's ear and healed
him.

52 Then Jesus spoke to the chief priests,
the officers of the temple guard, and the
elders. They had all come for him. "Am
I leading a band of armed men against
you?" he asked. "Do you have to come
with swords and clubs? 53 Every day I
was with you in the temple courtyard.
And you didn't lay a hand on me. But
this is your hour. This is when darkness
rules."

Peter Says He Does Not Know Jesus

54 Then the men arrested Jesus and
led him away. They took him into the
high priest's house. Peter followed from
far away. 55 Some people there started a
fire in the middle of the courtyard. Then
they sat down together. Peter sat down
with them. 56 A female servant saw him
sitting there in the firelight. She looked
closely at him. Then she said, "This man
was with Jesus."

57 But Peter said he had not been with
him. "Woman, I don't know him," he
said.

58 A little later someone else saw Peter.
"You also are one of them," he said.

"No," Peter replied. "I'm not!"

59 About an hour later, another person
spoke up. "This fellow must have been
with Jesus," he said. "He is from Galilee."

60 Peter replied, "Man, I don't know
what you're talking about!" Just as he
was speaking, the rooster crowed. 61 The
Lord turned and looked right at Peter.

Then Peter remembered what the Lord
had spoken to him. "The rooster will
crow today," Jesus had said. "Before it
does, you will say three times that you
don't know me." 62 Peter went outside.
He broke down and cried.

The Guards Make Fun of Jesus

63 There were men guarding Jesus.
They began laughing at him and beating him. 64 They blindfolded him. They
said, "Prophesy! Who hit you?" 65 They
also said many other things to make
fun of him.

Jesus Is Brought to Pilate and Herod

66 At dawn the elders of the people
met together. These included the chief
priests and the teachers of the law. Jesus
was led to them. 67 "If you are the Messiah," they said, "tell us."

Jesus answered, "If I tell you, you will
not believe me. 68 And if I asked you,
you would not answer. 69 But from now
on, the Son of Man will be seated at the
right hand of the mighty God."

70 They all asked, "Are you the Son
of God then?"

He replied, "You say that I am."

71 Then they said, "Why do we need
any more witnesses? We have heard it
from his own lips."

23 Then the whole group got up
and led Jesus off to Pilate. 2 They
began to bring charges against Jesus.
They said, "We have found this man
misleading our people. He is against
paying taxes to Caesar. And he claims
to be Messiah, a king."

3 So Pilate asked Jesus, "Are you the
king of the Jews?"

"You have said so," Jesus replied.

4 Then Pilate spoke to the chief priests
and the crowd. He announced, "I find
no basis for a charge against this man."

5 But they kept it up. They said, "His
teaching stirs up the people all over
Judea. He started in Galilee and has
come all the way here."

6 When Pilate heard this, he asked if
the man was from Galilee. 7 He learned
that Jesus was from Herod's area of authority. So Pilate sent Jesus to Herod. At
that time Herod was also in Jerusalem.

8 When Herod saw Jesus, he was
very pleased. He had been wanting
to see Jesus for a long time. He had
heard much about him. He hoped to
see Jesus perform a sign of some kind.
9 Herod asked him many questions, but
Jesus gave him no answer. 10 The chief
priests and the teachers of the law were
standing there. With loud shouts they
brought charges against him. 11 Herod
and his soldiers laughed at him and
made fun of him. They dressed him in
a beautiful robe. Then they sent him
back to Pilate. 12 That day Herod and
Pilate became friends. Before this time
they had been enemies.

13 Pilate called together the chief
priests, the rulers and the people. 14 He
said to them, "You brought me this
man. You said he was turning the people against the authorities. I have questioned him in front of you. I have found
no basis for your charges against him.
15 Herod hasn't either. So he sent Jesus
back to us. As you can see, Jesus has
done nothing that is worthy of death.
16-17 So I will just have him whipped and
let him go."

18 But the whole crowd shouted, "Kill
this man! But let Barabbas go!" 19 Barabbas had been thrown into prison. He
had taken part in a struggle in the city
against the authorities. He had also
committed murder.

20 Pilate wanted to let Jesus go. So he
made an appeal to the crowd again.
21 But they kept shouting, "Crucify him!
Crucify him!"

22 Pilate spoke to them for the third
time. "Why?" he asked. "What wrong
has this man done? I have found no
reason to have him put to death. So I will
just have him whipped and let him go."

23 But with loud shouts they kept calling for Jesus to be crucified. The people's
shouts won out. 24 So Pilate decided to
give them what they wanted. 25 He set
free the man they asked for. The man
had been thrown in prison for murder
and for fighting against the authorities.
Pilate handed Jesus over to them so
they could carry out their plans.

Jesus Is Nailed to a Cross

26 As the soldiers led Jesus away, they
took hold of Simon. Simon was from
Cyrene. He was on his way in from the
country. They put a wooden cross on
his shoulders. Then they made him carry it behind Jesus. 27 A large number

of people followed Jesus. Some were women whose hearts were filled with sorrow. They cried loudly because of him. 28 Jesus turned and said to them, "Daughters of Jerusalem, do not weep for me. Weep for yourselves and for your children. 29 The time will come when you will say, 'Blessed are the women who can't have children! Blessed are those who never gave birth or nursed babies!' 30 It is written,

" 'The people will say to the
mountains, "Fall on us!"
They'll say to the hills, "Cover
us!" ' *(Hosea 10:8)*

31 People do these things when trees are green. So what will happen when trees are dry?"

32 Two other men were also led out with Jesus to be killed. Both of them had broken the law. 33 The soldiers brought them to the place called the Skull. There they nailed Jesus to the cross. He hung between the two criminals. One was on his right and one was on his left. 34 Jesus said, "Father, forgive them. They don't know what they are doing." The soldiers divided up his clothes by casting lots.

35 The people stood there watching. The rulers even made fun of Jesus. They said, "He saved others. Let him save himself if he is God's Messiah, the Chosen One."

36 The soldiers also came up and poked fun at him. They offered him wine vinegar. 37 They said, "If you are the king of the Jews, save yourself."

38 A written sign had been placed above him. It read,

THIS IS THE KING OF THE JEWS.

39 One of the criminals hanging there made fun of Jesus. He said, "Aren't you the Messiah? Save yourself! Save us!"

40 But the other criminal scolded him. "Don't you have any respect for God?" he said. "Remember, you are under the same sentence of death. 41 We are being punished fairly. We are getting just what our actions call for. But this man hasn't done anything wrong."

42 Then he said, "Jesus, remember me when you come into your kingdom."

43 Jesus answered him, "What I'm about to tell you is true. Today you will be with me in paradise."

Jesus Dies

44 It was now about noon. Then darkness covered the whole land until three o'clock. 45 The sun had stopped shining. The temple curtain was torn in two. 46 Jesus called out in a loud voice, "Father, into your hands I commit my life." After he said this, he took his last breath.

47 The Roman commander saw what had happened. He praised God and said, "Jesus was surely a man who did what was right." 48 The people had gathered to watch this sight. When they saw what happened, they felt very sad. Then they went away. 49 But all those who knew Jesus stood not very far away, watching these things. They included the women who had followed him from Galilee.

Jesus Is Buried

50 A man named Joseph was a member of the Jewish Council. He was a good and honest man. 51 Joseph had not agreed with what the leaders had decided and done. He was from Arimathea, a town in Judea. He himself was waiting for God's kingdom. 52 Joseph went to Pilate and asked for Jesus' body. 53 Joseph took it down and wrapped it in linen cloth. Then he placed it in a tomb cut in the rock. No one had ever been buried there. 54 It was Preparation Day. The Sabbath day was about to begin.

55 The women who had come with Jesus from Galilee followed Joseph. They saw the tomb and how Jesus' body was placed in it. 56 Then they went home. There they prepared spices and perfumes. But they rested on the Sabbath day in order to obey the Law.

Jesus Rises From the Dead

24 It was very early in the morning on the first day of the week. The women took the spices they had prepared. Then they went to the tomb. 2 They found the stone rolled away from it. 3 When they entered the tomb, they did not find the body of the Lord Jesus. 4 They were wondering about this. Suddenly two men in clothes as bright as lightning stood beside them. 5 The women were terrified. They bowed down with their faces to the ground. Then the men said to them, "Why do you look for the living among the dead? 6 Jesus is not here! He has risen! Remember how he

told you he would rise. It was while he
was still with you in Galilee. 7 He said,
'The Son of Man must be handed over
to sinful people. He must be nailed to a
cross. On the third day he will rise from
the dead.' " 8 Then the women remembered Jesus' words.

9 They came back from the tomb.
They told all these things to the 11
apostles and to all the others. 10 Mary
Magdalene, Joanna, Mary the mother
of James, and the others with them
were the ones who told the apostles.
11 But the apostles did not believe the
women. Their words didn't make any
sense to them. 12 But Peter got up and
ran to the tomb. He bent over and saw
the strips of linen lying by themselves.
Then he went away, wondering what
had happened.

On the Road to Emmaus

13 That same day two of Jesus' followers were going to a village called
Emmaus. It was about seven miles
from Jerusalem. 14 They were talking
with each other about everything that
had happened. 15 As they talked about
those things, Jesus himself came up and
walked along with them. 16 But God kept
them from recognizing him.

17 Jesus asked them, "What are you
talking about as you walk along?"

They stood still, and their faces were
sad. 18 One of them was named Cleo-
pas. He said to Jesus, "Are you the only
person visiting Jerusalem who doesn't
know? Don't you know about the things
that have happened there in the last
few days?"

19 "What things?" Jesus asked.

"About Jesus of Nazareth," they replied. "He was a prophet. He was powerful in what he said and did in the sight
of God and all the people. 20 The chief
priests and our rulers handed Jesus over
to be sentenced to death. They nailed
him to a cross. 21 But we had hoped that
he was the one who was going to set
Israel free. Also, it is the third day since
all this happened. 22 Some of our women
amazed us too. Early this morning they
went to the tomb. 23 But they didn't find
his body. So they came and told us what
they had seen. They saw angels, who
said Jesus was alive. 24 Then some of
our friends went to the tomb. They saw
it was empty, just as the women had
said. They didn't see Jesus' body there."

25 Jesus said to them, "How foolish
you are! How long it takes you to believe all that the prophets said! 26 Didn't
the Messiah have to suffer these things
and then receive his glory?" 27 Jesus
explained to them what was said about
himself in all the Scriptures. He began
with Moses and all the Prophets.

28 They approached the village where
they were going. Jesus kept walking as
if he were going farther. 29 But they tried
hard to keep him from leaving. They
said, "Stay with us. It is nearly evening.
The day is almost over." So he went in
to stay with them.

30 He joined them at the table. Then
he took bread and gave thanks. He
broke it and began to give it to them.
31 Their eyes were opened, and they recognized him. But then he disappeared
from their sight. 32 They said to each
other, "He explained to us what the
Scriptures meant. Weren't we excited as
he talked with us on the road?"

33 They got up and returned at once
to Jerusalem. There they found the 11
disciples and those with them. They
were all gathered together. 34 They were
saying, "It's true! The Lord has risen!
He has appeared to Simon!" 35 Then the
two of them told what had happened to
them on the way. They told how they
had recognized Jesus when he broke
the bread.

Jesus Appears to the Disciples

36 The disciples were still talking
about this when Jesus himself suddenly
stood among them. He said, "May you
have peace!"

37 They were surprised and terrified.
They thought they were seeing a ghost.
38 Jesus said to them, "Why are you troubled? Why do you have doubts in your
minds? 39 Look at my hands and my
feet. It's really me! Touch me and see.
A ghost does not have a body or bones.
But you can see that I do."

40 After he said that, he showed them
his hands and feet. 41 But they still did
not believe it. They were amazed and
filled with joy. So Jesus asked them,
"Do you have anything here to eat?"
42 They gave him a piece of cooked fish.
43 He took it and ate it in front of them.

44 Jesus said to them, "This is what
I told you while I was still with you.
Everything written about me in the Law
of Moses, the Prophets and the Psalms
must come true."

45 Then he opened their minds so they
could understand the Scriptures. 46 He
told them, "This is what is written. The
Messiah will suffer. He will rise from the
dead on the third day. 47 His followers
will preach in his name. They will tell
others to turn away from their sins and
be forgiven. People from every nation
will hear it, beginning at Jerusalem.
48 You have seen these things with your
own eyes. 49 I am going to send you
what my Father has promised. But for
now, stay in the city. Stay there until
you have received power from heaven."

Jesus Is Taken Up Into Heaven

50 Jesus led his disciples out to the
area near Bethany. Then he lifted up
his hands and blessed them. 51 While
he was blessing them, he left them. He
was taken up into heaven. 52 Then they
worshiped him. With great joy, they
returned to Jerusalem. 53 Every day
they went to the temple, praising God.

JOHN

Author: John

John was one of Jesus' disciples and friends. Throughout Jesus' ministry of traveling and teaching, John was right there with him. John knew and loved Jesus, and Jesus knew and loved John. In fact, John felt so loved by Jesus that throughout this book he called himself "the disciple Jesus loved" (John 13:23). John was there when Jesus died, and he testified about Jesus' resurrection from the dead.

John's Gospel also tells of Jesus' life, death, and resurrection, and John wanted his readers to know this: Jesus is the Messiah, and he can change your life forever. You see, John didn't just want people to agree that Jesus was the promised Savior; he wanted them to know Jesus personally and experience the salvation that Jesus came to bring. John's Gospel helps us see not only how Jesus fulfilled all of God's promises from the Old Testament but also how Jesus *is* the expression of God's love to the world.

Gospels & Acts

The Word Became a Human Being

1 In the beginning, the Word was
already there. The Word was with
God, and the Word was God. 2 He was
with God in the beginning. 3 All things
were made through him. Nothing that
has been made was made without him.
4 Life was in him, and that life was the
light for all people. 5 The light shines in
the darkness. But the darkness has not
overcome the light.
6 There was a man sent from God. His
name was John. 7 He came to be a witness about that light. He was a witness
so that all people might believe. 8 John
himself was not the light. He came only
as a witness to the light.
9 The true light that gives light to
everyone was coming into the world.
10 The Word was in the world. And the
world was made through him. But the
world did not recognize him. 11 He came
to what was his own. But his own people
did not accept him. 12 Some people did
accept him and did believe in his name.
He gave them the right to become children of God. 13 To be a child of God has
nothing to do with human parents.
Children of God are not born because
of human choice or because a husband
wants them to be born. They are born
because of what God does.
14 The Word became a human being.
He made his home with us. We have
seen his glory. It is the glory of the One
and Only, who came from the Father.
And the Word was full of grace and
truth.
15 John was a witness about the Word.
John cried out and said, "This was the
one I was talking about. I said, 'He who
comes after me is more important than
I am. He is more important because
he existed before I was born.' " 16 God
is full of grace. From him we have all
received grace in place of the grace already given. 17 In the past, God gave us
grace through the law of Moses. Now,
grace and truth come to us through
Jesus Christ. 18 No one has ever seen God.
But the One and Only is God and is at
the Father's side. The one at the Father's
side has shown us what God is like.

in John?

God is the Great I Am. He gives us everything we need to walk in his ways as we learn about and follow him.

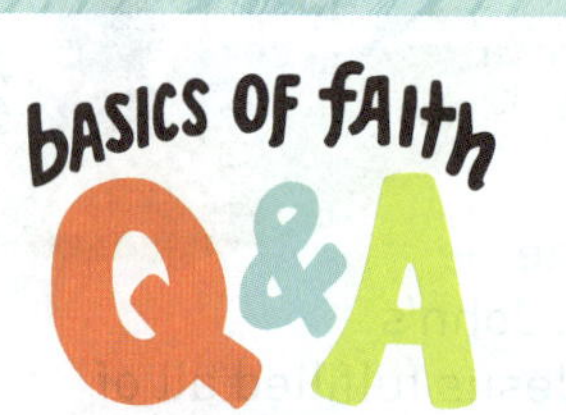

Was there ever a time when God did not exist?

God has no beginning or end. He is eternal, which means he has always existed.

Can you find the following verse?

JOHN 1:1

John the Baptist Says That He Is Not the Messiah

19 The Jewish leaders in Jerusalem
sent priests and Levites to ask John who
he was. John spoke the truth to them.
20 He did not try to hide the truth. He
spoke to them openly. He said, "I am
not the Messiah."
21 They asked him, "Then who are
you? Are you Elijah?"
He said, "I am not."
"Are you the Prophet we've been expecting?" they asked.
"No," he answered.
22 They asked one last time, "Who are
you? Give us an answer to take back
to those who sent us. What do you say
about yourself?"

[23]John replied, using the words of Isaiah the prophet. John said, "I'm the messenger who is calling out in the desert, 'Make the way for the Lord straight.'" *(Isaiah 40:3)*

[24]The Pharisees who had been sent
[25]asked him, "If you are not the Messiah, why are you baptizing people? Why are you doing that if you aren't Elijah or the Prophet we've been expecting?"

[26]"I baptize people with water," John replied. "But someone is standing among you whom you do not know.
[27]He is the one who comes after me. I am not good enough to untie his sandals."

[28]This all happened at Bethany on the other side of the Jordan River. That was where John was baptizing.

What John Says About Jesus

[29]The next day John saw Jesus coming toward him. John said, "Look! The Lamb of God! He takes away the sin of
the world! [30]This is the one I was talking about. I said, 'A man who comes after me is more important than I am. That's because he existed before I was born.'
[31]I did not know him. But God wants to make it clear to Israel who this person is. That's the reason I came baptizing with water."

[32]Then John told them, "I saw the Holy Spirit come down from heaven like a dove. The Spirit remained on Jesus. [33]I
myself did not know him. But the one who sent me to baptize with water told me, 'You will see the Spirit come down and remain on someone. He is the one who will baptize with the Holy Spirit.'
[34]I have seen it happen. I am a witness that this is God's Chosen One."

John's Disciples Follow Jesus

[35]The next day John was there again
with two of his disciples. [36]He saw Jesus walking by. John said, "Look! The Lamb of God!"

[37]The two disciples heard him say
this. So they followed Jesus. [38]Then
Jesus turned around and saw them following. He asked, "What do you want?"

They said, "Rabbi, where are you staying?" Rabbi means Teacher.

[39]"Come," he replied. "You will see."

So they went and saw where he was staying. They spent the rest of the day with him. It was about four o'clock in the afternoon.

[40]Andrew was Simon Peter's brother. Andrew was one of the two disciples who heard what John had said. He had
also followed Jesus. [41]The first thing
Andrew did was to find his brother

MY GOD IS... DIVINE

Simply said, God is God. He is holy and sovereign, having all power and rightly ruling over all things.

Have you ever wondered why people can't do the things God can do? Have you ever wished you could speak something into existence, like God did in the book of Genesis? Or have you ever wished you could make a bunch of food from just a little bit of food, like Jesus did two different times for the crowds of people who listened to him teach (see Matthew 14:13–24; 15:29–39)? We can't do any of these things in our own power because we are not divine. God alone is divine, which means there is no other God. There is no one else in all the universe who is divine.

Simon. He told him, "We have found
the Messiah." Messiah means Christ.
42 And he brought Simon to Jesus.
Jesus looked at him and said, "You
are Simon, son of John. You will be
called Cephas." Cephas means Peter,
or Rock.

Jesus Chooses Philip and Nathanael

43 The next day Jesus decided to leave
for Galilee. He found Philip and said to
him, "Follow me."
44 Philip was from the town of Bethsaida. So were Andrew and Peter. 45 Philip found Nathanael and told him, "We
have found the one whom Moses wrote
about in the Law. The prophets also
wrote about him. He is Jesus of Nazareth, the son of Joseph."
46 "Nazareth! Can anything good
come from there?" Nathanael asked.
"Come and see," said Philip.
47 Jesus saw Nathanael approaching.
Here is what Jesus said about him. "He
is a true Israelite. Nothing about him
is false."
48 "How do you know me?" Nathanael
asked.
Jesus answered, "I saw you while you
were still under the fig tree. I saw you
there before Philip called you."
49 Nathanael replied, "Rabbi, you
are the Son of God. You are the king
of Israel."
50 Jesus said, "You believe because I
told you I saw you under the fig tree.
You will see greater things than that."
51 Then he said to the disciples, "What
I'm about to tell you is true. You will see
heaven open. You will see the angels of
God going up and coming down on the
Son of Man."

Jesus Changes Water Into Wine

2 On the third day there was a wedding. It took place at Cana in Galilee. Jesus' mother was there. 2 Jesus and
his disciples had also been invited to
the wedding. 3 When the wine was gone,
Jesus' mother said to him, "They have
no more wine."
4 "Dear woman, why are you telling
me about this?" Jesus replied. "The time
for me to show who I really am isn't
here yet."
5 His mother said to the servants, "Do
what he tells you."
6 Six stone water jars stood nearby.
The Jews used water from that kind of
jar for special washings. They did that
to make themselves pure and "clean."
Each jar could hold 20 to 30 gallons.
7 Jesus said to the servants, "Fill the
jars with water." So they filled them
to the top.
8 Then he told them, "Now dip some
out. Take it to the person in charge of
the dinner."
They did what he said. 9 The person
in charge tasted the water that had
been turned into wine. He didn't realize where it had come from. But the
servants who had brought the water
knew. Then the person in charge called
the groom to one side. 10 He said to him,
"Everyone brings out the best wine
first. They bring out the cheaper wine
after the guests have had too much
to drink. But you have saved the best
until now."
11 What Jesus did here in Cana in
Galilee was the first of his signs. Jesus
showed his glory by doing this sign. And
his disciples believed in him.
12 After this, Jesus went down to
Capernaum. His mother and brothers
and disciples went with him. They all
stayed there for a few days.

Jesus Clears Out the Temple Courtyard

13 It was almost time for the Jewish
Passover Feast. So Jesus went up to
Jerusalem. 14 In the temple courtyard
he found people selling cattle, sheep
and doves. Others were sitting at tables
exchanging money. 15 So Jesus made
a whip out of ropes. He chased all
the sheep and cattle from the temple
courtyard. He scattered the coins of
the people exchanging money. And
he turned over their tables. 16 He told
those who were selling doves, "Get these
out of here! Stop turning my Father's
house into a market!" 17 His disciples
remembered what had been written.
It says, "My great love for your house
will destroy me." *(Psalm 69:9)*
18 Then the Jewish leaders asked him,
"What sign can you show us to prove
your authority to do this?"
19 Jesus answered them, "When you
destroy this temple, I will raise it up
again in three days."

20 They replied, "It has taken 46 years
to build this temple. Are you going to
raise it up in three days?" 21 But the
temple Jesus had spoken about was his
body. 22 His disciples later remembered
what he had said. That was after he had
been raised from the dead. Then they
believed the Scripture. They also believed the words that Jesus had spoken.
23 Meanwhile, he was in Jerusalem at
the Passover Feast. Many people saw the
signs he was doing. And they believed
in his name. 24 But Jesus did not fully
trust them. He knew what people are
like. 25 He didn't need anyone to tell him
what people are like. He already knew
why people do what they do.

Jesus Teaches Nicodemus

3 There was a Pharisee named Nicodemus. He was one of the Jewish
rulers. 2 He came to Jesus at night
and said, "Rabbi, we know that you
are a teacher who has come from God.
We know that God is with you. If he
weren't, you couldn't do the signs you
are doing."
3 Jesus replied, "What I'm about to
tell you is true. No one can see God's
kingdom unless they are born again."
4 "How can someone be born when
they are old?" Nicodemus asked. "They
can't go back inside their mother! They
can't be born a second time!"
5 Jesus answered, "What I'm about to
tell you is true. No one can enter God's
kingdom unless they are born with water and the Holy Spirit. 6 People give
birth to people. But the Spirit gives birth
to spirit. 7 You should not be surprised
when I say, 'You must all be born again.'
8 The wind blows where it wants to. You
hear the sound it makes. But you can't
tell where it comes from or where it is
going. It is the same with everyone who
is born with the Spirit."
9 "How can this be?" Nicodemus
asked.
10 "You are Israel's teacher," said
Jesus. "Don't you understand these
things? 11 What I'm about to tell you
is true. We speak about what we know.
We are witnesses about what we have
seen. But still you people do not accept what we say. 12 I have spoken to
you about earthly things, and you do
not believe. So how will you believe if
I speak about heavenly things? 13 No
one has ever gone into heaven except
the one who came from heaven. He is
the Son of Man. 14 Moses lifted up the
snake in the desert. In the same way,
the Son of Man must also be lifted up.
15 Then everyone who believes may have
eternal life in him."
16 God so loved the world that he gave
his one and only Son. Anyone who believes in him will not die but will have
eternal life. 17 God did not send his Son
into the world to judge the world. He
sent his Son to save the world through
him. 18 Anyone who believes in him is
not judged. But anyone who does not
believe is judged already. They have not
believed in the name of God's one and
only Son. 19 Here is the judgment. Light
has come into the world, but people
loved darkness instead of light. They
loved darkness because what they did
was evil. 20 Everyone who does evil
deeds hates the light. They will not
come into the light. They are afraid that
what they do will be seen. 21 But anyone
who lives by the truth comes into the
light. They live by the truth with God's
help. They come into the light so that
it will be easy to see their good deeds.

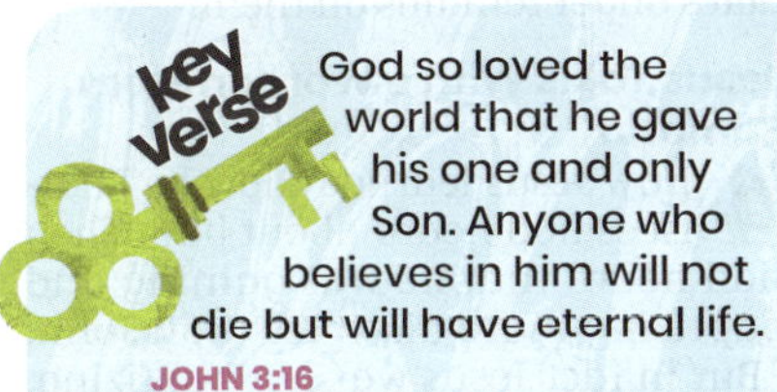

John the Baptist Is a Witness About Jesus

22 After this, Jesus and his disciples
went out into the countryside of Judea.
There he spent some time with them.
And he baptized people there. 23 John
was also baptizing. He was at Aenon
near Salim, where there was plenty of
water. People were coming and being
baptized. 24 This was before John was
put in prison. 25 Some of John's disciples and a certain Jew began to argue.
They argued about special washings
to make people "clean." 26 They came
to John and here is what they said to
him. "Rabbi, that man who was with

you on the other side of the Jordan River
is baptizing people. He is the one you
told us about. Everyone is going to him."
27 John replied, "A person can receive
only what God gives them from heaven.
28 You yourselves are witnesses that I
said, 'I am not the Messiah. I was sent
ahead of him.' 29 The bride belongs to
the groom. The friend who helps the
groom waits and listens for him. He is
full of joy when he hears the groom's
voice. That joy is mine, and it is now
complete. 30 He must become more important. I must become less important.
31 "The one who comes from above
is above everything. The one who is
from the earth belongs to the earth and
speaks like someone from the earth. The
one who comes from heaven is above
everything. 32 He is a witness to what he
has seen and heard. But no one accepts
what he says. 33 Anyone who has accepted it has said, 'Yes. God is truthful.' 34 The
one whom God has sent speaks God's
words. That's because God gives the Holy
Spirit without limit. 35 The Father loves
the Son and has put everything into his
hands. 36 Anyone who believes in the
Son has eternal life. Anyone who does
not believe in the Son will not have life.
God's anger remains on them."

Jesus Talks With a Woman From Samaria

4 Now Jesus learned that the Pharisees had heard about him. They
had heard that he was gaining and
baptizing more disciples than John.
2 But in fact Jesus was not baptizing.
His disciples were. 3 So Jesus left Judea
and went back again to Galilee.
4 Jesus had to go through Samaria.
5 He came to a town in Samaria called
Sychar. It was near the piece of land
Jacob had given his son Joseph. 6 Jacob's
well was there. Jesus was tired from the
journey. So he sat down by the well. It
was about noon.
7 A woman from Samaria came to get
some water. Jesus said to her, "Will you
give me a drink?" 8 His disciples had
gone into the town to buy food.
9 The Samaritan woman said to him,
"You are a Jew. I am a Samaritan woman. How can you ask me for a drink?"
She said this because Jews don't have
anything to do with Samaritans.
10 Jesus answered her, "You do not
know what God's gift is. And you do not
know who is asking you for a drink. If
you did, you would have asked him.
He would have given you living water."
11 "Sir," the woman said, "you don't
have anything to get water with. The
well is deep. Where can you get this
living water? 12 Our father Jacob gave
us the well. He drank from it himself. So
did his sons and his livestock. Are you
more important than he is?"
13 Jesus answered, "Everyone who
drinks this water will be thirsty again.
14 But anyone who drinks the water I
give them will never be thirsty. In fact,
the water I give them will become a
spring of water in them. It will flow up
into eternal life."
15 The woman said to him, "Sir, give
me this water. Then I will never be
thirsty. And I won't have to keep coming
here to get water."
16 He told her, "Go. Get your husband
and come back."
17 "I have no husband," she replied.
Jesus said to her, "You are right when
you say you have no husband. 18 The
fact is, you have had five husbands.
And the man you live with now is not
your husband. What you have just said
is very true."
19 "Sir," the woman said, "I can see
that you are a prophet. 20 Our people
have always worshiped on this mountain. But you Jews claim that the place
where we must worship is in Jerusalem."
21 Jesus said, "Woman, believe me. A
time is coming when you will not worship the Father on this mountain or in
Jerusalem. 22 You Samaritans worship
what you do not know. We worship what
we do know. Salvation comes from the
Jews. 23 But a new time is coming. In
fact, it is already here. True worshipers
will worship the Father in the Spirit and
in truth. They are the kind of worshipers
the Father is looking for. 24 God is spirit.
His worshipers must worship him in the
Spirit and in truth."
25 The woman said, "I know that
Messiah is coming." Messiah means
Christ. "When he comes, he will explain
everything to us."
26 Then Jesus said, "The one you're
talking about is the one speaking to
you. I am he."

The Disciples Join Jesus Again

27 Just then Jesus' disciples returned.
They were surprised to find him talking
with a woman. But no one asked, "What
do you want from her?" No one asked,
"Why are you talking with her?"
28 The woman left her water jar and
went back to the town. She said to the
people, 29 "Come. See a man who told
me everything I've ever done. Could
this be the Messiah?" 30 The people came
out of the town and made their way
toward Jesus.
31 His disciples were saying to him,
"Rabbi, eat something!"
32 But he said to them, "I have food
to eat that you know nothing about."
33 Then his disciples asked each other,
"Did someone bring him food?"
34 Jesus said, "My food is to do what
my Father sent me to do. My food is
to finish his work. 35 Don't you have a
saying? You say, 'It's still four months
until harvest time.' But I tell you, open
your eyes! Look at the fields! They are
ripe for harvest right now. 36 Even now
the one who gathers the crop is getting
paid. They are already harvesting the
crop for eternal life. So the one who
plants and the one who gathers can now
be glad together. 37 Here is a true saying.
'One plants and another gathers.' 38 I
sent you to gather what you have not
worked for. Others have done the hard
work. You have gathered the benefits
of their work."

Many Samaritans Believe in Jesus

39 Many of the Samaritans from the
town of Sychar believed in Jesus. They
believed because of what the woman
had said about him. She said, "He told
me everything I've ever done." 40 Then
the Samaritans came to him and tried
to get him to stay with them. So he
stayed two days. 41 Because of what
he said, many more people became
believers.
42 They said to the woman, "We no
longer believe just because of what you
said. We have now heard for ourselves.
We know that this man really is the
Savior of the world."

Jesus Heals an Official's Son

43 After the two days, Jesus left for Galilee. 44 He himself had pointed out that
a prophet is not respected in his own
country. 45 When he arrived in Galilee,
the people living there welcomed him.
They had seen everything he had done
in Jerusalem at the Passover Feast. That
was because they had also been there.
46 Once more, Jesus visited Cana in
Galilee. Cana is where he had turned
the water into wine. A royal official
was there. His son was sick in bed at
Capernaum. 47 The official heard that
Jesus had arrived in Galilee from Judea.
So he went to Jesus and begged him to
come and heal his son. The boy was
close to death.
48 Jesus told him, "You people will
never believe unless you see signs and
wonders."
49 The royal official said, "Sir, come
down before my child dies."
50 "Go," Jesus replied. "Your son will
live."
The man believed what Jesus said,
and so he left. 51 While he was still on
his way home, his slaves met him. They
gave him the news that his boy was
living. 52 He asked what time his son got
better. They said to him, "Yesterday, at
one o'clock in the afternoon, the fever
left him."
53 Then the father realized what had
happened. That was the exact time
Jesus had said to him, "Your son will
live." So he and his whole family became believers.
54 This was the second sign that Jesus
did after coming from Judea to Galilee.

Jesus Heals a Man at the Pool

5 Some time later, Jesus went up to
Jerusalem for one of the Jewish
feasts. 2 In Jerusalem near the Sheep
Gate is a pool. In the Aramaic language
it is called Bethesda. It is surrounded by
five rows of columns with a roof over
them. 3-4 Here a great number of disabled people used to lie down. Among
them were those who were blind, those
who could not walk, and those who
could hardly move. 5 One person was
there who had not been able to walk
for 38 years. 6 Jesus saw him lying there.
He knew that the man had been in that
condition for a long time. So he asked
him, "Do you want to get well?"
7 "Sir," the disabled man replied, "I
have no one to help me into the pool
when an angel stirs up the water. I try

ETERNAL

There has never been a time when God did not exist. God was never born, meaning he has no beginning, and there will never be a time when God stops existing, meaning he has no end. God has always been and will always be.

Do you ever wonder what existed before God created the world—before the creation of the moon and the sun, land and ocean, animals and people? The only thing that existed before the world began was God (see Psalm 90:2). He alone existed as Father, Son, and Spirit. We can trust that God knows all things because he has lived forever and ever and ever.

to get in, but someone else always goes
down ahead of me."
8 Then Jesus said to him, "Get up! Pick
up your mat and walk." 9 The man was
healed right away. He picked up his mat
and walked.
This happened on a Sabbath day.
10 So the Jewish leaders said to the man
who had been healed, "It is the Sabbath
day. The law does not allow you to carry
your mat."
11 But he replied, "The one who made
me well said to me, 'Pick up your mat
and walk.' "
12 They asked him, "Who is this fellow?
Who told you to pick it up and walk?"
13 The one who was healed had no
idea who it was. Jesus had slipped away
into the crowd that was there.
14 Later Jesus found him at the temple. Jesus said to him, "See, you are well
again. Stop sinning, or something worse
may happen to you." 15 The man went
away. He told the Jewish leaders it was
Jesus who had made him well.

The Authority of the Son

16 Jesus was doing these things on
the Sabbath day. So the Jewish leaders
began to oppose him. 17 Jesus defended
himself. He said to them, "My Father is
always doing his work. He is working
right up to this day. I am working too."
18 For this reason the Jewish leaders
tried even harder to kill him. According
to them, Jesus was not only breaking
the law of the Sabbath day. He was
even calling God his own Father. He
was making himself equal with God.
19 Jesus answered, "What I'm about to
tell you is true. The Son can do nothing
by himself. He can do only what he sees
his Father doing. What the Father does,
the Son also does. 20 This is because the
Father loves the Son. The Father shows
him everything he does. Yes, and the
Father will show the Son even greater works than these. And you will be
amazed. 21 The Father raises the dead
and gives them life. In the same way,
the Son gives life to anyone he wants
to. 22 Also, the Father does not judge
anyone. He has given the Son the task
of judging. 23 Then all people will honor
the Son just as they honor the Father.
Whoever does not honor the Son does
not honor the Father, who sent him.
24 "What I'm about to tell you is true.
Anyone who hears my word and believes him who sent me has eternal
life. They will not be judged. They have
crossed over from death to life. 25 What
I'm about to tell you is true. A time is
coming for me to give life. In fact, it
has already begun. The dead will hear
the voice of the Son of God. Those who
hear it will live. 26 The Father has life in
himself. He has allowed the Son also to

have life in himself. 27 And the Father
has given him the authority to judge.
This is because he is the Son of Man.
28 "Do not be amazed at this. A time is
coming when all who are in their graves
will hear his voice. 29 They will all come
out of their graves. People who have
done what is good will rise and live
again. People who have done what is
evil will rise and be found guilty. 30 I
can do nothing by myself. I judge only
as I hear. And my judging is fair. I do
not try to please myself. I try to please
the one who sent me.

Being a Witness About Jesus

31 "If I am a witness about myself,
what I say is not true. 32 There is someone else who is a witness in my favor.
And I know that what he says about
me is true.
33 "You have sent people to John the
Baptist. He has been a witness to the
truth. 34 I do not accept what a person
says. I only talk about what John says
so that you can be saved. 35 John was
like a lamp that burned and gave light.
For a while you chose to enjoy his light.
36 "What I say about myself is more
important than what John says about
me. I am doing the works the Father
gave me to finish. These works are a
witness that the Father has sent me.
37 The Father who sent me is himself a
witness about me. You have never heard
his voice. You have never seen what he
really looks like. 38 And his word does
not live in you. That's because you do
not believe the one he sent. 39 You study
the Scriptures carefully. You study them
because you think they will give you
eternal life. The Scriptures you study
are a witness about me. 40 But you
refuse to come to me and receive life.
41 "I do not accept praise from human
beings. 42 But I know you. I know that
you do not have love for God in your
hearts. 43 I have come in my Father's
name, and you do not accept me. But if
someone else comes in his own name,
you will accept him. 44 You accept praise
from one another. But you do not seek
the praise that comes from the only
God. So how can you believe?
45 "Do not think I will bring charges
against you in front of the Father. Moses
is the one who does that. And he is the
one you build your hopes on. 46 Do you
believe Moses? Then you should believe
me. He wrote about me. 47 But you do
not believe what he wrote. So how are
you going to believe what I say?"

Jesus Feeds the Five Thousand

6 Some time after this, Jesus crossed
over to the other side of the Sea
of Galilee. It is also called the Sea of
Tiberias. 2 A large crowd of people followed him. They had seen the signs he
had done by healing sick people. 3 Then
Jesus went up on a mountainside. There
he sat down with his disciples. 4 The
Jewish Passover Feast was near.
5 Jesus looked up and saw a large
crowd coming toward him. So he said
to Philip, "Where can we buy bread for
these people to eat?" 6 He asked this
only to test Philip. He already knew
what he was going to do.
7 Philip answered him, "Suppose we
were able to buy enough bread for each
person to have just a bite. That would
take more than half a year's pay!"
8 Another of his disciples spoke up.
It was Andrew, Simon Peter's brother.
He said, 9 "Here is a boy with five small
loaves of barley bread. He also has two
small fish. But how far will that go in
such a large crowd?"
10 Jesus said, "Have the people sit
down." There was plenty of grass in
that place, and they sat down. About
5,000 men were there. 11 Then Jesus took
the loaves and gave thanks. He handed
out the bread to those who were seated.
He gave them as much as they wanted.
And he did the same with the fish.
12 When all of them had enough to eat,
Jesus spoke to his disciples. "Gather the
leftover pieces," he said. "Don't waste
anything." 13 So they gathered what was
left over from the five barley loaves.
They filled 12 baskets with the pieces
left by those who had eaten.
14 The people saw the sign that Jesus
did. Then they began to say, "This must
be the Prophet who is supposed to come
into the world." 15 But Jesus knew that
they planned to come and force him to
be their king. So he went away again
to a mountain by himself.

Jesus Walks on the Water

16 When evening came, Jesus' disciples
went down to the Sea of Galilee. 17 There

they got into a boat and headed across the lake toward Capernaum. By now it was dark. Jesus had not yet joined them. 18 A strong wind was blowing, and the water became rough. 19 They rowed about three or four miles. Then they saw Jesus coming toward the boat. He was walking on the water. They were frightened. 20 But he said to them, "It is I. Don't be afraid." 21 Then they agreed to take him into the boat. Right away the boat reached the shore where they were heading.

22 The next day the crowd that had stayed on the other side of the lake realized something. They saw that only one boat had been there. They knew that Jesus had not gotten into it with his disciples. And they knew that the disciples had gone away alone. 23 Then some boats arrived from Tiberias. It was near the place where the people had eaten the bread after the Lord gave thanks. 24 The crowd realized that Jesus and his disciples were not there. So they got into boats and went to Capernaum to look for Jesus.

Jesus Is the Bread of Life

25 They found him on the other side of the lake. They asked him, "Rabbi, when did you get here?"

26 Jesus answered, "What I'm about to tell you is true. You are not looking for me because you saw the signs I did. You are looking for me because you ate the loaves until you were full. 27 Do not work for food that spoils. Work for food that lasts forever. That is the food the Son of Man will give you. For God the Father has put his seal of approval on him."

28 Then they asked him, "What does God want from us? What works does he want us to do?"

29 Jesus answered, "God's work is to believe in the one he has sent."

30 So they asked him, "What sign will you give us? What will you do so we can see it and believe you? 31 Long ago our people ate the manna in the desert. It is written in Scripture, 'The Lord gave them bread from heaven to eat.' " *(Exodus 16:4; Nehemiah 9:15; Psalm 78:24,25)*

32 Jesus said to them, "What I'm about to tell you is true. It is not Moses who has given you the bread from heaven. It is my Father who gives you the true bread from heaven. 33 The bread of God is the bread that comes down from heaven. He gives life to the world."

34 "Sir," they said, "always give us this bread."

35 Then Jesus said, "I am the bread of life. Whoever comes to me will never go hungry. And whoever believes in me will never be thirsty. 36 But it is just as I told you. You have seen me, and you still do not believe. 37 Everyone the Father gives me will come to me. I will never send away anyone who comes to me. 38 I have not come down from heaven to do what I want to do. I have come to do what the one who sent me wants me to do. 39 The one who sent me doesn't want me to lose anyone he has given me. He wants me to raise them up on the last day. 40 My Father wants all who look to the Son and believe in him to have eternal life. I will raise them up on the last day."

41 Then the Jews there began to complain about Jesus. That was because he said, "I am the bread that came down from heaven." 42 They said, "Isn't this Jesus, the son of Joseph? Don't we know his father and mother? How can he now say, 'I came down from heaven'?"

43 "Stop complaining among yourselves," Jesus answered. 44 "No one can come to me unless the Father who sent me brings them. Then I will raise them up on the last day. 45 It is written in the Prophets, 'God will teach all of them.' *(Isaiah 54:13)* Everyone who has heard the Father and learned from him comes to me. 46 No one has seen the Father except the one who has come from God. Only he has seen the Father. 47 What I'm about to tell you is true. Everyone who believes has life forever. 48 I am the bread of life. 49 Long ago your people ate the manna in the desert, and they still died. 50 But here is the bread that comes down from heaven. A person can eat it and not die. 51 I am the living bread that came down from heaven. Everyone who eats some of this bread will live forever. This bread is my body. I will give it for the life of the world."

52 Then the Jews began to argue sharply among themselves. They said, "How can this man give us his body to eat?"

53 Jesus said to them, "What I'm
about to tell you is true. You must eat
the Son of Man's body and drink his
blood. If you don't, you have no life in
you. 54 Anyone who eats my body and
drinks my blood has eternal life. I will
raise them up on the last day. 55 My
body is real food. My blood is real drink.
56 Anyone who eats my body and drinks
my blood remains in me. And I remain
in them. 57 The living Father sent me,
and I live because of him. In the same
way, those who feed on me will live
because of me. 58 This is the bread that
came down from heaven. Long ago your
people ate manna and died. But whoever eats this bread will live forever." 59 He
said this while he was teaching in the
synagogue in Capernaum.

Many Disciples Leave Jesus

60 Jesus' disciples heard this. Many
of them said, "This is a hard teaching.
Who can accept it?"

61 Jesus was aware that his disciples
were complaining about his teaching.
So he said to them, "Does this upset you?
62 Then what if you see the Son of Man
go up to where he was before? 63 The
Holy Spirit gives life. The body means
nothing at all. The words I have spoken
to you are full of the Spirit. They give
life. 64 But there are some of you who
do not believe." Jesus had known from
the beginning which of them did not believe. And he had known who was going
to hand him over to his enemies. 65 So
he continued speaking. He said, "This
is why I told you that no one can come
to me unless the Father helps them."

66 From this time on, many of his
disciples turned back. They no longer
followed him.

67 "You don't want to leave also, do
you?" Jesus asked the 12 disciples.

68 Simon Peter answered him, "Lord,
who can we go to? You have the words of
eternal life. 69 We have come to believe
and to know that you are the Holy One
of God."

70 Then Jesus replied, "Didn't I choose
you, the 12 disciples? But one of you is
a devil!" 71 He meant Judas, the son of
Simon Iscariot. Judas was one of the 12
disciples. But later he was going to hand
Jesus over to his enemies.

Jesus Goes to the Feast of Booths

7 After this, Jesus went around in
Galilee. He didn't want to travel
around in Judea. That was because the
Jewish leaders there were looking for
a way to kill him. 2 The Jewish Feast of
Booths was near. 3 Jesus' brothers said
to him, "Leave Galilee and go to Judea.
Then your disciples there will see the
works that you do. 4 No one who wants
to be well known does things in secret.
Since you are doing these things, show
yourself to the world." 5 Even Jesus' own
brothers did not believe in him.

6 So Jesus told them, "The time for me
to show who I really am is not here yet.
For you, any time would be the right
time. 7 The people of the world can't hate
you. But they hate me. This is because I
am a witness that their works are evil.
8 You go to the feast. I am not going up
to this feast. This is because my time
has not yet fully come." 9 After he said
this, he stayed in Galilee.

10 But when his brothers had left for
the feast, he went also. But he went
secretly, not openly. 11 At the feast the
Jewish leaders were watching for Jesus.
They were asking, "Where is he?"

12 Many people in the crowd were
whispering about him. Some said, "He
is a good man."

Others replied, "No. He fools the people." 13 But no one would say anything
about him openly. They were afraid of
the leaders.

Jesus Teaches at the Feast

14 Jesus did nothing until halfway
through the feast. Then he went up to
the temple courtyard and began to
teach. 15 The Jews there were amazed.
They asked, "How did this man learn so
much without being taught?"

16 Jesus answered, "What I teach is
not my own. It comes from the one who
sent me. 17 Here is how someone can
find out whether my teaching comes
from God or from me. That person must
choose to do what God wants them to
do. 18 Whoever speaks on their own does
it to get personal honor. But someone
who works for the honor of the one who
sent him is truthful. Nothing about him
is false. 19 Didn't Moses give you the law?
But not one of you obeys the law. Why
are you trying to kill me?"

20 “You are controlled by demons,”
the crowd answered. “Who is trying
to kill you?”
21 Jesus said to them, “I did one miracle, and you are all amazed. 22 Moses
gave you circumcision, and so you circumcise a child on the Sabbath day.
But circumcision did not really come
from Moses. It came from Abraham.
23 You circumcise a boy on the Sabbath
day. You think that if you do, you won't
break the law of Moses. Then why are
you angry with me? I healed a man's
entire body on the Sabbath day! 24 Stop
judging only by what you see. Judge in
the right way.”

People Don't Agree About Who Jesus Is

25 Then some of the people of Jerusalem began asking questions. They
said, “Isn't this the man some people
are trying to kill? 26 Here he is! He is
speaking openly. They aren't saying
a word to him. Have the authorities
really decided that he is the Messiah?
27 But we know where this man is from.
When the Messiah comes, no one will
know where he is from.”
28 Jesus was still teaching in the temple courtyard. He cried out, “Yes, you
know me. And you know where I am
from. I am not here on my own authority. The one who sent me is true. You do
not know him. 29 But I know him. I am
from him, and he sent me.”
30 When he said this, they tried to
arrest him. But no one laid a hand on
him. The time for him to show who he
really was had not yet come. 31 Still,
many people in the crowd believed in
him. They said, “How will it be when the
Messiah comes? Will he do more signs
than this man?”
32 The Pharisees heard the crowd
whispering things like this about him.
Then the chief priests and the Pharisees
sent temple guards to arrest him.
33 Jesus said, “I am with you for only
a short time. Then I will go to the one
who sent me. 34 You will look for me,
but you won't find me. You can't come
where I am going.”
35 The Jews said to one another,
“Where does this man plan to go? Does
he think we can't find him? Will he go
where our people live scattered among
the Greeks? Will he go there to teach
the Greeks? 36 What did he mean when
he said, ‘You will look for me, but you
won't find me’? And what did he mean
when he said, ‘You can't come where I
am going’?”
37 It was the last and most important
day of the feast. Jesus stood up and
spoke in a loud voice. He said, “Let anyone who is thirsty come to me and drink.
38 Does anyone believe in me? Then, just
as Scripture says, rivers of living water
will flow from inside them.” 39 When he
said this, he meant the Holy Spirit. Those
who believed in Jesus would receive the
Spirit later. Up to that time, the Spirit
had not been given. This was because
Jesus had not yet received glory.
40 The people heard his words. Some
of them said, “This man must be the
Prophet we've been expecting.”
41 Others said, “He is the Messiah.”
Still others asked, “How can the
Messiah come from Galilee? 42 Doesn't
Scripture say that the Messiah will come
from the family line of David? Doesn't it
say that he will come from Bethlehem,
the town where David lived?” 43 So the
people did not agree about who Jesus
was. 44 Some wanted to arrest him. But
no one laid a hand on him.

The Jewish Leaders Do Not Believe

45 Finally the temple guards went
back to the chief priests and the Pharisees. They asked the guards, “Why
didn't you bring him in?”
46 “No one ever spoke the way this
man does,” the guards replied.
47 “You mean he has fooled you also?”
the Pharisees asked. 48 “Have any of the
rulers or Pharisees believed in him?
49 No! But this mob knows nothing
about the law. There is a curse on them.”
50 Then Nicodemus, a Pharisee, spoke.
He was the one who had gone to Jesus
earlier. He asked, 51 “Does our law find a
man guilty without hearing him first?
Doesn't it want to find out what he is
doing?”
52 They replied, “Are you from Galilee
too? Look into it. You will find that a
prophet does not come out of Galilee.”
53 Then they all went home. 1 But

8 Jesus went to the Mount of Olives.
2 At sunrise he arrived again in
the temple courtyard. All the people

gathered around him there. He sat down
to teach them. 3 The teachers of the law
and the Pharisees brought in a woman.
She had been caught committing adultery. They made her stand in front of
the group. 4 They said to Jesus, "Teacher,
this woman was caught sleeping with a
man who was not her husband. 5 In the
Law, Moses commanded us to kill such
women by throwing stones at them.
Now what do you say?" 6 They were
trying to trap Jesus with that question.
They wanted to have a reason to bring
charges against him.

But Jesus bent down and started to
write on the ground with his finger.
7 They kept asking him questions. So
he stood up and said to them, "Has any
one of you not sinned? Then you be
the first to throw a stone at her." 8 He
bent down again and wrote on the
ground.

9 Those who heard what he had said
began to go away. They left one at a
time, the older ones first. Soon only
Jesus was left. The woman was still
standing there. 10 Jesus stood up and
asked her, "Woman, where are they?
Hasn't anyone found you guilty?"

11 "No one, sir," she said.

"Then I don't find you guilty either,"
Jesus said. "Go now and leave your life
of sin."

Challenge to What Jesus Says About Himself

12 Jesus spoke to the people again.
He said, "I am the light of the world.
Anyone who follows me will never walk
in darkness. They will have that light.
They will have life."

13 The Pharisees argued with him.
"Here you are," they said, "appearing
as your own witness. But your witness
does not count."

14 Jesus answered, "Even if I am a
witness about myself, what I say does
count. I know where I came from. And
I know where I am going. But you have
no idea where I come from or where I
am going. 15 You judge by human standards. I don't judge anyone. 16 But if I
do judge, what I decide is true. This is
because I am not alone. I stand with
the Father, who sent me. 17 Your own
Law says that the witness of two people
proves the truth about something. 18 I
am a witness about myself. The other
witness about me is the Father, who
sent me."

19 Then they asked him, "Where is
your father?"

"You do not know me or my Father,"
Jesus replied. "If you knew me, you
would know my Father also." 20 He
spoke these words while he was teaching in the temple courtyard. He was
near the place where the offerings were
put. But no one arrested him. That's
because the time for him to die had
not yet come.

Challenge to Who Jesus Claims to Be

21 Once more Jesus said to them, "I
am going away. You will look for me,
and you will die in your sin. You can't
come where I am going."

22 This made the Jews ask, "Will he
kill himself? Is that why he says, 'You
can't come where I am going'?"

23 But Jesus said, "You are from below.
I am from heaven. You are from this
world. I am not from this world. 24 I told
you that you would die in your sins.
This will happen if you don't believe
that I am he. If you don't believe, you
will certainly die in your sins."

25 "Who are you?" they asked.

"Just what I have been telling you
from the beginning," Jesus replied. 26 "I
have a lot to say that will judge you.
But the one who sent me can be trusted.
And I tell the world what I have heard
from him."

27 They did not understand that Jesus
was telling them about his Father. 28 So
Jesus said, "You will lift up the Son of
Man. Then you will know that I am he.
You will also know that I do nothing on
my own. I speak just what the Father
has taught me. 29 The one who sent me
is with me. He has not left me alone,
because I always do what pleases him."
30 Even while Jesus was speaking, many
people believed in him.

Challenge to the Claim to Be Children of Abraham

31 Jesus spoke to the Jews who had believed him. "If you obey my teaching,"
he said, "you are really my disciples.
32 Then you will know the truth. And
the truth will set you free."

33 They answered him, "We are Abraham's children. We have never been slaves of anyone. So how can you say that we will be set free?"

34 Jesus replied, "What I'm about to tell you is true. Everyone who sins is a slave of sin. 35 A slave has no lasting place in the family. But a son belongs to the family forever. 36 So if the Son of Man sets you free, you will really be free. 37 I know that you are Abraham's children. But you are looking for a way to kill me. You have no room for my word. 38 I am telling you what I saw when I was with my Father. You are doing what you have heard from your father."

39 "Abraham is our father," they answered.

Jesus said, "Are you really Abraham's children? If you are, you will do what Abraham did. 40 But you are looking for a way to kill me. I am a man who has told you the truth I heard from God. Abraham didn't do the things you want to do. 41 You are doing what your own father does."

"We have the right to claim to be God's children," they objected. "The only Father we have is God himself."

42 Jesus said to them, "If God were your Father, you would love me. I have come here from God. I have not come on my own. God sent me. 43 Why aren't my words clear to you? Because you can't really hear what I say. 44 You belong to your father, the devil. You want to obey your father's wishes. From the beginning, the devil was a murderer. He has never obeyed the truth. There is no truth in him. When he lies, he speaks his natural language. He does this because he is a liar. He is the father of lies. 45 But because I tell the truth, you don't believe me! 46 Can any of you prove I am guilty of sinning? Am I not telling the truth? Then why don't you believe me? 47 Whoever belongs to God hears what God says. The reason you don't hear is that you don't belong to God."

Jesus Makes Claims About Himself

48 The Jews answered Jesus, "Aren't we right when we say you are a Samaritan? Aren't you controlled by a demon?"

49 "I am not controlled by a demon," said Jesus. "I honor my Father. You do not honor me. 50 I am not seeking glory for myself. But there is one who brings glory to me. He is the judge. 51 What I'm about to tell you is true. Whoever obeys my word will never die."

52 Then they cried out, "Now we know you are controlled by a demon! Abraham died. So did the prophets. But you say that whoever obeys your word will never die. 53 Are you greater than our father Abraham? He died. So did the prophets. Who do you think you are?"

54 Jesus replied, "If I bring glory to myself, my glory means nothing. You claim that my Father is your God. He is the one who brings glory to me. 55 You do not know him. But I know him. If I said I did not, I would be a liar like you. But I do know him. And I obey his word. 56 Your father Abraham was filled with joy at the thought of seeing my day. He saw it and was glad."

57 "You are not even 50 years old," they said to Jesus. "And you have seen Abraham?"

58 "What I'm about to tell you is true," Jesus answered. "Before Abraham was born, I am!" 59 When he said this, they picked up stones to kill him. But Jesus hid himself. He slipped away from the temple area.

Jesus Heals a Man Born Blind

9 As Jesus went along, he saw a man who was blind. He had been blind since he was born. 2 Jesus' disciples asked him, "Rabbi, who sinned? Was this man born blind because he sinned? Or did his parents sin?"

3 "It isn't because this man sinned," said Jesus. "It isn't because his parents sinned. He was born blind so that God's power could be shown by what's going to happen. 4 While it is still day, we must do the works of the one who sent me. Night is coming. Then no one can work. 5 While I am in the world, I am the light of the world."

6 After he said this, he spit on the ground. He made some mud with the spit. Then he put the mud on the man's eyes. 7 "Go," he told him. "Wash in the Pool of Siloam." Siloam means Sent. So the man went and washed. And he came home able to see.

8 His neighbors and people who had seen him earlier begging asked

questions. "Isn't this the same man who
used to sit and beg?" they asked. 9 Some
claimed that he was.

Others said, "No. He only looks like
him."

But the man who had been blind kept
saying, "I am the man."

10 "Then how were your eyes opened?"
they asked.

11 He replied, "The man they call Jesus
made some mud and put it on my eyes.
He told me to go to Siloam and wash. So
I went and washed. Then I could see."

12 "Where is this man?" they asked
him.

"I don't know," he said.

The Pharisees Want to Know How the Blind Man Was Healed

13 They brought to the Pharisees the
man who had been blind. 14 The day
Jesus made the mud and opened the
man's eyes was a Sabbath day. 15 So the
Pharisees also asked him how he was
able to see. "He put mud on my eyes,"
the man replied. "Then I washed. And
now I can see."

16 Some of the Pharisees said, "Jesus
has not come from God. He does not
keep the Sabbath day."

But others asked, "How can a sinner
do such signs?" So the Pharisees did not
agree with one another.

17 Then they turned again to the blind
man. "What do you have to say about
him?" they asked. "It was your eyes
he opened."

The man replied, "He is a prophet."

18 They still did not believe that the
man had been blind and now could see.
So they sent for his parents. 19 "Is this
your son?" they asked. "Is this the one
you say was born blind? How is it that
now he can see?"

20 "We know he is our son," the parents answered. "And we know he was
born blind. 21 But we don't know how
he can now see. And we don't know who
opened his eyes. Ask him. He is an adult.
He can speak for himself." 22 His parents
said this because they were afraid of the
Jewish leaders. The leaders had already
made this decision about Jesus. Anyone
who said Jesus was the Messiah would
be put out of the synagogue. 23 That was
why the man's parents said, "He is an
adult. Ask him."

24 Again the Pharisees called the man
who had been blind to come to them.
"Give glory to God by telling the truth!"
they said. "We know that the man who
healed you is a sinner."

25 He replied, "I don't know if he is a
sinner or not. I do know one thing. I was
blind, but now I can see!"

26 Then they asked him, "What did he
do to you? How did he open your eyes?"

27 He answered, "I have already told
you. But you didn't listen. Why do you
want to hear it again? Do you want to
become his disciples too?"

28 Then they began to attack him
with their words. "You are this fellow's
disciple!" they said. "We are disciples
of Moses! 29 We know that God spoke to
Moses. But we don't even know where
this fellow comes from."

30 The man answered, "That is really
surprising! You don't know where he
comes from, and yet he opened my
eyes. 31 We know that God does not listen
to sinners. He listens to the godly person
who does what he wants them to do.
32 Nobody has ever heard of anyone
opening the eyes of a person born blind.
33 If this man had not come from God,
he could do nothing."

34 Then the Pharisees replied, "When
you were born, you were already deep
in sin. How dare you talk like that to us!"
And they threw him out of the synagogue.

People Who Can't See the Truth

35 Jesus heard that the Pharisees had
thrown the man out of the synagogue.
When Jesus found him, he said, "Do you
believe in the Son of Man?"

36 "Who is he, sir?" the man asked.
"Tell me, so I can believe in him."

37 Jesus said, "You have now seen him.
In fact, he is the one speaking with you."

38 Then the man said, "Lord, I believe."
And he worshiped him.

39 Jesus said, "I have come into this
world to judge it. I have come so that
people who are blind will see. I have
come so that people who can see will
become blind."

40 Some Pharisees who were with him
heard him say this. They asked, "What?
Are we blind too?"

41 Jesus said, "If you were blind, you
would not be guilty of sin. But since you
claim you can see, you remain guilty.

The Good Shepherd and His Sheep

10 "What I'm about to tell you Pharisees is true. What if someone does not enter the sheep pen through the gate but climbs in another way? That person is a thief and a robber. 2 The one who enters through the gate is the shepherd of the sheep. 3 The gatekeeper opens the gate for him. The sheep listen to his voice. He calls his own sheep by name and leads them out. 4 When he has brought out all his own sheep, he goes on ahead of them. His sheep follow him because they know his voice. 5 But they will never follow a stranger. In fact, they will run away from him. They don't recognize a stranger's voice." 6 Jesus told this story. But the Pharisees didn't understand what he was telling them.

7 So Jesus said again, "What I'm about to tell you is true. I am like a gate for the sheep. 8 All who have come before me are thieves and robbers. But the sheep have not listened to them. 9 I'm like a gate. Anyone who enters through me will be saved. They will come in and go out. And they will find plenty of food. 10 A thief comes only to steal and kill and destroy. I have come so they may have life. I want them to have it in the fullest possible way.

11 "I am the good shepherd. The good shepherd gives his life for the sheep. 12 The hired man is not the shepherd and does not own the sheep. So when the hired man sees the wolf coming, he leaves the sheep and runs away. Then the wolf attacks the flock and scatters it. 13 The man runs away because he is a hired man. He does not care about the sheep.

14 "I am the good shepherd. I know my sheep, and my sheep know me. 15 They know me just as the Father knows me and I know the Father. And I give my life for the sheep. 16 I have other sheep that do not belong to this sheep pen. I must bring them in too. They also will listen to my voice. Then there will be one flock and one shepherd. 17 The reason my Father loves me is that I give up my life. But I will take it back again. 18 No one takes it from me. I give it up myself. I have the authority to give it up. And I have the authority to take it back again. I received this command from my Father."

19 The Jews who heard these words could not agree with one another. 20 Many of them said, "He is controlled by a demon. He has gone crazy! Why should we listen to him?"

21 But others said, "A person controlled by a demon does not say things like this. Can a demon open the eyes of someone who is blind?"

Another Challenge to Jesus' Claims

22 Then came the Feast of Hanukkah at Jerusalem. It was winter. 23 Jesus was in the temple courtyard walking in Solomon's Porch. 24 The Jews who were gathered there around Jesus spoke to him. They said, "How long will you keep us waiting? If you are the Messiah, tell us plainly."

25 Jesus answered, "I did tell you. But you do not believe. The works that I do in my Father's name are a witness for me. 26 But you do not believe, because you are not my sheep. 27 My sheep listen to my voice. I know them, and they follow me. 28 I give them eternal life, and they will never die. No one will steal them out of my hand. 29 My Father, who has given them to me, is greater than anyone. No one can steal them out of my Father's hand. 30 I and the Father are one."

31 Again the Jews who had challenged him picked up stones to kill him. 32 But Jesus said to them, "I have shown you many good works from the Father. Which good work are you throwing stones at me for?"

33 "We are not throwing stones at you for any good work," they replied. "We are stoning you for saying a very evil thing. You are only a man. But you claim to be God."

34 Jesus answered them, "Didn't God say in your Law, 'I have said you are "gods" '? *(Psalm 82:6)* 35 We know that Scripture is always true. God spoke to some people and called them 'gods.' 36 If that is true, what about the one the Father set apart as his very own? What about this one the Father sent into the world? Why do you charge me with saying a very evil thing? Is it because I said, 'I am God's Son'? 37 Don't believe me unless I do the works of my Father. 38 But what if I do them? Even if you don't believe me, believe these works. Then you will know and understand

that the Father is in me and I am in the Father." 39 Again they tried to arrest him. But he escaped from them.

40 Then Jesus went back across the Jordan River. He went to the place where John had been baptizing in the early days. There he stayed. 41 Many people came to him. They said, "John never performed a sign. But everything he said about this man was true." 42 And in that place many believed in Jesus.

Lazarus Dies

11 A man named Lazarus was sick. He was from Bethany, the village where Mary and her sister Martha lived. 2 Mary would later pour perfume on the Lord. She would also wipe Jesus' feet with her hair. It was her brother Lazarus who was sick in bed. 3 So the sisters sent a message to Jesus. "Lord," they told him, "the one you love is sick."

4 When Jesus heard this, he said, "This sickness will not end in death. No, it is for God's glory. God's Son will receive glory because of it." 5 Jesus loved Martha and her sister and Lazarus. 6 So after he heard Lazarus was sick, he stayed where he was for two more days. 7 And then he said to his disciples, "Let us go back to Judea."

8 "But Rabbi," they said, "a short time ago the Jews there tried to kill you with stones. Are you still going back?"

9 Jesus answered, "Aren't there 12 hours of daylight? Anyone who walks during the day won't trip and fall. They can see because of this world's light. 10 But when they walk at night, they'll trip and fall. They have no light."

11 After he said this, Jesus went on speaking to them. "Our friend Lazarus has fallen asleep," he said. "But I am going there to wake him up."

12 His disciples replied, "Lord, if he's sleeping, he will get better." 13 Jesus had been speaking about the death of Lazarus. But his disciples thought he meant natural sleep.

14 So then he told them plainly, "Lazarus is dead. 15 For your benefit, I am glad I was not there. Now you will believe. But let us go to him."

16 Then Thomas, who was also called Didymus, spoke to the rest of the disciples. "Let us go also," he said. "Then we can die with Jesus."

Jesus Comforts the Sisters of Lazarus

17 When Jesus arrived, he found out that Lazarus had already been in the tomb for four days. 18 Bethany was less than two miles from Jerusalem. 19 Many Jews had come to Martha and Mary. They had come to comfort them because their brother was dead. 20 When Martha heard that Jesus was coming, she went out to meet him. But Mary stayed at home.

21 "Lord," Martha said to Jesus, "I wish you had been here! Then my brother would not have died. 22 But I know that even now God will give you anything you ask for."

23 Jesus said to her, "Your brother will rise again."

24 Martha answered, "I know he will rise again. This will happen when people are raised from the dead on the last day."

25 Jesus said to her, "I am the resurrection and the life. Anyone who believes in me will live, even if they die. 26 And whoever lives by believing in me will never die. Do you believe this?"

27 "Yes, Lord," she replied. "I believe that you are the Messiah, the Son of God. I believe that you are the one who is supposed to come into the world."

28 After she said this, she went back home. She called her sister Mary to one side to talk to her. "The Teacher is here," Martha said. "He is asking for you." 29 When Mary heard this, she got up quickly and went to him. 30 Jesus had not yet entered the village. He was still at the place where Martha had met him. 31 Some Jews had been comforting Mary in the house. They noticed how quickly she got up and went out. So they followed her. They thought she was going to the tomb to mourn there.

32 Mary reached the place where Jesus was. When she saw him, she fell at his feet. She said, "Lord, I wish you had been here! Then my brother would not have died."

33 Jesus saw her crying. He saw that the Jews who had come along with her were crying also. His spirit became very sad, and he was troubled. 34 "Where have you put him?" he asked.

"Come and see, Lord," they replied.

35 Jesus wept.

36 Then the Jews said, "See how much he loved him!"

37 But some of them said, "He opened the eyes of the blind man. Couldn't he have kept this man from dying?"

Jesus Raises Lazarus From the Dead

38 Once more Jesus felt very sad. He came to the tomb. It was a cave with a stone in front of the entrance. 39 "Take away the stone," he said.

"But, Lord," said Martha, the sister of the dead man, "by this time there is a bad smell. Lazarus has been in the tomb for four days."

40 Then Jesus said, "Didn't I tell you that if you believe, you will see God's glory?"

41 So they took away the stone. Then Jesus looked up. He said, "Father, I thank you for hearing me. 42 I know that you always hear me. But I said this for the benefit of the people standing here. I said it so they will believe that you sent me."

43 Then Jesus called in a loud voice. He said, "Lazarus, come out!" 44 The dead man came out. His hands and feet were wrapped with strips of linen. A cloth was around his face.

Jesus said to them, "Take off the clothes he was buried in and let him go."

The Plan to Kill Jesus

45 Many of the Jews who had come to visit Mary saw what Jesus did. So they believed in him. 46 But some of them went to the Pharisees. They told the Pharisees what Jesus had done. 47 Then the chief priests and the Pharisees called a meeting of the Sanhedrin.

"What can we do?" they asked. "This man is performing many signs. 48 If we let him keep on doing this, everyone will believe in him. Then the Romans will come. They will take away our temple and our nation."

49 One of the Jewish leaders spoke up. His name was Caiaphas. He was high priest at that time. He said, "You don't know anything at all! 50 You don't realize what is good for you. It is better if one man dies for the people than if the whole nation is destroyed."

51 He did not say this on his own because he was high priest at that time. He prophesied that Jesus would die for the Jewish nation. 52 He also prophesied that Jesus would die for God's children scattered everywhere. He would die to bring them together and make them one. 53 So from that day on, the Jewish rulers planned to kill Jesus.

54 Jesus no longer moved around openly among the people of Judea. Instead, he went away to an area near the desert. He went to a village called Ephraim. There he stayed with his disciples.

55 It was almost time for the Jewish Passover Feast. Many people went up from the country to Jerusalem. They went there for the special washing that would make them pure before the Passover Feast. 56 They kept looking for Jesus as they stood in the temple courtyard. They asked one another, "What do you think? Isn't he coming to the feast at all?" 57 But the chief priests and the Pharisees had given orders. They had commanded anyone who found out where Jesus was staying to report it. Then they could arrest him.

Mary Pours Perfume on Jesus at Bethany

12 It was six days before the Passover Feast. Jesus came to Bethany, where Lazarus lived. Lazarus was the one Jesus had raised from the dead. 2 A dinner was given at Bethany to honor Jesus. Martha served the food. Lazarus was among the people at the table with Jesus. 3 Then Mary took about a pint of pure nard. It was an expensive perfume. She poured it on Jesus' feet and wiped them with her hair. The house was filled with the sweet smell of the perfume.

4 But Judas Iscariot didn't like what Mary did. He was one of Jesus' disciples. Later he was going to hand Jesus over to his enemies. Judas said, 5 "Why wasn't this perfume sold? Why wasn't the money given to poor people? It was worth a year's pay." 6 He didn't say this because he cared about the poor. He said it because he was a thief. Judas was in charge of the money bag. He used to help himself to what was in it.

7 "Leave her alone," Jesus replied. "The perfume was meant for the day I am buried. 8 You will always have the poor among you. But you won't always have me."

9 Meanwhile a large crowd of Jews
found out that Jesus was there, so they
came. But they did not come only because of Jesus. They also came to see
Lazarus. After all, Jesus had raised him
from the dead. 10 So the chief priests
made plans to kill Lazarus too. 11 Because of Lazarus, many of the Jews
were starting to follow Jesus. They were
believing in him.

Jesus Comes to Jerusalem as King

12 The next day the large crowd that
had come for the feast heard that Jesus
was on his way to Jerusalem. 13 So they
took branches from palm trees and
went out to meet him. They shouted,

"Hosanna!"

"Blessed is the one who comes in
the name of the Lord!" *(Psalm 118:25,26)*

"Blessed is the king of Israel!"

14 Jesus found a young donkey and
sat on it. This is just as it is written in
Scripture. It says,

15 "City of Zion, do not be afraid.
See, your king is coming.
He is sitting on a donkey's colt."
(Zechariah 9:9)

16 At first, Jesus' disciples did not understand all this. They realized it only
after he had received glory. Then they
realized that these things had been
written about him. They realized that
these things had been done to him.
17 A crowd had been with Jesus when
he called Lazarus from the tomb and
raised him from the dead. So they continued to tell everyone about what had
happened. 18 Many people went out to
meet him. They had heard that he had
done this sign. 19 So the Pharisees said
to one another, "This isn't getting us
anywhere. Look how the whole world
is following him!"

Jesus Tells About His Coming Death

20 There were some Greeks among the
people who went up to worship during
the feast. 21 They came to ask Philip for
a favor. Philip was from Bethsaida in
Galilee. "Sir," they said, "we would like to
see Jesus." 22 Philip went to tell Andrew.
Then Andrew and Philip told Jesus.
23 Jesus replied, "The time has come for
the Son of Man to receive glory. 24 What
I'm about to tell you is true. Unless a
grain of wheat falls to the ground and
dies, it remains only one seed. But if it
dies, it produces many seeds. 25 Anyone
who loves their life will lose it. But anyone who hates their life in this world will
keep it and have eternal life. 26 Anyone
who serves me must follow me. And
where I am, my servant will also be. My
Father will honor the one who serves me.
27 "My soul is troubled. What should I
say? 'Father, keep me from having to go
through with this'? No. This is the very
reason I have come to this point in my
life. 28 Father, bring glory to your name!"

Then a voice came from heaven. It
said, "I have brought glory to my name.
I will bring glory to it again." 29 The
crowd there heard the voice. Some said
it was thunder. Others said an angel had
spoken to Jesus.
30 Jesus said, "This voice was for your
benefit, not mine. 31 Now it is time for
the world to be judged. Now the prince
of this world will be thrown out. 32 And I
am going to be lifted up from the earth.
When I am, I will bring all people to
myself." 33 He said this to show them
how he was going to die.
34 The crowd spoke up. "The Law tells
us that the Messiah will remain forever,"
they said. "So how can you say, 'The Son
of Man must be lifted up'? Who is this
'Son of Man'?"
35 Then Jesus told them, "You are going to have the light just a little while
longer. Walk while you have the light.
Do this before darkness catches up with
you. Whoever walks in the dark does not
know where they are going. 36 While you
have the light, believe in it. Then you
can become children of light." When
Jesus had finished speaking, he left and
hid from them.

Some Jews Believe and Some Don't

37 Jesus had performed so many signs
in front of them. But they still would
not believe in him. 38 This happened as
Isaiah the prophet had said it would.
He had said,

"Lord, who has believed what we've
been saying?
Who has seen the Lord's saving
power?" *(Isaiah 53:1)*

39 For this reason, they could not believe. As Isaiah says in another place,

40 "The Lord has blinded their eyes.
He has closed their minds.
So they can't see with their eyes.
They can't understand with their minds.
They can't turn to the Lord. If they could, he would heal them." *(Isaiah 6:10)*

41 Isaiah said this because he saw Jesus' glory and spoke about him.

42 At the same time that Jesus did those signs, many of the Jewish leaders believed in him. But because of the Pharisees, they would not openly admit they believed. They were afraid they would be thrown out of the synagogue. 43 They loved praise from people more than praise from God.

44 Then Jesus cried out, "Whoever believes in me does not believe in me only. They also believe in the one who sent me. 45 The one who looks at me sees the one who sent me. 46 I have come into the world to be its light. So no one who believes in me will stay in darkness.

47 "I don't judge a person who hears my words but does not obey them. I didn't come to judge the world. I came to save the world. 48 But there is a judge for anyone who does not accept me and my words. These words I have spoken will judge them on the last day. 49 I did not speak on my own. The Father who sent me commanded me to say all that I have said. 50 I know that his command leads to eternal life. So everything I say is just what the Father has told me to say."

Jesus Washes His Disciples' Feet

13 It was just before the Passover Feast. Jesus knew that the time had come for him to leave this world. It was time for him to go to the Father. Jesus loved his disciples who were in the world. So he now loved them to the very end.

2 They were having their evening meal. The devil had already tempted Judas, son of Simon Iscariot. He had urged Judas to hand Jesus over to his enemies. 3 Jesus knew that the Father had put everything under his power. He also knew he had come from God and was returning to God. 4 So he got up from the meal and took off his outer clothes. He wrapped a towel around his waist. 5 After that, he poured water into a large bowl. Then he began to wash his disciples' feet. He dried them with the towel that was wrapped around him.

6 He came to Simon Peter. "Lord," Peter said to him, "are you going to wash my feet?"

7 Jesus replied, "You don't realize now what I am doing. But later you will understand."

8 "No," said Peter. "You will never wash my feet."

Jesus answered, "Unless I wash you, you can't share life with me."

9 "Lord," Simon Peter replied, "not just my feet! Wash my hands and my head too!"

10 Jesus answered, "People who have had a bath need to wash only their feet. The rest of their body is clean. And you are clean. But not all of you are." 11 Jesus knew who was going to hand him over to his enemies. That was why he said not every one was clean.

12 When Jesus finished washing their feet, he put on his clothes. Then he returned to his place. "Do you understand what I have done for you?" he asked them. 13 "You call me 'Teacher' and 'Lord.' You are right. That is what I am. 14 I, your Lord and Teacher, have washed your feet. So you also should wash one another's feet. 15 I have given you an example. You should do as I have done for you. 16 What I'm about to tell you is true. A slave is not more important than his master. And a messenger is not more important than the one who sends him. 17 Now you know these things. So you will be blessed if you do them.

Jesus Tells What Judas Will Do

18 "I am not talking about all of you. I know the ones I have chosen. But this will happen so that this passage of Scripture will come true. It says, 'The one who shared my bread has turned against me.' *(Psalm 41:9)*

19 "I am telling you now, before it happens. When it does happen, you will believe that I am who I am. 20 What I'm about to tell you is true. Anyone who accepts someone I send accepts me. And anyone who accepts me accepts the one who sent me."

21 After he had said this, Jesus' spirit
was troubled. He said, "What I'm about
to tell you is true. One of you is going to
hand me over to my enemies."
22 His disciples stared at one another.
They had no idea which one of them he
meant. 23 The disciple Jesus loved was
next to him at the table. 24 Simon Peter
motioned to that disciple. He said, "Ask
Jesus which one he means."
25 The disciple was leaning back
against Jesus. He asked him, "Lord,
who is it?"
26 Jesus answered, "It is the one I will
give this piece of bread to. I will give it
to him after I have dipped it in the dish."
He dipped the piece of bread. Then he
gave it to Judas, son of Simon Iscariot.
27 As soon as Judas took the bread, Satan
entered into him.
So Jesus told him, "Do quickly what
you are going to do." 28 But no one at
the meal understood why Jesus said
this to him. 29 Judas was in charge of
the money. So some of the disciples
thought Jesus was telling him to buy
what was needed for the feast. Others
thought Jesus was talking about giving
something to poor people. 30 As soon as
Judas had taken the bread, he went out.
And it was night.

Peter Will Say He Does Not Know Jesus

31 After Judas was gone, Jesus spoke.
He said, "Now the Son of Man receives
glory. And he brings glory to God. 32 If
the Son brings glory to God, God himself
will bring glory to the Son. God will do
it at once.
33 "My children, I will be with you only
a little longer. You will look for me. Just
as I told the Jews, so I am telling you
now. You can't come where I am going.
34 "I give you a new command. Love
one another. You must love one another,
just as I have loved you. 35 If you love
one another, everyone will know you
are my disciples."
36 Simon Peter asked him, "Lord,
where are you going?"
Jesus replied, "Where I am going you
can't follow now. But you will follow
me later."
37 "Lord," Peter asked, "why can't I
follow you now? I will give my life for
you."
38 Then Jesus answered, "Will you
really give your life for me? What I'm
about to tell you is true. Before the
rooster crows, you will say three times
that you don't know me!

Jesus Comforts His Disciples

14 "Do not let your hearts be troubled. You believe in God. Believe
in me also. 2 There are many rooms
in my Father's house. If this were not
true, would I have told you that I am
going there? Would I have told you that
I would prepare a place for you there?
3 If I go and do that, I will come back.
And I will take you to be with me. Then
you will also be where I am. 4 You know
the way to the place where I am going."

Jesus Is the Way to the Father

5 Thomas said to him, "Lord, we don't
know where you are going. So how can
we know the way?"
6 Jesus answered, "I am the way and
the truth and the life. No one comes
to the Father except through me. 7 If
you really know me, you will know my
Father also. From now on, you do know
him. And you have seen him."
8 Philip said, "Lord, show us the Father. That will be enough for us."
9 Jesus answered, "Don't you know
me, Philip? I have been among you such
a long time! Anyone who has seen me
has seen the Father. So how can you say,
'Show us the Father'? 10 Don't you believe
that I am in the Father? Don't you believe
that the Father is in me? The words I say
to you I do not speak on my own authority. The Father lives in me. He is the one
who is doing his work. 11 Believe me when
I say I am in the Father. Also believe that
the Father is in me. Or at least believe
what the works I have been doing say
about me. 12 What I'm about to tell you
is true. Anyone who believes in me will
do the works I have been doing. In fact,
they will do even greater things. That's
because I am going to the Father. 13 And
I will do anything you ask in my name.
Then the Father will receive glory from
the Son. 14 You may ask me for anything
in my name. I will do it.

Jesus Promises That the Holy Spirit Will Come

15 "If you love me, obey my commands. 16 I will ask the Father. And he

will give you another friend to help you
and to be with you forever. 17 That friend
is the Spirit of truth. The world can't accept him. That's because the world does
not see him or know him. But you know
him. He lives with you, and he will be in
you. 18 I will not leave you like children
who don't have parents. I will come to
you. 19 Before long, the world will not
see me anymore. But you will see me.
Because I live, you will live also. 20 On
that day you will realize that I am in
my Father. You will know that you are
in me, and I am in you. 21 Anyone who
has my commands and obeys them
loves me. My Father will love the one
who loves me. I too will love them. And
I will show myself to them."

22 Then Judas spoke. "Lord," he said,
"why do you plan to show yourself only
to us? Why not also to the world?" The
Judas who spoke those words was not
Judas Iscariot.

23 Jesus replied, "Anyone who loves
me will obey my teaching. My Father
will love them. We will come to them
and make our home with them. 24 Anyone who does not love me will not obey
my teaching. The words you hear me
say are not my own. They belong to the
Father who sent me.

25 "I have spoken all these things
while I am still with you. 26 But the Father will send the Friend in my name to
help you. The Friend is the Holy Spirit.
He will teach you all things. He will
remind you of everything I have said
to you. 27 I leave my peace with you. I
give my peace to you. I do not give it to
you as the world does. Do not let your
hearts be troubled. And do not be afraid.

28 "You heard me say, 'I am going
away. And I am coming back to you.'
If you loved me, you would be glad I
am going to the Father. The Father is
greater than I am. 29 I have told you now
before it happens. Then when it does
happen, you will believe. 30 I will not
say much more to you. The prince of this
world is coming. He has no power over
me. 31 But he comes so that the world
may learn that I love the Father. They
must also learn that I do exactly what
my Father has commanded me to do.

"Come now. Let us leave.

If I'm saved by grace, why do I need to obey God?

When you trust in God for salvation, his Spirit comes and lives inside of you, giving you the ability to love and obey him. Genuine faith means a growing desire to do things God's way.

Can you find the following verse?

JOHN 14:21

The Vine and the Branches

15 "I am the true vine. My Father is
the gardener. 2 He cuts off every
branch joined to me that does not bear
fruit. He trims every branch that does
bear fruit. Then it will bear even more
fruit. 3 You are already clean because
of the word I have spoken to you. 4 Remain joined to me, just as I also remain
joined to you. No branch can bear fruit
by itself. It must remain joined to the
vine. In the same way, you can't bear
fruit unless you remain joined to me.

5 "I am the vine. You are the branches.
If you remain joined to me, and I to
you, you will bear a lot of fruit. You
can't do anything without me. 6 If you
don't remain joined to me, you are
like a branch that is thrown away and
dries up. Branches like those are picked
up. They are thrown into the fire and
burned. 7 If you remain joined to me
and my words remain in you, ask for
anything you wish. And it will be done
for you. 8 When you bear a lot of fruit,
it brings glory to my Father. It shows
that you are my disciples.

9 "Just as the Father has loved me,
I have loved you. Now remain in my
love. 10 If you obey my commands,
you will remain in my love. In the

same way, I have obeyed my Father's
commands and remain in his love. 11 I
have told you this so that you will have
the same joy that I have. I also want
your joy to be complete. 12 Here is my
command. Love one another, just as I
have loved you. 13 No one has greater
love than the one who gives their life
for their friends. 14 You are my friends
if you do what I command. 15 I do not
call you slaves anymore. Slaves do not
know their master's business. Instead,
I have called you friends. I have told
you everything I learned from my Father. 16 You did not choose me. Instead,
I chose you. I appointed you so that you
might go and bear fruit that will last. I
also appointed you so that the Father
will give you what you ask for. He will
give you whatever you ask for in my
name. 17 Here is my command. Love
one another.

The World Hates the Disciples

18 "My disciples, does the world hate
you? Remember that it hated me first.
19 If you belonged to the world, it would
love you like one of its own. But you do
not belong to the world. I have chosen
you out of the world. That is why the
world hates you. 20 Remember what
I told you. I said, 'A slave is not more
important than his master.' *(John 13:16)*
If people hated me and tried to hurt me,
they will do the same to you. If they
obeyed my teaching, they will obey
yours also. 21 They will treat you like
that because of my name. They do not
know the one who sent me. 22 If I had not
come and spoken to them, they would
not be guilty of sin. But now they have
no excuse for their sin. 23 Whoever hates
me hates my Father also. 24 I did works
among them that no one else did. If I
hadn't, they would not be guilty of sin.
But now they have seen those works.
And still they have hated both me and
my Father. 25 This has happened so that
what is written in their Law would come
true. It says, 'They hated me without
any reason.' *(Psalms 35:19; 69:4)*

The Work of the Holy Spirit

26 "I will send the Friend to you from
the Father. He is the Spirit of truth, who
comes out from the Father. When the
Friend comes to help you, he will be a
witness about me. 27 You must also be
witnesses about me. That's because you
have been with me from the beginning.

16 "I have told you all this so that
you will not turn away from the
truth. 2 You will be thrown out of the
synagogue. In fact, the time is coming
when someone may kill you. And they
will think they are doing God a favor.
3 They will do things like that because
they do not know the Father or me.
4 Why have I told you this? So that when
their time comes, you will remember
that I warned you about them. I didn't
tell you this from the beginning because
I was with you. 5 But now I am going to
the one who sent me. None of you asks
me, 'Where are you going?' 6 Instead,
you are filled with sadness because I
have said these things. 7 But what I'm
about to tell you is true. It is for your
good that I am going away. Unless I go
away, the Friend will not come to help
you. But if I go, I will send him to you.
8 When he comes, he will prove that
the world's people are guilty. He will
prove their guilt concerning sin and
godliness and judgment. 9 The world is
guilty as far as sin is concerned. That's
because people do not believe in me.
10 The world is guilty as far as godliness
is concerned. That's because I am going
to the Father, where you can't see me
anymore. 11 The world is guilty as far as
judgment is concerned. That's because
the devil, the prince of this world, has
already been judged.

12 "I have much more to say to you. It
is more than you can handle right now.
13 But when the Spirit of truth comes,
he will guide you into all the truth. He
will not speak on his own. He will speak
only what he hears. And he will tell you
what is still going to happen. 14 He will
bring me glory. That's because what
he receives from me he will show to
you. 15 Everything that belongs to the
Father is mine. That is why I said what
the Holy Spirit receives from me he will
show to you."

The Disciples' Sadness Will Turn Into Joy

16 Jesus continued, "In a little while,
you will no longer see me. Then after a
little while, you will see me."

17 After they heard this, some of his
disciples spoke to one another. They

said, "What does he mean by saying,
'In a little while, you will no longer see
me. Then after a little while, you will see
me'? And what does he mean by saying,
'I am going to the Father'?" 18 They kept
asking, "What does he mean by 'a little
while'? We don't understand what he
is saying."

19 Jesus saw that they wanted to ask
him about these things. So he said to
them, "Are you asking one another
what I meant? Didn't you understand
when I said, 'In a little while, you will
no longer see me. Then after a little
while, you will see me'? 20 What I'm
about to tell you is true. You will weep
and mourn while the world is full of joy.
You will be sad, but your sadness will
turn into joy. 21 A woman giving birth
to a baby has pain. That's because her
time to give birth has come. But when
her baby is born, she forgets the pain.
She forgets because she is so happy that
a baby has been born into the world.
22 That's the way it is with you. Now
it's your time to be sad. But I will see
you again. Then you will be full of joy.
And no one will take away your joy.
23 When that day comes, you will no
longer ask me for anything. What I'm
about to tell you is true. My Father will
give you anything you ask for in my
name. 24 Until now you have not asked
for anything in my name. Ask, and you
will receive what you ask for. Then your
joy will be complete.

25 "I have not been speaking to you
plainly. But a time is coming when I
will speak clearly. Then I will tell you
plainly about my Father. 26 When that
day comes, you will ask for things in
my name. I am not saying I will ask the
Father instead of you asking him. 27 No,
the Father himself loves you because
you have loved me. He also loves you
because you have believed that I came
from God. 28 I came from the Father and
entered the world. Now I am leaving the
world and going back to the Father."

29 Then Jesus' disciples said, "Now
you are speaking plainly. You are using
examples that are clear. 30 Now we can
see that you know everything. You don't
even need anyone to ask you questions.
This makes us believe that you came
from God."

31 "Do you believe now?" Jesus replied.
32 "A time is coming when you will be
scattered and go to your own homes. In
fact, that time is already here. You will
leave me all alone. But I am not really
alone. My Father is with me.

33 "I have told you these things, so
that you can have peace because of me.
In this world you will have trouble. But
be encouraged! I have won the battle
over the world."

Jesus Prays for Himself

17 After Jesus said this, he looked toward heaven and prayed. He said,

"Father, the time has come. Bring
glory to your Son. Then your Son
will bring glory to you. 2 You gave
him authority over all people. He
gives eternal life to all those you
have given him. 3 And what is eternal life? It is knowing you, the only
true God, and Jesus Christ, whom
you have sent. 4 I have brought you
glory on earth. I have finished the
work you gave me to do. 5 So now,
Father, give glory to me in heaven
where your throne is. Give me the
glory I had with you before the
world began.

Jesus Prays for His Disciples

6 "I have shown you to the disciples you gave me out of the world.
They were yours. You gave them
to me. And they have obeyed your
word. 7 Now they know that everything you have given me comes
from you. 8 I gave them the words
you gave me. And they accepted
them. They knew for certain that I
came from you. They believed that
you sent me. 9 I pray for them. I
am not praying for the world. I am
praying for those you have given
me, because they are yours. 10 All
I have is yours, and all you have
is mine. Glory has come to me because of my disciples. 11 I will not
remain in the world any longer.
But they are still in the world, and
I am coming to you. Holy Father,
keep them safe by the power of
your name. It is the name you gave
me. Keep them safe so they can
be one, just as you and I are one.
12 While I was with them, I guarded

them. I kept them safe through the name you gave me. None of them has been lost, except the one who was headed for ruin. It happened so that Scripture would come true.
13 "I am coming to you now. But I say these things while I am still in the world. I say them so that those you gave me can have the same joy
that I have. 14 I have given them your word. The world has hated them. That's because they are not part of
the world any more than I am. 15 I
do not pray that you will take them out of the world. I pray that you will keep them safe from the evil one.
16 They do not belong to the world,
just as I do not belong to it. 17 Use
the truth to make them holy. Your
word is truth. 18 You sent me into
the world. In the same way, I have
sent them into the world. 19 I make
myself holy for them so that they too can be made holy by the truth.

Jesus Prays for All Believers

20 "I do not pray only for them. I pray also for everyone who will believe in me because of their message.
21 Father, I pray they will be one, just as you are in me and I am in you. I want them also to be in us. Then the world will believe that you
have sent me. 22 I have given them
the glory you gave me. I did this so they would be one, just as we are
one. 23 I will be in them, just as you
are in me. This is so that they may be brought together perfectly as one. Then the world will know that you sent me. It will also show the world that you have loved those you gave me, just as you have loved me.
24 "Father, I want those you have given me to be with me where I am. I want them to see my glory, the glory you have given me. You gave it to me because you loved me before the world was created.
25 "Father, you are holy. The world does not know you, but I know you. Those you have given
me know you have sent me. 26 I
have shown you to them. And I will continue to show you to them. Then the love you have for me will be in them. I myself will be in them."

Jesus Is Arrested

18 When Jesus had finished praying, he left with his disciples. They crossed the Kidron Valley. On the other side there was a garden. Jesus and his disciples went into it.
2 Judas knew the place. He was going to hand Jesus over to his enemies. Jesus had often met in that place with his
disciples. 3 So Judas came to the garden.
He was guiding a group of soldiers and some officials. The chief priests and the Pharisees had sent them. They were carrying torches, lanterns and weapons.
4 Jesus knew everything that was going to happen to him. So he went out and asked them, "Who do you want?"
5 "Jesus of Nazareth," they replied.
"I am he," Jesus said. Judas, who was going to hand Jesus over, was standing
there with them. 6 When Jesus said, "I
am he," they moved back. Then they fell to the ground.
7 He asked them again, "Who do you want?"
"Jesus of Nazareth," they said.
8 Jesus answered, "I told you I am he. If you are looking for me, then let these
men go." 9 This happened so that the
words Jesus had spoken would come true. He had said, "I have not lost anyone God has given me." *(John 6:39)*
10 Simon Peter had a sword and pulled it out. He struck the high priest's slave and cut off his right ear. The slave's name was Malchus.
11 Jesus commanded Peter, "Put your sword away! Shouldn't I drink the cup of suffering the Father has given me?"
12 Then the group of soldiers, their commander and the Jewish officials
arrested Jesus. They tied him up 13 and
brought him first to Annas. He was the father-in-law of Caiaphas, the high
priest at that time. 14 Caiaphas had
advised the Jewish leaders that it would be good if one man died for the people.

Peter Says He Is Not Jesus' Disciple

15 Simon Peter and another disciple were following Jesus. The high priest knew the other disciple. So that disciple went with Jesus into the high priest's
courtyard. 16 But Peter had to wait
outside by the door. The other disciple came back. He was the one the high priest knew. He spoke to the servant

woman who was on duty there. Then
he brought Peter in.
17 She asked Peter, "You aren't one of
Jesus' disciples too, are you?"
"I am not," he replied.
18 It was cold. The slaves and officials
stood around a fire. They had made it
to keep warm. Peter was also standing
with them. He was warming himself.

The High Priest Questions Jesus

19 Meanwhile, the high priest questioned Jesus. He asked him about his
disciples and his teaching.
20 "I have spoken openly to the
world," Jesus replied. "I always taught
in synagogues or at the temple, where
all the Jews come together. I didn't say
anything in secret. 21 Why question me?
Ask the people who heard me. They
certainly know what I said."
22 When Jesus said that, one of the
officials nearby slapped him in the face.
"Is this any way to answer the high
priest?" he asked.
23 "Have I said something wrong?"
Jesus replied. "If I have, then tell everyone what it was. But if I spoke the truth,
why did you hit me?" 24 Annas sent him,
tied up, to Caiaphas, the high priest.

Peter Again Says He Is Not Jesus' Disciple

25 Meanwhile, Simon Peter was still
standing there warming himself by the
fire. So they asked him, "You aren't one
of Jesus' disciples too, are you?"
He said, "I am not."
26 One of the high priest's slaves was
a relative of the man whose ear Peter
had cut off. He said to Peter, "Didn't I see
you with Jesus in the garden?" 27 Again
Peter said no. At that exact moment a
rooster began to crow.

Jesus Is Brought to Pilate

28 Then the Jewish leaders took
Jesus from Caiaphas to the palace of
the Roman governor. By now it was
early morning. The Jewish leaders did
not want to be made "unclean." They
wanted to be able to eat the Passover
meal. So they did not enter the palace.
29 Pilate came out to them. He asked,
"What charges are you bringing against
this man?"
30 "He has committed crimes," they
replied. "If he hadn't, we would not have
handed him over to you."
31 Pilate said, "Take him yourselves.
Judge him by your own law."
"But we don't have the right to put
anyone to death," they complained.
32 This happened so that what Jesus said
about how he was going to die would
come true.
33 Then Pilate went back inside the
palace. He ordered Jesus to be brought
to him. Pilate asked him, "Are you the
king of the Jews?"
34 "Is that your own idea?" Jesus
asked. "Or did others talk to you about
me?"
35 "Am I a Jew?" Pilate replied. "Your
own people and chief priests handed
you over to me. What have you done?"
36 Jesus said, "My kingdom is not from
this world. If it were, those who serve me
would fight. They would try to keep the
Jewish leaders from arresting me. My
kingdom is from another place."
37 "So you are a king, then!" said
Pilate.
Jesus answered, "You say that I
am a king. In fact, that's the reason
I was born. I was born and came into
the world to be a witness to the truth.
Everyone who is on the side of truth
listens to me."
38 "What is truth?" Pilate replied. Then
Pilate went out again to the Jews gathered there. He said, "I find no basis for
any charge against him. 39 But you have
a practice at Passover time. At that time,
you ask me to set one prisoner free for
you. Do you want me to set 'the king of
the Jews' free?"
40 They shouted back, "No! Not him!
Give us Barabbas!" Barabbas had taken
part in an armed struggle against the
country's rulers.

Jesus Is Sentenced to Be Crucified

19 Then Pilate took Jesus and had
him whipped. 2 The soldiers twisted thorns together to make a crown.
They put it on Jesus' head. Then they
put a purple robe on him. 3 They went
up to him again and again. They kept
saying, "We honor you, king of the
Jews!" And they slapped him in the face.
4 Once more Pilate came out. He said
to the Jews gathered there, "Look, I am

bringing Jesus out to you. I want to let you know that I find no basis for a charge against him." 5 Jesus came out wearing the crown of thorns and the purple robe. Then Pilate said to them, "Here is the man!"

6 As soon as the chief priests and their officials saw him, they shouted, "Crucify him! Crucify him!"

But Pilate answered, "You take him and crucify him. I myself find no basis for a charge against him."

7 The Jewish leaders replied, "We have a law. That law says he must die. He claimed to be the Son of God."

8 When Pilate heard that, he was even more afraid. 9 He went back inside the palace. "Where do you come from?" he asked Jesus. But Jesus did not answer him. 10 "Do you refuse to speak to me?" Pilate said. "Don't you understand? I have the power to set you free or to nail you to a cross."

11 Jesus answered, "You were given power from heaven. If you weren't, you would have no power over me. So the one who handed me over to you is guilty of a greater sin."

12 From then on, Pilate tried to set Jesus free. But the Jewish leaders kept shouting, "If you let this man go, you are not Caesar's friend! Anyone who claims to be a king is against Caesar!"

13 When Pilate heard that, he brought Jesus out. Pilate sat down on the judge's seat. It was at a place called the Stone Walkway. In the Aramaic language it was called Gabbatha. 14 It was about noon on Preparation Day in Passover Week.

"Here is your king," Pilate said to the Jews.

15 But they shouted, "Take him away! Take him away! Crucify him!"

"Should I crucify your king?" Pilate asked.

"We have no king but Caesar," the chief priests answered.

16 Finally, Pilate handed Jesus over to them to be nailed to a cross.

Jesus Is Nailed to a Cross

So the soldiers took charge of Jesus. 17 He had to carry his own cross. He went out to a place called the Skull. In the Aramaic language it was called Golgotha. 18 There they nailed Jesus to the cross. Two other men were crucified with him. One was on each side of him. Jesus was in the middle.

19 Pilate had a notice prepared. It was fastened to the cross. It read,

JESUS OF NAZARETH, THE KING
OF THE JEWS.

20 Many of the Jews read the sign. That's because the place where Jesus was crucified was near the city. And the sign was written in the Aramaic, Latin and Greek languages. 21 The chief priests of the Jews argued with Pilate. They said, "Do not write 'The King of the Jews.' Write that this man claimed to be king of the Jews."

22 Pilate answered, "I have written what I have written."

23 When the soldiers crucified Jesus, they took his clothes. They divided them into four parts. Each soldier got one part. All that was left was Jesus' long, inner robe. It did not have any seams. It was made out of one piece of cloth from top to bottom.

24 "Let's not tear it," they said to one another. "Let's cast lots to see who will get it."

This happened so that Scripture would come true. It says,

"They divided up my clothes
among them.
They cast lots for what I was
wearing." *(Psalm 22:18)*

So that is what the soldiers did.

25 Jesus' mother stood near his cross. So did his mother's sister, Mary the wife of Clopas, and Mary Magdalene. 26 Jesus saw his mother there. He also saw the disciple he loved standing nearby. Jesus said to his mother, "Dear woman, here is your son." 27 He said to the disciple, "Here is your mother." From that time on, the disciple took her into his home.

Jesus Dies

28 Later, Jesus knew that everything had now been finished. He also knew that what Scripture said must come true. So he said, "I am thirsty." 29 A jar of wine vinegar was there. So they soaked a sponge in it. They put the sponge on the stem of a hyssop plant. Then they lifted it up to Jesus' lips. 30 After Jesus

drank he said, "It is finished." Then he
bowed his head and died.
31 It was Preparation Day. The next
day would be a special Sabbath day. The
Jewish leaders did not want the bodies
left on the crosses during the Sabbath
day. So they asked Pilate to have the
legs broken and the bodies taken down.
32 The soldiers came and broke the legs
of the first man who had been crucified
with Jesus. Then they broke the legs of
the other man. 33 But when they came
to Jesus, they saw that he was already
dead. So they did not break his legs.
34 Instead, one of the soldiers stuck his
spear into Jesus' side. Right away, blood
and water flowed out. 35 The man who
saw it has been a witness about it. And
what he has said is true. He knows that
he tells the truth. He is a witness so that
you also may believe. 36 These things
happened in order that Scripture would
come true. It says, "Not one of his bones
will be broken." *(Exodus 12:46; Numbers
9:12; Psalm 34:20)* 37 Scripture also says,
"They will look to the one they have
pierced." *(Zechariah 12:10)*

Jesus Is Buried

38 Later Joseph asked Pilate for Jesus'
body. Joseph was from the town of Arimathea. He was a follower of Jesus. But
he followed Jesus secretly because he
was afraid of the Jewish leaders. After
Pilate gave him permission, Joseph
came and took the body away. 39 Nicodemus went with Joseph. He was the
man who had earlier visited Jesus at
night. Nicodemus brought some mixed
spices that weighed about 75 pounds.
40 The two men took Jesus' body. They
wrapped it in strips of linen cloth, along
with the spices. That was the way the
Jews buried people. 41 At the place where
Jesus was crucified, there was a garden.
A new tomb was there. No one had ever
been put in it before. 42 That day was the
Jewish Preparation Day, and the tomb
was nearby. So they placed Jesus there.

The Tomb Is Empty

20 Early on the first day of the
week, Mary Magdalene went
to the tomb. It was still dark. She saw
that the stone had been moved away
from the entrance. 2 So she ran to Simon Peter and another disciple, the one
Jesus loved. She said, "They have taken
the Lord out of the tomb! We don't know
where they have put him!"
3 So Peter and the other disciple started
out for the tomb. 4 Both of them were running. The other disciple ran faster than
Peter. He reached the tomb first. 5 He bent
over and looked in at the strips of linen
lying there. But he did not go in. 6 Then
Simon Peter came along behind him. He
went straight into the tomb. He saw the
strips of linen lying there. 7 He also saw
the funeral cloth that had been wrapped
around Jesus' head. The cloth was still
lying in its place. It was separate from the
linen. 8 The disciple who had reached the
tomb first also went inside. He saw and
believed. 9 They still did not understand
from Scripture that Jesus had to rise from
the dead. 10 Then the disciples went back
to where they were staying.

Jesus Appears to Mary Magdalene

11 But Mary stood outside the tomb
crying. As she cried, she bent over to
look into the tomb. 12 She saw two angels dressed in white. They were seated
where Jesus' body had been. One of
them was where Jesus' head had been
laid. The other sat where his feet had
been placed.
13 They asked her, "Woman, why are
you crying?"
"They have taken my Lord away,"
she said. "I don't know where they have
put him." 14 Then she turned around and
saw Jesus standing there. But she didn't
realize that it was Jesus.
15 He asked her, "Woman, why are
you crying? Who are you looking for?"
She thought he was the gardener. So
she said, "Sir, did you carry him away?
Tell me where you put him. Then I will
go and get him."
16 Jesus said to her, "Mary."
She turned toward him. Then she
cried out in the Aramaic language,
"Rabboni!" Rabboni means Teacher.
17 Jesus said, "Do not hold on to me.
I have not yet ascended to the Father.
Instead, go to those who believe in me.
Tell them, 'I am ascending to my Father
and your Father, to my God and your
God.' "
18 Mary Magdalene went to the disciples with the news. She said, "I have
seen the Lord!" And she told them that
he had said these things to her.

Jesus Appears to His Disciples

19 On the evening of that first day of the week, the disciples were together. They had locked the doors because they were afraid of the Jewish leaders. Jesus came in and stood among them. He said, "May peace be with you!" 20 Then he showed them his hands and his side. The disciples were very happy when they saw the Lord.

21 Again Jesus said, "May peace be with you! The Father has sent me. So now I am sending you." 22 He then breathed on them. He said, "Receive the Holy Spirit. 23 If you forgive anyone's sins, their sins are forgiven. If you do not forgive them, they are not forgiven."

Jesus Appears to Thomas

24 Thomas was one of the 12 disciples. He was also called Didymus. He was not with the other disciples when Jesus came. 25 So they told him, "We have seen the Lord!"

But he said to them, "First I must see the nail marks in his hands. I must put my finger where the nails were. I must put my hand into his side. Only then will I believe."

26 A week later, Jesus' disciples were in the house again. Thomas was with them. Even though the doors were locked, Jesus came in and stood among them. He said, "May peace be with you!" 27 Then he said to Thomas, "Put your finger here. See my hands. Reach out your hand and put it into my side. Stop doubting and believe."

28 Thomas said to him, "My Lord and my God!"

29 Then Jesus told him, "Because you have seen me, you have believed. Blessed are those who have not seen me but still have believed."

The Purpose of John's Gospel

30 Jesus performed many other signs in front of his disciples. They are not written down in this book. 31 But these are written so that you may believe that Jesus is the Messiah, the Son of God. If you believe this, you will have life because you belong to him.

Jesus and the Miracle of Many Fish

21 After this, Jesus appeared to his disciples again. It was by the Sea of Galilee. Here is what happened. 2 Simon Peter and Thomas, who was also called Didymus, were there together. Nathanael from Cana in Galilee and the sons of Zebedee were with them. So were two other disciples. 3 "I'm going out to fish," Simon Peter told them. They said, "We'll go with you." So they went out and got into the boat. That night they didn't catch anything.

4 Early in the morning, Jesus stood on the shore. But the disciples did not realize that it was Jesus.

5 He called out to them, "Friends, don't you have any fish?"

"No," they answered.

6 He said, "Throw your net on the right side of the boat. There you will find some fish." When they did, they could not pull the net into the boat. There were too many fish in it.

7 Then the disciple Jesus loved said to Simon Peter, "It is the Lord!" As soon as Peter heard that, he put his coat on. He had taken it off earlier. Then he jumped into the water. 8 The other disciples followed in the boat. They were towing the net full of fish. The shore was only about 100 yards away. 9 When they landed, they saw a fire of burning coals. There were fish on it. There was also some bread.

10 Jesus said to them, "Bring some of the fish you have just caught." 11 So Simon Peter climbed back into the boat. He dragged the net to shore. It was full of large fish. There were 153 of them. But even with that many fish the net was not torn. 12 Jesus said to them, "Come and have breakfast." None of the disciples dared to ask him, "Who are you?" They knew it was the Lord. 13 Jesus came, took the bread and gave it to them. He did the same thing with the fish. 14 This was the third time Jesus appeared to his disciples after he was raised from the dead.

Jesus Gives Peter His Task

15 When Jesus and the disciples had finished eating, Jesus spoke to Simon Peter. He asked, "Simon, son of John, do you love me more than these others do?"

"Yes, Lord," he answered. "You know that I love you."

Jesus said, "Feed my lambs."

16 Again Jesus asked, "Simon, son of John, do you love me?"

He answered, "Yes, Lord. You know
that I love you."

Jesus said, "Take care of my sheep."
17 Jesus spoke to him a third time.
He asked, "Simon, son of John, do you
love me?"

Peter felt bad because Jesus asked
him the third time, "Do you love me?"
He answered, "Lord, you know all
things. You know that I love you."

Jesus said, "Feed my sheep. 18 What
I'm about to tell you is true. When you
were younger, you dressed yourself.
You went wherever you wanted to go.
But when you are old, you will stretch
out your hands. Someone else will dress
you. Someone else will lead you where
you do not want to go." 19 Jesus said this
to point out how Peter would die. His
death would bring glory to God. Then
Jesus said to him, "Follow me!"
20 Peter turned around. He saw that
the disciple Jesus loved was following
them. He was the one who had leaned
back against Jesus at the supper. He had
said, "Lord, who is going to hand you
over to your enemies?" 21 When Peter
saw that disciple, he asked, "Lord, what
will happen to him?"
22 Jesus answered, "Suppose I want
him to remain alive until I return. What
does that matter to you? You must follow me." 23 Because of what Jesus said,
a false report spread among the believers. The story was told that the disciple
Jesus loved wouldn't die. But Jesus did
not say he would not die. He only said,
"Suppose I want him to remain alive
until I return. What does that matter
to you?"
24 This is the disciple who is a witness
about these things. He also wrote them
down. We know that what he says is
true.
25 Jesus also did many other things.
What if every one of them were written
down? I suppose that even the whole
world would not have room for the
books that would be written.

ACTS

Author: Luke

Luke wrote not only the Gospel of Luke but also the book of Acts. In the Gospel of Luke, he wanted to show God's people what Jesus did in his life and tell about his death and resurrection. In the book of Acts, Luke wanted to show God's people how Jesus established his church to be a witness, or example, to the world.

Acts tells how God built the early church, or gathering of believers. These people had heard that the Messiah had come and believed that anyone could be saved if they put their faith in Jesus. Acts explains what the people learned about working together and how God sent the Holy Spirit to lead, guide, and counsel them (see Acts 2:1–4). They became known as Christians (see Acts 11:26). This was an exciting time in the life of God's people! They didn't all have the same background—some were Jews who believed that Jesus was the Savior they had been waiting for all along, and others were Gentiles (non-Jews) who had heard about Jesus and put their faith in him. Each of them was given the mission of telling others the good news about Jesus. These Christians gathered together to learn and grow in their faith as they walked by God's Spirit, obeying his commands.

Gospels & Acts

Jesus Is Taken Up Into Heaven

1 Theophilus, I wrote about Jesus in
my earlier book. I wrote about all he
did and taught 2 until the day he was
taken up to heaven. Before Jesus left,
he gave orders to the apostles he had
chosen. He did this through the Holy
Spirit. 3 After his suffering and death,
he appeared to them. In many ways he
proved that he was alive. He appeared
to them over a period of 40 days. During
that time he spoke about God's kingdom. 4 One day Jesus was eating with
them. He gave them a command. "Do
not leave Jerusalem," he said. "Wait for
the gift my Father promised. You have
heard me talk about it. 5 John baptized
with water. But in a few days you will
be baptized with the Holy Spirit."

6 Then the apostles gathered around
Jesus and asked him a question. "Lord,"
they said, "are you going to give the
kingdom back to Israel now?"

7 He said to them, "You should not be
concerned about times or dates. The Father has set them by his own authority.
8 But you will receive power when the
Holy Spirit comes on you. Then you will
tell people about me in Jerusalem, and
in all Judea and Samaria. And you will
even tell other people about me from
one end of the earth to the other."

9 After Jesus said this, he was taken
up to heaven. The apostles watched
until a cloud hid him from their sight.

10 While he was going up, they kept
on looking at the sky. Suddenly two
men dressed in white clothing stood
beside them. 11 "Men of Galilee," they
said, "why do you stand here looking
at the sky? Jesus has been taken away
from you into heaven. But he will come
back in the same way you saw him go."

Matthias Is Chosen to Take the Place of Judas Iscariot

12 The apostles returned to Jerusalem
from the hill called the Mount of Olives.
It is just over half a mile from the city.
13 When they arrived, they went upstairs
to the room where they were staying.
Here is a list of those who were there.

Peter, John, James and Andrew,
Philip and Thomas,
Bartholomew and Matthew,
James son of Alphaeus, Simon the
Zealot and Judas son of James

in Acts?

God is the Wonderful Counselor. God sent his Spirit to guide and direct his people as he builds his church.

14 They all came together regularly to
pray. The women joined them too. So did
Jesus' mother Mary and his brothers.

15 In those days Peter stood up among
the believers. About 120 of them were
there. 16 Peter said, "Brothers and sisters,
a long time ago the Holy Spirit spoke
through David. He spoke about Judas
Iscariot. What the Scripture said would
happen had to come true. Judas was the
guide for the men who arrested Jesus.
17 But Judas was one of us. He shared
with us in our work for God."

18 Judas bought a field with the payment he received for the evil thing he
had done. He fell down headfirst in the
field. His body burst open. All his insides
spilled out. 19 Everyone in Jerusalem
heard about this. So they called that
field Akeldama. In their language, Akeldama means the Field of Blood.

20 Peter said, "Here is what is written
in the Book of Psalms. It says,

" 'May his home be deserted.
May no one live in it.' *(Psalm 69:25)*

The Psalms also say,

" 'Let someone else take his place as
leader.' *(Psalm 109:8)*

21 So we need to choose someone to take
his place. It will have to be a man who
was with us the whole time the Lord
Jesus was living among us. 22 That time
began when John was baptizing. It ended when Jesus was taken up from us. The
one we choose must join us in telling
people that Jesus rose from the dead."

PAUL'S MISSIONARY JOURNEYS

CITIES PAUL VISITED

Paul personally experienced the grace and mercy of God and wanted everyone to know about the Savior, Jesus. Paul knew that the gospel of Jesus was life-changing. Paul traveled to different cities preaching to everyone who would listen that Jesus was the only way to be made right with God. He taught the Jews that Jesus was the Messiah their ancestors had been waiting for, and he taught Gentiles (non-Jews) that Jesus was the Savior who welcomed them into the family of God.

During his life and ministry, Paul went on three missionary journeys. On these three journeys he helped start many new churches full of new Christians. Later, when he traveled to a new city or region, he would write letters to those churches he had helped start. This is how we got many of the letters in the New Testament!

To read about Paul's first missionary journey, turn to page 1249.
To read about Paul's second missionary journey, turn to page 1254.
To read about Paul's third missionary journey, turn to page 1259.

23 So they suggested the names of two
men. One was Joseph, who was called
Barsabbas. He was also called Justus.
The other man was Matthias. 24 Then the
believers prayed. They said, "Lord, you
know everyone's heart. Show us which
of these two you have chosen. 25 Show
us who should take the place of Judas as
an apostle. He gave up being an apostle
to go where he belongs." 26 Then they
cast lots. Matthias was chosen. So he
was added to the 11 apostles.

The Holy Spirit Comes at Pentecost

2 When the day of Pentecost came, all
the believers gathered in one place.
2 Suddenly a sound came from heaven. It
was like a strong wind blowing. It filled
the whole house where they were sitting.
3 They saw something that looked like
fire in the shape of tongues. The flames
separated and came to rest on each of
them. 4 All of them were filled with the
Holy Spirit. They began to speak in languages they had not known before. The
Spirit gave them the ability to do this.
5 Godly Jews from every country in
the world were staying in Jerusalem.
6 A crowd came together when they
heard the sound. They were bewildered
because each of them heard their own
language being spoken. 7 The crowd was
really amazed. They asked, "Aren't all
these people who are speaking Galileans?
8 Then why do we each hear them speaking in our own native language? 9 We are
Parthians, Medes and Elamites. We live
in Mesopotamia, Judea and Cappadocia.
We are from Pontus, Asia, 10 Phrygia and
Pamphylia. Others of us are from Egypt
and the parts of Libya near Cyrene. Still
others are visitors from Rome. 11 Some of
the visitors are Jews. Others have accepted the Jewish faith. Also, Cretans and
Arabs are here. We hear all these people
speaking about God's wonders in our
own languages!" 12 They were amazed
and bewildered. They asked one another,
"What does this mean?"
13 But some people in the crowd made
fun of the believers. "They've had too
much wine!" they said.

Peter Speaks to the Crowd

14 Then Peter stood up with the 11
apostles. In a loud voice he spoke to
the crowd. "My fellow Jews," he said,
"let me explain this to you. All of you
who live in Jerusalem, listen carefully
to what I say. 15 You think these people
are drunk. But they aren't. It's only nine
o'clock in the morning! 16 No, here is
what the prophet Joel meant. 17 He said,

" 'In the last days, God says,
I will pour out my Holy Spirit on
all people.
Your sons and daughters will
prophesy.
Your young men will see visions.
Your old men will have dreams.
18 In those days, I will pour out my
Spirit on my servants.
I will pour out my Spirit on both
men and women.
When I do, they will prophesy.
19 I will show wonders in the heavens
above.
I will show signs on the earth
below.

The Holy Spirit Is Our Comforter

When Jesus was getting ready to return to heaven after the resurrection, his friends and disciples were worried. What would they do without Jesus living with them, traveling alongside them, and talking with them? They would miss their friend and Savior so much! But Jesus made them a promise. He told them that the Father would send the Holy Spirit to be their Comforter (see John 14:26). And guess what? The Holy Spirit came (see Acts 2:1–4)! All who put their faith in Jesus are given the Holy Spirit, who brings comfort, wise advice, and a sense of belonging to Jesus as we follow him.

There will be blood and fire and
clouds of smoke.
20 The sun will become dark.
The moon will turn red like blood.
This will happen before the
coming of the great and
glorious day of the Lord.
21 Everyone who calls
on the name of the Lord will be
saved.' *(Joel 2:28–32)*

22 "Fellow Israelites, listen to this!
Jesus of Nazareth was a man who
had God's approval. God did miracles,
wonders and signs among you through
Jesus. You yourselves know this. 23 Long
ago God planned that Jesus would be
handed over to you. With the help of
evil people, you put Jesus to death. You
nailed him to the cross. 24 But God raised
him from the dead. He set him free from
the suffering of death. It wasn't possible for death to keep its hold on Jesus.
25 David spoke about him. He said,

" 'I know that the Lord is always
with me.
Because he is at my right hand,
I will always be secure.
26 So my heart is glad and joy is on
my tongue.
My whole body will be full of hope.
27 You will not leave me in the place
of the dead.
You will not let your holy one rot
away.
28 You always show me the path that
leads to life.
You will fill me with joy when I
am with you.' *(Psalm 16:8–11)*

29 "Fellow Israelites, you can be sure
that King David died. He was buried. His
tomb is still here today. 30 But David was
a prophet. He knew that God had made
a promise to him. God had promised
that he would make someone in David's
family line king after him. 31 David saw
what was coming. So he spoke about the
Messiah rising from the dead. He said
that the Messiah would not be left in
the place of the dead. His body wouldn't
rot in the ground. 32 God has raised this
same Jesus back to life. We are all witnesses of this. 33 Jesus has been given a
place of honor at the right hand of God.
He has received the Holy Spirit from the
Father. This is what God had promised.
It is Jesus who has poured out what you
now see and hear. 34 David did not go
up to heaven. But he said,

" 'The Lord said to my Lord,
"Sit at my right hand.
35 I will put your enemies
under your control." ' *(Psalm 110:1)*

36 "So be sure of this, all you people
of Israel. You nailed Jesus to the cross.
But God has made him both Lord and
Messiah."
37 When the people heard this, it had a
deep effect on them. They said to Peter
and the other apostles, "Brothers, what
should we do?"
38 Peter replied, "All of you must turn
away from your sins and be baptized
in the name of Jesus Christ. Then your
sins will be forgiven. You will receive the
gift of the Holy Spirit. 39 The promise is
for you and your children. It is also for
all who are far away. It is for all whom
the Lord our God will choose."
40 Peter said many other things to
warn them. He begged them, "Save
yourselves from these evil people."
41 Those who accepted his message were
baptized. About 3,000 people joined the
believers that day.

The Believers Share Their Lives Together

42 The believers studied what the
apostles taught. They shared their lives
together. They ate and prayed together.
43 Everyone was amazed at what God
was doing. They were amazed when the
apostles performed many wonders and
signs. 44 All the believers were together. They shared everything they had.
45 They sold property and other things
they owned. They gave to anyone who
needed something. 46 Every day they met
together in the temple courtyard. They
ate meals together in their homes. Their
hearts were glad and sincere. 47 They
praised God. They were respected by all
the people. Every day the Lord added to
their group those who were being saved.

key verse The believers studied what the apostles taught. They shared their lives together. They ate and prayed together. ACTS 2:42

Peter Heals a Beggar Who Can't Walk

3 One day Peter and John were going up to the temple. It was three o'clock in the afternoon. It was the time for prayer. 2 A man unable to walk was being carried to the temple gate called Beautiful. He had been that way since he was born. Every day someone put him near the gate. There he would beg from people going into the temple courtyards. 3 He saw that Peter and John were about to enter. So he asked them for money. 4 Peter looked straight at him, and so did John. Then Peter said, "Look at us!" 5 So the man watched them closely. He expected to get something from them.

6 Peter said, "I don't have any silver or gold. But I'll give you what I do have. In the name of Jesus Christ of Nazareth, get up and walk." 7 Then Peter took him by the right hand and helped him up. At once the man's feet and ankles became strong. 8 He jumped to his feet and began to walk. He went with Peter and John into the temple courtyards. He walked and jumped and praised God. 9 All the people saw him walking and praising God. 10 They recognized him as the same man who used to sit and beg at the temple gate called Beautiful. They were filled with wonder. They were amazed at what had happened to him.

Peter Speaks to the People at the Temple

11 The man was holding on to Peter and John. All the people were amazed. They came running to them at the place called Solomon's Porch. 12 When Peter saw this, he said, "Fellow Israelites, why does this surprise you? Why do you stare at us? It's not as if we've made this man walk by our own power or godliness. 13 The God of our fathers, Abraham, Isaac and Jacob, has done this. God has brought glory to Jesus, who serves him. But you handed Jesus over to be killed. Pilate had decided to let him go. But you spoke against Jesus when he was in Pilate's court. 14 You spoke against the Holy and Blameless One. You asked for a murderer to be set free instead. 15 You killed the one who gives life. But God raised him from the dead. We are witnesses of this. 16 This man whom you see and know was made strong because of faith in Jesus' name. Faith in Jesus has healed him completely. You can see it with your own eyes.

17 "My fellow Israelites, I know you didn't realize what you were doing. Neither did your leaders. 18 But God had given a promise through all the prophets. And this is how he has made his promise come true. He said that his Messiah would suffer. 19 So turn away from your sins. Turn to God. Then your sins will be wiped away. The time will come when the Lord will make everything new. 20 He will send the Messiah. Jesus has been appointed as the Messiah for you. 21 Heaven must receive him until the time when God makes everything new. He promised this long ago through his holy prophets. 22 Moses said, 'The Lord your God will raise up for you a prophet like me. He will be one of your own people. You must listen to everything he tells you. 23 Anyone who does not listen to him will be completely cut off from their people.' *(Deuteronomy 18:15,18,19)*

24 "Beginning with Samuel, all the prophets spoke about this. They said these days would come. 25 What the prophets said was meant for you. The covenant God made with your people long ago is yours also. He said to Abraham, 'All nations on earth will be blessed through your children.' *(Genesis 22:18; 26:4)* 26 God raised up Jesus, who serves him. God sent him first to you. He did it to bless you. He wanted to turn each of you from your evil ways."

Peter and John Are Taken to the Sanhedrin

4 Peter and John were speaking to the people. The priests, the captain of the temple guard, and the Sadducees came up to the apostles. 2 They were very upset by what the apostles were teaching the people. The apostles were saying that people can be raised from the dead. They said this can happen because Jesus rose from the dead. 3 So the temple authorities arrested Peter and John. It was already evening, so they put them in prison until the next day. 4 But many who heard the message believed. The number of men who believed grew to about 5,000.

5 The next day the rulers, the elders
and the teachers of the law met in Jerusalem. 6 Annas, the high priest, was
there. So were Caiaphas, John, Alexander and other people in the high
priest's family. 7 They had Peter and
John brought to them. They wanted
to question them. "By what power did
you do this?" they asked. "And through
whose name?"
8 Peter was filled with the Holy Spirit.
He said to them, "Rulers and elders of
the people! 9 Are you asking us to explain our actions today? Do you want to
know why we were kind to a man who
couldn't walk? Are you asking how he
was healed? 10 Then listen to this, you
and all the people of Israel! You nailed
Jesus Christ of Nazareth to the cross.
But God raised him from the dead. It
is through Jesus' name that this man
stands healed in front of you. 11 Scripture says that Jesus is

" 'the stone you builders did not
accept.
But it has become the most
important stone of all.'
(Psalm 118:22)

12 You can't be saved by believing in
anyone else. God has given people no
other name under heaven that will save
them."
13 The leaders saw how bold Peter and
John were. They also realized that Peter
and John were ordinary men with no
training. This surprised the leaders. They
realized that these men had been with
Jesus. 14 The leaders could see the man
who had been healed. He was standing
there with them. So there was nothing
they could say. 15 They ordered Peter
and John to leave the Sanhedrin. Then
they talked things over. 16 "What can we
do with these men?" they asked. "Everyone living in Jerusalem knows they
have performed an unusual miracle. We
can't say it didn't happen. 17 We have to
stop this thing. It must not spread any
further among the people. We have to
warn these men. They must never speak
to anyone in Jesus' name again."
18 Once again the leaders called in
Peter and John. They commanded them
not to speak or teach at all in Jesus'
name. 19 But Peter and John replied,
"Which is right from God's point of view?

basics of faith Q&A

Can anyone besides Jesus save people?

Jesus is the only true Savior.
He is the only way to God.

Can you find the following verse?

ACTS 4:12

Should we listen to you? Or should we listen to God? You be the judges! 20 There's
nothing else we can do. We have to speak
about the things we've seen and heard."
21 The leaders warned them again.
Then they let them go. They couldn't
decide how to punish Peter and John.
They knew that all the people were
praising God for what had happened.
22 The man who had been healed by the
miracle was over 40 years old.

The Believers Pray

23 Peter and John were allowed to
leave. They went back to their own
people. They reported everything the
chief priests and the elders had said
to them. 24 The believers heard this.
Then they raised their voices together
in prayer to God. "Lord and King," they
said, "you made the heavens, the earth
and the sea. You made everything in
them. 25 Long ago you spoke by the Holy
Spirit. You spoke through the mouth
of our father David, who served you.
You said,

" 'Why are the nations angry?
Why do the people make useless
plans?
26 The kings of the earth rise up.
The rulers of the earth gather
together
against the Lord
and against his anointed king.'
(Psalm 2:1,2)

27 In fact, Herod and Pontius Pilate
met with the Gentiles in this city. They
also met with the people of Israel. All
of them made plans against your holy
servant Jesus. He is the one you anointed. 28 They did what your power and
purpose had already decided should
happen. 29 Now, Lord, consider the bad
things they say they are going to do.
Help us to be very bold when we speak
your word. 30 Stretch out your hand to
heal. Do signs and wonders through
the name of your holy servant Jesus."

31 After they prayed, the place where
they were meeting was shaken. They
were all filled with the Holy Spirit. They
were bold when they spoke God's word.

The Believers Share What They Own

32 All the believers were agreed in
heart and mind. They didn't claim
that anything they had was their
own. Instead, they shared everything
they owned. 33 With great power the
apostles continued their teaching. They
were telling people that the Lord Jesus
had risen from the dead. And God's
grace was working powerfully in all of
them. 34 So there were no needy persons
among them. From time to time, those
who owned land or houses sold them.
They brought the money from the sales.
35 They put it down at the apostles' feet.
It was then given out to anyone who
needed it.

36 Joseph was a Levite from Cyprus.
The apostles called him Barnabas. The
name Barnabas means Son of Help.
37 Barnabas sold a field he owned. He
brought the money from the sale. He
put it down at the apostles' feet.

Ananias and Sapphira

5 A man named Ananias and his
wife, Sapphira, also sold some
land. 2 He kept part of the money for
himself. Sapphira knew he had kept
it. He brought the rest of it and put it
down at the apostles' feet.

3 Then Peter said, "Ananias, why did
you let Satan fill your heart? He made
you lie to the Holy Spirit. You have kept
some of the money you received for the
land. 4 Didn't the land belong to you
before it was sold? After it was sold,
you could have used the money as you
wished. What made you think of doing
such a thing? You haven't lied just to
people. You've also lied to God."

5 When Ananias heard this, he fell
down and died. All who heard what
had happened were filled with fear.
6 Some young men came and wrapped
up his body. They carried him out and
buried him.

7 About three hours later, the wife of
Ananias came in. She didn't know what
had happened. 8 Peter asked her, "Tell
me. Is this the price you and Ananias
sold the land for?"

"Yes," she said. "That's the price."

9 Peter asked her, "How could you
agree to test the Spirit of the Lord? Listen! You can hear the steps of the men
who buried your husband. They are at
the door. They will carry you out also."

10 At that moment she fell down at
Peter's feet and died. Then the young
men came in. They saw that Sapphira
was dead. So they carried her out and
buried her beside her husband. 11 The
whole church and all who heard about
these things were filled with fear.

The Apostles Heal Many People

12 The apostles did many signs and
wonders among the people. All the
believers used to meet together at
Solomon's Porch. 13 No outsider dared
to join them. But the people thought
highly of them. 14 More and more men
and women believed in the Lord. They
joined the other believers. 15 So people
brought those who were sick into the
streets. They placed them on beds and
mats. They hoped that at least Peter's
shadow might fall on some of them as
he walked by. 16 Crowds even gathered
from the towns around Jerusalem.
They brought their sick people. They
also brought those who were suffering
because of evil spirits. All of them were
healed.

The Apostles Are Treated Badly

17 The high priest and all his companions were Sadducees. They were
very jealous of the apostles. 18 So they
arrested them and put them in the public jail. 19 But during the night an angel
of the Lord came. He opened the doors
of the jail and brought the apostles out.
20 "Go! Stand in the temple courtyard,"
the angel said. "Tell the people all about
this new life."

21 Early the next day they did as they had been told. They entered the temple courtyard. There they began to teach the people.

The high priest and his companions arrived. They called the Sanhedrin together. The Sanhedrin was a gathering of all the elders of Israel. They sent for the apostles who were in jail. 22 The officers arrived at the jail. But they didn't find the apostles there. So they went back and reported it. 23 "We found the jail locked up tight," they said. "The guards were standing at the doors. But when we opened the doors, we didn't find anyone inside." 24 When the captain of the temple guard and the chief priests heard this report, they were bewildered. They wondered what would happen next.

25 Then someone came and said, "Look! The men you put in jail are standing in the temple courtyard. They are teaching the people." 26 So the captain went with his officers and brought the apostles back. But they didn't use force. They were afraid the people would kill them by throwing stones at them.

27 They brought the apostles to the Sanhedrin. The high priest questioned them. 28 "We gave you clear orders not to teach in Jesus' name," he said. "But you have filled Jerusalem with your teaching. You want to make us guilty of this man's death."

29 Peter and the other apostles replied, "We must obey God instead of people! 30 You had Jesus killed by nailing him to a cross. But the God of our people raised Jesus from the dead. 31 Now Jesus is Prince and Savior. God has proved this by giving Jesus a place of honor with him. He did it to turn Israel away from their sins and forgive them. 32 We are telling people about these things. And so is the Holy Spirit. God has given the Spirit to those who obey him."

33 When the leaders heard this, they became very angry. They wanted to put the apostles to death. 34 But a Pharisee named Gamaliel stood up in the Sanhedrin. He was a teacher of the law. He was honored by all the people. He ordered the apostles to be taken outside for a little while. 35 Then Gamaliel spoke to the Sanhedrin. "Men of Israel," he said, "think carefully about what you plan to do to these men. 36 Some time ago Theudas appeared. He claimed he was really somebody. About 400 people followed him. But he was killed. All his followers were scattered. So they accomplished nothing. 37 After this, Judas from Galilee came along. This was in the days when the Romans made a list of all the people. Judas led a gang of men against the Romans. He too was killed. All his followers were scattered. 38 So let me give you some advice. Leave these men alone! Let them go! If their plans and actions only come from people, they will fail. 39 But if their plans come from God, you won't be able to stop these men. You will only find yourselves fighting against God."

40 His speech won the leaders over. They called the apostles in and had them whipped. The leaders ordered them not to speak in Jesus' name. Then they let the apostles go.

41 The apostles were full of joy as they left the Sanhedrin. They considered it an honor to suffer shame for the name of Jesus. 42 Every day they taught in the temple courtyards and from house to house. They never stopped telling people the good news that Jesus is the Messiah.

Seven Leaders Are Chosen

6 In those days the number of believers was growing. The Greek Jews complained about the non-Greek Jews. They said that the widows of the Greek Jews were not being taken care of. They weren't getting their fair share of food each day. 2 So the 12 apostles gathered all the believers together. They said, "It wouldn't be right for us to give up teaching God's word. And we'd have to stop teaching to wait on tables. 3 Brothers and sisters, choose seven of your men. They must be known as men who are wise and full of the Holy Spirit. We will turn this important work over to them. 4 Then we can give our attention to prayer and to teaching God's word."

5 This plan pleased the whole group. They chose Stephen. He was full of faith and of the Holy Spirit. Philip, Procorus, Nicanor, Timon and Parmenas were chosen too. The group also chose Nicolas from Antioch. He had accepted

the Jewish faith. 6 The group brought
them to the apostles. Then the apostles
prayed and placed their hands on them.
7 So God's word spread. The number
of believers in Jerusalem grew quickly.
Also, a large number of priests began
to obey Jesus' teachings.

Stephen Is Arrested

8 Stephen was full of God's grace and
power. He did great wonders and signs
among the people. 9 But members of
the group called the Synagogue of the
Freedmen began to oppose him. Some
of them were Jews from Cyrene and
Alexandria. Others were Jews from
Cilicia and Asia Minor. They all began
to argue with Stephen. 10 But he was too
wise for them. That's because the Holy
Spirit gave Stephen wisdom whenever
he spoke.

11 Then in secret they talked some
men into lying about Stephen. They
said, "We heard Stephen speak evil
things against Moses and against God."
12 So the people were stirred up. The
elders and the teachers of the law were
stirred up too. They arrested Stephen
and brought him to the Sanhedrin.
13 They found witnesses who were willing to tell lies. These liars said, "This
fellow never stops speaking against this
holy place. He also speaks against the
law. 14 We have heard him say that this
Jesus of Nazareth will destroy this place.
He says Jesus will change the practices
that Moses handed down to us."

15 All who were sitting in the Sanhedrin looked right at Stephen. They
saw that his face was like the face of
an angel.

Stephen Speaks to the Sanhedrin

7 Then the high priest questioned
Stephen. "Is what these people are
saying true?" he asked.

2 "Brothers and fathers, listen to me!"
Stephen replied. "The God of glory appeared to our father Abraham. At that
time Abraham was still in Mesopotamia. He had not yet begun living in
Harran. 3 'Leave your country and your
people,' God said. 'Go to the land I will
show you.' *(Genesis 12:1)*

4 "So Abraham left the land of Babylonia. He settled in Harran. After his
father died, God sent Abraham to this
land where you are now living. 5 God
didn't give him any property here. He
didn't even give him enough land to set
his foot on. But God made a promise to
him and to all his family after him. He
said they would possess the land. The
promise was made even though at that
time Abraham had no child. 6 Here is
what God said to him. 'For 400 years
your family after you will be strangers
in a country not their own. They will be
slaves and will be treated badly. 7 But
I will punish the nation that makes
them slaves,' God said. 'After that, they
will leave that country and worship
me here.' *(Genesis 15:13,14)* 8 Then God
made a covenant with Abraham. God
told him that circumcision would show
who the members of the covenant were.
Abraham became Isaac's father. He
circumcised Isaac eight days after he
was born. Later, Isaac became Jacob's
father. Jacob had 12 sons. They became
the founders of the 12 tribes of Israel.

9 "Jacob's sons were jealous of their
brother Joseph. So they sold him as a
slave. He was taken to Egypt. But God
was with him. 10 He saved Joseph from
all his troubles. God made Joseph wise.
He helped him to become the friend of
Pharaoh, the king of Egypt. So Pharaoh
made Joseph ruler over Egypt and his
whole palace.

11 "There was not enough food for all
Egypt and Canaan. This brought great
suffering. Jacob and his sons couldn't
find food. 12 But Jacob heard that there
was grain in Egypt. So he sent his sons
on their first visit. 13 On their second visit, Joseph told his brothers who he was.
Pharaoh learned about Joseph's family.
14 After this, Joseph sent for his father
Jacob and his whole family. The total
number of people was 75. 15 Then Jacob
went down to Egypt. There he and his
family died. 16 Some of their bodies were
brought back to Shechem. They were
placed in a tomb Abraham had bought.
He had purchased it from Hamor's sons
at Shechem. He had purchased it for a
certain amount of money.

17 "In Egypt the number of our people
grew and grew. It was nearly time for
God to make his promise to Abraham
come true. 18 Then 'a new king came to
power in Egypt. Joseph didn't mean
anything to him.' *(Exodus 1:8)* 19 The
king was very evil and dishonest with

our people. He treated them badly. He forced them to throw out their newborn babies to die.

20 “At that time Moses was born. He was not an ordinary child. For three months he was taken care of by his family. 21 Then he was placed outside. But Pharaoh’s daughter took him home. She brought him up as her own son. 22 Moses was taught all the knowledge of the people of Egypt. He became a powerful speaker and a man of action.

23 “When Moses was 40 years old, he decided to visit the people of Israel. They were his own people. 24 He saw one of them being treated badly by an Egyptian. So he went to help him. He got even by killing the man. 25 Moses thought his own people would realize that God was using him to save them. But they didn’t. 26 The next day Moses saw two Israelites fighting. He tried to make peace between them. ‘Men, you are both Israelites,’ he said. ‘Why do you want to hurt each other?’

27 “But the man who was treating the other one badly pushed Moses to one side. He said, ‘Who made you ruler and judge over us? 28 Are you thinking of killing me as you killed the Egyptian yesterday?’ *(Exodus 2:14)* 29 When Moses heard this, he escaped to Midian. He lived there as an outsider. He became the father of two sons there.

30 “Forty years passed. Then an angel appeared to Moses in the flames of a burning bush. This happened in the desert near Mount Sinai. 31 When Moses saw the bush, he was amazed. He went over for a closer look. There he heard the Lord say, 32 ‘I am the God of your fathers. I am the God of Abraham, Isaac and Jacob.’ *(Exodus 3:6)* Moses shook with fear. He didn’t dare to look.

33 “Then the Lord said to him, ‘Take off your sandals. You must do this because the place where you are standing is holy ground. 34 I have seen my people beaten down in Egypt. I have heard their groans. I have come down to set them free. Now come. I will send you back to Egypt.’ *(Exodus 3:5,7,8,10)*

35 “This is the same Moses the two men of Israel would not accept. They had said, ‘Who made you ruler and judge?’ But God himself sent Moses to rule the people of Israel and set them free. He spoke to Moses through an angel. The angel had appeared to him in the bush. 36 So Moses led them out of Egypt. He did wonders and signs in Egypt, at the Red Sea, and for 40 years in the desert.

37 “This is the same Moses who spoke to the Israelites. ‘God will send you a prophet,’ he said. ‘He will be like me. He will come from your own people.’ *(Deuteronomy 18:15)* 38 Moses was with the Israelites in the desert. He was with the angel who spoke to him on Mount Sinai. Moses was with our people of long ago. He received living words to pass on to us.

39 “But our people refused to obey Moses. They would not accept him. In their hearts, they wished they were back in Egypt. 40 They told Aaron, ‘Make us a god who will lead us. This fellow Moses brought us up out of Egypt. But we don’t know what has happened to him!’ *(Exodus 32:1)* 41 That was the time they made a statue to be their god. It was shaped like a calf. They brought sacrifices to it. They even enjoyed what they had made with their own hands. 42 But God turned away from them. He let them go on worshiping the sun, moon and stars. This agrees with what is written in the book of the prophets. There it says,

“ ‘People of Israel, did you bring me
sacrifices and offerings
for 40 years in the desert?
43 You have taken with you the shrine
of your false god Molek.
You have taken with you the star
of your false god Rephan.
You made statues of those gods
to worship.
So I will send you away from your
country.’ *(Amos 5:25–27)*
God sent them to Babylon and
even farther.

44 “Long ago our people were in the desert. They had with them the holy tent. The tent was where the tablets of the covenant law were kept. Moses had made the holy tent as God had commanded him. Moses made it like the pattern he had seen. 45 Our people received the tent from God. Then they brought it with them when they took the land of Canaan. God drove out the nations that were in their way. At that time Joshua was Israel’s leader. The tent

remained in the land until David's time. 46 David was blessed by God. So David asked if he could build a house for the God of Jacob. 47 But it was Solomon who built the temple for God.

48 "But the Most High God does not live in houses made by human hands. As God says through the prophet,

49 " 'Heaven is my throne.
  The earth is under my control.
What kind of house will you build
  for me?
  says the Lord.
  Where will my resting place be?
50 Didn't my hand make all these
  things?' *(Isaiah 66:1,2)*

51 "You stubborn people! You won't obey! You won't listen! You are just like your people of long ago! You always oppose the Holy Spirit! 52 Was there ever a prophet your people didn't try to hurt? They even killed those who told about the coming of the Blameless One. And now you have handed him over to his enemies. You have murdered him. 53 The law you received was given by angels. But you haven't obeyed it."

Stephen Is Killed

54 When the members of the Sanhedrin heard this, they became very angry. They were so angry they ground their teeth at Stephen. 55 But he was full of the Holy Spirit. He looked up to heaven and saw God's glory. He saw Jesus standing at God's right hand. 56 "Look!" he said. "I see heaven open. The Son of Man is standing at God's right hand."

57 When the Sanhedrin heard this, they covered their ears. They yelled at the top of their voices. They all rushed at him. 58 They dragged him out of the city. They began to throw stones at him to kill him. The people who had brought false charges against Stephen took off their coats. They placed them at the feet of a young man named Saul.

59 While the members of the Sanhedrin were throwing stones at Stephen, he prayed. "Lord Jesus, receive my spirit," he said. 60 Then he fell on his knees. He cried out, "Lord! Don't hold this sin against them!" When he had said this, he died.

8 And Saul had agreed with the Sanhedrin that Stephen should die.

The Church Is Treated Badly and Scattered

On that day the church in Jerusalem began to be attacked and treated badly. All except the apostles were scattered throughout Judea and Samaria. 2 Godly Jews buried Stephen. They mourned deeply for him. 3 But Saul began to destroy the church. He went from house to house. He dragged away men and women and put them in prison.

Philip Goes to Samaria

4 The believers who had been scattered preached the word everywhere they went. 5 Philip went down to a city in Samaria. There he preached about the Messiah. 6 The crowds listened to Philip and saw the signs he did. All of them paid close attention to what he said. 7 Evil spirits screamed and came out of many people. Many people who were disabled or who couldn't walk were healed. 8 So there was great joy in that city.

Simon the Evil Magician

9 A man named Simon lived in the city. For quite a while he had practiced evil magic there. He amazed all the people of Samaria. He claimed to be someone great. 10 And all the people listened to him, from the least important of them to the most important. They exclaimed, "It is right to call this man the Great Power of God!" 11 He had amazed them for a long time with his evil magic. So they followed him. 12 But Philip announced the good news of God's kingdom and the name of Jesus Christ. So men and women believed and were baptized. 13 Simon himself believed and was baptized. He followed Philip everywhere. He was amazed by the great signs and miracles he saw.

14 The apostles in Jerusalem heard that people in Samaria had accepted God's word. So they sent Peter and John to Samaria. 15 When they arrived there, they prayed for the new believers. They prayed that they would receive the Holy Spirit. 16 The Holy Spirit had not yet come on any of them. They had only been baptized in the name of the Lord Jesus.

17 Then Peter and John placed their hands on them. And they received the Holy Spirit.

18 Simon watched as the apostles placed their hands on them. He saw that the Spirit was given to them. So he offered money to Peter and John. 19 He said, "Give me this power too. Then everyone I place my hands on will receive the Holy Spirit."

20 Peter answered, "May your money be destroyed with you! Do you think you can buy God's gift with money? 21 You have no part or share in this holy work. Your heart is not right with God. 22 Turn away from this evil sin of yours. Pray to the Lord. Perhaps he will forgive you for having such a thought in your heart. 23 I see that you are very bitter. You are a prisoner of sin."

24 Then Simon answered, "Pray to the Lord for me. Pray that nothing you have said will happen to me."

25 Peter and John continued to preach the word of the Lord and tell people about Jesus. Then they returned to Jerusalem. On the way they preached the good news in many villages in Samaria.

Philip and the Man From Ethiopia

26 An angel of the Lord spoke to Philip. "Go south to the desert road," he said. "It's the road that goes down from Jerusalem to Gaza." 27 So Philip started out. On his way he met an Ethiopian official. The man had an important position in charge of all the wealth of the Kandake. Kandake means queen of Ethiopia. This official had gone to Jerusalem to worship. 28 On his way home he was sitting in his chariot. He was reading the Book of Isaiah the prophet. 29 The Holy Spirit told Philip, "Go to that chariot. Stay near it."

30 So Philip ran up to the chariot. He heard the man reading Isaiah the prophet. "Do you understand what you're reading?" Philip asked.

31 "How can I?" he said. "I need someone to explain it to me." So he invited Philip to come up and sit with him.

32 Here is the part of Scripture the official was reading. It says,

"He was led like a sheep to be
killed.
Just as lambs are silent while
their wool is being cut off,
he did not open his mouth.
33 When he was treated badly, he was
refused a fair trial.
Who can say anything about his
children?
His life was cut off from the
earth." *(Isaiah 53:7,8)*

34 The official said to Philip, "Tell me, please. Who is the prophet talking about? Himself, or someone else?" 35 Then Philip began with that same part of Scripture. He told him the good news about Jesus.

36-37 As they traveled along the road, they came to some water. The official said, "Look! Here is water! What can stop me from being baptized?" 38 He gave orders to stop the chariot. Then both Philip and the official went down into the water. Philip baptized him. 39 When they came up out of the water, the Spirit of the Lord suddenly took Philip away. The official did not see him again. He went on his way full of joy. 40 Philip was seen next at Azotus. From there he traveled all around. He preached the good news in all the towns. Finally he arrived in Caesarea.

Saul Becomes a Believer

9 Meanwhile, Saul continued to oppose the Lord's followers. He said they would be put to death. He went to the high priest. 2 He asked the priest for letters to the synagogues in Damascus. He wanted to find men and women who belonged to the Way of Jesus. The letters would allow him to take them as prisoners to Jerusalem. 3 On his journey, Saul approached Damascus. Suddenly a light from heaven flashed around him. 4 He fell to the ground. He heard a voice speak to him, "Saul! Saul! Why are you opposing me?"

5 "Who are you, Lord?" Saul asked.

"I am Jesus," he replied. "I am the one you are opposing. 6 Now get up and go into the city. There you will be told what you must do."

7 The men traveling with Saul stood there. They weren't able to speak. They had heard the sound. But they didn't see anyone. 8 Saul got up from the ground.

He opened his eyes, but he couldn't see.
So they led him by the hand into Da-
mascus. 9 For three days he was blind.
He didn't eat or drink anything.

10 In Damascus there was a believer
named Ananias. The Lord called out
to him in a vision. "Ananias!" he said.

"Yes, Lord," he answered.

11 The Lord told him, "Go to the house
of Judas on Straight Street. Ask for a
man from Tarsus named Saul. He is
praying. 12 In a vision Saul has seen
a man come and place his hands on
him. That man's name is Ananias. In
the vision, Ananias placed his hands
on Saul so he could see again."

13 "Lord," Ananias answered, "I've
heard many reports about this man.
They say he has done great harm to
your holy people in Jerusalem. 14 Now
he has come here to arrest all those
who worship you. The chief priests have
given him authority to do this."

15 But the Lord said to Ananias, "Go!
I have chosen this man to work for
me. He will announce my name to the
Gentiles and to their kings. He will also
announce my name to the people of
Israel. 16 I will show him how much he
must suffer for me."

17 Then Ananias went to the house and
entered it. He placed his hands on Saul.
"Brother Saul," he said, "you saw the Lord
Jesus. He appeared to you on the road as
you were coming here. He has sent me
so that you will be able to see again. You
will be filled with the Holy Spirit." 18 Right
away something like scales fell from
Saul's eyes. And he could see again. He
got up and was baptized. 19 After eating
some food, he got his strength back.

Saul in Damascus and Jerusalem

Saul spent several days with the
believers in Damascus. 20 Right away
he began to preach in the synagogues.
He taught that Jesus is the Son of God.
21 All who heard him were amazed. They
asked, "Isn't he the man who caused
great trouble in Jerusalem? Didn't he
make trouble for those who worship
Jesus? Hasn't he come here to take them
as prisoners to the chief priests?" 22 But
Saul grew more and more powerful. The
Jews living in Damascus couldn't believe
what was happening. Saul proved to
them that Jesus is the Messiah.

23 After many days, the Jews had a
meeting. They planned to kill Saul.
24 But he learned about their plan. Day
and night they watched the city gates
closely in order to kill him. 25 But his
followers helped him escape by night.
They lowered him in a basket through
an opening in the wall.

26 When Saul came to Jerusalem, he
tried to join the believers. But they were
all afraid of him. They didn't believe he
was really one of Jesus' followers. 27 But
Barnabas took him to the apostles. He
told them about Saul's journey. He said
that Saul had seen the Lord. He told how
the Lord had spoken to Saul. Barnabas
also said that Saul had preached without fear in Jesus' name in Damascus.
28 So Saul stayed with the believers. He
moved about freely in Jerusalem.
He spoke boldly in the Lord's name.
29 He talked and argued with the Greek
Jews. But they tried to kill him. 30 The
other believers heard about this. They
took Saul down to Caesarea. From there
they sent him off to Tarsus.

31 Then the church throughout Judea,
Galilee and Samaria enjoyed a time of
peace. The church was strengthened
and grew larger. That's because they
worshiped the Lord and the Holy Spirit
helped them.

Peter Heals Aeneas and Dorcas

32 Peter traveled around the country.
He went to visit the Lord's people who
lived in Lydda. 33 There he found a disabled man named Aeneas. For eight
years the man had spent most of his
time in bed. 34 "Aeneas," Peter said to
him, "Jesus Christ heals you. Get up! Roll
up your mat!" So Aeneas got up right
away. 35 Everyone who lived in Lydda
and Sharon saw him. They turned to
the Lord.

36 In Joppa there was a believer
named Tabitha. Her name in the Greek
language is Dorcas. She was always
doing good and helping poor people.
37 About that time she became sick and
died. Her body was washed and placed
in a room upstairs. 38 Lydda was near
Joppa. The believers heard that Peter
was in Lydda. So they sent two men to
him. They begged him, "Please come
at once!"

39 Peter went with them. When he
arrived, he was taken upstairs to the
room. All the widows stood around him
crying. They showed him the robes and
other clothes Dorcas had made before
she died.
40 Peter sent them all out of the room.
Then he got down on his knees and
prayed. He turned toward the dead
woman. He said, "Tabitha, get up."
She opened her eyes. When she saw
Peter, she sat up. 41 He took her by the
hand and helped her to her feet. Then he
called the believers and especially the
widows. He brought her to them. They
saw that she was alive. 42 This became
known all over Joppa. Many people
believed in the Lord. 43 Peter stayed in
Joppa for some time. He stayed with
Simon, a man who worked with leather.

Cornelius Calls for Peter

10 A man named Cornelius lived
in Caesarea. He was a Roman
commander in the Italian Regiment.
2 Cornelius and all his family were faithful and worshiped God. He gave freely
to people who were in need. He prayed
to God regularly. 3 One day about three
o'clock in the afternoon he had a vision.
He saw clearly an angel of God. The angel came to him and said, "Cornelius!"
4 Cornelius was afraid. He stared at
the angel. "What is it, Lord?" he asked.
The angel answered, "Your prayers
and gifts to poor people are like an offering to God. So he has remembered
you. 5 Now send men to Joppa. Have
them bring back a man named Simon.
He is also called Peter. 6 He is staying
with another Simon, a man who works
with leather. His house is by the sea."
7 The angel who spoke to him left.
Then Cornelius called two of his servants. He also called a godly soldier
who was one of his attendants. 8 He told
them everything that had happened.
Then he sent them to Joppa.

Peter Has a Vision

9 It was about noon the next day.
The men were on their journey and
were approaching the city. Peter went
up on the roof to pray. 10 He became
hungry. He wanted something to eat.
While the meal was being prepared,
Peter had a vision. 11 He saw heaven
open up. There he saw something that
looked like a large sheet. It was being
let down to earth by its four corners.
12 It had all kinds of four-footed animals
in it. It also had reptiles and birds in it.
13 Then a voice told him, "Get up, Peter.
Kill and eat."
14 "No, Lord! I will not!" Peter replied.
"I have never eaten anything that is not
pure and 'clean.'"
15 The voice spoke to him a second
time. It said, "Do not say anything is
not pure that God has made 'clean.'"
16 This happened three times. Right
away the sheet was taken back up to
heaven.
17 Peter was wondering what the vision meant. At that very moment the
men sent by Cornelius found Simon's
house. They stopped at the gate 18 and
called out. They asked if Simon Peter
was staying there.
19 Peter was still thinking about the
vision. The Holy Spirit spoke to him.
"Simon," he said, "three men are looking for you. 20 Get up and go downstairs.
Don't let anything keep you from going
with them. I have sent them."
21 Peter went down and spoke to the
men. "I'm the one you're looking for,"
he said. "Why have you come?"
22 The men replied, "We have come
from Cornelius, the Roman commander.
He is a good man who worships God.
All the Jewish people respect him. A
holy angel told him to invite you to his
house. Then Cornelius can hear what
you have to say." 23 Then Peter invited
the men into the house to be his guests.

Peter Goes to the House of Cornelius

The next day Peter went with the
three men. Some of the believers from
Joppa went along. 24 The following day
he arrived in Caesarea. Cornelius was
expecting them. He had called together
his relatives and close friends. 25 When
Peter entered the house, Cornelius met
him. As a sign of respect, he fell at Peter's feet. 26 But Peter made him get
up. "Stand up," he said. "I am only a
man myself."
27 As he was talking with Cornelius,
Peter went inside. There he found a
large group of people. 28 He said to
them, "You know that it is against our
law for a Jew to enter a Gentile home.
A Jew shouldn't have any close contact

with a Gentile. But God has shown me that I should not say anyone is not pure and 'clean.' 29 So when you sent for me, I came without asking any questions. May I ask why you sent for me?"

30 Cornelius answered, "Three days ago at this very hour I was in my house praying. It was three o'clock in the afternoon. Suddenly a man in shining clothes stood in front of me. 31 He said, 'Cornelius, God has heard your prayer. He has remembered your gifts to poor people. 32 Send someone to Joppa to get Simon Peter. He is a guest in the home of another Simon, who works with leather. He lives by the sea.' 33 So I sent for you right away. It was good of you to come. Now we are all here. And God is here with us. We are ready to listen to everything the Lord has commanded you to tell us."

34 Then Peter began to speak. "I now realize how true it is that God treats everyone the same," he said. 35 "He accepts people from every nation. He accepts anyone who has respect for him and does what is right. 36 You know the message God sent to the people of Israel. It is the good news of peace through Jesus Christ. He is Lord of all. 37 You know what has happened all through the area of Judea. It started in Galilee after John preached about baptism. 38 You know how God anointed Jesus of Nazareth with the Holy Spirit and with power. Jesus went around doing good. He healed all who were under the devil's power. God was with him.

39 "We are witnesses of everything he did in the land of the Jews and in Jerusalem. They killed him by nailing him to a cross. 40 But on the third day God raised him from the dead. God allowed Jesus to be seen. 41 But he wasn't seen by all the people. He was seen only by us. We are witnesses whom God had already chosen. We ate and drank with him after he rose from the dead. 42 He commanded us to preach to the people. He told us to tell people that he is the one appointed by God to judge the living and the dead. 43 All the prophets tell about him. They say that all who believe in him have their sins forgiven through his name."

44 While Peter was still speaking, the Holy Spirit came on all who heard the message. 45 Some Jewish believers had come with Peter. They were amazed because the gift of the Holy Spirit had been poured out even on the Gentiles. 46 They heard them speaking in languages they had not known before. They also heard them praising God.

Then Peter said, 47 "Surely no one can keep these people from being baptized with water. They have received the Holy Spirit just as we have." 48 So he ordered that they be baptized in the name of Jesus Christ. Then they asked Peter to stay with them for a few days.

Peter Explains His Actions

11 The apostles and the believers all through Judea heard that Gentiles had also received God's word. 2 Peter went up to Jerusalem. There the Jewish believers found fault with him. 3 They said, "You went into the house of Gentiles. You ate with them."

4 Starting from the beginning, Peter told them the whole story. 5 "I was in the city of Joppa praying," he said. "There I had a vision. I saw something that looked like a large sheet. It was being let down from heaven by its four corners. It came down to where I was. 6 I looked into it and saw four-footed animals of the earth. There were also wild animals, reptiles and birds. 7 Then I heard a voice speaking to me. 'Get up, Peter,' the voice said. 'Kill and eat.'

8 "I replied, 'No, Lord! I will not! Nothing that is not pure and "clean" has ever entered my mouth.'

9 "A second time the voice spoke from heaven. The voice said, 'Do not say anything is not pure that God has made "clean."' 10 This happened three times. Then the sheet was pulled up into heaven.

11 "Just then three men stopped at the house where I was staying. They had been sent to me from Caesarea. 12 The Holy Spirit told me not to let anything keep me from going with them. These six brothers here went with me. We entered the man's house. 13 He told us how he had seen an angel appear in his house. The angel said, 'Send to Joppa for Simon Peter. 14 He has a message to bring to you. You and your whole family will be saved through it.'

[15]“As I began to speak, the Holy Spirit came on them. He came just as he had come on us at the beginning. [16]Then I remembered the Lord’s words. ‘John baptized with water,’ he had said. ‘But you will be baptized with the Holy Spirit.’ [17]God gave them the same gift he gave those of us who believed in the Lord Jesus Christ. So who was I to think that I could stand in God’s way?”

[18]When they heard this, they didn’t object anymore. They praised God. They said, “So then, God has allowed even Gentiles to turn away from their sins. He did this so that they could live.”

The Believers in Antioch

[19]Some believers had been scattered by the suffering that unbelievers had caused them. They were scattered after Stephen was killed. Those believers traveled as far as Phoenicia, Cyprus and Antioch. But they spread the word only among Jews. [20]Some believers from Cyprus and Cyrene went to Antioch. There they began to speak to Greeks also. They told them the good news about the Lord Jesus. [21]The Lord’s power was with them. Large numbers of people believed and turned to the Lord.

[22]The church in Jerusalem heard about this. So they sent Barnabas to Antioch. [23]When he arrived and saw what the grace of God had done, he was glad. He told them all to remain true to the Lord with all their hearts. [24]Barnabas was a good man. He was full of the Holy Spirit and of faith. Large numbers of people came to know the Lord.

[25]Then Barnabas went to Tarsus to look for Saul. [26]He found him there. Then he brought him to Antioch. For a whole year Barnabas and Saul met with the church. They taught large numbers of people. At Antioch the believers were called Christians for the first time.

[27]In those days some prophets came down from Jerusalem to Antioch. [28]One of them was named Agabus. He stood up and spoke through the Spirit. He said there would not be nearly enough food anywhere in the Roman world. This happened while Claudius was the emperor. [29]The believers decided to provide help for the brothers and sisters living in Judea. All of them helped as much as they could. [30]They sent their gift to the elders through Barnabas and Saul.

An Angel Helps Peter Escape From Prison

12 About this time, King Herod arrested some people who belonged to the church. He planned to make them suffer greatly. [2]He had James killed with a sword. James was John’s brother. [3]Herod saw that the death of James pleased some Jews. So he arrested Peter also. This happened during the Feast of Unleavened Bread. [4]After Herod arrested Peter, he put him in prison. Peter was placed under guard. He was watched by four groups of four soldiers each. Herod planned to put Peter on public trial. It would take place after the Passover Feast.

[5]So Peter was kept in prison. But the church prayed hard to God for him.

[6]It was the night before Herod was going to bring him to trial. Peter was sleeping between two soldiers. Two chains held him there. Lookouts stood guard at the entrance. [7]Suddenly an angel of the Lord appeared. A light shone in the prison cell. The angel struck Peter on his side. Peter woke up. “Quick!” the angel said. “Get up!” The chains fell off Peter’s wrists.

[8]Then the angel said to him, “Put on your clothes and sandals.” Peter did so. “Put on your coat,” the angel told him. “Follow me.” [9]Peter followed him out of the prison. But he had no idea that what the angel was doing was really happening. He thought he was seeing a vision. [10]They passed the first and second guards. Then they came to the iron gate leading to the city. It opened for them by itself. They went through it. They walked the length of one street. Suddenly the angel left Peter.

[11]Then Peter realized what had happened. He said, “Now I know for sure that the Lord has sent his angel. He set me free from Herod’s power. He saved me from everything the Jewish people were hoping would happen.”

[12]When Peter understood what had happened, he went to Mary’s house. Mary was the mother of John Mark. Many people had gathered in her home. They were praying there. [13]Peter knocked at the outer entrance. A

servant named Rhoda came to answer
the door. 14 She recognized Peter's voice.
She was so excited that she ran back
without opening the door. "Peter is at
the door!" she exclaimed.
15 "You're out of your mind," they said
to her. But she kept telling them it was
true. So they said, "It must be his angel."
16 Peter kept on knocking. When they
opened the door and saw him, they were
amazed. 17 Peter motioned with his hand
for them to be quiet. He explained how
the Lord had brought him out of prison.
"Tell James and the other brothers and
sisters about this," he said. Then he went
to another place.
18 In the morning the soldiers were
bewildered. They couldn't figure out
what had happened to Peter. 19 So Herod
had them look everywhere for Peter. But
they didn't find him. Then Herod questioned the guards closely. He ordered
that they be put to death.

Herod Dies

Then Herod went from Judea to
Caesarea and stayed there. 20 He had
been quarreling with the people of Tyre
and Sidon. So they got together and
asked for a meeting with him. This was
because they depended on the king's
country to supply them with food. They
gained the support of Blastus and then
asked for peace. Blastus was a trusted
personal servant of the king.
21 The appointed day came. Herod was
seated on his throne. He was wearing
his royal robes. He made a speech to
the people. 22 Then they shouted, "This
is the voice of a god. It's not the voice of
a man." 23 Right away an angel of the
Lord struck Herod down. Herod had not
given praise to God. So he was eaten by
worms and died.
24 But God's word continued to spread
and many people believed the message.

Barnabas and Saul Are Sent Off

25 Barnabas and Saul finished their
task. Then they returned from Jerusalem. They took John Mark with them.
13 1 In the church at Antioch there
were prophets and teachers.
Among them were Barnabas, Simeon,
and Lucius from Cyrene. Simeon was
also called Niger. Another was Manaen.
He had been brought up with Herod, the
ruler of Galilee. Saul was among them
too. 2 While they were worshiping the
Lord and fasting, the Holy Spirit spoke.
"Set apart Barnabas and Saul for me,"
he said. "I have appointed them to do
special work." 3 The prophets and teachers fasted and prayed. They placed their
hands on Barnabas and Saul. Then they
sent them off.

Events on Cyprus

4 Barnabas and Saul were sent on
their way by the Holy Spirit. They
went down to Seleucia. From there
they sailed to Cyprus. 5 They arrived
at Salamis. There they preached God's
word in the Jewish synagogues. John
was with them as their helper.
6 They traveled all across the island
until they came to Paphos. There they
met a Jew named Bar-Jesus. He was
an evil magician and a false prophet.
7 He was an attendant of Sergius Paulus, the governor. Paulus was a man
of understanding. He sent for Barnabas and Saul. He wanted to hear God's
word. 8 But the evil magician named
Elymas opposed them. The name Elymas means Magician. He tried to keep
the governor from becoming a believer.
9 Saul was also known as Paul. He was
filled with the Holy Spirit. He looked
straight at Elymas. He said to him,
10 "You are a child of the devil! You are
an enemy of everything that is right!
You cheat people. You use all kinds of
tricks. Won't you ever stop twisting the
right ways of the Lord? 11 Now the Lord's
hand is against you. You are going to
go blind. For a while you won't even be
able to see the light of the sun."
Right away mist and darkness came
over him. He tried to feel his way
around. He wanted to find someone
to lead him by the hand. 12 When the
governor saw what had happened, he
believed. He was amazed at what Paul
was teaching about the Lord.

Paul Preaches in Pisidian Antioch

13 From Paphos, Paul and his companions sailed to Perga in Pamphylia.
There John Mark left them and returned
to Jerusalem. 14 From Perga they went
on to Pisidian Antioch. On the Sabbath
day they entered the synagogue and
sat down. 15 The Law and the Prophets
were read aloud. Then the leaders of
the synagogue sent word to Paul and

PAUL'S FIRST MISSIONARY JOURNEY

ACTS 13:1—14:28

Paul's first missionary journey began in Antioch (modern-day Syria). There, God called Paul and his friend and ministry partner Barnabas to go spread the good news about Jesus. Their primary mission (we think) was to preach about Jesus in Jewish synagogues (places where Jews worshiped), telling the Jews that the Messiah had come.

Paul and Barnabas sailed from Seleucia to the island of Cyprus and preached in a couple of cities there. Then they traveled to the cities (in modern-day Turkey) of Perga, Antioch (Pisidian), Iconium, Lystra, and Derbe. After retracing their steps, they sailed from the port city of Attalia back to Antioch. When they proclaimed that Jesus was the Messiah, they were often opposed by the Jewish leaders. But on this journey, Paul and Barnabas saw a huge number of Gentiles (non-Jews) put their faith in Jesus.

Paul also connected with believers in a region called Galatia. He later wrote a letter to the believers in Galatia too, which is now the book of Galatians in the Bible.

his companions. They said, "Brothers,
do you have any words of instruction
for the people? If you do, please speak."
16 Paul stood up and motioned with
his hand. Then he said, "Fellow Israelites, and you Gentiles who worship
God, listen to me! 17 The God of Israel
chose our people who lived long ago. He
blessed them greatly while they were
in Egypt. With his mighty power he led
them out of that country. 18 He put up
with their behavior for about 40 years
in the desert. 19 And he destroyed seven
nations in Canaan. Then he gave the
land to his people as their rightful share.
20 All this took about 450 years.

"After this, God gave them judges
until the time of Samuel the prophet.
21 Then the people asked for a king. He
gave them Saul, son of Kish. Saul was
from the tribe of Benjamin. He ruled for
40 years. 22 God removed him and made
David their king. Here is God's witness
about him. 'David, son of Jesse, is a man
dear to my heart,' he said. 'David will
do everything I want him to do.'
23 "From this man's family line God has
brought to Israel the Savior Jesus. This
is what he had promised. 24 Before Jesus
came, John preached that we should
turn away from our sins and be baptized.
He preached this to all Israel. 25 John was
coming to the end of his work. 'Who do
you suppose I am?' he said. 'I am not
the one you are looking for. But there
is someone coming after me. I am not
good enough to untie his sandals.'
26 "Listen, fellow children of Abraham! Listen, you Gentiles who worship
God! This message of salvation has been
sent to us. 27 The people of Jerusalem
and their rulers did not recognize Jesus.
By finding him guilty, they made the
prophets' words come true. These are
read every Sabbath day. 28 The people
and their rulers had no reason at all
for sentencing Jesus to death. But they
asked Pilate to have him killed. 29 They
did everything that had been written
about Jesus. Then they took him down
from the cross. They laid him in a tomb.
30 But God raised him from the dead.
31 For many days he was seen by those
who had traveled with him from Galilee
to Jerusalem. Now they are telling our
people about Jesus.
32 "We are telling you the good news.
What God promised our people long
ago 33 he has done for us, their children.
He has raised up Jesus. This is what is
written in the second Psalm. It says,

" 'You are my son.
Today I have become your
father.' *(Psalm 2:7)*

34 God raised Jesus from the dead. He
will never rot in the grave. As God has
said,

" 'Holy and sure blessings were
promised to David.
I will give them to you.'
(Isaiah 55:3)

35 In another place it also says,

" 'You will not let your holy one rot
away.' *(Psalm 16:10)*

36 "David carried out God's purpose
while he lived. Then he died. He was
buried with his people. His body rotted
away. 37 But the one whom God raised
from the dead did not rot away.
38 "My friends, here is what I want
you to know. I announce to you that
your sins can be forgiven because of
what Jesus has done. 39 Through him
everyone who believes is set free from
every sin. Moses' law could not make
you right in God's eyes. 40 Be careful!
Don't let what the prophets spoke about
happen to you. They said,

41 " 'Look, you who make fun of the
truth!
Wonder and die!
I am going to do something in your
days
that you would never believe.
You wouldn't believe it even if
someone told you.' "
(Habakkuk 1:5)

42 Paul and Barnabas started to leave
the synagogue. The people invited them
to say more about these things on the
next Sabbath day. 43 The people were
told they could leave the service. Many
Jews followed Paul and Barnabas. Many
Gentiles who faithfully worshiped the
God of the Jews did the same. Paul and
Barnabas talked with them. They tried
to get them to keep living in God's grace.
44 On the next Sabbath day, almost
the whole city gathered. They gathered

to hear the word of the Lord. 45 When
the Jews saw the crowds, they became
very jealous. They began to disagree
with what Paul was saying. They said
evil things against him.
46 Then Paul and Barnabas answered
them boldly. "We had to speak God's
word to you first," they said. "But you
don't accept it. You don't think you are
good enough for eternal life. So now
we are turning to the Gentiles. 47 This
is what the Lord has commanded us
to do. He said,

> "'I have made you a light for the
> Gentiles.
> You will bring salvation to the
> whole earth.'" *(Isaiah 49:6)*

48 When the Gentiles heard this, they
were glad. They honored the word of
the Lord. All who were appointed for
eternal life believed.
49 The word of the Lord spread through
the whole area. 50 But the Jewish leaders
stirred up the important women who
worshiped God. They also stirred up the
men who were leaders in the city. The
Jewish leaders tried to get the women
and men to attack Paul and Barnabas.
They threw Paul and Barnabas out of
that area. 51 Paul and Barnabas shook
the dust off their feet. This was a warning to the people who had opposed
them. Then Paul and Barnabas went
on to Iconium. 52 The believers were filled
with joy and with the Holy Spirit.

Paul and Barnabas Preach in Iconium

14 At Iconium, Paul and Barnabas
went into the Jewish synagogue
as usual. They spoke there with great
power. Large numbers of Jews and
Greeks became believers. 2 But the Jews
who refused to believe stirred up some of
the Gentiles who were there. They turned
them against the two men and the new
believers. 3 So Paul and Barnabas spent
a lot of time there. They spoke boldly for
the Lord. He gave them the ability to do
signs and wonders. In this way the Lord
showed that they were telling the truth
about his grace. 4 The people of the city
did not agree with one another. Some
were on the side of the Jews. Others were
on the side of the apostles. 5 Jews and
Gentiles alike planned to treat Paul and
Barnabas badly. Their leaders agreed.
They planned to kill them by throwing
stones at them. 6 But Paul and Barnabas
found out about the plan. They escaped
to the Lycaonian cities of Lystra and
Derbe and to the surrounding area.
7 There they continued to preach the
good news.

Paul Preaches in Lystra

8 In Lystra there sat a man who
couldn't walk. He hadn't been able to
use his feet since the day he was born.
9 He listened as Paul spoke. Paul looked
right at him. He saw that the man had
faith to be healed. 10 So he called out,
"Stand up on your feet!" Then the man
jumped up and began to walk.
11 The crowd saw what Paul had done.
They shouted in the Lycaonian language. "The gods have come down to
us in human form!" they exclaimed.
12 They called Barnabas Zeus. Paul was
the main speaker. So they called him
Hermes. 13 Just outside the city was the
temple of the god Zeus. The priest of
Zeus brought bulls and wreaths to the
city gates. He and the crowd wanted to
offer sacrifices to Paul and Barnabas.
14 But the apostles Barnabas and Paul
heard about this. So they tore their
clothes. They rushed out into the crowd.
They shouted, 15 "Friends, why are you
doing this? We are only human, just like
you. We are bringing you good news.
Turn away from these worthless things.
Turn to the living God. He is the one who
made the heavens and the earth and the
sea. He made everything in them. 16 In
the past, he let all nations go their own
way. 17 But he has given proof of what
he is like. He has shown kindness by
giving you rain from heaven. He gives
you crops in their seasons. He provides
you with plenty of food. He fills your
hearts with joy." 18 Paul and Barnabas
told them all these things. But they had
trouble keeping the crowd from offering
sacrifices to them.
19 Then some Jews came from Antioch and Iconium. They won the crowd
over to their side. They threw stones
at Paul. They thought he was dead, so
they dragged him out of the city. 20 The
believers gathered around Paul. Then he
got up and went back into the city. The
next day he and Barnabas left for Derbe.

Paul and Barnabas Return to Antioch

21 Paul and Barnabas preached the
good news in the city of Derbe. They
won large numbers of followers. Then
they returned to Lystra, Iconium and
Antioch. 22 There they helped the believers gain strength. They told them to
remain faithful to what they had been
taught. "We must go through many
hard times to enter God's kingdom,"
they said. 23 Paul and Barnabas appointed elders for them in each church.
The elders had trusted in the Lord. Paul
and Barnabas prayed and fasted. They
placed the elders in the Lord's care.
24 After going through Pisidia, Paul and
Barnabas came into Pamphylia. 25 They
preached the good news in Perga. Then
they went down to Attalia.

26 From Attalia they sailed back to
Antioch. In Antioch they had been put
in God's care to preach the good news.
They had now completed the work God
had given them to do. 27 When they
arrived at Antioch, they gathered the
church together. They reported all that
God had done through them. They told
how he had opened a way for the Gentiles to believe. 28 And they stayed there
a long time with the believers.

Church Leaders Meet in Jerusalem

15 Certain people came down from
Judea to Antioch. Here is what
they were teaching the believers. "Moses commanded you to be circumcised,"
they said. "If you aren't, you can't be
saved." 2 But Paul and Barnabas didn't
agree with this. They argued strongly
with them. So Paul and Barnabas were
appointed to go up to Jerusalem. Some
other believers were chosen to go with
them. They were told to ask the apostles
and elders about this question. 3 The
church sent them on their way. They
traveled through Phoenicia and Samaria. There they told how the Gentiles
had turned to God. This news made all
the believers very glad. 4 When they
arrived in Jerusalem, the church welcomed them. The apostles and elders
welcomed them too. Then Paul and
Barnabas reported everything God had
done through them.

5 Some of the believers were Pharisees.
They stood up and said, "The Gentiles
must be circumcised. They must obey
the law of Moses."

6 The apostles and elders met to
consider this question. 7 After they had
talked it over, Peter got up and spoke
to them. "Brothers," he said, "you know
that some time ago God chose me. He
appointed me to take the good news to
the Gentiles. He wanted them to hear the
good news and believe. 8 God knows the
human heart. By giving the Holy Spirit
to the Gentiles, he showed that he accepted them. He did the same for them
as he had done for us. 9 God showed
that there is no difference between
us and them. That's because he made
their hearts pure because of their faith.
10 Now then, why are you trying to test
God? You test him when you put a heavy
load on the shoulders of Gentiles. Our
people of long ago couldn't carry that
load. We can't either. 11 No! We believe
we are saved through the grace of our
Lord Jesus. The Gentiles are saved in
the same way."

12 Everyone became quiet as they listened to Barnabas and Paul. They were
telling about the signs and wonders
God had done through them among the
Gentiles. 13 When they finished, James
spoke up. "Brothers," he said, "listen to
me. 14 Simon Peter has explained to us
what God has now done. He has chosen
some of the Gentiles to be among his
very own people. 15 The prophets' words
agree with that. They say,

16 " 'After this I will return
and set up again David's fallen
tent.
I will rebuild what was destroyed.
I will make it what it used to be.
17 Then everyone else can look to the
Lord.
This includes all the Gentiles who
belong to me, says the Lord.
The Lord is the one who does these
things.' *(Amos 9:11,12)*
18 The Lord does things that have
been known from long ago.

19 "Now here is my decision. We should
not make it hard for the Gentiles who
are turning to God. 20 Here is what we
should write to them. They must not
eat food that has been made impure by
being offered to statues of gods. They
must not commit sexual sins. They must

not eat the meat of animals that have
been choked to death. And they must
not drink blood. 21These laws of Moses
have been preached in every city from
the earliest times. They are read out
loud in the synagogues every Sabbath
day."

A Letter Is Written to Gentile Believers

22Then the apostles, the elders and
the whole church decided what to do.
They would choose some of their own
men who were leaders among the
believers. They would send them to
Antioch with Paul and Barnabas. So
they chose Judas Barsabbas and Silas.
They were leaders among the believers.
23Here is the letter they sent with them.

The apostles and elders, your brothers, are writing this letter.

We are sending it to the Gentile believers in Antioch, Syria and Cilicia.

Greetings.

24We have heard that some of
our people came to you and caused
trouble. You were upset by what
they said. But we had given them
no authority to go. 25So we all
agreed to send our dear friends
Barnabas and Paul to you. We
chose some other men to go with
them. 26Barnabas and Paul have
put their lives in danger. They did
it for the name of our Lord Jesus
Christ. 27So we are sending Judas
and Silas with them. What they say
will agree with this letter. 28Here
is what seemed good to the Holy
Spirit and to us. We will not give
you a load that is too heavy. So
here are a few basic rules. 29Don't
eat food that has been offered to
statues of gods. Don't drink blood.
Don't eat the meat of animals that
have been choked to death. And
don't commit sexual sins. You will
do well to keep away from these
things.

Farewell.

30So the men were sent down to Antioch. There they gathered the church
together. They gave the letter to them.
31The people read it. They were glad for
its message of hope. 32Judas and Silas
were prophets. They said many things
to give strength and hope to the believers. 33-34Judas and Silas stayed there
for some time. Then the believers sent
them away with the blessing of peace.
They sent them back to those who had
sent them out. 35Paul and Barnabas
remained in Antioch. There they and
many others taught and preached the
word of the Lord.

Paul and Barnabas Do Not Agree

36Some time later Paul spoke to Barnabas. "Let's go back to all the towns
where we preached the word of the
Lord," he said. "Let's visit the believers
and see how they are doing." 37Bar-
nabas wanted to take John Mark with
them. 38But Paul didn't think it was wise
to take him. Mark had deserted them
in Pamphylia. He hadn't continued
with them in their work. 39Barnabas
and Paul strongly disagreed with each
other. So they went their separate ways.
Barnabas took Mark and sailed for Cyprus. 40But Paul chose Silas. The believers asked the Lord to give his grace
to Paul and Silas as they went. 41Paul
traveled through Syria and Cilicia. He
gave strength to the churches there.

Timothy Joins Paul and Silas

16 Paul came to Derbe. Then he went
on to Lystra. A believer named
Timothy lived there. His mother was
Jewish and a believer. His father was
a Greek. 2The believers at Lystra and
Iconium said good things about Timothy. 3Paul wanted to take him along on
the journey. So he circumcised Timothy
because of the Jews who lived in that
area. They all knew that Timothy's father was a Greek. 4Paul and his companions traveled from town to town.
They reported what the apostles and
elders in Jerusalem had decided. The
people were supposed to obey what
was in the report. 5So the churches were
made strong in the faith. The number
of believers grew every day.

Paul's Vision of the Man From Macedonia

6Paul and his companions traveled
all through the area of Phrygia and
Galatia. The Holy Spirit had kept them
from preaching the word in Asia Minor.

2

PAUL'S SECOND MISSIONARY JOURNEY

ACTS 15:39—18:22

After staying for a while in Antioch, Paul wanted to go on another journey with Barnabas. But they had a disagreement and decided to travel separately, not together. Barnabas went back to Cyprus with Mark, and Paul went with a friend named Silas. On this trip, Paul and Silas were joined by Timothy, a younger man whom Paul would disciple, or teach about Jesus.

As Paul, Silas, and Timothy were traveling, the Holy Spirit gave Paul a vision, a picture in his mind (like a dream but when you're awake), showing him that they were to go to a region called Macedonia (in modern-day Greece). While they were in Philippi, a city in Macedonia, a woman named Lydia listened as Paul shared the gospel with her, and she put her faith in Jesus.

On another day, Paul commanded an evil spirit to come out of a slave girl. This made her owners angry with Paul and Silas because the slave girl was making her owners money by telling people what was going to happen in the future. Her owners dragged Paul and Silas to the city leaders, who threw them into prison. While in prison, Paul and Silas prayed and sang songs of praise to God. As they were praying and singing, God miraculously sent an earthquake to loosen their chains and swing the prison doors wide open! Paul and Silas told the jailer about Jesus. And that day, the jailer and his whole family put their faith in Jesus. (For the whole story, read Acts 16:16–40.)

As Paul, Silas, and Timothy continued to travel and share the gospel, they met many people who followed Jesus, including a couple named Aquila and Priscilla who also were working to spread the gospel. Finally, Paul traveled back to Antioch, where his journey had begun.

7 They came to the border of Mysia. From there they tried to enter Bithynia. But the Spirit of Jesus would not let them. 8 So they passed by Mysia. Then they went down to Troas. 9 During the night Paul had a vision. He saw a man from Macedonia standing and begging him. "Come over to Macedonia!" the man said. "Help us!" 10 After Paul had seen the vision, we got ready at once to leave for Macedonia. We decided that God had called us to preach the good news there.

Lydia Becomes a Believer in Philippi

11 At Troas we got into a boat. We sailed straight for Samothrace. The next day we went on to Neapolis. 12 From there we traveled to Philippi, a Roman colony. It is an important city in that part of Macedonia. We stayed there several days.

13 On the Sabbath day we went outside the city gate. We walked down to the river. There we expected to find a place of prayer. We sat down and began to speak to the women who had gathered together. 14 One of the women listening was from the city of Thyatira. Her name was Lydia, and her business was selling purple cloth. She was a worshiper of God. The Lord opened her heart to accept Paul's message. 15 She and her family were baptized. Then she invited us to her home. "Do you consider me a believer in the Lord?" she asked. "If you do, come and stay at my house." She succeeded in getting us to go home with her.

Paul and Silas Are Thrown Into Prison

16 One day we were going to the place of prayer. On the way we were met by a female slave. She had a spirit that helped her tell people what was going to happen. She earned a lot of money for her owners by doing this. 17 She followed Paul and the rest of us around. She shouted, "These men serve the Most High God. They are telling you how to be saved." 18 She kept this up for many days. Finally Paul became upset. Turning around, he spoke to the spirit that was in her. "In the name of Jesus Christ," he said, "I command you to come out of her!" At that very moment the spirit left the woman.

19 Her owners realized that their hope of making money was gone. So they grabbed Paul and Silas. They dragged them into the market place to face the authorities. 20 They brought them to the judges. "These men are Jews," her owners said. "They are making trouble in our city. 21 They are suggesting practices that are against Roman law. These are practices we can't accept or take part in."

22 The crowd joined the attack against Paul and Silas. The judges ordered that Paul and Silas be stripped and beaten with rods. 23 They were whipped without mercy. Then they were thrown into prison. The jailer was commanded to guard them carefully. 24 When he received these orders, he put Paul and Silas deep inside the prison. He fastened their feet so they couldn't get away.

25 About midnight Paul and Silas were praying. They were also singing hymns to God. The other prisoners were listening to them. 26 Suddenly there was a powerful earthquake. It shook the prison from top to bottom. All at once the prison doors flew open. Everyone's chains came loose. 27 The jailer woke up. He saw that the prison doors were open. He pulled out his sword and was going to kill himself. He thought the prisoners had escaped. 28 "Don't harm yourself!" Paul shouted. "We are all here!"

29 The jailer called out for some lights. He rushed in, shaking with fear. He fell down in front of Paul and Silas. 30 Then he brought them out. He asked, "Sirs, what must I do to be saved?"

31 They replied, "Believe in the Lord Jesus. Then you and everyone living in your house will be saved." 32 They spoke the word of the Lord to him. They also spoke to all the others in his house. 33 At that hour of the night, the jailer took Paul and Silas and washed their wounds. Right away he and everyone who lived with him were baptized. 34 The jailer brought them into his house. He set a meal in front of them. He and everyone who lived with him were filled with joy. They had become believers in God.

35 Early in the morning the judges sent their officers to the jailer. They ordered him, "Let those men go." 36 The jailer told Paul, "The judges have ordered me

to set you and Silas free. You can leave now. Go in peace."

37 But Paul replied to the officers. "They beat us in public," he said. "We weren't given a trial. And we are Roman citizens! They threw us into prison. And now do they want to get rid of us quietly? No! Let them come themselves and personally lead us out."

38 The officers reported this to the judges. When the judges heard that Paul and Silas were Roman citizens, they became afraid. 39 So they came and said they were sorry. They led them out of the prison. Then they asked them to leave the city. 40 After Paul and Silas came out of the prison, they went to Lydia's house. There they met with the brothers and sisters. They told them to be brave. Then they left.

Paul and Silas Arrive in Thessalonica

17 Paul and those traveling with him passed through Amphipolis and Apollonia. They came to Thessalonica. A Jewish synagogue was there. 2 Paul went into the synagogue as he usually did. For three Sabbath days in a row he talked with the Jews about the Scriptures. 3 He explained and proved that the Messiah had to suffer and rise from the dead. "This Jesus I am telling you about is the Messiah!" he said. 4 His words won over some of the Jews. They joined Paul and Silas. A large number of Greeks who worshiped God joined them too. So did quite a few important women.

5 But other Jews were jealous. So they rounded up some evil people from the market place. Forming a crowd, they started all kinds of trouble in the city. The Jews rushed to Jason's house. They were looking for Paul and Silas. They wanted to bring them out to the crowd. 6 But they couldn't find them. So they dragged Jason and some other believers to the city officials. "These men have caused trouble all over the world," they shouted. "Now they have come here. 7 Jason has welcomed them into his house. They are all disobeying Caesar's commands. They say there is another king. He is called Jesus." 8 When the crowd and the city officials heard this, they became very upset. 9 They made Jason and the others give them money. The officials did this to make sure they would return to the court. Then they let Jason and the others go.

Paul and Silas Are Sent to Berea

10 As soon as it was night, the believers sent Paul and Silas away to Berea. When they arrived, they went to the Jewish synagogue. 11 The Berean Jews were very glad to receive Paul's message. They studied the Scriptures carefully every day. They wanted to see if what Paul said was true. So they were more noble than the Thessalonian Jews. 12 Because of this, many of the Berean Jews believed. A number of important Greek women also became believers. And so did many Greek men.

13 But the Jews in Thessalonica found out that Paul was preaching God's word in Berea. So some of them went there too. They stirred up the crowds and got them all worked up. 14 Right away the believers sent Paul to the coast. But Silas and Timothy stayed in Berea. 15 The believers who went with Paul took him to Athens. Then they returned with orders that Silas and Timothy were supposed to join him as soon as they could.

Paul Preaches in Athens

16 Paul was waiting for Silas and Timothy in Athens. He was very upset to see that the city was full of statues of gods. 17 So he went to the synagogue. There he talked both with Jews and with Greeks who worshiped God. Each day he spoke with anyone who happened to be in the market place. 18 A group of Epicurean and Stoic thinkers began to argue with him. Some of them asked, "What is this fellow chattering about?" Others said, "He seems to be telling us about gods we've never heard of." They said this because Paul was preaching the good news about Jesus. He was telling them that Jesus had risen from the dead. 19 They took him to a meeting of the Areopagus. There they said to him, "What is this new teaching you're giving us? 20 You have some strange ideas we've never heard before. We would like to know what they mean." 21 All the people of Athens spent their time talking about and listening to the latest ideas. People from other lands who lived there did the same.

22 Then Paul stood up in the meeting of the Areopagus. He said, "People of Athens! I see that you are very religious in every way. 23 As I walked around, I looked carefully at the things you worship. I even found an altar with

TO AN UNKNOWN GOD

written on it. So you don't know what you are worshiping. Now I am going to tell you about this 'unknown god.'

24 "He is the God who made the world. He also made everything in it. He is the Lord of heaven and earth. He doesn't live in temples built by human hands. 25 He is not served by human hands. He doesn't need anything. Instead, he himself gives life and breath to all people. He also gives them everything else they have. 26 From one man he made all the people of the world. Now they live all over the earth. He decided exactly when they should live. And he decided exactly where they should live. 27 God did this so that people would seek him. And perhaps they would reach out for him and find him. They would find him even though he is not far from any of us. 28 'In him we live and move and exist.' As some of your own poets have also said, 'We are his children.'

29 "Yes, we are God's children. So we shouldn't think that God is made out of gold or silver or stone. He isn't a statue planned and made by clever people. 30 In the past, God didn't judge people for what they didn't know. But now he commands all people everywhere to turn away from their sins. 31 He has set a day when he will judge the world fairly. He has appointed a man to be its judge. God has proved this to everyone by raising that man from the dead."

32 They heard Paul talk about the dead being raised. Some of them made fun of this idea. But others said, "We want to hear you speak about this again." 33 So Paul left the meeting of the Areopagus. 34 Some of the people became followers of Paul and believed in Jesus. Dionysius was one of them. He was a member of the Areopagus. A woman named Damaris also became a believer. And so did some others.

Paul Goes to Corinth

18 After this, Paul left Athens and went to Corinth. 2 There he met a Jew named Aquila, who was a native of Pontus. Aquila had recently come from Italy with his wife Priscilla. The emperor Claudius had ordered all Jews to leave Rome. Paul went to see Aquila and Priscilla. 3 They were tentmakers, just as he was. So he stayed and worked with them. 4 Every Sabbath day he went to the synagogue. He was trying to get both Jews and Greeks to believe in the Lord.

5 Silas and Timothy came from Macedonia. Then Paul spent all his time preaching. He was a witness to the Jews that Jesus was the Messiah. 6 But they opposed Paul. They treated him badly. So he shook out his clothes in protest. Then he said to them, "God's judgment against you will be your own fault! Don't blame me for it! From now on I will go to the Gentiles."

7 Then Paul left the synagogue and went to the house next door. It was the house of Titius Justus, a man who worshiped God. 8 Crispus was the synagogue leader. He and everyone living in his house came to believe in the Lord. Many others who lived in Corinth heard Paul. They too believed and were baptized.

9 One night the Lord spoke to Paul in a vision. "Don't be afraid," he said. "Keep on speaking. Don't be silent. 10 I am with you. No one will attack you and harm you. I have many people in this city." 11 So Paul stayed in Corinth for a year and a half. He taught them God's word.

12 At that time Gallio was governor of Achaia. The Jews of Corinth got together and attacked Paul. They brought him into court. 13 They made a charge against Paul. They said, "This man is talking people into worshiping God in wrong ways. Those ways are against the law."

14 Paul was about to give reasons for his actions. But just then Gallio spoke to them. He said, "You Jews don't claim that Paul has committed a great or small crime. If you did, it would make sense for me to listen to you. 15 But this is about your own law. It is a question of words and names. Settle the matter yourselves. I will not be a judge of

such things." 16 So he made them leave.
17 Then the crowd there turned against
Sosthenes, the synagogue leader. They
beat him up in front of the governor.
But Gallio didn't care at all.

Priscilla and Aquila Teach Apollos

18 Paul stayed in Corinth for some
time. Then he left the brothers and sisters and sailed for Syria. Priscilla and
Aquila went with him. Before he sailed,
he had his hair cut off at Cenchreae. He
did this because he had made a promise to God. 19 They arrived at Ephesus.
There Paul said goodbye to Priscilla
and Aquila. He himself went into the
synagogue and talked with the Jews.
20 The Jews asked him to spend more
time with them. But he said no. 21 As
he left, he made them a promise. "If
God wants me to," he said, "I will come
back." Then he sailed from Ephesus.
22 When he landed at Caesarea, he went
up to Jerusalem. There he greeted the
church. He then went down to Antioch.

23 Paul spent some time in Antioch.
Then he left and traveled all over Galatia and Phrygia. He gave strength to
all the believers there.

24 At that time a Jew named Apollos
came to Ephesus. He was an educated
man from Alexandria. He knew the
Scriptures very well. 25 Apollos had
been taught the way of the Lord. He
spoke with great power. He taught the
truth about Jesus. But he only knew
about John's baptism. 26 He began to
speak boldly in the synagogue. Priscilla and Aquila heard him. So they
invited him to their home. There they
gave him a better understanding of
the way of God.

27 Apollos wanted to go to Achaia. The
brothers and sisters agreed with him.
They wrote to the believers there. They
asked them to welcome him. When he
arrived, he was a great help to those
who had become believers by God's
grace. 28 In public meetings, he argued
strongly against Jews who disagreed
with him. He proved from the Scriptures
that Jesus was the Messiah.

Paul Goes to Ephesus

19 While Apollos was at Corinth,
Paul took the road to Ephesus.
When he arrived, he found some believers there. 2 He asked them, "Did
you receive the Holy Spirit when you
became believers?"

"No," they answered. "We haven't
even heard that there is a Holy Spirit."

3 So Paul asked, "Then what baptism
did you receive?"

"John's baptism," they replied.

4 Paul said, "John baptized people,
calling them to turn away from their
sins. He told them to believe in the
one who was coming after him. Jesus
is that one." 5 After hearing this, they
were baptized in the name of the Lord
Jesus. 6 Paul placed his hands on them.
Then the Holy Spirit came on them.
They spoke in languages they had not
known before. They also prophesied.
7 There were about 12 men in all.

8 Paul entered the synagogue. There
he spoke boldly for three months. He
gave good reasons for believing the
truth about God's kingdom. 9 But some
of them wouldn't listen. They refused to
believe. In public they said evil things
about the Way of Jesus. So Paul left
them. He took the believers with him.
Each day he talked with people in the
lecture hall of Tyrannus. 10 This went
on for two years. So all the Jews and
Greeks who lived in Asia Minor heard
the word of the Lord.

11 God did amazing miracles through
Paul. 12 Even handkerchiefs and aprons
that had touched him were taken to
those who were sick. When this happened, their sicknesses were healed
and evil spirits left them.

13 Some Jews went around driving
out evil spirits. They tried to use the
name of the Lord Jesus to set free those
who were controlled by demons. They
said, "In Jesus' name I command you
to come out. He is the Jesus that Paul is
preaching about." 14 Seven sons of Sceva
were doing this. Sceva was a Jewish
chief priest. 15 One day the evil spirit answered them, "I know Jesus. And I know
about Paul. But who are you?" 16 Then
the man who had the evil spirit jumped
on Sceva's sons. He overpowered them
all. He gave them a terrible beating.
They ran out of the house naked and
bleeding.

17 The Jews and Greeks living in
Ephesus heard about this. They were
all overcome with fear. They held the
name of the Lord Jesus in high honor.

3

PAUL'S THIRD MISSIONARY JOURNEY

ACTS 18:23—21:17

Paul's third missionary journey was very similar to his second journey. He visited many churches in Galatia and Macedonia where he had previously taught and ministered. While in these regions, Paul traveled to various cities where he preached in the synagogues and performed miracles by the power of the Spirit.

Paul also spent time in the city of Ephesus, where he discovered that some of the new Christians had not heard about the Holy Spirit and baptism in Jesus' name. He took time to teach them about baptism to help them better understand, and eventually he said goodbye to his dear friends and fellow workers in Ephesus. Paul later wrote the believers in Ephesus a letter, which is now the book of Ephesians in the Bible.

[18] Many who believed now came and
openly admitted what they had done.
[19] A number of those who had practiced evil magic brought their scrolls
together. They set them on fire out in
the open. They added up the value of
the scrolls. The scrolls were worth more
than someone could earn in two life-
times. [20] The word of the Lord spread
everywhere. It became more and more
powerful.
[21] After all this had happened, Paul
decided to go to Jerusalem. He went
through Macedonia and Achaia. "After
I have been to Jerusalem," he said, "I
must visit Rome also." [22] He sent Timothy and Erastus, two of his helpers, to
Macedonia. But he stayed a little longer
in Asia Minor.

Trouble in Ephesus

[23] At that time many people became
very upset about the Way of Jesus.
[24] There was a man named Demetrius who made things out of silver. He
made silver models of the temple of
the goddess Artemis. He brought in
a lot of business for the other skilled
workers there. [25] One day he called
them together. He also called others
who were in the same kind of business.
"My friends," he said, "you know that
we make good money from our work.
[26] You have seen and heard what this
fellow Paul is doing. He has talked to
large numbers of people here in Ephesus. Almost everywhere in Asia Minor
he has led people away from our gods.
He says that the gods made by human
hands are not gods at all. [27] Our work
is in danger of losing its good name.
People's faith in the temple of the great
goddess Artemis will be weakened. Now
she is worshiped all over Asia Minor
and the whole world. But soon she will
be robbed of her greatness."
[28] When they heard this, they became
very angry. They began shouting,
"Great is Artemis of the Ephesians!"
[29] Soon people were making trouble
in the whole city. They all rushed into
the theater. They dragged Gaius and
Aristarchus along with them. These two
men had come with Paul from Macedonia. [30] Paul wanted to appear in front
of the crowd. But the believers wouldn't
let him. [31] Some of the officials in Asia
Minor were friends of Paul. They sent
him a message, begging him not to go
into the theater.
[32] The crowd didn't know what was
going on. Some were shouting one
thing and some another. Most of the
people didn't even know why they were
there. [33] The Jews in the crowd pushed
Alexander to the front. They tried to
tell him what to say. But he motioned
for them to be quiet. He was about to
give the people reasons for his actions.
[34] But then they realized that he was a
Jew. So they all shouted the same thing
for about two hours. "Great is Artemis
of the Ephesians!" they yelled.
[35] The city clerk quieted the crowd
down. "People of Ephesus!" he said.
"The city of Ephesus guards the temple of the great Artemis. The whole
world knows this. They know that
Ephesus guards her statue, which fell
from heaven. [36] These facts can't be
questioned. So calm down. Don't do
anything foolish. [37] These men haven't
robbed any temples. They haven't
said evil things against our female
god. But you have brought them here
anyhow. [38] Demetrius and the other
skilled workers may feel they have
been wronged by someone. Let them
bring charges. The courts are open. We
have our governors. [39] Is there anything else you want to bring up? Settle
it in a court of law. [40] As it is, we are in
danger of being charged with a crime.
We could be charged with causing all
this trouble today. There is no reason
for it. So we wouldn't be able to explain
what has happened." [41] After he said
this, he sent the people away.

Paul Travels Through Macedonia and Greece

20 All the trouble came to an end.
Then Paul sent for the believers. After encouraging them, he said
goodbye. He then left for Macedonia.
[2] He traveled through that area, speaking many words of hope to the people.
Finally he arrived in Greece. [3] There he
stayed for three months. He was just
about to sail for Syria. But some Jews
were making plans against him. So
he decided to go back through Macedonia. [4] Sopater, son of Pyrrhus, from
Berea went with him. Aristarchus and

Secundus from Thessalonica, Gaius
from Derbe, and Timothy went too.
Tychicus and Trophimus from Asia
Minor also went with him. 5 These men
went on ahead. They waited for us at
Troas. 6 But we sailed from Philippi after
the Feast of Unleavened Bread. Five
days later we joined the others at Troas.
We stayed there for seven days.

Eutychus Is Raised From the Dead at Troas

7 On the first day of the week we met
to break bread and eat together. Paul
spoke to the people. He kept on talking
until midnight because he planned to
leave the next day. 8 There were many
lamps in the room upstairs where we
were meeting. 9 A young man named
Eutychus was sitting in a window. He
sank into a deep sleep as Paul talked
on and on. Sound asleep, Eutychus fell
from the third floor. When they picked
him up from the ground, he was dead.
10 Paul went down and threw himself
on the young man. He put his arms
around him. "Don't be alarmed," he
told them. "He's alive!" 11 Then Paul
went upstairs again. He broke bread
and ate with them. He kept on talking
until daylight. Then he left. 12 The people took the young man home. They
were greatly comforted because he
was alive.

Paul Says Goodbye to the Ephesian Elders

13 We went on ahead to the ship. We
sailed for Assos. There we were going
to take Paul on board. He had planned
it this way because he wanted to go to
Assos by land. 14 So he met us there.
We took him on board and went on to
Mitylene. 15 The next day we sailed from
there. We arrived near Chios. The day
after that we crossed over to Samos. We
arrived at Miletus the next day. 16 Paul
had decided to sail past Ephesus. He
didn't want to spend time in Asia Minor.
He was in a hurry to get to Jerusalem. If
he could, he wanted to be there by the
day of Pentecost.

17 From Miletus, Paul sent for the elders of the church at Ephesus. 18 When
they arrived, he spoke to them. "You
know how I lived the whole time I was
with you," he said. "From the first day
I came into Asia Minor, 19 I served the
Lord with tears and without pride. I
served him when I was greatly tested.
I was tested by the evil plans of the
Jews who disagreed with me. 20 You
know that nothing has kept me from
preaching whatever would help you.
I have taught you in public and from
house to house. 21 I have told both Jews
and Greeks that they must turn away
from their sins to God. They must have
faith in our Lord Jesus.

22 "Now I am going to Jerusalem. The
Holy Spirit compels me. I don't know
what will happen to me there. 23 I only
know that in every city the Spirit warns
me. He tells me that I will face prison
and suffering. 24 But my life means
nothing to me. My only goal is to finish
the race. I want to complete the work
the Lord Jesus has given me. He wants
me to tell others about the good news
of God's grace.

25 "I have spent time with you preaching about the kingdom. I know that
none of you will ever see me again. 26 So
I tell you today that I am not guilty if
any of you don't believe. 27 I haven't
let anyone keep me from telling you
everything God wants you to do. 28 Keep
watch over yourselves. Keep watch over
all the believers. The Holy Spirit has
made you leaders over them. Be shepherds of God's church. He bought it with
his own blood. 29 I know that after I
leave, wild wolves will come in among
you. They won't spare any of the sheep.
30 Even men from your own people will
rise up and twist the truth. They want
to get the believers to follow them. 31 So
be on your guard! Remember that for
three years I never stopped warning
you. Night and day I warned each of
you with tears.

32 "Now I trust God to take care of you.
I commit you to the message about his
grace. It can build you up. Then you will
share in what God plans to give all his
people. 33 I haven't longed for anyone's
silver or gold or clothing. 34 You yourselves know that I have used my own
hands to meet my needs. I have also
met the needs of my companions. 35 In
everything I did, I showed you that we
must work hard and help the weak. We
must remember the words of the Lord
Jesus. He said, 'It is more blessed to give
than to receive.' "

[36]Paul finished speaking. Then he got
down on his knees with all of them and
prayed. [37]They all wept as they hugged
and kissed him. [38]Paul had said that
they would never see him again. That's
what hurt them the most. Then they
went with him to the ship.

Paul Continues His Journey to Jerusalem

21 After we had torn ourselves
away from the Ephesian el-
ders, we headed out to sea. We sailed
straight to Kos. The next day we went
to Rhodes. From there we continued on
to Patara. [2]We found a ship crossing
over to Phoenicia. So we went on board
and headed out to sea. [3]We came near
Cyprus and passed to the south of it.
Then we sailed on to Syria. We landed
at Tyre. There our ship was supposed
to unload. [4]We looked for the believers
there and stayed with them for seven
days. The believers tried to keep Paul
from going on to Jerusalem. They were
led by the Holy Spirit to do this. [5]When
it was time to leave, we continued on
our way. All the believers, including
their whole families, went with us out
of the city. There on the beach we got
down on our knees to pray. [6]We said
goodbye to each other. Then we went
on board the ship. And they returned
home.

[7]Continuing on from Tyre, we landed at Ptolemais. There we greeted the
brothers and sisters. We stayed with
them for a day. [8]The next day we left
and arrived at Caesarea. We stayed
at the house of Philip the evangelist.
He was one of the seven deacons. [9]He
had four unmarried daughters who
prophesied.

[10]We stayed there several days. Then
a prophet named Agabus came down
from Judea. [11]He came over to us. Then
he took Paul's belt and tied his own
hands and feet with it. He said, "The
Holy Spirit says, 'This is how the Jewish leaders in Jerusalem will tie up the
owner of this belt. They will hand him
over to the Gentiles.' "

[12]When we heard this, we all begged
Paul not to go up to Jerusalem. [13]He
asked, "Why are you crying? Why are
you breaking my heart? I'm ready to be
put in prison. In fact, I'm ready to die
in Jerusalem for the Lord Jesus." [14]We
couldn't change his mind. So we gave
up. We said, "May what the Lord wants
to happen be done."

[15]After this, we started on our way
to Jerusalem. [16]Some of the believers from Caesarea went with us. They
brought us to Mnason's home. We were
supposed to stay there. Mnason was
from Cyprus. He was one of the first
believers.

Paul Arrives in Jerusalem

[17]When we arrived in Jerusalem, the
brothers and sisters gave us a warm
welcome. [18]The next day Paul and the
rest of us went to see James. All the
elders were there. [19]Paul greeted them.
Then he reported everything God had
done among the Gentiles through his
work.

[20]When they heard this, they praised
God. Then they spoke to Paul. "Brother,"
they said, "you see that thousands of
Jews have become believers. All of them
try very hard to obey the law. [21]They
have been told that you teach Jews to
turn away from the Law of Moses. You
teach this to the Jews who live among
the Gentiles. They think that you teach
those Jews not to circumcise their children. They think that you teach them
to give up our Jewish ways. [22]What
should we do? They will certainly hear
that you have come. [23]So do what we
tell you. There are four men with us
who have made a promise to God.
[24]Take them with you. Join them in
the Jewish practice that makes people
pure and 'clean.' Pay their expenses
so they can have their heads shaved.
Then everyone will know that these
reports about you are not true in any
way. They will know that you yourself
obey the law. [25]We have already given
written directions to the believers who
are not Jews. They must not eat food
that has been offered to statues of gods.
They must not drink blood. They must
not eat the meat of animals that have
been choked to death. And they must
not commit sexual sins."

[26]The next day Paul took the men
with him. They all made themselves
pure and "clean" in the usual way.
Then Paul went to the temple. There
he reported the date when the days

of cleansing would end. At that time
the proper offering would be made for
each of them.

Paul Is Arrested

27 The seven days of cleansing were
almost over. Some Jews from Asia Minor
saw Paul at the temple. They stirred
up the whole crowd and grabbed Paul.
28 "Fellow Israelites, help us!" they
shouted. "This is the man who teaches everyone in all places against our
people. He speaks against our law and
against this holy place. Besides, he has
brought Greeks into the temple. He has
made this holy place 'unclean.'" 29 They
said this because they had seen Trophimus the Ephesian in the city with Paul.
They thought Paul had brought him
into the temple.

30 The whole city was stirred up. People came running from all directions.
They grabbed Paul and dragged him
out of the temple. Right away the temple gates were shut. 31 The people were
trying to kill Paul. But news reached the
commander of the Roman troops. He
heard that people were making trouble
in the whole city of Jerusalem. 32 Right
away he took some officers and soldiers
with him. They ran down to the crowd.
The people causing the trouble saw the
commander and his soldiers. So they
stopped beating Paul.

33 The commander came up and arrested Paul. He ordered him to be held
with two chains. Then he asked who
Paul was and what he had done. 34 Some
in the crowd shouted one thing, some
another. But the commander couldn't
get the facts because of all the noise.
So he ordered that Paul be taken into
the fort. 35 Paul reached the steps. But
then the mob became so wild that he
had to be carried by the soldiers. 36 The
crowd that followed kept shouting, "Get
rid of him!"

Paul Speaks to the Crowd

37 The soldiers were about to take Paul
into the fort. Then he asked the commander, "May I say something to you?"

"Do you speak Greek?" he replied.
38 "Aren't you the Egyptian who turned
some of our people against their leaders? Didn't you lead 4,000 terrorists out
into the desert some time ago?"

39 Paul answered, "I am a Jew from
Tarsus in Cilicia. I am a citizen of an
important city. Please let me speak to
the people."

40 The commander told him he could.
So Paul stood on the steps and motioned
to the crowd. When all of them were
quiet, he spoke to them in the Aramaic
22 language. 1 "Brothers and fathers," Paul began, "listen to me
now. I want to give you reasons for my
actions."

2 When they heard that he was speaking to them in Aramaic, they became
very quiet.

Then Paul said, 3 "I am a Jew. I was
born in Tarsus in Cilicia, but I grew up
here in Jerusalem. I studied with Gamaliel. I was well trained by him in the law
given to our people long ago. I wanted
to serve God as much as any of you do
today. 4 I hurt the followers of the Way
of Jesus. I sent many of them to their
death. I arrested men and women. I
threw them into prison. 5 The high priest
and the whole Council can be witnesses
of this themselves. I even had some
official letters they had written to their
friends in Damascus. So I went there
to bring these people as prisoners to
Jerusalem to be punished.

6 "I had almost reached Damascus.
About noon a bright light from heaven
suddenly flashed around me. 7 I fell to
the ground and heard a voice speak to
me. 'Saul! Saul!' it said. 'Why are you
opposing me?'

8 " 'Who are you, Lord?' I asked.

" 'I am Jesus of Nazareth,' he replied.
'I am the one you are opposing.' 9 The
light was seen by my companions. But
they didn't understand the voice of the
one speaking to me.

10 " 'What should I do, Lord?' I asked.

" 'Get up,' the Lord said. 'Go into Damascus. There you will be told everything you have been given to do.' 11 The
brightness of the light had blinded me.
So my companions led me by the hand
into Damascus.

12 "A man named Ananias came to see
me. He was a godly Jew who obeyed the
law. All the Jews living there respected
him very much. 13 He stood beside me
and said, 'Brother Saul, receive your
sight!' At that very moment I was able
to see him.

14 "Then he said, 'The God of our people has chosen you. He wanted to tell
you his plans for you. You have seen
the Blameless One. You have heard
words from his mouth. 15 Now you will
tell everyone about what you have seen
and heard. 16 So what are you waiting
for? Get up and call on his name. Be
baptized. Have your sins washed away.'
17 "I returned to Jerusalem and was
praying at the temple. Then it seemed
to me that I was dreaming. 18 I saw the
Lord speaking to me. 'Quick!' he said.
'Leave Jerusalem at once. The people
here will not accept what you tell them
about me.'
19 " 'Lord,' I replied, 'these people
know what I used to do. I went from one
synagogue to another and put believers
in prison. I also beat them. 20 Stephen
was a man who told other people about
you. I stood there when he was killed.
I had agreed that he should die. I even
guarded the coats of those who were
killing him.'
21 "Then the Lord said to me, 'Go. I
will send you far away to people who
are not Jews.' "

Paul the Roman Citizen

22 The crowd listened to Paul until he
said this. Then they shouted, "Kill him!
He isn't fit to live!"
23 They shouted and threw off their
coats. They threw dust into the air. 24 So
the commanding officer ordered that
Paul be taken into the fort. He gave
orders for Paul to be whipped and questioned. He wanted to find out why the
people were shouting at him like this.
25 A commander was standing there as
they stretched Paul out to be whipped.
Paul said to him, "Does the law allow
you to whip a Roman citizen who hasn't
even been found guilty?"
26 When the commander heard this,
he went to the commanding officer and
reported it. "What are you going to do?"
the commander asked. "This man is a
Roman citizen."
27 So the commanding officer went
to Paul. "Tell me," he asked. "Are you a
Roman citizen?"
"Yes, I am," Paul answered.
28 Then the officer said, "I had to pay
a lot of money to become a citizen."
"But I was born a citizen," Paul replied.
29 Right away those who were about
to question him left. Even the officer
was alarmed. He realized that he had
put Paul, a Roman citizen, in chains.

Paul Is Taken to the Sanhedrin

30 The commanding officer wanted
to find out exactly what the Jews had
against Paul. So the next day he let Paul
out of prison. He ordered a meeting of
the chief priests and all the members
of the Sanhedrin. Then he brought Paul
and had him stand in front of them.
23 Paul looked straight at the
Sanhedrin. "My brothers," he
said, "I have always done my duty
to God. To this day I feel that I have
done nothing wrong." 2 Ananias the
high priest heard this. So he ordered
the men standing near Paul to hit him
on the mouth. 3 Then Paul said to him,
"You pretender! God will hit you! You
sit there and judge me by the law. But
you yourself broke the law when you
commanded them to hit me!"
4 Those who were standing near Paul
spoke to him. They said, "How dare you
talk like that to God's high priest!"
5 Paul replied, "Brothers, I didn't realize he was the high priest. It is written,
'Do not speak evil about the ruler of
your people.' " *(Exodus 22:28)*
6 Paul knew that some of them were
Sadducees and the others were Pharisees. So he called out to the members of
the Sanhedrin. "My brothers," he said, "I
am a Pharisee. I come from a family of
Pharisees. I believe that people will rise
from the dead. That's why I am on trial."
7 When he said this, the Pharisees and
the Sadducees started to argue. They
began to take sides. 8 The Sadducees say
that people will not rise from the dead.
They don't believe there are angels or
spirits either. But the Pharisees believe
all these things.
9 People were causing trouble and
making a lot of noise. Some of the
teachers of the law who were Pharisees
stood up. They argued strongly. "We
find nothing wrong with this man," they
said. "What if a spirit or an angel has
spoken to him?" 10 The people arguing
were getting out of control. The commanding officer was afraid that Paul
would be torn to pieces by them. So he
ordered the soldiers to go down and

take him away from them by force.
The officer had told them to bring Paul
into the fort.
11 The next night the Lord stood near
Paul. He said, "Be brave! You have told
people about me in Jerusalem. You
must do the same in Rome."

The Plan to Kill Paul

12 The next morning some Jews gathered secretly to make plans against
Paul. They made a promise to themselves. They promised that they would
not eat or drink anything until they
killed him. 13 More than 40 men took
part in this plan. 14 They went to the
chief priests and the elders. They said,
"We have made a special promise to
God. We will not eat anything until we
have killed Paul. 15 Now then, you and
the Sanhedrin must make an appeal
to the commanding officer. Ask him to
bring Paul to you. Pretend you want
more facts about his case. We are ready
to kill him before he gets here."
16 But Paul's nephew heard about this
plan. So he went into the fort and told
Paul.
17 Then Paul called one of the commanders. He said to him, "Take this
young man to the commanding officer.
He has something to tell him." 18 So the
commander took Paul's nephew to the
officer.
The commander said, "Paul, the prisoner, sent for me. He asked me to bring
this young man to you. The young man
has something to tell you."
19 The commanding officer took the
young man by the hand. He spoke to
him in private. "What do you want to
tell me?" the officer asked.
20 He said, "Some Jews have agreed to
ask you to bring Paul to the Sanhedrin
tomorrow. They will pretend they want
more facts about him. 21 Don't give in to
them. More than 40 of them are waiting in hiding to attack him. They have
promised that they will not eat or drink
anything until they have killed him.
They are ready now. All they need is
for you to bring Paul to the Sanhedrin."
22 The commanding officer let the
young man go. But he gave him a
warning. "Don't tell anyone you have
reported this to me," he said.

Paul Is Taken to Caesarea

23 Then the commanding officer
called for two of his commanders. He
ordered them, "Gather a company of
200 soldiers, 70 horsemen and 200 men
armed with spears. Get them ready to
go to Caesarea at nine o'clock tonight.
24 Provide horses for Paul so that he
may be taken safely to Governor Felix."
25 Here is the letter the officer wrote.

> 26 I, Claudius Lysias, am writing
> this letter.
>
> I am sending it to His Excellency,
> Governor Felix.
>
> Greetings.
>
> 27 The Jews grabbed Paul. They
> were about to kill him. But I came
> with my soldiers and saved him.
> I had learned that he is a Roman
> citizen. 28 I wanted to know why
> they were bringing charges against
> him. So I brought him to their
> Sanhedrin. 29 I found out that the
> charge against him was based on
> questions about their law. But there
> was no charge against him worthy
> of death or prison. 30 Then I was
> told about a plan against the man.
> So I sent him to you at once. I also
> ordered those bringing charges
> against him to present their case
> to you.

31 The soldiers followed their orders.
During the night they took Paul with
them. They brought him as far as An-
tipatris. 32 The next day they let the
horsemen go on with him. The soldiers
returned to the fort. 33 The horsemen arrived in Caesarea. They gave the letter
to the governor. Then they handed Paul
over to him. 34 The governor read the
letter. He asked Paul where he was from.
He learned that Paul was from Cilicia.
35 So he said, "I will hear your case when
those bringing charges against you get
here." Then he ordered that Paul be kept
under guard in Herod's palace.

Paul's Trial in Front of Felix

24 Five days later Ananias the
high priest went down to
Caesarea. Some elders and a lawyer
named Tertullus went with him. They
brought their charges against Paul to
the governor. 2 So Paul was called in.

Tertullus began to bring the charges
against Paul. He said to Felix, "We have
enjoyed a long time of peace while you
have been ruling. You are a wise leader.
You have made this a better nation.
3 Most excellent Felix, we gladly admit
this everywhere and in every way. And
we are very thankful. 4 I don't want
to bother you. But would you be kind
enough to listen to us for a short time?
5 "We have found that Paul is a troublemaker. This man stirs up trouble
among Jews all over the world. He is
a leader of those who follow Jesus of
Nazareth. 6-7 He even tried to make our
temple impure. So we arrested him.
8 Question him yourself. Then you will
learn the truth about all these charges
we are bringing against him."
9 The other Jews said the same thing.
They agreed that the charges were true.
10 The governor motioned for Paul
to speak. Paul said, "I know that you
have been a judge over this nation for
quite a few years. So I am glad to explain my actions to you. 11 About 12 days
ago I went up to Jerusalem to worship.
You can easily check on this. 12 Those
bringing charges against me did not
find me arguing with anyone at the
temple. I wasn't stirring up a crowd in
the synagogues or anywhere else in
the city. 13 They can't prove to you any
of the charges they are making against
me. 14 It is true that I worship the God
of our people. I am a follower of the
Way of Jesus. Those bringing charges
against me call it a cult. I believe everything that is in keeping with the Law.
I believe everything that is in keeping
with what is written in the Prophets. 15 I
have the same hope in God that these
men themselves have. I believe that
both the godly and the ungodly will rise
from the dead. 16 So I always try not to
do anything wrong in the eyes of God
or in the eyes of people.
17 "I was away for several years. Then
I came to Jerusalem to bring my people
gifts for those who were poor. I also
came to offer sacrifices. 18 They found
me doing this in the temple courtyard. I
had already been made pure and 'clean'
in the usual way. There was no crowd
with me. I didn't stir up any trouble.
19 But there are some other Jews who
should be here in front of you. They
are from Asia Minor. They should bring
charges if they have anything against
me. 20 Let the Jews who are here tell
you what crime I am guilty of. After
all, I was put on trial by the Sanhedrin.
21 Perhaps they blame me for what I said
when I was on trial. I shouted, 'I believe
that people will rise from the dead. That
is why I am on trial here today.'"
22 Felix knew all about the Way of
Jesus. So he put off the trial for the time
being. "Lysias the commanding officer
will come," he said. "Then I will decide
your case." 23 He ordered the commander to keep Paul under guard. He told him
to give Paul some freedom. He also told
him to allow Paul's friends to take care
of his needs.
24 Several days later Felix came
with his wife Drusilla. She was a Jew.
Felix sent for Paul and listened to him
speak about faith in Christ Jesus. 25 Paul
talked about how to live a godly life.
He talked about how people should
control themselves. He also talked
about the time when God will judge
everyone. Then Felix became afraid.
"That's enough for now!" he said. "You
may leave. When I find the time, I will
send for you." 26 He was hoping that
Paul would offer him some money to
let him go. So he often sent for Paul and
talked with him.
27 Two years passed. Porcius Festus
took the place of Felix. But Felix wanted
to do the Jews a favor. So he left Paul
in prison.

Paul's Trial in Front of Festus

25 Three days after Festus arrived,
he went up from Caesarea to
Jerusalem. 2 There the chief priests
and the Jewish leaders came to Festus.
They brought their charges against
Paul. 3 They tried very hard to get Festus to have Paul taken to Jerusalem.
They asked for this as a favor. They
were planning to hide and attack Paul
along the way. They wanted to kill him.
4 Festus answered, "Paul is being held
at Caesarea. Soon I'll be going there
myself. 5 Let some of your leaders come
with me. If the man has done anything
wrong, they can bring charges against
him there."
6 Festus spent eight or ten days in
Jerusalem with them. Then he went

down to Caesarea. The next day he called the court together. He ordered Paul to be brought to him. 7 When Paul arrived, the Jews who had come down from Jerusalem stood around him. They brought many strong charges against him. But they couldn't prove that these charges were true.

8 Then Paul spoke up for himself. He said, "I've done nothing wrong against the law of the Jews or against the temple. I've done nothing wrong against Caesar."

9 But Festus wanted to do the Jews a favor. So he said to Paul, "Are you willing to go up to Jerusalem? Are you willing to go on trial there? Are you willing to face these charges in my court?"

10 Paul answered, "I'm already standing in Caesar's court. This is where I should go on trial. I haven't done anything wrong to the Jews. You yourself know that very well. 11 If I am guilty of anything worthy of death, I'm willing to die. But the charges brought against me by these Jews are not true. No one has the right to hand me over to them. I make my appeal to Caesar!"

12 Festus talked it over with the members of his court. Then he said, "You have made an appeal to Caesar. To Caesar you will go!"

Festus Talks With King Agrippa

13 A few days later King Agrippa and Bernice arrived in Caesarea. They came to pay a visit to Festus. 14 They were spending many days there. So Festus talked with the king about Paul's case. He said, "There's a man here that Felix left as a prisoner. 15 When I went to Jerusalem, the Jewish chief priests and the elders brought charges against the man. They wanted him to be found guilty.

16 "I told them that this is not the way Romans do things. We don't judge people before they have faced those bringing charges against them. They must have a chance to argue against the charges for themselves. 17 When the Jewish leaders came back with me, I didn't waste any time. I called the court together the next day. I ordered the man to be brought in. 18 Those bringing charges against him got up to speak. But they didn't charge him with any of the crimes I had expected. 19 Instead, they argued with him about their own beliefs. They didn't agree about a man named Jesus. They said Jesus was dead, but Paul claimed Jesus was alive. 20 I had no idea how to look into such matters. So I asked Paul if he would be willing to go to Jerusalem. There he could be tried on these charges. 21 But Paul made an appeal to have the Emperor decide his case. So I ordered him to be held until I could send him to Caesar."

22 Then Agrippa said to Festus, "I would like to hear this man myself."

Festus replied, "Tomorrow you will hear him."

Paul in Front of Agrippa

23 The next day Agrippa and Bernice arrived. They were treated like very important people. They entered the courtroom. The most important military officers and the leading men of the city came with them. When Festus gave the command, Paul was brought in. 24 Festus said, "King Agrippa, and everyone else here, take a good look at this man! A large number of Jews have come to me about him. They came to me in Jerusalem and also here in Caesarea. They keep shouting that he shouldn't live any longer. 25 I have found that he hasn't done anything worthy of death. But he made his appeal to the Emperor. So I decided to send him to Rome. 26 I don't have anything certain to write about him to His Majesty. So I have brought him here today. Now all of you will be able to hear him. King Agrippa, it will also be very good for you to hear him. As a result of this hearing, I will have something to write. 27 It doesn't make sense to send a prisoner on to Rome without listing the charges against him."

26 Agrippa said to Paul, "You may now present your case."

So Paul motioned with his hand. Then he began to present his case. 2 "King Agrippa," he said, "I am happy to be able to stand here today. I will answer all the charges brought against me by the Jews. 3 I am very pleased that you are familiar with Jewish ways. You know the kinds of things they argue about. So I beg you to be patient as you listen to me.

4 “The Jewish people all know how I
have lived ever since I was a child. They
know all about me from the beginning
of my life. They know how I lived in my
own country and in Jerusalem. 5 They
have known me for a long time. So if
they wanted to, they could tell you how
I have lived. I have lived by the rules of
the Pharisees. Those rules are harder to
obey than those of any other Jewish
group. 6 Today I am on trial because
of the hope I have. I believe in what
God promised our people of long ago.
7 It is the promise that our 12 tribes are
hoping to see come true. Because of
this hope they serve God with faithful
and honest hearts day and night. King
Agrippa, it is also because of this hope
that these Jews are bringing charges
against me. 8 Why should any of you
think it is impossible for God to raise
the dead?

9 “I believed that I should oppose
the name of Jesus of Nazareth. So I
did everything I could to oppose his
name. 10 That's just what I was doing in
Jerusalem. On the authority of the chief
priests, I put many of the Lord's people
in prison. I agreed that they should
die. 11 I often went from one synagogue
to another to have them punished. I
tried to force them to speak evil things
against Jesus. All I wanted to do was
hurt them. I even went looking for them
in the cities of other lands.

12 “On one of these journeys I was on
my way to Damascus. I had the authority and commission of the chief
priests. 13 About noon, King Agrippa, I
was on the road. I saw a light coming
from heaven. It was brighter than the
sun. It was shining around me and my
companions. 14 We all fell to the ground.
I heard a voice speak to me in the Aramaic language. ‘Saul! Saul!’ it said.
‘Why are you opposing me? It is hard
for you to go against what you know
is right.’

15 “Then I asked, ‘Who are you, Lord?’

“ ‘I am Jesus,’ the Lord replied. ‘I am
the one you are opposing. 16 Now get
up. Stand on your feet. I have appeared
to you to appoint you to serve me. And
you must tell other people about me.
You must tell others that you have seen
me today. You must also tell them that
I will show myself to you again. 17 I will
save you from your own people and
from the Gentiles. I am sending you to
them 18 to open their eyes. I want you
to turn them from darkness to light. I
want you to turn them from Satan's
power to God. I want their sins to be
forgiven. They will be forgiven when
they believe in me. They will have their
place among God's people.’

19 “So then, King Agrippa, I obeyed
the vision that appeared from heaven.
20 First I preached to people in Damascus. Then I preached in Jerusalem and
in all Judea. And then I preached to
the Gentiles. I told them to turn away
from their sins to God. The way they
live must show that they have turned
away from their sins. 21 That's why
some Jews grabbed me in the temple
courtyard and tried to kill me. 22 But
God has helped me to this day. So I
stand here and tell you what is true.
I tell it to everyone, both small and
great. I have been saying nothing
different from what the prophets and
Moses said would happen. 23 They said
the Messiah would suffer. He would be
the first to rise from the dead. He would
bring the message of God's light. He
would bring it to his own people and
to the Gentiles.”

24 While Paul was still presenting his
case, Festus interrupted. “You are out
of your mind, Paul!” he shouted. “Your
great learning is driving you crazy!”

25 “I am not crazy, most excellent Festus,” Paul replied. “What I am saying is
true and reasonable. 26 The king is familiar with these things. So I can speak
openly to him. I am certain he knows
everything that has been going on. After all, it was not done in secret. 27 King
Agrippa, do you believe the prophets?
I know you do.”

28 Then Agrippa spoke to Paul. “Are
you trying to talk me into becoming a
Christian?” he said. “Do you think you
can do that in such a short time?”

29 Paul replied, “I don't care if it takes
a short time or a long time. I pray to God
for you and all who are listening to me
today. I pray that you may become like
me, except for these chains.”

30 The king stood up. The governor
and Bernice and those sitting with them
stood up too. 31 They left the room and
began to talk with one another. “Why

should this man die or be put in prison?"
they said. "He has done nothing worthy
of that!"
32 Agrippa said to Festus, "This man
could have been set free. But he has
made an appeal to Caesar."

Paul Sails for Rome

27 It was decided that we would
sail for Italy. Paul and some
other prisoners were handed over to a
Roman commander named Julius. He
belonged to the Imperial Guard. 2 We
boarded a ship from Adramyttium. It
was about to sail for ports along the
coast of Asia Minor. We headed out to
sea. Aristarchus was with us. He was a
Macedonian from Thessalonica.
3 The next day we landed at Sidon.
There Julius was kind to Paul. He let
Paul visit his friends so they could give
him what he needed. 4 From there we
headed out to sea again. We passed
the calmer side of Cyprus because the
winds were against us. 5 We sailed across
the open sea off the coast of Cilicia and
Pamphylia. Then we landed at Myra in
Lycia. 6 There the commander found a
ship from Alexandria sailing for Italy.
He put us on board. 7 We moved along
slowly for many days. We had trouble
getting to Cnidus. The wind did not let
us stay on course. So we passed the
calmer side of Crete, opposite Salmone.
8 It was not easy to sail along the coast.
Then we came to a place called Fair
Havens. It was near the town of Lasea.
9 A lot of time had passed. Sailing
had already become dangerous. By
now it was after the Day of Atonement,
a day of fasting. So Paul gave them a
warning. 10 "Men," he said, "I can see
that our trip is going to be dangerous.
The ship and everything in it will be lost.
Our own lives will be in danger also."
11 But the commander didn't listen to
what Paul said. Instead, he followed the
advice of the pilot and the ship's owner.
12 The harbor wasn't a good place for
ships to stay during winter. So most of
the people decided we should sail on.
They hoped we would reach Phoenix.
They wanted to spend the winter there.
Phoenix was a harbor in Crete. It faced
both southwest and northwest.

The Storm

13 A gentle south wind began to blow.
The ship's crew thought they saw their
chance to leave safely. So they pulled up
the anchor and sailed along the shore
of Crete. 14 Before very long, a wind
blew down from the island. It had the
force of a hurricane. It was called the
Northeaster. 15 The ship was caught by
the storm. We could not keep it sailing
into the wind. So we gave up and were
driven along by the wind. 16 We passed
the calmer side of a small island called
Cauda. We almost lost the lifeboat that
was tied to the side of the ship. 17 So the
men lifted the lifeboat on board. Then
they tied ropes under the ship itself
to hold it together. They were afraid
it would get stuck on the sandbars of
Syrtis. So they lowered the sea anchor
and let the ship be driven along. 18 We
took a very bad beating from the storm.
The next day the crew began to throw
the ship's contents overboard. 19 On the
third day, they even threw the ship's
tools and supplies overboard with their
own hands. 20 The sun and stars didn't
appear for many days. The storm was
terrible. So we gave up all hope of being
saved.
21 The men had not eaten for a long
time. Paul stood up in front of them.
"Men," he said, "you should have taken
my advice not to sail from Crete. Then
you would have avoided this harm and
loss. 22 Now I beg you to be brave. Not
one of you will die. Only the ship will
be destroyed. 23 I belong to God and
serve him. Last night his angel stood
beside me. 24 The angel said, 'Do not
be afraid, Paul. You must go on trial in
front of Caesar. God has shown his grace
by sparing the lives of all those sailing
with you.' 25 Men, continue to be brave. I
have faith in God. It will happen just as
he told me. 26 But we must run the ship
onto the beach of some island."

The Ship Is Destroyed

27 On the 14th night the wind was
still pushing us across the Adriatic
Sea. About midnight the sailors had
a feeling that they were approaching
land. 28 They measured how deep the
water was. They found that it was 120
feet deep. A short time later they measured the water again. This time it was

90 feet deep. 29 They were afraid we would crash against the rocks. So they dropped four anchors from the back of the ship. They prayed that daylight would come. 30 The sailors wanted to escape from the ship. So they let the lifeboat down into the sea. They pretended they were going to lower some anchors from the front of the ship. 31 But Paul spoke to the commander and the soldiers. "These men must stay with the ship," he said. "If they don't, you can't be saved." 32 So the soldiers cut the ropes that held the lifeboat. They let it drift away.

33 Just before dawn Paul tried to get them all to eat. "For the last 14 days," he said, "you have wondered what would happen. You have gone without food. You haven't eaten anything. 34 Now I am asking you to eat some food. You need it to live. Not one of you will lose a single hair from your head." 35 After Paul said this, he took some bread and gave thanks to God. He did this where they all could see him. Then he broke it and began to eat. 36 All of them were filled with hope. So they ate some food. 37 There were 276 of us on board. 38 They ate as much as they wanted. They needed to make the ship lighter. So they threw the rest of the grain into the sea.

39 When daylight came, they saw a bay with a sandy beach. They didn't recognize the place. But they decided to run the ship onto the beach if they could. 40 So they cut the anchors loose and left them in the sea. At the same time, they untied the ropes that held the rudders. They lifted the sail at the front of the ship to the wind. Then they headed for the beach. 41 But the ship hit a sandbar. So the front of it got stuck and wouldn't move. The back of the ship was broken to pieces by the pounding of the waves.

42 The soldiers planned to kill the prisoners. They wanted to keep them from swimming away and escaping. 43 But the commander wanted to save Paul's life. So he kept the soldiers from carrying out their plan. He ordered those who could swim to jump overboard first and swim to land. 44 The rest were supposed to get there on boards or other pieces of the ship. That is how everyone reached land safely.

On Shore at Malta

28 When we were safe on shore, we found out that the island was called Malta. 2 The people of the island were unusually kind. It was raining and cold. So they built a fire and welcomed all of us. 3 Paul gathered some sticks and put them on the fire. A poisonous snake was driven out by the heat. It fastened itself on Paul's hand. 4 The people of the island saw the snake hanging from his hand. They said to one another, "This man must be a murderer. He escaped from the sea. But the female god Justice won't let him live." 5 Paul shook the snake off into the fire. He was not harmed. 6 The people expected him to swell up. They thought he would suddenly fall dead. They waited for a long time. But they didn't see anything unusual happen to him. So they changed their minds. They said he was a god.

7 Publius owned property nearby. He was the chief official on the island. He welcomed us to his home. For three days he took care of us. He treated us with kindness. 8 His father was sick in bed. The man suffered from fever and dysentery. So Paul went in to see him. Paul prayed for him. He placed his hands on him and healed him. 9 Then the rest of the sick people on the island came. They too were healed. 10 The people of the island honored us in many ways. When we were ready to sail, they gave us the supplies we needed.

Paul Arrives in Rome

11 After three months we headed out to sea. We sailed in a ship from Alexandria that had stayed at the island during the winter. On the front of the ship the figures of twin gods were carved. Their names were Castor and Pollux. 12 We landed at Syracuse and stayed there for three days. 13 From there we sailed to Rhegium. The next day the south wind came up. The day after that, we reached Puteoli. 14 There we found some believers. They invited us to spend a week with them. At last we came to Rome. 15 The believers there had heard we were coming. They traveled as far as the Forum of Appius and the Three Taverns to meet us. When Paul saw these people, he thanked God for them and

was encouraged by them. 16 When we
got to Rome, Paul was allowed to live
by himself. But a soldier guarded him.

Paul Preaches in Rome

17 Three days later Paul called a meeting of the local Jewish leaders. When
they came, Paul spoke to them. He
said, "My brothers, I have done nothing
against our people. I have also done
nothing against what our people of
long ago practiced. But I was arrested
in Jerusalem. I was handed over to the
Romans. 18 They questioned me. And
they wanted to let me go. They saw
I wasn't guilty of any crime worthy
of death. 19 But the Jews objected, so
I had to make an appeal to Caesar. I
certainly did not mean to bring any
charge against my own people. 20 I
share Israel's hope. That is why I am
held with this chain. So I have asked
to see you and talk with you."

21 They replied, "We have not received
any letters from Judea about you. None
of our people here from Judea has reported or said anything bad about you. 22 But
we want to hear what your ideas are. We
know that people everywhere are talking
against those who believe as you do."

23 They decided to meet Paul on a certain day. At that time even more people
came to the place where he was staying.
From morning until evening, he told
them about God's kingdom. Using the
Law of Moses and the Prophets, he tried
to get them to believe in Jesus. 24 Some
believed what he said, and others did
not. 25 They didn't agree with one another. They began to leave after Paul had
made a final statement. He said, "The
Holy Spirit was right when he spoke to
your people long ago. Through Isaiah
the prophet the Spirit said,

26 " 'Go to your people. Say to them,
"You will hear but never
understand.
You will see but never know what
you are seeing."
27 These people's hearts have become
stubborn.
They can barely hear with their
ears.
They have closed their eyes.
Otherwise they might see with their
eyes.
They might hear with their ears.
They might understand with
their hearts.
They might turn, and then I would
heal them.' *(Isaiah 6:9,10)*

28-29 "Here is what I want you to know.
God has sent his salvation to the Gentiles. And they will listen!"

30 For two whole years Paul stayed
there in a house he rented. He welcomed
all who came to see him. 31 He preached
boldly about God's kingdom. He taught
people about the Lord Jesus Christ. And
no one could keep him from teaching
and preaching about these things.

Letters & Revelation
ROMANS
1 CORINTHIANS
2 CORINTHIANS
GALATIANS
EPHESIANS
PHILIPPIANS
COLOSSIANS
1 THESSALONIANS
2 THESSALONIANS
1 TIMOTHY
2 TIMOTHY
TITUS
PHILEMON
HEBREWS
JAMES
1 PETER
2 PETER
1 JOHN
2 JOHN
3 JOHN
JUDE
REVELATION

The Letters and Revelation were mostly written by apostles, or people who had seen Jesus firsthand. They taught new Christians how to live out their faith in their everyday lives.

After the first Christians put their faith in Jesus, they had some big questions: *How do we live our lives now? What does it mean to follow Jesus? How do we worship Jesus together when we are so different from each other?* These are important questions, and God didn't leave them (or us!) without answers.

The Letters talk about the gospel, what it means to be a Christian and how Christians can share their faith with others. Revelation encourages new Christians to remember that Jesus is worth everything.

We know we are reading Letters because these books were named after either the person who wrote them or the person (or group of people) they were written to. They often include the name of the author or audience within the first few verses (similar to the way we address a letter with "To" and "From"). Revelation reveals truth about Jesus and his promise to return to take all who believe in him to heaven to live with him forever.

ROMANS

Author: Paul

The book of Romans is a letter that was written to the church in Rome by a man named Paul. The Roman Empire was the largest empire in the world, and its rulers were not followers of Jesus. Paul was a devout Jew who saw new followers of Jesus as a threat. He wanted the Jews to keep following the old commands; he didn't believe that Jesus was the Savior God had promised. Paul persecuted Christians—he threw them in jail for believing that Jesus was the Savior. One day God revealed to Paul that Jesus was the Messiah the Jewish people had been waiting for all along (see Acts 9:1–19). From that day forward, Paul became a missionary for Jesus, telling anyone who would listen that Jesus was the Savior.

Letters & Revelation

The Christians living in Rome included both Jews and Gentiles who believed in Jesus. Because they had grown up differently, they sometimes argued about how they were to love and worship God. Paul wrote this letter to the believers in Rome, encouraging them to be unified and reminding them of the one very big thing they had in common: their belief that Jesus was the King of the world and that he had changed each of their lives for the better.

1 I, Paul, am writing this letter. I serve Christ Jesus. I have been appointed to be an apostle. God set me apart to tell others his good news. 2 He promised the good news long ago. He announced it through his prophets in the Holy Scriptures. 3 The good news is about God's Son. He was born into the family line of King David. 4 By the Holy Spirit, he was appointed to be the mighty Son of God. God did this by raising him from the dead. He is Jesus Christ our Lord. 5 We received grace because of what Jesus did. He made us apostles to the Gentiles. We must invite all of them to obey God by trusting in Jesus. We do this to bring glory to him. 6 You also are among those Gentiles who are appointed to belong to Jesus Christ.

7 I am sending this letter to all of you in Rome. You are loved by God and appointed to be his holy people.

May God our Father and the Lord Jesus Christ give you grace and peace.

Paul Longs to Visit Rome

8 First, I thank my God through Jesus Christ for all of you. People all over the world are talking about your faith. 9 I serve God with my whole heart. I preach the good news about his Son. God knows that I always remember you 10 in my prayers. I pray that now at last it may be God's plan to open the way for me to visit you.

11 I long to see you. I want to make you strong by giving you a gift from the Holy Spirit. 12 I want us to encourage one another in the faith we share. 13 Brothers and sisters, I want you to know that I planned many times to visit you. But until now I have been kept from coming. My work has produced results among the other Gentiles. In the same way, I want to see results among you.

14 I have a duty both to Greeks and to non-Greeks. I have a duty both to wise people and to foolish people. 15 So I really want to preach the good news also to you who live in Rome.

16 I want to preach it because I'm not ashamed of the good news. It is God's power to save everyone who believes. It is meant first for the Jews. It is meant also for the Gentiles. 17 The good news shows God's power to make people right with himself. God's power to be made right with him is given to the person who has faith. It happens by faith from beginning to end. It is written, "The one who is right with God will live by faith." *(Habakkuk 2:4)*

key verse

I want to preach it because I'm not ashamed of the good news. It is God's power to save everyone who believes. It is meant first for the Jews. It is meant also for the Gentiles.

ROMANS 1:16

God's Anger Against Sinners

18 God shows his anger from heaven. It is against all the godless and evil things people do. They are so evil that they say no to the truth. 19 The truth about God is plain to them. God has made it plain. 20 Ever since the world was created it has been possible to see the qualities of God that are not seen. I'm talking about his eternal power and about the fact that he is God. Those things can be seen in what he has made. So people have no excuse for what they do.

21 They knew God. But they didn't honor him as God. They didn't thank him. Their thinking became worthless. Their foolish hearts became dark. 22 They claimed to be wise. But they made fools of themselves. 23 They would rather have statues of gods than the glorious God who lives forever. Their statues of gods are made to look like people, birds, animals and reptiles.

24 So God let them go. He allowed them to do what their sinful hearts wanted to. He let them commit sexual sins. They made one another's bodies impure by what they did. 25 They chose a lie instead of the truth about God. They worshiped and served created things. They didn't worship the Creator. But he is praised forever. Amen.

26 So God let them continue to have their shameful desires. Their women committed sexual acts that were not natural. 27 In the same way, the men turned away from their natural love for women. They burned with sexual desire

in Romans?

God is the Good Father. Those who put their faith in Jesus are brought into the family of God, no matter where they come from or what they have done.

for each other. Men did shameful things with other men. They suffered in their bodies for all the wrong things they did.

[28]They didn't think it was important to know God. So God let them continue to have evil thoughts. They did things they shouldn't do. [29]They are full of every kind of sin, evil and ungodliness. They want more than they need. They commit murder. They want what belongs to other people. They fight and cheat. They hate others. They say mean things about other people. [30]They tell lies about them. They hate God. They are rude and proud. They brag. They think of new ways to do evil. They don't obey their parents. [31]They do not understand. They can't be trusted. They are not loving and kind. [32]They know that God's commands are right. They know that those who do evil things should die. But they continue to do those very things. They also approve of others who do them.

God Judges Fairly

2 If you judge someone else, you have no excuse for it. When you judge another person, you are judging yourself. You do the same things you blame others for doing. [2]We know that when God judges those who do evil things, he judges fairly. [3]Though you are only a human being, you judge others. But you yourself do the same things. So how do you think you will escape when God judges you? [4]Do you disrespect God's great kindness and favor? Do you disrespect God when he is patient with you? Don't you realize that God's kindness is meant to turn you away from your sins?

[5]But you are stubborn. In your heart you are not sorry for your sins. You are storing up anger against yourself. The day of God's anger is coming. Then his way of judging fairly will be shown. [6]God "will pay back each person in keeping with what they have done." *(Psalm 62:12; Proverbs 24:12)* [7]God will give eternal life to those who keep on doing good. They want glory, honor, and life that never ends. [8]But there are others who only look out for themselves. They don't accept the truth. They go astray. God will pour out his great anger on them. [9]There will be trouble and suffering for everyone who does evil. That is meant first for the Jews. It is also meant for the Gentiles. [10]But there will be glory, honor and peace for everyone who does good. That is meant first for the Jews. It is also meant for the Gentiles. [11]God treats everyone the same.

[12]Some people do not know God's law when they sin. They will not be judged by the law when they die. Others do know God's law when they sin. They will be judged by the law. [13]Hearing the law does not make a person right with God. People are considered to be right with God only when they obey the law. [14]Gentiles do not have the law. Sometimes they just naturally do what the law requires. They are a law for themselves. This is true even though they don't have the law. [15]They show that what the law requires is written on their hearts. The way their minds judge them proves this fact. Sometimes their thoughts find them guilty. At other times their thoughts find them not guilty. [16]This will happen on the day God appoints Jesus Christ to judge people's secret thoughts. That's part of my good news.

The Jews and the Law

[17]Suppose you call yourself a Jew. You trust in the law. You brag that you know God. [18]You know what God wants. You agree with what is best because the law teaches you. [19]You think you know so much more than the people you teach.

You think you're helping blind people. You think you are a light for those in the dark. 20 You think you can make foolish people wise. You act like you're teaching little children. You think that the law gives you all knowledge and truth. 21 You claim to teach others, but you don't even teach yourself! You preach against stealing. But you steal! 22 You say that people should not commit adultery. But you commit adultery! You hate statues of gods. But you rob temples! 23 You brag about the law. But when you break it, you rob God of his honor! 24 It is written, "The Gentiles say evil things against God's name because of you." *(Isaiah 52:5; Ezekiel 36:22)*

25 Circumcision has value if you obey the law. But if you break the law, it is just as if you hadn't been circumcised. 26 And sometimes those who aren't circumcised do what the law requires. Won't God accept them as if they had been circumcised? 27 Many are not circumcised physically, but they obey the law. They will prove that you are guilty. You are breaking the law, even though you have the written law and are circumcised.

28 A person is not a Jew if they are a Jew only on the outside. And circumcision is more than just something done to the outside of a man's body. 29 No, a person is a Jew only if they are a Jew on the inside. And true circumcision means that the heart has been circumcised by the Holy Spirit. The person whose heart has been circumcised does more than obey the written law. The praise that matters for that kind of person does not come from other people. It comes from God.

God Is Faithful

3 Is there any advantage in being a Jew? Is there any value in being circumcised? 2 There is great value in every way! First of all, the Jews have been given the very words of God.

3 What if some Jews were not faithful? Will the fact that they weren't faithful keep God from being faithful? 4 Not at all! God is true, even if every human being is a liar. It is written,

"You are right when you
sentence me.
You are fair when you judge me."
(Psalm 51:4)

5 Doesn't the fact that we are wrong prove more clearly that God is right? Then what can we say? Can we say that God is not fair when he brings his anger down on us? As you can tell, I am just using human ways of thinking. 6 God is certainly fair! If he weren't, how could he judge the world? 7 Someone might argue, "When I lie, it becomes clearer that God is truthful. It makes his glory shine more brightly. Why then does he find me guilty of sin?" 8 Why not say, "Let's do evil things so that good things will happen"? Some people actually lie by reporting that this is what we say. They are the ones who will rightly be found guilty.

No One Is Right With God

9 What should we say then? Do we Jews have any advantage? Not at all! We have already claimed that Jews and Gentiles are sinners. Everyone is under the power of sin. 10 It is written,

"No one is right with God, no one at
all.
11 No one understands.
No one trusts in God.
12 All of them have turned away.
They have all become worthless.
No one does anything good,
no one at all." *(Psalms 14:1–3;
53:1–3; Ecclesiastes 7:20)*
13 "Their throats are like open graves.
With their tongues they tell lies."
(Psalm 5:9)
"The words from their lips are like
the poison of a snake." *(Psalm
140:3)*
14 "Their mouths are full of curses
and bitterness." *(Psalm 10:7)*
15 "They run quickly to commit
murder.
16 They leave a trail of harmful
actions.
17 They do not know how to live in
peace." *(Isaiah 59:7,8)*
18 "They don't have any respect for
God." *(Psalm 36:1)*

19 What the law says, it says to those who are ruled by the law. Its purpose is to shut every mouth and make the whole world accountable to God. 20 So no one will be considered right with God by obeying the law. Instead, the law makes us more aware of our sin.

Becoming Right With God by Faith

21 But now God has shown us his saving power without the help of the law. But the Law and the Prophets tell us about this. 22 We are made right with God by putting our faith in Jesus Christ. This happens to all who believe. It is no different for the Jews than for the Gentiles. 23 Everyone has sinned. No one measures up to God's glory. 24 The free gift of God's grace makes us right with him. Christ Jesus paid the price to set us free. 25 God gave Christ as a sacrifice to pay for sins through the spilling of his blood. So God forgives the sins of those who have faith. God did all this to prove that he does what is right. He is a God of mercy. So he did not punish for their sins the people who lived before Jesus lived. 26 God did all this to prove in our own time that he does what is right. He also makes right with himself those who believe in Jesus.

27 So who can brag? No one! Are people saved by the law that requires them to obey? Not at all! They are saved because of the law that requires faith. 28 We firmly believe that a person is made right with God because of their faith. They are not saved by obeying the law. 29 Or is God the God of Jews only? Isn't he also the God of Gentiles? Yes, he is their God too. 30 There is only one God. When those who are circumcised believe in him, he makes them right with himself. Suppose those who are not circumcised believe in him. Then God also will make them right with himself. 31 Does faith make the law useless? Not at all! We agree with the law.

Abraham's Faith Made Him Right With God

4 What should we say about these things? What did Abraham, the father of our people, discover about being right with God? 2 Did he become right with God because of something he did? If so, he could brag about it. But he couldn't brag to God. 3 What do we find in Scripture? It says, "Abraham believed God. God accepted Abraham's faith, and so his faith made him right with God." *(Genesis 15:6)*

4 When a person works, their pay is not considered a gift. It is owed to them. 5 But things are different with God. He makes ungodly people right with himself. If people trust in him, their faith is accepted even though they do not work. Their faith makes them right with God. 6 King David says the same thing. He tells us how blessed people are when God makes them right with himself. They are blessed because they don't have to do anything in return. David says,

7 "Blessed are those
whose lawless acts are forgiven.
Blessed are those
whose sins are taken away.
8 Blessed is the person
whose sin the Lord never counts
against them." *(Psalm 32:1,2)*

9 Is that blessing only for those who are circumcised? Or is it also for those who are not circumcised? We have been saying that God accepted Abraham's faith. So his faith made him right with God. 10 When did it happen? Was it after Abraham was circumcised, or before? It was before he was circumcised, not after! 11 He was circumcised as a sign of the covenant God had made with him. It showed that his faith had made him right with God before he was circumcised. So Abraham is the father of all believers who have not been circumcised. God accepts their faith. So their faith makes them right with him. 12 And Abraham is also the father of those

Is there anyone who has not sinned?

Everyone has sinned, except for Jesus. He is the only one who lived a sinless life because he was God in the flesh.

Can you find the following verses?

ROMANS 3:23–24

who are circumcised and believe. So just being circumcised is not enough. Those who are circumcised must also follow the steps of our father Abraham. He had faith before he was circumcised.

13 Abraham and his family received a promise. God promised that Abraham would receive the world. It would not come to him because he obeyed the law. It would come because of his faith, which made him right with God. 14 Do those who depend on the law receive the promise? If they do, faith would mean nothing. God's promise would be worthless. 15 The law brings God's anger. Where there is no law, the law can't be broken.

16 The promise is based on God's grace. The promise comes by faith. All of Abraham's children will certainly receive the promise. And it is not only for those who are ruled by the law. Those who have the same faith that Abraham had are also included. He is the father of us all. 17 It is written, "I have made you a father of many nations." *(Genesis 17:5)* God considers Abraham to be our father. The God that Abraham believed in gives life to the dead. Abraham's God also creates things that did not exist before.

18 When there was no reason for hope, Abraham believed because he had hope. He became the father of many nations, exactly as God had promised. God said, "That is how many children you will have." *(Genesis 15:5)* 19 Abraham did not become weak in his faith. He accepted the fact that he was past the time when he could have children. At that time Abraham was about 100 years old. He also realized that Sarah was too old to have children. 20 But Abraham kept believing in God's promise. He became strong in his faith. He gave glory to God. 21 He was absolutely sure that God had the power to do what he had promised. 22 That's why "God accepted Abraham because he believed. So his faith made him right with God." *(Genesis 15:6)* 23 The words "God accepted Abraham's faith" were written not only for Abraham. 24 They were written also for us. We believe in the God who raised Jesus our Lord from the dead. So God will accept our faith and make us right with himself. 25 Jesus was handed over to die for our sins. He was raised to life in order to make us right with God.

Peace and Hope

5 We have been made right with God because of our faith. Now we have peace with him because of our Lord Jesus Christ. 2 Through faith in Jesus we have received God's grace. In that grace we stand. We are full of joy because we expect to share in God's glory. 3 And that's not all. We are full of joy even when we suffer. We know that our suffering gives us the strength to go on. 4 The strength to go on produces character. Character produces hope. 5 And hope will never bring us shame. That's because God's love has been poured into our hearts. This happened through the Holy Spirit, who has been given to us.

6 At just the right time Christ died for ungodly people. He died for us when we had no power of our own. 7 It is unusual for anyone to die for a godly person. Maybe someone would be willing to die for a good person. 8 But here is how God has shown his love for us. While we were still sinners, Christ died for us.

9 The blood of Christ has made us right with God. So we are even more sure that Jesus will save us from God's anger. 10 Once we were God's enemies. But we have been brought back to him because his Son has died for us. Now that God has brought us back, we are even more secure. We know that we will be saved because Christ lives. 11 And that is not all. We are full of joy in God because of our Lord Jesus Christ. Because of him, God has brought us back to himself.

Death Through Adam, Life Through Christ

12 Sin entered the world because one man sinned. And death came because of sin. Everyone sinned, so death came to all people.

13 Before the law was given, sin was in the world. This is certainly true. But people are not judged for sin when there is no law. 14 Death ruled from the time of Adam to the time of Moses. Death ruled even over those who did not sin as Adam did. He broke God's command. But Adam also became a pattern of the Messiah. The Messiah was the one who was going to come.

15 God's gift can't be compared with Adam's sin. Many people died because of the sin of that one man. But it was

even more sure that God's grace would also come through one man. That man is Jesus Christ. God's gift of grace was more than enough for the whole world.
[16]The result of God's gift is different from the result of Adam's sin. That one sin brought God's judgment. But after many sins, God's gift made people right with him.
[17]One man sinned, and death ruled over all people because of his sin. What will happen is even more sure than this. Those who receive the rich supply of God's grace will rule with Christ. They will rule in his kingdom. They have received God's gift and have been made right with him. This will happen because of what the one man, Jesus Christ, has done.

[18]So one man's sin brought guilt to all people. In the same way, one right act made people right with God. That one right act gave life to all people.
[19]Many people were made sinners because one man did not obey. But one man did obey. That is why many people will be made right with God.

[20]The law was given so that sin would increase. But where sin increased, God's grace increased even more.
[21]Sin ruled and brought death. But grace rules in the lives of those who are right with God. The grace of God brings eternal life. That's because of what Jesus Christ our Lord has done.

Living a New Life in Christ

6 What should we say then? Should we keep on sinning so that God's grace can increase?
[2]Not at all! As far as sin is concerned, we are dead. So how can we keep on sinning?
[3]All of us were baptized into Christ Jesus. Don't you know that we were baptized into his death?
[4]By being baptized, we were buried with Christ into his death. Christ has been raised from the dead by the Father's glory. And like Christ we also can live a new life.

[5]By being baptized, we have been joined with him in a death like his. So we will certainly also be joined with him in a resurrection like his.
[6]We know that what we used to be was nailed to the cross with him. That happened so our bodies that were ruled by sin would lose their power. So we are no longer slaves of sin.
[7]That's because those who have died have been set free from sin.

[8]We died with Christ. So we believe that we will also live with him.
[9]We know that Christ was raised from the dead and will never die again. Death

KIND

God is always thinking about us. In fact, he delights in us—the people he has made—and wants to provide generously for us. God gives us good gifts and cares about the things we care about (see James 1:17).

Can you think of something good God has given you? Perhaps a new friend, a warm blanket, or the courage to be in a new classroom. God is always kind toward us, and his Spirit gently leads us to follow him.

God also proves his kindness by inviting all people to know him. He welcomes all who come to him through Jesus. As we grow in our relationship with God, his kindness shines through us so we can bless others.

My GOD IS...

doesn't control him anymore. 10 When
he died, he died once and for all time.
He did this to break the power of sin.
Now that he lives, he lives in the power
of God.
11 In the same way, consider yourselves to be dead as far as sin is concerned. Now you believe in Christ Jesus.
So consider yourselves to be alive as far
as God is concerned. 12 So don't let sin
rule your body, which is going to die.
Don't obey its evil desires. 13 Don't give
any part of yourself to serve sin. Don't
let any part of yourself be used to do
evil. Instead, give yourselves to God.
You have been brought from death to
life. So give every part of yourself to
God to do what is right. 14 Sin will no
longer control you like a master. That's
because the law does not rule you. God's
grace has set you free.

Slaves to Right Living

15 What should we say then? Should
we sin because we are not ruled by
the law but by God's grace? Not at all!
16 Don't you know that when you give
yourselves to obey someone you become that person's slave? If you are
slaves of sin, then you will die. But if you
are slaves who obey God, then you will
live a godly life. 17 You used to be slaves
of sin. But thank God that with your
whole heart you obeyed the teachings
you were given! 18 You have been set
free from sin. You have become slaves
to right living.
19 Because you are human, you find
this hard to understand. So I am using
an everyday example to help you understand. You used to give yourselves
to be slaves to unclean living. You were
becoming more and more evil. Now
give yourselves to be slaves to right
living. Then you will become holy.
20 Once you were slaves of sin. At that
time right living did not control you.
21 What benefit did you gain from doing
the things you are now ashamed of?
Those things lead to death! 22 You have
been set free from sin. God has made
you his slaves. The benefit you gain
leads to holy living. And the end result
is eternal life. 23 When you sin, the pay
you get is death. But God gives you the
gift of eternal life. That's because of
what Christ Jesus our Lord has done.

Jesus Is Our Redeemer

Sin separates us from God. Sometimes sin is referred to as *debt*. Debt is when you owe someone money, but you don't have the money to pay them. Only God can pay for our debt of sin. We can't earn our way back to God on our own. We need a redeemer, or a rescuer, to buy us back from sin and make us right with God.

Jesus is the Redeemer whom God promised to send. Jesus died in our place, and by his righteousness, he redeems us, or pays the debt we cannot pay (see Colossians 2:14). We are made right with God through Jesus, and we are given power through the Holy Spirit to resist sin and live for the glory of God.

An Example From Marriage

7 Brothers and sisters, I am speaking
to you who know the law. Don't you
know that the law has authority over
someone only as long as they live? 2 For
example, by law a married woman remains married as long as her husband
lives. But suppose her husband dies.
Then the law that joins her to him no longer applies. 3 But suppose that married
woman sleeps with another man while
her husband is still alive. Then she is
called a woman who commits adultery.
But suppose her husband dies. Then she
is free from that law. She is not guilty of
adultery if she marries another man.
4 My brothers and sisters, when Christ
died you also died as far as the law is
concerned. Then it became possible for

you to belong to him. He was raised
from the dead. Now our lives can be
useful to God. 5 The power of sin used to
control us. The law stirred up sinful desires in us. So the things we did resulted
in death. 6 But now we have died to what
used to control us. We have been set free
from the law. Now we serve in the new
way of the Holy Spirit. We no longer
serve in the old way of the written law.

The Law and Sin

7 What should we say then? That the
law is sinful? Not at all! Yet I wouldn't
have known what sin was unless the
law had told me. The law says, "Do not
want what belongs to other people."
(Exodus 20:17; Deuteronomy 5:21) If the
law hadn't said that, I would not have
known what it was like to want what belongs to others. 8 But the commandment
gave sin an opportunity. Sin caused me
to want all kinds of things that belong
to others. A person can't sin by breaking
a law if that law doesn't exist. 9 Before
I knew about the law, I was alive. But
then the commandment came. Sin
came to life, and I died. 10 I found that
the commandment that was supposed
to bring life actually brought death.
11 When the commandment gave sin the
opportunity, sin tricked me. It used the
commandment to put me to death. 12 So
the law is holy. The commandment also
is holy and right and good.

13 Did what is good cause me to die?
Not at all! Sin had to be recognized for
what it really is. So it used what is good
to bring about my death. Because of
the commandment, sin became totally
sinful.

14 We know that the law is holy. But I
am not. I have been sold to be a slave
of sin. 15 I don't understand what I do.
I don't do what I want to do. Instead, I
do what I hate to do. 16 I do what I don't
want to do. So I agree that the law is
good. 17 As it is, I am no longer the one
who does these things. It is sin living
in me that does them. 18 I know there is
nothing good in my desires controlled
by sin. I want to do what is good, but I
can't. 19 I don't do the good things I want
to do. I keep on doing the evil things I
don't want to do. 20 I do what I don't want
to do. But I am not really the one who is
doing it. It is sin living in me that does it.

21 Here is the law I find working in me.
When I want to do good, evil is right
there with me. 22 Deep inside me I find
joy in God's law. 23 But I see another law
working in me. It fights against the law
of my mind. It makes me a prisoner of
the law of sin. That law controls me.
24 What a terrible failure I am! Who will
save me from this sin that brings death
to my body? 25 I give thanks to God who
saves me. He saves me through Jesus
Christ our Lord.

So in my mind I am a slave to God's
law. But sin controls my desires. So I am
a slave to the law of sin.

The Holy Spirit Gives Life

8 Those who belong to Christ Jesus
are no longer under God's judgment. 2 Because of what Christ Jesus
has done, you are free. You are now
controlled by the law of the Holy Spirit
who gives you life. The law of the Spirit
frees you from the law of sin that brings
death. 3 The written law was made weak
by the power of sin. But God did what
the written law could not do. He made
his Son to be like those who live under
the power of sin. God sent him to be an
offering for sin. Jesus suffered God's
judgment against our sin. 4 Jesus does
for us everything the holy law requires.
The power of sin should no longer control the way we live. The Holy Spirit
should control the way we live.

5 So don't live under the control of sin.
If you do, you will think about what sin
wants. Live under the control of the Holy
Spirit. If you do, you will think about
what the Spirit wants. 6 The thoughts of
a person ruled by sin bring death. But
the mind ruled by the Spirit brings life
and peace. 7 The mind ruled by the power of sin is at war with God. It does not
obey God's law. It can't. 8 Those who are
under the power of sin can't please God.

9 But you are not ruled by the power
of sin. Instead, the Holy Spirit rules over
you. This is true if the Spirit of God lives in
you. Anyone who does not have the Spirit
of Christ does not belong to Christ. 10 If
Christ lives in you, you will live. Though
your body will die because of sin, the
Spirit gives you life. The Spirit does this
because you have been made right with
God. 11 The Spirit of the God who raised
Jesus from the dead is living in you. So

the God who raised Christ from the dead
will also give life to your bodies. He will do
this because of his Spirit who lives in you.
[12]Brothers and sisters, we have a duty.
Our duty is not to live under the power
of sin. [13]If you live under the power of
sin, you will die. But by the Spirit's power
you can put to death the sins you commit. Then you will live.
[14]Those who are led by the Spirit of
God are children of God. [15]The Spirit
you received doesn't make you slaves.
Otherwise you would live in fear again.
Instead, the Holy Spirit you received
made you God's adopted child. By the
Spirit's power we call God *Abba*. Abba
means Father. [16]The Spirit himself joins
with our spirits. Together they tell us
that we are God's children. [17]As his children, we will receive all that he has for
us. We will share what Christ receives.
But we must share in his sufferings if
we want to share in his glory.

Suffering Now and Glory in the Future

[18]What we are suffering now is nothing compared with our future glory.
[19]Everything God created looks forward
to the future. That will be the time when
his children appear in their full and
final glory. [20]The created world was
held back from fulfilling its purpose. But
this was not the result of its own choice.
It was planned that way by the one who
held it back. God planned [21]to set the
created world free. He didn't want it
to rot away. Instead, God wanted it to
have the same freedom and glory that
his children have.
[22]We know that all that God created
has been groaning. It is in pain as if it
were giving birth to a child. The created
world continues to groan even now.
[23]And that's not all. We have the Holy
Spirit as the promise of future blessing.
But we also groan inside ourselves. We
do this as we look forward to the time
when God adopts us as full members
of his family. Then he will give us everything he has for us. He will raise our
bodies and give glory to them. [24]That's
the hope we had when we were saved.
But hope that can be seen is no hope at
all. Who hopes for what they already
have? [25]We hope for what we don't have
yet. So we are patient as we wait for it.
[26]In the same way, the Holy Spirit
helps us when we are weak. We don't
know what we should pray for. But the
Spirit himself prays for us. He prays
through groans too deep for words.
[27]God, who looks into our hearts, knows
the mind of the Spirit. And the Spirit
prays for God's people just as God wants
him to pray.
[28]We know that in all things God
works for the good of those who love
him. He appointed them to be saved
in keeping with his purpose. [29]God
planned that those he had chosen
would become like his Son. In that way,
Christ will be the first and most honored among many brothers and sisters.
[30]And those God has planned for, he has
also appointed to be saved. Those he
has appointed, he has made right with
himself. To those he has made right
with himself, he has given his glory.

We Are More Than Winners

[31]What should we say then? Since
God is on our side, who can be against
us? [32]God did not spare his own Son.
He gave him up for us all. Then won't
he also freely give us everything else?
[33]Who can bring any charge against
God's chosen ones? God makes us right
with himself. [34]Then who can sentence
us to death? No one. Christ Jesus is at the
right hand of God and is also praying
for us. He died. More than that, he was
raised to life. [35]Who can separate us
from Christ's love? Can trouble or hard
times or harm or hunger? Can naked-
ness or danger or war? [36]It is written,

> "Because of you, we face death all
> day long.
> We are considered as sheep to be
> killed." *(Psalm 44:22)*

[37]No! In all these things we are more
than winners! We owe it all to Christ,
who has loved us. [38]I am absolutely sure
that not even death or life can separate
us from God's love. Not even angels or
demons, the present or the future, or
any powers can separate us. [39]Not even
the highest places or the lowest, or anything else in all creation can separate
us. Nothing at all can ever separate us
from God's love. That's because of what
Christ Jesus our Lord has done.

Paul Mourns for Israel

9 I speak the truth in Christ. I am not
lying. My mind tells me that what I
say is true. It is guided by the Holy Spirit.
2 My heart is full of sorrow. My sadness
never ends. 3 I am so concerned about
my people, who are members of my
own race. I am ready to be cursed, if that
would help them. I am even willing to
be separated from Christ. 4 They are the
people of Israel. They have been adopted
as God's children. God's glory belongs to
them. So do the covenants. They received
the law. They were taught to worship in
the temple. They were given the promises. 5 The founders of our nation belong
to them. The Messiah comes from their
family line. He is God over all. May he
always be praised! Amen.

God's Free Choice

6 I do not mean that God's word has
failed. Not everyone in the family line
of Israel really belongs to Israel. 7 Not
everyone in Abraham's family line is
really his child. Not at all! Scripture
says, "Your family line will continue
through Isaac." *(Genesis 21:12)* 8 In other
words, God's children are not just in
the family line of Abraham. Instead,
they are the children God promised to
him. They are the ones considered to be
Abraham's children. 9 God promised, "I
will return at the appointed time. Sarah
will have a son." *(Genesis 18:10,14)*

10 And that's not all. Rebekah's children
were born at the same time by the same
father. He was our father Isaac. 11 Here
is what happened. Rebekah's twins had
not even been born. They hadn't done
anything good or bad yet. So they show
that God's purpose is based firmly on
his free choice. 12 It was not because of
anything they did but because of God's
choice. So Rebekah was told, "The older
son will serve the younger one." *(Genesis 25:23)* 13 It is written, "I chose Jacob
instead of Esau." *(Malachi 1:2,3)*

14 What should we say then? Is God
unfair? Not at all! 15 He said to Moses,

"I will have mercy on whom I have
mercy.
I will show love to those I love."
(Exodus 33:19)

16 So it doesn't depend on what people
want or what they do. It depends on
God's mercy. 17 In Scripture, God says
to Pharaoh, "I had a special reason for
making you king. I decided to use you
to show my power. I wanted my name
to become known everywhere on earth."
(Exodus 9:16) 18 So God does what he
wants to do. He shows mercy to one
person and makes another stubborn.

19 One of you will say to me, "Then
why does God still blame us? Who can
oppose what he wants to do?" 20 But you
are a mere human being. So who are you
to talk back to God? Scripture says, "Can
what is made say to the one who made
it, 'Why did you make me like this?' "
(Isaiah 29:16; 45:9) 21 Isn't the potter free
to make different kinds of pots out of the
same lump of clay? Some are for special
purposes. Others are for ordinary use.

22 What if God chose to show his great
anger? What if he chose to make his
power known? But he put up with the
people he was angry with. They were
made to be destroyed. 23 What if he
put up with them to show the riches of
his glory to other people? Those other
people are the ones he shows his mercy
to. He made them to receive his glory.
24 We are those people. He has chosen
us. We do not come only from the Jewish
race. Many of us are not Jews. 25 God
says in Hosea,

"I will call those who are not my
people 'my people.'
I will call the one who is not my
loved one 'my loved one.' "
(Hosea 2:23)

26 He also says,

"Once it was said to them,
'You are not my people.'
In that very place they will be
called 'children of the living
God.' " *(Hosea 1:10)*

27 Isaiah cries out concerning Israel.
He says,

"The number of people from Israel
may be like the sand by the
sea.
But only a few of them will be
saved.
28 The Lord will carry out his
sentence.
He will be quick to carry it out on
earth, once and for all." *(Isaiah
10:22,23)*

29 Earlier Isaiah had said,

"The Lord who rules over all
left us children and
grandchildren.
If he hadn't, we would have become
like Sodom.
We would have been like
Gomorrah." *(Isaiah 1:9)*

Israel Does Not Believe

30 What should we say then? Gentiles
did not look for a way to be right with
God. But they found it by having faith.
31 The people of Israel tried to obey the
law to make themselves right with God.
But they didn't reach their goal of being
right with God. 32 Why not? Because they
tried to do it without faith. They tried
to be right with God by what they did.
They tripped over the stone that causes
people to trip and fall. 33 It is written,

"Look! In Zion I am laying a stone
that causes people to trip.
It is a rock that makes them fall.
The one who believes in him will
never be put to shame." *(Isaiah
8:14; 28:16)*

10 Brothers and sisters, with all
my heart I long for the people
of Israel to be saved. I pray to God for
them. 2 I can tell you for certain that
they really want to serve God. But how
they are trying to do it is not based
on knowledge. 3 They didn't know that
God's power makes people right with
himself. They tried to get right with
God in their own way. They didn't do
it in God's way. 4 Christ has fulfilled
everything the law was meant to do.
So now everyone who believes can be
right with God.

5 Moses writes about how the law
could help a person do what God requires. He writes, "The person who does
these things will live by them." *(Leviticus 18:5)* 6 But the way to do what God
requires must begin by having faith in
him. Scripture says, "Do not say in your
heart, 'Who will go up into heaven?' "
(Deuteronomy 30:12) That means to go
up into heaven and bring Christ down.
7 "And do not say, 'Who will go down
into the grave?' " *(Deuteronomy 30:13)*
That means to bring Christ up from the
dead. 8 But what does it say? "The message is near you. It's in your mouth and
in your heart." *(Deuteronomy 30:14)* This
means the message about faith that we
are preaching. 9 Say with your mouth,
"Jesus is Lord." Believe in your heart
that God raised him from the dead.
Then you will be saved. 10 With your
heart you believe and are made right
with God. With your mouth you say
what you believe. And so you are saved.
11 Scripture says, "The one who believes
in him will never be put to shame."
(Isaiah 28:16) 12 There is no difference
between those who are Jews and those
who are not. The same Lord is Lord of
all. He richly blesses everyone who calls
on him. 13 Scripture says, "Everyone
who calls on the name of the Lord will
be saved." *(Joel 2:32)*

14 How can they call on him unless
they believe in him? How can they believe in him unless they hear about
him? How can they hear about him unless someone preaches to them? 15 And
how can anyone preach without being
sent? It is written, "How beautiful are
the feet of those who bring good news!"
(Isaiah 52:7)

16 But not all the people of Israel
accepted the good news. Isaiah says,
"Lord, who has believed our message?"
(Isaiah 53:1) 17 So faith comes from hearing the message. And the message that
is heard is the message about Christ.
18 But I ask, "Didn't the people of Israel
hear?" Of course they did. It is written,

"Their voice has gone out into the
whole earth.
Their words have gone out from
one end of the world to the
other." *(Psalm 19:4)*

19 Again I ask, "Didn't Israel understand?" First, Moses says,

"I will use people who are not a
nation to make you jealous.
I will use a nation that has no
understanding to make you
angry." *(Deuteronomy 32:21)*

20 Then Isaiah boldly speaks about what
God says. God said,

"I was found by those who were not
trying to find me.
I made myself known to those
who were not asking for me."
(Isaiah 65:1)

[21]But Isaiah also speaks about what
God says concerning Israel. God said,

"All day long I have held out my
hands.
I have held them out to a
stubborn people who do not
obey me." *(Isaiah 65:2)*

The Israelites Who Are Faithful

11 So here is what I ask. Did God turn
his back on his people? Not at all!
I myself belong to Israel. I am one of
Abraham's children. I am from the tribe
of Benjamin. [2]God didn't turn his back on
his people. After all, he chose them. Don't
you know what Scripture says about Elijah? He complained to God about Israel.
[3]He said, "Lord, they have killed your
prophets. They have torn down your
altars. I'm the only one left. And they
are trying to kill me." *(1 Kings 19:10,14)*
[4]How did God answer him? God said, "I
have kept 7,000 people for myself. They
have not bowed down to Baal." *(1 Kings
19:18)* [5]Some are also faithful today. They
have been chosen by God's grace. [6]And
if they are chosen by grace, then they
can't work for it. If that were true, grace
wouldn't be grace anymore.

[7]What should we say then? The people of Israel did not receive what they
wanted so badly. Those Israelites who
were chosen did receive it. But the rest
of the people were made stubborn. [8]It
is written,

"God made it hard for them to
understand.
He gave them eyes that could not
see.
He gave them ears that could not
hear.
And they are still like that today."
(Deuteronomy 29:4; Isaiah 29:10)

[9]David says,

"Let their feast be a trap and a
snare.
Let them trip and fall. Let them
get what's coming to them.
[10]Let their eyes grow dark so they
can't see.
Let their backs be bent forever."
(Psalm 69:22,23)

Two Kinds of Olive Branches

[11]Again, here is what I ask. The Israelites didn't trip and fall once and for
all time, did they? Not at all! Because
Israel sinned, the Gentiles can be saved.
That will make Israel jealous of them.
[12]Israel's sin brought riches to the world.
Their loss brings riches to the Gentiles.
So then what greater riches will come
when all Israel turns to God!

[13]I am talking to you who are not
Jews. I am the apostle to the Gentiles.
So I take pride in the work I do for God
and others. [14]I hope somehow to stir
up my own people to want what you
have. Perhaps I can save some of them.
[15]When they were not accepted, it became possible for the whole world to
be brought back to God. So what will
happen when they are accepted? It will
be like life from the dead. [16]The first
handful of dough that is offered is holy.
This makes all of the dough holy. If the
root is holy, so are the branches.

[17]Some of the natural branches have
been broken off. You are a wild olive
branch. But you have been joined to
the tree with the other branches. Now
you enjoy the life-giving sap of the olive
tree root. [18]So don't think you are better
than the other branches. Remember,
you don't give life to the root. The root
gives life to you. [19]You will say, "Some
branches were broken off so that I could
be joined to the tree." [20]That's true.
But they were broken off because they
didn't believe. You stand only because
you do believe. So don't be proud, but
tremble. [21]God didn't spare the natural
branches. He won't spare you either.

[22]Think about how kind God is! Also
think about how firm he is! He was
hard on those who stopped following
him. But he is kind to you. So you must
continue to live in his kindness. If you
don't, you also will be cut off. [23]If the
people of Israel do not continue in their
unbelief, they will again be joined to the
tree. God is able to join them to the tree
again. [24]After all, weren't you cut from
a wild olive tree? Weren't you joined to
an olive tree that was taken care of? And
wasn't that the opposite of how things
should be done? How much more easily
will the natural branches be joined to
their own olive tree!

All Israel Will Be Saved

[25]Brothers and sisters, here is a mystery I want you to understand. It will

keep you from being proud. Part of
Israel has refused to obey God. That
will continue until the full number of
Gentiles has entered God's kingdom.
26 In this way all Israel will be saved.
It is written,

"The God who saves will come from
Mount Zion.
He will remove sin from Jacob's
family.
27 Here is my covenant with them.
I will take away their sins."
(Isaiah 59:20,21; 27:9; Jeremiah 31:33,34)

28 As far as the good news is concerned,
the people of Israel are enemies. This is
for your good. But as far as God's choice is
concerned, the people of Israel are loved.
This is because of God's promises to the
founders of our nation. 29 God does not
take back his gifts. He does not change
his mind about those he has chosen. 30 At
one time you did not obey God. But now
you have received mercy because Israel
did not obey. 31 In the same way, Israel
has not been obeying God. But now they
receive mercy because of God's mercy to
you. 32 God has found everyone guilty of
not obeying him. So now he can have
mercy on everyone.

Praise to God

33 How very rich are God's wisdom
and knowledge!
How he judges is more than we
can understand!
The way he deals with people is
more than we can know!
34 "Who can ever know what the Lord
is thinking?
Or who can ever give him
advice?" *(Isaiah 40:13)*
35 "Has anyone ever given anything
to God,
so that God has to pay them
back?" *(Job 41:11)*
36 All things come from him.
All things are directed by him.
All things are for his praise.
May God be given the glory
forever! Amen.

Living as a Holy Sacrifice to God

12 Brothers and sisters, God has
shown you his mercy. So I am
asking you to offer up your bodies to
him while you are still alive. Your bodies
are a holy sacrifice that is pleasing to
God. When you offer your bodies to God,
you are worshiping him in the right
way. 2 Don't live the way this world lives.
Let your way of thinking be completely
changed. Then you will be able to test
what God wants for you. And you will
agree that what he wants is right. His
plan is good and pleasing and perfect.

Serving One Another in the Body of Christ

3 God's grace has been given to me. So
here is what I say to every one of you.
Don't think of yourself more highly
than you should. Be reasonable when
you think about yourself. Keep in mind
the faith God has given to each of you.
4 Each of us has one body with many
parts. And the parts do not all have the
same purpose. 5 So also we are many
persons. But in Christ we are one body.
And each part of the body belongs to
all the other parts. 6 We all have gifts.
They differ according to the grace God
has given to each of us. Do you have the
gift of prophecy? Then use it according
to the faith you have. 7 If your gift is
serving, then serve. If it is teaching,
then teach. 8 Is it encouraging others?
Then encourage them. Is it giving to
others? Then give freely. Is it being a
leader? Then work hard at it. Is it showing mercy? Then do it cheerfully.

Love in Action

9 Love must be honest and true. Hate
what is evil. Hold on to what is good.
10 Love one another deeply. Honor others more than yourselves. 11 Stay excited
about your faith as you serve the Lord.
12 When you hope, be joyful. When you
suffer, be patient. When you pray, be
faithful. 13 Share with the Lord's people
who are in need. Welcome others into
your homes.

14 Bless those who hurt you. Bless
them, and do not curse them. 15 Be joyful
with those who are joyful. Be sad with
those who are sad. 16 Agree with one
another. Don't be proud. Be willing to be
a friend of people who aren't considered
important. Don't think that you are
better than others.

17 Don't pay back evil with evil. Be
careful to do what everyone thinks is
right. 18 If possible, live in peace with
everyone. Do that as much as you can.

19 My dear friends, don't try to get even.
Leave room for God to show his anger.
It is written, "I am the God who judges
people. I will pay them back," *(Deuteronomy 32:35)* says the Lord. 20 Do just
the opposite. Scripture says,

"If your enemies are hungry, give
them food to eat.
If they are thirsty, give them
something to drink.
By doing those things, you will
pile up burning coals on their
heads." *(Proverbs 25:21,22)*

21 Don't let evil overcome you. Overcome
evil by doing good.

Obey Those in Authority

13 All of you must obey those who
rule over you. There are no
authorities except the ones God has
chosen. Those who now rule have been
chosen by God. 2 So whoever opposes the
authorities opposes leaders whom God
has appointed. Those who do that will
be judged. 3 If you do what is right, you
won't need to be afraid of your rulers.
But watch out if you do what is wrong!
You don't want to be afraid of those
in authority, do you? Then do what is
right, and you will be praised. 4 The one
in authority serves God for your good.
But if you do wrong, watch out! Rulers
don't carry a sword for no reason at all.
They serve God. And God is carrying
out his anger through them. The ruler
punishes anyone who does wrong. 5 You
must obey the authorities. Then you
will not be punished. You must also
obey them because you know it is right.
6 That's also why you pay taxes. The
authorities serve God. Ruling takes up
all their time. 7 Give to everyone what
you owe them. Do you owe taxes? Then
pay them. Do you owe anything else to
the government? Then pay it. Do you
owe respect? Then give it. Do you owe
honor? Then show it.

Love Fulfills the Law

8 Pay everything you owe. But you
can never pay back all the love you
owe one another. Whoever loves other
people has done everything the law
requires. 9 Here are some commandments to think about. "Do not commit
adultery." "Do not commit murder." "Do
not steal." "Do not want what belongs
to others." *(Exodus 20:13–15,17; Deuteronomy 5:17–19,21)* These and all other commands are included in one command.
Here's what it is. "Love your neighbor
as you love yourself." *(Leviticus 19:18)*
10 Love does not harm its neighbor. So
love does everything the law requires.

The Day Is Near

11 When you do these things, keep in
mind the times we are living in. The
hour has already come for you to wake
up from your sleep. The full effects of
our salvation are closer now than when
we first believed in Christ. 12 The dark
night of evil is nearly over. The day of
Christ's return is almost here. So let us
get rid of the works of darkness that
harm us. Let us do the works of light
that protect us. 13 Let us act as we should,
like people living in the daytime. Have
nothing to do with wild parties, and
don't get drunk. Don't take part in
sexual sins or evil conduct. Don't fight
with each other or be jealous of anyone.
14 Instead, put on the Lord Jesus Christ
as if he were your clothing. Don't think
about how to satisfy sinful desires.

The Weak and the Strong

14 Accept the person whose faith
is weak. Don't argue with them
where you have differences of opinion.
2 One person's faith allows them to eat
anything. But another person eats only
vegetables because their faith is weak.
3 The person who eats everything must
not look down on the one who does not.
And the one who doesn't eat everything
must not judge the person who does.
That's because God has accepted them.
4 Who are you to judge someone else's
servant? Whether they are faithful or
not is their own master's concern. And
they will be faithful, because the Lord
has the power to make them faithful.
5 One person considers one day to
be more holy than another. Another
person thinks all days are the same.
Each of them should be absolutely sure
in their own mind. 6 Whoever thinks
that one day is special does so to honor
the Lord. Whoever eats meat does so to
honor the Lord. They give thanks to God.
And whoever doesn't eat meat does so
to honor the Lord. They also give thanks
to God. 7 We don't live for ourselves only.
And we don't die for ourselves only. 8 If

we live, we live to honor the Lord. If we
die, we die to honor the Lord. So whether
we live or die, we belong to the Lord.
9 Christ died and came back to life. He
did this to become the Lord of both the
dead and the living.
10 Now then, who are you to judge
your brother or sister? Why do you act
like you're better than they are? We
will all stand in God's courtroom to be
judged. 11 It is written,

"'You can be sure that I live,' says
the Lord.
'And you can be just as sure that
everyone will kneel down in
front of me.
Every tongue will have to tell the
truth about God.'" *(Isaiah 45:23)*

12 So we will all have to explain to God
the things we have done.
13 Let us stop judging one another.
Instead, decide not to put anything in
the way of a brother or sister. Don't put
anything in their way that would make
them trip and fall. 14 I am absolutely
sure that nothing is "unclean" in itself.
The Lord Jesus has convinced me of this.
But someone may consider a thing to
be "unclean." If they do, it is "unclean"
for them. 15 Your brother or sister may
be upset by what you eat. If they are,
you are no longer acting as though you
love them. So don't destroy them by
what you eat. Remember that Christ
died for them. 16 So suppose you know
something is good. Then don't let it be
spoken of as if it were evil. 17 God's kingdom is not about eating or drinking. It
is about doing what is right and having
peace and joy. All this comes through
the Holy Spirit. 18 Those who serve Christ
in this way are pleasing to God. They
are pleasing to people too.
19 So let us do all we can to live in
peace. And let us work hard to build
up one another. 20 Don't destroy the
work of God because of food. All food is
"clean." But it's wrong to eat anything
that might cause problems for someone
else's faith. 21 Don't eat meat if it causes
your brother or sister to sin. Don't drink
wine or do anything else that will make
them sin.
22 Whatever you believe about these
things, keep between yourself and God.
Blessed is the person who doesn't feel
guilty for what they do. 23 But whoever
has doubts about what they eat is guilty
if they eat. That's because their eating
is not based on faith. Everything that
is not based on faith is sin.

15 We who have strong faith
should help the weak with their
problems. We should not please only
ourselves. 2 Each of us should please
our neighbors. Let us do what is good
for them in order to build them up.
3 Even Christ did not please himself. It
is written, "The bad things people have
said about you have been aimed at me
also." *(Psalm 69:9)* 4 Everything written
in the past was written to teach us. The
Scriptures give us strength to go on.
They encourage us and give us hope.
5 Our God is a God who strengthens
and encourages you. May he give you
the same attitude toward one another
that Christ Jesus had. 6 Then you can
give glory to God with one mind and
voice. He is the God and Father of our
Lord Jesus Christ.
7 Christ has accepted you. So accept
one another in order to bring praise to
God. 8 I tell you that Christ has become
a servant of the Jews. He teaches us
that God is true. He shows us that God
will keep the promises he made to the
founders of our nation. 9 Jesus became
a servant of the Jews. He did this so that
the Gentiles might give glory to God for
his mercy. It is written,

"I will praise you among the
Gentiles.
I will sing the praises of your
name." *(2 Samuel 22:50; Psalm
18:49)*

10 Again it says,

"You Gentiles, be full of joy.
Be joyful together with God's
people." *(Deuteronomy 32:43)*

11 And again it says,

"All you Gentiles, praise the Lord.
Let all the nations sing praises to
him." *(Psalm 117:1)*

12 And Isaiah says,

"The Root of Jesse will grow up
quickly.
He will rule over the nations.
The Gentiles will put their hope
in him." *(Isaiah 11:10)*

[13] May the God who gives hope fill you with great joy. May you have perfect peace as you trust in him. May the power of the Holy Spirit fill you with hope.

Paul Serves the Gentiles

[14] My brothers and sisters, I am sure that you are full of goodness. You are filled with knowledge and able to teach one another. [15] But I have written to you very boldly about some things. I wanted to remind you of them again. The grace of God has allowed me [16] to serve Christ Jesus among the Gentiles. I have the duty of a priest to preach God's good news. Then the Gentiles will become an offering that pleases God. The Holy Spirit will make the offering holy.

[17] Because I belong to Christ Jesus, I can take pride in my work for God. [18] I will speak about what Christ has done through me. I won't try to speak about anything else. He has been leading the Gentiles to obey God. He has been doing this by what I have said and done. [19] He has given me power to do signs and wonders. I can do these things by the power of the Spirit of God. From Jerusalem all the way around to Illyricum I have finished preaching. In those places, I preached the good news about Christ. [20] I have always wanted to preach the good news where Christ was not known. I don't want to build on what someone else has started. [21] It is written,

> "Those who were not told about
> him will understand.
> Those who have not heard will
> know what it all means." *(Isaiah 52:15)*

[22] That's why I have often been kept from coming to you.

Paul Plans to Visit Rome

[23] Now there is no more place for me to work in those areas. For many years I have wanted to visit you. [24] So I plan to see you when I go to Spain. I hope to visit you while I am passing through. And I hope you will help me on my journey there. But first I want to enjoy being with you for a while. [25] Now I am on my way to Jerusalem to serve the Lord's people there. [26] The believers in Macedonia and Achaia were pleased to take an offering. It was for those who were poor among the Lord's people in Jerusalem. [27] They were happy to do it. And of course they owe it to them. The Gentiles have shared in the Jews' spiritual blessings. So the Gentiles should share their earthly blessings with the Jews. [28] I want to finish my task. I want to make sure that the poor in Jerusalem have received this offering. Then I will go to Spain. On my way I will visit you. [29] I know that when I come to you, I will come with the full blessing of Christ.

[30] Brothers and sisters, I ask you to join me in my struggle. Join me by praying to God for me. I ask this through the authority of our Lord Jesus Christ. Pray for me with the love the Holy Spirit provides. [31] Pray that I will be kept safe from those in Judea who do not believe. I am taking the offering to Jerusalem. Pray that it will be welcomed by the Lord's people there. [32] Then I will come to you with joy just as God has planned. We will be renewed by being together. [33] May the God who gives peace be with you all. Amen.

Personal Greetings

16 I would like you to welcome our sister Phoebe. She is a deacon of the church in Cenchreae. [2] I ask you to receive her as one who belongs to the Lord. Receive her in the way God's people should. Give her any help she may need from you. She has been a great help to many people, including me.

[3] Greet Priscilla and Aquila. They work together with me in serving Christ Jesus. [4] They have put their lives in danger for me. I am thankful for them. So are all the Gentile churches.

[5] Greet also the church that meets in the house of Priscilla and Aquila.

Greet my dear friend Epenetus. He was the first person in Asia Minor to become a believer in Christ.

[6] Greet Mary. She worked very hard for you.

[7] Greet Andronicus and Junia, my fellow Jews. They have been in prison with me. They are leaders among the apostles. They became believers in Christ before I did.

[8] Greet Ampliatus, my dear friend in the Lord.

[9] Greet Urbanus. He works together with me in serving Christ. And greet my dear friend Stachys.

10 Greet Apelles. He remained faithful to Christ even when he was tested.

Greet those who live in the house of Aristobulus.

11 Greet Herodion, my fellow Jew.

Greet the believers who live in the house of Narcissus.

12 Greet Tryphena and Tryphosa. Those women work hard for the Lord.

Greet my dear friend Persis. She is another woman who has worked very hard for the Lord.

13 Greet Rufus. He is a chosen believer in the Lord. And greet his mother. She has been like a mother to me too.

14 Greet Asyncritus, Phlegon and Hermes. Greet Patrobas, Hermas and the other brothers and sisters with them.

15 Greet Philologus, Julia, Nereus and his sister. Greet Olympas and all of the Lord's people who are with them.

16 Greet one another with a holy kiss.

All the churches of Christ send their greetings.

17 I am warning you, brothers and sisters, to watch out for those who try to keep you from staying together. They want to trip you up. They teach you things opposite to what you have
learned. Stay away from them. 18 People
like that are not serving Christ our Lord. They are serving only themselves. With smooth talk and with words they don't mean they fool people who don't know
any better. 19 Everyone has heard that
you obey God. So you have filled me with joy. I want you to be wise about what is good. And I want you to have nothing to do with what is evil.

20 The God who gives peace will soon crush Satan under your feet.

May the grace of our Lord Jesus be with you.

21 Timothy works together with me. He sends his greetings to you. So do Lucius, Jason and Sosipater, my fellow Jews.

22 I, Tertius, wrote down this letter. I greet you as a believer in the Lord.

23-24 Gaius sends you his greetings. He has welcomed me and the whole church here into his house.

Erastus is the director of public works here in the city. He sends you his greetings. Our brother Quartus also greets you.

25 May God receive glory. He is able to strengthen your faith. He does this in keeping with the good news and the message I preach. It is the message about Jesus Christ. This message is in keeping with the mystery hidden for a
very long time. 26 The mystery has now
been made known through the writings of the prophets. The eternal God commanded that it be made known. God wanted all the Gentiles to obey him by
trusting in him. 27 May the only wise
God receive glory forever through Jesus Christ. Amen.

1 CORINTHIANS

Author: Paul

On one of Paul's missionary journeys, he traveled to the city of Corinth. There he shared the good news about Jesus and helped the new Christians start a church. But after Paul left Corinth, he kept hearing troubling reports: The Corinthian Christians weren't living like people who loved God. They were living in disobedience—lying, cheating, being unfaithful, and more.

In response, Paul wrote them two letters. The first was about how to live as faithful followers of Jesus. He told them that the way they were living was inconsistent with God's ways and that they had the Holy Spirit to help them do the right things. He also reminded them that the gospel changed everything—how they treated others, how they expressed their freedom, and how they worked.

Letters & Revelation

Paul wanted the people in Corinth to know that they were no longer slaves to sin but were welcomed into the family of God through Jesus. As a family, they were to care and sacrifice for one another and to make things right when they wronged one another. Paul wanted them to experience the unity God called them to as a church, and he wanted them to help each other live for Jesus, even when it was hard.

1 I, Paul, am writing this letter. I have been chosen to be an apostle of Christ Jesus just as God planned. Our brother Sosthenes joins me in writing.

2 We are sending this letter to you, the members of God's church in Corinth. You have been made holy because you belong to Christ Jesus. God has chosen you to be his holy people. He has done the same for all people everywhere who pray to our Lord Jesus Christ. Jesus is their Lord and ours.

3 May God our Father and the Lord Jesus Christ give you grace and peace.

Paul Gives Thanks

4 I always thank my God for you. I thank him because of the grace he has given to you who belong to Christ Jesus. 5 You have been blessed in every way because of him. You have been blessed in all your speech and knowledge. 6 God has shown that what we have spoken to you about Christ is true. 7 There is no gift of the Holy Spirit that you don't have. You are full of hope as you wait for our Lord Jesus Christ to come again. 8 God will also keep you strong in faith to the very end. Then you will be without blame on the day our Lord Jesus Christ returns. 9 God is faithful. He has chosen you to share life with his Son, Jesus Christ our Lord.

Taking Sides in the Church

10 Brothers and sisters, I make my appeal to you. I do this in the name of our Lord Jesus Christ. I ask that all of you agree with one another in what you say. I ask that you don't take sides. I ask that you are in complete agreement in all that you think. 11 My brothers and sisters, I have been told you are arguing with one another. Some people from Chloe's house have told me this. 12 Here is what I mean. One of you says, "I follow Paul." Another says, "I follow Apollos." Another says, "I follow Peter." And still another says, "I follow Christ."

13 Does Christ take sides? Did Paul die on the cross for you? Were you baptized in the name of Paul? 14 I thank God that I didn't baptize any of you except Crispus and Gaius. 15 No one can say that you were baptized in my name. 16 It's true that I also baptized those who live in the house of Stephanas. Besides that, I don't remember if I baptized anyone else. 17 Christ did not send me to baptize. He sent me to preach the good news. He commanded me not to preach with wisdom and fancy words. That would take all the power away from the cross of Christ.

Christ Is God's Power and Wisdom

18 The message of the cross seems foolish to those who are lost and dying. But it is God's power to us who are being saved. 19 It is written,

"I will destroy the wisdom of those
who are wise.
I will do away with the cleverness
of those who think they are so
smart." *(Isaiah 29:14)*

20 Where is the wise person? Where is the teacher of the law? Where are the great thinkers of our time? Hasn't God made the wisdom of the world foolish? 21 God wisely planned that the world would not know him through its own wisdom. It pleased God to use the foolish things we preach to save those who believe. 22 Jews require signs. Greeks look for wisdom. 23 But we preach about Christ and his death on the cross. That is very hard for Jews to accept. And everyone else thinks it's foolish. 24 But there are those God has chosen, both Jews and Greeks. To them Christ is God's power and God's wisdom. 25 The foolish things of God are wiser than human wisdom. The weakness of God is stronger than human strength.

26 Brothers and sisters, think of what you were when God chose you. Not many of you were considered wise by human standards. Not many of you were powerful. Not many of you belonged to important families. 27 But God chose the foolish things of the world to shame the wise. God chose the weak things of the world to shame the strong. 28 God chose the things of this world that are common and looked down on. God chose things considered unimportant to do away with things considered important. 29 So no one can boast to God. 30 Because of what God has done, you belong to Christ Jesus. He has become God's wisdom for us. He makes us right with God. He makes us holy and sets us free. 31 It is written, "The one who boasts should boast about what the Lord has done." *(Jeremiah 9:24)*

2 And this was the way it was with
me, brothers and sisters. When I
came to you, I didn't come with fancy
words or human wisdom. I preached
to you the truth about God's love. 2 My
goal while I was with you was to talk
about only one thing. And that was
Jesus Christ and his death on the cross.
3 When I came to you, I was weak and
very afraid and trembling all over. 4 I
didn't preach my message with clever
and compelling words. Instead, my
preaching showed the Holy Spirit's power. 5 This was so that your faith would be
based on God's power. Your faith would
not be based on human wisdom.

God's Wisdom Through the Holy Spirit

6 The words we speak to those who
have grown in the faith are wise. Our
words are different from the wisdom
of this world. Our words are different
from those of the rulers of this world.
These rulers are becoming less and less
powerful. 7 No, we announce God's wisdom. His wisdom is a mystery that has
been hidden. But before time began,
God planned that his wisdom would
bring us heavenly glory. 8 None of the
rulers of this world understood God's
wisdom. If they had, they would not
have nailed the Lord of glory to the
cross. 9 It is written that

"no eye has seen,
no ear has heard,
and no human mind has known."
(Isaiah 64:4)
God has prepared these things
for those who love him.

10 God has shown these things to us
through his Spirit.

The Spirit understands all things. He
understands even the deep things of
God. 11 Who can know the thoughts of
another person? Only a person's own
spirit can know them. In the same
way, only the Spirit of God knows God's
thoughts. 12 What we have received is
not the spirit of the world. We have received the Spirit who is from God. The
Spirit helps us understand what God has
freely given us. 13 That is what we speak
about. We don't use words taught to us
by people. We use words taught to us by
the Holy Spirit. We use the words taught

in 1 Corinthians?

God is the Everlasting One. He gives us a new life when we follow him, and the work we do with him matters for eternity.

by the Spirit to explain spiritual truths.
14 The person without the Spirit doesn't
accept the things that come from the
Spirit of God. These things are foolish
to them. They can't understand them.
In fact, such things can't be understood
without the Spirit's help. 15 The person
who has the Spirit can judge all things.
But no human being can judge those
who have the Spirit. It is written,

16 "Who can ever know what is in the
Lord's mind?
Can anyone ever teach him?"
(Isaiah 40:13)

But we have the mind of Christ.

The Church and Its Leaders

3 Brothers and sisters, I couldn't
speak to you as people who live
by the Holy Spirit. I had to speak to you
as people who were still following the
ways of the world. You aren't growing
as Christ wants you to. You are still
like babies. 2 The words I spoke to you
were like milk, not like solid food. You
weren't ready for solid food yet. And
you still aren't ready for it. 3 You are still
following the ways of the world. Some
of you are jealous. Some of you argue.
So aren't you following the ways of the
world? Aren't you acting like ordinary
human beings? 4 One of you says, "I
follow Paul." Another says, "I follow
Apollos." Aren't you acting like ordinary
human beings?

5 After all, what is Apollos? And what
is Paul? We are only people who serve.

We helped you to believe. The Lord has
given each of us our own work to do. 6 I
planted the seed. Apollos watered it.
But God has been making it grow. 7 So
the one who plants is not important.
The one who waters is not important.
It is God who makes things grow. He
is the important one. 8 The one who
plants and the one who waters have
the same purpose. The Lord will give
each of them a reward for their work.
9 We work together to serve God. You
are like God's field. You are like his
building.

10 God has given me the grace to lay
a foundation as a wise builder. Now
someone else is building on it. But each
one should build carefully. 11 No one can
lay any other foundation than what has
already been laid. That foundation is
Jesus Christ. 12 A person may build on
it using gold, silver, jewels, wood, hay
or straw. 13 But each person's work will
be shown for what it is. On judgment
day it will be brought to light. It will
be put through fire. The fire will test
how good each person's work is. 14 If
the building doesn't burn up, God will
give the builder a reward for the work.
15 If the building burns up, the builder
will lose everything. The builder will
be saved, but only like one escaping
through the flames.

16 Don't you know that you yourselves
are God's temple? Don't you know that
God's Spirit lives among you? 17 If anyone destroys God's temple, God will destroy that person. God's temple is holy.
And you all together are that temple.

18 Don't fool yourselves. Suppose
some of you think you are wise by
the standards of the world. Then you
should become "fools" so that you
can become wise. 19 The wisdom of
this world is foolish in God's eyes. It
is written, "God catches wise people in
their own evil plans." *(Job 5:13)* 20 It is
also written, "The Lord knows that the
thoughts of wise people don't amount
to anything." *(Psalm 94:11)* 21 So no more
bragging about human leaders! All
things are yours. 22 That means Paul
or Apollos or Peter or the world or life
or death or the present or the future.
All are yours. 23 You are joined to Christ
and belong to him. And Christ is joined
to God.

True Apostles of Christ

4 So here is how you should think of
us. We serve Christ. We are trusted
with the mysteries God has shown us.
2 Those who have been given a trust must
prove that they are faithful. 3 I care very
little if I am judged by you or by any
human court. I don't even judge myself.
4 I don't feel I have done anything wrong.
But that doesn't mean I'm not guilty.
The Lord judges me. 5 So don't judge
anything before the appointed time.
Wait until the Lord returns. He will bring
to light what is hidden in the dark. He
will show the real reasons why people do
what they do. At that time each person
will receive their praise from God.

6 Brothers and sisters, I have used
myself and Apollos as examples to help
you. You can learn from us the meaning
of the saying, "Don't go beyond what is
written." Then you won't be proud that
you follow one of us instead of the other.
7 Who makes you different from anyone
else? What do you have that you did not
receive? And if you did receive it, why
do you brag as though you did not?

8 You already have everything you
want, don't you? Have you already become rich? Have you already begun to
rule? And did you do that without us? I
wish that you really had begun to rule.
Then we could also rule with you! 9 It
seems to me that God has put us apostles
on display at the end of a parade. We are
like people sentenced to die in front of
a crowd. We have been made a show for
the whole creation to see. Angels and
people are staring at us. 10 We are fools
for Christ. But you are so wise in Christ!
We are weak. But you are so strong! You
are honored. But we are looked down on!
11 Up to this very hour we are hungry and
thirsty. We are dressed in rags. We are
being treated badly. We have no homes.
12 We work hard with our own hands.
When others curse us, we bless them.
When we are attacked, we put up with
it. 13 When others say bad things about
us, we answer with kind words. We have
become the world's garbage. We are everybody's trash, right up to this moment.

Paul Warns Against Pride

14 I am not writing this to shame you.
You are my dear children, and I want
to warn you. 15 Suppose you had 10,000

believers in Christ watching over you.
You still wouldn't have many fathers.
I became your father by serving Christ
Jesus and telling you the good news.
16 So I'm asking you to follow my example. 17 That's the reason I have sent
Timothy to you. He is like a son to me,
and I love him. He is faithful in serving
the Lord. He will remind you of my way
of life in serving Christ Jesus. And that
agrees with what I teach everywhere
in every church.
18 Some of you have become proud.
You act as if I weren't coming to you.
19 But I will come very soon, if that's
what the Lord wants. Then I will find out
how those proud people are talking. I
will also find out what power they have.
20 The kingdom of God is not a matter
of talk. It is a matter of power. 21 Which
do you want? Should I come to you to
correct and punish you? Or should I
come in love and with a gentle spirit?

Throw Out the Evil Person!

5 It is actually reported that there is
sexual sin among you. I'm told that
a man is sleeping with his father's wife.
Even people who don't know God don't
let that kind of sin continue. 2 And you
are proud! Shouldn't you be very sad instead? Shouldn't you have thrown out of
your church the man doing this? 3 Even
though I am not right there with you, I
am with you in spirit. And because I am
with you in spirit, I have already judged
the man doing this. I have judged him
in the name of our Lord Jesus. 4 So when
you come together, I will be with you
in spirit. The power of our Lord Jesus
will also be with you. 5 When you come
together like this, hand this man over
to Satan. Then the power of sin in his
life will be destroyed. His spirit will be
saved on the day the Lord returns.
6 Your bragging is not good. It is like
yeast. Don't you know that just a little
yeast makes the whole batch of dough
rise? 7 Get rid of the old yeast. Then
you can be like a new batch of dough
without yeast. That is what you really
are. That's because Christ, our Passover
Lamb, has been offered up for us. 8 So
let us keep the Feast, but not with the
old bread made with yeast. The yeast
I'm talking about is hatred and evil.
Let us keep the Feast with bread made
without yeast. Let us keep it with bread
that is honesty and truth.
9 I wrote a letter to you to tell you to
stay away from people who commit
sexual sins. 10 I didn't mean the people of this world who sin in this way.
I didn't mean those who always want
more and more. I didn't mean those
who cheat or who worship statues of
gods. In that case you would have to
leave this world! 11 But here is what I am
writing to you now. You must stay away
from anyone who claims to be a believer
but does evil things. Stay away from
anyone who commits sexual sins. Stay
away from anyone who always wants
more and more things. Stay away from
anyone who worships statues of gods.
Stay away from anyone who tells lies
about others. Stay away from anyone
who gets drunk or who cheats. Don't
even eat with people like these.

Jesus Is the Lamb of God

In the Old Testament, God told his people to offer a perfect, spotless lamb as an offering for their sin. In the New Testament, Jesus *became* the perfect, spotless lamb because he lived a sinless life (see 1 Peter 1:19). In other words, Jesus died in our place, taking upon himself the death that our sin required. He was the final offering made for sin, so God's people no longer need to sacrifice lambs for their sins. Instead, all people are welcomed into the family of God. This is the Good News: Jesus died in our place so we could live with God forever!

12 Is it my business to judge those outside the church? Aren't you supposed to
judge those inside the church? 13 God will
judge those outside. Scripture says, "Get
rid of that evil person!" *(Deuteronomy
17:7; 19:19; 21:21; 22:21,24; 24:7)*

Do Not Take Believers to Court

6 Suppose one of you wants to bring
a charge against another believer.
Should you take it to ungodly people to
be judged? Why not take it to the Lord's
people? 2 Or don't you know that the
Lord's people will judge the world? Since
this is true, aren't you able to judge
small cases? 3 Don't you know that we
will judge angels? Then we should be
able to judge the things of this life even
more! 4 So suppose you disagree with
one another in matters like this. Who
do you ask to decide which of you is
right? Do you ask people who live in
a way the church disapproves of? Of
course not! 5 I say this to shame you.
Is it possible that no one among you is
wise enough to judge matters between
believers? 6 Instead, one believer goes to
court against another. And this happens
in front of unbelievers!

7 When you take another believer to
court, you have lost the battle already.
Why not be treated wrongly? Why not
be cheated? 8 Instead, you yourselves
cheat and do wrong. And you do it to
your brothers and sisters. 9 Don't you
know that people who do wrong will not
receive God's kingdom? Don't be fooled.
Those who commit sexual sins will not
receive the kingdom. Neither will those
who worship statues of gods or commit
adultery. Neither will men who sleep
with other men. 10 Neither will thieves or
those who always want more and more.
Neither will those who are often drunk
or tell lies or cheat. People who live like
that will not receive God's kingdom.
11 Some of you used to do those things.
But your sins were washed away. You
were made holy. You were made right
with God. All of this was done in the
name of the Lord Jesus Christ. It was
also done by the Spirit of our God.

Sexual Sins

12 Some of you say, "I have the right
to do anything." But not everything is
helpful. Again some of you say, "I have
the right to do anything." But I will not
be controlled by anything. 13 Some of
you say, "Food is for the stomach, and
the stomach is for food. And God will
destroy both of them." But the body
is not meant for sexual sins. The body
is meant for the Lord. And the Lord is
meant for the body. 14 By his power
God raised the Lord from the dead. He
will also raise us up. 15 Don't you know
that your bodies belong to the body of
Christ? Should I take what belongs to
Christ and join it to a prostitute? Never!
16 When you join yourself to a prostitute,
you become one with her in body. Don't
you know this? Scripture says, "The two
will become one." *(Genesis 2:24)* 17 But
whoever is joined to the Lord becomes
one with him in spirit.

18 Keep far away from sexual sins.
All the other sins a person commits are
outside the body. But sexual sins are
sins against their own body. 19 Don't
you know that your bodies are temples
of the Holy Spirit? The Spirit is in you,
and you have received the Spirit from
God. You do not belong to yourselves.
20 Christ has paid the price for you. So
use your bodies in a way that honors
God.

key verses Don't you know that your bodies are temples of the Holy Spirit? The Spirit is in you, and you have received the Spirit from God. You do not belong to yourselves. Christ has paid the price for you. 1 CORINTHIANS 6:19–20

Advice for Those Who Are Married

7 Now I want to deal with the things
you wrote me about. Some of you
say, "It is good for a man not to sleep
with a woman." 2 But since sexual sin
is happening, each man should sleep
with his own wife. And each woman
should sleep with her own husband.
3 A husband should satisfy his wife's
needs. And a wife should satisfy her
husband's needs. 4 The wife's body does
not belong only to her. It also belongs
to her husband. In the same way, the
husband's body does not belong only
to him. It also belongs to his wife. 5 You

shouldn't stop giving yourselves to each
other. You might possibly do this when
you both agree to it. And you should
only agree to it to give yourselves time
to pray. Then you should come together
again. In that way, Satan will not tempt
you when you can't control yourselves.
6 I say those things to you as my advice,
not as a command. 7 I wish all of you
were single like me. But you each have
your own gift from God. One has this
gift, and another has that one.

8 I speak now to those who are not
married. I also speak to widows. It is
good for you to stay single like me.
9 But if you can't control yourselves,
you should get married. It is better to
get married than to burn with desire.

10 I give a command to those who are
married. It is a direct command from
the Lord, not from me. A wife must not
leave her husband. 11 But if she does, she
must not get married again. Or she can
go back to her husband. And a husband
must not divorce his wife.

12 I also have something to say to everyone else. It is from me, not a direct
command from the Lord. Suppose a
brother has a wife who is not a believer. If she is willing to live with him, he
must not divorce her. 13 And suppose
a woman has a husband who is not
a believer. If he is willing to live with
her, she must not divorce him. 14 The
unbelieving husband has been made
holy through his wife. The unbelieving
wife has been made holy through her
believing husband. If that were not the
case, your children would not be pure
and "clean." But as it is, they are holy.

15 But if the unbeliever leaves, let that
person go. In that case, the believer does
not have to stay married to the unbeliever. God wants us to live in peace.
16 Wife, how do you know if you will
save your husband? Husband, how do
you know if you will save your wife?

Stay as You Were When God Chose You

17 But each believer should live in
whatever situation the Lord has given
them. Stay as you were when God chose
you. That's the rule all the churches
must follow. 18 Was a man already circumcised when God chose him? Then he
should not become uncircumcised. Was
he uncircumcised when God chose him?
Then he should not be circumcised.
19 Being circumcised means nothing.
Being uncircumcised means nothing.
Doing what God commands is what
counts. 20 Each of you should stay as
you were when God chose you.

21 Were you a slave when God chose
you? Don't let it trouble you. But if you
can get your master to set you free,
do it. 22 The person who was a slave
when the Lord chose them is now the
Lord's free person. The one who was
free when God chose them is now a
slave of Christ. 23 Christ has paid the
price for you. Don't become slaves of
human beings. 24 Brothers and sisters,
each person is accountable to God. So
each person should stay as they were
when God chose them.

Advice for Those Who Are Not Married

25 Now I want to say something about
virgins. I have no direct command from
the Lord. But I give my opinion. Because
of the Lord's mercy, I give it as one who
can be trusted. 26 Times are hard for you
right now. So I think it's good for a man
to stay as he is. 27 Are you engaged to a
woman? Then don't try to get out of it.
Are you free from such a promise? Then
don't look for a wife. 28 But if you do
marry someone, you have not sinned.
And if a virgin marries someone, she
has not sinned. But those who marry
someone will have many troubles in
this life. I want to save you from this.

29 Brothers and sisters, what I mean
is that the time is short. From now
on, those who have a husband or wife
should live as if they did not. 30 Those
who mourn should live as if they did
not. Those who are happy should live
as if they were not. Those who buy
something should live as if it were not
theirs to keep. 31 Those who use the
things of the world should not become
all wrapped up in them. The world as
it now exists is passing away.

32 I don't want you to have anything
to worry about. A single man is concerned about the Lord's matters. He
wants to know how he can please the
Lord. 33 But a married man is concerned
about the matters of this world. He
wants to know how he can please his

wife. 34 His concerns pull him in two directions. A single woman or a virgin is concerned about the Lord's matters. She wants to serve the Lord with both body and spirit. But a married woman is concerned about the matters of this world. She wants to know how she can please her husband. 35 I'm saying those things for your own good. I'm not trying to hold you back. I want you to be free to live in a way that is right. I want you to give yourselves completely to the Lord.

36 Suppose someone is worried that he is not acting with honor toward the virgin he has promised to marry. Suppose his desires are too strong, and he feels that he should marry her. He should do as he wants. He is not sinning. They should get married. 37 But suppose the man has decided not to marry the virgin. And suppose he has no compelling need to get married and can control himself. If he has made up his mind not to get married, he also does the right thing. 38 So then, the man who marries the virgin does the right thing. But the man who doesn't marry her does a better thing.

39 A woman has to stay married to her husband as long as he lives. If he dies, she is free to marry anyone she wants to. But the one she marries must belong to the Lord. 40 In my opinion, she is happier if she stays single. And I also think that I am led by the Spirit of God in saying this.

Food Sacrificed to Statues of Gods

8 Now I want to deal with food sacrificed to statues of gods. We know that "We all have knowledge." But knowledge makes people proud, while love builds them up. 2 Those who think they know something still don't know as they should. 3 But whoever loves God is known by God.

4 So then, here is what I say about eating food sacrificed to statues of gods. We know that "a god made by human hands is really nothing at all in the world." We know that "there is only one God." 5 There may be so-called gods either in heaven or on earth. In fact, there are many "gods" and many "lords." 6 But for us there is only one God. He is the Father. All things came from him, and we live for him. And there is only one Lord. He is Jesus Christ. All things came because of him, and we live because of him.

7 But not everyone knows this. Some people still think that statues of gods are real gods. They might eat food sacrificed to statues of gods. When they do, they think of it as food sacrificed to real gods. And because those people have a weak sense of what is right and wrong, they feel guilty. 8 But food doesn't bring us close to God. We are no worse if we don't eat. We are no better if we do eat.

9 But be careful how you use your rights. Be sure you don't cause someone weaker than you to fall into sin. 10 Suppose you, with all your knowledge, are eating in a temple of one of those gods. And suppose someone who has a weak sense of what is right and wrong sees you. Won't that person become bold and eat what is sacrificed to statues of gods? 11 If so, then your knowledge destroys that weak brother or sister for whom Christ died. 12 Suppose you sin against them in this way. Then you harm their weak sense of what is right and wrong. By doing this, you sin against Christ. 13 So suppose what I eat causes my brother or sister to fall into sin. Then what should I do? I will never eat meat again. In that way, I will not cause them to fall.

Paul's Rights as an Apostle

9 Am I not free? Am I not an apostle? Haven't I seen Jesus our Lord? Aren't you the result of my work for the Lord? 2 Others may not think of me as an apostle. But I am certainly one to you! You are the proof that I am the Lord's apostle.

3 That is what I say to stand up for myself when people judge me. 4 Don't we have the right to eat and drink? 5 Don't we have the right to take a believing wife with us when we travel? The other apostles do. The Lord's brothers do. Peter does. 6 Or are Barnabas and I the only ones who have to do other work for a living? Are we the only ones who can't just do the work of apostles all the time?

7 Who serves as a soldier but doesn't get paid? Who plants a vineyard but doesn't eat any of its grapes? Who takes care of a flock but doesn't drink

any of the milk? 8 Do I say this only on
human authority? The Law says the
same thing. 9 Here is what is written
in the Law of Moses. "Do not stop an
ox from eating while it helps separate
the grain from the straw." *(Deuteronomy
25:4)* Is it oxen that God is concerned
about? 10 Doesn't he say that for us? Yes,
it was written for us. Whoever plows and
separates the grain hopes to share the
harvest. And it is right for them to hope
for this. 11 We have planted spiritual seed
among you. Is it too much to ask that
we receive from you some things we
need? 12 Others have the right to receive
help from you. Don't we have even more
right to do so?

But we didn't use that right. No, we
have put up with everything. We didn't
want to keep the good news of Christ
from spreading.

13 People who serve in the temple get
their food from the temple. Don't you
know this? People who serve at the
altar eat from what is offered on the
altar. Don't you know this? 14 So those
who preach the good news should also
receive their living from their work.
That is what the Lord has commanded.

BASICS OF FAITH Q&A

How can I do what is right when I'm tempted to do what is wrong?

God says you will never be tempted beyond your ability to do what is right. This is because followers of Jesus have his Spirit living in them to help them walk in God's ways.

Can you find the following verse?

1 CORINTHIANS 10:13

15 But I haven't used any of those
rights. And I'm not writing because I
hope you will do things like that for me.
I would rather die than allow anyone to
take away my pride in my work. 16 But
when I preach the good news, I can't
brag. I have to preach it. How terrible
it will be for me if I do not preach the
good news! 17 If I preach because I want
to, I get a reward. If I preach because I
have to, I'm only doing my duty. 18 Then
what reward do I get? Here is what it is. I
am able to preach the good news free of
charge. And I can do this without using
all my rights as a person who preaches
the good news.

Paul Uses His Freedom to Share the Good News

19 I am free and don't belong to anyone. But I have made myself a slave
to everyone. I do it to win as many as
I can to Christ. 20 To the Jews I became
like a Jew. That was to win the Jews.
To those under the law I became like
one who was under the law. I did this
even though I myself am not under the
law. That was to win those under the
law. 21 To those who don't have the law
I became like one who doesn't have the
law. I did this even though I am not free
from God's law. I am under Christ's law.
Now I can win those who don't have the
law. 22 To those who are weak I became
weak. That was to win the weak. I have
become all things to all people. I have
done this so that in all possible ways I
might save some. 23 I do all this because
of the good news. And I want to share
in its blessings.

Training to Win the Prize

24 In a race all the runners run. But
only one gets the prize. You know that,
don't you? So run in a way that will get
you the prize. 25 All who take part in the
games train hard. They do it to get a
crown that will not last. But we do it to
get a crown that will last forever. 26 So
I do not run like someone who doesn't
run toward the finish line. I do not fight
like a boxer who hits nothing but air.
27 No, I train my body and bring it under
control. Then after I have preached to
others, I myself will not break the rules.
If I did break them, I would fail to win
the prize.

GLORIOUS

God is full of beauty and splendor because of who he is in his unchanging, eternal nature and perfect character.

Have you ever seen a beautiful sunset and thought to yourself, "Wow! That is amazing! I can hardly take it all in!" Or maybe you've looked at the stars in the sky on a clear night and thought, "This is amazing! I can't even understand how incredible this sight is!" That is just a small picture of what it is like to behold God's glory—we can't take it all in.

God's holiness and greatness are beyond our understanding. This is why the writers of the book of Psalms over and over again compare God to things that are unimaginably beautiful—the night sky, the sunrise, the ocean, and more (see Psalm 8:1). God's glory is magnificent!

Warnings From Israel's History

10 Brothers and sisters, I want you to
know something about our peo-
ple who lived long ago. They were all led
by the cloud. They all walked through
the Red Sea. 2 They were all baptized into
Moses in the cloud and in the sea. 3 They
all ate the same spiritual food. 4 They all
drank the same spiritual water. They
drank from the spiritual rock that went
with them. That rock was Christ. 5 But
God was not pleased with most of them.
Their bodies were scattered in the desert.
6 Now those things happened as examples for us. They are supposed to keep
us from wanting evil things. The people
of Israel wanted these evil things. 7 So
don't worship statues of gods, as some
of them did. It is written, "The people sat
down to eat and drink. Then they got
up to dance wildly in front of their god."
(Exodus 32:6) 8 We should not commit
sexual sins, as some of them did. In one
day 23,000 of them died. 9 We should
not test the Messiah, as some of them
did. They were killed by snakes. 10 Don't
speak against God. That's what some of
the people of Israel did. And they were
killed by the destroying angel.
11 Those things happened to them
as examples for us. They were written
down to warn us. That's because we are
living at the time when God's work is
being completed. 12 So be careful. When
you think you are standing firm, you
might fall. 13 You are tempted in the
same way all other human beings are.
God is faithful. He will not let you be
tempted any more than you can take.
But when you are tempted, God will
give you a way out. Then you will be
able to deal with it.

Sharing in the Lord's Supper

14 My dear friends, run away from
statues of gods. Don't worship them.
15 I'm talking to people who are reasonable. Judge for yourselves what I
say. 16 We give thanks for the cup at
the Lord's Supper. When we do, aren't
we sharing in the blood of Christ? When
we break the bread, aren't we sharing
in the body of Christ? 17 Just as there is
one loaf, so we who are many are one
body. We all share the one loaf.
18 Think about the people of Israel. Don't those who eat the offerings
share in the altar? 19 Do I mean that
food sacrificed to a statue of a god is

anything? Do I mean that a statue of
a god is anything? 20 No! But what is
sacrificed by those who worship statues
of gods is really sacrificed to demons. It
is not sacrificed to God. I don't want you
to be sharing with demons. 21 You can't
drink the cup of the Lord and the cup
of demons too. You can't have a part in
both the Lord's table and the table of
demons. 22 Are we trying to make the
Lord jealous? Are we stronger than he is?

The Believer's Freedom

23 You say, "I have the right to do anything." But not everything is helpful.
Again you say, "I have the right to do
anything." But not everything builds us
up. 24 No one should look out for their
own interests. Instead, they should look
out for the interests of others.

25 Eat anything sold in the meat
market. Don't ask if it's right or wrong.
26 Scripture says, "The earth belongs to
the Lord. And so does everything in it."
(Psalm 24:1)

27 Suppose an unbeliever invites you
to a meal and you want to go. Then eat
anything that is put in front of you.
Don't ask if it's right or wrong. 28 But
suppose someone says to you, "This
food has been sacrificed to a statue of
a god." Then don't eat it. Keep in mind
the good of the person who told you.
And don't eat because of a sense of
what is right and wrong. 29 I'm talking
about the other person's sense of what
is right and wrong, not yours. Why is
my freedom being judged by what
someone else thinks? 30 Suppose I give
thanks when I eat. Then why should I be
blamed for eating food I thank God for?

31 So eat and drink and do everything
else for the glory of God. 32 Don't do anything that causes another person to
trip and fall. It doesn't matter if that
person is a Jew or a Greek or a member
of God's church. 33 Follow my example.
I try to please everyone in every way.
I'm not looking out for what is good for
me. I'm looking out for the interests
of others. I do it so that they might be
11 saved. 1 Follow my example, just
as I follow the example of Christ.

Proper Worship

2 I praise you for being faithful in
remembering me. I also praise you for
staying true to the teachings of the past.
You have stayed true to them, just as
I gave them to you. 3 But I want you to
know that the head of every man is
Christ. The head of the woman is the
man. And the head of Christ is God.
4 Every man who prays or prophesies
with his head covered brings shame on
his head. 5 But every woman who prays
or prophesies with her head uncovered
brings shame on her head. It is the same
as having her head shaved. 6 What if a
woman does not cover her head? She
might as well have her hair cut off. But
it is shameful for her to cut her hair or
shave her head. So she should cover
her head.

7 A man should not cover his head.
He is the likeness and glory of God. But
woman is the glory of man. 8 Man did
not come from woman. Woman came
from man. 9 Also, man was not created
for woman. Woman was created for
man. 10 That's why a woman should
have authority over her own head. She
should have this because of the angels.
11 But here is how things are for those
who belong to the Lord. Woman is not
independent of man. And man is not
independent of woman. 12 Woman came
from man, and man is born from woman. But everything comes from God.

13 You be the judge. Is it proper for
a woman to pray to God without covering her head? 14 Suppose a man has
long hair. Doesn't the very nature of
things teach you that it is shameful?
15 And suppose a woman has long hair.
Doesn't the very nature of things teach
you that it is her glory? Long hair is
given to her as a covering. 16 If anyone
wants to argue about this, we don't have
any other practice. And God's churches
don't either.

Celebrating the Lord's Supper in the Right Way

17 In the following matters, I don't
praise you. Your meetings do more
harm than good. 18 First, here is what
people are telling me. When you come
together as a church, you take sides.
And in some ways I believe it. 19 Do you
really think you need to take sides? You
probably think God favors one side over
the other! 20 So when you come together,
it is not the Lord's Supper you eat. 21 As
you eat, some of you go ahead and eat

your own private meals. Because of this, one person stays hungry and another gets drunk. 22 Don't you have homes to eat and drink in? You are shaming those in the church who have nothing. Do you think so little of God's church that you do this? What should I say to you? Should I praise you? Certainly not about the Lord's Supper!

23 I passed on to you what I received from the Lord. On the night the Lord Jesus was handed over to his enemies, he took bread. 24 When he had given thanks, he broke it. He said, "This is my body. It is given for you. Every time you eat it, do it in memory of me." 25 In the same way, after supper he took the cup. He said, "This cup is the new covenant in my blood. Every time you drink it, do it in memory of me." 26 You eat the bread and drink the cup. When you do this, you are announcing the Lord's death until he comes again.

27 Eat the bread or drink the cup of the Lord in the right way. Don't do it in a way that isn't worthy of him. If you do, you will be guilty. You'll be guilty of sinning against the body and blood of the Lord. 28 Everyone should take a careful look at themselves before they eat the bread and drink from the cup. 29 Whoever eats and drinks must recognize the body of Christ. If they don't, judgment will come upon them. 30 That is why many of you are weak and sick. That is why a number of you have died. 31 We should think more carefully about what we are doing. Then we would not be found guilty for this. 32 When the Lord judges us in this way, he corrects us. Then in the end we will not be judged along with the rest of the world.

33 My brothers and sisters, when you come together to eat, you should all eat together. 34 Anyone who is hungry should eat something at home. Then when you come together, you will not be judged.

When I come, I will give you more directions.

Gifts of the Holy Spirit

12 Brothers and sisters, I want you to know about the gifts of the Holy Spirit. 2 You know that at one time you were unbelievers. You were somehow drawn away to worship statues of gods that couldn't even speak. 3 So I want you to know that no one who is speaking with the help of God's Spirit says, "May Jesus be cursed." And without the help of the Holy Spirit no one can say, "Jesus is Lord."

4 There are different kinds of gifts. But they are all given to believers by the same Spirit. 5 There are different ways to serve. But they all come from the same Lord. 6 There are different ways the Spirit works. But the same God is working in all these ways and in all people.

7 The Holy Spirit is given to each of us in a special way. That is for the good of all. 8 To some people the Spirit gives a message of wisdom. To others the same Spirit gives a message of knowledge. 9 To others the same Spirit gives faith. To others that one Spirit gives gifts of healing. 10 To others he gives the power to do miracles. To others he gives the ability to prophesy. To others he gives the ability to tell the spirits apart. To others he gives the ability to speak in different kinds of languages they had not known before. And to still others he gives the ability to explain what was said in those languages. 11 All the gifts are produced by one and the same Spirit. He gives gifts to each person, just as he decides.

One Body but Many Parts

12 There is one body, but it has many parts. But all its many parts make up one body. It is the same with Christ. 13 We were all baptized by one Holy Spirit. And so we are formed into one body. It didn't matter whether we were Jews or Gentiles, slaves or free people. We were all given the same Spirit to drink. 14 So the body is not made up of just one part. It has many parts.

15 Suppose the foot says, "I am not a hand. So I don't belong to the body." By saying this, it cannot stop being part of the body. 16 And suppose the ear says, "I am not an eye. So I don't belong to the body." By saying this, it cannot stop being part of the body. 17 If the whole body were an eye, how could it hear? If the whole body were an ear, how could it smell? 18 God has placed each part in the body just as he wanted it to be. 19 If all the parts were the same, how could

there be a body? 20 As it is, there are many parts. But there is only one body.

21 The eye can't say to the hand, "I don't need you!" The head can't say to the feet, "I don't need you!" 22 In fact, it is just the opposite. The parts of the body that seem to be weaker are the ones we can't do without. 23 The parts that we think are less important we treat with special honor. The private parts aren't shown. But they are treated with special care. 24 The parts that can be shown don't need special care. But God has put together all the parts of the body. And he has given more honor to the parts that didn't have any. 25 In that way, the parts of the body will not take sides. All of them will take care of one another. 26 If one part suffers, every part suffers with it. If one part is honored, every part shares in its joy.

27 You are the body of Christ. Each one of you is a part of it. 28 First, God has placed apostles in the church. Second, he has placed prophets in the church. Third, he has placed teachers in the church. Then he has given to the church miracles and gifts of healing. He also has given the gift of helping others and the gift of guiding the church. God also has given the gift of speaking in different kinds of languages. 29 Is everyone an apostle? Is everyone a prophet? Is everyone a teacher? Do all work miracles? 30 Do all have gifts of healing? Do all speak in languages they had not known before? Do all explain what is said in those languages? 31 But above all, you should want the more important gifts.

Love Is Necessary

But now I will show you the best way of all.

13 Suppose I speak in the languages of human beings or of angels. If I don't have love, I am only a loud gong or a noisy cymbal. 2 Suppose I have the gift of prophecy. Suppose I can understand all the secret things of God and know everything about him. And suppose I have enough faith to move mountains. If I don't have love, I am nothing at all. 3 Suppose I give everything I have to poor people. And suppose I give myself over to a difficult life so I can brag. If I don't have love, I get nothing at all.

4 Love is patient. Love is kind. It does not want what belongs to others. It does not brag. It is not proud. 5 It does not dishonor other people. It does not look out for its own interests. It does not easily become angry. It does not keep track of other people's wrongs. 6 Love is not happy with evil. But it is full of joy when the truth is spoken. 7 It always protects. It always trusts. It always hopes. It never gives up.

8 Love never fails. But prophecy will pass away. Speaking in languages that had not been known before will end. And knowledge will pass away. 9 What we know now is not complete. What we prophesy now is not perfect. 10 But when what is complete comes, the things that are not complete will pass away. 11 When I was a child, I talked like a child. I thought like a child. I had the understanding of a child. When I became a man, I put the ways of childhood behind me. 12 Now we see only a dim likeness of things. It is as if we were seeing them in a foggy mirror. But someday we will see clearly. We will see face to face. What I know now is not complete. But someday I will know completely, just as God knows me completely.

13 The three most important things to have are faith, hope and love. But the greatest of them is love.

Worship in a Way That Helps People Understand

14 Follow the way of love. You should also want the gifts the Holy Spirit gives. Most of all, you should want the gift of prophecy. 2 Anyone who speaks in a language they had not known before doesn't speak to people. They speak only to God. In fact, no one understands them. What they say by the Spirit remains a mystery. 3 But the person who prophesies speaks to people. That person prophesies to make people stronger, to give them hope, and to comfort them. 4 Anyone who speaks in other languages builds up only themselves. But the person who prophesies builds up the church. 5 I would like all of you to speak in other languages. But I would rather have you prophesy. The person who prophesies is more helpful than those who speak in other languages. But that is not the

case if someone explains what was said
in the other languages. Then the whole
church can be built up.
6 Brothers and sisters, suppose I were
to come to you and speak in other languages. What good would I be to you?
None! I would need to come with new
truth or knowledge. Or I would need
to come with a prophecy or a teaching. 7 Here are some examples. Certain
objects make sounds. Take a flute or a
harp. No one will know what the tune is
unless different notes are played. 8 Also,
if the trumpet call isn't clear, who will
get ready for battle? 9 It's the same with
you. You must speak words that people
understand. If you don't, no one will
know what you are saying. You will just
be speaking into the air. 10 It is true that
there are all kinds of languages in the
world. And they all have meaning. 11 But
if I don't understand what someone is
saying, I am a stranger to the person
speaking. And that person is a stranger
to me. 12 It's the same with you. You
want the gifts of the Spirit. So try to do
your best in using gifts that build up
the church.
13 So here is what the person who
speaks in languages they had not
known before should do. They should
pray that they can explain what they
say. 14 If I pray in another language,
my spirit prays. But my mind does not
pray. 15 So what should I do? I will pray
with my spirit. But I will also pray with
my understanding. I will sing with my
spirit. But I will also sing with my understanding. 16 Suppose you are praising God in the Spirit. And suppose there
are visitors among you who want to
know what's going on. How can they say
"Amen" when you give thanks? They
don't know what you are saying. 17 You
are certainly giving thanks. But no one
else is being built up.
18 I thank God that I speak in other
languages more than all of you do.
19 In the church, I wouldn't want to
speak 10,000 words in an unfamiliar
language. I'd rather speak five words
in a language people could understand.
Then I would be teaching others.
20 Brothers and sisters, stop thinking
like children. Be like babies as far as
evil is concerned. But be grown up in
your thinking. 21 In the law it is written,

"With unfamiliar languages
and through the lips of outsiders
I will speak to these people.
But even then they will not listen
to me." *(Isaiah 28:11,12)*
That is what the Lord says.

22 So speaking in other languages is
a sign for those who don't believe. It
is not a sign for those who do believe.
But prophecy is not for those who don't
believe. It is for those who believe.
23 Suppose the whole church comes
together and everyone speaks in other languages. And suppose visitors or
unbelievers come in. Won't they say you
are out of your minds? 24 But suppose
unbelievers or visitors come in while
everyone is prophesying. Then they
will feel guilty about their sin. They
will be judged by all. 25 The secrets of
their hearts will be brought out into the
open. They will fall down and worship
God. They will exclaim, "God is really
here among you!"

Proper Worship

26 Brothers and sisters, what should
we say then? When you come together, each of you brings something. You
bring a hymn or a teaching or a message from God. You bring a message
in another language or explain what
was said in that language. Everything
must be done to build up the church.
27 No more than two or three people
should speak in another language. And
they should speak one at a time. Then
someone must explain what was said.
28 If there is no one to explain, the person speaking should keep quiet in the
church. They can speak to themselves
and to God.
29 Only two or three prophets are supposed to speak. Others should decide if
what is being said is true. 30 What if a
message from God comes to someone
else who is sitting there? Then the one
who is speaking should stop. 31 Those
who prophesy can all take turns. In
that way, everyone can be taught and
be given hope. 32 Those who prophesy
should control their speaking. 33 God
is not a God of disorder. He is a God of
peace, just as in all the churches of the
Lord's people.
34 Women should remain silent in
church meetings. They are not allowed

to speak. They must follow the lead of
those who are in authority, as the law
says. 35 If they have a question about
something, they should ask their own
husbands at home. It is shameful for
women to speak in church meetings.
36 Or did the word of God begin with
you? Or are you the only people it has
reached? 37 Suppose anyone thinks they
are a prophet. Or suppose they think
they have other gifts given by the Holy
Spirit. They should agree that what I am
writing to you is the Lord's command.
38 But anyone who does not recognize
this will not be recognized.
39 Brothers and sisters, you should
want to prophesy. And don't stop people
from speaking in languages they had
not known before. 40 But everything
should be done in a proper and orderly
way.

Christ Rose From the Dead

15 Brothers and sisters, I want to
remind you of the good news I
preached to you. You received it and
have put your faith in it. 2 Because you
believed the good news, you are saved.
But you must hold firmly to the message I preached to you. If you don't, you
have believed it for nothing.
3 What I received I passed on to you.
And it is the most important of all. Here
is what it is. Christ died for our sins, just
as Scripture said he would. 4 He was buried. He was raised from the dead on the
third day, just as Scripture said he would
be. 5 He appeared to Peter. Then he appeared to the 12 apostles. 6 After that, he
appeared to more than 500 brothers and
sisters at the same time. Most of them
are still living. But some have died. 7 He
appeared to James. Then he appeared
to all the apostles. 8 Last of all, he also
appeared to me. I was like someone who
wasn't born at the right time.
9 I am the least important of the
apostles. I'm not even fit to be called an
apostle. I tried to destroy God's church.
10 But because of God's grace I am what
I am. And his grace was not wasted on
me. No, I have worked harder than all
the other apostles. But I didn't do the
work. God's grace was with me. 11 So this
is what we preach, whether I or the other
apostles who preached to you. And that
is what you believed.

Believers Will Rise From the Dead

12 We have preached that Christ has
been raised from the dead. So how
can some of you say that no one rises
from the dead? 13 If no one rises from
the dead, then not even Christ has been
raised. 14 And if Christ has not been
raised, what we preach doesn't mean
anything. Your faith doesn't mean anything either. 15 More than that, we would
be lying about God. We are witnesses
that God raised Christ from the dead.
But he did not raise him if the dead are
not raised. 16 If the dead are not raised,
then Christ has not been raised either.
17 And if Christ has not been raised, your
faith doesn't mean anything. Your sins
have not been forgiven. 18 Those who
have died believing in Christ are also
lost. 19 Do we have hope in Christ only
for this life? Then people should pity us
more than anyone else.
20 But Christ really has been raised
from the dead. He is the first of all those
who will rise from the dead. 21 Death
came because of what a man did. Rising
from the dead also comes because of
what a man did. 22 Because of Adam,
all people die. So because of Christ, all
will be made alive. 23 But here is the
order of events. Christ is the first of those
who rise from the dead. When he comes
back, those who belong to him will be
raised. 24 Then the end will come after
Christ destroys all rule, authority and
power. Then he will hand over the kingdom to God the Father. 25 Christ must
rule until he has put all his enemies
under his control. 26 The last enemy that
will be destroyed is death. 27 Scripture
says that God "has put everything under his control." *(Psalm 8:6)* It says that
"everything" has been put under him.
But it is clear that this does not include
God himself. That's because God put
everything under Christ. 28 When he has
done that, the Son also will be under
God's rule. God put everything under the
Son. In that way, God will be all in all.
29 Suppose no one rises from the
dead. Then what will people do who
are baptized for the dead? Suppose the
dead are not raised at all. Then why are
people baptized for them? 30 And why
would we put ourselves in danger every
hour? 31 I face death every day. That's
the truth. And here is something you

can be just as sure of. I take pride in
what Christ Jesus our Lord has done for
you through my work. 32 Did I fight wild
animals in Ephesus with nothing more
than human hopes? Then what have I
gotten for it? If the dead are not raised,

> "Let us eat and drink,
> because tomorrow we will die."
> *(Isaiah 22:13)*

33 Don't let anyone fool you. "Bad companions make a good person bad."
34 You should come back to your senses
and stop sinning. Some of you don't
know anything about God. I say this
to make you ashamed.

The Body That Rises From the Dead

35 But someone will ask, "How are the
dead raised? What kind of body will
they have?" 36 How foolish! What you
plant doesn't come to life unless it dies.
37 When you plant something, it isn't a
completely grown plant that you put in
the ground. You only plant a seed. Maybe it's wheat or something else. 38 But
God gives the seed a body just as he
has planned. And to each kind of seed
he gives its own body. 39 Not all earthly
creatures are the same. People have one
kind of body. Animals have another.
Birds have another kind. Fish have still
another. 40 There are also heavenly bodies as well as earthly bodies. Heavenly
bodies have one kind of glory. Earthly
bodies have another. 41 The sun has one
kind of glory. The moon has another
kind. The stars have still another. And
one star's glory is different from that
of another star.

42 It will be like that with bodies that
are raised from the dead. The body that
is planted does not last forever. The
body that is raised from the dead lasts
forever. 43 It is planted without honor.
But it is raised in glory. It is planted in
weakness. But it is raised in power. 44 It
is planted as an earthly body. But it is
raised as a spiritual body.

Just as there is an earthly body, there
is also a spiritual body. 45 It is written,
"The first man Adam became a living
person." *(Genesis 2:7)* The last Adam
became a spirit that gives life. 46 What
is spiritual did not come first. What is
earthly came first. What is spiritual
came after that. 47 The first man came
from the dust of the earth. The second
man came from heaven. 48 Those who
belong to the earth are like the one
who came from the earth. And those
who are spiritual are like the heavenly
man. 49 We are like the earthly man.
And we will be like the heavenly man.

50 Brothers and sisters, here is what
I'm telling you. Bodies made of flesh
and blood can't share in the kingdom of
God. And what dies can't share in what
never dies. 51 Listen! I am telling you a
mystery. We will not all die. But we will
all be changed. 52 That will happen in
a flash, as quickly as you can wink an
eye. It will happen at the blast of the last
trumpet. Then the dead will be raised
to live forever. And we will be changed.
53 Our natural bodies don't last forever.
They must be dressed with what does
last forever. What dies must be dressed
with what does not die. 54 In fact, that is
going to happen. What does not last will
be dressed with what lasts forever. What
dies will be dressed with what does not
die. Then what is written will come true.
It says, "Death has been swallowed up.
It has lost the battle." *(Isaiah 25:8)*

> 55 "Death, where is the victory you
> thought you had?
> Death, where is your sting?"
> *(Hosea 13:14)*

56 The sting of death is sin. And the
power of sin is the law. 57 But let us give
thanks to God! He gives us the victory
because of what our Lord Jesus Christ
has done.

58 My dear brothers and sisters, remain strong in the faith. Don't let anything move you. Always give yourselves
completely to the work of the Lord.
Because you belong to the Lord, you
know that your work is not worthless.

The Offering for the Lord's People

16 Now I want to deal with the offering of money for the Lord's
people. Do what I told the churches in
Galatia to do. 2 On the first day of every week, each of you should put some
money away. The amount should be
in keeping with how much money you
make. Save the money so that you
won't have to take up an offering when
I come. 3 When I arrive, I will send some
people with your gift to Jerusalem. They

will be people you consider to be good.
And I will give them letters that explain
who they are. 4 If it seems good for me
to go also, they will go with me.

What Paul Asks for Himself

5 After I go through Macedonia, I
will come to you. I will only be passing
through Macedonia. 6 But I might stay
with you for a while. I might even spend
the winter. Then you can help me on my
journey everywhere I go. 7 I don't want
to see you now while I am just passing
through. Instead, I hope to spend some
time with you, if the Lord allows it. 8 But
I will stay at Ephesus until the day of
Pentecost. 9 A door has opened wide for
me to do some good work here. There
are many people who oppose me.

10 Timothy will visit you. Make sure
he has nothing to worry about while he
is with you. He is doing the work of the
Lord, just as I am. 11 No one should treat
him badly. Send him safely on his way
so he can return to me. I'm expecting
him to come back along with the others.

12 I want to say something about our
brother Apollos. I tried my best to get
him to go to you with the others. But
he didn't want to go right now. He will
go when he can.

13 Be on your guard. Remain strong
in the faith. Be brave. 14 Be loving in
everything you do.

15 You know that the first believers
in Achaia were from the family of
Stephanas. They have spent all their
time serving the Lord's people. Brothers and sisters, I am asking you 16 to
follow the lead of people like them.
Follow everyone who joins in the task
and works hard at it. 17 I was glad when
Stephanas, Fortunatus and Achaicus arrived. They have supplied me with what
you couldn't give me. 18 They renewed
my spirit, and yours also. People like
them are worthy of honor.

Final Greetings

19 The churches in Asia Minor send
you greetings.

Aquila and Priscilla greet you warmly
because of the Lord's love. So does the
church that meets in their house.

20 All the brothers and sisters here
send you greetings.

Greet one another with a holy kiss.

21 I, Paul, am writing this greeting
with my own hand.

22 If anyone does not love the Lord, let
a curse be on that person! Come, Lord!

23 May the grace of the Lord Jesus be
with you.

24 I give my love to all of you who
belong to Christ Jesus. Amen.

2 CORINTHIANS

Author: Paul

After Paul wrote his first letter to the church in Corinth, he wrote a second letter to further teach them that the ways of God are not the ways of the world. Paul talked about how encouraged he was to hear from his friend Titus that many of the Christians in Corinth had repented and were seeking to live godly lives. He warned them to watch out for people who would lead them away from God and urged them to hold tightly to the truth of the gospel.

Paul also addressed questions from those in Corinth who wondered about Paul's ability to teach and lead them in the ways of Christ. Some people were saying that Paul was weak and that he might not be the best person for the job. But Paul reminded them that God does not value the things that the world values. In fact, God reveals his power through human weakness (see 2 Corinthians 12:9). Being a witness for Jesus does not require a lot of money, strength, or skill. All that is needed is a heart that loves God and willingly obeys him. The book of 2 Corinthians reminds Christians that we give God glory by loving, surrendering, and living obediently.

Letters & Revelation

in 2 Corinthians?

God is the Ultimate Encourager. He showed us how to love and forgive one another by sending his Son, Jesus, to be the perfect example.

1 I, Paul, am writing this letter. I am
an apostle of Christ Jesus just as God
planned. Timothy our brother joins me
in writing.

We are sending this letter to you, the
members of God's church in Corinth. It
is also for all God's holy people everywhere in Achaia.

2 May God our Father and the Lord
Jesus Christ give you grace and peace.

Praise to the God Who Gives Comfort

3 Give praise to the God and Father
of our Lord Jesus Christ! He is the Father who gives tender love. All comfort
comes from him. 4 He comforts us in all
our troubles. Now we can comfort others
when they are in trouble. We ourselves
receive comfort from God. 5 We share
very much in the sufferings of Christ. So
we also share very much in his comfort.
6 If we are having trouble, it is so that
you will be comforted and renewed. If
we are comforted, it is so that you will
be comforted. Then you will be able
to put up with the same suffering we
have gone through. 7 Our hope for you
remains firm. We know that you suffer
just as we do. In the same way, God
comforts you just as he comforts us.

8 Brothers and sisters, we want you
to know about the hard times we had
in Asia Minor. We were having a lot of
trouble. It was far more than we could
stand. We even thought we were going
to die. 9 In fact, we felt as if we were
under the sentence of death. But that
happened so that we would not depend
on ourselves but on God. He raises the
dead to life. 10 God has saved us from
deadly dangers. And he will continue
to do it. We have put our hope in him.
He will continue to save us. 11 You must
help us by praying for us. Then many
people will give thanks because of what
will happen to us. They will thank God
for his kindness to us in answer to the
prayers of many.

Paul Changes His Plans

12 Here is what we take pride in. Our
sense of what is right and wrong tells
us how we have acted. We have lived
with honor and godly honesty. We have
depended on God's grace and not on
the world's wisdom. We lived that way
most of all when we were dealing with
you. 13 We are writing only what you
can read and understand. And here is
what I hope. 14 Up to this point you have
understood some of the things we have
said. But now here is what I hope for
when the Lord Jesus returns. I hope that
your pride in us will be the same as our
pride in you. When this happens, you
will understand us completely.

15 Because I was sure of this, I wanted
to visit you first. Here is how I thought
you would be helped twice. 16 I planned
to visit you on my way to Macedonia.
I would have come back to you from
there. Then you would have sent me on
my way to Judea. 17 When I planned all
this, was I ready to change my mind for
no good reason? No. I don't make my
plans the way the world makes theirs.
In the same breath the world says both,
"Yes! Yes!" and "No! No!"

18 But just as sure as God is faithful,
our message to you is not "Yes" and
"No." 19 Silas, Timothy and I preached to
you about the Son of God, Jesus Christ.
Our message did not say "Yes" and "No"
at the same time. The message of Christ
has always been "Yes." 20 God has made
a great many promises. They are all
"Yes" because of what Christ has done.
So through Christ we say "Amen." We
want God to receive glory. 21 He makes
both us and you remain strong in the
faith because we belong to Christ. He
anointed us. 22 He put his Spirit in our

hearts and marked us as his own. We can now be sure that he will give us everything he promised us.
23 I call God to be my witness. May he take my life if I'm lying. I wanted to spare you, so I didn't return to Corinth.
24 Your faith is not under our control. You remain strong in your own faith. But we work together with you for your
2 joy. 1 So I made up my mind that I would not make another painful visit to you. 2 If I make you sad, who is going to make me glad? Only you, the people I made sad. 3 What I wrote to you I wrote for a special reason. When I came, I didn't want to be troubled by those who should make me glad. I was sure that all of you would share my joy. 4 I was very troubled when I wrote to you. My heart was sad. My eyes were full of tears. I didn't want to make you sad. I wanted to let you know that I love you very deeply.

Forgive Those Who Make You Sad

5 Suppose someone has made us sad. In some ways, he hasn't made me sad so much as he has made all of you sad. But I don't want to put this too strongly. 6 He has been punished because most of you decided he should be. This punishment is enough. 7 Now you should forgive him and comfort him. Then he won't be sad more than he can stand. 8 So I'm asking you to tell him again that you still love him. 9 I wrote to you for another special reason. I wanted to see if you could stand the test. I wanted to see if you could obey everything asked of you.
10 Anyone you forgive I also forgive. Was there anything to forgive? If so, I have forgiven it for your benefit, knowing that Christ is watching. 11 We don't want Satan to outsmart us. We know how he does his evil work.

Serving Under the New Covenant

12 I went to Troas to preach the good news about Christ. There I found that the Lord had opened a door of opportunity for me. 13 But I still had no peace of mind. I couldn't find my brother Titus there. So I said goodbye to the believers at Troas and went on to Macedonia.

14 Give thanks to God! He always leads us as if we were prisoners in Christ's victory parade. Through us, God spreads the knowledge of Christ everywhere like perfume. 15 God considers us to be the pleasing smell that Christ is spreading. He is spreading it among people who are being saved and people who are

VICTORIOUS

My GOD IS...

God will have the ultimate and final victory in this life and in the life to come. God's Word, the Bible, tells us that there is a spiritual battle between God and God's enemy, Satan. Satan wants God's place of power and authority. He wants to take the glory that belongs to God alone. But the enemy is not equal to God. The Bible assures us that God will have the final victory!

When Jesus died on the cross and rose again, God defeated Satan. God promised that one day his victory will be complete for all eternity.

We can trust that even when things in this world look bad—when we see those whom we love suffering or when we feel the effects of sin and brokenness—God has the ultimate victory and one day will destroy sin and death forever (see 1 Corinthians 15:55–57).

dying. 16 To those who are dying, we are the smell of death. To those who are being saved, we are the perfume of life. Who is able to do this work? 17 Unlike many people, we aren't selling God's word to make money. In fact, it is just the opposite. Because of Christ we speak honestly before God. We speak like people God has sent.

3 Are we beginning to praise ourselves again? Some people need letters that speak well of them. Do we need those kinds of letters, either to you or from you? 2 You yourselves are our letter. You are written on our hearts. Everyone knows you and reads you. 3 You make it clear that you are a letter from Christ. You are the result of our work for God. You are a letter written not with ink but with the Spirit of the living God. You are a letter written not on tablets made out of stone but on human hearts.

4 Through Christ, we can be sure of this before God. 5 In ourselves we are not able to claim anything for ourselves. The power to do what we do comes from God. 6 He has given us the power to serve under a new covenant. The covenant is not based on the written Law of Moses. It comes from the Holy Spirit. The written Law kills, but the Spirit gives life.

The Greater Glory of the New Covenant

7 The Law was written in letters on stone. Even though it was a way of serving God, it led to death. But even that way of serving God came with glory. The glory lasted for only a short time. Even so, the people of Israel couldn't look at Moses' face very long. 8 Since all this is true, won't the work of the Holy Spirit be even more glorious? 9 The law that condemns people to death had glory. How much more glory does the work of the Spirit have! His work makes people right with God. 10 The glory of the old covenant is nothing compared with the far greater glory of the new. 11 The glory of the old lasts for only a short time. How much greater is the glory of the new! It will last forever.

12 Since we have that kind of hope, we are very bold. 13 We are not like Moses. He used to cover his face with a veil. That was to keep the people of Israel from seeing the end of what was passing away. 14 But their minds were made stubborn. To this day, the same veil remains when the old covenant is read. The veil has not been removed. Only faith in Christ can take it away. 15 To this day, when the Law of Moses is read, a veil covers the minds of those who hear it. 16 But when anyone turns to the Lord, the veil is taken away. 17 Now the Lord is the Holy Spirit. And where the Spirit of the Lord is, freedom is also there. 18 None of our faces are covered with a veil. All of us can see the Lord's glory and think deeply about it. So we are being changed to become more like him so that we have more and more glory. And this glory comes from the Lord, who is the Holy Spirit.

A Treasure in Clay Jars

4 So because of God's mercy, we have work to do. He has given it to us. And we don't give up. 2 Instead, we have given up doing secret and shameful things. We don't twist God's word. In fact, we do just the opposite. We present the truth plainly. In the sight of God, we make our appeal to everyone's sense of what is right and wrong. 3 Suppose our good news is covered with a veil. Then it is veiled to those who are dying. 4 The god of this world has blinded the minds of those who don't believe. They can't see the light of the good news that makes Christ's glory clear. Christ is the likeness of God. 5 The message we preach is not about ourselves. Our message is about Jesus Christ. We say that he is Lord. And we say that we serve you because of Jesus. 6 God said, "Let light shine out of darkness." *(Genesis 1:3)* He made his light shine in our hearts. His light gives us the light to know God's glory. His glory is shown in the face of Christ.

7 Treasure is kept in clay jars. In the same way, we have the treasure of the good news in these earthly bodies of ours. That shows that the mighty power of the good news comes from God. It doesn't come from us. 8 We are pushed hard from all sides. But we are not beaten down. We are bewildered. But that doesn't make us lose hope. 9 Others make us suffer. But God does not desert us. We are knocked down.

But we are not knocked out. 10 We always carry around the death of Jesus in our bodies. In that way, the life of Jesus can be shown in our bodies. 11 We who are alive are always in danger of death because we are serving Jesus. This happens so that his life can also be shown in our earthly bodies. 12 Death is at work in us. But life is at work in you.

13 It is written, "I believed, and so I have spoken." *(Psalm 116:10)* We have that same spirit of faith. So we also believe and speak. 14 We know that God raised the Lord Jesus from the dead. And he will also raise us up with Jesus. And he will present both you and us to himself. 15 All this is for your benefit. God's grace is reaching more and more people. So they will become more and more thankful. They will give glory to God.

16 We don't give up. Our bodies are becoming weaker and weaker. But our spirits are being renewed day by day. 17 Our troubles are small. They last only for a short time. But they are earning for us a glory that will last forever. It is greater than all our troubles. 18 So we don't spend all our time looking at what we can see. Instead, we look at what we can't see. That's because what can be seen lasts only a short time. But what can't be seen will last forever.

Waiting for Our New Bodies

5 We know that the earthly tent we live in will be destroyed. But we have a building made by God. It is a house in heaven that lasts forever. Human hands did not build it. 2 During our time on earth we groan. We long to put on our house in heaven as if it were clothing. 3 Then we will not be naked. 4 While we live in this tent of ours, we groan under our heavy load. We don't want to be naked. Instead, we want to be fully dressed with our house in heaven. What must die will be swallowed up by life. 5 God has formed us for that very purpose. He has given us the Holy Spirit as a down payment. The Spirit makes us sure of what is still to come.

6 So here is what we can always be certain about. As long as we are at home in our bodies, we are away from the Lord. 7 We live by believing, not by seeing. 8 We are certain about that. We would rather be away from our bodies and at home with the Lord. 9 So we try our best to please him. We want to please him whether we are at home in our bodies or away from them. 10 We must all stand in front of Christ to be judged. Each one of us will be judged for what we do while in our bodies. We'll be judged for the good things and the bad things. Then each of us will receive what we are supposed to get.

Christ Brings Us Back to God

11 We know what it means to have respect for the Lord. So we try to help other people to understand it. What we are is plain to God. I hope it is also plain to your way of thinking. 12 We are not trying to make an appeal to you again. But we are giving you a chance to take pride in us. Some people take pride in their looks rather than what's in their hearts. If you take pride in us, you will be able to answer them. 13 Are we "out of our minds," as some people say? If so, it is because we want to serve God. Does what we say make sense? If so, it is because we want to serve you. 14 Christ's love controls us. We are sure that one person died for everyone. And so everyone died. 15 Christ died for everyone. He died so that those who live should not live for themselves anymore. They should live for Christ. He died for them and was raised again.

16 So from now on we don't look at anyone the way the world does. At one time we looked at Christ in that way. But we don't anymore. 17 When anyone lives in Christ, the new creation has come. The old is gone! The new is here! 18 All this is from God. He brought us back to himself through Christ's death on the cross. And he has given us the task of bringing others back to him through Christ. 19 God was bringing the world back to himself through Christ. He did not hold people's sins against them. God has trusted us with the message

When anyone lives in Christ, the new creation has come. The old is gone! The new is here!

2 CORINTHIANS 5:17

that people may be brought back to
him. 20 So we are Christ's official messengers. It is as if God were making his
appeal through us. Here is what Christ
wants us to beg you to do. Come back
to God! 21 Christ didn't have any sin. But
God made him become sin for us. So we
can be made right with God because of
what Christ has done for us.

6 We work together with God. So we are
asking you not to receive God's grace
and then do nothing with it. 2 He says,

"When I had mercy on you, I heard
you.
On the day I saved you, I helped
you." *(Isaiah 49:8)*

I tell you, now is the time God has mercy. Now is the day he saves.

Paul's Sufferings

3 We don't put anything in anyone's
way. So no one can find fault with our
work for God. 4 Instead, we make it clear
that we serve God in every way. We serve
him by standing firm in troubles, hard
times and suffering. 5 We don't give up
when we are beaten or put in prison.
When people stir up trouble in the streets,
we continue to serve God. We work hard
for him. We go without sleep and food.
6 We remain pure. We understand completely what it means to serve God. We
are patient and kind. We serve him in
the power of the Holy Spirit. We serve
him with true love. 7 We speak the truth.
We serve in the power of God. We hold
the weapons of godliness in the right
hand and in the left. 8 We serve God in
times of glory and shame. We serve him
whether the news about us is bad or good.
We are true to our calling. But people
treat us as if we were pretenders. 9 We are
known, but people treat us as if we were
unknown. We are dying, but we continue
to live. We are beaten, but we are not
killed. 10 We are sad, but we are always
full of joy. We are poor, but we make
many people rich. We have nothing, but
we own everything.

11 Believers at Corinth, we have spoken
freely to you. We have opened our hearts
wide to you. 12 We are not holding back
our love from you. But you are holding
back your love from us. 13 I speak to you
as if you were my children. It is only fair
that you open your hearts wide to us also.

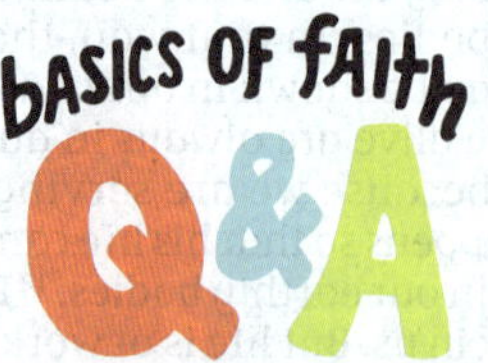

How can I be made right with God?

Jesus lived a perfect, sinless life. He died in your place to take away your sin and give you his righteousness. By receiving him as Lord and Savior, you can be made right with God.

Can you find the following verse?

2 CORINTHIANS 5:21

Paul Warns Against Worshiping False Gods

14 Do not be joined to unbelievers.
What do right and wrong have in
common? Can light and darkness be
friends? 15 How can Christ and Satan
agree? Or what does a believer have in
common with an unbeliever? 16 How
can the temple of the true God and the
statues of other gods agree? We are the
temple of the living God. God has said,

"I will live with them.
I will walk among them.
I will be their God.
And they will be my people."
(Leviticus 26:12; Jeremiah 32:38; Ezekiel 37:27)

17 So,

"Come out from among them
and be separate,
says the Lord.
Do not touch anything that is not
pure and 'clean.'
Then I will receive you." *(Isaiah 52:11; Ezekiel 20:34,41)*

18 And,

"I will be your Father.
You will be my sons and daughters,
says the Lord who rules over all."
(2 Samuel 7:14; 7:8)

7 Dear friends, we have these promises from God. So let us make ourselves pure from everything that makes our bodies and spirits impure. Let us be completely holy. We want to honor God.

Paul Has Joy When the Church Turns Away From Sin

2 Make room for us in your hearts. We haven't done anything wrong to anyone. We haven't caused anyone to sin. We haven't taken advantage of anyone. 3 I don't say this to judge you. I have told you before that you have an important place in our hearts. We would live or die with you. 4 I have spoken to you very honestly. I am very proud of you. I am very happy. Even with all our troubles, my joy has no limit.

5 When we came to Macedonia, we weren't able to rest. We were attacked no matter where we went. We had battles on the outside and fears on the inside. 6 But God comforts those who are sad. He comforted us when Titus came. 7 We were comforted not only when he came but also by the comfort you had given him. He told us how much you longed for me. He told us about your deep sadness and concern for me. That made my joy greater than ever.

8 Even if my letter made you sad, I'm not sorry I sent it. At first I was sorry. I see that my letter hurt you, but only for a little while. 9 Now I am happy. I'm not happy because you were made sad. I'm happy because your sadness led you to turn away from your sins. You became sad just as God wanted you to. So you were not hurt in any way by us. 10 Godly sadness causes us to turn away from our sins and be saved. And we are certainly not sorry about that! But worldly sadness brings death. 11 Look at what that godly sadness has produced in you. You are working hard to clear yourselves. You are angry and alarmed. You are longing to see me. You are concerned. You are ready to make sure that the right thing is done. In every way you have proved that you are not guilty in that matter. 12 So even though I wrote to you, it wasn't because of the one who did the wrong. It wasn't because of the one who was hurt either. Instead, I wrote you so that in the sight of God you could see for yourselves how faithful you are to us. 13 All this encourages us.

We were also very glad to see how happy Titus was. You have all renewed his spirit. 14 I had bragged about you to him. And you have not let me down. Everything we said to you was true. In the same way, our bragging about you to Titus has also turned out to be true. 15 His love for you is even greater when he remembers that you all obeyed his teaching. You received him with fear and trembling. 16 I am glad I can have complete faith in you.

Giving Freely to the Lord's People

8 Brothers and sisters, we want you to know about the grace that God has given to the churches in Macedonia. 2 They have suffered a great deal. But in their suffering, their joy was more than full. Even though they were very poor, they gave very freely. 3 I tell you that they gave as much as they could. In fact, they gave even more than they could. Completely on their own, 4 they begged us for the chance to share in serving the Lord's people in that way. 5 They did more than we expected. First they gave themselves to the Lord. Then they gave themselves to us because that was what God wanted. 6 Titus had already started collecting money from you. So we asked him to help you finish making your kind gift. 7 You do well in everything else. You do well in faith and in speaking. You do well in knowledge and in complete commitment. And you do well in the love we have helped to start in you. So make sure that you also do well in the grace of giving to others.

8 I am not commanding you to do it. But I want to test you. I want to find out if you really love God. I want to compare your love with that of others. 9 You know the grace shown by our Lord Jesus Christ. Even though he was rich, he became poor to help you. Because he became poor, you can become rich.

10 Here is my opinion about what is best for you in that matter. Last year you were the first to give. You were also the first to want to give. 11 So finish the work. Then your desire to do it will be matched by your finishing it. Give on the basis of what you have. 12 Do you really want to give? Then the gift is

measured by what someone has. It is
not measured by what they don't have.
[13]We don't want others to have it easy
at your expense. We want things to be
equal. [14]Right now you have plenty in
order to take care of what they need.
Then they will have plenty to take care
of what you need. The goal is to even
things out. [15]It is written, "The one who
gathered a lot didn't have too much.
And the one who gathered a little had
enough." *(Exodus 16:18)*

Paul Sends Titus to Corinth to Receive the Offering

[16]God put into the heart of Titus the
same concern I have for you. Thanks
should be given to God for this. [17]Titus
welcomed our appeal. He is also excited
about coming to you. It was his own
idea. [18]Along with Titus, we are sending another brother. All the churches
praise him for his service in telling the
good news. [19]He was also chosen by
the churches to go with us as we bring
the offering. We are in charge of it.
We want to honor the Lord himself.
We want to show how ready we are to
help. [20]We want to keep anyone from
blaming us for how we take care of that
large gift. [21]We are trying hard to do
what both the Lord and people think
is right.
[22]We are also sending another one of
our brothers with them. He has often
proved to us in many ways that he is
very committed. He is now even more
committed because he has great faith in
you. [23]Titus is my helper. He and I work
together among you. Our brothers are
messengers from the churches. They
honor Christ. [24]So show them that you
really love them. Show them why we
are proud of you. Then the churches
can see it.

9 I don't need to write to you about
giving to the Lord's people. [2]I know
how much you want to help. I have been
bragging about it to the people in Macedonia. I have been telling them that
since last year you who live in Achaia
were ready to give. You are so excited that it has stirred up most of them
to take action. [3]But I am sending the
brothers. Then our bragging about you
in this matter will have a good reason.
You will be ready, just as I said you
would be. [4]Suppose people from Macedonia come with me and find out that
you are not prepared. Then we, as well
as you, would be ashamed of being so
certain. [5]So I thought I should try to get
the brothers to visit you ahead of time.
They will finish the plans for the large
gift you had promised. Then it will be
ready as a gift freely given. It will not
be given by force.

Paul's Advice to Give Freely

[6]Here is something to remember.
The one who plants only a little will
gather only a little. And the one who
plants a lot will gather a lot. [7]Each of
you should give what you have decided
in your heart to give. You shouldn't give
if you don't want to. You shouldn't give
because you are forced to. God loves
a cheerful giver. [8]And God is able to
shower all kinds of blessings on you.
So in all things and at all times you
will have everything you need. You
will do more and more good works.
[9]It is written,

"They have spread their gifts
around to poor people.
Their good works continue
forever." *(Psalm 112:9)*

[10]God supplies seed for the person who
plants. He supplies bread for food.
God will also supply and increase the
amount of your seed. He will increase
the results of your good works. [11]You
will be made rich in every way. Then
you can always give freely. We will take
your many gifts to the people who need
them. And they will give thanks to God.
[12]Your gifts meet the needs of the
Lord's people. And that's not all. Your
gifts also cause many people to thank
God. [13]You have shown yourselves to
be worthy by what you have given. So
other people will praise God because
you obey him. That proves that you
really believe the good news about
Christ. They will also praise God because
you share freely with them and with
everyone else. [14]Their hearts will be
filled with love for you when they pray
for you. God has given you grace that
is better than anything. [15]Let us give
thanks to God for his gift. It is so great
that no one can tell how wonderful it
really is!

Paul Speaks Up for His Service to the Church

10 Christ is humble and free of pride. Because of this, I make my appeal to you. I, Paul, am the one you call "shy" when I am face to face with you. But when I am away from you, you think I am "bold" toward you. 2 I am coming to see you. Please don't make me be as bold as I expect to be toward some people. They think that I live the way the people of this world live. 3 I do live in the world. But I don't fight my battles the way the people of the world do. 4 The weapons I fight with are not the weapons the world uses. In fact, it is just the opposite. My weapons have the power of God to destroy the camps of the enemy. 5 I destroy every claim and every reason that keeps people from knowing God. I keep every thought under control in order to make it obey Christ. 6 Until you have obeyed completely, I will be ready to punish you every time you don't obey.

7 You are judging only by how things look on the surface. Suppose someone is sure they belong to Christ. Then they should consider again that we belong to Christ just as much as they do. 8 Do I brag too much about the authority the Lord gave me? If I do, it's because I want to build you up, not tear you down. And I'm not ashamed of that kind of bragging. 9 Don't think that I'm trying to scare you with my letters. 10 Some say, "His letters sound important. They are powerful. But in person he doesn't seem like much. And what he says doesn't amount to anything." 11 People like that have a lot to learn. What I say in my letters when I'm away from you, I will do in my actions when I'm with you.

12 I don't dare to compare myself with those who praise themselves. I'm not that kind of person. They measure themselves by themselves. They compare themselves with themselves. When they do that, they are not wise. 13 But I won't brag more than I should. God himself has given me an opportunity for serving. I will only brag about what I have done with that opportunity. This opportunity for serving also includes you. 14 I am not going too far in my bragging. I would be going too far if I hadn't come to where you live. But I did get there with the good news about Christ. 15 And I won't brag about work done by others. If I did, I would be bragging more than I should. As your faith continues to grow, I hope that my work among you will greatly increase. 16 Then I will be able to preach the good news in the areas beyond you. I don't want to brag about work already done in someone else's territory. 17 But, "The one who brags should brag about what the Lord has done." *(Jeremiah 9:24)* 18 Those who praise themselves are not accepted. Those the Lord praises are accepted.

Paul and Those Who Pretend to Be Apostles

11 I hope you will put up with me in a little foolish bragging. Yes, please put up with me! 2 My jealousy for you comes from God himself. I promised to give you to only one husband. That husband is Christ. I wanted to be able to give you to him as if you were a pure virgin. 3 But Eve's mind was tricked by the snake's clever lies. And here's what I'm afraid of. Your minds will also somehow be led astray. They will be led away from your true and pure love for Christ. 4 Suppose someone comes to you and preaches about a Jesus different from the Jesus we preached about. Or suppose you receive a spirit different from the Spirit you received before. Or suppose you receive a different message of good news. Suppose it was different from the one you accepted earlier. You put up with those kinds of things easily enough.

5 I don't think I'm in any way less important than those "super-apostles." 6 It's true that I haven't been trained as a speaker. But I do have knowledge. I've made that very clear to you in every way. 7 I preached God's good news to you free of charge. When I did that, I was putting myself down in order to lift you up. Was this a sin? 8 I received help from other churches so I could serve you. This was almost like robbing them. 9 When I was with you and needed something, I didn't cause you any expense. The believers who came from Macedonia gave me what I needed. I haven't caused you

any expense at all. And I won't ever do
it. 10 I'm sure that the truth of Christ is
in me. And I'm just as sure that nobody
in Achaia will keep me from bragging.
11 Why? Because I don't love you? No!
God knows I do!

12 And I will keep on doing what I'm
doing. That will stop those who claim
they have things to brag about. They
think they have a chance to be considered equal with us. 13 People like that are
false apostles. They are workers who tell
lies. They only pretend to be apostles
of Christ. 14 That comes as no surprise.
Even Satan himself pretends to be an
angel of light. 15 So it doesn't surprise
us that Satan's servants also pretend
to be serving God. They will finally get
exactly what they deserve.

Paul Brags About His Sufferings

16 I will say it again. Don't let anyone
think I'm a fool. But if you do, put up
with me just as you would put up with
a fool. Then I can do a little bragging.
17 When I brag about myself like this, I'm
not talking the way the Lord would. I'm
talking like a fool. 18 Many are bragging
the way the people of the world do. So
I will brag like that too. 19 You are so
wise! You gladly put up with fools! 20 In
fact, you even put up with anyone who
makes you a slave or uses you. You put
up with those who take advantage of
you. You put up with those who claim
to be better than you. You put up with
those who slap you in the face. 21 I'm
ashamed to have to say that I was too
weak for that!

Whatever anyone else dares to brag
about, I also dare to brag about. I'm
speaking like a fool! 22 Are they Hebrews? So am I. Do they belong to the
people of Israel? So do I. Are they Abraham's children? So am I. 23 Are they serving Christ? I am serving him even more.
I'm out of my mind to talk like this! I
have worked much harder. I have been
in prison more often. I have suffered
terrible beatings. Again and again I
almost died. 24 Five times the Jews gave
me 39 strokes with a whip. 25 Three times
I was beaten with sticks. Once they tried
to kill me by throwing stones at me.
Three times I was shipwrecked. I spent
a night and a day in the open sea. 26 I
have had to keep on the move. I have
been in danger from rivers. I have been
in danger from robbers. I have been
in danger from my fellow Jews and in
danger from Gentiles. I have been in
danger in the city, in the country, and at
sea. I have been in danger from people
who pretended they were believers. 27 I
have worked very hard. Often I have
gone without sleep. I have been hungry
and thirsty. Often I have gone without food. I have been cold and naked.
28 Besides everything else, every day I
am concerned about all the churches.
It is a very heavy load. 29 If anyone is
weak, I feel weak. If anyone is led into
sin, I burn on the inside.

30 If I have to brag, I will brag about
the things that show how weak I am.
31 I am not lying. The God and Father
of the Lord Jesus knows this. May God
be praised forever. 32 In Damascus the
governor who served under King Are-
tas had their city guarded. He wanted
to arrest me. 33 But I was lowered in a
basket from a window in the wall. So I
escaped from the governor.

Paul's Vision and His Painful Problem

12 We can't gain anything by bragging. But I have to do it anyway.
I am going to tell you what I've seen. I
want to talk about what the Lord has
shown me. 2 I know a believer in Christ
who was taken up to the third heaven
14 years ago. I don't know if his body
was taken up or not. Only God knows.
3 I don't know if that man was in his
body or out of it. Only God knows. But
I do know that 4 he was taken up to
paradise. He heard things there that
couldn't be put into words. They were
things that no one is allowed to talk
about. 5 I will brag about a man like
that. But I won't brag about myself. I
will brag only about how weak I am.
6 Suppose I decide to brag. That would
not make me a fool, because I would
be telling the truth. But I don't brag, so
that no one will think more of me than
they should. People should judge me
by what I do and say. 7 God has shown
me amazing and wonderful things.
People should not think more of me
because of it. So I wouldn't become
proud of myself, I was given a problem. This problem caused pain in my

body. It is a messenger from Satan to make me suffer. 8 Three times I begged the Lord to take it away from me. 9 But he said to me, "My grace is all you need. My power is strongest when you are weak." So I am very happy to brag about how weak I am. Then Christ's power can rest on me. 10 Because of how I suffered for Christ, I'm glad that I am weak. I am glad in hard times. I am glad when people say mean things about me. I am glad when things are difficult. And I am glad when people make me suffer. When I am weak, I am strong.

Paul's Concern for the People of Corinth

11 I have made a fool of myself. But you made me do it. You should have praised me. Even though I am nothing, I am in no way less important than the "super-apostles." 12 While I was with you, I kept on showing you the actions of a true apostle. These actions include signs, wonders and miracles. 13 How were you less important than the other churches? The only difference was that I didn't cause you any expense. Forgive me for that wrong!

14 Now I am ready to visit you for the third time. I won't cause you any expense. I don't want what you have. What I really want is you. After all, children shouldn't have to save up for their parents. Parents should save up for their children. 15 So I will be very happy to spend everything I have for you. I will even spend myself. If I love you more, will you love me less? 16 In any case, I haven't caused you any expense. But I'm so tricky! I have caught you by tricking you! Or so you think! 17 Did I take advantage of you through any of the men I sent to you? 18 I asked Titus to go to you. And I sent our brother with him. Titus didn't take advantage of you, did he? Didn't we walk in the same footsteps by the same Spirit?

19 All this time, have you been thinking that I've been speaking up for myself? No, I've been speaking with God as my witness. I've been speaking like a believer in Christ. Dear friends, everything I do is to help you become stronger. 20 I'm afraid that when I come I won't find you as I want you to be. I'm afraid that you won't find me as you want me to be. I'm afraid there will be arguing, jealousy and fits of anger. I'm afraid each of you will focus only on getting ahead. Then you will tell lies about each other. You will talk about each other. I'm afraid you will be proud and cause trouble. 21 I'm afraid that when I come again my God will put me to shame in front of you. Then I will be sad about many who sinned earlier and have not turned away from it. They have not turned away from uncleanness, sexual sins and wild living. They have done all those things.

Final Warnings

13 This will be my third visit to you. Scripture says, "Every matter must be proved by the words of two or three witnesses." *(Deuteronomy 19:15)* 2 I already warned you during my second visit. I now say it again while I'm away. When I return, I won't spare those who sinned earlier. I won't spare any of the others either. 3 You are asking me to prove that Christ is speaking through me. He is not weak in dealing with you. He is powerful among you. 4 It is true that Christ was nailed to the cross because he was weak. But Christ lives by God's power. In the same way, we share his weakness. But by God's power we will live with Christ as we serve you.

5 Take a good look at yourselves to see if you are really believers. Test yourselves. Don't you realize that Christ Jesus is in you? Unless, of course, you fail the test! 6 I hope you will discover that I haven't failed the test. 7 I pray to God that you won't do anything wrong. I don't pray so that people will see that I have passed the test. Instead, I pray this so that you will do what is right, even if it seems I have failed. 8 I can't do anything to stop the truth. I can only work for the truth. 9 I'm glad when I am weak but you are strong. I pray that there will be no more problems among you. 10 That's why I write these things before I come to you. Then when I do come, I won't have to be hard on you when I use my authority. The Lord gave me the authority to build you up. He didn't give it to me to tear you down.

Final Greetings

[11]Finally, brothers and sisters, be joyful!
Work to make things right with one another. Help one another and agree with one another. Live in peace. And the God who gives love and peace will be with you.
[12]Greet one another with a holy kiss.
[13]All God's people here send their greetings.
[14]May the grace shown by the Lord Jesus Christ be with you all. May the love that God has given us be with you. And may the sharing of life brought about by the Holy Spirit be with you all.

GALATIANS

Author: Paul

When Paul was traveling as a missionary teaching people about Jesus, he came to a region called Galatia. There he told many people—both Jews and Gentiles—the Good News. That little group of Christians grew until there were multiple churches in Galatia. These new Christians were eager to follow Jesus and grow in knowing and loving him together!

After Paul left, however, other teachers started telling the new Christians that Jesus wasn't enough for salvation. They said Christians needed to follow the Old Testament laws as well. This confused the Christians in Galatia. Were they really saved by grace through faith in Jesus alone? Or did they need to do something else to be made right with God? Paul wrote the church a letter to remind them that faith in Jesus was all they needed to be saved. Paul reminded them that no one can be made right with God in their own efforts; no one can measure up to God's standards on their own. Paul encouraged them to trust God for salvation and rely on the Holy Spirit to transform their hearts. The fact that salvation can't be earned through good works is what makes the gospel beautiful—changing people from the inside out.

Letters & Revelation

1 I, Paul, am writing this letter. I am
an apostle. People have not sent me.
No human authority has sent me. I
have been sent by Jesus Christ and by
God the Father. God raised Jesus from
the dead. 2 All the brothers and sisters
who are with me join me in writing.

We are sending this letter to you, the
members of the churches in Galatia.

3 May God our Father and the Lord
Jesus Christ give you grace and peace.
4 Jesus gave his life for our sins. He set
us free from this evil world. That was
what our God and Father wanted. 5 Give
glory to God for ever and ever. Amen.

There Is No Other Good News

6 I am amazed. You are so quickly deserting the one who chose you. He chose
you to live in the grace that Christ has
provided. You are turning to a different
"good news." 7 What you are accepting
is really not the good news at all. It
seems that some people have gotten
you all mixed up. They are trying to
twist the good news about Christ. 8 But
suppose even we should preach a different "good news." Suppose even an angel
from heaven should preach it. Suppose
it is different from the good news we
gave you. Then let anyone who does
that be cursed by God. 9 I have already
said it. Now I will say it again. Suppose
someone preaches a "good news" that
is different from what you accepted.
That person should be cursed by God.
10 Am I now trying to get people to think
well of me? Or do I want God to think well
of me? Am I trying to please people? If I
were, I would not be serving Christ.

Paul Was Appointed by God

11 Brothers and sisters, here is what
I want you to know. The good news I
preached does not come from human
beings. 12 No one gave it to me. No one
taught it to me. Instead, I received it
from Jesus Christ. He showed it to me.
13 You have heard how I lived earlier
in my Jewish way of life. With all my
strength I attacked the church of God.
I tried to destroy it. 14 I was moving
ahead in my Jewish way of life. I went
beyond many of my people who were
my own age. I held firmly to the teachings passed down by my people. 15 But
God set me apart from before the time

in Galatians?

God is the Highest Authority. He is the only one who can set us free from our sin. There is nothing we can do to earn our salvation.

I was born. He showed me his grace by
appointing me. He was pleased 16 to
show his Son in my life. He wanted
me to preach about Jesus among the
Gentiles. When God appointed me, I
decided right away not to ask anyone
for advice. 17 I didn't go up to Jerusalem
to see those who were apostles before I
was. Instead, I went into Arabia. Later
I returned to Damascus.
18 Then after three years I went up to
Jerusalem. I went there to get to know
Peter. I stayed with him for 15 days. 19 I
didn't see any of the other apostles.
I only saw James, the Lord's brother.
20 Here is what you can be sure of. And
God is even a witness to it. What I am
writing you is not a lie.
21 Then I went to Syria and Cilicia.
22 The members of Christ's churches in
Judea did not know me in a personal
way. 23 They only heard others say, "The
man who used to attack us has changed.
He is now preaching the faith he once
tried to destroy." 24 And they praised
God because of me.

Paul Is Accepted by the Apostles

2 Then after fourteen years, I went up
again to Jerusalem. This time I went
with Barnabas. I took Titus along also.
2 I went because God showed me what
he wanted me to do. I spoke in private
to those who are respected as leaders. I
told them the good news that I preach
among the Gentiles. I wanted to be sure
I wasn't running my race for no purpose.

And I wanted to know that I had not
been running my race for no purpose.
3 Titus was with me. He was a Greek. But
even he was not forced to be circumcised.
4 This matter came up because some people had slipped in among us. They had
pretended to be believers. They wanted
to find out about the freedom we have
because we belong to Christ Jesus. They
wanted to make us slaves again. 5 We
didn't give in to them for a moment. We
did this so that the truth of the good news
would be kept safe for you.

6 Some people in Jerusalem were
thought to be important. But it makes
no difference to me what they were. God
does not treat people differently. Those
people added nothing to my message.
7 In fact, it was just the opposite. They
recognized the task I had been trusted
with. It was the task of preaching the
good news to the Gentiles. My task was
like Peter's task. He had been trusted
with the task of preaching to the Jews.
8 God was working in Peter as an apostle
to the Jews. God was also working in me
as an apostle to the Gentiles. 9 James,
Peter and John are respected as pillars
in the church. They recognized the special grace given to me. So they shook my
hand and the hand of Barnabas. They
wanted to show they accepted us. They
agreed that we should go to the Gentiles.
They would go to the Jews. 10 They asked
only one thing. They wanted us to continue to remember poor people. That
was what I had wanted to do all along.

Paul Opposes Peter

11 When Peter came to Antioch, I told
him to his face that I was against what
he was doing. He was clearly wrong.
12 He used to eat with the Gentiles. But
certain men came from a group sent by
James. When they arrived, Peter began
to draw back. He separated himself
from the Gentiles. That's because he
was afraid of the circumcision group
sent by James. 13 Peter's actions were not
honest, and other Jews in Antioch joined
him. Even Barnabas was led astray.

14 I saw what they were doing. It was
not in line with the truth of the good
news. So I spoke to Peter in front of them
all. "You are a Jew," I said. "But you live
like one who is not. So why do you force
Gentiles to follow Jewish ways?"

15 We are Jews by birth. We are not
sinful Gentiles. 16 Here is what we know.
No one is made right with God by obeying the law. It is by believing in Jesus
Christ. So we too have put our faith in
Christ Jesus. This is so we can be made
right with God by believing in Christ.
We are not made right by obeying the
law. That's because no one can be made
right with God by obeying the law.

17 We are seeking to be made right
with God through Christ. As we do, what
if we find that we who are Jews are also
sinners? Does that mean that Christ
causes us to sin? Certainly not! 18 Suppose I build again what I had destroyed.
Then I would really be breaking the law.

19 By the law, I died as far as the law is
concerned. I died so that I might live for
God. 20 I have been crucified with Christ.
I don't live any longer, but Christ lives
in me. Now I live my life in my body by
faith in the Son of God. He loved me and
gave himself for me. 21 I do not get rid of
the grace of God. What if a person could
become right with God by obeying the
law? Then Christ died for nothing!

Faith or Obeying the Law

3 You foolish people of Galatia! Who
has put you under an evil spell?
When I preached, I clearly showed you
that Jesus Christ had been nailed to the
cross. 2 I would like to learn just one
thing from you. Did you receive the
Holy Spirit by obeying the law? Or did
you receive the Spirit by believing what
you heard? 3 Are you so foolish? You
began by the Holy Spirit. Are you now
trying to finish God's work in you by
your own strength? 4 Have you experienced so much for nothing? And was it
really for nothing? 5 So I ask you again,
how does God give you his Spirit? How
does he work miracles among you? Is
it by doing what the law says? Or is it
by believing what you have heard? 6 In
the same way, Abraham "believed God.
God was pleased with Abraham because
he believed. So his faith made him right
with God." *(Genesis 15:6)*

7 So you see, those who have faith are
children of Abraham. 8 Long ago, Scripture knew that God would make the
Gentiles right with himself. He would
do this by their faith in him. He announced the good news ahead of time

to Abraham. God said, "All nations will
be blessed because of you." *(Genesis 12:3;
18:18; 22:18)* 9 So those who depend on
faith are blessed along with Abraham.
He was the man of faith.
10 All who depend on obeying the law
are under a curse. It is written, "May
everyone who doesn't continue to do
everything written in the Book of the
Law be under God's curse." *(Deuteronomy 27:26)* 11 We know that no one who
depends on the law is made right with
God. This is because "the one who is
right with God will live by faith." *(Habakkuk 2:4)* 12 The law is not based on faith.
In fact, it is just the opposite. It teaches
that "the person who does these things
will live by them." *(Leviticus 18:5)* 13 Christ
set us free from the curse of the law. He
did it by becoming a curse for us. It is
written, "Everyone who is hung on a
pole is under God's curse." *(Deuteronomy
21:23)* 14 Christ Jesus set us free so that
the blessing given to Abraham would
come to the Gentiles through Christ.
He did it so that we might receive the
promise of the Holy Spirit. The promised
Spirit comes by believing in Christ.

The Law and the Promise

15 Brothers and sisters, let me give
you an example from everyday life. No
one can get rid of an official agreement
between people. No one can add to it.
It can't be changed after it has been
made. It is the same with God's covenant agreement. 16 The promises were
given to Abraham. They were also given
to his seed. Scripture does not say, "and
to seeds." That means many people. It
says, "and to your seed." *(Genesis 12:7;
13:15; 24:7)* That means one person. And
that one person is Christ. 17 Here is what
I mean. The law came 430 years after
the promise. But the law does not get
rid of God's covenant and promise. The
covenant had already been made by
God. So the law does not do away with
the promise. 18 The great gift that God
has for us does not depend on the law. If
it did, it would no longer depend on the
promise. But God gave it to Abraham as
a free gift through a promise.
19 Then why was the law given at all?
It was added because of human sin. And
it was supposed to control us until the
promised Seed had come. The law was
given through angels, and a go-between
was put in charge of it. 20 A go-between
means that there is more than one side
to an agreement. But God didn't use a
go-between when he made his promise
to Abraham.
21 So is the law opposed to God's promises? Certainly not! What if a law had
been given that could give life? Then
people could become right with God
by obeying the law. 22 But Scripture has
locked up everything under the control
of sin. It does so in order that what was
promised might be given to those who
believe. The promise comes through
faith in Jesus Christ.

Children of God

23 Before faith in Christ came, we were
guarded by the law. We were locked up
until this faith was made known. 24 So the
law was put in charge of us until Christ
came. He came so that we might be made
right with God by believing in Christ.
25 But now faith in Christ has come. So
the law is no longer in charge of us.
26 So in Christ Jesus you are all children of God by believing in Christ. 27 This
is because all of you who were baptized
into Christ have put on Christ. You have
put him on as if he were your clothes.
28 There is no Jew or Gentile. There is no
slave or free person. There is no male or
female. That's because you are all one
in Christ Jesus. 29 You who belong to
Christ are Abraham's seed. So you will
receive what God has promised.

4 Here is what I have been saying.
As long as your own children are
young, they are no different from slaves
in your house. They are no different,
even though they will own all the property. 2 People are in charge of the property. And other people are in charge of
the children. The children remain under
their care until they become adults. At
that time their fathers give them the
property. 3 It is the same with us. When
we were children, we were slaves to the
basic spiritual powers of the world. 4 But
then the chosen time came. God sent his
Son. A woman gave birth to him. He was
born under the authority of the law. 5 He
came to set free those who were under
the authority of the law. He wanted
us to be adopted as children with all
the rights children have. 6 Because you

are his children, God sent the Spirit of
his Son into our hearts. He is the Holy
Spirit. By his power we call God *Abba*.
Abba means Father. 7 So you aren't a
slave any longer. You are God's child.
Because you are his child, God gives you
the rights of those who are his children.

Paul's Concern for the Believers in Galatia

8 At one time you didn't know God.
You were slaves to gods that are really
not gods at all. 9 But now you know God.
Even better, God knows you. So why are
you turning back to those weak and
worthless powers? Do you want to be
slaves to them all over again? 10 You
are observing special days and months
and seasons and years! 11 I am afraid for
you. I am afraid that somehow I have
wasted my efforts on you.

12 I make my appeal to you, brothers
and sisters. I'm asking you to become
like me. After all, I became like you.
You didn't do anything wrong to me.
13 Remember when I first preached the
good news to you? Remember I did that
because I was sick. 14 And my sickness
was hard on you. But you weren't mean
to me. You didn't make fun of me. Instead, you welcomed me as if I were
an angel of God. You welcomed me as
if I were Christ Jesus himself. 15 So why
aren't you treating me the same way
now? Suppose you could have torn out
your own eyes and given them to me.
Then you would have done it. I am a
witness to this. 16 Have I become your
enemy now by telling you the truth?

17 Those people are trying hard to win
you over. But it is not for your good. They
want to take you away from us. They
want you to commit yourselves to them.
18 It is fine to be committed to something,
if the purpose is good. And you shouldn't
be committed only when I am with you.
You should always be committed. 19 My
dear children, I am in pain for you like I
was when we first met. I have pain like
a woman giving birth. And my pain will
continue until Christ makes you like himself. 20 I wish I could be with you now. I
wish I could change my tone of voice. As
it is, I don't understand you.

Hagar and Sarah

21 You who want to be under the authority of the law, tell me something.
Don't you know what the law says? 22 It
is written that Abraham had two sons.
The slave woman gave birth to one of
them. The free woman gave birth to the
other one. 23 Abraham's son by the slave
woman was born in the usual way. But
his son by the free woman was born
because of God's promise.

24 These things are examples. The two
women stand for two covenants. One
covenant comes from Mount Sinai. It
gives birth to children who are going
to be slaves. It is Hagar. 25 Hagar stands
for Mount Sinai in Arabia. She stands
for the present city of Jerusalem. That's
because she and her children are slaves.
26 But the Jerusalem that is above is
free. She is our mother. 27 It is written,

"Be glad, woman,
  you who have never had
    children.
Shout for joy and cry out loud,
  you who have never had labor
    pains.
The woman who is all alone has
    more children
  than the woman who has a
    husband." *(Isaiah 54:1)*

28 Brothers and sisters, you are children because of God's promise just as
Isaac was. 29 At that time, the son born
in the usual way tried to hurt the other
son. The other son was born by the power of the Holy Spirit. It is the same now.
30 But what does Scripture say? "Get rid
of the slave woman. Get rid of her son.
The slave woman's son will never have a
share of the family's property. He'll never share it with the free woman's son."
(Genesis 21:10) 31 Brothers and sisters, we
are not the slave woman's children. We
are the free woman's children.

Christ Sets Us Free

5 Christ has set us free to enjoy our
freedom. So remain strong in the
faith. Don't let the chains of slavery
hold you again.

2 Here is what I, Paul, say to you.
Don't let yourselves be circumcised.
If you do, Christ won't be of any value
to you. 3 I say it again. Every man who
lets himself be circumcised must obey
the whole law. 4 Some of you are trying
to be made right with God by obeying the law. You have been separated
from Christ. You have fallen away from
God's grace. 5 But we long to be made
completely holy because of our faith
in Christ. Through the Holy Spirit we
wait for this in hope. 6 Circumcision and
uncircumcision aren't worth anything
to those who believe in Christ Jesus. The
only thing that really counts is faith
that shows itself through love.

7 You were running a good race. Who
has kept you from obeying the truth?
8 The God who chooses you does not
keep you from obeying the truth. 9 You
should know that "just a little yeast
works its way through the whole batch
of dough." 10 The Lord makes me certain that you will see the truth of this.
The one who has gotten you all mixed
up will have to pay the price. This
will happen no matter who has done
it. 11 Brothers and sisters, I no longer
preach that people must be circumcised.
If I did, why am I still being opposed? If
I preached that, then the cross wouldn't
upset anyone. 12 So then, what about
troublemakers who try to get others to
be circumcised? I wish they would go
the whole way! I wish they would cut
off everything that marks them as men!

Living by the Holy Spirit's Power

13 My brothers and sisters, you were
chosen to be free. But don't use your
freedom as an excuse to live under the
power of sin. Instead, serve one another
in love. 14 The whole law is fulfilled by
obeying this one command. "Love your
neighbor as you love yourself." *(Leviticus 19:18)* 15 If you say or do things that
harm one another, watch out! You could
end up destroying one another.

16 So I say, live by the Holy Spirit's power. Then you will not do what your desires
controlled by sin want you to do. 17 The
desires controlled by sin do not want
what the Spirit delights in. And the Spirit
does not want what the desires controlled
by sin delight in. The two are at war with
each other. That's why you are not supposed to do whatever you want. 18 But
if you are led by the Spirit, you are not
under the authority of the law.

19 The result of sin's control in our lives
is clear. It includes sexual sins, impure
acts and wild living. 20 It includes worshiping statues of gods and worshiping
evil powers. It also includes hatred and
fighting, jealousy and fits of anger. Sinful desire is interested only in getting
ahead. It stirs up trouble. It separates
people into their own little groups. 21 It
wants what others have. It gets drunk
and takes part in wild parties. It does
many things of that kind. I warn you
now as I did before. People who live
like this will not receive God's kingdom.

22 But the fruit the Holy Spirit produces is love, joy and peace. It is being
patient, kind and good. It is being faithful 23 and gentle and having control of
oneself. There is no law against things
of that kind. 24 Those who belong to
Christ Jesus have nailed their sinful
desires to his cross. They don't want
these things anymore. 25 Since we live
by the Spirit, let us keep in step with the
Spirit. 26 Let us not become proud. Let us
not make each other angry. Let us not
want what belongs to others.

What will my life look like when the Holy Spirit lives inside of me?

The Holy Spirit will develop God's character in your life, which the Bible calls "fruit." As a result, you'll begin to think and do things that honor God and show others who he is.

Can you find the following verses?

GALATIANS 5:22–23

Do Good to Everyone

6 Brothers and sisters, what if someone is caught in a sin? Then you
who live by the Spirit should correct
that person. Do it in a gentle way. But
be careful. You could be tempted too.
2 Carry one another's heavy loads. If
you do, you will fulfill the law of Christ.
3 If anyone thinks they are somebody
when they are nobody, they are fooling themselves. 4 Each person should
test their own actions. Then they can
take pride in themselves. They won't
be comparing themselves to someone
else. 5 Each person should carry their
own load. 6 But those who are taught
the word should share all good things
with their teacher.

7 Don't be fooled. You can't outsmart
God. A man gathers a crop from what
he plants. 8 Some people plant to please
their desires controlled by sin. From
these desires they will harvest death.
Others plant to please the Holy Spirit.
From the Spirit they will harvest eternal
life. 9 Let us not become tired of doing
good. At the right time we will gather a
crop if we don't give up. 10 So when we
can do good to everyone, let us do it.
Let's try even harder to do good to the
family of believers.

Not Circumcision but the New Creation

11 Look at the big letters I'm using as I
write to you with my own hand!

12 Some people are worried about how
things look on the outside. They are
trying to force you to be circumcised.
They do it for only one reason. They
don't want to suffer by being connected
with the cross of Christ. 13 Even those
who are circumcised don't obey the law.
But they want you to be circumcised.
Then they can brag about what has
been done to your body. 14 I never want
to brag about anything except the cross
of our Lord Jesus Christ. Through that
cross the ways of the world have been
crucified as far as I am concerned. And
I have been crucified as far as the ways
of the world are concerned. 15 Circumcision and uncircumcision don't mean
anything. What really counts is that the
new creation has come. 16 May peace
and mercy be given to all who follow
this rule. May peace and mercy be given
to the Israel that belongs to God.

17 From now on, let no one cause trouble for me. My body has marks that
show I belong to Jesus.

18 Brothers and sisters, may the grace
of our Lord Jesus Christ be with your
spirit. Amen.

EPHESIANS

Author: Paul

The Romans put Paul in prison for telling people about Jesus. While in prison, Paul wrote a letter to a group of Christians in the city of Ephesus. This was a big city full of people from all over the world who practiced different religions. In his letter, Paul reminded the Ephesians that God's plan of salvation was for the entire world—God was making for himself a family of people from every nation.

Letters & Revelation

Paul wanted to write the Ephesians a letter both to encourage them and to teach them. In the first part of his letter, Paul talked about what it means to be saved and how those who put their faith in Jesus are brought into the family of God. Paul encouraged the Ephesians to embrace their new identity as Jesus followers. In the second part of his letter, Paul explained how to live out a new identity in Christ. He shared how Jesus made a way for diverse groups of people to live united. He didn't just want them to know *about* Jesus; he wanted their knowledge of Jesus to transform the way they lived. Paul taught them how the gospel message changed everything about their day-to-day lives.

1 I, Paul, am writing this letter. I am
an apostle of Christ Jesus just as God
planned.

I am sending this letter to you, God's holy people in Ephesus. Because you belong to Christ Jesus, you are faithful.

2 May God our Father and the Lord
Jesus Christ give you grace and peace.

Praise God for His Spiritual Blessings in Christ

3 Give praise to the God and Father of
our Lord Jesus Christ. He has blessed
us with every spiritual blessing. Those
blessings come from the heavenly
world. They belong to us because we
belong to Christ. 4 God chose us to belong to Christ before the world was
created. He chose us to be holy and
without blame in his eyes. He loved
us. 5 So he decided long ago to adopt
us. He adopted us as his children with
all the rights children have. He did it
because of what Jesus Christ has done.
It pleased God to do it. 6 All those things
bring praise to his glorious grace. God
freely gave us his grace because of the
One he loves. 7 We have been set free because of what Christ has done. Because
he bled and died our sins have been
forgiven. We have been set free because
God's grace is so rich. 8 He poured his
grace on us. By giving us great wisdom
and understanding, 9 he showed us the
mystery of his plan. It was in keeping
with what he wanted to do. It was what
he had planned through Christ. 10 It
will all come about when history has
been completed. God will then bring
together all things in heaven and on
earth under Christ.

11 We were also chosen to belong to
him. God decided to choose us long ago
in keeping with his plan. He works out
everything to fit his plan and purpose.
12 We were the first to put our hope in
Christ. We were chosen to bring praise to
his glory. 13 You also became believers in
Christ. That happened when you heard
the message of truth. It was the good
news about how you could be saved.
When you believed, he stamped you
with an official mark. That official mark
is the Holy Spirit that he promised.
14 The Spirit marks us as God's own. We
can now be sure that someday we will
receive all that God has promised. That
will happen after God sets all his people
completely free. All these things will
bring praise to his glory.

Paul Prays and Gives Thanks

15 I have heard about your faith in the
Lord Jesus. I have also heard about your
love for all God's people. That is why 16 I
have not stopped thanking God for you.
I always remember you in my prayers.
17 I pray to the God of our Lord Jesus
Christ. God is the glorious Father. I keep
asking him to give you the wisdom and
understanding that come from the Holy
Spirit. I want you to know God better.
18 I pray that you may understand more
clearly. Then you will know the hope
God has chosen you to receive. You will
know that what God will give his holy
people is rich and glorious. 19 And you
will know God's great power. It can't
be compared with anything else. His
power works for us who believe. It is the
same mighty strength 20 God showed.
He showed this when he raised Christ
from the dead. God seated him at his
right hand in his heavenly kingdom.
21 There Christ sits far above all who
rule and have authority. He also sits
far above all powers and kings. He is
above every name that is appealed to
in this world and in the world to come.
22 God placed all things under Christ's
rule. He appointed him to be ruler over
everything for the church. 23 The church
is Christ's body and is filled by Christ.
He fills everything in every way.

in Ephesians?

God is the Eternal Reward. He saved us by grace and gives us opportunities to serve him.

God Has Given Us New Life Through Christ

2 You were living in your sins and lawless ways. But in fact you were dead. 2 You used to live as sinners when you followed the ways of this world. You served the one who rules over the spiritual forces of evil. He is the spirit who is now at work in those who don't obey God. 3 At one time we all lived among them. Our desires were controlled by sin. We tried to satisfy what they wanted us to do. We followed our desires and thoughts. God was angry with us like he was with everyone else. That's because of the kind of people we all were. 4 But God loves us deeply. He is full of mercy. 5 So he gave us new life because of what Christ has done. He gave us life even when we were dead in sin. God's grace has saved you. 6 God raised us up with Christ. He has seated us with him in his heavenly kingdom. That's because we belong to Christ Jesus. 7 He has done it to show the riches of his grace for all time to come. His grace can't be compared with anything else. He has shown it by being kind to us. He was kind to us because of what Christ Jesus has done. 8 God's grace has saved you because of your faith in Christ. Your salvation doesn't come from anything you do. It is God's gift. 9 It is not based on anything you have done. No one can brag about earning it. 10 We are God's creation. He created us to belong to Christ Jesus. Now we can do good works. Long ago God prepared these works for us to do.

God's New Family of Jews and Gentiles

11 You who are not Jews by birth, here is what I want you to remember. You are called "uncircumcised" by those who call themselves "circumcised." But they have only been circumcised in their bodies by human hands. 12 Before you believed in Christ, you were separated from him. You were not considered to be citizens of Israel. You were not included in what the covenants promised. You were without hope and without God in the world. 13 At one time you were far away from God. But now you belong to Christ Jesus. He spilled his blood for you. This has brought you near to God.

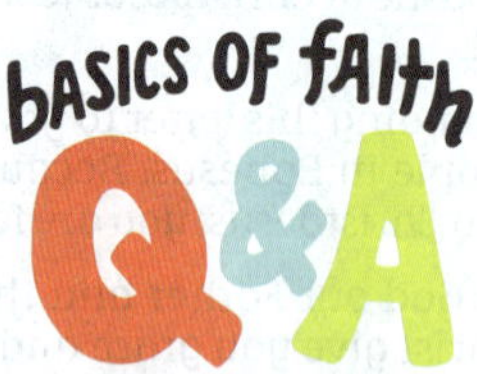

What is grace?

Grace is a gift no one deserves. By God's grace, he offers salvation to all people everywhere. No one can earn salvation, but we can receive it by grace.

Can you find the following verses?

EPHESIANS 2:8–9

14 Christ himself is our peace. He has made Jews and Gentiles into one group of people. He has destroyed the hatred that was like a wall between us. 15 Through his body on the cross, Christ set aside the law with all its commands and rules. He planned to create one new people out of Jews and Gentiles. He wanted to make peace between them. 16 He planned to bring both Jews and Gentiles back to God as one body. He planned to do this through the cross. On that cross, Christ put to death their hatred toward one another. 17 He came and preached peace to you who were far away. He also preached peace to those who were near. 18 Through Christ we both come to the Father by the power of one Holy Spirit.

19 So you are no longer outsiders and strangers. You are citizens together with God's people. You are also members of God's family. 20 You are a building that is built on the apostles and prophets. They are the foundation. Christ Jesus himself is the most important stone in the building. 21 The whole building is held together by him. It rises to become a holy temple because it belongs to the Lord. 22 And because you belong to him, you too are being built together. You are being made into a house where God lives through his Spirit.

God's Wonderful Plan for the Gentiles

3 I, Paul, am a prisoner because of Christ Jesus. I am in prison because of my work among you who are Gentiles.

2 I am sure you have heard that God appointed me to share his grace with you. 3 I'm talking about the mystery God showed me. I have already written a little about it. 4 By reading about this mystery, you will be able to understand what I know. You will know about the mystery of Christ. 5 The mystery was not made known to people of other times. But now the Holy Spirit has made this mystery known to God's holy apostles and prophets. 6 Here is the mystery. Because of the good news, God's promises are for Gentiles as well as for Jews. Both groups are parts of one body. They share in the promise. It belongs to them because they belong to Christ Jesus.

7 I now serve the good news because God gave me his grace. His power is at work in me. 8 I am by far the least important of all the Lord's holy people. But he gave me the grace to preach to the Gentiles about the unlimited riches that Christ gives. 9 God told me to make clear to everyone how the mystery came about. In times past it was kept hidden in the mind of God, who created all things. 10 He wanted the rulers and authorities in the heavenly world to come to know his great wisdom. The church would make it known to them. 11 That was God's plan from the beginning. He has fulfilled his plan through Christ Jesus our Lord. 12 Through him and through faith in him we can approach God. We can come to him freely. We can come without fear. 13 So here is what I'm asking you to do. Don't lose hope because I am suffering for you. It will lead to the time when God will give you his glory.

Paul Prays for the Ephesians

14 I bow in prayer to the Father because of my work among you. 15 From the Father every family in heaven and on earth gets its name. 16 I pray that he will use his glorious riches to make you strong. May his Holy Spirit give you his power deep down inside you. 17 Then Christ will live in your hearts because you believe in him. And I pray that your love will have deep roots. I pray that it will have a strong foundation. 18 May you have power together with all the Lord's holy people to understand Christ's love. May you know how wide and long and high and deep it is. 19 And may you know his love, even though it can't be known completely. Then you will be filled with everything God has for you.

IMMEASURABLE

My GOD IS...

God has no limits (see Psalm 147:5). He is so great that he cannot be measured.

Think of some of the ways you can be measured. When you go to the doctor's office, a nurse measures your height to see if you've grown taller. Each year on your birthday, you measure how many years have passed since you were born. Humans can be measured in all sorts of ways, but God cannot be measured.

We can't measure God's height to see how big he is because God is limitless. And we can't measure his age because he has no beginning and will have no end.

20 God is able to do far more than we
could ever ask for or imagine. He does
everything by his power that is working
in us. 21 Give him glory in the church and
in Christ Jesus. Give him glory through
all time and for ever and ever. Amen.

Growing Up Together in the Body of Christ

4 I am a prisoner because of the Lord.
So I am asking you to live a life
worthy of what God chose you for. 2 Don't
be proud at all. Be completely gentle.
Be patient. Put up with one another in
love. 3 The Holy Spirit makes you one in
every way. So try your best to remain as
one. Let peace keep you together. 4 There
is one body and one Spirit. You were
appointed to one hope when you were
chosen. 5 There is one Lord, one faith
and one baptism. 6 There is one God and
Father of all. He is over everything. He is
through everything. He is in everything.

7 But each one of us has received a
gift of grace. These gifts are given to us
by Christ. 8 That is why Scripture says,

> "When he went up to his place on
> high,
> he took many prisoners.
> He gave gifts to his people."
> *(Psalm 68:18)*

9 What does "he went up" mean? It can
only mean that he also came down to
the lower, earthly places. 10 The one
who came down is the same one who
went up. He went up higher than all
the heavens. He did it in order to fill all
creation. 11 So Christ himself gave the gift
of the apostles to the church. He gave
the prophets and those who preach the
good news. And he also gave the pastors
and teachers as a gift to the church. 12 He
gave all these people so that they might
prepare God's people to serve. Then the
body of Christ will be built up. 13 That
will continue until we all become one
in the faith. We will also become one in
the knowledge of God's Son. Then we
will be grown up in the faith. We will
receive everything that Christ has for us.

14 We will no longer be babies in the
faith. We won't be like ships tossed
around by the waves. We won't be blown
here and there by every new teaching. We
won't be blown around by cleverness and
tricks. Certain people use them to hide
their evil plans. 15 Instead, we will speak
the truth in love. So we will grow up in
every way to become the body of Christ.
Christ is the head of the body. 16 He makes
the whole body grow and build itself up
in love. Under the control of Christ, each
part of the body does its work. It supports
the other parts. In that way, the body is
joined and held together.

Teachings for Living as Christians

17 Here is what I'm telling you. I am
speaking for the Lord as I warn you. You
must no longer live as the Gentiles do.
Their thoughts don't have any purpose.
18 They can't understand the truth. They
are separated from the life of God. That's
because they don't know him. And they
don't know him because their hearts are
stubborn. 19 They have lost all feeling for
what is right. So they have given themselves over to all kinds of evil pleasures.
They take part in every kind of unclean
act. And they are full of greed.

20 But that is not the way of life in
Christ that you learned about. 21 You
heard about Christ and were taught
about life in him. What you learned
was the truth about Jesus. 22 You were
taught not to live the way you used to.

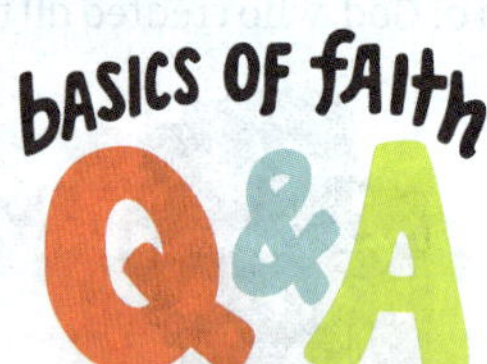

Why do I have to go to church?

Church is a gathering of people who put their faith in Jesus. God created people to need one another. By spending time worshiping God together, serving one another, and learning more about who God is, God's people honor him and become more like him.

Can you find the following verse?

EPHESIANS 4:16

You must get rid of your old way of life. That's because it has been made impure by the desire for things that lead you astray. 23 You were taught to be made new in your thinking. 24 You were taught to start living a new life. It is created to be truly good and holy, just as God is.

25 So each of you must get rid of your lying. Speak the truth to your neighbor. We are all parts of one body. 26 Scripture says, "When you are angry, do not sin." *(Psalm 4:4)* Do not let the sun go down while you are still angry. 27 Don't give the devil a chance. 28 Anyone who has been stealing must never steal again. Instead, they must work. They must do something useful with their own hands. Then they will have something to give to people in need.

29 Don't let any evil talk come out of your mouths. Say only what will help to build others up and meet their needs. Then what you say will help those who listen. 30 Do not make God's Holy Spirit mourn. The Holy Spirit is the proof that you belong to God. And the Spirit is the proof that God will set you completely free. 31 Get rid of all hard feelings, anger and rage. Stop all fighting and lying. Don't have anything to do with any kind of hatred. 32 Be kind and tender to one another. Forgive one another, just as God forgave you because of what Christ has done.

5 1 You are the children that God dearly loves. So follow his example. 2 Lead a life of love, just as Christ did. He loved us. He gave himself up for us. He was a sweet-smelling offering and sacrifice to God.

3 There should not be even a hint of sexual sin among you. Don't do anything impure. And do not always want more and more. These are not the things God's holy people should do. 4 There must not be any bad language or foolish talk or dirty jokes. They are out of place. Instead, you should give thanks. 5 Here is what you can be sure of. Those who give themselves over to sexual sins are lost. So are people whose lives are impure. The same is true of those who always want more and more. People who do these things might as well worship statues of gods. No one who does them will receive a share in the kingdom of Christ and of God. 6 Don't let anyone fool you with worthless words. People who say things like that aren't obeying God. He is angry with them. 7 So don't go along with people like that.

8 At one time you were in the dark. But now you are in the light because of what the Lord has done. Live like children of the light. 9 The light produces what is completely good, right and true. 10 Find out what pleases the Lord. 11 Have nothing to do with the acts of darkness. They don't produce anything good. Show what they are really like. 12 It is shameful even to talk about what people who don't obey do in secret. 13 But everything the light shines on can be seen. And everything that the light shines on becomes a light. 14 That is why it is said,

"Wake up, sleeper.
  Rise from the dead.
  Then Christ will shine on you."

15 So be very careful how you live. Do not live like people who aren't wise. Live like people who are wise. 16 Make the most of every opportunity. The days are evil. 17 So don't be foolish. Instead, understand what the Lord wants. 18 Don't fill yourself up with wine. Getting drunk will lead to wild living. Instead, be filled with the Holy Spirit. 19 Speak to one another with psalms, hymns and songs from the Spirit. Sing and make music from your heart to the Lord. 20 Always give thanks to God the Father for everything. Give thanks to him in the name of our Lord Jesus Christ.

Teachings for Christian Families

21 Follow the lead of one another because of your respect for Christ.

22 Wives, follow the lead of your own husbands as you follow the Lord. 23 The husband is the head of the wife, just as Christ is the head of the church. The church is Christ's body. He is its Savior. 24 The church follows the lead of Christ. In the same way, wives should follow the lead of their husbands in everything.

25 Husbands, love your wives. Love them just as Christ loved the church. He gave himself up for her. 26 He did it to make her holy. He made her clean by washing her with water and the word. 27 He did it to bring her to himself as a brightly shining church. He wants a church that has no stain or wrinkle or

any other flaw. He wants a church that is holy and without blame. [28] In the same way, husbands should love their wives. They should love them as they love their own bodies. Any man who loves his wife loves himself. [29] After all, no one ever hated their own body. Instead, they feed and care for their body. And this is what Christ does for the church. [30] We are parts of his body. [31] Scripture says, "That's why a man will leave his father and mother and be joined to his wife. The two will become one." *(Genesis 2:24)* [32] That is a deep mystery. But I'm talking about Christ and the church. [33] A husband also must love his wife. He must love her just as he loves himself. And a wife must respect her husband.

6 Children, obey your parents as believers in the Lord. Obey them because it's the right thing to do. [2] Scripture says, "Honor your father and mother." That is the first commandment that has a promise. [3] "Then things will go well with you. You will live a long time on the earth." *(Deuteronomy 5:16)*

[4] Fathers, don't make your children angry. Instead, instruct them and teach them the ways of the Lord as you raise them.

[5] Slaves, obey your masters here on earth. Respect them and honor them with a heart that is true. Obey them just as you would obey Christ. [6] Don't obey them only to please them when they are watching. Do it because you are slaves of Christ. Be sure your heart does what God wants. [7] Serve your masters with all your heart. Work as serving the Lord and not as serving people. [8] You know that the Lord will give each person a reward. He will give it to them in keeping with the good they do. It doesn't matter whether they are a slave or not.

[9] Masters, treat your slaves in the same way. When you warn them, don't be too hard on them. You know that the God who is their Master and yours is in heaven. And he treats everyone the same.

God's Armor for Believers

[10] Finally, let the Lord make you strong. Depend on his mighty power. [11] Put on all of God's armor. Then you can remain strong against the devil's evil plans. [12] Our fight is not against human beings. It is against the rulers, the

key verses Finally, let the Lord make you strong. Depend on his mighty power. Put on all of God's armor. Then you can remain strong against the devil's evil plans. **EPHESIANS 6:10–11**

authorities and the powers of this dark world. It is against the spiritual forces of evil in the heavenly world. [13] So put on all of God's armor. Evil days will come. But you will be able to stand up to anything. And after you have done everything you can, you will still be standing. [14] So remain strong in the faith. Put the belt of truth around your waist. Put the armor of godliness on your chest. [15] Wear on your feet what will prepare you to tell the good news of peace. [16] Also, pick up the shield of faith. With it you can put out all the flaming arrows of the evil one. [17] Put on the helmet of salvation. And take the sword of the Holy Spirit. The sword is God's word.

[18] At all times, pray by the power of the Spirit. Pray all kinds of prayers. Be watchful, so that you can pray. Always keep on praying for all the Lord's people. [19] Pray also for me. Pray that whenever I speak, the right words will be given to me. Then I can be bold as I tell the mystery of the good news. [20] Because of the good news, I am being held by chains as the Lord's messenger. So pray that I will be bold as I preach the good news. That's what I should do.

Final Greetings

[21] Tychicus is a dear brother. He is faithful in serving the Lord. He will tell you everything about me. Then you will know how I am and what I am doing. [22] That's why I am sending him to you. I want you to know how we are. And I want him to encourage you.

[23] May God the Father and the Lord Jesus Christ give peace to the brothers and sisters. May they also give the believers love and faith.

[24] May grace be given to everyone who loves our Lord Jesus Christ with a love that will never die.

PHILIPPIANS

Author: Paul

The Philippians were dear friends of Paul who had learned from him and were working to spread the gospel. While Paul was in prison in Rome, the church of Philippi sent Epaphroditus to visit Paul. In response, Paul, with the help of Timothy, wrote them this letter.

In his letter, Paul expressed how thankful he was for the church in Philippi. He told them he loved and missed them and hoped to see them again one day. The Christians in Philippi were experiencing persecution, or unfair treatment, for their new faith. They looked at their lives of suffering and wondered, "Is this really what it means to have a new life in Jesus?" Paul reminded them that following Jesus sometimes means being disliked, just like Jesus was. He encouraged them not to be afraid but always to live in a way that honored Jesus—because Jesus is better than anything. Paul also told them that even when they were struggling, they could have joy. They could view their hardships as opportunities to show Jesus' love and power. Through the Philippians' trials and Paul's imprisonment, the world was going to see the goodness of Jesus Christ. And that, Paul said, made every hard thing worth it.

Letters & Revelation

1 We, Paul and Timothy, are writing this letter. We serve Christ Jesus.

We are sending this letter to you, all God's holy people in Philippi. You belong to Christ Jesus. We are also sending this letter to your leaders and deacons.

2 May God our Father and the Lord Jesus Christ give you grace and peace.

Paul Prays and Gives Thanks

3 I thank my God every time I remember you. 4 In all my prayers for all of you, I always pray with joy. 5 I am happy because you have joined me in spreading the good news. You have done so from the first day until now. 6 God began a good work in you. And I am sure that he will carry it on until it is completed. That will be on the day Christ Jesus returns.

7 It is right for me to feel this way about all of you. I love you with all my heart. I may be held by chains, or I may be standing up for the truth of the good news. Either way, all of you share in God's grace together with me. 8 God is my witness that I long for all of you. I love you with the love that Christ Jesus gives.

9 I pray that your love will grow more and more. And let it be based on knowledge and understanding. 10 Then you will be able to know what is best. Then you will be pure and without blame for the day that Christ returns. 11 You will be filled with the fruit of right living produced by Jesus Christ. All these things bring glory and praise to God.

Paul Spreads the Good News While in Prison

12 Brothers and sisters, here is what I want you to know. What has happened to me has actually helped to spread the good news. 13 One thing has become clear. I am being held by chains because I am a witness for Christ. All the palace guards and everyone else know it. 14 And because I am a prisoner, most of the believers have become bolder in the Lord. They now dare even more to preach the good news without fear.

15 It's true that some preach about Christ because they are jealous. But others preach about Christ to help me in my work. 16 The last group acts out of love. They know I have been put here to be a witness for the good news. 17 But the others preach about Christ only to get ahead. They preach Christ for the wrong reasons. They think they can stir up trouble for me while I am being held by chains. 18 But what does it matter? Here is the important thing. Whether for right or wrong reasons, Christ is being preached about. That makes me very glad.

And I will continue to be glad. 19 I know that you are praying for me. I also know that God will give me the Spirit of Jesus Christ to help me. So no matter what happens, I'm sure I will still be set free. 20 I completely expect and hope that I won't be ashamed in any way. I'm sure I will be brave enough. Now as always Christ will receive glory because of what happens to me. He will receive glory whether I live or die. 21 For me, life finds all its meaning in Christ. Death also has its benefits. 22 Suppose I go on living in my body. Then I will be able to carry on my work. It will bear a lot of fruit. But what should I choose? I don't know! 23 I can't decide between the two. I long to leave this world and be with Christ. That is better by far. 24 But it is more important for you that I stay alive. 25 I'm sure of this. So I know I will remain with you. And I will continue with all of you to help you grow in your faith. I will also continue to help you be joyful in what you have been taught. 26 I'm sure I will be with you again. Then you will be able to boast in Christ Jesus even more because of me.

Living to Honor the Good News

27 No matter what happens, live in a way that brings honor to the good news

in Philippians?

God is the Redeemer. When our hearts ache or we are going through difficult times, God promises to be near.

about Christ. Then I will know that you
remain strong together in the one Spirit.
I will know this if I come and see you or
only hear about you. I will know that you
work together as one person. I will know
that you work to spread the teachings
about the good news. 28 So don't be afraid
in any way of those who oppose you.
This will show them that they will be destroyed and that you will be saved. That's
what God will do. 29 Here is what he has
given you to do for Christ. You must not
only believe in him. You must also suffer
for him. 30 You are going through the
same struggle you saw me go through.
As you have heard, I am still struggling.

Being Humble Like Christ

2 So does belonging to Christ help you
in any way? Does his love comfort
you at all? Do you share anything in
common because of the Holy Spirit?
Has Christ ever been gentle and loving
toward you? 2 If any of these things has
happened to you, then agree with one
another. Have the same love. Be one
in spirit and in the way you think and
act. By doing this, you will make my
joy complete. 3 Don't do anything only
to get ahead. Don't do it because you
are proud. Instead, be humble. Value
others more than yourselves. 4 None of
you should look out just for your own
good. Each of you should also look out
for the good of others.

5 As you deal with one another, you
should think and act as Jesus did.

6 In his very nature he was God.
Jesus was equal with God. But
Jesus didn't take advantage of
that fact.
7 Instead, he made himself nothing.
He did this by taking on the
nature of a servant.
He was made just like human
beings.
8 He appeared as a man.
He was humble and obeyed God
completely.
He did this even though it led to
his death.
Even worse, he died on a cross!
9 So God lifted him up to the highest
place.
God gave him the name that is
above every name.
10 When the name of Jesus is spoken,
everyone will kneel down to
worship him.
Everyone in heaven and on earth
and under the earth will kneel
down to worship him.
11 Everyone's mouth will say that
Jesus Christ is Lord.
And God the Father will receive
the glory.

Live Without Complaining

12 My dear friends, you have always
obeyed God. You obeyed while I was
with you. And you have obeyed even
more while I am not with you. So continue to work out your own salvation.
Do it with fear and trembling. 13 God is
working in you. He wants your plans
and your acts to fulfill his good purpose.

14 Do everything without complaining
or arguing. 15 Then you will be pure and
without blame. You will be children of
God without fault among sinful and
evil people. Then you will shine among
them like stars in the sky. 16 You will
shine as you hold on tight to the word
of life. Then I will be able to boast about
you on the day Christ returns. I can
be happy that I didn't run or work for
nothing. 17 But my life might even be
poured out like a drink offering on your
sacrifices. I'm talking about the way
you serve because you believe. Even
so, I am glad. I am joyful with all of
you. 18 So you too should be glad and
joyful with me.

Timothy and Epaphroditus

19 I hope to send Timothy to you soon
if the Lord Jesus allows it. Then I will be
encouraged when I receive news about
you. 20 I have no one else like Timothy.
He will truly care about how you are
doing. 21 All the others are looking out
for their own interests. They are not
looking out for the interests of Jesus
Christ. 22 But you know that Timothy
has proved himself. He has served with
me like a son with his father in spreading the good news. 23 So I hope to send
him as soon as I see how things go with
me. 24 And I'm sure I myself will come
soon if the Lord allows it.

25 But I think it's necessary to send
Epaphroditus back to you. He is my
brother in the Lord. He is a worker and
a soldier of Christ together with me. He

is also your messenger. You sent him to
take care of my needs. 26 He longs for all
of you. He is troubled because you heard
he was sick. 27 He was very sick. In fact, he
almost died. But God had mercy on him.
He also had mercy on me. God spared me
sadness after sadness. 28 So I want even
more to send him to you. Then when
you see him again, you will be glad.
And I won't worry so much. 29 So then,
welcome him as a brother in the Lord
with great joy. Honor people like him.
30 He almost died for the work of Christ.
He put his life in danger to make up for
the help you yourselves couldn't give me.

Do Not Trust in Who You Are or What You Can Do

3 Further, my brothers and sisters,
be joyful because you belong to
the Lord! It is no trouble for me to write
about some important matters to you
again. If you know about them, you
will have a safe path to follow. 2 Watch
out for those dogs. They are people who
do evil things. When they circumcise, it
is nothing more than a useless cutting
of the body. 3 But we have been truly
circumcised. We serve God by the power
of his Spirit. We boast about what Christ
Jesus has done. We don't put our trust in
who we are or what we can do. 4 I have
many reasons to trust in who I am and
what I have done. Someone else may

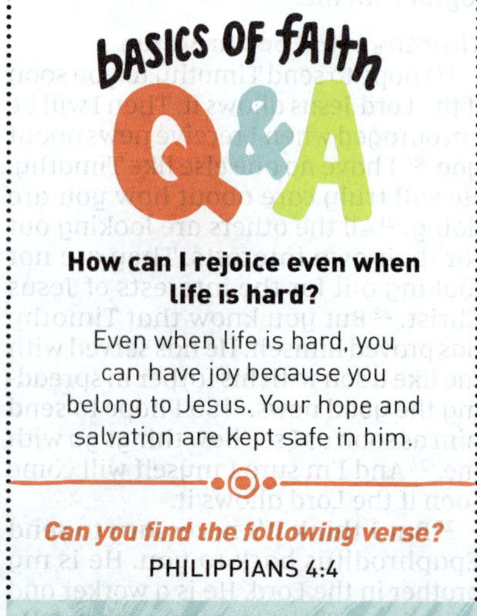

How can I rejoice even when life is hard?

Even when life is hard, you can have joy because you belong to Jesus. Your hope and salvation are kept safe in him.

Can you find the following verse?

PHILIPPIANS 4:4

think they have reasons to trust in these
things. But I have even more.
5 I was circumcised on the eighth day.
I am part of the people of Israel. I am
from the tribe of Benjamin. I am a pure
Hebrew. As far as the law is concerned,
I am a Pharisee. 6 As far as being committed is concerned, I opposed and
attacked the church. As far as keeping
the law is concerned, I kept it perfectly.
7 I thought things like that were really
something great. But now I consider
them to be nothing because of Christ.
8 Even more, I consider everything
to be nothing compared to knowing
Christ Jesus my Lord. To know him is
worth much more than anything else.
Because of him I have lost everything.
But I consider all of it to be garbage
so I can know Christ better. 9 I want to
be joined to him. Being right with God
does not come from my obeying the
law. It comes because I believe in Christ.
It comes from God because of faith.
10 I want to know Christ better. Yes, I
want to know the power that raised
him from the dead. I want to join him
in his sufferings. I want to become like
him by sharing in his death. 11 Then by
God's grace I will rise from the dead.
12 I have not yet received all these
things. I have not yet reached my goal.
Christ Jesus took hold of me so that I
could reach that goal. So I keep pushing
myself forward to reach it. 13 Brothers
and sisters, I don't consider that I have
taken hold of it yet. But here is the one
thing I do. I forget what is behind me. I
push hard toward what is ahead of me.
14 I push myself forward toward the goal
to win the prize. God has appointed me
to win it. The heavenly prize is Christ
Jesus himself.

Following Paul's Example

15 So all of us who are grown up in the
faith should see things this way. Maybe
you think differently about something.
But God will make it clear to you. 16 Only
let us live up to what we have already
reached.
17 Brothers and sisters, join together
in following my example. You have us
as a model. So pay close attention to
those who live as we do. 18 I have told
you these things many times before.
Now I tell you again with tears in my
eyes. Many people live like enemies of

the cross of Christ. 19 The only thing they have coming to them is death. Their stomach is their god. They brag about what they should be ashamed of. They think only about earthly things. 20 But we are citizens of heaven. And we can hardly wait for a Savior from there. He is the Lord Jesus Christ. 21 He has the power to bring everything under his control. By his power he will change our earthly bodies. They will become like his glorious body.

Remain Strong in the Lord

4 My brothers and sisters, in this way remain strong in the Lord. I love you and long for you. Dear friends, you are my joy and my crown.

2 Here is what I'm asking Euodia and Syntyche to do. I'm asking them to work together in the Lord. That's because they both belong to the Lord. 3 My true companion, here is what I ask you to do. Help these women, because they have served at my side. They have worked with me to spread the good news. So have Clement and the rest of those who have worked together with me. Their names are all written in the book of life.

Final Commands

4 Always be joyful because you belong to the Lord. I will say it again. Be joyful! 5 Let everyone know how gentle you are. The Lord is coming soon. 6 Don't worry about anything. No matter what happens, tell God about everything. Ask and pray, and give thanks to him. 7 Then God's peace will watch over your hearts and your minds. He will do this because you belong to Christ Jesus. God's peace can never be completely understood.

8 Finally, my brothers and sisters, always think about what is true. Think about what is noble, right and pure. Think about what is lovely and worthy of respect. If anything is excellent or worthy of praise, think about those kinds of things. 9 Do what you have learned or received or heard from me. Follow my example. The God who gives peace will be with you.

Paul Gives Thanks for the Philippians' Gifts

10 At last you are concerned about me again. That makes me very happy. We belong to the Lord. I know that you were concerned. But you had no chance to show it. 11 I'm not saying this because I need anything. I have learned to be content no matter what happens to me. 12 I know what it's like not to have what I need. I also know what it's like to have more than I need. I have learned the secret of being content no matter what happens. I am content whether I am well fed or hungry. I am content whether I have more than enough or not enough. 13 I can do all this by the power of Christ. He gives me strength.

I can do all this by the power of Christ. He gives me strength.
PHILIPPIANS 4:13

14 But it was good of you to share in my troubles. 15 And you believers at Philippi know what happened when I left Macedonia. Not one church helped me in the matter of giving and receiving. You were the only one that did. That was in the early days when you first heard the good news. 16 Even when I was in Thessalonica, you sent me help when I needed it. And you did it more than once. 17 It is not that I want your gifts. What I really want is what is best for you. 18 I have received my full pay and have more than enough. I have everything I need. That's because Epaphroditus brought me the gifts you sent. They are a sweet-smelling offering. They are a gift that God accepts. He is pleased with it. 19 My God will meet all your needs. He will meet them in keeping with his wonderful riches. These riches come to you because you belong to Christ Jesus.

20 Give glory to our God and Father for ever and ever. Amen.

Final Greetings

21 Greet all God's people. They belong to Christ Jesus.

The brothers and sisters who are with me send greetings.

22 All God's people here send you greetings. Most of all, those who live in the palace of Caesar send you greetings.

23 May the grace of the Lord Jesus Christ be with your spirit. Amen.

COLOSSIANS

Author: Paul

While Paul was in prison, another missionary named Epaphras told Paul about a group of new Christians in a city called Colossae. Epaphras was teaching these Christians about Jesus. However, these Christians were often tempted to go back to living like they did before they knew Jesus. They were being pressured by nonbelievers to give up their faith. At times, it seemed easier to give in and live the way they did before they believed in Jesus.

Letters & Revelation

Even though Paul had never met the Christians in Colossae, he, along with Timothy, wrote the Colossians this letter to encourage them. Paul told them that Jesus is worth more than anything. Paul also reminded them of everything Jesus did—especially how he defeated death by dying on the cross and rising from the grave. Through Christ's life, death, and resurrection, a new and better way of living was possible. Paul told the Colossians that he and Timothy were praying that God would fill them with wisdom and that the Holy Spirit would help them understand what it means to follow Jesus. When God saves us, he transforms us by his power so that we will live holy lives that humbly serve others and bring him glory.

1 I, Paul, am writing this letter. I am
an apostle of Christ Jesus just as God
planned. Our brother Timothy joins me
in writing.

2 We are sending this letter to you,
our brothers and sisters in Colossae.
You belong to Christ. You are holy and
faithful.

May God our Father give you grace
and peace.

Paul Prays and Gives Thanks

3 We always thank God, the Father of
our Lord Jesus Christ, when we pray for
you. 4 We thank him because we have
heard about your faith in Christ Jesus.
We have also heard that you love all
God's people. 5 Your faith and love are
based on the hope you have. What you
hope for is stored up for you in heav-
en. You have already heard about it.
You were told about it when the true
message was given to you. I'm talking
about the good news 6 that has come to
you. In the same way, the good news
is bearing fruit. It is bearing fruit and
growing all over the world. It has been
doing that among you since the day
you heard it. That is when you really
understood God's grace. 7 You learned
the good news from Epaphras. He is
dear to us. He serves Christ together
with us. He faithfully works for Christ
and for us among you. 8 He also told
us about your love that comes from
the Holy Spirit.
9 That's why we have not stopped
praying for you. We have been praying
for you since the day we heard about
you. We keep asking God to fill you with
the knowledge of what he wants. We
pray he will give you the wisdom and
understanding that the Spirit gives.
10 Then you will be able to lead a life
that is worthy of the Lord. We pray that
you will please him in every way. So we
want you to bear fruit in every good
thing you do. We pray that you will
grow to know God better. 11 We want
you to be very strong, in keeping with
his glorious power. We want you to be
patient. We pray that you will never
give up. 12 We want you to give thanks
with joy to the Father. He has made you
fit to have what he will give to all his
holy people. You will all receive a share

in Colossians?

God is the Greatest Treasure. Anything we sacrifice or give up to follow Jesus is nothing compared to his goodness toward us.

in the kingdom of light. 13 He has saved
us from the kingdom of darkness. He
has brought us into the kingdom of the
Son he loves. 14 Because of what the Son
has done, we have been set free. Because
of him, all our sins have been forgiven.

The Son of God Is Better Than Everything Else

15 The Son is the exact likeness of God,
who can't be seen. The Son is first, and
he is over all creation. 16 All things were
created in him. He created everything
in heaven and on earth. He created
everything that can be seen and everything that can't be seen. He created
kings, powers, rulers and authorities. All
things have been created by him and
for him. 17 Before anything was created,
he was already there. He holds everything together. 18 And he is the head of
the body, which is the church. He is the
beginning. He is the first to be raised
from the dead. That happened so that
he would be far above everything. 19 God
was pleased to have his whole nature
living in Christ. 20 God was pleased to
bring all things back to himself. That's
because of what Christ has done. These
things include everything on earth and
in heaven. God made peace through
Christ's blood, by his death on the cross.
21 At one time you were separated
from God. You were enemies in your
minds because of your evil ways. 22 But
because Christ died, God has brought

SOVEREIGN

God is the rightful Ruler over all things. Though there are many earthly rulers, such as kings, presidents, and leaders, God was never appointed or elected as king. No one could make him king because he *is already* the rightful King over everything.

God's sovereignty means he is in charge of all creation. Everything is under his control (see Psalm 50:10–12). This is a good thing because he sees and knows everything. He is present in all creation, and there is no end to his reign. God is a good King, and he will be King over all forever!

you back to himself. Christ's death
has made you holy in God's sight. So
now you don't have any flaw. You are
free from blame. 23 But you must keep
your faith steady and firm. You must
not move away from the hope the
good news holds out to you. This is the
good news that you heard. It has been
preached to every creature under heav-
en. I, Paul, now serve the good news.

Paul's Work for the Church

24 I am happy because of what I am
suffering for you. My suffering joins
with and continues the sufferings of
Christ. I suffer for his body, which is the
church. 25 I serve the church. God appointed me to bring the complete word
of God to you. 26 That word contains the
mystery that has been hidden for many
ages. But now it has been made known
to the Lord's people. 27 God has chosen
to make known to them the glorious
riches of that mystery. He has made it
known among the Gentiles. And here
is what it is. Christ is in you. He is your
hope of glory.

28 Christ is the one we preach about.
With all the wisdom we have, we warn
and teach everyone. When we bring
them to God, we want them to be like
Christ. We want them to be grown up as
people who belong to Christ. 29 That's
what I'm working for. I work hard with
all the strength of Christ. His strength
works powerfully in me.

2 I want you to know how hard I am
working for you. I'm concerned for
those who are in Laodicea. I'm also concerned for everyone who has not met me
in person. 2 My goal is that their hearts
may be encouraged and strengthened.
I want them to be joined together in
love. Then their understanding will be
rich and complete. They will know the
mystery of God. That mystery is Christ.
3 All the treasures of wisdom and knowledge are hidden in him. 4 But I don't
want anyone to fool you with words that
only sound good. 5 So even though I am
away from you in body, I am with you
in spirit. And I am glad to see that you
are controlling yourselves. I am happy
that your faith in Christ is so strong.

Having All Things in Christ

6 You received Christ Jesus as Lord. So
keep on living your lives in him. 7 Have
your roots in him. Build yourselves up
in him. Grow strong in what you believe, just as you were taught. Be more
thankful than ever before.

8 Make sure no one controls you. They
will try to control you by using false reasoning that has no meaning. Their ideas
depend on human teachings. They also
depend on the basic spiritual powers of
this world. They don't depend on Christ.

9 God's whole nature is living in Christ in human form. 10 Because you belong to Christ, you have been made complete. He is the ruler over every power and authority. 11 When you received Christ, your circumcision was not done by human hands. Instead, your circumcision was done by Christ. He put away the person you used to be. At that time, sin's power ruled over you. 12 When you were baptized, you were buried together with Christ. And you were raised to life together with him when you were baptized. You were raised to life by believing in God's work. God himself raised Jesus from the dead.

13 At one time you were dead in your sins. Your desires controlled by sin were not circumcised. But God gave you new life together with Christ. He forgave us all our sins. 14 He wiped out what the law said that we owed. The law stood against us. It judged us. But he has taken it away and nailed it to the cross. 15 He took away the weapons of the powers and authorities. He made a public show of them. He won the battle over them by dying on the cross.

Freedom From Human Rules

16 So don't let anyone judge you because of what you eat or drink. Don't let anyone judge you about holy days. I'm talking about special feasts and New Moons and Sabbath days. 17 They are only a shadow of the things to come. But what is real is found in Christ. 18 Some people enjoy pretending they aren't proud. They worship angels. But don't let people like that judge you. These people tell you every little thing about what they have seen. They are proud of their useless ideas. That's because their minds are not guided by the Holy Spirit. 19 They aren't connected anymore to the head, who is Christ. But the whole body grows from the head. The muscles and tendons hold the body together. And God causes it to grow.

20 Some people still follow the basic spiritual powers of the world. But you died with Christ as far as these powers are concerned. So why do you act as if you still belong to the world? Here are the rules you follow. 21 "Do not handle! Do not taste! Do not touch!" 22 Rules like these are about things that will pass away soon. They are based on merely human rules and teachings. 23 It is true that these rules seem wise. Because of them, people give themselves over to their own kind of worship. They pretend they are humble. They treat their bodies very badly. But rules like these don't help. They don't stop people from chasing after sinful pleasures.

Teachings About Holy Living

3 You have been raised up with Christ. So think about things that are in heaven. That is where Christ is. He is sitting at God's right hand. 2 Think about things that are in heaven. Don't think about things that are only on earth. 3 You died. Now your life is hidden with Christ in God. 4 Christ is your life. When he appears again, you also will appear with him in heaven's glory.

key verse

You have been raised up with Christ. So think about things that are in heaven. That is where Christ is. He is sitting at God's right hand.

COLOSSIANS 3:1

5 So put to death anything that comes from sinful desires. Get rid of sexual sins and impure acts. Don't let your feelings get out of control. Remove from your life all evil desires. Stop always wanting more and more. You might as well be worshiping statues of gods. 6 God's anger is going to come because of these things. 7 That's the way you lived at one time in your life. 8 But now here are the kinds of things you must also get rid of. You must get rid of anger, rage, hate and lies. Let no dirty words come out of your mouths. 9 Don't lie to one another. You have gotten rid of your old way of life and its habits. 10 You have started living a new life. Your knowledge of how that life should have the Creator's likeness is being made new. 11 Here there is no Gentile or Jew. There is no difference between those who are circumcised and those who are not. There is no rude outsider, or even a Scythian. There is no slave or free person. But Christ is everything. And he is in everything.

12 You are God's chosen people. You
are holy and dearly loved. So put on
tender mercy and kindness as if they
were your clothes. Don't be proud. Be
gentle and patient. 13 Put up with one
another. Forgive one another if you are
holding something against someone.
Forgive, just as the Lord forgave you.
14 And over all these good things put
on love. Love holds them all together
perfectly as if they were one.
15 Let the peace that Christ gives rule
in your hearts. As parts of one body,
you were appointed to live in peace.
And be thankful. 16 Let the message
about Christ live among you like a rich
treasure. Teach and correct one another
wisely. Teach one another by singing
psalms and hymns and songs from the
Spirit. Sing to God with thanks in your
hearts. 17 Do everything you say or do in
the name of the Lord Jesus. Always give
thanks to God the Father through Christ.

Teachings About Christian Families

18 Wives, follow the lead of your husbands. That's what the Lord wants you
to do.
19 Husbands, love your wives. Don't
be mean to them.
20 Children, obey your parents in everything. That pleases the Lord.
21 Fathers, don't make your children
bitter. If you do, they will lose hope.
22 Slaves, obey your earthly masters
in everything. Don't do it just to please
them when they are watching you.
Obey them with an honest heart. Do
it out of respect for the Lord. 23 Work at
everything you do with all your heart.
Work as if you were working for the
Lord, not for human masters. 24 Work
because you know that you will finally
receive as a reward what the Lord wants
you to have. You are slaves of the Lord
Christ. 25 Anyone who does wrong will be
paid back for what they do. God treats
everyone the same.

4 Masters, give your slaves what is
right and fair. Do it because you
know that you also have a Master in
heaven.

More Teachings

2 Give a lot of time and effort to prayer.
Always be watchful and thankful. 3 Pray
for us too. Pray that God will give us an
opportunity to preach our message.
Then we can preach the mystery of
Christ. Because I preached it, I am being
held by chains. 4 Pray that I will preach
it clearly, as I should. 5 Be wise in the
way you act toward outsiders. Make
the most of every opportunity. 6 Let
the words you speak always be full of
grace. Learn how to make your words
what people want to hear. Then you will
know how to answer everyone.

Final Greetings

7 Tychicus will tell you all the news
about me. He is a dear brother. He is
a faithful worker. He serves the Lord
together with us. 8 I am sending him to
you for one reason. I want you to know
what is happening here. I want him to
encourage you and make your hearts
strong. 9 He is coming with Onesimus,
our faithful and dear brother. He is one
of you. They will tell you everything
that is happening here.

10 Aristarchus is in prison with me. He
sends you his greetings. So does Mark,
the cousin of Barnabas. You have been
given directions about him. If he comes
to you, welcome him.
11 Jesus, who is called Justus, also
sends greetings. They are the only Jews

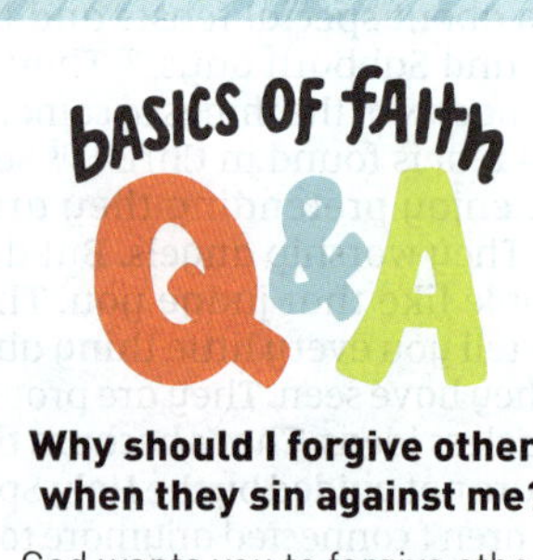

Why should I forgive others when they sin against me?

God wants you to forgive others because of how much he has forgiven you. God always forgives you when you ask, and you grow to be more like him when you freely forgive others.

Can you find the following verse?

COLOSSIANS 3:13

who have worked together with me
for God's kingdom. They have been a
comfort to me.
12 Epaphras sends greetings. He is
one of you. He serves Christ Jesus. He is
always praying hard for you. He prays
that you will hold on tightly to all that
God has in mind for us. He prays that
you will keep growing in your knowledge of what God wants. He also prays
that you will be completely sure about
it. 13 I am happy to tell you that he is
working very hard for you. He is also
working hard for everyone in Laodicea
and Hierapolis.
14 Our dear friend Luke, the doctor,
sends greetings. So does Demas.

15 Give my greetings to the brothers
and sisters in Laodicea. Also give my
greetings to Nympha and the church
that meets in her house.

16 After this letter has been read to you,
send it on. Be sure that it is also read
to the church in Laodicea. And be sure
that you read the letter from Laodicea.

17 Tell Archippus, "Be sure that you
complete the work the Lord gave you
to do."

18 I, Paul, am writing this greeting
with my own hand. Remember that
I am being held by chains. May grace
be with you.

1 THESSALONIANS

Author: Paul

In the book of Acts, we learn about Paul and his coworker Silas going to the city of Thessalonica to teach the Thessalonians the Good News. As a result of their visit, many of the Thessalonians began to follow Jesus. But the local rulers didn't like that these new Christians were following King Jesus because they wanted to be the only rulers over the people. They treated the new Jesus followers badly, forcing Paul and Silas to flee from the city for safety (see Acts 17:1–10).

Letters & Revelation

Timothy visited Paul, reporting that the Thessalonians were standing strong in their faith despite persecution. Paul was delighted to hear this news and wrote the Thessalonians two letters in response. In this first letter, he rejoiced because the believers were growing in their faith! Paul encouraged them to keep living in a way that pleased God and reminded them to put their hope in Jesus' return. This is also known as the "day of the Lord" (1 Thessalonians 5:2), the day when Jesus will establish his forever kingdom. In the meantime, Paul reminded the Thessalonians that following Jesus meant responding to their enemies with love and mercy. This kind of response was one of the ways the message of the gospel would spread!

1 I, Paul, am writing this letter. Silas and Timothy join me in writing.

We are sending this letter to you, the members of the church in Thessalonica. You belong to God the Father and the Lord Jesus Christ.

May grace and peace be given to you.

Paul Gives Thanks for the Thessalonians' Faith

2 We always thank God for all of you. We keep on praying for you. 3 We remember you when we pray to our God and Father. Your work is produced by your faith. Your service is the result of your love. Your strength to continue comes from your hope in our Lord Jesus Christ.

4 Brothers and sisters, you are loved by God. We know that he has chosen you. 5 Our good news didn't come to you only in words. It came with power. It came with the Holy Spirit's help. He gave us complete faith in what we were preaching. You know how we lived among you for your good. 6 We and the Lord were your examples. You followed us. You welcomed our message even when you were suffering terribly. You welcomed it with the joy the Holy Spirit gives. 7 So you became a model to all the believers in the lands of Macedonia and Achaia. 8 The Lord's message rang out from you. That was true not only in Macedonia and Achaia. Your faith in God has also become known everywhere. So we don't have to say anything about it. 9 The believers themselves report the kind of welcome you gave us. They tell about how you turned away from statues of gods. And you turned to serve the living and true God. 10 They tell about how you are waiting for his Son to come from heaven. God raised him from the dead. He is Jesus. He saves us from God's anger, and his anger is sure to come.

Paul's Work for God in Thessalonica

2 Brothers and sisters, you know that our visit to you produced results. 2 You know what happened earlier in the city of Philippi. We suffered, and people treated us very badly there. But God gave us the boldness to tell you his good news. We preached to you even when people strongly opposed us. 3 The

in 1 Thessalonians?

God is the All-Powerful Savior. Jesus came for the first time as a baby, and he will come again as the victorious King.

appeal we make is based on truth. It comes from a pure heart. We are not trying to trick you. 4 In fact, it is just the opposite. God has approved us to preach. He has trusted us with the good news. We aren't trying to please people. We want to please God. He tests our hearts. 5 As you know, we never praised you if we didn't mean it. We didn't put on a mask to cover up any sinful desire. God is our witness that this is true. 6 We were not expecting people to praise us. We were not looking for praise from you or anyone else. Yet as Christ's apostles, we could have used our authority over you. 7 Instead, we were like young children when we were with you.

As a mother feeds and cares for her little children, 8 we cared for you. We loved you so much. So we were happy to share with you God's good news. We were also happy to share our lives with you. 9 Brothers and sisters, I am sure you remember how hard we worked. We labored night and day while we preached to you God's good news. We didn't want to cause you any expense. 10 You are witnesses of how we lived among you believers. God is also a witness that we were holy and godly and without blame. 11 You know that we treated each of you as a father treats his own children. 12 We gave you hope and strength. We comforted you. We really wanted you to live in a way that is worthy of God. He chooses you to enter his glorious kingdom.

13 We never stop thanking God for the
way you received his word. You heard
it from us. But you didn't accept it as a
human word. You accepted it for what
it really is. It is God's word. It is really at
work in you who believe. 14 Brothers and
sisters, you became like the members
of God's churches in Judea. They are
believers in Christ Jesus, just as you
are. Your own people made you suffer.
You went through the same things the
church members in Judea suffered from
the Jews. 15 The Jews who killed the Lord
Jesus and the prophets also forced us
to leave. They do not please God. They
are enemies of everyone. 16 They try to
keep us from speaking to the Gentiles.
These Jews don't want the Gentiles to
be saved. In this way, these Jews always
increase their sins to the limit. God's
anger has come on them at last.

Paul Wants to See the Believers in Thessalonica

17 Brothers and sisters, we were separated from you for a short time. Apart
from you, we were like children without
parents. We were no longer with you in
person. But we kept you in our thoughts.
We really wanted to see you. So we tried
very hard to do so. 18 We wanted to come
to you. Again and again I, Paul, wanted
to come. But Satan blocked our way.
19 What is our hope? What is our joy?
When our Lord Jesus returns, what is
the crown we will delight in? Isn't it you?
20 Yes, you are our glory and our joy.

3 We couldn't wait any longer. So we
thought it was best to be left by ourselves in Athens. 2 We sent our brother
Timothy to give you strength and hope
in your faith. He works together with us
in God's service to spread the good news
about Christ. 3 We sent him so that no
one would be upset by times of testing.
You know very well that we have to
go through times of testing. 4 In fact,
when we were with you, here is what
we kept telling you. We were telling
you that our enemies would make us
suffer. As you know very well, it has
turned out that way. 5 That's the reason
I sent someone to find out about your
faith. I couldn't wait any longer. I was
afraid that Satan had tempted you in
some way. Then our work among you
would have been useless.

Timothy Brings a Good Report

6 But Timothy has come to us from
you just now. He has brought good
news about your faith and love. He
has told us that you always have happy
memories of us. He has also said that
you desire to see us, just as we desire
to see you. 7 Brothers and sisters, in all
our trouble and suffering your faith
encouraged us. 8 Now we really live,
because you are standing firm in the
Lord. 9 How can we thank God enough
for you? We thank God because of all
the joy we have in his presence. We have
this joy because of you. 10 Night and
day we pray very hard that we will see
you again. We want to give you what
is missing in your faith.

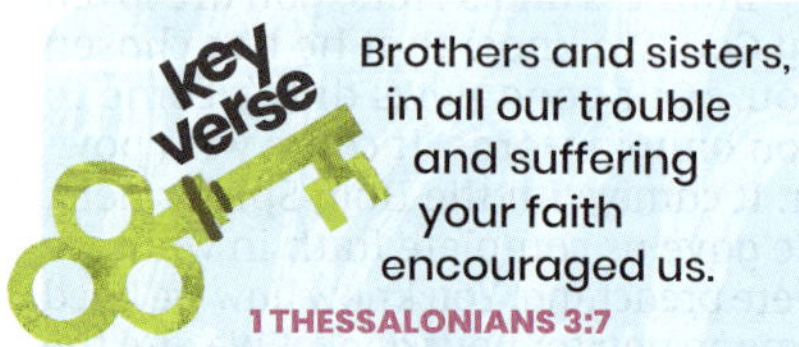

11 Now may a way be opened up for
us to come to you. May our God and
Father himself and our Lord Jesus do
this. 12 May the Lord make your love
grow. May it be like a rising flood. May
your love for one another increase. May
it also increase for everyone else. May it
be just like our love for you. 13 May the
Lord give you strength in your hearts.
Then you will be holy and without
blame in the sight of our God and Father. May that be true when our Lord
Jesus comes with all his holy ones.

Living in a Way That Pleases God

4 Now I want to talk about some
other matters, brothers and sisters.
We taught you how to live in a way that
pleases God. In fact, that is how you are
living. In the name of the Lord Jesus
we ask and beg you to do it more and
more. 2 You know the directions we gave
you. They were given by the authority
of the Lord Jesus.

3 God wants you to be made holy. He
wants you to stay away from sexual
sins. 4 He wants all of you to learn to
control your own bodies. You must live
in a way that is holy. You must live with

honor. 5 Don't desire to commit sexual sins like people who don't know God. 6 None of you should sin against your brother or sister by doing that. You should not take advantage of your brother or sister. The Lord will punish everyone who commits these kinds of sins. We have already told you and warned you about this. 7 That's because God chose us to live pure lives. He wants us to be holy. 8 Suppose someone refuses to accept our teaching. They are not turning their back on us. They are turning their back on God. This same God gives you his Holy Spirit.

9 We don't need to write to you about your love for one another. God himself has taught you to love one another. 10 In fact, you do love all God's family all around Macedonia. Brothers and sisters, we are asking you to love one another more and more. 11 And do everything you can to live a quiet life. You should mind your own business. And work with your hands, just as we told you to. 12 Then unbelievers will have respect for your everyday life. And you won't have to depend on anyone.

What Happens to Believers Who Have Died

13 Brothers and sisters, we want you to know what happens to those who die. We don't want you to mourn, as other people do. They mourn because they don't have any hope. 14 We believe that Jesus died and rose again. When he returns, many who believe in him will have died already. We believe that God will bring them back with Jesus. 15 This agrees with what the Lord has said. When the Lord comes, many of us will still be alive. We tell you that we will certainly not go up before those who have died. 16 The Lord himself will come down from heaven. We will hear a loud command. We will hear the voice of the leader of the angels. We will hear a blast from God's trumpet. Many who believe in Christ will have died already. They will rise first. 17 After that, we who are still alive and are left will be caught up together with them. We will be taken up in the clouds. We will meet the Lord in the air. And we will be with him forever. 18 So encourage one another with these words of comfort.

The Day of the Lord Is Coming

5 Brothers and sisters, we don't have to write to you about times and dates. 2 You know very well how the day of the Lord will come. It will come like a thief in the night. 3 People will be saying that everything is peaceful and safe. Then suddenly they will be destroyed. It will happen like birth pains coming on a pregnant woman. None of the people will escape.

4 Brothers and sisters, you are not in darkness. So that day should not surprise you as a thief would. 5 All of you are children of the light. You are children of the day. We don't belong to the night. We don't belong to the darkness. 6 So let us not be like the others. They are asleep. Instead, let us be wide awake and in full control of ourselves. 7 Those who sleep, sleep at night. Those who get drunk, get drunk at night. 8 But we belong to the day. So let us control ourselves. Let us put on our chest the armor of faith and love. Let us put on the hope of salvation like a helmet. 9 God didn't choose us to receive his anger. He chose us to receive salvation because of what our Lord Jesus Christ has done. 10 Jesus died for us. Some will be alive when he comes. Others will be dead. Either way, we will live together with him. 11 So encourage one another with the hope you have. Build each other up. In fact, that's what you are doing.

Final Teachings

12 Brothers and sisters, we ask you to accept the godly leaders who work hard among you. They care for you in the Lord. They correct you. 13 Have a lot of respect for them. Love them because of what they do. Live in peace with one another. 14 Brothers and sisters, we are asking you to warn certain people. These people don't want to work. Instead, they make trouble. We are also asking you to encourage those who have lost hope. Help those who are weak. Be patient with everyone. 15 Make sure that no one pays back one wrong act with another. Instead, always try to do what is good for each other and for everyone else.

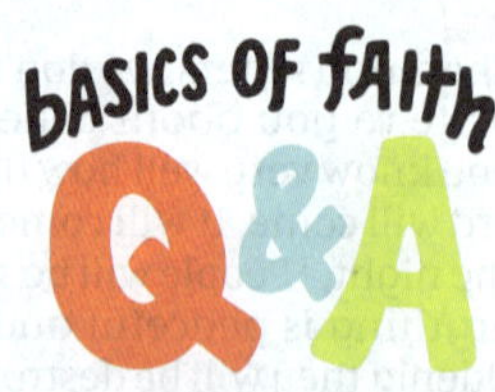

Where can I find peace?

Peace is found in God alone. Jesus made it possible for people to have peace with God. When you put your trust in Jesus, the Holy Spirit guides you to live at peace with others.

Can you find the following verse?

1 THESSALONIANS 5:23

16 Always be joyful. 17 Never stop
praying. 18 Give thanks no matter
what happens. God wants you to thank
him because you believe in Christ
Jesus.
19 Don't try to stop what the Holy Spirit is doing. 20 Don't treat prophecies as
if they weren't important. 21 But test all
prophecies. Hold on to what is good.
22 Say no to every kind of evil.
23 God is the God who gives peace.
May he make you holy through and
through. May your whole spirit, soul
and body be kept free from blame. May
you be without blame from now until
our Lord Jesus Christ comes. 24 The God
who has chosen you is faithful. He will
do all these things.

25 Brothers and sisters, pray for us.

26 Greet all God's people with a holy
kiss.

27 While the Lord is watching, here is
what I command you. Have this letter
read to all the brothers and sisters.

28 May the grace of our Lord Jesus
Christ be with you.

2 THESSALONIANS

Author: Paul

After Paul sent his first letter, he heard that things had gotten worse in Thessalonica—the Christians were being mistreated more, and they were confused about the day of the Lord. Paul wrote this second letter to help the Thessalonians understand how the hope of Jesus' return could give them strength to endure persecution. He reminded them that God saw them in their suffering and would be faithful to protect them from the evil one.

Paul also encouraged the Thessalonians by explaining that while they were waiting for the Lord's return, God was working in their lives to make them more like Jesus. Paul wanted them to remain hopeful and persevere because the hope God gives is good. God had not left them to suffer unfair treatment on their own but had given them his Spirit to dwell within them. Paul urged them not to become lazy or grow weary but to keep sharing the Good News because the day of the Lord was drawing near. They didn't need to live in fear; rather, they could live confidently, knowing God loved them and Jesus would come again.

Letters & Revelation

1 I, Paul, am writing this letter. Silas
and Timothy join me in writing.

We are sending this letter to you, the
members of the church in Thessalonica.
You belong to God our Father and the
Lord Jesus Christ.

2 May God the Father and the Lord
Jesus Christ give you grace and peace.

Paul Prays and Gives Thanks

3 Brothers and sisters, we should always thank God for you. That is only
right, because your faith is growing
more and more. We also thank God that
the love you all have for one another is
increasing. 4 So among God's churches
we brag about the fact that you don't
give up easily. We brag about your faith
in all the suffering and testing you are
going through.
5 All of this proves that when God
judges, he is fair. So you will be considered worthy to enter God's kingdom.
You are suffering for his kingdom. 6 God
is fair. He will pay back trouble to those
who give you trouble. 7 He will help you
who are troubled. And he will also help
us. All these things will happen when
the Lord Jesus appears from heaven. He
will come in blazing fire. He will come
with his powerful angels. 8 He will punish those who don't know God. He will
punish those who don't obey the good
news about our Lord Jesus. 9 They will
be destroyed forever. They will be shut
out of heaven. They will never see the
glory of the Lord's strength. 10 All these
things will happen when he comes. On
that day his glory will be seen in his
holy people. Everyone who has believed
will be amazed when they see him. This
includes you, because you believed the
witness we gave you.
11 Keeping this in mind, we never stop
praying for you. Our God has chosen
you. We pray that he will make you
worthy of his choice. We pray he will
make every good thing you want to do
come true. We pray that he will do this
by his power. We pray that he will make
perfect all that you have done by faith.
12 We pray this so that the name of our
Lord Jesus will receive glory through
what you have done. We also pray that
you will receive glory through what he
has done. We pray all these things in
keeping with the grace of our God and
the Lord Jesus Christ.

The Man of Sin

2 Brothers and sisters, we want to ask
you something. It has to do with
the coming of our Lord Jesus Christ.
It concerns the time when we will go
to be with him. 2 What if you receive a
message that is supposed to have come
from us? What if it says that the day of
the Lord has already come? If it does,
we ask you not to become easily upset
or alarmed. Don't be upset whether that
message is spoken or written or prophesied. 3 Don't let anyone trick you in any
way. That day will not come until people rise up against God. It will not come
until the man of sin appears. He is a
marked man. He is headed for ruin. 4 He
will oppose everything that is called
God. He will oppose everything that is
worshiped. He will give himself power
over everything. He will set himself up
in God's temple. He will announce that
he himself is God.
5 Don't you remember? When I was
with you, I used to tell you these things.
6 Now you know what is holding back
the man of sin. He is held back so that
he can make his appearance at the right
time. 7 The secret power of sin is already
at work. But the one who now holds
back that power will keep doing it until
he is taken out of the way. 8 Then the
man of sin will appear. The Lord Jesus
will overthrow him with the breath of
his mouth. The glorious brightness of

in 2 Thessalonians?

God is the Giver of Strength. He provides his people with the energy they need to accomplish his good will.

How do I know that God will make all things right?

God sees everything, and he promises to be just and fair. When bad things happen, you can trust that Jesus will return and make all things right.

Can you find the following verses?

2 THESSALONIANS 1:6–7

Jesus' coming will destroy the man of
sin. 9 The coming of the man of sin will
fit how Satan works. The man of sin
will show his power through all kinds
of signs and wonders. These signs and
wonders will lead people astray. 10 So
people who are dying will be fooled
by this evil. These people are dying
because they refuse to love the truth.
The truth would save them. 11 So God will
fool them completely. Then they will
believe the lie. 12 Many will not believe
the truth. They will take pleasure in
evil. They will be judged.

Remain Strong in the Faith

13 Brothers and sisters, we should
always thank God for you. The Lord
loves you. That's because God chose
you as the first to be saved. Salvation
comes through the Holy Spirit's work.
He makes people holy. It also comes
through believing the truth. 14 He chose
you to be saved by accepting the good
news that we preach. And you will share
in the glory of our Lord Jesus Christ.

15 Brothers and sisters, remain strong
in the faith. Hold on to what we taught
you. We passed our teachings on to you
by what we preached and wrote.

16 Our Lord Jesus Christ and God
our Father loved us. By his grace God
gave us comfort that will last forever.
The hope he gave us is good. May our
Lord Jesus Christ and God our Father
17 comfort your hearts. May they make
you strong in every good thing you do
and say.

Paul Asks for Prayer

3 Now I want to talk about some other
matters. Brothers and sisters, pray
for us. Pray that the Lord's message will
spread quickly. Pray that others will
honor it just as you did. 2 And pray that
we will be saved from sinful and evil
people. Not everyone is a believer. 3 But
the Lord is faithful. He will strengthen
you. He will guard you from the evil
one. 4 We trust in the Lord. So we are
sure that you are doing the things we
tell you to do. And we are sure that you
will keep on doing them. 5 May the Lord
fill your hearts with God's love. May
Christ give you the strength to go on.

Brothers and sisters, in all our trouble and suffering your faith encouraged us.

1 THESSALONIANS 3:7

Paul Warns Those Who Do Not Want to Work

6 Brothers and sisters, here is a command we give you. We give it in the
name of the Lord Jesus Christ. Keep
away from every believer who doesn't
want to work and makes trouble. Keep
away from any believer who doesn't live
up to the teaching you received from
us. 7 You know how you should follow
our example. We worked when we were
with you. 8 We didn't eat anyone's food
without paying for it. In fact, it was
just the opposite. We worked night and
day. We worked very hard so that we
wouldn't cause any expense to any of
you. 9 We worked, even though we have
the right to receive help from you. We
did it in order to be a model for you to
follow. 10 Even when we were with you,
we gave you a rule. We said, "Anyone
who won't work shouldn't be allowed
to eat."

11 We hear that some people among
you don't want to work and are making trouble. They aren't really busy.

Instead, they are bothering others. [12] We belong to the Lord Jesus Christ. So we strongly command people like that to settle down. They have to earn the food they eat. [13] Brothers and sisters, don't ever get tired of doing what is good.

[14] Keep an eye on anyone who doesn't obey the teachings in our letter. Don't have anything to do with that person. Then they will feel ashamed. [15] But don't think of them as an enemy. Instead, warn them as you would warn another believer.

Final Greetings

[16] May the Lord who gives peace give you peace at all times and in every way. May the Lord be with all of you.

[17] I, Paul, write this greeting in my own handwriting. That's how I prove that I am the author of all my letters. I always do it that way.

[18] May the grace of our Lord Jesus Christ be with you all.

1 TIMOTHY

Author: Paul

On one of Paul's missionary journeys, he met a young man named Timothy. Paul knew that Timothy had genuine faith and would help spread the good news about Jesus around the world, so Paul took Timothy with him as he continued to travel and teach people about Jesus. Timothy helped Paul start a church in Ephesus, and when the time came for Paul to leave Ephesus, Timothy stayed to lead and teach the church. Later, Paul heard that things weren't going very well for the church in Ephesus—there were false teachers who were saying confusing and untrue things about what it meant to follow Jesus. So Paul wrote Timothy two letters. In this first letter, Paul encouraged the church community and leaders to remember the gospel and remain faithful to Scripture. He shared his own story of how God showed him grace and mercy. Then Paul reminded Timothy that helping the church in Ephesus was a God-given mission and urged him to remain confident in the Lord, even when things were hard. Paul also gave Timothy practical advice for how the church in Ephesus could grow and mature in their faith through prayer, good teaching, and godly leadership.

Letters & Revelation

in 1 Timothy?

God is the Gentle Shepherd. God never leaves his people alone but tenderly guides them, providing just enough for each day.

1 I, Paul, am writing this letter. I am an apostle of Christ Jesus, just as God our Savior commanded. Christ Jesus also commanded it. We have put our hope in him.

2 Timothy, I am sending you this letter. You are my true son in the faith.

May God the Father and Christ Jesus our Lord give you grace, mercy and peace.

Paul Warns Timothy to Oppose False Teachers

3 Timothy, stay there in Ephesus. That is what I told you to do when I went into Macedonia. I want you to command certain people not to teach things that aren't true. 4 And command them not to spend their time on stories that are made up. They must not waste time on family histories that never end. These things only lead to fights about ideas. They don't help God's work move forward. His work is done by faith. 5 Love is the purpose of my command. Love comes from a pure heart. It comes from a good sense of what is right and wrong. It comes from faith that is honest and true. 6 Some have turned from these teachings. They would rather talk about things that have no meaning. 7 They want to be teachers of the law. And they are very sure about that law. But they don't know what they are talking about.

8 We know that the law is good if it is used properly. 9 We also know that the law isn't made for godly people. It is made for those who break the law. It is for those who refuse to obey. It is for ungodly and sinful people. It is for those who aren't holy and who don't believe. It is for those who kill their fathers or mothers. It is for murderers. 10 It is for those who commit sexual sins. It is for those who commit homosexual acts. It is for people who buy and sell slaves. It is for liars. It is for people who tell lies in court. It is for those who are a witness to things that aren't true. And it is for anything else that is the opposite of true teaching. 11 True teaching agrees with the good news about the glory of the blessed God. He trusted me with that good news.

The Lord Pours Out His Grace on Paul

12 I am thankful to Christ Jesus our Lord. He has given me strength. I thank him that he considered me faithful. I thank him for appointing me to serve him. 13 I used to speak evil things against Jesus. I tried to hurt his followers. I really pushed them around. But God showed me mercy anyway. I did those things without knowing any better. I wasn't a believer. 14 Our Lord poured out more and more of his grace on me. Along with it came faith and love from Christ Jesus.

15 Here is a saying that you can trust. It should be accepted completely. Christ Jesus came into the world to save sinners. And I am the worst sinner of all. 16 But for that very reason, God showed me mercy. And I am the worst of sinners. He showed me mercy so that Christ Jesus could show that he is very patient. I was an example for those who would come to believe in him. Then they would receive eternal life. 17 The eternal King will never die. He can't be seen. He is the only God. Give him honor and glory for ever and ever. Amen.

Paul Commands Timothy

18 My son Timothy, I am giving you this command. It is in keeping with the prophecies once made about you. By remembering them, you can fight the battle well. 19 Then you will hold on to faith. You will hold on to a good sense of what is right and wrong. Some have not accepted this knowledge of right and wrong. So they have destroyed their faith. They are like a ship that

has sunk. 20 Hymenaeus and Alexander are among them. I have handed them over to Satan. That will teach them not to speak evil things against God.

Teachings About Worship

2 First, I want you to pray for all people. Ask God to help and bless them. Give thanks for them. 2 Pray for kings. Pray for everyone who is in authority. Pray that we can live peaceful and quiet lives. And pray that we will be godly and holy. 3 This is good, and it pleases God our Savior. 4 He wants all people to be saved. He wants them to come to know the truth. 5 There is only one God. And there is only one go-between for God and human beings. He is the man Christ Jesus. 6 He gave himself to pay for the sins of all people. We have been told this message at just the right time. 7 I was appointed to be a messenger and an apostle to preach the good news. I am telling the truth. I'm not lying. God appointed me to be a true and faithful teacher of the Gentiles.

8 So I want the men in every place to pray. I want them to lift up holy hands. I don't want them to be angry when they pray. I don't want them to argue. 9 In the same way, I want the women to be careful how they dress. They should wear clothes that are right and proper. They shouldn't wear their hair in very fancy styles. They shouldn't wear gold or pearls. They shouldn't wear clothes that cost a lot of money. 10 Instead, they should put on good works as if good works were their clothes. This is proper for women who claim to worship God.

11 When a woman is learning, she should be quiet. She should follow her leaders in every way. 12 I do not let women teach or take authority over a man. They must be quiet. 13 That's because Adam was made first. Then Eve was made. 14 Adam was not the one who was tricked. The woman was tricked and became a sinner. 15 Will women be saved by having children? Only if they keep on believing, loving, and leading a holy life in a proper way.

Rules for Choosing Leaders and Deacons

3 Here is a saying you can trust. If anyone wants to be a leader in the church, they want to do a good work for God and people. 2 A leader must be free from blame. He must be faithful to his wife. In anything he does, he must not go too far. He must control himself. He must be worthy of respect. He must welcome people into his home. He must be able to teach. 3 He must not get drunk. He must not push people around. He must be gentle. He must not be a person who likes to argue. He must not love money. 4 He must manage his own family well. He must make sure that his children obey him. And he must do this in a way that gains him respect. 5 Suppose someone doesn't know how to manage his own family. Then how can he take care of God's church? 6 The leader must not be a new believer. If he is, he might become proud. Then he would be judged just like the devil. 7 The leader must also be respected by those who are outside the church. Then he will not be put to shame. He will not fall into the devil's trap.

8 In the same way, deacons must be worthy of respect. They must be honest and true. They must not drink too much wine. They must not try to get money by cheating people. 9 They must hold on to the deep truths of the faith. Even their own minds tell them to do that. 10 First they must be tested. Then let them serve as deacons if there is nothing against them.

Do all people worship the same God?

The God of the Bible is the one true God. He is the only God who exists. Any other gods that people worship are false gods.

Can you find the following verse?

1 TIMOTHY 2:5

11 In the same way, the women must be worthy of respect. They must not say things that harm others. In anything they do, they must not go too far. They must be worthy of trust in everything. 12 A deacon must be faithful to his wife. He must manage his children and family well. 13 Those who have served well earn the full respect of others. They also become more sure of their faith in Christ Jesus.

Paul's Reasons for Giving Instructions to Timothy

14 I hope I can come to you soon. But now I am writing these instructions to you. 15 Then if I have to put off my visit, you will know how people should act in God's family. The family of God is the church of the living God. It is the pillar and foundation of the truth. 16 There is no doubt that true godliness comes from this great mystery.

Jesus came as a human being.
 The Holy Spirit proved that he
  was the Son of God.
He was seen by angels.
 He was preached among the
  nations.
People in the world believed in him.
 He was taken up to heaven in
  glory.

4 The Holy Spirit clearly says that in the last days some people will leave the faith. They will follow spirits that will fool them. They will believe things that demons will teach them. 2 Teachings like those come from liars who pretend to be what they are not. Their sense of what is right and wrong has been destroyed. It's as though it has been burned with a hot iron. 3 They do not allow people to get married. They order them not to eat certain foods. But God created those foods. So people who believe and know the truth should receive them and give thanks for them. 4 Everything God created is good. You shouldn't turn anything down. Instead, you should thank God for it. 5 The word of God and prayer make it holy.

6 Point out these things to the brothers and sisters. Then you will serve Christ Jesus well. You will show that you've grown in the truths of the faith. You will show that you've been trained by the good teaching you've obeyed. 7 Don't have anything to do with godless stories and silly tales. Instead, train yourself to be godly. 8 Training the body has some value. But being godly has value in every way. It promises help for the life you are now living and the life to come. 9 This is the truth you can trust and accept completely. 10 This is why we work and try so hard. It's because we have put our hope in the living God. He is the Savior of all people. Most of all, he is the Savior of those who believe.

11 Command and teach these things. 12 Don't let anyone look down on you because you are young. Set an example for the believers in what you say and in how you live. Also set an example in how you love and in what you believe. Show the believers how to be pure. 13 Until I come, spend your time reading Scripture out loud to one another. Spend your time preaching and teaching. 14 Don't fail to use the gift the Holy Spirit gave you. He gave it to you through a prophecy from God. It was given when the elders placed their hands on you.

key verse

Don't let anyone look down on you because you are young. Set an example for the believers in what you say and in how you live.

1 TIMOTHY 4:12

15 Keep on doing these things. Give them your complete attention. Then everyone will see how you are coming along. 16 Be careful of how you live and what you believe. Never give up. Then you will save yourself and those who hear you.

Instructions About Widows, Elders and Slaves

5 Correct an older man in a way that shows respect. Make an appeal to him as if he were your father. Treat younger men as if they were your brothers. 2 Treat older women as if they were your mothers. Treat younger women as if they were your sisters. Be completely pure in the way you treat them.

3 Take care of the widows who really
need help. 4 But suppose a widow has
children or grandchildren. They should
first learn to put their faith into practice. They should care for their own
family. In that way they will pay back
their parents and grandparents. That
pleases God. 5 A widow who really needs
help and is left all alone puts her hope
in God. Night and day she keeps on
praying. Night and day she asks God
for help. 6 But a widow who lives for
pleasure is dead even while she is still
living. 7 Give these instructions to the
people. Then no one can be blamed.
8 Everyone should provide for their own
relatives. Most of all, everyone should
take care of their own family. If they
don't, they have left the faith. They
are worse than someone who doesn't
believe.

9 No widow should be put on the list
of widows unless she is more than 60
years old. She must also have been
faithful to her husband. 10 She must
be well known for the good things she
does. That includes bringing up children. It includes inviting guests into
her home. It includes washing the feet
of the Lord's people. It includes helping those who are in trouble. A widow
should spend her time doing all kinds
of good things.

11 Don't put younger widows on that
kind of list. They might want pleasure
more than they want Christ. Then they
would want to get married again. 12 If
they do that, they will be judged. They
have broken their first promise. 13 Besides, they get into the habit of having
nothing to do. They go around from
house to house. They waste their time.
They also bother other people and
say things that make no sense. They
shouldn't say those things. 14 So here
is the advice I give to younger widows.
Get married. Have children. Take care of
your own homes. Don't give the enemy
the chance to tell lies about you. 15 In
fact, some have already turned away
to follow Satan.

16 Suppose a woman is a believer
and takes care of widows. She should
continue to help them. She shouldn't
let the church pay the expenses. Then
the church can help the widows who
really need it.

17 The elders who do the church's work
well are worth twice as much honor.
That is true in a special way of elders
who preach and teach. 18 Scripture says,
"Do not stop an ox from eating while
it helps separate the grain from the
straw." *(Deuteronomy 25:4)* Scripture
also says, "Workers are worthy of their
pay." *(Luke 10:7)* 19 Don't believe a charge
against an elder unless two or three
witnesses bring it. 20 But those elders
who are sinning should be corrected in
front of everyone. This will be a warning to the others. 21 I command you to
follow these instructions. I command
you in the sight of God and Christ Jesus
and the chosen angels. Treat everyone
the same. Don't favor one person over
another.

22 Don't be too quick to place your
hands on others to set them apart to
serve God. Don't take part in the sins
of others. Keep yourself pure.

23 Stop drinking only water. If your
stomach is upset, drink a little wine. It
can also help the other sicknesses you
often have.

24 The sins of some people are easy
to see. They are already being judged.
Others will be judged later. 25 In the
same way, good works are easy to see.
But even good works that are hard to
see can't stay hidden forever.

6 All who are forced to serve as slaves
should consider their masters worthy of full respect. Then people will not
speak evil things against God's name
and against what we teach. 2 Some
slaves have masters who are believers. They shouldn't show their masters
disrespect just because they are also
believers. Instead, they should serve
them even better. That's because their
masters are loved by them as believers.
These masters are committed to caring
for their slaves.

People Who Teach Lies or Love Money

These are the things you are to teach.
Try hard to get the believers to do them.
3 Suppose someone teaches something
different than I have taught. Suppose
that person doesn't agree with the true
teaching of our Lord Jesus Christ. Suppose they don't agree with godly teaching. 4 Then that person is proud and

doesn't understand anything. They like
to argue more than they should. They
can't agree about what words mean. All
of this results in wanting what others
have. It causes fighting, harmful talk,
and evil distrust. 5 It stirs up trouble all
the time among people whose minds
are twisted by sin. The truth they once
had has been taken away from them.
They think they can get rich by being
godly.

6 You gain a lot when you live a godly
life. But you must be happy with what
you have. 7 We didn't bring anything
into the world. We can't take anything
out of it. 8 If we have food and clothing,
we will be happy with that. 9 People
who want to get rich are tempted. They
fall into a trap. They are tripped up by
wanting many foolish and harmful
things. Those who live like that are
dragged down by what they do. They
are destroyed and die. 10 Love for money causes all kinds of evil. Some people
want to get rich. They have wandered
away from the faith. They have wounded themselves with many sorrows.

Paul Gives a Final Command to Timothy

11 But you are a man of God. Run away
from all these things. Try hard to do
what is right and godly. Have faith, love
and gentleness. Hold on to what you believe. 12 Fight the good fight along with
all other believers. Take hold of eternal
life. You were chosen for it when you
openly told others what you believe.
Many witnesses heard you. 13 God gives
life to everything. Christ Jesus told the
truth when he was a witness in front of
Pontius Pilate. In the sight of God and
Christ, I give you a command. 14 Obey
it until our Lord Jesus Christ appears.
Obey it completely. Then no one can
find fault with it or you. 15 God will bring
Jesus back at a time that pleases him.
God is the blessed and only Ruler. He is
the greatest King of all. He is the most
powerful Lord of all. 16 God is the only
one who can't die. He lives in light that
no one can get close to. No one has seen
him. No one can see him. Honor and
power belong to him forever. Amen.

17 Command people who are rich in
this world not to be proud. Tell them
not to put their hope in riches. Wealth

GENEROUS

My GOD is...

God willingly and joyfully gives good gifts to others even when it costs him a whole lot.

Have you ever given a friend or family member a gift? When we've worked hard to be able to buy a gift at the store or spent a lot of time and attention to make a gift, we feel excited about giving someone our gift. We want them to enjoy it! This desire to give is called *generosity*, and it comes from God. He delights in giving to others, and he is generous to give us exactly what we need (see Romans 8:32).

God was very generous when Jesus willingly went to the cross to pay for the sins of the world. That gift cost Jesus his life, and yet he generously gave up his life for us.

is so uncertain. Command those who
are rich to put their hope in God. He
richly provides us with everything to
enjoy. 18 Command the rich to do what
is good. Tell them to be rich in doing
good things. They must give freely.
They must be willing to share. 19 In this
way, they will store up true riches for
themselves. It will provide a firm basis
for the next life. Then they will take hold
of the life that really is life.

20 Timothy, guard what God has
trusted you with. Turn away from godless chatter. Stay away from opposing
ideas that are falsely called knowledge.
21 Some people believe them. By doing
that they have turned away from the
faith.

May God's grace be with you all.

2 TIMOTHY

Author: Paul

Timothy continued to lead the church in Ephesus, but it wasn't easy. Paul wrote Timothy a second letter, encouraging him to persevere despite suffering and hardship. Paul used his own life as an example to remind Timothy that when things were difficult, God was right there with him. God never left Paul or Timothy alone in their suffering! Instead, God stayed with them, and through his Spirit, he gave them everything they needed to remain faithful, even when they were mistreated.

Letters & Revelation

False teachers continued to be a problem in Ephesus. They taught things that didn't align with the truth. Though Timothy was young, Paul encouraged him to set an example of righteous living, trusting that the Lord would raise up others who could work alongside him. Paul wanted Timothy to know that God would work through him and others who were devoted to serving the Lord. In this second letter to Timothy, which is likely the last letter from Paul, he urged Timothy to study Scripture and preach the gospel, because it is good news both now and in the life to come!

1 I, Paul, am writing this letter. I am an apostle of Christ Jesus just as God planned. He sent me to tell about the promise of life found in Christ Jesus.

2 Timothy, I am sending you this letter. You are my dear son.

May God the Father and Christ Jesus our Lord give you grace, mercy and peace.

Paul Gives Thanks

3 I thank God, whom [illegible] as did our
[illegible] God, knowing
[illegible] one is right. Night and
[illegible] thank God for you. Night and day
I always remember you in my prayers.
4 I remember your tears. I long to see
you so that I can be filled with joy. 5 I
remember your honest and true faith. It
was alive first in your grandmother Lois
and in your mother Eunice. And I am
certain that it is now alive in you also.

Paul Encourages Timothy to Be Faithful

6 This is why I remind you to help
God's gift grow, just as a small spark
grows into a fire. God put his gift in you
when I placed my hands on you. 7 God
gave us his Spirit. And the Spirit doesn't
make us weak and fearful. Instead,
the Spirit gives us power and love. He
helps us control ourselves. 8 So don't
be ashamed of the message about our
Lord. And don't be ashamed of me, his
prisoner. Instead, join with me as I suffer for the good news. God's power will
help us do that. 9 God has saved us. He
has chosen us to live a holy life. It wasn't
because of anything we have done. It
was because of his own purpose and
grace. Through Christ Jesus, God gave us
this grace even before time began. 10 It
has now been made known through the
coming of our Savior, Christ Jesus. He
has broken the power of death. Because
of the good news, he has brought life
out into the light. That life never dies.
11 I was appointed to announce the good
news. I was appointed to be an apostle
and a teacher. 12 That's why I'm suffering the way I am. But this gives me no
reason to be ashamed. That's because I
know who I have believed in. I am sure
he is able to take care of what I have
given him. I can trust him with it until
the day he returns as judge.

13 Follow what you heard from me as
the pattern of true teaching. Follow it
with faith and love because you belong
to Christ Jesus. 14 Guard the truth of the
good news that you were trusted with.
Guard it with the help of the Holy Spirit
who lives in us.

Examples of Faithful and Unfaithful People

15 You know that all the believers in
Asia Minor have deserted me. They include Phygelus and Hermogenes.

in 2 Timothy?

God is the Persevering One. Even when things in life are difficult or challenging, God never abandons or gives up on us.

Can I talk to God?

Prayer is talking to God. You can pray and talk to God at any time of the day or night. God promises that he hears your prayers.

Can you find the following verse?

2 TIMOTHY 1:3

TRUTHFUL

God never li/s. He never bends the truth or
says anythin/that is false. All that God says is
honest and rue. But Satan is the enemy of God
and the faier of lies (see John 8:44). He tries
to get pele to believe his lies instead of
followi God's tru

We ca know God's truth by
minds with God's words, which are found
in the Bible. We can talk to God through
prayer and listen for his voice.

Are there any lies you might be believing? Do you sometimes feel afraid, as though God is not with you? You can replace that lie with the truth from God's Word, which says that God is with us everywhere we go (see Joshua 1:9).

God's truthfulness makes him trustworthy. We, too, can be trustworthy by being truthful like God.

16 May the Lord show mercy to all
who live in the house of Onesiphorus.
He often encouraged me. He was not
ashamed that I was being held by
chains. 17 In fact, it was just the opposite. When he was in Rome, he looked
everywhere for me. At last he found me.
18 May Onesiphorus find mercy from the
Lord on the day Jesus returns as judge!
You know very well how many ways
Onesiphorus helped me in Ephesus.

Paul Again Encourages Timothy to Be Faithful

2 My son, be strong in the grace that
is yours in Christ Jesus. 2 You have
heard me teach in front of many witnesses. Pass on to people you can trust
the things you've heard me say. Then
they will be able to teach others also.
3 Like a good soldier of Christ Jesus, join
with me in suffering. 4 A soldier does
not take part in things that don't have
anything to do with the army. Instead,
he tries to please his commanding officer. 5 It is the same for anyone who
takes part in a sport. They don't receive
the winner's crown unless they play by
the rules. 6 The farmer who works hard
should be the first to receive a share of
the crops. 7 Think about what I'm saying. The Lord will help you understand
what all of it means.

8 Remember Jesus Christ. He came
from David's family line. He was raised
from the dead. That is my good news.
9 I am suffering for it. I have even been
put in chains like someone who has
committed a crime. But God's word is
not held back by chains. 10 So I put up
with everything for the good of God's
chosen people. Then they also can be
saved. Christ Jesus saves them. He gives
them glory that will last forever.
11 Here is a saying you can trust.

If we died with him,
we will also live with him.
12 If we don't give up,
we will also rule with him.
If we say we don't know him,
he will also say he doesn't
know us.
13 Even if we are not faithful,
he remains faithful.
He must be true to himself.

TITUS

Author: Paul

The good news about Jesus traveled all the way to a little island called Crete. Crete was known for being populated with people who were unkind, selfish, and dishonest. But even in Crete, Paul shared the Good News, and some of the Cretans put their faith in Jesus. The gospel changed everything for the new Christians, and soon churches began to gather. Paul left one of his coworkers, Titus, to help guide the people of Crete in their new faith. Unfortunately, the unkind, selfish, and dishonest ways of the people began to spread in the churches, and the Christians struggled to live as Jesus followers. In response, Paul wrote this letter to Titus to share with the churches what it meant to live like Jesus. Paul taught that the ways of Jesus are different from the ways of the world. He said that how the believers lived should make others want to know God too. Doing good out of gratitude and love for God would draw other Cretans to the truth of the gospel.

Letters & Revelation

1 I, Paul, am writing this letter. I serve God, and I am an apostle of Jesus Christ. God sent me to help his chosen people believe in Christ more and more. God sent me to help them understand even more the truth that leads to godly living. 2 That belief and understanding lead to the hope of eternal life. Before time began, God promised to give that life. And he does not lie. 3 Now, at just the right time, he has made his promise clear. He did this through the preaching that he trusted me with. God our Savior has commanded all these things.

4 Titus, I am sending you this letter. You are my true son in the faith we share.

May God the Father and Christ Jesus our Savior give you grace and peace.

Choosing Elders Who Love What Is Good

5 I left you on the island of Crete. I did this because there were some things that hadn't been finished. I wanted you to put them in order. I also wanted you to appoint elders in every town. I told you how to do it. 6 An elder must be without blame. He must be faithful to his wife. His children must be believers. They must not give anyone a reason to say that they are wild and don't obey. 7 A church leader takes care of God's family. That's why he must be without blame. He must not look after only his own interests. He must not get angry easily. He must not get drunk. He must not push people around. He must not try to get money by cheating people. 8 Instead, a church leader must welcome people into his home. He must love what is good. He must control his mind and feelings. He must do what is right. He must be holy. He must control the desires of his body. 9 The message as it has been taught can be trusted. He must hold firmly to it. Then he will be able to use true teaching to comfort others and build them up. He will be able to prove that people who oppose it are wrong.

Warning People Who Fail to Do Good

10 Many people refuse to obey God. All they do is talk about things that mean nothing. They try to fool others. No one does these things more than the circumcision group. 11 They must be stopped. They are making trouble for entire families. They do this by teaching things they shouldn't. They do these things to cheat people. 12 One of Crete's own prophets has a saying. He says, "People from Crete are always liars. They are evil beasts. They don't want to work. They live only to eat." 13 This saying is true. So give a strong warning to people who refuse to obey God. Then they will understand the faith correctly. 14 Then they will pay no attention to Jewish stories that aren't true. They won't listen to the mere human commands of people who turn away from the truth. 15 To people who are pure, all things are pure. But to those who have twisted minds and don't believe, nothing is pure. In fact, their minds and their sense of what is right and wrong are twisted. 16 They claim to know God. But their actions show they don't know him. They are hated by God. They refuse to obey him. They aren't fit to do anything good.

in Titus?

God is the Loving One. He knew we could not save ourselves, so he mercifully offered us salvation through his Son, Jesus.

Doing Good Because of the Good News

2 But what you teach must agree with true teaching. 2 Tell the older men that in anything they do, they must not go too far. They must be worthy of respect. They must control themselves. They must have true faith. They must love others. They must not give up.

[3]In the same way, teach the older
women to lead a holy life. They must
not tell lies about others. They must
not let wine control them. Instead,
they must teach what is good. [4]Then
they can advise the younger women
to love their husbands and children.
[5]The younger women must control
themselves and be pure. They must take
good care of their homes. They must be
kind. They must follow the lead of their
husbands. Then no one will be able to
speak evil things against God's word.
[6]In the same way, help the young
men to control themselves. [7]Do what
is good. Set an example for them in
everything. When you teach, be honest
and serious. [8]No one can question the
truth. So teach what is true. Then those
who oppose you will be ashamed. That's
because they will have nothing bad to
say about us.
[9]Teach slaves to obey their masters
in everything they do. Tell them to try
to please their masters. They must not
talk back to them. [10]They must not steal
from them. Instead, they must show
that they can be trusted completely.
Then they will make the teaching about
God our Savior appealing in every way.
[11]God's grace has now appeared. By
his grace, God offers to save all people.
[12]His grace teaches us to say no to godless ways and sinful desires. We must
control ourselves. We must do what
is right. We must lead godly lives in
today's world. [13]That's how we should
live as we wait for the blessed hope God
has given us. We are waiting for Jesus
Christ to appear in his glory. He is our
great God and Savior. [14]He gave himself
for us. By doing that, he set us free from
all evil. He wanted to make us pure. He
wanted us to be his very own people. He
wanted us to desire to do what is good.

What do followers of Jesus hope for most?

Our greatest hope is the return of Jesus. He promised to come again and make all things new.

Can you find the following verse?

TITUS 2:13

ZEALOUS

God intensely loves and desires to protect his people. He wants us to know what is true, and he longs for us to worship him alone (see James 4:5).

A spiritual battle is taking place in this world, and God knows that all kinds of distractions constantly try to pull our attention away from him. But because God is zealous for us, he will overcome evil and accomplish his purposes.

Being zealous for God by obeying him and telling others about Jesus' love for them is one way we can be faithful to God. We can encourage one another to be devoted to God and put our trust in his love and protection.

15 These are the things you should
teach. Encourage people and give them
hope. Correct them with full authority.
Don't let anyone look down on you.

Do What Is Good Because You Are Saved

3 Remind God's people to obey rulers and authorities. Remind them
to be ready to do what is good. 2 Tell
them not to speak evil things against
anyone. Remind them to live in peace.
They must consider the needs of others.
They must always be gentle toward
everyone.
3 At one time we too acted like fools.
We didn't obey God. We were tricked. We
were controlled by all kinds of desires
and pleasures. We were full of evil. We
wanted what belongs to others. People
hated us, and we hated one another.
4 But the kindness and love of God our
Savior appeared. 5 He saved us. It wasn't
because of the good things we had done.
It was because of his mercy. He saved
us by washing away our sins. We were
born again. The Holy Spirit gave us
new life. 6 God poured out the Spirit on
us freely. That's because of what Jesus
Christ our Savior has done. 7 His grace
made us right with God. So now we have
received the hope of eternal life as God's
children. 8 You can trust this saying.
These things are important. Treat them
that way. Then those who trust in God
will be careful to commit themselves to
doing good. These things are excellent.
They are for the good of everyone.
9 But keep away from foolish dis-
agreements. Don't argue about family

histories. Don't make trouble. Don't
fight about what the law teaches. Don't
argue about things like that. It doesn't
do any good. It doesn't help anyone.
10 Warn anyone who tries to get believers to separate from one another. Warn
that person more than once. After that,
have nothing to do with them. 11 You
can be sure that people like this are
twisted and sinful. Their own actions
judge them.

Final Words

12 I will send Artemas or Tychicus to
you. Then do your best to come to me
at Nicopolis. I've decided to spend the
winter there. 13 Do everything you can
to help Zenas the lawyer and Apollos.
Send them on their way. See that they
have everything they need.

14 Our people must learn to commit
themselves to doing what is good. Then
they can provide for people when they
are in great need. If they do that, their
lives won't turn out to be useless.

15 Everyone who is with me sends you
greetings.
Greet those who love us in the faith.

May God's grace be with you all.

PHILEMON

Author: Paul

Paul wrote this letter to Philemon, a wealthy leader and partner in spreading the gospel. Philemon had household servants, but at some point his servant Onesimus wronged him and ran away. Onesimus met Paul, who shared the gospel with him, and Onesimus became a Christian. We don't know exactly what Onesimus did to wrong Philemon, but we do know this: Both of them believed Jesus was their Savior and King, which changed everything.

Paul wanted Onesimus to return to Philemon and make things right with him, but he didn't send Onesimus back to Philemon empty-handed; he sent Onesimus with a letter. In the letter, Paul encouraged Philemon to represent the forgiveness Jesus offers by forgiving Onesimus and accepting him as a dear brother. The power of the gospel is that through Christ, we are called to love one another and work together to live at peace with everyone. Paul asked Philemon to see Onesimus not as a servant but as an equal, joined together in the family of faith.

Letters & Revelation

1 I, Paul, am writing this letter. I am
a prisoner because of Christ Jesus. Our
brother Timothy joins me in writing.

Philemon, we are sending you this
letter. You are our dear friend. You work
together with us. 2 We are also sending
it to our sister Apphia and to Archippus.
He is a soldier of Christ together with
us. And we are sending it to the church
that meets in your home.

3 May God our Father and the Lord
Jesus Christ give you grace and peace.

Paul Prays and Gives Thanks

4 I always thank my God when I remember you in my prayers. 5 That's
because I hear about your love for all
God's people. I also hear about your
faith in the Lord Jesus. 6 I pray that
what we share by believing will help
you understand even more. Then you
will completely understand every good
thing we share by believing in Christ.
7 Your love has given me great joy. It has
encouraged me. My brother, you have
renewed the hearts of the Lord's people.

I always thank my God when I remember you in my prayers.
PHILEMON 4

Paul Makes an Appeal for Onesimus

8 Because of the authority Christ has
given me, I could be bold. I could order
you to do what you should do anyway.
9 But we love each other. And I would
rather appeal to you on the basis of
that love. I, Paul, am an old man. I am
now also a prisoner because of Christ
Jesus. 10 I am an old man, and I'm in
prison. This is how I make my appeal
to you for my son Onesimus. He became
a son to me while I was being held in
chains. 11 Before that, he was useless to
you. But now he has become useful to
you and to me.

12 I'm sending Onesimus back to you.
All my love for him goes with him. 13 I'm
being held in chains because of the good
news. So I would have liked to keep
Onesimus with me. And he could take
your place in helping me. 14 But I didn't
want to do anything unless you agreed.
Any favor you do must be done because
you want to do it, not because you have
to. 15 Onesimus was separated from you
for a little while. Maybe that was so
you could have him back forever. 16 You
could have him back not as a slave.
Instead, he would be better than a slave.
He would be a dear brother. He is very

in Philemon?

God is the Just King. He does not play favorites and treats his children with fairness.

How do I follow Jesus when life gets hard?

You can be encouraged by the example of others who followed Jesus even when it meant they were disliked or treated unfairly. Their love and commitment to walking with Jesus no matter what is a reminder that Jesus is worth any hard thing you may go through.

Can you find the following verse?
PHILEMON 7

dear to me but even more dear to you.
He is dear to you not only as another
human being. He is also dear to you as
a brother in the Lord.

17 Do you think of me as a believer
who works together with you? Then
welcome Onesimus as you would
welcome me. 18 Has he done anything
wrong to you? Does he owe you anything? Then charge it to me. 19 I'll pay it
back. I, Paul, am writing this with my
own hand. I won't even mention that
you owe me your life. 20 My brother,
we both belong to the Lord. So I wish
I could receive some benefit from you.
Renew my heart. We know that Christ
is the one who really renews it. 21 I'm
sure you will obey. So I'm writing to
you. I know you will do even more
than I ask.

22 There is one more thing. Have a
guest room ready for me. I hope I can
return to all of you in answer to your
prayers.

23 Epaphras sends you greetings. Together with me, he is a prisoner because
of Christ Jesus.

24 Mark, Aristarchus, Demas and Luke
work together with me. They also send
you greetings.

25 May the grace of the Lord Jesus
Christ be with your spirit.

HEBREWS

Author: We don't know.

Even though we don't know who wrote the book of Hebrews, we do know that the author knew the Old Testament. The book is organized like a sermon, or message, that was intended to be read aloud. Hebrews was probably meant to be read to Christians who were facing persecution, or suffering mistreatment, for their new faith to assure them that the good news about Jesus is the best news ever! No one and nothing can ever compare to the glory of the risen Savior. Jesus is the new high priest who fulfills the laws of the old covenant, thereby making way for the new covenant. His death and resurrection make him superior to the old ways of offering sacrifices for sins. Because of Jesus' ultimate sacrifice, Christians can have confidence and stand firm in their faith.

Letters & Revelation

The book of Hebrews reminds Christians that God has been faithful to his people—from Abraham to Moses to the prophets—and reassures them that God never breaks his promises. By making a list of Old Testament people who responded to God in faith, the author was highlighting that God has been faithful in every generation (see Hebrews 11). Therefore, God's people can have confidence in his goodness and courage to live out their faith in Jesus just like those who have gone before them.

God Speaks His Final Word Through His Son

1 In the past, God spoke to our people through the prophets. He spoke at many times. He spoke in different ways. [2] But in these last days, he has spoken to us through his Son. He is the one whom God appointed to receive all things. God also made everything through him. [3] The Son is the shining brightness of God's glory. He is the exact likeness of God's being. He uses his powerful word to hold all things together. He provided the way for people to be made pure from sin. Then he sat down at the right hand of the King, the Majesty in heaven. [4] So he became higher than the angels. The name he received is more excellent than theirs.

The Son Is Greater Than the Angels

[5] God never said to any of the angels,

"You are my Son.
Today I have become your Father." *(Psalm 2:7)*

Or,

"I will be his Father.
And he will be my Son." *(2 Samuel 7:14; 1 Chronicles 17:13)*

[6] God's first and only Son is over all things. When God brings him into the world, he says,

"Let all God's angels worship him." *(Deuteronomy 32:43)*

[7] Here is something else God says about the angels.

"God makes his angels to be like spirits.
He makes those who serve him to be like flashes of lightning." *(Psalm 104:4)*

[8] But here is what he says about the Son.

"You are God. Your throne will last for ever and ever.
Your kingdom will be ruled by justice.
[9] You have loved what is right and hated what is evil.
So your God has placed you above your companions.
He has filled you with joy by pouring the sacred oil on your head." *(Psalm 45:6,7)*

[10] He also says,

"Lord, in the beginning you made the earth secure. You placed it on its foundations.
The heavens are the work of your hands.
[11] They will pass away. But you remain.
They will all wear out like a piece of clothing.
[12] You will roll them up like a robe.
They will be changed as a person changes clothes.
But you remain the same.
Your years will never end." *(Psalm 102:25–27)*

[13] God never said to an angel,

"Sit at my right hand
until I put your enemies under your control." *(Psalm 110:1)*

[14] All angels are spirits who serve. God sends them to serve those who will receive salvation.

in Hebrews?

God is the Promise Keeper. God has not made a single promise that he has not kept. He does what he says he is going to do.

A Warning to Pay Attention

2 So we must pay the most careful attention to what we have heard. Then we will not drift away from it. [2] Even the message God spoke through angels had to be obeyed. Every time people broke the Law, they were punished. Every time they didn't obey, they were punished. [3] Then how will we escape if we don't pay attention to God's great salvation? The Lord first announced this salvation. Those who

MERCIFUL

My GOD IS...

When the first humans sinned, all humanity was separated from God. Our relationship with God was broken, and the penalty, or punishment, for that separation was death—both physical death and the eternal death of being separated from God forever. The penalty for sin was too much for any person to pay; no one could live a perfect life or offer the perfect sacrifice our sins required. But God mercifully sent his Son, Jesus, to die in our place.

Now we can receive eternal life through Jesus, and we can receive God's mercy for each day. He wants to draw near to us and will always forgive us when we ask (see James 4:8). Just as God has forgiven us, we can be merciful to others by forgiving them and choosing to be kind.

heard him gave us the message about it.
4 God showed that this message is true
by signs and wonders. He showed that
it's true by different kinds of miracles.
God also showed that this message is
true by the gifts of the Holy Spirit. God
gave them out as it pleased him.

Jesus Was Made Fully Human

5 God has not put angels in charge
of the world that is going to come. We
are talking about that world. 6 There
is a place where someone has spoken
about this. He said,

"What are human beings that you
think about them?
What is a son of man that you
take care of him?
7 You made them a little lower than
the angels.
You placed on them a crown of
glory and honor.
8 You have put everything under
their control." *(Psalm 8:4–6)*

So God has put everything under his
Son. Everything is under his control.
We do not now see everything under his
control. 9 But we do see Jesus already
given a crown of glory and honor. He
was made lower than the angels for a
little while. He suffered death. By the
grace of God, he tasted death for everyone. That is why he was given his crown.
10 God has made everything. He is now
bringing his many sons and daughters
to share in his glory. It is only right that
Jesus is the one to lead them into their
salvation. That's because God made him
perfect by his sufferings. 11 And Jesus,
who makes people holy, and the people he makes holy belong to the same
family. So Jesus is not ashamed to call
them his brothers and sisters. 12 He says,

"I will announce your name to my
brothers and sisters.
I will sing your praises among
those who worship you."
(Psalm 22:22)

13 Again he says,

"I will put my trust in him."
(Isaiah 8:17)

And again he says,

"Here I am. Here are the children
God has given me." *(Isaiah 8:18)*

14 Those children have bodies made
out of flesh and blood. So Jesus became

human like them in order to die for
them. By doing this, he could break the
power of the devil. The devil is the one
who rules over the kingdom of death.
15 Jesus could set people free who were
afraid of death. All their lives they were
held as slaves by that fear. 16 It is certainly Abraham's children that he helps.
He doesn't help angels. 17 So he had to be
made like people, fully human in every
way. Then he could serve God as a kind
and faithful high priest. And then he
could pay for the sins of the people by
dying for them. 18 He himself suffered
when he was tempted. Now he is able
to help others who are being tempted.

Jesus Is Greater Than Moses

3 Holy brothers and sisters, God
chose you to be his people. So
keep thinking about Jesus. We embrace
him as our apostle and our high priest.
2 Moses was faithful in everything he
did in the house of God. In the same
way, Jesus was faithful to the God who
appointed him. 3 The person who builds
a house has greater honor than the
house itself. In the same way, Jesus
has been found worthy of greater hon-
or than Moses. 4 Every house is built
by someone. But God is the builder of
everything. 5 "Moses was faithful as
one who serves in the house of God."
(Numbers 12:7) He was a witness to what
God would say in days to come. 6 But
Christ is faithful as the Son over the
house of God. And we are his house if
we hold tightly to what we are certain
about. We must also hold tightly to the
hope we boast in.

A Warning Against Unbelief

7 The Holy Spirit says,

"Listen to his voice today.
8 If you hear it, don't be stubborn.
You were stubborn when you
opposed me.
You did that when you were
tested in the desert.
9 There your people of long ago
tested me.
Yet for 40 years they saw what I
did.
10 That is why I was angry with them.
I said, 'Their hearts are always
going astray.
They have not known my ways.'
11 So when I was angry, I made a
promise.
I said, 'They will never enjoy
the rest I planned for them.'"
(Psalm 95:7–11)

12 Brothers and sisters, make sure that
none of you has a sinful heart. Do not
let an unbelieving heart turn you away
from the living God. 13 But build one
another up every day. Do it as long as
there is still time. Then none of you will
become stubborn. You won't be fooled
by sin's tricks. 14 We belong to Christ if
we hold tightly to the faith we had at
first. But we must hold it tightly until
the end. 15 It has just been said,

"Listen to his voice today.
If you hear it, don't be stubborn.
You were stubborn when you
opposed me." *(Psalm 95:7,8)*

16 Who were those who heard and
refused to obey? Weren't they all the
people Moses led out of Egypt? 17 Who
was God angry with for 40 years? Wasn't
it with those who sinned? They died in
the desert. 18 God promised that those
people would never enjoy the rest he
planned for them. God gave his word
when he made that promise. Didn't he
make that promise to those who didn't
obey? 19 So we see that they weren't able
to enter. That's because they didn't
believe.

God's People Enter His Sabbath Rest

4 God's promise of enjoying his rest
still stands. So be careful that none
of you fails to receive it. 2 The good news
was announced to our people of long
ago. It has also been preached to us.
The message they heard didn't have
any value for them. That's because
they didn't share the faith of those who
obeyed. 3 Now we who have believed
enjoy that rest. God said,

"When I was angry, I made a
promise.
I said, 'They will never enjoy
the rest I planned for them.'"
(Psalm 95:11)

Ever since God created the world, his
works have been finished. 4 Somewhere
he spoke about the seventh day. He
said, "On the seventh day God rested

from all his works." *(Genesis 2:2)* [5] In the part of Scripture I talked about earlier God spoke. He said, "They will never enjoy the rest I planned for them." *(Psalm 95:11)*

[6] It is still true that some people will enjoy this rest. But those who had the good news announced to them earlier didn't go in. That's because they didn't obey. [7] So God again chose a certain day. He named it Today. He did this when he spoke through David a long time later. Here is what was written in the Scripture already given.

"Listen to his voice today.
 If you hear it, don't be stubborn."
 (Psalm 95:7,8)

[8] Suppose Joshua had given them rest. If he had, God would not have spoken later about another day. [9] So there is still a Sabbath rest for God's people. [10] God rested from his work. Those who enjoy God's rest also rest from their works. [11] So let us make every effort to enjoy that rest. Then no one will die by disobeying as they did.

[12] The word of God is alive and active. It is sharper than any sword that has two edges. It cuts deep enough to separate soul from spirit. It can separate bones from joints. It judges the thoughts and purposes of the heart. [13] Nothing God created is hidden from him. His eyes see everything. He will hold us responsible for everything we do.

Jesus Is the Great High Priest

[14] We have a great high priest. He has gone up into heaven. He is Jesus the Son of God. So let us hold firmly to what we say we believe. [15] We have a high priest who can feel it when we are weak and hurting. We have a high priest who has been tempted in every way, just as we are. But he did not sin. [16] So let us boldly approach God's throne of grace. Then we will receive mercy. We will find grace to help us when we need it.

5 Every high priest is chosen from among the people. He is appointed to act for the people. He acts for them in whatever has to do with God. He offers gifts and sacrifices for their sins. [2] Some people have gone astray without knowing it. He is able to deal gently with them. He can do that because he himself is weak. [3] That's why he has to offer sacrifices for his own sins. He must also do it for the sins of the people. [4] And no one can take this honor for himself. Instead, he receives it when he is appointed by God. That is just how it was for Aaron.

[5] It was the same for Christ. He did not take for himself the glory of becoming a high priest. But God said to him,

"You are my Son.
 Today I have become your
 Father." *(Psalm 2:7)*

[6] In another place God said,

"You are a priest forever,
 just like Melchizedek." *(Psalm 110:4)*

[7] Jesus prayed while he lived on earth. He made his appeal with sincere cries and tears. He prayed to the God who could save him from death. God answered Jesus because he truly honored God. [8] Jesus was God's Son. But by suffering he learned what it means to obey. [9] In this way he was made perfect. Eternal salvation comes from him. He saves all those who obey him. [10] God appointed him to be the high priest, just like Melchizedek.

A Warning Against Falling Away

[11] We have a lot to say about this. But it is hard to make it clear to you. That's because you are no longer trying to understand. [12] By this time you should be teachers. But in fact, you need someone to teach you all over again. You need even the simple truths of God's word. You need milk, not solid food. [13] Anyone who lives on milk is still a baby. That person does not want to learn about living a godly life. [14] Solid food is for those who are grown up. They have trained themselves to tell the difference between good and evil. That shows they have grown up.

6 So let us move beyond the simple teachings about Christ. Let us grow up as believers. Let us not start all over again with the basic teachings. They taught us that we need to turn away from doing things that lead to death. They taught us that we must have faith in God. [2] These basic teachings taught us about different ways of becoming "clean." They taught us about placing

Why should I read the Bible?

The Bible shows you who God is and what he is like so that you can know him. The Bible also teaches you how you can be more like Jesus through the power of the Holy Spirit.

Can you find the following verse?

HEBREWS 4:12

hands of blessing on people. They
taught us that people will rise from
the dead. They taught us that God will
judge everyone. And they taught us
that what he decides will last forever.
3 If God permits, we will go beyond those
teachings and grow up.
4 What if some people fall away from
the faith? It won't be possible to bring
them back. It is true that they have
seen the light. They have tasted the
heavenly gift. They have shared in the
Holy Spirit. 5 They have tasted the good
things of God's word. They have tasted
the powers of the age to come. 6 But they
have fallen away from the faith. So it
won't be possible to bring them back.
They won't be able to turn away from
their sins. They are losing everything.
That's because they are nailing the Son
of God to the cross all over again. They
are bringing shame on him in front of
everyone. 7 Some land drinks the rain
that falls on it. It produces a crop that is
useful to those who farm the land. That
land receives God's blessing. 8 But other
land produces only thorns and weeds.
That land isn't worth anything. It is in
danger of coming under God's curse. In
the end, it will be burned.
9 Dear friends, we have to say these
things. But we are sure of better things
in your case. We are talking about the
things that have to do with being saved.
10 God is fair. He will not forget what
you have done. He will remember the
love you have shown him. You showed
it when you helped his people. And you
show it when you keep on helping them.
11 We want each of you to be faithful to
the very end. If you are, then what you
hope for will fully happen. 12 We don't
want you to slow down. Instead, be like
those who have faith and are patient.
They will receive what God promised.

God Keeps His Promise

13 When God made his promise to
Abraham, God gave his word. There
was no one greater than himself to
promise by. So he promised by making
an appeal to himself. 14 He said, "I will
certainly bless you. I will give you many
children." *(Genesis 22:17)* 15 Abraham was
patient while he waited. Then he received what God promised him.
16 People promise things by someone
greater than themselves. Giving your
word makes a promise certain. It puts
an end to all arguing. 17 So God gave
his word when he made his promise.
He wanted to make it very clear that
his purpose does not change. He wanted those who would receive what was
promised to know this. 18 When God
made his promise, he gave his word. He
did this so we would have good reason
not to give up. Instead, we have run to
take hold of the hope set before us. This
hope is set before us in God's promise.
So God made his promise and gave his
word. These two things can't change.
He couldn't lie about them. 19 Our hope
is certain. It is something for the soul
to hold on to. It is strong and secure.
It goes all the way into the Most Holy
Room behind the curtain. 20 That is
where Jesus has gone. He went there
to open the way ahead of us. He has
become a high priest forever, just like
Melchizedek.

Melchizedek the Priest

7 Melchizedek was the king of Salem.
He was the priest of God Most High.
He met Abraham, who was returning
from winning a battle over some kings.
Melchizedek blessed him. 2 Abraham
gave him a tenth of everything. First,
the name Melchizedek means "king

of what is right." Also, "king of Salem" means "king of peace." 3 Melchizedek has no father or mother. He has no family line. His days have no beginning. His life has no end. He remains a priest forever. In this way, he is like the Son of God.

4 Think how great Melchizedek was! Even our father Abraham gave him a tenth of what he had captured. 5 Now the law lays down a rule for the sons of Levi who become priests. They must collect a tenth from the people. They must collect it from the other Israelites. They must do this, even though all of them belong to the family line of Abraham. 6 Melchizedek did not trace his family line from Levi. But he collected a tenth from Abraham. Melchizedek blessed the one who had received the promises. 7 Without a doubt, the more important person blesses the less important one. 8 In the one case, the tenth is collected by people who die. But in the other case, it is collected by the one who is said to be living. 9 Levi collects the tenth. But we might say that Levi paid the tenth through Abraham. 10 That's because when Melchizedek met Abraham, Levi was still in Abraham's body.

Jesus Is Like Melchizedek

11 The law that was given to the people called for the priestly system. That system began with Levi. Suppose the priestly system could have made people perfect. Then why was there still a need for another priest to come? And why did he need to be like Melchizedek? Why wasn't he from Aaron's family line? 12 A change of the priestly system requires a change of law. 13 We are talking about a priest who is from a different tribe. No one from that tribe has ever served at the altar. 14 It is clear that our Lord came from the family line of Judah. Moses said nothing about priests who were from the tribe of Judah. 15 But suppose another priest like Melchizedek appears. Then what we have said is even more clear. 16 He has not become a priest because of a rule about his family line. He has become a priest because of his powerful life. His life can never be destroyed. 17 Scripture says,

"You are a priest forever,
just like Melchizedek." *(Psalm 110:4)*

18 The old rule is set aside. It was weak and useless. 19 The law didn't make anything perfect. Now a better hope has been given to us. That hope brings us near to God.

20 The change of priestly system was made with a promise. Others became priests without any promise. 21 But Jesus became a priest with a promise. God said to him,

"The Lord has given his word and
made a promise.
He will not change his mind. He
has said,
'You are a priest forever.' "
(Psalm 110:4)

22 Because God gave his word, Jesus makes certain the promise of a better covenant.

23 There were many priests in Levi's family line. Death kept them from continuing in office. 24 But Jesus lives forever. So he always holds the office of priest. 25 People now come to God through him. And he is able to save them completely and for all time. Jesus lives forever. He prays for them.

26 A high priest like that really meets our need. He is holy, pure and without blame. He isn't like other people. He does not sin. He is lifted high above the heavens. 27 He isn't like the other high priests. They need to offer sacrifices day after day. First they bring offerings for their own sins. Then they do it for the sins of the people. But Jesus gave one sacrifice for the sins of the people. He gave it once and for all time. He did it by offering himself. 28 The law appoints as high priests men who are weak. But God's promise came after the law. By his promise the Son was appointed. The Son has been made perfect forever.

The High Priest of a New Covenant

8 Here is the main point of what we are saying. We have a high priest like that. He sat down at the right hand of the throne of the King, the Majesty in heaven. 2 He serves in the sacred tent. The Lord set up the true holy tent. A mere human being did not set it up.

3 Every high priest is appointed to offer gifts and sacrifices. So this priest also had to have something to offer. 4 What if he were on earth? Then he would not be

a priest. There are already priests who
offer the gifts required by the law. [5]They
serve at a sacred tent. But it is only a
copy and shadow of what is in heaven.
That's why God warned Moses when he
was about to build the holy tent. God
said, "Be sure to make everything just
like the pattern I showed you on the
mountain." *(Exodus 25:40)* [6]But Jesus
has been given a greater work to do for
God. He is the go-between for the new
covenant. This covenant is better than
the old one. The new covenant is based
on better promises.

[7]Suppose nothing had been wrong
with that first covenant. Then no one
would have looked for another covenant. [8]But God found fault with the
people. He said,

"The days are coming, announces
 the Lord.
I will make a new covenant
with the people of Israel.
I will also make it with the
 people of Judah.
[9]It will not be like the covenant
I made with their people of long
 ago.
That was when I took them by the
 hand.
I led them out of Egypt.
My new covenant will be different
 because they didn't remain
 faithful to my old covenant.
So I turned away from them,
 announces the Lord.
[10]This is the covenant I will establish
 with the people of Israel
 after that time, says the Lord.
I will put my laws in their minds.
I will write them on their hearts.
I will be their God.
And they will be my people.
[11]People will not teach their neighbor
 anymore.
They will not say to one another,
 'Know the Lord.'
That's because everyone will
 know me.
From the least important to the
 most important,
all of them will know me.
[12]I will forgive their evil ways.
I will not remember their sins
 anymore." *(Jeremiah 31:31–34)*

[13]God called this covenant "new." So
he has done away with the first one.
And what is out of date and has been
done away with will soon disappear.

Worship in the Holy Tent on Earth

9 The first covenant had rules for
worship. It also had a sacred tent
on earth. [2]A holy tent was set up. The
lampstand was in the first room. So was
the table with its holy bread. That was
called the Holy Room. [3]Behind the second curtain was a room called the Most
Holy Room. [4]It had the golden altar for
incense. It also had the wooden chest
called the ark of the covenant. The ark
was covered with gold. It held the gold
jar of manna. It held Aaron's walking
stick that had budded. It also held the
stone tablets. The words of the covenant
were written on them. [5]The cherubim
were above the ark. God showed his
glory there. The cherubim spread their
wings over the place where sin was paid
for. But we can't say everything about
these things now.

[6]That's how everything was arranged
in the holy tent. The priests entered it
at regular times. They went into the
outer room to do their work for God and
others. [7]But only the high priest went
into the inner room. He went in only
once a year. He never entered without
taking blood with him. He offered the
blood for himself. He also offered it
for the sins the people had committed
because they didn't know any better.
[8]Here is what the Holy Spirit was showing us. He was telling us that God had
not yet clearly shown the way into the
Most Holy Room. It would not be clearly
shown as long as the first holy tent was
still being used. [9]That's an example
for the present time. It shows us that
the gifts and sacrifices people offered
were not enough. They were not able to
remove the worshiper's feelings of guilt.
[10]They deal only with food and drink
and different kinds of special washings.
They are rules people had to obey only
until the new covenant came.

The Blood of Christ

[11]But Christ came to be the high priest
of the good things already here now.
When he came, he went through the
greater and more perfect holy tent. This
tent was not made with human hands.

In other words, it is not a part of this
creation. 12 He did not enter by spilling
the blood of goats and calves. He entered the Most Holy Room by spilling
his own blood. He did it once and for
all time. In this way, he paid the price
to set us free from sin forever. 13 The
blood of goats and bulls is sprinkled
on people. So are the ashes of a young
cow. They are sprinkled on people the
law called "unclean." The people are
sprinkled to make them holy. That
makes them "clean" on the outside.
14 But Christ offered himself to God
without any flaw. He did this through
the power of the eternal Holy Spirit.
So how much cleaner will the blood
of Christ make us! It washes away our
feelings of guilt for committing sin. Sin
always leads to death. But now we can
serve the living God.

15 That's why Christ is the go-between
of a new covenant. Now those God calls
to himself will receive the eternal gift
he promised. They will receive it now
that Christ has died to save them. He
died to set them free from the sins they
committed under the first covenant.

16 What happens when someone
leaves a will? It is necessary to prove
that the person who made the will
has died. 17 A will is in effect only when
somebody has died. It never takes effect
while the one who made it is still living.
18 That's why even the first covenant was
not put into effect without the spilling
of blood. 19 Moses first announced every
command of the law to all the people.
Then he took the blood of calves. He
also took water, bright red wool and
branches of a hyssop plant. He sprinkled the Book of the Covenant. He also
sprinkled all the people. 20 He said, "This
is the blood of the covenant God has
commanded you to keep." *(Exodus 24:8)*
21 In the same way, he sprinkled the
holy tent with blood. He also sprinkled
everything that was used in worship
there. 22 In fact, the law requires that
nearly everything be made "clean" with
blood. Without the spilling of blood, no
one can be forgiven.

23 So the copies of the heavenly things
had to be made pure with these sacrifices. But the heavenly things themselves
had to be made pure with better sacrifices. 24 Christ did not enter a sacred tent
made with human hands. That tent was
only a copy of the true one. He entered
heaven itself. He did it to stand in front
of God for us. He is there right now. 25 The
high priest enters the Most Holy Room
every year. He enters with blood that
is not his own. But Christ did not enter heaven to offer himself again and
again. 26 If he had, he would have had
to suffer many times since the world
was created. But he has appeared once
and for all time. He has come at the time
when God's work is being completed.
He has come to do away with sin by
offering himself. 27 People have to die
once. After that, God will judge them.
28 In the same way, Christ was offered
up once. He took away the sins of many
people. He will also come a second time.
At that time he will not suffer for sin.
Instead, he will come to bring salvation
to those who are waiting for him.

Christ's Sacrifice Is Once and for All Time

10 The law is only a shadow of the
good things that are coming. It
is not the real things themselves. The
same sacrifices have to be offered over
and over again. They must be offered
year after year. That's why the law can
never make perfect those who come
near to worship. 2 If the law could,
wouldn't the sacrifices have stopped
being offered? The worshipers would
have been made "clean" once and for all
time. They would not have felt guilty for
their sins anymore. 3 But those offerings
remind people of their sins every year.
4 It isn't possible for the blood of bulls
and goats to take away sins.

5 So when Christ came into the world,
he said,

"You didn't want sacrifices and
offerings.
Instead, you prepared a body
for me.
6 You weren't pleased
with burnt offerings and sin
offerings.
7 Then I said, 'Here I am. It is written
about me in the book.
I have come to do what you
want, my God.' " *(Psalm 40:6–8)*

8 First Christ said, "You didn't want sacrifices and offerings. You didn't want

burnt offerings and sin offerings. You
weren't pleased with them." He said
this even though they were offered in
keeping with the law. 9 Then he said,
"Here I am. I have come to do what you
want." He did away with the shadow of
the good things that were coming. He
did it to put in place the good things
themselves. 10 We have been made holy
by what God wanted. We have been
made holy because Jesus Christ offered
his body once and for all time.

11 Day after day every priest stands
and does his special duties. He offers the
same sacrifices again and again. But
they can never take away sins. 12 Jesus
our priest offered one sacrifice for sins
for all time. Then he sat down at the
right hand of God. 13 And since that time,
he waits for his enemies to be put under
his control. 14 By that one sacrifice he
has made perfect forever those who are
being made holy.

15 The Holy Spirit also speaks to us
about this. First he says,

16 "This is the covenant I will make
with them
after that time, says the Lord.
I will put my laws in their hearts.
I will write my laws on their
minds." *(Jeremiah 31:33)*

17 Then he adds,

"I will not remember their sins
anymore.
I will not remember the evil
things they have done."
(Jeremiah 31:34)

18 Where these sins have been forgiv-
en, an offering for sin is no longer
necessary.

An Appeal and Warning to Remain Faithful

19 Brothers and sisters, we are not
afraid to enter the Most Holy Room.
We enter boldly because of the blood
of Jesus. 20 His way is new because he
lives. It has been opened for us through
the curtain. I'm talking about his body.
21 We also have a great priest over the
house of God. 22 So let us come near to
God with a sincere heart. Let us come
near boldly because of our faith. Our
hearts have been sprinkled. Our minds
have been cleansed from a sense of
guilt. Our bodies have been washed
with pure water. 23 Let us hold firmly
to the hope we claim to have. The God
who promised is faithful. 24 Let us consider how we can stir up one another
to love. Let us help one another to do
good works. 25 And let us not give up
meeting together. Some are in the habit
of doing this. Instead, let us encourage
one another with words of hope. Let us
do this even more as you see Christ's
return approaching.

26 What if we keep sinning on purpose? What if we do it even after we
know the truth? Then there is no offering for our sins. 27 All we can do is to
wait in fear for God to judge. His blazing
fire will burn up his enemies. 28 Suppose
someone did not obey the law of Moses.
And suppose two or three witnesses
made charges against them. That person would die without mercy. 29 People
who deserve even more punishment
include those who have hated the Son
of God. They include people who have
said no to him. They include people who
have treated as unholy the blood of the
covenant that makes them holy. They
also include people who have disrespected the Holy Spirit who brings God's
grace. Don't you think people like this
should be punished more than anyone
else? 30 We know the God who said, "I
am the God who judges people. I will
pay them back." *(Deuteronomy 32:35)*
Scripture also says, "The Lord will judge
his people." *(Deuteronomy 32:36; Psalm
135:14)* 31 It is a terrible thing to fall into
the hands of the living God.

32 Remember those earlier days after
you received the light. You remained
strong in a great battle that was full of
suffering. 33 Sometimes people spoke
badly about you in front of others.
Sometimes you were treated badly. At
other times you stood side by side with
people being treated like this. 34 You
suffered along with people in prison.
When your property was taken from
you, you accepted it with joy. You knew
that God had given you better and more
lasting things. 35 So don't throw away
your bold faith. It will bring you rich
rewards.

36 You need to be faithful. Then you
will do what God wants. You will receive
what he has promised.

37 “In just a little while,
he who is coming will come.
He will not wait any longer.”

38 And,

“The one who is right with God will
live by faith.
And I am not pleased with
the one who pulls back.”
(Habakkuk 2:3,4)

39 But we don’t belong to the people who
pull back and are destroyed. We belong
to the people who believe and are saved.

Faith That Produces Action

11 Faith is being sure of what we hope
for. It is being sure of what we do
not see. 2 That is what the people of long
ago were praised for.

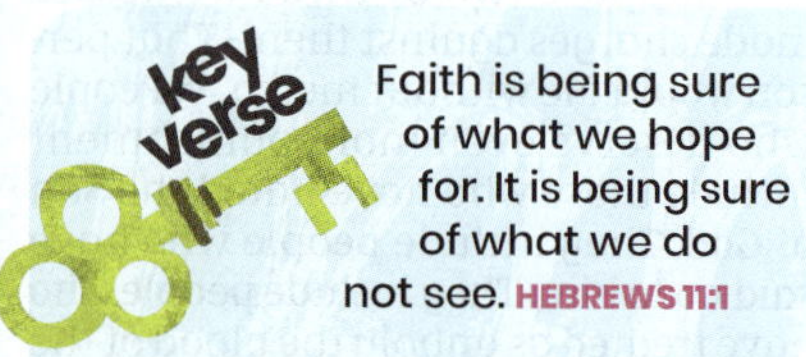

Faith is being sure of what we hope for. It is being sure of what we do not see. HEBREWS 11:1

3 We have faith. So we understand
that everything was made when God
commanded it. That’s why we believe
that what we see was not made out of
what could be seen.
4 Abel had faith. So he brought to God a
better offering than Cain did. Because of
his faith Abel was praised as a godly man.
God said good things about his offerings.
Because of his faith Abel still speaks. He
speaks even though he is dead.
5 Enoch had faith. So he was taken
from this life. He didn’t die. “He couldn’t
be found, because God had taken him
away.” *(Genesis 5:24)* Before God took
him, Enoch was praised as one who
pleased God. 6 Without faith it is impossible to please God. Those who come
to God must believe that he exists. And
they must believe that he rewards those
who look to him.
7 Noah had faith. So he built an ark
to save his family. He built it because
of his great respect for God. God had
warned him about things that could not
yet be seen. Because of his faith Noah
showed the world that it was guilty.
Because of his faith he was considered
right with God.
8 Abraham had faith. So he obeyed
God. God called him to go to a place he
would later receive as his own. So he
went. He did it even though he didn’t
know where he was going. 9 Because of
his faith he made his home in the land
God had promised him. Abraham was
like an outsider in a strange country.
He lived there in tents. So did Isaac and
Jacob. They received the same promise
he did. 10 Abraham was looking forward
to the city that has foundations. He was
waiting for the city that God planned
and built. 11 And Sarah had faith. So
God made it possible for her to become
a mother. She became a mother even
though she was too old to have children. But Sarah believed that the God
who made the promise was faithful.
12 Abraham was past the time when he
could have children. But many children

God Is the Creator

Everything that exists was made by God’s limitless power. When you and I create, we use things that already exist to make something new. We use fabric and thread to make a blanket, or we use flour and eggs to make chocolate chip cookies. Everything we make uses things that God has already created.

In the beginning, when God created, he simply spoke words and everything came into being. Think about this: Before God created, nothing existed but God. He created the things we can see and even things we cannot see (see Colossians 1:16). Everything that exists was created through God’s life-giving power and endless creativity.

came from that one man. They were
as many as the stars in the sky. They
were as many as the grains of sand on
the seashore. No one could count them.
13 All these people were still living by
faith when they died. They didn't receive the things God had promised. They
only saw them and welcomed them
from a long way off. They openly said
that they were outsiders and strangers
on earth. 14 People who say things like
that show that they are looking for a
country of their own. 15 What if they had
been thinking of the country they had
left? Then they could have returned to
it. 16 Instead, they longed for a better
country. They wanted a heavenly one.
So God is pleased when they call him
their God. In fact, he has prepared a
city for them.
17 Abraham had faith. So when God
tested him, Abraham offered Isaac as
a sacrifice. Abraham had held on tightly to the promises. But he was about
to offer his one and only son. 18 God
had said to him, "Your family line will
continue through Isaac." *(Genesis 21:12)*
Even so, Abraham was going to offer
him up. 19 Abraham did this, because
he believed that God could even raise
the dead. In a way, he did receive Isaac
back from death.
20 Isaac had faith. So he blessed Jacob
and Esau. He told them what was ahead
for them.
21 Jacob had faith. So he blessed each
of Joseph's sons. He blessed them when
he was dying. Because of his faith he
worshiped God. Jacob worshiped as he
leaned on the top of his walking stick.
22 Joseph had faith. So he spoke to the
people of Israel about how they would
leave Egypt someday. When his death
was near, he spoke about where to bury
his bones.
23 Moses' parents had faith. So they
hid him for three months after he was
born. They saw he was a special child.
They were not afraid of the king's
command.
24 Moses had faith. So he refused to be
called the son of Pharaoh's daughter.
That happened after he had grown up.
25 He chose to be treated badly together
with the people of God. He chose not
to enjoy sin's pleasures. They only last
for a short time. 26 He suffered shame

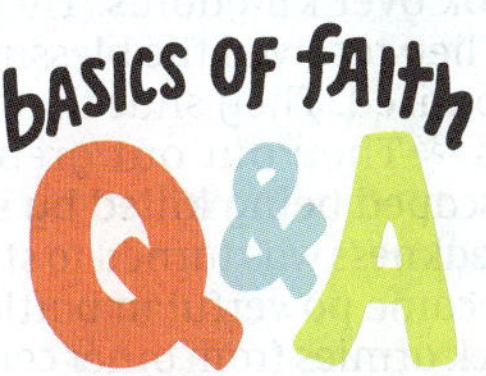

How can I know if I'm pleasing God?

No matter how good you are, the only way you can please God is through faith. God asks his people to live by faith and believe that he will do everything he says he will do.

Can you find the following verse?

HEBREWS 11:6

because of Christ. He thought it had
great value. Moses considered it better
than the riches of Egypt. He was looking
ahead to his reward. 27 Because of his
faith, Moses left Egypt. It wasn't because
he was afraid of the king's anger. He
didn't let anything stop him. That's
because he saw the God who can't be
seen. 28 Because of his faith, Moses was
the first to keep the Passover Feast. He
commanded the people of Israel to
sprinkle blood on their doorways. He
did it so that the destroying angel would
not touch their oldest sons.
29 The people of Israel had faith. So
they passed through the Red Sea. They
went through it as if it were dry land.
The Egyptians tried to do it also. But
they drowned.
30 Israel's army had faith. So the walls
of Jericho fell down. It happened after
they had marched around the city for
seven days.
31 Rahab, the prostitute, had faith.
So she welcomed the spies. That's why
she wasn't killed with those who didn't
obey God.
32 What more can I say? I don't have
time to tell about all the others. I don't
have time to talk about Gideon, Barak,
Samson and Jephthah. I don't have time
to tell about David and Samuel and

the prophets. 33 Because of their faith
they took over kingdoms. They ruled
fairly. They received the blessings God
had promised. They shut the mouths
of lions. 34 They put out great fires.
They escaped being killed by swords.
Their weakness was turned to strength.
They became powerful in battle. They
beat back armies from other countries.
35 Women received back their dead. The
dead were raised to life again. There
were others who were made to suffer
greatly. But they refused to be set free.
They did this so that after death they
would be raised to an even better life.
36 Some were made fun of and even
whipped. Some were held by chains.
Some were put in prison. 37 Some were
killed with stones. Some were sawed
in two. Some were killed by swords.
They went around wearing the skins
of sheep and goats. They were poor.
They were attacked. They were treated
badly. 38 The world was not worthy of
them. They wandered in deserts and
mountains. They lived in caves. They
lived in holes in the ground.

39 All these people were praised
because they had faith. But none of
them received what God had promised. 40 That's because God had planned
something better for us. So they would
only be made perfect together with us.

12 A huge cloud of witnesses is all
around us. So let us throw off
everything that stands in our way. Let
us throw off any sin that holds on to
us so tightly. And let us keep on running the race marked out for us. 2 Let
us keep looking to Jesus. He is the one
who started this journey of faith. And he
is the one who completes the journey of
faith. He paid no attention to the shame
of the cross. He suffered there because
of the joy he was looking forward to.
Then he sat down at the right hand of
the throne of God. 3 He made it through
these attacks by sinners. So think about
him. Then you won't get tired. You won't
lose hope.

God Trains His Children

4 You struggle against sin. But you
have not yet fought to the point of spilling your blood. 5 Have you completely
forgotten this word of hope? It speaks to
you as a father to his children. It says,

"My son, think of the Lord's
training as important.
Do not lose hope when he
corrects you.
6 The Lord trains the one he loves.
He corrects everyone he accepts
as his son." *(Proverbs 3:11,12)*

7 Put up with hard times. God uses
them to train you. He is treating you
as his children. What children are not
trained by their parents? 8 God trains
all his children. But what if he doesn't
train you? Then you are not really his
children. You are not God's true sons
and daughters at all. 9 Besides, we have
all had human fathers who trained us.
We respected them for it. How much
more should we be trained by the Father of spirits and live! 10 Our parents
trained us for a little while. They did
what they thought was best. But God
trains us for our good. He does this
so we may share in his holiness. 11 No
training seems pleasant at the time.
In fact, it seems painful. But later on
it produces a harvest of godliness and
peace. It does this for those who have
been trained by it.

12 So put your hands to work.
Strengthen your legs for the journey.
13 "Make level paths for your feet to walk
on." *(Proverbs 4:26)* Then those who
have trouble walking won't be disabled.
Instead, they will be healed.

A Warning and an Appeal

14 Try your best to live in peace with
everyone. Try hard to be holy. Without
holiness no one will see the Lord. 15 Be
sure that no one misses out on God's
grace. See to it that a bitter plant doesn't
grow up. If it does, it will cause trouble.
And it will make many people impure.
16 See to it that no one commits sexual
sins. See to it that no one is godless
like Esau. He sold the rights to what
he would receive as the oldest son. He
sold them for a single meal. 17 As you
know, after that he wanted to receive
his father's blessing. But he was turned
away. With tears he tried to get the
blessing. But he couldn't change what
he had done.

The Mountain of Fear and the Mountain of Joy

18 You haven't come to a mountain that can be touched. You haven't come to a mountain burning with fire. You haven't come to darkness, gloom and storm. 19 You haven't come to a blast from God's trumpet. You haven't come to a voice speaking to you. When people heard that voice long ago, they begged it not to say anything more to them. 20 What God commanded was too much for them. He said, "If even an animal touches the mountain, it must be killed with stones." *(Exodus 19:12,13)* 21 The sight was terrifying. Moses said, "I am trembling with fear." *(Deuteronomy 9:19)*

22 But you have come to Mount Zion. You have come to the city of the living God. This is the heavenly Jerusalem. You have come to a joyful gathering of angels. There are thousands and thousands of them. 23 You have come to the church of God's people. God's first and only Son is over all things. God's people share in what belongs to his Son. Their names are written in heaven. You have come to God, who is the Judge of all people. You have come to the spirits of godly people who have been made perfect. 24 You have come to Jesus. He is the go-between of a new covenant. You have come to the sprinkled blood. It promises better things than the blood of Abel.

25 Be sure that you don't say no to the one who speaks. People did not escape when they said no to the one who warned them on earth. And what if we turn away from the one who warns us from heaven? How much less will we escape! 26 At that time his voice shook the earth. But now he has promised, "Once more I will shake the earth. I will also shake the heavens." *(Haggai 2:6)* 27 The words "once more" point out that what can be shaken can be taken away. I'm talking about created things. Then what can't be shaken will remain.

28 We are receiving a kingdom that can't be shaken. So let us be thankful. Then we can worship God in a way that pleases him. Let us worship him with deep respect and wonder. 29 Our "God is like a fire that burns everything up." *(Deuteronomy 4:24)*

Final Appeals

13 Keep on loving one another as brothers and sisters. 2 Don't forget to welcome outsiders. By doing that, some people have welcomed angels without knowing it. 3 Keep on remembering those in prison. Do this as if you were together with them in prison. And remember those who are treated badly as if you yourselves were suffering.

4 All of you should honor marriage. You should keep the marriage bed pure. God will judge the person who commits adultery. He will judge everyone who commits sexual sins. 5 Don't be controlled by love for money. Be happy with what you have. God has said,

"I will never leave you.
I will never desert you."
(Deuteronomy 31:6)

6 So we can say boldly,

"The Lord helps me. I will not be afraid.
What can mere human beings do to me?" *(Psalm 118:6,7)*

7 Remember your leaders. They spoke God's word to you. Think about the results of their way of life. Copy their faith. 8 Jesus Christ is the same yesterday and today and forever.

9 Don't let all kinds of strange teachings lead you astray. It is good that God's grace makes our hearts strong. Don't try to grow strong by eating foods that the law requires. They have no value for the people who eat them. 10 The priests, who are Levites, worship at the holy tent. But we have an altar that they have no right to eat from.

11 The high priest carries the blood of animals into the Most Holy Room. He brings their blood as a sin offering. But the bodies are burned outside the camp. 12 Jesus also suffered outside the city gate. He suffered to make the people holy by spilling his own blood. 13 So let us go to him outside the camp. Let us be willing to suffer the shame he suffered. 14 Here we do not have a city that lasts. But we are looking for the city that is going to come.

15 So let us never stop offering to God our praise through Jesus. Let us talk openly about our faith in him. Then our words will be like an offering to God.

16 Don't forget to do good. Don't forget to share with others. God is pleased with those kinds of offerings.

17 Trust in your leaders. Put yourselves under their authority. Do this, because they keep watch over you. They know they are accountable to God for everything they do. Do this, so that their work will be a joy. If you make their work a heavy load, it won't do you any good.

18 Pray for us. We feel sure we have done what is right. We desire to live as
we should in every way. 19 I beg you to
pray that I may return to you soon.

Final Blessing and Greetings

20 Our Lord Jesus is the great Shepherd of the sheep. The God who gives peace brought him back from the dead. He did it because of the blood of the eternal covenant. Now may God
21 supply you with everything good. Then you can do what he wants. May he do in us what is pleasing to him. We can do it only with the help of Jesus Christ. Give him glory for ever and ever. Amen.

22 Brothers and sisters, I beg you to accept my word. It tells you to be faithful. Accept my word because I have written to you only a short letter.

23 I want you to know that our brother Timothy has been set free. If he arrives soon, I will come with him to see you.

24 Greet all your leaders. Greet all the Lord's people.

The believers from Italy send you their greetings.

25 May grace be with you all.

JAMES

Author: James

This book was written by Jesus' half brother James, who was living in Jerusalem. After Jesus' death, resurrection, and return to heaven, James became a leader in the church. He believed that the gospel of Jesus compels believers to live lives marked by justice, mercy, and faith, to name a few characteristics, and he wanted the way that Jesus followers live to align with the things they believe. James's letter contains his wise teachings on how to live as a Christian.

The book of James is similar to the books of Wisdom in the Old Testament. God showed his wisdom through Jesus, and his Spirit enables Christians to lead wise and holy lives set apart from the ways of the world. In his letter, James wrote that Christians shouldn't just read God's Word but also apply it to their everyday lives. This means believers are to control what comes out of their mouths, to live in ways that honor God, and to treat all people with kindness and humility. These are just a few of the practical, everyday kinds of ways that the message of Jesus transforms those who choose to follow him. James's letter describes many more ways Jesus transforms our lives!

Letters & Revelation

1

I, James, am writing this letter. I
serve God and the Lord Jesus Christ.

I am sending this letter to you, the
12 tribes scattered among the nations.

Greetings.

Facing All Kinds of Trouble

2 My brothers and sisters, you will
face all kinds of trouble. When you do,
think of it as pure joy. 3 Your faith will
be tested. You know that when this happens it will produce in you the strength
to continue. 4 And you must allow this
strength to finish its work. Then you
will be all you should be. You will have
everything you need. 5 If any of you
needs wisdom, you should ask God for
it. He will give it to you. God gives freely
to everyone and doesn't find fault. 6 But
when you ask, you must believe. You
must not doubt. That's because a person
who doubts is like a wave of the sea. The
wind blows and tosses them around.
7 They shouldn't expect to receive anything from the Lord. 8 This kind of person can't make up their mind. They can
never decide what to do.

9 Here's what believers who are in
low positions in life should be proud of.
They should be proud that God has giv-
en them a high position in the kingdom.
10 But rich people should take pride in
their low positions. That's because they
will fade away like wild flowers. 11 The
sun rises. Its burning heat dries up the
plants. Their blossoms fall. Their beauty is destroyed. In the same way, rich
people will fade away. They fade away
even as they go about their business.

12 Blessed is the person who keeps on
going when times are hard. After they
have come through hard times, this
person will receive a crown. The crown
is life itself. The Lord has promised it to
those who love him.

13 When a person is tempted, they
shouldn't say, "God is tempting me."
God can't be tempted by evil. And he
doesn't tempt anyone. 14 But each person is tempted by their own evil desires.
These desires lead them on and drag
them away. 15 When these desires are
allowed to remain, they lead to sin.
And when sin is allowed to remain and
grow, it leads to death.

16 My dear brothers and sisters, don't
let anyone fool you. 17 Every good and

key verse

If any of you needs wisdom, you should ask God for it. He will give it to you. God gives freely to everyone and doesn't find fault. JAMES 1:5

My GOD IS... WISE

God knows what is best because he created the whole world for our good and his glory (see Job 12:13). Since God created the whole world, he has the right to decide how things work. Just as a builder knows the right way for a building to be used, God knows the right way for us to live.

God gives us directions for how to live in his creation. His directions, or commands, display his wisdom. Each command invites us to know and live in God's wisdom.

As a perfect, loving, and wise Father, God desires for us to grow both in relationship with him and in relationship with each other.

in James?

God is the Ever-Present Father. Not only is he with us every day, but he seeks to transform us each day as we live by faith.

perfect gift is from God. This kind of
gift comes down from the Father who
created the heavenly lights. These
lights create shadows that move. But
the Father does not change like these
shadows. 18 God chose to give us new
birth through the message of truth. He
wanted us to be the first harvest of his
new creation.

Listen to the Word and Do What It Says

19 My dear brothers and sisters, pay
attention to what I say. Everyone
should be quick to listen. But they
should be slow to speak. They should
be slow to get angry. 20 Human anger
doesn't produce the holy life God wants.
21 So get rid of everything that is sinful.
Get rid of the evil that is all around us.
Don't be too proud to accept the word
that is planted in you. It can save you.
22 Don't just listen to the word. You
fool yourselves if you do that. You must
do what it says. 23 Suppose someone
listens to the word but doesn't do what
it says. Then they are like a person who
looks at their face in a mirror. 24 After
looking at themselves, they leave. And
right away they forget what they look
like. 25 But suppose someone takes a
good look at the perfect law that gives
freedom. And they keep looking at it.
Suppose they don't forget what they've
heard, but they do what the law says.
Then this person will be blessed in what
they do.

26 Suppose people think their beliefs
and how they live are both right. But
they don't control what they say. Then
they are fooling themselves. Their beliefs and way of life are not worth anything at all. 27 Here are the beliefs and
way of life that God our Father accepts
as pure and without fault. When widows are in trouble, take care of them.
Do the same for children who have no
parents. And don't let the world make
you impure.

Treat Everyone the Same

2 My brothers and sisters, you are
believers in our glorious Lord Jesus
Christ. So treat everyone the same.
2 Suppose a man comes into your meeting wearing a gold ring and fine clothes.
And suppose a poor man in dirty old
clothes also comes in. 3 Would you show
special attention to the man wearing
fine clothes? Would you say, "Here's a
good seat for you"? Would you say to
the poor man, "You stand there"? Or "Sit
on the floor by my feet"? 4 If you would,
aren't you treating some people better
than others? Aren't you like judges who
have evil thoughts?
5 My dear brothers and sisters, listen
to me. Hasn't God chosen those who are
poor in the world's eyes to be rich in
faith? Hasn't he chosen them to receive

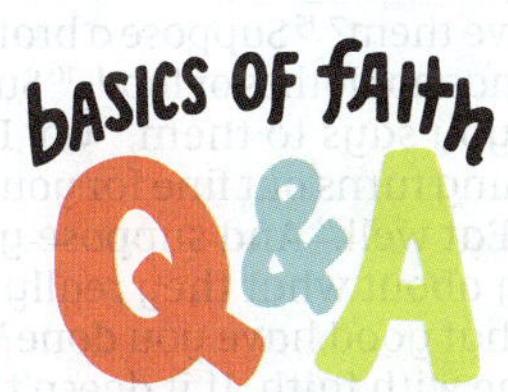

Should I treat poor people and rich people the same?

It doesn't matter if a person has a lot of money or is very poor. We should treat all people the same because God tells believers in him to love everyone.

Can you find the following verses?

JAMES 2:1–4

the kingdom? Hasn't he promised it to
those who love him? [6] But you have
disrespected poor people. Aren't rich
people taking advantage of you? Aren't
they dragging you into court? [7] Aren't
they speaking evil things against the
worthy name of Jesus? Remember, you
belong to him.
[8] The royal law is found in Scripture.
It says, "Love your neighbor as you love
yourself." *(Leviticus 19:18)* If you really
keep this law, you are doing what is
right. [9] But you sin if you don't treat
everyone the same. The law judges you
because you have broken it. [10] Suppose
you keep the whole law but trip over
just one part of it. Then you are guilty
of breaking all of it. [11] God said, "Do
not commit adultery." *(Exodus 20:14;
Deuteronomy 5:18)* He also said, "Do not
commit murder." *(Exodus 20:13; Deuteronomy 5:17)* Suppose you don't commit
adultery but do commit murder. Then
you have broken the law.
[12] Speak and act like people who are
going to be judged by the law that gives
freedom. [13] Those who have not shown
mercy will not receive mercy when they
are judged. To show mercy is better than
to judge.

Show Your Faith by What You Do

[14] Suppose a person claims to have
faith but doesn't act on their faith. My
brothers and sisters, can this kind of
faith save them? [15] Suppose a brother or
a sister has no clothes or food. [16] Suppose
one of you says to them, "Go. I hope
everything turns out fine for you. Keep
warm. Eat well." And suppose you do
nothing about what they really need.
Then what good have you done? [17] It is
the same with faith. If it doesn't cause
us to do something, it's dead.
[18] But someone will say, "You have
faith. I do good deeds."
Show me your faith that doesn't cause
you to do good deeds. And I will show
you my faith by the goods deeds I do.
[19] You believe there is one God. Good!
Even the demons believe that. And they
tremble!
[20] You foolish person! Do you want
proof that faith without good deeds is
useless? [21] Our father Abraham offered
his son Isaac on the altar. Wasn't he
considered to be right with God because
of what he did? [22] So you see that what
he believed and what he did were
working together. What he did made
his faith complete. [23] That is what Scripture means where it says, "Abraham
believed God. God accepted Abraham
because he believed. So his faith made
him right with God." *(Genesis 15:6)* And
that's not all. God called Abraham his
friend. [24] So you see that a person is
considered right with God by what they
do. It doesn't happen only because they
believe.
[25] Didn't God consider even Rahab the
prostitute to be right with him? That's
because of what she did for the spies.
She gave them a place to stay. Then she
sent them off in a different direction.
[26] A person's body without their spirit
is dead. In the same way, faith without
good deeds is dead.

Control What You Say

3 My brothers and sisters, most of
you shouldn't become teachers.
That's because you know that those of
us who teach will be held more accountable. [2] All of us get tripped up in many
ways. Suppose someone is never wrong
in what they say. Then they are perfect.
They are able to keep their whole body
under control.
[3] We put a small piece of metal in the
mouth of a horse to make it obey us. We
can control the whole animal with it.
[4] And how about ships? They are very
big. They are driven along by strong
winds. But they are steered by a very
small rudder. It makes them go where
the captain wants to go. [5] In the same
way, the tongue is a small part of a
person's body. But it talks big. Think
about how a small spark can set a big
forest on fire. [6] The tongue is also a fire.
The tongue is the most evil part of the
body. It makes the whole body impure.
It sets a person's whole way of life on
fire. And the tongue itself is set on fire
by hell.
[7] People have tamed all kinds of wild
animals, birds, reptiles and sea creatures. And they still tame them. [8] But
no one can tame the tongue. It is an
evil thing that never rests. It is full of
deadly poison.
[9] With our tongues we praise our
Lord and Father. With our tongues we

curse people. We do it even though people have been created to be like God.
10 Praise and cursing come out of the
same mouth. My brothers and sisters, it
shouldn't be this way. 11 Can fresh water
and salt water flow out of the same
spring? 12 My brothers and sisters, can
a fig tree produce olives? Can a grape-
vine produce figs? Of course not. And
a saltwater spring can't produce fresh
water either.

Two Kinds of Wisdom

13 Is anyone among you wise and understanding? That person should show
it by living a good life. A wise person
isn't proud when they do good deeds.
14 But suppose your hearts are jealous
and bitter. Suppose you are concerned
only about getting ahead. Then don't
brag about it. And don't say no to the
truth. 15 Wisdom like this doesn't come
down from heaven. It belongs to the
earth. It doesn't come from the Holy
Spirit. It comes from the devil. 16 Are
you jealous? Are you concerned only
about getting ahead? Then your life will
be a mess. You will be doing all kinds
of evil things.

17 But the wisdom that comes from
heaven is pure. That's the most important thing about it. And that's not all. It
also loves peace. It thinks about others.
It obeys. It is full of mercy and good
fruit. It is fair. It doesn't pretend to be
what it is not. 18 Those who make peace
plant it like a seed. They will harvest a
crop of right living.

Obey God

4 Why do you fight and argue among
yourselves? Isn't it because of your
sinful desires? They fight within you.
2 You want something, but you don't
have it. So you kill. You want what
others have, but you can't get what
you want. So you argue and fight. You
don't have what you want, because you
don't ask God. 3 When you do ask for
something, you don't receive it. That's
because you ask for the wrong reason.
You want to spend your money on your
sinful pleasures.

4 You are not faithful to God. Don't
you know that to be a friend of the
world is to hate God? So anyone who
chooses to be the world's friend becomes
God's enemy. 5 Don't you know what
Scripture says? God wants the spirit in
us to belong only to him. God caused
this spirit to live in us. Don't you think
Scripture has a reason for saying this?
6 But God continues to give us more
grace. That's why Scripture says,

> "God opposes those who are proud.
> But he gives grace to those who
> are humble." *(Proverbs 3:34)*

7 So obey God. Stand up to the devil.
He will run away from you. 8 Come near
to God, and he will come near to you.
Wash your hands, you sinners. Make
your hearts pure, you who can't make
up your minds. 9 Be full of sorrow. Cry
and weep. Change your laughter to
mourning. Change your joy to sadness.
10 Be humble in front of the Lord. And
he will lift you up.

11 My brothers and sisters, don't
speak against one another. Anyone
who speaks against a brother or sister
speaks against the law. And anyone
who judges another believer judges the
law. When you judge the law, you are
not keeping it. Instead, you are acting
as if you were its judge. 12 There is only
one Lawgiver and Judge. He is the God
who is able to save life or destroy it. But
who are you to judge your neighbor?

Bragging About Tomorrow

13 Now listen, you who say, "Today
or tomorrow we will go to this or that
city. We will spend a year there. We will
buy and sell and make money." 14 You
don't even know what will happen tomorrow. What is your life? It is a mist
that appears for a little while. Then it
disappears. 15 Instead, you should say,
"If it pleases the Lord, we will live and
do this or that." 16 As it is, you brag. You
brag about the evil plans your pride
produces. This kind of bragging is evil.
17 So suppose someone knows the good
deeds they should do. But suppose they
don't do them. By not doing these good
deeds, they sin.

A Warning to Rich People

5 You rich people, listen to me. Cry
and weep, because you will soon
be suffering. 2 Your riches have rotted.
Moths have eaten your clothes. 3 Your
gold and silver have lost their brightness. Their dullness will be a witness
against you. Your wanting more and

more will eat your body like fire. You
have stored up riches in these last days.
4 You have even failed to pay the workers who mowed your fields. Their pay
is crying out against you. The cries of
those who gathered the harvest have
reached the ears of the Lord. He rules
over all. 5 You have lived an easy life
on earth. You have given yourselves
everything you wanted. You have made
yourselves fat like cattle that will soon
be butchered. 6 You have judged and
murdered people who aren't guilty.
And they weren't even opposing you.

Be Patient When You Suffer

7 Brothers and sisters, be patient until
the Lord comes. See how the farmer
waits for the land to produce its rich
crop. See how patient the farmer is for
the fall and spring rains. 8 You too must
be patient. You must remain strong. The
Lord will soon come back. 9 Brothers
and sisters, don't find fault with one
another. If you do, you will be judged.
And the Judge is standing at the door!
10 Brothers and sisters, think about
the prophets who spoke in the name of
the Lord. They are an example of how
to be patient when you suffer. 11 As you
know, we think that people who don't
give up are blessed. You have heard
that Job was patient. And you have
seen what the Lord finally did for him.
The Lord is full of tender mercy and
loving concern.
12 My brothers and sisters, here is
what is most important. Don't make
a promise by giving your word. Don't
promise by heaven or earth. And don't
promise by anything else to back up
what you say. All you need to say is
a simple "Yes" or "No." If you do more
than this, you will be judged.

The Prayer of Faith

13 Is anyone among you in trouble? Then that person should pray. Is
anyone among you happy? Then that
person should sing songs of praise. 14 Is
anyone among you sick? Then that
person should send for the elders of the
church to pray over them. They should
ask the elders to anoint them with olive
oil in the name of the Lord. 15 The prayer
offered by those who have faith will
make the sick person well. The Lord will
heal them. If they have sinned, they
will be forgiven. 16 So confess your sins
to one another. Pray for one another so
that you might be healed. The prayer
of a godly person is powerful. Things
happen because of it.
17 Elijah was a human being, just as
we are. He prayed hard that it wouldn't
rain. And it didn't rain on the land for
three and a half years. 18 Then he prayed
again. That time it rained. And the
earth produced its crops.
19 My brothers and sisters, suppose
one of you wanders away from the
truth. And suppose someone brings
that person back. 20 Then here is what
I want you to remember. Anyone who
keeps a sinner from going astray will
save them from death. God will erase
many sins by forgiving them.

1 PETER

Author: Peter

Peter was a disciple and friend of Jesus. Years after Jesus' return to heaven, Peter heard that communities of new Christians throughout Asia Minor (known today as Turkey) were facing persecution for their faith. Nonbelievers were causing believers to suffer because of their faith. Peter wrote the believers two letters encouraging them to persevere, to keep believing, even in hard times.

In this first letter, Peter assured the believers that they had hope because of their salvation. Even though they were being persecuted and treated unfairly, Peter reminded them that they hadn't lost their very best treasure: Jesus. He, too, suffered for doing good. Peter described for his readers the benefits of living for God, who has far better things to offer than the things of this world. Peter also explained that following God requires surrender and a willingness to serve. Choosing to follow Jesus means living right even when suffering, because that's how others see genuine faith. God's people may not always be understood in this world, but they can endure hard times by keeping their eyes fixed on their eternal treasure.

Letters & Revelation

1 I, Peter, am writing this letter. I am an apostle of Jesus Christ.

I am sending this letter to you, God's chosen people. You are people who have had to wander in the world. You are scattered all over the areas of Pontus, Galatia, Cappadocia, Asia and Bithynia. 2You have been chosen in keeping with what God the Father had planned. That happened through the Spirit's work to make you pure and holy. God chose you so that you might obey Jesus Christ. God wanted you to be in a covenant relationship with him. He established this relationship by the blood of Christ.

May more and more grace and peace be given to you.

Peter Praises God for a Living Hope

3Give praise to the God and Father of our Lord Jesus Christ. In his great mercy he has given us a new birth and a living hope. This hope is living because Jesus Christ rose from the dead. 4He has given us new birth so that we might share in what belongs to him. This is a gift that can never be destroyed. It can never spoil or even fade away. It is kept in heaven for you. 5Through faith you are kept safe by God's power. Your salvation is going to be completed. It is ready to be shown to you in the last days. 6Because you know all this, you have great joy. You have joy even though you may have had to suffer for a little while. You may have had to suffer sadness in all kinds of trouble. 7Your troubles have come in order to prove that your faith is real. Your faith is worth more than gold. That's because gold can pass away even when fire has made it pure. Your faith is meant to bring praise, honor and glory to God. This will happen when Jesus Christ returns. 8Even though you have not seen him, you love him. Though you do not see him now, you believe in him. You are filled with a glorious joy that can't be put into words. 9You are receiving the salvation of your souls. This salvation is the final result of your faith.

10The prophets searched very hard and with great care to find out about this salvation. They spoke about the grace that was going to come to you. 11They wanted to find out when and how this salvation would come. The

in 1 Peter?

God is the Spotless Lamb. He is perfect in all his ways, and he alone is worthy of all honor, glory, and praise.

Spirit of Christ in them was telling them about the sufferings of the Messiah. These were his sufferings that were going to come. The Spirit of Christ was also telling them about the glory that would follow. 12It was made known to the prophets that they were not serving themselves. Instead, they were serving you when they spoke about the things that you have now heard. Those who have preached the good news to you have told you these things. They have done it with the help of the Holy Spirit sent from heaven. Even angels long to look into these things.

Be Holy

13So be watchful, and control yourselves completely. In this way, put your hope in the grace that lies ahead. This grace will be brought to you when Jesus Christ returns. 14You should obey your Father. You shouldn't give in to evil desires. They controlled your life when you didn't know any better. 15The God who chose you is holy. So you should be holy in all that you do. 16It is written, "Be holy, because I am holy." *(Leviticus 11:44,45; 19:2)*

17You call on a Father who judges each person's work without favoring one over another. So live as outsiders during your time here. Live with the highest respect for God. 18You were set free from an empty way of life. This way of life was handed down to you by your own people of long ago. You know that you were not bought with things

that can pass away, like silver or gold.
19 Instead, you were bought with the
priceless blood of Christ. He is a perfect
lamb. He doesn't have any flaws at all.
20 He was chosen before God created the
world. But he came into the world for
your sake in these last days. 21 Because
of what Christ has done, you believe in
God. It was God who raised him from
the dead. And it was God who gave him
glory. So your faith and hope are in God.
22 You have made yourselves pure by
obeying the truth. So you have an honest and true love for each other. So love
one another deeply, from your hearts.
23 You have been born again by means
of the living word of God. His word lasts
forever. You were not born again from a
seed that will die. You were born from a
seed that can't die. 24 It is written,

"All people are like grass.
All their glory is like the flowers
in the field.
The grass dries up. The flowers fall
to the ground.
25 But the word of the Lord lasts
forever." *(Isaiah 40:6–8)*

And this is the word that was preached
to you.

2 So get rid of every kind of evil, and
stop telling lies. Don't pretend to
be something you are not. Stop wanting what others have, and don't speak
against one another. 2 Like newborn babies, you should long for the pure milk
of God's word. It will help you grow up
as believers. 3 You can do this now that
you have tasted how good the Lord is.

The Living Stone and a Chosen People

4 Christ is the living Stone. People
did not accept him, but God chose
him. God places the highest value on
him. 5 You also are like living stones.
As you come to Christ, you are being
built into a house for worship. There
you will be holy priests. You will offer
spiritual sacrifices. God will accept them
because of what Jesus Christ has done.
6 In Scripture it says,

"Look! I am placing a stone in Zion.
It is a chosen and very valuable
stone.
It is the most important stone in
the building.
The one who trusts in him
will never be put to shame."
(Isaiah 28:16)

God is set apart from all creation and pure in all his ways. He has never done anything wrong, and he never will do anything wrong. God cannot make mistakes, and he has no faults or flaws.

People, on the other hand, struggle with sin. We don't naturally want to **trust** God and live by faith. But God said that **we** can be holy, or set apart as special, by receiving Jesus as Lord and following his example (see 1 Corinthians 1:30).

Have you ever looked in a mirror and seen yourself looking back at you? If you wiggle your nose or stick your hand in the air, you see your action reflected in the mirror. We can reflect God's goodness and holiness to others by choosing to follow Jesus.

My GOD is...

[7] This stone is very valuable to you who believe. But to people who do not believe,

> "The stone the builders did not accept
> has become the most important stone of all." *(Psalm 118:22)*

[8] And,

> "It is a stone that causes people to trip.
> It is a rock that makes them fall." *(Isaiah 8:14)*

They trip and fall because they do not obey the message. That is also what God planned for them.

[9] But God chose you to be his people. You are royal priests. You are a holy nation. You are God's special treasure. You are all these things so that you can give him praise. God brought you out of darkness into his wonderful light. [10] Once you were not a people. But now you are the people of God. Once you had not received mercy. But now you have received mercy.

key verse But God chose you to be his people. You are royal priests. You are a holy nation. You are God's special treasure. You are all these things so that you can give him praise. **1 PETER 2:9**

Living Godly Lives Among People Who Don't Believe

[11] Dear friends, you are outsiders and those who wander in this world. So I'm asking you not to give in to your sinful desires. They fight against your soul. [12] People who don't believe might say you are doing wrong. But lead good lives among them. Then they will see your good deeds. And they will give glory to God on the day he comes to judge.

[13] Follow the lead of every human authority. Do this for the Lord's sake. Obey the emperor. He is the highest authority. [14] Obey the governors. The emperor sends them to punish those who do wrong. He also sends them to praise those who do right. [15] By doing good you will put a stop to the talk of foolish people. They don't know what they are saying. [16] Live as free people. But don't use your freedom to cover up evil. Live as people who are God's slaves. [17] Show proper respect to everyone. Love the family of believers. Have respect for God. Honor the emperor.

[18] Slaves, obey your masters out of deep respect for God. Obey not only those who are good and kind. Obey also those who are not kind. [19] Suppose a person suffers pain unfairly because they want to obey God. This is worthy of praise. [20] But suppose you receive a beating for doing wrong, and you put up with it. Will anyone honor you for this? Of course not. But suppose you suffer for doing good, and you put up with it. God will praise you for this. [21] You were chosen to do good even if you suffer. That's because Christ suffered for you. He left you an example that he expects you to follow. [22] Scripture says,

> "He didn't commit any sin.
> No lies ever came out of his mouth." *(Isaiah 53:9)*

[23] People shouted at him and made fun of him. But he didn't do the same thing back to them. When he suffered, he didn't say he would make them suffer. Instead, he trusted in the God who judges fairly. [24] "He himself carried our sins" in his body on the cross. *(Isaiah 53:5)* He did it so that we would die as far as sins are concerned. Then we would lead godly lives. "His wounds have healed you." *(Isaiah 53:5)* [25] "You were like sheep wandering away." *(Isaiah 53:6)* But now you have returned to the Shepherd. He is the one who watches over your souls.

3 Wives, follow the lead of your own husbands. Suppose some of them don't believe God's word. Then let them be won to Christ without words by seeing how their wives behave. [2] Let them see how pure you are. Let them see that your lives are full of respect for God. [3] Fancy hairstyles don't make you beautiful. Wearing gold jewelry or fine clothes doesn't make you beautiful. [4] Instead, your beauty comes from inside you. It is the beauty of a gentle and quiet spirit. Beauty like this doesn't fade away. God places great value on it. [5] This is how the holy women of the past used to make themselves beautiful. They put their hope in God. And they followed the lead of their own husbands. [6] Sarah was like that. She obeyed Abraham. She called him her master. Do you want to be like her? Then do what is right. And don't give in to fear.

[7] Husbands, consider the needs of your wives. They are weaker than you. So treat them with respect. Honor them as those who will share with you the gracious gift of life. Then nothing will stand in the way of your prayers.

Suffering for Doing Good

[8] Finally, I want all of you to agree with one another. Be understanding. Love one another. Be kind and tender. Be humble. [9] Don't pay back evil with evil. Don't pay back unkind words with unkind words. Instead, pay back evil with kind words. This is what you have been chosen to do. You will receive a blessing by doing this. [10] Scripture says,

"Suppose someone wants to love life
and see good days.
Then they must keep their tongues from speaking evil.
They must keep their lips from telling lies.
[11] They must turn away from evil and do good.
They must look for peace and go after it.
[12] The Lord's eyes look on godly people, and he blesses them.
His ears are open to their prayers.
But the Lord doesn't bless those who do evil." *(Psalm 34:12–16)*

[13] Who is going to hurt you if you really want to do good? [14] But suppose you do suffer for doing what is right. Even then you will be blessed. Scripture says, "Don't fear what others say they will do to hurt you. Don't be afraid." *(Isaiah 8:12)* [15] But make sure that in your hearts you honor Christ as Lord. Always be ready to give an answer to anyone who asks you about the hope you have. Be ready to give the reason for it. But do it gently and with respect. [16] Live so that you don't have to feel you've done anything wrong. Some people may say evil things about your good conduct

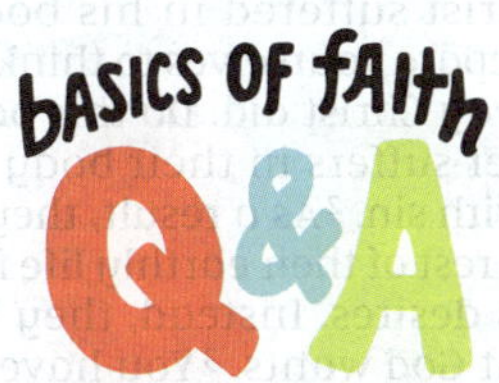

What do I say if someone treats me unkindly for following Jesus?

God calls you to share the hope you have in Jesus with others. And he says you should always be gentle and respectful toward others, even if they treat you unkindly.

Can you find the following verses?

1 PETER 3:14–15

as believers in Christ. If they do, they will be put to shame for speaking like this about you. [17] God may want you to suffer for doing good. That's better than suffering for doing evil. [18] Christ also suffered once for sins. The one who did what is right suffered for those who don't do right. He suffered to bring you to God. His body was put to death. But the Holy Spirit brought him back to life. [19] After that, Christ went and made an announcement to the spirits in prison. [20] Long ago these spirits did not obey. That was when God was patient while Noah was building the ark. And only a few people went into the ark. In fact, there were only eight. Those eight people were saved through water. [21] The water of the flood is a picture. It is a picture of the baptism that now saves you too. This baptism has nothing to do with removing dirt from your body. Instead, it promises God that you will keep a clear sense of right and wrong. This baptism saves you by the same power that raised Jesus Christ from the dead. [22] He has gone into heaven. He is at God's right hand. Angels, authorities and powers are under his control.

Living for God

4 Christ suffered in his body. So prepare yourselves to think in the same way Christ did. Do this because whoever suffers in their body is finished with sin. 2 As a result, they don't live the rest of their earthly life for evil human desires. Instead, they live to do what God wants. 3 You have spent enough time in the past doing what ungodly people choose to do. You lived a wild life. You longed for evil things. You got drunk. You went to wild parties. You worshiped statues of gods, which the Lord hates. 4 Ungodly people are surprised that you no longer join them in what they do. They want you to join them in their wild and wasteful living. So they say bad things about you. 5 But they will have to explain their actions to God. He is ready to judge those who are alive and those who are dead. 6 That's why the good news was preached even to people who are now dead. It was preached to them for two reasons. It was preached so that their bodies might be judged. This judgment is made by human standards. But the good news was also preached so that their spirits might live. This life comes by means of God's power.

7 The end of all things is near. So be watchful and control yourselves. Then you may pray. 8 Most of all, love one another deeply. Love erases many sins by forgiving them. 9 Welcome others into your homes without complaining. 10 God's gifts of grace come in many forms. Each of you has received a gift in order to serve others. You should use it faithfully. 11 If anyone speaks, they should do it as one speaking God's words. If anyone serves, they should do it with the strength God provides. Then in all things God will be praised through Jesus Christ. Glory and power belong to him for ever and ever. Amen.

Suffering for Being a Christian

12 Dear friends, don't be surprised by the terrible things happening to you. The trouble you are having has come to test you. So don't feel as if something strange were happening to you. 13 Instead, be joyful that you are taking part in Christ's sufferings. Then you will have even more joy when Christ returns in glory. 14 Suppose people say bad things about you because you believe in Christ. Then you are blessed, because God's Spirit rests on you. He is the Spirit of glory. 15 If you suffer, it shouldn't be because you are a murderer. It shouldn't be because you are a thief or someone who does evil things. It shouldn't be because you interfere with other people's business. 16 But suppose you suffer for being a Christian. Then don't be ashamed. Instead, praise God because you are known by the name of Christ. 17 It is time for judgment to begin with the household of God. And since it begins with us, what will happen to people who don't obey God's good news? 18 Scripture says,

"Suppose it is hard for godly people
to be saved.
Then what will happen to
ungodly people and sinners?"
(Proverbs 11:31)

19 Here is what people who suffer because of God's plan should do. They should commit themselves to their faithful Creator. And they should continue to do good.

To Older and Younger Believers

5 I'm speaking to the elders among you. I was a witness of Christ's sufferings. And I will also share in the glory that is going to come. I'm making my appeal to you as one who is an elder together with you. 2 Be shepherds of God's flock, the believers under your care. Watch over them, though not because you have to. Instead, do it because you want to. That's what God wants you to do. Don't do it because you want to get money in dishonest ways. Do it because you really want to serve. 3 Don't act as if you were a ruler over those under your care. Instead, be examples to the flock. 4 The Chief Shepherd will come again. Then you will receive the crown of glory. It is a crown that will never fade away.

5 In the same way, I'm speaking to you who are younger. Follow the lead of those who are older. All of you, put on a spirit free of pride toward one another. Put it on as if it were your clothes. Do this because Scripture says,

"God opposes those who are proud.
But he gives grace to those who
are humble." *(Proverbs 3:34)*

6 So make yourselves humble. Put yourselves under God's mighty hand. Then
he will honor you at the right time.
7 Turn all your worries over to him. He
cares about you.
8 Be watchful and control yourselves.
Your enemy the devil is like a roaring
lion. He prowls around looking for
someone to swallow up. 9 Stand up
to him. Remain strong in what you
believe. You know that you are not
alone in your suffering. The family of
believers throughout the world is going
through the same thing.
10 God always gives you all the grace
you need. So you will only have to suffer
for a little while. Then God himself will
build you up again. He will make you
strong and steady. And he has chosen
you to share in his eternal glory because
you belong to Christ. 11 Give him the
power for ever and ever. Amen.

Final Greetings

12 I consider Silas to be a faithful
brother. With his help I have written
you this short letter. I have written it
to encourage you. And I have written
to speak the truth about the true grace
of God. Remain strong in it.

13 The members of the church in Babylon send you their greetings. They
were chosen together with you. Mark,
my son in the faith, also sends you his
greetings.
14 Greet each other with a kiss of
friendship.

May God give peace to all of you who
believe in Christ.

2 PETER

Author: Peter

After his first letter, Peter wrote a second letter to the churches spread throughout Asia Minor. In this letter, Peter reminded the suffering believers that the grace of God changes everything. God could use their suffering to make them more like him by the power of the Holy Spirit.

Letters & Revelation

Peter also wanted to encourage the believers with two important truths. The first was that Jesus really rose from the dead. Some people were teaching that Jesus didn't rise from the dead, but Peter wrote that God holds all power. The second truth Peter reminded them of was that Jesus was coming back soon. Peter wanted the believers to know that God had kept his first promise to send the Savior, and he would also keep his promise to return and make all things right!

Peter encouraged the believers to hold on to the hope of Jesus' return. This would give them the confidence they needed to live for God. These two truths—the resurrection of Jesus and his promised return—give us the grace and strength we need to endure anything as we follow Jesus our whole lives!

1 I, Simon Peter, am writing this letter.
I serve Jesus Christ. I am his apostle.
I am sending this letter to you. You
are those who have received a faith as
valuable as ours. You received it because our God and Savior Jesus Christ
does what is right.
2 May more and more grace and
peace be given to you. May they come
to you as you learn more about God
and about Jesus our Lord.

Showing That God Has Chosen You

3 God's power has given us everything
we need to lead a godly life. All of this
has come to us because we know the
God who chose us. He chose us because
of his own glory and goodness. 4 He has
also given us his very great and valuable promises. He did it so you could
share in his nature. You can share in it
because you've escaped from the evil in
the world. This evil is caused by sinful
desires.
5 So you should try very hard to add
goodness to your faith. To goodness,
add knowledge. 6 To knowledge, add
the ability to control yourselves. To the
ability to control yourselves, add the
strength to keep going. To the strength
to keep going, add godliness. 7 To godliness, add kindness for one another.
And to kindness for one another, add
love. 8 All these things should describe
you more and more. They will make
you useful and fruitful as you know
our Lord Jesus Christ better. 9 But what
if these things don't describe someone
at all? Then that person can't see very
well. In fact, they are blind. They have
forgotten that their past sins have been
washed away.
10 My brothers and sisters, try very
hard to show that God has appointed
you to be saved. Try hard to show that
he has chosen you. If you do everything
I have just said, you will never trip and
fall. 11 You will receive a rich welcome
into the kingdom that lasts forever. It
is the kingdom of our Lord and Savior
Jesus Christ.

Prophecy of Scripture Comes From God

12 So I will always remind you of these
things. I'll do it even though you know
them. I'll do it even though you now

in 2 Peter?

God is the Peacemaker.
He welcomes everyone
from around the
entire globe to have a
relationship with him.

have deep roots in the truth. 13 I think it
is right for me to remind you. It is right
as long as I live in this tent. I'm talking
about my body. 14 I know my tent will
soon be removed. Our Lord Jesus Christ
has made that clear to me. 15 I hope that
you will always be able to remember
these things after I'm gone. I will try
very hard to see that you do.
16 We told you about the time our Lord
Jesus Christ came with power. But we
didn't make up clever stories when we
told you about it. With our own eyes
we saw him in all his majesty. 17 God
the Father gave him honor and glory.
The voice of the Majestic Glory came
to him. It said, "This is my Son, and I
love him. I am very pleased with him."
(Matthew 17:5; Mark 9:7; Luke 9:35) 18 We
ourselves heard this voice that came
from heaven. We were with him on the
sacred mountain.
19 We also have the message of the
prophets. This message can be trusted
completely. You must pay attention to
it. The message is like a light shining
in a dark place. It will shine until the
day Jesus comes. Then the Morning
Star will rise in your hearts. 20 Above
all, here is what you must understand.
No prophecy in Scripture ever came
from a prophet's own understanding of
things. 21 Prophecy never came simply
because a prophet wanted it to. Instead,
the Holy Spirit guided the prophets as
they spoke. So, although prophets are
human, prophecy comes from God.

False Teachers Will Be Destroyed

2 But there were also false prophets among the people. In the same way there will be false teachers among you. In secret they will bring in teachings that will destroy you. They will even turn against the Lord and Master who died to pay for their sins. So they will quickly destroy themselves. [2] Many people will follow their lead. These people will do the same evil things the false teachers do. They will cause people to think badly about the way of truth. [3] These teachers are never satisfied. They want to get something out of you. So they make up stories to take advantage of you. They have been under a sentence of death for a long time. The God who will destroy them has not been sleeping.

[4] God did not spare angels when they sinned. Instead, he sent them to hell. He chained them up in dark prisons. He will keep them there until he judges them. [5] God did not spare the world's ungodly people long ago. He brought the flood on them. But Noah preached about the right way to live. God kept him safe. He also saved seven others. [6] God judged the cities of Sodom and Gomorrah. He burned them to ashes. He made them an example of what is going to happen to ungodly people. [7] God saved Lot, a man who did what was right. Lot was shocked by the evil conduct of people who didn't obey God's laws. [8] That good man lived among them day after day. He saw and heard the evil things they were doing. They were breaking God's laws. And the godly spirit of Lot was deeply troubled. [9] Since all this is true, then the Lord knows how to save godly people. He knows how to keep them safe in times of testing. The Lord also knows how to keep ungodly people under guard. He will do so until the day they will be judged and punished. [10] Most of all, this is true of people who follow desires that come from sin's power. These people hate to be under authority.

They are bold and proud. So they aren't even afraid to speak evil things against heavenly beings. [11] Now angels are stronger and more powerful than these people. But even angels don't speak evil things against heavenly beings. They don't do this when they bring judgment on them from the Lord. [12] These people speak evil about things they don't understand. They are like wild animals who can't think. Instead, they do what comes naturally to them. They are born only to be caught and destroyed. Just like animals, these people too will die.

[13] They will be paid back with harm for the harm they have done. Their idea of pleasure is to have wild parties in the middle of the day. They are like dirty spots and stains. They enjoy their sinful pleasures while they eat with you. [14] They stare at women who are not their wives. They want to sleep with them. They never stop sinning. They trap those who are not firm in their faith. They have mastered the art of getting what they want. God has placed them under his judgment. [15] They have left God's way. They have wandered off. They follow the way of Balaam, son of Beor. He loved to get paid for doing his evil work. [16] But a donkey corrected him for the wrong he did. Animals don't speak. But the donkey spoke with a human voice. It tried to stop the prophet from doing a very dumb thing.

[17] These people are like springs without water. They are like mists driven by a storm. The blackest darkness is reserved for them. [18] They speak empty, bragging words. They make their appeal

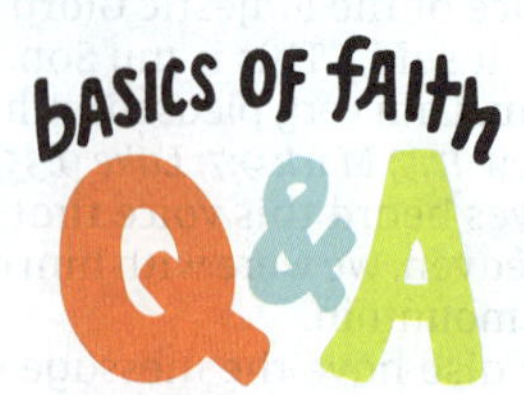

Who does God want to save through faith in Jesus?

God wants everyone to turn from their sin and put their faith in Jesus. God patiently waits for people to repent because he loves us.

Can you find the following verse?

2 PETER 3:9

to the evil desires that come from sin's
power. They tempt new believers who
are just escaping from the company of
sinful people. 19 They promise to give
freedom to these new believers. But they
themselves are slaves to sinful living.
That's because "people are slaves to anything that controls them." 20 They may
have escaped the sin of the world. They
may have come to know our Lord and
Savior Jesus Christ. But what if they are
once again caught up in sin? And what
if it has become their master? Then they
are worse off at the end than they were
at the beginning. 21 Suppose they had
not known the way of godliness. This
would have been better than to know
godliness and then turn away from
it. The way of godliness is the sacred
command passed on to them. 22 What
the proverbs say about them is true.
"A dog returns to where it has thrown
up." *(Proverbs 26:11)* And, "A pig that is
washed goes back to rolling in the mud."

The Day of the Lord

3 Dear friends, this is now my second letter to you. I have written
both of them as reminders. I want to
encourage you to think in a way that
is pure. 2 I want you to remember the
words the holy prophets spoke in the
past. Remember the command our Lord
and Savior gave through your apostles.

3 Most of all, here is what you must
understand. In the last days people
will make fun of the truth. They will
laugh at it. They will follow their own
evil desires. 4 They will say, "Where is
this 'return' he promised? Everything
goes on in the same way it has since
our people of long ago died. In fact, it
has continued this way since God first
created everything." 5 Long ago, God's
word brought the heavens into being.
His word separated the earth from the
waters. And the waters surrounded it.
But these people forget things like that
on purpose. 6 The waters also flooded
the world of that time. And so they destroyed the world. 7 By God's word the
heavens and earth of today are being
reserved for fire. They are being kept
for the day when God will judge. Then
ungodly people will be destroyed.

8 Dear friends, here is one thing you
must not forget. With the Lord a day is
like a thousand years. And a thousand
years are like a day. 9 The Lord is not
slow to keep his promise. He is not slow
in the way some people understand
it. Instead, he is patient with you. He
doesn't want anyone to be destroyed.
Instead, he wants all people to turn
away from their sins.

10 But the day of the Lord will come
like a thief. The heavens will disappear
with a roar. Fire will destroy everything
in them. God will judge the earth and
everything done in it.

11 So everything will be destroyed in
this way. And what kind of people should
you be? You should lead holy and godly
lives. 12 Live like this as you look forward
to the day of God. Living like this will
make the day come more quickly. On
that day fire will destroy the heavens. Its
heat will melt everything in them. 13 But
we are looking forward to a new heaven
and a new earth. Godliness will live there.
All this is in keeping with God's promise.

14 Dear friends, I know you are looking forward to this. So try your best to
be found pure and without blame. Be
at peace with God. 15 Remember that
while our Lord is waiting patiently to
return, people are being saved. Our dear
brother Paul also wrote to you about
this. God made him wise to write as he
did. 16 Paul writes the same way in all
his letters. He speaks about what I have
just told you. His letters include some
things that are hard to understand.
People who don't know better and aren't
firm in the faith twist what he says.
They twist the other Scriptures too. So
they will be destroyed.

17 Dear friends, you have already been
warned about this. So be on your guard.
Then you won't be led astray by people
who don't obey the law. Instead, you
will remain safe. 18 Grow in the grace
and knowledge of our Lord and Savior
Jesus Christ.

Glory belongs to him both now and
forever. Amen.

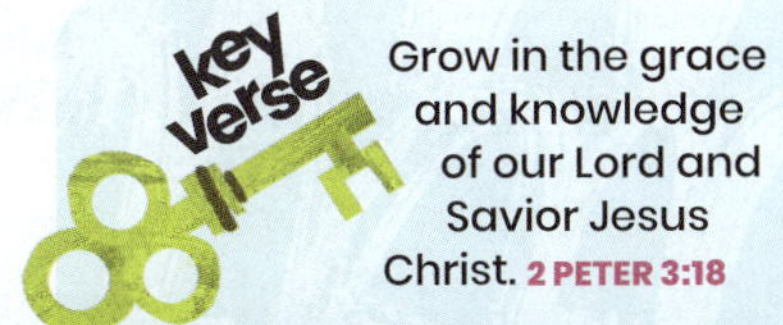

1 JOHN

Author: John

The books of 1, 2, and 3 John were written to a group of new Christians who were learning what it meant to follow Jesus and live out their faith in him. John wrote these three letters to help them understand the gospel.

In this first letter, John exposed false teachings and reminded his readers that Jesus was the Son of God who came and walked the earth. John wrote that Jesus was with the Father since the beginning of the world and eternal life comes only through faith in him. John also explained how Christians are to walk in the light. Living in hidden sin is like walking in the darkness, but living honestly before God is like walking in the light (see 1 John 1:5–7). No one can walk in the light in their own power, but everyone is invited to trust in Jesus, who empowers believers by the Holy Spirit to walk in holiness. John's letter also encourages Christians to love one another because God loves them. Trusting in Jesus for salvation, as well as loving one another as Jesus does, unites Christians in a special way. And this joining together with other believers is how God builds his church!

Letters & Revelation

The Word of Life Became a Human Being

1 Here is what we announce to everyone about the Word of life. The Word
was already here from the beginning.
We have heard him. We have seen him
with our eyes. We have looked at him.
Our hands have touched him. 2 This
life has appeared. We have seen him.
We are witnesses about him. And we
announce to you this same eternal life.
He was already with the Father. He has
appeared to us. 3 We announce to you
what we have seen and heard. We do
it so you can share life together with
us. And we share life with the Father
and with his Son, Jesus Christ. 4 We are
writing this to make our joy complete.

Walking in the Light

5 Here is the message we have heard
from him and announce to you. God
is light. There is no darkness in him at
all. 6 Suppose we say that we share life
with God but still walk in the darkness.
Then we are lying. We are not living out
the truth. 7 But suppose we walk in the
light, just as he is in the light. Then we
share life with one another. And the
blood of Jesus, his Son, makes us pure
from all sin.
8 Suppose we claim we are without
sin. Then we are fooling ourselves. The
truth is not in us. 9 But God is faithful
and fair. If we confess our sins, he will
forgive our sins. He will forgive every
wrong thing we have done. He will

in 1 John?

God is the Giver of Life. He loved us first and invites all of us to turn away from sin and have fullness of life.

MY GOD IS... SIMPLE

All of God's attributes, or character qualities, exist together in perfect harmony—like how our fingers work together to hold a spoon, or how the different parts of a bike work together so that you can ride it down the street. His attributes do not compete against one another, nor are they individual parts of who he is. Rather all of God's attributes exist equally within himself.

In our relationships with one another, we may think that love and justice, or fairness, can't exist together. Or we might think that being honest and living peacefully is not possible. But all of God's attributes work together in perfect harmony and are never in conflict. In other words, God is God and is one with himself (see Deuteronomy 6:4). As we continue learning about who God is, we can trust that all of God's attributes work together, because God is simple.

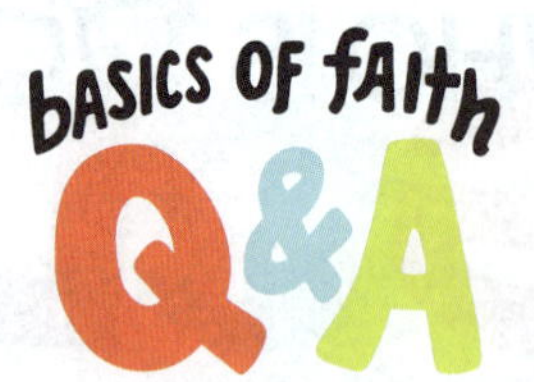

What should I do when I know I have sinned?

God invites you to confess your sin to him. Confession is agreeing with God that you have disobeyed his commands. The good news is that God promises to forgive your sins and make you pure.

Can you find the following verse?

1 JOHN 1:9

make us pure. 10 If we claim we have
not sinned, we are calling God a liar.
His word is not in us.

2 My dear children, I'm writing this
to you so that you will not sin. But
suppose someone does sin. Then we
have a friend who speaks to the Father
for us. He is Jesus Christ, the Blameless
One. 2 He gave his life to pay for our sins.
But he not only paid for our sins. He also
paid for the sins of the whole world.

Instructions About Loving and Hating Other Believers

3 We know that we have come to know
God if we obey his commands. 4 Suppose someone says, "I know him." But
suppose this person does not do what
God commands. Then this person is a
liar and is not telling the truth. 5 But if
anyone obeys God's word, then that
person truly loves God. Here is how we
know we belong to him. 6 Those who
claim to belong to him must live just
as Jesus did.

7 Dear friends, I'm not writing you a
new command. Instead, I'm writing one
you have heard before. You have had it
since the beginning. 8 But I am writing
what amounts to a new command. Its
truth was shown in how Jesus lived. It
is also shown in how you live. That's
because the darkness is passing away.
And the true light is already shining.

9 Suppose someone claims to be in the
light but hates a brother or sister. Then
they are still in the darkness. 10 Anyone
who loves their brother and sister lives
in the light. There is nothing in them to
make them fall into sin. 11 But anyone who
hates a brother or sister is in the darkness.
They walk around in the darkness. They
don't know where they are going. The
darkness has made them blind.

Reasons for Writing

12 Dear children, I'm writing to you
because your sins have been
forgiven.
They have been forgiven because
of what Jesus has done.
13 Fathers, I'm writing to you
because you know the one who is
from the beginning.
Young men, I'm writing to you
because you have won the battle
over the evil one.

14 Dear children, I'm writing to you
because you know the Father.
Fathers, I'm writing to you
because you know the one who is
from the beginning.
Young men, I'm writing to you
because you are strong.
God's word lives in you.
You have won the battle over the
evil one.

Do Not Love the World

15 Do not love the world or anything
in it. If anyone loves the world, love for
the Father is not in them. 16 Here is what
people who belong to this world do. They
try to satisfy what their sinful desires
want to do. They long for what their sinful
eyes look at. They take pride in what they
have and what they do. All of this comes
from the world. None of it comes from the
Father. 17 The world and its evil desires are
passing away. But whoever does what
God wants them to do lives forever.

Warnings About Saying No to the Son

18 Dear children, we are living in the
last days. You have heard that the great
enemy of Christ is coming. But even now
many enemies of Christ have already
come. That's how we know that these

ALL-KNOWING

My GOD IS...

There is nothing God doesn't know, because all knowledge belongs to him.

Do you sometimes get overwhelmed by how much there is to learn? We, as created beings, have limited knowledge, and we have to learn in order to gain more knowledge. But that's not true of God.

God has all knowledge; he has never needed anyone to teach him anything. God knows the answer to every math problem, he can solve the trickiest riddles, and he knows the punch line to every joke! And more importantly, he knows everything about *you* (see Psalm 139:1–4,13–16). He knows how many hairs you have on your head and how many freckles cover your nose; he knows the thoughts you think in your brain, and he knows what makes you happy, sad, or afraid. God knows everything about you because God is all-knowing.

are the last days. 19 These enemies left
our community of believers. They didn't
really belong to us. If they had belonged
to us, they would have remained with
us. But by leaving they showed that
none of them belonged to us.
20 You have received the Spirit from
the Holy One. And all of you know the
truth. 21 I'm not writing to you because
you don't know the truth. I'm writing
because you do know it. I'm writing
to you because no lie comes from the
truth. 22 Who is the liar? It is anyone
who says that Jesus is not the Christ.
The person who says this is the great
enemy of Christ. They say no to the
Father and the Son. 23 The person who
says no to the Son doesn't belong to the
Father. But anyone who says yes to the
Son belongs to the Father also.
24 Make sure that you don't forget
what you have heard from the beginning. Then you will remain joined to
the Son and to the Father. 25 And here
is what God has promised us. He has
promised us eternal life.
26 I'm writing these things to warn
you. I am warning you about people
trying to lead you astray. 27 But you
have received the Holy Spirit from God.
He continues to live in you. So you don't
need anyone to teach you. God's Spirit
teaches you about everything. What
he says is true. He doesn't lie. Remain
joined to Christ, just as you have been
taught by the Spirit.

God's Children and Sin

28 Dear children, remain joined to
Christ. Then when he comes, we can be
bold. We will not be ashamed to meet
him when he comes.
29 You know that God is right and always does what is right. And you know
that everyone who does what is right
is God's child.

3 See what amazing love the Father
has given us! Because of it, we are
called children of God. And that's what
we really are! The world doesn't know
us because it didn't know him. 2 Dear
friends, now we are children of God. He
still hasn't let us know what we will be.
But we know that when Christ appears,
we will be like him. That's because we
will see him as he really is. 3 Christ is
pure. All who hope to be like him make
themselves pure.
4 Everyone who sins breaks the law.
In fact, breaking the law is sin. 5 But you

know that Christ came to take our sins away. And there is no sin in him. [6] No one who remains joined to him keeps on sinning. No one who keeps on sinning has seen him or known him.

[7] Dear children, don't let anyone lead you astray. The person who does what is right is holy, just as Christ is holy. [8] The person who does what is sinful belongs to the devil. That's because the devil has been sinning from the beginning. But the Son of God came to destroy the devil's work. [9] Those who are God's children will not keep on sinning. God's very nature remains in them. They can't go on sinning. That's because they are God's children. [10] Here is how you can tell the difference between God's children and the devil's children. Anyone who doesn't do what is right isn't God's child. And anyone who doesn't love their brother or sister isn't God's child either.

More Instructions About Loving and Hating One Another

[11] From the beginning we have heard that we should love one another. [12] Don't be like Cain. He belonged to the evil one. He murdered his brother. And why did he murder him? Because the things Cain had done were wrong. But the things his brother had done were right. [13] My brothers and sisters, don't be surprised if the world hates you. [14] We know that we have left our old dead way of life. And we have entered into new life. We know this because we love one another. Anyone who doesn't love still lives in their old condition. [15] Anyone who hates their brother or sister is a murderer. And you know that no murderer has eternal life.

[16] We know what love is because Jesus Christ gave his life for us. So we should give our lives for our brothers and sisters. [17] Suppose someone sees a brother or sister in need and is able to help them. And suppose that person doesn't take pity on these needy people. Then how can the love of God be in that person? [18] Dear children, don't just talk about love. Put your love into action. Then it will truly be love.

[19] Here's how we know that we hold to the truth. And here's how we put our hearts at rest, knowing that God is watching. [20] If our hearts judge us, we know that God is greater than our hearts. And he knows everything. [21] Dear friends, if our hearts do not judge us, we can be bold with God. [22] And he will give us anything we ask. That's because we obey his commands. We do what pleases him. [23] God has commanded us to believe in the name of his Son, Jesus Christ. He has also commanded us to love one another. [24] The one who obeys God's commands remains joined to him. And he remains joined to them. Here is how we know that God lives in us. We know it because of the Holy Spirit he gave us.

Jesus Came as a Human Being

4 Dear friends, do not believe every spirit. Test the spirits to see if they belong to God. Many false prophets have gone out into the world. [2] Here is how you can recognize the Spirit of God. Every spirit agreeing that Jesus Christ came in a human body belongs to God. [3] But every spirit that doesn't agree with this does not belong to God. You have heard that the spirit of the great enemy of Christ is coming. Even now it is already in the world.

[4] Dear children, you belong to God. You have not accepted the teachings of the false prophets. That's because the one who is in you is powerful. He is more powerful than the one who is in the world. [5] False prophets belong to the world. So they speak from the world's point of view. And the world listens to them. [6] We belong to God. And those who know God listen to us. But those who don't belong to God don't listen to us. That's how we can tell the difference between the Spirit of truth and the spirit of lies.

We Love Because God Loved Us

[7] Dear friends, let us love one another, because love comes from God. Everyone who loves has become a child of God and knows God. [8] Anyone who does not love does not know God, because God is love. [9] Here is how God showed his love among us. He sent his one and only Son into the world. He sent him so we could receive life through him. [10] Here is what love is. It is not that we loved God. It is that he loved us and sent his Son to give his life to pay for our sins. [11] Dear friends, since God loved us this much, we should also love one another. [12] No one has ever seen God. But if we love one another, God lives in us. His love is made complete in us.

13 Here's how we know that we are joined to him and he to us. He has given us his Holy Spirit. 14 The Father has sent his Son to be the Savior of the world. We have seen it and are witnesses to it. 15 God lives in anyone who agrees that Jesus is the Son of God. This kind of person remains joined to God. 16 So we know that God loves us. We depend on it.

God is love. Anyone who leads a life of love is joined to God. And God is joined to them. 17 Suppose love is fulfilled among us. Then we can be without fear on the day God judges the world. Love is fulfilled among us when in this world we are like Jesus. 18 There is no fear in love. Instead, perfect love drives away fear. That's because fear has to do with being punished. The one who fears does not have perfect love.

19 We love because he loved us first. 20 Suppose someone claims to love God but hates a brother or sister. Then they are a liar. They don't love their brother or sister, whom they have seen. So they can't love God, whom they haven't seen. 21 Here is the command God has given us. Anyone who loves God must also love their brother and sister.

Faith in God's Son Who Became a Human Being

5 Everyone who believes that Jesus is the Christ is a child of God. And everyone who loves the Father loves his children as well. 2 Here is how we know that we love God's children. We know it when we love God and obey his commands. 3 In fact, here is what it means to love God. We love him by obeying his commands. And his commands are not hard to obey. 4 That's because everyone who is a child of God has won the battle over the world. Our faith has won the battle for us. 5 Who is it that has won the battle over the world? Only the person who believes that Jesus is the Son of God.

6 Jesus Christ was born as we are, and he died on the cross. He wasn't just born as we are. He also died on the cross. The Holy Spirit is a truthful witness about him. That's because the Spirit is the truth. 7 There are three that are witnesses about Jesus. 8 They are the Holy Spirit, the birth of Jesus, and the death of Jesus. And the three of them agree. 9 We accept what people say when they are witnesses. But it's more important when God is a witness. That's because it is what God says about his Son. 10 Whoever believes in the Son of God accepts what God says about him. Whoever does not believe God is calling him a liar. That's because they have not believed what God said about his Son. 11 Here is what God says about the Son. God has given us eternal life. And this life is found in his Son. 12 Whoever belongs to the Son has life. Whoever doesn't belong to the Son of God doesn't have life.

Final Words

13 I'm writing these things to you who believe in the name of the Son of God. I'm writing so you will know that you have eternal life. 14 Here is what we can be sure of when we come to God in prayer. If we ask anything in keeping with what he wants, he hears us. 15 If we know that God hears what we ask for, we know that we have it.

16 Suppose you see any brother or sister commit a sin. But this sin is not the kind that leads to death. Then you should pray, and God will give them life. I'm talking about someone whose sin does not lead to death. But there is a sin that does lead to death. I'm not saying you should pray about that sin. 17 Every wrong thing we do is sin. But there are sins that do not lead to death.

18 We know that those who are children of God do not keep on sinning. The Son of God keeps them safe. The evil one can't harm them. 19 We know that we are children of God. We know that the whole world is under the control of the evil one. 20 We also know that the Son of God has come. He has given us understanding. So we can know the God who is true. And we belong to the true God by belonging to his Son, Jesus Christ. He is the true God and eternal life.

21 Dear children, keep away from statues of gods.

2 JOHN

Author: John

John wrote the book of 2 John to remind Christians to stand firm in the gospel and love one another. His letter includes a warning: Watch out for people who don't follow Christ's teachings. He didn't want Christians to believe those who were teaching that Jesus was not the Messiah. He wanted the believers to hold on to the truth and not let anyone convince them, or change their mind, to give up their faith. John told his readers to use discernment (the wisdom God gives his people) because he didn't want them to listen to teachers who weren't following God. Disobeying God is not worth the cost, but living in obedience to Jesus is worth everything. John encouraged Christians to continue growing in faith and walking in love. He urged them to hold tightly to the truth of the gospel while living out their faith in their everyday lives.

Letters & Revelation

1 I, the elder, am writing this letter.

I am sending it to the lady chosen by God and to her children. I love all of you because of the truth. I'm not the only one who loves you. So does everyone who knows the truth. 2 I love you because of the truth that is alive in us. This truth will be with us forever.

3 God the Father and Jesus Christ his Son will give you grace, mercy and peace. These blessings will be with us because we love the truth.

4 It has given me great joy to find some of your children living by the truth. That's just what the Father commanded us to do. 5 Dear lady, I'm not writing you a new command. I'm writing a command we've had from the beginning. I'm asking that we love one another. 6 The way we show our love is to obey God's commands. He commands you to lead a life of love. That's what you have heard from the beginning.

I'm writing a command we've had from the beginning. I'm asking that we love one another. 2 JOHN 5

7 I say this because many people have tried to fool others. These people have gone out into the world. They don't agree that Jesus Christ came in a human body. People like this try to trick others. These people are like the great enemy of Christ. 8 Watch out that you don't lose what we have worked for. Make sure that you get your full reward. 9 Suppose someone thinks they know more than we do. So they don't follow Christ's teaching. Then that person doesn't belong to God. But whoever follows Christ's teaching belongs to the Father and the Son. 10 Suppose someone comes to you and doesn't teach these truths. Then don't take them into your house or welcome them. 11 Anyone who welcomes them shares in their evil work.

in 2 John?

God is the Kind Friend. His great love spills over into the lives of those who follow him. In return, those who follow him love him and love others.

12 I have a lot to write to you. But I don't want to use paper and ink. I hope I can visit you instead. Then I can talk with you face to face. That will make our joy complete.

13 The children of your sister, who is chosen by God, send their greetings.

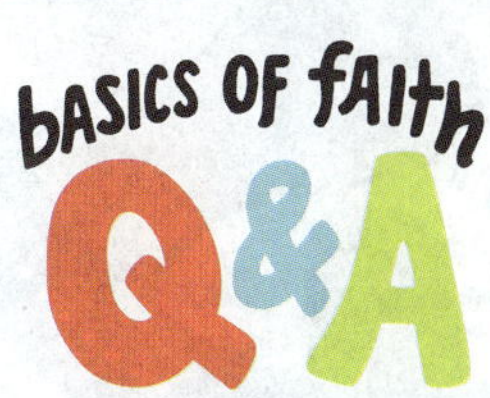

What does it mean to love God?

As you grow in knowing God, you'll grow in loving him and others too. To love God means you don't just *feel* love toward God but take action by obeying his commands.

Can you find the following verse?

2 JOHN 6

3 JOHN

Author: John

The book of 3 John is John's third and final letter. In it, he reminded a group of Christians to welcome people who were working to spread the gospel. John said that Christians will stand out in the world when they love one another, spend time together, and practice hospitality. He told these new believers that they were a family, each united to Jesus in salvation, and as they loved one another, they would be living out the message of the gospel. But that's not all. John also told them they would show how Jesus had changed their lives by the way they welcomed people. God calls his followers to love him and to love others—and this includes warmly welcoming others into our homes and into our lives. John told his readers that by loving God and loving others, the gospel of Jesus would continue to spread and their faith would be strengthened!

Letters & Revelation

1 I, the elder, am writing this letter.

I am sending it to you, my dear friend
Gaius. I love you because of the truth.

2 Dear friend, I know that your spiritual life is going well. I pray that you also
may enjoy good health. And I pray that
everything else may go well with you.
3 Some believers came to me and told
me that you are faithful to the truth.
They told me that you continue to live
by it. This news gave me great joy. 4 I
have no greater joy than to hear that
my children are living by the truth.
5 Dear friend, you are faithful in what
you are doing for the brothers and sisters. You are faithful even though they
are strangers to you. 6 They have told
the church about your love. Please help
them by sending them on their way in a
manner that honors God. 7 They started
on their journey to serve Jesus Christ.
They didn't receive any help from those
who aren't believers. 8 So we should
welcome people like them. We should
work together with them for the truth.
9 I wrote to the church. But Diotrephes
will not welcome us. He loves to be the
first in everything. 10 So when I come,
I will point out what he is doing. He is
saying evil things that aren't true about
us. Even this doesn't satisfy him. So
he refuses to welcome other believers.
He also keeps others from welcoming
them. In fact, he throws them out of
the church.
11 Dear friend, don't be like those
who do evil. Be like those who do
good. Anyone who does what is good
belongs to God. Anyone who does what
is evil hasn't really seen or known God.
12 Everyone says good things about
Demetrius. He lives in keeping with the
truth. We also say good things about
him. And you know that what we say
is true.

13 I have a lot to write to you. But I
don't want to write with pen and ink.
14 I hope I can see you soon. Then we
can talk face to face.

15 May you have peace.

The friends here send their greetings.
Greet each one of the friends there.

How do I know if someone is telling me God's truth?

God's Word, the Bible, is truth. You can know truth by reading God's Word. The more you read God's Word, the better you'll be at knowing when someone *isn't* speaking truth.

Can you find the following verse?

3 JOHN 4

in 3 John?

God is the Joyful One. He will guide his people in truth because those who follow his ways bring him the greatest joy.

Dear friend, don't be like those who do evil. Be like those who do good.

3 JOHN 11

JUDE

Author: Jude

Jude was a half brother of Jesus. At first, Jude didn't believe Jesus was the Messiah, but he saw how Jesus could change a person's whole life—both here on earth and for eternity. After Jesus ascended into heaven, Jude became a teacher and leader in the early church. One day he heard that a group of Christians was being led astray by false teachers. These teachers were telling the new Christians that because God is gracious, they could do whatever they wanted—they didn't need to obey. Their message was this: *God doesn't care what you do! Because God will forgive your sins, you don't have to obey his commands anymore!*

Letters & Revelation

This false teaching was causing believers to turn away from the true teachings of Jesus. Jude wrote these believers a letter to help them understand something very important: Because of God's grace, our sins are forgiven and we get to live our lives for Jesus. He doesn't save us just so we can live free from sin in eternity but so we can live free from sin now. We can enjoy life with Jesus now and forever!

1 I, Jude, am writing this letter. I serve
Jesus Christ. I am a brother of James.

I am sending this letter to you who
have been chosen by God. You are loved
by God the Father. You are kept safe for
Jesus Christ.

2 May more and more mercy, peace
and love be given to you.

A Warning Against the Sin of Ungodly People

3 Dear friends, I really wanted to write
to you about the salvation we share.
But now I feel I should write and ask
you to stand up for the faith. God's holy
people were trusted with it once and for
all time. 4 Certain people have secretly
slipped in among you. Long ago it was
written that they would be judged. They
are ungodly people. They misuse the
grace of our God as an excuse for sexual
sins. They say no to Jesus Christ, our
only Lord and King.
5 I want to remind you about some
things you already know. The Lord
saved his people. At one time he
brought them out of Egypt. But later
he destroyed those who did not believe.
6 Some of the angels didn't stay where
they belonged. They didn't keep their
positions of authority. The Lord has
kept those angels in darkness. They
are held by chains that last forever.
On judgment day, God will judge them.
7 The people of Sodom and Gomorrah
and the towns around them also did evil
things. They freely committed sexual
sins. They committed sins of the worst
possible kind. There is a fire that never
goes out. Those people are an example
of those who are punished with it.
8 In the very same way, these ungodly
people act on their evil dreams. So they
make their own bodies impure. They
don't accept authority. And they say
evil things against heavenly beings.
9 But even Michael, the leader of the
angels, didn't dare to say these things.
He didn't even say these things when he
argued with the devil about the body of
Moses. Michael didn't dare to judge the
devil. He didn't say the devil was guilty
of saying evil things. Instead, Michael
said, "May the Lord judge you!" 10 But
these people say evil things against
whatever they don't understand. And

in Jude?

God is the Faithful Protector. He promises to protect his children eternally and gives them the Holy Spirit to guide them.

the very things they do understand
will destroy them. That's because they
are like wild animals that can't think
for themselves. Instead, they do what
comes naturally to them.
11 How terrible it will be for them!
They have followed the way of Cain.
They have rushed into the same mistake Balaam made. They did it because
they loved money. They are like Korah.
He turned against his leaders. These
people will certainly be destroyed, just
as Korah was.
12 These ungodly people are like stains
at the meals you share. They have no
shame. They are shepherds who feed
only themselves. They are like clouds
without rain. They are blown along by
the wind. They are like trees in the fall.
Since they have no fruit, they are pulled
out of the ground. So they die twice.
13 They are like wild waves of the sea.
Their shame rises up like foam. They
are like falling stars. God has reserved
a place of very black darkness for them
forever.
14 Enoch was the seventh man in the
family line of Adam. He gave a prophecy about these people. He said, "Look!
The Lord is coming with thousands and
thousands of his holy ones. 15 He is coming to judge everyone. He is coming
to sentence all of them. He will judge
them for all the ungodly acts they have
done. They have done them in ungodly
ways. He will sentence ungodly sinners

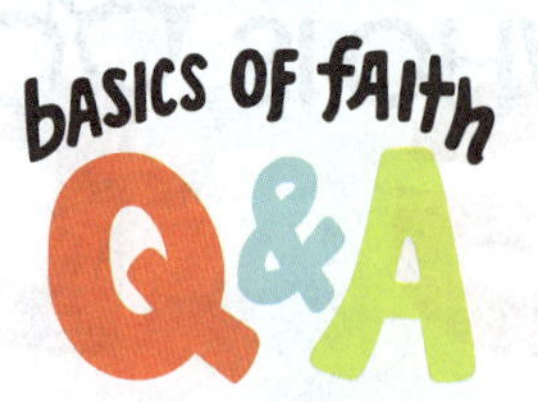

When will Jesus return?

No one knows exactly when Jesus will return, but the Bible encourages us to wait. His Spirit is working to invite all people to follow him.

Can you find the following verse?

JUDE 21

for all the things they have said to oppose him." 16 These people complain
and find fault with others. They follow
their own evil desires. They brag about
themselves. They praise others to get
what they want.

Remain in God's Love

17 Dear friends, remember what the
apostles of our Lord Jesus Christ said
would happen. 18 They told you, "In the
last days, some people will make fun
of the truth. They will follow their own
ungodly desires." 19 They are the people
who separate you from one another.
They do only what comes naturally.
They are not led by the Holy Spirit.
20 But you, dear friends, build yourselves up in your most holy faith. Let
the Holy Spirit guide and help you when
you pray. 21 And by doing these things,
remain in God's love as you wait. You
are waiting for the mercy of our Lord
Jesus Christ to bring you eternal life.

Remain in God's love. JUDE 21

22 Show mercy to those who doubt.
23 Save others by pulling them out of
the fire. To others, show mercy mixed
with fear of sin. Hate even the clothes
that are stained by the sins of those
who wear them.

Praise to God

24 Give praise to the God who is able
to keep you from falling into sin. He
will bring you into his heavenly glory
without any fault. He will bring you
there with great joy. 25 Give praise to
the only God our Savior. Glory, majesty, power and authority belong to
him. Give praise to him through Jesus
Christ our Lord. His praise was before
all time, continues now, and will last
forever. Amen.

REVELATION

Author: John (but we don't know which one!)

The book of Revelation is about a vision God gave John of what it will be like when King Jesus returns to bring his kingdom to earth forever. On that day, Jesus will completely defeat and destroy death and wickedness—sin will be demolished. Those who put their faith in Jesus will be brought safely into God's presence. Anyone who didn't believe that Jesus is King will be removed from God's presence forever. In heaven, no one will ever be sad, no one will ever get sick, and no one will ever pass away. Everything that sin broke, Jesus will restore. He will fulfill every single one of God's promises and make all things new.

John ends this book with the best news ever: Jesus is coming back! The entire Bible—every page of the Old Testament and every page of the New Testament—is true. God has kept all his promises in the past, and we can trust him to keep all his promises in the future because God fulfilled his best promise in sending Jesus Christ to be our Savior and forever King!

Letters & Revelation

The Revelation Is Given

1 This is the revelation from Jesus
Christ. God gave it to him to show
those who serve God what will happen
soon. God made it known by sending
his angel to his servant John. 2 John is
a witness to everything he saw. What
he saw is God's word and what Jesus
Christ has said. 3 Blessed is the one who
reads out loud the words of this prophecy. Blessed are those who hear it and
think everything it says is important.
The time when these things will come
true is near.

Greetings and Praise to God

4 I, John, am writing this letter.

I am sending it to the seven churches
in Asia Minor.

May grace and peace come to you
from God. He is the one who is, and who
was, and who will come. May grace and
peace come to you from the seven spirits.
These spirits are in front of God's throne.
5 May grace and peace come to you from
Jesus Christ. He is the faithful witness,
so what he has shown can be trusted. He
was the first to rise from the dead. He
rules over the kings of the earth.

Glory and power belong to Jesus
Christ who loves us! He has set us free
from our sins by pouring out his blood
for us. 6 He has made us members of his
royal family. He has made us priests
who serve his God and Father. Glory
and power belong to Jesus Christ for
ever and ever! Amen.

7 "Look! He is coming with the
clouds!" *(Daniel 7:13)*
"Every eye will see him.
Even those who pierced him will
see him."
All the nations of the earth
"will mourn because of him."
(Zechariah 12:10)

This will really happen! Amen.

8 "I am the Alpha and the Omega, the
Beginning and the End," says the Lord
God. "I am the God who is, and who was,
and who will come. I am the Mighty One."

John's Vision of Christ

9 I, John, am a believer like you. I
am a friend who suffers like you. As
members of Jesus' royal family, we can
put up with anything that happens
to us. I was on the island of Patmos
because I taught God's word and what
Jesus said. 10 The Holy Spirit gave me
a vision on the Lord's Day. I heard a
loud voice behind me that sounded
like a trumpet. 11 The voice said, "Write
on a scroll what you see. Send it to the
seven churches in Asia Minor. They are
Ephesus, Smyrna, Pergamum, Thyatira,
Sardis, Philadelphia and Laodicea."

12 I turned around to see who was
speaking to me. When I turned, I saw
seven golden lampstands. 13 In the middle of them was someone who looked
"like a son of man." *(Daniel 7:13)* He was
dressed in a long robe with a gold strip
of cloth around his chest. 14 The hair on
his head was white like wool, as white
as snow. His eyes were like a blazing
fire. 15 His feet were like bronze metal
glowing in a furnace. His voice sounded
like rushing waters. 16 He held seven
stars in his right hand. Coming out of
his mouth was a sharp sword with two
edges. His face was like the sun shining
in all its brightness.

17 When I saw him, I fell at his feet
as if I were dead. Then he put his right
hand on me and said, "Do not be afraid.
I am the First and the Last. 18 I am the
Living One. I was dead. But now look!
I am alive for ever and ever! And I hold
the keys to Death and Hell.

19 "So write down what you have seen.
Write about what is happening now and
what will happen later. 20 Here is the
meaning of the mystery of the seven
stars you saw in my right hand. They
are the angels of the seven churches.
And the seven golden lampstands you
saw stand for the seven churches.

The Letter to the Church in Ephesus

2 "Here is what I command you to
write to the church in Ephesus.

Here are the words of Jesus, who
holds the seven stars in his right
hand. He also walks among the
seven golden lampstands. He says,

2 'I know what you are doing.
You work long and hard. I know
you can't put up with evil people.
You have tested those who claim to

in Revelation?

God is the Forever King.
He will come again, and
his kingdom will have
no end!

be apostles but are not. You have
found out that they are liars. 3 You
have been faithful and have put up
with a lot of trouble because of me.
You have not given up.
4 'But here is something I hold
against you. You have turned away
from the love you had at first.
5 Think about how far you have
fallen! Turn away from your sins.
Do the things you did at first. If
you don't, I will come to you and
remove your lampstand from its
place. 6 But you do have this in
your favor. You hate the way the
Nicolaitans act. I hate it too.
7 'Whoever has ears should listen
to what the Holy Spirit says to the
churches. Here is what I will do for
anyone who has victory over sin.
I will let that person eat from the
tree of life in God's paradise.'

The Letter to the Church in Smyrna

8 "Here is what I command you to
write to the church in Smyrna.

Here are the words of Jesus, who is the First and the Last. He is the one who died and came to life again. He says,

9 'I know that you suffer and are
poor. But you are rich! Some people say they are Jews but are not.
I know that their words are evil.
Their worship comes from Satan.
10 Don't be afraid of what you are
going to suffer. I tell you, the devil
will put some of you in prison to
test you. You will be treated badly for ten days. Be faithful, even
if it means you must die. Then I
will give you life as your crown
of victory.
11 'Whoever has ears should listen
to what the Holy Spirit says to the
churches. Here is what I will do for
anyone who has victory over sin. I
will not let that person be hurt at
all by the second death.'

The Letter to the Church in Pergamum

12 "Here is what I command you to
write to the church in Pergamum.

Here are the words of Jesus, who has the sharp sword with two edges. He says,

13 'I know that you live where Satan has his throne. But you remain
faithful to me. You did not give up
your faith in me. You didn't give
it up even in the days of Antipas.
Antipas, my faithful witness, was
put to death in your city, where
Satan lives.
14 'But I have a few things against
you. Some of your people follow
the teaching of Balaam. He taught
Balak to lead the people of Israel
into sin. So they ate food that had
been offered to statues of gods. And
they committed sexual sins. 15 You
also have people who follow the
teaching of the Nicolaitans. 16 So
turn away from your sins! If you
don't, I will come to you soon. I will
fight against those people with the
sword that comes out of my mouth.
17 'Whoever has ears should listen
to what the Holy Spirit says to the
churches. Here is what I will do for
anyone who has victory over sin. I
will give that person hidden manna
to eat. I will also give each of them a
white stone with a new name written on it. Only the one who receives
this name will know what it is.'

The Letter to the Church in Thyatira

18 "Here is what I command you to
write to the church in Thyatira.

Here are the words of the Son of God. He is Jesus, whose eyes are

like blazing fire. His feet are like
polished bronze. He says,

[19]'I know what you are doing. I
know your love and your faith.
I know how well you have served. I
know you don't give up easily. In
fact, you are doing more now than
you did at first.
[20]'But here is what I have against
you. You put up with that woman
Jezebel. She calls herself a prophet.
With her teaching, she has led my
servants into sexual sin. She has
tricked them into eating food offered to statues of gods. [21]I've given
her time to turn away from her
sinful ways. But she doesn't want
to. [22]She lay down to commit her
sin so I will make her lie down in
suffering. Those who commit adultery with her will suffer greatly too.
Their only way out is to turn away
from what she taught them to do.
[23]I will strike her children dead.
Then all the churches will know
that I search hearts and minds. I
will pay each of you back for what
you have done.
[24]'I won't ask the rest of you in
Thyatira to do anything else. You
don't follow the teaching of Jezebel.
You haven't learned what some
people call Satan's deep secrets.
[25]Just hold on to what you have
until I come.
[26]'Here is what I will do for anyone who has victory over sin. I will
do it for anyone who carries out
my plans to the end. I will give
that person authority over the nations. [27]It is written, "They will rule
them with an iron scepter. They
will break them to pieces like clay
pots." *(Psalm 2:9)* Their authority
is like the authority I've received
from my Father. [28]I will also give
the morning star to all who have
victory. [29]Whoever has ears should
listen to what the Holy Spirit says
to the churches.'

The Letter to the Church in Sardis

3 "Here is what I command you to
write to the church in Sardis.

Here are the words of Jesus, who
holds the seven spirits of God. He
has the seven stars in his hand.
He says,

'I know what you are doing. People think you are alive, but you are
dead. [2]Wake up! Strengthen what
is left, or it will die. You have not
done all that my God wants you to
do. [3]So remember what you have
been taught and have heard. Hold
firmly to it. Turn away from your
sins. If you don't wake up, I will
come like a thief. You won't know
when I will come to you.
[4]'But you have a few people in
Sardis who are pure. They aren't
covered with evil like dirty clothes.
They will walk with me, dressed in
white, because they are worthy.
[5]Here is what I will do for anyone
who has victory over sin. I will dress
that person in white like those worthy people. I will never erase their
names from the book of life. I will
speak of them by name to my Father and his angels. [6]Whoever has
ears should listen to what the Holy
Spirit says to the churches.'

The Letter to the Church in Philadelphia

[7]"Here is what I command you to
write to the church in Philadelphia.

Here are the words of Jesus, who
is holy and true. He holds the key
of David. No one can shut what he
opens. And no one can open what
he shuts. He says,

[8]'I know what you are doing.
Look! I have put an open door in
front of you. No one can shut it. I
know that you don't have much
strength. But you have obeyed my
word. You have not said no to me.
[9]Some people claim they are Jews
but are not. They are liars. Their
worship comes from Satan. I will
make them come and fall down at
your feet. I will make them say in
public that I have loved you. [10]You
have kept my command to remain
strong in the faith no matter what
happens. So I will keep you from
the time of suffering. That time is
going to come to the whole world.
It will test those who live on the
earth.

11 'I am coming soon. Hold on to
what you have. Then no one will
take away your crown. 12 Here is
what I will do for anyone who has
victory over sin. I will make that
person a pillar in the temple of my
God. They will never leave it again.
I will write the name of my God on
them. I will write the name of the
city of my God on them. This is the
new Jerusalem, which is coming
down out of heaven from my God.
I will also write my new name on
them. 13 Whoever has ears should
listen to what the Holy Spirit says
to the churches.'

The Letter to the Church in Laodicea

14 "Here is what I command you to
write to the church in Laodicea.

Here are the words of Jesus,
who is the Amen. What he speaks
is faithful and true. He rules over
what God has created. He says,

15 'I know what you are doing. I
know you aren't cold or hot. I wish
you were either one or the other!
16 But you are lukewarm. You aren't
hot or cold. So I am going to spit
you out of my mouth. 17 You say, "I
am rich. I've become wealthy and
don't need anything." But you don't
realize how pitiful and miserable
you have become. You are poor,
blind and naked. 18 So here's my
advice. Buy from me gold made
pure by fire. Then you will become
rich. Buy from me white clothes to
wear. Then you will be able to cover
the shame of your naked bodies.
And buy from me healing lotion
to put on your eyes. Then you will
be able to see.

19 'I warn and correct those I love.
So be sincere, and turn away from
your sins. 20 Here I am! I stand at
the door and knock. If anyone
hears my voice and opens the door,
I will come in. I will eat with that
person, and they will eat with me.
21 'Here is what I will do for anyone who has victory over sin. I will
give that person the right to sit with
me on my throne. In the same way,
I had victory. Then I sat down with
my Father on his throne. 22 Whoever has ears should listen to what the
Holy Spirit says to the churches.' "

The Throne in Heaven

4 After this I looked, and there in
front of me was a door standing
open in heaven. I heard the voice I had
heard before. It sounded like a trumpet. The voice said, "Come up here. I
will show you what must happen after this." 2 At once the Holy Spirit gave
me a vision. There in front of me was
a throne in heaven with someone sitting
on it. 3 The one who sat there shone like
jasper and ruby. Around the throne
was a rainbow shining like an emerald.
4 Twenty-four other thrones surrounded
that throne. Twenty-four elders were
sitting on them. The elders were dressed
in white. They had gold crowns on their
heads. 5 From the throne came flashes
of lightning, rumblings and thunder.
Seven lamps were blazing in front of
the throne. These stand for the seven
spirits of God. 6 There was something
that looked like a sea of glass in front
of the throne. It was as clear as crystal.
In the inner circle, around the throne,
were four living creatures. They were
covered with eyes, in front and in back.
7 The first creature looked like a lion. The
second looked like an ox. The third had
a man's face. The fourth looked like a
flying eagle. 8 Each of the four living
creatures had six wings. Each creature
was covered all over with eyes. It had
eyes even under its wings. Day and
night, they never stop saying,

" 'Holy, holy, holy
is the Lord God who rules over all.'
(Isaiah 6:3)
He was, and he is, and he will come."

9 The living creatures give glory, honor
and thanks to the one who sits on the
throne. He lives for ever and ever. 10 At
the same time, the 24 elders fall down
and worship the one who sits on the
throne. He lives for ever and ever. They
lay their crowns in front of the throne.
They say,

11 "You are worthy, our Lord and God!
You are worthy to receive glory
and honor and power.
You are worthy because you
created all things.

They were created and they
exist.
This is the way you planned it."

The Scroll and the Lamb

5 Then I saw a scroll in the right hand
of the one sitting on the throne.
The scroll had writing on both sides.
It was sealed with seven seals. 2 I saw
a mighty angel calling out in a loud
voice. He said, "Who is worthy to break
the seals and open the scroll?" 3 But no
one in heaven or on earth or under the
earth could open the scroll. No one could
even look inside it. 4 I cried and cried.
That's because no one was found who
was worthy to open the scroll or look
inside. 5 Then one of the elders said to
me, "Do not cry! The Lion of the tribe
of Judah has won the battle. He is the
Root of David. He is able to break the
seven seals and open the scroll."

6 Then I saw a Lamb that looked as if
he had been put to death. He stood at the
center of the area around the throne. The
Lamb was surrounded by the four living
creatures and the elders. He had seven
horns and seven eyes. The eyes stand
for the seven spirits of God, which are
sent out into all the earth. 7 The Lamb
went and took the scroll. He took it from
the right hand of the one sitting on the
throne. 8 Then the four living creatures
and the 24 elders fell down in front of the
Lamb. Each one had a harp. They were
holding golden bowls full of incense.
They stand for the prayers of God's people. 9 Here is the new song they sang.

"You are worthy to take the scroll
and break open its seals.
You are worthy because you were
put to death.
With your blood you bought
people for God.
They come from every tribe,
people and nation,
no matter what language they
speak.
10 You have made them members of a
royal family.
You have made them priests to
serve our God.
They will rule on the earth."

11 Then I looked and heard the voice
of millions and millions of angels. They
surrounded the throne. They surrounded
the living creatures and the elders. 12 In
a loud voice they were saying,

"The Lamb, who was put to death,
is worthy!
He is worthy to receive power
and wealth and wisdom and
strength!
He is worthy to receive honor and
glory and praise!"

13 All creatures in heaven, on earth,
under the earth, and on the sea were
speaking. The whole creation was
speaking. I heard all of them say,

"Praise and honor belong
to the one who sits on the throne
and to the Lamb!
Glory and power belong to God for
ever and ever!"

14 The four living creatures said, "Amen."
And the elders fell down and worshiped.

Jesus Is the Lion of Judah

Judah was one of the 12 sons of Jacob. The tribe of Judah refers to all the people, or descendants, who were born into Judah's family. Jacob proclaimed that a victorious king would be one of the descendants from the tribe of Judah (see Genesis 49:9–10). Many years later, Jesus was born into the tribe of Judah. He is described as a lion who defends his people from their enemies just like a lion courageously defends its young cubs (see Revelation 5:5). Jesus is powerful and strong and will defeat our ultimate enemies, sin and death, when he returns. Jesus, the Lion of Judah, is coming back!

The Seals of the Scroll Are Broken

6 I watched as the Lamb broke open
the first of the seven seals. Then I
heard one of the four living creatures
say in a voice that sounded like thunder, "Come!" 2 I looked, and there in
front of me was a white horse! Its rider
held a bow in his hands. He was given
a crown. He rode out like a hero on his
way to victory.

3 The Lamb broke open the second
seal. Then I heard the second living
creature say, "Come!" 4 Another horse
came out. It was red like fire. Its rider
was given power to take peace from
the earth. He was given power to make
people kill each other. He was given a
large sword.

5 The Lamb broke open the third seal.
Then I heard the third living creature
say, "Come!" I looked, and there in front
of me was a black horse! Its rider was
holding a pair of scales in his hand.
6 Next, I heard what sounded like a voice
coming from among the four living
creatures. It said, "Two pounds of wheat
for a day's pay. And six pounds of barley
for a day's pay. And leave the olive oil
and the wine alone!"

7 The Lamb broke open the fourth
seal. Then I heard the voice of the
fourth living creature say, "Come!" 8 I
looked, and there in front of me was a
pale horse! Its rider's name was Death.
Following close behind him was Hell.
They were given power over a fourth
of the earth. They were given power to
kill people by swords. They could also
use hunger, sickness and the earth's
wild animals to kill.

9 The Lamb broke open the fifth seal.
I saw souls under the altar. They were
the souls of people who had been killed.
They had been killed because of God's
word and their faithful witness. 10 They
called out in a loud voice. "How long,
Lord and King, holy and true?" they
asked. "How long will you wait to judge
those who live on the earth? How long
will it be until you pay them back for
killing us?" 11 Then each of them was
given a white robe. "Wait a little longer,"
they were told. "There are still more of
your believing brothers and sisters who
will be killed. They will be killed just as
you were."

12 I watched as the Lamb broke open
the sixth seal. There was a powerful
earthquake. The sun turned black like
the clothes people wear when they're
sad. Those clothes are made out of
goat's hair. The whole moon turned as
red as blood. 13 The stars in the sky fell
to earth. They dropped like figs from a
tree shaken by a strong wind. 14 The sky
rolled back like a scroll. Every mountain
and island was moved out of its place.

15 Everyone hid in caves and among
the rocks of the mountains. This included the kings of the earth, the princes
and the generals. It included rich people
and powerful people. It also included
everyone else, both slaves and people
who were free. 16 They called out to the
mountains and rocks, "Fall on us! Hide
us from the face of the one who sits on
the throne! Hide us from the anger of
the Lamb! 17 The great day of their anger
has come. Who can live through it?"

144,000 People Are Marked With the Seal of the Living God

7 After this I saw four angels. They
were standing at the four corners
of the earth. They were holding back
the four winds of the earth. This kept
the winds from blowing on the land
or the sea or on any tree. 2 Then I saw
another angel coming up from the east.
He brought the official seal of the living
God. He called out in a loud voice to the
four angels. They had been allowed to
harm the land and the sea. 3 "Do not
harm the land or the sea or the trees," he
said. "Wait until we mark with this seal
the foreheads of those who serve our
God." 4 Then I heard how many people
were marked with the seal. There were
144,000 from all the tribes of Israel.

5 From the tribe of Judah, 12,000
were marked with the seal.
From the tribe of Reuben, 12,000.
From the tribe of Gad, 12,000.
6 From the tribe of Asher, 12,000.
From the tribe of Naphtali, 12,000.
From the tribe of Manasseh,
12,000.
7 From the tribe of Simeon, 12,000.
From the tribe of Levi, 12,000.
From the tribe of Issachar, 12,000.
8 From the tribe of Zebulun, 12,000.
From the tribe of Joseph, 12,000.
From the tribe of Benjamin, 12,000.

The Huge Crowd Wearing White Robes

[9]After this I looked, and there in front
of me was a huge crowd of people. They
stood in front of the throne and in front
of the Lamb. There were so many that
no one could count them. They came
from every nation, tribe and people.
That's true no matter what language
they spoke. They were wearing white
robes. In their hands they were holding
palm branches. [10]They cried out in a
loud voice,

"Salvation belongs to our God,
who sits on the throne.
Salvation also belongs to the
Lamb."

[11]All the angels were standing around
the throne. They were standing around
the elders and the four living creatures.
They fell down on their faces in front of
the throne and worshiped God. [12]They
said,

"Amen!
May praise and glory
and wisdom be given to our God for
ever and ever.
Give him thanks and honor and
power and strength.
Amen!"

[13]Then one of the elders spoke to me.
"Who are these people dressed in white
robes?" he asked. "Where did they come
from?"

[14]I answered, "Sir, you know."

He said, "They are the ones who have
come out of the time of terrible suffering. They have washed their robes and
made them white in the blood of the
Lamb. [15]So

"they are in front of the throne of
God.
They serve him day and night in
his temple.
The one who sits on the throne
will be with them to keep them
safe.
[16]'Never again will they be hungry.
Never again will they be thirsty.
The sun will not beat down on
them.' *(Isaiah 49:10)*
The heat of the desert will not
harm them.
[17]The Lamb, who is at the center of
the area around the throne,
will be their shepherd.
'He will lead them to springs of
living water.' *(Isaiah 49:10)*
'And God will wipe away every
tear from their eyes.'"
(Isaiah 25:8)

The Seventh Seal and the Gold Cup

8 The Lamb opened the seventh seal.
Then there was silence in heaven
for about half an hour.

[2]I saw the seven angels who stand
in front of God. Seven trumpets were
given to them.

[3]Another angel came and stood at
the altar. He had a shallow gold cup
for burning incense. He was given a lot
of incense to offer on the golden altar.
The altar was in front of the throne.
With the incense he offered the prayers
of all God's people. [4]The smoke of the
incense rose up from the angel's hand.
The prayers of God's people rose up
together with it. The smoke and the
prayers went up in front of God. [5]Then
the angel took the gold cup and filled
it with fire from the altar. He threw it
down on the earth. There were rumblings and thunder, flashes of lightning,
and an earthquake.

The Trumpets

[6]Then the seven angels who had the
seven trumpets got ready to blow them.

[7]The first angel blew his trumpet.
Hail and fire mixed with blood were
thrown down on the earth. A third of
the earth was burned up. A third of the
trees were burned up. All the green grass
was burned up.

[8]The second angel blew his trumpet. Something that looked like a huge
mountain on fire was thrown into the
sea. A third of the sea turned into blood.
[9]A third of the living creatures in the sea
died. A third of the ships were destroyed.

[10]The third angel blew his trumpet.
Then a great star fell from the sky. It
looked like a blazing torch. It fell on a
third of the rivers and on the springs of
water. [11]The name of the star is Worm-
wood. A third of the water turned bitter.
Many people died from it.

[12]The fourth angel blew his trumpet.
Then a third of the sun was struck. A
third of the moon was struck. A third

[8]A second angel followed him. He said, "'Fallen! Babylon the Great has fallen!' *(Isaiah 21:9)* The city of Babylon made all the nations drink the strong wine of her terrible sins."

[9]A third angel followed them. He said in a loud voice, "There will be trouble for anyone who worships the beast and its statue! There will be trouble for anyone who has its mark on their forehead or their hand! [10]They, too, will drink the wine of God's great anger. His wine has been poured full strength into the cup of his anger. They will be burned with flaming sulfur. The holy angels and the Lamb will see it happen. [11]The smoke of their terrible suffering will rise for ever and ever. Day and night, there will be no rest for anyone who worships the beast and its statue. There will be no rest for anyone who receives the mark of its name." [12]God's people need to be very patient. They are the ones who obey God's commands. And they remain faithful to Jesus.

[13]Then I heard a voice from heaven. "Write this," it said. "Blessed are the dead who die as believers in the Lord from now on."

"Yes," says the Holy Spirit. "They will rest from their labor. What they have done will not be forgotten."

The Harvest of the Earth

[14]I looked, and there in front of me was a white cloud. Sitting on the cloud was one who looked "like a son of man." *(Daniel 7:13)* He wore a gold crown on his head. In his hand was a sharp, curved blade for cutting grain. [15]Then another angel came out of the temple. He called in a loud voice to the one sitting on the cloud. "Take your blade," he said. "Cut the grain. The time has come. The earth is ready to be harvested." [16]So the one sitting on the cloud swung his blade over the earth. And the earth was harvested.

[17]Another angel came out of the temple in heaven. He too had a sharp, curved blade. [18]Still another angel came from the altar. He was in charge of the fire on the altar. He called out in a loud voice to the angel who had the sharp blade. "Take your blade," he said, "and gather the bunches of grapes from the earth's vine. Its grapes are ripe." [19]So the angel swung his blade over the earth. He gathered its grapes. Then he threw them into a huge winepress. The winepress stands for God's anger. [20]In the winepress outside the city, the grapes were stomped on. Blood flowed out of the winepress. It spread over the land for about 180 miles. It rose as high as the horses' heads.

Seven Angels With Seven Plagues

15 I saw in heaven another great and wonderful sign. Seven angels were about to bring the seven last plagues. The plagues would complete God's anger. [2]Then I saw something that looked like a sea of glass glowing with fire. Standing beside the sea were those who had won the battle over the beast. They had also overcome its statue and the number of its name. They held harps given to them by God. [3]They sang the song of God's servant Moses and of the Lamb. They sang,

"Lord God who rules over all,
 everything you do is great and wonderful.
King of the nations,
 your ways are true and fair.
[4]Lord, who will not have respect for you?
 Who will not bring glory to your name?
You alone are holy.
All nations will come
 and worship you.
They see that the things you do are right."

[5]After this I looked, and I saw the temple in heaven. And it was opened. The temple is the holy tent where the tablets of the covenant law were kept. [6]Out of the temple came the seven angels who were bringing the seven plagues. They were dressed in clean, shining linen. They wore gold strips of cloth around their chests. [7]Then one of the four living creatures gave seven golden bowls to the seven angels. The bowls were filled with the anger of God, who lives for ever and ever. [8]The temple was filled with smoke that came from the glory and power of God. No one could enter the temple at that time. They had to wait until the seven plagues of the seven angels were completed.

The Seven Bowls of God's Great Anger

16 Then I heard a loud voice from
the temple speaking to the seven
angels. "Go," it said. "Pour out the seven
bowls of God's great anger on the earth."
2 The first angel went and poured out
his bowl on the land. Ugly and painful sores broke out on people. Those
people had the mark of the beast and
worshiped its statue.
3 The second angel poured out his
bowl on the sea. It turned into blood
like the blood of a dead person. Every
living thing in the sea died.
4 The third angel poured out his bowl
on the rivers and springs of water. They
became blood. 5 Then I heard the angel
who was in charge of the waters. He
said,

"Holy One, the way you judge is
fair.
You are the God who is and who
was.
6 Those who worship the beast have
poured out blood.
They have poured out the life's
blood of your holy people and
your prophets.
So you have given blood to drink to
those who worship the beast.
That's exactly what they should
get."

7 Then I heard the altar reply. It said,

"Lord God who rules over all,
the way you judge is true and
fair."

8 The fourth angel poured out his
bowl on the sun. The sun was allowed
to burn people with fire. 9 They were
burned by the blazing heat. So they
spoke evil things against the name of
God, who controlled these plagues. But
they refused to turn away from their
sins. They did not give glory to God.
10 The fifth angel poured out his bowl
on the throne of the beast. The kingdom
of the beast became very dark. People chewed on their tongues because
they were suffering so much. 11 They
spoke evil things against the God of
heaven. They did this because of their
pains and their sores. But they refused
to turn away from the sins they had
committed.

12 The sixth angel poured out his
bowl on the great river Euphrates. Its
water dried up to prepare the way for
the kings from the East. 13 Then I saw
three evil spirits that looked like frogs.
They came out of the mouths of the
dragon, the beast and the false prophet.
14 They are spirits of demons that perform signs. They go out to gather the
kings of the whole world for battle. This
battle will take place on the great day
of the God who rules over all.

15 "Look! I am coming like a thief!
Blessed is anyone who stays awake
and keeps their clothes on. Then
they will be ready. They will not
be caught naked and so be put to
shame."

16 Then the evil spirits gathered the
kings together. In the Hebrew language,
the place where the kings met is called
Armageddon.
17 The seventh angel poured out his
bowl into the air. Out of the temple
came a loud voice from the throne. It
said, "It is done!" 18 Then there came
flashes of lightning, rumblings, thunder
and a powerful earthquake. There has
never been an earthquake as terrible
as this. One like this hasn't happened
while human beings have lived on
earth. 19 The great city split into three
parts. The cities of the nations crumbled
and fell. God remembered Babylon the
Great. He gave Babylon the cup filled
with the wine of his terrible anger. 20 Every island ran away. The mountains
could not be found. 21 Huge hailstones
weighing about 100 pounds each fell
from the sky. The hail crushed people.
And they spoke evil things against God
because of the plague. That's because
the plague of hail was so terrible.

Babylon the Great Prostitute Sits on the Beast

17 One of the seven angels who had
the seven bowls came to me. He
said, "Come. I will show you how the
great prostitute will be punished. She is
the one who sits by many waters. 2 The
kings of the earth took part in her evil
ways. The people living on earth were
drunk with the wine of her terrible sins."
3 Then in a vision the angel carried
me away to a desert. There the Holy

Spirit showed me a woman sitting on a bright red beast. It was covered with names that say evil things about God. It had seven heads and ten horns.
4 The woman was dressed in purple and bright red. She was gleaming with gold, jewels and pearls. In her hand she held a golden cup filled with things that God hates. It was filled with her terrible, dirty sins.
5 The name written on her forehead was a mystery. Here is what it said.

THE GREAT CITY OF BABYLON
THE MOTHER OF PROSTITUTES
THE MOTHER OF EVERYTHING ON EARTH THAT GOD HATES

6 I saw that the woman was drunk with the blood of God's holy people. They are the ones who are witnesses about Jesus.

When I saw her, I was very amazed.
7 Then the angel said to me, "Why are you amazed? I will explain to you the mystery of the woman. And I will explain the mystery of the beast she rides on. The beast is the one who has the seven heads and ten horns.
8 The beast that you saw used to exist and now does not. Yet it will come up out of the Abyss and be destroyed. Some people on the earth will be amazed when they see the beast. Their names have not been written in the book of life from the time the world was created. They will be amazed at the beast. That's because it will come again even though it used to exist and now does not.

9 "Here is a problem that you have to be wise to understand. The seven heads are seven hills that the woman sits on.
10 They are also seven kings. Five have fallen, one is ruling, and the other has still not come. When he does come, he must remain for only a little while.
11 The beast who used to exist, and now does not, is an eighth king. He belongs to the other seven. He will be destroyed.

12 "The ten horns you saw are ten kings. They have not yet received a kingdom. But for one hour they will receive authority to rule together with the beast.
13 They have only one purpose. So they will give their power and authority to the beast.
14 They will make war against the Lamb. But the Lamb will have victory over them. That's because he is the most powerful Lord of all and the greatest King of all. His appointed, chosen and faithful followers will be with him."

15 Then the angel spoke to me. "You saw the waters the prostitute sits on," he said. "They stand for all the nations of the world, no matter what their race or language is.
16 The beast and the ten horns you saw will hate the prostitute. They will destroy her and leave her naked. They will eat her flesh and burn her with fire.
17 God has put it into their hearts to carry out his purpose. So they agreed to give the beast their royal authority. They will give him this authority until God's words come true.
18 The woman you saw stands for the great city of Babylon. That city rules over the kings of the earth."

Weeping When Babylon Falls

18 After these things I saw another angel coming down from heaven. He had great authority. His glory filled the earth with light.
2 With a mighty voice he shouted,

"'Fallen! Babylon the Great has fallen!' *(Isaiah 21:9)*
She has become a place where demons live.
She has become a den for every evil spirit.
She has become a place where every 'unclean' bird is found.
She has become a place where every 'unclean' and hated animal is found.
3 All the nations have drunk the strong wine of her terrible sins.
The kings of the earth took part in her evil ways.
The traders of the world grew rich from her great wealth."

Warning to Run From Babylon's Judgment

4 Then I heard another voice from heaven. It said,

"'Come out of her, my people.' *(Jeremiah 51:45)*
Then you will not take part in her sins.
You will not suffer from any of her plagues.
5 Her sins are piled up to heaven.
God has remembered her crimes.

[6] Do to her as she has done to others.
Pay her back double for what she has done.
Pour her a double dose of what she has poured for others.
[7] Give her as much pain and suffering
as the glory and wealth she gave herself.
She brags to herself,
'I rule on a throne like a queen.
I am not a widow.
I will never mourn.' *(Isaiah 47:7,8)*
[8] But she will be plagued by death, sadness and hunger.
In a single day she will suffer all these plagues.
She will be burned up by fire.
That's because the Lord God who judges her is mighty.

How Terrible When Babylon Falls!

[9] "The kings of the earth who committed terrible sins with her will weep.
They will mourn because they used
to share her riches. They will see the
smoke rising as she burns. [10] They
will be terrified by her suffering. They
will stand far away from her. And
they will cry out,

" 'How terrible! How terrible it is for you, great city!
How terrible for you, mighty city of Babylon!
In just one hour you have been destroyed!'

[11] "The traders of the world will weep
and mourn over her. No one buys what
they sell anymore. [12] Here is what they
had for sale.

"Gold, silver, jewels, pearls.
Fine linen, purple, silk, bright red cloth.
Every kind of citron wood.
All sorts of things made out of ivory, valuable wood, bronze, iron, marble.
[13] Cinnamon, spice, incense, myrrh, frankincense.
Wine, olive oil, fine flour, wheat.
Cattle, sheep, horses, carriages, and human beings sold as slaves.

[14] "The merchants will say, 'The pleasure you longed for has left you. All
your riches and glory have disappeared
forever.' [15] The traders who sold these
things became rich because of Babylon.
When she suffers, they will stand far
away. Her suffering will terrify them.
They will weep and mourn. [16] They will
cry out,

" 'How terrible! How terrible it is for you, great city,
dressed in fine linen, purple and bright red!
How terrible for you, great city,
gleaming with gold, jewels and pearls!
[17] In just one hour your great wealth has been destroyed!'

"Every sea captain and all who travel
by ship will stand far away. So will the
sailors and all who earn their living
from the sea. [18] They will see the smoke
rising as Babylon burns. They will ask,
'Was there ever a city like this great
city?' [19] They will throw dust on their
heads. They will weep and mourn. They
will cry out,

" 'How terrible! How terrible it is for you, great city!
All who had ships on the sea became rich because of her wealth!
In just one hour she has been destroyed!'
[20] "You heavens, be glad for this!
You people of God, be glad!
You apostles and prophets, be glad!
God has judged her
with the judgment she gave to you."

Babylon's Judgment Is Final

[21] Then a mighty angel picked up a
huge rock. It was the size of a large millstone. He threw it into the sea. Then
he said,

"That is how
the great city of Babylon will be thrown down.
Never again will it be found.
[22] The songs of musicians will never be heard in you again.
Gone will be the music of harps, flutes and trumpets.
No worker of any kind
will ever be found in you again.

The sound of a millstone
will never be heard in you again.
23 The light of a lamp
will never shine in you again.
The voices of brides and grooms
will never be heard in you again.
Your traders were among the
world's most important people.
By your magic spell all the
nations were led astray.
24 You were guilty of the murder
of prophets and God's holy
people.
You were guilty of the blood of
all who have been killed on the
earth."

Three Hallelujahs for the Fall of Babylon!

19 After these things I heard a roar
in heaven. It sounded like a huge
crowd shouting,

"Hallelujah!
Salvation and glory and power
belong to our God.
2 The way he judges is true and
fair.
He has judged the great prostitute.
She made the earth impure with
her terrible sins.
God has paid her back for killing
those who served him."

3 Again they shouted,

"Hallelujah!
The smoke from her fire goes up for
ever and ever."

4 The 24 elders and the four living
creatures bowed down. They worshiped
God, who was sitting on the throne.
They cried out,

"Amen! Hallelujah!"

5 Then a voice came from the throne.
It said,

"Praise our God,
all you who serve him!
Praise God, all you who have
respect for him,
both great and small!"

6 Then I heard the noise of a huge
crowd. It sounded like the roar of rushing waters and like loud thunder. The
people were shouting,

"Hallelujah!
Our Lord God is the King who
rules over all.
7 Let us be joyful and glad!
Let us give him glory!
It is time for the Lamb's wedding.
His bride has made herself ready.
8 Fine linen, bright and clean,
was given to her to wear."

Fine linen stands for the right things
that God's holy people do.

9 Here is what the angel told me to
write. "Blessed are those invited to the
wedding supper of the Lamb!" Then
he added, "These are the true words
of God."
10 When I heard this, I fell at his feet to
worship him. But he said to me, "Don't
do that! I serve God, just as you do. I am
God's servant, just like believers who
hold firmly to what Jesus has taught.
Worship God! The Spirit of prophecy
tells the truth about Jesus."

Jesus Is the King of kings

Jesus is the true Ruler over every earthly ruler who ever has existed or ever will exist.

This world has a lot of kings. The people of every nation have someone who leads them, and people often fight about who gets to rule earthly nations. But God's Word tells us that Jesus is the King over every other king (see Revelation 17:14). He is perfectly sovereign and has all power. Jesus is not the King because anyone voted to make him king or because he was born into a royal family. Jesus is King because he is God.

The Heavenly Warrior Has Victory Over the Beast

11 I saw heaven standing open. There in front of me was a white horse. Its rider is called Faithful and True. When he judges or makes war, he is always fair. 12 His eyes are like blazing fire. On his head are many crowns. A name is written on him that only he knows. 13 He is dressed in a robe dipped in blood. His name is the Word of God. 14 The armies of heaven were following him, riding on white horses. They were dressed in fine linen, white and clean. 15 Coming out of the rider's mouth is a sharp sword. He will strike down the nations with the sword. Scripture says, "He will rule them with an iron scepter." *(Psalm 2:9)* He stomps on the grapes of God's winepress. The winepress stands for the terrible anger of the God who rules over all. 16 Here is the name that is written on the rider's robe and on his thigh.

THE GREATEST KING OF ALL AND THE MOST POWERFUL LORD OF ALL

17 I saw an angel standing in the sun. He shouted to all the birds flying high in the air, "Come! Gather together for the great supper of God. 18 Come and eat the dead bodies of kings, generals, and other mighty people. Eat the bodies of horses and their riders. Eat the bodies of all people, free and slave, great and small."

19 Then I saw the beast and the kings of the earth with their armies. They had gathered together to make war against the rider on the horse and his army. 20 But the beast and the false prophet were captured. The false prophet had done signs for the beast. In this way the false prophet had tricked some people. Those people had received the mark of the beast and had worshiped its statue. The beast and the false prophet were thrown alive into the lake of fire. The lake of fire burns with sulfur. 21 The rest were killed by the sword that came out of the rider's mouth. All the birds stuffed themselves with the dead bodies.

The Thousand Years

20 I saw an angel coming down out of heaven. He had the key to the Abyss. In his hand he held a heavy chain. 2 He grabbed the dragon, that old serpent. The serpent is also called the devil, or Satan. The angel put him in chains for 1,000 years. 3 Then he threw him into the Abyss. He locked it and sealed him in. This was to keep Satan from causing the nations to believe his lies anymore. Satan will be locked away until the 1,000 years are ended. After that, he must be set free for a short time.

4 I saw thrones. Those who had been given authority to judge were sitting on them. I also saw the souls of those whose heads had been cut off. They had been killed because they had spoken what was true about Jesus. They had also been killed because of the word of God. They had not worshiped the beast or its statue. They had not received its mark on their foreheads or hands. They came to life and ruled with Christ for 1,000 years. 5 This is the first resurrection. The rest of the dead did not come to life until the 1,000 years were ended. 6 Blessed and holy are those who share in the first resurrection. The second death has no power over them. They will be priests of God and of Christ. They will rule with him for 1,000 years.

Satan Is Judged

7 When the 1,000 years are over, Satan will be set free from his prison. 8 He will

What will we do in heaven?

Heaven will probably be like the Garden of Eden before Adam and Eve sinned. We will be with God, doing the things God told Adam and Eve to do, like caring for the world and working together. There will be great joy!

Can you find the following verses?

REVELATION 21:3–4

go out to cause the nations to believe
lies. He will gather them from the four
corners of the earth. He will bring Gog
and Magog together for battle. Their
troops are as many as the grains of
sand on the seashore. 9They marched
across the whole earth. They surrounded the place where God's holy people
were camped. It was the city he loves.
But fire came down from heaven and
burned them up. 10The devil had caused
them to believe lies. He was thrown
into the lake of burning sulfur. That is
where the beast and the false prophet
had been thrown. They will all suffer
day and night for ever and ever.

The Dead Are Judged

11I saw a great white throne. And I
saw God sitting on it. When the earth
and sky saw his face, they ran away.
There was no place for them. 12I saw
the dead, great and small, standing in
front of the throne. Books were opened.
Then another book was opened. It was
the book of life. The dead were judged
by what they had done. The things they
had done were written in the books.
13The sea gave up the dead that were
in it. And Death and Hell gave up their
dead. Each person was judged by what
they had done. 14Then Death and Hell
were thrown into the lake of fire. The
lake of fire is the second death. 15Any-
one whose name was not written in
the book of life was thrown into the
lake of fire.

A New Heaven and a New Earth

21 I saw "a new heaven and a new
earth." *(Isaiah 65:17)* The first heav-
en and the first earth were completely
gone. There was no longer any sea. 2I
saw the Holy City, the new Jerusalem.
It was coming down out of heaven from
God. It was prepared like a bride beauti-
fully dressed for her husband. 3I heard
a loud voice from the throne. It said,
"Look! God now makes his home with
the people. He will live with them. They
will be his people. And God himself will
be with them and be their God. 4'He will
wipe away every tear from their eyes.
There will be no more death.' *(Isaiah
25:8)* And there will be no more sadness.
There will be no more crying or pain.
Things are no longer the way they used
to be."

5He who was sitting on the throne
said, "I am making everything new!"
Then he said, "Write this down. You
can trust these words. They are true."

6He said to me, "It is done. I am the
Alpha and the Omega, the Beginning
and the End. I will give water to anyone who is thirsty. The water will come

LOVING

My GOD IS...

God's love is the greatest gift of all. He loves you more than you can imagine! Do you know *why* he loves you so much? He doesn't love you because you work really hard or do good things. Nope. He loves you because you belong to him. He made you, and because you believe in Jesus, you are part of his family.

Nothing you do will make God love you any more or any less. He loves you just as you are. Can you think of things that make you feel loved? Now can you think of ways that you can love others? We are loving God when we are loving toward others (see 1 John 4:7,12).

from the spring of the water of life. It
doesn't cost anything! 7 Those who have
victory will receive all this from me. I
will be their God, and they will be my
children. 8 But others will be thrown into
the lake of fire that burns with sulfur.
Those who are afraid and those who do
not believe will be there. Murderers and
those who make themselves impure will
join them. Those who commit sexual
sins and those who practice witchcraft
will go there. Those who worship statues
of gods and all who tell lies will be there
too. The lake of fire is the second death."

The New Jerusalem is the Bride of the Lamb

9 One of the seven angels who had
the seven bowls came and spoke to me.
The bowls were filled with the seven
last plagues. The angel said, "Come. I
will show you the bride, the wife of the
Lamb." 10 Then he carried me away in
a vision. The Spirit took me to a huge,
high mountain. He showed me Jerusalem, the Holy City. It was coming down
out of heaven from God. 11 It shone with
the glory of God. It gleamed like a very
valuable jewel. It was like a jasper, as
clear as crystal. 12 The city had a huge,
high wall with 12 gates. Twelve angels
were at the gates, one at each of them.
On the gates were written the names of
the 12 tribes of Israel. 13 There were three
gates on the east and three on the north.
There were three gates on the south
and three on the west. 14 The wall of
the city had 12 foundations. Written on
them were the names of the 12 apostles
of the Lamb.

15 The angel who talked with me had a
gold measuring rod. He used it to measure the city, its gates and its walls.
16 The city was laid out like a square.
It was as long as it was wide. The angel measured the city with the rod. It
was 1,400 miles long. It was as wide
and high as it was long. 17 The angel
measured the wall as human beings
measure things. It was 200 feet thick.
18 The wall was made out of jasper. The
city was made out of pure gold, as pure
as glass. 19 The foundations of the city
walls were decorated with every kind
of jewel. The first foundation was made
out of jasper. The second was made out
of sapphire. The third was made out of
agate. The fourth was made out of emerald. 20 The fifth was made out of onyx.
The sixth was made out of ruby. The
seventh was made out of chrysolite. The
eighth was made out of beryl. The ninth
was made out of topaz. The tenth was
made out of turquoise. The eleventh
was made out of jacinth. The twelfth
was made out of amethyst. 21 The 12
gates were made from 12 pearls. Each
gate was made out of a single pearl. The
main street of the city was made out of
gold. It was gold as pure as glass that
people can see through clearly.

22 I didn't see a temple in the city.
That's because the Lamb and the Lord
God who rules over all are its temple.
23 The city does not need the sun or
moon to shine on it. God's glory is its
light, and the Lamb is its lamp. 24 The
nations will walk by the light of the
city. The kings of the world will bring
their glory into it. 25 Its gates will never
be shut, because there will be no night
there. 26 The glory and honor of the nations will be brought into it. 27 Only what
is pure will enter the city. No one who
causes people to believe lies will enter
it. No one who does shameful things
will enter it either. Only those whose
names are written in the Lamb's book
of life will enter the city.

The Earth Is Made Like New Again

22 Then the angel showed me the
river of the water of life. It was
as clear as crystal. It flowed from the
throne of God and of the Lamb. 2 It
flowed down the middle of the city's
main street. On each side of the river
stood the tree of life, bearing 12 crops
of fruit. Its fruit was ripe every month.
The leaves of the tree bring healing
to the nations. 3 There will no longer
be any curse. The throne of God and
of the Lamb will be in the city. God's
servants will serve him. 4 They will see
his face. His name will be on their foreheads. 5 There will be no more night.
They will not need the light of a lamp
or the light of the sun. The Lord God
will give them light. They will rule for
ever and ever.

John and the Angel

6 The angel said to me, "You can trust
these words. They are true. The Lord
is the God who gives messages to the

prophets. He sent his angel to show his servants the things that must soon take place."

7 "Look! I am coming soon! Words of prophecy are written in this book. Blessed is the person who obeys them."

8 I, John, am the one who heard and saw these things. After that, I fell down to worship at the feet of the angel. He is the one who had been showing me
these things. 9 But he said to me, "Don't do that! I serve God, just as you do. I am God's servant, just like the other prophets. And I serve God along with all who obey the words of this book. Worship God!"

10 Then he told me, "Do not seal up the words of the prophecy in this book.
These things are about to happen. 11 Let
the person who does wrong keep on doing wrong. Let the evil person continue to be evil. Let the person who does right keep on doing what is right. And let the holy person continue to be holy."

The Revelation Ends With Warnings and Blessings

12 "Look! I am coming soon! I bring my rewards with me. I will reward each
person for what they have done. 13 I am
the Alpha and the Omega. I am the First and the Last. I am the Beginning and the End.

14 "Blessed are those who wash their robes. They will have the right to come to the tree of life. They will be allowed to go through the gates into the city.
15 Outside the city are those who are impure. These people include those who practice witchcraft. Outside are also those who commit sexual sins and murder. Outside are those who worship statues of gods. And outside is everyone who loves and does what is false.

16 "I, Jesus, have sent my angel to give you this witness for the churches. I am the Root and the Son of David. I am the bright Morning Star."

17 The Holy Spirit and the bride say, "Come!" And the person who hears should say, "Come!" Anyone who is thirsty should come. Anyone who wants to take the free gift of the water of life should do so.

18 I am warning everyone who hears the words of the prophecy of this book. Suppose someone adds anything to them. Then God will add to that person the plagues told about in this book.
19 Suppose someone takes away any words from this book of prophecy. Then God will take away from that person the blessings told about in this book. God will take away their share in the tree of life. God will also take away their place in the Holy City.

20 Jesus is a witness about these things. He says, "Yes. I am coming soon."

Amen. Come, Lord Jesus!

21 May the grace of the Lord Jesus be with God's people. Amen.

Glossary

GLOSSARY

ANGEL OF THE LORD: Since no one can see God and live, the angel of the Lord in the Old Testament is a special messenger from God who represents God and meets face-to-face with certain people, like Gideon (see Judges 6:12). The angel of the Lord wants to draw people near to God.

ANGELS: Angels in the Bible are mighty warriors who worship God and carry out his commands. Angels appear to God's people throughout Scripture to deliver messages for God or to act on God's behalf. Angels worship God in heaven, giving God the glory he deserves and saying, "Holy, holy, holy is the Lord God" (Revelation 4:8).

ASCENSION: The ascension is when Jesus returned (or ascended) to the Father after his death and resurrection. When Jesus' ministry on earth was completed, he went up to heaven, and, as he did, he sent his disciples into all the world to share the good news of the gospel (see Acts 1:8–9).

ATONEMENT: Atonement is the act of restoring a broken relationship. Through sin, all of humanity's relationship with God is broken. God is holy, and sin cannot exist in his presence. But God provided a way for his people to be made right with him again by sending his Son to be the atonement for their sins (see Romans 5:11). Jesus died in our place, and rose again, to pay the penalty of our sin and restore our relationship with God.

BAPTISM: Baptism is an act of obedience practiced by Christians in every generation. It is a public declaration of faith in God, a way of telling those in our faith community that we believe in God's promises and desire to follow him with our whole self. In baptism, Christians go underneath water, which symbolizes Jesus' death in our place, and are raised up out of the water again, symbolizing the newness of life that comes from following Jesus (see Romans 6:4). Some churches baptize through sprinkling, but the meaning is the same.

BELIEVE: To believe something is to agree that it is true and to live our life as if it is true. Christians believe that Jesus is the Savior who forgives our sins and makes us right with God (see Romans 10:9). When we believe, we agree with God that Jesus is our Savior, and we live in a way that shows the world that he has changed our lives.

CHURCH: The church is the people of God. The church isn't a building where worship happens, but it is the gathering of worshipers who have chosen to follow Jesus. Accepting Jesus as Savior is a personal decision that brings each individual together with others who follow Jesus—the family of God called the church.

COMMAND: Throughout the Bible God gives his people instructions for how to live life in a way that honors him. These are called *commands*, and they show God's people how to give God glory, live life the best way, and mirror God's character.

COMMUNION: Before Jesus went to the cross, he took bread and broke it and told his disciples that it represented his body, which would be broken for them in death. He also took a cup of wine, telling them that it represented his blood that would be poured out for the forgiveness of sin (see Matthew 26:26–30). Jesus commanded his disciples (and us today) to remember his death and resurrection in the same way, by taking bread and wine or juice, called *communion*, or the Lord's Supper. This meal reminds Christians that Jesus died for our sins and promised that when he returns again, we will feast with him in the new heaven and new earth.

CONDEMNATION: Condemnation is when someone's actions are sinful and deserve punishment. God said that sin would bring death. This is why Scripture says that sin deserves God's judgment, rightly separating us from God (see Isaiah 59:2). The good news is that because of Jesus, we can be free from God's judgment (see Romans 8:1).

CONFESSION: When we disobey God's commands, we sin, and our sin separates us from God and others. The first step in making things right is confession. Confession happens when we agree with God that our sin is wrong; we tell him that we have failed to live up to his perfect standards (see Psalm 32:5).

COVENANT: Throughout the Bible God makes special agreements with his people called covenants. When God enters into a covenant with his people, he gives them both promises and commands, and he marks them as his special people (see Genesis 9:8–17; 22:17; Exodus 20–23; 2 Samuel 7:16; Luke 22:20).

CREATION: God made the entire world by speaking it into existence (see Genesis 1:1—2:3). Everything we can see and even things we cannot see (like the center of the earth or faraway stars) was made by him and is part of his creation. The most special thing God created was people, whom he made in his image.

CRUCIFIXION: The crucifixion is when Jesus died in our place to pay the penalty for our sins (see Matthew 27:27–56). He was nailed by his wrists and feet to a wooden cross, and he hung on the cross until he gave up his spirit to the Father and died. The crucifixion was essential for our salvation and is a reminder of how much God loves us—so much that he would give his own Son to suffer in our place.

DOCTRINE: Doctrine is how we talk about what we believe. Christians believe the Bible is true and that it teaches us about God and his character (see 2 Timothy 3:16–17). Everything the Bible says about a certain topic, such as salvation or the Holy Spirit, is called doctrine.

ETERNITY: When something is eternal, it goes on forever and ever. Eternity will have no end! God has promised to take his people to be with him forever either when we die or when Jesus returns (see Revelation 21:3).

FAITH: To have faith means to have confidence in someone or something (see Hebrews 11:1). Christians have faith in Jesus to save us from our sins, and we have faith that God's Word is true. Christians follow God in faith, even when we don't have all the answers to our questions or when we can't see what the future holds.

FAITHFUL: To be faithful means to be reliable and trustworthy; someone who is faithful will always keep their promises and do what they say they will do. God is faithful, and he always keeps his promises (see 1 Corinthians 1:9). God invites and commands Christians to be faithful to his Word and his ways, just as he is faithful to us.

FALL, THE: When the first man and woman (Adam and Eve) disobeyed God, they sinned. Sin broke everything—man and woman's relationship with God, their relationship with each other, and their relationship with all creation. (You can read this story in Genesis 3.) Ever since the first sin was committed, all humans have been born sinful. We are born wanting to disobey God, and we all act on that desire by disobeying God's commands. *The fall* is the name given to the story in Genesis of the first sin because it was then that all humanity fell into sin.

FRUIT OF THE SPIRIT: The Holy Spirit lives within all who put their faith in Jesus. The Bible uses the term "fruit" when it talks about how the Spirit of God helps us mirror God's character. Just as fruit takes time to grow, God's Spirit, over time, grows God's character in our lives. The fruit of the Spirit is love, joy, peace, patience, kindness, goodness, faithfulness, gentleness, and self-control (see Galatians 5:22–23).

GENEROSITY: To be generous is to give more than expected. God has given us many good gifts, including the best gift of all—salvation through his Son, Jesus. God also instructs, or teaches, his people to be generous with others by sharing our time, words of encouragement, and our things with others.

GENTILES: The word *Gentiles* refers to non-Jews. It is the word that identifies those who were not born into Abraham's family line—the nation of Israel.

GLORY: Glory is the honor that is owed to someone for who they are or what they have done. God is worthy of all glory and honor, and when we worship and obey him, we glorify him as God (see Revelation 4:11).

GOD THE FATHER: God is triune, meaning he is three persons in one. The first person of the Trinity is God the Father. He spoke the world into existence, sent Jesus as the promised Savior, cares for his people, and hears his people's prayers.

GOD THE SON / JESUS CHRIST: The second person of the Trinity is God the Son, or Jesus. He was present at creation and through him all things were made (see Colossians 1:15–17). Jesus Christ was born to a virgin mother, Mary, and came to earth in a human body. He lived a sinless life, suffered, and died in our place. On the third day, he rose from the dead. He is now at the right hand of God the Father, and one day he will return.

GOD THE SPIRIT / HOLY SPIRIT: The third person of the Trinity is God the Holy Spirit. The Spirit was present at creation, gives glory to the Son, and lives inside all Christians who put their faith in Jesus. The Holy Spirit is the great Helper for all believers (see John 14:26).

GOODNESS: God is the only one who is ultimately good. We see his goodness in how he cares for creation and his people. We also see it in Jesus, who was sinless. No person can be good on their own, but the Bible teaches us that the goodness of God helps us know our need for a Savior and opens our eyes to see that Jesus is the Savior we need (see Romans 3:10–12).

GOSPEL: The gospel is the story of how Jesus' death and resurrection made it possible for people, who were separated from God through sin, to have a relationship with God. It is also known as the Good News because all who put their faith in Jesus Christ are saved by grace through faith.

GRACE: Grace is God's free gift that we cannot earn and do not deserve. God's best gift of grace to us is the gift of salvation through Jesus (see Ephesians 2:18–19)!

HONOR: To honor someone is to treat them with respect. The Bible teaches us that we honor God by living our lives according to his commands, and we honor others by treating them the way we also want to be treated (see 1 John 5:1–5; Luke 6:31).

HOPE: Hope is expecting with great confidence that a certain something is going to happen. The Bible promises us that we have an eternal hope in Jesus—that he will save us, that he will return again, and that one day, sin and death will be no more. We live in hope when we live with the expectation that God will keep all his promises.

IDOL / IDOLATRY: An idol is something that we worship instead of God. Throughout the Bible many people worshiped false gods, or idols. The Bible teaches us to stay away from having idols in our hearts—things or people we love more than God or worship in place of God (see 1 John 5:21).

IMAGE OF GOD: When God created the world, he made man and woman in a special way. He said that men and women would bear his image. This means that humans are like God in a way that the rest of creation is not like God (see Genesis 1:26). Every person deserves to be treated with love and respect because every person who has ever lived or ever will live is made in the image of God.

INCARNATION: The incarnation refers to the time when Jesus (the second person of the Trinity) became man (see Philippians 2:6–7). Jesus was fully man and fully God! He didn't just look human; he really was fully human! And Jesus didn't just claim to be God or do God-like things; he really was fully God! At the incarnation, Jesus became fully man while remaining fully God.

JOY: Joy is a fruit of the Spirit that is developed in us when we follow Jesus. Joy means we are content, or satisfied, even when things are hard because we are trusting in God's goodness. The Bible says we can be joyful and talk to God about anything (see 1 Thessalonians 5:16–17).

JUSTICE: To be just is to be completely fair. God is perfectly just. Often in our world we see things that are unjust—unfair laws and unfair treatment of people. But God has promised that one day he will return and establish perfect and eternal justice for all.

JUSTIFICATION: Justification is the process by which someone becomes righteous in God's sight. Although all people have sinned against God, Jesus' death and resurrection have provided the way for us to be made right with God (see Romans 3:23).

KINDNESS: Even though God doesn't need us, he loves us and wants to have a relationship with us. In his kindness, he sent his Son, Jesus, to pay the penalty for our sin. He shows his kindness by offering us salvation, providing for our needs, being with us when we're hurting, and giving us good gifts to enjoy.

KINGDOM OF GOD: This world has many kings and rulers, but the Bible teaches that Jesus is the one true and eternal King (see John 18:36–37). Jesus' kingdom came into this world through his death and resurrection, and he will fully establish his kingdom when he returns to reign forever.

LOVE: Love is a deep feeling of affection that moves someone to action. The Bible tells us that love shows itself when we are patient and kind and choose not to brag or be envious or prideful. Love is also sacrificial and not self-seeking, which means it's looking out for other people's needs first. Love always rejoices in the truth rather than in wrongdoing (see 1 Corinthians 13:4–7). Love is a fruit of the Spirit; it is how Christians relate to God and to each other.

MERCY: Mercy is when we do not receive the punishment we do deserve. Although our sins deserve death, God showed us mercy by putting our punishment on Jesus, who died in our place (see Ephesians 2:4).

MIRACLE: A miracle is something done in God's power that no human could do. It is a surprising, supernatural event that God brings about both to bless his people and to point them to himself.

NEIGHBOR: Most people today would say that our neighbor is whoever lives right next door to us, or maybe all the people who live near our home. But the Bible tells us that every person we meet is our neighbor, and God commands us to love our neighbors as ourselves. God says we should point them to him and share with them the good news about Jesus (see Luke 10:25–37).

NEW HEAVEN AND NEW EARTH: Jesus has promised that one day he will come again and make all things right. When he does, he will establish the new heaven and new earth. In the new heaven and new earth, God will live with his people, sin will be destroyed, and pain and death will be no more.

OBEY: To obey is to follow a command or direction by someone who has the right to be in charge. God has the right to be in charge of us—his creation—and he wants us to do what he teaches us in his Word, the Bible. God wants us to trust him and follow his commands because he loves us and we love him (see 1 John 4:19).

OLD AND NEW TESTAMENTS: The Bible is a collection of sixty-six books. These books are grouped into two testaments, the Old Testament and the New Testament. Throughout both testaments, God tells one continuous story of how he saved his people from their sin through Jesus Christ.

PATIENCE: Patience is the ability to endure something very hard without getting angry or upset. To be patient is to calmly wait for something we really want, trusting that God is in control. Patience is not natural to us as humans, but it is a fruit of the Spirit that God grows in our hearts (see Galatians 5:22).

PEACE: Peace is staying calm on the inside even when chaos is happening on the outside. Peace comes from trusting God even when life is confusing, difficult, or scary. Peace is a fruit of the Spirit (see Galatians 5:22).

PERSEVERE: To persevere means to keep going even when things get hard or something gets in our way. Christians are called to keep following Jesus even when others oppose us or when doing the right thing is not easy (see James 1:12). Perseverance comes from God.

PHARISEE: In the New Testament, Pharisees were religious leaders. They often tried hard to follow the rules of God's law on the outside but failed to let God's love change their hearts on the inside.

PRIDE: Pride is a sin that lives in human hearts. Pride is thinking that we are better than other people or thinking that we can save ourselves.

PRIEST: Throughout the Old Testament God gave his people priests. Priests stood before God on the people's behalf, presenting the people's requests to God and making sacrifices for the people's sins. Jesus is our high priest because he offered the final sacrifice for our sins (see Hebrews 4:14). Now, Jesus represents all believers as righteous to God and gives us the ability to talk directly to God.

PSALM: A psalm is a song that points us to God. In the Old Testament, the psalms collected in the book of Psalms were written and used by God's people to sing praises to him, to cry out to him for help, and to remind them of who God is.

RECONCILED: When a relationship between two people is broken or not at peace, the Bible tells us they need to be reconciled (see Matthew 5:23–24). When two people are reconciled, the broken relationship is repaired and finds new life. Christians are reconciled to God through Jesus.

REDEMPTION: Redemption is saving something by buying it back and restoring it. Sin created a debt to God that we could not pay. We had no hope of redeeming ourselves. But Jesus took our place by dying on the cross. He rose again to buy us back from bondage to sin and to restore us to right relationship with God (see 1 Peter 1:18–19).

REPENTANCE: Repentance is acknowledging before God that we are not perfect like he is. Repentance is telling God that we are sorry for our sin and, by the help of the Holy Spirit, committing to walk away from sin and toward obedience to God's Word.

RESURRECTION: Jesus died on the cross in our place, but that isn't where the story ends! Three days after he died, he rose again, just as he promised he would (see Matthew 28:6). This is called the resurrection, and it is when Jesus displayed his power over death and the grave. He also promised that all who trust in him to forgive their sins will be raised as he was raised and will enjoy eternal life with him.

SABBATH: The Sabbath is the day of rest that God commanded his people to observe in the Mosaic Law (see Exodus 20:8). Just as God rested on the seventh day of creation, God calls his people to rest on the seventh day of the week. Many Christians rest on Sunday. Resting for a full day reminds us that we are not God and that we need him for all things. When Jesus came, he fulfilled the Sabbath by providing the ultimate rest for our souls (see Matthew 12:8).

SACRIFICE: A sacrifice is the act of surrendering something as an offering to God. In the Old Testament, animals were sacrificed to God (put to death) in the place of someone who had sinned. In the New Testament, Jesus offered himself as the sacrifice for our sins, and we are to give him back offerings, or sacrifices, of our time, worship, and talents.

SALVATION: Salvation is being rescued from something terrible—harm, loss, or even death. The Bible teaches us that Jesus Christ is our Savior who rescues us from the worst thing imaginable—spiritual death, which is eternal separation from him (see Acts 4:12). Jesus saves us from spiritual death and welcomes us into eternal life with God.

SANCTIFICATION: Sanctification is how God makes us more like himself. God invites and commands us to mirror his character in the world (his communicable attributes, or ways we can be like him). We cannot do this in our own power. When we put our trust in Jesus, God gives us his Spirit as the Helper we need to become more like Jesus.

SCRIPTURE: *Scripture* is another word for the Bible. Scripture is God's self-revelation. It is the primary place where God tells us who he is and what he is like. Scripture is made up of sixty-six books; it includes the Old and New Testaments and six different genres.

SELF-CONTROL: Self-control is the ability to manage our actions or emotions. It is the ability to be careful about what we say and to do the right thing when we really want to do the wrong thing. Self-control is a fruit of the Spirit (see 2 Timothy 1:7).

SIN: To sin is to miss the mark, like an arrow missing a target. God has set a perfect standard, and he himself is that standard. Anything we say, think, or do that falls short of his perfect standard is sin because it misses the mark. Sin separates us from God, which is why God sent Jesus to pay the penalty for our sin and make us right with God.

THEOLOGY: Theology is everything we know and believe about God. The best way to learn about God is by reading and studying the Bible and asking questions. This helps grow our understanding of God's holiness and love.

TRUTH: Truth is based on facts or reality; it is accurate. God's Word is true, and Jesus himself is the Truth (see John 14:6). The Bible is also full of stories of events that really happened.

WILL: A person's will is their inner drive to make a certain decision or take a specific action. When we talk about a person's will, we are talking about what they want most. The Bible teaches us that God's will is for "all people to be saved" (1 Timothy 2:4).

WISDOM: Wisdom is knowing what the right thing to do is, knowing *when* to do the right thing, and actually *doing* the right thing. In the Bible we learn that God's wisdom is the foundation of the world and that God gives wisdom freely to anyone who asks for it (see James 1:5).

WORD OF GOD: In the Old Testament, God spoke to his people through prophets and angels. Then, for 400 years, God was silent. In the New Testament, God spoke by sending Jesus into the world to save his people from their sins (see Hebrews 1:1–2).

Jesus is called the Word of God because he broke the silence. The Bible is also referred to as the Word of God.

WORKS: Works are the things we do in order to accomplish a bigger goal. The Bible talks about two kinds of "works" that we can pursue: works of the law and works of the Spirit. Works of the law are things we do to try to save ourselves, but we cannot save ourselves. Works of the Spirit are things God does within us by his Spirit that form us into the people he wants us to be (see Galatians 5:22–25). Works of the Spirit bring about true salvation.

WORSHIP: Christians worship God when they show him honor, or reverence, and love. Some of the ways we worship God are talking to him in prayer, reading his Word, singing songs to him, and obeying his commands.

YAHWEH: Yahweh is one of God's most special names in the whole Bible. It comes from the Hebrew verb "I AM" and is God's unique way of telling his people that he is self-existent (see Exodus 3:13–15). This means that God always has existed and always will exist. Whenever we see the word "LORD" in the Bible, we know that the name being used for God is Yahweh.

ZION: Zion is another name for the city of Jerusalem, where God's presence dwelled among his people in the temple (see Psalm 132:13). Zion is remembered by God's people as a place of his glory. It reminds Christians today that one day Jesus will return and take us to live in the glory of his presence forever.

A NOTE REGARDING THE TYPE

This Bible was set in the Zondervan NIrV Typeface, commissioned by Zondervan, a division of HarperCollins Christian Publishing, and designed in Aarhus, Denmark, by Klaus E. Krogh and Heidi Rand Sorensen of 2K/DENMARK. Like the New International Version (NIV), the New International Reader's Version (NIrV) achieves great accuracy through rigorous faithfulness to the original languages combined with faithfulness to contemporary language. As the NIrV is based on the NIV translation and maintains the original intent of the NIV, the same typeface is utilized within NIV and NIrV Bibles—a distinctive Bible typeface that is uncompromisingly beautiful, clear, and readable at any size.

Maps

Map 1: WORLD OF THE PATRIARCHS

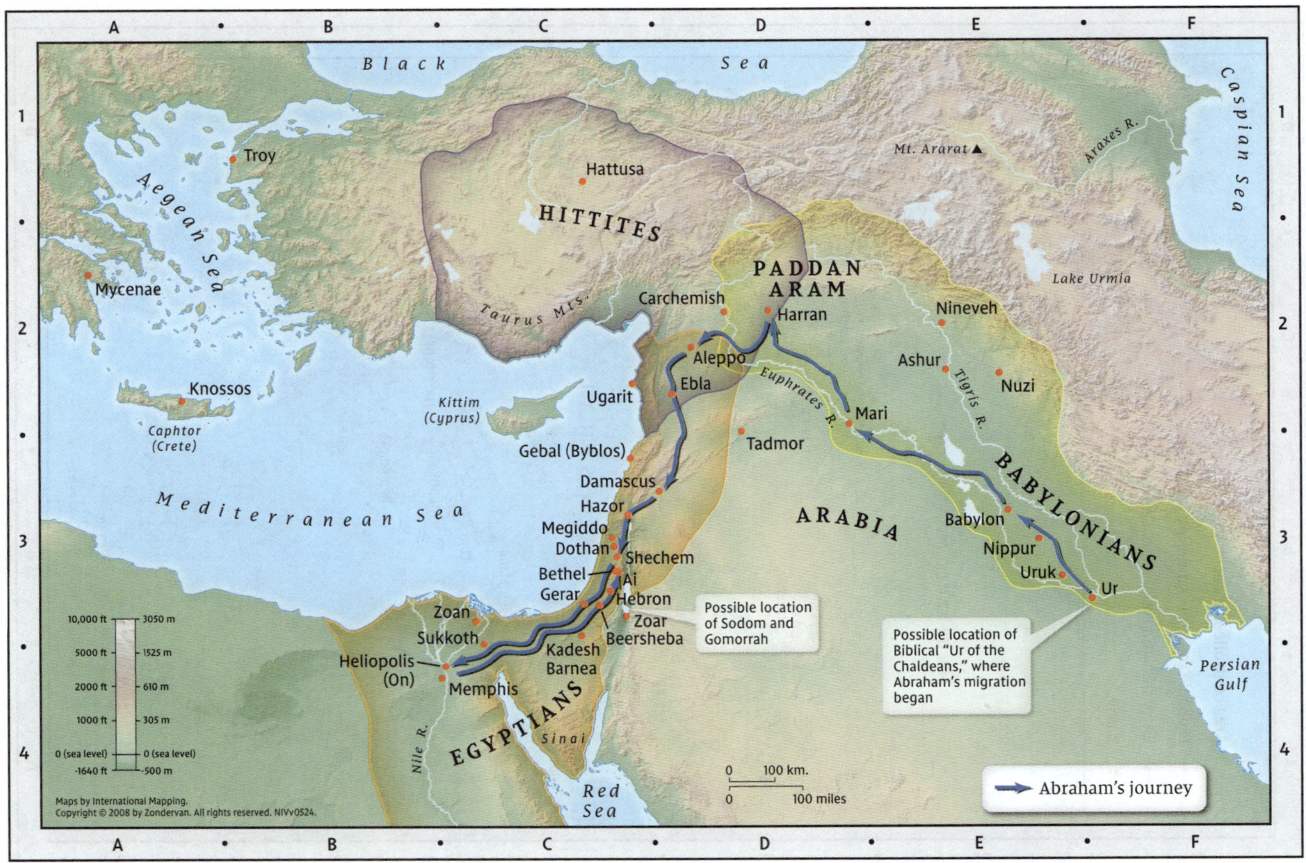

Maps by International Mapping.
Copyright © 2008 by Zondervan. All rights reserved. NIVv0524.

Map 2: EXODUS AND CONQUEST OF CANAAN

Copyright © 2008 by Zondervan. All rights reserved. NIVv0524.

Map 3: LAND OF THE TWELVE TRIBES

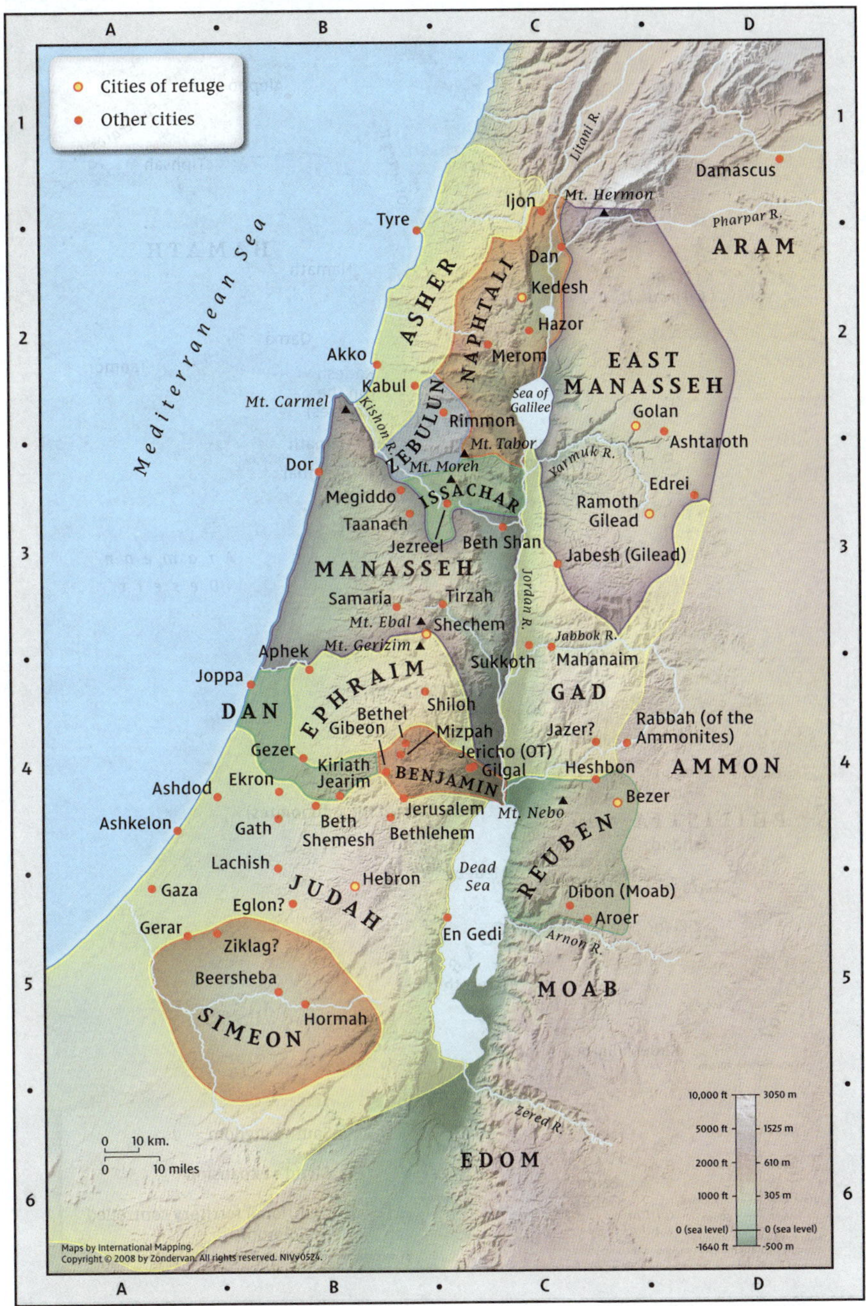

Map 4: KINGDOM OF DAVID AND SOLOMON

Copyright © 2008 by Zondervan. All rights reserved. NIVv0524.

Map 5: JESUS' MINISTRY

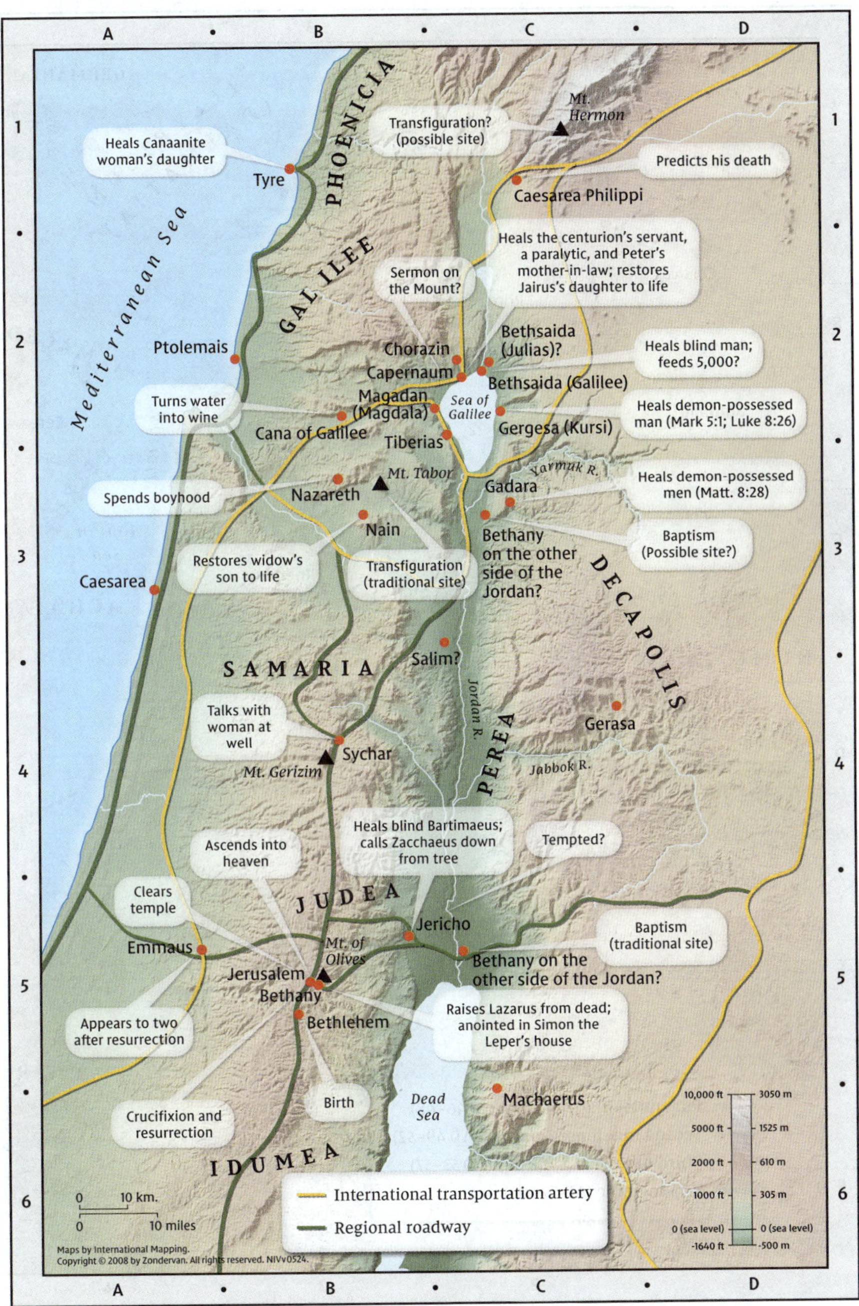

Maps by International Mapping.
Copyright © 2008 by Zondervan. All rights reserved. NIVv0524.

Map 6: PAUL'S MISSIONARY JOURNEYS

5
6
7
8
A
B
C
D
E
F
DACIA
MOESIA
THRACE
ONIA
Black Sea
10,000 ft
3050 m
5000 ft
1525 m
2000 ft
610 m
1000 ft
305 m
0 (sea level)
0 (sea level)
-1640 ft
-500 m
Amphipolis
Philippi
Thessalonica
Neapolis
Samothrace
Apollonia?
Mt. Olympus
BITHYNIA & PONTUS
Troas
Assos
Mitylene
MYSIA
ASIA
Pergamum
Thyatira
GALATIA
CAPPADOCIA
Aegean Sea
Chios
LYDIA
Sardis
Delphi
Smyrna
Ephesus
Philadelphia
PISIDIA
LYCAONIA
Antioch (Pisidian)
COMMAGENE
Athens
Iconium
Samos
Laodicea
Colossae
PAMPHYLIA
Lystra
Derbe
Euphrates R.
Cenchreae
Corinth
Sparta
Patmos
Miletus
LYCIA
Attalia
CILICIA
Tarsus
Issus
SYRIA
Kos
Cnidus
Patara
Myra
Seleucia Pieria
Aleppo
Antioch (Syrian)
Crete
Rhodes
Perga
Phoenix
Salmone
Lasea
Cyprus
Cauda
Fair Havens
Salamis
Paphos
PHOENICIA
ABILENE
Mediterranean Sea
Sidon
Tyre
Damascus
Ptolemais
Caesarea
JUDEA
Jordan R.
Jerusalem
Dead Sea
ENAICA
ARABIA
EGYPT
Nile R.
0
200 km.
0
200 miles
Red Sea

Map 7: JERUSALEM IN THE TIME OF JESUS

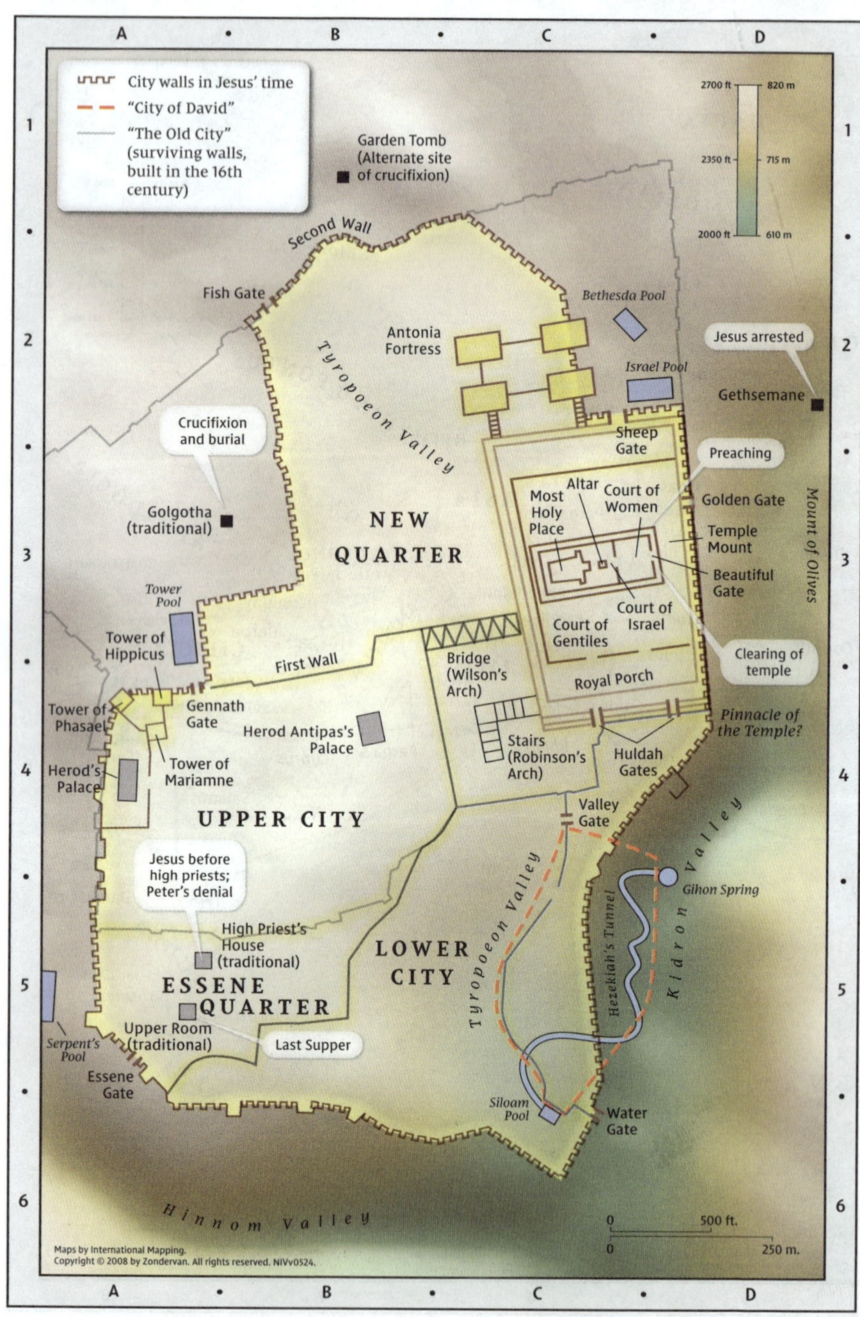

Maps by International Mapping.
Copyright © 2008 by Zondervan. All rights reserved. NIVv0524.